BIO 11
Human Anatomy

Irvine Valley College

McGraw Hill create®

create.mheducation.com

create

ISBN-13: 9781307579000

ISBN-10: 1307579000

Contents

About the Authors

Courtesy of Janyce McKinley

MICHAEL P. MCKINLEY received his undergraduate degree from the University of California, and both MS and PhD degrees from Arizona State University. In 1978, he accepted a postdoctoral fellowship at the University of California at San Francisco (UCSF) Medical School in the laboratory of Dr. Stanley Prusiner, where he worked for 12 years investigating prions and prion-diseases. In 1980, he became a member of the anatomy faculty at the UCSF Medical School, where he taught medical histology for 10 years while continuing to do research on prions. During this time, he was an author or co-author of more than 80 scientific papers.

Michael was a member of the biology faculty at Glendale Community College from 1991 to 2012, where he taught undergraduate anatomy and physiology, general biology, and genetics. Between 1991 and 2000, he also participated in Alzheimer disease research and served as director of the Brain Donation Program at the Sun Health Research Institute, as well as teaching developmental biology and human genetics at Arizona State University, West. His vast experience in histology, neuroanatomy, and cell biology greatly shaped the related content in *Human Anatomy.* He retired from active teaching in 2012 and continues to be an active member of the Human Anatomy and Physiology Society (HAPS). Michael is coauthor of the McKinley/O'Loughlin/Bidle: *Anatomy & Physiology: An Integrative Approach,* Third Edition, textbook. He resides in Tempe, AZ, with his wife Jan.

Courtesy of Indiana University

VALERIE DEAN O'LOUGHLIN received her undergraduate degree from the College of William and Mary, and her PhD in biological anthropology from Indiana University. She is Professor of Anatomy at Indiana University School of Medicine–Bloomington, where she teaches human gross anatomy to medical students, basic human anatomy to undergraduates, and human anatomy for medical imaging evaluation to undergraduate and graduate students. She also teaches a graduate pedagogical methods course and mentors PhD students pursuing anatomy education research. She is a fellow of the American Association of Anatomists (AAA), a President Emeritus of the Human Anatomy and Physiology Society (HAPS), and a current member of the HAPS Steering Committee. She received the AAA Basmajian Award for excellence in teaching gross anatomy and outstanding accomplishments in scholarship in education, and in 2018 she was awarded the AAA Henry Gray Distinguished Educator Award. In 2014 she received the Scholar Educator award from the Indiana University School of Medicine, which recognizes a single faculty member who approaches teaching through a scholarly lens. Valerie is coauthor of the McKinley/O'Loughlin/Bidle:*Anatomy & Physiology: An Integrative Approach,* Third Edition, textbook.

Courtesy of Medicine Hat College

ELIZABETH E. PENNEFATHER-O'BRIEN received her undergraduate degree from the University of Alberta, Edmonton, Alberta, Canada, and her MA and PhD degrees in biological anthropology from Indiana University, Bloomington. She is the Dean of Science and Health at Medicine Hat College in Alberta, where she taught anatomy and physiology to nursing and paramedic students for 14 years. She has also taught physiology and biology for nonmajors. Elizabeth is active in several professional organizations, including sitting on the board of the Human Anatomy and Physiology Society (HAPS). In 2012, Elizabeth was one of five inaugural recipients of the College Sector Educator Awards bestowed by the Society of Teaching and Learning in Higher Education (STLHE). She is recognized as a 3M Teaching Fellow.

Preface

What Makes This Book Special?

Human anatomy is a fascinating field with many layers of complexity. The subject is difficult to teach, and students can often be overwhelmed by its massive amount of material. Our goal in writing *Human Anatomy* was to create a textbook that guides students on a clearly written and expertly illustrated beginner's path through the human body. For all six editions it has been of paramount importance to make this book enjoyable to read, easy to understand, pedagogically efficient, and visually engaging. The following pages highlight the enhancements we've made to the sixth edition, as well as the hallmark features that define this book.

New to the Sixth Edition

New research findings, shifting terminology, technological advancements, and the evolving needs of students and instructors in the classroom require textbook authors to continually monitor and revise their content. Throughout the sixth edition, changes have been made to incorporate the latest information, update terminology, and improve wording to make discussions easier for students to read and understand. Highlights of these revisions are as follows.

Global Changes

The Sixth Edition received some global changes to increase student understanding and success.

- Additional Learning Strategies are added to each chapter, and are consecutively numbered, for easier reference
- All major concepts are addressed by a measurable Learning Objective
- Data from McGraw-Hill's LearnSmart program was used to clarify and edit text in areas where students most need support
- *What Did You Learn?* questions are revised to be more challenging and provide more active learning experiences such as drawing, preparing flowcharts, or making tables of concepts
- When possible, images or photos are added to most *Clinical Views* and *Learning Strategies*
- Each End of Chapter section is extensively revised, including:
    - *Challenge Yourself* section now includes a prompt for students to actively write or type their answers in a separate document to reinforce learning before checking their answers
    - *Challenge Yourself* questions are aligned to cover all chapter Learning Objectives
    - *Multiple Choice* and *Content Review* questions are edited to be more challenging and to review more global aspects
    - All chapters now have three *Developing Critical Reasoning* questions

In addition to these changes, all chapters were thoroughly edited to respond to reviewers' comments and suggestions. Chapter-specific changes are as follows:

Chapter 1 A First Look at Anatomy

- New Clinical View 1.1: Clinicians' Use of Scientific Method
- New Clinical View 1.2: Etiology (Causes) and Pathogenesis (Development) of Disease
- Modified section 1.4e to clarify discussion of pelvic brim
- Edited Clinical View 1.3: Medical Imaging Procedures
- Revised figures: 1.1a, 1.1b, 1.4, 1.5
- Revised tables: 1.1, 1.4

Chapter 2 The Cell: Basic Unit of Structure and Function

- New Learning Strategy 2.2 on receptors and ligands
- Modified section 2.1b to clarify discussion of the general cell function of reproduction
- Edited Clinical View 2.3: Adrenoleukodystrophy (ALD) to include more recent treatment
- Adapted Clinical View 2.5: Characteristics of Cancer Cells to include an image of a dividing cervical cancer cell
- Revised figures: 2.1, 2.5, 2.9–2.13, 2.15, 2.19, 2.20
- Revised table 2.2

Chapter 3 Embryology

- New Clinical View 3.7: Preterm (Premature) Birth
- Revised Clinical View 3.6 to include information on both Amniocentesis and Chorionic Villus Sampling
- Edited Clinical View 3.5: Congenital Malformations
- Edited text in sections 3.2 (discussion of fertilization), 3.3 (clarified concept of capacitation), 3.4g (clarified peak development period)
- Revised figures: 3.1, 3.3, 3.5, 3.6, 3.7
- Revised tables: 3.2, 3.3, 3.4

Chapter 4 Tissue Level of Organization

- Revised Clinical View 4.1: Stem Cells
- Edited Clinical View 4.2: What Are You Planning to Do with Your Baby's Umbilical Cord?
- Modified Clinical View 4.4: Gangrene
- Edited Clinical View 4.5: Tissue Transplantation
- Modified section 4.1a discussion on polarity to include apical surface modifications
- Adapted section 4.1f to change the discussion order of secretion types
- Edited section 4.4a to clarify use of terms *involuntary* and *autorhythmic*
- Revised figures: 4.1b, 4.2, 4.4, 4.7, 4.8
- Revised tables: 4.1, 4.11, 4.13

Chapter 5 Integumentary System

- New Learning Strategy 5.2 and accompanying photo comparing dermal papillae and epidermal ridges to egg crate foam

- Edited section 5.1b on metabolic regulation
- Revised section 5.2a description of stratum spinosum
- Modified section 5.5 to clarify discussion of epidermal derivatives
- Removed Clinical View 5.3 on dermatoglyphics, and incorporated selected information into the text
- Added new photos for selected Clinical View boxes
- Clinical View 5.6: Treatments for Aging Skin is updated to include information about dermal fillers, with a new photo of a Botox treatment
- Revised figures: 5.3, 5.4, 5.9, 5.10
- Revised tables: 5.3, 5.4

Chapter 6 Cartilage and Bone

- Enhanced Clinical View 6.3: Achondroplastic Dwarfism with the inclusion of a photo
- Revised Clinical View 6.5: Bone Scans
- Edited Clinical View 6.6: Osteoporosis
- Revised figures: 6.4, 6.8, 6.9, 6.12, 6.13, 6.16

Chapter 7 Axial Skeleton

- Section 7.1 discussion of basal view of the skull edited
- Clinical View 7.3: Spinal Curvature Abnormalities was adapted to incorporate the terms *hyperkyphosis* and *hyperlordosis* to describe abnormal curvatures
- Modified Clinical View 7.4: Herniated Discs
- Revised figures: 7.7, 7.9, 7.15, 7.23

Chapter 8 Appendicular Skeleton

- Adapted Clinical View 8.1: Fracture of the Clavicle to add an illustration
- Modified Clinical View 8.2: Colles Fracture to add an illustration
- Expanded Clinical View 8.4: Pott Fracture to include an illustration
- Revised figures: 8.2, 8.4, 8.9, 8.10, 8.11

Chapter 9 Articulations

- New Learning Strategy 9.2 on gomphosis
- New Learning Strategy 9.3 relating to the movements at selected joints
- Edited Clinical Views 9.1–9.9 to be more concise; Clinical View 9.9: Arthritis contains updated treatment information; new photos are added to Clinical Views 9.1 and 9.6; several photos in other Clinical Views were replaced
- Removed previous Clinical View on Joint Replacement; pertinent text is now included in section 9.6 (disease and aging of the joints)
- Revised discussions in section 9.4a (general anatomy of synovial joints) on cartilage, bursae throughout the body, and Hilton's law with regard to innervation of joints
- Edited discussion of glenohumeral joint in section 9.5b to emphasize that it is the muscles, not the ligaments, that provide support to the joint
- Expanded discussion of the elbow joint in section 9.5b to include discussion on Tommy John surgery to emphasize the importance of the ulnar collateral ligament in this joint
- Revised figures: 9.7, 9.11
- Edited table 9.2, figure 9.7, and the text to emphasize that hyperextension is a movement beyond the normal range of motion
- Edited tables 9.3–9.5 to ensure consistent discussion of movement

Chapter 10 Muscle Tissue and Organization

- New Learning Strategy 10.1 on the connective tissue components of muscle
- Expanded Learning Strategy 10.3 to include a figure
- New Learning Strategy 10.4 on motor unit recruitment
- Updated Clinical View 10.1: Tendonitis
- Enhanced Clinical View 10.3: Muscular Paralysis and Neurotoxins with a figure
- Revised Clinical View 10.5: Anabolic Steroids and Other Performance-Enhancing Compounds
- Updated Clinical View 10.6: Neuromuscular Diseases
- Enhanced our discussion of levers in section 10.7 by adding text and a figure

Chapter 11 Axial Muscles

- Modified Learning Strategy 11.1
- Extensively editedClinical View 11.2: Strabismus, including new photos
- Edited section 11.15, figure 11.15, and table 11.12 to replace the outdated reference to "urogenital diaphragm " with the names of the muscles composing this structure
- Revised figure 11.15
- Revised tables: 11.8, 11.10, 11.12

Chapter 12 Appendicular Muscles

- Added photo to Clinical View 12.1: Paralysis of the Serratus Anterior Muscle ("Winged Scapula")
- Removed Clinical View 12.5: Anatomic Snuffbox
- Modified Clinical View 12.5: Thigh Muscle Injuries to include figure
- Expanded Clinical View 12.6: Plantar Fasciitis to include figure
- Updated Clinical View 12.7: Shin Splints and Compartment Syndrome
- Enhanced Learning Strategy 12.5 with a new figure
- Edited section 12.1b to include discussion of short head of biceps brachii
- Updated terminology: actions versus functions of muscles; intermuscular septum; radial and ulnar deviation
- Edited section 12.2c to note the variability of presence of fibularis tertius
- Revised figures: 12.1, 12.2, 12.4, 12.5, 12.16
- Revised tables: 12.1, 12.2, 12.4, 12.6, 12.8

Chapter 13 Surface Anatomy

- New *What Did You Learn?* section at the end of section 13.1
- New Learning Strategy 13.2 to help distinguish the anterior and lateral cervical regions of the neck
- New Learning Strategy 13.3 to help students remember which side of the lower limb originates the small and great saphenous veins
- Modified section 13.2 to discuss six regions of the face
- Clinical View 13.1: Lip Color as a Diagnostic Tool includesa new photo
- Updated section 13.3 and figure 13.2 the discussion on the regions of the neck, using the *Terminologia Anatomica*-approved terms *anterior, lateral, and posterior cervical regions of the neck;* the terms *anterior triangle* and *posterior triangle* are replaced

- Revised section 13.6d (foot) to clarify discussion on where to take the pulse of the dorsalis pedis artery

Chapter 14 Nervous Tissue

- New Learning Strategy 14.1 on functions of dendrites and axons
- New Learning Strategy 14.3 on myelin
- Significantly revised Clinical View 14.1: Neuroplasticity and Neurogenesis, including differentiation between the CNS and the PNS
- Enhanced Clinical View 14.2: Tumors of the Central Nervous System with a new image
- Added new Clinical View 14.3: Nervous System Disorders Affecting Myelin
- Revised Clinical View 14.4: Treating Spinal Cord Injuries
- Modified Clinical View 14.5: Amyotrophic Lateral Sclerosis
- Updated Clinical View 14.6: Neural Tube Defects
- Edited section 14.2a to update discussion on anaxonic neurons
- Edited section 14.2b to include current information on astrocyte function, and neuron-to-glial -cell ratios
- Edited section 14.6a
- Edited section 14.7 to use the term *neuronal circuits* instead of *neuronal pools,* and to clarify examples
- Revised figures: 14.10, 4.12
- Revised tables: 14.1, 14.4

Chapter 15 Brain and Cranial Nerves

- Modified all Clinical Views, with new photos added when appropriate
- Clarified section 15.2 regarding the meninges and the falx cerebri
- Retitled Clinical View 15.1 Meningitis and Encephalitis, and included information on both for comparison, as some people confuse the two ailments
- New Learning Strategy 15.2 notes the cerebral lobes share the same name as the skull bone that overlies each lobe
- Edited and updated Section 15.3b discussion of sensory homunculus per medical neuroscience research to state there is extensive overlap of body regions in this structure (and thus it is not as precise as the motor homunculus)
- Extensively updated Clinical View 15.5 to discuss functional brain regions and provide up-to-date information from the Human Connectome Project about updated brain maps. It includes new photos from the Human Connectome Project.
- Removed section 15.3b and figure 15.11:discussion and portrayal of gnostic area, due to debate by neuroscientists about this region's borders and functions
- Edited, clarified, and updated section 15.3d and table 15.5 : discussion on cerebral nuclei per latest neuroscience research
- New Learning Strategy 15.3 to help the reader remember the functions of the superior and inferior colliculi
- Revised section 15.5 (brainstem)
- Updated section 15.6 (cerebellum) to discuss additional non-motor functions of the cerebellum
- New Learning Strategy 15.4 on the cerebellar peduncle and how it connects to the brainstem
- Revised section 15.7 (limbic system) to include information about neurogenesis in the hippocampus
- Revised figures: 15.11, 15.13, 15.19, 15.20, 15.22

Chapter 16 Spinal Cord and Spinal Nerves

- Significantly updated Clinical View 16.1: Lumbar Puncture and Epidural Injection to include the similarities and differences between the two
- Updated terminology in Clinical View 16.2: Shingles (Herpes Zoster)
- Revised Clinical View 16.3: Brachial Plexus Injuries text, with an added figure
- Enhanced Clinical View 16.4: Sacral Plexus Nerve Injuries with a new figure
- New Learning Strategy 16.3 distinguishes vertebral foramina from intervertebral foramina
- Expanded section 16.4g to include a paragraph on sural nerves
- Modified section 16.5b to change terminology from *Golgi tendon reflex* to *tendon reflex*
- Revised figures: 16.2, 16.3; removed figure 16.4
- Revised tables: 16.3, 16.4

Chapter 17 Pathways and Integrative Functions

- New Learning Strategy 17.1 distinguishes between a tract and a pathway
- Revised section 17.1 based on recent research on the sensory homunculus
- New Learning Strategy 17.3 on location of sensory pathways and their common primary neuron—posterior root ganglion
- Clarified section 17.2a discussion of sensory pathways
- New Learning Strategy 17.4 distinguishes medial pathway from lateral pathway
- Updated Clinical View 17.1: Cerebrovascular Accident to include information about transient ischemic attacks
- Retitled Clinical View 17.2 as Epilepsy, Lobectomy, and Hemispherectomies, with updated text
- Updated Clinical View 17.6: Alzheimer Disease: The "Long Goodbye"
- Revised figures: 17.9, 17.10, 17.12

Chapter 18 Autonomic Nervous System

- New Learning Strategy 18.2 on functions of parasympathetic versus sympathetic nervous system
- New Learning Strategy 18.3 on remembering splanchnic nerves
- Added new Clinical View 18.1: Autonomic Nervous System and Cardiovascular Disease
- Enhanced Clinical View 18.2: Raynaud Syndrome with a new figure
- Expanded Clinical View 8.4: Autonomic Dysreflexia expanded to include bladder/bowel care in spinal cord injuries and a new figure
- Edited section 18.3 reference to the PNS decreasing force of contraction in the heart
- Revised section 18.5c on lack of ANS influence on skeletal muscle blood vessels, and to discuss the receptors for the ANS
- Revised figures: 18.1, 18.3, 18.4, 18.5, 18.7, 18.8, 18.9
- Revised tables: 18.1, 18.2, 18.3, 18.4, 18.5

Chapter 19 Senses: General and Special

- Reordered and edited sections 19.3 and 19.4 to discuss olfaction prior to gustation
- Added photos to selected Learning Strategies

- Clarified discussion in section 19.1a is edited on tonic vs. phasic receptors
- Clarified text in section 19.2 contains clarified text on encapsulated tactile receptors
- New Learning Strategy 19.2 highlights similarities between olfactory and gustation receptors
- New Learning Strategy 19.3 helps to recall the differences between rods and cones
- New Learning Strategy 19.4 details that semicircular ducts detect angular movements of the head
- New Clinical View 19.9: Are Earbuds Bad for Your Health?
- Revised figures: 19.2, 19.5, 19.6 (previously 19.8), 19.11, 19.12, 19.13, 19.14, 19.17, 19.26
- Revised table 19.4

Chapter 20 Endocrine System

- Enhanced Learning Strategy 20.1 with a new figure
- Updated Clinical View 20.1: Disorders of Growth Hormone Secretion
- Modified Clinical View 20.2: Hypophysectomy to include figure
- Clinical View 20.3: Disorders of Thyroid Hormone Secretion includes updated photos
- Edited section 20.3a to clarify the portal system and what it is in general before discussing the specific portal system
- Reordered and edited section 20.3a discussion of mammotropic cells and prolactin
- Edited section 20.9a to clarify renin secretion
- Revised figures: 20.1, 20.6, 20.10, 20.12, 20.13, 20.14, 20.15; removed figure 20.13
- Revised tables: 20.1, 20.2, 20.3, 20.4, 20.6, 20.7, 20.8

Chapter 21 Blood

- Edited section 21.1b (functions of blood) to clarify discussion on pH, and movement of fluid and nutrients
- Added new section 21.2b (other solutes in plasma) and expanded complement information in table 21.1
- Added new photos to selected Clinical Views
- Modified Clinical View 21.2 to focus on anemia; includes a new photo
- New Clinical View 21.4: Whole Blood versus Plasma Donations
- Edited section 21.3b (leukocytes) and section 21.3c (platelets)
- Included the embryonic period in section 21.4 (hematopoiesis)
- Added discussion in section 21.4 about alternative models for hematopoiesis
- Revised figures: 21.7, 21.10
- Revised table 21.1

Chapter 22 Heart

- New Learning Strategy 22.2 on coronary circulation
- New Learning Strategy 22.4 on pressure and blood flow
- Enhanced Clinical View 22.1: Pericarditis with a new figure
- Revised Clinical View 22.4: Angina Pectoris and Myocardial Infarction to include a figure
- Edited section 22.1c to clarify the role of serous fluid in the pericardial cavity
- Modified sections 22.2b and 22.2c for clarity
- Revised section 22.4b's discussion on gap junctions and desmosomes
- Edited terminology from *isovolumetric* to *isovolumic* in section 22.6a and figure 22.14
- Revised figures: 22.1, 22.2, 22.5, 22.9, 22.14
- Revised table 22.2

Chapter 23 Vessels and Circulation

- Modified and repositioned Learning Strategy 23.3 to before section 23.3a, where the named vessels are first discussed
- Added examples to section 23.1 (anatomy of blood vessels) to illuminate the difference between arterial and venous anastomoses
- Revised section 23.1a to explain the difference between arteries and veins
- Clarified section 23.1b regarding vasoconstriction of all artery types to varying degrees
- Edited the discussion of section 23.1c (capillaries) about precapillary sphincters and capillary beds
- Revised section 23.3 to include a new section on blood flow through the spinal cord
- New Learning Strategy 23.5 helps recall where the great saphenous vein is located
- Rewrote and expanded section 23.6
- Revised figures: 23.4, 23.8

Chapter 24 Lymphatic System

- Terminology is modified throughout the chapter: *lymphoid* is used to reference organs, structures, and cells; *lymphatic* is used when referring to the system, vessels, ducts, trunks, capillaries, and movement of lymph
- New Learning Strategy 24.1 on movement of lymph into capillaries
- New Learning Strategy 24.3 on functions of different types of lymphocytes
- Edited section 24.2c and section 24.3a
- Replaced photos in several Clinical View boxes
- Revised figures: 24.1, 24.5, 24.6, 24.7, 24.8, 24.10

Chapter 25 Respiratory System

- Edited/corrected the discussion in sections 25.1, 25.2 and 25.3, in table 25.2, and in selected figures to clarify the division between the upper and lower respiratory tracts, so the larynx is included with discussion of the upper respiratory tract
- Larynx (previously section 25.3a) moved to section 25.2d (so it is grouped with other upper respiratory tract structures)
- New photos added to Learning Strategies and Clinical Views, when appropriate
- In section 25.2b, more detail added regarding the function of the paranasal sinuses
- Revised Clinical View 25.3 to focus on aspirated bodies and the Heimlich maneuver; includes new photo of how to perform the Heimlich maneuver; discussion of bronchoscopy removed as this clinical procedure is no longer commonly used
- Expanded section 25.3c (bronchial tree) to explain why less cartilage is needed in the bronchial tree compared to the trachea, and that bronchoconstriction and bronchodilation are controlled by the ANS
- Modified sections 25.6a and 25.7a
- Revised figures: 25.1, 25.4, 25.7, 25.8, 25.9, 25.10

Chapter 26 Digestive System

- New Learning Strategy 26.1 on mixing/segmentation
- Revised section 26.1a to employ the term *segmentation*
- Edited section 26.2c to update secretion types in salivary glands
- Edited sections 26.4a and 26.4b
- Replaced photos in Clinical Views 26.2, 26.3, 26.4, 26.5, 26.6
- Edited text in Clinical View 26.5: Gallstones (Cholelithiases) to distinguish between cholelithiasis and choledocholithiasis
- Enhanced Clinical View 26.8: Intestinal Disorders with a new figure
- Revised figures: 26.6, 26.11, 26.21

Chapter 27 Urinary System

- New Learning Strategy 27.1 on the main function of the kidneys
- New Learning Strategy 27.2 to help visualize the retroperitoneal nature of the kidneys
- Edited section 27.2d (nephrons) and table 27.2 to clarify that nutrients normally are reabsorbed at the proximal convoluted tubule
- New Learning Strategy 27.4 uses the analogy of a conveyor belt to explain filtration, secretion, and reabsorption
- New Learning Strategy 27.5 to help recall that aldosterone helps us retain sodium
- Updated terminology in section 27.2f (juxtaglomerular apparatus) using *granular cells* to replace *juxtaglomerular cells*
- New Learning Strategy 27.6 on how to ID transitional epithelium
- Edited section 27.3c discussion of external urethral sphincter to remove reference to the outdated term *urogenital diaphragm*
- Revised figures: 27.7, 27.8, 27.10, 27.11

Chapter 28 Reproductive System

- Added subheads to better organize ovarian cycle phase discussion
- Updated section 28.2a for more current discussion of the follicular phase
- Edited section 28.2c for easier readability
- Updated Clinical View 28.1 to add a figure
- Replaced photos in Clinical Views 28.2, 28.5
- Updated Clinical View 28.2: Cervical Cancer with current information
- Added figures to Clinical View 28.3: Endometriosis, Clinical View 28.6: Benign Prostatic Hyperplasia and Prostate Cancer, and Clinical View 28.8: Sexually Transmitted Infections
- Updated Clinical View 28.4: Contraception Methods
- Modified Clinical View 28.5: Breast Cancer
- Revised figures: 28.4, 28.6, 28.11, 28.13, 28.16

Themes and Distinctive Topic Approaches

Through our teaching experience, we have developed a few approaches that really seem to help students grasp certain topics or spark their interest. Thus, we have tried to incorporate these successful ideas from our own courses into our book.

- **Embryology.** Learning about embryologic events can increase understanding of the adult anatomy. For this reason, chapter 3, Embryology, appears early in the book. In addition, "systems embryology" sections in each systems chapter (e.g., integumentary system, digestive system) provide a brief but thorough overview of the developmental processes for that particular system.
- **Forensic Anthropology.** Forensic examples are a great way to reinforce learning, and students enjoy the "real-life" application of anatomic knowledge in forensic analysis. The skeletal system chapters (6–9) feature discussions on topics such as determining age of death by evaluating epiphyseal plates and the pubic symphysis, and determining sex by noting differences in the skull and pelvis.
- **Surface Anatomy.** To best serve our audience, we have dedicated a full chapter (13) to surface anatomy. This chapter contains beautiful photographs and clear, concise text as well as numerous Clinical Views that illustrate the importance of surface anatomy landmarks and how they are used daily in health care.
- **Nervous System.** In order to understand the workings of the nervous system, it is best to learn how the brain controls all aspects of the nervous system. Thus, in this text we examine the brain first, followed by a chapter comparing its similarities, differences, and relationships to the spinal cord. It seemed appropriate to use central nervous system terminology to describe the brain first and then the spinal cord. Additionally, because the nuclei of the cranial nerves are housed within the brain, we felt it made more sense to present the cranial nerves along with the brain.
- **Arteries and Veins.** Arteries and veins are covered in unison by region. For example, we present the arteries and veins of the upper limb together. This approach emphasizes to students that the arteries often have corresponding veins and that both are responsible for the blood flow in a general region.

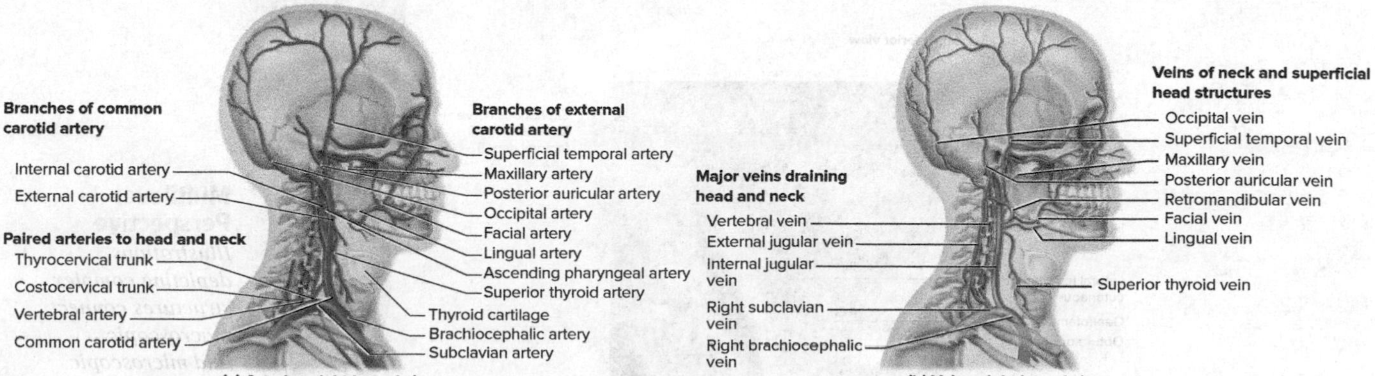
Branches of common carotid artery
Internal carotid artery
External carotid artery
Paired arteries to head and neck
Thyrocervical trunk
Costocervical trunk
Vertebral artery
Common carotid artery
Branches of external carotid artery
Superficial temporal artery
Maxillary artery
Posterior auricular artery
Occipital artery
Facial artery
Lingual artery
Ascending pharyngeal artery
Superior thyroid artery
Thyroid cartilage
Brachiocephalic artery
Subclavian artery
Major veins draining head and neck
Vertebral vein
External jugular vein
Internal jugular vein
Right subclavian vein
Right brachiocephalic vein
Veins of neck and superficial head structures
Occipital vein
Superficial temporal vein
Maxillary vein
Posterior auricular vein
Retromandibular vein
Facial vein
Lingual vein
Superior thyroid vein

(a) Arteries, right lateral view **(b) Veins, right lateral view**

Accurate and Engaging Illustrations

Because anatomy is a visual subject, quality illustrations are crucial to understanding and retention. The brilliant illustrations in *Human Anatomy* bring the study of anatomy to life! Drawn by a team of medical illustrators, all figures have been carefully rendered to convey realistic, three-dimensional detail. Each drawing has been meticulously reviewed for accuracy and consistency, and precisely labeled to coordinate with the text discussions. *Human Anatomy* also features a beautiful collection of cadaver dissection images, bone photographs, surface anatomy shots, and histology micrographs. These detailed images capture the intangible characteristics of human anatomy that can only be conveyed in human specimens, and help familiarize students with the appearance of structures they will encounter in lab.

View Orientation

Reference diagrams clarify the view or plane an illustration represents.

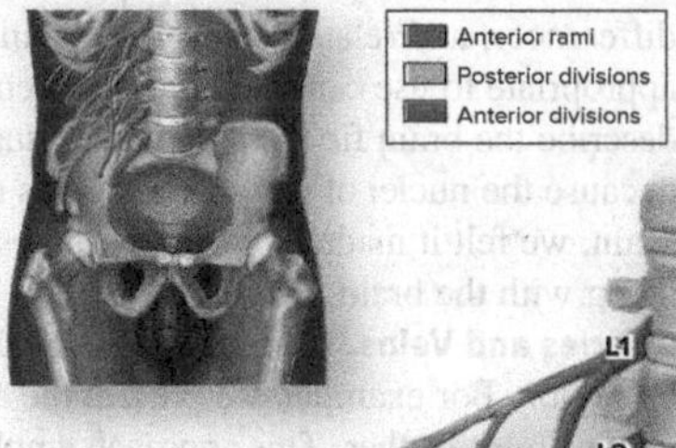

Anterior rami
Posterior divisions
Anterior divisions

Color Coding

Many illustrations use color coding to organize information and clarify concepts for visual learners.

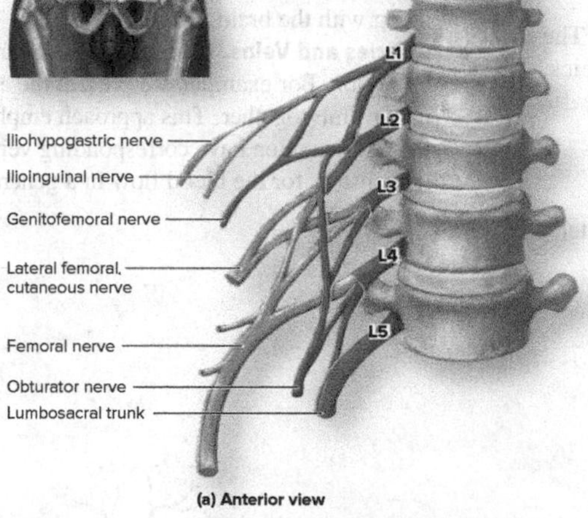

L1
L2
L3
L4
L5
Iliohypogastric nerve
Ilioinguinal nerve
Genitofemoral nerve
Lateral femoral cutaneous nerve
Femoral nerve
Obturator nerve
Lumbosacral trunk

(a) Anterior view

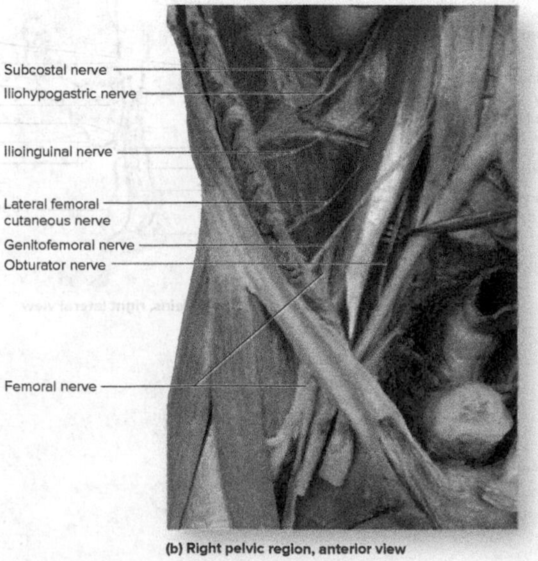

Subcostal nerve
Iliohypogastric nerve
Ilioinguinal nerve
Lateral femoral cutaneous nerve
Genitofemoral nerve
Obturator nerve
Femoral nerve

(b) Right pelvic region, anterior view

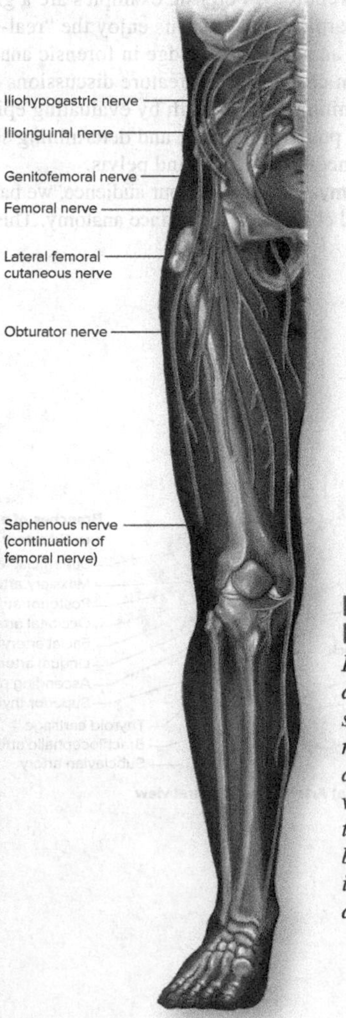

Iliohypogastric nerve
Ilioinguinal nerve
Genitofemoral nerve
Femoral nerve
Lateral femoral cutaneous nerve
Obturator nerve
Saphenous nerve (continuation of femoral nerve)

(c) Right lower limb, anterior view

Multilevel Perspective

Illustrations depicting complex structures connect macroscopic and microscopic views to show the relationships between increasingly detailed drawings.

(b) ©McGraw-Hill Education/Christine Eckel, photographer

Complementary Views

Drawings paired with photographs enhance visualization of structures. Labels on art and photos mirror each other whenever possible, making it easy to correlate structures between views.

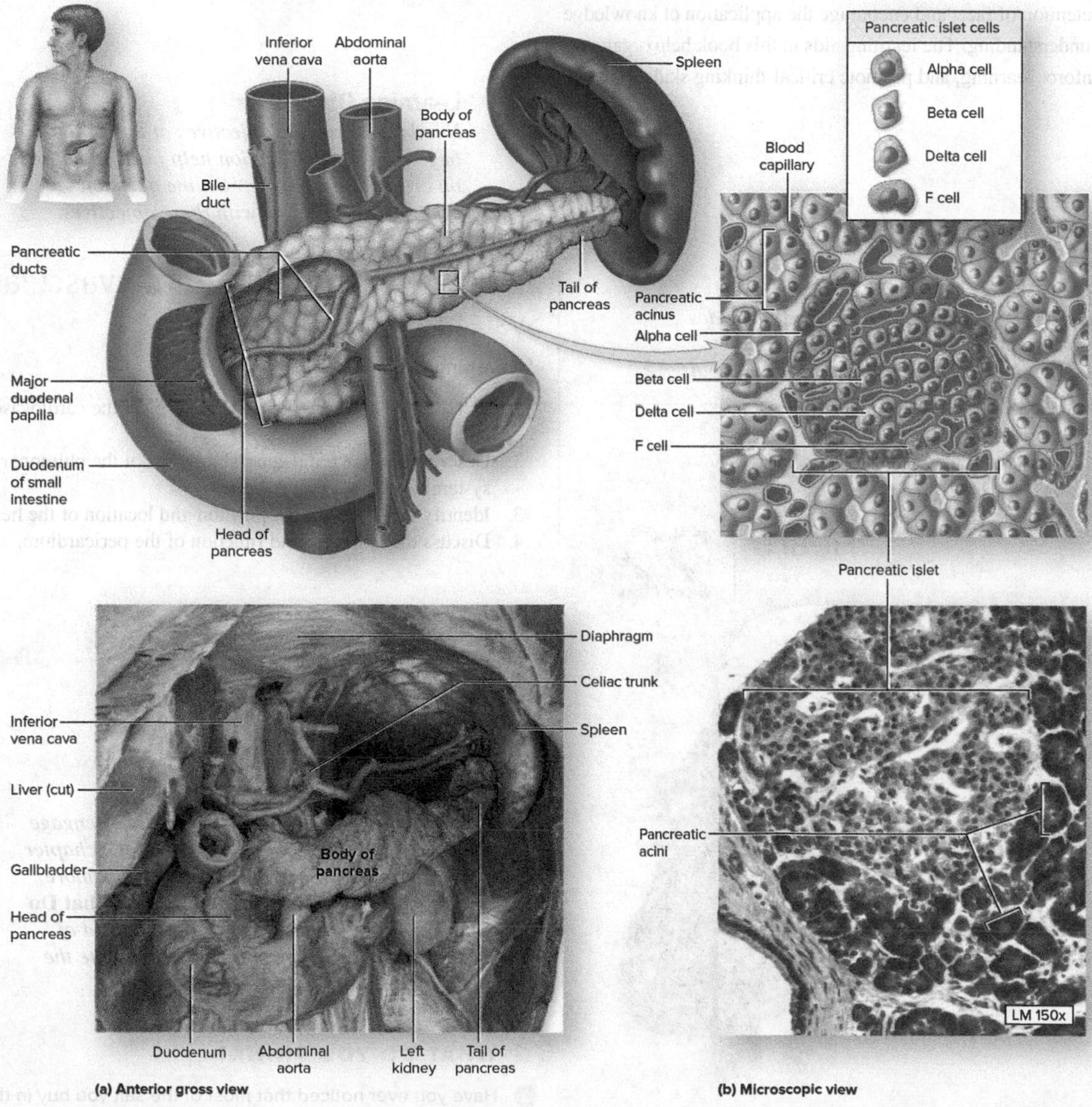

(a) Anterior gross view **(b) Microscopic view**

(a) ©McGraw-Hill Education/Christina Eckel, photographer;
(b) ©McGraw-Hill Education/Alvin Telser, photographer

Cadaver Dissections

Expertly dissected specimens are preserved in richly colored photos that reveal incredible detail. Many unique views show relationships between anatomic structures from a new perspective.

Histology Micrographs

Light micrographs, as well as scanning and transmission electron micrographs, are used in conjunction with illustrations to present a true picture of microscopic anatomy. Magnifications provide a reference point for the sizes of the structures shown in the micrographs.

Helpful Pedagogical Tools

Human Anatomy is built around a pedagogical framework designed to foster retention of facts and encourage the application of knowledge that leads to understanding. The learning aids in this book help organize studying, reinforce learning, and promote critical-thinking skills.

Learning Objectives
Numbered learning objectives at the beginning of each section help focus attention on critical information. Online question banks are correlated with these objectives.

Chapter Outline
Each chapter begins with an outline that provides a quick snapshot of the chapter contents and organization. Headings are numbered throughout the chapter for easy reference.

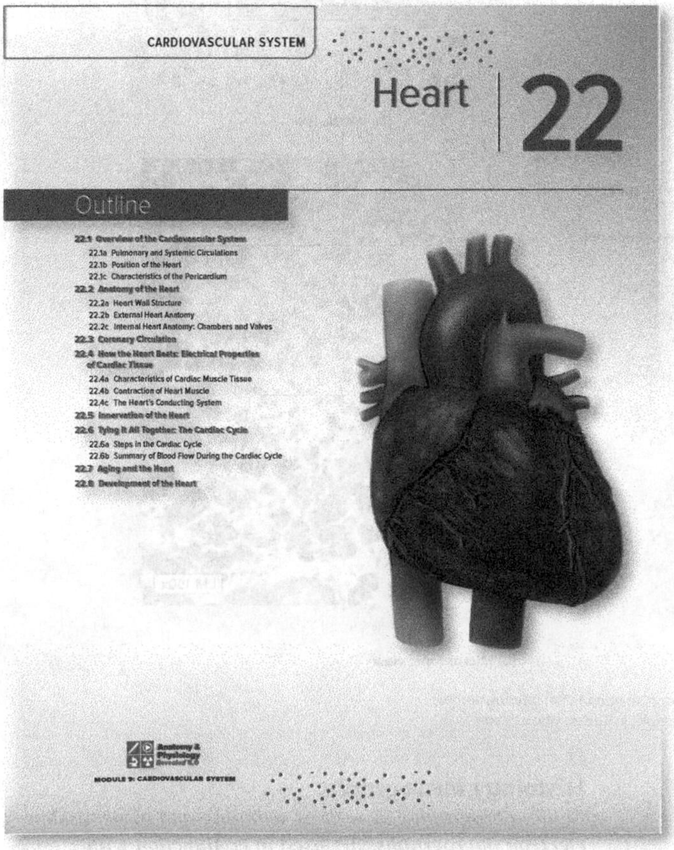
CARDIOVASCULAR SYSTEM
Heart
22
Outline
22.1 Overview of the Cardiovascular System
22.1a Pulmonary and Systemic Circulations
22.1b Position of the Heart
22.1c Characteristics of the Pericardium
22.2 Anatomy of the Heart
22.2a Heart Wall Structure
22.2b External Heart Anatomy
22.2c Internal Heart Anatomy: Chambers and Valves
22.3 Coronary Circulation
22.4 How the Heart Beats: Electrical Properties of Cardiac Tissue
22.4a Characteristics of Cardiac Muscle Tissue
22.4b Contraction of Heart Muscle
22.4c The Heart's Conducting System
22.5 Innervation of the Heart
22.6 Tying It All Together: The Cardiac Cycle
22.6a Steps in the Cardiac Cycle
22.6b Summary of Blood Flow During the Cardiac Cycle
22.7 Aging and the Heart
22.8 Development of the Heart

22.1 Overview of the Cardiovascular System

✓ **Learning Objectives**

1. Identify and describe the basic features of the cardiovascular system.
2. Describe and trace the general patterns of the pulmonary and systemic circulations.
3. Identify and describe the position and location of the heart.
4. Discuss the structure and function of the pericardium.

What Do You Think?
These critical thinking questions actively engage students in application or analysis of the chapter material and encourage students to think more globally about the content. Answers to **What Do You Think?** *questions are given at the end of each chapter, allowing students to evaluate the logic used to solve the problem.*

WHAT DO YOU THINK?

2 Have you ever noticed that most of the salt you buy in the grocery store is labeled as "iodized"? Why is iodine added to our salt?

Clinical View 21.3

Rh Incompatibility and Pregnancy

The potential presence of anti-D antibodies is especially important in pregnant women who are Rh negative and have an Rh positive fetus. An Rh incompatibility may result during the pregnancy if the mother has previously been exposed to Rh positive blood (such as can occur with a previously carried Rh positive fetus, typically at the time of childbirth). As a result of the prior exposure, the mother has anti-D antibodies that may cross the placenta and destroy the fetal erythrocytes, resulting in severe illness or death. The illness that occurs in the newborn is called **hemolytic disease of the newborn (HDN),** or *erythroblastosis fetalis.* The newborn typically presents with *anemia* and *hyperbilirubinemia* (increased bilirubin in the blood) due to erythrocyte destruction. In severe cases, the infant may develop heart failure and must be given a blood transfusion to survive.

Giving a pregnant Rh negative woman special immunoglobulins (e.g., RhoGAM) between weeks 28–32 of her pregnancy and at birth prevents the mother from developing anti-D anitbodies. Specifically, these immunoglobulins bind to fetal erythrocyte surface antigens—and in so doing, prevent the mother's immune system from recognizing Rh antigens and being stimulated to produce anti-D antibodies.

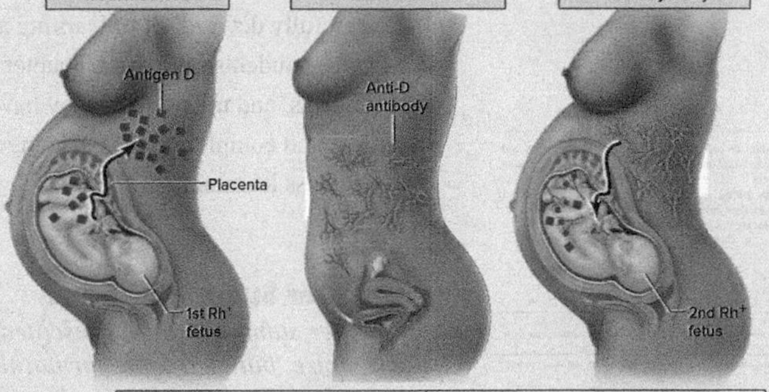

	Mother Rh Blood Types		Fetus Rh Blood Types	
	Pregnancy #1	Pregnancy #2	Pregnancy #1	Pregnancy #2
Blood type	Rh negative	Rh negative	Rh positive	Rh positive
Erythrocytes	No antigen D	No antigen D	Antigen D	Antigen D
Plasma	No anti-D antibodies	Anti-D antibodies (due to prior exposure)	No anti-D antibodies	No anti-D antibodies Anti-D antibodies from mother cross placenta and attack fetal erythrocytes causing **hemolytic disease of the newborn**

Hemolytic disease of the newborn.

Clinical View

Sometimes an example of what can go wrong in the body helps crystallize understanding of the "norm." **Clinical Views** *provide insights into health or disease processes. These essays expand upon topics covered in the text and provide relevant background information for students pursuing health-related careers.*

In contrast to the ABO blood group, where antibodies may be found in the blood even without prior exposure to a foreign antigen, antibodies to the Rh factor termed **anti-D antibodies** appear in the blood only when an Rh negative individual is exposed to Rh positive blood. This exposure to Rh positive blood most often occurs as a result of an inappropriate blood transfusion. Therefore, individuals who are Rh positive never exhibit anti-D antibodies, because they possess the Rh antigen on their erythrocytes. Only individuals who are Rh negative can exhibit anti-D antibodies, and that can occur only after exposure to Rh antigens.

The ABO and Rh blood types are usually reported together. For example, types AB and Rh⁺ together are reported as AB⁺. However, remember that ABO and Rh blood types are independent of each other, and neither of them interacts with or influences the presence or activities of the other group.

WHAT DID YOU LEARN?

5. Why does an erythrocyte lack cellular organelles, and how is this related to its life span?
6. How do transferrin and ferritin participate in recycling erythrocyte components after the cells break down?
7. Should a person with blood type A donate blood to a person with blood type AB? Why or why not?

What Did You Learn?

Review questions at the end of each section prompt students to test their comprehension of key concepts. These mini self-tests help students determine whether they have a sufficient grasp of the information before moving on to the next section of the chapter.

Learning Strategy 14.3

Recall from Section 2.3a: "Composition and Structure of Membranes" that the plasma membrane is composed of lipids and proteins. Similar to flattening and rolling up a tube of toothpaste to get the toothpaste out, the myelinating cell (neurolemmocyte or oligodendrocyte) is flattened and rolled up, leaving only the lipid bilayers of plasma membrane, which make the myelin.

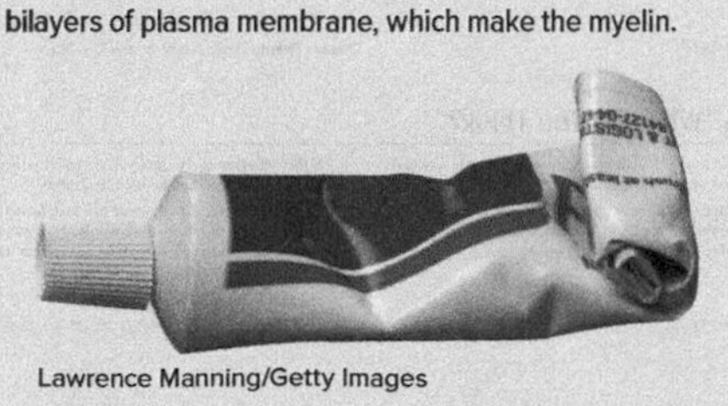

Lawrence Manning/Getty Images

Learning Strategy

Many anatomy instructors provide students with everyday analogies, mnemonics, and other useful tips to help them understand and remember the information. **Learning Strategy** *boxes throughout each chapter offer tried-and-tested practical learning strategies that students can apply as they read. These tips are not just useful—they can also be fun!*

End-of-Chapter Tools

A carefully devised set of learning aids at the end of each chapter helps students review the chapter content, evaluate their grasp of key concepts, and utilize what they have learned. Reading the chapter summary and completing the Challenge Yourself exercises is a great way to assess learning.

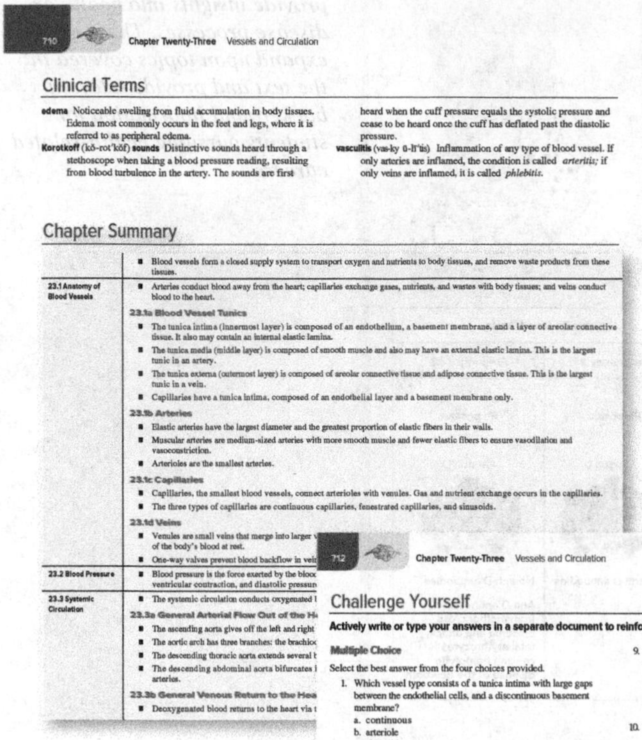

710 Chapter Twenty-Three Vessels and Circulation

Clinical Terms

edema Noticeable swelling from fluid accumulation in body tissues. Edema most commonly occurs in the feet and legs, where it is referred to as peripheral edema.

Korotkoff (kŏ-rot′kŏf) **sounds** Distinctive sounds heard through a stethoscope when taking a blood pressure reading, resulting from blood turbulence in the artery. The sounds are first heard when the cuff pressure equals the systolic pressure and cease to be heard once the cuff has deflated past the diastolic pressure.

vasculitis (vas-ky ū-lī′tis) Inflammation of any type of blood vessel. If only arteries are inflamed, the condition is called *arteritis;* if only veins are inflamed, it is called *phlebitis.*

Chapter Summary

	■ Blood vessels form a closed supply system to transport oxygen and nutrients to body tissues, and remove waste products from these tissues.
23.1 Anatomy of Blood Vessels	■ Arteries conduct blood away from the heart; capillaries exchange gases, nutrients, and wastes with body tissues; and veins conduct blood to the heart. **23.1a Blood Vessel Tunics** ■ The tunica intima (innermost layer) is composed of an endothelium, a basement membrane, and a layer of areolar connective tissue. It also may contain an internal elastic lamina. ■ The tunica media (middle layer) is composed of smooth muscle and also may have an external elastic lamina. This is the largest tunic in an artery. ■ The tunica externa (outermost layer) is composed of areolar connective tissue and adipose connective tissue. This is the largest tunic in a vein. ■ Capillaries have a tunica intima, composed of an endothelial layer and a basement membrane only. **23.1b Arteries** ■ Elastic arteries have the largest diameter and the greatest proportion of elastic fibers in their walls. ■ Muscular arteries are medium-sized arteries with more smooth muscle and fewer elastic fibers to ensure vasodilation and vasoconstriction. ■ Arterioles are the smallest arteries. **23.1c Capillaries** ■ Capillaries, the smallest blood vessels, connect arterioles with venules. Gas and nutrient exchange occurs in the capillaries. ■ The three types of capillaries are continuous capillaries, fenestrated capillaries, and sinusoids. **23.1d Veins** ■ Venules are small veins that merge into larger v… of the body's blood at rest. ■ One-way valves prevent blood backflow in vei…
23.2 Blood Pressure	■ Blood pressure is the force exerted by the bloo… ventricular contraction, and diastolic pressur…
23.3 Systemic Circulation	■ The systemic circulation conducts oxygenated b… **23.3a General Arterial Flow Out of the H…** ■ The ascending aorta gives off the left and right… ■ The aortic arch has three branches: the brachio… ■ The descending thoracic aorta extends several b… ■ The descending abdominal aorta bifurcates i… arteries. **23.3b General Venous Return to the Hea…** ■ Deoxygenated blood returns to the heart via t…

Chapter Summary Tables

Chapter summaries are presented in a concise, bulleted table format that provides a basic overview of each chapter. Section and page references make it easy to look up topics for review.

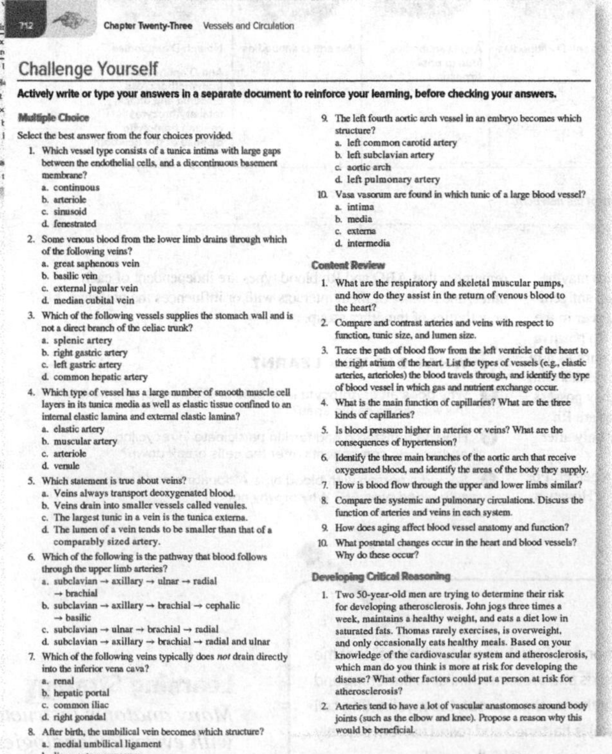

712 Chapter Twenty-Three Vessels and Circulation

Challenge Yourself

Actively write or type your answers in a separate document to reinforce your learning, before checking your answers.

Multiple Choice

Select the best answer from the four choices provided.

1. Which vessel type consists of a tunica intima with large gaps between the endothelial cells, and a discontinuous basement membrane?
   a. continuous
   b. arteriole
   c. sinusoid
   d. fenestrated
2. Some venous blood from the lower limb drains through which of the following veins?
   a. great saphenous vein
   b. basilic vein
   c. external jugular vein
   d. median cubital vein
3. Which of the following vessels supplies the stomach wall and is not a direct branch of the celiac trunk?
   a. splenic artery
   b. right gastric artery
   c. left gastric artery
   d. common hepatic artery
4. Which type of vessel has a large number of smooth muscle cell layers in its tunica media as well as elastic tissue confined to an internal elastic lamina and external elastic lamina?
   a. elastic artery
   b. muscular artery
   c. arteriole
   d. venule
5. Which statement is true about veins?
   a. Veins always transport deoxygenated blood.
   b. Veins drain into smaller vessels called venules.
   c. The largest tunic in a vein is the tunica externa.
   d. The lumen of a vein tends to be smaller than that of a comparably sized artery.
6. Which of the following is the pathway that blood follows through the upper limb arteries?
   a. subclavian → axillary → ulnar → radial → brachial
   b. subclavian → axillary → brachial → cephalic → basilic
   c. subclavian → ulnar → brachial → radial
   d. subclavian → axillary → brachial → radial and ulnar
7. Which of the following veins typically does *not* drain directly into the inferior vena cava?
   a. renal
   b. hepatic portal
   c. common iliac
   d. right gonadal
8. After birth, the umbilical vein becomes which structure?
   a. medial umbilical ligament
   b. ligamentum venosum
   c. ligamentum arteriosum
   d. round ligament of the liver
9. The left fourth aortic arch vessel in an embryo becomes which structure?
   a. left common carotid artery
   b. left subclavian artery
   c. aortic arch
   d. left pulmonary artery
10. Vasa vasorum are found in which tunic of a large blood vessel?
   a. intima
   b. media
   c. externa
   d. intermedia

Content Review

1. What are the respiratory and skeletal muscular pumps, and how do they assist in the return of venous blood to the heart?
2. Compare and contrast arteries and veins with respect to function, tunic size, and lumen size.
3. Trace the path of blood flow from the left ventricle of the heart to the right atrium of the heart. List the types of vessels (e.g., elastic arteries, arterioles) the blood travels through, and identify the type of blood vessel in which gas and nutrient exchange occur.
4. What is the main function of capillaries? What are the three kinds of capillaries?
5. Is blood pressure higher in arteries or veins? What are the consequences of hypertension?
6. Identify the three main branches of the aortic arch that receive oxygenated blood, and identify the areas of the body they supply.
7. How is blood flow through the upper and lower limbs similar?
8. Compare the systemic and pulmonary circulations. Discuss the function of arteries and veins in each system.
9. How does aging affect blood vessel anatomy and function?
10. What postnatal changes occur in the heart and blood vessels? Why do these occur?

Developing Critical Reasoning

1. Two 50-year-old men are trying to determine their risk for developing atherosclerosis. John jogs three times a week, maintains a healthy weight, and eats a diet low in saturated fats. Thomas rarely exercises, is overweight, and only occasionally eats healthy meals. Based on your knowledge of the cardiovascular system and atherosclerosis, which man do you think is more at risk for developing the disease? What other factors could put a person at risk for atherosclerosis?
2. Arteries tend to have a lot of vascular anastomoses around body joints (such as the elbow and knee). Propose a reason why this would be beneficial.

Challenge Yourself

This battery of matching, multiple-choice, short answer, and critical-thinking questions is designed to test students on all levels of learning, from basic comprehension to synthesis of concepts.

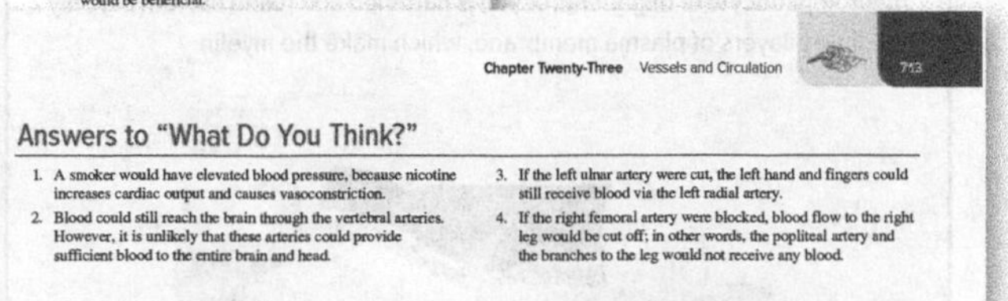

Chapter Twenty-Three Vessels and Circulation 713

Answers to "What Do You Think?"

1. A smoker would have elevated blood pressure, because nicotine increases cardiac output and causes vasoconstriction.
2. Blood could still reach the brain through the vertebral arteries. However, it is unlikely that these arteries could provide sufficient blood to the entire brain and head.
3. If the left ulnar artery were cut, the left hand and fingers could still receive blood via the left radial artery.
4. If the right femoral artery were blocked, blood flow to the right leg would be cut off; in other words, the popliteal artery and the branches to the leg would not receive any blood.

Answers to What Do You Think?

The **What Do You Think?** *questions are answered at the end of each chapter.*

Laboratory Resources

Eckel's Human Anatomy Laboratory Manual, 3rd Edition

The *Human Anatomy Laboratory Manual,* by Christine Eckel of University of Indiana, is expressly written to supplement and expand upon content covered in the lecture course—not to repeat it. This highly customizable, hands-on learning tool guides students through human anatomy lab exercises using observation, touch, dissection, and practical activities such as sketching, labeling, and coloring. The manual focuses on human specimens and also includes common animal dissections such as cow bone, cow eye, sheep brain, and sheep heart.

Supplemental resources include Connect®, assignable and auto-gradable Pre- and Post-Lab questions, LearnSmart Prep, Anatomy & Physiology REVEALED 4.0, and a full eBook.

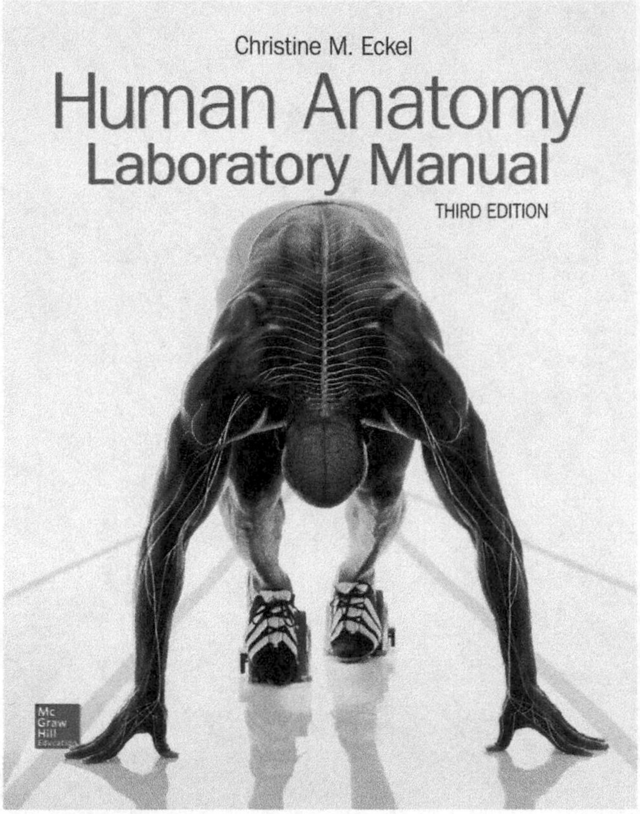

Mike Powell/The Image Bank/Getty Images

Broyles' Workbook to Accompany Anatomy & Physiology REVEALED

The *Workbook to Accompany Anatomy and Physiology Revealed 4.0,* third edition, by Robert Broyles, is a workbook/study guide designed to help students get the most they can out of Anatomy and Physiology REVEALED 4.0 (APR), and out of their anatomy and physiology course. The Table of Contents closely follows APR and is organized along the lines of a typical Anatomy and Physiology course. The individual exercises include art from APR and also have review questions, tables, coloring exercises, terminology quiz questions, and reminders on key content.

For additional details and customization opportunities, please contact your Learning Technology Representative.

ACKNOWLEDGMENTS

Many people worked with us to produce this text. Thanks go to our book team members at McGraw-Hill who attended to the many tasks involved in bringing this edition and its supporting materials to market: Matthew Garcia, Portfolio Manager; Donna Nemmers, Product Developer; Jessica Portz and Brent dela Cruz, Content Project Managers; David Hash, Designer; and Lori Hancock, Content Licensing Specialist. Over the span of six editions, we have been fortunate to work with the following individuals who contributed their specific talents to various tasks: Christine Eckel, cadaver dissection and photography; Jw Ramsey, surface anatomy photography; Al Telser, photomicroscopy; Mark Braun, clinical consultant; and Frank Baker, language consultant.

Reviewers have evaluated the fifth edition and provided invaluable comments and suggestions to help us continually improve this textbook. We thank the fifth edition reviewers for their recommendations, which have helped us to improve this sixth edition.

Also, in this edition, we are very pleased to have been able to incorporate real student data points and input, derived from thousands of our LearnSmart users, to help guide our revision. LearnSmart Heat Maps provided a quick visual snapshot of usage of portions of the text and the relative difficulty students experienced in mastering the content. With these data, we were able to hone not only our text content but also the LearnSmart probes.

Finally, we could not have performed this effort were it not for the love and support of our families. They provided us with the encouragement we needed, were forgiving when our book schedules made it seem as if we were working all the time, and made sacrifices along with us in order to see this project to fruition.

Reviewers

Stephanie Bender
Grand Valley State University

Sandi Brown
Johnson County Community College

Diep Burbridge
Long Beach City College

William E. Cullinan
Marquette University

Barbara E. Davis
Eastern Kentucky University

Danielle Dodenhoff
California State University—Bakersfield

John Fitzsimmons
Michigan State University

Allan Forsman
East Tennessee State University

Eric Green
Salt Lake Community College

Karri Haen Whitmer
Iowa State University

Lyon H. Hough
Missouri State University

Elizabeth O. Lobo
Cuesta College

Tyler Morris
Missouri State University

Natalie Reynolds
Carl Albert State College

Clinical Views

Chapter 1 | A First Look at Anatomy
1.1 Clinicians' Use of Scientific Method
1.2 Etiology (Causes) and Pathogenesis (Development) of Disease
1.3 Medical Imaging Procedures

Chapter 2 | The Cell: Basic Unit of Structure and Function
2.1 Cystic Fibrosis and Chloride Channels
2.2 Tay-Sachs Disease
2.3 Adrenoleukodystrophy (ALD)
2.4 MELAS and Mitochondria
2.5 Characteristics of Cancer Cells

Chapter 3 | Embryology
3.1 Nondisjunction
3.2 Chromosomal Abnormalities and Spontaneous Abortion (Miscarriage)
3.3 Twinning
3.4 Infertility and Infertility Treatments
3.5 Congenital Malformations
3.6 Amniocentesis and Chorionic Villus Sampling
3.7 Preterm (Premature) Birth

Chapter 4 | Tissue Level of Organization
4.1 Stem Cells
4.2 What Are You Planning to Do with Your Baby's Umbilical Cord?
4.3 Systemic Lupus Erythematosus
4.4 Gangrene
4.5 Tissue Transplantation

Chapter 5 | Integumentary System
5.1 Tattoos
5.2 UV Radiation, Sunscreens, and Sunless Tanners
5.3 Nail Disorders
5.4 Acne and Acne Treatments
5.5 Burns
5.6 Treatments for Aging Skin
5.7 Psoriasis

Chapter 6 | Cartilage and Bone
6.1 Osteitis Deformans
6.2 Forensic Anthropology: Determining Age at Death
6.3 Achondroplastic Dwarfism
6.4 Rickets
6.5 Bone Scans
6.6 Osteoporosis

Chapter 7 | Axial Skeleton
7.1 Craniosynostosis and Plagiocephaly
7.2 Cleft Lip and Cleft Palate
7.3 Spinal Curvature Abnormalities
7.4 Herniated Discs
7.5 Sternal Foramen
7.6 Variations in Rib Development

Chapter 8 | Appendicular Skeleton
8.1 Fracture of the Clavicle
8.2 Colles Fracture
8.3 Scaphoid Fractures
8.4 Pott Fracture
8.5 Pathologies of the Foot
8.6 Limb Malformations

Chapter 9 | Articulations
9.1 Costochondritis
9.2 "Cracking Knuckles"
9.3 TMJ Disorders
9.4 Shoulder Joint Dislocations
9.5 Subluxation of the Head of the Radius
9.6 Fracture of the Femoral Neck
9.7 Knee Ligament and Cartilage Injuries
9.8 Ankle Sprains
9.9 Arthritis

Chapter 10 | Muscle Tissue and Organization
10.1 Tendonitis
10.2 Mitochondrial Myopathies

Introduction

A First Look at Anatomy 1

Outline

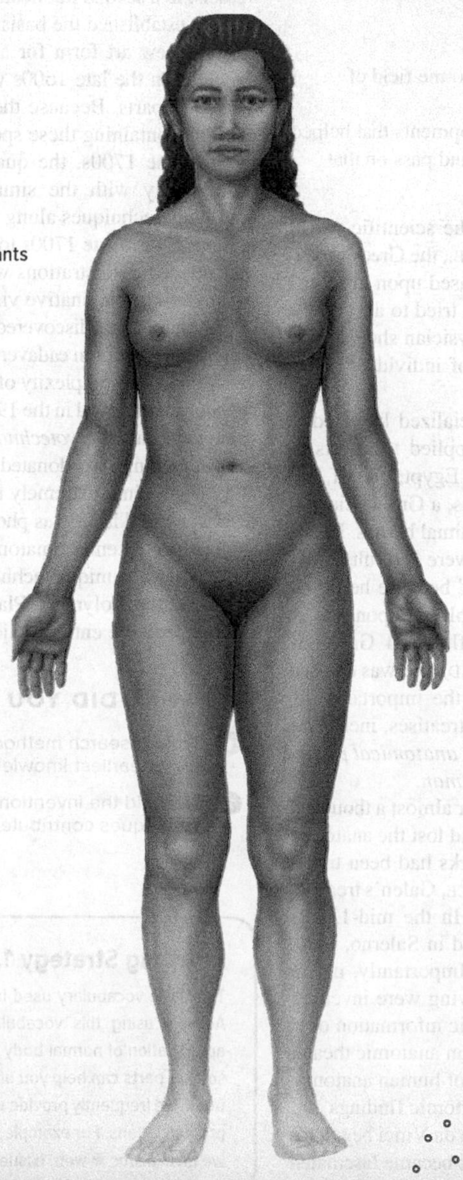

Anatomy & Physiology Revealed 4.0

MODULE 1: BODY ORIENTATION

You are about to embark on an exciting adventure in the world of human anatomy, investigating the structure and organization of an incredible machine, the human body. Human anatomy is an applied science that provides the basis for understanding health and physical performance. In this book, you will find that structure and function are inseparable, and you will discover what happens when the body works normally, as well as how it is affected by injury or disease.

Learning Strategy 1.1

Throughout these chapters, boxed elements like this provide helpful analogies, mnemonics, and other learning strategies to help you better understand and learn the material. Look for these boxes throughout each chapter.

1.1 History of Human Anatomy

✓ Learning Objectives

1. Explain the contributions of early scientists to the field of human anatomy.
2. Describe the significant technological developments that helped expand the study of human body structures and pass on that knowledge.

For several centuries BCE., the main centers of the scientific world were in ancient Greece and Egypt. Around 400 BCE., the Greek physician Hippocrates developed a medical practice based upon observations and studies of the human body. Hippocrates tried to accurately describe disease symptoms and thought that a physician should treat the body as a whole rather than as a collection of individual parts. Hippocrates is called the "Father of Medicine."

The ancient Egyptians had developed specialized knowledge in some areas of human anatomy, which they applied to efforts to mummify their deceased leaders. In Alexandria, Egypt, one of the great anatomy teachers in 300 BCE was Herophilus, a Greek scientist who was the first to publicly dissect human and animal bodies. Many of the early descriptions of anatomic structures were a result of his efforts. He is known as the "Father of Anatomy" because he based his conclusions (such as that blood vessels carry blood) upon human dissection. The work of Herophilus greatly influenced Galen of Pergamum, who lived between 130 and 200 CE (AD) and was dubbed the "Prince of Physicians" because he stressed the importance of experimentation in medicine. Galen wrote many treatises, including *On the movement of the chest and of the lung, On anatomical procedure,* and *On the uses of the parts of the body of man.*

Advancements in anatomy were curtailed for almost a thousand years from 200 to 1200 CE. Western Europeans had lost the anatomic treatises attributed to Galen. However, these works had been translated into Arabic by Islamic scholars. After 1200 CE, Galen's treatises began to be translated from Arabic into Latin. In the mid-1200s, the first European medical school was established in Salerno, Italy. There, human bodies were dissected in public. Importantly, in the mid-1400s, movable type and copperplate engraving were invented, thus providing a means for disseminating anatomic information on a larger scale. Just before 1500 CE, in Padua, Italy, an anatomic theater opened and became the centerpiece for the study of human anatomy.

Illustrations became a way of recording anatomic findings and passing on that knowledge (**figure 1.1**). Leonardo da Vinci began his study of the human body around 1500 CE. Da Vinci became fascinated with the human body when he performed dissections to improve his drawing and painting techniques. In the mid-1500s, Andreas Vesalius, a Belgian physician and anatomist, began a movement in medicine and anatomy that was characterized by "refined observations." He organized the medical school classroom in a way that brought students close to the operating table. His dissections of the human body and descriptions of his findings helped correct misconceptions that had existed for 2000 years. Vesalius was called the "Reformer of Anatomy" because he promoted the idea of "living anatomy." His text, *De Humani Corporis Fabrica,* was the first anatomically accurate medical textbook, and the fine engravings in the book were produced from his personal sketches.

William Harvey was an Englishman who studied medicine at the University of Padua in Italy in the early 1600s, a time when this was the center for western European medical instruction. In 1628 he published a book, entitled *An Anatomical Study of the Motion of the Heart and of the Blood in Animals,* that described how blood was pumped from the heart to the body and then back to the heart. His ideas on recirculation formed the basis for modern efforts to study the heart and blood vessels. In a second publication, *Essays on the Generation of Animals,* Harvey established the basis for modern embryology.

A new art form for anatomy, called the preserved specimen, appeared in the late 1600s when anatomists began to collect bodies and body parts. Because these were real specimens, viewers of the exhibits containing these specimens were astonished.

In the 1700s, the quality of anatomic illustrations improved dramatically with the simultaneous development of etching and engraving techniques along with mezzotint that provided beauty and texture. By the late 1700s to early 1800s, anatomists began to ensure that scientific illustrations were as accurate and realistic as possible by removing imaginative visual elements from artistic efforts.

Anatomists discovered in the early 1800s that cross sections obtained from frozen cadavers and parts of cadavers provided incredible insight into the complexity of the human body. The nature of the frozen specimens improved in the 1900s with advancements in this field, which came to be called *cryotechnology.* In the late 1980s, the Visible Human Project began. Two donated bodies were deep-frozen in blue gelatin, and then cut into extremely thin cross sections from head to toe. Each newly exposed layer was photographed digitally for computer analysis.

More recently, anatomists have been using a technique called *plastination,* a unique technology that preserves anatomic specimens using reactive polymers. Plastination may preserve individual organs or may preserve entire bodies for observation and study.

WHAT DID YOU LEARN?

1. What research method that is still used today formed the basis of our earliest knowledge about human body structure?
2. How did the invention of movable type and engraving techniques contribute to the science of human anatomy?

Learning Strategy 1.2

The basic vocabulary used in anatomy is derived from Greek and Latin. Actively using this vocabulary will enhance your understanding and appreciation of normal body structure and function. Breaking a word into smaller parts can help you understand and remember its meaning. In this book, we frequently provide word derivations for new terms following their pronunciations. For example, in the case of histology, the study of tissues, we give (*histos* = web, tissue, *logos* = study).

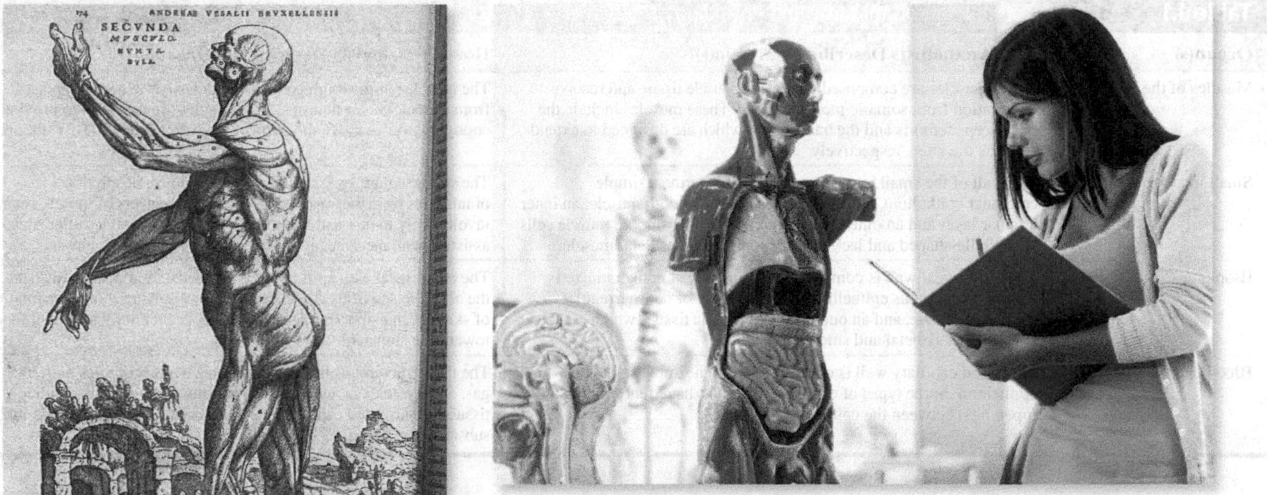

(a) Anatomic drawing by Vesalius

(b) 3D anatomic models

Figure 1.1

Aids for Anatomic Study. (*a*) Early anatomists, such as Andreas Vesalius, recorded the findings from their dissections of the human body by making detailed drawings. (*b*) Many anatomy classrooms, like the one shown here, utilize three-dimensional anatomic models for studying purposes.

(a) Source: Digital image courtesy of the Getty's Open Content Program; (b) ©Fotostorm/Getty Images

1.2 Definition of Anatomy

✓ Learning Objectives

3. Explain the similarities and differences between anatomy and physiology.
4. List the steps involved in the scientific method and explain how the scientific method has been used in the fields of anatomy and physiology.
5. Describe microscopic anatomy and its subdivisions.
6. Define gross anatomy and compare and contrast its subdisciplines.

Anatomy is the study of structure. The word *anatomy* is derived from Greek and means "to cut apart." Anatomists, scientists who study anatomy, examine the relationships among parts of the body as well as the structure of individual organs. Often the anatomy of specific body parts suggests their functions. The scientific discipline that studies the function of body structures is called **physiology.** A special relationship exists between anatomy and physiology because structure and function cannot be completely separated. The examples in **table 1.1** illustrate the differences and the interrelationships between anatomy (structure) and physiology (function).

Anatomists and physiologists are professionals who use the scientific method to explain and understand the workings of the body. The **scientific method** refers to a systematic and rigorous process by which scientists:

- Examine natural events (or phenomena) through observation.
- Develop a hypothesis (possible explanation) for explaining these phenomena.
- Experiment and test the hypothesis through the collection of data.
- Determine if the data support the hypothesis, or if the hypothesis needs to be rejected or modified.

For example, early anatomists and physiologists used the scientific method to explain how blood circulates through the body. Today, we continue to use the scientific method for a variety of topics, such as to understand how the brain stores memories or explain how cancer may spread throughout the body.

The discipline of anatomy is an extremely broad field that can be divided into two general categories: microscopic anatomy and gross anatomy.

1.2a Microscopic Anatomy

Microscopic anatomy examines structures that cannot be viewed by the unaided eye. For most such studies, scientists prepare individual cells or thin slices of some part of the body and examine them by

Clinical View 1.1

Clinicians' Use of Scientific Method

Clinicians regularly apply the principles of the scientific method when interacting with patients. When a patient comes in for an appointment, the first thing the clinician does is gather information. The clinician obtains the patient's weight, medical history, blood pressure, and other vital signs. Then the clinician asks about the patient's specific complaint(s) and completes a physical examination. Based on the information gathered, the clinician forms a hypothesis—a tentative explanation of any specific symptoms the patient may be experiencing. To test the hypothesis, the clinician may order medical tests and evaluate the test results. Based on the information gathered, the clinician draws a conclusion to make a diagnosis. The clinician treats the patient based on the diagnosis, and additional information is gathered as the patient's response to the treatment is monitored. In some cases, additional tests and information may result in the clinician adjusting the diagnosis as needed.

Table 1.1 Comparison of Anatomy and Physiology

Organ(s)	How Anatomists Describe the Organ(s)	How Physiologists Describe the Organ(s)
Muscles of the thigh	These muscles are composed of skeletal muscle tissue and receive innervation from somatic motor neurons. These muscles include the quadriceps femoris and the hamstrings, which are designed to extend and flex the knee, respectively.	The muscles of the thigh contract voluntarily via nerve impulses from somatic motor neurons. The muscles are designed to provide enough power to move the parts of the lower limbs while walking.
Small intestine	The wall of the small intestine contains an innermost simple columnar epithelium, as well as two layers of smooth muscle: an inner circular layer and an outer longitudinal layer. The smooth muscle cells are spindle-shaped and lack the striations seen in skeletal muscle.	The simple columnar epithelium is designed for absorption of nutrients from the small intestine. The two layers of muscle contract involuntarily to mix and move materials in the small intestine, thus assisting with mechanical digestion and absorption of nutrients.
Esophagus	The esophageal wall is composed of an innermost nonkeratinized stratified squamous epithelium, a middle layer of dense irregular connective tissue, and an outer layer of muscle tissue (which contains a mixture of skeletal and smooth muscle).	The esophageal wall epithelium is protective and helps withstand the abrasive activities associated with swallowing food. The mixture of skeletal and smooth muscle contracts sequentially to propel food toward the stomach.
Blood capillaries	The blood capillary wall is composed of a thin simple squamous epithelium. Some types of capillary walls also have fenestrations (openings) between the epithelial cells.	The thin structure of the blood capillary walls promotes nutrient, gas, and waste exchange between the blood and the surrounding tissues. Fenestrated capillaries are designed to allow for additional substance exchange.

microscope. Even so, there are limits to the magnification possible based upon the sophistication of the equipment used.

Figure 1.2 illustrates how the microscope has evolved from the primitive form first developed in the seventeenth century to a modern microscope commonly found in anatomy labs today. Specialized subdivisions of microscopic anatomy are defined by the dimensional range of the material being examined. For example, **cytology** (sī-tol′ō-jē; *kytos* = hollow (cell), *logos* = study), or *cellular anatomy,* is the study of single body cells and their internal structures, whereas **histology** (his-tol′ō-jē; *histos* = web or tissue, *logos* = study) is the study of tissues. Histology takes a wider approach to microscopic anatomy by examining how groups of specialized cells and their products function for a common purpose.

1.2b Gross Anatomy

Gross anatomy, also called *macroscopic anatomy,* investigates the structure and relationships of large body parts that are visible to the unaided eye, such as the intestines, stomach, brain, heart, and kidneys. In these macroscopic investigations, preserved specimens or their parts are often cut open (dissected) for examination. There are several approaches to gross anatomy:

- **Comparative anatomy** examines the similarities and differences in the anatomy of different species.
- **Developmental anatomy** investigates the changes in structure within an individual from conception through maturity.
- **Embryology** (em-br ē-ol′ō-jē; *embryon* = young one) is concerned specifically with developmental changes occurring prior to birth.
- **Regional anatomy** examines all the structures in a particular region of the body as one complete unit—for example, the skin,

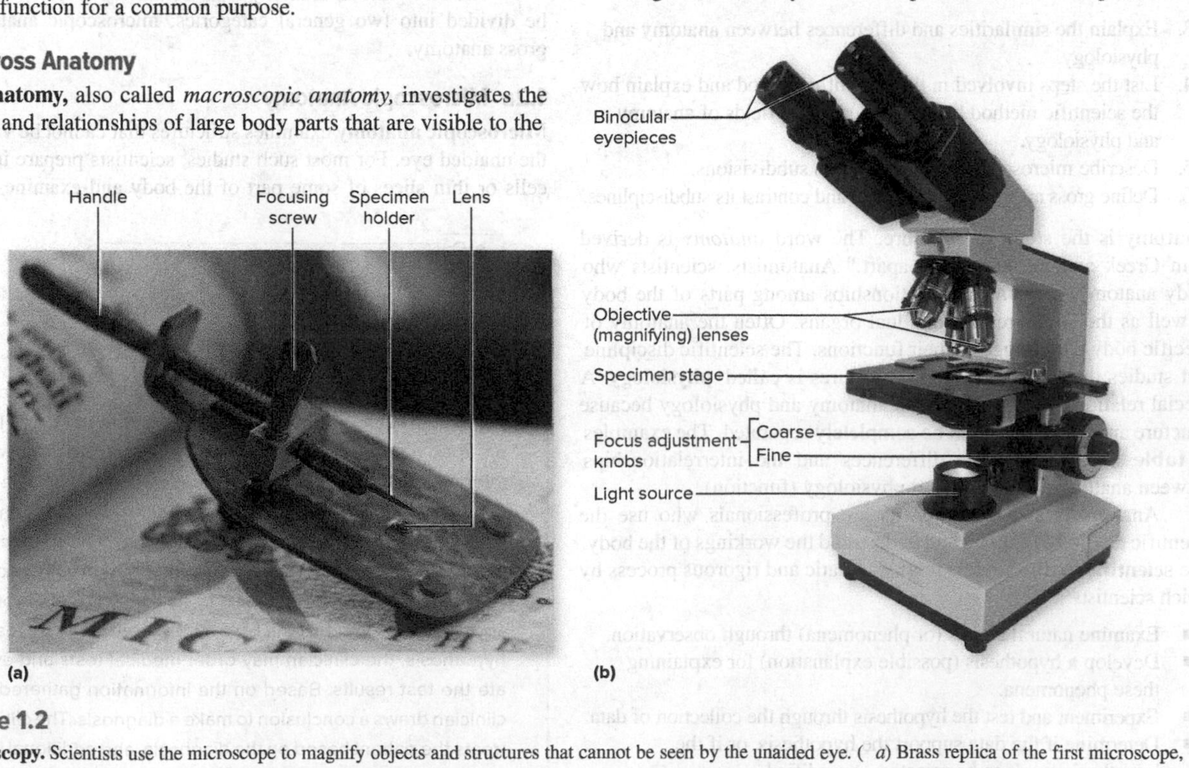
Handle
Focusing screw
Specimen holder
Lens
(a)
Binocular eyepieces
Objective (magnifying) lenses
Specimen stage
Focus adjustment knobs
Coarse
Fine
Light source
(b)

Figure 1.2

Microscopy. Scientists use the microscope to magnify objects and structures that cannot be seen by the unaided eye. (*a*) Brass replica of the first microscope, invented by Antoni van Leeuwenhoek. (*b*) A typical microscope used by students today will have adjustment knobs for coarse and fine focus and a light source to illuminate the tissue being studied.

(a) ©Tetra Images/Alamy Stock Photo; (b) ©Comstock/Getty Images connective tissue and fat, bones, muscles, nerves, and blood vessels of the neck.

- **Surface anatomy** examines both superficial anatomic markings and internal body structures as they relate to the skin covering them. Health-care professionals use surface features to identify and locate specific bony processes at joints as well as to obtain a pulse or a blood sample from a patient.
- **Systemic anatomy** studies the gross anatomy of each system in the body. For example, studying the urinary system would involve examining the kidneys, where urine is formed, along with the organs of urine transport (ureters and urethra) and storage (urinary bladder).

Several specialized branches of anatomy focus on the diagnosis of medical conditions or the advancement of basic scientific research:

- **Pathologic** (path'ō-loj'ik; *pathos* = disease) **anatomy** examines all anatomic changes resulting from disease.
- **Radiographic anatomy** studies the relationships among internal structures that may be visualized by specific medical imaging procedures, such as ultrasound, magnetic resonance imaging (MRI), or x-ray.
- **Surgical anatomy** investigates the anatomic landmarks used before and after surgery. For example, prior to back surgery, the location of the L_4 vertebra is precisely identified by drawing an imaginary line between the hip bones. The intersection of this line with the vertebral column shows the location of L_4.

Although you might at first assume that the field of anatomy has already been completely described, it is not fixed. Anatomic studies are ongoing, and the success of the discipline depends upon precise observation, thorough description, and correct use of terminology. These tools are essential to your eventual mastery of the discipline.

WHAT DID YOU LEARN?

3. What is the relationship between anatomy and physiology?
4. What are some of the subdisciplines of gross anatomy?

Clinical View 1.2

Etiology (Causes) and Pathogenesis (Development) of Disease

All health-care professionals must understand both how body structures function normally and how disease or injury can affect them. Throughout the chapters in this book, Clinical View boxes introduce you to selected pathologies and indicate how these pathologies affect the body's anatomy and physiology.

1.3 Structural Organization of the Body

✓ Learning Objectives

7. Rank the major levels of organization in the human body, from least to most complex.
8. Describe the characteristics common to all forms of life.
9. List the 11 organ systems of the body and their major organs.

Anatomists recognize several levels of increasingly complex organization in humans, as illustrated in **figure 1.3**. The **chemical level** is

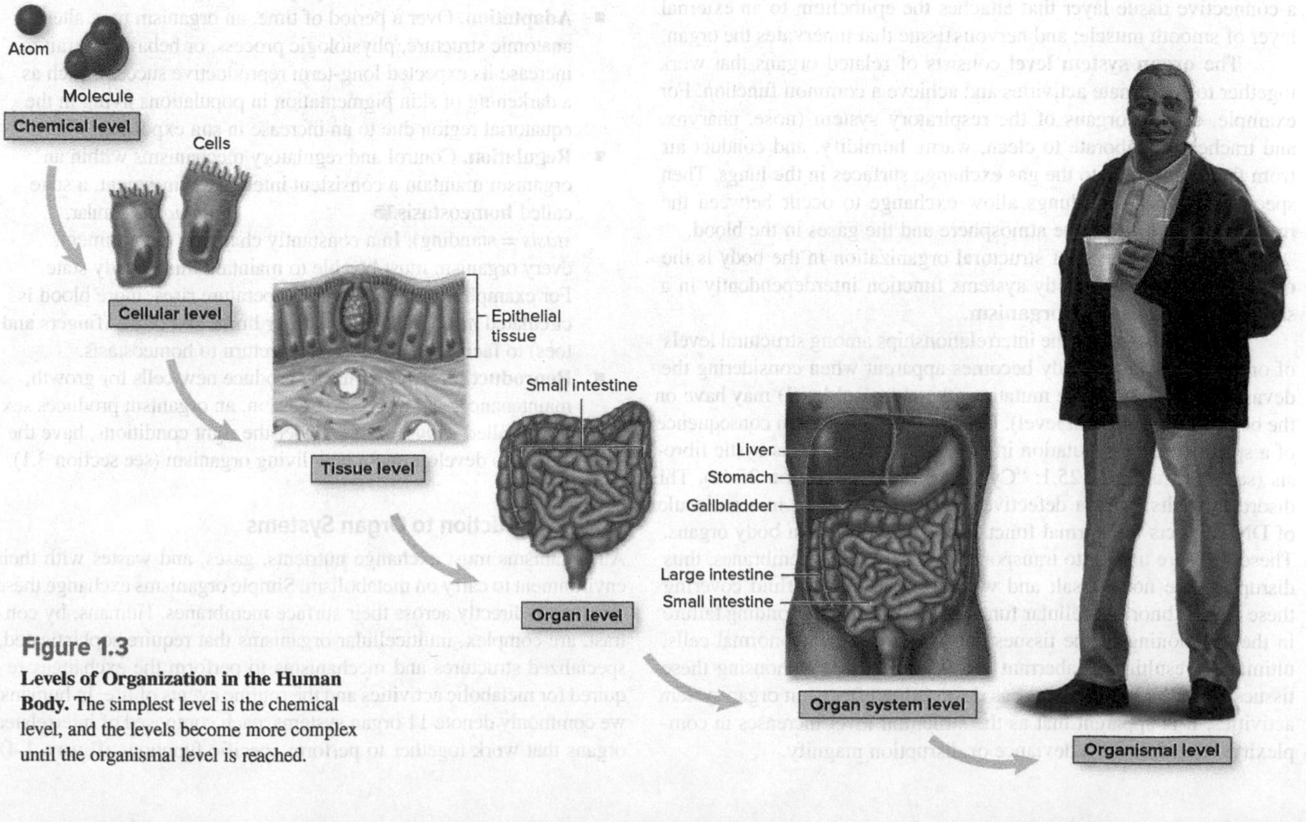
Atom
Molecule
Chemical level
Cells
Cellular level
Epithelial tissue
Tissue level
Small intestine
Organ level
Liver
Stomach
Gallbladder
Large intestine
Small intestine
Organ system level
Organismal level

Figure 1.3
Levels of Organization in the Human Body. The simplest level is the chemical level, and the levels become more complex until the organismal level is reached.

the simplest level, and it involves atoms and molecules. **Atoms** are the smallest units of matter. When two or more atoms combine, they form a **molecule.** Examples of molecules include a sugar, a water molecule, or a vitamin. More complex molecules are called **macromolecules** and include some proteins and the deoxyribonucleic acid (DNA) molecules. Macromolecules form **organelles,** which are microscopic structures found within cells.

The **cellular level** consists of **cells,** which are the smallest living structures and serve as the basic units of structure and function in organisms. Cells and their components are formed from the atoms and molecules from the chemical level. The structures of cells vary widely, reflecting the specializations needed for their different functions. For example, a skeletal muscle cell may be very long and contain numerous organized protein filaments that aid in muscle contraction, whereas a simple squamous epithelial cell (found in the lung air sac lining) is small and flattened to allow for efficient diffusion of respiratory gases.

Groups of similar cells with a common function form the next stage in the hierarchy, the **tissue level. Tissues** are precise organizations of similar cells that perform specialized functions. The four types of tissues and their general roles in the human body are (1) epithelial tissue (covers exposed surfaces and lines body cavities); (2) connective tissue (protects, supports, and interconnects body parts and organs); (3) muscle tissue (produces movement); and (4) nervous tissue (conducts impulses for internal communication).

At the **organ level,** different tissue types combine to form an organ, such as the small intestine, brain, lungs, stomach, or heart. **Organs** contain two or more tissue types that work together to perform specific, complex functions. The small intestine, for example, has different structural and organizational relationships within its tissues that work together to process and absorb digested nutrients. Thus, the small intestine shown in figure 1.3 exhibits all four tissue types: an internal lining composed of simple columnar epithelium; a connective tissue layer that attaches the epithelium to an external layer of smooth muscle; and nervous tissue that innervates the organ.

The **organ system level** consists of related organs that work together to coordinate activities and achieve a common function. For example, several organs of the respiratory system (nose, pharynx, and trachea) collaborate to clean, warm, humidify, and conduct air from the atmosphere to the gas exchange surfaces in the lungs. Then special air sacs in the lungs allow exchange to occur between the respiratory gases from the atmosphere and the gases in the blood.

The highest level of structural organization in the body is the **organismal level.** All body systems function interdependently in a single living human, the **organism.**

The importance of the interrelationships among structural levels of organization in the body becomes apparent when considering the devastating effects a gene mutation (the chemical level) may have on the body (the organismal level). For example, a common consequence of a specific genetic mutation in an individual's DNA is cystic fibrosis (see Clinical View 25.1: "Cystic Fibrosis" in section 25.1a). This disorder results when a defective or abnormal region in a molecule of DNA affects the normal function of cells in certain body organs. These cells are unable to transport salt across their membranes, thus disrupting the normal salt and water balance in the fluid covering these cells. Abnormal cellular function causes a corresponding failure in the functioning of the tissues composed of these abnormal cells, ultimately resulting in aberrant activity in the organ housing these tissues as well. Organ failure has devastating effects on organ system activities. It is apparent that as the structural level increases in complexity, the effects of a deviance or disruption magnify.

WHAT DO YOU THINK?

1. At which level of organization is the stomach? At which level is the digestive system?

1.3a Characteristics of Living Things

Life is neither defined by a single property nor exemplified by one characteristic only. The cell is the smallest structural unit that exhibits the characteristics of living things (organisms), and it is the smallest living portion of the human body. Several properties are common to all organisms, including humans:

- **Organization.** All organisms exhibit a complex structure and order. As mentioned earlier in this section, the human body has several increasingly complex levels of organization.
- **Metabolism.** All organisms carry out various chemical reactions, collectively termed **metabolism.** These chemical reactions include breaking down ingested nutrients into digestible particles, using the cells' own energy to perform certain functions, and contracting and relaxing muscles to move the body. Metabolic activities such as ingesting nutrients and expelling wastes enable the body to continue acquiring the energy needed for life's activities.
- **Growth and development.** During their lifetime, organisms assimilate materials from their environment and exhibit increased size (growth) and increased specialization as related to form and function (development). As the human body grows in size, structures such as the brain become more complex and sophisticated.
- **Responsiveness.** All organisms sense and respond to changes in their internal or external environment. For example, a stimulus to the skin of the hand, such as extremely hot or cold temperature, causes a human to withdraw the hand from the stimulus, so as to prevent injury or damage.
- **Adaptation.** Over a period of time, an organism may alter an anatomic structure, physiologic process, or behavioral trait to increase its expected long-term reproductive success, such as a darkening of skin pigmentation in populations living in the equatorial region due to an increase in sun exposure.
- **Regulation.** Control and regulatory mechanisms within an organism maintain a consistent internal environment, a state called **homeostasis** *homoios* = similar, *stasis* = standing). In a constantly changing environment, every organism must be able to maintain this "steady state." For example, when the body temperature rises, more blood is circulated near the surfaces of our limbs and digits (fingers and toes) to facilitate heat loss and a return to homeostasis.
- **Reproduction.** All organisms produce new cells for growth, maintenance, and repair. In addition, an organism produces sex cells (called *gametes*) that, under the right conditions, have the ability to develop into a new living organism (see section 3.1).

1.3b Introduction to Organ Systems

All organisms must exchange nutrients, gases, and wastes with their environment to carry on metabolism. Simple organisms exchange these substances directly across their surface membranes. Humans, by contrast, are complex, multicellular organisms that require sophisticated, specialized structures and mechanisms to perform the exchanges required for metabolic activities and the routine events of life. In humans, we commonly denote 11 organ systems, each composed of interrelated organs that work together to perform specific functions (**figure 1.4**).

Figure 1.4

Organ Systems. Locations and major components of the 11 organ systems of the human body. (In Skeletal System and Muscular System, selected examples of bones and muscles are shown.) (*a*) Integumentary system, (*b*) skeletal system, (*c*) muscular system, (*d*) nervous system, (*e*) endocrine system, (*f*) cardiovascular system, (*g*) lymphatic system, (*h*) respiratory system, (*i*) digestive system, (*j*) urinary system, (*k*) male reproductive system, and (*l*) female reproductive system. APR

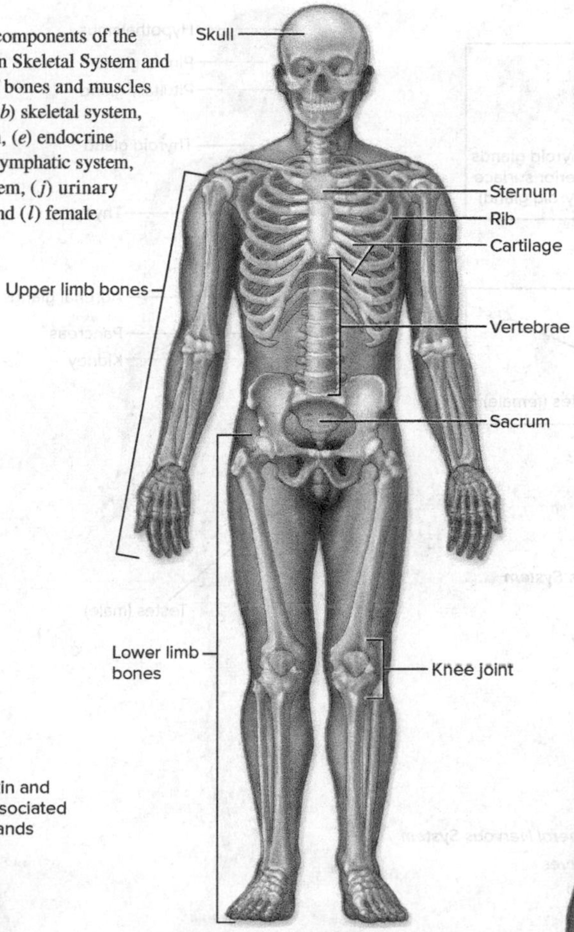
Skull
Sternum
Rib
Cartilage
Upper limb bones
Vertebrae
Sacrum
Lower limb bones
Knee joint

(b) Skeletal System (Chapters 6–9)

Provides support and protection, site of hemopoiesis (blood cell production), stores calcium and phosphorus, provides sites for muscle attachments.

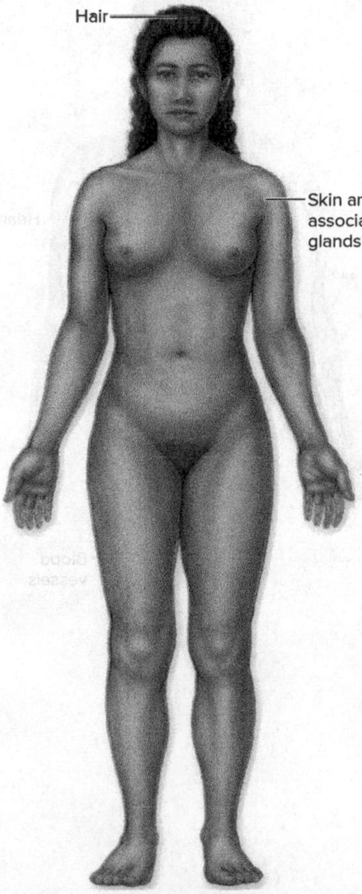
Hair
Skin and associated glands

(a) Integumentary System (Chapter 5)

Provides protection, regulates body temperature, site of cutaneous receptors, synthesizes vitamin D, prevents water loss.

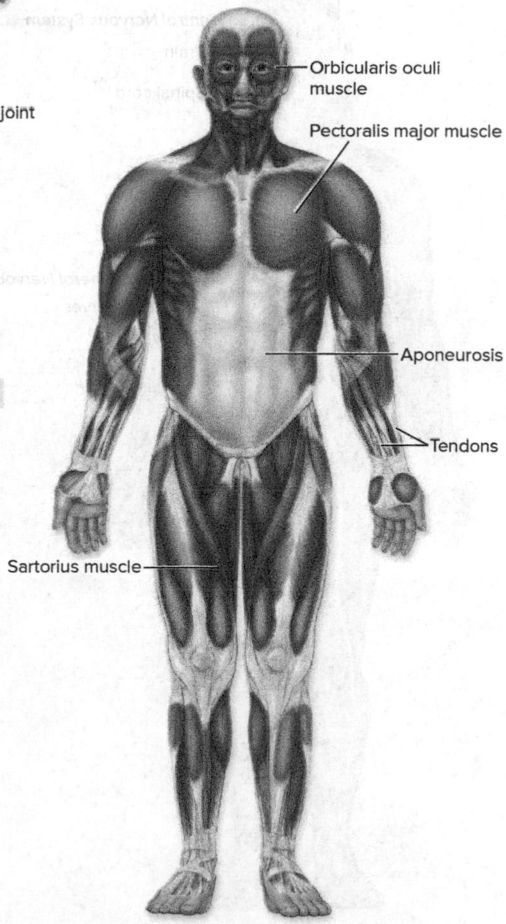
Orbicularis oculi muscle
Pectoralis major muscle
Aponeurosis
Tendons
Sartorius muscle

(c) Muscular System (Chapters 10–12)

Produces body movement, generates heat when muscles contract.

Figure 1.4
Organ Systems. ***(continued)***

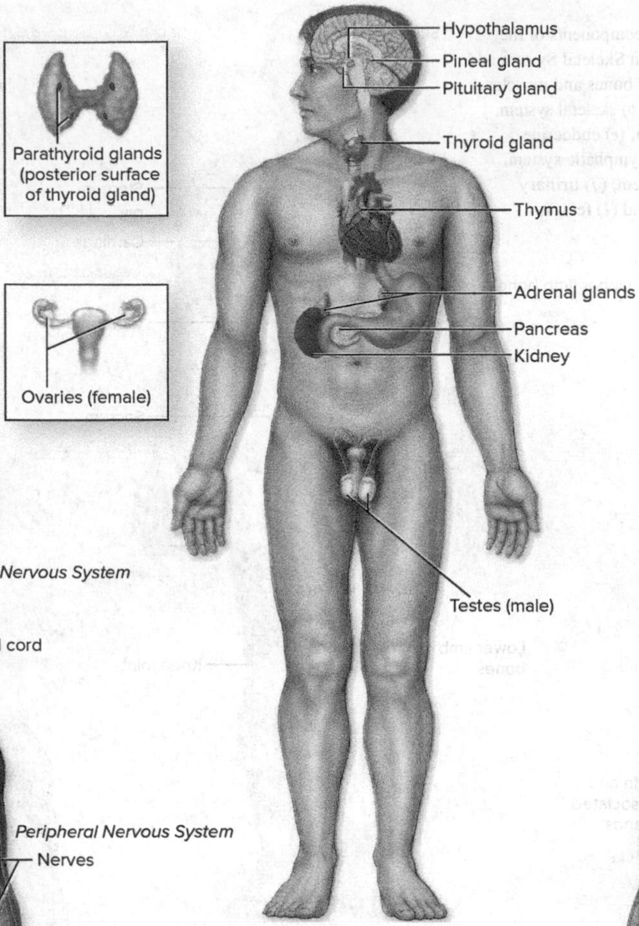
Parathyroid glands (posterior surface of thyroid gland)
Ovaries (female)
Hypothalamus
Pineal gland
Pituitary gland
Thyroid gland
Thymus
Adrenal glands
Pancreas
Kidney
Testes (male)

(e) Endocrine System (Chapter 20)
Consists of glands and cell clusters that secrete hormones, some of which regulate body and cellular growth, chemical levels in the body, and reproductive functions.

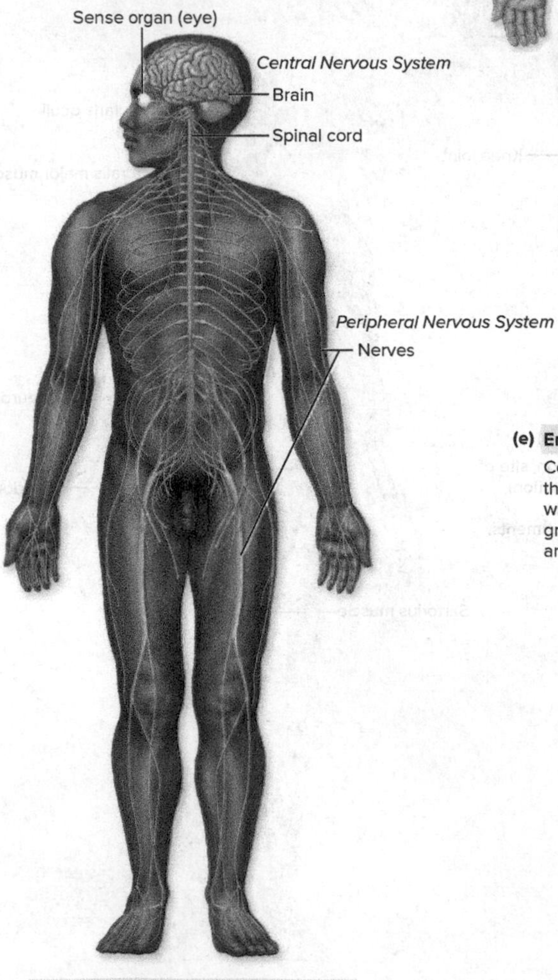
Sense organ (eye)
Central Nervous System
Brain
Spinal cord
Peripheral Nervous System
Nerves

(d) Nervous System (Chapters 14–19)
A regulatory system that controls body movement, responds to sensory stimuli, and helps control all other systems of the body. Also responsible for consciousness, intelligence, and memory.

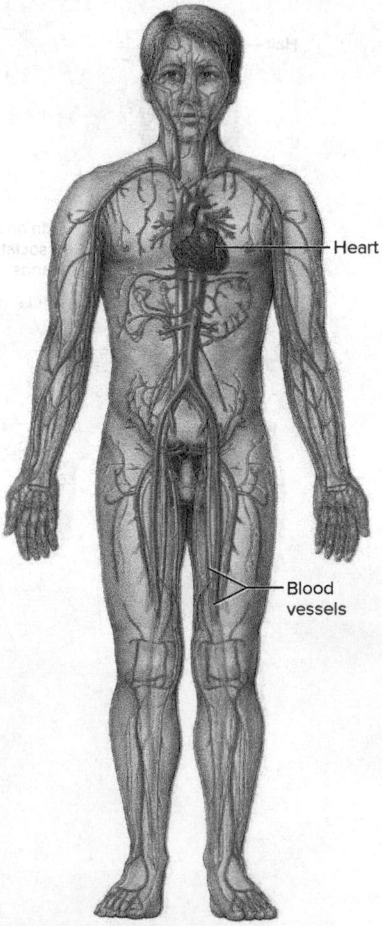
Heart
Blood vessels

(f) Cardiovascular System (Chapters 21–23)
Consists of the heart (a pump), blood, and blood vessels; the heart moves blood through blood vessels to distribute hormones, nutrients, and gases, and pick up waste products.

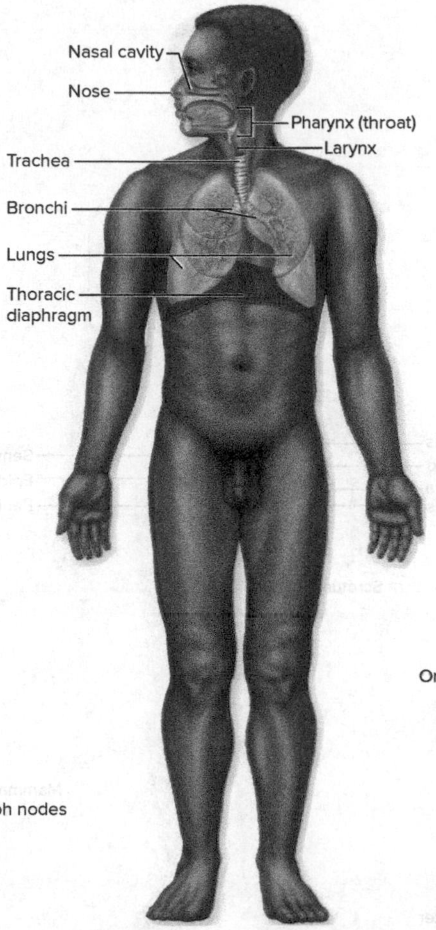
Nasal cavity
Nose
Pharynx (throat)
Larynx
Trachea
Bronchi
Lungs
Thoracic diaphragm

(h) Respiratory System (Chapter 25)
Responsible for exchange of gases (oxygen and carbon dioxide) between blood and the air in the lungs.

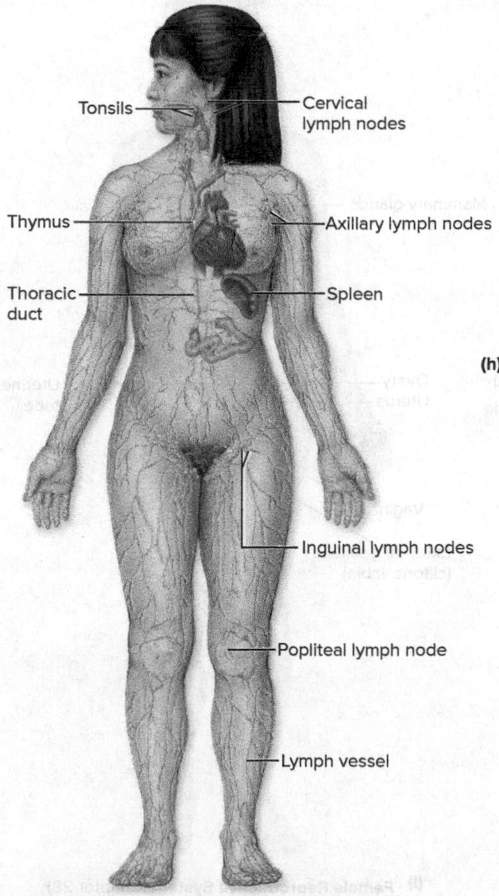
Tonsils
Cervical lymph nodes
Thymus
Axillary lymph nodes
Thoracic duct
Spleen
Inguinal lymph nodes
Popliteal lymph node
Lymph vessel

(g) Lymphatic System (Chapter 24)
Transports and filters lymph (interstitial fluid transported through lymph vessels) and initiates an immune response when necessary.

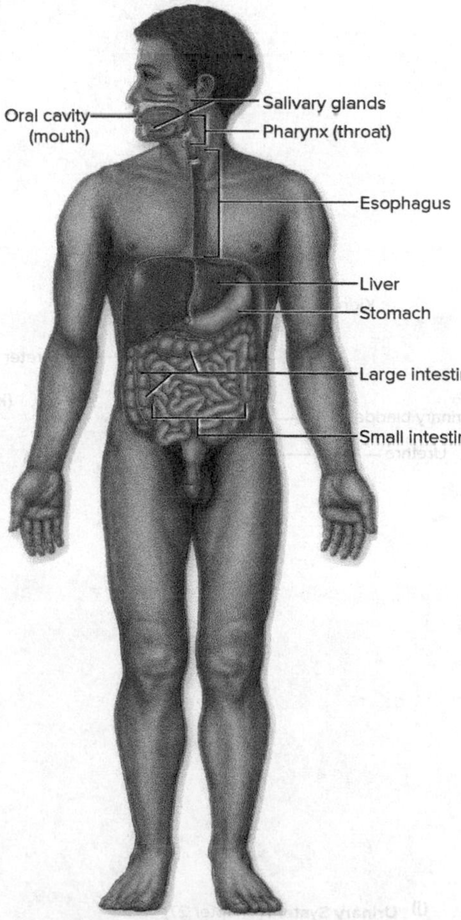
Oral cavity (mouth)
Salivary glands
Pharynx (throat)
Esophagus
Liver
Stomach
Large intestine
Small intestine

(i) Digestive System (Chapter 26)
Mechanically and chemically digests food materials, absorbs nutrients, and expels waste products.

Figure 1.4
Organ Systems. ***(continued)***

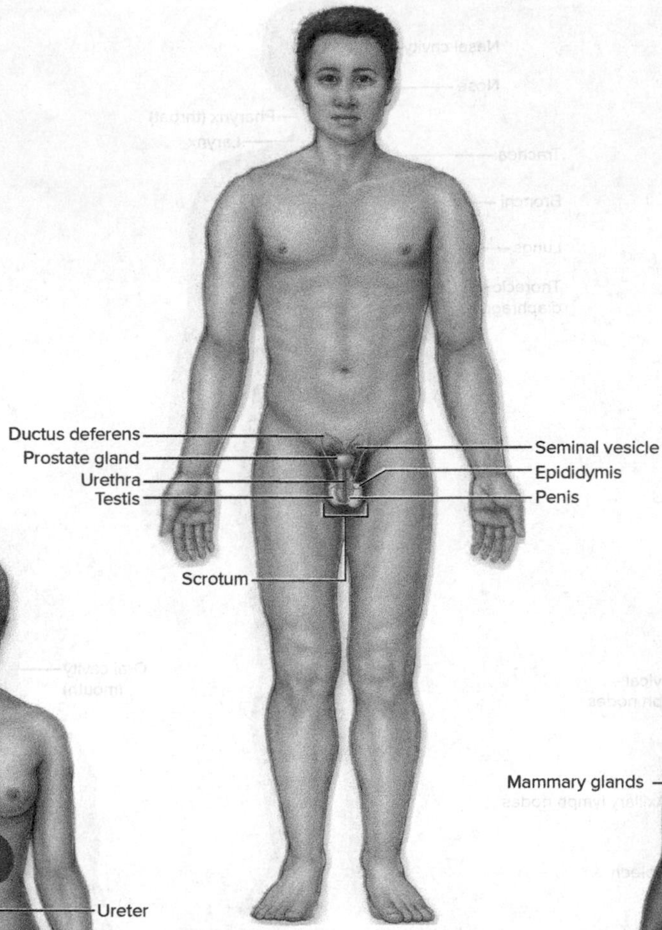
Ductus deferens
Prostate gland
Urethra
Testis
Scrotum
Seminal vesicle
Epididymis
Penis

(k) Male Reproductive System (Chapter 28)
Produces male sex cells (sperm) and male hormones (e.g., testosterone); transfers sperm to the female.

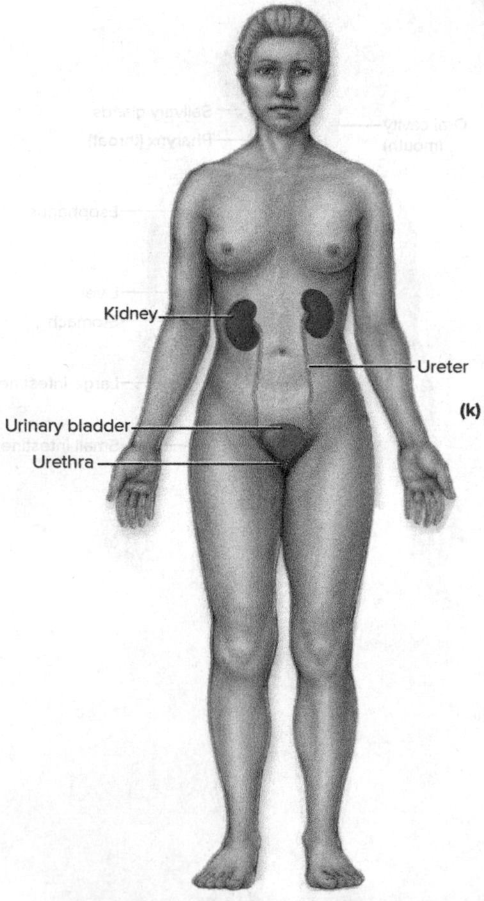
Kidney
Ureter
Urinary bladder
Urethra

(j) Urinary System (Chapter 27)
Filters the blood and removes waste products from the blood, concentrates waste products in the form of urine, and expels urine from the body.

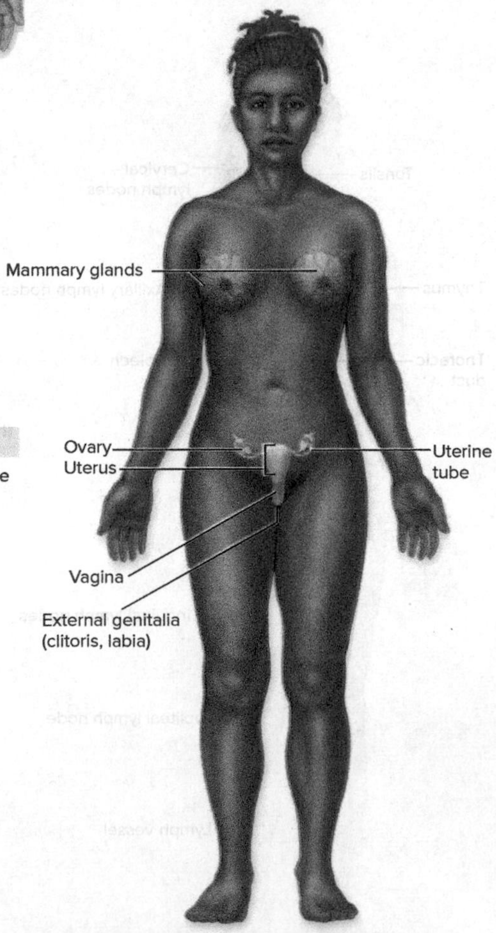
Mammary glands
Ovary
Uterus
Uterine tube
Vagina
External genitalia (clitoris, labia)

(l) Female Reproductive System (Chapter 28)
Produces female sex cells (oocytes) and female hormones (e.g., estrogen and progesterone), receives sperm from male, site of fertilization of oocyte, site of growth and development of embryo and fetus, and produces and secretes breast milk for nourishment of newborn.

Thus, a human body maintains homeostasis, or internal equilibrium, through the intricate interworkings of all its organ systems. Subsequent chapters examine each of these organ systems in detail.

WHAT DID YOU LEARN?

5 Which level of organization consists of similar cells that work together to perform a common function?

6 List four characteristics common to all organisms.

7 List the 11 anatomic body systems and some representative organs in each.

1.4 Precise Language of Anatomy

✓ Learning Objectives

10. Demonstrate the anatomic position and explain its significance.
11. Use correct terminology to define the three common anatomic planes.
12. Compare and contrast the proper terms to describe directions in the body.
13. Define the terms that describe major regions of the body.
14. Explain the terms that identify the body cavities and their subdivisions.
15. Describe the composition and function of a serous membrane.
16. Identify and list the nine regions and four quadrants of the abdominopelvic cavity.

All of us are interested in our own bodies, but we are often stymied by the seeming mountain of terminology that must be scaled before we can speak the language of anatomy correctly. For the sake of accuracy, anatomists must adhere to a set of proper terms, rather than the descriptive words of everyday conversation. For example, to properly describe human anatomic landmarks, we cannot use such common phrases as *in front of, behind, above,* or *below*. That is, it would be inaccurate to say, "The heart is above the stomach," because the heart appears to be above the stomach when a person is standing erect—but not when the person is lying on his or her back. Therefore, anatomists and health-care providers identify and locate body structures using descriptive terms based upon the premise that the body is in the anatomic position, defined in section 1.4a.

Learning Strategy 1.3

You should always rely on two resource books while using this human anatomy text: *Stedman's Medical Dictionary,* which defines all medical terms, and *Terminologia Anatomica,* which uses the proper anatomic terms and organizes them for all the body systems. Cultivating a familiarity with these resources—and with the origins of terminology—will help you acquire the vocabulary necessary for succeeding in this discipline.

1.4a Anatomic Position

Descriptions of any region or body part require an initial point of reference and the use of directional indicators. In the **anatomic position,** an individual stands upright with the feet parallel and flat on the floor. The head is level, and the eyes look forward toward the observer. The arms are at either side of the body with the palms facing forward and the thumbs pointing away from the body. (Refer to the model in the chapter-opening figure; she is standing in the anatomic position.) By visualizing the body in anatomic position, all observers have a common point of reference when describing and discussing its regions. All of the functional and directional terms used in this book refer to the body in anatomic position. APR

1.4b Sections and Planes

Anatomists refer to real or imaginary "slices" of the body, called sections or planes, to examine its internal anatomy and describe the position of one body part relative to another. The term *section* implies an actual cut or slice to expose the internal anatomy, whereas the word *plane* implies an imaginary flat surface passing through the body. The three major anatomic planes through the body or individual organs are the coronal, transverse, and midsagittal planes (**figure 1.5**).

A **coronal** (kōr′ō-năl; *korone* = crown) **plane,** also called a *frontal plane,* is a vertical plane that divides the body into *anterior* (front) and *posterior* (back) parts. When a coronal plane is taken through the trunk, the anterior portion contains the chest, and the posterior portion contains the back.

A **transverse plane,** also called a *cross-sectional plane* or *horizontal plane,* cuts perpendicularly along the long axis of the body or organ. The body or organ is separated into both *superior* (upper) and *inferior* (lower) parts, and the relationship of neighboring organs at a particular level is revealed. Computed tomography (CT) scans provide transverse sectional images of the body for study (see Clinical View 1.3: "Medical Imaging Procedures" in section 1.4f).

A **midsagittal plane** (mid′saj′i-ăl; *sagittow* = arrow), or *median plane,* extends through the body or organ vertically and divides

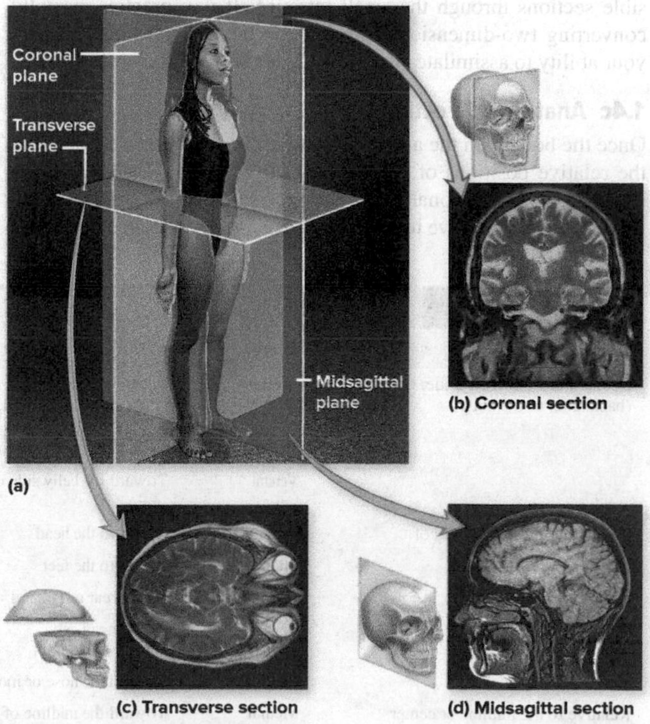

Figure 1.5

Anatomic Position and Body Planes. (*a*) In the anatomic position, the body is upright, and the forearms are positioned so the palms are facing anteriorly. A plane is an imaginary surface that slices the body into specific sections. The three major anatomic planes of reference are the (*b*) coronal, (*c*) transverse, and (*d*) midsagittal planes. APR

(a) ©McGraw-Hill Education/Joe DeGrandis, photographer; (b) ©CGinspiration/iStock/Getty Images; (c) ©Trevor Lush/The Image Bank/Getty Images; (d) ©Roxana Wegner/Getty Images the structure into right and left halves. A plane that is parallel to the midsagittal plane, but either to the left or right of it, is termed a **sagittal plane.** Thus, a sagittal plane divides a structure into right and left portions that may or may not be equal. Although there is only one midsagittal plane, an infinite number of sagittal planes are possible. A midsagittal or sagittal plane is often used to show internal body parts, especially in the head and thoracic organs.

In addition to the coronal, transverse, and midsagittal planes, there are numerous minor planes called the **oblique** (ob-lēk′) **planes** that pass through the specimen at an angle. (For an example, see **figure 1.6**, second section from the top.)

Interpreting body sections has become increasingly important for health-care professionals. Technical advances in medical imaging (see Clinical View 1.3: "Medical Imaging Procedures" in section 1.4f) have produced spectacular sectional images. To determine the shape of any object within a section, we must be able to reconstruct its three-dimensional shape by observing many continuous sections. Just as sections of a curved, twisting tube may have significantly different appearances depending upon where the section is taken, sectioning the body or an organ along different planes often results in very different views. For example, all sections (coronal, transverse, and midsagittal) through most regions of the abdominal cavity will exhibit multiple profiles of the long, twisted tube that is the small intestine. These sections will appear as circles, ovals, long tubes with parallel sides, a figure "8," and maybe a solid region because the section is through the wall only. Figure 1.6 shows the results of several possible sections through the small intestine. If you practice mentally converting two-dimensional images into three-dimensional shapes, your ability to assimilate anatomic information will advance quickly.

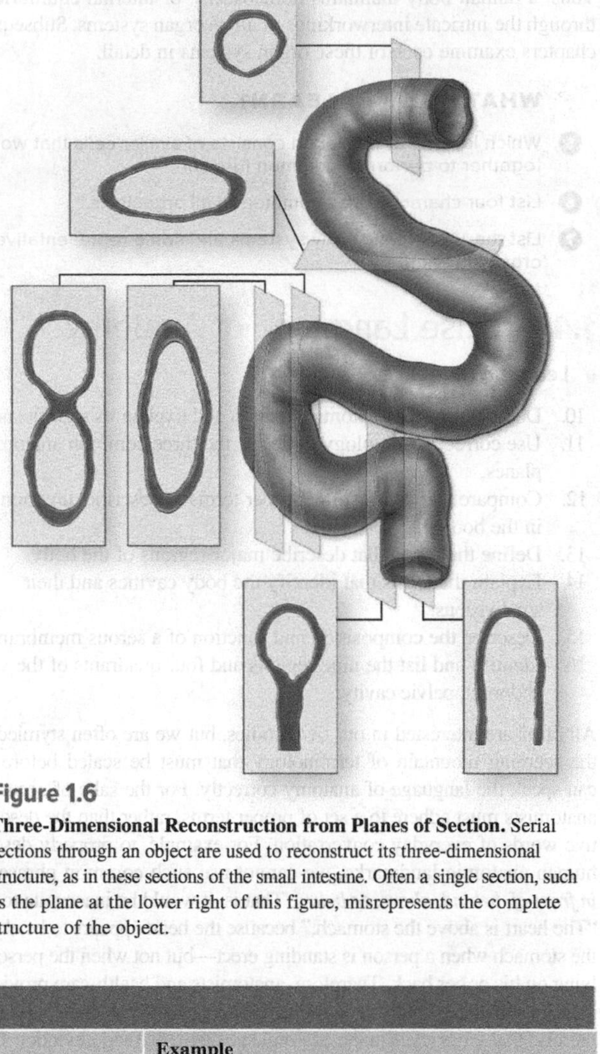

Figure 1.6

Three-Dimensional Reconstruction from Planes of Section. Serial sections through an object are used to reconstruct its three-dimensional structure, as in these sections of the small intestine. Often a single section, such as the plane at the lower right of this figure, misrepresents the complete structure of the object.

1.4c Anatomic Directions

Once the body is in the anatomic position, we can precisely describe the relative positions of various structures by using specific directional terms. Directional terms are precise and brief, and most of them have a correlative term that means just the opposite. **Table 1.2**

Table 1.2 Anatomic Directional Terms

Direction	Term	Meaning	Example
Relative to front (belly side) or back (back side) of the body	Anterior	In front of; toward the front surface	The stomach is *anterior* to the spinal cord.
	Posterior	In back of; toward the back surface	The heart is *posterior* to the sternum.
	Dorsal	Toward the back side of the human body	The spinal cord is on the *dorsal* side of the body.
	Ventral	Toward the belly side of the human body	The umbilicus (navel, belly button) is on the *ventral* side of the body.
Relative to the head or tail of the body	Superior	Closer to the head	The chest is *superior* to the pelvis.
	Inferior	Closer to the feet	The stomach is *inferior* to the heart.
	Caudal	At the rear or tail end	The abdomen is *caudal* to the head.
	Cranial (cephalic)	At the head end	The shoulders are *cranial* to the feet.
	Rostral	Toward the nose or mouth	The frontal lobe is *rostral* to the occipital lobe.
Relative to the midline or center of the body	Medial	Toward the midline of the body	The lungs are *medial* to the shoulders.
	Lateral	Away from the midline of the body	The arms are *lateral* to the heart.
	Ipsilateral	On the same side	The right arm is *ipsilateral* to the right leg.
	Contralateral	On the opposite side	The right arm is *contralateral* to the left leg.
	Deep	On the inside, internal to another structure	The heart is *deep* to the rib cage.
	Superficial	On the outside, external to another structure	The skin is *superficial* to the biceps brachii muscle.
Relative to point of attachment of the appendage	Proximal	Closest to point of attachment to trunk	The elbow is *proximal* to the hand.
	Distal	Furthest from point of attachment to trunk	The wrist is *distal* to the elbow.

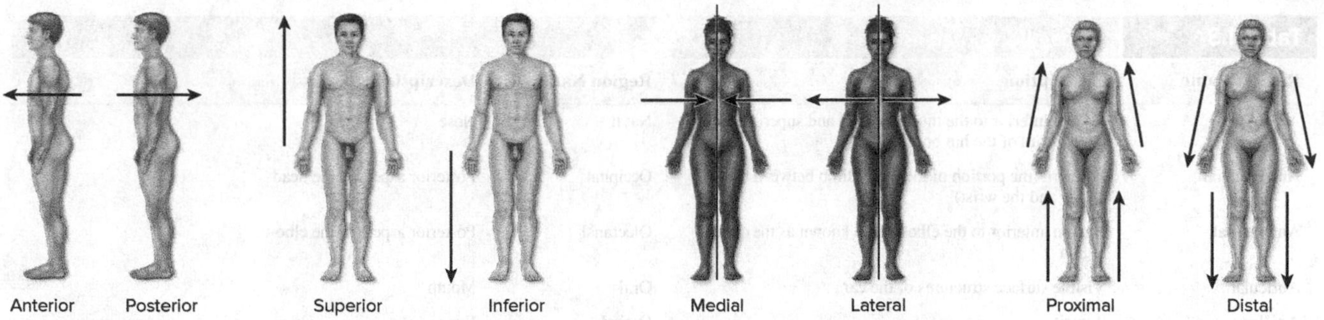
Anterior
Posterior
Superior
Inferior
Medial
Lateral
Proximal
Distal

Figure 1.7

Directional Terms in Anatomy. Directional terms precisely describe the location and relative relationships of body parts. This image visually represents eight of the most common directional terms used in anatomy. See also table 1.2. APR

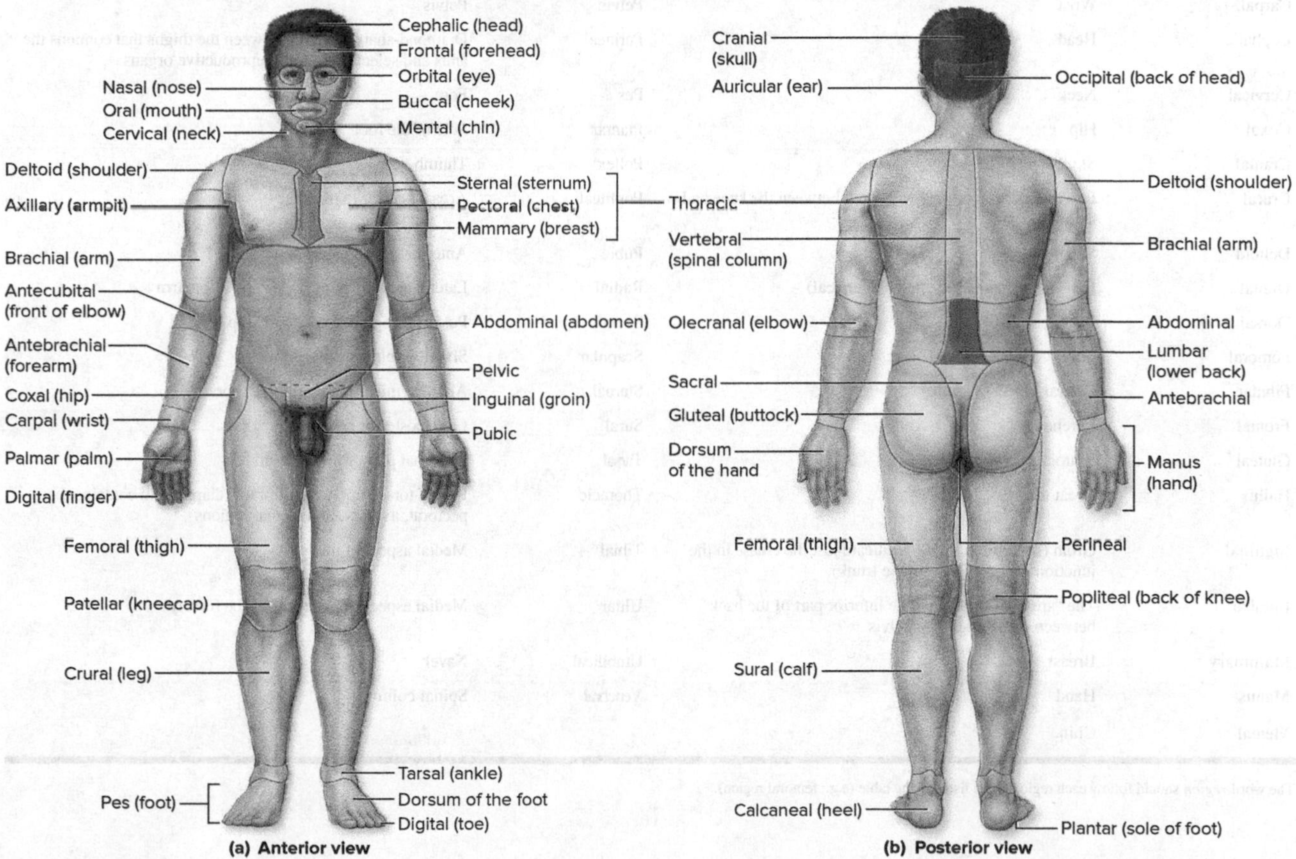
Cephalic (head)
Frontal (forehead)
Orbital (eye)
Nasal (nose)
Buccal (cheek)
Oral (mouth)
Mental (chin)
Cervical (neck)
Deltoid (shoulder)
Sternal (sternum)
Axillary (armpit)
Pectoral (chest)
Mammary (breast)
Thoracic
Brachial (arm)
Antecubital (front of elbow)
Abdominal (abdomen)
Antebrachial (forearm)
Pelvic
Coxal (hip)
Inguinal (groin)
Carpal (wrist)
Pubic
Palmar (palm)
Digital (finger)
Femoral (thigh)
Patellar (kneecap)
Crural (leg)
Tarsal (ankle)
Pes (foot)
Dorsum of the foot
Digital (toe)
(a) Anterior view
Cranial (skull)
Auricular (ear)
Occipital (back of head)
Deltoid (shoulder)
Vertebral (spinal column)
Brachial (arm)
Olecranal (elbow)
Abdominal
Lumbar (lower back)
Sacral
Antebrachial
Gluteal (buttock)
Dorsum of the hand
Manus (hand)
Femoral (thigh)
Perineal
Popliteal (back of knee)
Sural (calf)
Calcaneal (heel)
Plantar (sole of foot)
(b) Posterior view

Figure 1.8

Key Body Regions. (*a*) Anterior and (*b*) posterior views identify the key regions of the body. The word *region* should follow each of the terms listed in the figure (e.g., femoral region). Their common names appear in parentheses. APR

and **figure 1.7** describe some important and commonly used directional terms. Studying the table and the figure together will maximize your understanding of anatomic directions and aid your study of anatomy throughout the rest of this book.

1.4d Regional Anatomy

The human body is partitioned into two main regions, called the axial and appendicular regions. The **axial** (ak′sē-ăl) **region** includes the head, neck, and trunk; it forms the main vertical axis of the body. Our limbs, or appendages, attach to the body's axis and make up the **appendicular** (ap′en-dik′ū-lăr) **region.** Several specific terms are used to identify the anatomic areas within these two regions. **Figure 1.8** and **table 1.3** identify the major regional terms and some additional minor ones. (Not all regions are shown in figure 1.8.)

Table 1.3 Human Body Regions[1]

Region Name	Description	Region Name	Description
Abdominal	Region inferior to the thorax (chest) and superior to the pelvic brim of the hip bones	Nasal	Nose
Antebrachial	Forearm (the portion of the upper limb between the elbow and the wrist)	Occipital	Posterior aspect of the head
Antecubital	Region anterior to the elbow; also known as the cubital region	Olecranal	Posterior aspect of the elbow
Auricular	Visible surface structures of the ear	Oral	Mouth
Axillary	Armpit	Orbital	Eye
Brachial	Arm (the portion of the upper limb between the shoulder and the elbow)	Palmar	Palm of the hand
Buccal	Cheek	Patellar	Kneecap
Calcaneal	Heel of the foot	Pectoral	Chest, includes the mammary region
Carpal	Wrist	Pelvic	Pelvis
Cephalic	Head	Perineal	Diamond-shaped region between the thighs that contains the anus and selected external reproductive organs
Cervical	Neck	Pes	Foot
Coxal	Hip	Plantar	Sole of the foot
Cranial	Skull	Pollex	Thumb
Crural	Leg (the portion of the lower limb between the knee and the ankle)	Popliteal	Area posterior to the knee
Deltoid	Shoulder	Pubic	Anterior region of the pelvis
Digital	Fingers or toes (also called phalangeal)	Radial	Lateral aspect (thumb side) of the forearm
Dorsal	Back	Sacral	Posterior region between the hip bones
Femoral	Thigh	Scapular	Shoulder blade
Fibular	Lateral aspect of the leg	Sternal	Anterior middle region of the thorax
Frontal	Forehead	Sural	Calf (posterior part of the leg)
Gluteal	Buttock	Tarsal	Proximal part of foot and ankle
Hallux	Great toe	Thoracic	Part of torso superior to thoracic diaphragm; contains the pectoral, axillary, and sternal regions
Inguinal	Groin (sometimes used to indicate just the crease in the junction of the thigh with the trunk)	Tibial	Medial aspect of the leg
Lumbar	The "small of the back": the inferior part of the back between the ribs and the pelvis	Ulnar	Medial aspect (pinky side) of the forearm
Mammary	Breast	Umbilical	Navel
Manus	Hand	Vertebral	Spinal column
Mental	Chin		

[1] The word *region* should follow each region name listed in the table (e.g., femoral region).

1.4e Body Cavities and Membranes

Internal organs and organ systems are housed within separate enclosed spaces, or cavities. These body cavities are named according to the bones that surround them or the organs they contain. For purposes of discussion, the axial region is subdivided into two areas: the posterior aspect and the ventral cavity.

Posterior Aspect

The **posterior aspect** has two enclosed cavities (**figure 1.9*a***). A **cranial cavity** is formed by the cranium, and so it also goes by the name *endocranium*. It houses the brain. A **vertebral** (ver′te-br ăl) **canal** is formed by the individual bones of the vertebral column and contains the spinal cord. These two cavities are encased in bone and thus are physically and developmentally different from the ventral cavity. The term *dorsal body cavity* has been used by others to describe this posterior aspect, but is not used here because of these differences between the posterior aspect and the ventral cavity.

Ventral Cavity

The **ventral cavity** is the larger, anteriorly placed cavity in the body. The ventral cavity is partitioned into a superior **thoracic** (thō-ras′ik) **cavity** and an inferior **abdominopelvic** (ab-dom ′i-nō-pel′vik) **cavity** by the thoracic **diaphragm** (figure 1.9).

Both the thoracic and abdominopelvic cavities are lined by thin **serous membranes,** which are composed of two layers. A **parietal** (pă-rī′ĕ-tăl) **layer** typically lines the internal surface of the

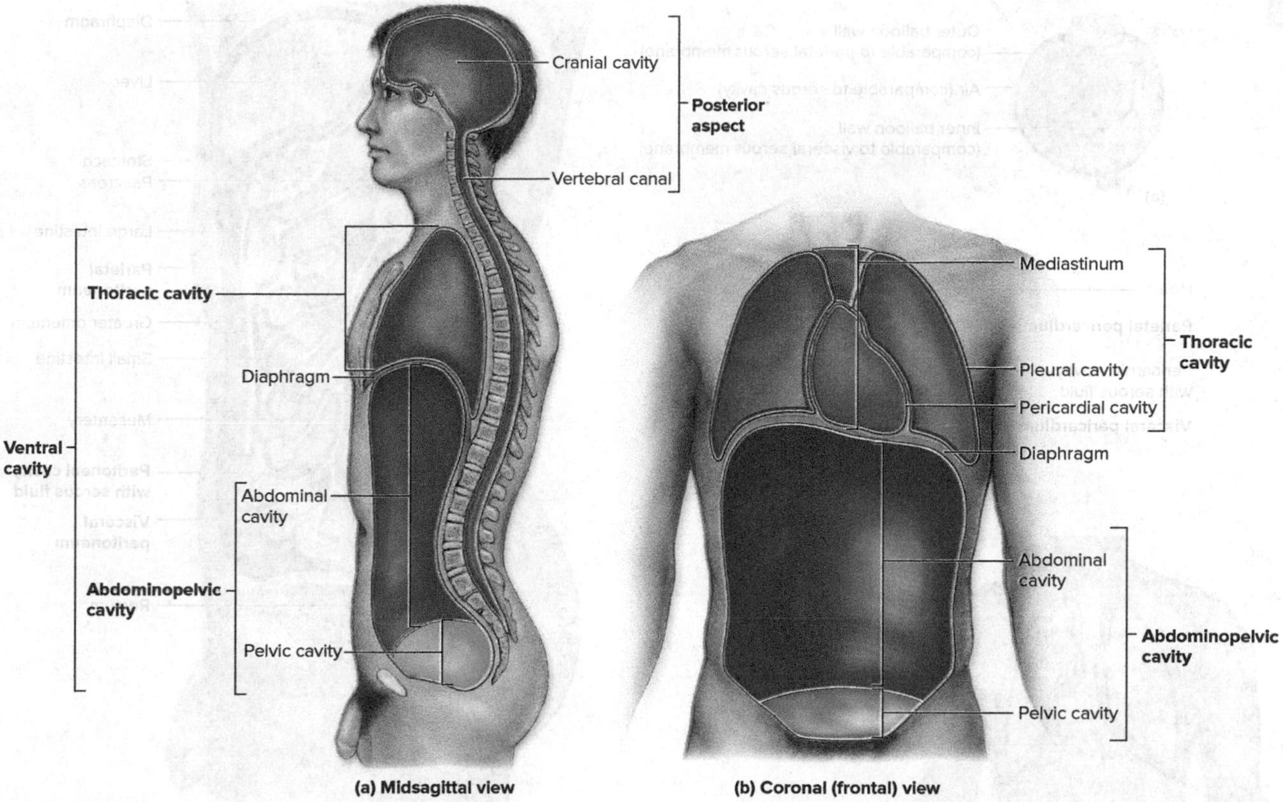
Cranial cavity
Posterior aspect
Vertebral canal
Thoracic cavity
Diaphragm
Ventral cavity
Abdominal cavity
Abdominopelvic cavity
Pelvic cavity
(a) Midsagittal view
Mediastinum
Thoracic cavity
Pleural cavity
Pericardial cavity
Diaphragm
Abdominal cavity
Abdominopelvic cavity
Pelvic cavity
(b) Coronal (frontal) view

Figure 1.9

Body Cavities. The body is composed of two main spaces: the posterior aspect and the ventral cavity. Many vital organs are housed within these spaces. (*a*) A midsagittal view shows both the posterior aspect and the ventral cavity. (*b*) A coronal view shows the relationship between the thoracic and abdominopelvic cavities within the ventral cavity. APR

body wall, whereas a **visceral** (vis′er-ăl) **layer** covers the external surface of organs (**viscera**) within the cavity. Between the parietal and visceral layers of the serous membrane is a potential space called the **serous cavity** (a potential space is capable of becoming a larger cavity). Serous membranes secrete a liquid called **serous fluid** within a serous cavity. Serous fluid has the consistency of oil and serves as a lubricant. In a living human, the organs (e.g., heart, lungs, stomach, and intestines) move and rub against each other and the body wall. This constant movement causes friction. The serous fluid's lubricant properties reduce this friction and help the organs move smoothly against both one another and the body wall.

WHAT DO YOU THINK?

2 Try this experiment to determine the value of serous fluid: First, rub the palms of your hands quickly against one another. The sound you hear and the heat you feel are consequences of the friction being produced. Now put lotion (our version of serous fluid) on the palms of your hands and repeat the experiment. Do you still hear the noise and feel heat from your hands? What do you think would happen to your body organs if there were no serous fluid?

Figure 1.10*a* provides a helpful analogy for visualizing the serous membrane layers. The closed fist is comparable to an organ, and the balloon is comparable to a serous membrane. When a fist is pushed into the wall of the balloon, the inner balloon wall that surrounds the fist is comparable to the visceral layer of the serous membrane. The outer balloon wall is comparable to the parietal layer of the serous membrane. The thin, air-filled space within the balloon, between the two "walls," is comparable to the serous cavity. The organ is not *inside* the serous cavity; it is actually *outside* this cavity and merely covered by the visceral layer of the serous membrane!

Thoracic Cavity The median space in the thoracic cavity is called the **mediastinum** (me′d ē-as-tī′nŭm) (see figure 1.9*b*). It contains the heart, thymus, esophagus, trachea, and major blood vessels.

Within the mediastinum, the heart is enclosed by a two-layered serous membrane called the **pericardium** (see figure 1.10*b*). The **parietal pericardium** (per-i-kar′d ē-ŭm; *peri* = around, *kardia* = heart) is the outermost layer and forms the sac around the heart; the **visceral pericardium** (also called *epicardium*; *epi* = upon) forms the heart's external surface. The **pericardial cavity** is the potential space between the parietal and visceral pericardia; it contains serous fluid (see section 22.1c).

The right and left sides of the thoracic cavity contain the lungs, which are lined by a two-layered serous membrane called the **pleura** (plūr′ă) (see figure 1.10*c*). The outer layer of this serous membrane is the **parietal pleura;** it lines the internal surface of the thoracic wall. The inner layer of this serous membrane is the **visceral pleura;** it covers the external surface of the lung. The narrow, moist, potential space between the parietal and visceral layers is called the **pleural cavity,** and it contains serous fluid (see section 25.4a).

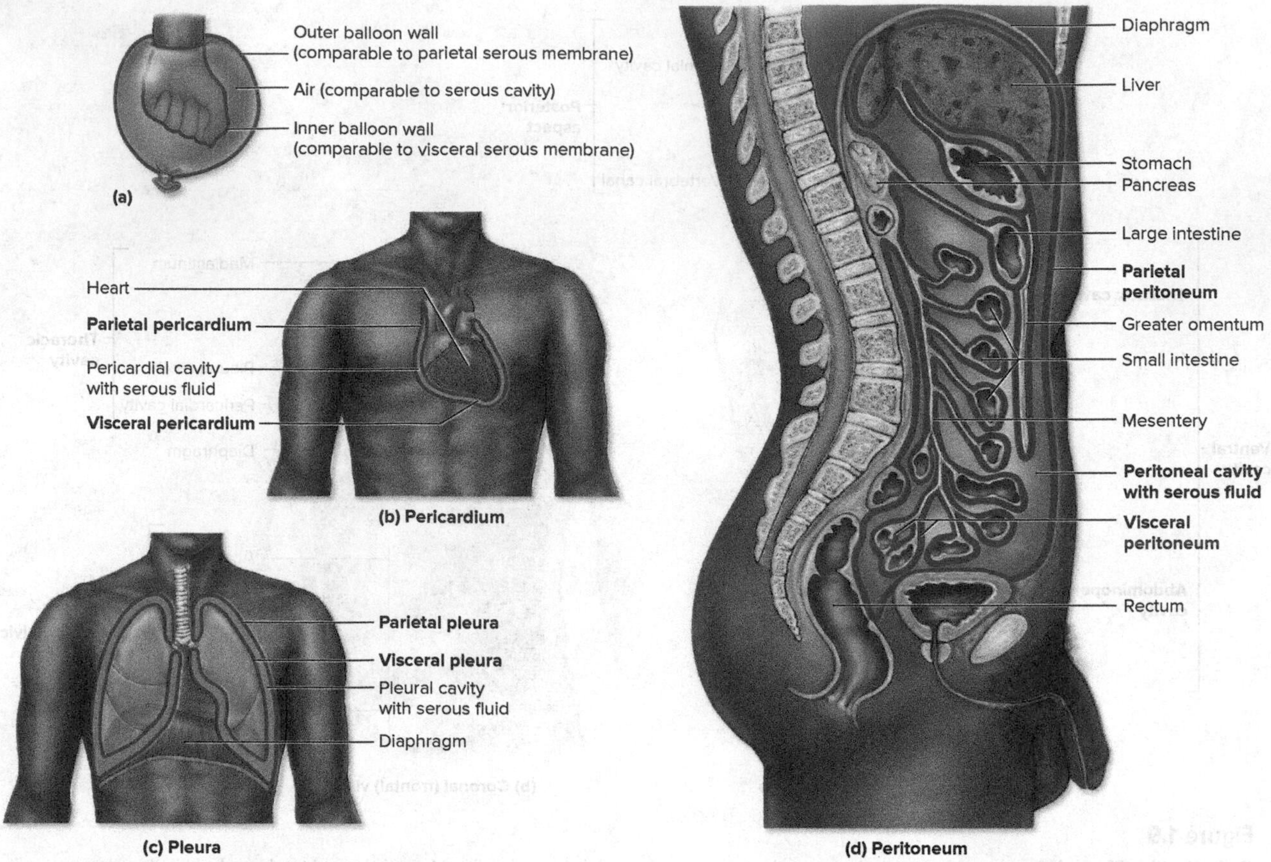

Figure 1.10

Serous Membranes in the Thoracic and Abdominopelvic Body Cavities. Serous membranes have two layers: the lining of the inside of the cavity (parietal layer) and the lining of the outside of an organ within the cavity (visceral layer). (*a*) The parietal and visceral serous membranes are similar to the inner and outer walls of a balloon that wrap around a fist, where the fist represents the body organ. (*b*) Parietal and visceral layers of the pericardium surround the pericardial cavity around the heart. (*c*) Parietal and visceral layers of the pleura surround the pleural cavity between the lungs and the chest wall. (*d*) Parietal and visceral layers of the peritoneum surround the peritoneal cavity that lies between the abdominopelvic organs and the body wall. APR

Abdominopelvic Cavity The abdominopelvic cavity consists of an **abdominal cavity,** which is superior to the pelvic brim of the hip bones (see section 8.3b), and a **pelvic cavity** that is inferior to the pelvic brim. The abdominal cavity contains most of the organs of the digestive system, as well as the kidneys and ureters of the urinary system. The organs of the pelvic cavity consist of the distal part of the large intestine, the urinary bladder and urethra, and the internal reproductiveorgans.

The **peritoneum** (per′i-tō-nē′ŭm; *periteino* = to stretch over) is a moist, two-layered serous membrane that lines the abdominopelvic cavity (see figure 1.10*d*). The **parietal peritoneum,** the outer layer of this serous membrane, lines the internal walls of the abdominopelvic cavity, whereas the **visceral peritoneum,** the inner layer of this serous membrane, ensheathes the external surfaces of most of the digestive organs. The potential space between these serous membrane layers in the abdominopelvic cavity is the **peritoneal cavity,** where the lubricating serous fluid is located (see section 26.4a). APR

Table 1.4 summarizes the characteristics of the body cavities.

1.4f Abdominopelvic Regions and Quadrants

To accurately describe organ location in the larger abdominopelvic cavity, anatomists and health-care professionals commonly partition the cavity into smaller, imaginary compartments. Nine compartments, called **abdominopelvic regions,** are delineated by using two transverse planes and two sagittal planes. The nine regions are arranged into three rows (superior, middle, and inferior) and three columns (left, middle, and right) (**figure 1.11*a***). Each region has a specific name:

- The **epigastric** (ep-i-gas′trik; *epi* = above, *gaster* = belly) **region,** the superior region in the middle column of the abdomen, typically contains part of the liver, part of the stomach, the duodenum, part of the pancreas, and both adrenal glands.
- The **umbilical** (ŭm-bil′i-kăl; *umbilicus* = navel) **region,** the middle region in the middle column of the abdomen, typically contains the transverse colon (middle part), part of the small intestine, and the branches of the blood vessels to the lower limbs.

Table 1.4	Body Cavities	
Posterior Aspect Cavities	**Description**	**Serous Membrane**
Cranial cavity	Formed by the cranium; houses the brain	None
Vertebral canal	Formed by the vertebral column; contains the spinal cord	None
Ventral Cavities	**Description**	**Serous Membrane**
THORACIC CAVITY	Chest cavity; bordered anteriorly and laterally by chest wall and inferiorly by diaphragm	
Mediastinum	Contains the pericardial cavity, heart, thymus, trachea, esophagus, and major blood vessels	None
Pericardial	Central region associated with the heart	Pericardium
Pleural	Lateral regions associated with the lungs	Pleura
ABDOMINOPELVIC CAVITY	Composed of two parts: abdominal and pelvic cavities	
Abdominal	Bordered superiorly by the diaphragm and inferiorly by the pelvic brim of the hip bones (see section 8.3b). Associated with the abdominal viscera, including stomach, spleen, liver, pancreas, small intestine, most of large intestine, kidneys, ureters	Peritoneum
Pelvic	Region located inferior to the pelvic brim of the hip bones (see section 8.3b). Associated with the pelvic viscera, including urinary bladder and urethra, internal reproductive organs, some of the large intestine	Peritoneum

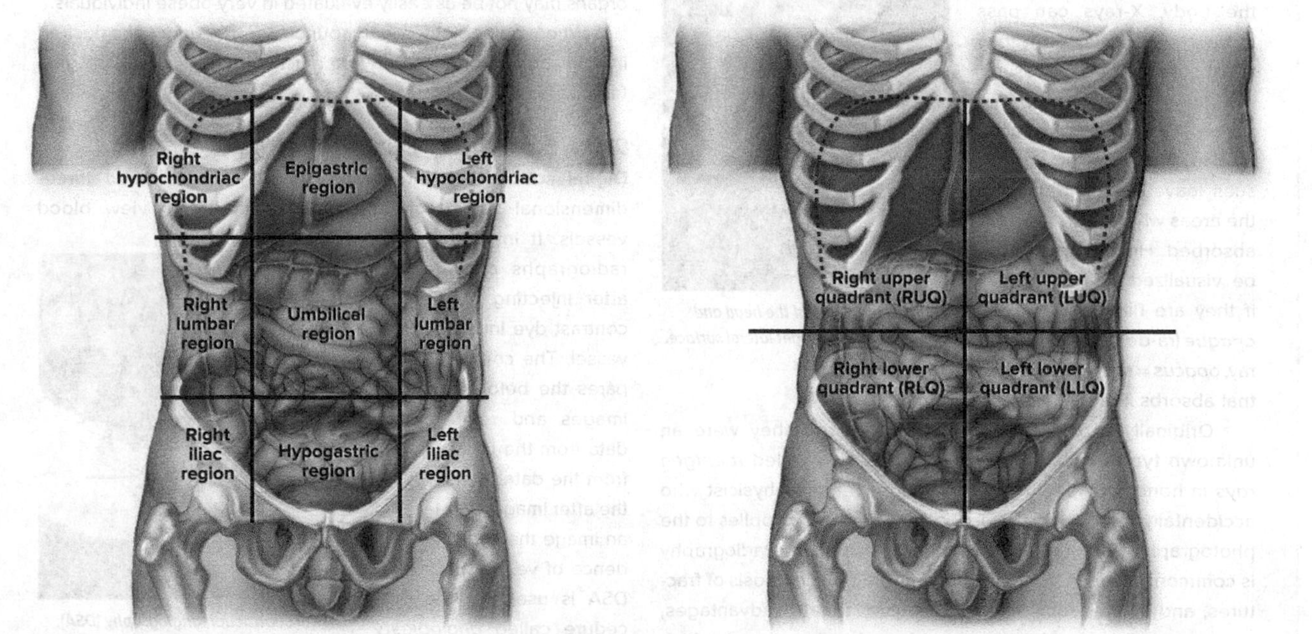

Figure 1.11
Abdominopelvic Regions and Quadrants. The abdominopelvic cavity can be subdivided into *(a)* nine regions or *(b)* four quadrants for purposes of description or identification. APR

- The **hypogastric** (hī-pō-gas′trik; *hypo* = under, *gaster* = belly) **region,** the inferior region in the middle column of the abdomen, typically contains part of the small intestine, the urinary bladder, and the sigmoid colon of the large intestine.
- The **right** and **left hypochondriac** (hī-pō-kon′drē-ak; *hypo* = under, *chondros* = cartilage) **regions** are the superior regions lateral to the epigastric region. The right hypochondriac region typically contains part of the liver, the gallbladder, and part of the right kidney; the left hypochondriac region typically contains part of the stomach, the spleen, the left colic flexure of the large intestine, and part of the left kidney.
- The **right** and **left lumbar regions** are the middle regions lateral to the umbilical region. The right lumbar region typically contains the ascending colon and the right colic flexure of the large intestine, the superior part of the cecum, part of the right kidney, and part of the small intestine; the left

Clinical View 1.3

Medical Imaging Procedures

To extend their ability to visualize internal body structures noninvasively (without inserting an instrument into the body), health-care professionals have taken advantage of various medical imaging techniques. Many of these techniques have quickly advanced health care and modern medicine. Some of the most common techniques are radiography, sonography, computed tomography, digital subtraction angiography, dynamic spatial reconstruction, magnetic resonance imaging, and positron emission tomography.

Radiography

Radiography (rā′dē-og′ră-fē; *radius* = ray, *grapho* = to write) is the primary method of obtaining a clinical image of a body part for diagnostic purposes. A beam of **x-rays,** which are a form of high-energy radiation, penetrates solid structures within the body. X-rays can pass through soft tissues, but they are absorbed by dense tissues, including bone, teeth, and tumors. Film images produced by x-rays passing through tissues leave the film lighter in the areas where the x-rays are absorbed. Hollow organs can be visualized by radiography if they are filled with a ***radiopaque*** (rā-dē-ō-pāk′; *radius* = ray, *opacus* = shady) substance that absorbs x-rays.

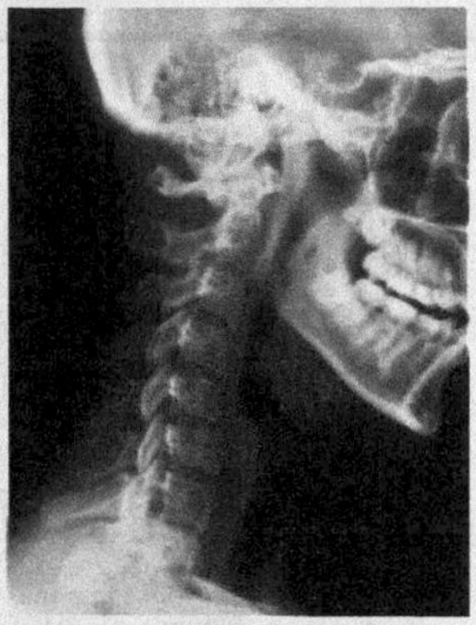

Radiograph (x-ray) of the head and neck, viewed from right lateral surface.
©HT-Pix/Getty Images

Originally, x-rays got their name because they were an unknown type of radiation, but they are also called *roentgen rays* in honor of Wilhelm Roentgen, the German physicist who accidentally discovered them. The term *x-ray* also applies to the photograph (radiograph) made by this technique. Radiography is commonly used in dentistry, mammography, diagnosis of fractures, and chest examination. In terms of their disadvantages, x-rays sometimes produce images of overlapping organs, which can be confusing, and they are unable to reveal slight differences in tissue density.

Ultrasound

The second most widely used imaging method is **ultrasound**, also known as *sonography* (sō-nog′ră-fē; *sonus* = sound, *grapho* = to write). Generally, a technician slowly moves a small, handheld device called a **transducer** across the body surface. This device produces high-frequency ultrasound waves and then receives signals that are reflected from internal organs. Ultrasound is the imaging choice in obstetrics to show the location of the placenta and help evaluate fetal age, position, and development. Ultrasound avoids the harmful effects of x-rays, and the equipment is inexpensive and portable. Many physicians are using handheld ultrasounds and are able to keep the device in a pocket and thus examine patients in their rooms. Ultrasound can visualize most organ systems and is used frequently in the ER to determine if someone has experienced internal bleeding. Cardiologists utilize ultrasound to evaluate the function and competency of the heart valves, and to determine if heart function has been compromised. Anesthesiologists use ultrasound to help guide them with anesthetic needle insertion. The primary disadvantage of ultrasound is that it does not produce as sharp an image as other methods, and some organs may not be as easily evaluated in very obese individuals.

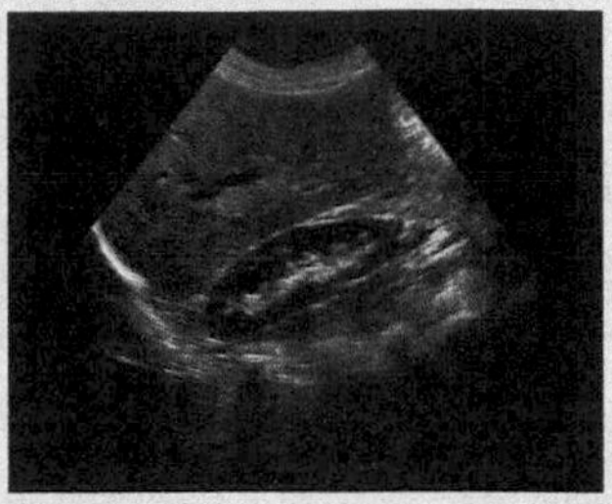

Ultrasound of the liver and right kidney.
©flik47/iStock/Getty Images

When radiography or ultrasound cannot produce the desired images, other more detailed (but much more expensive) imaging techniques are available.

Digital Subtraction Angiography (DSA)

Digital subtraction angiography (DSA) is a modified three-dimensional x-ray technique used primarily to view blood vessels. It involves taking radiographs prior to and after injecting an opaque contrast dye into the blood vessel. The computer compares the before and after images and removes the data from the before image from the data generated by the after image, thus leaving an image that indicates evidence of vessel blockages. DSA is useful in the procedure called *angioplasty* (an′jē-ō-plas-tē; *angos* = a vessel, *plastos* = formed), in which a physician directs a **catheter** (a flexible tube) through the blood vessels and puts a stent in the area where the vessel is blocked. The image produced by the DSA allows the physician to accurately guide the catheter to the blockage. A drawback of DSA is that it is an invasive procedure—a contrast must be injected, and a catheter is inserted into the vessel. For vessel image production, DSA is being more frequently replaced by the noninvasive techniques CTA (CT angiography) or MRA (MR angiography), both of which produce

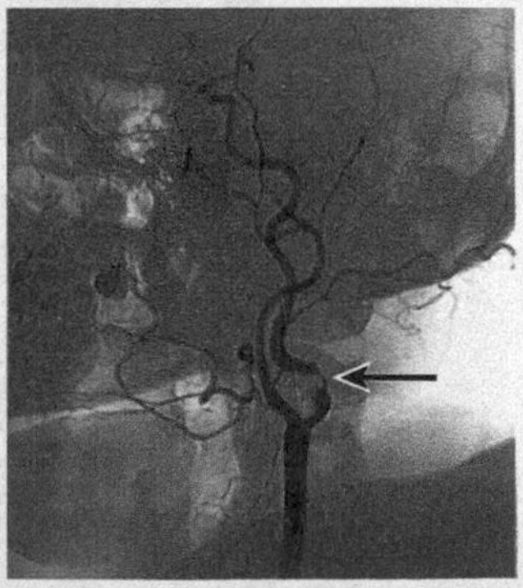

Digital subtraction angiography (DSA), anterior view with the head turned laterally, shows the head and neck vessels and highlights a narrowing (black arrow) in the patient's internal carotid artery.
©Science Photo Library/Alamy Stock Photo

higher-quality images of the vessels and neither of which requires the use of a catheter. (CTs and MRIs are discussed next.)

Computed Tomography (CT)[1]

A **computed tomography (CT)** (tō-mog′ră-fē; *tomos* = a section) scan, previously termed a *computerized axial tomography* (*CAT*) scan, is a more sophisticated application of x-rays. A patient is slowly moved through a doughnut-shaped machine, while low-intensity x-rays are emitted on one side of the cylinder, passed through the body, collected by detectors, and then processed and analyzed by a computer. These signals produce an image of the body that is about the thickness of a dime. Continuous thin "slices" are used to reconstruct a three-dimensional image of a particular tissue or organ. By providing images of thin sections of the body, there is little overlap of organs and the image is much sharper than one obtained by a conventional x-ray. CT scanning is useful for identifying tumors, aneurysms, kidney stones, cerebral hemorrhages, and other abnormalities.

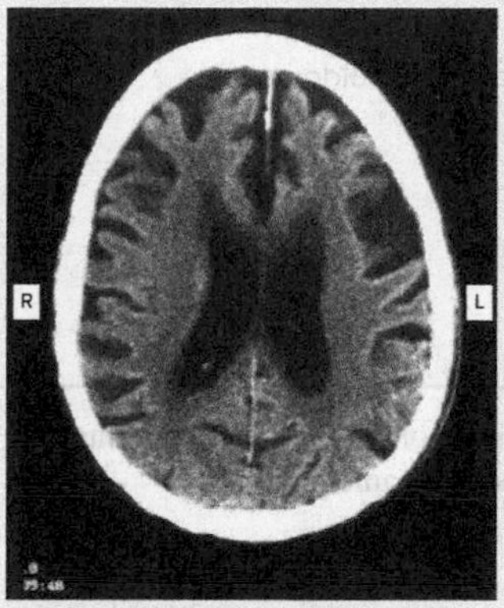

Computed tomographic (CT) scan, transverse section of the brain of an 84-year-old individual suffering from Alzheimer disease.

Magnetic Resonance Imaging (MRI)[1]

Magnetic resonance imaging (MRI), previously called *nuclear magnetic resonance* (*NMR*) *imaging*, was developed as a noninvasive technique to visualize soft tissues. The patient is placed in a supine position within a cylindrical chamber that is surrounded by a large electromagnet. The magnet generates a strong magnetic field that causes protons (hydrogen atoms) in the tissues to align. Thereafter, upon exposure to radio waves, the protons absorb additional energy and align in a different direction. The hydrogen atoms abruptly realign themselves to the magnetic field immediately after the radio waves are turned off. This results in the release of the atoms' excess energy at different rates, depending upon the type of tissue. A computer analyzes the emitted energy to produce an image of the body. MRI is better than CT for distinguishing between soft tissues, such as the white and gray matter of the nervous system. However, dense structures (bone) do not show up as well in MRI. Formerly, another disadvantage of MRI was that patients felt claustrophobic, while isolated within the closed cylinder. However, newer MRI technology has improved the hardware and lessened this effect. An advance in MRI, called **functional MRI (fMRI)**, provide the means to map brain function based upon local oxygen concentration differences in blood flow. Increased blood flow relates to brain activity and is detected by a decrease in deoxyhemoglobin (the form of hemoglobin lacking oxygen) in the blood.

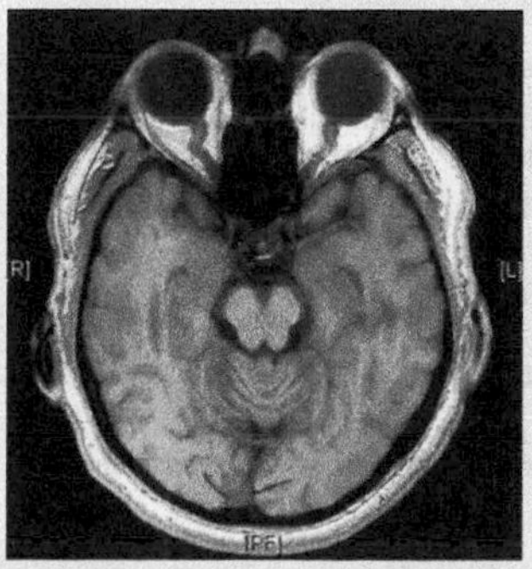

Magnetic resonance imaging (MRI) scan of the head at the level of the eyes, viewed in transverse section.

Positron Emission Tomography (PET)

The **positron emission tomography (PET)** scan is used both to analyze the metabolic state of a tissue at a given moment in time and to determine which tissues are most active. The procedure begins with an injection of radioactively labeled glucose (sugar), which emits particles called *positrons* (like electrons, but with a positive charge). Collisions between a positron and an electron cause the release of gamma rays that can be detected by sensors and analyzed by computer. The result is a brilliant color image that shows which tissues were using the most glucose at that moment. In cardiology, the image can reveal the extent of damaged heart tissue. Because damaged heart tissue consumes little or no glucose, the tissue appears dark. Alternatively, PET scans have been used to illustrate activity levels in the brain and, in so doing, have been useful in examining the effects of neurologic ailments (e.g., schizophrenia, Alzheimer disease). The PET scan is an example of nuclear medicine, which uses radioactive isotopes to form anatomic images of the body. PET scans are used to detect whether certain cancers have metastasized throughout the body, because cancerous cells will take up more glucose and show up as a "hot spot" on the scan.

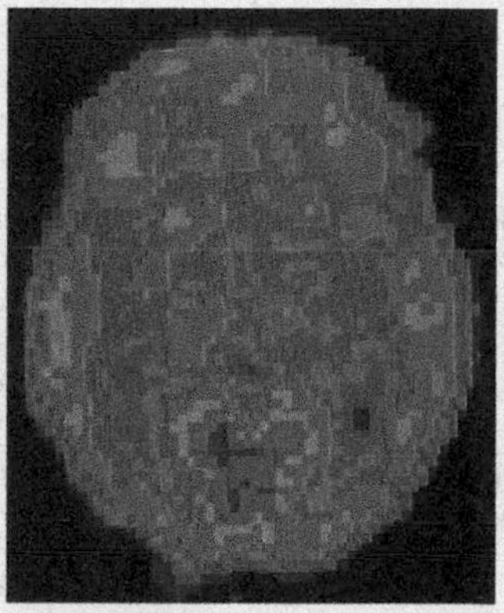

Positron emission tomography (PET) scan of the brain of an unmedicated schizophrenic patient. Red areas indicate high glucose use (metabolic activity). The visual center at the posterior region of the brain was especially active when the scan was made. Viewed in transverse section.

[1]CT and MRI films taken in the transverse plane are usually, but not always, read from an inferior view. So, the right side of the body is on the left side of the image, and the left side of the body is on the right side of the image. Thus, when reading a CT or MRI scan in transverse section, check the orientation of the image. Often, there may be L and R letters to let you know which side of the film corresponds to the left or right side of the patient.

lumbar region contains the descending colon, part of the left kidney, and part of the small intestine.

- The **right** and **left iliac** (il′ē-ak; *eileo* = to twist) **regions** are the inferior regions lateral to the hypogastric region. The right iliac region typically contains the inferior end of the cecum, the appendix, and part of the small intestine; the left iliac region contains the junction of parts of the colon as well as part of the small intestine.

Some health-care professionals prefer to partition the abdomen more simply into four quadrants (figure 1.11*b*). They use these areas to locate aches, pains, injuries, or other abnormalities. Imaginary transverse and midsagittal planes pass through the umbilicus to divide the abdominopelvic cavity into these four quadrants: right upper quadrant (RUQ), left upper quadrant (LUQ), right lower quadrant (RLQ), and left lower quadrant (LLQ).

WHAT DID YOU LEARN?

8. What type of plane would separate the nose and mouth into superior and inferior structures?
9. If a physician makes an incision into a body cavity just superior to the diaphragm and inferior to the neck, what body cavity will be exposed?
10. Sketch the torso of the body and label the 4 abdominal quadrants. Sketch another torso and label the 9 abdominal regions.
11. Use a directional term to describe the following:
    The elbow is ______ to the wrist.
    The neck is ______ to the shoulders.

Clinical Terms

auscultation A diagnostic method that involves listening to the sounds produced by various body structures.

palpation Using the hands to detect organs, masses, or infiltration of a body part during a physical examination.

Chapter Summary

1.1 History of Human Anatomy	■ The earliest studies of human anatomy date back to 400–300 BCE and were based upon evidence gleaned from dissection. ■ Anatomic studies revived in Europe during the Middle Ages and advances in printing and engraving techniques led to Andreas Vesalius's illustrated and anatomically accurate textbook in the 1500s as well as to important books by William Harvey in the next century. ■ Later technological advances, including preserved specimens, cryotechnology, and plastination, have continued to improve and help disseminate knowledge about human body structure.
1.2 Definition of Anatomy	■ Anatomy is the study of the structure of individual body organs and their relationships to one another. ■ Physiology is the study of the functions of body structures. **1.2a Microscopic Anatomy** ■ Microscopic anatomy includes cytology, the study of cells, and histology, the study of tissues. **1.2b Gross Anatomy** ■ Gross anatomy includes numerous subdisciplines, such as regional anatomy, systemic anatomy, and surface anatomy. ■ Developmental anatomy investigates the changes in form that occur continuously from conception through physical maturity. Embryology is the study of the processes and developmental changes that occur prior to birth. ■ Some anatomic specialties important to health-care providers are pathologic anatomy, radiographic anatomy, and surgical anatomy. ■ The human body is organized in an increasingly complex series of interacting levels: the chemical level, the cellular level, the tissue level, the organ level, the organ system level, and the organismal level.
1.3 Structural Organization of the Body	**1.3a Characteristics of Living Things** ■ All living organisms exhibit several common properties: organization, metabolism, growth and development, responsiveness, adaptation, regulation, and reproduction. **1.3b Introduction to Organ Systems** ■ The organ systems of the body function together to maintain a constant internal environment, a state called homeostasis. ■ Clear, exact terminology accurately describes body structures and helps us identify and locate them.
1.4 Precise Language of Anatomy	**1.4a Anatomic Position** ■ The anatomic position is used as a standard reference point. **1.4b Sections and Planes** ■ Three planes describe relationships among the parts of the three-dimensional human body: the coronal (or frontal) plane, the transverse (cross-sectional or horizontal) plane, and the midsagittal (or median) plane.

1.4c Anatomic Directions

- Specific directional terms indicate relative body locations (see table 1.2).

1.4d Regional Anatomy

- Specific anatomic terms identify body regions (see table 1.3 and figure 1.8).

1.4e Body Cavities and Membranes

- Body cavities are spaces that enclose organs and organ systems. The posterior aspect of the body contains two cavities: the cranial cavity and the vertebral canal. The ventral cavity is separated into a superior thoracic cavity and an inferior abdominopelvic cavity.
- The ventral cavity is lined by thin serous membranes. A parietal layer lines the internal body wall surface, and a visceral layer lines the external surface of the organs.
- The thoracic cavity is composed of three separate spaces: a central space called the mediastinum, and two lateral spaces, the pleural cavities.
- Within the mediastinum is a space called the pericardial cavity.
- The abdominopelvic cavity is composed of two subdivisions: the abdominal cavity and the pelvic cavity.

1.4f Abdominopelvic Regions and Quadrants

- Regions and quadrants are two aids for describing locations of the viscera in the abdominopelvic area of the body. There are nine abdominopelvic regions and four abdominopelvic quadrants.

Challenge Yourself

Actively write or type your answers in a separate document to reinforce your learning, before checking your answers.

Multiple Choice

Select the best answer from the four choices provided.

1. Cutting a midsagittal section through the body separates which parts of the body?
   a. anterior and posterior portions
   b. superior and inferior portions
   c. proximal and distal portions
   d. right and left halves
2. When you palpate your sternum and recognize that it overlies the heart, or you palpate your clavicle (collarbone) and realize that the brachial plexus (a collection of nerves) underlies it, you are practicing which of the following anatomical specialties?
   a. microscopic anatomy
   b. surface anatomy
   c. pathologic anatomy
   d. systemic anatomy
3. Which of the following regions corresponds to the forearm?
   a. cervical
   b. antebrachial
   c. femoral
   d. pes
4. What term describes the state of maintaining a constant internal environment in the body?
   a. reproduction
   b. homeostasis
   c. responsiveness
   d. growth
5. Which level of organization is composed of two or more tissue types that work together to perform a common function?
   a. cellular
   b. tissue
   c. organ
   d. organismal
6. Which body cavity is located inferior to the diaphragm and superior to the pelvic brim of the hip bones?
   a. abdominal cavity
   b. thoracic cavity
   c. pleural cavity
   d. pelvic cavity
7. What is the term used to refer to a body structure that is below, or at a lower level than, another structure?
   a. ventral
   b. medial
   c. inferior
   d. distal
8. Which organ system filters waste products from the blood and excretes those waste products through the urethra to the outside of the body?
   a. cardiovascular
   b. respiratory
   c. lymphatic
   d. urinary
9. Which region refers to the anterior portion of the knee?
   a. patellar
   b. popliteal
   c. pes
   d. inguinal
10. Which serous membrane covers the surface of the lung?
    a. parietal pleura
    b. visceral pleura
    c. parietal peritoneum
    d. visceral peritoneum

Content Review

1. What are the differences between cytology and histology?
2. Compare and contrast the fields of anatomy and physiology, and explain how the fields may differ in their description of the small intestine.
3. What are the basic steps involved in the scientific method, and how does a clinician utilize the scientific method when treating a patient?
4. What are the 11 organ systems in the human body?
5. Describe the body in the anatomic position. Why is the anatomic position used?
6. Compare and contrast the use of the terms *medial* and *lateral* with the terms *proximal* and *distal*. How do these terms differ?
7. List the anatomic term that describes each of the following body regions: forearm, wrist, chest, armpit, thigh, and foot.
8. What are the two body cavities within the posterior aspect, and what does each cavity contain?
9. Describe the structure and the function of serous membranes in the body.
10. List the 4 abdominal quadrants and the 9 abdominal regions. Then list which abdominal regions are in which quadrant (note that some regions may be in more than one quadrant).

Developing Critical Reasoning

1. If a person becomes ill and the symptoms indicate infection by a parasitic organism, treatment will depend upon correct diagnosis of the problem. What category of anatomic study would be most appropriate for identifying an infectious agent in the blood or muscle tissue? What kinds of effects would an infection in the blood or muscle tissue have?
2. Lynn was knocked off her bicycle during a race. She damaged a nerve in her antebrachial region, suffered an abrasion in her patellar region, and broke bones in her sacral and brachial regions. Explain where each of these injuries is located.
3. Your grandmother is being seen by a radiologist to diagnose a possible tumor in her small intestine. Explain to your grandmother what imaging techniques would best determine whether a tumor exists, and which imaging techniques would be inadequate for determining the placement of the tumor.

Answers to "What Do You Think?"

1. The stomach is at the organ level, whereas the digestive system is at the organ system level.
2. When you put lotion on your hands, the heat and the noise lessen considerably because friction is reduced. If the thoracic and abdominopelvic cavities didn't have the lubricating serous fluid, friction would build up, and you would feel pain whenever your organs moved. For example, the illness *pleurisy* (inflammation of the pleura) makes it very painful to breathe, because the pleura is inflamed and the serous fluid cannot lubricate the membranes.

Design Element: Pencil Icon: Slavojub Pantelic/Shutterstock

The Cell: Basic Unit of Structure and Function 2

Outline

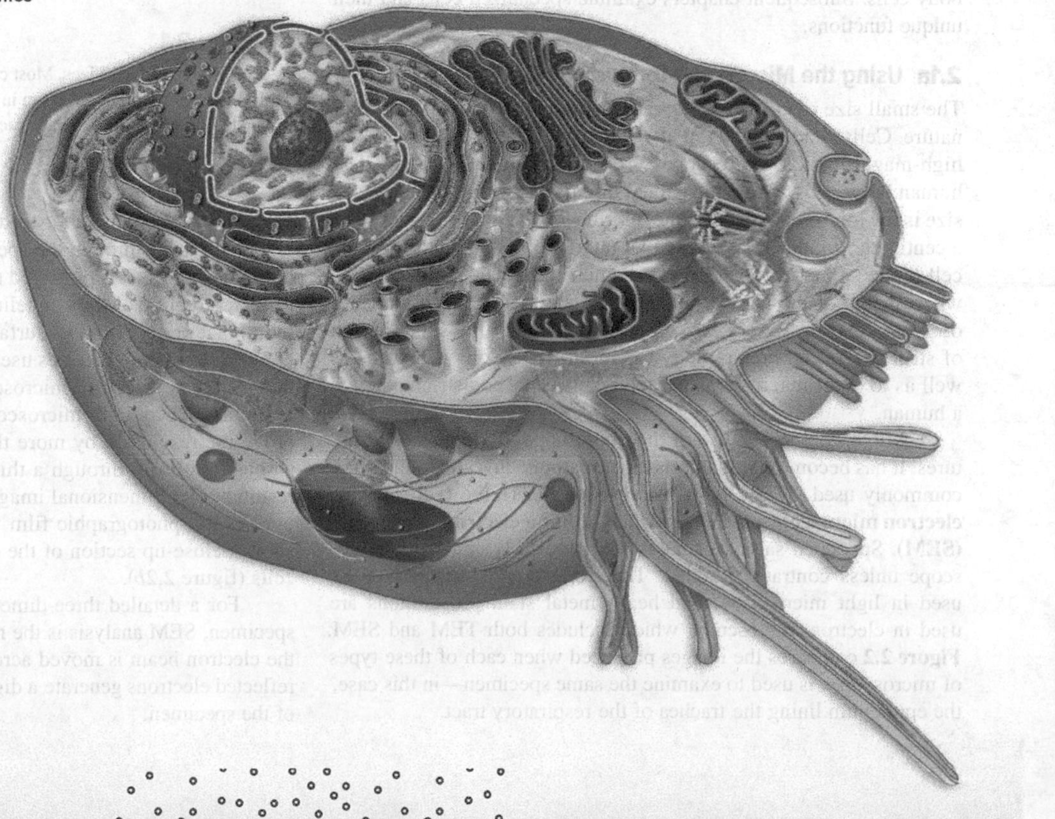

Anatomy & Physiology Revealed 4.0

MODULE 2: CELLS & CHEMISTRY

Cells are the structural and functional units of all organisms, including humans. An adult human body contains about 75 trillion cells. Most cells are composed of characteristic parts that work together to allow them to perform specific body functions. There are about 200 different types of cells in the human body, but all of them share certain common characteristics:

- All cells perform the general housekeeping functions necessary to sustain life. Each cell must obtain nutrients and other materials essential for survival from its surrounding fluids. Recall from section 1.3a that the total of all the chemical reactions that occur in cells is called metabolism.
- Cells must dispose of the wastes they produce. If a cell didn't remove its waste products, this waste would build up in the cell and lead to its death.
- The shape and integrity of a cell is maintained by both its internal contents and its surrounding membrane.
- Cell function and physical characteristics are determined by the genetic material housed in the nucleus.
- Most cells are capable of undergoing cell division to make more cells of the same type.

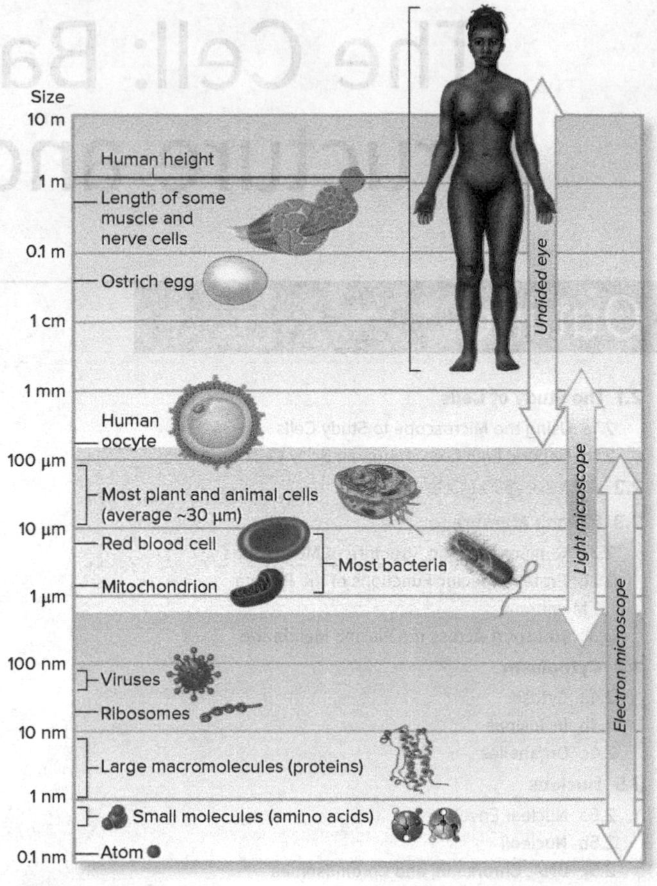

Figure 2.1

The Range of Cell Sizes. Most cells in the human body are between 1 micrometer (μm) and 100 μm in diameter. Individual cells are viewed by light microscopy; subcellular structures are studied by electron microscopy.

2.1 The Study of Cells

✓ Learning Objectives

1. Compare and contrast the advantages and disadvantages of LM, TEM, and SEM.
2. Describe the general functions of human body cells.

The study of cells is called **cytology.** Throughout this chapter, we will examine the generalized structures and functions shared by all body cells. Subsequent chapters examine specialized cells and their unique functions.

2.1a Using the Microscope to Study Cells

The small size of cells is the greatest obstacle to determining their nature. Cells were discovered after microscopes were invented, and high-magnification microscopes are required to see the smallest human body cells. The dimensional unit often used to measure cell size is the micrometer (μm). One micrometer is equal to 1/10,000 of a centimeter (about 1/125,000 of an inch). For example, a red blood cell (called an erythrocyte) has a diameter of about 7 μm to 8 μm, whereas one of the largest human cells, an oocyte, has a diameter of about 120 μm. **Figure 2.1** compares the size of the smallest unit of structure in the human body (an atom) to various cell types as well as to other macroscopic structures, such as an ostrich egg and a human.

Microscopy is the use of the microscope to view small structures. It has become a valuable asset in anatomic investigations. Most commonly used are the **light microscope (LM),** the **transmission electron microscope (TEM),** and the **scanning electron microscope (SEM).** Specimen samples cannot be seen clearly under the microscope unless contrast is added. Therefore, colored-dye stains are used in light microscopy, and heavy-metal stain preparations are used in electron microscopy, which includes both TEM and SEM. **Figure 2.2** compares the images produced when each of these types of microscopes is used to examine the same specimen—in this case, the epithelium lining the trachea of the respiratory tract.

The LM produces a two-dimensional image for study by passing visible light through the specimen. Glass lenses focus and magnify the image as it is projected toward the eye. Figure 2.2*a* shows the cellular structure of the epithelium as well as the hairlike structures (cilia) that project from its surface.

Electron microscopes use a beam of electrons to "illuminate" the specimen. Electron microscopes easily exceed the magnification obtained by light microscopy, but more importantly, they improve the resolution by more than a thousandfold. A TEM directs an electron beam through a thin-cut section of the specimen. The resultant two-dimensional image is focused onto a screen for viewing or onto photographic film to record the image. The TEM can show a close-up section of the cilia on the surface of the epithelial cells (figure 2.2*b*).

For a detailed three-dimensional image of the surface of the specimen, SEM analysis is the method of choice (figure 2.2*c*). Here, the electron beam is moved across the surface of the specimen, and reflected electrons generate a digital image of the surface topography of the specimen.

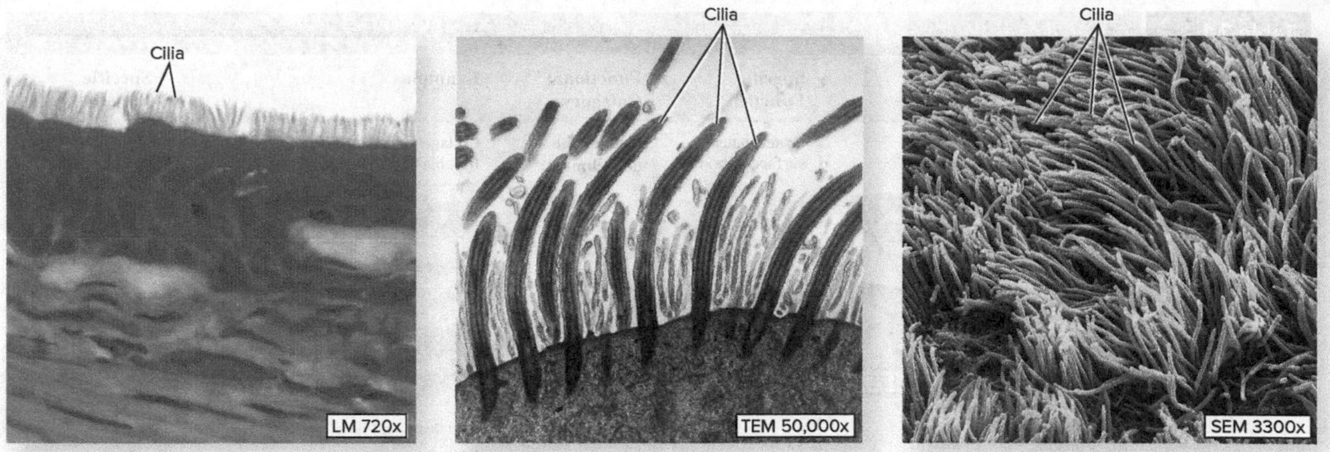
Cilia
LM 720x
Cilia
TEM 50,000x
Cilia
SEM 3300x

(a) (b) (c)

Figure 2.2

Microscopic Techniques for Cellular Studies. Different techniques are used to investigate cellular anatomy. (*a*) A light microscope (LM) shows hairlike structures, termed cilia, that project from the free membrane surfaces of the cells lining the trachea of the respiratory tract. (*b*) A transmission electron microscope (TEM) reveals the two-dimensional ultrastructure of the cilia on the same type of cells. (*c*) A scanning electron microscope (SEM) shows the three-dimensional image of the cilia-covered surface of the same type of cells.

2.1b General Functions of Human Body Cells

Besides differing in size, cells also vary in shape, which may be flat, cylindrical, oval, or quite irregular. Often, cells' functions are reflected in either their size or their shape. Among the general functions of cells are the following:

- **Covering.** Epithelial cells form a sheet to cover surfaces. For example, skin cells cover the external body surface.
- **Lining.** Epithelial cells line the internal surfaces of our organs, such as the small intestine.
- **Storage.** Some body cells, such as hepatocytes (liver cells) and adipocytes (fat cells), store nutrients or energy reserves for the body.
- **Movement.** Muscle cells are composed of contractile proteins that cause the muscle to shorten (contract), thereby allowing movement to occur. Skeletal muscle cells attach to the skeleton so that when these cells contract, they move the skeleton. In contrast, when the muscle cells in the heart wall contract, they are able to pump blood throughout the body.
- **Connection.** Multiple cell types occur in connective tissues, which help connect and support other tissues. For example, fibroblast cells produce protein fibers that are found in ligaments, the connective tissue that binds bone to bone.
- **Defense.** Many cell types protect the body against pathogens or antigens (anything perceived as foreign in the body). White blood cells (called leukocytes) are designed to recognize foreign material (antigens) and attack them. The process of attacking the foreign materials is called an immune response.
- **Communication.** Nerve cells (called *neurons*) transmit nerve impulses from one part of the body to another. The nerve impulse carries information between neurons within the nervous system, sensory information to the brain for processing, or motor information to make a muscle contract or a gland secrete.
- **Reproduction.** Some cells function solely to produce new individuals. For example, within the gonads, the sex cells (sperm and oocytes) are produced. They are specialized cells designed to join together and initiate the formation of a new individual. Additionally, some cells divide to provide new cells that can specialize—such as cells within red bone marrow, which continually produce new blood cells. These types of cells are called *stem cells* and are discussed in more detail in Clinical View 4.1: "Stem Cells" in Section 4.1f.

Table 2.1 summarizes the types of cellular functions as they relate to cell type. Now that we have mentioned that cells come in a variety of shapes and sizes and have different functions, let us examine the structures common to almost all cells.

WHAT DID YOU LEARN?

1. Describe an advantage of using TEM rather than LM to study intracellular structure.
2. What are some basic functions of human body cells?

Table 2.1 Selected Common Types of Cells and Their Functions

Functional Category	Example	Specific Function	Functional Category	Example	Specific Function
Covering	Epidermal cells of skin 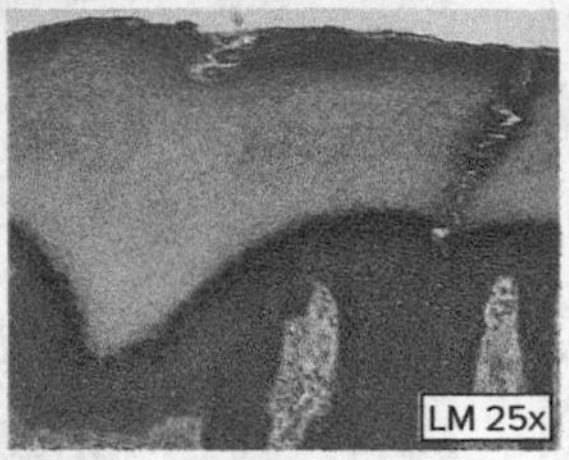 LM 25x ©Ed Reschke/Photolibrary/ Getty Images	Protect outer surface of body	Connection (attachment)	Collagen (protein) fibers from fibroblasts 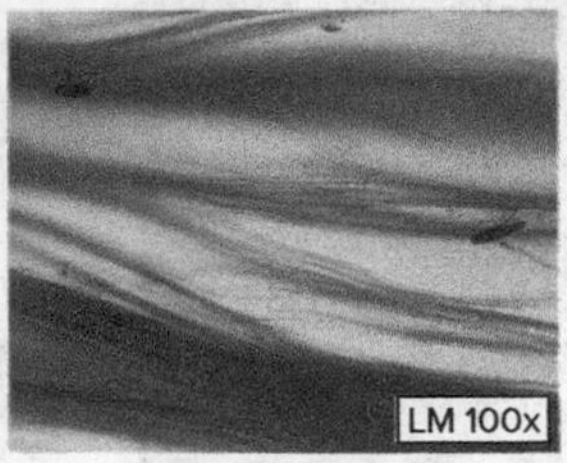 LM 100x ©Ed Reschke/Photolibrary/ Getty Images	Form ligaments that attach bone to bone
Lining	Epithelial cells in small intestine 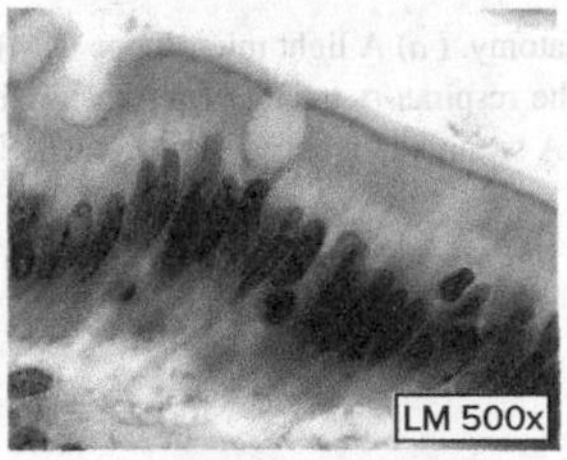 LM 500x ©McGraw-Hill Education/Al Telser, photographer	Regulate nutrient movement into body tissues	Defense	Lymphocytes 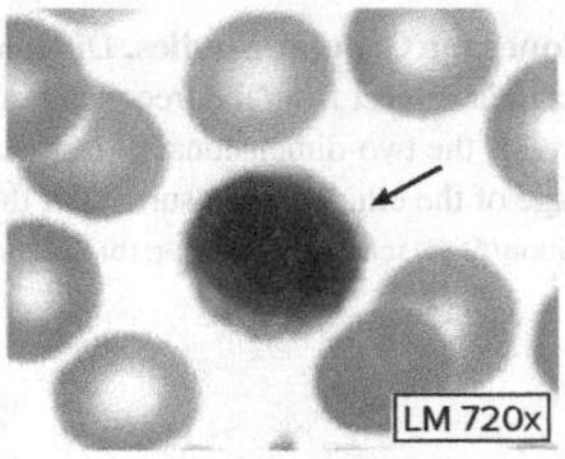 LM 720x ©McGraw-Hill Education/Al Telser, photographer	Produce antibodies to target antigens or invading cells
Storage	Adipocytes (fat cells) Hepatocytes (liver cells) 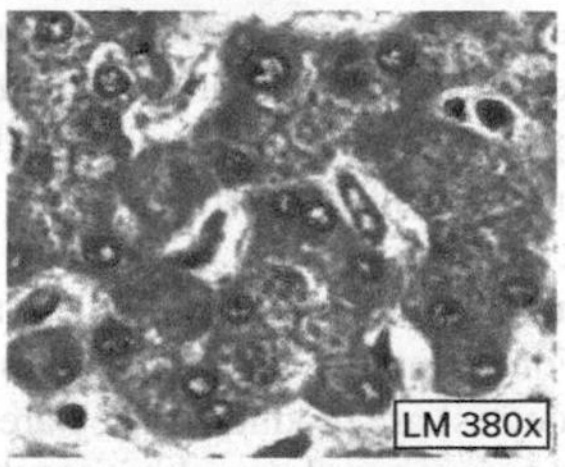 LM 380x ©McGraw-Hill Education/Al Telser, photographer	Store lipid reserves Store carbohydrate nutrients as glycogen	Communication	Neurons (nerve cells) 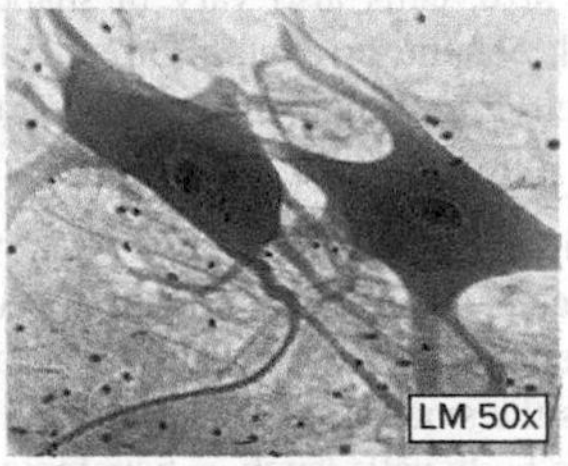 LM 50x ©Ed Reschke/Photolibrary/Getty Images	Send information between regions of the brain
Movement	Cardiac (heart) muscle cells Skeletal muscle cells  LM 500x ©McGraw-Hill Education/Al Telser, photographer	Pump blood Move skeleton	Reproduction	Bone marrow stem cells Sperm and oocyte cells 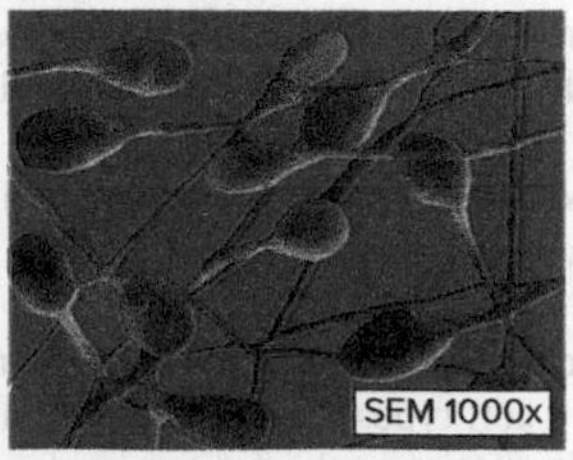 SEM 1000x ©Ed White/Taxi/Getty Images	Produce new blood cells Produce a new individual

2.2 A Prototypical Cell

✓ Learning Objectives

3. Identify and describe the main components of a typical cell: the plasma membrane, cytoplasm, and nucleus.
4. Describe the contents of a prototypical cell.

The generalized cell in **figure 2.3** isn't an actual body cell, but rather a representation of a cell that combines features of several different types of body cells. Almost all mature human cells share the same three basic constituents, which can be described in terms of the prototypical cell:

- **Plasma membrane.** The plasma membrane, sometimes called the cell membrane, forms the outer, limiting barrier separating the internal contents of the cell from the external environment.
- **Cytoplasm.** Cytoplasm (sī′tō-plazm; *kytos* = a hollow [cell], *plasma* = a thing formed) is a general term for all cellular contents located between the plasma membrane and the nucleus. The three components of the cytoplasm are cytosol (a viscous fluid), inclusions (nonfunctional, temporary structures that store cellular products), and organelles (tiny structures that perform specific cellular functions).
- **Nucleus.** The nucleus (nū′klē-ŭs; *nux* = the kernel or inside of a thing) is the cell's control center. It controls protein synthesis (production of new proteins), and in so doing, it directs the functional and structural characteristics of the cell.

Sections 2.3, 2.4, and 2.5 describe the contents and specific functions of the plasma membrane, the cytoplasm, and the nucleus. As you read these descriptions, it may help to refer to **table 2.2**, which summarizes this information.

WHAT DID YOU LEARN?

3. Briefly describe the three main constituents of a cell.

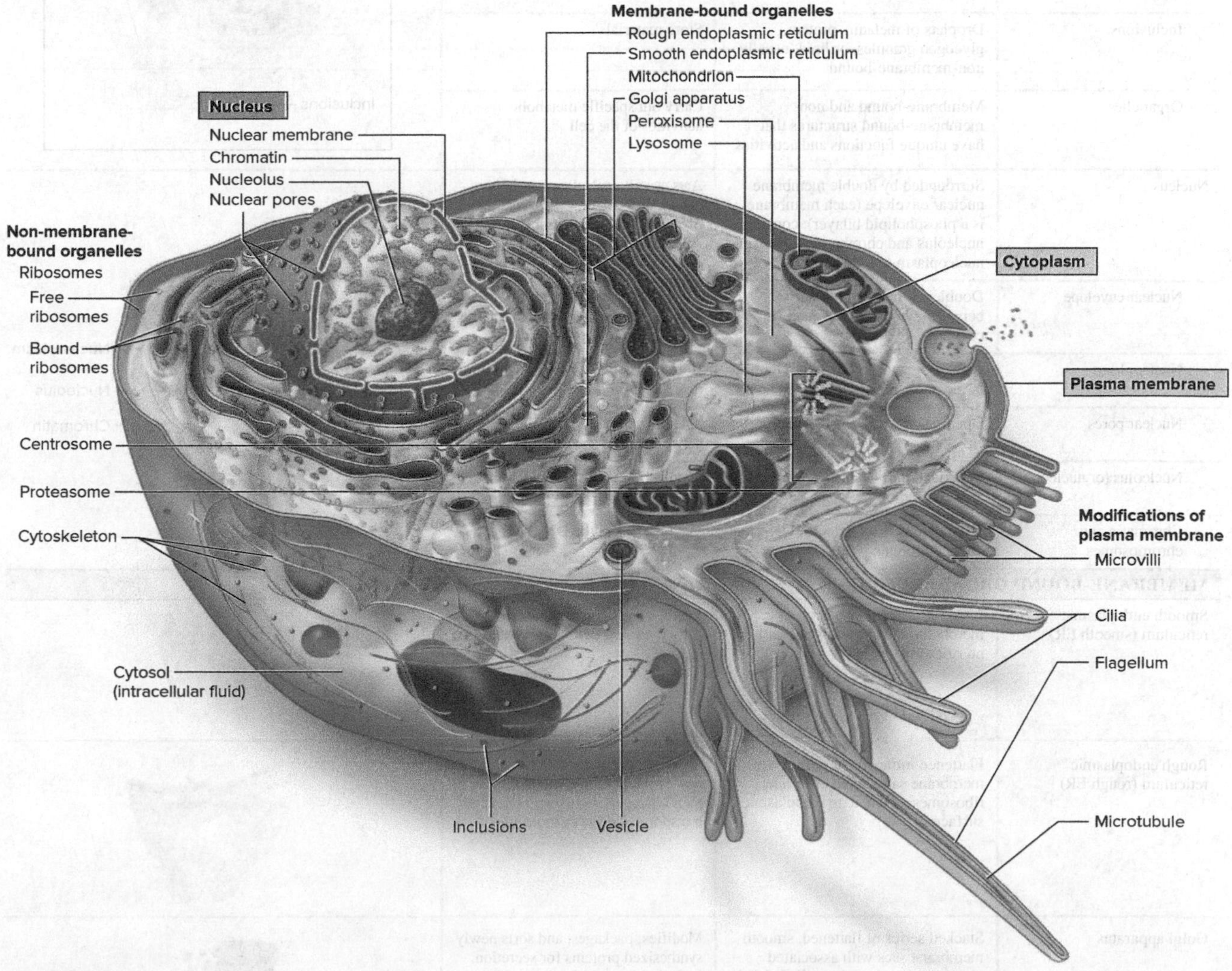
Membrane-bound organelles
Rough endoplasmic reticulum
Smooth endoplasmic reticulum
Mitochondrion
Golgi apparatus
Peroxisome
Lysosome
Nucleus
Nuclear membrane
Chromatin
Nucleolus
Nuclear pores
Non-membrane-bound organelles
Ribosomes
Free ribosomes
Bound ribosomes
Centrosome
Proteasome
Cytoskeleton
Cytosol (intracellular fluid)
Inclusions
Vesicle
Cytoplasm
Plasma membrane
Modifications of plasma membrane
Microvilli
Cilia
Flagellum
Microtubule

Figure 2.3

The Structure of a Cell. This generalized cell illustrates most of the common features found in mature human cells, which include the plasma membrane, nucleus, and cytoplasm. Composing the cytoplasm is cytosol and organelles that are either membrane-bound or non-membrane-bound. Some cells also contain inclusions, which are temporary stores of specific molecules. APR

Table 2.2 Components of the Cell

Component	Structure(s)	Function(s)	Appearance
MAJOR CELL COMPONENTS			
Plasma (cell) membrane	Phospholipid bilayer containing cholesterol, proteins (integral and peripheral), and some carbohydrates (externally)	Contains receptors for communication; forms intercellular connections; acts as physical barrier to enclose cell contents; regulates material movement into and out of the cell	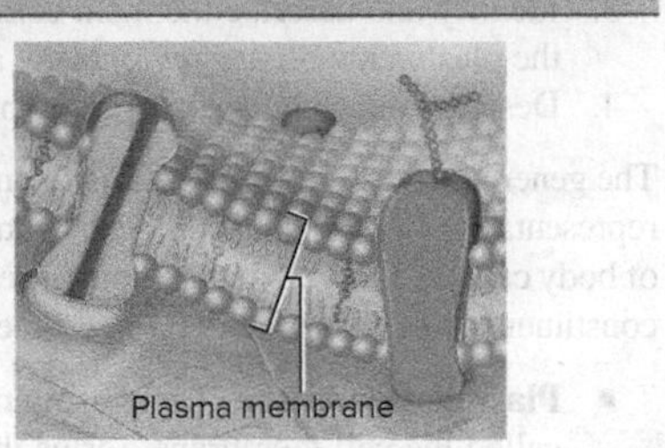
Cytoplasm	Contains cytosol (a viscous fluid), inclusions, and organelles	Place of many metabolic processes of the cell; stores nutrients and dissolved solutes	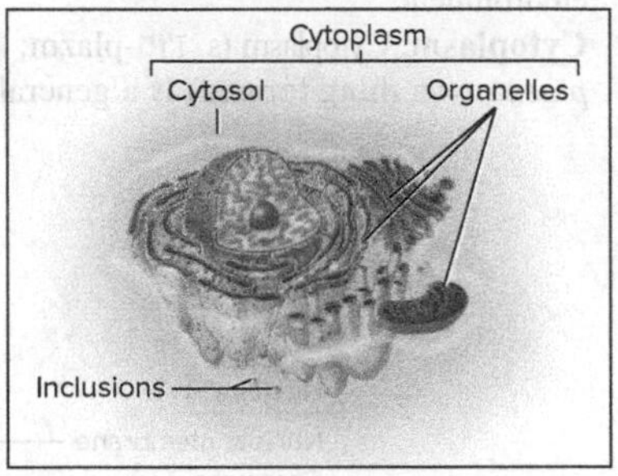
Cytosol	Viscous fluid medium with dissolved solutes (ions, nutrients, proteins, carbohydrates, lipids, and other small molecules)	Provides support for organelles; serves as viscous medium through which diffusion occurs	
Inclusions	Droplets of melanin, protein, glycogen granules, or lipid; usually non-membrane-bound	Store materials	
Organelles	Membrane-bound and non-membrane-bound structures that have unique functions and activities	Carry out specific metabolic activities of the cell	
Nucleus	Surrounded by double membrane nuclear envelope (each membrane is a phospholipid bilayer); contains nucleolus and chromatin within nucleoplasm (a fluid)	Acts as cell control center; houses genetic information (DNA); site of ribosome subunit assembly	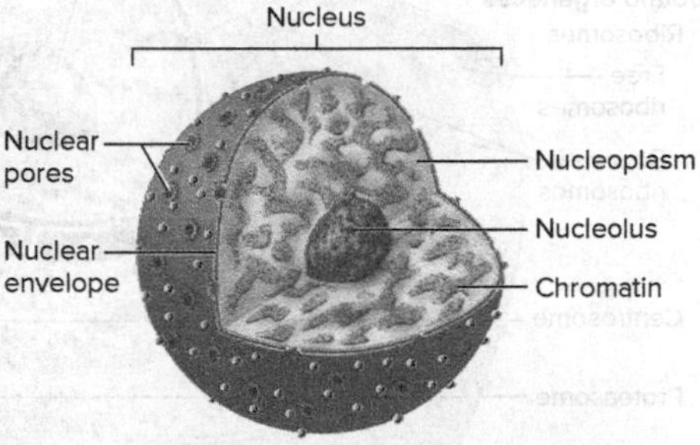
Nuclear envelope	Double membrane boundary between cytoplasm and nuclear contents	Physical barrier that controls movement of materials between the nucleus and the cytoplasm	
Nucleoplasm	A fluid or semifluid medium housed in the nucleus	Houses dissolved solutes including nucleotides and proteins	
Nuclear pores	Openings through the nuclear envelope	Allow for passage of materials between nucleus and cytoplasm	
Nucleolus (or nucleoli)	Spherical, dark-staining, dense granular region in the nucleus	Synthesizes rRNA and assembles ribosomes in the nucleus	
Chromatin and chromosomes	Filamentous association of DNA and histone proteins	Site of genes in the DNA	
MEMBRANE-BOUND ORGANELLES			
Smooth endoplasmic reticulum (smooth ER)	Interconnected network of membrane tubules and vesicles; no ribosome	Synthesizes lipids; metabolizes carbohydrates; detoxifies drugs, alcohol	
Rough endoplasmic reticulum (rough ER)	Flattened intracellular network of membrane sacs called cisternae; ribosomes attached on cytoplasmic surface	Synthesizes proteins for secretion, new proteins for the plasma membrane, and lysosomal enzymes; transports and stores molecules	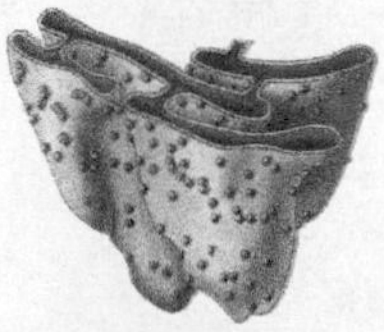
Golgi apparatus	Stacked series of flattened, smooth membrane sacs with associated transport vesicles (also called shuttle vesicles)	Modifies, packages, and sorts newly synthesized proteins for secretion, inclusion in new plasma membrane, or lysosomal enzyme synthesis	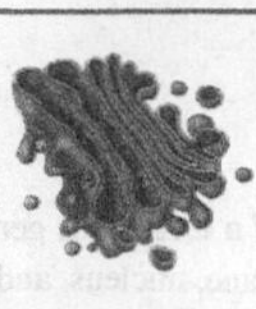

Table 2.2	Components of the Cell *(continued)*		
Component	**Structure(s)**	**Function(s)**	**Appearance**
MEMBRANE-BOUND ORGANELLES *(continued)*			
Lysosomes	Membrane sacs with digestive enzymes	Digest materials or microbes ingested by the cell; remove old/damaged organelles; self-destruct (autolyze)	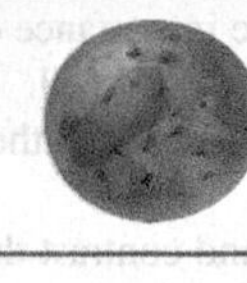
Peroxisomes	Membrane-enclosed sacs; usually contain large amounts of specific enzymes to break down harmful substances	Convert hydrogen peroxide formed during metabolism to water	
Mitochondria	Double membrane structures with cristae; fluid matrix contents at center	Synthesize most ATP during cellular respiration; "powerhouses of cell"	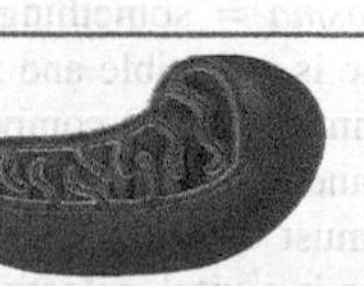
NON-MEMBRANE-BOUND ORGANELLES			
Ribosomes	Dense cytoplasmic granules with two subunits (large and small); may be free in cytoplasm (free ribosomes) or bound to rough ER (bound ribosomes)	Synthesize proteins for: 1. use in the cell (free ribosomes) 2. secretion, incorporation into plasma membrane, or lysosomes (bound ribosomes)	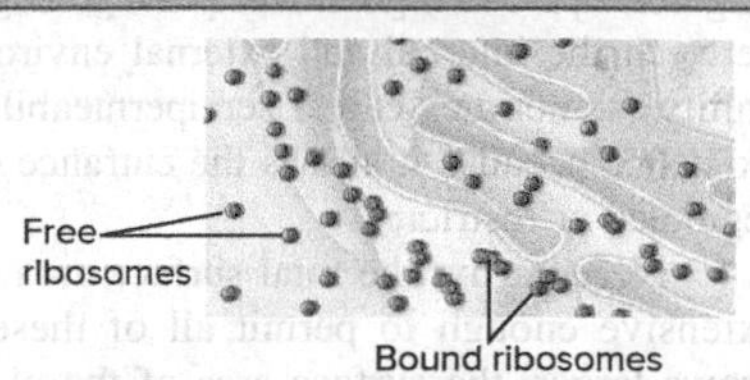
Cytoskeleton	Organized network of protein filaments or hollow tubules throughout the cell	Provides structural support; facilitates cytoplasmic streaming, organelle and cellular motility, transport of materials, chromosomal movement and cell division	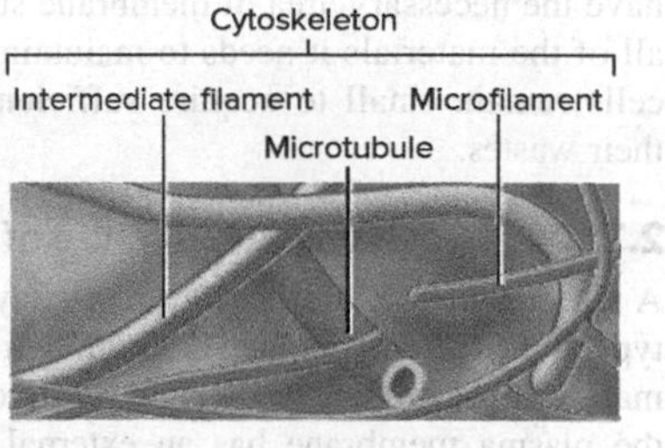
Microfilaments	Actin protein monomers formed into filaments	Maintain cell shape; aid in muscle contraction and intracellular movement; separate dividing cells	
Intermediate filaments	Various protein components	Provide structural support; stabilize cell junctions	
Microtubules	Hollow cylinders of tubulin protein; able to lengthen and shorten	Support cell; hold organelles in place; maintain cell shape and rigidity; direct organelle movement within cell and cell motility as cilia and flagella; move chromosomes at cell division	
Centrosome	Amorphous region adjacent to nucleus; contains a pair of centrioles	Organizes microtubules; participates in spindle formation during cell division	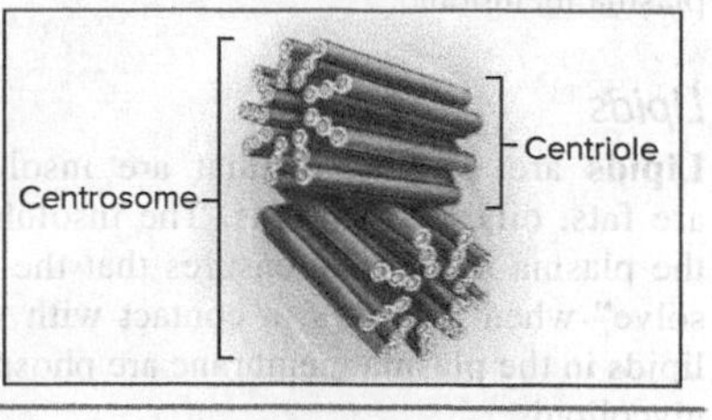
Centrioles	Paired perpendicular cylindrical bodies; composed of microtubule triplets	Organize microtubules during cell division for movement and separation of chromosomes	
Cilia	Short, membrane-attached projections containing microtubules; occur in large numbers on some mucous membrane surfaces	Move fluid, mucus, and materials over the cell surface	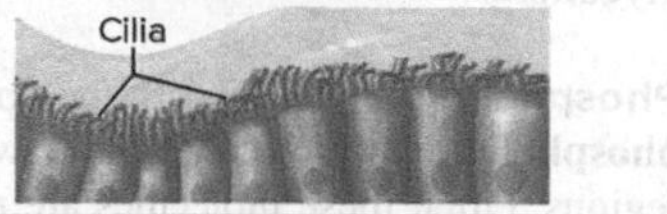
Flagellum	Long, singular membrane extension containing microtubules	Propels sperm in human male	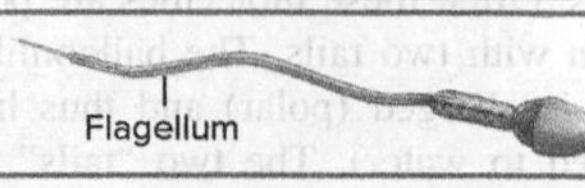
Microvilli	Numerous thin membrane folds projecting from the free cell surface	Increase membrane surface area for absorption and/or secretion	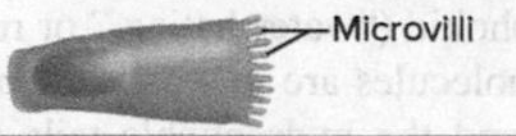

2.3 Plasma Membrane

✓ **Learning Objectives**

5. Describe the structure of the plasma membrane.
6. Explain the importance of selective permeability of the plasma membrane for the cell.
7. Identify and describe the specific types of passive and active transport.
8. Compare and contrast the use of the specific types of passive and active transport.

The **plasma membrane,** or *cell membrane,* forms the thin outer border of the cell. Also sometimes called the *plasmalemma* (plaz′m ă-lem′ă; *plasma* = something formed, *lemma* = husk), the plasma membrane is a flexible and fluid molecular layer that separates the internal (intracellular) components of a cell from the external environment and extracellular materials. All materials that enter or leave the cell must cross the plasma membrane. Therefore, the plasma membrane is a vital, selectively permeable barrier that functions as a "gatekeeper" to regulate the passage of gases, nutrients, and wastes between the internal and external environments. Selective permeability (sometimes called semipermeability) is essential to a cell's existence because it allows the entrance or exit of substances to be regulated or restricted.

Necessarily, the total surface area of the membrane must be extensive enough to permit all of these movements. As the cell grows larger, the surface area of the plasma membrane increases by square units, whereas the volume of cytoplasm within the cell increases by cubic units. If a cell becomes too large, it does not have the necessary area of membrane surface required to transport all of the materials it needs to maintain life processes. Thus, most cells remain small to acquire sufficient nutrients and dispose of their wastes.

2.3a Composition and Structure of Membranes

A plasma membrane is not a rigid layer of molecules. Rather, a typical plasma membrane is a fluid matrix composed of an approximately equal mixture, by weight, of lipids and proteins. In addition, the plasma membrane has an external carbohydrate (sugar) coat, called the **glycocalyx** (glī′kō-kā′liks; *glykys* = sweet, *kalyx* = husk). The following discussion explains how these components form the plasma membrane.

Lipids

Lipids are compounds that are insoluble in water; examples are fats, oils, and steroids. The insolubility of the lipids within the plasma membrane ensures that the membrane will not "dissolve" when it comes in contact with water. The three types of lipids in the plasma membrane are phospholipids, cholesterol, and glycolipids.

Phospholipids Most of the plasma membrane lipids are **phospholipids,** which contain both water-soluble and water-insoluble regions. Often these molecules are portrayed in the membrane as a balloon with two tails. The balloonlike "head" contains phosphate, which is charged (polar) and thus hydrophilic ("water-loving," or attracted to water). The two "tails" are uncharged (nonpolar) and hydrophobic ("water-hating," or repelled by water). When phospholipid molecules are in water, the hydrophilic heads interact with the water and the hydrophobic tails interact with each other, forming two parallel sheets. The tails form the internal environment of the membrane, which is hydrophobic and keeps charged particles from crossing the membrane. This basic structure of the plasma membrane is called the **phospholipid bilayer (figure 2.4)**. It ensures that **intracellular fluid (ICF)** (fluid within the cell) remains inside the cell, and **extracellular fluid (ECF)** (fluid outside the cell) remains outside. One type of ECF is **interstitial fluid,** the thin layer of fluid that bathes the external surface of a cell.

Cholesterol **Cholesterol,** a type of lipid called a steroid, amounts to about 20% of the plasma membrane lipids. Cholesterol is scattered within the hydrophobic internal region of the phospholipid bilayer, where it strengthens the membrane and stabilizes it at temperature extremes. Cholesterol is primarily a nonpolar molecule but has a polar hydroxyl, which allows this molecule to associate with both the phospholipid polar heads and the phospholipid nonpolar tails.

Glycolipids **Glycolipids,** lipids with attached carbohydrate groups, form about 5% to 10% of the membrane lipids. They are located only on the outer layer of the membrane, where they are exposed to the extracellular fluid. The carbohydrate portion of the glycolipid molecule is a component of the glycocalyx, which functions in cell–cell recognition, intracellular adhesion, and communication.

Proteins

The other common molecular structures within the plasma membrane are proteins. Proteins make up about half of the plasma membrane by weight. **Proteins** are complex, diverse molecules composed of chains of smaller molecules called *amino acids.* Proteins play various structural and functional roles within the cell and within the body. Resident proteins determine the specific functions of the plasma membrane. Plasma membrane proteins are of two types: integral and peripheral.

Integral proteins are embedded within, and can extend through the phospholipid bilayer. Some integral proteins act as **membrane channels,** providing a pore (hole) in the membrane through which specific substances pass. Other integral proteins, termed **receptors,** serve as binding sites for molecules outside of the cell. Hydrophobic regions within the integral proteins interact with the hydrophobic interior of the membrane. In contrast, the hydrophilic regions of the integral proteins are exposed to the aqueous environments on either side of the membrane.

Peripheral proteins are not embedded in the phospholipid bilayer. They are attached loosely either to the external or internal

Learning Strategy 2.1

Think of the glycoproteins and glycolipids as similar to your student ID card. This personal identification item supplies information about you and lets the school know you are supposed to be there. If a person doesn't have a student ID card, he or she is not allowed access to certain school facilities. Similarly, the glycoprotein and glycolipid molecules allow other cells in the body to recognize this cell and not confuse it with a foreign substance that must be destroyed.

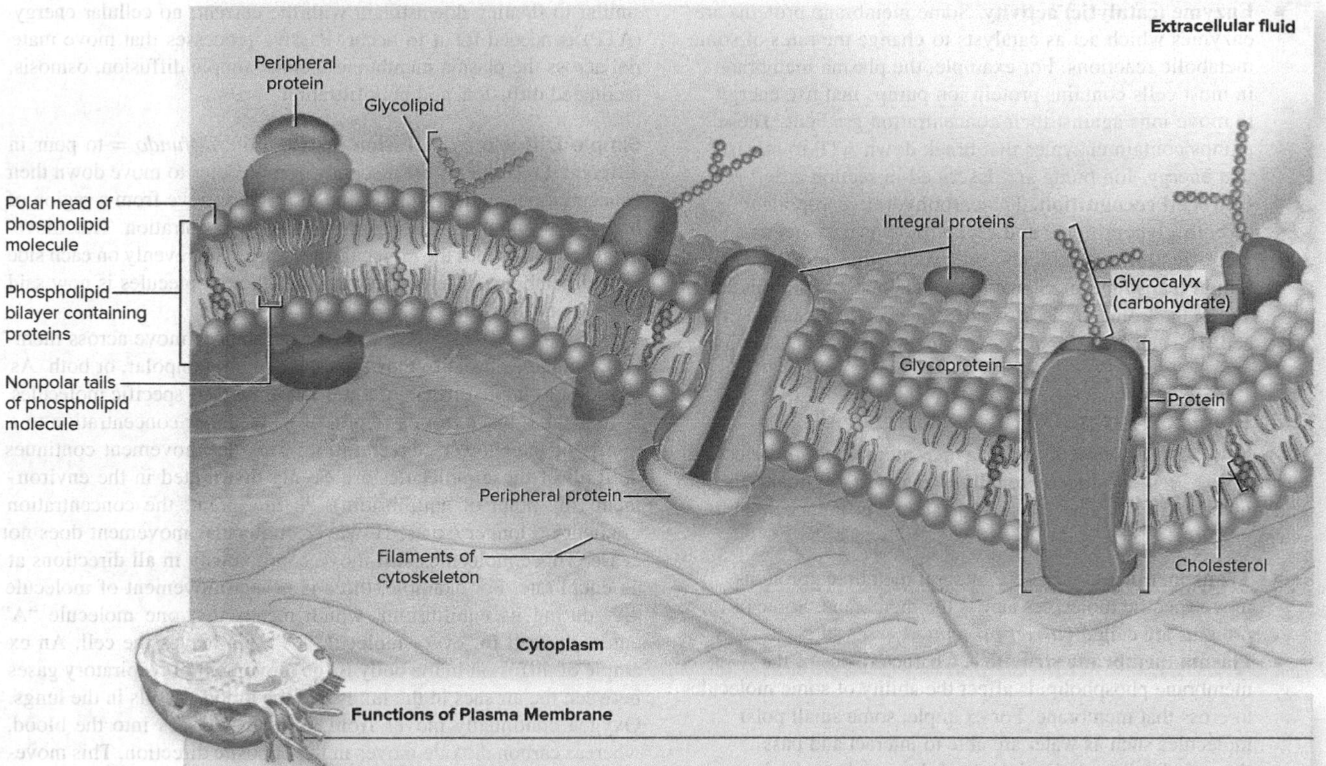

Functions of Plasma Membrane

1. **Communication:** Contains receptors that recognize and respond to molecular signals
2. **Intercellular connection:** Establishes a flexible boundary, protects cellular contents, and supports cell structure
3. **Physical barrier:** Phospholipid bilayer separates substances inside and outside the cell
4. **Selective permeability:** Regulates entry and exit of ions, nutrients, and waste molecules through the membrane

Figure 2.4
Structure of the Plasma Membrane. The plasma membrane is a phospholipid bilayer with cholesterol and proteins. These proteins are integral or peripheral to the membrane. Also present are carbohydrates chains attached either to phospholipids, forming a glycolipid, or to a protein, forming a glycoprotein. **APR**

surface of the membrane, often to integral proteins. Peripheral proteins can "float" and move about the bilayer, much like a beach ball floating on the surface in a swimming pool.

Both integral and peripheral membrane proteins may serve as **enzymes,** which are also called catalysts. Enzymes are molecules that are important for functional or metabolic activities in the cell because they change the rate of a reaction without being affected by the reaction itself.

Many integral membrane proteins are **glycoproteins** (proteins with attached carbohydrate groups). They form about 90% of all the membrane molecules that have carbohydrates attached to their external surface. The carbohydrate groups attached to both glycoproteins and the previously mentioned glycolipids form the fuzzy glycocalyx on the external surface of the plasma membrane.

WHAT DO YOU THINK?

1. What is the benefit to the cell of having a plasma membrane that is selectively permeable? What are some disadvantages of having a selectively permeable plasma membrane?

2.3b Protein-Specific Functions of the Plasma Membrane

The proteins of the plasma membrane perform a variety of important activities that promote its overall functions, including the following:

- **Transport.** A transmembrane protein is an integral protein that spans the plasma membrane completely. This protein assists the movement of a particular substance across the membrane. Sometimes the transport of material across the membrane requires cellular energy. A molecule called **ATP (adenosine triphosphate)** provides the energy for that transport. ATP releases energy when the bond that attaches its third phosphate to the rest of the molecule is broken.
- **Intercellular connection.** Junctions form between some neighboring cells when proteins in the membranes of each cell attach (discussed in section 4.1c) These junctions secure the cells to each other.
- **Anchorage for the cytoskeleton.** Cell shape is maintained by the attachment of structural proteins inside the cell (the cytoskeleton) to membrane proteins.

- **Enzyme (catalytic) activity.** Some membrane proteins are enzymes which act as catalysts to change the rates of some metabolic reactions. For example, the plasma membrane in most cells contains protein ion pumps that use energy to move ions against their concentration gradient. These pumps contain enzymes that break down ATP to release that energy. Ion pump are described in section 2.3c.
- **Cell–cell recognition.** The carbohydrate components of both glycoproteins and glycolipids usually act as identification molecules to other cell types in the body.
- **Signal transduction.** Signal transduction is the transmission of a message from a molecule outside the cell to the inside of the cell. The cell then responds by changing its internal activities.

2.3c Transport Across the Plasma Membrane

As we've just discussed, the plasma membrane is selectively permeable, so it is able to regulate transport of materials into and out of the cell. The following factors influence membrane permeability:

- **Transport proteins.** These integral membrane proteins move specific molecules across the membrane. Some of these proteins are called *carrier proteins.*
- **Plasma membrane structure.** Characteristics of the membrane phospholipids affect the ability of some molecules to cross that membrane. For example, some small polar molecules such as water are able to interact and pass through the phospholipids in the bilayer, whereas other polar molecules, such as simple sugars, cannot.
- **Concentration gradient.** Materials move more rapidly when their concentrations are significantly different between two compartments. For example, if intracellular fluid has a low concentration of a permeable substance, and the extracellular fluid has a high concentration of that substance, it would pass more quickly through the membrane into the cell.
- **Ionic charge.** An **ion** (atom with a net negative or positive charge) may either be repulsed or attracted to the membrane structures, influencing rate of molecular movement across the membrane. For example, if the inside of the cell has a net negative charge, a negative ion might be repelled by the intracellular environment, whereas a positive ion might be attracted to the intracellular environment.
- **Lipid solubility.** Materials that are lipid-soluble readlily pass through the membrane. For example, small nonpolar molecules called fatty acids move through the hydrophobic interior of the phospholipid bilayer and enter the cytoplasm of the cell, whereas larger, charged polar molecules, such as simple sugars or amino acids, are prevented from moving through the plasma membrane.
- **Molecular size.** Smaller molecules move across the plasma membrane readily, whereas larger molecules need special transport systems to move them across the membrane.

Passive Transport

The processes of transporting substances across plasma membranes are classified as either passive or active. **Passive transport** moves substances across a plasma membrane without the expenditure of energy by the cell. Materials move along a concentration gradient, meaning that they flow from a region of higher concentration of the material to a region of lower concentration. Passive transport is similar to floating downstream with the current; no cellular energy (ATP) is needed for it to occur. Passive processes that move material across the plasma membrane include simple diffusion, osmosis, facilitated diffusion, and bulk filtration.

Simple Diffusion **Diffusion** (di-fy ū'zhŭn; *diffundo* = to pour in different directions) is the tendency of molecules to move down their concentration gradient; that is, the molecules move from a region of higher concentration to a region of lower concentration. This movement continues until the molecules are spread out evenly on each side of the membrane. The concentration of these molecules is now said to be at **equilibrium.**

Simple diffusion occurs when substances move across membranes unaided because they are either small, nonpolar, or both. As a result of simple diffusion, a **net movement** of specific molecules or ions takes place from a region of their higher concentration to a region of their lower concentration. This net movement continues until all of those molecules are evenly distributed in the environment (the point of equilibrium). At this point, the concentration gradient no longer exists. However, molecular movement does not cease. Those molecules still move continuously in all directions at an equal rate. For example, there is no net movement of molecule "A" during its equilibrium, which means that one molecule "A" enters the cell for every molecule "A" that leaves the cell. An example of diffusion in the body is the movement of respiratory gases between the air sacs in the lungs and the blood vessels in the lungs. Oxygen continually moves from the lung air sacs into the blood, whereas carbon dioxide moves in the opposite direction. This movement guarantees that the blood will receive oxygen and eliminate carbon dioxide as part of normal respiration. The process of simple diffusion can occur without the presence of a membrane. Thus, it also occurs within the cell to distribute substances throughout the cytoplasm. APR

Osmosis **Osmosis** (os-m ō'sis; *osmos* = a thrusting) is a special type of simple diffusion in which water diffuses from one side of the selectively permeable membrane to the other. The net movement of water across a semipermeable membrane continues from a region of high water concentration to a region of low water concentration until equilibrium is established. In the body, the movement of water between the blood and the extracellular fluid around cells occurs by osmosis. APR

Facilitated Diffusion **Facilitated diffusion** requires the participation of transport proteins that help specific substances move across the plasma membrane. These substances are either large molecules or molecules that are insoluble in lipids. The molecule to be moved binds to the transport protein in the membrane. This binding helps alter the shape of both the transport protein and the molecule to be moved, thus permitting it to pass through the membrane. For example, glucose and some amino acids move across the membrane by this means. Facilitated diffusion differs from simple diffusion in that a specific protein is required to aid transport. APR

Bulk Filtration **Bulk filtration,** or *bulk movement,* involves the diffusion of solvents and solutes together across the selectively permeable membrane. **Solvents** are liquids that have substances called **solutes** dissolved within them. For example, water is a solvent if a solute such as salt or sugar is dissolved in it. Bulk filtration occurs when fluid and certain solutes are transported from the blood into the extracellular fluid. It works in this way: **Hydrostatic pressure** (hī′drō-stat′ik presh′ŭr) (fluid pressure exerted by blood pushing against the inside wall of a blood vessel) forces both water and small solutes from the blood across the plasma membranes of cells lining the capillaries (the smallest type of blood vessel). Only smaller molecules (glucose) and ions (such as sodium [Na^+] and potassium [K^+]) can be forced across the membrane by hydrostatic pressure. The largest molecules (called macromolecules) and large solid particles in the solvent must be transported through the membrane by the process of active transport, which we examine next.

Active Transport

Active transport is the movement of a substance across a plasma membrane *against* a concentration gradient, so materials must be moved from an area of low concentration to an area of high concentration. It is similar to swimming upstream against a current, where you must exert energy (swim) to move against the water flow. To move materials against their concentration gradient, active transport requires cellular energy in the form of ATP (adenosine triphosphate) and sometimes a transport protein as well. ATP is continually synthesized by mitochondria, cell structures described in section 2.4c. Active transport methods include ion pumps and several processes collectively known as bulk transport.

Ion Pumps Active transport mechanisms that use transport proteins to move ions across the membrane are called **ion pumps.** Ion pumps are a major factor in a cell's ability to maintain its internal concentrations of ions. One type of ion pump is the **sodium-potassium pump.** This transport mechanism is an example of an exchange pump, because it moves one ion type into the cell and simultaneously removes another type of ion from the cell (**figure 2.5**). For example, compared to their extracellular fluid, some human cells have much higher concentrations of potassium ions and much lower concentrations of sodium ions. The plasma membrane uses the sodium-potassium pump to maintain these steep concentration gradient differences by continuously removing sodium ions from the cell and moving potassium ions into the cell. Figure 2.5 shows how the cell expends energy in the form of ATP to maintain these sodium and potassium levels.

Bulk Transport Macromolecules, such as large proteins and polysaccharides, cannot move across the plasma membrane via ion pumps or with the assistance of normal transport proteins. Instead, larger molecules or bulk structures move across the membrane via the active transport processes called exocytosis and endocytosis.

In **exocytosis** (ek′s ō-sī-tō′sis; *exo* = outside, *kytos* = a hollow [cell], *osis* = condition of), large molecules are secreted *from* the cell (**figure 2.6**). Typically, the material for secretion is packaged within intracellular transport **vesicles** (ves′i-k ăl; *vesica* = bladder), which move toward the plasma membrane. When the vesicle and plasma membrane come into contact, the lipid molecules of the vesicle and plasma membrane bilayers rearrange themselves so that the two membranes fuse. The fusion of these lipid bilayers requires the cell to expend energy in the form of ATP. Following fusion, the vesicle contents are released to the outside of the cell. An example of this process occurs in the pancreas, where cells release digestive enzymes into a pancreatic duct for transport to the small intestine.

By contrast, large particulate substances and macromolecules are taken *into* the cell via **endocytosis** (en′d ō-sī-tō′sis; *endon* = within). The steps of endocytosis are similar to those of exocytosis, only in reverse. In endocytosis, extracellular macromolecules and large particulate matter are packaged in a vesicle that forms at the cell surface for internalization into the cell. A small area of plasma membrane folds inward to form a pocket, or **invagination** (in-vaj′i-nā′shŭn; *in* = in, *vagina* = a sheath), which deepens and pinches off as the lipid bilayer fuses. This fusion of the lipid bilayer is the energy-expending step. A new intracellular vesicle is formed containing material that was formerly outside the cell. There are three types of endocytosis: phagocytosis, pinocytosis, and receptor-mediated endocytosis (**figure 2.7**).

Phagocytosis (fag′ō-sī-tō′sis; *phago* = to eat, *kytos* = a hollow [cell], *osis* = condition) means "cellular eating." It is a nonspecific process that occurs when a cell engulfs or captures a large particle external to the cell by forming membrane extensions, called **pseudopodia** (sing., *pseudopodium*; sū′dō-pō′dē-ŭm, -pō′dē-ă; *pous* = foot), or *false feet,* to surround the particle (figure 2.7*a*). Once the particle is engulfed by the pseudopodia, it is packaged within an enclosed membrane sac. If large enough, this sac is classified as a **vacuole** (vak′y ū-ōl; *vacuum* = an empty space). The contents of the vacuole are broken down chemically (digested) after it fuses with a *lysosome* (lī′sō-sōm; *lysis* = a loosening, *soma* = body), which contains specific digestive enzymes that split large molecules into smaller ones. Only a few types of cells are able to perform phagocytosis. For example, phagocytosis occurs regularly when a white blood cell engulfs and digests a bacterium.

Clinical View 2.1

Cystic Fibrosis and Chloride Channels

The inherited disease **cystic fibrosis (CF)** involves defective plasma membrane proteins that affect chloride ion (Cl^-) channels in the membrane. These channels are transport proteins that use facilitated diffusion to move chloride ions across the plasma membrane. The genetic defect that causes CF results in the formation of abnormal chloride channel proteins in the membranes of cells lining the respiratory passageways and ducts in glands, such as the pancreas. The primary defect in these chloride channels results in an abnormal flow of chloride ions across the membrane, causing salt to be trapped within the cytoplasm of affected cells. Ultimately, the normal osmotic flow of water across the plasma membrane breaks down. The concentration of salt within the cytoplasm of these cells causes an increase in the osmotic flow of water into the cell, thereby resulting in thickening of the mucus in the respiratory passageways and the pancreatic ducts. The aggregation of thickened mucus plugs the airways of the lungs, leading to breathing problems and increasing the risk of infection. Therefore, a single genetic and biochemical defect in a transport protein produces significant health problems. The effect of CF on the lungs is continued with Clinical View 25.1: "Cystic Fibrosis" in section 25.1a.

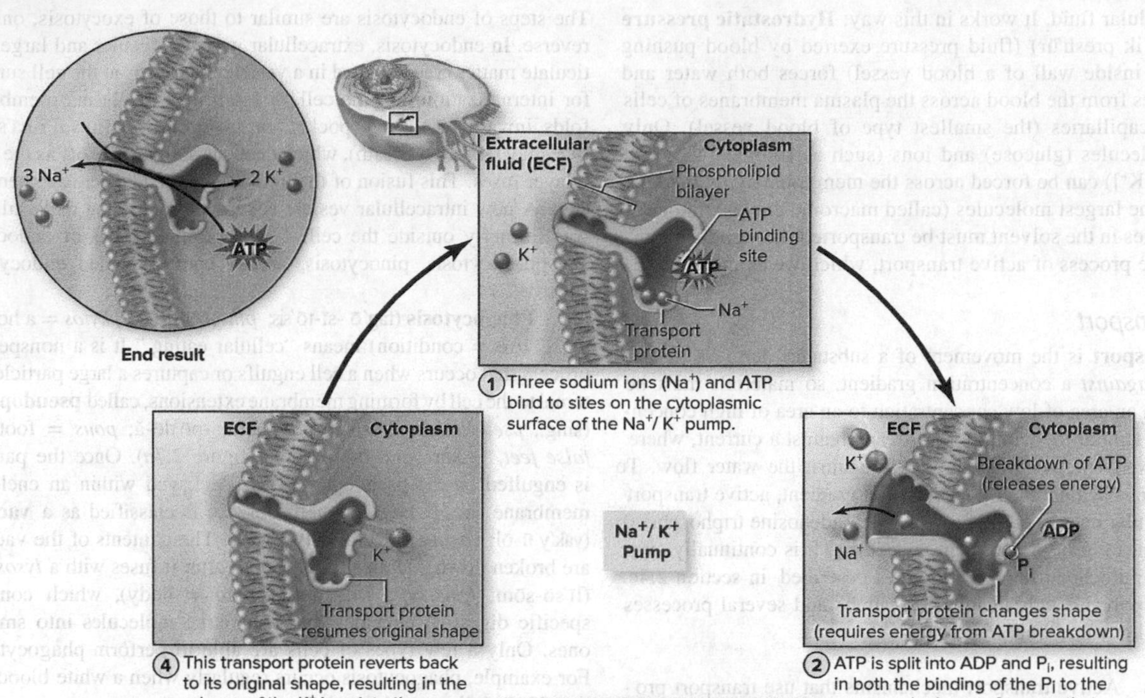
3 Na+
2 K+
ATP
End result
Extracellular fluid (ECF)
Cytoplasm
Phospholipid bilayer
ATP binding site
K+
ATP
Na+
Transport protein
1 Three sodium ions (Na+) and ATP bind to sites on the cytoplasmic surface of the Na+/ K+ pump.
ECF
Cytoplasm
K+
Breakdown of ATP (releases energy)
ADP
Na+
Pi
Transport protein changes shape (requires energy from ATP breakdown)
2 ATP is split into ADP and Pi, resulting in both the binding of the Pi to the pump and release of energy that causes the Na+/ K+ pump to change conformation (shape) and release the Na+ ions into the extracellular fluid.
Na+/ K+ Pump
ECF
Cytoplasm
K+
Transport protein resumes original shape
4 This transport protein reverts back to its original shape, resulting in the release of the K+ ions into the cytoplasm. The Na+/ K+ pump is now ready to begin the process again.
ECF
Cytoplasm
K+
Na+
Pi
3 Two K+ ions from the extracellular fluid then bind to sites on the outer cellular surface of the Na+/ K+ pump. At the same time, the Pi produced earlier by ATP hydrolysis is released into the cytoplasm.

Figure 2.5

Sodium-Potassium Pump. A sodium-potassium pump is a transport protein that uses ATP to transport Na^+ and K^+ ions in opposite directions through the membrane from a region of low concentration to a region of high concentration. This continuous, active transport process can be broken down into four steps. APR

Pinocytosis (pin′ō-sī-tō′sis [or pī′nō-]; *pineo* = to drink, *kytos* = a hollow [cell], *osis* = condition) is known as "cellular drinking." This process occurs when the cell internalizes a very small droplet of extracellular fluid into tiny internal vesicles (figure 2.7*b*). This process is nonspecific because all solutes dissolved in the droplet are taken into the cell. Most cells perform this type of transport across the membrane. Pinocytosis is similar to bulk filtration in that both types of transport move similar materials. However, it differs from bulk filtration because pinocytosis moves materials against a concentration gradient. An example of pinocytosis occurs within cells that form a capillary (tiny blood vessel) wall, where vesicles fill with a fluid droplet containing small solutes from the blood, carry this droplet to the other side of the cell, and then expel its contents outside the capillary wall.

Receptor-mediated endocytosis is the movement of specific molecules from the extracellular fluid into a cell by way of a newly formed vesicle. This process begins when molecules in the extracellular fluid bind to their specific integral membrane protein receptors. (Recall that a membrane receptor is a protein that acts as a binding site for molecules outside the cell.) This process is different from the nonspecific transport mechanisms discussed earlier in this section. It is considered a specific mechanism because the endocytosis is stimulated by the binding of the specific molecules to their specific membrane receptors. The receptor proteins then cluster in one region of the membrane to begin the process of endocytosis. The plasma membrane housing the bound specific molecules from the extracellular fluid folds inward to form a pocket, or invagination (figure 2.7*c*). This membrane pocket deepens and pinches off as the lipid bilayers fuse. The fusion of these lipid bilayers requires the cell to expend energy in the form of ATP. An example of receptor-mediated endocytosis occurs when human cells contain receptors that bind to and internalize cholesterol, which is

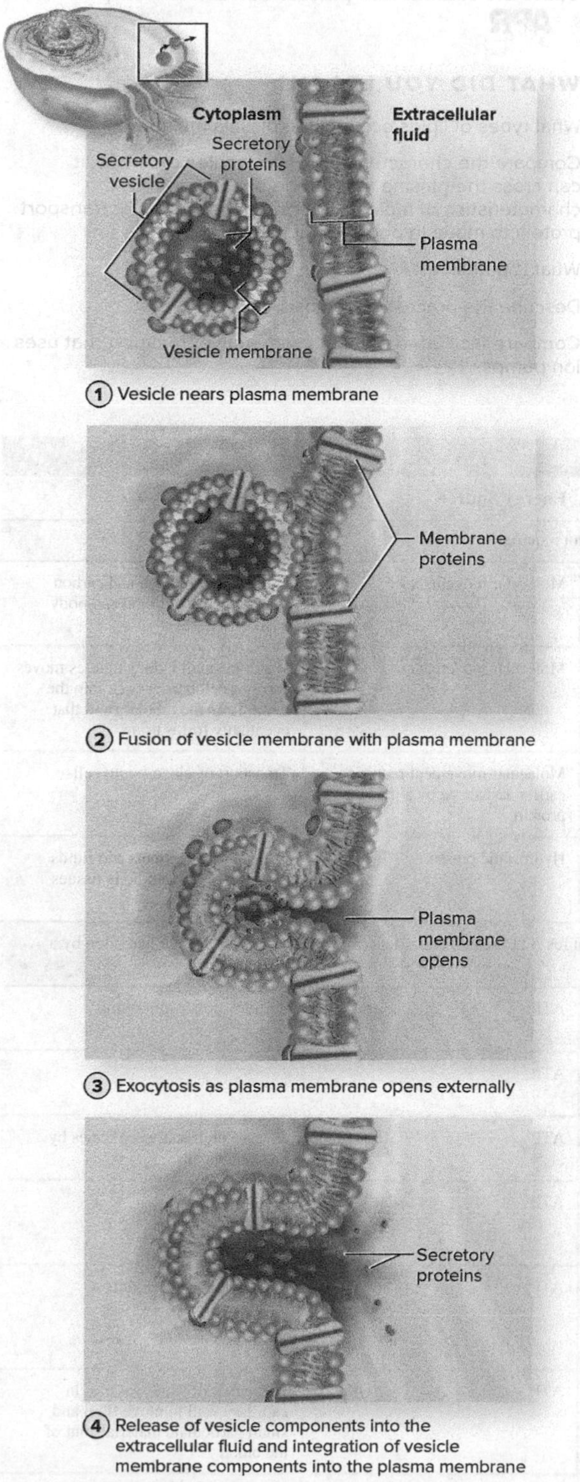

Cytoplasm
Extracellular fluid
Secretory vesicle
Secretory proteins
Plasma membrane
Vesicle membrane
1 Vesicle nears plasma membrane
Membrane proteins
2 Fusion of vesicle membrane with plasma membrane
Plasma membrane opens
3 Exocytosis as plasma membrane opens externally
Secretory proteins
4 Release of vesicle components into the extracellular fluid and integration of vesicle membrane components into the plasma membrane

Figure 2.6

Exocytosis. In exocytosis, the cell secretes bulk volumes of materials into the extracellular fluid. This continuous process is shown in four steps.

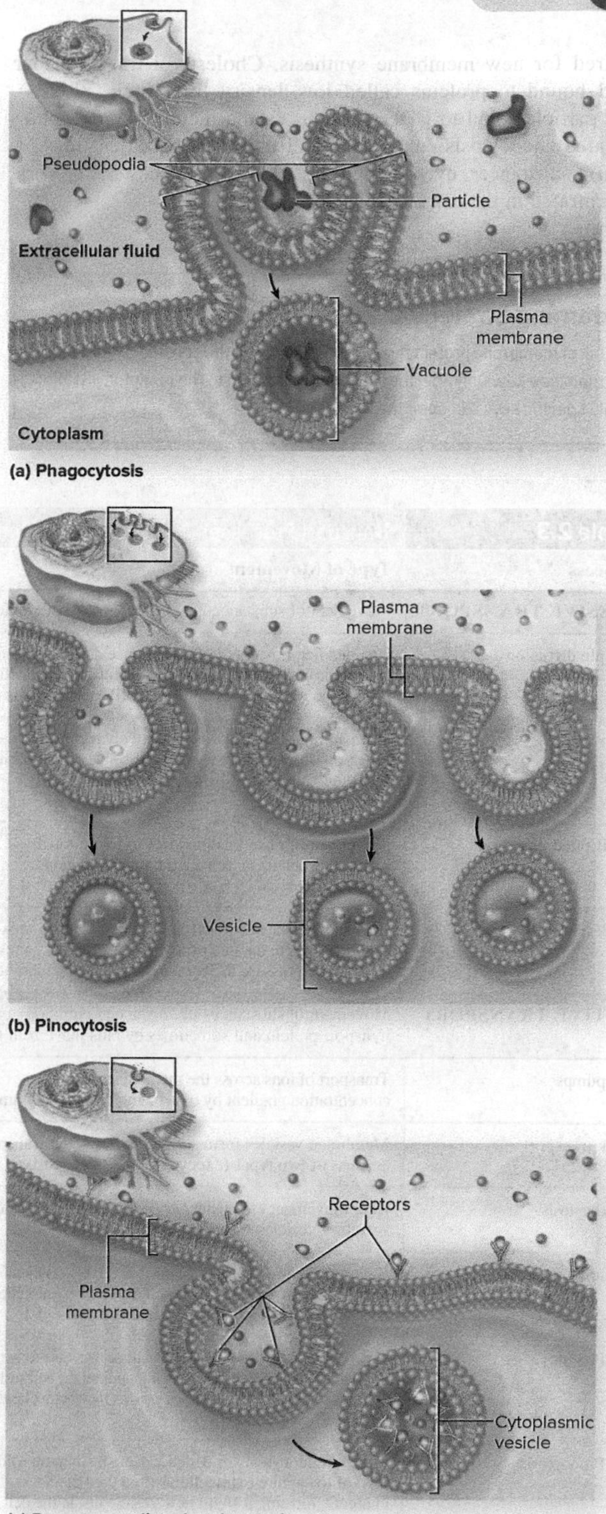

Pseudopodia
Particle
Extracellular fluid
Plasma membrane
Vacuole
Cytoplasm
(a) Phagocytosis
Plasma membrane
Vesicle
(b) Pinocytosis
Receptors
Plasma membrane
Cytoplasmic vesicle
(c) Receptor-mediated endocytosis

Figure 2.7

Three Forms of Endocytosis. Endocytosis is a process whereby the cell acquires materials from the extracellular fluid. (*a*) Phagocytosis occurs when membrane extensions, termed pseudopodia, engulf a particle and internalize it into a vacuole. (*b*) Pinocytosis is the incorporation of droplets of extracellular fluid into the cell via the formation of small vesicles. (*c*) In receptor-mediated endocytosis, receptors with specific molecules bound to them aggregate within the membrane, and then an invagination forms around them to create a cytoplasmic vesicle.

required for new membrane synthesis. Cholesterol travels in our blood bound to proteins called low-density lipoproteins (LDLs). LDL particles bind to LDL receptors in the membrane. Receptor-mediated endocytosis enables the cell to obtain bulk quantities of specific substances, even though those substances may not be very concentrated in the extracellular fluid.

Learning Strategy 2.2

Think of membrane protein receptors as a lock and the substance that binds to them as a key. Only specific substances can bind to the receptor, just like only specific keys can open the lock.

Table 2.3 summarizes passive and active transport mechanisms. APR

WHAT DID YOU LEARN?

4. What types of lipids occur in the plasma membrane?
5. Compare the characteristics of molecules or ions that can cross the plasma membrane unaided versus the characteristics of molecules or ions that require a transport protein to move in or out of the cell.
6. What is diffusion?
7. Describe the process of osmosis.
8. Compare facilitated diffusion with active transport that uses ion pumps.

Table 2.3 Transport Processes Across a Plasma Membrane

Process	Type of Movement	Energy Source	Example
PASSIVE TRANSPORT	Movement of substance *along* a concentration gradient; ATP not required		
Simple diffusion	Unaided net movement of a substance due to molecular motion down its concentration gradient across selectively permeable membrane; continues until equilibrium is reached	Molecular movement	Exchange of oxygen and carbon dioxide between blood and body tissues
Osmosis	Diffusion of water across a selectively permeable membrane; direction is determined by relative solute concentrations; continues until equilibrium is reached	Molecular movement	Water in small kidney tubules moves across a cell barrier back into the blood from the tubular fluid that eventually forms urine
Facilitated diffusion	Movement of materials too large to pass through membrane channels; relies on transport proteins	Molecular movement requiring carrier assistance by a transport protein	Transport of glucose into cells
Bulk filtration	Bulk movement of solvents and solutes from an area of high concentration to an area of low concentration as a result of hydrostatic pressure differences across the membrane	Hydrostatic pressure	Transport of nutrients and fluids from the blood into body tissues
ACTIVE TRANSPORT	Movement of substances *against* a concentration gradient; requires ATP; requires assistance to move across the membrane, often by a transport protein and sometimes by bulk movement in vesicles.		
Ion pumps	Transport of ions across the membrane against a concentration gradient by transmembrane protein pumps	ATP	Sodium-potassium pump
Bulk transport	Membrane vesicles form around materials for transport; consists of two types (exocytosis and endocytosis)	ATP	
Exocytosis	Bulk movement of substances *out* of the cell by fusion of secretory vesicles with the plasma membrane	ATP	Release of digestive enzymes by pancreatic cells
Endocytosis	Bulk movement of substances *into* a cell by vesicles forming at the plasma membrane; consists of three types (phagocytosis, pinocytosis, and receptor-mediated endocytosis)	ATP	
Phagocytosis	Type of endocytosis in which particulate materials move into a cell after being engulfed by pseudopodia at the cell surface; vesicles form at the inside of the plasma membrane; large sacs are called vacuoles	ATP	White blood cell engulfs a bacterium
Pinocytosis	Type of endocytosis in which plasma membrane folds inward to capture extracellular fluid droplet and its dissolved contents, forming a small new vesicle inside the cell	ATP	Formation of small vesicles in capillary wall to move fluid and small particulate materials out of the blood
Receptor-mediated endocytosis	Type of endocytosis in which specific molecule-receptor complexes in the plasma membrane stimulate the clustering of bound molecule-receptor complexes; vesicles containing specific molecules bound to receptors in the membrane stimulate internalization of the bound molecules	ATP	Uptake of cholesterol into cells

2.4 Cytoplasm

✓ Learning Objectives

9. Describe the three parts of a cell's cytoplasm.
10. Identify and describe the structures and functions of cellular organelles.

Cytoplasm is a nonspecific term for all of the materials contained within the plasma membrane and surrounding the nucleus. The cytoplasm includes three separate parts: cytosol, inclusions, and organelles (except the nucleus).

2.4a Cytosol

The **cytosol** (sī′tō-sol; *kytos* = a hollow [cell], *sol* = abbrev. of soluble), also called the *cytoplasmic matrix* or *intracellular fluid,* is the viscous, syruplike fluid of the cytoplasm. It has a high water content and contains many dissolved solutes, including ions, nutrients, proteins, carbohydrates, lipids, and other small molecules. Many cytoplasmic proteins are the enzymes that act as catalysts in cellular reactions. The cytosol's carbohydrates and lipids serve as an energy source for the cell. Many of the small molecules in the cytosol are the building blocks of large macromolecules. For example, amino acids are small molecules dissolved in the cytosol that the cell uses to synthesize new proteins.

2.4b Inclusions

The cytosol of some cells contains **inclusions,** a large and diverse group of chemical substances that these cells store temporarily. Most inclusions are not bound by a membrane. Cellular inclusions include pigments, such as melanin; protein crystals; and nutrient stores, such as glycogen and triglycerides. **Melanin** (mel′ă-nin; *melas* = black), a stored pigment in some skin, hair, and eye cells, protects the body from the sun's ultraviolet light. **Glycogen** is a polysaccharide (a type of carbohydrate [sugar]) that is stored primarily in liver and skeletal muscle cells.

2.4c Organelles

Organelles (ŏr′g ăn-el; *organon* = organ, *elle* = the diminutive suffix), meaning "little organs," are complex, organized structures with unique, characteristic shapes. Each type of organelle performs a different function for the cell. Collectively, the specialized functions of all organelles are essential for normal cellular structure and activities. These unique structures permit the cell to carry on different activities simultaneously. This division of labor prevents interference between cellular activities and promotes maximal functional efficiency in the cell. Organelles assume specific roles in growth, repair, and cellular maintenance. Different cell types vary in organelle distribution and numbers, depending on the cell function. Two categories of organelles are recognized: membrane-bound organelles and non-membrane-bound organelles.

Membrane-Bound Organelles

Some organelles are surrounded by a membrane and thus are called **membrane-bound organelles,** or *membranous organelles.* This membrane is similar to the plasma membrane surrounding the cell in that it is composed of a phospholipid bilayer with diverse associated proteins. Every membrane exhibits a unique protein-lipid composition, which confers a unique function(s) to that membrane. The membrane separates the organelle's contents from the cytosol so that the activities of the organelle can proceed without disrupting other cellular activities. Membrane-bound organelles include the endoplasmic reticulum, the Golgi apparatus, lysosomes, peroxisomes, and mitochondria.

Endoplasmic Reticulum The **endoplasmic reticulum** (re-tik′y ū-lŭm; *rete* = net) (ER) is an extensive intracellular membrane network throughout the cytoplasm. ER is composed of two distinct regions that differ in structure and function: smooth endoplasmic reticulum (smooth ER, or SER) and rough endoplasmic reticulum (rough ER, or RER; **figure 2.8**). The amount of either kind of ER varies, depending upon the specific functions of the cell.

Smooth ER is continuous with the rough ER. Smooth ER walls do not have the rough appearance of rough ER, because there are no ribosomes attached to the membranes. Smooth ER resembles multiple interconnected branches of tubules. The smooth ER of various cell types functions in diverse metabolic processes, including synthesis, transport, and storage of lipids; metabolism of carbohydrates; and detoxification of drugs, alcohol, and poisons. The amount of smooth ER is greater in cells that synthesize steroid hormones. In addition, the liver contains abundant amounts of smooth ER to process digested nutrients and detoxify drugs and alcohol.

Rough ER is responsible for producing, transporting, and storing proteins associated with a membrane. Rough ER consists of parallel membranes enclosing spaces called **cisternae** (sis-ter′nē; *cisterna* = cistern). Ribosomes are the small structures attached to the cytoplasmic sides (called faces) of these membranes. These ribosomes are called bound ribosomes because they are attached to the membrane surface of the ER, thus forming the rough ER. These ribosomes synthesize the proteins targeted for cell export, insertion into the plasma membrane, or inclusion within a lysosome as a catalyst. As new proteins are synthesized by the bound ribosomes, they pass through the membrane of the rough ER and enter its cisternae, where their original structure changes by either adding other molecules or removing part of what was originally synthesized. These modified proteins are packaged into small, enclosed membrane sacs that pinch off from the ER. These sacs, termed **transport vesicles,** shuttle proteins from the rough ER to another organelle, the Golgi apparatus (discussed later in this section), for further modification. For a seamless interaction and transition between organelles, transport vesicles, and the plasma membrane, the membranes of each structure have the same general lipid and protein composition and organization. The amount of rough ER is greater in cells producing large amounts of protein for secretion, such as a cell in the pancreas that secretes enzymes for digesting materials in the small intestine.

Golgi Apparatus The **Golgi apparatus,** also called the *Golgi complex,* is a center for modifying, packaging, and sorting materials that arrive from the rough ER in transport vesicles. The Golgi apparatus is especially extensive and active in cells specialized for secretion.

The Golgi apparatus is composed primarily of a series of cisternae, which are arranged in a stack (**figure 2.9*a***). The edges of each sac bulge, and many small transport vesicles are clustered around the expanded edges of the individual sacs. The vesicles concentrated at

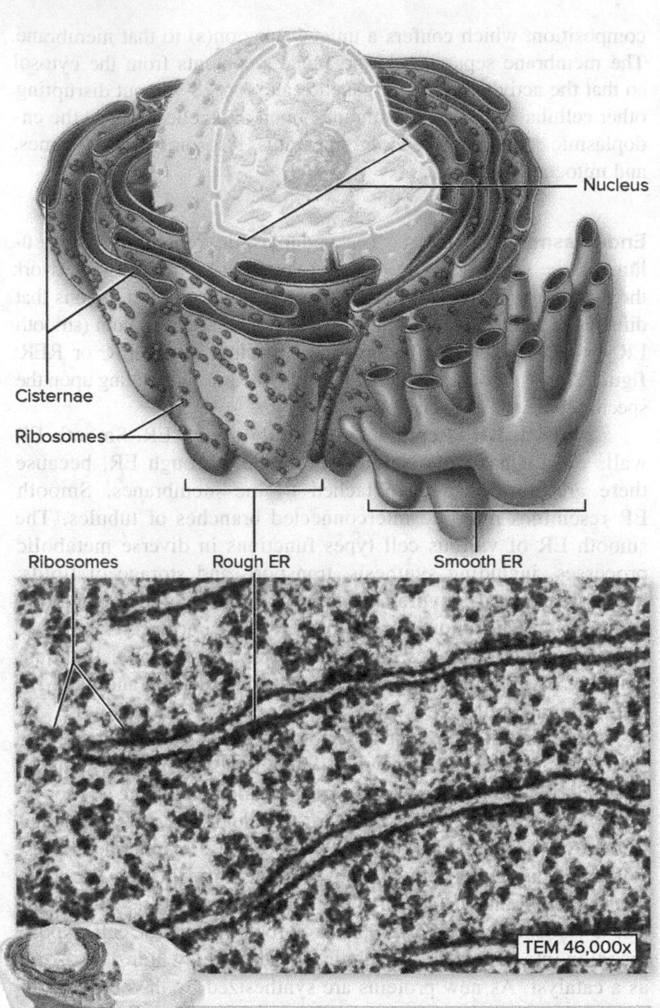

Nucleus
Cisternae
Ribosomes
Ribosomes
Rough ER
Smooth ER
TEM 46,000x

Functions of Endoplasmic Reticulum

1. **Synthesis:** Provides a place for chemical reactions
   a. Smooth ER is the site of lipid synthesis and carbohydrate metabolism
   b. Rough ER synthesizes proteins for secretion, incorporation into the plasma membrane, and as enzymes within lysosomes
2. **Transport:** Moves molecules through cisternal space from one part of the cell to another; sequestered away from the cytoplasm
3. **Storage:** Stores newly synthesized molecules
4. **Detoxification:** Smooth ER detoxifies drugs, alcohol, and poisons

Figure 2.8

Endoplasmic Reticulum (ER). A drawing and TEM show that the ER is a membranous network of flattened membrane sacs (cisternae) and interconnected tubules that is continuous with the nuclear envelope. Smooth ER, which is not shown on this TEM, consists of even-surfaced, interconnected tubules, and it lacks associated ribosomes. Rough ER, by contrast, is composed of cisternal membranes with ribosomes attached to their cytoplasmic surfaces. However, the two types of ER are continuous.

the periphery of the Golgi apparatus are active in transporting and transferring material between the individual sacs of the Golgi apparatus as well as between the Golgi apparatus and other cellular structures.

The Golgi apparatus exhibits a distinct polarity: The membranes of the cisternae at opposite ends of a stack differ in thickness and molecular composition. These two poles of the Golgi apparatus are called the **receiving region** (or *cis-face*) and the **shipping region** (or *trans-face*), respectively. The diameter of the flattened sac is larger in the receiving region than in the shipping region. The products of the rough ER move through the Golgi apparatus via transport vesicles, going from the receiving region to the shipping region. Normally, materials move through the Golgi apparatus as shown in figure 2.9*b* and described here:

1. Newly synthesized proteins in the rough ER cisternae are sequestered into a transport vesicle.
2. The vesicle pinches off the rough ER and travels to the Golgi apparatus.
3. Newly arrived transport vesicles fuse with the receiving region of the Golgi apparatus.
4. Protein modification occurs as the proteins are moved by transport vesicles sequentially through the Golgi apparatus cisternae from the receiving region to the shipping region.
5. Modified proteins are packaged in secretory vesicles.
6. Vesicles leaving the shipping region become (a) lysosomes, which contain proteins called digestive enzymes, (b) secretory vesicles that undergo exocytosis, or (c) new parts of the plasma membrane.

Lysosomes **Lysosomes** (lī′sō-sōm; *lysis* = a loosening, *soma* = body) are membrane sacs formed by the Golgi apparatus **(figure 2.10)**. Lysosomes contain enzymes used by the cell to digest waste products and ingested macromolecules. These enzymes break down large molecules, such as proteins, fats, polysaccharides, and nucleic acids, into smaller molecules. Lysosomes are sometimes referred to as the "garbagemen" of the cell because they digest and remove waste products.

Some substances digested by lysosomal enzymes enter the cell by endocytosis. Lysosomes fuse with endocytic vesicles, and their enzymes combine with the internalized materials. The products resulting from these digestive activities are released from the lysosome into the cytosol, where they are recycled for various future uses. For example, a large protein is broken down into its component amino acids, which may be used to synthesize a new, different protein needed by that cell.

Lysosomes also remove the cell's damaged parts. An internal membrane encloses these damaged structures, and then it fuses with the lysosomes. Thus, old organelles are removed via a process called **autophagy** (aw-tof′ă-jē; *autos* = self, *phago* = to eat). When a cell is damaged or dies, enzymes from all lysosomes are eventually released into the cell, resulting in the rapid digestion of the cell itself. This process is called **autolysis** (aw-tol′i-sis; *autos* = self, *lysis* = dissolution). There are specific types of autophagy named for the organelle or macromolecule that is being degraded.

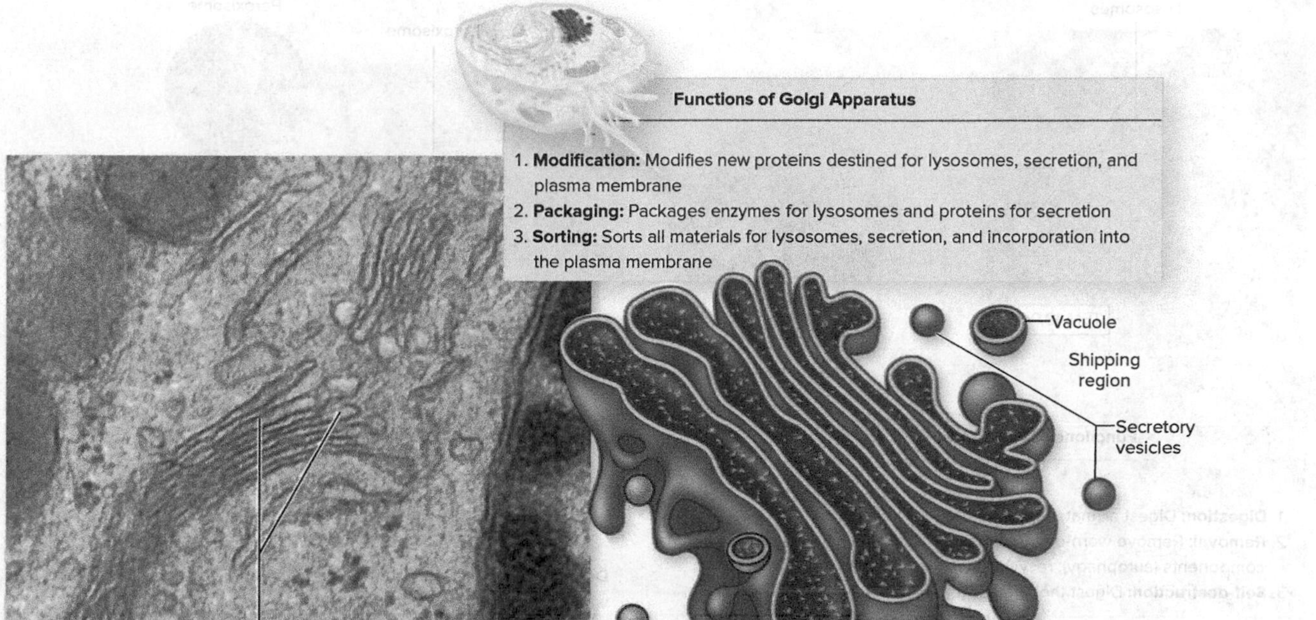
Functions of Golgi Apparatus
1. Modification: Modifies new proteins destined for lysosomes, secretion, and plasma membrane
2. Packaging: Packages enzymes for lysosomes and proteins for secretion
3. Sorting: Sorts all materials for lysosomes, secretion, and incorporation into the plasma membrane
TEM 34,000x
(a)
Cisternae
Vacuole
Shipping region
Secretory vesicles
Transport vesicle
Lumen of cisterna filled with secretory product
Transport vesicle
Rough endoplasmic reticulum (rough ER)
Golgi apparatus
Membrane protein transport vesicles
Protein incorporation in plasma membrane
Extracellular fluid
Secretory vesicles
Plasma membrane
Shipping region
Receiving region
Exocytosis
Lysosomes
Transport vesicles
Cytoplasm
Synthesis, Modification, and Shipping of Proteins
1 Rough ER synthesizes protein that is released in a transport vesicle.
2 Vesicle from the rough ER moves to the Golgi apparatus.
3 Vesicle fuses with Golgi apparatus at the receiving region.
4 Proteins are modified as they move through Golgi apparatus (e.g., addition of carbohydrate).
5 Modified proteins are packaged and released within secretory vesicle from the shipping region.
6 Secretory vesicles (6a) merge with the plasma membrane to insert molecules into the plasma membrane (6b), or release contents by exocytosis. They may also serve as lysosomes (6c).

(b) Movement of materials through the Golgi apparatus

Figure 2.9

Golgi Apparatus. Each Golgi apparatus is composed of several flattened membrane sacs (cisternae), with some associated transport vesicles at the periphery of these sacs. The arrangement of sacs exhibits both structural and functional polarity. (*a*) A TEM and a drawing provide different views of the Golgi apparatus along with a list of its functions. (*b*) The receiving region receives incoming transport vesicles from the rough ER; large vesicles carrying finished product exit the shipping region. The progress through the Golgi apparatus is described in six steps.

(a) ©EM Research Services, Newcastle University

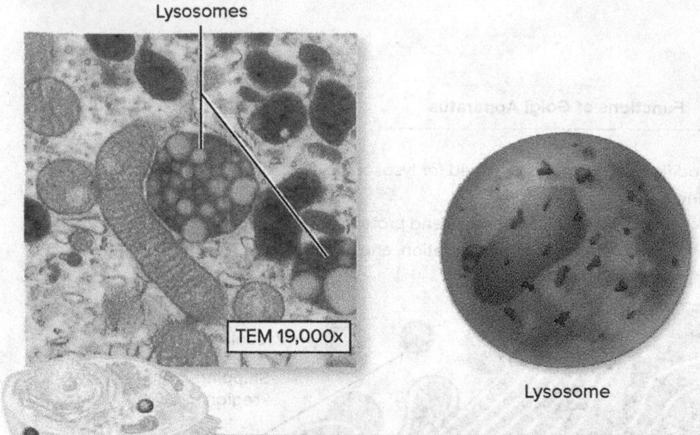
Lysosomes
TEM 19,000x
Lysosome

Functions of Lysosomes

1. **Digestion:** Digest all materials that enter cell by endocytosis
2. **Removal:** Remove worn-out or damaged organelles and cellular components (autophagy); recycle small molecules for resynthesis
3. **Self-destruction:** Digest the remains (autolysis) after cellular death

Figure 2.10

Lysosomes. A drawing and TEM show lysosomes, which are membrane-bound, spherical sacs in the cytoplasm of a cell. Lysosomes house enzymes for intracellular digestion, as well as performing the other functions listed here. APR

©EM Research Services, Newcastle University

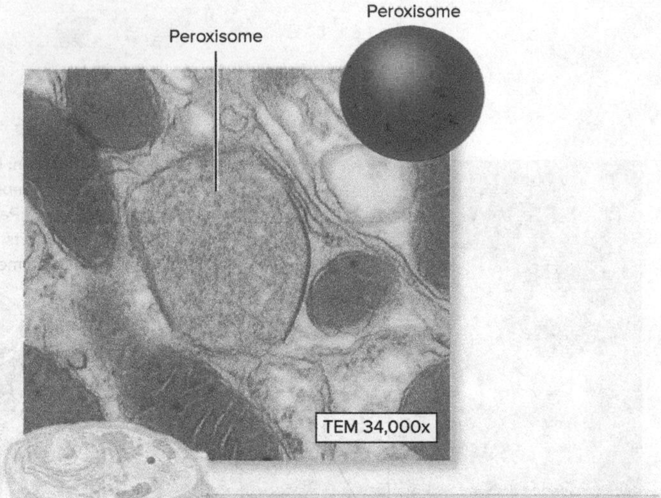
Peroxisome
Peroxisome
TEM 34,000x

Function of Peroxisomes

Detoxification: Detoxify harmful substances; convert hydrogen peroxide to water; break down fatty acid molecules

Figure 2.11

Peroxisomes. A drawing and a TEM show a peroxisome in a cell. Peroxisomes are small, membrane-bound organelles that degrade harmful substances, including hydrogen peroxide, during cellular reactions. They also break down fatty acid molecules.

(a) ©EM Research Services, Newcastle University; (b) ©Electronic Publishing Services, Inc., NY/McGraw-Hill Education

WHAT DO YOU THINK?

2. What would happen to a cell if it didn't contain any lysosomes (or if its lysosomes weren't functioning)? Would the cell be able to survive?

Clinical View 2.2

Tay-Sachs Disease

Tay-Sachs disease is a rare, inherited lysosomal storage disease that results in the buildup of fatty material in nerve cells. Healthy, properly functioning lysosomes are essential for the health of the cells and the whole body. Tay-Sachs disease occurs because one of the approximately 50 different lysosomal enzymes is missing or nonfunctional. Lysosomes in affected individuals lack an enzyme that is needed to break down a complex membrane lipid. As a result, the complex lipid accumulates within cells. The cellular signs of Tay-Sachs disease are swollen lysosomes due to accumulation of the complex lipid that cannot be digested. Affected infants appear normal at birth, but begin to show signs of the disease by the age of 6 months. The nervous system exhibits the most damage with development of paralysis, blindness, and deafness followed by death by the age of 4. Unfortunately, there is no treatment or cure for this deadly disease.

Peroxisomes **Peroxisomes** (pĕ-rok′si-sōm) are membrane-enclosed sacs that are usually smaller in diameter than lysosomes (**figure 2.11**). They are formed by pinching off vesicles from the rough ER. Peroxisomes use oxygen to catalytically detoxify specific harmful substances either produced by the cell or taken into the cell. For example, the peroxisome is able to convert hydrogen peroxide (a toxic compound) that is sometimes produced by cells into water before it can damage the cell. It does this using the enzyme catalase, which is a component of the peroxisome. Peroxisomes are most abundant in liver cells, where they break down fatty acids and detoxify some toxic materials, such as alcohol, that are absorbed in the gastrointestinal tract.

Mitochondria **Mitochondria** (mī′to-kon′drē-ă; sing., *mitochondrion*, mī-tō-kon′drē-on′; *mitos* = thread, *chondros* = granule) are organelles with a double membrane that are involved in producing large amounts of the cell's energy currency, ATP. For this reason, mitochondria are called the "powerhouses" of the cell. A mitochondrion is completely surrounded by an outer membrane, while a second, or inner membrane, is folded internally into the space at the center of the organelle. These folds, called **cristae** (kris′ tă, -tē; *crista* = crest), increase the surface area that is exposed to the internal fluid contents, termed the **matrix** (**figure 2.12**). Inner membrane proteins, including enzymes for ATP synthesis, are on the cristae.

The number of mitochondria in a cell depends upon the cell's energy needs. Because mitochondria can self-replicate, the numbers of mitochondria are greater in cells that have a high energy demand.

Clinical View 2.3

Adrenoleukodystrophy (ALD)

Adrenoleukodystrophy is a rare inherited disorder that is caused when a membrane protein is missing in the peroxisome. In the healthy state, this protein transports into the peroxisome an enzyme that controls the breakdown of very-long-chain fatty acids, which are part of the neutral fats in our diets. When the enzyme cannot enter the peroxisome because the transport protein is missing, the peroxisomes cannot function normally, and so the very-long-chain fatty acids accumulate in cells of the central nervous system, eventually stripping these cells of their myelin covering. The absence of this myelin covering prevents the normal transmission of messages through the nerve cell, and the messages "short-circuit." The very-long-chain fatty acids also build up in the adrenal glands, causing them to malfunction.

ALD exists in several forms, but the most severe kind affects young boys between the ages of 4 and 10. There is no cure for ALD, and it is deadly if not treated. Dietary modification (to reduce the amounts of very-long-chain fatty acids in the diet) and use of oleic acid/rapeseed oil blend helps control the very-long-chain fatty acid buildup. Some research has indicated that statins (medicines that control cholesterol levels) may help prevent the buildup of the very-long-chain fatty acids. A recent clinical trial has shown promise using gene therapy to treat individuals with ALD.

For example, muscle cells with a high rate of energy usage have a large number of mitochondria in their cytoplasm. Mitochondria numbers increase with increased demands for ATP. Additionally, mitochondria contain a circular chromosome (chromosomes are described in section 2.5c). In the mitochondria, this piece of DNA contains genes for producing mitochondrial proteins. Mitochondrial shape also varies among cells. Interestingly, the head of a sperm contains no mitochondria because that portion has no energy need. Instead, there are mitochondria in the midpiece of the sperm, the region responsible for propelling the sperm.

WHAT DO YOU THINK?

3 While examining a cell by microscope, you note that the cell has few mitochondria. What does this imply about the cell's energy requirements?

Non-Membrane-Bound Organelles

Organelles that are always in direct contact with the cytosol are called either **non-membrane-bound organelles** or *nonmembranous organelles*.

Ribosomes **Ribosomes** (rī′bō-sōm; *ribos* = reference to a 5-carbon sugar, *soma* = body) are very small, dense granules that are responsible for protein production (synthesis). Each ribosome has a small subunit and a large subunit (**figure 2.13*a***); the small subunit is about one-half the size of the large subunit. The parts of the subunits are formed in the nucleus, and the subunits are assembled within the cytosol at the time when a new protein is about to be synthesized. Once ribosomes are assembled, those that float freely within the cytosol of the cell are called **free ribosomes,** whereas those that are attached to the rough endoplasmic reticulum are called **bound ribosomes** (figure 2.13*b*). Free ribosomes are responsible for the synthesis of proteins that remain within the cytosol of the cell. Bound ribosomes produce proteins that are exported outside the cell, incorporated into the plasma membrane, or housed as enzymes within a new lysosome.

Cytoskeleton The **cytoskeleton** is composed of protein subunits organized either as filaments or hollow tubes. The cytoskeleton has three separate components—microfilaments, intermediate filaments, and microtubules—which differ in their structures and functions (**figure 2.14**).

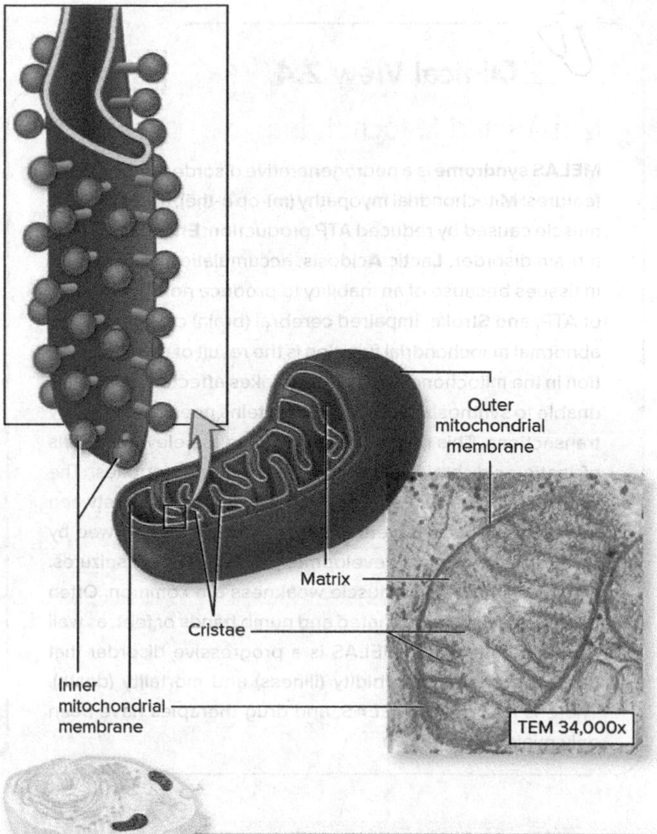

Function of Mitochondria

Energy synthesis: Produce ATP by cellular respiration for energy needs of the cell; called the "powerhouses" of the cell

Figure 2.12
Mitochondria. A drawing and TEM show a mitochondrion. Mitochondria are double-membrane-bound organelles that produce ATP for cellular work.
©EM Research Services, Newcastle University

Clinical View 2.4

MELAS and Mitochondria

MELAS syndrome is a neurogenerative disorder named for its features: **M**itochondrial myopathy (mī-op'ă-thē), a weakness in muscle caused by reduced ATP production; **E**ncephalopathy, a brain disorder; **L**actic **A**cidosis, accumulation of lactic acid in tissues because of an inability to produce normal amounts of ATP; and **S**troke, impaired cerebral (brain) circulation. The abnormal mitochondrial function is the result of a single mutation in the mitochondrial DNA that makes affected individuals unable to synthesize some of the proteins needed for energy transactions. This mutation also leads to the elevated levels of lactic acid, brain pathology, and recurring strokes. The syndrome typically first presents with stroke (often between the ages of 4 and 15 years), a symptom that is followed by episodes of fatigue, developmental delays, and seizures. Low muscle tone and muscle weakness are common. Often patients have uncoordinated and numb hands or feet, as well as diabetes mellitus. MELAS is a progressive disorder that has a high rate of morbidity (illness) and mortality (death). There is no cure for MELAS, and drug therapies have been only minimally effective.

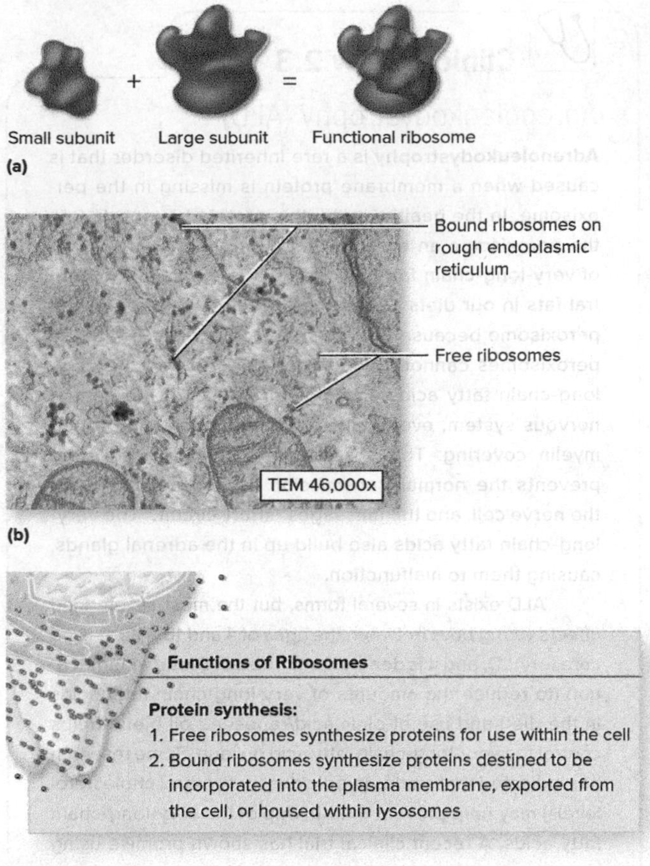

Small subunit
Large subunit
Functional ribosome
(a)
Bound ribosomes on rough endoplasmic reticulum
Free ribosomes
TEM 46,000x
(b)
Functions of Ribosomes
Protein synthesis:
1. Free ribosomes synthesize proteins for use within the cell
2. Bound ribosomes synthesize proteins destined to be incorporated into the plasma membrane, exported from the cell, or housed within lysosomes

Figure 2.13

Ribosomes. Ribosomes are small, dense, cytoplasmic granules where proteins are synthesized within the cell. (*a*) Ribosomes consist of both small and large subunits. (*b*) A TEM shows bound and free ribosomes in the cell cytoplasm.

(b) ©EM Research Services, Newcastle University

Microfilaments (mī'krō-fil'ă-ment; *micros* = small) are the smallest components of the cytoskeleton. They are about 7 nanometers (nm) in diameter and are composed of thin protein filaments (actin proteins) organized into two intertwined strands. They form an interlacing network on the cytoplasmic side of the plasma membrane. Microfilaments help maintain cell shape, support changes in cell shape, participate in muscle contraction, separate the two cells formed during cell division, and facilitate cytoplasmic streaming, which is the movement of the cytoplasm associated with changing cell shape.

Intermediate filaments are between 8 nm and 12 nm in diameter, and are more rigid than microfilaments. They support cells structurally and stabilize junctions between cells. Their protein component differs, depending upon the cells in which they occur in the body.

Microtubules (mī'krō-tū'byūl; *micros* = small, *tubus* = tube) are hollow tubules, about 25 nm in diameter, composed of long chains of a protein called tubulin. Microtubules radiate from the centrosome (discussed next) and help hold organelles in place, maintain cell shape and rigidity, direct organelle movement between different regions of the cell, provide a means of cell motility using structures called cilia or flagella, and move chromosomes during the process of cell division. Microtubules are not permanent structures, and they can be elongated or shortened as needed to complete their functions.

Centrosome and Centrioles Closely adjacent to the nucleus in most cells is a nonmembranous, spherical structure called the **centrosome.** The matrix of this region is a microtubule organization center that supports the growth and elongation of microtubules. Within the region of the centrosome are a pair of cylindrical **centrioles** (sen'trē-ōl; *kentron* = a point, center) that lie perpendicular to one another. Each centriole is composed of nine sets of three closely aligned microtubules, called microtubule triplets, that are arranged in a circle (**figure 2.15**). The centrioles replicate immediately prior to cell division (mitosis). During mitosis (described in section 2.6b), they are responsible for organizing microtubules that are a part of the mitotic spindle. Some of these microtubules attach to chromosomes to facilitate their movement.

Cilia and Flagella **Cilia** (sil'ē-ă; sing., *cilium*, sil'ē-ŭm; an eyelash) and **flagella** (flă-jel'ă; sing., *flagellum*, flă-jel'ŭm; a whip) are projections extending from the cell. They are composed of cytoplasm and supportive microtubules enclosed by the plasma membrane.

Cilia are found in large numbers on some cell surfaces exposed to the external environment (**figure 2.16*a***). For example, cells with cilia line parts of the respiratory passageways. Here, these ciliated cells are always associated with mucin-secreting goblet cells. Mucus that is formed from the secreted mucin appears as a sticky film on the free surface of ciliated cells. The beating of the cilia

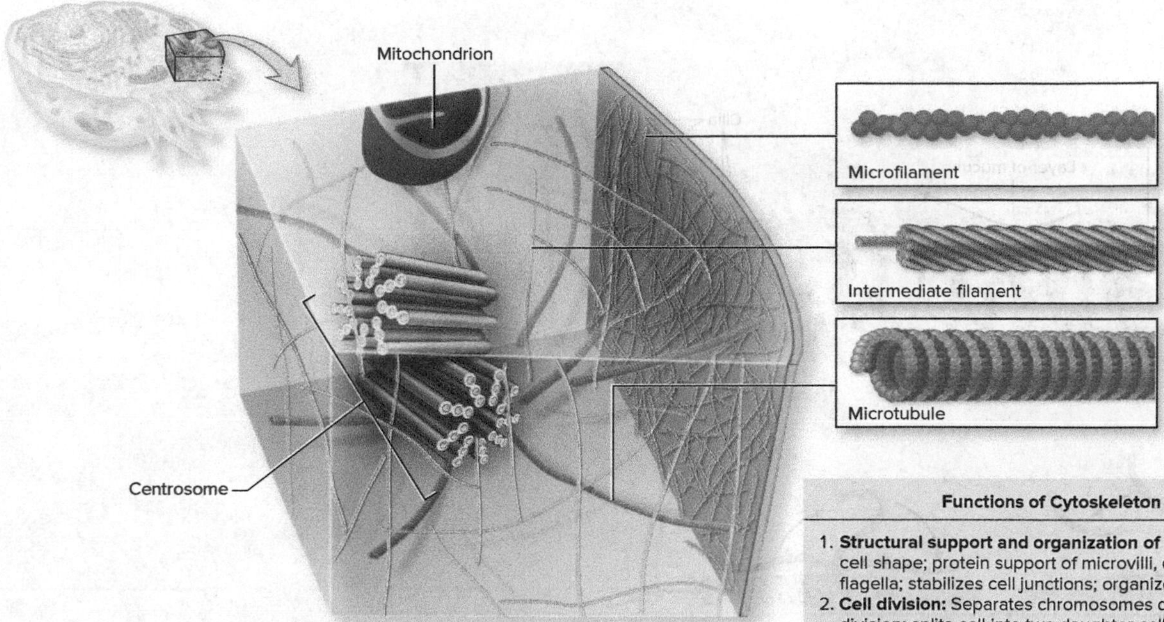
Mitochondrion
Microfilament
Intermediate filament
Microtubule
Centrosome

Functions of Cytoskeleton

1. **Structural support and organization of cell:** Maintains cell shape; protein support of microvilli, cilia, and flagella; stabilizes cell junctions; organizes organelles
2. **Cell division:** Separates chromosomes during cell division; splits cell into two daughter cells (cytokinesis)
3. **Movement:** Facilitates cytoplasmic streaming; involved in movement of vesicles within a cell; participates in muscle contraction

Figure 2.14

The Cytoskeleton. Filamentous proteins form the cytoskeleton. They help give the cell its shape and coordinate cellular movements. The three cytoskeletal elements are microfilaments, intermediate filaments, and microtubules. APR

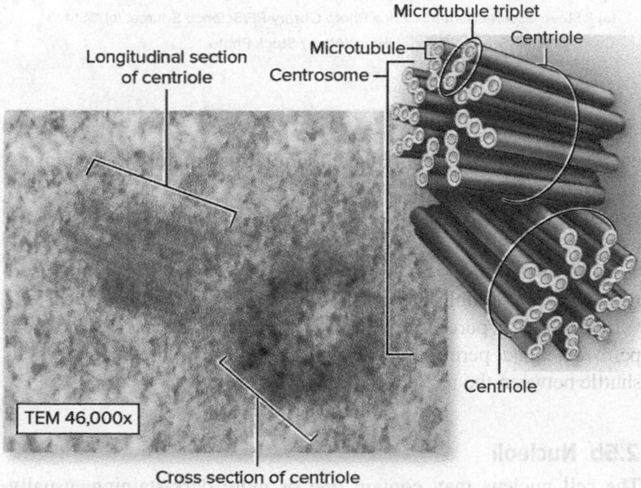
Microtubule triplet
Centriole
Longitudinal section of centriole
Microtubule
Centrosome
Centriole
TEM 46,000x
Cross section of centriole

Functions of Centrosomes and Centrioles

1. **Microtubule support:** Organizes microtubules and supports their growth in nondividing cells
2. **Cell division:** Directs formation of mitotic spindle in dividing cells

Figure 2.15

Centrosome and Centrioles. A drawing and TEM show that a region of the cytoplasm called the centrosome surrounds a centriole pair.

©EM Research Services, Newcastle University

moves the mucus and any adherent particulate material along the cell surface toward the throat, where it may then be expelled from the body.

Flagella are similar to cilia in basic structure; however, they are longer and usually appear alone (figure 2.16*c*). The function of a flagellum is to help propel or move an entire cell. In humans, the only example of a cell with a flagellum is the sperm.

Microvilli **Microvilli** are thin, microscopic projections extending from the surface of the plasma membrane. They are much smaller than cilia, much more densely packed together, and do not have powered movement (see figure 2.3). The main function of microvilli is to increase the surface area of the plasma membrane. In essence, these projections create a more extensive plasma membrane surface for molecules to travel across. Just as not all cells have cilia, not all cells have microvilli. Cells with microvilli occur throughout the small intestine, where increased surface area is needed to absorb digested nutrients.

WHAT DID YOU LEARN?

9 Describe the characteristics of the cytosol.

10 Explain the functions of lysosomes, mitochondria, and centrioles.

11 Contrast the fates of proteins synthesized on free ribosomes versus those synthesized on bound ribosomes.

12 What is the function of cilia?

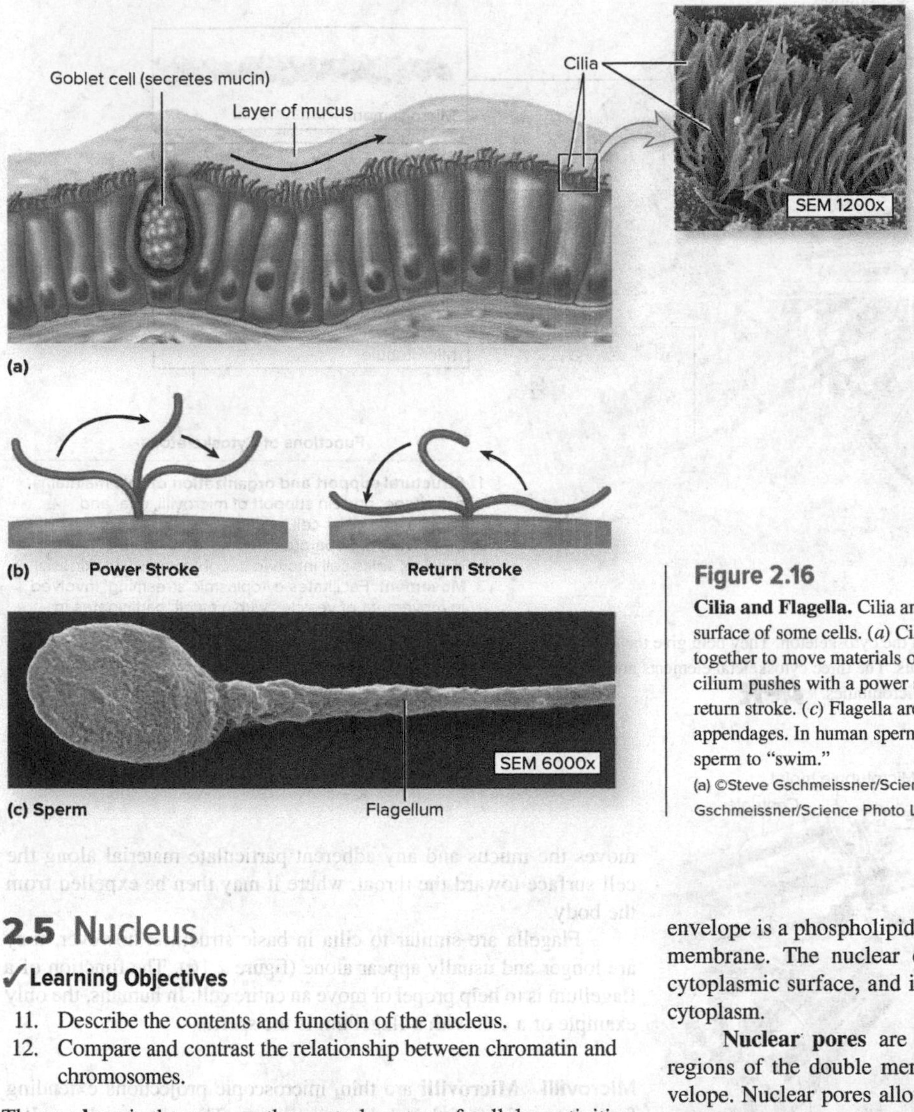
Goblet cell (secretes mucin)
Layer of mucus
Cilia
SEM 1200x
(a)
(b)
Power Stroke
Return Stroke
SEM 6000x
(c) Sperm
Flagellum

Figure 2.16

Cilia and Flagella. Cilia and flagella are appendages extending from the surface of some cells. (*a*) Cilia usually occur in large numbers; they work together to move materials or fluids along the surface of a cell. (*b*) A single cilium pushes with a power stroke and returns to its original position with a return stroke. (*c*) Flagella are longer than cilia, and usually occur as single appendages. In human sperm, the flagellum is the apparatus that enables the sperm to "swim."

(a) ©Steve Gschmeissner/Science Photo Library RF/Science Source; (c) ©Steve Gschmeissner/Science Photo Library/Alamy Stock Photo

2.5 Nucleus

✓ Learning Objectives

11. Describe the contents and function of the nucleus.
12. Compare and contrast the relationship between chromatin and chromosomes.

The **nucleus** is the core, or the control center, of cellular activities. Usually, it is the largest structure within the cell, averaging about 5 μm to 7 μm in diameter (**figure 2.17**). Generally, its shape mirrors the shape of the cell. For example, a cuboidal cell has a spherical nucleus in the center of the cell, whereas a thin, elongated cell's nucleus is elongated in the same direction as the cell itself. Some cells contain uniquely shaped nuclei. For example, neutrophils, a type of white blood cell, have a multilobed nucleus—one that has three or more bulges.

The nucleus contains three basic structures: a nuclear envelope, nucleoli, and chromatin.

2.5a Nuclear Envelope

The nucleus is enclosed by a double membrane structure called the **nuclear envelope,** which separates the cytoplasm from the **nucleoplasm** (the fluid within the nucleus). The nuclear envelope encloses a narrow perinuclear space between its double-layered membrane. This boundary controls the entry and exit of materials between the nucleus and the cytoplasm. Each layer of the nuclear envelope is a phospholipid bilayer, similar in structure to the plasma membrane. The nuclear envelope has ribosomes attached to its cytoplasmic surface, and it is continuous with the rough ER in the cytoplasm.

Nuclear pores are open passageways that penetrate fused regions of the double membrane throughout the entire nuclear envelope. Nuclear pores allow the nuclear membrane to be selectively permeable and permit most ions and water-soluble molecules to shuttle between the nucleus and the cytoplasm.

2.5b Nucleoli

The cell nucleus may contain one or more dark-staining, usually spherical bodies called **nucleoli** (figure 2.17). (The singular term is *nucleolus* [nū-klē′ō-lŭs; pl., *nucleoli*, nū-klē′ō-lī].) Nucleoli are made up of RNA, enzymes, and other proteins. Nucleoli are responsible for making the small and large subunits of ribosomes. These subunits are exported outside the nucleus into the cytoplasm, where they are then assembled to form ribosomes. You can think of the ribosomal subunits as puzzle pieces that are made in the nucleolus. Arrangement of the puzzle pieces into one complete puzzle (ribosome) occurs in the cytoplasm.

Not all cells contain a nucleolus. The presence and number of nucleoli indicate the protein synthetic activity of a cell. For example, nerve cells contain nucleoli because they produce many

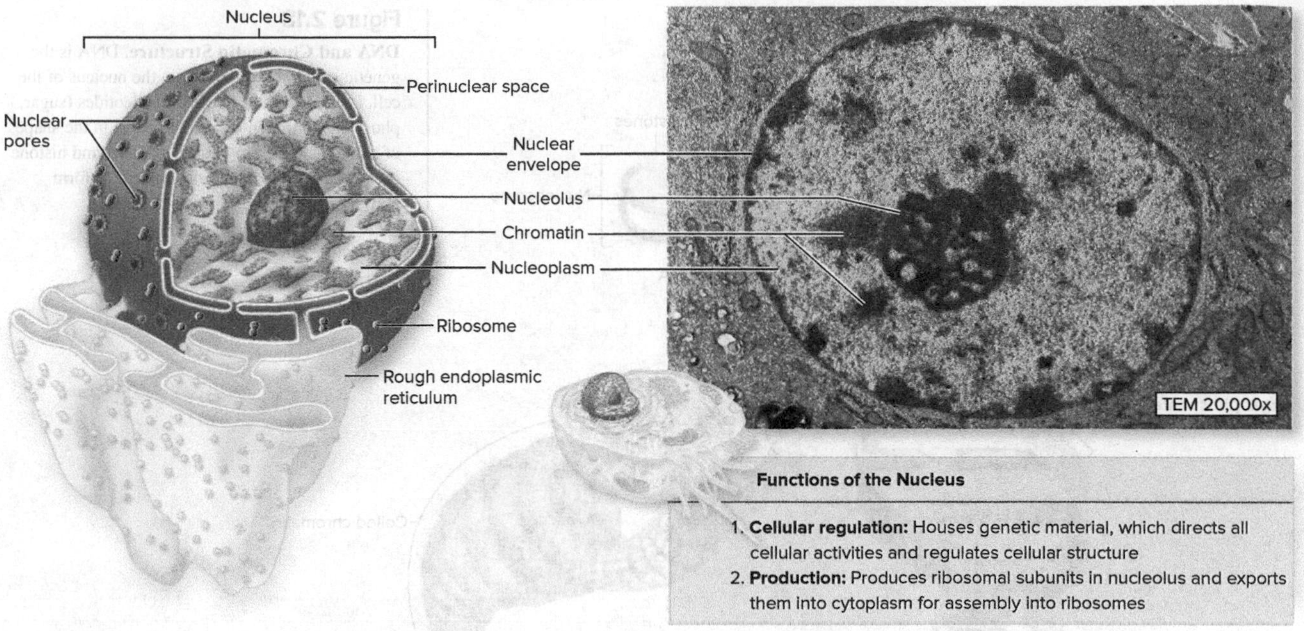
Nucleus
Perinuclear space
Nuclear pores
Nuclear envelope
Nucleolus
Chromatin
Nucleoplasm
Ribosome
Rough endoplasmic reticulum
TEM 20,000x
Functions of the Nucleus
1. Cellular regulation: Houses genetic material, which directs all cellular activities and regulates cellular structure
2. Production: Produces ribosomal subunits in nucleolus and exports them into cytoplasm for assembly into ribosomes

Figure 2.17

Nucleus. A drawing and TEM compare the structures of the nucleus within a cell. Control of cellular activities is centered in the nucleus.

proteins. In contrast, sperm have no nucleoli because they produce no proteins.

2.5c DNA, Chromatin, and Chromosomes

The nucleus houses **deoxyribonucleic acid (DNA),** an enormous macromolecule that contains the genetic material of the cell. The DNA within the nucleus, termed **nuclear DNA,** is much more complex than the DNA in mitochondria. DNA is organized into discrete units called **genes.** Genes provide the instructions for the production of specific proteins, and thereby direct all of the cell's activities.

DNA is in the shape of a double helix, or a ladder twisted into a spiral shape. The building blocks that form this double helix are called **nucleotides** (nū′klē-ō-tīd; *nucleus* = a little nut or kernel) (**figure 2.18*a***). A nucleotide contains a sugar (called a deoxyribose sugar), a phosphate molecule, and a nitrogen-containing base. There are four different types of nucleotides, each having one of four different bases: adenine (A), cytosine (C), guanine (G), and thymine (T). These nucleotides are arranged to form the unique double-helical shape of DNA. If you think of the DNA as a ladder, the sugar and phosphate components of the nucleotides form the vertical "struts" of the ladder, while pairs of nucleotide bases interconnected by weak hydrogen bonds form the horizontal "rungs." The base guanine interconnects only with the base cytosine, whereas the base adenine pairs only with the base thymine. The specific order of the bases in the nucleotides "codes for" specific proteins the body needs.

When a cell is not dividing, the DNA and its associated proteins are in the form of an unwound, finely filamented mass called **chromatin** (krō′ma-tin; *chroma* = color). Dark-staining chromatin in the nucleus of a nondividing cell is condensed chromatin. Other, light-staining regions of the nucleus contain chromatin that is uncoiled and spread out in fine strands of DNA and protein. When the cell is not dividing, the DNA remains unwound in fine, uncoiled chromatin, so that the genes within the DNA can direct the production of cellular proteins. This is not possible when the DNA is condensed and organized into a chromosome at the time of cell division.

Once the cell begins to divide, the chromatin rearranges itself in more precise and identifiable elongated structures called chromosomes. The **chromosome** (krō′mō-sōm; *chroma* = color, *soma* = body) is the most organized level of genetic material. Each chromosome contains a single, long molecule of DNA and associated proteins. Chromosomes become visible only when the cell is dividing. As a cell prepares for division, the DNA and protein in the chromatin coil, wrap, and twist to form the chromosomes, which resemble relatively short, thick rods. The long DNA double helix winds around a cluster of special nuclear proteins called **histones,** forming a complex known as a **nucleosome** (figure 2.18*b*). The degree of coiling of the DNA around the histone proteins ultimately determines the length and thickness of the chromosome.

WHAT DID YOU LEARN?

13. What is the function of the nuclear envelope?
14. What is the difference between chromatin and chromosomes?

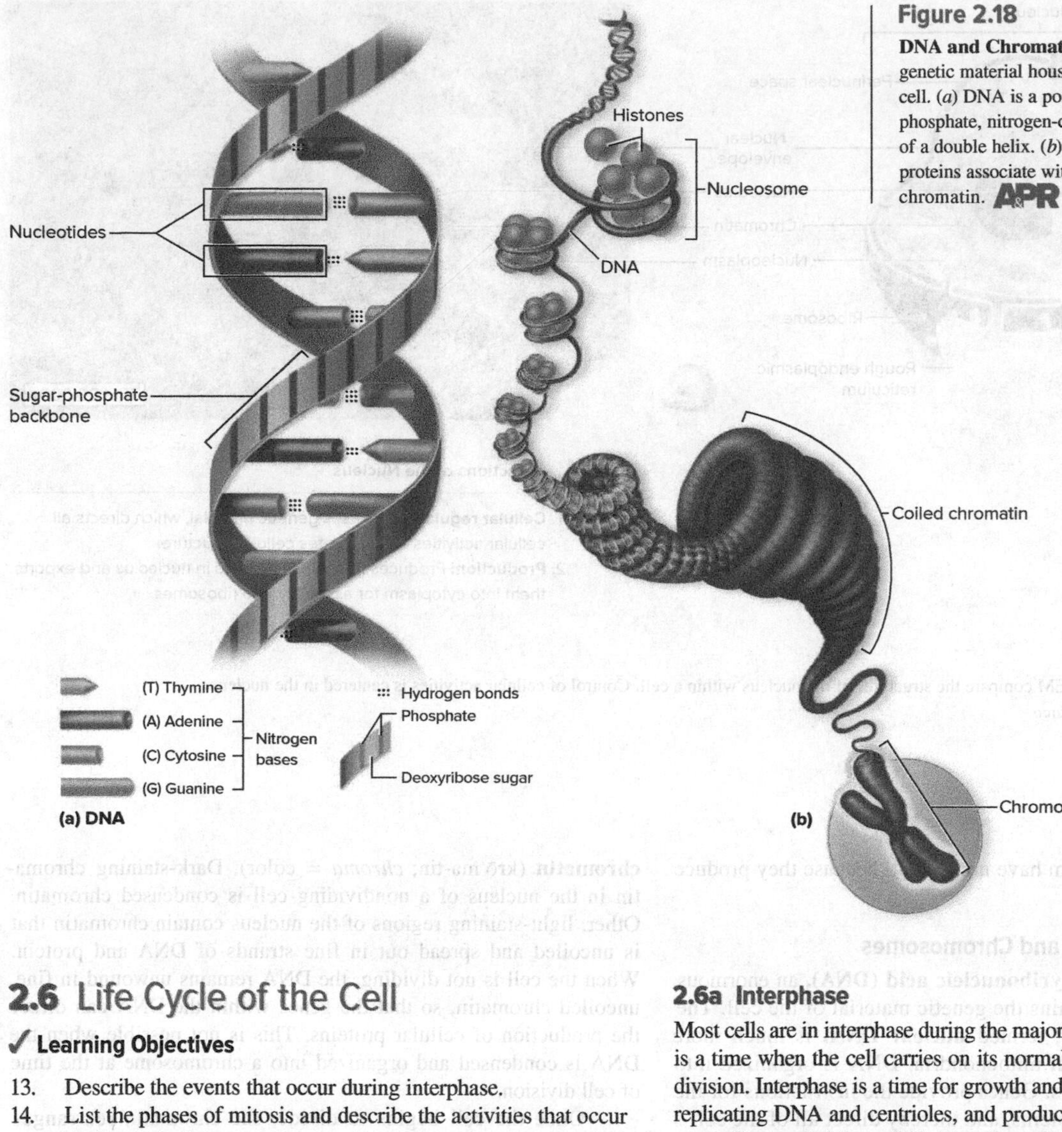
Histones
Nucleosome
Nucleotides
DNA
Sugar-phosphate backbone
Coiled chromatin
(T) Thymine
(A) Adenine
(C) Cytosine
(G) Guanine
Nitrogen bases
Hydrogen bonds
Phosphate
Deoxyribose sugar
(a) DNA
(b)
Chromosome

Figure 2.18

DNA and Chromatin Structure. DNA is the genetic material housed within the nucleus of the cell. (*a*) DNA is a polymer of nucleotides (sugar, phosphate, nitrogen-containing base) in the shape of a double helix. (*b*) Strands of DNA and histone proteins associate within the nucleus to form chromatin. APR

2.6 Life Cycle of the Cell

✓ Learning Objectives

13. Describe the events that occur during interphase.
14. List the phases of mitosis and describe the activities that occur during each phase.

Producing the trillions of cells that form a human body—and replacing the aging, damaged, or dead ones—requires continuous cell division. In cell division, one cell divides to produce two identical cells, called **daughter cells.** There are two types of cell division: mitosis and meiosis. **Mitosis** (mī-tō′sis; *mitos* = thread) is the cell division process that takes place in the **somatic cells,** which are all of the cells in the body except the sex cells. (Meiosis occurs in the sex cells, which give rise to sperm or oocytes, and is discussed in section 3.2 .)

The **cell cycle** has two phases: interphase and the mitotic (M) phase. **Interphase** is the time between cell divisions when the cell maintains and carries out normal metabolic activities and may also prepare for division. The **mitotic (M) phase** is the time when the cell divides into two cells (**figure 2.19**).

The lives of cells vary, depending upon their specific type and their environment. For example, blood cells and epithelial skin cells are replaced frequently, so the cells that produce them undergo frequent cell division. Other cells, such as most nerve cells, undergo cell division infrequently or not at all. However, all somatic cells that divide go through both interphase and mitotic phase.

2.6a Interphase

Most cells are in interphase during the majority of their lives. Interphase is a time when the cell carries on its normal activities and prepares for division. Interphase is a time for growth and making new cellular parts, replicating DNA and centrioles, and producing the proteins, RNA, and organelles needed for cell division. Interphase is divided into three distinct phases: G_1, S, and G_2 (figure 2.19).

G_1 Phase

During the **G_1 phase** (the first "growth" or gap stage), cells grow, produce new organelles, carry out their specific metabolic activities, and produce proteins required for division. Near the end of G_1, the centrioles begin to replicate in preparation for cell division. Nondividing cells remain in a state of arrested development termed G_0. Most nerve cells appear to be in this state and do not enter cell division.

S Phase

The **S phase** ("synthesis" phase) is the next period of interphase for cells that will eventually be dividing. During this short phase, each DNA molecule replicates (makes an exact copy of itself) completely. Replication is in preparation for cell division and provides for the partitioning of all of the hereditary material of a parent cell into two identical daughter cells. A parent DNA molecule has two strands of DNA that are complementary, meaning that each base on one strand is paired with a specific partner: Adenine (A) pairs with thymine (T), and cytosine (C) pairs with guanine (G) (see figure 2.18*a*). The first

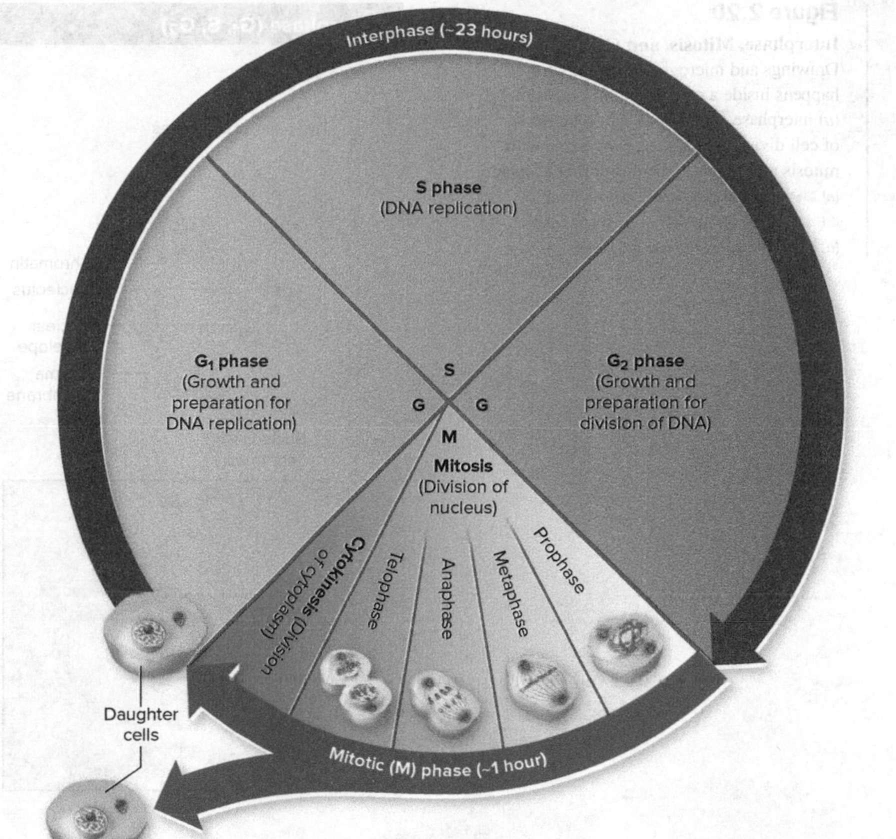

Interphase (~23 hours)
S phase
(DNA replication)
G1 phase
(Growth and
preparation for
DNA replication)
G2 phase
(Growth and
preparation for
division of DNA)
S
G
G
M
Mitosis
(Division of
nucleus)
Prophase
Metaphase
Anaphase
Telophase
Cytokinesis
(Division
of cytoplasm)
Daughter
cells
Mitotic (M) phase (~1 hour)

Figure 2.19

The Cell Cycle. The cell cycle includes two basic phases: interphase and the mitotic (M) phase. Interphase is a growth period that is subdivided into G_1, S, and G_2. The mitotic phase includes mitosis, the process of nuclear division, and cytokinesis, the division of the cytoplasm. Note that this figure does not accurately reflect the relative time a cell would spend in each phase. APR

steps in replication are the unwinding of the helix followed by the separation, or "unzipping," of the two strands of DNA in the parent molecule. Once separated, each parent strand serves as a template for the order of bases in the new complementary strand according to the base-pairing pattern just described. Each new DNA molecule now consists of one parent strand and one new strand. APR

G_2 Phase

The last part of interphase, called the **G_2 phase** (or the second "growth" or gap phase), is brief. During this phase, centriole replication is completed, organelle production continues, and enzymes needed for cell division are synthesized.

2.6b Mitotic (M) Phase

Cell division is necessary to provide the large number of cells essential for the growth and survival of a human. Cells divide at different rates through specific stages in their life cycle. Following interphase, cells enter the M (mitotic) phase (**figure 2.20**). Two distinct events occur during this phase: **mitosis,** or division of the nucleus, followed by **cytokinesis** (sī'tō-ki-nē'sis; *kytos* = cell, *kinesis* = movement), division of the cytoplasm.

Mitotic cell division produces two daughter cells that are identical to the original (parent) cell. The nucleus divides such that the replicated DNA molecules of the original parent cell are apportioned into the two new daughter cells, with each receiving an identical copy of the DNA of the original cell.

Four consecutive phases take place during mitosis: prophase, metaphase, anaphase, and telophase. Each phase merges smoothly into the next in a nonstop process. The duration of mitosis varies according to cell type, but it typically lasts about 2 hours.

Prophase

Prophase is the first stage of mitosis (figure 2.20*b*). Chromatin becomes supercoiled into relatively short, dense chromosomes, which are more maneuverable during cell division than the long, delicate chromatin strands. Remember that the DNA replicated itself during interphase, so during prophase each chromosome (called a **replicated chromosome** or a *double-stranded chromosome*) contains two copies of its DNA. A replicated chromosome consists of two genetically identical structures, called **sister chromatids.** Each sister chromatid is composed of an identical DNA double helix, and the two sister chromatids are joined together by proteins at a constricted region called the **centromere** (sen'tr ō-mēr; *kentron* = center, *meros* = part).

During prophase, the nucleolus breaks down and disappears. The replicated chromosomes form a big puffy ball within the nucleus. Elongated microtubules called **spindle fibers** begin to grow from the centrioles, and this event pushes the two centriole pairs apart. Eventually, the centrioles come to lie at opposite poles of the cell. The end of prophase is marked by the dissolution of the nuclear envelope, which permits the replicated chromosomes to move freely into and through the cytoplasm.

Metaphase

Metaphase occurs when the replicated chromosomes line up along the equatorial plate of the cell (figure 2.20*c*). Spindle fibers grow from each centriole toward the replicated chromosomes, and some attach to the

Figure 2.20

Interphase, Mitosis, and Cytokinesis. Drawings and micrographs depict what happens inside a cell during the stages of (*a*) interphase and (*b–e*) the mitotic phase of cell division. Cytokinesis overlaps with mitosis and generally begins during anaphase.

(a) ©Michael Abbey/Science Source; (b-d) ©Ed Reschke/Photolibrary/Getty Images; (e) ©Michael Abbey/Science Source

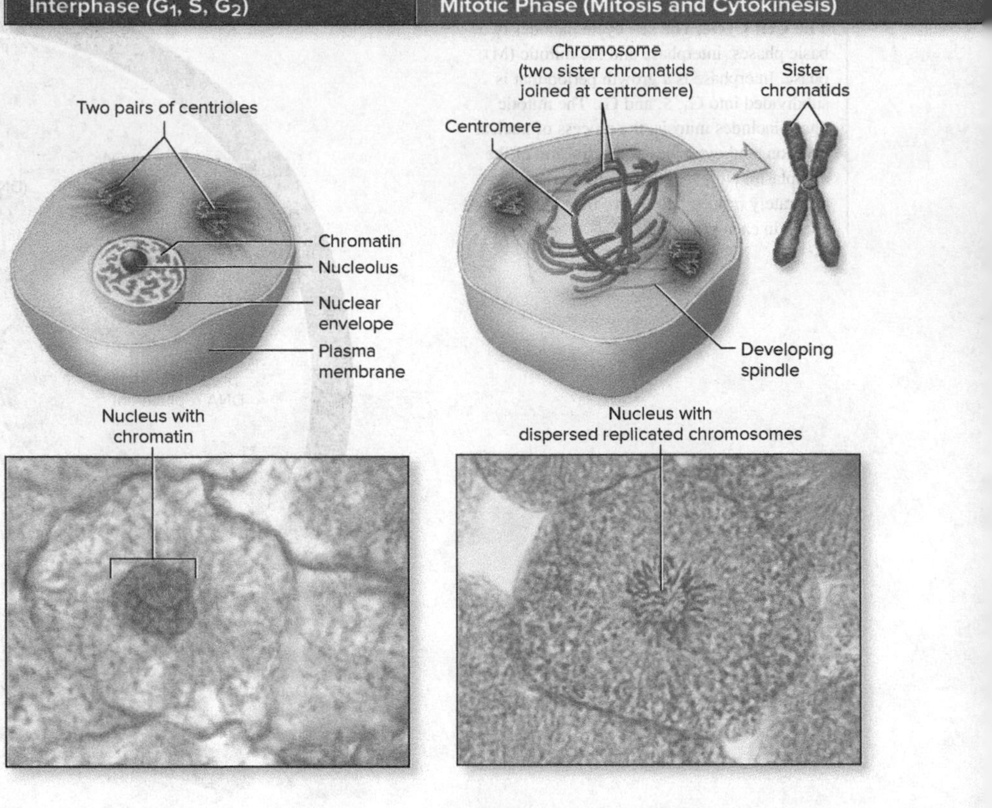

Interphase (G_1, S, G_2)
Mitotic Phase (Mitosis and Cytokinesis)
Two pairs of centrioles
Chromatin
Nucleolus
Nuclear envelope
Plasma membrane
Nucleus with chromatin
Chromosome (two sister chromatids joined at centromere)
Sister chromatids
Centromere
Developing spindle
Nucleus with dispersed replicated chromosomes

(a) Interphase

Synthesis of cellular components.

Replication of DNA and duplication of centrioles (if cell is to undergo mitosis).

(b) Prophase

Chromosomes appear due to coiling of chromatin.

Nucleolus breaks down.

Spindle fibers begin to form from centrioles.

Centrioles move toward opposing cell poles.

Nuclear envelope breaks down at the end of this stage.

centromere of each replicated chromosomes. The collection of spindle fibers extending from the centrioles to the replicated chromosomes forms an oval-structured array termed the **mitotic spindle.** This arrangement remains in place until the next phase begins.

Anaphase

Anaphase begins as spindle fibers pull sister chromatids apart at the centromere (figure 2.20 *d*). The spindle fibers shorten, and each "reels in" a chromatid, like a fishing line reeling in a fish. After the chromatids are pulled apart, each chromatid is called a **single chromosome** (or *single-stranded chromosome*), as each forms its own unique centromere. Thus, a pair of single chromosomes is pulled apart from sister chromatids, and each migrates to the opposite end of the cell (cell pole). As each single chromosome migrates toward the cell pole, its centromere leads the way, and the arms of the chromosome trail behind. In most cases, cytokinesis, the division of the cytoplasm, begins in late anaphase.

Telophase

Telophase begins once a group of single chromosomes arrives at each cell pole (figure 2.20*e*). A new nuclear envelope forms around each set of chromosomes, and the chromosomes begin to uncoil and return to the form of dispersed threads of chromatin. The mitotic spindle breaks up and disappears. Each new nucleus forms nucleoli.

Telophase signals the end of nuclear division and it overlaps with cytokinesis. A contractile ring of protein filaments at the periphery of the cell equator pinches the mother cell into two separate cells. The resulting **cleavage furrow** indicates where the cytoplasm is dividing. The two new daughter cells then enter the interphase of their life cycle, and the process continues.

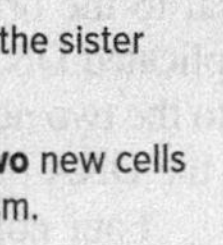

Learning Strategy 2.3

Use these to help you remember some of the hallmark events that occur during each phase of mitosis:

- The **p** in **p**rophase stands for the **puffy** ball of replicated chromosomes that forms in the center of the cell.
- The **m** in **m**etaphase stands for **middle:** During this phase, the replicated chromosomes align along the **middle** of the cell.
- The **a** in **a**naphase stands for **apart:** During this phase, the sister chromatids are pulled **apart**.
- The **t** in **t**elophase stands for **two:** During this phase, **two** new cells begin to form as a cleavage furrow divides the cytoplasm.

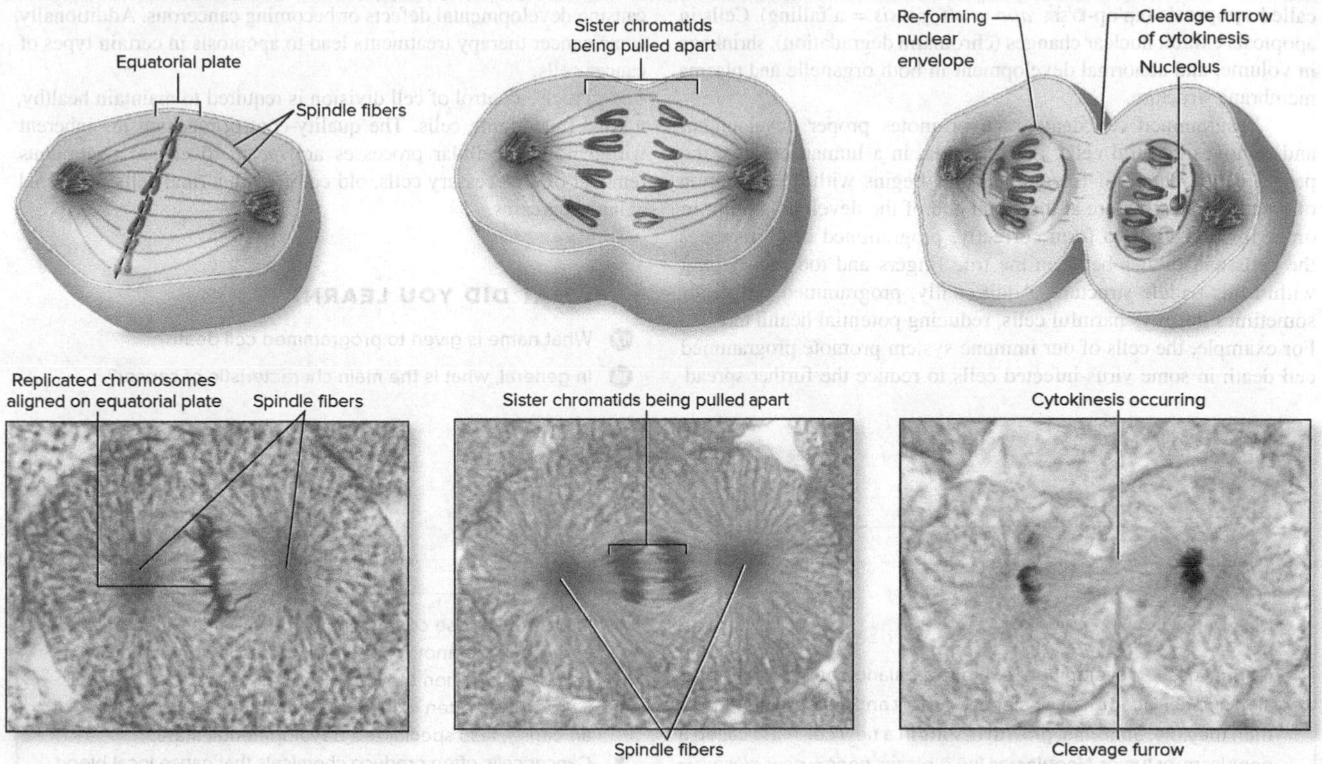
Equatorial plate
Spindle fibers
Sister chromatids being pulled apart
Re-forming nuclear envelope
Cleavage furrow of cytokinesis
Nucleolus
Replicated chromosomes aligned on equatorial plate
Spindle fibers
Sister chromatids being pulled apart
Cytokinesis occurring
Spindle fibers
Cleavage furrow

(c) Metaphase
Spindle fibers attach to the centromeres of the chromosomes extending from the centrioles.
Chromosomes are aligned at the equatorial plate of the cell by spindle fibers.

(d) Anaphase
Sister chromatids are separated by spindle fibers and moved toward opposite ends of the cell.
Each sister chromatid is now a single-stranded chromosome with its own centromere.
Cytokinesis begins.

(e) Telophase
Chromosomes uncoil to form chromatin.
A nucleolus re-forms within each nucleus.
Spindle fibers break up and disappear.
New nuclear envelope forms around each set of chromosomes.
Cytokinesis continues as cleavage furrow deepens.

WHAT DID YOU LEARN?

15 Observation shows that most cells are suspended in interphase for most of their lives. Identify the parts of interphase, and describe an event that occurs during each part.

16 Draw the stages of mitosis in order of occurrence. Describe a unique activity associated with each stage.

2.7 Aging and the Cell

✓ Learning Objectives

15. Describe the effects of aging on cells.
16. Explain two causes of cell death.

Aging is a normal, continuous process that often exhibits obvious body signs. However, at the cellular level, changes within cells due to aging are neither obvious nor well understood. Often, reduced metabolic functions of normal cells have wide-ranging effects throughout the body, including cells' decreased ability to maintain homeostasis. These signs of aging reflect a reduced number of normal functional body cells, and may even suggest abnormal function in the remaining cells. Affected cells may exhibit alteration in either the structure or the number of specific organelles. For example, if mitochondrial function begins to fail, the cell's ability to synthesize ATP will diminish. Additionally, changes in the distribution and structure of the chromatin and chromosomes within the nucleus may occur. Often, both chromatin and chromosomes clump, shrink, or fragment as a result of repeated divisions.

Many cancers (e.g., prostate cancer) appear with greater frequency in elderly individuals. Cancer is essentially caused by cells that undergo uncontrolled cell division and fail to "turn off" the cell division process. Thus, as we age, the whole mechanism of cell division becomes more faulty, making cancers more prevalent. Further, pregnant women over the age of 35 are at greater risk for giving birth to a child with a birth defect than are younger pregnant women. One reason for this greater risk is that older women's sex cells (oocytes) are older, and their mechanisms for completing sex cell division and maturation may not operate properly.

Essentially, cells die by one of two mechanisms: (1) They are killed by harmful agents or mechanical damage, in a process called **necrosis** (nĕ-krō'sis; *nekrosis* = death), wherein the damage is irreversible and there is an inflammatory response; or (2) they are induced to commit suicide, a process of programmed cell death called **apoptosis** (ap′op-tō′sis; *apo* = off, *ptosis* = a falling). Cells in apoptosis exhibit nuclear changes (chromatin degradation), shrinkage in volume, and abnormal development in both organelle and plasma membrane structure.

Programmed cell death both promotes proper development and removes harmful cells. For example, in a human embryo, the proper development of fingers and toes begins with the formation of a paddlelike structure at the distal end of the developing limb. In order for our digits to form correctly, programmed death removes the cells and tissues between the true fingers and toes developing within this paddle structure. Additionally, programmed cell death sometimes destroys harmful cells, reducing potential health threats. For example, the cells of our immune system promote programmed cell death in some virus-infected cells to reduce the further spread of infection. Often, cells with damaged DNA appear to promote events leading to apoptosis, presumably to prevent these cells from causing developmental defects or becoming cancerous. Additionally, some cancer therapy treatments lead to apoptosis in certain types of cancer cells.

Precise control of cell division is required to maintain healthy, normal-functioning cells. The quality-control mechanisms inherent within normal cellular processes are meant to ensure continuous removal of unnecessary cells, old cells, or abnormal cells as normal aging progresses.

WHAT DID YOU LEARN?

17 What name is given to programmed cell death?

18 In general, what is the main characteristic of cancer?

Clinical View 2.5

Characteristics of Cancer Cells

Normal tissue development exhibits a balance between cell division and cell death. If this balance is upset and cells multiply faster than they die, abnormal growth results in a new cell mass called a neoplasm, or tumor. **Neoplasms** (nē′ō-plazm; *neos* = new, *plasma* = thing formed) are classified as benign or malignant.

Benign (bē-nīn′; *benignus* = kind) **neoplasms** usually grow slowly and are confined within a connective tissue capsule. Cells within these tumors **dedifferentiate**—that is, they revert to a less specialized state and cause an increase in their own vascular supply to support their growth. These tumors are usually not lethal, but they have the potential to become life-threatening if they compress brain tissue, nerves, blood vessels, or airways.

Malignant (mă-lig′nănt; *maligno* = to do maliciously) **neoplasms** are unencapsulated, contain cells that dedifferentiate, increase their vascular supply, grow rapidly, and are able to spread easily to other organs by way of the blood or lymph, a phenomenon called ***metastasis*** (mĕ-tas′tă-sis; *meta* = in the midst of, *stasis* = a placing).

Cancer is the general term used to describe a group of diseases characterized by various types of malignant neoplasms. Cancer cells resemble undifferentiated or primordial cell types. Generally, they do not mature before they divide and are not capable of maintaining normal function. They use energy very inefficiently, and their growth comes at the expense of normal cells and tissues. The characteristics of cancer include the following:

- Cancer cells lose control of their cell cycle. Cells divide too frequently and grow out of control.
- Cancer cells lose contact inhibition, meaning that they overgrow one another and lack the ability to stop growing and dividing when they crowd other cells.
- Cancer cells often exhibit dedifferentiation and revert to an earlier, less specialized developmental state.
- Cancer cells often produce chemicals that cause local blood vessel formation (a process called *angiogenesis*), resulting in increased blood vessels in the developing tumor.
- Cancer cells have the ability to squeeze into any space, a property called *invasiveness*. This permits cancer cells to leave their place of origin and travel elsewhere in the body.
- Cancer cells acquire the ability to metastasize—that is, spread to other organs in the body.

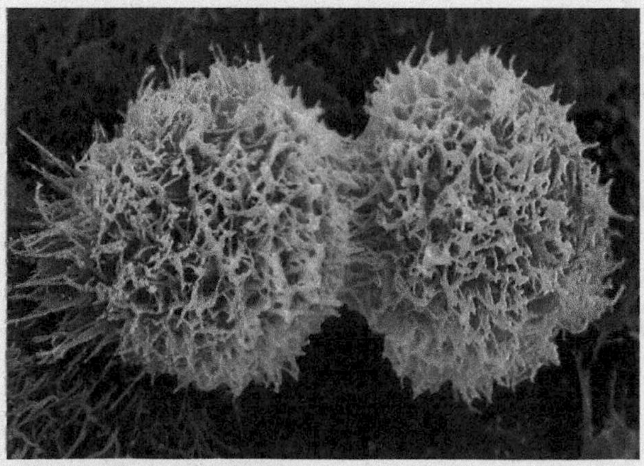

SEM of a cervical cancer cell dividing.

Clinical Terms

anaplasia Obvious loss of cellular or structural differentiation and change in cells' orientation to each other and to blood vessels; seen in most malignant neoplasms.

dysplasia (dis-plā′zē-ă; *dys* = bad, *plasis* = a molding) Abnormal development of a tissue; a pathologic condition resulting in a change in the shape, size, and organization of adult cells; development of cellular and tissue elements that are not normal.

hyperplasia Increase in the normal number of cells within a tissue or organ; an excessive proliferation of normal cells; does not include tumor formation.

hypertrophy Generalized increase in the bulk or size of a part of an organ, not as a consequence of tumor formation.

metaplasia Abnormal transformation of a fully differentiated adult tissue into a differentiated tissue of another kind.

Chapter Summary

2.1 The Study of Cells

- Cytology is the study of anatomy at the cellular level.

2.1a Using the Microscope to Study Cells

- Variations in magnification and resolution exist when comparing light microscopy (LM) and electron microscopy (TEM and SEM).

2.1b General Functions of Human Body Cells

- Cells vary in shape and size, often related to various cellular functions.

2.2 A Prototypical Cell

- A cell is surrounded by a thin layer of extracellular fluid. Interstitial fluid is a type of extracellular fluid forming a thin layer on the outside of the cell. Most mature human cells have an outer boundary called the plasma (cell) membrane, general cell contents termed cytoplasm, and a nucleus that serves as the cell's control center.

2.3 Plasma Membrane

- The plasma membrane acts as a gatekeeper to regulate movement of material into and out of the cell.

2.3a Composition and Structure of Membranes

- Plasma membranes are composed of an approximately equal mixture of lipids and proteins.
- The primary membrane lipids are phospholipids, arranged as a bilayer.
- Membrane proteins are of two types: integral proteins and peripheral proteins. Some integral membrane proteins have carbohydrate molecules attached to their external surfaces.
- The glycocalyx is the carbohydrate component of the plasma membrane attached either to lipid (glycolipid) or protein (glycoprotein) components. It functions in cell–cell recognition and communication.

2.3b Protein-Specific Functions of the Plasma Membrane

- Plasma membrane proteins function in transport, intercellular attachment, cytoskeleton anchorage, catalytic (enzyme) activity, cell–cell recognition, and signal transduction.

2.3c Transport Across the Plasma Membrane

- Plasma membrane permeability is influenced by transport proteins, membrane structure, concentration gradient across the membrane, ionic charge, lipid solubility of materials, and molecular size.
- Passive transport is the movement of a substance across a membrane at no energy cost to the cell; it includes diffusion (simple diffusion, osmosis, and facilitated diffusion) and bulk filtration.
- All active transport processes require energy in the form of ATP. Two active processes are ion pumps and bulk transport in vesicles (exocytosis and endocytosis).
- Bulk transport includes exocytosis, a mechanism to export packaged materials from the cell, and endocytosis, a mechanism by which materials are imported into the cell.

2.4 Cytoplasm

- The cytoplasm is all the material between the plasma membrane and the nucleus. It contains cytosol, inclusions, and organelles.

2.4a Cytosol

- Cytosol is a viscous intracellular fluid containing ions, nutrients, and other molecules necessary for cell metabolism.

2.4b Inclusions

- Inclusions are storage bodies in the cytoplasm.

2.4c Organelles

- Membrane-bound organelles include endoplasmic reticulum (both rough and smooth), the Golgi apparatus, lysosomes, peroxisomes, and mitochondria.
- Non-membrane-bound organelles include ribosomes (both free and bound), the cytoskeleton, the centrosome, and centrioles, cilia, flagella, and microvilli.

(continued on next page)

Chapter Summary *(continued)*

2.5 Nucleus	■ The nucleus is the cell's control center. **2.5a Nuclear Envelope** ■ The nuclear envelope is a double membrane boundary surrounding the nucleus, separating the cytoplasm from the nucleoplasm. Nuclear pores are openings that penetrate the nuclear envelope and permit direct communication with the cytosol. **2.5b Nucleoli** ■ A nucleolus is a dark-staining, usually spherical body in the nucleus that produces the subunits that will form ribosomes. **2.5c DNA, Chromatin, and Chromosomes** ■ Chromatin is the name of the fine, uncoiled strands of DNA in the nucleus. As the cell prepares to divide, the DNA strands begin to coil and wind to form large, microscopically identifiable structures termed chromosomes.
2.6 Life Cycle of the Cell	■ Cell division in somatic cells is called mitosis, and cell division in sex cells (sperm and oocytes) is called meiosis. **2.6a Interphase** ■ Somatic cells spend the majority of their time in interphase, a time of maintenance and growth that occurs between cell divisions. **2.6b Mitotic (M) Phase** ■ The division of the somatic cell nucleus is called mitosis, whereas the division of the cytoplasm following mitosis is called cytokinesis. Both mitosis and cytokinesis represent the mitotic phase. ■ Four consecutive phases make up mitosis: prophase, metaphase, anaphase, and telophase (see figure 2.20).
2.7 Aging and the Cell	■ Aging is a normal process that is often marked by changes in normal cells. ■ Cells may be killed by harmful agents or mechanical damage, or they may undergo programmed cell death, called apoptosis.

Challenge Yourself

Actively write or type your answers in a separate document to reinforce your learning, before checking your answers.

Multiple Choice

Select the best answer from the four choices provided.

1. What is the best way to visualize microtubules within a nerve cell?
   a. light microscope
   b. telescope
   c. transmission electron microscope
   d. scanning electron microscope
2. Which of the following describes integral membrane proteins?
   a. They permit water movement only into or out of the cell.
   b. They transport only large proteins into the cell.
   c. They extend across the phospholipid bilayer.
   d. They are attached to the external plasma membrane surface.
3. How do active transport and facilitated diffusion differ?
   a. Facilitated diffusion expends ATP.
   b. Facilitated diffusion moves molecules from an area of higher concentration to one of lower concentration.
   c. Facilitated diffusion does not require a carrier protein for transport.
   d. Facilitated diffusion moves molecules in vesicles across a semipermeable membrane.
4. A cell uses which type of transport to move glucose (a polar molecule) from high concentration to low concentration?
   a. simple diffusion
   b. facilitated diffusion
   c. ion pump
   d. endocytosis
5. Which structure increases the outer surface area of the plasma membrane to increase absorption?
   a. centrioles
   b. cilia
   c. microvilli
   d. flagella
6. Which statement describes the major functions of the Golgi apparatus?
   a. The Golgi apparatus controls diffusion and osmosis.
   b. The Golgi apparatus detoxifies substances and removes waste products.
   c. The Golgi apparatus synthesizes new proteins for the cytoplasm.
   d. The Golgi apparatus packages, sorts, and modifies new molecules.
7. Interphase of the cell cycle is divided into which of the following parts?
   a. prophase, metaphase, anaphase, and telophase
   b. G_1, S, and G_2
   c. mitosis and cytokinesis
   d. S and mitosis
8. Which organelle provides most of the ATP needed by the cell?
   a. endoplasmic reticulum
   b. mitochondrion
   c. lysosome
   d. Golgi apparatus

9. During which phase of mitosis do the sister chromatids begin to move apart from each other at the middle of the cell?
   a. prophase
   b. metaphase
   c. anaphase
   d. telophase
10. A peroxisome uses oxygen to do which of the following?
   a. detoxify harmful substances
   b. make ATP
   c. help make proteins
   d. package secretory materials

Content Review

1. Describe the three main components common to all cells, and briefly discuss the composition of each region.
2. Describe the structure and the function of the plasma membrane.
3. What is meant by passive transport of materials into a cell? Describe the passive processes by which substances enter and leave cells.
4. How does active transport differ from passive transport? What are the three specific forms of the active transport mechanism termed endocytosis?
5. Discuss the two categories of organelles and the main differences between these groups.
6. Compare and contrast the structure and functions of the SER and the RER.
7. Identify the three parts of the cytoskeleton, and describe the structure and function of each component.
8. What are the basic components of the nucleus, and what are their functions?
9. What is interphase? What role does it serve in the cell cycle?
10. Identify the phases of mitosis, and briefly discuss the events that occur during each phase.

Developing Critical Reasoning

1. You place some cells into a solution of unknown content and then note them on a microscope slide. After a short period, all of the cells appear shrunken, and their plasma membranes look wrinkled. What took place, and why?
2. Why is it efficient for some organelles to be enclosed by a membrane similar to a plasma membrane?
3. Longtime cigarette smokers often cough. Why do you think that is? What cell structure do you think might be involved? Explain.

Answers to "What Do You Think?"

1. A selectively permeable plasma membrane allows some materials to enter the cell and blocks the entry of other materials that may be detrimental to the cell. However, a selectively permeable plasma membrane may inadvertently block some beneficial material. In these cases, active transport methods (e.g., endocytosis) are needed to bring the material into the cell.
2. Most cells would not be able to function without lysosomes. Lysosomes are necessary for breaking down and removing waste products. If lysosomes do not function properly, the waste products build up in the cell and cause cell death.
3. The number of mitochondria is positively related to the metabolic activity of the cell. A cell with few mitochondria is probably not as active metabolically as a cell with numerous mitochondria.

Design Element: Pencil Icon: Slavojub Pantelic/Shutterstock

REPRODUCTIVE SYSTEM

3 | Embryology

Outline

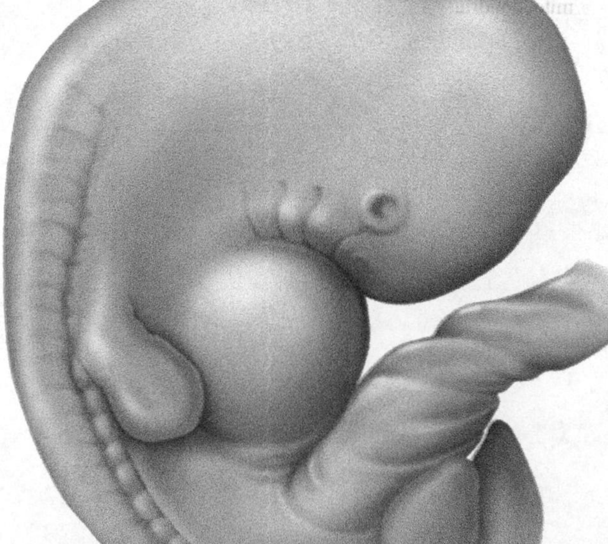

Anatomy & Physiology Revealed 4.0

MODULE 14: REPRODUCTIVE SYSTEM

Like all organisms, humans undergo development, a series of progressive changes that accomplishes two major functions: differentiation and reproduction. **Differentiation** leads to the formation and organization of all the diverse cell types in the body. **Reproduction** ensures that new individuals are produced from generation to generation. Development continues throughout the life of a human, but in this chapter we focus on the developmental events that occur prior to birth, a discipline known as **embryology** (em′brē-ol′ŏ-jē; *embryon* = a young one, *logos* = study).

3.1 Overview of Embryology

✓ Learning Objectives

1. Identify and describe the major events of the three prenatal periods.
2. Describe the processes that make up embryogenesis.

Embryology deals with the developmental events that occur during the **prenatal period,** the first 38 weeks of human development that begin with the fertilization of the secondary oocyte and end with birth.[1] The prenatal period is broken down into the following shorter periods:

- The **pre-embryonic period** is the first 2 weeks of development (the first 2 weeks after fertilization), when the single cell produced by fertilization (the zygote) becomes a spherical, multicellular structure (a blastocyst). This period ends when the blastocyst implants in the lining of the uterus.
- The **embryonic period** includes the third through eighth weeks of development. It is a remarkably active time during which rudimentary versions of the major organ systems appear in the body, which is now called an embryo.
- The **fetal** (fē′tăl; *fetus* = offspring) **period** includes the remaining 30 weeks of development prior to birth, when the organism is called a *fetus*. During the fetal period, the fetus continues to grow, and its organs increase in complexity.

The developmental processes that occur in the pre-embryonic and embryonic periods are known collectively as **embryogenesis.** **Figure 3.1** shows the three stages of embryogenesis:

- **Cleavage.** The zygote undergoes mitotic cell division to form a multicellular structure called a blastocyst.

[1]Some physicians refer to a 40-week gestation period, or pregnancy. This time frame is measured from a woman's last period to the birth of the newborn. In this time frame, fertilization does not occur until week 2 (when a woman ovulates)! So why refer to a 40-week gestation? Physicians use this reference because a woman knows when her last period was, but she may not know the day she ovulated and had a secondary oocyte fertilized. Even when the date of conception is known, normal pregnancy length may vary up to 37 days from this average.

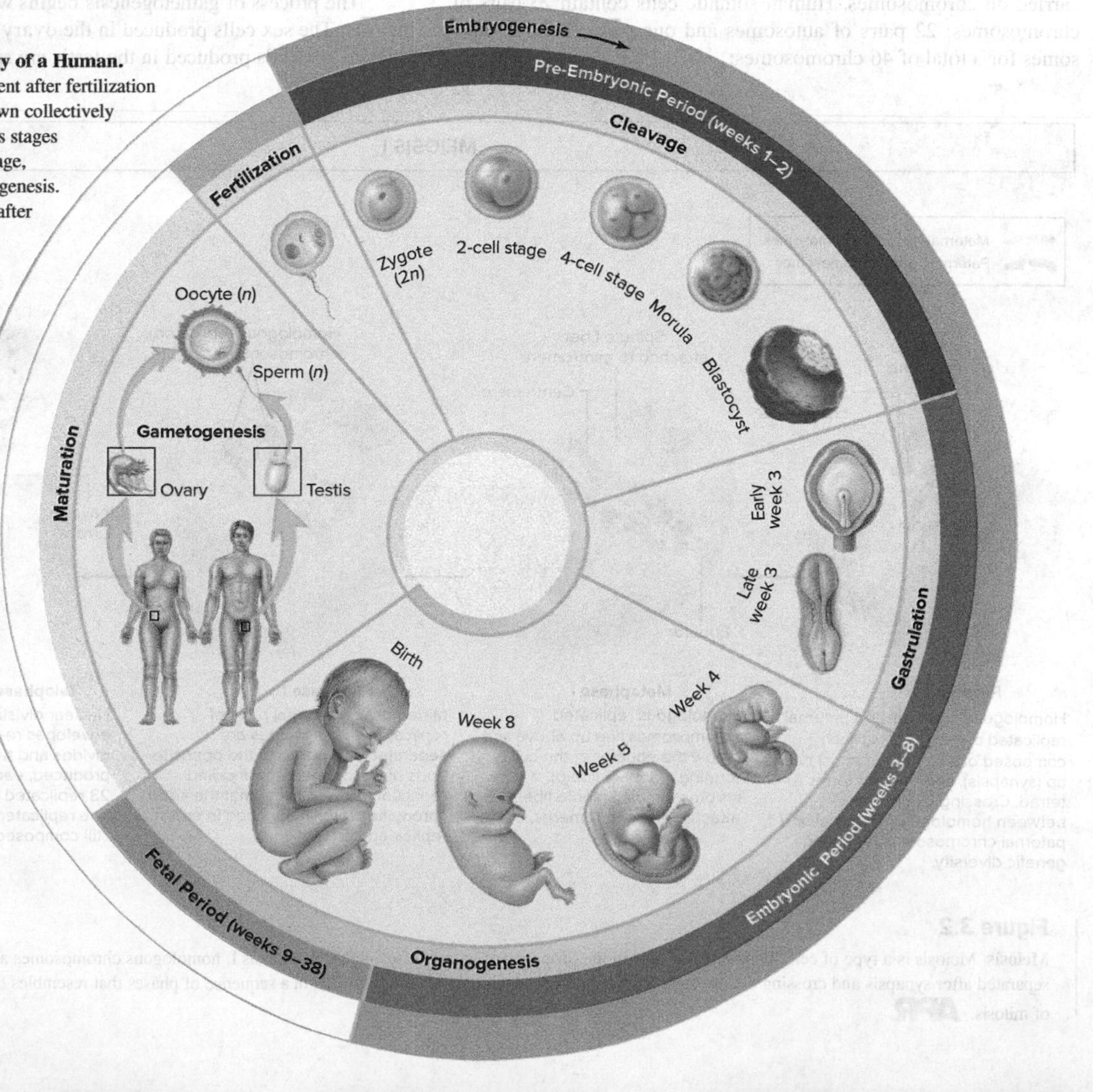
Embryogenesis
Pre-Embryonic Period (weeks 1–2)
Cleavage
Fertilization
Zygote (2n)
2-cell stage
4-cell stage
Morula
Blastocyst
Oocyte (n)
Sperm (n)
Gametogenesis
Ovary
Testis
Maturation
Early week 3
Late week 3
Gastrulation
Birth
Week 4
Week 8
Week 5
Embryonic Period (weeks 3–8)
Fetal Period (weeks 9–38)
Organogenesis

Figure 3.1

Developmental History of a Human. The stages of development after fertilization through week 8 are known collectively as embryogenesis and its stages are separated into cleavage, gastrulation, and organogenesis. The fetal period occurs after week 8 until birth, and this period continues with organogenesis. Gametogenesis occurs in the sexually mature adult.

- **Gastrulation.** The blastocyst cells form three primary germ layers, which are the basic cellular structures from which all body tissues develop.
- **Organogenesis.** The three primary germ layers arrange themselves in ways that give rise to all organs in the body.

Following birth, an individual spends a great portion of his or her life undergoing maturation. During this stage, the body grows and develops, and the sex organs become mature. The sex organs (ovaries or testes) then begin to produce sex cells, or **gametes** (gam′ēt; *gameo* = to marry), through a process called **gametogenesis.**

3.2 Gametogenesis

✓ Learning Objectives

3. Compare and contrast meiosis and mitosis with respect to types of cells involved and number of cells produced.
4. Identify and describe the events that occur during meiosis.

Gametogenesis is necessary for the reproductive phase of development. When humans reproduce, they pass on their traits to a new individual. As mentioned in section 2.5c, hereditary information is carried on chromosomes. Human somatic cells contain 23 pairs of chromosomes: 22 pairs of autosomes and one pair of sex chromosomes for a total of 46 chromosomes:

- **Autosomes** contain genetic information for most human characteristics, such as eye color, hair color, height, and skin pigmentation. A pair of similar autosomes are called **homologous chromosomes** (hō-mol′ō-gŭs; *homos* = same, *logos* = relation).
- The pair of **sex chromosomes** primarily determines whether an individual is genetically female (they will have two X chromosomes) or genetically male (they will have one X chromosome and one Y chromosome).

One member of each pair of chromosomes (be they autosomes or sex chromosomes) is inherited from each parent. In other words, if you examined one of your body cells, you would discover that 23 of the chromosomes came from your mother, and the other 23 chromosomes in this same cell came from your father. A cell that contains 23 pairs of chromosomes is said to be **diploid** (dip′loyd; *diploos* = double) and to have $2n$ chromosomes, where n is the unpaired chromosome number.

If the gametes were diploid, then each new individual would receive two sets of paired chromosomes, or $4n$. This situation is not what happens in nature, and it is not compatible in life. The gametes from either sex are **haploid** (hap′loyd; *haplos* = simple, *eidos* = appearance) because they contain 23 chromosomes only, not 23 pairs, and thus their chromosome number is designated as $1n$, or just n.

The process of gametogenesis begins with cell division, called meiosis. The sex cells produced in the ovary are secondary oocytes, whereas sex cells produced in the testis are sperm.

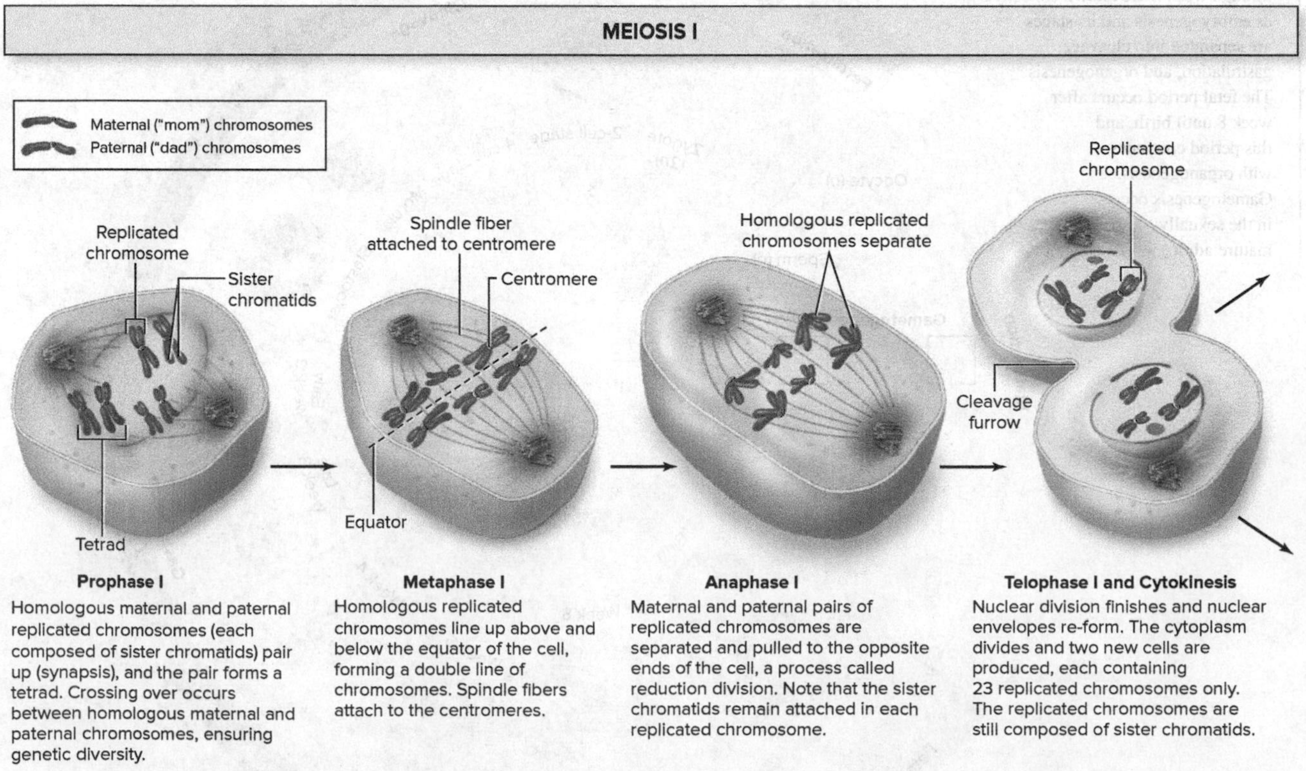
MEIOSIS I
Maternal ("mom") chromosomes
Paternal ("dad") chromosomes
Replicated chromosome
Sister chromatids
Tetrad
Spindle fiber attached to centromere
Centromere
Equator
Homologous replicated chromosomes separate
Replicated chromosome
Cleavage furrow
Prophase I
Homologous maternal and paternal replicated chromosomes (each composed of sister chromatids) pair up (synapsis), and the pair forms a tetrad. Crossing over occurs between homologous maternal and paternal chromosomes, ensuring genetic diversity.
Metaphase I
Homologous replicated chromosomes line up above and below the equator of the cell, forming a double line of chromosomes. Spindle fibers attach to the centromeres.
Anaphase I
Maternal and paternal pairs of replicated chromosomes are separated and pulled to the opposite ends of the cell, a process called reduction division. Note that the sister chromatids remain attached in each replicated chromosome.
Telophase I and Cytokinesis
Nuclear division finishes and nuclear envelopes re-form. The cytoplasm divides and two new cells are produced, each containing 23 replicated chromosomes only. The replicated chromosomes are still composed of sister chromatids.

Figure 3.2

Meiosis. Meiosis is a type of cell division that results in the formation of gametes (sex cells). In meiosis I, homologous chromosomes are separated after synapsis and crossing over occurs. In meiosis II, sister chromatids are separated in a sequence of phases that resembles the steps of mitosis. APR

3.2a Meiosis

Meiosis (mī-ō′sis; *meiosis* = lessening) is sex cell division; it begins with a diploid parent cell and produces four haploid daughter cells called *gametes.* Mitosis (somatic cell division, described in section 2.6) and meiosis (sex cell division) differ in the following ways:

- Mitosis produces *two* daughter cells that are genetically *identical* to the parent cell. In contrast, meiosis produces *four* daughter cells that are genetically *different* from the parent cell.
- Mitosis produces daughter cells that are *diploid,* whereas meiosis produces daughter cells that are *haploid.*
- Meiosis includes a process called **crossing over,** whereby genetic material is exchanged between homologous chromosomes.

WHAT DO YOU THINK?

1. How does crossing over relate to genetic diversity among individual sex cells?

Crossing over helps "shuffle the genetic deck of cards," so to speak. Thus, crossing over is a means of combining different genes from both parents on one of the homologous chromosomes. Crossing over does not occur in mitosis.

Meiosis begins with a diploid parent cell located in the gonad (ovary or testis). In this cell, 23 chromosomes came from the organism's mother (23 maternal chromosomes), and 23 came from the father (23 paternal chromosomes). To produce haploid gametes, this parent cell must undergo meiosis.

The cell phase called interphase occurs prior to meiosis. During interphase, the DNA in each chromosome is replicated, or duplicated, in the parent cell. These **replicated chromosomes** (also known as *double-stranded chromosomes*) are composed of two identical structures called **sister chromatids** (krō′mă-tid; *chromo* = color, *id* = resembling). Each sister chromatid contains an identical copy of DNA at this point. The sister chromatids are attached at a specialized region termed the **centromere.**

Note that sister chromatids are not the same as a "pair" of chromosomes. A chromosome composed of sister chromatids resembles a written letter X, whereas a homologous pair of chromosomes is composed of a matching maternal chromosome and paternal chromosome, which are not attached at a centromere. Therefore, after interphase, there are 23 pairs of replicated chromosomes. To assist you with this terminology, please refer to **table 3.1**.

Once the DNA is replicated in interphase, the phases of meiosis begin (**figure 3.2**). Meiosis is comprised of two separate sequential events: meiosis I and meiosis II.

Meiosis I: Reduction Division

During **meiosis** I (also known as the *first meiotic division*), the homologous pairs of chromosomes are separated when the cell divides. The result is two cells, each of which contains 23 chromosomes only (not 23 pairs) that consist of duplicated sister chromatids held together at a centromere. Because meiosis I results in the reduction of the number of chromosomes in the daughter cells, it is also called *reduction division.* Meiosis I consists of four phases plus cytokinesis, described next.

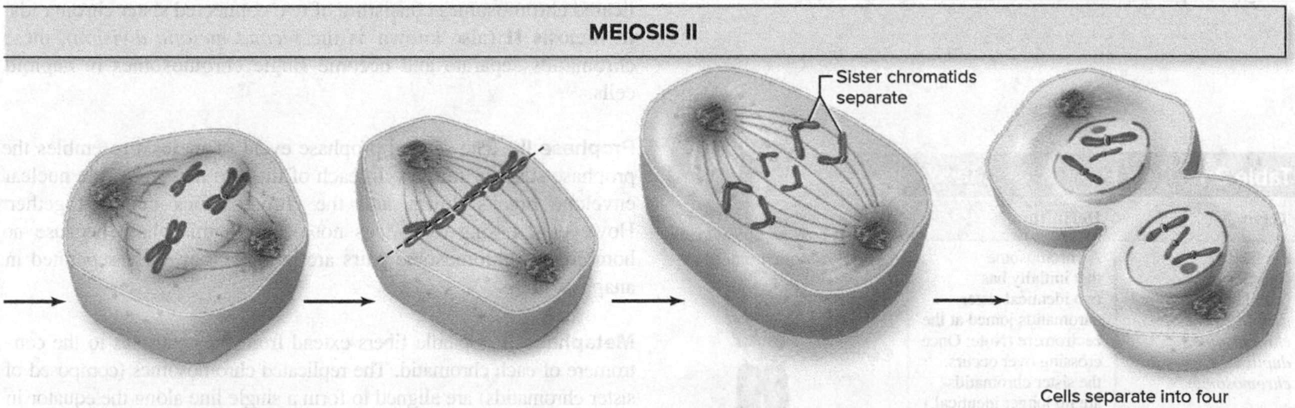

Prophase II
Nuclear envelope breaks down, and replicated chromosomes cluster together. (There is no crossing over in prophase II.)

Metaphase II
Spindle fibers extend from the centrioles to each sister chromatid in each chromosome and align the replicated chromosomes along the equator of the cell.

Anaphase II
Sister chromatids of each replicated chromosome are pulled apart at the centromere. Sister chromatids (now called single chromosomes) migrate to opposite ends of the cell.

Telophase II and Cytokinesis
Nuclear division finishes, and the nuclear envelopes re-form. The four new daughter cells that are produced each contain 23 single chromosomes only.

Prophase I Homologous replicated chromosomes in the parent cell pair up to form a **tetrad.** (Keep in mind that each chromosome here consists of two sister chromatids.) The process by which homologous chromosomes pair up is called **synapsis** (si-nap′sis; *syn* = together).

As the maternal and paternal chromosomes come close together, crossing over occurs. The homologous chromosomes within each tetrad exchange genetic material at this time. A portion of the genetic material in a sister chromatid of a maternal chromosome is exchanged with the same portion of genetic material in a sister chromatid of a paternal chromosome. This shuffling of the genetic material ensures continued genetic diversity in new organisms. (Note that after crossing over, the sister chromatids in a replicated chromosome are no longer identical.) Prophase I ends with the breakdown of the nuclear envelope.

Metaphase I The homologous pairs of each tetrad line up on either side of the midline or equator of the cell, forming a double line of chromosomes. This alignment of paired chromosomes is random with respect to whether the original maternal or paternal chromosome of a pair is on one side of the equator or the other. For example, some maternal chromosomes may be to the left of the equator, while the remaining maternal chromosomes may be to the right. This random alignment of homologous chromosomes is called **independent assortment.**

Spindle fibers formed by microtubules extend from centrioles at opposite ends of the cell and attach to the centromere of each homologous replicated chromosome.

Table 3.1 Cell Division Terminology

Term	Definition	Image
Replicated chromosome (also known as a *double-stranded chromosome, duplicated chromosome*)	A chromosome that initially has two identical sister chromatids joined at the centromere (Note: Once crossing over occurs, the sister chromatids are no longer identical.)	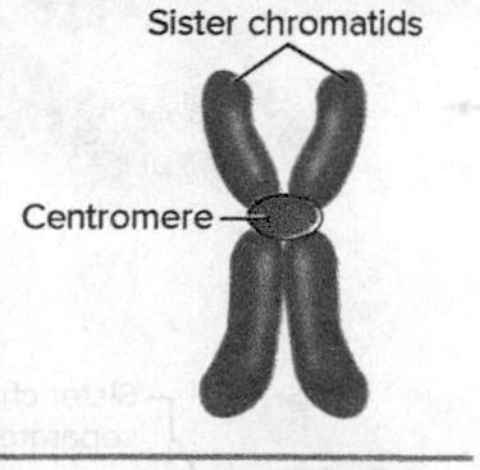
Pair of chromosomes	A homologous maternal chromosome and a paternal chromosome	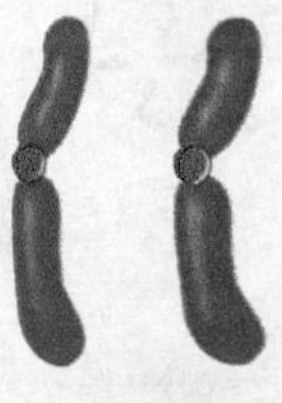
Single chromosome (also known as a *single-stranded chromosome*)	A chromosome (previously formed from a single chromatid) and a centromere	

Anaphase I The homologous pairs of chromosomes separate and are pulled to the opposite ends of the cell. Thus, a maternal chromosome consisting of two sister chromatids is pulled to one side of the cell, while the homologous paternal chromosome is pulled to the opposite side. The process by which maternal and paternal chromosome pairs are separated and move to opposite ends of the cell is referred to as **reduction division,** because each daughter cell receives only one-half the starting number of chromosomes (only 23 chromosomes of the original 23 pairs). Note that the pairs of chromosomes are no longer together; however, each replicated chromosome still consists of two sister chromatids. In addition, recognize that not all maternal chromosomes are pulled to the same side of the cell; because of independent assortment, there is a random alignment of maternal and paternal chromosomes.

Telophase I and Cytokinesis The replicated chromosomes arrive at opposite ends of the cell, and then a nuclear membrane may re-form around these chromosomes. A cleavage furrow forms in the cell, and the cell cytoplasm divides (cytokinesis) to produce two new cells. Each daughter cell now contains 23 replicated chromosomes only, but each replicated chromosome is still composed of two sister chromatids bound together.

The two cells formed in this stage must undergo another round of cell division, meiosis II, to separate the sister chromatids.

Meiosis II: Separation of Sister Chromatids

After meiosis I, the two daughter cells formed each contain 23 replicated chromosomes consisting of two connected sister chromatids. In **meiosis II** (also known as the *second meiotic division*), these chromatids separate and become single chromosomes in haploid cells.

Prophase II The second prophase event of meiosis resembles the prophase stage of mitosis. In each of the two new cells, the nuclear envelope breaks down, and the chromosomes collect together. However, crossing over does not occur in this phase because no homologous chromosome pairs are present; they were separated in anaphase I.

Metaphase II Spindle fibers extend from the centrioles to the centromere of each chromatid. The replicated chromosomes (composed of sister chromatids) are aligned to form a single line along the equator in the middle of the cell.

Anaphase II The sister chromatids of each replicated chromosome are pulled apart at the centromere and are now separated. Each sister chromatid is now called a **single chromosome** (or *single-stranded chromosome*) and is pulled to the opposite pole of the cell.

Learning Strategy 3.1

Meiosis I (the first meiotic division) randomly separates maternal and paternal *pairs* of replicated (double-stranded) chromosomes, whereas meiosis II (the second meiotic division) separates replicated chromosomes into single chromosomes. Also, meiosis II is very similar to mitosis. Thus, if you remember the steps of mitosis, you can figure out the steps of meiosis II.

Telophase II and Cytokinesis The single chromosomes arrive at opposite ends of the cell. Nuclear membranes re-form, a cleavage furrow forms, and the cytoplasm in both cells divides.

These meiotic processes produce four daughter cells from the original single cell. These daughter cells are haploid, because they contain 23 chromosomes only, not 23 pairs. Twenty-two of these are autosomes, and one is a sex chromosome.

These daughter cells mature into secondary oocytes in the ovaries, and they mature into sperm in the testes. These processes are described in more detail later in this chapter.

3.2b Oocyte Development (Oogenesis)

In ovaries, the sex cell produced is called the **secondary oocyte,** and the process of oocyte development is called **oogenesis** (ō′ō-jen′ĕ-sis; *oon* = egg, *genesis* = origin). This cell will have 22 autosomes and one X chromosome. Oogenesis is discussed in greater detail in section 28.2a, but we provide a brief summary here.

The parent cells, or *stem cells,* that produce oocytes are called **oogonia** (ō′ō-gō′nē-ă), and they reside in the ovaries. Oogonia are diploid cells that undergo meiosis. In a fetus with ovaries, all the oogonia start the process of meiosis and form **primary oocytes** prior to birth. Primary oocytes are arrested in prophase I and remain this way until puberty (i.e., the individual begins regular menstruation cycles). Then, each month, a number of primary oocytes begin to mature; usually only one becomes a secondary oocyte.

When the primary oocyte completes the first meiotic division (prophase I, metaphase I, anaphase I, and telophase I), two cells are produced. However, the division of the cytoplasm is grossly unequal. The cell we call the **secondary oocyte** receives the bulk of the cytoplasm and is the cell that is arrested in metaphase II. The diameter of

Clinical View 3.1

Nondisjunction

Normally, the two members of a homologous chromosome pair separate during meiosis I, and paired sister chromatids separate during meiosis II. In **nondisjunction,** these entities fail to separate properly, and both members of a homologous chromosome pair move into one cell, or both sister chromatids move into one cell. As a result of nondisjunction, one gamete may receive two copies of a single chromosome and thus have 24 chromosomes, while the other gamete would receive none of a specific chromosome and would have only 22 chromosomes. If either of these cells unites with a normal gamete at fertilization, the resulting individual will have either 47 chromosomes **(trisomy)** or 45 chromosomes **(monosomy).** Trisomy means the individual has three copies of a chromosome, whereas monosomy means an individual has only one copy of a chromosome.

Most trisomies and monosomies are lethal to the embryo, but a few trisomies that involve smaller chromosomes allow survival. A trisomy disorder is named according to the specific chromosome that has three copies. The most well known is **trisomy 21,** also known as **Down syndrome.** A person with trisomy 21 typically has some form of intellectual disability, slanting epicanthal folds (eye creases), heart defects, poor muscle tone, and short stature. Many, but not all, cases of Down syndrome occur due to nondisjunction in the formation of the oocyte. The incidence of Down syndrome increases with the mother's age, suggesting that nondisjunction problems may occur as the mother (and her sex cells) age; however, cases are known in which the nondisjunction occurs in formation of sperm. (A less common cause of Down syndrome is the result of part of chromosome 21 translocating [attaching] to chromosome 14.)

(a) Nondisjunction during meiosis can lead to abnormalities in chromosome number.
(b) Down syndrome (trisomy 21) is one possible consequence of nondisjunction. Individuals with Down syndrome have certain characteristic facial features and may have mental and/or physical abnormalities.
(b) Disability Images/Blend Images LLC

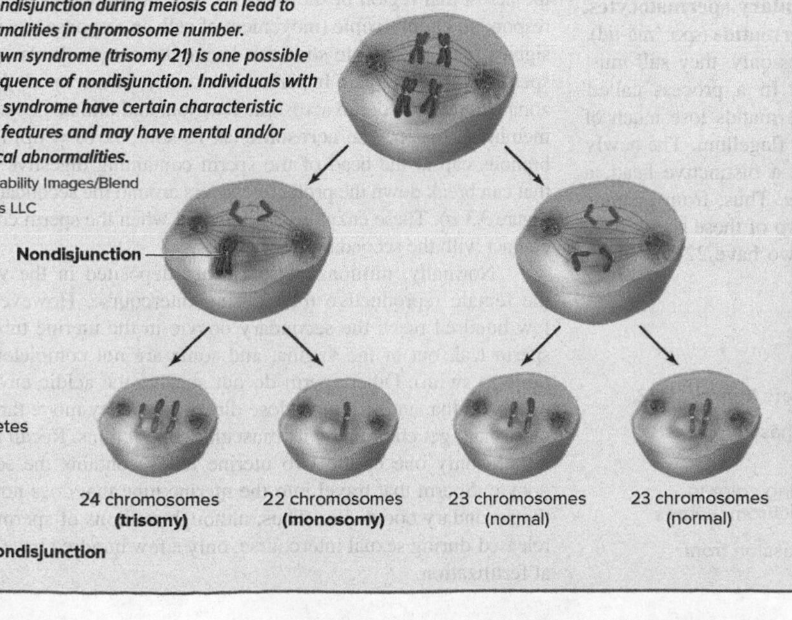
Meiosis
Nondisjunction
Gametes
24 chromosomes
(trisomy)
22 chromosomes
(monosomy)
23 chromosomes
(normal)
23 chromosomes
(normal)

(a) Nondisjunction

(b) Individual with Down Syndrome

the secondary oocyte varies, but is typically 100 to 120 micrometers (μm) (see figure 2.1). The second cell, which receives only a tiny bit of the cytoplasm, is called a **polar body.** The polar body is a nonfunctional cell that eventually degenerates.

Thus, only the secondary oocyte (and not the polar body) has the potential to be fertilized. The secondary oocyte is **ovulated** (expelled from the ovary into the uterine tube). Surrounding the ovulated oocyte are two other components—cuboidal cells that form the **corona radiata** (kō-rō′nă rā-dē-ă′tă; radiate crown) and a thin ring of proteins and glycoproteins called the **zona pellucida** (pe-lū′sid-ă; *pellucid* = allowing the passage of light). The corona radiata and the zona pellucida form protective layers around the secondary oocyte.

The further development of the secondary oocyte varies, depending upon whether or not it is fertilized by a sperm. If the secondary oocyte is not fertilized, it degenerates about 24 hours after ovulation, still arrested in metaphase II. If the secondary oocyte is fertilized, it first finishes the process of meiosis. Two new cells are produced, and as before, the division of the cytoplasm is unequal. The cell that receives very little cytoplasm becomes another polar body and eventually degenerates. The cell that receives the majority of the cytoplasm becomes an **ovum** (ō′vŭm; egg). It is the ovum pronucleus that combines with the sperm pronucleus to produce the diploid fertilized cell, or zygote.

Typically, only one secondary oocyte is expelled (ovulated) from one of the two ovaries each month. This is in stark contrast to sex cell production in testes, which produce and release millions of gametes (sperm) throughout the entire month.

3.2c Sperm Development (Spermatogenesis)

The sex cell produced in testes is called a **sperm (spermatozoon;** pl., spermatozoa), and the process of sperm development is called **spermatogenesis.** Spermatogenesis is discussed in greater detail in section 28.3c, but we provide a brief summary here.

The parent or stem cells that produce sperm are called **spermatogonia** (sper′mă-tō-gō′nē-ă; *sperma* = seed, *gone* = generation). Spermatogonia are diploid cells that reside in the male gonads, the testes. Each spermatogonium first divides by mitosis to make an exact copy of itself, a new cell called a **primary spermatocyte.** Each primary spermatocyte divides into two **secondary spermatocytes,** and each secondary spermatocyte into two **spermatids** (sper′mă-tid). Although spermatids contain 23 chromosomes only, they still must undergo further changes to form a sperm. In a process called **spermiogenesis** (sper′mē-ō-jen′ĕ-sis), the spermatids lose much of their cytoplasm and grow a long tail called a flagellum. The newly formed sperm are haploid cells that exhibit a distinctive head, a midpiece, and a tail, as shown in **figure 3.3*a*.** Thus, from a single spermatocyte, four new sperm are formed. Two of these sperm have 22 autosomes and one X chromosome, and two have 22 autosomes and one Y chromosome. APR

WHAT DID YOU LEARN?

1. What are two ways in which meiosis differs from mitosis?
2. What is crossing over, and during what phase of meiosis does it occur?
3. Draw each of the stages of meiosis, using color to differentiate the maternal and paternal chromosomes.
4. Make a flowchart that shows the progression from spermatogonium to sperm.

3.3 Pre-embryonic Period

✓ Learning Objectives

5. Describe the major events of fertilization.
6. Explain the effects of cleavage.
7. Explain the major steps involved in implantation.
8. Describe the extraembryonic membranes and their functions.
9. Identify and describe the components of the placenta.

The pre-embryonic period in human development begins with fertilization, when sperm and the ovum unite to form a single diploid cell called the **zygote** (zī′gōt; *zygotes* = yoked). The zygote is the same size as the secondary oocyte, which typically is between 100 and 120 μm in diameter. Within the first 2 weeks, the zygote undergoes mitotic cell divisions, and the number of cells increases, forming a **pre-embryo.** The pre-embryonic stage of development spans the time from fertilization in the uterine tube through completion of implantation (burrowing and embedding) into the wall of the uterus. **Table 3.2** traces the sequence of these events.

3.3a Fertilization

Fertilization is the process whereby two sex cells fuse to form a new cell containing genetic material derived from both parents. Besides combining sperm and ovum genetic material, fertilization restores the diploid number of chromosomes, determines the genetic sex of the organism, and initiates cleavage (discussed later in this section). Fertilization occurs in the widest part of the uterine tube, called the ampulla. Following ovulation, the secondary oocyte remains viable in the female reproductive tract for no more than 24 hours, whereas sperm remain viable for an average of 3 to 4 days after ejaculation.

Upon arrival in the female reproductive tract, sperm are not yet capable of fertilizing the secondary oocyte. Before they can successfully do so, sperm must undergo **capacitation** (kă-pas′i-tā′shŭn; *capacitas* = capable of), which is a period of physiological change during which the sperm attain the ability to fertilize a secondary oocyte. Capacitation takes place in the female reproductive tract, and typically lasts several hours. During this time, a glycoprotein coat and some proteins are removed from the sperm plasma membrane that overlies the acrosomal region of the sperm. Capacitation allows the sperm to respond to **chemotropic** (movement of cells in response to a chemical) signals from the oocyte so it can locate the oocyte. It also gives the sperm an ability to gain hyperactive motility, interact with the oocyte zona pellucida, undergo acrosome reaction, and initiate oocyte plasma membrane fusion. The **acrosome** (ak′rō-sōm; *akros* = tip) is a membranous cap at the head of the sperm containing digestive enzymes that can break down the protective layers around the secondary oocyte (figure 3.3 *a*). These enzymes are released when the sperm comes into contact with the secondary oocyte.

Normally, millions of sperm are deposited in the vagina of the female reproductive tract during intercourse. However, only a few hundred reach the secondary oocyte in the uterine tube. Many sperm leak out of the vagina, and some are not completely motile (able to swim). Other sperm do not survive the acidic environment of the vagina, and still more lose direction as they move through the uterus and get churned by its muscular contractions. Recall that each month, only one of the two uterine tubes contains the secondary oocyte. Sperm that travel into the uterine tube that does not contain the secondary oocyte die. Thus, although millions of sperm may be released during sexual intercourse, only a few hundred have a chance at fertilization.

Table 3.2 Chronology of Events in Pre-embryonic Development

Developmental Stage	Time of Occurrence	Location	Event(s)
Fertilization 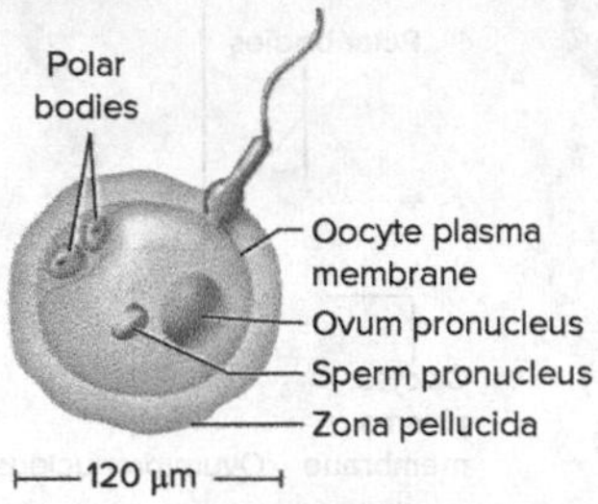 Polar bodies Oocyte plasma membrane Ovum pronucleus Sperm pronucleus Zona pellucida 120 µm	Within 12–24 hours after ovulation	Ampulla of uterine tube	Sperm penetrates secondary oocyte; secondary oocyte completes meiosis II and becomes an ovum; ovum and sperm pronuclei fuse
Zygote 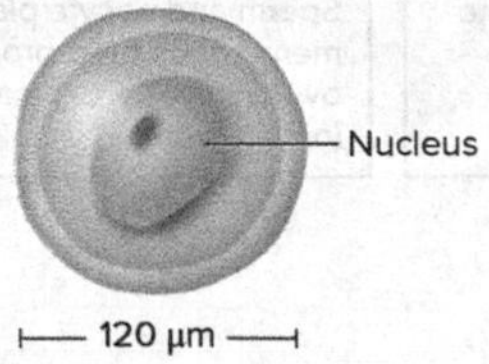 Nucleus 120 µm	At the end of fertilization	Ampulla of uterine tube	Diploid cell produced when ovum and sperm pronuclei fuse
Cleavage 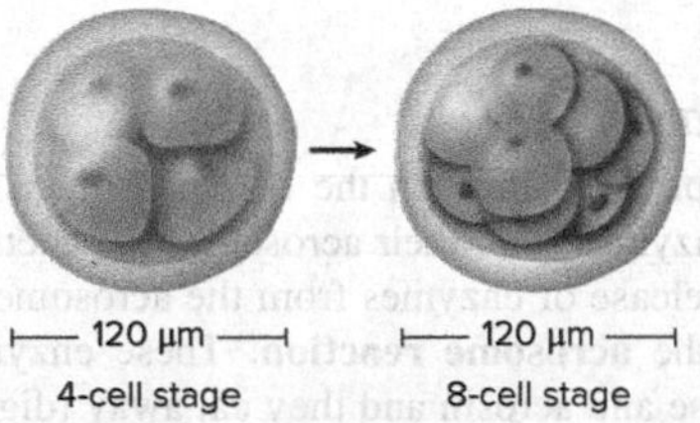 120 µm 4-cell stage 120 µm 8-cell stage	30 hours to day 3 post-fertilization	Uterine tube	Zygote undergoes cell division by mitosis to increase cell number, but overall size of the structure remains constant
Morula 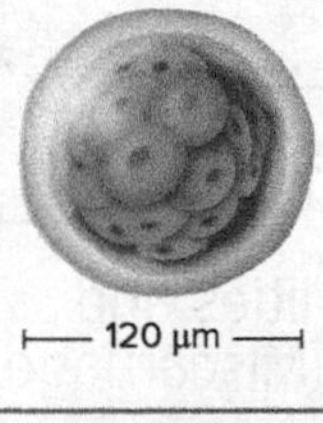 120 µm	Days 3–4 post-fertilization	Uterine tube	Structure formed resembles a solid ball of cells; 16 or more cells are present, but there is no change in diameter from original zygote
Blastocyst 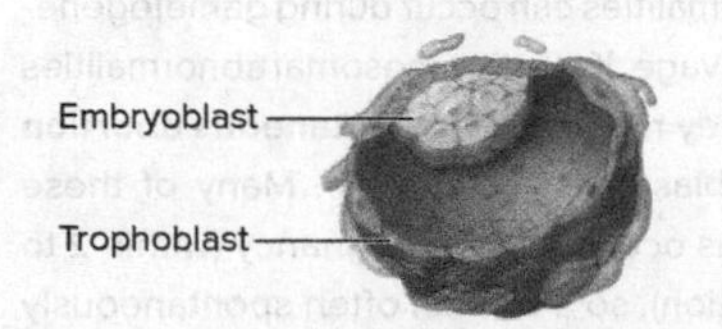 Embryoblast Trophoblast 120 µm	Days 5–6	Uterus	Hollow ball of cells; outer ring of the ball formed by trophoblast; inner cell mass (embryoblast) is cell cluster inside blastocyst
Implantation 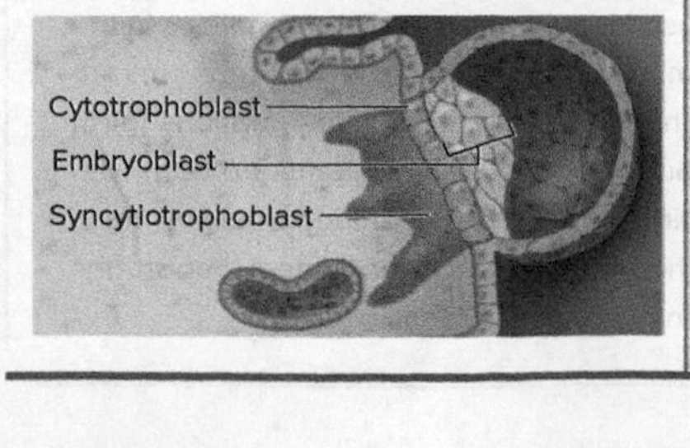 Cytotrophoblast Embryoblast Syncytiotrophoblast	Begins late first week and is complete by end of second week	Functional layer of endometrium (inner lining) of uterus	Blastocyst adheres to uterine lining; trophoblast cells and functional layer together begin to form the placenta

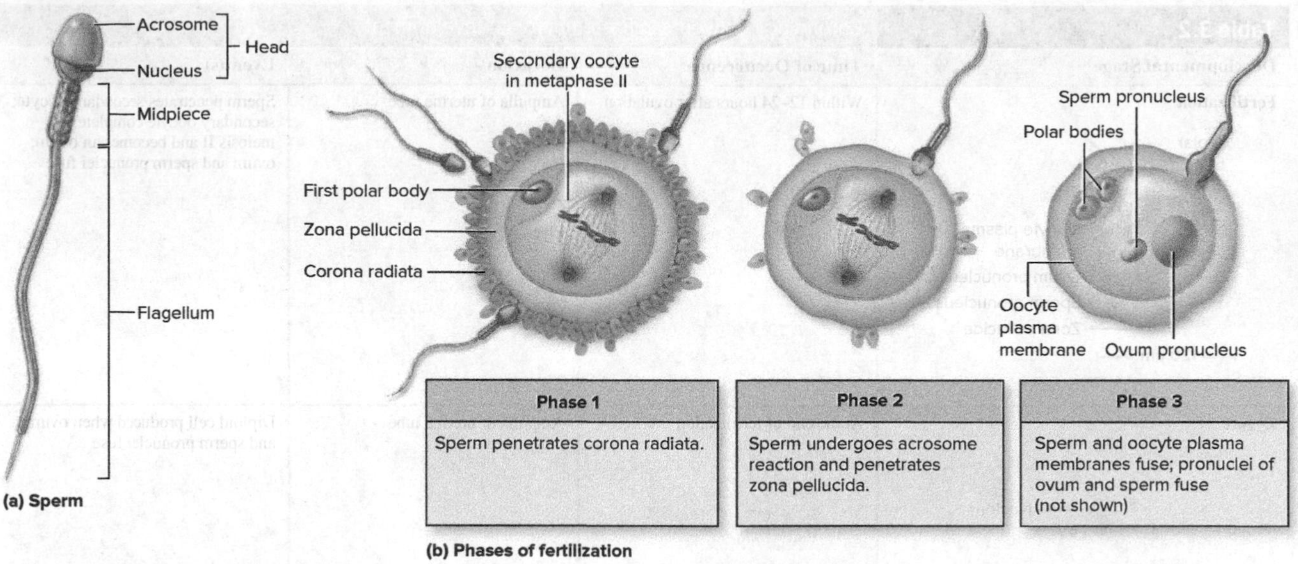
Acrosome
Head
Nucleus
Midpiece
Flagellum
(a) Sperm
Secondary oocyte in metaphase II
First polar body
Zona pellucida
Corona radiata
Sperm pronucleus
Polar bodies
Oocyte plasma membrane
Ovum pronucleus
Phase 1
Sperm penetrates corona radiata.
Phase 2
Sperm undergoes acrosome reaction and penetrates zona pellucida.
Phase 3
Sperm and oocyte plasma membranes fuse; pronuclei of ovum and sperm fuse (not shown)
(b) Phases of fertilization

Figure 3.3

Fertilization of a Secondary Oocyte in Humans. A secondary oocyte is ovulated in a "developmentally arrested" state at metaphase II in meiosis. (*a*) Diagrammatic representation of a normal sperm. (*b*) Schematic representation of the three phases of fertilization.

Once sperm reach the secondary oocyte, the race is on to see which sperm can fertilize the oocyte first. Only the first sperm to enter the secondary oocyte is able to fertilize it; the remaining sperm are prevented from penetrating the oocyte.

WHAT DO YOU THINK?

2 Rarely, two sperm may penetrate a secondary oocyte. Do you think this fertilized cell will survive for long? Why or why not?

Some causes of infertility (inability to achieve or maintain pregnancy) are due to immune system reactions related to the sperm or oocyte. Some genetic males (and more rarely, some genetic females) develop anti-sperm **antibodies,** which are substances (specialized proteins) that mark and target the sperm for destruction by the immune system (see section 24.3a). It is believed that individuals develop these antibodies against their sperm when the blood-testis barrier (a protective barrier between the testis and the blood vessels traveling through it) is breached, such as due to severe trauma to the testis or reversal of a vasectomy. In other immune-related fertility problems, the woman's body perceives the sperm and/or the fertilized oocyte as something foreign that must be destroyed. Researchers are examining ways to prevent these immune-related infertility problems from occurring.

The phases of fertilization are corona radiata penetration, zona pellucida penetration, and fusion of the sperm and oocyte plasma membranes (figure 3.3*b*).

Corona Radiata Penetration

The sperm that successfully reach the secondary oocyte are initially prevented entry by both the corona radiata and the zona pellucida. When sperm reach the corona radiata, their motility allows the sperm to push through the cell layers. Once the sperm penetrate the corona radiata, they then encounter the more solid zona pellucida.

Zona Pellucida Penetration

Once the sperm make a pathway through the corona radiata, the sperm release digestive enzymes from their acrosomes to penetrate the zona pellucida. This release of enzymes from the acrosome by exocytosis is known as the **acrosome reaction.** These enzymes are primarily hyaluronidase and acrosin and they eat away (digest)

Clinical View 3.2

Chromosomal Abnormalities and Spontaneous Abortion (Miscarriage)

Abnormalities in chromosome number, shape, or form occur regularly. These abnormalities can occur during gametogenesis, fertilization, or cleavage. If the chromosomal abnormalities are severe enough, they result in the **spontaneous abortion (miscarriage)** of the blastocyst or embryo. Many of these spontaneous abortions occur early in pregnancy (within 2 to 3 weeks after fertilization), so a woman often spontaneously aborts without realizing she was ever pregnant.

Some estimates propose that about 50% of all pregnancies terminate as a result of spontaneous abortion; perhaps half of these are caused by chromosomal abnormalities in the developing organism. As a consequence, fewer organisms are stillborn or born with severe congenital malformations (birth defects). Thus, although 2% to 3% of all infants are born with some type of major birth defect, this percentage would be much higher if not for the high frequency of spontaneous abortions very early in pregnancy.

a portion of the zona pellucida. After the first sperm successfully penetrates the zona pellucida and its nucleus enters the secondary oocyte, immediate changes occur to both the zona pellucida and the oocyte so that no other sperm can enter the oocyte. The cortical reaction alters the zona pellucida by the exocytosis of oocyte cortical granules, leading to a modification of the zona pellucida to block polyspermy. In essence, the zona pellucida hardens and sperm receptors in the zona pellucida are deactivated preventing other sperm from binding to and ultimately digesting their way through this layer. This process is necessary to ensure that only one sperm fertilizes the oocyte.

On very rare occasions, two or more sperm nuclei simultaneously enter the secondary oocyte, a phenomenon called **polyspermy** (pol′ē-spěr′mē; *polys* = many). Polyspermy is immediately fatal because it causes the fertilized oocyte to have 23 triplets (if two sperm enter) or 23 quadruplets (if three sperm enter) of chromosomes, instead of the normal 23 pairs of chromosomes.

Fusion of Sperm and Oocyte Plasma Membranes

When the sperm and oocyte plasma membranes come into contact, they immediately fuse. Only the nucleus of the sperm enters the cytoplasm of the secondary oocyte. Once the nucleus of the sperm enters the secondary oocyte, the secondary oocyte completes the second meiotic division and forms an ovum.

Once meiosis is complete, the nucleus of the sperm and the nucleus of the ovum are called **pronuclei** (*pro* = before, precursor of) because they have a haploid number of chromosomes. These pronuclei come together and fuse, forming a single nucleus that contains a diploid number (23 pairs) of chromosomes. The single diploid cell formed is the *zygote*.

3.3b Cleavage

Following fertilization, the zygote begins the process of becoming a multicellular organism. After the zygote divides once and reaches the 2-cell stage, a series of mitotic divisions, called **cleavage** (klēv′ij), results in an increase in cell number but not an increase in the overall size of the structure. The diameter of the structure remains about 120 µm, so the mitotic divisions produce greater numbers of smaller cells to fit in this structure. The structure will not increase in *size* until it implants in the uterine wall and derives a source of nourishment from the mother (**figure 3.4**).

Before the 8-cell stage, cells are not tightly bound together, but after the third cleavage division, the cells become tightly compacted into a ball, which is accompanied by the formation of tight and gap junctions. The process by which contact between cells is increased to the maximum is called **compaction.** These cells now divide again, forming a 16-cell stage, the **morula** (mōr′ū-lă, *morus* = mulberry). The cells of the morula continue to divide further.

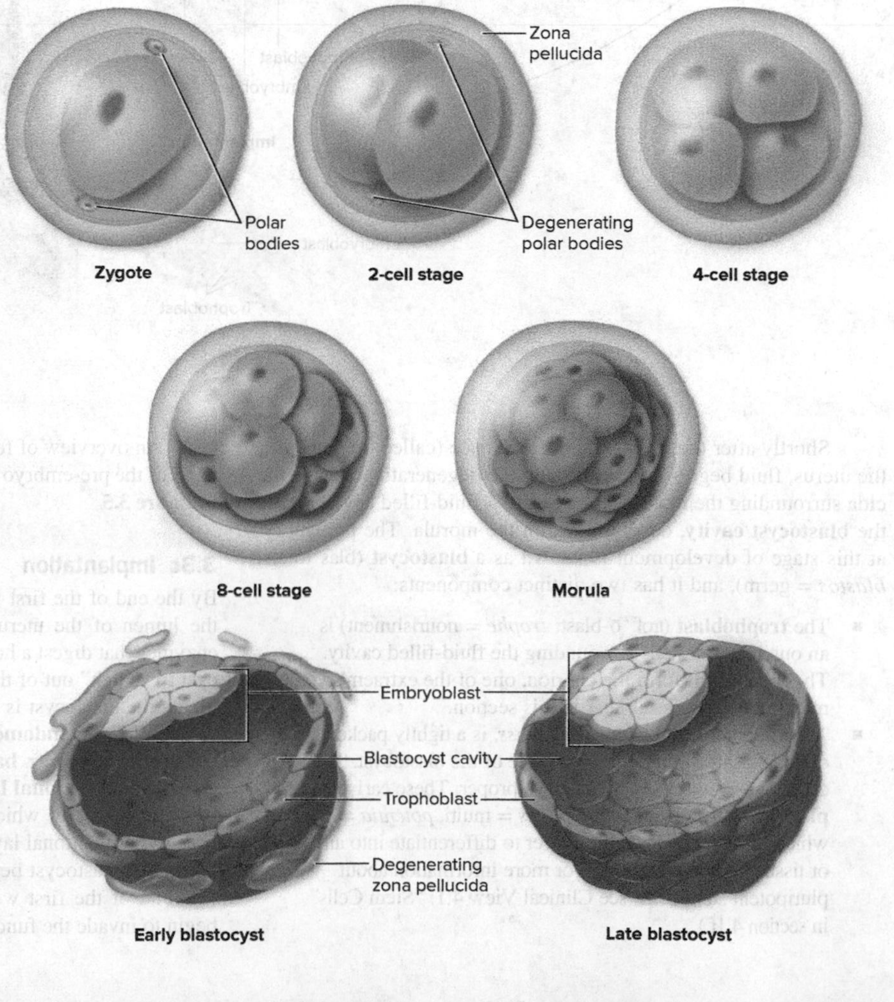
Zona pellucida
Polar bodies
Degenerating polar bodies
Zygote
2-cell stage
4-cell stage
8-cell stage
Morula
Embryoblast
Blastocyst cavity
Trophoblast
Degenerating zona pellucida
Early blastocyst
Late blastocyst

Figure 3.4

Cleavage in the Pre-embryo. Shortly after fertilization, the zygote begins to undergo a series of cell divisions, termed cleavage. Divisions increase the number of cells in the pre-embryo, but the pre-embryo remains the same size. During each succeeding division, the cells are smaller than those in the previous generation, until they reach the size of most cells of the body.

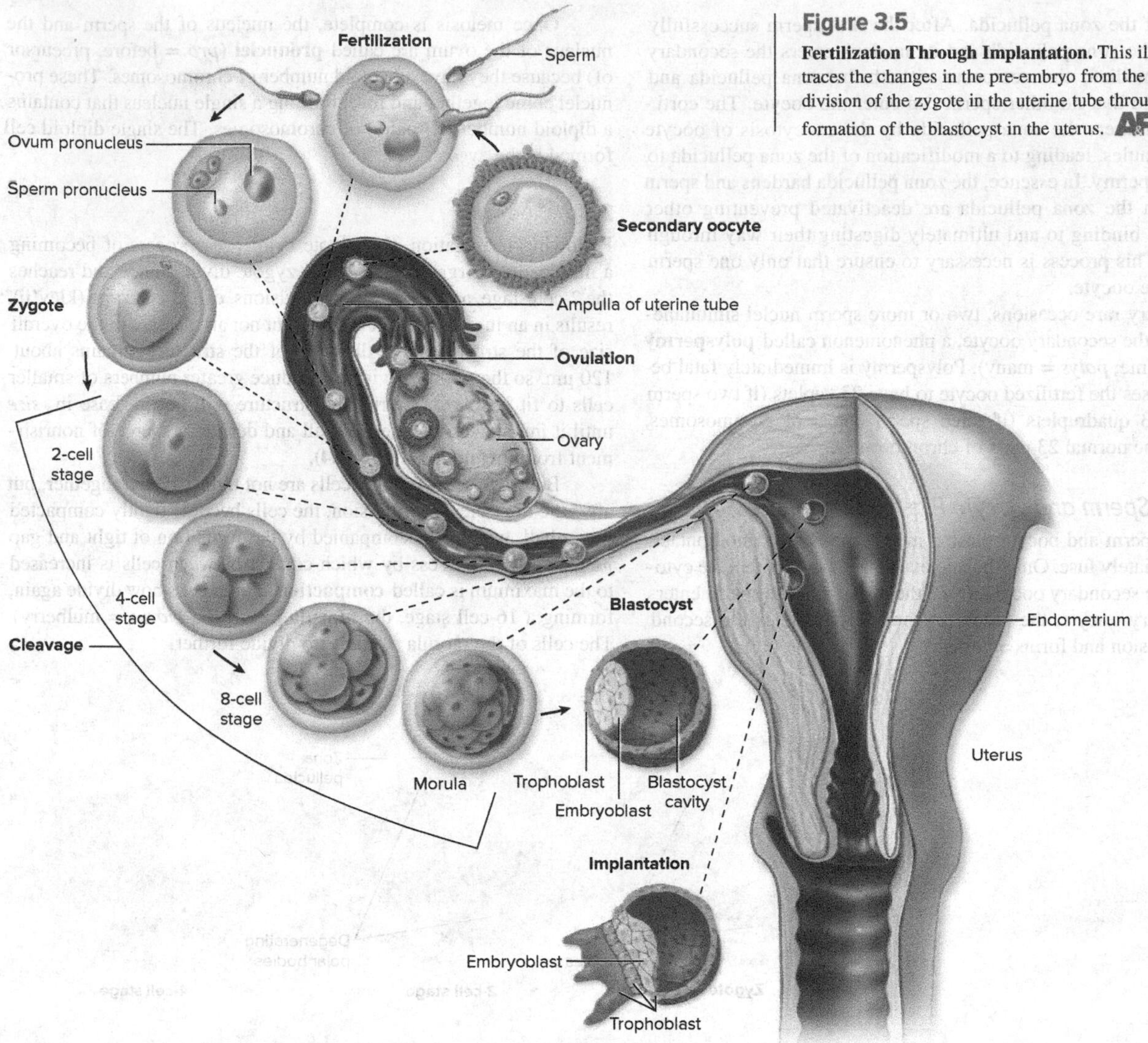
Fertilization
Sperm
Ovum pronucleus
Sperm pronucleus
Secondary oocyte
Zygote
Ampulla of uterine tube
Ovulation
Ovary
2-cell stage
4-cell stage
Cleavage
8-cell stage
Blastocyst
Endometrium
Uterus
Morula
Trophoblast
Embryoblast
Blastocyst cavity
Implantation
Embryoblast
Trophoblast

Figure 3.5

Fertilization Through Implantation. This illustration traces the changes in the pre-embryo from the first cleavage division of the zygote in the uterine tube through the formation of the blastocyst in the uterus. APR

Shortly after the morula enters the space (called the lumen) of the uterus, fluid begins to leak through the degenerating zona pellucida surrounding the morula. As a result, a fluid-filled cavity, called the **blastocyst cavity,** develops within the morula. The pre-embryo at this stage of development is known as a **blastocyst** (blas′tō-sist; *blastos* = germ), and it has two distinct components:

- The **trophoblast** (trof′ō-blast; *trophe* = nourishment) is an outer ring of cells surrounding the fluid-filled cavity. These cells will form the chorion, one of the extraembryonic membranes discussed later in this section.
- The **embryoblast,** or *inner cell mass,* is a tightly packed group of cells located only within one side of the blastocyst. The embryoblast will form the embryo proper. These early cells are **pluripotent** (plū-rip′ŏ-tĕnt; *pluris* = multi, *potentia* = power), which means they have the power to differentiate into any cell or tissue type in the body. (For more information about pluripotent stem cells, see Clinical View 4.1: "Stem Cells" in section 4.1f.)

An overview of fertilization and cleavage, including the movement of the pre-embryo from the uterine tube into the uterus, is given in **figure 3.5**.

3.3c Implantation

By the end of the first week after fertilization, the blastocyst enters the lumen of the uterus. During this time the blastocyst secretes enzymes that digest a hole in the zona pellucida, allowing the blastocyst to "hatch" out of the zona pellucida. Once outside the zona pellucida the blastocyst is able to invade the inner lining of the uterine wall, called the **endometrium** (see section 28.2c). The endometrium consists of a deeper **basal layer,** the *stratum basalis,* and a more superficial **functional layer,** the *stratum functionalis.* **Implantation** is the process by which the blastocyst burrows into and embeds within the functional layer of the endometrium.

The blastocyst begins the implantation process by about day 7 (the end of the first week of development), when trophoblast cells begin to invade the functional layer of the endometrium **(figure 3.6)**.

Simultaneously, the trophoblast subdivides into two layers: a **cytotrophoblast** (sī'tō-trof'ō-blast; *kytos* = a hollow [cell]), which is the inner cellular layer of the trophoblast, and a **syncytiotrophoblast** (sin-sish'ē-ō-trō' fo-blast), which is the outer, thick layer of the trophoblast where no plasma membranes between individual cells are visible. Over the next few days, the syncytiotrophoblast cells burrow into the functional layer of the endometrium and bring with them the rest of the blastocyst. By day 9, the blastocyst has completely burrowed into the uterine wall and makes contact with the pools of nutrients in the uterine glands that supply the developing organism. Thus, implantation begins during the first week of development and is not complete until the second week.

The syncytiotrophoblast is responsible for producing a hormone called **human chorionic gonadotropin (hCG).** This hormone signals the female reproductive system that fertilization and implantation have occurred. Thus, the corpus luteum does not degenerate but rather persists for another 3 months, producing large amounts of estrogen and progesterone that thicken and maintain the uterine lining.

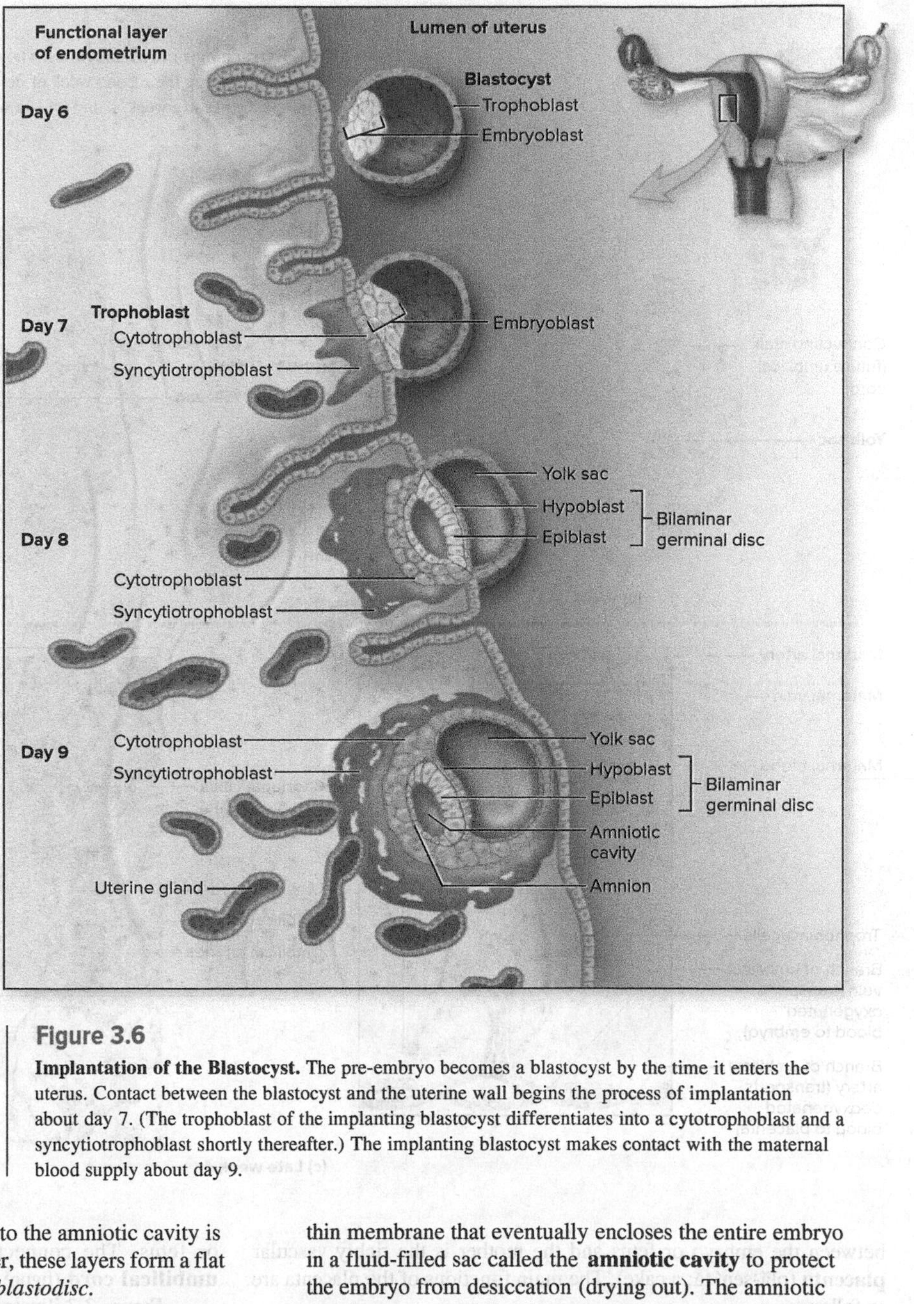

Figure 3.6

Implantation of the Blastocyst. The pre-embryo becomes a blastocyst by the time it enters the uterus. Contact between the blastocyst and the uterine wall begins the process of implantation about day 7. (The trophoblast of the implanting blastocyst differentiates into a cytotrophoblast and a syncytiotrophoblast shortly thereafter.) The implanting blastocyst makes contact with the maternal blood supply about day 9.

3.3d Formation of the Bilaminar Germinal Disc and the Extraembryonic Membranes

During the second week of development, as the blastocyst is undergoing implantation, changes also occur to the embryoblast portion of the blastocyst (the inner cell mass described in section 3.3b). By day 8, the cells of the embryoblast begin to differentiate into two layers. A layer of small, cuboidal cells adjacent to the blastocyst cavity is termed the **hypoblast** layer, and a layer of columnar cells adjacent to the amniotic cavity is called the **epiblast** layer (figure 3.6). Together, these layers form a flat disc termed a **bilaminar germinal disc,** or *blastodisc.*

The bilaminar germinal disc and trophoblast also produce **extraembryonic membranes** to mediate between them and the environment **(figure 3.7)**. They first appear during the second week of development and continue to develop during the embryonic and fetal periods. They protect the embryo and assist the embryo in vital functions such as nutrition, gas exchange, and removal and storage of waste materials. These extraembryonic membranes are as follows:

- The **yolk sac** is the first extraembryonic membrane to develop. It is formed from and continuous with the hypoblast layer. In humans, it does not store yolk as it does in eggs of birds and reptiles, but it is an important site for early blood cell and blood vessel formation.
- The **amnion** (am' nē-on; *amnios* = lamb) is formed from and continuous with the epiblast layer. The amnion is a thin membrane that eventually encloses the entire embryo in a fluid-filled sac called the **amniotic cavity** to protect the embryo from desiccation (drying out). The amniotic membrane is specialized to secrete the amniotic fluid that bathes the embryo.
- The **chorion** (kōr' ē-on; membrane covering the fetus) is the outermost extraembryonic membrane and is formed from both the rapidly growing cytotrophoblast cells and syncytiotrophoblast. These cells blend with the functional layer of the endometrium and eventually form the placenta, the site of exchange between the embryo and the mother.

3.3e Development of the Placenta

Recall that the blastocyst is about the same size as the initial zygote, but the blastocyst contains many more cells than the zygote. To develop into an embryo and fetus, the blastocyst must receive nutrients and respiratory gases from the maternal blood supply. The connection

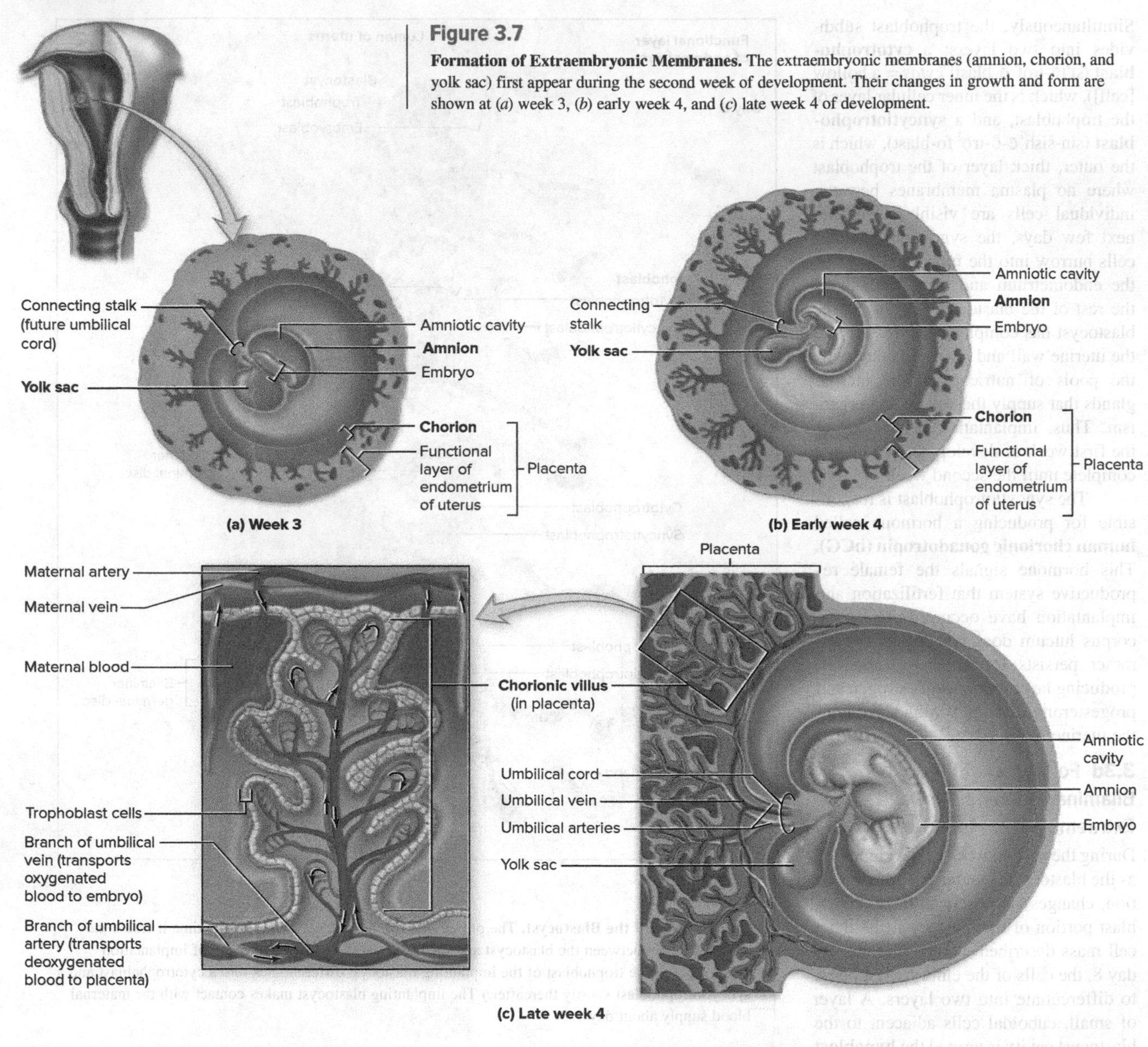

Figure 3.7

Formation of Extraembryonic Membranes. The extraembryonic membranes (amnion, chorion, and yolk sac) first appear during the second week of development. Their changes in growth and form are shown at (*a*) week 3, (*b*) early week 4, and (*c*) late week 4 of development.

between the embryo or fetus and the mother is the richly vascular **placenta** (plă-sen′ tă; a cake). The main functions of the placenta are as follows:

- Exchange of nutrients, waste products, and respiratory gases between the maternal and fetal blood
- Transmission of maternal antibodies (immune system substances that target viruses or bacteria) to the developing embryo or fetus
- Production of hormones (primarily estrogen and progesterone) to maintain and build the uterine lining

The placenta begins to form during the second week of development. The fetal portion of the placenta develops from the chorion, while the maternal portion of the placenta forms from the functional layer of the uterus. The early organism is connected to the placenta via a structure called the **connecting stalk.** This connecting stalk eventually contains the umbilical arteries and veins that distribute blood through the embryo or fetus. The connecting stalk is the precursor to the future **umbilical cord** (figure 3.7 *c*).

Figure 3.7 illustrates how the components of the placenta become better defined during the embryonic period. Fingerlike structures called **chorionic villi** form from the chorion. The chorionic villi contain branches of the umbilical vessels. Adjacent to the chorionic villi is the functional layer of the endometrium, which contains maternal blood. Note that fetal blood and maternal blood do not mix; however, the bloodstreams are so close to one another that exchange of gases and nutrients can occur. Also, undesirable substances like drugs, alcohol, and nicotine can cross the placental barrier and cause damage to the fetus.

Although the placenta first forms during the pre-embryonic period, most of its growth and development occur during the fetal period. It takes about 3 months for the placenta to become fully formed and able to produce sufficient amounts of estrogen and progesterone to maintain and build the uterine lining. Within these first 3 months,

Clinical View 3.3

Twinning

There are two common types of twinning: dizygotic and monozygotic. **Dizygotic twins** (commonly known as *fraternal* twins or *nonidentical* twins) occur when two secondary oocytes become fertilized and are implanted in the uterine wall at about the same time. They result from multiple ovulations, which can be induced by drugs commonly used in patients with infertility. Dizygotic twins may or may not be the same sex. Epidemiologic studies demonstrate that there is a genetic predisposition for dizygotic twinning—thus, nonidentical twins tend to run in families.

Monozygotic twins (also known as *identical* twins) arise from a single secondary oocyte fertilized by a single sperm. At some stage up to 8 days of gestation, the embryonic cells separate into two parts, each of which gives rise to a complete embryo. If separation occurs after 8 days, the embryos are likely to remain attached and become conjoined twins, but this is rare. Depending upon the stage at which the zygote divides, monozygotic twins may share the same amnion (known as *monoamniotic*) or not (*diamniotic*). Diamniotic monozygotic twins may share the same placenta (known as *monochorionic*) or not (*dichorionic*). All monoamniotic twins are monochorionic. Monozygotic twins are genetically identical. It appears that monozygotic twins do not run in families but are, rather, random events.

a structure called the **corpus luteum** (in the ovary of the mother) produces the estrogen and progesterone (corpus luteum will be discussed in more detail in section 28.2a). When the placenta matures, it resembles a disc in shape and adheres firmly to the wall of the uterus. Immediately after the baby is born, the placenta is also expelled from the uterus. The expelled placenta is often called the *afterbirth*.

WHAT DID YOU LEARN?

5. How is a secondary oocyte different from an ovum?
6. What are some factors or events that can prevent sperm from reaching the secondary oocyte?
7. List the four extraembryonic membranes and explain the function of each.
8. What are the main functions of the placenta?

Learning Strategy 3.2

The *second week* of development may be thought of as the "period of twos," because many paired structures develop:

- A *two-layered* (epiblast and hypoblast) germinal disc forms.
- *Two membranes* (the yolk sac and the amnion) develop on either side of the bilaminar germinal disc.
- The placenta develops from *two* components that merge (the chorion and the functional layer of the endometrium of the uterus).

3.4 Embryonic Period

✓ Learning Objectives

10. Explain the processes that occur during gastrulation.
11. Identify and describe the three primary germ layers.
12. List the major structures formed from each of the primary germ layers.
13. Compare and contrast the processes of cephalocaudal and transverse folding of the embryo.
14. Describe the steps involved in neurulation.
15. Define teratogens and explain when and how teratogens may affect organogenesis.

The embryonic period begins with the process called gastrulation, whereby the three primary germ layers (ectoderm, mesoderm, and endoderm) form. Once gastrulation is complete, a process called organogenesis occurs, whereby the basic structure of all organs are formed. By the end of the embryonic period (week 8), the main organ systems have been established, and the major features of the external body form are recognizable. **Table 3.3** summarizes the events that occur during the embryonic period.

Table 3.3 Events in Embryonic Development

Developmental Week	Events
Week 3 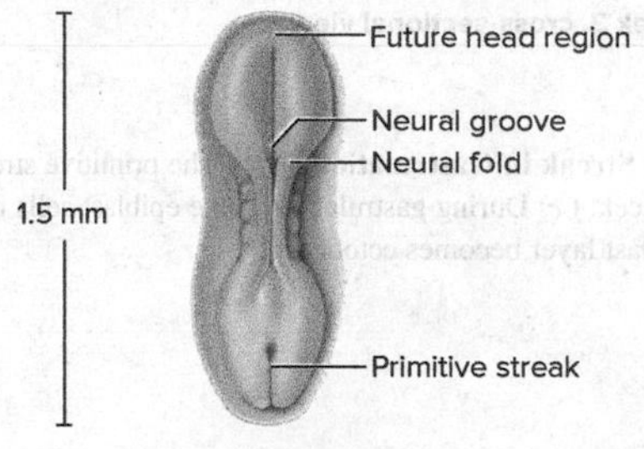 1.5 mm Future head region Neural groove Neural fold Primitive streak **Superior/dorsal view**	Primitive streak appears Gastrulation occurs Notochord develops Neurulation begins Length: 1.5 millimeters (mm)
Week 4 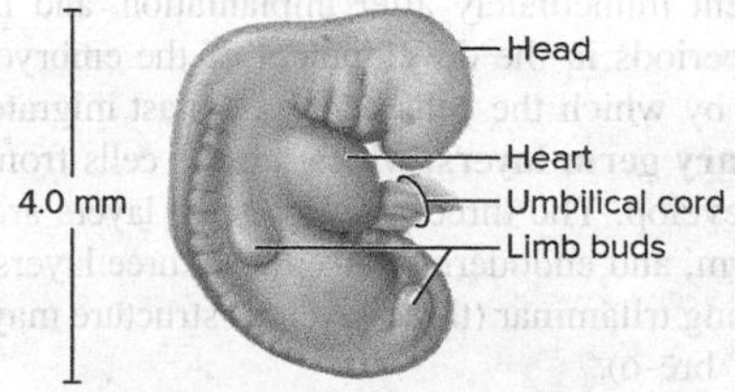 4.0 mm Head Heart Umbilical cord Limb buds **Lateral view**	Cephalocaudal and lateral folding produce a cylindrical embryo Basic human body plan is established Derivatives of the three germ layers begin to form Limb buds appear Crown-rump length: 4.0 mm
Weeks 5–8 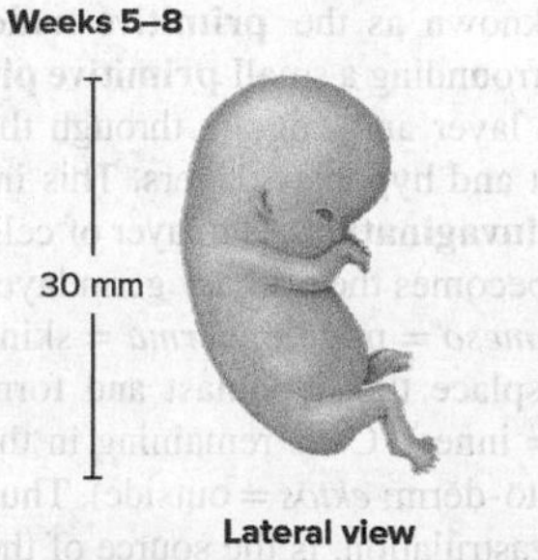 30 mm **Lateral view**	Head enlarges Eyes, ears, and nose appear Major organ systems are formed by the end of week 8 (although some may not be fully functional yet) Crown-rump length (by the end of week 8): 30 mm

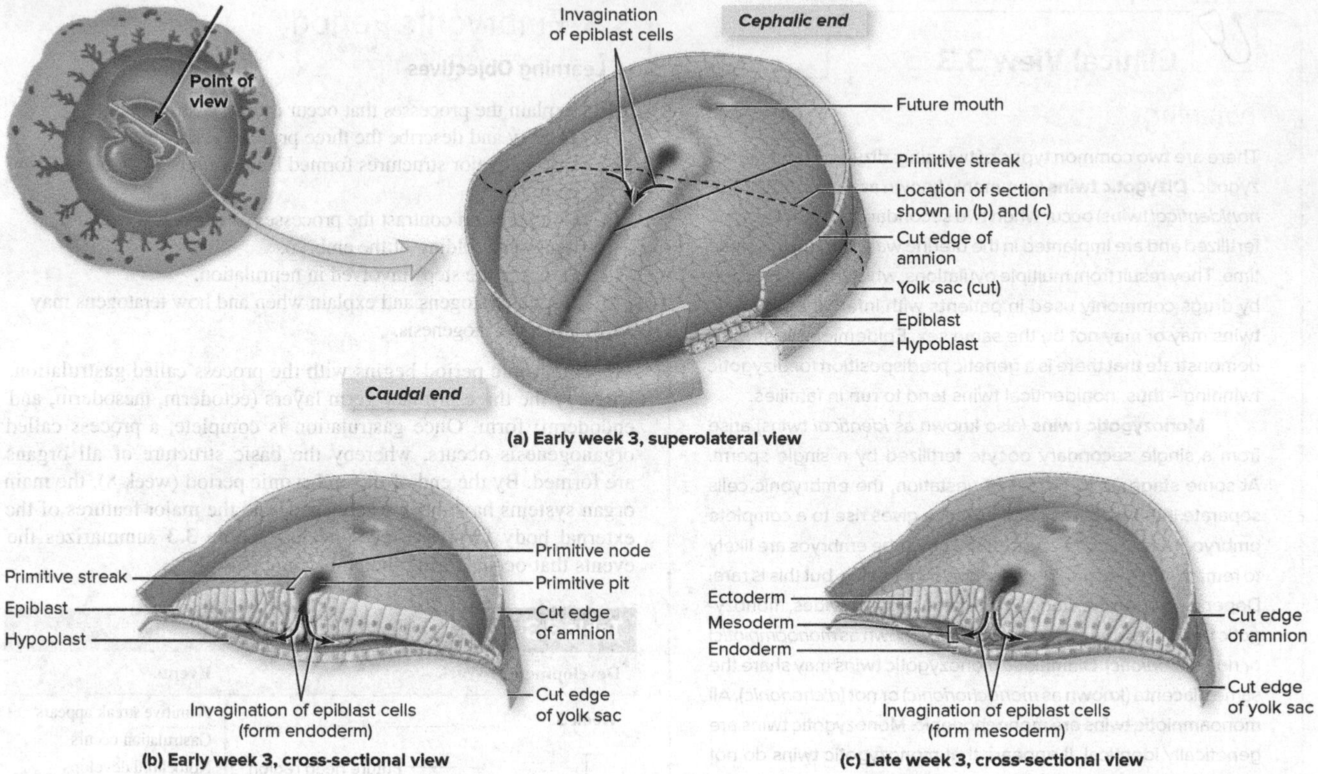

Figure 3.8

The Role of the Primitive Streak in Gastrulation. (*a, b*) The primitive streak is a raised groove on the epiblast surface of the bilaminar germinal disc that appears early in the third week. (*c*) During gastrulation, some epiblast cells migrate and go through the primitive streak to form the endoderm and mesoderm layers. The remaining epiblast layer becomes ectoderm.

3.4a Gastrulation

Gastrulation (gas′ trū-lā′ shŭn; *gaster* = belly) occurs during the third week of development immediately after implantation, and is one of the most critical periods in the development of the embryo. Gastrulation is a process by which the cells of the epiblast migrate and form the three **primary germ layers,** which are the cells from which all body tissues develop. The three primary germ layers are called ectoderm, mesoderm, and endoderm. Once these three layers have formed, the developing trilaminar (three-layered) structure may be called an **embryo** (em′ brē-ō).

Gastrulation begins with formation of the **primitive streak,** a thin depression on the surface of the epiblast (**figure 3.8*a, b***). The cephalic (head) end of the streak, known as the **primitive node,** consists of a slightly elevated area surrounding a small **primitive pit.**

Cells detach from the epiblast layer and migrate through the primitive streak between the epiblast and hypoblast layers. This inward movement of cells is known as **invagination.** The layer of cells that forms between these two layers becomes the primary germ layer known as **mesoderm** (mez′ ō-dĕrm; *meso* = middle, *derma* = skin). Other migrating cells eventually displace the hypoblast and form the **endoderm** (en′ dō-dĕrm; *endo* = inner). Cells remaining in the epiblast then form the **ectoderm** (ek′ tō-dĕrm; *ektos* = outside). Thus, the epiblast, through the process of gastrulation, is the source of the three primary germ layers, from which all body tissues and organs eventually derive (figure 3.8*c*).

3.4b Folding of the Embryonic Disc

The 3-week embryo is a flattened, disc-shaped structure. For this reason, the structure is also referred to as an **embryonic disc (figure 3.9)**. So how does this flattened structure turn into a three-dimensional human?

The shape transformation begins during the late third and fourth weeks of development, when certain regions of the embryo grow faster than others. As a result of this differential growth, the embryonic disc starts to fold on itself and become more cylindrical. **Figure 3.10** illustrates the two types of folding that occur: cephalocaudal folding and transverse folding.

Learning Strategy 3.3

The *third week* of development produces an embryo with *three* primary germ layers: ectoderm, mesoderm, and endoderm.

Clinical View 3.4

Infertility and Infertility Treatments

Infertility refers to the inability to conceive and maintain a pregnancy. Typically, it is defined medically as the inability to conceive after at least 1 year of regular sexual intercourse without protection.

Contrary to popular belief, the causes of infertility are equally split between genetic females and males. One of the most common causes of female infertility is blocked uterine tubes due to pelvic inflammatory disease or complications from endometriosis (see Clinical View 28.3: "Endometriosis" in section 28.2c and Clinical View 28.8: "Sexually Transmitted Infections" in section 28.3g). Ovulation disorders (e.g., abnormal follicle-stimulating hormone [FSH] and luteinizing hormone [LH] secretion or polycystic ovarian syndrome) are another common cause of female infertility. Some men (and more rarely, some women) develop **anti-sperm antibodies,** substances that mark and target the sperm for destruction by the immune system. Other male-related causes of infertility include low sperm count, morphologically abnormal sperm, or impaired sperm delivery. Obesity, alcohol intake, drug use, smoking, exposure to certain environmental chemicals, and higher levels of stress have been associated with an increased risk of infertility in both genetic males and genetic females. In some cases, the cause for infertility remains unknown.

Several potential treatments are available for infertility, depending upon the initial cause:

- **Intrauterine insemination,** also known as *artificial insemination,* consists of injection of specially prepared sperm directly into the uterus through the vagina. Prior to injection, the sperm are prepared in the lab and stimulated to undergo capacitation.
- **Clomiphene citrate** (Clomid) is an oral medication that competes for estrogen receptors in the hypothalamus, pituitary, and ovaries—and in so doing, it reduces the negative feedback effects of the body's own estrogens on the ovarian cycle. Thus, follicular development and ovulation is stimulated. Clomid sometimes is associated with multiple pregnancies and ovarian hyperstimulation.
- **Menotropins,** also known as *human menopausal gonadotropins* (e.g., Repronex, Menopur, and Pergonal), are a combination of FSH and LH hormones to stimulate both follicular development and ovulation. Pure **follicle-stimulating hormone (FSH)** (Gonal-F) is another injected medication that stimulates follicular development. These medications may have multiple adverse effects, including multiple pregnancy (from too many follicles being stimulated), ectopic pregnancy, miscarriages, and ovarian hyperstimulation syndrome.
- **Bromocriptine** (Parlodel) is an oral medication used to treat high prolactin levels seen in some infertile women. When prolactin levels drop, normal follicular development may ensue.

If pregnancy does not ensue after about 6 months of treatment with medications, or with multiple intrauterine insemination attempts, a couple may wish to explore the more complex **assisted reproductive technologies (ARTs).** These technologies may cost tens of thousands of dollars and have variable success rates. Among the ARTs are the following:

- **In vitro fertilization (IVF)** is a procedure by which preovulatory oocytes are surgically extracted from the ovaries and each is injected with a prepared sperm in the lab. Prior to this process, medications (such as the ones previously listed) are taken to stimulate the ovaries to produce multiple mature follicles. One or more fertilized oocytes (now multicellular pre-embryos) are then surgically implanted in the uterus, and any remaining fertilized pre-embryos are cryopreserved (frozen) for future use. This procedure may have a success rate ranging from 10% to 35%, depending upon the age of the mother and other factors. One complication of IVF is multiple pregnancies, due to the fact that usually two or more pre-embryos are transferred during any one procedure.
- **Donor oocytes** may be retrieved from a donor surgically. The oocytes may be fertilized with sperm in vitro and then placed in the future mother's uterus. Alternatively, the donor oocytes may be injected into the future mother's uterine tube with sperm (a process referred to as **gamete intrafallopian transfer**), in the hopes that the sperm will fertilize one or more of the donor oocytes.
- Likewise, **donor embryos** may be given to, and used by, an infertile couple. These embryos often were cryopreserved from another couple who may have undergone IVF.

Some infertility treatments have a greater likelihood of multiple births, which can be risky for both mother and the developing fetuses.
Nancy R. Cohen/Getty Images

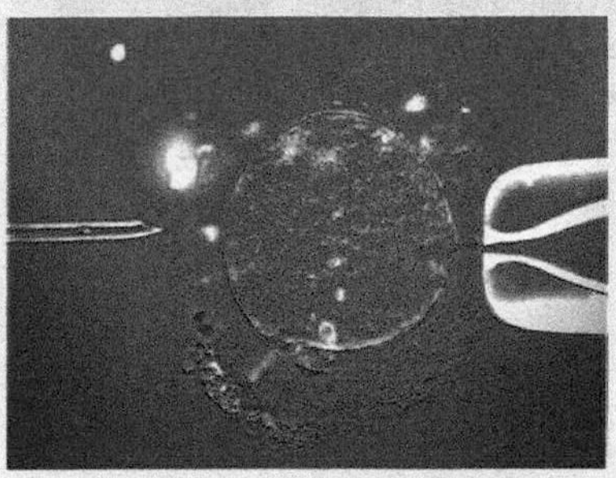

In vitro fertilization (IVF), shown in this photo, is a procedure where a sperm is injected directly into the secondary oocyte.
Zephyr/Science Photo Library/Getty Images

Some infertile couples have chosen to have a **surrogate mother.** This surrogate may be impregnated with a pre-embryo from the infertile couple, or she may use her own oocyte and donated sperm. However, the use of surrogates is fraught with ethical and legal complications; for example, the surrogate and the couple may fight for legal rights to the baby, or the couple may have issues with respect to how the surrogate is caring for herself during the pregnancy.

Many of these infertility treatments have come under ethical and legal scrutiny. For example, is it ethical to impregnate a woman with multiple pre-embryos? Who has legal rights to cryopreserved embryos, and who decides about their fate if the couple disagrees? If a couple uses a surrogate mother, and that same couple later divorces, could one person in the couple claim sole custody because that person is the only parent biologically related to the child? The medical advances of infertility treatments have outpaced their regulation and oversight, and medical ethicists will continue to debate these issues for years to come.

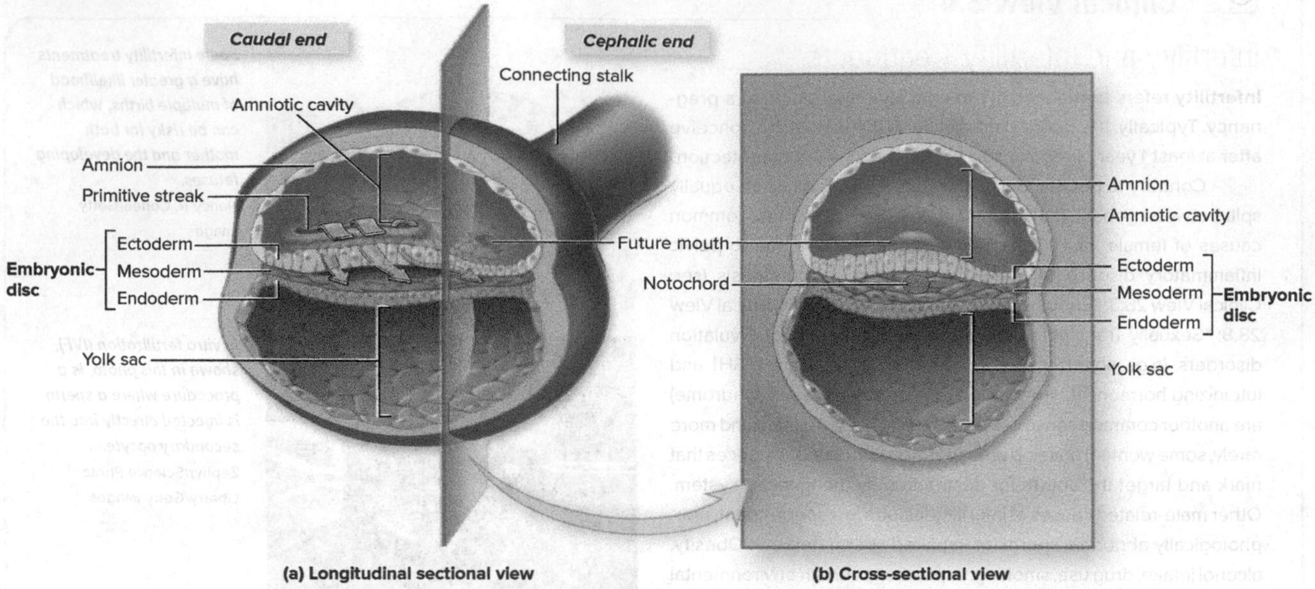

Figure 3.9

Formation of the Embryonic Disc. Gastrulation produces a trilaminar embryonic disc that contains three primary germ layers: endoderm, mesoderm, and ectoderm.

Cephalocaudal (sef′ ă-lō-kaw′ dăl) **folding** occurs in the cephalic (head) and caudal (tail) regions of the embryo. Essentially, the embryonic disc and amnion grow very rapidly, but the yolk sac does not grow at all. This differential growth causes the head and tail regions to fold on themselves.

Transverse folding (or *lateral folding*) occurs when the left and right sides of the embryo curve and migrate toward the midline. As these sides come together, they restrict and start to pinch off the yolk sac. Eventually, the sides of the embryonic disc fuse in the midline and form a cylindrical embryo. Thus, the ectoderm is now solely along the entire exterior of the embryo, and the endoderm is confined to the internal region of the embryo. As this midline fusion occurs, the yolk sac pinches off from most of the endoderm (with the exception of one small region of communication called the vitelline duct).

Thus, cephalocaudal folding helps form the future head and buttocks region of the embryo, whereas transverse folding forms a cylindrical trunk or torso region of the embryo. Let us now examine the specific derivatives of these primary germ layers.

3.4c Differentiation of Ectoderm

After the embryo undergoes cephalocaudal and transverse folding, the ectoderm is located on the external surface of the now-cylindrical embryo. The ectoderm is responsible for forming nervous system tissue as well as many externally placed structures, including the epidermis of the skin and epidermal derivatives such as hair and nails. The process of nervous system formation from the ectoderm is called neurulation.

Neurulation

A cylindrical mass of mesoderm called the **notochord** (nō′ tō-kōrd; *notos* = back, *chorde* = cord, string) forms immediately internal and parallel to the primitive streak (see figure 3.9*b*). The notochord influences some of the overlying ectoderm to begin to form nervous tissue via a process called **induction,** in which one structure influences or induces another structure to change form. The inductive action that transforms a flat layer of ectodermal cells into a hollow nervous system tube is termed **neurulation** (nū′ rū-lā′ shŭn; *neuron* = nerve, *-ulus* = small one) **(figure 3.11)**.

In the third week of development, much of the ectoderm forms a thickened layer of cells called the **neural plate.** By the end of the third week, the lateral edges of this plate elevate to form **neural folds,** and the depression between the folds forms the **neural groove.** The neural folds approach each other gradually in the midline and fuse. Fusion of these folds produces a cylindrical **neural tube** (figure 3.11 *c*). This fusion begins in the middle of the neural folds and proceeds in both cephalic and caudal directions. The cylindrical neural tube eventually forms the brain and spinal cord. Neurulation is complete by the end of the fourth week of development.

As the neural folds migrate toward each other and fuse, some cells along the lateral border of folds begin to dissociate from adjacent cells. Collectively, these cells are known as the **neural crest cell,** or simply *neural crest.* Neural crest cells migrate throughout the body and give rise to a vast, heterogeneous array of structures. Among the structures neural crest cells give rise to are melanocytes (pigment cells of the skin), the adrenal medulla (inner portion of the adrenal gland), some skeletal and muscular components of the head, spinal ganglia (specific nervous system structures), and a portion of the developing heart.

Not all ectodermal cells form the neural plate. The ectodermal cells covering the embryo after neurulation form the epidermis, the external layer of skin. Ectoderm also forms most exocrine glands, hair, nails, tooth enamel, and sensory organs. In general, ectoderm gives rise to those organs and structures that maintain contact with the outside world **(figure 3.12)**.

3.4d Differentiation of Mesoderm

Mesoderm subdivides into the following five categories:

- The tightly packed midline group of mesodermal cells, also called *chordamesoderm,* forms the notochord. Recall that the notochord serves as the basis for the central body axis and the axial skeleton, and induces the formation of the neural tube.
- **Paraxial mesoderm** is found on both sides of the neural tube. The paraxial mesoderm then forms **somites** (sō′mīt;

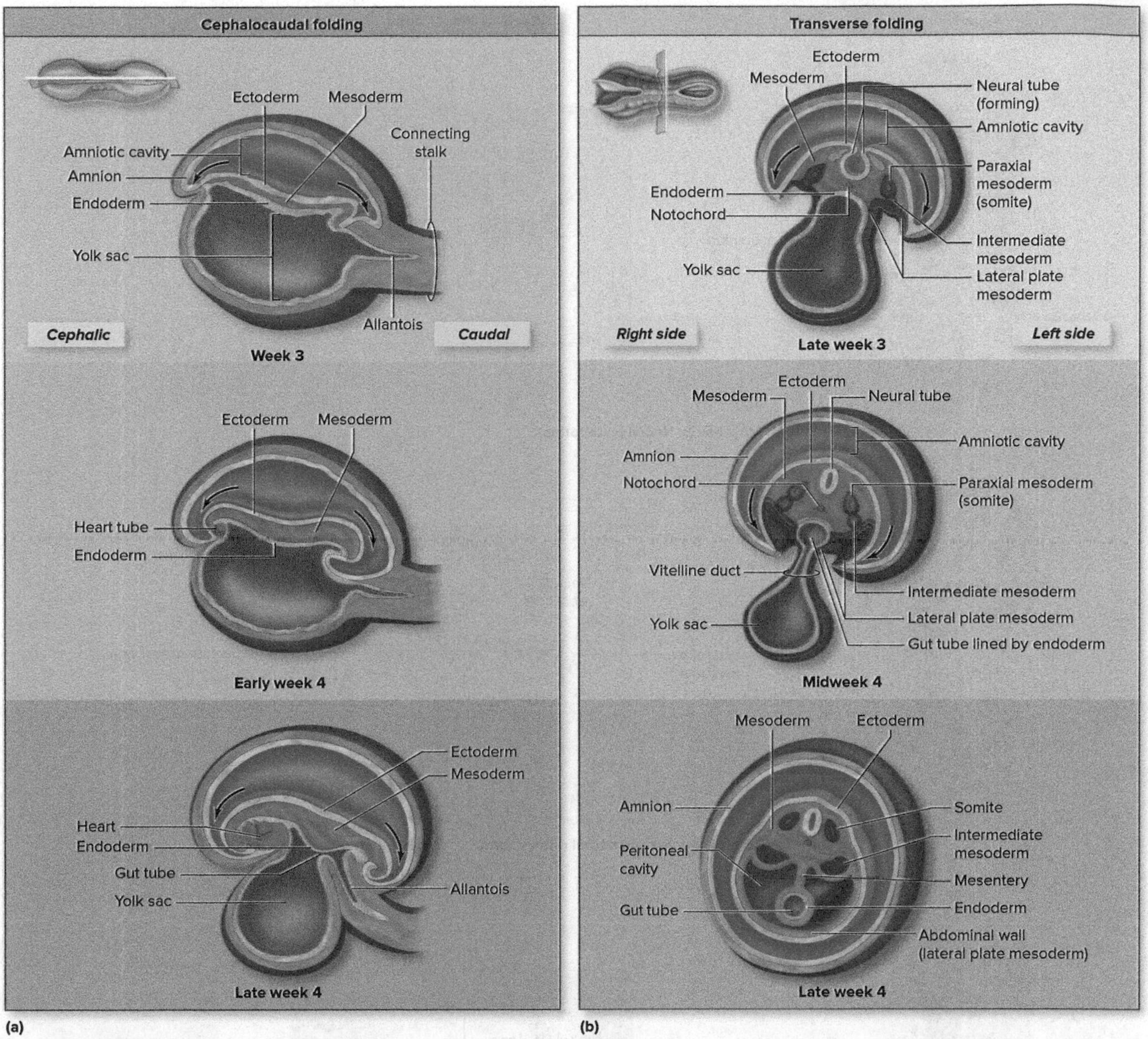

Figure 3.10

Folding of the Embryonic Disc. During the third and fourth weeks of development, the flat embryo folds in both (*a*) cephalocaudal and (*b*) transverse (lateral) directions. The sequence of cephalocaudal folding is shown in the left column, and transverse folding is shown in the right column.

soma = body), which are blocklike masses responsible for the formation of the axial skeleton, most muscle (including limb musculature), and most of the cartilage, dermis, and connective tissues of the body (see figure 3.11).

- Lateral to the paraxial mesoderm are cords of **intermediate mesoderm,** which forms most of the urinary system and the reproductive system.
- The most lateral layers of mesoderm on both sides of the neural tube remain thin and are called the **lateral plate mesoderm.** These give rise to most of the components of the cardiovascular system, the serous membranes that line the body cavities, the thoracic and abdominal body walls, and all the connective tissue components of the limbs.
- The last region of mesoderm, called the **head mesenchyme** (mes′eng-k īm), forms connective tissues and musculature of the face.

The derivatives of the mesoderm are listed and illustrated in figure 3.12.

3.4e Differentiation of Endoderm

Endoderm becomes the innermost tissue when the embryo undergoes transverse folding. Among the structures formed by embryonic endoderm are the linings of the gastrointestinal (GI), respiratory, urinary, and reproductive tracts (figure 3.12). Endoderm also forms the thyroid gland, parathyroid glands, thymus, and portions of the palatine tonsils, as well as most of the liver, gallbladder, and pancreas.

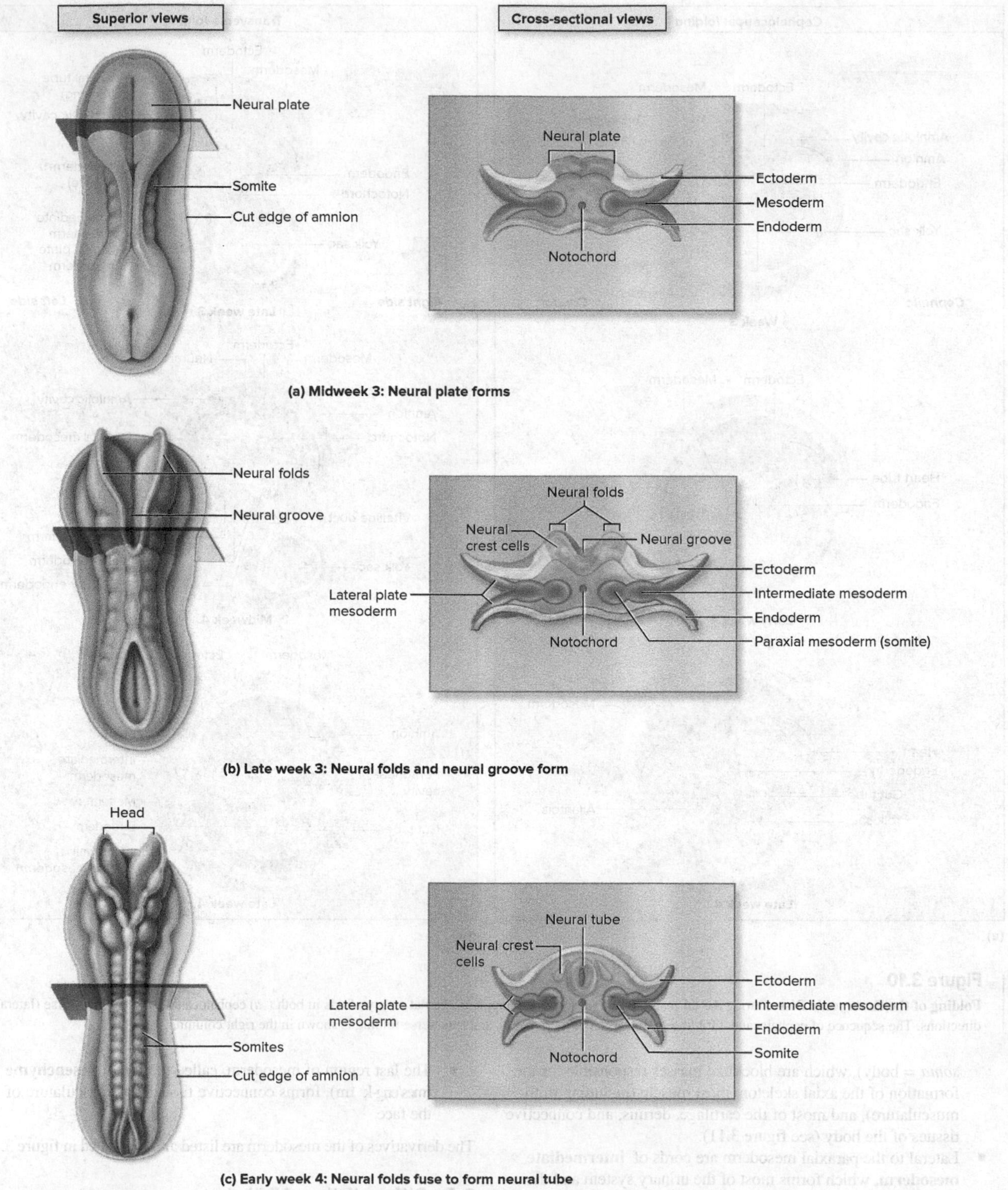
Superior views
Cross-sectional views
Neural plate
Somite
Cut edge of amnion
Neural plate
Ectoderm
Mesoderm
Endoderm
Notochord
(a) Midweek 3: Neural plate forms
Neural folds
Neural groove
Neural folds
Neural crest cells
Neural groove
Lateral plate mesoderm
Ectoderm
Intermediate mesoderm
Endoderm
Notochord
Paraxial mesoderm (somite)
(b) Late week 3: Neural folds and neural groove form
Head
Neural tube
Neural crest cells
Lateral plate mesoderm
Ectoderm
Intermediate mesoderm
Endoderm
Somite
Notochord
Somites
Cut edge of amnion
(c) Early week 4: Neural folds fuse to form neural tube

Figure 3.11

Neurulation. Superior and cross-sectional views show the developing embryo during neural tube formation. (*a*) Ectoderm thickens in the midline, forming the neural plate. (*b*) The neural plate develops a depression called the neural groove and two elevations called the neural folds. (*c*) Neural folds fuse to form the neural tube, while neural crest cells pinch off the neural folds and migrate to various areas of the body.

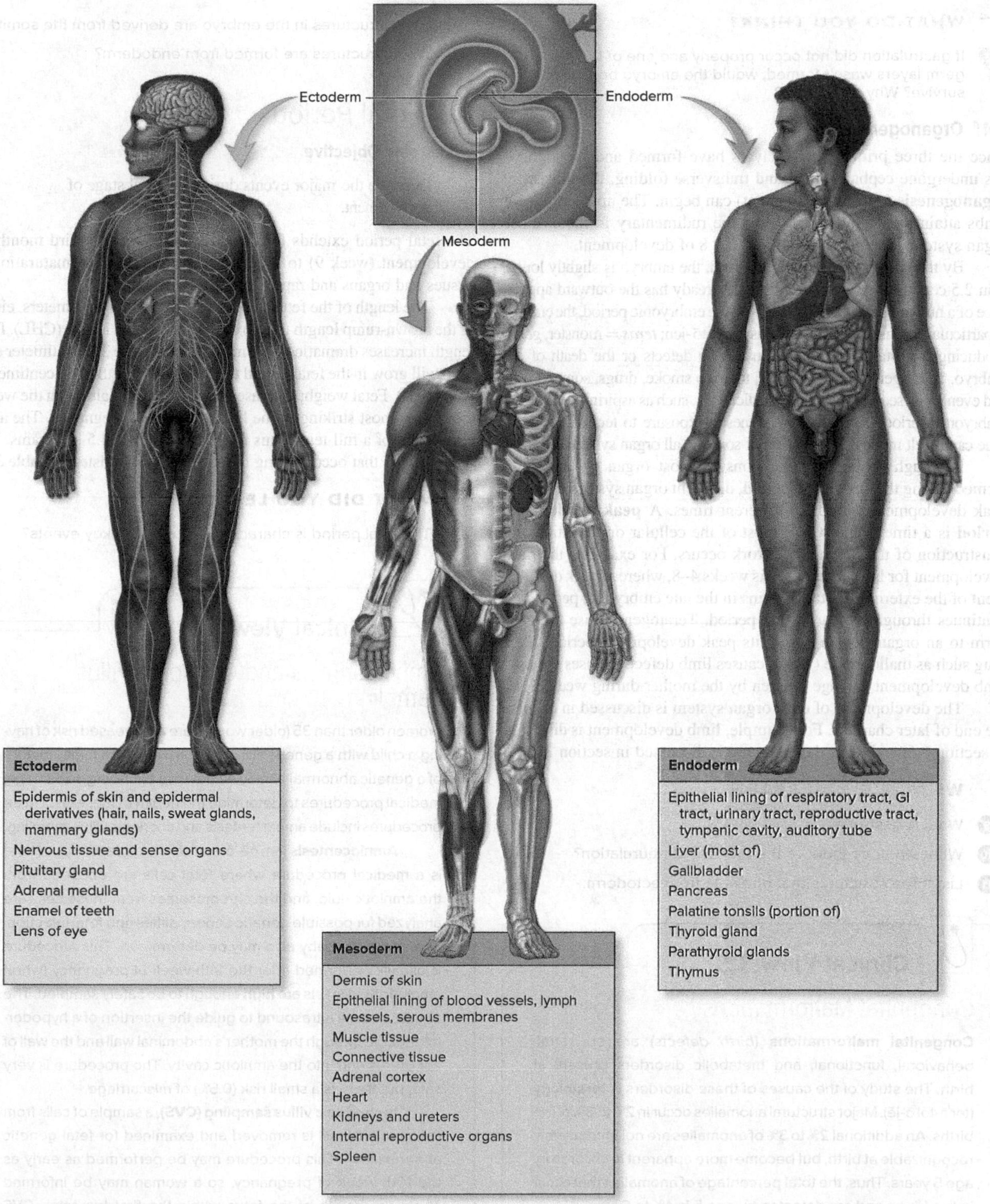
Ectoderm
Endoderm
Mesoderm
Ectoderm
Epidermis of skin and epidermal derivatives (hair, nails, sweat glands, mammary glands)
Nervous tissue and sense organs
Pituitary gland
Adrenal medulla
Enamel of teeth
Lens of eye
Mesoderm
Dermis of skin
Epithelial lining of blood vessels, lymph vessels, serous membranes
Muscle tissue
Connective tissue
Adrenal cortex
Heart
Kidneys and ureters
Internal reproductive organs
Spleen
Endoderm
Epithelial lining of respiratory tract, GI tract, urinary tract, reproductive tract, tympanic cavity, auditory tube
Liver (most of)
Gallbladder
Pancreas
Palatine tonsils (portion of)
Thyroid gland
Parathyroid glands
Thymus

Figure 3.12

The Three Primary Germ Layers and Their Derivatives. Ectoderm, mesoderm, and endoderm give rise to all of the tissues in the body.

WHAT DO YOU THINK?

3. If gastrulation did not occur properly and one of the primary germ layers wasn't formed, would the embryo be able to survive? Why or why not?

3.4f Organogenesis

Once the three primary germ layers have formed and the embryo has undergone cephalocaudal and transverse folding, the process of **organogenesis** (organ development) can begin. The upper and lower limbs attain their adult shapes, and the rudimentary forms of most organ systems have developed by week 8 of development.

By the end of the embryonic period, the embryo is slightly longer than 2.5 centimeters (1 inch), and yet it already has the outward appearance of a human (see figure 3.1). During the embryonic period, the embryo is particularly sensitive to **teratogens** (ter′ă-tō-jen; *teras* = monster, *gen* = producing), substances that can cause birth defects or the death of the embryo. Teratogens include alcohol, tobacco smoke, drugs, some viruses, and even some seemingly benign medications, such as aspirin. Because the embryonic period includes organogenesis, exposure to teratogens at this time can result in the malformation of some or all organ systems.

Although rudimentary versions of most organ systems have formed during the embryonic period, different organ systems undergo peak development periods at different times. A **peak development period** is a time frame where most of the cellular organization and construction of the organ framework occurs. For example, the peak development for limb maturation is weeks 4–8, whereas peak development of the external genitalia begins in the late embryonic period and continues through the early fetal period. Teratogens cause the most harm to an organ system during its peak development period. So, a drug such as thalidomide (which causes limb defects) causes the most limb development damage if taken by the mother during weeks 4–8.

The development of each organ system is discussed in detail at the end of later chapters. For example, limb development is discussed in section 8.6, and heart development is discussed in section 22.8.

WHAT DID YOU LEARN?

9. What is gastrulation?
10. What structure induces the process of neurulation?
11. List three structures that originate from ectoderm.

Clinical View 3.5

Congenital Malformations

Congenital malformations (*birth defects*) are structural, behavioral, functional, and metabolic disorders present at birth. The study of the causes of these disorders is **teratology** (ter′ă-tol′ō-jē). Major structural anomalies occur in 2% to 3% of live births. An additional 2% to 3% of anomalies are not immediately recognizable at birth, but become more apparent in children by age 5 years. Thus, the total percentage of anomalies that occur in live births and are detected by age 5 is 4% to 6%.

In 40% to 60% of all congenital malformations, the cause is unknown. Of the remainder, genetic factors, such as chromosomal abnormalities and mutant genes, account for about 15%; environmental factors produce about 10%; and a combination of genetic and environmental influences produces 20% to 25%.

12. What structures in the embryo are derived from the somites?
13. What structures are formed from endoderm?

3.5 Fetal Period

✓ Learning Objective

16. Describe the major events during the fetal stage of development.

The fetal period extends from the beginning of the third month of development (week 9) to birth. It is characterized by maturation of tissues and organs and rapid growth of the body.

The length of the fetus is usually measured in centimeters, either as the crown-rump length (CRL) or the crown-heel length (CHL). Fetal length increases dramatically in months 3 to 5. The 2.5-centimeter embryo will grow in the fetal period to an average length of 53 centimeters (21 inches). Fetal weight increases steadily as well, although the weight increase is most striking in the last 2 months of pregnancy. The average weight of a full-term fetus ranges from 2.5 to 4.5 kilograms. The major events that occur during the fetal period are listed in **table 3.4**.

WHAT DID YOU LEARN?

14. The fetal period is characterized by which key events?

Clinical View 3.6

Amniocentesis and Chorionic Villus Sampling

Women older than 35 (older women are at increased risk of having a child with a genetic abnormalities) or with a family history of a genetic abnormality may be advised to undergo additional medical procedures to determine the health of the fetus. These procedures include amniocentesis and chorionic villus sampling.

Amniocentesis (am′nē-ō-sen-tē′sis; *kentesis* = puncture) is a medical procedure where fetal cells are obtained from the amniotic fluid, and the chromosomes from these cells are analyzed for possible genetic abnormalities and fetal infection. The sex of the baby also may be determined. This procedure is usually performed after the 14th week of pregnancy (when amniotic fluid levels are high enough to be safely sampled. The physician uses ultrasound to guide the insertion of a hypodermic needle through the mother's abdominal wall and the wall of her uterus and into the amniotic cavity. The procedure is very safe, but there is a small risk (0.5%) of miscarriage.

In **chorionic villus sampling (CVS)**, a sample of cells from the chorionic villi is removed and examined for fetal genetic abnormalities. This procedure may be performed as early as the 10th week of pregnancy, so a woman may be informed about the health of the fetus within the first trimester. CVS can identify the sex of the fetus and examine for most genetic abnormalities, except for spina bifida and other neural tube defects (these defects can be determined only by detecting abnormal levels of a protein in the amniotic fluid). There is a slightly higher miscarriage rate for CVS (1.0%).

Table 3.4 Fetal Stage of Development

Time Period	Major Events
Weeks 9–12 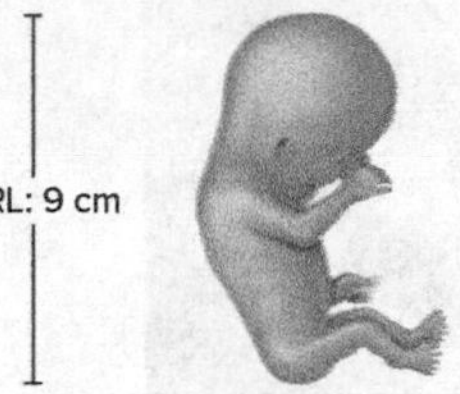 CRL: 9 cm	Primary ossification centers appear in most bones Reproductive organs begin to develop Coordination between nerves and muscles for movement of limbs occurs Brain enlarges Body elongates Epidermis and dermis of the skin become more fully developed Permanent kidney develops Palate (roof of mouth) develops Average head circumference at 12 weeks: 6.8 centimeters (cm) Average crown-rump length at 12 weeks: 9 cm Average weight: 28 grams (g)
Weeks 13–16 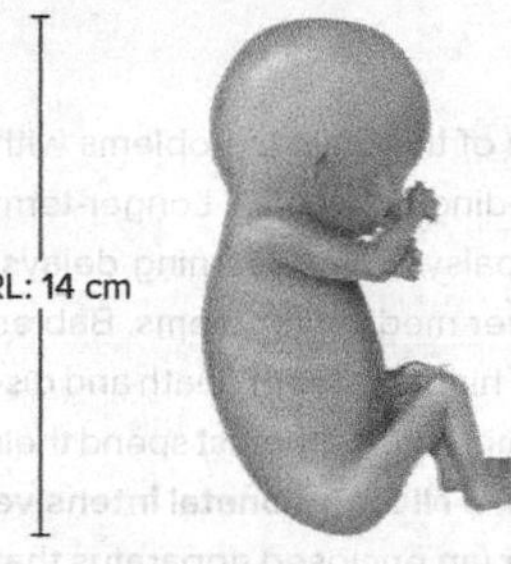 CRL: 14 cm	Body grows rapidly Ossification in the skeleton continues Limbs become more proportionate in length to body Brain and skull continue to enlarge Average head circumference at 16 weeks: 12.3 cm Average crown-rump length at 16 weeks: 14 cm Average weight: 170 g
Weeks 17–20 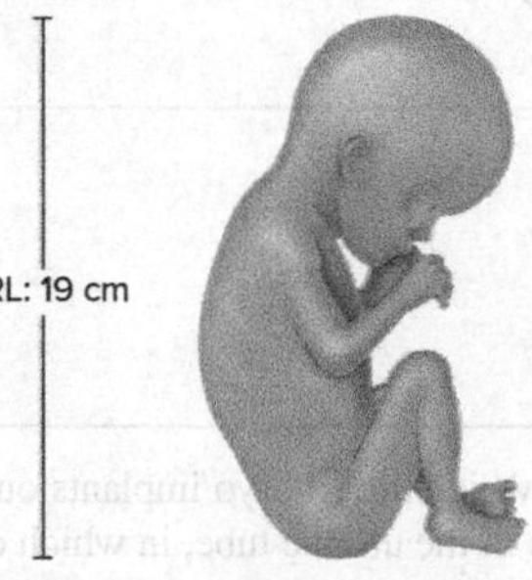 CRL: 19 cm	Muscle movements become stronger and more frequent Lanugo covers skin Vernix caseosa covers skin Limbs near final proportions Brain and skull continue to enlarge Average head circumference at 20 weeks: 17.45 cm Average crown-rump length at 20 weeks: 19 cm Average weight: 454 g
Weeks 21–38 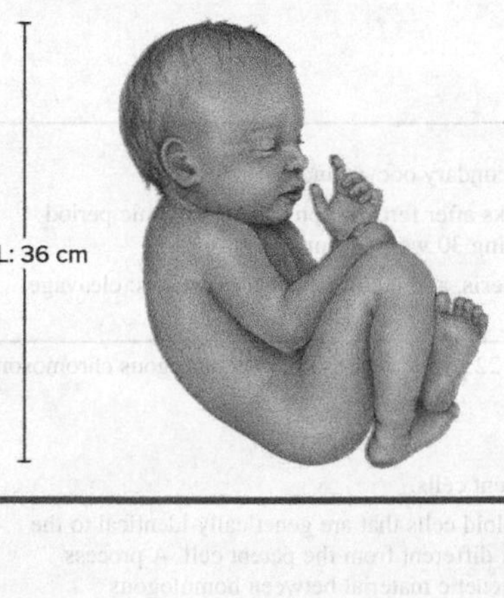 CRL: 36 cm	Body gains major amount of weight Subcutaneous fat is deposited Eyebrows and eyelashes appear Eyelids open Testes descend into scrotum (month 9) Blood cells form in marrow only Average head circumference at 38 weeks: 33.5 cm Average crown-rump length at 38 weeks: 36 cm Average *total* length at 38 weeks: 53 cm Average weight: 2.5–4.5 kilograms (kg)

Clinical View 3.7

Preterm (Premature) Birth

Preterm (premature) birth is when a baby is born before the start of the 37th week of pregnancy. In the United States, approximately 10% of all infants born are preterm. Risk factors for preterm birth include low socioeconomic status, ethnicity (black women are more likely to deliver preterm), teen pregnancy, pregnancy over age 35, tobacco and/or drug use, increased stress, carrying more than one fetus, infection, and prior preterm pregnancy.

The earliest surviving preterm birth thus far was at 21 weeks, but preterm births earlier than 24 weeks usually either do not survive or have severe medical issues. The earlier a baby is born, the greater the risk that the child will have developmental delays and medical problems. The lungs, brain, and liver are still developing extensively in the last trimester, so premature birth especially affects these organs. Mildly or moderately preterm births (those born between weeks 32 and 37) have better prognoses than severely preterm births (prior to 32 weeks). Thus, every additional day the fetus can remain in the mother's uterus increases its chances of survival.

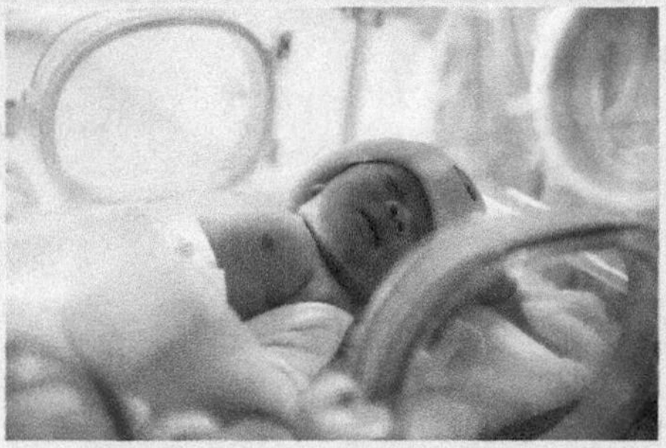

A preterm infant sleeps in a neonatal incubator.
Naypong/Shutterstock

A premature baby (often nicknamed a **preemie**) typically is of very low birth weight (less than 5 lbs. for a mildly preterm baby, and sometimes as little as 1–2 lb for a baby delivered at 32 weeks). Short-term complications for a premature baby include **jaundice** (yellowish skin color due to the liver not being able to process bilirubin effectively), breathing difficulties (which are more severe, the younger the preemie is, due to the immaturity of the lungs), problems with regulating body temperature, and feeding difficulties. Longer-term complications may include cerebral palsy and/or learning delays, vision and hearing problems, and other medical problems. Babies born earlier than 32 weeks have much higher rates of death and disability than later preterm babies. Preemies typically must spend their first weeks or months in the hospital in a **NICU (neonatal intensive care unit)** and in a neonatal **incubator** (an enclosed apparatus that assists in regulating body temperature). They will stay in the NICU until they have gained enough weight and are able to breathe and feed without medical intervention.

Clinical Terms

congenital anomaly A malformation or deformity present at birth.

ectopic pregnancy A pregnancy in which the embryo implants outside the uterus; commonly occurs in the uterine tube, in which case it is called a *tubal pregnancy*.

Chapter Summary

3.1 Overview of Embryology	■ Embryology is the study of development between the fertilization of the secondary oocyte and birth. ■ The prenatal period is subdivided into the pre-embryonic period (the 2 weeks after fertilization), the embryonic period (between 3 and 8 weeks after fertilization), and the fetal period (the remaining 30 weeks prior to birth). ■ The process that takes place during the prenatal period is called embryogenesis, and it consists of three stages: cleavage, gastrulation, and organogenesis.
3.2 Gametogenesis	■ Human somatic cells contain a diploid number (23 pairs) of chromosomes: 22 pairs of autosomes (homologous chromosomes) and one pair of sex chromosomes. **3.2a Meiosis** ■ Meiosis is sex cell division that produces haploid gametes from diploid parent cells. ■ Mitosis and meiosis differ in the following ways: Mitosis produces two diploid cells that are genetically identical to the parent cell, whereas meiosis produces four haploid cells that are genetically different from the parent cell. A process called crossing over occurs only in meiosis and results in the exchange of genetic material between homologous chromosomes. ■ Meiosis involves two rounds of division. In meiosis I, crossing over occurs, and pairs of homologous chromosomes separate. In meiosis II, sister chromatids separate in the same way they do in mitosis.

	3.2b Oocyte Development (Oogenesis) ■ Oogenesis occurs in the ovaries and produces a single secondary oocyte, which has 22 autosomes and one X chromosome. **3.2c Sperm Development (Spermatogenesis)** ■ Spermatogenesis occurs in the testes and produces four haploid cells (sperm) from each diploid primary spermatocyte. Two of these sperm have 22 autosomes and one X chromosome, and two have 22 autosomes and one Y chromosome.
3.3 Pre-embryonic Period	■ A pre-embryo develops during the first 2 weeks after fertilization. **3.3a Fertilization** ■ Fertilization is the process whereby two sex cells fuse to form a new organism. ■ Sperm are not capable of fertilizing the secondary oocyte until they undergo capacitation, a conditioning period for sperm after their deposition within the female reproductive tract. ■ The acrosome at the tip of the sperm contains digestive enzymes that penetrate the protective layers around the secondary oocyte. ■ The phases of fertilization are corona radiata penetration, zona pellucida penetration, and fusion of the sperm and oocyte plasma membranes. ■ When a sperm penetrates the secondary oocyte, the secondary oocyte completes meiosis II and becomes an ovum. The pronuclei of the ovum and sperm fuse and form a single diploid cell called a zygote. **3.3b Cleavage** ■ The series of mitotic divisions of the zygote is called cleavage. ■ After the third cleavage division, the pre-embryo cells form a compressed ball of cells held together by tight junctions, a process called compaction. ■ At the 16-cell stage, the ball of cells is called a morula. ■ Upon arrival in the uterine lumen, the pre-embryo develops a single central fluid-filled cavity and is called a blastocyst. Cells within the blastocyst form the embryoblast (inner cell mass), which gives rise to the embryo proper. The outer ring of cells forms the trophoblast, which contributes to the placenta. **3.3c Implantation** ■ Implantation consists of attachment, cell changes in the trophoblast and uterine epithelium, and invasion of the endometrial wall. ■ The trophoblast subdivides into a cytotrophoblast (the inner cellular layer of the trophoblast) and a syncytiotrophoblast (the outer, thick layer). **3.3d Formation of the Bilaminar Germinal Disc and the Extraembryonic Membranes** ■ During the implantation of the blastocyst into the endometrium of the uterus, cells of the embryoblast differentiate into two layers: the hypoblast and the epiblast. Together, these two layers form a flat disc called a bilaminar germinal disc. ■ The yolk sac is the site for the formation of the first blood cells and blood vessels. ■ The amnion is a thin ectodermal membrane that eventually encloses the entire embryo in a fluid-filled sac. ■ The chorion is the embryonic contribution to the placenta. **3.3e Development of the Placenta** ■ The main functions of the placenta are the exchange of metabolic products and respiratory gases between the fetal and maternal blood, transmission of maternal antibodies, and hormone production.
3.4 Embryonic Period	■ The embryonic period extends from weeks 3 to 8. **3.4a Gastrulation** ■ Gastrulation produces three primary germ layers: ectoderm, mesoderm, and endoderm. **3.4b Folding of the Embryonic Disc** ■ The embryonic disc undergoes cephalocaudal and transverse folding, beginning late in the third week. **3.4c Differentiation of Ectoderm** ■ The development of ectoderm into the entire nervous system is called neurulation. ■ Neurulation is an example of induction, a complex process whereby a structure stimulates a response from another tissue or group of cells. ■ Besides the nervous system, derivatives of the ectoderm include most exocrine glands, tooth enamel, epidermis, and the sense organs. **3.4d Differentiation of Mesoderm** ■ The notochord is formed by chordamesoderm. ■ Paraxial mesoderm forms somites, which eventually give rise to the axial skeleton and most muscle, cartilage, dermis, and connective tissues. ■ Intermediate mesoderm forms most of the urinary system and the reproductive system. ■ Lateral plate mesoderm gives rise to most of the cardiovascular system, body cavity linings, and most limb structures. ■ Head mesenchyme forms connective tissues and musculature of the face.

(continued on next page)

Chapter Summary *(continued)*

	3.4e Differentiation of Endoderm ■ Endoderm gives rise to the inner lining of the digestive, respiratory, and urinary tracts as well as the thyroid, parathyroid, and thymus glands, portions of the palatine tonsils, and most of the liver, gallbladder, and pancreas.
	3.4f Organogenesis ■ Almost all of organogenesis (organ development) occurs during the embryonic period. ■ During the embryonic period, the embryo is very sensitive to teratogens, substances that can cause birth defects or the death of the embryo.
3.5 Fetal Period	■ The time from the beginning of the third month to birth is known as the fetal period. It is characterized by maturation of tissues and organs and rapid growth.

Challenge Yourself

Actively write or type your answers in a separate document to reinforce your learning, before checking your answers.

Multiple Choice

Select the best answer from the four choices provided.

1. During which period of development does organogenesis begin?
   a. cleavage
   b. embryonic period
   c. pre-embryonic period
   d. fetal period
2. What is the outer layer of the blastocyst that attaches to the wall of the uterus at implantation called?
   a. amnion
   b. yolk sac
   c. embryoblast
   d. trophoblast
3. Which process occurs at about day 3 after fertilization, and is where the cells of the pre-embryo adhere tightly to each other and increase their surface contact?
   a. implantation
   b. compaction
   c. gastrulation
   d. neurulation
4. Somites develop from which of the following?
   a. paraxial mesoderm
   b. intermediate mesoderm
   c. lateral plate mesoderm
   d. head mesenchyme
5. During gastrulation, cells from which layer of the bilaminar germinal disc migrate and form the three primary germ layers?
   a. notochord
   b. hypoblast
   c. epiblast
   d. mesoblast
6. Which stage of development is part of embryogenesis?
   a. fertilization
   b. fetal period
   c. cleavage
   d. gametogenesis
7. At the end of telophase I of meiosis, the genetic material is in what form?
   a. 23 chromosomes only, and each chromosome contains 2 chromatids
   b. 23 pairs of chromosomes, and each chromosome contains 2 chromatids
   c. 23 chromosomes only, and each chromosome contains 1 chromatid only
   d. 23 pairs of chromosomes, and each chromosome contains 1 chromatid only
8. Which structure is an extraembryonic membrane that is the fetal contribution to the placenta?
   a. amnion
   b. chorion
   c. morula
   d. yolk sac
9. When does capacitation occur?
   a. when sperm move through the uterine tubes
   b. when sperm are mixed with secretions from the testes
   c. when sperm are deposited within the female reproductive tract
   d. when sperm are traveling through the penis
10. What term is used to describe the beginning of the formation of the brain and spinal cord?
    a. cephalocaudal folding
    b. organogenesis
    c. neurulation
    d. gastrulation

Content Review

1. Briefly describe the process of meiosis, mentioning a hallmark event that occurs during each phase.
2. What are the three phases of fertilization?
3. Describe the implantation of the blastocyst into the uterine wall.
4. What is the function of the chorion?
5. Compare and contrast meiosis and mitosis with respect to cell type, number of cells produced, and numbers of chromosomes in the daughter cells.
6. Describe the process of gastrulation and the formation of the primary germ layers.
7. Explain how the cylindrical body shape of the human embryo is derived from the flat embryonic disc.
8. List the five regions of the mesoderm, and identify some major body parts derived from each region.
9. Explain why teratogens are especially harmful to the developing organism during the embryonic period. What events occur during this period?
10. Describe the general differences between the embryonic period and the fetal period.

Developing Critical Reasoning

1. Jennifer is 37 years old and is just over 3 months pregnant. She is the mother of three healthy children. Her obstetrician recommends that she be checked to see if her developing fetus is trisomic. What procedure is used to check for trisomy in the fetus? If a trisomic condition is detected, what is the most common cause, and how did it occur?
2. In the late 1960s, a number of pregnant women in Europe and Canada were prescribed a drug called thalidomide , a sleeping aid which was prescribed off-label to relieve morning sickness. Many of these women gave birth to children with amelia (no limbs) or meromelia (malformed upper and/ or lower limbs). It was later discovered that thalidomide is a teratogen that can cause limb defects in an unborn baby. Based upon this information, during what period of their pregnancy (pre-embryonic, embryonic, or fetal) do you think these women took thalidomide? During which of these periods would thalidomide cause the most harm to limb development?
3. A 22-year-old woman consumes large quantities of alcohol at a party and loses consciousness. Three weeks later, she misses her second consecutive period, and a pregnancy test is positive. Should she be concerned about the effects of her binge drinking episode on her baby?

Answers to "What Do You Think?"

1. Crossing over helps "shuffle" the genetic material between maternal and paternal chromosomes in the cell. Moving genetic material between these chromosomes forms genetically diverse sex cells that have the potential to produce a human being with its own unique array of traits.
2. If two sperm penetrate the secondary oocyte, the condition called polyspermy occurs. In this case, the fertilized cell contains 23 triplets of chromosomes, instead of the normal 23 pairs of chromosomes. In humans, no cell with 23 triplets of chromosomes can survive, so this fertilized cell will not survive.
3. If gastrulation did not occur properly and one of the primary germ layers wasn't formed, the embryo would not be able to survive. Each of the primary germ layers forms tissues that are vital for life, and without all of these tissues, there is no way the embryo could survive.

Design Element: Pencil Icon: Slavojub Pantelic/Shutterstock

TISSUES

4 Tissue Level of Organization

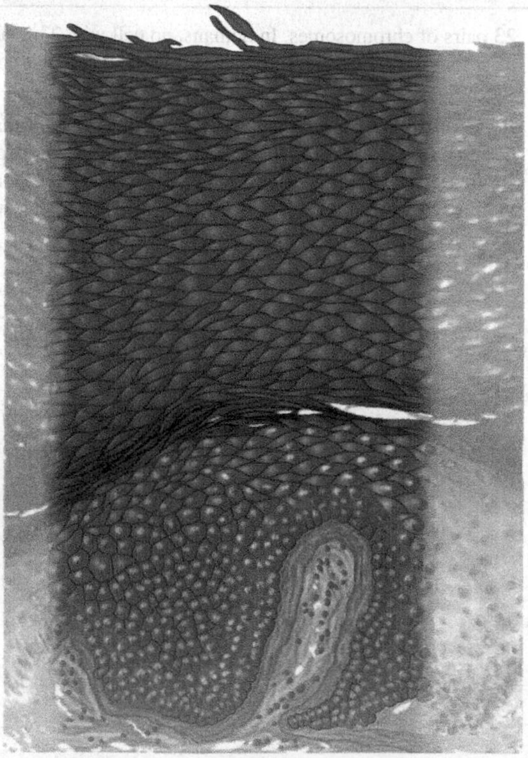

Outline

Anatomy & Physiology Revealed 4.0

MODULE 3: TISSUES

The human body is composed of trillions of cells, which are organized into more complex units called tissues. **Tissues** are groups of similar cells and extracellular products that carry out a common function, such as providing protection or facilitating body movement. The study of tissues and their relationships within organs is called **histology.**

There are four principal types of tissues in the body: epithelial tissue, connective tissue, muscle tissue, and nervous tissue. Tissues are formed from the three primary germ layers (ectoderm, mesoderm, and endoderm). The four tissue types vary in terms of the structure and function of their specialized cells, as well as the presence of an **extracellular matrix** (mā'triks; *matrix* = womb) that not only is produced by the cells but surrounds them. The extracellular matrix is composed of varying amounts of water, protein fibers, and dissolved molecules (e.g., glucose, oxygen). Its consistency ranges from fluid to quite solid. Epithelial, muscle, and nervous tissues have relatively little extracellular matrix. In contrast, connective tissue types contain varying amounts of extracellular matrix that differ in the volume, the relative amounts of noncellular components, and the consistency (ratio of fluid to solid). The section on connective tissue (see section 4.2) is immediately followed by a discussion of body membranes (see section 4.3), because most of these structures are composed of an epithelial sheet and an underlying connective tissue layer.

As we examine each of the four classes of tissues in this chapter, it may help you to refer to **table 4.1**, which summarizes their characteristics and functions. This chapter is a transition between chapter 2, which investigated the nature of cells, and later chapters, which examine tissue interactions in organs and organ systems.

4.1 Epithelial Tissue

✓ **Learning Objectives**

1. Explain the general characteristics and functions of epithelial tissue.
2. Describe the specialized features of an epithelium.
3. Explain the structure and function of each type of epithelial tissue.
4. Identify and describe where each type of epithelial tissue is found in the body.
5. Classify exocrine glands based on their form and structure, secretion type, and secretion methods.

Epithelial (ep'i-th ē'lē-ăl; *epi* = upon, *thēlē* = nipple) **tissue** covers or lines every body surface and all body cavities; thus it forms both the external and internal lining of many organs, and it constitutes the majority of glands. An **epithelium** (pl., epithelia) is composed of one or more layers of closely packed cells between two compartments having different components. There is little to no extracellular matrix between epithelial cells; additionally, no blood vessels penetrate an epithelium.

4.1a Characteristics of Epithelial Tissue

All epithelia exhibit several common characteristics, some of which are shown in **figure 4.1**:

- **Cellularity.** Epithelial tissue is composed almost entirely of cells. The cells of an epithelium are bound closely together by different types of intercellular junctions. A minimal amount of extracellular matrix separates the cells.
- **Polarity.** Every epithelium has an **apical** (ap'i-k ăl) **surface** (free or top surface), which is exposed either to the external environment or to some internal body space. This surface may have some modifications, such as cilia or microvilli (see section 2.4c). **Lateral surfaces** have intercellular junctions (see section 4.1c). Additionally, each epithelium has **abasal** (bā'săl) **surface** (fixed or bottom surface) where the epithelium is attached to the underlying connective tissue.
- **Attachment to a basement membrane.** At the basal surface of an epithelium, the epithelial layer is bound to a thin basement membrane, a complex molecular structure produced by both the epithelium and the underlying connective tissue.
- **Avascularity.** All epithelial tissues lack blood vessels. Epithelial cells obtain nutrients either directly across the apical surface or by diffusion across the basal surface from the underlying connective tissue.
- **Innervation.** Epithelia are richly innervated to detect changes in the environment at a particular body or organ surface region. Most nervous tissue is in the underlying connective tissue.
- **High regeneration capacity.** Because epithelial cells have an apical surface that is exposed to the environment, they are frequently damaged or lost by abrasion. However, damaged or

Table 4.1 Overview of Tissue Types

Type	General Characteristics	General Functions	Primary Germ Layer Derivative	Examples of Subtypes and Their Locations
Epithelial tissue	Cellular, polar, attached to a basement membrane, avascular, innervated, high regeneration capacity	Covers surfaces; lines insides of organs and body cavities	Ectoderm, mesoderm, or endoderm	Simple columnar epithelium: Lining of digestive tract Stratified squamous epithelium: Epidermis of skin Transitional epithelium: Lining of urinary bladder
Connective tissue	Diverse types; all contain cells, protein fibers, and ground substance	Protects, binds together, and supports organs	Mesoderm	Adipose connective tissue: Fat Dense regular connective tissue: Ligaments and tendons Dense irregular connective tissue: Dermis of skin Hyaline cartilage: Articular cartilage in some joints Fluid connective tissue: Blood and lymph
Muscle tissue	Contractile; can be voluntary or involuntary, and receives input from the nervous or endocrine systems.	Facilitates movement of skeleton or organ walls	Mesoderm	Skeletal muscle: Muscles attached to bones Cardiac muscle: Muscle layer in heart Smooth muscle: Muscle layer in digestive tract
Nervous tissue	Neurons: Excitable, high metabolic rate, extreme longevity, nonmitotic Glial cells: Nonexcitable, mitotic	Neurons: Control activities, process information Glial cells: Support and protect neurons	Ectoderm	Neurons: Brain, spinal cord, and nerves Glial cells: Brain, spinal cord, and nerves

lost epithelial cells generally are replaced as fast as they are lost because epithelia have a high regeneration capacity. The continual replacement occurs through the mitotic divisions of the deepest epithelial cells (called *stem cells*), which are found within the epithelium near its basement membrane.

4.1b Functions of Epithelial Tissue

Epithelia may have several functions, although no single epithelium performs all of them. These functions include:

- **Physical protection.** Epithelial tissues protect both exposed and internal surfaces from dehydration, abrasion, and destruction by physical, chemical, or biological agents.
- **Selective permeability.** All substances that enter or leave the body must pass through an epithelium; thus, epithelial cells act as "gatekeepers." Sometimes an epithelium exhibits a range of permeability; that is, it may be relatively impermeable to some substances, at the same time promoting and assisting the passage of other molecules by absorption or secretion.
- **Secretion.** Some epithelial cells, called exocrine glands, are specialized to produce secretions. Individual gland cells may be scattered among other cell types in an epithelium, or a large group of epithelial secretory cells may form a gland to produce specific secretions (see section 4.1f).
- **Sensation.** Epithelial tissues are innervated by nerve endings to detect changes in the external environment at their surface. These sensory nerve endings and those in the underlying connective tissue continuously supply information to the nervous system concerning touch, pressure, temperature, and pain. For example, receptors in the epithelium of the skin respond to pressure by stimulating adjacent sensory nerves. Additionally, several organs contain a specialized epithelium, called a *neuroepithelium,* that houses specific cells responsible for the senses of taste, smell, vision, hearing, and equilibrium (as described in sections 19.3 to 19.6).

WHAT DO YOU THINK?

1. Why do you think epithelial tissue does not contain blood vessels? Can you think of an epithelial function that could be compromised if blood vessels were running through the tissue?

4.1c Specialized Structures of Epithelial Tissue

Because epithelial tissues are located at all free surfaces in the body, they exhibit distinct structural specializations. An epithelium rests on a layer of connective tissue and adheres firmly to it which secures the epithelium in place and prevents it from tearing. Between the epithelium and the underlying connective tissue is a thin extracellular layer called the **basement membrane.** The basement membrane can be seen as a single layer beneath epithelium with light microscopy (figure 4.1a). However, it actually consists of three layers when examined using electron microscopy : the lamina lucida, the lamina densa, and the reticular lamina. The **two laminae** closest to the epithelium contain collagen fibers as well as specific proteins and carbohydrates some of which are secreted by the epithelial cells. Cells in the underlying connective tissue secrete the **reticular lamina,** which contains protein fibers and carbohydrates. Together, these components of the basement membrane strengthen the attachment and form a selective molecular barrier between the epithelium and the underlying connective tissue.

The basement membrane has the following functions:

- Provides physical support for the epithelium
- Anchors the epithelium to the connective tissue
- Acts as a barrier to regulate the movement of large molecules between the epithelium and the underlying connective tissue

Intercellular Junctions

Epithelial cells are strongly bound together by specialized connections in the plasma membranes of their lateral surfaces called **intercellular junctions.** There are four types of junctions: tight junctions, adhering junctions, desmosomes, and gap junctions (figure 4.1*b*). Each of these types of junctions has a specialized structure.

Tight Junctions **Tight junctions,** also called *zonula* (zō′nyū-lă) *occludens* ("occluding belt"), encircle epithelial cells near their apical surface and completely attach each cell to its neighbors. Plasma membrane proteins among neighboring cells fuse, so the apical surfaces of the cells are tightly connected everywhere around the cell. This seals off the intercellular space and prevents substances from passing between the epithelial cells. The tight junction forces almost all materials to move *through,* rather than *between,* the epithelial cells in order to cross the epithelium. Thus, epithelia control whatever enters and leaves the body. For example, in the small intestine, tight junctions prevent digestive enzymes that degrade molecules from moving between epithelial cells into underlying connective tissue.

Adhering Junctions **Adhering junctions,** also called *zonula adherens* ("adhesion belt"), form completely around the cell. This type of junction occurs when extensive zones of microfilaments extend from the cytoplasm into the plasma membrane, forming a supporting and strengthening belt within the plasma membrane that completely encircles the cell immediately adjacent to all of its neighbors. Typically, adhering junctions are located deep to the tight junctions; the anchoring of the microfilament proteins within this belt provides the only means of junctional support for the apical surface of the cell. The ultra-strong tight junctions are needed only near the apical surface and not along the entire length of the cell. Once neighboring cells are fused together by the tight junctions near the apical surface, the adhering junctions support the apical surface and provide for a small space between neighboring cells in the direction of the basal surface. Thus, the junction affords a passageway between cells for materials that have already passed through the apical surface of the epithelial cell and can then exit through the membranes on the lateral surface and continue their journey toward the basement membrane.

Desmosomes A **desmosome** (dez′m ō-sōm; *desmos* = a band, *soma* = body), also called a *macula adherens* ("adhering spot"), is like a button or snap between adjacent epithelial cells. Each cell contributes half of the complete desmosome. It is a small region that holds cells together and provides resistance to mechanical stress at a single point, but it does not totally encircle the cell. In contrast to tight junctions, which encircle the cell to secure it to its neighbors everywhere around its periphery, the desmosome attaches a cell to its neighbors only at potential stress points. The neighboring cells are separated by a small space that is spanned by a fine web of protein filaments. These filaments anchor into a thickened protein plaque located at the internal surface of the plasma membrane. On the cytoplasmic side of each plaque, intermediate

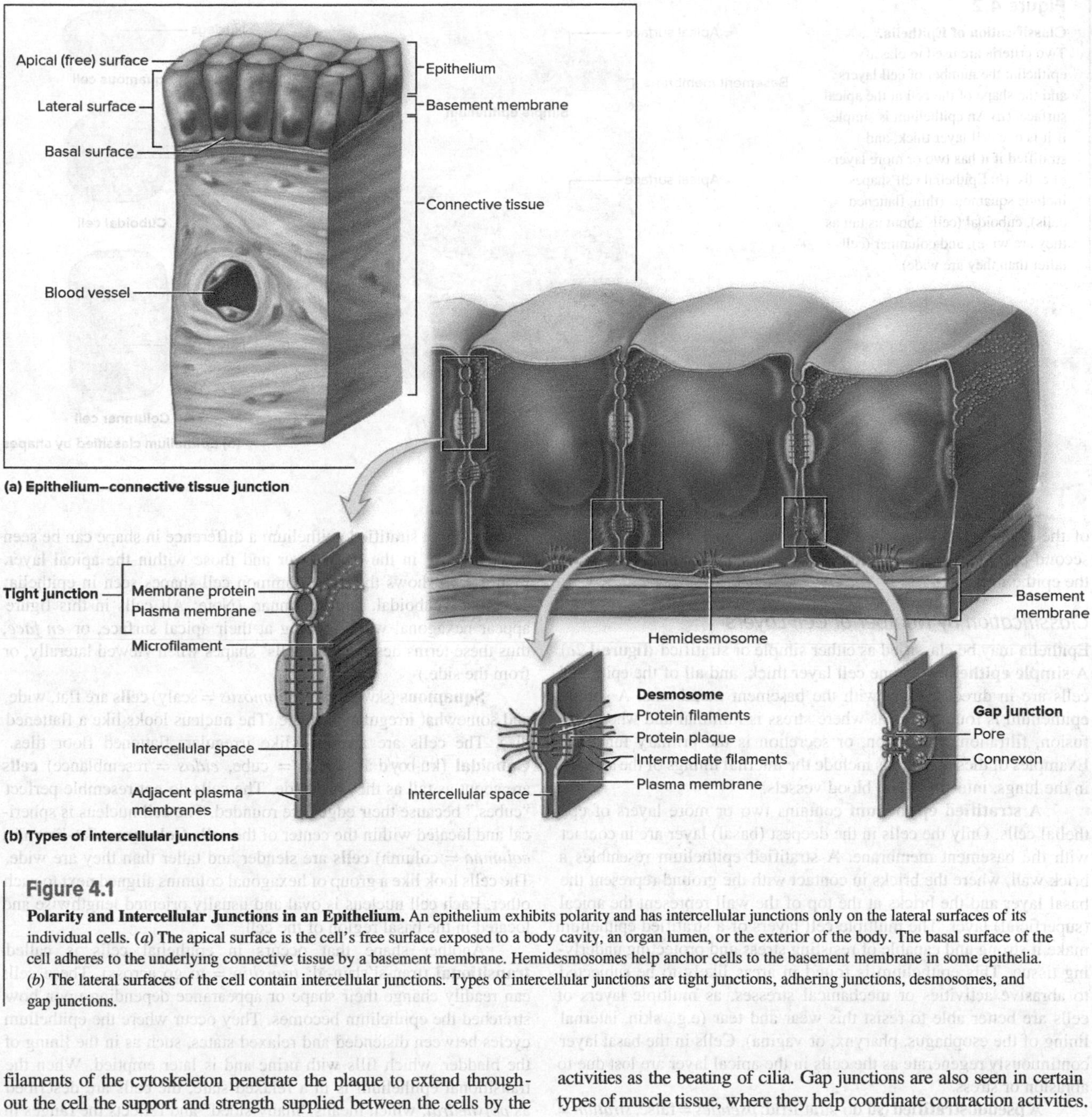

Figure 4.1
Polarity and Intercellular Junctions in an Epithelium. An epithelium exhibits polarity and has intercellular junctions only on the lateral surfaces of its individual cells. (*a*) The apical surface is the cell's free surface exposed to a body cavity, an organ lumen, or the exterior of the body. The basal surface of the cell adheres to the underlying connective tissue by a basement membrane. Hemidesmosomes help anchor cells to the basement membrane in some epithelia. (*b*) The lateral surfaces of the cell contain intercellular junctions. Types of intercellular junctions are tight junctions, adhering junctions, desmosomes, and gap junctions.

filaments of the cytoskeleton penetrate the plaque to extend throughout the cell the support and strength supplied between the cells by the desmosome. The basal cells of some epithelial tissue exhibit structures called **hemidesmosomes,** half-desmosomes that anchor them to the underlying basement membrane.

Gap Junctions A **gap junction** is formed across the intercellular gap between neighboring cells. This gap (about 2 nanometers in length) is bridged by structures called **connexons** (kō-neks′ŏnz). Each connexon consists of six transmembrane proteins, arranged in a circular fashion to form a tiny, fluid-filled tunnel or **pore.** Gap junctions provide a direct passageway for small molecules traveling between neighboring cells. Ions, glucose, amino acids, and other small solutes can pass directly from the cytoplasm of one cell into the neighboring cell through these channels. The flow of ions between cells coordinates such cellular activities as the beating of cilia. Gap junctions are also seen in certain types of muscle tissue, where they help coordinate contraction activities.

WHAT DID YOU LEARN?

1. Describe the basement membrane, its origins, and its functions.
2. Which intercellular junction ensures that epithelial cells act as "gatekeepers"?
3. What type of intercellular junction provides resistance to mechanical stress at a single point?

4.1d Classification of Epithelial Tissue

The body contains many different kinds of epithelia, and the classification of each type is indicated by a two-part name. The first part

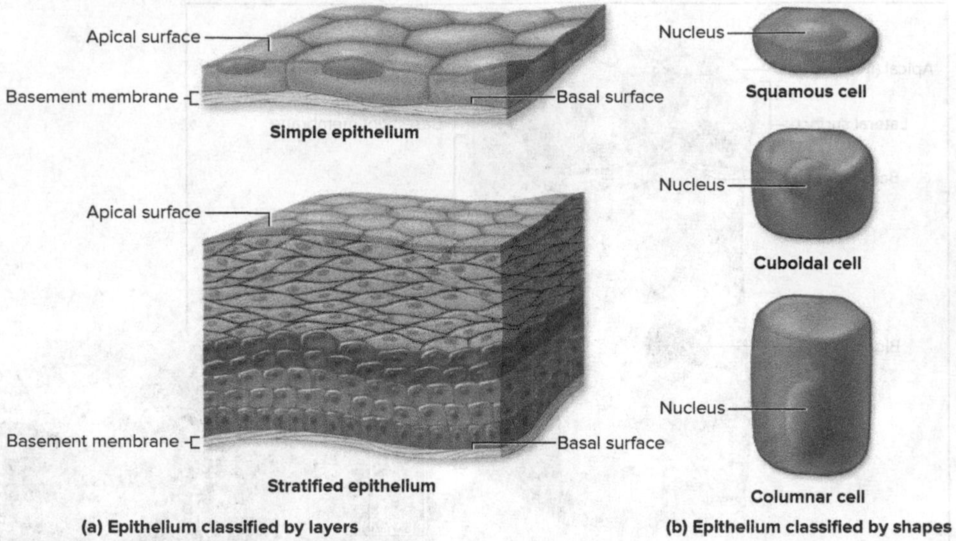

Figure 4.2

Classification of Epithelia. Two criteria are used to classify epithelia: the number of cell layers and the shape of the cell at the apical surface. (*a*) An epithelium is simple if it is one cell layer thick, and stratified if it has two or more layers of cells. (*b*) Epithelial cell shapes include squamous (thin, flattened cells), cuboidal (cells about as tall as they are wide), and columnar (cells taller than they are wide).

of the name refers to the *number* of epithelial cell layers, and the second part describes the *shape* of the cells at the apical surface of the epithelium.

Classification by Number of Cell Layers

Epithelia may be classified as either simple or stratified (**figure 4.2*a***). A **simple epithelium** is one cell layer thick, and all of the epithelial cells are in direct contact with the basement membrane. A simple epithelium is found in areas where stress is minimal and where diffusion, filtration, absorption, or secretion is the primary function. Examples of these locations include the internal linings of the air sacs in the lungs, intestines, and blood vessels.

A **stratified epithelium** contains two or more layers of epithelial cells. Only the cells in the deepest (basal) layer are in contact with the basement membrane. A stratified epithelium resembles a brick wall, where the bricks in contact with the ground represent the basal layer and the bricks at the top of the wall represent the apical (superficial) layer. The multiple cell layers of a stratified epithelium make it strong and capable of resisting stress and protecting underlying tissue. This epithelium is found in areas likely to be subjected to abrasive activities or mechanical stresses, as multiple layers of cells are better able to resist this wear and tear (e.g., skin, internal lining of the esophagus, pharynx, or vagina). Cells in the basal layer continuously regenerate as the cells in the apical layer are lost due to abrasion or stress.

A **pseudostratified** (sū'do-strat'i-fīd; *pseudes* = false, *stratum* = layer) **epithelium** appears layered (stratified) because the cells' nuclei are distributed at different levels between the apical and basal surfaces. All of these epithelial cells are attached to the basement membrane, but some of them do not reach its apical surface. Because all the cells are attached to the basement membrane, we have classified pseudostratified epithelium as a type of simple epithelium. A ciliated pseudostratified epithelium lines the nasal cavity and the respiratory passageways.

Classification by Cell Shape

Epithelia are also classified by the shape of the cell at the apical surface. In a simple epithelium, all of the cells display the same shape. However, in a stratified epithelium a difference in shape can be seen between cells in the basal layer and those within the apical layer. Figure 4.2*b* shows the three common cell shapes seen in epithelia: squamous, cuboidal, and columnar. (Note: All cells in this figure appear hexagonal when looking at their apical surface, or *en face*; thus these terms describe the cells' shapes when viewed laterally, or from the side.)

Squamous (skwā'mŭs; *squamosus* = scaly) **cells** are flat, wide, and somewhat irregular in shape. The nucleus looks like a flattened disc. The cells are arranged like irregular, flattened floor tiles. **Cuboidal** (kū-boy'd ăl; *kybos* = cube, *eidos* = resemblance) **cells** are about as tall as they are wide. The cells do not resemble perfect "cubes," because their edges are rounded. The cell nucleus is spherical and located within the center of the cell. **Columnar** (kō-lŭm'năr; *columna* = column) **cells** are slender and taller than they are wide. The cells look like a group of hexagonal columns aligned next to each other. Each cell nucleus is oval and usually oriented lengthwise and located in the basal region of the cell.

Another shape that occurs in epithelial cells is called **transitional** (tran-si'shŭn-ăl; *transitio* = to go across). These cells can readily change their shape or appearance depending upon how stretched the epithelium becomes. They occur where the epithelium cycles between distended and relaxed states, such as in the lining of the bladder, which fills with urine and is later emptied. When the transitional epithelium is in a relaxed state, the cells are described as *polyhedral,* which means "many-sided" and reflects the ranges in shape that are possible in this type of epithelium. When transitional epithelium is stretched, the surface cells resemble squamous cells.

4.1e Types of Epithelium

Using the classification system just described, epithelium can be broken down into the primary types shown in **figure 4.3**. In this section, we describe the characteristics of these types of epithelium and show how each appears using light microscopy.

Simple Squamous Epithelium

A **simple squamous epithelium** consists of a single layer of flattened cells **(table 4.2*a*)**. When viewed *en face*, the irregularly shaped cells

Learning Strategy 4.1

In your anatomy lab, you may be asked to identify a particular type of epithelium using light microscopy.

1. Is the epithelium one layer or many layers thick? If it is one layer thick, you are looking at some type of simple epithelium. If it is many layers thick, you are looking at some type of stratified epithelium or one of the unusual types of epithelium (such as pseudostratified or transitional).
2. What is the shape of the cells? If the cells (or at least the apical layer of cells) are flattened, you are looking at some type of squamous epithelium.

Your answer to question 1 gives you the first part of the epithelium's name (e.g., simple). Your answer to question 2 gives you the second part of the epithelium's name (e.g., squamous). Put these answers together, and you will have the name of the tissue (simple squamous epithelium, in this case).

display a spherical to oval nucleus, and they appear tightly bound together. Each squamous cell resembles a fried egg, with the nucleus representing the yolk. This epithelium is extremely delicate and highly specialized to allow rapid movement of molecules and ions across its surface by membrane transport processes (see section 2.3c). Simple squamous epithelium is found only in protected regions where moist surfaces reduce friction and abrasion. For example, in the lining of the lung air sacs (alveoli), the thin epithelium is well suited for the exchange of oxygen and carbon dioxide between the blood and inhaled air. This type of epithelium is also found lining the lumen (inside space) of blood vessel walls, where it allows for rapid exchange of nutrients and waste between the blood and the interstitial fluid surrounding the blood vessels.

Simple squamous epithelia that line closed internal body cavities and all circulatory structures have special names. The simple squamous epithelium that lines the lumen of the blood and lymphatic vessels and the heart and its chambers is termed **endothelium** (en′d ō-thē′lē-ŭm; *endon* = within). **Mesothelium** (mez′ō-thē′lē-ŭm; *mesos* = middle) is the simple squamous epithelium of the **serous membrane** (discussed in section 1.4e) that lines the internal walls of the pericardial, pleural, and peritoneal cavities as well as the external surfaces of the organs within those cavities. Mesothelium gets its name from the primary germ layer mesoderm, from which it is derived.

Simple Cuboidal Epithelium

A **simple cuboidal epithelium** consists of a single layer of cells that are as tall as they are wide (table 4.2*b*). A spherical nucleus is located in the center of the cell. A simple cuboidal epithelium functions primarily for absorption and secretion. It forms the walls of kidney tubules, where it participates in the reabsorption of nutrients, ions, and water that are filtered out of the blood plasma. It also forms the ducts of exocrine glands, which secrete materials. Simple cuboidal epithelium covers the surface of the ovary and also lines the follicles of the thyroid gland.

Simple Columnar Epithelium

A **simple columnar epithelium** is composed of a single layer of tall, narrow cells. The nucleus is oval, oriented lengthwise, and located within the basal region of the cell. Active movement of molecules occurs across this type of epithelium by either absorption or secretion. Simple columnar epithelium has two forms; one type has no cilia, whereas the apical surface of the other type is lined by cilia.

Nonciliated simple columnar epithelium often contains **microvilli** and a scattering of unicellular glands called **goblet cells** (table 4.2 *c*). Recall that microvilli are tiny, cytoplasmic projections on the apical surface of the cell that increase the surface area for secretion and absorption (see table 2.2). You cannot distinguish individual microvilli with light microscopy; rather, the microvilli collectively appear as a more darkly stained, fuzzy structure known as a **brush border.** Goblet cells secrete **mucin** (myū′sin; *mucus* = mucus), a glycoprotein that when hydrated (mixed with water) forms mucus. Nonciliated simple columnar epithelium lines most of the digestive tract, from the stomach to the anal canal.

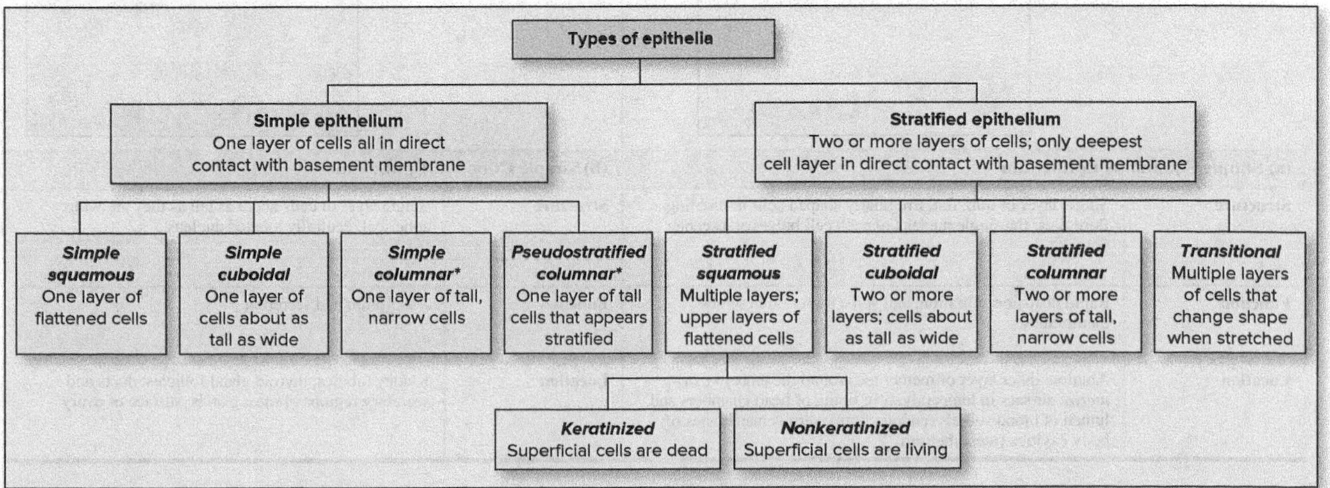

Figure 4.3

Organization and Relationship of Epithelia Types. Epithelia are classified by (1) the number of cell layers and (2) the cell shape at the surface.

Table 4.2 Simple Epithelia

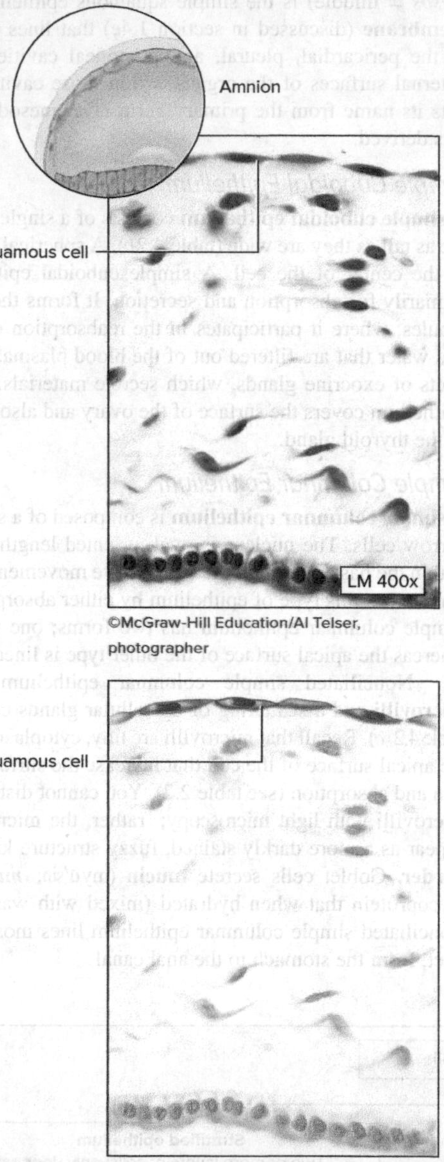

Amnion
Simple squamous cell
LM 400x
Simple squamous cell

©McGraw-Hill Education/Al Telser, photographer

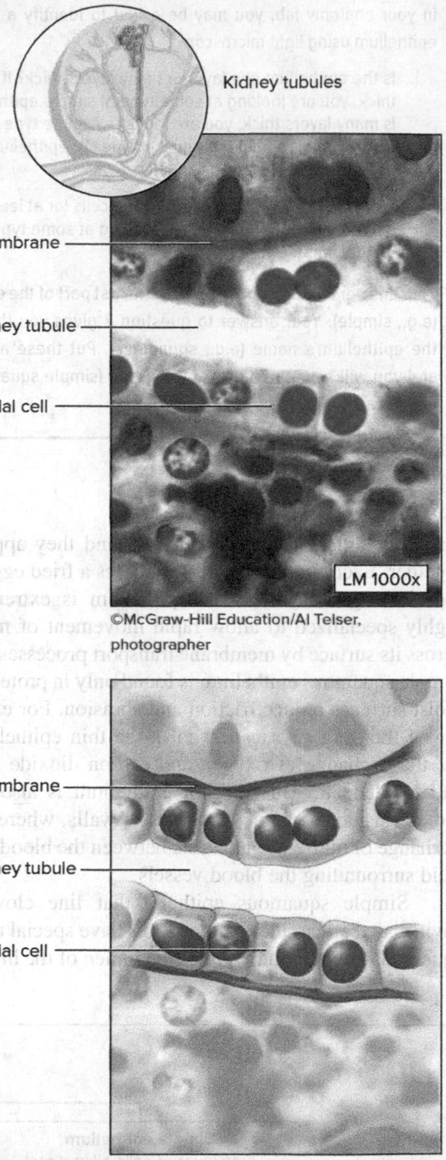

Kidney tubules
Basement membrane
Lumen of kidney tubule
Simple cuboidal cell
LM 1000x
Basement membrane
Lumen of kidney tubule
Simple cuboidal cell

©McGraw-Hill Education/Al Telser, photographer

(a) Simple Squamous Epithelium		**(b) Simple Cuboidal Epithelium**	
Structure	Single layer of thin, flat, irregularly shaped cells resembling floor tiles; the single nucleus of each cell bulges at its center	**Structure**	Single layer of cells about as tall as they are wide; spherical, centrally located nucleus
Function	Rapid diffusion, filtration, and some secretion in serous membranes	**Function**	Absorption and secretion
Location	Amnion, inner layer of membrane around the embryo (*in utero*); air sacs in lungs (alveoli); lining of heart chambers and lumen of blood vessels (endothelium); serous membranes of body cavities (mesothelium)	**Location**	Kidney tubules; thyroid gland follicles; ducts and secretory regions of most glands; surface of ovary

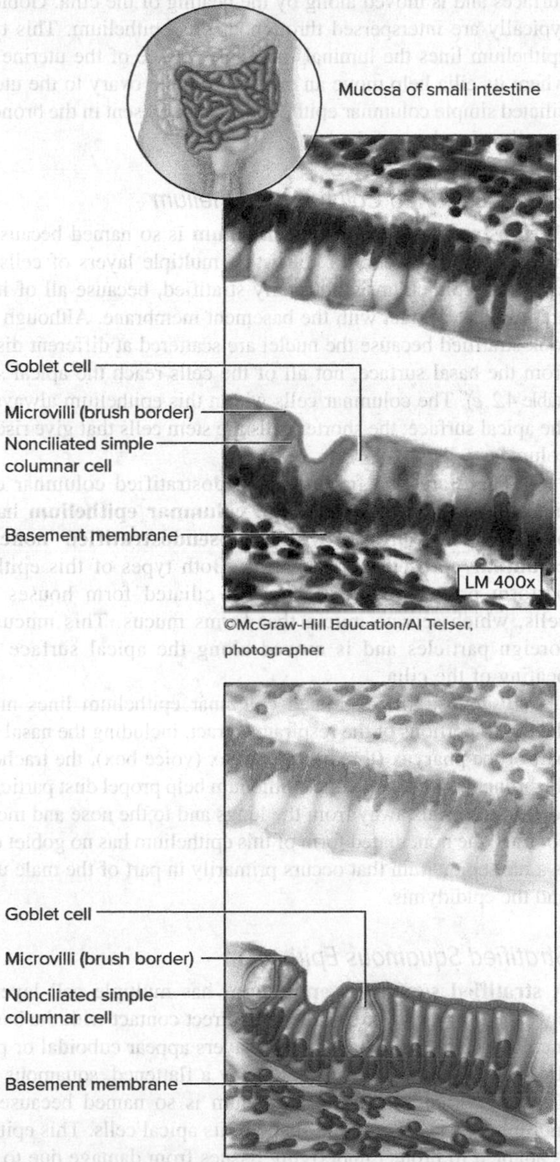
Mucosa of small intestine
Goblet cell
Microvilli (brush border)
Nonciliated simple columnar cell
Basement membrane
LM 400x
Goblet cell
Microvilli (brush border)
Nonciliated simple columnar cell
Basement membrane

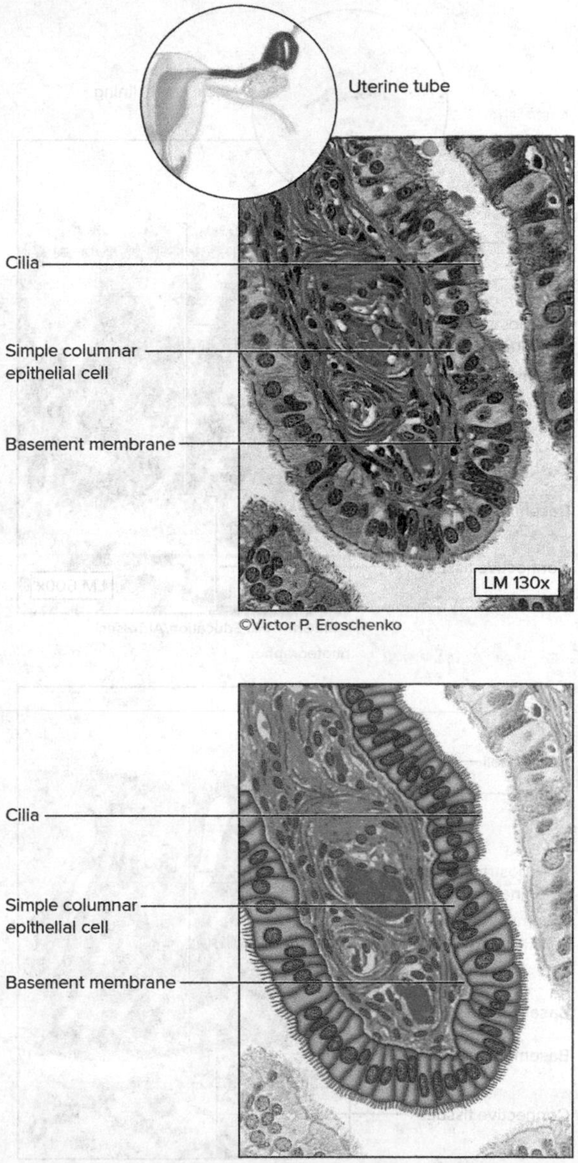
Uterine tube
Cilia
Simple columnar epithelial cell
Basement membrane
LM 130x
Cilia
Simple columnar epithelial cell
Basement membrane

(c) Nonciliated Simple Columnar Epithelium		**(d) Ciliated Simple Columnar Epithelium**	
Structure	Single layer of tall, narrow cells; oval-shaped nucleus oriented lengthwise in the basal region of the cell; apical regions of cells have microvilli; may contain goblet cells that secrete mucin	**Structure**	Single layer of tall, narrow, ciliated cells; oval-shaped nucleus oriented lengthwise in the basal region of the cell; goblet cells may be present
Function	Absorption and secretion; secretion of mucin	**Function**	Secretion of mucin and movement of mucus along apical surface of epithelium by action of cilia; oocyte movement through uterine tube
Location	Lining of most of digestive tract; lining of stomach does not contain goblet cells	**Location**	Lining of uterine tubes and larger bronchioles of respiratory tract

(continued on next page)

Table 4.2 Simple Epithelia *(continued)*

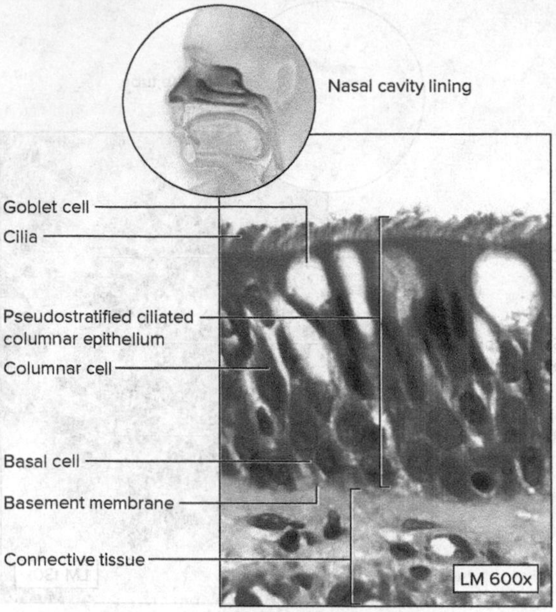
Nasal cavity lining
Goblet cell
Cilia
Pseudostratified ciliated columnar epithelium
Columnar cell
Basal cell
Basement membrane
Connective tissue
LM 600x

©McGraw-Hill Education/Al Telser, photographer

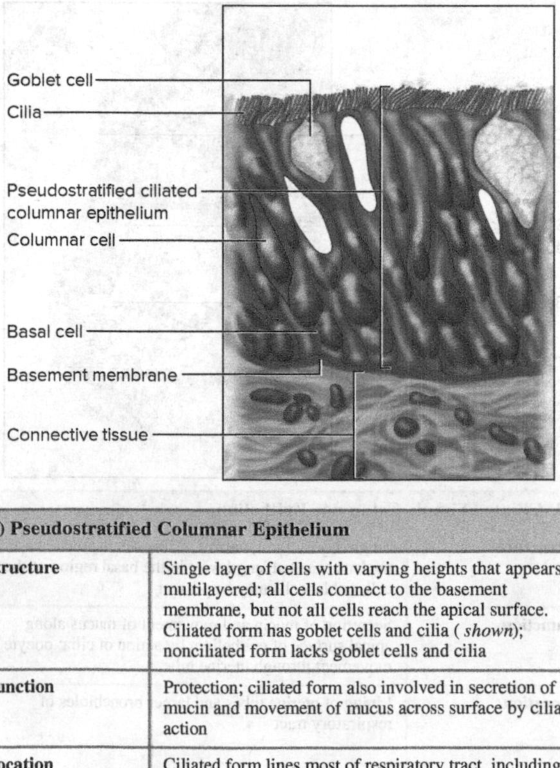
Goblet cell
Cilia
Pseudostratified ciliated columnar epithelium
Columnar cell
Basal cell
Basement membrane
Connective tissue

(e) Pseudostratified Columnar Epithelium	
Structure	Single layer of cells with varying heights that appears multilayered; all cells connect to the basement membrane, but not all cells reach the apical surface. Ciliated form has goblet cells and cilia (*shown*); nonciliated form lacks goblet cells and cilia
Function	Protection; ciliated form also involved in secretion of mucin and movement of mucus across surface by ciliary action
Location	Ciliated form lines most of respiratory tract, including nasal cavity, part of pharynx, larynx, trachea, bronchi. Nonciliated form is rare; lines epididymis and part of male urethra

Ciliated simple columnar epithelium has cilia that project from the apical surfaces of the cells (table 4.2*d*). Mucus covers these apical surfaces and is moved along by the beating of the cilia. Goblet cells typically are interspersed throughout this epithelium. This type of epithelium lines the luminal (internal) surface of the uterine tubes, where its cilia help move an oocyte from the ovary to the uterus. A ciliated simple columnar epithelium is also present in the bronchioles (smaller air tubes) of the lung.

Pseudostratified Columnar Epithelium

Pseudostratified columnar epithelium is so named because upon first glance, it appears to consist of multiple layers of cells. However, this epithelium is not really stratified, because all of its cells are in direct contact with the basement membrane. Although it may look stratified because the nuclei are scattered at different distances from the basal surface, not all of the cells reach the apical surface (table 4.2 *e*). The columnar cells within this epithelium always reach the apical surface; the shorter cells are stem cells that give rise to the columnar cells.

There are two forms of pseudostratified columnar epithelium: **Pseudostratified ciliated columnar epithelium** has cilia on its apical surface, whereas **pseudostratified nonciliated columnar epithelium** lacks cilia. Both types of this epithelium perform protective functions. The ciliated form houses goblet cells, which secrete mucin that forms mucus. This mucus traps foreign particles and is moved along the apical surface by the beating of the cilia.

Pseudostratified ciliated columnar epithelium lines much of the larger portions of the respiratory tract, including the nasal cavity, part of the pharynx (throat), the larynx (voice box), the trachea, and the bronchi. The cilia in this epithelium help propel dust particles and foreign materials away from the lungs and to the nose and mouth. In contrast, the nonciliated form of this epithelium has no goblet cells. It is a rare epithelium that occurs primarily in part of the male urethra and the epididymis.

Stratified Squamous Epithelium

A **stratified squamous epithelium** has multiple cell layers, and only the deepest layer of cells is in direct contact with the basement membrane. The cells in the basal layers appear cuboidal or polyhedral, whereas the apical cells display a flattened, squamous shape. Thus, stratified squamous epithelium is so named because of its multiple cell layers and the shape of its apical cells. This epithelium is adapted to protect underlying tissues from damage due to activities that are abrasive and cause friction. Stem cells in the basal layer continuously divide to produce a new stem cell and a committed cell that gradually moves toward the surface to replace the cells lost during protective activities. This type of epithelium exists in two forms: keratinized and nonkeratinized.

Learning Strategy 4.2

If you are having trouble distinguishing cilia from microvilli with light microscopy, recall that cilia appear like fine hairs extending from the apical surface of the cell, whereas microvilli are extensive folds of the plasma membrane that appear as a fuzzy, darkened brush border at the apical surface.

In **keratinized** (ker′ă-ti-nīzd; *keras* = horn) **stratified squamous epithelium,** the apical surface is composed of layers of cells that are dead; these cells lack nuclei and all organelles and are filled with **keratin,** a tough, protective, fibrous protein. It is obvious that the superficial cells lack nuclei when they are viewed with light microscopy **(table 4.3*a*)**. New committed cells produced in the basal region of the epithelium migrate toward the apical surface. During their migration, they fill with

Table 4.3 Stratified Epithelia

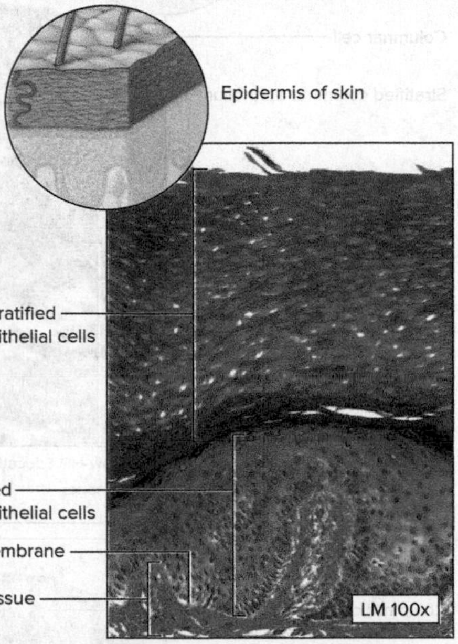
Epidermis of skin
Keratinized stratified squamous epithelial cells
Living stratified squamous epithelial cells
Basement membrane
Connective tissue
LM 100x

©McGraw-Hill Education/Al Telser, photographer

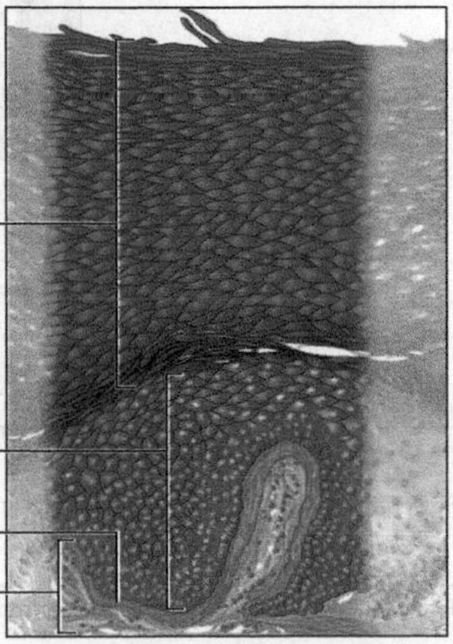
Keratinized stratified squamous epithelial cells
Living stratified squamous epithelial cells
Basement membrane
Connective tissue

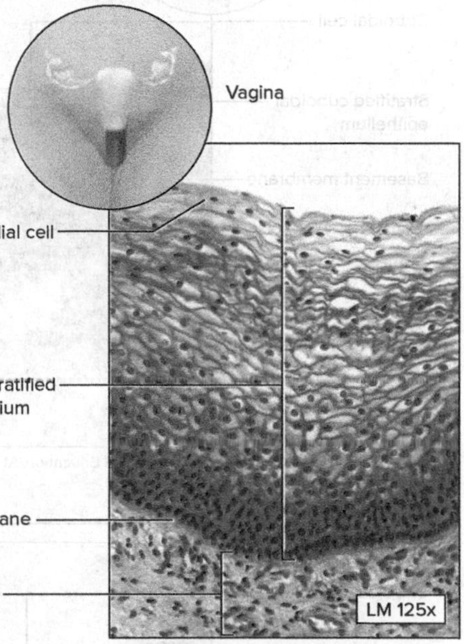
Vagina
Squamous epithelial cell
Nonkeratinized stratified squamous epithelium
Basement membrane
Connective tissue
LM 125x

©McGraw-Hill Education/Al Telser, photographer

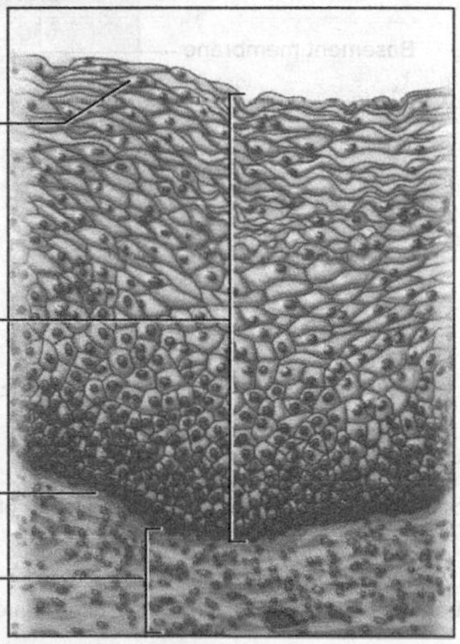
Squamous epithelial cell
Nonkeratinized stratified squamous epithelium
Basement membrane
Connective tissue

(a) Keratinized Stratified Squamous Epithelium	
Structure	Multiple layers of cells; basal cells typically are cuboidal or polyhedral, whereas apical (superficial) cells are squamous; more superficial cells are dead and filled with the protein keratin
Function	Protection of underlying tissue
Location	Epidermis of skin

(b) Nonkeratinized Stratified Squamous Epithelium	
Structure	Multiple layers of cells; basal cells typically are cuboidal or polyhedral, whereas apical (superficial) cells are squamous; surface cells are alive and kept moist
Function	Protection of underlying tissue
Location	Lining of vagina, oral cavity, part of pharynx, esophagus, and anus

(continued on next page)

Table 4.3 Stratified Epithelia *(continued)*

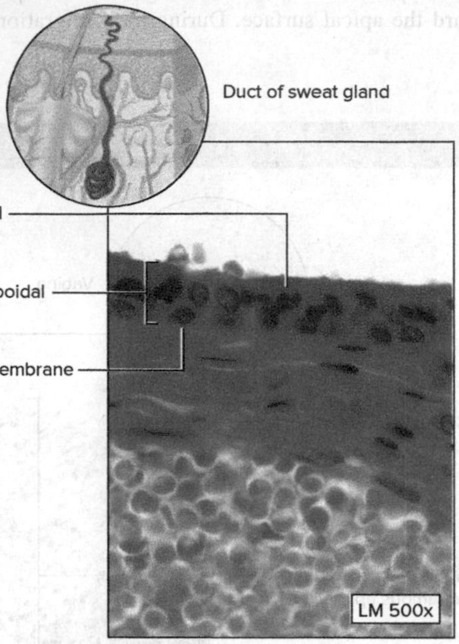
Duct of sweat gland
Cuboidal cell
Stratified cuboidal epithelium
Basement membrane
LM 500x

©McGraw-Hill Education/Al Telser, photographer

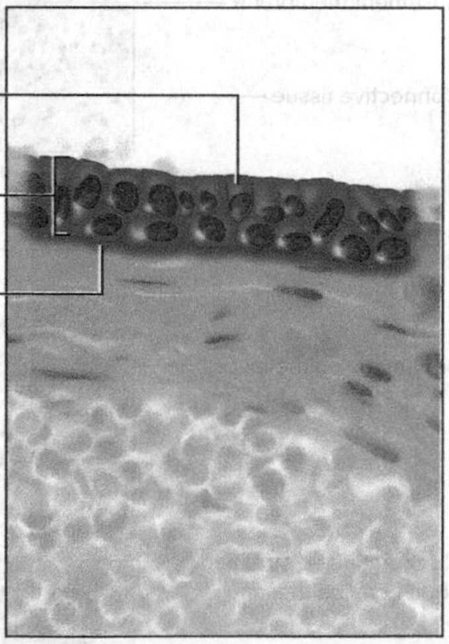
Cuboidal cell
Stratified cuboidal epithelium
Basement membrane

(c) Stratified Cuboidal Epithelium	
Structure	Two or more layers of cells; cells at the apical surface are cuboidal
Function	Protection and secretion
Location	Found in large ducts in most exocrine glands and in some parts of the male urethra

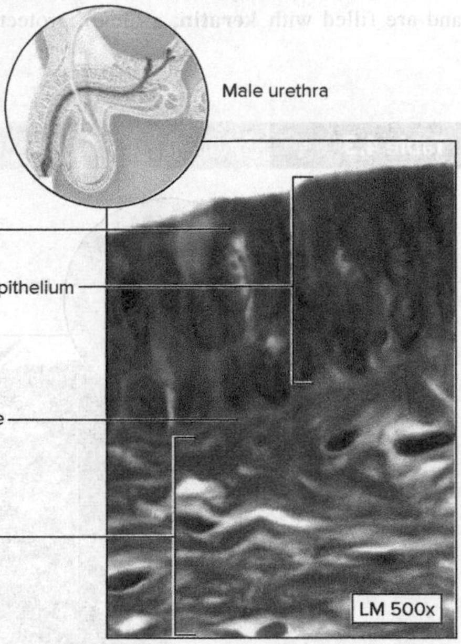
Male urethra
Columnar cell
Stratified columnar epithelium
Basement membrane
Connective tissue
LM 500x

©McGraw-Hill Education/Al Telser, photographer

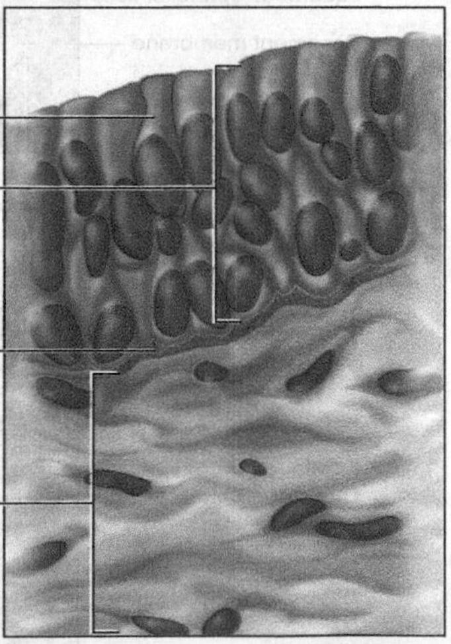
Columnar cell
Stratified columnar epithelium
Basement membrane
Connective tissue

(d) Stratified Columnar Epithelium	
Structure	Two or more layers of cells; cells at the apical surface are columnar
Function	Protection and secretion
Location	Rare; found in some regions of the male urethra and in large ducts of some exocrine glands

keratin, lose their organelles and nuclei, and die. However, the keratin in these dead cells makes them very strong. Thus, there is a tradeoff with the appearance of keratin, in that the tissue becomes very strong, but the cells must die as a result. The epidermis (outer layer) of the skin consists of keratinized stratified squamous epithelium.

The cells in **nonkeratinized stratified squamous epithelium** remain alive all the way to its apical surface, and they are kept

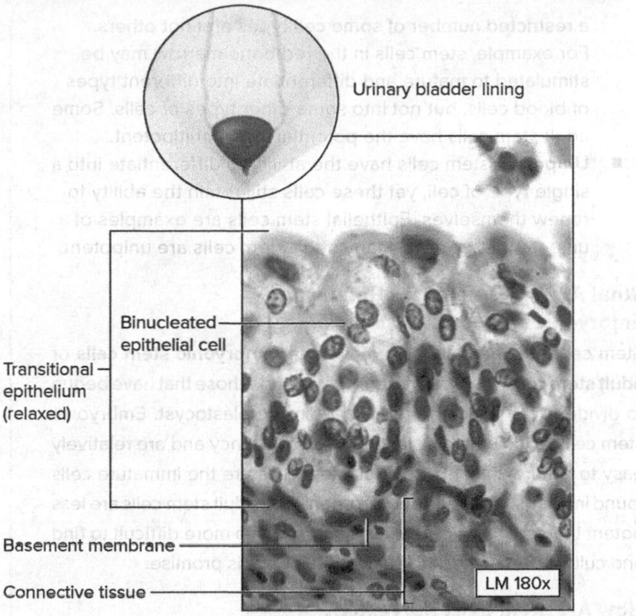
Urinary bladder lining
Binucleated epithelial cell
Transitional epithelium (relaxed)
Basement membrane
Connective tissue
LM 180x

©McGraw-Hill Education/Al Telser, photographer

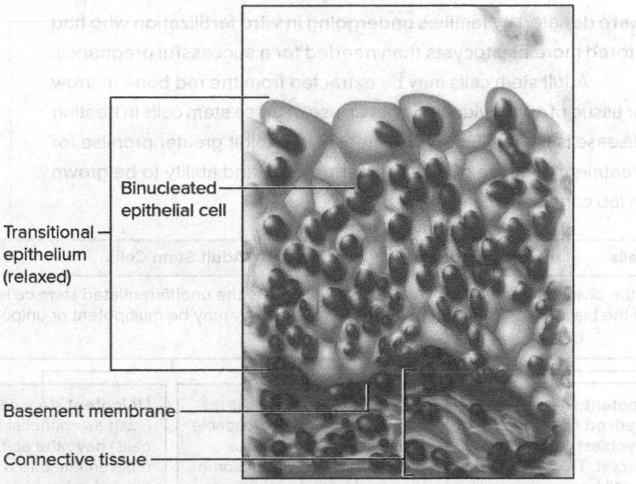
Binucleated epithelial cell
Transitional epithelium (relaxed)
Basement membrane
Connective tissue

(e) Transitional Epithelium	
Structure	Epithelial appearance varies, depending on whether the tissue is stretched or relaxed; shape of cells at apical surface changes; some cells may be binucleated
Function	Distension and relaxation to accommodate urine volume changes in bladder, ureters, and urethra
Location	Lining of urinary bladder, ureters, and part of urethra

moist with secretions such as saliva or mucus. These cells lack keratin. Because all of the cells are still alive, the flattened nuclei characteristic of squamous cells are visible even in the most superficial cells (table 4.3*b*). Nonkeratinized stratified squamous epithelium lines the vagina, the oral cavity (mouth), part of the pharynx (throat), the esophagus, and the anus.

Stratified Cuboidal Epithelium

A **stratified cuboidal epithelium** contains two or more layers of cells, and the apical cells tend to be cuboidal in shape (table 4.3*c*). This type of epithelium forms the walls of the larger ducts of most exocrine glands, such as the sweat glands in the skin. Although the function of stratified cuboidal epithelium is mainly protective, it also serves to strengthen the wall of gland ducts.

Stratified Columnar Epithelium

A **stratified columnar epithelium** is relatively rare in the body. It consists of two or more layers of cells, but only the apical surface cells are columnar in shape (table 4.3*d*). This type of epithelium is found in the membranous segment of the male urethra and in the large ducts of the salivary glands.

Transitional Epithelium

A **transitional epithelium** varies in appearance, depending upon whether it is in a relaxed or a stretched state (table 4.3*e*). In a relaxed state, the basal cells appear almost cuboidal, and the apical cells are large and rounded. During stretching, the transitional epithelium thins, and the apical cells continue to flatten, becoming almost squamous. In this distended state, it may be difficult to distinguish a transitional epithelium from a squamous epithelium. However, one distinguishing feature of transitional epithelium is the presence of a handful of **binucleated** (containing two nuclei) **cells.** This epithelium lines the urinary bladder, an organ that changes shape as it fills with urine. It also lines the ureters and the proximal part of the urethra. Transitional epithelium permits stretching and ensures that toxic urine does not seep into the underlying tissues and structures of these organs. APR

WHAT DO YOU THINK?

2 What types of epithelium are well suited for protection?

4.1f Glands

As epithelial tissue develops in the embryo, small invaginations from this epithelium into the underlying connective tissue give rise to specialized secretory structures called glands. **Glands** are either individual cells or multicellular organs composed predominantly of epithelial tissue. They secrete substances either for use elsewhere in the body or for elimination from the body. Glandular secretions include mucin, electrolytes, hormones, enzymes, and waste products.

Endocrine and Exocrine Glands

Glands are classified as either endocrine or exocrine, depending upon whether they have a duct connecting the secretory cells to the surface of an epithelium.

Endocrine (en′dō-krin; *endon* = within, *krino* = to separate) **glands** lack ducts and secrete their products directly into the interstitial fluid and blood. The secretions of endocrine glands, called *hormones,* act as chemical messengers to influence cell activities elsewhere in the body. Endocrine glands are discussed in depth in section 20.1.

Clinical View 4.1

Stem Cells

Why All the Interest in Stem Cells?

Stem cells are immature, undifferentiated cells. These cells are able to divide into two cells, one of which is another stem cell, and the other a cell that could differentiate into a specialized, mature cell with a unique function. Stem cells have generated interest in the scientific and medical communities because of their potential for repair or replacement of damaged or dying tissue. Stem cells have long been used for bone marrow replacement and skin grafts. Research into the use of stem cells for treatment of Parkinson disease, Alzheimer disease, spinal cord injuries, and type 1 diabetes mellitus is ongoing.

What Are the Two Basic Characteristics of Stem Cells?

All stem cells exhibit two characteristics: self-renewal and potency. **Self-renewal** refers to their ability to divide repeatedly to produce both new cells for maturation and new stem cells. **Potency** is the potential for differentiation. Different stem cells have varying ability to differentiate into almost any type of cell. Stem cells exhibit four levels of potency: totipotency, pluripotency, multipotency, and unipotency.

- **Totipotent** stem cells have a "total potential," meaning that they exhibit the ability to differentiate into any cell type within an organism. A totipotent cell is produced when a secondary oocyte is fertilized by a sperm, giving rise to a zygote. The first few cell divisions of the zygote result in equally totipotent cells. Thus, only embryonic (and not adult) stem cells have the potential to be totipotent.
- **Pluripotent** stem cells are derived from totipotent stem cells. These stem cells are formed from the embryoblast portion (inner cell mass) of the **blastocyst.** The blastocyst is a ball of cells that develops during the first week of development from the zygote. The embryoblast is the portion of the blastocyst that will eventually become an embryo and then a fetus. Pluripotent stem cells can form cells in any of the tissue layers of the embryo, but they cannot form structures such as the placenta. Embryonic genes can be introduced into adult specialized cells to reprogram them to function like embryonic stem cells. These cells are called **induced pluripotent stem cells (iPSCs).**
- **Multipotent** stem cells are derived from pluripotent stem cells. They have the capability to differentiate into a restricted number of some cell types and not others. For example, stem cells in the red bone marrow may be stimulated to mature and differentiate into different types of blood cells, but not into some other types of cells. Some adult stem cells have the potential to be multipotent.
- **Unipotent** stem cells have the ability to differentiate into a single type of cell, yet these cells still retain the ability to renew themselves. Epithelial stem cells are examples of unipotent stem cells. Many adult stem cells are unipotent.

What Are the Differences Between Embryonic and Adult Stem Cells?

Stem cells may be categorized as either **embryonic stem cells** or **adult stem cells.** Embryonic stem cells include those that have begun to divide in the zygote and the cells in the blastocyst. Embryonic stem cells exhibit the greatest degree of potency and are relatively easy to culture. In contrast, adult stem cells are the immature cells found in postnatal (already born) organisms. Adult stem cells are less potent than embryonic stem cells and are also more difficult to find and culture. Research in the use of iPSCs holds promise.

How Are Stem Cells Harvested?

Most embryonic stem cells must be harvested from a structure no more differentiated than a blastocyst. Most of these blastocysts were donated by families undergoing in vitro fertilization who had stored more blastocysts than needed for a successful pregnancy.

Adult stem cells may be extracted from the red bone marrow or tissue of an individual. However, use of these stem cells in treating disease is limited. Embryonic stem cells exhibit greater promise for treatment because of their greater potency and ability to be grown in lab conditions.

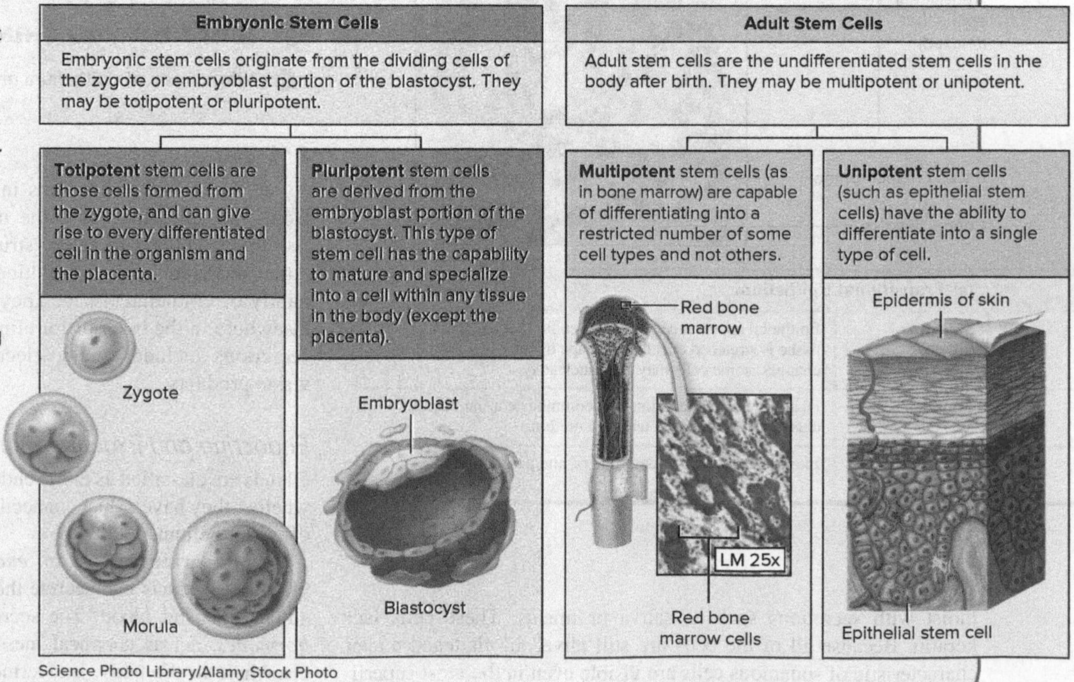
Embryonic Stem Cells
Embryonic stem cells originate from the dividing cells of the zygote or embryoblast portion of the blastocyst. They may be totipotent or pluripotent.
Totipotent stem cells are those cells formed from the zygote, and can give rise to every differentiated cell in the organism and the placenta.
Pluripotent stem cells are derived from the embryoblast portion of the blastocyst. This type of stem cell has the capability to mature and specialize into a cell within any tissue in the body (except the placenta).
Zygote
Morula
Embryoblast
Blastocyst
Adult Stem Cells
Adult stem cells are the undifferentiated stem cells in the body after birth. They may be multipotent or unipotent.
Multipotent stem cells (as in bone marrow) are capable of differentiating into a restricted number of some cell types and not others.
Unipotent stem cells (such as epithelial stem cells) have the ability to differentiate into a single type of cell.
Red bone marrow
LM 25x
Red bone marrow cells
Epidermis of skin
Epithelial stem cell

Science Photo Library/Alamy Stock Photo

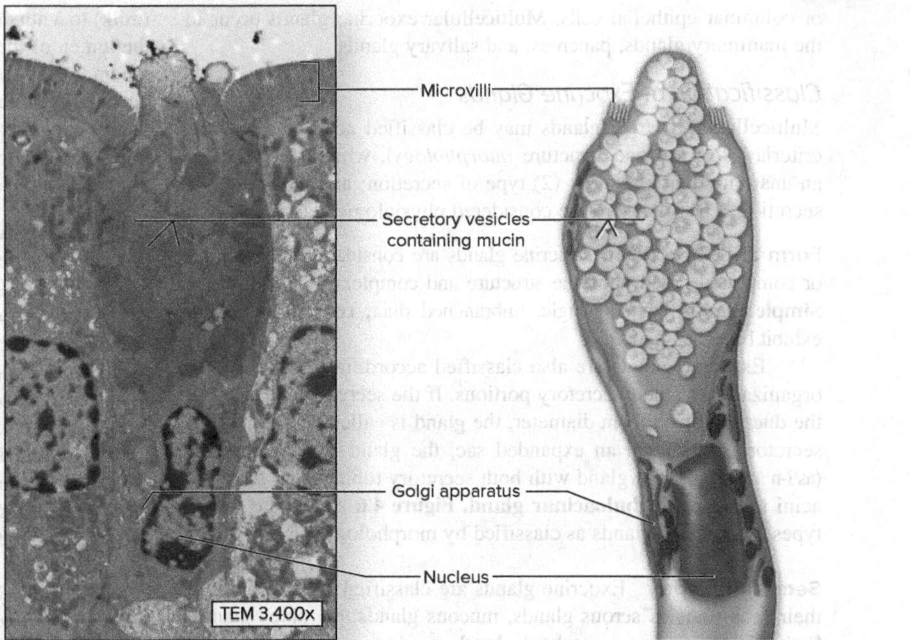
Microvilli
Secretory vesicles containing mucin
Golgi apparatus
Nucleus
TEM 3,400x
(a)
(b)

Figure 4.4
Goblet Cell: A Unicellular Exocrine Gland. (*a*) Transmission electron micrograph and (*b*) diagram of a goblet cell in the small intestine.
(a) EM Research Services/Newcastle University

Exocrine (ek′s ō-krin; *exo* = outside) **glands** typically originate from an invagination of epithelium that burrows into the deeper connective tissues. These glands usually maintain their contact with the epithelial surface by means of a **duct,** an epithelium-lined tube through which secretions of the gland are discharged onto the epithelial surface. This duct may secrete materials onto the surface of the skin (e.g., sweat from sweat glands or milk from mammary glands) or onto an epithelial surface lining an internal passageway (e.g., enzymes from the pancreas into the small intestine or saliva from the salivary glands into the oral cavity).

Exocrine Gland Structure

An exocrine gland may be unicellular or multicellular. A unicellular exocrine gland is an individual exocrine cell located within an epithelium that is predominantly nonsecretory. Unicellular exocrine glands do not contain a duct, and they are located close to the surface of the epithelium in which they reside. The most common type of unicellular exocrine gland is the goblet cell (**figure 4.4**). It is usually found in both a simple columnar epithelium and pseudostratified ciliated columnar epithelium. For example, the respiratory tract is lined mainly by pseudostratified ciliated columnar epithelium, which also contains some mucin-secreting goblet cells. Mucus then coats the inner surface of the respiratory passageway to cover and protect its lining and to help warm, humidify, and cleanse the inhaled air before it reaches the gas exchange surfaces in the lungs.

Multicellular exocrine glands are composed of numerous cells that work together to produce a secretion and secrete it onto the surface of an epithelium. The gland consists of secretory portions, often **acini** (as′i-n ī; sing., as′i-n ŭs; *acinus* = grape), that produce the secretion, and one or more smaller ducts (the conducting portion), which merge to eventually form a larger duct that transports the secretion to the epithelial surface (**figure 4.5**).

Most multicellular exocrine glands are enclosed within a fibrous **capsule.** Extensions of this capsule, called **septa** or *trabeculae,* partition the gland internally into compartments called **lobes.** Further subdivisions of the septa within each lobe form microscopic **lobules** (lob′y ūl). The septa contain ducts, blood vessels, and nerves supplying the gland. The connective tissue framework of the gland is called the **stroma.** The stroma supports and organizes the **parenchyma** (pă-reng′ki-mă), the functional cells of the gland that produce and secrete the gland products. These cells are usually simple cuboidal

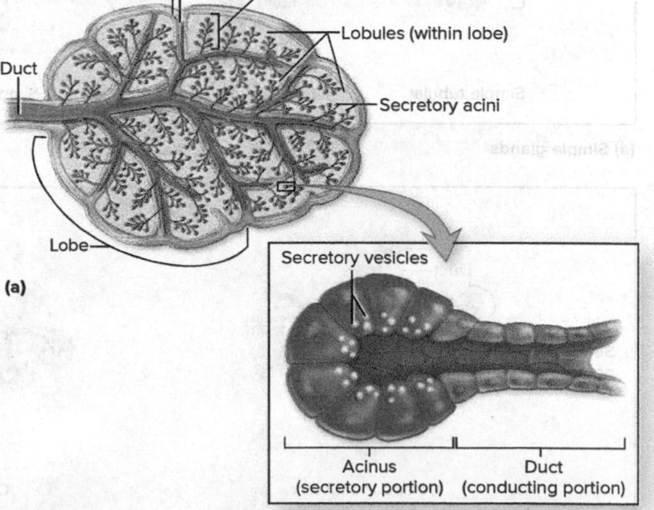
Stroma
Septum
Capsule
Parenchyma
Lobules (within lobe)
Duct
Secretory acini
Lobe
(a)
Secretory vesicles
Acinus
(secretory portion)
Duct
(conducting portion)
(b)

Figure 4.5
General Structure of Multicellular Exocrine Glands. (*a*) Exocrine glands have a connection called a duct that leads to an organ or body surface. Inside the gland, the duct branches repeatedly, following the connective tissue septa, until its finest divisions end on secretory acini. (*b*) The acinus is the secretory portion of the gland, and the duct is the conducting portion.

or columnar epithelial cells. Multicellular exocrine glands occur in the mammary glands, pancreas, and salivary glands.

Classification of Exocrine Glands

Multicellular exocrine glands may be classified according to three criteria: (1) form and structure (*morphology*), which is considered an anatomic classification; (2) type of secretion; and (3) method of secretion. The latter two are considered physiologic classifications.

Form and Structure Exocrine glands are considered either simple or compound based upon the structure and complexity of their ducts. **Simple glands** have a single, unbranched duct; **compound glands** exhibit branched ducts.

Exocrine glands are also classified according to the shape or organization of their secretory portions. If the secretory portion and the duct are of uniform diameter, the gland is called **tubular.** If the secretory cells form an expanded sac, the gland is called **acinar** (as′i-n ăr). Finally, a gland with both secretory tubules and secretory acini is called a **tubuloacinar gland. Figure 4.6** shows the several types of exocrine glands as classified by morphology.

Secretion Types Exocrine glands are classified by the nature of their secretions as serous glands, mucous glands, or mixed glands. **Serous** (sē′rŭs; *serum* = whey) **glands** produce and secrete a non-viscous, watery fluid, such as sweat, milk, tears, or digestive juices. This fluid carries wastes (sweat) to the surface of the skin, nutrients (milk) to a nursing infant, or digestive enzymes from the pancreas to the lumen of the small intestine. **Mucous** (myū′kŭs) **glands** secrete mucin, which forms mucus when mixed with water. Mucous glands occur in such places as the roof of the oral cavity and the surface of the tongue. **Mixed glands,** such as the two pairs of salivary glands inferior to the oral cavity, contain both serous and mucous cells, and produce a mixture of the two types of secretions.

Secretion Methods Glands are also classified by their mechanism of discharging secretory product as merocrine glands, holocrine glands, or apocrine glands (**figure 4.7**).

Merocrine (mer′ō-krin; *meros* = share) **glands** package their secretions in structures called *secretory vesicles* and release their secretion by exocytosis. The cells remain intact and are not damaged in any way by producing the secretion. Lacrimal (tear) glands, salivary glands, sweat glands, the exocrine glands of the pancreas, and the gastric glands of the stomach are examples of merocrine glands. Some merocrine glands are also called *eccrine glands,* to denote a type of sweat gland in the skin that is not connected to a hair follicle (see section 5.5c). APR

Apocrine (ap′ō-krin; *apo* = away from or off) **glands** are composed of cells that accumulate their secretory products within the apical portion of their cytoplasm. Secretion occurs when the cell's apical portion pinches off, releasing cytoplasmic content. Thereafter, the cell repairs itself in order to repeat its secretory activity. Mammary glands and ceruminous glands are apocrine glands. APR

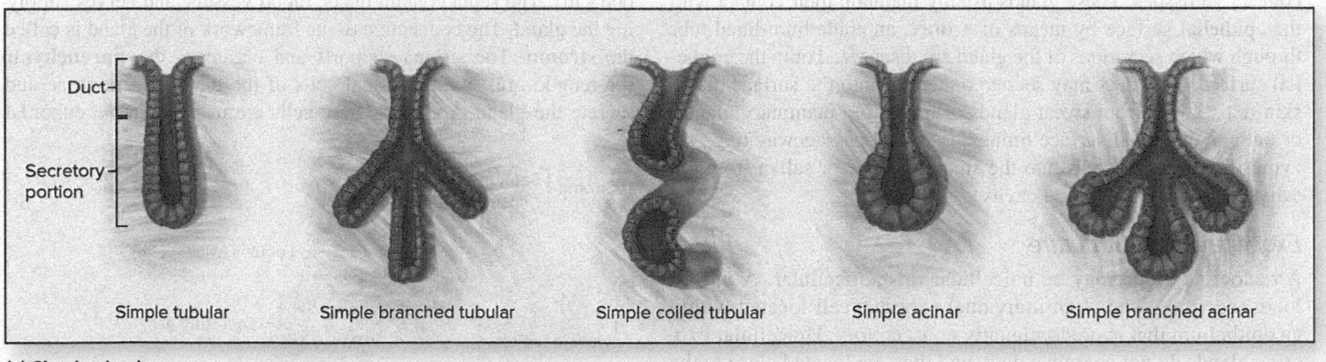
Duct
Secretory portion
Simple tubular
Simple branched tubular
Simple coiled tubular
Simple acinar
Simple branched acinar

(a) Simple glands

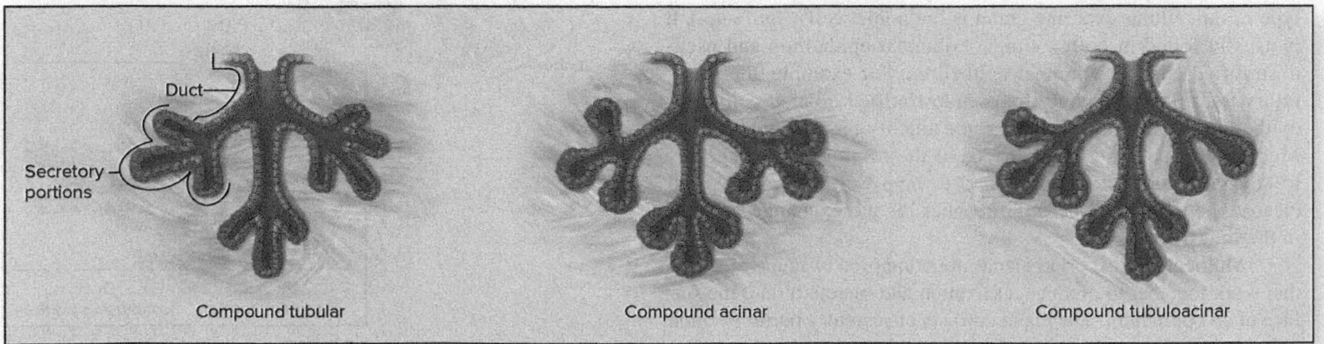
Duct
Secretory portions
Compound tubular
Compound acinar
Compound tubuloacinar

(b) Compound glands

Figure 4.6

Structural Classification of Multicellular Exocrine Glands. (*a*) Simple glands have unbranched ducts, whereas (*b*) compound glands have ducts that branch. These glands also exhibit different forms: Tubular glands have secretory cells in a space with a uniform diameter, acinar glands have secretory cells arranged in saclike acini, and tubuloacinar glands have secretory cells in both acinar and tubular regions.

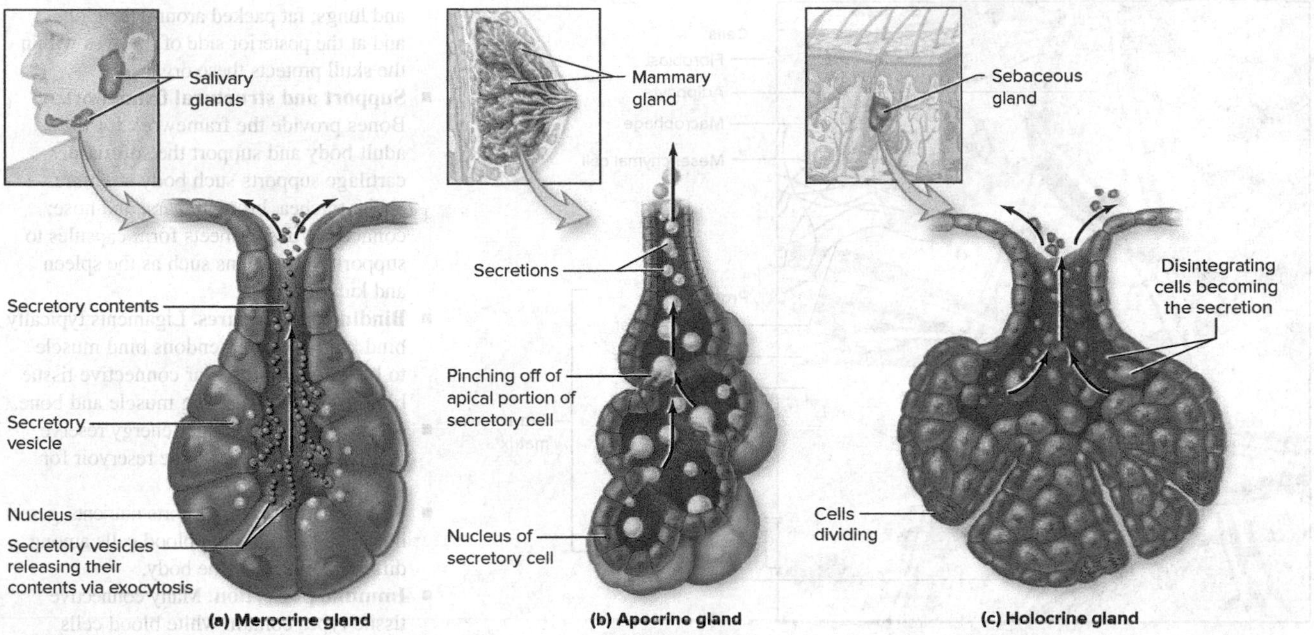

Figure 4.7

Modes of Exocrine Secretion. Exocrine glands use different processes to release their secretory products. (*a*) Merocrine glands secrete products by means of exocytosis at the apical surface of the secretory cells. (*b*) Apocrine gland secretion occurs with the "decapitation" of the apical surface of the cell and the subsequent release of secretory product and some cellular fragments. (*c*) Holocrine gland secretion is produced through the destruction of the secretory cell. Lost cells are replaced by cell division at the base of the gland.

Holocrine (hol′ō-krin; *holos* = whole) **glands** are formed from cells that accumulate a product and then the entire cell disintegrates. Thus, a holocrine secretion is a viscous mixture of cell fragments and the product the cell synthesized prior to its destruction. The ruptured, dead cells are continuously replaced by other epithelial cells undergoing mitosis. The oil-producing glands (sebaceous glands) in the skin are an example of holocrine glands. (So the oily secretion you feel on your skin is actually composed of ruptured, dead cells!)

WHAT DID YOU LEARN?

4 What two main characteristics are used to classify epithelial tissues?

5 Draw the following epithelial tissue types: (a) simple squamous epithelium, (b) simple cuboidal epithelium, (c) simple columnar epithelium, (d) pseudostratified columnar epithelium, (e) stratified squamous epithelium, and (f) transitional epithelium.

6 What are the differences between endocrine glands and exocrine glands?

7 What are the three types of exocrine glands (classified by secretion type), and how does each produce its secretions?

4.2 Connective Tissue

✓ Learning Objectives

6. Explain the characteristics and functions of connective tissue.
7. Describe the characteristics of embryonic connective tissue.
8. Compare connective tissue proper, supporting connective tissue, and fluid connective tissue.
9. Locate and describe where each type of connective tissue is found in the body.

Learning Strategy 4.3

The *apo* part of "apocrine" sounds like "a part." Secretions produced when a part of the cell is pinched off come from apocrine glands. The *hol* part of "holocrine" sounds like the word "whole." *Hol*ocrine gland secretions are produced when the *whole* cell ruptures, dies, and becomes the secretion.

Connective tissue is the most diverse, abundant, widely distributed, and microscopically variable of the tissues. Connective tissue is designed to support, protect, and bind organs. As its name implies, it is the "glue" that binds body structures together. The diversity of connective tissue is obvious when examining some of its types. Connective tissue includes the fibrous tendons and ligaments, body fat, the cartilage that connects the ends of ribs to the sternum, the bones of the skeleton, and the blood.

4.2a Characteristics of Connective Tissue

Although the types of connective tissue are diverse, all of them share three basic components: cells, protein fibers, and ground substance (**figure 4.8**). Their diversity is due to varying proportions of these components as well as to differences in the types and amounts of protein fibers.

Cells

Each type of connective tissue contains specific types of cells. For example, connective tissue proper contains fibroblasts, fat contains

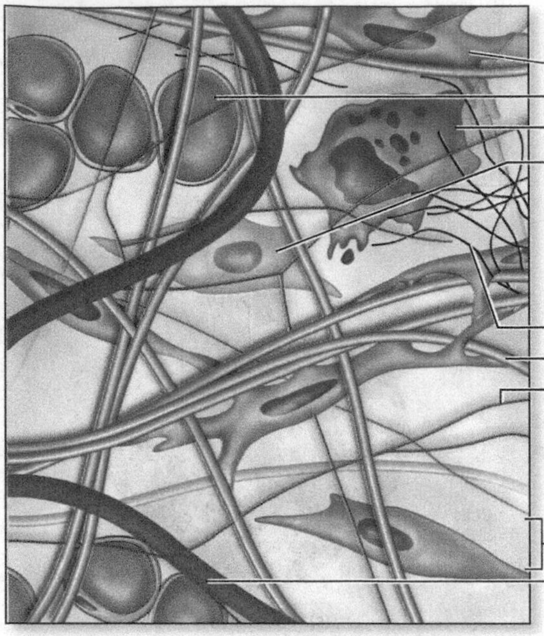
Cells
Fibroblast
Adipocyte
Macrophage
Mesenchymal cell
Protein fibers
Reticular fiber
Collagen fiber
Elastic fiber
Extracellular matrix
Ground substance
Blood vessel

Figure 4.8

Connective Tissue Components and Organization. Connective tissue is composed of cells and an extracellular matrix of protein fibers and ground substance.

adipocytes, cartilage contains chondrocytes, and bone contains osteocytes. Most connective tissue cells are not in direct contact with each other, but are scattered throughout the tissue. This differs markedly from epithelial tissue, whose cells crowd closely together with little to no extracellular matrix surrounding them.

Protein Fibers

Most connective tissue contains protein fibers throughout. These fibers strengthen and support connective tissue. The type and abundance of these fibers indicate to what extent the particular connective tissue is responsible for strength and support. Three types of protein fibers occur in connective tissue: collagen fibers, which are strong and stretch-resistant; elastic fibers, which are flexible and resilient; and reticular fibers, which form an interwoven framework.

Ground Substance

Both the cells and the protein fibers reside within a material called *ground substance.* This nonliving material is produced by the connective tissue cells. It primarily consists of protein and carbohydrate molecules and variable amounts of water. The ground substance may be viscous (as in blood), semisolid (as in cartilage), or solid (as in bone). The viscosity of this ground substance affects movement of cells and other materials through the tissue. Together, the ground substance and the protein fibers form an **extracellular matrix.** Most connective tissues are composed primarily of an extracellular matrix, with relatively small proportions of cells.

4.2b Functions of Connective Tissue

As a group, the many types of connective tissue perform a wide variety of functions, including the following:

- **Physical protection.** The bones of the cranium, sternum, and thoracic cage protect delicate organs, such as the brain, heart, and lungs; fat packed around the kidneys and at the posterior side of the eyes within the skull protects these organs.
- **Support and structural framework.** Bones provide the framework for the adult body and support the soft tissues; cartilage supports such body structures as the trachea, bronchi, ears, and nose; connective tissue sheets form capsules to support body organs such as the spleen and kidneys.
- **Binding of structures.** Ligaments typically bind bone to bone; tendons bind muscle to bone; dense irregular connective tissue binds skin to underlying muscle and bone.
- **Storage.** Fat is the major energy reserve in the body; bone is a large reservoir for calcium and phosphorus.
- **Transport.** Blood transports nutrients, gases, hormones, wastes, and blood cells among different regions of the body.
- **Immune protection.** Many connective tissue types contain white blood cells (leukocytes), which protect the body against disease and mount an immune response when the body is exposed to something foreign. Additionally, the extracellular matrix is a viscous material that interferes with the movement and spread of disease-causing organisms.

WHAT DO YOU THINK?

3 Why does connective tissue contain fewer cells than epithelium? Can you think of some reasons related to the functions of connective tissue?

4.2c Development of Connective Tissue

The primary germ layer, mesoderm, forms all connective tissues. There are two types of embryonic connective tissue: mesenchyme and mucous connective tissue. In the developing embryo, **mesenchyme** (mes'eng-k īm; *mesos* = middle, *enkyma* = infusion) is the first type of connective tissue to emerge. It has star-shaped (stellate) or spindle-shaped mesenchymal cells dispersed within a gel-like ground substance that contains fine, immature protein fibers **(table 4.4*a*)**. In fact, there is proportionately more ground substance than mesenchymal cells in this type of embryonic connective tissue. Mesenchyme is the source of all other connective tissues. Adult connective tissues often house numerous mesenchymal (stem) cells that support the repair of the tissue following damage or injury.

A second type of embryonic connective tissue is **mucous connective tissue** (*Wharton's jelly*). The immature protein fibers in mucous connective tissue are more numerous than those within mesenchyme (table 4.4*b*). Mucous connective tissue is located within the umbilical cord only.

4.2d Classification of Connective Tissue

The connective tissue types present after birth are classified into three broad categories: connective tissue proper, supporting connective tissue, and fluid connective tissue. **Figure 4.9** provides an overview of these tissue types and the subcategories within them, each of which is described in detail next.

Table 4.4 Types of Embryonic Connective Tissue

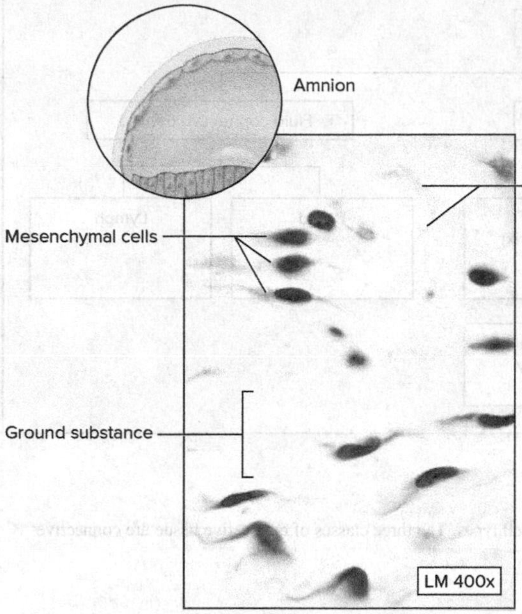

©McGraw-Hill Education/Al Telser, photographer

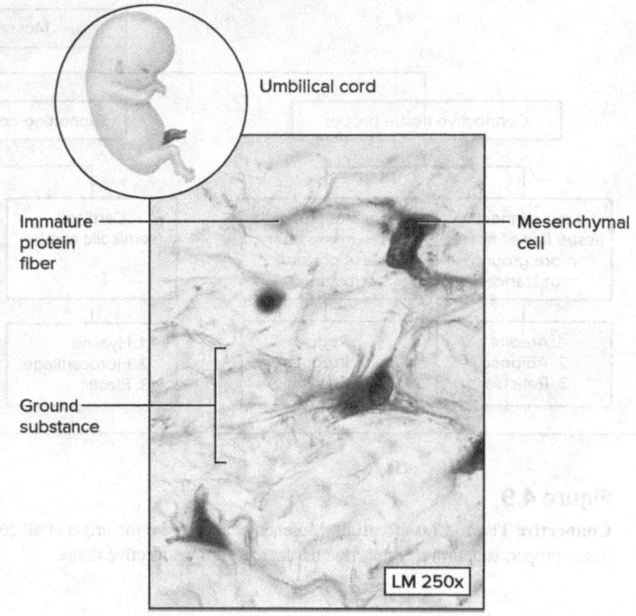

©Ed Reschke

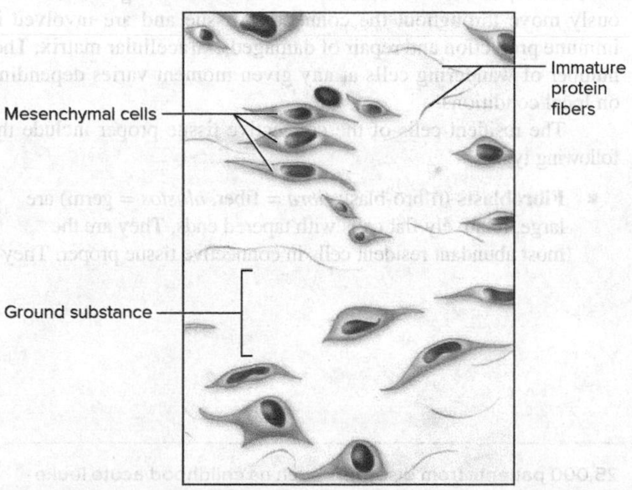

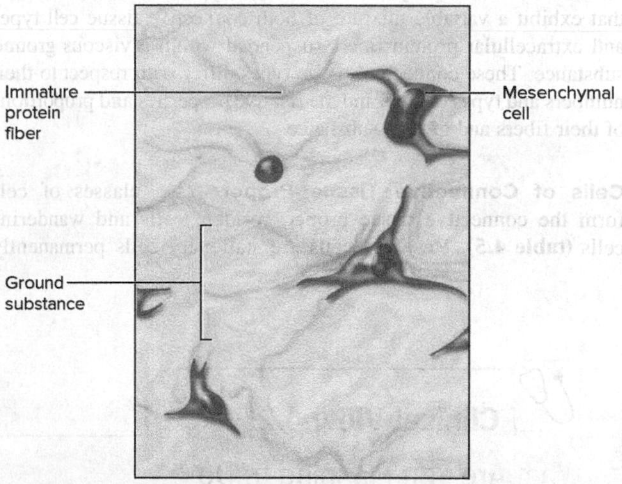

(a) Mesenchyme		(b) Mucous Connective Tissue	
Structure	Ground substance is a viscous gel with some immature protein fibers; mesenchymal cells are stellate or spindle-shaped	**Structure**	Mesenchymal cells scattered within a viscous, gel-like ground substance; immature protein fibers present
Function	Common origin for all other connective tissue types	**Function**	Support of structures in umbilical cord attaching fetus to mother
Location	Throughout the body of the embryo, fetus, and adult	**Location**	Umbilical cord of fetus

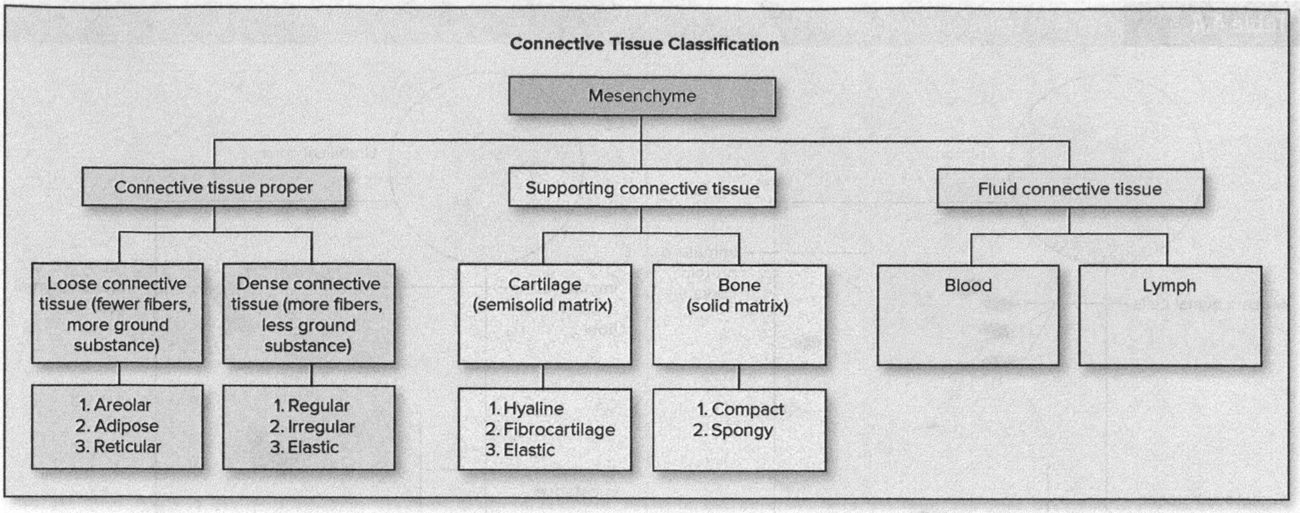

Figure 4.9

Connective Tissue Classification. Mesenchymal cells are the origin of all connective tissue cell types. The three classes of connective tissue are connective tissue proper, supporting connective tissue, and fluid connective tissue.

Connective Tissue Proper

Connective tissue proper includes those types of connective tissue that exhibit a variable mixture of both connective tissue cell types and extracellular protein fibers suspended within a viscous ground substance. These connective tissue types differ with respect to their numbers and types of cells and the relative properties and proportions of their fibers and ground substance.

Cells of Connective Tissue Proper Two classes of cells form the connective tissue proper: resident cells and wandering cells **(table 4.5)**. **Resident cells** are stationary cells permanently contained within the connective tissue. They help support, maintain, and repair the extracellular matrix. **Wandering cells** continuously move throughout the connective tissue and are involved in immune protection and repair of damaged extracellular matrix. The number of wandering cells at any given moment varies depending on local conditions.

The resident cells of the connective tissue proper include the following types:

- **Fibroblasts** (fī′brō-blast; *fibra* = fiber, *blastos* = germ) are large, relatively flat cells with tapered ends. They are the most abundant resident cells in connective tissue proper. They

Clinical View 4.2

What Are You Planning to Do with Your Baby's Umbilical Cord?

A baby's umbilical cord blood contains 10 times the number of stem cells found in a child's bone marrow, and these cells can be used to treat a variety of life-threatening diseases. More importantly, stem cells are easy to collect because leftover blood in the placenta and umbilical cord is a ready, and often discarded, source.

Cord blood (CB) can easily be harvested immediately following the birth of a baby. The specimen can be shipped to a CB bank for testing, processing, and storage. The cells are carefully banked in a cryogenic vault for optimal preservation. Researchers have found that CB stem cells are more tolerated by unrelated recipients than stem cells harvested from other body regions, so potentially they can have widespread benefits. Umbilical cord blood transplants (UCBT) have cured over 25,000 patients from disorders such as childhood acute leukemia and metabolic disorders, leukemia, lymphoma, and genetic disorders. It has potential use for cardiovascular disease and neurological disorders.

As this technology improves, there are still drawbacks. Each CB sample contains relatively few stem cells. It takes longer for the UCBT cells to grow and make healthy cells. The immune system also takes longer to recover, so there is an increased chance of infection. Also, harvesting and storing CB in private banks can be costly.

The odds of a child needing a cord blood stem cell transplant are about 4 in 10,000, or about 0.04%. Also, for many conditions it is not recommended to use the person's own CB. Instead of banking CB for a child's future use, public banking of CB for the general population use appears to be of more benefit.

Table 4.5	Cells of Connective Tissue Proper	
Type of Cell	**Appearance**	**Function**
Resident Cells		Maintain and repair extracellular matrix; store materials
Fibroblasts	Abundant, large, relatively flat cells, often with tapered ends	Produce fibers and ground substance of the extracellular matrix
Adipocytes	Fat cells with a single large lipid droplet; cellular components pushed to one side	Store lipid reserves
Fixed macrophages	Large cells derived from monocytes in blood; reside in extracellular matrix after leaving the blood	Phagocytize foreign materials
Mesenchymal cells	Stellate or spindle-shaped embryonic stem cells	Divide in response to injury to produce new connective tissue cells
Wandering Cells		Repair damaged extracellular matrix; active in immune response
Mast cells	Small cells with a granule-filled cytoplasm	Release histamine and heparin to stimulate local inflammation
Plasma cells	Small cells with a distinct nucleus derived from activated B-lymphocytes	Form antibodies that bind to foreign substances, bacteria, viruses
Free macrophages	Mobile phagocytic cells formed from monocytes of the blood	Phagocytize foreign materials
Other leukocytes	White blood cells that enter connective tissue	Attack foreign materials (lymphocytes) or directly combat bacteria (neutrophils)

produce the fibers and ground substance components of the extracellular matrix.

- **Adipocytes** (ad′i-p ō-sīt; *adip* = fat) are also called *fat cells.* They often appear in small clusters within some types of connective tissue proper. If a larger cluster of these cells dominates an area, the connective tissue is called adipose connective tissue.
- **Fixed macrophages** (mak′r ō-fāj; *makros* = large, *phago* = to eat) are relatively large, irregular-shaped cells with numerous surface folds and projections. They are derived from one type of leukocyte (called a monocyte) and dispersed throughout the extracellular matrix, where they phagocytize damaged cells or pathogens. When the fixed macrophages encounter foreign materials, the cells release chemicals that stimulate the immune system and lure numerous wandering cells involved in body defense to the foreign materials.
- **Mesenchymal cells** are a type of embryonic stem cell contained within connective tissue. As a result of local injury or connective tissue damage, mesenchymal stem cells divide. One of the cells produced is the replacement mesenchymal cell, and the other becomes a committed cell that moves into the damaged or injured area and differentiates into the type of connective tissue cell that is needed.

The wandering cells of the connective tissue proper are primarily types of **leukocytes** (lū′kō-sīt; *leukos* = white), also called *white blood cells.* As you will learn in greater detail in section 21.3b, there are several different types of leukocytes, and each type performs certain functions that help us overcome illness or fight foreign invaders in our bodies. Connective tissue proper contains specific types of wandering cells, including the following:

- **Mast cells.** These small, mobile cells contain a granule-filled cytoplasm. They are usually found close to blood vessels; they secrete heparin to inhibit blood clotting, and histamine to dilate blood vessels and increase blood flow.
- **Plasma cells.** When B-lymphocytes (a type of white blood cell) are activated by exposure to foreign materials, the cells become plasma cells. These cells are small "factories" that synthesize disease-fighting proteins called **antibodies** (an′t ē-bod′ ē; *anti* = against, *bodig* = corpus). Usually, plasma cells are found in the intestinal walls, spleen, and lymph nodes.
- **Free macrophages.** These mobile, phagocytic cells are formed from monocytes (a type of white blood cell) that migrate out of the bloodstream. They wander through connective tissue and engulf and destroy any bacteria, foreign particles, or damaged cells and debris they encounter.
- **Other leukocytes.** In addition to the leukocytes just mentioned, other leukocytes migrate through the blood vessel walls into the connective tissue where they spend most of their time. The majority of these leukocytes are neutrophils, a type of white blood cell that seeks out and phagocytizes bacteria. The rest are lymphocytes, which attack and destroy foreign materials.

Protein Fibers of Connective Tissue Proper As mentioned previously, the three types of protein fibers in connective tissue proper are collagen fibers, elastic fibers, and reticular fibers. Fibroblasts synthesize the components of all three fiber types, and then secrete these protein subunits into the interstitial fluid. The subunits combine or aggregate within the matrix and form the completed fiber.

Collagen (kol′lă-jen; *koila* = glue, *gen* = producing) **fibers** are long, unbranched, "cablelike" extracellular fibers composed of the protein collagen. They are strong, flexible, and resistant to stretching. Collagen forms about 25% of the body's protein, making it the most abundant protein in the body. In fresh tissue, collagen fibers appear white, and thus they are often called *white fibers.* In tissue sections stained with hematoxylin and eosin to give contrast, they appear pink. The parallel structure and arrangement of collagen bundles in tendons and ligaments allows them to withstand enormous forces in one direction.

Elastic (ē-las′tik; *elastreo* = drive) **fibers** contain the protein elastin and are thinner than collagen fibers. They stretch easily, branch, rejoin, and appear wavy. The coiled structure of elastin allows it to stretch and recoil like a rubber band when the deforming force is withdrawn. Elastic fibers permit the skin, lungs, and arteries to return to their normal shape after being stretched. Fresh

Table 4.6	Connective Tissue Proper		
Type	**Structure**	**Function**	**Location**
Loose Connective Tissue	Relatively fewer cells and fibers than in dense connective tissue; fibers are loosely arranged		
Areolar connective tissue	Fibroblasts; lesser amounts of collagen and elastic fibers; viscous ground substance	Packs around and binds organs	Surrounding nerves, vessels; subcutaneous layer
Adipose connective tissue	Adipocytes	Protects; stores fat; insulates	Subcutaneous layer; surrounding kidney and selected other organs
Reticular connective tissue	Meshwork of reticular fibers	Forms stroma of lymphatic organs	Stroma of spleen, liver, lymph nodes, bone marrow
Dense Connective Tissue	Higher proportion of fibers to ground substance; protein fibers densely packed together		
Dense regular connective tissue	Densely packed collagen fibers are parallel to direction of stress	Provides great strength and flexibility primarily in a single direction	Tendons and ligaments
Dense irregular connective tissue	Densely packed collagen fibers are interwoven; fibers are irregularly clumped together and project in all directions	Provides tensile strength in all directions	Dermis of skin; capsules of organs
Elastic connective tissue	Elastic and collagen fibers are arranged irregularly	Provides framework and supports organs	Walls of large arteries

elastic fibers have a yellowish color and are called yellow fibers. In tissue sections, elastic fibers are visible only when stained with special stains, such as Verhoff stain, which makes elastic fibers appear black.

Reticular (re-tik′y ū-lăr; *reticulum* = small net) **fibers** are thinner than collagen fibers. They contain the same protein subunits that collagen has, but their subunits are combined in a different way and they are coated with a glycoprotein (a protein with some carbohydrate attached to it). These fibers form a branching, interwoven framework that is tough but flexible. Reticular fibers are especially abundant in the **stroma,** a structural connective tissue framework in organs such as the lymph nodes, spleen, and liver. The meshlike arrangement of the reticular fibers permits them to physically support organs and resist external forces that may damage the organ's cells and blood vessels.

Ground Substance of Connective Tissue Proper The cellular and fibrous components of the connective tissue proper are suspended within the ground substance, a colorless, featureless, viscous solution. Ground substance usually has a gelatinous, almost rubbery consistency due to the mixture of its component molecules, which vary both in their size and in their proportions of proteins and carbohydrates. The different molecules in the ground substance are called glycosaminoglycans, proteoglycans, and structural glycoproteins. Note that this viscous ground substance is not static. Fluid, molecules, and cells constantly travel through this material as they move among cells, blood vessels, and lymph vessels.

Categories of Connective Tissue Proper

Connective tissue proper is divided into two broad categories: loose connective tissue and dense connective tissue (**table 4.6**). This classification is based upon the relative proportions of cells, protein fibers, and ground substance.

Loose Connective Tissue **Loose connective tissue** contains relatively fewer cells and protein fibers than dense connective tissue. The protein fibers in loose connective tissue are loosely arranged rather than tightly packed together. Usually, this tissue occupies the spaces between and around organs. Loose connective tissues support the overlying epithelia and provide cushioning around organs, support and surround blood vessels and nerves, store lipids, and provide a medium for the diffusion of materials. Thus, loose connective tissues act as the body's "packing material." There are three types of loose connective tissue: areolar connective tissue, adipose connective tissue, and reticular connective tissue.

Areolar (ă-rē′ō-lăr) **connective tissue** is highly variable in appearance and the least specialized connective tissue in the body **(table 4.7*a*)**. It has a loosely organized array of collagen and elastic fibers and an abundant distribution of blood vessels. Areolar connective tissue contains all of the cell types of connective tissue proper, although the predominant cell is the fibroblast. A viscous ground substance occupies the spaces between fibers and accounts for most of the volume of areolar connective tissue. The ground substance cushions shocks, and the loosely organized fibers ensure that this type of connective tissue can be distorted without damage. Additionally, the elastic properties of this tissue promote independent movements. For instance, under the dermis of the skin is a superficial layer of areolar connective tissue, thus tugging on the skin of the leg, for example, does not affect the underlying muscle.

Areolar connective tissue is found nearly everywhere in the body. It surrounds nerves, blood vessels, and individual muscle cells. It is also a major component of the subcutaneous layer deep to the skin.

Adipose connective tissue (commonly known as *fat*) is a loose connective tissue composed primarily of cells called **adipocytes** (table 4.7 *b*). Adipocytes (white fat) usually range from 70 μm to 120 μm in diameter. In life, adipocytes are filled with one lipid droplet. On a histology slide, the lipid has been extracted during preparation, so all that is left is the plasma membrane of the adipocyte, with the nucleus pushed to the side of a round, clear space looking much like a ring.

Adipose connective tissue serves as packing around structures and provides padding, cushions shocks, and acts as an insulator to slow heat loss through the skin. Adipose connective tissue is commonly found throughout the body in such diverse locations as a fat capsule surrounding the kidney, the pericardial and abdominopelvic cavities, and the subcutaneous layer.

Clinical View 4.3

Systemic Lupus Erythematosus

Systemic lupus erythematosus (SLE), also known simply as *lupus,* is an autoimmune disorder that causes chronic inflammation of body tissues, which cycles between relapses and remissions. It can affect many organs, but the most commonly affected parts of the body are the skin, joints, kidneys, nervous system, and blood cells. Symptoms include joint pain, fatigue, nonspecific fever, sunlight sensitivity, and hair loss. About 50% of the affected individuals exhibit a malar, or "butterfly," rash over the bridge of their nose and their cheeks. During childbearing years, about 11 times more women than men are diagnosed with SLE. Twin studies have shown that there is a genetic component to this disorder, but it is still unknown what causes SLE. Worldwide studies of incidence suggest that there are strong indications of environmental influences. There is no cure for SLE, only treatment of the symptoms. Treatment is tailored to the individual, and early detection and monitoring of individuals with this disorder can improve quality of life.

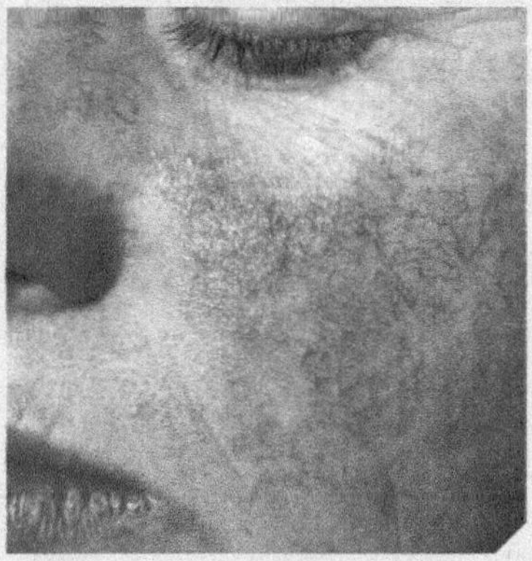

Classic malar rash of SLE.
BSIP/Science Source

Fat is a primary energy store for the body. The amount of stored fat fluctuates as the adipose cells either increase their amount of stored fat (called *lipogenesis*) or decrease their amount of stored fat (called *lipolysis*). But although there is a constant turnover of the stored fat, an equilibrium is usually reached, and the amount of stored fat and the number of adipocytes are normally quite stable in an individual. Although adipocytes cannot divide, mesenchymal cells can provide additional fat cells if the body has excess nutrients. Thus, even after a surgical procedure to reduce the amount of body fat, such as liposuction, the mesenchymal stem cells may replace adipocytes to store excess fat in the body.

Reticular connective tissue contains a meshwork of reticular fibers, fibroblasts, and leukocytes (table 4.7*c*). This connective tissue forms the stroma of many lymphatic organs, such as the spleen, thymus, lymph nodes, and bone marrow.

Dense Connective Tissue **Dense connective tissue** is composed primarily of protein fibers and has proportionately less ground substance than does loose connective tissue. Dense connective tissue is sometimes called *collagenous tissue* because collagen fibers are the dominant fiber type. There are three categories of dense connective tissue: (1) dense regular connective tissue, (2) dense irregular connective tissue, and (3) elastic connective tissue.

Dense regular connective tissue has collagen fibers that are packed tightly and aligned parallel to an applied force (**table 4.8*a***). This tissue type is found in tendons and ligaments, where stress is applied in a single direction. Dense regular connective tissue has few blood vessels, and thus it takes a long time to heal following injury, because a rich blood supply is necessary for good healing.

In **dense irregular connective tissue,** individual bundles of collagen fibers extend in all directions in a scattered meshwork. These bundles of collagen fibers appear in clumps throughout the tissue, rather than arranged in parallel as seen in dense regular connective tissue (table 4.8*b*). Dense irregular connective tissue provides support and resistance to stress in multiple directions.

An example of dense irregular connective tissue is the deep portion of the dermis, which lends strength to the skin and permits it to withstand applied forces from any direction. Dense irregular connective tissue also forms a supporting layer around cartilage (called the perichondrium) and around bone (called the periosteum), except at joints. In addition, it forms a thick, fibrous capsule that supports and houses internal organs, such as the liver, kidneys, and spleen.

Elastic connective tissue has branching elastic fibers and more fibroblasts than loose connective tissue in addition to packed collagen fibers (table 4.8*c*). The elastic fibers provide resilience and the ability to deform and then return to normal shape. Examples of structures composed of elastic connective tissue are the vocal cords, the suspensory ligament of the penis, and some ligaments of the spinal column. Elastic connective tissue also is present as wavy sheets in the walls of large and medium arteries.

WHAT DO YOU THINK?

4. What type of connective tissue have you damaged when you sprain your ankle? How does the tissue type relate to the length it takes your sprained ankle to heal?

Learning Strategy 4.4

Ask the following questions to help distinguish the types of connective tissue proper viewed with light microscopy:

1. Is the connective tissue loose or dense? Loose connective tissue has fewer protein fibers and relatively more ground substance. Dense connective tissue has more protein fibers and relatively little ground substance.
2. If the tissue is dense, are the protein fibers in clumps or in parallel? Protein fibers in clumps indicate dense irregular connective tissue. Protein fibers that run in parallel, like lasagna noodles stacked on top of one another, indicate dense regular connective tissue. Elastic connective tissue may resemble dense regular connective tissue, but its fibers are not as neatly arranged.
3. If the tissue is loose, what types of cells are present? Areolar connective tissue primarily contains fibroblasts, whereas adipose connective tissue contains adipocytes. The presence of numerous leukocytes may indicate reticular connective tissue.

Table 4.7 Connective Tissue Proper: Loose Connective Tissue

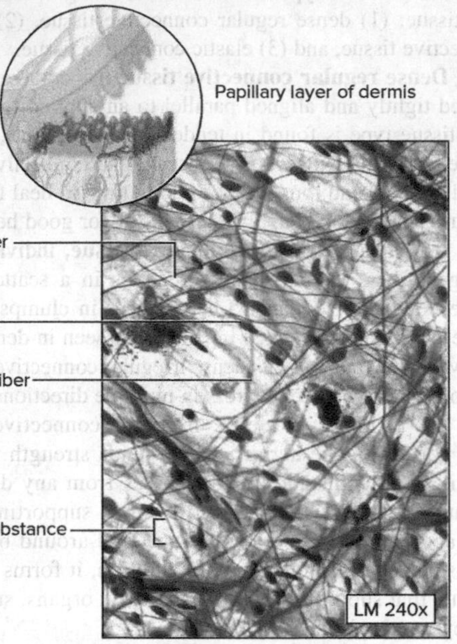
Papillary layer of dermis
Elastic fiber
Fibroblast
Collagen fiber
Ground substance
LM 240x

©McGraw-Hill Education/Al Telser, photographer

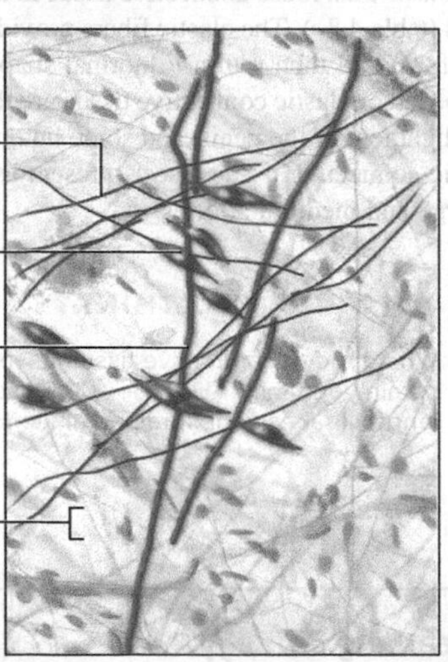
Elastic fiber
Fibroblast
Collagen fiber
Ground substance

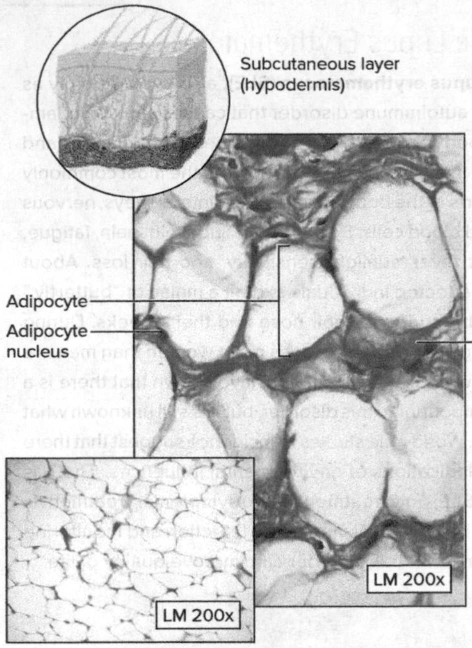
Subcutaneous layer (hypodermis)
Adipocyte
Adipocyte nucleus
Blood vessel
LM 200x
LM 200x

©McGraw-Hill Education/Al Telser, photographer

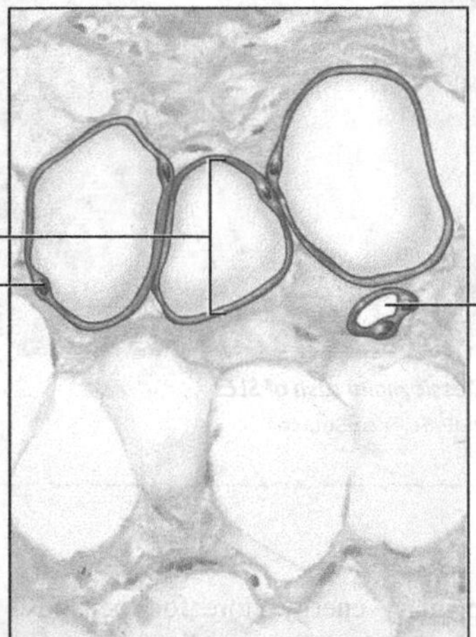
Adipocyte
Adipocyte nucleus
Blood vessel

(a) Areolar Connective Tissue		**(b) Adipose Connective Tissue**	
Structure	Abundant vascularized ground substance is gel-like; scattered fibroblasts; many blood vessels	**Structure**	Closely packed adipocytes (fat cells); nucleus squeezed to one side by large fat droplet
Function	Surrounds and protects tissues and organs; loosely binds epithelia to deeper tissues; provides nerve and blood vessel packing	**Function**	Stores energy; protects, cushions, and insulates
Location	Papillary layer of dermis, subcutaneous layer under skin; surrounds organs	**Location**	Subcutaneous layer; covers and surrounds some organs

Supporting Connective Tissue

Cartilage and bone are types of **supporting connective tissue** because they form a strong, durable framework that protects and supports the soft body tissues. The extracellular matrix in supporting connective tissue contains many protein fibers and a ground substance that ranges from semisolid to solid. In general, cartilage has a semisolid extracellular matrix, and bone has a solid extracellular matrix.

Cartilage **Cartilage** has a firm, gel-like extracellular matrix composed of both protein fibers and ground substance. Mature cartilage

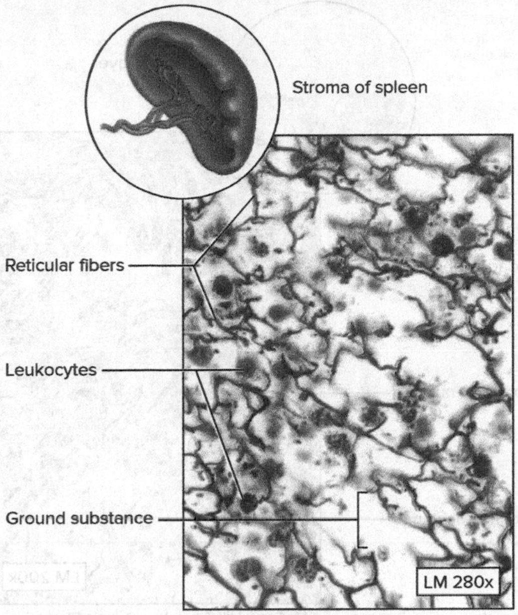
Stroma of spleen
Reticular fibers
Leukocytes
Ground substance
LM 280x

©McGraw-Hill Education/Al Telser, photographer

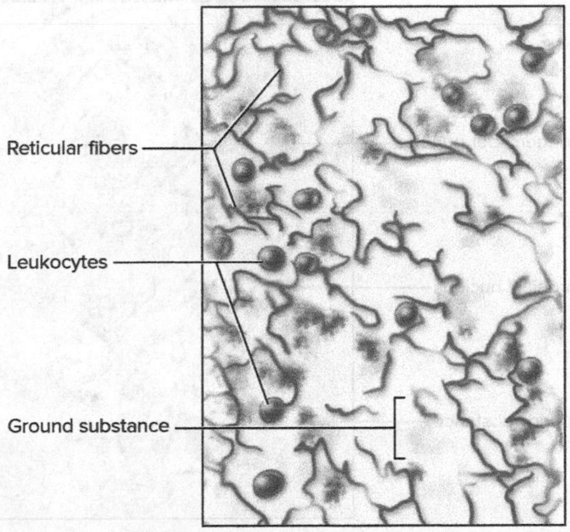
Reticular fibers
Leukocytes
Ground substance

(c) Reticular Connective Tissue	
Structure	Ground substance is gel-like liquid; scattered arrangement of reticular fibers, fibroblasts, and leukocytes
Function	Provides supportive framework for spleen, lymph nodes, thymus, bone marrow
Location	Forms stroma of spleen, lymph nodes, thymus, bone marrow

cells are called **chondrocytes** (kon′dr ō-sīt; *chondros* = gristle or cartilage, *cytos* = a hollow [cell]). They occupy small spaces called **lacunae** (lă-kū′nē; *lacus* = a hollow, a lake), within the extracellular matrix. The physical properties of cartilage vary with the extracellular matrix contents. Cartilage is stronger and more resilient than any previously discussed connective tissue type, and it provides more flexibility than bone. Collagen fibers within the matrix give cartilage its tensile strength; its resilience is attributed to elastic fibers and variations in the kinds and amounts of ground substance components, including water.

Cartilage is found in areas of the body that need support and must withstand deformation, such as the tip of the nose or the external part of the ear (auricle).

Chondrocytes produce a chemical that prevents blood vessel formation and growth within the extracellular matrix. Thus, mature cartilage is avascular, meaning without blood vessels. Therefore, the chondrocytes must exchange nutrients and waste products with blood vessels outside of the cartilage by diffusion. Cartilage usually has a covering called the **perichondrium** (per′i-kon′dr ē-ŭm; *peri* = around). Two distinct layers form the perichondrium: an outer, fibrous region of dense irregular connective tissue and an inner, cellular layer. The fibrous layer provides protection and mechanical support, and secures the perichondrium to the cartilage and to other structures. The cellular layer contains stem cells (chondroblasts) necessary for the growth and maintenance of the cartilage.

Types of Cartilage Three major types of cartilage occur in the body: hyaline cartilage, fibrocartilage, and elastic cartilage. The cartilage types exhibit differences in density and dispersal of chondrocytes within the extracellular matrix.

Hyaline (hī′ă-lin, -lēn; *hyalos* = glass) **cartilage** is the most common type of cartilage and also the weakest. It provides its support through flexibility and resilience. Hyaline cartilage is surrounded by perichondrium. It is named for its clear, glassy appearance under the microscope. The chondrocytes within their lacunae are irregularly scattered throughout the extracellular matrix **(table 4.9*a*)**. However, the collagen within the matrix is not readily seen by light microscopy. If the hyaline cartilage tissue is stained by hematoxylin and eosin and then examined with light microscopy, the tissue resembles carbonated grape soda, where the lacunae represent the bubbles in the soda.

Hyaline cartilage has many functions in addition to its primary one of supporting soft tissue. It forms most of the fetal skeleton and is a model for most future bone growth. The cartilage at the articular ends of long bones allows the bones in a joint to move freely and easily. Hyaline cartilage is found in many other areas of the body, including the nose, trachea, most of the larynx, costal cartilage (the cartilage attached to the ribs), and the articular ends of long bones.

Fibrocartilage (fī′brō-kar′ti-l ăj; *fibro* = fiber) has numerous coarse, readily visible fibers in its extracellular matrix (table 4.9*b*). The fibers are arranged as irregular bundles between large chondrocytes. There is only a sparse amount of ground substance, and often the chondrocytes are arranged in parallel rows. The densely interwoven collagen fibers contribute to the extreme durability of this type of cartilage. It has no perichondrium because stress applied at the surface of the fibrocartilage would destroy this tissue layer.

Fibrocartilage is found in the intervertebral discs (circular structures between adjacent vertebrae), the pubic symphysis (a pad of cartilage between the anterior parts of the pelvic bones), and the menisci (C-shaped cartilage pads) of the knee joint. In these locations, fibrocartilage acts as a shock absorber and resists compression.

Elastic cartilage is so named because it contains numerous elastic fibers in its matrix (table 4.9*c*). The higher concentration of elastic fibers in this cartilage causes it to appear yellow in fresh sections. The chondrocytes of elastic cartilage are almost indistinguishable from those of hyaline cartilage. They are typically closely

Table 4.8 Connective Tissue Proper: Dense Connective Tissue

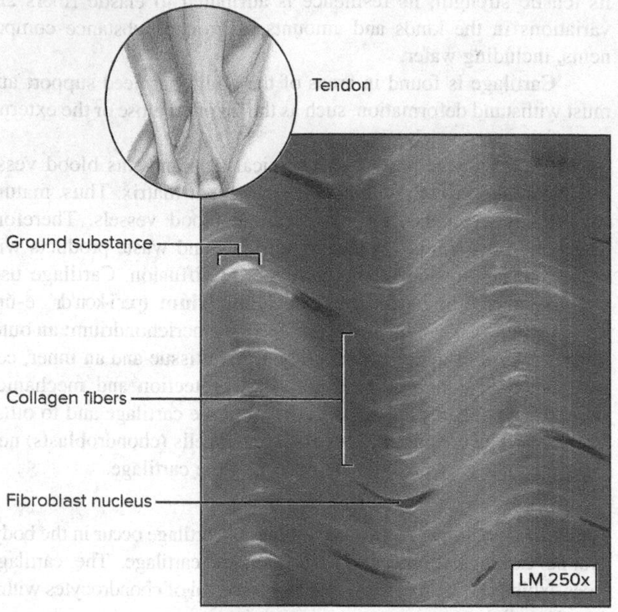

Tendon
Ground substance
Collagen fibers
Fibroblast nucleus
LM 250x

©Ed Reschke

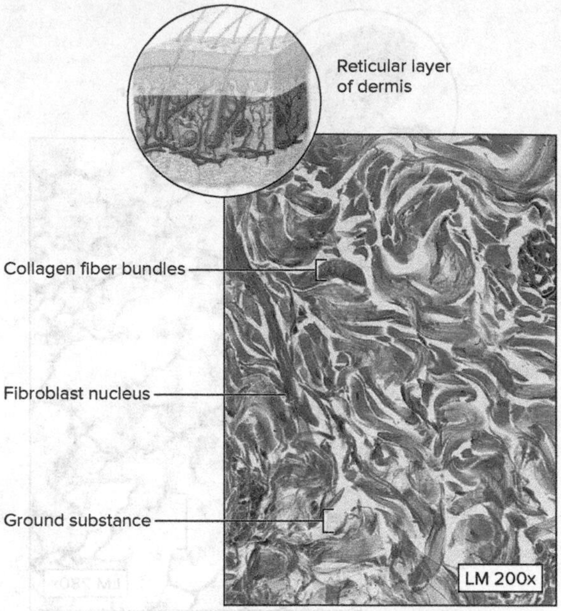

Reticular layer of dermis
Collagen fiber bundles
Fibroblast nucleus
Ground substance
LM 200x

©McGraw-Hill Education/Dennis Strete, photographer

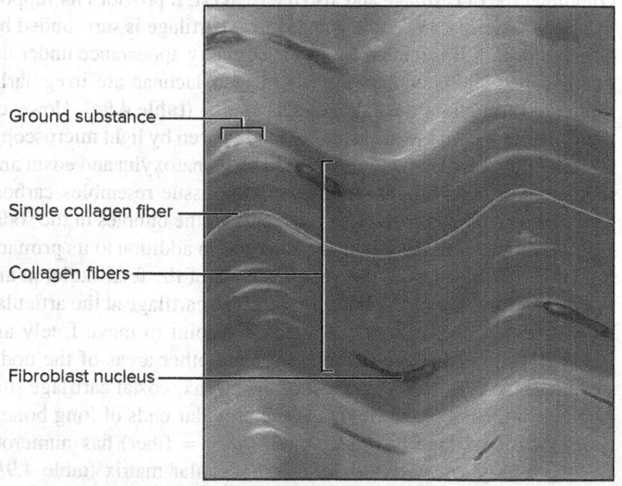

Ground substance
Single collagen fiber
Collagen fibers
Fibroblast nucleus

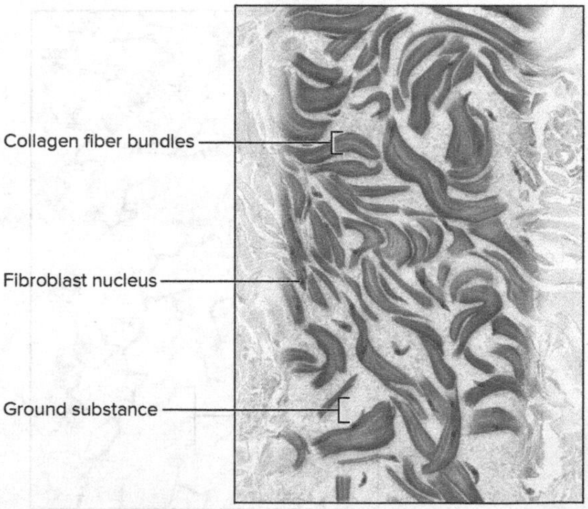

Collagen fiber bundles
Fibroblast nucleus
Ground substance

(a) Dense Regular Connective Tissue

Structure	Densely packed, parallel collagen fibers; fibroblast nuclei squeezed between layers of fibers; scarce ground substance
Function	Attaches muscle to bone and bone to bone; resists stress applied in one direction
Location	Tendons, most ligaments

(b) Dense Irregular Connective Tissue

Structure	Predominantly collagen fibers, randomly arranged and clumped together; fibroblasts in spaces among fibers; more ground substance than in dense regular connective tissue
Function	Withstands stresses applied in all directions; durable
Location	Dermis; periosteum covering bone; perichondrium covering cartilage, organ capsules

packed and surrounded by only a small amount of extracellular matrix. The elastic fibers are both denser and more highly branched in the central region of the extracellular matrix, where they form a weblike mesh around the chondrocytes within the lacunae. These fibers ensure that elastic cartilage is extremely resilient and flexible. Elastic cartilage is surrounded by a perichondrium.

Elastic cartilage is found in the epiglottis (a structure in the larynx that prevents swallowed food and fluids from entering the trachea) and in the external ear. You can see for yourself how flexible elastic cartilage is by performing this experiment: Fold your external ear over your finger, hold for 10 seconds, and release. You will notice that your ear springs back to its original shape because the elastic

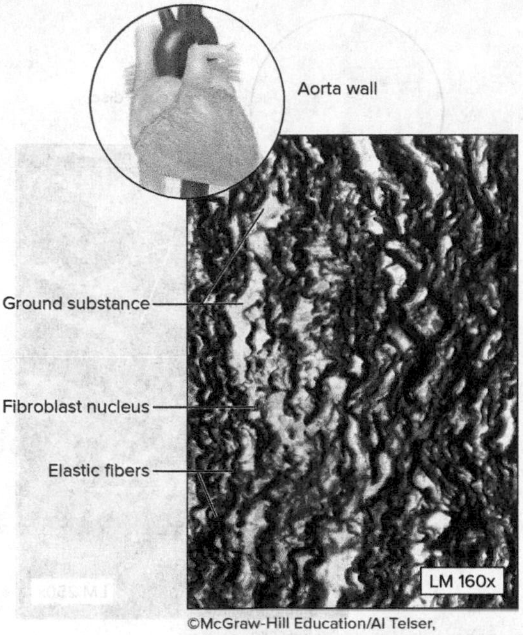
Aorta wall
Ground substance
Fibroblast nucleus
Elastic fibers
LM 160x

©McGraw-Hill Education/Al Telser, photographer

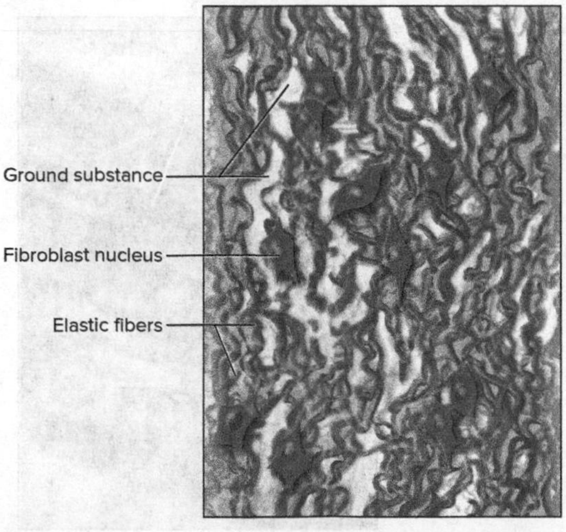
Ground substance
Fibroblast nucleus
Elastic fibers

(c) Elastic Connective Tissue	
Structure	Predominantly freely branching elastic fibers; fibroblasts occupy some spaces between fibers
Function	Allows stretching of some organs
Location	Walls of elastic arteries; trachea; bronchial tubes; true vocal cords; suspensory ligaments of penis

cartilage resists the deformational pressure you applied. (This also explains why our ears aren't permanently misshapen if we sleep on them in an unusual way!)

Bone **Bone connective tissue** (or *osseous connective tissue*) makes up the mass of most of the body structures referred to as "bones." Bone is more solid than cartilage and provides greater support. Section 6.3 provides a detailed description of the histology of bone connective tissue.

About one-third of the dry weight of bone is composed of organic components (collagen fibers and different protein-carbohydrate molecules), and two-thirds consists of inorganic components (a mixture of calcium salts, primarily calcium phosphate). Bone derives its remarkable properties from its combination of components: Its organic portions provide some flexibility and tensile strength, and its inorganic portions provide compressional strength. The minerals are deposited onto the collagen fibers, resulting in a structure that is strong and durable but not brittle. Almost all bone surfaces (except for the surfaces of the joints of long bones) are covered by a dense irregular connective tissue called the **periosteum** (per'ē-os'tē-ŭm; *osteon* = bone), which is similar to the perichondrium of cartilage.

There are two forms of bone connective tissue: compact bone and spongy bone. Both types are typically found in all bones of the body. **Compact bone** appears solid but is in fact perforated by a number of vascular canals. It usually forms the hard outer shell of the bone. **Spongy bone** (or *cancellous bone*) is located within the interior of a bone. Instead of being completely solid, spongy bone contains spaces, and the bone connective tissue forms a latticework structure that is very strong, yet lightweight. This design allows our bones to be both strong and lightweight at the same time.

Compact bone has an ordered histologic pattern **(table 4.10)**. It is formed from cylindrical structures called **osteons,** or *Haversian systems.* Osteons run parallel to the shafts of long bones. Each osteon contains concentric rings of bone called **lamellae** (lă-mel'ē; *lamina* = plate), which encircle a **central canal** (*Haversian canal*). Blood vessels and nerves travel through the central canals of osteons. Lacunae between neighboring concentric lamellae house bone cells, called **osteocytes** (os'tē-ō-sīt). Diffusion of nutrients and waste products cannot occur through the hard matrix of bone, so osteocytes must communicate with one another, and ultimately with the blood vessels in the central canal, through minute passageways in the matrix called **canaliculi** (kan-ă-lik'y ū-lī; *canalis* = canal). Together, all of the canaliculi form a branching network throughout compact bone for the exchange of materials between the blood vessels and the osteocytes within the lacunae.

Bone serves a variety of functions. Bones provide levers for movement when the muscles attached to them contract, and they protect soft tissues and vital body organs. The hard matrix of bone stores important minerals, such as calcium and phosphorus. Finally, many areas of spongy bone contain **hematopoietic** (hē'ma-tō-poy-et'ik; *hemat* = blood) **cells,** which form reticular connective tissue that is responsible for producing blood cells (a process called *hematopoiesis*). Thus, the connective tissue that produces our blood cells is stored within our spongy bone.

Fluid Connective Tissue

There are two types of fluid connective tissue: blood and lymph. **Blood** is a fluid connective tissue composed in part of cells and cell fragments called formed elements. These formed elements are **erythrocytes** (red blood cells), **leukocytes** (white blood cells), and **platelets** **(table 4.11)**. The erythrocytes transport oxygen and carbon dioxide between the lungs and the body tissues, while some leukocytes mount an adaptive immune response and others respond to foreign pathogens such as bacteria, viruses, fungi, and parasites. Platelets are involved in blood clotting.

Table 4.9 Supporting Connective Tissue: Cartilage

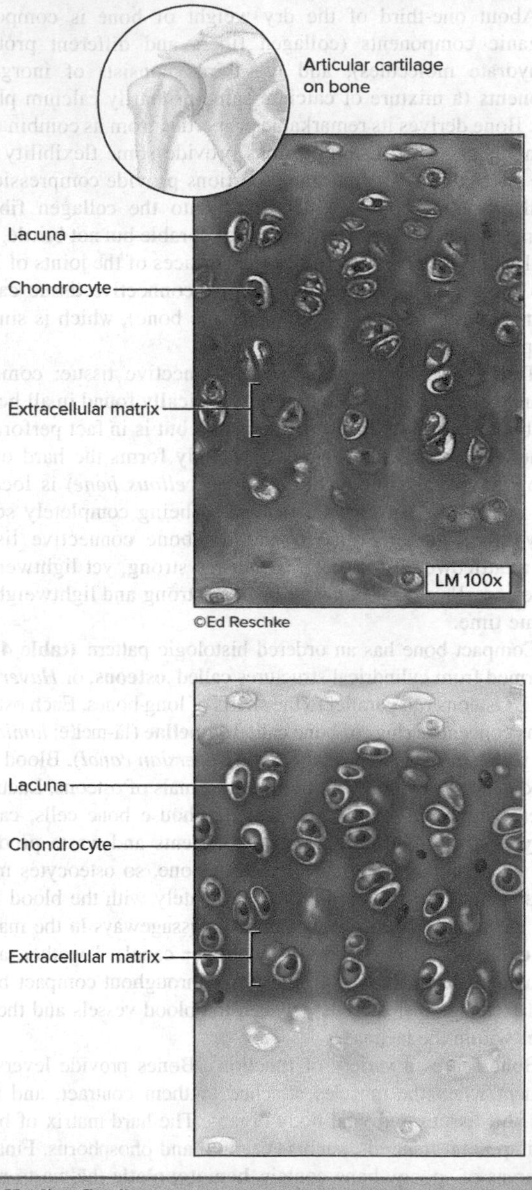
Articular cartilage on bone
Lacuna
Chondrocyte
Extracellular matrix
LM 100x
©Ed Reschke
Lacuna
Chondrocyte
Extracellular matrix

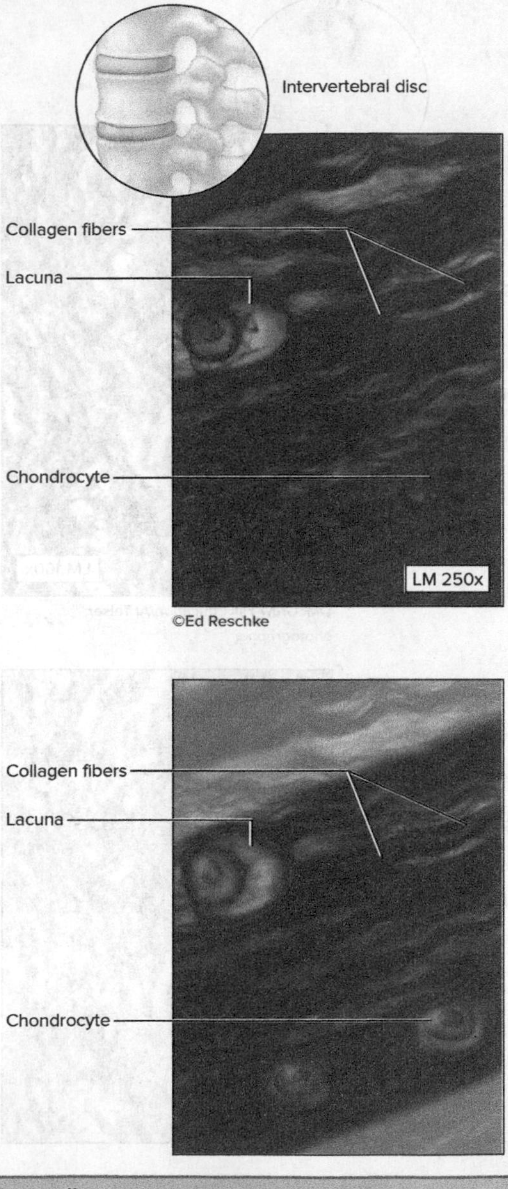
Intervertebral disc
Collagen fibers
Lacuna
Chondrocyte
LM 250x
©Ed Reschke
Collagen fibers
Lacuna
Chondrocyte

(a) Hyaline Cartilage	
Structure	Glassy-appearing matrix; lacunae house chondrocytes; usually covered by perichondrium
Function	Smooth surfaces for movement at joints; model for bone growth; supports soft tissue
Location	Covers articular ends of long bones; most of fetal skeleton; costal cartilage; most of the larynx, trachea, nose

(b) Fibrocartilage	
Structure	Readily visible, parallel collagen fibers in matrix; lacunae house chondrocytes; no perichondrium
Function	Resists compression; absorbs shock in some joints
Location	Intervertebral discs; pubic symphysis; menisci of knee joints

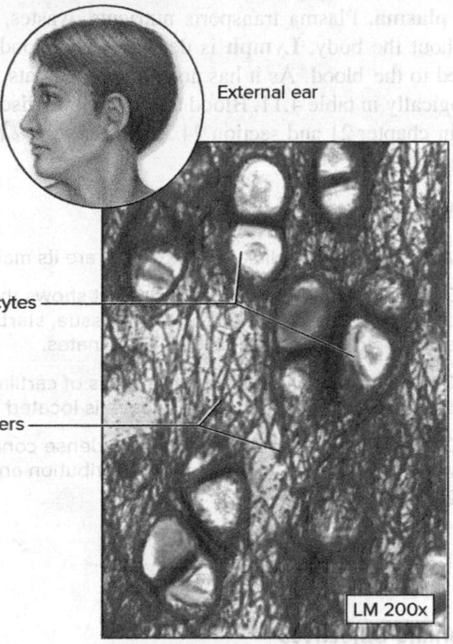
External ear
Chondrocytes
Elastic fibers
LM 200x

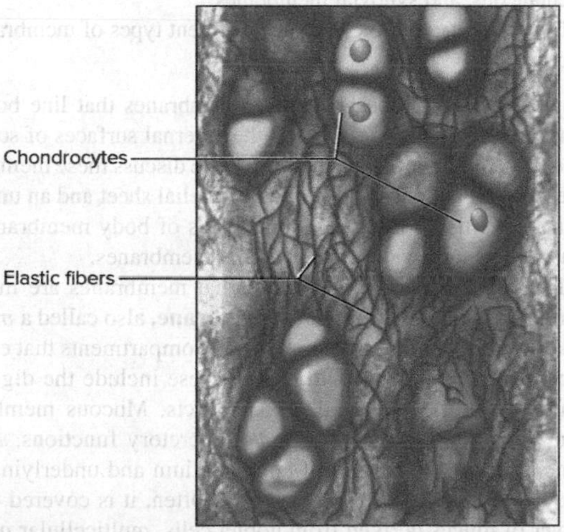
Chondrocytes
Elastic fibers

(c) Elastic Cartilage	
Structure	Contains abundant elastic fibers; elastic fibers form weblike mesh around lacunae; perichondrium present
Function	Maintains structure and shape while permitting extensive flexibility
Location	External ear; epiglottis of the larynx

Table 4.10 Supporting Connective Tissue: Bone

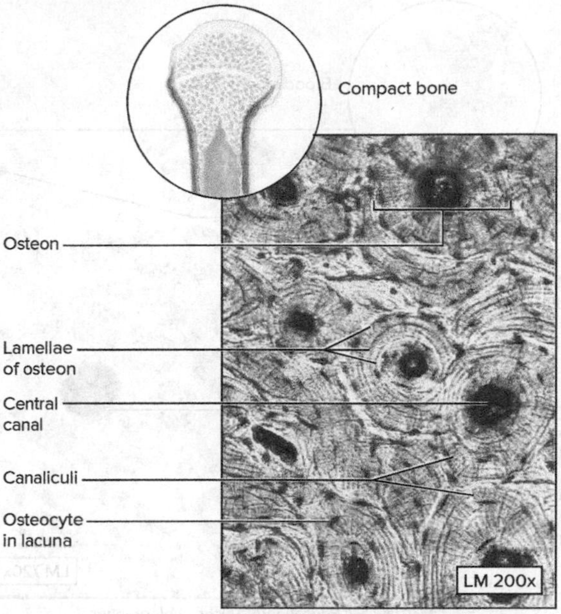
Compact bone
Osteon
Lamellae of osteon
Central canal
Canaliculi
Osteocyte in lacuna
LM 200x

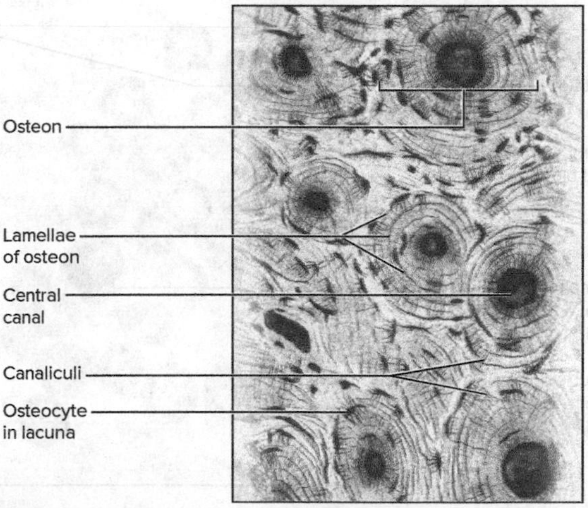
Osteon
Lamellae of osteon
Central canal
Canaliculi
Osteocyte in lacuna

Bone	
Structure	*Compact bone:* Calcified matrix arranged in osteons (concentric lamellae arranged around a central canal containing blood vessels) *Spongy bone:* Lacks the organization of compact bone; contains macroscopic spaces; bone arranged in a meshwork pattern
Function	Supports soft structures; protects vital organs; provides levers for movement; stores calcium and phosphorus. Spongy bone is the site of hematopoiesis.
Location	Bones of the body

Table 4.11 Fluid Connective Tissue: Blood[1]

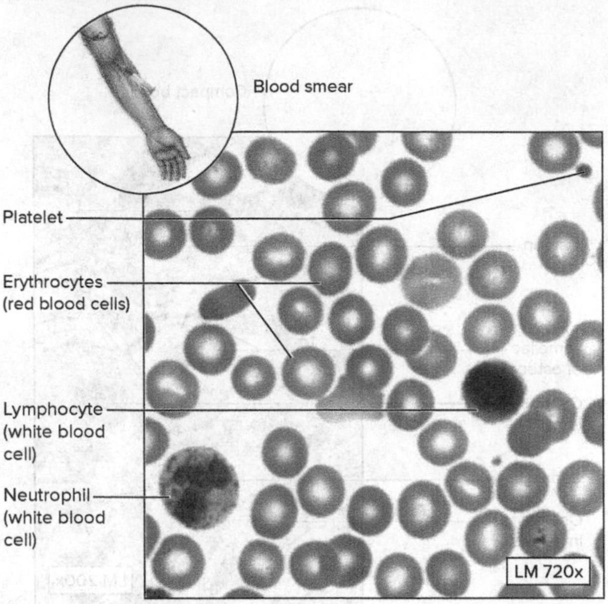
Blood smear
Platelet
Erythrocytes (red blood cells)
Lymphocyte (white blood cell)
Neutrophil (white blood cell)
LM 720x

©McGraw-Hill Education/Al Telser, photographer

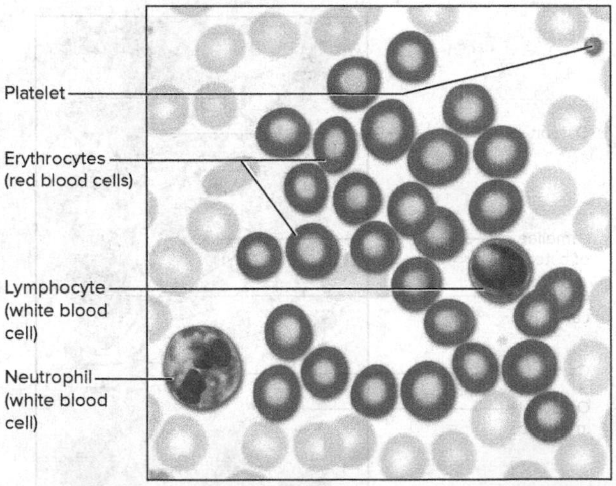
Platelet
Erythrocytes (red blood cells)
Lymphocyte (white blood cell)
Neutrophil (white blood cell)

Blood	
Structure	Contains erythrocytes, leukocytes, and platelets; soluble (dissolved) protein fibers and a watery ground substance form a fluid extracellular matrix called plasma
Function	Erythrocytes transport oxygen and some carbon dioxide. Leukocytes initiate and control immune response. Plasma contains clotting elements to stop blood loss. Platelets help with blood clotting. Plasma transports nutrients, wastes, and hormones throughout the body.
Location	Primarily within blood vessels (arteries, veins, capillaries) and the heart; leukocytes are also located in lymphatic organs and can migrate to infected or inflamed tissues in the body

[1] Lymph is not shown in this table as it has no formed elements and cannot be seen histologically.

Besides the formed elements, blood contains dissolved protein fibers in a watery ground substance. Together, the dissolved protein fibers and the watery ground substance form an extracellular matrix called **plasma.** Plasma transports nutrients, wastes, and hormones throughout the body. **Lymph** is derived from blood plasma and is returned to the blood. As it has no formed elements, it is not shown histologically in table 4.11. Blood and lymph are discussed in greater detail in chapter 21 and section 24.2, respectively. APR

WHAT DID YOU LEARN?

8 What is the extracellular matrix? What are its main components?

9 Draw your own table or flowchart that shows the classification of the different kinds of connective tissue, starting with the embryonic CT from which all CT originates.

10 Compare and contrast the three types of cartilage with respect to structure and where each is located in the body.

11 Compare loose connective tissue to dense connective tissue with respect to fiber density and distribution and amount of ground substance.

4.3 Body Membranes

✓ Learning Objectives

10. Explain the structure and function of mucous, serous, cutaneous, and synovial membranes.
11. Describe where in the body the different types of membranes occur.

The major cavities of the body have membranes that line both the internal surfaces of the cavities and the external surfaces of some of the viscera housed within those cavities. We discuss these membranes here because all but one consist of an epithelial sheet and an underlying connective tissue layer. The four types of body membranes are mucous, serous, cutaneous, and synovial membranes.

The two principal kinds of internal membranes are mucous and serous membranes. A **mucous membrane,** also called a *mucosa* (myū-kō′să), lines body passageways and compartments that eventually open to the external environment; these include the digestive, respiratory, reproductive, and urinary tracts. Mucous membranes perform absorptive, protective, and/or secretory functions. A mucous membrane is composed of an epithelium and underlying connective tissue called the lamina propria. Often, it is covered with a thin layer of mucus derived from goblet cells, multicellular mucous glands, or both. The mucus prevents the underlying layer of cells from drying out (a process called *desiccation*), provides lubrication, and traps bacteria and foreign particles to prevent them from invading the body.

A **serous membrane,** also termed a *serosa* (se-r ō′să), is composed of a simple squamous epithelium called **mesothelium** and a thin underlying layer of loose connective tissue. The mesothelium is so named because it is derived from mesoderm. Serous membranes produce a thin, watery **serous fluid,** or *transudate* (tranz′y ū-dāt; *trans* = across, *sudo* = to sweat), which is derived from blood plasma. Serous membranes are composed of two parts: a **parietal layer** that lines the body cavity and a **visceral layer** that covers organs. The parietal and visceral layers are in close contact; a thin layer of serous fluid between them reduces the friction between their opposing surfaces. Examples of serous membranes include the pericardium, the peritoneum, and the pleura.

The largest body membrane is the **cutaneous** (kyū-tā′nē-ŭs; *cutis* = skin) **membrane,** more commonly called the *skin*. The cutaneous membrane is composed of a keratinized stratified squamous epithelium (called the epidermis) and a layer of connective tissue (termed the dermis) upon which the epithelium rests (see sections 5.2 and 5.3). It differs from the other membranes discussed so far in that it is relatively dry. Its many functions include protecting internal organs and preventing water loss.

Some joints of the skeletal system are lined by a **synovial** (si-n ō′vē-ăl; *syn* = together, *ovum* = egg) **membrane,** which is composed of a well-vascularized areolar, fibrous, or adipose connective tissue under a superficial cellular lining. Some of the cells, called **synoviocytes,** secrete a **synovial fluid** that reduces friction in the joint cavity and distributes nutrients to the cartilage on the joint surfaces of the bone.

WHAT DO YOU THINK?

5 What type of body membrane is found on the external surface of your forearm?

WHAT DID YOU LEARN?

12 What is the function of mucous membranes?

13 Distinguish between the parietal and visceral layers of the serous membrane.

4.4 Muscle Tissue

✓ Learning Objectives

12. Explain the structure and function of skeletal, cardiac, and smooth muscle.
13. Identify and describe the body locations where each type of muscle tissue is found.

Muscle tissue is composed of specialized cells (fibers) that undergo internal changes that cause them to shorten. As muscle tissue shortens, it exerts physical forces on other tissues and organs to produce movement; these movements include voluntary motion of body parts, blood circulation, respiratory activities, propulsion of materials through the digestive tract, waste elimination, and thermoregulation. To perform these functions, muscle cells are very different from typical cells with respect to their cellular organization, cellular organelles, and other properties.

4.4a Classification of Muscle Tissue

The three histologic types of muscle in the body are skeletal muscle, cardiac muscle, and smooth muscle. The contraction mechanism is somewhat similar in all three, but they vary in their appearance, location, physiology, internal organization, and means of control by the nervous system. Specific details about the muscular system are discussed in chapter 10.

Skeletal Muscle Tissue

Skeletal muscle tissue is composed of cylindrical muscle cells called **skeletal muscle fibers** (table 4.12*a*). Individual skeletal muscle cells are slender and often long (sometimes the length of the entire muscle). Such long cells need more than one nucleus to control and carry out all cellular functions, so each skeletal muscle fiber is multinucleated; some contain hundreds of nuclei. These multiple nuclei form when smaller embryonic muscle cells fuse early in the development of the skeletal muscle fiber. The nuclei in skeletal muscle fibers are located at the edge of the cell (called the periphery), immediately internal to the plasma membrane.

Skeletal muscle is described as striated and voluntary. When this tissue is viewed with light microscopy, the cells of skeletal muscle exhibit alternating light and dark bands, termed **striations** (str ī-ā′shŭn; *striatus* = furrow), that reflect the overlapping pattern of parallel thick and thin contractile protein filaments inside the cell. Additionally, skeletal muscle is considered **voluntary** because it usually does not contract unless stimulated by the somatic (voluntary) nervous system. Skeletal muscle attaches to the bones of the skeleton and also forms muscles associated with the skin, such as the muscles of facial expression and those forming body sphincters that help control waste removal. When skeletal muscles contract and relax, they produce heat for the body, which is why we become warmer when we "work out" at the gym or fitness center.

Cardiac Muscle Tissue

Cardiac muscle tissue is confined to the thick middle layer of the heart wall (called the myocardium). Microscopically, cardiac muscle tissue resembles skeletal muscle in that both contain visible striations (table 4.12 *b*). However, several obvious cellular differences distinguish the two types. First, the typical cardiac muscle cell is much shorter than a typical skeletal muscle fiber. Second, a cardiac muscle cell contains only one or two centrally located nuclei. Third, the cardiac muscle cell often bifurcates (branches), thus resembling a Y in shape. Finally, cardiac muscle cells are connected by **intercalated discs** (in-ter′k ă-lā-tĕd; *intercalates* = inserted between), which have strong desmosomes and gap junctions between the cells. The intercalated discs promote the rapid transport of an electrical activity through many cardiac muscle cells at once, allowing the entire muscle wall to contract as a unit. When you view cardiac muscle tissue with light microscopy, the intercalated discs appear as thick, dark lines between the cells.

Cardiac muscle is responsible for the rhythmic heart contractions that pump blood throughout the blood vessels of the body. Cardiac muscle cells are **autorythmic** because they do not require nervous system activity to initiate a contraction; instead, specialized cardiac muscle cells in the heart wall initiate the contraction. Cardiac muscle is innervated by the autonomic nervous system, so is considered **involuntary**. Thus, cardiac muscle tissue is striated, autorythmic, and involuntary.

Smooth Muscle Tissue

Smooth muscle tissue is so named because it lacks the striations seen in the other two types of muscle tissue, so the cells appear smooth (table 4.12*c*). Smooth muscle tissue is also called *visceral muscle tissue* because it is found in the walls of most viscera, such as the stomach, urinary bladder, and blood vessels. The contraction of smooth muscle helps propel and control the movement of material through these organs. Smooth muscle cells are fusiform (spindle-shaped), which means they are thick in the middle and tapered at their ends. The cells are also relatively short. Each cell has one centrally placed nucleus. Smooth muscle is considered involuntary because it is innervated by the autonomic nervous system (see section 14.1b). We do not have conscious control over it. For example, you cannot stop your stomach from digesting your food or your blood vessels from transporting your blood. APR

WHAT DID YOU LEARN?

14 Draw the three types of muscle tissue, and label the characteristics of each.

15 Why is smooth muscle referred to as involuntary?

Table 4.12 Muscle Tissue

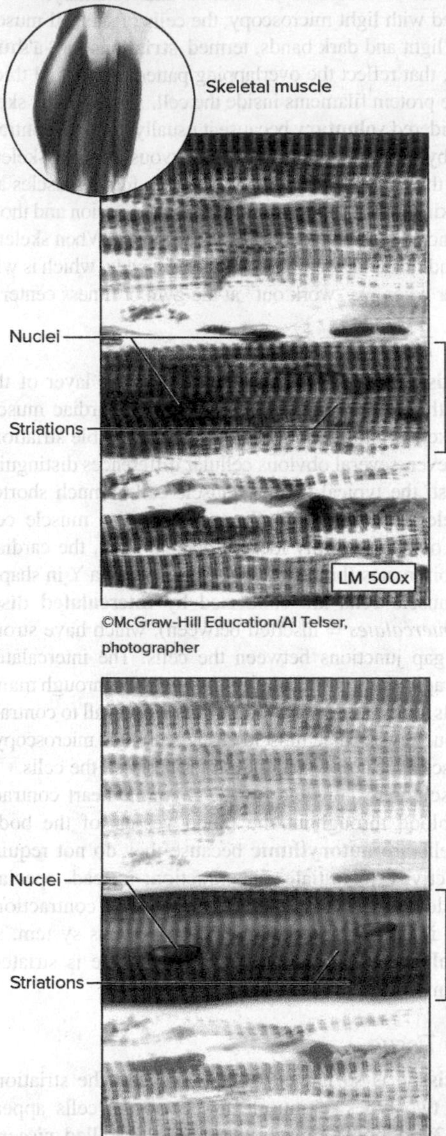
Skeletal muscle
Nuclei
Striations
Skeletal muscle fiber
LM 500x
Nuclei
Striations
Skeletal muscle fiber

©McGraw-Hill Education/Al Telser, photographer

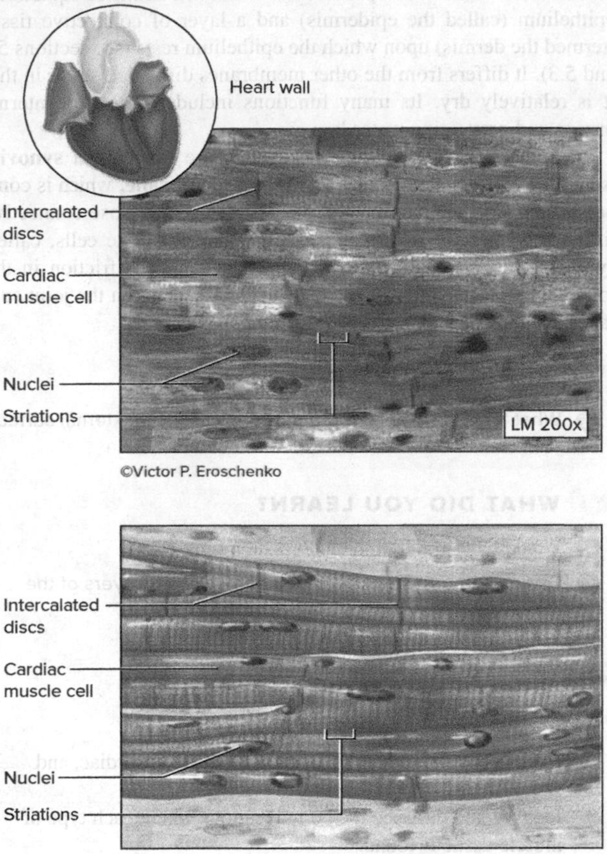
Heart wall
Intercalated discs
Cardiac muscle cell
Nuclei
Striations
LM 200x
Intercalated discs
Cardiac muscle cell
Nuclei
Striations

©Victor P. Eroschenko

(a) Skeletal Muscle Tissue		**(b) Cardiac Muscle Tissue**	
Structure	Fibers are long, cylindrical, striated, parallel, and unbranched; fibers are multinucleated with nuclei along periphery	**Structure**	Cells are short, bifurcated, and striated, with one or two centrally located nuclei; intercalated discs between cells
Function	Moves skeleton; responsible for voluntary body movements, locomotion, heat production	**Function**	Involuntary contraction and relaxation pump blood in heart
Location	Attaches to bones or sometimes to skin (e.g., facial muscles); also found in the voluntary sphincters—lips, urethra, anus	**Location**	Heart wall (myocardium)

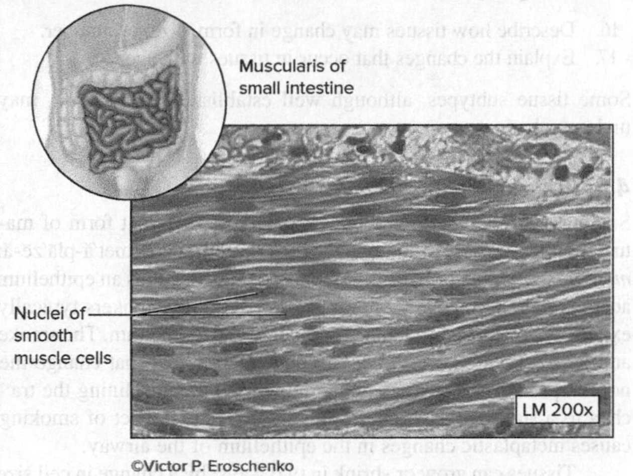
Muscularis of
small intestine
Nuclei of
smooth
muscle cells
LM 200x

©Victor P. Eroschenko

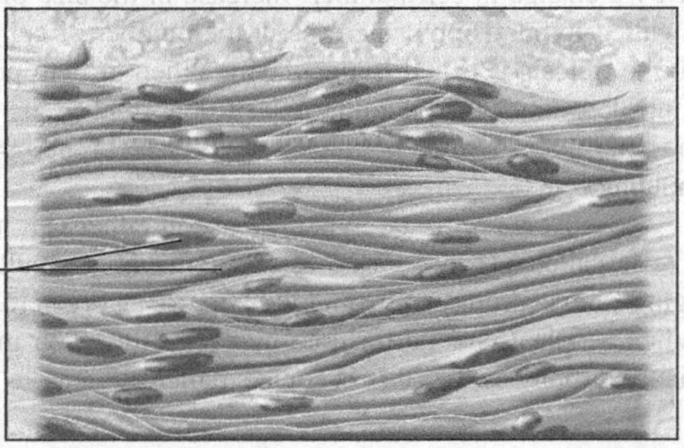
Nuclei of
smooth
muscle cells

(c) Smooth Muscle Tissue	
Structure	Cells are fusiform (spindle-shaped), short, nonstriated, and contain one centrally located nucleus
Function	Involuntary movements and motion; moves materials through internal organs
Location	Walls of hollow internal organs, such as vessels, airways, stomach, bladder, uterus

Learning Strategy 4.5

Ask the following questions to help distinguish the three types of muscle tissue with light microscopy:

1. What is the shape of the cell? Skeletal muscle fibers are long and cylindrical; smooth muscle cells are fusiform; and cardiac muscle cells are short and bifurcated.
2. Are the nuclei centrally located or at the periphery of the cell? Skeletal muscle nuclei are located at the periphery, whereas cardiac and smooth muscle cells have centrally located nuclei.
3. How many nuclei are present? A skeletal muscle fiber contains many nuclei at the periphery of the cylindrical fiber. A smooth muscle cell has one nucleus at the center of the cell. A cardiac muscle cell has one or two nuclei at its center.
4. Do the cells have striations? Smooth muscle cells have no striations, whereas cardiac and skeletal muscle cells do have striations.
5. Do you see intercalated discs? Only cardiac muscle has intercalated discs.

4.5 Nervous Tissue

✓ Learning Objectives

14. Explain the structure and function of nervous tissue.
15. Identify and describe where nervous tissue is found in the body.

Nervous tissue is sometimes termed *neural tissue*. It consists of cells called **neurons** (nū′ron), or *nerve cells*, and a larger number of different types of **glial cells** (or *supporting cells*) that support, protect, and provide a framework for neurons (**table 4.13**). This tissue will be discussed in detail in section 14.2, but we provide a brief description here.

4.5a Characteristics of Neurons

Neurons are specialized to detect stimuli, process information quickly, and rapidly transmit impulses from one region of the body to another. Each neuron has a prominent **cell body,** or soma, that houses the nucleus and most other organelles. The cell body is the "head" that controls the rest of the cell and produces proteins for the cell. Extending from the cell body are branches called nerve cell processes. The short, branched processes are **dendrites** (den′dr īts; *dendrites* = relating to a tree), which receive incoming signals from other cells and transmit the information to the cell body. The long nerve cell process extending from a cell body is the **axon** (ak′son; *axon* = axis), which carries outgoing signals to other cells. Due to the length of an axon, neurons are usually the longest cells in the body; some are longer than a meter. Much of the nervous tissue in the body is concentrated in the brain and spinal cord, the control centers for the nervous system. APR

WHAT DID YOU LEARN?

16 What are the two general types of cells found in nervous tissue, and what are the cells' functions?

Table 4.13 Nervous Tissue

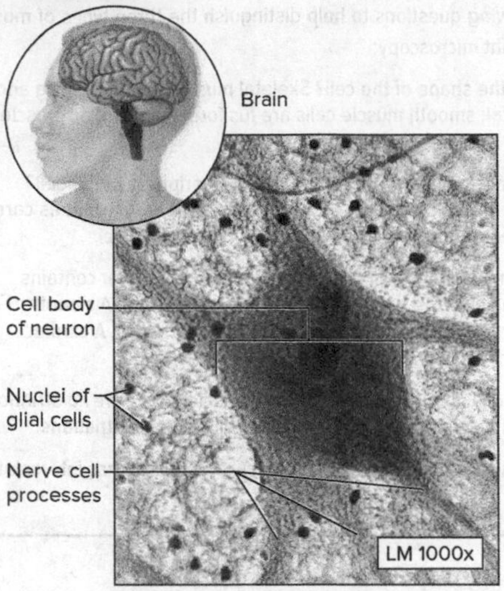
Brain
Cell body of neuron
Nuclei of glial cells
Nerve cell processes
LM 1000x

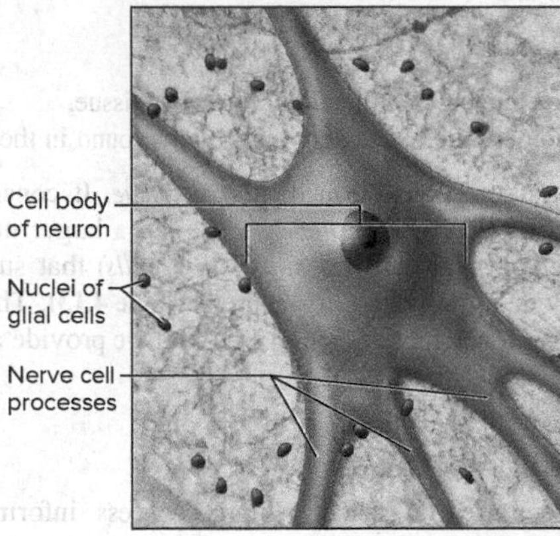
Cell body of neuron
Nuclei of glial cells
Nerve cell processes

Nervous Tissue	
Structure	Contains neurons with rounded or stellate cell bodies and an axon and dendrites extending from the cell body; glial cells lack such extensive fibrous processes
Function	*Neurons:* Responsible for control; information processing, storage, and retrieval; internal communication *Glial cells:* Support and protect neurons
Location	Brain, spinal cord, nerves

4.6 Tissue Change and Aging

✓ Learning Objectives

16. Describe how tissues may change in form, size, or number.
17. Explain the changes that occur in tissues with age.

Some tissue subtypes, although well established in an adult, may undergo changes.

4.6a Tissue Change

Sometimes a mature epithelium changes to a different form of mature epithelium, a phenomenon called **metaplasia** (met′ă-plā′zē-ă; *metaplasis* = transformation). Metaplasia may occur as an epithelium adapts to environmental conditions. For example, smokers typically experience metaplastic changes in the tracheal epithelium. The smoke and its by-products are the environmental stressors that change the normal pseudostratified ciliated columnar epithelium lining the trachea to a stratified squamous epithelium. Thus, the act of smoking causes metaplastic changes in the epithelium of the airway.

Tissues can grow or shrink in two ways: by a change in cell size or by a change in cell number. Increase in the size of existing cells is called **hypertrophy;** increase in the number of cells in the tissue due to mitosis is called **hyperplasia.** When growth proceeds out of control, a tumor that is composed of abnormal tissue develops, and the condition is termed **neoplasia** (nē′ō-plā′zē-ă; *neo* = new, *plasis* = molding).

Shrinkage of tissue by a decrease in either cell number or cell size is called **atrophy** (at′rō-fē). Atrophy may result from normal aging (senile atrophy) or from failure to use an organ (disuse atrophy). When people do not perform normal activities, their muscles exhibit disuse atrophy as the cells become smaller.

4.6b Tissue Aging

All tissues change as a result of aging. Proper nutrition, good health, normal circulation, and relatively infrequent wounds promote continued normal tissue functioning past middle age. Thereafter, the support, maintenance, and replacement of cells and extracellular matrix become less efficient. Physical damage, chemical changes, and physiologic changes can alter the structure and chemical composition of many tissues. For example, adequate intake of protein is required to enable the cells to continue synthesizing new proteins, the body's structural and functional building blocks. As individuals age, epithelia become thinner, and connective tissues lose their pliability and resilience. Because the amount of collagen in the body declines, tissue repair and wound healing lose efficiency. Bones become brittle; joint pains and broken bones are common. Muscle and nervous tissue begin to atrophy. Diet and circulation problems contribute to these tissue declines. Eventually, cumulative losses from relatively minor damage or injury contribute to major health problems.

Clinical View 4.4

Gangrene

Gangrene is the necrosis (death) of the soft tissues of a body part due to a diminished or obstructed arterial blood supply to that region. The body parts most commonly affected are the limbs, fingers, or toes. Gangrene is a major complication for diabetics, who often suffer from diminished blood flow to their upper and lower limbs as a consequence of their disease. There are several different forms of gangrene.

Intestinal gangrene usually occurs following an obstruction of the blood supply to the intestines. If the intestines are without sufficient blood, the tissue undergoes necrosis and gangrene. Untreated intestinal gangrene leads to death.

Dry gangrene is a form of gangrene in which the involved body part is desiccated, sharply demarcated, and shriveled, usually due to constricted blood vessels as a result of exposure to extreme cold. Dry gangrene can be a complication of frostbite or result from a variety of cardiovascular diseases that restrict blood flow, primarily to the hands and feet.

Wet gangrene is caused by a bacterial infection of tissues that have lost their blood and oxygen supply. The cells in the dying tissue rupture and release fluid. The wet environment allows bacteria to flourish, and they often produce a foul-smelling pus. The most common bacteria associated with wet gangrene are *Streptococcus, Staphylococcus, Enterobacter,* and *Klebsiella.* Wet gangrene must be treated quickly with antibiotics and removal of the necrotic tissue.

Gas gangrene is often mistaken for wet gangrene. However, the bacteria typically associated with gas gangrene are *Clostridrium.* This type of gangrene usually affects muscle tissue. As the bacteria invade the necrotic tissue, a release of gases from the tissue produces gas bubbles. These bubbles make a crackling sound in the tissue, especially if the patient is moved. Symptoms of fever, pain, and edema (localized swelling) occur within 72 hours of the initial trauma to the region. The treatment for gas gangrene is similar to that for wet gangrene.

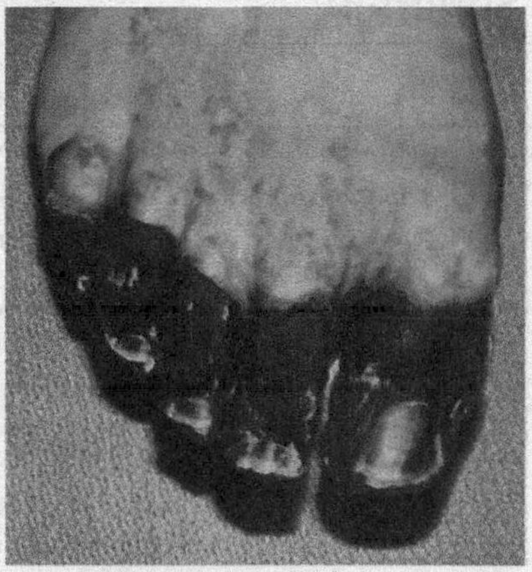

Dry gangrene of the foot.
Source: William Archibald/CDC

Clinical View 4.5

Tissue Transplantation

Grafting is the process of surgically transplanting healthy tissue to replace diseased, damaged, or defective tissue. The healthy tissue may be a person's own tissue or tissue from another individual or animal. There are four types of tissue grafts.

An **autograft** (aw´tō-graft; *autos* = self, *graef* = implant) is a tissue transplant from one site on a person to a different site on the same person. Autografts are often performed with skin, as healthy skin from one part of the body is grafted to another part of the body where the skin has been damaged by burns or chemicals. Because an autograft uses a person's own tissue, the body does not reject the tissue as foreign. However, autografts may not be feasible in certain situations, such as when the amount of skin damaged is so great that it would not be possible to transplant such a large portion of tissue.

A **syngenetic** (sin´jĕ-net´ik; *syn* = together) **graft,** also called an *isograft,* is a tissue transplant from one person to a genetically identical person (i.e., an identical twin). It is unlikely that the body will reject the syngenetic graft because it came from a genetically identical individual. However, very few of us have an identical twin, so this type of graft is not possible for most people.

An **allograft** (al´ō-graft; *allos* = other) is the transplantation of tissue from a person who is genetically different. Many tissue types have been used as allografts, including skin, muscle, bone, and cartilage. The term allograft also refers to the transplantation of organs or parts of organs, such as heart valves, kidneys, and the liver.

The patient and the organ donor must be as genetically similar as possible; traits such as blood type and other blood factors must match between patient and donor. The closer the match, the less likely the allograft will be rejected. The recipient of the transplanted organ(s) must take powerful immunosuppressant drugs, which help prevent the body from rejecting the organ. Unfortunately, these same drugs work by suppressing the immune system, making the transplant patient more susceptible to illness.

A **xenograft** (zen´ō-graft; *xeno* = foreign), also called a *heterograft* (het´ĕr-ō-graft; *heteros* = other), is a tissue transplant from an animal into a human. For example, porcine (pig) and bovine (cow) tissue have been successfully used to replace heart valves, blood vessels, and bone. Xenographs, like allographs, are prone to rejection.

Clinical Terms

adhesions Inflammatory bands that connect opposing serous surfaces.

biopsy Microscopic examination of tissue removed from the body for the purpose of diagnosing a disease. In a skin or muscle biopsy, a small piece of skin or muscle is removed, and the wound is sutured; in a needle biopsy, a tissue sample is removed from skin or an organ through an inserted needle; in an aspiration biopsy, cells are sucked into a syringe through a needle.

lesion (lē′zhŭn) Any localized wound, injury, or infection that affects tissue over a specific area rather than spread throughout the body.

liposuction A method of removing unwanted subcutaneous fat using a suction tube.

Chapter Summary

- There are four tissue types: epithelial tissue, connective tissue, muscle tissue, and nervous tissue.

4.1 Epithelial Tissue

- Epithelial tissue covers the surface of the body, lines body cavities, and forms secretory structures called glands.

4.1a Characteristics of Epithelial Tissue

- The characteristics of an epithelium include cellularity, polarity, attachment to a basement membrane, avascularity, innervation, and high regeneration ability.
- Epithelial cells have an apical (free) surface, junctions on lateral membranes that bind neighboring cells, and a basal surface, which is closest to the basement membrane.

4.1b Functions of Epithelial Tissue

- Epithelial tissues provide physical protection, control permeability, produce secretory products, and contain nerve cells that detect sensations. Gland cells are derived from epithelial cells and produce secretions.

4.1c Specialized Structures of Epithelial Tissue

- The four types of epithelial cell junctions are tight junctions, adhering junctions, desmosomes, and gap junctions.

4.1d Classification of Epithelial Tissue

- Epithelia are classified by two criteria: (1) number of cell layers, and (2) shape of apical surface cells.
- A simple epithelium has only one cell layer overlaying the basement membrane. A stratified epithelium is two or more layers of cells thick, and only the deepest (basal) layer is in direct contact with the basement membrane. Pseudostratified columnar epithelium appears stratified but is not; all cells are in contact with the basement membrane.

4.1e Types of Epithelium

- In a simple epithelium, the surface cells are thin and flat (squamous epithelium), about as tall as they are wide (cuboidal epithelium), or taller than they are wide (columnar epithelium).
- The shape of transitional epithelium cells changes between relaxed and distended states.

4.1f Glands

- Endocrine glands secrete hormones into the blood. Exocrine glands secrete their products through ducts onto the epithelial surface.
- Multicellular exocrine glands are classified by the structure of their ducts and the organization of the secretory portion of the gland.
- Serous glands produce nonviscous, watery fluids; mucous glands secrete mucin that forms mucus; and mixed glands produce both types of secretions.

4.2 Connective Tissue

- Connective tissue binds, protects, and supports the body organs.

4.2a Characteristics of Connective Tissue

- Connective tissue contains cells, protein fibers, and a ground substance. The protein fibers and ground substance together form the extracellular matrix.

4.2b Functions of Connective Tissue

- Connective tissue provides physical protection, support and structural framework, binding of structures, storage, transport, and immune protection.

4.2c Development of Connective Tissue

- All connective tissues are derived from two types of embryonic connective tissue: mesenchyme and mucous connective tissue.

4.2d Classification of Connective Tissue

- Loose connective tissue has a high volume of ground substance; it is easily distorted and serves to cushion shocks.
- Dense connective tissue consists primarily of large amounts of extracellular protein fibers.
- Supporting connective tissue (cartilage and bone) provides support and protection to the soft tissues and organs of the body.
- Blood and lymph are fluid connective tissues. Blood cells are called formed elements, and the dissolved protein fibers and watery ground substance form an extracellular matrix called plasma. Lymph is derived from plasma, and thus has no formed elements.

4.3 Body Membranes	■ Mucous membranes line cavities that communicate with the exterior. ■ Serous membranes line internal cavities and are delicate, moist, and very permeable. ■ The external body surface is covered by the cutaneous membrane, which is dry, keratinized, and relatively thick. ■ Synovial membranes line the inner surface of synovial joint cavities.
4.4 Muscle Tissue	■ Muscle tissue is composed of muscle cells, sometimes termed muscle fibers, which are capable of contractions resulting in cellular shortening along their longitudinal axes and producing movement, either of the skeleton or specific body parts. **4.4a Classification of Muscle Tissue** ■ Skeletal muscle tissue is composed of long, multinucleated, cylindrical fibers that are striated and voluntary. ■ Cardiac muscle tissue is located within the wall of the heart. It is composed of branched, short cells with one or two centrally located nuclei. It is striated, autorythmic, and involuntary. ■ Smooth muscle tissue is found in the walls of organs; it has short, tapered cells that are nonstriated and involuntary.
4.5 Nervous Tissue	■ Nervous tissue is composed of two specific cell types: neurons and glial cells. Neurons receive stimuli and transmit impulses in response. Glial cells interact with each other to form an extensive supporting framework for neurons and nervous tissue. Additionally, glial cells help provide nutrient support to the neuron. **4.5a Characteristics of Neurons** ■ Neurons have a prominent cell body, dendrites, and a long process called the axon.
4.6 Tissue Change and Aging	**4.6a Tissue Change** ■ Metaplasia is a change from one mature epithelial type to another in response to injury or stress. ■ Hypertrophy is an increase in cell size, whereas hyperplasia is an increase in cell number. **4.6b Tissue Aging** ■ When tissues age, repair and maintenance become less efficient, and the structure and chemical composition of many tissues are altered.

Challenge Yourself

Actively write or type your answers in a separate document to reinforce your learning, before checking your answers.

Multiple Choice

Select the best answer from the four choices provided.

1. The tissue that is responsible for control and internal communication in the body consists of which cell types?
   a. chondrocytes and osteocytes
   b. erythrocytes and leukocytes
   c. fibroblasts and mast cells
   d. neurons and glial cells
2. What is the predominant cell type in areolar connective tissue?
   a. mesenchymal cell
   b. fibroblast
   c. adipocyte
   d. satellite cell
3. Which body membrane functions to prevent desiccation and provide surface lubrication?
   a. cutaneous
   b. mucous
   c. serous
   d. synovial
4. Which of the following is a correct statement about a simple epithelium?
   a. It protects against mechanical abrasion.
   b. It may contain the protein keratin.
   c. It is adapted for diffusion and filtration.
   d. It is formed from multiple layers of epithelial cells.
5. Which of the following is a characteristic of an epithelium?
   a. It exhibits polarity.
   b. It has few cells and densely packed protein fibers.
   c. It is highly vascular.
   d. Its cells are long lived.
6. Which connective tissue type provides an abundantly resilient and flexible form to the structures it supports?
   a. elastic cartilage
   b. elastic connective tissue
   c. fibrocartilage
   d. dense regular connective tissue
7. What is the name for a change of cell size in a tissue?
   a. atrophy
   b. hyperplasia
   c. hyperthrophy
   d. metaplasia
8. Which epithelial tissue type lines the trachea (air tube)?
   a. simple columnar epithelium
   b. pseudostratified ciliated columnar epithelium
   c. simple squamous epithelium
   d. stratified squamous epithelium
9. Which muscle type consists of long, cylindrical, striated cells with multiple nuclei located at the periphery of the cell?
   a. smooth muscle
   b. cardiac muscle
   c. skeletal muscle
   d. involuntary muscle

10. Which type of gland releases its secretion by exocytosis?
    a. apocrine
    b. merocrine
    c. holocrine
    d. ceruminous

Content Review

1. What are some common characteristics of all types of epithelium?
2. Describe the types of intercellular junctions between epithelial cells. Where are these junctions located and what are their functions?
3. List the epithelial type that is found (a) lining the lumen of the stomach, (b) lining the oral cavity, (c) lining the urinary bladder, and (d) lining the tiny air sacs of the lungs.
4. What are the three secretion methods of exocrine glands, and how does each method work?
5. What characteristics are common to all connective tissues?
6. What are the main structural differences between dense regular and dense irregular connective tissue?
7. In what regions of the body would you expect to find hyaline cartilage, fibrocartilage, and elastic cartilage, and why would these supporting connective tissues be located in these regions?
8. Name the four types of body membranes, and identify a location of each type.
9. A significant structural feature in the microscopic study of cardiac muscle cells is the presence of gap junctions between neighboring cells. Why are these junctions so important?
10. What are the similarities and differences between skeletal muscle, cardiac muscle, and smooth muscle?

Developing Critical Reasoning

1. In the anatomy laboratory, a student makes the following observations about a tissue viewed with light microscopy: (1) The tissue contains some different types of scattered protein fibers—that is, they exhibit different widths, some are branched, some are long and unbranched, and their staining characteristics differ (some are seen only with specific stains). (2) Several cell types with different morphologies are scattered throughout the section, but these cells are not grouped tightly together. (3) The examined section has some "open spaces"—that is, places between cells and the observed fibers in the section that appear clear with no recognizable features. What type of tissue is the student observing? Where might this tissue be found in the body?
2. Your father is suffering from painful knee joints. He has been told that he either has the early stages of arthritis or some inherent joint problems. His friend recommends that he take a chemical supplement with his meals (chondroitin sulfate), which has been shown to help some people with joint aches and pains. This supplement stimulates growth and recovery of degenerated cartilage on the surfaces of bones in joints. Based on your knowledge of connective tissues, do you think the chondroitin sulfate supplements could help your father's knee problems?
3. As adults grow older, their skin becomes thinner and more fragile. Can you explain why this occurs?

Answers to "What Do You Think?"

1. If epithelium contained blood vessels, the "gatekeeper" function of selective permeability would be compromised. Materials would be able to enter the body by entering the blood without passing through the epithelium.
2. All types of stratified epithelium (stratified squamous, stratified columnar, stratified cuboidal) and transitional epithelium are suited for protection, because they have multiple layers of cells.
3. Connective tissue has fewer cells because it contains other materials, such as protein fibers and ground substance. The number of protein fibers in connective tissue is related to the strength and support the connective tissue gives. The ground substance can serve as a packing and binding material and can suspend the cells and protein fibers. Ground substance also allows for movement of molecules and cells through the tissue.
4. You have damaged dense regular connective tissue when you sprain your ankle. Recall that dense regular CT has poor vascularity. Tissues with poor vascularity take a long time to heal. That is why your ankle sprain doesn't heal as quickly as some other tissue injuries.
5. A cutaneous membrane is found on the external surface of your forearm.

Design Element: Pencil Icon: Slavojub Pantelic/Shutterstock

INTEGUMENTARY SYSTEM

Integumentary System 5

Outline

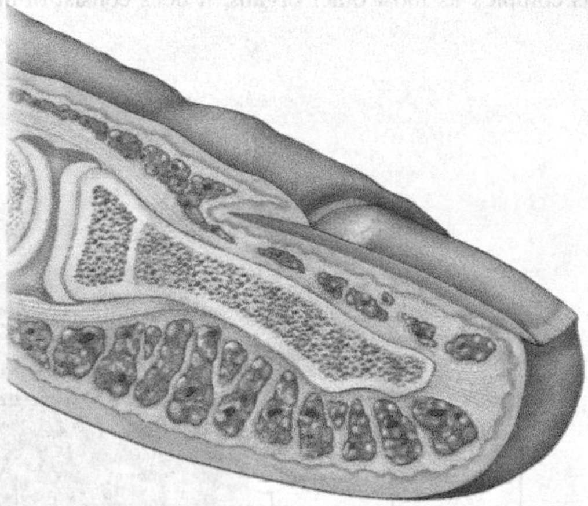

Anatomy & Physiology Revealed 4.0

MODULE 4: INTEGUMENTARY SYSTEM

The integument (in-teg′yū-ment; *integumentum* = a covering) is the skin that covers your body. Skin is also known as the **cutaneous** (kyū-tā′nē-ūs) **membrane,** or *cutaneous layer.* The **integumentary** (in-teg′yū-men′t ă-rē) **system** consists of the skin and its derivatives—nails, hair, sweat glands, and sebaceous glands. We are most conscious of this highly visible and overexamined body system, because it characterizes our self-image and reflects our emotions. Our skin is a vulnerable barrier to the outside world; it is subjected to trauma, harmful chemicals, pollutants, microbes, and damaging sunlight. Still, it usually remains strong and pliable, is easily cleaned, is self-renewing, and serves as a visual indicator of our physiology and health. Changes in the color of the skin may reflect body disorders or anomalies; skin changes or lesions sometimes indicate systemic infections or diseases. The scientific study and treatment of the integumentary system is called **dermatology** (der′mă-tol′ō-jē; *derma* = skin, *logos* = study).

5.1 Structure and Functions of the Integument

✓ Learning Objectives

1. Describe the general structure of the integument.
2. Explain the varied functions of the integument.

The integument is the body's largest organ. Although the integument is not as complex as most other organs, it does consist of different tissue types that collectively perform specific activities. Its surface is covered by an epithelium that protects underlying body layers. The connective tissues that underlie this epithelium contain blood vessels, which provide nutrients to the epithelial cells and give strength and resilience to the skin. Smooth muscle controls blood vessel diameter and hair position for these integumentary structures. Finally, nervous tissue supports and monitors sensory receptors in the skin, which provide information about touch, pressure, temperature, and pain.

5.1a Integument Structure

The integument covers the entire body surface, an area that ranges between about 1.5 and 2.0 square meters (m^2) and accounts for 7% to 8% of the body weight. Its thickness ranges between 1.5 and 4 millimeters (mm) or more, depending upon its location in the body. The integument consists of two distinct layers: a layer of stratified squamous epithelium called the epidermis, and a deeper layer of dense irregular and areolar (loose) connective tissue called the dermis (**figure 5.1**). Deep to the dermis is a layer composed of areolar and adipose connective tissue called the subcutaneous layer, or hypodermis. The subcutaneous layer is not part of the integumentary system; however, it is described in this chapter because it is closely involved with both the structure and function of the skin.

The integument meets the mucous membranes within the nostrils, lips, anus, urethral opening, and vaginal opening. At these sites, the transition is seamless, and the epithelial defenses remain intact and functional.

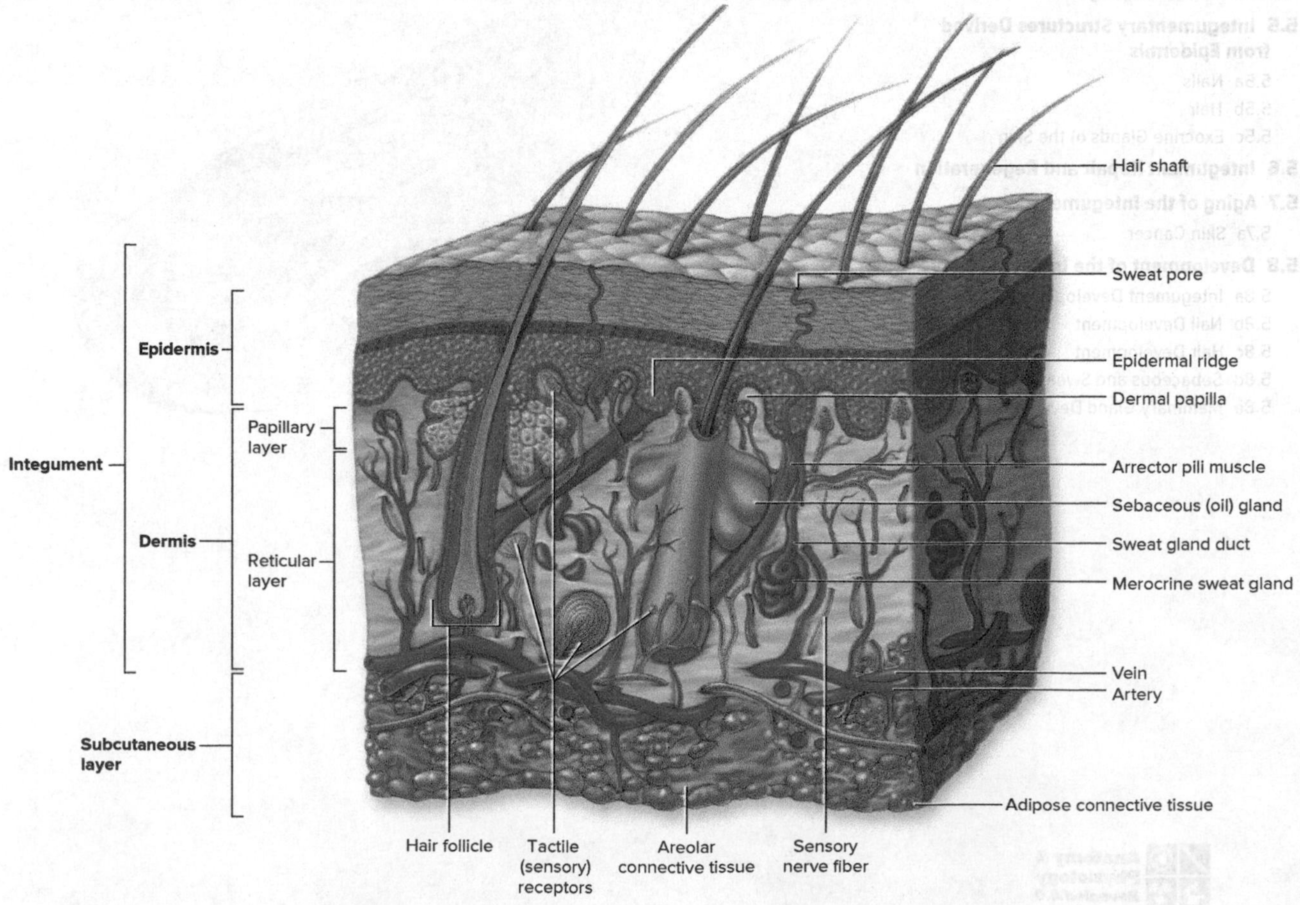

Figure 5.1

Layers of the Integument. A diagrammatic sectional view through the integument shows its relationship to the underlying subcutaneous layer. APR

5.1b Integument Functions

The integument is more than just a wrapping around the body. It serves many varied functions, including protection, prevention of water loss and water gain, temperature regulation, metabolic regulation, immune defense, sensory reception, and secretion.

Protection

The skin acts as a physical barrier that protects the entire body from physical injury, trauma, bumps, and scrapes. It also offers protection against harmful chemicals, toxins, microbes, and excessive heat or cold. Paradoxically, it can absorb certain chemicals and drugs (such as estrogen from a birth control patch or nicotine from a nicotine patch). Thus, the skin is said to be **selectively permeable** because some materials are able to pass through it, while others are effectively blocked. The epidermis is built to withstand stresses and regenerate itself continuously throughout a person's lifetime. The skin also protects deeper tissues from solar radiation, especially ultraviolet rays. When exposed to the sun, the melanocytes become more active and produce more melanin, thus giving the skin a darker, tanned look. Even when you get a sunburn, the deeper tissues (muscles and internal organs) remain unaffected.

Prevention of Water Loss and Water Gain

The epidermis is water-resistant and helps prevent unnecessary water loss or water gain. (If the skin were not water-resistant, each time you took a bath you would swell up like a sponge as your skin absorbed water!) Water cannot easily exit or enter the skin, unless it is specifically secreted by the sweat glands. The skin also prevents the water within the body cells and in the extracellular fluid (the fluid outside of cells) from leaking out. When the skin is severely burned, a primary danger is dehydration, because the individual has lost the protective skin barrier, and water can escape from body tissues.

Although the integument is water-resistant, it is not entirely waterproof. Some interstitial fluids slowly escape through the epidermis to the surface, where they evaporate into the surrounding air, a process called **transepidermal water loss (TEWL).** About 500 milliliters (mL) (about 1 pint) of water is lost daily by evaporation of moisture from the skin or from respiratory passageways during breathing. There are two main types of transepidermal water loss: insensible perspiration and sensible perspiration. **Insensible perspiration** is the release of water vapor from sweat glands under circumstances when we are not sweating. In contrast, **sensible perspiration** is visible sweating. On most parts of the skin, water vapor released from sweat glands during insensible perspiration mixes with sebaceous secretions (sebum), which produces a thin, slightly acidic film (pH 4–6) over the surface of the epidermis. This film helps slow down TEWL by forming an oily barrier over the surface of the skin. The acidic nature of the barrier also prevents the invasion of certain bacteria.

Temperature Regulation

Body temperature is influenced by vast capillary networks and sweat glands in the dermis. When the body is too warm and needs to dissipate heat, the diameter of the blood vessels in the dermis enlarges to permit more blood flow through the dermis, and sweat glands release fluid onto the skin surface. As relatively more blood flows through these dermal vessels, the warmth from the blood dissipates through the skin, and the body cools off by evaporation of the sweat. Conversely, when the body is cold and needs to conserve heat, the blood vessels in the dermis constrict to reduce blood flow. In an effort to conserve heat, more blood is shunted to deeper body tissues, and relatively less blood flows in the dermal blood vessels.

Metabolic Regulation

Vitamin D_3, also called **cholecalciferol** (kō′lē-kal-sif′er-ol), is produced by some epidermal cells when they are exposed to ultraviolet radiation. **Calcitriol** (kal′si-tr ī′ol) is synthesized from the cholecalciferol by some endocrine cells in the kidney (see section 20.9a). Calcitriol is the active form of vitamin D_3 and is considered a hormone. It increases absorption of calcium and phosphate from the small intestine into the blood, which results in a greater amount of the calcium being absorbed from the foods we eat. Thus, the synthesis of vitamin D_3 is important in regulating the levels of calcium and phosphate in the blood. As little as 15 minutes of direct sunlight a day may provide your body with its daily vitamin D requirement.

Immune Defense

The epidermis contains a small population of immune cells. These immune cells (derived from a type of white blood cell), called **epidermal dendritic** (den-drit′ik) **cells,** or *Langerhans cells,* play an important role in initiating an immune response by phagocytizing pathogens that have penetrated the epidermis and also against epidermal cancer cells.

Sensory Reception

The skin contains numerous sensory receptors. These receptors are associated with nerve endings that detect heat, cold, touch, pressure, texture, and vibration. For example, **tactile cells** (or *Merkel cells*) are large, specialized epithelial cells that stimulate specific sensory nerve endings when they are distorted by fine touch or pressure. Because your skin is responsible for perceiving many stimuli, it needs different sensory receptor types to detect, distinguish, and interpret these stimuli. For further details about the other types of sensory receptors in the skin, see section 19.2.

Secretion

Skin exhibits an excretory function when it secretes substances from the body during sweating. Sweating, or sensible perspiration, occurs when the body needs to cool itself off. Notice that sweat sometimes feels gritty because of the waste products being secreted onto the skin surface. These substances include water, salts, and urea, a nitrogen-containing waste product of body cells. In addition, the skin contains sebaceous glands that secrete an oily material called sebum, which lubricates the skin surface and hair.

WHAT DID YOU LEARN?

1. What are the two major layers of the integument and the general components of each?
2. In what ways does the skin protect us, and why is it said to be selectively permeable?

WHAT DO YOU THINK?

1. During the Industrial Revolution, as children spent little time outdoors and most of their time working in factories, increasing numbers of them developed a bone disorder called rickets. Rickets is caused by inadequate intake and absorption of vitamin D. Based upon your knowledge of skin function, why do you think these children developed rickets?

5.2 Epidermis

✓ Learning Objectives

3. Describe the structure, composition and arrangement, and functions of the epidermal strata.
4. Describe the composition, function, and locations of the epidermal cells.
5. Compare and contrast epidermal variations in thickness, color, and markings.

The epithelium of the integument is called the **epidermis** (ep′i-dĕrm′is; *epi* = on, *derma* = skin). The epidermis is a keratinized, stratified squamous epithelium. Like other epithelia, the epidermis is avascular, and it acquires its nutrients through diffusion from the underlying dermis.

5.2a Epidermal Strata

Careful examination of the epidermis, from the basement membrane to its surface, reveals several layers, or strata. From deep to superficial, these layers are the stratum basale, the stratum spinosum, the stratum granulosum, the stratum lucidum (found in thick skin only), and the stratum corneum (**figure 5.2**). The first three strata listed are composed of living keratinocytes, whereas the most superficial two strata contain dead keratinocytes.

Stratum Basale

The deepest epidermal layer is the **stratum basale** (strat′ŭm bah-sā′lē) (also known as the *stratum germinativum* or *basal layer*). This single layer of cells ranges from cuboidal to low columnar in appearance. It is tightly attached to an underlying basement membrane that separates the epidermis from the connective tissue of the adjacent dermis. Three types of cells occupy the stratum basale (figure 5.2*b*):

1. **Keratinocytes** (ke-rat′i-nō-sīt; *keras* = horn) are the most abundant cell type in the epidermis and occur throughout all epidermal strata. The stratum basale is dominated by large keratinocyte stem cells, which divide to provide both replacement stem cells and new keratinocytes that replace the dead keratinocytes shed from the surface. Their name is derived from their role in the synthesis of the protein **keratin** (ker′ă-tin) in the epidermal cells of the skin. Keratin is a family of fibrous structural proteins that are both tough and insoluble. Fibrous keratin molecules can twist and intertwine around each other to form helical intermediate filaments of the cytoskeleton (see section 2.4c). The keratins found in epidermal cells of the skin are called *cytokeratins*. Their structure in these cells gives skin its strength and makes the epidermis almost waterproof.
2. **Melanocytes** (mel′ă-nō-sīt; *melano* = black) have long, branching cytoplasmic processes and are scattered among the keratinocytes of the stratum basale. They produce and store the pigment **melanin** (mel′ă-nin) in response to ultraviolet (UV) light exposure. The cells' cytoplasmic processes transfer pigment granules, called **melanosomes** (mel′ă-nō-sōmes), by phagocytosis or exocytosis, into the keratinocytes within the basal layer and sometimes within more superficial layers. This pigment (black, brown, or yellow-brown) accumulates around the nucleus of the keratinocyte and shields the DNA within the nucleus from ultraviolet radiation. The darker tones of the skin result from melanin being produced by the melanocytes and from the darkening of melanin already present upon exposure to ultraviolet light.
3. **Tactile cells** (also known as *Merkel cells*) are few in number and found scattered among the cells within the stratum basale. Tactile cells are sensitive to touch, and when compressed, they release chemicals that stimulate sensory nerve endings, providing information about objects touching the skin (see section 19.2a).

Stratum Spinosum

Several layers of polygonal keratinocytes form the **stratum spinosum** (spi-nō′sŭm), or *spiny layer*. Each time a keratinocyte stem cell in the stratum basale divides, the new cell is pushed toward the external surface. Once this new cell enters the stratum spinosum, the cell begins

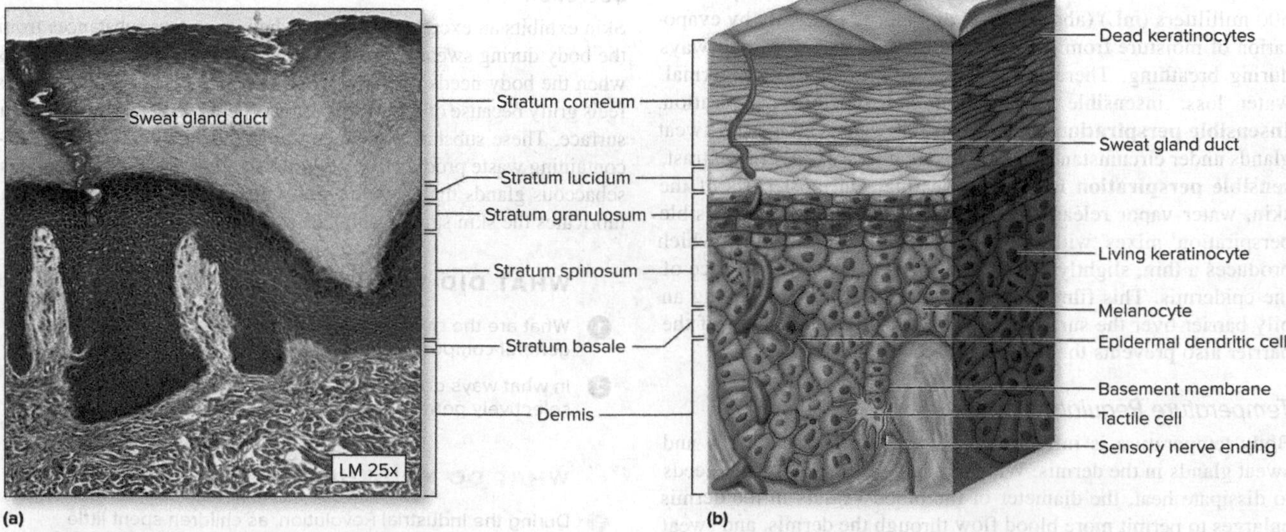
Sweat gland duct
Stratum corneum
Stratum lucidum
Stratum granulosum
Stratum spinosum
Stratum basale
Dermis
LM 25x
(a)
(b)
Dead keratinocytes
Sweat gland duct
Living keratinocyte
Melanocyte
Epidermal dendritic cell
Basement membrane
Tactile cell
Sensory nerve ending

Figure 5.2

Epidermal Strata. (*a*) Photomicrograph and (*b*) diagram compare the order and relationships of the epidermal strata in thick skin. **APR**

(a) Ed Reschke/Photolibrary/Getty Images

to differentiate into a nondividing, highly specialized keratinocyte. The nondividing keratinocytes in the stratum spinosum attach to their neighbors by many intercellular junctions called desmosomes (described in section 4.1c). The process of preparing epidermal tissue for observation on a microscope slide shrinks the cytoplasm of the cells in the stratum spinosum. Because the cytoskeletal elements and desmosomes remain intact, the shrunken stratum spinosum cells resemble miniature porcupines attached to their neighbors. These bridges between neighboring cells provide a spiny appearance, explaining the name of the layer.

In addition to the keratinocytes, the stratum spinosum also contains the fourth epidermal cell type, the epidermal dendritic cells (figure 5.2 *b*). Epidermal dendritic cells are immune cells that help fight infection in the epidermis. These cells are often present but not easily identifiable in both the stratum spinosum and the more superficial stratum granulosum. Their phagocytic activity initiates an immune response to protect the body against pathogens that have penetrated the superficial layers of the epidermis as well as against epidermal cancer cells.

Stratum Granulosum

The **stratum granulosum** (gran-ū-lō′sum), or *granular layer,* consists of three to five layers of keratinocytes superficial to the stratum spinosum. There are two types of granules in the stratum granulosum: *keratohyalin granules,* which are involved in the keratinization process, and *lamellar granules,* which fuse with the plasma membrane and extrude their contents (lipids primarily) into the extracellular space. The lipids are important in the prevention of water loss (by serving as a water barrier) and protective functions of the skin. Within this stratum begins a process called **keratinization** (ker′ă-tin-i-zā′shŭn), by which the keratinocytes fill up with the protein keratin. Several significant events occur during keratinization. As the cells pass through the stratum granulosum and true keratin filaments (intermediate filaments of the cytoskeleton) begin to develop, the cells become thinner and flatter. Their membranes thicken and become less permeable. The nucleus and all organelles disintegrate, and the cells start to die. Subsequently, the dehydrated material left within the cells forms a tightly interlocked layer of keratin fibers sandwiched between thickened phospholipid membranes. Keratinization is not complete until the cells reach the more superficial epidermal layers. A fully keratinized cell is dead (because it has neither a nucleus nor organelles), but it is strong because it contains keratin.

Stratum Lucidum

The **stratum lucidum** (lū′sĭ-dum), or *clear layer,* is a thin, translucent region about two to three cell layers thick that is superficial to the stratum granulosum. This stratum is found only in thick skin, such as the palms of the hands and the soles of the feet. Cells occupying this layer appear pale and featureless, and have indistinct boundaries. The keratinocytes within this layer are flattened and filled with the protein **eleidin** (ē-lē′ĭ-din), an intermediate product in the process of keratin maturation.

Stratum Corneum

The **stratum corneum** (kōr′nē-ŭm; *corneus* = horny), or *hornlike layer,* is the most superficial layer of the epidermis. It is the stratum you see when you look at your skin. The stratum corneum consists of about 20 to 30 layers of dead, scaly, interlocking keratinized cells called corneocytes (kōr′nē-ō-sīt). The dead cells are **anucleate** (lacking a nucleus) and tightly packed together.

A keratinized (or cornified) epithelium contains large amounts of keratin. After keratinocytes are formed from stem cells within the stratum basale, they change in structure and in their relationship to their neighbors as they move through the different strata until they eventually reach the stratum corneum and are sloughed off from its external surface. Migration of the keratinocyte to the stratum corneum from the stratum basale occurs during the first 2 weeks of the keratinocyte's life. The dead, keratinized cells usually remain for an additional 2 weeks in the exposed stratum corneum layer, providing a barrier for cells deeper in the epidermis before they are shed, washed away, or removed by abrasion. Overall, keratinocytes are present for about 1 month following their formation.

Learning Strategy 5.1

In your lab, you may be asked to identify a specific epidermal stratum. Answer the following questions to help identify these strata:

1. Is the epidermal stratum near the free surface of the epithelium or closer to the basal surface? Remember, the stratum corneum forms the free surface, and the stratum basale forms the deepest epidermal layer.
2. What is the shape of the cells? The stratum basale contains cells that are cuboidal to low columnar in shape; the stratum spinosum contains polygonal cells; and the stratum lucidum and stratum corneum contain squamous cells.
3. Do the keratinocytes have a nucleus, or are they anucleate (lacking a nucleus)? When the keratinocytes are still alive (as in the strata basale, spinosum, and granulosum), you will be able to see nuclei in the keratinocytes. The stratum lucidum and stratum corneum layers contain anucleate keratinocytes.
4. How many layers of cells are in the stratum? The stratum basale has only one layer of cells, and the stratum corneum contains 20 to 30 layers of cells. The other layers contain about 2 to 5 layers of cells.
5. Does the cytoplasm of the cells contain visible dark granules? If the answer is yes, you likely are looking at the stratum granulosum.

Clinical View 5.1

Tattoos

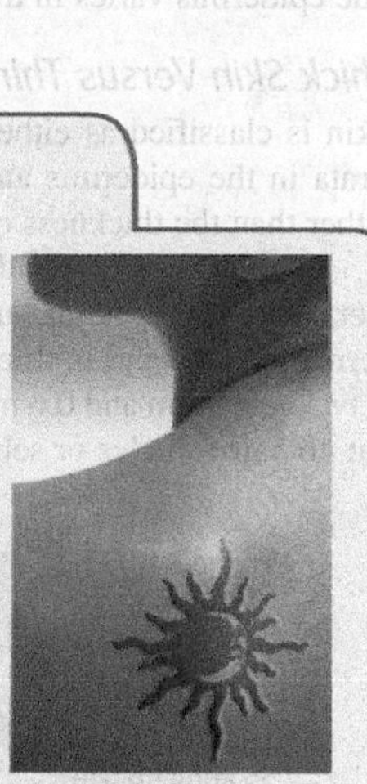

Ingram Publishing/SuperStock

Tattoos are permanent images produced on the integument through the process of injecting a dye into the dermis. The dermis doesn't have rapid cell turnover, so the injected dye remains in the area for a long time. Scar tissue surrounds the dye granules, which are too large for dendritic cells to ingest, and they become a permanent part of the dermis layer.

It is usually impossible to completely remove a tattoo, and some scarring may occur. Older methods include excision (cutting out the tattoo), **dermabrasion** (sanding down the tattooed skin), and **cryosurgery** (freezing the area of tattooed skin prior to its removal). Lasers are now used in some cases to break down the tattoo pigments. Newer tattoo inks have been introduced that allow for easier tattoo removal.

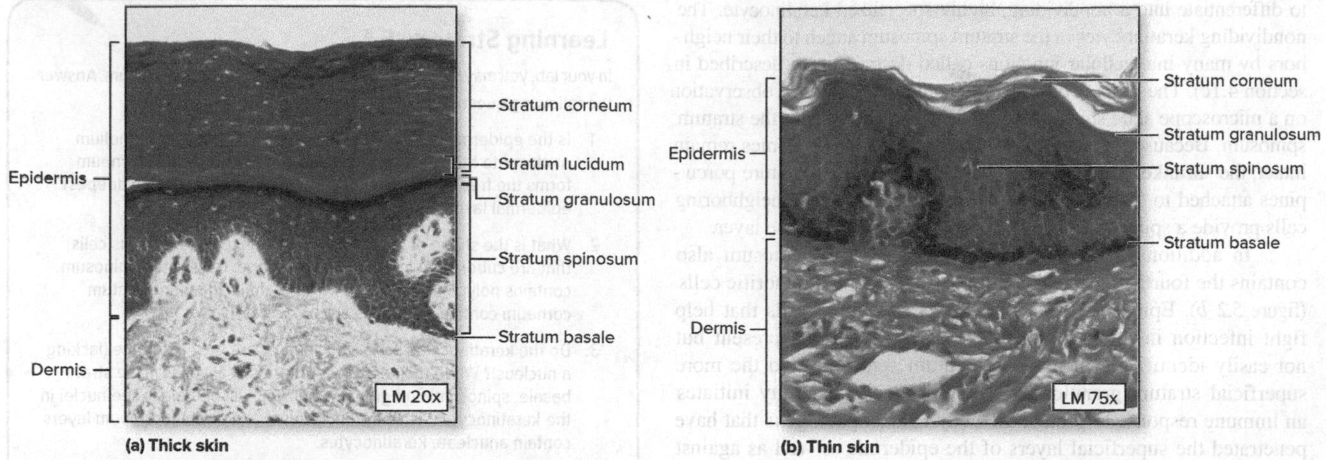

Figure 5.3

Thick Skin and Thin Skin. The stratified squamous epithelium of the epidermis varies in thickness, depending upon the region of the body in which it is located. (*a*) Thick skin contains all five epidermal strata and covers the soles of the feet and the palms of the hands. (*b*) Thin skin covers most body surfaces; it lacks a stratum lucidum.

(a) ©Lutz Slomianka; (b) Carolina Biological Supply Company/Phototake

The normally dry stratum corneum presents a thickened surface unsuitable for the growth of many microorganisms. Additionally, some secretions onto the surface of the epidermis from exocrine glands help prevent the growth of microorganisms on the epidermis, thus supporting its barrier function.

5.2b Variations in the Epidermis

The epidermis exhibits variations among different body regions within a single individual, as well as differences between individuals. The epidermis varies in thickness, coloration, and skin markings.

Thick Skin Versus Thin Skin

Skin is classified as either thick or thin based upon the number of strata in the epidermis and the relative thickness of the epidermis, rather than the thickness of the entire integument (**figure 5.3**).

Thick skin is found on the palms of the hands, the soles of the feet, and corresponding surfaces of the fingers and toes. All five epidermal strata occur in thick skin. The epidermis of thick skin ranges between 0.4 mm and 0.6 mm thick. Thick skin contains sweat glands, but no hair follicles or sebaceous (oil) glands. APR

Thin skin covers most of the body. The epidermis lacks the stratum lucidum, so it has only four layers. Thin skin contains the following accessories: hair follicles, sebaceous glands, and sweat glands. The epidermis of thin skin ranges from 0.075 mm to 0.150 mm thick. APR

WHAT DO YOU THINK?

2. Why does thick skin lack hair follicles and sebaceous glands? Think about the locations where thick skin is found and how the presence of hair follicles and sebaceous glands might interfere with the function of thick skin in those areas.

Skin Color

Normal skin color results from a combination of hemoglobin, melanin, and carotene. **Hemoglobin** (hē-mō-glō′bin; *haima* = blood) is an oxygen-binding protein present within red blood cells (see section 21.3a). Hemoglobin exhibits a bright red color upon binding to oxygen, giving blood vessels in the dermis a bright reddish tint that is most easily seen in the skin of lightly pigmented individuals.

Melanin is a pigment produced and stored in melanocytes (**figure 5.4**; see figure 5.2*b*). There are two types of melanin, *eumelanin*

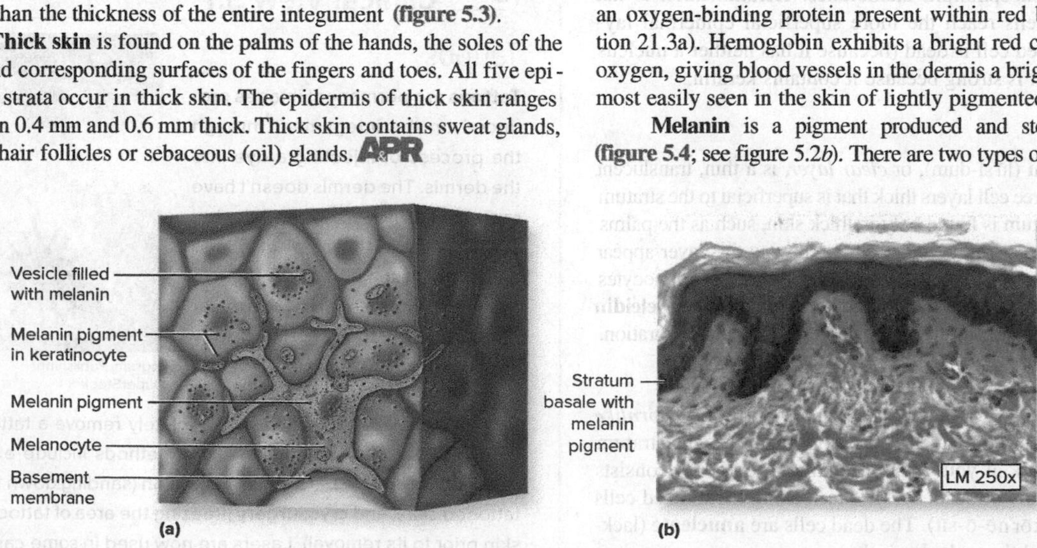

Figure 5.4

Production of Melanin by Melanocytes. Melanin gives a yellow to tan to brown color to the skin. (*a*) Vesicles in melanocytes transport the melanin pigment to the keratinocytes, where the pigment surrounds the nucleus. (*b*) Melanin is incorporated into the cells of the stratum basale.

(b) ©McGraw-Hill Education/Al Telser, photographer

Table 5.1	Abnormal Skin Colors	
Name	**Description**	**Cause(s)**
Albinism	Hair is white, skin is pale, irises of eyes are pink	Lack of melanin production; inherited recessive condition in which enzyme needed to synthesize melanin is nonfunctional, so melanocytes cannot produce melanin
Bronzing	Skin appears golden-brown, copper, or bronze in color	Glucocorticoid hormone deficiency in the adrenal cortex; Addison disease
Cyanosis	Skin appears bluish as a result of oxygen deficiency in circulating blood	Airway obstruction, emphysema, or respiratory arrest; also results from exposure to cold weather or from cardiac arrest with slow blood flow
Erythema	Skin appears abnormally red	Exercise, sunburn, excess heat, emotions (anger or embarrassment) resulting in increased blood flow in dilated blood vessels in the dermis
Hematoma	A bruise (visible pool of clotted blood) is observable through the skin	Usually due to trauma (a blow to the skin); also may be indicative of hemophilia or a nutritional or metabolic disorder
Jaundice	Skin and sclera (white of the eyes) appear yellowish	Elevated levels of bilirubin in the blood; often occurs when normal liver function is disrupted, and in premature infants whose liver function is not yet sufficient
Pallor	Skin appears ashen, pale due to white collagen fibers housed within the dermis	Decreased blood flow to the skin; occurs as a result of low blood pressure, cold temperature, emotional stress, severe anemia, or circulatory shock

and *pheomelanin,* and they occur in various ratios of yellow, reddish, tan, brown, and black shades. Recall that melanin is transferred in membrane-bound vesicles from melanocytes to keratinocytes in the stratum basale and stratum spinosum via phagocytosis or exocytosis. The keratinocytes that receive the melanin are displaced toward the stratum corneum, and thus melanocyte activity affects the color of the entire epidermis.

The amount of melanin in the skin is determined by both heredity and light exposure. All people have about the same *number* of melanocytes. However, melanocyte *activity* and the *color* of the melanin produced by these cells varies among individuals and ethnicities, resulting in different skin color tones. Darker-skinned individuals have melanocytes that produce relatively more and darker melanin than do lighter-skinned individuals. Further, these more active melanocytes package melanin into cells in the more superficial epidermal layers, such as the stratum granulosum. Recall that exposure to ultraviolet (UV) light stimulates melanocytes to produce more melanin.

Carotene (kar'ō-tēn) is a yellow-orange pigment that is acquired in the body by eating various yellow-orange vegetables, such as carrots, corn, and squash. Normally, carotene accumulates inside keratinocytes of the stratum corneum and within the subcutaneous layer. In the body, carotene is converted into vitamin A, which has an important function in normal vision. Additionally, carotene has been implicated in reducing the number of potentially dangerous molecules formed during normal metabolic activity and in improving immune cell number and activity.

Table 5.1 describes some abnormalities in skin color.

Clinical View 5.2

UV Radiation, Sunscreens, and Sunless Tanners

The sun generates three forms of ultraviolet radiation: **UVA (ultraviolet A), UVB (ultraviolet B),** and **UVC (ultraviolet C).** The wavelength of UVA ranges between 320 and 400 nanometers (nm), that of UVB ranges between 290 nm and 320 nm, and UVC ranges between 100 and 280 nm. In contrast, visible light ranges begin at about 400 nm (the deepest violet). UVC rays are absorbed by the upper atmosphere and do not reach the earth's surface; UVA and UVB rays do reach the surface and can affect individuals' skin color.

©McGraw-Hill Education/Jill Braaten, photographer

UVA light commonly is termed *tanning rays,* whereas UVB light often is called *burning rays.* Many tanning salons claim to provide a safe tan because they use only UVA rays. However, UVA rays can cause burning as well as tanning, and they also inhibit the immune system. Both UVA and UVB rays have been implicated in causing skin cancer. Thus, there is no such thing as a healthy suntan.

Sunscreens are lotions that contain materials that absorb or block UVA and UVB rays. Sunscreens can help protect the skin, not only for light-skinned people but also for those with darker skin colors—but *only* if they are used correctly. First, sunscreen must be applied liberally over all exposed body surfaces, and reapplied after being in the water or perspiring. Second, a sunscreen must have a high enough **SPF (sun protection factor).** SPF is a number determined experimentally by exposing subjects to a light spectrum. The amount of light that induces redness in sunscreen-protected skin, divided by the amount of light that induces redness in unprotected skin, equals the SPF. For example, a sunscreen with an SPF of 15 will delay the onset of a sunburn in a person who would otherwise burn in 10 minutes to 150 minutes. It is never safe, however, to assume that a sunscreen may protect you completely from the harmful rays of the sun.

Sunless tanners create a tanned, bronzed skin without UV light exposure. The most effective ones contain **dihydroxyacetone (DHA)** as their active ingredient. When applied to the epidermis, DHA interacts with the amino acids in the cells to produce a darkened, brownish color change. Because only the most superficial epidermal cells are affected, the color change is temporary and lasts about 5 to 7 days. Other sunless tanners on the market containing different chemicals do not appear to be as effective.

Most sunless tanners contain no sunscreen and offer no protection against UV rays. Thus, individuals who use sunless tanners should also apply sunscreen to protect their skin.

Skin Markings

A **nevus** (nē′vŭs; pl., nē′vī; *naevus* = mole, birthmark), commonly called a **mole,** is a harmless, localized overgrowth of melanin-forming cells. Almost everyone is born with a few nevi, and some people have as many as 20 or more. On rare occasions, a nevus may become malignant, typically as a consequence of excessive UV light exposure. Thus, nevi should be monitored for changes that may suggest malignancy. **Freckles** are yellowish or brown spots that represent localized areas of excessive melanocyte activity, not an increase in melanocyte numbers. A freckle's degree of pigmentation varies and depends upon both sun exposure and heredity.

A **hemangioma** (hē-man′j ē-ō′mă; *angio* = vessel, *oma* = tumor) is a congenital anomaly that results in skin discoloration due to blood vessels that proliferate and form a benign tumor. **Capillary hemangiomas,** or *strawberry-colored birthmarks,* appear in the skin as bright red to deep purple nodules that usually disappear in childhood. However, their development may occur in adults. **Cavernous hemangiomas,** also known as *port wine stains,* involve larger dermal blood vessels and may last a lifetime.

The contours of the skin surface follow ridge patterns, varying from small, conical pegs (in thin skin) to complex arches and whorls (in thick skin) called **friction ridges.** Friction ridges occur on the fingers (called *fingerprints*), palms, soles, and toes (**figure 5.5**). These ridges are formed from large folds and valleys of both the dermis and epidermis. With the help of moisture from merocrine sweat glands, friction ridges increase friction so that objects do not slip easily from our hands and our feet do not slip on the floor when we walk barefoot. Some researchers have suggested friction ridges also provide flexibility to the skin and allow it to deform without being damaged. When sweat and oil glands release their secretions, friction ridges can leave noticeable prints on touched surfaces. The study of friction ridge patterns is known as **dermatoglyphics** (*derma* = skin, *glyph* = carving). Friction ridge patterns are well formed by the fourth month of fetal development, and are a unique identifier because no two individuals share the same set of fingerprints. Thus, dermatoglyphics is a valuable identification tool for law enforcement.

Arch
Whorl
Loop
Combination

Figure 5.5

Friction Ridges of Thick Skin. Friction ridges form fingerprints, palm prints, and toe prints. Shown here are four basic fingerprint patterns.

WHAT DO YOU THINK?

3 Why are people's attempts to change their recognizable fingerprints usually not successful?

WHAT DID YOU LEARN?

3 Draw and label the five layers of the epidermis. Label the layer that is present only in thick skin.

4 Briefly describe the process of keratinization. Where does it begin? Why is it important?

5 List the epidermal cells, and for each cell type, list the layer(s) in which it is found.

6 What are the substances that contribute to skin color, and how specifically do they affect its color?

5.3 Dermis

✓Learning Objectives

6. Describe the organization and function of the layers of the dermis.
7. Describe nerve and blood supply to the dermis, and the role of the dermal blood supply in regulating body temperature.

The **dermis** (der′mis) lies deep to the epidermis and ranges in thickness from 0.5 mm to 3.0 mm. The dermis consists of two types of connective tissue: areolar and dense irregular. These connective tissue layers are composed of fibroblasts and primarily of collagen fibers, although both elastic and reticular fibers are also present. Other components of the dermis are blood vessels, sweat glands, sebaceous glands, hair follicles, nail roots, sensory nerve endings, and smooth muscle tissue (arrector pili). There are two major regions of the dermis: a superficial papillary layer and a deeper reticular layer (**figure 5.6**).

5.3a Papillary Layer of the Dermis

The **papillary** (pap′i-lār′ē) **layer** is the superficial region of the dermis directly adjacent to the epidermis. It is composed of areolar connective tissue, and it derives its name from the projections of the dermis toward the epidermis called **dermal papillae** (der′măl pă-pil′ē; sing., *papilla;* a nipple). The dermal papillae interlock with deep projections of epidermis called **epidermal ridges.** Together, the epidermal ridges and

Learning Strategy 5.2

Experiment with egg crate foam to better understand how the epidermal ridges and dermal papillae interlock. Use one layer of the egg crate foam as the epidermis, and another layer of the foam as the dermis. Put the two layers together so that the projections of one layer fit into the depressions/valleys of the other.

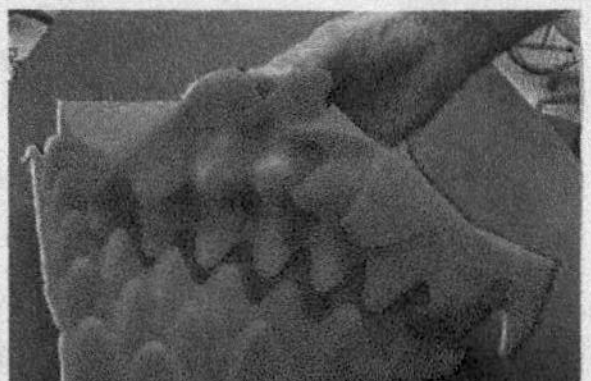

©Valerie Dean O'Loughlin, PhD

(The projections on the first piece of foam represent the dermal papillae, while the projections on the second piece of foam represent the epidermal ridges.) Note how the two layers now interlock tightly—which is what happens when the epidermal ridges and dermal papillae interlock in your integument.

Figure 5.6

Layers of the Dermis. The dermis is composed of a papillary layer and a reticular layer.

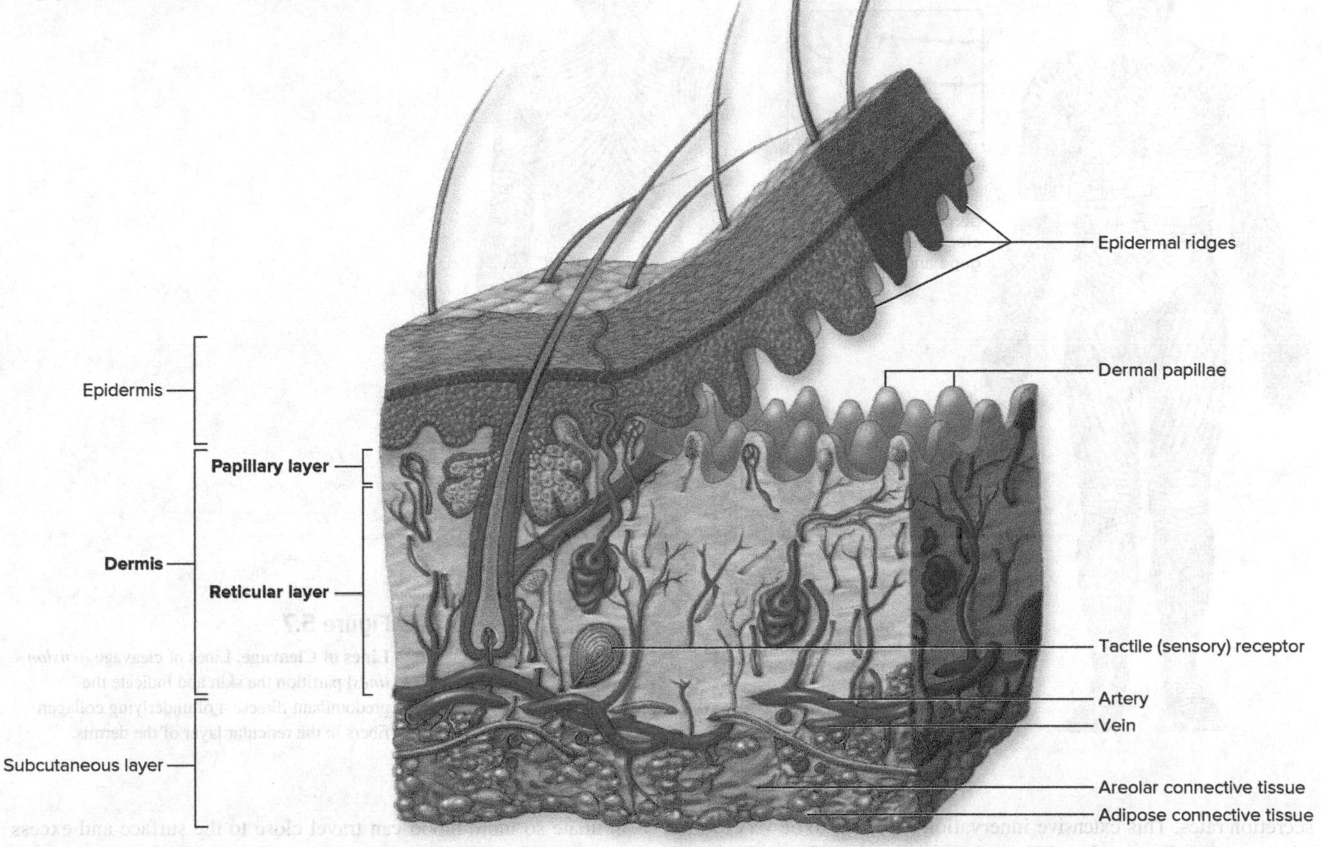

dermal papillae increase the area of contact between the epidermis and dermis and connect these layers. Each dermal papilla contains the capillaries that supply nutrients to the cells of the epidermis. Additionally, dermal papillae house sensory receptors, such as some of the receptors shown in figure 5.1, that continuously monitor touch on the surface of the epidermis. Section 19.2 discusses tactile receptors in detail.

5.3b Reticular Layer of the Dermis

The **reticular layer** forms the deeper, major portion of the dermis and extends from the thin, overlying papillary layer to the underlying subcutaneous layer. The reticular layer consists primarily of dense irregular connective tissue through which large bundles of collagen fibers project in all directions. These fibers are interwoven into a meshwork that surrounds the structures in the dermis, such as hair follicles, sebaceous glands, sweat glands, nerves, and blood vessels. The word *reticular* in the name of this layer means "network" and refers to the meshwork of collagen fibers. These interwoven collagen fiber bundles obscure any distinct boundary between the papillary and reticular layers.

5.3c Lines of Cleavage and Stretch Marks

The majority of the collagen and elastic fibers in the skin are oriented in parallel bundles at specific body locations. The alignment of fiber bundles within the dermis is a result of the direction of applied stress during routine movement; therefore, the function of the bundles is to resist stress. **Lines of cleavage** (*tension lines*) in the skin identify the predominant orientation of collagen fiber bundles (**figure 5.7**). These are clinically and surgically significant because any procedure resulting in a cut at right angles to a cleavage line usually is pulled open as a result of the recoil resulting from cut elastic fibers, often resulting in slow healing and increased scarring. In contrast, an incision made parallel to a cleavage line usually will remain closed. Therefore, surgical procedures should be planned to consider lines of cleavage, thus ensuring rapid healing and prevention of scarring.

Collagen fibers and elastic fibers together contribute to the physical characteristics of the skin. Whereas the collagen fibers impart tensile strength, elastic fibers allow some stretch and recoil in the dermis during normal movement activities. Stretching of the skin that may occur as a result of excessive weight gain or pregnancy often exceeds the elastic capabilities of the skin. When the skin is stretched beyond its capacity, some collagen fibers are torn and result in stretch marks, called **striae** (strī′ē; *stria* = furrow). Both the flexibility and thickness of the dermis are diminished by effects of exposure to ultraviolet light and aging, causing either sagging or wrinkled skin.

5.3d Innervation and Blood Supply

Innervation means to supply with nerves. Nerve fibers are extensively dispersed throughout the dermis, so the dermis is richly innervated. Nerve fibers in the skin monitor sensory receptors (such as tacile corpuscles and tactile cells) in the dermis and epidermis (see section 19.2), and they also control both blood flow and gland

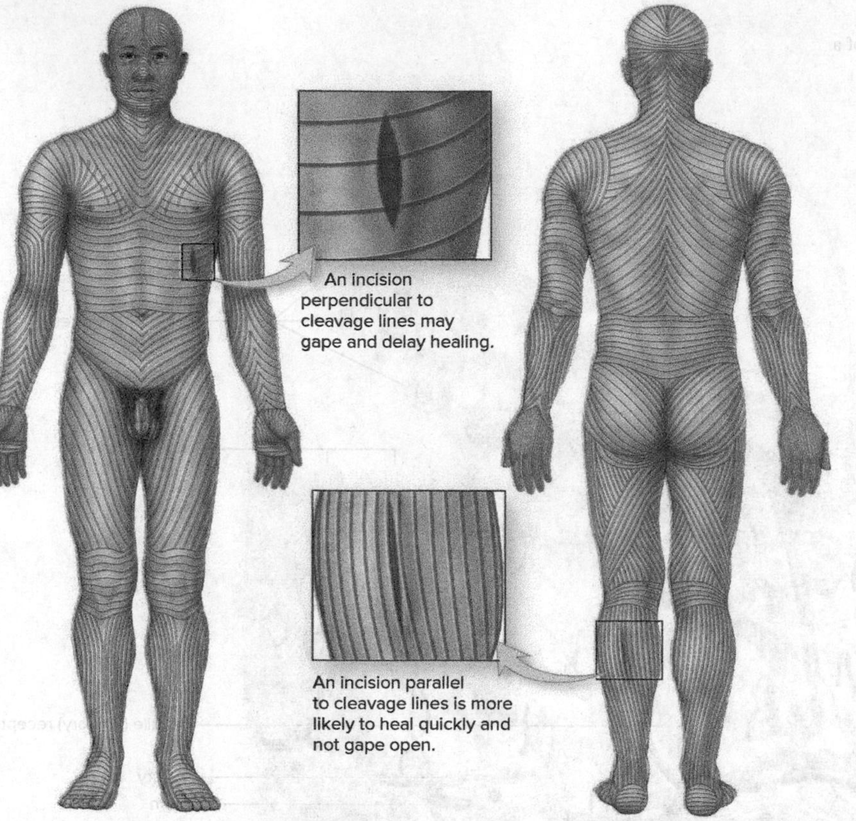
An incision
perpendicular to
cleavage lines may
gape and delay healing.
An incision parallel
to cleavage lines is more
likely to heal quickly and
not gape open.

Figure 5.7

Lines of Cleavage. Lines of cleavage (*tension lines*) partition the skin and indicate the predominant direction of underlying collagen fibers in the reticular layer of the dermis.

secretion rates. This extensive innervation allows us to be very aware of our surroundings and to differentiate among the different kinds of sensory signals from receptors in the skin.

Recall that all epithelia, including the epidermis, are avascular. Therefore, blood vessels within the dermis must supply nutrients to the living cells in the epidermis as well as to all structures in the dermis. The largest of these blood vessels lie along the border between the reticular layer of the dermis and the subcutaneous layer. Smaller vessels branch into the dermis to supply the hair follicles, sweat glands, sensory receptors, and other structures housed there. The smallest arterial vessels connect to capillary loops within the dermal papillae. Eventually, these capillaries drain into small vessels, forming a vessel network that merges into small veins draining the dermis.

Dermal blood vessels have an important role in regulating body temperature and blood pressure. **Vasoconstriction** (vā′sō-kon-strik′shŭn; *vas* = a vessel) means that the diameters of the vessels narrow, so relatively less blood can travel through them. Therefore, relatively more blood must travel in blood vessels that are deeper internal to the skin. The net effect of vasoconstriction of the dermal blood vessels is a shunting of blood *away* from the periphery of the body. If the body is cold, the dermal blood vessels vasoconstrict to conserve heat in the blood. This is why we are paler when we are exposed to cold temperatures.

Conversely, **vasodilation** of the dermal blood vessels means that the diameter of the vessels increases, so relatively more blood can travel through them. As more blood is shunted to these superficial blood vessels, the heat from the blood may be more easily dissipated through the skin. If the body is too warm, the dermal blood vessels vasodilate so more blood can travel close to the surface and excess heat can be lost. This additional blood flow in the dermis gives a more reddish or pinkish hue to the skin. Thus, your face may become flushed when you exercise because your dermal blood vessels are dilated in an attempt to release the excess heat you generated while working out. Because blood volume typically remains constant, any increase in circulation to the skin results in a decrease in circulation to other organs.

WHAT DID YOU LEARN?

7. Briefly describe the structure of epidermal ridges and dermal papillae. What is the importance of each, and how do they interact?
8. What is indicated by the lines of cleavage in the skin, and why are they medically important?
9. Why does your face become flushed when you exercise?

5.4 Subcutaneous Layer

✓ Learning Objective

8. Identify and describe the structure and function of the subcutaneous layer.

Deep to the integument is the **subcutaneous** (sŭb′kyū-tā′nē-ŭs; *sub* = beneath; *cutis* = skin) **layer,** also called the *hypodermis* or *superficial facia*. It is not considered a part of the integument. This layer consists of both areolar connective tissue and adipose connective tissue (see figure 5.1). In some locations of the body, adipose connective tissue

Table 5.2 Layers of the Integument and the Subcutaneous Layer APR

Layer	Specific Layer	Description
INTEGUMENT: EPIDERMIS		
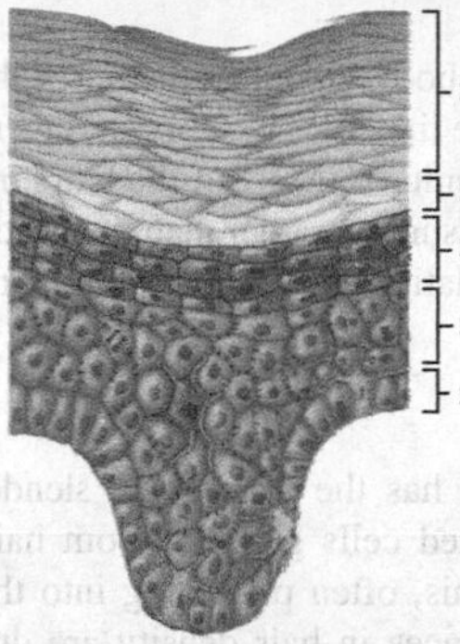	Stratum corneum	Most superficial layer of epidermis; 20–30 layers of dead, flattened, anucleate, keratin-filled keratinocytes
	Stratum lucidum	2–3 layers of anucleate, dead keratinocytes; seen only in thick skin (e.g., palms of hands, soles of feet)
	Stratum granulosum	3–5 layers of keratinocytes with distinct granules in the cytoplasm: keratinization begins in this layer
	Stratum spinosum	Several layers of keratinocytes attached to neighbors by desmosomes; epidermal dendritic cells present
	Stratum basale	Deepest, single layer of cuboidal to low columnar keratinocytes in contact with basement membrane; mitosis occurs here; also contains melanocytes and tactile cells
INTEGUMENT: DERMIS		
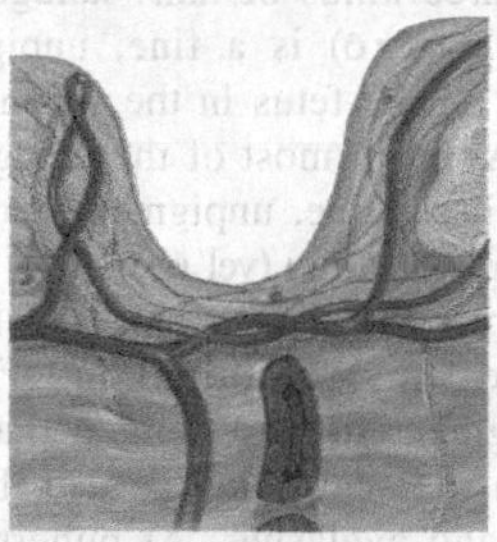	Papillary layer	Superficial layer of dermis that is in contact with epidermis; composed of areolar connective tissue; forms dermal papillae
	Reticular layer	Deeper layer of dermis; dense irregular connective tissue surrounding blood vessels, hair follicles, nerves, sweat glands, and sebaceous glands
SUBCUTANEOUS LAYER		
	No specific layers	Not considered part of the integument; deep to dermis; composed of areolar connective tissue and adipose connective tissue

predominates, and the subcutaneous layer is called **subcutaneous fat.** The connective tissue fibers of the reticular layer are extensively interwoven with those of the subcutaneous layer to stabilize the position of the skin and bind it to the underlying tissues. The subcutaneous layer pads and protects the body and its parts, acts as an energy reservoir, and provides thermal insulation.

Drugs are often injected into the subcutaneous layer because its excessive vascular network promotes rapid absorption. Normally, the subcutaneous layer is thicker in genetic females than in genetic males, and its regional distribution also differs between the sexes. Adult males tend to accumulate subcutaneous fat primarily at the neck, upper arms, abdomen, along the lower back, and over the buttocks, whereas adult females tend to accumulate subcutaneous fat primarily in the breasts, buttocks, hips, and thighs.

Table 5.2 reviews the layers of the integument and the subcutaneous layer.

WHAT DID YOU LEARN?

10 What are some functions of the subcutaneous layer?

5.5 Integumentary Structures Derived from Epidermis

✓ Learning Objectives

9. Describe the structure and functions of nails.
10. Describe the structure, distribution, and functions of hairs.
11. Describe how hair changes throughout life (i.e., the hair growth cycle).
12. Identify and describe the characteristics of sweat glands, sebaceous glands, and other glands found in the skin.

Nails, hair, and exocrine glands of the skin all are derived from the epithelium of the epidermis. These structures also are known as **epidermal derivatives,** or *epidermal appendages,* of the integument. Epidermal derivatives were formed during embryological development when the epidermis invaginated into the dermis; they are located in the dermis and may project through the epidermis to the surface. Both nails and hair are composed primarily of dead keratinocytes, whereas the exocrine glands are composed of living epithelial cells.

5.5a Nails

Nails are scalelike modifications of the stratum corneum layer of the epidermis that form on the dorsal tips of the fingers and toes. They protect the exposed distal tips when the fingers or toes are subjected to mechanical stress—for example, during running, kicking, or catching. Nails also help us grasp objects.

Each nail has a distal whitish **free edge,** a pinkish **nail body,** and a **nail root,** which is the proximal part embedded in the skin (**figure 5.8**). Together, these parts form the **nail plate.** The nail body covers a layer of epidermis that is called the **nail bed,** which contains only the deeper, living cell layers of the epidermis.

Most of the nail body appears pink because of the blood flowing in the underlying capillaries; the free edge of the nail appears white because there are no underlying capillaries. At the nail root and the proximal end of the nail body, the nail bed thickens to form the **nail matrix,** which is the actively growing part of the nail. The **lunula** (lū′nū-lă; *luna* = moon) is the whitish semilunar area of the proximal end of the nail body. It has a lighter appearance because a thickened stratum basale obscures the underlying blood vessels.

Along the lateral and proximal borders of the nail, folds of skin called **nail folds** overlap the nail. The **eponychium** (ep′ō-nik′ē-ŭm; *onyx* = nail), also known as the **cuticle** (kyū′ti-kil), is a narrow band of epidermis extending from the margin of the nail wall onto the nail body. The **hyponychium** (hī′pō-nik′ē-ŭm) is a region of thickened stratum corneum over which the free nail edge projects.

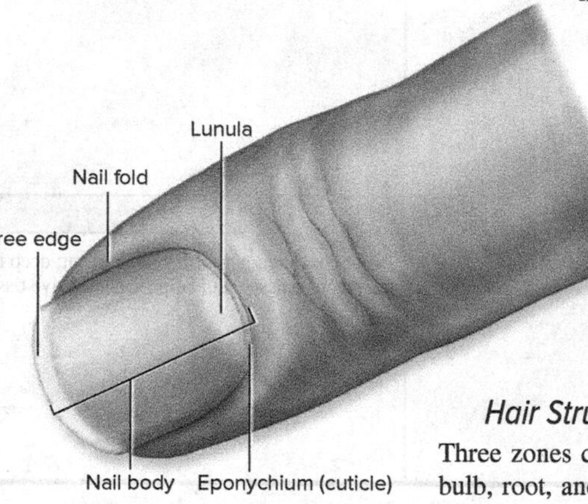
Lunula
Nail fold
Free edge
Nail body
Eponychium (cuticle)

(a)

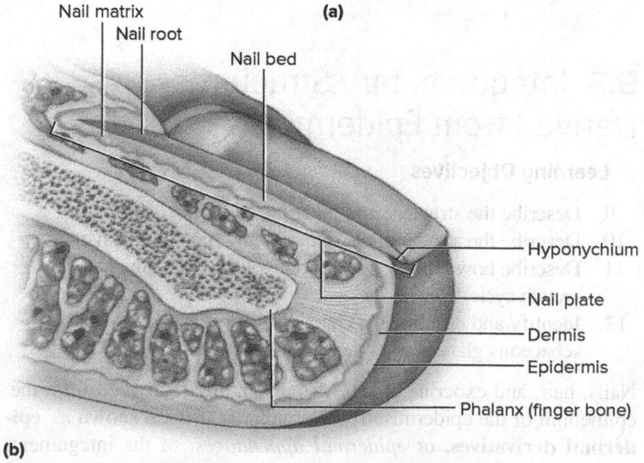
Nail matrix
Nail root
Nail bed
Hyponychium
Nail plate
Dermis
Epidermis
Phalanx (finger bone)

(b)

Figure 5.8

Structure of a Fingernail. Nails are formed from the stratum corneum of the epidermis. (*a*) Surface view of a fingernail. (*b*) Sagittal section showing the internal details of a fingernail. APR

5.5b Hair

Hair is found almost everywhere on the body except the palms of the hands, the sides and soles of the feet, the lips, the sides of the fingers and toes, and portions of the external genitalia. Most of the hairs on the human body are on the general body surface rather than the head. The general structure of hair and its relationship to the integument are shown in **figure 5.9**.

Hair Type and Distribution

A single hair is also called a *pilus*. It has the shape of a slender filament, and is composed of keratinized cells growing from hair follicles that extend deep into the dermis, often projecting into the underlying subcutaneous layer. Differences in hair density are due primarily to differences in its texture and pigmentation.

During our lives, we produce three kinds of hair: lanugo, vellus, and terminal hair. **Lanugo** (lă-nū′gō) is a fine, unpigmented, downy hair that first appears on the fetus in the second trimester of development. At birth, most of the lanugo has been replaced by similarly fine, unpigmented or lightly pigmented hair called **vellus** (vel′ŭs; *vellus* = fleece). Vellus is the primary human hair and is found on most of the body. **Terminal hair** is usually coarser, pigmented, and longer than vellus. It grows on the scalp, and is also the hair of eyebrows and eyelashes. At puberty, terminal hair replaces vellus in the axillary and pubic regions. Additionally, under the influence of testosterone, terminal hair forms a beard.

Hair Structure and Follicles

Three zones can be recognized along the length of a hair: the hair bulb, root, and shaft. The **hair bulb** consists of epithelial cells and is a swelling at the base where the hair originates in the dermis. The epithelium at the base of the bulb surrounds a small **hair papilla,** which is composed of a small amount of connective tissue containing tiny blood vessels and nerves. The **root** is the portion of the hair deep to the skin surface. The **shaft** is that portion of the hair that extends beyond the skin surface. The hair bulb contains living epithelial cells, whereas the root and shaft consist of dead epithelial cells.

Hair production involves a specialized type of keratinization that occurs in the **hair matrix.** Epithelial cells near the center of the hair matrix divide, producing new cells that are gradually pushed toward the surface. The **medulla,** not found in all hair types, is a remnant of the soft core of the matrix. It is composed of loosely arranged cells and air spaces, and contains flexible, soft keratin. Several layers of flattened cells closer to the outer surface of the developing hair form the relatively hard **cortex.** Multiple cell layers around the cortex form the **cuticle,** which coats the hair. The free edges of cuticle cells are directed externally.

The hair root extends from the hair bulb to the region where the hair shaft is completely mature. The entire hair root lies internal to the skin, and the hair shaft extends from the hair root to the exposed tip of the hair. The hair shaft's size, shape, and color can be highly variable.

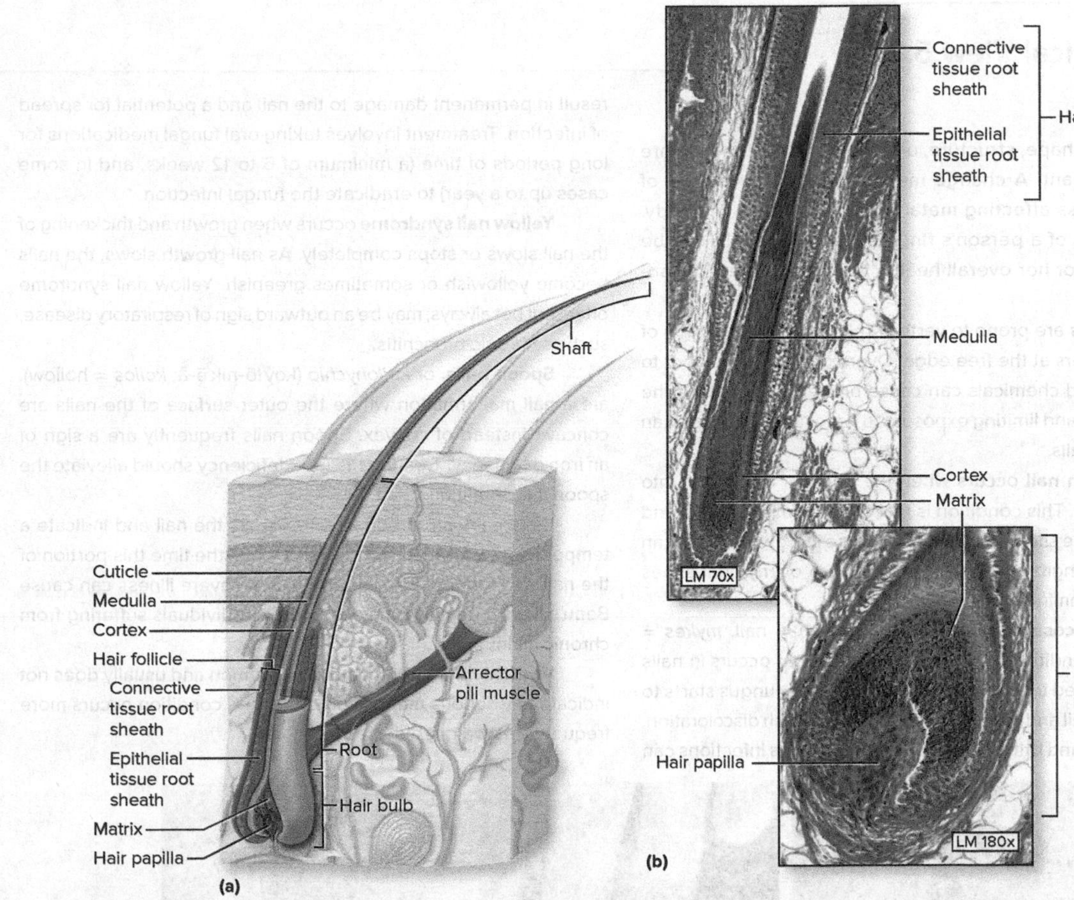

Figure 5.9

Hair. *(a)* A hair grows from a follicle extending from the dermis into the epidermis. Hair is a derivative of the epithelium. (*b*) Light micrographs of a hair follicle base.

(b) ©McGraw-Hill Education/Al Telser, photographer

The **hair follicle** (fol′i-k ĕl; *folliculus* = a small sac) is an oblique tube that surrounds the root hair. The follicle always extends into the dermis and sometimes into the subcutaneous layer. The cells of the follicle walls are organized into two principal concentric layers: an outer **connective tissue root sheath,** which originates from the dermis, and an inner **epithelial tissue root sheath,** which originates from the epidermis (figure 5.9 *b*).

Extending from the dermal papillae to the mid-region of the hair follicles are thin ribbons of smooth muscle that are collectively called the **arrector pili** (ă-rek′tōr pī′lī; *arrector* = to raise up, *pilus* = hair) **muscles.** The arrector pili muscles are usually stimulated in response to an emotional state, such as fear or rage, or exposure to cold temperatures. Upon stimulation, the arrector pili muscles contract, pulling on the follicles and elevating the hairs, to produce "goose bumps."

Functions of Hair

The millions of hairs distributed on the surface of the human body have important functions that include the following:

- **Protection.** The hair on the head protects the scalp from sunburn and injury. Hair within the nostrils entraps particles before they travel deeper into the respiratory system, whereas hairs within the external ear canal protect the ear from insects and foreign particles. Eyelashes protect the eyes, and eyebrows help prevent sweat on the forehead from dripping into the eyes.
- **Heat retention.** Hair on the head prevents the loss of conducted heat from the scalp to the surrounding air. Individuals who have lost their scalp hair release much more heat through the scalp than those who have a full head of hair.
- **Sensory reception.** Hair has associated tactile receptors (hair root plexuses) that detect light touch (see section 19.2a).
- **Visual identification.** Hair characteristics are important in determining age and sex, and in identifying individuals. (Hair analysis also assists in determining animal species.)

Hair Color

Hair color is a result of the synthesis of melanin in the matrix adjacent to the papillae. Variations in hair color reflect genetically determined differences in the structure of the melanin. Additionally, environmental and hormonal factors may influence the color of the hair. As people age, pigment production decreases, and thus hair

Clinical View 5.3

Nail Disorders

Changes in the shape, structure, or appearance of the nails are clinically significant. A change may indicate the existence of a disease process affecting metabolism throughout the body. In fact, the state of a person's fingernails and toenails can be indicative of his or her overall health. Nails are subject to various disorders.

Brittle nails are prone to vertical splitting and separation of the nail plate layers at the free edge. Overexposure to water or to certain household chemicals can cause brittle nails. Keeping the nails moisturized and limiting exposure to water and chemicals can alleviate brittle nails.

An **ingrown nail** occurs when the edge of a nail digs into the skin around it. This condition is first characterized by pain and inflammation at the site. If left untreated, some ingrown toenails can cause infection. Ingrown nails may result from overly tight shoes and improper trimming of the nails.

Onychomycosis (on′i-kō-mī-kō′sis; *onych* = nail, *mykes* = fungus, *osis* = condition) is a *fungal infection* that occurs in nails constantly exposed to warmth and moisture. The fungus starts to grow under the nail and eventually causes a yellowish discoloration, a thickened nail, and brittle, cracked edges. Fungus infections can result in permanent damage to the nail and a potential for spread of infection. Treatment involves taking oral fungal medications for long periods of time (a minimum of 6 to 12 weeks, and in some cases up to a year) to eradicate the fungal infection.

Yellow nail syndrome occurs when growth and thickening of the nail slows or stops completely. As nail growth slows, the nails become yellowish or sometimes greenish. Yellow nail syndrome often, but not always, may be an outward sign of respiratory disease, such as chronic bronchitis.

Spoon nails, or *koilonychia* (koy′lō-nik′ē-ă; *koilos* = hollow), are a nail malformation where the outer surface of the nails are concave instead of convex. Spoon nails frequently are a sign of an iron deficiency. Treating the iron deficiency should alleviate the spoon nail condition.

Beau's lines run horizontally across the nail and indicate a temporary interference with nail growth at the time this portion of the nail was formed. Injury to the nail or severe illness can cause Beau's lines. They also may be seen in individuals suffering from chronic malnutrition.

Vertical ridging of the nails is common and usually does not indicate any serious medical problem. The condition occurs more frequently as we get older.

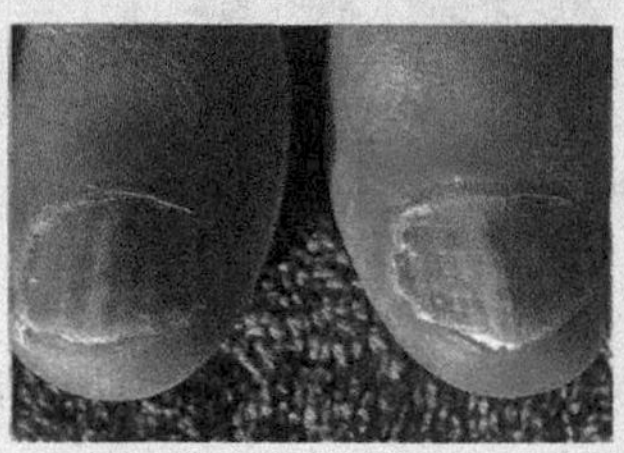

Onychomycosis
Source: Dr Edwin P Ewing, Jr./Centers for Disease Control and Prevention

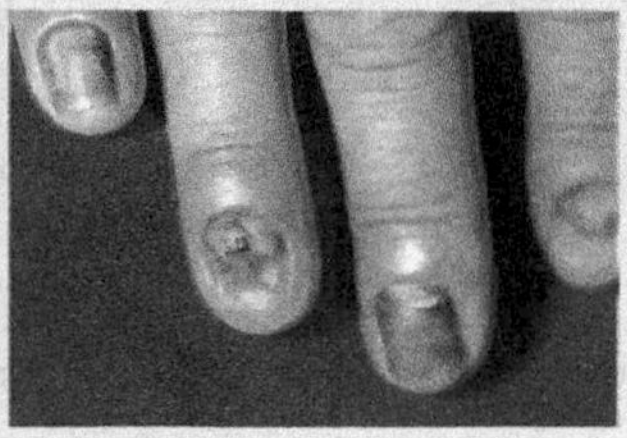

Yellow nail syndrome
©Visual DX

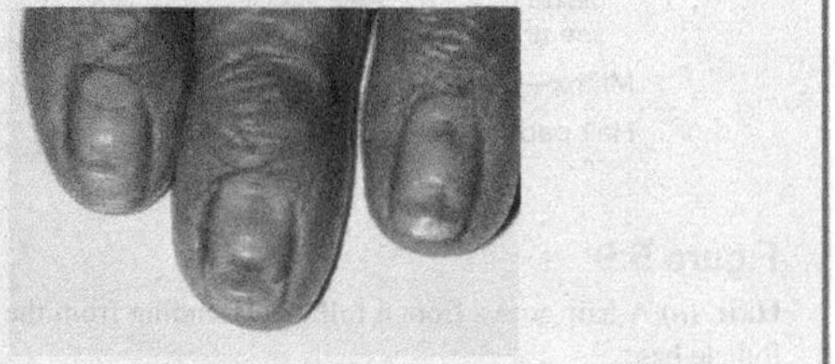

Beau's lines
©Dr. P. Marazzi/Science Source

becomes lighter in color. Gray hair results from the gradual reduction of melanin production within the hair follicle, whereas white hair signifies a complete stoppage of melanin production. Usually, hair color changes gradually.

Hair Growth Cycle

There are three stages of the hair growth cycle: anagen, catagen, and telogen:

1. The **anagen phase** is the active phase of growth where living cells of the hair bulb are rapidly growing, dividing, and transforming into hair. It is the longest part of the growth cycle and lasts from about 18 months to as much as 7 years, depending upon the genetics of the person (e.g., people who can grow long hair have the longest anagen phase of the cycle). On the scalp, during the anagen phase, each hair strand grows about one-third of a millimeter per day, or 0.5 to 1.0 centimeter per month. On a normal scalp, 80% to 95% of follicles are in anagen phase.
2. The **catagen phase** is a brief regression period where cell division ceases. The follicle undergoes involution and shrinks toward the scalp surface. This very short phase lasts for about 3 to 4 weeks.
3. The **telogen phase** is the resting phase and is usually the phase where the hair is shed (these hairs are the ones we find in our comb or brush). After 3 to 4 months in the telogen phase, the cells of the hair bulb are stimulated (stimulus unknown) to start regrowing, and the follicle reenters the anagen phase.

The hair growth rate and the duration of the hair growth cycle vary; however, the scalp normally loses between 10 and 100 hairs per day. Thus, this amount of hair loss shouldn't cause noticeable thinning of the scalp hair. Continuous losses that exceed 100 hairs per day often indicate a health problem. Sometimes hair loss may be temporary as a result of one or more of the following factors: certain medications, dietary factors, radiation, high fever, or stress. Thinning of the hair, called **alopecia** (al′ō-pē′shē-ă; *alopekia* = a disease like fox mange), can occur in both males and females, usually as a result of aging. In **diffuse hair loss,** hair is shed from all parts of the scalp. This condition primarily affects genetic females, and may be due to hormones, medications, or iron deficiency.

The condition called **male pattern baldness** causes loss of hair first from only the crown region of the scalp rather than uniformly. It is caused by a combination of genetic and hormonal influences. At puberty, the testes begin secreting large quantities of male sex hormones (primarily testosterone). Male sex hormones produce a typical pattern of underarm hair, facial hair, and chest hair. The relevant gene for male pattern baldness has two alleles, one for uniform hair growth and one for baldness. The baldness allele is dominant in genetic males and is expressed only in the presence of a high level of testosterone. In genetic females, the baldness allele is recessive. Thus, this trait is a *sex-influenced trait,* in which an allele is dominant in one sex (males) and recessive in the other (females). Changes in the level of the sex hormones circulating in the blood can affect hair development on the scalp, causing a shift from terminal hair to vellus production.

Excessive hairiness in areas of the body that normally do not have terminal hair is called **hirsutism** (her'sū-tizm; *hirsutus* = shaggy). This hair growth typically occurs on the face, chest, and back and may affect both sexes, but typically is more distressing for those who identify as female. Hirsutism most commonly is caused by an excess of male sex hormones called androgens, either through a medical condition (such as polycystic ovarian syndrome) or by certain medications that cause a rise in androgens.

5.5c Exocrine Glands of the Skin

The skin houses two types of exocrine glands: **sweat (sudoriferous) glands** and **sebaceous glands** (**figure 5.10*a***) (see section 4.1f). Sweat glands produce a watery solution that performs several specific functions. Sebaceous glands produce an oily material that coats hair shafts and the epidermal surface. **Table 5.3** compares the types of glands found in the skin.

Sweat (Sudoriferous) Glands

The two types of sweat glands in the skin are **merocrine sweat glands** and **apocrine sweat glands.** These sweat glands have a coiled, tubular secretory portion located either in the reticular layer of the dermis, or in the subcutaneous layer. A **sweat gland duct** transports the secretion to the surface of the epidermis (in a merocrine gland) or into a hair follicle (in an apocrine gland). The opening of the sweat gland duct on the epidermal surface is an indented region called a **sweat pore.**

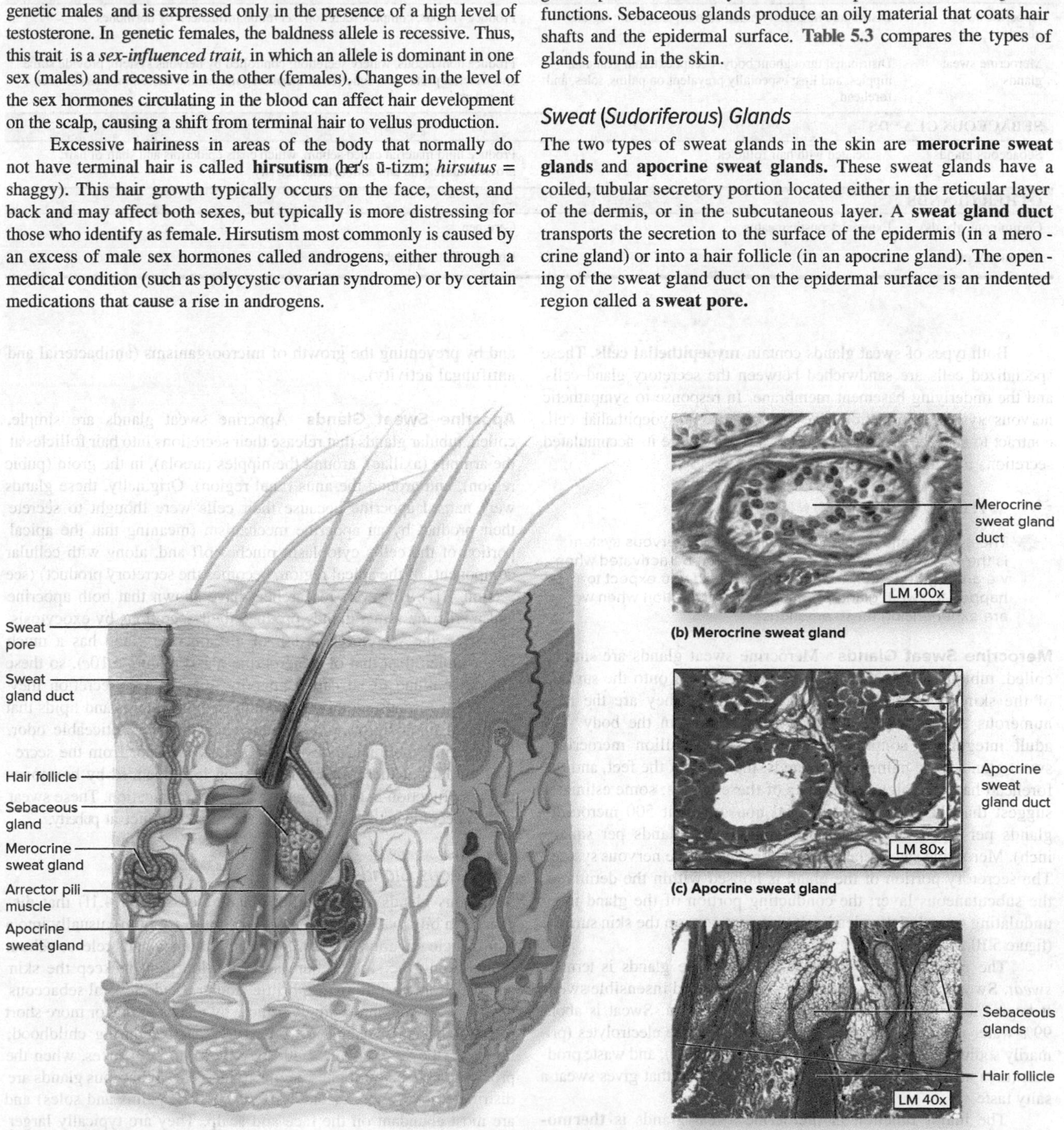

Figure 5.10

Exocrine Glands of the Skin. (*a*) The integument contains sweat glands and sebaceous glands. (*b*) Merocrine sweat glands have a duct with a narrow lumen that opens onto the skin surface through a pore. (*c*) Apocrine sweat glands exhibit a duct with a large lumen to convey secretion products into a hair follicle. (*d*) The cells of sebaceous glands are destroyed during the release of their oily secretion into the follicle.

(b) ©CNRI/Science Source; (c, d) ©McGraw-Hill Education/Alvin Telser, Ph.D., photographer

Table 5.3 Glands of the Skin

Type	Location	Products Secreted/Description
SWEAT (SUDORIFEROUS) GLANDS		
Apocrine sweat glands	Distributed in axillary, anal, areolar, and pubic regions	Produce viscous, complex secretion; secretion influenced by hormones
Merocrine sweat glands	Distributed throughout body, except external genitalia, nipples, and lips; especially prevalent on palms, soles, and forehead	Produce nonviscous, watery secretion; controlled by nervous system; provide some antibacterial protection; function in thermoregulation and excretion; flush surface of epidermis
SEBACEOUS GLANDS		
Sebaceous glands	Associated with hair follicles	Produce lipid material called sebum, which coats epidermis and shaft of hair; provide lubrication and antibacterial activity
OTHER GLANDS		
Ceruminous glands	External acoustic meatus	Cerumen
Mammary glands	Breasts	Breast milk to nourish offspring

Both types of sweat glands contain **myoepithelial cells.** These specialized cells are sandwiched between the secretory gland cells and the underlying basement membrane. In response to sympathetic nervous system stimulation (see section 18.2), myoepithelial cells contract to squeeze the gland, causing it to discharge its accumulated secretions into the duct.

WHAT DO YOU THINK?

4 The sympathetic division of the autonomic nervous system is the part of the nervous system that can be activated when we are frightened or nervous. What would you expect to happen to sweat gland production and secretion when we are experiencing these emotions?

Merocrine Sweat Glands Merocrine sweat glands are simple, coiled, tubular glands that release their secretion onto the surface of the skin by exocytosis (see section 2.3c). They are the most numerous and widely distributed sweat glands in the body. The adult integument contains between 3 and 4 million merocrine sweat glands. The palms of the hands, the soles of the feet, and the forehead have the highest numbers of these glands; some estimates suggest that the palm of each hand houses about 500 merocrine glands per square centimeter (or about 3000 glands per square inch). Merocrine sweat glands are controlled by the nervous system. The secretory portion of the gland is housed within the dermis or the subcutaneous layer; the conducting portion of the gland is an undulating or coiled duct leading to a sweat pore on the skin surface (figure 5.10 *b*).

The clear secretion produced by merocrine glands is termed *sweat.* Sweat comes in two varieties, sensible and insensible sweat. It begins as a protein-free filtrate of blood plasma. Sweat is about 99% water and 1% other chemicals, including some electrolytes (primarily sodium and chloride), metabolites (lactic acid), and waste products (urea and ammonia). It is the sodium chloride that gives sweat a salty taste.

The major function of merocrine sweat glands is **thermoregulation,** which is the regulation of body temperature by evaporation of fluid from the skin. Merocrine sweat gland secretions provide a means for the loss of both water and electrolytes. The secretions also may help eliminate a number of ingested drugs. Finally, merocrine sweat gland secretions provide some protection from environmental hazards both by diluting harmful chemicals and by preventing the growth of microorganisms (antibacterial and antifungal activity).

Apocrine Sweat Glands Apocrine sweat glands are simple, coiled, tubular glands that release their secretions into hair follicles at the armpits (axillae), around the nipples (areola), in the groin (pubic region), and around the anus (anal region). Originally, these glands were named apocrine because their cells were thought to secrete their product by an apocrine mechanism (meaning that the apical portion of the cell's cytoplasm pinches off and, along with cellular components of the apical region, becomes the secretory product) (see section 4.1f). However, researchers have shown that both apocrine and merocrine sweat glands produce their secretions by exocytosis. However, the secretory portion of an apocrine gland has a much larger lumen than that of a merocrine gland (figure 5.10*c*), so these glands continue to be called apocrine glands. The secretion they produce is viscous, cloudy, and composed of proteins and lipids that are acted upon by bacteria, producing a distinct, noticeable odor. (Underarm deodorant is designed to mask the odor from the secretory product of these glands.) Secretion is influenced by hormones and may function in both signaling and communication. These sweat glands become active and produce secretory product at puberty.

Sebaceous Glands

Sebaceous glands are holocrine glands (see section 4.1f) that discharge an oily, waxy secretion called **sebum** (sē′bŭm), usually into a hair follicle (figure 5.10*a, d*). Some sebaceous glands release sebum directly onto the skin. Sebum acts as a lubricant to keep the skin and hair from becoming dry, brittle, and cracked. Several sebaceous glands may open onto a single follicle by means of one or more short ducts. Sebaceous glands are relatively inactive during childhood; however, they are activated during puberty in both sexes, when the production of sex hormones begins to increase. Sebaceous glands are distributed over most of the body (except the palms and soles) and are most abundant on the face and scalp. They are typically larger on and around the nose where they secrete larger volumes of sebum.

Sebum has bactericidal (bacteria-killing) properties. However, under some conditions, bacteria can cause an infection within the sebaceous gland and produce a local inflammation called **folliculitis** (fŏ-lik′y ū-lī′tis). A blocked duct in a sebaceous gland often develops into a distinctive abscess called a **furuncle** (fū′rŭng-kĕl; *furunculus* =

a petty thief), or *boil*. A furuncle is usually treated by lancing (cutting it open) to facilitate normal drainage and healing.

Other Integumentary Glands

Some specialized glands of the integument are restricted to specific locations. Two important examples are the ceruminous glands and the mammary glands.

Ceruminous (sĕ-rū′mi-n ŭs; *cera* = wax) **glands** are true apocrine glands (see section 4.1f) located only in the external acoustic meatus (external ear canal), where their secretion mixes with both sebum and exfoliated keratinocytes to form waterproof earwax called **cerumen** (sĕ-rū′men). There are about 1000 to 2000 of these glands in the external acoustic meatus. They are simple, coiled, tubular glands with ducts leading to the surface of the skin. Ceruminous glands differ from sweat glands in that they secrete cerumen via the apocrine mechanism. Cerumen, together with tiny hairs along the ear canal, helps trap foreign particles or small insects and keeps them from reaching the eardrum. Cerumen also lubricates the external acoustic meatus and eardrum. In addition, cerumen contains lysozyme, an enzyme capable of destroying bacterial cell walls.

The **mammary glands** of the breasts are modified apocrine sweat glands (see section 4.1f). Both males and females have mammary glands, but these glands only become functional in pregnant females, when they produce a secretion (breast milk) that nourishes offspring. The development of the gland and the production of its secretory products are controlled by a complex interaction between gonadal and pituitary hormones. The structure and function of mammary glands are discussed in section 28.2f.

WHAT DID YOU LEARN?

11. Why is the nail body pinkish, while the free edge of a nail is white?
12. What are the major functions of hair?
13. Compare and contrast merocrine and apocrine sweat gland secretions.
14. What do sebaceous glands secrete, and what is the purpose of the secretion? How does sebaceous gland activity change as we mature?

Clinical View 5.4

Acne and Acne Treatments

Acne (ak′nē) is the term used to describe plugged sebaceous ducts. Acne typically becomes abundant beginning at puberty, because increases in hormone levels stimulate sebaceous gland secretion, making the pores more prone to blockage. Acne is prevalent during the teenage years, although any age group may experience acne.

The types of acne lesions include the following:

- **Comedo** (kom′ē-dō; pl., comedones). A sebaceous gland plugged with sebum. An open comedo is called a **blackhead,** because the plugged material has a dark, blackish appearance. A closed comedo is called a **whitehead,** because the top surface is whitish in color.
- **Papule** (pap′yūl) and **pustule** (pŭs′tyūl). Both are dome-shaped lesions. Papules typically are fluid-filled, form red elevations on the skin and do not contain pus. Papules may become pustules, which are filled with a mixture of white blood cells, dead skin cells, and bacteria (called pus).
- **Nodule** (nod′yūl). Similar to a pustule, but extending into the deeper skin layers and usually rupturing the hair follicle wall. Nodules can be prone to scarring.
- **Cyst** A large, fluid-filled nodule that can become severely inflamed and painful and can lead to scarring of the skin.

Many medicinal treatments are available for acne, depending upon the type and severity. The effectiveness of the following medications varies from individual to individual. These treatments include benzoyl peroxide, salicyclic (sal-i-sil′ik) acid, topical and oral antibiotics, topical vitamin A–like compounds (e.g., retinoids such as tretinoin [Retin-A]), and systemic retinoids such as isotretinoin (e.g., Accutane).

Other treatments include light chemical skin peels and comedo extraction by a dermatologist. Severe, untreated acne and picking at acne lesions can lead to scarring.

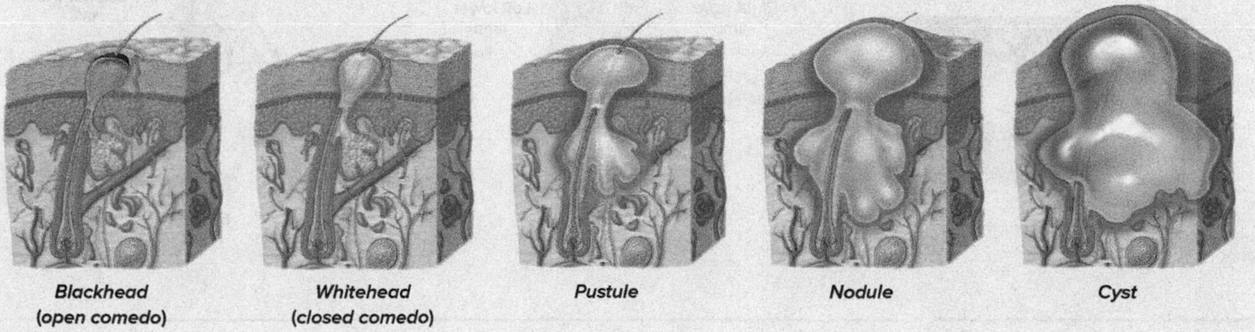
Blackhead (open comedo)
Whitehead (closed comedo)
Pustule
Nodule
Cyst

Clinical View 5.5

Burns

Burns are a major cause of accidental death and are usually caused by heat, radiation, harmful chemicals, sunlight, or electrical shock. The immediate threat to life results primarily from fluid loss, infection, and the effects of burned, dead tissue.

Burns are classified by depth of tissue involvement. First- and second-degree burns are called *partial-thickness burns;* third-degree burns are called *full-thickness burns.*

How Are First-, Second-, and Third-Degree Burns Distinguished?

First-degree burns involve only the epidermis and are characterized by redness, pain, and slight edema. An example is a mild sunburn. Treatment involves immersing the burned area in cool water or applying cool, wet compresses, possibly followed by covering the burn with sterile, nonadhesive bandages. The healing time averages about 3 to 5 days, and typically there is no scarring.

Second-degree burns involve the epidermis and part of the dermis. The skin also is blistered and painful. Examples include very severe sunburns (where the skin also blisters) or scalding from hot liquids or chemicals. Treatment is similar to that for first-degree burns, and care must be taken not to break the blisters, which would increase the risk of infection. Applying ointments to the blisters is not recommended, because the ointments can retain heat in the burned area. In addition, burned limbs should be elevated to prevent swelling. Healing times are about 2 to 4 weeks, and slight scarring may occur.

Third-degree burns involve the epidermis, dermis, and subcutaneous layer, which often are destroyed. Third-degree burns typically are caused by contact with corrosive chemicals or fire, or prolonged contact with extremely hot water. Dehydration is a major concern with a third-degree burn, because the entire portion of skin has been lost, and water cannot be retained in the area. Most third-degree burns require hospitalization. Skin grafting typically is needed for patients with third-degree burns, because the entire dermis and its vasculature are destroyed and regeneration is limited. A **skin graft** is a piece of skin transplanted from one part of the body to another to cover a destroyed area.

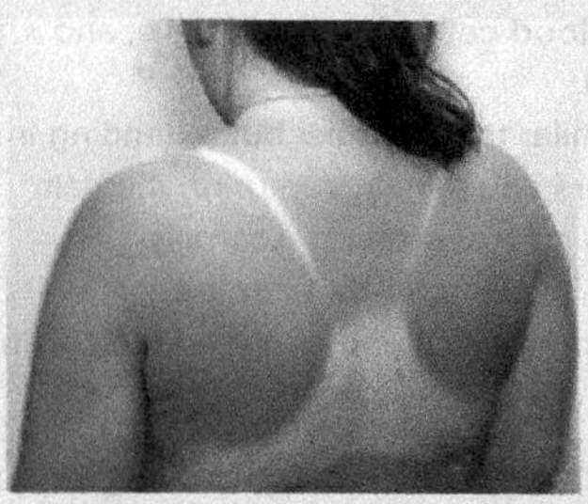

First-degree burn
©McGraw-Hill Education/Rick Brady, photographer

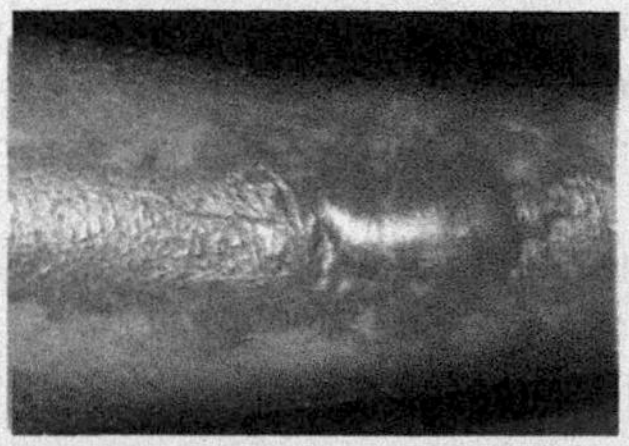

Second-degree burn
©Dr. P. Marazzi/Science Source

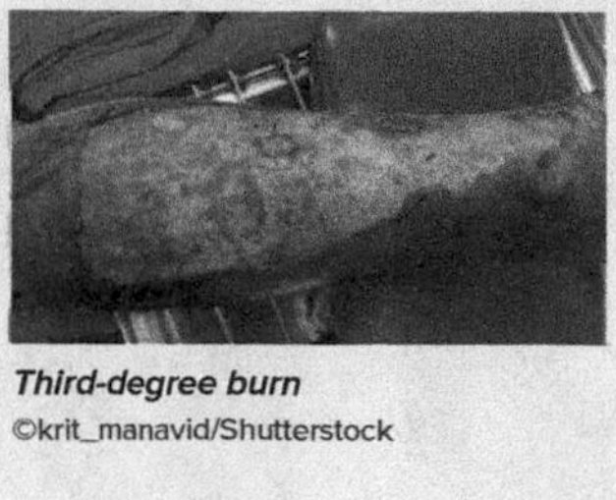

Third-degree burn
©krit_manavid/Shutterstock

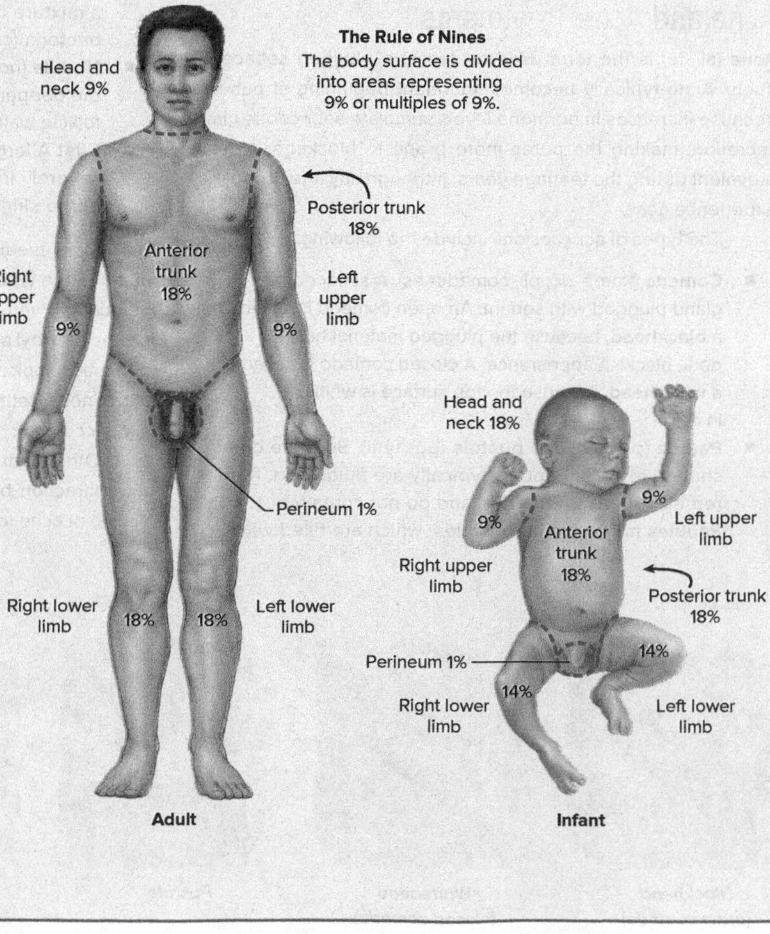
The Rule of Nines
The body surface is divided into areas representing 9% or multiples of 9%.
Head and neck 9%
Posterior trunk 18%
Anterior trunk 18%
Right upper limb
9%
Left upper limb
9%
Perineum 1%
Right lower limb
18%
18%
Left lower limb
Adult
Head and neck 18%
9%
9%
Left upper limb
Anterior trunk 18%
Right upper limb
Posterior trunk 18%
14%
Perineum 1%
14%
Right lower limb
Left lower limb
Infant

Skin grafts help prevent infection and dehydration in the affected area, and they also help minimize abnormal connective tissue fibrosis and disfigurement.

How Is the Overall Severity of a Burn Injury Determined?

The severity of a burn injury is measured not only by the degree of the burn, but also by the age of the patient, the general size of the burn, and the location of the burn. For example, a burn on the face may require more extensive treatment than a similar burn on an extremity. The **rule of nines** is used to estimate surface area of a burn. Simply put, most major body areas approximately account for some factor of 9% of the total body suface area. In adults, the anterior and posterior parts of the head and neck count 9% of the total body suface area each, each upper limb counts 9%, each lower limb (including the gluteal region) counts 18%, the anterior trunk counts 18%, the posterior trunk counts 18%, and the perineum is 1%. Estimating the surface area of a burn is critical for determining appropriate fluid replacement. The greater the surface area of the burn, the greater the volume of fluids that are lost, and these fluids must be replaced, either orally or intravenously.

Burns are considered very severe or critical if one of the following criteria is met:

1. Over 25% of the body has second-degree burns.
2. Over 10% of the body has third-degree burns.
3. Third-degree burns are present on the hands, feet, face, or perineum.

What Treatments Are Used for Burn Injuries?

In general, acute treatment involves managing fluid loss, relieving swelling, pain management, removing dead tissue and foreign material from the wound (debridement), controlling infection, and increasing caloric intake.

Swelling also may occur as the blood capillaries become more permeable ("leaky"), and fluid may collect in localized tissues, which exacerbates the overall fluid loss in the circulation. In severe cases, a procedure called an **escharatomy** (es-kă-rot'ŭ-mē) is performed, where an incision is made in the dermis to lessen the constriction caused by the swelling.

Pain medications may be given to alleviate any discomfort from the burn and resulting swelling. Antibiotics and other medications may be given to help limit and prevent infection.

Finally, individuals with severe burns become hypermetabolic as the body attempts to heal, and so their demand for nutrition greatly increases. The burn patient must be given additional caloric intake, sometimes as much as two to three times their normal caloric intake, to meet the demands. Typically, this supplementary nutrition is given through feeding tubes, IVs, or both.

5.6 Integument Repair and Regeneration

✓ Learning Objectives

13. Distinguish between regeneration and fibrosis.
14. Describe the process of wound healing.

The components of the integumentary system exhibit a tremendous ability to respond to stressors, trauma, and damage. Repetitive mechanical stresses applied to the integument stimulate mitotic activity in the stem cells of the stratum basale, resulting in a thickening of the epidermis and an improved ability to withstand stress. For example, walking about without shoes causes the soles of the feet to thicken, thus providing more protection for the underlying tissues.

Damaged tissues are normally repaired in one of two ways. The replacement of damaged or dead cells with the same cell type is called **regeneration.** This restores organ function. When regeneration is not possible because part of the organ is too severely damaged or its cells lack the capacity to divide, the body fills in the gap with scar tissue. This process, known as **fibrosis,** effectively binds the damaged parts back together. The replacement scar tissue is produced by fibroblasts and is composed primarily of collagen fibers. Some structural restoration occurs; however, functional activities are not restored. Fibrosis is the repair response in tissues subjected to severe injuries or burns. Both regeneration and fibrosis may occur in the healing of damage to the skin.

Figure 5.11 illustrates stages in wound healing of the skin:

1. Cut blood vessels initiate bleeding into the wound. The blood brings clotting proteins, numerous leukocytes (white blood cells), and antibodies.
2. A blood clot forms, temporarily patching the edges of the wound together and acting as a barrier to prevent the entry of pathogens into the body. Internal to the clot, macrophages and neutrophils (two types of leukocytes, see section 21.3b) clean the wound of cellular debris.
3. The cut blood vessels regenerate and grow in the wound. A soft mass deep in the wound becomes **granulation** (gran'ū-lā-shŭn) **tissue,** which is a vascular connective tissue that initially forms in a healing wound. Macrophages within the wound begin to remove the clotted blood. Fibroblasts produce new collagen fibers in the region.
4. Epithelial regeneration of the epidermis occurs due to division of epithelial cells at the edge of the wound. These new epithelial cells migrate over the wound, creeping internally to the now superficial remains of the clot (the scab). The connective tissue is replaced by fibrosis.

The skin repair and regeneration process is not rapid. The wider and deeper the surface affected, the longer it takes for skin to be repaired. Additionally, the area under repair usually is more susceptible to complications due to fluid loss and infection. Some integumentary system components that are not repaired following severe damage to the integument include hair follicles, exocrine glands, nerves, and the arrector pili muscle cells.

WHAT DID YOU LEARN?

15 Briefly list the 4 steps involved in wound healing.

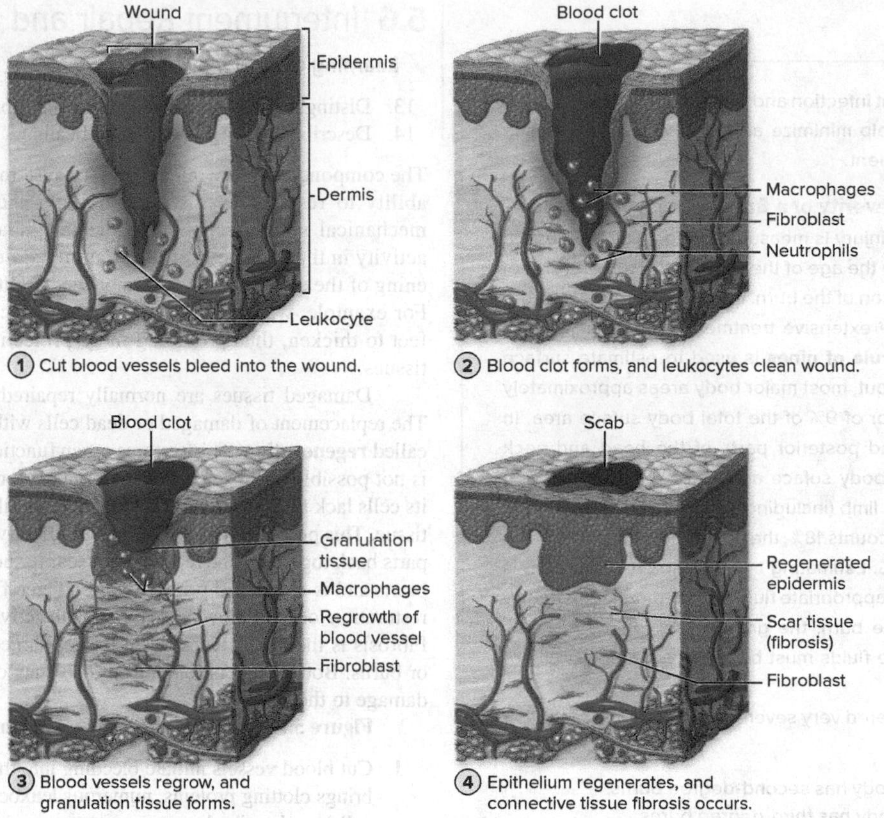
Wound
Epidermis
Dermis
Leukocyte
1 Cut blood vessels bleed into the wound.
Blood clot
Macrophages
Fibroblast
Neutrophils
2 Blood clot forms, and leukocytes clean wound.
Blood clot
Granulation tissue
Macrophages
Regrowth of blood vessel
Fibroblast
3 Blood vessels regrow, and granulation tissue forms.
Scab
Regenerated epidermis
Scar tissue (fibrosis)
Fibroblast
4 Epithelium regenerates, and connective tissue fibrosis occurs.

Figure 5.11
Stages in Wound Healing. Cut blood vessels in tissue initiate the multistep process of wound healing.

5.7 Aging of the Integument

✓ Learning Objectives

15. Describe the changes that occur in the skin during aging.
16. Identify the warning signs and characteristics of skin cancer.

Although some people develop acne when they enter puberty, most skin problems do not become obvious until an individual reaches middle age. Eventually, all components of the integumentary system are affected by age in the following ways:

- Skin repair processes take longer to complete because of the reduced number and activity of stem cells. Skin repair and regeneration that take 3 weeks in a healthy young person often take twice that time for a person in his or her 70s. Additionally, the reduced stem cell activity in the epidermis results in thinner skin that is less likely to protect against mechanical trauma.
- Collagen fibers in the dermis decrease in number and organization, and elastic fibers lose their elasticity. Also years of making particular facial expressions (e.g., squinting, smiling) produce crease lines in the integument. As a result, the skin forms wrinkles and becomes less resilient.
- The skin's immune responsiveness is diminished by a decrease in the number and efficiency of epidermal dendritic cells. This decreased immune response may be related to the appearance of longer dendritic processes and the decrease in molecules on their surface that recognize pathogens.
- Skin becomes drier and sometimes scaly because decreased sebaceous gland activity diminishes the amounts of natural skin lubricants.
- A decrease in melanocytes causes altered skin pigmentation. As a result, hair becomes gray or white, and sensitivity to sun exposure increases. Often, exposure to the sun or other forms of UV light leads to an increase in skin pigmentation in certain body areas. The resulting flat, brown or black spots are called **liver spots,** although they are unrelated to the liver.
- Sweat production diminishes as a result of decreased sweat gland activity.
- Dermal blood vessels lose some permeability as a result of decreased elasticity. Blood supply to the dermis is reduced as the extent of blood vessel distribution decreases. These vascular changes, along with glandular changes associated with aging, lead to impaired thermoregulation.
- Hair follicles either produce thinner hairs or stop production entirely.
- Integumentary production of vitamin D_3 decreases. If vitamin D_3 levels diminish significantly, the body is unable to absorb calcium and phosphorus from the digestive tract. The resulting declines in calcium and phosphorus concentrations affect muscle activity and bone density.
- Chronic overexposure to UV rays can damage the DNA in epidermal cells and accelerate aging.

5.7a Skin Cancer

Chronic overexposure to UV rays can damage the DNA in epidermal cells and accelerate aging. Specifically, research has indicated that chronic UV ray exposure can mutate the p53 gene in normal skin. This gene, when mutated, has been identified as a risk factor in many cancers (including skin cancer). Thus, UV overexposure is the predominant factor in the development of nearly all skin cancers. Skin cancer is the most common type of cancer. It occurs most frequently on the head and neck regions, followed by other regions commonly exposed to the sun. Fair-skinned individuals, especially those who experienced severe sunburns as children, are most at risk for skin cancer. However, skin cancer can arise in anyone of any age. Individuals should use sunscreen regularly and avoid prolonged exposure to the sun (see Clinical View 5.2: "UV Radiation, Sunscreens, and Sunless Tanners" in section 5.2b). An individual should regularly and thoroughly inspect his or her skin for any changes, such as an increase in the number or size of moles or the appearance of new skin lesions. In addition, an examination by a dermatologist should be part of everyone's routine health checkup. **Table 5.4** describes the three main types of skin cancer.

Clinical View 5.6

Treatments for Aging Skin

As a result of the aging process and exposure to UV radiation, skin begins to lose its resiliency and elasticity due to excessive cross-linking of collagen molecules in the dermis. Combined with years of repeated facial movements (e.g., frowning, squinting, and smiling), this contributes to wrinkle formation that accompanies skin aging. There are several treatments for aging skin, discussed here.

Laser Resurfacing

This procedure uses a focused laser (acronym for **l**ight **a**mplification by **s**timulated **e**mission of **r**adiation) to send out short impulses (each about a millisecond) of high-energy light into the epidermis and dermis. The procedure is most effective for improving skin texture and appearance, including wrinkles around the eyes and mouth. It is also effective on mild and moderate acne scars and to remove tattoos.

Fat Injections

In this procedure, also known as *fat transfer,* fat is liposuctioned from the abdominal area of the patient's body, and injected into the dermis and subcutaneous layer under the wrinkle or area to be augmented. This procedure is primarily used to add fullness to the face, lips, hands, and the buttocks. Some injected fat cells are lost in the procedure so doctors will usually inject a slightly greater volume than necessary, knowing that after a few weeks the final result will be more to the patient's liking.

Dermal Fillers

Substances referred to as **dermal fillers** are injected into the dermis and subcutaneous layer to plump up the skin. Most of these fillers contain **hyaluronic acid (HA),** which is a natural component of the integument. Some brand names of these fillers include Juvaderm and Restylane. The dermal fillers have a gel-like composition, and when injected into the dermis or subcutaneous layer beneath wrinkles, add volume and lift to the skin. The effects of dermal filler injections on the skin typically last 3–6 months.

Botulinum Toxin Type A (Botox) Injections

One popular treatment for wrinkles caused by repeated facial muscle expression is **botulinum toxin type A** (*Botox*). This medicine is derived from the toxin produced by the bacterium *Clostridium botulinum*. Although large doses of this toxin may be deadly, small therapeutic doses temporarily block nerve impulses to the facial expression muscles, thereby temporarily decreasing or eliminating the wrinkles they produce. The procedure is done in a doctor's office, where the doctor injects Botox in the specific facial muscles responsible for the wrinkles. An individual must repeat the procedure after about 4 months, as the muscles regain their function and may produce wrinkles again.

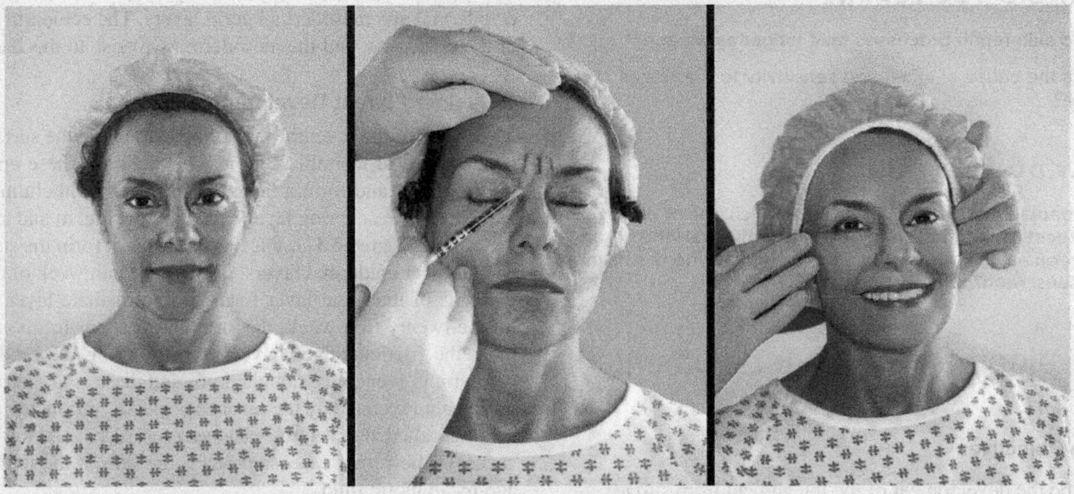

(left to right) Photos of a woman before, during, and after receiving Botox injections to smooth out frown lines.

Thinkstock/Comstock Images/Getty Images

Table 5.4	Skin Cancer
BASAL CELL CARCINOMA	
 Dr. P. Marazzi/Science Photo Library/Getty Images	■ Most common type of skin cancer ■ Least dangerous type because it seldom metastasizes ■ Originates in stratum basale ■ First appears as small, pearly white or pink shiny elevation with small blood vessels running along it; later a lesion may enlarge and develop central depression with pearly edge ■ Usually occurs on face ■ Treated by surgical removal of lesion
SQUAMOUS CELL CARCINOMA	
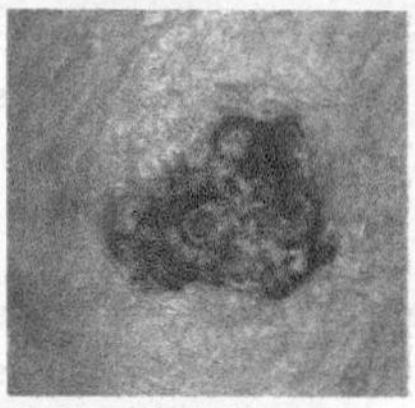 Science Photo Library/ Alamy Stock Photo	■ Arises from keratinocytes of stratum spinosum ■ Lesions usually appear on scalp, ears, lower lip, or back of hand ■ Early lesions are raised, reddened, scaly; later lesions form concave ulcers with elevated edges ■ Treated by surgical removal of lesion ■ May metastasize to other parts of the body
MALIGNANT MELANOMA	
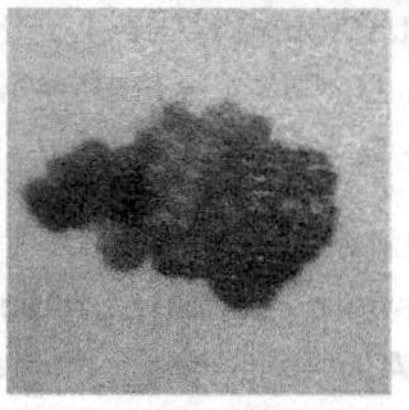 Source: National Cancer Institute (NCI)/U.S. Department of Health and Human Services (USHSS)	■ Most deadly type of skin cancer due to aggressive growth and metastasis ■ Arises from melanocytes, usually in a preexisting mole ■ Individuals at increased risk include those who have had severe sunburns, especially as children. ■ Characterized by change in mole diameter, color, shape of border, and symmetry ■ Survival rates improved by early detection and surgical removal of lesion ■ Advanced cases (metastasis of disease) are difficult to cure and are treated additionally with chemotherapy, interferon therapy, and radiation therapy. The usual signs of melanoma may be easily remembered using the ABCDE rule. Report any of the following changes in a birthmark or mole to your physician if you see any of the ABCDE characteristics, described below: **A** = Asymmetry: One-half of a mole or birthmark does not match the other. **B** = Border: Edges are notched, irregular, blurred, or ragged. **C** = Color: Color is not uniform; differing shades (usually brown or black and sometimes patches of white, blue, or red) may be seen. **D** = Diameter: Affected area is larger than 6 mm (about 1/4 inch) or is growing larger. **E** = Evolving: Change in the size, shape, or color of a mole. Or a change in symptoms, such as how a mole feels (how itchy or tender it feels) or what happens on the surface of a mole (especially bleeding).

WHAT DID YOU LEARN?

16 Why do skin repair processes take longer as we age?

17 What is the cause of increased sensitivity to the sun as we age?

WHAT DO YOU THINK?

5 If two people enjoy being in the sun, which one of them would you expect to get more wrinkles—the individual who has used sunscreen all his or her life, or the individual who has never used sunscreen? Why?

5.8 Development of the Integumentary System

✓ Learning Objectives

17. Describe the development of the integument from surface ectoderm and mesoderm.
18. Describe the development of epidermal derivatives.

The structures of the integumentary system are derived from the ectodermal and mesodermal germ layers. The ectoderm is the origin of the epidermis, and the mesoderm gives rise to the dermis.

5.8a Integument Development

By the end of the seventh week of development, the surface ectoderm is composed of a simple cuboidal epithelium. These epithelial cells divide, grow, and form a layer of squamous epithelium that flattens and becomes a covering layer called the **periderm** and an underlying **basal layer (figure 5.12).** The basal layer will form the stratum basale and all other epidermal layers. By the eleventh week of development, the cells of the basal layer form an intermediate layer of skin, and by the twenty-first week, the stratum corneum forms. Also by this time, the friction ridges have formed. During the fetal period, the periderm is eventually sloughed off, and these sloughed off cells mix with sebum secreted by the sebaceous glands, producing a waterproof coating called the **vernix caseosa** (ver′niks; varnish; kas-ē-ō′sa = cheese). The vernix caseosa protects the skin of the fetus from damage by amniotic fluid.

Although keratinocytes are formed from epidermal cells, melanocytes originate from specialized neural crest cells called

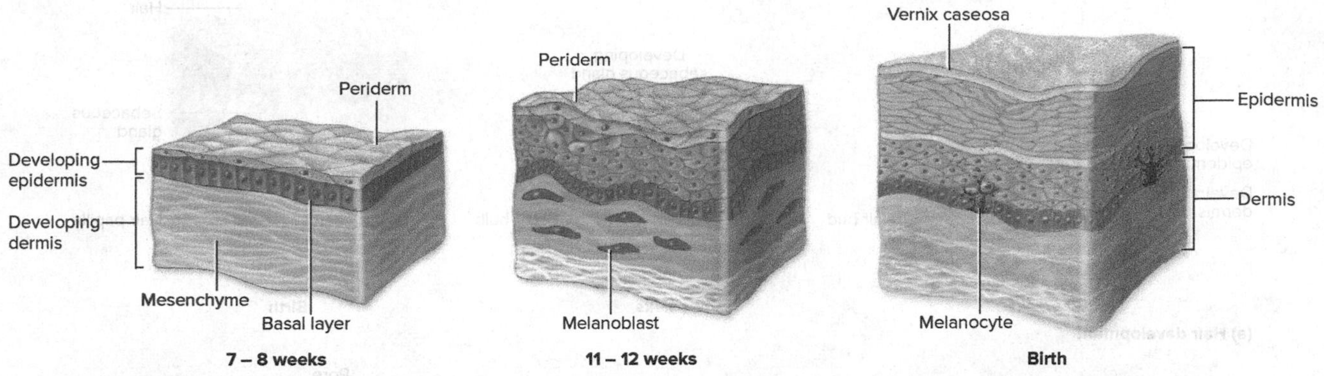

Figure 5.12

Integument Development. Skin structure becomes increasingly complex in the period from 7 weeks to birth.

melanoblasts, which arise from the ectoderm that also forms nervous tissue.

The dermis is derived from mesoderm. During the embryonic period, this mesoderm becomes mesenchyme, and at about 11 weeks, the mesenchymal cells begin to form the components of the dermis. The formation of collagen and elastic fibers causes folding at the boundary of the overlying epidermis and dermis, resulting in the formation of dermal papillae.

5.8b Nail Development

Fingernails and toenails start to form in the tenth week of development. The fingernails reach the tips of the fingers by 32 weeks, whereas the toenails become fully formed by about 36 weeks. Infants born prematurely may not have fully formed fingernails and toenails.

5.8c Hair Development

Hair development is illustrated in **figure 5.13*a*.** Hair follicles begin to appear between 9 and 12 weeks of development as pockets of cells called **hair buds** that invade the dermis from the overlying stratum basale of the epidermis. These buds differentiate into a hair bulb, hair papillae, sebaceous glands, and other structures associated with hair follicles. Eventually, hair grows due to continuous mitotic activity in the epithelial cells of the hair bulb. These hairs do not become easily recognizable in the fetus until about the twentieth week, when they appear as lanugo. They are replaced by vellus hairs after birth.

5.8d Sebaceous and Sweat Gland Development

Both sebaceous and sweat glands develop from the stratum basale of the epidermis (figure 5.13*b*). These glands originate from epidermis but start to grow and burrow into the underlying dermis. Sweat glands appear at about 20 weeks on the palms and soles and later in other regions. The secretory portion of these glands coils as the gland develops within the dermis. Sebaceous glands typically develop as epidermal outgrowths from the sides of a developing hair follicle. Sebaceous glands start to form sebum during the fetal period. As previously described, this sebum mixes with the cells of the sloughed off periderm to form the vernix caseosa.

5.8e Mammary Gland Development

A **primary mammary bud** first appears during the sixth week of development as an epidermal growth into the underlying dermal layer (figure 5.13 *c*). At about 16 weeks (the fourth month) of development, each primary mammary bud branches to form **secondary mammary buds,** which branch and elongate.

Late in the fetal period, the mammary gland develops an external epidermal depression called the **mammary pit.** The mammary pit forms the center around which the nipple tissue will grow.

Clinical View 5.7

Psoriasis

Psoriasis (sō-rī′-ă-sis; *psora* = itch) is a chronic autoimmune skin disease that has periods of flare-ups and remissions throughout a person's lifetime. A type of leukocyte called a T-lymphocyte mistakenly attacks the keratinocytes, causing rapid overgrowth and overproduction of new skin cells. The normal sloughing-off cycle of keratinocytes is thrown out of balance, and the proliferation of cells develops into patches of typically whitish, scaly skin (called *plaques*) that form on the epidermal surface. The plaques are not contagious, but for the affected individual they may cause severe itching, pain, and skin cracking and bleeding. Any part of the skin may be affected, but common areas of involvement include the scalp, the limbs, and the buttocks. Treatments for psoriasis include topical corticosteroids, ultraviolet light therapy, and certain oral medications (e.g., methotrexate) that may interfere with the production of skin cells.

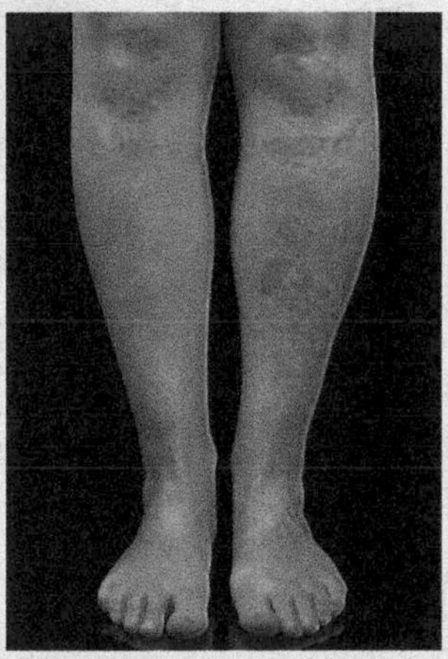

Multiple whitish plaques on the legs of a person with psoriasis.
Alamy Creativity/Alamy Stock Photo

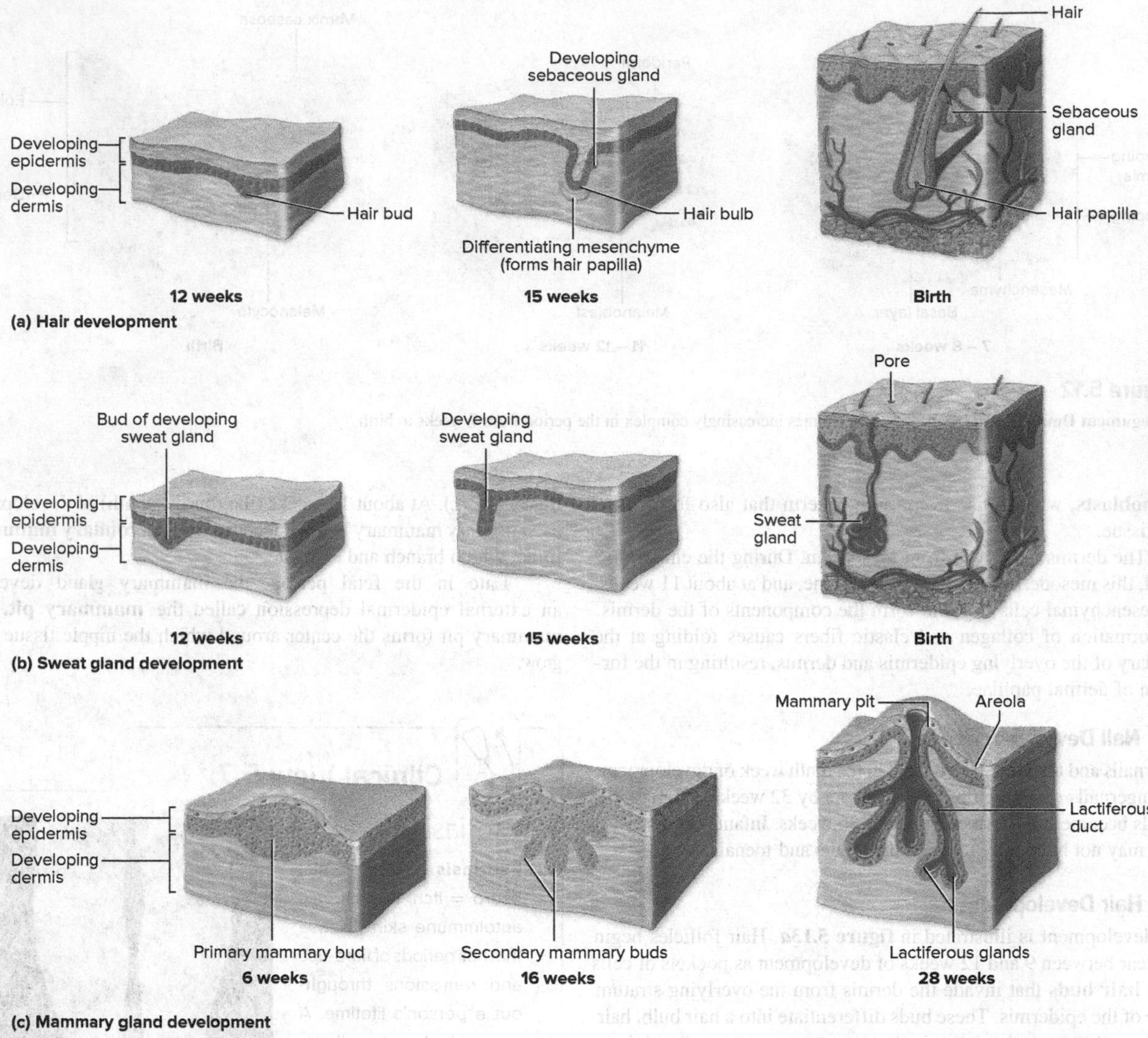
Developing epidermis
Developing dermis
Hair bud
12 weeks
Developing sebaceous gland
Hair bulb
Differentiating mesenchyme (forms hair papilla)
15 weeks
Hair
Sebaceous gland
Hair papilla
Birth
(a) Hair development
Bud of developing sweat gland
Developing epidermis
Developing dermis
12 weeks
Developing sweat gland
15 weeks
Pore
Sweat gland
Birth
(b) Sweat gland development
Developing epidermis
Developing dermis
Primary mammary bud
6 weeks
Secondary mammary buds
16 weeks
Mammary pit
Areola
Lactiferous duct
Lactiferous glands
28 weeks
(c) Mammary gland development

Figure 5.13

Hair, Sweat Gland, and Mammary Gland Development. Comparison of the development of hair, sweat glands, and mammary glands prior to and at birth.

Clinical Terms

athlete's foot A fungal infection of the skin, especially between the toes; causes itching, redness, and peeling. Also called *tinea pedis.*

blister A thin-walled, fluid-filled sac either internal to or within the epidermis; caused by a burn or by excessive friction.

cold sore Small, fluid-filled blister that is sensitive and painful to the touch; associated with the lips and the mucosa of the oral cavity; caused by herpes simplex type 1 virus, which infects nerve cells that supply the skin. Also called a *fever blister.*

dandruff Flaking of the epidermis of the scalp, resulting in white or gray scales in the hair.

eczema (ek′zĕ-mă) Noncontagious skin inflammation often characterized by itchy, red vesicles that may be scaly or crusty.

hives Eruption of reddish, raised areas on the skin, usually accompanied by extreme itching; causes include certain foods, specific drugs, or stress.

keloid (kē′loyd) Excess scar tissue caused by collagen formation during healing; often painful and tender.

pruritis (prū-rī′tŭs) Irritating, itching condition of the skin that may be caused by infection or exposure to various irritants, such as chemicals, cleaning solutions, or mites.

rosacea (rō-zā′shē-ă) Chronic skin disorder that results in redness and small, red, pus-filled bumps or pustules, mainly on the face. The cause of rosacea remains unknown but evidence indicates heredity and environmental factors are to blame.

wart A growth of epidermal cells that forms a roughened projection from the surface of the skin; caused by human papillomavirus.

Chapter Summary

	■ The integumentary system consists of the skin (integument) and its derivatives (nails, hair, sweat glands, and sebaceous glands).
5.1 Structure and Functions of the Integument	■ The integument is the body's largest organ. **5.1a Integument Structure** ■ The integument contains a superficial, stratified squamous epithelium called the epidermis, and a deeper, dense irregular connective tissue layer called the dermis. ■ Deep to the dermis is the subcutaneous layer, or hypodermis, which is not part of the integumentary system. **5.1b Integument Functions** ■ The integument's functions include providing mechanical protection and a physical barrier, preventing water gain and water loss and microbial invasion, regulating temperature, aiding metabolism, contributing to immune defense, perceiving sensations, and excreting wastes through secretion.
5.2 Epidermis	■ Four distinct cell types occur within the epidermis: keratinocytes, melanocytes, tactile cells, and epidermal dendritic cells. **5.2a Epidermal Strata** ■ The stratum basale is a single cell layer of stem cells adjacent to the basement membrane, separating the epidermis from the dermis. ■ The stratum spinosum contains multiple layers of keratinocytes attached together by desmosomes. ■ The stratum granulosum is composed of three to five layers of keratinocytes. The process of keratinization begins here. ■ The stratum lucidum is a thin, translucent layer of anucleate cells superficial to the stratum granulosum; it occurs only in the thick skin of the palms and soles. ■ The stratum corneum has numerous layers of dead, scaly, interlocking keratinized cells. **5.2b Variations in the Epidermis** ■ Normal skin color is a result of a combination of hemoglobin in the blood of the dermis and variable quantities of the pigments melanin and carotene.
5.3 Dermis	■ Components of the dermis include blood vessels, sweat glands, sebaceous glands, hair follicles, nail roots, sensory nerve endings, and muscular tissue. **5.3a Papillary Layer of the Dermis** ■ The papillary layer is composed of areolar connective tissue. Epidermal ridges interdigitate with dermal papillae at the boundary between the epidermis and dermis to interlock these layers and increase the area of contact between them. **5.3b Reticular Layer of the Dermis** ■ The reticular layer lies deep to the papillary layer; it consists of dense irregular connective tissue. **5.3c Lines of Cleavage and Stretch Marks** ■ Lines of cleavage in the skin indicate the predominant direction of the underlying bundles of collagen fibers. ■ Skin stretching due to weight gain or pregnancy causes stretch marks, called striae. **5.3d Innervation and Blood Supply** ■ Vasoconstriction of dermal blood vessels causes decreased circulation to the skin and a corresponding conservation of heat in the blood. Vasodilation of dermal blood vessels causes increased circulation to the skin and loss of excess heat.
5.4 Subcutaneous Layer	■ The subcutaneous layer consists of areolar connective tissue and adipose connective tissue.
5.5 Integumentary Structures Derived from Epidermis	■ The nails, hair, and exocrine glands of the skin are known as epidermal derivatives, or epidermal appendages, of the integument. **5.5a Nails** ■ Nails are formed from stratum corneum; they protect the exposed distal tips of the fingers and toes. **5.5b Hair** ■ Hairs project beyond the skin surface almost everywhere except over the palms of the hands, the sides and soles of the feet, the lips, the sides of the fingers and toes, and portions of the external genitalia. ■ Hair functions include protection, thermoregulation, facial expression, sensory reception, visual identification, and dispersal of pheromones. **5.5c Exocrine Glands of the Skin** ■ Merocrine sweat glands produce a thin, watery secretion called sweat (sensible perspiration). ■ Apocrine sweat glands produce a thick secretion that becomes odorous after exposure to bacteria on the skin surface. ■ Sebaceous glands discharge an oily sebum into hair follicles by holocrine secretion. ■ Ceruminous glands housed within the external ear canal are modified sweat glands; they produce a waxy product called cerumen. ■ Mammary glands are modified apocrine sweat glands that produce breast milk to nourish an infant.
5.6 Integument Repair and Regeneration	■ The skin can regenerate even after considerable damage, including trauma due to burns. ■ Severe damage to the dermis and accessory structures of the skin cannot be repaired. Often, fibrous scar tissue forms, and a graft is required.

(continued on next page)

Chapter Summary *(continued)*

5.7 Aging of the Integument	■ Changes to the skin due to aging include slower regeneration and repair, decreased numbers of collagen fibers and melanocytes, diminished immune responsiveness and sweat production, and increased dryness. **5.7a Skin Cancer** ■ UV rays from the sun pose the greatest risk for this most common type of cancer.
5.8 Development of the Integumentary System	■ The epidermis is derived from the ectoderm, and the dermis is derived from the mesoderm. **5.8a Integument Development** ■ Surface ectoderm forms a covering called periderm and an underlying basal layer. **5.8b Nail Development** ■ Nails form from thickened epithelial ridges called nail fields. **5.8c Hair Development** ■ Hair follicles form from hair buds that differentiate into hair bulbs, hair papillae, and sebaceous glands. **5.8d Sebaceous and Sweat Gland Development** ■ Both types of glands originate from the stratum basale of the epidermis. **5.8e Mammary Gland Development** ■ A primary mammary bud develops as an epidermal outgrowth in the underlying dermis: Each bud branches to form secondary mammary buds.

Challenge Yourself

Actively write or type your answers in a separate document to reinforce your learning before checking your answers.

Multiple Choice

Select the best answer from the four choices provided.

1. Which statement is true about sebaceous glands?
   a. They are located primarily in the axillary and pubic regions of the body.
   b. They release their product by holocrine secretion.
   c. They are located in the epidermis.
   d. The secretion is produced when a portion of the cytoplasm pinches off and becomes the secretion.
2. Which layer of the epidermis contains the cells that begin the process of keratinization?
   a. stratum corneum
   b. stratum basale
   c. stratum lucidum
   d. stratum granulosum
3. Which epidermal cell type is located in the stratum lucidum layer of the epidermis?
   a. melanocyte
   b. keratinocyte
   c. epidermal dendritic dell
   d. all of the above
4. Which of the following is *not* a function of the integument?
   a. acts as a physical barrier
   b. stores calcium in the dermis
   c. regulates temperature through vasoconstriction and vasodilation of dermal blood vessels
   d. participates in immune defense
5. What layer is correctly matched with the tissue that forms it?
   a. papillary layer of dermis; areolar connective tissue
   b. subcutaneous layer; dense irregular connective tissue
   c. reticular layer of dermis; stratified squamous epithelium
   d. epidermis; dense irregular connective tissue
6. Which statement is true about melanin and melanocytes?
   a. Melanin is produced by cells that are located in the stratum spinosum.
   b. Melanin is a pigment that accumulates inside keratinocytes.
   c. Darker-skinned individuals have more melanocytes than lighter-skinned individuals.
   d. Albinism is caused by a lack of melanocytes in the body.
7. The layer of squamous epithelium that forms by the seventh week of development to give rise to the integument is which of the following?
   a. mesenchyme
   b. periderm
   c. basal layer
   d. sebaceous layer
8. Which cells in a hair follicle are responsible for forming hair?
   a. papillary cells
   b. matrix cells
   c. medullary cells
   d. cortex cells
9. Which of the following skin markings, also known as a mole, is formed from an overgrowth of melanin-forming cells?
   a. capillary hemangioma
   b. freckle
   c. nevus
   d. cavernous hemangioma
10. Which part of a nail is its whitish semilunar proximal part?
   a. nail bed
   b. hyponchyium
   c. nail body
   d. lunula

Content Review

1. What effect does the protein keratin have on both the appearance and the function of the integument?
2. Why is the integument considered an organ?
3. List the layers of the epidermis from deep to superficial and compare their structure.
4. Compare and contrast the three types of hair produced during a person's lifetime.
5. Compare and contrast the papillary and reticular layers of the dermis with respect to their composition and the structures within each.
6. How do apocrine and merocrine sweat glands differ in structure and function?
7. Describe how the skin is involved in vitamin D production.
8. Describe how vasoconstriction and vasodilation of blood vessels in the dermis can regulate body temperature.
9. Describe the four steps in wound repair of the integument.
10. What are some effects of aging on the integument?

Developing Critical Reasoning

1. When you are outside on a cold day, your skin is much paler than normal. Later, you enter a warm room, and your face becomes flushed. What are the reasons for these changes in color?
2. Teri is a 14-year-old with a bad case of acne. Explain the probable cause of Teri's skin condition.
3. When he was a teenager, John spent every summer afternoon at the pool for many years. As he approached the age of 50, his skin was quite wrinkled, and he discovered some suspicious growths on his face. He visited a dermatologist, who removed these growths. What were the growths, and what probably caused them?

Answers to "What Do You Think?"

1. The children were not getting enough vitamin D in their diet, and they were spending all of their daylight hours indoors. Because the children weren't exposed to much sunlight, their skin could not synthesize vitamin D from the UV rays of the sun. Without adequate amounts of vitamin D, the children succumbed to rickets.
2. Thick skin is found on the palms of the hands and the soles of the feet. Secretions from sebaceous glands would make these areas slippery, which would interfere with grasping objects and walking. The presence of hair in these areas would interfere with these same functions.
3. Fingerprints are formed from folds of both epidermal and dermal tissue, so to physically "change" or remove fingerprints, you would have to destroy or damage both layers. This would be very painful, and permanent scarring or malformation would likely result.
4. When we are frightened or nervous, the sympathetic division of the autonomic nervous system is stimulated, which in turn stimulates the sweat glands to produce and release sweat. This is why our palms and other body regions become sweaty in nervous or frightening situations.
5. The person who has never used sunscreen is more likely to get wrinkles. Constant, unprotected exposure to UV rays can cause wrinkling and increased aging of the skin, and it also increases the risk of developing skin cancer.

Design Element: Pencil Icon: Slavojub Pantelic/Shutterstock

Skeletal System

6 Cartilage and Bone

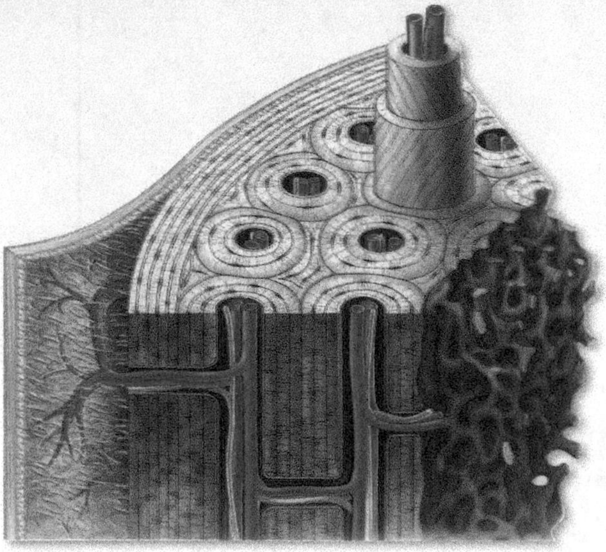

Outline

Anatomy & Physiology Revealed 4.0

MODULE 5: SKELETAL SYSTEM

Mention of the skeletal system conjures up images of dry, lifeless bones in various sizes and shapes. But the **skeleton** (skel′ĕ-tŏn; *skeletos* = dried) is much more than a supporting framework for the soft tissues of the body. The skeletal system is composed of dynamic living tissues; it interacts with all of the other organ systems and continually rebuilds and remodels itself. Our skeletal system includes the bones of the skeleton as well as cartilage, ligaments, and other connective tissues that stabilize or connect the bones. Bones support our weight and interact with muscles to produce precisely controlled movements. This interaction permits us to sit, stand, walk, and run. Further, our bones serve as vital reservoirs for calcium and phosphorus. We first examine the cartilage components of the skeleton before concentrating on the bone connective tissue.

6.1 Cartilage

✓ Learning Objectives

1. Explain the functions of cartilage.
2. Describe the function and distribution of hyaline cartilage, fibrocartilage, and elastic cartilage.
3. Explain both the interstitial and appositional growth of cartilage.

Cartilage is found throughout the human body (**figure 6.1**). Cartilage is a semirigid connective tissue that is weaker than bone, but more flexible and resilient (see section 4.2d). As with all connective tissue types, cartilage contains a population of cells scattered throughout a matrix of protein fibers embedded within a gel-like ground substance. **Chondroblasts** (kon′dr ō-blast; *chondros* = grit or gristle, *blastos* = germ) are the cells that produce the matrix of cartilage. Once they become encased within the matrix they have produced and secreted, the cells are called **chondrocytes** (kon′dr ō-sīt; *cyte* = cell) and occupy small spaces named **lacunae.** These mature cartilage cells maintain the matrix and ensure that it remains healthy and viable. Mature cartilage is avascular (not penetrated by blood vessels) so nutrients must diffuse through the matrix. The three different types of cartilage—hyaline, elastic, and fibrocartilage—are described in detail in section 4.2d, so only cartilage functions, locations, and growth will be discussed in this chapter.

6.1a Functions of Cartilage

Cartilage has three major functions in the body:

- Supporting tissues. For example, C-shaped hyaline cartilage rings in the trachea support the connective tissue and musculature of the tracheal wall; fibrocartilage provides both toughness and

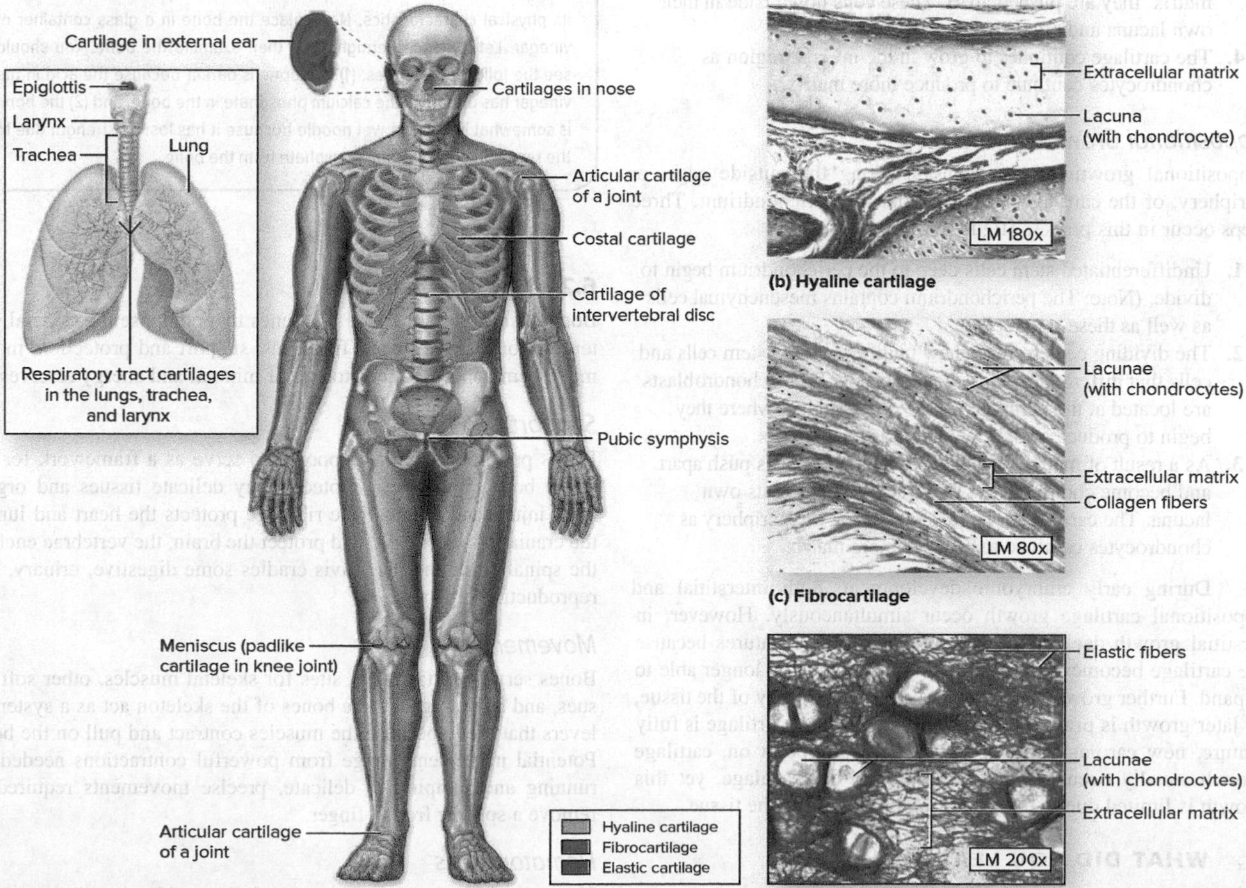

Cartilage in external ear
Epiglottis
Larynx
Trachea
Lung
Cartilages in nose
Articular cartilage of a joint
Costal cartilage
Cartilage of intervertebral disc
Respiratory tract cartilages in the lungs, trachea, and larynx
Pubic symphysis
Meniscus (padlike cartilage in knee joint)
Articular cartilage of a joint
Hyaline cartilage
Fibrocartilage
Elastic cartilage
(a)
Extracellular matrix
Lacuna (with chondrocyte)
LM 180x
(b) Hyaline cartilage
Lacunae (with chondrocytes)
Extracellular matrix
Collagen fibers
LM 80x
(c) Fibrocartilage
Elastic fibers
Lacunae (with chondrocytes)
Extracellular matrix
LM 200x
(d) Elastic cartilage

Figure 6.1

Distribution of Cartilage in an Adult. (*a*) Three types of cartilage occur within an adult. Photomicrographs show (*b*) hyaline cartilage, (*c*) fibrocartilage, and (*d*) elastic cartilage.

flexibility to the pubic symphysis and intervertebral discs; and flexible elastic cartilage supports the fleshy, external part of the ear called the auricle (aw′ri-kl; *auris* = ear).

- Providing a gliding surface at **articulations** (joints), where two bones meet.
- Providing a model for the formation of most of the bones in the body. Beginning in the embryonic period, cartilage serves as a "rough draft" form that is later replaced by bone tissue.

6.1b Growth Patterns of Cartilage

Cartilage grows in two ways. Growth from within the cartilage itself is termed **interstitial** (in′tĕr-stish′ ăl) **growth.** Growth along the cartilage's outside edge, or periphery, is called **appositional** (ap′ō-zish′ ŭn-ăl) **growth (figure 6.2).**

Interstitial Growth

Interstitial growth occurs within the internal regions of cartilage through a series of four steps (figure 6.2*a*):

1. Chondrocytes housed within lacunae are stimulated to undergo mitotic cell division.
2. Following cell division, two cells occupy a single lacuna; they are now called chondroblasts.
3. As chondroblasts begin to synthesize and secrete new cartilage matrix, they are pushed apart. These cells now reside in their own lacuna and are called chondrocytes.
4. The cartilage continues to grow in the internal region as chondrocytes continue to produce more matrix.

Appositional Growth

Appositional growth is an expansion along the outside edge, or periphery, of the cartilage, usually under the perichondrium. Three steps occur in this process (figure 6.2*b*):

1. Undifferentiated stem cells deep to the perichondrium begin to divide. (Note: The perichondrium contains mesenchymal cells as well as these stem cells.)
2. The dividing cells result in new undifferentiated stem cells and cells that differentiate into chondroblasts. These chondroblasts are located at the periphery of the old cartilage, where they begin to produce and secrete new cartilage matrix.
3. As a result of matrix formation, the chondroblasts push apart and become chondrocytes, with each occupying its own lacuna. The cartilage continues to grow at the periphery as chondrocytes continue to produce more matrix.

During early embryonic development, both interstitial and appositional cartilage growth occur simultaneously. However, interstitial growth declines rapidly as the cartilage matures because the cartilage becomes semirigid, and the matrix is no longer able to expand. Further growth can occur only at the periphery of the tissue, so later growth is primarily appositional. Once the cartilage is fully mature, new cartilage growth stops. From this point on, cartilage growth usually occurs only after injury to the cartilage, yet this growth is limited due to the lack of blood vessels in the tissue.

WHAT DID YOU LEARN?

1. Make a chart to summarize the three types of cartilage and their structures, functions, and locations.
2. Explain why appositional growth of cartilage can continue into adulthood when interstitial growth stops. How does this difference in growth relate to cartilage damage?

6.2 Bone

✓ Learning Objective

4. Explain the functions of bone.

The bones of the skeleton are complex, dynamic organs containing all tissue types. Their primary component is **bone connective tissue,** also called *osseous* (os′ē-ŭs) *connective tissue* (see section 4.2d). In addition, they contain connective tissue proper (periosteum), cartilage connective tissue (articular cartilage), smooth muscle tissue (forming the walls of blood vessels that supply bone), fluid connective tissue (blood), epithelial tissue (lining the inside opening of blood vessels), and nervous tissue (nerves that supply bone). The matrix of bone connective tissue is sturdy and rigid due to deposition of minerals in the matrix, a process called **calcification** (kal′si-fi-kā′shŭn), or *mineralization.*

Learning Strategy 6.1

You can do a quick overnight experiment to demonstrate what would happen to our body shape if the composition of our bones changed. Obtain the "wishbone" (fused clavicles) from a chicken or game hen and examine its physical characteristics. Next, place the bone in a glass container of vinegar. Let it stand overnight, and then examine the bone. You should see the following changes: (1) The bone is darker because the acid in the vinegar has dissolved the calcium phosphate in the bone, and (2) the bone is somewhat limp like a wet noodle because it has lost its strength due to the removal of the calcium phosphate from the bone.

6.2a Functions of Bone

Bone connective tissue and the bones that compose the skeletal system perform several basic functions: support and protection, movement, hematopoiesis, and storage of mineral and energy reserves.

Support and Protection

Bones provide structural support and serve as a framework for the entire body. Bones also protect many delicate tissues and organs from injury and trauma. The rib cage protects the heart and lungs, the cranial bones enclose and protect the brain, the vertebrae enclose the spinal cord, and the pelvis cradles some digestive, urinary, and reproductive organs.

Movement

Bones serve as attachment sites for skeletal muscles, other soft tissues, and some organs. The bones of the skeleton act as a system of levers that move because the muscles contract and pull on the bone. Potential movements range from powerful contractions needed for running and jumping to delicate, precise movements required to remove a splinter from a finger.

Hematopoiesis

Hematopoiesis (he′ma-tō-poy-ē′sis; *haima* = blood, *poiesi* = a making) is the process of production of formed elements in the blood. It occurs in a connective tissue called **red bone marrow,** which is located in some spongy bone. Red bone marrow contains stem cells that form all blood cells and platelets (see section 21.4).

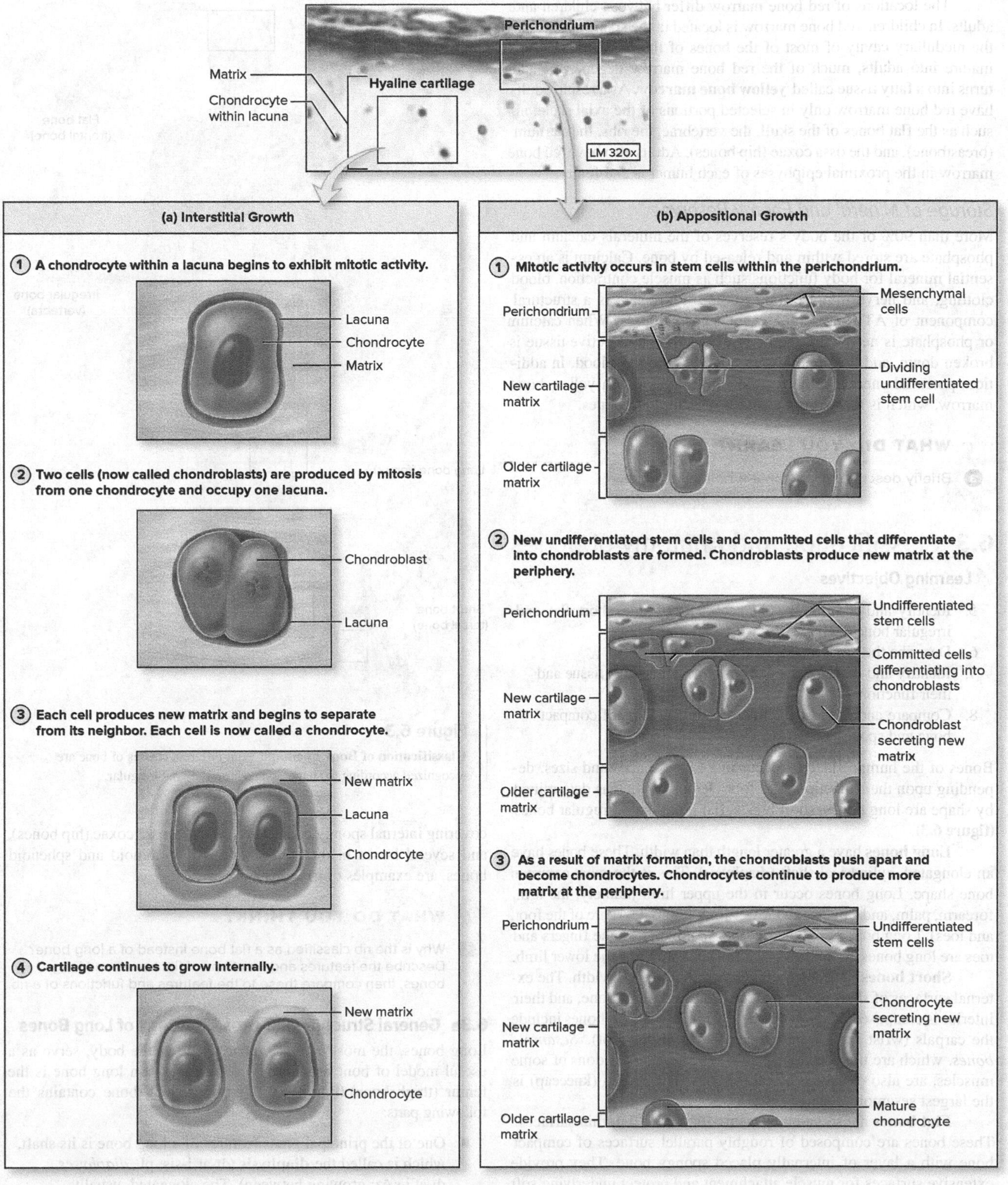
Perichondrium
Matrix
Hyaline cartilage
Chondrocyte within lacuna
LM 320x
(a) Interstitial Growth
1 A chondrocyte within a lacuna begins to exhibit mitotic activity.
Lacuna
Chondrocyte
Matrix
2 Two cells (now called chondroblasts) are produced by mitosis from one chondrocyte and occupy one lacuna.
Chondroblast
Lacuna
3 Each cell produces new matrix and begins to separate from its neighbor. Each cell is now called a chondrocyte.
New matrix
Lacuna
Chondrocyte
4 Cartilage continues to grow internally.
New matrix
Chondrocyte
(b) Appositional Growth
1 Mitotic activity occurs in stem cells within the perichondrium.
Perichondrium
Mesenchymal cells
Dividing undifferentiated stem cell
New cartilage matrix
Older cartilage matrix
2 New undifferentiated stem cells and committed cells that differentiate into chondroblasts are formed. Chondroblasts produce new matrix at the periphery.
Perichondrium
Undifferentiated stem cells
Committed cells differentiating into chondroblasts
New cartilage matrix
Chondroblast secreting new matrix
Older cartilage matrix
3 As a result of matrix formation, the chondroblasts push apart and become chondrocytes. Chondrocytes continue to produce more matrix at the periphery.
Perichondrium
Undifferentiated stem cells
Chondrocyte secreting new matrix
New cartilage matrix
Mature chondrocyte
Older cartilage matrix

Figure 6.2

Formation and Growth of Cartilage. Cartilage grows either (a) from within the tissue by interstitial growth or (b) at its periphery, or edge, by appositional growth. APR

(top) ©McGraw-Hill Education/Al Telser, photographer

The locations of red bone marrow differ between children and adults. In children, red bone marrow is located in the spongy bone and the medullary cavity of most of the bones of the body. As children mature into adults, much of the red bone marrow degenerates and turns into a fatty tissue called **yellow bone marrow.** As a result, adults have red bone marrow only in selected portions of the axial skeleton, such as the flat bones of the skull, the vertebrae, the ribs, the sternum (breastbone), and the ossa coxae (hip bones). Adults also have red bone marrow in the proximal epiphyses of each humerus and femur.

Storage of Mineral and Energy Reserves

More than 90% of the body's reserves of the minerals calcium and phosphate are stored within and released by bone. Calcium is an essential mineral for body functions such as muscle contraction, blood clotting, and nerve impulse transmission. Phosphate is a structural component of ATP, nucleotides, and phospholipids. When calcium or phosphate is needed by the body, some bone connective tissue is broken down, and the minerals are released into the blood. In addition, potential energy in the form of lipids is stored in yellow bone marrow, which is located in the shafts of adult long bones.

WHAT DID YOU LEARN?

3 Briefly describe at least four functions of bone.

6.3 Classification and Anatomy of Bones

✓ Learning Objectives

5. Identify and describe the characteristics of long, short, flat, and irregular bones.
6. Describe the gross anatomy of a long bone.
7. Identify and describe the cells of bone connective tissue and their functions.
8. Compare and contrast the microscopic anatomy of compact bone and spongy bone.

Bones of the human skeleton occur in various shapes and sizes, depending upon their function. The four classes of bone as determined by shape are long bones, short bones, flat bones, and irregular bones (**figure 6.3**).

Long bones have a greater length than width. These bones have an elongated, cylindrical shaft (diaphysis). This is the most common bone shape. Long bones occur in the upper limb (namely, the arm, forearm, palm, and fingers) and lower limb (thigh, leg, sole of the foot, and toes). Long bones vary in size; the small bones in the fingers and toes are long bones, as are the larger tibia and fibula of the lower limb.

Short bones have a length nearly equal to their width. The external surfaces of short bones are covered by compact bone, and their interior is composed of spongy bone. Examples of short bones include the carpals (wrist bones) and tarsals (bones in the foot). *Sesamoid bones,* which are tiny, seed-shaped bones along the tendons of some muscles, are also classified as short bones. The patella (kneecap) is the largest sesamoid bone.

Flat bones are so named because they have flat, thin surfaces. These bones are composed of roughly parallel surfaces of compact bone with a layer of internally placed spongy bone. They provide extensive surfaces for muscle attachment and protect underlying soft tissues. Flat bones form the roof of the skull, the scapulae (shoulder blades), the sternum (breastbone), and the ribs.

Irregular bones have elaborate, complex shapes and do not fit into any of the preceding categories. These bones have compact bone

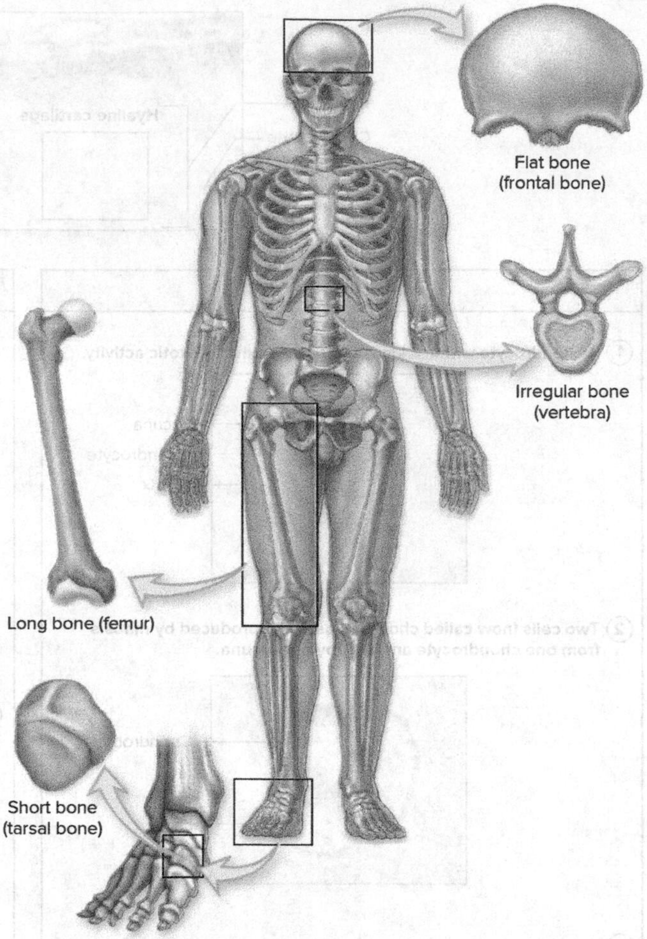
Flat bone
(frontal bone)
Irregular bone
(vertebra)
Long bone (femur)
Short bone
(tarsal bone)

Figure 6.3

Classification of Bone by Shape. Four different classes of bone are recognized according to shape: long, short, flat, and irregular.

covering internal spongy bone. The vertebrae, ossa coxae (hip bones), and several bones in the skull, such as the ethmoid and sphenoid bones, are examples of irregular bones.

WHAT DO YOU THINK?

1 Why is the rib classified as a flat bone instead of a long bone? Describe the features and functions of flat bones and long bones, then compare these to the features and functions of a rib.

6.3a General Structure and Gross Anatomy of Long Bones

Long bones, the most common bone shape in the body, serve as a useful model of bone structure. One example of a long bone is the femur (thigh bone) (**figure 6.4**). A typical long bone contains the following parts:

- One of the principal gross features of a long bone is its shaft, which is called the **diaphysis** (dī-af′i-sis; pl., *diaphyses,* dī-af′i-s ēz; growing between). The elongated, usually cylindrical diaphysis provides for the leverage and major weight support of a long bone.
- At each end of a long bone is an expanded, knobby region called the **epiphysis** (e-pif′i-sis; pl., *epiphyses,* e-pif′i-sēz;

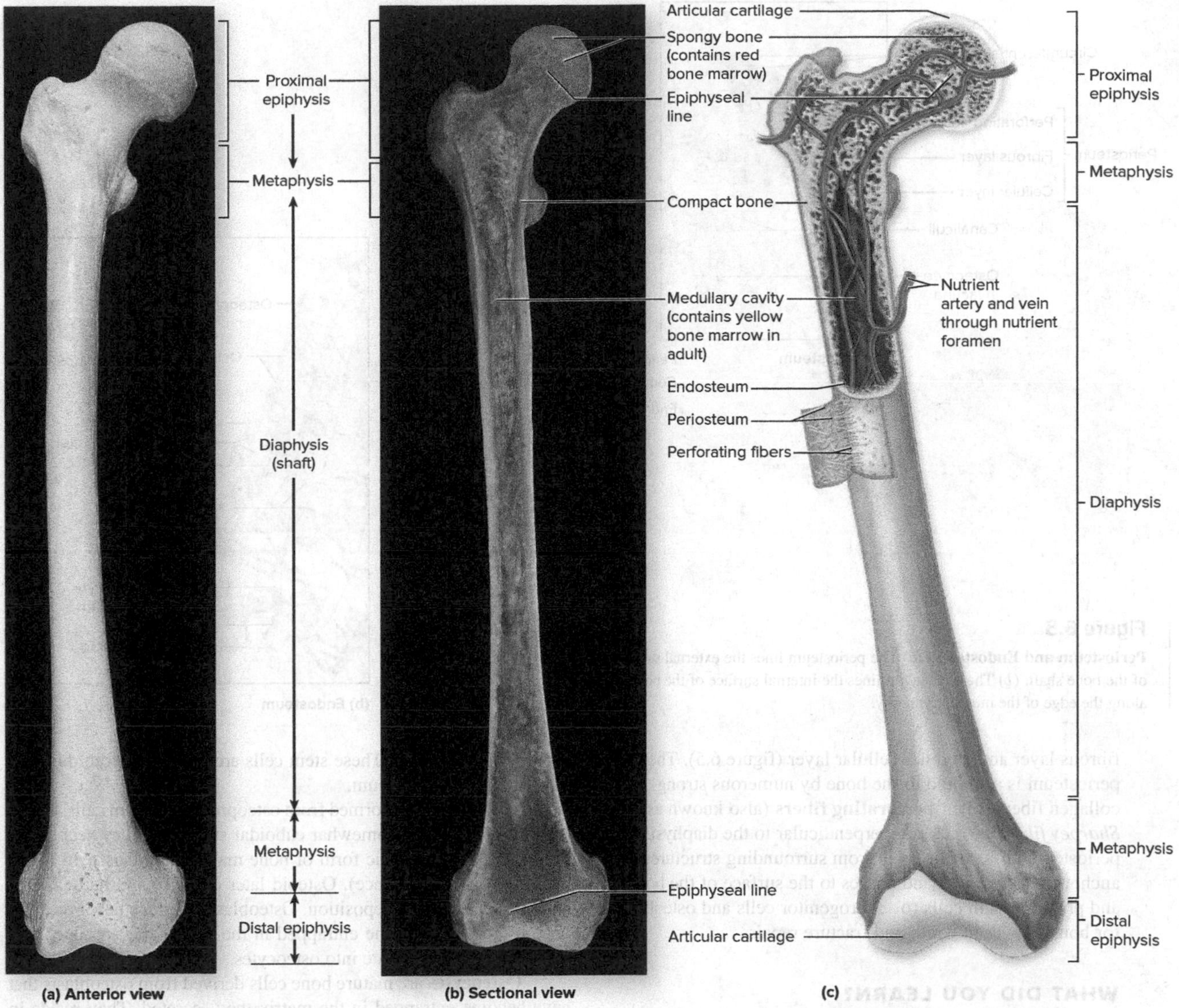

Figure 6.4

Gross Anatomy of a Long Bone. Long bones support soft tissues in the limbs. The femur, the bone of the thigh, is shown in both (*a*) anterior and (*b*) sectional views. (*c*) A drawing of a femur showing both compact and spongy bone. APR

(a) ©McGraw-Hill Education/Christine Eckel, photographer; (b) ©Elizabeth Pennefather-O'Brien

epi = upon, *physis* = growth). The epiphysis is enlarged to strengthen the joint and provide added surface area for bone-to-bone articulation as well as tendon and ligament attachment. It is composed of an outer layer of compact bone and an inner layer of spongy bone. A **proximal epiphysis** is the end of the bone closest to the body trunk, and a **distal epiphysis** is the end farthest from the trunk.

- The **metaphysis** (mĕ-taf′i-sis) is the region of a long bone where the bone widens and transfers forces between the diaphysis and the epiphysis. In a growing bone, this region contains the **epiphyseal** (growth) **plate,** thin layers of hyaline cartilage that provide for the continued lengthwise growth of the diaphysis. In adults, the remnant of the epiphyseal plate is a thin layer of compact bone called the **epiphyseal line.**
- The thin layer of hyaline cartilage covering the epiphysis at a joint surface is called **articular cartilage.** This cartilage helps reduce friction and absorb shock in movable joints.
- The hollow, cylindrical space within the diaphysis is called the **medullary cavity** (*marrow cavity*). In adults, it contains yellow bone marrow.
- The **endosteum** (en-dos′tē-ŭm; *endo* = within, *osteon* = bone) is an incomplete layer of cells that covers all internal surfaces of the bone, such as the medullary cavity. The endosteum contains osteoprogenitor cells, osteoblasts, and osteoclasts (**figure 6.5**), and is active during bone growth, repair, and remodeling.
- A tough sheath called **periosteum** (per′ē-os′tē-ŭm; *peri* = around) covers the outer surface of the bone, except for the areas covered by articular cartilage. Periosteum is formed by dense irregular connective tissue and consists of an outer

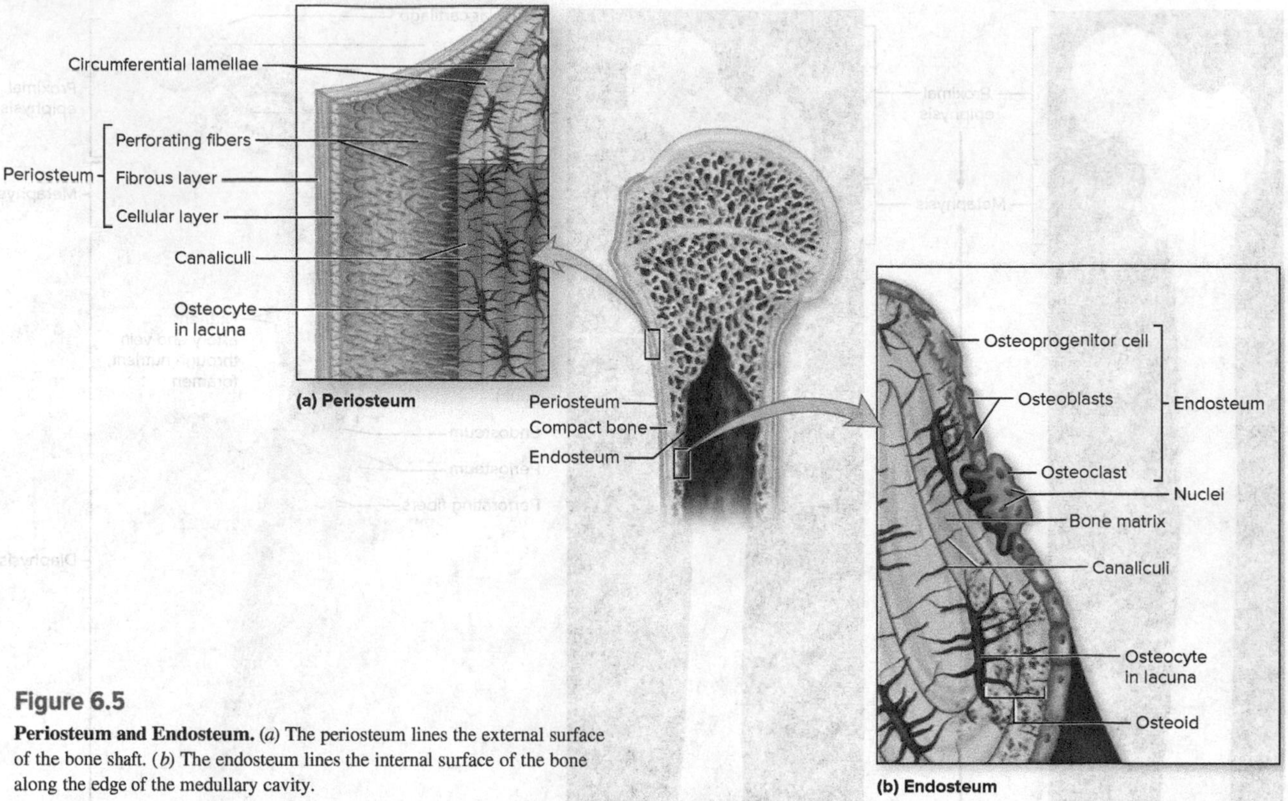

Figure 6.5

Periosteum and Endosteum. *(a)* The periosteum lines the external surface of the bone shaft. *(b)* The endosteum lines the internal surface of the bone along the edge of the medullary cavity.

fibrous layer and an inner cellular layer (figure 6.5). The periosteum is anchored to the bone by numerous strong collagen fibers called **perforating fibers** (also known as *Sharpey fibers*), which run perpendicular to the diaphysis. The periosteum protects the bone from surrounding structures, anchors blood vessels and nerves to the surface of the bone, and provides stem cells (osteoprogenitor cells and osteoblasts) for bone growth in width and fracture repair.

WHAT DID YOU LEARN?

4. What are the four classes of bone in terms of shape? Into which group would the os coxae (hip bone) be placed?
5. Draw a generalized long bone. Then on your drawing label the following: proximal epiphysis, distal epiphysis, diaphysis, articular cartilage, and periosteum.

Cells of Bone

Four types of cells occur in bone connective tissue: osteoprogenitor cells, osteoblasts, osteocytes, and osteoclasts(**figure 6.6**).

Osteoprogenitor (os′tē-ō-prō-jen′i-tōr; *osteo* = bone) **cells** are stem cells derived from mesenchyme. When they divide, they produce another stem cell and a "committed cell" that matures to become an osteoblast. These stem cells are located in both the periosteum and the endosteum.

Osteoblasts are formed from osteoprogenitor stem cells. Often, osteoblasts exhibit a somewhat cuboidal structure. They secrete the initial semisolid, organic form of bone matrix called **osteoid** (os′tē-oyd; *eidos* = resemblance). Osteoid later calcifies and hardens as a result of calcium salt deposition. Osteoblasts produce new bone, and once osteoblasts become entrapped in the matrix they produce and secrete, they differentiate into osteocytes.

Osteocytes are mature bone cells derived from osteoblasts that have become entrapped in the matrix they secreted. They reside in small spaces within the matrix called **lacunae.** Osteocytes maintain the bone matrix and detect mechanical stress on a bone. This information is communicated to osteoblasts, and may result in the deposition of new bone matrix at the surface.

Osteoclasts (os′tē-ō-klast′; *klastos* = broken) are large, multinuclear, phagocytic cells. They are derived from fused bone marrow cells similar to those that produce monocytes (described in section 21.3b). These cells exhibit a ruffled border where they contact the bone, which increases their surface area exposure to the bone. An osteoclast is often located within or adjacent to a depression or pit on the bone surface called a **resorption lacuna** (*Howship lacuna*). Osteoclasts are involved in an important process called **bone resorption** that takes place as follows: Osteoclasts secrete hydrochloric acid, which dissolves the mineral parts (calcium and phosphate) of the bone matrix, while lysosomes within the osteoclasts secrete enzymes that dissolve the organic part of the matrix. The release of the stored calcium and phosphate from the bone matrix is called **osteolysis** (os′tē-ol′i-sis; *lysis* = dissolution, loosening). The liberated calcium and phosphate ions enter the tissue fluid and then the blood.

> **Learning Strategy 6.2**
>
> A long bone is similar in shape to a barbell: The barbell's rounded ends represent the epiphyses, and its cylindrical handle is the diaphysis.

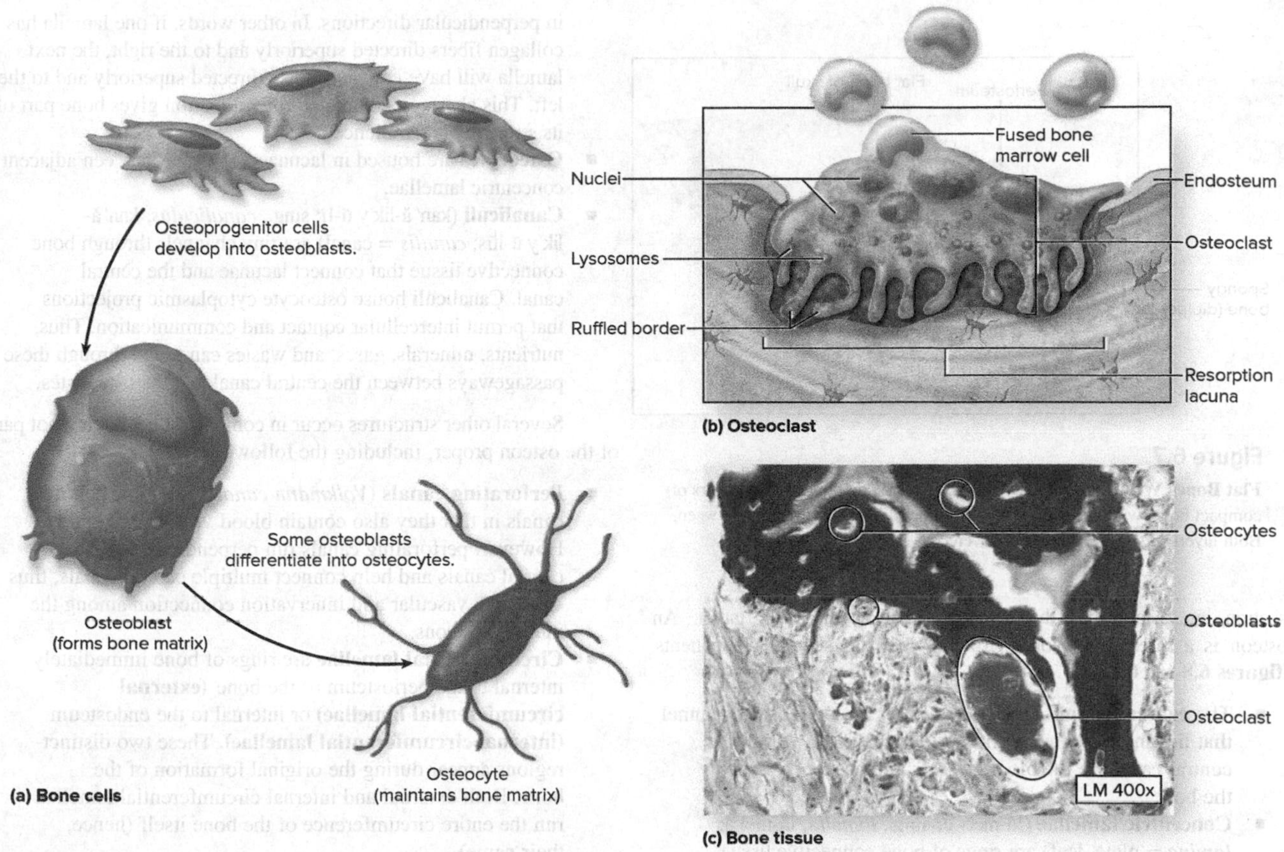

Figure 6.6

Types of Cells in Bone Connective Tissue. Four different types of cells occur in bone connective tissue. (*a*) Osteoprogenitor cells develop into osteoblasts, many of which differentiate to become osteocytes. (*b*) Bone marrow cells fuse to form osteoclasts. (*c*) A photomicrograph shows osteoblasts, osteocytes, and an osteoclast.

Osteoblasts add to bone matrix and osteoclasts remove the matrix, thus maintaining a delicate balance. Osteoblast and osteoclast activity are affected by hormonal levels (discussed in section 6.5a), the body's need for calcium and/or phosphorus, and gravitational or mechanical stressors to bone. For example, when a person wears orthodontic braces, osteoblasts and osteoclasts work together to modify the tooth-jaw junction, in response to the mechanical stress applied by the braces to the teeth and jaw. If osteoclasts resorb the bone to remove calcium salts at a faster rate than osteoblasts produce matrix to stimulate deposition, bones lose mass and become weaker; in contrast, when osteoblast activity outpaces osteoclast activity, bones have a greater mass.

Composition of the Bone Matrix

The matrix of bone connective tissue has both organic and inorganic components. About one-third of bone mass is composed of organic components called osteoid. It includes cells, collagen fibers, and ground substance. (The ground substance is the semisolid material that suspends and supports the collagen fibers.) The collagen fibers give a bone tensile strength by resisting stretching and twisting, and contribute to its overall flexibility. The inorganic components of the bone provide its compressional strength. Calcium phosphate, $Ca_3(PO_4)_2$, accounts for most of the inorganic components of bone. Calcium phosphate and calcium hydroxide interact to form crystals of **hydroxyapatite** (hī-drok′sē-ap-ă-tīt), which is $Ca_{10}(PO_4)_6(OH)_2$. These crystals deposit around the collagen fibers, leading to hardening of the extracellular matrix. The crystals also incorporate other salts, such as calcium carbonate, and ions, such as sodium, magnesium, sulfate, and fluoride, in the process of calcification.

Comparison of Compact and Spongy Bone

Two types of bone connective tissue are present in most of the bones of the body: **compact bone** (also called *dense* or *cortical bone*) and **spongy bone** (also called *cancellous* or *trabecular bone*). As their names imply, compact bone is solid and relatively dense, whereas spongy bone appears more porous, like a sponge. The arrangement of compact bone and spongy bone components differs at the microscopic level. In a long bone, compact bone forms the solid external walls of the bone, and spongy bone is located internally, primarily within the epiphyses. Spongy bone forms an open lattice of narrow plates of bone, called **trabeculae** (tră-bek′y ū-lē; sing., *trabecula*, tră-bek′y ū -lă; *trabs* = a beam). In a flat bone of the skull, the spongy bone, also called **diploë** (dip′l ō-ē; *diplous* = double), is sandwiched between two layers of compact bone (**figure 6.7**).

Compact Bone Microscopic Anatomy Compact bone has an organized structure when viewed with light microscopy. A cylindrical **osteon** (os′tē-on), or *Haversian system*, is the basic functional and structural unit of mature compact bone. Osteons run parallel to the diaphysis of the long bone. When viewed in cross

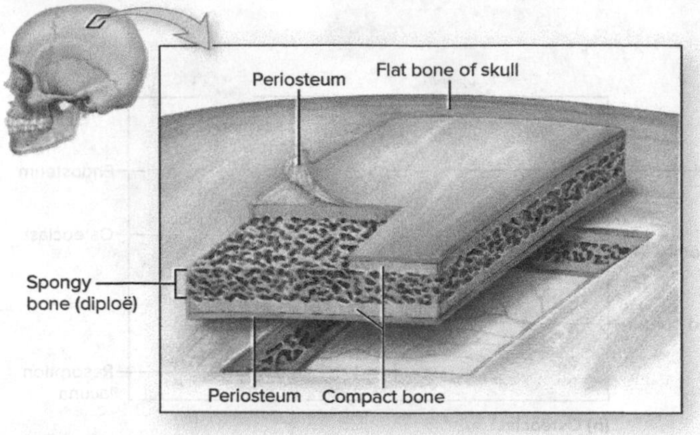

Figure 6.7

Flat Bones Within the Skull. These bones are composed of two layers of compact bone, with a region of spongy bone (diploë) sandwiched between. Both layers of compact bone are covered by periosteum.

section, an osteon has the appearance of a bull's-eye target. An osteon is a three-dimensional structure that has several components (**figures 6.8** and **6.9*a***).

- The **central canal** (*Haversian canal*) is a cylindrical channel that lies in the center of the osteon. Traveling within the central canal are the blood vessels and nerves that supply the bone.
- **Concentric lamellae** (lă-mel′- ē; sing., *lamella*, lă-mel′ă; *lamina* = plate, leaf) are rings of bone connective tissue that surround the central canal and form the bulk of the osteon. The numbers of concentric lamellae vary among osteons. Each lamella contains collagen fibers oriented in one direction; adjacent lamellae contain collagen fibers oriented in perpendicular directions. In other words, if one lamella has collagen fibers directed superiorly and to the right, the next lamella will have collagen fibers directed superiorly and to the left. This alternating collagen fiber direction gives bone part of its strength and resilience.
- **Osteocytes** are housed in lacunae and occur between adjacent concentric lamellae.
- **Canaliculi** (kan′ ă-lik′y ū-lī; sing., *canaliculus,* kan′ă-lik′y ū-lŭs; *canalis* = canal) are tiny channels through bone connective tissue that connect lacunae and the central canal. Canaliculi house osteocyte cytoplasmic projections that permit intercellular contact and communication. Thus, nutrients, minerals, gases, and wastes can travel through these passageways between the central canal and the osteocytes.

Several other structures occur in compact bone, but are not part of the osteon proper, including the following (see figure 6.8):

- **Perforating canals** (*Volkmann canals*) resemble central canals in that they also contain blood vessels and nerves. However, perforating canals run perpendicular to the central canals and help connect multiple central canals, thus creating a vascular and innervation connection among the multiple osteons.
- **Circumferential lamellae** are rings of bone immediately internal to the periosteum of the bone **(external circumferential lamellae)** or internal to the endosteum **(internal circumferential lamellae).** These two distinct regions appear during the original formation of the bone. Both external and internal circumferential lamellae run the entire circumference of the bone itself (hence, their name).
- **Interstitial lamellae** are the leftover parts of osteons that have been partially resorbed. They often look like a "bite" has been taken out of them. The interstitial lamellae are incomplete and typically have no central canal.

Clinical View 6.1

Osteitis Deformans

Osteitis deformans (*Paget disease of bone*) was first described by Sir James Paget in 1877. It is characterized by excessive bone resorption (excessive osteoclast activity) followed by excessive bone deposition (excessive osteoblast activity).

In osteitis deformans, the osteoclasts are five times larger than normal and may contain 20 or more nuclei (compared to about 3 to 5 nuclei in normal osteoclasts). These larger osteoclasts resorb bone at a higher rate. In response to this excessive bone resorption, the osteoblasts deposit additional bone, but this new bone is poorly formed and structurally unstable, making it more susceptible to deformation and fractures.

Osteitis deformans most commonly occurs in the bones of the pelvis, skull, vertebrae, femur (thigh bone), and tibia (leg bone). Initial symptoms include bone deformity and pain. Eventually, the lower limb bones may bow, and the skull often becomes thicker and enlarged.

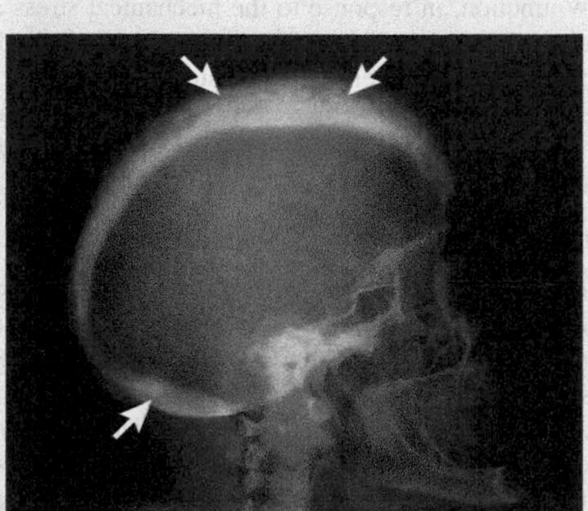

Lateral x-ray of a skull with osteitis deformans. White arrows indicate areas of excessive bone deposition.

SPL/Science Source

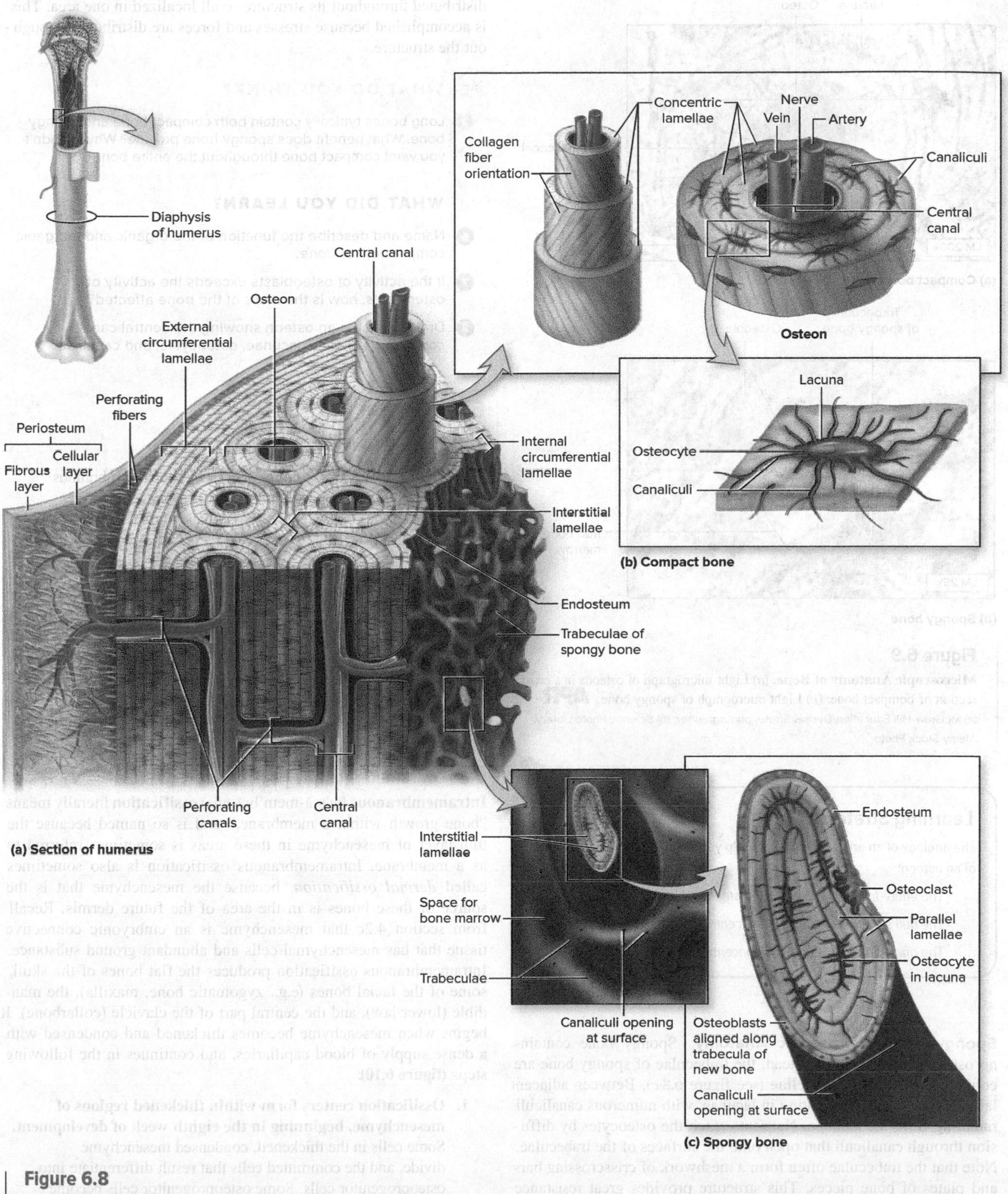

Diaphysis of humerus
Central canal
Osteon
External circumferential lamellae
Perforating fibers
Periosteum
Fibrous layer
Cellular layer
Internal circumferential lamellae
Interstitial lamellae
Endosteum
Trabeculae of spongy bone
Perforating canals
Central canal
(a) Section of humerus
Collagen fiber orientation
Concentric lamellae
Nerve
Vein
Artery
Canaliculi
Central canal
Osteon
Lacuna
Osteocyte
Canaliculi
(b) Compact bone
Interstitial lamellae
Space for bone marrow
Trabeculae
Canaliculi opening at surface
Endosteum
Osteoclast
Parallel lamellae
Osteocyte in lacuna
Osteoblasts aligned along trabecula of new bone
Canaliculi opening at surface
(c) Spongy bone

Figure 6.8

Components of Bone. (*a*) An expanded section of the humerus shows the distribution of osteons within (*b*) the compact bone and (*c*) the arrangement of trabeculae within spongy bone.

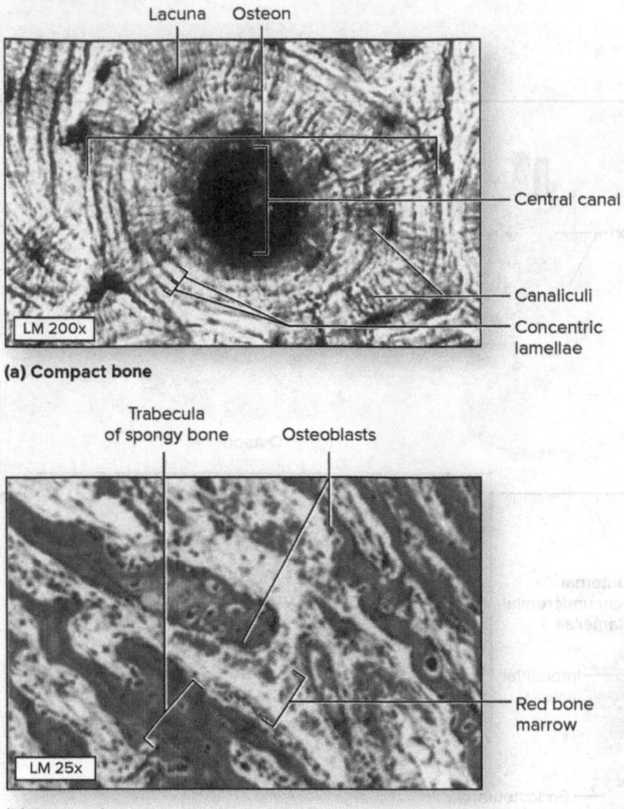
Lacuna
Osteon
Central canal
Canaliculi
Concentric lamellae
LM 200x
(a) Compact bone
Trabecula of spongy bone
Osteoblasts
Red bone marrow
LM 25x
(b) Spongy bone

Figure 6.9

Microscopic Anatomy of Bone. (*a*) Light micrograph of osteons in a cross section of compact bone. (*b*) Light micrograph of spongy bone. APR

(a) McGraw-Hill Education/Dennis Strete, photographer; (b) Science Photo Library/ Alamy Stock Photo

Learning Strategy 6.3

The analogy of an archery target can help you remember the components of an osteon:

The entire *target* represents the *osteon.*

The *bull's-eye* of the target is the *central canal.*

The *rings* of the target are the *concentric lamellae.*

Spongy Bone Microscopic Anatomy Spongy bone contains no osteons (figure 6.9*b*). Instead, the trabeculae of spongy bone are composed of **parallel lamellae** (see figure 6.8*c*). Between adjacent lamellae are osteocytes resting in lacunae, with numerous canaliculi radiating from the lacunae. Nutrients reach the osteocytes by diffusion through canaliculi that open onto the surfaces of the trabeculae. Note that the trabeculae often form a meshwork of crisscrossing bars and plates of bone pieces. This structure provides great resistance to stresses applied in many directions by distributing the stress throughout the entire framework. As an analogy, visualize the jungle gym climbing apparatus on a children's playground. It is capable of supporting the weight of numerous children whether they are distributed throughout its structure or all localized in one area. This is accomplished because stresses and forces are distributed throughout the structure.

WHAT DO YOU THINK?

2 Long bones typically contain both compact bone and spongy bone. What benefit does spongy bone provide? Why wouldn't you want compact bone throughout the entire bone?

WHAT DID YOU LEARN?

6 Name and describe the function of the organic and inorganic components of bone.

7 If the activity of osteoblasts exceeds the activity of osteoclasts, how is the mass of the bone affected?

8 Draw and label an osteon showing the central canal, concentric lamellae, lacunae, osteocytes, and canaliculi.

6.4 Ossification

✓ Learning Objectives

9. Describe and compare the processes of intramembranous ossification and endochondral ossification.
10. Explain the components of bone that enable it to grow and be remodeled.

Ossification (os'i-fi-kā'shŭn; *os* = bone, *facio* = to make), or *osteogenesis* (os'tē-ō-jen'ĕ-sis; *genesis* = beginning), refers to the formation and development of bone connective tissue. Ossification begins in the embryo and continues as the skeleton grows during childhood and adolescence. Even after the adult bones have formed, ossification continues. By the eighth through twelfth weeks of development, the skeleton begins forming from either thickened condensations of mesenchyme or a hyaline cartilage model of bone. Thereafter, these models are replaced by hard bone.

6.4a Intramembranous Ossification

Intramembranous (in'tr ă-mem'brā-nŭs) **ossification** literally means "bone growth within a membrane," and is so named because the thin layer of mesenchyme in these areas is sometimes referred to as a membrane. Intramembranous ossification is also sometimes called *dermal ossification,* because the mesenchyme that is the source of these bones is in the area of the future dermis. Recall from section 4.2c that mesenchyme is an embryonic connective tissue that has mesenchymal cells and abundant ground substance. Intramembranous ossification produces the flat bones of the skull, some of the facial bones (e.g., zygomatic bone, maxilla), the mandible (lower jaw), and the central part of the clavicle (collarbone). It begins when mesenchyme becomes thickened and condensed with a dense supply of blood capillaries, and continues in the following steps **(figure 6.10)**:

1. **Ossification centers form within thickened regions of mesenchyme, beginning in the eighth week of development.** Some cells in the thickened, condensed mesenchyme divide, and the committed cells that result differentiate into osteoprogenitor cells. Some osteoprogenitor cells become osteoblasts, which secrete the semisolid organic components of the bone matrix called osteoid. Multiple **ossification centers** develop within the thickened mesenchyme as the number of osteoblasts increases.

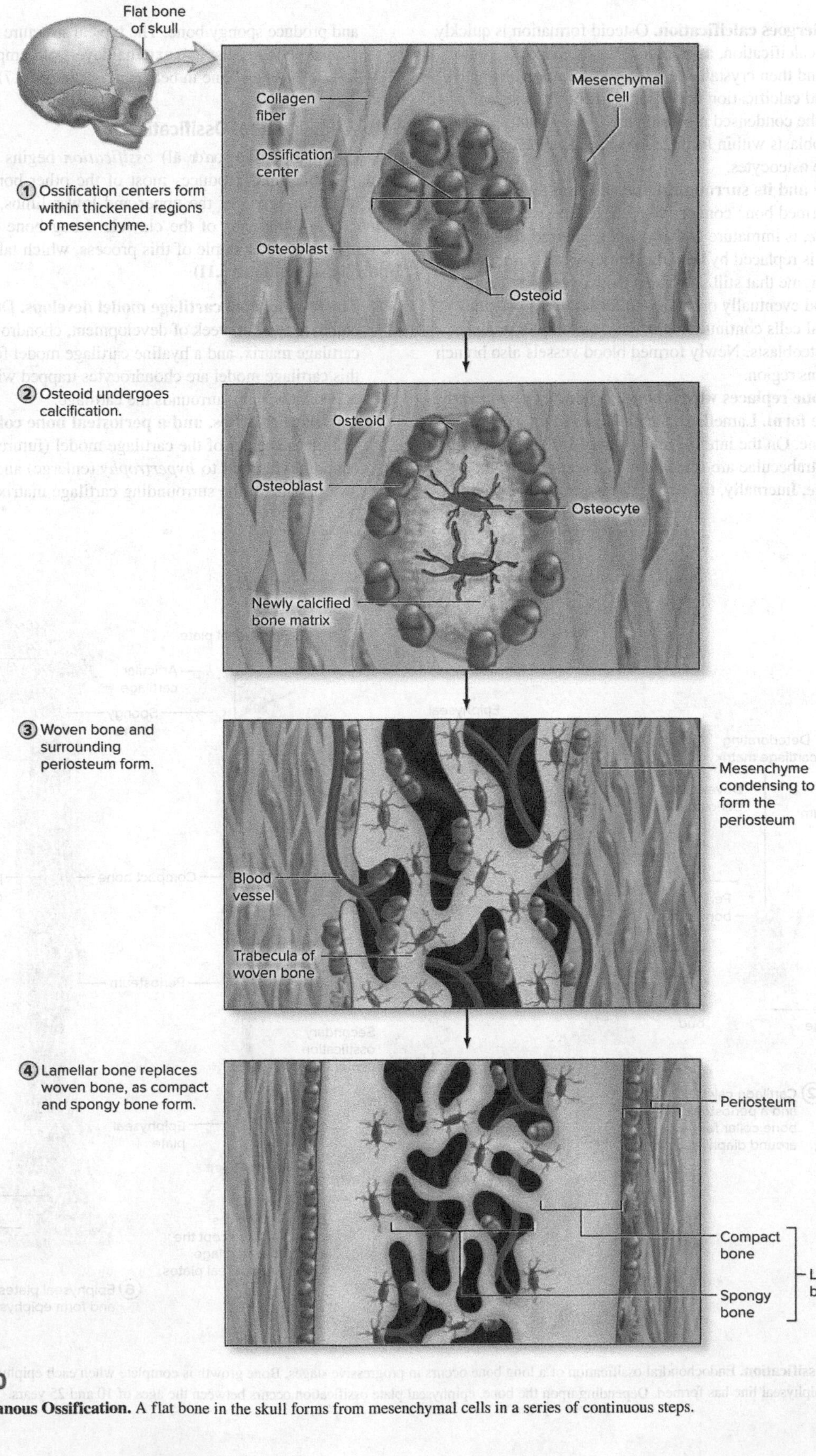
Flat bone of skull
Collagen fiber
Mesenchymal cell
Ossification center
① Ossification centers form within thickened regions of mesenchyme.
Osteoblast
Osteoid
② Osteoid undergoes calcification.
Osteoid
Osteoblast
Osteocyte
Newly calcified bone matrix
③ Woven bone and surrounding periosteum form.
Mesenchyme condensing to form the periosteum
Blood vessel
Trabecula of woven bone
④ Lamellar bone replaces woven bone, as compact and spongy bone form.
Periosteum
Compact bone
Spongy bone
Lamellar bone

Figure 6.10
Intramembranous Ossification. A flat bone in the skull forms from mesenchymal cells in a series of continuous steps.

2. **Osteoid undergoes calcification.** Osteoid formation is quickly followed by calcification, as calcium salts are deposited onto the osteoid and then crystallize (solidify). Both organic matrix formation and calcification occur simultaneously at several sites within the condensed mesenchyme. When calcification entraps osteoblasts within lacunae in the matrix, the entrapped cells become osteocytes.
3. **Woven bone and its surrounding periosteum form.** Initially, the newly formed bone connective tissue, called **woven bone** or *primary bone*, is immature and not well organized. Eventually, woven bone is replaced by **lamellar bone,** or *secondary bone.* The mesenchyme that still surrounds the woven bone begins to thicken and eventually organizes to form the periosteum. Mesenchymal cells continue to grow and develop to produce additional osteoblasts. Newly formed blood vessels also branch throughout this region.
4. **Lamellar bone replaces woven bone, as compact bone and spongy bone form.** Lamellar bone replaces the trabeculae of woven bone. On the internal and external surfaces, spaces between the trabeculae are filled, and the bone becomes compact bone. Internally, the trabeculae are modified slightly and produce spongy bone. The typical structure of a flat cranial bone results: two external layers of compact bone with a layer of spongy bone in between (see figure 6.7).

6.4b Endochondral Ossification

Endochondral (en'd ō-kon'dr ăl) *ossification* begins with a hyaline cartilage model and produces most of the other bones of the skeleton, including those of the upper and lower limbs, the pelvis, the vertebrae, and the ends of the clavicle. Long bone development in the limb is a good example of this process, which takes place in the following steps (**figure 6.11**):

1. **The fetal hyaline cartilage model develops.** During the eighth to twelfth week of development, chondroblasts secrete cartilage matrix, and a hyaline cartilage model forms. Within this cartilage model are chondrocytes trapped within lacunae. A perichondrium surrounds the cartilage.
2. **Cartilage calcifies, and a periosteal bone collar forms.** Within the center of the cartilage model (future diaphysis), chondrocytes start to *hypertrophy* (enlarge) and *resorb* (eat away) some of the surrounding cartilage matrix, producing

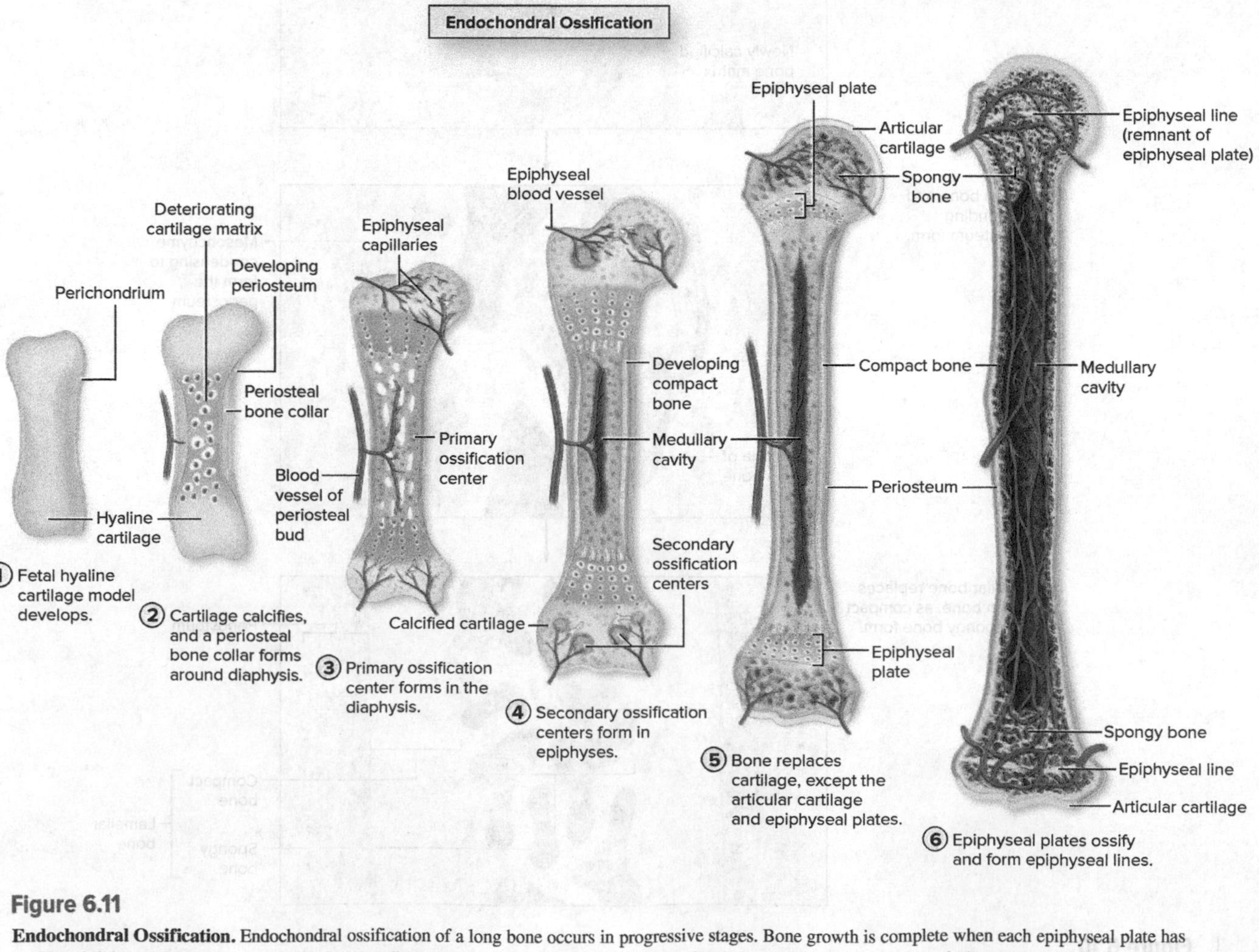

Figure 6.11

Endochondral Ossification. Endochondral ossification of a long bone occurs in progressive stages. Bone growth is complete when each epiphyseal plate has ossified and the epiphyseal line has formed. Depending upon the bone, epiphyseal plate ossification occurs between the ages of 10 and 25 years.

larger holes in the matrix. As these chondrocytes enlarge, the cartilage matrix begins to calcify. Chondrocytes in this region die and disintegrate because nutrients cannot diffuse to them through this calcified matrix. The result is a calcified cartilage shaft with large holes in the place where chondrocytes had been.

As the cartilage in the shaft is calcifying, blood vessels grow toward the cartilage and start to penetrate the perichondrium around the shaft. Stem cells within the perichondrium divide to form osteoblasts. As the osteoblasts develop, this supporting connective tissue becomes highly vascularized, and the perichondrium becomes a periosteum. The osteoblasts within the internal layer of the periosteum start secreting a layer of osteoid around the calcified cartilage shaft. The osteoid hardens and forms a **periosteal bone collar** around this shaft.

3. **The primary ossification center forms in the diaphysis.** A growth of capillaries and osteoblasts, called a *periosteal bud,* extends from the periosteum into the core of the cartilage shaft, invading the spaces left by the chondrocytes. The remains of the calcified cartilage serve as a template on which osteoblasts begin to produce osteoid. This region is called the **primary ossification center** because it is the first major center of bone formation. Bone development extends in both directions toward the epiphyses from the primary ossification center. Healthy bone tissue quickly replaces the calcified, degenerating cartilage in the shaft. Most, but not all, primary ossification centers have formed by the twelfth week of development.
4. **Secondary ossification centers form in the epiphyses.** The same basic process that formed the primary ossification center occurs later in the epiphyses. Beginning around the time of birth, the hyaline cartilage in the center of each epiphysis calcifies and begins to degenerate. Epiphyseal blood vessels and osteoprogenitor cells enter each epiphysis. **Secondary ossification centers** form as bone replaces calcified cartilage. Not all secondary ossification centers form at birth; some form later in childhood. As the secondary ossification centers form, osteoclasts resorb some bone matrix within the diaphysis, creating a hollow medullary cavity.
5. **Bone replaces cartilage, except the articular cartilage and epiphyseal plates.** By late stages of bone development, almost all of the hyaline cartilage is replaced by bone. Hyaline cartilage is found only as articular cartilage on the articular surface of each epiphysis, and as a region called the **epiphyseal** (ep'i-fiz'ē-ăl) **plate,** sandwiched between the diaphysis and the epiphysis.
6. **Lengthwise growth continues until the epiphyseal plates ossify and form epiphyseal lines.** Bone growth continues through puberty until ossification of the epiphyseal plates, indicating the bone has reached its adult length. Eventually, the only remnant of each epiphyseal plate is an internal thin line of compact bone called an **epiphyseal line.** Depending upon the bone, most epiphyseal plates fuse between the ages of 10 and 25. (The last epiphyseal plates to ossify are those of the clavicle in the late 20s.)

Table 6.1 shows a minimum comparison between intramembranous and endochondral bone formation. Although adult bone size has been reached, the bone continues to reshape itself throughout a person's lifetime in a constant process of bone resorption and deposition called bone remodeling (discussed in section 6.4d).

Table 6.1 Comparison of Intramembranous and Endochondral Ossification

	Intramembranous	Endochondral
Starting tissue	Mesenchyme	Hyaline cartilage
Initial development	8 weeks	8–12 weeks
Ossification centers	Multiple	Diaphysis first, then epiphyses
Examples of bones	Flat bones of skull, some facial bones, mandible, and central clavicle	Upper and lower limb bones, pelvis, vertebrae, ends of clavicle, ribs

WHAT DO YOU THINK?

3 Why does endochondral bone formation involve so many complex steps? Instead of having the hyaline cartilage model followed by the separate formation of the diaphysis and epiphyses, why can't bone simply be completely formed in the fetus?

Learning Strategy 6.4

Endochondral bone growth is a tough process to learn and understand. Before trying to remember every single detail, first learn these basics:

1. A hyaline cartilage model of bone forms.
2. Bone first replaces hyaline cartilage in the diaphysis.
3. Later, bone replaces hyaline cartilage in the epiphyses.
4. Eventually, bone replaces hyaline cartilage everywhere, except the epiphyseal plates and articular cartilage.
5. By a person's late 20s, the epiphyseal plates have ossified, and lengthwise bone growth is complete.

6.4c Epiphyseal Plate Morphology

Interstitial growth is dependent upon growth of cartilage within the epiphyseal plate. The epiphyseal plate exhibits five distinct microscopic zones, which are continuous from the first zone (zone 1) nearest the epiphysis to the last zone (zone 5) nearest the diaphysis (**figure 6.12**).

1. **Zone of resting cartilage.** This zone is farthest from the medullary cavity of the diaphysis and nearest the epiphysis. It is composed of small chondrocytes distributed throughout the cartilage matrix, and resembles mature, healthy hyaline cartilage. This region secures the epiphysis to the epiphyseal plate.
2. **Zone of proliferating cartilage.** Chondrocytes in this zone undergo rapid mitotic cell division, enlarge slightly, and become aligned like a stack of coins into longitudinal columns of flattened lacunae. These columns are parallel to the diaphysis.
3. **Zone of hypertrophic cartilage.** Chondrocytes cease dividing and begin to hypertrophy (enlarge) greatly. The walls of the lacunae become thin because the chondrocytes resorb matrix as they hypertrophy.
4. **Zone of calcified cartilage.** This zone usually is composed of two to three layers of cartilage. Minerals are deposited in the

Clinical View 6.2

Forensic Anthropology: Determining Age at Death

During endochondral ossification, the epiphyseal plates ossify, and fuse to and unite with the diaphysis in an orderly manner. The timings of these fusions are well known. If an epiphyseal plate has not yet ossified, the diaphysis and epiphysis are two separate pieces of bone. Thus, a skeleton that displays separate epiphyses and diaphyses (as opposed to whole fused bones) is that of a juvenile rather than an adult. Forensic anthropologists use this anatomic information to help determine the age of skeletal remains.

Fusion of an epiphyseal plate is progressive, and is usually scored as follows:

- **Open** (no bony fusion or union between the epiphysis and the other bone end)
- **Partial union** (some fusion between the epiphysis and the rest of the bone, but a distinct line of separation may be seen)
- **Complete union** (all visible aspects of the epiphysis are united to the rest of the bone)

When determining the age at death from skeletal remains, the skeleton will be older than the oldest complete union and younger than the youngest open center. For example, if one epiphyseal plate that typically fuses at age 17 is completely united, but another plate that typically fuses at age 19 is open, the skeleton is that of a person between the ages of 17 and 19.

Current standards for estimating age based upon epiphyseal plate fusion primarily have used male skeletal remains. Female epiphyseal plates tend to fuse about 1 to 2 years earlier than those of males, which needs to be considered when estimating the age of a female skeleton. Population differences also may exist with some epiphyseal plate unions. With these caveats in mind, the accompanying table lists standards for selected epiphyseal plate unions.

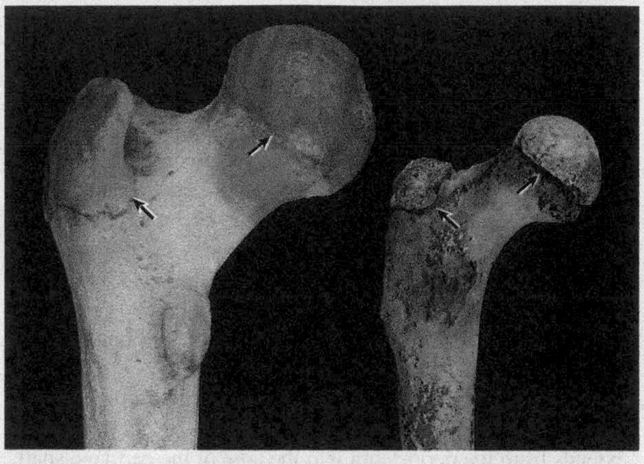

These two femora came from individuals of different ages. (Left) In partial union (arrows), the epiphyses are partially fused. This individual likely was between the ages of 15 and 23 at death. (Right) No fusion has occurred between the epiphyses and the diaphysis (see arrows), a category called open. This individual likely was younger than 15 years of age.

©David Hunt

Bone	Male Age at Epiphyseal Union (years)
Humerus, lateral epicondyle	11–16 (female: 9–13)
Humerus, medial epicondyle	11–16 (female: 10–15)
Humerus, head	14.5–23.5
Proximal radius	14–19
Distal radius	17–22
Distal fibula and tibia	14.5–19.5
Proximal tibia	15–22
Femur, head	14.5–23.5
Distal femur	14.5–21.5
Clavicle	19–30

matrix between the columns of lacunae; this calcification kills the chondrocytes and makes the matrix appear opaque.

5. **Zone of ossification**. The walls break down between lacunae in the columns, forming longitudinal channels. These spaces are invaded by capillaries and osteoprogenitor cells from the medullary cavity. The osteoprogenitor cells will become osteoblasts which will deposit new bone matrix on the remaining calcified cartilage matrix.

6.4d Growth of Bone

As with cartilage growth, a long bone's growth in length is called *interstitial growth*, and its growth in diameter or thickness is called *appositional growth*. Interstitial growth occurs within the epiphyseal plate as chondrocytes undergo mitotic cell division in zone 2 and chondrocytes hypertrophy in zone 3. These activities combine to push the zone of resting cartilage toward the epiphysis. It is the flexible matrix of hyaline cartilage that permits this growth. Once growth in length has occurred, new bone connective tissue is produced at the same rate in zone 5. Thus, growth in length is due to growth in hyaline cartilage connective tissue that is later replaced with bone (endochondral ossification).

The epiphyseal plate maintains its thickness in childhood as it is pushed away from the center of the shaft. At maturity, the rate of epiphyseal cartilage production slows, and the rate of osteoblast activity accelerates. As a result, the epiphyseal plate becomes narrower, until it disappears, and interstitial growth completely stops. The appearance of the remnant epiphyseal line signals the termination of lengthwise growth of the bone.

Appositional growth occurs within the periosteum (**figure 6.13**). In this process, osteoblasts in the inner cellular layer of the periosteum lay down bone matrix in layers parallel to the surface, called external circumferential lamellae. These lamellae are analogous to tree rings: As they increase in number, the structure widens. Thus, the bone becomes wider as new bone is laid down at the periphery. As this new bone is being laid down, osteoclasts along the medullary cavity resorb bone matrix, creating an expanding medullary cavity. The combined effects of

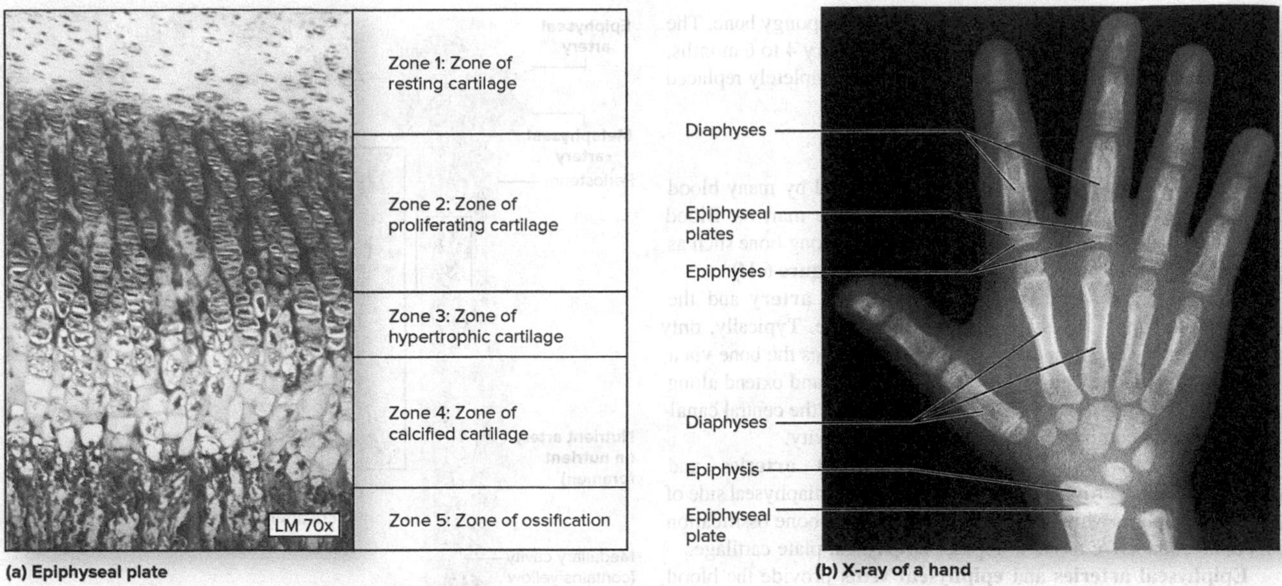
Zone 1: Zone of resting cartilage
Zone 2: Zone of proliferating cartilage
Zone 3: Zone of hypertrophic cartilage
Zone 4: Zone of calcified cartilage
Zone 5: Zone of ossification
LM 70x
(a) Epiphyseal plate
Diaphyses
Epiphyseal plates
Epiphyses
Diaphyses
Epiphysis
Epiphyseal plate
(b) X-ray of a hand

Figure 6.12

Epiphyseal Plate. (*a*) In a growing long bone, the epiphyseal plate, located at the boundary between the diaphysis and the epiphysis, exhibits five distinct but continuous zones. Zones 1–4 are cartilage, and zone 5 is bone. (*b*) An x-ray of a child's hand shows the cartilaginous epiphyseal plates as dark lines between the epiphysis and the diaphysis of long bones.

(a) Biophoto Associates/Science Source; (b) Puwadol Jaturawutthichai/stockdevil/123RF

bone growth at the periphery and bone resorption within the medullary cavity transform an infant bone into a larger version called an adult bone.

Bone Remodeling

Bone continues to grow and renew itself throughout life. The continual deposition of new bone connective tissue and the removal (resorption) of old bone connective tissue is called **bone remodeling.** Bone remodeling helps maintain calcium and phosphate levels in body fluids, and can be stimulated by stress on a bone (e.g., bone fracture, or exercise that builds up muscles that attach to bone). This ongoing process occurs at both the periosteal and endosteal surfaces of a bone. It either modifies the architecture of the bone or changes the total amount of minerals deposited in the skeleton. Prior to and throughout puberty, the formation of bone typically exceeds its resorption. In young adults, the processes of formation and resorption tend to occur at about the same rate. However, they become disproportionate in older adults when resorption of bone exceeds its formation.

It is estimated that about 20% of the adult human skeleton is replaced yearly. However, bone remodeling does not occur at the same rate everywhere in the skeleton. For example, the compact bone

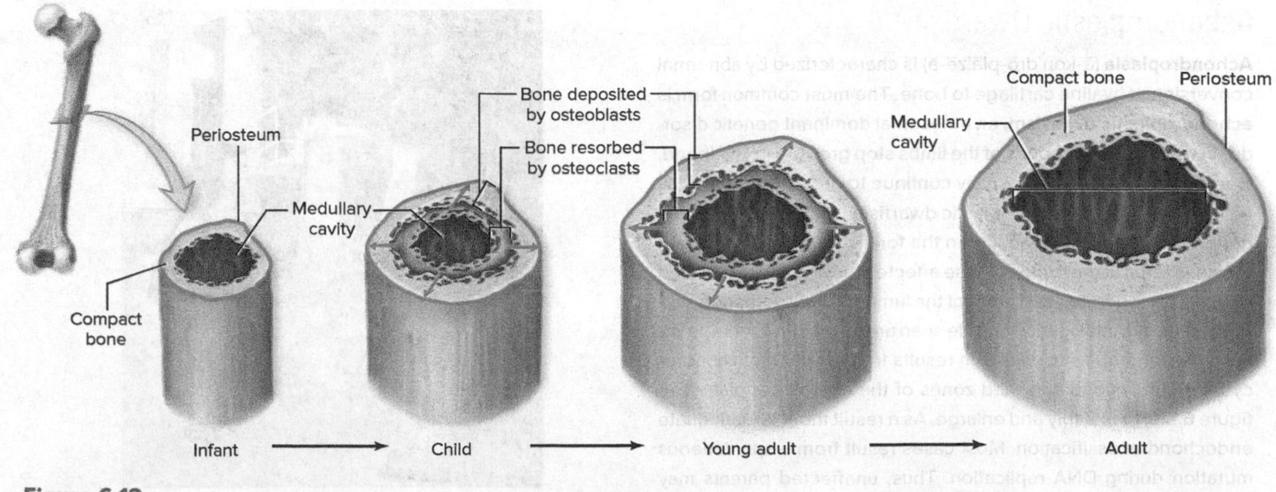
Periosteum
Medullary cavity
Compact bone
Bone deposited by osteoblasts
Bone resorbed by osteoclasts
Compact bone
Periosteum
Medullary cavity
Infant
Child
Young adult
Adult

Figure 6.13

Appositional Bone Growth. A bone increases in diameter as new bone is added to the surface. At the same time, some bone may be removed from the inner surface to enlarge the marrow cavity. APR in our skeleton is replaced at a slower rate than the spongy bone. The distal part of the femur (thigh bone) is replaced every 4 to 6 months, whereas the diaphysis of this bone may not be completely replaced during an individual's lifetime.

6.4e Blood Supply and Innervation

Bone is highly vascularized (meaning it is supplied by many blood vessels), especially in regions containing red bone marrow. Blood vessels enter bones from the periosteum. A typical long bone such as the humerus has four major sets of blood vessels (**figure 6.14**).

Nutrient blood vessels, called the **nutrient artery** and the **nutrient vein,** supply the diaphysis of a long bone. Typically, only one nutrient artery enters and one nutrient vein leaves the bone via a nutrient foramen in the bone. These vessels branch and extend along the length of the shaft toward the epiphyses and into the central canal of osteons within compact bone and the marrow cavity.

Metaphyseal blood vessels (**metaphyseal arteries** and **metaphyseal veins**) provide the blood supply to the diaphyseal side of the epiphyseal plate, which is the region where new bone ossification forms bone connective tissue to replace epiphyseal plate cartilage.

Epiphyseal arteries and **epiphyseal veins** provide the blood supply to the epiphyses of the bone. In early childhood, the cartilaginous epiphyseal plate separates the epiphyseal and metaphyseal vessels. However, once an epiphyseal plate ossifies and becomes an epiphyseal line, the epiphyseal vessels and metaphyseal vessels anastomose (interconnect) through channels formed in the epiphyseal line (see figure 6.14 for examples).

Periosteal blood vessels (**periosteal arteries** and **periosteal veins**) provide blood to the external circumferential lamellae and the superficial osteons within the compact bone at the external edge of the bone. These vessels and the accompanying periosteal nerves penetrate the diaphysis and enter the perforating canals at many locations.

Nerves that supply bones accompany blood vessels through the nutrient foramen and innervate the bone as well as its periosteum, endosteum, and marrow cavity. These are mainly sensory nerves that signal injuries to the skeleton.

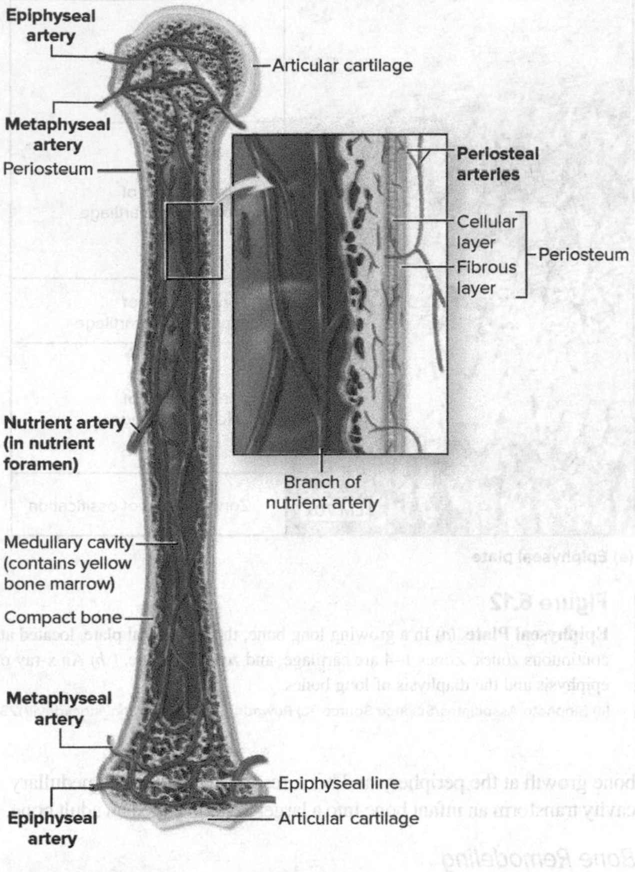

Figure 6.14

Arterial Supply to a Mature Bone. Four major sets of blood vessels supply the humerus, a long bone: nutrient arteries and veins, metaphyseal arteries and veins, epiphyseal arteries and veins, and periosteal arteries and veins.

Clinical View 6.3

Achondroplastic Dwarfism

Achondroplasia (ā-kon′drō-plā′zē-ă) is characterized by abnormal conversion of hyaline cartilage to bone. The most common form is **achondroplastic dwarfism,** an autosomal dominant genetic disorder in which the long bones of the limbs stop growing in childhood, whereas the other bones usually continue to grow normally. Thus, an individual with achondroplastic dwarfism is short in stature but generally has a large head. Often the forehead is prominent, and the nose is flat at the bridge. Those affected may have bowlegs and lordosis (exaggerated curvature of the lumbar spine). Although stature is affected, intelligence and life span are not in these individuals.

Achondroplastic dwarfism results from a failure of chondrocytes in the second and third zones of the epiphyseal plate (see figure 6.12a) to multiply and enlarge. As a result there is inadequate endochondral ossification. Most cases result from a spontaneous mutation during DNA replication. Thus, unaffected parents may have a child with achondroplastic dwarfism. Children of an affected parent also may inherit the disorder.

The individual on the right displays achondroplasia.

WHAT DID YOU LEARN?

9. What is intramembranous ossification? What bones form by this process?
10. Draw a generalized long bone and identify the locations of primary and secondary ossification centers.
11. How could a physician determine whether a patient had reached full height by examining x-rays of his or her bones?
12. Create a table listing the five zones in an epiphyseal plate as separate rows in a column. In the next column list the characteristics of each of these zones. In the final column, sketch what these zones look like to you to help you identify them.

6.5 Maintaining Homeostasis and Promoting Bone Growth

✓ Learning Objectives

11. Explain the effects of hormones, vitamins, and exercise on bone growth and maintenance.
12. Identify and describe basic types of bone fracture.
13. Describe the steps involved in healing bone fractures.

Bone growth, maintenance, and repair normally depend upon hormones, vitamins (table 6.2), and exercise.

6.5a Effects of Hormones

Hormones are molecules released from one cell into the blood and they travel throughout the body to affect other cells (see section 20.1a). Hormones control and regulate bone growth and maintenance by altering the rates of osteoblast and osteoclast activity. **Growth hormone,** also called *somatotropin* (sō′mă-tō-trō′pin), is produced by the anterior pituitary gland. It affects bone growth by stimulating the liver to form another hormone called **insulin-like growth factor (IGF),** also called *somatomedin* (sō′mă-tō-mē′din). Growth hormone and IGF directly stimulate growth of cartilage in the epiphyseal plate.

Thyroid hormone, secreted by the thyroid gland, stimulates bone growth by influencing the basal metabolic rate of bone cells. Together, growth hormone and thyroid hormone, if maintained in proper balance, regulate and maintain normal activity at the epiphyseal plates until puberty. If a child's growth hormone and/or thyroid hormone levels are chronically too low, then bone growth is adversely affected, and the child will be short in stature.

Two hormones regulate calcium levels in the blood. **Calcitonin** (kal′si-t ō′nin; *calx* = lime, *tonos* = stretching) is secreted by cells in the thyroid gland in response to elevated levels of calcium in the blood. Calcitonin promotes calcium deposition from blood into bone and inhibits osteoclast activity that resorbs bone.

Parathyroid hormone is produced and released by the parathyroid glands in response to reduced calcium levels in the blood. It stimulates osteoclasts to resorb bone and thereby increase calcium levels in the blood. Parathyroid hormone presence also influences the production of calcitriol in the kidneys. Together they increase the release of calcium from bone.

Sex hormones **(estrogen** and **testosterone),** which begin to be secreted in great amounts at puberty, dramatically accelerate bone growth. Sex hormones increase the rate of bone formation by osteoblasts in ossification centers within the epiphyseal plate, resulting in increased length of long bones and increased height. The high levels of sex hormones at puberty also lead to stopping growth at the epiphyseal plate. Eventually, more bone is produced at the epiphyseal plate, the thickness of the epiphyseal plate cartilage diminishes, and eventually it disappears altogether. The remnant of the epiphyseal plate is called the epiphyseal line. Sex hormones are normally reduced in older individuals, which may result in reduced bone mass.

Finally, *abnormal* amounts of certain hormones can affect bone maintenance and growth. Recall that chronically low levels of growth hormone and/or thyroid hormone in a child inhibit bone growth and result in short stature. Another example are the **glucocorticoids,** a group of hormones produced by the adrenal cortex. Normal glucocorticoid levels tend not to have any major effects on bone growth or mass. However, if glucocorticoid levels are chronically too high, they stimulate bone resorption and can lead to significant loss of bone mass. This result is particularly concerning for children on corticosteroid treatment for chronic disorders such as Crohn disease.

Table 6.2	Effects of Hormones and Vitamins on Bone Maintenance and Growth
HORMONES	
Growth hormone	Stimulates liver to produce the hormone insulin-like growth factor (somatomedin), which causes cartilage proliferation at epiphyseal plate and resulting bone elongation; too little growth hormone results in short stature in the child
Thyroid hormone	Stimulates bone growth by stimulating metabolic rate of osteoblasts; too little thyroid hormone results in short stature
Calcitonin	Promotes calcium deposition in bone and inhibits osteoclast activity
Parathyroid hormone	Increases blood calcium levels by encouraging bone resorption by osteoclasts
Sex hormones (estrogen and testosterone)	Stimulate osteoblasts; promote epiphyseal plate growth and eventual closure
Glucocorticoids	If levels are chronically too high, bone resorption occurs and significant bone mass is lost
VITAMINS	
Vitamin A	Activates osteoblasts
Vitamin C (ascorbic acid)	Promotes collagen production
Vitamin D	Promotes absorption of calcium and phosphate into blood; helps with calcification of bone

6.5b Effects of Vitamins

A continual dietary source of vitamins is required for normal bone growth and maintenance. For example, **vitamin A** activates osteoblasts, whereas **vitamin C** is required for normal synthesis of collagen, the primary organic component in the bone matrix. **Vitamin D** stimulates the absorption and transport of calcium and phosphate ions into the blood. As calcium and phosphate levels rise in the blood, calcitonin is secreted, which encourages the deposition of these minerals into bone.

6.5c Effects of Exercise

Mechanical stress, in the form of exercise, is required for normal bone remodeling. In response to mechanical stress, bone has the ability to increase its strength over a period of time by increasing the amounts of mineral salts deposited and collagen fibers synthesized.

Clinical View 6.4

Rickets

Rickets is a disease caused by a vitamin D deficiency in childhood and characterized by overproduction and deficient calcification of osteoid. Due to the lack of vitamin D, the digestive tract is unable to absorb calcium and phosphorus, minerals needed for the hardening of the osteoid during the formation of bone.

Rickets results in bones that are poorly calcified and exhibit too much flexibility. Patients with rickets acquire a bow-legged appearance as their weight increases and the bones in their legs bend. In addition to skeletal deformities, rickets is characterized by disturbances in growth, hypocalcemia (an abnormally low level of calcium in the blood), and sometimes tetany (cramps and muscle twitches), usually caused by low blood calcium. The condition is often accompanied by irritability, listlessness, and generalized muscular weakness. Fractures frequently occur in patients with rickets.

During the Industrial Revolution, the incidence of rickets increased as children were forced to work indoors in factories. These children had little exposure to sunlight and were usually malnourished as well. (Recall from section 5.1b that the body can manufacture its own vitamin D when the integument is exposed to sunlight.) Rickets continues to occur in some developing nations, and the incidence has increased in urban areas of the United States. Researchers have discovered that these children spend much of their time indoors and typically do not drink enough vitamin D-fortified milk, opting for soft drinks instead. So, unfortunately, a disease that is easily preventable is making a comeback in the United States due to poor dietary and lifestyle habits among the nation's youth.

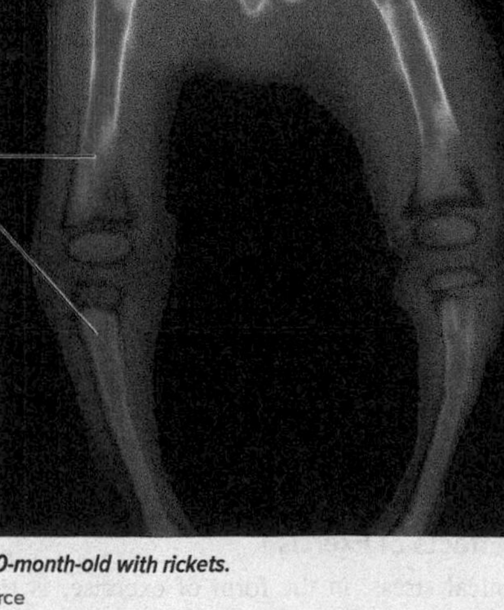
Bowing lower limb long bones

Radiograph of a 10-month-old with rickets.

Dr. LR/Science Source

Clinical View 6.5

Bone Scans

Bone scans are tests that can detect bone pathologies sooner than standard x-rays, while exposing the patient to only a fraction of the radiation of a normal x-ray. The patient is injected intravenously with a small amount of a radioactive tracer compound that is absorbed by bone. A scanning camera then detects and measures the radiation emitted from the bone. This information is converted into a diagram or photograph that can be read like an x-ray. In these films, normal bone tissue is a consistent gray color, whereas darker areas are "hot spots" indicating increased metabolism, and lighter areas are "cold spots" indicating decreased metabolism. Abnormalities that can be detected by a bone scan include fractures, decalcification of bone, osteomyelitis, degenerative bone disease, and osteitis deformans. Bone scans are also used to determine whether cancer has metastasized to bone, to identify bone infections, to monitor the progress of bone grafts and degenerative bone disorders, to evaluate unexplained bone pain or possible fracture, and to monitor response to therapy of a cancer that has spread to bone.

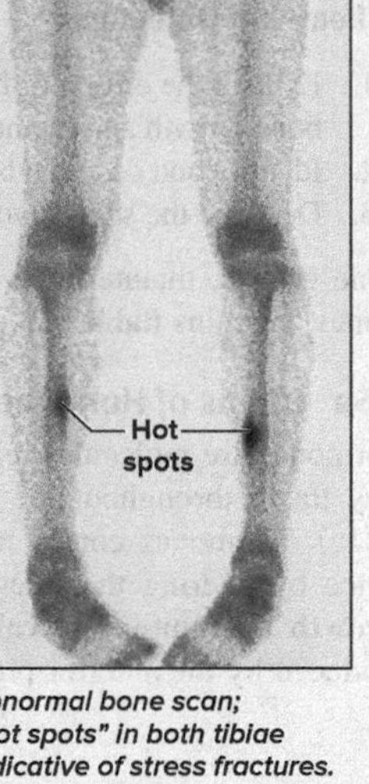
Hot spots

Abnormal bone scan; "hot spots" in both tibiae indicative of stress fractures.

John Pape/MedPix

Stress also increases the production of the hormone calcitonin, which helps inhibit bone resorption by osteoclasts and encourage bone deposition by osteoblasts.

Mechanical stresses that significantly affect bone result from repeated skeletal muscle contraction and gravitational forces. Typically, the bones of athletes become noticeably thicker as a result of repetitive and stressful exercise. Weight-bearing activities, such as weight lifting or walking, help build and retain bone mass. In contrast, lack of mechanical stress weakens bone through both demineralization of the bone matrix and reduction of collagen formation. For example, if a person has a fractured bone in a cast or is bedridden, the mass of the unstressed bone decreases in the immobilized limbs. While in space, astronauts must exercise so that the lesser gravity won't weaken their bones.

Research has shown that regular weight-bearing exercise can increase total bone mass in adolescents and young adults prior to its inevitable reduction later in life. In fact, studies have shown that even 70- and 80-year-olds who perform moderate weight training can increase their bone mass.

6.5d Fracture and Repair

Bone has great mineral strength, and yet it may break as a result of unusual stress or a sudden impact. Breaks in bones, called **fractures,** are classified in several ways. They can be named from the cause: stress, trauma, or pathology. A **stress fracture** is a thin break caused by recent increased physical activity in which the bone experiences repetitive loads (e.g., as seen in some runners). Stress fractures tend to occur in the weight-bearing bones (e.g., pelvis and lower limb). A traumatic fracture is a result of impact or excess stress to the bone, and a **pathologic fracture** usually occurs in bone that has been weakened by disease, such as when the vertebrae fracture in someone with osteoporosis (a bone condition discussed in Clinical View 6.6 "Osteoporosis" in section 6.7). Fractures are categorized by the amount of soft tissue damage associated with the fracture. In a **simple fracture,** the broken bone does not penetrate the skin, whereas in a **compound fracture,** one or both ends of the broken bone pierce the overlying skin and body tissues. Fractures are also known through eponyms (such as Colles or Pott), which have specific characteristics describing these fractures. Most often fractures are classified by the description of the fracture. **Figure 6.15** shows some of the different classifications of fractures. Often many fracture classifications are used to describe a single fracture. For instance, a Colles fracture is a complete, transverse fracture of the distal radius with posterior displacement.

The healing of a simple fracture takes about 2 to 3 months, whereas a compound fracture takes longer to heal. Fractures heal much more quickly in young children (average healing time, 3 weeks) and become slower to heal as we age. In the elderly, the normal thinning and weakening of bone increases the incidence of fractures, and some severe fractures never heal without surgical

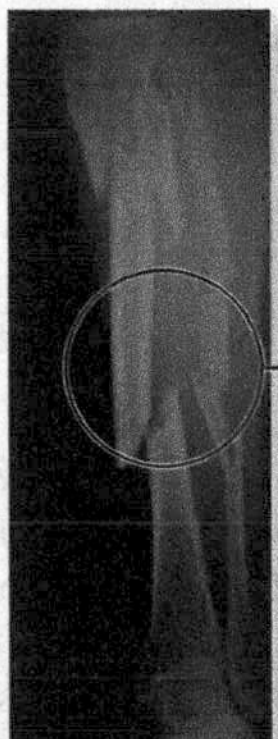

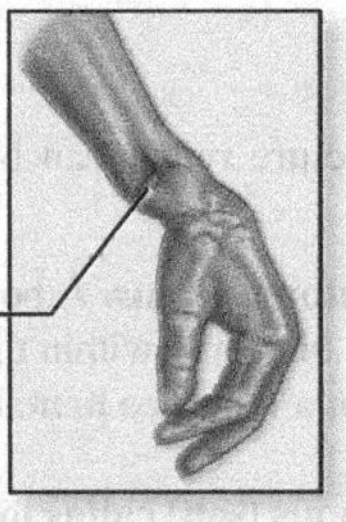

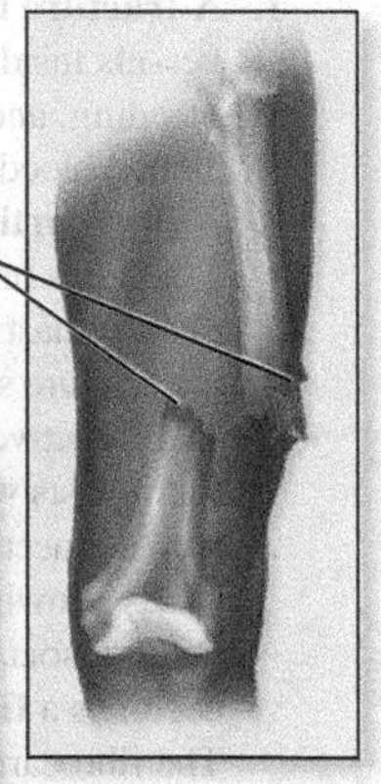

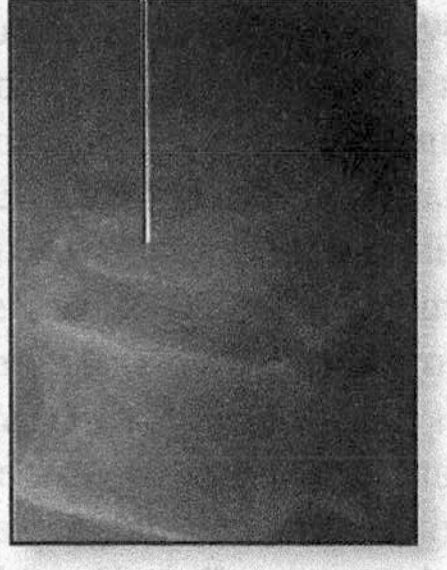

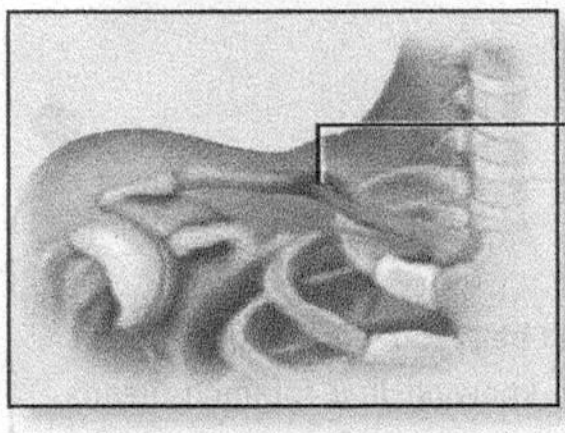

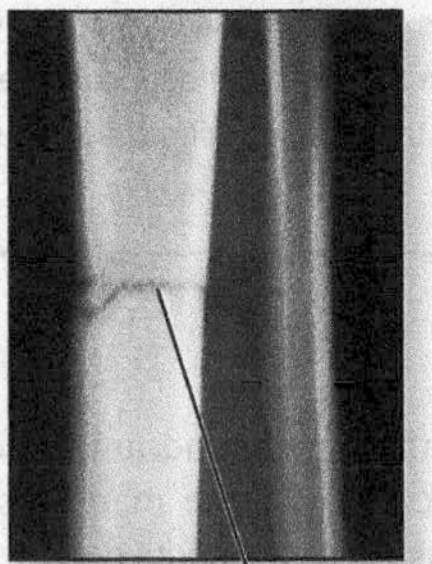

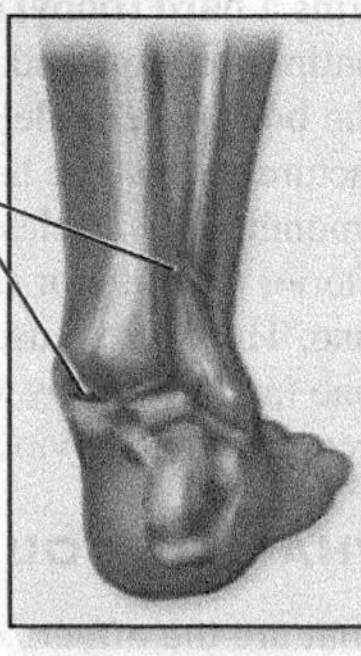

Classification of Bone Fractures

Fracture	Description
Avulsion	Complete severing of a body part (typically a toe or finger)
Colles	Fracture of the distal end of the lateral forearm bone (radius); produces a "dinner fork" deformity
Comminuted	Bone is splintered into several small pieces between the main parts
Complete	Bone is broken into two or more pieces
Compound (open)	Broken ends of the bone protrude through the skin
Compression	Bone is squashed (may occur in a vertebra during a fall)
Depressed	Broken part of the bone forms a concavity (as in skull fracture)
Displaced	Fractured bone parts are out of anatomic alignment
Epiphyseal	Epiphysis is separated from the diaphysis at the epiphyseal plate
Greenstick	Partial fracture; one side of bone breaks—the other side is bent
Hairline	Fine crack in which sections of bone remain aligned (common in skull)
Impacted	One fragment of bone is firmly driven into the other
Incomplete	Partial fracture extends only partway across the bone
Linear	Fracture is parallel to the long axis of the bone
Oblique	Diagonal fracture is at an angle
Pathologic	Weakening of a bone caused by disease process (e.g., cancer)
Pott	Fracture is at the distal ends of the tibia and fibula
Simple (closed)	Bone does not break through the skin
Spiral	Fracture spirals around axis of long bone; results from twisting stress
Stress	Thin fractures due to repeated, stressful impact such as running (These fractures often are difficult to see on x-rays, and a bone scan may be necessary to accurately identify their presence.)
Transverse	Fracture is at right angles to the long axis of the bone

Figure 6.15

Classification of Bone Fractures.

(top) Robert Destefano/Alamy Stock Photo; (middle) Sutthaburawonk/Getty Images; (bottom) Wellcome Images

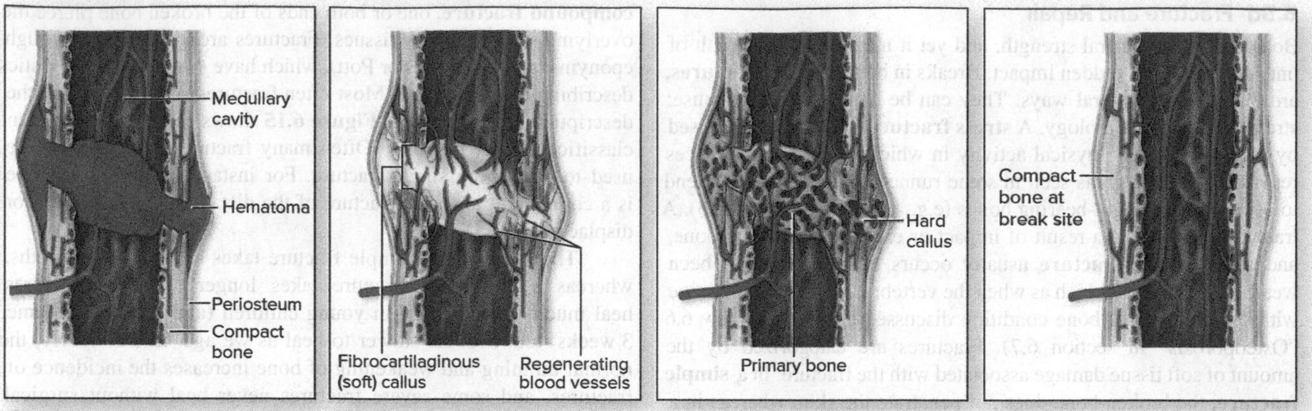
Medullary cavity
Hematoma
Periosteum
Compact bone
Fibrocartilaginous (soft) callus
Regenerating blood vessels
Hard callus
Primary bone
Compact bone at break site

① A fracture hematoma forms. ② A fibrocartilaginous (soft) callus forms. ③ A hard (bony) callus forms. ④ The bone is remodeled.

Figure 6.16

Fracture Repair. The repair of a bone fracture occurs in a series of steps.

intervention. Bone fracture repair can be described as a series of steps **(figure 6.16)**:

1. **A fracture hematoma forms.** A bone fracture tears blood vessels inside the bone and within the periosteum, causing bleeding, and then a **fracture hematoma** forms from the clotted blood.
2. **A fibrocartilaginous (soft) callus forms.** Regenerated blood capillaries infiltrate the fracture hematoma due to an increase in osteoblasts in both the periosteum and the endosteum near the fracture site. First, the fracture hematoma is reorganized into an actively growing connective tissue called a **procallus.** Fibroblasts within the procallus produce collagen fibers that help connect the broken ends of the bones. Chondroblasts in the newly growing connective tissue form a dense regular connective tissue associated with the cartilage. Eventually, the procallus becomes a **fibrocartilaginous (soft) callus** (kal'ŭs; hard skin). The fibrocartilaginous callus stage lasts at least 3 weeks.
3. **A hard (bony) callus forms.** Within a week, osteoprogenitor cells in areas adjacent to the fibrocartilaginous callus become osteoblasts and produce trabeculae of primary bone. The fibrocartilaginous callus is then replaced by this bone, which forms a **hard (bony) callus.** The trabeculae of the hard callus continue to grow and thicken for several months.
4. **The bone is remodeled.** Remodeling is the final phase of fracture repair. The hard callus persists for at least 3 to 4 months as osteoclasts remove excess bony material from both exterior and interior surfaces. Compact bone replaces primary bone. The fracture usually leaves a slight thickening of the bone (as detected by x-ray); however, in many instances healing occurs with no obvious thickening.

WHAT DID YOU LEARN?

13 What are the effects of growth hormone and parathyroid hormone on bone growth and/or bone mass?

14 List and describe vitamins that help regulate bone growth.

15 Describe the steps of fracture repair. List which fracture from Figure 6.15 you think would be most difficult to repair and which fracture would be easier, and state why.

6.6 Bone Markings

✓ Learning Objective

14. Identify the anatomic terms that describe the surface features of bone.

Distinctive **bone markings,** or *surface features,* characterize each bone in the body. Projections from the bone surface mark the point where tendons and ligaments attach. Sites of articulation between adjacent bones are smooth areas. Depressions, grooves, and tunnels through bones indicate sites where blood vessels and nerves travel. Anatomists use specific terms to describe these elevations and depressions **(figure 6.17)**.

Learning Strategy 6.5

Knowing the names of bone markings will help you learn about specific bones in chapters 7 and 8. For example, knowing that foramen means "hole" or "passageway" will tell you to look for a hole when trying to find the foramen magnum on the skull. Likewise, you can usually correctly assume that any smooth, oval prominence on a bone is called a condyle. Refer back to figure 6.17 frequently for assistance in learning the bones and their features.

For professional criminologists, pathologists, and anthropologists, bones can tell an intricate anatomic story. Bone markings on skeletal remains indicate where the soft tissue components once were, often allowing an individual's height, age, sex, and general appearance to be determined.

WHAT DID YOU LEARN?

16 List all the anatomic terms that are used to refer to a passageway or opening through a bone.

Figure 6.17

Bone Markings. Specific anatomic terms describe the characteristic identification marks for bones.

General Structure	Anatomic Term	Description
Articulating surfaces	Condyle	Large, smooth, rounded oval structure
	Facet	Small, flat, shallow surface
	Head	Prominent, rounded epiphysis
	Trochlea	Smooth, grooved, pulley-like process
Depressions	Alveolus (pl., *alveoli*)	Deep pit or socket in the maxillae or mandible
	Fossa (pl., *fossae*)	Flattened or shallow depression
	Sulcus	Narrow groove
Projections for tendon and ligament attachment	Crest	Narrow, prominent, ridgelike projection
	Epicondyle	Projection adjacent to a condyle
	Line	Low ridge
	Process	Any marked bony prominence
	Ramus (pl., *rami*)	Angular extension of a bone relative to the rest of the structure
	Spine	Pointed, slender process
	Trochanter	Massive, rough projection found only on the femur
	Tubercle	Small, round projection
	Tuberosity	Large, rough projection
Openings and spaces	Canal	Passageway through a bone
	Fissure	Narrow, slitlike opening through a bone
	Foramen (pl., *foramina*)	Rounded passageway through a bone
	Meatus	Passageway through a bone
	Sinus	Cavity or hollow space in a bone

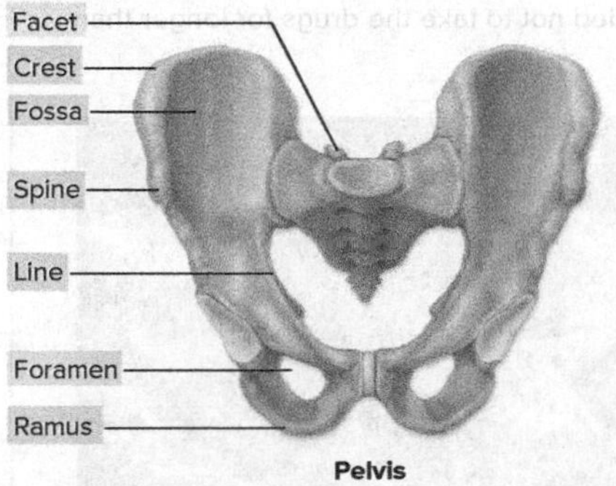

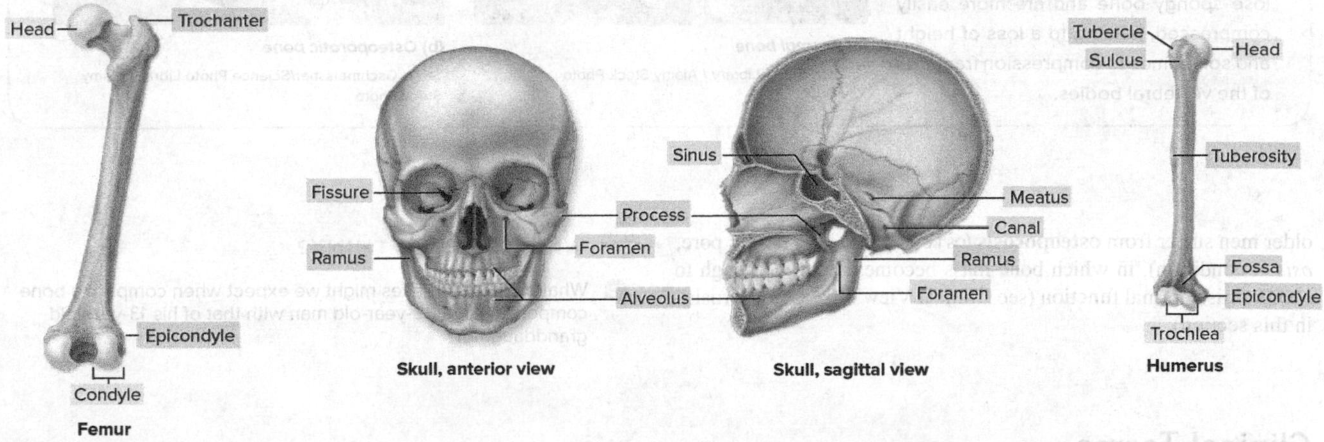

6.7 Aging of the Skeletal System

✓ Learning Objective

15. Explain the changes in bone architecture and bone mass related to age.

Aging affects bone connective tissue in two ways. First, the tensile strength of bone decreases due to a reduced rate of protein synthesis, which in turn results in decreased ability to produce the organic portion of bone matrix. Consequently, the percentage of inorganic minerals in the bone matrix increases, and the bones of the skeleton become brittle and susceptible to fracture.

Second, bone loses calcium and other minerals (demineralization). The bones of the skeleton become thinner and weaker, resulting in insufficient ossification, a condition called **osteopenia** (os′tē-ō-pē′nē-ă; *penia* = poverty). Aging causes all people to become slightly osteopenic. This reduction in bone mass may begin as early as 35–40 years of age, when osteoblast activity declines and osteoclast activity continues at previous levels. During each successive decade of their lives, women lose more of their skeletal mass than do men. Different parts of the skeleton are affected unequally. Vertebrae, jaw bones, and epiphyses lose large amounts of mass, resulting in reduced height, loss of teeth, and fragile limbs. A significant percentage of older women and a smaller proportion of

Clinical View 6.6

Osteoporosis

Osteoporosis, meaning "porous bones," is a disease that results in decreased bone mass and microarchitectural changes that lead to weakened bones that are prone to fracture. The occurrence of osteoporosis is greatest among the elderly, especially Caucasian women, and the severity is closely linked to age and the onset of menopause. Smoking is also a risk factor for osteoporosis. Postmenopausal women are at risk because (1) women have less bone mass than men, (2) women begin losing bone mass earlier and faster in life (sometimes as early as 35 years of age), and (3) postmenopausal women no longer produce significant amounts of estrogen, which appears to help protect against osteoporosis by stimulating bone growth. Although the condition does affect men, osteoporosis in men is typically less severe than in women.

The incidence of fractures increases in people with osteoporosis. The most frequent fracture sites are in the wrist, hip, and vertebral column, and usually as the result of a normal amount of stress. Wrist fractures occur at the distal end of the radius (Colles fracture), and hip fractures usually occur at the neck of the femur. The weight-bearing regions of the vertebrae lose spongy bone and are more easily compressed, leading to a loss of height and sometimes to compression fractures of the vertebral bodies.

The best treatment seems to be prevention. Young adults should maintain good nutrition and physical activity to ensure adequate bone density, thus allowing for the normal, age-related loss later in life. Calcium supplements with vitamin D may help maintain bone health, but by themselves will not stimulate new bone growth.

A class of medications called bisphosphonates (e.g., alendronate [Fosamax], risedronate [Actonel], ibandronate [Boniva]) may be prescribed to slow the progression of osteoporosis. These drugs work by interfering with osteoclast function and thus retarding the removal of bone during remodeling. Unfortunately, these drugs have also been implicated in increased risk of **osteonecrosis** (bone death) of the jaw and some other bone growth abnormalities, so patients are recommended not to take the drugs for longer than 5 years at a time.

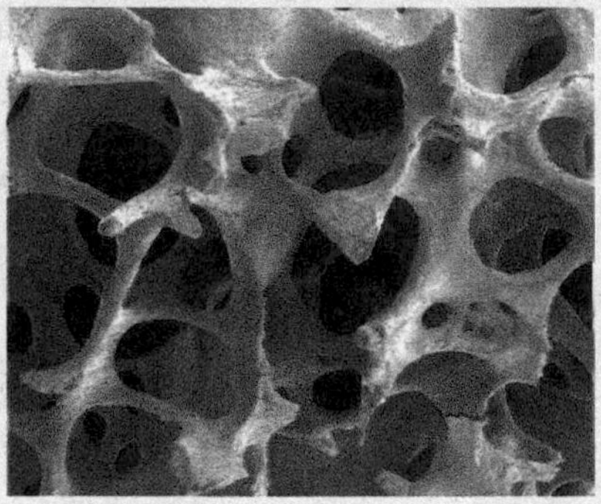

(a) *Normal bone*
Science Photo Library / Alamy Stock Photo

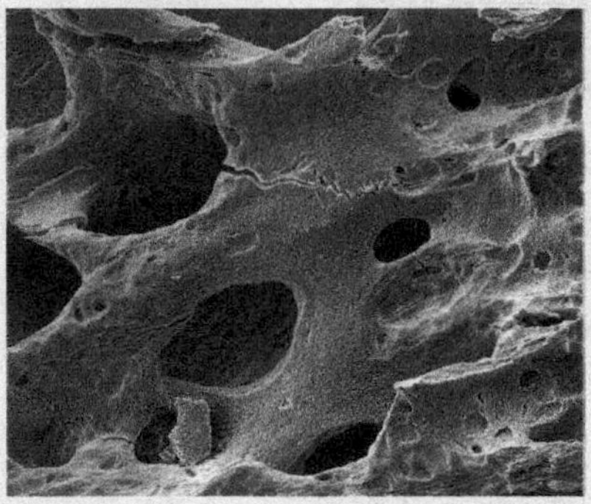

(b) *Osteoporotic bone*
Steve Gschmeissner/Science Photo Library/Alamy Stock Photo

older men suffer from **osteoporosis** (os′tē-ō-pō-rō′sis; *poros* = pore, *osis* = condition), in which bone mass becomes reduced enough to compromise normal function (see Clinical View 6.6: "Osteoporosis" in this section).

WHAT DO YOU THINK?

4 What major differences might we expect when comparing bone composition in a 65-year-old man with that of his 13-year-old granddaughter?

Clinical Terms

chondroma Benign (noncancerous) tumor derived from cartilage cells.

chondrosarcoma Malignant (cancerous) tumor derived from cartilage cells.

hyperostosis Excessive formation of bone tissue.

osteogenesis imperfecta Also known as *brittle bone disease*; inherited condition that affects collagen fiber distribution and organization. It occurs due to impaired osteoblast function, and results in abnormal bone growth, brittle bones, continuing deformation of the skeleton, and increased susceptibility to fracture.

osteoma Benign tumor in lamellar bone, often in the jaw or the skull.

osteomalacia Vitamin D deficiency disease in adults characterized by gradual softening and bending of the bones as a result of decreased mineral content; although bone mass is still present, it is demineralized.

osteomyelitis Infection and inflammation within both the bone marrow and neighboring regions of the bone.

osteosarcoma The most common and malignant bone sarcoma; arises from bone-forming cells (osteoblasts) and chiefly affects the ends of long bones.

Chapter Summary

	■ The skeletal system is composed of bones, cartilage that supports the bones, and ligaments that bind together, support, and stabilize bones.
6.1 Cartilage	■ Cartilage contains cells embedded within a matrix of protein fibers and a gel-like ground substance. **6.1a Functions of Cartilage** ■ Cartilage provides support for soft tissues, a sliding surface for bone, and a model for formation of most of the bones of the body. **6.1b Growth Patterns of Cartilage** ■ Cartilage growth includes both interstitial growth (growth from within preexisting cartilage) and appositional growth (growth around the periphery of cartilage).
6.2 Bone	■ Bones are organs that contain multiple tissue types, the most abundant being bone (osseous) connective tissue. **6.2a Functions of Bone** ■ Bone performs the following functions: support and protection, movement, hematopoiesis, and storage of minerals and energy.
6.3 Classification and Anatomy of Bones	■ Bones are categorized by shape as long, short, flat, or irregular. **6.3a General Structure and Gross Anatomy of Long Bones** ■ A long bone contains the following parts: diaphysis, epiphyses, metaphysis, articular cartilage, medullary cavity, periosteum, and endosteum. ■ Osteoblasts synthesize and secrete osteoid, the matrix of bone prior to its calcification. ■ Osteocytes are mature bone cells that reside in lacunae. ■ Osteoclasts are large, multinucleated cells involved in bone resorption. ■ An osteon is the basic unit of structure and function of mature compact bone. ■ An osteon contains a central canal that houses blood vessels and nerves, concentric bone layers called lamellae, osteocytes in lacunae, and thin channels called canaliculi.
6.4 Ossification	■ Ossification is the process of bone connective tissue formation. **6.4a Intramembranous Ossification** ■ In intramembranous ossification, bone forms from mesenchyme. **6.4b Endochondral Ossification** ■ Endochondral ossification uses a hyaline cartilage model that is gradually replaced by newly formed osseous tissue. **6.4c Epiphyseal Plate Morphology** ■ The epiphyseal plate contains five zones where cartilage grows and is replaced by bone. **6.4d Growth of Bone** ■ Lengthwise bone growth is called interstitial growth, whereas a bone increases in diameter through appositional growth at the periosteum. ■ The continual deposition of new bone tissue and resorption of old bone tissue is called bone remodeling. **6.4e Blood Supply and Innervation** ■ Four categories of blood vessels develop to supply a typical bone: nutrient vessels, metaphyseal vessels, epiphyseal vessels, and periosteal vessels.
6.5 Maintaining Homeostasis and Promoting Bone Growth	**6.5a Effects of Hormones** ■ Growth hormone, thyroid hormone, calcitonin, and sex hormones stimulate bone growth. ■ Parathyroid hormone stimulates osteoclast activity. **6.5b Effects of Vitamins** ■ Vitamins A and C are essential for bone growth and remodeling. Vitamin D is needed for calcium and phosphorus absorption and calcification of bone. **6.5c Effects of Exercise** ■ Stress in the form of exercise strengthens bone tissue by increasing the amounts of mineral salts deposited and collagen fibers synthesized. **6.5d Fracture and Repair** ■ A fracture is a break in a bone that can usually be healed if portions of the blood supply, endosteum, and periosteum remain intact.
6.6 Bone Markings	■ Specific names denote bone markings such as projections, elevations, depressions, and passageways.
6.7 Aging of the Skeletal System	■ Due to aging, the tensile strength of bone decreases, and bone loses calcium and other minerals (demineralization).

Challenge Yourself

Actively write or type your answers in a separate document to reinforce your learning, before checking your answers.

Multiple Choice

Select the best answer from the four choices provided.

1. What is the term for immature cells that produce osteoid?
   a. osteocytes
   b. osteoblasts
   c. osteoclasts
   d. osteons
2. Which structure is made of fibrocartilage?
   a. trachea
   b. larynx
   c. pubic symphysis
   d. fetal skeleton
3. What is the term for a small space in compact bone that houses an osteocyte?
   a. lamella
   b. lacuna
   c. canaliculus
   d. medullary cavity
4. Endochondral ossification begins within which type of tissue?
   a. dense regular connective tissue
   b. hyaline cartilage
   c. fibrocartilage
   d. mesenchyme
5. Increased presence of sex hormones at puberty have what effect on bone growth?
   a. Bone growth is not affected.
   b. Bone growth slows.
   c. Bone growth increases slowly.
   d. Bone growth increases rapidly.
6. When does an epiphyseal line appear?
   a. when epiphyseal plate growth is complete
   b. when growth at the epiphyseal plate begins
   c. when the diameter is increasing around the periphery of the bone
   d. when the primary ossification center first develops
7. What is the term for the condition of inadequate ossification that may accompany aging and is a result of reduced calcification?
   a. osteopenia
   b. osteomyelitis
   c. osteitis
   d. osteosarcoma
8. What type of fracture occurs at the distal end of the radius and produces a characteristic "dinner fork" deformity?
   a. displaced
   b. Colles
   c. Pott
   d. stress
9. The rib is an example of what class of bone?
   a. flat bone
   b. long bone
   c. irregular bone
   d. short bone
10. What is the term for large, rough projection of a bone?
   a. fossa
   b. tuberosity
   c. ramus
   d. tubercle

Content Review

1. Identify the three types of cartilage and describe the function of each type.
2. Compare and contrast interstitial and appositional growth of cartilage.
3. Describe the characteristics of articular cartilage, the medullary cavity, and endosteum in a long bone.
4. Compare and contrast osteoblasts, osteocytes, and osteoclasts.
5. Why is spongy bone able to withstand stress in an area such as the expanded end of a long bone?
6. What is ossification? What is the difference between intramembranous and endochondral ossification?
7. List the four types of arteries that occur in a long bone, and what portions of the bone each artery supplies.
8. Discuss the effect of exercise on bone mass.
9. What are the steps in fracture repair?
10. Describe the causes of a projection from a bone surface versus the causes of a depression in a bone surface.

Developing Critical Reasoning

1. Marty fell off his skateboard and suffered a broken leg. A cast was put on the leg for 6 weeks. After the bone healed and the cast was removed, an enlarged, bony bump remained at the region of the fracture. Eventually, this enlargement disappeared, and the leg regained its normal appearance. What happened from the time the cast was removed until the enlargement disappeared?
2. Elise is 14 and lives in an apartment in the city. She does not like outdoor activities, so she spends most of her spare time watching TV, playing video games, drinking soft drinks, and talking to friends on the phone. One afternoon, Elise tries to run down the stairs while talking on the phone, and falls, breaking her leg. Although she appears healthy, her leg takes longer to heal than expected. What might cause the longer healing time?
3. Connor is a healthy, active 7-year-old who fell while climbing on a bar apparatus in the playground, breaking his forearm near the wrist. The doctor told Connor's father that the fracture would require insertion of screws to align ends of the broken bones and ensure proper growth in the future. Why was the physician taking special care with the healing of this fracture?

Answers to "What Do You Think?"

1. Ribs are best classified as flat bones because they have parallel surfaces of compact bone with internally placed spongy bone. Flat bones tend to be relatively thin (like the rib) and are both light and strong. In contrast, long bones typically have a cylindrical diaphysis, whereas ribs are flattened.
2. Spongy bone is lighter and able to withstand stresses applied from many directions. In addition, hematopoietic tissue resides in the spaces within some spongy bone. Compact bone is very strong but weighs more than spongy bone. A bone made entirely of compact bone would be too heavy to move and too metabolically expensive to maintain, partly due to the increased musculature necessary to move it.
3. The numerous complex steps in endochondral bone formation ensure that a working bone may be formed for a newborn and later develop into a working adult bone. Having a bone collar, epiphyseal plates, and constant bone remodeling ensures that the bone can reshape itself, grow in both width and length, and develop a medullary cavity so that it will not weigh too much.
4. The 13-year-old will likely have several active epiphyseal plates (indicating that the bones are still growing in length), whereas the 65-year-old's bones will have stopped growing in length. Typically, the 65-year-old will have less bone mass and be at greater risk for osteopenia than the 13-year-old. (However, staying active will help the 65-year-old maintain bone mass and help ward off osteoporosis.)

Design Element: Pencil Icon: Slavojub Pantelic/Shutterstock

SKELETAL SYSTEM

7 Axial Skeleton

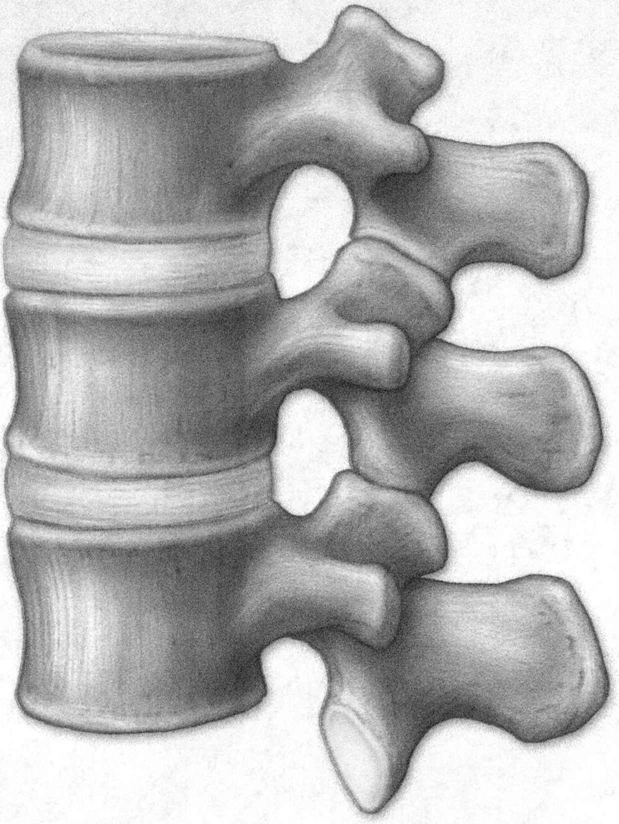

Outline

Anatomy & Physiology Revealed 4.0

MODULE 5: SKELETAL SYSTEM

The bones of the skeleton form an internal framework to support soft tissues, protect vital organs, bear the body's weight, and help us move. Without a bony skeleton, we would collapse into a formless mass. Typically, there are 206 bones in an adult skeleton, although this number varies in some individuals. A larger number of bones are present at birth, but the total number decreases with growth and maturity as some separate bones fuse. Bones differ in size, shape, weight, and even composition, and this diversity is directly related to the skeleton's many functions.

The skeletal system is divided into two parts: the axial skeleton and the appendicular skeleton. The **axial skeleton** is composed of the bones along the central axis of the body, which we commonly divide into three regions—the skull, the vertebral column, and the thoracic cage **(figure 7.1)**. The **appendicular skeleton** consists of the bones of the appendages (upper and lower limbs), as well as the bones that hold the limbs to the trunk of the body (the pectoral and pelvic girdles). The axial skeleton is the topic of this chapter; in chapter 8, we discuss the appendicular skeleton.

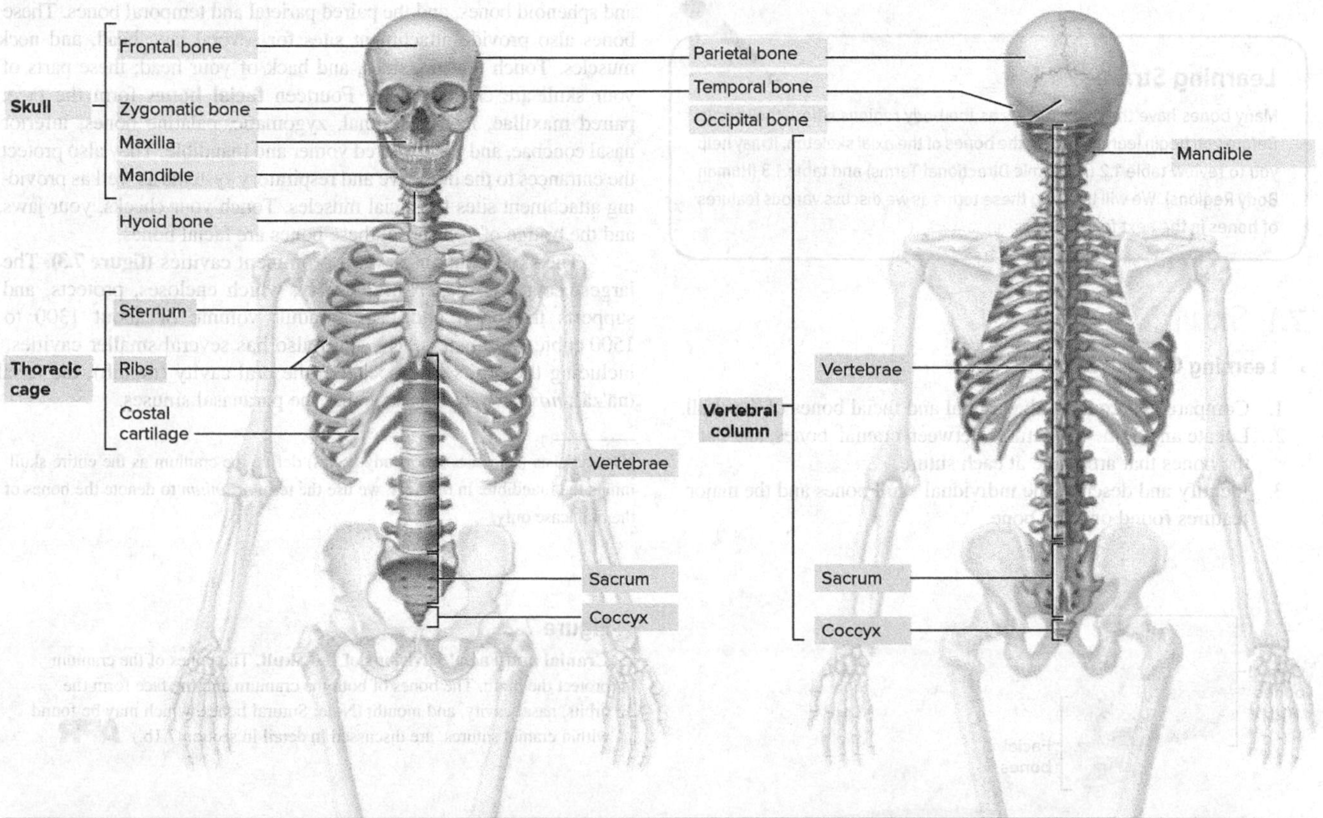

Bones of the Axial Skeleton (80)			
Skull (22)	Cranial bones (8) Frontal bone (1), parietal bones (2), temporal bones (2), occipital bone (1), sphenoid bone (1), ethmoid bone (1)	**Vertebral column (26)**	Cervical vertebrae (7) Thoracic vertebrae (12) Lumbar vertebrae (5)
	Facial bones (14) Zygomatic bones (2), lacrimal bones (2), nasal bones (2), vomer (1), inferior nasal conchae (2), palatine bones (2), maxillae (2), mandible (1)		Sacrum (1)
			Coccyx (1)
Associated bones of the skull (7)	Auditory ossicles (6) Malleus (2), incus (2), stapes (2) Hyoid bone (1)	**Thoracic cage (25)**	Sternum (1)
			Ribs (24)

(a) Anterior view **(b) Posterior view**

Figure 7.1

Axial Skeleton. (*a*) Anterior and (*b*) posterior views show the skeleton and highlight v the axial skeleton, which is composed of the skull, vertebral column, and thoracic cage. A table lists the bones within the axial skeleton. APR

The main function of the axial skeleton is to form a framework that supports and protects the organs. The axial skeleton also houses special sense organs (the organs for hearing, balance, taste, smell, and vision) and provides areas for the attachment of skeletal muscles. Additionally, the spongy bone of most of the axial skeleton contains hematopoietic tissue, which is responsible for blood cell formation.

We begin our examination of the axial skeleton by discussing its most complex structure, the skull.

Learning Strategy 7.1

Many bones have the same names as the body regions where they occur. Before you begin learning about the bones of the axial skeleton, it may help you to review table 1.2 (Anatomic Directional Terms) and table 1.3 (Human Body Regions). We will be using these terms as we discuss various features of bones in the next few chapters.

7.1 Skull

✓ Learning Objectives

1. Compare and contrast the cranial and facial bones of the skull.
2. Locate and name the sutures between cranial bones, and list the bones that articulate at each suture.
3. Identify and describe the individual skull bones and the major features found on each bone.
4. Describe the structure of the nasal complex and the paranasal sinuses.
5. Identify and describe the bones of the orbital complex.
6. List the bones associated with the skull, and describe their functions.

The **skull** is composed of both cranial and facial bones (**figure 7.2**). **Cranial bones** form the rounded **cranium** (krā′nē-ŭm; *kranion* = skull), which completely surrounds and encloses the brain.[1] Eight bones make up the cranium: the unpaired ethmoid, frontal, occipital, and sphenoid bones, and the paired parietal and temporal bones. These bones also provide attachment sites for several jaw, head, and neck muscles. Touch the top, sides, and back of your head; these parts of your skull are cranial bones. Fourteen **facial bones** form the face: paired maxillae, nasal, lacrimal, zygomatic, palatine bones, inferior nasal conchae, and the unpaired vomer and mandible. They also protect the entrances to the digestive and respiratory systems as well as providing attachment sites for facial muscles. Touch your cheeks, your jaws, and the bridge of your nose; these bones are facial bones.

The skull contains several prominent cavities (**figure 7.3**). The largest cavity is the **cranial cavity,** which encloses, protects, and supports the brain and has an adult volume of about 1300 to 1500 cubic centimeters. The skull also has several smaller cavities, including the orbits (eye sockets), the oral cavity (mouth), the nasal (nā′zăl; *nasus* = nose) cavity, and the paranasal sinuses.

[1] Osteologists (scientists who study bones) define the cranium as the entire skull minus the mandible. In this text, we use the term *cranium* to denote the bones of the braincase only.

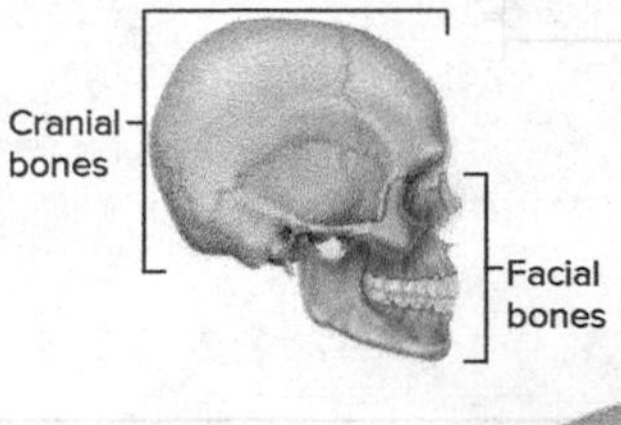
Cranial bones
Facial bones

Figure 7.2

Cranial and Facial Divisions of the Skull. The bones of the cranium protect the brain. The bones of both the cranium and the face form the orbits, nasal cavity, and mouth. (Note: Sutural bones, which may be found within cranial sutures, are discussed in detail in section 7.1b.) APR

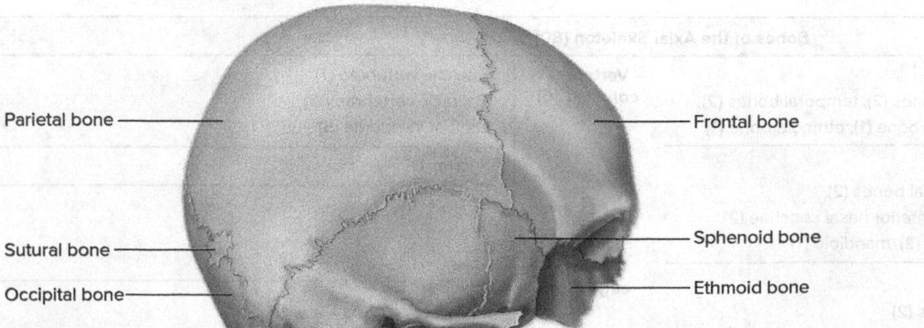
Parietal bone
Frontal bone
Sutural bone
Sphenoid bone
Occipital bone
Ethmoid bone
Temporal bone
Zygomatic bone
Nasal bone
Lacrimal bone
Vomer
Maxilla
Mandible

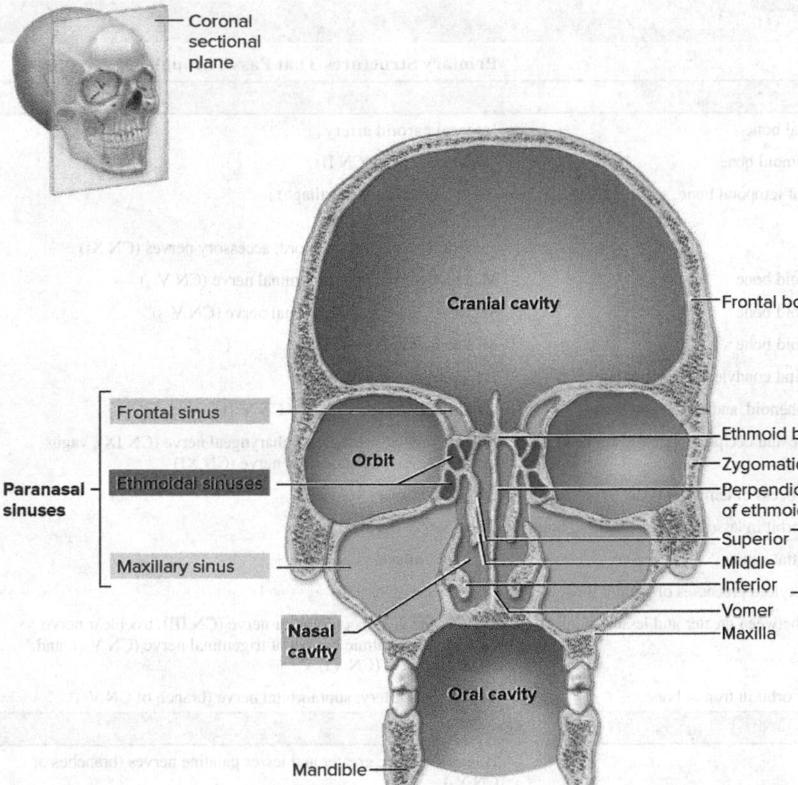
Coronal sectional plane
Cranial cavity
Frontal bone
Frontal sinus
Ethmoid bone
Orbit
Zygomatic bone
Paranasal sinuses
Ethmoidal sinuses
Perpendicular plate of ethmoid bone
Superior
Middle
Inferior
Nasal conchae
Maxillary sinus
Vomer
Maxilla
Nasal cavity
Oral cavity
Mandible

Figure 7.3

Major Cavities of the Skull. A coronal section diagram identifies the cavities within the skull. The sphenoidal sinus is not seen in this particular section.

WHAT DID YOU LEARN?

1. What are the two groups of skull bones?

7.1a Views of the Skull and Landmark Features

The skull is composed of multiple bones that exhibit complex shapes, and each bone articulates with at least one other. To best understand the complex nature of the skull, we first examine the skull as a whole and learn which bones are seen optimally from a particular view. Note that only some major features will be mentioned in this section. Later in this section we examine the individual skull bones in detail.

A cursory glance at the skull reveals numerous bone markings, such as canals, fissures, and foramina, which are passageways for blood vessels and nerves. The major foramina and canals of the cranial and facial bones are listed in **table 7.1**. Refer to this table as we examine the skull from various directions. (This table also will be important when we study individual nerves and blood vessels in sections 15.8 and 23.3, respectively.)

Anterior View

An anterior view best shows several major bones of the skull (**figure 7.4**). The *frontal bone* forms the forehead. Put your hand on your forehead; you are feeling your frontal bone. The left and right *orbits* (eye sockets) are formed from a complex articulation of multiple skull bones. Within the orbits are two large openings, called the *superior orbital fissure* and the *inferior orbital fissure.* Superior to the orbits are the *superciliary arches,* otherwise known as the brow ridges. The left and right *nasal bones* form the bony "bridge" of the nose. Superior to the nasal bones and between the orbits is a landmark area called the *glabella.*

The left and right *maxillae* join to form most of the upper jaw and the lateral boundaries of the nasal cavity. The maxillae also help form the floor of each orbit. Inferior to each orbit, within each maxilla, is an *infraorbital foramen,* which conducts blood vessels and nerves to the face. The lower jaw is formed by the *mandible.* The prominent "chin" of the mandible is called the *mental protuberance.*

An anterior view also shows the nasal cavity. Its inferior border is marked by a prominent *anterior nasal spine.* The thin ridge of bone that subdivides the nasal cavity into left and right halves helps form the *nasal septum.* Along the lateral walls of the nasal cavity are two scroll-shaped bones called the *inferior nasal conchae.*

Superior View

The superior view of the skull in **figure 7.5a** primarily shows four of the cranial bones: the frontal bone, both *parietal bones,* and the *occipital bone.* The articulation between the frontal and parietal bones is the *coronal suture,* so named because it runs along a coronal plane. The *sagittal suture* connects the left and right parietal bones almost exactly in the midline of the skull.

Along the posterior one-third of the sagittal suture are either a single *parietal foramen* or paired *parietal foramina.* These foramina conduct tiny emissary veins from the veins of the brain to the veins of the scalp. The number of parietal foramina can vary in individuals and between left and right sides of the same skull. The superior part of the *lambdoid suture* represents the articulation of the occipital bone with both parietal bones.

Posterior View

The posterior view of the skull in figure 7.5*b* shows part of the occipital bone and its lambdoid suture, as well as portions of the parietal and temporal bones. The *external occipital protuberance* is a bump on the back of the head. Palpate the back of your head; the size and

Table 7.1 Passageways Within the Skull

Passageway	Location	Primary Structures That Pass Through
CRANIAL BONES		
Carotid canal	Petrous part of temporal bone	Internal carotid artery
Cribriform foramina	Cribriform plate of ethmoid bone	Olfactory nerves (CN I)
Foramen lacerum	Between petrous part of temporal bone, sphenoid bone, and occipital bone	None (covered with cartilage)
Foramen magnum	Occipital bone	Vertebral arteries; spinal cord, accessory nerves (CN XI)
Foramen ovale	Greater wing of sphenoid bone	Mandibular branch of trigeminal nerve (CN V_3)
Foramen rotundum	Greater wing of sphenoid bone	Maxillary branch of trigeminal nerve (CN V_2)
Foramen spinosum	Greater wing of sphenoid bone	Middle meningeal vessels
Hypoglossal canal	Anteromedial to occipital condyle of occipital bone	Hypoglossal nerve (CN XII)
Inferior orbital fissure	Junction of maxilla, sphenoid, and zygomatic bones	Infraorbital nerve (branch of CN V_2)
Jugular foramen	Between temporal bone and occipital bone (posterior to carotid canal)	Internal jugular vein; glossopharyngeal nerve (CN IX), vagus nerve (CN X), and accessory nerve (CN XI)
Mastoid foramen	Posterior to mastoid process of temporal bone	Mastoid emissary veins
Optic canal	Posteromedial part of orbit in lesser wing of sphenoid bone	Optic nerve (CN II)
Parietal foramina	Parietal bone near sagittal suture	Parietal emissaryveins
Stylomastoid foramen	Between mastoid and styloid processes of temporal bone	Facial nerve (CN VII)
Superior orbital fissure	Posterior part of orbit between greater and lesser wings of sphenoid bone	Ophthalmic veins; oculomotor nerve (CN III), trochlear nerve (CN IV), ophthalmic branch of trigeminal nerve (CN V_1), and abducens nerve (CN VI)
Supraorbital foramen	Supraorbital margin of orbit in frontal bone	Supraorbital artery; supraorbital nerve (branch of CN V_1)
FACIAL BONES		
Greater and lesser palatine foramina	Palatine bone	Palatine vessels; greater and lesser palatine nerves (branches of CN V_2)
Incisive foramen	Posterior to incisor teeth in hard palate of maxilla	Nasopalatine nerve (branch of CN V_2)
Infraorbital foramen	Inferior to orbit in maxilla	Infraorbital artery: infraorbital nerve (branch of CN V_2)
Lacrimal groove	Lacrimal bone	Nasolacrimal duct
Mandibular foramen	Medial surface of ramus of mandible	Inferior alveolar blood vessels; inferior alveolar nerve (branch of CN V_3)
Mental foramen	Inferior to second premolar on anterolateral surface of mandible	Mental blood vessels; mental nerve (branch of CN V_3)

shape of this protuberance varies from large and angular to subtle and rounded (based upon genetic and hormonal sex.) Within the lambdoid suture there may be one or more *sutural (Wormian) bones.*

Lateral View

The lateral view of the skull in **figure 7.6** shows the following skull bones: one *parietal bone*, one *temporal bone*, one *zygomatic bone*, one *maxilla*, the *frontal bone*, the *mandible*, and portions of the *occipital bone*. The tiny *lacrimal bone* articulates with the nasal bone anteriorly and with the ethmoid bone posteriorly. A portion of the *sphenoid bone* articulates with the frontal, parietal, and tempo - ral bones. The region called the **pterion** (tē′rē-on; *ptéron* = wing), circled on figure 7.6, represents the H-shaped set of sutures of these four articulating bones.

The temporal process of the zygomatic bone and the zygomatic process of the temporal bone fuse to form the *zygomatic arch.* Put your fingers along the bony prominences ("apples") of your cheeks and move your fingers posteriorly to your ears; you are feeling the zygomatic arch. The zygomatic arch terminates superior to the point where the mandible articulates with the *mandibular fossa* of the temporal bone. This articulation is called the *temporomandibular joint.* By putting your finger anterior to your external ear opening and opening your jaw, you can feel that joint moving. The external ear opening overlies the *external acoustic meatus* of the skull. Posterior to this canal is the *mastoid process,* the bump you feel posterior to your ear lobe.

Sagittal Sectional View

Cutting the skull along a sagittal sectional plane reveals bones that form the nasal cavity and the endocranium (**figure 7.7**). The cranial cavity is formed from a complex articulation of the frontal, parietal, temporal, occipital, ethmoid, and sphenoid bones. Vessel impressions on the internal surface of the skull show up clearly. The*frontal sinus* (a space in the frontal bone) and the *sphenoidal sinus* (a space in the sphenoid bone) are visible.

A sagittal sectional view also shows the bones that form the nasal septum more clearly. The *perpendicular plate* forms the superior portion of the nasal septum, whereas the *vomer* forms the inferior portion. The ethmoid bone serves as a wall between the anterior floor of the cranial cavity and the roof of the nasal cavity. The *maxillae* and *palatine bones* form the hard palate, which acts as both the floor of the nasal cavity and part of the roof of the mouth. Move your tongue along the roof of your mouth; you are palpating the maxillae anteri - orly and the palatine bones posteriorly.

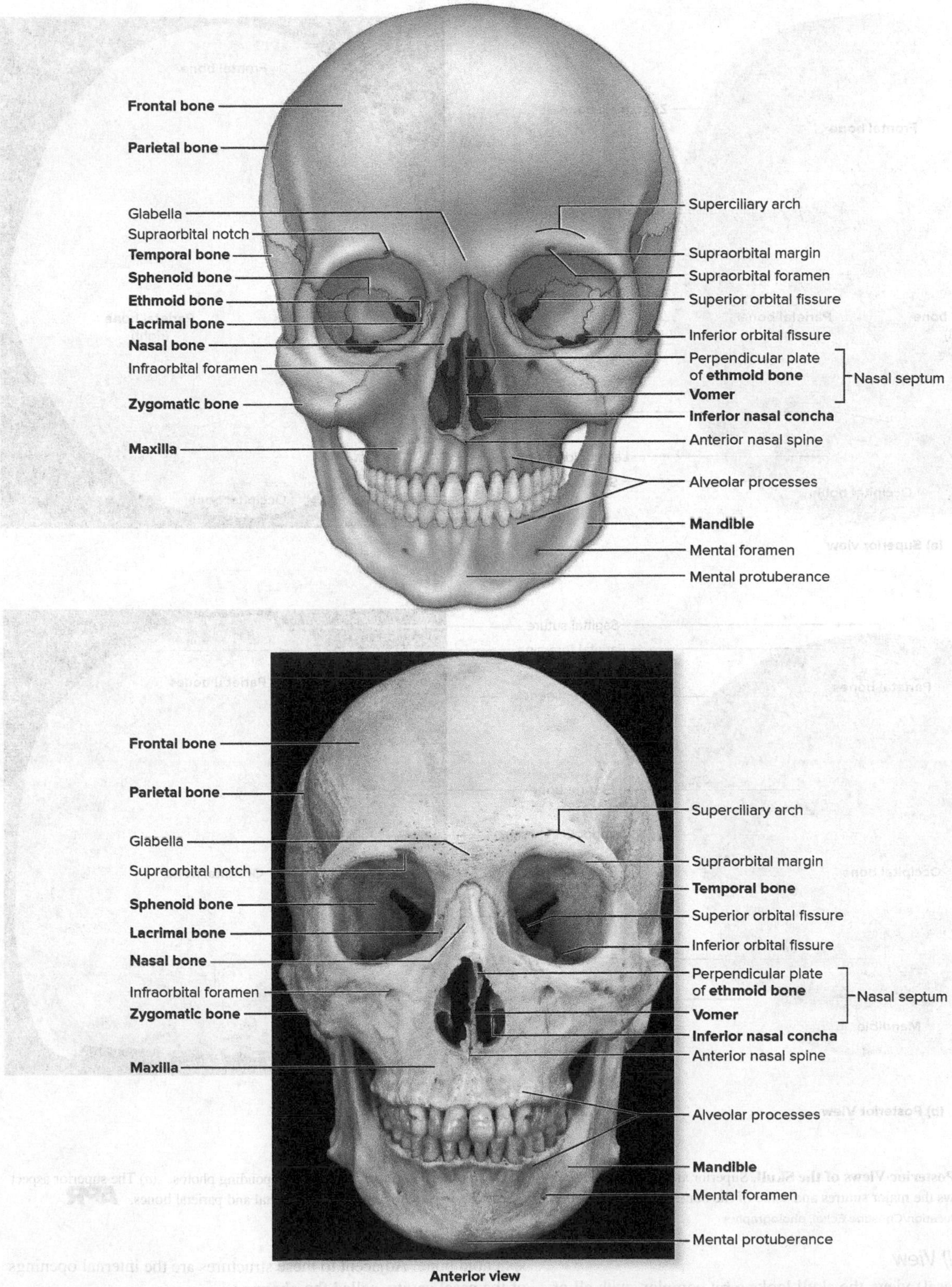

Figure 7.4

Anterior View of the Skull. An illustration and corresponding photo show the frontal bone, nasal bones, maxillae, and mandible are prominent in an anterior view of the skull. APR

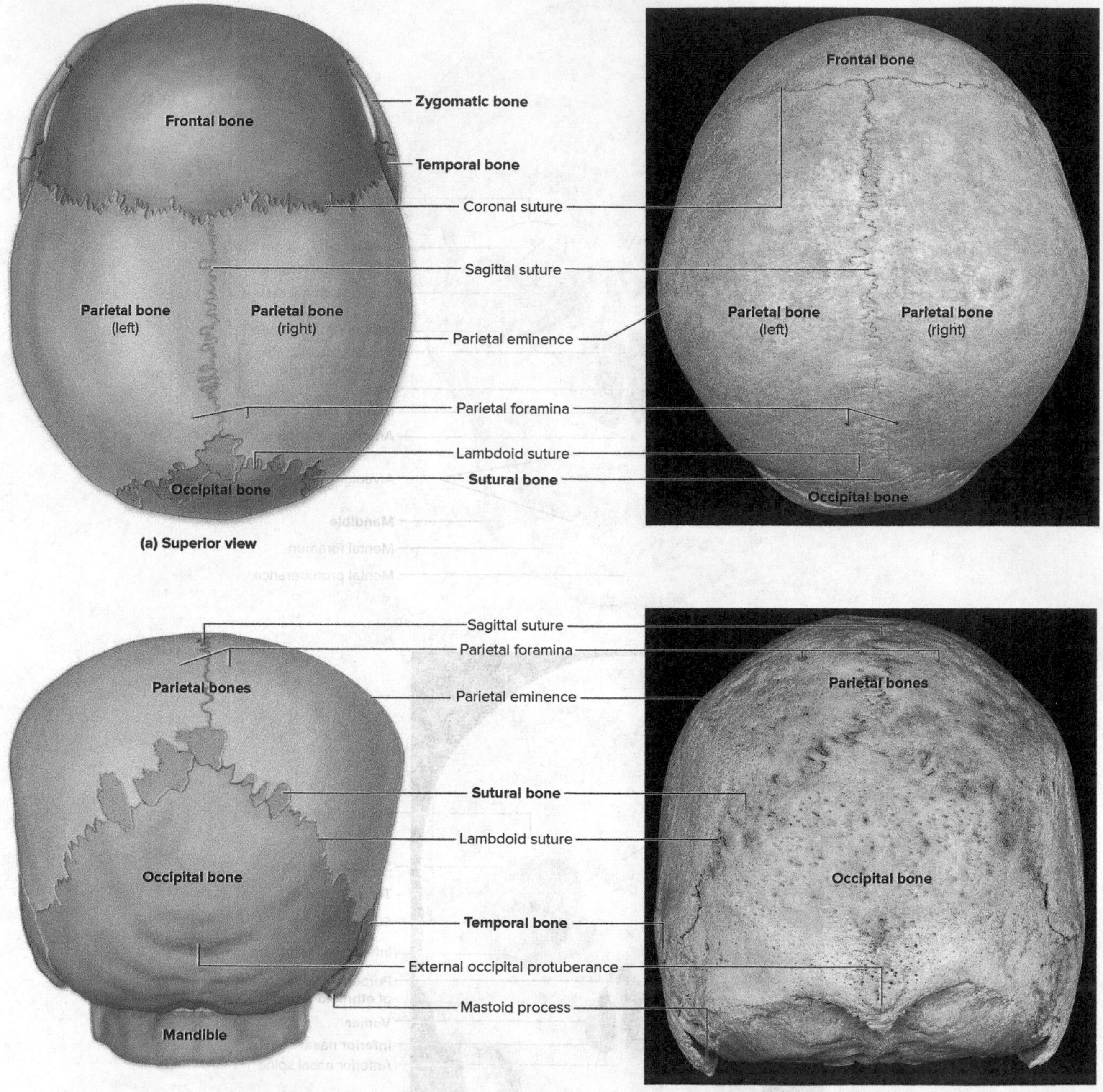
Frontal bone
Zygomatic bone
Temporal bone
Coronal suture
Sagittal suture
Parietal bone (left)
Parietal bone (right)
Parietal eminence
Parietal foramina
Lambdoid suture
Sutural bone
Occipital bone
(a) Superior view
Parietal bones
Temporal bone
External occipital protuberance
Mastoid process
Mandible
(b) Posterior View

Figure 7.5

Superior and Posterior Views of the Skull. Superior and posterior views of the skull are shown in drawings and corresponding photos. (*a*) The superior aspect of the skull shows the major sutures and some of the bones of the skull. (*b*) The posterior view is dominated by the occipital and parietal bones. **APR**

Inferior (Basal) View

In an inferior (basal) view, the skull looks a bit complex, with all of its foramina and weird-shaped bone features (**figure 7.8**). However, you will soon be able to recognize and distinguish some features that may be used as landmarks.

The most anterior structure is the *hard palate*. On the posterior aspect of either side of the palate are the *pterygoid processes* of the sphenoid bone. Adjacent to these structures are the internal openings of the nasal cavity, called the *choanae*.

Between the mandibular fossa and the pterygoid processes are several **foramina** (fō-ram′i-n ă; sing., *foramen*, fō′rā′men; *forare* = to bore) and canals. Closest to the pterygoid process is the *foramen ovale*, and lateral to this opening is the *foramen spinosum*. Posterior and lateral to these foramina is the **jugular** (jŭg′yū-lăr; *jugulum* = throat)

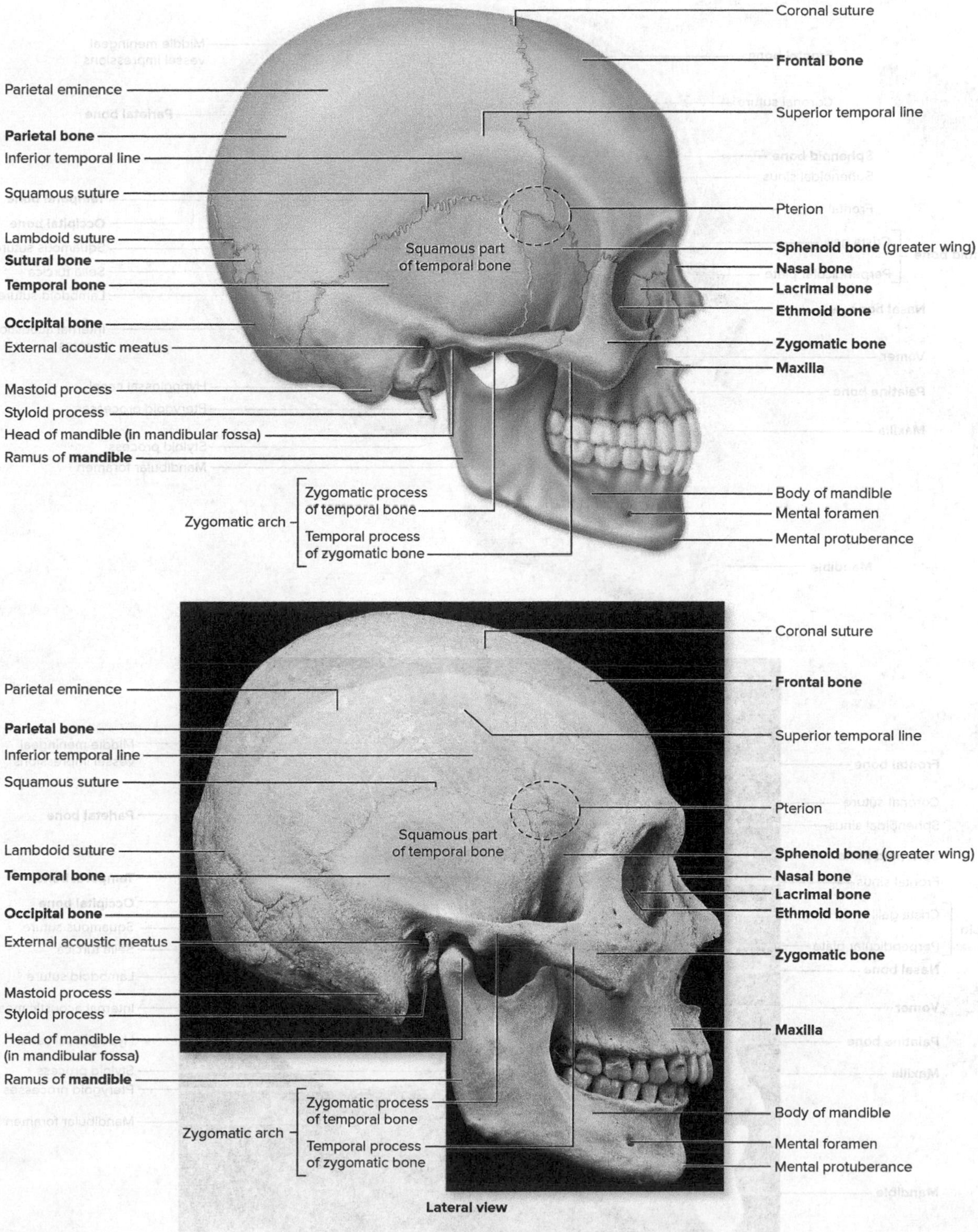
Coronal suture
Frontal bone
Parietal eminence
Superior temporal line
Parietal bone
Inferior temporal line
Squamous suture
Pterion
Lambdoid suture
Squamous part of temporal bone
Sphenoid bone (greater wing)
Sutural bone
Nasal bone
Temporal bone
Lacrimal bone
Ethmoid bone
Occipital bone
External acoustic meatus
Zygomatic bone
Maxilla
Mastoid process
Styloid process
Head of mandible (in mandibular fossa)
Ramus of mandible
Zygomatic process of temporal bone
Body of mandible
Zygomatic arch
Mental foramen
Temporal process of zygomatic bone
Mental protuberance
Coronal suture
Frontal bone
Parietal eminence
Parietal bone
Superior temporal line
Inferior temporal line
Squamous suture
Pterion
Squamous part of temporal bone
Lambdoid suture
Sphenoid bone (greater wing)
Temporal bone
Nasal bone
Lacrimal bone
Occipital bone
Ethmoid bone
External acoustic meatus
Zygomatic bone
Mastoid process
Styloid process
Maxilla
Head of mandible (in mandibular fossa)
Ramus of mandible
Zygomatic process of temporal bone
Body of mandible
Zygomatic arch
Temporal process of zygomatic bone
Mental foramen
Mental protuberance
Lateral view

Figure 7.6

Lateral View of the Skull. A diagram and corresponding photo show the lateral view of the skull, where the parietal, temporal, zygomatic, frontal, and occipital bones, as well as the maxilla and mandible, are clearly seen. APR

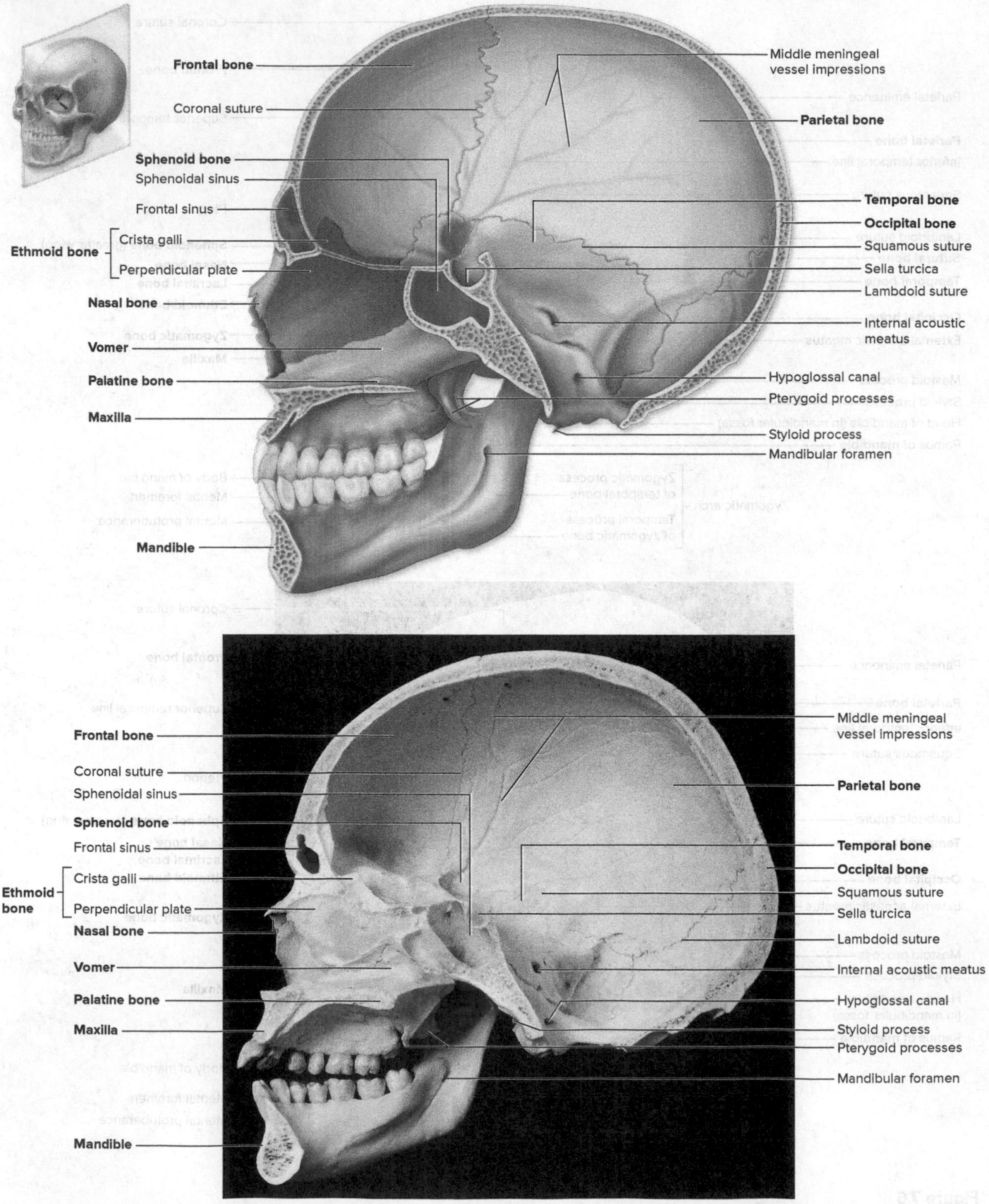
Frontal bone
Coronal suture
Sphenoid bone
Sphenoidal sinus
Frontal sinus
Ethmoid bone
Crista galli
Perpendicular plate
Nasal bone
Vomer
Palatine bone
Maxilla
Mandible
Middle meningeal vessel impressions
Parietal bone
Temporal bone
Occipital bone
Squamous suture
Sella turcica
Lambdoid suture
Internal acoustic meatus
Hypoglossal canal
Pterygoid processes
Styloid process
Mandibular foramen
Frontal bone
Coronal suture
Sphenoidal sinus
Sphenoid bone
Frontal sinus
Ethmoid bone
Crista galli
Perpendicular plate
Nasal bone
Vomer
Palatine bone
Maxilla
Mandible
Middle meningeal vessel impressions
Parietal bone
Temporal bone
Occipital bone
Squamous suture
Sella turcica
Lambdoid suture
Internal acoustic meatus
Hypoglossal canal
Styloid process
Pterygoid processes
Mandibular foramen
Sagittal section

Figure 7.7

Sagittal Section of the Skull. Some skull features are best seen in sagittal section, as shown here in both diagram and corresponding photo. Features such as the perpendicular plate of the ethmoid bone, the vomer, and the frontal and sphenoidal sinuses, as well as the internal relationships of the skull bones, are best seen in this view. APR

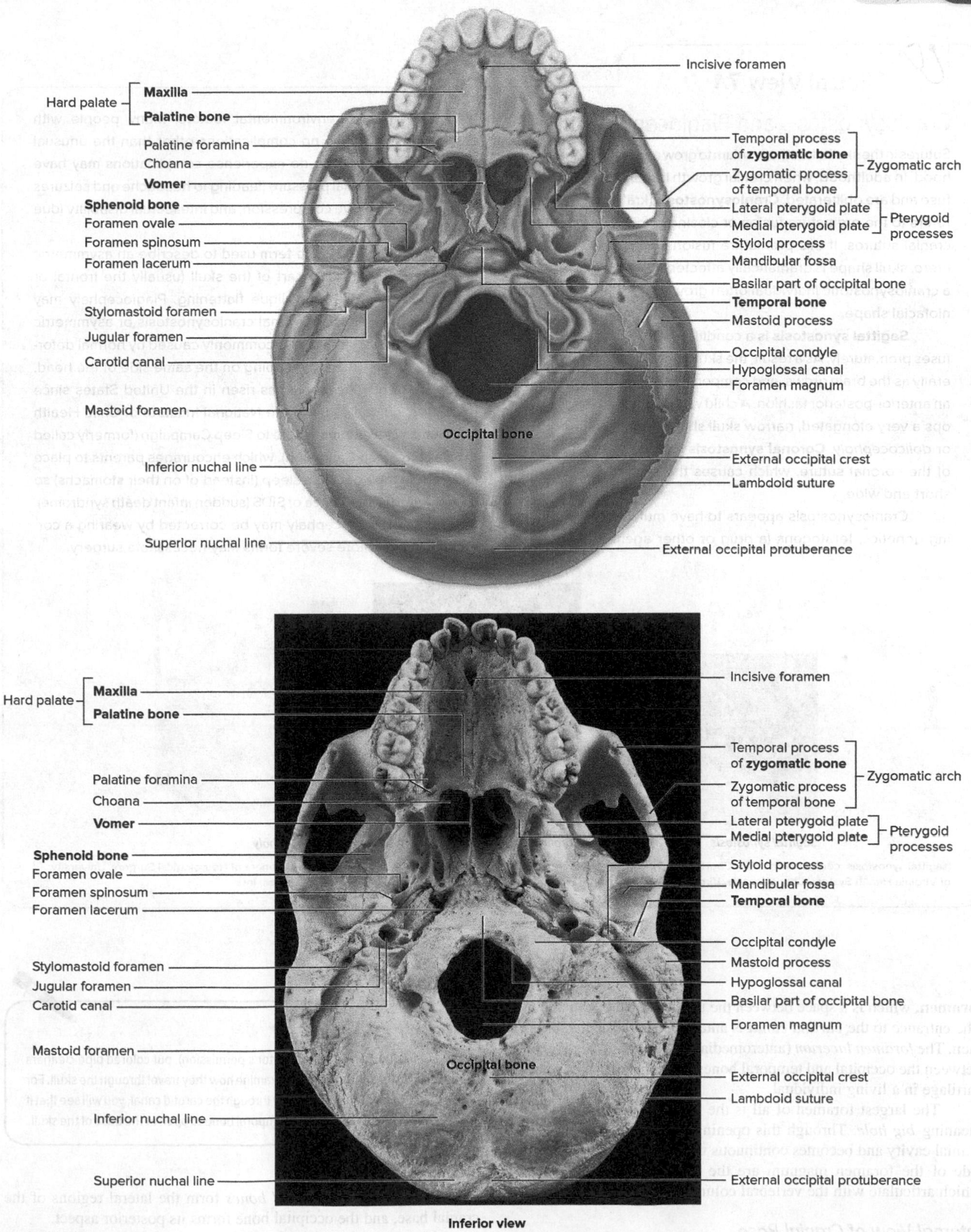

Figure 7.8

Inferior View of the Skull. A diagram and corresponding photo show the inferior aspect of the skull. The hard palate, sphenoid bone, parts of the temporal bone, and the occipital bone with its foramen magnum are readily visible when the mandible is removed in this inferior view. APR

Clinical View 7.1

Craniosynostosis and Plagiocephaly

Sutures in the skull allow the cranium to grow and expand during childhood. In adulthood, when cranial growth has stopped, the sutures fuse and are obliterated. **Craniosynostosis** (krā′nē-ō-sin′os-tō′sis) refers to the premature fusion or closing of one or more of these cranial sutures. If this premature fusion occurs early in life or *in utero*, skull shape is dramatically affected. If not surgically treated, a craniosynostotic individual often grows up with an unusual craniofacial shape.

Sagittal synostosis is a condition where the sagittal suture fuses prematurely. As a result, the skull cannot grow and expand laterally as the brain grows, and compensatory skull growth occurs in an anterior-posterior fashion. A child with sagittal synostosis develops a very elongated, narrow skull shape called **scaphocephaly,** or *dolicocephaly*. **Coronal synostosis** refers to premature fusion of the coronal suture, which causes the skull to be abnormally short and wide.

Craniosynostosis appears to have multiple causes, including genetics, teratogens (a drug or other agent that can cause birth defects), and environmental factors. Many people with craniosynostosis have no complications other than the unusual skull shape. Those who do experience complications may have increased intracranial pressure (leading to headache and seizures if severe), optic nerve compression, and intellectual disability (due to restricted brain growth).

Plagiocephaly is the term used to describe an asymmetric head shape, where one part of the skull (usually the frontal or occipital region) has an oblique flattening. Plagiocephaly may be caused by unilateral coronal craniosynostosis or asymmetric lambdoid synostosis. It also is commonly caused by normal deformational factors, such as sleeping on the same side of the head. Incidence of plagiocephaly has risen in the United States since the 1990s, primarily due to the National Institute of Child Health and Human Development Safe to Sleep Campaign (formerly called the Back to Sleep Campaign), which encourages parents to place children on their backs to sleep (instead of on their stomachs) so as to reduce the incidence of SIDS (sudden infant death syndrome). Mild forms of plagiocephaly may be corrected by wearing a corrective helmet; more severe forms may necessitate surgery.

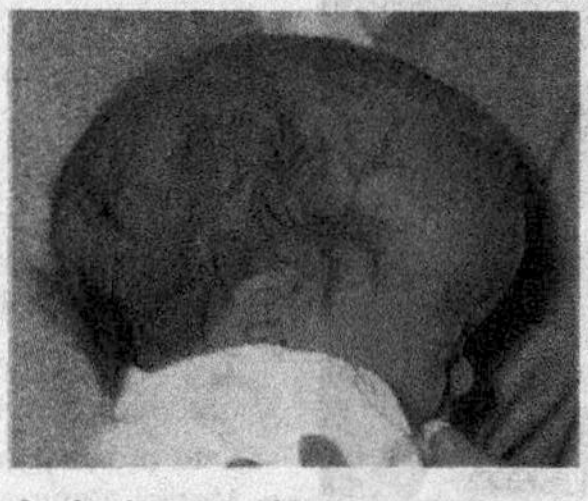

Sagittal synostosis

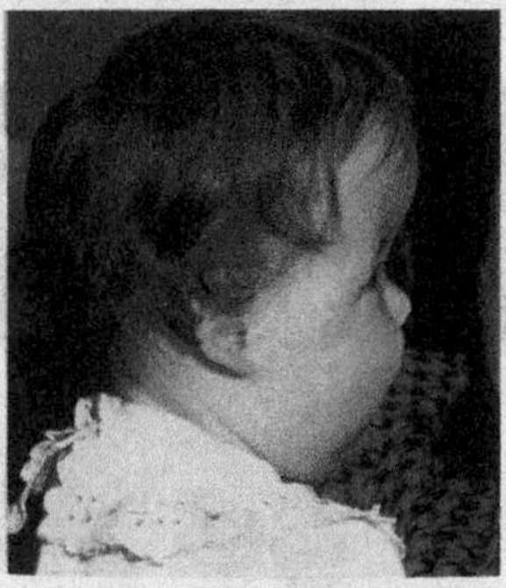

Coronal synostosis

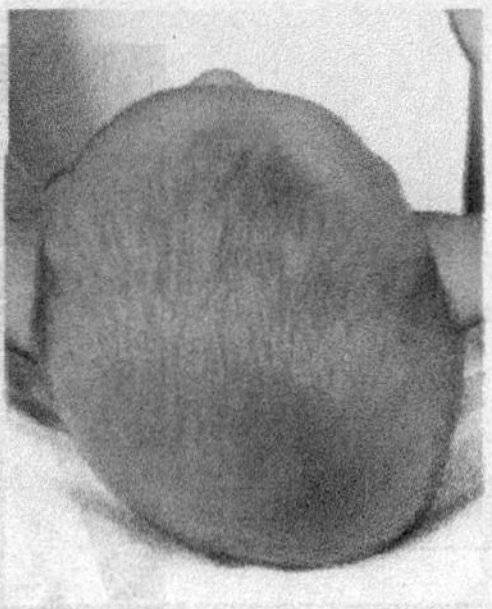

Plagiocephaly

(sagittal synostosis, coronal synostosis) Courtesy of Dr. John A. Jane, Sr., David D. Weaver Professor of Neurosurgery, Department of Neurological Surgery, University of Virginia Health System, Charlottesville, Virginia; (plagiocephaly) Used with permission and copyright of Cranial Technologies, Inc.

foramen, which is a space between the temporal and occipital bones. The entrance to the *carotid canal* is anteromedial to the jugular foramen. The *foramen lacerum* (anteromedial to the carotid canal) extends between the occipital and temporal bones. This opening is covered by cartilage in a living individual.

The largest foramen of all is the **foramen magnum,** literally meaning *big hole*. Through this opening, the spinal cord enters the cranial cavity and becomes continuous with the brainstem. On either side of the foramen magnum are the rounded occipital condyles, which articulate with the vertebral column.

Internal View of Cranial Base

When the superior part of the skull is cut and removed, the internal view of the cranial base (**figure 7.9**) reveals the *frontal bone* surrounding the delicate *cribriform plate* of the ethmoid bone. Posterior to the frontal bone are the *lesser wings* and the *greater wings* of the sphenoid bone. The *temporal bones* form the lateral regions of the cranial base, and the occipital bone forms its posterior aspect.

Many of the foramina labeled on the inferior view of the skull can also be seen from this internal view, but some new openings are visible as well. For example, left and right *optic canals* are located in the lesser wings of the sphenoid. The *internal acoustic meatus* is located more posteriorly in the temporal bone.

Learning Strategy 7.2

In your lab (and with your instructor's permission), put colored pipe cleaners through the cranial foramina to examine how they travel through the skull. For example, if you put a pipe cleaner through the carotid canal, you will see that it bends as it travels through the temporal bone to open at the base of the skull.

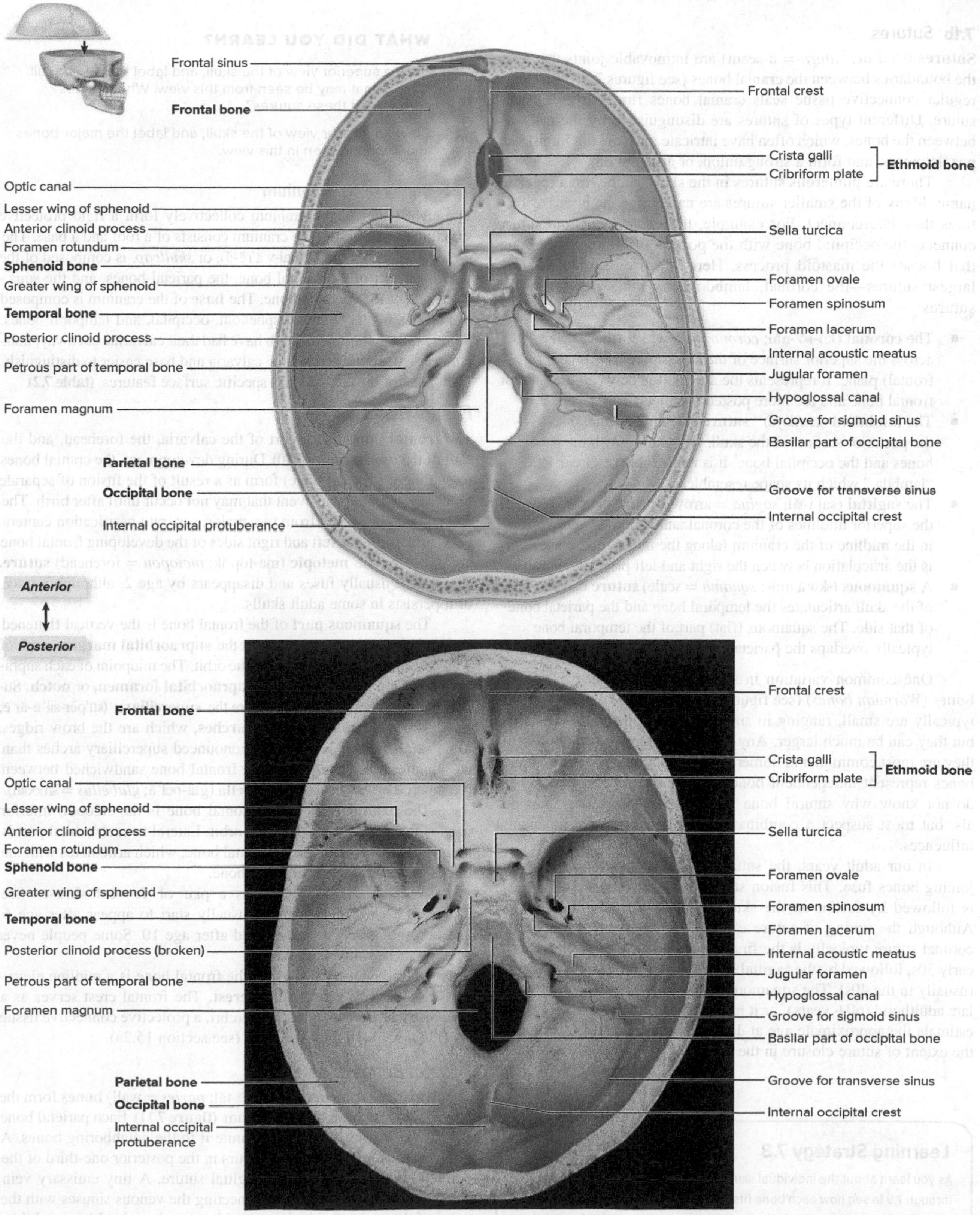

Frontal sinus
Frontal bone
Frontal crest
Crista galli
Cribriform plate
Ethmoid bone
Optic canal
Lesser wing of sphenoid
Anterior clinoid process
Foramen rotundum
Sphenoid bone
Greater wing of sphenoid
Temporal bone
Posterior clinoid process
Petrous part of temporal bone
Foramen magnum
Sella turcica
Foramen ovale
Foramen spinosum
Foramen lacerum
Internal acoustic meatus
Jugular foramen
Hypoglossal canal
Groove for sigmoid sinus
Basilar part of occipital bone
Parietal bone
Occipital bone
Internal occipital protuberance
Groove for transverse sinus
Internal occipital crest
Anterior
Posterior
Frontal crest
Frontal bone
Crista galli
Cribriform plate
Ethmoid bone
Optic canal
Lesser wing of sphenoid
Anterior clinoid process
Foramen rotundum
Sphenoid bone
Sella turcica
Greater wing of sphenoid
Foramen ovale
Foramen spinosum
Temporal bone
Foramen lacerum
Posterior clinoid process (broken)
Internal acoustic meatus
Jugular foramen
Petrous part of temporal bone
Hypoglossal canal
Foramen magnum
Groove for sigmoid sinus
Basilar part of occipital bone
Parietal bone
Groove for transverse sinus
Occipital bone
Internal occipital crest
Internal occipital protuberance
Sectioned skull, superior view

Figure 7.9

Superior View of the Endocranial Cavity of the Skull. When the calvarium is removed, the endocranial cavity of the skull may be seen in a superior view, as shown here in art and photo. In this view, the frontal, ethmoid, sphenoid, temporal, and occipital bones are prominent. APR

7.1b Sutures

Sutures (sū′chūr; *sutura* = a seam) are immovable joints that form the boundaries between the cranial bones (see figures 7.5–7.8). Dense regular connective tissue seals cranial bones firmly together at a suture. Different types of sutures are distinguished by the margins between the bones, which often have intricate interlocking forms, like puzzle pieces, and form a strong union, or articulation.

There are numerous sutures in the skull, each with a specific name. Many of the smaller sutures are named for the bones or features they interconnect. For example, the *occipitomastoid suture* connects the occipital bone with the portion of the temporal bone that houses the mastoid process. Here we discuss only the four largest sutures—the coronal, lambdoid, sagittal, and squamous sutures:

- The **coronal** (kō-rŏ′-năl; *corona* = crown) **suture** extends across the superior surface of the skull along a coronal (or frontal) plane. It represents the articulation between the anterior frontal bone and the more posterior parietal bones.
- The **lambdoid** (lam′doyd) **suture** extends like an arc across the posterior surface of the skull, articulating with the parietal bones and the occipital bone. It is named for the Greek letter "lambda," which its shape resembles.
- The **sagittal** (saj′i-tăl; *sagitta* = arrow) **suture** extends between the superior midlines of the coronal and lambdoid sutures. It is in the midline of the cranium (along the midsagittal plane) and is the articulation between the right and left parietal bones.
- A **squamous** (skw ā′mŭs; *squama* = scale) **suture** on each side of the skull articulates the temporal bone and the parietal bone of that side. The squamous (flat) part of the temporal bone typically overlaps the parietal bone.

One common variation in sutures is the presence of **sutural bones** (*Wormian bones*) (see figures 7.2, 7.5, and 7.6). Sutural bones typically are small, ranging in size from a tiny pebble to a quarter, but they can be much larger. Any suture may have sutural bones, but they are most common and numerous in the lambdoid suture. Sutural bones represent independent bone ossification centers. Researchers do not know why sutural bone incidence varies among individuals, but most suspect a combination of genetic and environmental influences.

In our adult years, the sutures typically disappear as the adjoining bones fuse. This fusion starts internally (endocranially) and is followed by fusion on the skull's external (ectocranial) surface. Although the timing of suture closure can be highly variable, the coronal suture typically is the first to fuse, usually in the late 20s to early 30s, followed by the sagittal suture and then the lambdoid suture (usually in the 40s). The squamous suture usually does not fuse until late adulthood (60+ years), or it may not fuse at all. Osteologists can estimate the approximate age at death of an individual by examining the extent of suture closure in the skull.

Learning Strategy 7.3

As you learn about the individual skull bones, be sure to review figures 7.4 through 7.9 to see how each bone fits within the various views of the whole skull. Comparing the individual bone images with the whole skull images will help you better understand the complex articulations among all of the cranial and facial bones.

WHAT DID YOU LEARN?

2. Draw a superior view of the skull, and label the three skull sutures that may be seen from this view. Which bones articulate at these sutures?
3. Draw an inferior view of the skull, and label the major bones and foramina seen in this view.

7.1c Bones of the Cranium

The eight bones of the cranium collectively form a rigid protective structure for the brain. The cranium consists of a roof and a base. The roof, called the **calvaria** (kal-v ā′rē-ă), or *skullcap,* is composed of the squamous part of the frontal bone, the parietal bones, and the squamous part of the occipital bone. The **base** of the cranium is composed of portions of the ethmoid, sphenoid, occipital, and temporal bones. Some skulls in the anatomy lab have had their calvariae cut away, making the distinction between the calvaria and base easier to distinguish. Each bone of the cranium has specific surface features **(table 7.2)**.

Frontal Bone

The **frontal bone** forms part of the calvaria, the forehead, and the roof of the orbits **(figure 7.10)**. During development, the cranial bones (including the frontal bone) form as a result of the fusion of separate ossification centers, an event that may not occur until after birth. The frontal bone is formed from two major, separate ossification centers. Soon after birth, the left and right sides of the developing frontal bone are united by the **metopic** (me-top′ik; *metopon* = forehead) **suture.** This suture usually fuses and disappears by age 2, although a trace of it persists in some adult skulls.

The **squamous part** of the frontal bone is the vertical flattened region. The squamous part ends at the **supraorbital margins,** each of which forms the superior ridge of the orbit. The midpoint of each supraorbital margin contains a single **supraorbital foramen,** or **notch.** Superior to the supraorbital margins are the **superciliary** (sū′pĕr-sil′ ē-ār′ē; *super* = above, *cilium* = eyelid) **arches,** which are the brow ridges. Male skulls tend to have more pronounced superciliary arches than do female skulls. The part of the frontal bone sandwiched between the superciliary arches is the **glabella** (glă-bel′ă; *glabellus* = smooth).

The **orbital part** of the frontal bone is the smooth, inferior portion that forms the roof of the orbit. Lateral to each orbital part is the **zygomatic process** of the frontal bone, which articulates with the frontal process of the zygomatic bone.

Within the frontal bone is a pair of **frontal sinuses** (see figure 7.9). The frontal sinuses usually start to appear after age 6 and become more fully developed after age 10. Some people never develop these sinuses at all.

On the internal surface of the frontal bone is a midline elevation of bone called the **frontal crest.** The frontal crest serves as a point of attachment for the falx cerebri, a protective connective tissue sheet that helps support the brain (see section 15.2a).

Parietal Bones

The right and left **parietal** (pă-rī′ĕ-tăl; *paries* = wall) **bones** form the lateral walls and roof of the cranium **(figure 7.11)**. Each parietal bone is bordered by four sutures that unite it to the neighboring bones. A **parietal foramen** sometimes occurs in the posterior one-third of the parietal bone, adjacent to the sagittal suture. A tiny emissary vein travels through this opening, connecting the venous sinuses with the veins of the scalp. On the lateral surface, each parietal bone exhibits a pair of faint ridges called the **superior** and **inferior temporal lines.** These lines arc across the surface of the parietal and frontal bones. They mark the attachment site of the large, fan-shaped temporalis

Table 7.2	Cranial Bones and Selected Features	
Bone(s) and Associated Passageways	**Bone Boundaries Within the Skull**	**Selected Features and Their Functions**
Frontal bone Supraorbital foramen	Forms superior and anterior parts of skull, part of anterior cranial fossa and orbit	**Frontal crest:** Attachment site for meninges to help stabilize brain within skull **Frontal sinuses:** Lighten bone, moisten inhaled air, and give resonance to voice **Orbital part:** Forms roof of orbit **Squamous part:** Attachment of scalp muscles **Supraorbital margin:** Forms protective superior border of orbit
Parietal bones Parietal foramina	Each forms most of lateral and superior walls of skull	**Inferior and superior temporal lines:** Attachment site for temporalis muscle **Parietal eminence:** Forms rounded prominence on each side of skull
Temporal bones Carotid canal External acoustic meatus Internal acoustic meatus Mastoid foramen Stylomastoid foramen Jugular foramen (with occipital bone)	Each forms inferolateral wall of the skull; forms part of middle cranial fossa; has three parts—petrous, squamous, and tympanic	**Mandibular fossa:** Articulates with mandible **Mastoid air cells:** Lighten mastoid process **Mastoid process:** Attachment site of some neck muscles to extend or rotate head **Petrous part:** Protects sensory structures in inner ear **Styloid process:** Attachment site for hyoid bone ligaments and muscles **Squamous part:** Attachment site of some jaw muscles **Zygomatic process:** Articulates with zygomatic bone to form zygomatic arch
Occipital bone Foramen magnum Hypoglossal canal Jugular foramen (with temporal bone)	Forms posteroinferior part of skull, including most of the posterior cranial fossa; forms part of base of skull	**External occipital crest:** Attachment site for ligaments **External occipital protuberance:** Attachment of muscles that move head **Inferior and superior nuchal lines:** Attachment of neck ligaments and muscles **Occipital condyles:** Articulate with first cervical vertebra (atlas)
Sphenoid bone Foramen lacerum (with temporal and occipital bones) Foramen ovale Foramen rotundum Foramen spinosum Optic canal Superior orbital fissure	Forms part of base of skull, posterior part of eye orbit, part of anterior and middle cranial fossae	**Body:** Houses sphenoidal sinuses **Sella turcica:** Houses pituitary gland **Optic canals:** House optic nerves (CN II) **Medial and lateral pterygoid plates:** Attachment site for two muscles of mastication (chewing muscles) **Lesser wings:** Form part of anterior cranial fossa; contain optic canal **Greater wings:** Form part of middle cranial fossa and orbit **Sphenoidal sinuses:** Moisten inhaled air and give resonance to voice
Ethmoid bone Cribriform foramina	Forms part of the anterior cranial fossa; part of nasal septum; roof and lateral walls of nasal cavity; part of medial wall of eye orbit	**Crista galli:** Attachment site for cranial dural septa to help stabilize brain within skull **Ethmoidal labyrinths:** Contain the ethmoidal sinuses and nasal conchae **Ethmoidal sinuses:** Lighten bone, moisten inhaled air, and give resonance to voice **Nasal conchae** (superior and middle)**:** Increase airflow turbulence in nasal cavity so air can be adequately moistened and cleaned by nasal mucosa **Orbital plate:** Forms part of medial wall of the orbit **Perpendicular plate:** Forms superior part of nasal septum

muscle that closes the mouth. Superior to these lines, the rounded, smooth parietal surface is called the **parietal eminence.** The internal surfaces of the parietal bones exhibit many grooves that accommodate some of the blood vessels within the cranium.

Temporal Bones

The paired **temporal bones** form the inferior lateral walls and part of the floor of the cranium (**figure 7.12**). Each temporal bone has a complex structure composed of three parts: the petrous, squamous, and tympanic parts.

The thick **petrous** (pet′rŭs; *patra* = a rock) **part** of the temporal bone houses sensory structures of the inner ear that provide information about hearing and balance. In figure 7.12*b*, observe the **internal acoustic meatus** (mē-ā′tŭs; a passage) (also called either the *internal auditory meatus,* or *internal auditory canal*). It provides a passageway for nerves and blood vessels to and from the inner ear (see section 19.6c). A**groove for the sigmoid** (sig′moyd; *sigma* = the letter S, *eidos* = resemblance) **sinus** runs along the inferior surface of the petrous region. The sigmoid sinus is a venous sinus (vein) that drains blood from the brain (see section 23.3c).

Externally, the prominent bulge on the inferior surface of the temporal bone is the **mastoid** (mas′toyd; *masto* = breast) **process,** an anchoring site for muscles that move the neck. Rather than being solid bone, it is filled with many small, interconnected air cells (called mastoid air cells) that communicate with the middle ear.

On the posteroinferior surface of the temporal bone, a **mastoid foramen** may be present near the mastoid process. Tiny emissary veins travel through this foramen to connect the venous sinuses inside the cranium with the veins on the scalp. A thin, pointed projection of bone, called the **styloid** (stī′loyd; *stylos* = pillar post) **process,** serves as an attachment site for several hyoid and tongue muscles. The**stylomastoid foramen** lies between the mastoid process and the styloid process (see figure 7.8). The facial nerve (CN VII) extends through the stylomastoid foramen to innervate the facial muscles (see section 15.8). The **carotid canal** (ka-rot′id; *karoo* = to put to sleep) is medial to the styloid process and transmits the internal carotid artery (see section 23.3c).

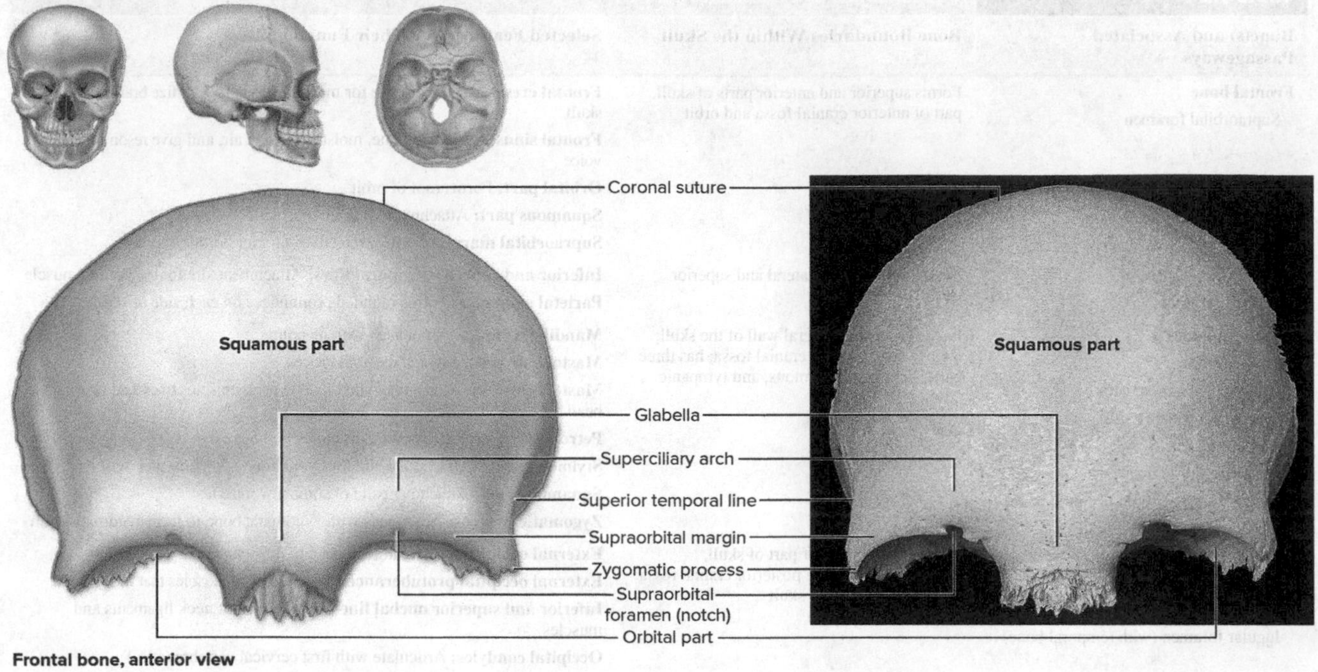

Figure 7.10

Anterior View of the Frontal Bone. The frontal bone forms the forehead and part of the orbits , and is shown in art and a photo .

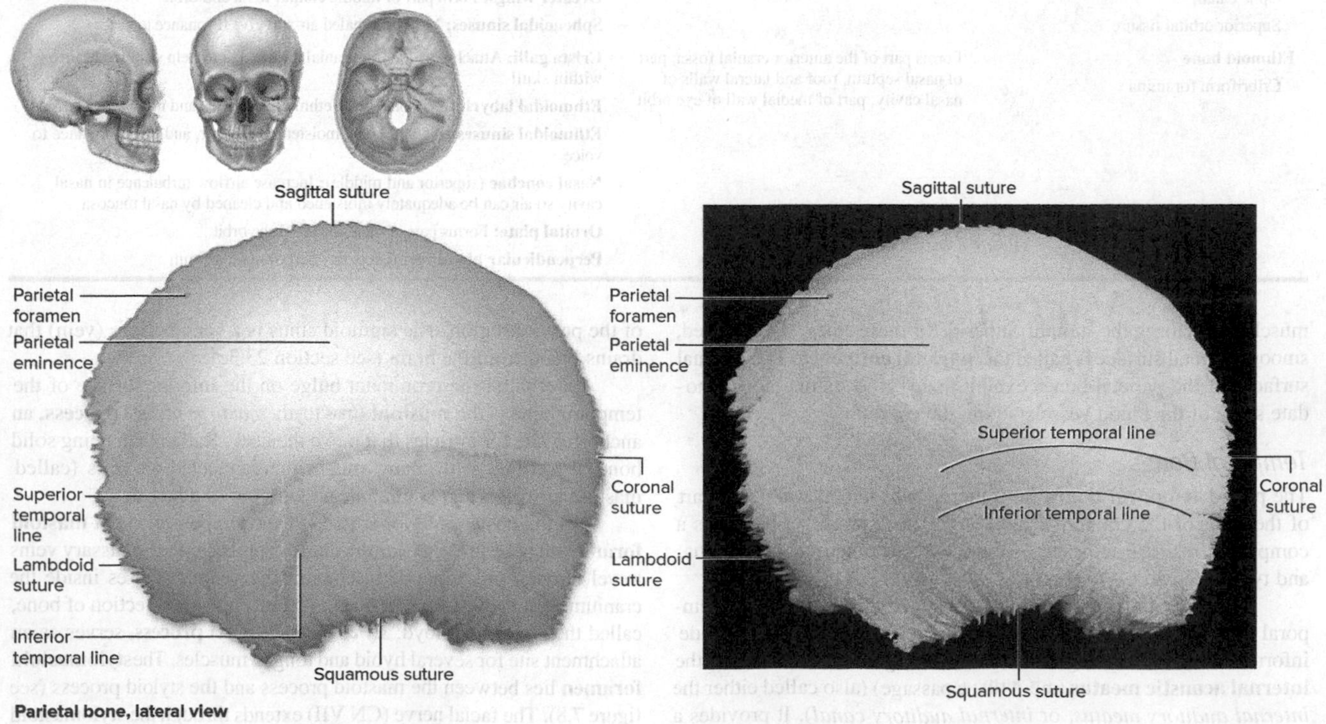

Figure 7.11

Lateral View of the Parietal Bone. The parietal bones form the lateral aspects of the skull , as seen in an image and a photo .

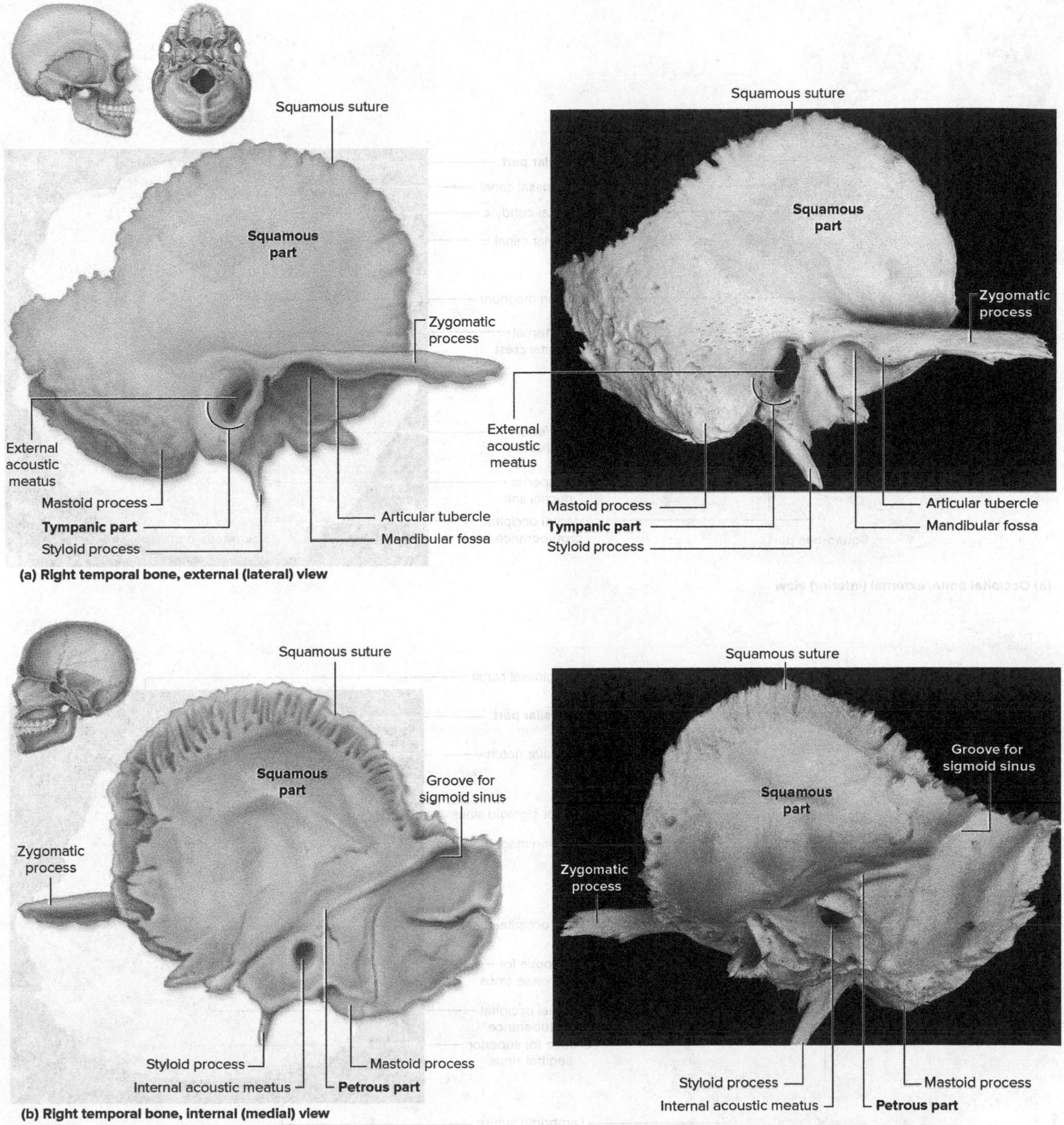
Squamous suture
Squamous part
Zygomatic process
External acoustic meatus
Mastoid process
Tympanic part
Styloid process
Articular tubercle
Mandibular fossa
(a) Right temporal bone, external (lateral) view
Squamous suture
Squamous part
Groove for sigmoid sinus
Zygomatic process
Styloid process
Internal acoustic meatus
Mastoid process
Petrous part
(b) Right temporal bone, internal (medial) view

Figure 7.12

Temporal Bone. The temporal bone is located adjacent to the ear. (*a*) External (lateral) view and (*b*) internal (medial) views of the right temporal bone are shown, using both images and photos of the bone. APR

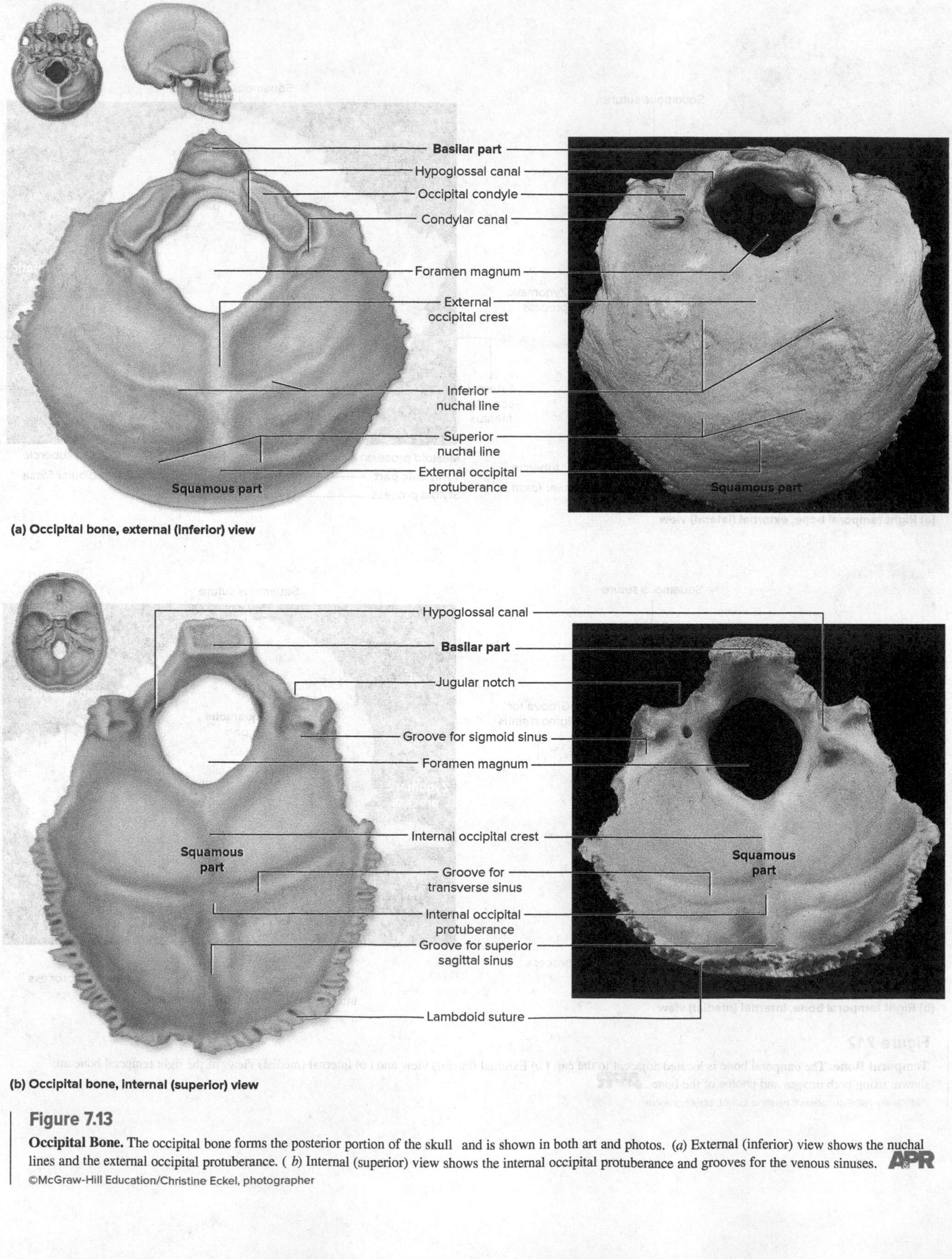
Basilar part
Hypoglossal canal
Occipital condyle
Condylar canal
Foramen magnum
External occipital crest
Inferior nuchal line
Superior nuchal line
External occipital protuberance
Squamous part
Squamous part
Hypoglossal canal
Basilar part
Jugular notch
Groove for sigmoid sinus
Foramen magnum
Internal occipital crest
Squamous part
Squamous part
Groove for transverse sinus
Internal occipital protuberance
Groove for superior sagittal sinus
Lambdoid suture

(a) Occipital bone, external (inferior) view

(b) Occipital bone, internal (superior) view

Figure 7.13

Occipital Bone. The occipital bone forms the posterior portion of the skull and is shown in both art and photos. (*a*) External (inferior) view shows the nuchal lines and the external occipital protuberance. (*b*) Internal (superior) view shows the internal occipital protuberance and grooves for the venous sinuses. APR

The **squamous part,** or *squama,* is the lateral flat surface of the temporal bone immediately inferior to the squamous suture (see figure 7.12). Immediately inferior to the squamous part, a prominent **zygomatic** (zī′gō-mat′ik; *zygoma* = a joining, a yoke) **process** curves laterally and anteriorly to unite with the **temporal process** of the **zygomatic bone.** The union of these processes forms the **zygomatic arch** (see figures 7.6 and 7.8). Each temporal bone articulates with the mandible inferior to the base of both zygomatic processes in a depression called the **mandibular** (man-dib′yū-lăr) **fossa.** Anterior to the mandibular fossa is a bump called the **articular tubercle.**

Immediately posterolateral to the mandibular fossa is the **tympanic** (tim-pan′ik; *tympanon* = drum) **part,** a small, bony ring surrounding the entrance to the **external acoustic meatus,** or *external auditory canal* (see figure 7.12).

Occipital Bone

The occipital bone is subdivided into a flattened **squamous part,** which forms the posterior region of the skull, and a median **basilar part,** which forms a portion of the base of the cranium (**figure 7.13**). Within the basilar part of the occipital bone is a large, circular opening called the **foramen magnum,** and lateral to this foramen are smooth knobs called **occipital** (ok-sip′i-tăl; *occiput* = back of head) **condyles.** The skull articulates with the first cervical vertebra at the occipital condyles. When you nod "yes," you are moving the occipital condyles against the vertebra. At the anteromedial edge of each condyle is a **hypoglossal canal** through which the hypoglossal nerve (CN XII) extends to supply the tongue muscles (see section 15.8). Posterior to each occipital condyle is a variable **condylar canal,** which transmits a vein.

Some prominent ridges appear on the external surface of the occipital bone. The **external occipital crest** projects in a posterior direction from the foramen magnum, ending in the **external occipital protuberance** (prō-tū′bĕr-ăns). Intersecting the external occipital crest are two horizontal ridges, the **superior** and **inferior nuchal** (nŭ′kăl) **lines.** These ridges are attachment sites for ligaments and neck muscles (see section 11.1g).

The portion of the occipital bone that helps form the jugular foramen is called the **jugular notch** (figure 7.13 *b*). The concave internal surface of the occipital bone closely follows the contours of the brain. Additionally, there are impressions named for the

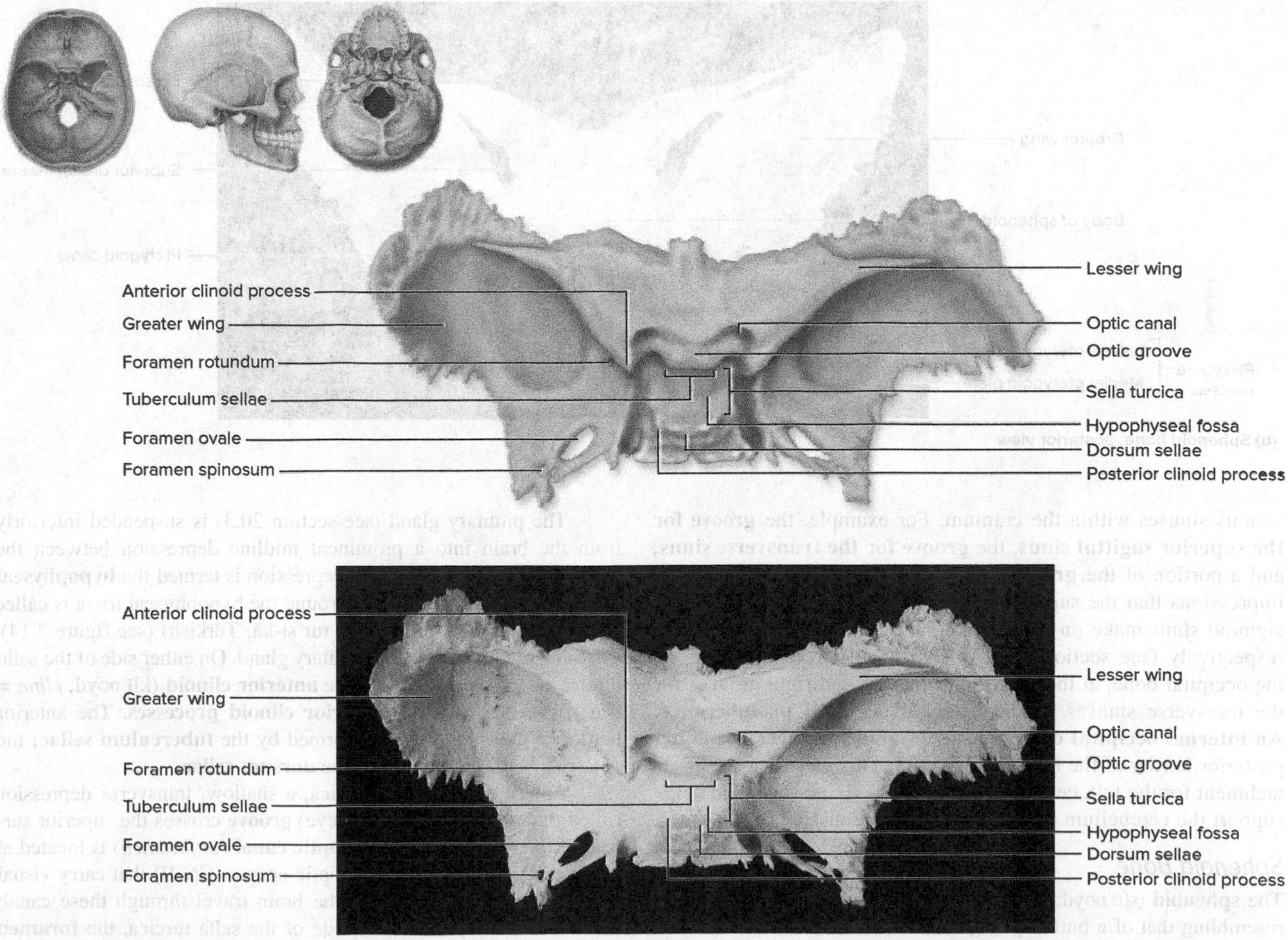

Anterior clinoid process
Greater wing
Foramen rotundum
Tuberculum sellae
Foramen ovale
Foramen spinosum
Lesser wing
Optic canal
Optic groove
Sella turcica
Hypophyseal fossa
Dorsum sellae
Posterior clinoid process
Anterior clinoid process
Greater wing
Foramen rotundum
Tuberculum sellae
Foramen ovale
Foramen spinosum
Lesser wing
Optic canal
Optic groove
Sella turcica
Hypophyseal fossa
Dorsum sellae
Posterior clinoid process

(a) Sphenoid bone, superior view

Figure 7.14

Sphenoid Bone. (*a*) Superior and (*b*) posterior views of the sphenoid (shown in both art and photos). The sphenoid bone is a butterfly-shaped bone that forms the centerpiece of the base of the cranium. APR

(continued on next page)

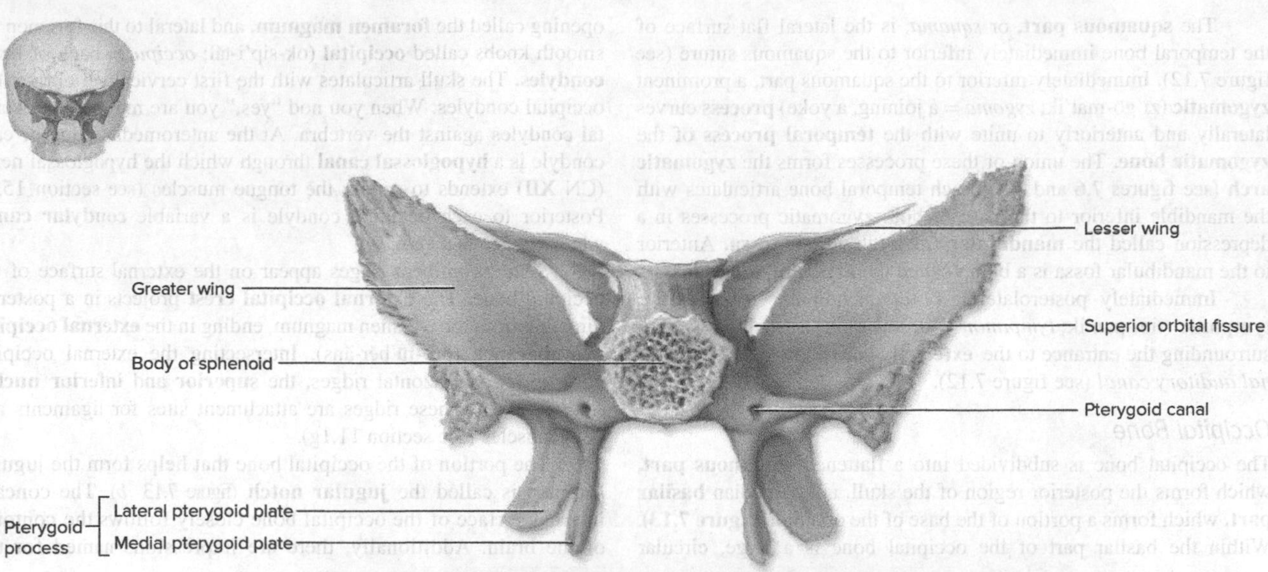

Lesser wing
Greater wing
Superior orbital fissure
Body of sphenoid
Pterygoid canal
Pterygoid process
Lateral pterygoid plate
Medial pterygoid plate

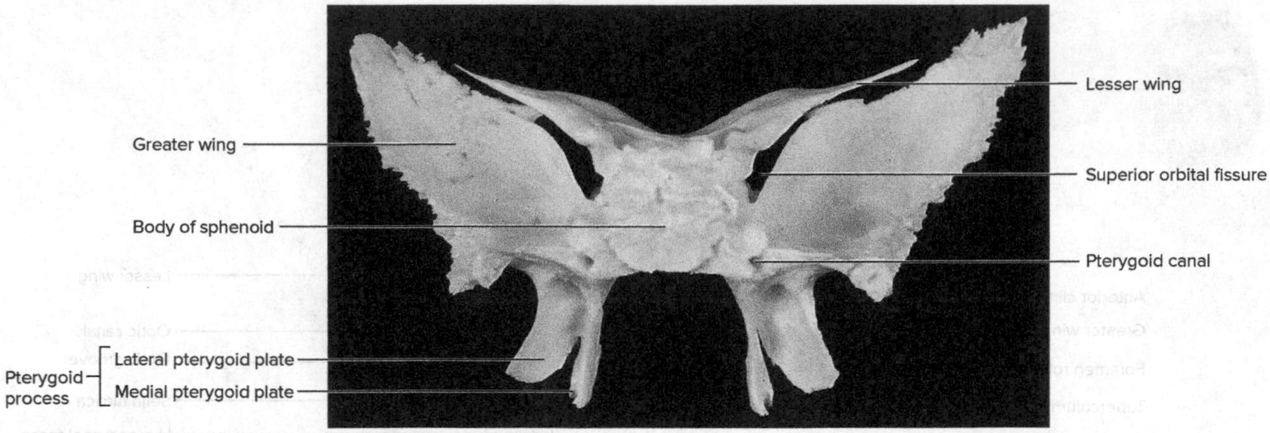

Lesser wing
Greater wing
Superior orbital fissure
Body of sphenoid
Pterygoid canal
Pterygoid process
Lateral pterygoid plate
Medial pterygoid plate

(b) Sphenoid bone, posterior view

venous sinuses within the cranium. For example, the **groove for the superior sagittal sinus,** the **groove for the transverse sinus,** and a portion of the **groove for the sigmoid sinus** represent the impressions that the superior sagittal sinus, transverse sinus, and sigmoid sinus make on the internal surface of the occipital bone, respectively (see section 23.3c). Also on the internal surface of the occipital bone, at the junction of the left and right grooves for the transverse sinuses, is the **internal occipital protuberance.** An **internal occipital crest** extends from the protuberance to the posterior border of the foramen magnum. This crest is a site of attachment for the falx cerebelli, a connective tissue sheet that helps support the cerebellum of the brain (see section 15.2a).

Sphenoid Bone

The **sphenoid** (sfē′noyd; wedge-shaped) **bone** has a complex shape, resembling that of a butterfly **(figure 7.14)**. It is often referred to as a "bridging bone," or the "keystone of the skull," because it unites the cranial and facial bones and articulates with almost every other bone of the skull **(figure 7.15)**. Medially, it has a thick **body,** which contains the **sphenoidal sinuses.** Laterally, it extends to form the **greater** and **lesser wings.** Although the sphenoid is relatively large, much of it is hidden by more superficial bones.

The pituitary gland (see section 20.3) is suspended inferiorly from the brain into a prominent midline depression between the greater and lesser wings. This depression is termed the **hypophyseal fossa,** and the bony enclosure around the hypophyseal fossa is called the **sella turcica** (sel′ă, saddle; tur′si-kă, Turkish) (see figure 7.14). The sella turcica houses the pituitary gland. On either side of the sella turcica are projections called the **anterior clinoid** (klī′noyd; *kline* = bed) **processes** and the **posterior clinoid processes.** The anterior border of the sella turcica is formed by the **tuberculum sellae;** the posterior border is formed by the **dorsum sellae.**

Anterior to the sella turcica, a shallow, transverse depression called the **optic** (op′tik; *ops* = eye) **groove** crosses the superior surface of the sphenoid bone. An **optic canal** (or *foramen*) is located at either end of this groove. The optic nerves (CN II) that carry visual information from the eyes to the brain travel through these canals (see section 15.8). On either side of the sella turcica, the **foramen rotundum** (rō-tŭn′dum; round), the **foramen ovale** (ō-văl′ē; oval), and the **foramen spinosum** (spī-nō′sŭm) penetrate the greater wings of the sphenoid bone. These openings transmit blood vessels to the meninges around the brain and nerves to structures of the orbit, face, and jaws. A **pterygoid canal** is located on either side of the body and transmits a nerve. The **pterygoid** (ter′i-goyd; *pteryx* = winglike)

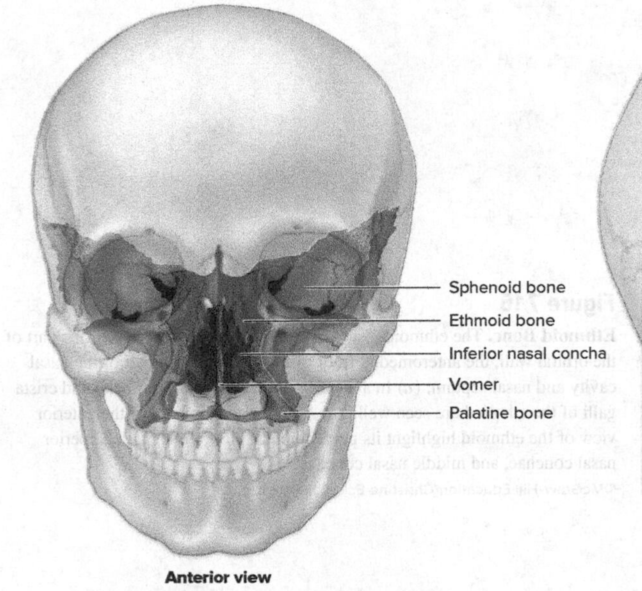
Sphenoid bone
Ethmoid bone
Inferior nasal concha
Vomer
Palatine bone
Anterior view

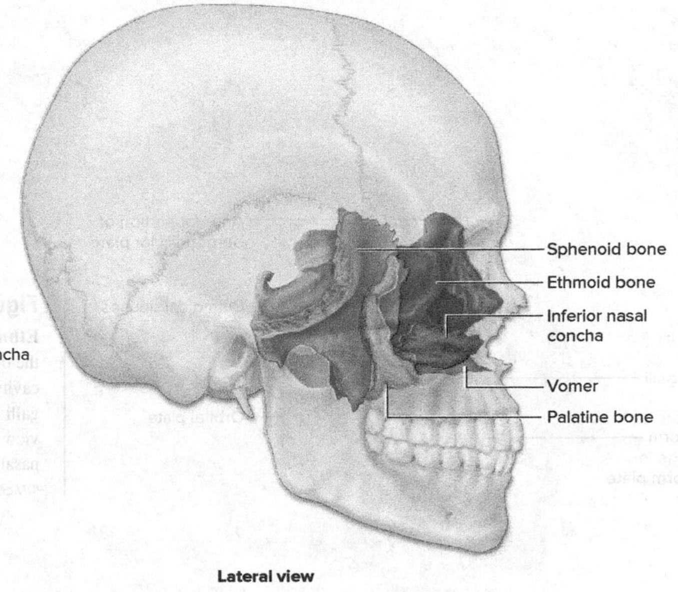
Sphenoid bone
Ethmoid bone
Inferior nasal concha
Vomer
Palatine bone
Lateral view

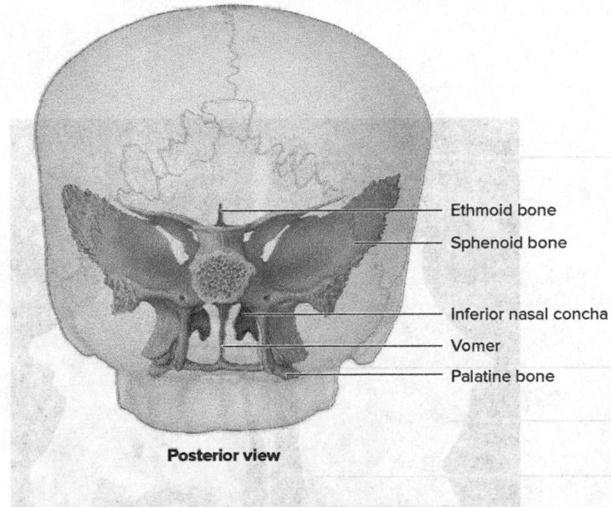
Ethmoid bone
Sphenoid bone
Inferior nasal concha
Vomer
Palatine bone
Posterior view

Figure 7.15

Articulations of the Sphenoid and Ethmoid Bones. Several bones of the skull, such as the sphenoid and ethmoid, are primarily located deep to other bones and can be seen only when the skull bones are disarticulated. This figure illustrates the positioning of these internal bones, relative to the externally placed skull bones , in three different views.

processes are vertical projections that begin at the boundary between the greater and lesser wings. Each pterygoid process forms a pair of **medial** and **lateral pterygoid plates,** which provide the attachment surfaces for some muscles that move the lower jaw and soft palate (see section 11.1c).

Ethmoid Bone

The irregularly shaped **ethmoid** (eth′moyd; *ethmos* = sieve) **bone** is positioned between the orbits (figure 7.15). It forms the anteromedial floor of the cranium, the roof of the nasal cavity, part of the medial wall of each orbit, and part of the nasal septum.

The superior part of the ethmoid bone exhibits a thin midsagittal elevation called the **crista** (kris′tă; crest) **galli** (gal′lē; cock) (**figure 7.16**). This bony crest is the point of attachment for the falx cerebri, a membranous sheet that helps support the brain (see section 15.2a). Immediately lateral to each side of the crista galli, the horizontal **cribriform** (krib′ri-fōrm; *cribrum* = sieve) **plate** has numerous perforations called the **cribriform foramina.** These foramina provide passageways for the olfactory nerves (CN I) (see section 15.8).

The paired **ethmoidal labyrinths** (*lateral masses*) contain tiny spaces called the **ethmoidal sinuses,** which open into both sides of the nasal cavity. The smooth part of each ethmoidal labyrinth is called the **orbital plate,** and forms part of the medial wall of the orbit. The ethmoidal labyrinths are partially composed of thin, scroll-like bones called the **superior** and the **middle nasal conchae** (kon′kē; sing., *concha,* kon′kă; shell). The inferior, midline projection of the ethmoid bone is called the **perpendicular plate,** and forms the superior part of the nasal septum.

Cranial Fossae

The contoured floor of the cranial cavity exhibits three curved depressions called the **cranial fossae** (**figure 7.17**). Their surfaces contain depressions for parts of the brain, grooves for blood vessels, and numerous foramina.

The **anterior cranial fossa** is the shallowest of the three depressions. It is formed by the frontal bone, the ethmoid bone, and the lesser wings of the sphenoid bone. The anterior cranial fossa houses the frontal lobes of the cerebral hemispheres. It ranges from the internal surface of the inferior part of the frontal bone (anteriorly) to the posterior edge of the lesser wings of the sphenoid bone (posteriorly).

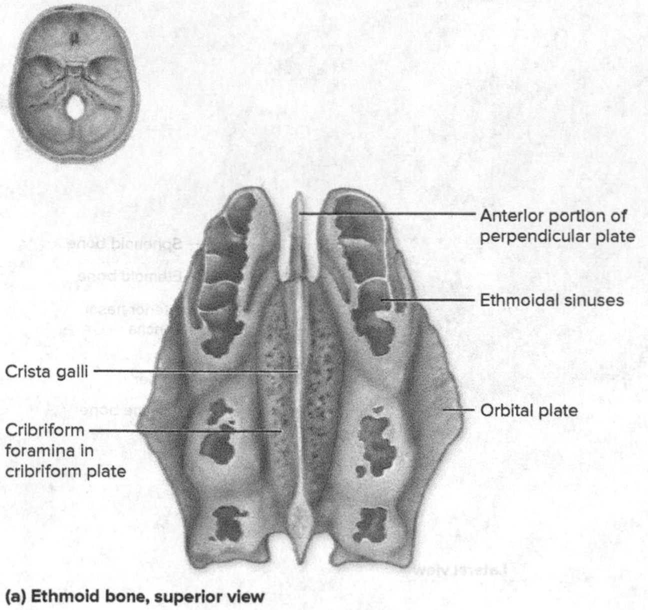

(a) Ethmoid bone, superior view

Figure 7.16

Ethmoid Bone. The ethmoid is an irregularly shaped bone that forms part of the orbital wall, the anteromedial floor of the cranium, and part of the nasal cavity and nasal septum. (*a*) In a superior view, the cribiform plate and crista galli of the ethmoid are seen well. (*b*) A drawing and photo of the anterior view of the ethmoid highlight its perpendicular plate, crista galli, superior nasal conchae, and middle nasal conchae. APR

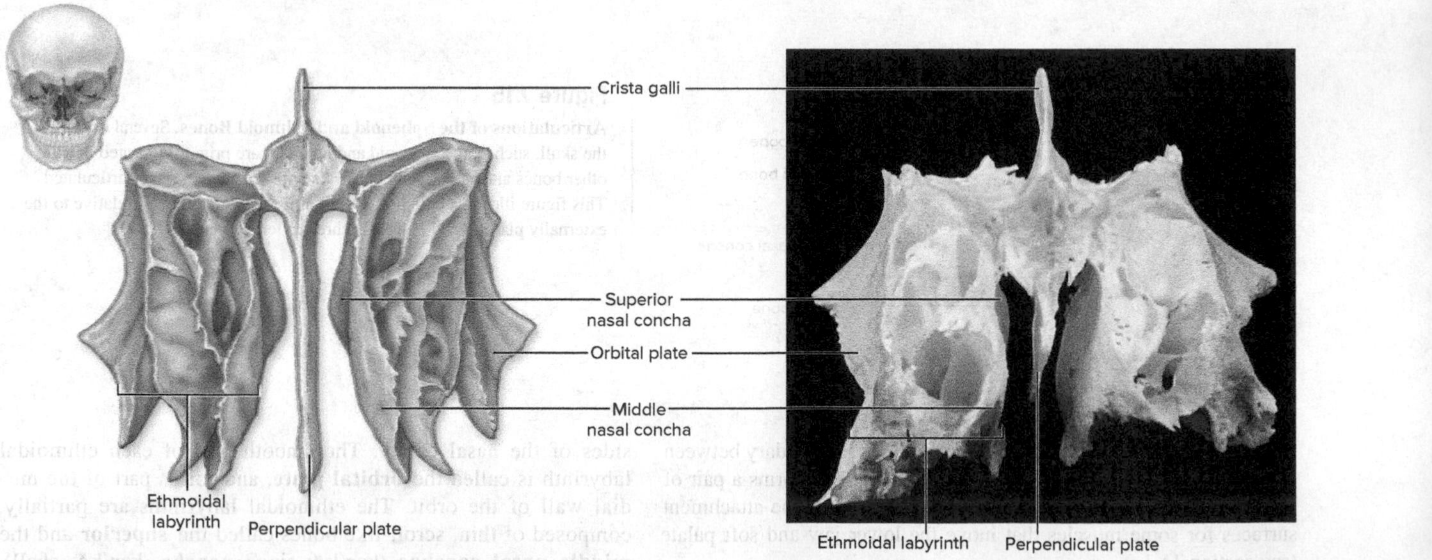

(b) Ethmoid bone, anterior view

The **middle cranial fossa** is inferior and posterior to the anterior cranial fossa. It ranges from the posterior edge of the lesser wings of the sphenoid bone (anteriorly) to the anterior part of the petrous part of the temporal bone (posteriorly). This fossa is formed by the parietal, sphenoid, and temporal bones. It houses the temporal lobes of the cerebral hemispheres and part of the brainstem.

The **posterior cranial fossa** is the most inferior and posterior cranial fossa. It extends from the posterior part of the petrous part of the temporal bones to the internal posterior surface of the skull. The posterior fossa is formed by the occipital, temporal, and parietal bones. This fossa houses the cerebellum and part of the brainstem.

WHAT DID YOU LEARN?

4. What are the three parts of the temporal bone?
5. What is the sella turcica, its function, and which bone has this feature?
6. What bones form the middle cranial fossa, and what structure is housed within it?

7.1d Bones of the Face

The **facial bones** (see figure 7.2) give shape and individuality to the face, form part of the orbit and nasal cavities, support the teeth, and provide for the attachment of muscles involved in facial expression

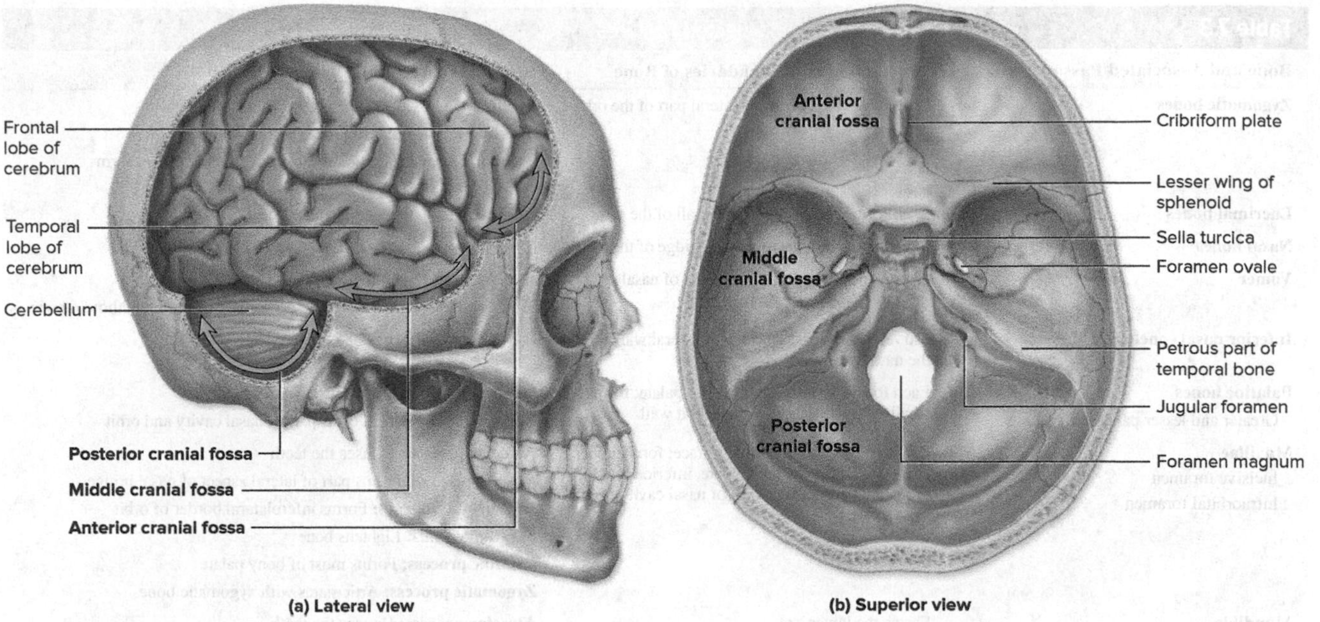
Frontal lobe of cerebrum
Temporal lobe of cerebrum
Cerebellum
Posterior cranial fossa
Middle cranial fossa
Anterior cranial fossa
(a) Lateral view
Anterior cranial fossa
Cribriform plate
Lesser wing of sphenoid
Sella turcica
Middle cranial fossa
Foramen ovale
Petrous part of temporal bone
Jugular foramen
Posterior cranial fossa
Foramen magnum
(b) Superior view

Figure 7.17

Cranial Fossae. (*a*) Lateral and (*b*) superior views show the three levels of depression in the cranium (anterior, middle, and posterior) that parallel the contours of the ventral surface of the brain.

and mastication. There are 14 facial bones, including the paired zygomatic bones, lacrimal bones, nasal bones, inferior nasal conchae, palatine bones, and maxillae, and the unpaired vomer and mandible **(table 7.3)**.

Zygomatic Bones

The **zygomatic bones,** commonly referred to as the "cheekbones," form part of the lateral wall of each orbit and the cheeks **(figure 7.18)**. A prominent **zygomatic arch** is formed by the articulation of the **temporal process** of each zygomatic bone with the zygomatic process of each temporal bone (see figure 7.6). The bone also has a **maxillary** (mak′si-lār-ē) **process,** which articulates with the zygomatic process of the maxilla, and a **frontal process,** which articulates with the frontal bone. The **orbital surface** of the zygomatic bone forms the lateral wall of the orbit.

Lacrimal Bones

The small, paired **lacrimal** (lak′ri-m ăl; *lacrima* = a tear) **bones** form part of the medial wall of each orbit (see figure 7.4). A small, depressed inferior opening called the **lacrimal groove** provides a passageway for the nasolacrimal duct, which drains tears into the nasal cavity (see section 19.5a).

Nasal Bones

The paired **nasal bones** form the bridge of the nose (see figure 7.4). The medial edge of each maxilla articulates with the lateral edge of a nasal bone. The nasal bones are often fractured by blows to the nose.

Vomer

The **vomer** (vō′mĕr; plowshare) has a triangular shape, and when viewed laterally, resembles a farming plow **(figure 7.19)**. It articulates along its midline with both the maxillae and the palatine bones. Its curved, thin, horizontal projection, called the **ala,** meaning "wing," articulates superiorly with the sphenoid bone. The **vertical plate** of the vomer articulates with the perpendicular plate of the ethmoid bone. Anteriorly, both the vomer and the perpendicular plate of the ethmoid bone form the bony nasal septum.

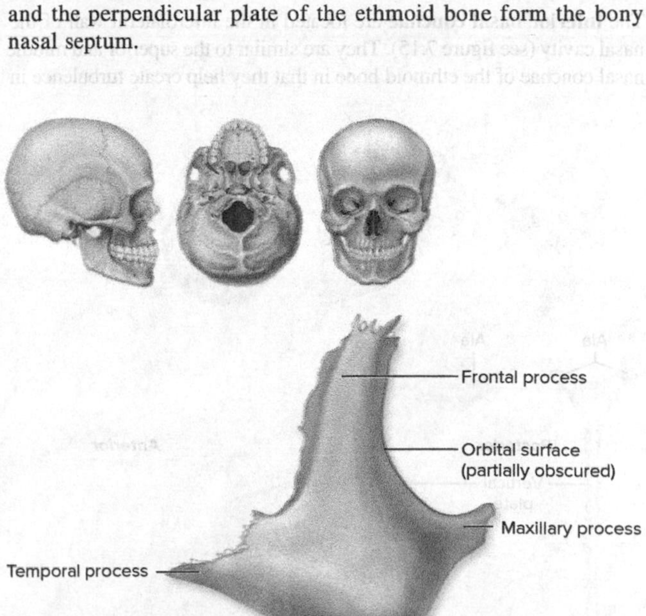
Frontal process
Orbital surface (partially obscured)
Maxillary process
Temporal process
Right zygomatic bone, lateral view

Figure 7.18

Zygomatic Bone. The zygomatic bone forms the cheek and part of the lateral wall of the orbit.

Table 7.3	Facial Bones and Selected Features	
Bone and Associated Passageways	**Description and Boundaries of Bone**	**Selected Features and Their Functions**
Zygomatic bones	Each forms the cheek and lateral part of the orbit	**Frontal process:** Articulates with frontal bone **Maxillary process:** Articulates with maxilla **Temporal process:** Articulates with temporal bone to form zygomatic arch
Lacrimal bones	Each forms part of the medial wall of the orbit	**Lacrimal groove:** Contains nasolacrimal duct
Nasal bones	Each forms the anterosuperior bridge of the nose	
Vomer	Forms inferior and posterior parts of nasal septum	**Ala:** Articulates with the sphenoid bone **Vertical plate:** Articulates with perpendicular plate of ethmoid bone
Inferior nasal conchae	Curved bones that project from lateral walls of the nasal cavity	Increase airflow turbulence in nasal cavity
Palatine bones Greater and lesser palatine foramina	Each forms posterior part of hard palate; forms small part of nasal cavity and orbit wall	**Horizontal plate:** Forms posterior part of palate **Perpendicular plate:** Forms part of nasal cavity and orbit
Maxillae Incisive foramen Infraorbital foramen	Each forms anterior portion of face; forms upper jaw and parts of the hard palate, inferior parts of orbits, and part of the walls of nasal cavity	**Alveolar process:** Houses the teeth **Frontal process:** Forms part of lateral aspect of nasal bridge **Infraorbital margin:** Forms inferolateral border of orbit **Maxillary sinus:** Lightens bone **Palatine process:** Forms most of bony palate **Zygomatic process:** Articulates with zygomatic bone
Mandible Mandibular foramen Mental foramen	Forms the lower jaw	**Alveolar process:** Houses the teeth **Coronoid process:** Attachment of temporalis muscle **Head of mandible:** Articulates with temporal bone **Mental protuberance:** Forms the chin **Mylohyoid line:** Attachment site for mylohyoid muscle

Inferior Nasal Conchae

The **inferior nasal conchae** are located in the inferolateral wall of the nasal cavity (see figure 7.15). They are similar to the superior and middle nasal conchae of the ethmoid bone in that they help create turbulence in inhaled air. However, inferior nasal conchae are separate bones, whereas the middle and superior nasal conchae are parts of the ethmoid bone.

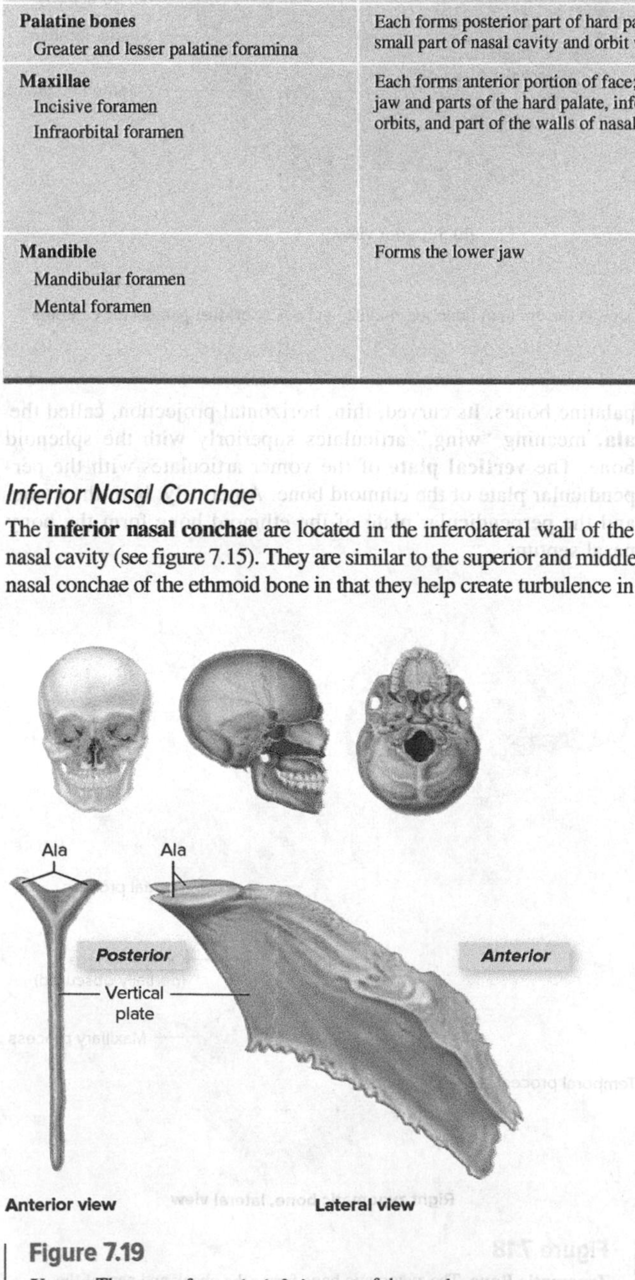
Ala
Ala
Posterior
Anterior
Vertical plate
Anterior view
Lateral view

Figure 7.19

Vomer. The vomer forms the inferior part of the nasal septum.

Palatine Bones

The **palatine** (pal′ă-tīn) **bones** are small bones with a distinct L shape. They form part of the hard palate, nasal cavity, and eye orbit (**figure 7.20**). The posterior portion of the hard palate is formed by the **horizontal plate** of the palatine bone, which articulates anteriorly with the palatine process of the maxilla. Greater and lesser **palatine foramina** perforate this horizontal plate (see figure 7.8). Nerves to the palate and upper teeth travel through these palatine formina. The **perpendicular plate** forms part of the lateral wall of the nasal cavity. The most superior part of the perpendicular plate has an **orbital process** that forms a small part of the medial floor of the orbit.

Maxillae

The paired **maxillae** (mak-sil′ ē; sing., *maxilla,* mak-sil′ ă; jawbone), also called *maxillary bones,* form the central part of the facial skeleton (**figure 7.21**). Left and right maxillae unite to form the upper jaw. Together, the united maxillae form a prominent **anterior nasal spine** along the inferior surface of the nasal cavity. Each maxilla contains an infraorbital margin and an inferior **orbital surface.** A large **infraorbital foramen** provides passage for a blood vessel and nerve (infraorbital artery and nerve). Within the orbit, this foramen extends along the **infraorbital groove.** The inferior portions of the maxillae contain the **alveolar** (al-vē′ō-lăr) **processes** that house the upper teeth.

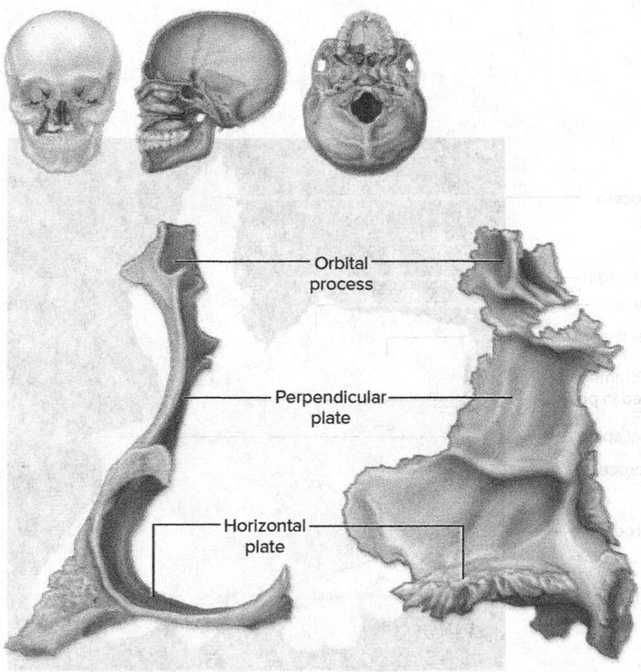
Orbital process
Perpendicular plate
Horizontal plate
Right palatine bone, anterior view
Right palatine bone, medial view

Figure 7.20

Palatine Bone. The L-shaped palatine bone forms part of the nasal complex and the hard palate. It is shown here in both anterior and medial views.

Clinical View 7.2

Cleft Lip and Cleft Palate

A **cleft lip** is the incomplete fusion of the upper jaw components of the developing embryo, resulting in a split upper lip extending from the mouth to the side of one nostril. Cleft lip may be unilateral (occurring on one side only) or bilateral (occurring on both sides). Cleft lip appears in 1 per 1000 births and tends to be more common in males. The etiology of cleft lip is multifactorial, in that both genetic and environmental factors appear to contribute to the condition.

Another anomaly that can develop is **cleft palate,** a congenital fissure in the midline of the palate. A cleft palate results when the left and right bones fuse incompletely or do not fuse at all. In the more severe cases, children experience swallowing and feeding problems because food can easily travel from the oral cavity into the nasal cavity. Cleft palate occurs in about 1 per 2500 births and tends to be more common in females. Like cleft lip, the etiology of cleft palate is multifactorial. Cleft palate sometimes occurs in conjunction with cleft lip.

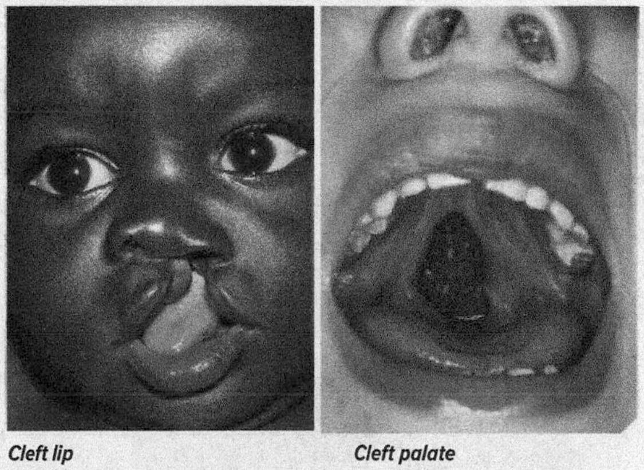

Cleft lip *Cleft palate*

(cleft lip) Dr. M.A. Ansary/Science Source; (cleft palate) Med. Mic. Sciences Cardiff Uni, Wellcome Images

Most of the hard palate is formed anteriorly by horizontal medial extensions of both maxillae, called **palatine processes** (see figure 7.21*b*). Near the anterior margin of the fused palatine processes, immediately posterior to the teeth called incisors, is an **incisive foramen.** This foramen is a passageway for branches of the nasopalatine nerve. Lateral to the nasal cavity, each maxilla contains a large, spacious cavity called the **maxillary sinus.** Laterally, each maxilla articulates with a zygomatic bone via a **zygomatic process.** Superiorly, the maxillae articulate with the frontal bones via **frontal processes** (see figure 7.21*a*).

Mandible

The **mandible** (man′di-bŭl) forms the entire lower jaw **(figure 7.22).** It supports the inferior teeth and provides attachment for the muscles of mastication. The mandible has a horizontal **body** and two vertical-to-oblique ascending posterior regions called the **rami** (rā′mī; sing., *ramus,* rā′mŭs). The teeth are supported by the **alveolar process** of the mandibular body. Each ramus intersects the body at a "corner" called the **angle of the mandible.** The point of the chin is the **mental** (*mentum* = chin) **protuberance.** On the anterolateral surface of the body, a **mental foramen** penetrates the body on each side of the chin to provide a passageway for nerves and blood vessels.

An **alveolar process** covers both the alveoli and the roots of the teeth medially in the mandible. On the medial aspect of the ramus, a prominent **mandibular foramen** provides a passageway for blood vessels and nerves that innervate the inferior teeth.

The posterior projection of each mandibular ramus, called the **condylar** (kon′di-l ăr) **process,** terminates at the **head of the mandible,** also called the *mandibular condyle* (kon′d īl). Each articulation of the head of the mandible with the mandibular fossa of the temporal bone is called the **temporomandibular joint (TMJ),** a mobile joint that allows us to move the lower jaw when we talk or chew (see section 9.5a). The anterior projection of the ramus, termed the **coronoid** (kōr′ŏ-noyd; *korōnē* = a crow) **process,** is the insertion point for the temporalis muscle, a powerful muscle involved in closing the mouth (see section 11.1c). The U-shaped depression between the two processes is called the **mandibular notch.**

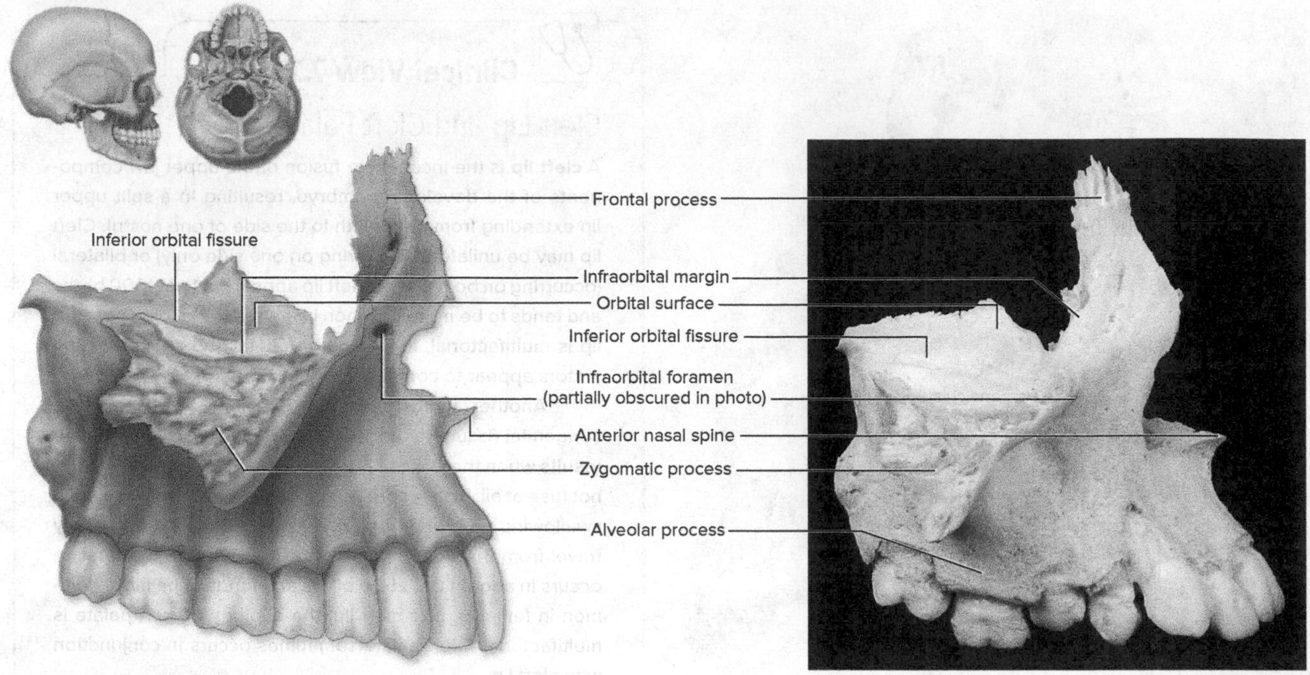
Frontal process
Inferior orbital fissure
Infraorbital margin
Orbital surface
Inferior orbital fissure
Infraorbital foramen
(partially obscured in photo)
Anterior nasal spine
Zygomatic process
Alveolar process

(a) Right maxilla, lateral view

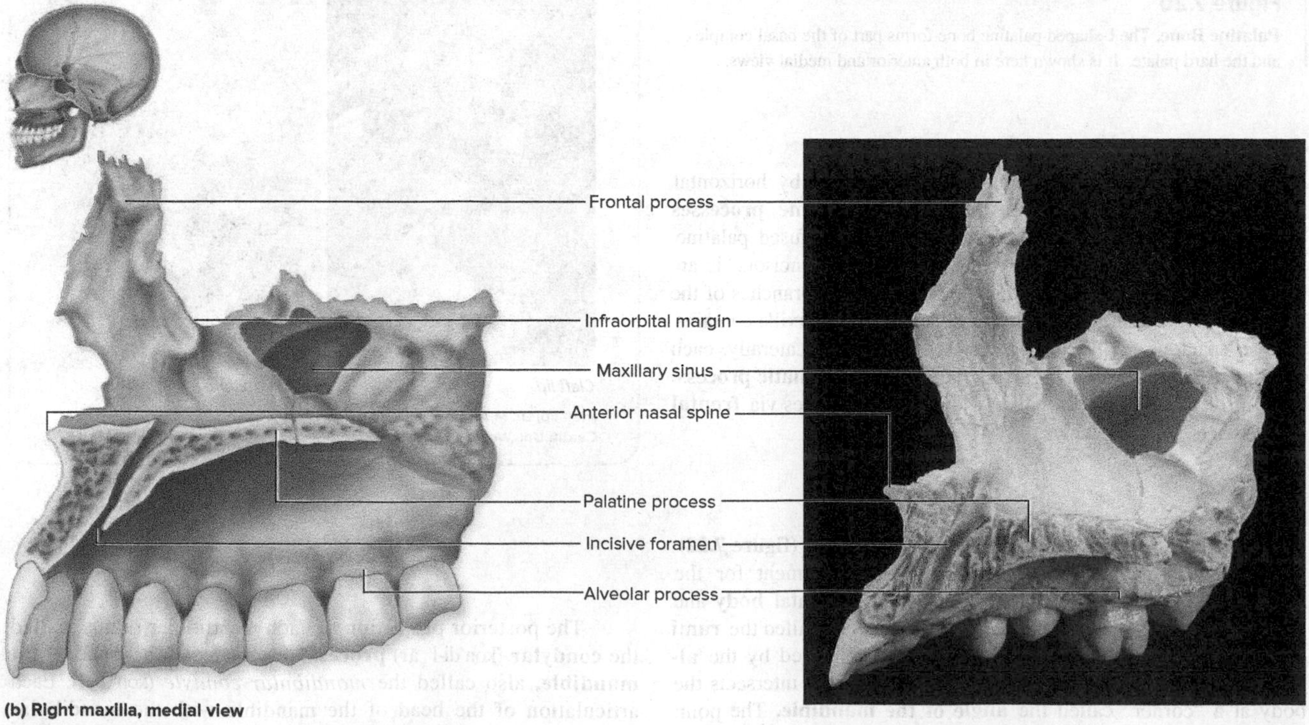
Frontal process
Infraorbital margin
Maxillary sinus
Anterior nasal spine
Palatine process
Incisive foramen
Alveolar process

(b) Right maxilla, medial view

Figure 7.21

Maxilla. Both maxillae form the upper jaw. (*a*) Lateral and (*b*) medial views show the right maxilla in both art and photos. APR

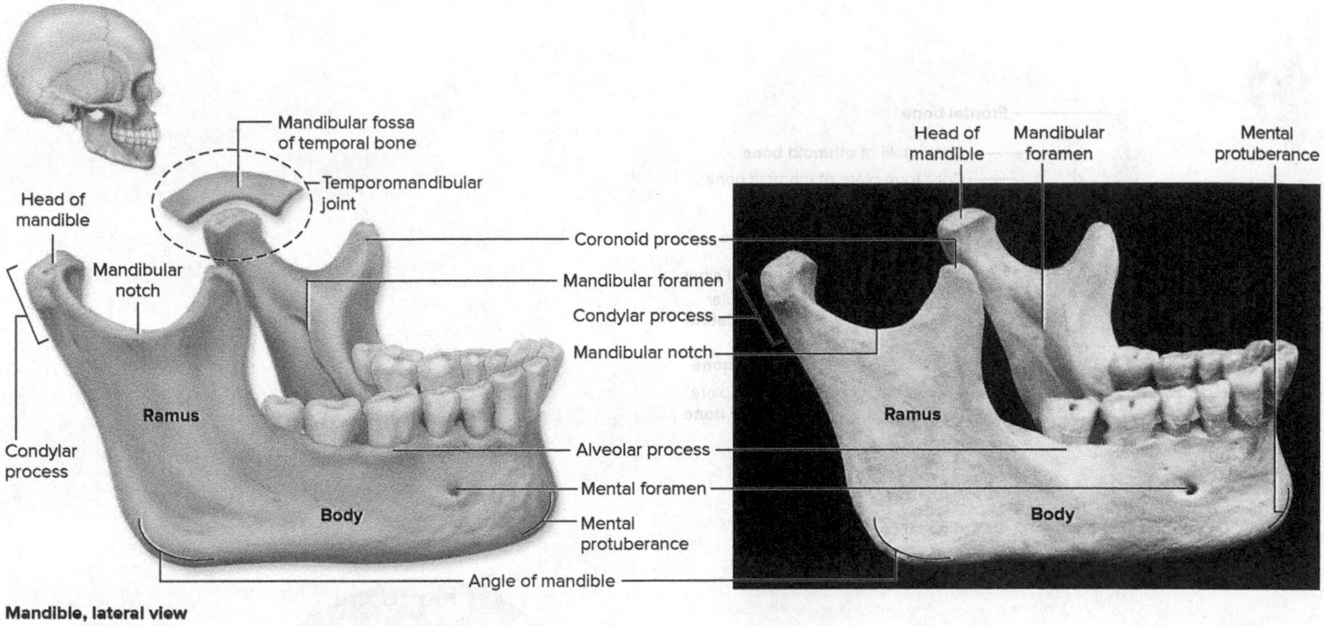

Figure 7.22

Mandible. The mandible, shown here in art and a photo, forms the lower jaw, and its articulation with the temporal bone forms the temporomandibular joint. APR

©McGraw-Hill Education/Christine Eckel, photographer

7.1e Nasal Complex

The **nasal complex** is composed of bones and cartilage that enclose the nasal cavity and the paranasal sinuses. These bones are shown in both sagittal section and coronal section, as in **figure 7.23**.

- The roof, or superior border, of the nasal complex is formed by the cribriform plate of the ethmoid bone and parts of the frontal and sphenoid bones.
- The floor, or inferior border, is formed by the palatine processes of the maxillae and the horizontal plates of the palatine bones.
- The lateral walls are formed by the ethmoid bone, maxillae, inferior nasal conchae, the perpendicular plates of the palatine bones, and the lacrimal bones.

Most of the anterior walls of the nasal cavity are formed by cartilage and the soft tissues of the nose, but the bridge of the nose is supported by the maxillae and the nasal bones (see section 25.2a).

7.1f Paranasal Sinuses

We have already described the ethmoidal, frontal, maxillary, and sphenoidal sinuses in connection with the bones where they occur. As a group, these air-filled chambers that open into the nasal cavities are called the **paranasal sinuses** (sī′nŭs; cavity, hollow) (**figure 7.24**). The sinuses have a mucous lining that helps to humidify and warm inhaled air. Additionally, the sinus spaces in some skull bones cause these skull bones to be lighter, and also provide resonance to the voice.

7.1g Orbital Complex

The bony cavities called orbits enclose and protect the eyes and the muscles that move them. The **orbital complex** consists of multiple bones that form each orbit (**figure 7.25**). The borders of the orbital complex are as follows:

- The roof of the orbit is formed from the orbital part of the frontal bone and the lesser wing of the sphenoid bone.
- The floor of the orbit is formed primarily by the orbital surface of the maxilla, although the zygomatic bone and orbital process of the palatine bone also contribute a portion.
- The medial wall is formed from the frontal process of the maxilla, the lacrimal bone, and the orbital plate of the ethmoid bone.
- The lateral wall of the orbit is formed from the orbital surface of the zygomatic bone, the greater wing of the sphenoid bone, and the zygomatic process of the frontal bone.
- The posterior wall of the orbit is formed primarily from the sphenoid bone.

7.1h Bones Associated with the Skull

The auditory ossicles and the hyoid bone are bones of the axial skeleton associated with the skull. Three tiny ear bones called **auditory ossicles** (os′i-k ĕl) are housed within the petrous part of each temporal bone. These bones—the **malleus** (mal′ ē-ŭs), the **incus** (ing′kŭs), and the **stapes** (stā′pēz)—are discussed in depth in section 19.6b.

The **hyoid bone** is a slender, curved bone located inferior to the skull between the mandible and the larynx (voice box)

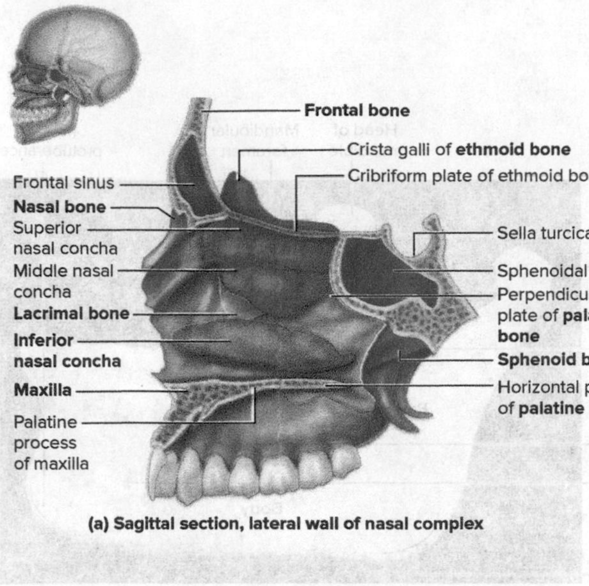
Frontal bone
Crista galli of ethmoid bone
Cribriform plate of ethmoid bone
Frontal sinus
Nasal bone
Superior nasal concha
Middle nasal concha
Lacrimal bone
Inferior nasal concha
Maxilla
Palatine process of maxilla
Sella turcica
Sphenoidal sinus
Perpendicular plate of palatine bone
Sphenoid bone
Horizontal plate of palatine bone
(a) Sagittal section, lateral wall of nasal complex

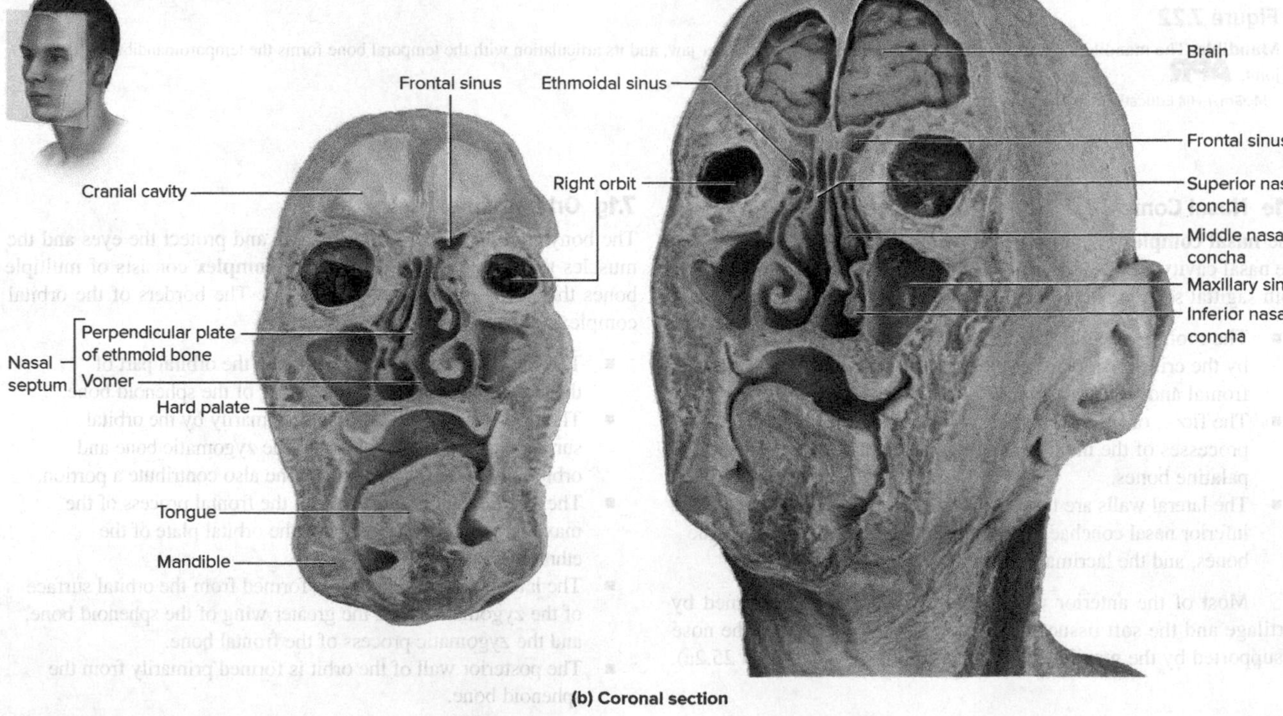
Frontal sinus
Ethmoidal sinus
Cranial cavity
Right orbit
Perpendicular plate of ethmoid bone
Nasal septum
Vomer
Hard palate
Tongue
Mandible
Brain
Frontal sinus
Superior nasal concha
Middle nasal concha
Maxillary sinus
Inferior nasal concha
(b) Coronal section

Figure 7.23

Nasal Complex. Multiple skull bones form the intricate nasal complex. (*a*) A sagittal section shows the right side of the nasal complex. (*b*) Cadaver photo of coronal sections through the head shows the nasal complex.

(**figure 7.26**). It does not articulate with any other bone in the skeleton. The hyoid has a midline **body** and two hornlike processes, the **greater cornu** (kōr′nū; pl., *cornua*, kor′n ū-ă; horn) and the **lesser cornu.** The cornua and body serve as attachment sites for tongue and anterior neck muscles and ligaments (see sections 11.1d and 11.1f).

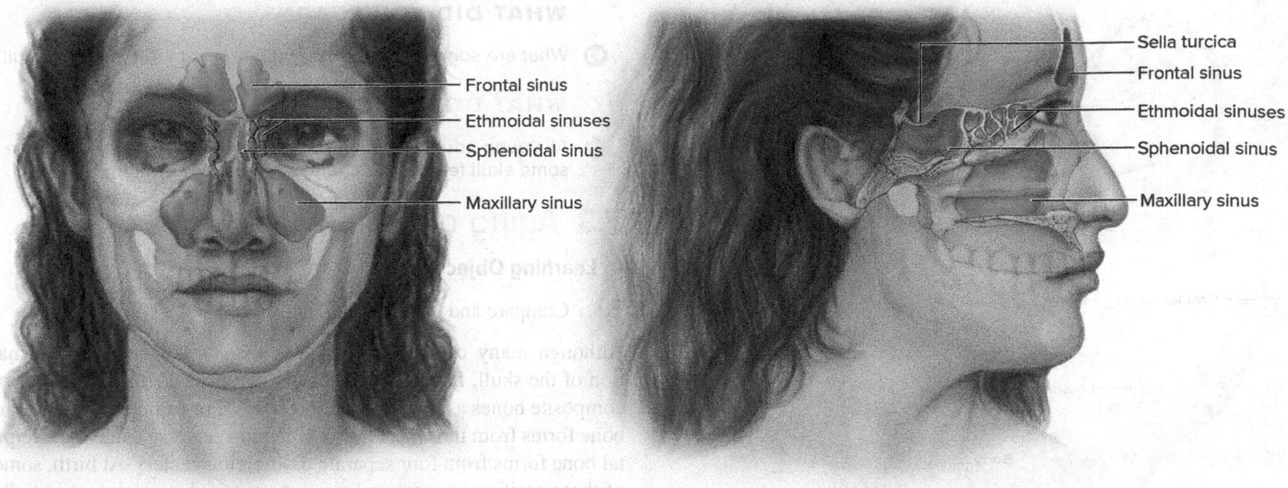
Frontal sinus
Ethmoidal sinuses
Sphenoidal sinus
Maxillary sinus
Anterior view
Sella turcica
Frontal sinus
Ethmoidal sinuses
Sphenoidal sinus
Maxillary sinus
Lateral view

Figure 7.24

Paranasal Sinuses. The paranasal sinuses are air-filled chambers within the frontal, ethmoid, and sphenoid bones and the maxillae. They act as extensions of the nasal cavity. APR

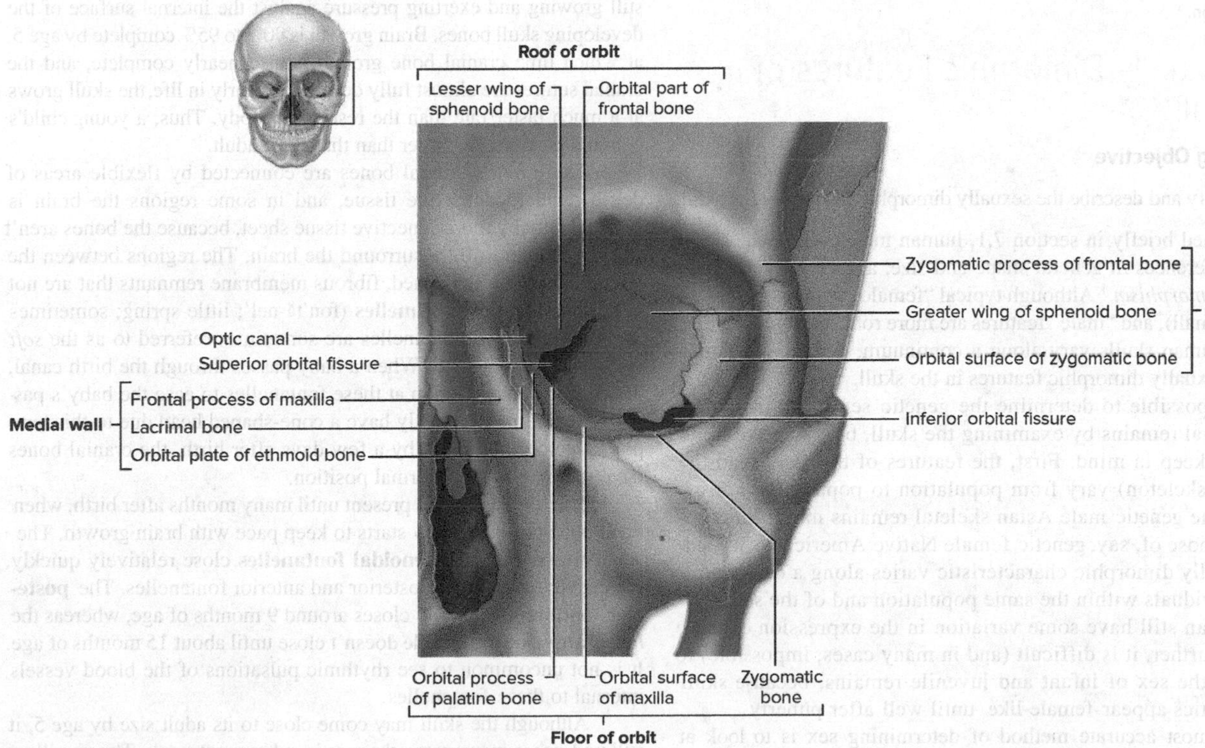
Roof of orbit
Lesser wing of sphenoid bone
Orbital part of frontal bone
Zygomatic process of frontal bone
Greater wing of sphenoid bone
Lateral wall
Orbital surface of zygomatic bone
Optic canal
Superior orbital fissure
Frontal process of maxilla
Medial wall
Lacrimal bone
Orbital plate of ethmoid bone
Inferior orbital fissure
Orbital process of palatine bone
Orbital surface of maxilla
Zygomatic bone
Floor of orbit

Figure 7.25

Left Orbit. Several bones compose the orbit of the eye. APR

WHAT DID YOU LEARN?

7. The hard palate is composed of what bones and their parts?
8. Identify the bones in which the paranasal sinuses are located.
9. Draw the bones of the orbital complex. What bones form the lateral wall of the orbit?

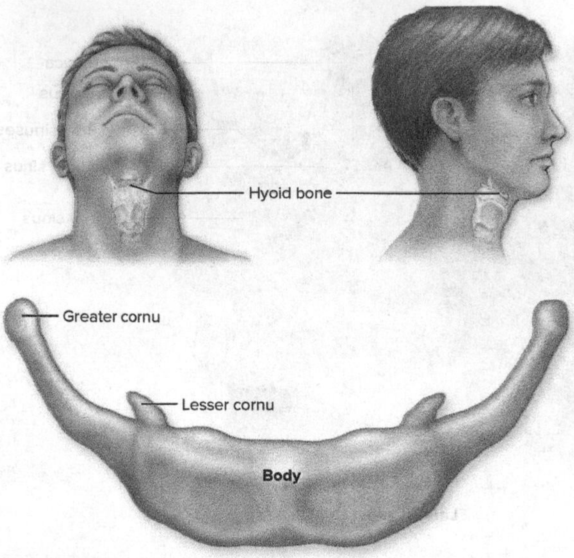
Hyoid bone
Greater cornu
Lesser cornu
Body
Hyoid bone, anterior view

Figure 7.26

Hyoid Bone. The hyoid bone is not in direct contact with any other bone of the skeleton.

7.2 Sexually Dimorphic Features of the Skull

✓ Learning Objective

7. Identify and describe the sexually dimorphic features of the skull.

As mentioned briefly in section 7.1, human male and female skulls display differences in general shape and size, a phenomenon known as *sexual dimorphism.*[1] Although typical "female" features are gracile (delicate, small), and "male" features are more robust (larger, sturdier, bulkier), human skulls vary along a continuum. **Table 7.4** summarizes the sexually dimorphic features in the skull.

It is possible to determine the genetic sex of an individual from skeletal remains by examining the skull, but there are some caveats to keep in mind. First, the features of the skull (and the remaining skeleton) vary from population to population. For example, some genetic male Asian skeletal remains may be less robust than those of, say, genetic female Native Americans. Second, each sexually dimorphic characteristic varies along a continuum. Thus, individuals within the same population and of the same genetic sex can still have some variation in the expression of these features. Further, it is difficult (and in many cases, impossible) to determine the sex of infant and juvenile remains, because skull characteristics appear female-like until well after puberty.

The most accurate method of determining sex is to look at multiple features on the skeleton and make a judgment based upon the majority of features present. For example, if a skull displays two female-like characteristics and four male-like characteristics, the skull will likely be classified as male. If your anatomy lab uses real skulls, use table 7.4 to determine the sex of the skull you are studying.

[1]For discussion of sexual dimorphism, we are using a combination of genetic sex combined with environmental factors, such as hormones, which result in the observable characteristics.

WHAT DID YOU LEARN?

10 What are some of the sexually dimorphic features of the skull?

WHAT DO YOU THINK?

1 All young adult skulls appear female-like. What factors cause some skull features to change in males by adulthood?

7.3 Aging of the Skull

✓ Learning Objective

8. Compare and contrast fetal, child, and adult skulls.

Although many centers of ossification are involved in the formation of the skull, fusion of the centers produces a smaller number of composite bones as development proceeds. For example, the ethmoid bone forms from three separate ossification centers, while the occipital bone forms from four separate ossification centers. At birth, some of these ossification centers have not yet fused, so an infant initially has two frontal bone elements, four occipital bone elements, and a number of sphenoid and temporal elements (**figure 7.27**).

The shape and structure of cranial elements differ in the skulls of infants and adults, causing variations in proportions and size. The most significant growth in the skull occurs before age 5, when the brain is still growing and exerting pressure against the internal surface of the developing skull bones. Brain growth is 90% to 95% complete by age 5, at which time cranial bone growth is also nearly complete, and the cranial sutures are almost fully developed. Early in life, the skull grows at a much faster rate than the rest of the body. Thus, a young child's cranium is relatively larger than that of an adult.

The infant's cranial bones are connected by flexible areas of dense regular connective tissue, and in some regions the brain is covered only by this connective tissue sheet, because the bones aren't yet big enough to fully surround the brain. The regions between the cranial bones are thickened, fibrous membrane remnants that are not yet ossified, called **fontanelles** (fon'tă-nel'; little spring; sometimes spelled *fontanels*). Fontanelles are sometimes referred to as the *soft spots* on a baby's head. When a baby passes through the birth canal, the cranial bones overlap at these fontanelles to ease the baby's passage. Newborns frequently have a cone-shaped head due to this temporary deformation, but by a few days after birth, the cranial bones have returned to their normal position.

The fontanelles are present until many months after birth, when skull bone growth finally starts to keep pace with brain growth. The small **mastoid** and **sphenoidal fontanelles** close relatively quickly, compared to the larger posterior and anterior fontanelles. The **posterior fontanelle** normally closes around 9 months of age, whereas the larger **anterior fontanelle** doesn't close until about 15 months of age. It is not uncommon to see rhythmic pulsations of the blood vessels internal to these fontanelles.

Although the skull may come close to its adult size by age 5, it still undergoes many more changes in subsequent years. The maxillary sinus becomes a bit more prominent beginning at age 5, and by age 10 the frontal sinus is becoming well formed. Later, the cranial sutures start to fuse and ossify. As a person ages, the teeth start to wear down from use, a process called *dental attrition.* Finally, if an individual loses some or all of his teeth, the alveolar processes of the maxillae and mandible regress, become less prominent, and eventually disappear.

WHAT DID YOU LEARN?

11 What are the two largest fontanelles, and when do they disappear?

Table 7.4 Sexually Dimorphic Features of the Skull

View	Female Skull	Male Skull
Anterior View	(photo below)	(photo below)
Lateral View	(photo below)	(photo below)

Anterior View — Female Skull

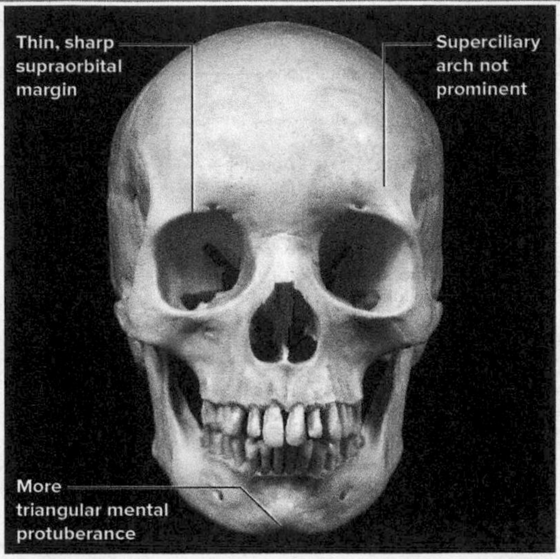
Thin, sharp supraorbital margin
Superciliary arch not prominent
More triangular mental protuberance

©McGraw-Hill Education/Christine Eckel, photographer

Anterior View — Male Skull

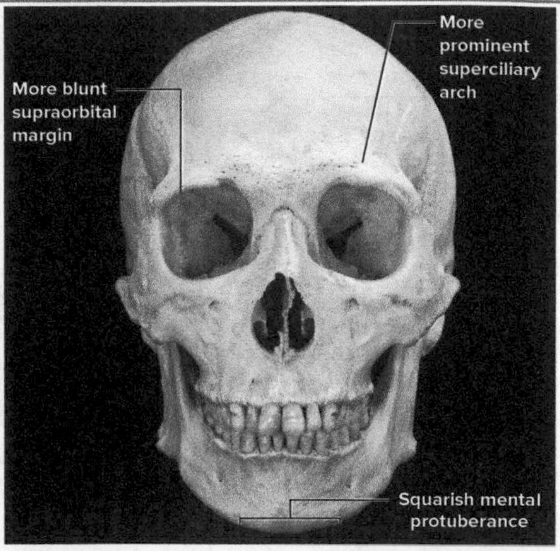
More prominent superciliary arch
More blunt supraorbital margin
Squarish mental protuberance

©McGraw-Hill Education/Christine Eckel, photographer

Lateral View — Female Skull

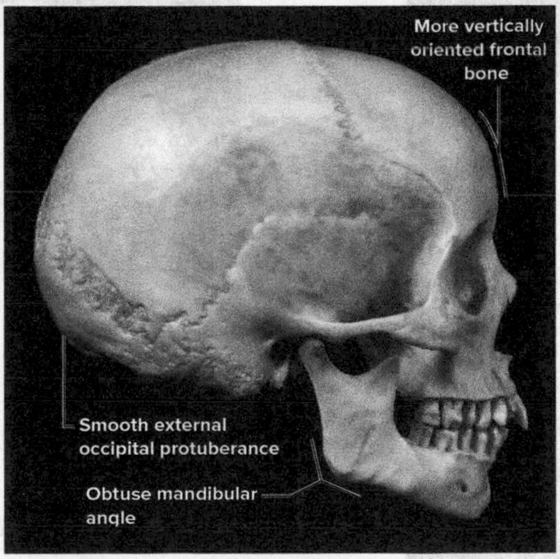
More vertically oriented frontal bone
Smooth external occipital protuberance
Obtuse mandibular angle

©McGraw-Hill Education/Christine Eckel, photographer

Lateral View — Male Skull

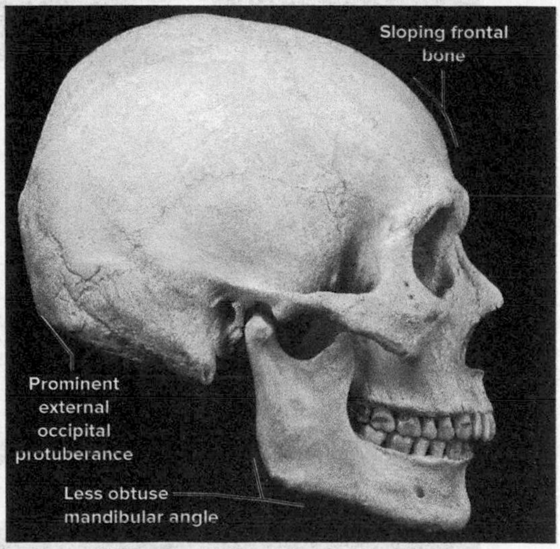
Sloping frontal bone
Prominent external occipital protuberance
Less obtuse mandibular angle

©McGraw-Hill Education/Christine Eckel, photographer

Skull Feature	Female-like Skull Characteristic	Male-like Skull Characteristic
General Size and Appearance	More gracile (delicate and small)	More robust (big and bulky), more prominent muscle markings
Nuchal Lines and External Occipital Protuberance	External surface of occipital bone is relatively smooth, with no major bony projections; external occipital protuberance typically is relatively rounded	Well-demarcated nuchal lines and typically prominent bump or "hook" for external occipital protuberance
Mastoid Process	Relatively small	Large, may project inferior to external acoustic meatus
Squamous Part of Frontal Bone	Usually more vertically oriented and rounded than in males	Exhibits a sloping angle
Supraorbital Margin	Thin, sharp border	Thick, rounded, blunt border
Superciliary Arches	Little or no prominence	More prominent and bulky
Mandible (general features)	Smaller and lighter	Larger, heavier, more robust
Mental Protuberance (chin)	More pointed and triangular-shaped, less forward projection	Squarish, more forward projection
Mandibular Angle	Typically greater than 125 degrees	Typically less obtuse and less than 125 degrees (closer to 90 degrees; angle edges may flare outward)
Sinuses	Smaller in total volume	Larger in total volume
Teeth	Relatively smaller	Relatively larger

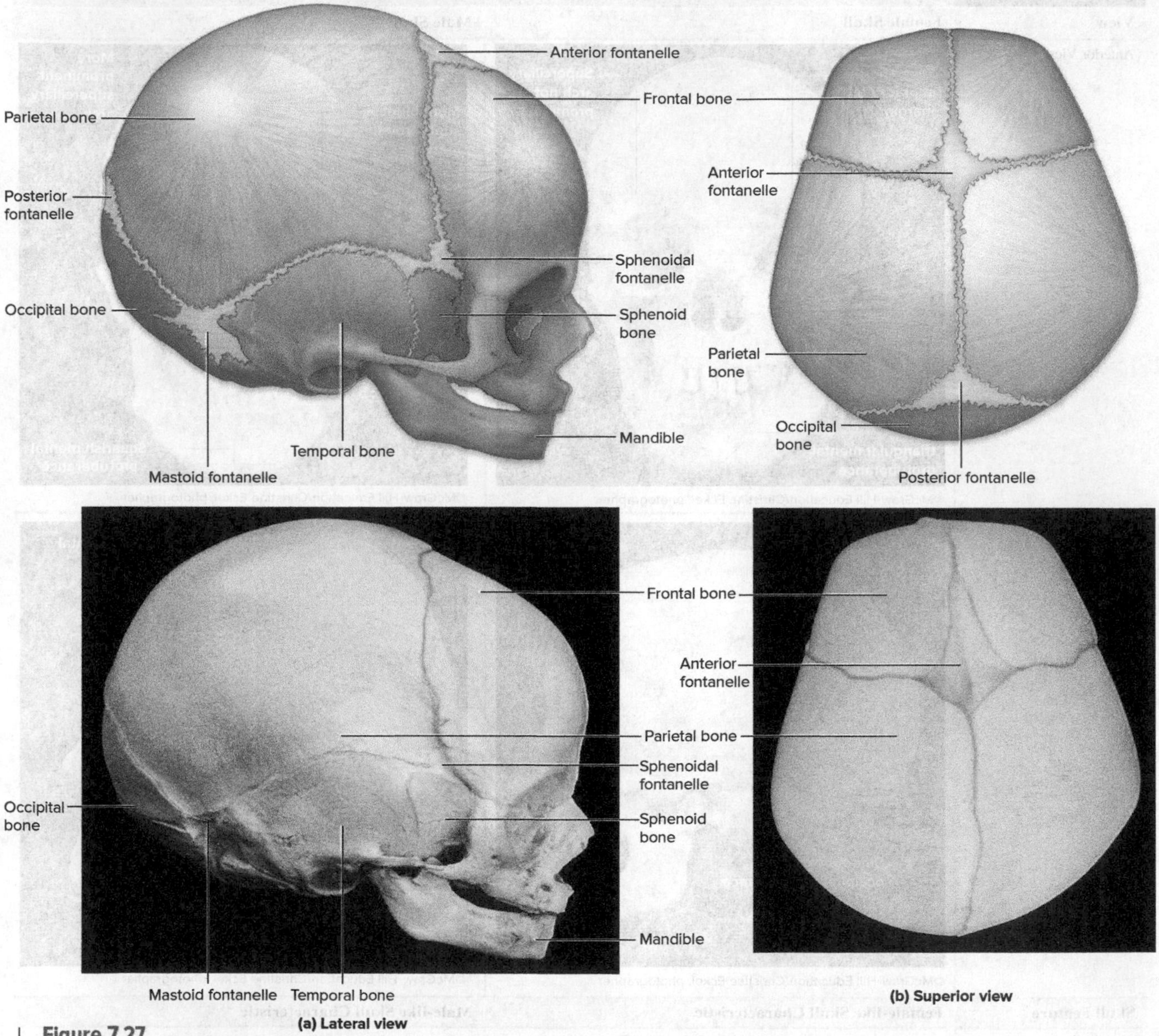
Anterior fontanelle
Frontal bone
Parietal bone
Posterior fontanelle
Sphenoidal fontanelle
Occipital bone
Sphenoid bone
Mandible
Temporal bone
Mastoid fontanelle
Anterior fontanelle
Parietal bone
Occipital bone
Posterior fontanelle
Frontal bone
Parietal bone
Sphenoidal fontanelle
Occipital bone
Sphenoid bone
Mandible
Mastoid fontanelle
Temporal bone
Frontal bone
Anterior fontanelle
(a) Lateral view
(b) Superior view

Figure 7.27

Fetal Skull. Art and photos of a fetal skull show how the flat bones are separated by fontanelles. These allow for the flexibility of the skull during birth and the growth of the brain after birth. *(a)* The mastoid and sphenoid fontanelles are best seen in lateral view, while *(b)* the anterior and posterior fontanelles are best seen in superior view.

7.4 Vertebral Column

✓ Learning Objectives

9. Describe the functions of the vertebral column.
10. Explain the general structure of the vertebral column.
11. Identify and describe the parts of a typical vertebra.
12. Compare and contrast the vertebrae from each region.

The adult **vertebral column** is composed of 26 bones, including 24 individual **vertebrae** (ver′tĕ-brē; sing., *vertebra,* ver′tĕ-bră) and the fused vertebrae that form both the sacrum and the coccyx. Each vertebra (except the first and the last) articulates with one superior vertebra and one inferior vertebra. The vertebral column has several functions:

- Provide vertical support for the body
- Support the weight of the head
- Help maintain upright body position
- Help transfer axial skeletal weight to the appendicular skeleton of the lower limbs
- House and protect the delicate spinal cord
- Provide a passageway for spinal nerves that connect to the spinal cord

7.4a Divisions of the Vertebral Column

The vertebral column is partitioned into five regions (**figure 7.28**). Vertebrae are identified by a capital letter that denotes their region, followed by a numerical subscript that indicates their sequence, going from superior to inferior:

- Seven **cervical** (ser′vī-kăl; *cervix* = neck) **vertebrae** (designated C_1–C_7) form the bones of the neck. The first cervical vertebra (C_1) articulates superiorly with the occipital condyles of the occipital bone of the skull. The seventh cervical vertebra (C_7) articulates inferiorly with the first thoracic vertebra.
- Twelve **thoracic vertebrae** (designated T_1–T_{12}) form the superior regions of the back, and each articulates laterally with one or two pairs of ribs. The twelfth thoracic vertebra articulates inferiorly with the first lumbar vertebra.
- Five **lumbar vertebrae** (L_1–L_5) form the inferior concave region ("small") of the back; L_5 articulates inferiorly with the sacrum.
- The **sacrum** (sā′krŭm) is formed from five sacral vertebrae (S_1–S_5), which fuse into a single bony structure by the mid to late 20s. The sacrum articulates with L_5 superiorly and with the first coccygeal vertebra inferiorly. In addition, the sacrum articulates laterally with the two ossa coxae (hip bones).
- The **coccyx** (kok′siks), commonly called the "tailbone," is formed from four **coccygeal vertebrae** (Co_1–Co_4) that start to unite during puberty. The first coccygeal vertebra (Co_1) articulates with the inferior end of the sacrum. When a person is much older, the coccyx may also fuse to the sacrum.

7.4b Spinal Curvatures

The vertebral column has some flexibility because it is not straight and rigid. When viewed from a lateral perspective, the adult vertebral column has four **spinal curvatures: the cervical curvature, thoracic curvature, lumbar curvature,** and **sacral curvature.** These spinal curvatures better support the weight of the body when standing than a straight spine could.

The spinal curvatures appear sequentially during fetal, newborn, and child developmental stages. The **primary curves** are the thoracic and sacral curvatures, which appear late in fetal development. These curves are also called *accommodation curves* because they accommodate the thoracic and abdominopelvic viscera. In the newborn, only these primary curves are present, and the vertebral column is C-shaped.

The **secondary curves** are the cervical and lumbar curvatures and appear after birth. These curves arch anteriorly and are also known as *compensation curves* because they help shift the trunk weight over the legs. The cervical curvature appears around 3–4 months of age, when the child is first able to hold up its head without support. The lumbar curvature appears by the first year of life, when the child is learning to stand and walk. These curves become accentuated as the child becomes more adept at walking and running.

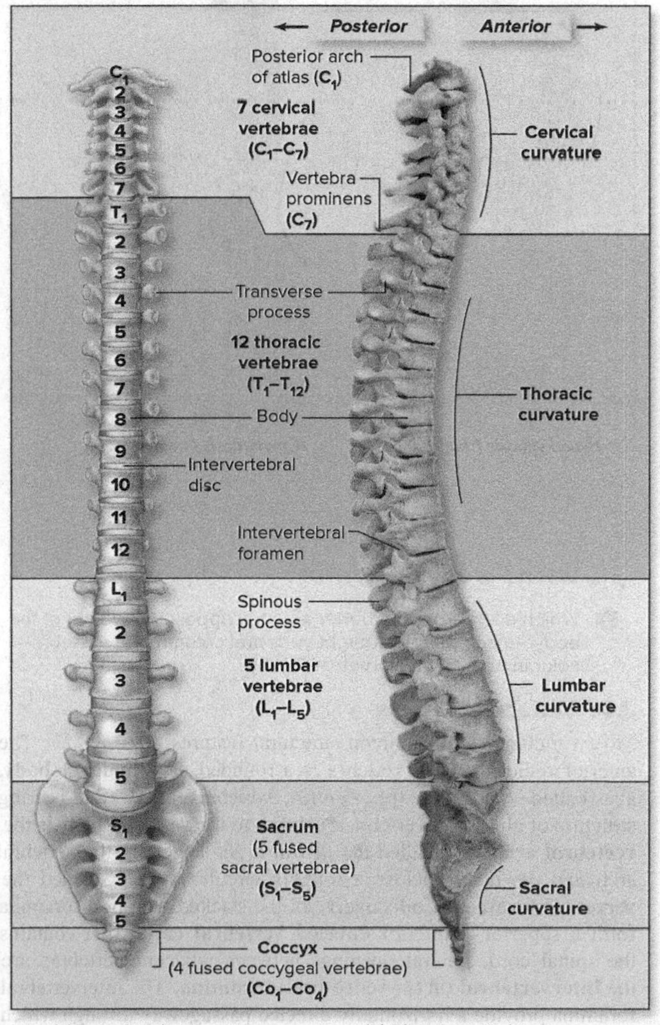

Figure 7.28
Vertebral Column. (*a*) Anterior and (*b*) right lateral views show the regions and curvatures in the vertebral column. APR

Clinical View 7.3

Spinal Curvature Abnormalities

Distortion of the normal spinal curvature may be caused by poor posture, disease, congenital defects in the structure of the vertebrae, or weakness or paralysis of muscles of the trunk. There are three main spinal curvature deformities: hyperkyphosis, hyperlordosis, and scoliosis.

Hyperkyphosis (kī-fō′sis) is an exaggerated thoracic curvature that is directed posteriorly, producing a "hunchback" look. Hyperkyphosis often results from osteoporosis, but it also occurs in individuals who experience any of the following: a vertebral compression fracture that affects the anterior region of the vertebral column, osteomalacia (a disease in which adult bones become demineralized), heavy weight lifting during adolescence, abnormal vertebral growth, or chronic contractions in muscles that insert on the vertebrae.

Hyperlordosis (lōr-dō′sis) is an exaggerated lumbar curvature, often called *swayback*, that is noted as a protrusion of the abdomen and buttocks. Hyperlordosis may have the same causes as hyperkyphosis, or it may result from the added abdominal weight associated with pregnancy or obesity.

Scoliosis (skō-lē-ō′sis) is the most common spinal curvature deformity. It is an abnormal lateral curvature of the spine that may develop during puberty, or rarely during fetal development when both the vertebral arch and body fail to form, or form incompletely, on one side of a vertebra. It can also be caused by unilateral muscular paralysis, or spasm, in the back, but most cases of scoliosis are idiopathic (i.e., the cause is not known). Mild cases of scoliosis may be treated in adolescence by wearing a back brace, whereas more severe cases may require surgical intervention. APR

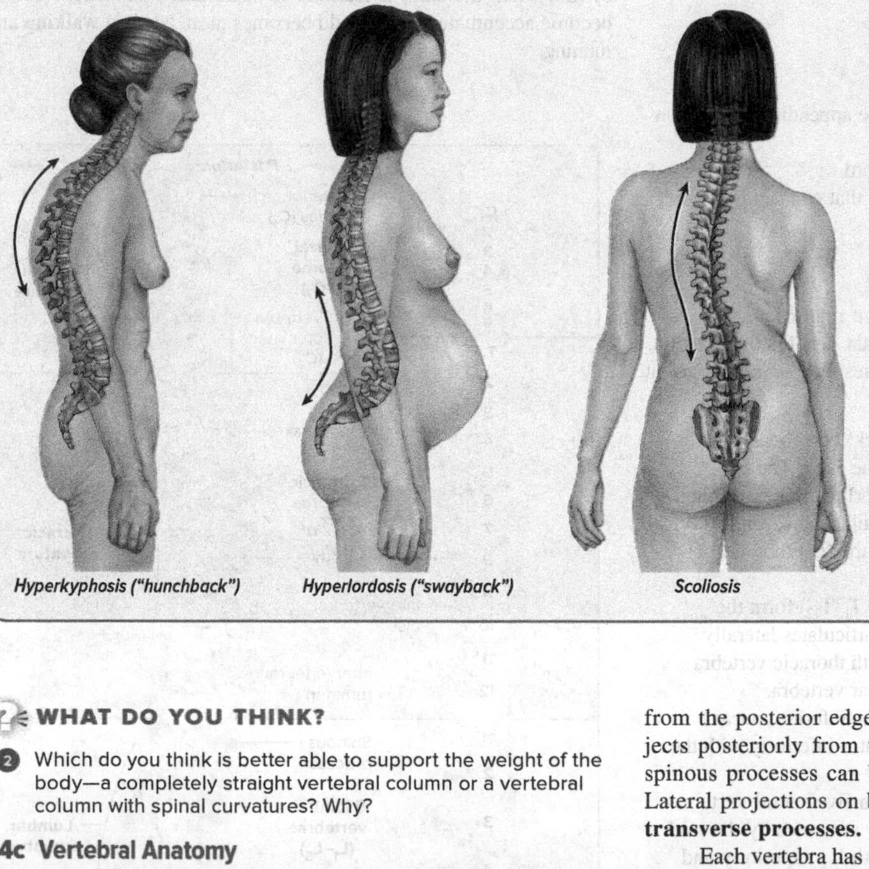

Hyperkyphosis ("hunchback") *Hyperlordosis ("swayback")* *Scoliosis*

WHAT DO YOU THINK?

2 Which do you think is better able to support the weight of the body—a completely straight vertebral column or a vertebral column with spinal curvatures? Why?

7.4c Vertebral Anatomy

Most vertebrae share common structural features (**figure 7.29**). The anterior region of each vertebra is a rounded or cylindrical **body,** also called a *centrum* (pl., *centra*), which is the weight-bearing structure of almost all vertebra. Posterior to the vertebral body is the **vertebral arch,** also called the *neural arch.* Together, the vertebral arch and the body enclose a roughly circular opening called the **vertebral foramen.** Collectively, all the stacked vertebral foramina form a superior-to-inferior directed **vertebral canal** that contains the spinal cord. Lateral openings between adjacent vertebrae are the **intervertebral** (in′tĕr-ver′tĕ-brăl) **foramina.** The intervertebral foramina provide a horizontally directed passageway through which spinal nerves travel to other parts of the body (see section 16.4).

The vertebral arch is composed of two pedicles and two laminae. The **pedicles** (ped′ī-kĕl; *pes* = foot) originate from the posterolateral margins of the body, whereas the **laminae** (lam′i-n ē; sing., *lamina,* lam′i-n ă; layer) extend posteromedially from the posterior edge of each pedicle. A **spinous process** projects posteriorly from the left and right laminae. Most of these spinous processes can be palpated through the skin of the back. Lateral projections on both sides of the vertebral arch are called **transverse processes.**

Each vertebra has **articular processes** on both its superior and inferior surfaces that project from the junction between the pedicles and laminae. The **inferior articular processes** of each vertebra articulate with the **superior articular processes** of the vertebra immediately inferior to it. Each articular process has a smooth surface, called an **articular facet** (fas′et, f ă-set′). The angles of these facets differ along the length of the vertebral column contributing to different movements along the vertebral column.

The vertebral bodies are interconnected by ligaments. Adjacent vertebral bodies are separated by pads of fibrocartilage called the **intervertebral discs.** Intervertebral discs are composed of an outer ring of fibrocartilage, called the **anulus fibrosus** (an′ū-lŭs fī-brō′sŭs), and an inner circular region, called the **nucleus pulposus.** The nucleus pulposus has a high water content, giving it a gelatinous consistency. Intervertebral discs make up about one-quarter of the entire vertebral column. They act as shock absorbers between the vertebral bodies, and also allow the vertebral

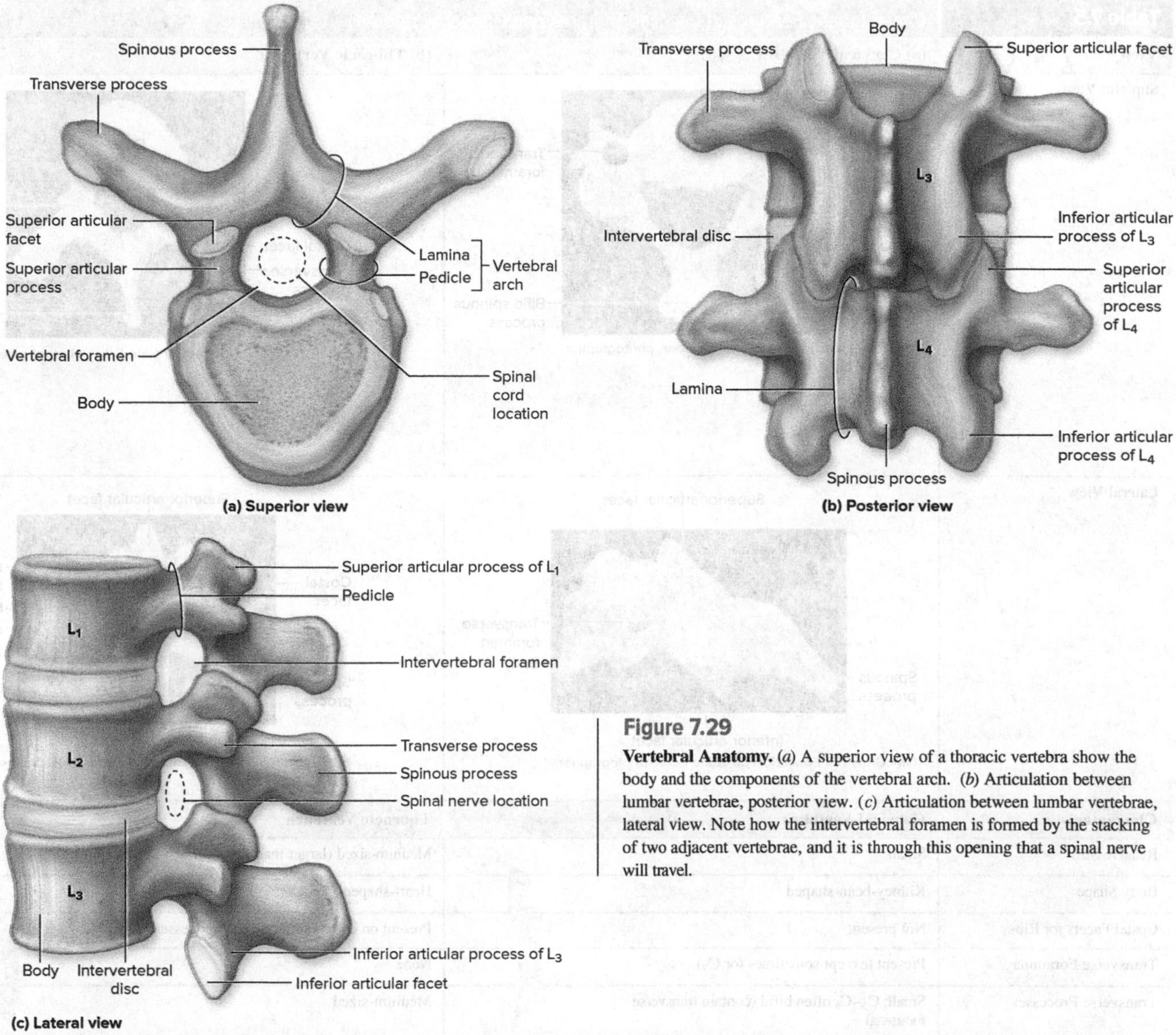

Figure 7.29

Vertebral Anatomy. (*a*) A superior view of a thoracic vertebra show the body and the components of the vertebral arch. (*b*) Articulation between lumbar vertebrae, posterior view. (*c*) Articulation between lumbar vertebrae, lateral view. Note how the intervertebral foramen is formed by the stacking of two adjacent vertebrae, and it is through this opening that a spinal nerve will travel.

column to bend. For example, when you bend your torso anteriorly, the intervertebral discs are compressed at the bending (anterior) surface and pushed out toward the opposite (posterior) surface.

Intervertebral discs are able to withstand a certain amount of compression. Over the course of a day, as body weight and gravity act on the vertebral column, the intervertebral discs become compressed and flattened. But while a person sleeps, lying horizontally, the intervertebral discs are able to spring back to their original shape.

In general, the vertebrae are smallest near the skull, and become gradually larger moving inferiorly through the body trunk as weight bearing increases. Thus, the cervical vertebrae are the smallest, followed by the thoracic, lumbar, and sacral vertebrae. Also, the vertebral foramen is largest in the cervical vertebrae and smallest in the sacral vertebrae.

Although vertebrae are divided into regions, there are no anatomically discrete "cutoffs" between the regions. For example, the most inferior cervical vertebra has some structural similarities to the most superior thoracic vertebra, as the two vertebrae are adjacent to one another. Likewise, the most inferior thoracic vertebra may look similar to the first lumbar vertebra. Despite this, there are basic characteristics that distinguish different types of vertebrae. We discuss these characteristics in the next sections. **Table 7.5** compares the characteristics of the cervical, thoracic, and lumbar vertebrae.

Cervical Vertebrae

The cervical vertebrae, C_1–C_7, are the most superiorly placed vertebrae (table 7.5*a*). They extend inferiorly from the occipital bone of the skull through the neck to the thorax. Because cervical vertebrae support only the weight of the head, their vertebral bodies are relatively small and light.

The body of a typical cervical vertebra (C_3–C_6) is relatively small compared to its foramen. The superior surface of a cervical

Table 7.5 Characteristic Features of Cervical, Thoracic, and Lumbar Vertebrae

View	(a) Cervical Vertebra	(b) Thoracic Vertebra
Superior View	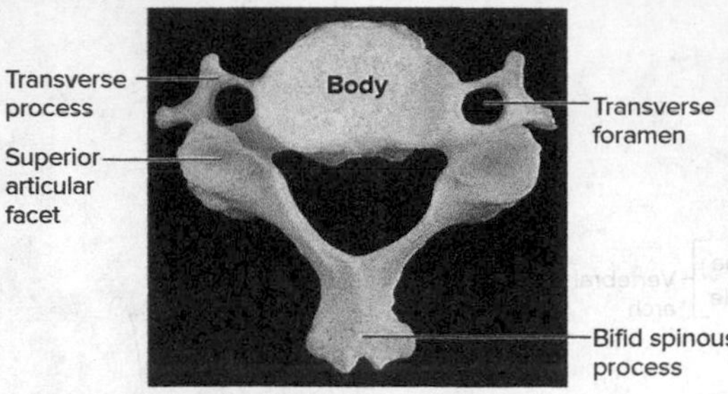 ©McGraw-Hill Education/Christine Eckel, photographer	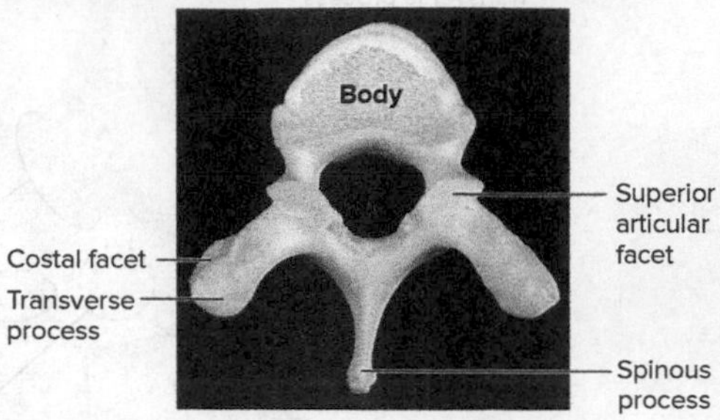 ©McGraw-Hill Education/Christine Eckel, photographer
Lateral View	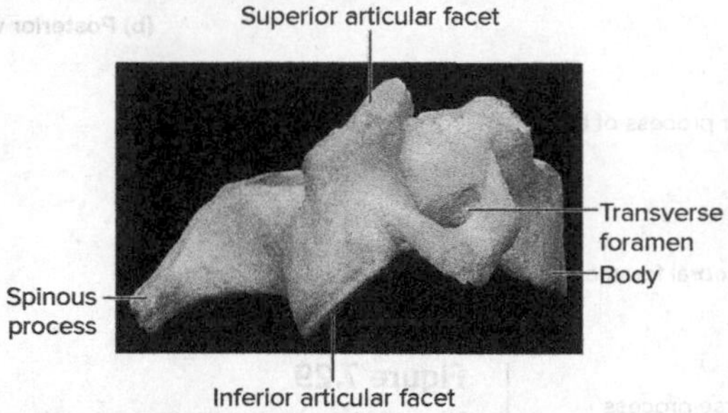 ©McGraw-Hill Education/Christine Eckel, photographer	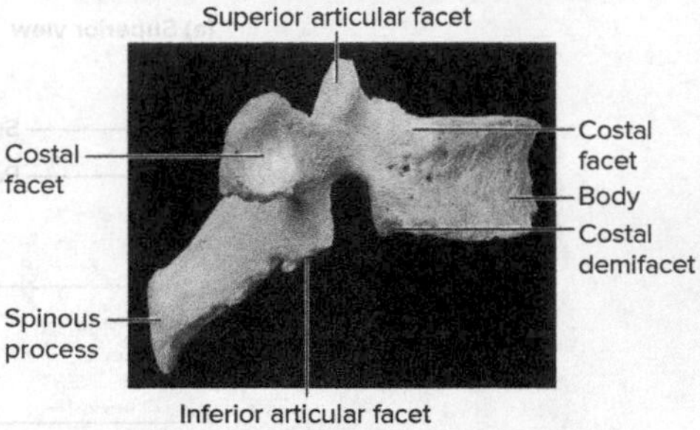 ©McGraw-Hill Education/Christine Eckel, photographer

Characteristic	Cervical Vertebra	Thoracic Vertebra
Relative Size	Small	Medium-sized (larger than cervical)
Body Shape	Kidney-bean-shaped	Heart-shaped
Costal Facets for Ribs	Not present	Present on body and transverse processes
Transverse Foramina	Present (except sometimes for C_7)	None
Transverse Processes	Small: C_3–C_6 often bifid (contain transverse foramina)	Medium-sized
Angle of Articular Facets		
1. Inferior	1. Anteroinferior	1. Anteromedial
2. Superior	2. Posterosuperior	2. Posterolateral
Spinous Process	Slender: C_2–C_6 are often bifid (Note: C_1 has no spinous process)	Long; most project inferiorly

vertebral body is concave from side to side, and it exhibits a superior slope from the posterior edge to the anterior edge. The spinous process is relatively short, usually less than the diameter of the vertebral foramen. The tip of each process, other than C_7, is usually bifurcated (bifid), meaning that the posterior end of the spinous process appears to be split in two. The transverse processes of the first six (and sometimes the seventh) cervical vertebrae are unique in that they contain prominent, round **transverse foramina,** which provide a protective bony passageway for the vertebral arteries and veins supplying the brain.

The head is a large, heavy structure that is precariously balanced upon the cervical vertebrae. Small muscles keep the head stable. However, if the body changes position suddenly—for example, due to a fall or the impact from a car crash—these "balancing" muscles cannot stabilize the head. A cervical dislocation called **whiplash** may result, characterized by injury to muscles and ligaments and potential injury to the spinal cord.

Atlas (C_1) The first cervical vertebra, called the **atlas** (at′las), supports the head via its articulation with the occipital condyles of the

(c) Lumbar Vertebra

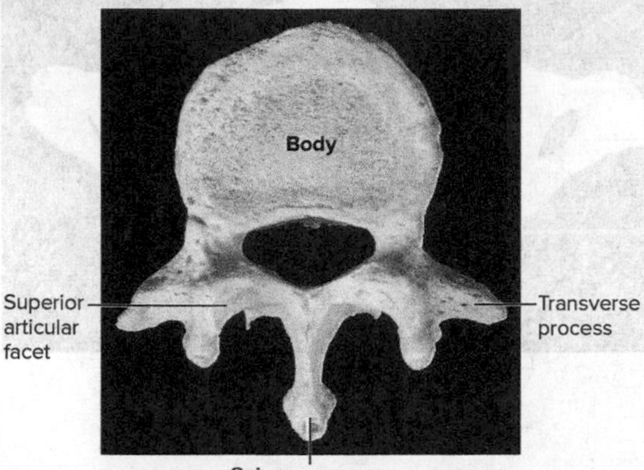

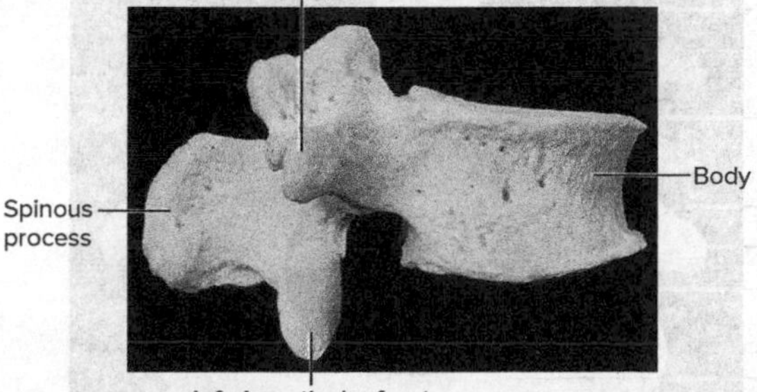

Lumbar Vertebra
Large (larger than thoracic)
Large, round or oval
Not present
None
Large, thick and blunt
1. Lateral
2. Medial
Short (thick and blunt); project posteriorly

occipital bone. This vertebra is named for the Greek mythological figure Atlas, who carried the world on his shoulders. The articulation between the occipital condyles and the atlas, called the atlanto-occipital joint, permits us to nod our heads "yes." The atlas is readily distinguished from the other vertebrae because it lacks a body and a spinous process. Instead, the atlas has lateral masses that are connected by semicircular **anterior** and **posterior arches,** each containing slight protuberances, the **anterior** and **posterior tubercles** (tū'bĕr-kĕl) (**figure 7.30*a***). The atlas has depressed, oval **superior articular facets** that articulate with the occipital condyles of the skull. The atlas also has **inferior articular facets** that articulate with the superior articular facets of the axis. Finally, the atlas has an **articular facet for dens** on its anterior arch where it articulates with the dens of the axis. APR

Axis (C_2) During development, the body of the atlas fuses to the body of the second cervical vertebra, called the **axis** (ak'sis) (figure 7.30 *b*). This fusion produces the most distinctive feature of the axis, the prominent **dens,** or *odontoid* (ō-don'toyd; *odont* = tooth) *process.* The dens rests in the articular facet for dens of the atlas, where it is held in place by a transverse ligament. The dens acts as a pivot for the rotation of both the atlas and the skull. This articulation between the atlas and axis, called the *atlantoaxial joint,* permits us to shake our heads "no" (figure 7.30*c*).

Because both the dens and the spinal cord occupy the vertebral foramen at the level of the axis, any trauma that dislocates the dens often results in severe injury. For example, an impact to the head or even severe shaking of a child can dislocate the dens and cause severe damage to the spinal cord. In an adult, a severe blow at or near the base of the skull is often equally dangerous because dislocation of the atlantoaxial joint can force the dens into the base of the brain, with fatal results. APR

Vertebra Prominens (C_7) The seventh cervical vertebra represents a transition to the thoracic vertebral region and has some features of thoracic vertebrae. The spinous process of C_7 is typically not bifurcated, and it is much larger and longer than the spinous processes of the other cervical vertebrae. This large spinous process is easily discerned and palpated through the skin, sometimes appearing as a slight protrusion between the shoulder blades and inferior to the neck (see section 13.4c). Thus, C_7 is called the **vertebra prominens** (prom'i-nens; prominent). If you drop your head forward (place your chin to your chest) and run your fingers down the back of your neck, it is the first bony lump you feel. APR

Thoracic Vertebrae

There are 12 thoracic vertebrae, designated T_1–T_{12}, and each vertebra articulates with the ribs (table 7.5*b*). The thoracic vertebrae lack the mobility of the other vertebrae due to their stabilizing articulation with the ribs. The thoracic vertebrae also lack the transverse foramina and bifid spinous processes of the cervical vertebrae, but they have their own distinctive characteristics. A thoracic vertebra has a heart-shaped body that is larger and more massive than the body of a cervical vertebra. Its spinous process is relatively pointed and long; in some thoracic vertebrae, it angles sharply in an inferior direction.

Thoracic vertebrae are distinguished from all other types of vertebrae by the presence of **costal facets** or **costal demifacets** (dem'ē; half) on the lateral side of the body and on the sides of the transverse processes. A costal facet is a circular depression that articulates with the entire head or tubercle of the rib, and a costal demifacet is a semicircular depression that articulates with either the superior or inferior edge of the head of the rib. The head of the rib articulates with the costal facet on the body of the thoracic vertebra. The tubercle of the rib articulates with the costal facets on the transverse processes of the vertebra.

The thoracic vertebrae vary slightly in terms of their transverse costal facets. Vertebrae T_1–T_{10} have transverse costal facets on their transverse processes; T_{11} and T_{12} lack these transverse costal facets because the eleventh and twelfth ribs do not have

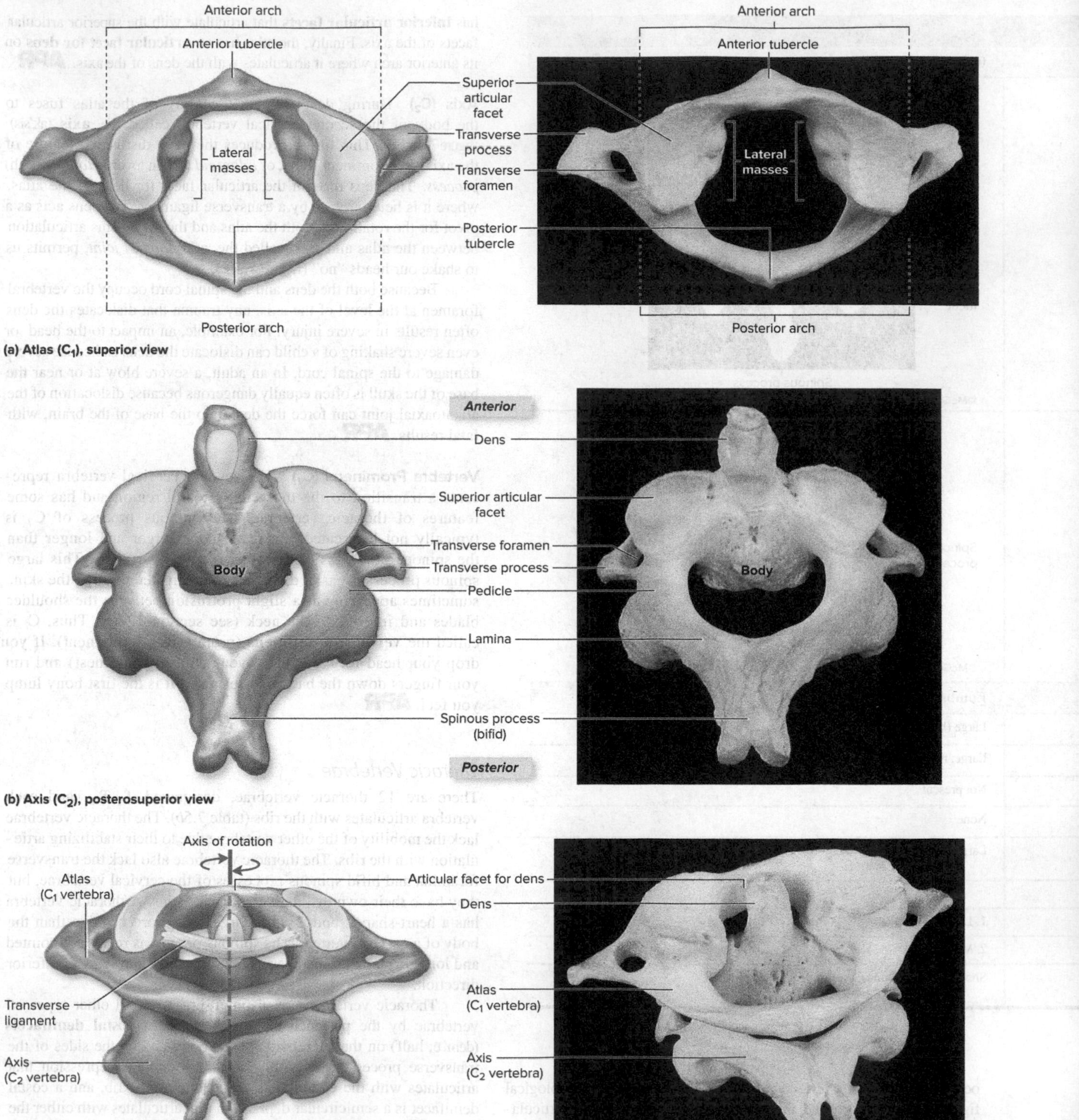

Figure 7.30

Cervical Vertebrae C_1 and C_2. The atlas (C_1) and the axis (C_2) differ in structure from a typical cervical vertebra, and are shown here in both art and photos. (*a*) Superior view of the atlas illustrates its lack of a body and spinous process. (*b*) The dens of the axis is best seen in posterosuperior view. (*c*) The articulation of the atlas and axis, called the atlantoaxial joint, allows for a rotational movement of the head, as when you shake your head "no."

Clinical View 7.4

Herniated Discs

A **herniated** (her'nē-āt'ĕd) **disc** occurs when the gelatinous nucleus pulposus protrudes into or through the anulus fibrosus. This herniation produces a "bulging" of the disc posterolaterally into the vertebral canal and pinches the spinal cord and/or nerves of the spinal cord. The cervical and lumbar intervertebral discs are the most common discs to be injured, because the vertebral column has a great deal of mobility in these regions, and the lumbar region bears increased weight. Cervical herniated discs can cause neck pain and pain down the upper limb, as the nerves that supply the upper limb originate in this region of the spinal cord. Lumbar herniated discs frequently cause low back pain. If the herniated lumbar disc starts to pinch nerve fibers, the patient may feel pain down the entire lower limb, a condition known as **sciatica** (see Clinical View 16.4: "Sacral Plexus Nerve Injuries" in section 16.5 for further information).

Treatment options for a herniated disc include nonsteroidal anti-inflammatory drugs (NSAIDs), steroid drugs, and physical therapy. Surgical treatments include **microdiscectomy,** a microsurgical technique whereby the herniated portion of the disc is removed, or **discectomy,** a more invasive technique in which the laminae of the nearby vertebrae and the back muscles are incised before removing the herniated portions of the disc.

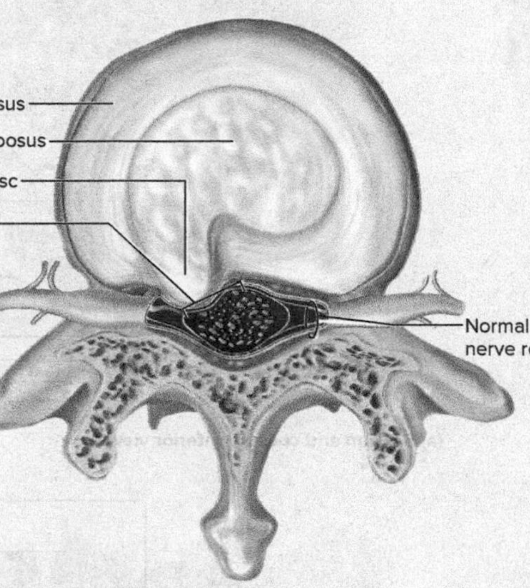
Anulus fibrosus
Nucleus pulposus
Herniated disc
Pinched left nerve roots
Normal right nerve roots

Superior view of a herniated disc.

tubercles (and thus do not articulate with the transverse processes). The costal facets on the *bodies* of the thoracic vertebrae also display variations:

- The body of vertebra T_1 bears a full costal facet for the first rib and a demifacet for the second rib.
- The bodies of vertebrae T_2–T_8 have two demifacets each: one on the superior edge of the body, and the other on the inferior edge of the body.
- The body of vertebra T_9 has only a superior demifacet for the articulation with the ninth rib.
- The bodies of vertebrae T_{10}–T_{12} have a single whole facet to articulate with their respective ribs. APR

Lumbar Vertebrae

The largest vertebrae are the lumbar vertebrae, and they bear most of the weight of the body. A typical lumbar vertebra body is thicker than those of all the other vertebrae, and its superior and inferior surfaces are oval or round, rather than heart-shaped (table 7.5*c*). The lumbar vertebrae are distinguished by the features they lack: A lumbar vertebra has neither transverse foramina nor costal facets. The transverse processes are thin and project dorsolaterally. The spinous processes are thick and project posteriorly, unlike the thoracic vertebrae spinous processes, which are long, slender, and point posteroinferiorly. APR

WHAT DO YOU THINK?

3 You are given a vertebra to identify. It has transverse foramina and a bifid spinous process. Is this a cervical, thoracic, or lumbar vertebra?

Sacrum

The sacrum is an anteriorly curved, somewhat triangular bone that forms the posterior wall of the pelvic cavity. The **apex** of the sacrum is a narrow, pointed portion of the bone that projects inferiorly, whereas the bone's broad superior surface forms its **base.** The lateral sacral curvature typically is more pronounced in males than in females.

The sacrum is composed of the five fused sacral vertebrae (**figure 7.31**). These vertebrae start to fuse shortly after puberty and are usually completely fused between ages 20 and 30. The horizontal lines of fusion that remain are called **transverse ridges.** Superiorly, the sacrum articulates with L_5 via a pair of **superior articular processes,** and inferiorly it articulates with the coccyx. The vertebral canal becomes much narrower and continues through the sacrum as the **sacral canal.** The sacral canal terminates in an inferior opening called the **sacral hiatus** (hī-ā'tŭs; *hio* = to yawn). The sacral hiatus represents an area where the laminae of the last sacral vertebra failed to fuse. On either side of the sacral hiatus are bony projections called the **sacral cornua.**

The anterosuperior edge of the first sacral vertebra bulges anteriorly into the pelvic cavity and is called the **promontory.** Four anterior lines cross the anterior surface of the sacrum, marking the lines of fusion of the sacral vertebrae. The paired **anterior sacral foramina** permit the passage of nerves to the pelvic organs. A dorsal ridge, termed the **median sacral crest,** is formed by the fusion of the spinous processes of individual sacral vertebrae. Also on the dorsal surface of the sacrum are four pairs of openings for spinal nerves, called the **posterior sacral foramina.** On each lateral surface of the sacrum is the **ala** (meaning "wing"). On the lateral surface of the ala is the **auricular surface,** which marks the site of articulation with the os coxae of the pelvic girdle, forming the strong **sacroiliac** (sā'krō-il'ē-ak) **joint** (see section 9.5c).

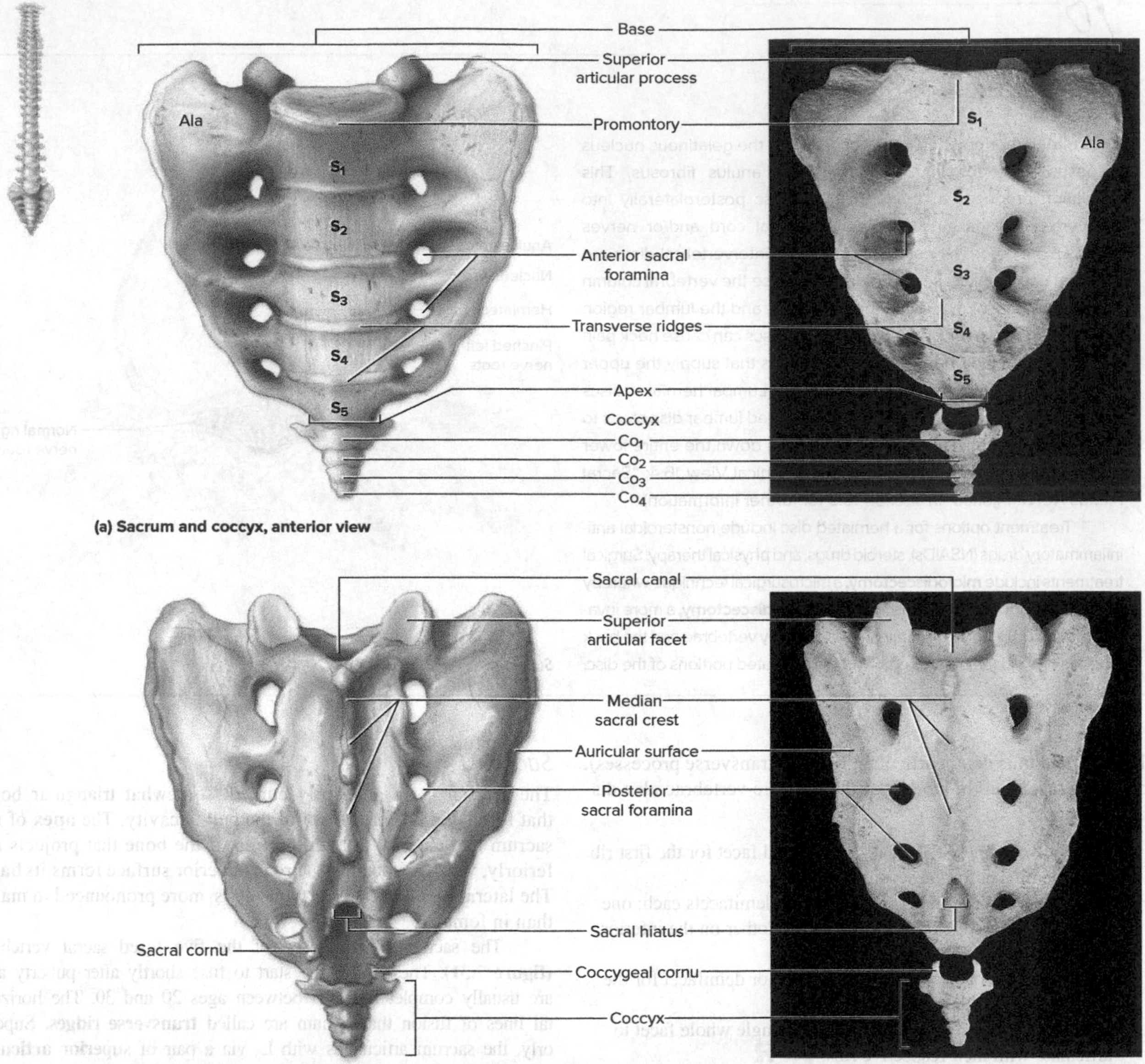

Base
Superior articular process
Ala
Promontory
S_1
S_2
Anterior sacral foramina
S_3
Transverse ridges
S_4
S_5
Apex
Coccyx
Co_1
Co_2
Co_3
Co_4
(a) Sacrum and coccyx, anterior view
Sacral canal
Superior articular facet
Median sacral crest
Auricular surface
Posterior sacral foramina
Sacral hiatus
Sacral cornu
Coccygeal cornu
Coccyx
(b) Sacrum and coccyx, posterior view

Figure 7.31

Sacrum and Coccyx. The sacrum is formed by the fusion of five sacral vertebrae, and the coccyx is formed by the fusion of four coccygeal vertebrae. (*a*) Anterior and (*b*) posterior views show the sacrum and the coccyx in both art and photo s. APR

Coccyx

Four small coccygeal vertebrae fuse to form the **coccyx** (figure 7.31 *a*). The individual vertebrae begin to fuse by about age 25. The coccyx is an attachment site for several ligaments and some muscles. The first and second coccygeal vertebrae have unfused vertebral arches and transverse processes. The prominent laminae of the first coccygeal vertebrae are known as the **coccygeal cornua,** which curve to meet the sacral cornua. Fusion of the coccygeal vertebrae is not complete until adulthood. In males, the coccyx tends to project anteriorly, but in females it tends to project more inferiorly, so as not to obstruct the birth canal. In very old individuals, the coccyx may fuse with the sacrum.

WHAT DID YOU LEARN?

12. Draw a typical vertebra. What characteristics are common to most vertebrae?
13. Make your own table that lists the characteristic features of cervical, thoracic, and lumbar vertebrae.
14. Compare the locations and functions of transverse foramina, intervertebral foramina, and the vertebral foramen.

7.5 Thoracic Cage

✓ Learning Objective

13. Describe the general structure of the sternum.
14. Describe the features of a typical rib, and distinguish among true, false, and floating ribs.
15. Explain how a rib articulates with a thoracic vertebra.

The bony framework of the chest is called the **thoracic cage;** it consists of the thoracic vertebrae posteriorly, the ribs laterally, and the sternum anteriorly (**figure 7.32**). The thoracic cage acts as a protective framework around vital organs, including the heart, lungs, trachea, and esophagus. It also provides attachment points for many muscles supporting the pectoral girdles (the bones that hold the upper limb in place), the chest, the neck, the shoulders, the back, and the muscles involved in respiration.

7.5a Sternum

The adult **sternum** (ster′nŭm; *sternon* = the chest), also called the *breastbone,* is a flat bone that forms in the anterior midline of the thoracic wall. Its shape has been likened to that of a sword. The sternum is composed of three parts: the manubrium, the body, and the xiphoid process.

The **manubrium** (mă-nū′brē-ŭm) is the widest and most superior portion of the sternum (the "handle" of the bony sword). Two **clavicular notches** articulate the sternum with the left and right clavicles. The shallow superior indentation between the clavicular notches is called the **suprasternal notch** (or *jugular notch*). A single pair of **costal notches** represent articulations for the first ribs' costal cartilages.

The **body** (or *gladiolus*) is the longest part of the sternum and forms its bulk (the "blade" of the bony sword). Individual costal cartilages from ribs 2–7 are attached to the body at indented articular costal notches. The body and the manubrium articulate at the **sternal angle,** a horizontal ridge that may be palpated under the skin. The sternal angle is an important landmark in that the costal cartilages of the second ribs attach there; thus, it may be used to count the ribs.

The **xiphoid** (zi′foyd; *xiphos* = sword) **process** represents the very tip of the sword blade. This small, inferiorly pointed projection is cartilaginous and often doesn't ossify until after age 40. The connection of the xiphoid process to the body of the sternum may be broken by an impact or strong pressure. The resulting internal projection of bone can severely damage the heart or liver.

7.5b Ribs

The ribs are elongated, curved, flat bones that articulate (connect) with the thoracic vertebrae and end in the anterior wall of the thorax (figure 7.32). Both males and females have the same number of ribs—12 pairs. Ribs 1–7 are called **true ribs.** At the anterior body wall, the true ribs articulate individually to the sternum by separate cartilaginous extensions called **costal** (kos′tăl; *costa* = rib) **cartilages.** The smallest true rib is the first.

Ribs 8–12 are called **false ribs** because their costal cartilages do not attach directly to the sternum. The costal cartilages of ribs 8–10 fuse to the costal cartilage of rib 7 and thus indirectly articulate with the sternum. The last two pairs of false ribs (ribs 11 and 12) are called **floating ribs** because they have no connection with the sternum.

The vertebral end of a typical rib articulates with the vertebral column at the **head** (or *capitulum*). The articular surface of the head is divided into **superior** and **inferior articular facets** by an interarticular **crest** (**figure 7.33*a***). The surfaces of these facets articulate with the costal facets on the bodies of the thoracic vertebrae. The **neck** of the rib lies between the head and the tubercle. The **tubercle** (or *tuberculum*) of the rib has an articular facet for the costal facet on the transverse process of the thoracic vertebra. Figure 7.33*b*, *c* illustrates how most of the ribs articulate with the thoracic vertebrae. Rib 1 articulates with vertebra T_1. The head of the rib articulates at a costal facet on the body, and the tubercle of the rib articulates at a transverse costal facet on the transverse process of T_1.

Ribs 2–9 articulate with vertebrae T_2–T_9. Each of these vertebrae has two demifacets on the lateral side of its body. The superior articular facet on the head of the rib articulates with the more superior vertebra, and the inferior articular facet articulates with the more

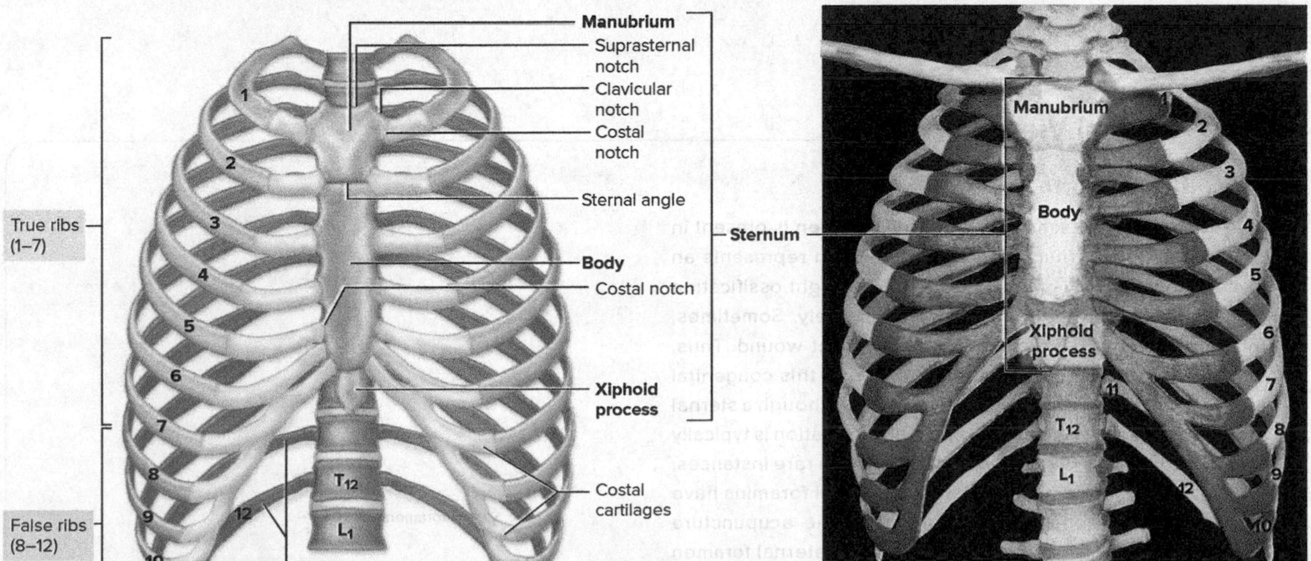

Figure 7.32

Thoracic Cage. Drawing and photograph show anterior views of the bones of the thoracic cage, which protect and enclose the organs in the thoracic cavity. APR

©McGraw-Hill Education/Christine Eckel, photographer

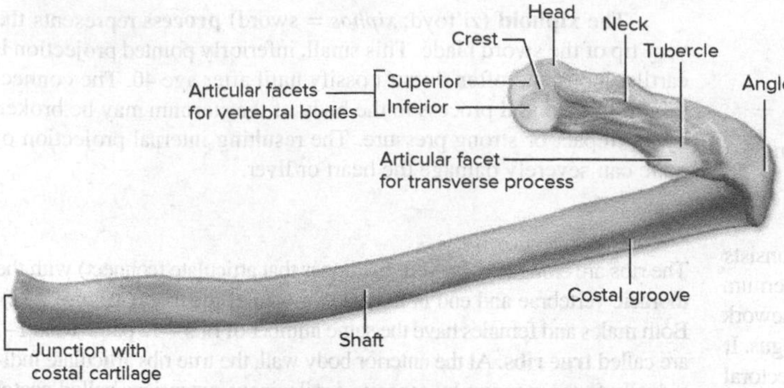

(a) Rib

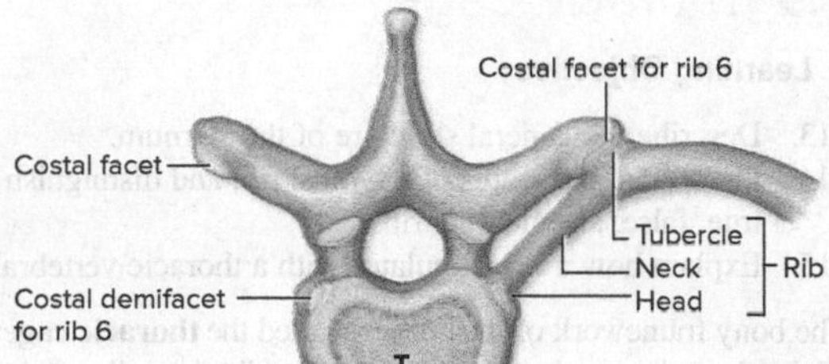

(b) Superior view

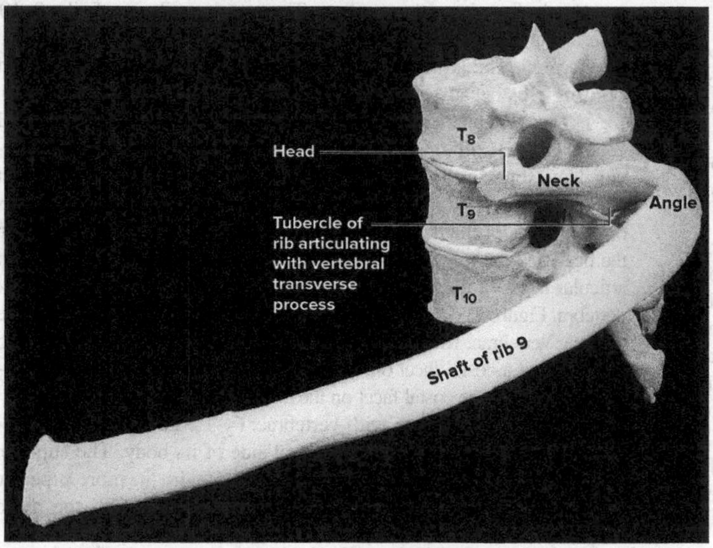

(c) Lateral view

Figure 7.33
Rib Anatomy and Articulation with Thoracic Vertebrae. Paired ribs attach to thoracic vertebrae posteriorly and extend anteroinferiorly to the anterior chest wall. (*a*) Features of ribs 2–10. (*b*) Superior and (*c*) lateral views show the articulation of a rib with a vertebra.
©McGraw-Hill Education/Christine Eckel, photographer

Clinical View 7.5

Sternal Foramen

In 4–10% of all adults, a midline **sternal foramen** is present in the body of the sternum. The sternal foramen represents an ossification anomaly—failure of the left and right ossification centers of the sternal body to fuse completely. Sometimes, this opening may be misidentified as a bullet wound. Thus, a crime scene investigator must be aware of this congenital anomaly when examining skeletal remains. Although a sternal foramen is usually clinically insignificant, its location is typically that of a commonly used acupuncture point. In rare instances, individuals with previously undetected sternal foramina have died after an acupuncture session, when the acupuncture needle was unwittingly inserted through the sternal foramen into the heart.

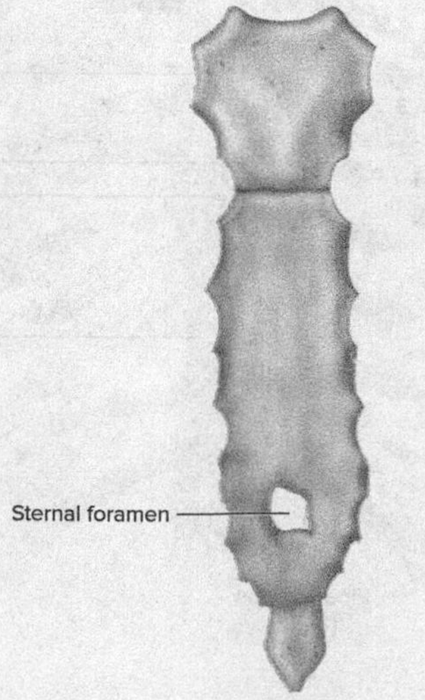

Location of a sternal foramen.

inferior vertebra. For example, the superior articular facet on the head of rib 2 articulates with the inferior costal demifacet on the body of T_1, and the inferior articular facet on the head of rib 2 articulates with the superior costal demifacet on the body of T_2. The tubercle of each rib articulates with the transverse costal facet on the transverse process of the corresponding vertebra. For example, the tubercle of rib 3 articulates with the transverse costal facet on the transverse process of T_3.

Ribs 10–12 articulate with vertebrae T_{10}–T_{12}. Each of these vertebrae has a whole costal facet on the lateral body to articulate with the head of its respective rib. Vertebra T_{10} also has transverse costal facets on its transverse processes to articulate with the tubercle of each rib 10. Ribs 11 and 12 do not have tubercles, so there are no costal facets on the transverse processes of T_{11} and T_{12}.

The **angle** (*border*) of the rib indicates the site where the tubular **shaft** (or *body*) begins curving anteriorly toward the sternum. A prominent **costal groove** along its inferior internal border marks the path of intercostal nerves and blood vessels to the thoracic wall (see section 16.4c).

WHAT DID YOU LEARN?

15 What are the three components of the sternum, and what ribs articulate directly with the sternum?

16 What parts of a rib articulate with a vertebra, and how do they articulate?

7.6 Aging of the Axial Skeleton

✓Learning Objective

16. Explain how the axial skeleton changes as we grow, mature, and age.

The general changes in the axial skeleton that take place with age have been described throughout this chapter. As mentioned before, many bones fuse when we age. Also, skeletal mass and density become reduced, and bones often become more porous and brittle, a condition known as osteoporosis (see Clinical View 6.6: "Osteoporosis," in section 6.7). Osteoporotic bones are susceptible to fracture, which is why elderly individuals are at greater risk for bone fractures.

In addition, articulating surfaces deteriorate, contributing to arthritic conditions. Whereas a younger individual has smooth, well-formed articular surfaces, those of an older individual may be rough, worn away, or covered with bony, spurlike growths, making movement at these surfaces painful and difficult. These changes begin in early childhood and continue throughout life.

WHAT DID YOU LEARN?

17 How do the articulating surfaces of bones change as we age?

7.7 Development of the Axial Skeleton

✓Learning Objective

17. Identify the major events in skeletal development prior to birth.

As mentioned in section 6.4, bone forms by either intramembranous ossification within a mesenchyme layer or endochondral ossification from hyaline cartilage models. **Figure 7.34** shows which bones are formed by which type of ossification.

The following bones of the skull are formed by intramembranous ossification: the flat bones of the skull (e.g., parietal, frontal, and part of the occipital bones), the zygomatic bones, the maxillae, and the mandible. Most of the bones at the base of the cranium (e.g., the sphenoid, part of the temporal bone, and part of the occipital bone) are formed by endochondral ossification. These bones become rather well formed by 12–20 weeks of development.

Almost all of the remaining bones of the skeleton form through endochondral ossification. (The exception is the clavicle, which is formed from a central membranous ossification center, whereas its ends are formed from endochondral ossification centers.)

The sternum develops from left and right cartilaginous **sternal bars (figure 7.35)** The sternal bars meet along the midline and start to fuse, beginning in the seventh week. Fusion commences at the superior end and finishes at the inferior end by the ninth week. Within these sternal bars, multiple bony ossification centers will develop.

Rib and vertebrae development are intertwined, as shown in **figure 7.36**. Recall from section 3.4d that blocks of mesoderm called **somites** are located on either side of the developing neural tube. A portion of each somite, called a **sclerotome** (sklē′rō-tōm), separates from the dermamyotome portion of the somite and is the origin of the vertebrae and ribs. The sclerotomes start to surround the neural tube during the fourth week of development. The sclerotomes later become cartilaginous and form portions of the vertebrae, including the **costal element** (or *costal process*) and the **transverse element.** For most vertebrae, the costal element and transverse element fuse to form the transverse process of the vertebra. However, in the thoracic region of the spinal cord, the costal element and transverse element remain separate. The transverse element in the developing thoracic vertebra forms the transverse process. The costal elements of the thoracic vertebrae elongate and form the ribs. This elongation of the costal elements starts during the fifth week of development, and ossification of the ribs occurs during the fetal period.

Clinical View 7.6

Variations in Rib Development

Variations in rib development are not uncommon. For example, in one out of every 200 people, the costal element of the seventh cervical vertebra elongates and forms a rudimentary **cervical rib.** Cervical ribs may compress the axillary artery and nerves extending toward the upper limb, producing tingling or pain. If a cervical rib continuously produces these symptoms, it is usually removed surgically. Less commonly, an extra pair of ribs may form from the costal elements of the first lumbar vertebra. These ribs tend to be asymptomatic.

Some individuals lack a pair of twelfth ribs, because their costal elements from the twelfth thoracic vertebra failed to elongate. Finally, **bifid ribs** occur in 1.2% of the world's population (and up to 8.4% of Samoans). A bifid rib splits into two separate portions when it reaches the sternum. Like most other variations in rib development, bifid ribs are typically asymptomatic and may be discovered only incidentally on a chest x-ray.

Within the cartilage of the developing vertebrae, multiple bony ossification centers form. At birth, only the body and the vertebral arch have ossified; it isn't until puberty that other secondary ossification centers, such as those in the tips of spinous and transverse processes, form. All secondary ossification centers fuse with the primary vertebral ossification centers by about age 25.

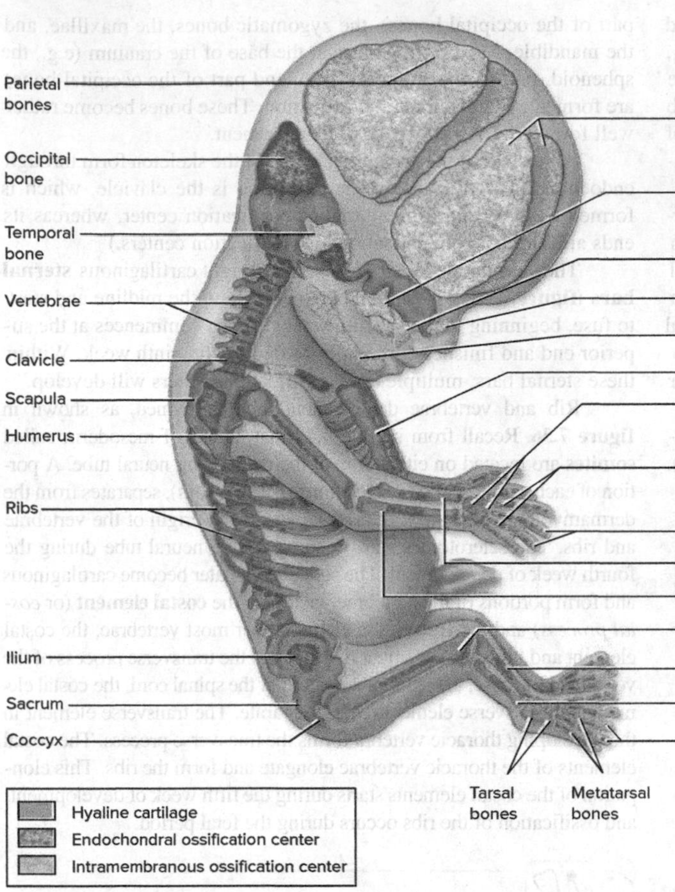
Parietal bones
Occipital bone
Temporal bone
Vertebrae
Clavicle
Scapula
Humerus
Ribs
Ilium
Sacrum
Coccyx
Frontal bones
Zygomatic bone
Maxilla
Nasal bone
Mandible
Sternum
Carpal bones
Metacarpal bones
Phalanges
Radius
Ulna
Femur
Tibia
Fibula
Phalanges
Tarsal bones
Metatarsal bones
Hyaline cartilage
Endochondral ossification center
Intramembranous ossification center

Figure 7.34

Development of the Axial Skeleton. Many centers of ossification for the axial skeleton are readily seen by the tenth week of development.

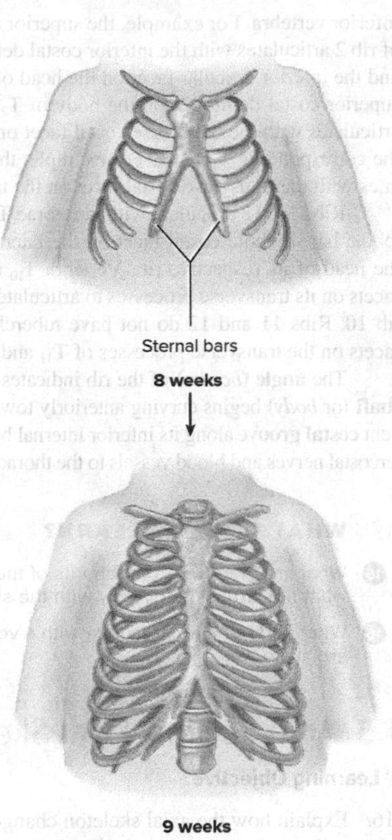
Sternal bars
8 weeks
9 weeks

Figure 7.35

Sternum Development. The sternum forms from the fusion of sternal bars.

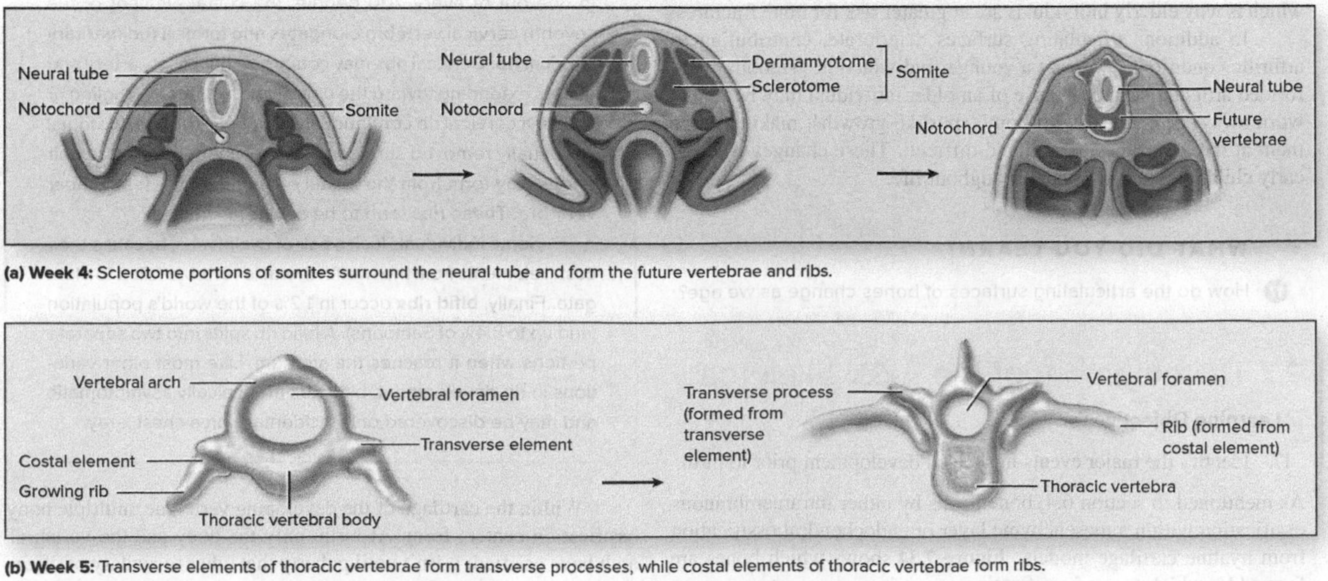
Neural tube
Notochord
Somite
Neural tube
Notochord
Dermamyotome
Sclerotome
Somite
Neural tube
Notochord
Future vertebrae
Vertebral arch
Vertebral foramen
Transverse element
Costal element
Growing rib
Thoracic vertebral body
Transverse process (formed from transverse element)
Vertebral foramen
Rib (formed from costal element)
Thoracic vertebra

(a) Week 4: Sclerotome portions of somites surround the neural tube and form the future vertebrae and ribs.

(b) Week 5: Transverse elements of thoracic vertebrae form transverse processes, while costal elements of thoracic vertebrae form ribs.

Figure 7.36

Rib and Vertebrae Development. Ribs and vertebrae form from portions of somites called sclerotomes.

Clinical Terms

sinusitis Inflammation of the mucous membrane of one or more paranasal sinuses.

spinal fusion Medical procedure used to stabilize part of the vertebral column; bone chips are inserted surgically as a tissue graft after a vertebra has been fractured or a disc has herniated.

Chapter Summary

	■ The axial skeleton includes the bones of the skull, the vertebral column, and the thoracic cage. ■ The appendicular skeleton includes the bones of the pectoral and pelvic girdles and the upper and lower limbs.
7.1 Skull	■ Cranial bones enclose the cranial cavity. Facial bones protect and support the entrances to the digestive and respiratory systems. **7.1a Views of the Skull and Landmark Features** ■ Anterior, superior, posterior, lateral, sagittal sectional, inferior (basal), and internal views show specific bones, foramina, processes, and bone landmarks. **7.1b Sutures** ■ Sutures are immovable joints that form boundaries between skull bones. **7.1c Bones of the Cranium** ■ The frontal bone forms the forehead and the superior region of the orbit. ■ Paired parietal bones form part of the superolateral surfaces of the cranium. ■ Paired temporal bones are on the lateral sides of the cranium. ■ The occipital bone forms part of the base of the skull and the back of the cranium. ■ The sphenoid bone contributes to the cranial base. ■ The ethmoid bone forms part of the orbit and the roof of the nasal cavity. **7.1d Bones of the Face** ■ The paired zygomatic bones form the cheeks. ■ The paired lacrimal bones are located in the anteromedial portion of each orbit. ■ The paired nasal bones form the bridge of the nose. ■ The vomer forms the inferior portion of the nasal septum. ■ The paired inferior nasal conchae attach to the lateral walls of the nasal cavity. ■ The paired palatine bones form the posterior portion of the hard palate. ■ The paired maxillae form the upper jaw and most of the hard palate. ■ The mandible is the lower jaw. **7.1e Nasal Complex** ■ The nasal complex is composed of bones and cartilage that enclose the nasal cavities and the paranasal sinuses. **7.1f Paranasal Sinuses** ■ Paranasal sinuses are hollow cavities in the maxillae, ethmoid, frontal, and sphenoid bones that connect with the nasal cavity. **7.1g Orbital Complex** ■ Seven bones form the orbit: the maxilla, frontal, lacrimal, ethmoid, sphenoid, palatine, and zygomatic bones. **7.1h Bones Associated with the Skull** ■ Auditory ossicles (malleus, incus, and stapes) are three tiny ear bones housed in each temporal bone. ■ The hyoid bone serves as a base for the attachment of several tongue and larynx muscles.
7.2 Sexually Dimorphic Features of the Skull	■ Female skulls tend to be more gracile, have more pointed (versus squared-off) chins, and have sharper orbital rims. ■ Male skulls tend to be more robust and have larger features as well as squared-off chins.
7.3 Aging of the Skull	■ Fontanelles permit the skulls of infants and young children to expand as the brain grows.
7.4 Vertebral Column	■ The vertebral column is composed of 26 vertebrae. **7.4a Divisions of the Vertebral Column** ■ There are 7 cervical vertebrae, 12 thoracic vertebrae, 5 lumbar vertebrae, the sacrum, and the coccyx.

(continued on next page)

Chapter Summary *(continued)*

	7.4b Spinal Curvatures ■ The adult spinal column exhibits four curvatures. The thoracic and sacral curvatures are called primary (accommodation) curves, and the cervical and lumbar curvatures are termed secondary (compensation) curves. **7.4c Vertebral Anatomy** ■ A typical vertebra has a body and a posterior vertebral arch. The vertebral arch is formed by pedicles and laminae. The vertebral foramen houses the spinal cord. ■ Between adjacent vertebrae are fibrocartilaginous intervertebral discs. ■ Cervical vertebrae typically have transverse foramina and bifid spinous processes. ■ Thoracic vertebrae typically have heart-shaped bodies, long spinous processes, costal facets on the body, and transverse processes that articulate with the ribs. ■ The lumbar vertebrae typically have large bodies, thick and blunt transverse processes, and short spinous processes .
7.5 Thoracic Cage	■ The skeleton of the thoracic cage is composed of the thoracic vertebrae, the ribs, and the sternum. **7.5a Sternum** ■ The sternum consists of a superiorly placed manubrium, a middle body, and an inferiorly placed xiphoid process. **7.5b Ribs** ■ Ribs 1–7 are called true ribs, and ribs 8–12 are called false ribs (while ribs 11–12 are also known as floating ribs).
7.6 Aging of the Axial Skeleton	■ Skeletal mass and density are often reduced with age, and articulating surfaces deteriorate, leading to arthritis.
7.7 Development of the Axial Skeleton	■ The flat bones of the skull are formed from intramembranous ossification, whereas almost all other bones of the skull are formed from endochondral ossification. ■ The sternum forms from two cartilaginous sternal bars that start to fuse during the eighth week of development. ■ Vertebrae and ribs are formed from the sclerotomes of developing somites.

Challenge Yourself

Actively write or type your answers in a separate document to reinforce your learning, before checking your answers.

Multiple Choice

Select the best answer from the four choices provided.

1. Which bones form the hard palate?
   a. mandible and maxillae
   b. palatine bones and mandible
   c. palatine bones and maxillae
   d. maxillae only
2. The bony portion of the nasal septum is formed by which bony structures?
   a. perpendicular plate of the ethmoid bone and vomer
   b. perpendicular plate of the ethmoid bone only
   c. nasal bones and perpendicular plate of the ethmoid bone
   d. vomer and sphenoid bones
3. The mandible articulates with which bone?
   a. occipital
   b. frontal
   c. temporal
   d. parietal
4. Some muscles that control the tongue and larynx are attached to which bone(s)?
   a. maxillae
   b. cervical vertebrae
   c. hyoid bone
   d. malleus bone
5. Which skull feature is considered 'male-like'?
   a. large mastoid process
   b. thin, sharp supraorbital margin
   c. triangular, pointed mental protuberance
   d. mandibular angle > 125 degrees
6. These spaces between an infant's skull bone allow for the compression of the skull bones during birth.
   a. ossification centers
   b. fontanelles
   c. foramina
   d. fossae
7. Which opening is found in the occipital bone?
   a. foramen rotundum
   b. hypoglossal canal
   c. foramen spinosum
   d. optic canal
8. Each temporal bone articulates with which of the following bones?
   a. frontal, temporal, occipital, and parietal bones only
   b. frontal, zygomatic, occipital, parietal, and sphenoid bones
   c. occipital, zygomatic, sphenoid, and parietal bones, and the mandible
   d. frontal, occipital, temporal, sphenoid, and parietal bones

9. Which vertebrae have a long spinous process that is angled inferiorly?
   a. cervical
   b. thoracic
   c. lumbar
   d. sacral
10. The clavicles articulate with which specific part of the sternum?
   a. manubrium
   b. xiphoid process
   c. body
   d. angle

Content Review

1. Explain the primary difference between a facial bone and a cranial bone. List the facial bones and list the cranial bones.
2. What are sutures, and how do they affect skull shape and growth?
3. With which bones does the occipital bone articulate?
4. Describe the embryonic components that form vertebrae and ribs.
5. Compare the superior, middle, and inferior nasal conchae. Are they part of another bone? Where in the nasal complex are they found?
6. Identify the seven bones that form the orbit, and discuss their arrangement.
7. What are the functions of the vertebral column?
8. Describe the first two cervical vertebrae and their unique structures, and discuss the functions these vertebrae perform in head movement.
9. What features are typically seen in thoracic vertebrae?
10. Describe similarities and differences among true, false, and floating ribs. How do these ribs articulate with the vertebrae?

Developing Critical Reasoning

1. Two patients see a doctor with complaints about lower back pain. The first is a construction worker who lifts bulky objects every day, and the second is an overweight teenager. Is there a common cause for these complaints? What might the doctor recommend?
2. Paul viewed his newborn daughter through the nursery window at the hospital and was distressed because the infant's skull was badly misshapen. A nurse told him not to worry—the shape of the infant's head would return to normal in a few days. What caused the misshapen skull, and what anatomic feature of the neonatal skull allows it to return to a more rounded shape?
3. A forensic anthropologist was asked to determine the sex of a skull found at a crime scene. How would she be able to discern this information?

Answers to "What Do You Think?"

1. Male sex hormones and increased growth beginning at puberty cause the skull to become more robust, with more prominent features and a more squared-off jaw.
2. A completely straight vertebral column would not be as well adapted for weight bearing as a vertebral column with spinal curvatures. The spinal curvatures support the weight of the body better by bringing that weight in line with the body axis and thus helping us walk upright. (Compare the spinal curvatures of a human to those of an animal that does not normally walk upright, such as a chimpanzee.)
3. A cervical vertebra typically has transverse foramina and a bifid spinous process.

Design Element: Pencil Icon: Slavojub Pantelic/Shutterstock

SKELETAL SYSTEM

8 Appendicular Skeleton

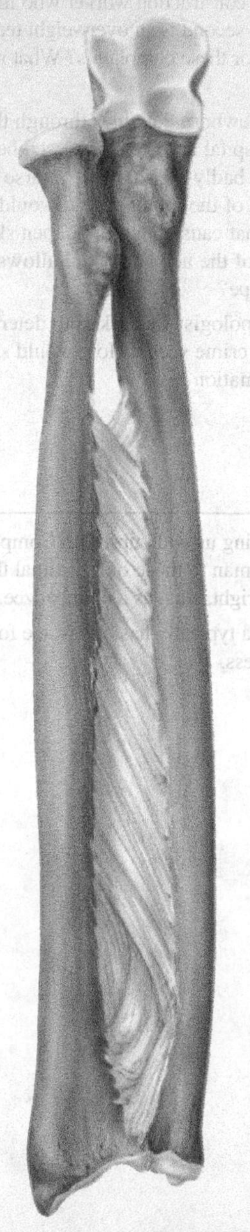

Outline

Anatomy & Physiology Revealed 4.0

MODULE 5: SKELETAL SYSTEM

One benefit of space travel is that it has helped advance our knowledge of human anatomy. We are amazed by video showing astronauts in space running on treadmills, riding stationary bicycles, jumping rope, and doing various other exercises. For astronauts—as for all of us—exercise is essential for maintaining bone mass and strength as well as muscle tone and strength. When we exercise on Earth, our contracting muscles work with and against gravity applying stress to the bones to which they are attached, thereby strengthening the bone and ultimately preventing it from becoming thin and brittle. Regular exercise prevents degenerative changes in the skeleton and helps us avoid serious health problems later in life.

When we exercise, we move the bones of the **appendicular skeleton,** which includes the bones of the upper and lower limbs, and the girdles of bones that hold and attach the upper and lower limbs to the axial skeleton (**figure 8.1**). The pectoral girdle consists of bones that hold the upper limbs in place, whereas the pelvic girdle consists of bones that hold the lower limbs in place. In this chapter, we examine the specific components of the appendicular skeleton and explore their interactions with other systems, such as the muscular and cardiovascular systems. Be sure to review figure 6.17 regarding bone markings before you proceed.

Learning Strategy 8.1

Many bones and bony features may be palpated (felt) underneath the skin. As you hold a bone in lab, try to palpate the same bone on your own body. In this way, you will understand how the bone is positioned, how it associates with other bones, and how it moves in a living body. In effect, you can use your body as a "bone study guide."

8.1 Pectoral Girdle

✓ Learning Objectives

1. Name the bones of the pectoral girdle and describe their functions.
2. Identify and describe the bone surface features of the pectoral girdle.

The **pectoral** (pek'tō-răl; *pectus* = breastbone) **girdle** (ger'd ĕl) articulates with the trunk and supports the upper limbs. A pectoral girdle consists of the left and right clavicles (collarbones) and the left and right scapulae (shoulder blades). It is the attachment site for many muscles that move the upper limbs. The pectoral girdle promotes upper limb mobility in two ways: (1) Because the scapula is not directly attached to the axial skeleton, it moves freely across the posterior surface of the thorax, permitting the arm to move with it; and (2) the shallow cavity of the shoulder joint permits a wide range of movement of the upper limb.

WHAT DO YOU THINK?

1. Why is the clavicle commonly known as the "collarbone"? Based upon this layman's term, can you figure out where the clavicle is located in your body?

8.1a Clavicle

The **clavicle** (klav'i-k ĕl; *clavis* = key) is an S-shaped bone that extends between the manubrium of the sternum and the acromion of the scapula (**figure 8.2**). It is the only direct connection between the pectoral girdle and the axial skeleton. Its **sternal end** (medial end) is roughly pyramidal in shape and articulates with the manubrium of the sternum, forming the sternoclavicular joint. The **acromial end** (lateral end) of the clavicle is broad and flattened. The acromial end articulates with the acromion of the scapula, forming the acromioclavicular joint.

You can palpate your own clavicle by first locating the superior aspect of your sternum and then moving your hand laterally. The curved bone you feel under your skin, and close to the collar of your shirt, is your clavicle.

The superior surface of the clavicle is relatively smooth, but the inferior surface is marked by grooves and ridges for muscle and ligament attachments. On the inferior surface, near the acromial end, is a rough tuberosity called the **conoid** (kō'noyd; *konoeides* = cone-shaped) **tubercle,** the attachment site for the coracoclavicular ligament. The inferiorly located prominence at the sternal end of the clavicle is called the **costal tuberosity,** the attachment of the shoulder's costoclavicular ligament.

8.1b Scapula

The **scapula** (skap'y ū-lă) is a broad, flat, triangular bone (**figure 8.3**). You can palpate your scapula by putting your hand on your superolateral back region and moving your shoulder; the bone you feel moving is the scapula. Several large projections extend from the scapula and provide surface area for muscle and ligament attachments. The **spine** of the scapula is a ridge of bone on the posterior aspect of the scapula. It is easily palpated under the skin. The spine is continuous with a larger, flattened, posterior process called the **acromion** (ă-krō'mē-on; *akron* = tip, *omos* = shoulder), which forms the bony tip of the shoulder. Palpate the superior region of your shoulder; the prominent bump you feel is the acromion. The acromion articulates with the acromial end of the clavicle. The **coracoid** (kōr'ă-koyd; *korakodes* = like a crow's beak) **process** is the smaller, more anterior projection.

The triangular shape of the scapula forms three sides, or borders. The **superior border** is the horizontal edge of the scapula superior to the spine of the scapula; the **medial border** (also called the *vertebral border*) is the edge of the scapula closest to the vertebrae;

Clinical View 8.1

Fracture of the Clavicle

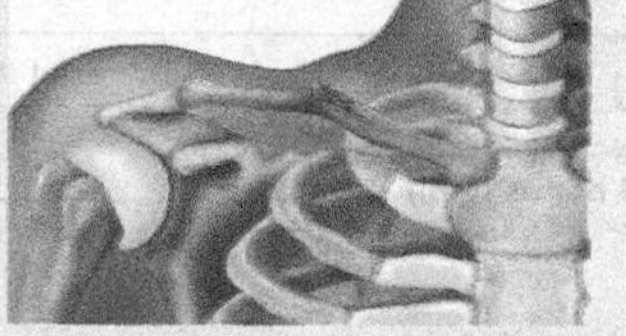

Diagram shows common fracture site for the clavicle.

The clavicle can fracture relatively easily because its S shape does not allow it to resist stress well. In addition, the sternoclavicular joint is incredibly strong, so if stress is placed on both the clavicle and the joint, the clavicle will fracture before the joint is damaged. A direct blow to the middle part of the clavicle, a fall onto the lateral border of the shoulder, or use of the arms to brace against a forward fall is often stress enough to fracture the clavicle. Because the clavicle has an anterior and posterior curve along its length between the medial and lateral edges, severe stress to the mid-region of the bone usually results in an anterior fracture. A posterior fracture may be more serious because bone splinters can penetrate the subclavian artery and vein, which lie immediately posterior and inferior to the clavicle and are the primary blood vessels supplying the upper limb.

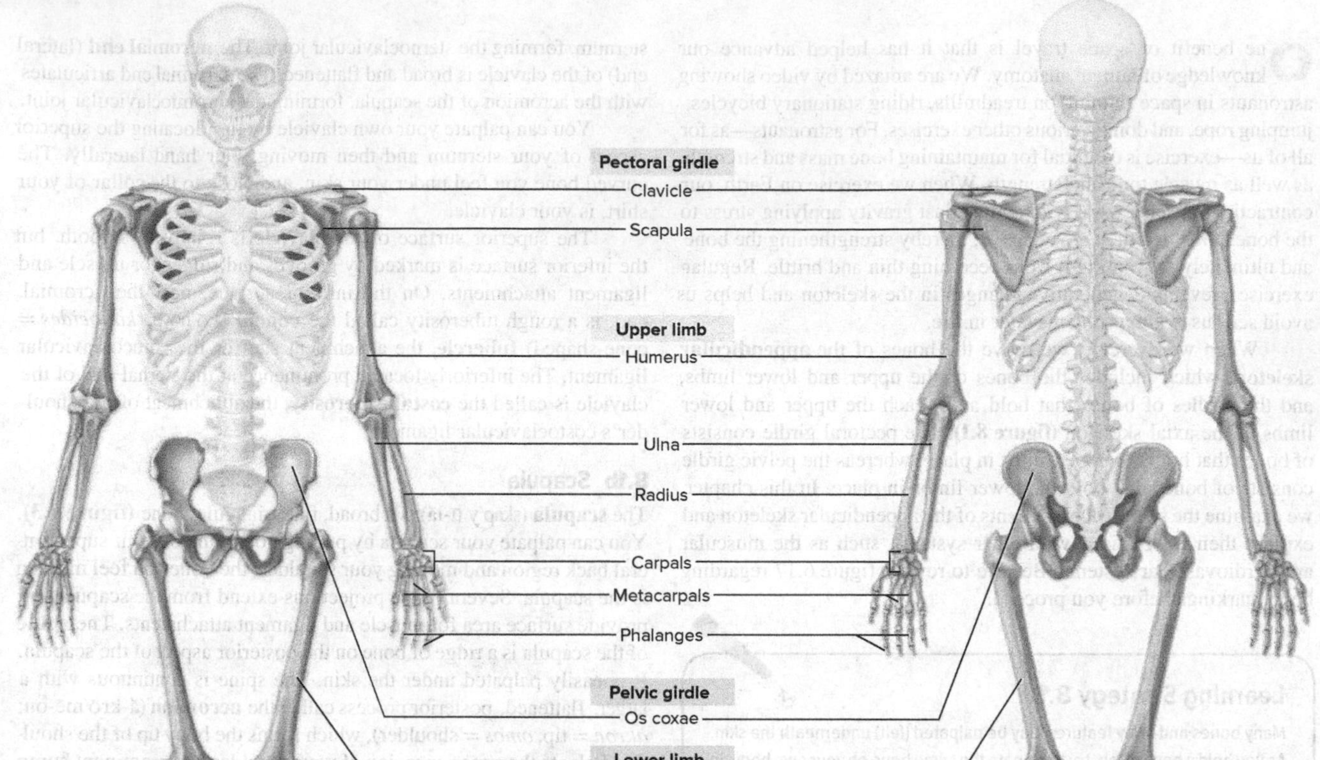

Pectoral girdle
Clavicle
Scapula
Upper limb
Humerus
Ulna
Radius
Carpals
Metacarpals
Phalanges
Pelvic girdle
Os coxae
Lower limb
Femur
Patella
Fibula
Tibia
Tarsals
Metatarsals
Phalanges
(a) Anterior view
(b) Posterior view

Bones of the Appendicular Skeleton (63 bones per each side of the body, 126 bones total)			
Pectoral girdle (4 bones total)	Clavicle (2)	**Pelvic girdle (2 bones total)**	Os coxae (2) Ilium, ischium, and pubis bones fuse to form the os coxae in early adolescence
	Scapula (2)		
Upper limbs (30 bones per each upper limb, 60 bones total)	Humerus (2)	**Lower limbs (30 bones per each lower limb, 60 bones total)**	Femur (2)
	Radius (2)		Patella (2)
	Ulna (2)		Tibia (2)
	Carpals (16) Scaphoid (2), lunate (2), triquetrum (2), pisiform (2), trapezium (2), trapezoid (2), capitate (2), hamate (2)		Fibula (2)
	Metacarpals (10)		Tarsals (14) Calcaneus (2), talus (2), navicular (2), cuboid (2), medial cuneiform (2), intermediate cuneiform (2), lateral cuneiform (2)
	Phalanges (28) Proximal phalanx (10), middle phalanx (8), distal phalanx (10)		Metatarsals (10)
			Phalanges (28) Proximal phalanx (10), middle phalanx (8), distal phalanx (10)

Figure 8.1

Appendicular Skeleton. (*a*) Anterior and (*b*) posterior views show drawings of the pectoral and pelvic girdles and the bones of the upper and lower limbs, all of which make up the appendicular skeleton. A table summarizes the appendicular bones of each region. APR

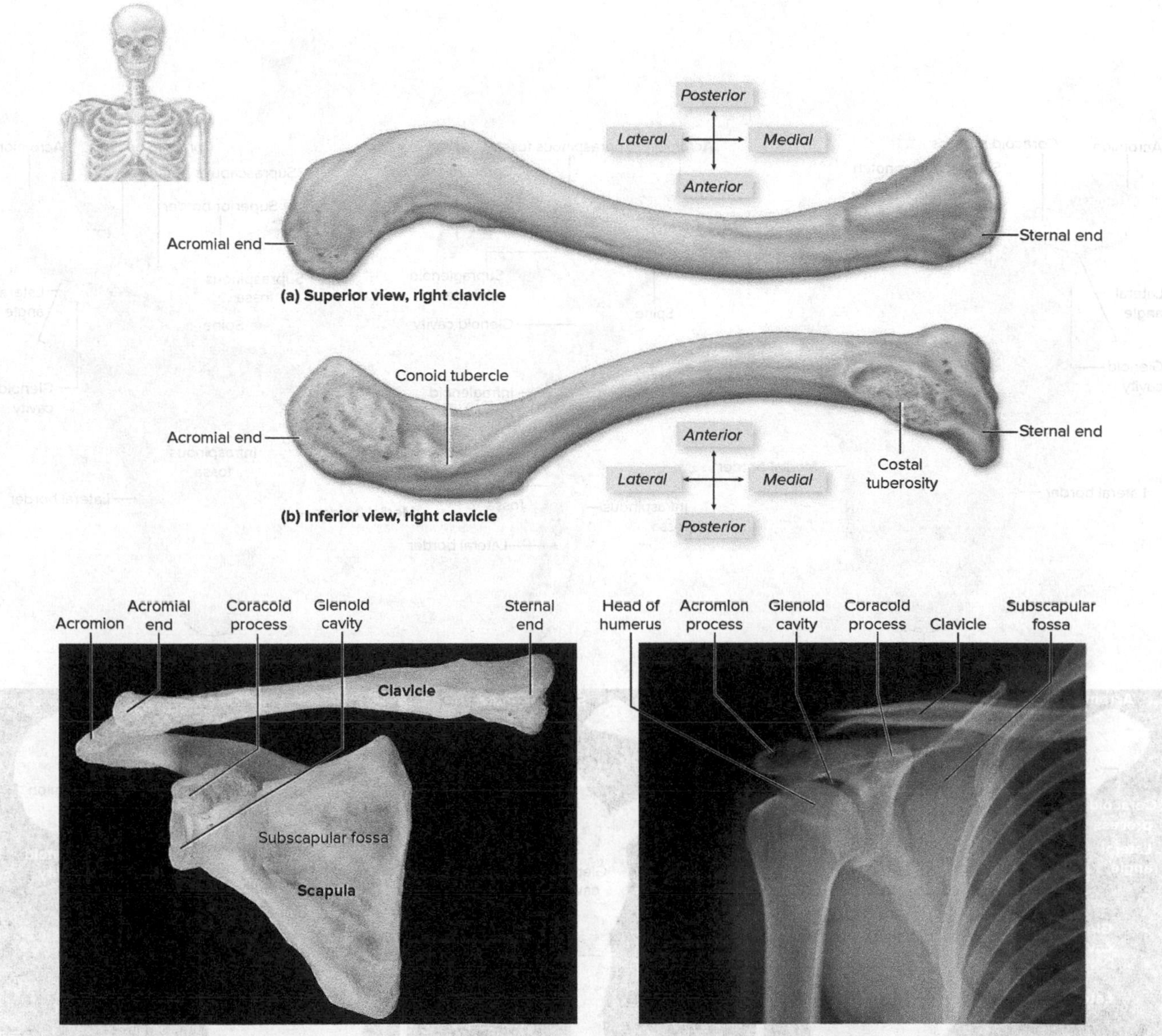
Posterior
Lateral
Medial
Anterior
Acromial end
Sternal end
(a) Superior view, right clavicle
Conoid tubercle
Acromial end
Anterior
Lateral
Medial
Posterior
Sternal end
Costal tuberosity
(b) Inferior view, right clavicle
Acromion
Acromial end
Coracoid process
Glenoid cavity
Sternal end
Clavicle
Subscapular fossa
Scapula
(c) Right scapula and clavicle articulation, anterior view
Head of humerus
Acromion process
Glenoid cavity
Coracoid process
Clavicle
Subscapular fossa
(d) Radiograph of right shoulder

Figure 8.2

Clavicle. The S-shaped clavicle is the only direct connection between the pectoral girdle and the axial skeleton. (*a*) Superior and (*b*) inferior views of the right clavicle are shown in the diagrams. (*c*) A photograph shows the anterior view of an articulated right clavicle and scapula. (*d*) A radiograph shows an articulated right clavicle and scapula.

(c) ©McGraw-Hill Education/Christine Eckel, photographer; (d) sanyanwuji/Getty Images

and the **lateral border** (also called the *axillary border*) is closest to the axilla (armpit). A conspicuous **suprascapular notch** (which in some individuals is a **suprascapular foramen**) in the superior border provides passage for the suprascapular nerve.

Between these borders are the superior, inferior, and lateral angles. The **superior angle** is the pointed part of the scapula between the superior and medial borders, whereas the **inferior angle** is located between the medial and lateral borders. The **lateral angle** is composed primarily of the cup-shaped, shallow **glenoid** (glē′noyd; resembling a socket) **cavity,** or *glenoid fossa,* which articulates with the humerus, the bone of the arm. Tubercles (tū′bĕr-kĕl) on the superior and inferior edges of the glenoid cavity serve as attachment sites for the muscles that position the shoulder and arm. Near the superior edge of the glenoid cavity is the **supraglenoid tubercle,** and near the inferior edge is the **infraglenoid tubercle.**

Learning Strategy 8.2

The acromial end of the clavicle is flattened and looks like the acromion of the scapula.

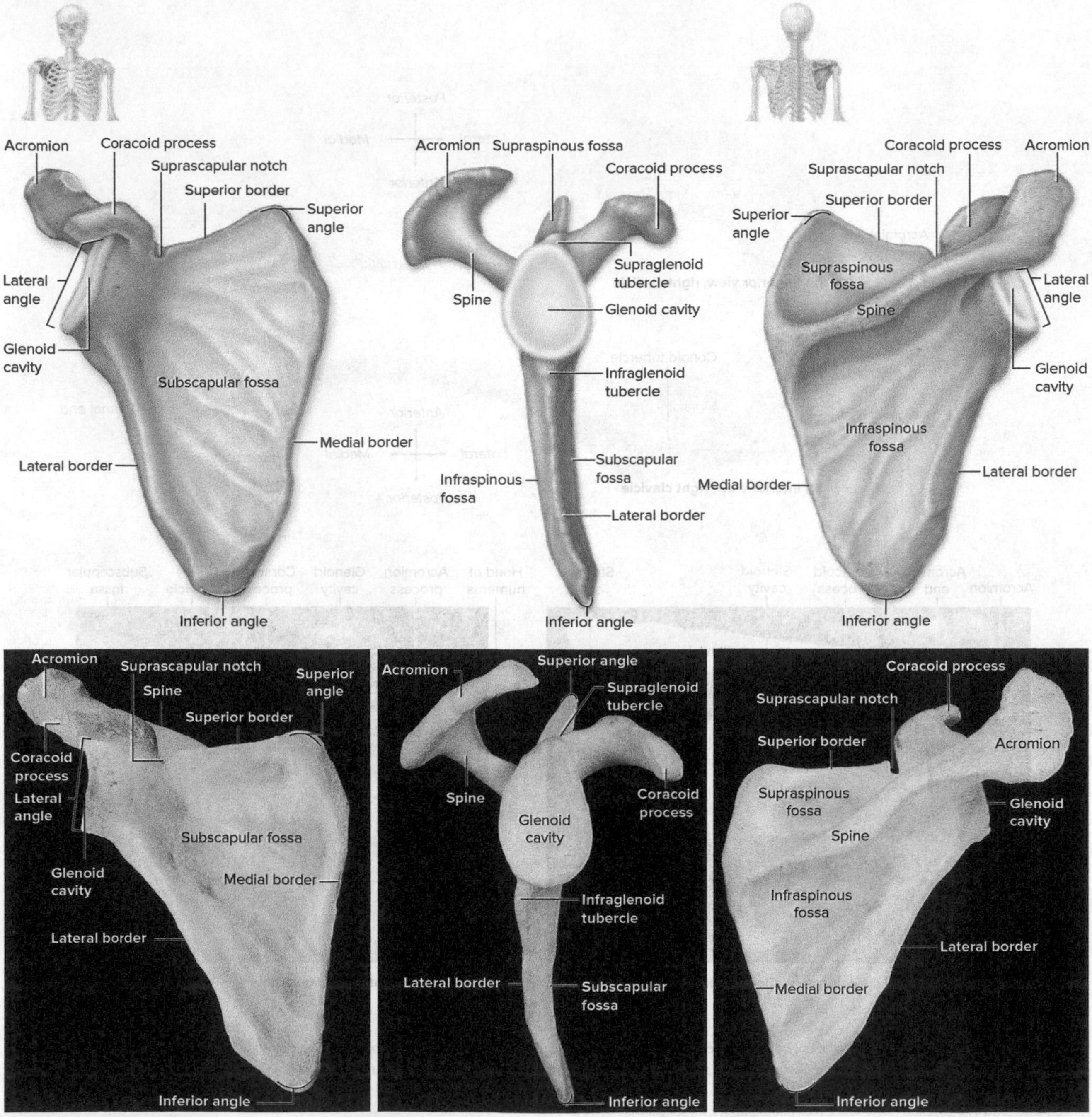

(a) Right scapula, anterior view **(b) Right scapula, lateral view** **(c) Right scapula, posterior view**

Figure 8.3

Scapula. The upper limb articulates with the pectoral girdle at the scapula, as shown in (*a*) anterior, (*b*) lateral, and (*c*) posterior views, in both drawing and photographs. **APR**

The scapula has several flattened regions of bone that provide surfaces for the attachment of some of the rotator cuff muscles, which help stabilize and move the shoulder joint. The broad, relatively smooth, anterior surface of the scapula is called the **subscapular** (sŭb-skap′yū-lăr; *sub* = under) **fossa** (fos′ă; pl., *fossae*, fos′ē). It is slightly concave and relatively featureless. A large muscle called the subscapularis overlies this fossa. The spine subdivides the posterior surface of the scapula into two shallow depressions, or fossae. The depression superior to the spine is the **supraspinous** (sū′pră-spī′n ŭs; *supra* = above) **fossa;** inferior to the spine is a broad, extensive surface called the **infraspinous fossa.** The supraspinatus and infraspinatus muscles, respectively, attach in these fossae (see section 12.1b).

WHAT DID YOU LEARN?

1. Sketch both the anterior and the posterior views of the scapula. Label the borders, angles, processes, fossae, and glenoid cavity.

8.2 Upper Limb

✓ Learning Objective

3. Name and describe the bones of the upper limb.
4. Identify the markings on the humerus, and explain how these markings relate to nearby soft tissue structures.
5. Identify the markings on the radius and the ulna, and explain how these markings relate to the soft-tissue structures nearby.
6. Identify and describe the carpals, metacarpals, and phalanges of the upper limb.

The upper limb consists of the brachium (arm), antebrachium (forearm), and hand. The complex structure of the hand in particular gives humans capabilities beyond those of most other vertebrates. Each upper limb contains 30 bones:

- 1 humerus, located in the brachium region
- 1 radius and 1 ulna, located in the antebrachium region
- 8 carpal bones, which form the wrist
- 5 metacarpal bones, which form the palm of the hand
- 14 phalanges, which form the fingers

8.2a Humerus

The **humerus** (hyū′mĕr-ŭs) is the longest and largest upper limb bone (**figure 8.4**). Its proximal end has a hemispherical **head** that articulates with the glenoid cavity of the scapula. Adjacent to the head are two tubercles. The prominent **greater tubercle** is positioned more laterally and helps form the rounded contour of the shoulder. The **lesser tubercle** is smaller and located more anteromedially. Between the two tubercles is the **intertubercular sulcus** (or *bicipital sulcus,* or bicipital groove), a depression that contains the tendon of the long head of the biceps brachii muscle (see section 12.1c).

Between the tubercles and the head of the humerus is the **anatomical neck,** an almost indistinct groove that marks the location of the former epiphyseal plate. The **surgical neck** is a narrowing of the bone immediately distal to the tubercles, at the transition from the head to the shaft. This feature is called the "surgical" neck because it is a common fracture site.

The **shaft** of the humerus has a roughened area, termed the **deltoid** (del′toyd; *deltoeides* = like the Greek letter Δ) **tuberosity** (tū′bĕr-os′i-tē), which extends along its lateral surface for about half the length of the humerus. The deltoid muscle of the shoulder attaches to this roughened surface (see section 12.1b). The **radial groove** (or *spiral groove*) is located adjacent to the deltoid tuberosity and is where the radial nerve (see section 16.4e) and some blood vessels travel.

Together, the bones of the humerus, radius, and ulna form the elbow joint (figure 8.4*b, c*). The **medial** and **lateral epicondyles** (ep′i-kon′d īl; *epi* = upon, *kondylos* = a knuckle) are bony side projections on the distal humerus that provide surfaces for muscle attachment. Palpate both sides of your elbow; the bumps you feel are the medial and lateral epicondyles. Traveling posterior to the medial epicondyle is the ulnar nerve (see section 16.4e), which supplies many intrinsic hand muscles.

The distal end of the humerus also has two smooth, curved surfaces for articulation with the bones of the forearm. The rounded **capitulum** (kă-pit′yū-lŭm; *caput* = head) is located laterally and articulates with the head of the radius. The pulley-shaped **trochlea** (trok′lē-ă; *trochileia* = a pulley) is located medially and articulates with the trochlear notch of the ulna. Additionally, the distal end of the humerus exhibits three depressions, two on its anterior surface and one on its posterior surface. The anterolaterally placed **radial fossa** accommodates the head of the radius, and the anteromedially placed **coronoid** (kōr′ŏ-noyd; *korōnē* = a crow, *eidos* = resembling) **fossa** accommodates the coronoid process of the ulna when the elbow is flexed. The posterior depression called the **olecranon** (ō-lek′r ă-non; *olene* = ulna, *kranion* = head) **fossa** accommodates the olecranon of the ulna when the elbow is extended.

8.2b Radius and Ulna

The radius and ulna are the bones of the forearm (**figure 8.5**). In anatomic position, these bones are parallel, and the **radius** (rā′dē-ŭs; spoke of a wheel, ray) is lateral. The proximal end of the radius has a distinctive disc-shaped **head** that articulates with the capitulum of the humerus. A narrow **neck** separates the radial head from the **radial tuberosity** (or *bicipital tuberosity*). The radial tuberosity is an attachment site for the biceps brachii muscle.

The **shaft** of the radius curves slightly and leads to a wide distal end where there is a laterally placed **styloid** (stī′loyd; *stylos* = pillar, post) **process.** This bony projection can be palpated on the lateral side of the wrist, just proximal to the thumb. On the distal medial surface of the radius is an **ulnar notch,** where the medial surface of the radius articulates with the distal end of the ulna (figure 8.5*c*).

The **ulna** (ŭl′nă) is the longer, medially placed bone of the forearm. At the proximal end of the ulna, a C-shaped **trochlear notch** interlocks with the trochlea of the humerus. The posterosuperior aspect of the trochlear notch has a prominent projection called the **olecranon.** The olecranon articulates with the olecranon fossa of the humerus and forms the posterior "bump" of the elbow. (Palpate your posterior elbow; the bump you feel is the olecranon.) The inferior lip of the trochlear notch, called the **coronoid process,** articulates with the humerus at the coronoid fossa. Lateral to the coronoid process, a smooth, curved **radial notch** accommodates the head of the radius and helps form the proximal radioulnar joint (figure 8.5*b*). Also at the proximal end of this bone is the **tuberosity of ulna.** At the distal end of the ulna, the shaft narrows and terminates in a knoblike **head** that has a posteromedial **styloid process.** The styloid process of the ulna may be palpated on the medial ("little finger" side) of the wrist.

Both the radius and the ulna exhibit **interosseous borders,** which face each other; the ulna's interosseous border projects laterally, whereas the radius's interosseous border projects medially. These interosseous borders are connected by an **interosseous membrane** (*interosseous ligament*), composed of dense regular connective tissue. This membrane helps keep the radius and ulna a fixed distance apart from one another and provides a pivot of rotation for the forearm. The bony joints that move during this rotation are the proximal and distal radioulnar joints (figure 8.5 *b, c*).

In anatomic position, the palm of the hand is facing anteriorly, and the bones of the forearm are said to be in **supination** (sū′pi-n ā′shŭn) (figure 8.5*d*). The radius and the ulna are parallel with one another. If you stand in anatomic position, so that you can view your own forearm, the radius is on the lateral (thumb) side of the forearm, whereas the ulna is on the medial (little finger) side of the forearm.

Learning Strategy 8.3

No matter what the position of the forearm (whether pronated or supinated), the distal end of the radius is always near the thumb, and the distal end of the ulna is always on the side of the little finger.

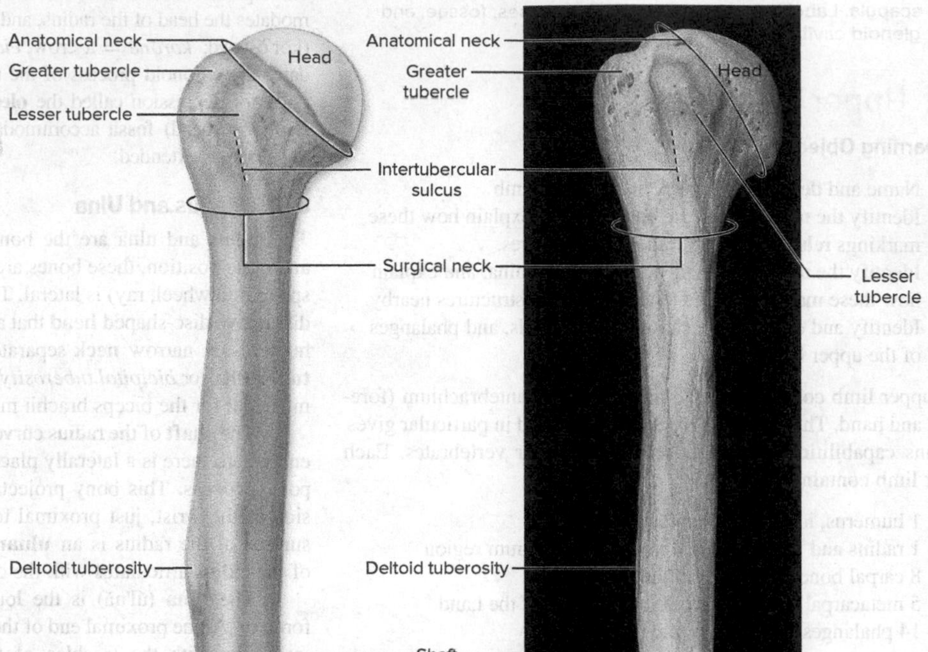
Anatomical neck
Greater tubercle
Lesser tubercle
Head
Anatomical neck
Greater tubercle
Head
Intertubercular sulcus
Surgical neck
Lesser tubercle
Deltoid tuberosity
Deltoid tuberosity
Shaft
Radial fossa
Radial fossa
Coronoid fossa
Coronoid fossa
Lateral epicondyle
Lateral epicondyle
Medial epicondyle
Medial epicondyle
Capitulum
Trochlea
Capitulum
Trochlea

(a) Right humerus, anterior view

Figure 8.4

Humerus and Elbow Joint. Diagrams and photographs show the right humerus is shown in (*a*) anterior and (*d*) posterior views. (*b*) Anterior and (*c*) posterior views of the elbow joint, which is formed by the humerus articulating with the radius and ulna , are shown in photographs only. APR

©McGraw-Hill Education/Christine Eckel, photographer

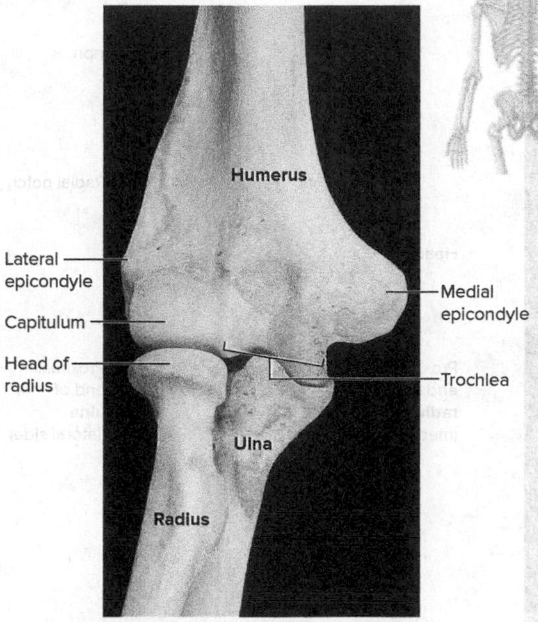
Humerus
Lateral epicondyle
Capitulum
Head of radius
Medial epicondyle
Trochlea
Ulna
Radius

(b) Right elbow joint, anterior view

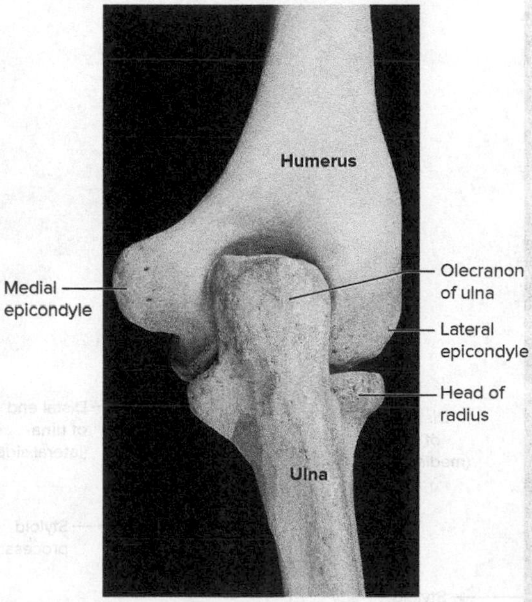
Humerus
Medial epicondyle
Olecranon of ulna
Lateral epicondyle
Head of radius
Ulna

(c) Right elbow joint, posterior view

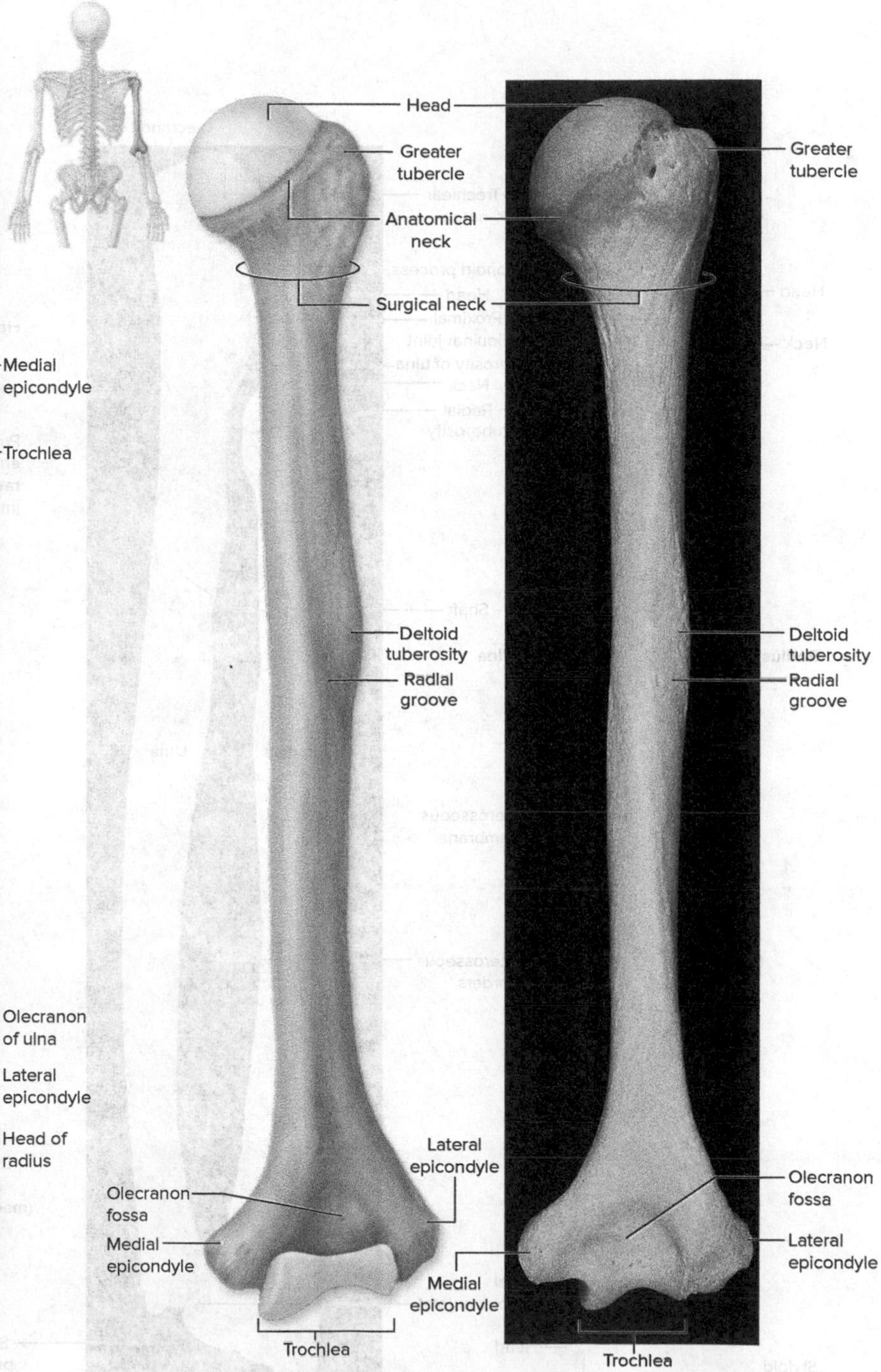
Head
Greater tubercle
Anatomical neck
Surgical neck
Greater tubercle
Deltoid tuberosity
Radial groove
Deltoid tuberosity
Radial groove
Lateral epicondyle
Olecranon fossa
Medial epicondyle
Medial epicondyle
Olecranon fossa
Lateral epicondyle
Trochlea
Trochlea

(d) Right humerus, posterior view

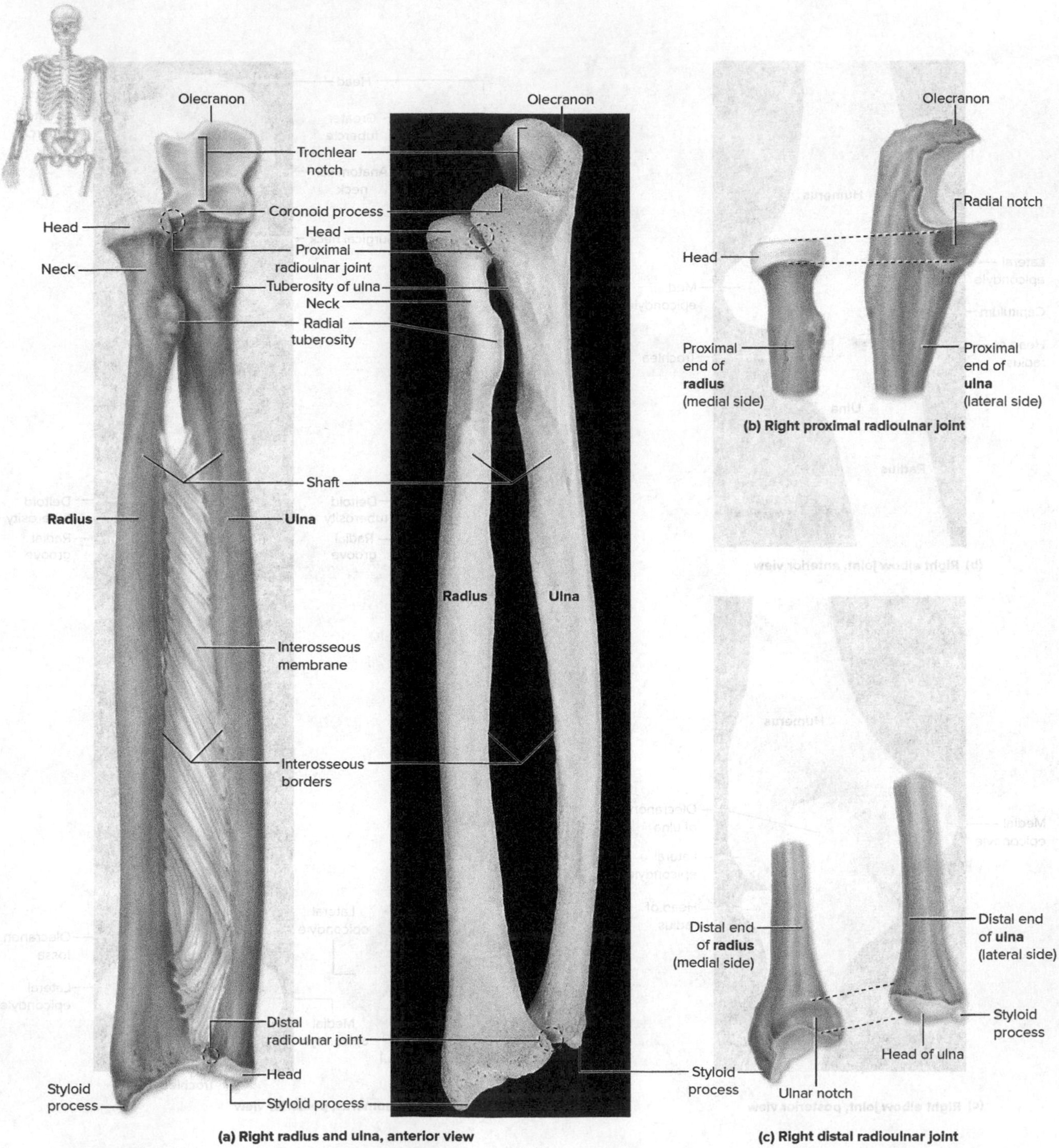
Olecranon
Trochlear notch
Coronoid process
Head
Proximal radioulnar joint
Neck
Tuberosity of ulna
Radial tuberosity
Shaft
Radius
Ulna
Interosseous membrane
Interosseous borders
Distal radioulnar joint
Styloid process
Radial notch
Proximal end of radius (medial side)
Proximal end of ulna (lateral side)
(b) Right proximal radioulnar joint
Distal end of radius (medial side)
Distal end of ulna (lateral side)
Head of ulna
Ulnar notch
(a) Right radius and ulna, anterior view
(c) Right distal radioulnar joint

Figure 8.5

Radius and Ulna. (*a*) Anterior view of the bones of the right forearm, shown in diagram and photo, along with diagrams (*b, c*) the proximal and distal radioulnar joints. (*d*) Supination and (*e*) pronation of the right forearm are shown in photos. (*f*) Posterior view of the right forearm, shown in photo and diagram. APR

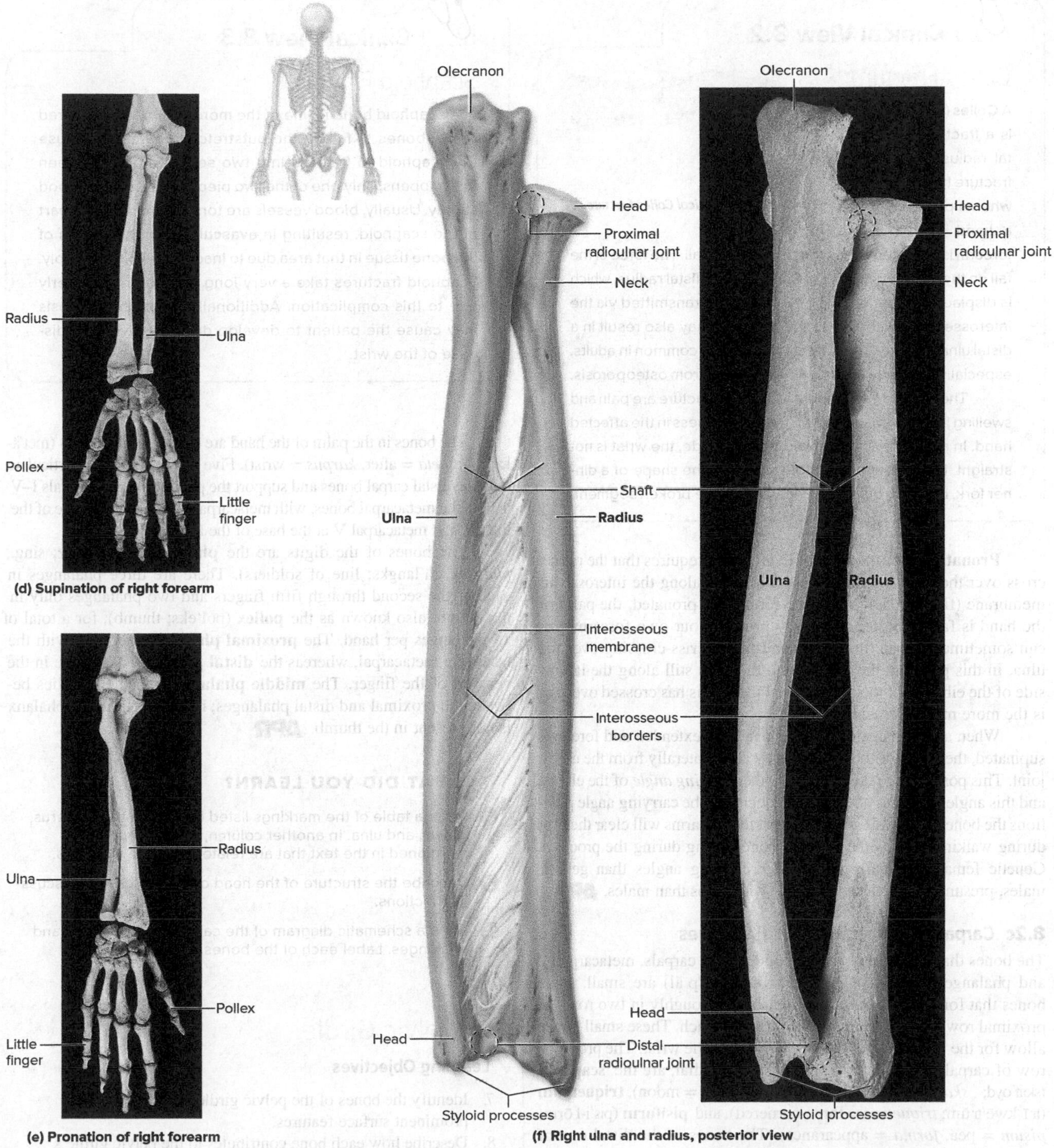
Radius
Ulna
Pollex
Little finger
Radius
Ulna
Pollex
Little finger
Olecranon
Head
Proximal radioulnar joint
Neck
Ulna
Radius
Shaft
Interosseous membrane
Interosseous borders
Head
Distal radioulnar joint
Styloid processes
Olecranon
Head
Proximal radioulnar joint
Neck
Ulna
Radius
Head
Styloid processes

(d) Supination of right forearm

(e) Pronation of right forearm

(f) Right ulna and radius, posterior view

Clinical View 8.2

Colles Fracture

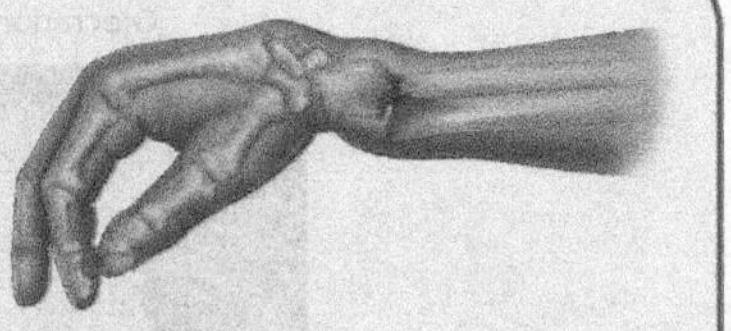

Diagram depicts typical Colles fracture.

A **Colles** (kol'ēz) **fracture** is a fracture of the distal radius. This type of fracture typically occurs when a person extends a hand (and thus the forearm is pronated) while trying to break a fall. The force of the fall on the outstretched hand fractures the distal radius, which is displaced posteriorly. The force can be transmitted via the interosseous membrane to the ulna and may also result in a distal ulna fracture. Colles fractures are very common in adults, especially in elderly individuals who suffer from osteoporosis.

The common symptoms of a Colles fracture are pain and swelling just proximal to the wrist and weakness in the affected hand. In addition, when viewed from the side, the wrist is not straight, but is bent at an angle similar to the shape of a dinner fork, because of the displacement of the broken segment.

Pronation (prō-nā'shŭn) of the forearm requires that the radius cross over the ulna and that both bones pivot along the interosseous membrane (figure 8.5*e*). When the forearm is pronated, the palm of the hand is facing posteriorly. Now pronate your own forearm; you can sometimes palpate the radius and feel it criss-crossing over the ulna. In this position, the head of the radius is still along the lateral side of the elbow, but the distal end of the radius has crossed over and is the more medial structure.

When an individual has the upper limbs extended and forearms supinated, the bones of the forearm may angle laterally from the elbow joint. This positioning is referred to as the *carrying angle* of the elbow, and this angle measures about 5 to 15 degrees. The carrying angle positions the bones of the forearms such that the forearms will clear the hips during walking (and as the forearm bones swing during the process). Genetic females typically have wider carrying angles than genetic males, presumably because they have wider hips than males. APR

8.2c Carpals, Metacarpals, and Phalanges

The bones that form the wrist and hand are the carpals, metacarpals, and phalanges (**figure 8.6**). The **carpals** (kar'p ăl) are small, short bones that form the wrist. They are arranged roughly in two rows (a proximal row and a distal row) of four bones each. These small bones allow for the multiple movements possible at the wrist. The proximal row of carpal bones, listed from lateral to medial, are the **scaphoid** (skaf'oyd; *skaphe* = boat), **lunate** (lū'nāt; *luna* = moon), **triquetrum** (trī-kwē'trŭm; *triquetrus* = three-cornered), and **pisiform** (pis'i-fōrm; *pisum* = pea, *forma* = appearance). The bones of the distal row of carpal bones are the most laterally placed **trapezium** (tra-pē'zē-ŭm; *trapeza* = table), **trapezoid** (trap' ĕ-zoyd), **capitate** (kap'i-tāt; *caput* = head), and **hamate** (ha'm āt; *hamus* = hook).

WHAT DO YOU THINK?

2. Why does each wrist have so many carpal bones (eight)? How does the number of carpal bones relate to the amount of movement in the wrist? Would your wrist be as freely movable if you had just one or two large carpal bones?

Clinical View 8.3

Scaphoid Fractures

The scaphoid bone is one of the more commonly fractured carpal bones. A fall on the outstretched hand may cause the scaphoid to fracture into two separate pieces. When this happens, only one of the two pieces maintains its blood supply. Usually, blood vessels are torn on the proximal part of the scaphoid, resulting in **avascular necrosis,** death of the bone tissue in that area due to inadequate blood supply. Scaphoid fractures take a very long time to heal properly due to this complication. Additionally, avascular necrosis may cause the patient to develop degenerative joint disease of the wrist.

The bones in the palm of the hand are called **metacarpals** (met'ă-kar'p ăl; *meta* = after, *karpus* = wrist). Five metacarpal bones articulate with the distal carpal bones and support the palm. Roman numerals I–V denote the metacarpal bones, with metacarpal I located at the base of the thumb, and metacarpal V at the base of the little finger.

The bones of the digits are the **phalanges** (fă-lan'jēz; sing., *phalanx*, fā'langks; line of soldiers). There are three phalanges in each of the second through fifth fingers and two phalanges only in the thumb, also known as the **pollex** (pol'eks; thumb), for a total of 14 phalanges per hand. The **proximal phalanx** articulates with the head of a metacarpal, whereas the **distal phalanx** is the bone in the very tip of the finger. The **middle phalanx** of each finger lies between the proximal and distal phalanges; however, a middle phalanx is not present in the thumb. APR

WHAT DID YOU LEARN?

2. Make a table of the markings listed in bold on the humerus, radius, and ulna. In another column, list the structures mentioned in the text that are related to those markings.
3. Describe the structure of the head of the radius, and discuss its functions.
4. Draw a schematic diagram of the carpals, metacarpals, and phalanges. Label each of the bones.

8.3 Pelvic Girdle

✓ Learning Objectives

7. Identify the bones of the pelvic girdle and describe their prominent surface features.
8. Describe how each bone contributes to the pelvic girdle's strength and function.
9. Identify and describe the sexually dimorphic features of the pelves.

The adult **pelvis** (pel'vis; pl., *pelves*, pel'vēz; basin) is composed of four bones: the sacrum, the coccyx, and the right and left **ossa coxae** (os'ă kok'să; sing., *os coxae*; hip bone), also known simply as the *hip bones* (**figure 8.7**). The pelvis protects and supports the viscera in the inferior part of the ventral body cavity. In contrast, the term **pelvic girdle** refers to the left and right ossa coxae only.

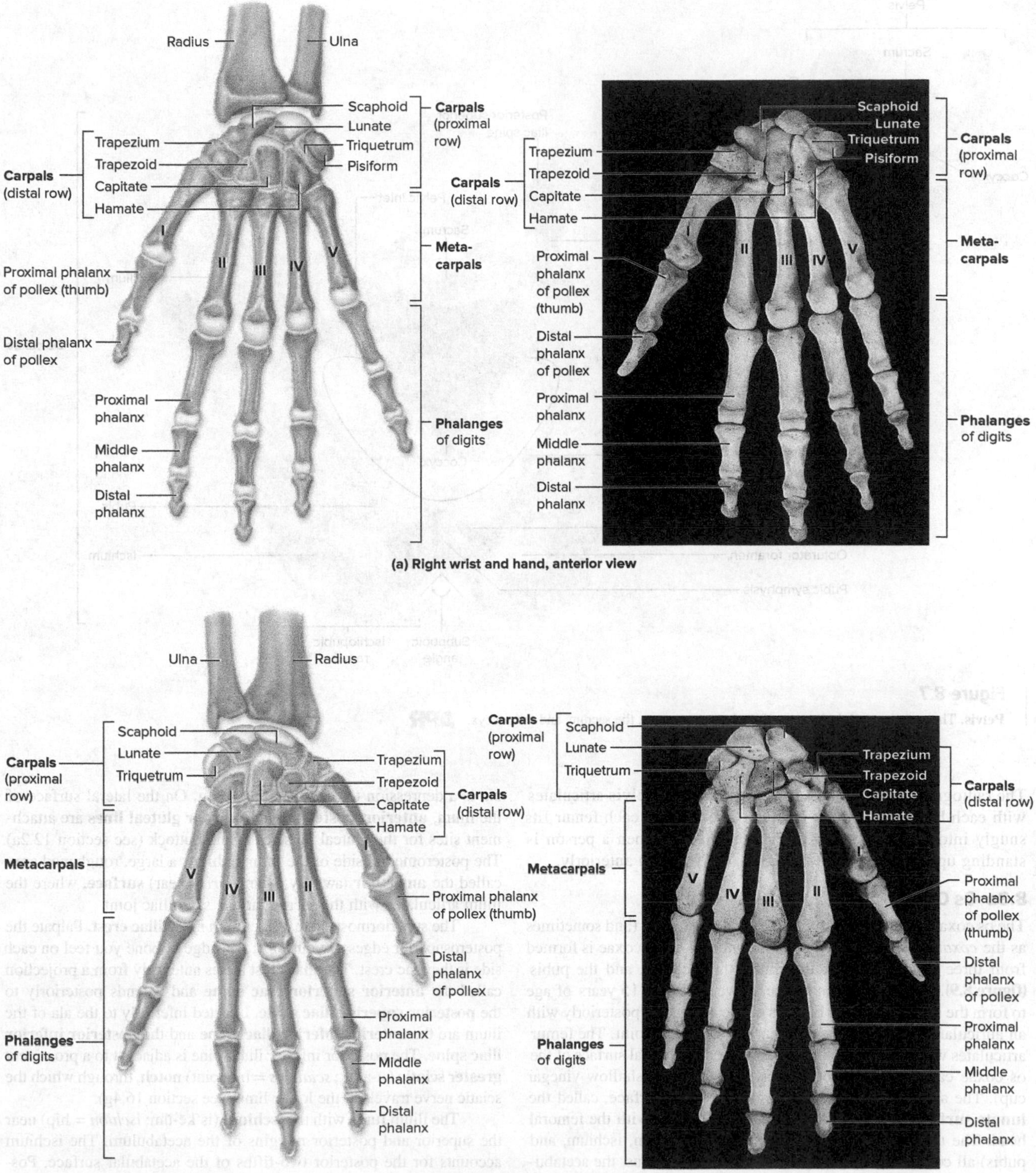

Figure 8.6

Bones of the Carpals, Metacarpals, and Phalanges. Diagrams and photos compare the carpal bones, which form the wrist, and the metacarpals and phalanges, which form the hand. (*a*) Anterior (palmar) and (*b*) posterior views of the right wrist and hand. APR

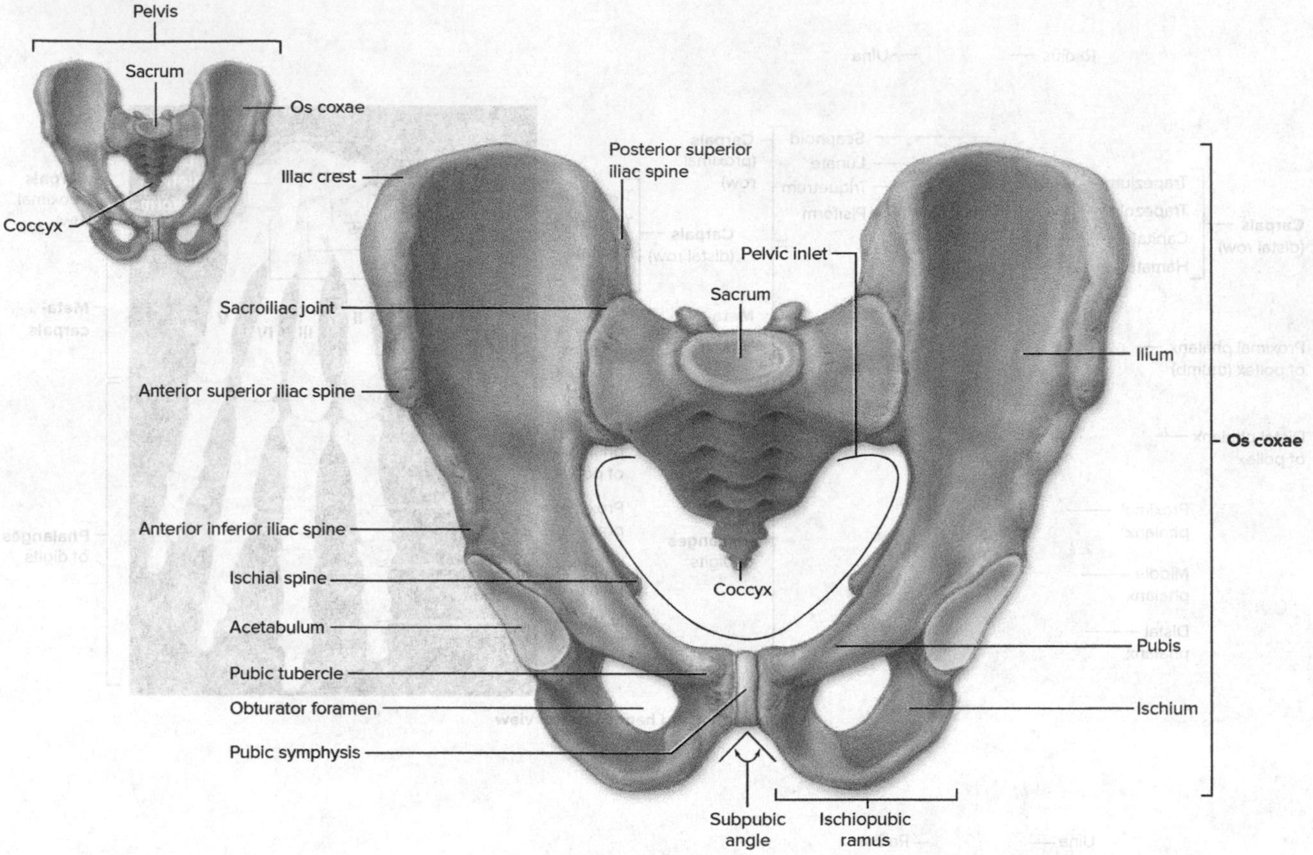

Figure 8.7

Pelvis. The complete pelvis consists of the two ossa coxae, the sacrum, and the coccyx. APR

The radiograph in **figure 8.8** illustrates how the pelvis articulates with each bone of the thigh (femur). The head of each femur fits snugly into the acetabulum of each os coxae. When a person is standing upright, the pelvis is angled (or "tipped") anteriorly.

8.3a Os Coxae

The os coxae is commonly referred to as the *hip bone* (and sometimes as the *coxal bone* or the *innominate bone*). Each os coxae is formed from three separate bones: the ilium, the ischium, and the pubis (**figure 8.9**). These three bones fuse between 13 and 15 years of age to form the single os coxae. Each os coxae articulates posteriorly with an auricular surface of the sacrum at the sacroiliac joint. The femur articulates with a deep, curved depression on the lateral surface of the os coxae called the **acetabulum** (as-ĕ-tab′y ū-lŭm; shallow vinegar cup). The acetabulum contains a smooth curved surface, called the **lunate surface,** which is C-shaped and articulates with the femoral head. The three bones that form the os coxae (ilium, ischium, and pubis) all contribute a portion to the acetabulum. Thus, the acetabulum represents a region where these bones have fused.

The largest of the three coxal bones is the **ilium** (il′ē-ŭm; groin, flank), which forms the superior region of the os coxae and the largest portion of the acetabular surface. The wide, fan-shaped portion of the ilium is called the **ala** (ā′lă; wing). The ala terminates inferiorly at a ridge called the **arcuate line** (ar′ky ū-āt; *arcuatus* = bowed) on the medial surface of the ilium. On the medial side of the ala is a depression termed the **iliac fossa.** On the lateral surface of the ilium, **anterior, posterior,** and **inferior gluteal lines** are attachment sites for the gluteal muscles of the buttock (see section 12.2a). The posteromedial side of the ilium exhibits a large, roughened area called the **auricular** (aw-rik′y ū-lăr; *auris* = ear) **surface,** where the ilium articulates with the sacrum at the sacroiliac joint.

The superiormost ridge of the ilium is the **iliac crest.** Palpate the posterosuperior edges of your hips; the ridge of bone you feel on each side is the iliac crest. The iliac crest arises anteriorly from a projection called the **anterior superior iliac spine** and extends posteriorly to the **posterior superior iliac spine.** Located inferiorly to the ala of the ilium are the **anterior inferior iliac spine** and the **posterior inferior iliac spine.** The posterior inferior iliac spine is adjacent to a prominent **greater sciatic** (sī-at′ik; *sciaticus* = hip joint) **notch,** through which the sciatic nerve travels to the lower limb (see section 16.4g).

The ilium fuses with the **ischium** (is′kē-ŭm; *ischion* = hip) near the superior and posterior margins of the acetabulum. The ischium accounts for the posterior two-fifths of the acetabular surface. Posterior to the acetabulum, the prominent triangular **ischial** (is′kē-ăl) **spine** projects medially. The bulky bone superior to the ischial spine is called the **ischial body.** The **lesser sciatic notch** is a semicircular depression inferior to the ischial spine. The posterolateral border of the ischium is a roughened projection called the **ischial tuberosity.** The ischial tuberosities are also called the *sitz bones* by some health professionals and fitness instructors, because they support the weight

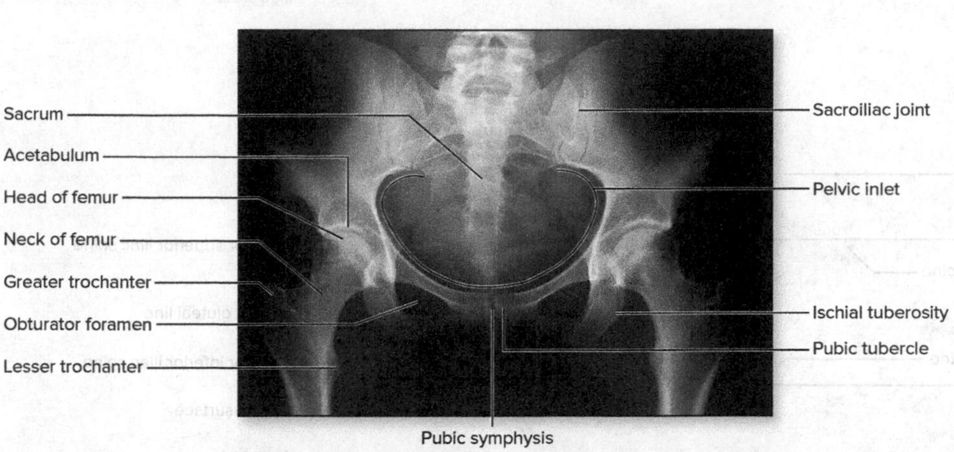
Sacrum
Acetabulum
Head of femur
Neck of femur
Greater trochanter
Obturator foramen
Lesser trochanter
Sacroiliac joint
Pelvic inlet
Ischial tuberosity
Pubic tubercle
Pubic symphysis

Figure 8.8

Pelvis and Femur Articulation. A radiograph shows an anterior view of the articulation between the pelvis and the femur.

Image Source/Getty Images

of the body when seated. If you palpate your buttocks while in a sitting position, you can feel the large ischial tuberosities. An elongated **ramus** (rā'mŭs; pl., *rami*, rā'mī) of the ischium extends from the ischial tuberosity toward its anterior fusion with the pubis.

The **pubis** (pyū'bis) fuses with the ilium and ischium at the acetabulum. The ischial ramus fuses anteriorly with the **inferior pubic ramus** to form the **ischiopubic ramus** (see figure 8.7). The **superior pubic ramus** originates at the anterior margin of the acetabulum. The **obturator** (ob'tū-rā'tŏr; *obturo* = to occlude) **foramen** is a space in the os coxae that is encircled by both pubic and ischial rami. A roughened ridge called the **pubic crest** is located on the anterosuperior surface of the superior ramus, and it ends at the **pubic tubercle.** The pubic tubercle is an attachment site for the inguinal ligament. A roughened area on the body of the pubis, called the **symphysial** (sim-fiz'ē-ăl; growing together) **surface,** or *pubic symphysis,* denotes the site of articulation between the pubic bones. On the medial surface of the pubis, the **pectineal** (pek-tin'ē-ăl; ridged or relating to the pubis) **line** originates and extends diagonally across the pubis to merge with the arcuate line.

WHAT DO YOU THINK?

3. Compare and contrast the glenoid cavity of the scapula with the acetabulum of the os coxae. Which girdle maintains stronger, more tightly fitting bony connections with its respective limbs—the pectoral girdle or the pelvic girdle?

8.3b True and False Pelves

The **pelvic brim** is a continuous oval ridge that extends from the pubic crest, pectineal line, and arcuate line to the rounded inferior edges of the sacral ala and promontory. This pelvic brim helps subdivide the entire pelvis into a true pelvis and a false pelvis (**figure 8.10**). The **true pelvis,** also known as the *lesser pelvis,* lies *inferior* to the pelvic brim. It encloses the pelvic cavity and forms a deep bowl that contains the pelvic organs. The **false pelvis,** also known as the *greater pelvis,* lies *superior* to the pelvic brim. It is enclosed by the ala of the iliac bones. It forms the inferior region of the abdominal cavity and houses the inferior abdominal organs.

The pelvis also has a superior and an inferior opening, and each has clinical significance. The **pelvic inlet,** also known as the *superior pelvic aperture,* is the superiorly positioned space enclosed by the pelvic brim. In other words, the pelvic brim is the bony oval *ridge* of bone, whereas the pelvic inlet is the *space* surrounded by the pelvic brim. The pelvic inlet is the opening at the boundary between the true pelvis and the false pelvis.

The **pelvic outlet,** also known as the *inferior pelvic aperture,* is the inferiorly placed opening bounded by the coccyx, the ischial tuberosities, and the inferior border of the pubic symphysis. The pelvic outlet is covered with muscles and skin and forms the body region called the **perineum** (per'i-nē'ŭm). The width and size of the pelvic outlet is especially important during childbirth, because the opening must be wide enough to accommodate the fetal head. Therefore, in genetic females, the ischial spines rarely project into the pelvic outlet. In males, the ischial spines often project into the pelvic outlet, thereby narrowing the diameter of this outlet.

8.3c Sexually Dimorphic Features of the Pelves

Although sexually dimorphic features are seen in the skull (see section 7.2), the most reliable indicator of sex is the pelvis, primarily the ossa coxae. The ossa coxae are the most sexually dimorphic bones of the body due to the requirements of pregnancy and childbirth.[1] For example, the female pelvis is shallower and wider than the male pelvis to accommodate an infant's head as it passes through the birth canal. Some of these differences are obvious, such as that males have narrower hips than females do. One reason for this difference is that the female ilium flares more laterally, and the male ilium projects more superiorly. Because the female pelvis is wider, the greater sciatic notch is much wider as well. In contrast, the male greater sciatic notch is much narrower and U-shaped. Females tend to have a **preauricular sulcus,** which is a depression/groove between the greater sciatic notch and the sacroiliac articulation. Males tend not to have this sulcus. The sacrum is usually shorter and wider in females. The coccyx projects more vertically in males, whereas the female coccyx has a posterior tilt.

The body of the pubis in females is much longer and almost rectangular in shape, compared to the shorter, triangular male pubic body. The **subpubic angle** (or *pubic arch*) is the angle formed when the left and right pubic bones are aligned at their pubic symphyses. Because females have much longer pubic bones, the corresponding subpubic angle is much wider and more convex, usually much greater than 100 degrees. The male pubic arch is much narrower and typically does not extend past 90 degrees.

[1] For discussion of sexual dimorphism, we are using a combination of genetic sex combined with environmental factors, such as hormones, which result in the observable characteristics.

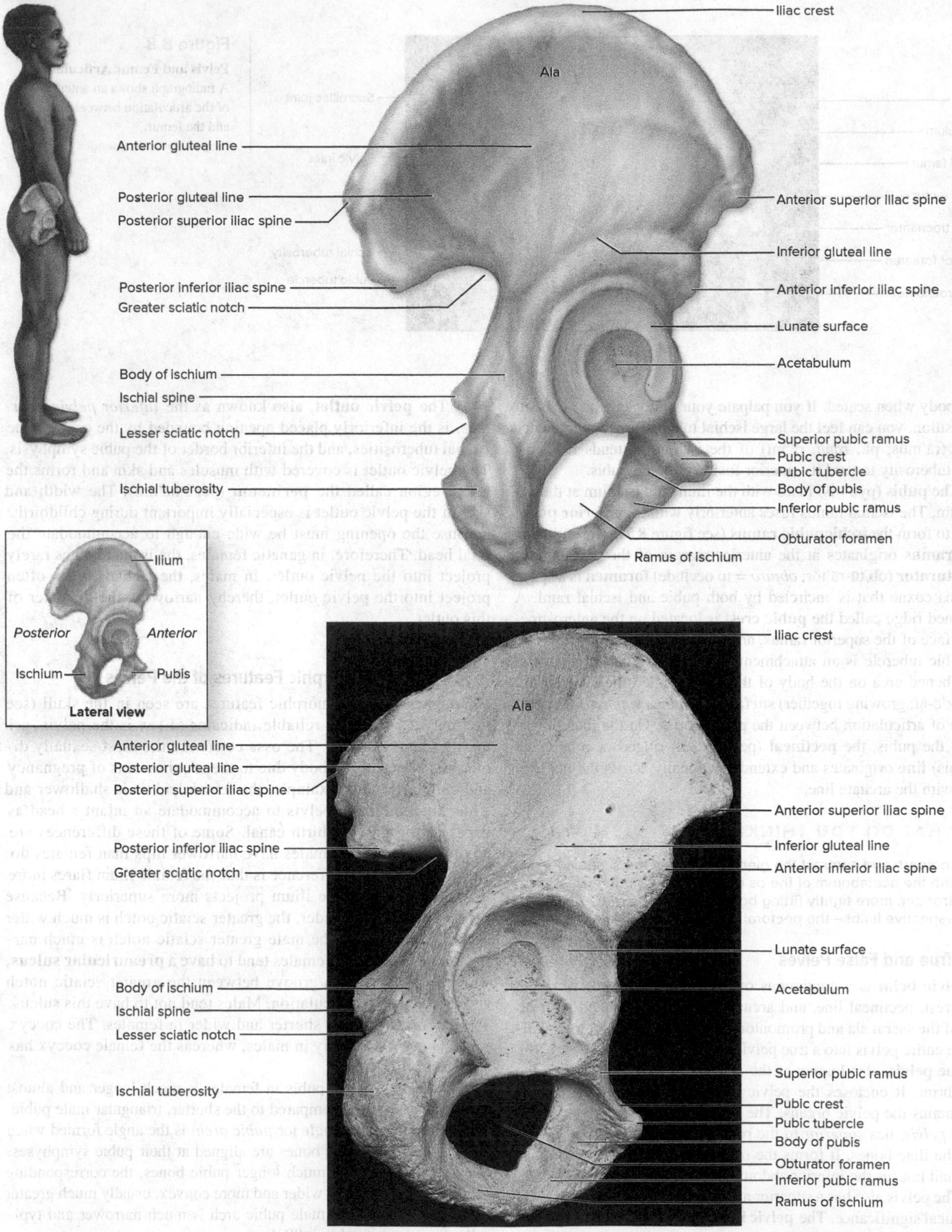
Iliac crest
Ala
Anterior gluteal line
Posterior gluteal line
Posterior superior iliac spine
Anterior superior iliac spine
Inferior gluteal line
Posterior inferior iliac spine
Greater sciatic notch
Anterior inferior iliac spine
Lunate surface
Acetabulum
Body of ischium
Ischial spine
Lesser sciatic notch
Superior pubic ramus
Pubic crest
Pubic tubercle
Ischial tuberosity
Body of pubis
Inferior pubic ramus
Obturator foramen
Ramus of ischium
Ilium
Posterior
Anterior
Ischium
Pubis
Lateral view
Iliac crest
Ala
Anterior gluteal line
Posterior gluteal line
Posterior superior iliac spine
Anterior superior iliac spine
Posterior inferior iliac spine
Inferior gluteal line
Greater sciatic notch
Anterior inferior iliac spine
Lunate surface
Body of ischium
Acetabulum
Ischial spine
Lesser sciatic notch
Superior pubic ramus
Ischial tuberosity
Pubic crest
Pubic tubercle
Body of pubis
Obturator foramen
Inferior pubic ramus
Ramus of ischium

(a) Right os coxae, lateral view

Figure 8.9

Os Coxae. Each os coxae of the pelvic girdle is formed by the fusion of three bones: an ilium, an ischium, and a pubis. Diagrams and photos show the features of these bones and their relationships in (*a*) lateral and (*b*) medial views.

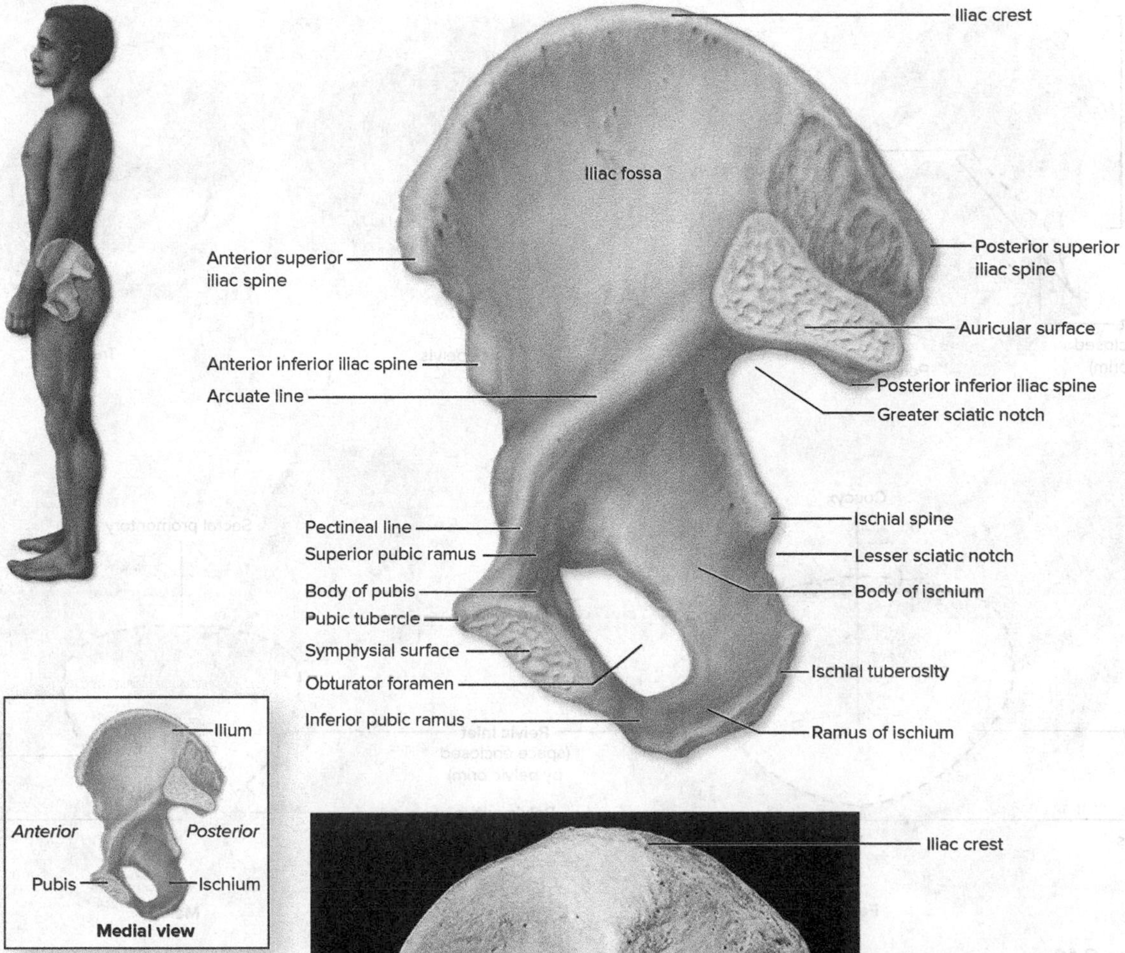
Iliac crest
Iliac fossa
Anterior superior iliac spine
Posterior superior iliac spine
Auricular surface
Anterior inferior iliac spine
Arcuate line
Posterior inferior iliac spine
Greater sciatic notch
Pectineal line
Ischial spine
Superior pubic ramus
Lesser sciatic notch
Body of pubis
Body of ischium
Pubic tubercle
Symphysial surface
Ischial tuberosity
Obturator foramen
Inferior pubic ramus
Ramus of ischium
Ilium
Anterior
Posterior
Pubis
Ischium
Medial view

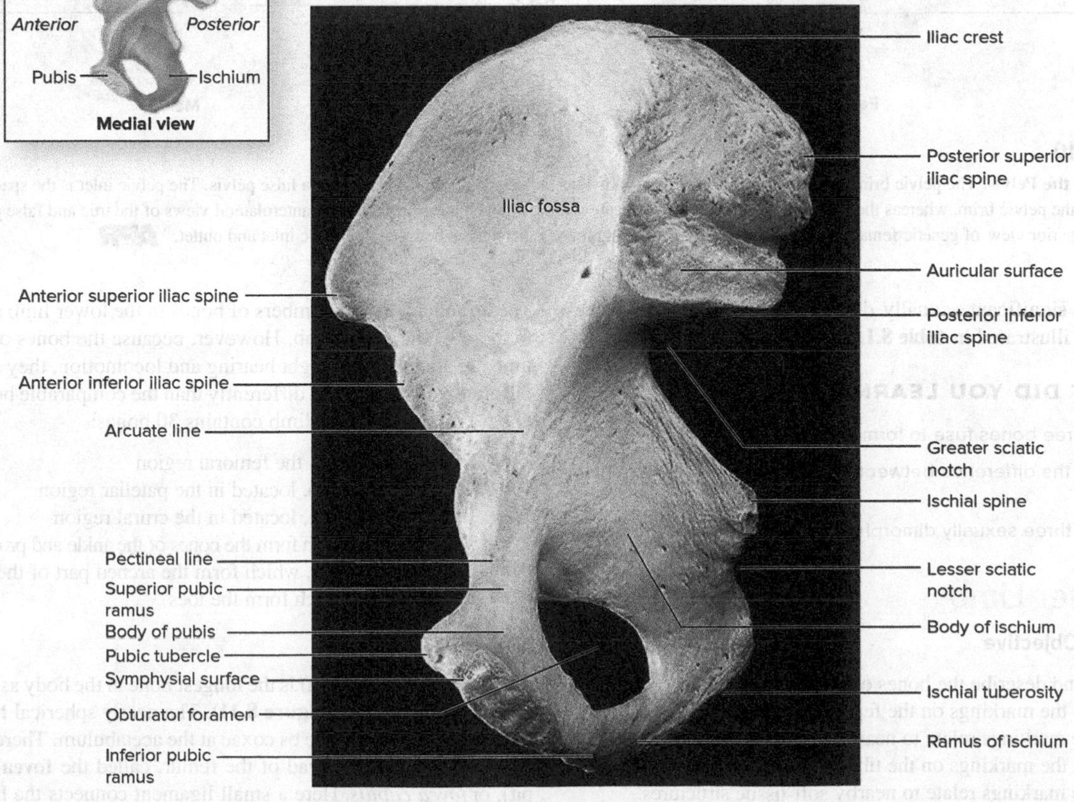
Iliac crest
Posterior superior iliac spine
Iliac fossa
Auricular surface
Anterior superior iliac spine
Posterior inferior iliac spine
Anterior inferior iliac spine
Arcuate line
Greater sciatic notch
Ischial spine
Pectineal line
Superior pubic ramus
Lesser sciatic notch
Body of pubis
Body of ischium
Pubic tubercle
Symphysial surface
Ischial tuberosity
Obturator foramen
Ramus of ischium
Inferior pubic ramus

(b) Right os coxae, medial view

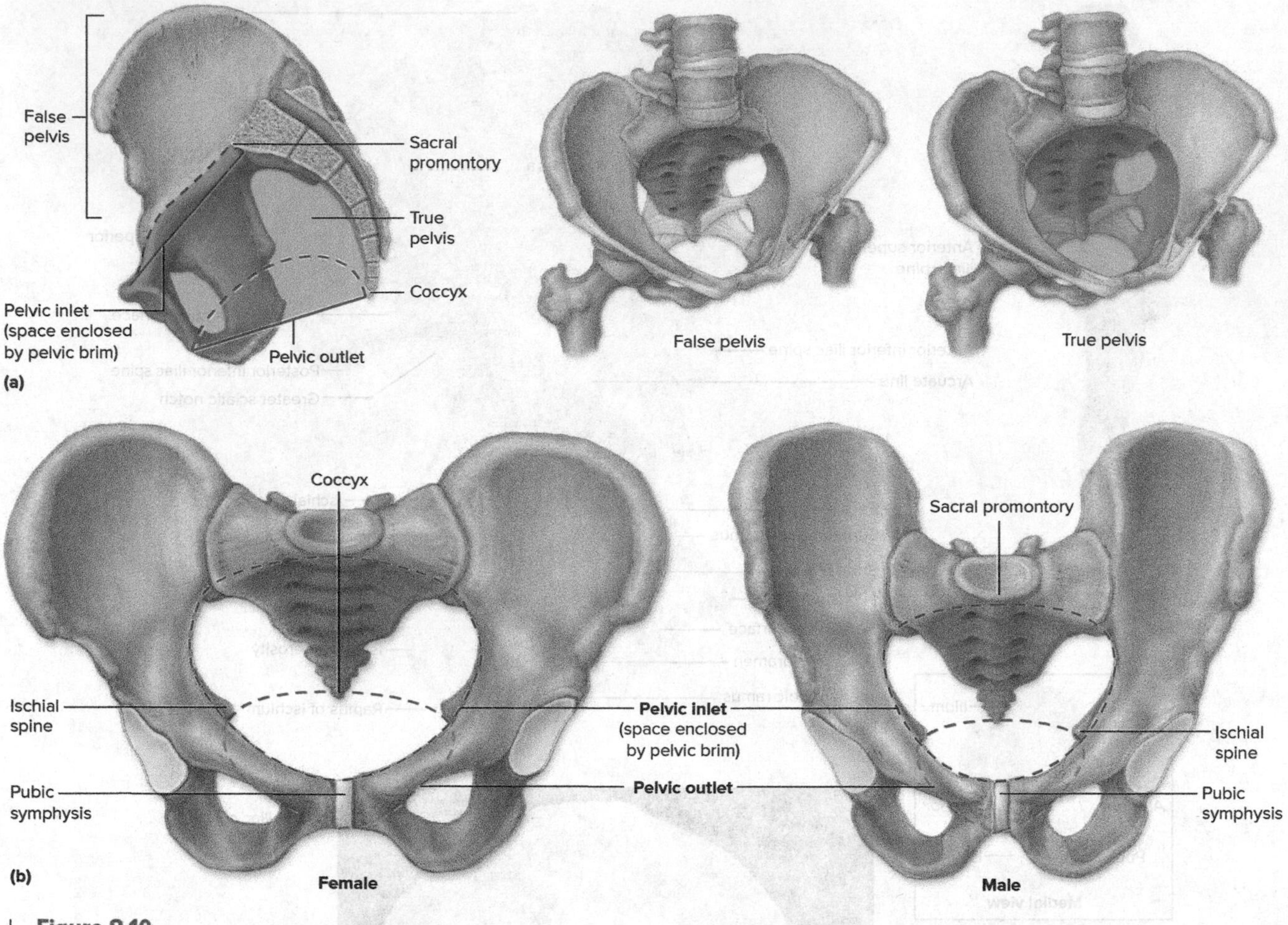
False pelvis
Sacral promontory
True pelvis
Coccyx
Pelvic inlet (space enclosed by pelvic brim)
Pelvic outlet
(a)
False pelvis
True pelvis
Coccyx
Sacral promontory
Ischial spine
Pelvic inlet (space enclosed by pelvic brim)
Ischial spine
Pubic symphysis
Pelvic outlet
Pubic symphysis
(b)
Female
Male

Figure 8.10

Features of the Pelvis. The pelvic brim is the oval bony ridge that subdivides the pelvis into a true pelvis and a false pelvis. The pelvic inlet is the space enclosed by the pelvic brim, whereas the pelvic outlet is the inferior opening in the true pelvis. (*a*) Medial and anterolateral views of the true and false pelves. (*b*) Anterosuperior view of genetic female and male pelves, demonstrating the sex differences between the pelvic inlet and outlet. APR

Several significant sexually dimorphic features of the pelves are listed and illustrated in **table 8.1**.

WHAT DID YOU LEARN?

5. What three bones fuse to form each os coxae?
6. What is the difference between the pelvic inlet and the pelvic outlet?
7. Explain three sexually dimorphic features of the pelves.

8.4 Lower Limb

✓ Learning Objective

10. Name and describe the bones of the lower limb.
11. Identify the markings on the femur and patella, and explain how the markings relate to nearby soft-tissue structures.
12. Identify the markings on the tibia and the fibula, and explain how the markings relate to nearby soft-tissue structures.
13. Identify and describe the tarsals, metatarsals, and phalanges of the lower limb.
14. Describe the three arches of the foot and explain their purpose.

The arrangement and numbers of bones in the lower limb are similar to those of the upper limb. However, because the bones of the lower limb are adapted for weight bearing and locomotion, they are shaped differently and articulate differently than the comparable bones of the upper limb. Each lower limb contains 30 bones:

- 1 femur, located in the femoral region
- 1 patella (kneecap), located in the patellar region
- 1 tibia and 1 fibula, located in the crural region
- 7 tarsal bones, which form the bones of the ankle and proximal foot
- 5 metatarsal bones, which form the arched part of the foot
- 14 phalanges, which form the toes

8.4a Femur

The **femur** (fē′mŭr; thigh) is the longest bone in the body as well as the strongest and heaviest (**figure 8.11**). The nearly spherical **head** of the femur articulates with the os coxae at the acetabulum. There is a small depression within the head of the femur, called the **fovea** (fō′vē-ă; a pit), or *fovea capitis.* Here a small ligament connects the head of the femur to the acetabulum. Distal to the head, an elongated, constricted **neck** joins the **shaft** of the femur at an angle, which brings the knees closer to the midline.

Table 8.1 Sexually Dimorphic Features of the Pelves

View	Female Pelvis	Male Pelvis
Medial View	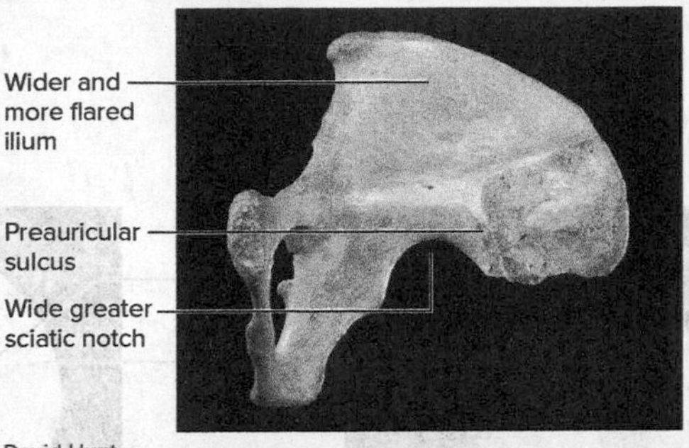 David Hunt	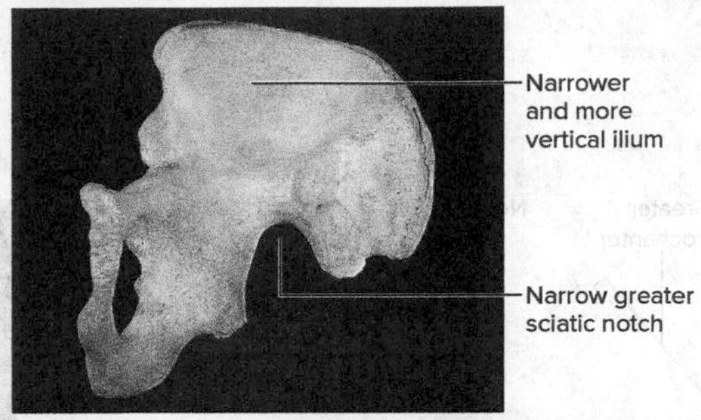 David Hunt
Anterior View	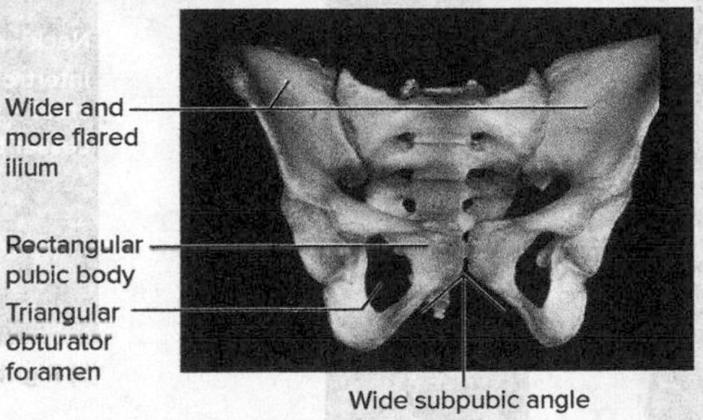 VideoSurgery/Science Source	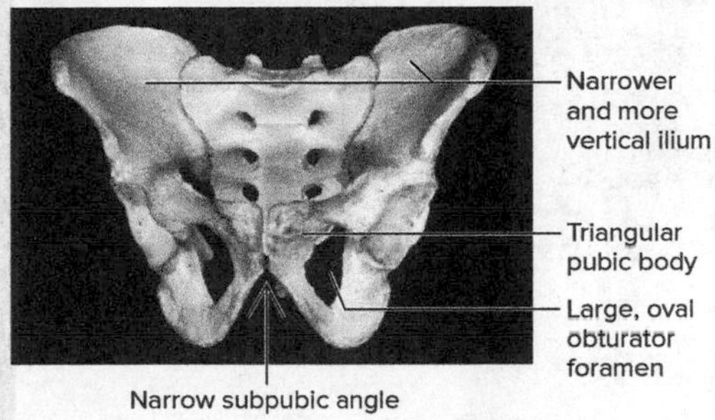 VideoSurgery/Science Source

Wider and more flared ilium
Preauricular sulcus
Wide greater sciatic notch

Narrower and more vertical ilium
Narrow greater sciatic notch

Wider and more flared ilium
Rectangular pubic body
Triangular obturator foramen
Wide subpubic angle

Narrower and more vertical ilium
Triangular pubic body
Large, oval obturator foramen
Narrow subpubic angle

Features	Female-like Characteristic(s)	Male-like Characteristic(s)
General Appearance	Less massive; gracile processes, less prominent muscle markings	More massive; more robust processes, more prominent muscle markings
General Width	Pelvic girdle is wider, more flared	Pelvic girdle is narrower and more vertically oriented, less flared
Pelvic Inlet	Spacious, wide, and oval	Heart-shaped
Acetabulum	Smaller	Larger
Greater Sciatic Notch	Wide and shallow	Narrow and U-shaped, deep
Ilium	Shallow: Does not project far above sacroiliac joint	Deep: Projects farther above sacroiliac joint
Obturator Foramen	Smaller and triangular	Larger and oval
Subpubic Angle	Broader, more convex, usually greater than 100 degrees	Narrow, V-shaped, usually less than 90 degrees
Body of Pubis	Longer, more rectangular	Shorter, triangular
Preauricular Sulcus	Usually present	Usually absent
Sacrum	Shorter and wider; flatter sacral curvature	Narrower and longer; more curved (greater sacral curvature)
Coccyx	Posterior tilt	Vertical
Ischiopubic Ramus	Narrow and sharp	Broad and flat
Ischial Spine	Rarely projects into pelvic outlet	Frequently rotated inward, projects into pelvic outlet

Two massive, rough processes originate near the proximal end of the femur and serve as insertion sites for the powerful gluteal and thigh muscles. The **greater trochanter** (trō-kan′tĕr; a runner) projects laterally from the junction of the neck and shaft. Stand up and palpate your lateral thigh, near the hip joint; the bony projection you feel is the greater trochanter. A **lesser trochanter** is located on the femur's posteromedial surface. The greater and lesser trochanters are connected on the posterior surface of the femur by a thick oblique ridge of bone called the **intertrochanteric** (in′tĕr-tr ō′kan-ter′ik) **crest.** Anteriorly, a raised **intertrochanteric line** extends between

Learning Strategy 8.4

As you learn the bones of the lower limb, compare and contrast them with their corresponding upper limb bones. For example, compare the femur with the humerus. Review how the two are similar, and then determine what features differ between them. This method will help you better remember and understand the bones and their features.

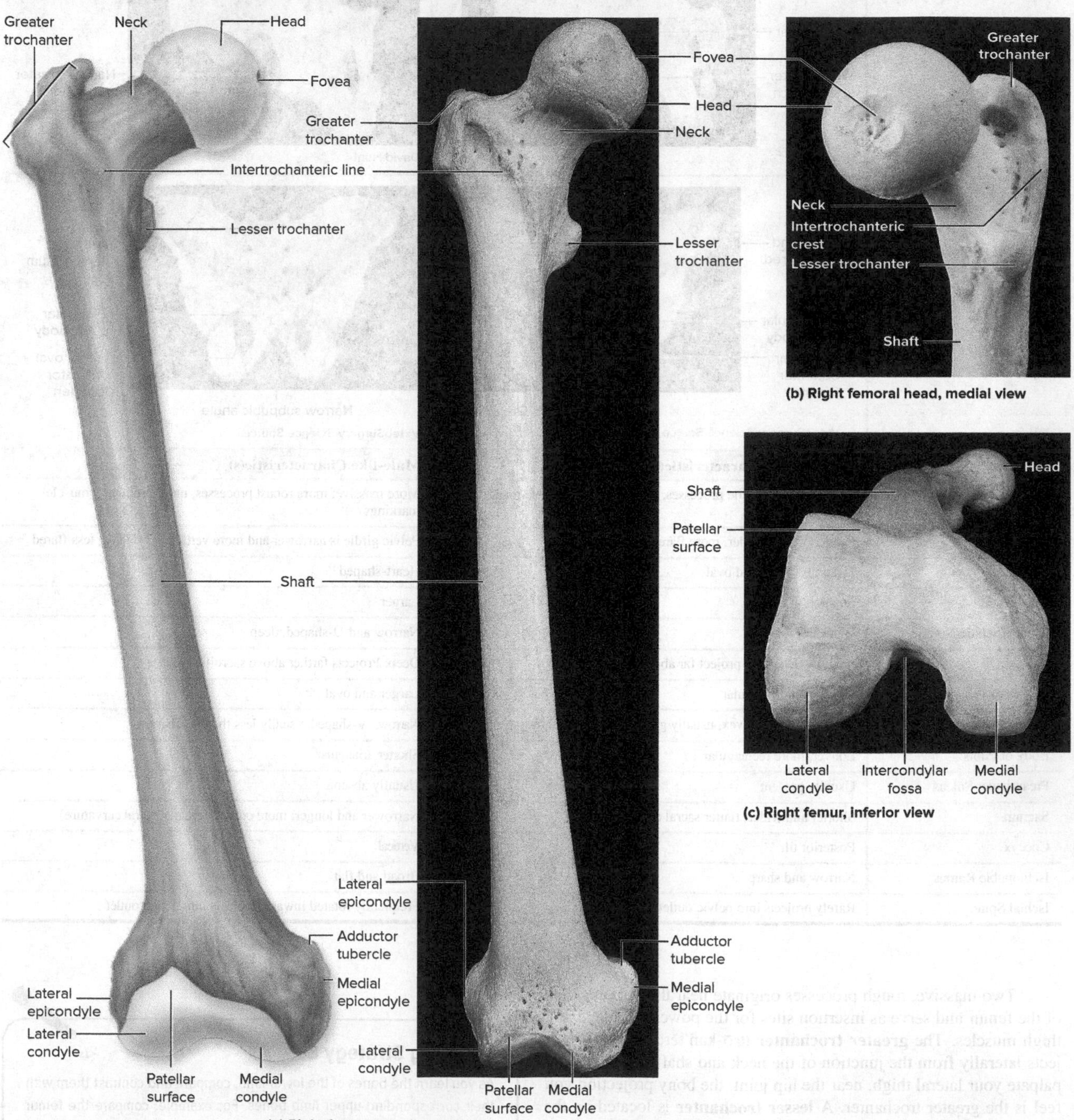
Greater trochanter
Neck
Head
Fovea
Intertrochanteric line
Lesser trochanter
Shaft
Lateral epicondyle
Adductor tubercle
Medial epicondyle
Lateral epicondyle
Lateral condyle
Patellar surface
Medial condyle
Fovea
Head
Greater trochanter
Neck
Lesser trochanter
Lateral condyle
Patellar surface
Medial condyle
Greater trochanter
Neck
Intertrochanteric crest
Lesser trochanter
Shaft
Head
Shaft
Patellar surface
Lateral condyle
Intercondylar fossa
Medial condyle

(a) Right femur, anterior view

(b) Right femoral head, medial view

(c) Right femur, inferior view

Figure 8.11

Femur. The femur is the bone of the femoral region. (*a*) Diagram and photo show an anterior view of the right femur. (*b*) Superomedial, (*c*) inferior, and (*d*) posterior views of the right femur. APR

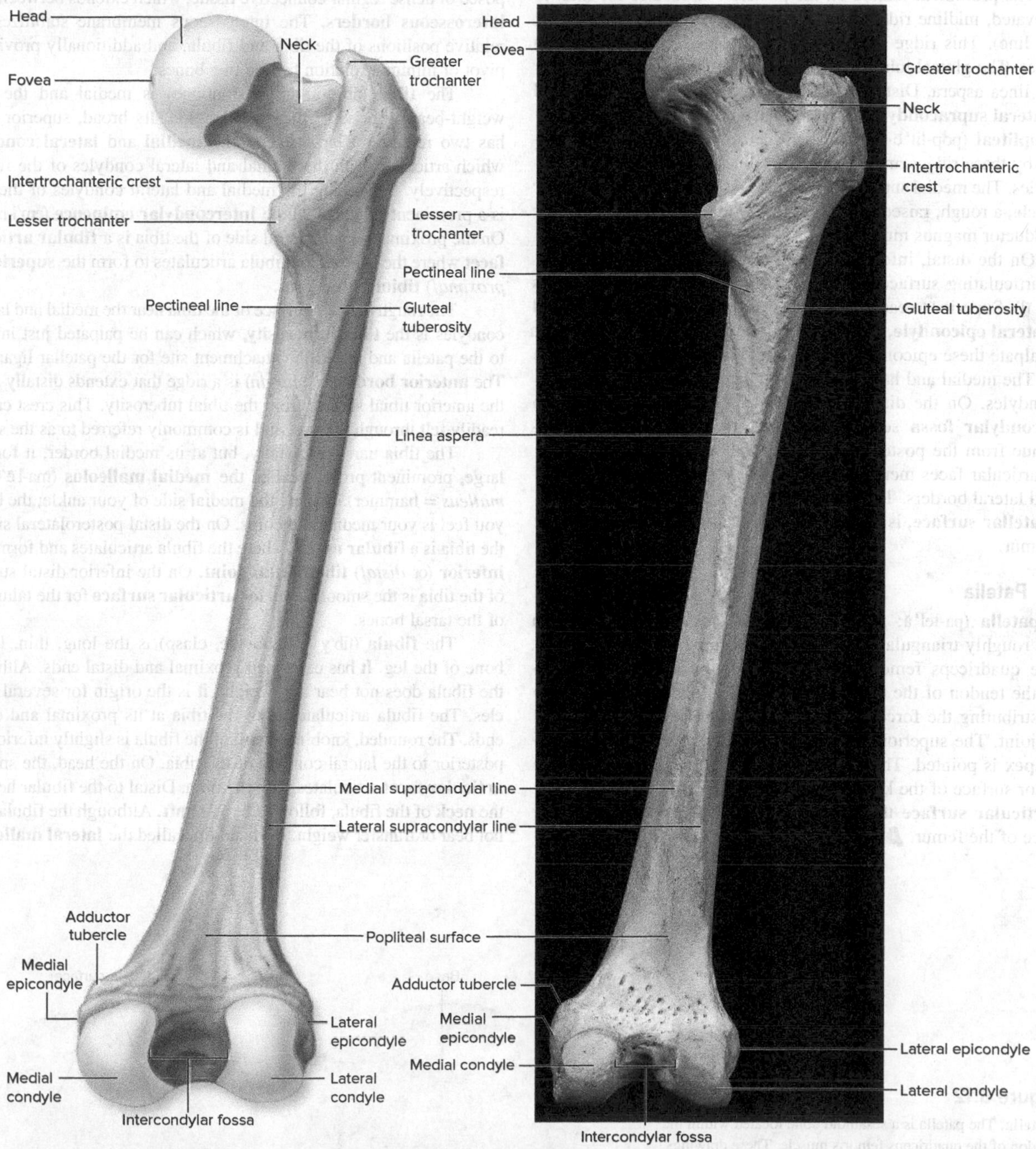
Head
Fovea
Neck
Greater trochanter
Intertrochanteric crest
Lesser trochanter
Pectineal line
Gluteal tuberosity
Linea aspera
Medial supracondylar line
Lateral supracondylar line
Adductor tubercle
Medial epicondyle
Popliteal surface
Lateral epicondyle
Medial condyle
Lateral condyle
Intercondylar fossa

(d) Right femur, posterior view

the two trochanters and marks the distal edge of the hip joint capsule. Inferior to the intertrochanteric crest, the **pectineal line** marks the attachment of the pectineus muscle, whereas the **gluteal** (glū́t ē-ăl; *gloutos* = buttock) **tuberosity** marks the attachment of the gluteus maximus muscle (see section 12.2a).

The prominent feature on the posterior surface of the shaft is an elevated, midline ridge called the **linea aspera** (lin′ ē-ă as′pĕr-ă; rough line). This ridge denotes the attachment site for many thigh muscles. The gluteal tuberosity and pectineal line merge proximally to the linea aspera. Distally, the linea aspera branches into **medial** and **lateral supracondylar lines.** A flattened triangular area, called the **popliteal** (pop-lit′ ē-ăl; *poples* = ham of knee) **surface,** is bordered by these ridges and an imaginary line between the distal epicondyles. The medial supracondylar ridge terminates in the **adductor tubercle,** a rough, raised projection that is the site of attachment for the adductor magnus muscle.

On the distal, inferior surface of the femur are two smooth, oval articulating surfaces called the **medial** and **lateral condyles** (kon′d īl). Superior to each condyle are projections called the **medial** and **lateral epicondyle,** respectively. When you flex your knee, you can palpate these epicondyles in the thigh on the sides of your knee joint. The medial and lateral supracondylar lines terminate at these epicondyles. On the distal posterior surface of the femur, a deep **intercondylar fossa** separates the two condyles. Both condyles continue from the posterior surface to the anterior surface, where their articular faces merge, producing an articular surface with elevated lateral borders. This smooth anteromedial depression, called the **patellar surface,** is the place where the patella articulates with the femur.

8.4b Patella

The **patella** (pa-tel′ă; *patina* = shallow disk), or *kneecap,* is a large, roughly triangular sesamoid bone located within the tendon of the quadriceps femoris muscle (**figure 8.12**). The patella allows the tendon of the quadriceps femoris to glide more smoothly by distributing the force placed on the tendon, and it protects the knee joint. The superior **base** of the patella is broad, and its inferior **apex** is pointed. The patella may be easily palpated along the anterior surface of the knee. The posterior aspect of the patella has an **articular surface** that articulates (connects) with the patellar surface of the femur. **APR**

8.4c Tibia and Fibula

Anatomists identify the part of the lower limb between the knee and the ankle as the crural region, or leg. The skeleton of the leg has two parallel bones, the thick, strong tibia and a slender fibula (**figure 8.13**). These two bones are connected by an **interosseous membrane** composed of dense regular connective tissue, which extends between their **interosseous borders.** The interosseous membrane stabilizes the relative positions of the tibia and fibula, and additionally provides a pivot of minimal rotation for the two bones.

The **tibia** (tib′ ē-ă; large shinbone) is medial and the only weight-bearing bone of the crural region. Its broad, superior head has two relatively flat surfaces, the **medial** and **lateral condyles,** which articulate with the medial and lateral condyles of the femur, respectively. Separating the medial and lateral condyles of the tibia is a prominent ridge called the **intercondylar eminence** (em′i-nens). On the proximal posterolateral side of the tibia is a **fibular articular facet** where the head of the fibula articulates to form the **superior** (or *proximal*) **tibiofibular joint.**

The rough anterior surface of the tibia near the medial and lateral condyles is the **tibial tuberosity,** which can be palpated just inferior to the patella and marks the attachment site for the patellar ligament. The **anterior border** (or *margin*) is a ridge that extends distally along the anterior tibial surface from the tibial tuberosity. This crest can be readily felt through the skin and is commonly referred to as the shin.

The tibia narrows distally, but at its medial border, it forms a large, prominent process called the **medial malleolus** (ma-lē′ō-lŭs; *malleus* = hammer). Palpate the medial side of your ankle; the bump you feel is your medial malleolus. On the distal posterolateral side of the tibia is a **fibular notch,** where the fibula articulates and forms the **inferior** (or *distal*) **tibiofibular joint.** On the inferior distal surface of the tibia is the smooth **inferior articular surface** for the talus, one of the tarsal bones.

The **fibula** (fib′y ū-lă; buckle, clasp) is the long, thin, lateral bone of the leg. It has expanded proximal and distal ends. Although the fibula does not bear any weight, it is the origin for several muscles. The fibula articulates with the tibia at its proximal and distal ends. The rounded, knoblike **head** of the fibula is slightly inferior and posterior to the lateral condyle of the tibia. On the head, the smooth **articular facet** articulates with the tibia. Distal to the fibular head is the **neck** of the fibula, followed by its **shaft.** Although the fibula does not bear or transfer weight, its distal tip, called the **lateral malleolus,**

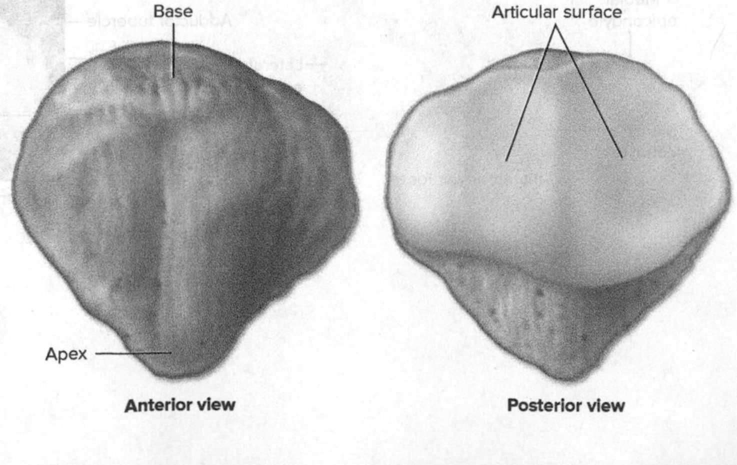
Base
Articular surface
Apex
Anterior view
Posterior view

Figure 8.12

Patella. The patella is a sesamoid bone located within the tendon of the quadriceps femoris muscle. These drawings show anterior and posterior views of the right patella.

Clinical View 8.4

Pott Fracture

A **Pott fracture** is a fracture of the distal tibia and often the fibula, involving the malleoli specifically. This fracture is a result of forced inversion (twisting or rolling) the ankle. It is a common sports injury as a result of jumping, or can occur simply by misjudging a step down a stair or off a curb. As the foot inverts, it damages the deltoid ligament and breaks the medial malleolus, which causes lateral movement of the foot damaging the lateral ligament and often breaks the fibular shaft just proximal to the lateral malleolus (see Clinical View 9.8: "Ankle Sprains" in section 9.5c).

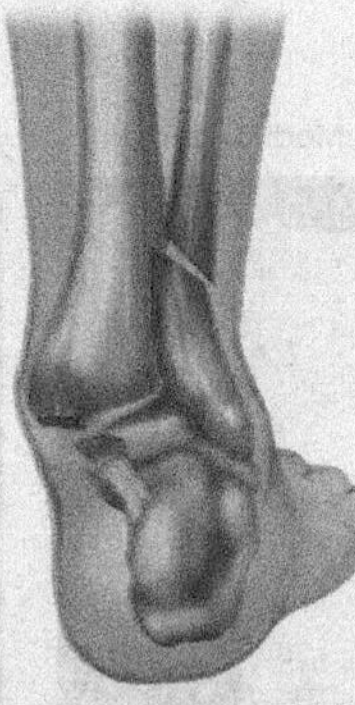

Diagram shows typical Pott fracture.

Symptoms include pain in the ankle, swelling, and bruising. Treatment depends upon the severity of the fracture and the amount of displacement of the bones. If there is displacement, then surgery is usually required. Otherwise, some form of immobilization and avoidance of weight-bearing exercise for several weeks is sufficient for proper healing.

extends laterally to the ankle joint, where it provides lateral stability. Palpate the lateral side of your ankle; the bump you feel is your lateral malleolus.

WHAT DO YOU THINK?

4. The medial and lateral malleoli of the leg are similar to what bony features of the forearm?

8.4d Tarsals, Metatarsals, and Phalanges

The bones that form the ankle and foot are the tarsals, metatarsals, and phalanges (**figure 8.14**). The seven **tarsals** (tar's ăl; *tarsus* = flat surface) of the ankle and proximal foot are analogous to the eight carpal bones of the wrist, although their shapes and arrangement are different. The tarsal bones are thoroughly integrated into the structure of the foot because they help the ankle bear the body's weight.

The calcaneus, talus, and navicular are considered the *proximal row* of tarsal bones. The largest tarsal bone is the **calcaneus** (kal-kā'nē-ŭs; heel), which forms the heel. Its posterior end is a rough, knob-shaped projection that is the point of attachment for the calcaneal (Achilles) tendon extending from the strong muscles on the posterior side of the leg. The superiormost and second-largest tarsal bone is the **talus** (tā'lŭs; ankle bone). The superior aspect of the talus articulates with the articular surface of the tibia. The **navicular** (nă-vik'y ū-lăr; *navis* = ship) **bone** is on the medial side of the ankle.

The distal row is formed by a group of four tarsal bones. The three **cuneiform** (kū'ne-i-f ōrm; *cuneus* = wedge) **bones** are wedge-shaped bones with articulations between them, positioned anterior to the navicular bone. They are named according to their position: **medial cuneiform, intermediate cuneiform,** and **lateral cuneiform bones.** The cuneiform bones articulate proximally with the anterior surface of the navicular bone. The laterally placed **cuboid** (kyū'boyd; *kybos* = cube) **bone** articulates at its medial surface with the lateral cuneiform and the calcaneus. The distal surfaces of the cuboid bone and the cuneiform bones articulate with the metatarsal bones of the foot.

WHAT DO YOU THINK?

5. What are some similarities and differences between the carpal bones and the tarsal bones?

The **metatarsal** (met'ă-tar's ăl) **bones** of the foot are five long bones similar in arrangement and name to the metacarpal bones of the hand. They form the sole of the foot and are identified with Roman numerals I–V, proceeding medially to laterally across the sole (figure 8.14). Metatarsals I through III articulate with the three cuneiform bones, and metatarsals IV and V articulate with the cuboid bone. Distally, each metatarsal bone articulates with a proximal phalanx. At the head of the first metatarsal are two tiny sesamoid bones, which insert on the tendons of the flexor hallucis brevis muscle and help these tendons move more freely by distributing the force more evenly along them.

The bones of the toes (like the bones of the fingers) are called **phalanges.** The toes contain 14 phalanges. The great toe is the **hallux** (hal' ŭks; *hallex* = great toe), and it has only two phalanges (proximal and distal); each of the other four toes has three phalanges (proximal, middle, and distal).

Arches of the Foot

Normally, the sole of the foot is arched, which helps it support the weight of the body and ensures that the blood vessels and nerves on the sole of the foot are not pinched when we are standing. The three arches of the foot are the medial longitudinal, lateral longitudinal, and transverse arches (**figure 8.15**).

The **medial longitudinal arch** (*arcus* = bow) is the highest of the three arches and extends from the heel to the great toe. It is formed from the calcaneus, talus, navicular, and cuneiform bones, and metatarsals I–III. The medial longitudinal arch prevents the medial side of the foot from touching the ground and gives our footprint its characteristic shape (figure 8.15*d*).

The **lateral longitudinal arch** is not as high as the medial arch, so the lateral part of the foot *does* contribute to a footprint. This arch extends between the little toe and the heel, and it is formed from the calcaneus and cuboid bones, and metatarsals IV and V.

The **transverse arch** runs perpendicular to the longitudinal arches. It is formed by the distal row of tarsals (cuboid and cuneiforms) and the bases of all five metatarsals. Note in figure 8.15*c* that the transverse arch is higher medially than laterally due to the medial longitudinal arch height.

The shape of these arches is maintained primarily by the foot bones themselves. These bones are shaped so that they can interlock and support their weight in an arch, much like the wedge-shaped blocks of an arched bridge can support the bridge without other mechanical supports. Secondarily, strong ligaments attach to the bones and contracting muscles pull on the tendons, thereby helping to maintain the shape of the foot arches.

WHAT DID YOU LEARN?

8. Where is the interosseous membrane of the leg located? What are its functions?
9. What are the names of the tarsal bones? Which tarsal bone articulates with the leg, and which tarsal bones articulate with the metatarsals of the foot?

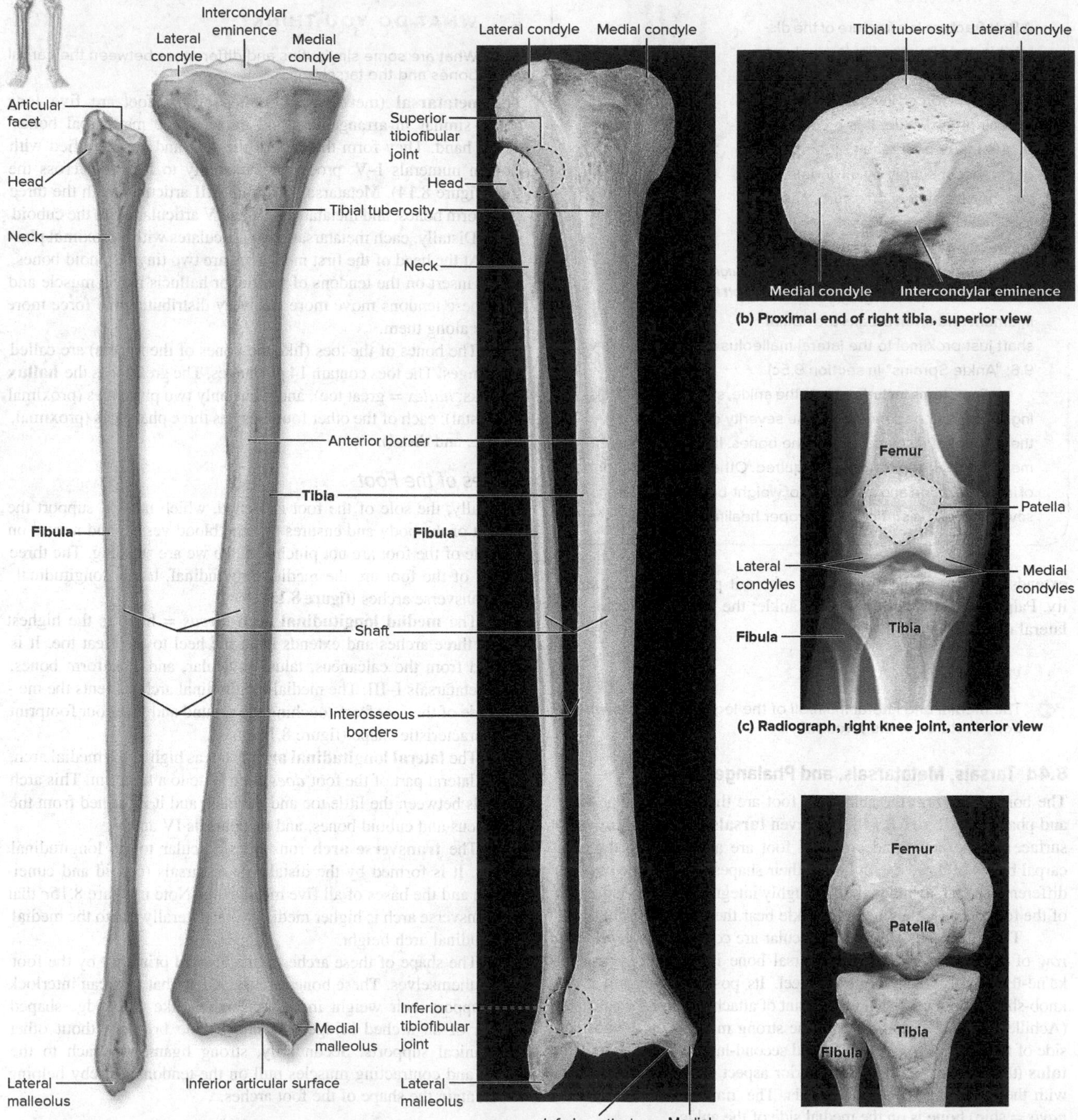
Intercondylar eminence
Lateral condyle
Medial condyle
Articular facet
Head
Neck
Superior tibiofibular joint
Head
Tibial tuberosity
Neck
Anterior border
Tibia
Fibula
Fibula
Shaft
Interosseous borders
Inferior tibiofibular joint
Medial malleolus
Lateral malleolus
Inferior articular surface
Lateral malleolus
Lateral condyle
Medial condyle
Inferior articular surface
Medial malleolus
Tibial tuberosity
Lateral condyle
Medial condyle
Intercondylar eminence
Femur
Patella
Lateral condyles
Medial condyles
Fibula
Tibia
Femur
Patella
Tibia
Fibula

(a) Right tibia and fibula, anterior view

(b) Proximal end of right tibia, superior view

(c) Radiograph, right knee joint, anterior view

(d) Right knee joint, anterior view

Figure 8.13

Tibia, Fibula, and Knee Joint. The tibia and fibula are the bones of the crural (leg) region. (*a*) Diagram and photo show an anterior view of the right tibia and fibula. (*b*) Proximal end of the right tibia. (*c, d*) Anterior view of the right knee joint. (*e*) Posterior view of the right tibia and fibula. (*f*) Posterior and (*g*) lateral views of the right knee joint. The fibula does not directly participate in the knee joint proper. APR

(a, b, d, e, f, g) ©McGraw-Hill Education/Christine Eckel, photographer; (c) Media for Medical/UIG/Getty Images

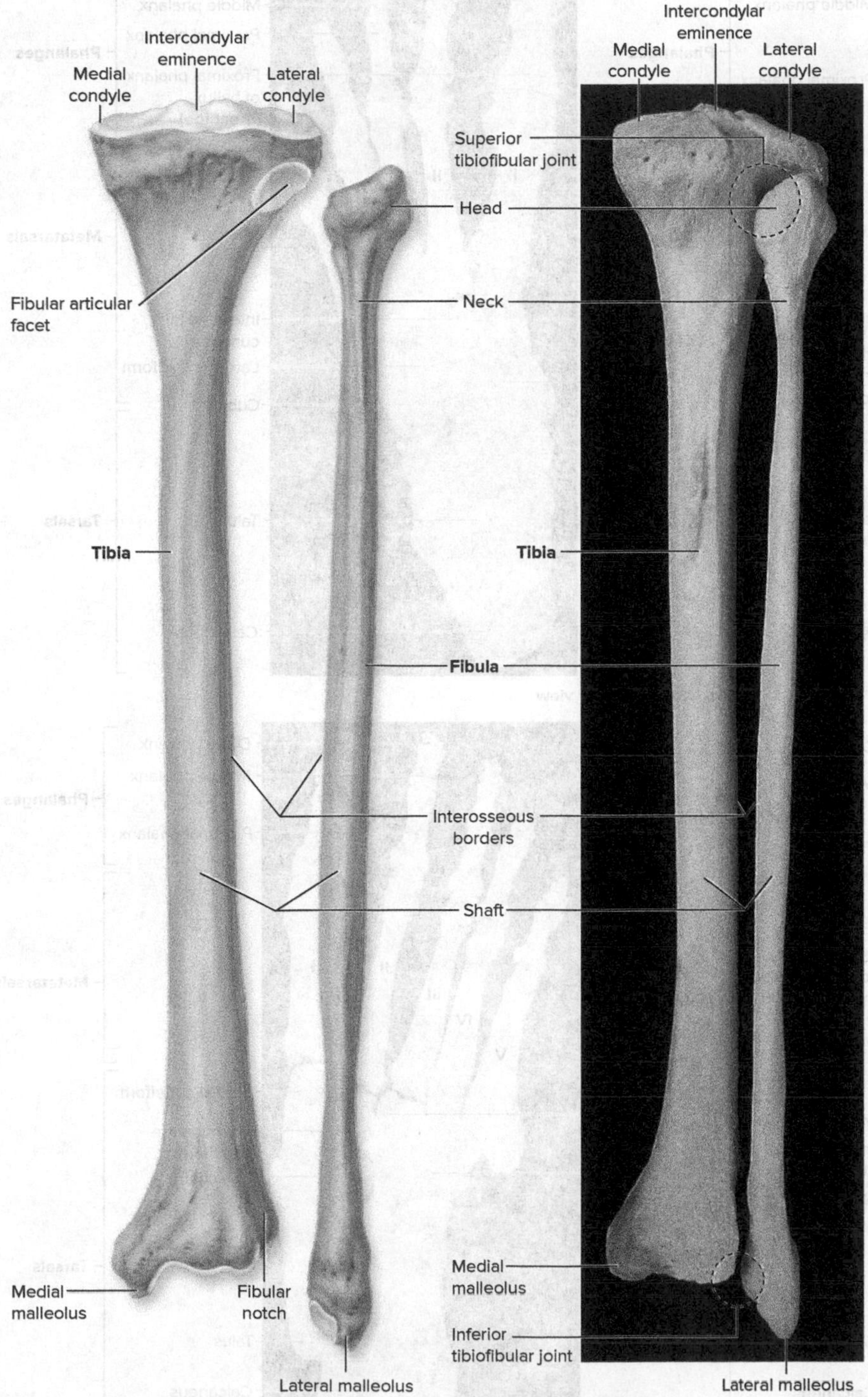
Intercondylar
eminence
Medial
condyle
Lateral
condyle
Fibular articular
facet
Superior
tibiofibular joint
Head
Neck
Tibia
Fibula
Interosseous
borders
Shaft
Medial
malleolus
Fibular
notch
Lateral malleolus
Inferior
tibiofibular joint
Lateral malleolus

(e) Right tibia and fibula, posterior view

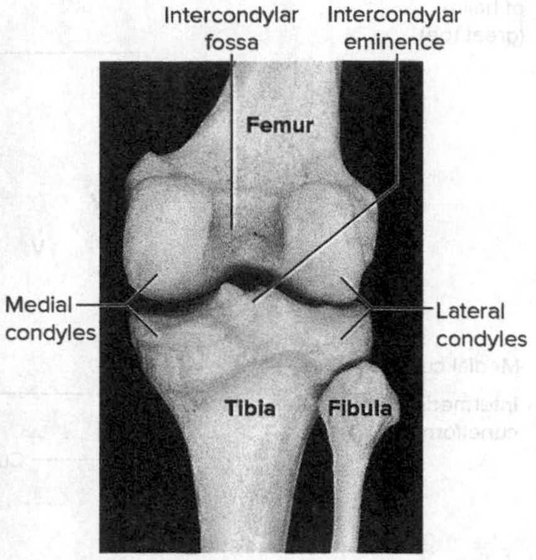
Intercondylar
fossa
Intercondylar
eminence
Femur
Medial
condyles
Lateral
condyles
Tibia
Fibula

(f) Right knee joint, posterior view

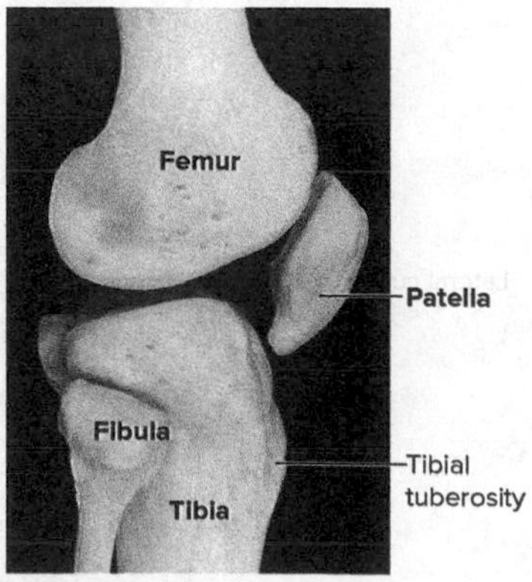
Femur
Patella
Fibula
Tibia
Tibial
tuberosity

(g) Right knee joint, lateral view

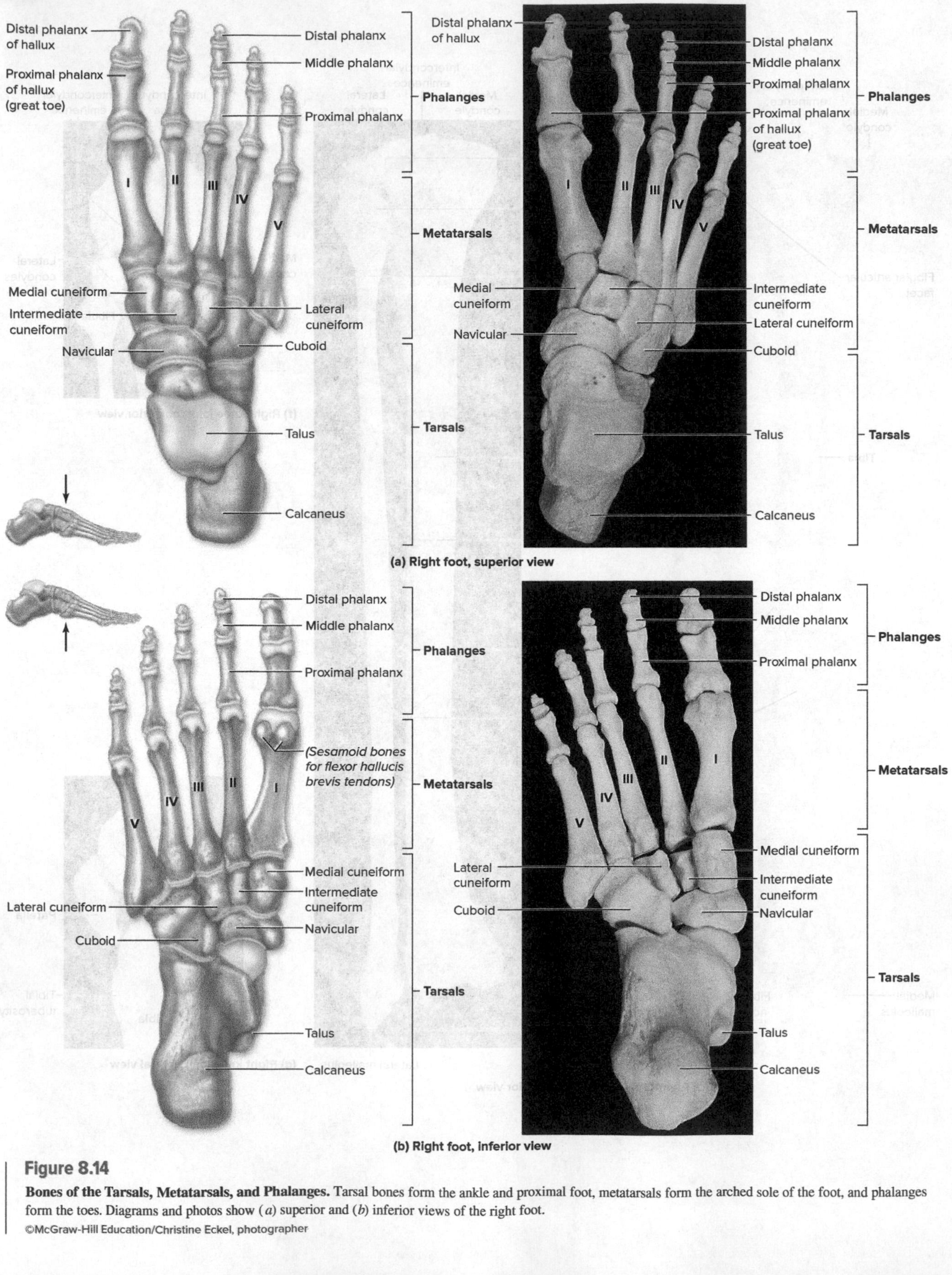

Distal phalanx of hallux
Proximal phalanx of hallux (great toe)
Distal phalanx
Middle phalanx
Proximal phalanx
Phalanges
I
II
III
IV
V
Metatarsals
Medial cuneiform
Intermediate cuneiform
Lateral cuneiform
Navicular
Cuboid
Tarsals
Talus
Calcaneus
Distal phalanx of hallux
Distal phalanx
Middle phalanx
Proximal phalanx
Proximal phalanx of hallux (great toe)
Phalanges
Metatarsals
Medial cuneiform
Intermediate cuneiform
Navicular
Lateral cuneiform
Cuboid
Talus
Tarsals
Calcaneus
(a) Right foot, superior view
Distal phalanx
Middle phalanx
Phalanges
Proximal phalanx
(Sesamoid bones for flexor hallucis brevis tendons)
Metatarsals
Medial cuneiform
Intermediate cuneiform
Lateral cuneiform
Navicular
Cuboid
Tarsals
Talus
Calcaneus
Distal phalanx
Middle phalanx
Phalanges
Proximal phalanx
Metatarsals
Lateral cuneiform
Medial cuneiform
Intermediate cuneiform
Cuboid
Navicular
Tarsals
Talus
Calcaneus
(b) Right foot, inferior view

Figure 8.14

Bones of the Tarsals, Metatarsals, and Phalanges. Tarsal bones form the ankle and proximal foot, metatarsals form the arched sole of the foot, and phalanges form the toes. Diagrams and photos show (*a*) superior and (*b*) inferior views of the right foot.

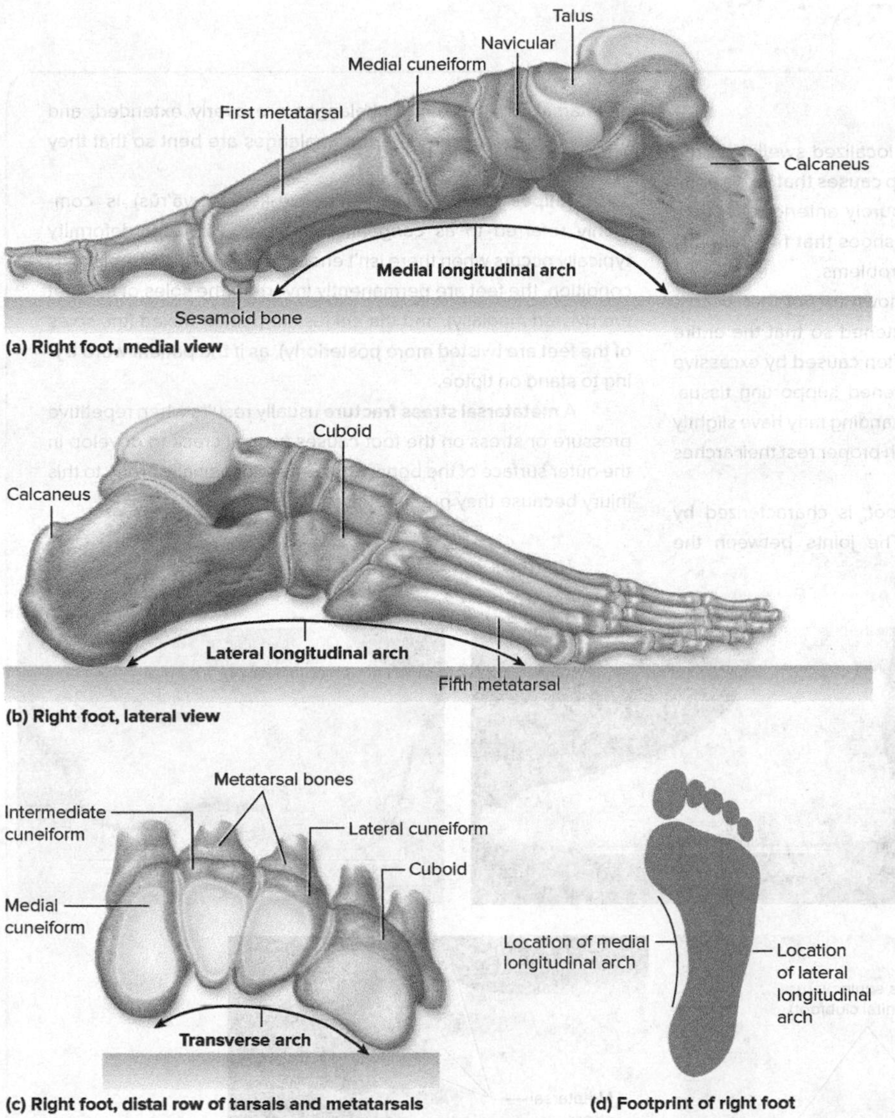
Talus
Navicular
Medial cuneiform
First metatarsal
Calcaneus
Medial longitudinal arch
Sesamoid bone
(a) Right foot, medial view
Cuboid
Calcaneus
Lateral longitudinal arch
Fifth metatarsal
(b) Right foot, lateral view
Metatarsal bones
Intermediate cuneiform
Lateral cuneiform
Cuboid
Medial cuneiform
Transverse arch
(c) Right foot, distal row of tarsals and metatarsals
Location of medial longitudinal arch
Location of lateral longitudinal arch
(d) Footprint of right foot

Figure 8.15

Arches of the Foot. The foot's two longitudinal arches and one transverse arch allow for better weight support. (*a*) Medial longitudinal arch. (*b*) Lateral longitudinal arch. (*c*) Transverse arch as seen in cross-sectional view. (*d*) A footprint illustrates the placement of the longitudinal arches.

8.5 Aging of the Appendicular Skeleton

✓ Learning Objective

15. Describe how the appendicular skeleton changes as we age.

As we age, skeletal mass and density decline, while erosion and porosity increase, potentially resulting in osteoporosis. Bones become more brittle and susceptible to fracture. Articulating surfaces deteriorate, contributing to osteoarthritis. Changes in the skeleton begin in childhood and continue throughout life. For example, most of the epiphyseal plates fuse between the ages of 10 and 25 years. Degenerative changes in the normal skeleton, such as a reduction in mineral content, don't begin until middle age. Measurable loss of calcium in men begins by age 45, but may start in some women as early as age 35.

The os coxae is not only a reliable indicator of sex, but it also can provide a good estimate of a skeleton's age at death. In particular, the pubic symphysis undergoes age-related changes. The pubic symphysis appears roughened or billowed in the teens and early 20s. Thereafter, the symphysis flattens and loses its billowing. In the 30s and 40s, the pubic symphysis develops a well-defined rim. Finally, as a person gets older, it begins to develop concavities and arthritic changes.

8.6 Development of the Appendicular Skeleton

✓ Learning Objective

16. Describe the events that occur during development of the appendicular skeleton.

As mentioned in section 6.4, bone forms by either intramembranous ossification or endochondral ossification. Many of the bones of the skull are formed from intramembranous ossification, whereas almost all of the remaining bones of the skeleton form through endochondral ossification. (The exception is the clavicle, which is formed from a

Clinical View 8.5

Pathologies of the Foot

A **bunion** (bŭn′yŭn; *buigne* = bump) is a localized swelling at the first metatarsophalangeal joint. This bump causes that toe to point toward the second toe instead of in a purely anterior direction. Bunions are usually caused by wearing shoes that fit too tightly and are among the most common foot problems.

Pes planus (pla′nus), commonly known as *flat feet*, occurs when the medial longitudinal arch is flattened so that the entire sole touches the ground. Pes planus is often caused by excessive weight, postural abnormalities, or weakened supporting tissue. Individuals who spend most of their day standing may have slightly fallen arches by the end of the day, but with proper rest their arches can return to normal shape.

Pes cavus (pes că′vus), or *clawfoot*, is characterized by excessively high longitudinal arches. The joints between the metatarsals and proximal phalanges are overly extended, and the joints between the different phalanges are bent so that they appear clawed.

Talipes equinovarus (tal′i-pēzē-kwē-nō-vā′rŭs) is commonly referred to as *congenital clubfoot*. This foot deformity typically occurs when there isn't enough room in the womb. In this condition, the feet are permanently inverted (the soles of the feet are twisted medially), and the ankles are plantar flexed (the soles of the feet are twisted more posteriorly), as if the patient were trying to stand on tiptoe.

A **metatarsal stress fracture** usually results when repetitive pressure or stress on the foot causes a small crack to develop in the outer surface of the bone. Runners are especially prone to this injury because they put repetitive stress on their feet.

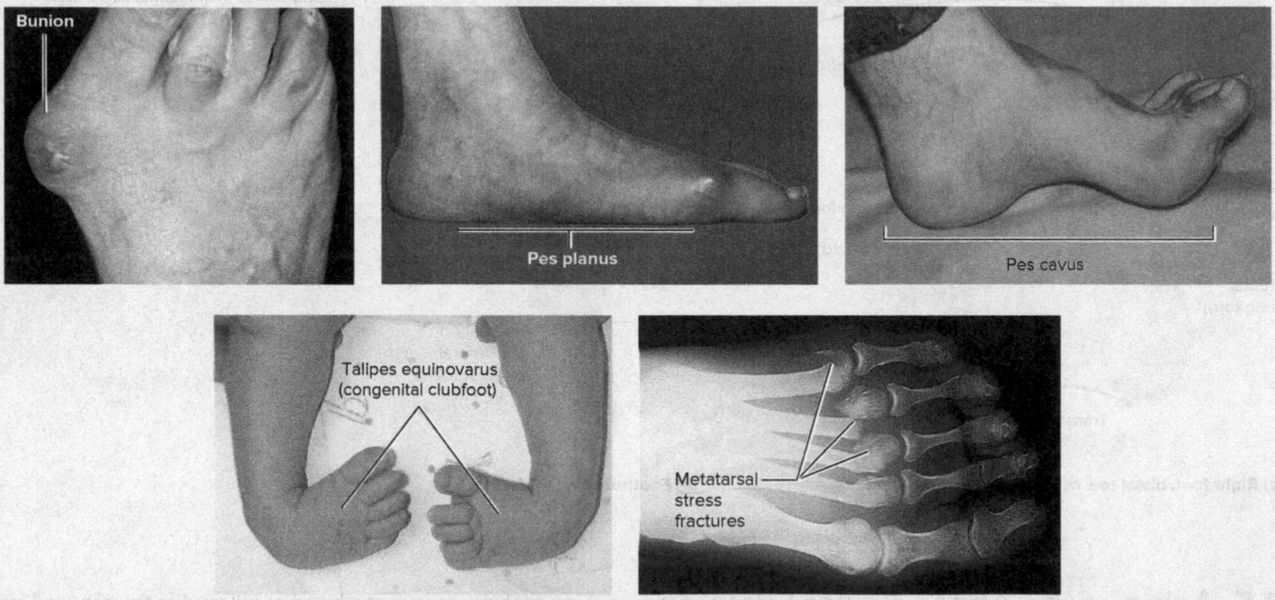

(bunion) Dr. P. Marazzi/Science Photo Library/Alamy Stock Photo; (pes planus) Bart's Medical Library/Phototake; (pes cavus) SPL/Science Source; (talipes equinovarus) Kevin Shea, M.D./Custom Medical Stock Photo/Newscom; (metatarsal stress fractures) ISM/Phototake

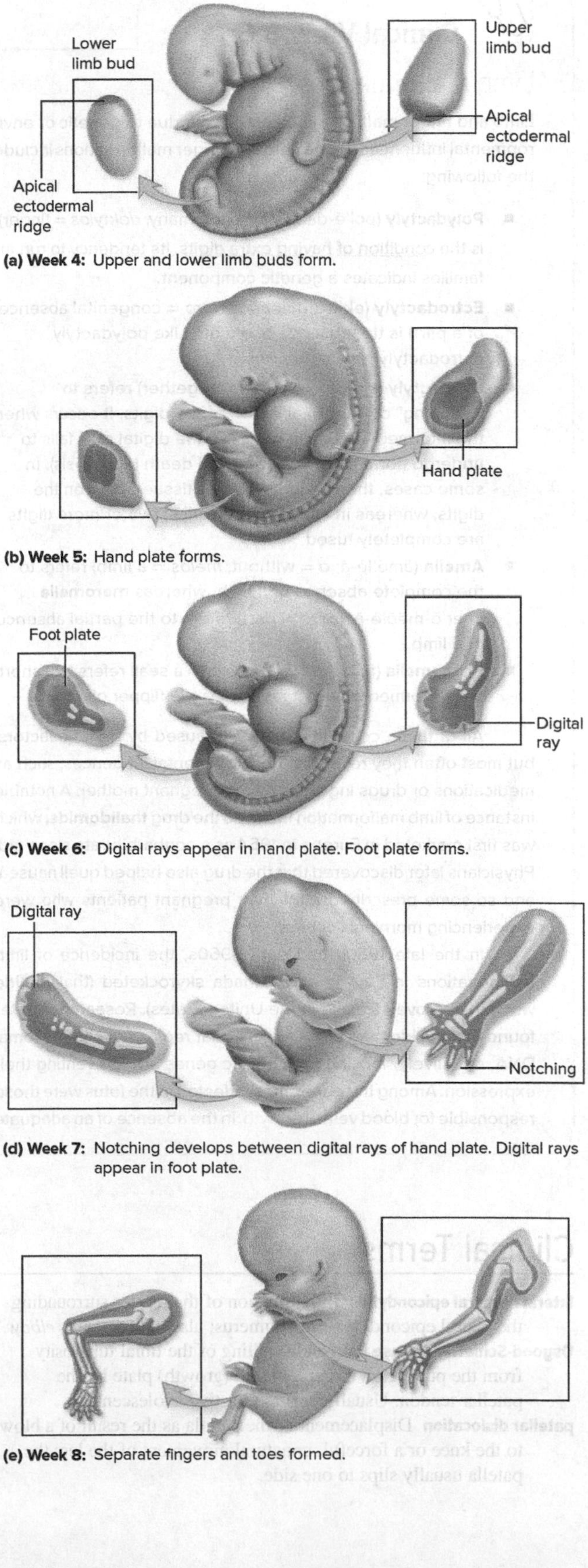

(a) **Week 4:** Upper and lower limb buds form.

(b) **Week 5:** Hand plate forms.

(c) **Week 6:** Digital rays appear in hand plate. Foot plate forms.

(d) **Week 7:** Notching develops between digital rays of hand plate. Digital rays appear in foot plate.

(e) **Week 8:** Separate fingers and toes formed.

Figure 8.16

Development of the Appendicular Skeleton. The upper and lower limbs develop between weeks 4 and 8. Upper limb development precedes corresponding lower limb development by 2 to 4 days.

central intramembranous ossification center; its ends are formed from endochondral ossification centers.)

The appendicular skeleton begins to develop during the fourth week, when **limb buds** appear as small ridges along the lateral sides of the embryo. The upper limb buds appear early in the fourth week (about day 26), and the lower limb buds appear a few days later (day 28) (**figure 8.16**). In general, the development of upper and lower limbs is similar. However, upper limb development precedes corresponding lower limb development by about 2 to 4 days. The upper and lower limbs form *proximodistally,* meaning that the more proximal parts of the limbs form first (in weeks 4–5), and the more distal parts differentiate later.

Early limb buds are composed of lateral plate mesoderm and covered by a layer of ectoderm. The lateral plate mesoderm later forms the bones, tendons, cartilage, and connective tissue of the limb, while the ectoderm forms the epidermis and the epidermal derivatives. The musculature of the limbs forms from somitic mesoderm that migrates to the developing limbs during the fifth week of development.

At the apex of each limb bud, part of the ectoderm forms an elevated thickening called the **apical ectodermal** (ek′tō-dĕr′măl) **ridge,** which plays a role in the differentiation and elongation of the limb. By mechanisms not completely understood, this ridge "signals" the underlying tissue to form the various components of the limb. Experiments on animals indicate that the limb fails to develop if the apical ectodermal ridge is removed. Thus, this ridge is vital for limb development and differentiation.

Initially, the limb buds are cylindrical. By the early fifth week, the distal portion of the upper limb bud forms a rounded, paddle-shaped **hand plate,** which later becomes the palm and fingers. In the lower limb bud, a corresponding **foot plate** forms during the sixth week. These plates develop longitudinal thickenings called **digital rays,** which eventually form the digits. The digital rays in the hand plate appear in the late sixth week, and the foot digital rays appear during the early seventh week. The digital rays are initially connected by intermediately placed tissue, which later undergoes programmed cell death (apoptosis). Thus, as this intermediate tissue dies, notching occurs between the digital rays, and separate digits are formed. This process occurs in the seventh week and is complete by the eighth week for both the fingers and the toes.

As the limb buds enlarge, bends appear where the future elbow and shoulder joints will develop. During the late seventh through early eighth weeks, the upper limb rotates laterally, so that the elbows are directed posteriorly, while the lower limb rotates medially, so that the knees are directed anteriorly. By week 8 of development, primary ossification centers begin to form in each bone. Hyaline cartilage is gradually replaced by bony tissue via the process of endochondral ossification (see section 6.4b). By week 12, the shafts of the limb bones are rapidly ossifying, but other developing bones remain as cartilage. All of these bones continue to develop throughout the fetal period and well into childhood.

Clinical View 8.6

Limb Malformations

Limb and finger malformations may occur due to genetic or environmental influences. Some limb and finger malformations include the following:

- **Polydactyly** (pol'ē-dak'ti-lē; *poly* = many, *daktylos* = finger) is the condition of having extra digits. Its tendency to run in families indicates a genetic component.
- **Ectrodactyly** (ek'trō-dak'ti-lē; *ectro* = congenital absence of a part) is the absence of a digit. Like polydactyly, ectrodactyly runs in families.
- **Syndactyly** (sin-dak'ti-lē; *syn* = together) refers to "webbing" or abnormal fusion of the digits. It occurs when the intermediate tissue between the digital rays fails to undergo normal programmed cell death (apoptosis). In some cases, there is merely extra tissue between the digits, whereas in more severe cases, two or more digits are completely fused.
- **Amelia** (ămē'lē-ă; *a* = without, *melos* = a limb) refers to the complete absence of a limb, whereas **meromelia** (mer'ō-mēōlē-ă; *mero* = part) refers to the partial absence of a limb.
- **Phocomelia** (fō'kō-mē'lē-ă; *phoke* = a seal) refers to a short, poorly formed limb that resembles the flipper of a seal.

All of these conditions may be caused by genetic factors, but most often they result from environmental influences, such as medications or drugs ingested by the pregnant mother. A notable instance of limb malformation involved the drug **thalidomide,** which was first marketed in Europe in 1954 as a nonbarbiturate sleep aid. Physicians later discovered that the drug also helped quell nausea, and so some prescribed it for their pregnant patients who were experiencing morning sickness.

In the late 1950s and early 1960s, the incidence of limb malformations in Europe and Canada skyrocketed (thalidomide was not approved for use in the United States). Researchers later found that thalidomide binds to particular regions of chromosomal DNA, effectively "locking up" specific genes and preventing their expression. Among the genes most affected in the fetus were those responsible for blood vessel growth. In the absence of an adequate vascular network, limb bud formation is disrupted. Researchers and clinicians discovered that if a pregnant female took thalidomide during weeks 4–8 of embryonic development (the time when the limbs are at their critical stage of development), limb formation was severely disrupted.

Thalidomide was taken off the market in the 1960s, but it has made a comeback as a treatment of multiple myeloma (a type of cancer of bone marrow cells), treating the symptoms of AIDS, and treating lupus (an autoimmune disease). It also is a very effective treatment for the more devastating effects of leprosy (which is prevalent in South America and other parts of the world). Unfortunately, although the drug now comes with extensive warnings and precautions, some patients ignore the warnings and others take the medication prescribed for someone else. As a result, there has been a resurgence of thalidomide babies born in South America in recent years. Thalidomide is the classic example of how teratogens can affect the delicate cycle of embryonic development, and why females of childbearing age should be sure they aren't pregnant before taking any medication.

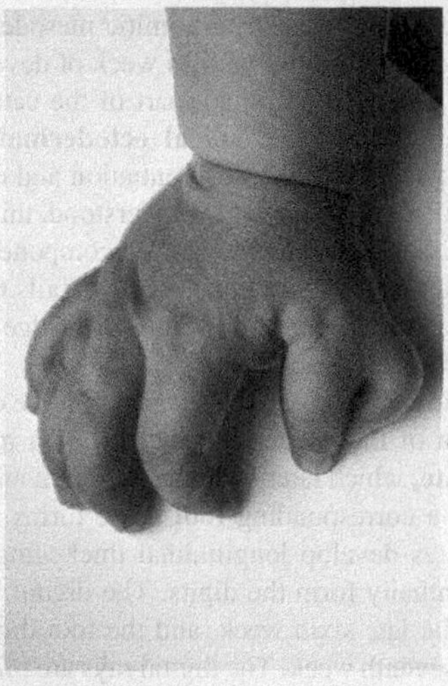

Photo of hand of child with polydactyly.
v.gi/Shutterstock

Clinical Terms

lateral humeral epicondylitis Inflammation of the tissues surrounding the lateral epicondyle of the humerus; also called *tennis elbow.*

Osgood-Schlatter disease Pain and swelling of the tibial tuberosity from the pulling on the epiphyseal (growth) plate by the patellar tendon. Usually occurs in active adolescents.

patellar dislocation Displacement of the patella as the result of a blow to the knee or a forceful, unnatural movement of the leg; the patella usually slips to one side.

patellofemoral syndrome Condition in which the patella doesn't track or align properly on the femur. Females are more prone to this condition because their hips are wider, and thus their femurs flare at a wider angle, affecting the knee joint as well. Due to a weakness of the vastus medialis portion of the quadriceps muscle, the patella is pulled laterally. Patients can alleviate the resulting knee pain by performing specific directed exercises to strengthen the vastus medialis muscle.

Chapter Summary

	■ The appendicular skeleton includes the bony supports (girdles) that attach the upper and lower limbs to the axial skeleton, as well as the bones of those limbs.
8.1 Pectoral Girdle	■ The pectoral girdle is composed of four bones: the left and right clavicles and scapulae. **8.1a Clavicle** ■ The clavicle is an S-shaped bone that forms the collarbone. **8.1b Scapula** ■ The scapula is commonly known as the *shoulder blade.*
8.2 Upper Limb	■ Each upper limb contains a humerus, radius, ulna, 8 carpals, 5 metacarpals, and 14 phalanges. **8.2a Humerus** ■ The head of the humerus articulates with the glenoid cavity of the scapula, whereas the trochlea and capitulum articulate with the radius and ulna at the elbow. **8.2b Radius and Ulna** ■ The radius and ulna are the bones of the forearm. **8.2c Carpals, Metacarpals, and Phalanges** ■ The carpal bones are the scaphoid, lunate, triquetrum, and pisiform (proximal row) and the trapezium, trapezoid, capitate, and hamate (distal row). ■ Five metacarpal bones form the bones in the palm of the hand. ■ The phalanges are the finger bones. Four of the fingers contain three phalanges; the pollex (thumb) has only two.
8.3 Pelvic Girdle	■ The pelvic girdle consists of two ossa coxae. The pelvis is composed of the two ossa coxae, the sacrum, and the coccyx. **8.3a Os Coxae** ■ Each os coxae forms through the fusion of an ilium, an ischium, and a pubis. The acetabulum is the socket that articulates with the head of the femur. **8.3b True and False Pelves** ■ The pelvic brim is an oval ridge of bone that divides the entire pelvis into a true (inferior) pelvis and a false (superior) pelvis. **8.3c Sexually Dimorphic Features of the Pelves** ■ The shapes and orientations of the pelvic bones differ between sexes.
8.4 Lower Limb	■ The lower limb is composed of the femur, patella, tibia, fibula, 7 tarsals, 5 metatarsals, and 14 phalanges. **8.4a Femur** ■ The femur has a rounded head and an elongated neck. The greater and lesser trochanters are projections near the head. ■ The medial and lateral condyles articulate with the condyles of the tibia. **8.4b Patella** ■ The patella is the kneecap. **8.4c Tibia and Fibula** ■ In the leg, the tibia is medially located. Its medial malleolus forms the medial bump of the ankle. ■ The fibula is the lateral leg bone. Its lateral malleolus forms the lateral bump of the ankle. **8.4d Tarsals, Metatarsals, and Phalanges** ■ The seven tarsal bones are the calcaneus, talus, navicular, three cuneiforms, and the cuboid. ■ When we stand, our weight is transferred along the longitudinal and transverse arches of the foot.
8.5 Aging of the Appendicular Skeleton	■ Some age-related changes in the skeleton are due to maturation and further development, whereas others reflect deterioration of bone tissue.
8.6 Development of the Appendicular Skeleton	■ The limbs first appear as limb buds during the fourth week. In general, lower limb development lags behind upper limb development by 2 to 4 days.

Challenge Yourself

Actively write or type your answers in a separate document to reinforce your learning, before checking your answers.

Multiple Choice

Select the best answer from the four choices provided.

1. The female pelvis typically has which of the following characteristics?
   a. narrow, U-shaped greater sciatic notch
   b. wide subpubic angle, greater than 100 degrees
   c. short, triangular pubic body
   d. smaller, heart-shaped pelvic inlet
2. Name the posterior surface depression at the distal end of the humerus.
   a. intercondylar fossa
   b. coronoid fossa
   c. olecranon fossa
   d. intertubercular groove
3. The spine of the scapula separates which two fossae?
   a. supraspinous, subscapular
   b. subscapular, infraspinous
   c. infraspinous, supraspinous
   d. supraspinous, glenoid
4. Which structure(s) of the femur articulate with the tibia?
   a. linea aspera
   b. medial and lateral condyles
   c. head of the femur
   d. greater trochanter of the femur
5. Which bony feature can be palpated on the dorsolateral side of the wrist?
   a. styloid process of radius
   b. head of ulna
   c. pisiform bone
   d. radial tuberosity
6. Identify the bone that articulates with the os coxae at the acetabulum.
   a. sacrum
   b. humerus
   c. femur
   d. tibia
7. Which of the following is a carpal bone?
   a. cuneiform
   b. cuboid
   c. trapezium
   d. talus
8. What bony features are you resting on when sitting upright?
   a. pubic bones
   b. ischial tuberosities
   c. sacroiliac joints
   d. iliac crest
9. Name the two prominent bumps you can palpate on the sides of your ankle.
   a. head of the fibula and the tibial tuberosity
   b. calcaneus and cuboid
   c. medial malleolus and lateral malleolus
   d. styloid processes
10. Which of the following bones make up the proximal row of the tarsals?
    a. talus, navicular, and cuboid
    b. talus, calcaneus, navicular
    c. talus, calcaneus, cuboid
    d. cuboid, navicular, and lateral cuneiform

Content Review

1. Compare the anatomic and functional features of the pectoral and pelvic girdles.
2. Identify and describe the borders of the scapula.
3. What is the difference between the anatomical neck and the surgical neck of the humerus?
4. Name and describe the placement of the eight carpal bones of the wrist.
5. How do the glenoid cavity and the acetabulum differ?
6. Name three features of the femur and the structures associated with these features.
7. Briefly describe changes to bone density as we age.
8. What is the function of the slender leg bone called the fibula?
9. Discuss the functions of the arches of the foot.
10. Discuss the development of the limbs. What primary germ layers form the limb bud? List the major events during each week of limb development.

Developing Critical Reasoning

1. A female in her first trimester of pregnancy sees her physician. She suffers from lupus and has read that the drug thalidomide has shown remarkable promise in treating the symptoms. Should the physician prescribe the drug for her at this time? Why or why not?
2. Forensic anthropologists are investigating portions of a human pelvis found in a cave. How can they tell the sex, relative age, and some physical characteristics of the individual based upon the pelvis alone?
3. Carlos wishes to enlist in the Army. During his physical, the physician tells him he has pes planus and will not be able to enlist because of it. What is pes planus, and why does the Army not accept individuals who have it?

Answers to "What Do You Think?"

1. The clavicle is called the "collarbone" because the collar of a shirt rests over this bone.
2. Eight cube-shaped carpal bones allow a great deal more movement than just one or two large carpal bones could because movement can occur between each joint among two or more bones. Having eight carpal bones results in many intercarpal joints where movement may occur, and hence many more possible movements.
3. The glenoid cavity of the scapula is flatter and shallower than the deep, curved acetabulum of the os coxae. The pelvic girdle (both ossa coxae) maintains stronger, more tightly fitting bony connections with the lower limbs than the pectoral girdle (scapulae and clavicles) does with the upper limbs.
4. The medial and lateral malleoli of the leg bones are analogous to the styloid processes of the radius and ulna. Both sets of bony features produce the bumps felt along the ankle and the wrist.
5. Both the carpal and the tarsal bones are short bones. The multiple bones (8 carpal bones, 7 tarsal bones) allow for a range of movement at the intercarpal or intertarsal joints. However, the wrist is more freely movable than the ankle and proximal foot, because the foot is adapted for weight bearing. The tarsal bones are larger and bulkier than the carpal bones.

Design Element: Pencil Icon: Slavojub Pantelic/Shutterstock

SKELETAL SYSTEM

9 Articulations

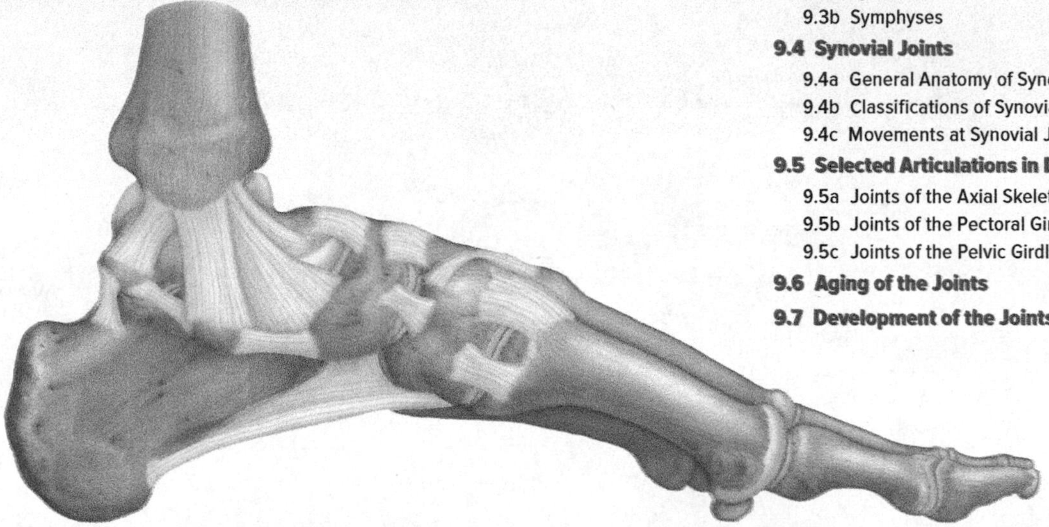

Outline

Anatomy & Physiology Revealed 4.0

MODULE 5: SKELETAL SYSTEM

Our skeleton protects vital organs and supports soft tissues. Its marrow cavity is the source of new blood cells. When it interacts with the muscular system, the skeleton helps the body move. Although bones are slightly flexible, they are too rigid to bend so they meet at joints, which anatomists call articulations. In this chapter, we examine how bones articulate and may allow some freedom of movement, depending upon the shapes and supporting structures of the various joints.

9.1 Articulations (Joints)

✓ Learning Objectives

1. Describe the general structure of articulations.
2. Explain the connection between mobility and stability of a joint.
3. Compare and contrast the structural and functional classifications of joints.

A **joint,** or **articulation** (ar-tik′y ū-lā′shŭn), is the place of contact between bones, between bone and cartilage, or between bones and teeth. Bones are said to **articulate** with each other at a joint. The scientific study of joints is called **arthrology** (ar-throl′ ō-jē; *arthron* = joint, *logos* = study).

The motion permitted at a joint ranges from no movement (e.g., where some skull bones interlock at a suture) to extensive movement (e.g., at the shoulder, where the arm connects to the scapula). The structure of each joint determines its mobility and its stability. There is an inverse relationship between mobility and stability in articulations. The more mobile a joint is, the less stable it is; and the more stable a joint is, the less mobile it is. **Figure 9.1** illustrates the "tradeoff" between mobility and stability for various joints.

Learning Strategy 9.1

You can figure out the names of most joints by piecing together the names of the bones that form them. For example, the *glenohumeral* joint is where the glenoid cavity of the scapula meets the head of the humerus, and the *sternoclavicular* joint is where the manubrium of the sternum articulates with the sternal end of the clavicle.

9.1a Classification of Joints

Joints are classified structurally on the basis of the type of connective tissue that binds the articulating surfaces of the bones, and whether a space occurs between the articulating bones:

- A **fibrous** (fī′brŭs) **joint** occurs where bones are held together by dense regular (fibrous) connective tissue.
- A **cartilaginous** (kar′ti-laj′i-nŭs; *cartilago* = gristle) **joint** occurs where bones are joined by cartilage.
- A **synovial** (si-n ō′vē-ăl) **joint** has a fluid-filled joint cavity that separates the cartilage-covered articulating surfaces of the bones. The articulating surfaces are enclosed within a capsule, and the bones are also joined by various ligaments.

Joints also are classified functionally based upon the extent of movement they permit:

- A **synarthrosis** (sin′ar-thr ō′sis; pl., sin′ar-thrō′sēz; *syn* = joined together, *osis* = condition) is an immobile joint. Two types of fibrous joints and one type of cartilaginous joint are synarthroses.
- An **amphiarthrosis** (am′fē-ar-thr ō′sis; pl., -sēz; *amphi* = around) is a slightly mobile joint. One type of fibrous joint and one type of cartilaginous joint are amphiarthroses.
- A **diarthrosis** (dī′ar-thr ō′sis; pl., -sēz; *di* = two) is a freely mobile joint. All synovial joints are diarthroses.

The following discussion of articulations is based upon their structural classification, with functional categories included as appropriate. As you read about the various types of joints, it may help you to refer to the summary of joint classifications in **table 9.1**.

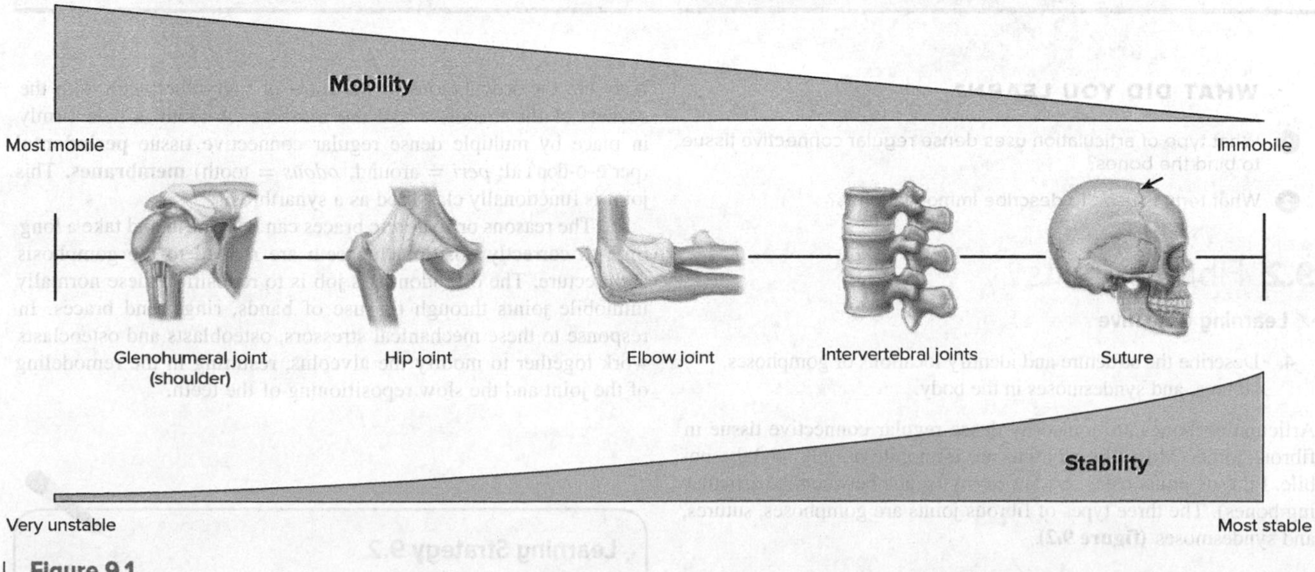
Mobility
Most mobile
Immobile
Glenohumeral joint (shoulder)
Hip joint
Elbow joint
Intervertebral joints
Suture
Stability
Very unstable
Most stable

Figure 9.1

Relationship Between Mobility and Stability in Joints. In every joint, there is a "tradeoff" between the relative amounts of mobility and stability. The more mobile the joint, the less stable it is. Conversely, the more stable the joint, the less mobile it is. In this diagram comparing the relationship of mobility and stability in selected joints, note how the glenohumeral (shoulder) joint is very mobile but not very stable, whereas a suture is immobile and yet very stable.

Table 9.1 Joint Classifications

Structural Classification	General Structural Characteristics	Structural Categories	Example(s)	Functional Classification
Fibrous (see figure 9.2)	Dense regular connective tissue holds together the ends of bones and bone parts; no joint cavity	**Gomphosis:** Periodontal membranes hold tooth to bony jaw	Tooth to jaw	Synarthrosis (immobile)
		Suture: Dense regular connective tissue connects skull bones	Lambdoid suture (connects occipital and parietal bones)	Synarthrosis (immobile)
		Syndesmosis: Dense regular connective tissue fibers (interosseous membrane) between bones	Articulation between radius and ulna, and between tibia and fibula	Amphiarthrosis (slightly mobile)
Cartilaginous (see figure 9.3)	Pad of cartilage is wedged between the ends of bones; no joint cavity	**Synchondrosis:** Hyaline cartilage between bones	Epiphyseal plates in growing bones; costochondral joints	Synarthrosis (immobile)
		Symphysis: Fibrocartilage between bones	Pubic symphysis; intervertebral disc articulations	Amphiarthrosis (slightly mobile)
Synovial (see figure 9.6)	Ends of bones covered with articular cartilage; joint cavity separates the articulating bones; joint enclosed by an articular capsule, lined by a synovial membrane; contains synovial fluid	*Uniaxial* **Plane joint:** Flattened or slightly curved faces slide across one another **Hinge joint:** Convex feature of one bone fits into concave depression of another bone **Pivot joint:** Bone with a rounded surface fits into a ring formed by a ligament and another bone	**Plane joint:** Intercarpal joints, intertarsal joints **Hinge joint:** Elbow joint, knee joint, IP (interphalangeal) joints **Pivot joint:** Atlantoaxial joint	Diarthrosis (freely mobile)
		Biaxial **Condylar joint:** Oval articular surface on one bone closely interfaces with a depressed oval surface on another bone **Saddle joint:** Saddle-shaped articular surface on one bone closely interfaces with a saddle-shaped surface on another bone	**Condylar joint:** MP (metacarpophalangeal or metatarsophalangeal) joints **Saddle joint:** Articulation between carpal and first metacarpal bone	Diarthrosis (freely mobile)
		Multiaxial (triaxial) **Ball-and-socket joint:** Round head of one bone rests within cup-shaped depression in another bone	**Ball-and-socket joint:** Glenohumeral joint, hip joint	Diarthrosis (freely mobile)

WHAT DID YOU LEARN?

1. What type of articulation uses dense regular connective tissue to bind the bones?
2. What term is used to describe immobile joints?

9.2 Fibrous Joints

✓ Learning Objective

4. Describe the structure and identify locations of gomphoses, sutures, and syndesmoses in the body.

Articulating bones are joined by dense regular connective tissue in fibrous joints. Most fibrous joints are immobile or only slightly mobile. Fibrous joints have no joint cavity (space between the articulating bones). The three types of fibrous joints are gomphoses, sutures, and syndesmoses **(figure 9.2)**.

9.2a Gomphoses

A **gomphosis** (gom-fō′sis; pl., -sēz; *gomphos* = bolt, *osis* = condition) resembles a "peg in a socket." The only gomphoses in the human body are the articulations of the roots of individual teeth with the sockets of the mandible and the maxillae. A tooth is held firmly in place by multiple dense regular connective tissue **periodontal** (per′ē-ō-don′t ăl; *peri* = around, *odous* = tooth) **membranes.** This joint is functionally classified as a synarthrosis.

The reasons orthodontic braces can be painful and take a long time to correctly position the teeth are related to the gomphosis architecture. The orthodontist's job is to reposition these normally immobile joints through the use of bands, rings, and braces. In response to these mechanical stressors, osteoblasts and osteoclasts work together to modify the alveolus, resulting in the remodeling of the joint and the slow repositioning of the teeth.

Learning Strategy 9.2

The first syllable of *gomphosis* (gom) sounds like the word *gum*, which is the tissue around the tooth socket.

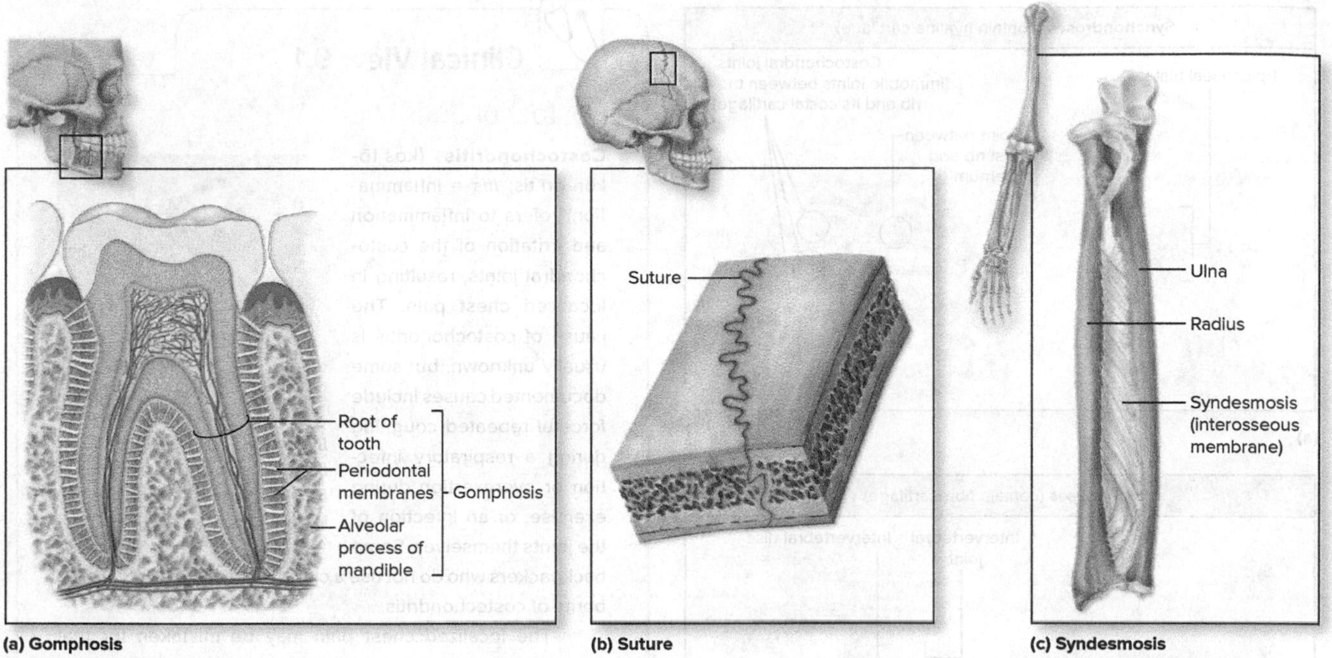
Root of tooth
Periodontal membranes
Gomphosis
Alveolar process of mandible
Suture
Ulna
Radius
Syndesmosis (interosseous membrane)
(a) Gomphosis
(b) Suture
(c) Syndesmosis

Figure 9.2

Fibrous Joints. Dense regular connective tissue binds the articulating bones in fibrous joints to prevent or severely restrict movement. (*a*) A gomphosis is the immobile joint between a tooth and the jaw. (*b*) A suture is an immobile joint between bones of the skull. (*c*) A syndesmosis permits slight mobility between the radius and the ulna. APR

9.2b Sutures

Sutures (sū′chūr; *sutura* = a seam) are fibrous joints that are immobile (synarthroses). They occur only between certain bones of the skull (see section 7.1b). Sutures have distinct, interlocking, usually irregular edges that both increase their strength and decrease the number of fractures at these articulations. In addition to joining bones, sutures permit the skull to grow as the brain increases in size during childhood. In an older adult, the dense regular connective tissue in the suture becomes ossified, fusing the skull bones together. When the bones have completely fused across the suture line, these obliterated sutures become **synostoses** (sin′os-t ō′sēz; sing., -sis). (See Clinical View 7.1: "Craniosynostosis and Plagiocephaly" in section 7.1a.)

9.2c Syndesmoses

Syndesmoses (sin′dez-mō′sēz; sing., -sis; *syndesmos* = a fastening) are fibrous joints in which articulating bones are joined by long strands of dense regular connective tissue only (figure 9.2). Because syndesmoses allow for slight mobility, they are classified as amphiarthroses. Syndesmoses occur between the radius and ulna (see section 8.2b), and between the tibia and fibula (see section 8.4c). The shafts of the two articulating bones are bound side by side by a broad ligamentous sheet called an **interosseous membrane** (or *interosseous ligament*). The interosseous membrane provides a pivot point where the radius and ulna (or the tibia and fibula) can move against one another.

WHAT DID YOU LEARN?

3. Describe the three types of fibrous joints, and list a place in the body where each type is found.

9.3 Cartilaginous Joints

Learning Objective

5. Describe the structure and identify locations of the two types of cartilaginous joints.

The articulating bones in cartilaginous joints are attached to each other by cartilage. These joints lack a joint cavity. The two types of cartilaginous joints are synchondroses and symphyses (**figure 9.3**).

9.3a Synchondroses

An articulation in which bones are joined by hyaline cartilage is called a **synchondrosis** (sin′kon-dr ō′sis; pl., -sēz; *chondros* = cartilage). Functionally, all synchondroses are immobile and thus are classified as synarthroses. The hyaline cartilage of epiphyseal plates in children forms synchondroses that bind the epiphyses and the diaphysis of long bones (see section 6.4b). When the hyaline cartilage stops growing, bone replaces the cartilage, and a synchondrosis no longer exists. APR

The *spheno-occipital synchondrosis* is found between the body of the sphenoid and the basilar part of the occipital bone (see section 7.1c). This synchondrosis fuses between 18 and 25 years of age, making it a useful tool for assessing the age of a skull.

Another synchondrosis is the attachment of the first rib to the sternum by costal cartilage (called the first sternocostal joint). Here, the first rib and its costal cartilage (formed from hyaline cartilage) are united firmly to the manubrium of the sternum to provide stability to the rib cage. A final example of synchondroses are the **costochondral** (kos′t ō-kon′dr ăl; *costa* = rib) **joints,** the

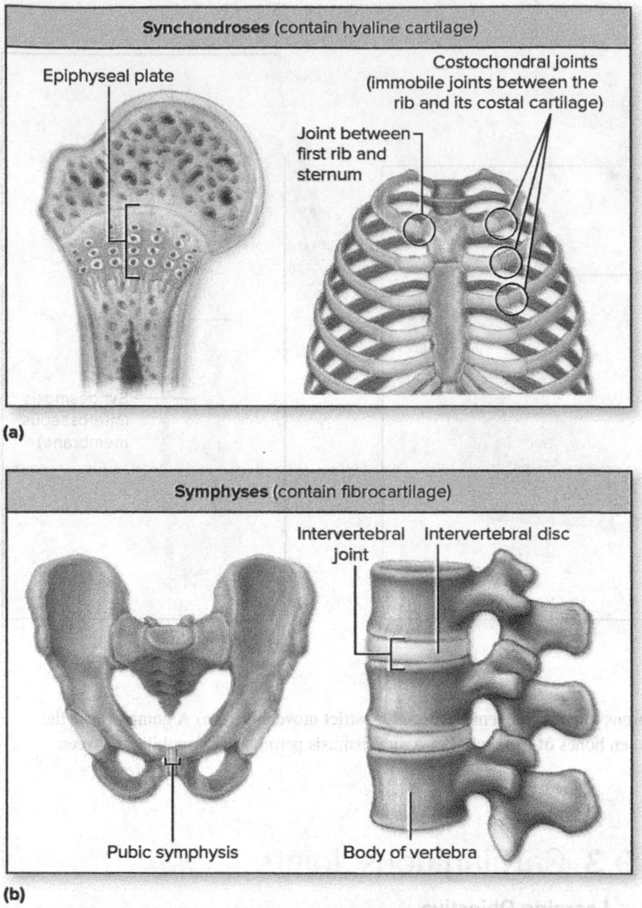

Figure 9.3
Cartilaginous Joints. Articulating bones are joined by cartilage. (*a*) Synchondroses are immobile joints that occur in an epiphyseal plate in a long bone and in the joint between a rib and the sternum. (*b*) Symphyses are amphiarthroses and occur in the intervertebral discs and the pubic symphysis. **APR**

joints between each bony rib and its respective costal cartilage. (The costochondral joints are different from the articulation between the sternum and the costal cartilage of ribs 2–7, which is a synovial joint, not a synchondrosis.)

WHAT DO YOU THINK?

1. Why is a synchondrosis a synarthrosis? Why would you want a synchondrosis to be immobile?

9.3b Symphyses

A **symphysis** (sim′fi-sis; pl., -sēz; growing together) has a pad of fibrocartilage between the articulating bones. The fibrocartilage resists compression and tension stresses and acts as a resilient shock absorber. All symphyses are amphiarthroses, meaning that they allow slight mobility.

One example of a symphysis is the pubic symphysis, which is located between the right and left pubic bones (see section 8.3a). During pregnancy, the pubic symphysis becomes more mobile to allow the pelvis to change shape slightly as the fetus passes through the birth canal.

Clinical View 9.1

Costochondritis

Costochondritis (kos′tō-kon-drī′tis; *itis* = inflammation) refers to inflammation and irritation of the costochondral joints, resulting in localized chest pain. The cause of costochondritis is usually unknown, but some documented causes include forceful repeated coughing during a respiratory infection or overexertion during exercise, or an infection of the joints themselves. Some backpackers who do not use a chest brace have experienced bouts of costochondritis.

By using the chest brace on his backpack, this hiker is protecting himself against costochondritis.
Maridav/Shutterstock

The localized chest pain may be mistaken for that caused by a myocardial infarction (heart attack). However, costochondritis is not a medical emergency and may be treated with NSAIDs (nonsteroidal anti-inflammatory drugs, such as aspirin).

Other examples of symphyses are the intervertebral joints, where the bodies of adjacent vertebrae are both separated and united by intervertebral discs (see section 7.4c). These intervertebral discs allow only slight movements between the adjacent vertebrae; however, the collective movements of all the intervertebral discs afford the spine considerable flexibility.

WHAT DID YOU LEARN?

4. Describe a symphysis. In what functional category is this type of joint placed, and why?

9.4 Synovial Joints

✓ Learning Objectives

6. Describe the general anatomy of synovial joints and their accessory structures.
7. Name the classes of synovial joints based upon the joint surface shapes, explain the types of movement permitted, and identify their locations in the body.
8. Define and describe dynamic movements that occur at synovial joints.

Synovial joints are freely mobile articulations (diarthroses). Unlike fibrous and cartilaginous joints, the bones in a synovial joint are separated by a space called a joint cavity. Most of the commonly known joints in the body are synovial joints, including the glenohumeral (shoulder) joint, the temporomandibular joint, the elbow joint, and the knee joint. Functionally, all synovial joints are classified as diarthroses, because all are freely mobile. Often, the terms *diarthrosis* and *synovial joint* are equated.

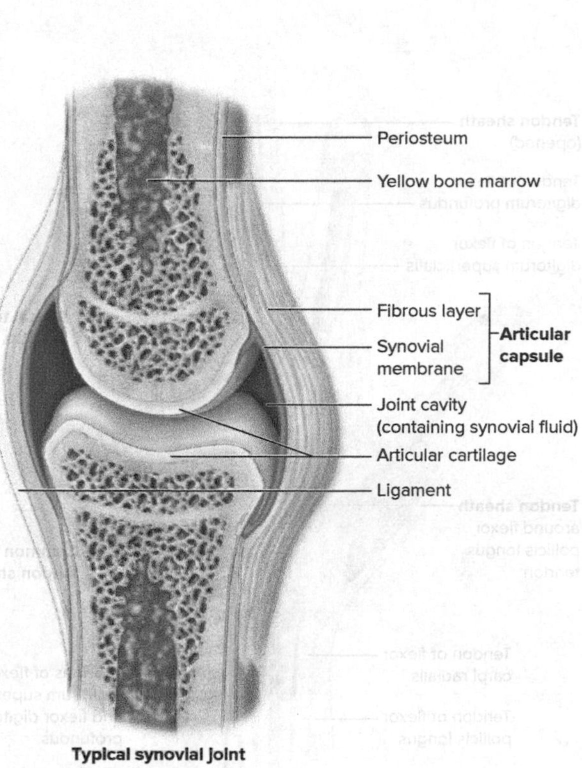
Periosteum
Yellow bone marrow
Fibrous layer
Synovial membrane
Articular capsule
Joint cavity (containing synovial fluid)
Articular cartilage
Ligament
Typical synovial joint

Figure 9.4

Synovial Joints. All synovial joints are diarthroses, and they permit a wide range of motion.

9.4a General Anatomy of Synovial Joints

All types of synovial joints have several basic, distinguishing features: an articular capsule, a joint cavity, synovial fluid, articular cartilage, ligaments, and nerves and blood vessels (**figure 9.4**).

Each synovial joint is composed of a double-layered capsule called the **articular** (ar-tik'y ū-lăr) **capsule** (or *joint capsule*). The outer layer is called the **fibrous layer,** whereas the inner layer is a **synovial membrane** (or *synovium*). The fibrous layer is formed from dense connective tissue, and it strengthens the joint to prevent the bones from being pulled apart. The synovial membrane is composed primarily of areolar connective tissue, covers all the internal joint surfaces not covered by cartilage, and lines the articular capsule.

All articulating bone surfaces in a synovial joint are covered by a thin layer of hyaline cartilage called **articular cartilage.** This cartilage has numerous functions: It reduces friction in the joint during movement, acts as a spongy cushion to absorb compression placed on the joint, and prevents damage to the articulating ends of the bones. This special hyaline cartilage lacks a perichondrium. Recall from section 4.2d that mature cartilage is avascular, so it does not have blood vessels to bring nutrients to and remove waste products from the cartilage. Thus, if cartilage is damaged, its avascularity is correlated with lack of or delayed healing of the tissue. However, the repetitious compression and expansion that occurs during exercise is vital to maintaining healthy articular cartilage because this action enhances its nutrition and waste removal.

Only synovial joints house a **joint cavity** (or *articular cavity*), a space that contains a small amount of synovial fluid. The cavity permits separation of the articulating bones. The articular cartilage and synovial fluid within the joint cavity reduce friction as bones move at a synovial joint.

Lining the joint cavity is the synovial membrane, which secretes a viscous, oily **synovial fluid.** Synovial fluid is composed of secretions from synovial membrane cells and a filtrate from blood plasma. Synovial fluid has three functions:

- Synovial fluid lubricates the articular cartilage on the articulating bones (in the same way that oil in a car engine lubricates the moving engine parts).
- Synovial fluid nourishes the articular cartilage's chondrocytes. The relatively small volume of synovial fluid must be circulated continually to provide nutrients and remove wastes to these cells. Whenever movement occurs at a synovial joint, the combined compression and re-expansion of the articular cartilage circulate the synovial fluid into and out of the cartilage matrix.
- Synovial fluid acts as a shock absorber, distributing stresses and force evenly across the articular surfaces when the pressure in the joint suddenly increases.

Ligaments (lig'ă-ment; *ligamentum* = a band) are composed of dense regular connective tissue. Ligaments connect one bone to another bone and strengthen and reinforce most synovial joints. **Extrinsic ligaments** are outside of and physically separate from the articular capsule, whereas **intrinsic ligaments** represent thickenings of the articular capsule itself. Intrinsic ligaments include *extracapsular ligaments* on the outer surface of the articular capsule and *intracapsular ligaments* within the articular capsule.

All synovial joints have numerous **sensory nerves** and **blood vessels** that innervate and supply the articular capsule and associated ligaments. The sensory nerves detect painful stimuli in the joint and report on the amount of movement and stretch in the joint. By monitoring stretching at a joint, the nervous system can detect changes in our posture and adjust body movements.

You can predict which specific nerves innervate a joint by using **Hilton's Law,** which states the nerves innervating a joint typically also innervate the muscles that move the joint or the skin that covers the joint. (You will learn these specific nerves when you get to sections 15.8 and 16.4.)

In addition to the main structures just described, synovial joints usually have the following accessory structures: bursae, fat pads, and tendons.

A **bursa** (ber'să; pl., *bursae*, ber'sē; a purse) is a fibrous, saclike structure that contains synovial fluid and is lined by a synovial

Clinical View 9.2

"Cracking Knuckles"

Stretching or pulling on a synovial joint, such as when a person "cracks their knuckles," causes the joint volume to immediately expand and the pressure on the fluid within the joint to decrease, so that a partial vacuum exists within the joint. As a result, the gases dissolved in the fluid become less soluble, and they form bubbles, a process called *cavitation.* When the joint is stretched to a certain point, the pressure in the joint drops even lower, so the bubbles in the fluid burst, resulting in a popping or cracking sound. Contrary to popular belief, cracking your knuckles does *not* cause arthritis.

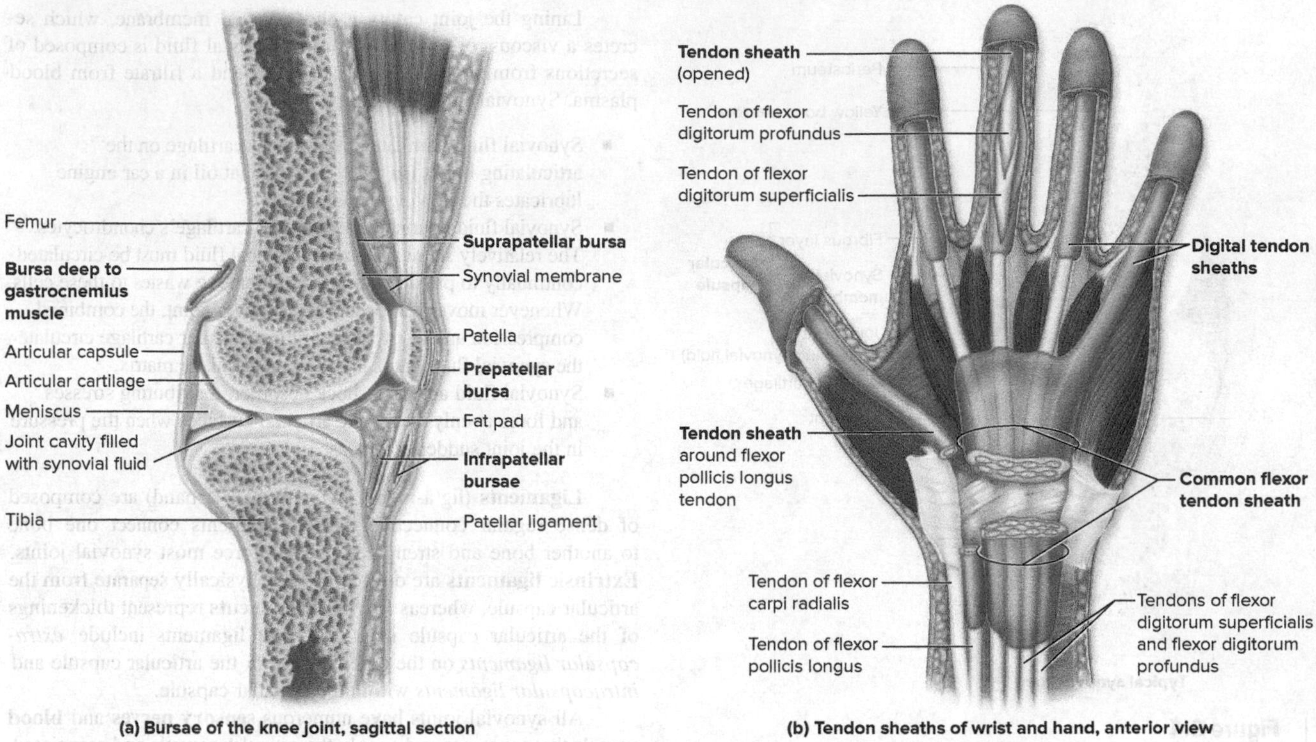

Figure 9.5

Bursae and Tendon Sheaths. Synovial-fluid-filled structures called bursae and tendon sheaths reduce friction where ligaments, muscles, tendons, and bones rub together. (*a*) The knee joint contains a number of bursae. (*b*) The wrist and hand contain numerous tendon sheaths (blue).

membrane (**figure 9.5*a***). Bursae occur around most synovial joints and also where bones, ligaments, muscles, skin, or tendons overlie each other and rub together. Bursae may be either connected to the joint cavity or completely separate from it. There are numerous bursae in the body, and they are designed to alleviate the friction resulting from the various body movements, such as a tendon or ligament rubbing against bone. An elongated bursa called a **tendon sheath** wraps around tendons where there may be excessive friction. Tendon sheaths are especially common in the confined spaces of the wrist and ankle (figure 9.5*b*).

Fat pads are often distributed along the margins of a synovial joint. They act as packing material and provide some protection for the joint. Often fat pads fill the spaces that form when bones move and the joint cavity changes shape.

Tendons (ten′d ŏn; *tendo* = extend) are not part of the synovial joint itself. Like a ligament, a tendon is composed of dense regular connective tissue. However, whereas a ligament binds bone to bone, a tendon attaches a muscle to a bone (see section 10.2b). When a muscle contracts, the tendon from that muscle moves the bone to which it is attached, thus creating movement at the joint. Tendons help stabilize joints because they pass across or around a joint providing mechanical support, and can limit the range or amount of movement permitted at a joint.

9.4b Classifications of Synovial Joints

Synovial joints are classified by the shapes of their articulating surfaces and the types of movement they allow. Movement of a bone at a synovial joint is best described with respect to three intersecting perpendicular planes or axes:

- A joint is said to be **uniaxial** (yū-nē-ak′s ē-ăl; *unus* = one) if the bone moves in just one plane or axis.
- A joint is **biaxial** (bī-ak′s ē-ăl; *bi* = double) if the bone moves in two planes or axes.
- A joint is **multiaxial** (or *triaxial* [trī-ak′s ē-ăl; *tri* = three]) if the bone moves in multiple planes or axes.

All synovial joints are diarthroses, although some are more mobile than others. From least mobile to most freely mobile, the six specific types of synovial joints are plane joints, hinge joints, pivot joints, condylar joints, saddle joints, and ball-and-socket joints (**figure 9.6**).

A **plane** (*planus* = *flat*) **joint,** also called a *planar* or *gliding joint,* is the simplest synovial articulation and the least mobile type of diarthrosis. This type of synovial joint is considered a uniaxial joint because only side-to-side movements are possible. The articular surfaces of the bones are flat, or planar. Examples of plane joints include the intercarpal and intertarsal joints (the joints between the carpal bones and tarsal bones, respectively).

A **hinge joint** is a uniaxial joint in which the convex surface of one articulating bone fits into a concave depression on the other bone in the joint. Movement is confined to a single axis, like the hinge of a door. An example is the elbow joint. The trochlear notch of the ulna fits directly into the trochlea of the humerus, so the forearm can be moved only anteriorly toward the arm or posteriorly away from the arm. Other hinge joints occur in the knee and the finger (interphalangeal [IP]) joints.

A **pivot** (piv′ŏt) **joint** is a uniaxial joint in which one articulating bone with a rounded surface fits into a ring formed by a ligament and another bone. The first bone rotates on its longitudinal axis relative to the second bone. An example is the proximal radioulnar joint, where the rounded head of the radius pivots along the ulna and permits the

Figure 9.6

Synovial Joints. The six types of synovial joints and their locations in the body are shown. APR

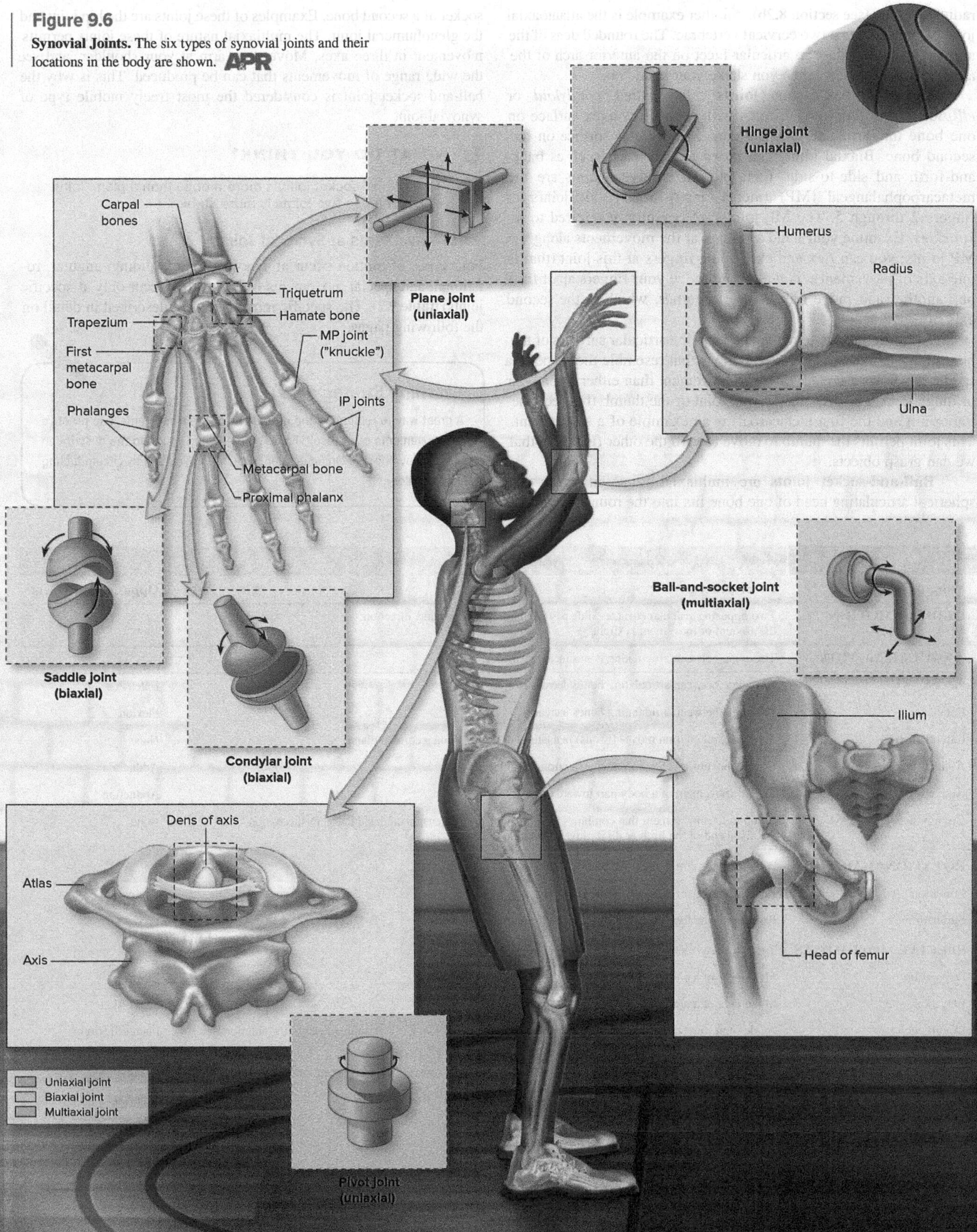

Hinge joint
(uniaxial)
Humerus
Radius
Ulna
Plane joint
(uniaxial)
Carpal bones
Triquetrum
Hamate bone
Trapezium
First metacarpal bone
MP joint
("knuckle")
Phalanges
IP joints
Metacarpal bone
Proximal phalanx
Saddle joint
(biaxial)
Condylar joint
(biaxial)
Ball-and-socket joint
(multiaxial)
Ilium
Head of femur
Dens of axis
Atlas
Axis
Uniaxial joint
Biaxial joint
Multiaxial joint
Pivot joint
(uniaxial)

radius to rotate (see section 8.2b). Another example is the atlantoaxial joint between the first two cervical vertebrae. The rounded dens of the axis fits snugly against an articular facet on the anterior arch of the atlas. This joint pivots when you shake your head "no."

Condylar (kon′di-l ăr) **joints,** also called *condyloid* or *ellipsoid joints,* are biaxial joints with an oval, convex surface on one bone that articulates with a concave articular surface on the second bone. Biaxial joints can move in two axes, such as back-and-forth and side-to-side. Examples of condylar joints are the metacarpophalangeal (MP) (met′ ă-kar′p ō-fă-lan′j ē-ăl) joints of fingers 2 through 5. The MP joints are commonly referred to as *knuckles.* Examine your hand and look at the movements along the MP joints; you can flex and extend the fingers at this joint (that is one axis of movement). You also can move your fingers apart from one another and move them closer together, which is the second axis of movement.

A **saddle joint** is so named because the articular surfaces of the bones have convex and concave regions that resemble the shape of a saddle. It allows a greater range of movement than either a condylar or hinge joint. The carpometacarpal joint of the thumb (between the trapezium and the first metacarpal) is an example of a saddle joint. This joint permits the thumb to move toward the other fingers so that we can grasp objects.

Ball-and-socket joints are multiaxial joints in which the spherical articulating head of one bone fits into the rounded, cuplike socket of a second bone. Examples of these joints are the hip joint and the glenohumeral joint. The multiaxial nature of these joints permits movement in three axes. Move your arm at your shoulder, and see the wide range of movements that can be produced. This is why the ball-and-socket joint is considered the most freely mobile type of synovial joint.

WHAT DO YOU THINK?

2 If a ball-and-socket joint is more mobile than a plane joint, which of these two joints is more stable?

9.4c Movements at Synovial Joints

Four types of motion occur at synovial joints: gliding, angular, rotational, and special movements (motions that occur only at specific joints) **(table 9.2)**. The specific movements are described in detail on the following pages.

Learning Strategy 9.3

A great way to remember the definitions of the movements is to practice the movements on yourself. For example, when you read the description for the movement of circumduction, practice on yourself by circumducting your shoulder.

Table 9.2 Movements at Synovial Joints APR

Movement	Description	Opposing Movement[1]
GLIDING MOTION	Two opposing articular surfaces slide past each other in almost any direction; the amount of movement is slight	
ANGULAR MOTION	The angle between articulating bones increases or decreases	
Flexion	The angle between articulating bones decreases	Extension
Extension	The angle between articulating bones increases	Flexion
Lateral flexion	The vertebral column moves (bends) in a lateral direction along a coronal plane	None
Abduction	Lateral movement of a body part away from the midline	Adduction
Adduction	Medial movement of a body part toward the midline	Abduction
Circumduction	A continuous movement that combines flexion, abduction, extension, and adduction in succession; the distal end of the limb or digit moves in a circle	None
ROTATIONAL MOTION	A bone pivots around its own longitudinal axis	
Pronation	Rotation of the forearm where the palm is turned posteriorly	Supination
Supination	Rotation of the forearm in which the palm is turned anteriorly	Pronation
SPECIAL MOVEMENTS	Types of movement that don't fit in the previous categories	
Depression	Movement of a body part inferiorly	Elevation
Elevation	Movement of a body part superiorly	Depression
Dorsiflexion	Ankle joint movement where the dorsum (superior surface) of the foot is brought closer to the anterior surface of the leg	Plantar flexion
Plantar flexion	Ankle joint movement whereby the sole of the foot is brought toward the posterior surface of the leg	Dorsiflexion
Inversion	Twisting motion of the foot that turns the sole medially or inward	Eversion
Eversion	Twisting motion of the foot that turns the sole laterally or outward	Inversion
Protraction	Anterior movement of a body part from anatomic position	Retraction
Retraction	Posterior movement of a body part from anatomic position	Protraction
Opposition	Special movement of the thumb across the palm toward the fingers to permit grasping and holding of an object	Reposition

[1] Some movements (e.g., circumduction) do not have an opposing movement.

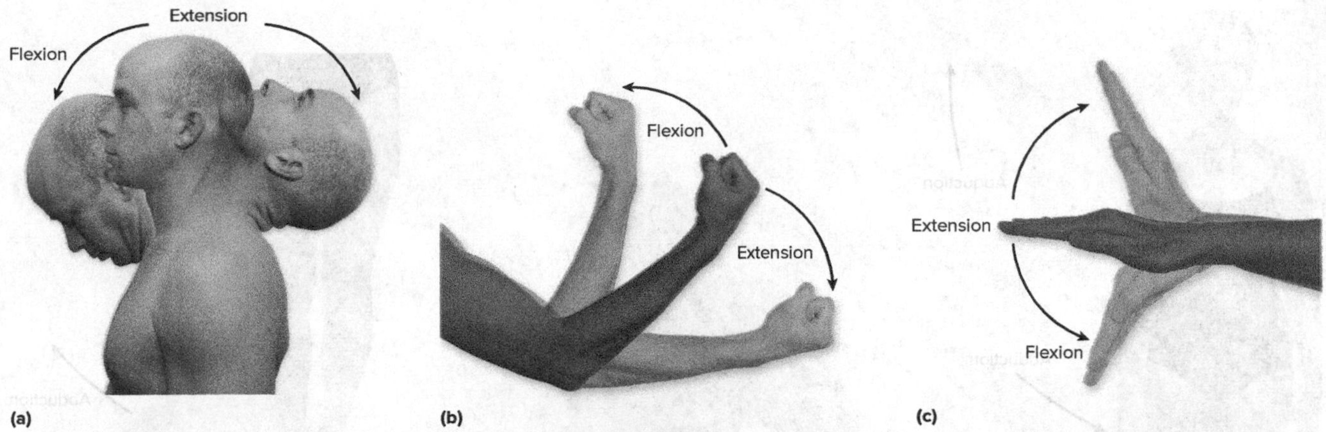

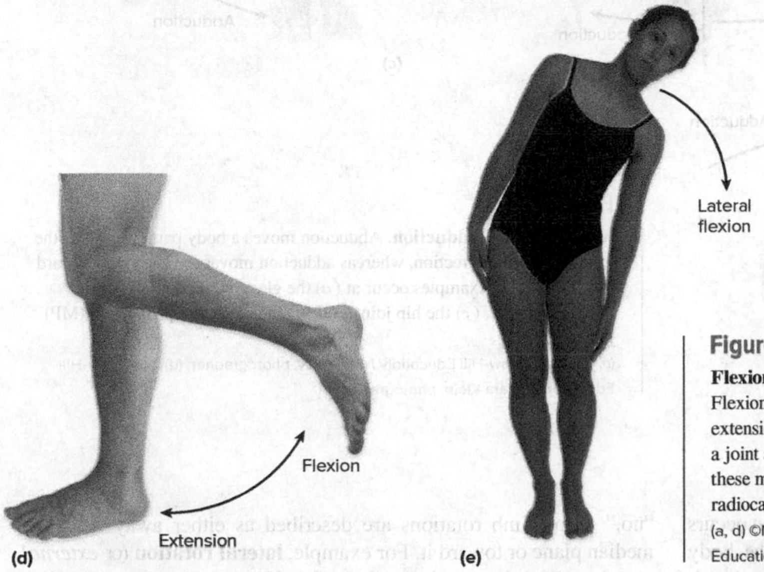

Figure 9.7

Flexion, Extension, and Lateral Flexion.

Flexion decreases the joint angle in an anterior-posterior (AP) plane, whereas extension increases the joint angle in the AP plane. Lateral flexion decreases a joint angle, but in a coronal plane. Examples of joints that allow some of these movements are (*a*) the atlanto-occipital joint, (*b*) the elbow joint, (*c*) the radiocarpal joint, (*d*) the knee joint, and (*e*) the intervertebral joints. APR

(a, d) ©McGraw-Hill Education/Tamara Klein, photographer; (b, c, e) ©McGraw-Hill Education/Jw Ramsey, photographer

Gliding Motion

Gliding is a simple movement in which two opposing surfaces slide slightly back-and-forth or side-to-side with respect to one another. In a gliding motion, the angle between the bones does not change, and only limited movement is possible in any direction. Gliding motion typically occurs along plane joints.

Angular Motion

Angular motion either increases or decreases the angle between two bones. These movements may occur at many of the synovial joints; they include the following specific types: flexion and extension, hyperextension, lateral flexion, abduction and adduction, and circumduction.

Flexion (flek′shŭn; *flecto* = to bend) is movement in an anterior-posterior (AP) plane of the body that *decreases* the angle between the articulating bones. Bones are brought closer together as the angle between them decreases. Examples include bending your fingers toward your palm to make a fist, bending your forearm toward your arm at the elbow, flexion at the shoulder when you raise an arm anteriorly, and flexion of the neck when you bend your head anteriorly to look down at your feet.

The opposite of flexion is **extension** (eks-ten′shŭn; *extensio* = a stretching out), which is movement in an anterior-posterior plane that *increases* the angle between the articulating bones. Extension is a straightening action that usually occurs in the sagittal plane of the body. Straightening your arm and forearm until the upper limb projects directly away from the anterior side of your body or straightening your fingers after making a clenched fist are examples of extension. Flexion and extension of various body parts are illustrated in **figure 9.7*a–d***.

Hyperextension (hī′pĕr-eks-ten′shŭn; *hyper* = above normal) is the extension of a joint beyond its normal range of motion. It may occur if someone has extensively mobile joints or has an injury at a joint.

Lateral flexion occurs when the trunk of the body moves in a coronal plane laterally away from the body. This type of movement occurs primarily between the vertebrae in the cervical and lumbar regions of the vertebral column (figure 9.7*e*).

Abduction (ab-d ŭk′sh ŭn), which means to "move away," is a lateral movement of a body part *away from* the body midline. Abduction occurs when either the arm or the thigh is moved laterally away from the body midline. Abduction of either the fingers or the toes means that you spread them apart, away from the longest digit, which is acting as the midline. Abducting the wrist (also known as *radial deviation*) involves pointing the hand and fingers laterally, away from the body. The opposite of abduction is **adduction** (ă-dŭk′sh ŭn), which means to "move toward," and is the medial

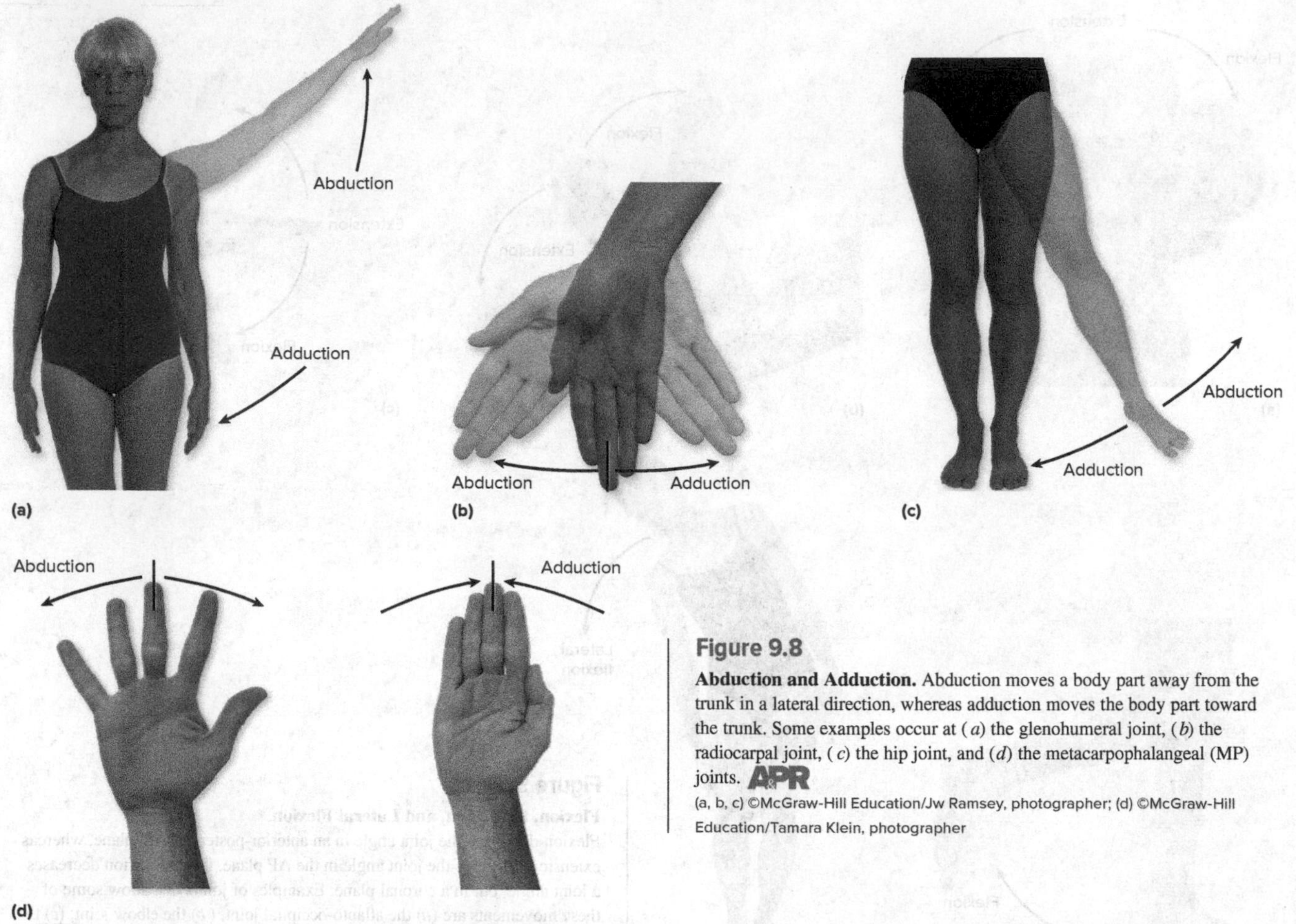

Figure 9.8

Abduction and Adduction. Abduction moves a body part away from the trunk in a lateral direction, whereas adduction moves the body part toward the trunk. Some examples occur at (*a*) the glenohumeral joint, (*b*) the radiocarpal joint, (*c*) the hip joint, and (*d*) the metacarpophalangeal (MP) joints. APR

(a, b, c) ©McGraw-Hill Education/Jw Ramsey, photographer; (d) ©McGraw-Hill Education/Tamara Klein, photographer

movement of a body part *toward* the body midline. Adduction occurs when you bring your raised arm or thigh back toward the body midline, or in the case of the digits, toward the midline of the hand. Adducting the wrist (also known as *ulnar deviation*) involves pointing the hand and fingers medially, toward the body. Abduction and adduction of various body parts are shown in **figure 9.8**.

Circumduction (ser′kŭm-dŭk′sh ŭn; *circum* = around, *duco* = to draw) is a sequence of movements in which the proximal end of an appendage remains relatively stationary, while the distal end makes a circular motion (**figure 9.9**). The resulting movement makes an imaginary cone shape. For example, when you draw a circle on the blackboard, your shoulder remains stationary while your hand moves. The tip of the imaginary cone is the stationary shoulder, while the rounded "base" of the cone is the circle the hand makes. Circumduction is a complex movement that occurs as a result of a continuous sequence of flexion, abduction, extension, and adduction.

WHAT DO YOU THINK?

3 When sitting upright in a chair, are your hip and knee joints flexed or extended?

Rotational Motion

Rotation is a pivoting motion in which a bone turns on its own longitudinal axis (**figure 9.10**). Rotational movement occurs at the atlantoaxial joint, which pivots when you rotate your head to gesture "no." Some limb rotations are described as either away from the median plane or toward it. For example, **lateral rotation** (or *external rotation*) turns the anterior surface of the femur or humerus laterally, whereas **medial rotation** (or *internal rotation*) turns the anterior surface of the femur or humerus medially.

Pronation (prō-nā′shŭn) is the medial rotation of the forearm so that the palm of the hand is directed posteriorly or inferiorly. The radius and ulna are crossed to form an X (see section 8.2b and figure 8.5*e*). **Supination** (sū′pi-n ā′shŭn; *supinus* = supine) occurs when the forearm rotates laterally so that the palm faces anteriorly or superiorly, and the radius is parallel with the ulna (see figure 8.5*d*). In the anatomic position, the forearm is supinated. Figure 9.10*d* illustrates pronation and supination.

Special Movements

Some motions occur only at specific joints and do not readily fit into any of the functional categories previously discussed. These special movements include depression and elevation, dorsiflexion and plantar flexion, inversion and eversion, protraction and retraction, and opposition.

Depression (*de* = away or down, *presso* = to press) is the inferior movement of a part of the body. Examples of depression include opening your mouth (by depressing the mandible) to chew food and the movement of your shoulders in an inferior direction. **Elevation** is the superior movement of a body part. Examples of elevation include the superior movement of the mandible while

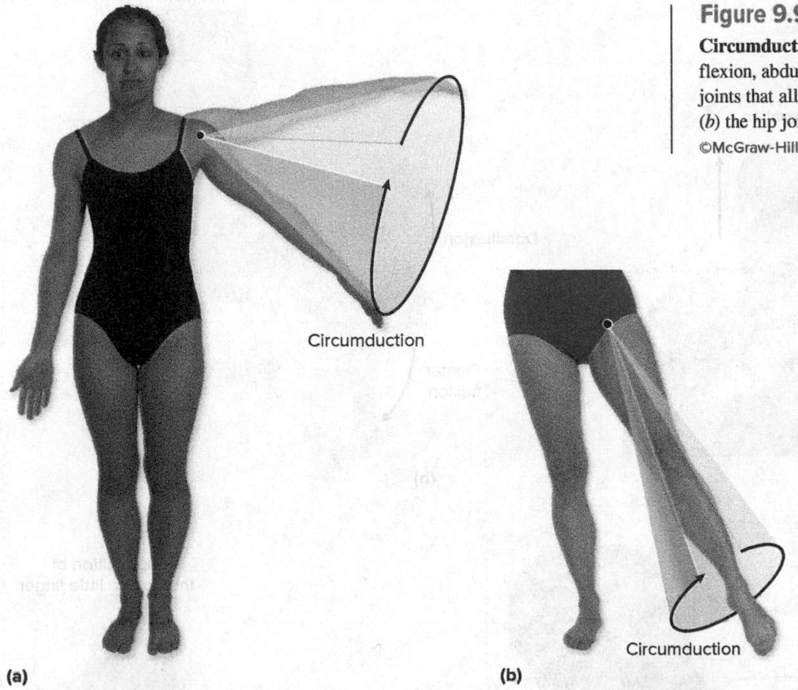
Circumduction
(a)
Circumduction
(b)

Figure 9.9

Circumduction. Circumduction is a complex movement that involves flexion, abduction, extension, and adduction in succession. Examples of joints that allow this movement are (*a*) the glenohumeral joint and (*b*) the hip joint. APR

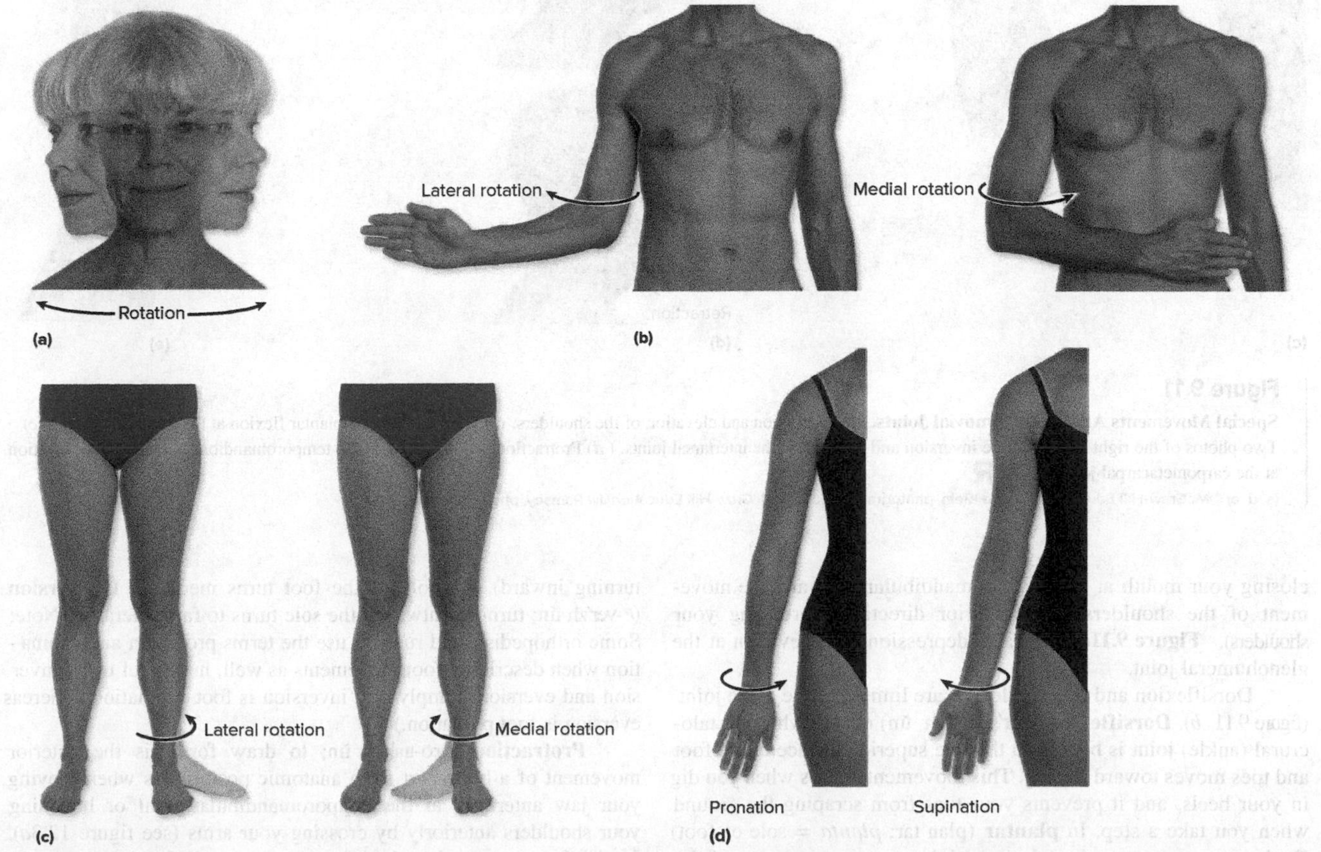
Rotation
(a)
Lateral rotation
Medial rotation
(b)
Lateral rotation
Medial rotation
(c)
Pronation
Supination
(d)

Figure 9.10

Rotational Movements. Rotation allows a bone to pivot on its longitudinal axis. Examples of joints that allow this movement are (*a*) the atlantoaxial joint, (*b*) the glenohumeral joint, and (*c*) the hip joint. (*d*) Pronation and supination occur at the forearm. APR

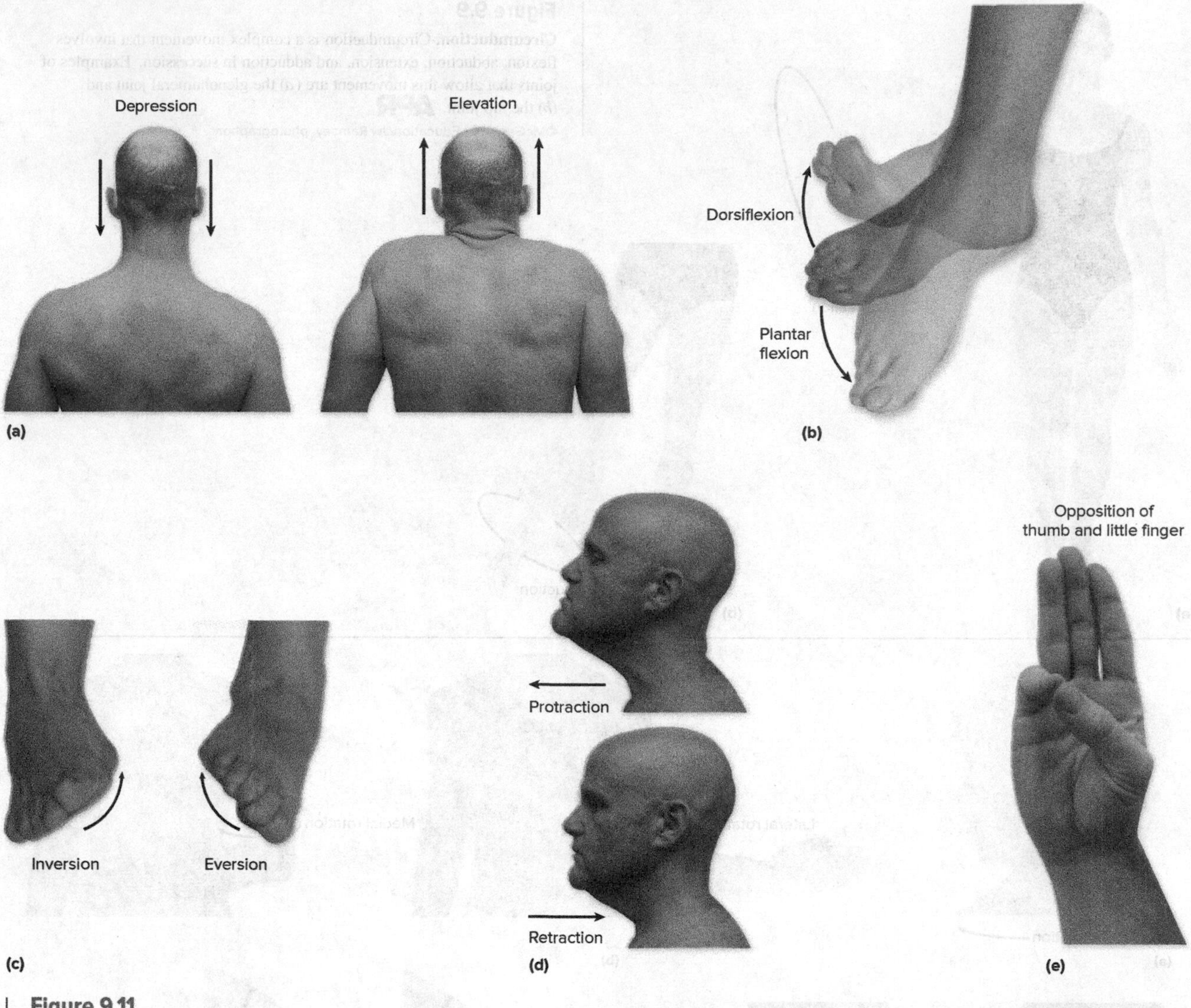
Depression
Elevation
(a)
Dorsiflexion
Plantar flexion
(b)
Inversion
Eversion
(c)
Protraction
Retraction
(d)
Opposition of thumb and little finger
(e)

Figure 9.11

Special Movements Allowed at Synovial Joints. (*a*) Depression and elevation of the shoulders. (*b*) Dorsiflexion and plantar flexion at the talocrural joint. (*c*) Two photos of the right foot illustrate inversion and eversion at the intertarsal joints. (*d*) Protraction and retraction at the temporomandibular joint. (*e*) Opposition at the carpometacarpal joints. APR

(a, d, e) ©McGraw-Hill Education/Tamara Klein, photographer; (b, c) ©McGraw-Hill Education/Jw Ramsey, photographer

closing your mouth at the temporomandibular joint and the movement of the shoulders in a superior direction (shrugging your shoulders). **Figure 9.11*a*** illustrates depression and elevation at the glenohumeral joint.

Dorsiflexion and plantar flexion are limited to the ankle joint (figure 9.11 *b*). **Dorsiflexion** (dōr′si-flek′sh ŭn) occurs when the talocrural (ankle) joint is bent such that the superior surface of the foot and toes moves toward the leg. This movement occurs when you dig in your heels, and it prevents your toes from scraping the ground when you take a step. In **plantar** (plan′tar; *planta* = sole of foot) **flexion,** movement at the talocrural joint permits extension of the foot so that the toes point inferiorly. When a ballerina is standing on her tiptoes (*en pointe*), her ankle joint is in full plantar flexion.

Inversion and eversion are movements that occur at the intertarsal joints of the foot only (figure 9.11*c*). In **inversion** (in-ver′zh ŭn; turning inward), the sole of the foot turns medially. In **eversion** (ē-ver′zh ŭn; turning outward), the sole turns to face laterally. (Note: Some orthopedists and runners use the terms pronation and supination when describing foot movements as well, instead of using inversion and eversion. Simply put, inversion is foot supination, whereas eversion is foot pronation.)

Protraction (prō-trak′sh ŭn; to draw forth) is the anterior movement of a body part from anatomic position, as when moving your jaw anteriorly at the temporomandibular joint or hunching your shoulders anteriorly by crossing your arms (see figure 12.3*a*). In the latter case, the clavicles move anteriorly due to movement at both the acromioclavicular and sternoclavicular joints. **Retraction** (rē-trak′sh ŭn; to draw back) is the posteriorly directed movement of a body part from anatomic position. Figure 9.11*d* illustrates protraction and retraction at the temporomandibular joint.

At the carpometacarpal joint, the thumb moves toward the palmar tips of the fingers as it crosses the palm of the hand. This movement is called **opposition** (op′ō-si′sh ŭn) (figure 9.11*l*). It enables the hand to grasp objects and is the most distinctive digital movement in humans. The opposite movement is called **reposition.**

> **Learning Strategy 9.4**
>
> When your mother tells you to "pull your shoulders back and stand up straight," you are *retracting* your shoulders. Conversely, when you are slumped forward in a chair, your shoulders are protracted.

WHAT DID YOU LEARN?

5. What are the basic characteristics of all types of synovial joints?
6. Compare and contrast the structure and motion permitted in saddle and condylar joints.
7. Describe the following types of movements, and give an example of each: (a) flexion, (b) circumduction, and (c) opposition. (Perform these movements to help you learn these terms.)

9.5 Selected Articulations in Depth

✓ Learning Objectives

9. Describe the characteristics of the major articulations of the axial skeleton.
10. Describe the characteristics of the major articulations of the upper limb.
11. Describe the characteristics of the major articulations of the lower limb.

In this section, we examine the structure and function of the more commonly known articulations of the axial and appendicular skeletons. For the axial skeleton, we present in-depth descriptions of the temporomandibular joint and the intervertebral articulations. **Table 9.3** summarizes the main features of these two areas and also provides comparable information about the other major joints of the axial skeleton.

9.5a Joints of the Axial Skeleton

Temporomandibular Joint

The **temporomandibular** (tem′p ŏ-rō-man-dib′y ū-lăr) **joint (TMJ)** is formed by the articulation of the head of the mandible with the articular tubercle of the temporal bone anteriorly and the mandibular fossa posteriorly. This small, complex articulation is the only mobile joint between skull bones. The temporomandibular joint has several unique anatomic features (**figure 9.12**). A loose **articular capsule** surrounds the joint and promotes an extensive range of motion. The TMJ is poorly stabilized, and thus a forceful anterior or lateral movement of the mandible can result in partial or complete dislocation of the mandible. The joint contains an **articular disc,** which is a thick pad of fibrocartilage separating the articulating bones and extending horizontally to divide the joint cavity into two separate chambers. As a result, the temporomandibular joint is really two synovial joints—one between the temporal bone and the articular disc, and a second between the articular disc and the mandible.

Several ligaments support this joint. The **sphenomandibular ligament** (an extracapsular ligament) is a thin band that extends anteriorly and inferiorly from the sphenoid to the medial surface of the mandibular ramus. The **stylomandibular ligament** (an extracapsular ligament) is a thick band that extends from the styloid process of the temporal bone to the mandibular angle. The **temporomandibular ligament** (or *lateral ligament*) is located

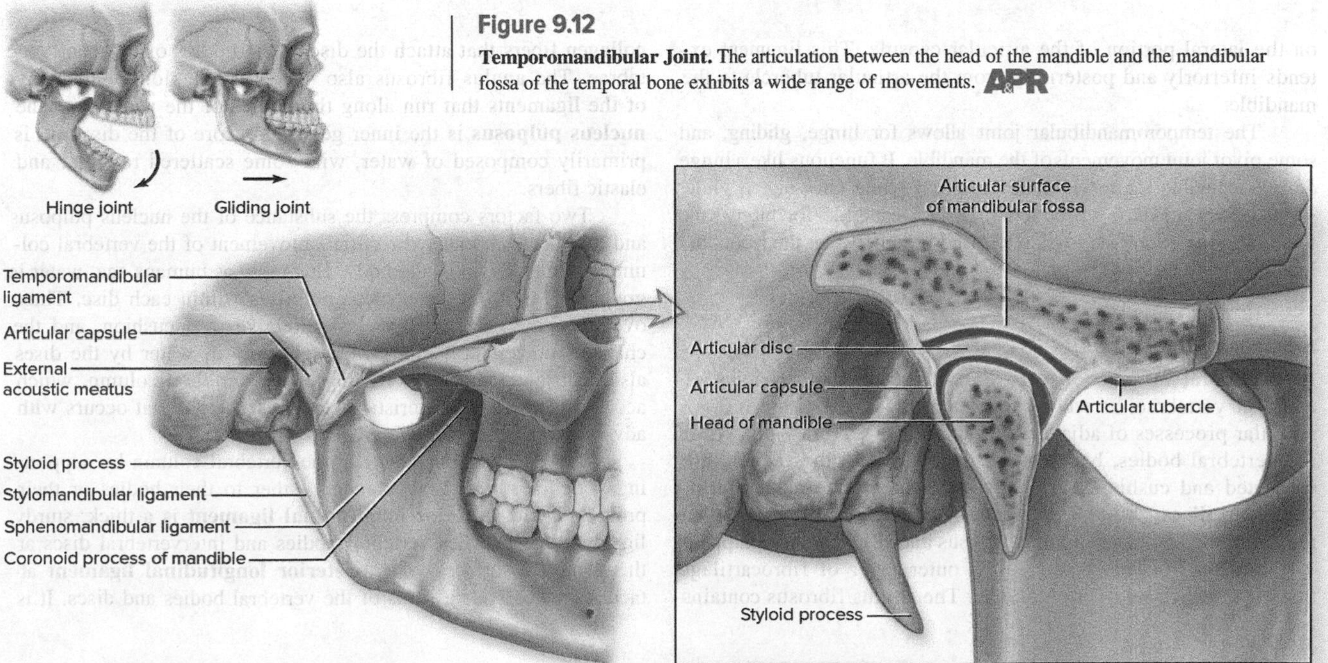
Hinge joint
Gliding joint
Temporomandibular ligament
Articular capsule
External acoustic meatus
Styloid process
Stylomandibular ligament
Sphenomandibular ligament
Coronoid process of mandible
Articular surface of mandibular fossa
Articular disc
Articular capsule
Head of mandible
Articular tubercle
Styloid process

Figure 9.12
Temporomandibular Joint. The articulation between the head of the mandible and the mandibular fossa of the temporal bone exhibits a wide range of movements. APR

Table 9.3 Axial Skeleton Joints

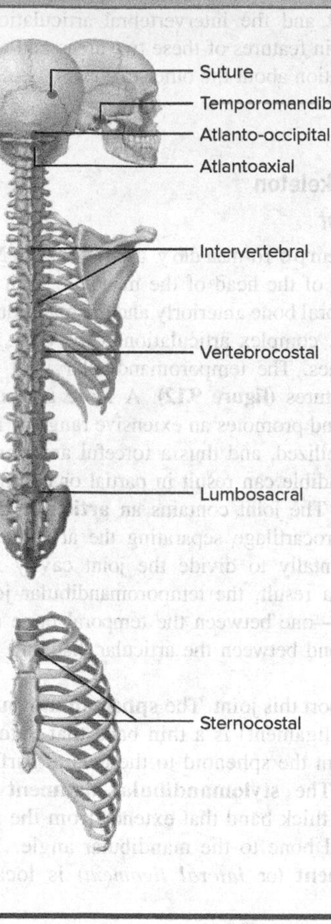
Suture
Temporomandibular
Atlanto-occipital
Atlantoaxial
Intervertebral
Vertebrocostal
Lumbosacral
Sternocostal

Joint	Articulation Components	Structural Classification
Suture	Adjacent skull bones	Fibrous joint
Temporomandibular	Head of mandible and mandibular fossa of temporal bone Head of mandible and articular tubercle of temporal bone	Synovial (hinge, plane) joints
Atlanto-occipital	Superior articular facets of atlas and occipital condyles of occipital bone	Synovial (condylar) joint
Atlantoaxial	Anterior arch of atlas and dens of axis	Synovial (pivot) joint
Intervertebral	Vertebral bodies of adjacent vertebrae Superior and inferior articular processes of adjacent vertebrae	Cartilaginous joint (symphysis) between vertebral bodies; synovial (plane) joint between articular processes
Vertebrocostal	Facets of heads of ribs and bodies of adjacent thoracic vertebrae and intervertebral discs between adjacent vertebrae Articular part of tubercles of ribs and facets of transverse processes of thoracic vertebrae	Synovial (plane) joint
Lumbosacral	Body of the fifth lumbar vertebra and base of the sacrum Inferior articular facets of fifth lumbar vertebra and superior articular facets of first sacral vertebra	Cartilaginous joint (symphysis) between lumbar body and base of sacrum; synovial (plane) joint between articular facets
Sternocostal	Sternum and first seven pairs of ribs	Cartilaginous joint (synchondrosis) between sternum and first ribs; synovial (plane) joint between sternum and ribs 2–7

on the lateral portion of the articular capsule. This ligament extends inferiorly and posteriorly from the articular tubercle to the mandible.

The temporomandibular joint allows for hinge, gliding, and some pivot joint movements of the mandible. It functions like a hinge during mandible depression and elevation while chewing. It glides slightly forward during protraction of the mandible for biting, and glides slightly from side-to-side to grind food between the teeth during chewing. APR

Intervertebral Articulations

Intervertebral articulations are located between the bodies of adjacent vertebrae, as well as between the superior and inferior articular processes of adjacent vertebrae (see section 7.4c). All of the vertebral bodies, between the axis (C_2) and the sacrum, are separated and cushioned by pads of fibrocartilage called **intervertebral discs (figure 9.13)**. Each intervertebral disc consists of two components: (1) an anulus fibrosus and (2) a nucleus pulposus. The **anulus fibrosus** is the tough outer layer of fibrocartilage that covers each intervertebral disc. The anulus fibrosus contains collagen fibers that attach the disc to the bodies of adjacent vertebrae. The anulus fibrosus also shares connections with many of the ligaments that run along the bodies of the vertebrae. The **nucleus pulposus** is the inner gelatinous core of the disc and is primarily composed of water, with some scattered reticular and elastic fibers.

Two factors compress the substance of the nucleus pulposus and displace it in every direction—movement of the vertebral column and the weight of the body. However, as humans age, water is gradually lost from the nucleus pulposus within each disc. Thus, over time the discs become less effective as a cushion, and the chances for vertebral injury increase. Loss of water by the discs also contributes to the shortening of the vertebral column, which accounts for the characteristic decrease in height that occurs with advanced age.

Several ligaments stabilize the vertebral column by supporting vertebrae through attachments either to their bodies or their processes. The **anterior longitudinal ligament** is a thick, sturdy ligament that attaches vertebral bodies and intervertebral discs at their anterior surfaces. The **posterior longitudinal ligament** attaches the posterior aspects of the vertebral bodies and discs. It is

Functional Classification	Description of Movement(s)
Synarthrosis	None
Diarthrosis	Depression, elevation, lateral displacement, protraction, retraction, slight rotation of mandible
Diarthrosis	Extension and flexion of the head; slight lateral flexion of head to sides
Diarthrosis	Head rotation
Amphiarthrosis between vertebral bodies; diarthrosis between articular processes	Extension, flexion, lateral flexion of vertebral column
Diarthrosis	Some slight gliding of the ribs
Amphiarthrosis between body and base; diarthrosis between articular facets	Extension, flexion, lateral flexion of vertebral column
Synarthrosis between sternum and first ribs; diarthrosis between sternum and ribs 2–7	No movement between sternum and first ribs; some gliding movement permitted between sternum and ribs 2–7

much thinner than the anterior longitudinal ligament, and it runs within the vertebral canal. Multiple **interspinous ligaments** interconnect the spinous processes of adjacent vertebrae. Their angled fibers merge with the supraspinous ligament. The **supraspinous ligament** interconnects the tips of the spinous processes from C_7 to the sacrum. The **ligamentum** (lig′ă-men′tŭm) nuchae (nū′kē; back of neck) is the part of the supraspinous ligament that extends between C_7 and the base of the skull. The ligamentum nuchae is very thick and sturdy, and helps stabilize the skull on the cervical vertebrae. The **ligamentum flavum** (flā′vŭm) connects the laminae of adjacent vertebrae.

A second type of intervertebral articulation occurs at the synovial joints between adjacent superior and inferior articular processes. The articular facets of the superior and inferior articular processes form plane joints that permit restricted gliding movements. An articular capsule surrounds these articular processes.

The movement possible between a single set of vertebrae is limited. However, when you add the movements of all the intervertebral joints of all the vertebrae together, an entire range of movements becomes possible, including flexion, extension, lateral flexion, and some rotation. APR

Clinical View 9.3

TMJ Disorders

The temporomandibular joint (TMJ) is subject to various disorders. The most common TMJ disorder occurs as a result of alternations in the ligaments that secure the joint, causing progressive internal displacement of the articular disc. As the articular disc is forced out of its normal position, a clicking or popping noise may be heard as the person opens or closes the mouth. Other symptoms may include headaches and sinus pressure as well as pain in such areas as the paranasal sinuses, tympanic membrane, oral cavity, eyes, and teeth.

TMJ disorders are often seen in people who habitually chew gum or grind or clench their teeth. The physician may prescribe a bite appliance for the patient to wear at night to prevent grinding and clenching of the teeth.

WHAT DO YOU THINK?

4 In which position does the anterior longitudinal ligament become taut: flexion or extension?

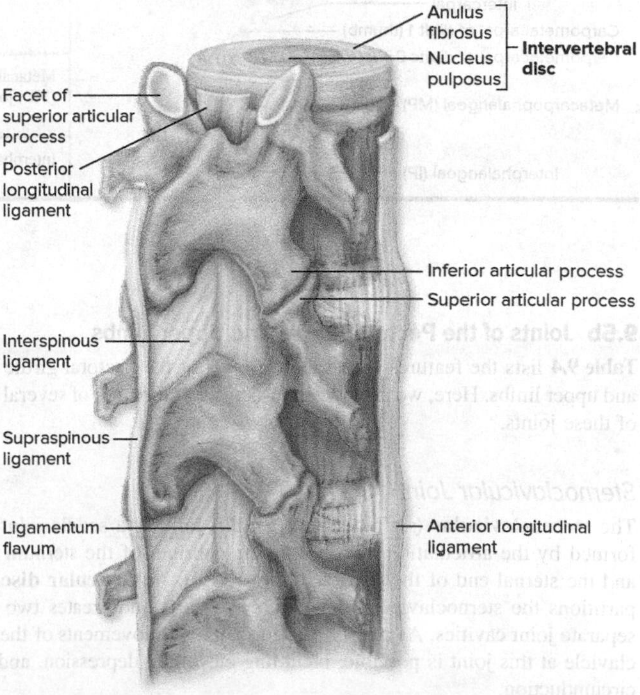

Figure 9.13
Intervertebral Articulations. Vertebrae articulate with adjacent vertebrae at both their superior and inferior articular processes. Intervertebral discs separate the bodies of adjacent vertebrae. APR

Table 9.4 Pectoral Girdle and Upper Limb Joints

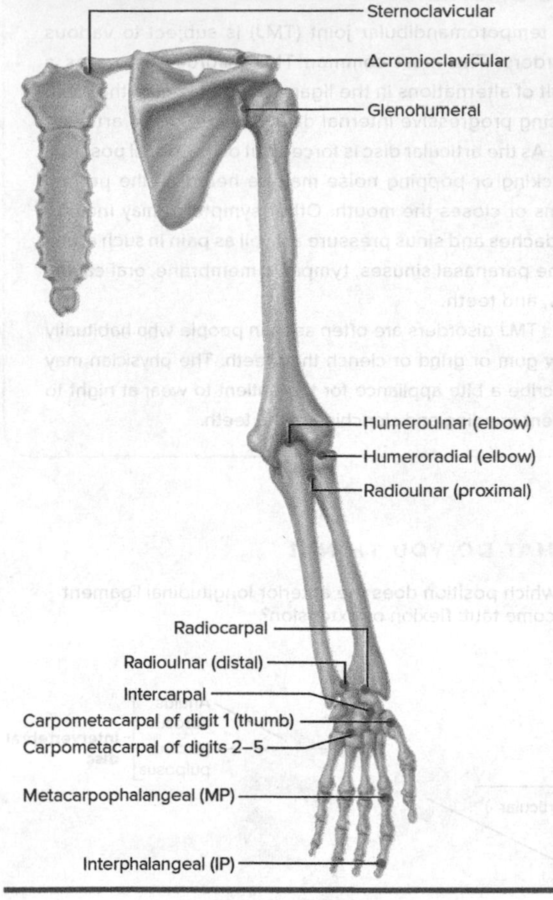
Sternoclavicular
Acromioclavicular
Glenohumeral
Humeroulnar (elbow)
Humeroradial (elbow)
Radioulnar (proximal)
Radiocarpal
Radioulnar (distal)
Intercarpal
Carpometacarpal of digit 1 (thumb)
Carpometacarpal of digits 2–5
Metacarpophalangeal (MP)
Interphalangeal (IP)

Joint	Articulation Components
Sternoclavicular	Manubrium of sternum and sternal end of clavicle
Acromioclavicular	Acromial end of clavicle and acromion of scapula
Glenohumeral	Glenoid cavity of scapula and head of humerus
Elbow	Humeroulnar joint: Trochlea of humerus and trochlear notch of ulna Humeroradial joint: Capitulum of humerus and head of radius
Radioulnar	Proximal joint: Head of radius and radial notch of ulna Distal joint: Distal end of ulna and ulnar notch of radius
Radiocarpal	Distal end of radius; lunate, scaphoid, and triquetrum
Intercarpal	Adjacent bones in proximal row of carpal bones Adjacent bones in distal row of carpal bones Adjacent bones between proximal and distal rows (midcarpal joints)
Carpometacarpal	Thumb: Trapezium (carpal bone) and first metacarpal Other digits: Carpals and metacarpals II–V
Metacarpophalangeal (MP) joints, or "knuckles"	Heads of metacarpals and bases of proximal phalanges
Interphalangeal (IP) joints	Heads of proximal and middle phalanges with bases of middle and distal phalanges, respectively

9.5b Joints of the Pectoral Girdle and Upper Limbs

Table 9.4 lists the features of the major joints of the pectoral girdle and upper limbs. Here, we provide an in-depth examination of several of these joints.

Sternoclavicular Joint

The **sternoclavicular** (ster′n ō-kla-vik′y ū-lăr) **joint** is a saddle joint formed by the articulation between the manubrium of the sternum and the sternal end of the clavicle (**figure 9.14**). An **articular disc** partitions the sternoclavicular joint into two parts and creates two separate joint cavities. As a result, a wide range of movements of the clavicle at this joint is possible, including elevation, depression, and circumduction.

Support and stability are provided to this articulation by the fibers of the articular capsule. The **anterior sternoclavicular ligament** and the **posterior sternoclavicular ligament** reinforce the capsule. In addition, two extracapsular ligaments also help strengthen the joint: (1) The clavicle is attached to the first rib by the strong, wide **costoclavicular ligament.** This ligament stabilizes the joint and prevents dislocation of the shoulder when the shoulder is elevated. (2) The **interclavicular ligament** runs along the sternal notch and attaches to each clavicle. It reinforces the superior regions of the adjacent capsules. This design makes the sternoclavicular joint very stable. If a person falls on an outstretched hand so that force is applied to the joint, the clavicle will fracture before this joint ever dislocates.

Acromioclavicular Joint

The **acromioclavicular** (ă-krō′mē-ō-kla-vik′y ū-lăr) **joint** is a plane joint between the acromion and the acromial end of the clavicle (**figure 9.15**). A fibrocartilaginous **articular disc** lies within the joint cavity between these two bones. This joint works with both the sternoclavicular joint and the glenohumeral joint to give the upper limb a full range of movement.

Several ligaments provide great stability to this joint. The articular capsule is strengthened superiorly by an **acromioclavicular ligament.**

Structural Classification	Functional Classification	Description of Movement(s)
Synovial (saddle)	Diarthrosis	Depression, elevation, circumduction of the clavicle
Synovial (plane)	Diarthrosis	Gliding of scapula on clavicle
Synovial (ball-and-socket)	Diarthrosis	Flexion, extension, abduction, adduction, circumduction, lateral rotation, and medial rotation of arm
Synovial (hinge)	Diarthrosis	Flexion and extension of forearm
Synovial (pivot)	Diarthrosis	Rotation of radius with respect to the ulna
Synovial (condylar)	Diarthrosis	Flexion, extension, abduction, adduction, and circumduction of wrist
Synovial (plane)	Diarthrosis	Gliding of the carpals
Synovial (saddle) at thumb; synovial (plane) at other digits	Diarthrosis	Flexion, extension, abduction, adduction, circumduction, and opposition at thumb; gliding at other digits
Synovial (condylar)	Diarthrosis	Flexion, extension, abduction, adduction, and circumduction of phalanges
Synovial (hinge)	Diarthrosis	Flexion and extension of phalanges

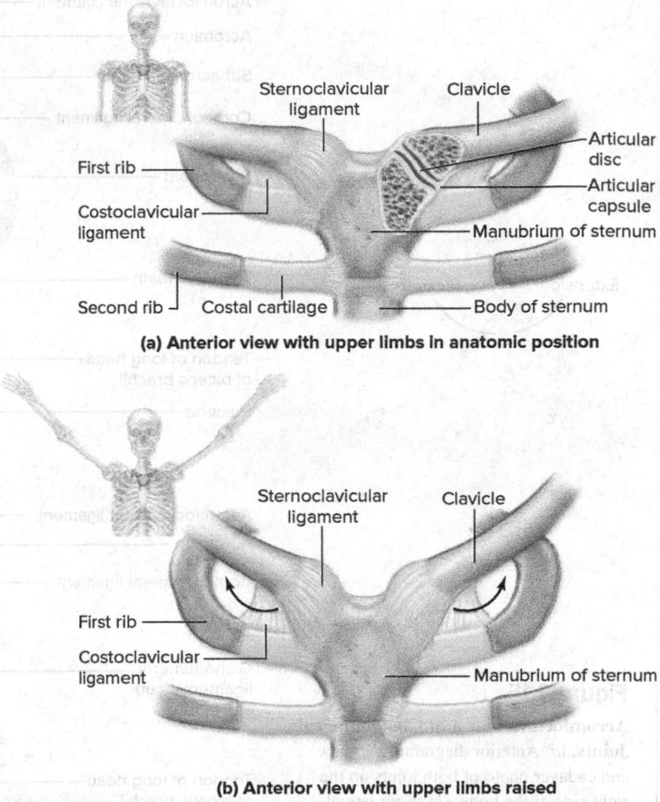

Figure 9.14

Sternoclavicular Joint. The sternoclavicular joint helps stabilize movements of the entire shoulder. The positioning of the joint is compared (*a*) with the upper limbs by the sides of the body and (*b*) with the upper limbs raised.

In addition, a very strong **coracoclavicular** (kōr′ă-kō-kla-vik′yū-lăr) **ligament** binds the clavicle to the coracoid process of the scapula. The coracoclavicular ligament is responsible for most of the stability of the joint, because it indirectly prevents the clavicle from losing contact with the acromion. If this ligament is torn (as occurs in severe shoulder separations; see Clinical View 9.4: "Shoulder Joint Dislocations" in this section), the acromion and clavicle no longer align properly.

Glenohumeral (Shoulder) Joint

The **glenohumeral** (glē′nō-hyū′mer-ăl) **joint** is commonly referred to as the shoulder joint. It is a ball-and-socket joint formed by the articulation of the head of the humerus and the glenoid cavity of the scapula (figure 9.15). It permits the greatest range of motion of any joint in the body, and so it is also the most unstable joint in the body and the one most frequently dislocated.

The fibrocartilaginous **glenoid labrum** encircles and covers the surface of the glenoid cavity. A relatively loose articular capsule attaches to the surgical neck of the humerus. The glenohumeral joint has several major ligaments. The **coracoacromial** (kōr′ă-kō-ă-krō′mē-ăl) **ligament** extends across the space between the coracoid process and the acromion. The large **coracohumeral** (kōr′ă-kō-hyū′mer-ăl) **ligament** is a thickening of the superior part of the joint capsule. It runs from the coracoid process to the humeral head. The **glenohumeral ligaments** are three thickenings of the anterior portion of the articular capsule. These ligaments are often indistinct or absent and provide only minimal support. In addition, the tendon of the long head of biceps brachii travels within the articular capsule and helps stabilize the humeral head in the joint.

Unlike other joints of the body (where ligaments provide most of the support), the ligaments of the glenohumeral joint do little to strengthen the joint. Instead, most of the glenohumeral joint's strength is due to the **rotator cuff** muscles surrounding it (see section 12.1b). The rotator cuff muscles (supraspinatus, infraspinatus, teres minor, and subscapularis) work as a group to hold the head of the humerus in the glenoid cavity. The tendons of these muscles

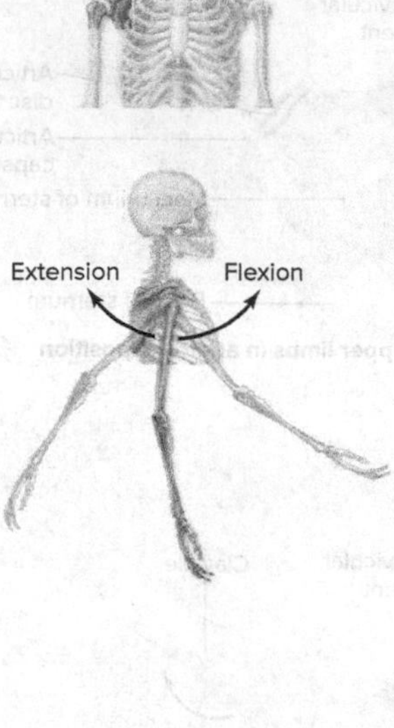
Extension
Flexion

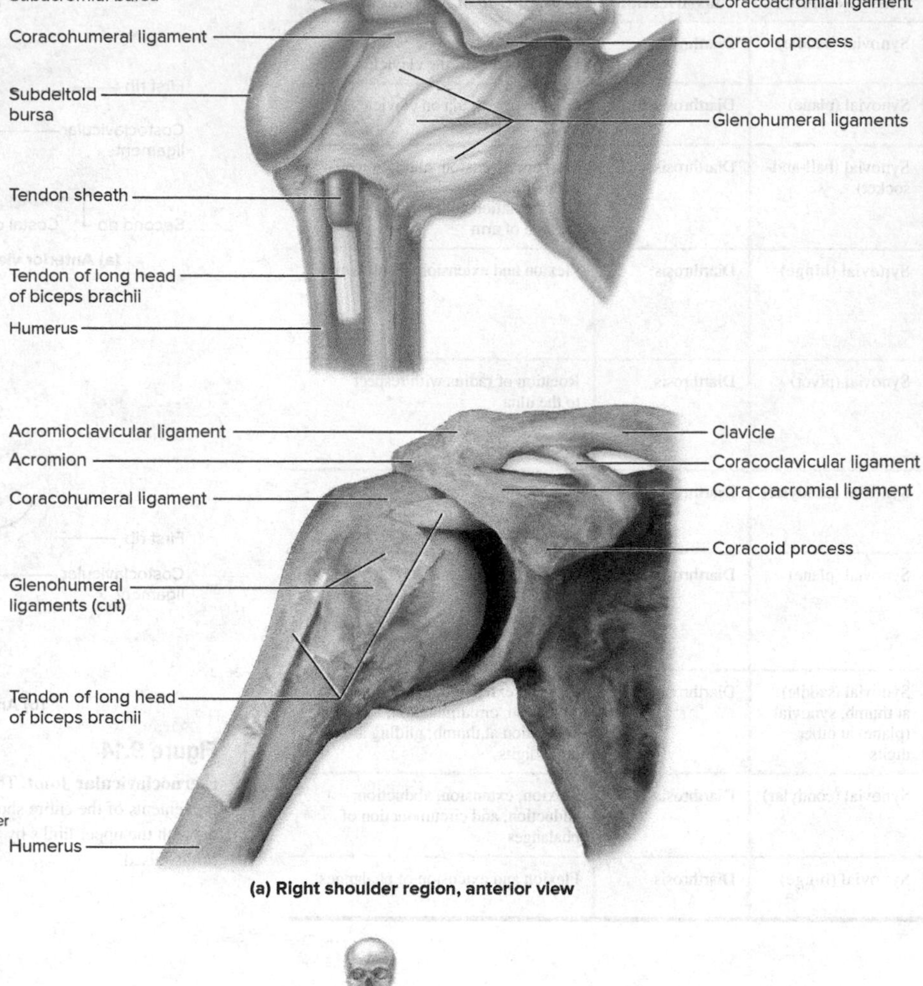
Acromioclavicular ligament
Acromion
Subacromial bursa
Coracohumeral ligament
Subdeltoid bursa
Tendon sheath
Tendon of long head of biceps brachii
Humerus
Clavicle
Coracoclavicular ligament
Coracoacromial ligament
Coracoid process
Glenohumeral ligaments
Acromioclavicular ligament
Acromion
Coracohumeral ligament
Glenohumeral ligaments (cut)
Tendon of long head of biceps brachii
Humerus
Clavicle
Coracoclavicular ligament
Coracoacromial ligament
Coracoid process

(a) Right shoulder region, anterior view

Figure 9.15

Acromioclavicular and Glenohumeral Joints. (*a*) Anterior diagrammatic view and cadaver photo of both joints on the right side of the body. (*b*) Right lateral view and (*c*) right coronal section show the articulating bones and supporting structures at the shoulder. APR

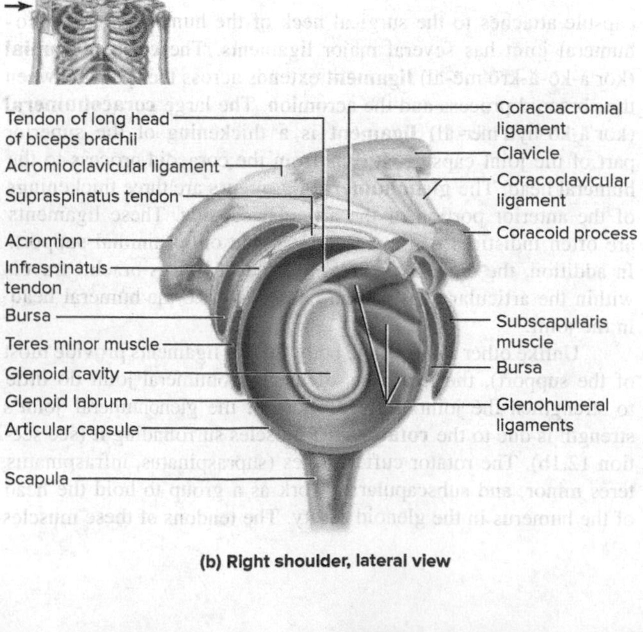
Tendon of long head of biceps brachii
Acromioclavicular ligament
Supraspinatus tendon
Acromion
Infraspinatus tendon
Bursa
Teres minor muscle
Glenoid cavity
Glenoid labrum
Articular capsule
Scapula
Coracoacromial ligament
Clavicle
Coracoclavicular ligament
Coracoid process
Subscapularis muscle
Bursa
Glenohumeral ligaments

(b) Right shoulder, lateral view

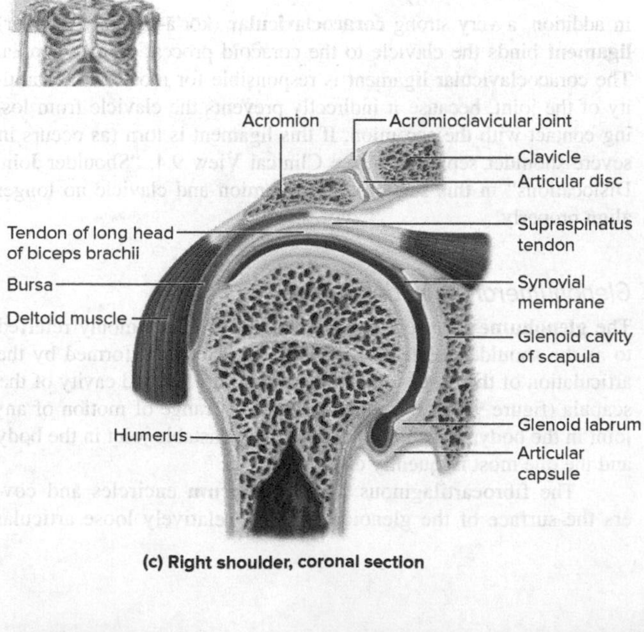
Acromion
Acromioclavicular joint
Clavicle
Articular disc
Supraspinatus tendon
Tendon of long head of biceps brachii
Bursa
Deltoid muscle
Synovial membrane
Glenoid cavity of scapula
Humerus
Glenoid labrum
Articular capsule

(c) Right shoulder, coronal section

encircle the joint (except for the inferior portion) and fuse with the articular capsule. Because the inferior portion of the joint lacks rotator cuff muscles, this area is weak and is the most likely site of injury.

Bursae help decrease friction at the specific places on the shoulder where both tendons and large muscles extend across the articular capsule. The shoulder has a relatively large number of bursae, several of which are shown in figure 9.15. APR

Elbow Joint

The **elbow joint** is a hinge joint composed primarily of two articulations: (1) the humeroulnar joint, where the trochlear notch of the ulna articulates with the trochlea of the humerus; and (2) the humeroradial joint, where the capitulum of the humerus articulates with the head of the radius. These joints are enclosed within a single articular capsule (**figure 9.16**).

The elbow is an extremely stable joint for several reasons. First, the articular capsule is fairly thick, and thus effectively protects the articulations. Second, the bony surfaces of the humerus and ulna interlock very well, and thus provide a solid bony support.

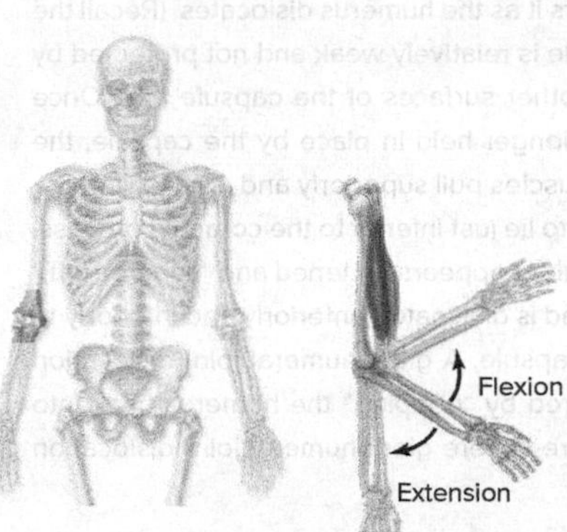

Figure 9.16

Elbow Joint. The elbow joint is a hinge joint. The right elbow is shown here in (*a*) anterior view, (*b*) lateral view, (*c*) medial view, and (*d*) sagittal section. APR

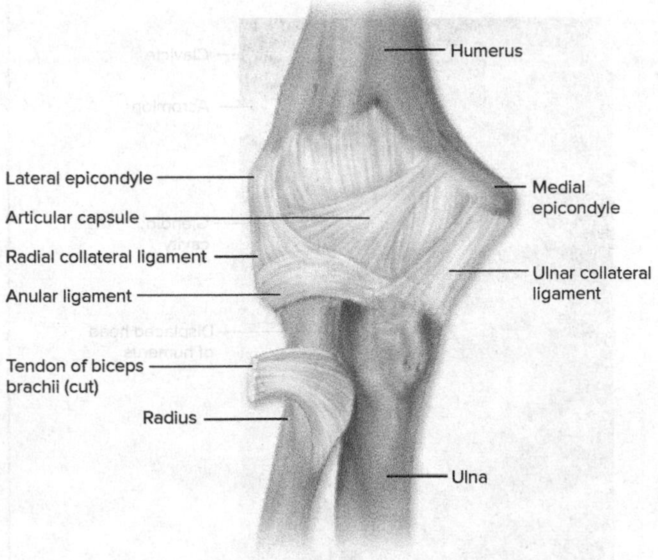

(a) Right elbow, anterior view

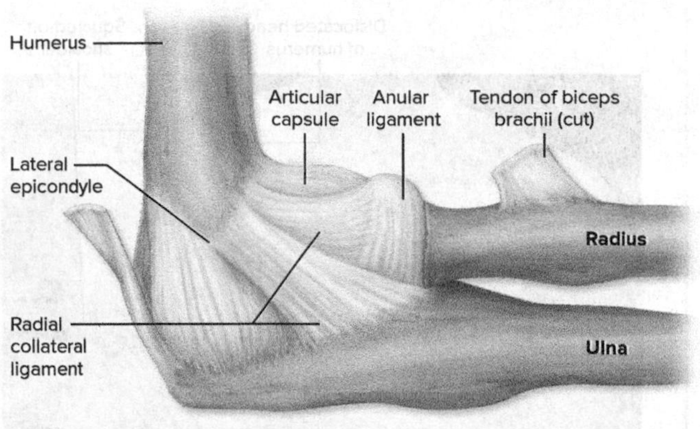

(b) Right elbow, lateral view

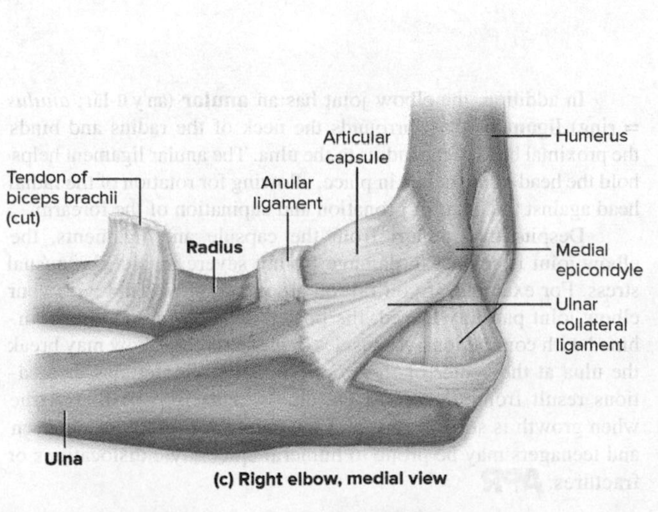

(c) Right elbow, medial view

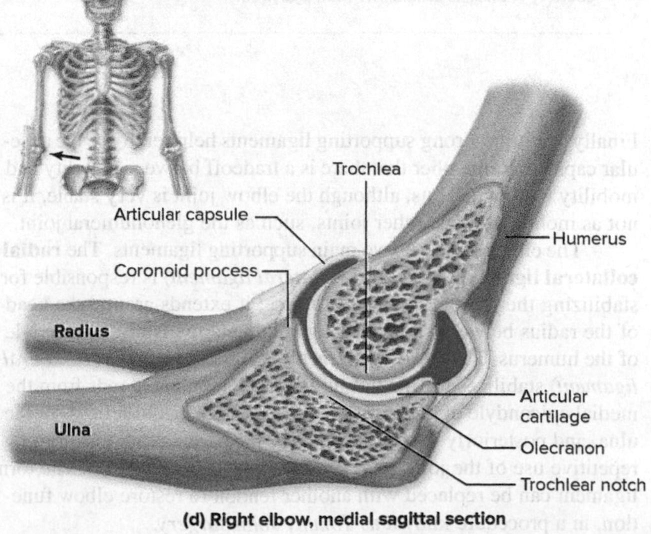

(d) Right elbow, medial sagittal section

Clinical View 9.4

Shoulder Joint Dislocations

Dislocation (dis′lō-kā′shŭn; *dis* = apart, *locatio* = placing), a joint injury in which the articulating bones have separated, is common in the shoulder. Although this injury can occur at any of the three shoulder joints described in the chapter, it is more common at the acromioclavicular joint or the glenohumoral joint.

The term **shoulder separation** refers to an acromioclavicular joint dislocation. This injury often results from a hard blow to the joint, as when a hockey player is "slammed into the boards" or one falls onto the shoulder. Symptoms include tenderness and edema (swelling) in the area of the joint. Additionally, the acromion will appear very prominent and pointed. Treatment can range from rest to surgery, depending upon the severity of the dislocation.

Glenohumeral joint dislocations are very common because this joint is very mobile and yet unstable. A glenohumeral joint dislocation usually occurs when a fully abducted humerus is struck hard—for example, when a quarterback is hit as he is about to release a football, or when a person falls on an outstretched hand. The initial blow pushes the humerus into the inferior part of the articular capsule and tears it as the humerus dislocates. (Recall the inferior part of the capsule is relatively weak and not protected by muscle tendons as the other surfaces of the capsule are.) Once the humeral head is no longer held in place by the capsule, the anterior thorax (chest) muscles pull superiorly and medially on the humeral head, causing it to lie just inferior to the coracoid process. The result is that the shoulder appears flattened and "squared-off," because the humeral head is dislocated anteriorly and inferiorly to the glenohumeral joint capsule. A glenohumeral joint dislocation sometimes can be repaired by "popping" the humerus back into the glenoid cavity. A more severe glenohumeral joint dislocation may need surgical repair.

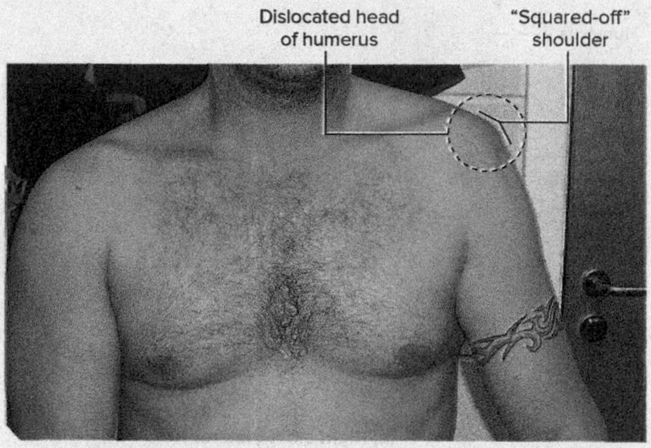
Dislocated head of humerus
"Squared-off" shoulder

Glenohumeral joint dislocation.
Courtesy of Dr. Mike Langran/www.ski-injury.com

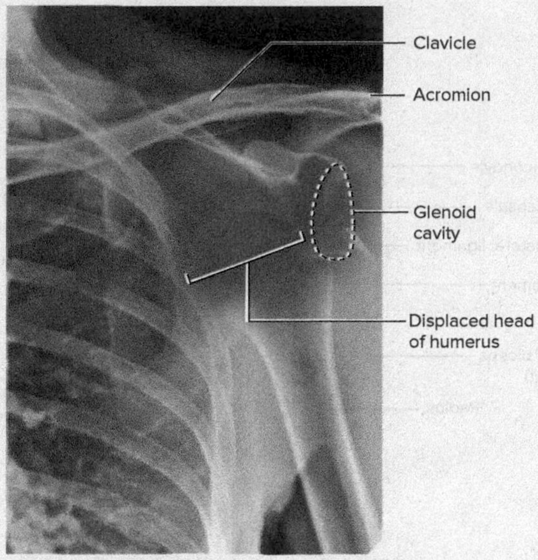
Clavicle
Acromion
Glenoid cavity
Displaced head of humerus

Colorized radiograph of a glenohumeral dislocation.
Science Photo Library/Alamy Stock Photo

Finally, multiple strong supporting ligaments help reinforce the articular capsule. Remember that there is a tradeoff between stability and mobility in a joint. Thus, although the elbow joint is very stable, it is not as mobile as some other joints, such as the glenohumeral joint.

The elbow joint has two main supporting ligaments. The **radial collateral ligament** (or *lateral collateral ligament*) is responsible for stabilizing the joint at its lateral surface; it extends around the head of the radius between the anular ligament and the lateral epicondyle of the humerus. The **ulnar collateral ligament** (or *medial collateral ligament*) stabilizes the medial side of the joint and extends from the medial epicondyle of the humerus to both the coronoid process of the ulna, and posteriorly to the olecranon. This ligament may be torn by repetitive use of the joint (e.g., as seen with some pitchers). The torn ligament can be replaced with another tendon to restore elbow function, in a procedure known as *Tommy John surgery.*

In addition, the elbow joint has an **anular** (an′y ū-lăr; *anulus* = ring) **ligament** that surrounds the neck of the radius and binds the proximal head of the radius to the ulna. The anular ligament helps hold the head of the radius in place, allowing for rotation of the radial head against the ulna for pronation and supination of the forearm.

Despite the support from the capsule and ligaments, the elbow joint is subject to damage from a severe impact or unusual stress. For example, if you fall on an outstretched hand with your elbow joint partially flexed, the posterior stress on the ulna combined with contractions of muscles that extend the elbow may break the ulna at the center of the trochlear notch. Sometimes dislocations result from stresses to the elbow. This is particularly true when growth is still occurring at the epiphyseal plate, so children and teenagers may be prone to humeral epicondyle dislocations or fractures. APR

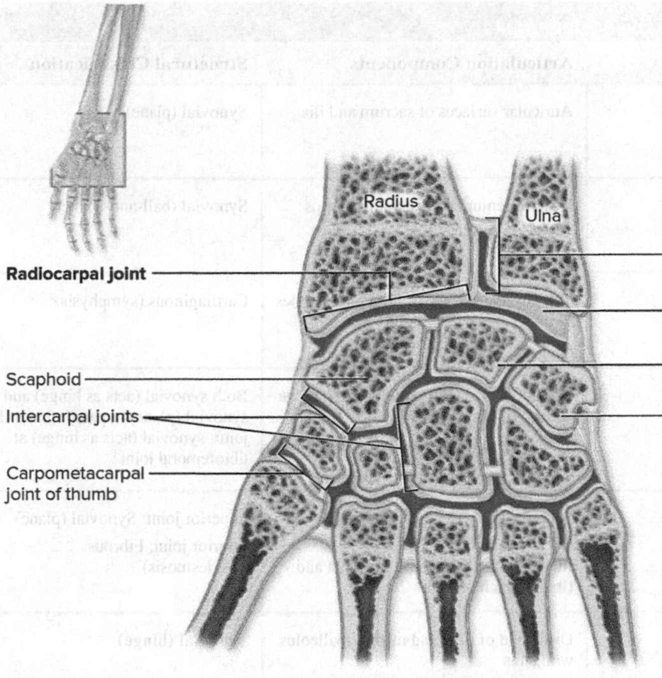

Figure 9.17

Radiocarpal Joint. A right coronal section depicts the condylar articulation between the radius and three proximal carpal bones. APR

Radiocarpal (Wrist) Joint

The **radiocarpal** (rā′dē-ō-kar′p ăl) **joint,** also known as the *wrist joint,* is an articulation among the three proximal carpal bones (scaphoid, lunate, and triquetrum), the distal articular surface of the radius, and a fibrocartilaginous **articular disc (figure 9.17).** This articular disc separates the ulna from the radiocarpal joint (which is why the ulna is not considered part of this joint). The entire wrist complex is ensheathed by an articular capsule that has reinforcing broad ligaments to support and stabilize the carpal bone positions. The radiocarpal joint is a condylar articulation that permits flexion, extension, adduction, abduction, and circumduction, but no rotation. Rotational movements (in the form of supination and pronation) occur at the distal and proximal radioulnar joints. APR

Additional movements in the wrist are made possible by **intercarpal articulations,** which are plane joints that permit gliding movements between the individual carpal bones.

WHAT DID YOU LEARN?

8. Describe the structural arrangement of the temporomandibular joint. What movements are allowed at this joint? What is the significance of its articular disc?
9. Which ligaments limit the relative mobility of the clavicle at the sternal end? At the acromial end?
10. Which structures are the primary stabilizers of the glenohumeral joint? How do these stabilizers differ from those found in other joints? Is there a part of the glenohumeral joint that is not well protected?
11. List the major elbow joint ligaments and explain each of their functions.

Clinical View 9.5

Subluxation of the Head of the Radius

The term **subluxation** refers to an incomplete dislocation, in which the contact between the bony joint surfaces is altered, but they are still in partial contact. In **subluxation of the head of the radius,** the head is pulled out of the anular ligament. The layman's terms for this injury include *pulled elbow, nursemaid's elbow,* or *slipped elbow.* This injury occurs commonly and almost exclusively in children (typically those younger than age 5), because a child's anular ligament is thin and the head of the radius is not fully formed. It may occur if an individual pulls suddenly on a child's pronated forearm, as shown in the corresponding photo.

Luckily, treatment is simple: The pediatrician applies a posteriorly placed pressure to the head of the radius while slowly supinating and extending the child's forearm. This movement literally screws the radial head back into the anular ligament.

Fuse/Getty Images

Table 9.5 Pelvic Girdle and Lower Limb Joints

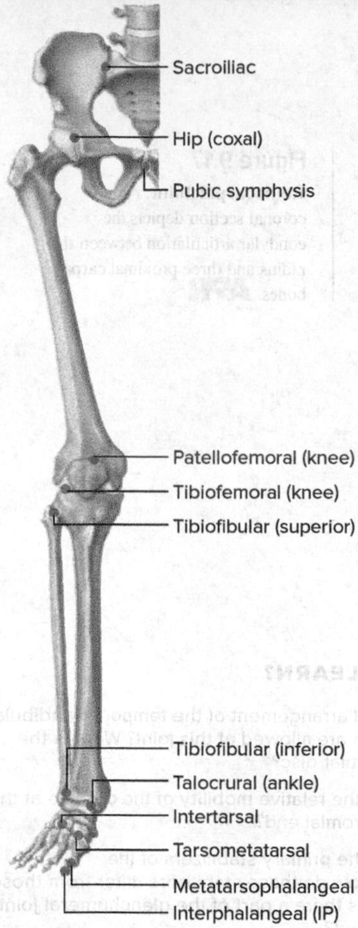
Sacroiliac
Hip (coxal)
Pubic symphysis
Patellofemoral (knee)
Tibiofemoral (knee)
Tibiofibular (superior)
Tibiofibular (inferior)
Talocrural (ankle)
Intertarsal
Tarsometatarsal
Metatarsophalangeal (MP)
Interphalangeal (IP)

Joint	Articulation Components	Structural Classification
Sacroiliac	Auricular surfaces of sacrum and ilia	Synovial (plane)
Hip (coxal)	Head of femur and acetabulum of os coxae	Synovial (ball-and-socket)
Pubic symphysis	Symphyseal surface of both pubic bones	Cartilaginous (symphysis)
Knee	Patellofemoral joint: Patella and patellar surface of femur Tibiofemoral joint: Condyles of femur and condyles of tibia	Both synovial (acts as hinge) and synovial (plane) at patellofemoral joint; synovial (acts as hinge) at tibiofemoral joint[1]
Tibiofibular	Superior joint: Head of fibula and lateral condyle of tibia Inferior joint: Distal end of fibula and fibular notch of tibia	Superior joint: Synovial (plane) Inferior joint: Fibrous (syndesmosis)
Talocrural (ankle)	Distal end of tibia and medial malleolus with talus Lateral malleolus of fibula and talus	Synovial (hinge)
Intertarsal	Between the tarsal bones	Synovial (plane)
Tarsometatarsal	Three cuneiforms (tarsal bones), cuboid, and bases of five metatarsal bones	Synovial (plane)
Metatarsophalangeal (MP) joints	Heads of metatarsals and bases of proximal phalanges	Synovial (condylar)
Interphalangeal (IP) joints	Heads of proximal and middle phalanges with bases of middle and distal phalanges, respectively	Synovial (hinge)

[1] Although anatomists classify the tibiofemoral joint as a hinge joint, some kinesiologists and exercise scientists prefer to classify the tibiofemoral joint as a modified condylar joint.

9.5c Joints of the Pelvic Girdle and Lower Limbs

Table 9.5 lists the features of the major joints of the pelvic girdle and lower limbs. Here, we provide an in-depth examination of several of these joints.

Hip (Coxal) Joint

The **hip joint,** also called the *coxal joint,* is the articulation between the head of the femur and the relatively deep, concave acetabulum of the os coxae (**figure 9.18**). A fibrocartilaginous **acetabular labrum** further deepens this socket. The hip joint's more extensive bony architecture is therefore much stronger and more stable than that of the glenohumeral joint. Conversely, the hip joint's increased stability means that it is less mobile than the glenohumeral joint. The hip joint must be more stable (and thus less mobile) because it supports the body weight.

The hip joint is secured by a strong articular capsule, several ligaments, and a number of powerful muscles. The articular capsule extends from the acetabulum to the trochanters of the femur, enclosing both the femoral head and neck. This arrangement prevents the head from moving away from the acetabulum. The ligamentous fibers of the articular capsule reflect around the neck of the femur. These reflected fibers, called **retinacular** (ret-i-nak′yū-lăr; *retinacula* = a band) **fibers,** provide additional stability to the capsule. Traveling through the retinacular fibers are retinacular arteries (branches of the deep femoral artery), which supply almost all of the blood to the head and neck of the femur.

The articular capsule is reinforced by three spiraling intracapsular ligaments. The **iliofemoral** (il′ē-ō-fem′ŏ-răl) **ligament** is a Y-shaped ligament that provides strong reinforcement for the anterior region of the articular capsule. The **ischiofemoral** (is-kē-ō-fem′ŏ-răl) **ligament** is a spiral-shaped, posteriorly located ligament. The **pubofemoral** (pyū′bō-fem′ŏ-răl) **ligament** is a triangular thickening of the capsule's inferior region. All of these spiraling ligaments become taut when the femur is extended at the hip joint, so the hip joint is most stable in the extended position. Try this experiment:

Functional Classification	Description of Movement(s)
Diarthrosis	Slight gliding of the hip bones; more movement during pregnancy and childbirth
Diarthrosis	Flexion, extension, abduction, adduction, circumduction, medial and lateral rotation of thigh
Amphiarthrosis	Very slight movements of the pubic bones; more movement during childbirth
Diarthrosis	Flexion, extension, lateral rotation of leg in flexed position, and slight medial rotation
Amphiarthrosis	Slight rotation of fibula during dorsiflexion of foot
Diarthrosis	Dorsiflexion and plantar flexion of the ankle
Diarthrosis	Eversion and inversion of foot
Diarthrosis	Slight gliding of the tarsals
Diarthrosis	Flexion, extension, abduction, adduction, and circumduction of proximal phalanges
Diarthrosis	Flexion and extension of phalanges

Flex your hip joint, and try to move the femur; you may notice a great deal of mobility. Now extend your hip joint (stand up), and try to move the femur. Because those ligaments are taut, you don't have as much mobility in the joint as you did when the hip joint was flexed.

Another tiny ligament, the **ligament of head of femur,** also called the *ligamentum teres,* originates along the acetabulum. Its attachment point is the center of the head of the femur. This ligament does not provide much strength to the joint; rather, it typically contains a small artery that supplies the head of the femur.

The combination of a deep bony socket, a strong articular capsule, supporting ligaments, and muscular padding gives the hip joint its stability. Movements possible at the hip joint include flexion, extension, abduction, adduction, rotation, and circumduction of the femur.

Knee Joint

The **knee joint** is the largest and most complex diarthrosis of the body (**figure 9.19**). It primarily functions as a hinge joint, but when the knee is flexed, it is also capable of slight rotation and lateral gliding. Structurally, the knee is composed of two separate articulations: (1) the **tibiofemoral** (tib′ē-ō-fem′ŏ-răl) **joint** is between the condyles of the femur and the condyles of the tibia, and (2) the **patellofemoral joint** is between the patella and the patellar surface of the femur.

Clinical View 9.6

Fracture of the Femoral Neck

Fracture of the femoral neck is a common and complex injury. Although this injury is often referred to as a "fractured hip," the os coxae isn't broken, just the femoral neck. When the femoral neck breaks, the pull of the lower limb muscles causes the leg to rotate laterally and shorten by several inches. Fractures of the femoral neck are of two types: intertrochanteric and subcapital.

Intertrochanteric fractures of the femoral neck occur distally to or outside the hip articular capsule—in other words, these fractures are *extracapsular.* The fracture line runs between the greater and lesser trochanters. This type of injury typically occurs in younger and middle-aged individuals, and usually in response to trauma.

Subcapital fractures (*or intracapsular fractures*) of the femoral neck occur within the hip articular capsule, very close to the head of the femur itself. This type of fracture usually occurs in elderly people whose bones have been weakened by osteoporosis.

Subcapital fractures result in tearing of the retinacular fibers and the retinacular arteries that supply the head and neck of the femur. The ligament to the head of the femur may be torn as well. As a result, the head and neck of the femur lose their blood supply. If a bone doesn't have an adequate blood supply, it develops **avascular necrosis,** which is death of the bone tissue due to lack of blood. Frequently, hip replacement surgery is needed. This surgery is not without risk, and many elderly patients do not survive because of postsurgical complications.

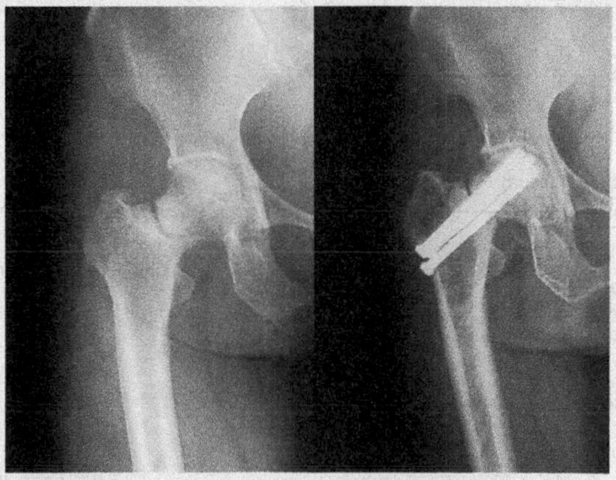

Radiographs showing a subcapital fracture of the femoral neck (left) and the same fracture, surgically reduced (right).
Suttha Burawonk/Shutterstock

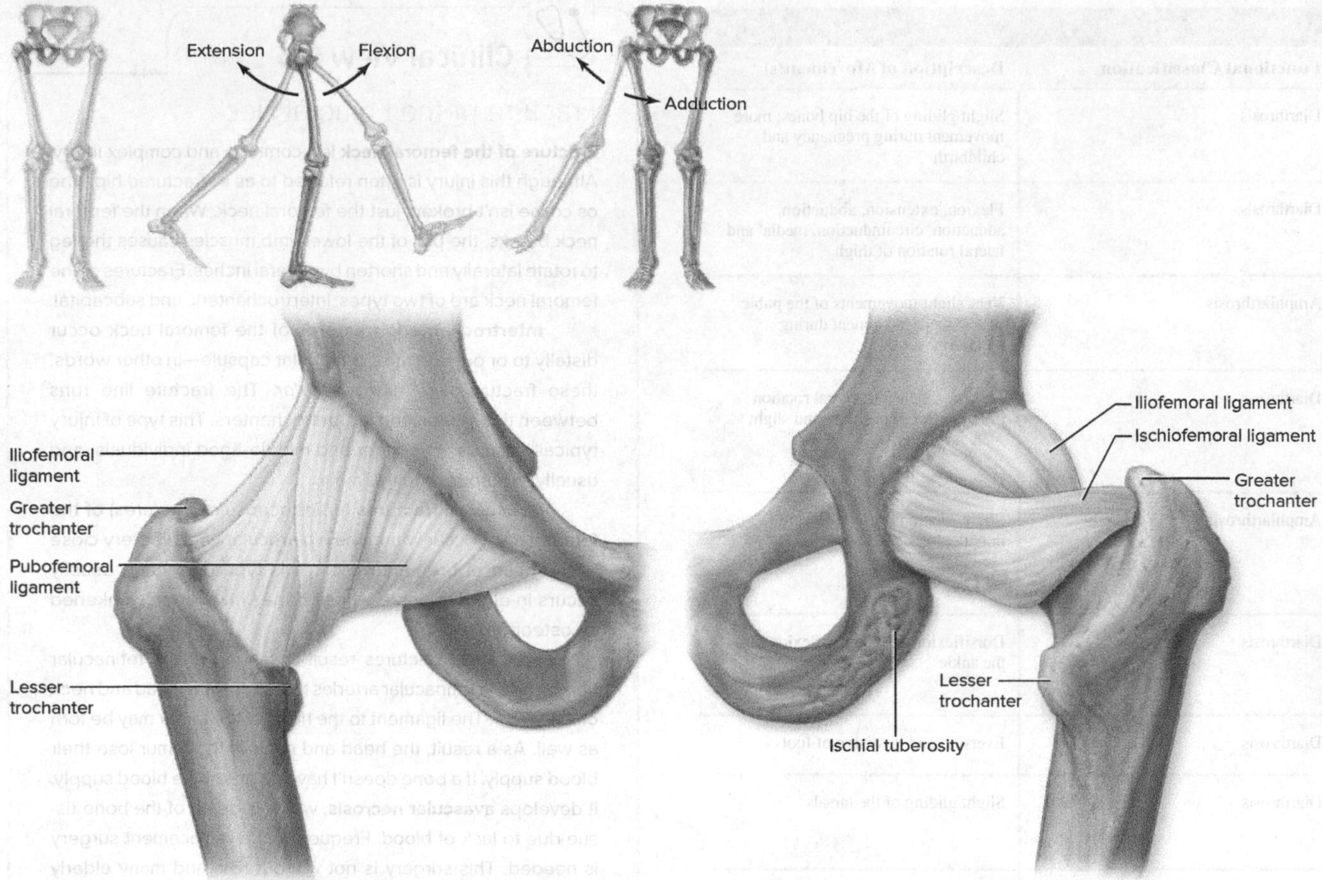
Extension
Flexion
Abduction
Adduction
Iliofemoral ligament
Greater trochanter
Pubofemoral ligament
Lesser trochanter
(a) Right hip, anterior view
Iliofemoral ligament
Ischiofemoral ligament
Greater trochanter
Lesser trochanter
Ischial tuberosity
(b) Right hip, posterior view
Acetabular labrum
Articular capsule
Acetabulum
Ligament of head of femur
Greater trochanter of femur
Retinacular fibers
Ischium
(c) Right hip, coronal section
Acetabular labrum
Ligament of head of femur
Head of femur
Articular capsule (cut)
(d) Right hip, anterior view, internal aspect of joint

Figure 9.18

Hip Joint. The hip joint is formed by the head of the femur and the acetabulum of the os coxae. The right hip joint is shown in (*a*) anterior view, (*b*) posterior view, and (*c*) coronal section. (*d*) Cadaver photo of the hip joint, with the articular capsule cut to show internal structures. APR

The knee joint has an articular capsule that encloses only the medial, lateral, and posterior regions of the knee joint. The articular capsule does not cover the anterior surface of the knee joint; rather, the quadriceps femoris muscle tendon passes over the anterior surface. The patella is embedded within this tendon, and the **patellar ligament** extends beyond the patella and continues to its attachment on the tibial tuberosity of the tibia. Thus, there is no single unified capsule in the knee, nor is there a common joint cavity. Posteriorly, the capsule is strengthened by several popliteal ligaments.

On either side of the joint are two collateral ligaments that become taut on extension and provide additional stability to the joint. The **fibular collateral ligament** (*lateral collateral ligament*) reinforces the lateral surface of the joint. This ligament runs from the femur to the fibula and prevents hyperadduction of the leg at the knee. (In other words, it prevents the leg from moving too far medially relative to the thigh.) The **tibial collateral ligament** (*medial collateral ligament*) reinforces the medial surface of the knee joint. This ligament runs from the femur to the tibia and prevents hyperabduction of the leg at the knee. (In other words, it prevents the leg from moving too far laterally relative to the thigh.) This ligament is attached to the medial meniscus of the knee joint as well, so an injury to the tibial collateral ligament usually affects the medial meniscus.

Deep to the articular capsule and within the knee joint itself are a pair of C-shaped fibrocartilage pads located on the condyles

Clinical View 9.7

Knee Ligament and Cartilage Injuries

Although the knee is capable of bearing much weight and has numerous strong supporting ligaments, it is highly vulnerable to injury, especially among athletes. Because the knee is reinforced by tendons and ligaments only, ligamentous injuries to the knee are very common.

The tibial collateral ligament is frequently injured when the leg is forcibly abducted at the knee, such as when a person's knee is hit on the lateral side. Because the tibial collateral ligament is attached to the medial meniscus, the medial meniscus may be injured as well.

Injury to the fibular collateral ligament can occur if the medial side of the knee is struck, resulting in hyperadduction of the leg at the knee. This type of injury is fairly rare, in part because the fibular collateral ligament is very strong and also because medial blows to the knee are not common.

The anterior cruciate ligament (ACL) can be injured when the leg is hyperextended—for example, if a runner's foot hits a hole. Because the ACL is rather weak compared to the other knee ligaments, it is especially prone to injury. To test for ACL injury, a physician gently tugs anteriorly on the tibia. In this so-called **anterior drawer test,** too much forward movement indicates an ACL tear.

Posterior cruciate ligament (PCL) injury can occur if the leg is hyperflexed or if the tibia is driven posteriorly on the femur. PCL injury occurs rarely, because this ligament is rather strong. To test for PCL injury, a physician gently pushes posteriorly on the tibia. In this **posterior drawer test,** too much posterior movement indicates a PCL tear.

The menisci also may be prone to injury. Tears in the meniscus may occur due to blows to the knee or due to general overuse of the joint. Because the menisci are composed of fibrocartilage, they cannot regenerate and often must be surgically treated.

The **unhappy triad** of injuries refers to a triple injury of the tibial collateral ligament, medial meniscus, and anterior cruciate ligament. This is the most common type of football injury. It occurs when a player is illegally "clipped" by a lateral blow to the knee, and the leg is forcibly abducted and laterally rotated.

The treatment of ligamentous knee injuries depends upon the severity and type of injury. Conservative treatment involves immobilizing the knee for a period of time to rest the joint. Surgical treatment can include repairing the torn ligaments or replacing the ligaments with a graft from another tendon or ligament (such as the quadriceps tendon). Many knee surgeries may be performed with arthroscopy. **Arthroscopy** is a type of conservative surgical treatment where a small incision is made in the knee and then an **arthroscope** (an instrument with a camera and light source) is inserted in the knee, allowing the surgeon to clearly see the surgical area without having to make large incisions.

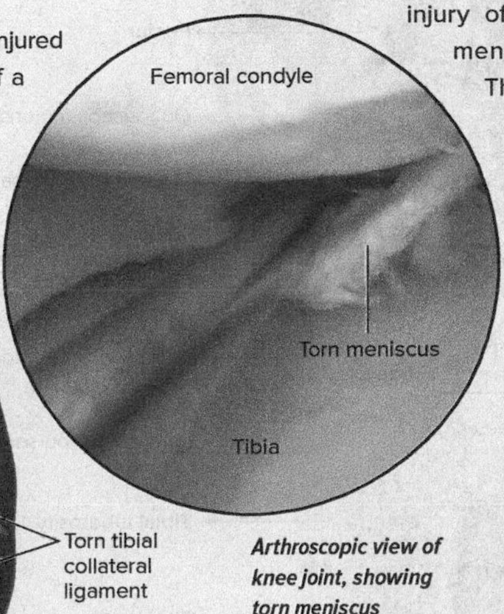
Femoral condyle
Torn meniscus
Tibia

Arthroscopic view of knee joint, showing torn meniscus
silkfactory/Getty Images

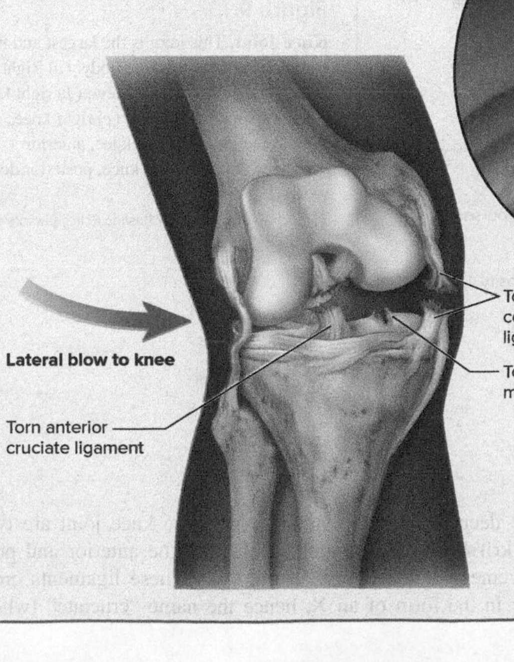
Torn tibial collateral ligament
Torn medial meniscus
Lateral blow to knee
Torn anterior cruciate ligament

"Unhappy triad" of injuries to the right knee.

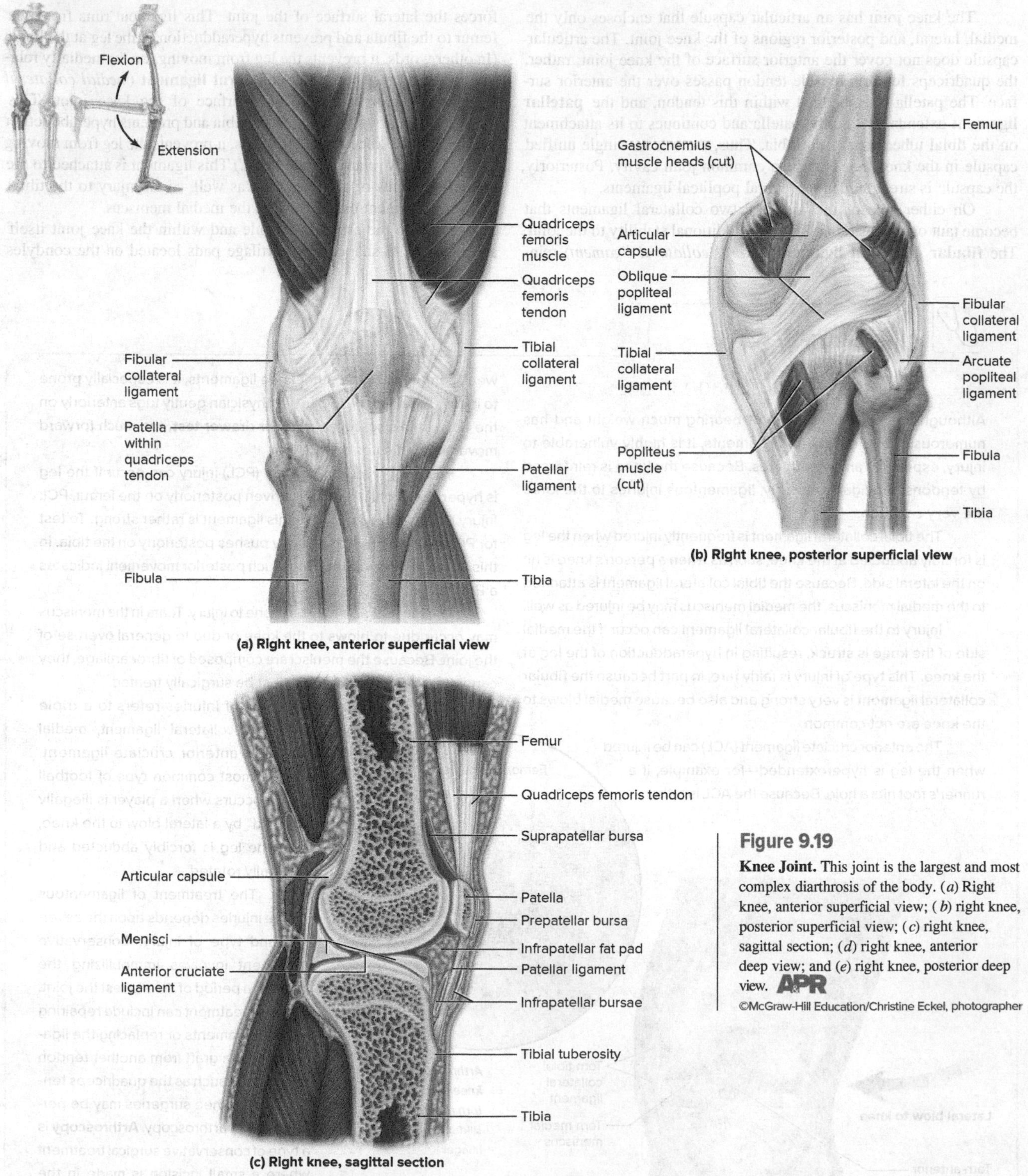
Flexion
Extension
Quadriceps femoris muscle
Quadriceps femoris tendon
Fibular collateral ligament
Tibial collateral ligament
Patella within quadriceps tendon
Patellar ligament
Fibula
Tibia
(a) Right knee, anterior superficial view
Femur
Gastrocnemius muscle heads (cut)
Articular capsule
Oblique popliteal ligament
Fibular collateral ligament
Tibial collateral ligament
Arcuate popliteal ligament
Popliteus muscle (cut)
Fibula
Tibia
(b) Right knee, posterior superficial view
Femur
Quadriceps femoris tendon
Suprapatellar bursa
Articular capsule
Patella
Prepatellar bursa
Menisci
Infrapatellar fat pad
Anterior cruciate ligament
Patellar ligament
Infrapatellar bursae
Tibial tuberosity
Tibia
(c) Right knee, sagittal section

Figure 9.19

Knee Joint. This joint is the largest and most complex diarthrosis of the body. (*a*) Right knee, anterior superficial view; (*b*) right knee, posterior superficial view; (*c*) right knee, sagittal section; (*d*) right knee, anterior deep view; and (*e*) right knee, posterior deep view. APR

of the tibia. These pads, called the **medial meniscus** and the **lateral meniscus,** partially stabilize the joint medially and laterally, act as cushions between articular surfaces, and continuously change shape to conform to the articulating surfaces as the femur moves.

Also deep to the articular capsule of the knee joint are two **cruciate** (krū′shē-āt) **ligaments,** which limit the anterior and posterior movement of the femur on the tibia. These ligaments cross each other in the form of an X, hence the name "cruciate" (which

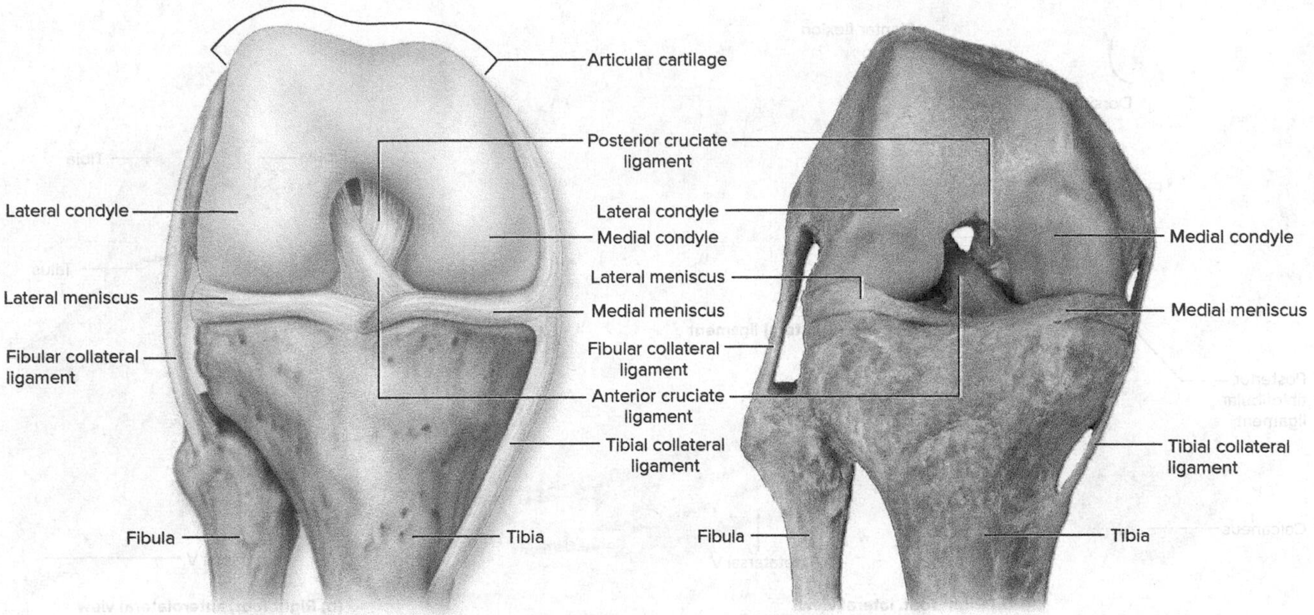
Articular cartilage
Posterior cruciate ligament
Lateral condyle
Lateral meniscus
Fibular collateral ligament
Lateral condyle
Medial condyle
Lateral meniscus
Medial meniscus
Fibular collateral ligament
Anterior cruciate ligament
Tibial collateral ligament
Medial condyle
Medial meniscus
Tibial collateral ligament
Fibula
Tibia
Fibula
Tibia

(d) Right knee, anterior deep view

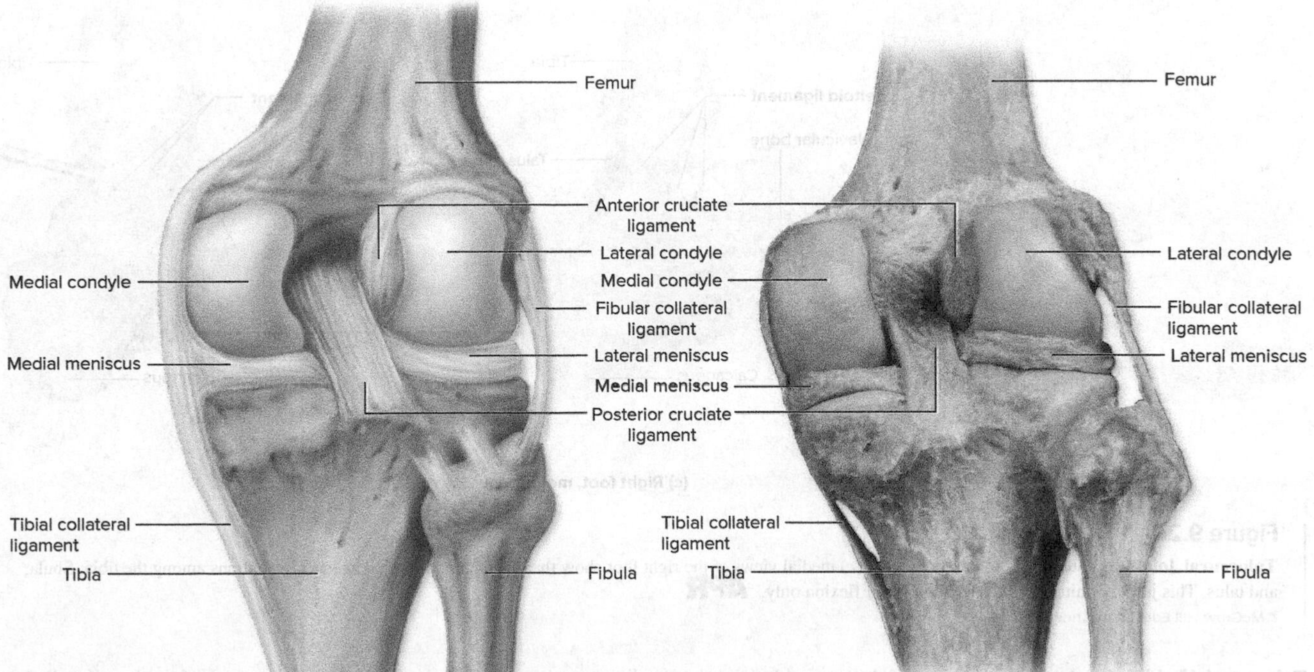
Femur
Femur
Anterior cruciate ligament
Lateral condyle
Medial condyle
Fibular collateral ligament
Lateral meniscus
Medial meniscus
Posterior cruciate ligament
Medial condyle
Medial meniscus
Lateral condyle
Fibular collateral ligament
Lateral meniscus
Tibial collateral ligament
Tibia
Fibula
Tibial collateral ligament
Tibia
Fibula

(e) Right knee, posterior deep view

means "cross"). The **anterior cruciate ligament (ACL)** runs from the posterior femur to the anterior side of the tibia. When the knee is extended, the ACL is pulled tight and prevents hyperextension of the leg at the knee joint. The ACL prevents the tibia from moving too far anteriorly on the femur. The **posterior cruciate ligament (PCL)** runs from the anteroinferior femur to the posterior side of the tibia. The PCL becomes taut on flexion, and so it prevents hyperflexion of the leg at the knee joint. The PCL also prevents posterior displacement of the tibia on the femur.

"Locking" the Knee Humans are bipedal animals, meaning that they walk on two feet. An important aspect of bipedal locomotion is the ability to "lock" the knees in the extended position and stand erect for long periods without tiring the leg muscles. At full extension, the tibia rotates laterally so as to tighten the anterior cruciate ligament and squeeze the meniscus between the tibia and femur. Muscular contraction by the popliteus muscle (see section 12.2c) unlocks the knee joint. Contraction of this muscle causes a slight rotational movement between the tibia and the femur. APR

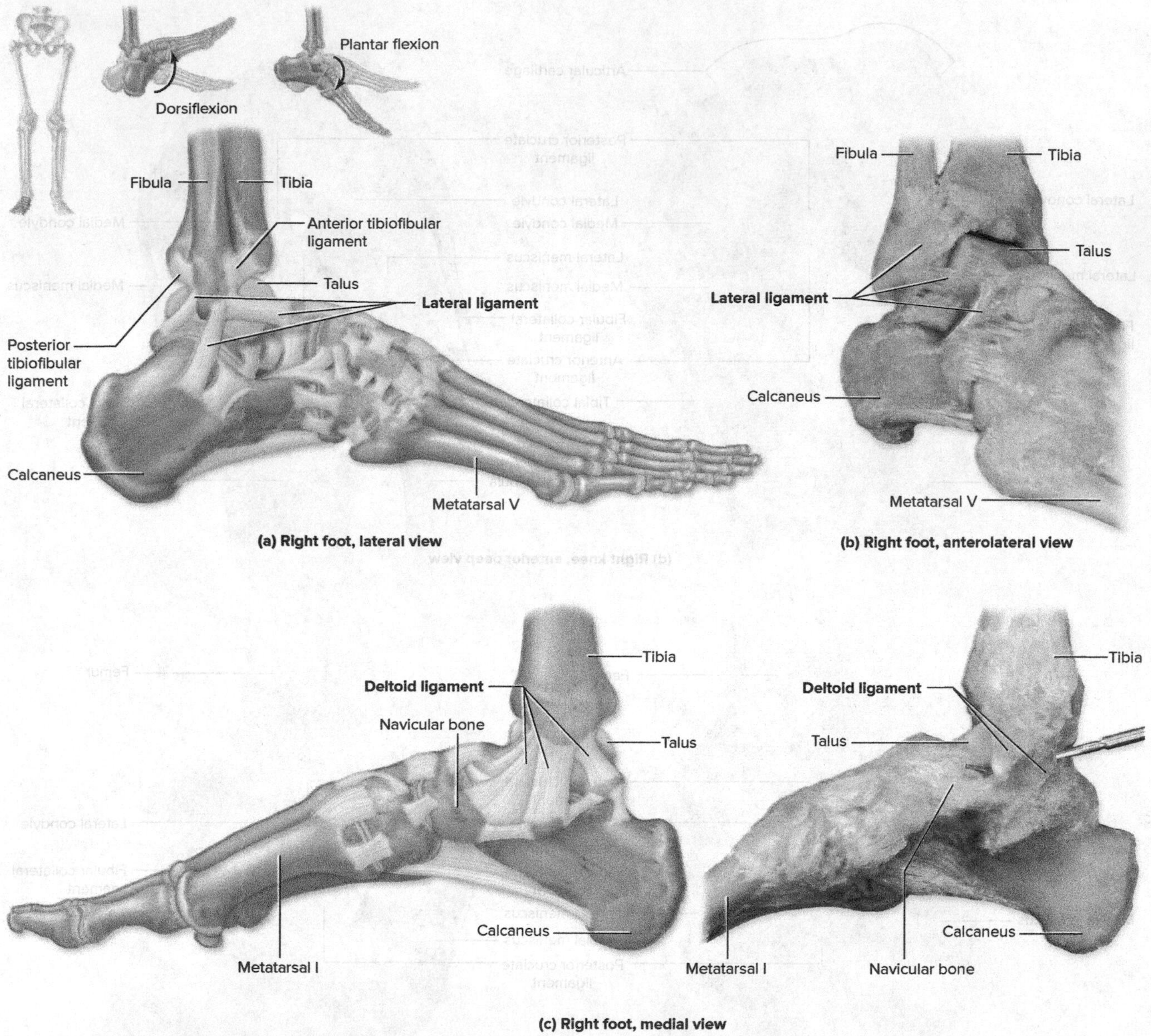

Figure 9.20

Talocrural Joint. (*a*) Lateral, (*b*) anterolateral, and (*c*) medial views of the right foot show that the talocrural joint contains articulations among the tibia, fibula, and talus. This joint permits dorsiflexion and plantar flexion only. APR

Talocrural (Ankle) Joint The **talocrural joint,** or ankle joint, is a highly modified hinge joint that permits dorsiflexion and plantar flexion of the foot at the ankle, and includes two articulations within one articular capsule. One of these articulations is between the distal end of the tibia and the talus, and the other is between the distal end of the fibula and the lateral aspect of the talus (**figure 9.20**). The medial and lateral malleoli of the tibia and fibula, respectively, form extensive medial and lateral margins and prevent the talus from sliding side-to-side.

The talocrural joint includes several distinctive anatomic features. An articular capsule covers the distal surfaces of the tibia, the medial malleolus, the lateral malleolus, and the talus. A multipart **deltoid ligament** (or *medial ligament*) binds the tibia to the foot on the medial side. This ligament prevents overeversion of the foot. The deltoid ligament is incredibly strong and rarely tears; in fact, it will pull the medial malleolus off the tibia before it ever ruptures! A much thinner, multipart **lateral ligament** binds the fibula to the foot on the lateral side. This ligament prevents overinversion of the foot. It is not as strong as the deltoid ligament, and is prone to sprains and tears (see Clinical View 9.8: "Ankle Sprains" in this section). Two **tibiofibular** (tib′ē-ō-fib′yū-lăr) **ligaments (anterior** and **posterior)** bind the tibia to the fibula. APR

Joints of the Foot

Four types of synovial joints occur in the foot: intertarsal joints, tarsometatarsal joints, metatarsophalangeal joints, and interphalangeal joints (**figure 9.21**). **Intertarsal joints** are the articulations between the tarsal bones. Some of these joints go by specific names (e.g.,

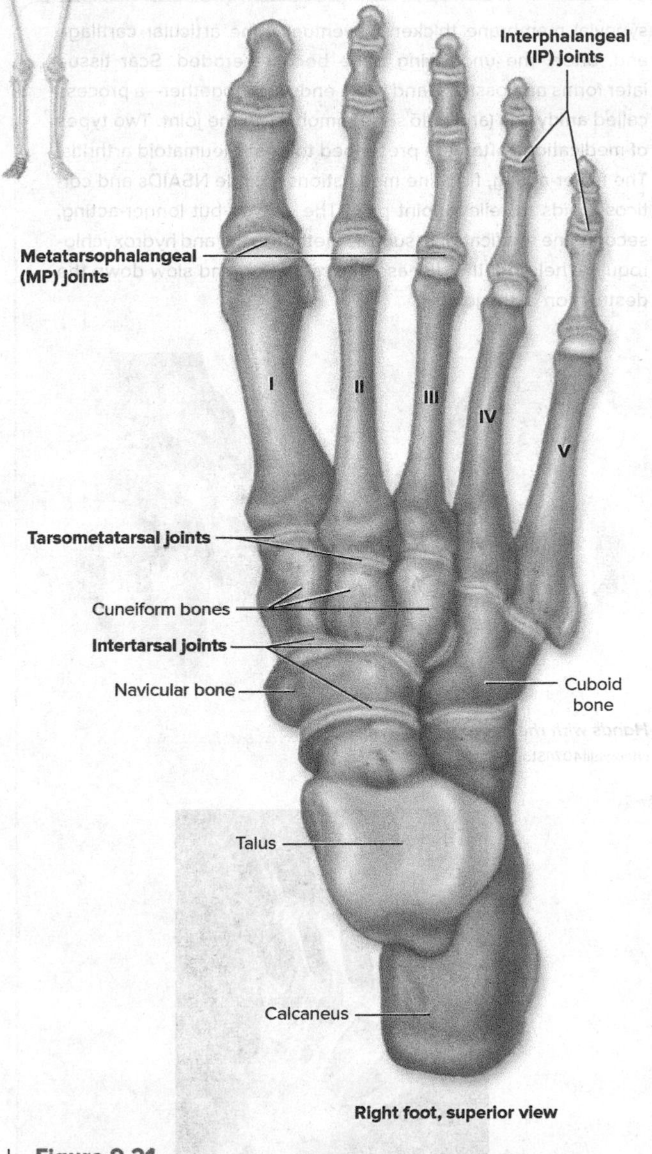

Figure 9.21

Joints of the Foot. The intertarsal, tarsometatarsal, metatarsophalangeal (MP), and interphalangeal (IP) joints help move the toes and foot. APR

talonavicular joint, calcaneocuboid joint). It is at the intertarsal joints that inversion and eversion of the foot occur (see figure 9.11). APR

The articulations between the tarsal and metatarsal bones form the **tarsometatarsal** (tar′s ō-met′ă-tar′s ăl) **joints.** These are plane articulations that permit some twisting and limited side-to-side movements of the tarsal bones. The medial, intermediate, and lateral cuneiform bones articulate with the first three metatarsals. The fourth and fifth metatarsals articulate with the cuboid.

The **metatarsophalangeal** (met′ă-tar′s ō-fă-lan′j ē-ăl) **joints,** also called the **MP joints,** are between the metatarsals and the phalanges of the toes. These are condylar joints, and they permit limited abduction and adduction of the toes, as well as flexion and extension of the toes.

Clinical View 9.8

Ankle Sprains

A **sprain** is a stretching or tearing of ligaments, without fracture or dislocation of the joint. An ankle sprain results when the foot is twisted, almost always due to **overinversion.** Fibers of the lateral ligaments are either stretched (in mild sprains) or torn (in more severe sprains), producing localized swelling and tenderness anteroinferior to the lateral malleolus. **Overeversion** sprains rarely occur due to the strength of the deltoid ligament. If overeversion *does* occur, a **Pott fracture** may result (described in Clinical View 8.4: "Pott Fracture" in section 8.4c). Remember from section 4.2d that ligaments are composed of dense regular connective tissue, which is poorly vascularized. Tissue that is poorly vascularized takes a long time to heal, and that is the case with ankle sprains. They are also prone to reinjury.

Finally, the **interphalangeal (IP) joints** occur between individual phalanges. Each interphalangeal joint is a hinge joint that permits flexion and extension only. APR

WHAT DID YOU LEARN?

12. Which ligaments support the hip joint?
13. List the intracapsular ligaments of the knee joint, and discuss their functions.
14. Compare the deltoid and lateral ligaments of the ankle joint. Which of these ligaments is stronger? What types of injuries are associated with these ligaments?

9.6 Aging of the Joints

✓ Learning Objective

12. Identify the effects of aging on the joints.

During a person's lifetime, the joints are subjected to extensive wear and tear. A joint's size, flexibility, and shape are affected and modified by use. Active joints develop larger and thicker capsules, and the supporting ligaments and bones increase in size. With age or injury, some joints may calcify or synostose. This can be seen in cartilaginous joints and along ligaments of synovial joints as bone formation along the joint margins.

Prior to the closure of the epiphyseal plates in early adulthood, some injuries to a young person may result in subluxation or fracture of an epiphysis, with potential adverse effects on the future development and health of the joint. After the epiphyseal plates close, injuries at the epiphyses typically result in sprains.

Arthritis is a disease that involves damage to articular cartilage (see Clinical View 9.9: "Arthritis" in this section). A highly prevalent problem that develops in an aging joint is osteoarthritis. The cause of the damage may vary, but it can be related to cumulative wear and tear at the joint surface.

Just as the strength of a bone is maintained by continual application of stress, the health of joints is directly related to moderate exercise. Exercise compresses the articular cartilages, causing

Clinical View 9.9

Arthritis

Arthritis (ar-thrī′tis) is a group of inflammatory or degenerative diseases of joints that occur in various forms. Each form presents the same symptoms: swelling of the joint, pain, and stiffness. Some common forms of arthritis are gouty arthritis, osteoarthritis, and rheumatoid arthritis.

Gouty arthritis is typically seen in middle-aged and older individuals, and is more common in males. Often called *gout,* this disease occurs as a result of an increased level of uric acid (a normal cellular waste product) in the blood. This abnormal level causes urate crystals to accumulate in the blood, synovial fluid, and synovial membranes. The body's inflammatory response to the urate crystals results in joint pain. Gout usually begins with an attack on a single joint (often in the great toe), and later progresses to other joints. Eventually, gouty arthritis may immobilize joints by causing fusion between the articular surfaces of the bones. Often, nonsteroidal anti-inflammatory drugs (NSAIDs) or colchicine (a medicine used to treat the symptoms of gout) are used to alleviate symptoms and reduce the inflammation. Patients are also advised to avoid dietary substances that may elevate uric acid levels (e.g., prepared meats like salamis, organ meat, shellfish, most alcohol), and they may be prescribed medications (e.g., Probenecid) to reduce uric acid levels in their blood.

Osteoarthritis (OA), also known as *degenerative arthritis,* is the most common type of arthritis. This chronic degenerative joint condition is termed *wear-and-tear arthritis* because of its prevalence in weight-bearing joints (e.g., hips, knees, spine) and its association with older adults. The entire joint is affected but the articular cartilage appears to break down first. Eventually, bone rubs against bone. Without the protective articular cartilage, movements at the joints become stiff and painful. Osteoarthritis is typically seen in older individuals, although more and more athletes are experiencing arthritis at an earlier age due to the repetitive stresses placed on their joints. NSAIDs, and sometimes corticosteroid injections into the joint, are used to alleviate the symptoms of osteoarthritis.

Rheumatoid (rū′mă-toyd) **arthritis (RA)** is typically seen in younger and middle-aged adults, and is much more prevalent in women. Rheumatoid arthritis is an *autoimmune disorder* in which the body's immune system targets its own tissues (i.e., the joint tissue) for attack.

Rheumatoid arthritis starts with synovial membrane inflammation. As a consequence, the joint swells, and the inflamed synovial membrane thickens; eventually, the articular cartilage and, often, the underlying bone become eroded. Scar tissue later forms and ossifies, and bone ends fuse together—a process called **anklyosis** (ang′ki-lō′sis)—immobilizing the joint. Two types of medications often are prescribed to treat rheumatoid arthritis. The faster-acting, first-line medications include NSAIDs and corticosteroids to relieve joint pain. The slower, but longer-acting, second-line medications, such as methotrexate and hydroxychloroquine, help put the disease into remission and slow down the destruction of the joints.

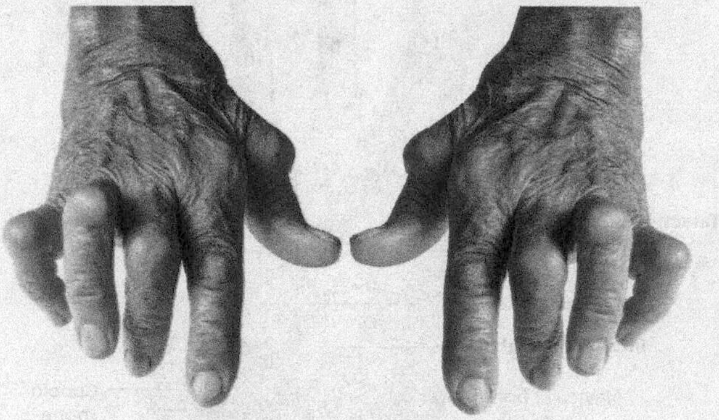

Hands with rheumatoid arthritis.
chaowalit407/iStock/Getty Images

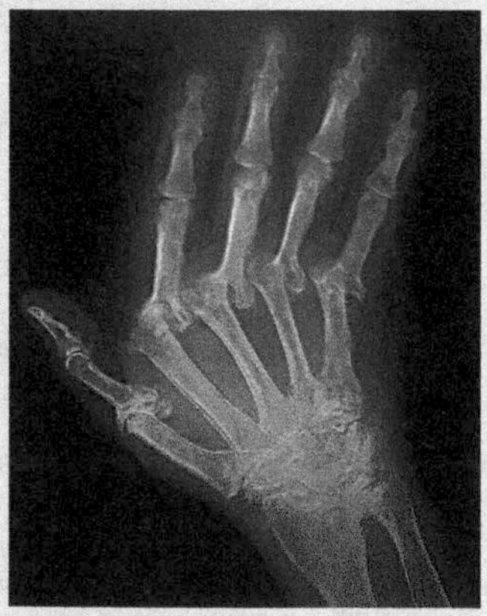

Colorized radiograph of a hand with rheumatoid arthritis.
Science Photo Library/Alamy Stock Photo

synovial fluid to be squeezed out of the cartilage and then pulled back inside the cartilage matrix. This flow of fluid gives the chondrocytes within the cartilage the nourishment required to maintain their health. Joints become stronger, and the rate of degeneration of the articular cartilage is reduced. Exercise also strengthens the muscles that support and stabilize the joint. However, extreme exercise should be avoided, because it aggravates potential joint problems and may worsen osteoarthritis. Athletes such as baseball player Nolan Ryan and Olympic cyclist Kristin Armstrong have experienced osteoarthritis at an early age due to extreme exercise. So the key is to keep your joints active and exercise, but try to avoid extreme exercise and repetitive movements.

If joint pain and arthritis become severe, and nonsurgical approaches fail to give relief, **arthroplasty** (ar′thrō-plas-tē, surgical joint replacement) may be performed. Arthroplasty is a surgical procedure that involves removing the damaged bone ends and replacing them with metal or plastic prosthetics.

WHAT DID YOU LEARN?

15 Define osteoarthritis, and discuss what contributes to it.

9.7 Development of the Joints

✓ Learning Objective

13. Describe how joints develop in the embryo and fetus.

Joints start to form by the sixth week of development and become better differentiated during the fetal period. Some of the mesenchyme around the developing bones develops into the connective tissues of the articulations. For example, in the area of future fibrous joints, the mesenchyme around the developing bones differentiates into dense regular connective tissue, and later joins the developing bones together. In cartilaginous joints, the mesenchyme differentiates either into fibrocartilage or hyaline cartilage.

The development of the synovial joints is more complex than that of fibrous and cartilaginous joints (**figure 9.22**). The mesenchyme around the articulating bones differentiates into the components of a synovial joint. The most *laterally* placed mesenchyme forms the articular capsule and supporting ligaments of the joint. Just medial to this region, the mesenchyme forms the synovial membrane, which then starts secreting synovial fluid into the joint cavity. The *centrally* located mesenchyme differentiates in one of three ways, depending upon the type of synovial joint:

- The centrally located mesenchyme is resorbed, and a **free joint cavity** forms. Examples of free joint cavities are the interphalangeal joints of the fingers and toes.
- The centrally located mesenchyme forms incomplete cartilaginous rings or blocks called **menisci,** which serve as shock absorbers in joints. The knee joint is a synovial joint that contains menisci.
- The centrally located mesenchyme condenses and forms a cartilaginous **articular disc** within the joint cavity. The articular disc assists the movement of the articulating bones. Examples of synovial joints with articular discs are the sternoclavicular joint, the acromioclavicular joint, and the radiocarpal joint.

Differentiation of the centrally located mesenchyme occurs by about the twelfth week of development, and the entire joint continues to differentiate throughout the fetal period.

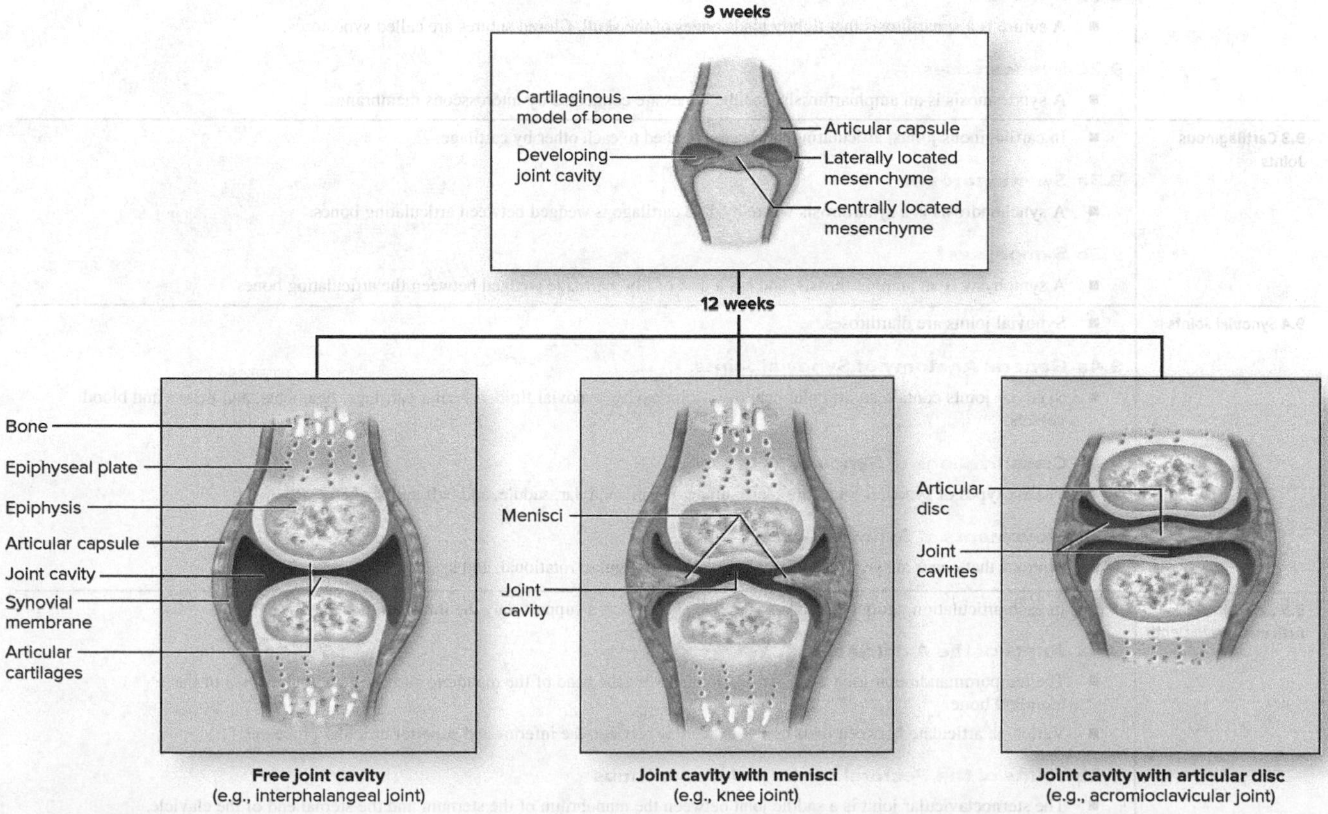

Figure 9.22

Development of the Synovial Joints. By 9 weeks of development, as the future bones are developing, a primitive model of the synovial joint cavities forms. Over the next several weeks, the synovial joints continue to differentiate. By 12 weeks, some have formed free joint cavities (e.g., the interphalangeal joints), while others have formed menisci (e.g., the knee joint). Still other joints have an articular disc (e.g., the acromioclavicular joint) that separates the articulating bones.

Clinical Terms

arthralgia (ar-thral′j ē-ă) Joint-associated pain that is not usually inflammatory.

bursitis Inflammation of a bursa.

chondromalacia (kon′dr ō-mă-lā′shē-ă) **patellae** Softening of the articular cartilage of the patella; sometimes considered a subtype of patellofemoral syndrome.

rheumatism (rū′mă-tizm) Any one of various conditions exhibiting joint pain or other symptoms of articular origin; often associated with muscular or skeletal system problems.

synovitis (sin′ ō-vī′tis) Inflammation of the synovial membrane of a joint.

Chapter Summary

9.1 Articulations (Joints)	■ Articulations occur where bones interact. Joints differ in structure, function, and the amount of movement they allow, which may be extensive, slight, or none at all. **9.1a Classification of Joints** ■ There are three structural categories of joints: fibrous, cartilaginous, and synovial. ■ The three functional categories of joints are synarthroses, which are immobile; amphiarthroses, which are slightly mobile; and diarthroses, which are freely mobile.
9.2 Fibrous Joints	■ In fibrous joints, articulating bones are interconnected by dense regular connective tissue. **9.2a Gomphoses** ■ A gomphosis is a synarthrosis between the tooth and either the mandible or the maxillae. **9.2b Sutures** ■ A suture is a synarthrosis that tightly binds bones of the skull. Closed sutures are called synostoses. **9.2c Syndesmoses** ■ A syndesmosis is an amphiarthrosis, and the bones are connected by interosseous membranes.
9.3 Cartilaginous Joints	■ In cartilaginous joints, articulating bones are attached to each other by cartilage. **9.3a Synchondroses** ■ A synchondrosis is a synarthrosis where hyaline cartilage is wedged between articulating bones. **9.3b Symphyses** ■ A symphysis is an amphiarthrosis, and has a disc of fibrocartilage wedged between the articulating bones.
9.4 Synovial Joints	■ Synovial joints are diarthroses. **9.4a General Anatomy of Synovial Joints** ■ Synovial joints contain an articular capsule, a joint cavity, synovial fluid, articular cartilage, ligaments, and nerves and blood vessels. **9.4b Classifications of Synovial Joints** ■ The six types of synovial joints are plane, hinge, pivot, condylar, saddle, and ball-and-socket. **9.4c Movements at Synovial Joints** ■ Motions that occur at synovial joints include gliding, angular, rotational, and special.
9.5 Selected Articulations in Depth	■ In each articulation, unique features of the articulating bones support only the intended movement. **9.5a Joints of the Axial Skeleton** ■ The temporomandibular joint is an articulation between the head of the mandible and the mandibular fossa of the temporal bone. ■ Vertebrae articulate between their bodies as well as between the inferior and superior articular processes. **9.5b Joints of the Pectoral Girdle and Upper Limbs** ■ The sternoclavicular joint is a saddle joint between the manubrium of the sternum and the sternal end of the clavicle. ■ The acromioclavicular joint is a plane synovial joint between the acromion and the acromial end of the clavicle. ■ The glenohumeral joint is a ball-and-socket joint between the glenoid cavity of the scapula and the head of the humerus.

	■ The elbow is a hinge joint. ■ The radiocarpal joint involves the distal radius and three proximal carpal bones.
	9.5c Joints of the Pelvic Girdle and Lower Limbs ■ The hip joint is a ball-and-socket joint between the head of the femur and the acetabulum of the os coxae. ■ The knee joint is primarily a hinge joint, but is capable of slight rotation and gliding. ■ The talocrural joint is a hinge joint that permits dorsiflexion and plantar flexion. ■ Intertarsal joints occur between the tarsal bones. ■ Tarsometatarsal joints are the articulations between the tarsal and metatarsal bones. ■ Metatarsophalangeal joints are the articulations between the metatarsals and the proximal phalanges. ■ Interphalangeal joints occur between individual phalanges.
9.6 Aging of the Joints	■ Osteoarthritis is a common joint problem that occurs with aging.
9.7 Development of the Joints	■ Joints begin to form during week 6 of development.

Challenge Yourself

Actively write or type your answers in a separate document to reinforce your learning, before checking your answers.

Multiple Choice

Select the best answer from the four choices provided.

1. Which joint in the body has the greatest range of mobility?
   a. knee
   b. hip
   c. glenohumeral
   d. elbow
2. What term describes a movement of the foot that turns the sole laterally?
   a. dorsiflexion
   b. inversion
   c. eversion
   d. plantar flexion
3. This joint has a pad of fibrocartilage between the bone ends, and is seen with intervertebral discs.
   a. gomphosis
   b. symphysis
   c. synchondrosis
   d. syndesmosis
4. Which ligament helps to maintain the alignment of the condyles between the femur and tibia and to limit the anterior movement of the tibia on the femur?
   a. tibial collateral ligament
   b. posterior cruciate ligament
   c. anterior cruciate ligament
   d. fibular collateral ligament
5. The glenohumeral joint is primarily stabilized by which structure(s)?
   a. coracohumeral ligament
   b. glenohumeral ligaments
   c. rotator cuff muscles that move the humerus
   d. scapula
6. Which statement is correct about the health of aging joints?
   a. The articular cartilage found in synovial joints repairs itself throughout our lifetime.
   b. Resting joints, and not subjecting them to exercise, is key to healthy joints.
   c. Extreme exercise in teen and young adult years can lead to osteoarthritis at earlier ages.
   d. Osteoarthritis is an autoimmune disorder of joints.
7. A metacarpophalangeal (MP) joint, which has oval articulating surfaces and permits movement in two planes, is what type of synovial joint?
   a. condylar
   b. plane
   c. hinge
   d. saddle
8. Which ligament is *not* associated with the intervertebral joints?
   a. anterior longitudinal ligament
   b. pubofemoral ligament
   c. ligamentum flavum
   d. supraspinous ligament
9. Which of the following is a function of synovial fluid?
   a. lubricates the joint
   b. provides nutrients for articular cartilage
   c. absorbs shock within the joint
   d. All of these are correct.
10. This type of fibrous joint allows for slight movement, and is located between the radius and the ulna.
    a. suture
    b. synchondrosis
    c. gomphosis
    d. syndesmosis

Content Review

1. Discuss the factors that influence both the stability and the mobility of a joint. What is the relationship between a joint's mobility and its stability?
2. Describe the structural differences between fibrous joints and cartilaginous joints.
3. Define the terms *synarthrosis, amphiarthrosis,* and *diarthrosis.* Make a table that categorizes the different types of fibrous, cartilaginous, and synovial joints, based upon these definitions.
4. Describe and explain the characteristics common to all synovial joints.
5. Compare a hinge joint and a pivot joint with respect to structure, function, and location within the body.
6. Describe and compare the movements of abduction, adduction, pronation, and supination.
7. Describe the basic anatomy of the hip joint.
8. What are the main supporting ligaments of the elbow joint?
9. How do synovial joints develop in the embryo and fetus?
10. What is the primary age-related change that can occur in a joint, and how does activity influence the health of the joint?

Developing Critical Reasoning

1. During soccer practice, Erin tripped over the outstretched leg of a teammate and fell directly onto her shoulder. She was taken to the hospital in excruciating pain. Examination revealed that the head of the humerus had moved inferiorly and anteriorly into the axilla. What happened to Erin in this injury?
2. While Lucas and Omar were watching a football game, a player was penalized for "clipping," meaning that he had hit an opposing player on the lateral knee, causing hyperabduction at the knee joint. Lucas asked Omar what the big deal was about "clipping." What joint is most at risk, and what kind of injuries can occur if a player gets "clipped"?
3. Carla, one of your classmates, says she is "double-jointed" and shows extensive extension of her thumb as proof. Based on your knowledge of articulations, is Carla correct in referring to herself as "double-jointed"? Why or why not?

Answers to "What Do You Think?"

1. A synchondrosis is designed to be a synarthrosis because as the bone ends are growing, they must not be allowed to move in relation to one another. For example, if the epiphysis and diaphysis move along the epiphyseal plate, bone growth is compromised and the bone becomes misshapen.
2. The plane joint, the least mobile of the two joints, must be more stable than the ball-and-socket joint.
3. When sitting upright in a chair, both the hip and knee joints are flexed.
4. The anterior longitudinal ligament becomes taut during extension, so it is taut when we are standing and more relaxed when we are sitting.

Muscular System

MUSCULAR SYSTEM

Muscle Tissue and Organization 10

Outline

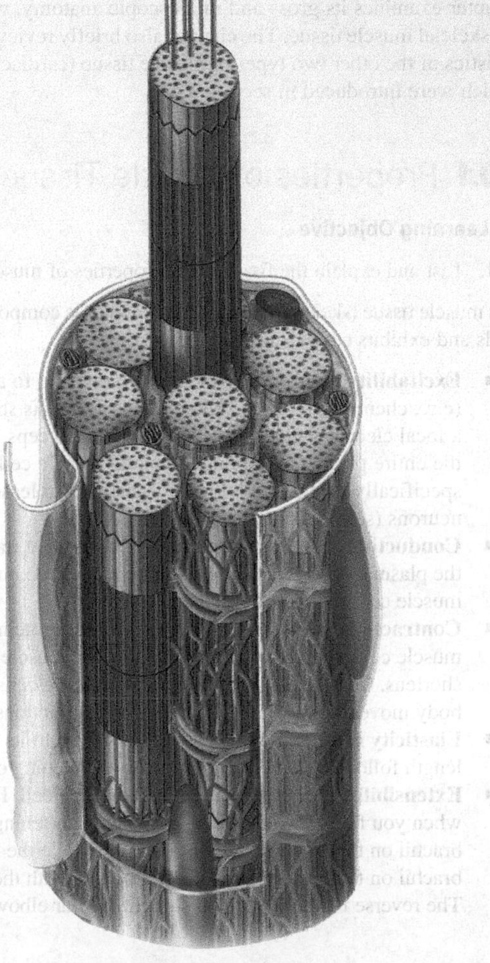

Anatomy & Physiology Revealed 4.0

MODULE 6: MUSCULAR SYSTEM

When most of us hear the word *muscle,* we think of the muscles that move the skeleton. These muscles are considered organs because they are composed not only of muscle tissue, but also of epithelial, connective, and nervous tissue. Over 700 skeletal muscles have been named and together they form the **muscular system.**

However, skeletal muscles are not the only places where muscle tissue is found. In fact, muscle tissue is distributed almost everywhere in the body and is responsible for the movement of materials within and throughout the body. Without this vital tissue, the food we eat would not be propelled along the gastrointestinal tract, the waste products we produce would not be rhythmically expelled, and our blood would not be pumped to body tissues.

To understand how muscle tissue performs these functions, this chapter examines its gross and microscopic anatomy, with emphasis on skeletal muscle tissue. The chapter also briefly reviews the characteristics of the other two types of muscle tissue (cardiac and smooth), which were introduced in section 4.4.

10.1 Properties of Muscle Tissue

✓ Learning Objective

1. List and explain the five unique properties of muscle tissue.

All muscle tissue (skeletal, cardiac, and smooth) is composed of muscle cells and exhibits certain common properties:

- **Excitability** is the ability of a cell to respond to a stimulus (e.g., chemical, stretch). When a muscle cell is stimulated, a local electrical change occurs that then sweeps across the entire plasma membrane. Skeletal muscle cells are specifically stimulated by neurotransmitter released from neurons (see section 10.3b).
- **Conductivity** involves an electrical change that travels along the plasma membrane during a muscle or nerve impulse. Both muscle cells and neurons exhibit conductivity.
- **Contractility** is exhibited when contractile proteins within muscle cells slide past one another and the muscle cell shortens. Contractility is what enables muscle cells to cause body movement and to perform the other functions of muscles.
- **Elasticity** is the ability of a muscle to return to its original length following either shortening or lengthening of the muscle.
- **Extensibility** is the lengthening of a muscle cell. For example, when you flex your elbow joint, you are shortening the biceps brachii on the anterior side of your arm, while the triceps brachii on the posterior side is lengthening with the motion. The reverse is true when you straighten your elbow joint.

WHAT DID YOU LEARN?

1. What are the properties of muscle tissue?

10.2 Characteristics of Skeletal Muscle Tissue

✓ Learning Objectives

2. Describe the many roles (functions) of skeletal muscle in the body.
3. Describe the levels of organization in a skeletal muscle.
4. Explain how muscles are attached to other body structures.
5. Outline and describe the components of muscle fibers.

Each skeletal muscle is an organ composed of the four tissue types: epithelial, connective, muscle, and nervous. A skeletal muscle is striated (marked by stripes or bands) and usually attached to one or more bones. Individual skeletal muscles vary widely in shape, ranging from elongated and flat to thick and triangular, or even circular. Because of their potentially extraordinary length, *skeletal muscle cells* are often referred to as **muscle fibers.** A single muscle may be composed of thousands of muscle fibers, and each fiber can be as long as the muscle itself. A small skeletal muscle fiber in a toe muscle may have a length of about 100 micrometers (μm) and a diameter of about 10 μm. In contrast, fibers in the muscle on the anterior side of the arm may extend up to 35 centimeters (cm) and have a diameter of about 100 μm (i.e., the same thickness as a fine strand of hair).

10.2a Functions of Skeletal Muscle Tissue

Skeletal muscles perform the following functions:

- **Body movement.** Bones of the skeleton move when muscles contract and pull on the tendons that attach the muscles to the bones. The integrated function of the muscles, bones, and joints can produce both the large movements involved in running and localized movements such as underlining a word in a book. Other types of body movements include those associated with producing facial expressions, speaking, breathing, and swallowing.
- **Maintain posture.** Contraction of specific skeletal muscles stabilizes joints and helps maintain the body's posture, such as holding the head and trunk erect. These postural muscles contract continuously when you are awake to keep you from collapsing.
- **Protect and support.** Some skeletal muscles are arranged in layers along the walls of the abdominal cavity and the floor of the pelvic cavity. These layers of muscle protect the internal organs and support their normal position within the abdominopelvic cavity.
- **Regulate elimination of materials.** Circular muscle bands, called **sphincters** (sfingk′ter; *sphincter* = a band), contract and relax to regulate passage of material. These skeletal muscle sphincters at the **orifices** (or′i-fis; *orificium* = opening) of the gastrointestinal and urinary tracts allow you to voluntarily control the expulsion of feces and urine, respectively.
- **Produce heat.** Energy is required for muscle tissue contraction, and heat is always produced by this energy use. Thus, muscles are like small furnaces that continuously generate heat and function to help maintain your normal body temperature. When you exercise, heat is produced by your working muscles and you feel warmer. When you shiver, your muscles are contracting and relaxing to produce heat.

10.2b Gross Anatomy of Skeletal Muscle

A skeletal muscle is composed of numerous skeletal muscle fibers, blood vessels and nerves, and connective tissue sheets that surround the muscle fibers and connect the muscle to bone. Although an individual muscle fiber runs the *length* of a muscle, it takes groupings of many muscle fibers to form the *width* of a muscle. If you look at a cross section (**figure 10.1**), each skeletal muscle is composed of **fascicles** (fas′i-kĕl; *fascis* = bundle), which are bundles of muscle fibers. Muscle fibers, in turn, contain cylindrical structures called myofibrils, which are composed of myofilaments. **Table 10.1** illustrates the levels of organization in a skeletal muscle.

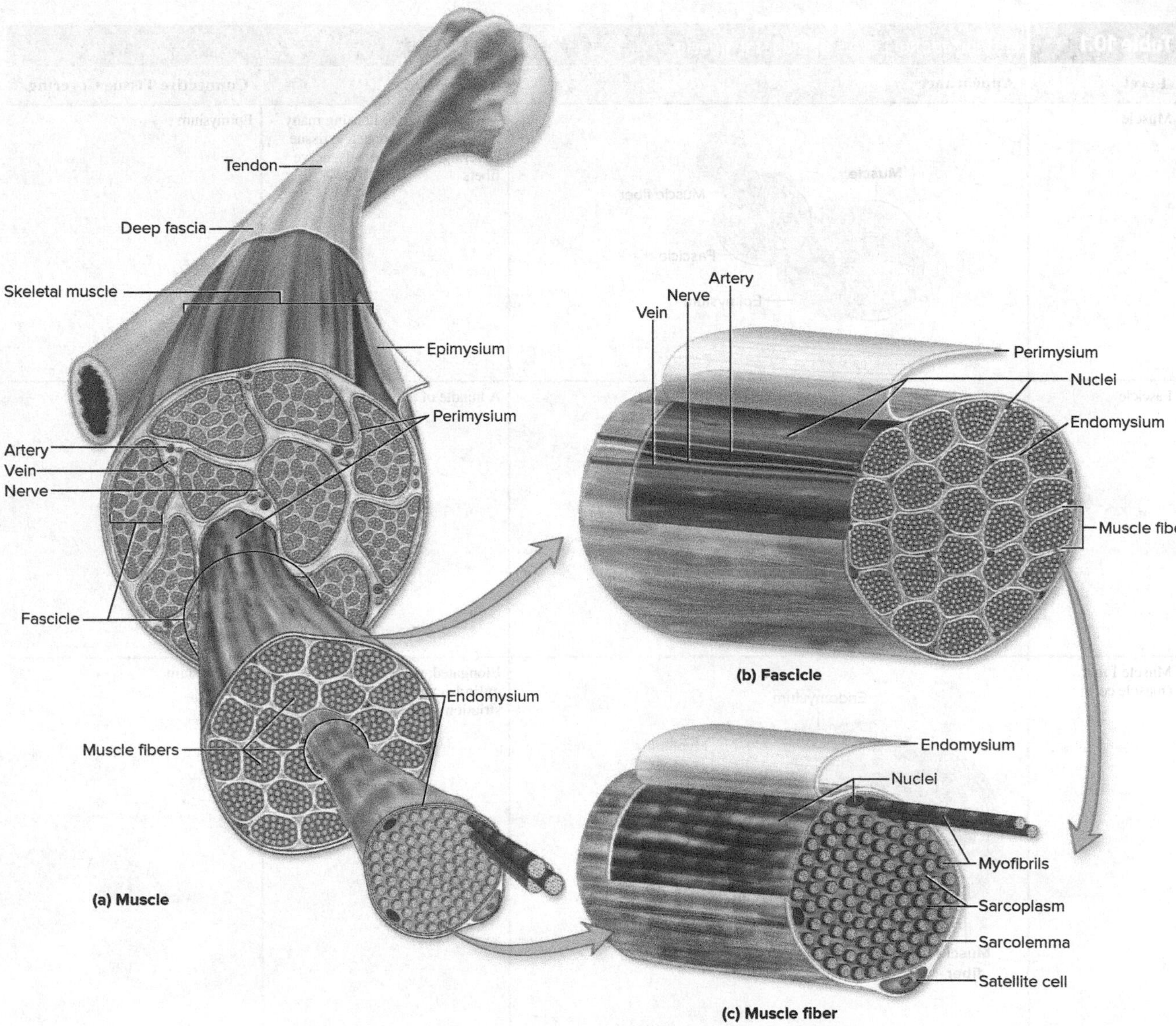
Tendon
Deep fascia
Skeletal muscle
Epimysium
Perimysium
Artery
Vein
Nerve
Fascicle
Endomysium
Muscle fibers
(a) Muscle
Artery
Nerve
Vein
Perimysium
Nuclei
Endomysium
Muscle fiber
(b) Fascicle
Endomysium
Nuclei
Myofibrils
Sarcoplasm
Sarcolemma
Satellite cell
(c) Muscle fiber

Figure 10.1

Structural Organization of Skeletal Muscle. *(a)* A skeletal muscle is ensheathed within a connective tissue layer called the epimysium. (*b)* Each fascicle (bundle of muscle fibers) is wrapped within a connective tissue layer called the perimysium. (*c)* Each muscle fiber is surrounded by a delicate connective tissue layer termed the endomysium. APR

Connective Tissue Components

Three layers of connective tissue occur within muscle: endomysium, perimysium, and epimysium. These layers, composed of collagen and elastic fibers, provide protection, sites for distribution of blood vessels and nerves, and a means of attachment to the skeleton.

The **endomysium** (en'd ō-mis' ē-ŭm, -miz'ē-ŭm; *endon* = within, *mys* = muscle) is the innermost connective tissue layer. It is a delicate, areolar connective tissue layer that surrounds and electrically insulates each muscle fiber. It contains reticular fibers to help bind together neighboring muscle fibers and support capillaries near these fibers.

The **perimysium** (per'i-mis' ē-ŭm, -miz'ē-ŭm; *peri* = around) surrounds the fascicles. The dense irregular connective tissue sheath of the perimysium contains extensive arrays of blood vessels and nerves (called *neurovascular bundles*) that branch to supply each individual fascicle.

The **epimysium** (ep'i-mis' ē-ŭm; *epi* = upon) is a layer of dense irregular connective tissue that surrounds the whole skeletal muscle.

Deep fascia (fash' ē-ă; band or filler), (also called *visceral* or *muscular fascia*), is an additional expansive sheet of dense irregular connective tissue that lies external to the epimysium, but often blends with it. It separates individual muscles, binds together muscles with similar functions, forms sheaths to help distribute nerves, blood vessels, and lymphatic vessels, and fills spaces between muscles. The deep fascia is internal to a layer called the **superficial fascia** (also called the *subcutaneous layer*). The superficial fascia is composed of areolar and adipose connective tissue that separates muscle from skin.

Table 10.1 Organizational Levels of Skeletal Muscle

Level	Appearance	Description	Connective Tissue Covering
Muscle	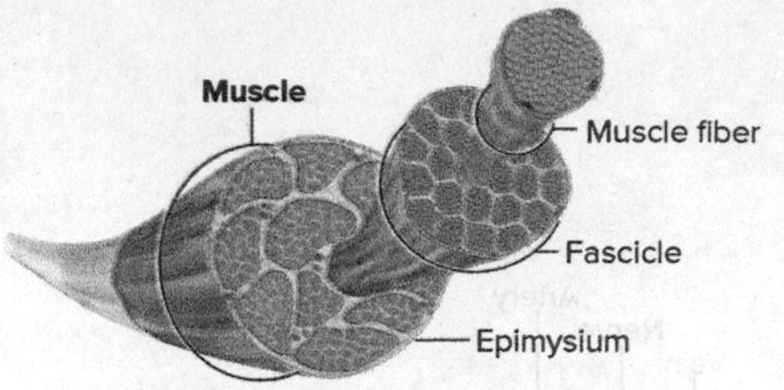	Multiple fascicles housing many muscle fibers, connective tissue coverings, blood vessels, nerve fibers	Epimysium
Fascicle	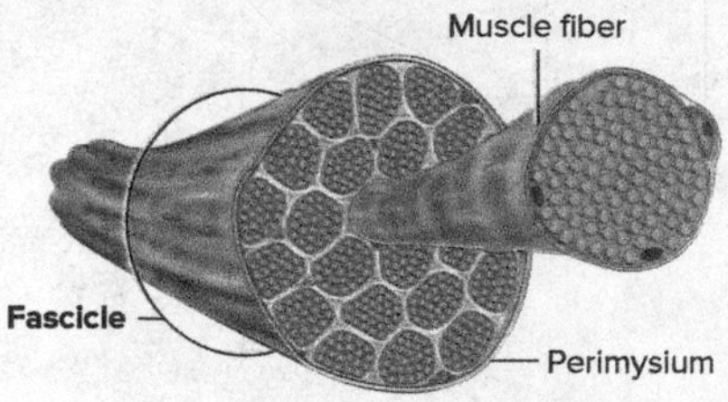	A bundle of muscle fibers	Perimysium
Muscle Fiber (muscle cell)	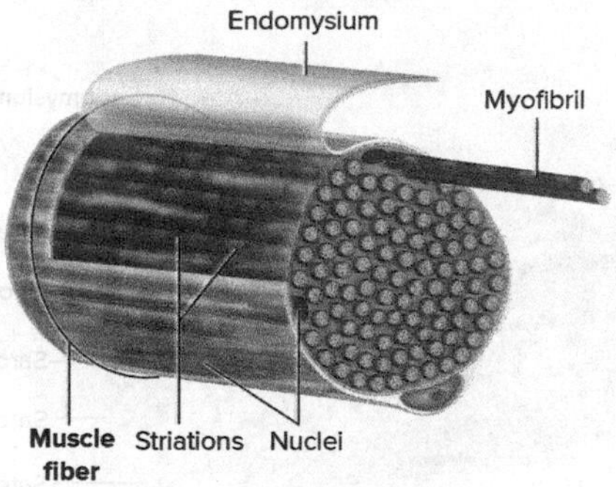	Elongated, multinucleated, cylindrical fiber (cell); exhibits striations; contains myofibrils	Endomysium
Myofibril	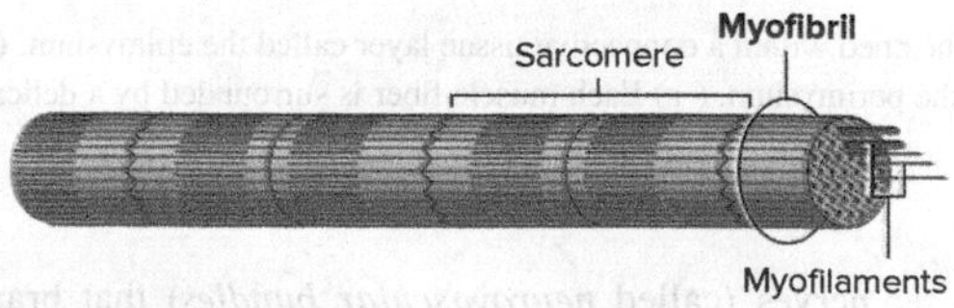	Long, cylindrical contractile element within muscle fiber; as long as the muscle fiber itself; composed of myofilaments; exhibits striations	None
Myofilaments	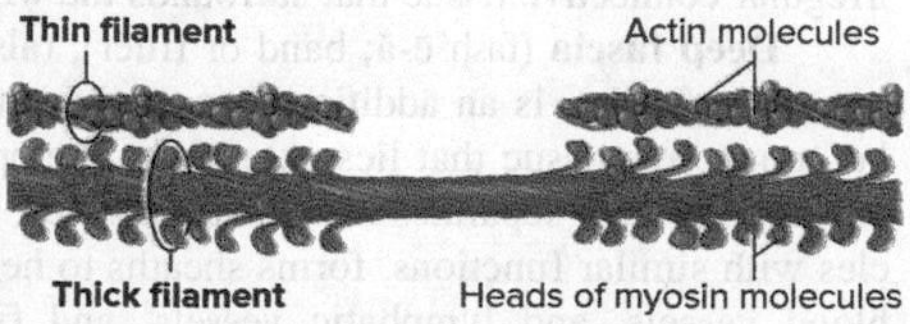	Short contractile proteins of two types: thick (composed of myosin) and thin (composed of actin, tropomyosin, and troponin)	None

Clinical View 10.1

Tendonitis

Tendonitis refers to inflammation of either a tendon or a synovial sheath surrounding the tendon. (The suffix *-itis* indicates an inflammatory process.) Tendonitis typically results from overuse or repetitive use of the tendon, as when someone spends too much time typing, and the synovial sheaths around the finger tendons inflame, resulting in swelling and pain.

Tendonitis can also be due to age-related changes or to an autoimmune condition such as rheumatoid arthritis. Although the cause of age-related tendonitis is not well understood, aging is known to cause a person's tendons to lose their elasticity and ability to glide smoothly. In rheumatoid arthritis, a person's immune system reacts against his or her own body. The same inflammatory process that damages the articular joints can injure the synovial sheaths of the tendons. Treatment of tendonitis includes rest, icing, and use of nonsteroidal anti-inflammatory agents (aspirin, ibuprofen, etc.).

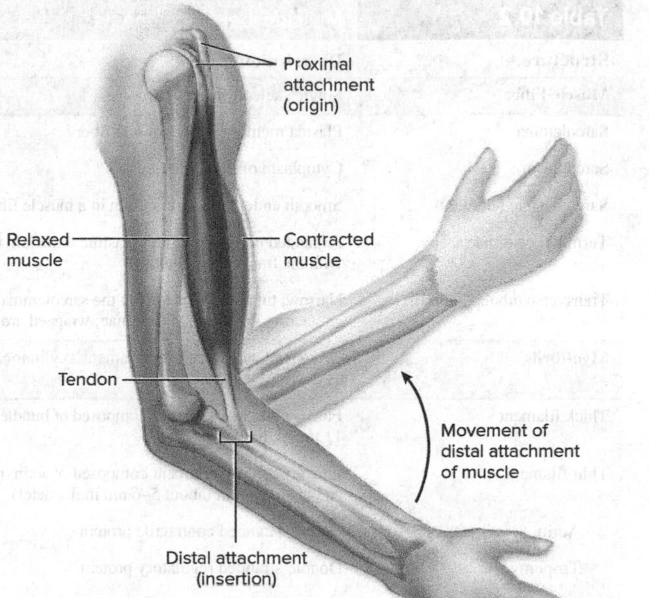

Figure 10.2
Muscle Attachments. In the appendicular skeleton, the proximal attachment is less mobile than the distal attachment, as shown in this view of the biceps brachii muscle.

Learning Strategy 10.1

The next time you go to the supermarket, examine a cut of steak, and compare it to skeletal muscle organization. An entire steak is equivalent to at least one skeletal muscle: The fat and connective tissue encircling the steak is the epimysium. Within the steak itself, a whitish, marbled texture is the perimysium, which encircles bundles of muscle fibers (fascicles). You won't be able to distinguish individual muscle fibers or the endomysium in the steak. (We hope you haven't been eating dinner as you have read this section—you may never eat steak again!)

Muscle Attachments At the ends of a muscle, the connective tissue layers merge to form a fibrous **tendon,** which attaches the muscle to bone, skin, or another muscle. Tendons usually have a thick, cordlike structure. Sometimes, the tendon forms a thin, flattened sheet, termed an **aponeurosis** (ap′ō-nū-rō′sis; *apo* = from, *neuron* = sinew).

Most skeletal muscles extend between bones and cross at least one mobile joint. Upon contraction, one of the bones moves while the other bone usually remains fixed. Often the less mobile attachment is called the *origin* and the more mobile attachment is called the *insertion*. The origin and insertion of muscles are not always easily determined by either movement or position, and some anatomists and clinicians are no longer using this terminology. Thus, we typically will use the terms **superior attachment** and **inferior attachment** when referring to the muscles moving the axial skeleton, and **proximal attachment** and **distal attachment** when referring to the muscles moving the appendicular skeleton. In muscles moving the axial skeleton, the superior attachment is often more mobile than the inferior attachment; thus, the superior portion of the body is pulled toward the inferior portion when the muscles contract as in flexing your neck or doing a crunch. In muscles moving the appendicular skeleton, the distal attachment is more mobile than the proximal attachment, and when muscles contract, the distal attachment moves toward the proximal attachment, as shown in **figure 10.2**. The biceps brachii muscle's proximal attachment is the scapula, and the distal attachment is the radius. As the biceps brachii contracts, the radius is pulled toward the scapula, causing the arm to flex at the elbow.

Blood Vessels and Nerves

An extensive network of blood vessels and nerve fibers extends through both the epimysium and the perimysium of skeletal muscle. The blood vessels deliver to the muscle fibers nutrients and oxygen needed for the production of ATP (adenosine triphosphate). They also remove waste products produced by the muscle fibers.

Skeletal muscles are classified as **voluntary muscles** because they are controlled by the somatic (voluntary) nervous system and we can consciously move our skeletal muscles. **Somatic motor neurons** extend from the brain and spinal cord to innervate skeletal muscle fibers. Each motor neuron has a long extension called an **axon** (ak′son; axis), or nerve fiber that branches extensively at its terminal end (see section 14.2a). The axon extends through all three connective tissue layers to almost make contact with an individual muscle fiber (i.e., there is a very small gap of about 30 nanometers between the motor neuron and muscle fiber). The junction between the axon and the muscle fiber is called a neuromuscular junction, and will be discussed in section 10.3b.

10.2c Microscopic Anatomy of Skeletal Muscle

Skeletal muscle fibers have many of the same components as the typical cells described in sections 2.2 through 2.5 but some of these components are named differently (**table 10.2**).

Table 10.2	Muscle Fiber Components	
Structure	**Description**	**Function**
Muscle Fiber	Single skeletal muscle cell	Metabolic activities; contraction
Sarcolemma	Plasma membrane of a muscle fiber	Surrounds muscle fiber and regulates entry and exit of materials
Sarcoplasm	Cytoplasm of a muscle fiber	Site of metabolic processes for normal muscle fiber activities
Sarcoplasmic reticulum	Smooth endoplasmic reticulum in a muscle fiber	Stores calcium ions needed for muscle contraction
Terminal cisternae	Expanded ends of the sarcoplasmic reticulum that are in contact with the transverse tubules	Site of calcium ion release to promote muscle contraction
Transverse tubule (T-tubule)	Narrow, tubular extensions of the sarcolemma into the sarcoplasm, contacting the terminal cisternae; wrapped around myofibrils	Quickly transports a muscle impulse from the sarcolemma throughout the entire muscle fiber
Myofibrils	Organized bundles of myofilaments; cylindrical structures as long as the muscle fiber itself.	Contain myofilaments that are responsible for muscle contraction
Thick filament	Fine protein myofilament composed of bundles of myosin (about 11 nm in diameter)	Binds to thin filament and causes contraction
Thin filament	Fine protein myofilament composed of actin, troponin, and tropomyosin (about 5–6 nm in diameter)	Thick filaments bind to it and cause contraction
Actin	Double-stranded contractile protein	Binding site for myosin to shorten a sarcomere
Tropomyosin	Double-stranded regulatory protein	Covers the active sites on actin, preventing myosin from binding to actin when muscle fiber is at rest
Troponin	Regulatory protein that holds tropomyosin in place and anchors to actin	When calcium ions bind to one of its subunits, troponin changes shape, causing the tropomyosin to move off the actin active site, and this permits myosin binding to actin
Connectin	Single molecular filament of a giant protein	Plays role in organization of the sarcomere and helps provide passive tension within sarcomere
Nebulin	Filament of giant protein	Possibly to regulate the length of the thin filament
Dystrophin	Protein complex	Anchors myofibrils adjacent to sarcolemma to proteins in the sarcolemma

For instance, the plasma membrane of a skeletal muscle fiber is called the **sarcolemma** (sar′k ō-lem′ă; *sarx* = flesh, *lemma* = husk), and the cytoplasm of the muscle fiber is called the **sarcoplasm** (sar′k ō-plazm) (**figure 10.3**). A typical muscle fiber contains abundant mitochondria (about 300 mitochondria per muscle fiber), because the fibers have a great demand for energy. They also contain lysosomes and other cellular organelles. Two main structures are unique to muscle fibers: T-tubules and sarcoplasmic reticulum.

Transverse (trans-vers′; *trans* = across, *versus* = to turn) **tubules,** or **T-tubules,** are deep invaginations of the sarcolemma that extend into the sarcoplasm of muscle fibers as a network of narrow membranous tubules. Muscle impulses generated when a nerve impulse reaches the sarcolemma travel rapidly along the sarcolemma and then spread internally along the membranes of the T-tubule network. The passage of this impulse helps stimulate and coordinate muscle contractions, as described in section 10.3c.

Muscle fibers contain another internal membrane complex called the **sarcoplasmic** (sar′k ō-plaz′mik) **reticulum** (re-tik′y ū-lŭm; *rete* = a net) (SR) that is similar to the smooth endoplasmic reticulum of other cells. The sarcoplasmic reticulum stores calcium ions needed to initiate muscle contraction. Some parts of the sarcoplasmic reticulum run parallel to the muscle fiber, whereas other parts appear as blind sacs perpendicular to the fiber's length. These blind sacs of the sarcoplasmic reticulum are called **terminal cisternae** (sis-ter′n ē; sing., sis-ter′nă). Pairs of terminal cisternae are immediately adjacent to each T-tubule; they are the reservoirs and specific sites for calcium ion release to initiate muscle contraction, and they interact with the T-tubules during muscle contraction. Together, the two terminal cisternae and the centrally placed T-tubule form a structure called a **triad** (figure 10.3*b*).

Recall from section 4.4a that skeletal muscle fibers are multinucleated. This increase in the number of nuclei occurs during development when groups of embryonic cells, termed **myoblasts** (mī′ō-blast; *blastos* = germ), fuse to form single muscle fibers (**figure 10.4**). During this fusion process, each myoblast nucleus contributes to the eventual total number of nuclei. Some myoblasts do not fuse with muscle fibers during development. These cells remain in adult skeletal muscle tissue as **satellite** (sat′ ĕ-līt) **cells**. If a skeletal muscle is injured, some satellite cells may be stimulated to differentiate and fuse with the damaged muscle fiber and assist, to a limited extent, in its repair and regeneration.

Myofibrils and Myofilaments

About 80% of the volume of a muscle fiber is composed of long, cylindrical structures termed **myofibrils** (mī′ ō-fī′bril) (figure 10.3*a*). A muscle fiber contains hundreds to thousands of myofibrils. Each myofibril is about 1 to 2 micrometers in diameter and extends the length of the entire muscle fiber. During contraction, the myofibrils shorten as their component proteins change position. Because myofibrils are attached to the ends of the muscle fiber, the shortening of the myofibrils during a contraction causes the fiber to shorten. Myofibrils consist of bundles of short **myofilaments** (mī′ō-fil′ă-ments; *filum* = thread). Whereas a single myofibril runs the length of the muscle fiber, it takes many

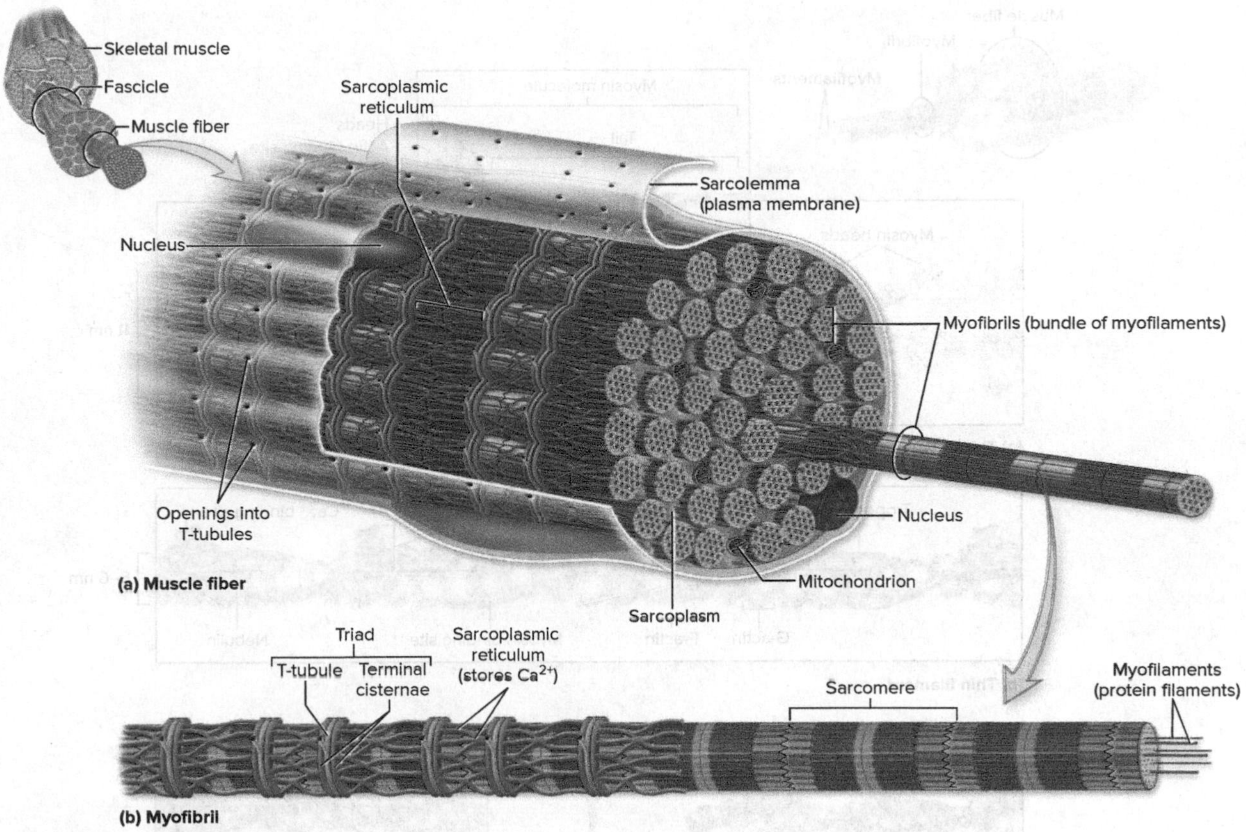

Figure 10.3

Formation, Structure, and Organization of a Muscle Fiber. *(a)* A muscle fiber is composed predominantly of myofibrils, which extend the length of the muscle fiber. *(b)* A myofibril is composed of bundles of myofilaments (protein filaments), and is enclosed within segments of the sarcoplasmic reticulum. The sarcoplasmic reticulum is a reservoir for calcium ions (Ca^{2+}).

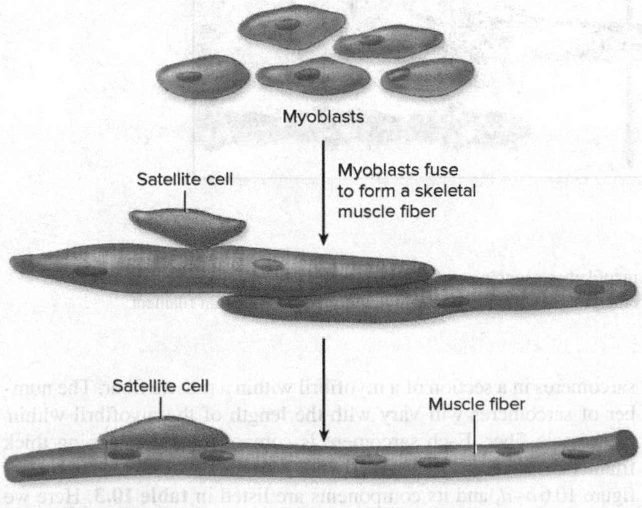

Figure 10.4

Development of Skeletal Muscle. Embryonic muscle cells called myoblasts fuse to form a single muscle fiber. Satellite cells are myoblasts that do not go on to form the skeletal muscle fiber. Instead, satellite cells remain with postnatal skeletal muscle tissue and assist in repair of muscles.

successive groupings of myofilaments to run the entire length of a myofibril.

Thick and Thin Filaments The bundles of myofilaments are classified as thick myofilaments (usually called thick filaments) and thin myofilaments (usually simply called thin filaments) (**figure 10.5**).

Thick filaments have a diameter of about 11 nanometers and are assembled from bundles of 200 to 500 **myosin** protein molecules. Each myosin molecule in a thick filament consists of two strands; each strand has a free, globular head and an attached, elongated tail. The tails of the two strands are intertwined. The myosin molecules are oriented so that their long tails extend toward the center of the thick filament and their heads extend toward the edges of the thick filament and project outward toward the surrounding thin filaments. During a contraction, myosin heads form **crossbridges** by binding thick filaments to actin in the thin filaments.

In contrast, **thin filaments** are only about 5 to 6 nanometers in diameter (about half the diameter of thick filaments). They are primarily composed of two strands of the protein **actin** twisted around each other to form a helical shape. In each helical strand of actin, many (300 to 400) small, spherical molecules are connected to form a long filament resembling a string of beads. Each spherical molecule is called *G (globular) actin,* and each filament composed of a strand of G-actin molecules is called *F (filamentous) actin.* Two regulatory

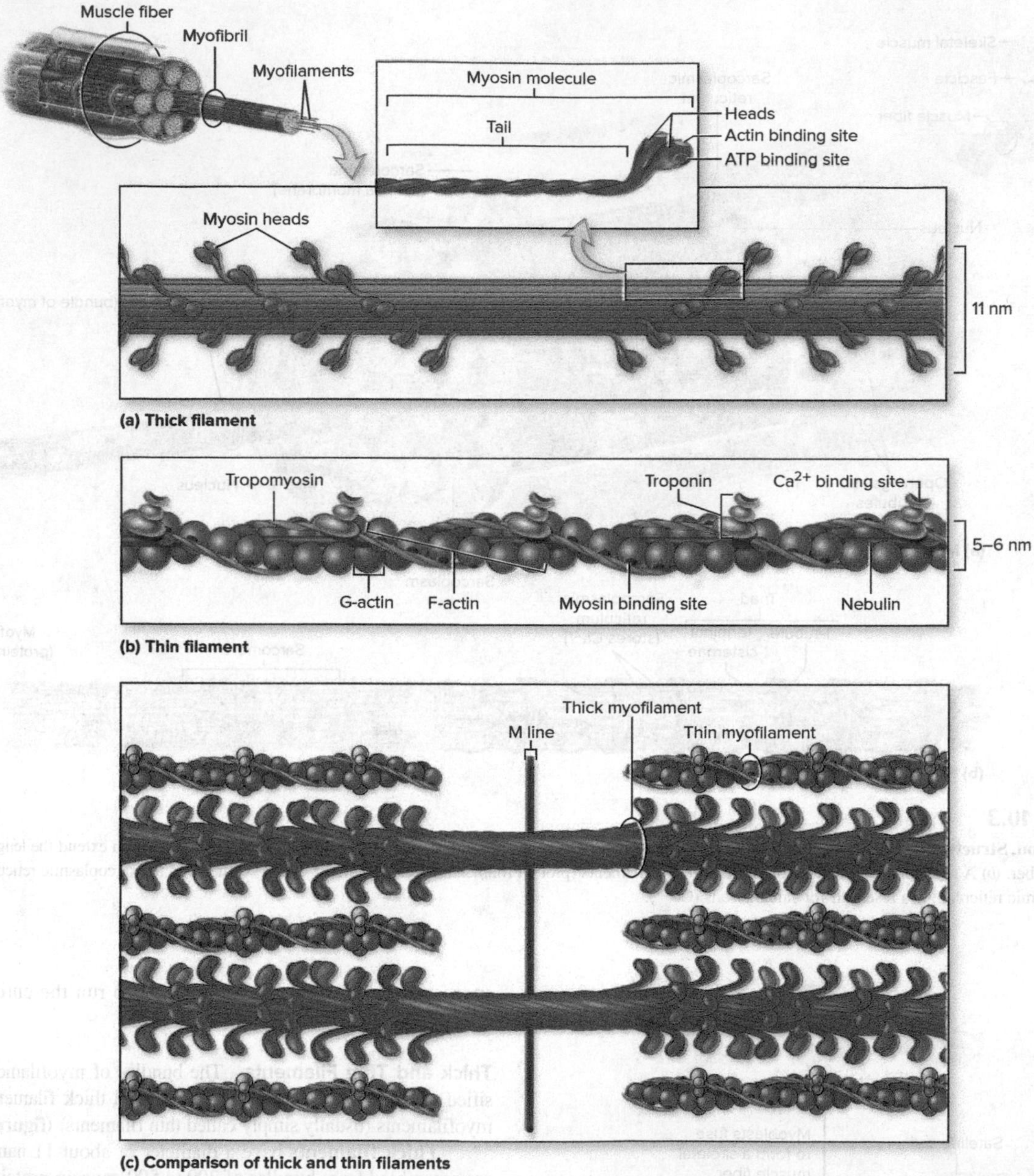

Figure 10.5

Molecular Structure of Thin and Thick Filaments. Contractile proteins form myofilaments within myofibrils. (*a*) A thick filament is composed of myosin protein molecules. (*b*) A thin filament is composed of actin, tropomyosin, and troponin proteins. Nebulin runs through the center of the thin filament. (*c*) Comparison of thick and thin filaments. APR

proteins, **tropomyosin** (trō′pō-mī′ō-sin) and **troponin** (trō′pō-nin), are part of the thin filaments. The tropomyosin molecule is a short, thin, twisted filament that covers small sections of the actin strands. The troponin attaches to actin and tropomyosin. It also provides a binding site for calcium ions.

Organization of a Sarcomere

Myofilaments within myofibrils are arranged in repeating microscopic cylindrical units (2 micrometers in length) called **sarcomeres** (sar′k ō-mēr; *meros* = part). A sarcomere is the *functional contractile unit* of a skeletal muscle fiber. **Figure 10.6*a*** shows several repeating sarcomeres in a section of a myofibril within a muscle fiber. The number of sarcomeres will vary with the length of the myofibril within the muscle fiber. Each sarcomere is composed of overlapping thick filaments and thin filaments. An individual sarcomere is shown in figure 10.6*b–d*, and its components are listed in **table 10.3**. Here we see that each sarcomere is delineated at both ends by Z discs. **Z discs** (also called *Z lines*) are composed of specialized proteins that are positioned perpendicular to the myofilaments and serve as anchors for the thin filaments. Although the Z disc appears as a flat disc when the myofibril is viewed in cross section, only the edge of the disc is visible in a side view, and it sometimes looks like a zigzagged line.

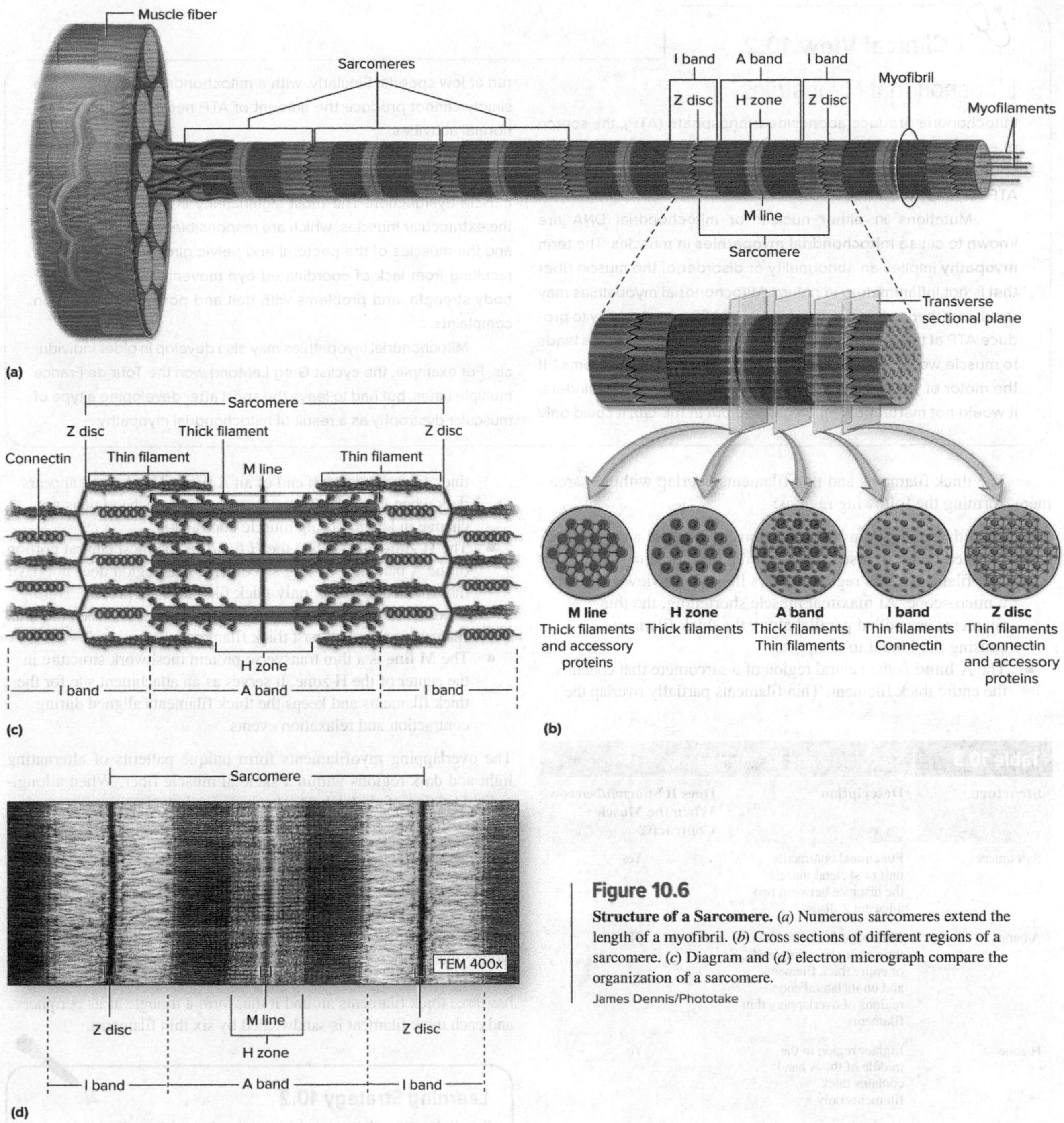
Muscle fiber
Sarcomeres
I band
A band
I band
Z disc
H zone
Z disc
Myofibril
Myofilaments
M line
Sarcomere
Transverse
sectional plane
(a)
M line
Thick filaments
and accessory
proteins
H zone
Thick filaments
A band
Thick filaments
Thin filaments
I band
Thin filaments
Connectin
Z disc
Thin filaments
Connectin
and accessory
proteins
(b)
Sarcomere
Z disc
Thick filament
Z disc
Connectin
Thin filament
M line
Thin filament
H zone
I band
A band
I band
(c)
Sarcomere
TEM 400x
Z disc
M line
Z disc
H zone
I band
A band
I band
(d)

Figure 10.6

Structure of a Sarcomere. *(a)* Numerous sarcomeres extend the length of a myofibril. *(b)* Cross sections of different regions of a sarcomere. *(c)* Diagram and *(d)* electron micrograph compare the organization of a sarcomere.

James Dennis/Phototake

Clinical View 10.2

Mitochondrial Myopathies

Mitochondria produce adenosine triphosphate (ATP), the source of energy for cell activities. Muscle fibers house numerous mitochondria because each fiber must produce abundant amounts of ATP for muscle contraction.

Mutations in either nuclear or mitochondrial DNA are known to cause **mitochondrial myopathies** in muscles. The term **myopathy** implies an abnormality or disorder of the muscle fiber that is not inflammatory in nature. Mitochondrial myopathies may result in either an inconsistent supply of ATP or an inability to produce ATP at the rate needed by the muscle fiber. Often, this leads to muscle weakness. It is as if the body has "engine problems." If the motor of your car suddenly worked on only half its cylinders, it would not matter how much gas you put in the car, it could only run at low speeds. Similarly, with a mitochondrial myopathy, cells simply cannot produce the amount of ATP necessary to carry on normal activities.

Mitochondrial myopathies typically occur in childhood or young adulthood, and are manifest by varying degrees of skeletal muscle dysfunction. The most significantly affected muscles are the extraocular muscles, which are responsible for eye movement, and the muscles of the pectoral and pelvic girdles. Double vision resulting from lack of coordinated eye movements, failing upper body strength, and problems with gait and posture are common complaints.

Mitochondrial myopathies may also develop in older individuals. For example, the cyclist Greg LeMond won the Tour de France multiple times, but had to leave the sport after developing a type of muscular dystrophy as a result of mitochondrial myopathy.

The thick filaments and thin filaments overlap within a sarcomere, forming the following regions:

- **I bands** extend from both directions of a Z disc and are bisected by the Z disc. These end regions contain only thin filaments; this region appears light when viewed with a microscope. At maximal muscle shortening, the thin filaments are pulled parallel along the thick filaments, causing the I band to disappear.
- The **A band** is the central region of a sarcomere that contains the entire thick filament. Thin filaments partially overlap the thick filament on each end of an A band. The A band appears dark when viewed with a microscope. The A band does not change in length during muscle contraction.
- The **H zone** (also called the *H band*) is the most central portion of the A band in a resting sarcomere. This region does not have thin filament overlap; only thick filaments are present. During maximal muscle shortening, this zone disappears when the thin filaments are pulled past thick filaments.
- The **M line** is a thin transverse protein meshwork structure in the center of the H zone. It serves as an attachment site for the thick filaments and keeps the thick filaments aligned during contraction and relaxation events.

Table 10.3 Sarcomere and Its Components

Structure	Description	Does It Shorten/Narrow When the Muscle Contracts?
Sarcomere	Functional contractile unit of skeletal muscle; the distance between two adjacent Z discs	Yes
A band	Dark band in the middle of the sarcomere; composed of entire thick filaments and on its lateral end regions of overlapping thin filaments	No
H zone	Lighter region in the middle of the A band; contains thick filaments only	Yes
M line	A thin transverse protein meshwork that appears as a dark protein disc in center of H zone where thick filaments attach	No
I band	Light band containing thin filaments only and connectin proteins	Yes
Z disc	Dark proteins called connectins in the center of the I band where thin filaments attach	No

The overlapping myofilaments form unique patterns of alternating light and dark regions within a skeletal muscle fiber. When a longitudinal section of skeletal muscle tissue is viewed in a microscope, it appears striated (striped) (see table 10.6). This striated appearance is due to both the size and density differences between thin filaments and thick filaments.

Figure 10.5*b* shows cross sections through various regions in a sarcomere. It presents the relative sizes, arrangements, and organization of thick and thin filaments at different locations within the sarcomere. Notice that in a cross section of an A band the arrangement of thick filaments relative to thin filaments is the following: Each thin filament has three thick filaments around it that form a triangle at its periphery, and each thick filament is sandwiched by six thin filaments.

Learning Strategy 10.2

The designations *A band* and *I band* are derived from ***A****nisotropic* and ***I****sotropic*, which refer to the appearance of these bands when viewed under polarized light (a type of light in which all wave vibrations are in one plane). **Anisotropic** (an-ī-sō-trop′ik) means the area appears dark when viewed under polarized light, whereas **isotropic** (ī-sō-trop′ik) means the area appears light when viewed under polarized light.

You can remember A bands and I bands in the following manner: The word *dark* contains the letter "A," just as the A bands are *dark* colored. In contrast, the word *light* contains the letter "I," reminding you that the I bands are *light* colored.

Other Structural and Functional Proteins There are other proteins that have structural and functional roles within muscle fibers. These include connectin, nebulin, and dystrophin.

Connectin (kon-nek′tin), also called *titin,* is a "cablelike" protein that extends from the Z discs to the M line through the core of each thick filament (see figure 10.6*b, c*). It stabilizes the position of the thick filament and maintains thick filament alignment within a sarcomere. Additionally, portions of the connectin molecules are coiled and "springlike," so that during contraction they are compressed to produce passive tension. This passive tension is released to return the sarcomere to its resting length. Thus, connectin contributes to muscle fiber elasticity.

Nebulin (neb′yū-lin) appears to be an actin-binding protein that is part of the I band of the sarcomere (figure 10.5*b*). Studies indicate that the length of nebulin is proportional to the length of the thin filament and helps determine thin filament length during sarcomere assembly.

Dystrophin (dis-trō′fin) is part of a protein complex that anchors myofibrils that are adjacent to the sarcolemma to proteins within the sarcolemma. These proteins of the sarcolemma also extend to the connective tissue of the endomysium that encloses the muscle fiber. Thus, dystrophin links internal myofilament proteins of a muscle fiber to external proteins. The genetic disorder of muscular dystrophy is caused by abnormal structure, or amounts, of dystrophin protein (see Clinical View 10.6: "Neuromuscular Diseases" in section 10.11).

WHAT DID YOU LEARN?

2. List and describe the connective tissue components of skeletal muscle.
3. Describe how muscle attachments are organized to work together for movement of an arm or movement of the head.
4. Compare and contrast myofibrils and myofilaments.
5. Draw and label the proteins seen in the thick filaments and thin filaments of a sarcomere.

10.3 Contraction of Skeletal Muscle Fibers

✓ Learning Objectives

6. Describe the structure of a neuromuscular junction.
7. Explain the process of skeletal muscle contraction.
8. Detail the structure and function of a motor unit.
9. Compare isometric and isotonic contractions.

A contracting skeletal muscle exerts tension on the attachment site of the muscle to produce movement. A muscle fiber typically shortens as all of its sarcomeres shorten in length when it contracts. The thick and thin protein filaments in sarcomeres interact to cause sacomere shortening and thus, muscle contraction. The mechanism for contraction is explained by the sliding filament theory.

10.3a The Sliding Filament Theory

According to the **sliding filament theory,** when a muscle contracts, thick and thin filaments slide past each other, and the sarcomere shortens (**figure 10.7**). The following changes occur within a sarcomere during a contraction:

- The width of the A band remains constant.
- The H zone disappears.
- The I bands narrow or shorten in length.
- The Z discs in one sarcomere move closer together.
- The sarcomere narrows or shortens in length.

Thick and thin filaments maintain their same length, whether the muscle is relaxed or contracted. However, during muscle fiber contraction, the relative position between the thick and thin filaments within the sarcomeres changes markedly. Thick filaments in neighboring sarcomeres move closer together, as do the thin filaments on either end of one sarcomere.

Learning Strategy 10.3

To help remember what shortens (and what stays the same length) during muscle contraction, try this experiment: Interlace your second through fifth fingers together—they represent the thick and thin filaments. Your thumbs (pointing upward) represent the Z discs. The distance between your thumbs is the sarcomere. Now slide your fingers toward each other. The distance between your thumbs (the sarcomere) shortens. Your thumbs (the Z discs) and your fingers (the thick and thin filaments) remain the same length. This illustrates that the filaments do not change *length*—only the *distance* between the Z discs is affected.

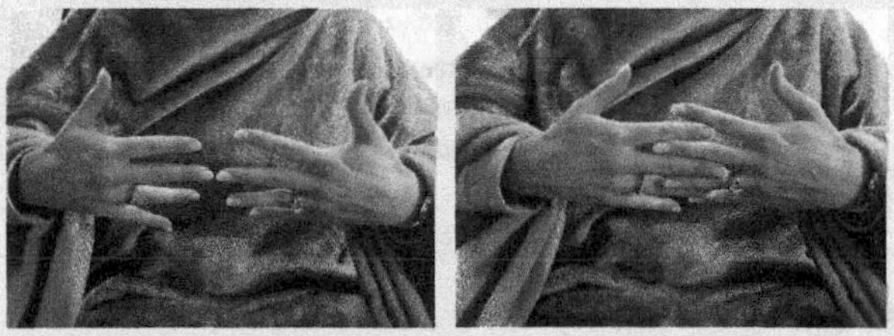

The photo on the left shows the thick and thin filaments (fingers) and the Z discs (thumbs) before contraction. The photo on the right shows the thick and thin filaments the same length but overlapping and the Z discs closer together.

©Elizabeth Pennefather-O'Brien

10.3b Neuromuscular Junctions

Recall from section 10.2b that motor neuron activity stimulates skeletal muscle contraction. Muscle contraction begins when a nerve impulse stimulates an impulse in a muscle fiber. Each muscle fiber is controlled by one motor neuron. The motor neuron transmits the effect of a nerve impulse to the muscle fiber at a **neuromuscular** (nū′rō-mŭs′kyū-lăr) **junction,** the point where a motor neuron meets a muscle fiber (**figure 10.8**). A neuromuscular junction has the following components:

- The **synaptic** (si-nap′tik; syn = with or together, *hapto* = to clasp) **knob** of the neuron is an expanded tip of an axon. When it nears the sarcolemma of a muscle fiber, it expands further to cover a relatively large surface area of the sarcolemma. A nerve impulse travels through the axon to the synaptic knob.
- The synaptic knob cytoplasm houses numerous **synaptic vesicles** (small membrane sacs) filled with molecules of the neurotransmitter **acetylcholine** (a-sē′til-kō′lēn) **(ACh).**
- The **synaptic cleft** is a narrow space separating the synaptic knob and the motor end plate.
- The **motor end plate** is a specialized region of the sarcolemma. It has folds and indentations to increase the membrane surface area covered by the synaptic knob.

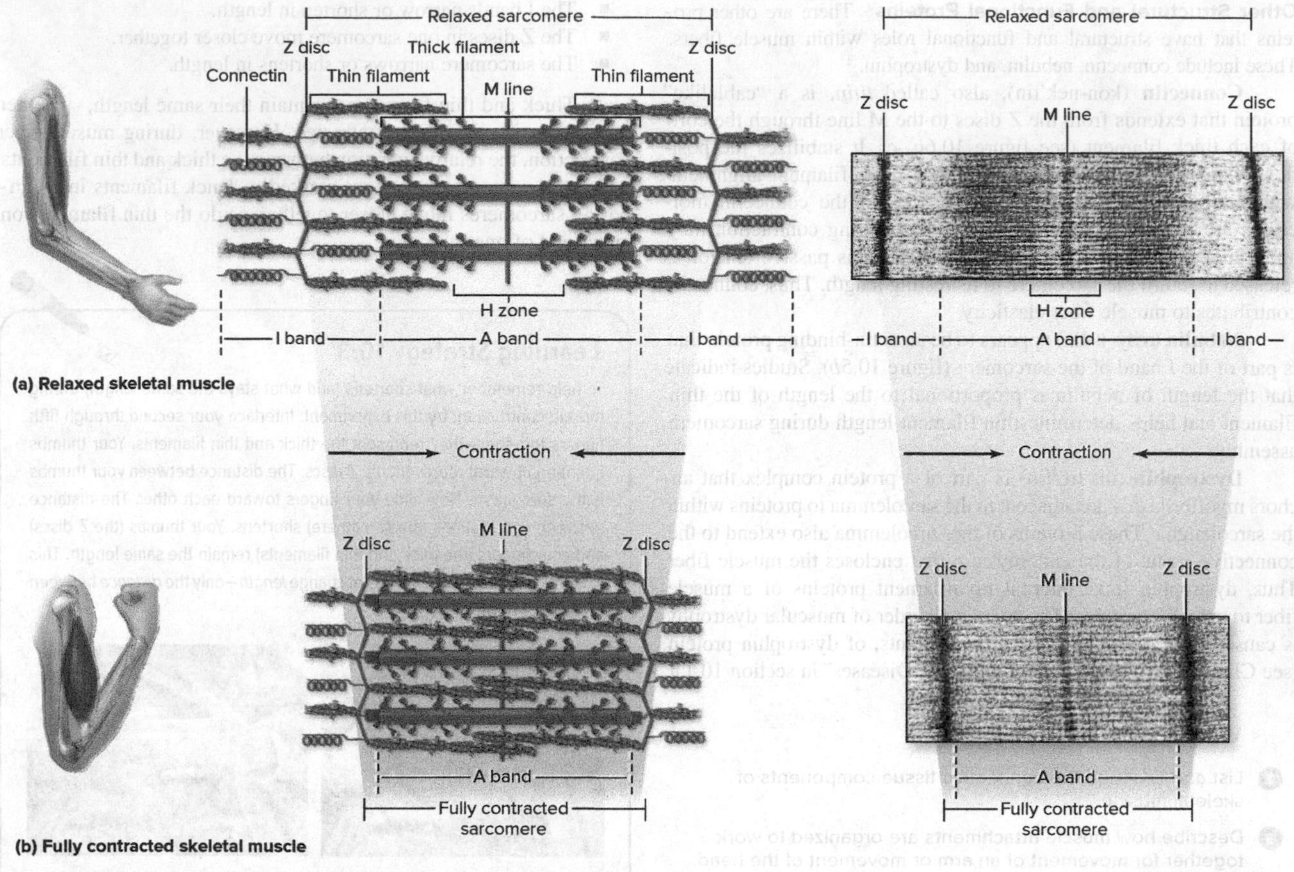

Relaxed sarcomere
Z disc
Thick filament
Z disc
Connectin
Thin filament
M line
Thin filament
H zone
I band
A band
I band
(a) Relaxed skeletal muscle
Relaxed sarcomere
Z disc
M line
Z disc
H zone
I band
A band
I band
Contraction
M line
Z disc
Z disc
A band
Fully contracted sarcomere
(b) Fully contracted skeletal muscle
Contraction
Z disc
M line
Z disc
A band
Fully contracted sarcomere

Figure 10.7

Sarcomere shortening. Illustrations and corresponding electron micrographs demonstrate sarcomere shortening during skeletal muscle contraction. (*a*) In a relaxed skeletal muscle, the A band, I band, and H zone are all visible. (*b*) In a fully contracted muscle, the sarcomere shortens, the Z discs move closer together, the I band narrows and may disappear, and the H zone disappears.

Dr. H.E. Huxley

- **ACh receptors** in the motor end plate act like doors that normally are closed. ACh is the only "key" to open these receptor doors.
- The enzyme **acetylcholinesterase** (a-sē′til-k ō′lin-es′ter- ās) **(AChE)**, which resides in the synaptic cleft, rapidly breaks down molecules of ACh that are released into the synaptic cleft. Thus, AChE is needed so that ACh will not continuously stimulate the muscle.

10.3c Physiology of Muscle Contraction

The arrival of a nerve impulse at the synaptic knob causes synaptic vesicles to release acetylcholine into the synaptic cleft **(figure 10.9)**. ACh attaches to receptors in the motor end plate. The binding of ACh causes the receptor to open, allowing sodium (Na^+) ions to enter the muscle fiber, initiating an **impulse** (a rapid, large voltage change) across the sarcolemma of the muscle fiber. This muscle impulse travels along the sarcolemma and into the muscle fiber via the T-tubules. The muscle impulse continues to spread throughout the muscle fiber as long as ACh keeps the receptors open. Usually ACh is quickly broken down and removed from the receptor by AChE.

Interaction Between the T-tubules and Terminal Cisternae

Recall from section 10.2c that T-tubules distribute the muscle impulse throughout the inside of the muscle fiber, and they are sandwiched by terminal cisternae, which are reservoirs storing the calcium ions required for muscle contraction. Spread of a muscle impulse along the T-tubule membrane causes calcium ions to leak out of the terminal cisternae into the sarcoplasm of the muscle fiber. These calcium ions diffuse throughout the sarcoplasm and attach to the troponin of the thin filaments.

Interactions Between Thick and Thin Filaments

Contraction of a muscle fiber requires that the myosin heads in the thick filament bind to active sites on G-actin molecules of the thin filaments (see figure 10.5). When the muscle fiber is in a relaxed state, the tropomyosin molecules cover these active sites, preventing interaction between thick filaments and thin filaments. However, when a calcium ion binds to troponin, the entire troponin molecule changes shape. As the troponin changes shape, it simultaneously moves the attached tropomyosin molecule, exposing the active sites on the G-actin molecules. Myosin is now able to bind to actin and form crossbridges.

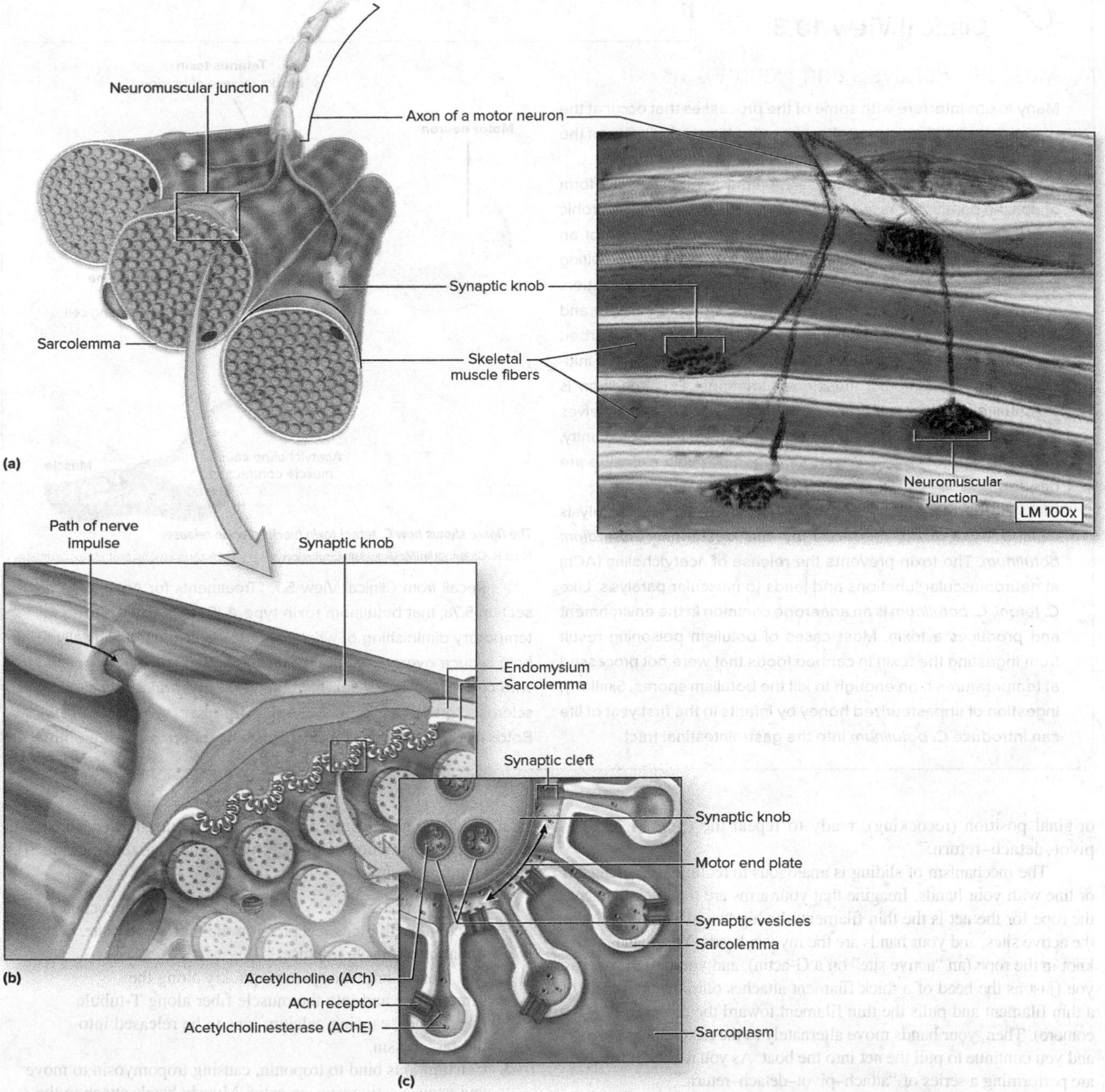
Neuromuscular junction
Axon of a motor neuron
Synaptic knob
Sarcolemma
Skeletal muscle fibers
(a)
Neuromuscular junction
LM 100x
Path of nerve impulse
Synaptic knob
Endomysium
Sarcolemma
Synaptic cleft
Synaptic knob
Motor end plate
Synaptic vesicles
Sarcolemma
(b)
Acetylcholine (ACh)
ACh receptor
Acetylcholinesterase (AChE)
Sarcoplasm
(c)

Figure 10.8

Neuromuscular Junction. (*a*) Diagram and light micrograph show the synaptic knob of an axon meeting a muscle fiber to form a neuromuscular junction. A (*b*) drawing and (*c*) micrograph show progressively enlarged views illustrate the components of a neuromuscular junction. APR

Dr. Thomas Caceci, Virginia-Maryland Regional College of Veterinary Medicine

When the stimulation from the nerve impulse ceases, calcium ions are pumped back into the sarcoplasmic reticulum and are no longer attached to troponin. Troponin returns to its original shape, which causes tropomyosin to once again block active sites on actin. Crossbridges can no longer form.

The Mechanism of Sliding As crossbridges form, the myosin heads pivot toward the center of the sarcomere. This action pulls the thin filaments toward the sarcomere center, causing the Z discs to move closer together as the sarcomere shortens. When the myosin head finishes pivoting, the crossbridge detaches and returns to its

Clinical View 10.3

Muscular Paralysis and Neurotoxins

Many toxins interfere with some of the processes that occur at the neuromuscular junction, resulting in muscular paralysis. Two of the conditions that can result are tetanus and botulism.

Tetanus (tet'ă-nŭs; *tetanos* = compulsive tension) is a form of spastic paralysis caused by a toxin produced by the anaerobic bacterium *Clostridium tetani*. The toxin blocks the release of an inhibitory neurotransmitter called glycine in the spinal cord, resulting in overstimulation of the muscles and excessive muscle contraction.

C. tetani is very common in soils and vegetable matter and can be infective if introduced into a wound. The toxin is absorbed into the blood and circulates to the nervous system where it initiates tetanic (spasmodic) muscle contractions. This condition is potentially life-threatening, and so we routinely immunize ourselves against it. These immunizations do not confer lifelong immunity, and booster shots every 10 years or upon possible exposure are needed.

Botulism (bot'yū-lizm) is a potentially fatal muscular paralysis caused by a toxin produced by the bacterium *Clostridium botulinum*. The toxin prevents the release of acetylcholine (ACh) at neuromuscular junctions and leads to muscular paralysis. Like *C. tetani*, *C. botulinum* is an anaerobe common in the environment and produces a toxin. Most cases of botulism poisoning result from ingesting the toxin in canned foods that were not processed at temperatures high enough to kill the botulism spores. Similarly, ingestion of unpasteurized honey by infants in the first year of life can introduce *C. botulinum* into the gastrointestinal tract.

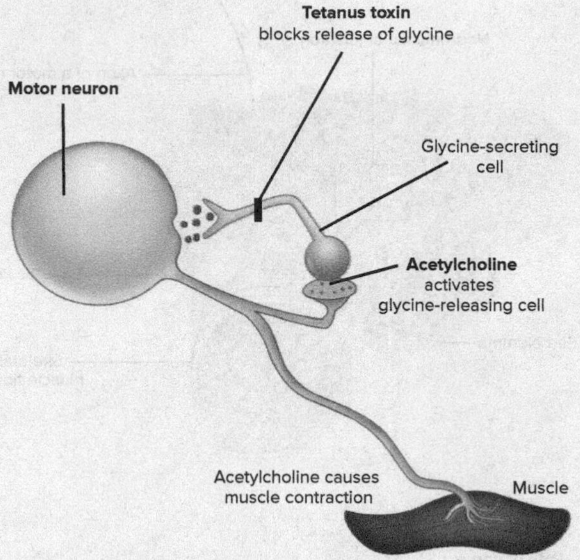

The figure shows how* C. tetani *toxin blocks glycine release.
Neal R. Chamberlin/McGraw-Hill Education

Recall from Clinical View 5.7: "Treatments for Aging Skin" in section 5.7a, that botulinum toxin type A (Botox) may be used for temporary diminishing of wrinkles. Botox is also used clinically to help reduce overcontraction of muscle (or spasticity) associated with certain disorders or conditions (e.g., cerebral palsy, multiple sclerosis, torticollis, changes following a stroke or spinal cord injury). Botox injections reduce muscle spasticity for up to 3 to 6 months.

original position (recocking), ready to repeat the cycle of "attach–pivot–detach–return."

The mechanism of sliding is analogous to reeling in a fishing net or line with your hands. Imagine that your arms are the thick filament, the rope for the net is the thin filament, the big "knots" in the rope are the active sites, and your hands are the myosin heads. Your hands grab a knot in the rope (an "active site" on a G-actin), and you pull the net past you (just as the head of a thick filament attaches onto the active site of a thin filament and pulls the thin filament toward the center of the sarcomere). Then, your hands move alternately to the next knot in the rope, and you continue to pull the net into the boat. As you reel in the net, you are performing a series of "attach–pivot–detach–return."

Energy to drive this myosin movement is provided in the form of ATP. Myosin head attachment and pivoting do not require energy, but ATP is needed for the myosin head crossbridge to detach from actin. Energy is released to power the detachment and recocking of the myosin head when ATP binds to the myosin head and is broken down into ADP (adenosine diphosphate) and P_i (phosphate). The return of the fiber to its resting length is completely passive and results from the pull of antagonistic muscles and from elastic forces in the contracting muscle fibers. APR

10.3d Muscle Contraction: A Summary

The events of muscle contraction have been called **excitation-contraction coupling,** meaning that the stimulation of a muscle fiber by a nerve impulse results in a series of events that culminates in muscle fiber contraction. These events are summarized in figure 10.9 and in the following list:

1. A nerve impulse causes ACh release at a neuromuscular junction. ACh binds receptors on the motor end plate, initiating a muscle impulse.
2. The muscle impulse spreads quickly along the sarcolemma and into the muscle fiber along T-tubule membranes, causing calcium ions to be released into the sarcoplasm.
3. Calcium ions bind to troponin, causing tropomyosin to move and expose active sites on actin. Myosin heads attach to the actin and form crossbridges.
4. Myosin heads go through cyclic "attach–pivot–detach–return" events as the thin filaments are pulled past the thick filaments. ATP is required to detach the myosin heads and complete the sequence of cyclic events. The sarcomere shortens, and the muscle contracts. The cyclic events continue as long as calcium ions remain bound to the troponin.
5. Calcium ions are moved back into the sarcoplasmic reticulum by ATP-driven ion pumps to reduce calcium concentration in the sarcoplasm, leading to relaxation. Termination of the muscle impulse results in the passive sliding of myofilaments back to their original state.

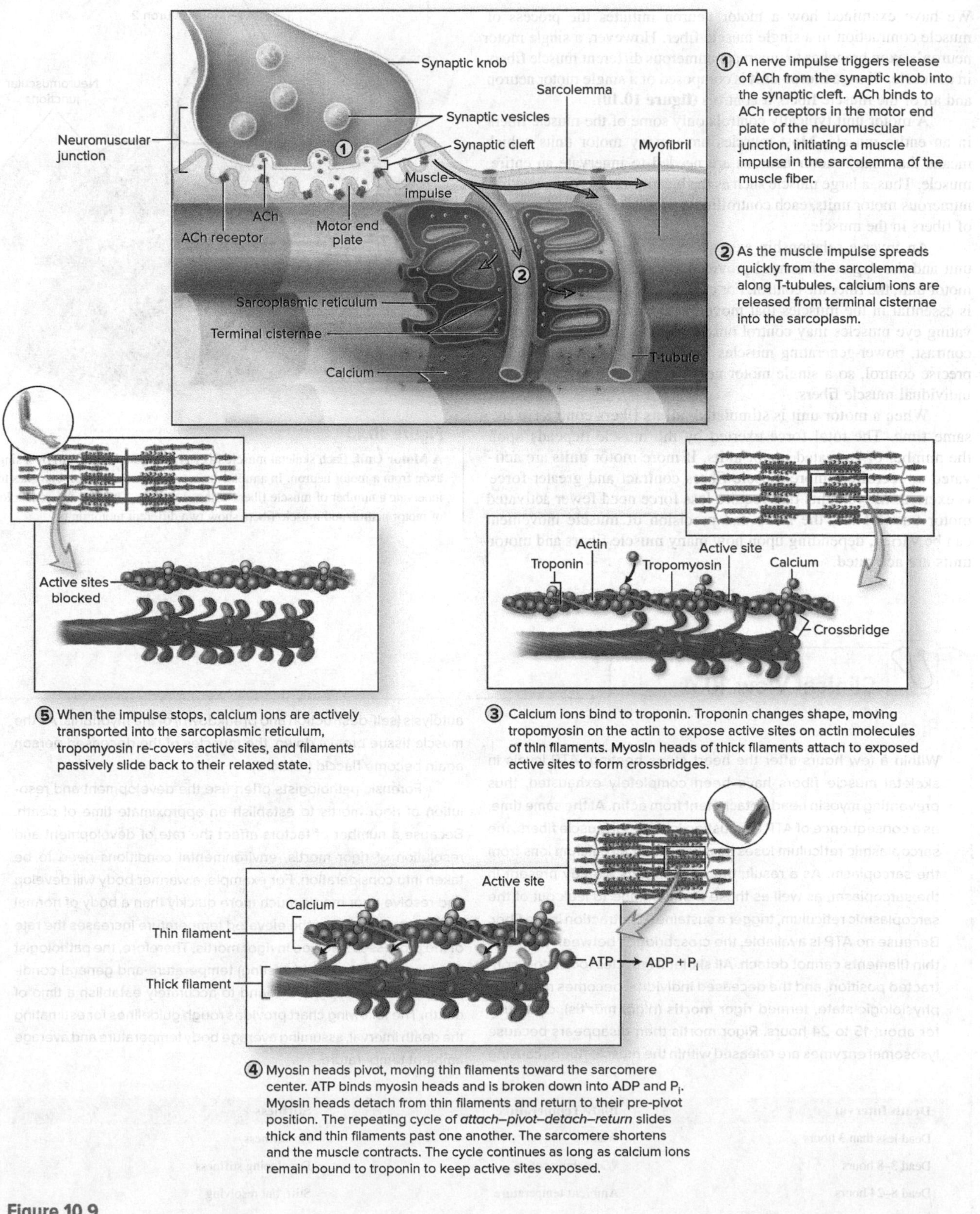
Synaptic knob
Sarcolemma
Synaptic vesicles
Neuromuscular junction
Synaptic cleft
Myofibril
Muscle impulse
ACh
ACh receptor
Motor end plate
Sarcoplasmic reticulum
Terminal cisternae
Calcium
T-tubule
① A nerve impulse triggers release of ACh from the synaptic knob into the synaptic cleft. ACh binds to ACh receptors in the motor end plate of the neuromuscular junction, initiating a muscle impulse in the sarcolemma of the muscle fiber.
② As the muscle impulse spreads quickly from the sarcolemma along T-tubules, calcium ions are released from terminal cisternae into the sarcoplasm.
Active sites blocked
Actin
Troponin
Tropomyosin
Active site
Calcium
Crossbridge
⑤ When the impulse stops, calcium ions are actively transported into the sarcoplasmic reticulum, tropomyosin re-covers active sites, and filaments passively slide back to their relaxed state.
③ Calcium ions bind to troponin. Troponin changes shape, moving tropomyosin on the actin to expose active sites on actin molecules of thin filaments. Myosin heads of thick filaments attach to exposed active sites to form crossbridges.
Active site
Calcium
Thin filament
Thick filament
ATP → ADP + P_i
④ Myosin heads pivot, moving thin filaments toward the sarcomere center. ATP binds myosin heads and is broken down into ADP and P_i. Myosin heads detach from thin filaments and return to their pre-pivot position. The repeating cycle of *attach–pivot–detach–return* slides thick and thin filaments past one another. The sarcomere shortens and the muscle contracts. The cycle continues as long as calcium ions remain bound to troponin to keep active sites exposed.

Figure 10.9
Events in Muscle Contraction. APR

10.3e Motor Units

We have examined how a motor neuron initiates the process of muscle contraction in a single muscle fiber. However, a single motor neuron's axon branches to innervate numerous different muscle fibers in a muscle. Thus, a **motor unit** is composed of a single motor neuron and all of the muscle fibers it controls (**figure 10.10**).

A motor unit typically controls only some of the muscle fibers in an entire muscle. Most muscles have many motor units, which means that many motor neurons are needed to innervate an entire muscle. Thus, a large muscle such as the biceps brachii of the arm has numerous motor units, each controlling a portion of the total number of fibers in the muscle.

An inverse relationship exists between the size of the motor unit and the degree of control provided. In general, the smaller the motor unit, the finer the control. For example, because precise control is essential in the muscles that move the eye, motor neurons innervating eye muscles may control only two or three muscle fibers. In contrast, power-generating muscles in our lower limbs require less precise control, so a single motor neuron controls several thousand individual muscle fibers.

When a motor unit is stimulated, all its fibers contract at the same time. The total force exerted by the muscle depends upon the number of activated motor units. If more motor units are activated or recruited, more muscle fibers contract and greater force is exerted. Movements that require less force need fewer activated motor units. Thus, the force and precision of muscle movement can be varied, depending upon how many muscle fibers and motor units are activated.

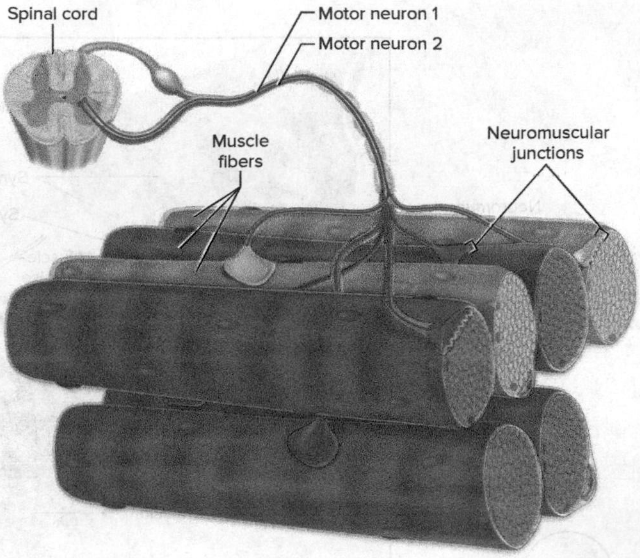

Figure 10.10

A Motor Unit. Each skeletal muscle fiber is innervated (supplied) by a single axon from a motor neuron. In a motor unit, a motor neuron axon branches to innervate a number of muscle fibers within a muscle. The two different colors of motor neuron and muscle fibers show two different motor units.

Clinical View 10.4

Rigor Mortis

Within a few hours after the heart stops beating, ATP levels in skeletal muscle fibers have been completely exhausted, thus preventing myosin head detachment from actin. At the same time, as a consequence of ATP exhaustion in skeletal muscle fibers, the sarcoplasmic reticulum loses its ability to recall calcium ions from the sarcoplasm. As a result, the calcium ions already present in the sarcoplasm, as well as those that continue to leak out of the sarcoplasmic reticulum, trigger a sustained contraction in the fiber. Because no ATP is available, the crossbridges between thick and thin filaments cannot detach. All skeletal muscles lock into a contracted position, and the deceased individual becomes rigid. This physiologic state, termed **rigor mortis** (ri'gŏr mōr'tis), continues for about 15 to 24 hours. Rigor mortis then disappears because lysosomal enzymes are released within the muscle fibers, causing autolysis (self-destruction and breakdown) of the myofibrils. As the muscle tissue breaks down, the muscles of the deceased person again become flaccid (relaxed).

Forensic pathologists often use the development and resolution of rigor mortis to establish an approximate time of death. Because a number of factors affect the rate of development and resolution of rigor mortis, environmental conditions need to be taken into consideration. For example, a warmer body will develop and resolve rigor mortis much more quickly than a body of normal temperature, because the elevated temperature increases the rate of the processes involved in rigor mortis. Therefore, the pathologist must know the ambient (existing) temperature and general conditions where the body was found to accurately establish a time of death. The following chart provides rough guidelines for estimating the death interval, assuming average body temperature and average ambient temperature.

Death Interval	Body Temperature	Stiffness
Dead less than 3 hours	Warm	No stiffness
Dead 3–8 hours	Warm, but cooling	Developing stiffness
Dead 8–24 hours	Ambient temperature	Stiff, but resolving
Dead 24–36 hours	Ambient temperature	No stiffness

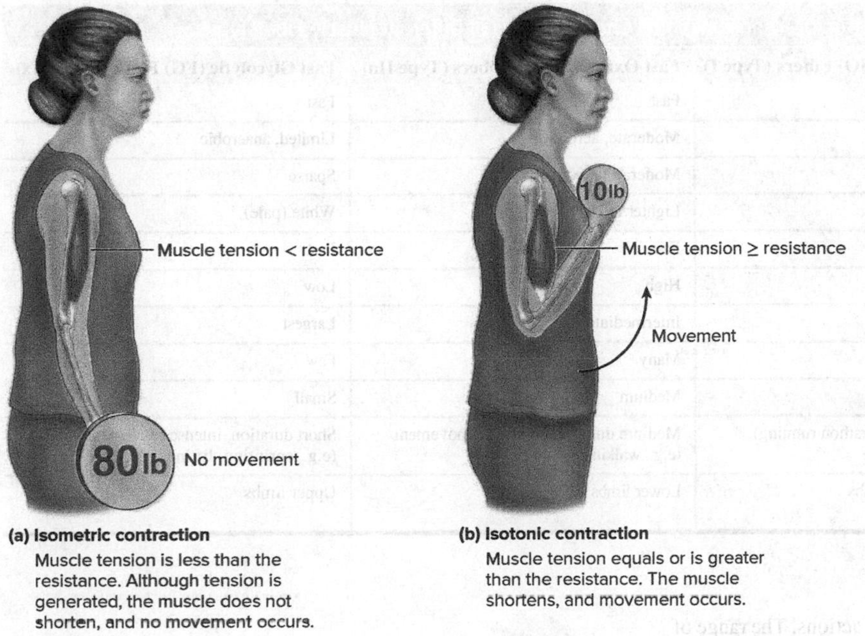
Muscle tension < resistance
80 lb
No movement
10 lb
Muscle tension ≥ resistance
Movement
(a) Isometric contraction
Muscle tension is less than the resistance. Although tension is generated, the muscle does not shorten, and no movement occurs.
(b) Isotonic contraction
Muscle tension equals or is greater than the resistance. The muscle shortens, and movement occurs.

Figure 10.11

Isometric Versus Isotonic Contraction. (*a*) When a muscle is isometrically contracted, its length does not change, but the muscle is tensed. (*b*) Isotonic muscle contraction causes the muscle to shorten and the body part to move.

> **Learning Strategy 10.4**
>
> The same muscles are used in picking up a pencil, a glass, a textbook, and a barbell. Different motor units activated or recruited allow this difference in force to be generated. It is similar to recruiting help to lift a couch.

WHAT DO YOU THINK?

1. What is the benefit of having multiple motor units in a skeletal muscle? Why wouldn't you simply want one motor unit to innervate all of the muscle fibers?

Muscle Tone and Contraction Types

Some motor units are always active, even when a muscle is at rest. These motor units produce tension but not enough tension to cause movement. **Muscle tone** is the resting tension in a skeletal muscle. Usually, motor units are stimulated randomly so that the attached tendon maintains a constant tension, but individual muscle fibers are afforded some relaxation time. This resting muscle tone stabilizes the position of bones and joints.

As stimulation begins and then increases in an active muscle, the fibers within the muscle begin to contract, generating tension in the muscle. The two types of muscle contraction are isometric and isotonic (**figure 10.11**).

During an **isometric** (ī′sō-met′rik; *iso* = same, *metron* = measure) **contraction,** the length of the muscle does not change because the tension produced by this contracting muscle never exceeds the resistance (load). For example, when a person tries to lift an extremely heavy object (such as picking up the back of a car off the ground), the arm muscles are isometrically contracted. Tension is generated, but it is not great enough to move the load.

In an **isotonic** (ī′sō-ton′ik; *tonos* = tension) **contraction,** the tension produced equals or is greater than the resistance, and then the muscle fibers shorten, resulting in movement. An example of isotonic contraction occurs when a person lifts a grocery bag out of the car. The tension generated in the appropriate muscles equals the load, and then the muscle fibers shorten. Most of the movements performed by individuals working out on weight machines produce isotonic contractions. Isotonic contractions are of two types. **Concentric contractions** actively shorten a muscle, as when we lift a baby from a crib. The load (weight of the baby) is less than the maximum tension that can be generated by the muscles in the arm; thus, the muscle shortens and the baby is raised up. **Eccentric contractions** actively lengthen a muscle when we are placing the baby back into the crib. The muscles in our arm are active while lengthening as we lay the baby down gently rather than just letting her "fall" into the crib.

Simply put, an isotonic contraction of the arm muscles allows you to lift a book from the table, whereas an isometric contraction of the arm muscles occurs when you push against a wall.

WHAT DID YOU LEARN?

6. Draw and label the structural relationship between a nerve fiber and a muscle fiber at the neuromuscular junction.
7. What is the function of calcium ions in skeletal muscle contraction?
8. Describe how thick and thin filaments interact during a muscle contraction.
9. Describe the difference between isometric and isotonic contractions, and give an example of each.

10.4 Types of Skeletal Muscle Fibers

✓ Learning Objectives

10. Identify and describe the characteristics of the three types of muscle fibers.
11. Explain the types of contractions facilitated by slow oxidative, fast oxidative, and fast glycolytic muscle fibers.

Table 10.4 Comparison of Structural and Functional Characteristics of Different Muscle Fiber Types

Fiber Characteristic	Slow Oxidative (SO) Fibers (Type I)	Fast Oxidative (FO) Fibers (Type IIa)	Fast Glycolytic (FG) Fibers (Type IIx)
ATP Use	Slow	Fast	Fast
Capacity to Make ATP	High, aerobic	Moderate, aerobic	Limited, anaerobic
Concentration of Capillaries	Extensive	Moderately extensive	Sparse
Color of Fibers	Dark red	Lighter red	White (pale)
Contraction Velocity	Slow	Fast	Fast
Resistance to Fatigue	Highest	High	Low
Fiber Diameter	Smallest	Intermediate	Largest
Number of Mitochondria	Many	Many	Few
Amount of Myoglobin	Large	Medium	Small
Primary Fiber Function	Endurance (e.g., marathon running), maintaining posture	Medium duration, moderate movement (e.g., walking, biking)	Short duration, intense movement (e.g., sprinting, lifting weights)
Muscles with a Large Abundance of Fiber Type	Trunk and lower limbs	Lower limbs	Upper limbs

Skeletal muscles must perform a wide variety of actions. The range of actions is determined by the types of fibers that form the muscle. The three types of muscle fibers are slow oxidative (type I), fast oxidative (type IIa), and fast glycolytic (type IIx). Their characteristics vary **(table 10.4)**. Each skeletal muscle typically contains a percentage of each of these muscle fiber types, as shown in **figure 10.12**.

- **Slow oxidative (SO) fibers,** also called *type I,* typically have half the diameter of other muscle fibers and contain slow myosin ATPase. These cells produce contractions that are slower and less powerful. However, they can contract over long periods of time without fatigue because ATP is supplied primarily through aerobic cellular respiration. These fibers appear dark red because of the presence of large amounts of myoglobin.
- **Fast oxidative (FO) fibers,** also called *intermediate fibers,* or *type IIa,* are the least numerous of the muscle fiber types. They are intermediate in size and contain fast myosin ATPase. They produce a fast, powerful contraction with ATP provided primarily through aerobic respiration. However, the vascular supply to fast oxidative fibers is less extensive than the network of capillaries serving SO fibers—thus, the delivery rate of nutrients and oxygen is lower. These fibers also contain myoglobin, but less than the amount found in SO fibers. Consequently, these fibers can be distinguished from SO fibers on a microscopic image because they appear a lighter red than SO fibers.
- **Fast glycolytic (FG) fibers,** also called *fast anaerobic fibers,* or *type IIx,* are the most prevalent muscle fiber type. They are largest in diameter, contain fast myosin ATPase, and provide both power and speed. However, they can contract for only short bursts because ATP is provided primarily through anaerobic cellular respiration. These fibers appear white because of the relative lack of myoglobin.

WHAT DO YOU THINK?

2 The next time you sit down to a turkey dinner, you may be asked if you prefer the "white meat" or the "dark meat." What can you say about the diameter of the muscle fibers of each type of meat? Which would be fast glycolytic fibers and which would be slow oxidative fibers? In life, which type of muscle would have had the greatest resistance to fatigue?

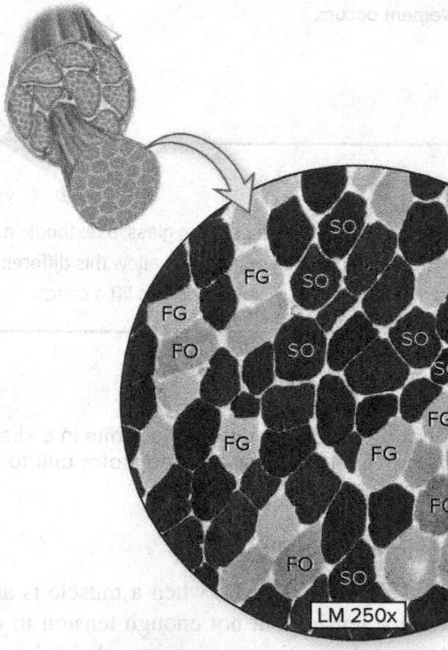

Figure 10.12
Comparison of Fiber Types in Skeletal Muscle. A cross section of a skeletal muscle using a specific staining technique demonstrates the types of fibers in the muscle. The fibers are distinguished by their shade of color. Fast glycolytic (FG) fibers are the lightest; slow oxidative (SO) fibers are the darkest; and fast oxidative (FO) fibers are less dark than the SO fibers.
G W Willis/Getty Images

10.4a Distribution of Slow Oxidative, Fast Oxidative, and Fast Glycolytic Fibers

The relative number of each of the slow and fast muscle fiber types varies in different skeletal muscles. Usually, skeletal muscles have a diverse number and composition of muscle fiber types. However, within a single motor unit, all fibers belong to the same type. Some muscles have no SO fibers, whereas others have no FG fibers. For example, SO fibers dominate many back and calf muscles, which contract almost continually to help us maintain an upright posture.

Clinical View 10.5

Anabolic Steroids and Other Performance-Enhancing Compounds

Anabolic (an'ă-bol'ik) **steroids** are synthetic substances that mimic the actions of natural testosterone. Anabolic steroids have only a few accepted medical uses—among them, the treatment of delayed puberty, certain types of impotence, and the wasting condition associated with HIV infection and other diseases. Because anabolic steroids stimulate the manufacture of muscle proteins, these compounds have become popular with some athletes as performance enhancers.

The stimulation of excessive muscle development requires relatively large doses of anabolic steroids, and the extra strength and speed gained come at a price. Many devastating side effects are associated with extended anabolic steroid use, including increased risk of heart disease and stroke, kidney damage, aggressive behavior, liver tumors, testicular atrophy, acne, and personality aberrations. Because anabolic steroids mimic the effects of testosterone, female athletes who use them often experience menstrual irregularities, growth of facial hair, and in extreme circumstances atrophy of the uterus and mammary glands; sterility has even been reported. Adding to these problems is the route of administration. Because many of these steroid preparations must be injected, the improper use or sharing of needles raises the possibility of transferring a disease such as AIDS or hepatitis. Therefore, the use of anabolic steroids as performance enhancers has been widely banned.

In addition to anabolic steroids, athletes have used other substances and some hormones, such as **growth homone (GH)** and **insulin-like growth factor 1 (IGF-1),** to increase muscle performance. Compounds such as creatine, branched-chain amino acids, and ephedrine have also been touted as increasing muscle size and power, but most research indicates this is not the case. In fact, ephedrine has been banned in the United States by the FDA after being linked to death in some individuals taking it.

Ingram Publishing

In contrast, there are no SO fibers in the muscles of the eye and hand, where swift but brief contractions are required.

The relative number of SO fibers compared to FG fibers in each muscle is determined by a person's genes, and their proportions determine an individual's endurance. For example, distance runners who have higher proportions of SO muscle fibers in their leg muscles are able to outperform runners who have a greater number of FG muscle fibers in their leg muscles.

Additionally, an individual has better proficiency in performing repeated contractions under aerobic conditions if he or she has a greater percentage of SO fibers in specific muscles. However, for brief periods of intense activity, such as sprinting or weight-lifting, the individual with a higher percentage of FG muscle fibers has the advantage.

The proportion of FO fibers changes with physical conditioning; if used repeatedly for endurance events, fast fibers can develop the appearance and functional capabilities of FO fibers. If used repeatedly for intense short-term activity, FO fibers can change their functional capabilities to FG fibers. Thus, physical conditioning enables athletes to improve both strength and endurance.

WHAT DID YOU LEARN?

10. Make a table listing the three types of muscle fibers in one column. In the next column, describe the anatomy of these fibers. In the last column, describe their functions.

10.5 Skeletal Muscle Fiber Organization

✓ Learning Objective

12. Describe the four fascicle organizational patterns in skeletal muscle.

As mentioned in section 10.2b, bundles of muscle fibers termed fascicles lie parallel to each other within each muscle. However, the organization of fascicles in different muscles often varies. There are four different patterns of fascicle arrangement: circular, parallel, convergent, and pennate **(table 10.5)**.

10.5a Circular Muscles

The fascicles in a **circular muscle** are concentrically arranged around an opening or recess. A circular muscle is also called a *sphincter*, because contraction of the muscle closes off the opening. Circular muscles are located at entrances and exits of internal passageways. An example is the orbicularis oris muscle that encircles the opening of the mouth.

10.5b Parallel Muscles

The fascicles in a **parallel muscle** run parallel to its long axis. Each muscle fiber in this type of skeletal muscle exhibits the functional characteristics of the entire parallel muscle. Parallel muscles have a central body, called the **belly,** or *gaster.* This muscle shortens when it contracts, and its body increases in diameter. Parallel muscles have high endurance but are not as strong as other muscle types. Examples of parallel muscles include the rectus abdominis (an anterior abdominal muscle that forms the "six-pack" of a well-sculpted abdomen), the biceps brachii of the arm, and the masseter that moves the mandible.

10.5c Convergent Muscles

A **convergent** (kon-ver'jent) **muscle** has widespread fascicles that converge on a common attachment site. This attachment site may be a single tendon, a tendinous sheet, or a slender band of collagen fibers known as a **raphe** (rā'fē; *rhaphe* = seam). These muscles are often triangular in shape, resembling a broad fan with a tendon at the tip. A convergent muscle is versatile—that is, the direction of its pull can be modified merely by activating a single group of fascicles at any one time. However, when the fibers in a convergent muscle all contract at once, they

Table 10.5 Skeletal Muscle Architecture

Pattern of Fascicles	Description	Example
Circular	Fascicles arranged concentrically around an opening Acts as a sphincter to close a passageway or opening (e.g., orbits, mouth, anus)	 Orbicularis oris
Parallel	Fascicles are parallel to the long axis of the muscle Body of muscle increases in diameter with contraction High endurance, not very strong	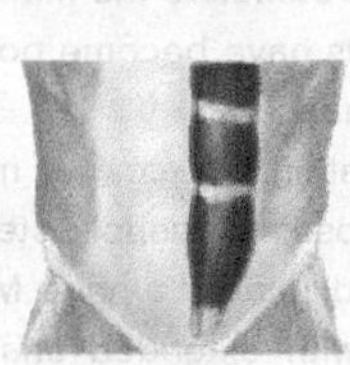 Rectus abdominis
Convergent	Triangular muscle with common attachment site Direction of pull of muscle can be changed Does not pull as hard as equal-sized parallel muscle	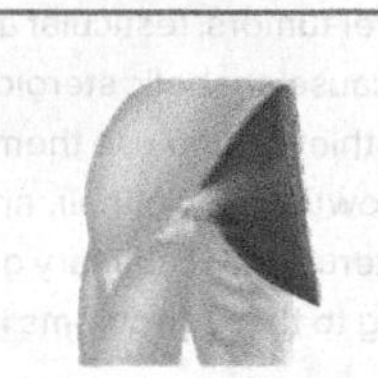 Pectoralis major
Pennate	Muscle body has one or more tendons Fascicles at oblique angle to tendon Pulls harder than a parallel muscle of equal size *Unipennate:* All fascicles on the same side of the tendon *Bipennate:* Fascicles on both sides of the tendon *Multipennate:* Tendon branches within the muscle	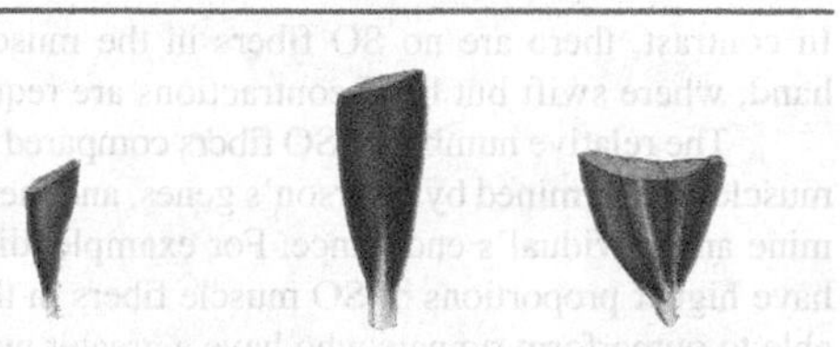 Extensor digitorum (unipennate) Rectus femoris (bipennate) Deltoid (multipennate)

do not pull as hard on the tendon as a parallel muscle of the same size because the muscle fibers on opposite sides of the tendon are not working together; rather, they are pulling in different directions. An example of a convergent muscle is the pectoralis major of the chest.

10.5d Pennate Muscles

Pennate (pen′āt; *penna* = feather) **muscles** are so named because the arrangement of the fascicles and the tendon(s) resembles a large feather. Pennate muscles have one or more tendons extending through their body, and the fascicles are arranged at an oblique angle to the tendon. Because pennate muscle fibers pull at an angle to the tendon, this type of muscle does not move its tendons as far as parallel muscles move their tendons. However, a contracting pennate muscle generates more tension than does a parallel muscle of the same size, and thus it is stronger.

There are three types of pennate muscles:

- In a **unipennate muscle,** all of the fascicles are on the same side of the tendon. The extensor digitorum, a long muscle that extends the fingers, is a unipennate muscle.
- A **bipennate muscle,** the most common type, has fascicles on both sides of the tendon. The palmar and dorsal interosseous muscles that attach to the metacarpals are composed of bipennate muscle that helps adduct and abduct the digits.
- A **multipennate muscle** has branches of the tendon within the muscle. The triangular deltoid that covers the superior surface of the shoulder joint is a multipennate muscle.

WHAT DID YOU LEARN?

11. Name the four main patterns of skeletal muscle fiber organization and describe how their arrangement affects their action.

10.6 Exercise and Skeletal Muscle

✓ Learning Objective

13. Explain what occurs during muscle atrophy and muscle hypertrophy.

Muscle building is a time-consuming endeavor that requires proper diet, specific workout regimens, and sufficient rest and recovery times between workouts. In contrast, the lack of sufficient exercise is detrimental to the health of skeletal muscle.

10.6a Muscle Hypertrophy

An increase in muscle fiber size is called **muscle hypertrophy.** Hypertrophy does not result in an increase in muscle fiber number, which would be termed *hyperplasia.* However, hypertrophy does result in an increase in the number of myofibrils per fiber in fast fibers. Muscle size may be increased by exercising. The repetitive, exhaustive stimulation of muscle fibers results in more mitochondria, larger glycogen reserves, and an increased ability to produce ATP. Ultimately, each muscle fiber develops more myofibrils, and each myofibril contains a larger number of myofilaments. An athlete who competes as a bodybuilder or weight lifter exhibits hypertrophied muscular development.

10.6b Muscle Atrophy

Muscle atrophy (at′rō-fē; *a* = without, *trophe* = nourishment) is a wasting of tissue that results in a reduction in muscle size, tone, and power. If a skeletal muscle experiences markedly reduced stimulation, it loses both mass and tone. The muscle becomes flaccid, and its fibers decrease in size and become weaker. Even a temporary reduction in muscle use can lead to muscular atrophy. For example, after a cast has been worn, the limb muscles under the cast exhibit reduced tone and size. Individuals who suffer damage to the nervous system or are paralyzed by spinal injuries gradually lose muscle tone and size in the areas affected. Although the muscle atrophy is initially reversible, dead or dying muscle fibers are not replaced. When extreme atrophy occurs, the loss of gross muscle function is permanent. For these reasons, physical therapy is required for patients who suffer temporary loss of mobility.

WHAT DID YOU LEARN?

12 What anatomic changes occur in a muscle fiber when it undergoes hypertrophy?

10.7 Levers and Joint Biomechanics

✓ Learning Objectives

14. Describe the characteristics of the three types of levers in the body.
15. Explain how interacting skeletal muscles can initiate or prevent movement.

If a skeletal muscle crosses a joint, its contractions may change the angular relationships of the bones in the joint, resulting in body movement. The location and nature of the muscular connection to the skeleton influences the speed, range, and force of movement.

When analyzing muscle contraction, anatomists often compare it to the mechanics of a lever; this practice of applying mechanical principles to biology is known as **biomechanics.** A **lever** (lev′ĕr, lē′ver; to lift) is an elongated, rigid object that rotates around a fixed point called the **fulcrum** (ful′kr ŭm). Opposing forces are applied to the lever: one is called the *effort* and one is called the *resistance.* Levers are used to change the speed and distance of movement produced by a force, the direction of an applied force, and the force strength. Rotation occurs when an effort applied to one point on the lever exceeds a resistance located at some other point. A seesaw is a familiar example of a lever.

The portion of a lever from the fulcrum to the point of effort is called the **effort arm,** and the segment from the fulcrum to the point of resistance is the **resistance arm (see figure 10.13)**. The ratio of the effort arm length to the resistance arm length determines the mechanical advantage of the lever. If the effort arm is longer than the resistance arm, more resistance can be overcome, thus it provides more mechanical advantage. As the effort arm shortens with respect to the resistance arm, less resistance can be overcome, but the range of motion and the speed at which movement can occur increases. For instance, if you are using a shovel to move a pile of dirt, you can lift more dirt if you place your lifting hand closer to the blade of the shovel (increasing the effort arm length), but the shovel has less range of motion **(see figure 10.14)**. If you place your lifting hand closer to the handle (decreasing effort arm length), you have much more range of motion, but cannot lift as much dirt.

In the body, a long bone acts as a lever, a joint serves as the fulcrum, and the effort is generated by a muscle attached to the long bone. Most joints in the human body are arranged such that the effort arm is close to the fulcrum, so we have speed and range of motion, but not great mechanical advantage.

10.7a Classes of Levers

Three classes of levers occur in the human body: first-class, second-class, and third-class (figure 10.13).

First-Class Levers

A **first-class lever** has a fulcrum in the middle, between the effort and the resistance. An example of a first-class lever is a pair of scissors. The effort is applied to the handle of the scissors, while the resistance is at the cutting end of the scissors. The fulcrum (pivot for movement) is along the middle of the scissors, between the handle and the cutting ends. In the body, an example of a first-class lever is the atlanto-occipital joint of the neck, where the muscles on the posterior side of the neck pull inferiorly on the nuchal lines of the skull and oppose the tendency of the head to tip anteriorly.

Second-Class Levers

The resistance in a **second-class lever** is between the fulcrum and the applied effort. A common example of this type of lever is lifting the handles of a wheelbarrow, allowing it to pivot on its wheel at the opposite end and lift a load in the middle. The load weight is the resistance, and the upward lift on the handle is the effort. A small force can balance a larger weight in this type of lever, because the force is always farther from the fulcrum than the resistance. In the body, second-class levers are rare, but one example occurs when the foot is plantar flexed so that a person can stand on tiptoe. The contraction of the calf muscle causes a pull superiorly by the calcaneal tendon attached to the calcaneus.

Third-Class Levers

In a **third-class lever,** an effort is applied between the resistance and the fulcrum, as when picking up a small object with a pair of forceps. Third-class levers are the most common levers in the body. One example is found at the elbow, where the fulcrum is the joint between the humerus and ulna, the effort is applied by the biceps brachii muscle, and the resistance is provided by any weight in the hand or by the weight of the forearm itself. In addition, the mandible acts as a third-class lever when you bite with your incisors on a piece of food. The temporomandibular joint is the fulcrum, and the temporalis muscle exerts the effort, while the resistance is the item of food being bitten.

WHAT DO YOU THINK?

3 What type of lever is the knee joint? Explain your answer.

10.7b Actions of Skeletal Muscles

Skeletal muscles generally do not function in isolation; rather, they work together to produce movements. Muscles are grouped according to their primary actions into three types: agonists, antagonists, and synergists.

An **agonist** (ag′on-ist; *agon* = a contest), also called a *prime mover,* is a muscle that contracts to produce a particular movement,

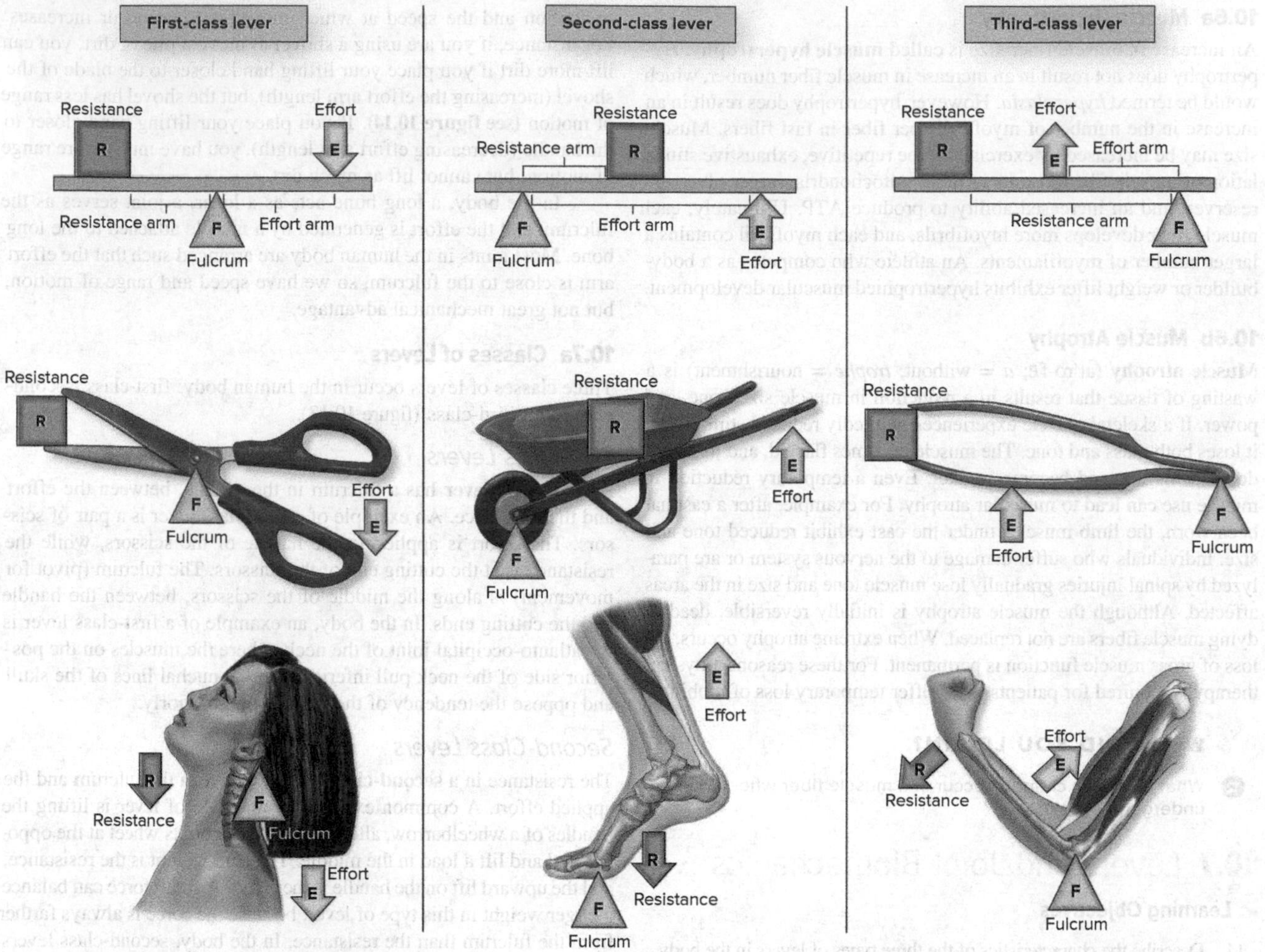

Figure 10.13

Classes of Levers. This comparison of the three classes of levers shows: (*top row*) relative position of each lever; (*middle row*) a mechanical example of each, and (*bottom row*) an anatomic example of each. First-class (*left*), second-class (*middle*), and third-class (*right*) levers are compared.

Figure 10.14

Mechanical Advantage. The longer the effort arm, the more the resistance that can be moved, as in this photo showing the man's hand close to the shovel blade to move more dirt.

Neil Guegan/Image Source

such as extending the forearm. The triceps brachii of the posterior arm is an agonist that causes forearm extension.

An **antagonist** (an-tag′ ō-nist; *anti* = against) is a muscle whose actions oppose those of the agonist. If the agonist produces extension, the antagonist produces flexion. The contraction of the agonist stretches the antagonist, and vice versa. As this movement occurs, the stretched muscle usually does not relax completely. Instead, the tension within the muscle being stretched is adjusted to control the speed of the movement and ensure that it is smooth. For example, when the triceps brachii acts as an agonist to extend the forearm, the biceps brachii on the anterior side of the humerus acts as an antagonist to stabilize the movement and produce the opposing action, which is flexion of the forearm.

A **synergist** (sin′ ĕr-jist; *ergon* = work) is a muscle that assists the agonist in performing its action. The contraction of a synergist usually either contributes to tension exerted close to the more mobile attachment of the muscle or stabilizes the less mobile attachment of the muscle. Usually, synergists are most useful at the start of a movement when the agonist is lengthened and cannot exert much power. Examples of synergistic muscles are the biceps brachii and the brachialis muscles of the arm. Both muscles work synergistically (together) to flex the elbow joint. Synergists may also assist an agonist by preventing movement at a joint and thereby stabilizing the origin of the agonist. In this case, these synergistic muscles are called *fixators*.

WHAT DID YOU LEARN?

13 Compare and contrast an agonist and a synergist.

10.8 The Naming of Skeletal Muscles

✓ Learning Objective

16. Explain how muscle names incorporate appearance, location, function, orientation, and/or unusual features.

Usually, the names of skeletal muscles provide clues to their identification. As **figure 10.15** shows, skeletal muscles are named according to the following criteria:

- **Muscle action.** Names that indicate the primary function or movement of the muscle include *flexor, extensor,* and *pronator.* These are such common actions that the names almost always contain other clues to the appearance or location of the muscle. For example, the pronator teres is a long, round muscle responsible for pronating the forearm.
- **Specific body regions.** The rectus femoris is on the thigh (*femur*), and the tibialis anterior is on the *anterior* surface of the *tibia*. Muscles that can be seen at the body surface are

Muscle action	
Adductor (adducts body part)	Adductor magnus
Abductor (abducts body part)	Abductor pollicis longus
Flexor (flexes a joint)	Flexor carpi radialis
Extensor (extends a joint)	Extensor hallucis longus
Specific body regions	
Oris (mouth)	Orbicularis oris
Cervicis (neck)	Semispinalis cervicis
Brachial (arm)	Biceps brachii
Carpi (wrist)	Flexor carpi ulnaris
Pollicis (thumb)	Opponens pollicis
Gluteal (buttocks)	Gluteus medius
Femoris (thigh)	Quadratus femoris
Hallucis (great toe)	Extensor hallucis longus
Anterior (toward the front of the body)	Tibialis anterior
Posterior or dorsal/dorsi (toward the back of the body)	Tibialis posterior Latissimus dorsi
Superior	Serratus posterior superior
Inferior	Serratus posterior inferior
Superficialis (superficial)	Flexor digitorum superficialis
Profundus (deep)	Flexor digitorum profundus
Muscle attachments	
Sternum and clavicle (cleido)	Sternocleidomastoid
Between the ribs	Intercostal
Subscapular fossa	Subscapularis
Fibula	Fibularis longus
Zygomatic bone	Zygomaticus major
Orientation of muscle fibers	
Rectus (straight)	Rectus abdominis
Oblique (angled)	External oblique
Orbicularis (circular)	Orbicularis oculi
Muscle shape and size	
Deltoid (triangular)	Deltoid
Quadratus (rectangular)	Pronator quadratus
Trapezius (trapezoidal)	Trapezius
Longus (long)	Abductor pollicis longus
Brevis (short)	Abductor pollicis brevis
Major (larger of two muscles)	Pectoralis major
Minor (smaller of two muscles)	Pectoralis minor
Maximus (largest)	Gluteus maximus
Medius (medium sized)	Gluteus medius
Minimus (smallest)	Gluteus minimus
Muscle heads / proximal tendons	
Biceps (two heads)	Biceps femoris
Triceps (three heads)	Triceps brachii
Quadriceps (four heads)	Quadriceps femoris

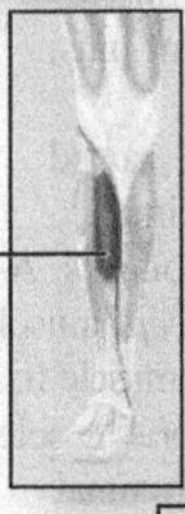
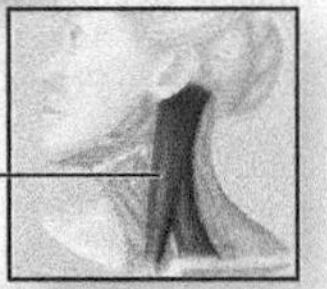
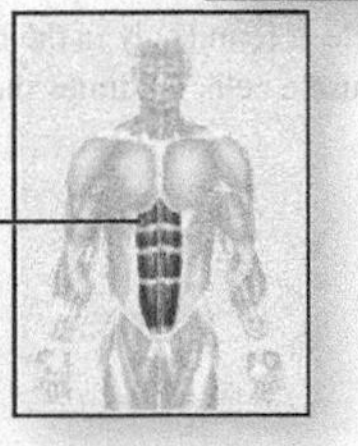
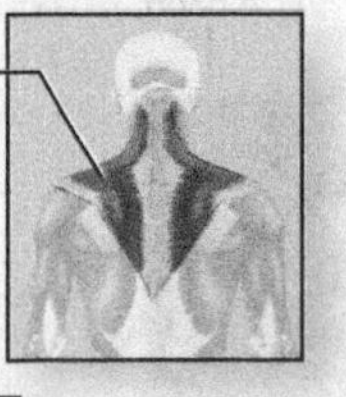

Figure 10.15
Muscle Naming. Muscles are named according to a variety of features.

often termed *superficialis* (sū′pĕr-fi′sh ē-ā′lis) or *externus* (eks-ter′n ŭs). In contrast, deeper or more internally placed muscles may have names such as *profundus* (prō-fŭn′dŭs; deep) or *internus*.

- **Muscle attachments.** Many muscle names identify their prominent attachments. Often, the first part of the name is the inferior attachment and the second part of the name is the superior attachment. For example, the sternocleidomastoid has inferior attachments on the *sternum* and clavicle (*cleido*) and a superior attachment on the *mastoid* process of the temporal bone.
- **Orientation of muscle fibers.** The rectus abdominis muscle is named for its lengthwise-running muscle fibers; *rectus* means "straight." Similarly, names such as *oblique* or *obliquus* (ob-lī′kwŭs) indicate muscles with fibers extending at an oblique angle to the longitudinal axis of the body.
- **Muscle shape and size.** Examples of shape in muscle names include deltoid, shaped like a triangle; orbicularis, a circle; rhomboid, a rhombus; and trapezius, a trapezoid. Short muscles are called *brevis* (brev′is); long muscles are called *longus* (lon′g ŭs) or *longissimus* (lon-jĭs′ĭ-mŭs; longest). *Teres* (ter′ēz, te′rēz) muscles are both long and round. Large muscles are called *magnus* (mag′n ŭs; big), *major* (mā′jŏr; bigger), or *maximus* (măk′sĭ-mŭs; biggest). Small muscles are called *minor* (mī′nŏr; smaller) or *minimus* (mĭ′nĭ-mŭs; smallest).
- **Muscle heads/proximal tendons.** Some muscles are named after specific features—for example, how many proximal tendons or how many muscle bellies or heads each contains. A *biceps* muscle has two heads/proximal tendons, a *triceps* muscle has three heads/proximal tendons, and a *quadriceps* muscle has four heads/proximal tendons. So the quadriceps femoris muscle is a muscle of the thigh that has four muscle heads/proximal tendons.

WHAT DID YOU LEARN?

14. List and explain at least four criteria used to determine how muscles are named.
15. The gluteus maximus muscle gets its name from which categories for naming muscles?

10.9 Characteristics of Cardiac and Smooth Muscle

✓ Learning Objective

17. Describe the similarities and differences among the three types of muscle tissue.

In addition to skeletal muscle, which we have just described in depth, two other types of muscle occur in the body: cardiac muscle and smooth muscle (see also section 4.4). Here we briefly review their characteristics and compare them to skeletal muscle.

10.9a Cardiac Muscle

Cardiac muscle cells are individual muscle cells arranged in thick bundles within the heart wall (**figure 10.16**). Cardiac muscle cells branch and are both shorter and thicker than skeletal muscle fibers. Individual cells are joined to adjacent muscle cells at junctions termed intercalated discs. **Intercalated** (in-ter′k ă-lā′ted) **discs** are unique to cardiac muscle; they are composed of desmosomes and gap junctions (see section 4.1c). These cells have only one or two nuclei. Cardiac muscle cells are striated because, like skeletal muscle fibers, cardiac muscle cells also contain sarcomeres. Cardiac muscle cells contain a large number of mitochondria, and use aerobic respiration almost exclusively to generate the ATP required for their unceasing work.

Cardiac muscle cells are **autorhythmic,** meaning that the individual cells can generate a muscle impulse without nervous stimulation. This feature of cardiac muscle cells is controlled by a specialized conducting

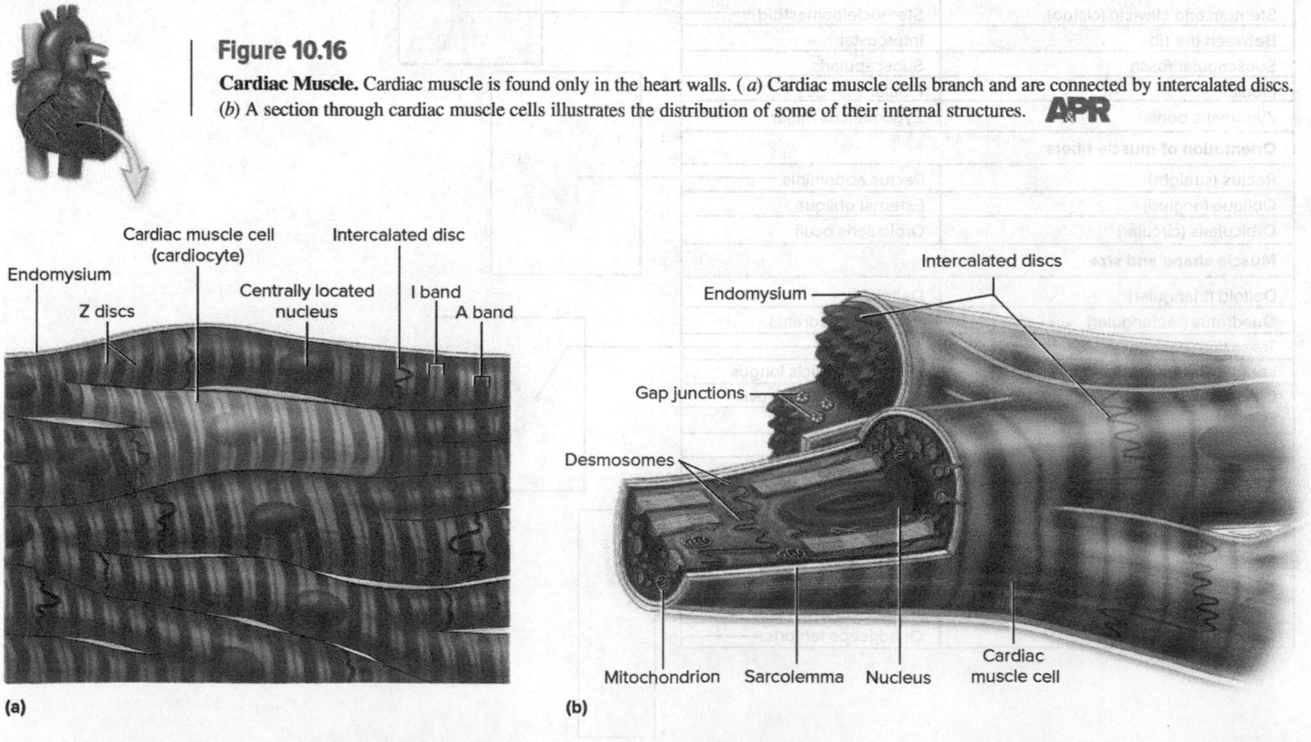

Figure 10.16

Cardiac Muscle. Cardiac muscle is found only in the heart walls. (*a*) Cardiac muscle cells branch and are connected by intercalated discs. (*b*) A section through cardiac muscle cells illustrates the distribution of some of their internal structures. APR system, which is responsible for our repetitious, rhythmic heartbeat (see section 22.4 for an in-depth discussion). The autonomic nervous system controls the rate of rhythmic contraction of cardiac muscle.

Cardiac muscle cells are dependent for their contraction upon calcium ions. Most of the calcium ions that stimulate the contraction of the cardiac muscle cells originate within the interstitial fluid bathing these cells, because their sarcoplasmic reticulum are less well developed and thus store fewer calcium ions than do skeletal muscle fibers.

10.9b Smooth Muscle

Smooth muscle is composed of short muscle cells that have a fusiform shape (widest at the middle of the cell and tapered at each end) **(figure 10.17)**. They have a single, centrally located nucleus. Although smooth muscle cells have both thick and thin filaments, they are not precisely aligned, so no visible striations or sarcomeres are present. Z discs are absent from smooth muscle cells; instead, thin filaments are attached to **dense bodies** by elements of the cytoskeleton. Dense bodies are small concentrations of protein scattered throughout the sarcoplasm and on the inner face of the sarcolemma. The sarcoplasmic reticulum is sparse, and transverse tubules and troponin are absent. Most of the calcium needed to activate smooth muscle contraction originates in the interstitial fluid around the cell.

The mechanism of smooth muscle contraction involves a calcium-binding protein called calmodulin. When the smooth muscle cells are inactive, no calcium enters from the interstitial fluid to bind to calmodulin; thus, smooth cells remain quiescent. However, when the cells are stimulated, calcium ions enter from the interstitial fluid, and the calmodulin activates a protein called myosin light-chain kinase (MLCK). MLCK then activates myosin ATPase, allowing crossbridge formation.

Smooth muscle contraction is slow, resistant to fatigue, and usually sustained for an extended period of time. These are important characteristics because smooth muscle in the walls of viscera and blood vessels must sustain an extended contraction without undergoing fatigue. Smooth muscle cells are resistant to fatigue because their ATP requirements are markedly reduced compared to the amount needed by skeletal muscle.

Smooth muscle contraction is under involuntary control. For example, we cannot voluntarily contract the smooth muscle in the walls of our digestive organs. Thus, smooth muscle cells contract and our stomach seems to "growl" at an inappropriate time. As with cardiac muscle, the autonomic nervous system is one way that the contraction of smooth muscle is controlled.

Skeletal, cardiac, and smooth muscle are compared in **table 10.6**.

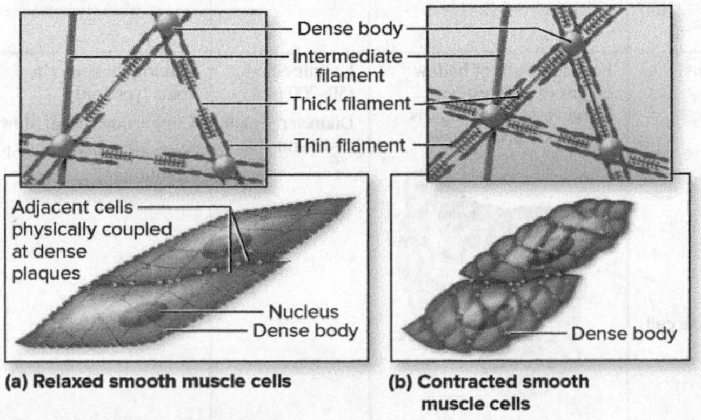

Dense body
Intermediate filament
Thick filament
Thin filament
Adjacent cells physically coupled at dense plaques
Nucleus
Dense body
Dense body
(a) Relaxed smooth muscle cells
(b) Contracted smooth muscle cells

Figure 10.17

Smooth Muscle. Smooth muscle is located in the walls of hollow organs and blood vessels. (*a*) Relaxed smooth muscle cells are elongated and fusiform. (*b*) Contracted smooth muscle cells are compact due to tension exerted by contractile proteins. APR

WHAT DID YOU LEARN?

16 Describe smooth muscle cell structure. What are dense bodies?

10.10 Aging and the Muscular System

✓ **Learning Objective**

18. Explain the effects of aging on skeletal muscle.

In a person's mid-30s, a slow, progressive loss of skeletal muscle mass begins as a direct result of increasing inactivity. The size and power of all muscle tissues also decrease. Often, the lost muscle mass is replaced by either adipose or fibrous connective tissue. Aging affects the muscular system in several specific ways.

First, the number of myofibrils and myofilaments in existing muscle fibers decreases. This muscular atrophy results in a decrease in muscle fiber volume. Second, skeletal muscle fibers decrease in diameter, usually due to this loss of myofibrils within the fiber. The consequences of decreased fiber diameter include a cutback in oxygen storage capacity because of less myoglobin, reduced glycogen reserves, and a decreased ability to produce ATP. Overall, muscle strength and endurance are impaired, and the individual has a tendency to fatigue quickly. Decreased cardiovascular performance often accompanies aging; thus, increased circulatory supply to active muscles occurs much more slowly in the elderly as they begin to exercise.

In addition, a person's tolerance for exercise lowers with age. Decreased muscle strength is compounded by a tendency toward rapid fatigue. The atrophy of muscle secondarily results in less tension generated by that muscle. Consequently, the muscle fatigues more readily while performing a specific amount of work.

As a person grows older, muscle tissue has a reduced capacity to recover from disease or injury. The number of satellite cells in skeletal muscle steadily decreases, and scar tissue often forms due to diminished repair capabilities. Finally, the elasticity of skeletal muscle also decreases as muscle mass is often replaced by dense regular (fibrous) connective tissue, a process called **fibrosis** (fī-brō′sis). The increasing amounts of dense regular connective tissue decrease the flexibility of muscle; an increase in collagen fibers can restrict movement and circulation.

All of us will eventually experience a decline in muscular performance, irrespective of our lifestyle or exercise patterns. But we can improve our chances of being in good shape later in life by striving for physical fitness early in life. Other benefits of regular exercise include strengthening our bones and increasing or maintaining bone mass, controlling body weight, and generally improving the quality of life. Exercise that is regular and moderate, rather than extremely demanding, is the most helpful type.

10.11 Development of the Muscular System

✓ **Learning Objective**

19. Describe the developmental events in muscle formation.

This brief examination of the development of the muscular system focuses primarily on skeletal muscle development. Skeletal muscle tissue formation is initiated during the fourth week of development from

Table 10.6 Muscle Tissue Types: General Comparisons

Muscle Tissue	Appearance and Shape of Cell	Location of Muscle	Cell Length/ Cell Diameter	Autorhythmicity/ Contraction Speed/ Nervous System Control
Skeletal Muscle	Long, cylindrical fiber; multiple peripheral nuclei internal to sarcolemma; striated 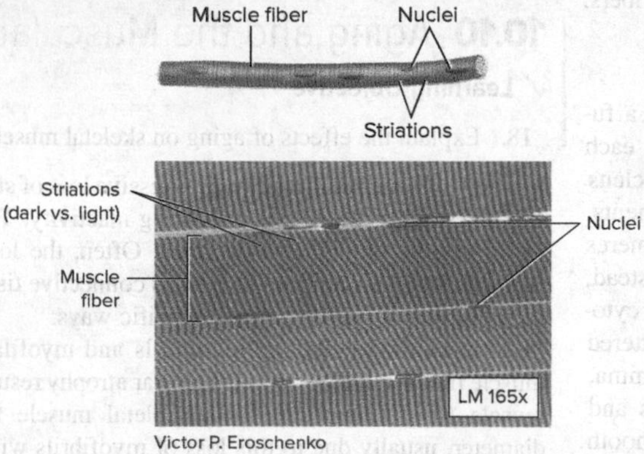	Attached to bones (usually via tendons) or to subcutaneous layer 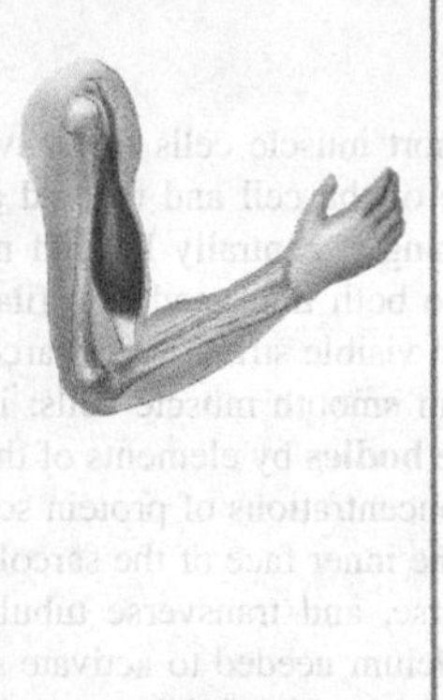	Length: Long (100 µm–30 cm) Diameter: Large (10–100 µm)	Autorhythmicity: No Contraction speed: Fast Nervous system control: Voluntary
Cardiac Muscle	Short, branched cell with 1 or 2 centrally located nuclei; intercalated discs between fibers; striated 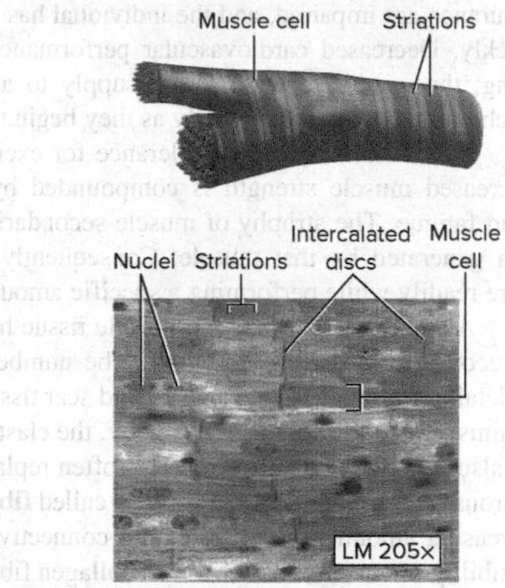	Only in heart wall 	Length: Short (50–100 µm) Diameter: Large (about 15 µm diameter)	Autorhythmicity: Yes Contraction speed: Moderate Nervous system control: Involuntary
Smooth Muscle	Spindle-shaped cell; a single centrally located nucleus; no striations 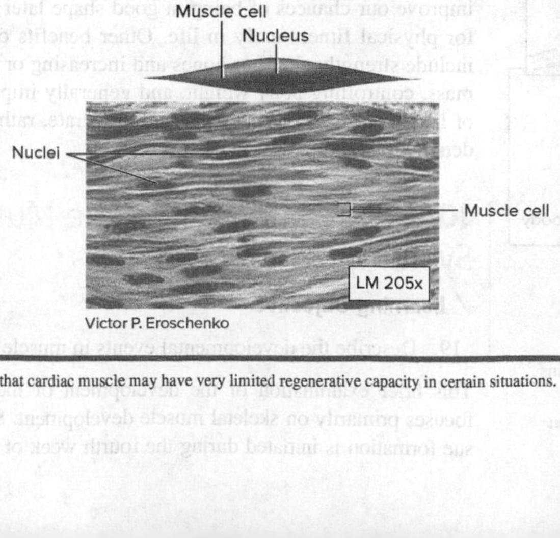	Found in walls of hollow organs (e.g., intestines, blood vessels); and in iris and ciliary body of eye 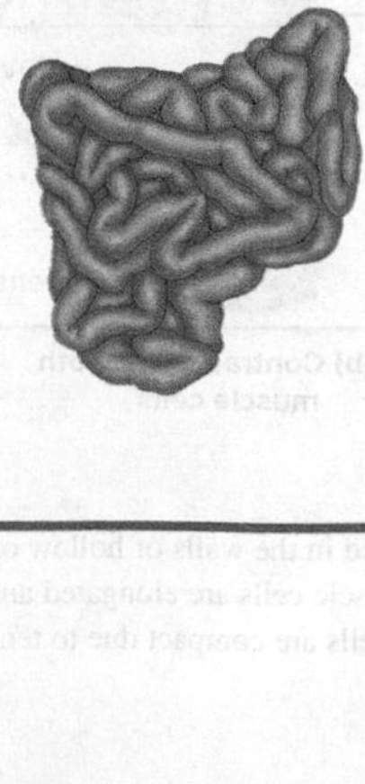	Length: Short (50–200 µm) Diameter: Small (5–10 µm)	Autorhythmicity: In some types only Contraction speed: Slow Nervous system control: Involuntary

[1] Some research indicates that cardiac muscle may have very limited regenerative capacity in certain situations.

	Connective Tissue Components	Calcium Source/ Junctions Between Cells/Neuromuscular Junctions	Presence of Myofibrils	Regeneration Capacity	Sarcomere Protein Organization	Sarcoplasmic Reticulum/Transverse Tubules
	Three layers: Epimysium, perimysium, endomysium 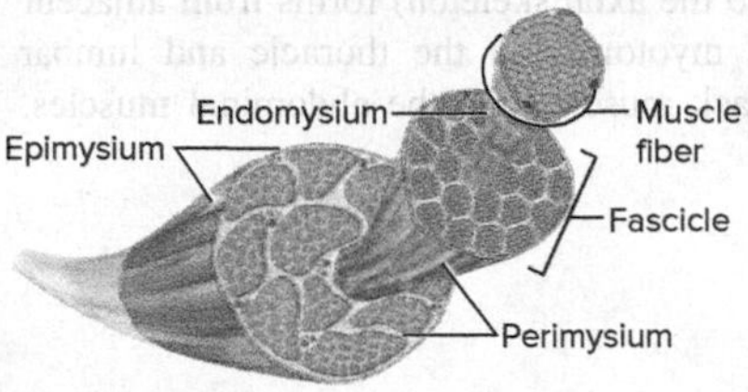	Calcium source: Sarcoplasmic reticulum Junctions between fibers: No junctions Neuromuscular junctions: Individual, one per fiber	Extensive	Very limited; requires satellite cells	Highly organized; revealed by striations	Sarcoplasmic reticulum: Abundant Transverse tubules: Extensive; aligned with A- and I-band junctions
	One layer of endomysium only 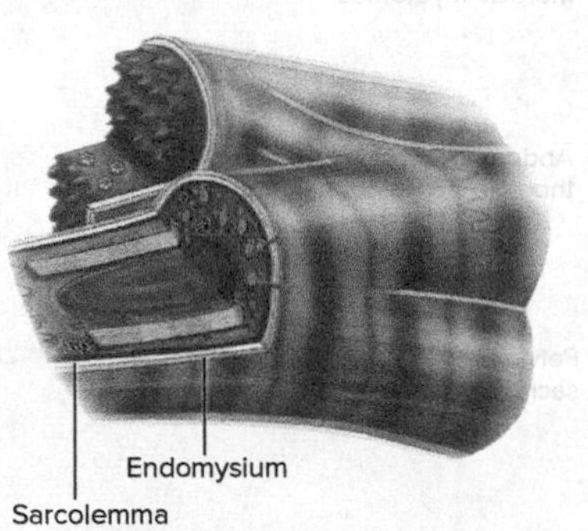	Calcium source: Sarcoplasmic reticulum and interstitial fluid Junctions between cells: Intercalated discs contain gap junctions and desmosomes Neuromuscular junctions: None (cardiac conduction system is responsible for transmitting nerve impulses throughout the muscle)	Extensive, but of irregular thickness	Very limited or none[1]	Highly organized; revealed by striations	Sarcoplasmic reticulum: Moderate Transverse tubules: Extensive; aligned with Z disc
	One layer of endomysium only 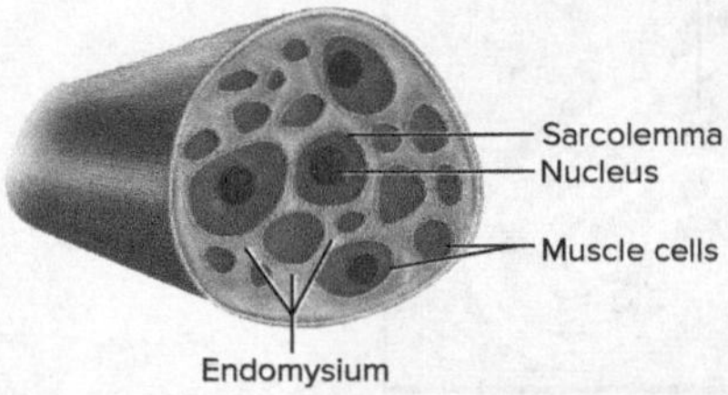	Calcium source: Sarcoplasmic reticulum and interstitial fluid Junctions between cells: Gap junctions in some types only Neuromuscular junctions: In some types only	None	Extensive	None	Sarcoplasmic reticulum: Almost none Transverse tubules: None

blocks of paraxial mesoderm that form structures called **somites** (sō′mīt) (see section 3.4d). The first somites appear in the cranial portion of the embryo at about day 20; new somites are formed caudally at regular intervals until the forty-fourth pair of somites appears on about day 30.

Cells within a somite differentiate into three distinct regions: (1) The **sclerotome** (sklē′rō-tōm; *skleros* = hard, *tome* = a cutting) separates from the rest of the somite and gives rise to the vertebral skeleton. (2) The **dermatome** (der′mă-tōm; *derma* = skin) forms the connective tissue of the skin. (3) The **myotome** (mī′ō-tōm) gives rise to the skeletal muscles. Myoblasts within the myotome begin rapid mitotic division (see figure 10.4). The number of cells continues to increase as myoblasts migrate and fuse into multinucleated **myotubules.** At about 9 weeks, primitive myofilaments extend through the myotubules. Growth in length continues via the addition of more myoblasts.

The myotomes give rise to virtually all skeletal muscles, except some muscles of the head (**figure 10.18**). The axial musculature (muscles that attach to the axial skeleton) forms from adjacent myotomes. For example, myotomes in the thoracic and lumbar regions form the lower back muscles and the abdominal muscles.

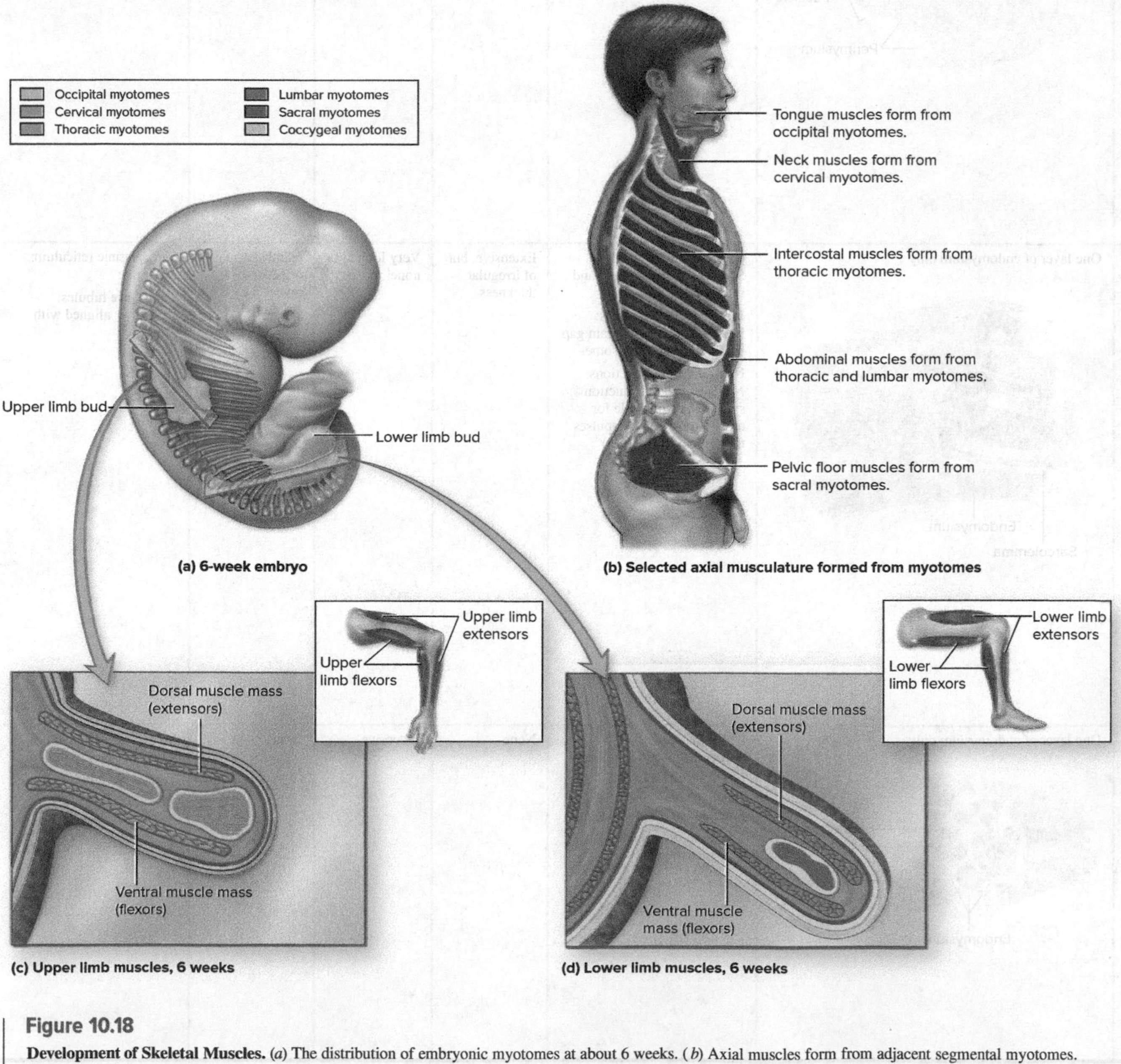
Occipital myotomes
Cervical myotomes
Thoracic myotomes
Lumbar myotomes
Sacral myotomes
Coccygeal myotomes
Upper limb bud
Lower limb bud
(a) 6-week embryo
Tongue muscles form from occipital myotomes.
Neck muscles form from cervical myotomes.
Intercostal muscles form from thoracic myotomes.
Abdominal muscles form from thoracic and lumbar myotomes.
Pelvic floor muscles form from sacral myotomes.
(b) Selected axial musculature formed from myotomes
Upper limb extensors
Upper limb flexors
Dorsal muscle mass (extensors)
Ventral muscle mass (flexors)
(c) Upper limb muscles, 6 weeks
Lower limb extensors
Lower limb flexors
Dorsal muscle mass (extensors)
Ventral muscle mass (flexors)
(d) Lower limb muscles, 6 weeks

Figure 10.18

Development of Skeletal Muscles. *(a)* The distribution of embryonic myotomes at about 6 weeks. *(b)* Axial muscles form from adjacent segmental myotomes. *(c)* Upper limb musculature forms from cervical and thoracic myotomes that migrate into the upper limb beginning in the fifth week of development. The myotomes split into two separate groups that later form the flexors and the extensors of the upper limb. *(d)* Lower limb musculature forms from lumbar and sacral myotomes that migrate into the lower limb beginning in the fifth week of development. The myotomes split into two separate groups that will form the flexors and extensors of the lower limb.

Clinical View 10.6

Neuromuscular Diseases

Disease or damage affecting somatic motor neurons, neuromuscular junctions, or muscle fibers often results in abnormal muscle functions, collectively termed **neuromuscular disease.** Some of these noninfectious disorders are fibromyalgia, muscular dystrophy, myasthenia gravis, and myofascial pain syndrome.

Fibromyalgia (fī′brō-mī-al′jē-ă; *algos* = pain) presents as a syndrome of chronic severe pain involving both the muscles and the skeleton, and accompanied by fatigue, morning stiffness, and sometimes psychological depression. No single cause has been determined, but a number of contributing factors have been identified, including alterations in brain neurotransmitters, stress and anxiety, sleep disturbances, and possibly endocrine abnormalities. Although the pain associated with this condition is body-wide, it most commonly affects the neck or lower back. About 1–2% of the population has this syndrome, and women are affected more frequently than men. Treatment consists of a combination of medication and self-care. Nonsteroidal anti-inflammatory medications (aspirin, ibuprofen, etc.) are useful for relieving pain and stiffness. Antidepressants and antiseizure medications are also known to help some people with this condition.

Muscular dystrophy (dis′trō-fē) is a collective term for several hereditary diseases in which the skeletal muscles degenerate, lose strength, and are gradually replaced by adipose and fibrous connective tissue. In a vicious cycle, the new connective tissues impede blood circulation, which further accelerates muscle degeneration.

Duchenne muscular dystrophy (DMD) is the most common form of muscular dystrophy. It results from the expression of a sex-linked recessive allele. DMD is almost exclusively a disease of males and occurs in about 1 in 3500 live births. For these individuals, muscular difficulties become apparent in early childhood. Walking is a problem; the child falls frequently and has difficulty standing up again. The hips are affected first, followed by the lower limbs, and eventually the abdominal and spinal muscles. Muscular atrophy causes shortening of the muscles, which results in postural abnormalities such as scoliosis (lateral curvature of the spine). DMD is an incurable disease, with patients confined to a wheelchair by adolescence. The DMD patient rarely lives beyond the age of 30, and death typically results from respiratory or heart complications.

Advances in gene therapy research may result in a treatment for DMD. Using an altered virus that carries the gene for **dystrophin,** an essential protein for muscle function that is missing in DMD patients, investigators have successfully stimulated the manufacture of the protein in laboratory mice that lack this gene. Although these early results provide great hope for treatment of humans, they are also cause for concern. Scientists recognize that the ability to deliver genes to every muscle fiber in the body through a single injection may also provide a means for performance enhancement in athletes.

Myasthenia gravis (mī′as-thē′nē-ă; *astheneia* = weakness) **(MG)** is an autoimmune disease that affects the neuromuscular junctions of skeletal muscle, and ultimately affects skeletal muscle function. The disease occurs in about 1 in 10,000 people, primarily women between 20 and 40 years of age. Antibodies attack the neuromuscular junctions, binding ACh receptors together into clusters. The abnormally clustered ACh receptors are removed from the muscle fiber sacrolemma by endocytosis, thus significantly diminishing the number of receptors on the muscle fiber. The resulting decreased ability to stimulate the muscle causes rapid fatigue and muscle weakness. Eye and facial muscles are often attacked first, resulting in double vision and drooping eyelids. These symptoms are usually followed by swallowing problems, limb weakness, and overall low physical stamina.

Some patients with MG have a normal life span, whereas others die quickly from paralysis of the respiratory muscles. Treatment often involves the use of cholinesterase inhibitors, immunosuppressive drugs, and thymectomy (removal of the thymus gland, which is abnormal in these patients). The cholinesterase inhibitors prevent ACh destruction by acetylcholinesterase, allowing for prolonged stimulation of the remaining ACh receptors in the muscle fiber membrane. Immunosuppressive drugs decrease the production of antibodies directed against the ACh receptors and thereby slow the attack on the neuromuscular junction.

Myofascial (mī′ō-fash′ē-ăl) **pain syndrome (MPS)** is a common disorder usually associated with excessive use of the postural muscles. Pain results when bands of muscle fibers tighten and then twitch after the overlying skin is stimulated. This "trigger point" stimulation of the pain is a widely recognized feature of MPS. Occasionally, the trigger points can produce autonomic nervous system changes, resulting in localized flushing of the skin, sweating, and even "goose bumps." Unlike some other neuromuscular disorders, MPS does not cause fatigue and morning stiffness. As many as 50% of people, between the ages of 30 and 60, may be affected by this disease. Massages, muscle stretching, and nonsteroidal anti-inflammatory drugs are effective in treating this condition.

Child with Duchenne muscular dystrophy.
Courtesy of Muscular Dystrophy Association (www.mda.org)

Some cervical myotomes form neck muscles, where the cervical vertebrae occur.

During the fifth week of development, portions of some of the somites migrate into the developing upper and lower limbs. The upper limb musculature forms from some cervical and thoracic myotomes. The lower limb musculature forms from some lumbar and sacral myotomes that migrate into the developing limb. As these myotomes migrate, the myotome group is subdivided into a **ventral muscle mass** (so named because this mass of muscles is close to the ventral, or belly, side of the embryo) and a **dorsal muscle mass** (located closer to the dorsal side of the embryo). The ventral muscle mass will form the future flexors of that limb. The biceps brachii muscle of the anterior arm is a ventral mass muscle, because this muscle flexes the elbow joint. The dorsal muscle mass will form the future extensors of that limb. The triceps brachii muscle of the posterior arm is a dorsal mass muscle, and this muscle extends the elbow joint. These muscle mass groups differentiate into individual skeletal muscles during the embryonic period.

Clinical Terms

"charley horse" Localized pain or muscle stiffness following the contusion of a muscle.

myoma (mī-ō′mă) Benign tumor of muscular tissue.

spasm (spazm) Sudden, involuntary contraction of one or more muscles.

strain To injure or tear a muscle as a result of either overuse or improper use.

tic Repeated contraction of certain muscles, resulting in stereotyped, individualized actions that can be voluntarily suppressed for only brief periods (e.g., clearing the throat, pursing the lips, or excessive blinking).

Chapter Summary

	■ Muscle tissue moves materials within and throughout the body. ■ The types of muscle tissue are skeletal muscle, cardiac muscle, and smooth muscle.
10.1 Properties of Muscle Tissue	■ Muscles exhibit excitability, contractility, elasticity, and extensibility.
10.2 Characteristics of Skeletal Muscle Tissue	■ Individual skeletal muscles vary in shape and are striated. **10.2a Functions of Skeletal Muscle Tissue** ■ Skeletal muscles produce body movement, maintain posture and body temperature, store and move materials, and provide support. **10.2b Gross Anatomy of Skeletal Muscle** ■ Skeletal muscles are ensheathed by three connective tissue layers: an inner endomysium, a middle perimysium, and an outer epimysium. ■ Tendons or aponeuroses attach muscle ends to other structures. **10.2c Microscopic Anatomy of Skeletal Muscle** ■ Muscle fibers are cylindrical and multinucleated, and have a plasma membrane (sarcolemma) that surrounds the cytoplasm (sarcoplasm). ■ T-tubules extend as sarcolemma invaginations into the sarcoplasm and conduct impulses for muscle contraction. ■ The sarcoplasmic reticulum (SR) is a specialized internal membrane system that stores calcium ions needed for muscle contraction. The calcium ions are housed in the terminal cisternae of the SR. A T-tubule together with the terminal cisternae at both its sides is called a triad. ■ Muscle fibers are filled with myofibrils that house thin and thick protein filaments called myofilaments. ■ Thin filaments are composed of actin (a contractile protein) and two regulatory proteins (tropomyosin and troponin). Thick filaments are made of myosin (a contractile protein). ■ Striations in a muscle fiber are alternating dark bands (A bands) and light bands (I bands) that result from thin and thick filament differences. The H zone is a light region in the middle of the A band. The Z disc is a protein attachment site for filaments in the middle of the I band; it appears as a thin, dark line. ■ The functional contractile unit of a muscle fiber is a sarcomere that extends between adjacent Z discs. Sarcomeres stack in each myofibril. ■ The M line is a thin transverse protein meshwork structure in the center of the H zone of a relaxed fiber.
10.3 Contraction of Skeletal Muscle Fibers	**10.3a The Sliding Filament Theory** ■ Thick and thin filaments slide past each other during a muscle contraction. A sarcomere shortens, but filament length does not change. **10.3b Neuromuscular Junctions** ■ Nerve impulses initiate impulses in muscle fibers. ■ The neuromuscular junction is the structure where axons of neurons transmit nerve impulses to muscle fibers.

10.3c Physiology of Muscle Contraction

- Nerve impulses in axons cause muscle impulses in the sarcolemma; these spread into T-tubules, causing calcium ions to be released from the terminal cisternae.
- Calcium ions bind troponin, resulting in tropomyosin movement away from the surface of actin.
- Myosin heads attach to actin (form crossbridges), pivot toward the center of the sarcomere, detach from actin, and recock to their original position.

10.3d Muscle Contraction: A Summary

- (1) A muscle impulse is generated; (2) calcium ions are released into the sarcoplasm; (3) calcium ions bind to troponin, causing tropomyosin to move off actin; (4) myosin heads attach, pivot, detach, and return, causing protein filaments to slide by each other; (5) the cycle continues as long as calcium ions bind to troponin. Rest occurs when muscle impulses cease.

10.3e Motor Units

- A motor unit is composed of a motor neuron and the muscle fibers it controls.
- Isometric contractions result in no muscle shortening; isotonic contractions result in muscle shortening.

10.4 Types of Skeletal Muscle Fibers

- The three muscle fiber types are slow oxidative, fast oxidative, and fast glycolic.

10.4a Distribution of Slow Oxidative, Fast Oxidative, and Fast Glycolytic Fibers

- Muscle function determines the presence of fiber types. Postural muscles have more slow oxidative fibers, whereas the muscles that move the eyes have more fast glycolic fibers.

10.5 Skeletal Muscle Fiber Organization

- Muscles are classified according to fiber arrangements.

10.5a Circular Muscles

- Circular muscles are composed of concentric fascicles, and occur at entrances and exits from the body or in internal passageways.

10.5b Parallel Muscles

- Parallel muscle fascicles are oriented parallel to the muscle long axes.

10.5c Convergent Muscles

- Convergent muscles are widespread fascicles joined at a single attachment site.

10.5d Pennate Muscles

- Pennate muscles are composed of one or more tendons extending through the muscle. Fascicles are oblique to the tendons. Subtypes are unipennate, bipennate, and multipennate.

10.6 Exercise and Skeletal Muscle

- Exercise and proper diet are required to increase skeletal muscle size.

10.6a Muscle Hypertrophy

- Muscular hypertrophy is an increase in muscle fiber size. Repetitive stimulation causes more myofibrils to develop.

10.6b Muscle Atrophy

- Muscles become flaccid and atrophied if stimulation is inadequate.

10.7 Levers and Joint Biomechanics

- Levers rotate around a fixed point to affect speed of movement, distance moved, direction of force, and strength of force.
- In the body, the joint acts as the fulcrum, the resistance is the weight of the body part, and the effort is the action of the muscle on the bone.

10.7a Classes of Levers

- Three classes of levers are defined by the arrangement of the fulcrum, resistance point, and effort arm. Third-class levers are the most common type of lever in the body.

10.7b Actions of Skeletal Muscles

- An agonist is a muscle that contracts to produce a particular movement. The antagonist opposes the agonist. The synergist assists the agonist.

10.8 The Naming of Skeletal Muscles

- Muscle names indicate muscle action, body regions, attachment sites, orientation, shape, size, heads, and tendon attachments.

10.9 Characteristics of Cardiac and Smooth Muscle

10.9a Cardiac Muscle

- Cardiac muscle is involuntary. Cardiac muscle cells occur in the wall of the heart and are autorhythmic. Intercalated discs are junctions between cardiac muscle cells.

10.9b Smooth Muscle

- Smooth muscle is involuntary; it has short, fusiform, nonstriated cells.

10.10 Aging and the Muscular System

- The aging process decreases the elasticity and diameter of muscle fibers, and reduces their ability to recover from disease or injury. Exercise tolerance decreases as the body ages.

10.11 Development of the Muscular System

- The development of skeletal muscle tissue is initiated during the fourth week of development. Blocks of mesoderm called somites form on either side of the neural tube. The myotome portion of the somites forms most skeletal muscle in the body.

Challenge Yourself

Actively write or type your answers in a separate document to reinforce your learning, before checking your answers.

Multiple Choice

Select the best answer from the four choices provided.

1. Which unit of muscle structure is composed of bundles of myofibrils, enclosed within a sarcolemma, and surrounded by a connective tissue covering called endomysium?
   a. myofibril
   b. fascicle
   c. myofilament
   d. muscle fiber
2. What happens to the myofibrils when a muscle contracts?
   a. They lengthen.
   b. They remain unchanged.
   c. They increase in diameter.
   d. They shorten.
3. Which of the following answers describes the arrangement of the fascicles in a convergent muscle?
   a. The fascicles are oblique to the tendon of the muscle.
   b. The fascicles are concentrically arranged.
   c. The fascicles run parallel to the long axis of the muscle.
   d. The fascicles are widespread over a broad area and joined at a common attachment site.
4. Which two properties of muscle cells are described by the the ability of the muscle cell to respond to a stimulus and return to its original length?
   a. conductivity and elasticity
   b. excitability and elasticity
   c. contractility and extensibility
   d. excitability and contractility
5. Which of the following groups of structures forms a triad in a muscle fiber?
   a. myosin, actin, and myofibrils
   b. one A band, one H zone, and one I band
   c. one transverse tubule and two terminal cisternae
   d. myofilaments, myofibrils, and sarcomeres
6. Which portion of a somite gives rise to skeletal muscle?
   a. dermatome
   b. scleroblast
   c. myotome
   d. satellite cell
7. What is a synaptic knob?
   a. A receptor for neurotransmitter in the neuromuscular junction
   b. A membrane sac holding the neurotransmitter
   c. The expanded tip of an axon at the neuromuscular junction
   d. The space that separates the neuron from the muscle fiber
8. Name the bundle of dense regular connective tissue that attaches a skeletal muscle to bone.
   a. tendon
   b. ligament
   c. endomysium
   d. fascicle
9. When biceps brachii assists brachialis to flex the elbow joint, biceps brachii is which of the following?
   a. antagonist
   b. synergist
   c. prime mover
   d. fixator
10. Which of the following changes in skeletal muscles is associated with aging?
    a. Muscle fibers increase in diameter.
    b. Muscles become more elastic.
    c. Muscle fibers increase their glycogen reserves.
    d. The number of satellite cells in muscle decreases.

Content Review

1. Compare the roles of the three concentric layers of connective tissue wrappings in the organization of skeletal muscle.
2. Describe the structure of tendons and aponeuroses, and discuss their purpose in the body.
3. Describe the structural relationships among the following in a resting muscle fiber: A band, H zone, M line.
4. Describe how flexion of the elbow joint is a third-class lever by identifying the fulcrum, the effort, and the resistance.
5. Describe in your own words the events that occur during skeletal muscle contraction.
6. Explain why the ratio of motor neurons to muscle fibers is greater in muscles that control eye movement than in postural muscles of the leg.
7. Briefly describe the differences between muscle atrophy and muscle hypertrophy. What might cause each condition?
8. Explain why athletes who excel at short sprints probably have fewer slow oxidative fibers in their leg muscles.
9. Explain what the following names tell us about muscles: longus, extensor, triceps, rectus, superficialis.
10. Describe the structure of intercalated discs in cardiac muscle cells, and briefly discuss their functions.

Developing Critical Reasoning

1. Paul broke his left radius playing football, and the doctor placed his forearm in a cast for 6 weeks. When the cast was removed, his left forearm was noticeably thinner and less well developed than his right forearm. How can you explain the noticeable decrease in mass in the left forearm?
2. Tessa and her laboratory partners were given the following assignment: Explain how the structure of myofilaments is related to their function, and then describe how the sliding filament theory allows for the shortening of a muscle fiber. If they asked for your help, how would you answer these questions?
3. Savannah and her 59-year-old grandfather spent a long day gardening. Pulling weeds, raking, and planting left both of them a bit sore. However, Savannah's grandfather was more stiff and sore, and it took him much longer to recover than Savannah. Why did Savannah and her grandfather react to this exertion differently?

Answers to "What Do You Think?"

1. If a muscle has multiple motor units, you can control the force and precision of the muscle contraction. The greater the number of motor units activated, the more forceful the contraction, because more muscle fibers are contracting. Likewise, a muscle can perform more precise movements if the motor units are controlling only a few muscle fibers.
2. The "white meat" of turkey contains large-diameter, fast glycolytic/muscle fibers that, in life, would have low resistance to fatigue. In contrast, the "dark meat" contains small-diameter, slow oxidative muscle fibers that would have great resistance to fatigue.
3. The knee joint is a third-class lever, because the fulcrum (bony knee joint) and the resistance (movement of the leg) are at either end, and the effort is applied by either the patellar ligament or hamstrings located between the two.

Design Element: Pencil Icon: Slavojub Pantelic/Shutterstock

MUSCULAR SYSTEM

11 Axial Muscles

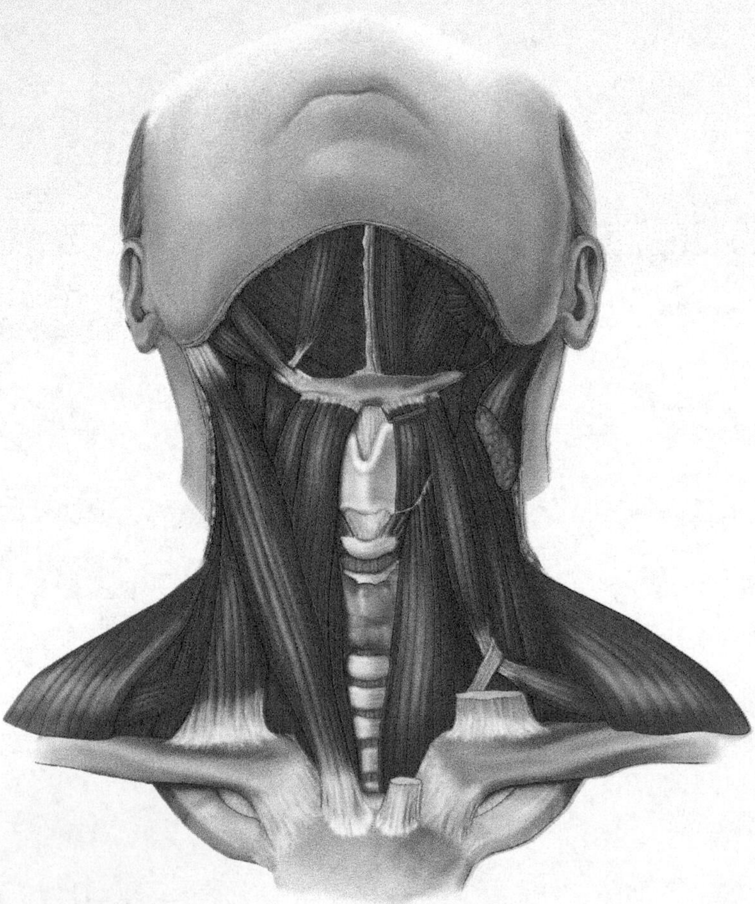

Outline

Anatomy & Physiology Revealed 4.0

MODULE 6: MUSCULAR SYSTEM

The artificial partitioning of the skeletal system into axial and appendicular divisions provides a useful guideline for subdividing the muscular system as well. **Axial muscles** have both their attachments on parts of the axial skeleton. Axial muscles support and move the head and spinal column, function in nonverbal communication by affecting facial features, move the mandible during chewing, assist in food processing and swallowing, aid breathing, and support and protect the abdominal and pelvic organs. The axial muscles are not responsible for stabilizing or moving the pectoral or pelvic girdles or their attached limbs; those are actions of the appendicular muscles (see chapter 12). Some muscles of both divisions are shown in **figure 11.1**.

Learning Strategy 11.1

The following suggestions may help you learn the muscles, whether axial or appendicular:

- Muscles often may be organized into groups based upon their location or action. Learning the muscles in groups is easiest.
- When studying a particular muscle, try to palpate it on yourself. Contract the muscle to sense its action and identify its regional location.
- Repeat the name of a muscle aloud to become familiar with its name. It is easier to remember and spell terms that you can pronounce.
- Associate visual images from models, cadavers, a photographic atlas, or dissected animals with muscle names. Connecting a muscle name with direct observation will help you remember it.
- Locate the attachments of muscles on an articulated skeleton. This helps you visualize the locations of muscles and understand how they produce particular actions.
- Learn the derivation of each muscle name because it usually describes the muscle's action, location, number of heads, orientation of muscle fibers, shape, or size.

Refer to figure 10.14 for examples of how some muscles are named.

The axial muscles are organized into five groups based upon their location:

- Muscles of the head and neck
- Muscles of the vertebral column
- Muscles of respiration
- Muscles of the abdominal wall
- Muscles of the pelvic floor

The discussion in this chapter has been organized according to these specific groups. For each group, tables provide information about muscle action, attachments, and innervation. (Note: The word *innervation* refers to the nerve(s) that supplies a muscle and stimulates it to contract. For further information about the nerves listed in the tables, see sections 15.8 and 16.4.)

Recall from section 10.2b about skeletal muscle attachments that we (along with many anatomists and clinicians) are replacing the terms *origin* and *insertion* with the terms *superior attachment* and *inferior attachment* (for most axial muscles), and *proximal attachment* and *distal attachment* for appendicular muscles. The reasons for this change are that the traditional origins and insertions are not always easily determined by either movement or position. In contrast, attachment locations are easier to identify and better describe the placement of the muscle. In this chapter, we primarily will use the terms *superior* and *inferior attachments*. In those exceptions where there is no clearly defined superior or inferior aspect of a muscle, slightly alternative terminology will be used and noted in the appropriate tables. The superior attachment usually is the more moveable attachment of the muscle, but there are many exceptions to this rule (e.g., the inferior attachment of the masseter muscle is the more moveable part of the muscle).

11.1 Muscles of the Head and Neck

✓ Learning Objectives

1. Identify and describe the major muscles involved in facial expression.
2. List the extrinsic muscles of the eye, and describe how each affects eye movement.
3. Name the muscles of mastication, and explain how each affects mandibular movement.
4. Describe the movements of the tongue, and compare its extrinsic and intrinsic muscles.
5. Identify and describe the muscles of the pharynx, and explain their actions during swallowing.
6. Explain the organization and distribution of the suprahyoid and infrahyoid muscles.
7. Identify and describe the muscles involved in the major movements of the head and neck.

The muscles of the head and neck are separated into several specific groups, based upon their location or general actions. Almost all of these muscles (except for a few muscles of the anterior neck) originate on either the skull or the hyoid bone.

11.1a Muscles of Facial Expression

The muscles of facial expression arise from the subcutaneous layer (deep to the skin) or on the skull bones (**figure 11.2**). These muscles insert on the subcutaneous layer deep to the skin, so when they contract, they contort the skin, causing it to move. All but one of these muscles are innervated by the seventh cranial nerve (CN VII), the facial nerve (see section 15.8).

The **epicranius** is composed of the **occipitofrontalis** muscle and a broad **epicranial aponeurosis,** also called the *galea aponeurotica*. The **frontal belly** of the occipitofrontalis is superficial to the frontal bone on the forehead. When this muscle contracts, it raises the eyebrows and wrinkles the skin of the forehead. The **occipital belly** of the occipitofrontalis covers the posterior side of the head. When this muscle contracts, it retracts the scalp slightly. Deep to the frontal belly is the **corrugator supercilii.** This muscle draws the eyebrows together and creates vertical wrinkle lines above the nose. The **orbicularis oculi** consists of circular muscle fibers that surround the orbit. When this muscle contracts, the eyelid closes, as when you wink, blink, or squint. The **levator palpebrae superioris** elevates the upper eyelid when you open your eyes. **APR**

Several muscles of facial expression are associated with the nose. The **nasalis** elevates the corners of the nostrils. When you "flare your nostrils," you are using the nasalis muscles. If you wrinkle your nose in distaste after smelling a foul odor, you have used your **procerus** muscle. This muscle is continuous with the frontalis muscle, and it runs over the bridge of the nose, where it produces transverse wrinkles when it contracts.

The mouth is the most expressive part of the face, and not surprisingly the muscles in that area are very diverse. The **orbicularis oris** consists of muscle fibers that encircle the opening of the mouth. When this muscle contracts, you close your mouth. When you "pucker up for a kiss," you are using this muscle. The **depressor labii inferioris** does what its name suggests—it pulls the lower lip inferiorly. The **depressor anguli oris** is considered the "frown" muscle, because

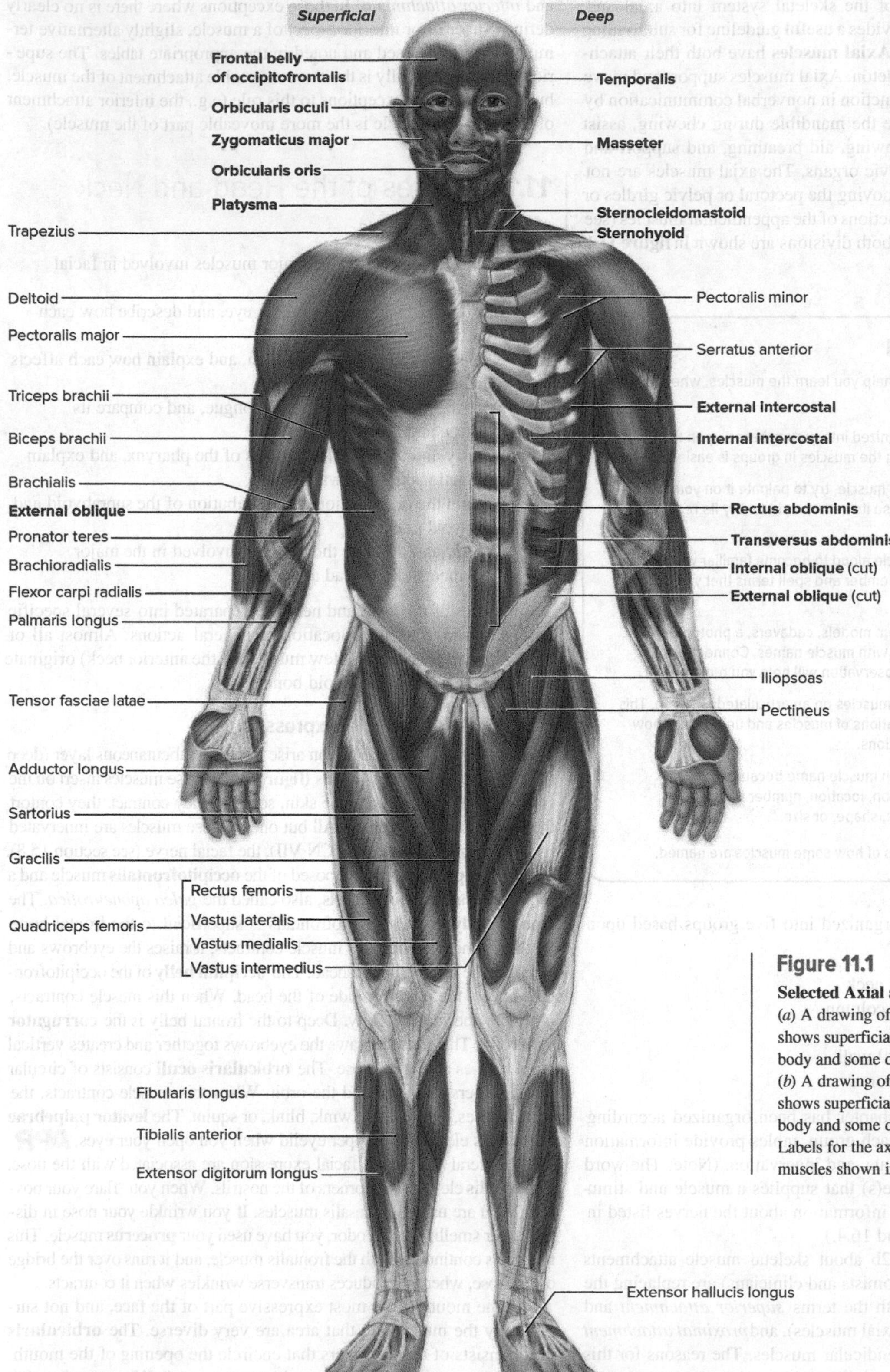

Superficial
Deep
Frontal belly of occipitofrontalis
Temporalis
Orbicularis oculi
Zygomaticus major
Masseter
Orbicularis oris
Platysma
Sternocleidomastoid
Sternohyoid
Trapezius
Deltoid
Pectoralis minor
Pectoralis major
Serratus anterior
Triceps brachii
External intercostal
Biceps brachii
Internal intercostal
Brachialis
External oblique
Rectus abdominis
Pronator teres
Transversus abdominis
Brachioradialis
Internal oblique (cut)
Flexor carpi radialis
External oblique (cut)
Palmaris longus
Iliopsoas
Tensor fasciae latae
Pectineus
Adductor longus
Sartorius
Gracilis
Rectus femoris
Vastus lateralis
Quadriceps femoris
Vastus medialis
Vastus intermedius
Fibularis longus
Tibialis anterior
Extensor digitorum longus
Extensor hallucis longus
(a) Anterior view

Figure 11.1

Selected Axial and Appendicular Muscles. (*a*) A drawing of an anterior view of the body shows superficial muscles on the right side of the body and some deeper muscles on the left side. (*b*) A drawing of the posterior view of the body shows superficial muscles on the left side of the body and some deeper muscles on the right side. Labels for the axial muscles are in bold; not all muscles shown in the figure are identified. **APR**

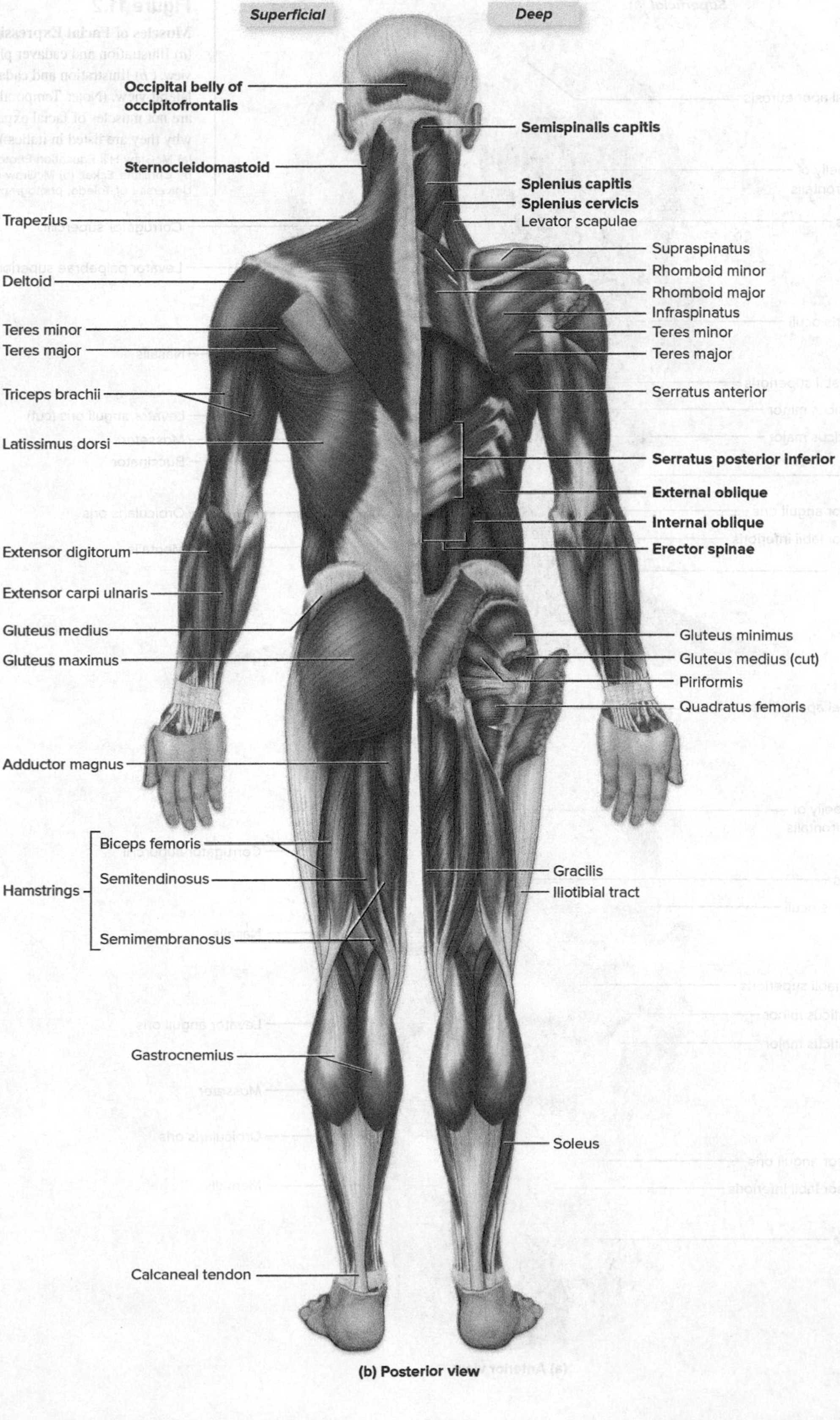
Superficial
Deep
Occipital belly of occipitofrontalis
Semispinalis capitis
Sternocleidomastoid
Splenius capitis
Splenius cervicis
Trapezius
Levator scapulae
Supraspinatus
Deltoid
Rhomboid minor
Rhomboid major
Infraspinatus
Teres minor
Teres minor
Teres major
Teres major
Triceps brachii
Serratus anterior
Latissimus dorsi
Serratus posterior inferior
External oblique
Internal oblique
Extensor digitorum
Erector spinae
Extensor carpi ulnaris
Gluteus medius
Gluteus minimus
Gluteus maximus
Gluteus medius (cut)
Piriformis
Quadratus femoris
Adductor magnus
Biceps femoris
Hamstrings
Semitendinosus
Gracilis
Iliotibial tract
Semimembranosus
Gastrocnemius
Soleus
Calcaneal tendon

(b) Posterior view

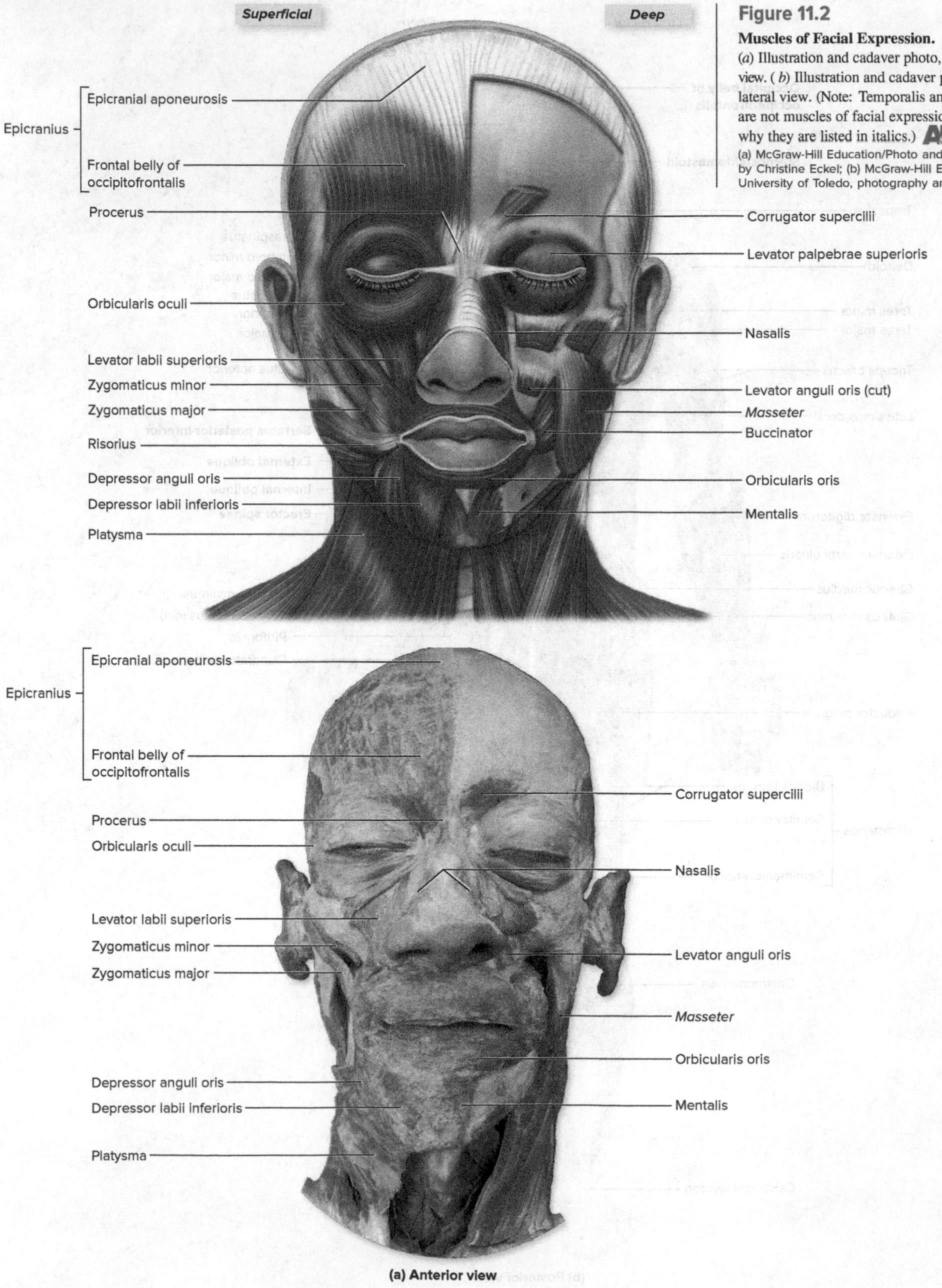
Superficial
Deep
Epicranius
Epicranial aponeurosis
Frontal belly of occipitofrontalis
Procerus
Corrugator supercilii
Levator palpebrae superioris
Orbicularis oculi
Nasalis
Levator labii superioris
Zygomaticus minor
Levator anguli oris (cut)
Zygomaticus major
Masseter
Buccinator
Risorius
Depressor anguli oris
Orbicularis oris
Depressor labii inferioris
Mentalis
Platysma
Epicranius
Epicranial aponeurosis
Frontal belly of occipitofrontalis
Corrugator supercilii
Procerus
Orbicularis oculi
Nasalis
Levator labii superioris
Zygomaticus minor
Levator anguli oris
Zygomaticus major
Masseter
Orbicularis oris
Depressor anguli oris
Depressor labii inferioris
Mentalis
Platysma
(a) Anterior view

Figure 11.2

Muscles of Facial Expression.
(*a*) Illustration and cadaver photo, anterior view. (*b*) Illustration and cadaver photo, lateral view. (Note: Temporalis and masseter are not muscles of facial expression, which is why they are listed in italics.) APR

(a) McGraw-Hill Education/Photo and Dissection by Christine Eckel; (b) McGraw-Hill Education/The University of Toledo, photography and dissection

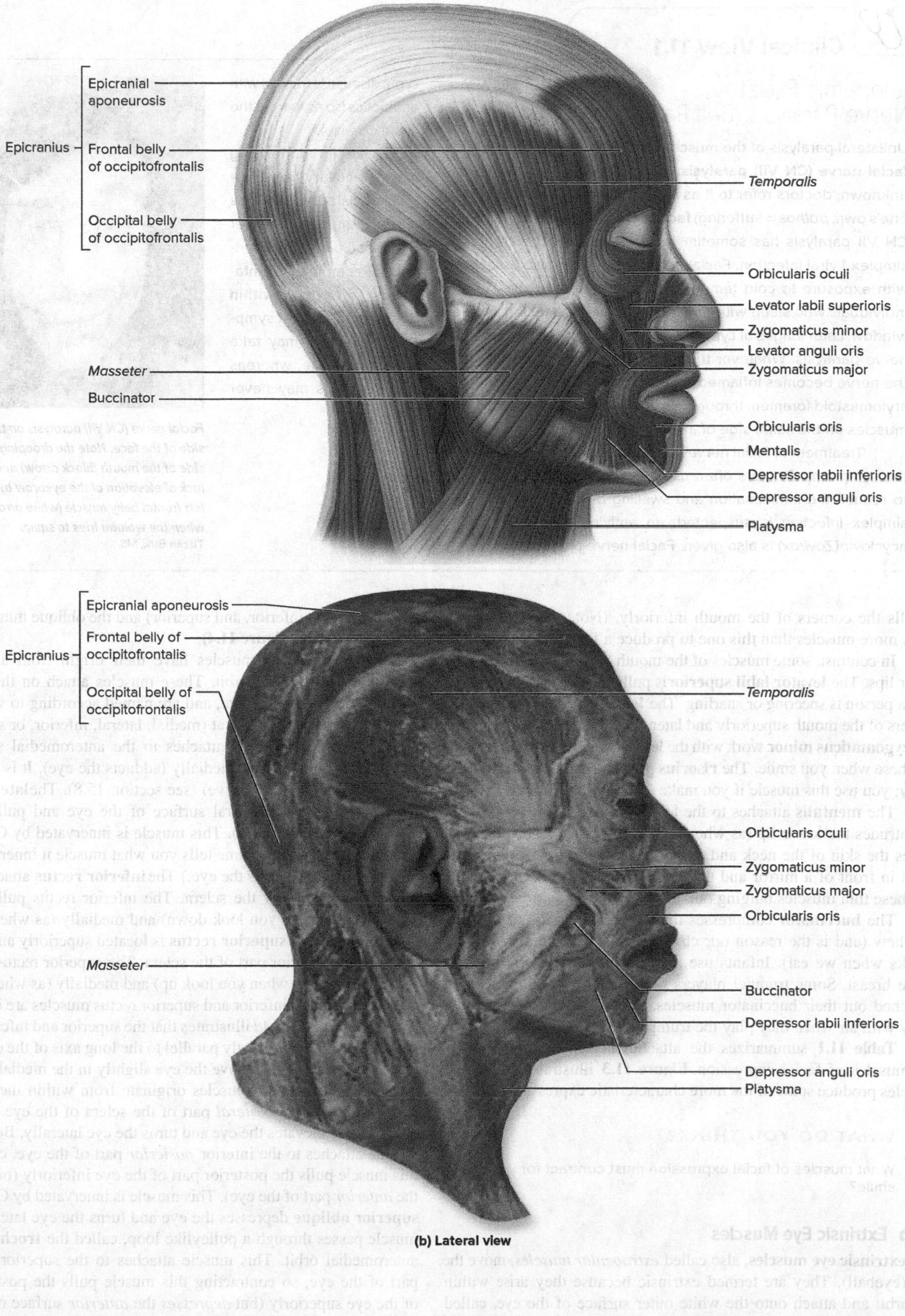
Epicranial aponeurosis
Epicranius
Frontal belly of occipitofrontalis
Occipital belly of occipitofrontalis
Temporalis
Orbicularis oculi
Levator labii superioris
Zygomaticus minor
Levator anguli oris
Zygomaticus major
Masseter
Buccinator
Orbicularis oris
Mentalis
Depressor labii inferioris
Depressor anguli oris
Platysma
Epicranial aponeurosis
Frontal belly of occipitofrontalis
Epicranius
Occipital belly of occipitofrontalis
Temporalis
Orbicularis oculi
Zygomaticus minor
Zygomaticus major
Orbicularis oris
Masseter
Buccinator
Depressor labii inferioris
Depressor anguli oris
Platysma

(b) Lateral view

Clinical View 11.1

Idiopathic Facial Nerve Paralysis (Bell Palsy)

Unilateral paralysis of the muscles of facial expression is termed **facial nerve (CN VII) paralysis.** If the cause of the condition is unknown, doctors refer to it as **idiopathic** (id′ē-ō-path′ik; *idios* = one's own; *pathos* = suffering) **facial nerve paralysis,** or *Bell palsy.* CN VII paralysis has sometimes been associated with herpes simplex 1 viral infection. Facial nerve paralysis is also associated with exposure to cold temperatures, and is commonly seen in individuals who sleep with one side of their head facing an open window. Later stages of Lyme disease may develop bilateral facial nerve paralysis. Whatever the underlying cause of the disease, the nerve becomes inflamed and compressed within the narrow stylomastoid foramen, through which the facial nerve travels. The muscles on the same side of the face are paralyzed as a result.

Treatment of facial nerve paralysis usually means alleviating the symptoms. Doctors often use prednisone (a type of steroid) to reduce the inflammation and swelling of the nerve. If herpes simplex infection is suspected, an antiviral medication called acyclovir (*Zovirax*) is also given. Facial nerve paralysis caused by Lyme disease is treated with antibiotics (so as to treat the Lyme disease).

Like its underlying cause, recovery from idiopathic facial nerve paralysis is equally mysterious. Over 50% of all patients experience a complete, spontaneous recovery within 30 days of their first symptoms. Recovery may take longer for some, whereas other patients may never recover.

Facial nerve (CN VII) paralysis on the left side of the face. Note the drooping left side of the mouth (black arrow) and the lack of elevation of the eyebrow by the left frontal belly muscle (white arrow) when the woman tries to smile.
Tirzah Birk, MS

it pulls the corners of the mouth inferiorly. (Note, however, that it takes more muscles than this one to produce a frown!) APR

In contrast, some muscles of the mouth elevate part or all of the upper lips. The **levator labii superioris** pulls the upper lip superiorly, as if a person is sneering or snarling. The **levator anguli oris** pulls the corners of the mouth superiorly and laterally. The **zygomaticus major** and **zygomaticus minor** work with the levator anguli oris muscles. You use these when you smile. The **risorius** pulls the corner of the lips laterally; you use this muscle if you make a closed-mouth smile. APR

The **mentalis** attaches to the lower lip, and when it contracts, it protrudes the lower lip (as when a person "pouts"). The **platysma** tenses the skin of the neck and pulls the lower lip inferiorly. If you stand in front of a mirror and tense the skin of your neck, you can see these thin muscles bulging out. APR

The **buccinator** compresses the cheek against the teeth when we chew (and is the reason our cheeks don't bulge like a squirrel's cheeks when we eat). Infants use the buccinator when they suckle at the breast. Some trumpet players (such as Dizzy Gillespie) have stretched out their buccinator muscles, allowing their cheeks to be puffy with air when they play the trumpet. APR

Table 11.1 summarizes the attachments and movements of the muscles of facial expression. **Figure 11.3** illustrates how these muscles produce some of the more characteristic expressions. APR

WHAT DO YOU THINK?

1. What muscles of facial expression must contract for you to smile?

11.1b Extrinsic Eye Muscles

The **extrinsic eye muscles,** also called *extraocular muscles,* move the eye (eyeball). They are termed extrinsic because they arise within the orbit and attach onto the white outer surface of the eye, called the sclera. There are six extrinsic eye muscles: the rectus muscles (medial, lateral, inferior, and superior) and the oblique muscles (inferior and superior) (**figure 11.4**).

The rectus eye muscles have their origin from a **common tendinous ring** in the orbit. These muscles attach on the *anterior* part of the sclera of the eye, and are named according to which side of the eye they are located at (medial, lateral, inferior, or superior).

The **medial rectus** attaches to the anteromedial surface of the eye and pulls the eye medially (adducts the eye). It is innervated by CN III (oculomotor nerve) (see section 15.8). The **lateral rectus** attaches to the anterolateral surface of the eye and pulls the eye laterally (abducts the eye). This muscle is innervated by CN VI (abducens). (This nerve's name tells you what muscle it innervates—the eye muscle that abducts the eye.) The **inferior rectus** attaches to the anteroinferior part of the sclera. The inferior rectus pulls the eye inferiorly (as when you look down) and medially (as when you look at your nose). The **superior rectus** is located superiorly and attaches to the anterosuperior part of the sclera. The superior rectus pulls the eye superiorly (as when you look up) and medially (as when you look at your nose). The inferior and superior rectus muscles are innervated by CN III. Figure 11.4*d* illustrates that the superior and inferior rectus muscles do not pull directly parallel to the long axis of the eye; that is why both muscles also move the eye slightly in the medial direction.

The oblique eye muscles originate from within the orbit and attach on the *posterolateral* part of the sclera of the eye. The **inferior oblique** elevates the eye and turns the eye laterally. Because this muscle attaches to the inferior *posterior* part of the eye, contracting this muscle pulls the posterior part of the eye inferiorly (but *elevates* the *anterior* part of the eye). This muscle is innervated by CN III. The **superior oblique** depresses the eye and turns the eye laterally. This muscle passes through a pulleylike loop, called the **trochlea,** in the anteromedial orbit. This muscle attaches to the superior *posterior* part of the eye, so contracting this muscle pulls the posterior part of the eye superiorly (but *depresses* the *anterior* surface of the eye). This muscle is innervated by CN IV (trochlear) (see section 15.8).

Table 11.1	Muscles of Facial Expression		
Region/Muscle	**Action(s)**	**Bony Attachment(s) (B)/Soft Tissue Attachment(s) (S)[1]**	**Innervation (see section 15.8)**
SCALP			
Epicranius (ep′i-kr ā′nē-ŭs) *epi* = over *cran* = skull		Composed of an epicranial aponeurosis and the occipitofrontalis muscle	
Frontal belly of occipitofrontalis (ok-sip′i-tō-frŏn-tā′lis) *front* = forehead	Moves scalp, eyebrows; wrinkles skin of forehead	B: Epicranial aponeurosis S: Skin and subcutaneous layer of forehead and eyebrows	CN VII (facial nerve)
Occipital belly of occipitofrontalis *occipito* = base of skull	Retracts scalp	B: Superior nuchal line S: Epicranial aponeurosis	CN VII (facial nerve)
NOSE			
Nasalis (nā′zā-lis) *nasus* = nose	Compresses bridge and depresses tip of nose; elevates corners of nostrils	B: Maxillae and alar cartilage of nose S: Dorsum of nose	CN VII (facial nerve)
Procerus (prō-sē′rŭs) *procerus* = long	Moves and wrinkles nose	B: Nasal bone and lateral nasal cartilage S: Aponeurosis at bridge of nose and skin of forehead	CN VII (facial nerve)
MOUTH			
Buccinator (buk′si-nā′tĕr) *bucco* = cheek	Compresses cheek; holds food between teeth during chewing ("trumpet-blowing" muscle)	B: Alveolar processes of mandible and maxillae S: Orbicularis oris	CN VII (facial nerve)
Depressor anguli oris (dē-pres′ŏr ang′gy ū-lī ŏr′ŭs) *depressor* = depresses *angul* = angle *or* = mouth	Draws corners of mouth inferiorly and laterally ("frown" muscle)	B: Body of mandible S: Skin at inferior corner (angle) of mouth	CN VII (facial nerve)
Depressor labii inferioris (lā′bē-ī in-fēr′ē-ōr-is) *labi* = lip *infer* = below	Draws lower lip inferiorly ("grimace" muscle)	B: Body of mandible lateral to midline S: Skin at inferior lip	CN VII (facial nerve)
Levator anguli oris (le-v ā′tŏr, le-v ā′tŏr) *leva* = raise	Draws corners of mouth superiorly and laterally ("smile" muscle)	B: Lateral maxilla S: Skin at superior corner of mouth	CN VII (facial nerve)
Levator labii superioris (sū-pēr′ē-ōr-is)	Opens lips; raises and furrows the upper lip ("Elvis" lip snarl)	B: Zygomatic bone; maxilla S: Skin and muscle of superior lip	CN VII (facial nerve)
Mentalis (men-tā′lis) *ment* = chin	Protrudes lower lip ("pout"); wrinkles chin	B: Central mandible S: Skin of chin	CN VII (facial nerve)
Orbicularis oris (ōr-bik′yū-lā′ris ōr′is) *orb* = circular *or* = mouth	Compresses and purses lips ("kiss" muscle)	B: Maxilla and mandible; blend with fibers from other facial muscles S: Encircling mouth; skin and muscles at angles to mouth	CN VII (facial nerve)
Risorius (rē-sōr′ē-ŭs) *risor* = laughter	Retracts corners of mouth, as in a closed-mouth smile	B: Deep fascia associated with masseter muscle S: Skin at angle of mouth	CN VII (facial nerve)
Zygomaticus major (zī′gō-mat′i-kŭs) *zygomatic* = cheekbone *major* = greater	Elevates corner of the mouth ("smile" muscle)	B: Zygomatic bone S: Skin at superolateral edge of mouth	CN VII (facial nerve)
Zygomaticus minor *minor* = lesser	Elevates corner of the mouth ("smile" muscle)	B: Zygomatic bone S: Skin of superior lip	CN VII (facial nerve)

(continued on next page)

Table 11.1	Muscles of Facial Expression *(continued)*		
Region/Muscle	**Action(s)**	**Bony Attachment(s) (B)/Soft Tissue Attachment(s) (S)[1]**	**Innervation (see section 15.8)**
EYE			
Corrugator supercilii (kŏr′ū-gā-ter sū′pĕr-sil′ ē-ī) *corrugo* = to wrinkle *cilium* = eyelid	Pulls eyebrows inferiorly and medially; creates vertical wrinkles above nose	B: Medial end of superciliary arch S: Skin superior to supraorbital margin and superciliary arch	CN VII (facial nerve)
Levator palpebrae superioris (see figure 19.9) (pal-p ē′brē) *levo* = to lift *palpebra* = eyelid	Elevates superior eyelid	B: Lesser wing of sphenoid bone S: Superior tarsal plate and skin of superior eyelid	CN III (oculomotor nerve)
Orbicularis oculi (ok′y ū-lī) *orb* = circular *ocul* = eye	Closes eye; produces winking, blinking, squinting ("squint" muscle)	B: Medial wall or margin of bony orbit S: Skin surrounding eyelids	CN VII (facial nerve)
NECK			
Platysma (plă-tiz′m ă) *platy* = flat	Pulls lower lip inferiorly; tenses skin of neck	B: Fascia of deltoid and pectoralis major muscles and acromion of scapula[2] S: Skin of cheek and mandible	CN VII (facial nerve)

[1] The muscles of facial expression typically originate on bone, and their more moveable insertion typically is on muscle, tendon, subcutaneous tissue, or integument. Thus, it is more appropriate to refer to *bony attachment* and *soft tissue attachment* for these muscles.

[2] Platysma is an exception to the "bony attachment" rule. Its traditional origin arises primarily from muscle.

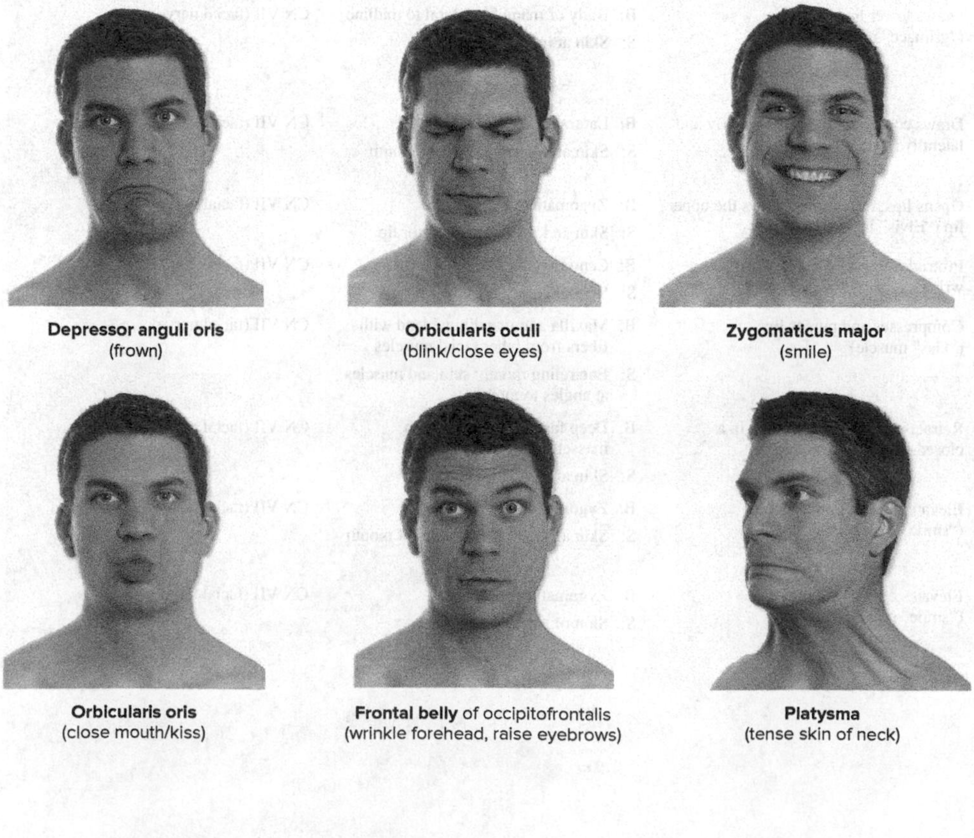
Depressor anguli oris (frown)
Orbicularis oculi (blink/close eyes)
Zygomaticus major (smile)
Orbicularis oris (close mouth/kiss)
Frontal belly of occipitofrontalis (wrinkle forehead, raise eyebrows)
Platysma (tense skin of neck)

Figure 11.3

Surface Anatomy of Some Muscles of Facial Expression. The movements of six of the most commonly used muscles of facial expression are shown in these photos.

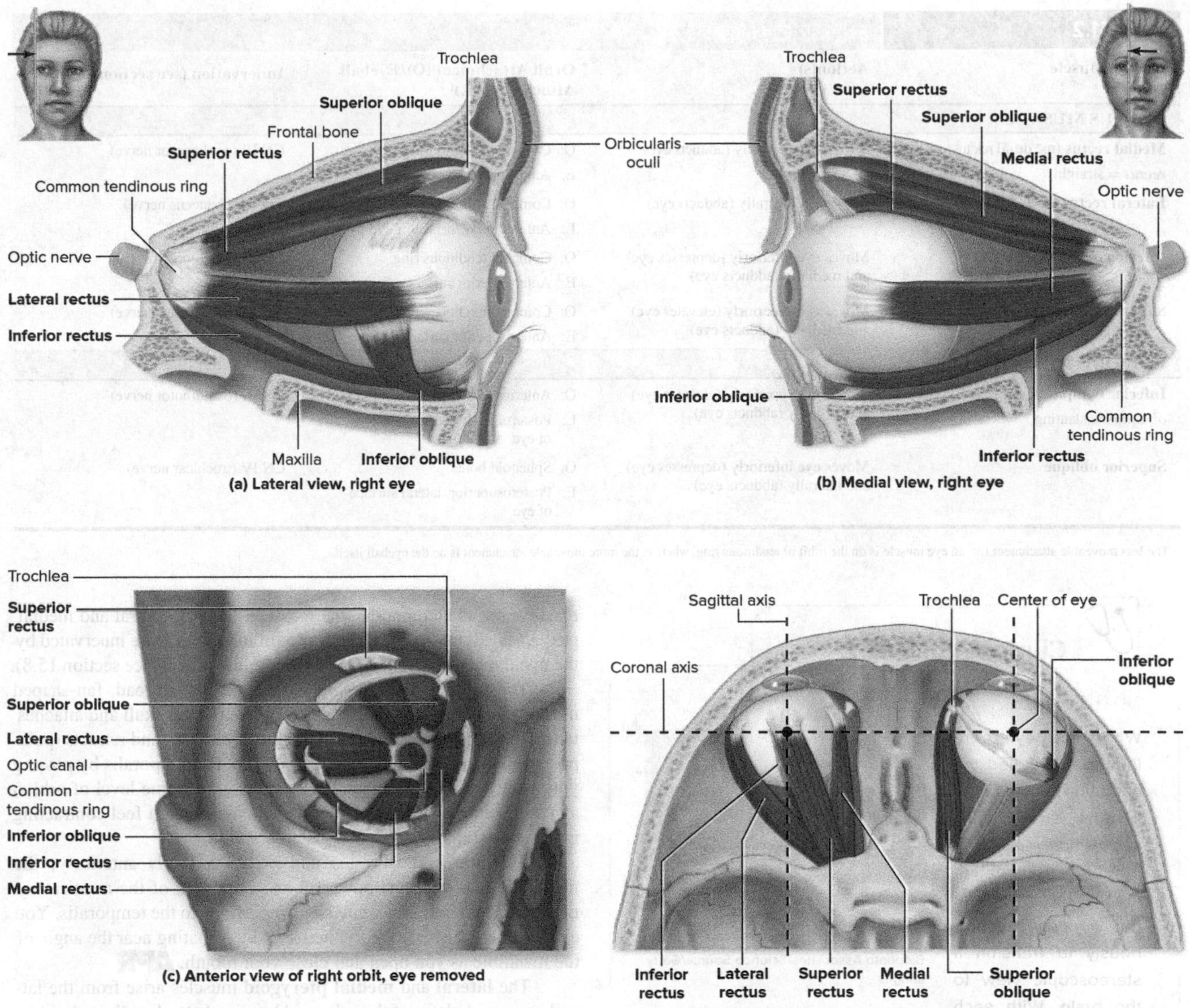
Trochlea
Superior oblique
Frontal bone
Superior rectus
Common tendinous ring
Optic nerve
Lateral rectus
Inferior rectus
Maxilla
Inferior oblique
(a) Lateral view, right eye
Orbicularis oculi
Trochlea
Superior rectus
Superior oblique
Medial rectus
Optic nerve
Inferior oblique
Common tendinous ring
Inferior rectus
(b) Medial view, right eye
Trochlea
Superior rectus
Superior oblique
Lateral rectus
Optic canal
Common tendinous ring
Inferior oblique
Inferior rectus
Medial rectus
(c) Anterior view of right orbit, eye removed
Sagittal axis
Trochlea
Center of eye
Coronal axis
Inferior oblique
Inferior rectus
Lateral rectus
Superior rectus
Medial rectus
Superior oblique
(d) Superior view, left and right orbits

Figure 11.4

Extrinsic Muscles of the Eye. The extrinsic eye muscles, listed in bold in the figures, control movements of the eye. (*a*) The attachments for the lateral, superior, and inferior rectus, as well as both the inferior and superior oblique muscles, appear prominently in a lateral view of the right eye. (*b*) The medial rectus muscle appears prominently in a medial view of the right eye. (*c*) Most of the eye muscles originate from a common tendinous ring, shown here in an anterior view of the right orbit. (*d*) A superior view of the left and right orbits illustrates the eyeball attachment differences between the rectus and oblique muscles, and how these differences affect their movement of the eye. APR

(This nerve's name is derived from the trochlea that holds the superior oblique in place.)

Table 11.2 compares the extrinsic muscles of the eye. APR

WHAT DID YOU LEARN?

1. Stand in front of a mirror and demonstrate the actions of the following muscles: zygomaticus major, orbicularis oris, platysma, orbicularis oculi, and depressor anguli oris. Then list what these muscles do.
2. List the extrinsic eye muscles, and describe the action of each muscle.
3. What is the common general attachment for the muscles of facial expression?

Learning Strategy 11.2

Remembering the innervation of the eye muscles can be difficult. Use the following "chemical formula" to help you learn the eye muscle innervation:

$$[(SO_4)(LR_6)]_3$$

In other words, the superior oblique **(SO)** is innervated by cranial nerve IV **(4)**, the lateral rectus **(LR)** is innervated by cranial nerve VI **(6)**, and the rest of the eye muscles are innervated by cranial nerve III **(3)**.

Table 11.2 Extrinsic Eye Muscles

Group/Muscle	Action(s)	Orbit Attachment (O)/Eyeball Attachment (E)[1]	Innervation (see section 15.8)
RECTUS MUSCLES			
Medial rectus (mē′dē-ăl rek′tus) *rectus* = straight	Moves eye medially (adducts eye)	O: Common tendinous ring E: Anteromedial surface of eye	CN III (oculomotor nerve)
Lateral rectus (lat′er- ăl)	Moves eye laterally (abducts eye)	O: Common tendinous ring E: Anterolateral surface of eye	CN VI (abducens nerve)
Inferior rectus (in-fē′rē-ōr)	Moves eye inferiorly (depresses eye) and medially (adducts eye)	O: Common tendinous ring E: Anteroinferior surface of eye	CN III (oculomotor nerve)
Superior rectus (sū-pēr′ē-ōr)	Moves eye superiorly (elevates eye) and medially (adducts eye)	O: Common tendinous ring E: Anterosuperior surface of eye	CN III (oculomotor nerve)
OBLIQUE MUSCLES			
Inferior oblique *obliquus* = slanting	Moves eye superiorly (elevates eye) and laterally (abducts eye)	O: Anterior orbital surface of maxilla E: Posteroinferior, lateral surface of eye	CN III (oculomotor nerve)
Superior oblique	Moves eye inferiorly (depresses eye) and laterally (abducts eye)	O: Sphenoid bone E: Posterosuperior, lateral surface of eye	CN IV (trochlear nerve)

[1] The less moveable attachment for an eye muscle is on the orbit or tendinous ring, whereas the more moveable attachment is on the eyeball itself.

Clinical View 11.2

Strabismus

When the eyes are improperly aligned, the condition is called **strabismus** (stra-biz′mŭs; *strabismos* = a squinting). The misalignment means the eyes are not working synchronously to transmit a stereoscopic view to the brain. With each eye sending a slightly different image, the brain becomes confused and ignores one of the images. The ignored eye becomes weaker and weaker over time, resulting in a condition termed *lazy eye.* If uncorrected, the lazy eye loses visual acuity, a condition termed **strabismic amblyopia** (am′blē-ō′pē-ă; *amblys* = dull, *ops* = eye).

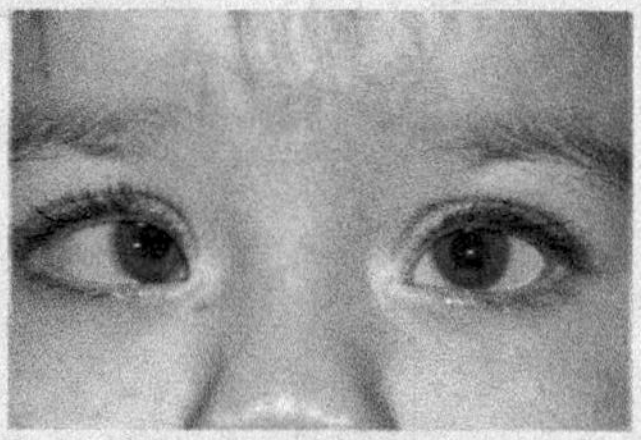

An individual with strabismus.
Biophoto Associates/Science Source/Getty Images

Causes of strabismus include birth injuries, selected eye diseases, damage to one of the nerves that innervate selected eye muscles, improper attachment of the extrinsic eye muscles, and heredity. Strabismus due to eye muscle weakness (and not nerve damage) may be treated by wearing a patch over the stronger eye. The weaker eye (*lazy eye*) is forced to be used, and the muscles for the eye may strengthen as a result.

11.1c Muscles of Mastication

The term **mastication** (mas′ti-kā′shŭn; *masticatus* = to chew) refers to the process of chewing. These muscles move the mandible at the temporomandibular joint. There are four paired muscles of mastication: the temporalis, the masseter, and the lateral and medial pterygoids (**figure 11.5**). The muscles of mastication are innervated by the mandibular division of CN V (trigeminal nerve) (see section 15.8).

The **temporalis** (or *temporal* muscle) is a broad, fan-shaped muscle that extends from the temporal lines of the skull and attaches to the coronoid process of the mandible. It elevates and retracts (pulls posteriorly) the mandible. You can palpate the temporalis by placing your fingers along your temple (lateral skull at same level of orbits) as you open and close your mouth. The muscle you feel contracting is the temporalis. APR

The **masseter** elevates and protracts (pulls anteriorly) the mandible. It is the most powerful and important of the masticatory muscles. This short, thick muscle is superficial to the temporalis. You can feel the contraction of the masseter by palpating near the angle of the mandible as you open and close your mouth. APR

The **lateral** and **medial pterygoid** muscles arise from the lateral pterygoid plates of the sphenoid bone and attach to the mandible. Both pterygoid muscles protract the mandible and move it from side to side during chewing. These movements maximize the efficiency of the teeth while chewing or grinding foods of various consistencies (see section 26.2d). The medial pterygoid also elevates the mandible.

Table 11.3 summarizes the characteristics of the muscles of mastication. APR

11.1d Muscles That Move the Tongue

The tongue is an agile, highly mobile organ (see section 26.2b). It consists of **intrinsic muscles** that curl, squeeze, and fold the tongue during chewing and speaking. Thus, the tongue itself acts like a big muscle.

The **extrinsic muscles** of the tongue attach from head and neck structures to the tongue. The extrinsic muscles end in the suffix *-glossus,* meaning tongue (**figure 11.6**). These extrinsic tongue muscles are used in various combinations to accomplish the precise, complex, and delicate tongue movements required for proper speech. Additionally, they manipulate food within the mouth in preparation for swallowing. Most of these muscles are innervated by CN XII, the hypoglossal nerve (see section 15.8).

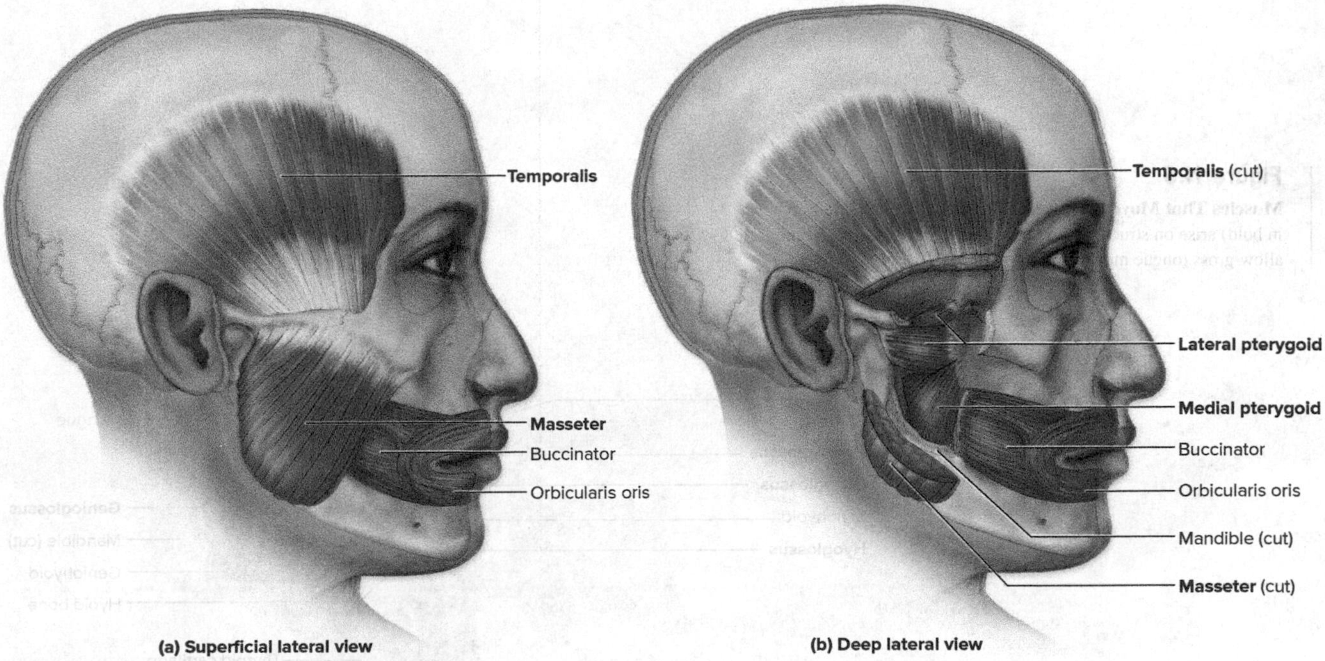
Temporalis
Masseter
Buccinator
Orbicularis oris
(a) Superficial lateral view
Temporalis (cut)
Lateral pterygoid
Medial pterygoid
Buccinator
Orbicularis oris
Mandible (cut)
Masseter (cut)
(b) Deep lateral view

Figure 11.5

Muscles of Mastication. (*a*) Superficial and (*b*) deep lateral views of the muscles of mastication (shown in bold), which move the mandible.

The left and right **genioglossus** muscles arise on the mandible and protract the tongue. You use these muscles when you stick out your tongue. The left and right **styloglossus** muscles arise from the styloid processes of the temporal bone. These muscles elevate and retract the tongue (pull the tongue posteriorly, back into the mouth). The left and right **hyoglossus** muscles attach to the hyoid bone and the sides of the tongue. These muscles depress and retract the tongue. The left and right **palatoglossus** muscles originate on the soft palate and elevate the posterior portion of the tongue.

Table 11.4 summarizes the characteristics of the muscles that move the tongue.

11.1e Muscles of the Pharynx

The **pharynx** (far′ingks), commonly called the *throat,* is a funnel-shaped tube that lies posterior to and extends inferiorly from both the oral and nasal cavities (see section 26.3). Several muscles help form this muscular tube or attach to it and aid in swallowing (**figure 11.7**). Most pharyngeal muscles are innervated by CN X (vagus nerve) (see section 15.8).

The primary pharyngeal muscles are the **pharyngeal constrictors (superior, middle, and inferior).** When a bolus of food enters the pharynx, these muscles contract sequentially to initiate swallowing and force the bolus inferiorly into the esophagus (see section 26.6). Other pharyngeal muscles help elevate or tense the palate when swallowing. These muscles are summarized in **table 11.5.**

Table 11.3 Muscles of Mastication

Muscle	Action(s)	Superior Attachment(s) (S)/ Inferior Attachment(s) (I)[1]	Innervation (see section 15.8)
Temporalis (tem′p ŏ-rā′lis) *tempora* = pertaining to temporal bone	Elevates and retracts mandible	S: Superior and inferior temporal lines I: Coronoid process of mandible	CN V_3 (trigeminal nerve, mandibular division)
Masseter (mas′ĕ-tĕr) *maseter* = chewer	Elevates and protracts mandible; prime mover of jaw closure	S: Zygomatic arch I: Ramus (lateral surface) and angle of mandible	CN V_3 (trigeminal nerve, mandibular division)
Medial pterygoid (ter′i-goyd)	Elevates and protracts mandible; produces side-to-side movement of mandible	S: Maxilla, palatine, and medial surface of lateral pterygoid plate I: Medial surface of mandibular ramus	CN V_3 (trigeminal nerve, mandibular division)
Lateral pterygoid *pterygoid* = winglike	Protracts mandible; produces side-to-side movement of mandible	S: Greater wing of sphenoid and lateral surface of lateral pterygoid plate I: Condylar process of mandible	CN V_3 (trigeminal nerve, mandibular division)

[1] The superior attachments of the mastication muscles are less moveable than the inferior attachments.

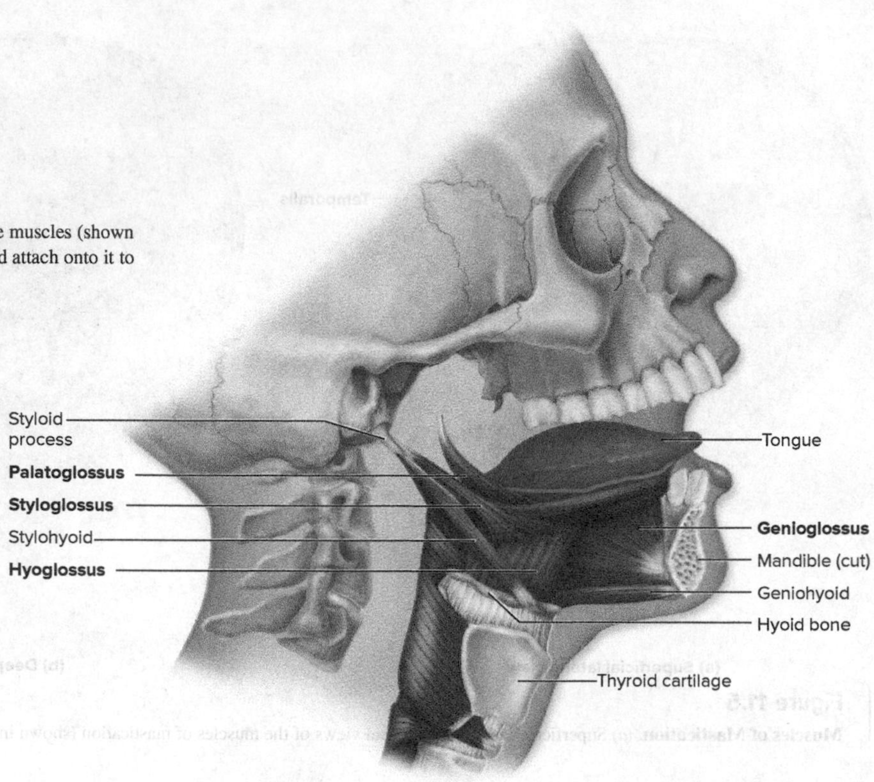

Right lateral view

Figure 11.6

Muscles That Move the Tongue. Extrinsic tongue muscles (shown in bold) arise on structures other than the tongue and attach onto it to allow gross tongue movement.

11.1f Muscles of the Anterior Neck

The muscles of the anterior neck are divided into the **suprahyoid muscles,** which are superior to the hyoid bone, and the **infrahyoid muscles,** which are inferior to the hyoid bone (**figure 11.8**).

The suprahyoid muscles are associated with the floor of the mouth. In general, these muscles act as a group to elevate the hyoid bone during swallowing or speaking. Some of these muscles perform additional actions: The **digastric** has two bellies, anterior and posterior. One belly extends from the mental protuberance to the hyoid, and the other continues from the hyoid to the mastoid portion of the temporal bone. The two bellies are united by an intermediate tendon that is held in position by a dense connective tissue sling. In addition to elevating the hyoid bone, this muscle can also depress the mandible. The **geniohyoid** arises from the mental spines of the mandible and attaches on the hyoid bone. This muscle elevates the hyoid bone. The broad, flat **mylohyoid** provides a muscular floor to the mouth. When this muscle contracts, it both elevates the hyoid bone and raises the floor of the mouth. The muscle fibers of the left and right mylohyoid are aligned in a V shape. The **stylohyoid** attaches to the styloid process of the skull and the hyoid. Upon contraction, it elevates the hyoid bone, causing the floor of the oral cavity to elongate during swallowing (see section 26.6).

Table 11.4 Muscles That Move the Tongue

Muscle	Action(s)	Head or Neck Attachment(s) (H)/ Tongue Attachment(s) (T)[1]	Innervation (see section 15.8)
Genioglossus (jĕ'nē-ō-glos'ŭs) *geni* = chin *glossus* = tongue	Protracts tongue	H: Mental spines of mandible T: Inferior region of tongue; hyoid bone	CN XII (hypoglossal nerve)
Styloglossus (stī'lō-glos'ŭs) *stylo* = pertaining to styloid process of temporal bone	Elevates and retracts tongue	H: Styloid process of temporal bone T: Sides and inferior aspect of tongue	CN XII (hypoglossal nerve)
Hyoglossus (hī'ō-glos'ŭs) *hyo* = pertaining to hyoid bone	Depresses and retracts tongue	H: Hyoid bone T: Inferolateral side of tongue	CN XII (hypoglossal nerve)
Palatoglossus (pal'ă-tō-glos'ŭs) *palato* = palate	Elevates posterior part of tongue	H: Anterior surface of soft palate T: Side and posterior aspect of tongue	CN X (vagus nerve) via pharyngeal plexus of nerves

[1] The tongue attachments are the more moveable parts of these muscles.

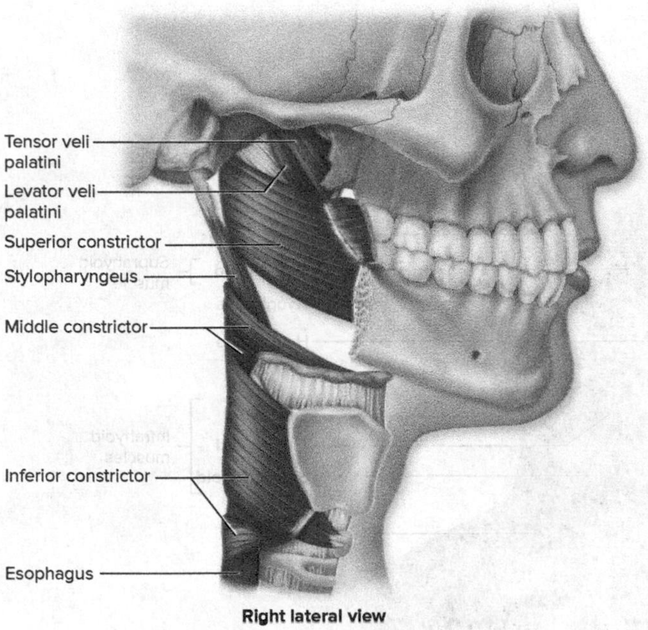

Figure 11.7

Pharyngeal Constrictors, Palate Muscles, and Laryngeal Elevators. A right lateral view of the head and neck reveals some of the muscles that constrict the pharynx when swallowing, move the palate, and elevate the larynx (palatopharyngeus and salpingopharyngeus not shown).

As swallowing ends, the infrahyoid muscles contract to move the hyoid bone and the larynx. In general, these muscles either depress the hyoid bone or depress the thyroid cartilage of the larynx. The **omohyoid** contains two thin muscle bellies anchored in place by a connective tissue "sling." This muscle is lateral to the sternohyoid and extends from the superior border of the scapula to the hyoid, where it depresses the hyoid bone. The **sternohyoid** extends from the sternum to the hyoid, where it depresses the hyoid bone. The **sternothyroid** is deep to the sternohyoid. It extends from the sternum to the thyroid cartilage of the larynx. It depresses the thyroid cartilage to return it to its original position after swallowing. The **thyrohyoid** extends from the thyroid cartilage of the larynx to the hyoid. It depresses the hyoid bone and elevates the thyroid cartilage to close off the larynx during swallowing. In addition, the omohyoid, sternohyoid, and thyrohyoid help anchor the hyoid so the digastric can depress the mandible.

Table 11.5 Muscles of the Pharynx[1]

Region/Muscle	Action(s)	Origin/Insertion[2]	Innervation (see section 15.8)
PALATE MUSCLES			
Levator veli palatini (vel'ī pal'ă-tē'nī) *levator* = elevates *velum* = veil	Elevates soft palate when swallowing	O: Petrous part of temporal bone I: Soft palate	CN X (vagus nerve)
Tensor veli palatini (ten's ŏr) *tensus* = to stretch	Tenses soft palate and opens auditory tube when swallowing or yawning	O: Sphenoid bone; region around auditory tube I: Soft palate	CN V_3 (trigeminal nerve, mandibular division)
PHARYNGEAL CONSTRICTORS			
Superior constrictor (kon-strik'tor, -tōr) *constringo* = to draw together	Constricts pharynx in sequence to force bolus into esophagus; superior is innermost	O: Pterygoid process of sphenoid bone; medial surface of mandible I: Posterior median raphe (muscle fiber union from both sides)	CN X (vagus nerve) via branches of pharyngeal plexus
Middle constrictor	Constricts pharynx in sequence	O: Hyoid bone I: Posterior median raphe	CN X (vagus nerve) via branches of pharyngeal plexus
Inferior constrictor	Constricts pharynx in sequence; inferior is outermost	O: Thyroid and cricoid cartilage I: Posterior median raphe	CN X (vagus nerve) via branches of pharyngeal plexus
LARYNGEAL (VOICE BOX) ELEVATORS			
Palatopharyngeus (pal'ă-tō-fa-rin'j ē-ŭs) *pharynx* = pharynx	Elevates pharynx and larynx	O: Soft palate I: Side of pharynx and thyroid cartilage of larynx	CN X (vagus nerve) via branches of pharyngeal plexus
Salpingopharyngeus (sal-ping'g ō-fă-rin'j ē-ŭs) *salpinx* = trumpet	Elevates pharynx and larynx; opens auditory tube	O: Auditory tube I: Blends with palatopharyngeus on lateral wall of pharynx	CN X (vagus nerve) via branches of pharyngeal plexus
Stylopharyngeus (stī'lō-far'in-j ē'ŭs) *stylo* = styloid process	Elevates pharynx and larynx	O: Styloid process of temporal bone I: Side of pharynx and thyroid cartilage of larynx	CN IX (glossopharyngeal nerve) via branches of pharyngeal plexus

[1] Only the pharyngeal constrictors are discussed in the text.

[2] Here, we keep the terms *origin* and *insertion* because the terms *superior attachment* and *inferior attachment* are not applicable for all of the muscles in this table.

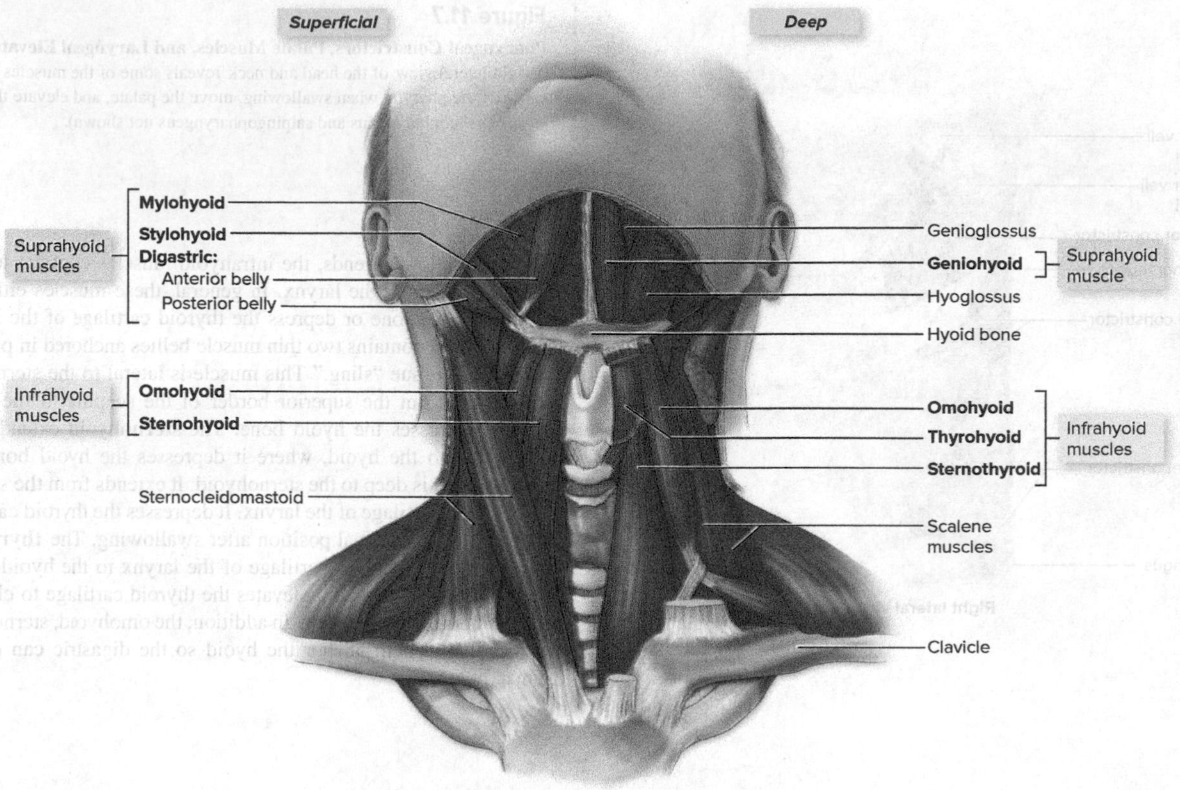

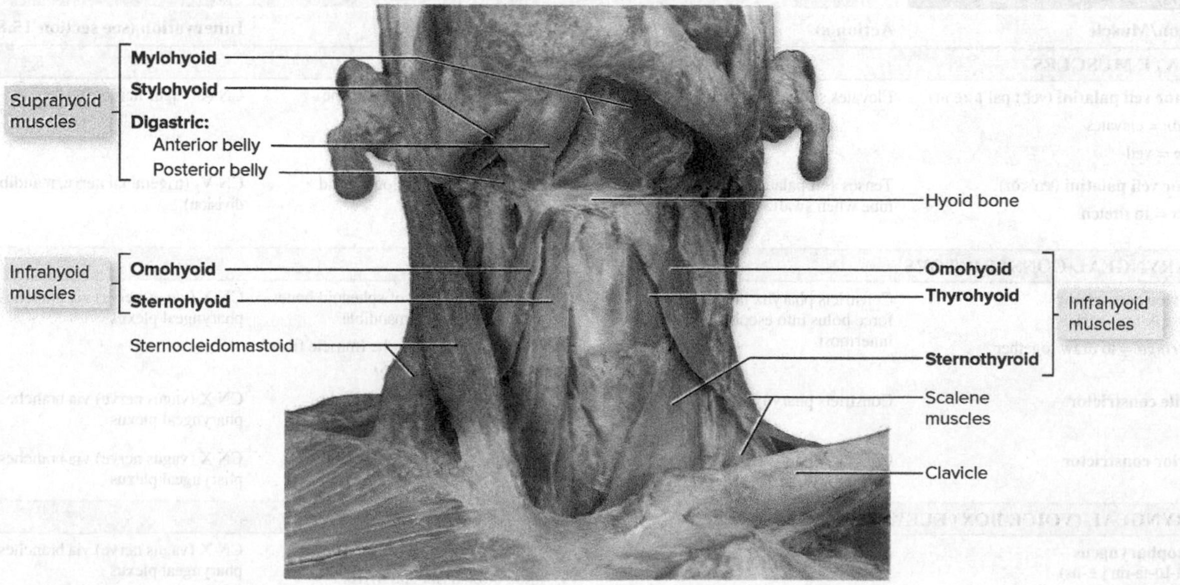

Anterior view

Figure 11.8

Muscles of the Anterior Neck. An illustration and a cadaver photo show the anterior neck muscles. The suprahyoid and infrahyoid muscles are in bold, and they move the hyoid bone and the thyroid cartilage. Superficial muscles are shown on the right side of the body, and deeper muscles are shown on the left side of the body. APR

Table 11.6 summarizes the characteristics of the muscles of the anterior neck. APR

WHAT DO YOU THINK?

2 Because muscles frequently are named for their attachment sites, what do you think the prefix *-omo* in "omohyoid" means?

11.1g Muscles That Move the Head and Neck

Muscles that move the head and neck arise from the vertebral column, the thoracic cage, and the pectoral girdle, and attach to bones of the cranium (**figure 11.9**; see figure 11.8).

Anterolateral Neck Muscles

The anterolateral neck muscles flex the head and/or neck. The main muscles in this group are the sternocleidomastoid and the three scalenes.

The **sternocleidomastoid** is a thick, cordlike muscle that extends from the sternum and clavicle to the mastoid process posterior to the ear. Contraction of both sternocleidomastoid muscles (called **bilateral contraction**) flexes the neck. Contraction of just one sternocleidomastoid muscle (called **unilateral contraction**) results in lateral flexion of the neck and rotation of the head to the opposite side. Thus, if the left sternocleidomastoid muscle contracts, it rotates the head to the right side of the body. The three **scalene muscles (anterior, middle,** and **posterior)** work with the sternocleidomastoid to flex the neck. In addition, the scalene muscles elevate the first and second ribs during forced inhalation.

Posterior Neck Muscles

Several muscles work together to extend the head and/or neck (**figure 11.10**). The trapezius attaches to the skull and helps extend the head and/or neck. The primary action of the trapezius is to help move the pectoral girdle, so it is discussed in greater detail in section 12.1a. When the left and right **splenius capitis, splenius cervicis, semispinalis capitis,** and **longissimus capitis** muscles bilaterally contract, they extend the neck. Unilateral contraction turns the head and neck to the same side. A group of muscles called the suboccipital muscles includes the **obliquus capitis superior, obliquus capitis inferior, rectus capitis posterior major,** and **rectus capitis posterior minor.** The obliquus muscles turn the head to the same side, whereas the rectus muscles extend the head and neck.

Table 11.7 summarizes the characteristics of the muscles of the head and neck.

WHAT DID YOU LEARN?

4 The masseter and temporalis work together to perform what common action? They work *opposite* one another with which actions?

5 Which muscle protracts the tongue?

6 Draw the suprahyoid and infrahyoid muscles. What is the common action of the suprahyoid muscles? of the infrahyoid muscles?

7 The unilateral contraction of which muscle causes lateral flexion of the neck and rotation of the head to the opposite side?

Table 11.6 Muscles of the Anterior Neck

Region/Muscle	Action(s)	Superior Attachment(s) (S)/ Inferior Attachment(s) (I)[1]	Innervation (sections 15.8 and 16.4d)
SUPRAHYOID MUSCLES			
Digastric (dī-gas′trik) *di* = two *gaster* = belly	Depresses mandible; elevates hyoid bone	S: Anterior belly, mandible near mental protuberance; posterior belly, mastoid process I: Hyoid bone via fascia sling	Anterior belly: CN V_3 (trigeminal nerve, mandibular division) Posterior belly: CN VII (facial nerve)
Geniohyoid (jĕ-nē-ō-hī′oyd) *hyoid* = hyoid bone	Elevates hyoid bone	S: Mental spines of mandible I: Hyoid bone	First cervical spinal nerve (C1) via CN XII (hypoglossal nerve)
Mylohyoid (mī′lō-hī′oyd) *myle* = molar	Elevates hyoid bone; elevates floor of mouth	S: Mylohyoid line of mandible I: Hyoid bone	CN V_3 (trigeminal nerve, mandibular division)
Stylohyoid (stī′lō-hī′oyd)	Elevates hyoid bone	S: Styloid process of temporal bone I: Hyoid bone	CN VII (facial nerve)
INFRAHYOID MUSCLES			
Omohyoid (ō′mō-hī′oyd) *omo* = shoulder	Depresses hyoid bone; fixes hyoid during opening of mouth	S: Hyoid bone I: Superior border of scapula	Cervical spinal nerves C1–C3 through ansa cervicalis (from cervical plexus)
Sternohyoid (ster′n ō-hī′oyd) *sterno* = sternum	Depresses hyoid bone	S: Hyoid bone I: Manubrium of sternum and medial end of clavicle	Cervical spinal nerves C1–C3 through ansa cervicalis (from cervical plexus)
Sternothyroid (ster′n ō-thī′royd) *thyro* = thyroid cartilage	Depresses thyroid cartilage of larynx	S: Thyroid cartilage of larynx I: Posterior surface of manubrium of sternum	Cervical spinal nerves C1–C3 through ansa cervicalis (from cervical plexus)
Thyrohyoid (thī′rō-hī′oyd)	Depresses hyoid bone and elevates thyroid cartilage of larynx	S: Hyoid bone I: Thyroid cartilage of larynx	First cervical spinal nerve C1 via CN XII (hypoglossal nerve)

[1] Note that with most of the infrahyoid muscles, the superior attachment is the more moveable part of each muscle, whereas the inferior attachment tends to be more moveable for the suprahyoid muscles.

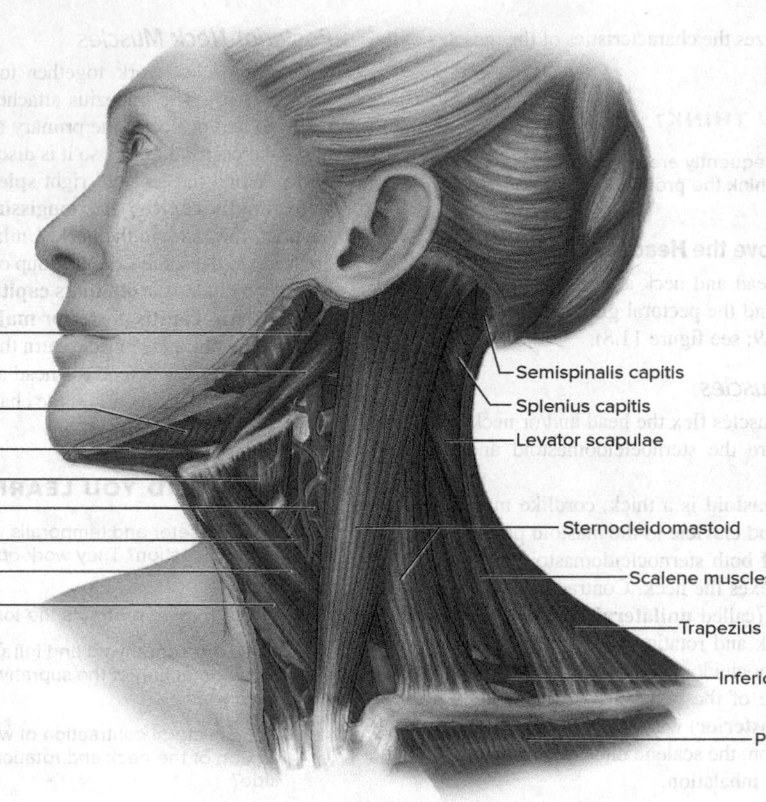
Stylohyoid
Posterior belly of digastric
Mylohyoid
Anterior belly of digastric
Thyrohyoid
Inferior constrictor
Sternothyroid
Superior belly of omohyoid
Sternohyoid
Semispinalis capitis
Splenius capitis
Levator scapulae
Sternocleidomastoid
Scalene muscles
Trapezius
Inferior belly of omohyoid
Platysma (cut)
Anterolateral view

Figure 11.9

Muscles That Move the Head and Neck. Anterolateral muscles collectively flex the neck, whereas posterior neck muscles extend the head and/or neck.

Clinical View 11.3

Congenital Muscular Torticollis

Congenital muscular torticollis (CMT), often known as *wryneck*, is a condition where a newborn presents with a shortened and tightened sternocleidomastoid muscle, which may persist into childhood. It is thought to be a result of trauma resulting from either a difficult birth or prenatal position of the fetus. The trauma causes a hematoma and fibrosing of the muscle tissue. Pediatricians also have seen an increase in acquired muscular torticollis among newborns who are kept in infant seats for extended periods of time outside of the car. Children with CMT often tilt their heads to the affected side and their chins to the unaffected side. Because the child typically favors a particular head position when sleeping, *plagiocephaly* (flattening of the head) often accompanies CMT.

CMT treatment typically involves stretching the affected muscle several times a day, changing sleeping positions, and making the child use the affected side more frequently. A newer approach to treatment of CMT is the use of botulinum toxin type A (Botox), which impairs contraction of the affected muscle, combined with stretching. In cases that do not respond to the treatments mentioned, sternocleidomastoid release surgery is recommended. The sternocleidomastoid is cut from at least one attachment point, repositioned, reattached, and Botox may be injected into the muscle. Recovery includes wearing a neck brace and physical therapy.

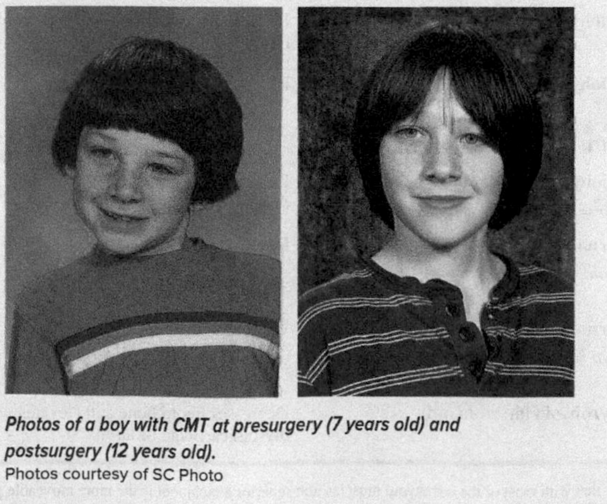

Photos of a boy with CMT at presurgery (7 years old) and postsurgery (12 years old).
Photos courtesy of SC Photo

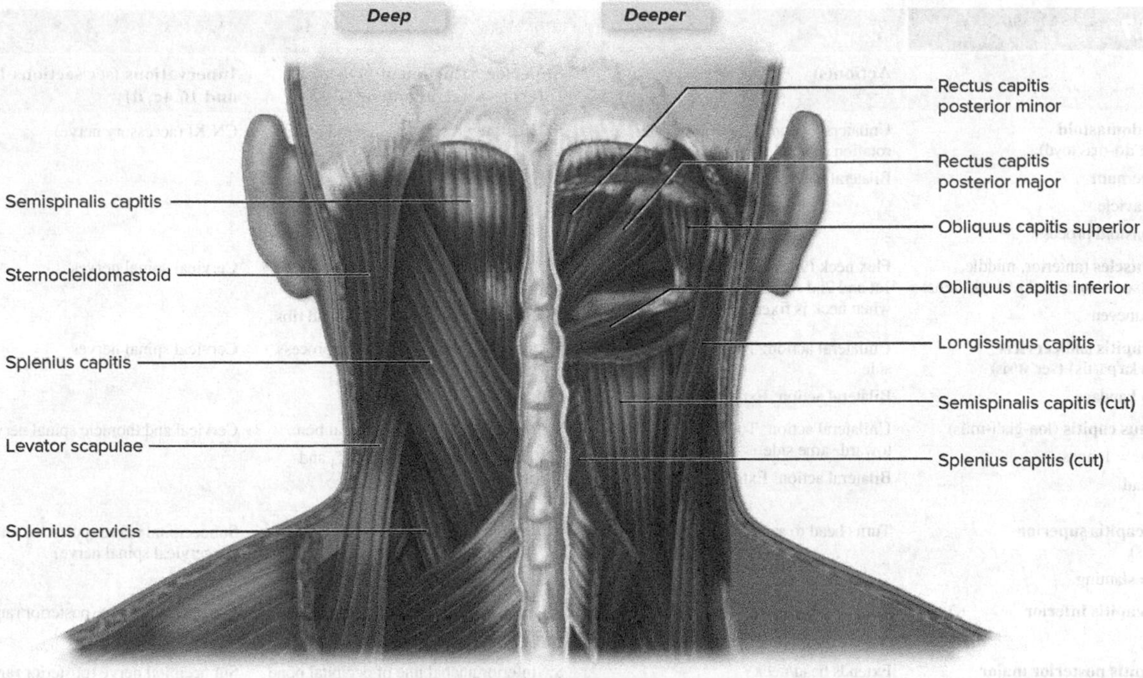

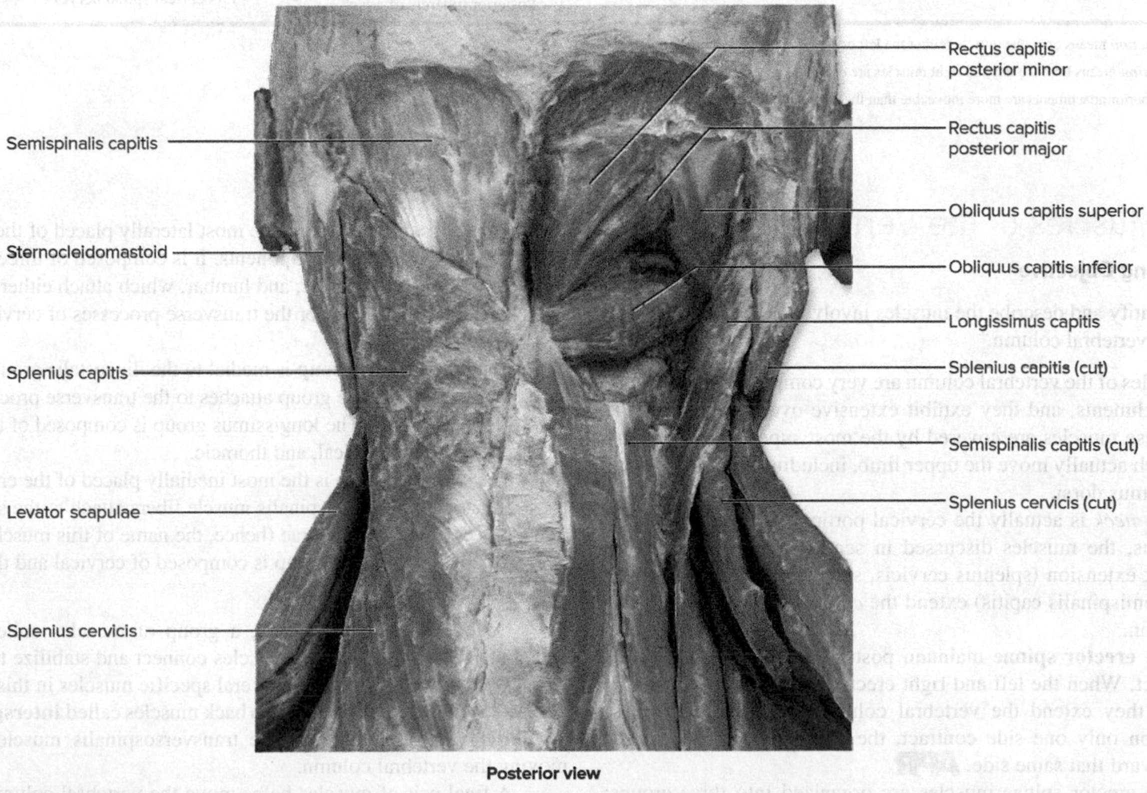

Figure 11.10

Posterior Neck Muscles. An illustration and a cadaver photo show the deep and deeper muscles of the posterior neck, which collectively extend and rotate the head and neck. APR

Table 11.7 Muscles That Move the Head and Neck

Muscle	Action(s)	Superior Attachment(s) (S)/ Inferior Attachment(s) (I)[3]	Innervations (see sections 15.8 and 16.4c, d)
Sternocleidomastoid (ster'n ō-klī'dō-mas'toyd) *sterno* = sternum *cleido* = clavicle *masto* = mastoid process	Unilateral action [1]: Lateral flexion, rotation of head to opposite side Bilateral action [2]: Flexes neck	S: Mastoid process of temporal bone I: Manubrium and sternal end of clavicle	CN XI (accessory nerve)
Scalene muscles (anterior, middle, posterior) (see also table 11.9) (skā'lēnz) *scalene* = uneven	Flex neck (when 1st rib is fixed); elevate 1st and 2nd ribs during forced inhalation when neck is fixed	S: Transverse processes of cervical vertebrae I: Superior surface of 1st and 2nd ribs	Cervical spinal nerves
Splenius capitis and **cervicis** (splē'nē-ŭs ka'pĭ-tis) (ser'vĭ'sis) *splenion* = bandage	Unilateral action: Turns head to same side Bilateral action: Extends head/neck	S: Occipital bone and mastoid process of temporal bone I: Ligamentum nuchae	Cervical spinal nerves
Longissimus capitis (lon-gis'i-mŭs) *longissimus* = longest *caput* = head	Unilateral action: Turns (rotates) head toward same side Bilateral action: Extends head/neck	S: Mastoid process of temporal bone I: Transverse process of T_1–T_4 and articular processes of C_4–C_7 vertebrae	Cervical and thoracic spinal nerves
Obliquus capitis superior (ob-lī'kwŭs) *obliquus* = slanting	Turns head to same side	S: Inferior nuchal line of occipital bone I: Transverse process of atlas	Suboccipital nerve (posterior ramus of 1st cervical spinal nerve)
Obliquus capitis inferior	Turns head to same side	S: Transverse process of atlas I: Spinous process of axis	Suboccipital nerve (posterior ramus of 1st cervical spinal nerve)
Rectus capitis posterior major	Extends head/neck	S: Inferior nuchal line of occipital bone I: Spinous process of axis	Suboccipital nerve (posterior ramus of 1st cervical spinal nerve)
Rectus capitis posterior minor	Extends head/neck	S: Inferior nuchal line of occipital bone I: Posterior tubercle of atlas	Suboccipital nerve (posterior ramus of 1st cervical spinal nerve)

[1] *Unilateral action* means only one muscle (either the left or right muscle) is contracting.

[2] *Bilateral action* means both the left and right muscles are contracting together.

[3] Here, the superior attachments are more moveable than the inferior attachments.

11.2 Muscles of the Vertebral Column

✓ Learning Objective

8. Identify and describe the muscles involved in the movements of the vertebral column.

The muscles of the vertebral column are very complex; they have multiple attachments, and they exhibit extensive overlap (**figure 11.11**). All of these muscles are covered by the most superficial back muscles, which actually move the upper limb, including the trapezius and the latissimus dorsi.

The *neck* is actually the cervical portion of the vertebral column. Thus, the muscles discussed in section 11.1g in connection with neck extension (splenius cervicis, splenius capitis, longissimus capitis, semispinalis capitis) extend the *cervical region* of the vertebral column.

The **erector spinae** maintain posture and help an individual stand erect. When the left and right erector spinae muscles contract together, they extend the vertebral column. If the erector spinae muscles on only one side contract, the vertebral column laterally flexes toward that same side. APR

The erector spinae muscles are organized into three groups; a series of multipart, overlapping muscles compose each of these groups. These muscles share a common tendinous connection from the posterior part of the iliac crest, posterior sacrum, and spinous processes of the lumbar vertebrae. The muscles are named based upon the body region with which they are associated.

- The **iliocostalis group** is the most laterally placed of the three erector spinae components. It is composed of three parts: cervical, thoracic, and lumbar, which attach either to the angles of the ribs or the transverse processes of cervical vertebrae.
- The **longissimus group** is medial to the iliocostalis group. The longissimus muscle group attaches to the transverse processes of the vertebrae. The longissimus group is composed of three parts: capitis, cervical, and thoracic.
- The **spinalis group** is the most medially placed of the erector spinae muscles. The spinalis muscle fibers attach to the spinous processes of the vertebrae (hence, the name of this muscle group). The spinalis group is composed of cervical and thoracic parts.

Deep to the erector spinae, a group of muscles collectively called the **transversospinalis** muscles connect and stabilize the vertebrae (**figure 11.12**). There are several specific muscles in this group (**table 11.8**). In addition, minor deep back muscles called **interspinales** and **intertransversarii** assist the transversospinalis muscles with moving the vertebral column.

A final pair of muscles helps move the vertebral column. The **quadratus lumborum** muscles are located primarily in the lumbar region (see figure 11.11). When the left and right quadratus lumborum muscles bilaterally contract, they extend the vertebral column. When either the left or right quadratus lumborum muscle unilaterally contracts, it laterally flexes the vertebral column.

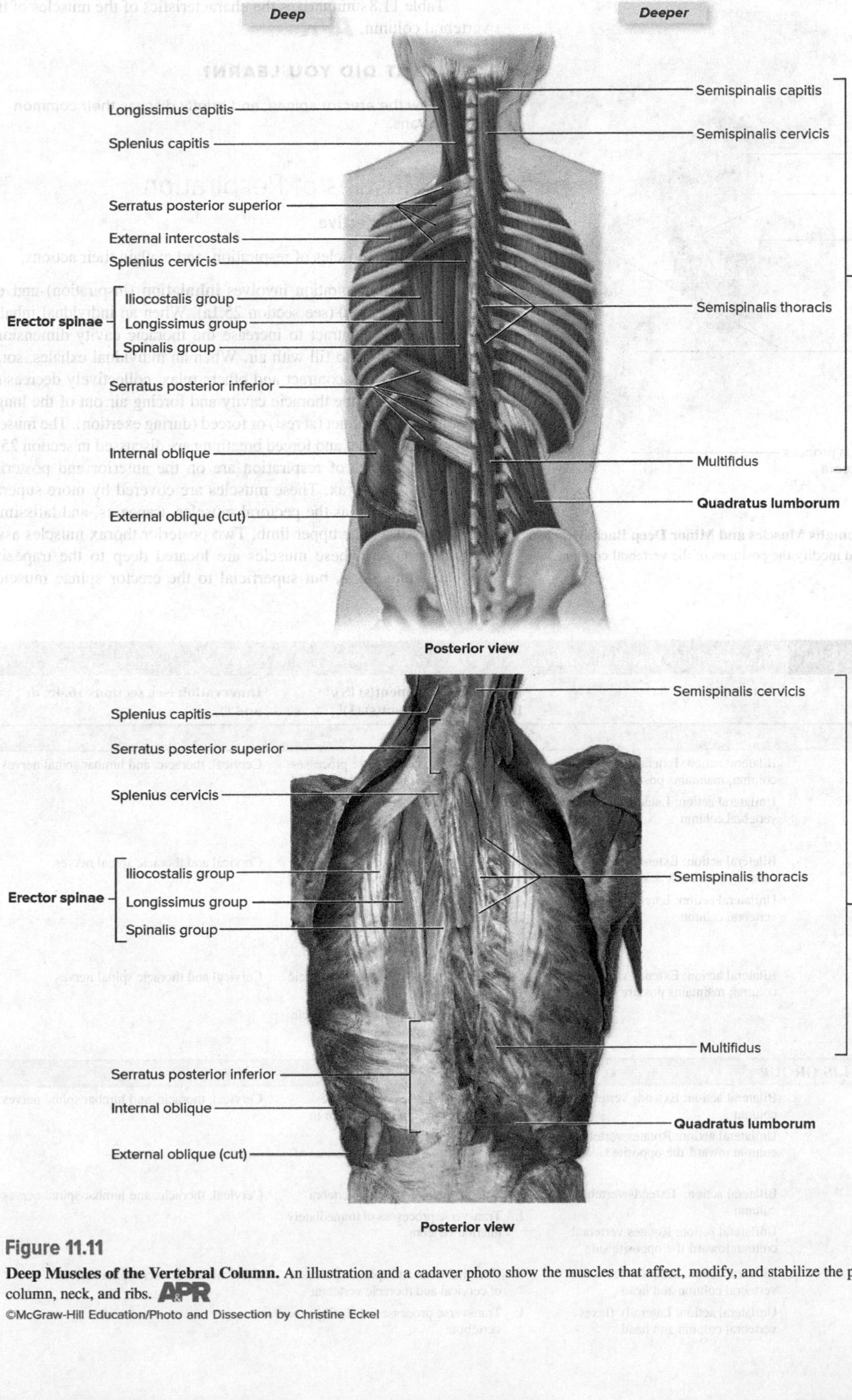
Deep
Deeper
Longissimus capitis
Splenius capitis
Serratus posterior superior
External intercostals
Splenius cervicis
Iliocostalis group
Erector spinae
Longissimus group
Spinalis group
Serratus posterior inferior
Internal oblique
External oblique (cut)
Semispinalis capitis
Semispinalis cervicis
Transversospinalis
Semispinalis thoracis
Multifidus
Quadratus lumborum
Posterior view
Semispinalis cervicis
Splenius capitis
Serratus posterior superior
Splenius cervicis
Iliocostalis group
Erector spinae
Longissimus group
Spinalis group
Semispinalis thoracis
Transversospinalis
Multifidus
Serratus posterior inferior
Internal oblique
Quadratus lumborum
External oblique (cut)
Posterior view

Figure 11.11

Deep Muscles of the Vertebral Column. An illustration and a cadaver photo show the muscles that affect, modify, and stabilize the positions of the vertebral column, neck, and ribs. APR

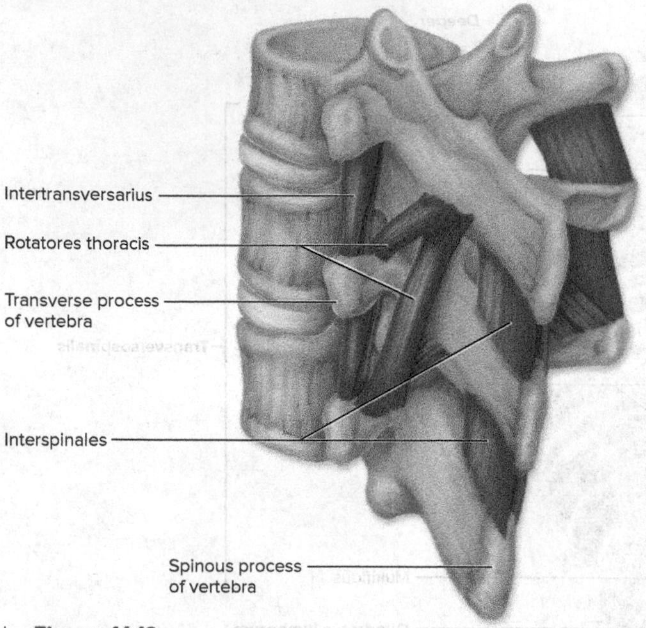

Intertransversarius
Rotatores thoracis
Transverse process of vertebra
Interspinales
Spinous process of vertebra

Figure 11.12

Selected Transversospinalis Muscles and Minor Deep Back Muscles. These muscles affect and modify the positions of the vertebral column.

Table 11.8 summarizes the characteristics of the muscles of the vertebral column. APR

WHAT DID YOU LEARN?

8. Draw the erector spinae, and briefly discuss their common actions.

11.3 Muscles of Respiration

✓ Learning Objective

9. Name the muscles of respiration, and explain their actions.

The process of respiration involves **inhalation** (inspiration) and **exhalation** (expiration) (see section 25.1a). When an individual inhales, several muscles contract to increase the thoracic cavity dimensions, allowing the lungs to fill with air. When an individual exhales, some respiratory muscles contract and others relax, collectively decreasing the dimensions of the thoracic cavity and forcing air out of the lungs. Breathing may be quiet (at rest) or forced (during exertion). The muscles responsible for quiet and forced breathing are discussed in section 25.6.

The muscles of respiration are on the anterior and posterior surfaces of the thorax. These muscles are covered by more superficial muscles (such as the pectoral muscles, trapezius, and latissimus dorsi) that move the upper limb. Two posterior thorax muscles assist with respiration. These muscles are located deep to the trapezius and latissimus dorsi, but superficial to the erector spinae muscles.

Table 11.8 Muscles of the Vertebral Column

Group/Muscle	Action(s)	Superior Attachment(s) (S)/ Inferior Attachment(s) (I)[1]	Innervation (see sections 16.4c, d, and f)
ERECTOR SPINAE			
Iliocostalis group (il-ē-ō-kos-tā'lis) *ilio* = ilium *cost* = rib	Bilateral action: Extends vertebral column; maintains posture Unilateral action: Laterally flexes vertebral column	S: Angles of ribs; transverse processes of cervical vertebrae I: Tendon from posterior part of iliac crest, posterior sacrum, and lumbar spinous processes	Cervical, thoracic, and lumbar spinal nerves
Longissimus group *longissimus* = longest	Bilateral action: Extends vertebral column; maintains posture Unilateral action: Laterally flexes vertebral column	S: Mastoid process of temporal bone and transverse processes of cervical and thoracic vertebrae I: Tendon from posterior part of iliac crest, posterior sacrum, and lumbar spinous processes	Cervical and thoracic spinal nerves
Spinalis group (spī-nā'lis) *spin* = spine	Bilateral action: Extends vertebral column; maintains posture	S: Spinous process of axis and thoracic vertebrae I: Lumbar spinous processes (thoracic part) and C_7 spinous process (cervical part)	Cervical and thoracic spinal nerves
TRANSVERSOSPINALIS GROUP			
Multifidus (mŭl-tif'i-dŭs) *multus* = much *findo* = to cleave	Bilateral action: Extends vertebral column Unilateral action: Rotates vertebral column toward the opposite side	S: Spinous processes of vertebrae located 2–4 segments superior to inferior attachment I: Sacrum and transverse processes of each vertebra	Cervical, thoracic, and lumbar spinal nerves
Rotatores (rō-tā'tōrz) *rotatus* = to revolve	Bilateral action: Extends vertebral column Unilateral action: Rotates vertebral column toward the opposite side	S: Spinous process of each vertebra I: Transverse processes of immediately inferior vertebra	Cervical, thoracic, and lumbar spinal nerves
Semispinalis group (sem'ē-spī-nā'lis)	Bilateral action: Extends cervical vertebral column and head Unilateral action: Laterally flexes vertebral column and head	S: Occipital bone and spinous processes of cervical and thoracic vertebrae I: Transverse processes of C_4–T_{12} vertebrae	Cervical and thoracic spinal nerves

Table 11.8 Muscles of the Vertebral Column *(continued)*

Group/Muscle	Action(s)	Superior Attachment(s) (S)/ Inferior Attachment(s) (I)[1]	Innervation (see sections 16.4c, d, and f)
MINOR DEEP BACK MUSCLES			
Interspinales (in′tĕr-spī-nă′lēz) *inter* = between	Extends vertebral column	S: Spinous process of each vertebra I: Spinous processes of more inferior vertebra	Cervical, thoracic, and lumbar spinal nerves
Intertransversarii (in′tĕr-trans′ver-s ăr′ē-ī)	Stabilizes vertebral column	S: Transverse process of each vertebra I: Transverse processes of more inferior vertebra	Cervical, thoracic, and lumbar spinal nerves
SPINAL EXTENSORS AND LATERAL FLEXORS			
Quadratus lumborum (quad-ră′tŭs lŭm-bōr′ŭm) *quad* = four-sided *lumb* = lumbar region	Bilateral action: Extends vertebral column Unilateral action: Laterally flexes vertebral column	S: 12th rib; transverse processes of lumbar vertebrae I: Iliaccrest	Thoracic and lumbar spinal nerves

[1] The superior attachments for vertebral column muscles are more moveable typically than the inferior attachments.

The **serratus posterior superior** attaches to ribs 2–5 (see figure 11.11) and elevates these ribs during forced inhalation, thereby increasing the lateral dimensions of the thoracic cavity. The **serratus posterior inferior** attaches to ribs 8–12 and depresses those ribs during forced exhalation.

Several groups of anterior thorax muscles change the dimensions of the thorax during respiration (**figure 11.13**). The scalene muscles (discussed in section 11.1g with other neck muscles) help elevate the first and second ribs during forced inhalation, thereby increasing the dimensions of the thoracic cavity.

The **external intercostals** extend inferomedially from the superior rib to the adjacent inferior rib. The external intercostals assist in expanding the thoracic cavity by elevating the ribs during inhalation. This movement is like lifting a bucket handle—that is, as the bucket handle (rib) is elevated, its distance from the center of the bucket (thorax) increases. Thus, contraction of the external intercostals increases the transverse dimensions of the thoracic cavity. The **internal intercostals** lie deep to the external intercostals, and their muscle fibers are at right angles to the external intercostals. The internal intercostals depress the ribs, but only during forced exhalation; normal exhalation takes no active muscular effort.

A small **transversus thoracis** extends across the inner surface of the thoracic cage and attaches to ribs 2–6. It helps depress the ribs.

Finally, the **diaphragm** is an internally placed, dome-shaped muscle that forms a partition between the thoracic and abdominopelvic cavities. It is the most important muscle associated with breathing. The muscle fibers of the diaphragm converge from its margins toward a fibrous **central tendon.** When the diaphragm contracts,

Clinical View 11.4

Paralysis of the Diaphragm

Injury to critical parts of the brain, spinal cord, or phrenic nerves can result in the loss of diaphragmatic innervation and cause paralysis. When the diaphragm becomes paralyzed, it cannot contract, and thus no air is exchanged in the lungs. The patient cannot breathe, and death is inevitable unless artificial breathing measures are implemented.

The most common cause of diaphragmatic paralysis today is spinal cord injury at or superior to the fourth cervical vertebra, where the motor neurons that innervate the diaphragm are located. In years past, infection with the poliovirus was a common cause of diaphragmatic paralysis, as the viral infection destroyed brain and spinal cord motor neurons. Prior to the development of the modern ventilator (a device to help the patient breathe) and other respiratory assistance techniques, the polio patient with diaphragmatic paralysis was placed in a device known as an **iron lung.** This was a chamber in which the air pressure surrounding the patient was cyclically decreased to facilitate inhalation and then increased to facilitate exhalation. Lying prone, with only the head extending from this large, tubular apparatus, a patient spent weeks or even months while the iron lung supplied the needed respiratory assistance.

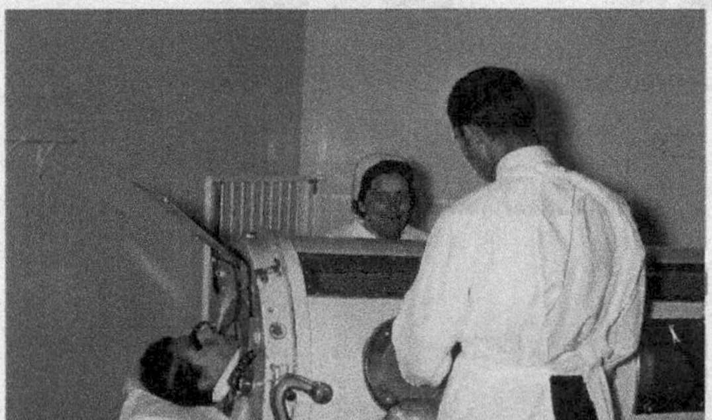

Due to a twentieth-century polio outbreak in the US, a patient with diaphragm paralysis resides in an iron lung.
Source: Centers for Disease Control and Prevention

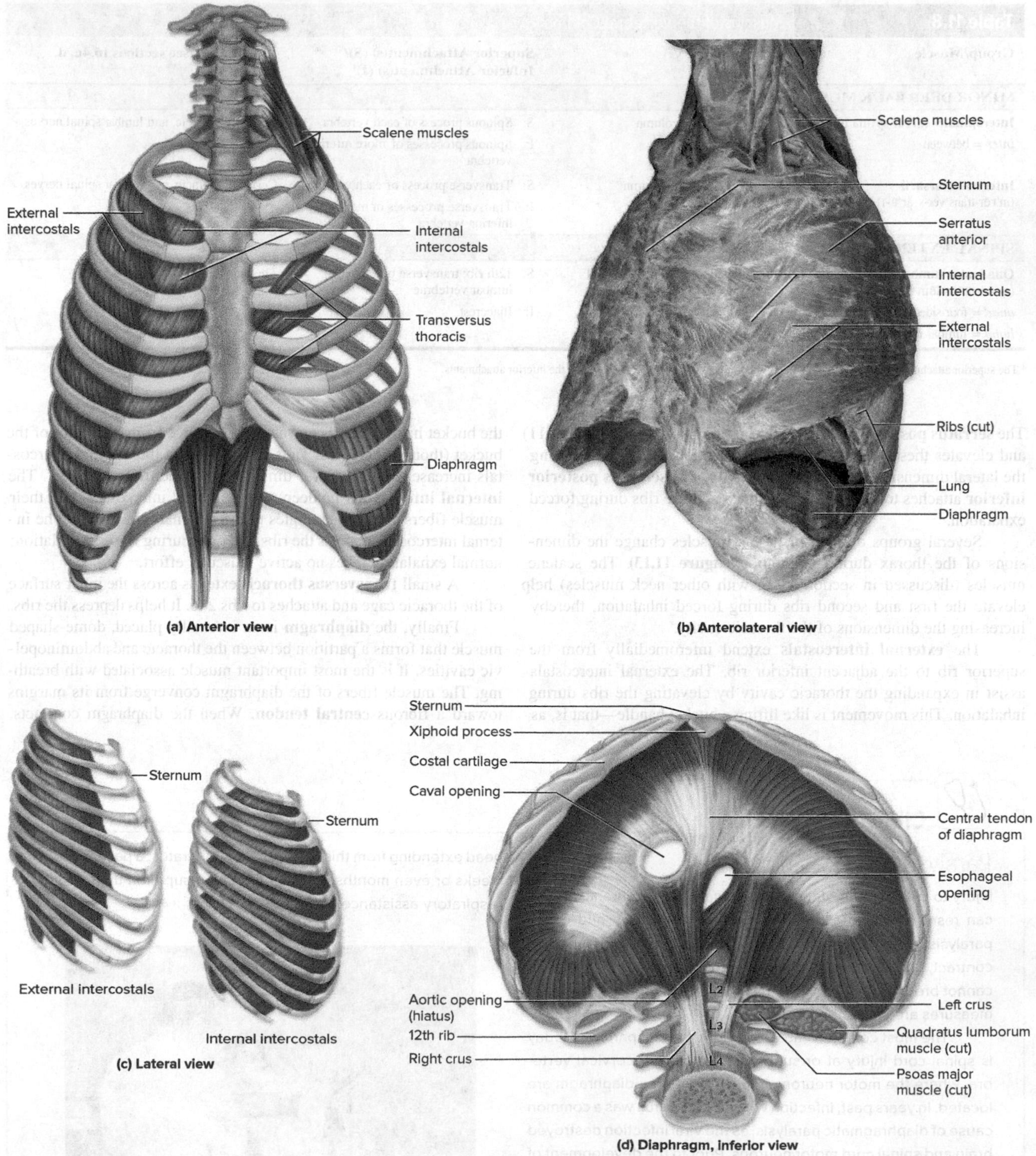
Scalene muscles
External intercostals
Internal intercostals
Transversus thoracis
Diaphragm
(a) Anterior view
Scalene muscles
Sternum
Serratus anterior
Internal intercostals
External intercostals
Ribs (cut)
Lung
Diaphragm
(b) Anterolateral view
Sternum
Sternum
External intercostals
Internal intercostals
(c) Lateral view
Sternum
Xiphoid process
Costal cartilage
Caval opening
Central tendon of diaphragm
Esophageal opening
L2
L3
L4
Aortic opening (hiatus)
12th rib
Right crus
Left crus
Quadratus lumborum muscle (cut)
Psoas major muscle (cut)
(d) Diaphragm, inferior view

Figure 11.13

Muscles of Respiration. The muscles of respiration contract rhythmically to alter the size of the thoracic cavity and facilitate respiration. (*a*) Anterior view. (*b*) A cadaver photo provides an anterolateral view, with the inferior ribs cut to expose the thoracic cavity and the superior surface of the diaphragm. (*c*) Lateral views demonstrate fiber directions of the external and internal intercostals. (*d*) Inferior view of the diaphragm. APR

Table 11.9	Muscles of Respiration		
Muscle	**Action(s)**	**Superior Attachment(s) (S)/ Inferior Attachment(s) (I)**[1]	**Innervation (see sections 16.4c, d)**
Serratus posterior superior (sĕr-ā'tŭs) *serratus* = a saw	Elevates ribs during forced inhalation	S: Spinous processes of C_7–T_3 vertebrae I: Lateral borders of ribs 2–5	Thoracic spinal nerves
Serratus posterior inferior	Depresses ribs during forced exhalation	S: Inferior borders of ribs 8–12 I: Spinous processes of T_{11}–L_2 vertebrae	Thoracic spinal nerves
Scalene muscles (anterior, middle, posterior) (described in table 11.7)			
External intercostals (in'tĕr-kos'tălz) *inter* = between *cost* = rib	Elevates ribs during inhalation	S: Superior border of inferior rib I: Inferior border of superior rib	Thoracic spinal nerves
Internal intercostals (in'ter-kos'talz)	Depresses ribs during forced exhalation; antagonistic to external intercostals	S: Superior border of inferior rib I: Inferior border of superior rib	Thoracic spinal nerves
Transversus thoracis (trans-ver's ŭs thō-ra'sis)	Depresses ribs during forced exhalation	S: Costal cartilages 2–6 I: Posterior surface of xiphoid process and inferior region of sternum	Thoracic spinal nerves
Diaphragm (dī'ă-fram) *dia* = across *phragm* = partition	Contraction causes flattening of diaphragm (moves inferiorly), and thus expansion of thoracic cavity; increases pressure in abdominopelvic cavity	S: Central tendon I: Inferior internal surface of ribs 7–12; xiphoid process of sternum and costal cartilages of inferior 6 ribs; lumbar vertebrae	Phrenic nerves (C3–C5)

[1] The superior attachment of these muscles is more moveable, except for serratus posterior superior and internal intercostals.

the central tendon is pulled inferiorly toward the abdominopelvic cavity, thereby increasing the vertical dimensions of the thoracic cavity. As it compresses the abdominopelvic cavity, it also increases intra-abdominal pressure, an event that is necessary for urination (see section 27.3b), defecation (see section 26.9c), and childbirth. Beyond respiration, diaphragm movements are also important in helping return venous blood to the heart from the inferior half of the body (see section 23.1d).

Table 11.9 summarizes the characteristics of the muscles of respiration. APR

WHAT DO YOU THINK?

3 After you've eaten a very large meal, it is sometimes difficult to take a big, deep breath. Why is it more difficult to breathe deeply with a full GI tract?

WHAT DID YOU LEARN?

9 Compare the external intercostals and the internal intercostals with respect to general location, muscle fiber direction, and action related to respiration.

10 Describe the movements of the diaphragm during respiration.

11.4 Muscles of the Abdominal Wall

✓ Learning Objective

10. Identify and describe the organization and actions of the muscles of the abdominal wall.

The anterolateral wall of the abdomen is reinforced by four pairs of muscles that collectively compress and hold the abdominal organs in place: the external oblique, internal oblique, transversus abdominis, and rectus abdominis (**figure 11.14**). This action increases intra-abdominal pressure, and so these muscles are used during forced exhalation. These muscles (except for transversus abdominis) also work together to flex the vertebral column.

The muscle fibers of the superficial **external oblique** are directed inferomedially. The external oblique is muscular along the lateral abdominal wall and forms an aponeurosis as it projects anteriorly. Inferiorly, the aponeurosis of the external oblique forms a strong, cordlike **inguinal ligament** that extends from the anterior superior iliac spine to the pubic tubercle. Immediately deep to the external oblique is the **internal oblique.** Its muscle fibers project superomedially, which is at right angles to the external oblique. Like the external oblique, this muscle forms an aponeurosis as it projects anteriorly. Unilaterally, the external and the opposite side's internal oblique work together to rotate the vertebral column (e.g., the left external oblique and the right internal oblique contract simultaneously to rotate the vertebral column to the left). APR

The deepest muscle is the **transversus abdominis,** whose fibers project transversely across the abdomen. The **rectus abdominis** is a long, straplike muscle that extends vertically the entire length of the anteromedial abdominal wall between the sternum and the pubic symphysis. It is partitioned into four segments by three fibrous **tendinous intersections,** which form the traditional "six-pack" of a muscular, toned abdominal wall. The rectus abdominis is enclosed within a fibrous sleeve called the **rectus sheath,** which is formed from the aponeuroses of the external oblique, internal oblique, and transversus abdominis muscles. The left and right rectus sheaths are connected by a vertical fibrous strip termed the **linea alba.** APR

Table 11.10 summarizes the characteristics of the muscles of the abdominal wall.

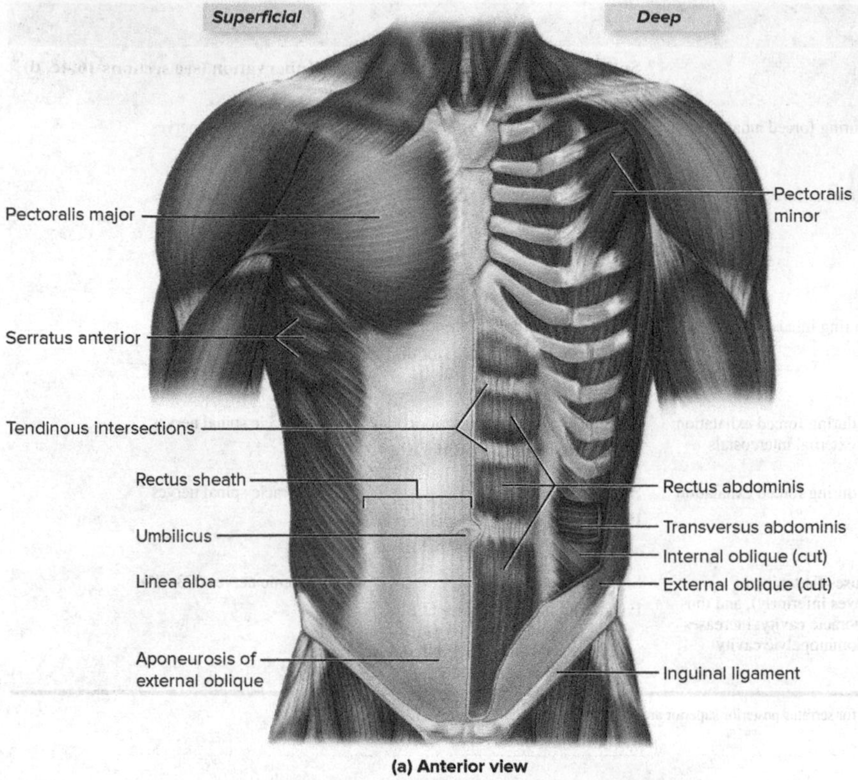

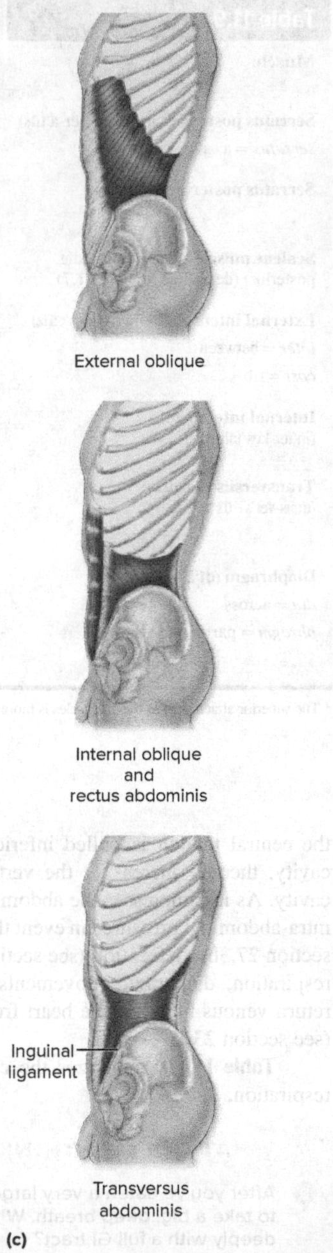

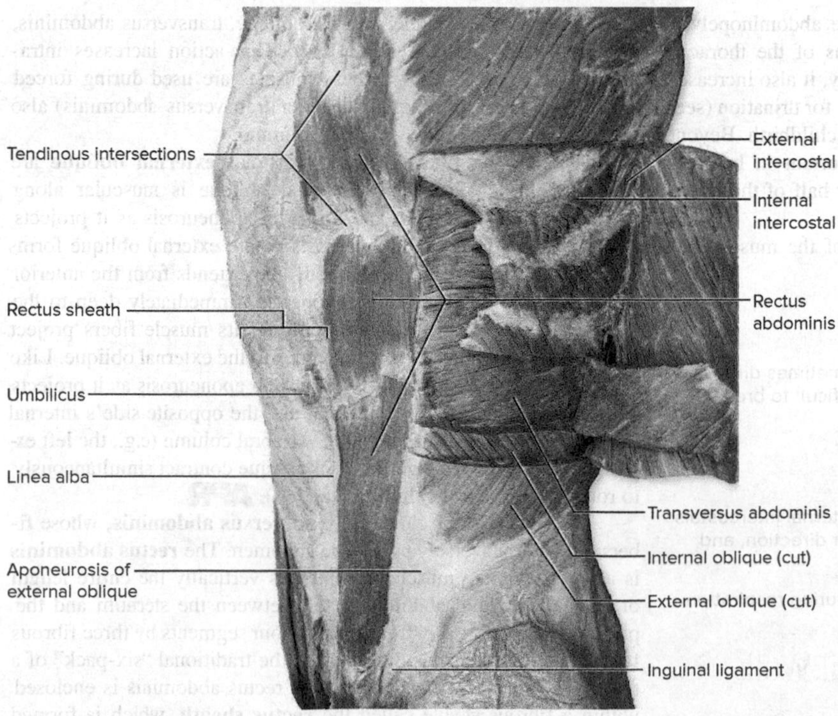

Figure 11.14

Muscles of the Abdominal Wall. The abdominal muscles compress abdominal contents , and most also flex the vertebral column. (*a*) An illustration provides an anterior view of some superficial and deep muscles. (*b*) A cadaver photo provides an anterolateral view of the muscles of the abdominal wall. (*c*) Diagrams show some individual abdominal muscles, ranging from superficial to deep. APR

©McGraw-Hill Education/Photo and Dissection by Christine Eckel

Table 11.10 Muscles of the Abdominal Wall

Muscle	Action(s)	Superior Attachment(s) (S)/ Inferior Attachment(s) (I)	Innervation (see sections 16.4c, f)
External oblique	Unilateral action: [1] Lateral flexion of vertebral column; rotation of vertebral column to same side Bilateral action: [2] Flexes vertebral column and compresses abdominal wall; used in forced exhalation	S: External and inferior borders of the inferior 8 ribs I: Linea alba by a broad aponeurosis; some to iliac crest	Spinal nerves T8–T12, L1
Internal oblique	Unilateral action: Lateral flexion of vertebral column; rotation of vertebral column to opposite side Bilateral action: Flexes vertebral column and compresses abdominal wall; used in forced exhalation	S: Lumbar fascia, inguinal ligament, and iliac crest I: Linea alba, pubic crest, inferior rib surfaces (last 4 ribs); costal cartilages of ribs 8–10	Spinal nerves T8–T12, L1
Transversus abdominis (ab-dom′i-nis)	Unilateral action: Lateral flexion of vertebral column Bilateral action: Compresses abdominal wall; used in forced exhalation	S: Iliac crest, cartilages of inferior 6 ribs; lumbar fascia; inguinal ligament I: Linea alba and pubic crest	Spinal nerves T8–T12, L1
Rectus abdominis	Flexes vertebral column; compresses abdominal wall; used in forced exhalation	S: Xiphoid process of sternum; inferior surfaces of ribs 5–7 I: Superior surface of pubis near symphysis	Spinal nerves T7–T12

[1] *Unilateral action* means only one muscle (either the left or right muscle) is contracting.

[2] *Bilateral action* means both the left and right muscles are contracting together.

Table 11.11 Muscle Actions on the Axial Skeleton

Extend the Head, Neck, and/or Vertebral Column	Flex the Head, Neck, and/or Vertebral Column	Laterally Flex the Vertebral Column	Rotate Head and/or Neck to One Side	Elevate the Ribs	Depress the Ribs
Splenius muscles[2]	Sternocleidomastoid[2]	Quadratus lumborum[1]	Sternocleidomastoid[1]	Serratus posterior superior	Serratus posterior inferior
Erector spinae[2] (iliocostalis, longissimus, spinalis)	Scalenes[2]	External oblique[1]	Splenius muscles[1]	External intercostals	Internal intercostals
Quadratus lumborum[2]	External oblique[2]	Internal oblique[1]	Longissimus capitis[1]	Scalene muscles (ribs 1 and 2 only)	Transversus thoracis
Transversospinalis group[2]	Internal oblique[2]	Transversus abdominis[1]	Obliquus capitis inferior[1]		
Minor deep back muscles[2]	Transversus abdominis[2]		Obliquus capitis superior[1]		
Rectus capitis posterior major and minor[2]	Rectus abdominis[2]				

[1] Unilateral action

[2] Bilateral action

We have seen that multiple muscles may work together to perform a common action. For example, several neck muscles and back muscles work together to extend the vertebral column. Learning muscles in groups according to common action helps most students assimilate the anatomy information. **Table 11.11** summarizes the actions of various axial muscles and groups them according to common action. A muscle that has multiple actions is listed in more than one group.

Learning Strategy 11.3

Knowing the direction of the oblique and intercostal muscle fibers can help you identify these specific muscles on models and cadavers:

- **The fibers of the external intercostals and external oblique muscles run in the same direction—inferomedially. This is the same direction that you put your hands in your pockets.**
- **The fibers of the internal intercostals and internal oblique muscles run perpendicular (in the opposite direction) to the external muscles—superomedially.**

WHAT DID YOU LEARN?

11. List the muscles of the abdominal wall from superficial to deep, and describe the directionality of each of their muscle fiber arrangements.

Clinical View 11.5

Hernias

The condition in which a portion of the viscera protrudes through a weakened point of the muscular wall of the abdominopelvic cavity is called a **hernia** (her′nē-ă; rupture). A significant medical problem may develop if the herniated portion of the intestine swells, becoming trapped. Blood flow to the trapped segment may diminish, causing that portion of the intestine to die. This condition, called a *strangulated intestinal hernia,* is very painful and can be life-threatening if not treated promptly.

Two common types of hernias are inguinal hernias and femoral hernias. An **inguinal hernia** is the most common type of hernia. The inguinal region is one of the weakest areas of the abdominal wall. Within this region is a canal (inguinal canal) that allows the passage of the spermatic cord in males (see section 28.3b), or a smaller structure called the *round ligament* in females (see section 28.2c). The inguinal canal, or the **superficial inguinal ring** associated with it, is often the site of a rupture or separation of the abdominal wall. Males are more likely to develop inguinal hernias than females, because their inguinal canals and superficial inguinal rings are larger to allow room for the spermatic cord. Rising pressure in the abdominopelvic cavity, as might develop while straining to lift a heavy object, provides the force to push a segment of the small intestine into the canal. (See Clinical View 13.3: "Testing for Inguinal Hernias" for further information and an image of an inguinal hernia.) There are two types of inguinal hernia:

- In a **direct inguinal hernia,** the loop of small intestine protrudes directly through the superficial inguinal ring, but not through the entire length of the inguinal canal, and creates a bulge in the lower anterior abdominal wall. This type of hernia is typically seen in middle-aged males with poorly developed abdominal muscles and protruding abdomens.
- In an **indirect inguinal hernia,** the herniation travels through the entire inguinal canal and may even extend all the way into the scrotum, because the path of the herniation follows the path of the spermatic cord. This type of hernia tends to occur in children who have a congenital anomaly called *patent process vaginalis,* in which the embryonic path taken by the testis into the scrotum fails to regress.

A **femoral hernia** occurs in the upper thigh, just inferior to the inguinal ligament, originating in a region called the femoral triangle. The medial part of the femoral triangle is relatively weak and prone to stress injury, thus allowing a loop of small intestine to protrude. Women more commonly develop femoral hernias because of the greater width of their femoral triangle, which equates to the wider hip span.

11.5 Muscles of the Pelvic Floor

✓ Learning Objective

11. Describe the general collective actions of the muscles of the pelvic floor.
12. Identify and describe the muscles that form the pelvic floor and perineum.

The floor of the pelvic cavity is formed by three layers of muscles and associated fasciae, collectively known as the **pelvic diaphragm.** (The term *diaphragm* refers to a muscle or group of muscles that covers or partitions an opening.) The pelvic diaphragm extends from the ischium and pubis of the ossa coxae across the pelvic outlet to the sacrum and coccyx. These muscles collectively form the pelvic floor and support the pelvic viscera **(figure 11.15)**.

The most superior (deepest) layer of the pelvic diaphram consists of the coccygeus and the levator ani. The **coccygeus** pulls the coccyx anteriorly after its posterior deflection during defecation or childbirth. The **external anal sphincter** (located within a region called the anal triangle) assists in defecation. The largest and most important collection of muscles in the pelvic floor is the **levator ani.** It supports the pelvic viscera and functions as a sphincter at the anorectal junction, urethra, and vagina. The levator ani is formed by the **iliococcygeus,** the **pubococcygeus,** and the **puborectalis** (not shown in figures). The puborectalis muscle forms a circular "sling" around the anorectal junction. When this muscle is contracted, it increases the bend or angle of the anorectal junction. When an individual wishes to defecate, the puborectalis muscle must be consciously relaxed to decrease the bend of the anorectal junction and allow for the easy passage of feces through the rectum.

The diamond-shaped region between the lower appendages is called the **perineum** (see section 28.1a). The perineum has four significant bony landmarks: the pubic symphysis anteriorly, the coccyx posteriorly, and both ischial tuberosities laterally. A transverse line drawn between the ischial tuberosities partitions the perineum into an anterior **urogenital triangle** that contains the external genitalia and urethra, and a posterior **anal triangle** that contains the anus (figure 11.15 *b, c*).

The urogenital triangle is subdivided into a superficial layer and a deep layer. The **superficial layer** of the urogenital triangle is composed of three muscles: **bulbospongiosus, ischiocavernosus,** and **superficial transverse perineal (table 11.12)**. The ischiocavernosus attaches to the pubic symphysis, whereas the bulbospongiosus and superficial transverse perineal muscles attach to a tendinous central structure called the **perineal body** (or *central tendon* of the perineum). The **deep layer** of the urogenital triangle is composed of two muscles: the **deep transverse perineal** and the **external urethral sphincter.**

Table 11.12 summarizes the characteristics of the muscles of the pelvic floor.

Figure 11.15

Muscles of the Pelvic Floor. The pelvic floor is composed of muscle layers that form the urogenital and anal triangles, extend across the pelvic outlet, and support the organs in the pelvic cavity (puborectalis not shown). (*a*) Superior view of the female pelvic cavity. Inferior views show (*b*) male and (*c*) female perineal regions. Muscles of the pelvic floor are in bold. APR

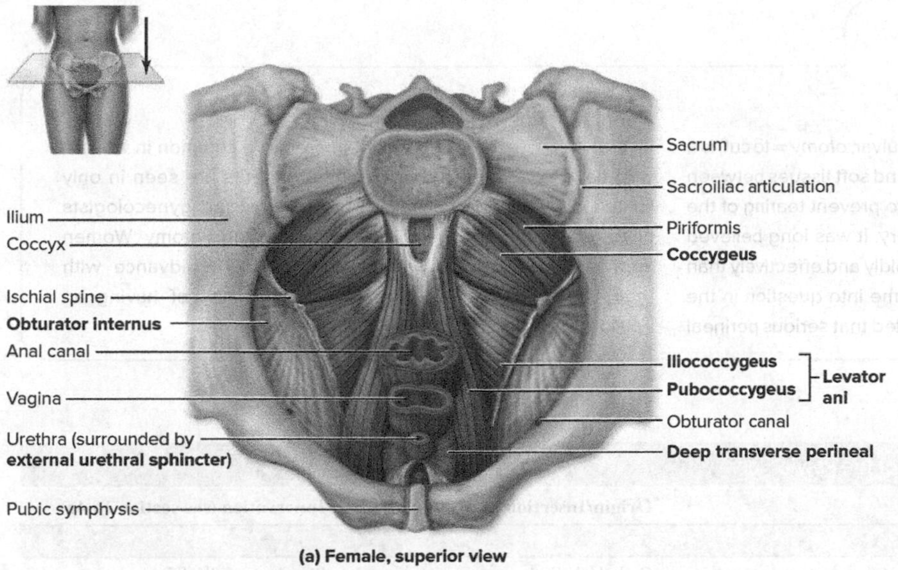

Sacrum
Sacroiliac articulation
Ilium
Piriformis
Coccyx
Coccygeus
Ischial spine
Obturator internus
Anal canal
Iliococcygeus
Pubococcygeus
Levator ani
Vagina
Obturator canal
Urethra (surrounded by **external urethral sphincter)**
Deep transverse perineal
Pubic symphysis
(a) Female, superior view

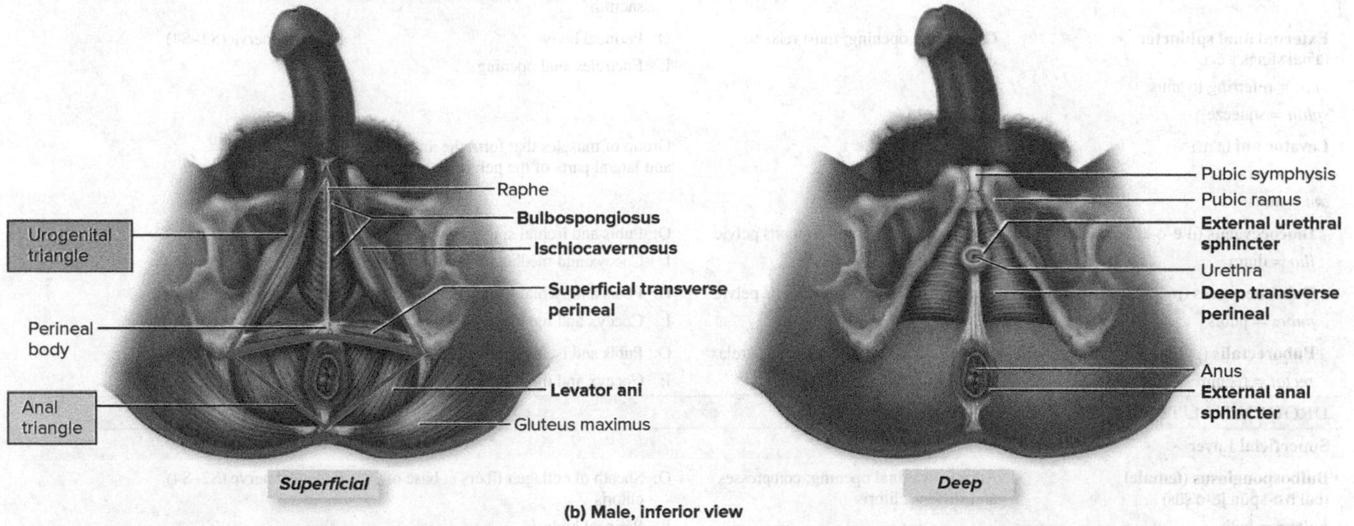

Raphe
Urogenital triangle
Bulbospongiosus
Ischiocavernosus
Superficial transverse perineal
Perineal body
Anal triangle
Levator ani
Gluteus maximus
Superficial
Pubic symphysis
Pubic ramus
External urethral sphincter
Urethra
Deep transverse perineal
Anus
External anal sphincter
Deep
(b) Male, inferior view

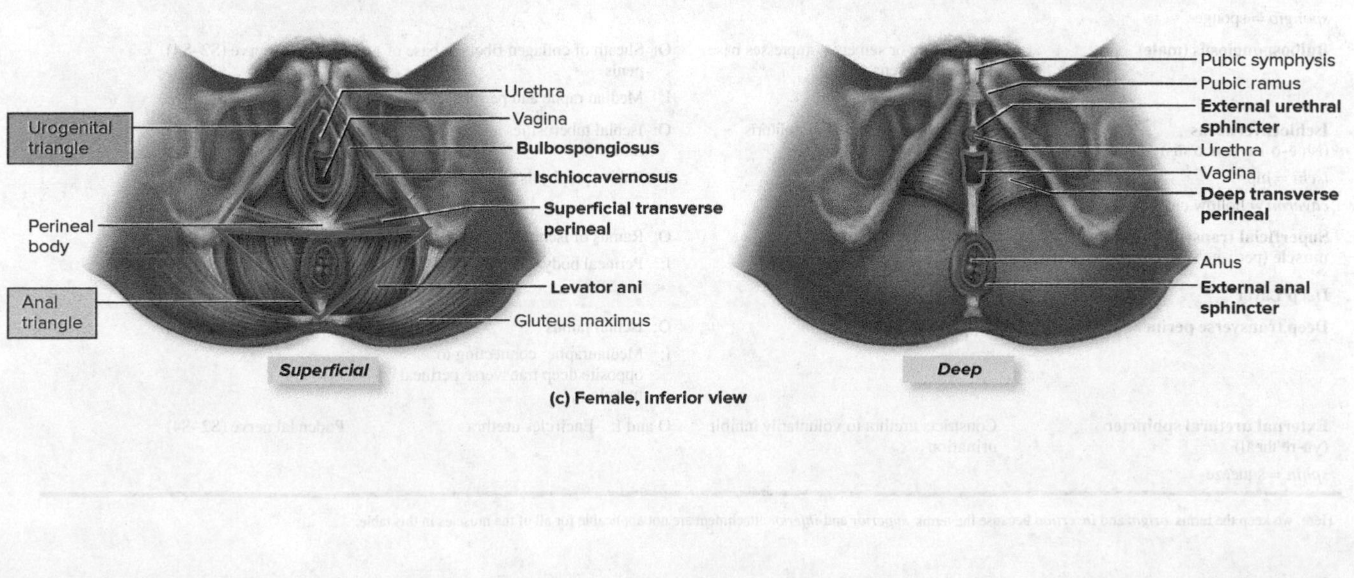

Urethra
Vagina
Urogenital triangle
Bulbospongiosus
Ischiocavernosus
Superficial transverse perineal
Perineal body
Levator ani
Anal triangle
Gluteus maximus
Superficial
Pubic symphysis
Pubic ramus
External urethral sphincter
Urethra
Vagina
Deep transverse perineal
Anus
External anal sphincter
Deep
(c) Female, inferior view

Clinical View 11.6

Episiotomy

An **episiotomy** (e-piz-ē-ot′ō-mē; *epicios* = vulvar, *otomy* = to cut) is a surgical incision made in the perineal skin and soft tissues between the vagina and the anus during childbirth to prevent tearing of the mother's tissues and to minimize fetal injury. It was long believed that a clean surgical incision heals more rapidly and effectively than a laceration or tear, but its routine use came into question in the late twentieth century. Studies have indicated that serious perineal lacerations, infection, and bleeding are more common in women who have had an episiotomy, and its benefits are seen in only limited deliveries. Now, many obstetricians and gynecologists have recommended against routine use of episiotomy. Women approaching childbirth are advised to talk in advance with their health-care provider about the necessity of having an episiotomy.

Table 11.12 Muscles of the Pelvic Floor

Group/Muscle	Action(s)	Origin/Insertion[1]	Innervation (see section 16.4g)
ANAL TRIANGLE			
Coccygeus (kok-sij′ ē-ŭs) *coccy* = coccyx	Forms pelvic floor and supports pelvic viscera	O: Ischial spine I: Lateral and inferior borders of sacrum	Spinal nerves (S4–S5)
External anal sphincter (ā′năl sfingk′t ĕr) *anal* = referring to anus *sphin* = squeeze	Closes anal opening; must relax to defecate	O: Perineal body I: Encircles anal opening	Pudendal nerve (S2–S4)
Levator ani (ā′nī) *levator* = raises *ani* = anus		Group of muscles that form the anterior and lateral parts of the pelvic diaphragm	
Iliococcygeus (il′ē-ō-kok-si′j ē-ŭs) *ilio* = ilium	Forms pelvic floor and supports pelvic viscera	O: Pubis and ischial spine I: Coccyx and median raphe	Pudendal nerve (S2–S4)
Pubococcygeus (pyū′bō-kok-si′j ē-ŭs) *pubes* = pubis	Forms pelvic floor and supports pelvic viscera	O: Pubis and ischial spine I: Coccyx and median raphe	Pudendal nerve (S2–S4)
Puborectalis (pyū′bō-rek′tăl-is) *rectal* = rectum	Supports anorectal junction; must relax to defecate	O: Pubis and ischial spine I: Coccyx and median raphe	Pudendal nerve (S2–S4)
UROGENITAL TRIANGLE			
Superficial Layer			
Bulbospongiosus (female) (bul′b ō-spŭn′jē-ō′sŭs) *bulbon* = bulb *spongio* = sponge	Narrows vaginal opening; compresses and stiffens clitoris	O: Sheath of collagen fibers at base of clitoris I: Perineal body	Pudendal nerve (S2–S4)
Bulbospongiosus (male)	Ejects urine or semen; compresses base of penis; stiffens penis	O: Sheath of collagen fibers at base of penis I: Median raphe and perineal body	Pudendal nerve (S2–S4)
Ischiocavernosus (ish′ē-ō-kav′er-n ō′sŭs) *ischi* = hip *caverna* = hollow chamber	Assists erection of penis or clitoris	O: Ischial tuberosities and ischial ramus I: Pubic symphysis	Pudendal nerve (S2–S4)
Superficial transverse perineal muscle (per′i-nē′ăl)	Supports pelvic organs	O: Ramus of ischium I: Perineal body	Pudendal nerve (S2–S4)
Deep Layer			
Deep transverse perineal muscle	Supports pelvic organs	O: Ischial ramus I: Medianraphe connecting to opposite deep transverse perineal muscle	Pudendal nerve (S2–S4)
External urethral sphincter (yū-rē′thr ăl) *sphin* = squeeze	Constricts urethra to voluntarily inhibit urination	O and I: Encircles urethra	Pudendal nerve (S2–S4)

[1] Here, we keep the terms *origin* and *insertion* because the terms *superior* and *inferior* attachment are not applicable for all of the muscles in this table.

Clinical Terms

linea nigra Condition sometimes seen in pregnancy, where the linea alba of the rectus sheath darkens (hence the term "nigra"), forming a line that extends along the midline of the abdomen.

rectus sheath separation Separation of the left and right rectus muscles/sheaths due to great expansion of the abdomen (as occurs in some pregnancies). If severe, the separation may have to be repaired surgically.

Chapter Summary

	■ The axial muscles attach to components of the axial skeleton, whereas the appendicular muscles stabilize or move components of the appendicular skeleton. ■ Axial musculature actions include supporting and positioning the head, vertebral column, and thoracic cage; controlling movements associated with respiration; and forming part of the floor of the pelvic cavity.
11.1 Muscles of the Head and Neck	■ Muscles of the head and neck are separated into groups based upon their specific activities. **11.1a Muscles of Facial Expression** ■ The muscles of facial expression arise from the skull and often attach to the skin. **11.1b Extrinsic Eye Muscles** ■ The six extrinsic eye muscles attach to the eye and control the movements and position of the eyes. **11.1c Muscles of Mastication** ■ The muscles of mastication move the mandible during chewing. **11.1d Muscles That Move the Tongue** ■ The muscles of the tongue are divided into intrinsic muscles and extrinsic muscles, which function during chewing, swallowing, and speaking. **11.1e Muscles of the Pharynx** ■ Muscles of the pharynx function in swallowing. **11.1f Muscles of the Anterior Neck** ■ Anterior neck muscles are the suprahyoid muscles, superior to the hyoid bone, and the infrahyoid muscles, inferior to the hyoid bone. These move the hyoid bone or thyroid cartilage during swallowing or speaking. **11.1g Muscles That Move the Head and Neck** ■ Muscles that move the head and neck arise from the vertebral column, the thoracic cage, and the pectoral girdle, and attach to bones of the cranium.
11.2 Muscles of the Vertebral Column	■ Deep back muscles extend the vertebral column.
11.3 Muscles of Respiration	■ The muscles of respiration are located on the anterior and posterior surfaces of the thorax and are covered by more superficial muscles. Their contraction either increases or decreases the size of the thoracic cavity.
11.4 Muscles of the Abdominal Wall	■ The muscles of the abdominal wall compress the abdomen, help hold the abdominal organs in place, and assist the stabilization and lateral flexion of the vertebral column.
11.5 Muscles of the Pelvic Floor	■ The muscles of the pelvic floor extend from the pubis and ischium anteriorly to the sacrum and coccyx posteriorly. They support the pelvic cavity organs and control the evacuation of waste materials from the digestive and urinary systems.

Challenge Yourself

Actively write or type your answers in a separate document to reinforce your learning, before checking your answers.

Multiple Choice

Select the best answer from the four choices provided.

1. What is the correct action of the geniohyoid muscle?
   a. depresses the hyoid bone
   b. elevates the floor of the mouth
   c. elevates the hyoid bone
   d. depresses the larynx

2. When the left and right ______ contract, they flex the neck.
   a. sternocleidomastoid
   b. longissimus group
   c. splenius
   d. rectus abdominis

3. When this large muscle contracts, the vertical dimensions of the thoracic cavity increase.
   a. external intercostal
   b. internal intercostal
   c. diaphragm
   d. transversus thoracis
4. Which of the following is a muscle of the pelvic floor, but *not* a muscle within the urogenital triangle?
   a. bulbospongiosus
   b. coccygeus
   c. superficial transverse perineal
   d. ischiocavernosus
5. Which eye muscle moves the eye medially?
   a. inferior rectus
   b. inferior oblique
   c. lateral rectus
   d. superior oblique
6. Which muscle allows you to stick out your tongue?
   a. palatoglossus
   b. genioglossus
   c. lateral pterygoid
   d. hyoglossus
7. Which of the following muscles is *least likely* (or least able) to laterally flex the vertebral column?
   a. external oblique
   b. quadratus lumborum
   c. spinalis
   d. internal oblique
8. Which muscle elevates and protracts the mandible?
   a. temporalis
   b. lateral pterygoid
   c. masseter
   d. medial pterygoid
9. What is one action of the transversus abdominis muscles?
   a. elevate the ribs
   b. compress the abdominal wall
   c. extend the vertebral column
   d. increase the dimensions of the thoracic cavity
10. Which muscle protrudes the lower lip (as when you "pout")?
   a. risorius
   b. levator labii superioris
   c. mentalis
   d. zygomaticus major

Content Review

1. Describe which muscles of facial expression you use to (a) smile and (b) frown.
2. Compare and contrast the actions of the extrinsic muscles of the tongue.
3. Discuss why the eye moves slightly medially during the contraction of either the superior or inferior rectus muscle.
4. Discuss the effect of contracting the three pharyngeal constrictors during swallowing.
5. Distinguish between suprahyoid and infrahyoid muscles, and describe the actions of each group.
6. Describe the differences in action between bilateral and unilateral contraction of the splenius muscles.
7. Describe the actions of the thoracic diaphragm.
8. What is the effect of contracting the abdominal oblique muscles?
9. Describe the three components of the erector spinae muscles with respect to placement, attachments, and actions.
10. What are the general actions of the pelvic diaphragm muscles, and what specific muscles form the pelvic diaphragm?

Developing Critical Reasoning

1. Albon is a 45-year-old male who characterizes himself as a "couch potato." He exercises infrequently and has a rounded abdomen ("beer belly"). While helping a friend move some heavy furniture, he felt a sharp pain deep within his abdominopelvic cavity. An emergency room resident told Albon that he had suffered an inguinal hernia. What is this injury, how did it occur, and how might Albon's poorly developed abdominal musculature have contributed to it?
2. While training on the balance beam, Pat slipped during her landing from a back flip and fell, straddling the beam. Although only slightly sore from the fall, she became concerned when she suddenly lost the ability to completely control her urination. What might have happened to Pat's pelvic floor structures during the fall?
3. Your 70-year-old grandfather tells you he wonders what causes his "crow's feet" (horizontal wrinkles by the lateral corners of his eyes). Based on your knowledge of skeletal muscle anatomy, how would you explain this phenomenon to your grandfather?

Answers to "What Do You Think?"

1. The zygomaticus major, zygomaticus minor, levator anguli oris, risorius, and levator labii superioris all contract when you smile.
2. Because the omohyoid attaches to the scapula, the prefix *-omo* means "shoulder."
3. When you breathe deeply, the diaphragm contracts and pushes down on the GI tract (abdominal viscera). If these viscera are bulging with food, the diaphragm has difficulty contracting fully, making it hard to take deep breaths.

Design Element: Pencil Icon: Slavojub Pantelic/Shutterstock

MUSCULAR SYSTEM

Appendicular Muscles 12

Outline

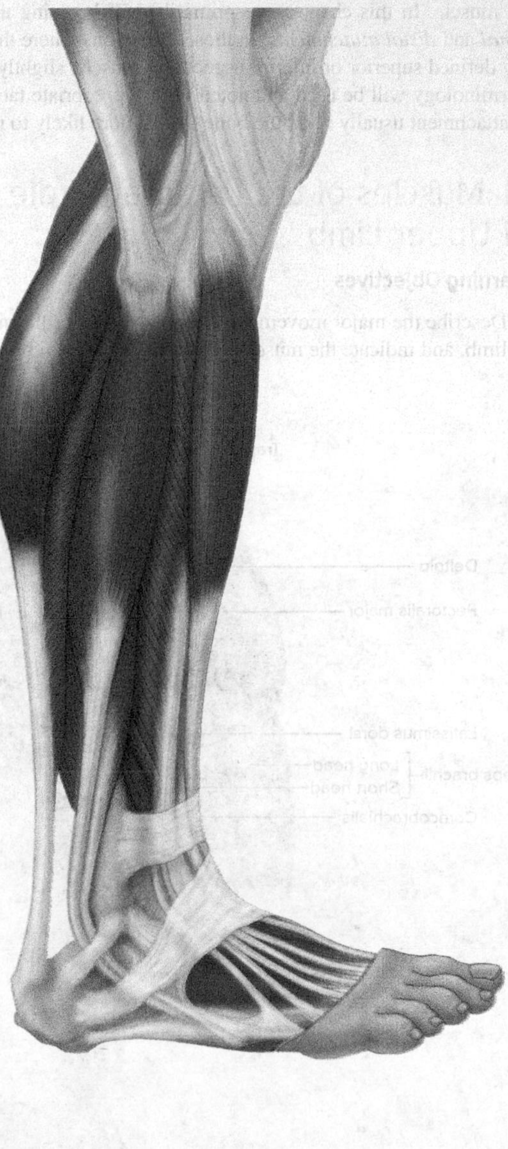

Anatomy & Physiology Revealed 4.0

MODULE 6: MUSCULAR SYSTEM

The **appendicular muscles** control the movements of the upper and lower limbs, and stabilize and control the movements of the pectoral and pelvic girdles. These muscles are organized into groups based upon their location in the body or the part of the skeleton they move. Beyond their individual activities, these muscles also work in groups that are either synergistic or antagonistic. Refer to figure 10.14 to review how muscles are named, and recall the first Learning Strategy from the chapter 11 introduction that gives suggestions for learning the muscles.

As discussed in section 10.2b, the terms *origin* and *insertion* will be replaced by the terms *superior attachment* and *inferior attachment* for axial muscles, and *proximal attachment* and *distal attachment* for appendicular muscles. Traditional origins and insertions are not always easily determined by either movement or position. In contrast, attachment locations are easier to identify and better describe the placement of the muscle. In this chapter, we primarily will be using the terms *proximal* and *distal attachments.* In those exceptions where there is no clearly defined superior or inferior aspect of a muscle, slightly alternative terminology will be used and noted in the appropriate tables. The distal attachment usually is on the bone that is more likely to move.

12.1 Muscles of the Pectoral Girdle and Upper Limb

✓ Learning Objectives

1. Describe the major movements of the pectoral girdle and upper limb, and indicate the muscles involved for each movement.
2. Identify and describe the muscles that move the scapula and their actions.
3. Name and describe the muscles of the glenohumeral joint, and explain how each moves the humerus.
4. Locate, name, and describe the muscles that move the elbow joints and their actions.
5. Describe the compartments of the arm and identify the muscles within each compartment and their actions.
6. Identify and describe the muscles that move the wrist joint, fingers, and thumb and their actions.
7. Describe the compartments of the forearm and identify the muscles within each compartment and their actions.
8. Identify and describe the intrinsic muscles of the hand and their actions.

Muscles that move the pectoral girdle and upper limb are organized into specific groups: (1) muscles that move the pectoral girdle; (2) muscles that move the glenohumeral joint/arm; (3) arm and forearm muscles that move the elbow joint/forearm; (4) forearm muscles that move the wrist joint, hand, and fingers; and (5) intrinsic muscles of the hand. Some of these muscles are superficial, and others are deep.

12.1a Muscles That Move the Pectoral Girdle

The muscles of the pectoral girdle attach the scapula and clavicle to the axial skeleton **(figures 12.1 and 12.2)**. These muscles both

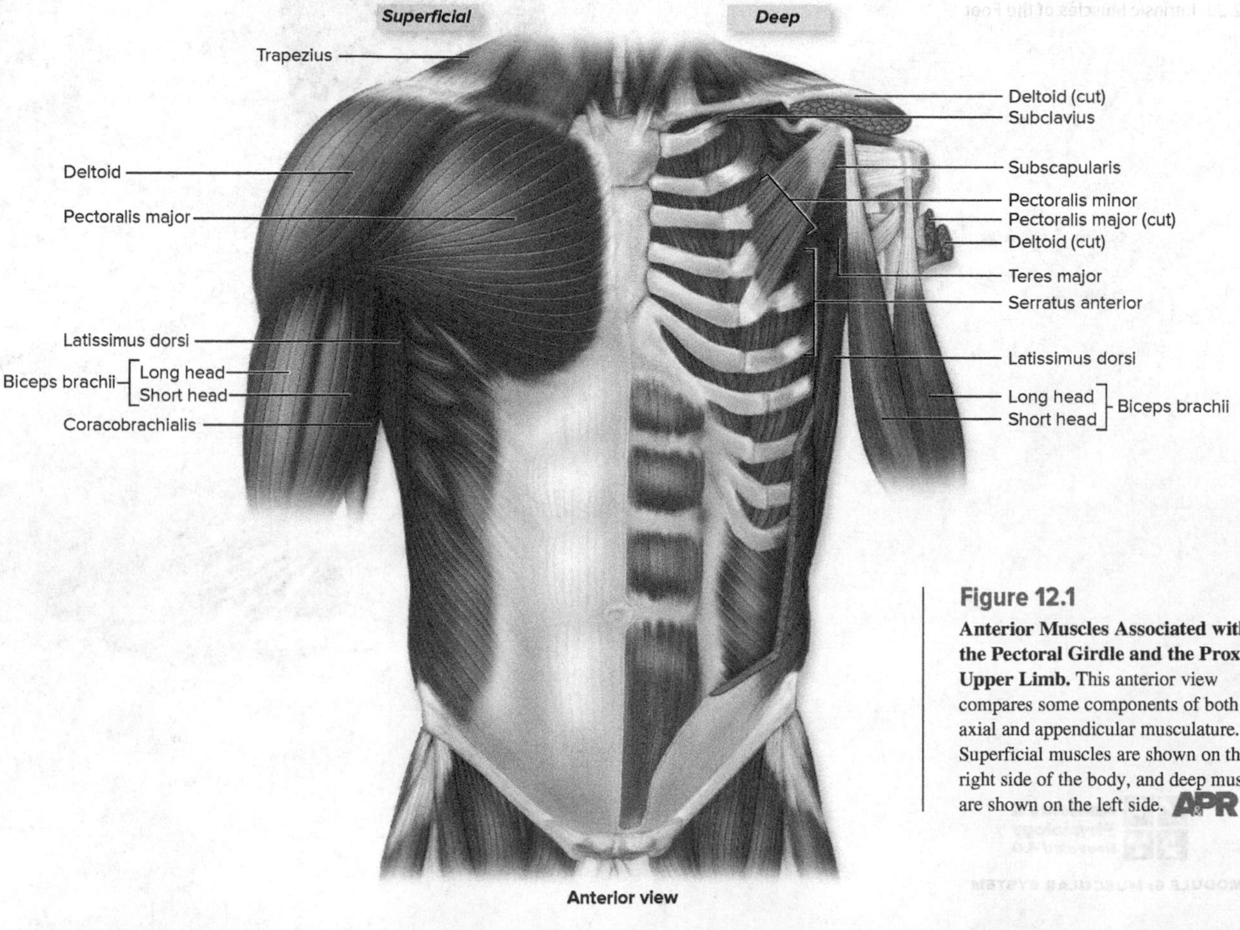
Superficial
Deep
Trapezius
Deltoid
Pectoralis major
Latissimus dorsi
Biceps brachii
Long head
Short head
Coracobrachialis
Deltoid (cut)
Subclavius
Subscapularis
Pectoralis minor
Pectoralis major (cut)
Deltoid (cut)
Teres major
Serratus anterior
Latissimus dorsi
Long head
Short head
Biceps brachii
Anterior view

Figure 12.1

Anterior Muscles Associated with the Pectoral Girdle and the Proximal Upper Limb. This anterior view compares some components of both the axial and appendicular musculature. Superficial muscles are shown on the right side of the body, and deep muscles are shown on the left side. APR

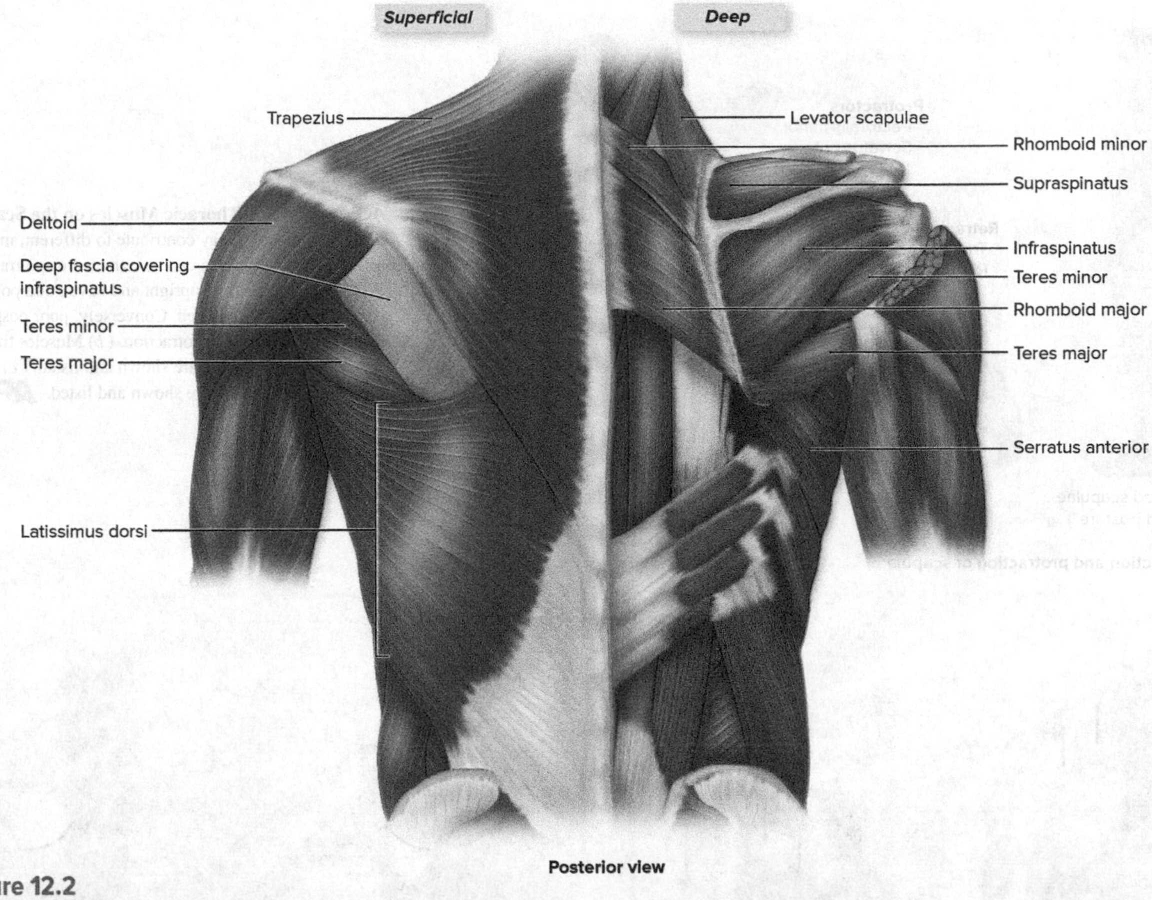

Figure 12.2

Posterior Muscles Associated with the Pectoral Girdle and the Proximal Upper Limb. This posterior view compares some components of both the axial and appendicular musculature. Only those muscles that move the scapula or the upper limb are labeled. Superficial muscles are shown on the left, and deep muscles are shown on the right. APR

Learning Strategy 12.1

When studying appendicular muscle action, remember these two basic rules:

1. If a muscle crosses over or spans a joint, it must move that joint. For example, because the biceps brachii crosses over the elbow joint, it must move the elbow joint.
2. Conversely, if a muscle doesn't cross over or span a joint, it cannot move that joint. For example, the deltoid is found in the shoulder, and it does not cross over the wrist joint. Therefore, there is no possible way the deltoid can move the wrist joint!

If you can visualize where a muscle is located in your body, you can usually figure out what type of movement the muscle performs.

stabilize the scapula (keep it from moving) and move it to increase the range of motion of the arm. Some of the superficial muscles of the thorax are grouped together according to the scapular movement they direct: elevation, depression, retraction, or protraction (**figure 12.3**). The muscles that move the pectoral girdle are classified according to their location in the thorax as either anterior or posterior thoracic muscles.

The anterior thoracic muscles are the pectoralis minor, serratus anterior, and subclavius (shown in **figure 12.4*a***). The **pectoralis minor** is a thin, flat, triangular muscle deep to the pectoralis major. This muscle helps depress and protract (pull anteriorly) the scapula. When your shoulders are hunched forward, the pectoralis minor muscle is contracting. The **serratus anterior** is a large, flat, fan-shaped muscle positioned between the ribs and the scapula. Its name is derived from the saw-toothed (serrated) appearance of its attachments to the ribs. This muscle is the agonist (prime mover) in scapula protraction, and thus works synergistically with the pectoralis minor. Serratus anterior also stabilizes or holds the scapula against the posterior side of the rib cage. It is a powerful superior rotator of the scapula and acts to move the glenoid cavity superiorly, as occurs when you abduct the upper limb. The **subclavius** is a small, cylindrical muscle named for its location inferior to the clavicle. It extends from the first rib to the clavicle, and its main action is to stabilize and depress the clavicle. APR

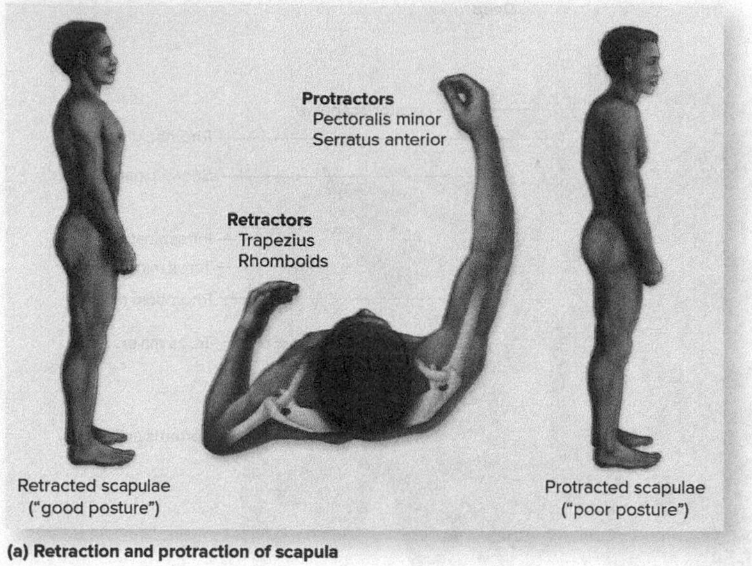
Protractors
Pectoralis minor
Serratus anterior
Retractors
Trapezius
Rhomboids
Retracted scapulae
("good posture")
Protracted scapulae
("poor posture")

(a) Retraction and protraction of scapula

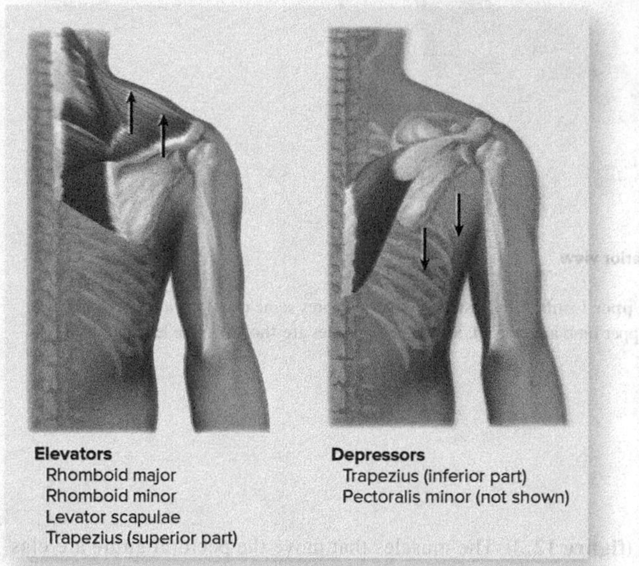
Elevators
Rhomboid major
Rhomboid minor
Levator scapulae
Trapezius (superior part)
Depressors
Trapezius (inferior part)
Pectoralis minor (not shown)

(b) Elevation and depression of scapula

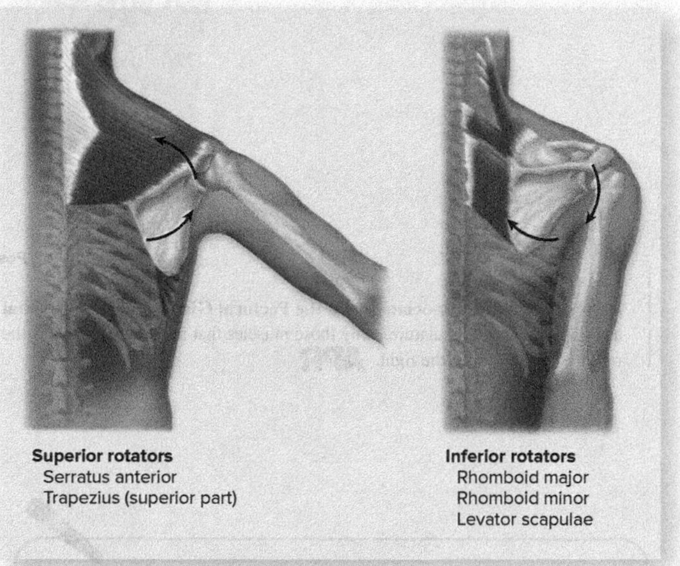
Superior rotators
Serratus anterior
Trapezius (superior part)
Inferior rotators
Rhomboid major
Rhomboid minor
Levator scapulae

(c) Superior and inferior rotation of scapula

Figure 12.3

Actions of Some Thoracic Muscles on the Scapula. Individual muscles may contribute to different, multiple actions. (*a*) The scapula can be retracted or protracted. When you are standing upright and have good posture, your scapulae are retracted. Conversely, poor posture demonstrates scapular protraction. (*b*) Muscles that elevate and depress the scapula are shown and listed. (*c*) Muscles that rotate the scapula are shown and listed. APR

The posterior thoracic muscles are the trapezius, levator scapulae, rhomboid minor, and rhomboid major (shown in figure 12.4*b*). The **trapezius** is a large, flat, diamond-shaped muscle that attaches medially to the skull and vertebral column and to the scapula and clavicle, laterally. In general, the trapezius can elevate, depress, retract, or rotate the scapula, depending upon which fibers of the muscle are contracting. The superior fibers of the trapezius elevate and superiorly rotate the scapula. The middle fibers work with the rhomboid muscles to retract the scapula, while the inferior fibers depress the scapula. APR

The **levator scapulae** is a narrow, elongated muscle that is deep to both the trapezius and sternocleidomastoid muscles. Its multiple heads attach superiorly to the transverse processes of the cervical vertebrae and attaches inferiorly to the superior angle of the scapula. As its name implies, its primary action is to elevate the scapula. It can also inferiorly rotate the scapula so that the glenoid cavity points inferiorly.

Both the **rhomboid minor** and the **rhomboid major** are located deep to the trapezius. These rhomboid muscles are parallel bands that run inferolaterally from the vertebrae to the scapula. Often they are indistinct from each other. They help elevate and retract (adduct) the scapula, as when you stand up straight with your shoulders back. The rhomboid muscles also inferiorly rotate the scapula. APR

Table 12.1 summarizes the characteristics of the thoracic muscles that move the pectoral girdle. APR

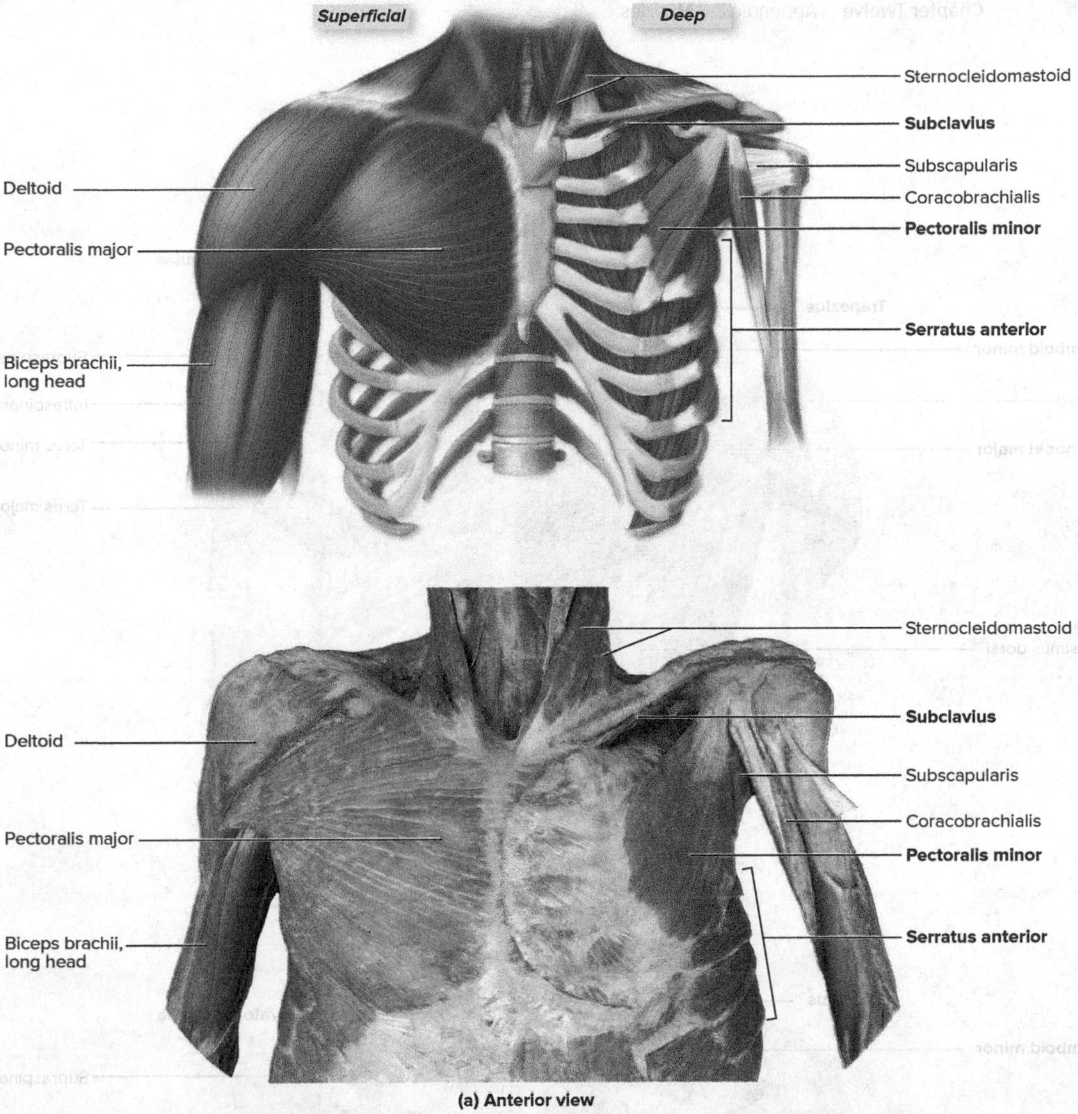
Superficial
Deep
Sternocleidomastoid
Subclavius
Subscapularis
Coracobrachialis
Pectoralis minor
Serratus anterior
Deltoid
Pectoralis major
Biceps brachii, long head
Sternocleidomastoid
Subclavius
Subscapularis
Coracobrachialis
Pectoralis minor
Serratus anterior
Deltoid
Pectoralis major
Biceps brachii, long head
(a) Anterior view

Figure 12.4

Muscles That Move the Pectoral Girdle and the Glenohumeral Joint/Arm. Illustrations and cadaver photos show (*a*) anterior and (*b*) posterior views of the muscles whose primary action is to move the pectoral girdle (scapula or clavicle), labeled in bold. Muscles that attach to the pectoral girdle but primarily move the arm are labeled but not in bold. On the anterior view (*a*) the superficial muscles are shown on the right side of the body and deep muscles on the left. On the posterior view (*b*) the superficial muscles are shown left and the deep muscles are shown on the right. APR

Clinical View 12.1

Paralysis of the Serratus Anterior Muscle ("Winged Scapula")

The serratus anterior muscle receives its innervation from the long thoracic nerve, which travels inferiorly along the anterolateral chest wall. Because of its location, the long thoracic nerve is occasionally damaged or cut during surgical removal of the breast (radical mastectomy). Damage to this nerve causes paralysis of the serratus anterior muscle. Recall that the serratus anterior is the primary protractor of the scapula, and under normal circumstances, its pull on the scapula is counterbalanced by the posterior thoracic (superficial back) muscles. Paralysis of the serratus anterior muscle leaves the posterior thoracic muscles unopposed. If a patient with this condition puts both arms anteriorly on a wall and then pushes, the scapula on the injured side will poke posteriorly like a bird's wing, a classic sign known as a **winged scapula.** The scapula on the unaffected side will remain in the expected anatomic position, close to the thoracic wall.

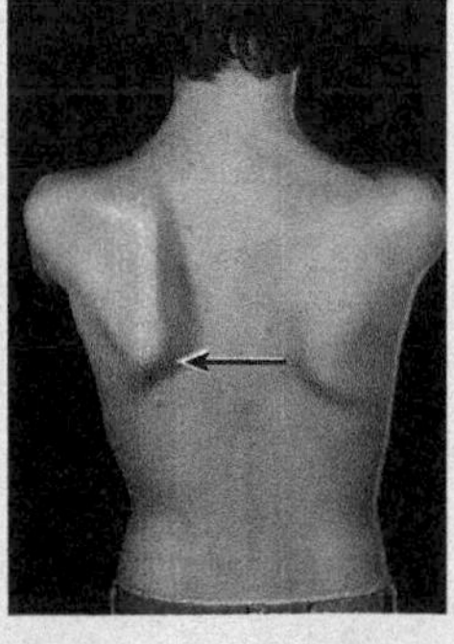

Winged left scapula indicated by arrow.

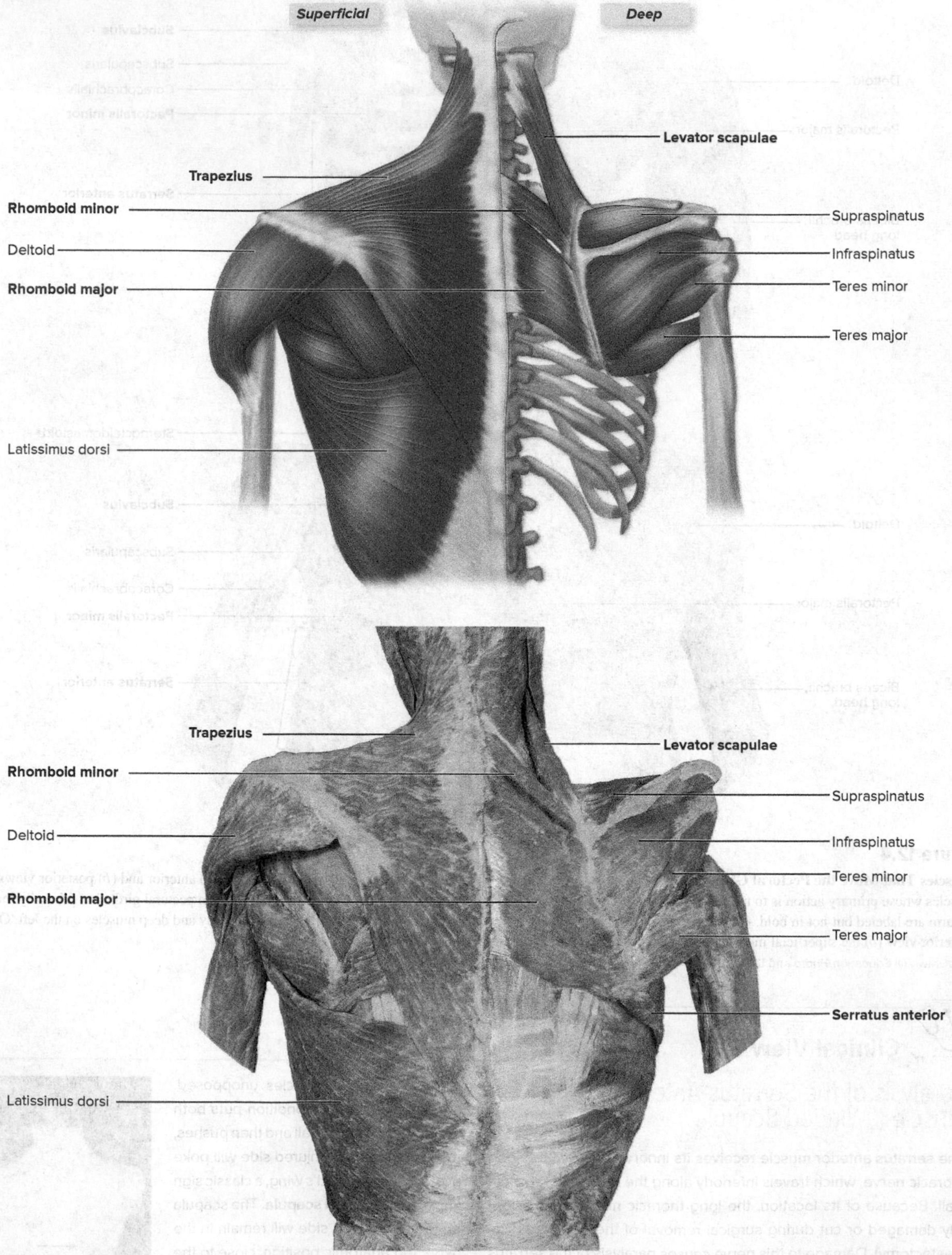
Superficial
Deep
Levator scapulae
Trapezius
Rhomboid minor
Supraspinatus
Deltoid
Infraspinatus
Rhomboid major
Teres minor
Teres major
Latissimus dorsi
Trapezius
Levator scapulae
Rhomboid minor
Supraspinatus
Deltoid
Infraspinatus
Teres minor
Rhomboid major
Teres major
Serratus anterior
Latissimus dorsi

(b) Posterior view

Figure 12.4

Muscles That Move the Pectoral Girdle and the Glenohumeral Joint/Arm. ***(continued)***

Table 12.1	Thoracic Muscles That Move the Pectoral Girdle		
Group/Muscle	**Actions**	**Attachments: Superior (S)/Inferior (I) or Medial (M)/Lateral (L)**[1]	**Innervation (see sections 15.8 and 16.4d, e)**
ANTERIOR MUSCLES			
Pectoralis minor (pek'tō-ra'lis mī'nŏr) *pectus* = chest	Protracts and depresses scapula	S: Coracoid process of scapula I: Ribs 3–5	Medial pectoral nerve (C8–T1)
Serratus anterior (ser-ā'tŭs an-tēr'ē-ōr) *serratus* = saw	Agonist in scapula protraction; superiorly rotates scapula (so glenoid cavity moves superiorly); stabilizes scapula	S: Medial border of scapula, anterior surface I: Ribs 1–8, anterior and superior margins	Long thoracic nerve (C5–C7)
Subclavius (sŭb-klā'vē-ŭs) *sub* = under *clav* = clavicle	Stabilizes and depresses clavicle	S: Inferior surface of clavicle I: Rib 1	Nerve to subclavius (C5–C6)
POSTERIOR MUSCLES			
Levator scapulae (lē-vā'tŏr, -tōr skap'yū-lē) *levator* = raises	Elevates scapula; inferiorly rotates scapula (pulls glenoid cavity inferiorly)	S: Transverse processes of C_1–C_4 I: Superior part of medial border of scapula	Cervical nerves (C3–C4) and dorsal scapular nerve (C5)
Rhomboid major (rom'boyd mā'jŏr) *rhomboid* = diamond-shaped	Elevates and retracts (adducts) scapula; inferiorly rotates scapula	M: Spinous processes of T_2–T_5 L: Medial border of scapula from spine to inferior angle	Dorsal scapular nerve (C5)
Rhomboid minor	Elevates and retracts (adducts) scapula; inferiorly rotates scapula	M: Spinous processes of C_7–T_1 L: Medial border of scapula superior to spine	Dorsal scapular nerve (C5)
Trapezius (tra-pē'zē-ŭs) *trapezion* = irregular four-sided figure	Superior fibers: Elevate and superiorly rotate scapula Middle fibers: Retract scapula Inferior fibers: Depress scapula	M: Occipital bone (superior nuchal line); ligamentum nuchae; spinous processes of C_7–T_{12} L: Clavicle; acromion process and spine of scapula	Accessory nerve (CN XI)

[1] Muscles that move the pectoral girdle do not adhere to any one set of attachment terms. We have tried to use terminology that best describes the muscle attachments.

12.1b Muscles That Move the Glenohumeral Joint/Arm

The phrases "moving the glenohumeral joint" and "moving the arm or humerus" mean the same thing. A movement such as flexion of the arm requires movement at the glenohumeral joint. Throughout this text, we refer to both the joint (where the movement is occurring) and the body region (that is being moved) to minimize any confusion you may have.

The glenohumeral joint is crossed by 11 muscles that attach to the arm (humerus) or the forearm (radius and ulna) (see figure 12.4). The **latissimus dorsi** and **pectoralis major** muscles are the primary attachments of the arm to the trunk. The latissimus dorsi is a broad, triangular muscle located on the inferior part of the back. Often, it is referred to as the "swimmer's muscle," because many of its actions are required for certain swimming strokes. It is the agonist for arm extension, and also adducts and medially rotates the arm. The pectoralis major is a large, thick, fan-shaped muscle that covers the superior part of the thorax. It is the agonist for arm flexion, and also adducts and medially rotates the arm. These muscles are antagonists with respect to arm flexion and arm extension, but work together (synergistically) when adducting and medially rotating the humerus. APR

The biceps brachii and triceps brachii, discussed in detail in section 12.1c with the muscles that move the elbow joint, also cross the glenohumeral joint. Specifically, the long head of the biceps brachii attaches proximally to the supraglenoid tubercle of the scapula, and the short head attaches proximally to the coracoid process of the scapula. The distal attachment for biceps brachii is the radial tuberosity and the bicipital aponeurosis. This muscle assists in flexing the arm. The long head of the triceps brachii attaches to the infraglenoid tubercle of the scapula proximally, and distally to the olecranon of the ulna. This part of the muscle helps extend and adduct the arm.

The seven remaining muscles that move the humerus at the glenohumeral joint are termed the *scapular muscles,* because their proximal attachment is almost entirely on the scapula. These muscles include the deltoid, coracobrachialis, teres major, and the four rotator cuff muscles.

The **deltoid** is a thick, powerful muscle that is the agonist for arm abduction and forms the rounded contour of the shoulder. There are three different proximal attachment points for the deltoid muscle fibers, and these different fiber groups all perform different functions: (1) The anterior fibers flex and medially rotate the arm. (2) The middle fibers abduct the arm; in fact, the deltoid is the prime abductor of the arm. (3) The posterior fibers extend and laterally rotate the arm. The **coracobrachialis** works as a synergist to the pectoralis major in flexing and adducting the arm. The **teres major** works

Learning Strategy 12.2

Generally speaking, muscles with proximal attachments anterior to the glenohumeral joint flex the arm (move it anteriorly), and those with proximal attachments posterior to the joint extend the arm (move it posteriorly).

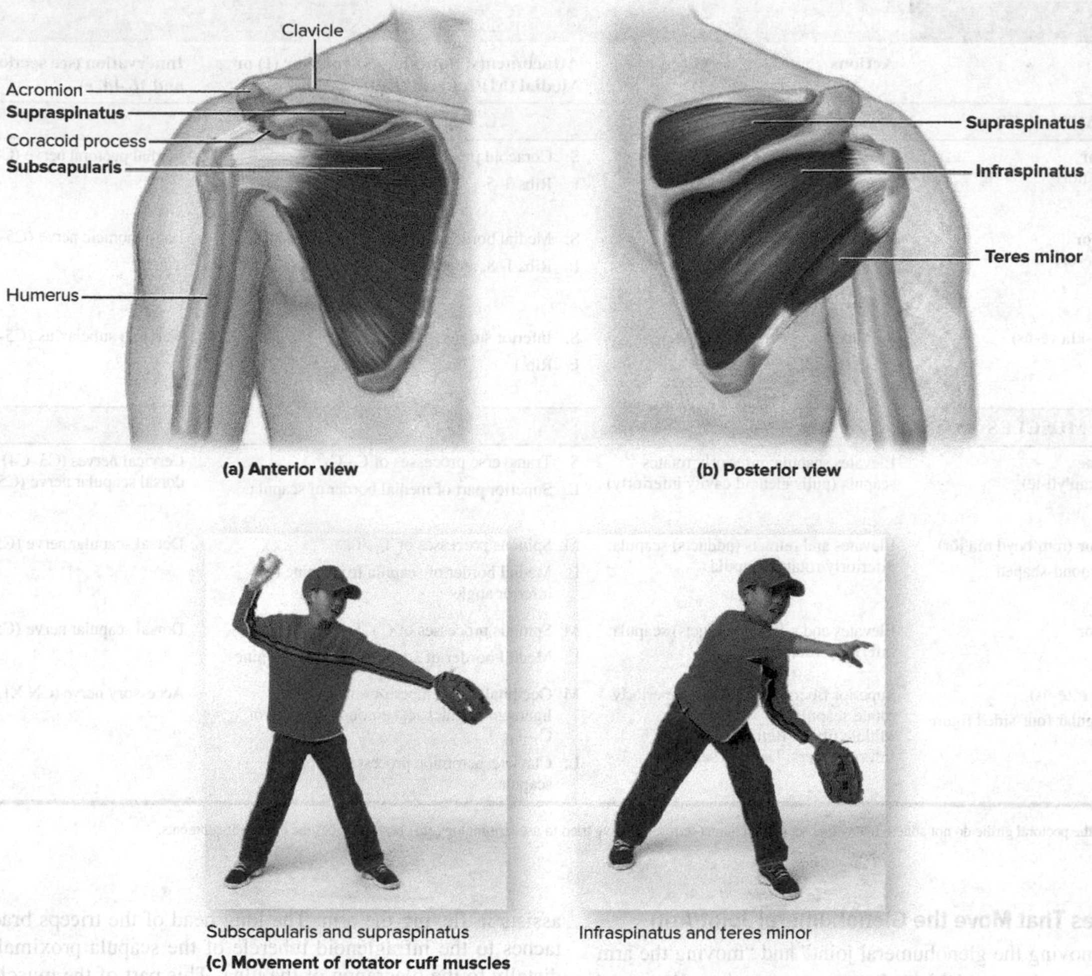

Figure 12.5

Rotator Cuff Muscles. The rotator cuff muscles reinforce the glenohumeral joint and secure the head of the humerus in the glenoid cavity. (*a*) The subscapularis is best seen in an anterior view of the right shoulder. (*b*) The supraspinatus, infraspinatus, and teres minor are best seen in a posterior view. (*c*) The two photos show that the subscapularis medially rotates the humerus (as when winding up for a pitch), the supraspinatus abducts the humerus (as when executing the pitch), and the infraspinatus and teres minor laterally rotate the humerus (as when completing the pitch and slowing down the pitching arm).

synergistically with the latissimus dorsi by extending, adducting, and medially rotating the arm. APR

Four **rotator cuff muscles** (subscapularis, supraspinatus, infraspinatus, and teres minor) provide strength and stability to the glenohumeral joint **(figure 12.5)**. The rotator cuff muscles attach the humerus to the scapula. The specific movements of each muscle are best learned when equating them to pitching a ball:

- The **subscapularis** is used when you wind up for a pitch. It medially rotates the arm. APR
- The **supraspinatus** is used when you start to execute the pitch, by helping abduct the arm. APR
- The **infraspinatus** and **teres minor** help slow down the pitching arm upon completion of the pitch. These two muscles adduct and laterally rotate the arm.

Table 12.2 summarizes the characteristics of the muscles that move the glenohumeral joint and arm. APR

WHAT DO YOU THINK?

1. Which rotator cuff muscle tends to suffer the most injuries, and why?

Learning Strategy 12.3

The four rotator cuff muscles also make up the acronym **SITS: S**upraspinatus, **I**nfraspinatus, **T**eres minor, and **S**ubscapularis.

Clinical View 12.2

Rotator Cuff Injuries

A **rotator cuff injury** is the result of trauma or disease to any portion of the rotator cuff musculature or tendons. Extensive and repetitive use of the rotator cuff muscles can cause tearing of muscle fibers or rupture of tendon attachments. Injury to the supraspinatus muscle is most common, likely because the tendon of this muscle may become impinged (pinched) inferior to the acromion when using the muscle.

This syndrome is especially common in baseball players because of the repetitive shoulder movements while pitching and throwing the ball. Painters also may experience rotator cuff injuries due to the repetitive overhead upper limb movements involved with their work.

Treatment depends upon severity of the injury and includes use of NSAIDs, corticosteroid shots, and physical therapy. Typically, severe rotator cuff injuries require surgical repair. Even after surgery, some individuals never regain full athletic use of the injured shoulder.

Table 12.2 Muscles That Move the Glenohumeral Joint/Arm

Group/Muscle	Action(s)	Proximal Attachment(s) (P)/ Distal Attachment(s) (D)	Innervation (see section 16.4e)
MUSCLES WITH AN AXIAL SKELETON ATTACHMENT			
Latissimus dorsi (lă-tis′i-mŭs dōr′sī) *latissimus* = widest *dorsi* = back	Agonist of arm extension; also adducts and medially rotates arm ("swimmer's muscle")	P: Spinous processes of T_7–T_{12}; ribs 8–12; iliac crest; thoracolumbar fascia D: Intertubercular sulcus of humerus	Thoracodorsal nerve (C6–C8)
Pectoralis major	Agonist of arm flexion; also adducts and medially rotates arm	P: Medial clavicle; costal cartilages of ribs 2–6; body of sternum D: Lateral part of intertubercular sulcus of humerus	Lateral pectoral (C5–C7) and medial pectoral (C8–T1) nerves
MUSCLES WITH A SCAPULA ATTACHMENT			
Deltoid (del′toyd) *delta* = triangular	Anterior fibers: Flex and medially rotate arm Middle fibers: Agonist of arm abduction Posterior fibers: Extend and laterally rotate arm	P: Acromial end of clavicle; acromion and spine of scapula D: Deltoid tuberosity of humerus	Axillary nerve (C5–C6)
Coracobrachialis (kōr′ă-kō-brā-kē-a′lis) *coraco* = coracoid *brachi* = arm	Adducts and flexes arm	P: Coracoid process of scapula D: Middle medial shaft of humerus	Musculocutaneous nerve (C5–C6 fibers)
Teres major (tĕr′ēz) *teres* = round	Extends, adducts, and medially rotates arm	P: Inferior lateral border and inferior angle of scapula D: Lesser tubercle and intertubercular groove of humerus	Lower subscapular nerve (C5–C6)
Triceps brachii (long head) (trī′seps brā′kē-ī) *triceps* = three heads	Extends and adducts arm	P: Infraglenoid tubercle of scapula D: Olecranon process of ulna	Radial nerve (C5–C7 fibers)
Biceps brachii (bī′seps)	Flexes arm (weakly)	P: Supraglenoid tubercle of scapula and coracoid process of scapula D: Radial tuberosity and bicipital aponeurosis	Musculocutaneous nerve (C5–C6 fibers)
Rotator cuff muscles (rō-tā′tōr kŭf) *rotatio* = to revolve	Collectively, these four muscles stabilize the glenohumeral joint		
Subscapularis (sŭb-skap′yū-lār′is) *sub* = under	Medially rotates arm	P: Subscapular fossa of scapula D: Lesser tubercle of humerus	Upper and lower subscapular nerves (C5–C6)
Supraspinatus (sū′pră-spī-nāt′ŭs) *supra* = above, over *spin* = spine	Abducts arm	P: Supraspinous fossa of scapula D: Greater tubercle of humerus	Suprascapular nerve (C5–C6)
Infraspinatus (in′fră-spī-nā′tŭs) *infra* = below	Adducts and laterally rotates arm	P: Infraspinous fossa of scapula D: Greater tubercle of humerus	Suprascapular nerve (C5–C6)
Teres minor	Adducts and laterally rotates arm	P: Upper dorsal lateral border of scapula (superior to teres major attachment) D: Greater tubercle of humerus	Axillary nerve (C5–C6)

Table 12.3 Summary of Muscle Actions at the Glenohumeral Joint/Arm

Abduction	Adduction	Extension	Flexion	Lateral Rotation	Medial Rotation
Deltoid (middle fibers)	**Latissimus dorsi**	**Latissimus dorsi**	**Pectoralis major**	**Infraspinatus**	**Subscapularis**
Supraspinatus	**Pectoralis major**	**Deltoid (posterior fibers)**	**Deltoid (anterior fibers)**	**Teres minor**	Deltoid (anterior fibers)
	Coracobrachialis	Teres major	Coracobrachialis	Deltoid (posterior fibers)	Latissimus dorsi
	Teres major	Long head of triceps brachii	(Biceps brachii)		Pectoralis major
	Teres minor				Teres major
	Infraspinatus				

Boldface indicates an agonist; others are synergists. Parentheses around an entire muscle name indicate only a slight effect.

Learning Strategy 12.4

The best way to remember the appendicular muscles is to group muscles that have similar actions. Note that a muscle that has multiple actions is in more than one group. The muscles that move the arm at the glenohumeral joint are grouped in **table 12.3** according to different types of actions. We recommend that you copy the columns multiple times and then test your knowledge by trying to write out all of the muscles in a group without looking at your notes. If you can list them all, you truly remember the information!

WHAT DID YOU LEARN?

1. What muscles are you using when you protract the scapula?
2. Determine the primary action of the levator scapulae by sketching the scapula and the attachment for the levator scapulae.
3. What muscles cause medial rotation of the arm and where do they attach to the humerus?
4. How can the deltoid extend and flex the arm?

12.1c Arm and Forearm Muscles That Move the Elbow Joint/Forearm

When you move the elbow joint, you move the bones of the forearm. Thus, the term "flexing the elbow joint" is synonymous with "flexing the forearm." Keep this in mind as we discuss the muscles that move the elbow joint and forearm.

The muscles in limbs are organized into **compartments,** which are separated by intermuscular septa and are surrounded by deep fascia. Each compartment houses functionally related skeletal muscles, as well as their associated nerves and blood vessels. The muscles of the arm may be subdivided into an **anterior compartment** and a **posterior compartment** (**figure 12.6**). The anterior compartment primarily contains elbow flexors, and the posterior compartment contains elbow extensors, so these compartments are also called the *flexor compartment* and the *extensor compartment,* respectively.

On the anterior side of the humerus are the principal flexors of the forearm: the biceps brachii and the brachialis (**figure 12.7**). The **biceps brachii** is a large, two-headed muscle on the anterior

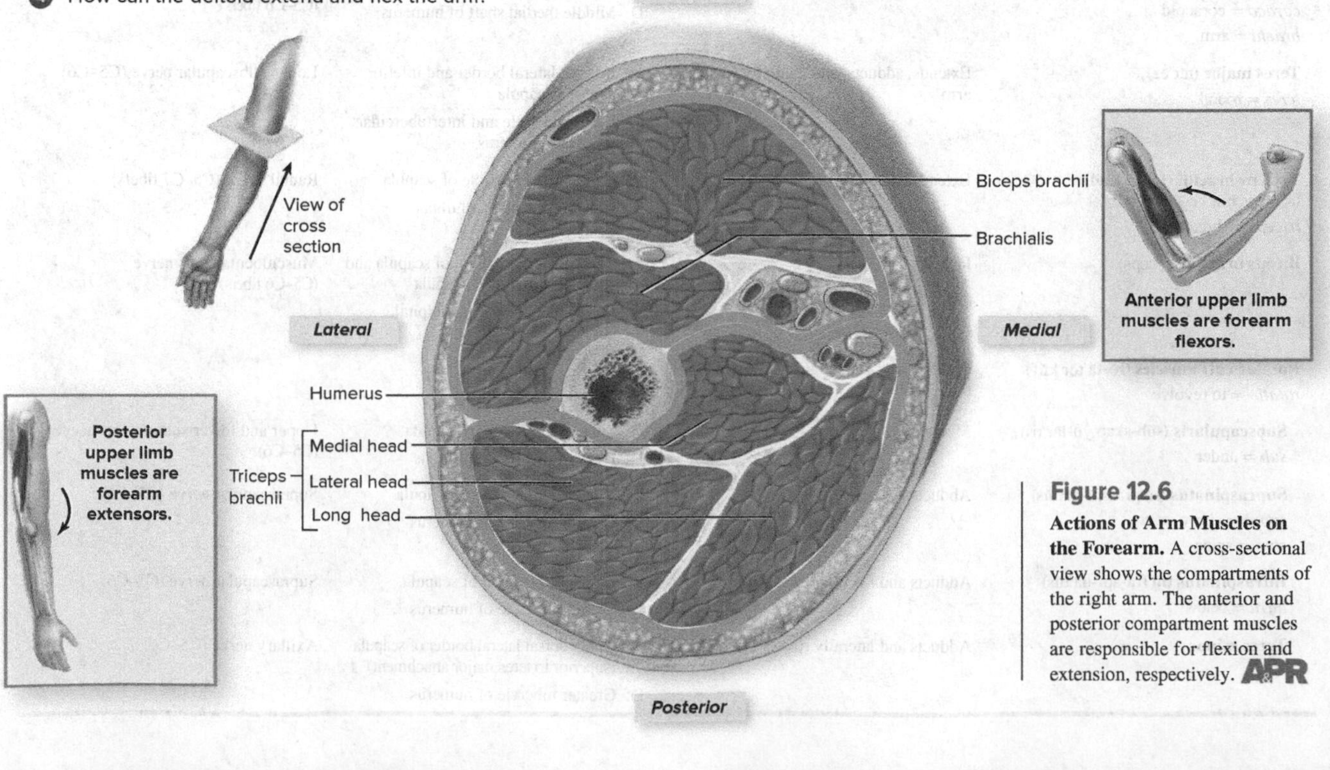

Anterior
View of cross section
Biceps brachii
Brachialis
Lateral
Medial
Anterior upper limb muscles are forearm flexors.
Humerus
Posterior upper limb muscles are forearm extensors.
Triceps brachii
Medial head
Lateral head
Long head
Posterior

Figure 12.6
Actions of Arm Muscles on the Forearm. A cross-sectional view shows the compartments of the right arm. The anterior and posterior compartment muscles are responsible for flexion and extension, respectively. APR

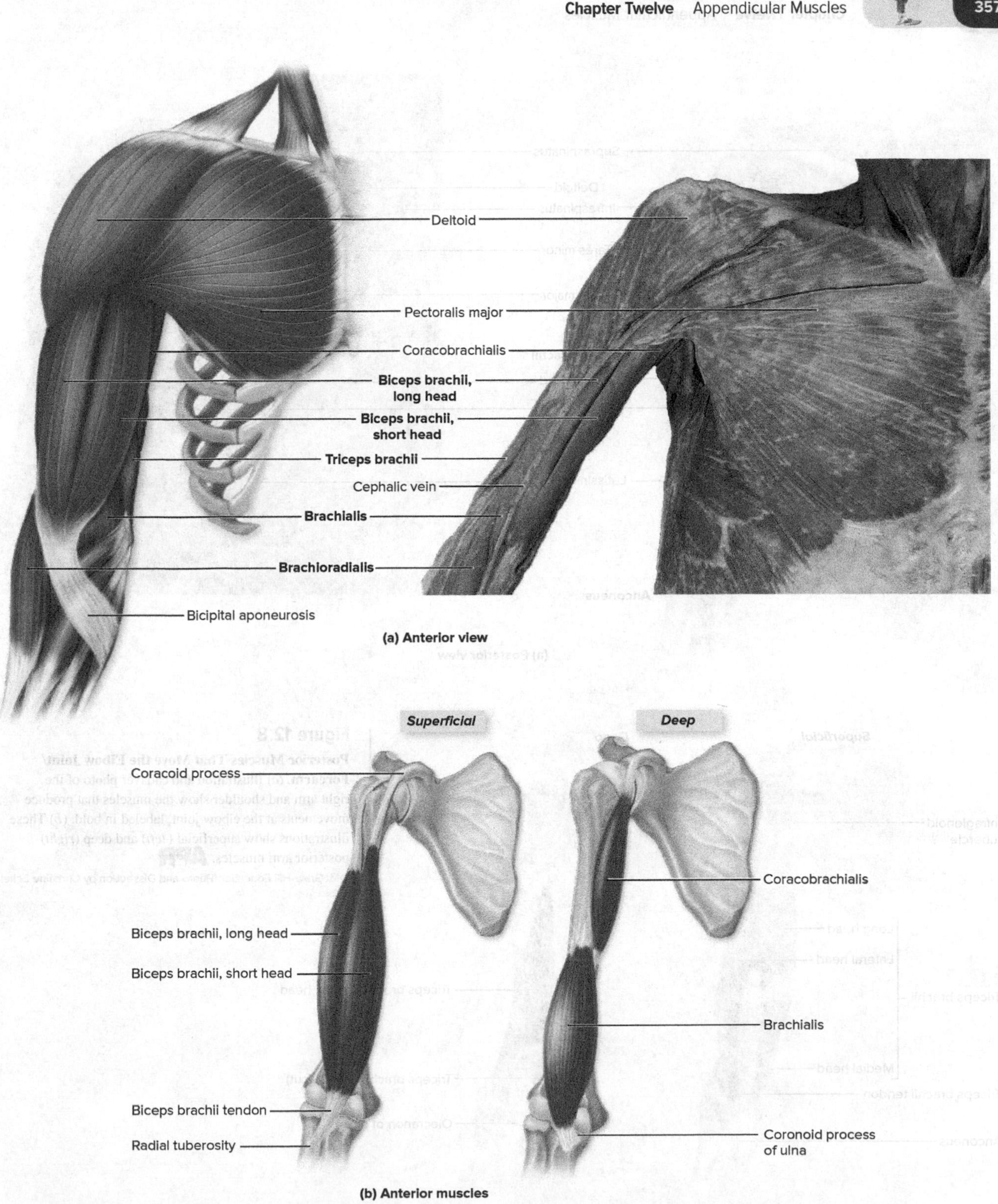
Deltoid
Pectoralis major
Coracobrachialis
Biceps brachii, long head
Biceps brachii, short head
Triceps brachii
Cephalic vein
Brachialis
Brachioradialis
Bicipital aponeurosis
(a) Anterior view
Superficial
Deep
Coracoid process
Biceps brachii, long head
Biceps brachii, short head
Biceps brachii tendon
Radial tuberosity
Coracobrachialis
Brachialis
Coronoid process of ulna
(b) Anterior muscles

Figure 12.7

Anterior Muscles That Move the Elbow Joint/Forearm. (*a*) Illustration and cadaver photo of the right arm and shoulder show the muscles that move the forearm at the elbow joint, labeled in bold. (*b*) These illustrations show superficial (*left*) and deep (*right*) anterior arm muscles. APR

©McGraw-Hill Education/Photo and Dissection by Christine Eckel

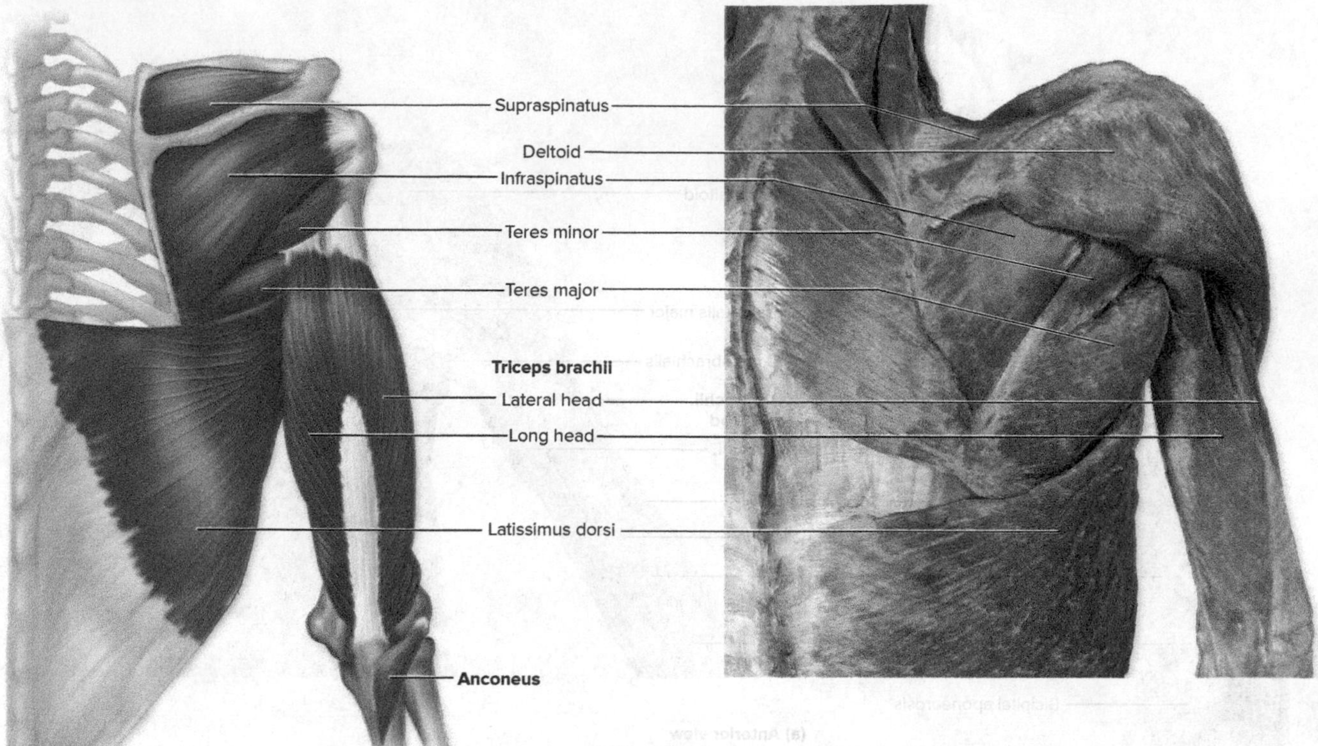

Supraspinatus
Deltoid
Infraspinatus
Teres minor
Teres major
Triceps brachii
Lateral head
Long head
Latissimus dorsi
Anconeus

(a) Posterior view

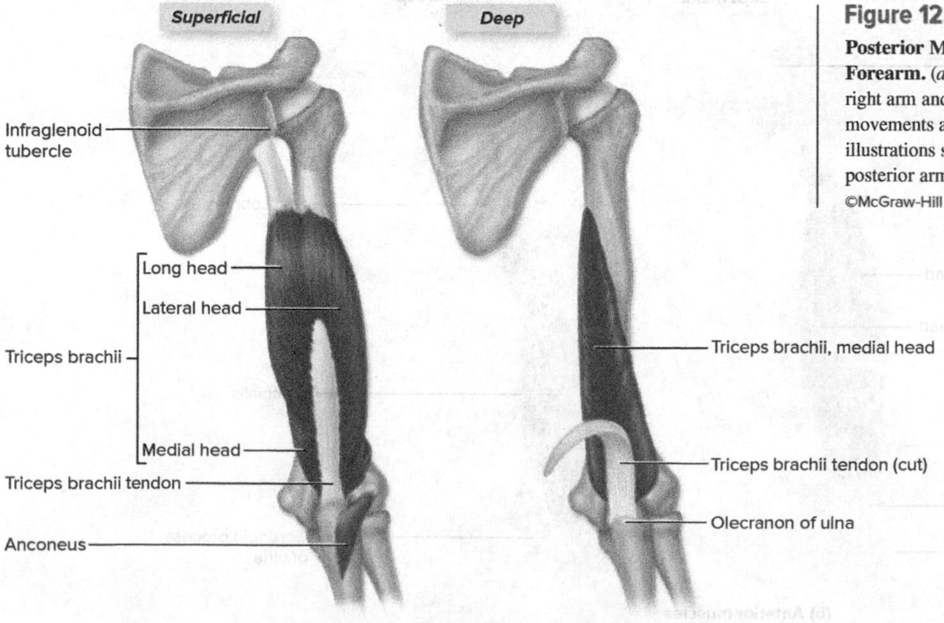

Superficial
Deep
Infraglenoid tubercle
Long head
Lateral head
Triceps brachii
Medial head
Triceps brachii tendon
Anconeus
Triceps brachii, medial head
Triceps brachii tendon (cut)
Olecranon of ulna

(b) Posterior muscles

Figure 12.8

Posterior Muscles That Move the Elbow Joint/Forearm. (*a*) Illustration and cadaver photo of the right arm and shoulder show the muscles that produce movements at the elbow joint, labeled in bold. (*b*) These illustrations show superficial (*left*) and deep (*right*) posterior arm muscles. APR

surface of the humerus. This muscle flexes the forearm and is a powerful supinator of the forearm when the elbow is flexed. (An example of this supination movement occurs when you tighten a screw with your right hand.) The tendons of both heads of the biceps brachii cross the shoulder joint, so this muscle helps flex the humerus as well (albeit weakly). The **brachialis** is deep to the biceps brachii and lies on the anterior surface of the humerus. It is the most powerful flexor of the forearm at the elbow. The **brachioradialis** is a prominent muscle on the lateral surface of the forearm that flexes the forearm at the elbow. APR

The posterior compartment of the arm contains two muscles that extend the forearm at the elbow: the triceps brachii and the anconeus (**figure 12.8**). The **triceps brachii** is the large, three-headed muscle on the posterior surface of the arm. It is the prime extensor of the forearm, and so its action is antagonistic to that of the biceps brachii. Only the long head of the triceps brachii crosses the gleno-humeral joint, where it helps extend the humerus. All three parts of this muscle merge to form a common attachment to the olecranon of the ulna. A weak elbow extensor is the small **anconeus** that crosses the posterolateral region of the elbow. APR

WHAT DO YOU THINK?

2. The brachialis is on the anterior surface of the arm. Without looking at the muscle tables, determine whether this muscle flexes or extends the elbow joint. How did you reach your conclusion?

Some forearm muscles pronate or supinate the forearm (**figure 12.9**). As their names imply, both the **pronator teres** and the **pronator quadratus** rotate the radius across the anterior surface of the ulna to pronate the forearm. These muscles are located in the anterior compartment of the forearm. They are antagonistic to the **supinator** in the posterior compartment of the forearm. The supinator works synergistically with the biceps brachii to supinate the forearm.

Table 12.4 summarizes the characteristics of the muscles that move the forearm, and **table 12.5** groups them according to common function. By learning these muscles as groups, you will have a better understanding of how they work together to perform specific functions. APR

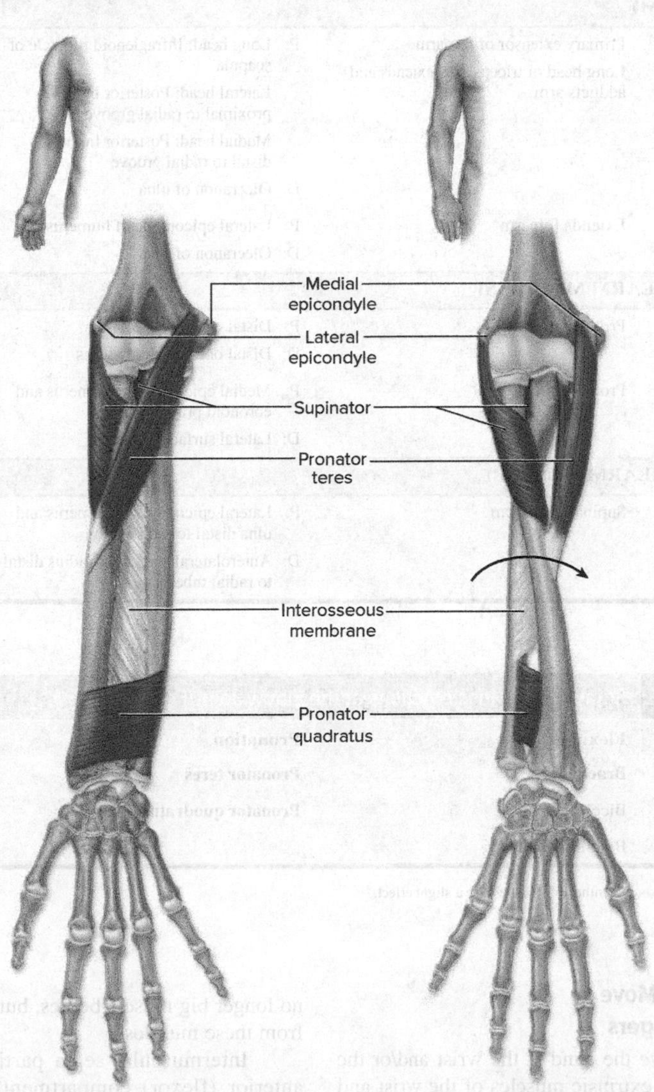
Medial epicondyle
Lateral epicondyle
Supinator
Pronator teres
Interosseous membrane
Pronator quadratus
Supination
Pronation

Figure 12.9
Forearm Muscles That Supinate and Pronate. A view of the right upper limb shows the supinator muscle supinates the forearm, whereas the pronator teres and pronator quadratus pronate the forearm. (The biceps brachii, an arm muscle not shown here, also supinates the forearm.) APR

Table 12.4 Muscles That Move the Forearm

Muscle	Action(s)	Proximal Attachment(s) (P)/ Distal Attachment(s) (D)	Innervation (see section 16.4e)
FLEXORS (ANTERIOR ARM)			
Biceps brachii *biceps* = two heads Long head Short head	Flexes forearm, powerful supinator of forearm; weakly flexes arm	P: Long head: Supraglenoid tubercle of scapula Short head: Coracoid process of scapula D: Radial tuberosity and bicipital aponeurosis	Musculocutaneous nerve (C5–C6 fibers)
Brachialis (brā′kē-al′is)	Primary flexor of forearm	P: Distal anterior surface of humerus D: Tuberosity and coronoid process of ulna	Musculocutaneous nerve (C5–C6 fibers)
Brachioradialis (brā′kē-ō-rā′dē-al′is)	Flexes forearm	P: Lateral supracondylar ridge of humerus D: Styloid process of radius	Radial nerve (C6–C7 fibers)
EXTENSORS (POSTERIOR ARM)			
Triceps brachii Long head Lateral head Medial head	Primary extensor of forearm Long head of triceps also extends and adducts arm	P: Long head: Infraglenoid tubercle of scapula Lateral head: Posterior humerus proximal to radial groove Medial head: Posterior humerus distal to radial groove D: Olecranon of ulna	Radial nerve (C5–C7 fibers)
Anconeus (ang-k ō′nē-ŭs) *ankon* = elbow	Extends forearm	P: Lateral epicondyle of humerus D: Olecranon of ulna	Radial nerve (C6–C8 fibers)
PRONATORS (ANTERIOR FOREARM MUSCLES)			
Pronator quadratus (prō-nā′tōr kwah-dr ā′tŭs)	Pronates forearm	P: Distal one-fourth of ulna D: Distal one-fourth of radius	Median nerve (C8–T1 fibers)
Pronator teres	Pronates forearm	P: Medial epicondyle of humerus and coronoid process of ulna D: Lateral surface of radius	Median nerve (C6–C7 fibers)
SUPINATOR (POSTERIOR FOREARM MUSCLE)			
Supinator (sū′pi-nā′tōr)	Supinates forearm	P: Lateral epicondyle of humerus and ulna distal to radial notch D: Anterolateral surface of radius distal to radial tuberosity	Radial nerve (C6–C8 fibers)

Table 12.5 Summary of Muscle Actions at the Elbow Joint/Forearm

Extension	Flexion	Pronation	Supination
Triceps brachii	**Brachialis**	**Pronator teres**	**Biceps brachii**
(Anconeus)	Biceps brachii	**Pronator quadratus**	Supinator
	Brachioradialis		

Boldface indicates an agonist; others are synergists. Parentheses indicate only a slight effect.

12.1d Forearm Muscles That Move the Wrist Joint, Hand, and Fingers

Most muscles in the forearm move the hand at the wrist and/or the fingers. These muscles are called extrinsic muscles of the wrist and hand, because the muscles attach proximally to the forearm, not the wrist or hand. Palpate your own forearm; it is bigger near the elbow because the bellies of these forearm muscles form the bulk of this region. Moving toward the wrist, the forearm thins because there are no longer big muscle bellies, but rather the long tendons that project from these muscles.

Intermuscular septa partition the forearm muscles into an anterior (flexor) compartment and a posterior (extensor) compartment (**figure 12.10**). Most of the **anterior compartment** muscles attach to the medial epicondyle of the humerus via a common flexor tendon. Muscles in the anterior compartment of the forearm flex the wrist, the metacarpophalangeal (MP) joints,

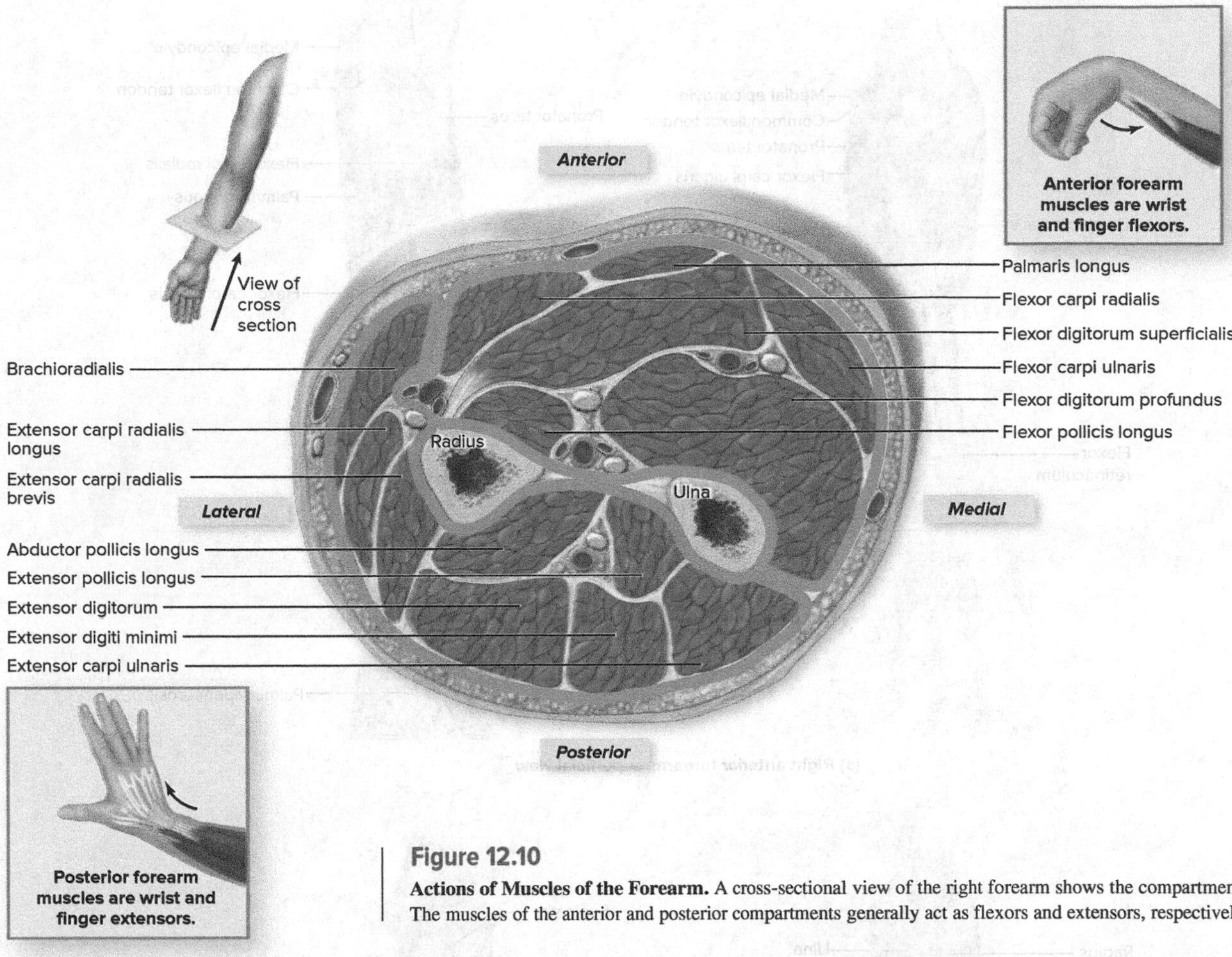
Anterior forearm muscles are wrist and finger flexors.
View of cross section
Anterior
Palmaris longus
Flexor carpi radialis
Flexor digitorum superficialis
Brachioradialis
Flexor carpi ulnaris
Flexor digitorum profundus
Extensor carpi radialis longus
Flexor pollicis longus
Radius
Extensor carpi radialis brevis
Ulna
Lateral
Medial
Abductor pollicis longus
Extensor pollicis longus
Extensor digitorum
Extensor digiti minimi
Extensor carpi ulnaris
Posterior
Posterior forearm muscles are wrist and finger extensors.

Figure 12.10

Actions of Muscles of the Forearm. A cross-sectional view of the right forearm shows the compartments. The muscles of the anterior and posterior compartments generally act as flexors and extensors, respectively.

Clinical View 12.3

Lateral Epicondylitis ("Tennis Elbow")

Lateral epicondylitis (ep′i-kon-di-lī′tis), or *tennis elbow,* is a painful condition resulting from trauma or overuse of the common extensor tendon of the posterior forearm muscles. The pain arises from the lateral epicondyle of the humerus, the attachment site of the common extensor tendon. Lateral epicondylitis most often results from the repeated forceful contraction of the forearm extensors. These are the muscles used to extend the hand at the wrist, as when pulling a heavy object from an overhead shelf, shoveling snow, or hitting a backhand shot in tennis.

Photo shows Serena Williams hitting a backhand shot.
Clive Brunskill/Getty Images

and/or the interphalangeal (IP) joints of the fingers. Most of the **posterior compartment** muscles attach to the lateral epicondyle of the humerus via a common extensor tendon. Muscles in the posterior compartment of the forearm extend the wrist, the MP joints, and/or the IP joints.

Note that not all anterior forearm muscles are flexors . Both the pronator teres and the pronator quadratus (see section 12.1c) are found in the anterior compartment of the forearm, but their primary action is pronation. Likewise, the supinator muscle is in the posterior compartment of the forearm, even though its primary action is supination, not extension.

The tendons of forearm muscles typically are surrounded by tendon (synovial) sheaths and held adjacent to the skeletal elements by strong fascial structures. At the wrist, the deep fascia of the forearm forms thickened, fibrous bands termed *retinacula.* The retinacula help hold the tendons close to the bone and prevent the tendons from "bowstringing" outward. The palmar (anterior) surface of the carpal bones is covered by the **flexor retinaculum (figure 12.11*a*)**. Flexor tendons of the digits and the median nerve pass through the tight space between the carpal bones and the flexor retinaculum, which is called the **carpal tunnel.** The **extensor retinaculum** is superficial to the dorsal surface of the carpal bones. Extensor tendons

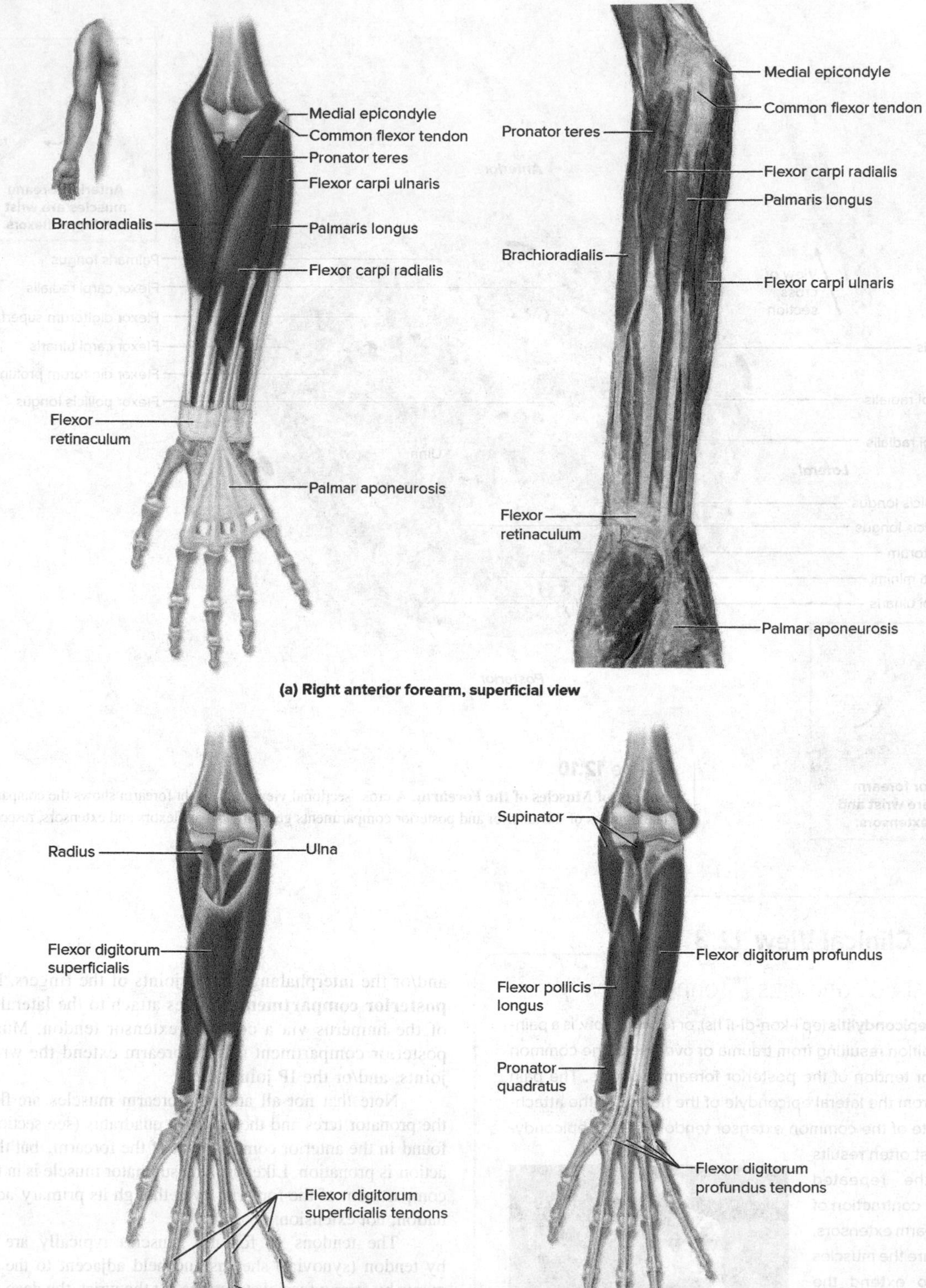
Medial epicondyle
Common flexor tendon
Pronator teres
Flexor carpi ulnaris
Brachioradialis
Palmaris longus
Flexor carpi radialis
Flexor retinaculum
Palmar aponeurosis
Medial epicondyle
Common flexor tendon
Pronator teres
Flexor carpi radialis
Palmaris longus
Brachioradialis
Flexor carpi ulnaris
Flexor retinaculum
Palmar aponeurosis
(a) Right anterior forearm, superficial view
Radius
Ulna
Flexor digitorum superficialis
Flexor digitorum superficialis tendons
Flexor digitorum profundus tendons
(b) Right anterior forearm, intermediate view
Supinator
Flexor digitorum profundus
Flexor pollicis longus
Pronator quadratus
Flexor digitorum profundus tendons
(c) Right anterior forearm, deep view

Figure 12.11

Anterior Forearm Muscles. The anterior forearm muscles pronate the forearm or flex the wrist and fingers. They may be subdivided into superficial, intermediate, and deep groups. (*a*) Illustration and cadaver photo show the superficial muscles of the right anterior forearm. Illustrations show (*b*) intermediate and (*c*) deep muscles of the right anterior forearm. **APR**

Clinical View 12.4

Carpal Tunnel Syndrome

The flexor retinaculum extends from the medial carpal bones to the lateral carpal bones, and the space between the carpal bones and the flexor retinaculum is the carpal tunnel. Through this narrow tunnel, numerous long muscle tendons extend to the fingers from the forearm. Accompanying these tendons is the median nerve, which innervates the skin on the lateral region of the hand and the muscles that move the thumb.

Any compression of either the median nerve or the tendons in the tunnel results in **carpal tunnel syndrome.** A common cause is inflammation of any component in the carpal tunnel—for example, swollen tendons as a result of overuse. Workers who repeatedly flex either their fingers or wrists, such as typists and computer programmers, experience this condition. In addition, females in their last trimester of pregnancy may develop carpal tunnel syndrome as increased water retention results in compression within the carpal tunnel.

Carpal tunnel syndrome is characterized by pain and **paresthesia** (par′es-thē′zē-ă; *aisthesis* = sensation), which is the feeling of "pins and needles." Sometimes, there is more extensive sensory loss as well as motor loss in the muscles of the hand supplied by the median nerve. The median nerve supplies the muscles of the thumb, so in severe cases of carpal tunnel syndrome, these muscles may atrophy as their nerve supply is diminished. Treatment of the syndrome includes supporting the hand in a splint and administering anti-inflammatory drugs (e.g., ibuprofen or prescription medicine). In chronic cases that do not respond to more conservative treatment, a surgeon can incise the flexor retinaculum and open the carpal tunnel, relieving the pressure.

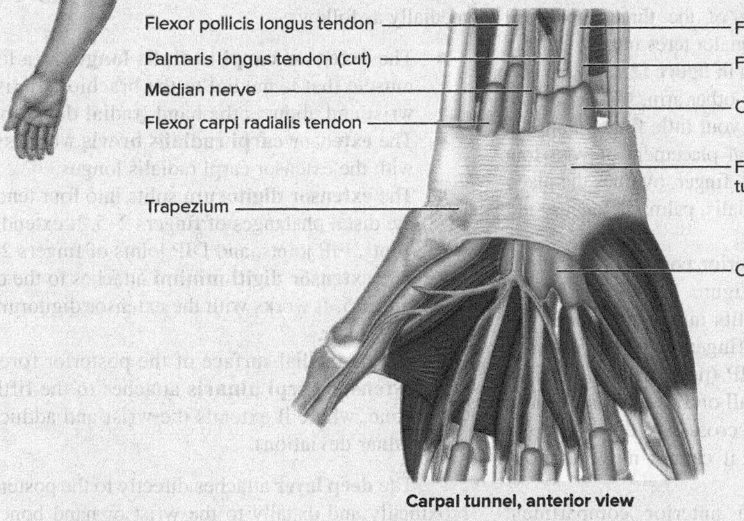

Flexor pollicis longus tendon
Palmaris longus tendon (cut)
Median nerve
Flexor carpi radialis tendon
Trapezium
Flexor digitorum superficialis tendon
Flexor digitorum profundus tendon
Common flexor synovial sheath
Flexor retinaculum covering carpal tunnel
Common flexor synovial sheath

Carpal tunnel, anterior view

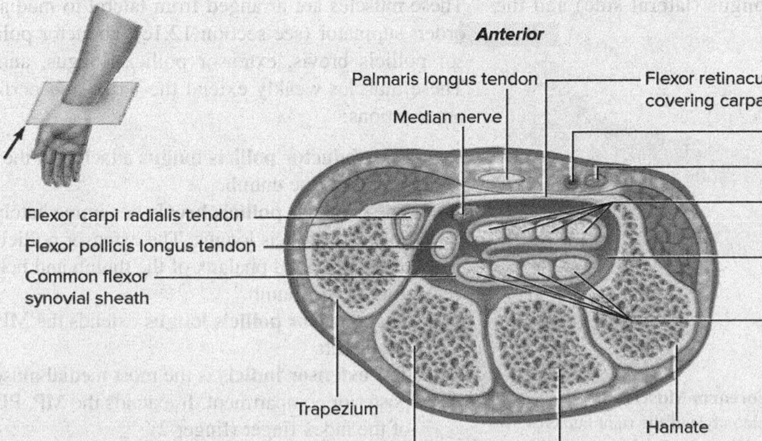

Anterior
View of cross section
Palmaris longus tendon
Median nerve
Flexor retinaculum covering carpal tunnel
Ulnar artery
Ulnar nerve
Flexor digitorum superficialis tendons
Flexor carpi radialis tendon
Flexor pollicis longus tendon
Carpal tunnel
Common flexor synovial sheath
Flexor digitorum profundus tendons
Trapezium
Hamate
Trapezoid
Capitate
Posterior

Carpal tunnel, transverse section

of the wrist and digits pass between the carpal bones and the extensor retinaculum.

The muscles of the **anterior compartment** of the forearm may be subdivided into a superficial layer, an intermediate layer, and a deep layer. The superficial and intermediate muscles share the common flexor tendon that attaches to the medial epicondyle of the humerus. The deep muscles attach directly to the forearm bones.

The **superficial layer** of anterior forearm muscles is arranged from the lateral to the medial surface of the forearm in the following order: pronator teres (described in section 12.1c), flexor carpi radialis, palmaris longus, and flexor carpi ulnaris (figure 12.11*a*).

The **flexor carpi radialis** extends diagonally across the anterior surface of the forearm. Its tendon is prominent on the lateral side of the forearm. This muscle flexes the wrist and abducts (radial deviation) the hand at the wrist. The **palmaris longus** is absent in about 10% of all individuals. This narrow, superficial muscle on the anterior surface of the forearm weakly assists in wrist flexion. On the anteromedial side of the forearm, the **flexor carpi ulnaris** both flexes the wrist and adducts (ulnar deviation) the hand at the wrist.

You can determine the positioning of the three superficial muscles of the anterior forearm and the pronator teres muscle on your own body by performing the exercise shown in **figure 12.12**. Wrap your thumb around the medial epicondyle of the other arm, so your thumb is positioned posterior to the elbow. Align your little finger along the medial border of your forearm. The natural placement of your four fingers, from your index finger to your little finger, overlies the placement of the pronator teres, flexor carpi radialis, palmaris longus, and flexor carpi ulnaris, respectively.

The **intermediate layer** in the anterior compartment of the forearm contains a single muscle (see figure 12.11*b*), the **flexor digitorum superficialis.** This muscle splits into four tendons that each attach to the middle phalanges of fingers 2–5. This muscle crosses over the wrist, MP joints, and PIP (proximal interphalangeal) joints of fingers 2–5; thus, it flexes all of these joints. Because the flexor digitorum superficialis does not cross over the DIP (distal interphalangeal) joints of these fingers, it cannot move the DIP joints. APR

The **deep layer** of the forearm anterior compartment muscles includes the flexor pollicis longus (lateral side) and the flexor digitorum profundus (medial side). Deep to both of these muscles is the pronator quadratus muscle (see section 12.1c and figure 12.11*c*).

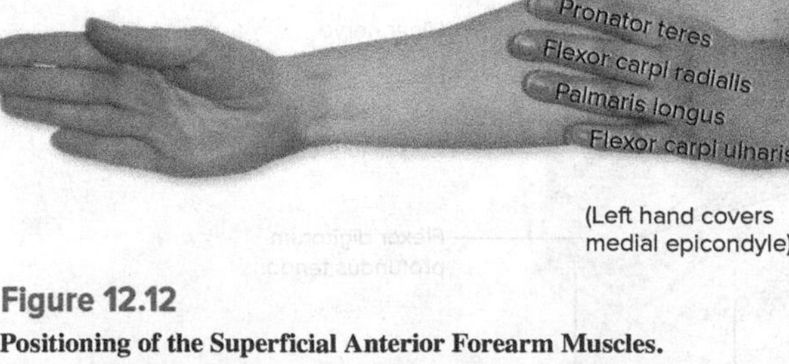

Figure 12.12

Positioning of the Superficial Anterior Forearm Muscles.
By positioning the left hand at the medial epicondyle of the right humerus, fingers 2–5 lay in the approximate position of the superficial muscles of the anterior forearm.

The **flexor pollicis longus** attaches to the distal phalanx of the thumb and flexes the MP and IP joints of the thumb. In addition, because this muscle crosses the wrist joint, it can weakly flex the wrist. The **flexor digitorum profundus** lies deep to the flexor digitorum superficialis. This muscle splits into four tendons that attach to the distal phalanges of fingers 2–5. At the level of the middle phalanges, the tendons of the flexor digitorum superficialis split to allow the flexor digitorum profundus tendons to pass to the tips of the fingers. The flexor digitorum profundus flexes the wrist, MP joints, PIP joints, and DIP joints of fingers 2–5.

Muscles of the **posterior compartment** of the forearm are primarily wrist and finger extensors. An exception is the supinator, which helps supinate the forearm. The posterior compartment muscles may be subdivided into a superficial layer and a deep layer.

The **superficial layer** of posterior forearm muscles proximally attach to a common extensor tendon on the lateral epicondyle of the humerus (**figure 12.13*a***). These muscles are positioned laterally to medially as follows:

- The **extensor carpi radialis longus** is a long, tapered muscle that is medial to the brachioradialis. It extends the wrist and abducts the hand (radial deviation) at the wrist.
- The **extensor carpi radialis brevis** works synergistically with the extensor carpi radialis longus.
- The **extensor digitorum** splits into four tendons that attach to the distal phalanges of fingers 2–5. It extends the wrist, MP joints, PIP joints, and DIP joints of fingers 2–5. APR
- The **extensor digiti minimi** attaches to the distal phalanx of finger 5. It works with the extensor digitorum to extend the little finger.
- On the medial surface of the posterior forearm, the **extensor carpi ulnaris** attaches to the fifth metacarpal bone, where it extends the wrist and adducts the hand (ulnar deviation).

The **deep layer** attaches directly to the posterior forearm bones proximally and distally to the wrist or hand bones (figure 12.13*b*). These muscles are arranged from lateral to medial in the following order: supinator (see section 12.1c), abductor pollicis longus, extensor pollicis brevis, extensor pollicis longus, and extensor indicis. These muscles weakly extend the wrist, and perform the following other actions:

- The **abductor pollicis longus** attaches to the first metacarpal. It abducts the thumb.
- The **extensor pollicis brevis** lies immediately medial to the abductor pollicis longus. The extensor pollicis brevis attaches to the proximal phalanx of the thumb and helps extend the MP joint of the thumb.
- The **extensor pollicis longus** extends the MP and IP joints of the thumb.
- The **extensor indicis** is the most medial muscle of the deep posterior compartment. It extends the MP, PIP, and DIP joints of the index finger (finger 2).

Table 12.6 summarizes the characteristics of the muscles that move the wrist joint, hand, and fingers.

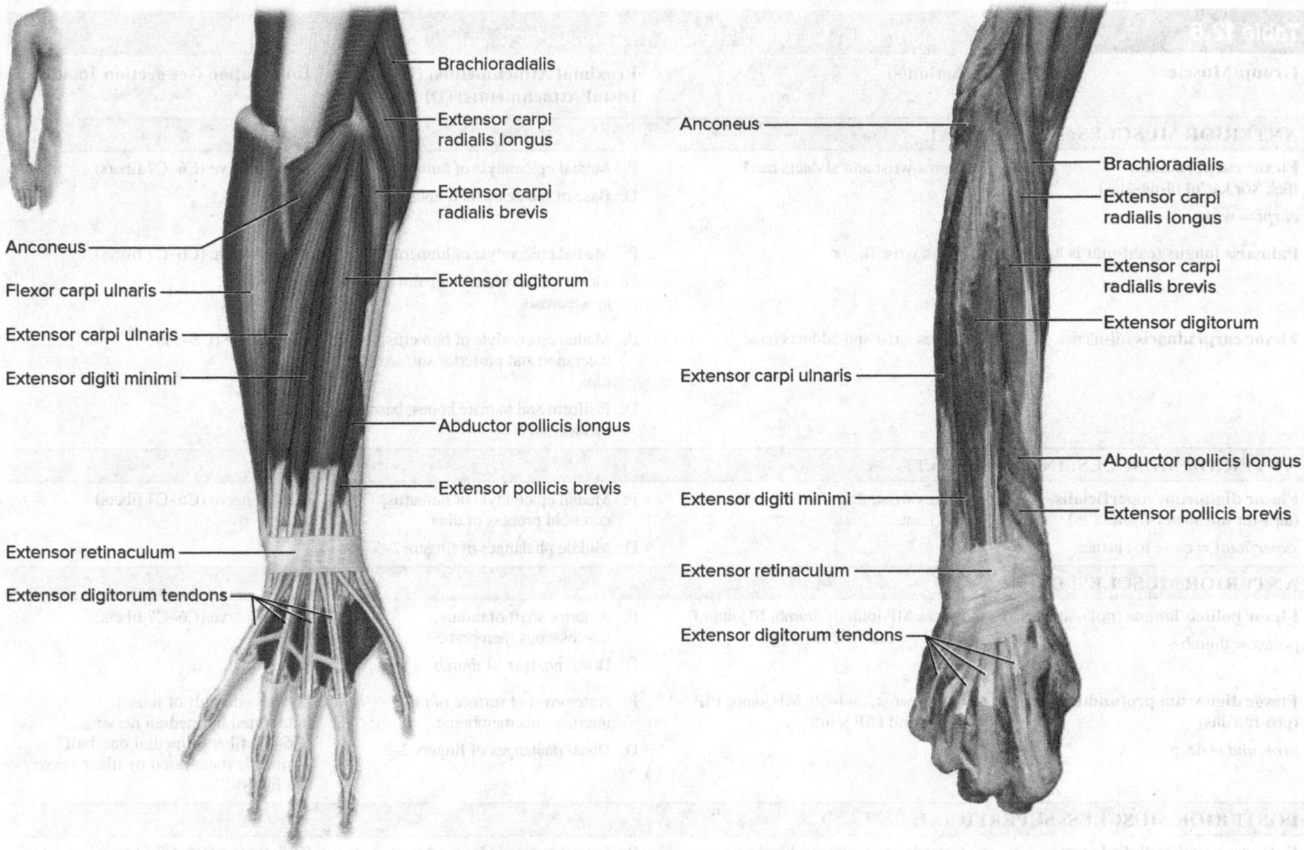

(a) Right posterior forearm, superficial views

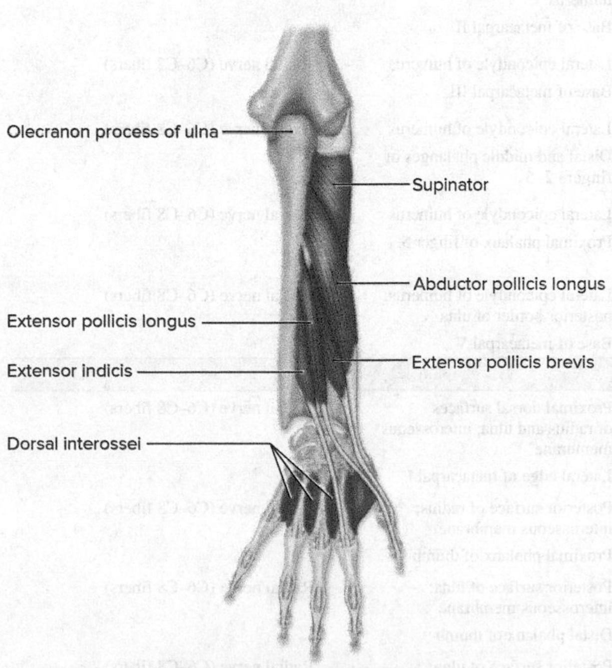

(b) Right posterior forearm, deep views

Figure 12.13

Posterior Forearm Muscles. The posterior forearm muscles supinate the forearm or extend the wrist or fingers. They may be subdivided into (*a*) superficial and (*b*) deep groups, as shown in the photo and illustrations of the right forearm. APR

©McGraw-Hill Education/Photo and Dissection by Christine Eckel

Table 12.6 Forearm Muscles That Move the Wrist Joint, Hand, and Fingers

Group/Muscle	Action(s)	Proximal Attachment(s) (P)/ Distal Attachment(s) (D)	Innervation (see section 16.4e)
ANTERIOR MUSCLES: SUPERFICIAL			
Flexor carpi radialis (flek'sŏr kar'pī rā-dē-āl'is) *carpi* = wrist	Flexes wrist and abducts hand	P: Medial epicondyle of humerus D: Base of metacarpals II and III	Median nerve (C6–C7 fibers)
Palmaris longus (pahl-mār'is lon'gŭs)	Weak wrist flexor	P: Medial epicondyle of humerus D: Flexor retinaculum and palmar aponeurosis	Median nerve (C6–C7 fibers)
Flexor carpi ulnaris (ŭl-nā'ris)	Flexes wrist and adducts hand	P: Medial epicondyle of humerus; olecranon and posterior surface of ulna D: Pisiform and hamate bones; base of metacarpal V	Ulnar nerve (C8–T1)
ANTERIOR MUSCLES: INTERMEDIATE			
Flexor digitorum superficialis (dij'i-tōr'ŭm sū'pĕr-fi'shē-ā'lis) *superficial* = close to surface	Flexes wrist, 2nd–5th MP joints, and PIP joints	P: Medial epicondyle of humerus, coronoid process of ulna D: Middle phalanges of fingers 2–5	Median nerve (C6–C7 fibers)
ANTERIOR MUSCLES: DEEP			
Flexor pollicis longus (pol'i-sis) *pollex* = thumb	Flexes MP joint of thumb, IP joint of thumb; weakly flexes wrist	P: Anterior shaft of radius; interosseous membrane D: Distal phalanx of thumb	Median nerve (C6–C7 fibers)
Flexor digitorum profundus (prō-fŭn'dŭs) *profound* = deep	Flexes wrist, 2nd–5th MP joints, PIP joints, and DIP joints	P: Anteromedial surface of ulna; interosseous membrane D: Distal phalanges of fingers 2–5	Lateral one-half of muscle innervated by median nerve (C6–C8 fibers), medial one-half of muscle innervated by ulnar nerve (C8 fibers)
POSTERIOR MUSCLES: SUPERFICIAL			
Extensor carpi radialis longus (eks-ten'sŏr, -sōr)	Extends wrist, abducts hand	P: Lateral supracondylar ridge of humerus D: Base of metacarpal II	Radial nerve (C6–C7 fibers)
Extensor carpi radialis brevis (brev'is) *brevis* = short	Extends wrist, abducts hand	P: Lateral epicondyle of humerus D: Base of metacarpal III	Radial nerve (C6–C7 fibers)
Extensor digitorum	Extends wrist, extends 2nd–5th MP joints, PIP joints, and DIP joints	P: Lateral epicondyle of humerus D: Distal and middle phalanges of fingers 2–5	Radial nerve (C6–C8 fibers)
Extensor digiti minimi (dij'i-tī mi'ni-mī) *digitus minimus* = little finger	Extends wrist, MP, and PIP joints of finger 5	P: Lateral epicondyle of humerus D: Proximal phalanx of finger 5	Radial nerve (C6–C8 fibers)
Extensor carpi ulnaris	Extends wrist, adducts hand	P: Lateral epicondyle of humerus; posterior border of ulna D: Base of metacarpal V	Radial nerve (C6–C8 fibers)
POSTERIOR MUSCLES: DEEP			
Abductor pollicis longus (ab-d ŭk'ter, -t ōr)	Abducts thumb, extends wrist (weakly)	P: Proximal dorsal surfaces of radius and ulna; interosseous membrane D: Lateral edge of metacarpal I	Radial nerve (C6–C8 fibers)
Extensor pollicis brevis	Extends MP joints of thumb, extends wrist (weakly)	P: Posterior surface of radius; interosseous membrane D: Proximal phalanx of thumb	Radial nerve (C6–C8 fibers)
Extensor pollicis longus	Extends MP and IP joints of thumb, extends wrist (weakly)	P: Posterior surface of ulna; interosseous membrane D: Distal phalanx of thumb	Radial nerve (C6–C8 fibers)
Extensor indicis (in'di-sis) *index* = forefinger	Extends MP, PIP, and DIP joints of finger 2, extends wrist (weakly)	P: Posterior surface of ulna; interosseous membrane D: Tendon of extensor digitorum	Radial nerve (C6–C8 fibers)

MP = metacarpophalangeal, PIP = proximal interphalangeal, DIP = distal interphalangeal

12.1e Intrinsic Muscles of the Hand

The intrinsic muscles of the hand are small muscles housed entirely within the palm, thus both proximal and distal attachments are within the hand (**figure 12.14**). These muscles are divided into three groups: (1) The **thenar group** forms the thick, fleshy mass (thenar eminence) at the base of the thumb. (2) The **hypothenar group** forms a smaller fleshy mass (hypothenar eminence) at the base of the little finger. (3) The **midpalmar group** occupies the space between the first two groups.

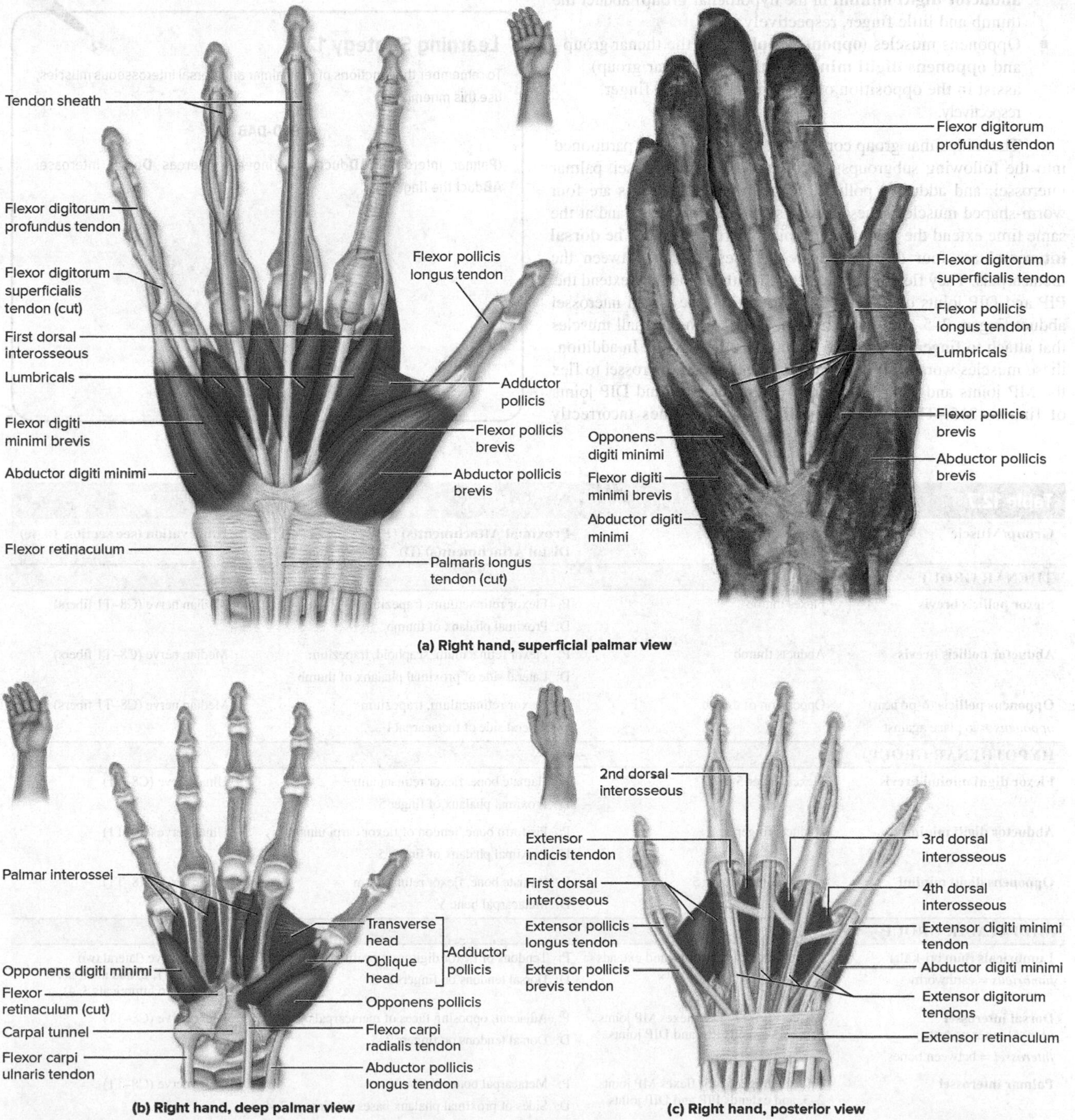
Tendon sheath
Flexor digitorum profundus tendon
Flexor digitorum superficialis tendon (cut)
First dorsal interosseous
Lumbricals
Flexor digiti minimi brevis
Abductor digiti minimi
Flexor retinaculum
Flexor pollicis longus tendon
Adductor pollicis
Flexor pollicis brevis
Abductor pollicis brevis
Palmaris longus tendon (cut)
Flexor digitorum profundus tendon
Flexor digitorum superficialis tendon
Flexor pollicis longus tendon
Lumbricals
Flexor pollicis brevis
Opponens digiti minimi
Abductor pollicis brevis
Flexor digiti minimi brevis
Abductor digiti minimi
(a) Right hand, superficial palmar view
Palmar interossei
Opponens digiti minimi
Flexor retinaculum (cut)
Carpal tunnel
Flexor carpi ulnaris tendon
Transverse head
Oblique head
Adductor pollicis
Opponens pollicis
Flexor carpi radialis tendon
Abductor pollicis longus tendon
(b) Right hand, deep palmar view
2nd dorsal interosseous
Extensor indicis tendon
First dorsal interosseous
Extensor pollicis longus tendon
Extensor pollicis brevis tendon
3rd dorsal interosseous
4th dorsal interosseous
Extensor digiti minimi tendon
Abductor digiti minimi
Extensor digitorum tendons
Extensor retinaculum
(c) Right hand, posterior view

Figure 12.14

Intrinsic Muscles of the Hand. These muscles allow the fine, controlled movements necessary for such activities as writing, typing, and playing a guitar. (*a*) The illustration and photo show palmar (anterior) views of the superficial muscles of the right hand. Illustrations show (*b*) palmar view of the deep muscles and (*c*) posterior (dorsal) view of the superficial muscles. APR

The thenar and hypothenar groups contain smaller muscles:

- Small flexors (**flexor pollicis brevis** in the thenar group and **flexor digiti minimi brevis** in the hypothenar group) flex the thumb and the little finger, respectively.
- Abductors (**abductor pollicis brevis** in the thenar group and **abductor digiti minimi** in the hypothenar group) abduct the thumb and little finger, respectively.
- Opponens muscles (**opponens pollicis** in the thenar group and **opponens digiti minimi** in the hypothenar group) assist in the opposition of the thumb and little finger, respectively.

The midpalmar group contains 12 muscles that are partitioned into the following subgroups: lumbricals, dorsal interossei, palmar interossei, and adductor pollicis. The **lumbrical muscles** are four worm-shaped muscles. These muscles flex the MP joints and at the same time extend the PIP and DIP joints of fingers 2–5. The **dorsal interossei** are four deep bipennate muscles located between the metacarpals. They flex the MP joints and at the same time extend the PIP and DIP joints of fingers 2–5. In addition, the dorsal interossei abduct fingers 2–5. The **palmar interossei** are three small muscles that attach to fingers 2, 4, and 5 and adduct the fingers. In addition, these muscles work with the lumbricals and dorsal interossei to flex the MP joints and at the same time extend the PIP and DIP joints of fingers 2–5. The **adductor pollicis** is sometimes incorrectly classified as a palmar interosseous muscle. As its name suggests, this muscle adducts the thumb.

The intrinsic muscles of the hand are summarized in **table 12.7** and a summary of muscle actions at the wrist and hand are listed in **table 12.8**.

Learning Strategy 12.5

To remember the functions of the palmar and dorsal interosseous muscles, use this mnemonic:

PAD-DAB

(**P**almar interossei **AD**duct the fingers, whereas **D**orsal interossei **AB**duct the fingers.)

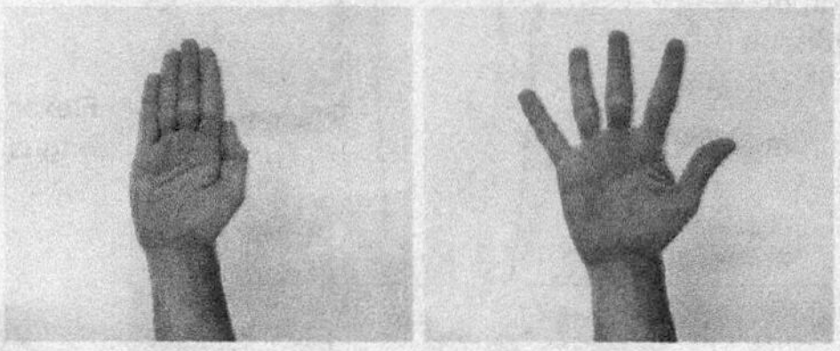

PAD DAB

©McGraw-Hill Education/Tamara Klein, photographer

Table 12.7 Intrinsic Muscles of the Hand

Group/Muscle	Action(s)	Proximal Attachment(s) (P)/ Distal Attachment(s) (D)	Innervation (see section 16.4e)
THENAR GROUP			
Flexor pollicis brevis	Flexes thumb	P: Flexor retinaculum, trapezium D: Proximal phalanx of thumb	Median nerve (C8–T1 fibers)
Abductor pollicis brevis	Abducts thumb	P: Flexor retinaculum, scaphoid, trapezium D: Lateral side of proximal phalanx of thumb	Median nerve (C8–T1 fibers)
Opponens pollicis (ŏ-pō′nens) *opponens* = to place against	Opposition of thumb	P: Flexor retinaculum, trapezium D: Lateral side of metacarpal I	Median nerve (C8–T1 fibers)
HYPOTHENAR GROUP			
Flexor digiti minimi brevis	Flexes finger 5	P: Hamate bone, flexor retinaculum D: Proximal phalanx of finger 5	Ulnar nerve (C8–T1)
Abductor digiti minimi	Abducts finger 5	P: Pisiform bone, tendon of flexor carpi ulnaris D: Proximal phalanx of finger 5	Ulnar nerve (C8–T1)
Opponens digiti minimi	Opposition of finger 5	P: Hamate bone, flexor retinaculum D: Metacarpal bone V	Ulnar nerve (C8–T1)
MIDPALMAR GROUP			
Lumbricals (lŭm′bri-kălz) *lumbricus* = earthworm	Flexes 2nd–5th MP joints and extends 2nd–5th PIP and DIP joints	P: Tendons of flexor digitorum profundus D: Dorsal tendons on fingers 2–5	Median nerve (lateral two lumbricals 1, 2) and ulnar nerve (medial two lumbricals 3, 4)
Dorsal interossei (dōr′săl in′tĕr-os′ē-ī) *interossei* = between bones	Abducts fingers 2–5; flexes MP joints 2–5, and extends PIP and DIP joints	P: Adjacent, opposing faces of metacarpals D: Dorsal tendons on fingers 2–5	Ulnar nerve (C8–T1)
Palmar interossei	Adducts fingers 2–5; flexes MP joints 2–5, and extends PIP and DIP joints	P: Metacarpal bones II, IV, V D: Sides of proximal phalanx bases for fingers 2, 4, and 5	Ulnar nerve (C8–T1)
Adductor pollicis (ă-dŭk′tōr)	Adducts thumb	P: Oblique head: capitate bone, bases of metacarpals II, III Transverse head: metacarpal III D: Medial side of proximal phalanx of thumb	Ulnar nerve (C8–T1)

Table 12.8	Summary of Muscle Actions at the Wrist and Hand		
Hand Abduction (Radial Deviation)	**Hand Adduction (Ulnar Deviation)**	**Wrist Extension**	**Wrist Flexion**
Flexor carpi radialis	Extensor carpi ulnaris	Extensor digitorum	Flexor carpi radialis
Extensor carpi radialis brevis	Flexor carpi ulnaris	Extensor carpi radialis brevis	Flexor carpi ulnaris
Extensor carpi radialis longus		Extensor carpi radialis longus	Flexor digitorum superficialis
		Extensor carpi ulnaris	Flexor digitorum profundus
		(Extensor indicis)	(Palmaris longus)
		(Extensor pollicis longus)	(Flexor pollicis longus)
		(Extensor pollicis brevis)	
		(Abductor pollicis longus)	
Finger Abduction	**Finger Adduction**	**IP Joint Extension**	**IP Joint Flexion**
Dorsal interossei	Palmar interossei	Extensor digitorum	Flexor digitorum profundus
Abductor pollicis longus	Adductor pollicis	Extensor indicis	Flexor digitorum superficialis
Abductor pollicis brevis		Extensor pollicis brevis	Flexor pollicis longus
Abductor digiti minimi		Extensor pollicis longus	Flexor pollicis brevis
		Extensor digiti minimi	Flexor digiti minimi
		Lumbricals	
		Dorsal Interossei	
		Palmar interossei	

Parentheses indicate only a slight effect.

WHAT DID YOU LEARN?

5. Identify the muscles that pronate and supinate the forearm.
6. Name the muscles that flex the forearm at the elbow.
7. What are the actions of the extensor carpi radialis muscles?
8. Sketch and label the intrinsic muscles of the hand that cause abduction of the fingers.

12.2 Muscles of the Pelvic Girdle and Lower Limb

✓ Learning Objectives

9. Describe the major movements at the pelvic girdle and lower limb, and identify the muscles involved.
10. Name and describe the muscles that move the thigh, and explain how each moves the femur.
11. Describe the compartments of the thigh, and identify the muscles within each compartment and their actions.
12. Identify and describe the muscles that move the leg.
13. Locate, name, and describe the muscles that move the ankle, foot, and toes.
14. Describe the compartments of the leg and identify the muscles within each compartment and their actions.
15. Identify and describe the intrinsic muscles of the foot and their actions.

The most powerful and largest muscles in the body are those of the lower limb. Several of these muscles cross and act upon two joints—the hip joint and the knee joint. We discuss first the muscles that move the thigh.

12.2a Muscles That Move the Hip Joint/Thigh

Note that in the subsequent discussion the phrases "moving the thigh" and "moving the hip joint" mean the same thing. The **fascia lata,** the deep fascia of the thigh, encircles the thigh muscles like a supportive stocking and tightly binds them. The fascia lata along with the intermuscular septa partition the thigh muscles into compartments, each with its own blood and nerve supply. The anterior compartment muscles either extend the knee or flex the thigh. The muscles of the medial compartment act as adductors of the thigh. Most muscles of the posterior compartment act as both flexors of the knee and extensors of the thigh. Some of these muscles also abduct the thigh. The muscle in the lateral thigh abducts the thigh.

Most muscles that act on the thigh attach proximally to the os coxae and distally to the femur. These muscles stabilize the highly mobile hip joint and support the body during standing and walking.

Multiple muscles attach to the anterior femur and flex the thigh at the hip (**figure 12.15*a***): The **psoas major** and the **iliacus** have different proximal attachments, but they share the common distal attachment to the lesser trochanter of the femur. Collectively, the two muscles merge and attach to the femur as the **iliopsoas.** These muscles work synergistically to flex the thigh. A long, thin muscle called the **sartorius** crosses over the anterior thigh and helps flex the thigh. The rectus femoris also flexes the thigh and is examined in section 12.2b. APR

Six muscles are located in the medial compartment of the thigh. Most of these muscles adduct the thigh, and some of them perform additional actions. The **adductor longus, adductor brevis, gracilis,** and **pectineus** also flex the thigh. A fifth muscle, the **adductor magnus,** also extends and laterally rotates the thigh. The **obturator externus** does not adduct the thigh, but it laterally rotates the thigh. APR

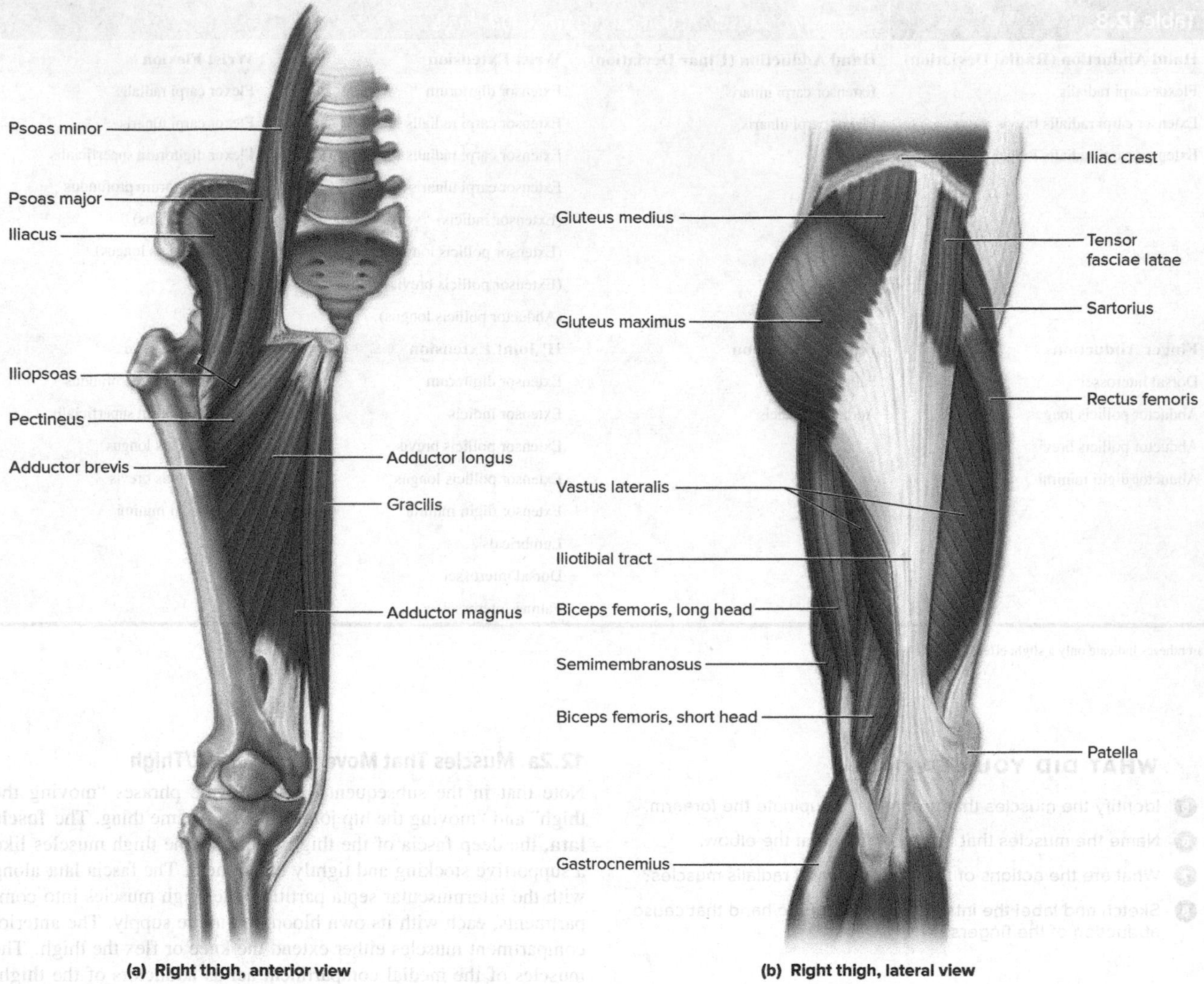
Psoas minor
Psoas major
Iliacus
Iliopsoas
Pectineus
Adductor brevis
Adductor longus
Gracilis
Adductor magnus
(a) Right thigh, anterior view
Iliac crest
Gluteus medius
Tensor fasciae latae
Sartorius
Gluteus maximus
Rectus femoris
Vastus lateralis
Iliotibial tract
Biceps femoris, long head
Semimembranosus
Biceps femoris, short head
Patella
Gastrocnemius
(b) Right thigh, lateral view

Figure 12.15

Muscles That Act on the Hip and Thigh. Illustrations show (*a*) deep anterior and, (*b*) lateral views of the right thigh. The illustration and photo show (*c*) deep posterior views of the right thigh. Most muscles that act on the thigh (femur) proximally attach to the os coxae. (Obturator externus not shown.) APR

On the lateral thigh is a single muscle called the **tensor fasciae latae** (figure 12.15*b*). It attaches to a lateral thickening of the fascia lata, called the **iliotibial tract** (or *iliotibial* [IT] *band*), which extends from the iliac crest to the lateral condyle of the tibia. The tensor fasciae latae abducts and medially rotates the thigh.

The posterior muscles that move the thigh include three gluteal muscles and the hamstring muscle group (figure 12.15*b, c*). The **gluteus maximus** is the largest of the three gluteal muscles and one of the largest muscles in the body. It is the chief extensor of the thigh, and it laterally rotates the thigh. Deep and lateral to the gluteus maximus is the **gluteus medius,** a powerful abductor of the thigh. This muscle also medially rotates the thigh. Intramuscular injections are often given in this muscle. The **gluteus minimus** is the smallest of the gluteal muscles and lies deep to gluteus medius. It works synergistically with gluteus medius to abduct and medially rotate the thigh. APR

Deep to the **gluteal muscles** are a group of muscles that laterally rotate the thigh and the hip joint, as when the legs are crossed with one ankle resting on the knee. These muscles are organized from superior to inferior within the posterior thigh as the **piriformis, superior gemellus, obturator internus, inferior gemellus,** and **quadratus femoris.**

Finally, the posterior thigh contains a group of muscles that are collectively referred to as the **hamstrings** because a ham is strung up by the tendons of these muscles while being smoked. The hamstring muscles are the biceps femoris, semimembranosus, and semitendinosus. These muscles share a common proximal attachment to the ischial tuberosity of the os coxae, and distally attach to the leg. Thus, these muscles move both the thigh and the knee. Their primary thigh movement is extension. These muscles will be discussed again in section 12.2b when we discuss movement at the knee joint and leg. APR

Table 12.9 summarizes the characteristics of the muscles that move the hip joint and thigh, and **table 12.10** groups these muscles according to their common actions on the hip joint and thigh. APR

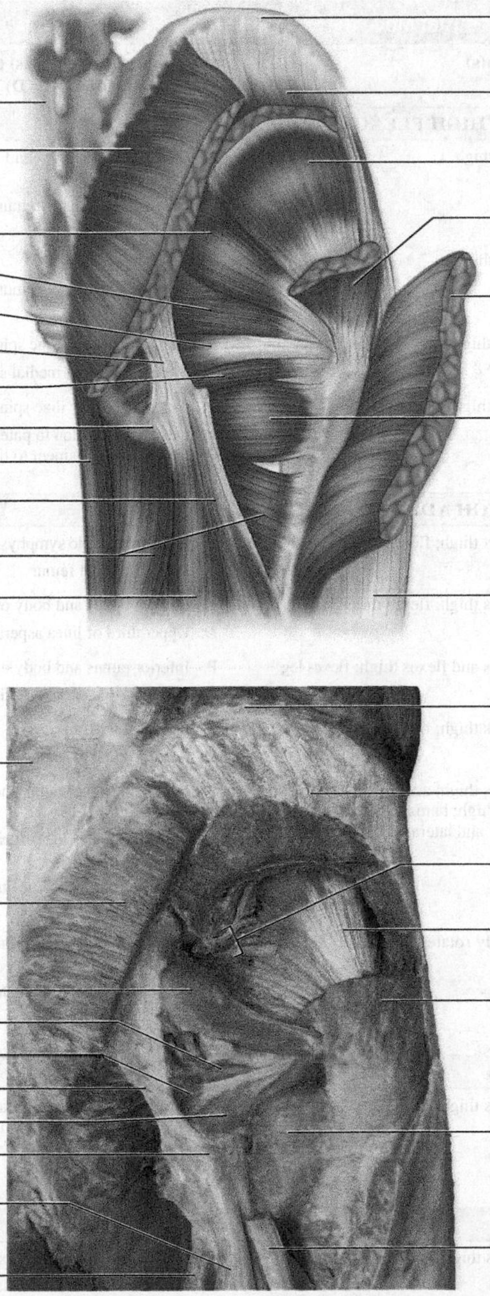

(c) Right thigh, deep posterior view

Figure 12.15
Muscles That Act on the Hip and Thigh. ***(continued)***

WHAT DID YOU LEARN?

9. What two muscles attach to the iliotibial tract?
10. What muscles adduct the thigh, and in what compartment of the thigh can you find them?
11. Name the muscles that laterally rotate the thigh, and identify their general attachment point on the femur.
12. Identify the muscles that extend the thigh.

Learning Strategy 12.6

In general, muscles in the same compartment tend to perform similar actions. So, the muscles in the anterior compartment of the thigh tend to flex the thigh and extend the leg, the muscles in the medial compartment tend to adduct the thigh, and the muscles in the posterior compartment tend to extend the thigh and flex the leg. (Note: There are exceptions to these rules, but this generalization will help as you start learning muscle actions.)

Table 12.9 Muscles That Move the Hip Joint/Thigh

Group/Muscle	Action(s)	Proximal Attachment(s) (P)/ Distal Attachment(s) (D)	Innervation (see sections 16.4f, g)
ANTERIOR THIGH COMPARTMENT (THIGH FLEXORS)			
Psoas major (sō′as mā′jŏr) *psoa* = loin muscle	Flexes thigh	P: Transverse processes and bodies of T_{12}–L_5 vertebrae D: Lesser trochanter of femur with iliacus	Branches of lumbar plexus (L2–L3)
Iliacus (il-ī′ă-kŭs) *iliac* = ilium	Flexes thigh	P: Iliacfossa D: Lesser trochanter of femur with psoas major	Femoral nerve (L2–L3 fibers)
Sartorius (sar-tō′rē-ŭs) *sartor* = tailor	Flexes thigh and rotates thigh laterally; flexes leg	P: Anterior superior iliac spine D: Tibial tuberosity, medial side	Femoral nerve (L2–L3 fibers)
Rectus femoris (rek′tŭs fem′ŏ-ris) *rectus* = straight *femoris* = femur	Flexes thigh, extends leg	P: Anterior inferior iliac spine D: Quadriceps tendon to patella and then patellar ligament to tibial tuberosity	Femoral nerve (L2–L4)
MEDIAL THIGH COMPARTMENT (THIGH ADDUCTORS)			
Adductor longus *adduct* = to move toward midline	Adducts thigh; flexes thigh	P: Pubis near pubic symphysis D: Linea aspera of femur	Obturator nerve (L2–L4)
Adductor brevis	Adducts thigh; flexes thigh	P: Inferior ramus and body of pubis D: Upper third of linea aspera of femur	Obturator nerve (L2–L3 fibers)
Gracilis (gras′i-lis) *gracilis* = slender	Adducts and flexes thigh; flexes leg	P: Inferior ramus and body of pubis D: Upper medial surface of tibia	Obturator nerve (L2–L4)
Pectineus (pek′tin′ē-ŭs) *pectin* = comb	Adducts thigh; flexes thigh	P: Pectineal line of pubis D: Pectineal line of femur	Femoral nerve (L2–L4) or obturator nerve (L2–L4)
Adductor magnus (mag′nŭs) *magnus* = large	Adducts thigh; adductor part of muscle flexes thigh; hamstring part of muscle extends and laterally rotates thigh	P: Inferior ramus of pubis and ischial tuberosity D: Hamstring part: Linea aspera of femur Adductor part: Adductor tubercle of femur	Adductor part: Obturator nerve (L2–L4) Hamstring part: Tibial division of sciatic nerve (L2–L4 fibers)
Obturator externus (ob′tū-rā′tŏr eks-ter′nŭs) *obturator* = any structure that occludes an opening *externus* = outside	Laterally rotates thigh	P: Margins of obturator foramen and obturator membrane D: Trochanteric fossa of posterior femur	Obturator nerve (L3–L4 fibers)
LATERAL THIGH (THIGH ABDUCTOR)			
Tensor fasciae latae (ten′sŏr fash′ă lā′tē) *tensor* = to make tense *fascia* = band *lata* = wide	Abducts thigh; medially rotates thigh	P: Iliac crest and lateral surface of anterior superior iliac spine D: Iliotibialband	Superior gluteal nerve (L4–S1)
GLUTEAL GROUP			
Gluteus maximus (glū′tē-ŭs mak′si-mŭs) *glutos* = buttock *maximus* = largest	Extends thigh; laterally rotates thigh	P: Iliac crest, sacrum, coccyx D: Iliotibial tract of fascia lata; linea aspera and gluteal tuberosity of femur	Inferior gluteal nerve (L5–S2)
Gluteus medius (mē′dē-ŭs) *medius* = middle	Abducts thigh; medially rotates thigh	P: Posterior iliac crest; lateral surface between posterior and anterior gluteal lines D: Greater trochanter of femur	Superior gluteal nerve (L4–S1)
Gluteus minimus (min′i-mŭs) *minimus* = smallest	Abducts thigh; medially rotates thigh	P: Lateral surface of ilium between inferior and anterior gluteal lines D: Greater trochanter of femur	Superior gluteal nerve (L4–S1)

Table 12.9 Muscles That Move the Hip Joint/Thigh *(continued)*

Group/Muscle	Action(s)	Proximal Attachment(s) (P)/ Distal Attachment(s) (D)	Innervation (see section 16.4g)
DEEP MUSCLES OF THE GLUTEAL REGION (LATERAL THIGH ROTATORS)			
Piriformis (pir′i-fōr′mis) *pirum* = pear *forma* = form	Laterally rotates thigh	P: Anterolateral surface of sacrum D: Greatertrochanter	Nerve to piriformis (S1–S2)
Superior gemellus (jĕ-mel′ŭs) *gemin* = twin, double	Laterally rotates thigh	P: Ischial spine and tuberosity D: Obturator internus tendon	Nerve to obturator internus (L5–S1)
Obturator internus (in-ter′nŭs) *internus* = inside	Laterally rotates thigh	P: Posterior surface of obturator membrane; margins of obturator foramen D: Greatertrochanter	Nerve to obturator internus (L5–S1)
Inferior gemellus	Laterally rotates thigh	P: Ischialtuberosity D: Obturator internus tendon	Nerve to quadratus femoris (L5–S1)
Quadratus femoris	Laterally rotates thigh	P: Lateral border of ischial tuberosity D: Intertrochanteric crest of femur	Nerve to quadratus femoris (L5–S1)
POSTERIOR THIGH (HAMSTRING) COMPARTMENT (THIGH EXTENSORS AND LEG FLEXORS)			
Biceps femoris Long head Short head	Extends thigh (long head only); flexes leg (both long head and short head); laterally rotates leg	P: Long head: Ischial tuberosity Short head: Linea aspera of femur D: Head of fibula	Long head: Tibial division of sciatic nerve (L4–S1 fibers) Short head: Common fibular division of sciatic nerve (L5–S1 fibers)
Semimembranosus (sem′ē-mem′bră-nō′sŭs) *semi* = half *membranosus* = membrane	Extends thigh and flexes leg; medially rotates leg	P: Ischialtuberosity D: Posterior surface of medial condyle of tibia	Tibial division of sciatic nerve (L4–S1 fibers)
Semitendinosus (sem′ē-ten′di-nō′sŭs) *tendinosus* = tendon	Extends thigh and flexes leg; medially rotates leg	P: Ischialtuberosity D: Proximal medial surface of tibia	Tibial division of sciatic nerve (L4–S1 fibers)

Table 12.10 Summary of Muscle Actions at the Hip Joint/Thigh

Abduction	Adduction	Extension	Flexion	Lateral Rotation	Medial Rotation
Gluteus medius	Adductor brevis, longus, magnus	**Gluteus maximus**	**Iliopsoas**	Adductor magnus (hamstring part)	Gluteus medius
Gluteus minimus	Gracilis	Adductor magnus (hamstring part)	Adductor brevis, longus, magnus (adductor part)	Gluteus maximus	Gluteus minimus
Tensor fasciae latae	Pectineus	Biceps femoris (long head)	Pectineus	Sartorius	Tensor fasciae latae
		Semimembranosus	Sartorius	Obturator externus	
		Semitendinosus	Rectus femoris	Obturator internus	
			Gracilis	Piriformis	
				Superior gemellus	
				Inferior gemellus	
				Quadratus femoris	

Boldface indicates an agonist; others are synergists.

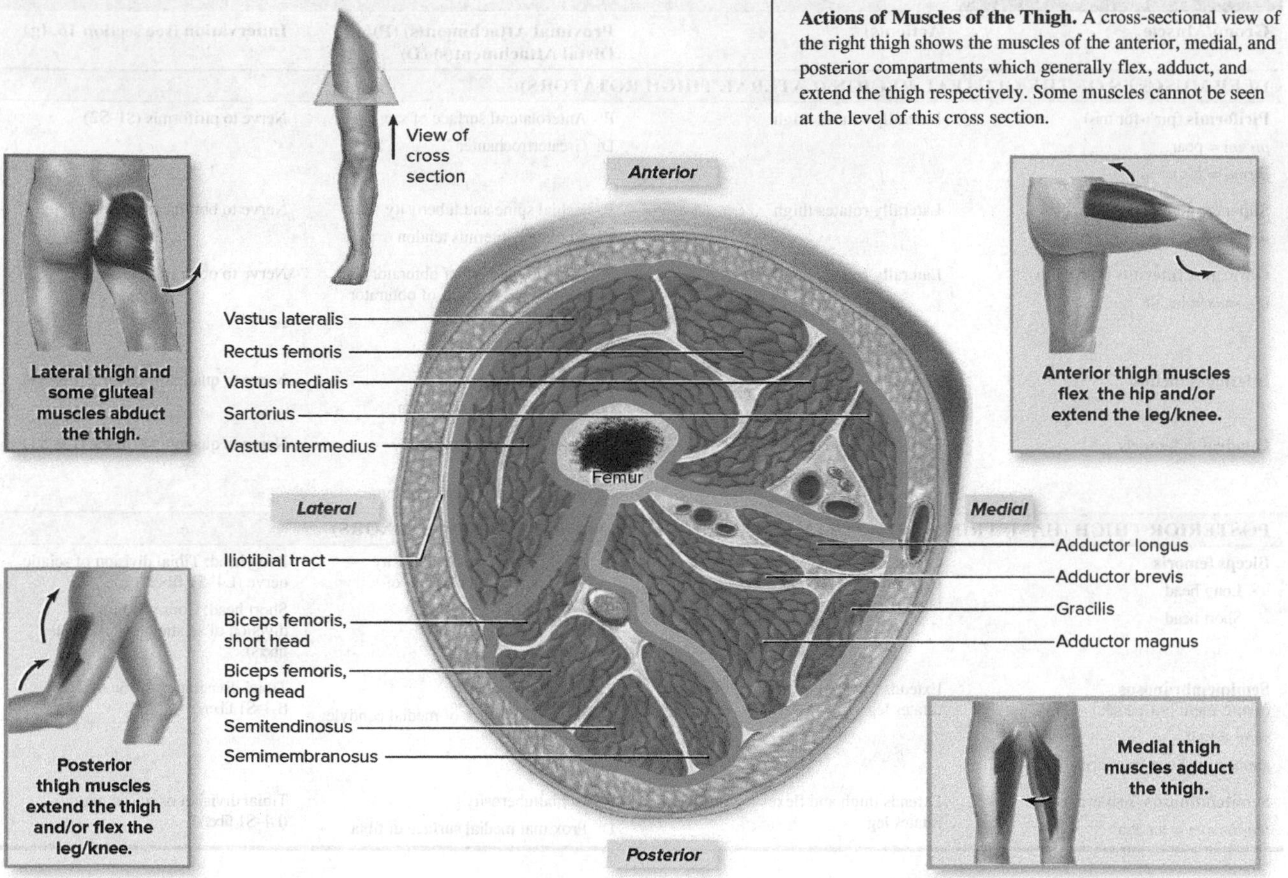
View of cross section
Anterior
Posterior
Lateral
Medial
Femur
Vastus lateralis
Rectus femoris
Vastus medialis
Sartorius
Vastus intermedius
Iliotibial tract
Biceps femoris, short head
Biceps femoris, long head
Semitendinosus
Semimembranosus
Adductor longus
Adductor brevis
Gracilis
Adductor magnus
Lateral thigh and some gluteal muscles abduct the thigh.
Anterior thigh muscles flex the hip and/or extend the leg/knee.
Posterior thigh muscles extend the thigh and/or flex the leg/knee.
Medial thigh muscles adduct the thigh.

Figure 12.16

Actions of Muscles of the Thigh. A cross-sectional view of the right thigh shows the muscles of the anterior, medial, and posterior compartments which generally flex, adduct, and extend the thigh respectively. Some muscles cannot be seen at the level of this cross section.

12.2b Thigh Muscles That Move the Knee Joint/Leg

The muscles that act on the knee form most of the mass of the thigh. Muscles in the thigh are separated by intermuscular septa into anterior, medial, and posterior compartments (**figure 12.16**).

The **anterior (extensor) compartment** of the thigh is composed of the large **quadriceps femoris,** the agonist of knee extension and the most powerful muscle in the body. The quadriceps femoris is a composite muscle with four heads, as shown on **figure 12.17**: **APR**

- The **rectus femoris** is on the anterior surface of the thigh; this muscle proximally attaches to the os coxae, and so it also flexes the thigh.
- The **vastus lateralis** forms the anterolateral surface of the thigh.
- The **vastus medialis** forms the anteromedial surface of the thigh.
- The **vastus intermedius** is positioned deep to the rectus femoris and sandwiched between the other two vastus muscles.

All four muscles converge on a single **quadriceps tendon,** which extends to the patella and then continues inferiorly as the **patellar ligament** and attaches to the tibial tuberosity. The patella becomes encased in this tendon and ligament. The quadriceps femoris is the great extensor muscle of the leg. It extends the knee when you stand up, take a step, or kick a ball, and it is very important in running, because it acts with the iliopsoas to flex the hip while the leg is off the ground.

The anterior compartment of the thigh contains another muscle worth noting. The long, straplike **sartorius** projects obliquely across the anterior surface of the thigh from the superolateral to the inferomedial side. It acts on both the hip and knee joints, flexing and laterally rotating the thigh while flexing the leg. This muscle is the longest in the body and is nicknamed the "tailor's muscle" because it helps us sit cross-legged, as tailors used to do.

The **medial (adductor) compartment** of the thigh is named for the muscles that adduct the thigh (see figures 12.15*a* and 12.17 *a*). The **gracilis** is part of this compartment and also flexes the leg, as it spans the knee joint.

The **posterior (flexor) compartment** of the thigh contains the three hamstring muscles (**figure 12.18**). These muscles also flex the leg. The **biceps femoris** is a two-headed muscle that attaches to the lateral side of the leg. This muscle also can laterally rotate the leg when the leg is flexed. The long head of the biceps femoris proximally attaches to the ischial tuberosity with the semimembranosus and semitendinosus. The short head of the biceps femoris proximal attachment is the linea aspera of the femur. The short head cannot move the thigh, but it does help the other hamstring muscles in flexing the leg. The **semimembranosus** is

Figure 12.17

Muscles of the Anterior Thigh. Muscles of the anterior thigh flex the thigh and extend the leg. (*a*) Illustration and cadaver photo show an anterior view of the right thigh. (*b*) Illustrations show individual muscles of the right anterior thigh. APR

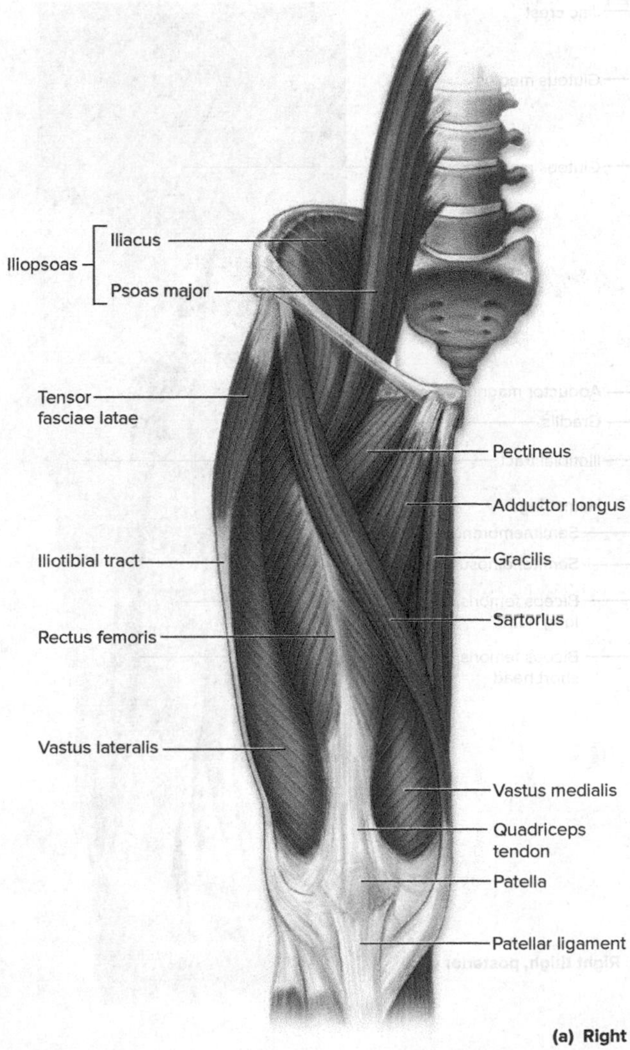
Iliopsoas
Iliacus
Psoas major
Tensor fasciae latae
Pectineus
Adductor longus
Iliotibial tract
Gracilis
Sartorius
Rectus femoris
Vastus lateralis
Vastus medialis
Quadriceps tendon
Patella
Patellar ligament

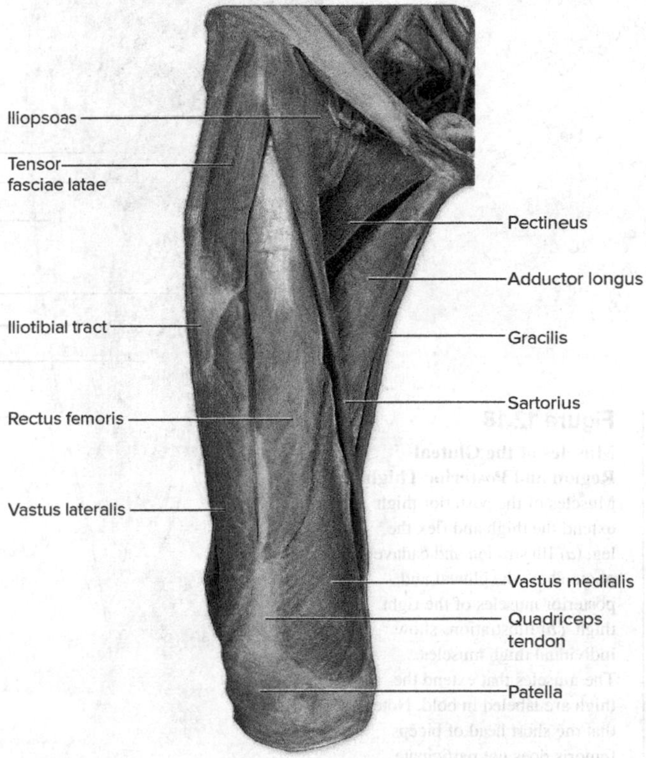
Iliopsoas
Tensor fasciae latae
Pectineus
Adductor longus
Iliotibial tract
Gracilis
Sartorius
Rectus femoris
Vastus lateralis
Vastus medialis
Quadriceps tendon
Patella

(a) Right thigh, anterior view

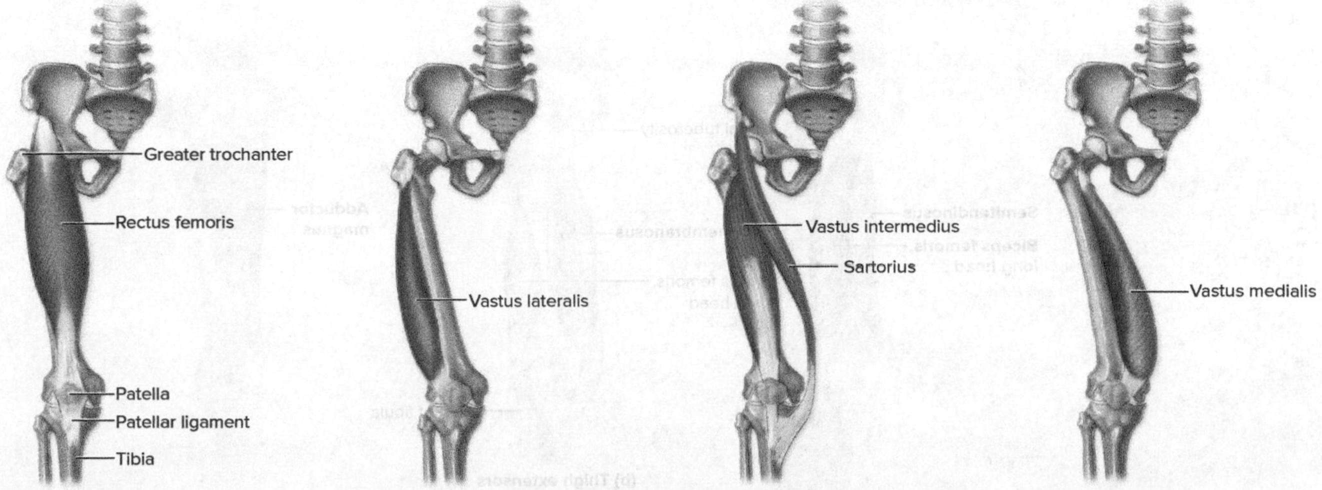
Greater trochanter
Rectus femoris
Patella
Patellar ligament
Tibia
Vastus lateralis
Vastus intermedius
Sartorius
Vastus medialis

(b) Anterior thigh muscles

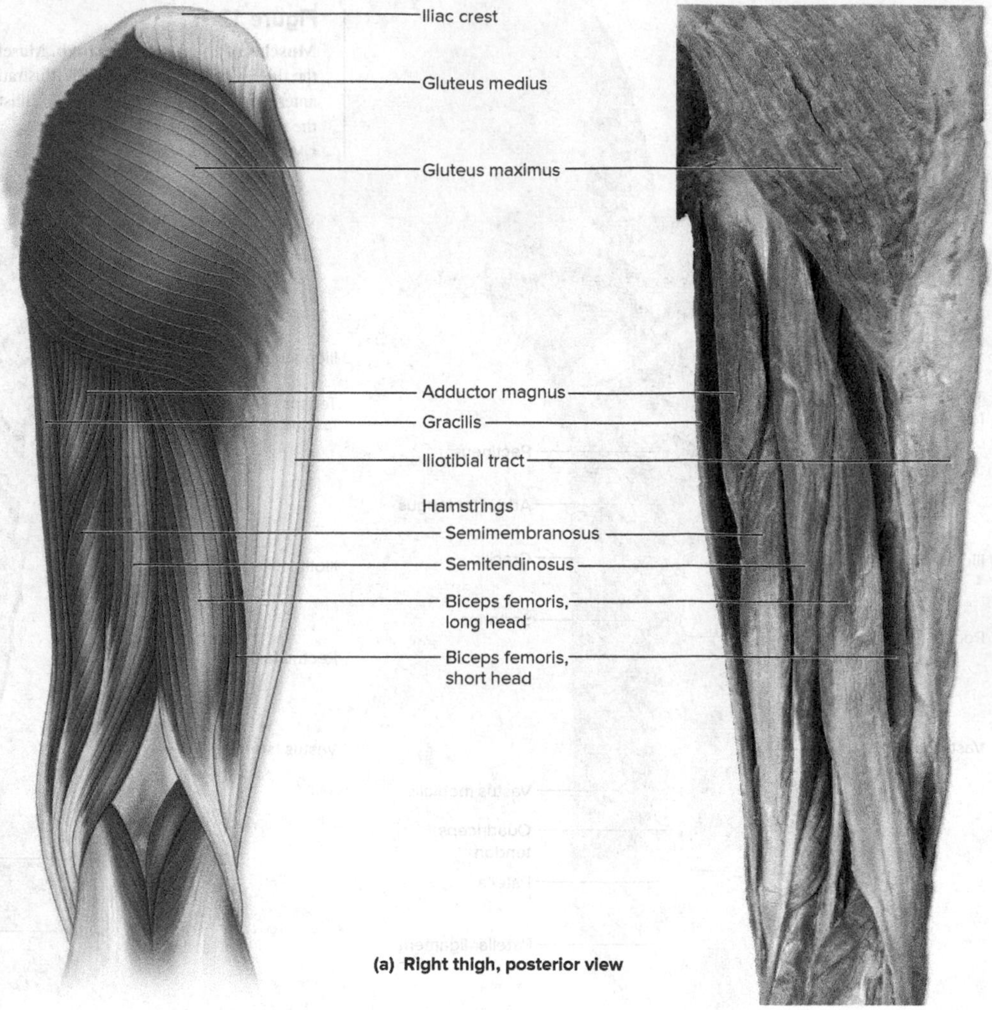
Iliac crest
Gluteus medius
Gluteus maximus
Adductor magnus
Gracilis
Iliotibial tract
Hamstrings
Semimembranosus
Semitendinosus
Biceps femoris, long head
Biceps femoris, short head

(a) Right thigh, posterior view

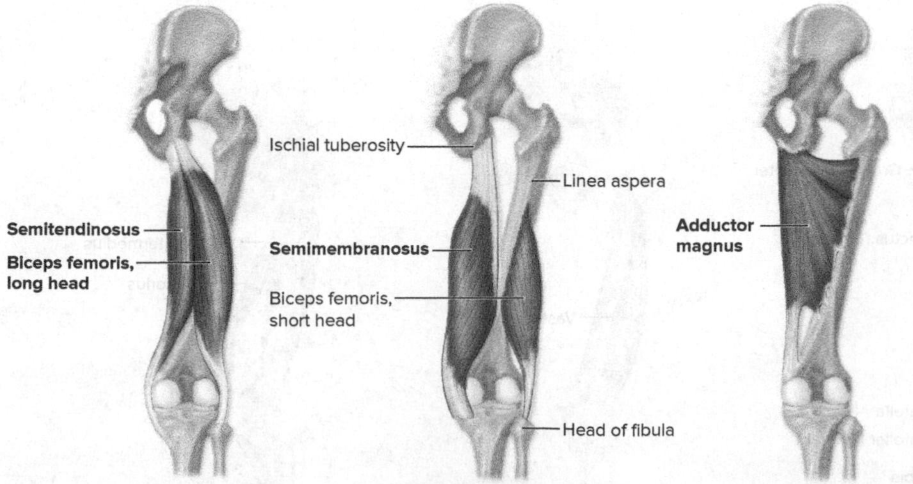
Ischial tuberosity
Linea aspera
Semitendinosus
Biceps femoris, long head
Semimembranosus
Biceps femoris, short head
Adductor magnus
Head of fibula

(b) Thigh extensors

Figure 12.18

Muscles of the Gluteal Region and Posterior Thigh. Muscles of the posterior thigh extend the thigh and flex the leg. (*a*) Illustration and cadaver photo show the gluteal and posterior muscles of the right thigh. (*b*) Illustrations show individual thigh muscles. The muscles that extend the thigh are labeled in bold. Note that the short head of biceps femoris does not participate in thigh extension. APR deep to the semitendinosus. It extends from the ischial tuberosity to the medial side of the leg. The **semitendinosus** is superficial to the semimembranosus and is attached to the medial leg. The semimembranosus and semitendinosus also medially rotate the leg when the leg is flexed.

Finally, several leg muscles span the knee joint and work to flex the leg. These muscles (gastrocnemius, plantaris, and popliteus) are discussed in the next section, as we examine muscles of the leg.

Table 12.11 summarizes the characteristics of the muscles that move the knee joint and leg.

WHAT DO YOU THINK?

3 Recall that if a muscle spans a joint, it must move the joint (and conversely, if a muscle doesn't span a joint, it cannot move that joint). Based upon this rule, would you expect the iliopsoas to flex the knee joint/leg? Why or why not?

12.2c Leg Muscles

The muscles that move the ankle, foot, and toes are housed within the leg and are called the **crural muscles.** Some of these muscles also help flex the leg. The deep fascia partitions the leg musculature into three compartments (anterior, lateral, and posterior), each with its own nerve and blood supply (figure 12.19).

Anterior compartment leg muscles dorsiflex the foot and/or extend the toes (figure 12.20). The **extensor digitorum longus** sends four long tendons to attach to the dorsal surface of toes 2–5. This muscle dorsiflexes the foot and extends toes 2–5. The **extensor hallucis longus** sends a tendon to the dorsum of the great toe (hallux), and so it dorsiflexes the foot and extends the great toe. The **fibularis tertius** (or *peroneus tertius*) extends from the extensor digitorum longus muscle. It dorsiflexes and weakly everts the foot. The presence of this muscle varies among populations and individuals. The **tibialis anterior** is the primary dorsiflexor of the foot at the ankle. This muscle attaches to the medial plantar side of the foot, so it also inverts the foot. Analogous to the wrist, tendons of the muscles within the anterior compartment are held tightly against the ankle by multiple deep fascia thickenings, collectively referred to as the **extensor retinaculum.**

The **lateral compartment** leg muscles contain two synergistic muscles that are very powerful evertors of the foot and weak plantar flexors (figure 12.21). The long, flat **fibularis longus** (or *peroneus longus*) is a superficial lateral muscle that covers the fibula. Its tendon attaches to the plantar side of the foot on the base of metatarsal I and the medial cuneiform. The **fibularis brevis** (or *peroneus brevis*) lies deep to the fibularis longus. Its tendon attaches to the base of the fifth metatarsal.

The **posterior compartment** of the leg is composed of seven muscles that are separated into superficial and deep groups (figure 12.22). The superficial muscles and most of the deep muscles plantar flex the foot at the ankle. The **superficial layer** of the posterior compartment contains three muscles: gastrocnemius, soleus, and plantaris. The **gastrocnemius** is the most superficial muscle. It has two thick muscle bellies, the lateral head and the medial head, that collectively form the prominence on the posterior part of the leg often referred to as the "calf." This muscle spans both the knee and the ankle joints; it flexes the leg and plantar flexes the foot. The tendon for the lateral head of gastrocnemius may have a normal variant sesamoid bone or cartilage called a fabella. The **soleus** is a broad, flat muscle deep to the gastrocnemius that resembles a flat fish. This muscle plantar flexes the foot. The **plantaris** is a small muscle that is absent in some individuals. It projects obliquely between the gastrocnemius and soleus muscles. This muscle is a weak leg flexor and plantar flexor of the foot.

The gastrocnemius and soleus are collectively known as the **triceps surae,** and together they are the most powerful plantar flexors of all of the leg muscles. These two muscles share a common distal attachment tendon, the **calcaneal tendon** (or *Achilles tendon*).

Clinical View 12.5

Thigh Muscle Injuries

The muscle groups in the lower limbs are prone to injury, especially in people who are physically active. Two examples of such injuries are groin pull and strained (or pulled) hamstrings.

A **groin pull** is caused by tearing, stretching, or straining the proximal attachments of the medial muscles of the thigh—the adductor muscles of the leg and/or the iliopsoas muscle. This type of injury most frequently results from activities that involve rapid accelerations, as are called for in football, baseball, tennis, running, and soccer.

Strained or **pulled hamstrings** are common in athletes who perform quick starts and stops, run very fast, or sustain sudden lateral or medial stress to the knee joint. The violent muscular exertion required to perform these running feats sometimes causes the hamstring tendons to be avulsed (torn away) from their attachment on the ischial tuberosity. The biceps femoris is especially susceptible to this type of stress injury. A *contusion* (bruising), blood vessel rupture, pain, hematoma formation (accumulation of blood in soft tissue), and tearing of muscle fibers may accompany hamstring damage. To prevent this type of injury, experts recommend that athletes warm up and perform stretching exercises prior to running.

Photo shows woman stretching her left hamstrings.
Big Cheese Photo/SuperStock

Table 12.11 Thigh Muscles That Move the Knee Joint/Leg

Group/Muscle	Action(s)	Proximal Attachment(s) (P)/ Distal Attachment(s) (D)	Innervation (see section 16.4f)
LEG EXTENSORS (ANTERIOR THIGH MUSCLES)			
Quadriceps Femoris			
Rectus femoris	Extends leg; flexes thigh	P: Anterior inferior iliac spine D: Quadriceps tendon to patella and then patellar ligament to tibial tuberosity	Femoral nerve (L2–L4)
Vastus intermedius (vas'tŭs in'tĕr-mē'dē-ŭs) *vastus* = great *intermedius* = intermediate	Extends leg	P: Anterolateral surface of femur D: Quadriceps tendon to patella and then patellar ligament to tibial tuberosity	Femoral nerve (L2–L4)
Vastus lateralis (lat-ĕr 'lis)	Extends leg	P: Greater trochanter and linea aspera D: Quadriceps tendon to patella and then patellar ligament to tibial tuberosity	Femoral nerve (L2–L4)
Vastus medialis (me'dē-ă'lis)	Extends leg	P: Intertrochanteric line and linea aspera of femur D: Quadriceps tendon to patella and then patellar ligament to tibial tuberosity	Femoral nerve (L2–L4)
LEG FLEXORS			
Sartorius	Flexes thigh and rotates thigh laterally; flexes leg and rotates leg medially	See table 12.9	See table 12.9
Gracilis	Flexes and adducts thigh; flexes leg	See table 12.9	See table 12.9
Hamstrings (biceps femoris, semimembranosus, semitendinosus)	Extend thigh and flex leg; rotate leg laterally	See table 12.9	See table 12.9

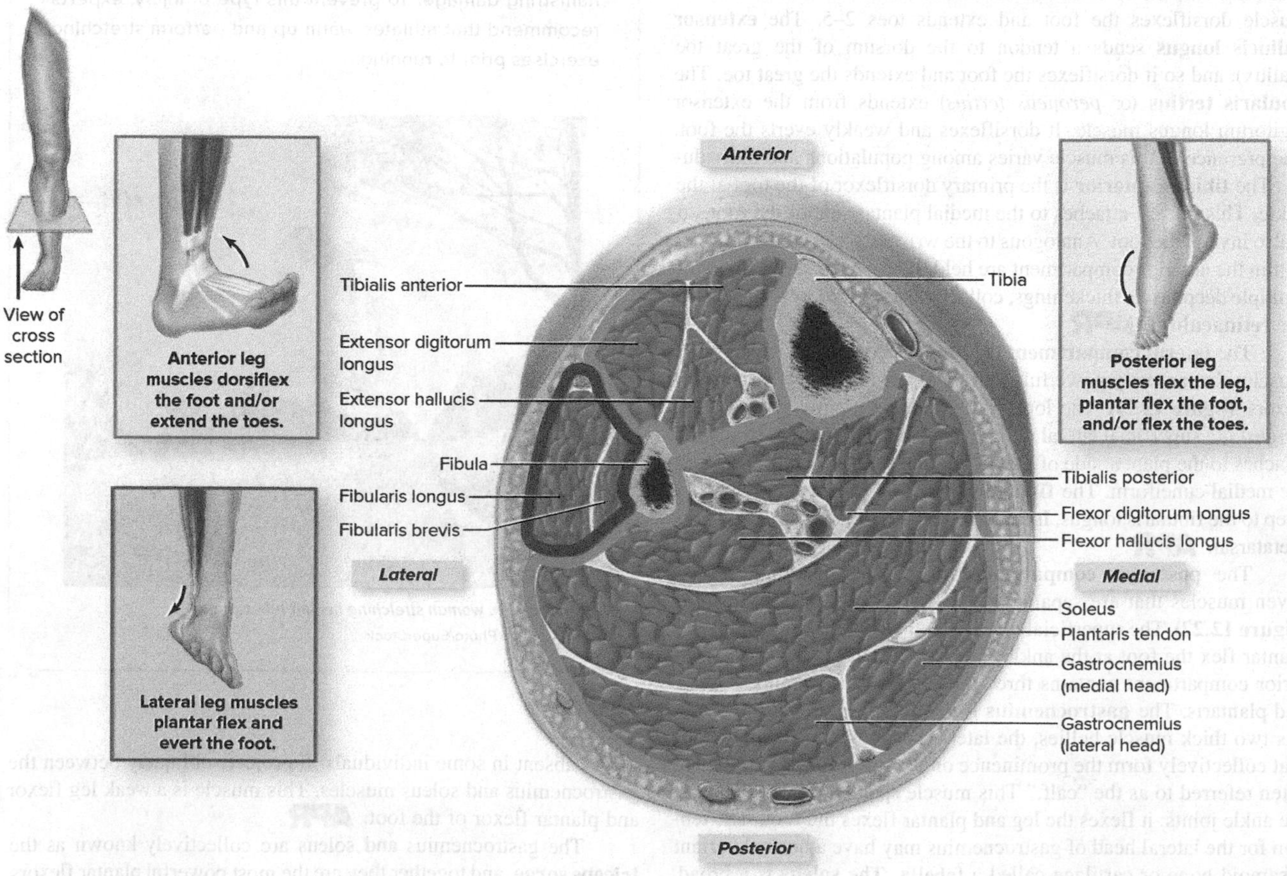

Figure 12.19

Actions of Muscles of the Leg. A cross-sectional view of the right leg shows the muscles of the anterior, lateral, and posterior compartments, which act to dorsiflex, evert, and plantar flex the foot, respectively.

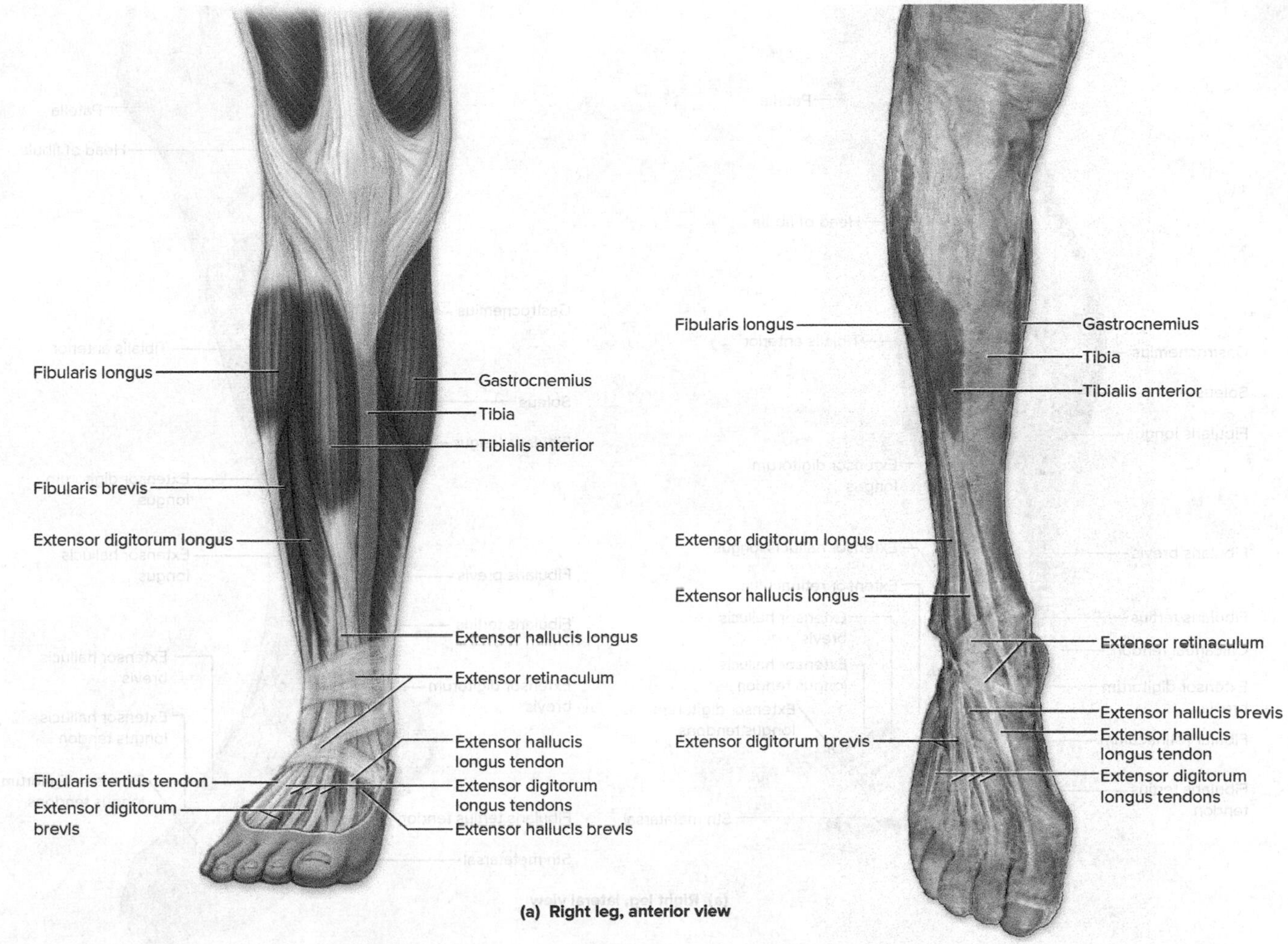
Fibularis longus
Gastrocnemius
Tibia
Tibialis anterior
Fibularis brevis
Extensor digitorum longus
Extensor hallucis longus
Extensor retinaculum
Extensor hallucis longus tendon
Fibularis tertius tendon
Extensor digitorum longus tendons
Extensor digitorum brevis
Extensor hallucis brevis
Fibularis longus
Gastrocnemius
Tibia
Tibialis anterior
Extensor digitorum longus
Extensor hallucis longus
Extensor retinaculum
Extensor hallucis brevis
Extensor digitorum brevis
Extensor hallucis longus tendon
Extensor digitorum longus tendons

(a) Right leg, anterior view

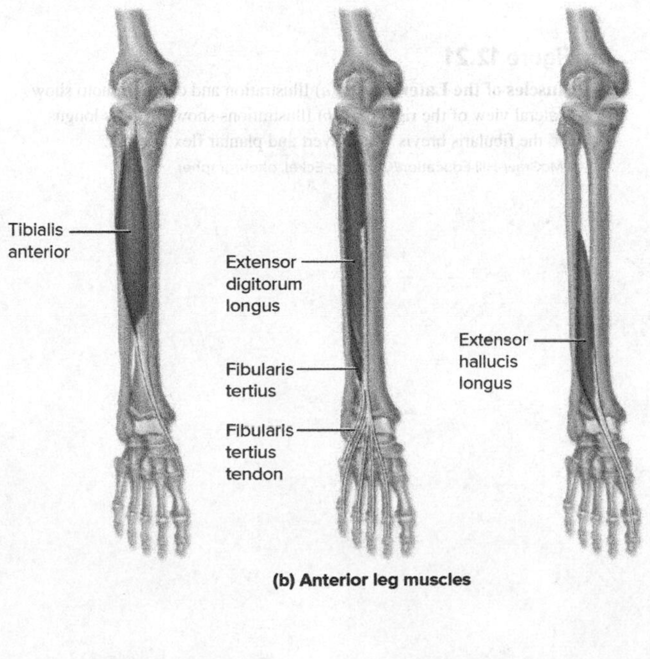
Tibialis anterior
Extensor digitorum longus
Fibularis tertius
Fibularis tertius tendon
Extensor hallucis longus

(b) Anterior leg muscles

Figure 12.20

Muscles of the Anterior Leg. The anterior muscles of the leg dorsiflex the foot and extend the toes. (*a*) Illustration and cadaver photo show an anterior view of the right leg. (*b*) Illustrations show individual muscles of the right anterior leg. APR

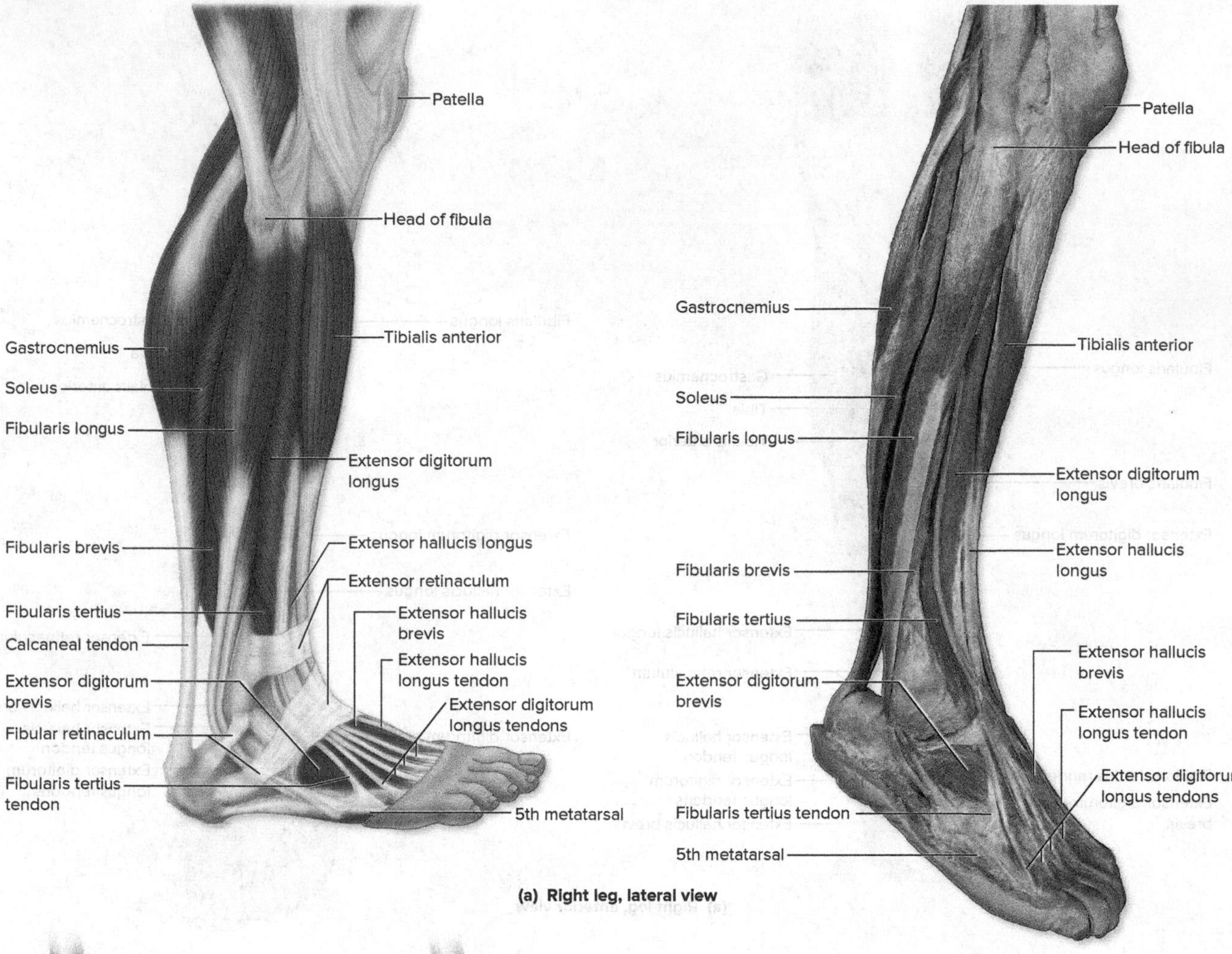
Patella
Head of fibula
Gastrocnemius
Tibialis anterior
Soleus
Fibularis longus
Extensor digitorum longus
Fibularis brevis
Extensor hallucis longus
Extensor retinaculum
Fibularis tertius
Extensor hallucis brevis
Calcaneal tendon
Extensor hallucis longus tendon
Extensor digitorum brevis
Extensor digitorum longus tendons
Fibular retinaculum
Fibularis tertius tendon
5th metatarsal
Patella
Head of fibula
Gastrocnemius
Tibialis anterior
Soleus
Fibularis longus
Extensor digitorum longus
Extensor hallucis longus
Fibularis brevis
Fibularis tertius
Extensor hallucis brevis
Extensor digitorum brevis
Extensor hallucis longus tendon
Extensor digitorum longus tendons
Fibularis tertius tendon
5th metatarsal

(a) Right leg, lateral view

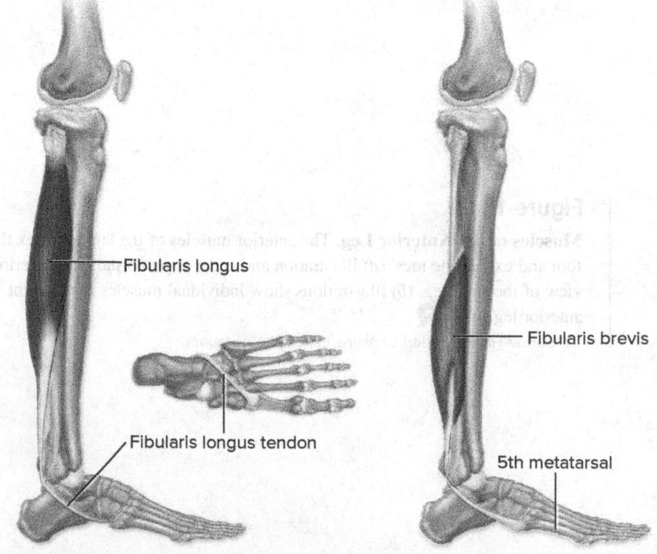
Fibularis longus
Fibularis brevis
Fibularis longus tendon
5th metatarsal

(b) Lateral leg muscles

Figure 12.21

Muscles of the Lateral Leg. (*a*) Illustration and cadaver photo show a lateral view of the right leg. (*b*) Illustrations show fibularis longus and the fibularis brevis which evert and plantar flex the foot.

©McGraw-Hill Education/Christine Eckel, photographer

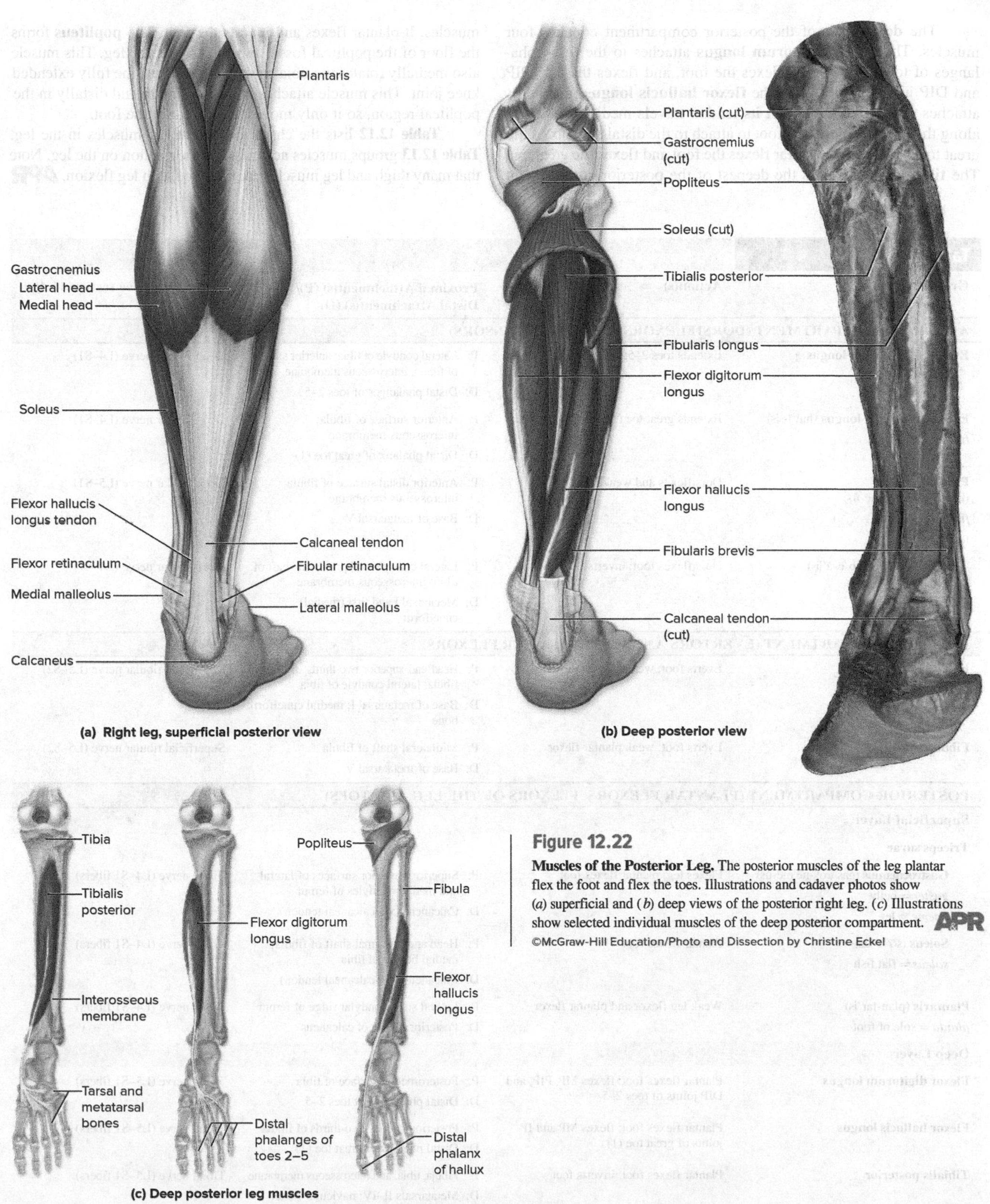
Plantaris
Gastrocnemius
Lateral head
Medial head
Soleus
Flexor hallucis longus tendon
Calcaneal tendon
Flexor retinaculum
Fibular retinaculum
Medial malleolus
Lateral malleolus
Calcaneus
(a) Right leg, superficial posterior view
Plantaris (cut)
Gastrocnemius (cut)
Popliteus
Soleus (cut)
Tibialis posterior
Fibularis longus
Flexor digitorum longus
Flexor hallucis longus
Fibularis brevis
Calcaneal tendon (cut)
(b) Deep posterior view
Tibia
Tibialis posterior
Interosseous membrane
Tarsal and metatarsal bones
Popliteus
Fibula
Flexor digitorum longus
Flexor hallucis longus
Distal phalanges of toes 2–5
Distal phalanx of hallux
(c) Deep posterior leg muscles

Figure 12.22

Muscles of the Posterior Leg. The posterior muscles of the leg plantar flex the foot and flex the toes. Illustrations and cadaver photos show (*a*) superficial and (*b*) deep views of the posterior right leg. (*c*) Illustrations show selected individual muscles of the deep posterior compartment. APR

The **deep layer** of the posterior compartment contains four muscles. The **flexor digitorum longus** attaches to the distal phalanges of toes 2–5, plantar flexes the foot, and flexes the MP, PIP, and DIP joints of toes 2–5. The **flexor hallucis longus** proximally attaches to the fibula, and yet its tendon travels medially and runs along the plantar side of the foot to attach to the distal phalanx of the great toe. This muscle plantar flexes the foot and flexes the great toe. The **tibialis posterior** is the deepest of the posterior compartment muscles. It plantar flexes and inverts the foot. The **popliteus** forms the floor of the popliteal fossa, and acts to flex the leg. This muscle also medially rotates the tibia slightly to "unlock" the fully extended knee joint. This muscle attaches both proximally and distally in the popliteal region, so it only moves the knee, not the foot.

Table 12.12 lists the characteristics of the muscles in the leg. **Table 12.13** groups muscles according to their action on the leg. Note that many thigh and leg muscles are involved with leg flexion. APR

Table 12.12 Leg Muscles

Group/Muscle	Action(s)	Proximal Attachment(s) (P)/ Distal Attachment(s) (D)	Innervation (see section 16.4g)
ANTERIOR COMPARTMENT (DORSIFLEXORS AND TOE EXTENSORS)			
Extensor digitorum longus	Extends toes 2–5; dorsiflexes foot	P: Lateral condyle of tibia; anterior surface of fibula; interosseous membrane D: Distal phalanges of toes 2–5	Deep fibular nerve (L4–S1)
Extensor hallucis longus (hal'ĭ-sis) *hallux* = great toe	Extends great toe (1); dorsiflexes foot	P: Anterior surface of fibula; interosseous membrane D: Distal phalanx of great toe (1)	Deep fibular nerve (L4–S1)
Fibularis tertius (fib'yū-lā'ris ter'shē-ŭs) *fibularis* = fibula *tertius* = third	Dorsiflexes and weakly everts foot	P: Anterior distal surface of fibula; interosseous membrane D: Base of metatarsal V	Deep fibular nerve (L5–S1)
Tibialis anterior (tib'ē-ā'lis)	Dorsiflexes foot; inverts foot	P: Lateral condyle and proximal shaft of tibia; interosseous membrane D: Metatarsal I and first (medial) cuneiform	Deep fibular nerve (L4–S1)
LATERAL COMPARTMENT (EVERTORS AND WEAK PLANTAR FLEXORS)			
Fibularis longus	Everts foot; weak plantar flexor	P: Head and superior two-thirds of shaft of fibula; lateral condyle of tibia D: Base of metatarsal I; medial cuneiform bone	Superficial fibular nerve (L5–S2)
Fibularis brevis	Everts foot; weak plantar flexor	P: Midlateral shaft of fibula D: Base of metatarsal V	Superficial fibular nerve (L5–S2)
POSTERIOR COMPARTMENT (PLANTAR FLEXORS, FLEXORS OF THE LEG AND TOES)			
Superficial Layer			
Triceps surae			
Gastrocnemius (gas'trok-nē'mē-ŭs) *gaster* = belly *kneme* = leg	Flexes leg; plantar flexes foot	P: Superior posterior surfaces of lateral and medial condyles of femur D: Calcaneus (via calcaneal tendon)	Tibial nerve (L4–S1 fibers)
Soleus (sō'lē-ŭs) *soleus* = flat fish	Plantar flexes foot	P: Head and proximal shaft of fibula; medial border of tibia D: Calcaneus (via calcaneal tendon)	Tibial nerve (L4–S1 fibers)
Plantaris (plan-tar'is) *planta* = sole of foot	Weak leg flexor and plantar flexor	P: Lateral supracondylar ridge of femur D: Posterior region of calcaneus	Tibial nerve (L4–S1 fibers)
Deep Layer			
Flexor digitorum longus	Plantar flexes foot; flexes MP, PIP, and DIP joints of toes 2–5	P: Posteromedial surface of tibia D: Distal phalanges of toes 2–5	Tibial nerve (L5–S1 fibers)
Flexor hallucis longus	Plantar flexes foot; flexes MP and IP joints of great toe (1)	P: Posterior inferior two-thirds of fibula D: Distal phalanx of great toe (1)	Tibial nerve (L5–S1 fibers)
Tibialis posterior	Plantar flexes foot; inverts foot	P: Fibula, tibia, and interosseous membrane D: Metatarsals II–IV; navicular bone; cuboid bone; all cuneiforms	Tibial nerve (L5–S1 fibers)
Popliteus (pop-lit'ē-ŭs) *poplit* = back of knee	Flexes leg; medially rotates tibia to unlock the knee	P: Lateral condyle of femur D: Posterior, proximal surface of tibia	Tibial nerve (L4–L5 fibers)

Table 12.13	Summary of Muscle Actions at the Knee Joint/Leg
Extension	**Flexion**
Quadriceps femoris:	Sartorius
Rectus femoris	Gracilis
Vastus lateralis	Adductor longus, brevis, magnus
Vastus intermedius	Biceps femoris
Vastus medialis	Semimembranosus
	Semitendinosus
	Gastrocnemius
	Popliteus
	(Plantaris)

Parentheses indicate only a slight effect.

12.2d Intrinsic Muscles of the Foot

The intrinsic muscles of the foot have both proximal and distal attachments within the foot. They support the arches and move the toes to aid locomotion. Most of these muscles are comparable to the intrinsic muscles of the hand, meaning that they have similar names and locations. However, the intrinsic muscles of the foot rarely perform all the precise movements their names suggest.

The intrinsic foot muscles form a dorsal group and a plantar group. The dorsal group contains only two muscles: the extensor hallucis brevis and the extensor digitorum brevis (see figures 12.20 and 12.21). The **extensor hallucis brevis** extends the MP joint of the great toe. The **extensor digitorum brevis** is deep to the tendons of the extensor digitorum longus, and it extends the MP, PIP, and DIP joints of toes 2–4.

Clinical View 12.6

Plantar Fasciitis

Plantar fasciitis (fas′ē-ī′tis, fash-) is an inflammation caused by chronic irritation of the plantar aponeurosis (fascia). Most often, the inflammation is greatest at the attachment of the plantar aponeurosis on the calcaneus bone. This condition is frequently caused by overexertion that stresses the plantar fascia. It also may be related to age, as loss of elasticity in the aponeurosis, which occurs with age, seems to be a factor in developing this condition. Other factors associated with plantar fasciitis include weight-bearing activities (e.g., lifting heavy objects, jogging, or walking), excessive body weight, improperly fitting shoes, and poor biomechanics (e.g., wearing high-heeled shoes or having flat feet). Because plantar fasciitis can occur as a consequence of repetitively pounding the feet on the ground, this condition has become the most common cause of heel pain in runners.

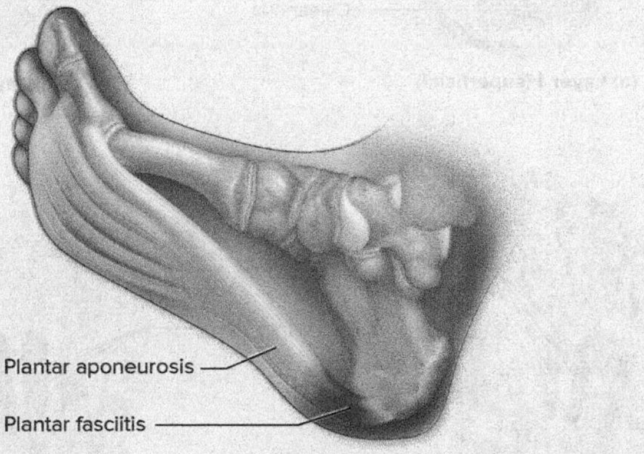

Location of plantar fascia, and pain associated with plantar fasciitis.

Clinical View 12.7

Shin Splints and Compartment Syndrome

Cross sections of the limbs reveal that the musculature is surrounded by deep fascia. This deep fascia is tough and unyielding; it wraps around the muscle like support hose, and it groups the muscles into compartments. Thus, the compartments of the leg (anterior, lateral, and posterior) are subdivided by this fascia along with the intermuscular septa. Sometimes problems develop within these compartments.

Shin splints, also called *shin splint syndrome*, refers specifically to soreness or pain somewhere along the length of the tibia. Causes of the syndrome include: (1) tendonitis involving muscles of the anterior compartment muscles of the leg, often the tibialis anterior muscle; and (2) inflammation of the periosteum, called periostitis. Shin splints often occurs in runners who are new to the sport, are poorly conditioned, wear ill-fitting shoes, or run on hard surfaces (concrete, asphalt).

Compartment syndrome occurs when the blood vessels within a limb compartment become compressed as a result of inflammation and swelling secondary to muscle strain, contusion, or overuse. More severe compartment syndrome can occur due to trauma to the limb compartment, such as a bone fracture or rupture of a blood vessel.

Because the deep fascia is tight and cannot stretch, swelling from muscles or any accumulating fluid or blood increases pressure in the compartment. Both the circulatory supply and the nerves of the compartment become compressed and compromised. The reduced blood flow (known as **ischemia** [is-kē′mē-ă; *isch* = to keep back, *haima* = blood]) leads to **hypoxia** (hī-pok′sē-ă; *hypo* = under, *oxo* = oxygen), which is a lack of oxygen within the compartment. If the blood flow is not restored, this situation can lead to death of nerves within 2 hours and death of skeletal muscle within 6 hours. Although the damaged nerves may regenerate after the compartment syndrome has been resolved, the loss of muscle cells is irreversible. Mild cases of compartment syndrome may be treated by immobilizing and resting the affected limb. In more severe cases, the fascia may have to be incised (cut) to relieve the pressure and decompress the affected compartment.

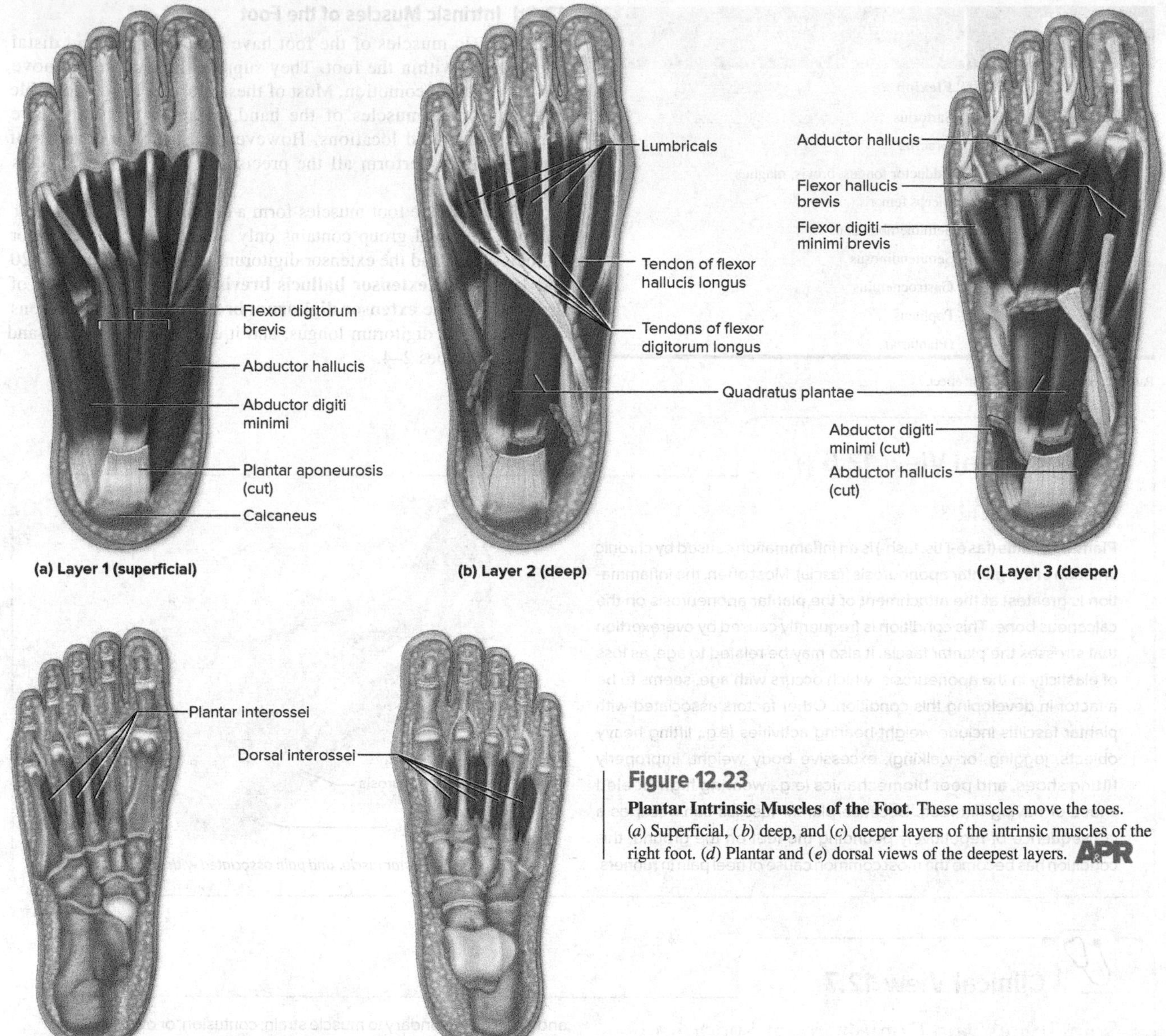

Figure 12.23
Plantar Intrinsic Muscles of the Foot. These muscles move the toes. (*a*) Superficial, (*b*) deep, and (*c*) deeper layers of the intrinsic muscles of the right foot. (*d*) Plantar and (*e*) dorsal views of the deepest layers. APR

WHAT DO YOU THINK?

4 The extensor digitorum brevis goes only to toes 2–4, so how is it possible to extend your little toe (toe 5)?

The plantar surface of the foot is supported by the **plantar aponeurosis** formed from the deep fascia of the foot. This aponeurosis extends between the phalanges of the toes and the calcaneus. It also encloses the plantar muscles of the foot.

The plantar muscles are grouped into four layers (**figure 12.23**). The first layer of muscles is the most superficial. It includes the **flexor digitorum brevis** that attaches to the middle phalanges of the toes, so it can flex the MP and PIP joints (but *not* the DIP joints) of toes 2–5. Also included in this layer are the **abductor hallucis,** which abducts the great toe (1), and the **abductor digiti minimi,** which abducts the small toe (5).

The second layer (deep to the first) consists of the thick, medial **quadratus plantae,** which attaches to the tendons of the flexor

Table 12.14	Intrinsic Muscles of the Foot		
Group/Muscle	**Action(s)**	**Proximal Attachment(s) (P)/ Distal Attachment(s) (D)**	**Innervation (see section 16.4g)**
DORSAL SURFACE (TOE EXTENSORS)			
Extensor hallucis brevis	Extends MP joint of great toe (1)	P: Calcaneus and inferior extensor retinaculum D: Proximal phalanx of great toe (1)	Deep fibular nerve (S1–S2 fibers)
Extensor digitorum brevis	Extends MP, PIP, and DIP joints of toes 2–4	P: Calcaneus and inferior extensor retinaculum D: Middle phalanges of toes 2–4	Deep fibular nerve (S1–S2 fibers)
PLANTAR SURFACE (TOE FLEXORS, ADDUCTORS, ABDUCTORS)			
Layer 1 (Superficial)			
Flexor digitorum brevis	Flexes MP and PIP joints of toes 2–5	P: Calcaneus D: Middle phalanges of toes 2–5	Medial plantar nerve (S2–S3)
Abductor hallucis	Abducts great toe (1)	P: Calcaneus D: Medial side of proximal phalanx of great toe (1)	Medial plantar nerve (S2–S3)
Abductor digiti minimi	Abducts toe 5	P: Calcaneus (inferior surface tuberosity) D: Lateral side of proximal phalanx of toe 5	Lateral plantar nerve (S2–S3)
Layer 2 (Deep)			
Quadratus plantae (plan′tē) *planta* = sole of foot	Pulls on flexor digitorum longus tendons to flex toes 2–5	P: Calcaneus, long plantar ligament D: Tendons of flexor digitorum longus	Lateral plantar nerve (S2–S3)
Lumbricals	Flexes MP joints and extends PIP and DIP joints of toes 2–5	P: Tendons of flexor digitorum longus D: Tendons of extensor digitorum longus	Medial plantar nerve (1st lumbrical); lateral plantar nerve (2nd–4th lumbricals)
Layer 3 (Deeper)			
Adductor hallucis	Adducts great toe (1)	P: Transverse head: Capsules of MP joints III–V Oblique head: Bases of metatarsals II–IV D: Lateral side of proximal phalanx of great toe (1)	Lateral plantar nerve (S2–S3)
Flexor hallucis brevis	Flexes MP joint of great toe (1)	P: Cuboid and lateral (3rd) cuneiform bones D: Proximal phalanx of great toe (1)	Medial plantar nerve (S2–S3)
Flexor digiti minimi brevis	Flexes MP joint of toe 5	P: MetatarsalV D: Proximal phalanx of toe 5	Lateral plantar nerve (S2–S3)
Layer 4 (Deepest)			
Dorsal interossei	Abducts toes	P: Adjacent sides of metatarsals D: Sides of proximal phalanges of toes 2–4	Lateral plantar nerve (S2–S3)
Plantar interossei	Adducts toes	P: Sides of metatarsals III–V D: Medial side of proximal phalanges of toes 3–5	Lateral plantar nerve (S2–S3)

digitorum longus. Note how the flexor digitorum longus tendons attach to the toes at an angle (figure 12.23*b*). The quadratus plantae pulls on the slanted flexor digitorum longus tendons in a posterior fashion so that toes 2–5 may be flexed properly, not at an angle. In addition, this layer contains the four **lumbrical muscles,** small muscles that attach to the tendons of the flexor digitorum longus and serve to flex the MP joints and extend the DIP and PIP joints of toes 2–5.

The third layer (deeper) contains the **adductor hallucis,** which adducts the great toe (1). Also in this layer are the medial **flexor hallucis brevis** and the lateral **flexor digiti minimi brevis,** which flex the great toe (1) and the small toe (5), respectively. The fourth layer (deepest) consists of four **dorsal interossei** and three **plantar interossei.** The dorsal interossei abduct the toes, while the plantar interossei adduct the toes.

Table 12.14 summarizes the characteristics of the intrinsic muscles of the foot, and **table 12.15** groups the leg and intrinsic foot muscles according to their common actions on the foot. APR

Table 12.15 Summary of Leg and Foot Muscle Actions at the Foot and Toes

FOOT			
Dorsiflexion	**Plantar Flexion**	**Eversion**	**Inversion**
Tibialis anterior	**Gastrocnemius**	**Fibularis longus**	**Tibialis posterior**
Extensor digitorum longus	**Soleus**	**Fibularis brevis**	**Tibialis anterior**
(Extensor hallucis longus)	Flexor digitorum longus	(Fibularis tertius)	
(Fibularis tertius)	Flexor hallucis longus		
	Tibialis posterior		
	(Fibularis longus)		
	(Fibularis brevis)		
	(Plantaris)		
TOES			
Extension	**Flexion**	**Abduction**	**Adduction**
Extensor digitorum longus	Flexor digitorum longus	Abductor hallucis	Adductor hallucis
Extensor hallucis longus	Flexor hallucis longus	Abductor digiti minimi	Plantar interossei
Extensor digitorum brevis	Flexor digitorum brevis	Dorsal interossei	
Extensor hallucis brevis	Flexor hallucis brevis		
	Flexor digiti minimi brevis		

Boldface indicates an agonist; others are synergists. Parentheses indicate only a slight effect.

WHAT DID YOU LEARN?

13 Name and provide the actions for the hamstring muscles?

14 Identify the muscles that extend the knee joint/leg.

15 What is the action of the muscles in the lateral compartment of the leg?

16 Identify the intrinsic muscles of the foot that extend the toes.

Clinical Terms

adductor strain Extreme thigh abduction results in pulled adductor muscles, especially the adductor longus.

hallux valgus (hal′ŭks val′gus; *valgus* = turned outward) Deviation of the tip of the great toe to the medial side of the foot away from the second toe.

Chapter Summary

- The appendicular muscles stabilize and help move the pectoral and pelvic girdles, and move the upper and lower limbs.

12.1 Muscles of the Pectoral Girdle and Upper Limb

- Five groups of muscles are associated with pectoral girdle and upper limb movement: muscles that move (1) the pectoral girdle; (2) the glenohumeral joint/arm; (3) the elbow joint/forearm; (4) the wrist joint, hand, and fingers; and (5) the intrinsic muscles of the hand.

12.1a Muscles That Move the Pectoral Girdle

- Anterior thoracic muscles protract, rotate, and/or depress the scapula; one anterior thoracic muscle depresses the clavicle.
- The posterior thoracic muscles elevate, retract, and/or rotate the scapula.

12.1b Muscles That Move the Glenohumeral Joint/Arm

- The pectoralis major flexes the arm, and the latissimus dorsi extends it, whereas both adduct and medially rotate it.
- Seven scapular muscles move the humerus, individually or together, causing abduction, adduction, extension, flexion, lateral rotation, or medial rotation of the arm.
- Collectively, the subscapularis, supraspinatus, infraspinatus, and teres minor are called the rotator cuff muscles. They provide strength and stability to the glenohumeral joint, and move the humerus.

12.1c Arm and Forearm Muscles That Move the Elbow Joint/Forearm

- The principal flexors are on the anterior side of the arm, and the principal extensors are on the posterior side of the arm.
- Muscles that move the forearm are the biceps brachii (flexes and supinates) and the triceps brachii (extends).
- The pronator teres and pronator quadratus cause pronation only of the forearm; the supinator opposes this movement.

12.1d Forearm Muscles That Move the Wrist Joint, Hand, and Fingers

- Strong fibrous bands, called the flexor retinaculum and the extensor retinaculum, hold tendon sheaths of the forearm muscles close to the skeletal elements of the wrist.
- Superficial muscles of the forearm function coordinately to flex the wrist; some also cause abduction and adduction of the wrist. The intermediate and deep anterior forearm muscles flex the wrist and the MP and IP joints.
- Extension of the wrist and fingers is provided by the extensor muscles of the forearm. Some also cause abduction or adduction of the hand. The deep posterior compartment muscles are primarily wrist and finger extensors.

12.1e Intrinsic Muscles of the Hand

- Intrinsic muscles of the hand are small muscles entirely within the hand and divided into three groups: (1) the thenar group, (2) the hypothenar group, and (3) the midpalmar group between the thenar and hypothenar groups.

12.2 Muscles of the Pelvic Girdle and Lower Limb

- Four groups of muscles are associated with the pelvis and lower limb: muscles that move (1) the hip joint/thigh, (2) the knee joint/leg, and (3) leg muscles, as well as (4) the intrinsic muscles of the foot.

12.2a Muscles That Move the Hip Joint/Thigh

- Muscles that act on the thigh (femur) proximally attach to the surface of the ossa coxae (pelvis) and distally attach to the femur.
- Anterior compartment muscles flex the thigh.
- There are three gluteal muscles: The gluteus maximus extends and laterally rotates the thigh; the gluteus medius and minimus are powerful abductors of the thigh.
- The deep gluteal muscles contain the lateral rotators of the thigh.
- The posterior compartment (hamstring) muscles extend the thigh.
- Medial compartment muscles adduct the thigh, and most also flex the thigh.
- The lateral muscle (tensor fasciae latae) abducts the thigh.

12.2b Thigh Muscles That Move the Knee Joint/Leg

- The quadriceps femoris extends the leg.
- The sartorius muscle flexes both the thigh and the leg.
- Some medial thigh muscles also flex the leg.
- The extensors of the thigh and flexors of the leg, termed the *hamstrings,* occupy the posterior compartment.

12.2c Leg Muscles

- The anterior compartment muscles dorsiflex the foot and extend the toes. One muscle also inverts the foot.
- Lateral compartment muscles evert and plantar flex the foot.
- Posterior compartment muscles plantar flex the foot.
- Deep posterior compartment muscles either flex the leg or plantar flex the foot, and either flex the toes or invert the foot.

12.2d Intrinsic Muscles of the Foot

- Dorsal muscles extend the toes.
- The four layers of plantar muscles flex, extend, abduct, and/or adduct the toes.

Challenge Yourself

Actively write or type your answers in a separate document to reinforce your learning, before checking your answers.

Multiple Choice

Select the best answer from the four choices provided.

1. The dorsal interossei muscles complete which of the following actions?
   a. adduct fingers 2–5
   b. abduct fingers 2–5
   c. flex the PIP and DIP joints
   d. extend the MP joints
2. The contraction of which of the following muscles causes medial rotation of the thigh?
   a. pectineus
   b. obturator externus
   c. gluteus minimus
   d. gracilis
3. What is the main action of the muscles in the anterior compartment of the leg?
   a. evert the foot
   b. dorsiflex the foot and extend the toes
   c. plantar flex the foot
   d. flex the toes
4. Which of the following muscles does *not* flex the forearm?
   a. brachialis
   b. biceps brachii
   c. brachioradialis
   d. anconeus
5. The quadriceps femoris is composed of which of the following muscles?
   a. biceps femoris, rectus femoris, vastus lateralis, and gracilis
   b. vastus lateralis, vastus medialis, rectus femoris, and vastus intermedius
   c. semimembranosus, semitendinosus, and biceps femoris
   d. popliteus, gracilis, and sartorius
6. Thumb opposition is caused by contraction of which muscle?
   a. flexor digiti minimi brevis
   b. opponens pollicis
   c. extensor pollicis longus
   d. adductor pollicis
7. Which muscle flexes the knee and causes a slight medial rotation to "unlock" the knee joint?
   a. sartorius
   b. soleus
   c. tensor fasciae latae
   d. popliteus
8. The latissimus dorsi and pectoralis major work synergistically in what action?
   a. extension of the humerus
   b. flexion of the humerus
   c. medial rotation of the humerus
   d. lateral rotation of the humerus
9. Which muscles attach to the ischial tuberosity and extend the thigh plus flex the leg?
   a. adductor muscles
   b. fibularis muscles
   c. hamstring muscles
   d. quadriceps muscles
10. Which muscle can abduct (radially deviate) the hand?
    a. abductor pollicis brevis
    b. flexor carpi radialis
    c. abductor magnus
    d. flexor carpi ulnaris

Content Review

1. The trapezius can perform what types of movements?
2. What movements are possible at the glenohumeral joint, and which muscles perform each of these movements?
3. Identify the compartments of the arm, the muscles in each compartment, and their function.
4. Compare and contrast the flexor digitorum superficialis and the flexor digitorum profundus; where does each attach distally, how are their tendons interrelated, and what muscle actions do they perform?
5. What is the primary function of the retinacula in a limb?
6. What muscles are responsible for thigh extension? Which of these is the agonist of thigh extension?
7. Which muscles abduct the thigh, and where are they located?
8. What leg muscles are contracted when you are sitting at your desk?
9. What leg muscles allow a ballet dancer to rise up and balance on her toes?
10. Which muscles are responsible for foot inversion, and what muscles are antagonists to those that invert the foot?

Developing Critical Reasoning

1. Edmund suffers an injury to the anterior compartment of his thigh that results in paralysis of the muscles of this compartment. What muscle movements will be compromised?
2. After falling while skateboarding, Karen had surgery on her elbow. During her recovery, she must visit the physical therapist to improve muscle function around the elbow. Develop a series of exercises that may improve all of Karen's elbow movements, and determine which muscles are being helped by each exercise.
3. Why is it more difficult for Eric to lift a heavy weight when his forearm is pronated than when it is in the supine position?

Answers to "What Do You Think?"

1. The supraspinatus muscle is the most commonly injured rotator cuff muscle, due in part to its location in the narrow space between the acromion and the humerus. Repetitive arm motions impinge (pinch) the muscle in this narrow space, and may eventually lead to tears of the muscle or tendon.
2. The brachialis is an anterior arm muscle. Since anterior arm muscles tend to flex the elbow joint, we can surmise that the brachialis flexes the elbow joint.
3. The iliopsoas cannot flex the leg, because this muscle does not cross over the knee joint.
4. Remember that there are leg muscles that also move the toes. In this case, the extensor digitorum longus (a leg muscle) attaches to toes 2–5 and helps move them all.

Design Element: Pencil Icon: Slavojub Pantelic/Shutterstock

BODY ORIENTATION

13 Surface Anatomy

Outline

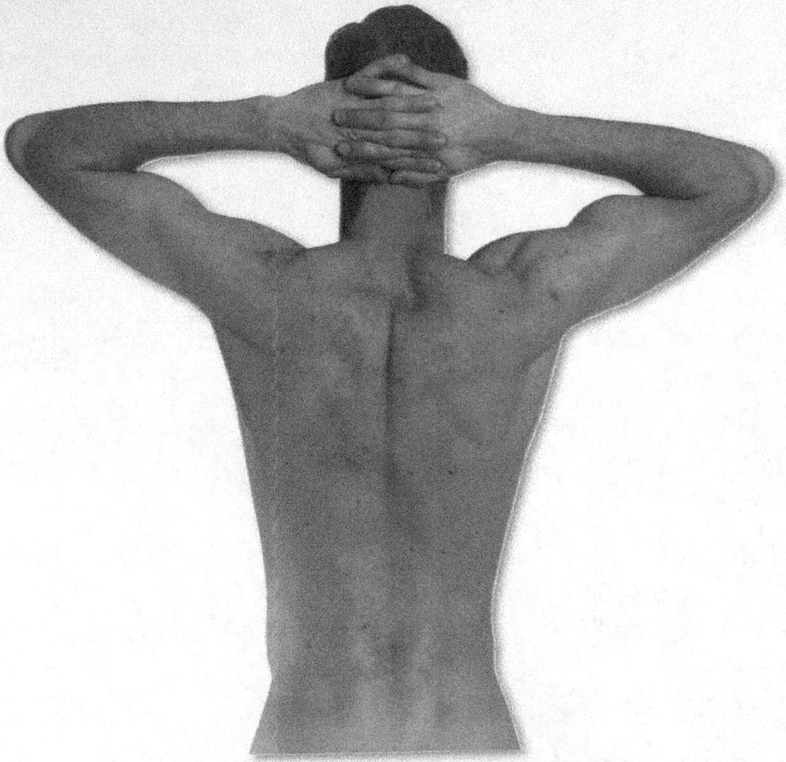

Anatomy & Physiology Revealed 4.0

MODULE 1: BODY ORIENTATION

Imagine this scenario: An unconscious patient has been brought to the emergency room. Although the patient cannot tell the ER physician what is wrong or "where it hurts," the doctor can assess some of the injuries by observing surface anatomy, including:

- Locating pulse points to determine the patient's heart rate and pulse strength
- Palpating the bones under the skin to determine if a fracture has occurred
- Passively moving the limbs to detect potential damage to muscles and tendons
- Examining skeletal and muscular landmarks to discover whether joints are dislocated

Examination of surface anatomy must often substitute for interviewing the patient, and when the health-care professional is a keen observer, it may be very accurate in assessing illness or injury.

13.1 A Regional Approach to Surface Anatomy

✓ Learning Objective

1. Explain the importance of surface anatomy in learning about internal structures and helping us diagnose and treat disease.

Surface anatomy is a branch of gross anatomy that examines shapes and markings on the surface of the body as they relate to deeper structures. An understanding of surface anatomy is essential for locating and identifying anatomic structures prior to studying internal gross anatomy. Health-care personnel use surface anatomy to help diagnose medical conditions and to treat patients, as when taking a pulse, inserting a needle or tube, or performing physical therapy. You have already begun your study of surface anatomy; each time we have asked you to palpate a part of your body and feel for a structure, you have examined your *own* surface anatomy.

Health-care professionals rely on four techniques when examining surface anatomy. Using **visual inspection,** they directly view the structure and markings of surface features. Through **palpation** (pal-pā'shŭn) (feeling with firm pressure or perceiving by the sense of touch), they precisely locate and identify anatomic features deep to the skin. Using **percussion** (per-kŭsh'ŭn), they tap firmly on specific body sites to detect resonating vibrations, and via **auscultation** (aws'kŭl-tā'shŭn), they listen to sounds emitted from organs.

In our discussion of surface anatomy in this chapter, the illustrations include some structures that we have discussed previously and other features yet to be discussed. We strongly suggest that you return to this chapter often as you explore and examine other body systems in subsequent chapters. In addition, before you begin, refer back to section 1.4 and review the discussion of body region names and abdominopelvic regions and quadrants. APR

Learning Strategy 13.1

When preparing for an anatomy exam, your best study aid is your own body. Palpating surface anatomy features on yourself will help you recall these features on an exam and, more importantly, give you a richer understanding of human anatomy.

WHAT DID YOU LEARN?

1. Define the following terms: *palpation*, *percussion*, and *ascultation*.

13.2 Head Region

✓ Learning Objective

2. Identify and describe the surface features of the cranial and facial regions.

The **head** is the most complex and highly integrated region of the body because it houses the brain, which communicates with and controls all of the body systems. The head is structurally and developmentally divided into the cranium and the face. **Figure 13.1** shows the regions and many of the surface anatomy structures of the head and neck.

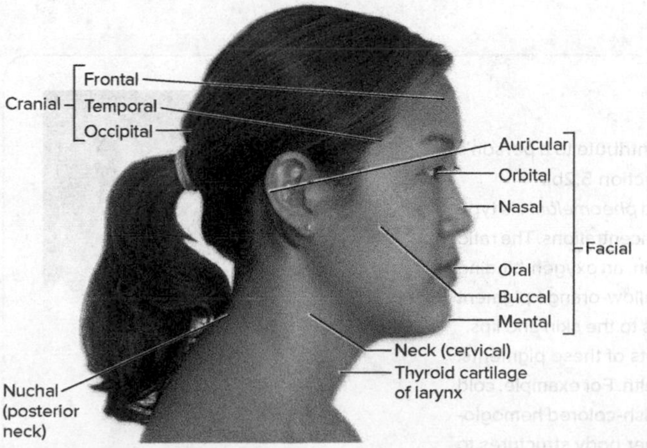

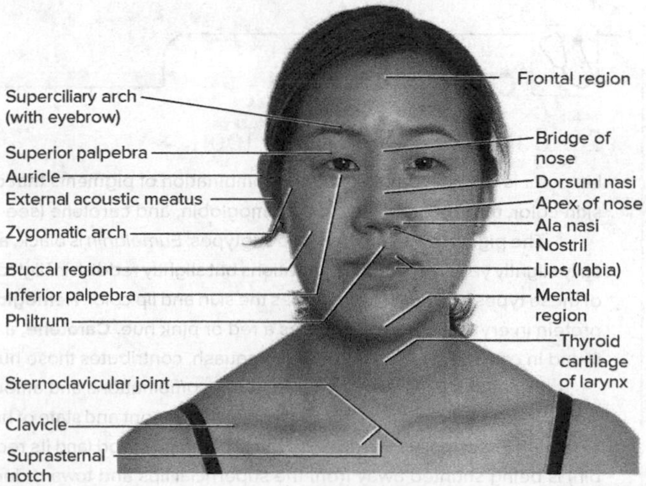

Figure 13.1

Head and Neck. The major regions of the head and neck are shown in (*a*) lateral view, and specific features are shown in (*b*) anterior view.

13.2a Cranium

The **cranium** (also called the **cranial region** or *braincase*) is covered by the scalp, which is composed of skin and subcutaneous tissue. The cranium can be subdivided into three regions, each having prominent surface anatomy features.

The **frontal region** of the cranium is the forehead. Covering this region is the **frontal belly** of the **occipitofrontalis** muscle. The frontal region terminates at the **superciliary arches.** You can feel these bony elevations immediately deep to your eyebrows.

Laterally, the scalp covers the sides of the skull in each **temporal region** and terminates just superior to the ear. The **temporalis** muscle is attached at the temporal region, and is easily palpable when the jaw is repeatedly clenched. Running over the temporalis muscle is the **superficial temporal artery.** You can feel the pulse of this artery just posterior to the orbits and anterior to the auricle of your ear.

The posterior part of the cranium is the **occipital** (ok-sip'i-t ăl) **region.** In the center of that region is the **external occipital protuberance,** a rounded or pointed projection (see figures 7.5 and 7.8). In section 7.2, you learned that larger, more robust individuals tend to have a more prominent, pointed external occipital protuberance than smaller, more gracile individuals. Palpate your own external occipital protuberance. Is it small and rounded, or somewhat larger and pointed? APR

WHAT DO YOU THINK?

1. Can you name some other facial muscles not already mentioned in this chapter that can be palpated easily under the skin?

13.2b Face

The **face** is divided into six regions: auricular, orbital, nasal, oral, buccal, and mental.

The **auricular** (aw-rik'y ū-lăr; *auris* = ear) **region** is composed of the visible surface structures of the ear as well as the ear's internal organs, which function in hearing and maintaining equilibrium (see section 19.6). The **auricle** (aw'ri-kl), or *pinna,* is the fleshy part of the external ear. Within the auricle is a tubular passage called the **external acoustic meatus.** The **mastoid process** is posterior and inferior to the auricle. Palpate your mastoid process; it should feel like a bony bump immediately posteroinferior to the ear.

The **orbital** (or *ocular*) **region** includes the **eyes** and associated structures (see section 19.5). Most orbital region surface features protect the eye. **Eyebrows** protect against sunlight and potential mechanical damage to the eyes; **eyelids (palpebrae;** pal'p ē-brē) close reflexively to protect against objects moving near the eye; and eyelashes prevent airborne particles from contacting the eyeball. The **superior palpebral fissure,** or upper eyelid crease, is palpated easily on most individuals, although many Asians do not have a superior palpebral fissure.

The **nasal region** contains the nose (see section 25.2a). The firm, narrow part of the nose that projects anteriorly between the eyes is the **bridge;** it is formed by the union of the nasal bones. Anteroinferior to the bridge is the fleshy part of the nose, called the **dorsum nasi** (nā'zē; *nasus* = nose). Farther anteroinferiorly is the tip of the nose, called the **apex.** The **nostrils,** or **external nares** (nā'ris; sing., *naris,* nā'ris), are the paired openings into the nose. The **ala nasi** (wing of the nose) forms the flared posterolateral margin of each nostril. APR

The **oral region** is inferior to the nasal region; it includes the buccal (cheek) region, the fleshy upper and lower **lips (labia),** and the structures of the **oral cavity** (mouth) that can be seen when the mouth is open (see section 26.2). Look in the mirror and observe the vertical depression between your nose and upper lip; this is called the **philtrum** (fil'tr ŭm; *philtron* = a love charm).

The **buccal** (bŭk'ăl) **region** refers to the cheek. Within this region is the buccinator muscle. Palpate the superolateral region of your cheek and locate your **zygomatic bone** and the **zygomatic arch.**

Finally, continuing in the inferior direction, look in the mirror and distinguish the **mental region,** which contains the **mentum,** or *chin.* Usually, the mentum ranges between pointed and almost triangular to a more "squared-off" shape (see section 7.2). APR

WHAT DID YOU LEARN?

2. Palpate your temporal region. Where is this region located and what features may be palpated in the region?

Clinical View 13.1

Lip Color as a Diagnostic Tool

Jack Hollingsworth/Blend Images LLC

Lip color is the collective result of a combination of pigments that contribute to a person's skin color, most notably melanin, hemoglobin, and carotene (see section 5.2b).

The pigment **melanin** has two subtypes: *Eumelanin* is black, and *pheomelanin* is typically slightly yellow in low concentrations but slightly reddish in high concentrations. The ratio of these types of melanin determines the skin and lip color. **Hemoglobin,** an oxygen-binding protein in erythrocytes, contributes a red or pink hue. **Carotene,** a yellow-orange pigment found in carrots, sweet potatoes, and squash, contributes those hues to the skin and lips.

Variations in lip color result from the combinations and amounts of these pigments. However, lip color is also affected by our environment and state of health. For example, cold weather causes our lips to appear "blue" because blood (and its reddish-colored hemoglobin) is being shunted away from the superficial lips and toward deeper body structures to conserve heat. Several health conditions also cause "blue lips." For instance, a patient who has anemia, pneumonia, emphysema, or certain disorders of the cardiovascular system could exhibit blueness or discoloration of the lips.

13.3 Neck Region

✓ Learning Objectives

3. Identify and describe the palpable structures in the neck.
4. List the three cervical regions of the neck, and describe the structures they contain.

The **neck,** also called the *cervical region* or *cervix* (ser′viks), is a complex region that connects the head to the trunk. The spinal cord, nerves, trachea, esophagus, and major vessels traverse this highly flexible area. In addition, the neck contains the larynx (voice box) and several important glands. For purposes of discussion, the neck can be subdivided into anterior, posterior, and lateral cervical regions.

The anterior region of the neck has several palpable landmarks, including the larynx, trachea, and sternal notch. The **larynx** (lar′ingks; voice box), found in the middle of the anterior neck, is composed of multiple cartilages (see section 25.3a). Its largest cartilage is the **thyroid cartilage,** which you can palpate as the big bulge on the anterior side of your neck. In post-pubescent males, the larynx has a noticeably pointed **laryngeal prominence** (commonly known as the *Adam's apple*) that may be visualized easily. Inferior to the larynx are the cricoid cartilage and **trachea** (air tube). The neck terminates at the **suprasternal notch** of the manubrium and the left and right clavicles. Palpate your anterior neck region: Moving inferiorly along the neck, you first feel the prominent thyroid cartilage, then the trachea with its hard, cartilaginous rings, and eventually the suprasternal notch and the clavicles.

The **posterior cervical region** *(nuchal region)* is the posterior aspect of the neck (see figure 13.1*a*). This region houses the spinal cord, cervical vertebrae, and the trapezius muscle. You can easily palpate the spinous process of the **vertebra prominens** (C_7), especially during neck flexion. Palpate your posterior cervical region; the bump you feel at the inferior boundary of this region is the vertebra prominens. As you move your fingers superiorly along the midline of the neck, you can palpate the **ligamentum nuchae,** a thick ligament that extends from C_7 to the nuchal lines of the skull.

The left and right sides of the neck contain the **sternocleidomastoid muscles.** Each sternocleidomastoid muscle partitions each side of the neck into two clinically important regions, an anterior cervical region and a lateral cervical region **(figure 13.2).** Each of these regions houses important structures that extend through the neck, and these triangles are further subdivided into smaller triangles.

Learning Strategy 13.2

To better distinguish the anterior and lateral cervical regions of the neck on your left side, flex your neck and turn your head to the right. That movement will make the left sternocleidomastoid muscle stand out (see section 11.1g) and better differentiate the regions.

The **anterior cervical region** *(anterior triangle)* is anterior to the sternocleidomastoid muscle and inferior to the mandible. This region is subdivided into four smaller triangles: the submental, submandibular, carotid, and muscular triangles.

The **submental triangle,** the most superiorly placed of the four triangles, is posteroinferior to the chin in the midline of the neck and partially bounded by the anterior belly of the digastric muscle. It contains some cervical lymph nodes and tiny veins. When you are ill, these lymph nodes (as well as some glands) may enlarge and become tender. A physician palpates these to determine if you have an infection that has been detected by immune cells within these nodes.

The **submandibular triangle** is inferior to the mandible and posterolateral to the submental triangle. It is bounded by the mandible and the bellies of the digastric muscle. If you palpate this triangle,

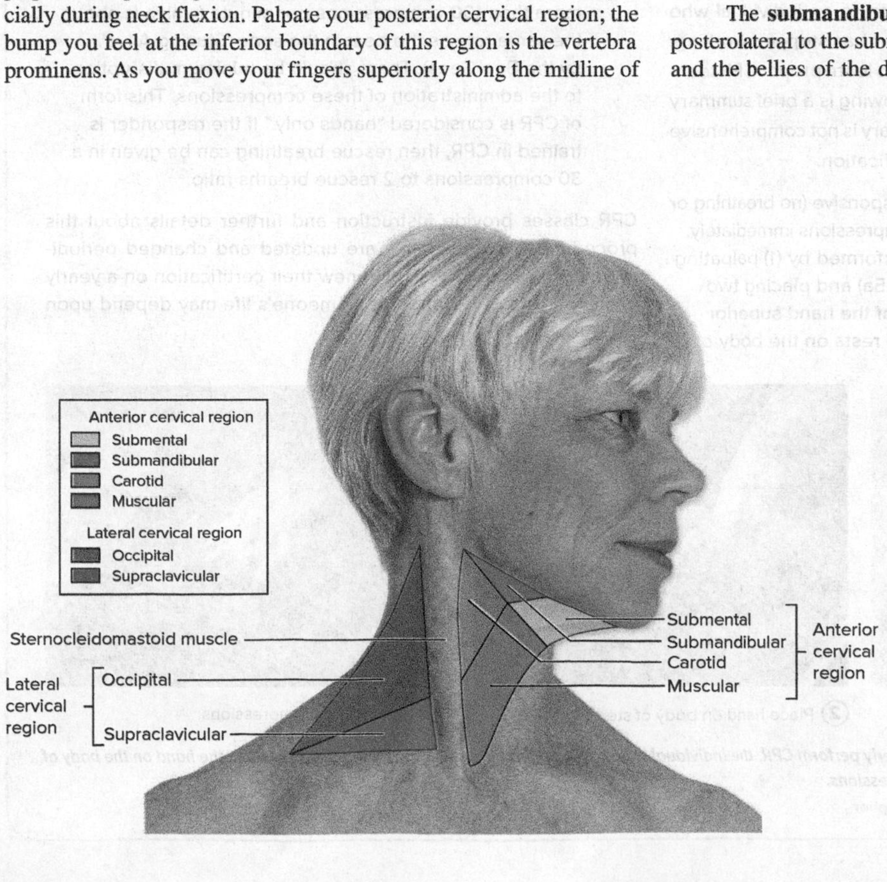

Figure 13.2
Anterior and Lateral Cervical Regions of the Neck. The sternocleidomastoid muscle is the landmark for separating the anterior and lateral cervical regions of the neck. These regions are further subdivided into smaller triangles, as shown.

©McGraw-Hill Education/Jw Ramsey, photographer

you can feel the **submandibular gland,** which is the bulge inferior to the mandible (see section 26.2c).

The **carotid** (ka-rot'id) **triangle** is bounded by the sternocleidomastoid, omohyoid, and posterior digastric muscles. Palpate this triangle until you feel the strong pulsation of an artery; that is the **common carotid artery** (see section 23.3c). This triangle also contains the internal jugular vein and some cervical lymph nodes, which may be easily palpated here as well.

The **muscular triangle** is the most inferior of the four triangles. It contains the **sternohyoid** and **sternothyroid muscles,** (see section 11.1f) as well as the lateral edges of the larynx and the **thyroid gland** (see section 20.4). Try to palpate the thyroid gland here. Also in this triangle are cervical lymph nodes. (Cervical lymph nodes are present throughout the neck, as we have indicated.)

The **lateral cervical region** *(posterior triangle)* is in the lateral region of the neck, posterior to the sternocleidomastoid muscle, superior to the clavicle inferiorly, and anterior to the trapezius muscle. This region is subdivided into two smaller triangles: the occipital and supraclavicular triangles.

The **occipital triangle** is the larger and more posteriorly placed of the two triangles. It is bounded by the omohyoid, trapezius, and sternocleidomastoid muscles. This important triangle contains the **external jugular vein** (which may be visible deep to the skin), the accessory nerve, the brachial plexus (a mass of nerves that innervates the upper limbs), and some lymph nodes.

The **supraclavicular** (sū'prā-kla-vik'yū-lăr) **triangle** also goes by the names *omoclavicular* and *subclavian.* It is bounded by the clavicle, omohyoid, and sternocleidomastoid muscles. It contains part of the subclavian vein and artery as well as some lymph nodes.

WHAT DID YOU LEARN?

3. What structures may be palpated along the anterior midline of the neck?
4. What muscle divides the neck into anterior and lateral cervical regions? What triangles are contained within these two cervical regions?

Clinical View 13.2

Surface Anatomy and CPR

All adults should learn the life-saving technique known as **cardiopulmonary resuscitation (CPR)**. CPR is a combination of chest compressions and rescue breathing given to an individual who is in *cardiac arrest,* meaning that the heart has stopped working. Classes are available for those who want to learn proper CPR techniques and obtain CPR certification. Following is a brief summary about CPR, but please note that this summary is not comprehensive and *not* a substitute for proper CPR certification:

- After dialing 9-1-1, if the adult is unresponsive (no breathing or no normal breathing) start chest compressions immediately.
- Chest compressions should be performed by (1) palpating the xiphoid process (see section 7.5a) and placing two fingers there; (2) placing the heel of the hand superior to the two fingers so that the hand rests on the body of the sternum; and (3) pressing down at least 2 inches on the body of the sternum, the place where the heart will receive maximum benefit.
- The compressions should be rapid and deep at a rate of more than 100 compressions per minute (which is about the same rate as the beat in the song 'Staying Alive', by the Bee Gees). There should be minimum disruption to the administration of these compressions. This form of CPR is considered "hands only." If the responder is trained in CPR, then rescue breathing can be given in a 30 compressions to 2 rescue breaths ratio.

CPR classes provide instruction and further details about this procedure. CPR guidelines are updated and changed periodically, so individuals need to renew their certification on a yearly basis. Become CPR certified: Someone's life may depend upon what you know!

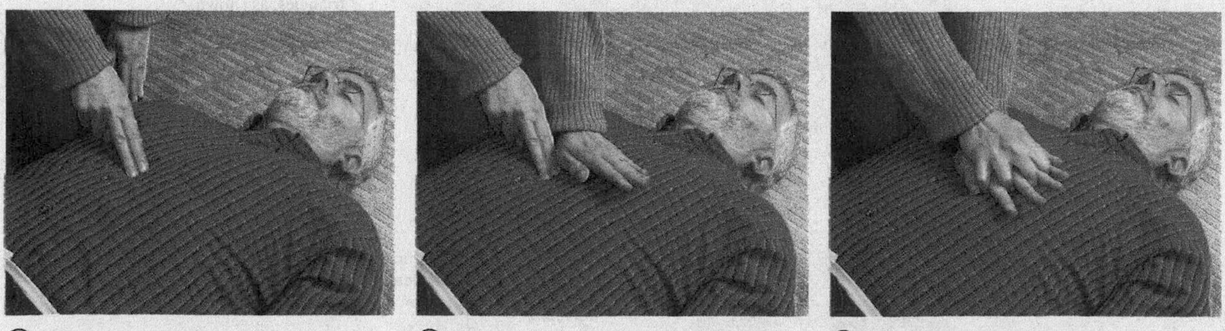

(1) Palpate xiphoid process. (2) Place hand on body of sternum. (3) Start chest compressions.

***Chest compression steps in CPR:** In order to properly perform CPR, the individual should first palpate the patient's xiphoid process, place the hand on the body of the patient's sternum, and then start chest compressions.*

13.4 Trunk Region

✓ Learning Objective

5. Identify and describe the surface features of the thorax, abdominopelvic region , and back.

The **trunk,** or *torso,* is partitioned into the **thorax** (chest), the **abdominopelvic region,** and the **back.** The surface anatomy of the trunk is particularly important in determining the location and condition of the viscera. However, some of the surface features may be obscured due to the age, sex, or body weight of an individual.

13.4a Thorax

The thorax is the superior portion of the trunk sandwiched between the neck superiorly and the abdomen inferiorly. It consists of the chest and the "upper back." On the anterior surface of the chest are the two dominating surface features of the thorax—the clavicles and the sternum—as well as several other important surface anatomy landmarks (**figure 13.3**).

The paired **clavicles** and the **suprasternal notch** represent the border between the thorax and the neck. Feel the clavicles on the superior anterior surface where they extend between the base of the neck on the right and left sides laterally to the shoulders. The left and right **costal margins** of the rib cage form the inferior boundary of the thorax. The **infrasternal angle** (*subcostal angle*) is where the costal margins join to form an inverted V at the xiphoid process. On a thin person, many of the **ribs** can be seen (see section 7.5b). Most of the ribs (with the exception of the first ribs) can be palpated.

The **sternum** is palpated readily as the midline bony structure in the thorax (see section 7.5a). Its three components (the **manubrium,** the **body,** and the **xiphoid process**) may also be palpated. The **sternal angle** can be felt as an elevation between the manubrium and the body. The sternal angle is clinically important because it is at the level of the costal cartilage of the second rib, where it is often used as a landmark for counting the ribs.

Each **breast** is located lateral to the sternum. The breast has a projection, the **nipple,** surrounded by a circular, colored region called the **areola** (see section 28.2f).

13.4b Abdominopelvic Region

The abdominopelvic region is the portion of the trunk that lies inferior to the rib cage. Surface anatomy features in this region may be difficult to palpate in some obese people. Some of the features in this region are shown in figure 13.3, and the abdominopelvic regions and quadrants are shown in figure 1.11 and discussed in section 1.4f.

On the anterior surface of the abdomen, the **umbilicus** (*navel*) is the prominent depression (if you have an "innie") or projection (if you have an "outie") in the midline of the abdominal wall. Also in the midline of the abdominal anterior surface is the **linea alba,** a tendinous structure that extends inferiorly from the xiphoid process to the pubic symphysis. If you view the anteroinferior surface of the abdomen, you can readily palpate the **pubic bones** in the pubic region, underneath the pubic hair (see section 8.3a).

Additionally, the abdominopelvic region houses several other readily seen structures. The left and right **rectus abdominis** muscles and their **tendinous intersections** are observable in individuals with well-developed abdominal musculature and low body fat (see section 11.4). These muscles and intersections are referred to as "six-pack abs." The superior aspect of the ilium (iliac crest) terminates anteriorly at the **anterior superior iliac spine.** Attached to the anterior superior iliac spine is the **inguinal ligament,** which forms the inferior boundary of the abdominal wall. The inguinal ligament terminates on a small

Clinical View 13.3

Testing for Inguinal Hernias

An **inguinal hernia** is a protrusion of intestine through a weak spot in the anterior abdominal wall, typically the superficial inguinal ring, located superolateral to the pubic tubercle. (Inguinal hernias are discussed in detail in the Clinical View 11.5: "Hernias" in section 11.4.)

First, the physician must find the superficial inguinal ring by locating both the inguinal ligament (found inferior to the ring) and the pubic tubercle (just inferior and medial to the ring). Once the ring is located, the physician inserts a finger in the depression formed by the superficial inguinal ring and into the inguinal canal, and asks the patient to turn their head and "cough." (Having the subject turn their head simply ensures that the patient doesn't cough in the physician's face.) The act of coughing increases intra-abdominal pressure, and would encourage a portion of intestine to poke through the ring if there was a problem. While the patient coughs, the physician palpates the superficial inguinal ring to make sure no intestine is protruding through it.

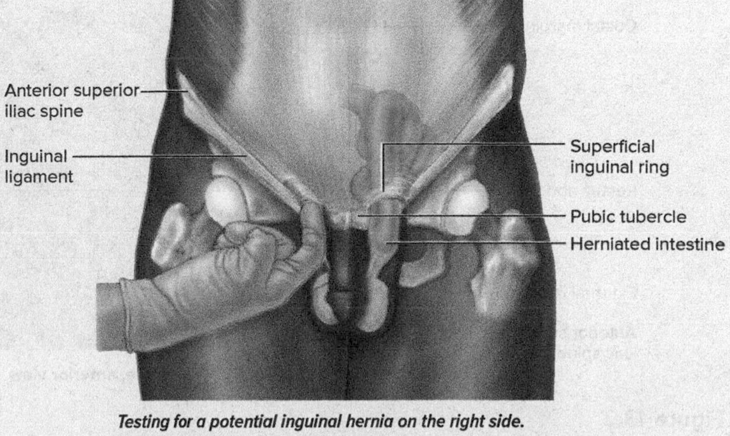

Testing for a potential inguinal hernia on the right side. Note the herniated intestine protruding through the left superficial inguinal ring.

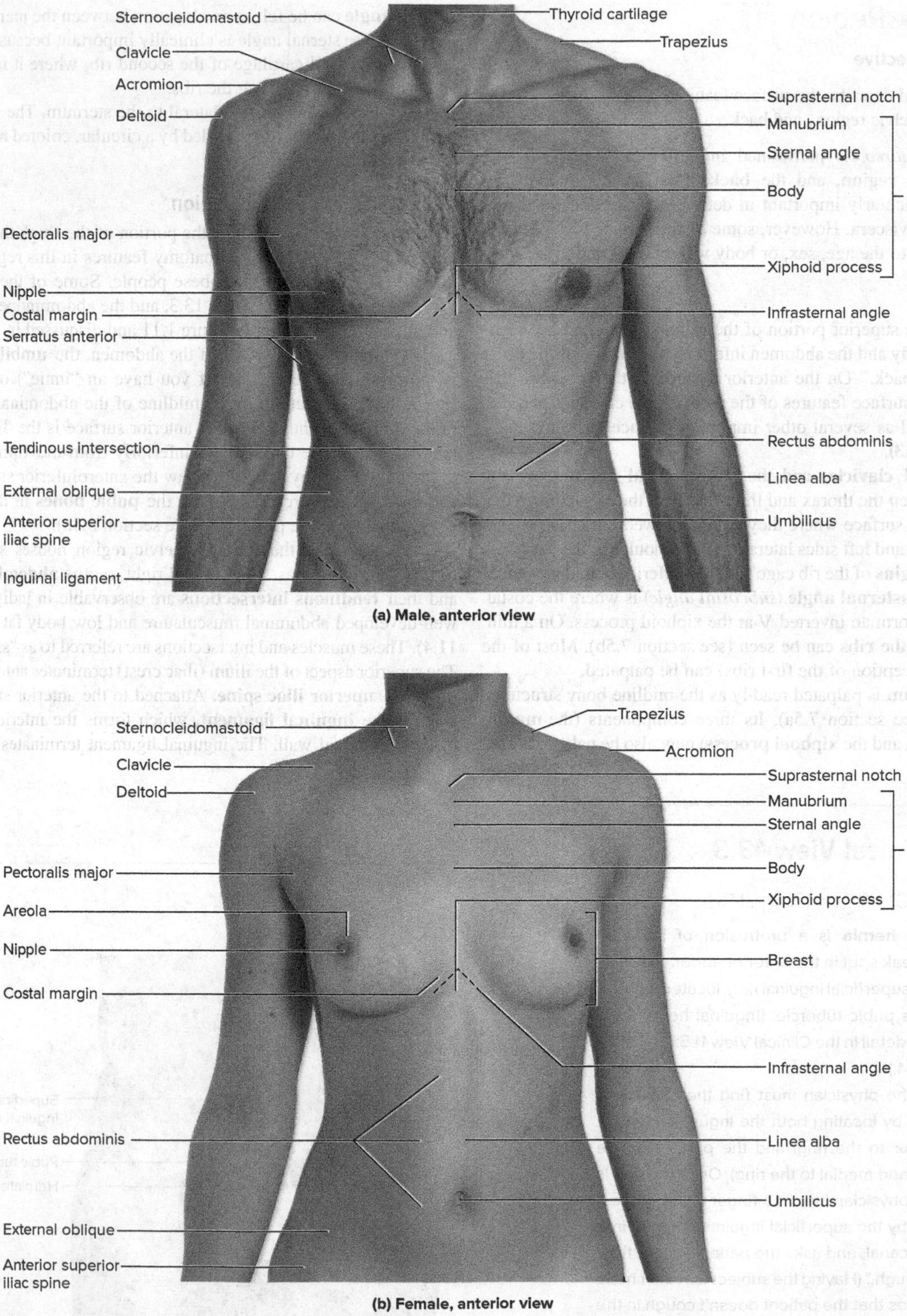
Sternocleidomastoid
Clavicle
Acromion
Deltoid
Thyroid cartilage
Trapezius
Suprasternal notch
Manubrium
Sternal angle
Body
Sternum
Xiphoid process
Pectoralis major
Nipple
Costal margin
Serratus anterior
Infrasternal angle
Tendinous intersection
Rectus abdominis
Linea alba
External oblique
Umbilicus
Anterior superior iliac spine
Inguinal ligament
(a) Male, anterior view
Trapezius
Sternocleidomastoid
Acromion
Clavicle
Deltoid
Suprasternal notch
Manubrium
Sternal angle
Sternum
Pectoralis major
Body
Xiphoid process
Areola
Nipple
Breast
Costal margin
Infrasternal angle
Rectus abdominis
Linea alba
Umbilicus
External oblique
Anterior superior iliac spine
(b) Female, anterior view

Figure 13.3

Anterior Trunk Regions. Anterior views show selected surface anatomy landmarks in (*a*) a male and (*b*) a female.

anterior, rounded projection on the pubis called the **pubic tubercle.** Superior to the medial portion of the inguinal ligament is the **superficial inguinal ring.** This "ring" is actually a superficial opening in the inferior anterior abdominal wall via the **inguinal canal,** and represents a weak spot in the wall. A physician can palpate the skin overlying the ring and the inguinal canal to detect an inguinal hernia.

13.4c Back

The surface anatomy features of the back appear in **figure 13.4**. At the superior midline surface of the back near the interface between the neck and back, the vertebra prominens is readily palpated, as discussed in section 7.4c. Moving inferiorly from the vertebra prominens in the midline, some vertebral spinous processes can be detected. The entire series of vertebral spines is visible when the vertebral column is flexed. When the back is extended, some of the inferior vertebral spines are obscured; instead, a vertically oriented indentation called the **median furrow** is all that can be seen along the inferior midline of the back.

Several prominent features of the posterior scapula are seen and easily palpated in some individuals, including the **lateral** and **medial borders** (see section 8.1b). The**spine of the scapula** is covered by the trapezius muscle, but it still may be palpated, especially when the back is flexed. The **triangle of auscultation** is a region bordered by three muscles: the rhomboid major, trapezius, and latissimus dorsi. When an individual flexes their vertebral column (so they are hunched over), this triangle becomes larger, and the sixth intercos - tal space becomes subcutaneous (lies directly internal to the skin). Thus, at this site a physician can hear respiratory sounds more readily through a stethoscope, without their being muffled by the muscles.

The **iliac crests** mark the superior surface of the ossa coxae (see section 8.3a). They originate along the abdominal wall and

Clinical View 13.4

Surface Anatomy and Lumbar Puncture

A **lumbar puncture,** sometimes called a *spinal tap,* is a procedure in which a needle is inserted into the vertebral canal for the purpose of giving an anesthetic or testing the fluid around the spinal cord for evidence of infection or hemorrhage. This procedure requires careful and precise use of surface anatomy features.

Because the adult spinal cord typically ends at the level of the L_1 vertebra (see section 16.1), a lumbar puncture must be performed inferior to this level to ensure that the spinal cord is not pierced by the needle. The typical location is between the L_3 and L_4 vertebrae. To locate this region, the physician must first palpate the iliac crests, the superiormost points of which are level with the spinous process of the L_4 vertebra. Once the physician has properly palpated the iliac crests, she can draw an imaginary horizontal line to the level of the L_4 vertebra to identify the correct spinous process (see figure 13.4). She can then insert the lumbar puncture needle either directly above or directly below the spinous process when the vertebral column is flexed. For further information about lumbar punctures, see Clinical View 16.1: "Lumbar Puncture and Epidural Injection" in section 16.2.

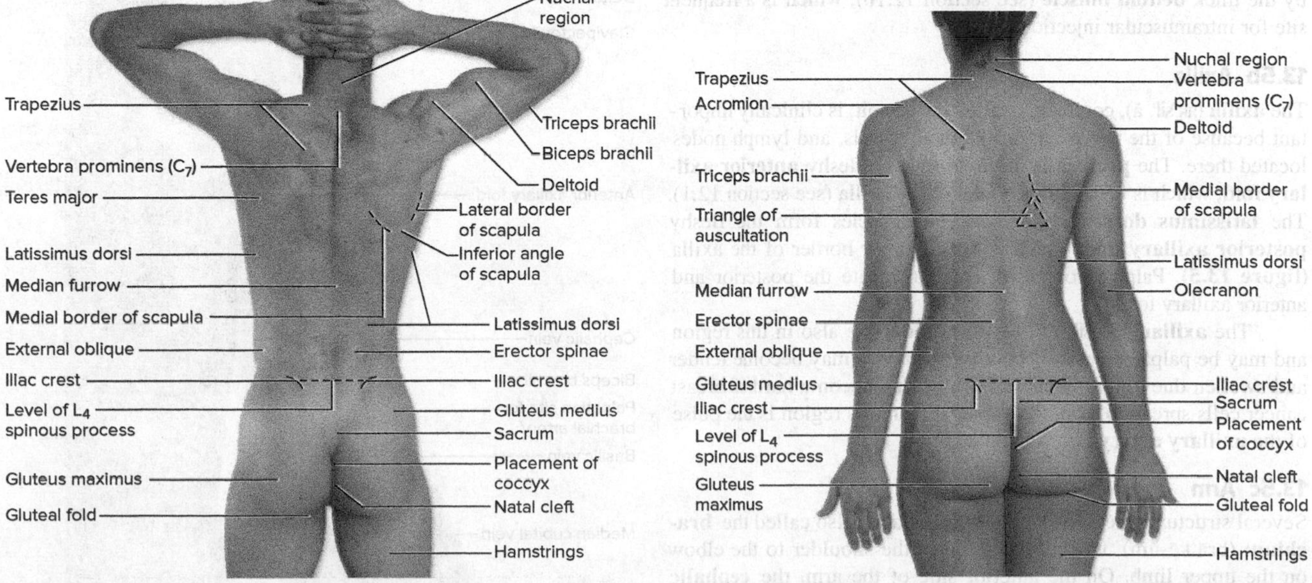

(a) Male, posterior view

(b) Female, posterior view

Figure 13.4

Posterior Trunk Regions. Posterior views show selected surface anatomy landmarks in (*a*) a male and (*b*) a female.

continue along the inferior border of the back. When the superior-most points of the iliac crests are palpated, drawing a horizontal line through them bisects the spinous process of the L_4 vertebra. (The iliac crests may be difficult to palpate in obese people.)

WHAT DID YOU LEARN?

5. What is the sternal angle, and what is its clinical significance?
6. The most superior levels of the iliac crests are at the same level as what bony structure? Why is this clinically important?
7. List the muscles that border the triangle of auscultation. What is the clinical significance of this triangle?

13.5 Shoulder and Upper Limb Region

✓ Learning Objectives

6. List and palpate on yourself the surface features of the shoulder and upper limb.
7. Identify and describe the locations where one can take an arterial pulse in the upper limb.

The anatomy of the shoulder and upper limb region is clinically important because of frequent trauma to these body regions. Additionally, vessels of the upper limb are often used as pressure sites and as sites for drawing blood, providing nutrients and fluids, and administering medicine.

13.5a Shoulder

The scapula, clavicle, and proximal part of the humerus collectively form the shoulder, and portions of each of these bones are important surface landmarks in this region (see figures 13.3 and 13.4). Anteriorly, the **clavicle** and **acromion** of the scapula may be palpated (see section 8.1). The acromion helps form the rounded, superior projection on your shoulder. The rounded curve of the shoulder is formed by the thick **deltoid muscle** (see section 12.1b), which is a frequent site for intramuscular injections.

13.5b Axilla

The **axilla** (ak'sil' ă), commonly called the armpit, is clinically important because of the nerves, axillary blood vessels, and lymph nodes located there. The **pectoralis major** forms the fleshy **anterior axillary fold,** which is the anterior border of the axilla (see section 12.1). The **latissimus dorsi** and **teres major** muscles form the fleshy **posterior axillary fold,** which is the posterior border of the axilla (**figure 13.5**). Palpate your own axilla to locate the posterior and anterior axillary folds.

The **axillary** (ak'sil- ār'ē) **lymph nodes** are also in this region and may be palpated easily. These lymph nodes may become tender and swollen due to an infection, or they may become hard if breast cancer cells spread to them. Also palpable in this region is the pulse of the **axillary artery** (see section 23.3h).

13.5c Arm

Several structures are clearly visible in the arm, also called the **brachium** (brā'kē-ŭm), which extends from the shoulder to the elbow on the upper limb. On the anterior side of the arm, the **cephalic vein** is evident in muscular individuals as it traverses along the anterolateral border of the entire upper limb. This vein terminates in a small surface depression, bordered by the deltoid and pectoralis major muscles, called the **clavipectoral triangle** (or *deltopectoral triangle*) (**figure 13.6**). The **basilic vein** is sometimes evident along

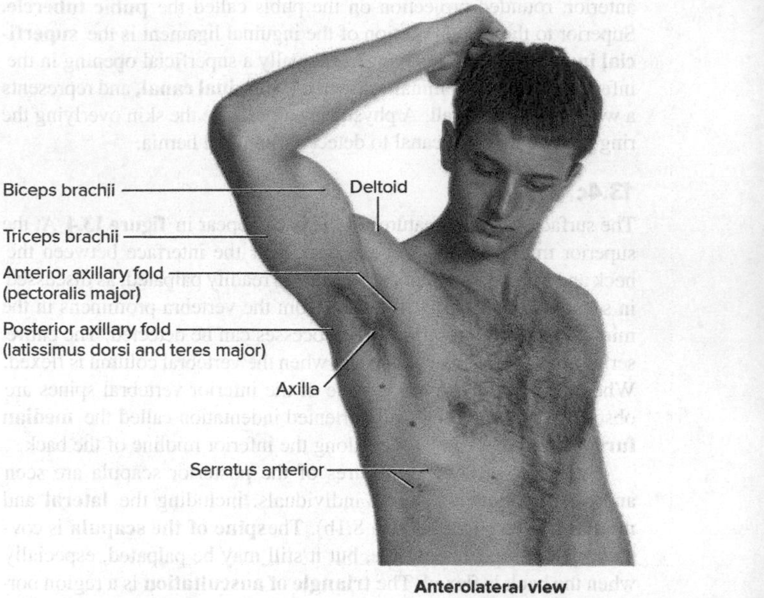
Biceps brachii
Deltoid
Triceps brachii
Anterior axillary fold
(pectoralis major)
Posterior axillary fold
(latissimus dorsi and teres major)
Axilla
Serratus anterior
Anterolateral view

Figure 13.5
Axilla and Trunk. An anterolateral view of the axilla and trunk.

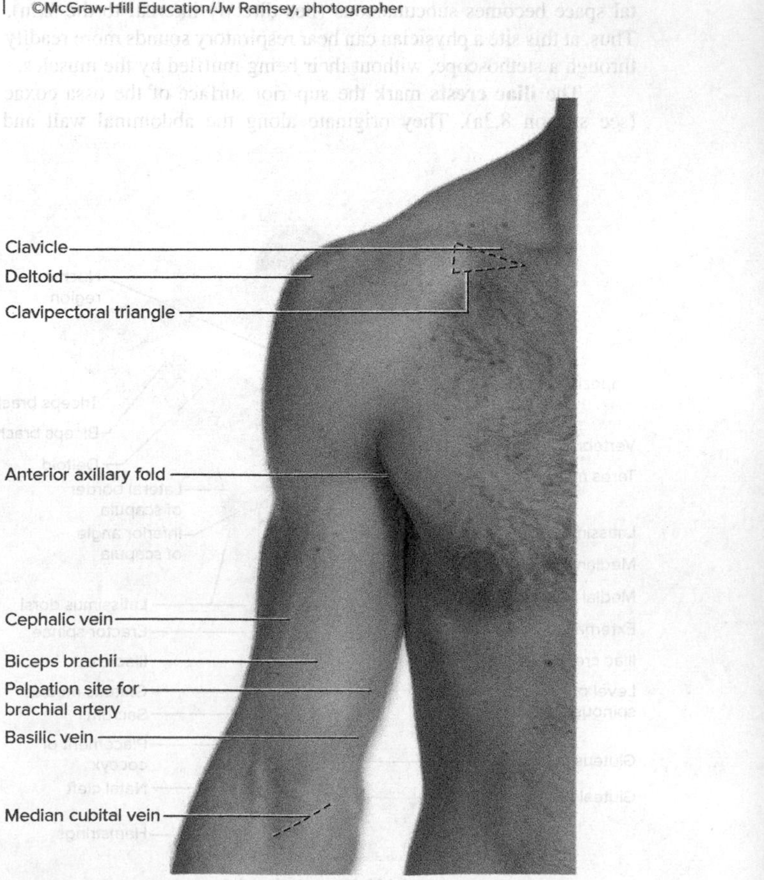
Clavicle
Deltoid
Clavipectoral triangle
Anterior axillary fold
Cephalic vein
Biceps brachii
Palpation site for
brachial artery
Basilic vein
Median cubital vein
Right brachium, anterior view

Figure 13.6
Arm. Anterior view shows the right shoulder and arm region.

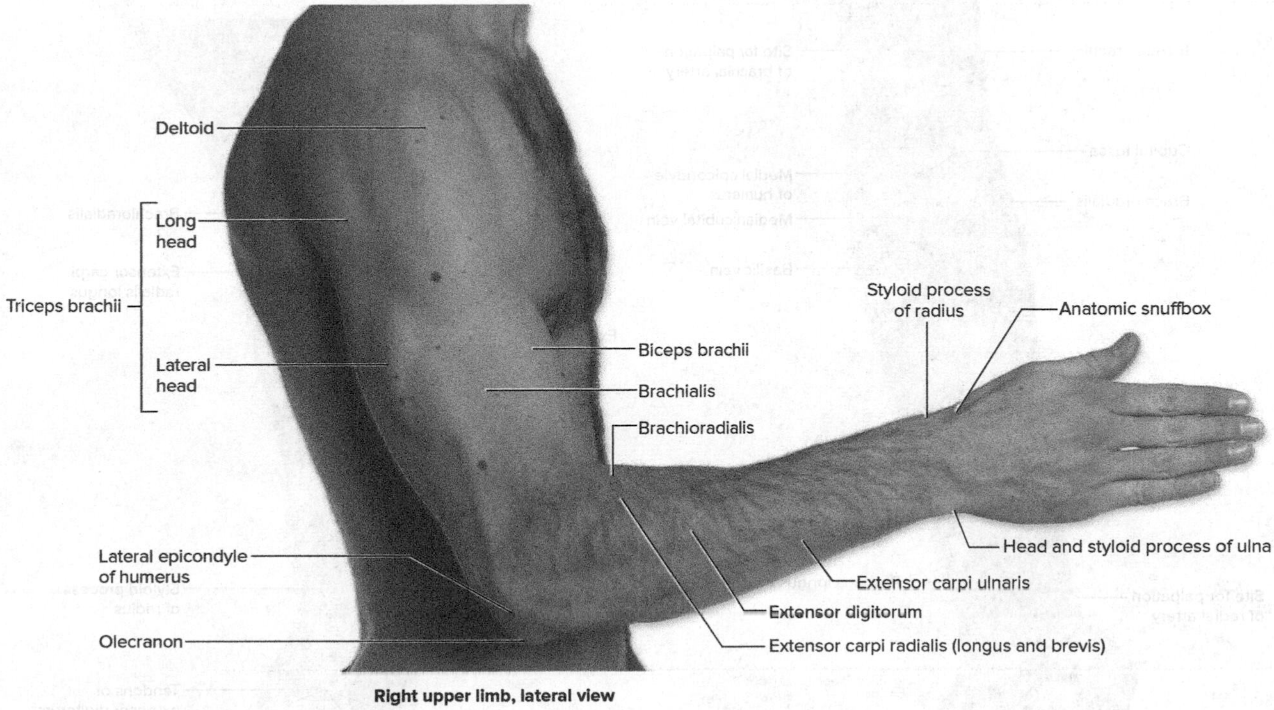

Figure 13.7

Upper Limb. Lateral view shows the right upper limb.

the medial side of the upper limb. The **brachial artery** becomes subcutaneous along the medial side of the brachium, and its pulse may be detected there. This region is clinically important in measuring blood pressure.

The **biceps brachii** muscle (see section 12.1c) becomes prominent when the elbow is flexed (**figure 13.7**). Located on the anterior surface of the elbow region, the **cubital fossa** is a depression within which the **median cubital vein** (see section 23.3h) connects the basilic and cephalic veins (see figure 13.6). The cubital fossa is a common site for **venipuncture** (removal of blood from a vein).

The bulk of the posterior surface of the brachium is formed by the **triceps brachii** muscle (see section 12.1c). Three bony prominences are readily identified in the distal region of the brachium near the elbow (**figure 13.8**; see also figure 13.7). The **lateral epicondyle** of the **humerus** is a rounded lateral projection at the distal end of the humerus (see section 8.2). The **olecranon** (ō-lek′r ă-non) of the ulna is palpated easily along the posterior aspect of the elbow. The **medial epicondyle** of the humerus is more prominent and may be easily palpated. The **ulnar nerve** traverses posterior and inferior to the medial epicondyle (see section 16.4e). When we hit our "funny bone," we actually are hitting or pinching the ulnar nerve as it travels posterior to the medial epicondyle.

13.5d Forearm

The radius, the ulna, and the muscles that control hand movements form the forearm, or **antebrachium** (an′t ē-brā′kē-ŭm) (figure 13.8). Palpate your own forearm. The proximal part of the forearm is bulkier, due to the fleshy bellies of the forearm muscles. The **head** of the **radius** may be palpated just distal to the lateral epicondyle of the humerus, especially when you pronate and supinate your forearm (see section 8.2b). As you palpate distally, the forearm becomes thinner because you are palpating the tendons of these muscles. The **styloid process** of the radius is readily palpable as the lateral bump along the wrist, whereas the **head** and **styloid process** of the **ulna** collectively form the medial prominence of the wrist.

The pulse of the **radial artery** (see section 23.3h) may be detected between the distal tendons of the flexor carpi radialis and the brachioradialis muscles (**figure 13.9**). The pulse of the **ulnar artery** is a bit more difficult to find. You can locate it by feeling for the medial bump in your hand that is the **pisiform bone** and then placing your fingers immediately lateral to the pisiform bone (see section 8.2c).

The tendons of the **extensor pollicis brevis, abductor pollicis longus,** and **extensor pollicis longus** muscles mark the boundary of the triangular **anatomic snuffbox.** You can palpate the pulse of the radial artery here as well. In addition, you can palpate the **scaphoid bone** in this region.

13.5e Hand

The most obvious surface anatomy features of the hand involve flexion creases, fingerprints, and fingernails (figure 13.9). Flexion creases are seen on the anterior surface of the hand for the **metacarpophalangeal (MP), proximal interphalangeal (PIP),** and **distal interphalangeal (DIP) joints.** Palpate the **thenar** (thē′nar) **eminence** (em′i-nens), the thickened, muscular region of the hand that forms the base of the thumb (see section 12.1e). The **hypothenar eminence** is the medial region of the palm immediately proximal to the little finger.

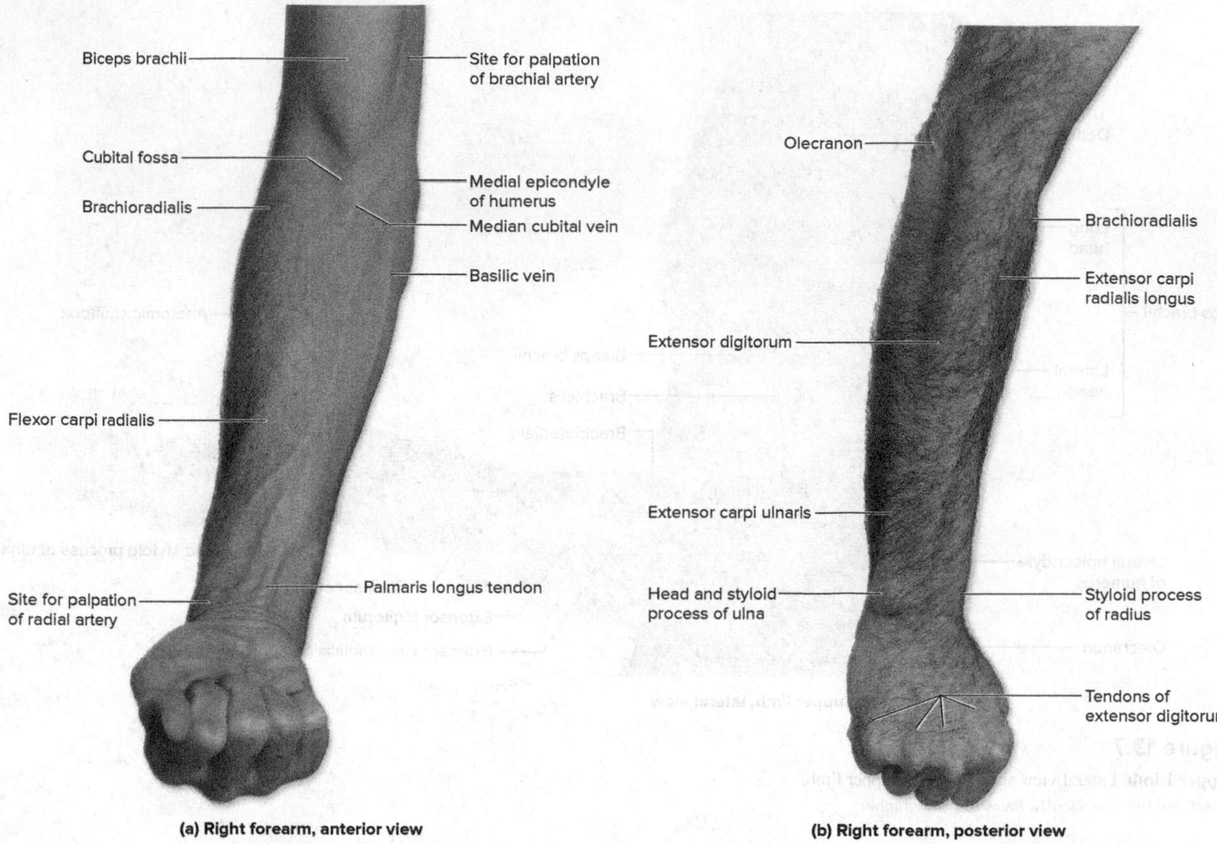
Biceps brachii
Site for palpation of brachial artery
Cubital fossa
Medial epicondyle of humerus
Brachioradialis
Median cubital vein
Basilic vein
Flexor carpi radialis
Palmaris longus tendon
Site for palpation of radial artery
(a) Right forearm, anterior view
Olecranon
Brachioradialis
Extensor carpi radialis longus
Extensor digitorum
Extensor carpi ulnaris
Head and styloid process of ulna
Styloid process of radius
Tendons of extensor digitorum
(b) Right forearm, posterior view

Figure 13.8

Forearm and Hand. (*a*) Anterior and (*b*) posterior views show the right forearm.

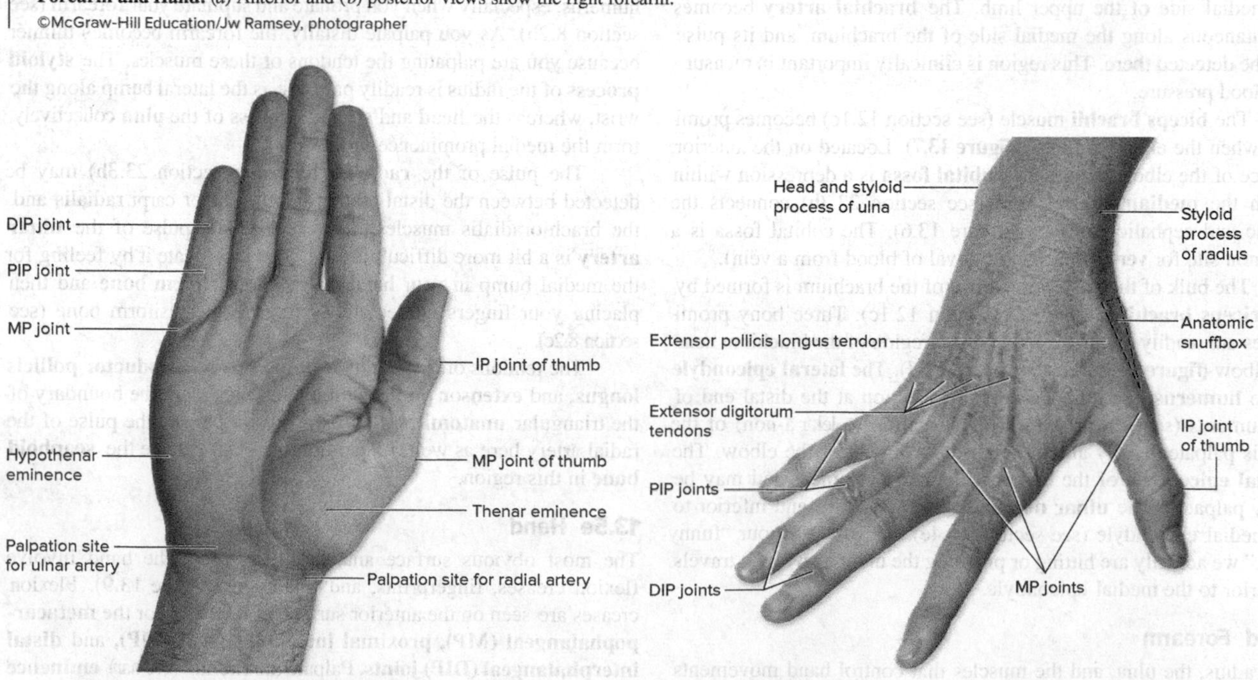
DIP joint
PIP joint
MP joint
IP joint of thumb
Hypothenar eminence
MP joint of thumb
Thenar eminence
Palpation site for ulnar artery
Palpation site for radial artery
(a) Right hand, palmar view
Head and styloid process of ulna
Styloid process of radius
Extensor pollicis longus tendon
Anatomic snuffbox
Extensor digitorum tendons
IP joint of thumb
PIP joints
DIP joints
MP joints
(b) Right hand, dorsal view

Figure 13.9

Wrist and Hand. (*a*) Palmar and (*b*) dorsal views of the right hand illustrate many surface anatomy features.

The tendons that extend to each of the fingers from the **extensor digitorum** muscle are readily seen on the posterior side of the hand when the digital joints are extended. Also on the posterior side of the hand, the MP joints ("knuckles") are formed by the distal ends of metacarpal bones II–V. Palpate each **phalanx** (fā′langks) and all the interphalangeal joints.

WHAT DID YOU LEARN?

8. What muscles form the anterior and posterior axillary folds?
9. Locate and palpate the cubital fossa. What structures are found in this depression?
10. Where is the pulse of the brachial artery taken? Palpate the pulse on yourself to confirm its location.

13.6 Lower Limb Region

✓ Learning Objectives

8. List and palpate on yourself the surface features of the gluteal region and lower limb.
9. Identify and describe the locations where one can take an arterial pulse in the lower limb.

The massive bones and strong muscles of the lower limbs are weight bearing and important with respect to locomotion, our ability to move from place to place.

13.6a Gluteal Region

The buttock could have been included in our discussion of the posterior region of the pelvis, but instead we discuss it here as the **gluteal** (glū′tē-ăl; *gloutos* = buttock) **region** (see section 12.2a). Several surface anatomy features are in this region (see figure 13.4).

The inferior border of the **gluteus maximus** muscle forms the **gluteal fold.** The **natal cleft** is a vertical depression that separates the buttocks into two prominences. In the inferior portion of each buttock, an **ischial** (is′kē-ăl) **tuberosity** can be palpated; these tuberosities support body weight when we are seated. The gluteus maximus muscle and some fat form most of the inferolateral "fleshy" part of the buttock. The **gluteus medius** muscle may be palpated only in the superolateral portion of each buttock. The **sciatic nerve** (see section 16.4g) isn't easily palpable, but knowledge of its location in the buttock region is essential for health-care providers who must give gluteal intramuscular injections. The sciatic nerve originates in the inferior medial quadrant of the buttock and travels inferiorly to the lower limb.

WHAT DO YOU THINK?

2. What muscle functions would be impaired if you accidentally pierced or injured the sciatic nerve?

13.6b Thigh

The thigh extends between the hip and the knee on each lower limb (**figure 13.10**). An extremely important element of thigh surface anatomy is a region called the **femoral triangle.** The femoral triangle is a region located inferior to the inguinal ligament and on the anteromedial surface in the superior portion of the thigh. It is bounded superiorly by the inguinal ligament, laterally by the sartorius muscle, and medially by the adductor longus muscle. The **femoral artery** travels through this triangle, making it an important arterial pressure

Clinical View 13.5

Gluteal Intramuscular Injections

An **intramuscular injection** delivers a medication into muscle, so it may be rapidly absorbed and transported through the bloodstream. The gluteal region is a preferred site for intramuscular (IM) injections because the gluteal muscles are quite thick and contain many blood vessels. However, health-care personnel must be careful not to accidentally inject the sciatic nerve or the superior and inferior gluteal vessels and nerves that supply the gluteal muscles. The sciatic nerve and the gluteal nerves and vessels are located primarily in the medial and inferior lateral part of the buttock. Therefore, the iliac crest is an important surface landmark for determining the safest place for a gluteal IM injection. Usually the injection is administered in the **superior lateral quadrant** of the buttock, about 5 to 7 centimeters inferior to the iliac crest. By placing the injection in the superior lateral quadrant, the health-care worker can be reasonably certain of not accidentally piercing an important nerve or blood vessel.

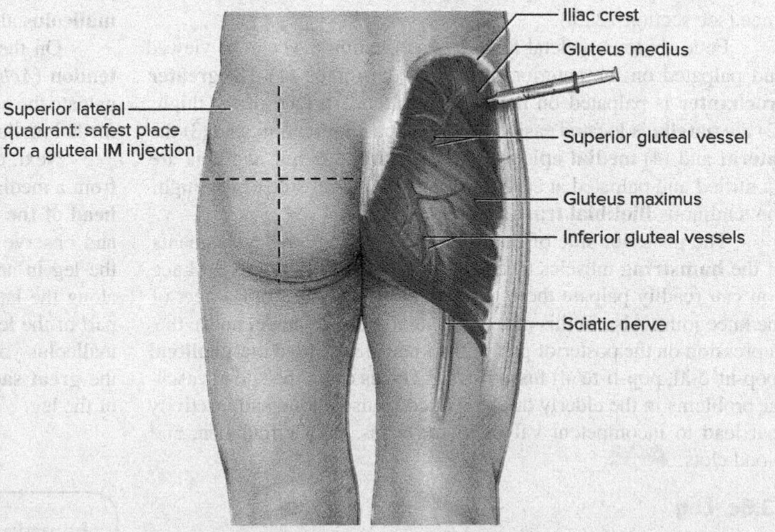

Proper placement of a gluteal intramuscular injection.

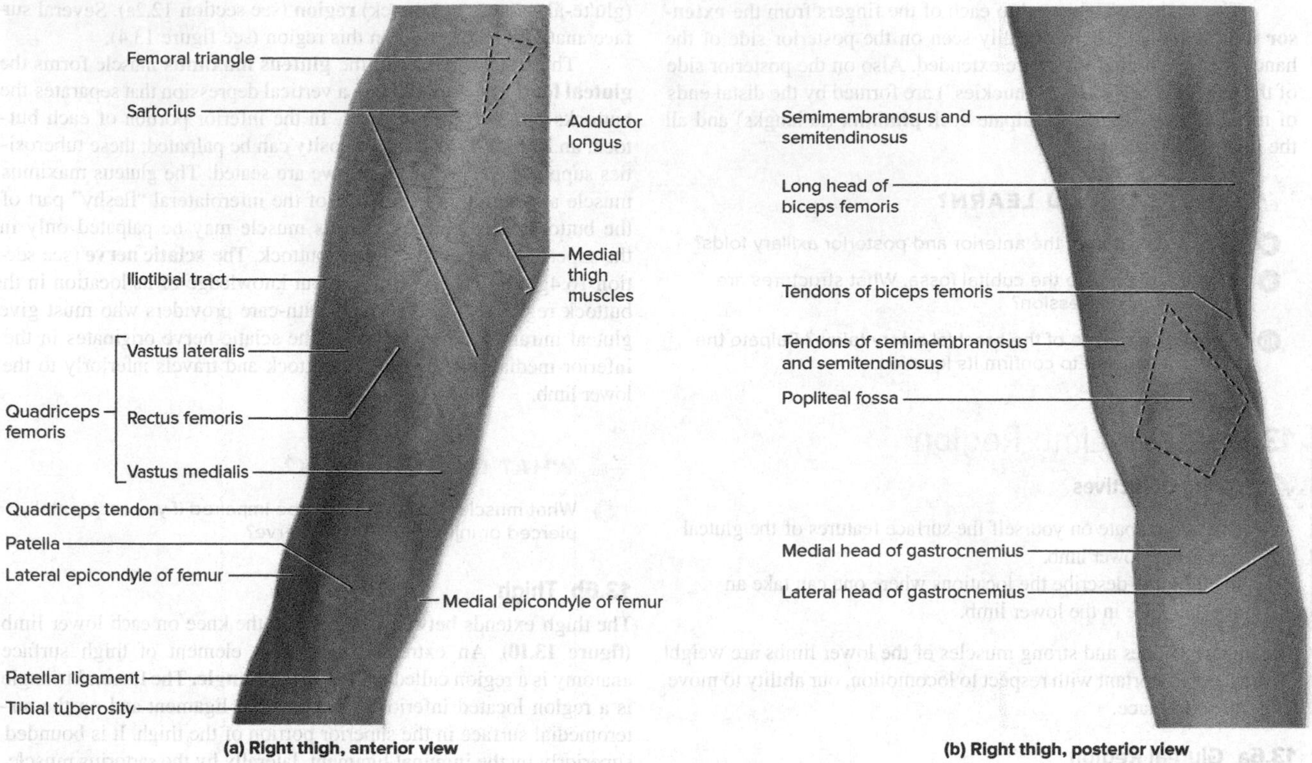

Femoral triangle
Sartorius
Adductor longus
Iliotibial tract
Medial thigh muscles
Quadriceps femoris
Vastus lateralis
Rectus femoris
Vastus medialis
Quadriceps tendon
Patella
Lateral epicondyle of femur
Medial epicondyle of femur
Patellar ligament
Tibial tuberosity
(a) Right thigh, anterior view
Semimembranosus and semitendinosus
Long head of biceps femoris
Tendons of biceps femoris
Tendons of semimembranosus and semitendinosus
Popliteal fossa
Medial head of gastrocnemius
Lateral head of gastrocnemius
(b) Right thigh, posterior view

Figure 13.10

Thigh and Knee. *(a)* An anterior view of the right thigh reveals the quadriceps femoris and patella, whereas *(b)* a posterior view illustrates the hamstrings.

point for controlling lower limb hemorrhage (bleeding). Now focus your attention on the distal part of your anterior thigh, and try to palpate three parts of the **quadriceps femoris** as they approach the knee (see section 12.2b).

Four obvious skeletal features (see section 8.4) can be viewed and palpated on the anterior surface of the thigh: (1) The **greater trochanter** is palpated on the superior lateral surface of the thigh; (2) the **patella** is located easily within the patellar tendon; and (3) the **lateral** and (4) **medial epicondyles** of both the femur and tibia are identified and palpated at each knee. On the lateral side of the thigh, the tendinous **iliotibial tract** may be palpated.

The posterior side of the thigh has the tendinous attachments of the **hamstring** muscles (see section 12.2a). By flexing your knee, you can readily palpate these tendons along the posterior aspect of the knee joint. Also in this part of the thigh near the knee, notice the depression on the posterior part of the knee joint, called the **popliteal** (pop-lit′ē-ăl, pop-li-tē′ăl) **fossa** (fos′ă). This is often the site of vascular problems in the elderly due to reduced muscle tone and inactivity that lead to incompetent valves in the veins, poor circulation, and blood clots. **APR**

13.6c Leg

Several skeletal features (see section 8.4c) are distinguishable as part of the surface anatomy of the leg, which extends from the knee to the foot (**figure 13.11**). From an anterior perspective, palpate the **tibial tuberosity** immediately inferior to the knee joint. Then, moving inferiorly, feel the **anterior border** of the tibia (called the "shin"), which is subcutaneous and palpable along its length. At the distal end of the leg, detect and palpate the **medial malleolus** and **lateral malleolus** along the sides of the ankle.

On the posterior side of the leg, palpate the strong **calcaneal tendon** (*Achilles tendon*) along the posteroinferior leg. Then try to palpate the pulse of the **posterior tibial artery,** posteroinferior to the medial malleolus of the tibia (see section 23.3i).

Next, examine the leg first from a lateral perspective and then from a medial perspective. The superior part of the lateral leg is the **head of the fibula.** Palpate this bony projection. Then look distally and observe the lateral malleolus that you palpated when viewing the leg in anterior view. The **small saphenous vein** is easily seen along the lateral malleolus, traveling superiorly along the posterior part of the leg. Switch over to a medial view and discern the medial malleolus you palpated earlier. Another superficial vein of the leg is the **great saphenous vein,** seen subcutaneously on the medial side of the leg.

Learning Strategy 13.3

The great saphenous vein is on the same side of the lower limb as the great (big) toe. The small saphenous vein is on the same side as the smallest toe.

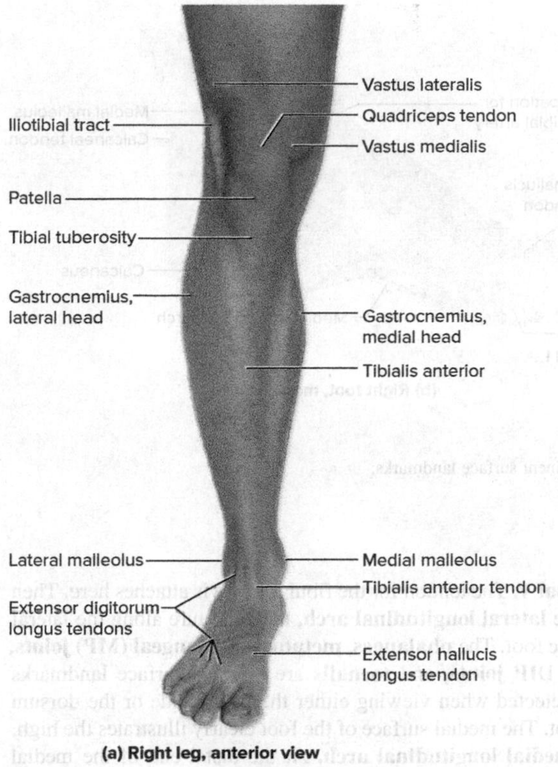
Vastus lateralis
Iliotibial tract
Quadriceps tendon
Vastus medialis
Patella
Tibial tuberosity
Gastrocnemius, lateral head
Gastrocnemius, medial head
Tibialis anterior
Lateral malleolus
Medial malleolus
Tibialis anterior tendon
Extensor digitorum longus tendons
Extensor hallucis longus tendon

(a) Right leg, anterior view

Figure 13.11

Leg. (*a*) Anterior, (*b*) posterior, and (*c*) lateral views of the right leg show the prominent surface landmarks.

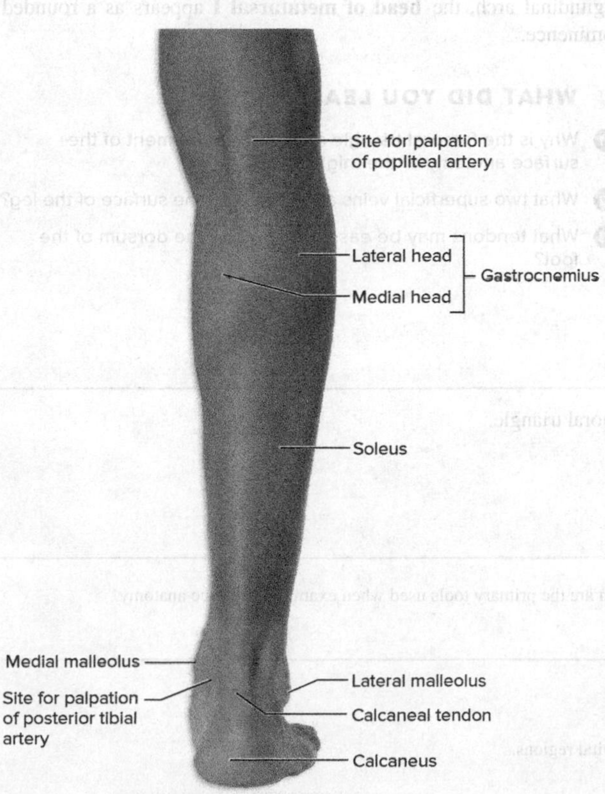
Site for palpation of popliteal artery
Lateral head
Medial head
Gastrocnemius
Soleus
Medial malleolus
Site for palpation of posterior tibial artery
Lateral malleolus
Calcaneal tendon
Calcaneus

(b) Right leg, posterior view

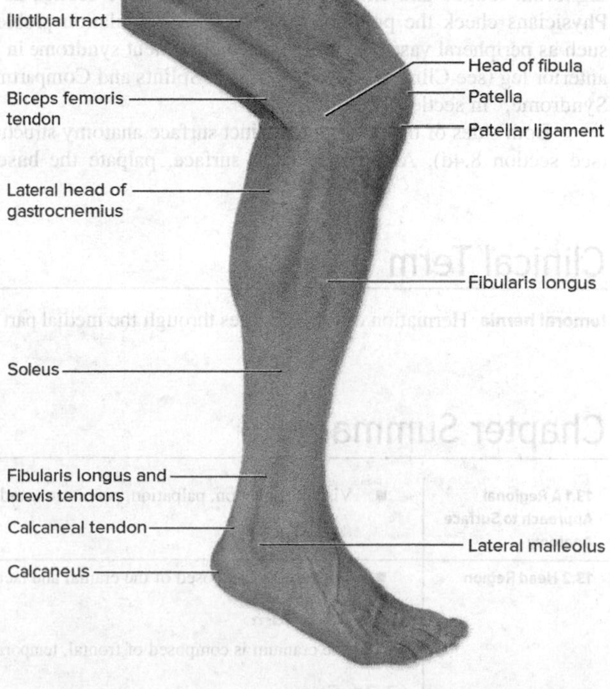
Iliotibial tract
Head of fibula
Patella
Biceps femoris tendon
Patellar ligament
Lateral head of gastrocnemius
Fibularis longus
Soleus
Fibularis longus and brevis tendons
Calcaneal tendon
Lateral malleolus
Calcaneus

(c) Right leg, lateral view

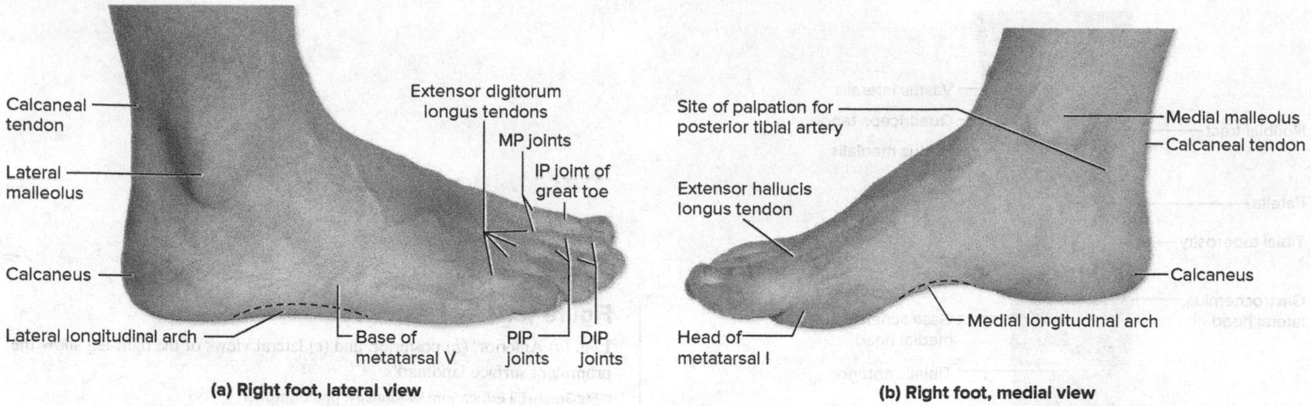

Figure 13.12

Ankle and Foot. (*a*) Lateral and (*b*) medial views of the right ankle and foot show the prominent surface landmarks.

13.6d Foot

In most individuals, numerous surface features of the foot can be clearly seen (**figure 13.12**; see figure 13.11*a*). On the superior side of the foot, also called the *dorsum,* palpate the tendons for the **tibialis anterior, extensor digitorum longus,** and **extensor hallucis longus** (see section 12.2c). Each of these tendons is clearly distinguished, especially when the foot is dorsiflexed. Move back toward the ankle, and palpate the **navicular bone** along the dorsum. You may feel the pulse of the **dorsalis pedis artery** on the dorsum of the proximal foot, distal to the ankle and between the tendons of the extensor digitorum longus and extensor hallucis longus (see section 23.3i). Physicians check the pulse of this artery for circulation problems such as peripheral vascular disease or compartment syndrome in the anterior leg (see Clinical View 12.7: "Shin Splints and Compartment Syndrome," in section 12.2d). APR

Both sides of the foot have distinct surface anatomy structures (see section 8.4d). Along the lateral surface, palpate the **base of metatarsal V.** The tendon for the fibularis brevis attaches here. Then notice the **lateral longitudinal arch,** the curvature along the lateral side of the foot. The **phalanges, metatarsophalangeal (MP) joints, PIP** and **DIP joints,** and **toenails** are obvious surface landmarks readily detected when viewing either the lateral side or the dorsum of the foot. The medial surface of the foot clearly illustrates the high, arched **medial longitudinal arch.** At the distal end of the medial longitudinal arch, the **head of metatarsal I** appears as a rounded prominence.

WHAT DID YOU LEARN?

11. Why is the femoral triangle an important element of the surface anatomy of the thigh?
12. What two superficial veins are viewed on the surface of the leg?
13. What tendons may be easily seen along the dorsum of the foot?

Clinical Term

femoral hernia Herniation of the intestines through the medial part of the femoral triangle.

Chapter Summary

13.1 A Regional Approach to Surface Anatomy	■ Visual inspection, palpation, percussion, and auscultation are the primary tools used when examining surface anatomy.
13.2 Head Region	■ The head is composed of the cranial and facial regions. **13.2a Cranium** ■ The cranium is composed of frontal, temporal, and occipital regions. **13.2b Face** ■ The facial region is composed of auricular, orbital, nasal, oral, and mental regions.
13.3 Neck Region	■ The sternocleidomastoid muscle subdivides the neck into anterior and lateral cervical regions. The posterior cervical region contains the trapezius muscle.

13.4 Trunk Region	■ The trunk is divided into the thorax, abdominopelvic region, and back. **13.4a Thorax** ■ Palpable structures of the thorax include the sternum, sternal angle, and ribs. **13.4b Abdominopelvic Region** ■ The important surface anatomy features of the abdominopelvic region include the linea alba, the umbilicus, and the inguinal ligaments. **13.4c Back** ■ The triangle of auscultation is an area where breathing sounds may be heard clearly with a stethoscope.
13.5 Shoulder and Upper Limb Region	■ The surface anatomy of the shoulder and upper limb is used for drawing blood, providing nutrients and fluids, and administering medicine. **13.5a Shoulder** ■ The scapula, the clavicle, and the humerus are palpable contributors to the structure of the shoulder. **13.5b Axilla** ■ The axilla, or armpit, is important clinically because of the blood vessels, nerves, and lymph nodes located there. **13.5c Arm** ■ The pulse of the brachial artery may be felt along the medial surface of the arm. **13.5d Forearm** ■ The styloid process of the radius and the head and styloid process of the ulna are readily palpable landmarks of the forearm. **13.5e Hand** ■ The thenar and hypothenar eminences are easily palpated on the anterior surface of the hand.
13.6 Lower Limb Region	■ The massive bones and strong muscles of the lower limbs are weight-bearers and serve in locomotion. **13.6a Gluteal Region** ■ The gluteal muscles form the prominences of the buttocks. **13.6b Thigh** ■ The femoral triangle and popliteal fossa are clinically important surface landmarks. **13.6c Leg** ■ The pulse of the posterior tibial artery is palpated posteroinferiorly from the medial malleolus. **13.6d Foot** ■ The pulse of the dorsalis pedis artery may be palpated on the medial dorsal side of the foot above the navicular bone, or along the dorsal interspace between the first and second metatarsals.

Challenge Yourself

Actively write or type your answers in a separate document to reinforce your learning, before checking your answers.

Multiple Choice

Select the best answer from the four choices provided.

1. Which structure can be palpated in the posterior cervical region?
   a. hyoid bone
   b. larynx
   c. cervical vertebra
   d. trachea
2. Which artery's pulse may be detected in a region bounded by the inguinal ligament, sartorius muscle, and adductor longus muscle?
   a. popliteal
   b. femoral
   c. anterior tibial
   d. posterior tibial
3. Which nerve is pinched when you "hit your funny bone"?
   a. ulnar nerve
   b. brachial nerve
   c. cephalic nerve
   d. radial nerve
4. Which of the following surface features may *not* be seen easily on obese people?
   a. philtrum
   b. auricle
   c. iliac crests
   d. natal cleft

5. An arterial pulse in the neck is best detected in which cervical triangle?
   a. carotid
   b. submandibular
   c. submental
   d. supraclavicular
6. The costal margin is the inferior edge of which structure?
   a. sternum
   b. clavicle
   c. rib cage
   d. linea alba
7. Eyebrows are located on which structure?
   a. ala nasi
   b. external occipital protuberance
   c. superciliary arches
   d. superior palpebral fissure
8. Which artery can be palpated between the tendons of the flexor carpi radialis and the brachioradialis?
   a. popliteal
   b. radial
   c. brachial
   d. femoral
9. The great and small saphenous veins are located in which anatomic region?
   a. forearm
   b. foot
   c. leg
   d. neck
10. Which muscle does *not* border the triangle of ascultation?
    a. trapezius
    b. rhomboid minor
    c. latissimus dorsi
    d. rhomboid major

Content Review

1. What is surface anatomy, and why is a knowledge of surface anatomy essential for health-care professionals?
2. Identify the six regions of the face, and specify a surface feature of each region.
3. Compare and contrast the anterior and lateral cervical regions with respect to their locations and the structures they contain.
4. Where is the superficial inguinal ring, and where can it be palpated? What is the ring's clinical significance?
5. Why must a physician know surface anatomy of the back to perform a lumbar puncture? What key surface anatomy features are used to do this procedure correctly?
6. What prominent features may be palpated at or near the elbow?
7. Identify and describe the tendons that can be discerned or palpated along the anterior surface of the wrist.
8. Discuss and describe the surface features that form the boundaries of a buttock.
9. Describe the location of the popliteal fossa, and discuss the clinical importance of this region.
10. Describe the anatomic locations where the following can be palpated: (a) the posterior tibial arteries, (b) the greater trochanter, (c) the medial malleolus and lateral malleolus, and (d) the tendinous attachments of the hamstring muscles.

Developing Critical Reasoning

1. Marcie went to the doctor and received an intramuscular injection in her right gluteal region. Afterward, Marcie had partial paralysis and lack of sensation in her right leg. What may have happened to Marcie during this injection?
2. Javier was hit hard in the lateral thoracic region. His doctor told him he had fractured his right sixth rib. How was the doctor able to determine which rib was fractured? What surface anatomy feature did he use to count the ribs?
3. When Louisa was sick with the flu, the doctor palpated her neck. What specific neck structures was the doctor palpating, and how do these structures relate to Louisa's infection?

Answers to "What Do You Think?"

1. Most of the muscles of facial expression may be palpated under the skin, including the orbicularis oculi, orbicularis oris, zygomaticus major, and platysma. In addition, you can palpate the masseter muscle, a muscle of mastication.
2. The sciatic nerve supplies the hamstrings, all leg muscles, and all muscles of the foot, so none of these muscles would work properly if the sciatic nerve were injured.

Nervous System

NERVOUS SYSTEM

Nervous Tissue 14

Outline

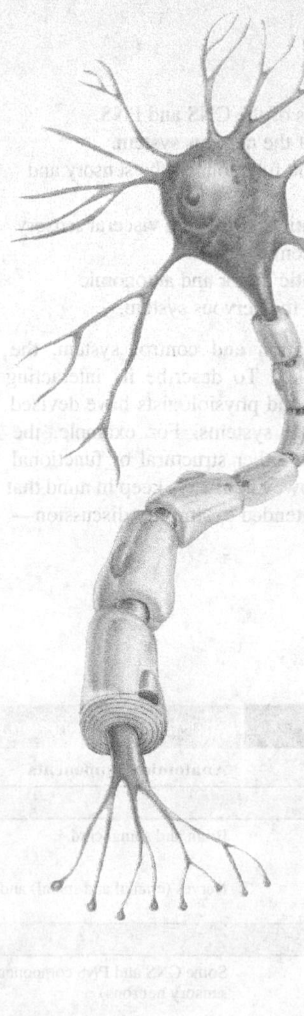

Anatomy & Physiology Revealed 4.0

MODULE 7: NERVOUS SYSTEM

Throughout the day, your body perceives and responds to multiple sensations. You smell spring flowers, feel the touch of a hand on your shoulder, and perceive your limbs moving. You control multiple muscle movements to walk, talk to the person sitting next to you, and hold this textbook. Other muscle movements occur without your voluntary input: Your heart beats, your stomach churns to digest your breakfast, and you jump at the sound of a honking horn. All of these sensations and muscle movements are interpreted and controlled by your **nervous system.** The nervous system is composed of all tissue types, but primarily of **nervous tissue**—neurons and glial cells (see section 4.5). This chapter introduces the study of the nervous system by first describing its overall organization and then investigating the components of nervous tissue.

14.1 Organization of the Nervous System

✓ Learning Objectives

1. Identify and describe the organs of the CNS and PNS.
2. Explain the general functions of the nervous system.
3. Identify and describe the specific functions of the sensory and motor nervous systems.
4. Compare and contrast the somatic sensory and visceral sensory components of the nervous system.
5. Compare and contrast the somatic motor and autonomic (visceral) motor components of the nervous system.

As the body's primary communication and control system, the nervous system is extremely complex. To describe its interacting structures and functions, anatomists and physiologists have devised specialized terms and organizational systems. For example, the nervous system may be divided into either structural or functional categories, as shown in **table 14.1**. However, always keep in mind that such artificial divisions are merely intended to simplify discussion—there is only one nervous system.

14.1a Structural Organization: Central and Peripheral Nervous Systems

The nervous system consists of two subdivisions: the central nervous system and the peripheral nervous system (**figure 14.1**). The **central nervous system (CNS)** includes the **brain** and **spinal cord.** The brain is protected and enclosed within the skull, whereas the spinal cord is housed and protected within the vertebral canal. The **peripheral** (pĕ-rif′ĕr-ăl) **nervous system (PNS)** includes the **cranial nerves** (nerves that extend from the brain), **spinal nerves** (nerves that extend from the spinal cord), and **ganglia** (gang′gl ē-ă; sing., *ganglion* = swelling), which are clusters of neuron cell bodies located outside the CNS.

14.1b Functional Organization: Sensory and Motor Nervous Systems

The nervous system has two functional divisions: the sensory nervous system and the motor nervous system (**figure 14.2**). Both divisions have CNS and PNS components, which together perform three general functions:

- **Collect information.** Specialized PNS structures called **receptors** (dendrite endings of sensory neurons or separate cells) detect changes in the internal or external environment (called *stimuli*) and pass them on to the CNS as sensory input (discussed in section 19.1).
- **Process and evaluate information.** After processing sensory input, the CNS determines what, if any, response is required.
- **Initiate response to information.** After selecting an appropriate response, the CNS initiates specific nerve impulses (rapid movements of an electrical charge along the neuron's plasma membrane of an axon), called motor output. Motor output travels through structures of the PNS to **effectors** (the cells that receive impulses from motor neurons: muscles or glands).

WHAT DO YOU THINK?

1. Why is the term *visceral* sometimes used to describe certain parts of the sensory and motor nervous systems?

Table 14.1 Structural and Functional Divisions of the Nervous System

Nervous System Organization	Anatomic Components	Description(s)
STRUCTURAL DIVISIONS		
Central nervous system (CNS)	Brain and spinal cord	Command center of nervous system that integrates and processes nervous information
Peripheral nervous system (PNS)	Nerves (cranial and spinal) and ganglia	Projects information to and receives information from CNS; mediates some reflexes
FUNCTIONAL DIVISIONS		
Sensory nervous system	Some CNS and PNS components (including sensory neurons)	Consists of all axons that transmit a nerve impulse *from* a peripheral structure *to* the CNS; includes pain, touch, temperature, and pressure ("input" information)
Somatic sensory		Transmits input from skin, fascia, joints, and skeletal muscle
Visceral sensory		Transmits input from viscera
Motor nervous system	Some CNS and PNS components (including motor neurons)	Consists of all axons that transmit a nerve impulse *from* the CNS *to* a muscle or gland ("output" information)
Somatic motor (somatic nervous system; SNS)		Transmit voluntary output to skeletal muscle
Autonomic motor (autonomic nervous system; ANS)		Transmit involuntary output to smooth muscle, cardiac muscle, and glands

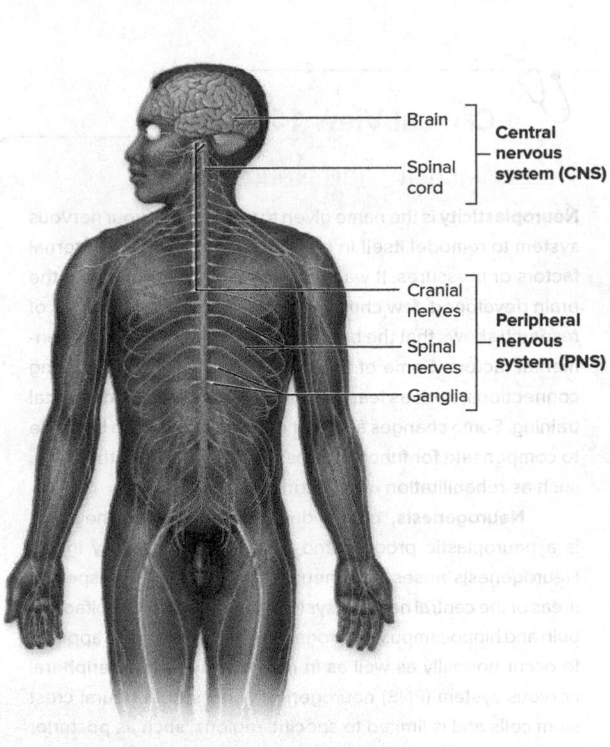

Figure 14.1

Structural Organization of the Nervous System. The central nervous system (CNS) is composed of the brain and spinal cord. The peripheral nervous system (PNS) is composed of cranial nerves, spinal nerves, and ganglia.

Sensory Nervous System

The **sensory** (or *afferent;* af′ĕr-ĕnt) **nervous system** is responsible for receiving sensory information *from* receptors and transmitting this information *to* the CNS. (The term *afferent* means "inflowing," which indicates that nerve impulses are transmitted to the CNS.) Thus, the sensory nervous system is responsible for **input.** The sensory nervous system contains both PNS and CNS components: Nerves of the PNS transmit the sensory information, and certain parts of the brain and spinal cord in the CNS interpret this information.

The sensory nervous system has two components: somatic sensory and visceral sensory. The **somatic sensory** components are the general somatic senses—touch, pain, pressure, vibration, temperature, and proprioception (sensing the position or movement of joints and limbs)—and the special senses (taste, vision, hearing, balance, and smell). These functions are considered *voluntary* because we have some control over them and we tend to be conscious of them. The **visceral sensory** components transmit nerve impulses from blood vessels and viscera to the CNS. The visceral receptors detect chemical composition of blood or stretch of an organ wall. These functions are said to be *involuntary* because most of the time you do not have voluntary control over them and are not conscious of them. However, you may become aware of visceral sensations when they are extreme—for example, if you have eaten too much and your stomach is bloated. (The various types of receptors are described in detail in section 19.1b.)

Motor Nervous System

The **motor** (or *efferent;* ef′ĕr-ent) **nervous system** is responsible for transmitting motor impulses *from* the CNS *to* effectors (muscles or glands). (The term *efferent* means "conducting outward," which indicates that nerve impulses are transmitted from the CNS.) Thus, the motor nervous system is responsible for **output.** The motor nervous system contains both CNS and PNS components: Parts of the brain and spinal cord (CNS) initiate nerve impulses, which travel through motor nerves that in turn transmit these impulses to effector organs.

The motor nervous system is subdivided into somatic motor and autonomic motor components. The **somatic motor** component **(somatic nervous system; SNS)** conducts nerve impulses from the CNS to the skeletal muscles, causing them to contract. The somatic motor component is often called the *voluntary nervous system* because the contractions of the skeletal muscles are under conscious control; for example, you exert voluntary control over your leg muscles as you press on the accelerator of your car.

The **autonomic motor** component is often called the **autonomic nervous system (ANS).** Because it innervates internal organs and regulates smooth muscle, cardiac muscle, and glands without our control, it is also known as the *visceral motor system* or the

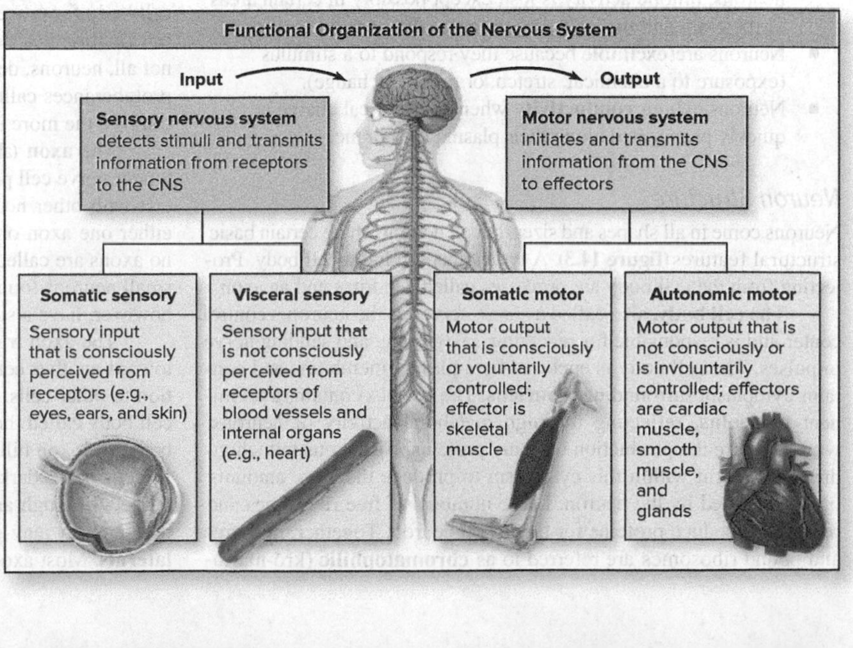

Figure 14.2

Functional Organization of the Nervous System. The nervous system is functionally divided into a sensory nervous system and a motor nervous system. Both of these parts of the nervous system contain somatic and visceral components.

involuntary nervous system. For example, we cannot voluntarily make our hearts stop beating, nor can we prevent our stomachs from growling. The autonomic nervous system has two further subdivisions—parasympathetic and sympathetic—which we examine in section 18.2.

WHAT DID YOU LEARN?

1. What three functions do the CNS and PNS perform? Draw a diagram to depict these functions.
2. Compare and contrast the meanings of afferent and efferent.

14.2 Cytology of Nervous Tissue

✓ Learning Objectives

6. Describe the basic characteristics common to all neurons.
7. Identify and describe the different structures of the neuron, including the cell body, dendrites, and axon.
8. Explain the structural and functional classifications of neurons.
9. Explain the differences among the various types of glial cells, and describe their structures and function.

Two distinct cell types form nervous tissue: neurons, which are excitable cells that are able to generate, transmit, and receive nerve impulses, and glial cells, which are nonexcitable cells that support and protect the neurons.

14.2a Neurons

The basic structural unit of the nervous system is the **neuron** (nū′ron). Neurons conduct nerve impulses from one part of the body to another. They have several special characteristics:

- Neurons have a **high metabolic rate.** Their survival depends upon continuous and abundant supplies of glucose and oxygen.
- Neurons have **extreme longevity.** Most neurons formed during fetal development are still functional in very elderly individuals.
- Neurons typically are **nonmitotic** (unable to divide and produce new neurons). During the fetal development of neurons, mitotic activity is lost, except possibly in certain areas of the brain and the sense organ for smell.
- Neurons are **excitable** because they respond to a stimulus (exposure to a chemical, stretch, or pressure change).
- Neurons exhibit **conductivity** when an electrical charge is quickly propagated along their plasma membrane.

Neuron Structure

Neurons come in all shapes and sizes, but all neurons share certain basic structural features (**figure 14.3**). A typical neuron has a cell body. Projecting from the cell body are processes called dendrites and an axon.

The **cell body,** also called a *soma,* serves as the neuron's control center and is responsible for receiving, integrating, and sending nerve impulses. The cell body is enclosed by a plasma membrane and contains cytoplasm surrounding a **nucleus.** The nucleus contains a prominent **nucleolus,** reflecting the high metabolic activity of neurons, which require the production of many proteins. Numerous mitochondria are present within this cytoplasm to produce the large amounts of ATP needed by the neuron. Large numbers of free ribosomes and rough ER produce proteins for the active neuron. Together, both free and bound ribosomes are referred to as **chromatophilic** (krō-mă-tō-fil′ik; *chromo* = color; *phileo* = to love) **substance,** because they stain darkly with basic dyes, or *Nissl bodies,* because they were first described by the German microscopist Franz Nissl. Cytologists believe that the chromatophilic substance, together with dendrites and cell bodies, account for the gray color of the gray matter, as seen in brain and spinal cord areas containing collections of neuron cell bodies.

Dendrites (den′drīt; *dendrites* = relating to a tree) tend to be shorter, smaller processes that branch off the cell body. Some neurons have only one dendrite, whereas others have many. Dendrites conduct information as electrical signals from other cells toward the cell body; in essence, they receive input and then transfer it to the cell body for processing. The more dendrites a neuron has, the more information that neuron can receive from other cells. On many, but not all, neurons, dendrite surface area is increased by small knoblike protuberances called dendritic spines. The more surface area a neuron has, the more interactions it can have with other cells.

The **axon** (ak′son; *axon* = axis), or *nerve fiber,* is typically a longer nerve cell process emanating from the cell body to make contact with other neurons, muscle cells, or gland cells. Neurons have either one axon or no axon at all. Neurons with only dendrites and no axons are called **anaxonic** (an-ak-son′ik; *an* = without). They are small neurons found only in the CNS as interneurons. Most neurons, however, have a single axon.

The axon transmits a nerve impulse away from the cell body toward another cell; in essence, the axon transmits output information to other cells. The axon extends from a triangular region of the cell body called the **axon hillock** (hil′lok). Unlike the rest of the cell body, the axon hillock is devoid of chromatophilic substance, and so it lacks those dark-staining regions when viewed under the microscope. Although an axon remains relatively unbranched for most of its length, it may give rise to a few side branches called **axon collaterals.** Most axons and their collaterals branch extensively at their

Clinical View 14.1

Neuroplasticity and Neurogenesis

Neuroplasticity is the name given to the ability of your nervous system to remodel itself in response to internal and external factors or pressures. It was previously thought that once the brain developed, few changes occurred. Several decades of research shows that the brain changes to respond to environmental factors. Some of these changes strengthen existing connections, such as learning, mental rehearsal, and musical training. Some changes allow for new connections to be made to compensate for functional loss in other areas of the brain, such as rehabilitation after a concussion or stroke.

Neurogenesis, or the development of new neurons, is a neuroplastic process and can be stimulated by injury. Neurogenesis arises from neural stem cells in very specific areas of the central nervous system (CNS), such as the olfactory bulb and hippocampus. Neurogenesis in these regions appears to occur normally as well as in response to injury. Peripheral nervous system (PNS) neurogenesis arises from neural crest stem cells and is limited to specific regions, such as posterior root ganglia and the enteric nervous system. Neurogenesis in the PNS appears to happen as a reaction to injury.

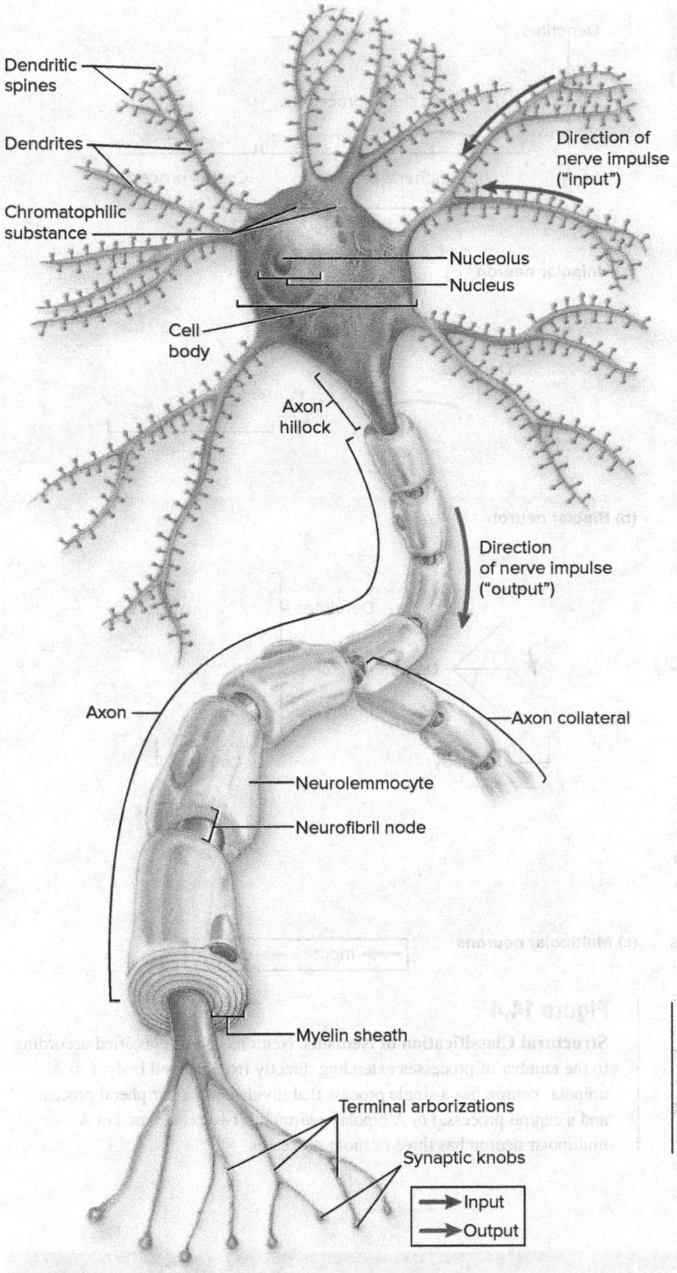

(a) Typical neuron components

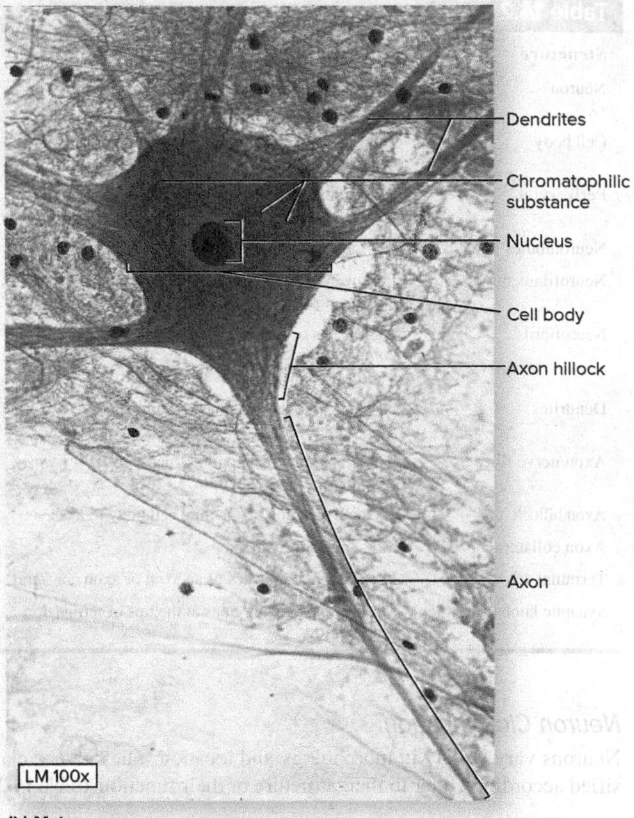

(b) Motor neuron

Figure 14.3

Structures in a Typical Neuron. (*a*) Input information (blue arrows) flows through dendrites to the cell body; output information (red arrow) flows through the axon to the next cell. (*b*) Photomicrograph of a large motor neuron. APR

(b) Ed Reschke

distal end into an array of fine terminal extensions called **terminal arborizations.** The extreme tips of these fine extensions are slightly expanded regions called **synaptic** (si-nap′tik) **knobs** (also called *synaptic bulbs, axon terminals, end bulbs,* or *terminal boutons*).

Learning Strategy 14.1

Sometimes the easiest way to remember functions is to simplify them. In the neuron, the dendrites receive and bring information to the cell body and the axons take information away from the cell body. Linking the words can help: Dendrites-to; axons-away.

Special terms denote other internal structures of a neuron. The cytoplasm within the cell body is called the **perikaryon** (per′i-kar′ē-on; *peri* = around, *karyon* = kernel), although some anatomists use that term to describe the whole cell body. The microtubules that form the cytoskeleton are called neurotubules. **Neurofilaments** (nū′rō-fil′ă-ment; *filamentum* = thread) are intermediate filaments that aggregate to form bundles called **neurofibrils** (nū′rō-fī′bril; *fibrilla* = fiber). Neurofibrils extend as a complex network into both the dendrites and axons, where their tensile strength provides support for these processes. **Table 14.2** reviews some of the terms used to describe neuron structures.

Table 14.2	Parts of a Neuron
Structure	**Description(s)**
Neuron	Structural and functional cell of the nervous system; sometimes called a nerve cell
Cell body	Nucleus and surrounding cytoplasm of a neuron (excluding its dendrites and axon)
Perikaryon	Most often refers to the cytoplasm within the cell body. Sometimes used to describe the entire cell body
Neurotubules	Microtubules that form the cytoskeleton
Neurofilaments	Intermediate filaments that aggregate to form bundles called neurofibrils
Neurofibrils	Aggregates of neurofilaments that extend as a complex network into dendrites and axons, their tensile strength provides support for these processes
Dendrites	Neuron processes that conduct information *to* the cell body ("input")
Axon/nerve fiber	Neuron process that conducts nerve impulses *away* from the cell body ("output")
Axon hillock	Triangular region connecting cell body to axon
Axon collaterals	Side branches of an axon
Terminal arborizations	Fine terminal branches of an axon or axon collateral
Synaptic knobs	Slightly expanded regions at the tips of terminal arborizations

Neuron Classification

Neurons vary widely in morphology and location. They can be classified according either to their structure or their function **(table 14.3)**.

Structural Classification Neurons are classified structurally into three types, based upon the number of neuron processes emanating directly from the cell body: unipolar, bipolar, or multipolar **(figure 14.4)**.

Unipolar neurons have a single, short process that emerges from the cell body and branches like a T. These neurons are also called *pseudounipolar* (sū′dō-yū′ni-p ō′lăr; *pseudo* = false, *uni* = one) because they start out as bipolar neurons during development, but their two processes fuse into a single process. The naming of the branched processes in unipolar neurons has been a source of confusion as it relates to the common definitions of dendrites and axons. It seems most appropriate to call the short, multiple-branched receptive endings dendrites. The combined **peripheral process** (from dendrites to the cell body) and **central process** (from the cell body into the

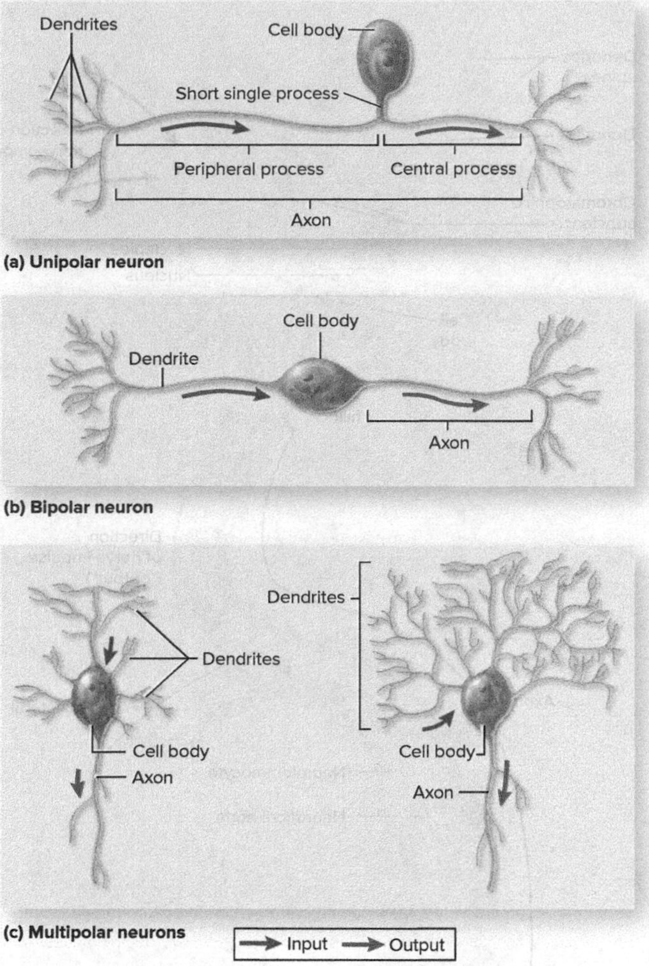

Figure 14.4

Structural Classification of Neurons. Neurons can be classified according to the number of processes extending directly from the cell body. (*a*) A unipolar neuron has a single process that divides into a peripheral process and a central process. (*b*) A bipolar neuron has two processes. (*c*) A multipolar neuron has three or more processes.

Table 14.3	Structural and Functional Classifications of Neurons	
Structural Classification	**Description(s)**	**Functional Example**
Unipolar neuron	Common type of sensory neuron; single short cell process extends directly from the cell body and looks like a T as a result of the fusion of two processes into one long axon	Most sensory neurons (detect stimuli in the form of touch, pressure, temperature, or chemicals)
Bipolar neuron	Relatively uncommon; two nerve cell processes extend directly from the cell body	Some special sense neurons (e.g., in olfactory epithelium of nose, retina of eye)
Multipolar neuron	Most common type of neuron; multiple nerve cell processes extend from cell body; typically one axon and many dendrites	Interneurons, motor neurons
Functional Classification	**Description(s)**	**Structural Example**
Sensory	Conducts nerve impulses *from* body *to* CNS	Most sensory neurons are unipolar; a few (e.g., some in olfactory epithelium and retina) are bipolar
Motor	Conducts nerve impulses *from* CNS *to* muscles or glands	Multipolar
Interneuron	Found only in CNS; facilitates communication between motor and sensory neurons	Multipolar

CNS) together denote the axon, because these processes generate and conduct impulses and are often myelinated. Most sensory neurons of the PNS are unipolar neurons.

Bipolar neurons have two processes that extend from the cell body—one axon and one dendrite. These neurons are relatively uncommon in humans and primarily limited to some of the special senses. For example, bipolar neurons are located in the olfactory epithelium of the nose and in the retina of the eye.

Multipolar neurons are the most common type of neuron. Multiple processes—many dendrites and a single axon—extend from the cell body. Examples of multipolar neurons include motor neurons that innervate muscle and glands. APR

Functional Classification Neurons are classified functionally into three types according to the direction the nerve impulse travels relative to the CNS: sensory neurons, motor neurons, or interneurons (**figure 14.5**).

Sensory neurons, or *afferent neurons,* transmit nerve impulses *from* sensory **receptors** *to* the CNS. These neurons are specialized to detect changes in their environment called **stimuli** (sing., *stimulus*). Stimuli can be in the form of touch, pressure, heat, light, or chemicals. Most sensory neurons are unipolar, although a few are bipolar (e.g., those in the olfactory epithelium of the nose and the retina of the eye, as previously mentioned). The cell bodies of unipolar sensory neurons are located outside the CNS and housed within structures called posterior (dorsal) root ganglia.

Motor neurons, or *efferent neurons,* transmit nerve impulses *from* the CNS *to* muscles or glands. They are called motor neurons because most of them extend to muscle cells, and the nerve impulses they transmit cause these cells to contract. The muscle and gland cells that receive nerve impulses from motor neurons are called effectors, because their stimulation produces a response or effect. The cell bodies of most motor neurons lie in the spinal cord, whereas the axons primarily travel in cranial or spinal nerves to muscles and glands. All motor neurons are multipolar.

Interneurons, or *association neurons,* lie entirely within the CNS and are multipolar structures. They receive nerve impulses from many other neurons and carry out the integrative function of the nervous system—that is, they retrieve, process, and store information and "decide" how the body responds to stimuli. Thus, interneurons facilitate communication between sensory and motor neurons. Figure 14.5 shows a sensory neuron transmitting stimuli (sensory information) to an interneuron, which then processes that information and signals the appropriate motor neuron(s) to transmit a nerve impulse to the muscle. Interneurons outnumber all other neurons in both their total number and different types; it is estimated that 99% of our neurons are interneurons. The number of interneurons activated during processing or storing increases dramatically with the complexity of the response.

Learning Strategy 14.2

It is sometimes difficult to remember the relationships between "afferent and sensory" and "efferent and motor" and their general locations. This mnemonic will help keep them straight in your mind: **SAME DAVE** (**S**ensory-**A**fferent, **M**otor-**E**fferent; **D**orsal-**A**fferent, **V**entral-**E**fferent). Don't forget that dorsal is posterior and ventral is anterior in humans.

14.2b Glial Cells

Glial (glī′ăl) **cells,** sometimes referred to as *neuroglia* (nū-rog′lē-ă; *glia* = glue), are located within both the CNS and the PNS. Glial cells differ from neurons in that they are smaller and capable of mitosis. Glial cells do not transmit nerve impulses, but they do assist neurons with their functions. Collectively, the glial cells physically protect and help nourish neurons, and provide an organized, supporting framework for all the nervous tissue. During development, glial cells form the framework that guides young migrating neurons to their destinations. Glial cells also play a role in learning and memory through their interaction with synapses between neurons.

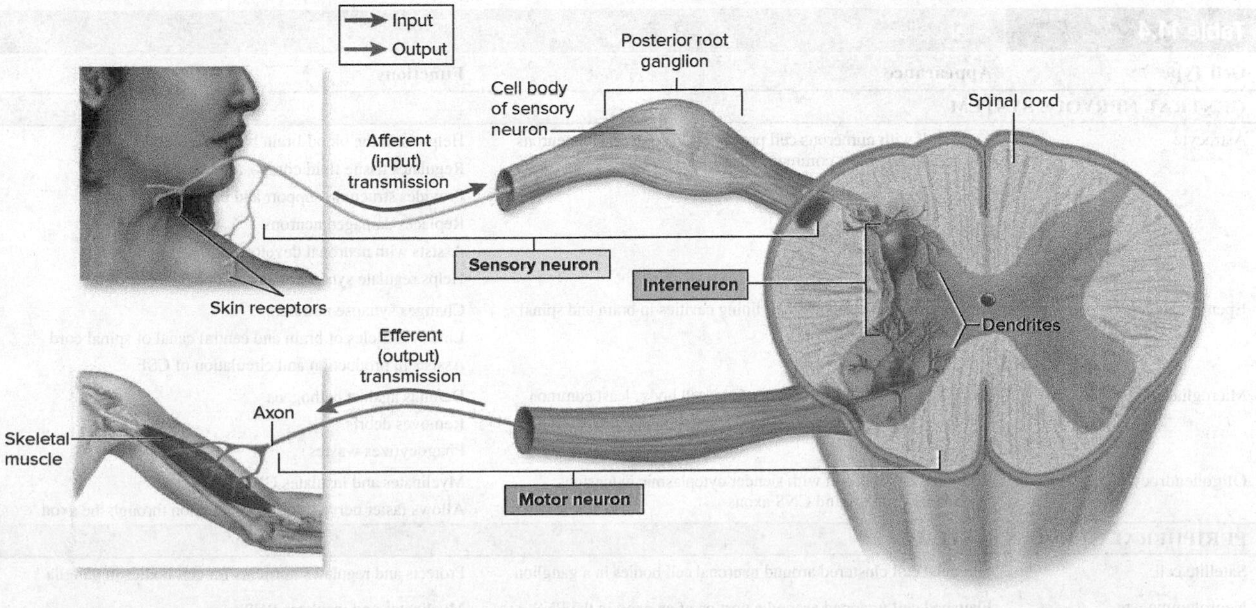

Figure 14.5
Functional Classification of Neurons. Sensory neurons transmit afferent (input) signals to the central nervous system. Interneurons process information within the CNS. Motor neurons transmit efferent (output) impulses from the CNS to effectors. APR

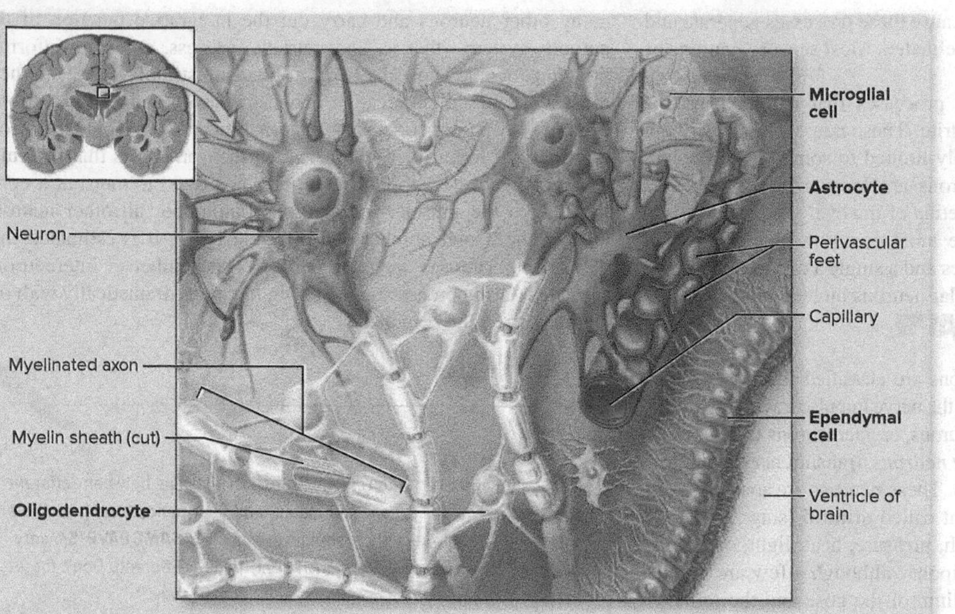
Neuron
Myelinated axon
Myelin sheath (cut)
Oligodendrocyte
Microglial cell
Astrocyte
Perivascular feet
Capillary
Ependymal cell
Ventricle of brain

Figure 14.6 **Cellular Organization of Nervous Tissue Within the CNS.** The four types of glial cells in the CNS are shown in relationship to a neuron.

There is scientific debate about the ratio of the number of glial cells to the number of neurons in the human brain. Past estimates suggest there are 100 billion neurons and 10 to 50 times that number of glial cells. Current estimates indicate that there are about 86 billion neurons and roughly the same number of glial cells in the human brain. Collectively, glial cells account for roughly half the volume of the nervous system. APR

WHAT DO YOU THINK?

2 If a person has a "brain tumor," is it more likely to have developed from neurons or from glial cells? Why?

Glial Cells of the CNS

Four types of glial cells occur in the central nervous system: astrocytes, ependymal cells, microglial cells, and oligodendrocytes **(figure 14.6)**. They can be distinguished on the basis of size, intracellular organization, and the presence of specific cytoplasmic processes **(table 14.4)**. All glial cells, except microglia, are derived from neural ectoderm. Microglia are derived from stem cells within red bone marrow that become monocytes (a type of white blood cell).

Astrocytes **Astrocytes** (as′trō-sīt; *astron* = star) exhibit a starlike shape due to many projections from their surface **(figure 14.7a)**. These

Table 14.4 Glial Cells

Cell Type	Appearance	Functions
CENTRAL NERVOUS SYSTEM		
Astrocyte	Large cell with numerous cell processes; in contact with neurons and capillaries; most common type of glial cell	Helps form the blood-brain barrier Regulates tissue fluid composition Provides structural support and organization to CNS Replaces damaged neurons Assists with neuronal development Helps regulate synaptic transmission Changes synapse numbers
Ependymal cell	Simple cuboidal epithelial cell lining cavities in brain and spinal cord; cilia on apical surface	Lines ventricles of brain and central canal of spinal cord Assists in production and circulation of CSF
Microglial cell	Small cell with slender branches from cell body; least common type of glial cell	Defends against pathogens Removes debris Phagocytizes wastes
Oligodendrocyte	Rounded, bulbous cell with slender cytoplasmic extensions; extensions wrap around CNS axons	Myelinates and insulates CNS axons Allows faster nerve impulse conduction through the axon
PERIPHERAL NERVOUS SYSTEM		
Satellite cell	Flattened cell clustered around neuronal cell bodies in a ganglion	Protects and regulates nutrients for cell bodies in ganglia
Neurolemmocyte	Flattened cell wrapped around a portion of an axon in the PNS	Myelinates and insulates PNS axons Allows for faster nerve impulse conduction through the axon

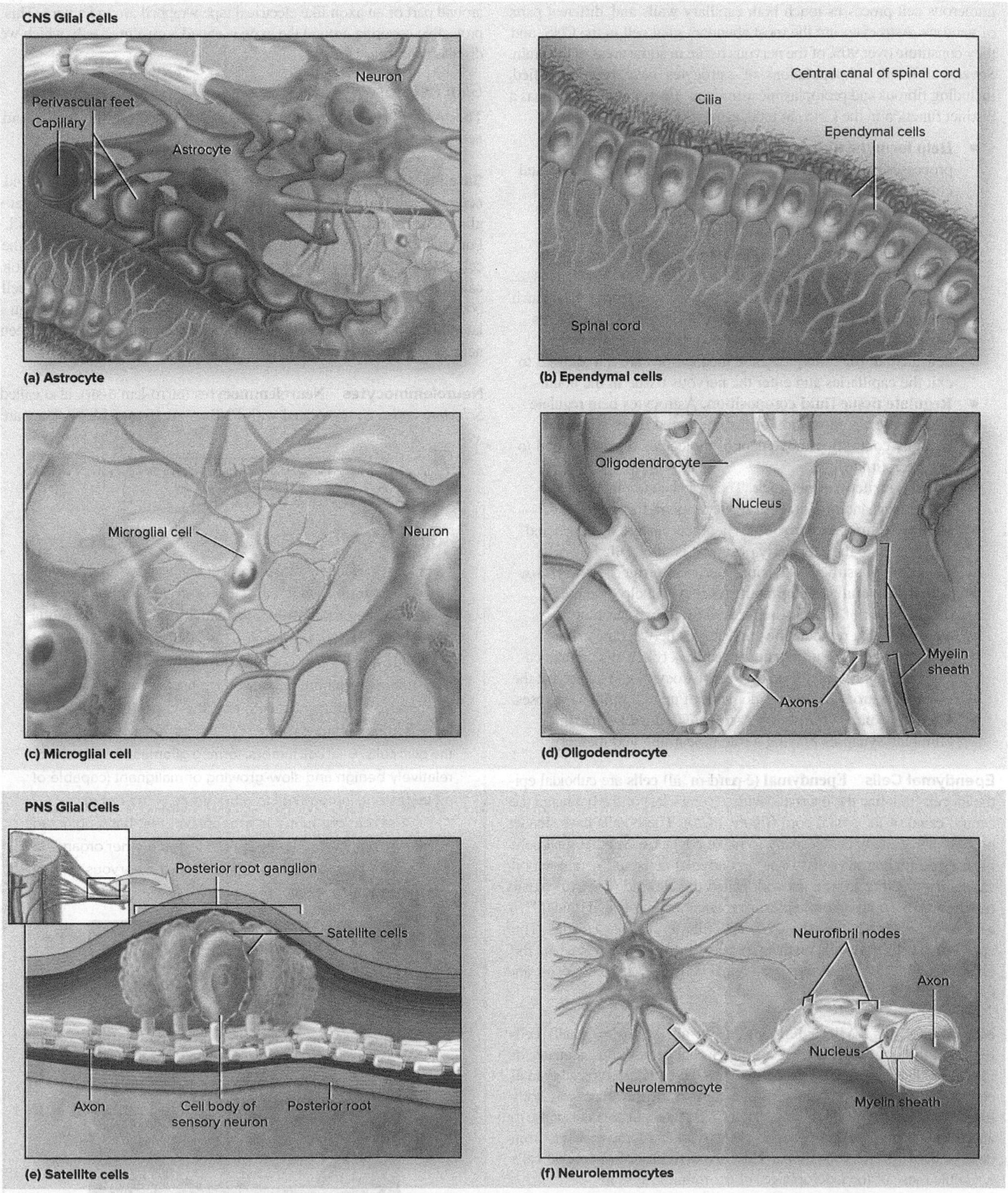

Figure 14.7

Glial Cells. (*a*) Astrocytes have perivascular feet (only a few are shown here to appreciate their morphology) that wrap completely around capillaries in the CNS. (*b*) Ependymal cells line the fluid-filled spaces in the brain and spinal cord. (*c*) Microglial cells phagocytize damaged neurons and cellular debris. (*d*) Oligodendrocytes myelinate axons in the CNS. (*e*) In the PNS, satellite cells surround neuron cell bodies in ganglia, such as the posterior root ganglion. (*f*) Neurolemmocytes myelinate axons in the PNS.

numerous cell processes touch both capillary walls and different parts of neurons. Astrocytes are the most abundant glial cell in the CNS, and they constitute over 90% of the nervous tissue in some areas of the brain. Several different subpopulations of astrocytes have been identified, including fibrous and protoplasmic astrocytes. Each subpopulation has a distinct function in the CNS. In total, astrocytes:

- **Help form the blood-brain barrier.** Ends of astrocyte processes called perivascular feet wrap completely around and cover the outer surface of capillaries in the brain. Together, the perivascular feet and the brain capillaries, which are less "leaky" than other capillaries in the body, contribute to a **blood-brain barrier (BBB)** that strictly controls substances entering the nervous tissue in the brain from the blood. This blood-brain barrier protects the delicate brain from toxins (such as certain waste products and drugs in the blood), but allows needed nutrients to pass through. Sometimes this barrier is detrimental; for example, some medications are not allowed to exit the capillaries and enter the nervous tissue in the brain.
- **Regulate tissue fluid composition.** Astrocytes help regulate the chemical composition of the interstitial fluid within the brain by controlling movement of molecules from the blood to the interstitial fluid.
- **Form a structural network.** The cytoskeleton in astrocytes strengthens and organizes nervous tissue in the CNS.
- **Replace damaged neurons.** When neurons are damaged and die, the space they formerly occupied is often filled by cells produced by astrocyte division, a process termed *astrocytosis.*
- **Assist neuronal development.** Astrocytes help direct the development of neurons in the fetal brain by secreting chemicals that regulate the connections between neurons.
- **Help regulate synaptic transmission.** A two-way communication pathway is established between astrocytes and neurons at the synapse. Astrocytes oversee domains of up to 2 million synapses.
- **Change synapse numbers.** Astrocytes can add synapses or eliminate synapses playing a role in learning and memory.

Ependymal Cells **Ependymal** (ĕ-pen′di-m ăl) **cells** are cuboidal epithelial cells that line the internal cavities (ventricles) of the brain and the central canal of the spinal cord (figure 14.7*b*). These cells have slender processes that branch extensively to make contact with other glial cells in the surrounding nervous tissue. Ependymal cells and nearby blood capillaries together form a network called the choroid (kor′oyd) plexus (see figure 15.7). The choroid plexus produces cerebrospinal fluid (CSF), a clear liquid that bathes the CNS and fills its internal cavities. The ependymal cells have cilia on their apical surfaces that help circulate the CSF. (Section 15.2c describes ependymal cells, the choroid plexus, and CSF in more detail.)

Microglial Cells **Microglial** (mī-krog′le-ăl; *micros* = small) **cells** represent the smallest percentage of CNS glial cells; some estimates of their prevalence are as low as 5%. Microglial cells are typically small cells that have slender branches extending from the main cell body (figure 14.7 *c*). They wander through the CNS and replicate in response to an infection. They perform phagocytic activity and remove debris from dead or damaged nervous tissue. Thus, the activities of microglial cells resemble those of the macrophages of the immune system.

Oligodendrocytes **Oligodendrocytes** (ol′i-gō-den′dr ō-sīt; *oligos* = few) are large cells with a bulbous body and slender cytoplasmic extensions or processes (figure 14.7*d*). The processes of oligodendrocytes ensheathe portions of many different axons, each repeatedly wrapping around part of an axon like electrical tape wrapped around a wire. This protective covering around the axon is called a myelin sheath, which we discuss in section 14.3a.

Glial Cells of the PNS

The two glial cell types in the PNS are satellite cells and neurolemmocytes.

Satellite Cells **Satellite cells** are flattened cells arranged around neuronal cell bodies in ganglia. (Recall from section 14.1a that a ganglion is a collection of neuron cell bodies located outside the CNS.) For example, figure 14.7*e* illustrates how satellite cells surround the cell bodies of sensory neurons located in a specific type of ganglion called a posterior root ganglion. Satellite cells physically separate cell bodies in a ganglion from their surrounding interstitial fluid, and regulate the continuous exchange of nutrients and waste products between neurons and their environment.

Neurolemmocytes **Neurolemmocytes** (nū′rō-lem′ō-sīt), also called *Schwann cells,* are associated with PNS axons (figure 14.7*f*). They are

Clinical View 14.2

Tumors of the Central Nervous System

Neoplasms resulting from unregulated cell growth, commonly known as **tumors,** sometimes occur in the central nervous system. A tumor that originates within the organ where it is found is called a *primary tumor.* Because mature neurons do not divide and are incapable of giving rise to tumors, primary CNS tumors originate in supporting tissues within the brain or spinal cord that have retained the capacity to undergo mitosis: the meninges (protective membranes of the CNS) or the glial cells. Glial cell tumors, termed **gliomas,** may be either relatively benign and slow-growing or malignant (capable of metastasizing [spreading] to other areas of the body).

A *secondary tumor* is a neoplasm that has originated at one site but subsequently spread to some other organ. For example, lung cancer can metastasize to the nervous system and form additional tumors.

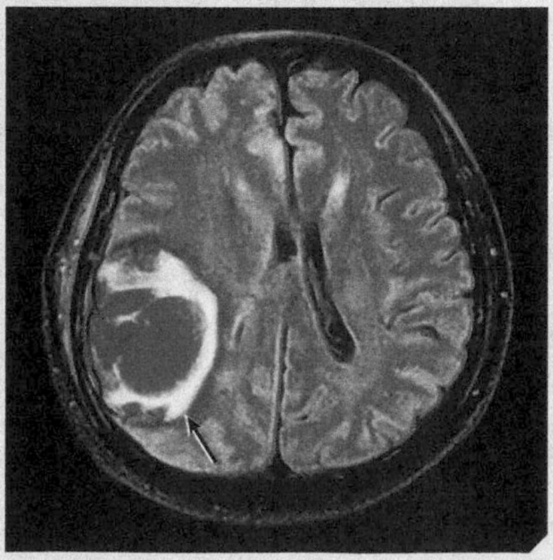

An MRI shows a tumor (colored in red) in the parietal lobe.
Puwadol Jaturawutthichai/Alamy Stock Photo

elongated, flattened cells that wrap around axons within the PNS, insulating the axon and forming a myelin sheath (described in section 14.3).

WHAT DID YOU LEARN?

3. Make a table or chart showing how dendrites and axons differ in terms of their structure, number, and general function?
4. Explain the role of astrocytes in the blood-brain barrier.
5. If a person suffers from meningitis (an inflammation of the coverings around the brain), which type of glial cell usually replicates in response to the infection?
6. What are satellite cells, where are they located, and what do they do?

14.3 Myelination of Axons

✓ Learning Objectives

10. Identify and describe the composition and function of a myelin sheath.
11. Describe and compare nerve impulse propagation in saltatory and continuous conduction.

The main activity of axons is nerve impulse conduction. A **nerve impulse** or *action potential* is the rapid movement of an electrical charge along an axon's plasma membrane. Neurons possess an electrical excitability—that is, the ability to respond to a stimulus and generate a nerve impulse. This impulse travels along the axon to stimulate either another neuron, muscle cell, or gland. The speed the impulse travels along an axon is affected by a process called myelination, which allows for faster propagation of action potentials.

14.3a Myelination

Myelination is the process by which part of an axon is wrapped with a **myelin sheath,** the insulating covering around the axon consisting of concentric layers of myelin. In the CNS, a myelin sheath forms from oligodendrocytes, and in the PNS, it forms from neurolemmocytes. Myelin consists of the plasma membranes of these glial cells and contains a large proportion of fats and a lesser amount of proteins. The high lipid content of the myelin sheath gives the axon a distinct, glossy-white appearance and serves to effectively insulate it.

Figure 14.8 illustrates the process of myelinating a PNS axon. The neurolemmocyte starts to encircle a 1 millimeter (mm) length portion of the axon, much as if you were wrapping a piece of tape around a portion of your pencil. As the neurolemmocyte continues to wrap around the axon, its cytoplasm and nucleus are squeezed to the periphery (the outside edge). The overlapping inner layers of the plasma membrane form the myelin sheath. Sometimes the name **neurilemma** is used to describe this delicate, thin outer membrane of the neurolemmocyte.

An oligodendrocyte in the CNS can myelinate a 1 millimeter length portion of *many* axons, not just one. **Figure 14.9*a*** shows oligodendrocytes myelinating portions of three different axons. The cytoplasmic extensions of the oligodendrocyte wrap successively around a portion of each axon, and successive plasma membrane layers form the myelin sheath.

In the PNS, a neurolemmocyte can myelinate a 1 millimeter length portion of a single axon only (figure 14.9*b*). Because most PNS axons are longer than 1 millimeter, it takes many neurolemmocytes to myelinate the entire axon. Figure 14.3*a* shows an axon that has seven neurolemmocytes wrapped around it. The axons in many of the nerves in the body have hundreds or thousands of neurolemmocytes covering their entire length.

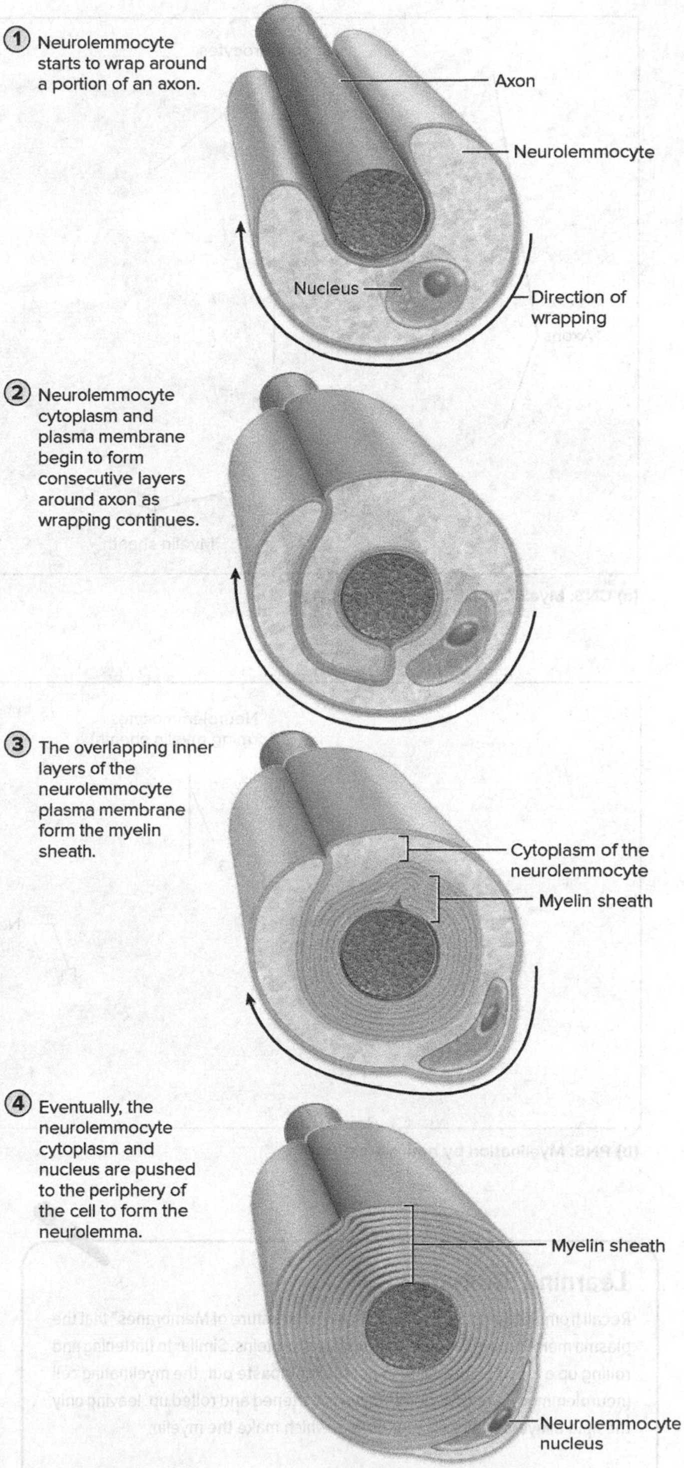

① Neurolemmocyte starts to wrap around a portion of an axon.
Axon
Neurolemmocyte
Nucleus
Direction of wrapping
② Neurolemmocyte cytoplasm and plasma membrane begin to form consecutive layers around axon as wrapping continues.
③ The overlapping inner layers of the neurolemmocyte plasma membrane form the myelin sheath.
Cytoplasm of the neurolemmocyte
Myelin sheath
④ Eventually, the neurolemmocyte cytoplasm and nucleus are pushed to the periphery of the cell to form the neurolemma.
Myelin sheath
Neurolemmocyte nucleus

Figure 14.8

Myelination of PNS Axons. A myelin sheath surrounds most axons. In the PNS, neurolemmocytes form both a myelin sheath and neurilemma in a series of sequential stages.

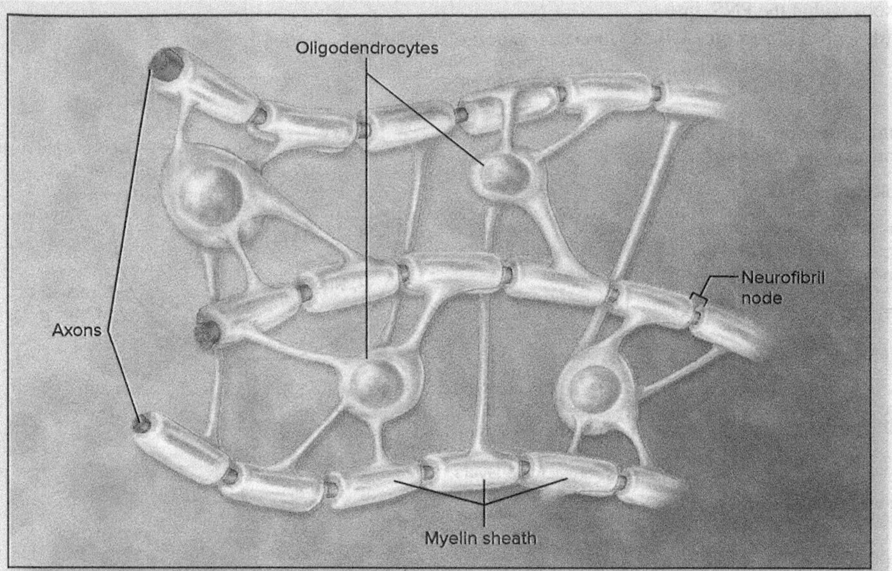

(a) CNS: Myelination by oligodendrocytes

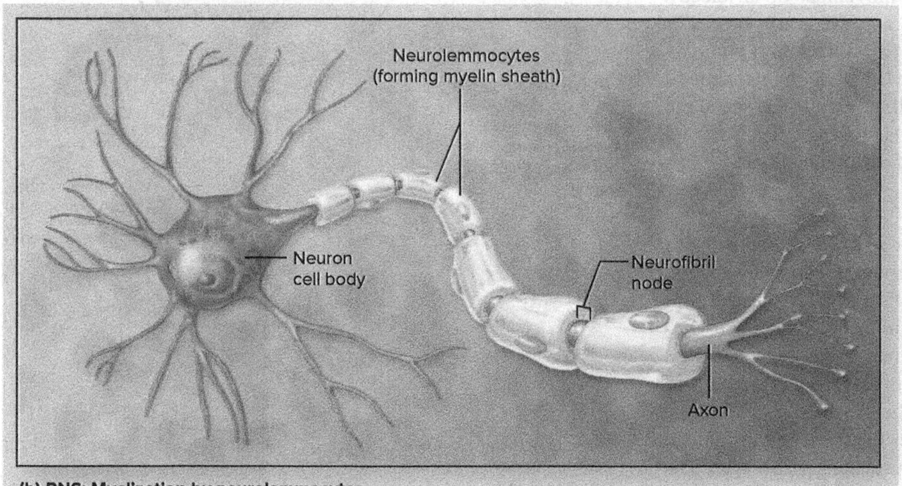

(b) PNS: Myelination by neurolemmocytes

Figure 14.9

Myelin Sheaths in the CNS and PNS. (*a*) In the CNS, several extensions from an oligodendrocyte wrap around small parts of multiple axons. (*b*) In the PNS, the neurolemmocyte ensheathes only one small part of a single axon. APR

Learning Strategy 14.3

Recall from Section 2.3a: "Composition and Structure of Membranes" that the plasma membrane is composed of lipids and proteins. Similar to flattening and rolling up a tube of toothpaste to get the toothpaste out, the myelinating cell (neurolemmocyte or oligodendrocyte) is flattened and rolled up, leaving only the lipid bilayers of plasma membrane, which make the myelin.

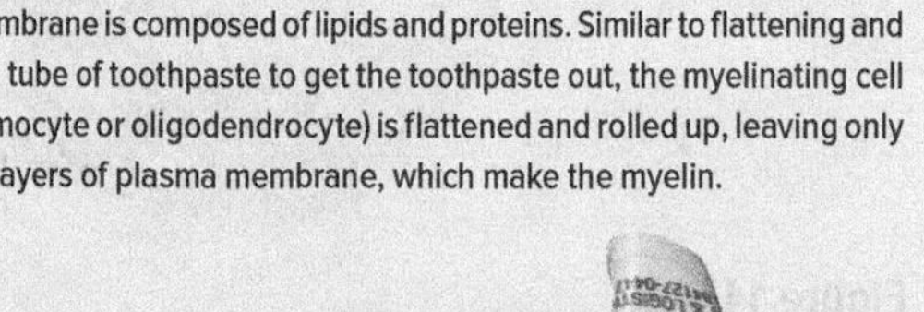

Lawrence Manning/Getty Images

Not all axons are myelinated. **Unmyelinated axons** in the PNS (shown in **figure 14.10**) are associated with a neurolemmocyte, but no myelin sheath covers them. In other words, the axon merely rests in a portion of the neurolemmocyte rather than being wrapped by successive layers of the plasma membrane. In the CNS, unmyelinated axons are not associated with oligodendrocytes.

14.3b Nerve Impulse Conduction

The myelin sheath insulates an axon. Note in figure 14.9 that small spaces interrupt the myelin sheath between adjacent oligodendrocytes or neurolemmocytes. These gaps are called **neurofibril nodes,** or *nodes of Ranvier.* At these nodes, and only at these nodes, can a change in voltage occur across the plasma membrane and result in the movement of a nerve impulse. Thus, in a myelinated axon, the nerve impulse seems to "jump" from neurofibril node to neurofibril node, a process called **saltatory conduction.** In an unmyelinated axon, the

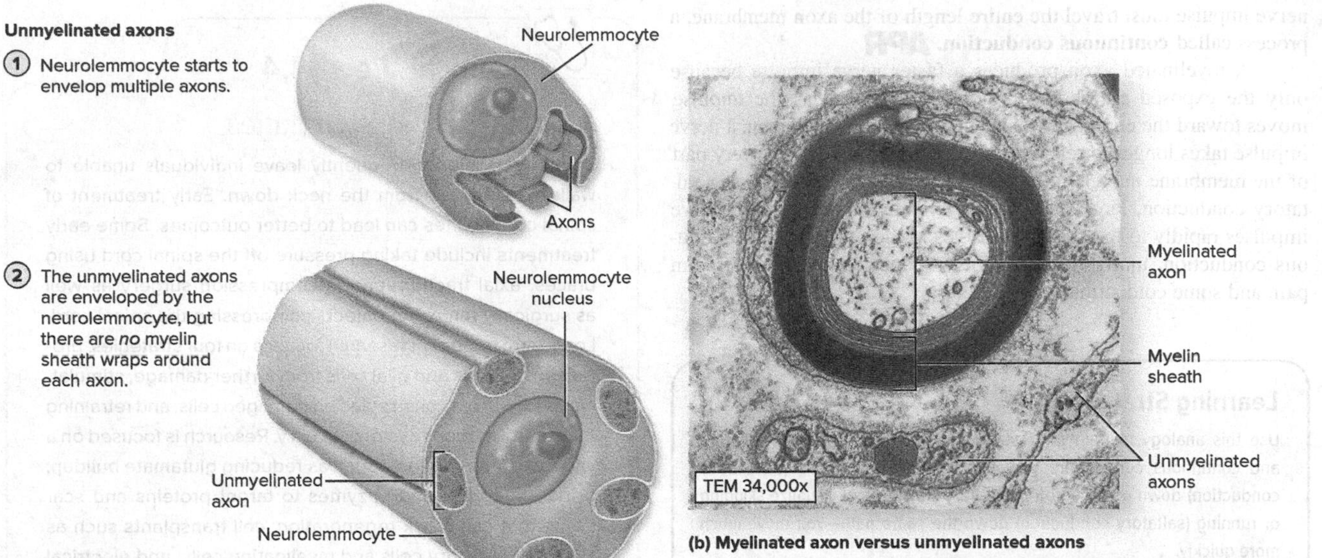
Unmyelinated axons
1 Neurolemmocyte starts to envelop multiple axons.
Neurolemmocyte
Axons
2 The unmyelinated axons are enveloped by the neurolemmocyte, but there are no myelin sheath wraps around each axon.
Neurolemmocyte nucleus
Unmyelinated axon
Neurolemmocyte
(a) Unmyelinated axon
Myelinated axon
Myelin sheath
Unmyelinated axons
TEM 34,000x
(b) Myelinated axon versus unmyelinated axons

Figure 14.10

Comparison of Unmyelinated and Myelinated Axons. (*a*) Unmyelinated axons are surrounded by a neurolemmocyte but are *not* wrapped in a myelin sheath. (*b*) An electron micrograph shows a myelinated axon and some unmyelinated axons.

(b) Dr. Dennis Emery, Iowa State University/McGraw-Hill Education

Clinical View 14.3

Nervous System Disorders Affecting Myelin

Multiple sclerosis (MS) is an autoimmune disorder of the central nervous system, where there is progressive demyelination of neurons accompanied by the destruction of oligodendrocytes. This disrupts the conduction of nerve impulses, leading to impaired sensory perception and motor coordination. Repeated inflammatory events at myelinated sites cause scarring (sclerosis), and over time some function is permanently lost. The disease is usually diagnosed in young adults between the ages of 15 and 45. It is more common in women than in men and appears to have strong geographic ties. MS progresses slowly, and most patients lead productive lives, especially during recurring periods of remission. Symptoms are diverse, because almost any myelinated site in the brain or spinal cord may be affected. Typical symptoms include vision problems, muscle weakness and spasms, urinary infections and bladder incontinence, and drastic mood changes.

Treatment depends upon the stage and severity of the disease and focuses on both the underlying immune system disorder as well as alleviation of symptoms. Steroids are useful during periods of acute symptoms, whereas interferons (natural proteins produced by the immune system) are used for prolonged therapy. Experiments have shown that one form of interferon lowers the activity of immune cells, reducing the number and severity of attacks.

Guillain-Barré syndrome (GBS) is a peripheral nervous system disorder in which inflammation causes loss of myelin from the peripheral nerves and spinal nerve roots. It is characterized by muscle weakness that begins in the distal limbs but rapidly advances to involve proximal muscles as well (ascending paralysis). Most cases of GBS are preceded by an acute, infectious respiratory or gastrointestinal illness. Both bacterial and viral vectors have been identified. GBS appears to be an immune-mediated condition, but steroids provide little improvement. Use of intravenous immunoglobulins (see section 24.3a) show better results, and most people recover almost all neurologic function on their own with little medical intervention.

This individual with multiple sclerosis uses two canes to assist with walking.

Don Emmert/AFP/Getty Images

nerve impulse must travel the entire length of the axon membrane, a process called **continuous conduction.** APR

A myelinated axon produces a faster nerve impulse because only the exposed membrane regions are affected as the impulse moves toward the end of the axon. In an unmyelinated axon, a nerve impulse takes longer to reach the end of the axon because every part of the membrane must be affected by the voltage change. Using saltatory conduction, large-diameter, myelinated axons conduct nerve impulses rapidly to the skeletal muscles in the limbs. Using continuous conduction, unmyelinated axons conduct nerve impulses from pain and some cold stimuli.

Learning Strategy 14.4

Use this analogy to help understand the difference between saltatory and continuous conduction: Visualize walking heel-to-toe (continuous conduction) down a path—you move very slowly. Now visualize skipping or running (saltatory conduction) down the same path—you move much more quickly.

Clinical View 14.4

Treating Spinal Cord Injuries

Spinal cord injuries frequently leave individuals unable to walk or paralyzed from the neck down. Early treatment of spinal cord injuries can lead to better outcomes. Some early treatments include taking pressure off the spinal cord using braces, axial traction, and decompression surgery as well as surgically removing objects compressing the spinal cord. Long-term treatment research focuses on four strategies: protecting neurons and glial cells from further damage, stimulating regrowth of axons, replacing damaged cells, and retraining the central nervous system circuitry. Research is focused on a variety of interventions, such as reducing glutamate buildup; using antibodies and enzymes to target proteins and scar tissue that can block regeneration; cell transplants such as stem cell olfactory cells and myelinating cells; and electrical stimulation in various forms. Hundreds of clinical trials are ongoing, so we must await their findings.

WHAT DO YOU THINK?

3 If myelinated axons produce faster nerve impulses than unmyelinated axons, why aren't all axons in the body myelinated?

WHAT DID YOU LEARN?

7 Explain the differences and similarities of myelination in the PNS and the CNS.

8 What are neurofibril nodes and what is their role?

14.4 Axon Regeneration

✓ Learning Objectives

12. Describe the conditions under which axons can regenerate.
13. Explain the events that occur after injury to a PNS axon.

PNS axons are vulnerable to cuts, crushing injuries, and other types of trauma. However, a damaged axon can regenerate if the cell body remains intact and a critical amount of neurilemma (see section 14.3a) remains. The success of PNS axon regeneration depends upon two primary factors: (1) the amount of damage, and (2) the distance between the site of the damaged axon and the structure it innervates. The possibility of repair is decreased with an increase in either of these two factors.

Neurolemmocytes play an active role in regeneration. This process is illustrated in **figure 14.11** and follows these stages:

1. The axon is severed by some type of trauma.
2. The portion of the axon proximal to the trauma seals off by membrane fusion and swells. The swelling is a result of axoplasmic flow (slow transport) from the neuron cell body through the axon. At the same time, the distal part of the axon severed from the cell body and the myelin sheath surrounding it breaks down—a process called **Wallerian** (waw-lē′rē-ăn) **degeneration.** Macrophages (phagocytic cells) remove the debris. However, the neurilemma in the distal region survives.
3. The neurilemma, in conjunction with the remaining endoneurium, forms a *regeneration tube.*
4. The axon regenerates and remyelination occurs. The regeneration tube guides the axon sprout as it begins to grow rapidly through the regeneration tube at a rate of about 2 to 5 millimeters per day. This occurs under the influence of nerve growth factors released by the neurolemmocytes.
5. Innervation is restored as the axon reestablishes contact with its original structure. The structure is either a receptor for sensory neurons or an effector for motor neurons to regain function of a muscle or a gland.

Potential regeneration of damaged neurons within the CNS is very limited for several reasons. First, oligodendrocytes do not release a nerve growth factor, and in fact they actively inhibit axon growth by producing and secreting several growth-inhibitory molecules. Second, the large number of axons crowded within the CNS tends to complicate regrowth activities. Finally, both astrocytes and connective tissue coverings may form some scar tissue that obstructs axon regrowth. (See Clinical View 14.4: "Treating Spinal Cord Injuries" in section 14.4.)

WHAT DID YOU LEARN?

9 What two primary factors determine PNS axon regeneration?

14.5 Nerves

✓ Learning Objectives

14. Describe the organization and structure of a nerve.
15. Explain how nerves are classified structurally and functionally.

A **nerve** is a cablelike bundle of parallel axons. Although a single axon typically must be viewed using a microscope, a nerve tends to be a macroscopic structure. **Figure 14.12** shows a typical nerve. Like a muscle, a nerve has three successive connective tissue wrappings:

- An individual axon in a myelinated neuron is surrounded by neurolemmocytes and then wrapped in the **endoneurium**

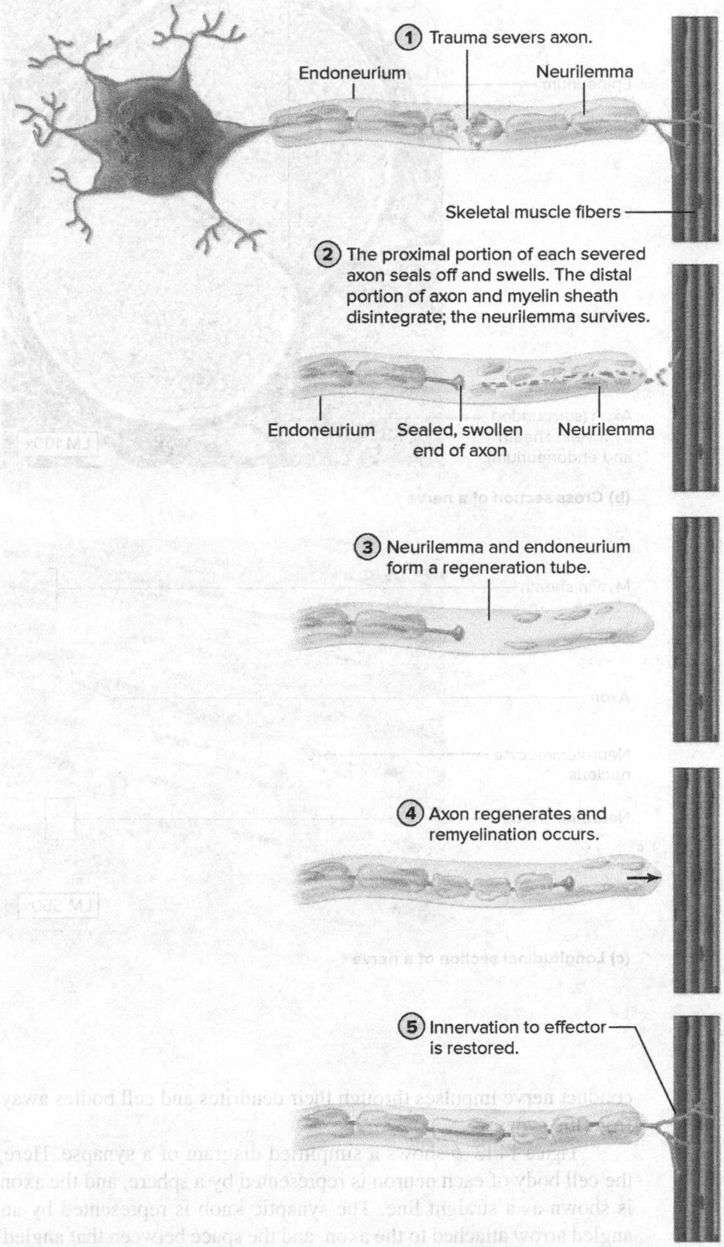

1 Trauma severs axon.
Endoneurium
Neurilemma
Skeletal muscle fibers
2 The proximal portion of each severed axon seals off and swells. The distal portion of axon and myelin sheath disintegrate; the neurilemma survives.
Endoneurium
Sealed, swollen end of axon
Neurilemma
3 Neurilemma and endoneurium form a regeneration tube.
4 Axon regenerates and remyelination occurs.
5 Innervation to effector is restored.

Figure 14.11

Regeneration of PNS Axons. Following injury to a peripheral nerve, the severed axons in the nerve may be repaired and grow out to reinnervate their effector cells (in this case, skeletal muscle fibers).

(en′d ō-nū′rē-ŭm; *endon* = within), a delicate layer of areolar connective tissue that separates and electrically isolates each axon. Also within this connective tissue layer are capillaries that supply each axon.

- Groups of axons are wrapped into separate bundles called **fascicles** (fas′i-k ĕl) by a cellular dense irregular connective tissue layer called the **perineurium** (per′i-nū′rē-ŭm; *peri* = around). This layer supports blood vessels supplying the capillaries within the endoneurium.
- All of the fascicles are bundled together by a superficial connective tissue covering termed the **epineurium** (ep′i-n ū′rē-ŭm; *epi* = upon). This thick layer of dense irregular connective tissue encloses the entire nerve, providing both support and protection to the fascicles within the layer.

Nerves are a component of the peripheral nervous system. Sensory neurons convey sensory information to the central nervous system, motor neurons convey motor impulses from the central nervous system to the muscles and glands. Mixed nerves convey both types of information.

WHAT DID YOU LEARN?

10. Sketch and label a peripheral nerve cross section, showing at least one myelinated axon within one fascicle, endoneurium, perineurium, and epineurium.
11. Regeneration of a severed axon has a better chance for success in the PNS than in the CNS. Why is regeneration in the CNS less likely to succeed?

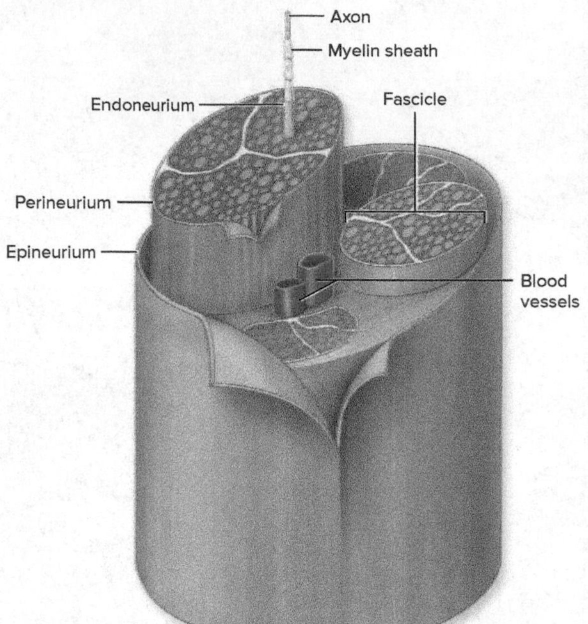

(a) Nerve composition

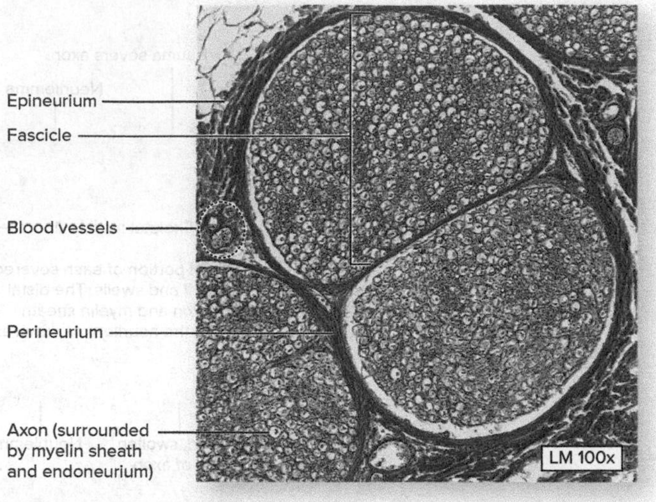

(b) Cross section of a nerve

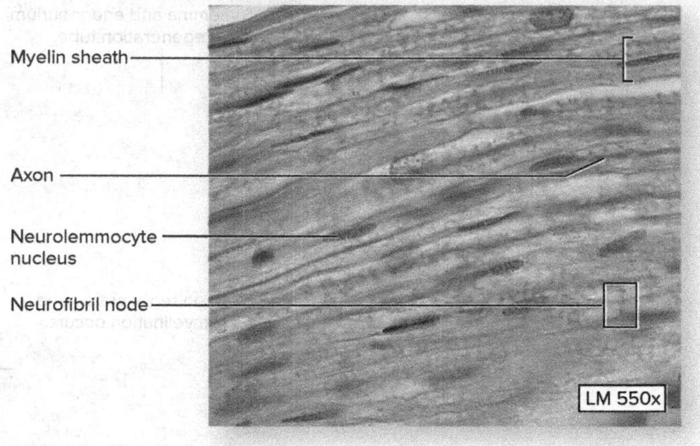

(c) Longitudinal section of a nerve

Figure 14.12

Nerve Structure. (*a*) A nerve is formed from many parallel axons wrapped by successive connective tissue layers. (*b*) LM shows a cross section of a nerve. (*c*) A photomicrograph shows a longitudinal section of a nerve.

(b) Science Photo Library/Alamy Stock Photo; (c) John F. Ash

14.6 Synapses

✓ Learning Objectives

16. Describe the components of the various types of synapses.
17. Summarize and explain the events that occur during the conduction of nerve impulses in electrical and chemical synapses.

Axons terminate as they contact other neurons, muscle cells, or gland cells at specialized junctions called **synapses** (sy-nap'sez; *syn* = together, *hapto* = to clasp) where the nerve impulse is transmitted to the other cell. **Figure 14.13*a*** shows an axon transmitting a nerve impulse to another neuron at a synapse. As the axon approaches the cell onto which it will terminate, it generally branches repeatedly into several unmyelinated terminal arborizations. Additionally, the synaptic endings usually form swellings called synaptic knobs at the ends of the axon branches. A typical synapse in the CNS consists of the close association of a **presynaptic** (prē'sin-ap'tik; *pre* = before) **neuron** and a **postsynaptic** (pōst'sin-ap'tik; *post* = after) **neuron** at a region where their plasma membranes are separated by a very narrow space called the **synaptic cleft.** Presynaptic neurons transmit nerve impulses through their axons toward a synapse; postsynaptic neurons conduct nerve impulses through their dendrites and cell bodies away from the synapse.

Figure 14.13 *b* shows a simplified diagram of a synapse. Here, the cell body of each neuron is represented by a sphere, and the axon is shown as a straight line. The synaptic knob is represented by an angled arrow attached to the axon, and the space between that angled arrow and the cell body of the next neuron is the synapse.

Axons may establish synaptic contacts with any portion of the surface of another neuron, except those regions covered by a myelin sheath. Three common types of synapses are axodendritic, axosomatic, and axoaxonic (figure 14.13*c*):

- The **axodendritic** (ak's ō-den-drit'ik) **synapse** is the most common type. It occurs between the synaptic knobs of a presynaptic neuron and the dendrites of the postsynaptic neuron. These specific connections occur either on the expanded tips of narrow dendritic spines or on the shaft of the dendrite.
- The **axosomatic** (ak's ō-sō-mat'ik) **synapse** occurs between synaptic knobs and the cell body of the postsynaptic neuron.
- The **axoaxonic** (ak's ō-ak-son'ik) **synapse** is the least common synapse and far less understood. It occurs between the synaptic

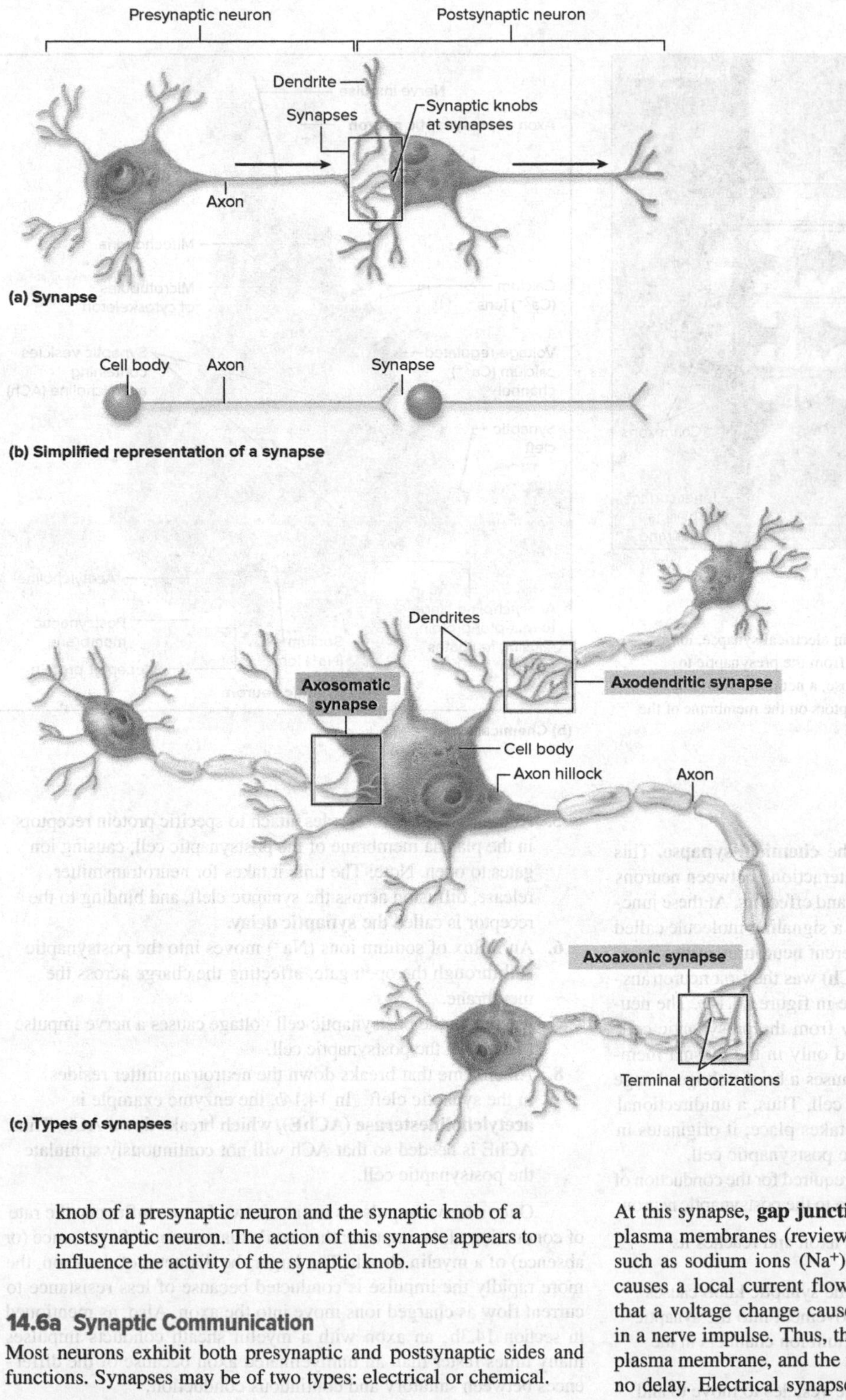

Figure 14.13

Synapses. Synapses are intercellular junctions where two excitable cells come in contact to exchange information. (*a*) A synapse occurs where the plasma membrane of a presynaptic neuron synaptic knob comes in close proximity to the plasma membrane of a postsynaptic neuron. Arrows indicate the direction of nerve impulse flow. (*b*) In this simplified representation of a synapse, the spheres represent the cell bodies of the presynaptic and postsynaptic cells, the line represents the axon, and the angled arrow represents the synaptic knobs. (*c*) An axodendritic synapse occurs between an axon and a dendrite; an axosomatic synapse occurs between an axon and a cell body; and an axoaxonic synapse is between an axon and another axon.

knob of a presynaptic neuron and the synaptic knob of a postsynaptic neuron. The action of this synapse appears to influence the activity of the synaptic knob.

14.6a Synaptic Communication

Most neurons exhibit both presynaptic and postsynaptic sides and functions. Synapses may be of two types: electrical or chemical.

Electrical Synapses

In an **electrical synapse,** the plasma membranes of the presynaptic and postsynaptic cells are bound tightly together. Electrical synapses are fast and secure, and they permit two-way signaling. At this synapse, **gap junctions** formed by connexons between both plasma membranes (review section 4.1c) facilitate the flow of ions, such as sodium ions (Na^+), between the cells **(figure 14.14*a*)**. This causes a local current flow between neighboring cells. Remember that a voltage change caused by movement of charged ions results in a nerve impulse. Thus, these cells act as if they shared a common plasma membrane, and the nerve impulse passes between them with no delay. Electrical synapses are not very common in the brains of mammals. In humans, for example, these synapses occur primarily between smooth muscle cells (such as the smooth muscle in the intestines), where quick, uniform innervation is essential. Electrical synapses are also located in cardiac muscle at the intercalated discs (see section 4.4a).

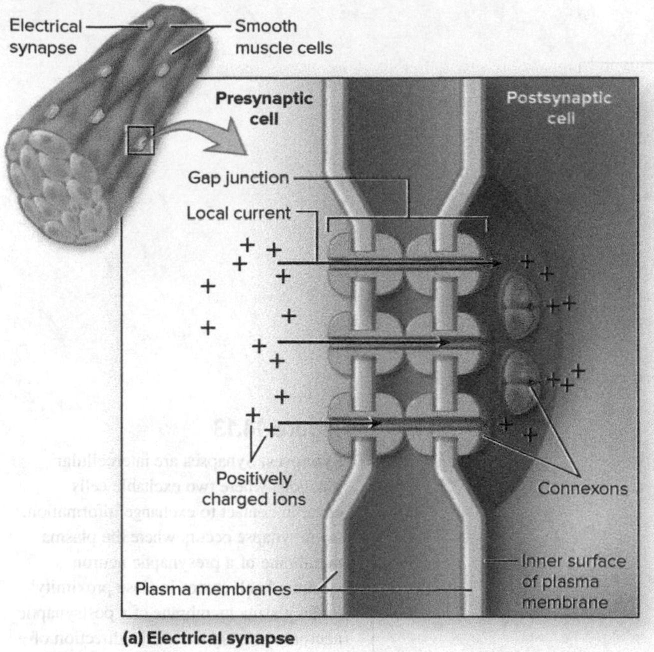

(a) Electrical synapse

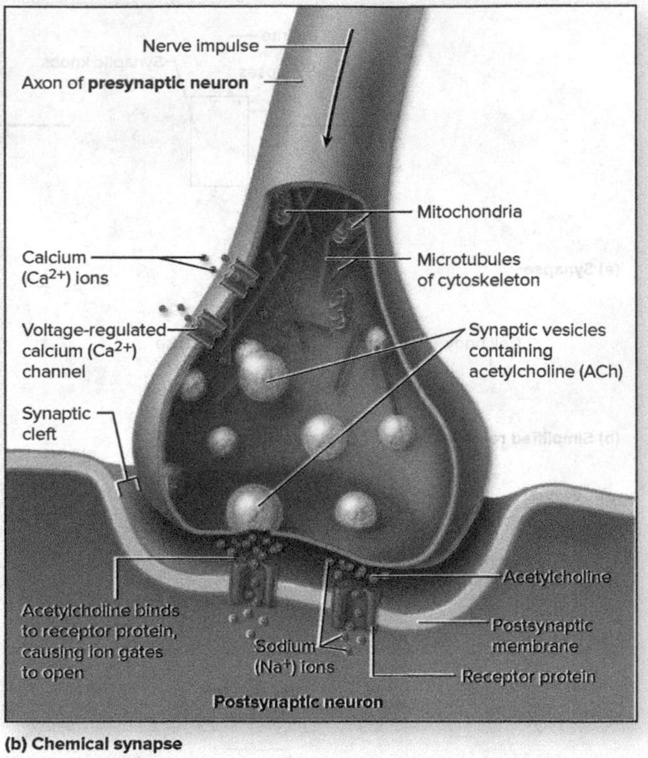

(b) Chemical synapse

Figure 14.14

Electrical and Chemical Synapses. *(a)* In an electrical synapse, ions pass through gap junctions between neurons from the presynaptic to the postsynaptic cell. *(b)* In a chemical synapse, a neurotransmitter is released from the presynaptic neuron to receptors on the membrane of the postsynaptic neuron. **APR**

Chemical Synapses

The most numerous type of synapse is the **chemical synapse.** This type of synapse facilitates most of the interactions between neurons and all communications between neurons and effectors. At these junctions, the presynaptic membrane releases a signaling molecule called a **neurotransmitter.** There are many different neurotransmitters used in the nervous system. **Acetylcholine (ACh)** was the first neurotransmitter to be identified and is our example in figure 14.14*b*. The neurotransmitter molecules are released only from the presynaptic cell. They then bind to receptor proteins found only in the plasma membrane of the postsynaptic cell, and this causes a brief voltage change across the membrane of the postsynaptic cell. Thus, a unidirectional flow of information and communication takes place; it originates in the presynaptic cell and is received by the postsynaptic cell.

A very precise sequence of events is required for the conduction of a nerve impulse from the presynaptic neuron to the postsynaptic neuron:

1. A nerve impulse travels through the axon and reaches its synaptic knob.
2. The arrival of the nerve impulse at the synaptic knob causes an increase in calcium ion (Ca^{2+}) movement into the synaptic knob through voltage-regulated calcium ion channels in the membrane.
3. Entering calcium ions cause synaptic vesicles to move to and bind to the inside surface of the membrane; neurotransmitter molecules (e.g.,ACh) within the synaptic vesicles are released into the synaptic cleft by exocytosis.
4. Neurotransmitter molecules diffuse across the synaptic cleft to the plasma membrane of the postsynaptic cell.
5. Neurotransmitter molecules attach to specific protein receptors in the plasma membrane of the postsynaptic cell, causing ion gates to open. Note: The time it takes for neurotransmitter release, diffusion across the synaptic cleft, and binding to the receptor is called the **synaptic delay.**
6. An influx of sodium ions (Na^+) moves into the postsynaptic cell through the open gate, affecting the charge across the membrane.
7. Change in the postsynaptic cell voltage causes a nerve impulse to begin in the postsynaptic cell.
8. An enzyme that breaks down the neurotransmitter resides in the synaptic cleft. In 14.14*b*, the enzyme example is **acetylcholinesterase (AChE),** which breaks down ACh. Thus, AChE is needed so that ACh will not continuously stimulate the postsynaptic cell.

Once a nerve impulse is initiated, two factors influence the rate of conduction of the impulse: the axon's diameter and the presence (or absence) of a myelin sheath. The larger the diameter of the axon, the more rapidly the impulse is conducted because of less resistance to current flow as charged ions move into the axon. Also, as mentioned in section 14.3b, an axon with a myelin sheath conducts impulses many times faster than an unmyelinated axon because of the differences between saltatory and continuous conduction.

WHAT DID YOU LEARN?

12 What are the two types of synaptic communication?

13 What factors influence the impulse conduction rate?

14.7 Neural Integration and Neural Circuits

✓ Learning Objective

18. Identify the four different neuronal circuits, and describe how each one functions.

The nervous system is able to coordinate and integrate nervous activity in part because billions of interneurons within the CNS are grouped in complex patterns called **neural circuits** (or *neuronal pathways* or *pools*). Neural circuits are defined based upon function, not anatomy, into four types: converging, diverging, reverberating, and parallel-after-discharge **(figure 14.15)**. A circuit may be localized, with its neurons confined to one specific location, or its neurons may be distributed in several different regions of the CNS. However, all neural circuits are restricted in their number of input sources and output destinations.

In a **converging circuit,** nerve impulses converge (come together) at a single postsynaptic neuron (figure 14.15*a*). This neuron receives input from several presynaptic neurons. For example, multiple

Clinical View 14.5

Amyotrophic Lateral Sclerosis

Amyotrophic lateral sclerosis (ALS; often called *Lou Gehrig disease* or *Charcot disease*) is a well-known motor neuron disease that typically progresses quickly and is fatal. (Stephen Hawking was the rare individual who lived with ALS for decades after his initial diagnosis.) It affects neurons in both the brain and the spinal cord, leading to progressive degeneration of the somatic motor system. ALS patients generally have weakened and atrophied muscles, especially in the hands and forearms. Additionally, they may experience speech impairment, breathing difficulties, and chewing and swallowing problems that result in choking or excessive drooling. However, the disease does not affect sensory abilities, such as hearing, sight, or smell. No effective treatment or cure exists.

ALS affects all sexes, but it occurs in males more often. About 90% to 95% of ALS cases occur in families with no previous history of the disease. In contrast, about 5% to 10% of cases are inherited and called *familial* (meaning that more members of the same family are affected than can be accounted for by chance).

Individual with amyotrophic lateral sclerosis.
Realistic Reflections

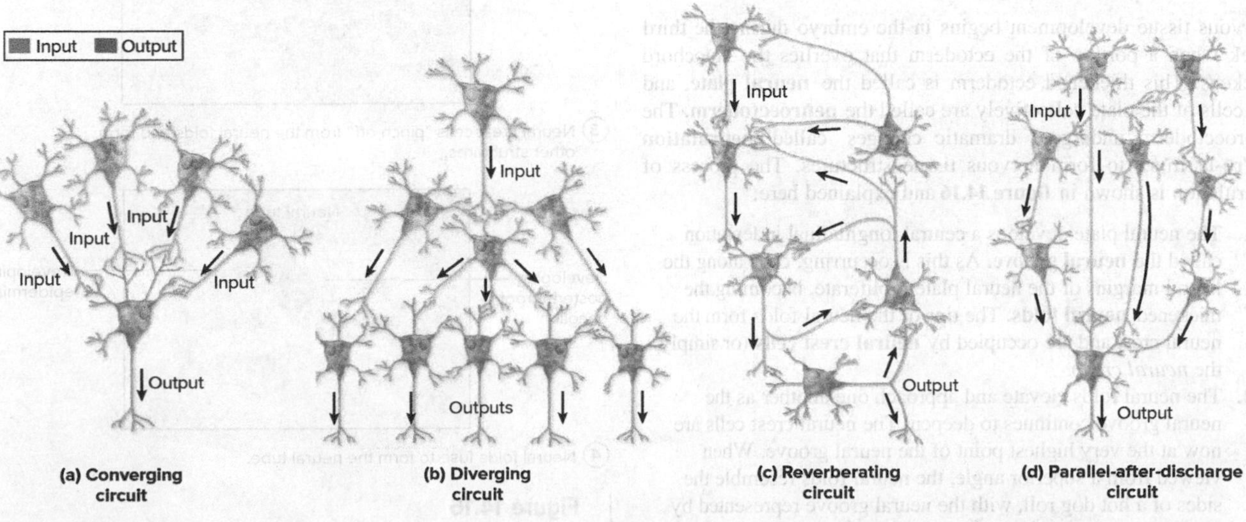

Figure 14.15

Neural Circuits. Neural circuits are groups of neurons arranged in specific patterns through which impulses are conducted and distributed. Four types of neural circuits are recognized: (*a*) converging circuit, (*b*) diverging circuit, (*c*) reverberating circuit, and (*d*) parallel-after-discharge circuit.

sensory neurons synapse on the neurons in the salivary nuclei in the brainstem, resulting in the production of saliva. The various inputs may originate from more than one stimulus—in this example, smelling food, seeing the time on the clock indicating dinnertime, hearing food preparation activities, or seeing pictures of food in a magazine. These multiple inputs lead to a single output, the production of saliva.

A **diverging circuit** spreads information from one presynaptic neuron to several postsynaptic neurons, or from one circuit to multiple circuits (figure 14.15*b*). For example, activation of a few neurons in the motor cortex of the brain can lead to excitation of thousands of muscle fibers in a muscle. In this case, a single or a few inputs lead to multiple outputs.

Reverberating circuits use feedback to produce a repeated, cyclical stimulation of the circuit, or a reverberation (figure 14.15*c*). Once activated, a reverberating circuit may continue to function until either inhibitory stimuli or synaptic fatigue breaks the cycle. (**Synaptic fatigue** occurs when repeated stimuli cause temporary inability of the presynaptic cell to meet demands of synaptic transmission as a result of a lack of neurotransmitter production.) The repetitious nature of a reverberating circuit ensures that we continue breathing while we are asleep.

In a **parallel-after-discharge circuit,** several neurons or neural circuits process the same information at one time. A single presynaptic neuron stimulates different groups of neurons, each of which passes the nerve impulse along a pathway that ultimately synapses with a common postsynaptic cell (figure 14.15*d*). This type of circuit is believed to be involved in higher-order thinking, such as the type needed to perform precise mathematical calculations.

WHAT DID YOU LEARN?

14 How is a diverging circuit different from a reverberating circuit?

14.8 Development of the Nervous System

✓ Learning Objective

19. Define and describe the early events in nervous system development.

Nervous tissue development begins in the embryo during the third week when a portion of the ectoderm that overlies the notochord thickens. This thickened ectoderm is called the **neural plate,** and the cells of the plate collectively are called the **neuroectoderm.** The neuroectoderm undergoes dramatic changes, called **neurulation** (nū′rū-lā′shŭn), to form nervous tissue structures. The process of neurulation is shown in **figure 14.16** and explained here:

1. The neural plate develops a central longitudinal indentation called the **neural groove.** As this is occurring, cells along the lateral margins of the neural plate proliferate, becoming the thickened **neural folds.** The tips of the neural folds form the neural crest and are occupied by **neural crest cells** (or simply, the *neural crest*).
2. The neural folds elevate and approach one another as the neural groove continues to deepen. The neural crest cells are now at the very highest point of the neural groove. When viewed from a superior angle, the neural folds resemble the sides of a hot dog roll, with the neural groove represented by the opening in the roll.
3. The neural crest cells "pinch off" from the neural folds and form other structures.

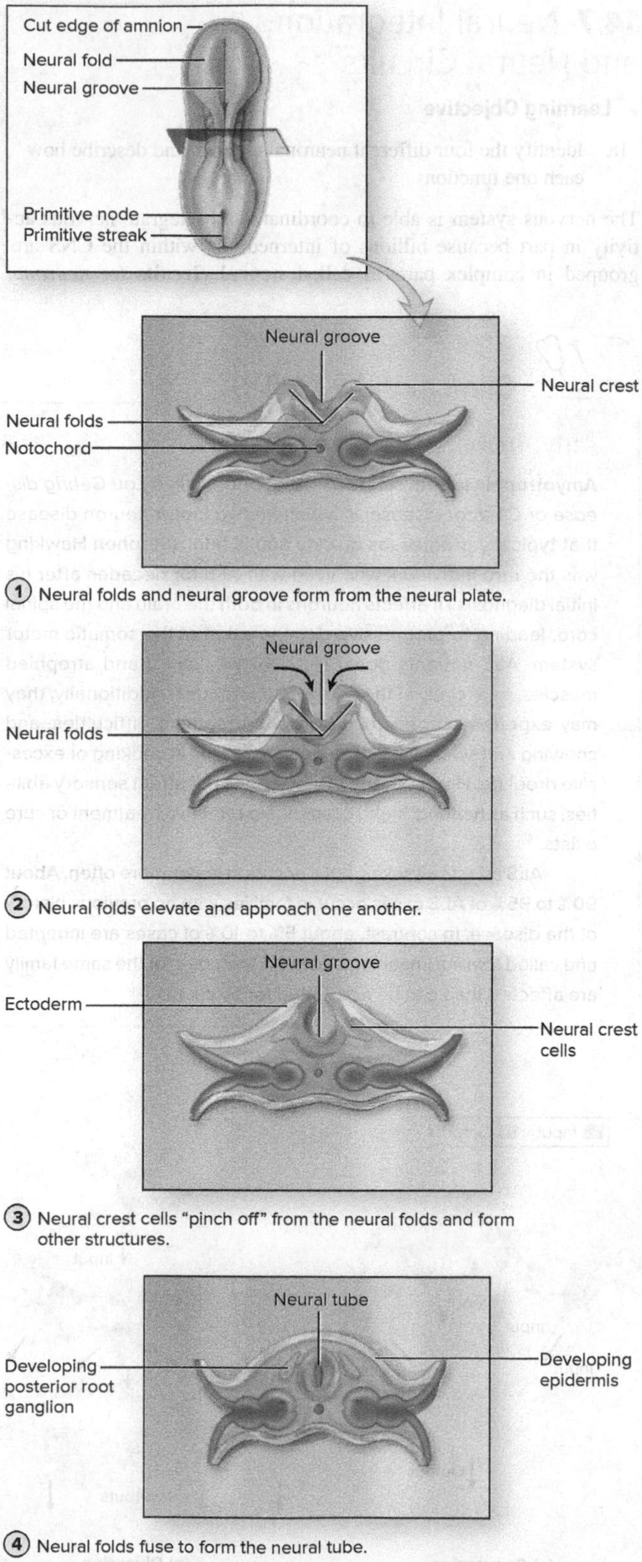

Figure 14.16

Nervous System Development. The process of neurulation begins in the third week, and the neural tube finishes closing by the end of week 4.

4. By the end of the third week, the neural folds have met and fused at the midline, and the neural groove starts to form a **neural tube,** which has an internal lumen called the **neural canal.** The neural tube initially fuses at its midline, and later the neural folds slightly superior and inferior to this midline fuse as well. Thus, the neural tube forms as the neural folds "zip" together both superiorly and inferiorly.

For a short time, the neural tube is open at both its ends. These openings, called **neuropores** (nū′rō-pōr), close during the end of the fourth week. The opening closest to the future head is the **cranial neuropore,** whereas the opening closest to the future buttocks region is the **caudal neuropore.** If these openings do not close, the developing human will have a neural tube defect (see Clinical View 14.6: "Neural Tube Defects" earlier in this section). The developing neural tube forms the central nervous system. In particular, the cranial part of the neural tube expands to form the brain (see section 15.1a), while the caudal part of the neural tube expands to form the spinal cord (see section 16.6). Also, please refer back to section 7.7 to review vertebral development.

Clinical View 14.6

Neural Tube Defects

Neural tube defects (NTDs) are serious developmental deformities of the brain, spinal cord, and meninges. The two basic categories of NTDs are anencephaly and spina bifida. Both conditions result from localized failure of the developing neural tube to close.

Anencephaly (an′en-sef′ă-lē; *an* = without, *enkephalos* = brain) is the substantial or complete absence of a brain as well as the bones making up the cranium. Infants with anencephaly rarely live longer than a few hours following birth. Fortunately, neural tube defects of this magnitude are rare, and are easily detected with prenatal ultrasound, thus alerting the parents to the condition.

Spina bifida (spī′nă bĭ′fid′ă; *spina* = spine, *bifidus* = cleft in two parts) occurs more frequently than anencephaly. This defect results when the caudal portion of the neural tube, often in the lumbar or sacral region, fails to close. Spina bifida has several forms, the most common and severe is **spina bifida cystica.** In spina bifida cystica, almost no vertebral arch forms, so the posterior aspect of the spinal cord in this region is left unprotected (**figures *a* and *b***). Typically, there is a large cystic structure in the back, filled with cerebrospinal fluid (CSF) and covered by a thin layer of skin or in some cases only by meninges (protective membranes around the spinal cord). Surgery is generally done promptly to close the defect, reduce the risk of infection, and preserve existing spinal cord function. Functional effects of spina bifida syndrome are determined by the anatomic level of spinal cord involvement. With early medical intervention, most children with spina bifida cystica live well into adulthood.

Spina bifida occulta is less serious, but much more common than the cystica variety. This condition is characterized by a partial defect of the vertebral arch, typically involving the vertebral lamina and spinous process (**figure *c***). People with this condition are generally asymptomatic, and it is detected incidentally during an x-ray for an unrelated reason. Estimates of the incidence of spina bifida occulta range as high as 17% of the population in some x-ray studies.

Although the risk of neural tube defects cannot be eliminated, it can be greatly reduced. Researchers have discovered that increased intake of the B vitamin **folic acid (folate)** by pregnant women is correlated with a decreased incidence of neural tube defects. Folic acid is critical to DNA formation and are necessary for cellular division and tissue differentiation. Thus, pregnant women are encouraged to take prenatal supplements containing high levels of this vitamin, and the food industry has begun fortifying many breads and grains with folate as well.

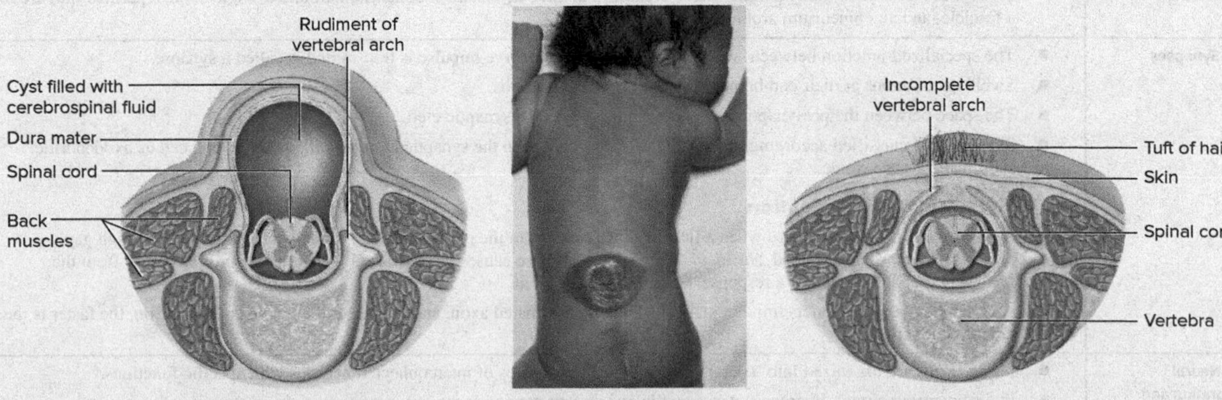

Spina bifida is a neural tube disorder that occurs in two forms: (a, b) spina bifida cystica; (c) spina bifida occulta. (See section 7.7 for a description of vertebral development.)

(b) Wellcome Photo Library, Wellcome Images

Clinical Terms

demyelination (dē-mī′e-lin- ā′shŭn) Progressive loss or destruction of myelin in the CNS and PNS with preservation of the axons; often leads to loss of sensation and/or motor control.

neuritis (nū-rī′tis) Inflammation of a nerve.

neuropathy (nū-rop′ă-thē) Classical term for a disorder affecting any segment of the nervous system.

neurotoxin (nū′rō-tok′sin) Any poison that acts specifically on nervous tissue.

Chapter Summary

14.1 Organization of the Nervous System	■ The nervous system includes all the nervous tissue in the body. **14.1a Structural Organization: Central and Peripheral Nervous Systems** ■ The central nervous system is composed of the brain and the spinal cord. ■ The peripheral nervous system is composed of the cranial nerves, spinal nerves, and ganglia. **14.1b Functional Organization: Sensory and Motor Nervous Systems** ■ The nervous system is functionally subdivided into a sensory nervous system that conveys sensory information to the CNS, and a motor nervous system that conducts motor commands to muscles and glands.
14.2 Cytology of Nervous Tissue	■ Neurons are excitable cells that transmit nerve impulses, and glial cells completely surround neurons and support them. **14.2a Neurons** ■ A generalized neuron has a cell body and processes called dendrites and an axon. They are classified structurally by the number of processes attached to the cell body (unipolar, bipolar, or multipolar) and functionally as sensory neurons, motor neurons, or interneurons. **14.2b Glial Cells** ■ Glial cells support neurons in the CNS. Astrocytes help form the blood-brain barrier and regulate tissue fluid composition; ependymal cells line CNS cavities and produce cerebrospinal fluid; microglial cells act as phagocytes in nervous tissue; and oligodendrocytes myelinate CNS axons. ■ In the PNS, satellite cells support neuron cell bodies in ganglia, and neurolemmocytes myelinate PNS axons.
14.3 Myelination of Axons	■ A nerve impulse is the rapid movement of a charge along a neuron's plasma membrane. **14.3a Myelination** ■ Oligodendrocytes (CNS) and neurolemmocytes (PNS) wrap around axons of neurons, forming a discontinuous myelin sheath along the axon, with small gaps called neurofibril nodes. **14.3b Nerve Impulse Conduction** ■ The myelin sheath insulates the axonal membrane, resulting in faster nerve impulse conduction. ■ Unmyelinated axons are associated with a neurolemmocyte but not ensheathed by it.
14.4 Axon Regeneration	■ Regeneration of damaged neurons is limited to PNS axons that are able to regrow under certain conditions.
14.5 Nerves	■ A nerve is a bundle of many parallel axons organized in three layers: an endoneurium around a single axon, a perineurium around a fascicle, and an epineurium around all of the fascicles.
14.6 Synapses	■ The specialized junction between two excitable cells where a nerve impulse is transmitted is called a synapse. ■ Swellings of axons at their end branches are called synaptic knobs. ■ The space between the presynaptic and postsynaptic cells is the synaptic cleft. ■ Synapses are classified according to the point of contact between the synaptic knob and the postsynaptic cell as axodendritic, axosomatic, or axoaxonic. **14.6a Synaptic Communication** ■ Synapses are termed *electrical* when a flow of ions passes from the presynaptic cell to the postsynaptic cell through gap junctions; synapses are termed *chemical* when a nerve impulse causes the release of a chemical neurotransmitter from the presynaptic cell that induces a response, in the postsynaptic cell. ■ A myelinated axon conducts impulses faster than an unmyelinated axon, and the larger the diameter of the axon, the faster is the rate of conduction.
14.7 Neural Integration and Neural Circuits	■ Interneurons are organized into neural circuits , which are groups of interconnected neurons with specific functions. ■ In a converging circuit, neurons synapse on the same postsynaptic neuron. ■ A diverging circuit spreads information to several neurons. ■ In a reverberating circuit, neurons continue to restimulate presynaptic neurons in the circuit. ■ A parallel-after-discharge circuit involves parallel pathways that process the same information over different amounts of time and deliver that information to the same output cell.

14.8 Development of the Nervous System	■ Nervous tissue development begins in the early embryo with the formation of the neural plate. As this plate grows and develops, a neural groove appears as a depression in the plate, prior to the elevation of neural folds along the lateral side of the plate. The fusion of the neural folds gives rise to a neural tube, from which the brain and spinal cord develop. ■ A neural tube defect can result if part of the neural tube fails to fuse.

Challenge Yourself

Actively write or type your answers in a separate document to reinforce your learning, before checking your answers.

Multiple Choice

Select the best answer from the four choices provided.

1. A mature neuron typically cannot undergo mitosis because it does not have which structure(s)?
   a. a nucleus
   b. ribosomes
   c. centrioles
   d. mitochondria
2. Which nervous system function and term are correctly paired?
   a. respond to information—receptor
   b. respond to information—effector
   c. collect information—effector
   d. collect information—stimuli
3. Which neurons are located only within the CNS?
   a. motor neurons
   b. unipolar neurons
   c. sensory neurons
   d. interneurons
4. Which structure or cell is responsible for increasing the propagation rate of a nerve impulse?
   a. motor neuron
   b. receptor
   c. neurolemmocyte
   d. ganglion
5. Which glial cells help produce CSF in the CNS?
   a. satellite cells
   b. microglial cells
   c. ependymal cells
   d. astrocytes
6. Which of the following is *not* a part of the CNS?
   a. microglial cell
   b. spinal cord
   c. neurolemmocyte
   d. brain
7. Which of these cells transmits, transfers, and processes a nerve impulse?
   a. neurolemmocyte
   b. astrocyte
   c. neuron
   d. oligodendrocyte
8. Which type of neural circuit is repeatedly stimulated by nerve impulse feedback?
   a. converging circuit
   b. diverging circuit
   c. reverberating circuit
   d. parallel-after-discharge circuit
9. Which structures facilitate interactions between presynaptic and postsynaptic membranes in an electrical synapse?
   a. neurofibril nodes
   b. gap junctions
   c. terminal arborizations
   d. neurotransmitters
10. Which of the following best describes an epineurium?
    a. a thick, dense irregular connective tissue layer enclosing the nerve
    b. a group of axons
    c. a delicate layer of areolar connective tissue
    d. a cellular layer of dense regular connective tissue

Content Review

1. What are the three structural types of neurons? How do they compare to the three functional types of neurons?
2. What is the function of sensory neurons?
3. Identify the principal types of glial cells, and briefly discuss the function of each type.
4. How does the myelin sheath differ between the CNS and the PNS?
5. Describe the procedure by which a PNS axon may repair itself.
6. Describe the arrangement and structure of the three coverings that surround axons in ANS nerves.
7. Clearly distinguish among the following: a neuron, an axon, and a nerve.
8. What are the differences between electrical and chemical synapses? Which is the more common type of synapse in humans?
9. Discuss the similarities and differences between converging and parallel-after-discharge circuits.
10. What are the basic developmental events that occur during neurulation?

Developing Critical Reasoning

1. Over a period of 6 to 9 months, Marianne began to experience vision problems as well as weakness and loss of fine control of the skeletal muscles in her leg. Blood tests revealed the presence of antibodies (immune system proteins) that attack myelin. Beyond the presence of the antibodies, what was the cause of Marianne's vision and muscular difficulties?
2. Surgeons were able to reattach an amputated limb, sewing both the nerves and the blood vessels back together. After the

surgery, which proceeded very well, the limb regained its blood supply almost immediately, but the limb remained motionless and the patient had no feeling in it for several months. Why did it take longer to reestablish innervation than circulation?

3. Brain trauma (stroke or injury) can cause death of neurons and glial cells. If neurons cannot undergo mitosis, explain processes that allow for nervous system function to be restored to some degree.

Answers to "What Do You Think?"

1. The term *visceral* refers to organs, especially thoracic and abdominal organs such as the heart, lungs, and gastrointestinal tract. Therefore, the parts of the sensory and motor nervous systems that innervate these viscera are called the visceral sensory and visceral motor (autonomic) nervous systems.
2. Tumors occur due to uncontrolled mitotic growth of cells. Because glial cells are mitotic and neurons typically are nonmitotic, a "brain tumor" almost always develops from glial cells.
3. A myelinated axon takes up more space than an unmyelinated axon. There simply isn't enough space in the body to hold myelin sheaths for every axon. Thus, the body conserves this space by myelinating only the axons that must transmit nerve impulses very rapidly.

Design Element: Pencil Icon: Slavojub Pantelic/Shutterstock

NERVOUS SYSTEM

Brain and Cranial Nerves 15

Outline

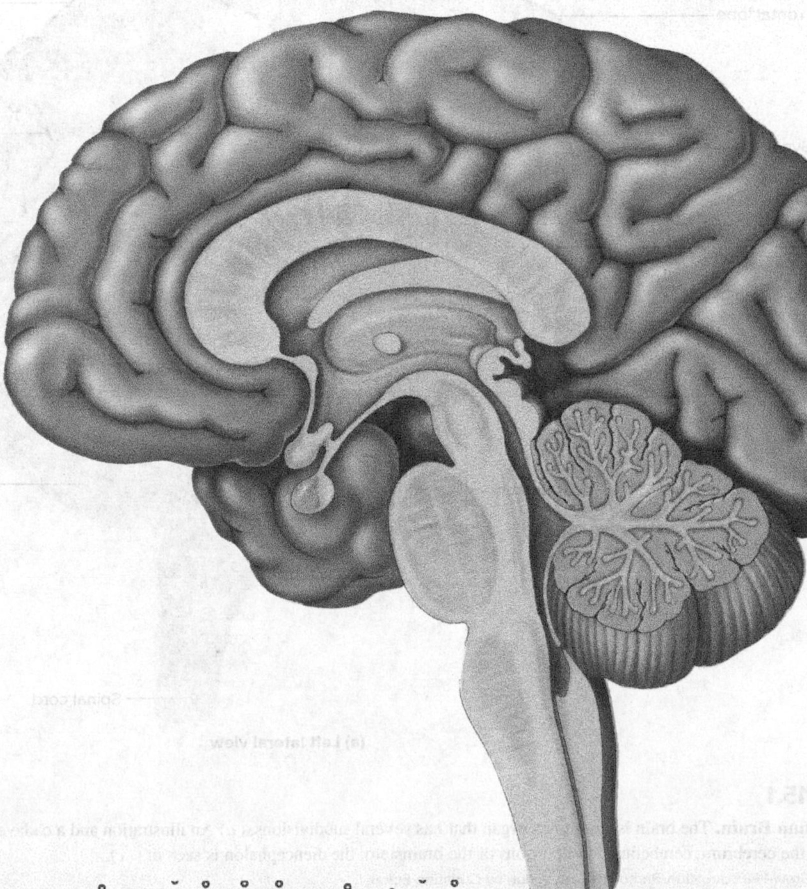

Anatomy & Physiology Revealed 4.0

MODULE 7: NERVOUS SYSTEM

About 4 to 6 million years ago, when the earliest humans were evolving, brain size was a mere 440 cubic centimeters (cc), not much larger than that of a modern chimpanzee. As humans have evolved, brain size has increased steadily and reached an average volume of 1200 cc to 1500 cc and an average weight of 1.35 to 1.4 kilograms. In addition, the texture of the outer surface of the brain (its hemispheres) has changed. Our skull size limits the size of the brain, so the tissue forming the brain's outer surface folded on itself so that more neurons could fit into the space within the skull. Although modern humans display variability in brain size, it isn't the *size* of the brain that determines intelligence, but the number of active synapses among neurons.

The brain is often compared to a computer because they both simultaneously receive and process enormous amounts of information, which they then organize, integrate, file, and store prior to making an appropriate output response. But in some ways this is a weak comparison, because no computer is capable of the multitude of continual adjustments that the brain's neurons perform. The brain can control numerous activities simultaneously, and it can also respond to various stimuli with an amazing degree of versatility.

15.1 Brain Development and Tissue Organization

✓ Learning Objectives

1. Describe the embryonic development of the divisions of the brain.
2. Compare and contrast the organization of gray and white matter in the brain.

The brain is composed of four major regions: the cerebrum, diencephalon, brainstem, and cerebellum. **Figure 15.1** shows the major parts of the adult brain from several views. Our discussion in this chapter focuses on these major brain regions. When viewed superiorly, the cerebrum is divided into two halves, called the left and right

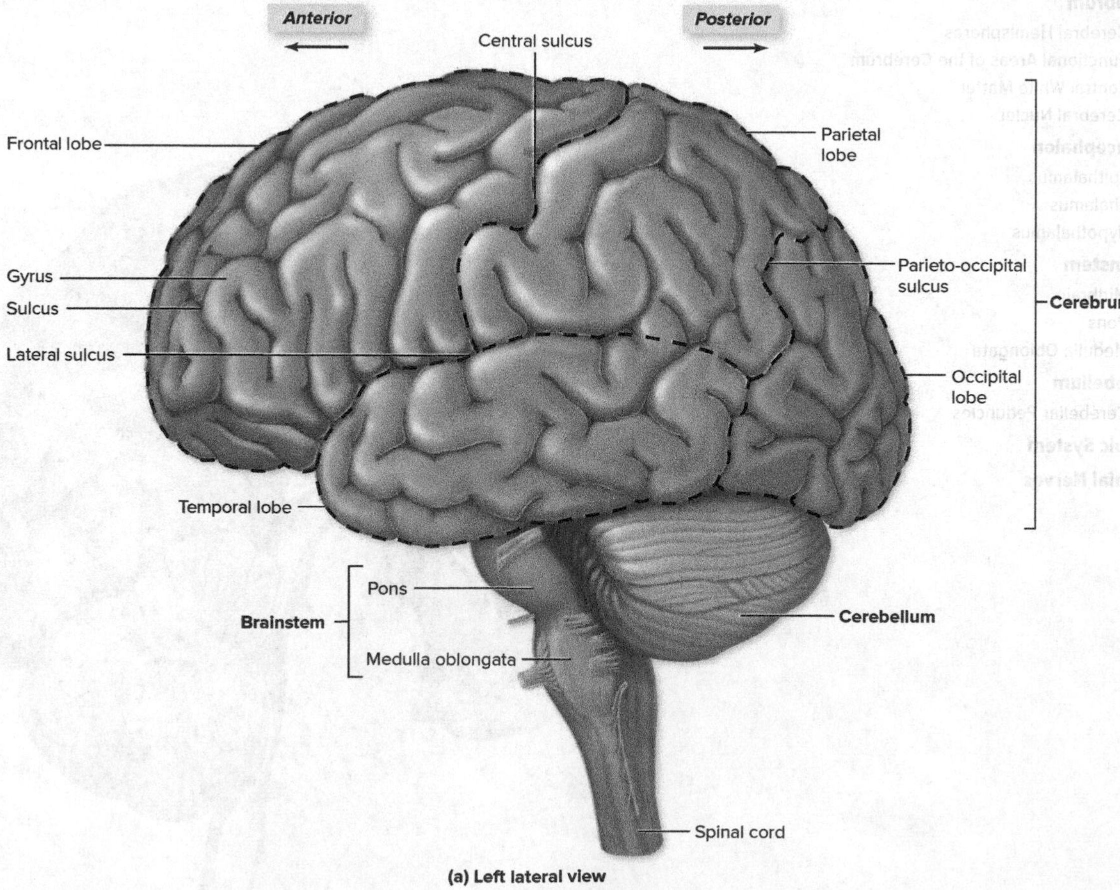

Figure 15.1

The Human Brain. The brain is a complex organ that has several subdivisions. (*a*) An illustration and a cadaver photo show left lateral views of the brain, revealing the cerebrum, cerebellum, and portions of the brainstem; the diencephalon is seen in (*c*).

cerebral hemispheres. Each hemisphere may be further subdivided into five functional areas called lobes. Four lobes are visible superficially, and one is seen only internally (see figure 15.11). The outer surface of an adult brain exhibits folds called **gyri** (jī'rī; sing., *gyrus; gyros* = circle) and shallow depressions between those folds called **sulci** (sŭl'sī; sing., *sulcus;* furrow, ditch). The brain is associated with 12 pairs of cranial nerves (see figure 15.24).

Two directional terms are often used to describe brain anatomy. **Anterior** is synonymous with *rostral* (meaning "toward the nose"), and **posterior** is synonymous with *caudal* (meaning "toward the tail"). (Please see section 1.4 to review all other directional terms that will be used in this chapter.)

15.1a Embryonic Development of the Brain

To understand how the structures of the adult brain are named and connected, it is essential to know how the brain develops. In the human embryo, the brain forms from the cranial (superior) part of the neural tube, which undergoes disproportionate growth rates in different regions. By the late fourth week of development, this growth has formed three **primary brain vesicles,** which eventually give rise to all the different regions of the adult brain. The names of these vesicles describe their relative positions in the developing head: The forebrain is called the **prosencephalon** (pros'en-sef'ă-lon; *proso* = forward, *enkephalos* = brain); the midbrain is called the **mesencephalon** (mes-en-sef'ă-lon; *mes* = middle); and the hindbrain is called the **rhombencephalon** (rom'ben-sef'ă-lon; *rhombo* = rhomboid) **(figure 15.2*a*)**.

By the fifth week of development, the three primary vesicles further develop into five secondary brain vesicles (figure 15.2*b*):

- The **telencephalon** (tel-en-sef'ă-lon; *tel* = head end) arises from the prosencephalon and eventually forms the cerebrum.
- The **diencephalon** (dī-en-sef'ă-lon; *dia* = through) arises from the prosencephalon and eventually forms the thalamus, hypothalamus, and epithalamus.
- The mesencephalon is the only primary vesicle that does not form a new secondary vesicle. After birth, it is renamed the midbrain.
- The **metencephalon** (met'en-sef'ă-lon; *meta* = after) arises from the rhombencephalon and eventually forms the pons and cerebellum.
- The **myelencephalon** (mī'el-en-sef'ă-lon; *myelos* = medulla) also derives from the rhombencephalon, and it eventually forms the medulla oblongata.

Table 15.1 summarizes the embryonic brain structures and their corresponding structures in the adult brain.

During the embryonic and fetal periods, the telencephalon grows rapidly and envelops the diencephalon. As the future brain develops, its surface becomes folded, especially in the telencephalon, leading to the formation of the adult sulci and gyri (see figure 15.1*a*). The bends and creases that occur in the developing brain determine the boundaries of the brain's cavities. Together, the bends, creases, and folds in the telencephalon surface are necessary to fit the massive

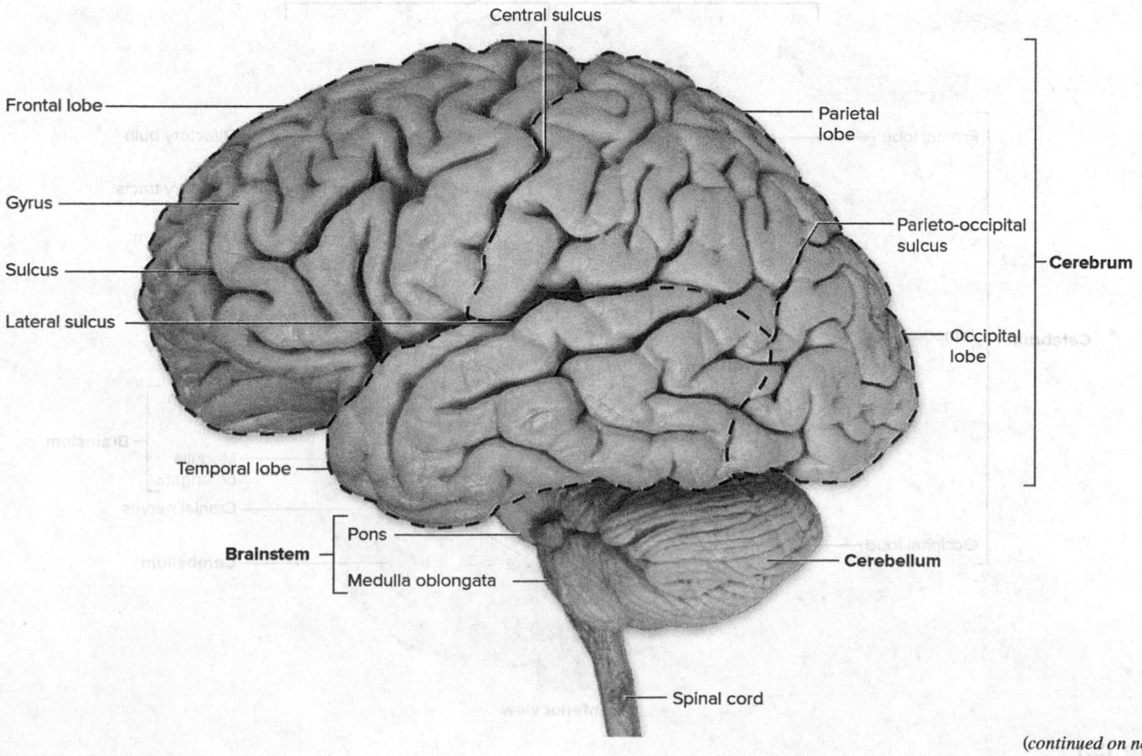
Central sulcus
Frontal lobe
Parietal lobe
Gyrus
Parieto-occipital sulcus
Sulcus
Cerebrum
Lateral sulcus
Occipital lobe
Temporal lobe
Pons
Brainstem
Medulla oblongata
Cerebellum
Spinal cord

(continued on next page)

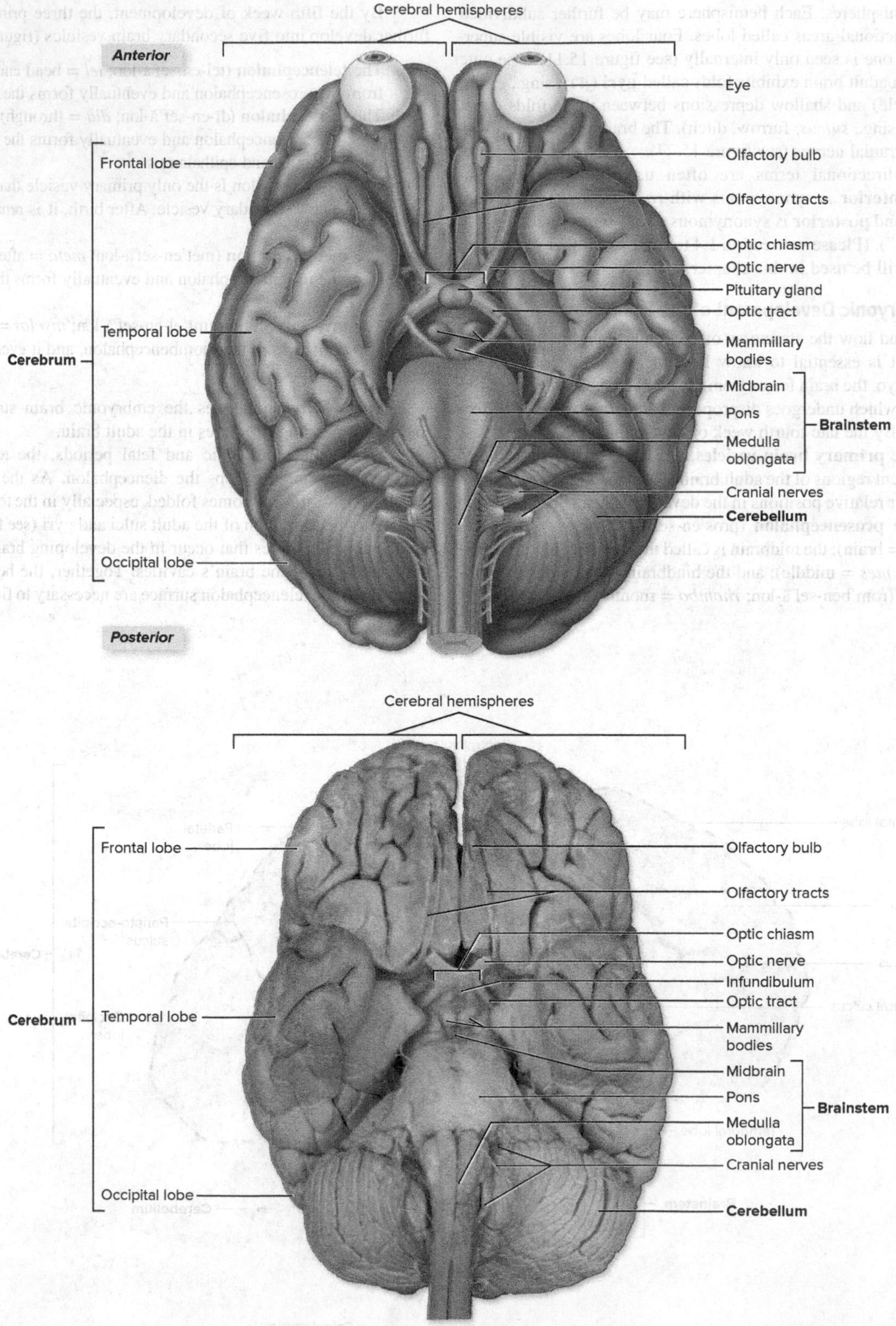
Cerebral hemispheres
Anterior
Eye
Frontal lobe
Olfactory bulb
Olfactory tracts
Optic chiasm
Optic nerve
Pituitary gland
Optic tract
Temporal lobe
Cerebrum
Mammillary bodies
Midbrain
Pons
Brainstem
Medulla oblongata
Cranial nerves
Cerebellum
Occipital lobe
Posterior
Cerebral hemispheres
Frontal lobe
Olfactory bulb
Olfactory tracts
Optic chiasm
Optic nerve
Infundibulum
Optic tract
Cerebrum
Temporal lobe
Mammillary bodies
Midbrain
Pons
Brainstem
Medulla oblongata
Cranial nerves
Occipital lobe
Cerebellum

(b) Inferior view

Figure 15.1

The Human Brain (*continued*). (*b*) An inferior view illustration and cadaver photo best illustrate the cranial nerves arising from the base of the brain. (*c*) Internal structures such as the thalamus and hypothalamus are best seen in midsagittal view. APR

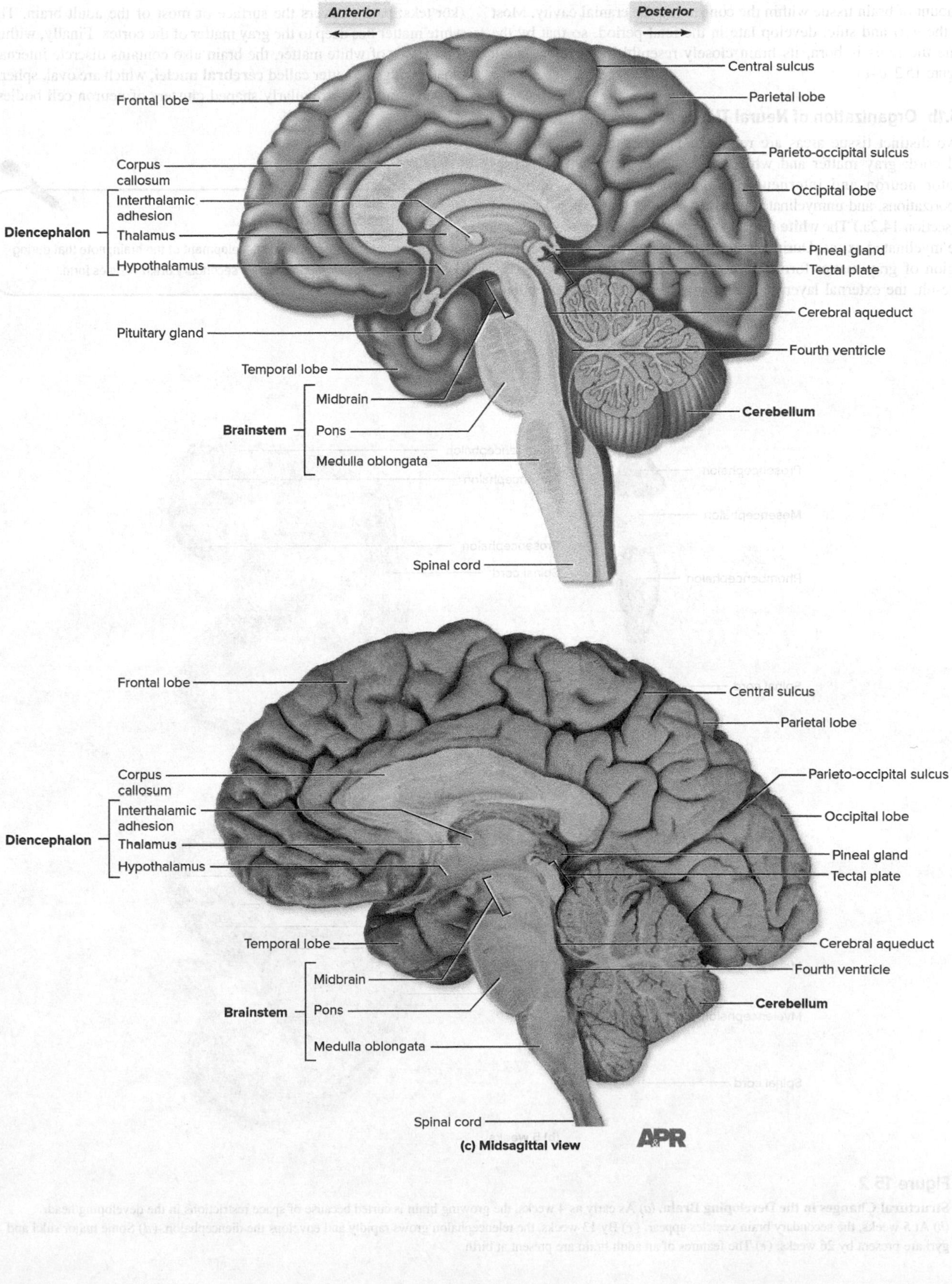
Anterior
Posterior
Central sulcus
Frontal lobe
Parietal lobe
Parieto-occipital sulcus
Corpus callosum
Occipital lobe
Interthalamic adhesion
Diencephalon
Thalamus
Pineal gland
Hypothalamus
Tectal plate
Cerebral aqueduct
Pituitary gland
Fourth ventricle
Temporal lobe
Midbrain
Cerebellum
Brainstem
Pons
Medulla oblongata
Spinal cord
Frontal lobe
Central sulcus
Parietal lobe
Corpus callosum
Parieto-occipital sulcus
Interthalamic adhesion
Occipital lobe
Diencephalon
Thalamus
Pineal gland
Hypothalamus
Tectal plate
Temporal lobe
Cerebral aqueduct
Fourth ventricle
Midbrain
Cerebellum
Brainstem
Pons
Medulla oblongata
Spinal cord

(c) Midsagittal view

amount of brain tissue within the confines of the cranial cavity. Most of the gyri and sulci develop late in the fetal period, so that by the time the fetus is born, its brain closely resembles that of an adult (figure 15.2 *c–e*).

15.1b Organization of Neural Tissue Areas in the Brain

Two distinct tissue areas are recognized within the brain and spinal cord: gray matter and white matter. The **gray matter** houses motor neuron and interneuron cell bodies, dendrites, terminal arborizations, and unmyelinated axons. (Origin of gray color described in section 14.2a.) The **white matter** derives its color from the myelin in the myelinated axons. During brain development, an outer, superficial region of gray matter forms from migrating peripheral neurons. As a result, the external layer of gray matter, called the cerebral **cortex** (kōr′teks; bark), covers the surface of most of the adult brain. The white matter lies deep to the gray matter of the cortex. Finally, within the masses of white matter, the brain also contains discrete internal clusters of gray matter called **cerebral nuclei,** which are oval, spherical, or sometimes irregularly shaped clusters of neuron cell bodies.

Learning Strategy 15.1

When reviewing the embryonic development of the brain, note that during the *fifth* week of development, *five* secondary brain vesicles form.

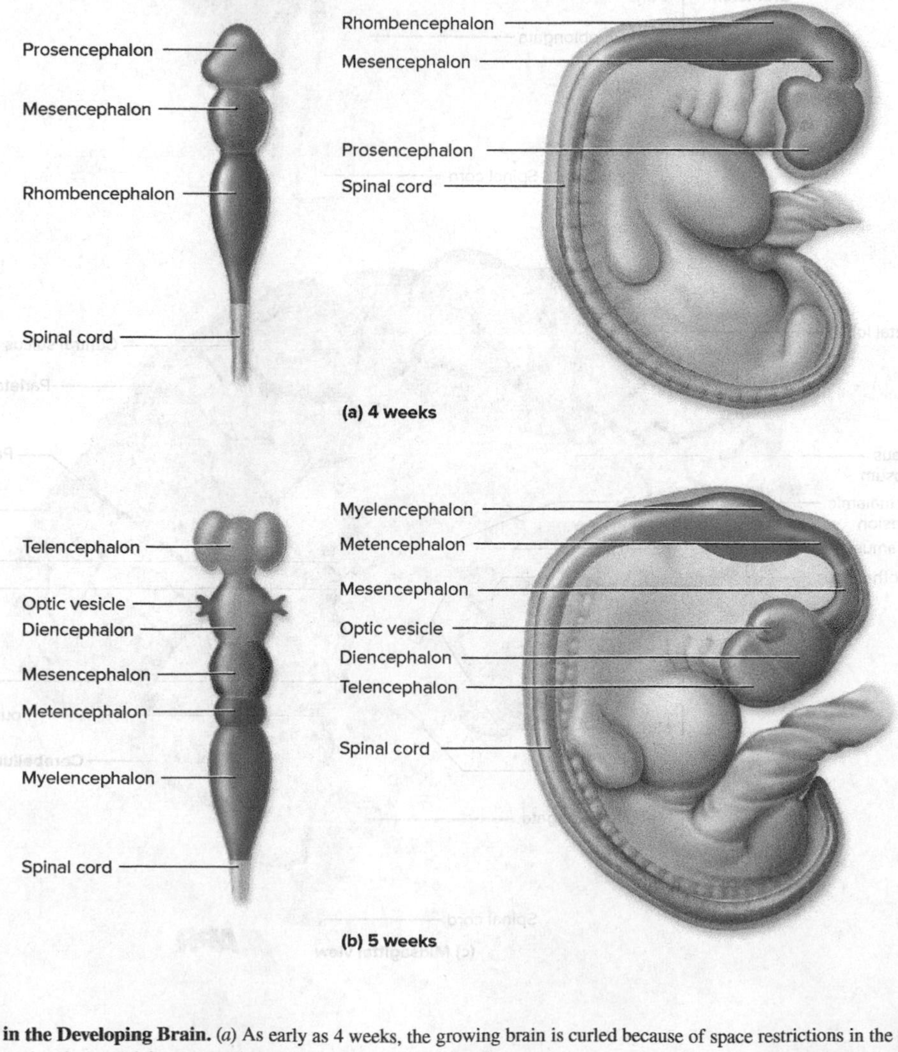

Figure 15.2

Structural Changes in the Developing Brain. (*a*) As early as 4 weeks, the growing brain is curled because of space restrictions in the developing head. (*b*) At 5 weeks, the secondary brain vesicles appear. (*c*) By 13 weeks, the telencephalon grows rapidly and envelops the diencephalon. (*d*) Some major sulci and gyri are present by 26 weeks. (*e*) The features of an adult brain are present at birth.

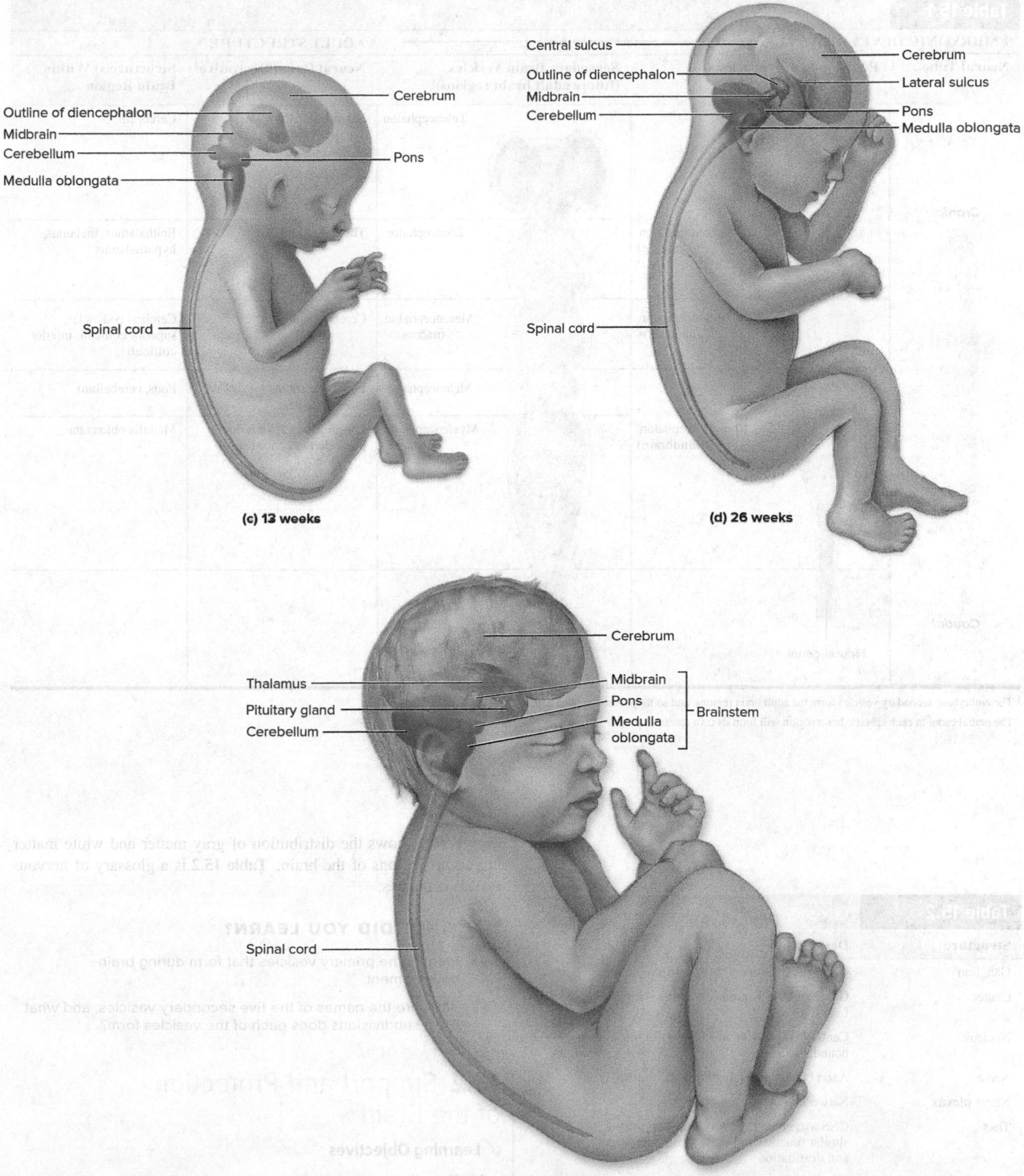
Outline of diencephalon
Midbrain
Cerebellum
Medulla oblongata
Cerebrum
Pons
Spinal cord
(c) 13 weeks
Central sulcus
Outline of diencephalon
Midbrain
Cerebellum
Cerebrum
Lateral sulcus
Pons
Medulla oblongata
Spinal cord
(d) 26 weeks
Cerebrum
Thalamus
Pituitary gland
Cerebellum
Midbrain
Pons
Medulla oblongata
Brainstem
Spinal cord

(e) Birth

Table 15.1 Major Brain Structures: Embryonic Through Adult

EMBRYONIC DEVELOPMENT →			ADULT STRUCTURE	
Neural Tube	**Primary Brain Vesicles**	**Secondary Brain Vesicles (future adult brain regions)[1]**	**Neural Canal Derivative[2]**	**Structure(s) Within Brain Region**
Cranial 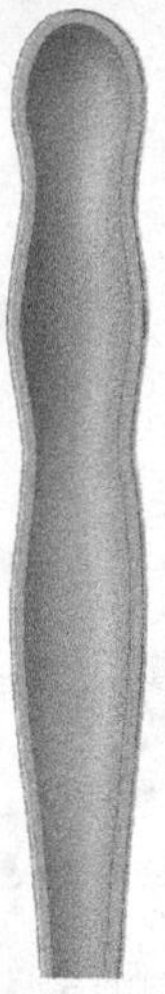 Caudal	 Neural canal	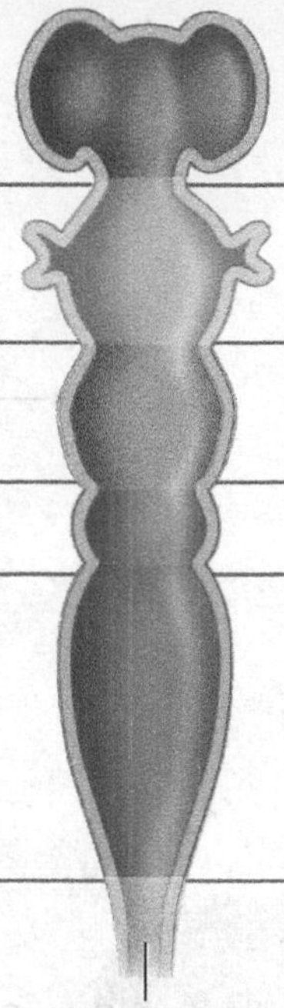 Neural canal		
	Prosencephalon (forebrain)	Telencephalon	Lateral ventricles	Cerebrum
		Diencephalon	Third ventricle	Epithalamus, thalamus, hypothalamus
	Mesencephalon (midbrain)	Mesencephalon (midbrain)	Cerebral aqueduct	Cerebral peduncles, superior colliculi, inferior colliculi
	Rhombencephalon (hindbrain)	Metencephalon	Fourth ventricle (superior part)	Pons, cerebellum
		Myelencephalon	Fourth ventricle (inferior part); part of central canal	Medulla oblongata

[1] The embryonic secondary vesicles form the adult brain regions, and so they share the same names.
[2] The neural canal in each specific brain region will form its own named "space."

Figure 15.3 shows the distribution of gray matter and white matter in various regions of the brain. Table 15.2 is a glossary of nervous system structures.

Table 15.2 Glossary of Nervous System Structures

Structure	Description
Ganglion	Cluster of neuron cell bodies within the PNS
Center	Group of CNS neuron cell bodies with a common function
Nucleus	Center in the CNS that displays discrete anatomic boundaries
Nerve	Axon bundle extending through the PNS
Nerve plexus	Network of nerves in PNS
Tract	CNS axon bundle in which the axons have a similar function and share a common origin and destination
Funiculus	Group of tracts in a specific area of the spinal cord
Pathway	Centers and tracts that connect the CNS with body organs and systems
Peduncle	A stalklike structure composed of tracts connecting two regions of the brain

WHAT DID YOU LEARN?

1. Identify the primary vesicles that form during brain development.
2. What are the names of the five secondary vesicles, and what brain subdivisions does each of the vesicles form?

15.2 Support and Protection of the Brain

✓ Learning Objectives

3. Describe the characteristics of the cranial meninges and the cranial dural septa.
4. Explain the origin, function, and pattern of cerebrospinal fluid circulation.
5. Describe the structure of the blood-brain barrier and how it protects the brain.

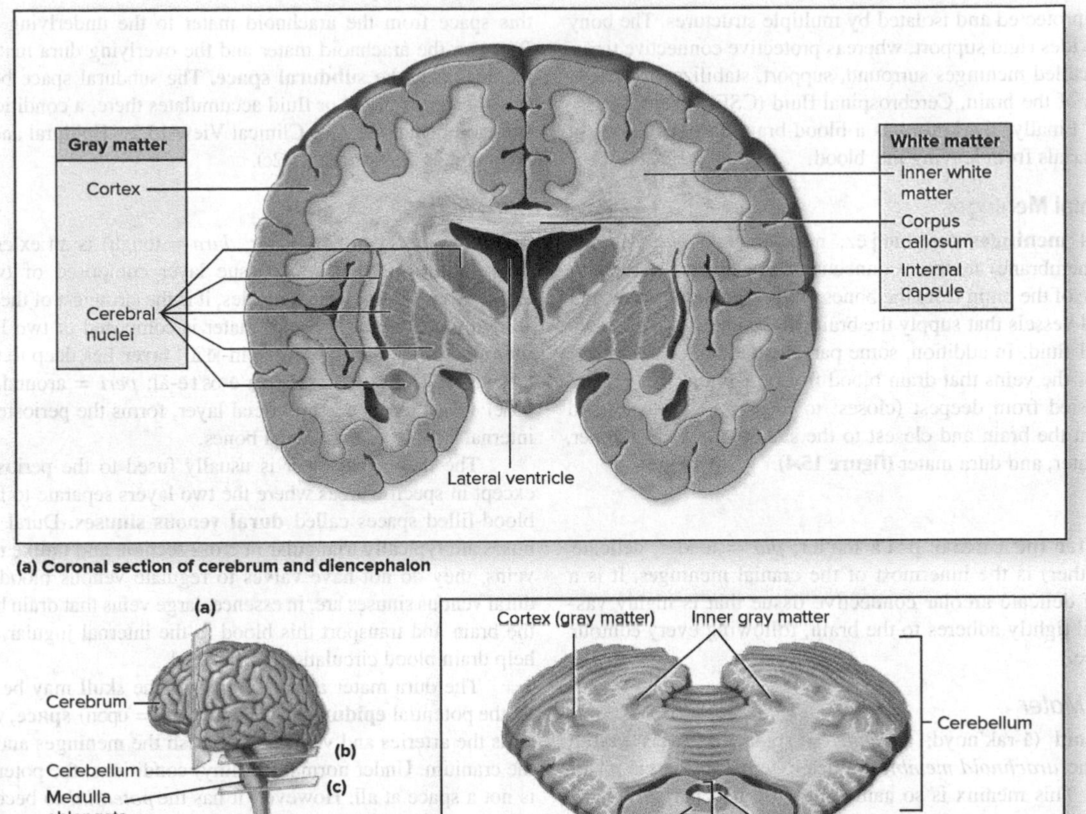

Figure 15.3

Gray and White Matter in the CNS. The gray matter represents regions containing neuron cell bodies, dendrites, terminal arborizations, and unmyelinated axons, whereas the white matter derives its color from myelinated axons. The distribution of gray and white matter is compared in (*a*) the cerebrum and diencephalon, (*b*) the cerebellum and brainstem, (*c*) the medulla oblongata, and (*d*) the spinal cord.

The brain is protected and isolated by multiple structures. The bony cranium provides rigid support, whereas protective connective tissue membranes called meninges surround, support, stabilize, and partition portions of the brain. Cerebrospinal fluid (CSF) acts as a cushioning fluid. Finally, the brain has a blood-brain barrier to prevent harmful materials from leaving the blood.

15.2a Cranial Meninges

The **cranial meninges** (mĕ-nin′j ēz, mē′nin-j ēz; sing., *meninx*, men′ingks; membrane) are three connective tissue layers that separate the soft tissue of the brain from the bones of the cranium, enclose and protect blood vessels that supply the brain, and contain and circulate cerebrospinal fluid. In addition, some parts of the cranial meninges form some of the veins that drain blood from the brain. The cranial meninges, listed from deepest (closest to the brain) to superficial (farthest from the brain and closest to the skull), are the pia mater, arachnoid mater, and dura mater (**figure 15.4**).

Pia Mater

The **pia mater** (pē′ă mah′ter, p ī′ă mā′ter; *pia* = tender, delicate, *mater* = mother) is the innermost of the cranial meninges. It is a thin layer of delicate areolar connective tissue that is highly vascularized and tightly adheres to the brain, following every contour of the surface.

Arachnoid Mater

The **arachnoid** (ă-rak′noyd; *arachne* = spider, cobweb) **mater,** also called the *arachnoid membrane,* lies external to the pia mater (fig15.4). This meninx is so named because it is partially composed of a delicate web of collagen and elastic fibers, termed the **arachnoid trabeculae.** Immediately deep to the arachnoid mater is the **subarachnoid space.** The arachnoid trabeculae extend through this space from the arachnoid mater to the underlying pia mater. Between the arachnoid mater and the overlying dura mater is a potential space, the **subdural space.** The subdural space becomes an actual space if blood or fluid accumulates there, a condition called a subdural hematoma (see Clinical View 15.2: "Epidural and Subdural Hematomas" in section 15.2c).

Dura Mater

The **dura mater** (dū′ră mā′tĕr; *dura* = tough) is an external tough, dense irregular connective tissue layer composed of two fibrous layers. As its Latin name indicates, it is the strongest of the meninges. Within the cranium, the dura mater is composed of two layers. The **meningeal** (mĕ-nin′j ē-ăl, men′in-jē′ăl) **layer** lies deep to the periosteal layer. The **periosteal** (per′ē-os′t ē-ăl; *peri* = around, *osteon* = bone) **layer,** the more superficial layer, forms the periosteum on the internal surface of the cranial bones.

The meningeal layer is usually fused to the periosteal layer, except in specific areas where the two layers separate to form large, blood-filled spaces called **dural venous sinuses.** Dural venous sinuses are typically triangular in cross section, and unlike most other veins, they do not have valves to regulate venous blood flow. The dural venous sinuses are, in essence, large veins that drain blood from the brain and transport this blood to the internal jugular veins that help drain blood circulation of the head.

The dura mater and the bones of the skull may be separated by the potential **epidural** (ep′i-d ū′răl; *epi* = upon) **space,** which contains the arteries and veins that nourish the meninges and bones of the cranium. Under normal (healthy) conditions, the potential space is not a space at all. However, it has the *potential* to become a *real* space and fill with fluid or blood as a result of trauma or disease (see Clinical View 15.2: "Epidural and Subdural Hematomas" in section 15.2c).

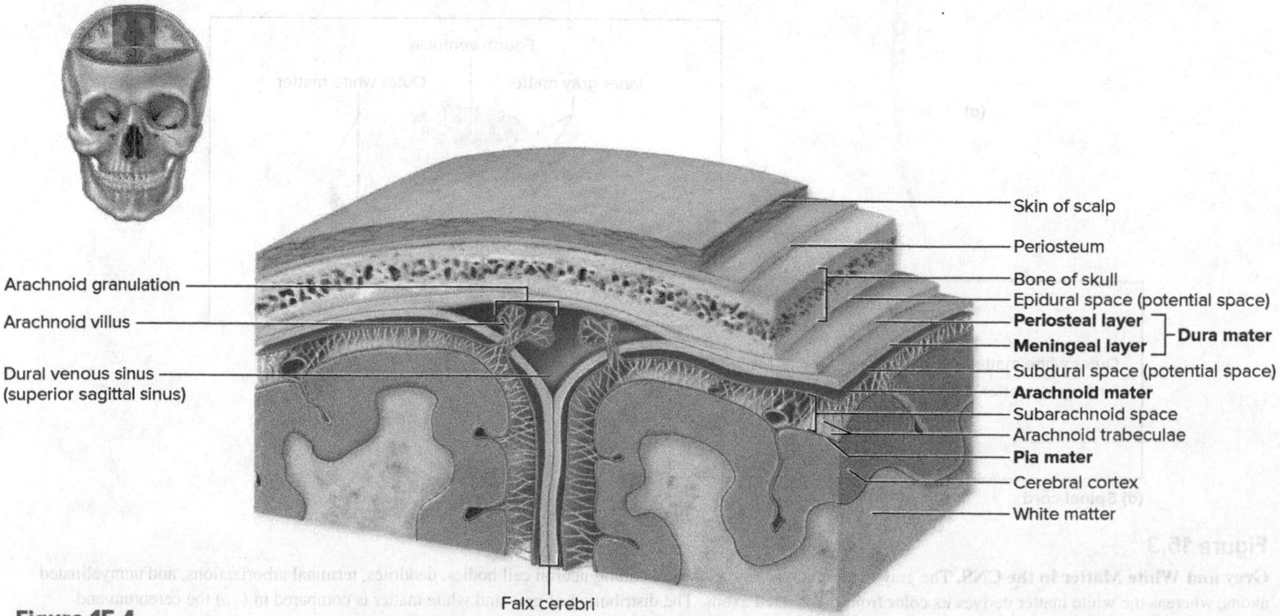

Figure 15.4

Cranial Meninges. A coronal section of the head depicts the organization of the three meningeal layers: the dura mater, the arachnoid mater, and the pia mater. In the midline, folds of the inner meningeal layer of the dura mater form the falx cerebri, which partitions the two cerebral hemispheres. The inner meningeal layer and the outer periosteal layer sometimes separate to form the dural venous sinuses, such as the dural venous sinus (superior sagittal sinus) (shown here), which drain blood away from the brain. APR

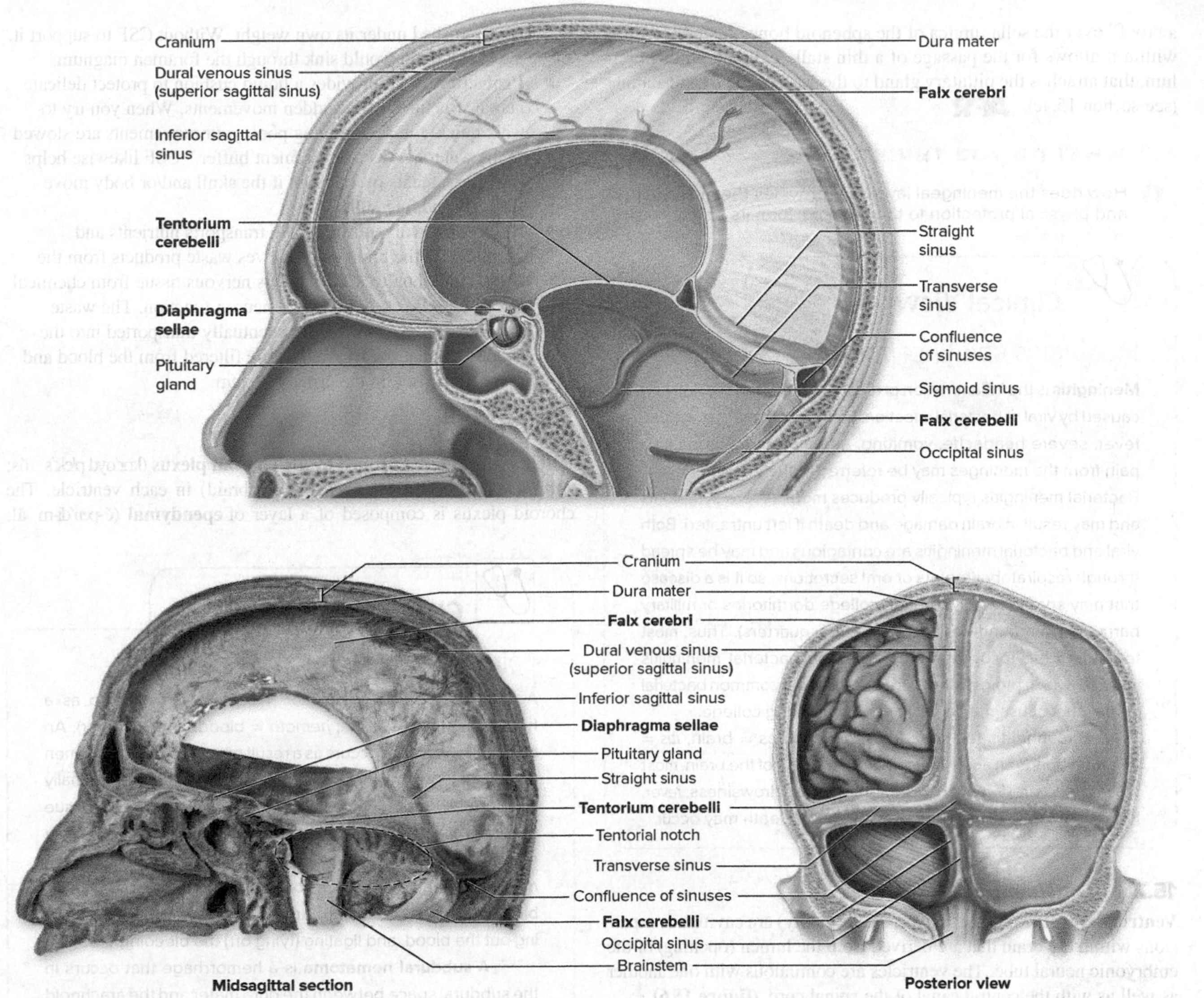

Figure 15.5

Cranial Dural Septa. An illustration and a cadaver photo of a midsagittal section of the skull show the orientation of the falx cerebri, falx cerebelli, tentorium cerebelli, and diaphragma sellae.

Cranial Dural Septa

The meningeal layer of the dura mater extends as flat partitions (septa) into the cranial cavity at four locations. Collectively, these double layers of dura mater are called **cranial dural septa.** These membranous partitions separate specific parts of the brain and provide additional stabilization and support to the entire brain. There are four cranial dural septa: the falx cerebri, tentorium cerebelli, falx cerebelli, and diaphragma sellae (**figure 15.5**).

The **falx cerebri** (fawlks s ē-rē′bri; *falx* = sickle, *cerebro* = brain), or *cerebral falx,* is the largest of the dural septa. This sickle-shaped vertical fold of dura is located in the midsagittal plane. The falx cerebri projects into the longitudinal fissure of the brain, which is between the left and right cerebral hemispheres. It attaches anteriorly to the crista galli of the ethmoid and posteriorly to the internal occipital crest of the skull. Running within the margins of the falx cerebri are two dural venous sinuses: the **superior sagittal sinus** and the **inferior sagittal sinus** (see figure 23.11*b*).

The **tentorium cerebelli** (ten-tō′rē-ŭm ser-e-bel′ī, or *cerebellar tentorium*) is a horizontally oriented fold of dura mater that separates the occipital and temporal lobes of the cerebrum from the cerebellum. It is named for the fact that it forms a dural "tent" over the cerebellum. The **transverse sinuses** run within its posterior border. The anterior surface of the tentorium cerebelli has a gap called the **tentorial notch** (or *tentorial incisure*) to allow for the passage of the brainstem.

Extending inferiorly from the tentorium cerebelli is the **falx cerebelli** (*cerebellar falx*), a sickle-shaped vertical partition that divides the left and right cerebellar hemispheres. A tiny **occipital sinus** (another dural venous sinus) runs in its posterior vertical border.

The smallest of the dural septa is the **diaphragma sellae** (dī′ă-frag′m ă sel′ē; *sella* = saddle), or *sellar diaphragm,* which forms a "roof" over the sella turcica of the sphenoid bone. A small opening within it allows for the passage of a thin stalk, called the infundibulum, that attaches the pituitary gland to the base of the hypothalamus (see section 15.4c). APR

WHAT DO YOU THINK?

1. How does the meningeal layer that provides the most support and physical protection to the brain perform its primary task?

Clinical View 15.1

Meningitis and Encephalitis

Meningitis is the inflammation of the meninges, and typically it is caused by viral or bacterial infection. Early symptoms may include fever, severe headache, vomiting, and a stiff neck (because pain from the meninges may be referred to the posterior neck). Bacterial meningitis typically produces more severe symptoms and may result in brain damage and death if left untreated. Both viral and bacterial meningitis are contagious and may be spread through respiratory droplets or oral secretions, so it is a disease that may spread rapidly through college dormitories or military barracks (where individuals live in close quarters). Thus, most teenagers are recommended to get the bacterial meningitis vaccine (which protects them against the most common bacterial strains that cause meningitis) prior to attending college.

Encephalitis (en-sef-ă-lī′ tis; *enkephalos* = brain, *itis* = inflammation) is an acute inflammatory disease of the brain, most often due to viral infection. Symptoms include drowsiness, fever, headache, neck pain, coma, and paralysis. Death may occur.

15.2b Brain Ventricles

Ventricles (ven′tri-k ĕl; *ventriculus* = little cavity) are cavities or expansions within the brain that are derived from the lumen (opening) of the embryonic neural tube. The ventricles are continuous with one another as well as with the central canal of the spinal cord **(figure 15.6)**.

There are four ventricles in the brain: Two **lateral ventricles** are in the cerebrum, separated by a thin medial partition called the **septum pellucidum** (pe-lū′si-dum; *pellucid* = transparent). Within the diencephalon is a smaller ventricle called the **third ventricle.** Each lateral ventricle communicates with the third ventricle through an opening called the **interventricular foramen** (formerly called the *foramen of Munro*). A narrow canal called the **cerebral aqueduct** (ak′we-d ŭkt; canal) (also called the *mesencephalic aqueduct* and *aqueduct of the midbrain* and formerly called the *aqueduct of Sylvius*), passes through the midbrain and connects the third ventricle with the tetrahedron-shaped **fourth ventricle.** The fourth ventricle is located between the pons/medulla and the cerebellum. The fourth ventricle narrows at its inferior end before it merges with the slender **central canal** in the spinal cord. All of the ventricles contain cerebrospinal fluid.

15.2c Cerebrospinal Fluid

Cerebrospinal (ser′ĕ-brō-spī′năl) **fluid (CSF)** is a clear, colorless liquid that circulates in the ventricles and subarachnoid space. CSF bathes the exposed surfaces of the central nervous system and completely surrounds the brain and spinal cord. CSF performs several important functions:

- **Buoyancy.** The brain floats in the CSF, which thereby supports more than 95% of its weight and prevents it from being crushed under its own weight. Without CSF to support it, the heavy brain would sink through the foramen magnum.
- **Protection.** CSF provides a liquid cushion to protect delicate neural structures from sudden movements. When you try to walk quickly in a swimming pool, your movements are slowed as the water acts as a "movement buffer." CSF likewise helps slow movements of the brain if the skull and/or body move suddenly and forcefully.
- **Environmental stability.** CSF transports nutrients and chemicals to the brain and removes waste products from the brain. Additionally, CSF protects nervous tissue from chemical fluctuations that would disrupt neuron function. The waste products and excess CSF are eventually transported into the venous circulation, where they are filtered from the blood and secreted in urine in the urinary system.

CSF Formation

Cerebrospinal fluid is formed by the **choroid plexus** (kor′oyd plek′s ŭs; *chorioeides* = membrane, *plexus* = a braid) in each ventricle. The choroid plexus is composed of a layer of **ependymal** (ĕ-pen′di-m ăl;

Clinical View 15.2

Epidural and Subdural Hematomas

A pooling of blood outside of a vessel is referred to as a **hematoma** (hē-mă-tō′mă; *hemato* = blood, *oma* = tumor). An **epidural hematoma** occurs as a result of a ruptured artery, when a pool of blood forms in the epidural space of the brain, usually due to a severe blow to the head. The adjacent brain tissue becomes distorted and compressed as a result of the hematoma continuing to increase in size. Severe neurologic injury and death may occur if the bleeding is not stopped and the accumulated blood removed by surgically drilling a hole in the skull, suctioning out the blood, and ligating (tying off) the bleeding vessel.

A **subdural hematoma** is a hemorrhage that occurs in the subdural space between the dura mater and the arachnoid mater. This type of hematoma typically results from ruptured veins caused by either fast or violent rotational motion of the head. Blood pools in this space and compresses the brain, although usually these events occur more slowly than with an epidural hematoma. Subdural hematomas are treated similarly to epidural hematomas.

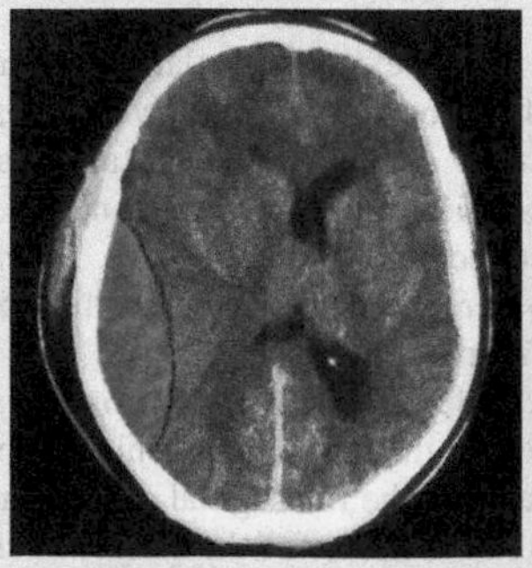

(a) Epidural hematoma (shaded in red on the CT).

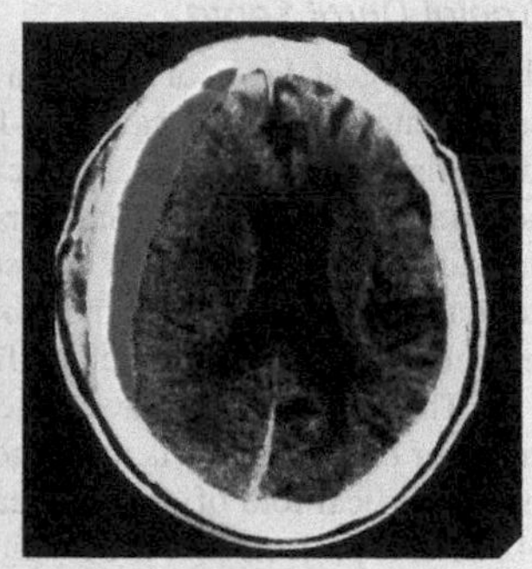

(b) Subdural hematoma (shaded in red on the CT).

(a) BSIP SA/Alamy Stock Photo; (b) Cultura RM/Alamy Stock Photo

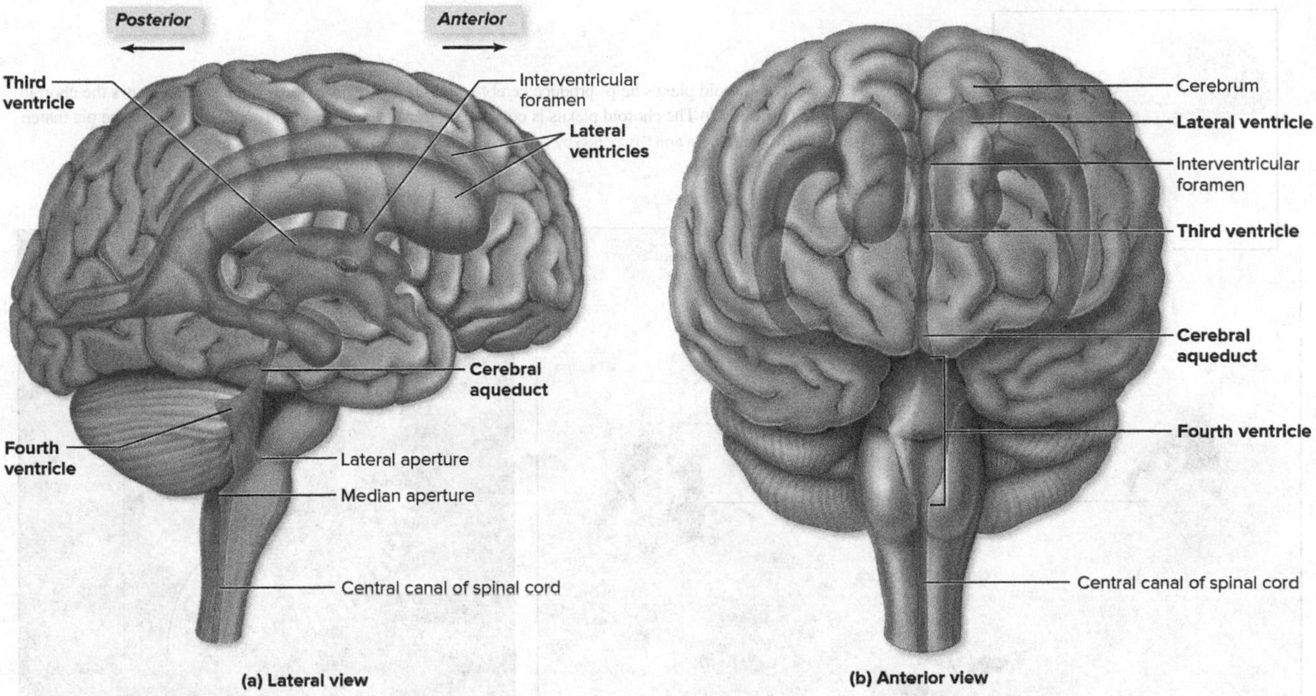

Figure 15.6

Ventricles of the Brain. The ventricles are formed from the embryonic neural canal. They are sites of production of cerebrospinal fluid (CSF), which transports chemical messengers, nutrients, and waste products. (*a*) Lateral and (*b*) anterior views show the positioning and relationships of the ventricles. APR

ependyma = an upper garment) **cells** and the capillaries that lie within the pia mater **(figure 15.7)**. CSF is formed from blood plasma (filtered from capillaries), and then this fluid is further modified by the ependymal cells. CSF is somewhat similar to blood plasma, although certain ion concentrations differ between the two types of fluid.

CSF Circulation

The choroid plexus produces CSF at a rate of about 500 milliliters (mL) per day. The CSF circulates through and eventually leaves the ventricles and enters the subarachnoid space, where the total volume of CSF at any given moment ranges between 100 mL and 160 mL.

Clinical View 15.3

Traumatic Brain Injuries: Concussion and Contusion

Traumatic brain injury (TBI) refers to the acute brain damage that occurs as a result of an accident or trauma. A **concussion** is the most common type of TBI. It is characterized by temporary, abrupt loss of consciousness after a blow to the head or the sudden stop of a moving head. Headache, drowsiness, lack of concentration, confusion, and amnesia (memory loss) may occur. Multiple concussions have a cumulative effect, causing the affected person to lose a small amount of mental ability with each episode. In fact, a history of multiple concussions has been related to long-term personality changes, depression, and intellectual decline. Athletes who are prone to concussions (such as football and soccer players) are at greater risk for these detrimental changes, so coaches and athletic trainers are being educated to be more cautious about letting an athlete play if a concussion is suspected.

A **contusion** is a TBI where there is bruising of the brain due to trauma that causes blood to leak from small vessels into the subarachnoid space (a fluid-filled space surrounding the brain). The bruising may appear on a computed tomography (CT) scan of the head. Usually, the person immediately loses consciousness (normally for no longer than 5 minutes). Respiration abnormalities and decreased blood pressure sometimes occur as well.

Of particular concern is a rare but serious condition called **second impact syndrome (SIS)**, where an individual experiences a second brain injury prior to the resolution of the first injury, and develops severe brain swelling and possible death as a result. For this reason, it is essential that the original TBI completely heals before an individual is allowed to resume a behavior that may put the individual at risk for another TBI. Both severe traumatic brain injury and repetitive TBIs may cause long-term cognitive deficits and motor impairment. Individuals may need physical, occupational, and speech therapy to regain a portion of these functions.

Interestingly, preliminary research has shown that TBI patients who received therapeutic progesterone made a greater and faster recovery than individuals with similar TBIs who did not receive the therapy. Thus, a reproductive hormone (progesterone) may also help the nervous system with its healing.

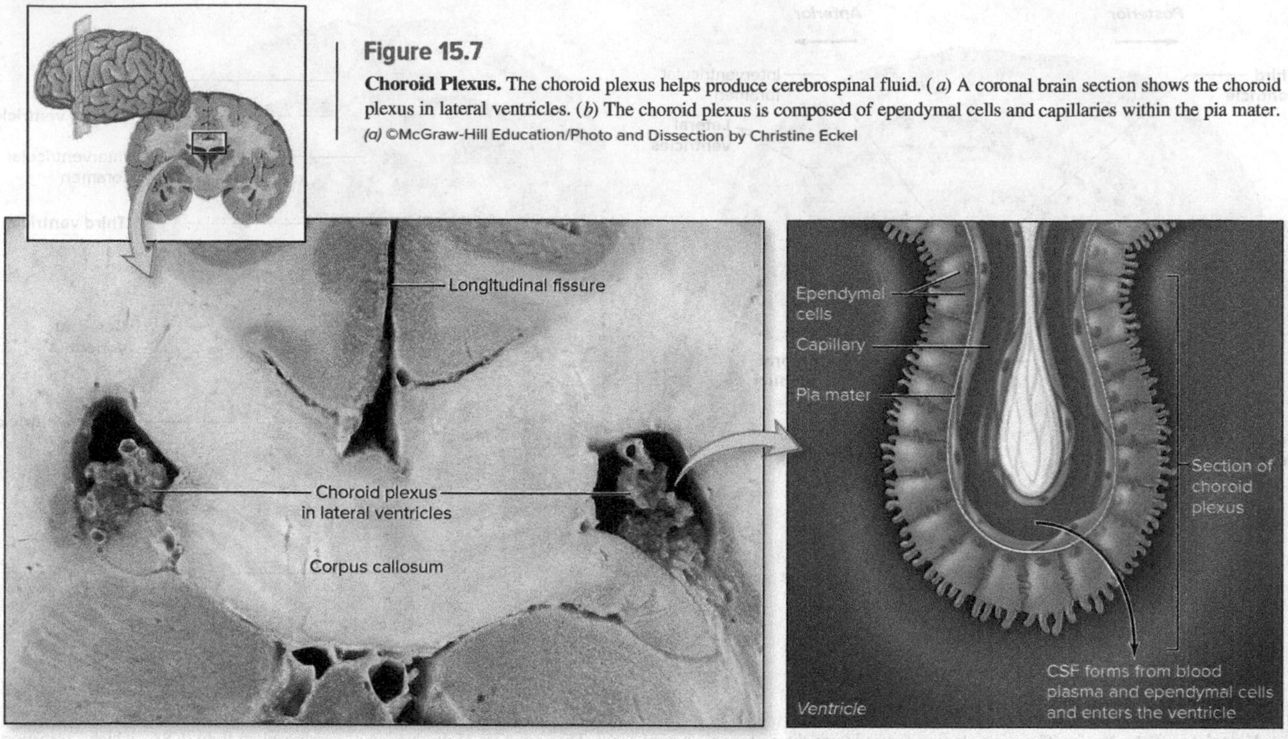
Longitudinal fissure
Choroid plexus
in lateral ventricles
Corpus callosum
Ependymal cells
Capillary
Pia mater
Section of choroid plexus
CSF forms from blood plasma and ependymal cells and enters the ventricle
Ventricle

(a) Coronal section of the brain, close-up

(b) Choroid plexus

Figure 15.7

Choroid Plexus. The choroid plexus helps produce cerebrospinal fluid. (*a*) A coronal brain section shows the choroid plexus in lateral ventricles. (*b*) The choroid plexus is composed of ependymal cells and capillaries within the pia mater.

(a) ©McGraw-Hill Education/Photo and Dissection by Christine Eckel

This means that excess CSF is continuously removed from the subarachnoid space so the fluid will not accumulate and compress and damage the nervous tissue. Fingerlike extensions of the arachnoid mater project through the dura mater into the dural venous sinuses to form **arachnoid villi** (vil′ ī; shaggy hair). Collections of arachnoid villi form **arachnoid granulations.** Excess CSF moves across the arachnoid mater membrane at the arachnoid villi to return to the blood within the dural venous sinuses. Within the subarachnoid space, cerebral arteries and veins are supported by the arachnoid trabeculae and surrounded by cerebrospinal fluid.

WHAT DO YOU THINK?

2 What would you predict happens if the amount of CSF produced begins to exceed the amount removed or drained at the arachnoid villi?

Figure 15.8 shows the process of CSF production, circulation, and removal, which consists of the following steps:

1. CSF is produced in the ventricles by the choroid plexus.
2. CSF flows from the lateral ventricles and third ventricle through the cerebral aqueduct into the fourth ventricle.
3. Most of the CSF in the fourth ventricle flows into the subarachnoid space by passing through openings in the roof of the fourth ventricle. These ventricular openings are the paired **lateral apertures** and the single **median aperture.** CSF also fills the central canal of the spinal cord.
4. As it travels through the subarachnoid space, CSF removes waste products and provides buoyancy for the brain and spinal cord.
5. As CSF accumulates within the subarachnoid space, it exerts pressure within the arachnoid villi. This pressure exceeds the pressure of blood in the venous sinuses. Thus, the arachnoid villi extending into the dural venous sinuses provide a conduit for a one-way flow of excess CSF to be returned into the blood within the dural venous sinuses.

15.2d Blood-Brain Barrier

Nervous tissue is protected from the general circulation by the **blood-brain barrier (BBB),** which strictly regulates what substances can enter the interstitial fluid of the brain (see section 14.2b). The blood-brain barrier keeps the neurons in the brain from being exposed to some normal substances, certain drugs, waste products in the blood, and variations in levels of normal substances (e.g., ions, hormones) that could adversely affect brain function.

Recall that the **perivascular feet** of astrocytes cover, wrap around, and completely envelop capillaries in the brain. Both the capillary endothelial cells and the astrocyte perivascular feet contribute to the blood-brain barrier (**figure 15.9**). The continuous basement membrane of the endothelial cells also is a significant barrier. Tight junctions between adjacent endothelial cells reduce capillary permeability and prevent materials from diffusing across the capillary wall. The astrocytes act as "gatekeepers" that permit materials to pass to the neurons after leaving the capillaries. Even so, the barrier is not absolute. Usually only lipid-soluble (dissolvable in fat) compounds, such as nicotine, alcohol, and some anesthetics, can diffuse across the endothelial plasma membranes and into the interstitial fluid of the CNS to reach the brain neurons.

The blood-brain barrier is markedly reduced or missing in three distinct locations in the CNS: the choroid plexus, the hypothalamus, and the pineal gland. The reasons for this are that the capillaries of the choroid plexus must be permeable to produce CSF, whereas the hypothalamus and pineal gland produce some hormones that must have ready access to the blood.

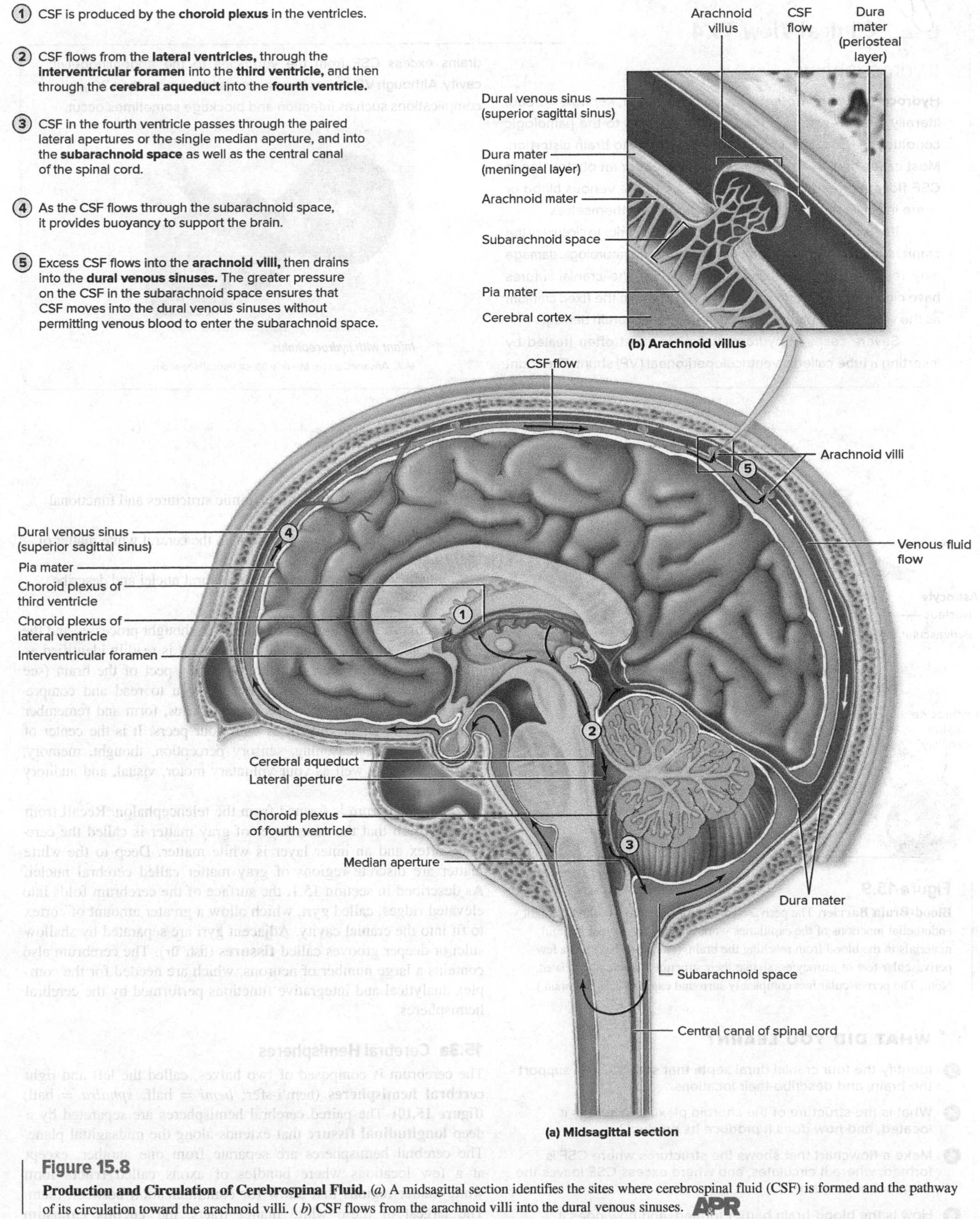

1 CSF is produced by the choroid plexus in the ventricles.
2 CSF flows from the lateral ventricles, through the interventricular foramen into the third ventricle, and then through the cerebral aqueduct into the fourth ventricle.
3 CSF in the fourth ventricle passes through the paired lateral apertures or the single median aperture, and into the subarachnoid space as well as the central canal of the spinal cord.
4 As the CSF flows through the subarachnoid space, it provides buoyancy to support the brain.
5 Excess CSF flows into the arachnoid villi, then drains into the dural venous sinuses. The greater pressure on the CSF in the subarachnoid space ensures that CSF moves into the dural venous sinuses without permitting venous blood to enter the subarachnoid space.
Arachnoid villus
CSF flow
Dura mater (periosteal layer)
Dural venous sinus (superior sagittal sinus)
Dura mater (meningeal layer)
Arachnoid mater
Subarachnoid space
Pia mater
Cerebral cortex
(b) Arachnoid villus
CSF flow
Arachnoid villi
Dural venous sinus (superior sagittal sinus)
Pia mater
Choroid plexus of third ventricle
Choroid plexus of lateral ventricle
Interventricular foramen
Venous fluid flow
Cerebral aqueduct
Lateral aperture
Choroid plexus of fourth ventricle
Median aperture
Dura mater
Subarachnoid space
Central canal of spinal cord
(a) Midsagittal section

Figure 15.8

Production and Circulation of Cerebrospinal Fluid. (*a*) A midsagittal section identifies the sites where cerebrospinal fluid (CSF) is formed and the pathway of its circulation toward the arachnoid villi. (*b*) CSF flows from the arachnoid villi into the dural venous sinuses. APR

Clinical View 15.4

Hydrocephalus

Hydrocephalus (hī′drō-sef′ă-lŭs; *hydro* = water, *kephale* = head) literally means "water on the brain" and refers to the pathologic condition of excessive CSF, which often leads to brain distortion. Most cases of hydrocephalus result from either an obstruction in CSF flow that restricts its reabsorption into the venous blood or some intrinsic problem with the arachnoid villi themselves.

If hydrocephalus develops in a young child, prior to closure of the cranial sutures, the head becomes enlarged, and neurologic damage may result. If hydrocephalus develops after the cranial sutures have closed, the brain may be compressed within the fixed cranium as the ventricles expand, resulting in permanent brain damage.

Severe cases of hydrocephalus are most often treated by inserting a tube called a ventriculoperitoneal (VP) shunt. The shunt drains excess CSF from the ventricles to the abdominopelvic cavity. Although VP shunts have been used for more than 30 years, complications such as infection and blockage sometimes occur.

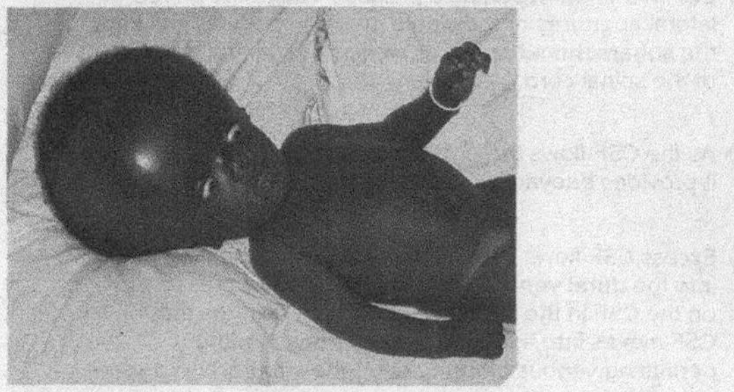

Infant with hydrocephalus.

M.A. Ansary/Custom Medical Stock Photo/Newscom

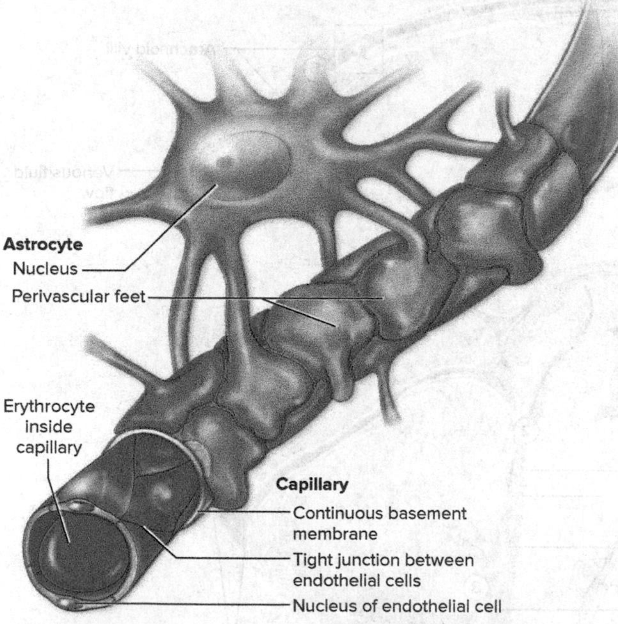

Astrocyte
Nucleus
Perivascular feet
Erythrocyte inside capillary
Capillary
Continuous basement membrane
Tight junction between endothelial cells
Nucleus of endothelial cell

Figure 15.9

Blood-Brain Barrier. The perivascular feet of the astrocytes and the tight endothelial junctions of the capillaries work together to prevent harmful materials in the blood from reaching the brain. (Here we show just a few perivascular feet of astrocytes, so that their structure may be appreciated. Note: The perivascular feet completely surround capillaries in the brain.)

WHAT DID YOU LEARN?

3. Identify the four cranial dural septa that stabilize and support the brain, and describe their locations.
4. What is the structure of the choroid plexus? Where is it located, and how does it produce its product?
5. Make a flowchart that shows the structures where CSF is formed, where it circulates, and where excess CSF leaves the subarachnoid space.
6. How is the blood-brain barrier formed, and how does it protect nervous tissue?

15.3 Cerebrum

✓ Learning Objectives

6. Identify and describe the anatomic structures and functional areas of the cerebrum.
7. Describe the tracts associated with the central white matter of the cerebrum.
8. Identify the components of the cerebral nuclei and describe their functions.

The **cerebrum** is the location of conscious thought processes and the origin of all complex intellectual functions. It is readily identified as the two large hemispheres on the superior aspect of the brain (see figure 15.1 *a, b*). Your cerebrum enables you to read and comprehend the words in this textbook, turn its pages, form and remember ideas, and talk about your ideas with your peers. It is the center of your intelligence, reasoning, sensory perception, thought, memory, and judgment, as well as your voluntary motor, visual, and auditory activities.

The cerebrum is formed from the telencephalon. Recall from section 15.1b that the outer layer of gray matter is called the cerebral cortex and an inner layer is white matter. Deep to the white matter are discrete regions of gray matter called cerebral nuclei. As described in section 15.1, the surface of the cerebrum folds into elevated ridges, called gyri, which allow a greater amount of cortex to fit into the cranial cavity. Adjacent gyri are separated by shallow sulci or deeper grooves called **fissures** (fish′ ŭr). The cerebrum also contains a large number of neurons, which are needed for the complex analytical and integrative functions performed by the cerebral hemispheres.

15.3a Cerebral Hemispheres

The cerebrum is composed of two halves, called the left and right **cerebral hemispheres** (hem′i-sfēr; *hemi* = half, *sphaira* = ball) **(figure 15.10)**. The paired cerebral hemispheres are separated by a deep **longitudinal fissure** that extends along the midsagittal plane. The cerebral hemispheres are separate from one another, except at a few locations where bundles of axons called **tracts** form white matter regions that allow for communication between them. The largest of these white matter tracts, the **corpus callosum** (kōr′pŭs kal-lō′sŭm; *corpus* = body, *callosum* = hard), connects the

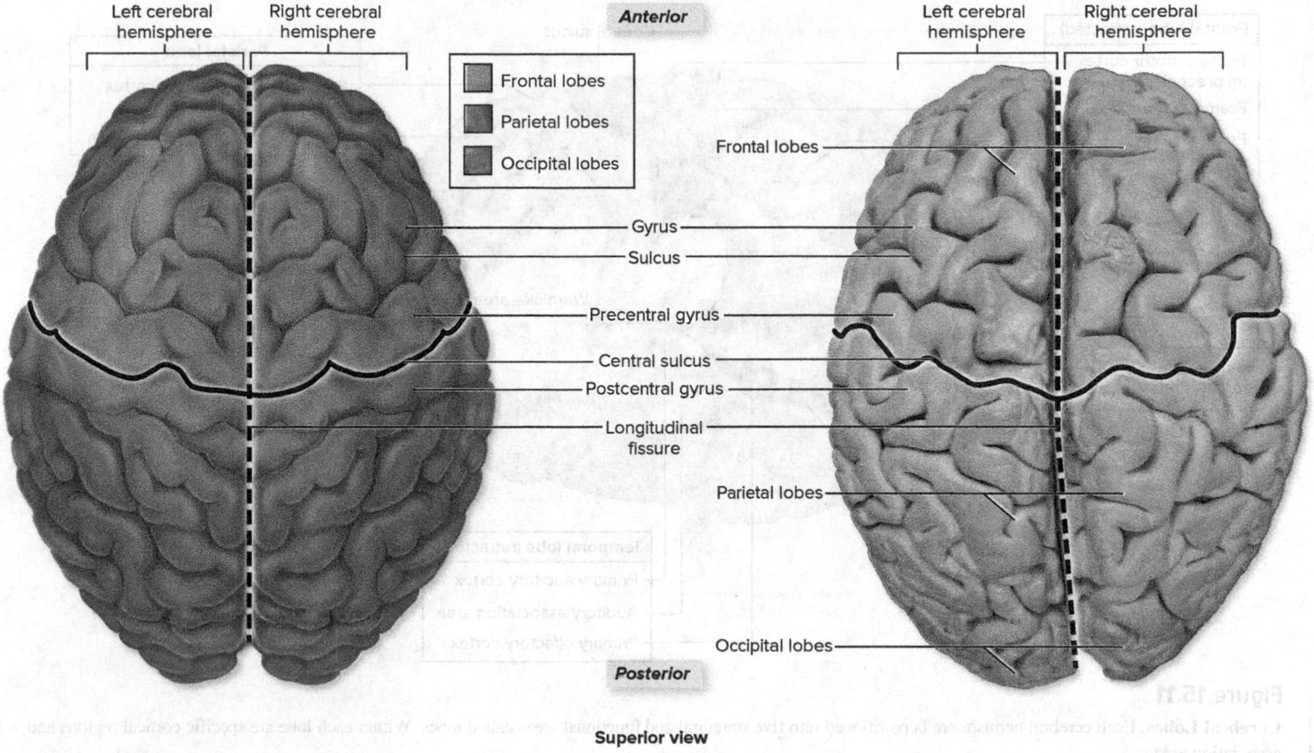

Figure 15.10

Cerebral Hemispheres. Superior views comparing an illustration and a cadaver photo show the cerebral hemispheres, where our conscious activities, memories, behaviors, plans, and ideas are initiated and controlled. APR

hemispheres (see a midsagittal section of the corpus callosum in figure 15.1 *c*). The corpus callosum provides the main communications link between these hemispheres.

Three points should be kept in mind with respect to the cerebral hemispheres:

- In most cases, it is difficult to assign a precise function to a specific region of the cerebral cortex. Considerable overlap and indistinct boundaries permit a single region of the cortex to exhibit several different functions. Additionally, some aspects of cortical function, such as memory or consciousness, cannot easily be assigned to any single region.
- With few exceptions, both cerebral hemispheres receive their sensory information from and project motor commands to the opposite side of the body. The right cerebral hemisphere controls the left side of the body, and vice versa.
- The two hemispheres appear as anatomic mirror images, but they display some functional differences, termed **hemispheric lateralization.** For example, the portions of the brain that are responsible for controlling speech and understanding verbalization are frequently located in the left hemisphere. These differences primarily affect higher-order functions, which are addressed in section 17.4.

WHAT DO YOU THINK?

3 In the past, one treatment for severe epilepsy was to cut the corpus callosum, thus confining epileptic seizures to just one cerebral hemisphere. How would cutting the corpus callosum affect communication between the left and right hemispheres?

Lobes of the Cerebrum

Each cerebral hemisphere is divided into five anatomically and functionally distinct lobes. The first four lobes—frontal, parietal, temporal, and occipital—are superficially visible **(figure 15.11)**. The fifth lobe, the insula, is not visible at the surface of the hemispheres. Each lobe exhibits specific cortical regions and association areas.

Learning Strategy 15.2

Four of the cerebral lobes—frontal, parietal, temporal, and occipital—each share the same name as the skull bone that overlies them.

The **frontal lobe** (lōb) lies deep to the frontal bone and forms the anterior part of the cerebral hemisphere. The frontal lobe ends posteriorly at a deep groove called the **central sulcus** that marks the boundary with the parietal lobe. The inferior border of the frontal lobe is marked by the **lateral sulcus,** a deep groove that separates the frontal and parietal lobes from the temporal lobe. An important anatomic feature of the frontal lobe is the **precentral gyrus,** which is a mass of nervous tissue immediately anterior to the central sulcus. The frontal lobe is primarily concerned with voluntary motor functions, concentration, verbal communication, decision making, planning, and personality.

The **parietal lobe** lies internal to the parietal bone and forms the superoposterior part of each cerebral hemisphere. It terminates anteriorly at the central sulcus, posteriorly at a relatively indistinct **parieto-occipital sulcus,** and laterally at the lateral sulcus. An

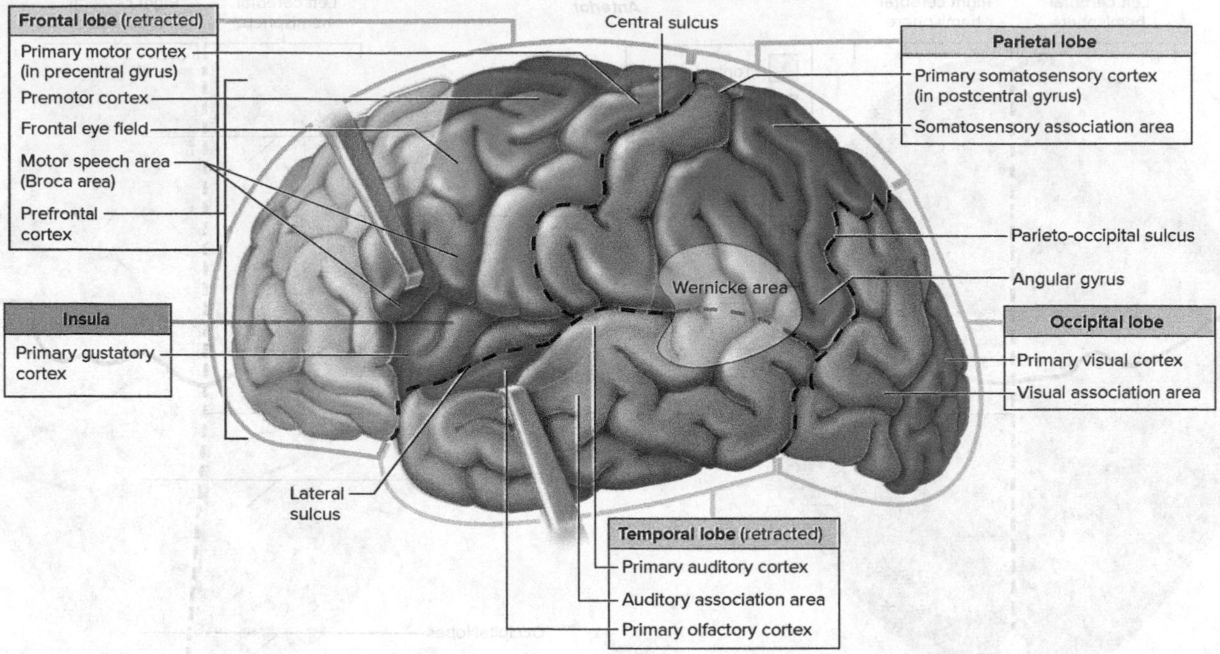

Figure 15.11

Cerebral Lobes. Each cerebral hemisphere is partitioned into five structural and functional areas called lobes. Within each lobe are specific cortical regions and association areas.

important anatomic feature of this lobe is the **postcentral gyrus,** which is a mass of nervous tissue immediately posterior to the central sulcus. The parietal lobe is involved with general sensory functions, such as evaluating the shape and texture of objects being touched.

The **temporal lobe** lies inferior to the lateral sulcus and underlies the temporal bone. This lobe is involved with hearing and smell.

The **occipital lobe** forms the posterior region of each hemisphere and immediately underlies the occipital bone. This lobe is responsible for processing incoming visual information and storing visual memories.

The **insula** (in′s ū-lă; inland) is a small lobe deep to the lateral sulcus. It can be viewed by laterally reflecting (pulling aside) the temporal lobe. The insula's lack of accessibility has prevented aggressive studies of its function, but it is apparently involved in interoceptive awareness, emotional responses, empathy, and the interpretation of taste.

Table 15.3 summarizes the lobes of the cerebrum and their subdivisions.

15.3b Functional Areas of the Cerebrum

Research has shown that specific structural areas of the cerebral cortex have distinct motor and sensory functions. In contrast, some higher mental functions, such as language and memory, are dispersed over large areas. Three categories of functional areas are recognized: motor areas that control voluntary motor functions; sensory areas that provide conscious awareness of sensation; and association areas that primarily integrate and store information. Although many structural areas have been identified, there is still much that is not known or understood about the brain.

Motor Areas

The cortical areas that control motor functions are housed within the frontal lobes. The **primary motor cortex,** also called the *somatic motor area,* is located within the precentral gyrus of the frontal lobe (figure 15.11). Neurons there control voluntary skeletal muscle activity. The axons of these neurons project contralaterally (to the opposite side) to the brainstem and spinal cord. Thus, the left primary motor cortex controls the right-side voluntary muscles, and vice versa.

The primary motor cortex innervation to various body parts can be diagrammed as a **motor homunculus** (hō-mŭngk′y ū-lŭs; diminutive man) on the precentral gyrus (**figure 15.12**, *left*). The bizarre, distorted proportions of the homunculus body reflect the amount of cortex dedicated to the motor activity of each body part. For example, the hands are represented by a much larger area of cortex than the trunk, because the hand muscles perform much more detailed, precise movements than the trunk muscles do. From a functional perspective, more motor activity is devoted to the hand in humans than in other animals because our hands are adapted for the precise, fine motor movements needed to manipulate the environment, and many motor units are devoted to muscles that move the hand and fingers.

The **motor speech area,** previously called the *Broca area,* is located in most individuals within the inferolateral portion of the left frontal lobe (see figure 15.11). This region is responsible for controlling the muscular movements necessary for vocalization.

The **frontal eye field** is on the superior surface of the middle frontal gyrus, which is immediately anterior to the premotor cortex in the frontal lobe. These cortical areas control and regulate the eye movements needed for reading and coordinating binocular vision (vision in which both eyes are used together). Some investigators include the frontal eye fields within the premotor area, thus considering the frontal eye fields part of the motor association cortex.

Sensory Areas

The cortical areas within the parietal, temporal, and occipital lobes typically are involved with conscious awareness of sensation. Each of the major senses has a distinct cortical area.

The **primary somatosensory cortex** is housed within the postcentral gyrus of the parietal lobes. Neurons in this cortex receive general somatic sensory information from touch, pressure, pain, and temperature

Table 15.3 Cerebral Lobes

Lobe	Cortices and Association Areas Within Lobe	Primary Functions
Frontal	Primary motor cortex (located within precentral gyrus) Premotor cortex Motor speech area (Broca area) (usually found only on the left frontal lobe) Frontal eye fields	Higher intellectual functions (concentration, decision making, planning); personality; verbal communication; voluntary motor control of skeletal muscles
Parietal	Primary somatosensory cortex (located within postcentral gyrus) Somatosensory association area Part of Wernicke area	Sensory interpretation of textures and shapes; understanding speech and formulating words to express thoughts and emotions
Temporal	Primary auditory cortex Primary olfactory cortex Auditory association area Part of Wernicke area	Interpretation and storage of auditory and olfactory sensations; understanding speech
Occipital	Primary visual cortex Visual association areas	Conscious perception of visual stimuli; integration of eye-focusing movements; correlation of visual images with previous visual experiences
Insula	Primary gustatory cortex	Interpretation of taste; memory

Clinical View 15.5

Mapping Functional Brain Regions

Scientists and physicians have long been interested in developing functional brain maps that correlate specific parts of the cerebral cortex with specific functions. Among the first to develop such a map was Korbinian Brodmann. He studied the comparative anatomy of the mammalian brain cortex in the early 1900s and produced a map that shows the specific areas of the cerebral cortex where certain functions occur. Brodmann developed a numbering system that correlates with his map and shows that similar cognitive functions are usually sequential. For example, areas 3, 1, and 2 represent the primary somatosensory cortex; area 17 overlaps the primary visual cortex; and areas 44 and 45 form the motor speech area. In 1907 Brodmann published his Brodmann areas map of 52 specialized brain regions (figure *a*).

With the advent of new and more sophisticated medical imaging techniques, researchers have been able to update and revise the functional brain areas map. The Human Connectome Project (HCP; https://www.humanconnectome.org/), a consortium of researchers from three universities in the United States and the United Kingdom, examined the brains of 1200 volunteers using multimodal MRI techniques. The data collected by the HCP were analyzed and used to develop a modern map of the human brain, the first version of which was published in 2016. This map includes 97 additional functional brain areas (figure *b*) and better delineates some of the brain regions first mapped by Brodmann. The HCP continues to revise and update its functional brain map.

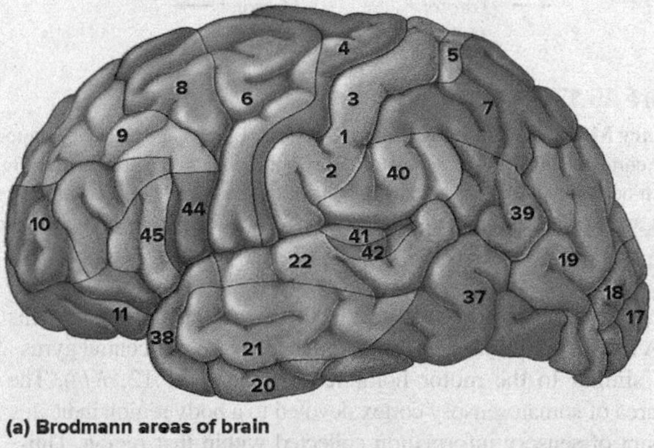

(a) Brodmann areas of brain

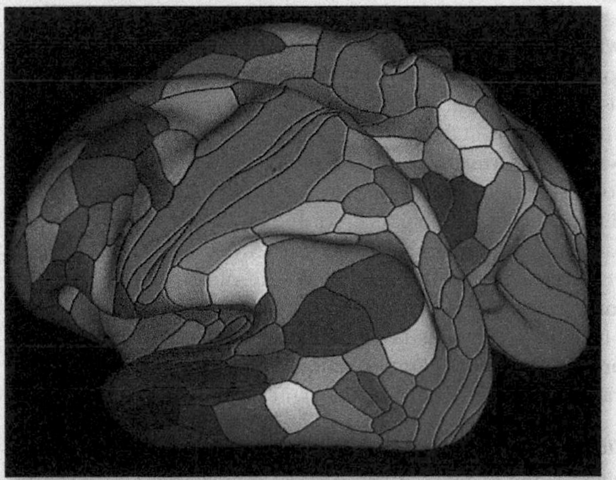

(b) Multimodal MRI of functional brain areas

A comparison of (a) Brodmann's map of the brain, showing selected Brodmann areas, and (b) a multimodal MRI from the Human Connectome Project, highlighting both previously known and newly discovered functional brain regions.

Dr. Matthew Glasser

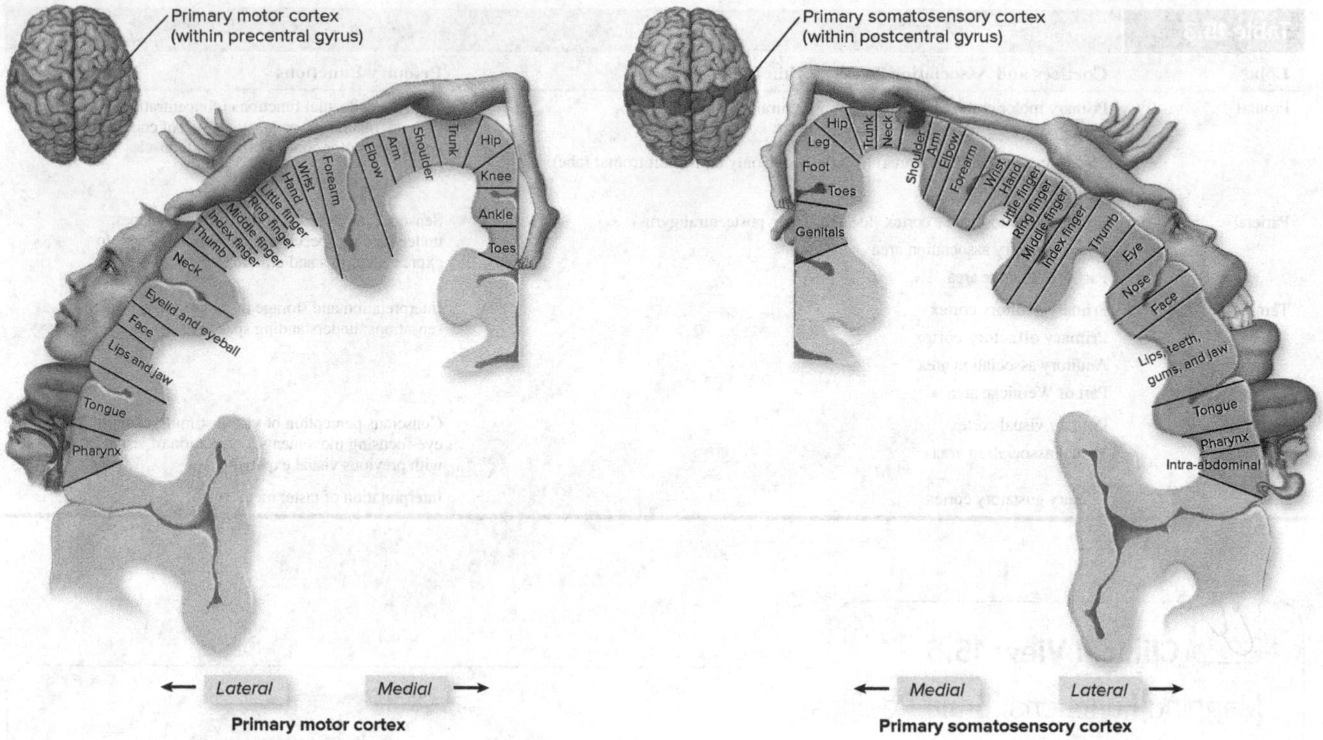

Figure 15.12

Primary Motor and Somatosensory Cortices. Body maps called the motor homunculus and the sensory homunculus illustrate the topography of the primary motor cortex and the primary somatosensory cortex in coronal section. The figure of the body (homunculus) depicts the nerve distributions; the size and location of each body region indicates relative innervation. Each cortex occurs on both sides of the brain but, for clarity, only the homunculus of the left primary motor cortex and the right primary somatosensory cortex are shown in this illustration.

receptors. We typically are conscious of the sensations received by this cortex. A **sensory homunculus** may be traced on the postcentral gyrus surface, similar to the motor homunculus (figure 15.12, *right*). The surface area of somatosensory cortex devoted to a body region indicates the amount of sensory information collected within that region. Thus, the lips, fingers, and genital region occupy larger portions of the homunculus, whereas the trunk of the body has proportionately fewer receptors, so its homunculus region is smaller. (However, the sensory homunculus shown is not as precise in real life, and there is extensive overlap between nearby body regions in the primary somatosensory cortex.)

Sensory information for sight, sound, taste, and smell arrives at other cortical regions (see figure 15.11). The **primary visual cortex,** located in the occipital lobe, receives and processes incoming visual information. The **primary auditory cortex,** located in the temporal lobe, receives and processes auditory information. The **primary gustatory** (gŭs′tă-tō′rē; *gustatio* = taste) **cortex** is in the insula and is involved in processing taste information. Finally, the **primary olfactory** (ol-fak′t ŏ-rē; *olfactus* = to smell) **cortex,** located in the temporal lobe, provides conscious awareness of smells.

Association Areas

The primary motor and sensory cortical regions are connected to adjacent **association areas** that either process and interpret incoming data or coordinate a motor response (see figure 15.11). Association areas integrate new sensory inputs with memories of past experiences. Descriptions of the main association areas are as follows:

The **premotor cortex,** also called the *somatic motor association area,* is located in the frontal lobe, immediately anterior to the precentral gyrus. It permits us to process motor information and is primarily responsible for coordinating learned, skilled motor activities, such as moving the eyes in a coordinated fashion when reading a book or playing the piano. An individual who has sustained trauma to this area would still be able to understand written letters and words, but would have difficulty reading because his or her eyes couldn't follow the lines on a printed page.

The **somatosensory association area** is located in the parietal lobe and lies immediately posterior to the primary somatosensory cortex. It interprets sensory information and is responsible for integrating and interpreting sensations to determine the texture, temperature, pressure, and shape of objects. The somatosensory association area allows us to identify objects while our eyes are closed. For example, we can tell the difference between the coarse feel of a handful of dirt, the smooth, round shape of a marble, and the thin, flat, rounded surface of a coin because those textures have already been stored in the somatosensory association area.

The **auditory association area** is located within the temporal lobe, posteroinferior to the primary auditory cortex. Within this area, the cortical neurons interpret the characteristics of sound and store memories of sounds heard in the past. The next time an annoying song is playing over and over in your head, you will know that this auditory association area is responsible (so try to hear a favorite song before turning off the music from your computer or phone).

The **visual association area** is located in the occipital lobe and surrounds the primary visual area. It enables us to process visual information by analyzing color, movement, and form, and to use this information to identify the things we see. For example, when we look at a face, the primary visual cortex receives bits of visual information, but the visual association area is responsible for integrating all of this information into a recognizable picture of a face.

A functional brain region acts like a multi-association area between lobes for integrating information from individual association areas. One functional brain region is the **Wernicke area** (see figure 15.11), which is typically located only within the left hemisphere, where it overlaps the parietal and temporal lobes. The Wernicke area is involved in recognizing, understanding, and comprehending spoken or written language. As you may expect, the Wernicke area and the motor speech area must work together in order for fluent communication to occur.

WHAT DO YOU THINK?

4 On January 8, 2011, then-U.S. Representative Gabrielle Giffords was critically injured by a gunshot wound to the head (reportedly an assassination attempt on her). After the shooting, she was able to understand verbal communication but was unable to respond verbally. In this context, what side of the brain did the bullet penetrate, and which functional brain region likely was most damaged?

Higher-Order Processing Centers

Other association areas are called higher-order processing areas. These centers process incoming information from several different association areas and ultimately direct either extremely complex motor activity or complicated analytical functions in response. Both cerebral hemispheres house higher-order processing centers involving such functions as speech, cognition, understanding spatial relationships, and general interpretation (see section 17.4).

15.3c Central White Matter

The **central white matter** lies deep to the gray matter of the cerebral cortex and is composed primarily of myelinated axons. Most of these axons are grouped into bundles called tracts, which are classified as association tracts, commissural tracts, or projection tracts (**figure 15.13**).

Association tracts connect different regions of the cerebral cortex within the same hemisphere. Short association tracts are composed of **arcuate** (ar′ky ū-āt; *arcuatus* = bowed) **fibers;** they connect neighboring gyri within the same lobe. The longer association tracts, which are composed of **longitudinal fasciculi** (fa-sik′y ū-lī; *fascis* = bundle), connect gyri in different lobes of the same hemisphere. An example of an association tract composed of arcuate fibers is the tract that connects the primary motor cortex (of the frontal lobe) with the premotor or motor association area (also within the frontal lobe). An example of a longitudinal fasciculi is the tract that connects the Wernicke area to the motor speech area.

Commissural (kom′i-sy ūr′ăl; *committo* = combine) **tracts** extend between the cerebral hemispheres through axonal bridges called commissures. The prominent commissural tracts that link the left and right cerebral hemispheres include the large, C-shaped **corpus callosum** and the smaller **anterior** and **posterior commissures.**

Projection tracts link the cerebral cortex to the inferior brain regions and the spinal cord. Examples of projection tracts are the corticospinal tracts that carry motor signals from the cerebrum to the brainstem and spinal cord. The packed group of axons in these tracts passing to and from the cortex between the cerebral nuclei is called the **internal capsule.**

Clinical View 15.6

Autism Spectrum Disorder

Autism spectrum disorder (ASD), also known simply as *autism,* is a widely variable disorder of neural development that affects 1 in 88 children in the United States alone. It typically is recognized in early childhood, but diagnosis may be difficult until a child is older. Since 2013, the phrase *autism spectrum disorder* is used to group and describe a variety of similar disorders including autistic disorder, childhood disintegrative disorder, and Asperger syndrome. ASD varies in severity among those affected (hence the term *spectrum* in its name), but all are characterized by some form of social and communication difficulties. Some children may experience delays in language acquisition or may be completely nonverbal. Social interaction is difficult, ranging from inability to reciprocate interest during a conversation to being withdrawn into the child's "own world." Intelligence also varies widely, from severe cognitive delay to possessing savantlike skills in focused areas like math or music.

Individuals with ASD often are highly sensitive to stimuli such as loud noises or unfamiliar people, and may struggle in adjusting to changes in routine. Discomfort due to overstimulation or frustration in the inability to communicate can lead to tantrums or "meltdowns." Other behaviors and traits commonly associated with ASD include repetitive motions like hand flapping or rocking, resistance to changes in routine (e.g., insisting on wearing the same shirt or eating the same meal each day), inability to engage in pretend play, inability to gauge the feelings of others, and intense interest in a particular activity or subject.

ASD is believed to stem from an inability of the brain to process information between neurons. However, the specific mechanisms and causes of the condition are not well understood or agreed upon. Genetic factors are thought to be involved, in part because autism affects males four times more often than females, and it often manifests in siblings. Biochemical and environmental factors have also been explored as potential causes, but few definitive answers exist. The disturbing aspect of this condition is that the number of cases has steadily increased since the late 1980s. The ability to detect the condition has improved, which may have increased the incidence of diagnosis.

A fraudulent paper published in 1988 claimed that the measles, mumps, and rubella (MMR) vaccine was linked to an increased risk of developing autism. In the years that followed, the paper was shown to have manipulated data and the study was inherently flawed, resulting in a retraction of the paper and the author (who was an MD) losing his medical license for serious professional misconduct. Numerous studies since then have shown no link between vaccines and developing autism. Unfortunately, the misconception that vaccines cause ASD still persists among some and has led to both a decline in vaccination rates and an increase in disease outbreaks as a result.

Treatment for ASD includes proven methods of speech and behavioral therapy, as well as holistic approaches that involve various diets, supplements, and experimental procedures. Some children with autism will go on to develop skills and live independent lives, whereas others will not. The biggest predictors for independence in adulthood are level of intelligence and ability to communicate.

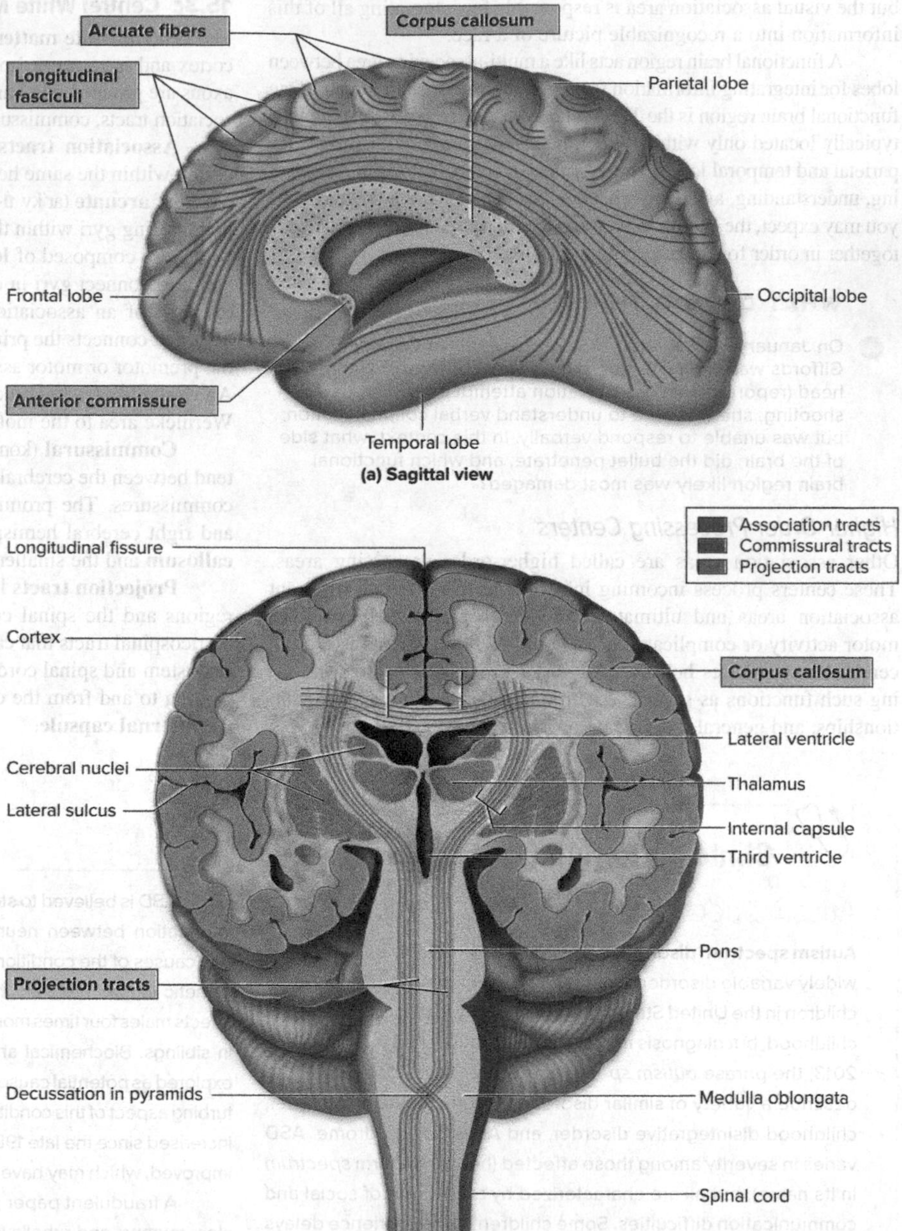
Arcuate fibers
Corpus callosum
Longitudinal fasciculi
Parietal lobe
Frontal lobe
Occipital lobe
Anterior commissure
Temporal lobe
(a) Sagittal view
Association tracts
Commissural tracts
Projection tracts
Longitudinal fissure
Cortex
Corpus callosum
Lateral ventricle
Cerebral nuclei
Thalamus
Lateral sulcus
Internal capsule
Third ventricle
Pons
Projection tracts
Decussation in pyramids
Medulla oblongata
Spinal cord
(b) Coronal section

Figure 15.13
Central White Matter Tracts. White matter tracts are composed of both myelinated and unmyelinated axons. Three major groups of axons are recognized based on their distribution. (*a*) A sagittal view shows arcuate fibers and longitudinal fasciculi association tracts, which extend between gyri within one hemisphere. (*b*) A coronal view shows how commissural tracts extend between cerebral hemispheres, whereas projection tracts extend between the hemispheres and the brainstem.

Table 15.4 White Matter Tracts in the Cerebrum

Tracts	Distribution of Axons	Examples
Association tracts	Connect separate cortical areas within the same hemisphere	Arcuate fibers, longitudinal fasciculi
Arcuate fibers	Connect neighboring gyri within a single cerebral lobe	Tracts connecting primary motor cortex (frontal lobe) to motor association area (frontal lobe)
Longitudinal fasciculi	Connect gyri between different cerebral lobes of the same hemisphere	Tracts connecting Wernicke area (parietal/temporal lobes) and motor speech area (frontal lobe)
Commissural tracts	Connect corresponding lobes of the right and left hemispheres	Corpus callosum, anterior commissure, posterior commissure
Projection tracts	Connect cerebral cortex to the diencephalon, brainstem, cerebellum, and spinal cord	Corticospinal tracts (motor axons traveling from cerebral cortex to spinal cord; sensory axons traveling from spinal cord to cerebrum)

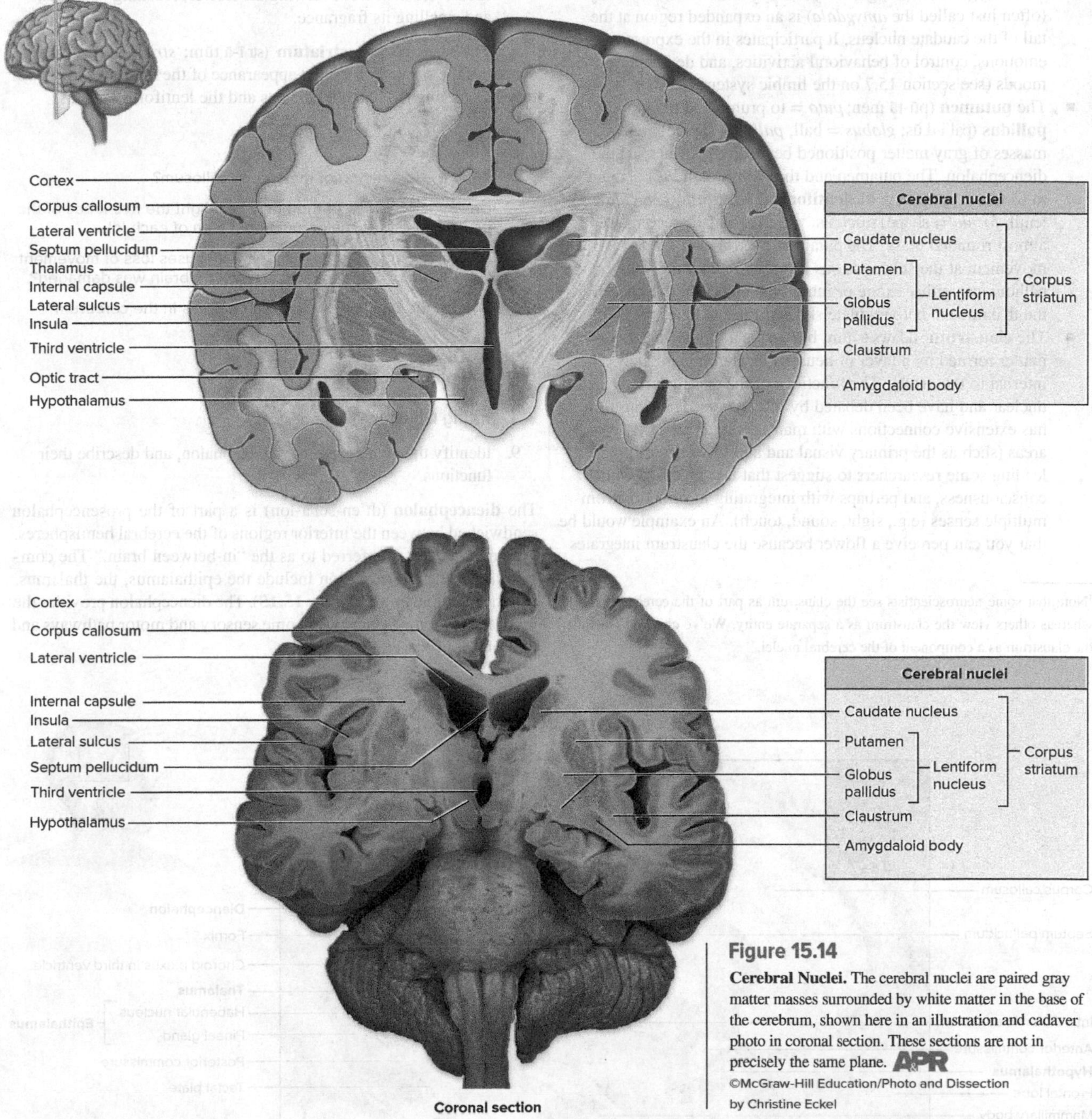
Cortex
Corpus callosum
Lateral ventricle
Septum pellucidum
Thalamus
Internal capsule
Lateral sulcus
Insula
Third ventricle
Optic tract
Hypothalamus
Cerebral nuclei
Caudate nucleus
Putamen
Globus pallidus
Lentiform nucleus
Corpus striatum
Claustrum
Amygdaloid body
Cortex
Corpus callosum
Lateral ventricle
Internal capsule
Insula
Lateral sulcus
Septum pellucidum
Third ventricle
Hypothalamus
Cerebral nuclei
Caudate nucleus
Putamen
Globus pallidus
Lentiform nucleus
Corpus striatum
Claustrum
Amygdaloid body
Coronal section

Figure 15.14

Cerebral Nuclei. The cerebral nuclei are paired gray matter masses surrounded by white matter in the base of the cerebrum, shown here in an illustration and cadaver photo in coronal section. These sections are not in precisely the same plane. APR

Table 15.4 summarizes the characteristics of the three white matter tracts of the cerebrum.

15.3d Cerebral Nuclei

The **cerebral nuclei** (also called the *basal nuclei;* and sometimes erroneously referred to as *basal ganglia*) are paired, irregular masses of gray matter buried deep within the central white matter in the basal region of the cerebral hemispheres inferior to the floor of the lateral ventricle (**figure 15.14**; see figure 15.3*a*). (These masses of gray matter are sometimes incorrectly called the basal ganglia. However, the term *ganglion* is best restricted to clusters of neuron cell bodies *outside* the CNS, whereas a *nucleus* is a collection of cell bodies *within* the CNS.)

Cerebral nuclei have the following components:

- The C-shaped **caudate** (kaw′d āt; *caud* = tail) **nucleus** has an enlarged head and a slender, arching tail that parallels the swinging curve of the lateral ventricle. When a person begins to walk, the neurons in this nucleus stimulate the appropriate muscles to produce the pattern and rhythm of arm and leg movements associated with walking.

- The **amygdaloid** (ă-mig′d ă-loyd; *amygdala* = almond) **body** (often just called the *amygdala*) is an expanded region at the tail of the caudate nucleus. It participates in the expression of emotions, control of behavioral activities, and development of moods (see section 15.7 on the limbic system).
- The **putamen** (pū-tā′men; *puto* = to prune) and the **globus pallidus** (pal′i-d ŭs; *globus* = ball, *pallidus* = pale) are two masses of gray matter positioned between the insula and the diencephalon. The putamen and the globus pallidus combine to form a larger body, the **lentiform** (len′ti-f ōrm; *lenticula* = lentil, *forma* = shape) **nucleus,** which is usually a compact, almost rounded mass. The putamen controls muscular movement at the subconscious level, whereas the globus pallidus can either excite or inhibit the anterior group nuclei of the thalamus to help regulate skeletal muscle tone.
- The **claustrum**[1] (klaws′tr ŭm; barrier) is a thin sliver of gray matter formed by a layer of neurons located immediately internal to the insula. The functions of the claustrum are unclear and have been debated by researchers. The claustrum has extensive connections with many cerebral cortex areas (such as the primary visual and auditory cortices), leading some researchers to suggest that it is involved with consciousness, and perhaps with integrating information from multiple senses (e.g., sight, sound, touch). An example would be that you can perceive a flower because the claustrum integrates the information from viewing the flower, touching its petals, and smelling its fragrance.

[1]Note that some neuroscientists see the claustrum as part of the cerebral nuclei, whereas others view the claustrum as a separate entity. We've chosen to include the claustrum as a component of the cerebral nuclei.

The term **corpus striatum** (str ī-ā′tŭm; *striatus* = furrowed) describes the striated or striped appearance of the internal capsule as it passes among the caudate nucleus and the lentiform nucleus.

WHAT DID YOU LEARN?

7. What is the function of the corpus callosum?
8. Draw a lateral view of the brain. Highlight the five lobes of the brain, and list the major functional area of each lobe.
9. An athlete suffers a head injury that causes loss of movement in his left leg. What specific area of the brain was damaged?
10. What is the function of association areas in the cerebrum?

15.4 Diencephalon

✓ Learning Objective

9. Identify the divisions of the diencephalon, and describe their functions.

The **diencephalon** (dī′en-sef′ă-lon) is a part of the prosencephalon sandwiched between the inferior regions of the cerebral hemispheres. This region is often referred to as the "in-between brain." The components of the diencephalon include the epithalamus, the thalamus, and the hypothalamus (**figure 15.15**). The diencephalon provides the relay and switching centers for some sensory and motor pathways and for control of visceral activities.

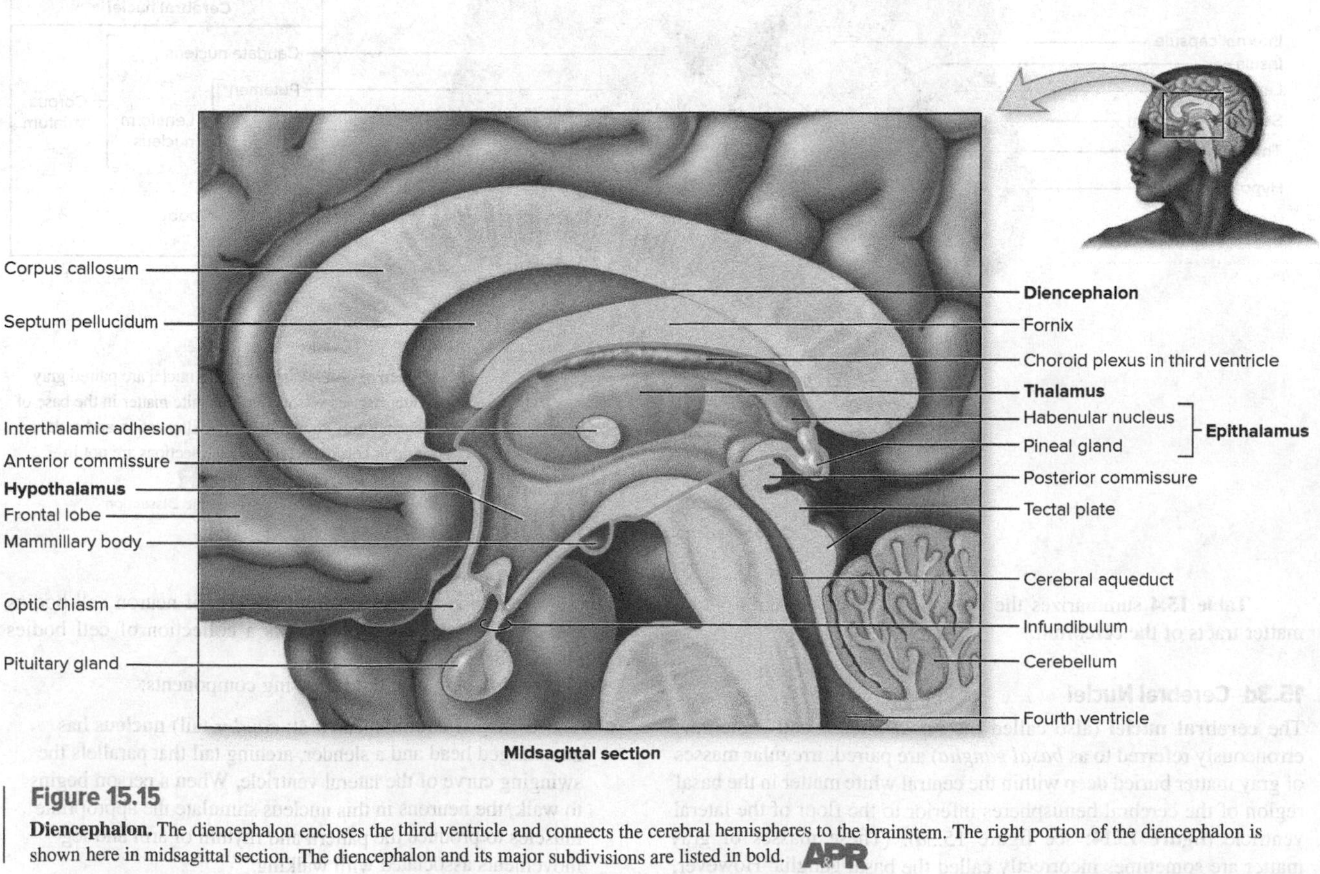

Figure 15.15

Diencephalon. The diencephalon encloses the third ventricle and connects the cerebral hemispheres to the brainstem. The right portion of the diencephalon is shown here in midsagittal section. The diencephalon and its major subdivisions are listed in bold. APR

15.4a Epithalamus

The **epithalamus** (ep′i-thal′ ă-mŭs) partially forms the posterior roof of the diencephalon and covers the third ventricle. The posterior portion of the epithalamus houses the pineal gland and the habenular nuclei. The **pineal** (pin′ē-ăl; *pineus* = pinecone-like) **gland** (or *pineal body*) is an endocrine gland. It secretes the hormone **melatonin,** which appears to help regulate day–night cycles known as the body's **circadian rhythm.** (Some companies are marketing the sale of melatonin in pill form as a cure for jet lag, although this "cure" has yet to be proven.) The **habenular** (hă-ben′yū-lăr; *habena* = strap) **nuclei** help relay signals from the *limbic system* (described in section 15.7) to the midbrain and are involved in visceral and emotional responses to odors.

15.4b Thalamus

The **thalamus** (thal′ ă-mŭs; bed) refers to paired oval masses of gray matter that lie on each side of the third ventricle (**figure 15.16**). The thalamus forms the superolateral walls of the third ventricle. When viewed in midsagittal section, the thalamus is located between the anterior commissure and the pineal gland. The **interthalamic adhesion** (or *intermediate mass*) is a small, midline mass of gray matter that connects the right and left thalamic bodies.

Each part of the thalamus is a gray matter mass composed of about a dozen major **thalamic nuclei;** axons from these nuclei project to specific regions of the cerebral cortex (figure 15.16*b*). Sensory impulses from all the conscious senses except olfaction converge on the thalamus and synapse in at least one of its nuclei. The major functions of each group of nuclei are detailed in **table 15.5**.

The thalamus is the principal and final relay point for sensory information that will be processed and projected to the primary somatosensory cortex. Only a relatively small portion of the sensory information that arrives at the thalamus is forwarded to the cerebrum because the thalamus acts as an information filter. For example, the thalamus is responsible for filtering out the sounds and sights in a busy

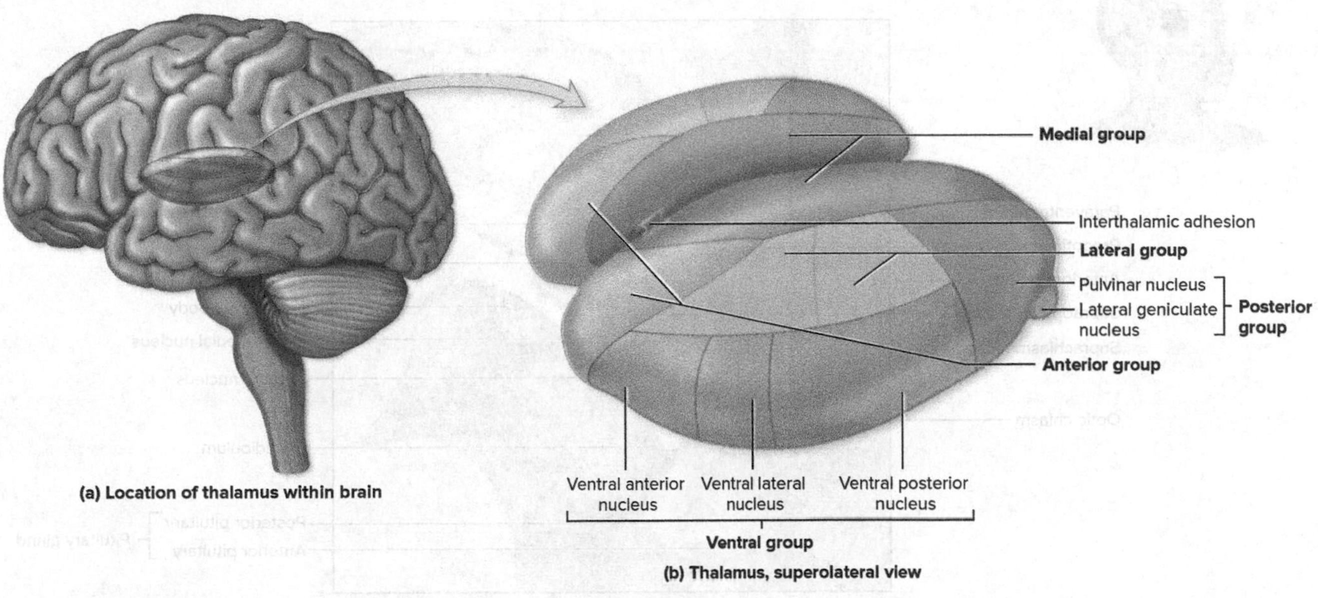
(a) Location of thalamus within brain
Medial group
Interthalamic adhesion
Lateral group
Pulvinar nucleus
Lateral geniculate nucleus
Posterior group
Anterior group
Ventral anterior nucleus
Ventral lateral nucleus
Ventral posterior nucleus
Ventral group
(b) Thalamus, superolateral view

Figure 15.16

Thalamus. (*a*) Lateral view of the brain identifies the approximate internal location of the thalamus. (*b*) The thalamus is composed of clusters of nuclei organized into groups, as shown in this enlarged view. Not all of the nuclei may be seen from this angle.

Table 15.5 Functions Controlled by Thalamic Nuclei

Nuclei Group	Function(s)
Anterior group	Changes motor cortex excitability (by connections with the globus pallidus of the cerebral nuclei) and modifies mood
Lateral group	Controls sensory flow to parietal lobes and emotional information to cingulate gyrus
Medial group	Sends signals about conscious awareness of emotional states to frontal lobes
Posterior group	Lateral geniculate nuclei: Relay visual information from optic tract to visual cortex and midbrain Medial geniculate nuclei: Relay auditory information from inner ear to auditory cortex Pulvinar nuclei: Integrate and relay sensory information for projection to association areas of cerebral cortex
Ventral group	Ventral anterior nuclei: Relay somatic motor information from cerebral nuclei and cerebellum to primary motor cortex and premotor cortex of frontal lobe Ventral lateral nuclei: Same as ventral anterior nuclei Ventral posterior nuclei: Relay sensory information to primary somatosensory cortex of parietal lobe

dorm cafeteria when you are trying to study. The thalamus also "clues in" the cerebrum about where this sensory information came from. For example, the thalamus lets the cerebrum know that a nerve impulse it receives came from the eye, indicating that the information is visual.

WHAT DO YOU THINK?

5 If there were no thalamus, how would the cerebrum's interpretation of sensory stimuli be affected?

15.4c Hypothalamus

The **hypothalamus** (hī′pō-thal′ ă-mŭs; *hypo* = under) is the anteroinferior region of the diencephalon. A thin, stalklike **infundibulum** (in′f ŭn-dib′y ū-lŭm; funnel) extends inferiorly from the hypothalamus to attach to the pituitary gland (**figure 15.17**).

Functions of the Hypothalamus

The hypothalamus has numerous functions, which are controlled by specific nuclei as listed in **table 15.6**. Functions of the hypothalamus include:

- **Master control of the autonomic nervous system.** The hypothalamus is a major autonomic integration center. In essence, it is the "president" of the corporation known as the autonomic nervous system (see section 18.6). It projects descending axons to autonomic nuclei in the inferior brainstem that influence heart rate, blood pressure, digestive activities, and respiration.
- **Master control of the endocrine system.** The hypothalamus is also "president" of another "corporation"—the endocrine system (see section 20.2)—overseeing most but not all of that

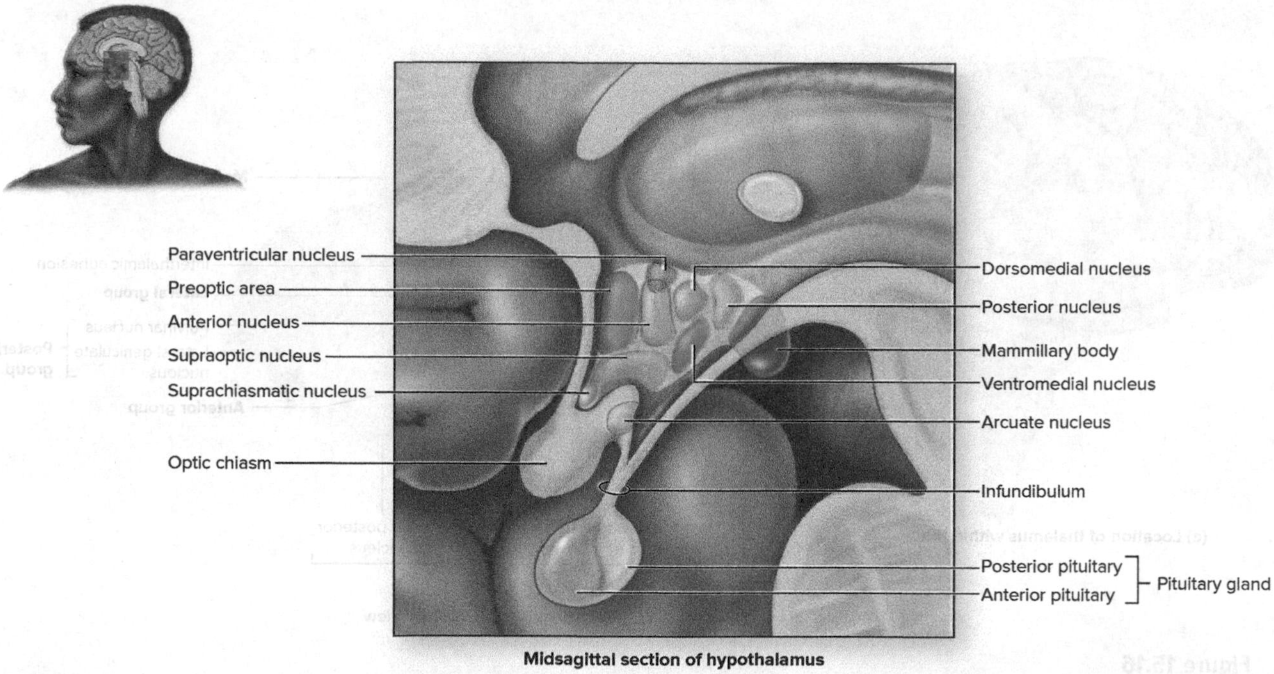

Figure 15.17
Hypothalamus. The hypothalamus is located anteroinferior to the thalamus and is organized into multiple nuclei.

Table 15.6 Functions Controlled by Selected Hypothalamic Structures

Nucleus or Hypothalamic Region	Function(s)
Anterior nucleus	"Thirst center" (stimulates fluid intake); autonomic control center
Arcuate nucleus	Regulates appetite, releases gonadotropin-releasing hormone, releases growth hormone-releasing hormone, and releases prolactin-inhibiting hormone
Mammillary body	Processes sensations related to olfaction; controls swallowing
Paraventricular nucleus	Produces oxytocin primarily
Preoptic area	"Thermostat" (regulates body temperature)
Suprachiasmatic nucleus	Regulates sleep–wake (circadian) rhythm
Supraoptic nucleus	Produces antidiuretic hormone (ADH) primarily
Ventromedial nucleus	"Satiety center" (produces hunger and satiety sensations)

system's functions. The hypothalamus secretes hormones that control secretory activities in the anterior pituitary gland. In turn, subsequent normal secretions from the pituitary gland control metabolism, growth, stress responses, and reproduction. Additionally, the hypothalamus produces two hormones that are transported through axons in the infundibulum and then stored and released in the posterior pituitary: Antidiuretic hormone reduces water loss at the kidneys, and oxytocin stimulates smooth muscle contractions in the uterus, mammary gland, and prostate gland.

- **Regulation of body temperature.** The body's thermostat is located within the hypothalamus. Neurons in the preoptic area detect altered blood temperatures and signal other hypothalamic nuclei, which control the mechanisms that heat or cool the body (shivering and sweating, respectively).
- **Control of emotional behavior.** The hypothalamus is located at the center of the limbic system, the part of the brain that controls emotional responses, such as pleasure, aggression, fear, rage, contentment, and the sex drive.
- **Control of food intake.** Neurons within the ventromedial nucleus monitor levels of nutrients such as glucose and amino acids in the blood and produce sensations of hunger.
- **Control of water intake.** Specific neurons within the anterior nucleus continuously monitor the blood solute (dissolved substances) concentration. High solute concentration stimulates both the intake of fluid and the production of antidiuretic hormone by neurons in the supraoptic nucleus and paraventricular nucleus (see section 20.2).
- **Regulation of sleep–wake (circadian) rhythms.** The suprachiasmatic nucleus directs the pineal gland when to secrete melatonin. Thus, both work to regulate circadian rhythms.

WHAT DID YOU LEARN?

11 Where is the epithalamus? What is the location and function of the pineal gland in relation to the epithalamus?

12 Describe the structure and the general function of the thalamus.

13 How does the hypothalamus regulate our water intake?

15.5 Brainstem

✓ Learning Objective

10. Identify the components of the brainstem, and describe their functions.

The **brainstem** connects the prosencephalon and cerebellum to the spinal cord. Three regions form the brainstem: the superiorly placed midbrain, the pons, and the inferiorly placed medulla oblongata (figure 15.18). The brainstem is a bidirectional passageway for all tracts extending between the cerebrum and the spinal cord. It also contains many autonomic centers and reflex centers required for our survival, and it houses nuclei of many of the cranial nerves.

15.5a Midbrain

The **midbrain** is the superior portion of the brainstem. Extending through the midbrain is the **cerebral aqueduct** connecting the third and fourth ventricles; it is surrounded by a region called the **periaqueductal gray matter** (figure 15.19). The nuclei of two cranial nerves that control some eye movements are housed in the midbrain: the oculomotor nerve (CN III) and the trochlear nerve (CN IV). The midbrain contains several major regions.

Cerebral peduncles (pe'd ŭng'kĕl; *pedunculus* = little foot) are motor tracts located on the anterolateral surfaces of the mesencephalon. Somatic motor axons descend (project inferiorly) from the primary motor cortex, through these peduncles, to the spinal cord. In addition, the midbrain is the final destination of the **superior cerebellar peduncles** connecting the cerebellum to the midbrain.

The **tegmentum** (teg-men't ŭm; covering structure) is sandwiched between the substantia nigra (described in the next paragraph) and the periaqueductal gray matter. The tegmentum contains the pigmented **red nuclei** and the reticular formation (to be discussed in section 17.4f). The reddish color of the nuclei is due to both blood vessel density and iron pigmentation in the neuronal cell bodies. The tegmentum integrates information from the cerebrum and cerebellum and issues involuntary motor commands to the erector spinae muscles of the back to help maintain posture while standing, bending at the waist, or walking.

The **substantia nigra** (sŭb-stan'sh ē-ă nī'gră; *niger* = black) consists of bilaterally symmetrical nuclei within the midbrain. It is best seen in cross section (figure 15.19). Its name derives from its almost black appearance, which is due to melanin pigmentation. The substantia nigra is squeezed between the cerebral peduncles and the tegmentum. The medial lemniscus (see section 15.5c on the medulla oblongata) is a band of axons immediately posterior to the substantia nigra. The substantia nigra houses clusters of neurons that produce the neurotransmitter dopamine, which affects brain processes that control movement, emotional response, and ability to experience pleasure and pain. These neurons are dark-hued due to the melanin they contain. Degeneration of these cells in the substantia nigra is a key characteristic in Parkinson disease (see Clinical View 15.8: "Brain Disorders" in section 15.7).

The **tectum** (tek't ŭm; roof) is the posterior region of the midbrain dorsal to the cerebral aqueduct. It contains two pairs of sensory nuclei, the superior and inferior colliculi, which are collectively called the **tectal plate** (*quadrigeminal* [kwah'dri-jem'i-n ăl] *plate* or *corpora quadrigemina*) (see figure 15.18b). These nuclei are relay stations in the processing pathway of visual and auditory sensations. The **superior colliculi** (ko-lik'yū-lī; sing., *colliculus;* mound) are the superior nuclei. They are called *visual reflex centers* because they help visually track moving objects and control reflexes such as turning the eyes and head in response to a visual stimulus. For example, the superior colliculi are at work when you think you see a large animal running at you and turn suddenly toward the image. The paired **inferior colliculi** are the *auditory reflex centers.* They control the turning of your head and eyes in unison toward an unexpected sound. For example, the inferior colliculi are at work when you hear the loud "BANG!" of a car backfiring and you turn suddenly toward the noise.

Learning Strategy 15.3

Just as the eyes are superior to the ears, the superior colliculi (which control visual reflexes) are superior to the inferior colliculi (which control auditory reflexes).

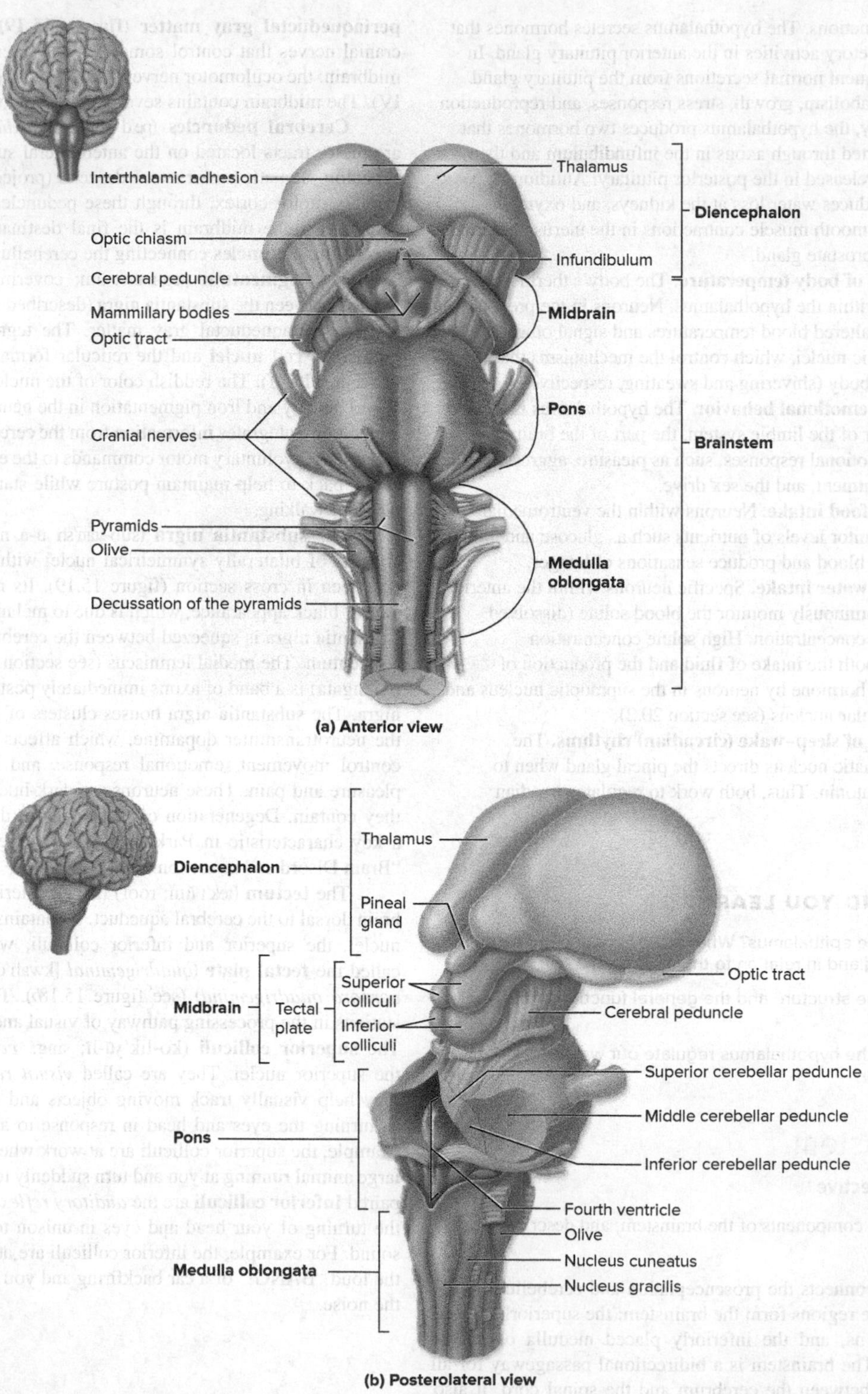
Thalamus
Interthalamic adhesion
Diencephalon
Optic chiasm
Infundibulum
Cerebral peduncle
Mammillary bodies
Midbrain
Optic tract
Pons
Cranial nerves
Brainstem
Pyramids
Olive
Medulla oblongata
Decussation of the pyramids
(a) Anterior view
Thalamus
Diencephalon
Pineal gland
Superior colliculi
Midbrain
Tectal plate
Inferior colliculi
Optic tract
Cerebral peduncle
Superior cerebellar peduncle
Middle cerebellar peduncle
Pons
Inferior cerebellar peduncle
Fourth ventricle
Olive
Nucleus cuneatus
Medulla oblongata
Nucleus gracilis
(b) Posterolateral view

Figure 15.18

Brainstem. (*a*) Anterior and (*b*) posterolateral views show the locations of the midbrain, pons, and medulla oblongata within the brainstem.

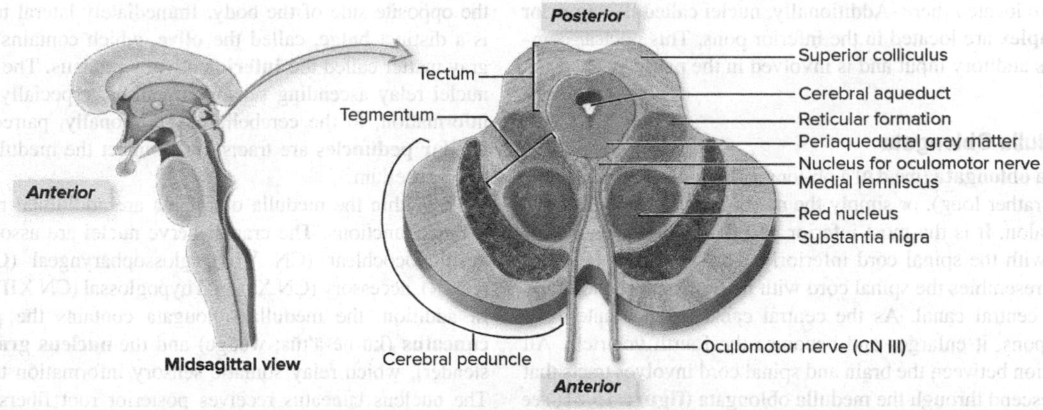

Figure 15.19

Midbrain. Components of the midbrain are shown in cross-sectional view.

15.5b Pons

The **pons** (ponz; bridge) is a bulging region on the anterior part of the brainstem that forms from part of the metencephalon (**figure 15.20**; see figure 15.18). Housed within the pons are sensory and motor tracts that connect to the brain and spinal cord. In addition, the **middle cerebellar peduncles** are transverse groups of fibers that connect the pons to the cerebellum. The pons houses the autonomic structure called the **pontine respiratory center** (previously called the *pneumotaxic* [nū′mō-tak′sik] *center*). This vital center, along with the medullary respiratory center within the medulla oblongata, regulates the skeletal muscles of breathing.

The pons houses sensory and motor cranial nerve nuclei for the trigeminal (CN V), abducens (CN VI), and facial (CN VII) cranial nerves. Some of the nuclei for the vestibulocochlear cranial nerve

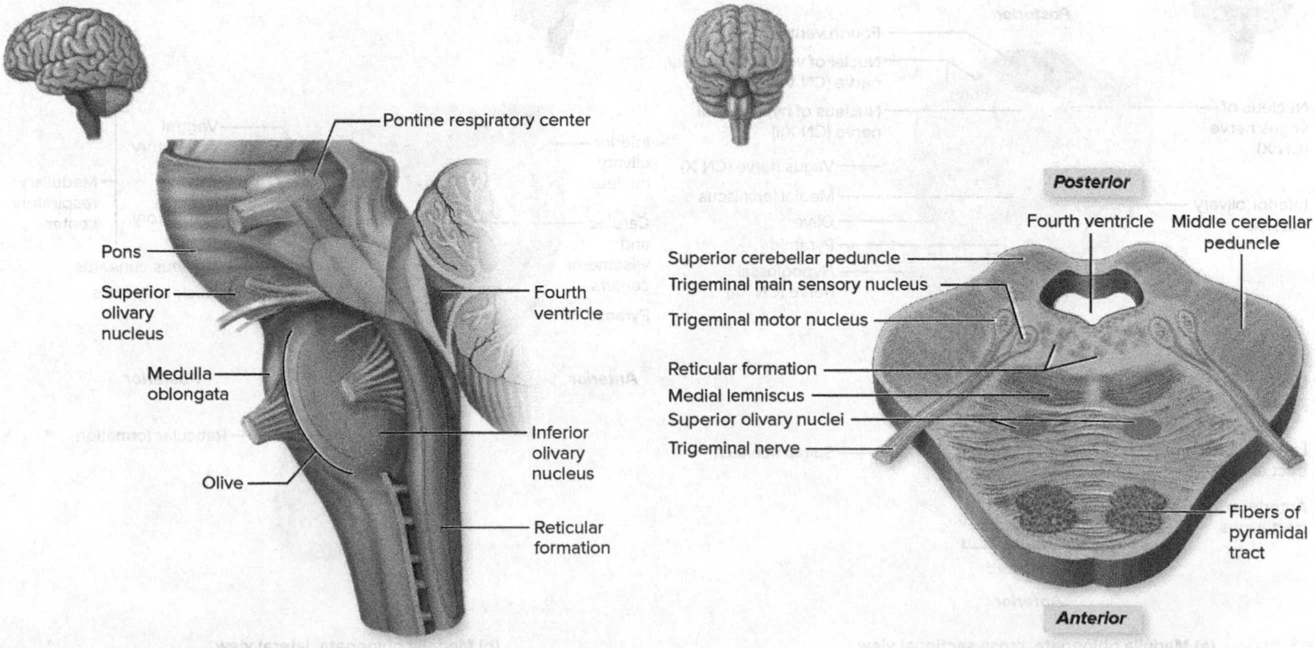

Figure 15.20

Pons. The pons is a bulge on the ventral side of the hindbrain that contains nerve tracts, nuclei, and part of the reticular formation. (*a*) A partially cut-away longitudinal section identifies the pontine respiratory center and the superior olivary nucleus. (*b*) A cross section through the pons shows the superior olivary nuclei, fiber tracts, and some cranial nerve nuclei.

(CN VIII) are located there. Additionally, nuclei called the **superior olivary complex** are located in the inferior pons. This nuclear complex receives auditory input and is involved in the pathway for sound localization.

15.5c Medulla Oblongata

The **medulla oblongata** (me-d ūl'ă ob-long-gah'tă; marrow or middle; *oblongus* = rather long), or simply the **medulla,** is formed from the myelencephalon. It is the most inferior part of the brainstem and is continuous with the spinal cord inferiorly. The posterior portion of the medulla resembles the spinal cord with its flattened, round shape and narrow central canal. As the central canal extends anteriorly toward the pons, it enlarges and becomes the fourth ventricle. All communication between the brain and spinal cord involves tracts that ascend or descend through the medulla oblongata (**figure 15.21**; see figures 15.18 and 15.20).

Several external landmarks are visible on the medulla oblongata. The anterior surface exhibits two longitudinal ridges called the **pyramids** (pir'ă-mid), which house the motor projection tracts called the corticospinal (pyramidal) tracts. In the posterior region of the medulla, most of these axons cross to the opposite side of the brain at a point called the **decussation of the pyramids** (dē-kŭ-sā'shŭn; *decussate* = to cross in the form of an X). As a result of the crossover, each cerebral hemisphere controls the voluntary movements of the opposite side of the body. Immediately lateral to each pyramid is a distinct bulge, called the **olive,** which contains a large fold of gray matter called the **inferior olivary nucleus.** The inferior olivary nuclei relay ascending sensory impulses, especially proprioceptive information, to the cerebellum. Additionally, paired **inferior cerebellar peduncles** are tracts that connect the medulla oblongata to the cerebellum.

Within the medulla oblongata are additional nuclei that have various functions. The cranial nerve nuclei are associated with the vestibulocochlear (CN VIII), glossopharyngeal (CN IX), vagus (CN X), accessory (CN XI), and hypoglossal (CN XII) cranial nerves. In addition, the medulla oblongata contains the paired **nucleus cuneatus** (kū-nē-ā'tŭs; wedge) and the **nucleus gracilis** (gras'i-lis; slender), which relay somatic sensory information to the thalamus. The nucleus cuneatus receives posterior root fibers corresponding to sensory innervation from the upper limb of the same side. The nucleus gracilis receives posterior root fibers carrying sensory information from the lower limb of the same side. Bands of myelinated fibers composing a **medial lemniscus** exit these nuclei and decussate in the inferior region of the medulla oblongata. The medial lemniscus projects through the brainstem to the ventral posterior nucleus of the thalamus.

Finally, the medulla oblongata contains several **autonomic nuclei,** which regulate functions vital for life. Autonomic nuclei

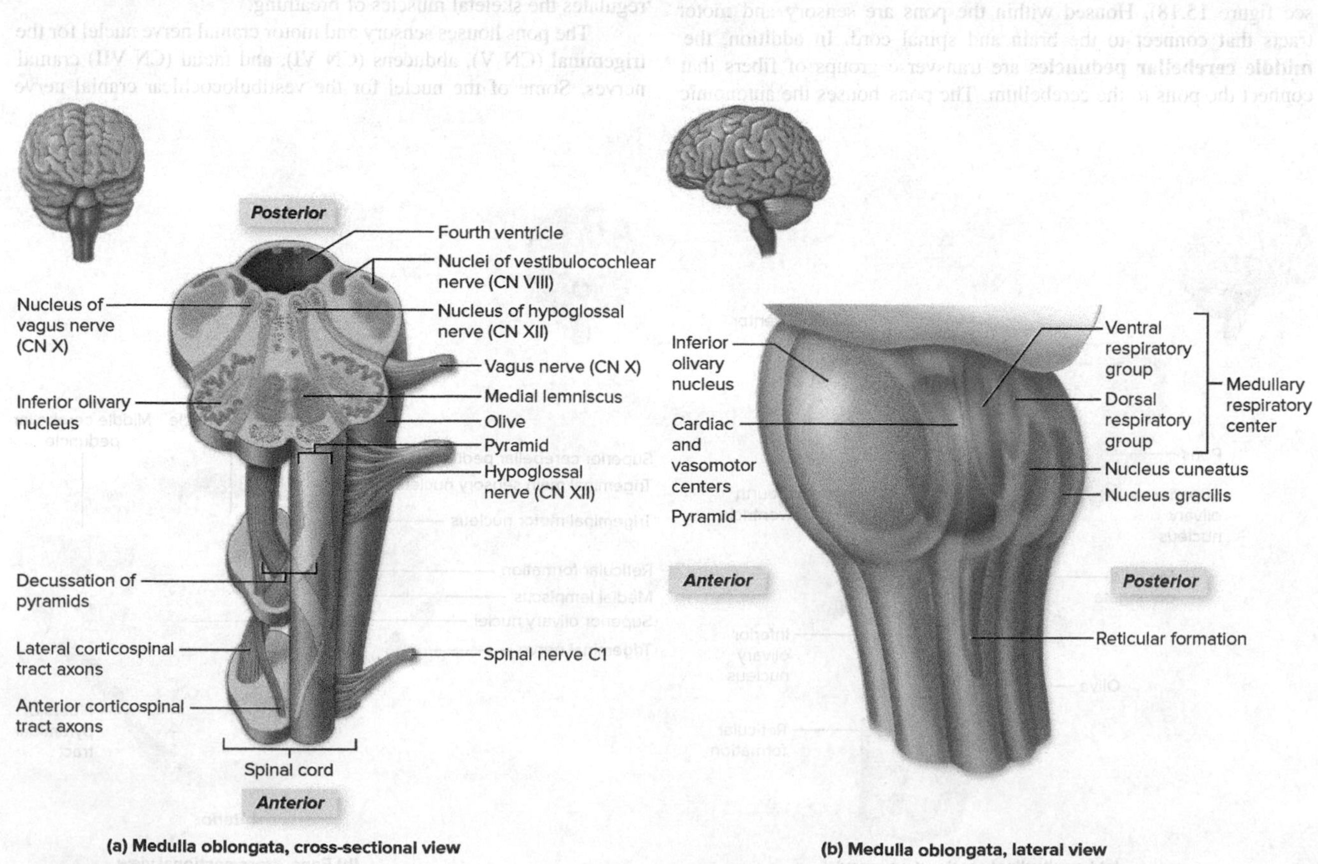

(a) Medulla oblongata, cross-sectional view

(b) Medulla oblongata, lateral view

Figure 15.21

Medulla Oblongata. The medulla oblongata connects the brain to the spinal cord. (*a*) A cross section illustrates important internal structures and decussations of the pyramids. (*b*) The medulla contains several nuclei that are involved in regulating the heart and respiratory rates and in receiving and sending sensory information about upper and lower limb movements. APR group together to form centers in the medulla oblongata. Following are the most important autonomic centers in the medulla oblongata and their functions:

- The **cardiac center** regulates both the heart's rate and its strength of contraction.
- The **vasomotor center** controls blood pressure by regulating the contraction and relaxation of smooth muscle in the walls of the smallest arteries (called arterioles) to alter vessel diameter. Blood pressure increases when vessel walls constrict and lowers when vessel walls dilate.
- The **medullary respiratory center,** which regulates the respiratory rate, is composed of a ventral respiratory group and a dorsal respiratory group. These groups are influenced by the pontine respiratory center in the pons.
- Other nuclei in the medulla oblongata are involved in coughing, sneezing, salivating, swallowing, gagging, and vomiting. **APR**

WHAT DID YOU LEARN?

14. Where are the superior and inferior colliculi located, and what are their functions?
15. Describe where the vasomotor center is located, and explain its function.

WHAT DO YOU THINK?

6. Based on your understanding of the medulla oblongata's functions, would you expect severe injury to the medulla oblongata to cause death, or merely be disabling? Why?

15.6 Cerebellum

✓ Learning Objectives

11. Describe the structure and functions of the cerebellum.
12. Identify and describe the peduncles that connect the cerebellum and the brainstem.

The **cerebellum** (ser-e-bel'ŭm; little brain) is the second largest part of the brain, and it develops from the metencephalon. The cerebellum has a complex, highly convoluted surface covered by a layer of cerebellar cortex. The folds of the cerebellar cortex are called **folia** (fō'lē-ă; *folium* = leaf) **(figure 15.22)**. The cerebellum is composed of left and right **cerebellar hemispheres.** Each hemisphere consists of two lobes, the **anterior lobe** and the **posterior lobe,** which are separated by the **primary fissure.** Along the midline, a narrow band of cortex known as the **vermis** (ver'mis; worm) separates the left and right cerebellar hemispheres (figure 15.22*b*). Slender **flocculonodular** (flok'yū-lō-nod'y ū-lăr; *flocculo* = wool-like tuft) **lobes** lie anterior and inferior to each cerebellar hemisphere (not shown).

The cerebellum is partitioned internally into three regions: an outer gray matter layer of cortex, an internal region of white matter, and the deepest gray matter layer, which is composed of cerebellar nuclei. The white matter of the cerebellum is called the **arbor vitae** (ar'b ōr vī'tē; tree of life) because its distribution pattern resembles the branches of a tree.

The cerebellum coordinates and "fine-tunes" skeletal muscle movements and ensures that skeletal muscle contraction follows the correct pattern leading to smooth, coordinated movements. The cerebellum stores memories of previously learned movement

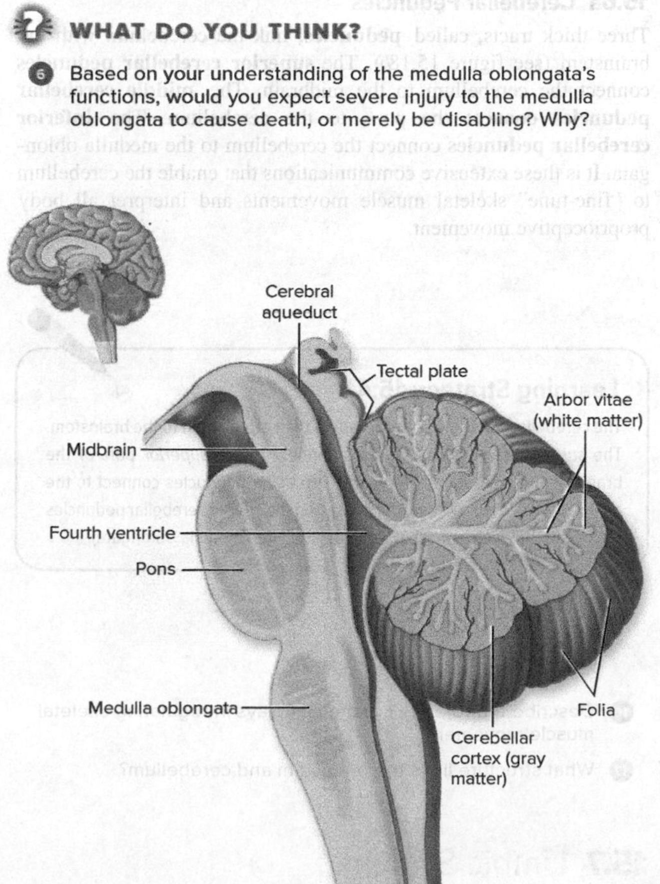

Cerebral aqueduct
Tectal plate
Arbor vitae (white matter)
Midbrain
Fourth ventricle
Pons
Medulla oblongata
Folia
Cerebellar cortex (gray matter)

(a) Midsagittal section

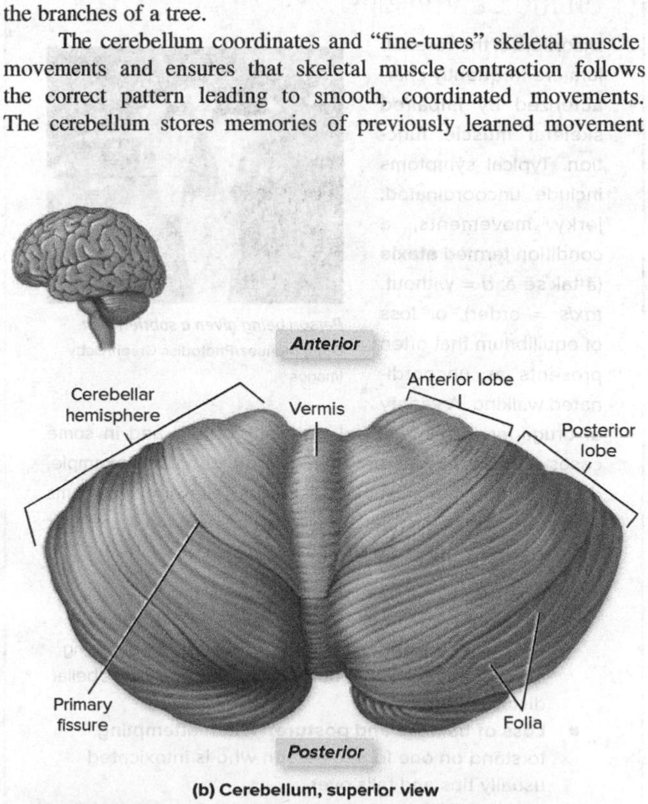

Anterior
Anterior lobe
Cerebellar hemisphere
Vermis
Posterior lobe
Primary fissure
Folia
Posterior

(b) Cerebellum, superior view

Figure 15.22

Cerebellum. The cerebellum lies posterior to the pons and medulla oblongata of the brainstem. (*a*) A midsagittal section shows the relationship of the cerebellum to the brainstem. (*b*) A superior view compares the anterior and posterior lobes of the cerebellum.

patterns. This function is performed indirectly, by regulating activity along both the voluntary and involuntary motor pathways at the cerebral cortex, cerebral nuclei, and motor centers in the brainstem. The cerebrum initiates a movement and sends a "rough draft" of the movement to the cerebellum, which then coordinates and fine-tunes it. For example, the controlled, precise movements a pianist makes when playing a concerto are due to fine-tuning by the cerebellum. Without the cerebellum, the pianist's movements would be choppy and sloppy, as in banging an entire hand across the keyboard.

In addition, the cerebellum has several other functions. It adjusts skeletal muscle activity to maintain equilibrium and posture. It also receives proprioceptive (sensory) information from the muscles and joints and uses this information to regulate the body's position (see section 19.1). For example, you are able to balance on one foot because the cerebellum takes the proprioceptive information from the body joints and "maps out" a muscle tone plan to keep the body upright. Finally, because proprioceptive information is sent from the cerebellum to the cerebrum, the cerebrum knows the position of each body joint and its muscle tone, even if the person is not looking at the joint. For example, if you close your eyes, you are still aware of which body joints are flexed and which are extended because the cerebrum gives you this awareness.

The cerebellum is more than just a coordinator of proprioceptive information and motor function, however. More recent research has shown that the cerebellum helps regulate behavioral expression and cognitive skills, as well as language processing and retrieval. fMRI studies have shown interconnections between the cerebellum and parts of the cerebral cortex that control these behaviors, further strengthening the argument that the cerebellum assists with these functions that were previously thought to be solely under the control of the cerebrum. Finally, clinical case studies have shown that many individuals who have cerebellar injury have problems with language production and word choice, cognitive skills, and/or behavioral (mood and emotion) expression. Clinicians use the diagnosis of **cerebellar cognitive affective syndrome (CCAS)** to describe patients with cerebellar damage who subsequently display deficits with language, cognition, and behavior/mood (i.e., affect).

Clinical View 15.7

Effects of Alcohol and Drugs on the Cerebellum

Person being given a sobriety test.
Doug Menuez/Photodisc Green/Getty Images

Disorders of the cerebellum are frequently characterized by impaired skeletal muscle function. Typical symptoms include uncoordinated, jerky movements, a condition termed **ataxia** (ă-tak′sē-ă; *a* = without, *taxis* = order), or loss of equilibrium that often presents as uncoordinated walking. A variety of drugs, especially alcohol, can temporarily, and in some cases permanently, impair cerebellar function. For example, drinking too much alcohol leads to the following symptoms of impaired cerebellar function, which are used in the classic sobriety tests performed by police officers:

- **Disturbance of gait.** A person under the influence of alcohol rarely walks in a straight line, but appears to sway and stagger. In addition, falling and bumping into objects are likely, due to the temporary cerebellar disturbance.
- **Loss of balance and posture.** When attempting to stand on one foot, a person who is intoxicated usually tips and falls over.
- **Inability to detect proprioceptive information.** When asked to close the eyes and touch the nose, an intoxicated person frequently misses the mark. This reaction is due to reduced ability to sense proprioceptive information, compounded by uncoordination of skeletal muscles.

15.6a Cerebellar Peduncles

Three thick tracts, called **peduncles,** link the cerebellum with the brainstem (see figure 15.18*b*). The **superior cerebellar peduncles** connect the cerebellum to the midbrain. The **middle cerebellar peduncles** connect the pons to the cerebellum. The **inferior cerebellar peduncles** connect the cerebellum to the medulla oblongata. It is these extensive communications that enable the cerebellum to "fine-tune" skeletal muscle movements and interpret all body proprioceptive movement.

Learning Strategy 15.4

The cerebellar peduncles are named for their attachment to the brainstem. The *superior* cerebellar peduncles connect to the *superior* part of the brainstem (the midbrain), the *middle* cerebellar penducles connect to the *middle* part of the brainstem (the pons), and the *inferior* cerebellar peduncles connect to the *inferior* part of the brainstem (the medulla oblongata).

WHAT DID YOU LEARN?

16 Describe the role the cerebellum plays in regulating skeletal muscle movement.

17 What structure links the brainstem and cerebellum?

15.7 Limbic System

✓ Learning Objective

13. Identify the structures of the limbic system, and describe their functions.

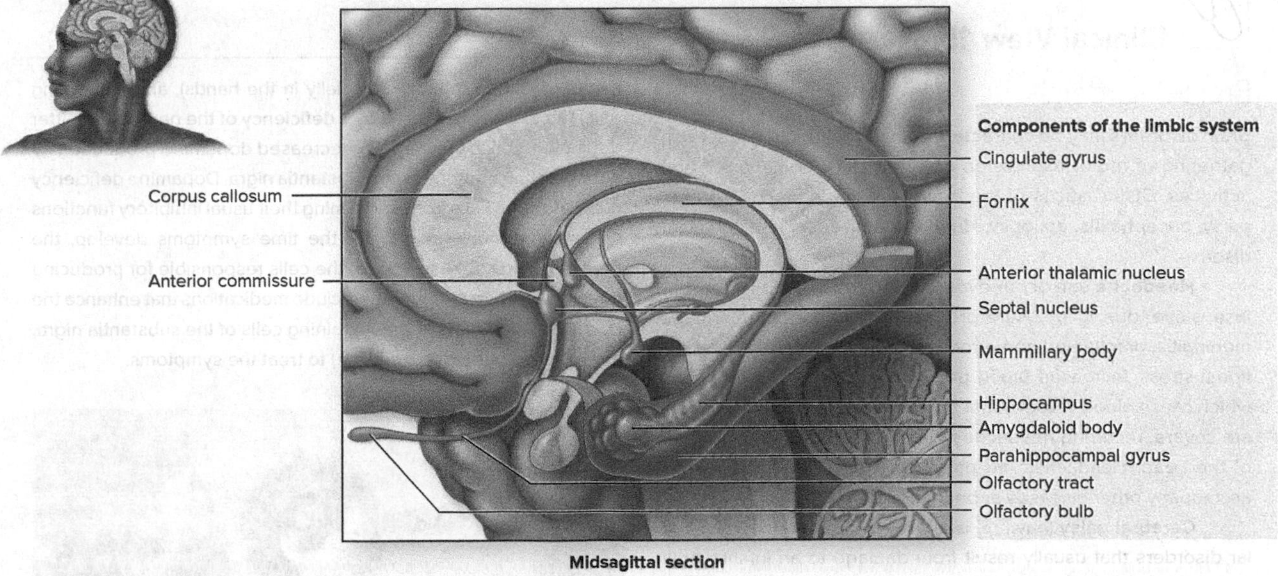
Components of the limbic system
Cingulate gyrus
Fornix
Anterior thalamic nucleus
Septal nucleus
Mammillary body
Hippocampus
Amygdaloid body
Parahippocampal gyrus
Olfactory tract
Olfactory bulb
Corpus callosum
Anterior commissure
Midsagittal section

Figure 15.23
Limbic System. The components of the limbic system are shown here in midsagittal section with three-dimensional reconstruction. The limbic system affects behavior and emotions.

The brain has two important systems that work together for a common function, even though their structures are scattered throughout the brain. These systems are the limbic system and the reticular formation, a loosely organized gray matter core in the brainstem. We will discuss the limbic system here; the reticular formation will be described in section 17.4f.

The **limbic** (lim′bik) **system** is composed of multiple cerebral and diencephalic structures that collaboratively process and experience emotions. It is a collective name for the human brain structures that are involved in motivation, emotion, and memory with an emotional association. The limbic system affects memory formation by integrating past memories of physical sensations with emotional states.

The structures of the limbic system form a ring or border around the diencephalon (*limbus* = border). Although neuroanatomists continue to debate the components of the limbic system, the brain structures commonly recognized are shown in **figure 15.23** and listed here:

- The **cingulate** (sin′gy ū-lāt; *cingulum* = girdle, to surround) **gyrus** is an internal mass of cerebral cortex located within the longitudinal fissure and superior to the corpus callosum. This mass of tissue may be seen only in sagittal section, and it surrounds the diencephalon. It receives input from the other components of the limbic system. It focuses attention on emotionally significant events and appears to bring them into consciousness.
- The **parahippocampal gyrus** is a mass of cortical tissue in the temporal lobe. Its function is associated with the hippocampus.
- The **hippocampus** (hip′ō-kam′p ŭs; seahorse) is a nucleus located superior to the parahippocampal gyrus that connects to the diencephalon via a structure called the fornix. As its name implies, this nucleus is shaped like a seahorse. Both the hippocampus and the parahippocampal gyrus are essential in storing memories and forming long-term memory. Researchers have found evidence of neurogenesis (the formation of new neurons; see section 14.2a) in the hippocampus of many animal species, including humans.
- The **amygdaloid body** connects to the hippocampus. The amygdaloid body is involved in several aspects of emotion, especially fear. It can also help store and code memories based on how a person emotionally perceives them—for example, as related to fear, extreme happiness, or sadness.
- The **olfactory bulbs, olfactory tracts,** and **olfactory cortex** are part of the limbic system as well, since particular odors can provoke certain emotions or be associated with certain memories.
- The **fornix** (fōr′niks; arch) is a thin tract of white matter that connects the hippocampus with other diencephalon limbic system structures.
- Various nuclei in the diencephalon, such as the **anterior thalamic nuclei,** the **habenular nuclei,** the **septal nuclei,** and the **mammillary** (mam′i-l ār′ē; *mammilla* = nipple) **bodies,** interconnect other parts of the limbic system and contribute to its overall function.

WHAT DID YOU LEARN?

18 Describe how the hippocampus and the olfactory structures participate in limbic system function.

Clinical View 15.8

Brain Disorders

Brain disorders may be characterized by a malfunction in sensory gathering or motor expression or by some combination of both activities. Disturbances of the brain include headache, cerebral palsy, encephalitis, epilepsy, Huntington disease, and Parkinson disease.

Headache can occur even though the brain itself is pain-insensitive, due to pressure produced by tumors, hemorrhage, meningitis, or inflamed nerve roots. More typical causes are emotional stress, increased blood pressure, and food allergies, all of which cause blood vessel diameter changes. **Migraine headaches** are severe, recurring headaches that usually affect only one side of the head. Headaches are not a brain disorder, but they may accompany other diseases or brain disorders.

Cerebral palsy (pawl′zē) is actually a group of neuromuscular disorders that usually result from damage to an infant's brain before, during, or immediately after birth. Three forms of cerebral palsy involve impairment of skeletal motor activity to some degree: *athetoid,* characterized by slow, involuntary, writhing hand movements; *ataxic,* marked by lack of muscular coordination; and *spastic,* exhibiting increased muscular tone. Intellectual impairment and speech difficulties may accompany this disorder.

Epilepsy (ep′i-lep′sē; *epilepsia* = seizure) is characterized by recurring attacks of motor, sensory, or psychological malfunction, with or without unconsciousness or convulsive movements. During an epileptic seizure, neurons in the brain fire at unpredictable times, even without a stimulus. The term epilepsy does not apply to a specific disease; rather, epilepsy refers to a group of symptoms with many causes. Some epileptic events may be *grand mal* seizures, which affect motor areas of the brain and cause severe spasms and loss of consciousness. Others may be *petit mal* seizures, which affect sensory areas and do not lead to convulsions or prolonged unconsciousness.

Huntington disease is an autosomal dominant hereditary disease that affects the cerebral nuclei. It causes rapid, jerky, involuntary movements that usually start unilaterally in the face, but over months and years progress to the arms and legs. Progressive intellectual deterioration also occurs, including personality changes, memory loss, and irritability. The disease has an onset age of 35–40, and is fatal within 10 to 20 years.

Parkinson disease is a slow-progressing neurologic condition that affects muscle movement and balance. Parkinson patients exhibit stiff posture, an expressionless face, slow voluntary movements, a resting tremor (especially in the hands), and a shuffling gait. The disease is caused by a deficiency of the neurotransmitter dopamine, which results from decreased dopamine production by degenerating neurons in the substantia nigra. Dopamine deficiency prevents brain cells from performing their usual inhibitory functions within the cerebral nuclei. By the time symptoms develop, the person has lost 80% to 90% of the cells responsible for producing dopamine. Current treatments include medications that enhance the amount of dopamine in the remaining cells of the substantia nigra, and medications (e.g., rasagiline) to treat the symptoms.

A young boy with cerebral palsy is able to move with the help of a specialized walker.

Jaren Jai Wicklund/Shutterstock

Learning Strategy 15.5

Developing a code or phrase called a **mnemonic** (nē-mon′ik; *mnemonikos* = pertaining to memory) may help you remember the cranial nerves. Mnemonics you devise yourself will be the most relevant to you, but here is a sample mnemonic for the cranial nerves:

oh	(olfactory)
once	(optic)
one	(oculomotor)
takes	(trochlear)
the	(trigeminal)
anatomy	(abducens)
final	(facial)
very	(vestibulocochlear)
good	(glossopharyngeal)
vacations	(vagus)
are	(accessory)
heavenly!	(hypoglossal)

15.8 Cranial Nerves

✓ Learning Objectives

14. List the names and identify the locations of the twelve cranial nerves.
15. Describe the main functions of each cranial nerve.

Cranial nerves are part of the peripheral nervous system and originate on the inferior surface of the brain. There are 12 pairs of cranial nerves. They are numbered according to their positions, beginning with the most anteriorly placed nerve and using Roman numerals, sometimes preceded by the prefix *CN* (**figure 15.24**). The name of each nerve generally has some relation to its function. Thus, the 12 pairs of cranial nerves are the olfactory (CN I), optic (CN II), oculomotor (CN III), trochlear (CN IV), trigeminal (CN V), abducens (CN VI), facial (CN VII), vestibulocochlear (CN VIII), glossopharyngeal (CN IX), vagus (CN X), accessory (CN XI), and hypoglossal (CN XII).

Each cranial nerve is composed of many axons. Some cranial nerves (e.g., CN XII, hypoglossal nerve) are composed of motor axons only, whereas other cranial nerves (e.g., CN II, optic nerve)

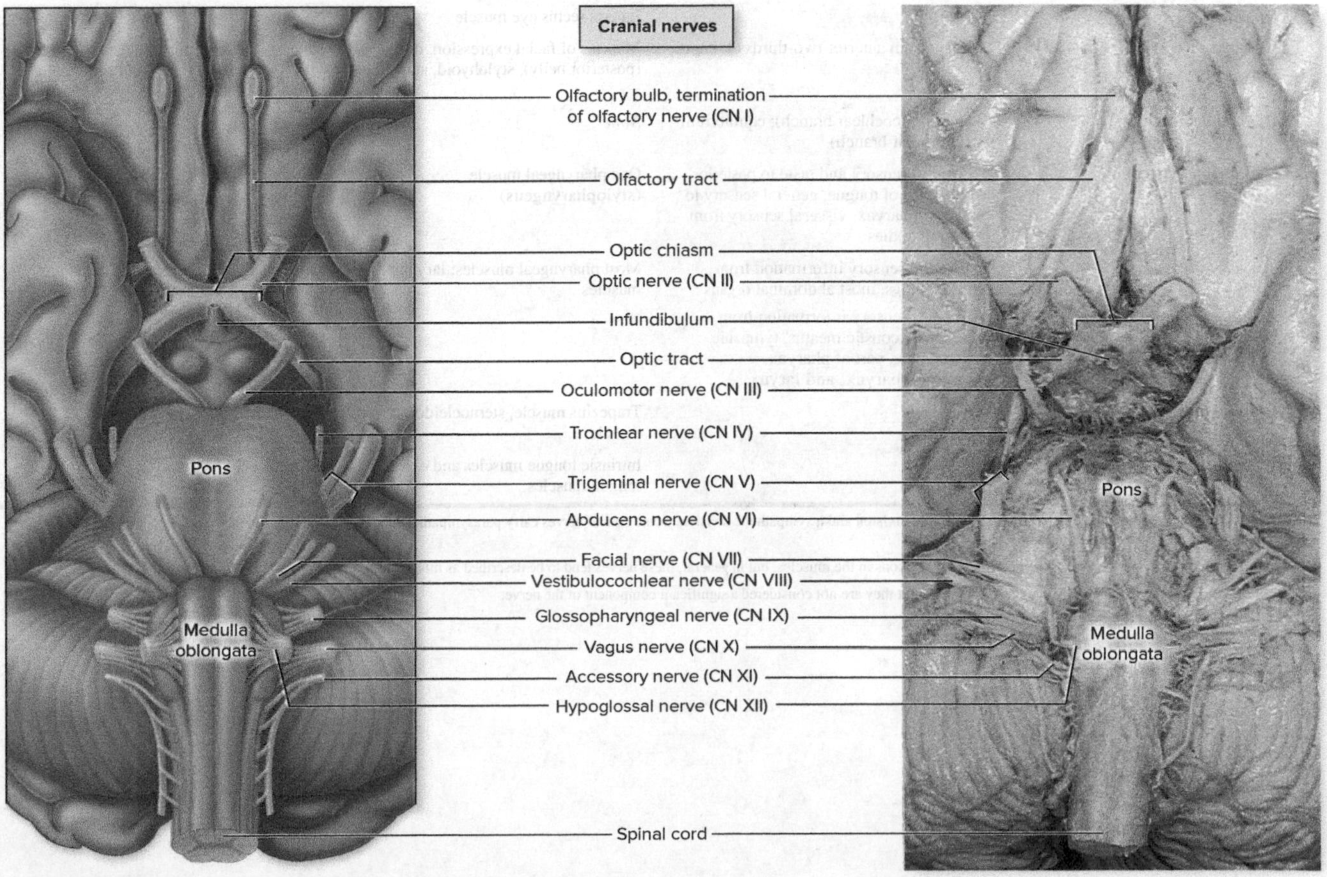
Cranial nerves
Olfactory bulb, termination of olfactory nerve (CN I)
Olfactory tract
Optic chiasm
Optic nerve (CN II)
Infundibulum
Optic tract
Oculomotor nerve (CN III)
Trochlear nerve (CN IV)
Pons
Trigeminal nerve (CN V)
Abducens nerve (CN VI)
Facial nerve (CN VII)
Vestibulocochlear nerve (CN VIII)
Glossopharyngeal nerve (CN IX)
Medulla oblongata
Vagus nerve (CN X)
Accessory nerve (CN XI)
Hypoglossal nerve (CN XII)
Spinal cord

Figure 15.24

Cranial Nerves. A diagram and a photo of the inferior surface of the brain show the 12 pairs of cranial nerves. APR are composed of sensory axons only. Still other cranial nerves (e.g., CN V, trigeminal nerve) are composed of both sensory and motor axons. **Tables 15.7** and **15.8** list whether a cranial nerve has somatic motor, parasympathetic motor, and/or sensory components.

Table 15.7 summarizes the main sensory and motor functions of each cranial nerve. For easier reference, each main function of a nerve is color-coded. Blue represents a sensory function, and pink stands for a somatic motor function; orange denotes a parasympathetic motor function (see section 18.3). Table 15.8 lists the individual cranial nerves and discusses their functions, origins, and pathways. The color-coding in table 15.7 carries over to table 15.8, so you can easily determine whether a cranial nerve has sensory and/or motor components.

Table 15.7 Primary Functions of Cranial Nerves

Cranial Nerve	Sensory Function(s)	Somatic Motor Function(s)	Parasympathetic Motor (Autonomic) Function(s)[1]
I (olfactory)	Olfaction (smell)	*None*	*None*
II (optic)	Vision	*None*	*None*
III (oculomotor)	*None*[2]	Four extrinsic eye muscles (medial rectus, superior rectus, inferior rectus, inferior oblique); levator palpebrae superioris muscle (elevates eyelid)	Innervates sphincter pupillae muscle in eye to make pupil constrict; contracts ciliary muscles to make lens of eye more rounded (as needed for near vision)
IV (trochlear)	*None*[2]	Superior oblique eye muscle	*None*
V (trigeminal)	General sensory from anterior scalp, nasal cavity, nasopharynx, entire face, most of oral cavity, teeth, anterior two-thirds of tongue; part of auricle of ear; meninges	Muscles of mastication, mylohyoid, digastric (anterior belly), tensor tympani, tensor veli palatini	*None*
VI (abducens)	*None*[2]	Lateral rectus eye muscle	*None*
VII (facial)	Taste from anterior two-thirds of tongue	Muscles of facial expression, digastric (posterior belly), stylohyoid, stapedius	Increases secretion from lacrimal gland of eye, submandibular and sublingual salivary glands
VIII (vestibulocochlear)	Hearing (cochlear branch); equilibrium (vestibular branch)	*None*[3]	*None*
IX (glossopharyngeal)	General sensory and taste to posterior one-third of tongue, general sensory to part of pharynx, visceral sensory from carotid bodies	One pharyngeal muscle (stylopharyngeus)	Increases secretion from parotid salivary gland
X (vagus)	Visceral sensory information from heart, lungs, most abdominal organs General sensory information from external acoustic meatus, tympanic membrane, part of pharynx, laryngopharynx, and larynx	Most pharyngeal muscles; laryngeal muscles	Innervates smooth muscle and glands of heart, lungs, larynx, trachea, most abdominal organs
XI (accessory)	*None*[2]	Trapezius muscle, sternocleidomastoid muscle	*None*
XII (hypoglossal)	*None*[2]	Intrinsic tongue muscles and extrinsic tongue muscles	*None*

[1] The autonomic nervous system contains a parasympathetic division and a sympathetic division. Some cranial nerves carry parasympathetic axons and are listed in this table. Detailed information about these divisions is found in chapter 18.

[2] These nerves do contain some tiny proprioceptive sensory axons in the muscles, but in general, these nerves tend to be described as motor only.

[3] A few motor axons travel with this nerve to the inner ear, but they are not considered a significant component of the nerve.

Table 15.8 Cranial Nerves

CN I OLFACTORY NERVE (ol-fak′tō-rē; *olfacio* = to smell)

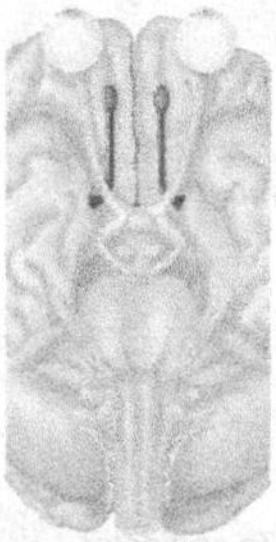
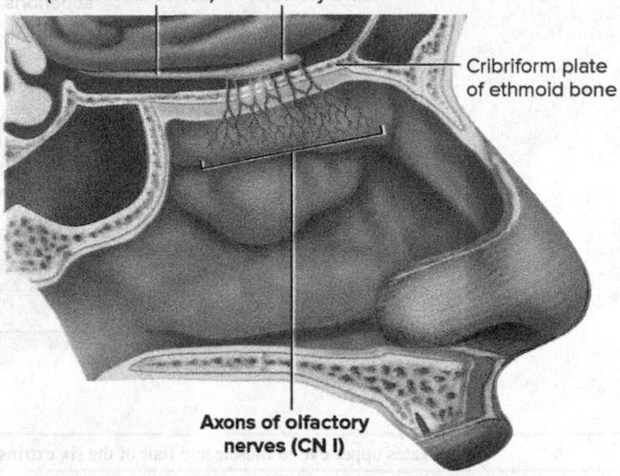
Olfactory tract
(to cerebral cortex)
Olfactory bulb
Cribriform plate
of ethmoid bone
Axons of olfactory
nerves (CN I)

Description	Conducts olfactory (smell) sensations to brain; only type of nervous tissue to regenerate
Sensory function	Olfaction (smell)
Origin	Receptors (bipolar neurons) in olfactory mucosa of nasal cavity
Pathway	Travels through the cribriform foramina of ethmoid bone and synapses in the olfactory bulbs, which are located in the anterior cranial fossa. Within the olfactory bulb, the axons synapse with a smaller number of neurons, the axons of which form the olfactory tract and project to olfactory cortex
Conditions caused by nerve damage	Anosmia (partial or total loss of smell)

CN II OPTIC NERVE (op′tik; *ops* = eye)

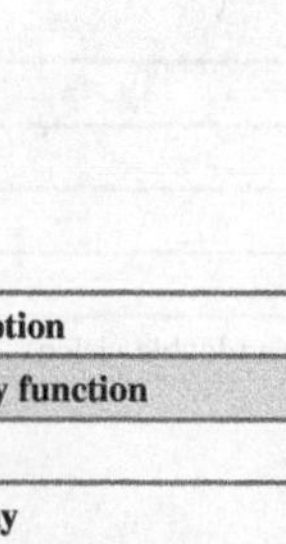
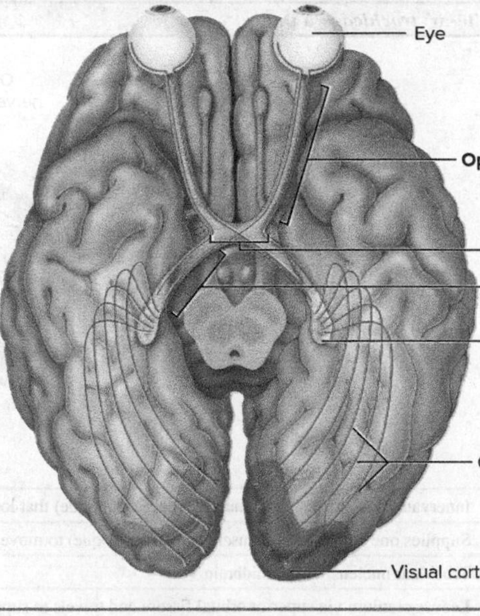
Eye
Optic nerve (CN II)
Optic chiasm
Optic tract
Lateral geniculate
nucleus of thalamus
Optic projection axons
Visual cortex (in occipital lobe)

Description	Special sensory nerve of vision that is an outgrowth of the brain; more appropriately called a brain tract
Sensory function	Vision
Origin	Retina of the eye
Pathway	Enters cranium via optic canal of sphenoid bone; left and right optic nerves unite at optic chiasm; optic tract travels to lateral geniculate nucleus of thalamus; finally, information is forwarded to the occipital lobe
Conditions caused by nerve damage	Anopsia (visual defects)

(continued on next page)

Table 15.8 Cranial Nerves *(continued)*

CN III OCULOMOTOR NERVE (ok′yū-lō-mō′tōr; *oculus* = eye, *motorius* = moving)

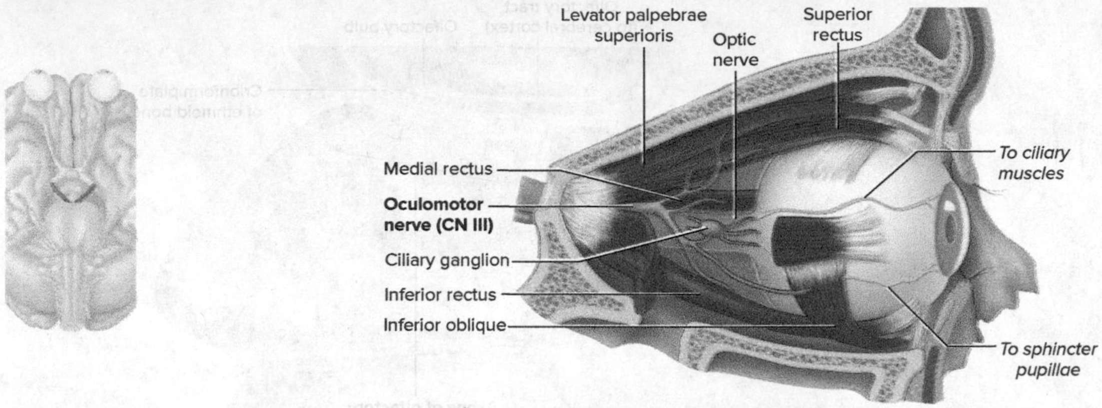

Description	Innervates upper eyelid muscle and four of the six extrinsic eye muscles
Somatic motor function	Supplies four extrinsic eye muscles (superior rectus, inferior rectus, medial rectus, inferior oblique) that move eye Supplies levator palpebrae superioris muscle to elevate eyelid
Parasympathetic motor function	Innervates sphincter pupillae muscle of iris to make pupil constrict Contracts ciliary muscles to make lens of eye more spherical (as needed for near vision)
Origin	Oculomotor and Edinger Westphal nuclei within midbrain
Pathway	Leaves cranium via superior orbital fissure and travels to eye and eyelid. (Parasympathetic fibers travel to ciliary ganglion, and postganglionic parasympathetic fibers then travel to iris and ciliary muscle.)
Conditions caused by nerve damage	Ptosis (upper eyelid droop); paralysis of most eye muscles, leading to strabismus (eyes not in parallel/deviated improperly), diplopia (double vision), focusing difficulty

CN IV TROCHLEAR NERVE (trok′lē-ar; *trochlea* = a pulley)

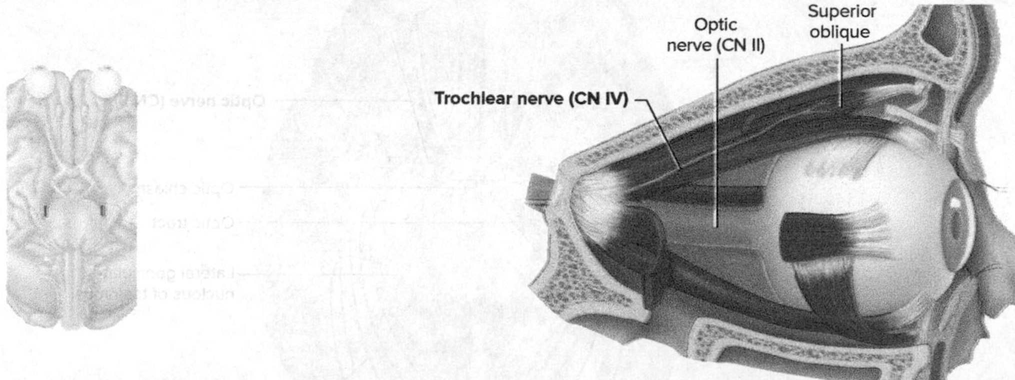

Description	Innervates one extrinsic eye muscle (superior oblique) that loops through a pulley-shaped ligament
Somatic motor function	Supplies one extrinsic eye muscle (superior oblique) to move eye inferiorly and laterally
Origin	Trochlear nucleus within midbrain
Pathway	Leaves cranium via superior orbital fissure and travels to superior oblique muscle
Conditions caused by nerve damage	Paralysis of superior oblique, leading to strabismus (eyes not in parallel/deviated improperly), diplopia (double vision)

Table 15.8 Cranial Nerves *(continued)*

CN V TRIGEMINAL NERVE (trī-jem′i-năl; *trigeminous* = threefold)

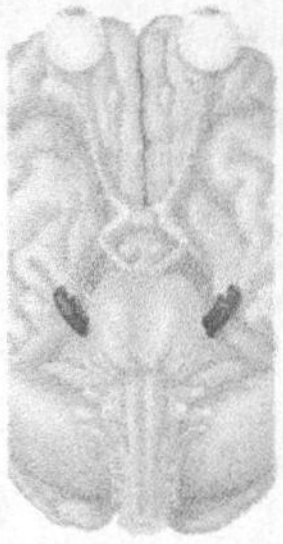

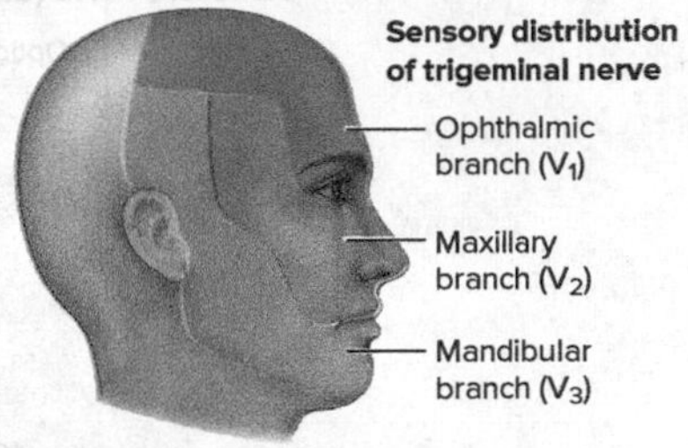
Sensory distribution
of trigeminal nerve
Ophthalmic
branch (V_1)
Maxillary
branch (V_2)
Mandibular
branch (V_3)

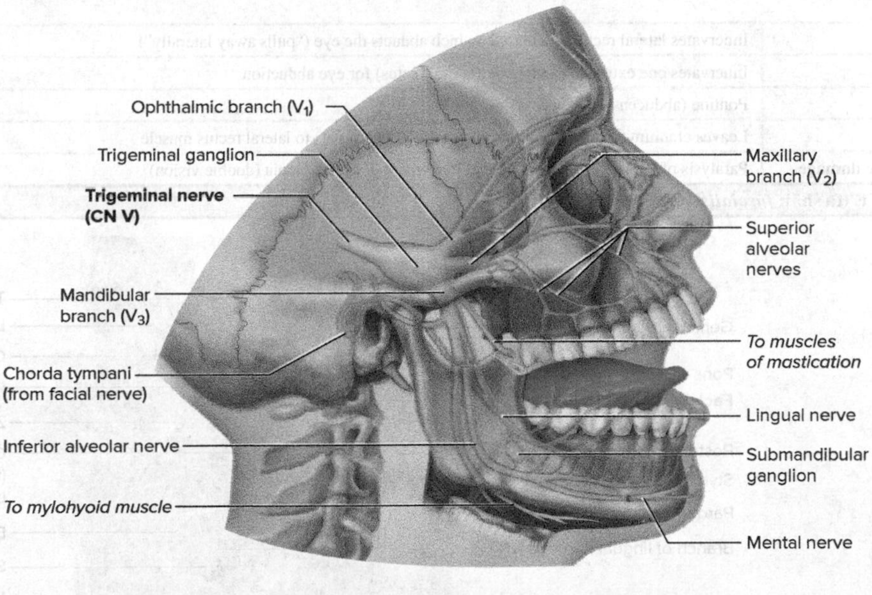
Ophthalmic branch (V_1)
Trigeminal ganglion
Trigeminal nerve
(CN V)
Mandibular
branch (V_3)
Chorda tympani
(from facial nerve)
Inferior alveolar nerve
To mylohyoid muscle
Maxillary
branch (V_2)
Superior
alveolar
nerves
To muscles
of mastication
Lingual nerve
Submandibular
ganglion
Mental nerve

Description	This nerve consists of three divisions: ophthalmic (V_1), maxillary (V_2), and mandibular (V_3); receives sensory impulses from face, oral cavity, nasal cavity, and anterior scalp, and innervates muscles of mastication
Sensory function	Sensory stimuli for this nerve are touch, temperature, and pain. V_1: Conducts sensory impulses from cornea, nose, forehead, anterior scalp, meninges V_2: Conducts sensory impulses from nasal mucosa, palate, gums, cheek, meninges V_3: Conducts sensory impulses from anterior two-thirds of tongue, meninges; skin of chin, lower jaw, lower teeth; one-third from sensory axons of auricle of ear
Somatic motor function	Innervates muscles of mastication (temporalis, masseter, lateral and medial pterygoids), mylohyoid, anterior belly of digastric, tensor tympani muscle, and tensor veli palatini
Origin	Nucleus in the pons
Pathway	V_1: Sensory axons enter cranium via superior orbital fissure and travel to trigeminal ganglion before entering pons V_2: Sensory axons enter cranium via foramen rotundum and travel to trigeminal ganglion before entering pons V_3: Motor axons leave pons and exit cranium via foramen ovale to supply muscles. Sensory axons travel through foramen ovale to trigeminal ganglion before entering pons
Conditions caused by nerve damage	Trigeminal neuralgia (tic douloureux) is caused by inflammation of the sensory components of the trigeminal nerve and results in intense, pulsating pain lasting from minutes to several hours

(continued on next page)

Table 15.8 Cranial Nerves *(continued)*

CN VI ABDUCENS NERVE (ab-dū′senz; to move away from)

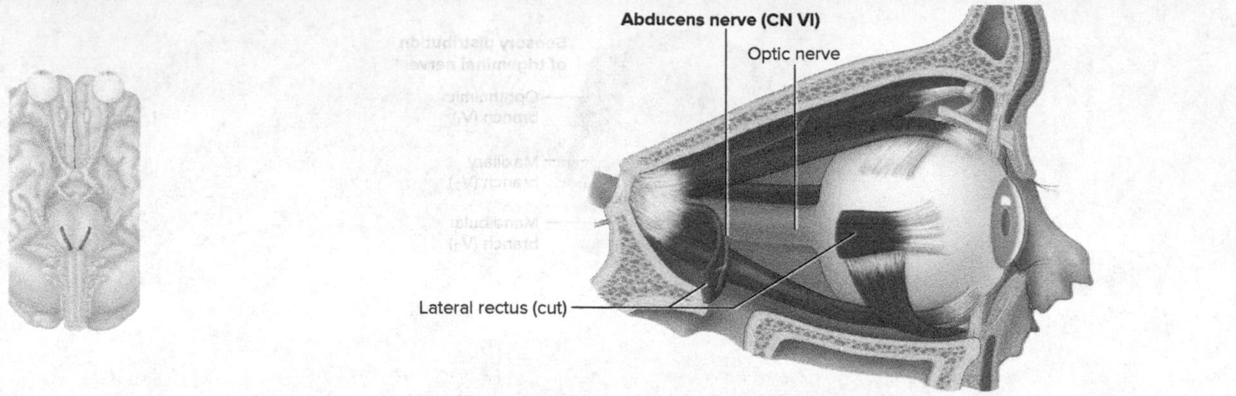
Abducens nerve (CN VI)
Optic nerve
Lateral rectus (cut)

Description	Innervates lateral rectus eye muscle, which abducts the eye ("pulls away laterally")
Somatic motor function	Innervates one extrinsic eye muscle (lateral rectus) for eye abduction
Origin	Pontine (abducens) nucleus in pons
Pathway	Leaves cranium through superior orbital fissure and travels to lateral rectus muscle
Conditions caused by nerve damage	Paralysis of lateral rectus limits lateral movement of eye; diplopia (double vision)

CN VII FACIAL NERVE (fā′shăl; *fascialis* = of the face)

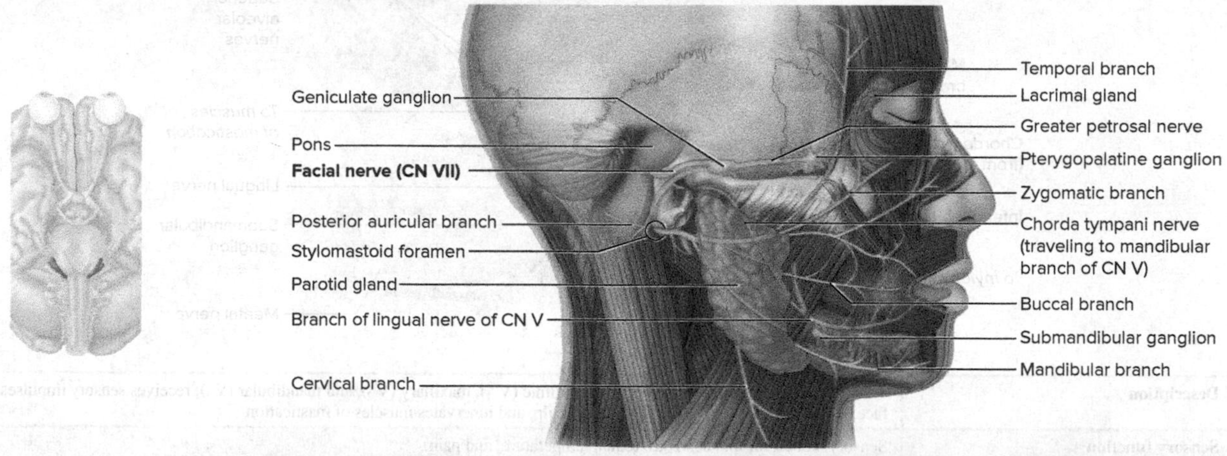
Geniculate ganglion
Pons
Facial nerve (CN VII)
Posterior auricular branch
Stylomastoid foramen
Parotid gland
Branch of lingual nerve of CN V
Cervical branch
Temporal branch
Lacrimal gland
Greater petrosal nerve
Pterygopalatine ganglion
Zygomatic branch
Chorda tympani nerve (traveling to mandibular branch of CN V)
Buccal branch
Submandibular ganglion
Mandibular branch

Description	Innervates muscles of facial expression, lacrimal (tear) gland, and most salivary glands; conducts taste sensations from anterior two-thirds of tongue
Sensory function	Taste from anterior two-thirds of tongue
Somatic motor function	The five major motor branches (temporal, zygomatic, buccal, mandibular, and cervical) innervate the muscles of facial expression, the posterior belly of the digastric muscle, and the stylohyoid and stapedius muscles
Parasympathetic motor function	Increases secretions of the lacrimal gland of the eye as well as the submandibular and sublingual salivary glands
Origin	Nuclei within the pons
Pathway	Sensory axons travel from the tongue via the chorda tympani branch of the facial nerve through a tiny foramen to enter the skull, and axons synapse at the geniculate ganglion of the facial nerve. Somatic motor axons leave the pons and enter the temporal bone through the internal acoustic meatus, project through temporal bone, and emerge through stylomastoid foramen to supply the musculature. Parasympathetic motor axons leave the pons, enter the internal acoustic meatus, leave with either the greater petrosal nerve or chorda tympani nerve, and travel to an autonomic ganglion before innervating their respective glands
Conditions caused by nerve damage	Decreased tearing (dry eye) and decreased salivation (dry mouth); loss of taste sensation to anterior two-thirds of tongue and/or facial nerve palsy (also known as Bell palsy) characterized by paralyzed facial muscles, lack of obicularis oculi contraction, sagging at corner of mouth—for a more complete description, see Clinical View 11.1: "Idiopathic Facial Nerve Paralysis (Bell Palsy)" in section 11.1a.

Table 15.8 Cranial Nerves (*continued*)

CN VIII VESTIBULOCOCHLEAR NERVE (ves-tib′ū-lō-kok′lē-ăr; relating to the vestibule and cochlea of the ear)

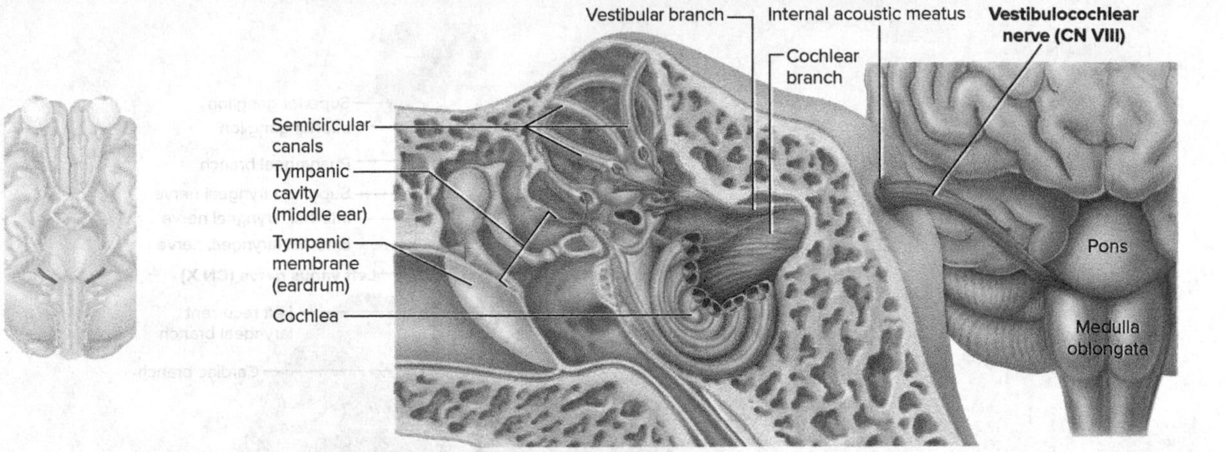

Description	Conducts equilibrium and auditory sensations to brain; formerly called the auditory or acoustic nerve
Sensory function	Vestibular branch conducts impulses for equilibrium, whereas cochlear branch conducts impulses for hearing
Origin	Vestibular branch: Hair cells in the vestibule of the inner ear Cochlear branch: Cochlea of the inner ear
Pathway	Sensory cell bodies of the vestibular branch are located in the vestibular ganglion, whereas sensory cell bodies of the cochlear branch are located in the spiral ganglion near the cochlea. The vestibular and cochlear branches merge, and together enter cranial cavity through internal acoustic meatus and travel to junction of the pons and the medulla oblongata
Conditions caused by nerve damage	Lesions in vestibular branch produce loss of balance, nausea, vomiting, and dizziness; lesions in cochlear branch result in deafness (loss of hearing)

CN IX GLOSSOPHARYNGEAL NERVE (glos′ō-fă-rin′jē-ăl; *glossa* = tongue)

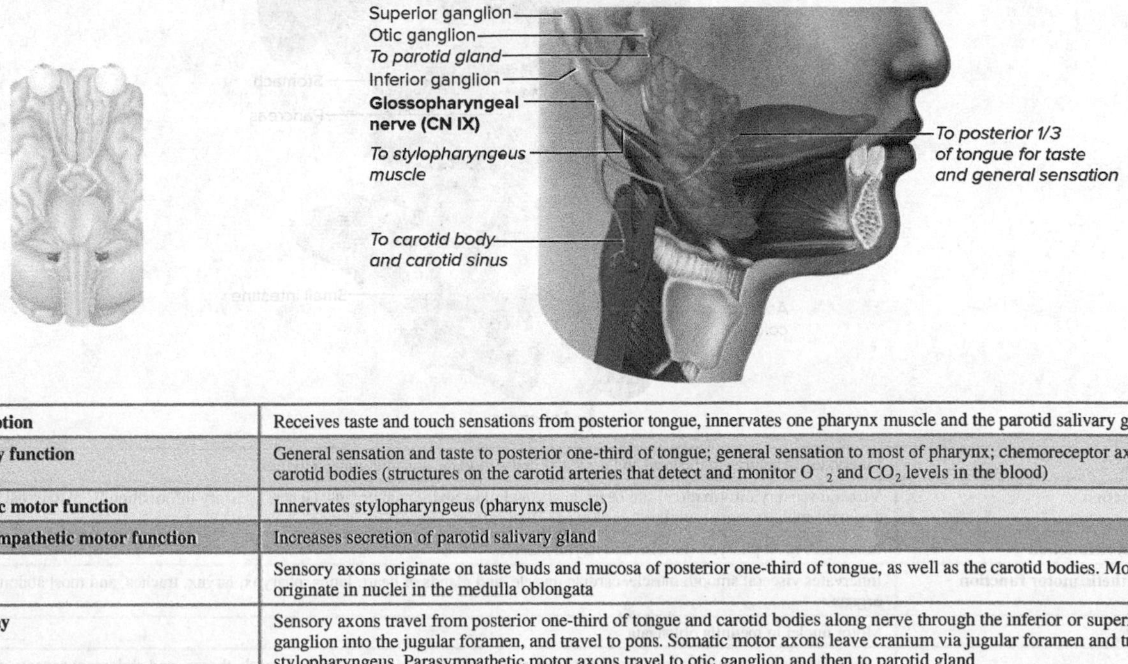

Description	Receives taste and touch sensations from posterior tongue, innervates one pharynx muscle and the parotid salivary gland
Sensory function	General sensation and taste to posterior one-third of tongue; general sensation to most of pharynx; chemoreceptor axons to carotid bodies (structures on the carotid arteries that detect and monitor O_2 and CO_2 levels in the blood)
Somatic motor function	Innervates stylopharyngeus (pharynx muscle)
Parasympathetic motor function	Increases secretion of parotid salivary gland
Origin	Sensory axons originate on taste buds and mucosa of posterior one-third of tongue, as well as the carotid bodies. Motor axons originate in nuclei in the medulla oblongata
Pathway	Sensory axons travel from posterior one-third of tongue and carotid bodies along nerve through the inferior or superior ganglion into the jugular foramen, and travel to pons. Somatic motor axons leave cranium via jugular foramen and travel to stylopharyngeus. Parasympathetic motor axons travel to otic ganglion and then to parotid gland
Conditions caused by nerve damage	Reduced salivary secretion (dry mouth); loss of taste sensations to posterior one-third of tongue

(*continued on next page*)

Table 15.8 Cranial Nerves *(continued)*

CN X VAGUS NERVE (vā′gŭs; wandering)

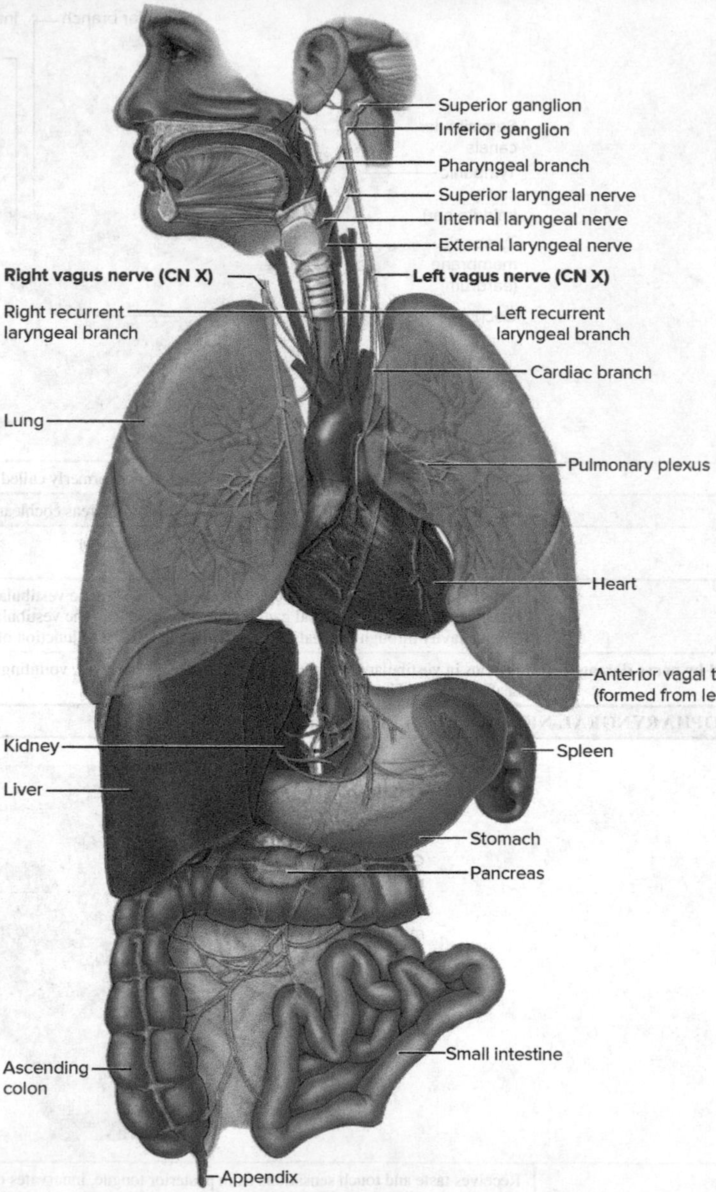
Superior ganglion
Inferior ganglion
Pharyngeal branch
Superior laryngeal nerve
Internal laryngeal nerve
External laryngeal nerve
Right vagus nerve (CN X)
Left vagus nerve (CN X)
Right recurrent laryngeal branch
Left recurrent laryngeal branch
Cardiac branch
Lung
Pulmonary plexus
Heart
Anterior vagal trunk (formed from left vagus)
Kidney
Spleen
Liver
Stomach
Pancreas
Small intestine
Ascending colon
Appendix

Description	Innervates structures in the head and neck and in the thoracic and abdominal cavities
Sensory function	Visceral sensory information from heart, lungs, and most abdominal organs. General sensory information from external acoustic meatus, eardrum, laryngopharynx, and larynx
Somatic motor function	Innervates most pharynx muscles and larynx muscles
Parasympathetic motor function	Innervates visceral smooth muscle, cardiac muscle, and glands of heart, lungs, pharynx, larynx, trachea, and most abdominal organs
Origin	Motor nuclei in medulla oblongata
Pathway	Leaves cranium via jugular foramen before traveling and branching extensively in neck, thorax, and abdomen; sensory neuron cell bodies are located in the superior and inferior ganglia associated with the nerve
Conditions caused by nerve damage	Paralysis leads to a variety of larynx problems, including hoarseness, monotone voice, or complete loss of voice. Other lesions may cause difficulty in swallowing or impaired gastrointestinal system mobility

Table 15.8 Cranial Nerves (continued)

CN XI ACCESSORY NERVE (ak-ses′ō-rē; *accedo* = to move toward)

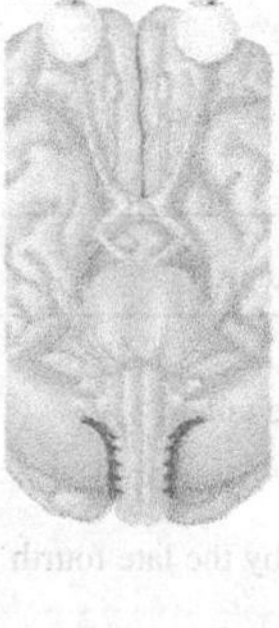

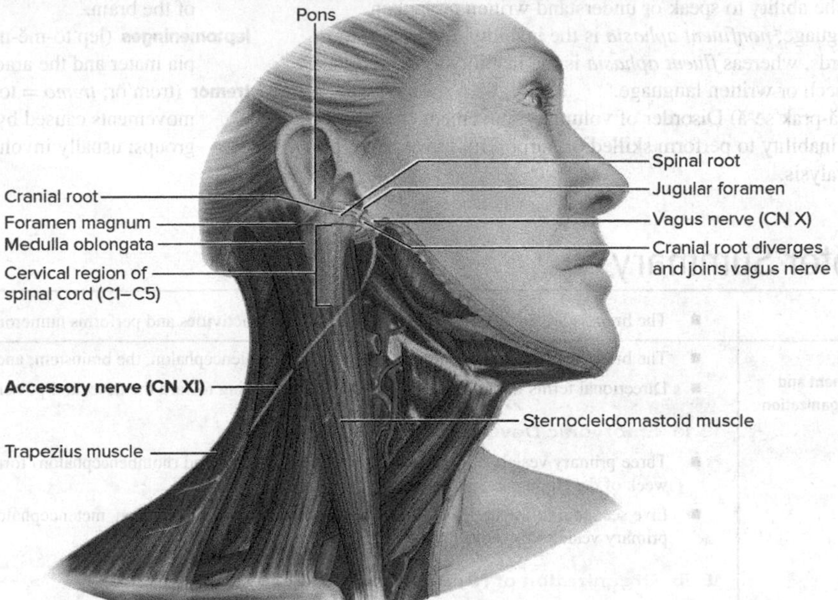
Pons
Spinal root
Jugular foramen
Vagus nerve (CN X)
Cranial root diverges
and joins vagus nerve
Cranial root
Foramen magnum
Medulla oblongata
Cervical region of
spinal cord (C1–C5)
Accessory nerve (CN XI)
Sternocleidomastoid muscle
Trapezius muscle

Description	Innervates trapezius, sternocleidomastoid, and some pharynx muscles; formerly called the *spinal accessory nerve*
Somatic motor function	Cranial root: Travels with CN X fibers to pharynx Spinal root: Innervates trapezius and sternocleidomastoid
Origin	Cranial root: Motor nuclei in medulla oblongata Spinal root: Motor nuclei in spinal cord
Pathway	Spinal root travels superiorly to enter skull through foramen magnum; there, cranial and spinal roots merge and leave the skull via jugular foramen. Once outside the skull, cranial root splits to travel with CN X (vagus) to innervate pharynx muscles, and spinal root travels to sternocleidomastoid and trapezius
Conditions caused by nerve damage	Paralysis of trapezius and sternocleidomastoid, resulting in difficulty in elevating shoulder (trapezius function) or turning head to opposite site (sternocleidomastoid function)

CN XII HYPOGLOSSAL NERVE (hī-pō-glos′ăl; *hypo* = below, *glossus* = tongue)

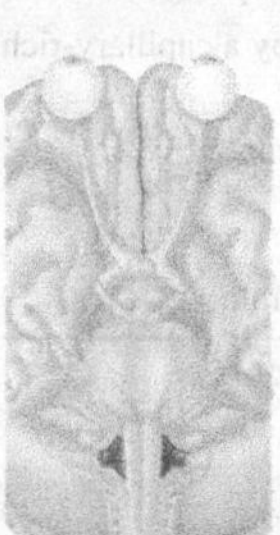

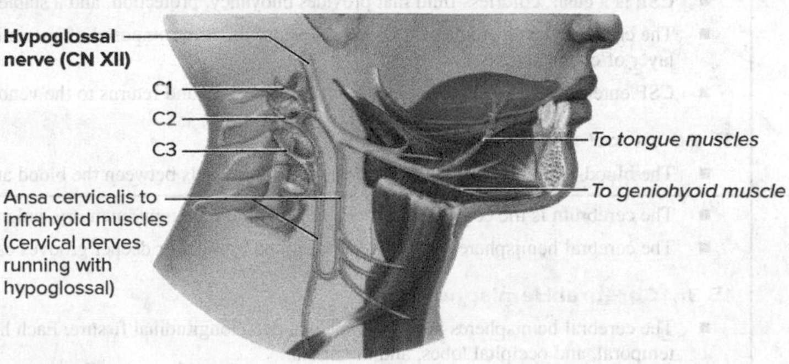
Hypoglossal
nerve (CN XII)
C1
C2
C3
To tongue muscles
To geniohyoid muscle
Ansa cervicalis to
infrahyoid muscles
(cervical nerves
running with
hypoglossal)

Description	Innervates intrinsic and extrinsic tongue muscles; name means "under the tongue"
Somatic motor function	Innervates intrinsic and extrinsic tongue muscles
Origin	Hypoglossal nucleus in medulla oblongata
Pathway	Leaves cranium via hypoglossal canal; travels inferior to mandible and to inferior surface of tongue
Conditions caused by nerve damage	Swallowing and speech difficulties due to impaired tongue movement; if a single hypoglossal nerve (either left or right) is paralyzed, a protruded (stuck out) tongue deviates to the side of the damaged nerve

Clinical Terms

aphasia (ă-fā′zē-ă; *a* = without, *phasis* = speech) Loss or impairment in the ability to speak or understand written or spoken language; *nonfluent aphasia* is the inability to properly form words, whereas *fluent aphasia* is the inability to comprehend speech or written language.

apraxia (ă-prak′sē-ă) Disorder of voluntary movement characterized by inability to perform skilled or purposeful movements, but no paralysis.

encephalopathy (en-sef′ă-lop′ă-thē; *pathos* = suffering) Any disorder of the brain.

leptomeninges (lep′tō-mĕ-nin′jēz) A medical term used to refer to the pia mater and the arachnoid mater together.

tremor (trem′ŏr; *tremo* = to tremble) Repetitive oscillatory movements caused by irregular contraction of opposing muscle groups; usually involuntary.

Chapter Summary

	■ The brain is a complex organ that controls all of our activities and performs numerous functions simultaneously.
15.1 Brain Development and Tissue Organization	■ The brain has four major regions: the cerebrum, the diencephalon, the brainstem, and the cerebellum. ■ Directional terms in brain anatomy are anterior, meaning toward the nose, and posterior, meaning toward the tail. **15.1a Embryonic Development of the Brain** ■ Three primary vesicles (prosencephalon, mesencephalon, and rhombencephalon) form from the neural tube by the late fourth week of development. ■ Five secondary vesicles (telencephalon, diencephalon, mesencephalon, metencephalon, and myelencephalon) form from the primary vesicles by the fifth week of development. **15.1b Organization of Neural Tissue Areas in the Brain** ■ Gray matter is made up of neuron and interneuron cell bodies, dendrites, terminal arborizations, and unmyelinated axons; white matter derives its white color from the myelin in myelinated axons.
15.2 Support and Protection of the Brain	■ The brain is protected and isolated by the cranium, the cranial meninges, the cerebrospinal fluid, and a blood-brain barrier. **15.2a Cranial Meninges** ■ The cranial meninges are the pia mater, arachnoid mater, and dura mater. ■ Dura mater septa project between the major parts of the brain to stabilize its position within the cranium. These septa are the falx cerebri, tentorium cerebelli, falx cerebelli, and diaphragma sellae. **15.2b Brain Ventricles** ■ Fluid-filled spaces in the brain are the paired lateral ventricles, the third ventricle, cerebral aqueduct, and the fourth ventricle. **15.2c Cerebrospinal Fluid** ■ CSF is a clear, colorless fluid that provides buoyancy, protection, and a stable environment for the brain and spinal cord. ■ The choroid plexus produces CSF in each ventricle. It is composed of specialized ependymal cells covered by a capillary-rich layer of connective tissue. ■ CSF enters the subarachnoid space from the ventricles and returns to the venous circulation through the arachnoid villi. **15.2d Blood-Brain Barrier** ■ The blood-brain barrier regulates movement of materials between the blood and the interstitial fluid of the brain.
15.3 Cerebrum	■ The cerebrum is the center of our sensory perception, thought, memory, judgment, and voluntary motor actions. ■ The cerebral hemispheres contain gyri separated by sulci or deeper grooves called fissures. **15.3a Cerebral Hemispheres** ■ The cerebral hemispheres are separated by a deep longitudinal fissure. Each hemisphere contains five lobes: the frontal, parietal, temporal, and occipital lobes, and the insula. **15.3b Functional Areas of the Cerebrum** ■ The primary motor cortex in the frontal lobe directs voluntary movements. A motor speech area is responsible for the motor functions involved in speaking. ■ The primary somatosensory cortex in the parietal lobe collects somatic sensory information from various general sensory receptors. **15.3c Central White Matter** ■ The central white matter contains three major groups of axons: association tracts, commissural tracts, and projection tracts. **15.3d Cerebral Nuclei** ■ The cerebral nuclei are located within the central white matter in the cerebral hemispheres. They include the caudate nucleus, amygdaloid body, putamen and globus pallidus, and claustrum.

15.4 Diencephalon	■ The diencephalon has processing and relay centers to integrate the sensory and motor pathways. **15.4a Epithalamus** ■ The epithalamus partially forms the posterior roof of the diencephalon; it contains the pineal gland and habenular nuclei. **15.4b Thalamus** ■ The thalamus is the principal and final relay point for integrating, assimilating, and amplifying sensory impulses sent to the cerebral cortex. **15.4c Hypothalamus** ■ The hypothalamus houses control and integrative centers, and oversees endocrine and autonomic nervous system functions.
15.5 Brainstem	■ The brainstem is composed of three regions: the midbrain, pons, and medulla oblongata. **15.5a Midbrain** ■ The midbrain is the superior portion of the brainstem containing the cerebral peduncles, substantia nigra, tegmentum, tectal plate, and nuclei for two cranial nerves. **15.5b Pons** ■ The pons is an anterior bulge in the metencephalon containing axon tracts, nuclei for involuntary control of respiration, nuclei for four cranial nerves, and nuclei that process and relay commands arriving through the middle cerebellar peduncles. **15.5c Medulla Oblongata** ■ The medulla oblongata connects the brain to the spinal cord. It contains sensory processing centers, autonomic reflex centers, and nuclei for four cranial nerves.
15.6 Cerebellum	■ The cerebellum helps maintain posture and balance, and establishes patterned muscular contractions. **15.6a Cerebellar Peduncles** ■ Three paired cerebellar peduncles (superior, middle, and inferior) are thick fiber tracts that connect the cerebellum with different parts of the brainstem.
15.7 Limbic System	■ The limbic system and the reticular formation are functional brain systems whose components are widely scattered in the brain, but whose activities combine for a common function. ■ The limbic system includes a group of cortical structures that surround the corpus callosum and thalamus near the anterior region of the diencephalon. They function in memory and emotional behavior.
15.8 Cranial Nerves	■ Twelve nerve pairs, called cranial nerves, project from the brain. Each nerve has a specific name and is designated by a Roman numeral.

Challenge Yourself

Actively write or type your answers in a separate document to reinforce your learning, before checking your answers.

Multiple Choice

Select the best answer from the four choices provided.

1. Which cranial nerve has three divisions (ophthalmic, maxillary, and mandibular)?
   a. accessory (CN XI)
   b. glossopharyngeal (CN IX)
   c. trigeminal (CN V)
   d. hypoglossal (CN XII)
2. The subdivision of the brain that does *not* initiate somatic motor movements, but instead coordinates and fine-tunes those movements is which of the following?
   a. medulla oblongata
   b. cerebrum
   c. cerebellum
   d. diencephalon
3. The visual reflex center is housed within which structure?
   a. cerebellum
   b. superior colliculus
   c. hypothalamus
   d. pons
4. After a severe blow to the head, a patient suddenly does not experience sensations of hunger and seems unable to tell if he is dehydrated. The attending physician should suspect damage to or a lesion within what general region of the brain?
   a. frontal lobe
   b. medulla oblongata
   c. Wernicke area
   d. hypothalamus
5. Which of the following statements is ***true*** about the blood-brain barrier?
   a. It prevents all toxic substances from reaching brain tissue.
   b. It is formed from the perivascular feet of microglia and ependymal cells.
   c. It is deficient in the regions of the choroid plexus, hypothalamus, and pineal gland.
   d. It produces and circulates cerebrospinal fluid.
6. Which structures are descending motor tracts on the anterolateral surface of the midbrain?
   a. olives
   b. inferior colliculi
   c. cerebral peduncles
   d. tegmenta

7. Which cerebral lobe is located immediately posterior to the central sulcus and superior to the lateral sulcus?
   a. frontal lobe
   b. temporal lobe
   c. parietal lobe
   d. insula
8. Which specific area of the brain may be impaired if you cannot tell the difference between a smooth and a rough surface, using your hands only?
   a. precentral gyrus
   b. postcentral gyrus
   c. motor speech area
   d. prefrontal cortex
9. Which structures are the isolated, innermost gray matter areas near the base of the cerebrum, inferior to the lateral ventricles?
   a. auditory association areas
   b. cerebral nuclei
   c. substantia nigra
   d. corpus callosum fibers
10. Which type of white matter tracts connect corresponding lobes of the left and right cerebral hemispheres?
    a. commisural tracts
    b. longitudinal fasciculi
    c. projection tracts
    d. arcuate fibers

Content Review

1. List the five secondary brain vesicles, and describe which adult brain structures are formed from each.
2. Describe (a) how and where the cerebrospinal fluid is formed, (b) its subsequent circulation, and (c) how and where it is reabsorbed into the vascular system.
3. What is the difference between the primary motor cortex and the premotor cortex (in terms of both location and function)? How do these two cortices work together?
4. What activities occur in the visual association area of the cerebrum?
5. What structures form the cerebral nuclei, and what are their functions?
6. Where is the thalamus located and what does it do?
7. What are the major functions of the cerebellum?
8. What are the general functions of the limbic system, and what are its components?
9. Name each cranial nerve that innervates (1) the lacrimal glands and most of the salivary glands, (2) the lateral rectus eye muscles, and (3) the intrinsic and extrinsic tongue muscles.
10. During surgery to remove a tumor from the occipital lobe of the left cerebrum, a surgeon must cut into the brain to reach the tumor. List in order (starting with the covering skin) all layers that must be "cut through" to reach the tumor.

Developing Critical Reasoning

1. Shannon felt strange when she awoke one morning. She could not hold a pen in her right hand when trying to write an entry in her diary, and her muscles were noticeably weaker on the right side of her body. Additionally, her husband noticed that she was slurring her speech, so he took her to the emergency room. What does the ER physician suspect has occurred? Where in the brain might the physician suspect that abnormal activity or perhaps a lesion is located, and why?
2. Parkinson disease is the result of decreased levels of the neurotransmitter dopamine in the brain. However, these patients can't take dopamine in drug form because the drug cannot reach the brain. What anatomic structure prevents the drug from reaching the brain? How could these same anatomic structures be beneficial to an individual under different circumstances?
3. During a robbery at his convenience store, Dustin was shot in the right cerebral hemisphere. He survived, although some specific functions were impaired. Would Dustin have been more likely or less likely to have survived if he had been shot in the brainstem? Why?

Answers to "What Do You Think?"

1. The dura mater provides the most support and physical protection. This layer is the thickest and most durable of the cranial meninges. It is composed of dense irregular connective tissue, and it anchors the brain "in place" via the cranial dural septa.
2. If CSF production exceeds the amount removed, a pathologic condition called hydrocephalus occurs. This excess volume of CSF often results in brain distortion and subsequent damage to the brain.
3. Cutting the corpus callosum dramatically reduces communication between the right and left cerebral hemispheres, but some communication is maintained via the much smaller anterior and posterior commissures.
4. The bullet probably penetrated the left side, as both the motor speech and Wernicke areas are usually found on the left side of the brain. Her ability to understand indicated that there was less damage to the Wernicke area. Thus, the more severely damaged functional brain region was the motor speech area. Since then, Gabrielle Giffords recovered some of her ability to speak, read, and write.
5. If there were no thalamus, the cerebrum would still receive sensory stimuli, but the information would not be decoded first. So, the cerebrum would not be able to distinguish taste information from touch or vision information.
6. Severe injury to the medulla oblongata would most likely cause death, because the medulla oblongata is responsible for basic reflex and life functions, including breathing and heartbeat.

Design Element: Pencil Icon: Slavojub Pantelic/Shutterstock

NERVOUS SYSTEM

Spinal Cord and Spinal Nerves 16

Outline

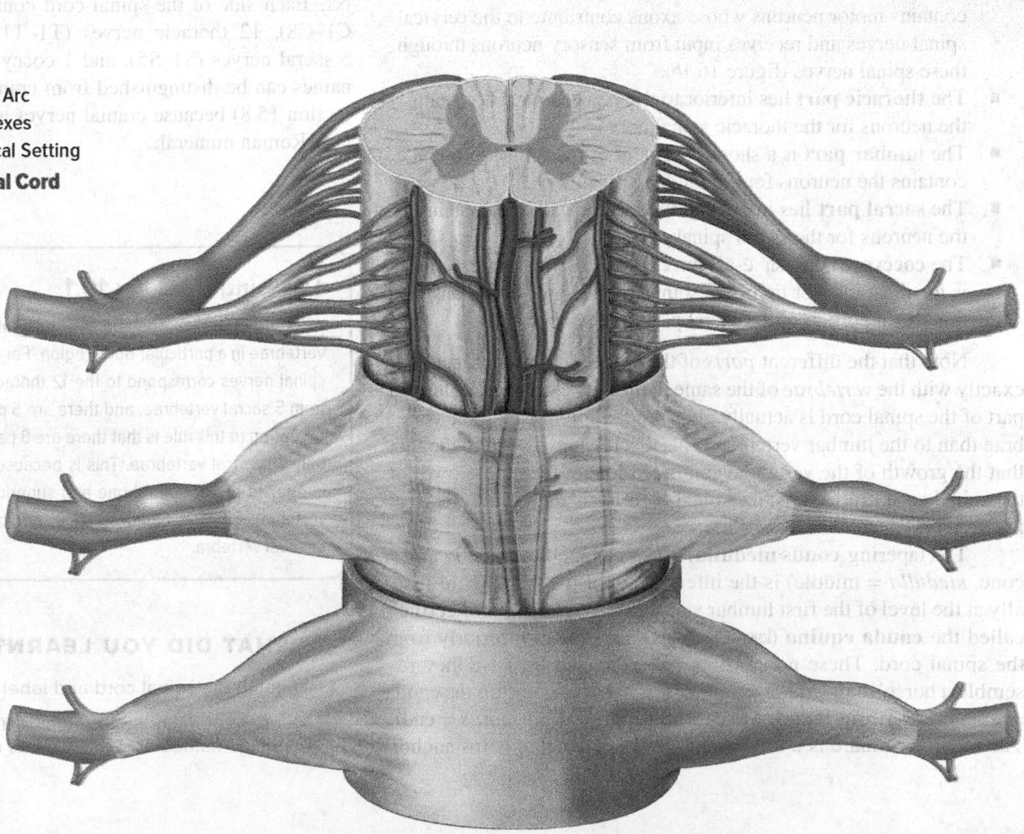

Anatomy & Physiology Revealed 4.0

MODULE 7: NERVOUS SYSTEM

The spinal cord provides a vital link between the brain and the rest of the body, and yet it exhibits some functional independence from the brain. The spinal cord and its attached spinal nerves serve two important functions. First, they are a pathway for sensory and motor impulses. Second, the spinal cord and spinal nerves are responsible for reflexes, which are our quickest reactions to a stimulus. In this chapter, we describe the anatomy of the spinal cord and the integrative activities that occur there.

16.1 Gross Anatomy of the Spinal Cord

✓ Learning Objectives

1. Describe the structure of the spinal cord.
2. Identify and describe the different regions and features of the spinal cord.
3. Explain the basic functions of the spinal cord.

A typical adult spinal cord is approximately 3/4 of an inch (19 millimeters) in diameter and ranges between 16 to 18 inches (41 to 45 centimeters) in length. It extends inferiorly from the medulla oblongata through the foramen magnum and the vertebral canal, ending at the inferior border of the L_1 vertebra. The spinal cord may be subdivided into the following five parts (**figure 16.1*a***):

- The **cervical part** is the superiormost region of the spinal cord. It is continuous with the medulla oblongata. The cervical part contains motor neurons whose axons contribute to the cervical spinal nerves and receives input from sensory neurons through these spinal nerves (figure 16.1*b*).
- The **thoracic part** lies inferior to the cervical part. It contains the neurons for the thoracic spinal nerves.
- The **lumbar part** is a shorter segment of the spinal cord that contains the neurons for the lumbar spinal nerves.
- The **sacral part** lies inferior to the lumbar part and contains the neurons for the sacral spinal nerves.
- The **coccygeal** (kok-sij′ ē-ăl) **part** (not shown in figure 16.1) is the most inferior tip of the spinal cord. (Some texts consider this part a portion of the sacral part of the spinal cord.)

Note that the different *parts* of the spinal cord do not match up exactly with the *vertebrae* of the same name. For example, the lumbar part of the spinal cord is actually closer to the inferior thoracic vertebrae than to the lumbar vertebrae. This discrepancy is due to the fact that the growth of the vertebrae continued longer than the growth of the spinal cord itself. Thus, the spinal cord in an adult is shorter than the vertebral canal that houses it.

The tapering **conus medullaris** (kō′nŭs med′ū-lăr′is; *kōnos* = cone, *medulla* = middle) is the inferior end of the spinal cord (usually at the level of the first lumbar vertebra). Nerve roots collectively called the **cauda equina** (kaw′d ă ē-kwī′nă) project inferiorly from the spinal cord. These nerve roots are so named because they resemble a horse's tail (*cauda* = tail, *equus* = horse). Within the cauda equina is the **filum terminale** (fī′lŭm ter′mi-n ăl; *terminus* = end). The filum terminale is a thin strand of pia mater that helps anchor the conus medullaris to the coccyx. Figure 16.1*c* shows the conus medullaris and the cauda equina.

Viewed in cross section, the spinal cord is roughly cylindrical, but slightly flattened both posteriorly and anteriorly. Its external surface has two longitudinal depressions: A narrow groove, the **posterior** (or *dorsal*) **median sulcus,** dips internally on the posterior surface, and a slightly wider groove, the **anterior** (or *ventral*) **median fissure,** is viewed on its anterior surface.

Cross-sectional views of the spinal cord vary, depending upon the part from which the section was taken (**table 16.1**). These subtle differences make identifying specific spinal cross sections a bit easier. For example, the diameter of the spinal cord changes along its length because the amount of gray matter and white matter and the function of the cord vary in different parts. Therefore, the spinal cord parts that control the upper and lower limbs are larger because more neuron cell bodies are located there, and more space is occupied by axons and dendrites. The **cervical enlargement,** located in the inferior cervical part of the spinal cord, contains the neurons that innervate the upper limbs. The **lumbosacral enlargement** extends through the lumbar and sacral parts of the spinal cord and innervates the lower limbs.

The spinal cord is associated with 31 pairs of spinal nerves that connect the CNS to receptors and effectors (muscles and glands). Spinal nerves are considered *mixed nerves* because they contain both motor and sensory axons. Spinal nerves are identified by the first letter of the spinal cord part to which they attach combined with a number. Each side of the spinal cord contains 8 cervical nerves (called C1–C8), 12 thoracic nerves (T1–T12), 5 lumbar nerves (L1–L5), 5 sacral nerves (S1–S5), and 1 coccygeal nerve (Co1). Spinal nerve names can be distinguished from cranial nerve names (discussed in section 15.8) because cranial nerves are designated by CN followed by a Roman numeral.

Learning Strategy 16.1

With one exception, the number of spinal nerves matches the number of vertebrae in a particular body region. For example, the 12 pairs of thoracic spinal nerves correspond to the 12 thoracic vertebrae. The sacrum forms from 5 sacral vertebrae, and there are 5 pairs of sacral spinal nerves. The exception to this rule is that there are 8 pairs of cervical spinal nerves, but only 7 cervical vertebrae. This is because the first cervical pair emerges inferior to the occipital bone and superior to the atlas (the first cervical vertebra), and the eighth cervical nerve arises inferior to the seventh cervical vertebra.

WHAT DID YOU LEARN?

1. Sketch the spinal cord and label its parts and features.
2. State the total number of pairs of spinal nerves, and list the specific names of spinal nerves according to their region.

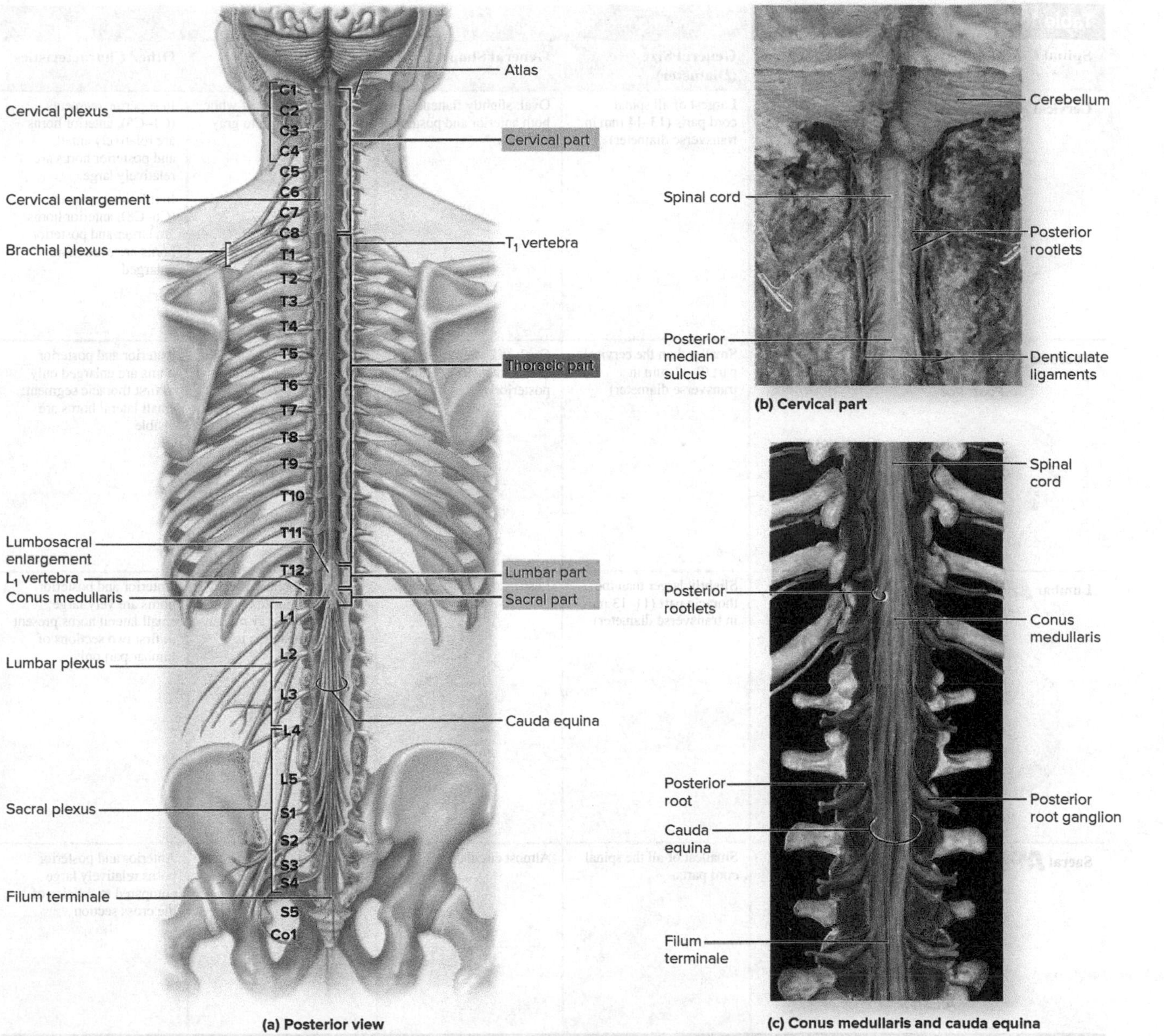
Atlas
Cervical plexus
C1
C2
C3
C4
C5
C6
C7
C8
Cervical part
Cervical enlargement
T_1 vertebra
Brachial plexus
T1
T2
T3
T4
T5
T6
T7
T8
T9
T10
T11
T12
Thoracic part
Lumbosacral enlargement
L_1 vertebra
Conus medullaris
Lumbar part
Sacral part
L1
L2
L3
L4
L5
Lumbar plexus
Cauda equina
Sacral plexus
S1
S2
S3
S4
S5
Co1
Filum terminale
(a) Posterior view
Cerebellum
Spinal cord
Posterior rootlets
Posterior median sulcus
Denticulate ligaments
(b) Cervical part
Spinal cord
Posterior rootlets
Conus medullaris
Posterior root
Posterior root ganglion
Cauda equina
Filum terminale
(c) Conus medullaris and cauda equina

Figure 16.1

Gross Anatomy of the Spinal Cord. The spinal cord extends inferiorly from the medulla oblongata through the vertebral canal. (*a*) The vertebral arches have been removed to reveal the anatomy of the adult spinal cord and its spinal nerves. (*b*) Cadaver photo of the cervical part of the spinal cord. (*c*) Cadaver photo of the conus medullaris and the cauda equina. APR

Table 16.1 Cross Sections of Representative Parts of the Spinal Cord

Spinal Cord Part	General Size (Diameter)	General Shape	White Matter/ Gray Matter Ratio	Other Characteristics
Cervical APR 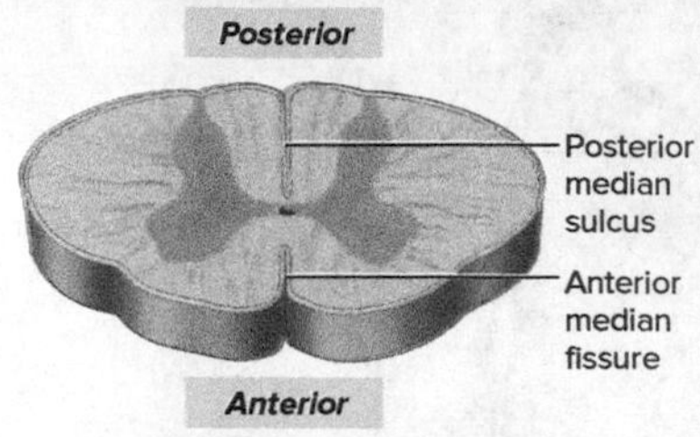 Posterior Posterior median sulcus Anterior median fissure Anterior	Largest of all spinal cord parts (13–14 mm in transverse diameter)	Oval; slightly flattened on both anterior and posterior surfaces	Large proportion of white matter compared to gray matter	In superior segments (C1–C5), anterior horns are relatively small, and posterior horns are relatively large In inferior segments (C6–C8), anterior horns are larger and posterior horns are even more enlarged
Thoracic APR 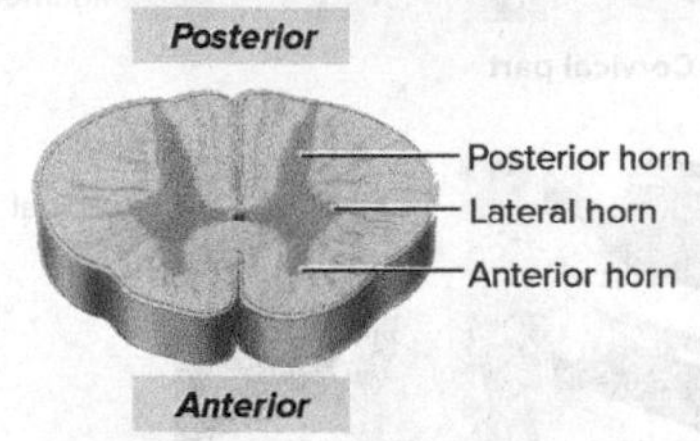 Posterior Posterior horn Lateral horn Anterior horn Anterior	Smaller than the cervical part (9–11 mm in transverse diameter)	Oval; still slightly flattened anteriorly and posteriorly	Larger proportion of white matter than gray matter	Anterior and posterior horns are enlarged only in first thoracic segment; small lateral horns are visible
Lumbar APR 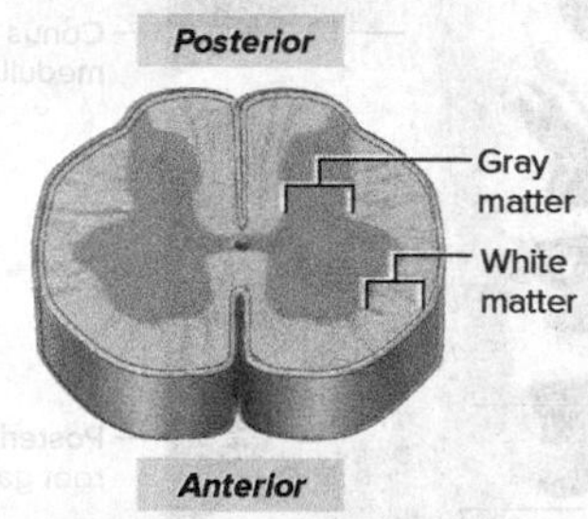 Posterior Gray matter White matter Anterior	Slightly larger than the thoracic part (11–13 mm in transverse diameter)	Less oval, almost circular	Relative amount of white matter is reduced both in proportion to gray matter and in comparison to cervical part	Anterior and posterior horns are very large; small lateral horns present in first two sections of lumbar part only
Sacral APR 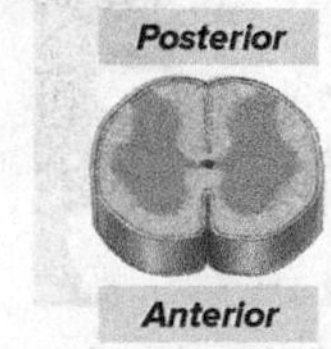 Posterior Anterior	Smallest of all the spinal cord parts.	Almost circular	Proportion of gray matter to white matter is largest in this spinal cord part	Anterior and posterior horns relatively large compared to the size of the cross section

16.2 Spinal Cord Meninges

✓ **Learning Objective**

4. Explain the arrangement and functions of the spinal meninges.

The spinal cord is protected and encapsulated by **spinal cord meninges,** which are continuous with the cranial meninges described in section 15.2a. In addition, spaces between some of the meninges have clinical significance. The structures and spaces (both real and potential) that encircle the spinal cord, listed from outermost to innermost, are as follows: vertebra, epidural space, dura mater, subdural space, arachnoid mater, subarachnoid space, and pia mater (**figure 16.2**).

The **epidural** (ep′i-d ū′răl) **space** lies between the dura mater and the periosteum covering the inner walls of the vertebra, and houses areolar connective tissue, blood vessels, and adipose connective tissue. Epidural anesthesia is administered into this space (see Clinical View 16.1: "Lumbar Puncture and Epidural Injection" in section 16.2). Deep to the epidural space is the outermost of the meninges, the **dura mater.** The spinal dura mater consists of a single meningeal layer, which differs from cranial dura mater's two layers. The dura mater provides stability to the spinal cord. In addition, at each intervertebral foramen, the dura mater extends between adjacent vertebrae and fuses with the connective tissue layers that surround the spinal nerves.

WHAT DO YOU THINK?

1. Why doesn't the spinal dura mater have two layers as the cranial dura mater does? What structures that are formed from cranial dura mater must be missing around the spinal cord?

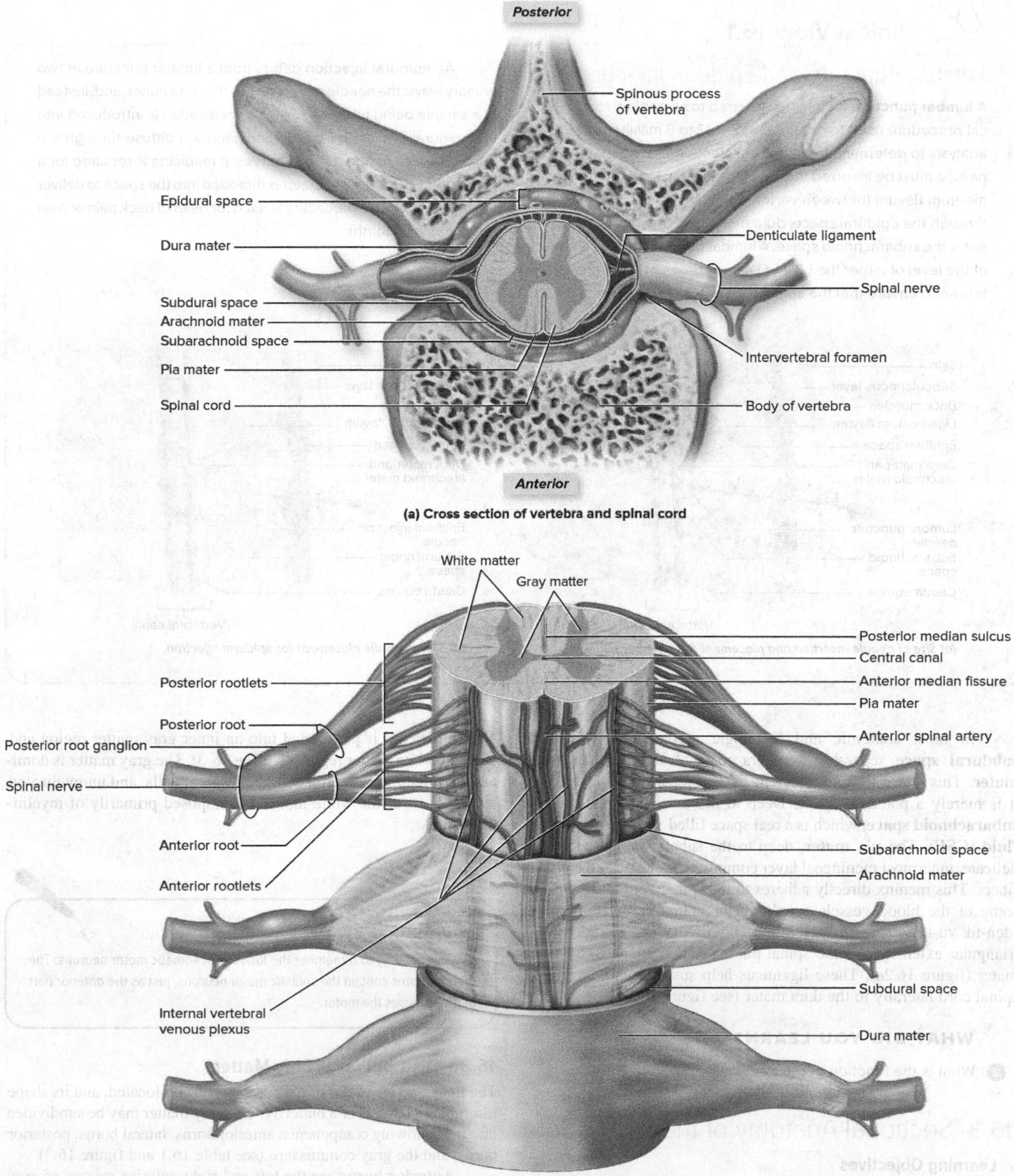
Posterior
Spinous process of vertebra
Epidural space
Dura mater
Denticulate ligament
Spinal nerve
Subdural space
Arachnoid mater
Subarachnoid space
Intervertebral foramen
Pia mater
Spinal cord
Body of vertebra
Anterior
(a) Cross section of vertebra and spinal cord
White matter
Gray matter
Posterior median sulcus
Central canal
Posterior rootlets
Anterior median fissure
Pia mater
Posterior root
Anterior spinal artery
Posterior root ganglion
Spinal nerve
Anterior root
Subarachnoid space
Arachnoid mater
Anterior rootlets
Subdural space
Internal vertebral venous plexus
Dura mater
(b) Anterior view

Figure 16.2

Spinal Meninges and Structure of the Spinal Cord. (*a*) A cross section of the spinal cord shows the relationship between the meningeal layers and the superficial landmarks of the spinal cord and vertebral column. (*b*) Anterior view shows the spinal cord, meninges, and some of the blood vessels that supply the spinal cord. The anterior and posterior spinal arteries provide much of the arterial blood to the cord, and the internal vertebral venous plexuses drain blood away from the spinal cord.

Clinical View 16.1

Lumbar Puncture and Epidural Injection

A **lumbar puncture** (commonly referred to as a *spinal tap*) is a clinical procedure used to obtain a sample (3 to 9 milliliters) of CSF for analysis to determine if there is an infection or CNS disorder. The needle must be inserted through the skin, back muscles, and ligamentum flavum (between vertebrae). Then the needle must pass through the epidural space, dura mater, and arachnoid mater, and enter the subarachnoid space. A lumbar puncture typically is made at the level of either the L3 and L4 vertebrae or the L4 and L5 vertebrae to ensure that the spinal cord is not pierced by the needle.

An **epidural injection** differs from a lumbar puncture in two primary ways: the needle never pierces the dura mater, and, instead of a sample being taken for analysis, medication is introduced into the epidural space. The medication can then diffuse through the epidural space to affect spinal nerves. If medicine is required for a longer period of time, a catheter is threaded into the space to deliver the medication. This procedure is used for relief of back pain or pain from labor (childbirth).

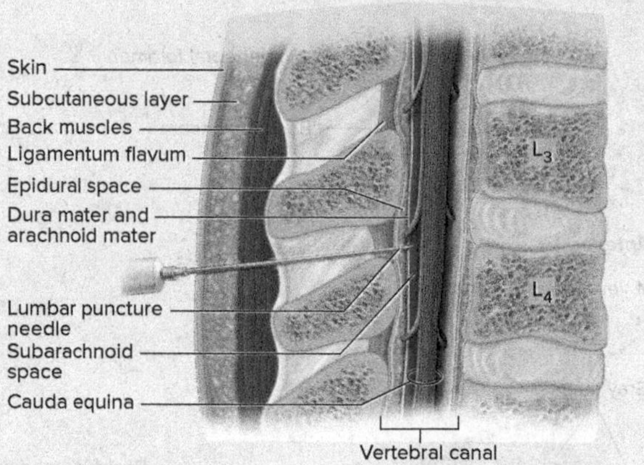
Skin
Subcutaneous layer
Back muscles
Ligamentum flavum
Epidural space
Dura mater and arachnoid mater
Lumbar puncture needle
Subarachnoid space
Cauda equina
L3
L4
Vertebral canal

(a) Site of needle insertion and placement for a lumbar puncture.

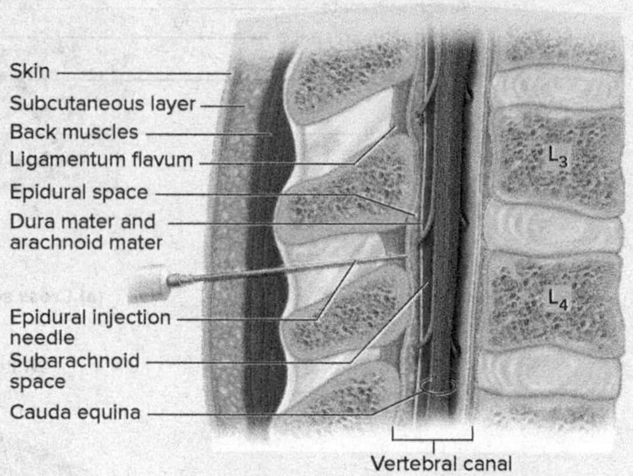
Skin
Subcutaneous layer
Back muscles
Ligamentum flavum
Epidural space
Dura mater and arachnoid mater
Epidural injection needle
Subarachnoid space
Cauda equina
L3
L4
Vertebral canal

(b) Site of needle placement for epidural injection.

In most anatomic and histologic preparations, a narrow **subdural space** separates the dura mater from the **arachnoid mater.** This space is found only in tissue preparations, and in life it is merely a potential space. Deep to the arachnoid mater is the **subarachnoid space,** which is a real space filled with **cerebrospinal fluid (CSF).** The **pia mater,** deep to the subarachnoid space, is a delicate, innermost meningeal layer composed of elastic and collagen fibers. This meninx directly adheres to the spinal cord and supports some of the blood vessels supplying the spinal cord. **Denticulate** (den-tik′yū-lāt; *dentatus* = toothed) **ligaments** are paired, lateral triangular extensions of the spinal pia mater that attach to the dura mater (figure 16.2*a*). These ligaments help suspend and anchor the spinal cord laterally to the dura mater (see figure 16.1*b*).

WHAT DID YOU LEARN?

3. What is the function of the denticulate ligaments?

16.3 Sectional Anatomy of the Spinal Cord

✓ Learning Objectives

5. Describe the internal anatomy of the spinal cord.
6. Identify and explain the distribution of gray matter and white matter in the spinal cord.
7. Compare the functions of gray matter and white matter with respect to their composition.

The spinal cord is partitioned into an inner gray matter region and an outer white matter region (**figure 16.3**). The gray matter is dominated by dendrites, neuron cell bodies, glial cells, and unmyelinated axons, whereas the white matter is composed primarily of myelinated axons.

Learning Strategy 16.2

Use this analogy to remember the location of somatic motor neurons: The *anterior* horns contain the somatic motor neurons, just as the *anterior* part of a car houses the motor.

16.3a Distribution of Gray Matter

The **gray matter** in the spinal cord is centrally located, and its shape resembles a letter H or a butterfly. The gray matter may be subdivided into the following components: anterior horns, lateral horns, posterior horns, and the gray commissure (see table 16.1 and figure 16.3).

Anterior horns are the left and right anterior masses of gray matter. The anterior horns primarily house the *cell bodies of somatic motor neurons,* which innervate skeletal muscle. **Lateral horns** occur in the T1–L2 parts of the spinal cord only. The lateral horns contain the *cell bodies of autonomic motor neurons,* which innervate cardiac muscle, smooth muscle, and glands. **Posterior horns** are the left and

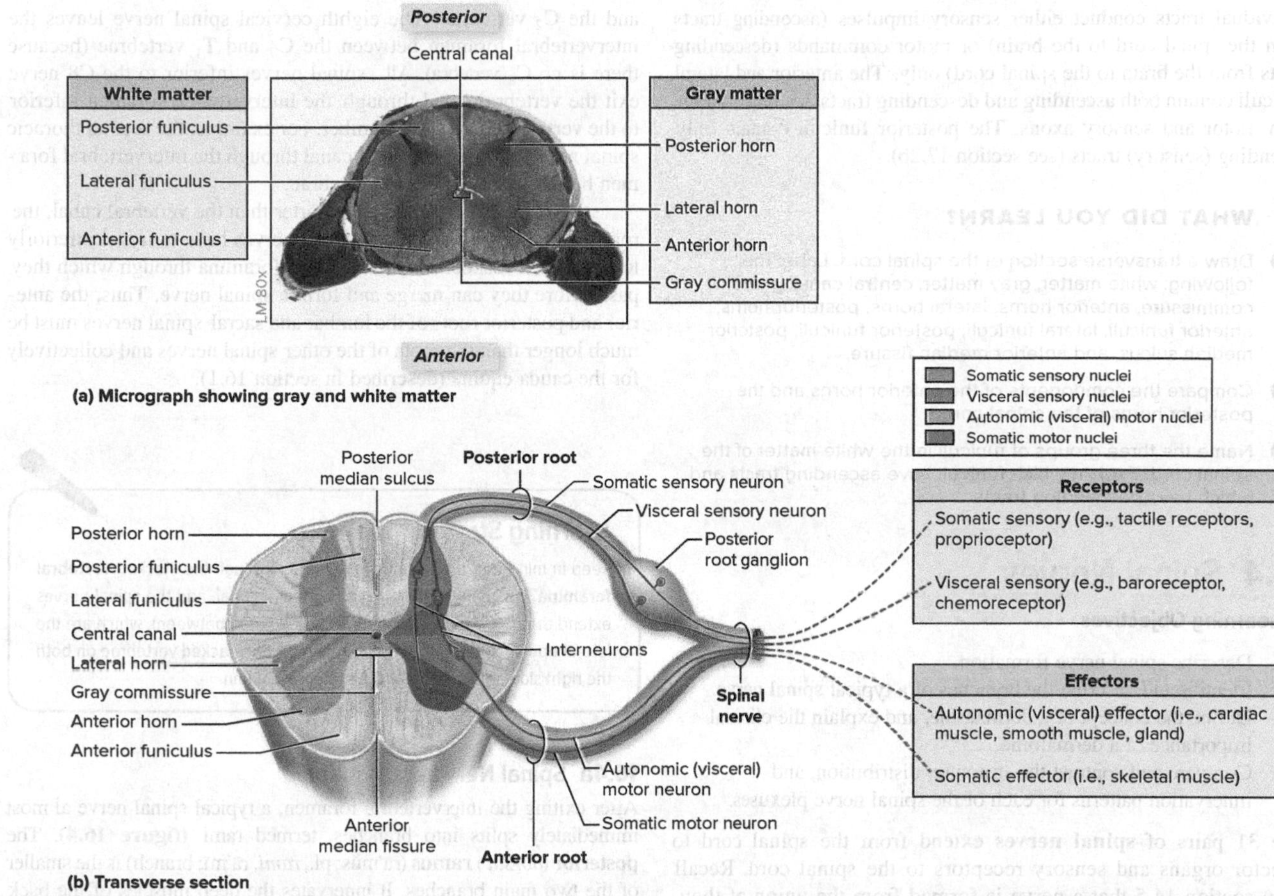
Posterior
Central canal
White matter
Posterior funiculus
Lateral funiculus
Anterior funiculus
Gray matter
Posterior horn
Lateral horn
Anterior horn
Gray commissure
LM 80x
Anterior
(a) Micrograph showing gray and white matter
Posterior median sulcus
Posterior root
Somatic sensory neuron
Visceral sensory neuron
Posterior root ganglion
Posterior horn
Posterior funiculus
Lateral funiculus
Central canal
Lateral horn
Gray commissure
Anterior horn
Anterior funiculus
Interneurons
Spinal nerve
Autonomic (visceral) motor neuron
Somatic motor neuron
Anterior median fissure
Anterior root
(b) Transverse section
Somatic sensory nuclei
Visceral sensory nuclei
Autonomic (visceral) motor nuclei
Somatic motor nuclei
Receptors
Somatic sensory (e.g., tactile receptors, proprioceptor)
Visceral sensory (e.g., baroreceptor, chemoreceptor)
Effectors
Autonomic (visceral) effector (i.e., cardiac muscle, smooth muscle, gland)
Somatic effector (i.e., skeletal muscle)

Figure 16.3

Cross Section of Spinal Cord and Spinal Roots. (*a*) Micrograph showing histology of a cross section of the spinal cord. (*b*) Illustration of a cross section of the spinal cord and spinal roots. The collections of neuron cell bodies within the CNS form specific nuclei. Neurons and their respective nuclei are color-coded on the drawing.

(a) Ed Reschke/Getty Images

right posterior masses of gray matter. The *axons of sensory neurons* and the *cell bodies of interneurons* are located in the posterior horns. (The cell bodies of these sensory neurons are not found in the posterior horns; rather, they are located in the posterior root ganglia, which are mentioned in section 16.4.) The **gray commissure** (kom′i-shūr; *commissura* = a seam) is a horizontal bar of gray matter that surrounds a narrow **central canal.** The gray commissure primarily contains unmyelinated axons and serves as a communication route between the right and left sides of the gray matter.

Within these regions of gray matter are various functional groups of neuron cell bodies called **nuclei** (nū′klē-ī) (figure 16.3*b*). **Sensory nuclei** in the posterior horns contain interneuron cell bodies. **Somatic sensory nuclei** receive information from sensory receptors, such as pain or pressure receptors in the skin, and **visceral sensory nuclei** receive information from sensory receptors such as the stretch receptors in the smooth muscle walls of viscera. **Motor nuclei** in the anterior and lateral horns contain motor neuron cell bodies that send nerve impulses to muscles and glands. The **somatic motor nuclei** in the anterior horns innervate skeletal muscle, whereas the **autonomic motor nuclei** in the lateral horns innervate smooth muscle, cardiac muscle, and glands.

16.3b Distribution of White Matter

The white matter of the spinal cord is external to the gray matter. White matter on each side of the cord is also partitioned into three regions, each called a **funiculus** (fū-nik′yū-lŭs; pl., *funiculi*,[1] fū-nik′yū-lī; *funis* = cord) (see figure 16.3*a*). A **posterior funiculus** lies between the posterior gray horns on the posterior side of the cord and the posterior median sulcus. The white matter region on each lateral side of the spinal cord is the **lateral funiculus.** The **anterior funiculus** is composed of tracts of white matter that occupy the space on each anterior side of the cord between the anterior gray horns and the anterior median fissure; the anterior funiculi are interconnected by the **white commissure.**

The axons within each white matter funiculus are organized into smaller structural units called **tracts** (*tractus* = a drawing out) or **fasciculi** (fa-sik′ū-lī; *fascis* = bundle), to be described in chapter 17.

[1] Note: Anterior and lateral funiculi were formerly called *columns*. The Federative Committee on Anatomical Terminology (FCAT) now states that the term *column* refers to structures within the gray matter of the spinal cord, whereas *funiculus* refers to the white matter regions.

Individual tracts conduct either sensory impulses (ascending tracts from the spinal cord to the brain) or motor commands (descending tracts from the brain to the spinal cord) only. The anterior and lateral funiculi contain both ascending and descending tracts, so they contain both motor and sensory axons. The posterior funiculi contain only ascending (sensory) tracts (see section 17.2b).

WHAT DID YOU LEARN?

4. Draw a transverse section of the spinal cord. Label the following: white matter, gray matter, central canal, gray commissure, anterior horns, lateral horns, posterior horns, anterior funiculi, lateral funiculi, posterior funiculi, posterior median sulcus, and anterior median fissure.
5. Compare the components of the anterior horns and the posterior horns of the spinal cord.
6. Name the three groups of funiculi in the white matter of the spinal cord. Explain which funiculi have ascending tracts and which have descending tracts.

16.4 Spinal Nerves

✓ Learning Objectives

8. Describe spinal nerve formation.
9. Identify and describe the branches of a typical spinal nerve.
10. Define the concept of a dermatome, and explain the clinical importance of a dermatome.
11. Compare and contrast the structure, distribution, and innervation patterns for each of the spinal nerve plexuses.

The 31 pairs of **spinal nerves** extend from the spinal cord to effector organs and sensory receptors to the spinal cord. Recall from section 14.5 that a nerve is formed from the union of thousands of motor and sensory axons, and contains three types of successive connective tissue wrappings: endoneurium, perineurium, and epineurium (see figure 14.12). Motor axons in a spinal nerve originate from the spinal cord (see figures 16.2 and 16.4). Anteriorly, multiple **anterior rootlets** arise from the spinal cord and merge to form a single **anterior root** (or *ventral root*), which contains motor axons only. These motor axons arise from cell bodies in the anterior and lateral horns of the spinal cord. Likewise, the posterior aspect of the spinal cord contains multiple **posterior rootlets** that enter the posterior aspect of the spinal cord. These rootlets were derived from a single **posterior root** (or *dorsal root*), which contains sensory axons only. The cell bodies of these sensory neurons are located in a **posterior root ganglion,** which is attached to the posterior root (see figures 16.2*b* and 16.4).

Each anterior root and its corresponding posterior root unite within the intervertebral foramen to become a spinal nerve. Thus, all spinal nerves are mixed nerves because each spinal nerve contains both motor axons (from the anterior root) and sensory axons (from the posterior root). You can compare a spinal nerve to a cable composed of multiple wires. The "wires" within a spinal nerve are the motor and sensory axons, and each "wire'" transmits in only one direction.

Cervical spinal nerves exit the vertebral canal through the intervertebral foramen superior to the cervical vertebra of the same number. For example, the second cervical spinal nerve exits the vertebral canal through the intervertebral foramen between the C_1 and the C_2 vertebrae. The eighth cervical spinal nerve leaves the intervertebral foramen between the C_7 and T_1 vertebrae (because there is no C_8 vertebra). All spinal nerves inferior to the C8 nerve exit the vertebral canal through the intervertebral foramen inferior to the vertebra of the same number. For example, the second thoracic spinal nerve exits the vertebral canal through the intervertebral foramen between the T_2 and T_3 vertebrae.

Because the spinal cord is shorter than the vertebral canal, the roots of the lumbar and sacral spinal nerves have to travel inferiorly to reach their respective intervertebral foramina through which they pass before they can merge and form a spinal nerve. Thus, the anterior and posterior roots of the lumbar and sacral spinal nerves must be much longer than the roots of the other spinal nerves and collectively for the cauda equina (described in section 16.1).

Learning Strategy 16.3

Keep in mind that the spinal cord extends through the stacked **vertebral foramina,** which medially form the vertebral canal, and the spinal nerves extend through **intervertebral foramina** (*inter* = between), which are the lateral openings formed between two adjacent stacked vertebrae on both the right side and left side of the vertebral column.

16.4a Spinal Nerve Distribution

After exiting the intervertebral foramen, a typical spinal nerve al most immediately splits into branches, termed rami (**figure 16.4**). The **posterior** (*dorsal*) **ramus** (rā'mŭs; pl., *rami*, rā'mī; branch) is the smaller of the two main branches. It innervates the deep muscles of the back (e.g., erector spinae and transversospinalis) and the skin of the back.

The **anterior** (*ventral*) **ramus** is the larger of the two main branches. The anterior ramus splits into multiple other branches, which innervate the anterior and lateral portions of the trunk, the upper limbs, and the lower limbs. Many of the anterior rami go on to form nerve plexuses, which are described in sections 16.4b and 16.4d through 16.4g.

Additional rami, called the **rami communicantes,** are also associated with spinal nerves. These rami contain axons associated with the autonomic nervous system (ANS). Each set of rami communicantes extends between the spinal nerve and a ball-like structure called the **sympathetic trunk ganglion.** These ganglia are interconnected and form a beaded necklace–like structure called the **sympathetic trunk.** The rami communicantes, the sympathetic trunk, and the rest of the autonomic nervous system are described in detail in chapter 18. **APR**

WHAT DO YOU THINK?

2. Why is an anterior ramus so much larger than a posterior ramus? (Hint: Think about what structures each innervates.)

Dermatomes

A **dermatome** (der'mă-tōm; *derma* = skin, *tome* = a cutting) is a specific segment of skin supplied by a single spinal nerve. All spinal nerves except C1 innervate a segment of skin, and each area of the skin that is innervated by a specific spinal nerve has been mapped. Thus, the skin of the body may be divided into sensory segments that

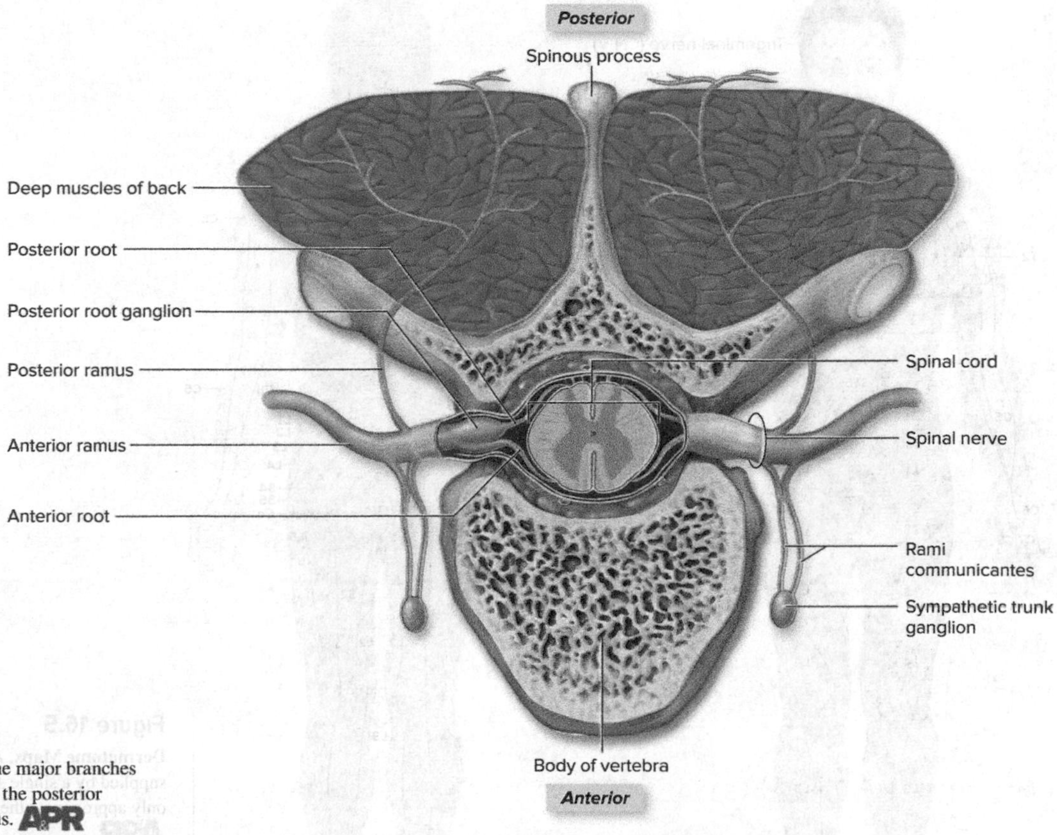

Figure 16.4
Spinal Nerve Branches. The major branches of a typical spinal nerve are the posterior ramus and the anterior ramus. **APR**

Clinical View 16.2

Shingles (Herpes Zoster)

Some adults (usually after age 50) experience a reactivation of their childhood varicella-zoster (chickenpox) infection, a condition termed **shingles** (shing′gĕlz). Psychological stress, other infections (such as a cold or the flu), and even a sunburn can trigger the development of shingles. During the initial infection, the varicella-zoster virus sometimes leaves the skin and invades the posterior root ganglia. There, the virus remains latent until adulthood, when it becomes reactivated and proliferates, traveling through the sensory axons to the dermatome. (The word *shingles* is derived from the Latin word *cingulum,* meaning "girdle," reflecting the dermatomal pattern of its spread.) The virus gives rise to a rash and blisters along the dermatome, which are often accompanied by intense burning or tingling pain. Antiviral medication (e.g., acyclovir) may reduce the severity and duration of symptoms of shingles. Additionally, older adults may receive a vaccine for shingles, which may help prevent or reduce the severity of the disease.

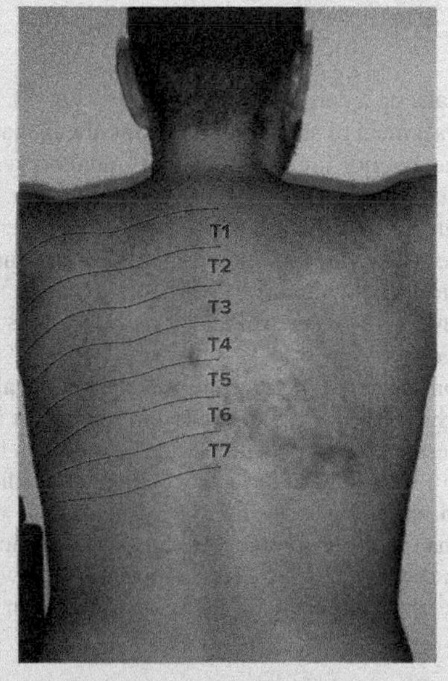

Typical dermatomal spread of a shingles rash in a 49-year-old man.

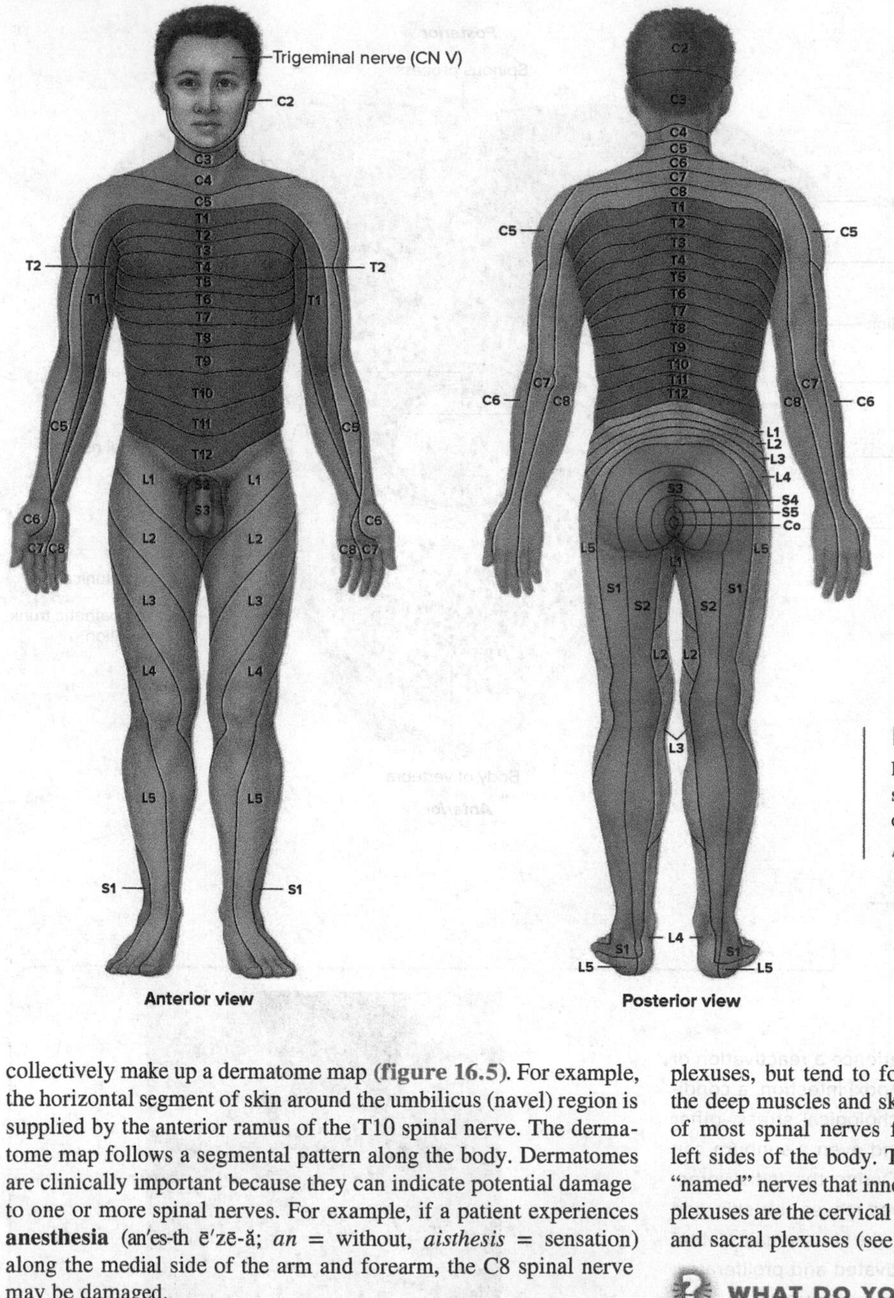

Figure 16.5

Dermatome Maps. A dermatome is an area of skin supplied by a single spinal nerve. These diagrams only approximate the dermatomal distribution.

APR

collectively make up a dermatome map (**figure 16.5**). For example, the horizontal segment of skin around the umbilicus (navel) region is supplied by the anterior ramus of the T10 spinal nerve. The dermatome map follows a segmental pattern along the body. Dermatomes are clinically important because they can indicate potential damage to one or more spinal nerves. For example, if a patient experiences **anesthesia** (an′es-th ē′zē-ă; *an* = without, *aisthesis* = sensation) along the medial side of the arm and forearm, the C8 spinal nerve may be damaged.

Dermatomes are also involved in **referred visceral pain,** a phenomenon in which pain or discomfort from one organ is mistakenly referred to a dermatome. For example, the appendix is innervated by axons from the T10 regions of the spinal cord, so appendicitis typically causes referred visceral pain to the T10 dermatome in the umbilicus region rather than in the abdominopelvic region of the appendix itself. Thus, pain in a dermatome may arise from an organ nowhere near the dermatome. Referred visceral pain is explored further in section 19.1b and figure 19.4.

16.4b Nerve Plexuses

A **nerve plexus** (plek′sŭs; a braid) is a network of interweaving anterior rami of spinal nerves. (Note: The posterior rami of spinal nerves are smaller than their anterior counterparts and do not form plexuses, but tend to follow a segmental pattern as they innervate the deep muscles and skin of the neck and back.) The anterior rami of most spinal nerves form nerve plexuses on both the right and left sides of the body. These nerve plexuses then split into multiple "named" nerves that innervate various body structures. The principal plexuses are the cervical plexuses, brachial plexuses, lumbar plexuses, and sacral plexuses (see figure 16.1).

WHAT DO YOU THINK?

3 What is the benefit of having an intricate nerve plexus, rather than a single nerve that innervates a structure?

Nerve plexuses are organized such that axons from each anterior ramus extend to body structures through several different branches. In addition, each terminal branch of the plexus houses axons from several different spinal nerves. Most of the named nerves from a plexus are composed of axons from multiple spinal nerves. Thus, damage to a single segment of the spinal cord or damage to a single spinal nerve generally does not result in complete loss of innervation to a particular muscle or region of skin.

Most of the thoracic spinal nerves, as well as nerves S5–Co1, do not form plexuses. We discuss the thoracic spinal nerves (called intercostal nerves) first, followed by the individual nerve plexuses.

16.4c Intercostal Nerves

The anterior rami of spinal nerves T1–T11 are called **intercostal nerves** because they travel in the intercostal space sandwiched between two adjacent ribs **(figure 16.6)**. (T12 is called a **subcostal nerve,** because it arises below the ribs, not between two ribs.) The innervation pattern of the T1–T12 nerves is as follows: With the exception of T1, the intercostal nerves do not form plexuses. A portion of the anterior ramus of T1 helps form the brachial plexus, but a branch of it travels within the first intercostal space. The anterior ramus of nerve T2 emerges from its intervertebral foramen and innervates the intercostal muscles of the second intercostal space. Additionally, a branch of T2 conducts sensory impulses from the skin covering the axilla and the medial surface of the arm. Anterior rami of nerves T3–T6 follow the costal grooves of the ribs to innervate the intercostal muscles and receive sensations from the anterior and lateral chest wall. Anterior rami of nerves T7–T12 innervate not only the inferior intercostal spaces, but also the abdominal muscles and their overlying skin.

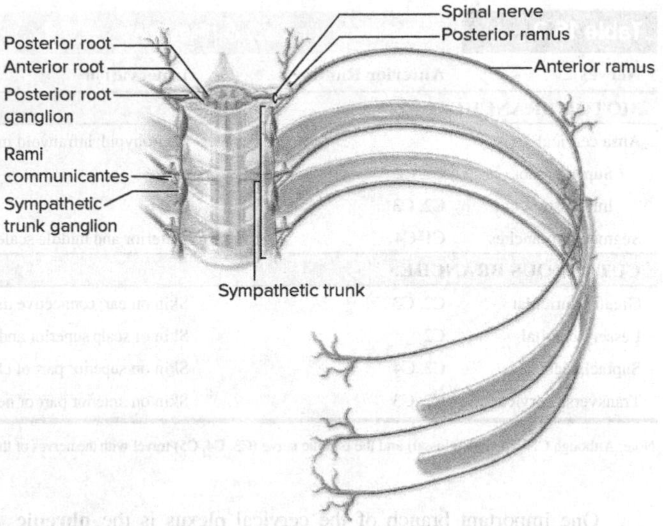

Figure 16.6

Intercostal Nerves. Intercostal nerves are the anterior rami of the T1–T11 spinal nerves. They are typically distributed as shown here.

Learning Strategy 16.4

This mnemonic will help you remember the nerves that innervate the diaphragm: **C three, four, and five keep the diaphragm alive.**

16.4d Cervical Plexuses

The left and right **cervical plexuses** are located deep on each side of the neck, immediately lateral to cervical vertebrae C_1–C_4 **(figure 16.7)**. They are formed primarily by the anterior rami of spinal nerves C1–C4. The fifth cervical spinal nerve is not considered part of the cervical plexus, although it contributes some axons to one of the plexus branches. Branches of the cervical plexuses innervate anterior neck muscles (see table 11.6) as well as the skin of the neck and portions of the head and shoulders. The branches of the cervical plexuses are described in detail in **table 16.2**.

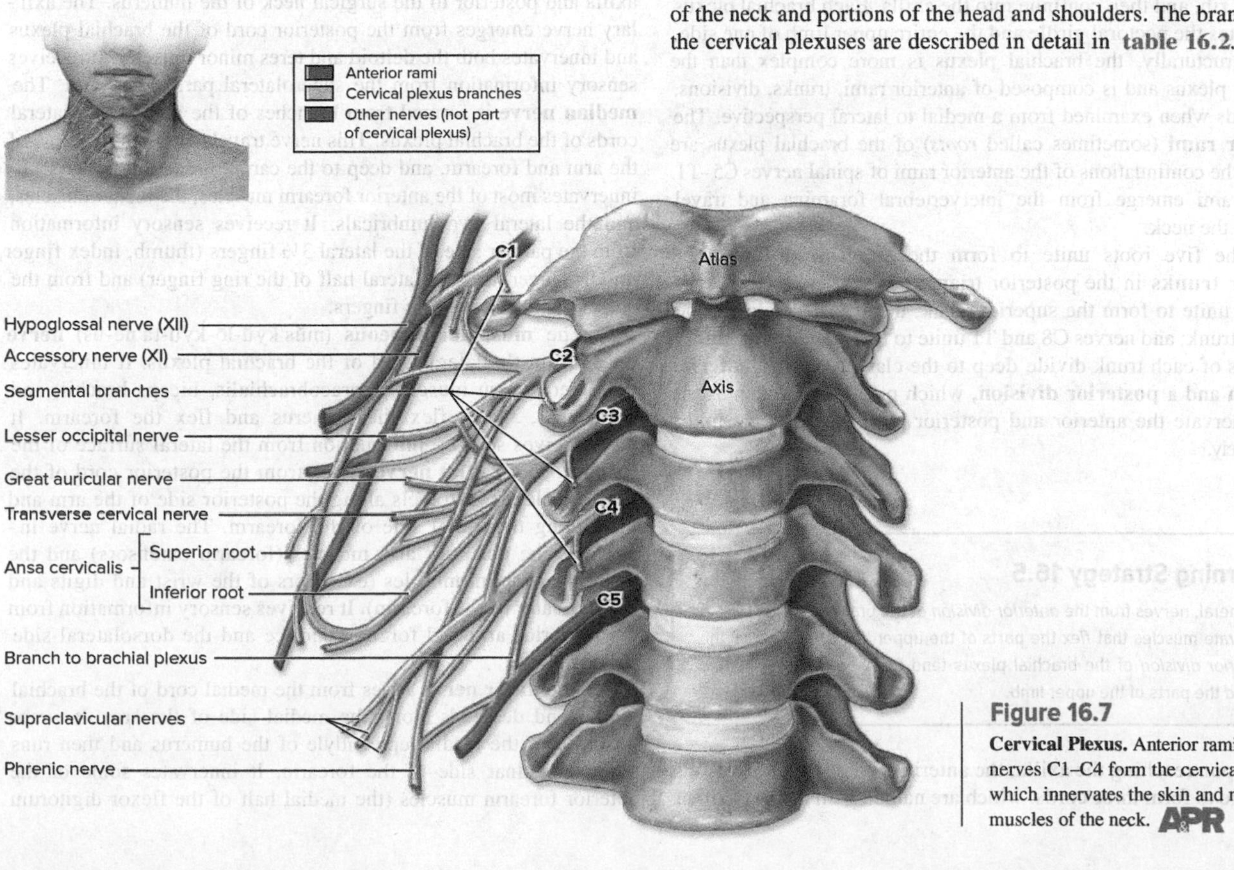

Figure 16.7

Cervical Plexus. Anterior rami of nerves C1–C4 form the cervical plexus, which innervates the skin and many muscles of the neck. APR

Table 16.2 Branches of the Cervical Plexuses

Nerves	Anterior Rami	Innervation
MOTOR BRANCHES		
Ansa cervicalis		Geniohyoid; infrahyoid muscles (omohyoid, sternohyoid, sternothyroid, and thyrohyoid)
Superior root	C1, C2	
Inferior root	C2, C3	
Segmental branches	C1–C4	Anterior and middle scalenes
CUTANEOUS BRANCHES		
Greater auricular	C2, C3	Skin on ear; connective tissue capsule covering parotid gland
Lesser occipital	C2	Skin of scalp superior and posterior to ear
Supraclavicular	C3, C4	Skin on superior part of chest and shoulder
Transverse cervical	C2, C3	Skin on anterior part of neck

Note: Although CN XII (hypoglossal) and the phrenic nerve (C3, C4, C5) travel with the nerves of the cervical plexus, the hypoglossal and phrenic nerves are not considered part of the plexus.

One important branch of the cervical plexus is the **phrenic** (fren′ik; *phren* = diaphragm) **nerve.** Although not part of the cervical plexus per se, the phrenic nerve receives some fibers from the cervical plexus. The phrenic nerve is formed primarily from the C4 nerve and some contributing axons from C3 and C5. The phrenic nerve travels through the thoracic cavity to innervate the diaphragm.

16.4e Brachial Plexuses

The left and right **brachial plexuses** are networks of nerves that supply the upper limb. Each brachial plexus is formed by the anterior rami of spinal nerves C5–T1 **(figure 16.8)**. The components of the brachial plexus extend laterally from the neck, pass superior to the first rib, and then continue into the axilla. Each brachial plexus innervates the pectoral girdle and the entire upper limb of one side.

Structurally, the brachial plexus is more complex than the cervical plexus and is composed of anterior rami, trunks, divisions, and cords when examined from a medial to lateral perspective. The **anterior rami** (sometimes called *roots*) of the brachial plexus are simply the continuations of the anterior rami of spinal nerves C5–T1. These rami emerge from the intervertebral foramina and travel through the neck.

The five roots unite to form the **superior, middle,** and **inferior trunks** in the posterior triangle of the neck. Nerves C5 and C6 unite to form the superior trunk; nerve C7 remains as the middle trunk; and nerves C8 and T1 unite to form the inferior trunk. Portions of each trunk divide deep to the clavicle into an **anterior division** and a **posterior division,** which primarily contain axons that innervate the anterior and posterior parts of the upper limb, respectively.

Learning Strategy 16.5

In general, nerves from the *anterior division* of the brachial plexus tend to innervate muscles that *flex* the parts of the upper limb. Nerves from the *posterior division* of the brachial plexus tend to innervate muscles that *extend* the parts of the upper limb.

Upon reaching the axilla, the anterior and posterior divisions converge to form three cords, which are named with respect to their position near the axillary artery. The **posterior cord** is posterior to the axillary artery and is formed by the posterior divisions of the superior, middle, and inferior trunks; therefore, it contains portions of C5–T1 nerves. The **medial cord** is medial to the axillary artery and is formed by the anterior division of the inferior trunk; it contains portions of nerves C8–T1. The **lateral cord** is lateral to the axillary artery and is formed from the anterior divisions of the superior and middle trunks; thus, it contains portions of nerves C5–C7.

Finally, five major **terminal branches** emerge from the three cords: the axillary, median, musculocutaneous, radial, and ulnar nerves **(table 16.3)**. The **axillary nerve** traverses through the axilla and posterior to the surgical neck of the humerus. The axillary nerve emerges from the posterior cord of the brachial plexus and innervates both the deltoid and teres minor muscles. It receives sensory information from the superolateral part of the arm. The **median nerve** is formed from branches of the medial and lateral cords of the brachial plexus. This nerve travels along the midline of the arm and forearm, and deep to the carpal tunnel in the wrist. It innervates most of the anterior forearm muscles, the thenar muscles, and the lateral two lumbricals. It receives sensory information from the palmar side of the lateral 3½ fingers (thumb, index finger, middle finger, and the lateral half of the ring finger) and from the dorsal tips of these same fingers.

The **musculocutaneous** (mŭs′kyū-lō-kyū-tā′nē-ŭs) **nerve** arises from the lateral cord of the brachial plexus. It innervates the anterior arm muscles (coracobrachialis, biceps brachii, and brachialis), which flex the humerus and flex the forearm. It also receives sensory information from the lateral surface of the forearm. The **radial nerve** arises from the posterior cord of the brachial plexus. It travels along the posterior side of the arm and then along the radial side of the forearm. The radial nerve innervates the posterior arm muscles (forearm extensors) and the posterior forearm muscles (extensors of the wrist and digits and the supinator of the forearm). It receives sensory information from the posterior arm and forearm surface and the dorsolateral side of the hand.

The **ulnar nerve** arises from the medial cord of the brachial plexus and descends along the medial side of the arm. It wraps posterior to the medial epicondyle of the humerus and then runs along the ulnar side of the forearm. It innervates some of the anterior forearm muscles (the medial half of the flexor digitorum

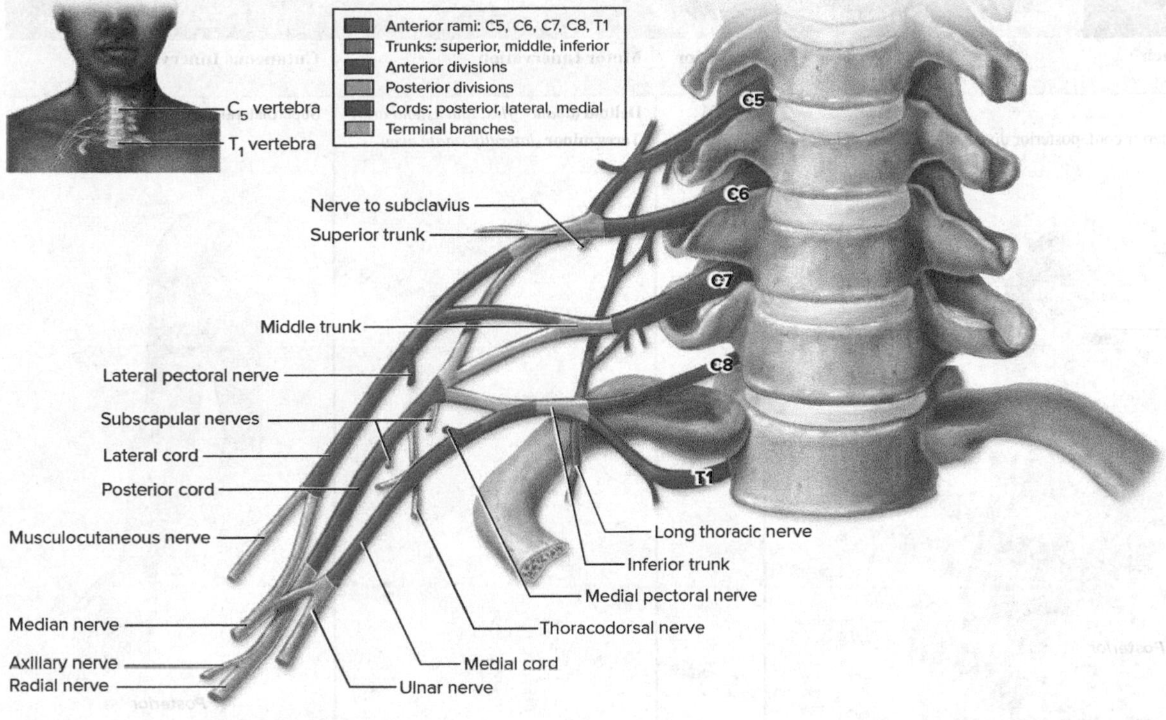
Anterior rami: C5, C6, C7, C8, T1
Trunks: superior, middle, inferior
Anterior divisions
Posterior divisions
Cords: posterior, lateral, medial
Terminal branches
C5 vertebra
T1 vertebra
C5
C6
C7
C8
T1
Nerve to subclavius
Superior trunk
Middle trunk
Lateral pectoral nerve
Subscapular nerves
Lateral cord
Posterior cord
Musculocutaneous nerve
Median nerve
Axillary nerve
Radial nerve
Ulnar nerve
Medial cord
Thoracodorsal nerve
Medial pectoral nerve
Inferior trunk
Long thoracic nerve

(a) Anterior view

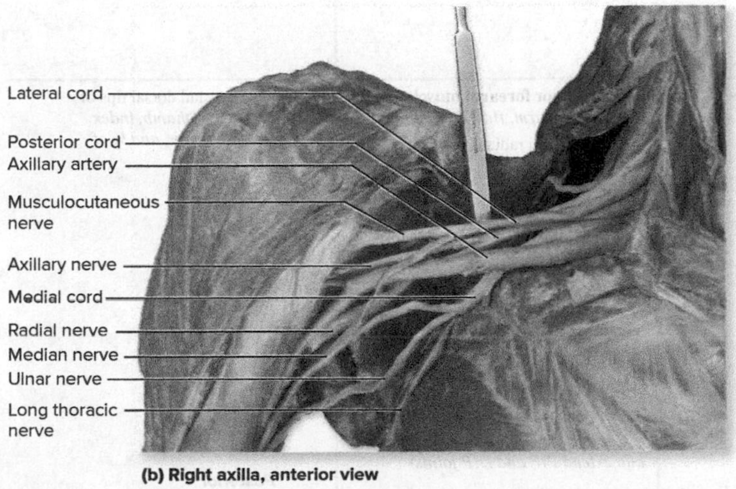
Lateral cord
Posterior cord
Axillary artery
Musculocutaneous nerve
Axillary nerve
Medial cord
Radial nerve
Median nerve
Ulnar nerve
Long thoracic nerve

(b) Right axilla, anterior view

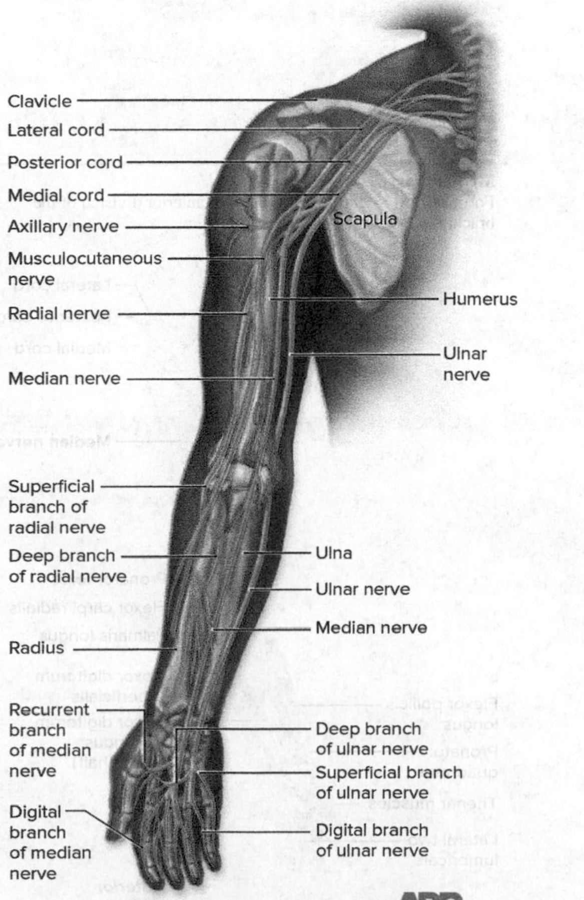
Clavicle
Lateral cord
Posterior cord
Medial cord
Axillary nerve
Scapula
Musculocutaneous nerve
Humerus
Radial nerve
Ulnar nerve
Median nerve
Superficial branch of radial nerve
Deep branch of radial nerve
Ulna
Ulnar nerve
Median nerve
Radius
Recurrent branch of median nerve
Deep branch of ulnar nerve
Superficial branch of ulnar nerve
Digital branch of median nerve
Digital branch of ulnar nerve

(c) Right upper limb, anterior view APR

Figure 16.8

Brachial Plexus. Anterior rami of nerves C5–T1 form the brachial plexus, which innervates the upper limb. (*a*) Rami, trunks, divisions, and cords form the subdivisions of this plexus. (*b*) A cadaver dissection photo shows and identifies major nerves from the right brachial plexus. (*c*) Complete pathways of main brachial plexus branches are shown in an anterior view of the right upper limb. APR

(b) Christine Eckel/McGraw-Hill Education

Table 16.3 Branches of the Brachial Plexus

Terminal Branch	Anterior Rami	Motor Innervation	Cutaneous Innervation
Axillary Nerve Formed from posterior cord, posterior division of the brachial plexus	C5, C6	**Deltoid** (*abduct, flex, and extend arm*) **Teres minor** (*laterally rotate arm*)	Superolateral arm
Median Nerve Formed from medial and lateral cords, anterior division of the brachial plexus	C6–T1	**Most anterior forearm muscles** (*pronate forearm, flex wrist, digits*) Flexor carpi radialis Flexor digitorum superficialis Pronator teres Pronator quadratus Lateral ½ of flexor digitorum profundus Flexor pollicis longus **Thenar (thumb) muscles** (*move thumb*) Flexor pollicis brevis Abductor pollicis brevis Opponens pollicis **Lateral 2 lumbricals** (*flex MP joints and extend PIP and DIP joints*)	Palmar aspects and dorsal tips of lateral 3½ digits (*thumb, index finger, middle finger, and ½ of ring finger*)

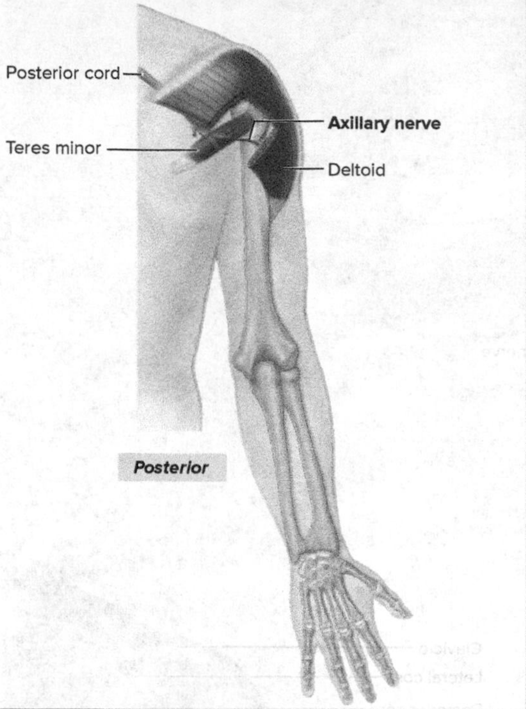
Posterior cord
Teres minor
Axillary nerve
Deltoid
Posterior

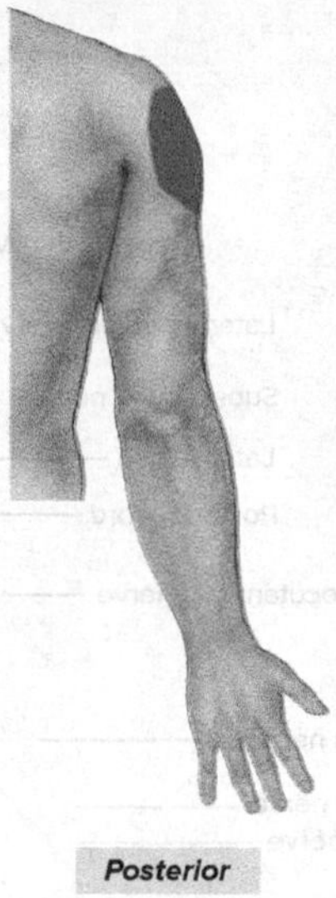
Posterior

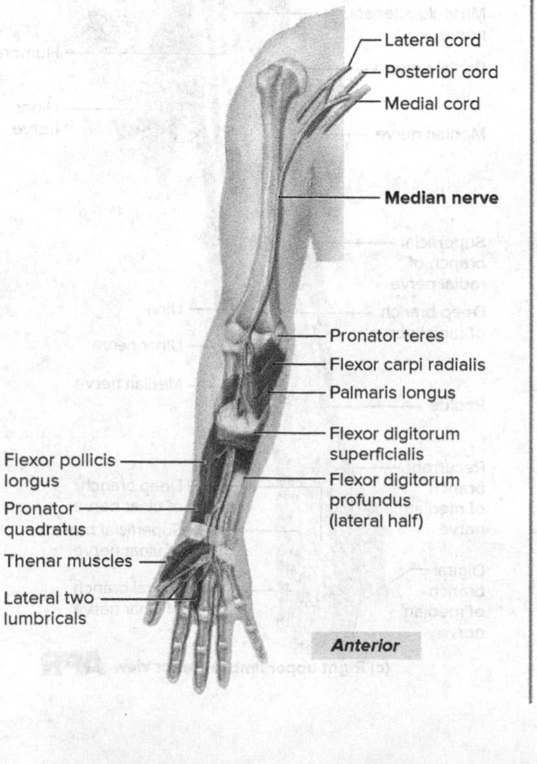
Lateral cord
Posterior cord
Medial cord
Median nerve
Pronator teres
Flexor carpi radialis
Palmaris longus
Flexor digitorum superficialis
Flexor digitorum profundus (lateral half)
Flexor pollicis longus
Pronator quadratus
Thenar muscles
Lateral two lumbricals
Anterior

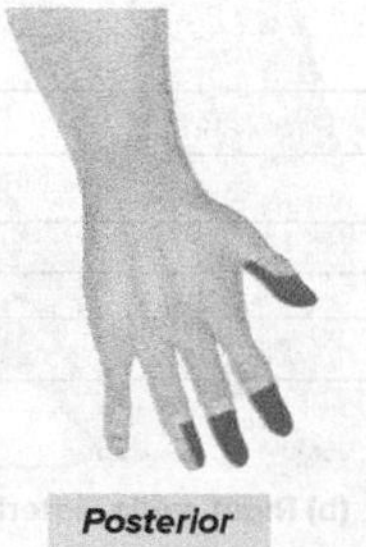
Posterior

Anterior

Table 16.3 Branches of the Brachial Plexus *(continued)*

<table>
<tr><th>Terminal Branch</th><th>Anterior Rami</th><th>Motor Innervation</th><th>Cutaneous Innervation</th></tr>
<tr>
<td>Musculocutaneous Nerve
Formed from the lateral cord, anterior division of the brachial plexus
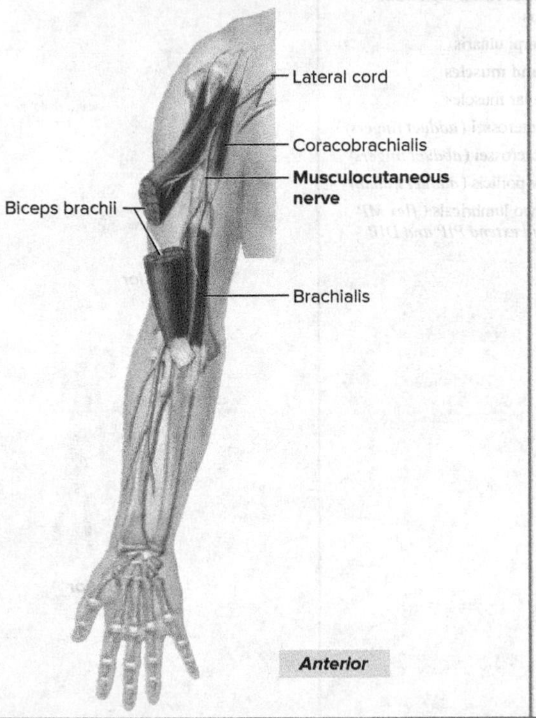
</td>
<td>C5–C7</td>
<td>Anterior arm muscles (flex arm, flex forearm, supinate forearm)
Coracobrachialis
Biceps brachii
Brachialis</td>
<td>Lateral region of forearm

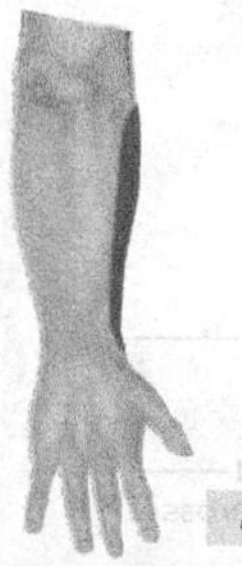
</td>
</tr>
<tr>
<td>Radial Nerve
Formed from the posterior cord, posterior division of the brachial plexus
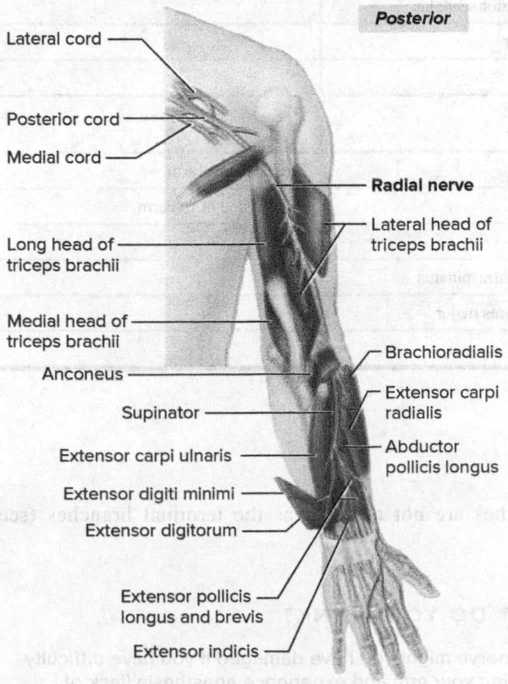
</td>
<td>C5–T1</td>
<td>Posterior arm muscles
(extend forearm)
Triceps brachii
Anconeus
Posterior forearm muscles
(supinate forearm, extend wrist, digits, one muscle that abducts thumb)
Supinator
Extensor carpi radialis muscles
Extensor digitorum
Extensor carpi ulnaris
Extensor pollicis longus
Extensor pollicis brevis
Abductor pollicis longus
Extensor digiti minimi
Extensor indicis
Brachioradialis (flex forearm)</td>
<td>Posterior region of arm
Posterior region of forearm
Dorsal aspect of lateral 3 ½ digits (except their distal tips)
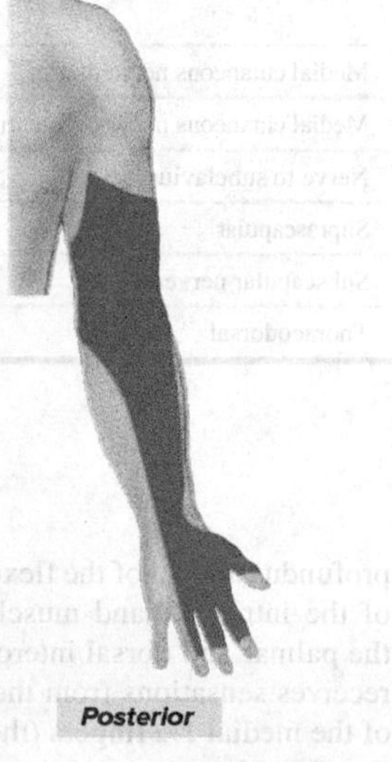
</td>
</tr>
</table>

(continued on next page)

Table 16.3 Branches of the Brachial Plexus *(continued)*

Terminal Branch	Anterior Rami	Motor Innervation	Cutaneous Innervation
Ulnar Nerve Formed from the medial cord, anterior division of the brachial plexus	C8–T1	**Anterior forearm muscles** (*flex wrist and digits*) Medial ½ of flexor digitorum profundus Flexor carpi ulnaris **Intrinsic hand muscles** Hypothenar muscles Palmar interossei (*adduct fingers*) Dorsal interossei (*abduct fingers*) Adductor pollicis (*adduct thumb*) Medial two lumbricals (*flex MP joints and extend PIP and DIP joints*)	Dorsal and palmar aspects of medial 1½ digits (*little finger, medial aspect of ring finger*)

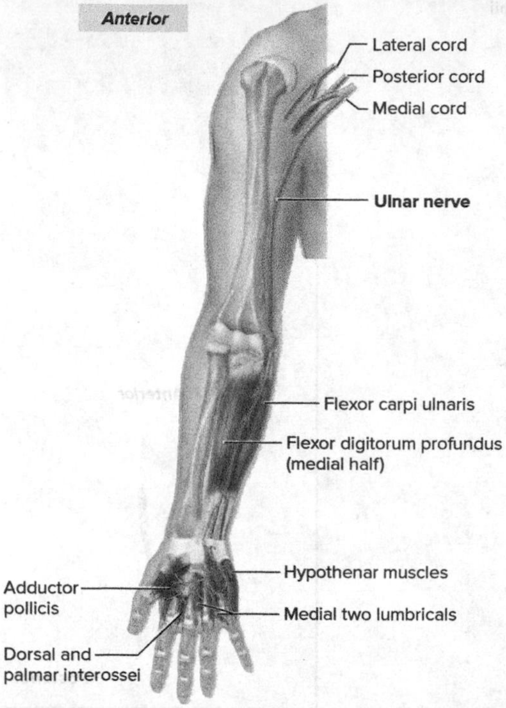

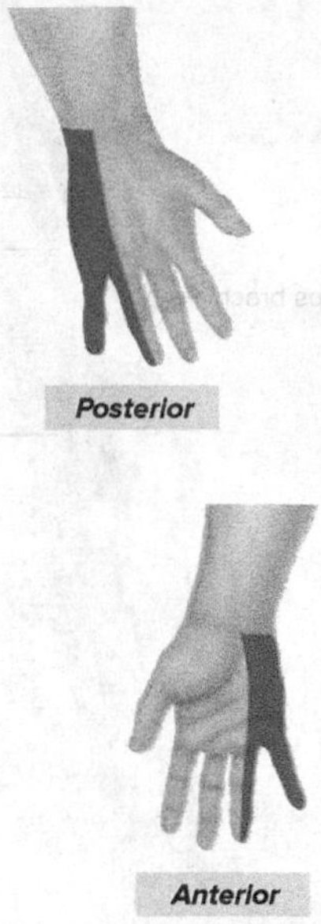

Smaller Branches of the Brachial Plexus	Anterior Rami	Motor Innervation	Cutaneous Innervation
Dorsal scapular	C5	Rhomboids, levator scapulae	
Long thoracic	C5–C7	Serratus anterior	
Lateral pectoral	C5–C7	Pectoralis major	
Medial pectoral	C8–T1	Pectoralis major Pectoralis minor	
Medial cutaneous nerve of arm	C8–T1		Medial side of arm
Medial cutaneous nerve of forearm	C8–T1		Medial side of forearm
Nerve to subclavius	C5–C6	Subclavius	
Suprascapular	C5–C6	Supraspinatus, infraspinatus	
Subscapular nerves	C5–C6	Subscapularis, teres major	
Thoracodorsal	C6–C8	Latissimus dorsi	

profundus and all of the flexor carpi ulnaris). It also innervates most of the intrinsic hand muscles, including the hypothenar muscles, the palmar and dorsal interossei, and the medial two lumbricals. It receives sensations from the skin of the dorsal and palmar aspects of the medial 1½ fingers (the little finger and the medial half of the ring finger).

The brachial plexus also gives off numerous other nerves that innervate portions of the upper limb and pectoral girdle. These branches are not as large as the terminal branches (see table 16.3).

WHAT DO YOU THINK?

4. Which nerve might you have damaged if you have difficulty abducting your arm and experience anesthesia (lack of sensation) along the superolateral arm?

Clinical View 16.3

Brachial Plexus Injuries

Injuries to parts of the brachial plexus are fairly common, especially in individuals aged 15–25. Minor plexus injuries are treated by simply resting the limb. More severe brachial plexus injuries may require nerve grafts or nerve transfers; for very severe injuries, no effective treatment exists.

Axillary Nerve Injury

The axillary nerve can be compressed within the axilla, or it can be damaged if the surgical neck of the humerus is broken (recall that the axillary nerve travels posterior to the surgical neck of the humerus). A patient whose axillary nerve is damaged has great difficulty abducting the arm due to paralysis of the deltoid muscle, as well as anesthesia (lack of sensation) along the superolateral skin of the arm.

Radial Nerve Injury

The radial nerve is especially subject to injury during humeral shaft fractures or in injuries to the lateral elbow. Nerve damage results in paralysis of the extensor muscles of the forearm, wrist, and fingers. A common clinical sign of radial nerve injury is *wrist drop,* meaning that the patient is unable to extend his or her wrist. The patient also experiences anesthesia along the posterior arm, the forearm, and the part of the hand normally supplied by this nerve.

Posterior Cord Injury

The posterior cord of the brachial plexus (which includes the axillary and radial nerves) may be injured by improper use of crutches, a condition called **crutch palsy.** Similarly, the posterior cord can be compressed if a person drapes the upper limb over the back of a chair for an extended period of time. Because this can happen if someone passes out in a drunken stupor, this condition is also referred to as *drunkard's paralysis.*

Improper placement of a crutch in axilla can lead to posterior cord injury.
JGI/Blend Images

Median Nerve Injury

The median nerve may be impinged on or compressed as a result of carpal tunnel syndrome (see Clinical View 12.4: "Carpal Tunnel Syndrome" in section 12.1d) or by any deep laceration of the wrist. Median nerve injury often results in paralysis of the thenar group of muscles. The classic sign of median nerve injury is the **ape hand deformity,** which develops over time as the thenar eminence wastes away until the hand eventually resembles that of an ape (apes lack well-developed thumb muscles). The lateral two lumbricals are also paralyzed, and sensation is lost in the part of the hand supplied by the median nerve.

Ulnar Nerve Injury

The ulnar nerve may be injured by fractures or dislocations of the elbow because of this nerve's close proximity to the medial epicondyle of the humerus. When you "hit your funny bone," you have actually hit your ulnar nerve. Most of the intrinsic hand muscles are paralyzed, so the person is unable to adduct or abduct the fingers. In addition, the person experiences sensory loss along the medial side of the hand. A clinician can test for ulnar nerve injury by having a patient hold a piece of paper tightly between the fingers as the doctor tries to pull it away. If the person has weak interossei muscles, the paper can be easily extracted.

Superior Trunk Injury

The superior trunk of the brachial plexus can be injured by excessive separation of the neck and shoulder, as when a person riding a motorcycle is flipped from the bike and lands on the side of the head. A superior trunk injury affects the C5 and C6 anterior rami, so any brachial plexus branch that has these nerves is also affected to some degree.

Inferior Trunk Injury

The inferior trunk of the brachial plexus can be injured if the arm is excessively abducted, as when a neonate's arm is pulled too hard during delivery. Inferior trunk injuries also may happen when grasping something above the head to break a fall—for example, grabbing a branch to keep from falling out of a tree. An inferior trunk injury involves the C8 and T1 anterior rami, so any brachial plexus branch that is formed from these nerves (such as the ulnar nerve) also is affected to some degree.

16.4f Lumbar Plexuses

The left and right **lumbar plexuses** are formed from the anterior rami of spinal nerves L1–L4 located lateral to the L_1–L_4 vertebrae and along the psoas major muscle in the posterior abdominal wall (**figure 16.9**). The lumbar plexus is structurally less complex than the brachial plexus. However, like the brachial plexus, the lumbar plexus is subdivided into an anterior division and a posterior division. The primary nerves of the lumbar plexus are listed in **table 16.4**.

The main nerve of the posterior division of the lumbar plexus is the **femoral nerve.** This nerve supplies the anterior thigh muscles, such as the quadriceps femoris (leg extensor) and the sartorius and iliopsoas (thigh flexors). It also receives sensory information from the anterior and inferomedial thigh as well as the medial aspect of the leg.

The main nerve of the anterior division is the **obturator nerve,** which travels through the obturator foramen to the medial thigh. There, the nerve innervates the medial thigh muscles (which adduct

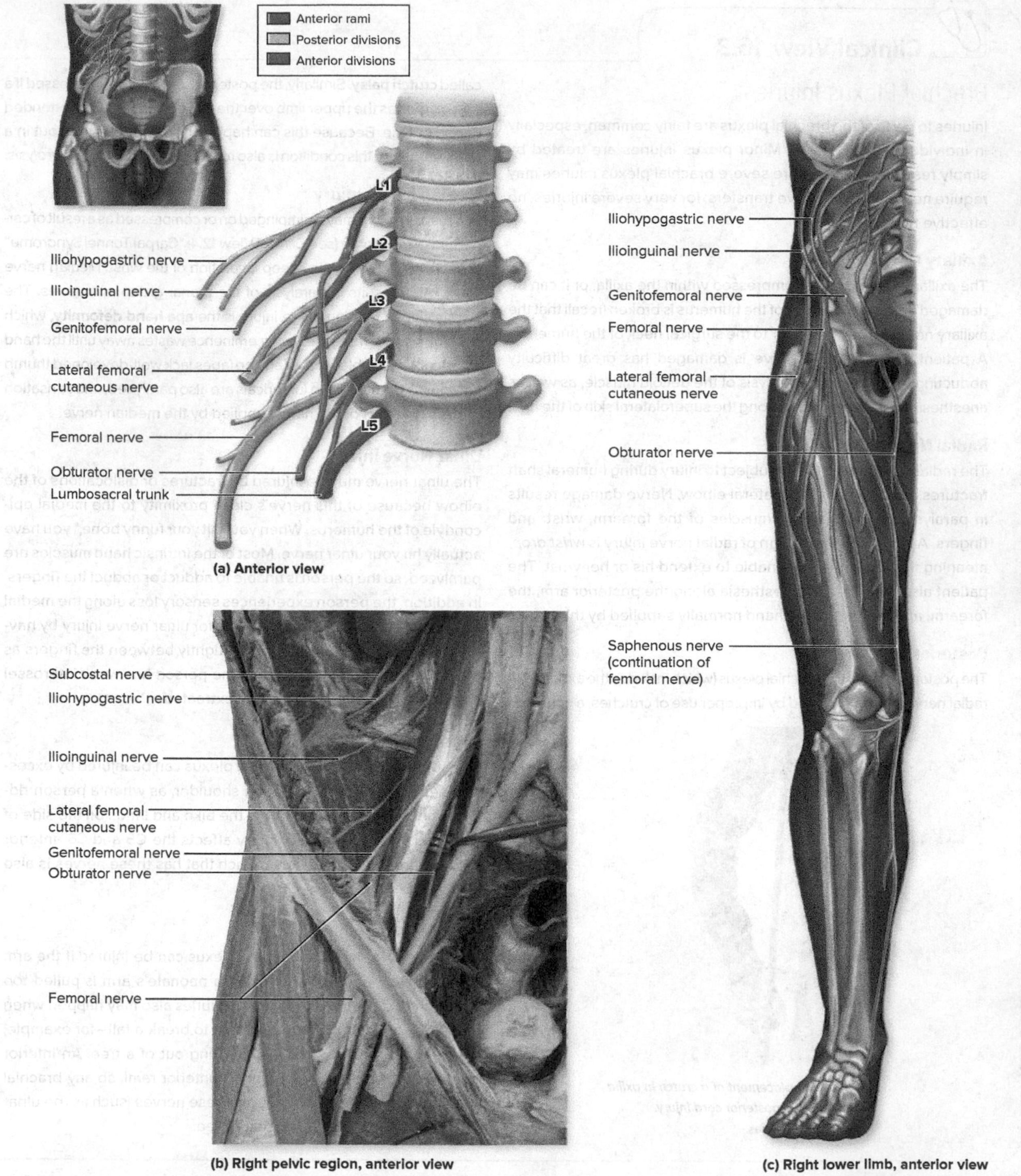

Anterior rami
Posterior divisions
Anterior divisions
L1
L2
L3
L4
L5
Iliohypogastric nerve
Ilioinguinal nerve
Genitofemoral nerve
Lateral femoral cutaneous nerve
Femoral nerve
Obturator nerve
Lumbosacral trunk
(a) Anterior view
Subcostal nerve
Iliohypogastric nerve
Ilioinguinal nerve
Lateral femoral cutaneous nerve
Genitofemoral nerve
Obturator nerve
Femoral nerve
(b) Right pelvic region, anterior view
Iliohypogastric nerve
Ilioinguinal nerve
Genitofemoral nerve
Femoral nerve
Lateral femoral cutaneous nerve
Obturator nerve
Saphenous nerve (continuation of femoral nerve)
(c) Right lower limb, anterior view

Figure 16.9

Lumbar Plexus. (*a*) Anterior rami of nerves L1–L4 form the lumbar plexus. (*b*) Cadaver photo shows the components of the lumbar plexus. (*c*) Pathways of lumbar plexus nerves. APR

<table>
<tr><th colspan="4">Table 16.4 Branches of the Lumbar Plexus</th></tr>
<tr><th>Main Branch</th><th>Anterior Rami</th><th>Motor Innervation</th><th>Cutaneous Innervation</th></tr>
<tr>
<td>Femoral Nerve
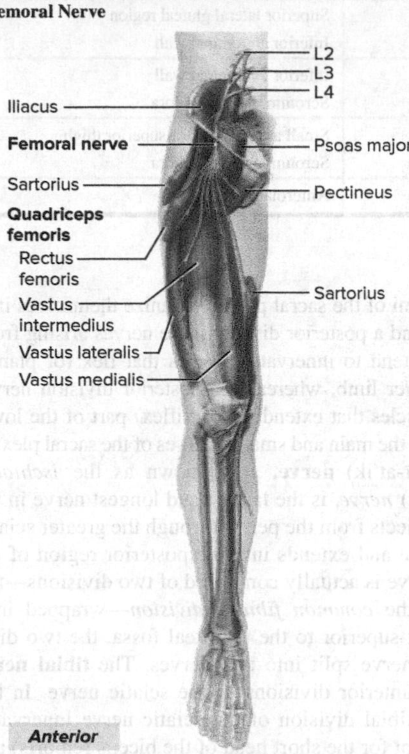
L2
L3
L4
Iliacus
Femoral nerve
Psoas major
Sartorius
Pectineus
Quadriceps femoris
Rectus femoris
Sartorius
Vastus intermedius
Vastus lateralis
Vastus medialis
Anterior</td>
<td>L2–L4</td>
<td>Anterior thigh muscles
Quadriceps femoris (extend leg)
Rectus femoris
Vastus lateralis
Vastus intermedius
Vastus medialis
Iliopsoas (flex thigh)
Sartorius (flex thigh and leg)
Pectineus[1] (flex thigh)</td>
<td>Anterior thigh
Inferomedial thigh
Medial side of leg
Most medial aspect of foot
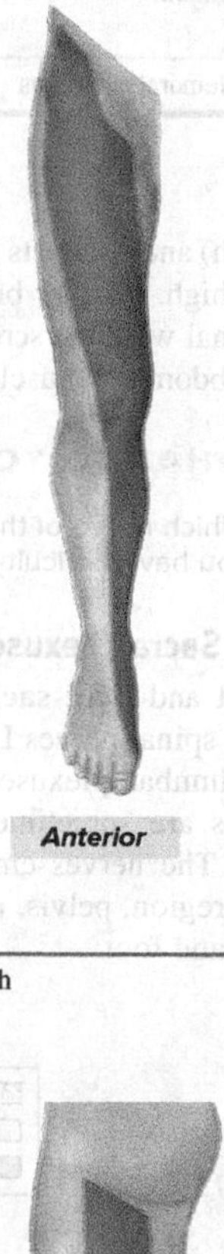
Anterior</td>
</tr>
<tr>
<td>Obturator Nerve
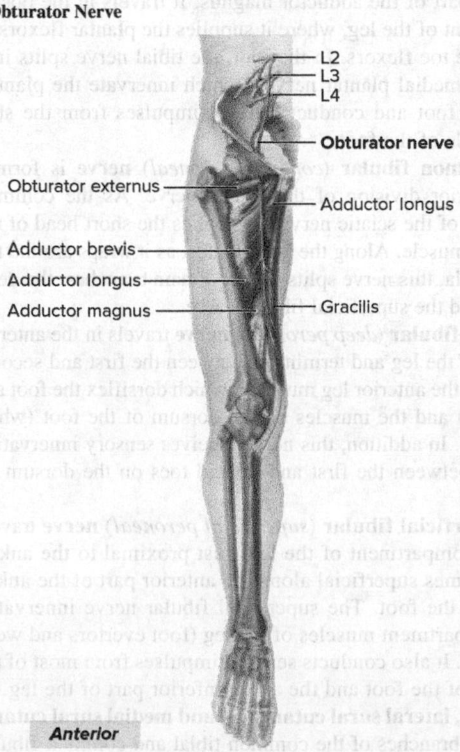
L2
L3
L4
Obturator nerve
Obturator externus
Adductor longus
Adductor brevis
Adductor longus
Adductor magnus
Gracilis
Anterior</td>
<td>L2–L4</td>
<td>Medial thigh muscles (adduct and flex thigh)
Adductors
Gracilis
Pectineus[1]
Obturator externus (laterally rotate thigh)</td>
<td>Superomedial thigh
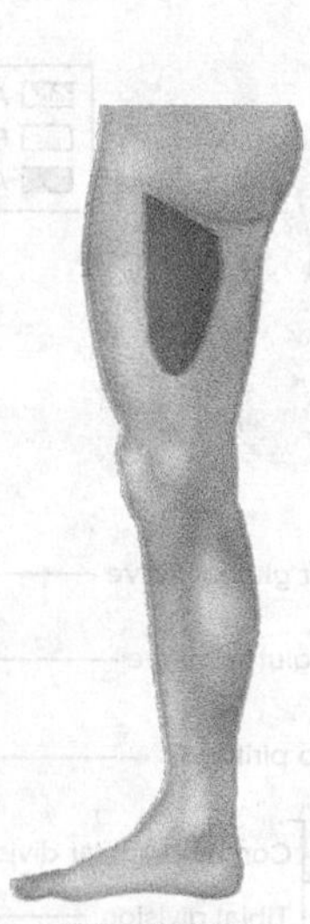
Medial</td>
</tr>
</table>

[1] Pectineus may be innervated by the femoral nerve, obturator nerve, or branches from both nerves.

(*continued on next page*)

Table 16.4 Branches of the Lumbar Plexus *(continued)*

Smaller Branches of the Lumbar Plexus	Anterior Rami	Motor Innervation	Cutaneous Innervation
Iliohypogastric	L1	Partial innervation to abdominal muscles (*flex vertebral column*)	Superior lateral gluteal region Inferior abdominal wall
Ilioinguinal	L1	Partial innervation to abdominal muscles (*flex vertebral column*)	Inferior abdominal wall Scrotum or labia majora
Genitofemoral	L1, L2		Small area in anterior superior thigh Scrotum or labia majora
Lateral femoral cutaneous	L2, L3		Anterolateral thigh

the thigh) and conducts sensory impulses from the superomedial skin of the thigh. Smaller branches of each lumbar plexus innervate the abdominal wall, the scrotum and the labia, and the inferior portions of the abdominal muscles (table 16.4).

WHAT DO YOU THINK?

5 Which nerve of the lumbar plexus might you have damaged if you have difficulty extending your knee?

16.4g Sacral Plexuses

The left and right **sacral plexuses** are formed from the anterior rami of spinal nerves L4–S4 and are located immediately inferior to the lumbar plexuses **(figure 16.10)**. The lumbar and sacral plexuses are sometimes considered together as the *lumbosacral plexus*. The nerves emerging from a sacral plexus innervate the gluteal region, pelvis, perineum, posterior thigh, and almost all of the leg and foot.

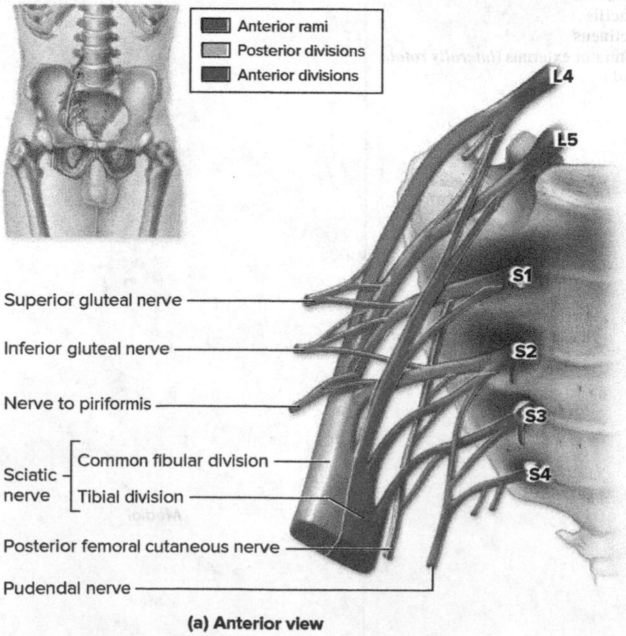

Anterior rami
Posterior divisions
Anterior divisions
L4
L5
S1
S2
S3
S4
Superior gluteal nerve
Inferior gluteal nerve
Nerve to piriformis
Sciatic nerve
Common fibular division
Tibial division
Posterior femoral cutaneous nerve
Pudendal nerve

(a) Anterior view

Figure 16.10

Sacral Plexus. Anterior rami of nerves L4, L5, and S1–S4 form the sacral plexus. (*a*) The sacral plexus has six rami and both anterior and posterior divisions.

The anterior rami of the sacral plexus organize themselves into an anterior division and a posterior division. The nerves arising from the anterior division tend to innervate muscles that flex (or plantar flex) parts of the lower limb, whereas the posterior division nerves tend to innervate muscles that extend (or dorsiflex) part of the lower limb. **Table 16.5** lists the main and smaller nerves of the sacral plexus.

The **sciatic** (sī-at′ik) **nerve,** also known as the *ischiadic* (is-kē-ad′ik; hip joint) *nerve,* is the largest and longest nerve in the body. This nerve projects from the pelvis through the greater sciatic notch of the os coxae and extends into the posterior region of the thigh. The sciatic nerve is actually composed of two divisions—the *tibial division* and the *common fibular division*—wrapped in a common sheath. Just superior to the popliteal fossa, the two divisions of the sciatic nerve split into two nerves. The **tibial nerve** is formed from the anterior divisions of the sciatic nerve. In the posterior thigh, the tibial division of the sciatic nerve innervates the hamstrings (except for the short head of the biceps femoris) and the hamstring part of the adductor magnus. It travels in the posterior compartment of the leg, where it supplies the plantar flexors of the foot and the toe flexors. In the foot, the tibial nerve splits into the lateral and medial plantar nerves, which innervate the plantar muscles of the foot and conduct sensory impulses from the skin covering the sole of the foot.

The **common fibular** (*common peroneal*) **nerve** is formed from the posterior division of the sciatic nerve. As the common fibular division of the sciatic nerve, it supplies the short head of the biceps femoris muscle. Along the lateral knee, as it wraps around the neck of the fibula, this nerve splits into two main branches: the deep fibular nerve and the superficial fibular nerve.

The **deep fibular** (*deep peroneal*) **nerve** travels in the anterior compartment of the leg and terminates between the first and second toes. It supplies the anterior leg muscles (which dorsiflex the foot and extend the toes) and the muscles on the dorsum of the foot (which extend the toes). In addition, this nerve receives sensory innervation from the skin between the first and second toes on the dorsum of the foot.

The **superficial fibular** (*superficial peroneal*) **nerve** travels in the lateral compartment of the leg. Just proximal to the ankle, this nerve becomes superficial along the anterior part of the ankle and dorsum of the foot. The superficial fibular nerve innervates the lateral compartment muscles of the leg (foot evertors and weak plantar flexors). It also conducts sensory impulses from most of the dorsal surface of the foot and the anteroinferior part of the leg.

The **sural, lateral sural cutaneous, and medial sural cutaneous nerves** are branches of the common tibial and common fibular nerves (figure 16.10). These nerves provide sensory information from the skin of the posterior lateral calf, lateral leg, and foot.

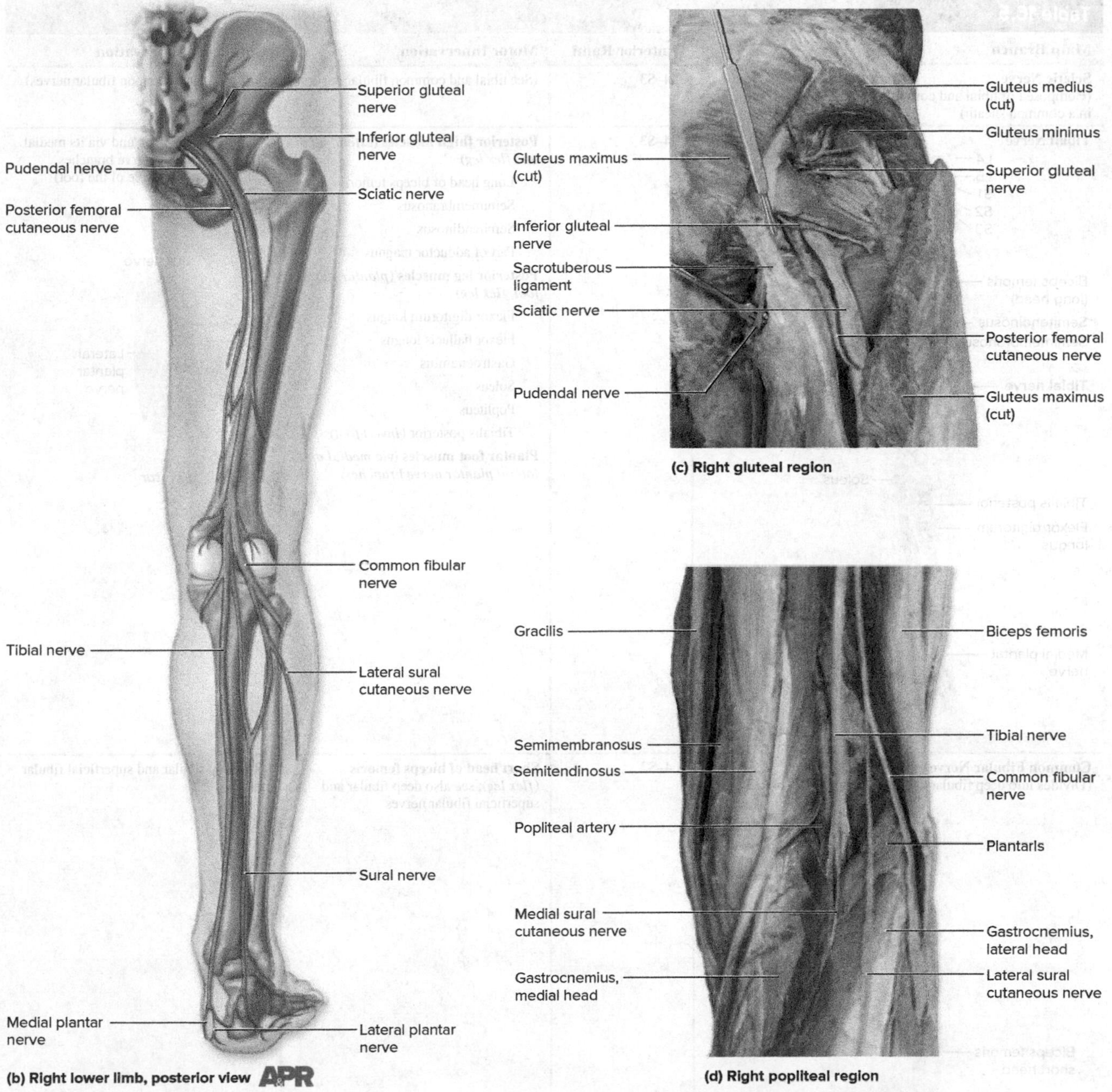
Superior gluteal nerve
Inferior gluteal nerve
Pudendal nerve
Sciatic nerve
Posterior femoral cutaneous nerve
Common fibular nerve
Tibial nerve
Lateral sural cutaneous nerve
Sural nerve
Medial plantar nerve
Lateral plantar nerve
(b) Right lower limb, posterior view
APR
Gluteus medius (cut)
Gluteus minimus
Gluteus maximus (cut)
Superior gluteal nerve
Inferior gluteal nerve
Sacrotuberous ligament
Sciatic nerve
Posterior femoral cutaneous nerve
Pudendal nerve
Gluteus maximus (cut)
(c) Right gluteal region
Gracilis
Biceps femoris
Semimembranosus
Tibial nerve
Semitendinosus
Common fibular nerve
Popliteal artery
Plantaris
Medial sural cutaneous nerve
Gastrocnemius, lateral head
Gastrocnemius, medial head
Lateral sural cutaneous nerve
(d) Right popliteal region

Figure 16.10

Sacral Plexus *(continued)* (*b*) A posterior view shows the distribution of nerves of the sacral plexus. (*c*, *d*) Cadaver photos reveal the major sacral plexus nerves of the right gluteal and popliteal regions.

WHAT DID YOU LEARN?

7. Where is a posterior root ganglion located, and what does it contain?
8. Identify the nerve plexuses, from superior to inferior, and list which spinal nerve anterior rami form each of them.
9. Sketch and label the cervical plexus and the brachial plexus.
10. Sketch and label the lumbar and sacral plexuses.

16.5 Reflexes

✓ Learning Objectives

12. Identify and describe the properties of a reflex.
13. List the structures and describe the steps involved in a reflex arc.
14. Explain how reflexes are used as diagnostic indicators.

Table 16.5 Branches of the Sacral Plexus

<table>
<tr><th>Main Branch</th><th>Anterior Rami</th><th>Motor Innervation</th><th>Cutaneous Innervation</th></tr>
<tr><td>Sciatic Nerve
(Composed of tibial and common fibular divisions wrapped in a common sheath)</td><td>L4–S3</td><td>(See tibial and common fibular nerves)</td><td>(See tibial and common fibular nerves)</td></tr>
<tr><td>Tibial Nerve
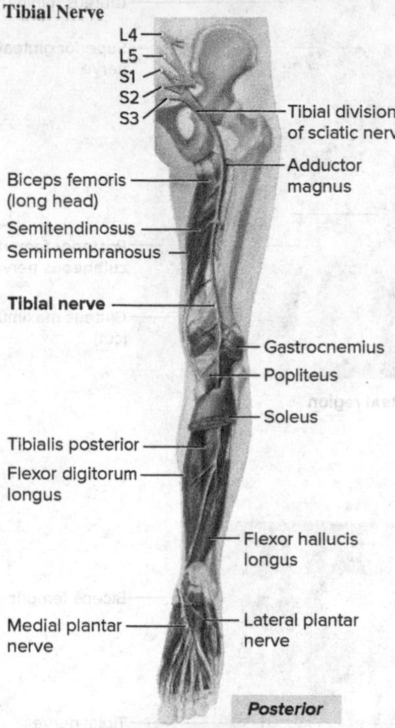
</td><td>L4–S3</td><td>Posterior thigh muscles (extend thigh and flex leg)
Long head of biceps femoris
Semimembranosus
Semitendinosus
Part of adductor magnus
Posterior leg muscles (plantar flex foot, flex leg)
Flexor digitorum longus
Flexor hallucis longus
Gastrocnemius
Soleus
Popliteus
Tibialis posterior (invert foot)
Plantar foot muscles (via medial and lateral plantar nerve branches)</td><td>Branches to the heel, and via its medial and lateral plantar nerve branches (which supply the sole of the foot)
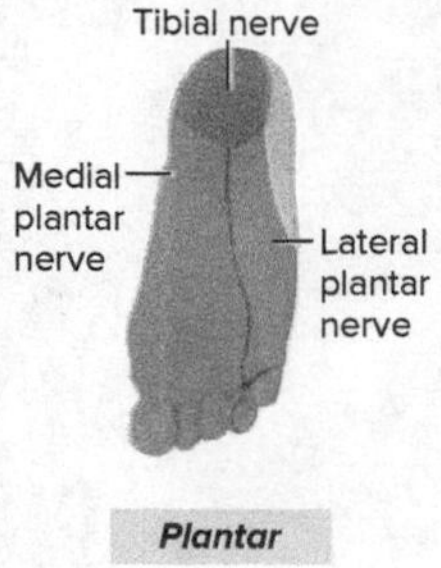
</td></tr>
<tr><td>Common Fibular Nerve
(Divides into deep fibular and superficial fibular branches)
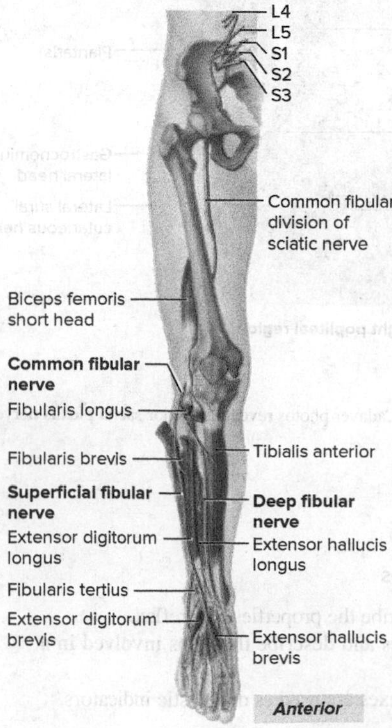
</td><td>L4–S2</td><td>Short head of biceps femoris (flex leg); see also deep fibular and superficial fibular nerves</td><td>(See deep fibular and superficial fibular nerves)</td></tr>
</table>

Table 16.5 Branches of the Sacral Plexus *(continued)*

Main Branch	Anterior Rami	Motor Innervation	Cutaneous Innervation
Deep Fibular Nerve 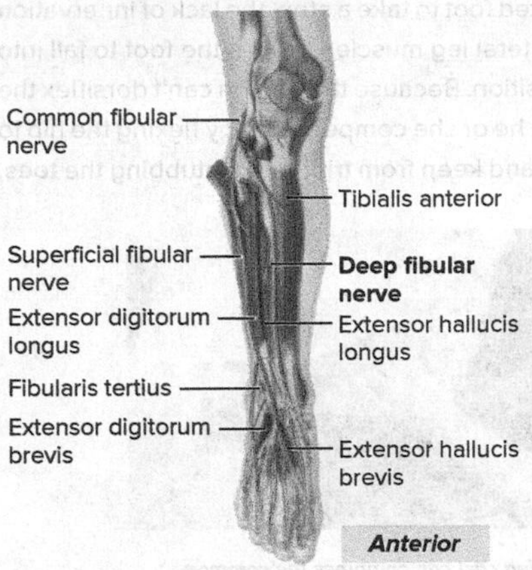	L4–S1	**Anterior leg muscles** (*dorsiflex foot, extend toes*) Tibialis anterior (*invert foot*) Extensor hallucis longus Extensor digitorum longus Fibularis tertius **Dorsum foot muscles** (*extend toes*) Extensor hallucis brevis Extensor digitorum brevis	Dorsal interspace between first and second toes 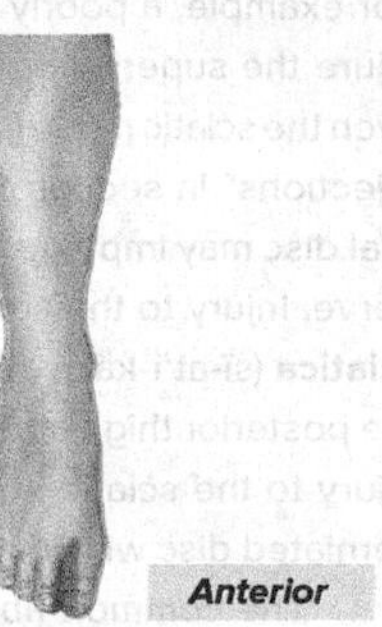
Superficial Fibular Nerve 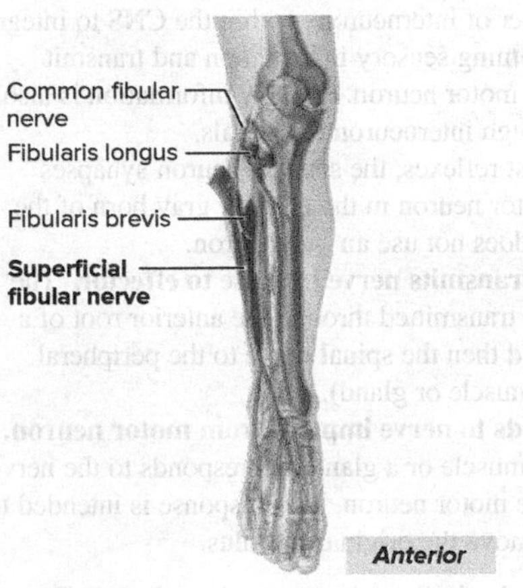	L5–S2	**Lateral leg muscles** (*evert foot, plantar flex foot*) Fibularis longus Fibularis brevis	Anteroinferior part of leg; most of dorsum of foot 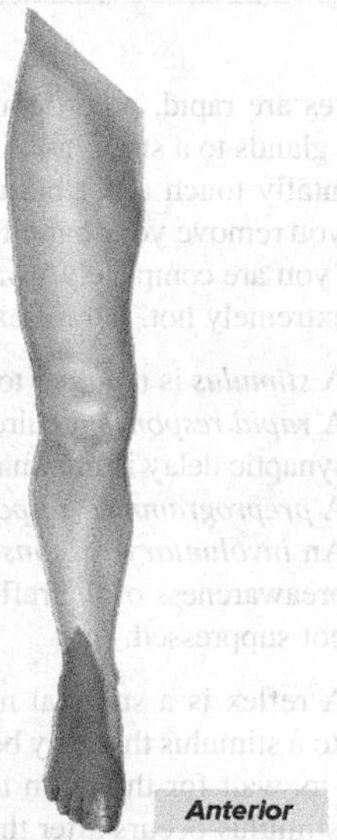

Smaller Branches of the Sacral Plexus	Anterior Rami	Motor Innervation	Cutaneous Innervation
Inferior gluteal nerve	L5–S2	Gluteus maximus (*extend thigh*)	
Superior gluteal nerve	L4–S1	Gluteus medius, gluteus minimus, and tensor fasciae latae (*abduct thigh*)	
Posterior femoral cutaneous nerve	S1–S3		Skin on posterior thigh
Pudendal nerve	S2–S4	Muscles of perineum, external anal sphincter, external urethral sphincter	Skin on external genitalia

Clinical View 16.4

Sacral Plexus Nerve Injuries

Some branches of the sacral plexus are readily subject to injury. For example, a poorly placed gluteal intramuscular injection can injure the superior or inferior gluteal nerves, and in some cases even the sciatic nerve (see Clinical View 13.5: "Gluteal Intramuscular Injections" in section 13.6a). Additionally, a herniated intervertebral disc may impinge on the nerve branches that form the sciatic nerve. Injury to the sciatic nerve produces a condition known as **sciatica** (sī-at′i-kă), which is characterized by extreme pain down the posterior thigh and leg. This pain does not go away unless the injury to the sciatic nerve is remedied. For example, repairing a herniated disc will alleviate the compression on the sciatic nerve.

The common fibular nerve may be injured due to fracture of the neck of the fibula or compression from a leg cast that is too tight. Compression of the nerve compromises it and its branches (superficial fibular, deep fibular), paralyzing the anterior and lateral leg muscles and leaving the person unable to dorsiflex and evert the foot. One classic sign of fibular nerve injury is *foot drop*. As a person lifts the affected foot to take a step, the lack of innervation of the anterior and lateral leg muscles causes the foot to fall into the plantar flexed position. Because the person can't dorsiflex the foot to walk normally, he or she compensates by flexing the hip to lift the affected area and keep from tripping or stubbing the toes.

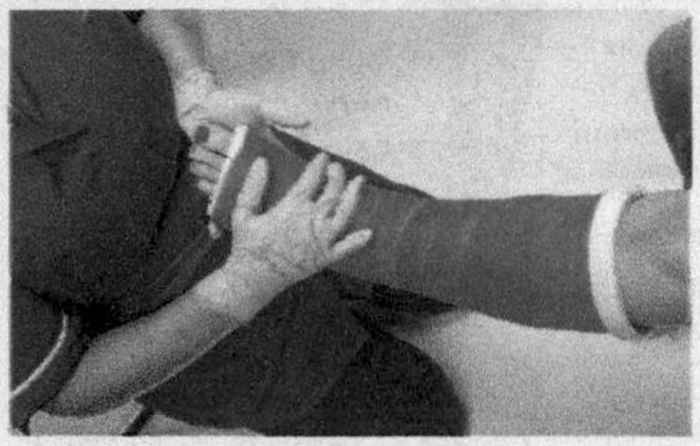

A tight leg cast can compress the common fibular nerve.
Richard Pinder/Shutterstock

Reflexes are rapid, preprogrammed, involuntary responses of muscles or glands to a stimulus. An example of a reflex occurs when you accidentally touch a hot burner on a stove. Instantly and automatically, you remove your hand from the stimulus (the hot burner), even before you are completely aware that your hand was touching something extremely hot. All reflexes have similar properties:

- A *stimulus* is required to initiate a reflex.
- A *rapid response* requires that few neurons are involved and synaptic delay is minimal.
- A *preprogrammed response* occurs the same way every time.
- An *involuntary response* requires no conscious intent or preawareness of the reflex activity. Thus, reflexes are usually not suppressed.

A reflex is a survival mechanism; it allows us to quickly respond to a stimulus that may be detrimental to our well-being without having to wait for the brain to process the information. Awareness of the stimulus occurs after the reflex action has been completed, in time to correct or avoid a potentially dangerous situation. (This is possible because sensory input has reached the cerebral cortex.)

16.5a Components of a Reflex Arc

A **reflex arc** is the neural circuit of a single reflex. It always begins at a receptor in the PNS, communicates with the CNS, and ends at a peripheral effector, such as a muscle or gland. The number of intermediate steps varies, depending upon the complexity of the reflex. Generally, five steps are involved in a simple reflex arc, as illustrated in **figure 16.11** and described here:

1. **Stimulus activates sensory receptor.** Sensory receptors (dendritic endings of a sensory neuron) respond to both external and internal stimuli, such as temperature, pressure, or tactile changes.
2. **Nerve impulse travels through sensory neuron to the CNS.** Sensory neurons conduct impulses from the receptor into the spinal cord (or brain).
3. **Information from nerve impulse is processed in the integration center by interneurons.** More complex reflexes may use a number of interneurons within the CNS to integrate and process incoming sensory information and transmit information to a motor neuron. Sensory information is also sent to the brain through interneuron collaterals.

   In the simplest reflexes, the sensory neuron synapses directly on a motor neuron in the anterior gray horn of the spinal cord and does not use an interneuron.
4. **Motor neuron transmits nerve impulse to effector.** The nerve impulse is transmitted through the anterior root of a motor neuron and then the spinal nerve to the peripheral effector organ (muscle or gland).
5. **Effector responds to nerve impulse from motor neuron.** An effector is a muscle or a gland that responds to the nerve impulse from the motor neuron. This response is intended to counteract or remove the original stimulus.

Reflex arcs may be ipsilateral or contralateral. A reflex arc is termed **ipsilateral** (ip-si-lat′ĕr-ăl; *ipse* = same, *latus* = side) when both the receptor and effector organs of the reflex are on the same side of the spinal cord. For example, an ipsilateral effect occurs when the muscles in your left arm contract to pull your left hand away from a hot object. A reflex arc is **contralateral** (kon-tr ă-lat′er- ăl; *contra* = opposite) when the sensory impulses from a receptor organ cross over through the spinal cord to activate effector organs in the opposite limb. For example, a contralateral effect occurs when you step on a sharp object with your left foot and then contract the muscles in your right leg to maintain balance as you withdraw your left leg from the damaging object.

Reflexes also may be monosynaptic or polysynaptic (**figure 16.12**). A **monosynaptic** (mon′ō-si-nap′tik; *monos* = single) **reflex** is the simplest of all reflexes. The sensory axons synapse directly on the motor neurons, whose axons project to the effector. Interneurons are not involved in processing this reflex. Very minor synaptic delay is incurred in the single synapse of this reflex arc, resulting in a very prompt reflex response. An example of a monosynaptic reflex is the **patellar** (knee-jerk) **reflex.** By tapping the patellar ligament with a reflex hammer, the muscle spindles in the quadriceps muscles are stretched. The brief stimulus causes a

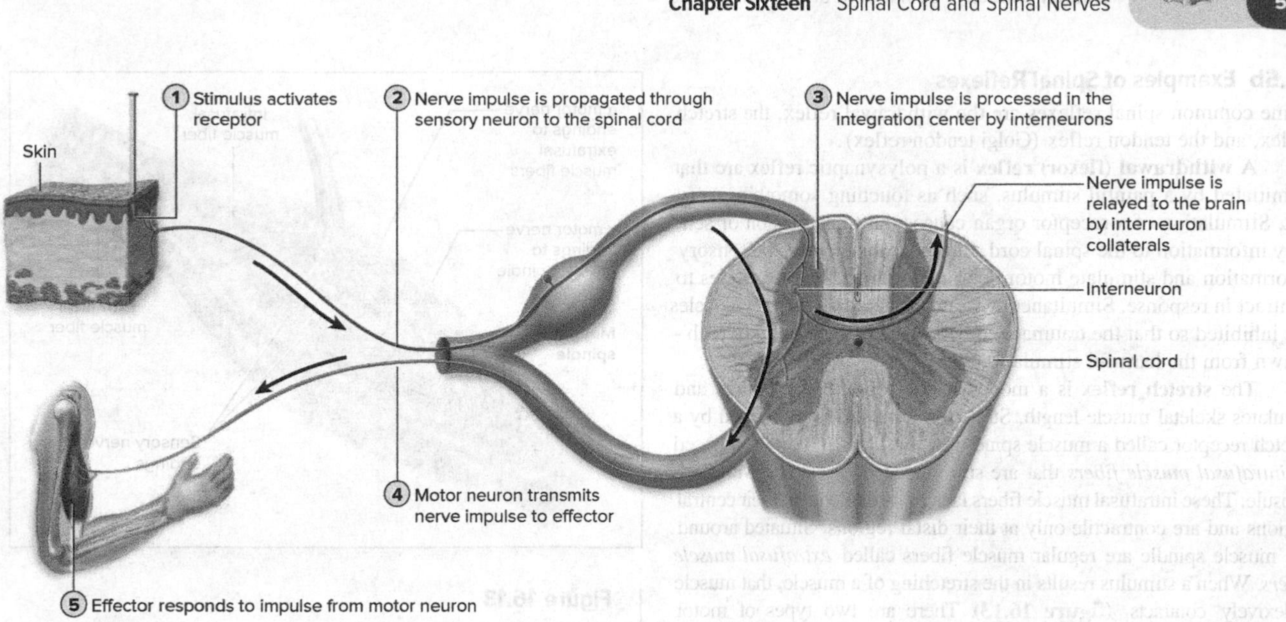

Figure 16.11

Simple Reflex Arc. A reflex arc is a nerve pathway composed of neurons that control rapid, subconscious, preprogrammed responses to a stimulus. **APR**

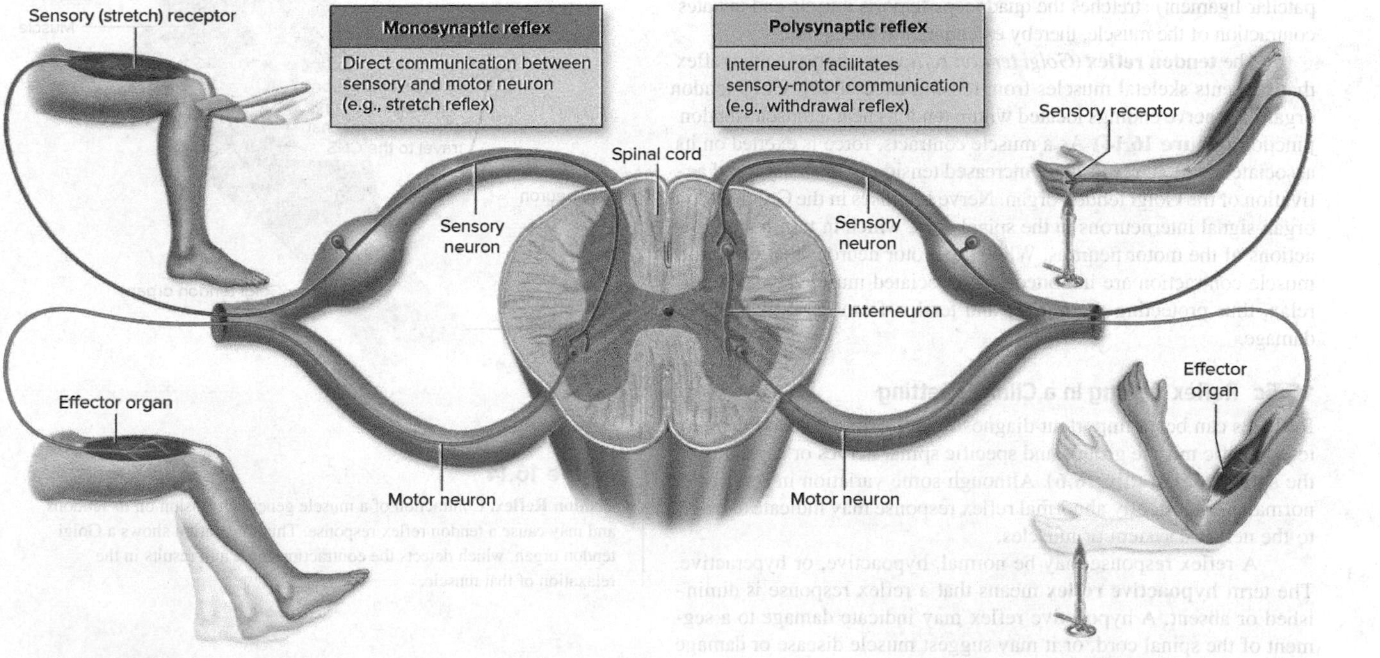

Figure 16.12

Monosynaptic and Polysynaptic Reflexes. The minimal number of neurons and the pathways of a monosynaptic reflex (*left*) are compared to those of a polysynaptic reflex (*right*).

reflexive contraction that occurs unopposed and produces a noticeable kick of the leg.

Polysynaptic (pol′ē-sin-ap′tik; *polys* = many) **reflexes** have more complex neural pathways that exhibit a number of synapses involving interneurons within the reflex arc. Because this reflex arc has more components, there is a more prolonged delay between stimulus and response. An example of a polysynaptic reflex is the crossed-extensor reflex, which is the reflex that supports postural muscle activity when you withdraw your foot from a painful stimulus, as in the previous example. Contraction of the extensor muscles in the other limb occurs by polysynaptic reflexes to enable you to maintain balance.

16.5b Examples of Spinal Reflexes

Some common spinal reflexes are the withdrawal reflex, the stretch reflex, and the tendon reflex (Golgi tendon reflex).

A **withdrawal (flexor) reflex** is a polysynaptic reflex arc that is initiated by a painful stimulus, such as touching something very hot. Stimulation of a receptor organ causes the transmission of sensory information to the spinal cord. Interneurons receive the sensory information and stimulate motor neurons to direct flexor muscles to contract in response. Simultaneously, antagonistic (extensor) muscles are inhibited so that the traumatized body part may be quickly withdrawn from the harmful stimulation.

The **stretch reflex** is a monosynaptic reflex that monitors and regulates skeletal muscle length. Stretch in a muscle is monitored by a stretch receptor called a muscle spindle. A muscle spindle is composed of *intrafusal muscle fibers* that are surrounded by a connective tissue capsule. These intrafusal muscle fibers lack myofilaments in their central regions and are contractile only at their distal regions. Situated around the muscle spindle are regular muscle fibers called *extrafusal muscle fibers.* When a stimulus results in the stretching of a muscle, that muscle reflexively contracts (**figure 16.13**). There are two types of motor neurons innervating a muscle: *alpha (α) motor neurons* and *gamma (γ) motor neurons.* Alpha motor neurons directly affect the lengthening or shortening of muscles by stimulating extrafusal muscle fibers. Gamma motor neurons are important in keeping muscle spindles taut by stimulating intrafusal muscle fibers, thereby allowing firing of alpha neurons to continue to discharge, leading to muscle contraction. The patellar (knee-jerk) reflex is an example of a stretch reflex. The stimulus (the tap on the patellar ligament) stretches the quadriceps femoris muscle and initiates contraction of the muscle, thereby extending the knee joint.

The **tendon reflex** (*Golgi tendon reflex*) is a polysynaptic reflex that prevents skeletal muscles from tensing excessively. Golgi tendon organs are nerve endings located within tendons near a muscle–tendon junction (**figure 16.14**). As a muscle contracts, force is exerted on its associated tendon, resulting in increased tension in the tendon and activation of the Golgi tendon organ. Nerve impulses in the Golgi tendon organ signal interneurons in the spinal cord, which in turn inhibit the actions of the motor neurons. When the motor neurons that cause the muscle contraction are inhibited, the associated muscle is allowed to relax, thus protecting the muscle and tendon from excessive tension damage.

16.5c Reflex Testing in a Clinical Setting

Reflexes can be an important diagnostic tool. Clinicians use them to test specific muscle groups and specific spinal nerves or segments of the spinal cord (**table 16.6**). Although some variation in reflexes is normal, a consistently abnormal reflex response may indicate damage to the nervous system or muscles.

A reflex response may be normal, hypoactive, or hyperactive. The term **hypoactive reflex** means that a reflex response is diminished or absent. A hypoactive reflex may indicate damage to a segment of the spinal cord, or it may suggest muscle disease or damage to the neuromuscular junction. A **hyperactive reflex** refers to an abnormally strong response. It may indicate damage somewhere in either the brain or spinal cord, especially if it is accompanied by **clonus** (klō′nŭs; tumult), rhythmic oscillations between flexion and extension when the muscle reflex is tested.

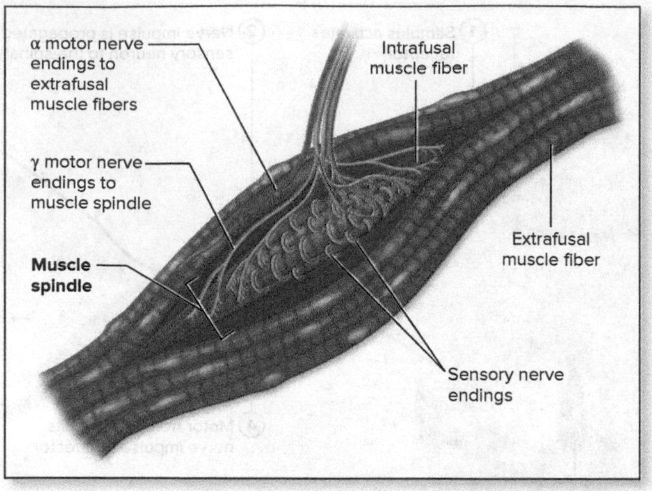

Figure 16.13

Stretch Reflexes. A stretch reflex is a simple monosynaptic reflex involving two neurons. A stretching force detected by a muscle spindle results in the contraction of that muscle.

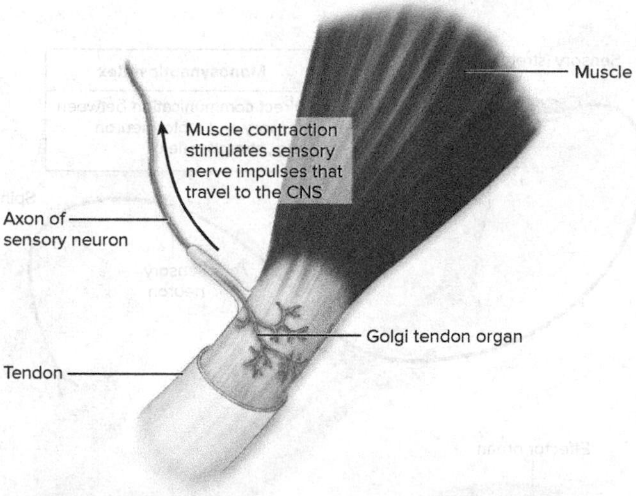

Figure 16.14

Tendon Reflex. Contraction of a muscle generates tension on its tendons, and may cause a tendon reflex response. This illustration shows a Golgi tendon organ, which detects the contraction force and results in the relaxation of that muscle.

WHAT DID YOU LEARN?

11. List the five steps in a reflex arc.
12. What is the major difference between monosynaptic reflexes and polysynaptic reflexes?

Table 16.6 Some Clinically Important Reflexes

Reflex	Spinal Nerve Segment(s) Tested	Normal Action(s) of Effector
Biceps reflex	C5, C6	Flexes elbow when biceps brachii tendon is tapped
Triceps reflex	C6, C7	Extends elbow when triceps brachii tendon is tapped
Abdominal reflexes	T8–T12	Contract abdominal muscles when one side of the abdominal wall is briskly stroked
Cremasteric reflex	L1, L2	Elevates testis (due to contraction of cremaster muscle in scrotum) when medial side of thigh is briskly stroked
Patellar (knee-jerk) reflex	L2–L4	Extends knee when patellar ligament is tapped
Ankle (Achilles) reflex	S1	Plantar flexes ankle when calcaneal tendon is tapped
Plantar reflex	L5, S1	Plantar flexes foot; flexes toes when plantar side of foot is briskly stroked [1]

[1] This is the *normal* reflex response in adults; in adults with spinal cord damage and in normal infants, the **Babinski sign** occurs, which is extension of the great toe and fanning of the other toes.

16.6 Development of the Spinal Cord

✓ Learning Objective

15. Explain how the spinal cord and spinal nerves develop in the embryo.

Recall from section 3.4c that the central nervous system forms primarily from the embryonic **neural tube,** and the cranial and spinal nerves form primarily from **neural crest cells** that have split off from the developing neural tube (see figure 3.11). The cranial (superior) part of the neural tube expands and develops into the brain, whereas the caudal (inferior) part of the neural tube forms the spinal cord. The following discussion focuses on the caudal part of the neural tube and its nearby neural crest cells.

As the caudal part of the neural tube differentiates and specializes, the spinal cord begins to develop (**figure 16.15**). However, this developmental process is much less complex than that for the brain. A hollow **neural canal** in the neural tube develops into the central canal of the spinal cord. The neural canal doesn't "shrink" in size; rather, the neural tube around it grows at a rapid rate. Thus, as the neural tube walls grow and expand, the neural canal in the newborn appears as a tiny hole called the central canal.

During the fourth and fifth weeks of embryonic development, the walls of the neural tube start to grow rapidly and unevenly. Part of the neural tube forms the white matter of the spinal cord, while other components form gray matter. By the sixth week of development, a horizontal groove called the **sulcus limitans** (lim′i-tanz; *limes* = boundary) forms in the lateral walls of the central canal (figure 16.1 5*b*). The sulcus limitans also represents a dividing point in the neural tube as two specific regions become evident on each side: the basal plates and the alar plates.

The **basal plates** lie anterior to the sulcus limitans. The basal plates develop into the anterior and lateral horns, motor structures of the gray matter. They also form the anterior part of the gray commissure. The **alar** (ā′lăr; *ala* = wing) **plates** lie posterior to the sulcus limitans. By about the ninth week of development, the alar plates develop into posterior horns, sensory structures of the gray matter. They also form the posterior part of the gray commissure.

During the embryonic period, the spinal cord extends the length of the vertebral canal. However, during the fetal period, the growth of the vertebral column (and its vertebral canal) outpaces that of the spinal cord. By the sixth fetal month, the spinal cord is at the level of the S_1 vertebra, whereas a newborn's spinal cord ends at about the L_3 vertebra. By adulthood, the spinal cord length extends only to the level of the L_1 vertebra. This disproportionate growth explains why the lumbar, sacral, and coccygeal regions of the spinal cord and its associated nerve roots do not lie next to their respective vertebrae.

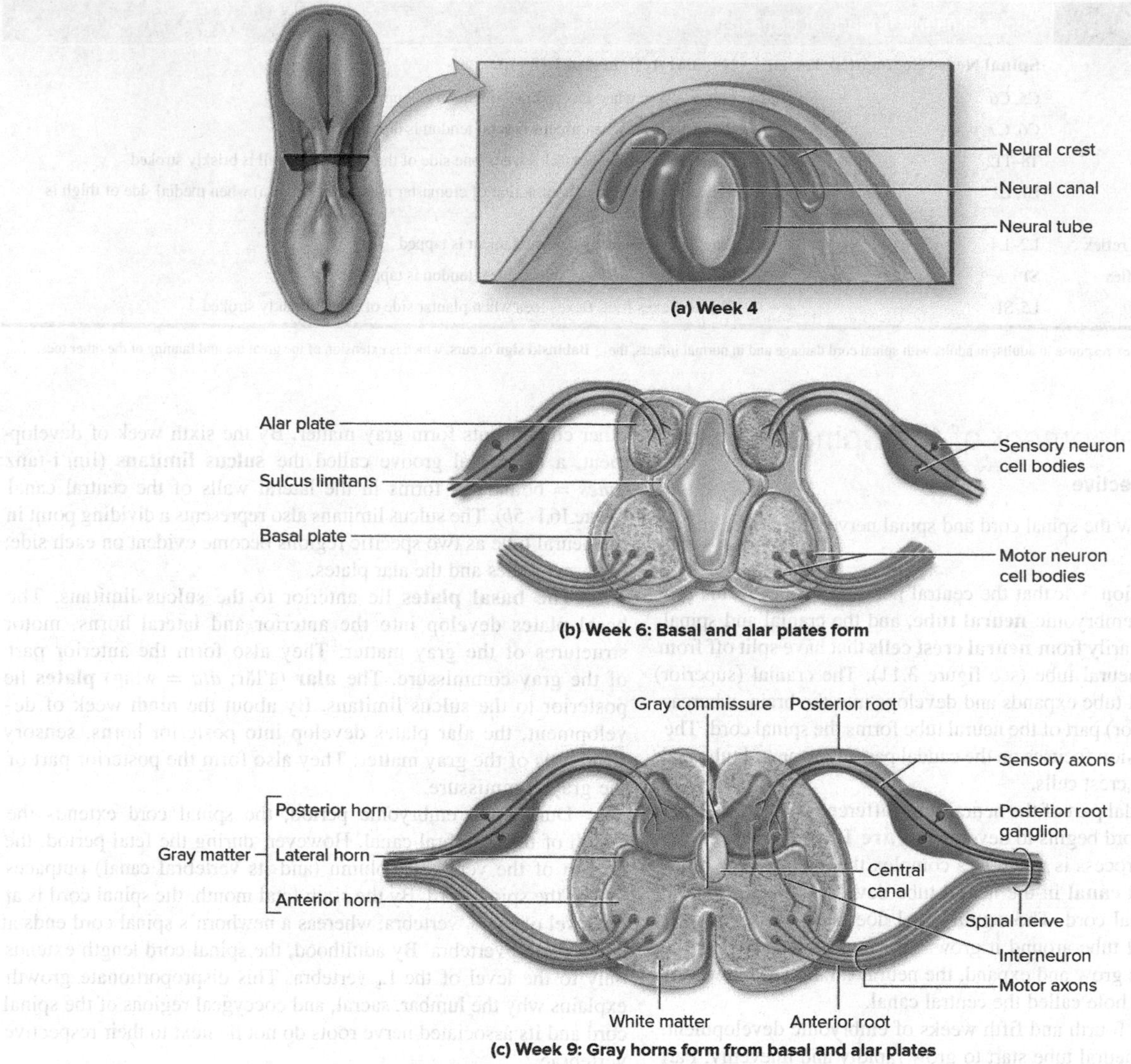
Neural crest
Neural canal
Neural tube
(a) Week 4
Alar plate
Sulcus limitans
Basal plate
Sensory neuron cell bodies
Motor neuron cell bodies
(b) Week 6: Basal and alar plates form
Gray commissure
Posterior root
Sensory axons
Posterior horn
Gray matter
Lateral horn
Anterior horn
Posterior root ganglion
Central canal
Spinal nerve
Interneuron
Motor axons
White matter
Anterior root
(c) Week 9: Gray horns form from basal and alar plates

Figure 16.15

Spinal Cord Development. The spinal cord begins development as a tubular extension of the brain. (*a*) A cross section shows the structures of the neural tube of an embryo in week 4 of development. Transverse sections show (*b*) the formation of the basal and alar plates at week 6 and (*c*) the developing spinal cord at week 9.

Clinical Terms

hemiplegia (hem′ē-plē′jē-ă; *hemi* = one-half, *plege* = stroke) Paralysis of the upper and lower limbs on one side of the body only, usually as a result of a stroke (cerebrovascular accident).

myelitis (mī′ĕ-lī′tis; *myelos* = medulla, marrow) Inflammation of the spinal cord.

paraplegia (par′ă-plē′jē-ă) Paralysis that results in loss of motor control in both lower limbs.

quadriplegia (kwah′dri-plē′jē-ă; *quattor* = four) Paralysis of both the upper and the lower limbs.

Chapter Summary

	■ The spinal cord and its attached spinal nerves serve as a pathway for sensory and motor impulses and are responsible for reflexes.
16.1 Gross Anatomy of the Spinal Cord	■ The adult spinal cord extends inferiorly from the brain through the vertebral canal and ends at the level of the L_1 vertebra. ■ Thirty-one pairs of spinal nerves connect the spinal cord to the body: 8 pairs of cervical nerves, 12 pairs of thoracic nerves, 5 pairs of lumbar nerves, 5 pairs of sacral nerves, and 1 pair of coccygeal nerves.
16.2 Spinal Cord Meninges	■ An outer epidural space separates the tough dura mater membrane from the inner walls of the vertebral canal. ■ The subarachnoid space, which is internal to the arachnoid mater, houses the cerebrospinal fluid. ■ The pia mater is the innermost meningeal layer. It is bound laterally to the spinal dura mater by paired denticulate ligaments.
16.3 Sectional Anatomy of the Spinal Cord	■ Gray matter is centrally located and H-shaped; peripheral to the gray matter is the white matter, which is composed primarily of myelinated axons. **16.3a Distribution of Gray Matter** ■ Gray matter is composed of three horns: anterior (cell bodies of somatic motor neurons), lateral (cell bodies of autonomic motor neurons), and posterior (sensory axons and interneurons). ■ The gray commissure connects the left and right sides of the gray matter and contains the axons of interneurons that extend between opposite sides of the spinal cord. **16.3b Distribution of White Matter** ■ The white matter is organized into three pairs of funiculi, each composed of specific tracts. Sensory information moves through ascending tracts to the brain, and motor information is carried by descending tracts from the brain to the spinal cord.
16.4 Spinal Nerves	■ Spinal nerves originate from anterior and posterior rootlets. **16.4a Spinal Nerve Distribution** ■ Spinal nerves have two branches: a posterior ramus innervates the skin and deep muscles of the back, and an anterior ramus innervates the anterior and lateral portions of the trunk and the limbs. **16.4b Nerve Plexuses** ■ A nerve plexus is a network of interwoven anterior rami. **16.4c Intercostal Nerves** ■ The anterior rami of spinal nerves T1–T11 form the intercostal nerves. Nerve T12 is called the subcostal nerve. **16.4d Cervical Plexuses** ■ The cervical plexus is formed from the anterior rami of C1–C4. It innervates the neck and portions of the head and shoulders. **16.4e Brachial Plexuses** ■ The brachial plexus innervates the upper limb and is formed from the anterior rami of C5–T1. **16.4f Lumbar Plexuses** ■ The lumbar plexus innervates the anterior and medial thigh and the skin of the medial leg. It is formed from the anterior rami of L1–L4. **16.4g Sacral Plexuses** ■ The sacral plexus innervates most of the lower limb and is formed from the anterior rami of L4–S4.
16.5 Reflexes	■ A reflex is a rapid, automatic, involuntary motor response of muscles or glands to a stimulus. **16.5a Components of a Reflex Arc** ■ The five steps involved in a reflex arc are (1) activation of a receptor by a stimulus, (2) impulse conduction to the CNS, (3) integration and processing of information by interneurons, (4) stimulation of a motor neuron, and (5) effector organ response. ■ The simplest reflex arc is a monosynaptic reflex, in which the sensory neuron synapses directly with the motor neuron. A polysynaptic reflex involves a sensory neuron, a motor neuron, and at least one interneuron connecting the sensory and motor neurons. **16.5b Examples of Spinal Reflexes** ■ A withdrawal reflex is polysynaptic and activates flexor muscles to immediately remove a body part from a painful stimulus. ■ A stretch reflex is monosynaptic and regulates skeletal muscle length and tone. ■ A tendon reflex is polysynaptic and prevents excessive tension in a muscle by inhibiting the contraction of the muscle, allowing it to relax. **16.5c Reflex Testing in a Clinical Setting** ■ Testing differentiates between hypoactive and hyperactive reflexes, and can help diagnose nervous system or muscular disorders.
16.6 Development of the Spinal Cord	■ The neural tube forms basal plates and alar plates. The basal plates form the anterior horns, lateral horns, and the anterior part of the gray commissure, while the alar plates form the posterior horns and the posterior part of the gray commissure.

Challenge Yourself

Actively write or type your answers in a separate document to reinforce your learning, before checking your answers.

Multiple Choice

Select the best answer from the four choices provided.

1. What is the tapered inferior end of the spinal cord called?
   a. conus medullaris
   b. filum terminale
   c. cauda equina
   d. posterior root
2. The anterior root of a spinal nerve contains what structures?
   a. axons of both motor and sensory neurons
   b. axons of sensory neurons only
   c. interneurons
   d. axons of motor neurons only
3. Identify the meningeal layer immediately deep to the subdural space.
   a. pia mater
   b. arachnoid mater
   c. epidural space
   d. dura mater
4. What is the name for the region of the spinal cord where axons cross from one side to the other?
   a. lateral horn
   b. posterior horn
   c. gray commissure
   d. anterior horn
5. Which plexus does the radial nerve originate from?
   a. cervical
   b. lumbar
   c. sacral
   d. brachial
6. Which structure provides motor innervation to the deep back muscles and receives sensory information from the skin of the back?
   a. anterior ramus
   b. anterior root
   c. posterior ramus
   d. posterior root
7. Lower limbs are supplied by neurons from which portion of the spinal cord?
   a. lumbosacral enlargement
   b. thoracic region
   c. cervical enlargement
   d. filum terminale
8. What is found in the epidural space?
   a. fat, connective tissue, and blood vessels
   b. fat, connective tissue, and CSF
   c. dura mater
   d. CSF
9. Which structures make up the majority of the white matter of the spinal cord?
   a. unmyelinated axons
   b. neurolemmocytes and satellite cells
   c. myelinated axons
   d. cell bodies of neurons
10. An individual was in a car accident and now has anesthesia from his lateral right arm through his right thumb. What structure may be affected?
   a. trigeminal nerve
   b. spinal nerve L1
   c. spinal nerve C6
   d. spinal nerve C8

Content Review

1. Identify the spinal cord parts, which spinal nerves are associated with them, and their relationship to the corresponding vertebrae.
2. Where is the epidural space? What is housed there?
3. List the three gray matter horns on each side of the spinal cord, and discuss the neuronal composition of each. In addition, list which types of nuclei (motor or sensory) are located in each horn.
4. Where are the cervical plexuses located, and what do they innervate?
5. What are the main terminal branches of the brachial plexus, and what muscles do these terminal branches innervate?
6. What anterior rami form the lumbar plexus, and what are some nerves formed from this plexus?
7. What muscles do the tibial and common fibular nerves innervate?
8. What is a reflex? How does it differ from a muscle movement that you consciously control, as when you consciously contract your biceps brachii muscle?
9. What are the differences between withdrawal, stretch, and tendon reflexes?
10. Where are the basal plates of the neural tube, and what does each form?

Developing Critical Reasoning

1. Arthur dove off a small cliff into water that was shallower than he expected and hit his head on a submerged object. He is now a quadriplegic, meaning that both his upper and lower limbs are paralyzed. Approximately where is the location of his injury? What is the likelihood that Arthur will recover from this injury? (You may want to review section 14.4 and Clinical View 14.4: "Treating Spinal Cord Injuries" in section 14.5 to answer the latter question.)
2. Jessica was knocked off her bicycle and fractured the medial epicondyle of her elbow. The neurologist detected swelling and increased pressure around Jessica's injury, and suspected that a nerve might be damaged as well. What nerve is likely damaged, and what other symptoms would the neurologist expect as a result of this injury?
3. During a very active game of tennis, Morgan felt something snap in her calcaneal tendon. Which reflex failed? Explain what that reflex does?

Answers to "What Do You Think?"

1. The two layers of the cranial dura mater split to form the dural venous sinuses, which are large veins that drain blood away from the brain. The spinal cord lacks dural venous sinuses, but has smaller veins that travel in the epidural space around the spinal cord.
2. An anterior ramus is larger than a posterior ramus because the posterior rami only innervate deep back muscles and the skin of the back, whereas the anterior rami innervate almost all other body structures (e.g., the limbs and the anterior and lateral trunk).
3. A nerve plexus houses axons from several different spinal nerves. Thus, damage to a single segment of the spinal cord or damage to a single spinal nerve generally does not result in complete loss of innervation to a particular muscle or region of skin.
4. Anesthesia along the upper lateral arm and difficulty abducting the arm indicate damage to the axillary nerve.
5. Difficulty extending the knee indicates damage to the femoral nerve.

NERVOUS SYSTEM

17 Pathways and Integrative Functions

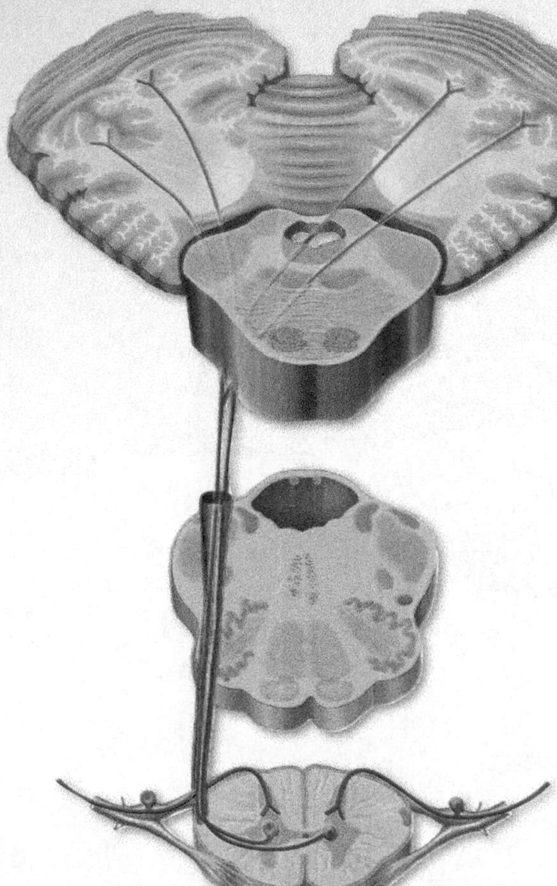

Outline

Anatomy & Physiology Revealed 4.0

MODULE 7: NERVOUS SYSTEM

This chapter focuses on the brain's higher-order activities—such as memory and learning—which are dependent upon the proper functioning of both sensory and motor pathways in the nervous system.

17.1 General Characteristics of Nervous System Pathways

✓ **Learning Objective**

1. Identify and describe the shared characteristics of sensory and motor pathways in the spinal cord.

The CNS communicates with body structures through **pathways.** These pathways conduct either sensory or motor information; processing and integration occur continuously along them. These pathways travel through the white matter of the brainstem and/or spinal cord as they connect various CNS regions with cranial and spinal nerves.

A pathway consists of both a tract and nucleus. **Tracts** are groups or bundles of axons that travel together within the CNS. Each tract may work with multiple groups of nuclei in the CNS. A **nucleus** is a collection of neuron cell bodies that display discrete anatomic boundaries located within the CNS (see table 15.2).

Nervous system pathways are sensory or motor. **Sensory pathways** are also called *ascending pathways* because the sensory information gathered by sensory receptors ascends through the spinal cord to the brain, whereas **motor pathways** are also called *descending pathways* because they transmit motor information that descends from the brain through the spinal cord to muscles or glands.

Learning Strategy 17.1

Be aware of the subtle difference between a tract and a pathway:

Tract: Myelinated axons that relay nerve signals from a common origin to a common destination (e.g., spinothalamic tract, which relays nerve signals from the spinal cord to the thalamus).

Pathway: A more general term that includes all of the neurons (and associated structures) that relay nerve signals between the brain and the body. Spinal pathways include components within the brain (e.g., cerebrum), and components of the spinal cord (identified as either fasciculi or tracts).

Most of the nervous system pathways we discuss in this chapter share several general characteristics:

- **Common location of neuron components.** The neuron cell bodies are located in one of three general places: ganglia within the peripheral nervous system, gray horns within the spinal cord, or nuclei within the brain along the pathway. In contrast, the axons of these neurons extend through the spinal cord and brain as tracts.
- **Paired tracts.** All pathways are composed of paired tracts. A pathway on the left side of the CNS has a corresponding tract on the right side of the CNS. Because each tract innervates structures on only one side of the body, both left and right tracts are needed to innervate both the left and right sides of the body.
- **Two or more neurons.** Most pathways are composed of a series of two or three neurons that work together. Sensory pathways have primary neurons, secondary neurons, and sometimes tertiary neurons that facilitate the pathway's functioning. In contrast, motor pathways use an upper motor neuron and a lower motor neuron. The cell bodies are located in the nuclei associated with each pathway. We discuss the specific neurons in greater detail later in this chapter.
- **Decussation of pathways.** Most pathways **decussate** (dē-kŭs′ āt; *decusseo* = to make in the form of an X) (cross over) from one side of the body to the other side at some point along their length. This crossover process, called *decussation,* means that the left side of the brain processes information from the right side of the body, and vice versa. For example, when you write with your right hand, the left side of your brain is controlling those right-sided muscles. The term **contralateral** is used to mean the opposite side, whereas the term **ipsilateral** means the same side. Over 90% of all pathways decussate, although the point at which decussation occurs can vary slightly from pathway to pathway.

WHAT DO YOU THINK?

1. What is a possible reason why most pathways decussate (cross over) from one side of the body to the other?

WHAT DID YOU LEARN?

1. What are the common shared characteristics of motor and sensory pathways?

Learning Strategy 17.2

Pathways and tracts are named according to their origin and terminal destination. For example, sensory pathways usually begin with the prefix *spino-*, indicating that they originate in the spinal cord. So the tract that originates in the spinal cord and terminates in the cerebellum is called the *spinocerebellar tract.* Motor pathways begin with either *cortico-*, indicating an origin in the cerebral cortex, or the name of a brainstem nucleus, such as *rubro-*, indicating an origin within the red nucleus of the midbrain. Tracts that terminate in the spinal cord have the suffix *-spinal* as part of their name. Thus, both *corticospinal* and *rubrospinal* denote motor tracts.

17.2 Sensory Pathways

✓ **Learning Objectives**

2. Identify the locations and describe the relationships of primary, secondary, and tertiary neurons.
3. Compare and contrast the three major somatosensory pathways.

Sensory pathways are ascending pathways that conduct proprioceptive information from the limbs to the brain and the sensations of touch, temperature, pressure, and pain. *Somatosensory pathways* process stimuli received from receptors within the skin, muscles, and joints, whereas *viscerosensory pathways* process stimuli received from the internal organs (viscera).

The multiple types of body sensations detected by the somatosensory system are grouped into three spinal cord pathways, each with a different brain destination: (1) Discriminative touch permits us to describe textures and shapes of unseen objects and includes pressure, touch, and vibration perception. (2) Temperature and pain allow us to detect those sensations, as well as the sensation of an itch.

(3) Proprioception allows us to detect the position of joints, amount of stretch in muscles, and tension in tendons. (Note: Visceral sensory pathways will be discussed in section 19.1b.)

Sensory receptors detect stimuli and then conduct nerve impulses to the central nervous system. Sensory pathway centers within either the spinal cord or the brainstem process and filter the incoming sensory information. These centers determine whether the incoming sensory stimulus should be transmitted to the cerebrum or terminated. Consequently, not all incoming impulses reach the cerebral cortex and our conscious awareness. For example, when you sit in a chair, you initially are aware of its pressure on your gluteal region, but after a short while that conscious awareness dissipates.

17.2a Functional Anatomy of Sensory Pathways

Sensory pathways utilize a series of two or three neurons to transmit stimulus information from the body periphery to the brain **(table 17.1)**. These neurons are named the primary neuron, secondary neuron, and tertiary neuron.

The first neuron in this chain is the **primary neuron** (or *first-order neuron*). The dendrites of this sensory neuron are part of the receptor that detects a specific stimulus. The cell bodies of primary neurons reside in the posterior root ganglia of spinal nerves or the sensory ganglia of cranial nerves. The axon of the primary neuron projects to a secondary neuron within the CNS.

The **secondary neuron** (or *second-order neuron*), the second neuron in this chain, is an interneuron. The cell body of this neuron resides within either the posterior horn of the spinal cord or a brainstem nucleus. The axon of a secondary neuron projects either to the thalamus for conscious sensations or to the cerebellum for unconscious proprioception. The axon of the secondary neuron arriving in the thalamus synapses with the tertiary neuron, the third neuron in the chain.

The **tertiary neuron** (or *third-order neuron*) is an interneuron whose cell body resides within the thalamus. Recall that the thalamus is the central processing and coding center for almost all sensory information; thus, it makes sense (pun intended!) that the last neuron in a sensory pathway chain resides in the thalamus.

There are three major types of **somatosensory pathways.** Each of these pathways has specific tracts that extend through the spinal cord **(figure 17.1)**. The posterior funiculus–medial lemniscal pathway relays sensory input through the fasciculus gracilis and fasciculus cuneatus. The anterolateral pathway relays sensory input through the lateral and anterior spinothalamic tracts. The spinocerebellar pathway relays sensory input through the anterior and posterior spinocerebellar tracts. Each of these pathways is described in detail next.

Table 17.1 Neurons Used in Sensory Pathways

Neuron	Functional Classification	Cell Body Origin(s)	Projects To:
Primary	Sensory neuron	Posterior root ganglia of spinal nerves; sensory ganglia of cranial nerves	Secondary neuron
Secondary	Interneuron	Posterior horn of a brainstem nucleus	Thalamus or cerebellum
Tertiary	Interneuron	Thalamus	Cerebral cortex

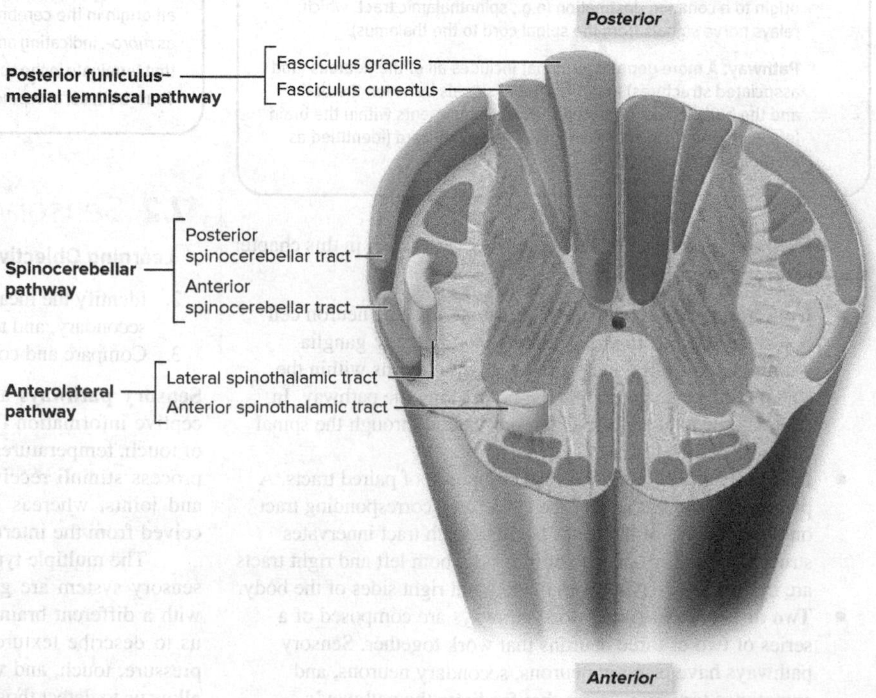

Figure 17.1
Sensory Pathways in the Spinal Cord.
The major sensory (ascending) pathways are bilaterally symmetrical tracts and shown here in different shades of blue. The major motor tracts (descending pathways) are indicated in pale red and will be described in section 17.3a.

> **Learning Strategy 17.3**
>
> The anterior and lateral funiculi contain both motor and sensory pathways, whereas the posterior funiculi contain sensory pathways only. Note that for all sensory pathways, their primary neurons are located in posterior root ganglia.

Posterior Funiculus–Medial Lemniscal Pathway

The **posterior funiculus–medial lemniscal pathway** (or *posterior column pathway*) projects through the spinal cord, brainstem, and diencephalon before terminating within the cerebral cortex (**figure 17.2**). Its name derives from two components: the tracts within the spinal cord, collectively called the **posterior funiculus** (fyū-nik'yū-lŭs; *funis* = cord); and the tracts within the brainstem, collectively called the **medial lemniscus** (lem-nis'k ŭs; *lemniskos* = ribbon). This pathway conducts sensory stimuli concerned with proprioceptive information about limb position as well as discriminative touch, precise pressure, and vibration sensations.

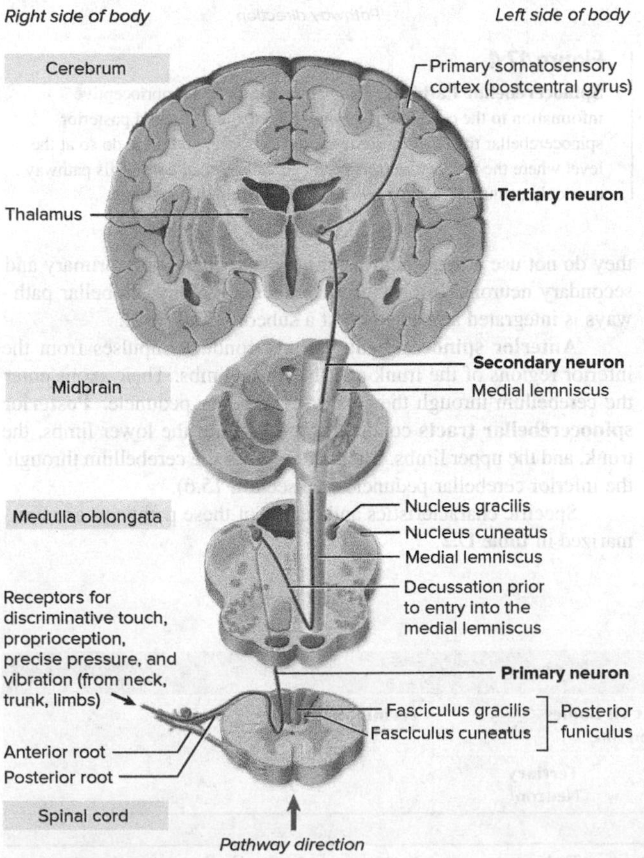
Right side of body
Left side of body
Cerebrum
Primary somatosensory cortex (postcentral gyrus)
Tertiary neuron
Thalamus
Secondary neuron
Medial lemniscus
Midbrain
Medulla oblongata
Nucleus gracilis
Nucleus cuneatus
Medial lemniscus
Decussation prior to entry into the medial lemniscus
Receptors for discriminative touch, proprioception, precise pressure, and vibration (from neck, trunk, limbs)
Primary neuron
Fasciculus gracilis
Fasciculus cuneatus
Posterior funiculus
Anterior root
Posterior root
Spinal cord
Pathway direction

Figure 17.2
Posterior Funiculus–Medial Lemniscal Pathway. This pathway conducts sensory information about limb position, fine touch, precise pressure, and vibration. This pathway is bilaterally symmetrical; to avoid confusion, only sensory input from the right side of the body is shown here. Decussation of axons occurs in the medulla oblongata. The primary neuron is purple, the secondary neuron is royal blue, and the tertiary neuron is navy blue.

The posterior funiculus–medial lemniscal pathway uses a chain of three neurons to signal the brain about a specific stimulus. Axons of the primary neurons traveling in spinal nerves reach the CNS through the posterior roots of spinal nerves. Upon entering the spinal cord, these axons ascend within a specific posterior funiculus, either the **fasciculus cuneatus** (kū'nē-ā-tŭs; *cuneus* = wedge) or the **fasciculus gracilis** (gras'i-lis).

The fasciculus cuneatus and fasciculus gracilis are both part of the posterior funiculus-medial lemniscal pathway, and both conduct sensory impulses about proprioceptive information and general sensory information. They differ in what regions of the body they receive information from: the fasciculus cuneatus receives information from the upper limb, superior trunk, neck, and posterior head, whereas the fasciculus gracilis receives information from the inferior trunk and lower limbs. The cell bodies of their sensory neurons are located in different locations of the medulla oblongata as well—the fasciculus cuneatus secondary neurons originate in the nucleus cuneatus (of the medulla oblongata), whereas the fasciculus gracilis secondary neurons originate in the nucleus gracilis (of the medulla oblongata).

Sensory axons from primary neurons that are ascending within the posterior funiculi synapse on secondary neuron cell bodies. These secondary neurons then project axons to relay the incoming sensory information to the thalamus on the opposite side of the brain through the medial lemniscus. Decussation occurs after secondary neuron axons exit their specific nuclei and before they enter the medial lemniscus.

The axons of the secondary neurons synapse on cell bodies of the tertiary neurons within the thalamus, where the ascending sensory information is sorted according to the region of the body involved. Axons from these tertiary neurons conduct sensory information to a specific location of the primary somatosensory cortex (within the postcentral gyrus, see section 15.3b).

Anterolateral Pathway

The **anterolateral pathway** (or *spinothalamic pathway*) is located in the anterior and lateral white funiculi of the spinal cord (**figure 17.3**). It is composed of both the **anterior spinothalamic tract** and the **lateral spinothalamic tract.** Axons projecting from primary neurons enter the spinal cord and synapse on secondary neurons within the posterior horns. The anterior spinothalamic tract conducts stimuli related to crude touch and pressure, whereas the lateral spinothalamic tract conducts stimuli for pain and temperature.

Axons of the secondary neurons in the anterolateral pathway decussate through the anterior white commissure, which is located anterior to the gray commissure, before ascending toward the brain. This decussation occurs through the **anterior white commissure,** located anterior to the gray commissure. Secondary neuron axons synapse on tertiary neurons located within the thalamus. Axons from the tertiary neurons then conduct stimulus information to the appropriate region of the primary somatosensory cortex (see section 15.3b).

Spinocerebellar Pathway

The **spinocerebellar pathway** conducts proprioceptive information to the cerebellum for processing to coordinate body movements. Its name derives from the origin (spinal cord) and destination (cerebellum) of the secondary neurons of this pathway.

The spinocerebellar pathway is composed of anterior and posterior spinocerebellar tracts; these are the major routes for transmitting postural input to the cerebellum (**figure 17.4**). Sensory input arriving at the cerebellum through these tracts is critical for regulating posture and balance and for coordinating skilled movements. These spinocerebellar tracts are different from the other sensory pathways in that

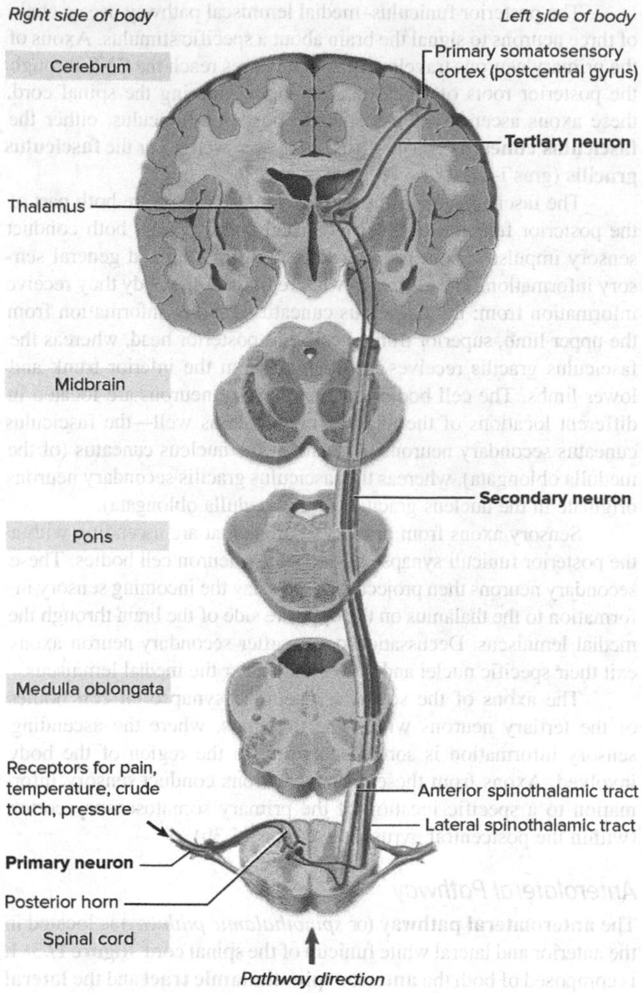
Right side of body
Left side of body
Cerebrum
Primary somatosensory cortex (postcentral gyrus)
Tertiary neuron
Thalamus
Midbrain
Secondary neuron
Pons
Medulla oblongata
Receptors for pain, temperature, crude touch, pressure
Anterior spinothalamic tract
Lateral spinothalamic tract
Primary neuron
Posterior horn
Spinal cord
Pathway direction

Figure 17.3

Anterolateral Pathway. This pathway conducts crude touch, pressure, pain, and temperature sensations toward the brain. Decussation of axons occurs at the level where the primary neuron axon enters the spinal cord. The primary neuron is purple, the secondary neuron is royal blue, and the tertiary neuron is navy blue.

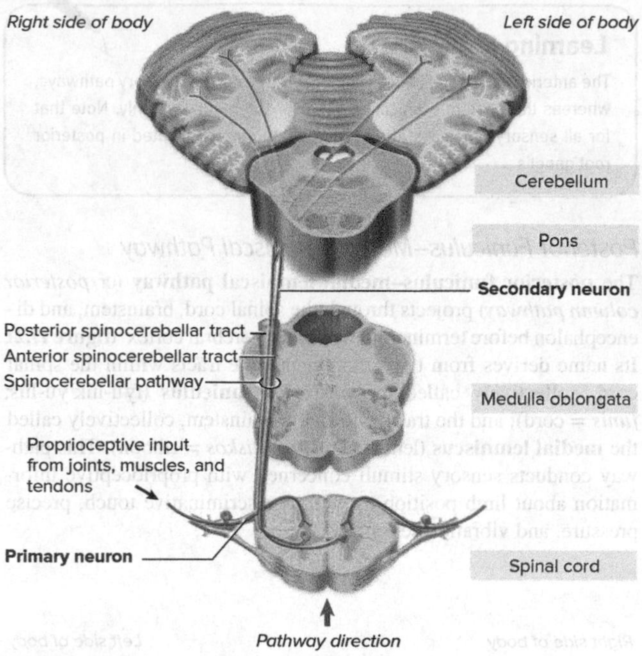
Right side of body
Left side of body
Cerebellum
Pons
Secondary neuron
Posterior spinocerebellar tract
Anterior spinocerebellar tract
Spinocerebellar pathway
Medulla oblongata
Proprioceptive input from joints, muscles, and tendons
Primary neuron
Spinal cord
Pathway direction

Figure 17.4

Spinocerebellar Pathway. This pathway conducts proprioceptive information to the cerebellum through both the anterior and posterior spinocerebellar tracts. Only some axons decussate, and these do so at the level where the primary neuron axon enters the spinal cord. This pathway uses only primary (purple) and secondary (royal blue) neurons.

they do not use tertiary neurons; rather, they have only primary and secondary neurons. Information conducted in spinocerebellar pathways is integrated and acted on at a subconscious level.

Anterior spinocerebellar tracts conduct impulses from the inferior regions of the trunk and the lower limbs. Their axons enter the cerebellum through the superior cerebellar peduncle. **Posterior spinocerebellar tracts** conduct impulses from the lower limbs, the trunk, and the upper limbs. Their axons enter the cerebellum through the inferior cerebellar peduncle (see section 15.6).

Specific characteristics and details of these pathways are summarized in **table 17.2**.

Table 17.2 Principal Sensory Spinal Cord Pathways

Sensory Pathway	Origin(s) of Pathway Neuron	Location of Neuron Cell Bodies and Decussation Site			Termination	Function
		Primary Neuron	Secondary Neuron	Tertiary Neuron		
POSTERIOR FUNICULUS–MEDIAL LEMNISCAL PATHWAY						
Fasciculus cuneatus	Upper limb, superior trunk, neck, posterior head	Posterior root ganglion	Nucleus cuneatus Axons decussate prior to entry into medial lemniscus	Thalamus	Nucleus cuneatus of medulla oblongata	Conduct sensory impulses for proprioceptive information discriminative touch, precise pressure, and vibration sensation
Fasciculus gracilis	Lower limb, inferior trunk	Posterior root ganglion	Nucleus gracilis Axons decussate prior to entry into medial lemniscus	Thalamus	Nucleus gracilis of medulla oblongata	Same as fasciculus cuneatus

Table 17.2 Principal Sensory Spinal Cord Pathways (continued)

Sensory Pathway	Origin(s) of Pathway Neuron	Location of Neuron Cell Bodies and Decussation Site			Termination	Function
		Primary Neuron	Secondary Neuron	Tertiary Neuron		
ANTEROLATERAL PATHWAY						
Anterior spinothalamic	Posterior horn interneurons	Posterior root ganglion	Posterior horn interneurons Axons decussate within spinal cord at level of entry	Thalamus	Primary somatosensory cortex	Conducts sensory impulses for crude touch and pressure
Lateral spinothalamic	Posterior horn interneurons	Posterior root ganglion	Posterior horn interneurons Axons decussate within spinal cord at level of entry	Thalamus	Primary somatosensory cortex	Conducts sensory impulses for pain and temperature
SPINOCEREBELLAR PATHWAY						
Anterior spinocerebellar	Posterior horn interneurons	Posterior root ganglion	Posterior horn interneurons Some axons decussate in spinal cord and pons, whereas others do not decussate	None	Cerebellum	Conducts proprioceptive impulses from inferior regions of trunk and lower limbs
Posterior spinocerebellar	Posterior horn interneurons	Posterior root ganglion	Posterior horn interneurons Axons do not decussate	None	Cerebellum	Conducts proprioceptive impulses from lower limbs, regions of trunk and upper limbs

WHAT DO YOU THINK?

2. You have learned that most sensory impulses never reach our conscious awareness. Why? What would be the drawback to being consciously aware of almost all sensory impulses?

WHAT DID YOU LEARN?

2. What information is conducted by sensory pathways, and how do somatosensory and viscerosensory pathways differ?
3. Compare primary and secondary neurons in the sensory pathways in terms of the location of their cell bodies and the neurons they synapse with.
4. In what ways do the fasciculus cuneatus and fasciculus gracilis differ?

17.3 Motor Pathways

✓ Learning Objectives

4. Identify and describe the key features and regional anatomy of motor pathways.
5. Compare and contrast the characteristics of direct and indirect motor pathways.
6. Describe how cerebral nuclei and the cerebellum function in motor activities.

Motor pathways are descending pathways in the brain and spinal cord that control the activities of skeletal muscle.

17.3a Functional Anatomy of Motor Pathways

Motor pathways are formed from the cerebral nuclei, the cerebellum, descending projection tracts, and motor neurons (**figure 17.5**). Motor neurons within these pathways either synapse directly on motor neurons in the CNS or on interneurons that, in turn, synapse on motor neurons.

There are at least two motor neurons in the somatic motor pathway: an upper motor neuron and a lower motor neuron (**table 17.3**).

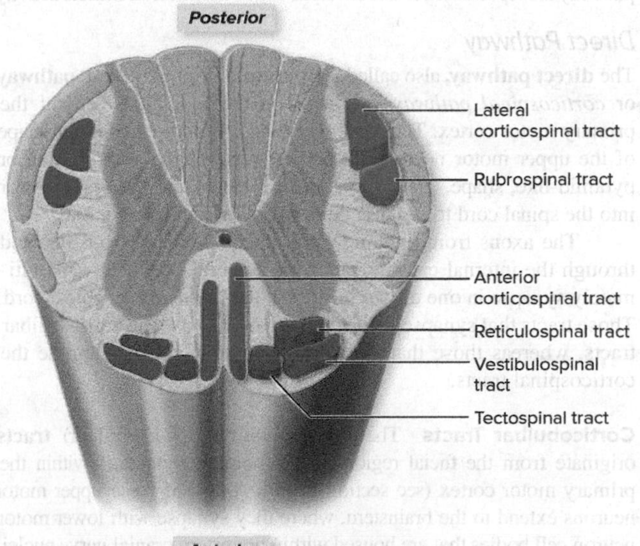

Figure 17.5
Motor Pathways in the Spinal Cord. Bilaterally symmetrical motor pathways descend from both the cortex and the brainstem into the spinal cord. Tract names indicate their point of origin and the spinal cord as their destination. Motor pathways are shown in shades of red and orange; sensory pathways are shown in blue.

Table 17.3 Neurons Used in Motor Pathways

Neuron	Cell Body Origin	Projects To:	Activity
Upper motor neuron	Cerebral cortex or brainstem nucleus	Lower motor neuron	May be either excitatory or inhibitory
Lower motor neuron	Brainstem nucleus or anterior horn of spinal cord	Skeletal muscle	Excitatory only

These neurons are involved in voluntary movements. The cell body of an **upper motor neuron** is housed within either the cerebral cortex or a nucleus within the brainstem. Axons of the upper motor neuron synapse either directly on lower motor neurons or on interneurons that synapse directly on lower motor neurons. The cell body of a **lower motor neuron** is housed either within the anterior horn of the spinal cord or within a brainstem cranial nerve nucleus. Axons of the lower motor neurons exit the CNS and project to the skeletal muscle to be innervated.

The two types of motor neurons perform different activities: The activity of the upper motor neuron either excites or inhibits the lower motor neuron, but the activity of the lower motor neuron is always excitatory because its axon connects directly to the skeletal muscle fibers. The cell bodies of motor neurons and most interneurons involved in the innervation and control of limb and trunk muscles reside in the spinal cord anterior horn and the gray matter zone between the anterior horn and the posterior horn. The neurons that innervate the head and neck are located in the motor nuclei of cranial nerves and in the reticular formation (introduced in section 15.7 and discussed in this chapter in section 17.4f).

Motor neuron axons form two types of somatic motor pathways: the direct pathway and indirect pathway. The direct pathway is responsible for conscious control of skeletal muscle activity, and the indirect pathway is responsible for unconscious control of skeletal muscle activity.

Direct Pathway

The **direct pathway,** also called the **pyramidal** (pi-ram′i-dăl) **pathway** or *corticospinal pathway,* originates in the pyramidal cells of the primary motor cortex. The name *pyramidal* is derived from the shape of the upper motor neuron cell bodies, which have a tetrahedral, or pyramid-like, shape. Their axons project either into the brainstem or into the spinal cord to synapse directly on lower motor neurons.

The axons from pyramidal cell upper motor neurons descend through the internal capsule, enter the cerebral peduncles, and ultimately synapse in one of two locations: the brainstem or spinal cord. Those tracts that synapse in the brainstem compose the corticobulbar tracts, whereas those that synapse in the spinal cord compose the corticospinal tracts.

Corticobulbar Tracts The **corticobulbar** (kōr′ti-k ō-bŭl′bar) **tracts** originate from the facial region of the motor homunculus within the primary motor cortex (see section 15.3b). Axons of these upper motor neurons extend to the brainstem, where they synapse with lower motor neuron cell bodies that are housed within brainstem cranial nerve nuclei (see section 15.8). The term *bulbar* means resembling a bulb and is used to indicate the rhombencephalon in the brainstem (see section 15.1a). Axons of these lower motor neurons help form the cranial nerves (see section 15.8). Thus, note that these tracts differ from the others that we are about to discuss in that (1) they do not pass through the spinal cord, and (2) they involve cranial nerves (and not spinal nerves).

Corticospinal Tracts The **corticospinal** (kor′ti-k ō-spī′năl; *spinalis* = backbone) **tracts** descend from the cerebral cortex through the brainstem and form a pair of thick anterior bulges in the medulla oblongata called the pyramids (see section 15.5c). Then they continue into the spinal cord to synapse on lower motor neurons in the anterior horn of the spinal cord (**figure 17.6**). The corticospinal tracts are composed of two components: lateral and anterior corticospinal tracts. These tracts differ in several significant ways, including their point of decussation, location within the spinal cord, and the specific muscles they innervate.

The **lateral corticospinal tracts** include about 85% of the axons of the upper motor neurons that decussate within the pyramids of the medulla oblongata and then form the lateral corticospinal tracts in the lateral funiculi of the spinal cord. These tracts contain axons that innervate both lower motor neurons of the anterior horn of the spinal cord and interneurons within the spinal cord. Axons of the lower motor neurons innervate skeletal muscles that control skilled movements in the *limbs,* such as playing a guitar, dribbling a soccer ball, or typing on your computer keyboard.

The **anterior corticospinal tracts** represent the remaining 15% of the axons of upper motor neurons that extend through the medulla oblongata. The axons of these neurons do not decussate at the level of the medulla oblongata; instead, they decussate at the level of a spinal cord segment through the anterior gray commissure. They subsequently

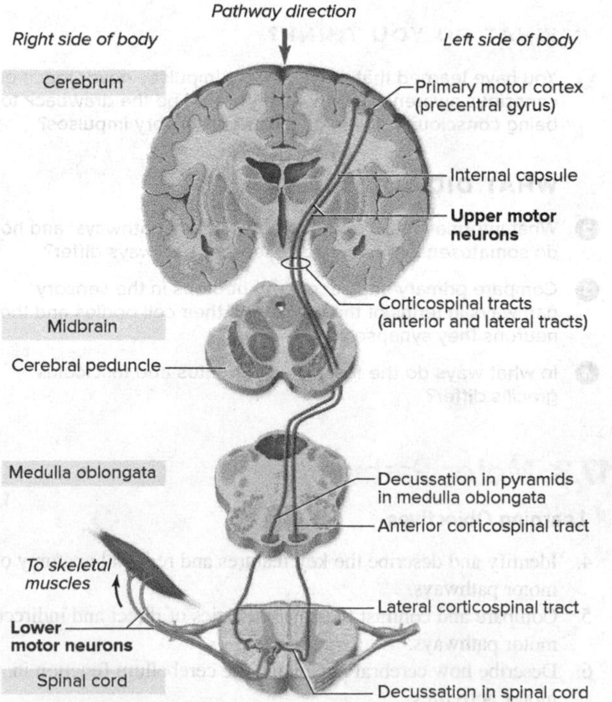

Figure 17.6

Corticospinal Tracts. Corticospinal tracts originate as collections of motor neurons within the motor cortex of the cerebrum and synapse on motor neurons within the anterior horns of the spinal cord to control voluntary motor activity. The upper motor neurons are red, and the lower motor neurons are dark orange. APR synapse either with interneurons or with lower motor neurons in the anterior horn of the spinal cord. Axons of the lower motor neurons innervate *axial* skeletal muscle.

Indirect Pathway

Several nuclei within the midbrain initiate motor commands for activities that occur at a subconscious or reflexive level. These nuclei and their associated tracts constitute the **indirect pathway,** so named because upper motor neurons originate within brainstem nuclei and take a complex, circuitous route before finally conducting the motor impulse into the spinal cord. Motor impulses conducted by axons of the upper motor neurons in the indirect pathway descend from specific brainstem nuclei into major tracts of the spinal cord and terminate on either interneurons or lower motor neurons (**figure 17.7**).

The indirect pathway modifies or helps control the pattern of somatic motor activity by exciting or inhibiting the lower motor neurons that innervate the muscles. Interaction among these motor pathway components occurs both within the brain and at the level of the motor neurons.

The different tracts of the indirect pathway are grouped according to their primary functions. The **lateral pathway** regulates and controls precise, discrete movements and tone in flexor muscles of the limbs—for example, the type of movement required to gently lay a baby in her crib. This pathway consists of the **rubrospinal** (rū′brō-spī′năl; *rubro* = red) **tracts** that originate in the red nucleus of the midbrain.

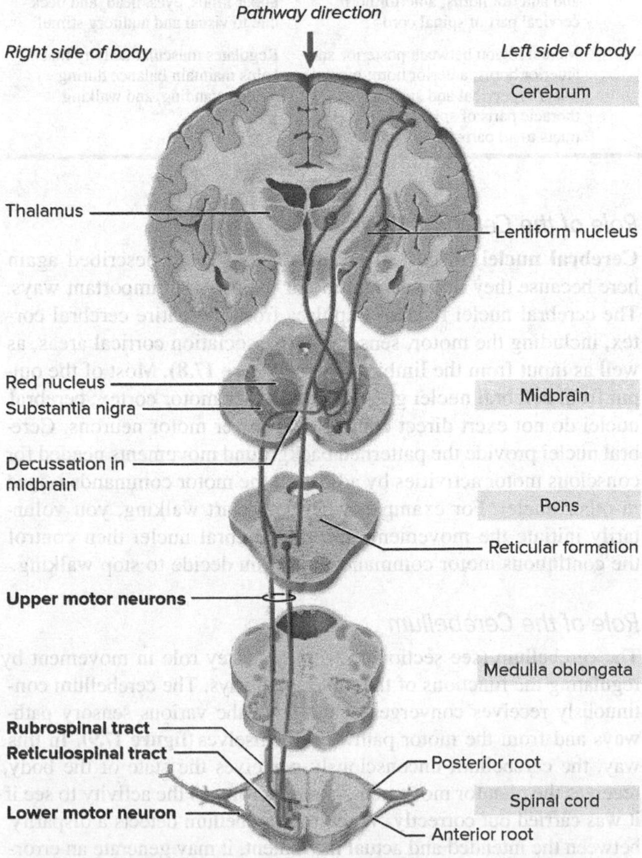
Pathway direction
Right side of body
Left side of body
Cerebrum
Thalamus
Lentiform nucleus
Red nucleus
Substantia nigra
Midbrain
Decussation in midbrain
Pons
Reticular formation
Upper motor neurons
Medulla oblongata
Rubrospinal tract
Reticulospinal tract
Posterior root
Spinal cord
Lower motor neuron
Anterior root

Figure 17.7
Indirect Motor Pathways in the Spinal Cord. These motor pathways originate from neurons housed within the brainstem. The upper motor neurons are red, and the lower motor neuron is dark orange.

Clinical View 17.1

Cerebrovascular Accident

A **cerebrovascular accident (CVA,** or **stroke)** is caused by reduced blood supply to a part of the brain due to a blocked or damaged arterial blood vessel. If a *thrombus* (a blood clot within the blood vessel) forms at a narrowed region of a cerebral artery, it can completely block the lumen of the artery. On occasion, a CVA also results from an *embolus* (a blood clot that formed someplace else) that breaks free, travels through the vascular system, and becomes lodged in a cerebral blood vessel. An especially serious form of stroke results when a weakened blood vessel in the brain ruptures and hemorrhages, quickly leading to unconsciousness and death.

Symptoms of a CVA include loss or blurring of vision, weakness or slight numbness, headache, dizziness, and walking difficulties. Depending upon the location of the blockage, the person may experience regional sensory loss, motor loss, or both. For example, a patient who suddenly exhibits speech difficulties and loss of motor control of the right arm may be experiencing a CVA that affects the left hemisphere's motor speech area as well as the precentral gyrus (see section 15.3b) in the region of the motor homunculus upper limb. If the obstruction lasts longer than about 10 minutes, tissue in the brain may die. A massive stroke can leave a person completely paralyzed and without sensation over as much as half the body.

A brief episode of lost sensation or motor ability may be caused by a **transient ischemic attach (TIA),** or *mini-stroke*. A TIA results from a temporary clot in a cerebral blood vessel that dissolves or dissipates in a matter of minutes. However, TIAs indicate increased risk for future strokes.

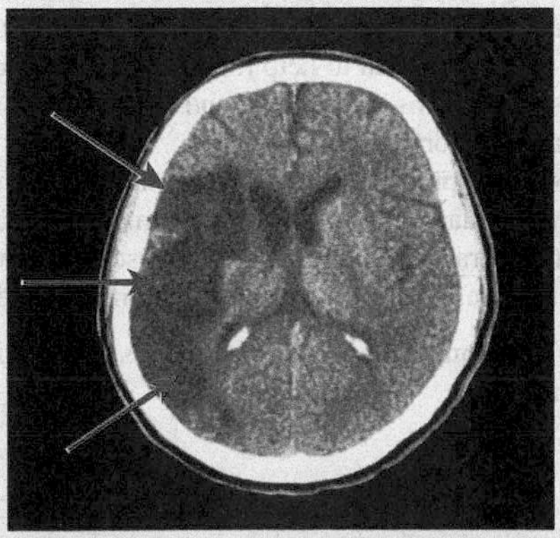

A CT scan of an individual who suffered a stroke in the right cerebral hemisphere (yellow arrows). Affected brain tissue is darker in color than nearby healthy brain tissue.
Puwadol Jaturawutthichai/Alamy Stock Photo

Table 17.4	Principal Motor Spinal Cord Pathways			
Motor Pathway	**Manner of Decussation**	**Destination of Upper Motor Neurons**	**Termination Site(s)**	**Function**
DIRECT PATHWAY				
Corticobulbar tracts	All cranial nerve motor nuclei receive bilateral (both ipsilateral and contralateral) input except CN VI, VII to the lower face, and XII. These receive only contralateral input	Brainstem only	Cranial nerve nuclei; reticular formation	Voluntary movement of cranial muscles
Lateral corticospinal tracts	All decussate at the pyramids	Lateral funiculus	Gray matter region between posterior and anterior horns; anterior horn; all levels of spinal cord	Voluntary movement of limb muscles
Anterior corticospinal tracts	Decussation occurs in spinal cord at level of lower motor neuron cell body	Anterior funiculus	Gray matter region between posterior and anterior horns; anterior horn; cervical part of spinal cord	Voluntary movement of axial muscles
INDIRECT PATHWAY				
Lateral Pathway				
Rubrospinal tract	Decussate at ventral tegmentum	Lateral funiculus	Lateral region between posterior and anterior horns; anterior horn; cervical part of spinal cord	Regulates and controls precise, discrete movements and tone in flexor muscles of the limbs
Medial Pathway				
Reticulospinal tract	No decussation (ipsilateral)	Anterior funiculus	Medial region between posterior and anterior horns; anterior horn; all parts of spinal cord	Controls more unskilled automatic movements related to posture and maintaining balance
Tectospinal tract	Decussate at dorsal tegmentum	Anterior funiculus	Medial region between posterior and anterior horns; anterior horn; cervical part of spinal cord	Regulates positional changes of the upper limbs, eyes, head, and neck due to visual and auditory stimuli
Vestibulospinal tract	Some decussate (contralateral) and some do not (ipsilateral)	Anterior funiculus	Medial region between posterior and anterior horns; anterior horn; medial tracts to cervical and superior thoracic parts of spinal cord; lateral tracts to all parts of spinal cord	Regulates muscular activity that helps maintain balance during sitting, standing, and walking

The **medial pathway** regulates reflexive tone and gross movements of the muscles of the head, neck, proximal parts of the limbs, and trunk. The medial pathway consists of three groups of tracts: reticulospinal tracts, tectospinal tracts, and vestibulospinal tracts.

- The **reticulospinal** (re-tik-y ū-lō-spī′năl) **tracts** originate from the reticular formation in the midbrain. They help control reflexive movements related to posture and maintaining balance.
- The **tectospinal** (tek-t ō-spī′năl) **tracts** conduct motor commands away from the superior and inferior colliculi in the tectum of the midbrain to help regulate reflexive positional changes of the arms, eyes, head, and neck as a consequence of visual and auditory stimuli.
- The **vestibulospinal** (ves-tib′y ū-lō-spī′năl) **tracts** originate within vestibular nuclei of the brainstem. Impulses conducted within these tracts regulate reflexive muscular activity that helps maintain balance during sitting, standing, and walking.

Table 17.4 summarizes the characteristics of the principal types of motor pathways.

Learning Strategy 17.4

The medial pathway regulates movement of muscle located in more medial regions of the body (e.g., head, neck, trunk, proximal limbs), whereas the lateral pathway regulates muscle movement located more distally (limb movement only).

Role of the Cerebral Nuclei

Cerebral nuclei, discussed in section 15.3d, are described again here because they interact with motor pathways in important ways. The cerebral nuclei receive impulses from the entire cerebral cortex, including the motor, sensory, and association cortical areas, as well as input from the limbic system **(figure 17.8).** Most of the output from cerebral nuclei goes to the primary motor cortex; cerebral nuclei do not exert direct control over lower motor neurons. Cerebral nuclei provide the patterned background movements needed for conscious motor activities by adjusting the motor commands issued in other nuclei. For example, when you start walking, you voluntarily initiate the movement, and the cerebral nuclei then control the continuous motor commands until you decide to stop walking.

Role of the Cerebellum

The cerebellum (see section 15.6) plays a key role in movement by regulating the functions of the motor pathways. The cerebellum continuously receives convergent input from the various sensory pathways and from the motor pathways themselves **(figure 17.9).** In this way, the cerebellum unconsciously perceives the state of the body, receives the plan for movement, and then follows the activity to see if it was carried out correctly. When the cerebellum detects a disparity between the intended and actual movement, it may generate an error-correcting signal. This signal is transmitted to both the premotor and primary motor cortices via the thalamus and the brainstem. Descending pathways then transmit these error-correcting signals to the motor neurons. Thus, the cerebellum influences and controls movement by indirectly affecting the excitability of motor neurons. The cerebellum

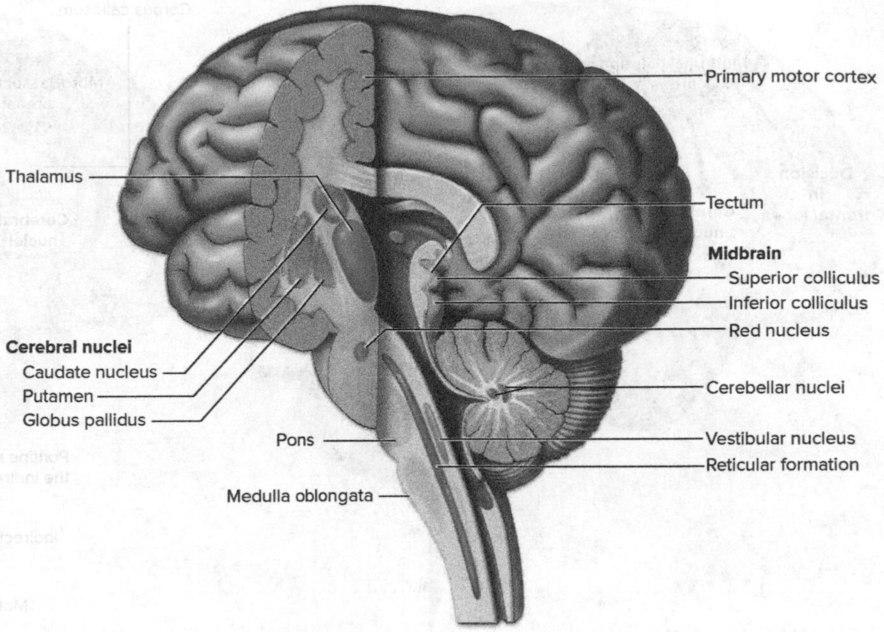

Primary motor cortex
Thalamus
Tectum
Midbrain
Superior colliculus
Inferior colliculus
Red nucleus
Cerebral nuclei
Caudate nucleus
Putamen
Globus pallidus
Cerebellar nuclei
Pons
Vestibular nucleus
Reticular formation
Medulla oblongata

Figure 17.8

Cerebral Nuclei and Selected Indirect Motor System Components. A partially cut-away brain diagram shows the general physical location of the cerebral nuclei and some structures of the indirect motor system.

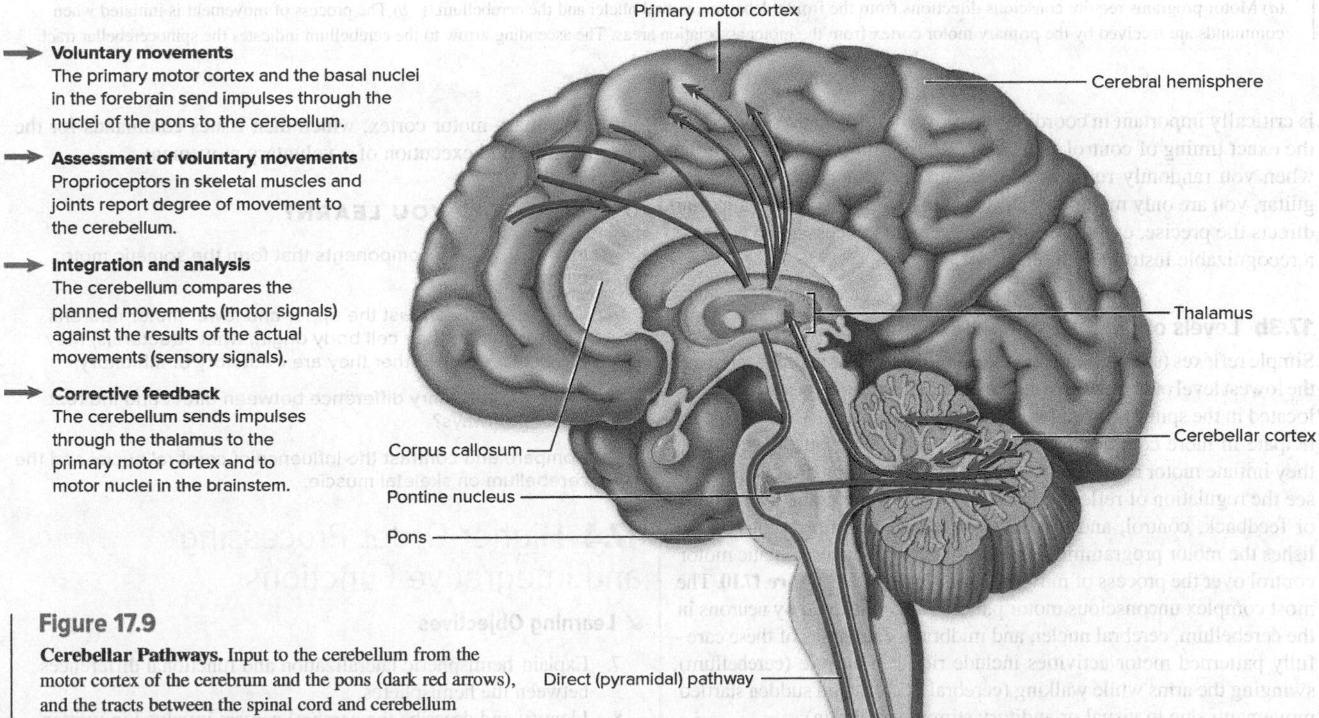

Primary motor cortex
Voluntary movements
The primary motor cortex and the basal nuclei in the forebrain send impulses through the nuclei of the pons to the cerebellum.
Assessment of voluntary movements
Proprioceptors in skeletal muscles and joints report degree of movement to the cerebellum.
Integration and analysis
The cerebellum compares the planned movements (motor signals) against the results of the actual movements (sensory signals).
Corrective feedback
The cerebellum sends impulses through the thalamus to the primary motor cortex and to motor nuclei in the brainstem.
Cerebral hemisphere
Thalamus
Cerebellar cortex
Corpus callosum
Pontine nucleus
Pons
Direct (pyramidal) pathway
Sagittal section

Figure 17.9

Cerebellar Pathways. Input to the cerebellum from the motor cortex of the cerebrum and the pons (dark red arrows), and the tracts between the spinal cord and cerebellum (blue arrow). Within the cerebellum, the integration and analysis of input information occurs (green arrows). Output from the cerebellum (yellow arrows) extends through the cerebellar peduncles (not shown).

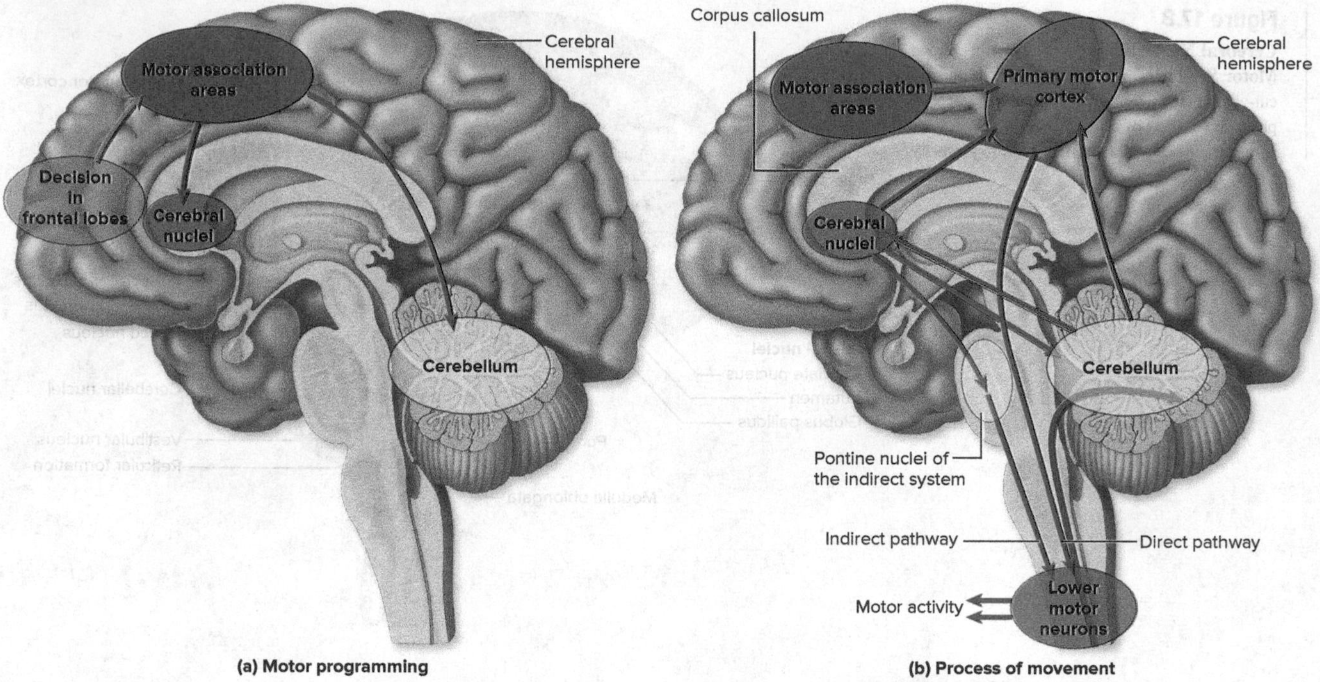

Figure 17.10

Somatic Motor Control. Several regions of the brain participate in the control and modification of motor programming to produce somatic motor activities. (*a*) Motor programs require conscious directions from the frontal lobes to cerebral nuclei and the cerebellum. (*b*) The process of movement is initiated when commands are received by the primary motor cortex from the motor association areas. The ascending arrow to the cerebellum indicates the spinocerebellar tract.

is critically important in coordinating movements because it specifies the exact timing of control signals to different muscles. For example, when you randomly run your fingers up and down the strings of a guitar, you are only making noise, not music. It is the cerebellum that directs the precise, exquisite finger movements necessary to produce a recognizable instrumental piece.

17.3b Levels of Processing and Motor Control

Simple reflexes (see section 16.5) that stimulate motor neurons represent the lowest level of motor control. The nuclei controlling these reflexes are located in the spinal cord and the brainstem. Brainstem nuclei also participate in more complex reflexes. Upon receipt of sensory impulses, they initiate motor responses to control motor neurons directly or oversee the regulation of reflex centers elsewhere in the brain. The pattern of feedback, control, and modification between brain regions establishes the motor programming that ultimately produces somatic motor control over the process of movement as illustrated in **figure 17.10**. The most complex unconscious motor patterns are controlled by neurons in the cerebellum, cerebral nuclei, and midbrain. Examples of these carefully patterned motor activities include riding a bicycle (cerebellum), swinging the arms while walking (cerebral nuclei), and sudden startled movements due to visual or auditory stimuli (midbrain).

Highly variable and complex voluntary motor patterns are controlled by the cerebral cortex and occupy the highest level of processing and motor control. Motor commands may be conducted to specific motor neurons directly, or they may be conveyed indirectly by altering the activity of a reflex control center. Figure 17.10*b* diagrammatically illustrates some steps involved in the interactions between the cerebral nuclei, motor association areas, and cerebellum, and the primary motor cortex, which then issues commands for the programming and execution of a voluntary movement.

WHAT DID YOU LEARN?

5. Identify the CNS components that form the somatic motor pathways.
6. Compare and contrast the upper and lower motor neurons with respect to their cell body origin, what structure(s) they project to, and whether they are excitatory or inhibitory.
7. What is the primary difference between direct and indirect motor pathways?
8. Compare and contrast the influence of cerebral nuclei and the cerebellum on skeletal muscle.

17.4 Higher-Order Processing and Integrative Functions

✓ Learning Objectives

7. Explain hemispheric lateralization and functional differences between the hemispheres.
8. Identify and describe the cerebral centers involved in written and spoken language.
9. Describe the brain regions and structures involved in cognition, memory storage, and recall.
10. Describe the brain structures involved with consciousness, and explain how an electroencephalogram interprets consciousness.
11. Explain the main characteristics of sleep, and compare and contrast non-REM versus REM sleep.

Higher-order mental functions encompass learning, memory, reasoning, and consciousness. These functions occur within the cortex of the cerebrum and involve multiple brain regions connected by complicated networks and arrays of axons. Both conscious and unconscious processing of information are involved in higher-order mental functions, and they may be continually adjusted or modified.

17.4a Development and Maturation of Higher-Order Processing

From infancy on, our motor control and processing capabilities become increasingly complex as we grow and mature. During the first year of life, the number of cortical neurons continues to increase. The myelination of most CNS axons continues throughout the first 2 years. (As a result, pediatricians recommend that infants and toddlers drink whole milk instead of skim milk, so their bodies will have adequate fat intake to support the development of myelin and the brain in general.) The brain grows rapidly in size and complexity so that by the age of 5, brain growth is about 95% complete. (The rest of the body doesn't reach its adult size until puberty.)

As the CNS continues to develop, some neurons expand their number of connections, providing the increased number of synaptic junctions required for increasingly complex reflex activities and processing. During this same period, the brain will "prune" various synaptic connections, so only the most commonly used connections will remain. Some CNS axons remain unmyelinated until about age 25 (e.g., some of the axons in the prefrontal cortex). In general, the axons of PNS neurons continue to myelinate past puberty. A person's ability to carry out higher-order mental functions is a direct result of the level of nervous system maturation.

17.4b Hemispheric Lateralization

Anatomically, the left and right cerebral hemispheres appear identical, but careful examination reveals a number of differences. Humans tend to have shape asymmetry of the frontal and occipital lobes of the brain, called **petalias.** Right-handed individuals tend to have right frontal petalias, meaning that the right frontal lobe projects farther than the left frontal lobe, and left occipital petalias, meaning that the left occipital lobe projects farther than the right occipital lobe. Conversely, left-handed individuals tend to have the reverse pattern (left frontal–right occipital petalias). The hemispheres also differ with respect to some of their functions. Each hemisphere tends to be specialized for certain tasks, a phenomenon called **hemispheric lateralization** (lat'er-al-ī-zā'shŭn), or *cerebral lateralization.* Higher-order centers in both hemispheres tend to have different but complementary functions.

In most people, the left hemisphere is the **categorical hemisphere.** It usually contains the Wernicke area and the motor speech area. It is specialized for language abilities, and is also important in performing sequential and analytical reasoning tasks, such as those required in science and mathematics. This hemisphere appears to direct or partition information into smaller fragments for analysis. The term *categorical hemisphere* reflects this hemisphere's function in categorization and identification.

The other hemisphere (the right in most people) is called the **representational hemisphere,** because it is concerned with visuospatial relationships and analyses. It is the seat of imagination and insight, musical and artistic skill, perception of patterns and spatial relationships, and comparison of sights, sounds, smells, and tastes.

Both cerebral hemispheres remain in constant communication through commissures, especially the corpus callosum, which contains hundreds of millions of axons that project between the hemispheres (**figure 17.11**).

Lateralization of the cerebral hemispheres develops early in life (prior to 5–6 years of age). In a young child, the functions of a damaged or removed hemisphere are often taken over by the other hemisphere before lateralization is complete. Some aspects of lateralization differ between males and females. Women have a thicker posterior part of the corpus callosum due to additional commissural axons in this region. Adult males tend to exhibit more lateralization than females and suffer more functional loss when one hemisphere is damaged.

Hemispheric lateralization is highly correlated with handedness. Right-handed individuals tend to have a slightly different lateralization pattern than those who are left-handed. Neuroanatomic research indicates that the petalia patterns just described differ between left-handed and right-handed individuals. In about 95% of the population, the left hemisphere is the categorical hemisphere, thus correlating with the 90% incidence of right-handed individuals in the population. However, the correlation is not nearly as strict among left-handed people, who may have either hemisphere as their categorical hemisphere. Interestingly, a thicker corpus callosum in left-handers suggests that more signals may be relayed between their hemispheres. Finally, the left hemisphere is the speech-dominant hemisphere; it controls speech in almost all right-handed people as well as in many left-handed ones.

17.4c Language

The higher-order processes involved in language include reading, writing, speaking, and understanding words. Recall from section 15.3b that two important cortical areas involved in language are the Wernicke area and the motor speech area (Broca area) (**figure 17.12**). The **Wernicke area** is involved in interpreting what we read or hear, and being able to produce understandable speech (and not simply speak "jibberish"). In contrast, the **motor speech area** receives axons originating from the Wernicke area and then helps regulate the precise motor activities required for us to speak. Immediately posterior to the Wernicke area is the **angular gyrus,** a region that processes the words we read into a form that we can speak (figure 17.12*a*). First, the Wernicke area sends a speech plan to the motor speech area, which initiates a specific patterned motor program that is transmitted to the primary motor cortex. Next, upper motor neurons in the primary motor cortex (pyramidal cells) signal the lower motor neurons, which then innervate the muscles of the cheeks, larynx, lips, and tongue to produce speech.

The Wernicke area is in the categorical hemisphere in most people. In the representational hemisphere, a cortical region opposite the Wernicke area recognizes the emotional content of speech. A lesion in this area of the cerebrum can make a person unable to understand emotional nuances, such as bitterness or happiness, in spoken words. A lesion in the cortical region of the representational hemisphere opposite the motor speech area results in **aprosodia,** which causes dull, emotionless speech. (Do not immediately assume that some of your instructors have aprosodia, if you frequently experience boring lectures.)

There are several speech disorders that affect the interpretation, processing, and execution of language (including sign language). For example, **apraxia of speech** is a motor function disorder. An individual is consciously aware of what she wants to say but is unable to coordinate and execute the motor commands needed to produce

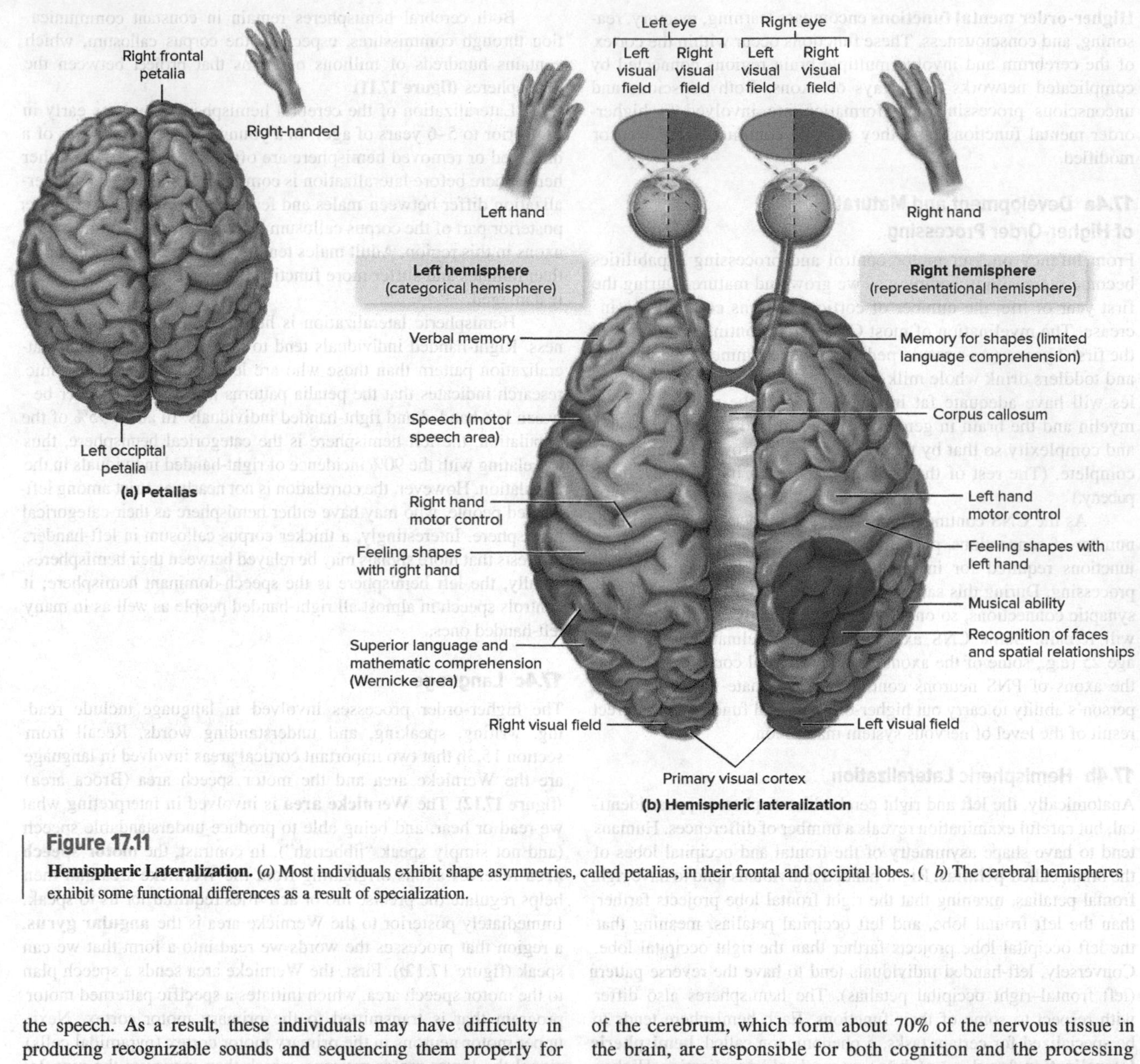
Right frontal petalia
Right-handed
Left occipital petalia
(a) Petalias
Left eye
Right eye
Left visual field
Right visual field
Left visual field
Right visual field
Left hand
Right hand
Left hemisphere (categorical hemisphere)
Right hemisphere (representational hemisphere)
Verbal memory
Memory for shapes (limited language comprehension)
Corpus callosum
Speech (motor speech area)
Left hand motor control
Right hand motor control
Feeling shapes with right hand
Feeling shapes with left hand
Musical ability
Recognition of faces and spatial relationships
Superior language and mathematic comprehension (Wernicke area)
Right visual field
Left visual field
Primary visual cortex
(b) Hemispheric lateralization

Figure 17.11

Hemispheric Lateralization. *(a)* Most individuals exhibit shape asymmetries, called petalias, in their frontal and occipital lobes. (*b*) The cerebral hemispheres exhibit some functional differences as a result of specialization.

the speech. As a result, these individuals may have difficulty in producing recognizable sounds and sequencing them properly for normal speech. In contrast, an individual with **aphasia** (a-fā′zē-ă; speechlessness) has difficulty understanding speech or writing or is unable to produce comprehensible speech. Aphasic individuals may have consistent difficulties finding the correct words and may use nonsense words to describe certain objects. Often, they may not realize that others cannot understand what they are saying. Many cases of aphasia are due to head injury or strokes that damage brain centers responsible for interpreting language. Speech-language pathologists (SLPs) work extensively with those suffering from either apraxia of speech or aphasia to help them improve language understanding and production.

17.4d Cognition

Mental processes such as awareness, knowledge, memory, perception, problem solving, decision making, information processing, and thinking are collectively called **cognition** (kog-ni′shŭn; *cognitio* = to become acquainted with). The association areas of the cerebrum, which form about 70% of the nervous tissue in the brain, are responsible for both cognition and the processing and integration of information between sensory input and motor output areas.

Various studies of individuals suffering from brain lesions (caused by cancer, infection, stroke, and trauma) have helped us determine the functions of the association areas of the cerebrum. For example, the frontal association area (prefrontal cortex) integrates information from the sensory, motor, and association areas to enable the individual to think, plan, and execute appropriate behavior. Thus, an individual with a frontal lobe lesion exhibits personality abnormalities. If a person loses the ability to detect and identify stimuli (termed loss of awareness) on one side of the body or in the limbs on that side, the primary somatosensory area in the hemisphere opposite the affected side of the body has been damaged. An individual who has **agnosia** (ag-nō′zē-ă; *a* = without, *gnosis* = knowledge) displays an inability either to recognize or understand the meaning of various stimuli. For example, a lesion in the temporal lobe may result in the inability either to recognize

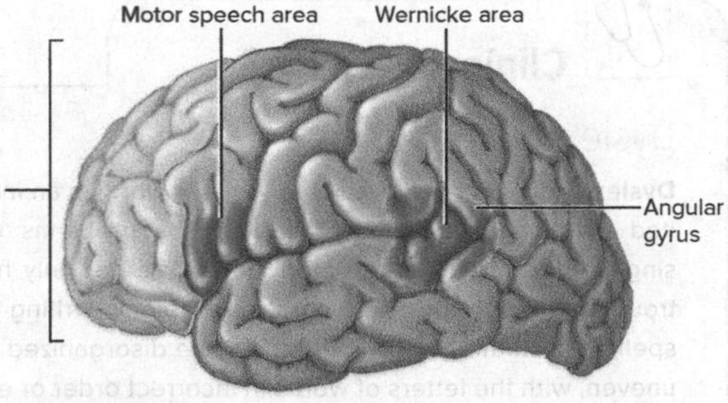

(a) Lateral view

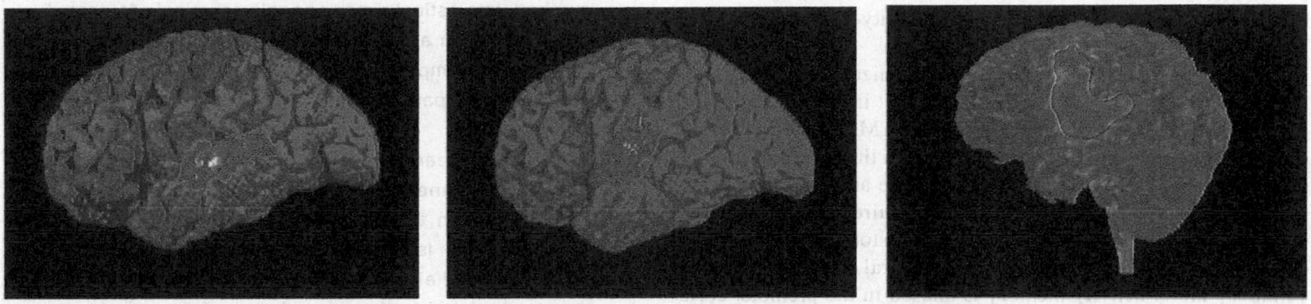

(1) Auditory information about a sentence travels to the primary auditory cortex. The Wernicke area then interprets the sentence.

(2) Information from the Wernicke area travels to the motor speech area.

(3) Information travels from the motor speech area to the primary motor cortex, where motor commands involving muscles used for speech are given.

(b) PET scans

Figure 17.12

Functional Areas Within the Cerebral Cortex. (*a*) In this left lateral view of the brain, the cortical areas involved with speech are highlighted and are the Wernicke area, the motor speech area, the angular gyrus, and the prefrontal cortex. (*b*) PET scans show the areas of the brain that are most active during speech.

(b1-b3) WDCN/Univ. College London/Science Source

Clinical View 17.2

Epilepsy, Lobectomy, and Hemispherectomy

Epilepsy is a disorder in which neurons emit nerve impulses too frequently and rapidly, causing seizures that detrimentally affect motor and sensory function. The seizure activity almost always originates on one side of the brain. Most seizures may be controlled by anticonvulsant medications, but if medications are ineffective, surgery may be the next therapy. Because the most common source of seizures is the temporal lobe, patients may undergo a **temporal lobectomy.** If the seizure source is in a different part of the brain, either an extratemporal lobectomy or a corpus callosotomy may be attempted. In severe cases, a cerebral **hemispherectomy** (hem′ē-sfēr-ek′to-mē) may be performed, in which the entire cerebral hemisphere responsible for the seizure activity is surgically removed. When a hemisphere is removed, additional cerebrospinal fluid fills the space it previously occupied. About 90% to 95% of epilepsy patients experience long-term seizure control following hemispherectomy.

Although brain function does not return to complete normalcy following a hemispherectomy, the remaining hemisphere takes over some of the functions of the missing hemisphere. The younger the individual, the better the chances that the other hemisphere can take over functions previously performed by the missing hemisphere.

or understand the meanings of sounds or words. Specific symptoms of agnosia vary, depending upon the location of the lesion within the cerebrum.

17.4e Memory

Memory is a versatile element of human cognition involving different lengths of time and different storage capacities. Storing and retrieving information requires higher-order mental functions and depends upon complex interactions among different brain regions. On a broader scale, in addition to memory, information management by the brain entails both learning (the acquisition of new information) and forgetting (the elimination of trivial or nonuseful information).

Neuroscientists classify memory in various ways. For example, **sensory memory** occurs when we form important associations based upon sensory input from the environment, such as the sounds coming from a crowded cafeteria, the smell from the food line, and the bright lights from the room. Sensory memory typically lasts for seconds at most.

Short-term memory (STM) follows sensory memory. It is generally characterized by limited capacity (about seven small segments of information) and brief duration (ranging from seconds to hours). Suppose that, in a Friday morning anatomy and physiology lecture, your instructor lists the general functions of the cerebral lobes on the board. Unless you study this information over the weekend, you will probably not recall it by Monday's lecture.

Some short-term memory, if adequately repeated and assessed, may be converted to long-term memory. Once information is placed into **long-term memory (LTM),** it may exist for limitless periods of time. So, for example, if over the weekend you read and recopy your lecture notes, review the text and figures in the book, and prepare note cards, you will have stored the information about the cerebral lobes as LTM. Not only will you be well prepared for your next examination, but you also may even remember this information for years to come. (However, information in LTM needs to be retrieved occasionally or it can be "lost," and our ability to store and retrieve information declines with aging.)

It appears that our brain must organize complex information in short-term memory prior to storing it in long-term memory **(figure 17.13)**. Conversion from STM to LTM is called **encoding,** or *memory consolidation*. Encoding requires the proper functioning of two components of the limbic system: the amygdaloid body and the hippocampus. The hippocampus is required for the formation of STM, whereas long-term memories are stored primarily in the corresponding association areas of the cerebral cortex. For example, voluntary motor activity memory is housed in the premotor cortex and the cerebellum, and memory of sounds is stored in the auditory association area.

Because STM and LTM involve different anatomic structures, loss of the ability to form STM does not affect the maintenance or accessibility of LTM.

WHAT DO YOU THINK?

3 What types of study habits best convert short-term memories into long-term memories? Do you practice these habits when you study for your exams?

17.4f Consciousness

Consciousness includes an awareness of sensation, voluntary control of motor activities, and activities necessary for higher mental processing. Levels of consciousness exist on a continuum. The highest state of consciousness and cortical activity is **alertness,** in which the individual is responsive, aware of self, and well-oriented to person, place, and time.

Consciousness involves the simultaneous activity of large areas of the cerebral cortex. Projecting vertically through the core of the midbrain, pons, and medulla is a loosely organized core of gray

Clinical View 17.3

Dyslexia

Dyslexia (dis-lek'sē-ā; *dys* = bad, *lexis* = word) is an inherited learning disability characterized by problems with single-word decoding. Affected individuals not only have trouble reading, but may also have problems writing and spelling accurately. Their writing may be disorganized and uneven, with the letters of words in incorrect order or even completely reversed. Occasionally, the ability to recognize and interpret the meaning of pictures and objects is also impaired. Interestingly, many people seemingly "outgrow" this condition, or at least develop improved reading ability over time. This improvement may reflect neural maturation or retraining of parts of the brain to better decode words and symbols.

Some researchers have postulated that dyslexia is a form of **disconnect syndrome,** in which transfer of information between the cerebral hemispheres through the corpus callosum is impaired. Genetic studies of a Finnish family identified a defective gene on chromosome 15 that appeared related to the transmission of dyslexia from a father to three of his children. Further research is ongoing to determine the environmental and genetic factors involved in dyslexia.

Randy Faris/Getty Images

Figure 17.13

Model of Information Processing. Cognitive psychologists have proposed a model to show the relationships between sensory memory and short-term memory. Long-term memory develops later.

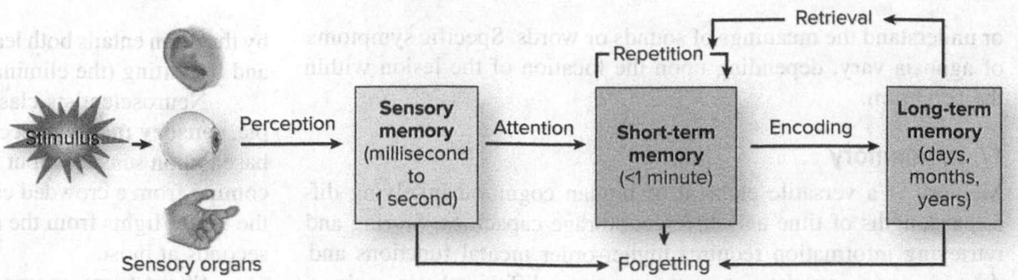

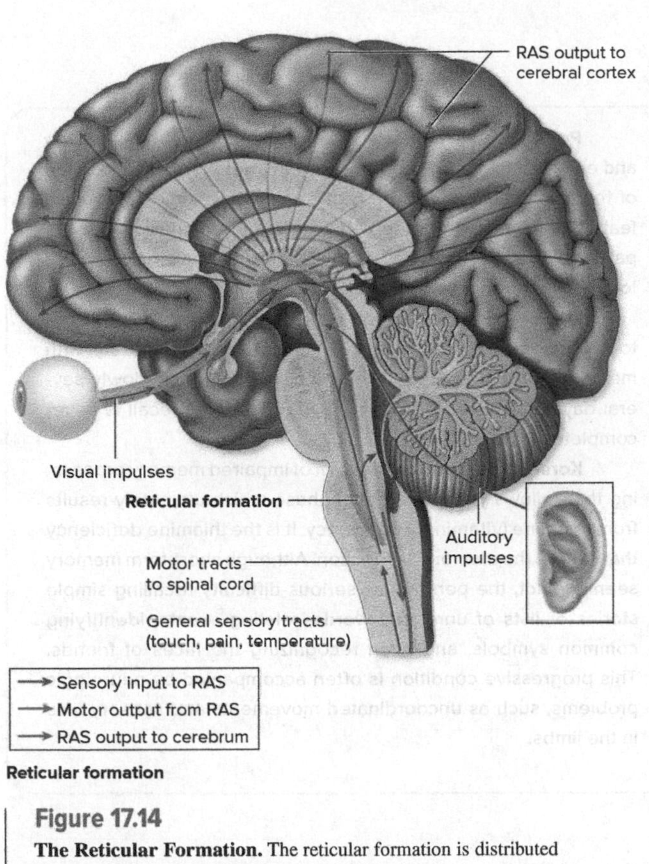
RAS output to cerebral cortex
Visual impulses
Reticular formation
Auditory impulses
Motor tracts to spinal cord
General sensory tracts (touch, pain, temperature)
Sensory input to RAS
Motor output from RAS
RAS output to cerebrum
Reticular formation

Figure 17.14

The Reticular Formation. The reticular formation is distributed throughout the brainstem. The reticular formation receives and processes various types of stimuli (blue arrow). It participates in cyclic activities such as arousing the cortex to consciousness (purple arrow) and controlling the sleep-wake cycle. Some outputs from the reticular formation influence muscle activity (red arrow).

matter called the **reticular formation (figure 17.14)**. The reticular formation extends slightly into the diencephalon and the spinal cord as well. This functional brain system has both motor and sensory components.

The motor component of the reticular formation communicates with the spinal cord and is responsible for regulating muscle tone (especially when the muscles are at rest). The motor component of the reticular formation also assists in autonomic motor functions, such as respiration, blood pressure, and heart rate, by working with the autonomic centers in the medulla and pons.

The sensory component of the reticular formation is responsible for alerting the cerebrum to incoming sensory information. This component, also known as the **reticular activating system (RAS),** contains sensory axons that project to the cerebral cortex. The RAS processes visual, auditory, and touch stimuli and uses this information to keep us in a state of mental alertness. Additionally, the RAS arouses us from sleep. The sound of an alarm clock can awaken us because the RAS receives various sensory stimuli and sends it to the cerebrum, thereby arousing it. Conversely, little or no stimuli (e.g., when you are in bed with the lights out, and no sounds are disturbing you) allow you to sleep, because the RAS is not stimulated to act.

17.4g Electroencephalogram

An **electroencephalogram (EEG)** is a diagnostic test where electrodes are attached to the head to record the electrical activity of the brain **(figure 17.15)**. This procedure is performed to investigate sleep disorders, brain lesions, and to determine if an individual is in a coma or a persistent vegetative state (see Clinical View 17.5: "Pathologic States of Consciousness," in section 17.5). EEGs also may evaluate a **seizure,** which is an event of abnormal electrical activity in the brain. There are different types of seizures, some of which may result in a brief blackout, and others that may result in shaking and muscle spasms. **Epilepsy** is the condition where a person experiences repeated seizures over time (see Clinical View 17.2:"Epilepsy, Lobectomy, and Hemispherectomy" in section 17.4d).

An EEG measures and plots four types of brain waves (i.e., alpha, beta, theta, and delta). The distribution and frequency of these waves varies, depending upon whether the person is a child or an adult and if the individual is in a deep sleep, having a seizure, or is experiencing a pathologic state of consciousness. For example, alpha and beta waves are typically seen in an awake or alert state, whereas theta and delta waves are more common during sleep. The presence of theta and delta waves in an awake adult is suggestive of a brain abnormality. Each electrode attached to a person's head will register a brain wave over that region of the head, so a patient's EEG printout will show multiple brain waves over a period of time.

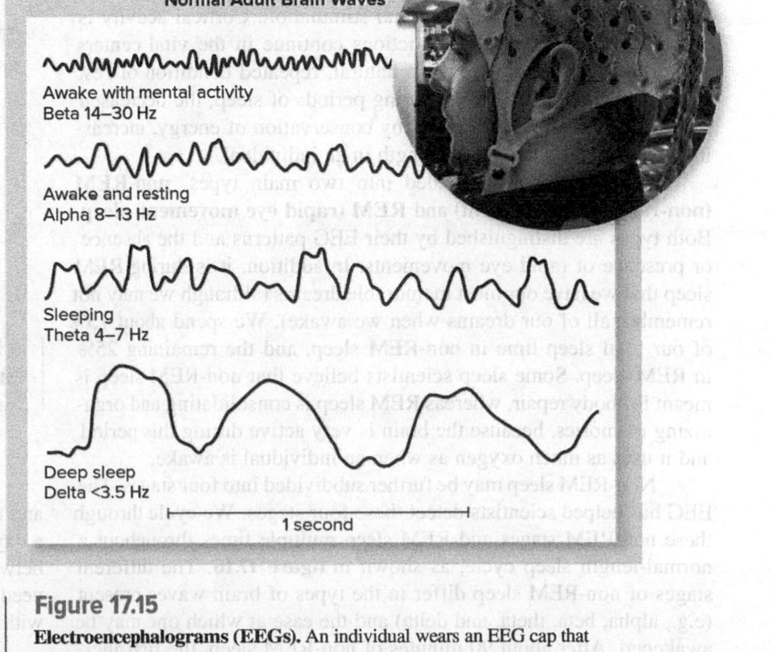
Normal Adult Brain Waves
Awake with mental activity
Beta 14–30 Hz
Awake and resting
Alpha 8–13 Hz
Sleeping
Theta 4–7 Hz
Deep sleep
Delta <3.5 Hz
1 second

Figure 17.15

Electroencephalograms (EEGs). An individual wears an EEG cap that contains multiple electrodes to record brain wave activity, and a sample EEG recording is shown.

Daniel Mihailescu/AFP/Getty Images

Clinical View 17.4

Amnesia

Amnesia (am-nē′zē-ă; forgetfulness) refers to complete or partial loss of memory. Most often, amnesia is temporary and affects only a portion of a person's experiences. Causes of amnesia range from psychological trauma to direct brain injury, such as a severe blow to the head or even a cerebrovascular accident (CVA). There are several types of amnesia.

Anterograde (an′ter-ō-grād; moving ahead) **amnesia** is a form in which a person finds it hard or even impossible to process and/or store ongoing events, although his or her memories from the past are intact and retrievable. Because day-to-day events are forgotten so quickly, the world is always new to the person with anterograde amnesia. Some medications, including general anesthetics, illicit drugs, and even alcohol, temporarily disrupt memory processing, resulting in temporary anterograde amnesia immediately following their use.

In **retrograde** (ret′rō-grād; behind) **amnesia,** the person loses memories of past events. Short-term retrograde amnesia may follow a blow to the head, as might occur in an auto accident or a football game. These patients often experience a memory gap spanning as much as 20 minutes immediately preceding the event.

Posttraumatic amnesia follows a head injury. The duration and extent of the amnesia depend upon the severity and location of the brain damage. Posttraumatic amnesia commonly involves features of both retrograde and anterograde amnesia, with the patient exhibiting decreased ability to recall past events as well as to process current events.

Hysterical amnesia covers episodes of memory loss linked to psychological trauma. The condition is usually temporary, with memories of the traumatic event typically returning slowly several days afterward. For some people, however, recall is never complete.

Korsakoff syndrome is a form of impaired memory processing that follows years of alcohol abuse which ultimately results from thiamine (vitamin B_1) deficiency. It is the thiamine deficiency that causes the memory disfunction. Although short-term memory seems intact, the person has serious difficulty recalling simple stories or lists of unrelated words, relating events, identifying common symbols, and even recognizing the faces of friends. This progressive condition is often accompanied by neurologic problems, such as uncoordinated movements and sensory loss in the limbs.

17.4h Sleep

People normally alternate between periods of alertness and **sleep,** which is the natural, temporary absence of consciousness from which a person can be aroused by normal stimulation. Cortical activity is depressed during sleep, but functions continue in the vital centers within the brainstem. Sleep is a natural, repeated condition of rest for both the body and mind. During periods of sleep, the decreased body activities are accompanied by conservation of energy, increasing growth, and renewal of strength in an individual.

Sleep may be subdivided into two main types, **non-REM (non-rapid eye movement)** and **REM (rapid eye movement) sleep.** Both types are distinguished by their EEG patterns and the absence or presence of rapid eye movements. In addition, it is during REM sleep that we have our most memorable dreams (although we may not remember all of our dreams when we awake). We spend about 75% of our total sleep time in non-REM sleep, and the remaining 25% in REM sleep. Some sleep scientists believe that non-REM sleep is meant for body repair, whereas REM sleep is consolidating and organizing memories, because the brain is very active during this period and it uses as much oxygen as when an individual is awake.

Non-REM sleep may be further subdivided into four stages. The EEG has helped scientists detect these four stages. We cycle through these non-REM stages and REM sleep multiple times throughout a normal-length sleep cycle, as shown in **figure 17.16**. The different stages of non-REM sleep differ in the types of brain waves present (e.g., alpha, beta, theta, and delta) and the ease at which one may be awakened. After about 90 minutes of non-REM sleep, the first incidence of REM sleep occurs and typically lasts about 10 minutes. The body then cycles back into non-REM sleep and then a longer period of REM sleep.

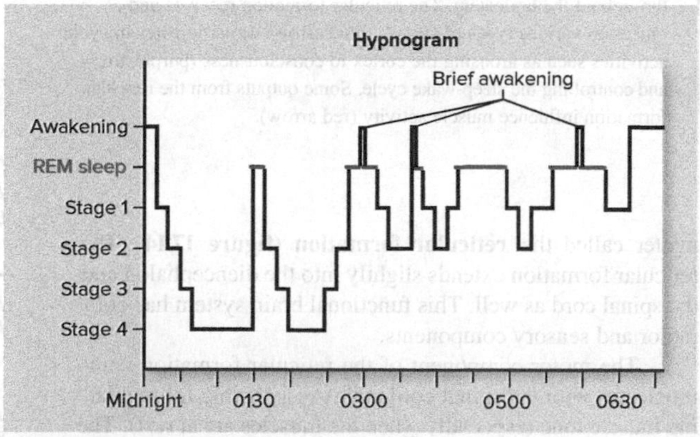

Figure 17.16
Hypnogram. A hypnogram documents the length of time a person is in each sleep stage.

The amount of sleep a person needs varies based upon our age and our health. Infants typically need up to 17 to 18 hours of sleep a day, and this number drops as we get older. Teens typically need between 8.5 and 9.5 hours of sleep a night, whereas the average adult needs about 7 to 8 hours of sleep. Lack of sleep has been associated with depression, impaired memory, and decreased immune function.

The term **insomnia** refers to the difficulty in falling asleep and staying asleep. Insomnia becomes more prevalent as we age, and certain medications may interfere with sleep (including how frequently we experience REM sleep) as well. **Sleep apnea** is where a person experiences

Clinical View 17.5

Pathologic States of Unconsciousness

The level of consciousness of a healthy person varies greatly during a 24-hour period, ranging from wide awake and alert to deep sleep. When a person is asleep, he or she is technically unconscious, but not pathologically so. Prior to entering the sleep state, an individual becomes **lethargic** (leth'ăr-jik), a normal level of reduced alertness and awareness associated with an inclination to sleep.

Other unconscious conditions are pathologic. A brief loss of consciousness, termed **fainting,** or **syncope** (sin'kō-pē), often signals inadequate cerebral blood flow due to low blood pressure, as might follow hemorrhage or sudden emotional stress. **Stupor** (stū'pŏr; *stupeo* = to be stunned) is a moderately deep level of unconsciousness from which the person can be aroused only by extreme repeated or painful stimuli. A stupor may be associated with metabolic disorders such as low blood sugar, diseases of the liver or kidney, CVA or other brain trauma, or drug use.

A **coma** is a deep and profound state of unconsciousness from which the person cannot be aroused, even by repeated or painful stimuli. A person in a coma is alive, but unable to respond to the environment. A coma may result from severe head injury or CVA, marked metabolic failure (as occurs in advanced liver and kidney disease), very low blood sugar, or drug use. To gauge the depth of a coma, and possibly identify the cause, the physician performs a detailed neurologic exam.

A **persistent vegetative state (PSV)** is a condition in which the person has lost his or her thinking ability and awareness of the environment, but noncognitive brain functions continue, such as the brainstem's monitoring of heart rate, breathing, and the sleep-wake cycle. People in a persistent vegetative state are unable to speak and do not respond to commands. However, some people in this state exhibit spontaneous movements, such as moving their eyes, grimacing, crying, and even laughing.

repeated breathing interruptions during sleep. These breathing interruptions cause the individual to wake repeatedly throughout the night, so the individual is at risk to a variety of ailments associated with lack of sleep. Sleep apnea may be treated with a **CPAP (continuous positive airway pressure) machine,** where air is pumped through a mask that the patient wears during sleep so as to keep the airways open and allow the individual to sleep uninterrupted.

WHAT DID YOU LEARN?

9. Distinguish between the activities controlled by the left and right cerebral hemispheres.
10. What is the function of the Wernicke area?
11. What is cognition?
12. What is meant by encoding with respect to memory formation?
13. How does the reticular activating system relate to the reticular formation, and how do both relate to consciousness?
14. What are the main differences between non-REM and REM sleep?

17.5 Aging and the Nervous System

✓ Learning Objective

12. List and describe the effects of aging on the nervous system.

Noticeable effects of aging on the brain and nervous system commence at about 30 years of age. Structural changes occur in nervous tissue, in the blood vessels of the brain, and in the brain's gross appearance. However, it must be emphasized that although aging may result in some brain atrophy, recognizable changes in brain size may not necessarily occur. Functional changes in the brain affect its performance and the body's ability to maintain homeostasis. Structural and functional changes overlap somewhat because, for example, a decrease in a blood vessel's carrying capacity (a structural change) often results in diminished metabolic activity in a particular brain region (a functional change).

Structurally, at the tissue level the number of neurons in the brain diminishes. Neurons that die are not replaced; thus, the amount of gray matter decreases. Superficial observation confirms that overall weight is reduced in older individuals. Loss of neurons causes a reduction in the number of synaptic connections, which adversely affects brain function due to diminished communication between neurons. Reduction in the number of sensory neurons leads to diminished ability to detect and discriminate among external stimuli such as pain, light touch, pressure, and postural changes. Because the affected individual cannot appropriately assess the immediate environment, he or she may exhibit reduced control and coordination of movement. Physical injury is also possible, due to the inability to assess and avoid harmful stimuli, such as a hot object or a noxious odor.

In addition, blood flow to specific brain regions decreases because deposited lipids and atherosclerotic plaques often cause narrowing of the internal walls of blood vessels. The resulting diminished nutrient supply affects nervous tissue performance.

Ultimately, any decrease in the number of neurons, the number of interneuronal synapses, or the supply of nutrients and removal of wastes impairs a person's cognitive capacity.

Clinical View 17.6

Alzheimer Disease: The "Long Goodbye"

Alzheimer disease (AD) has become the leading cause of dementia in the developed world. (**Dementia** refers to a general loss of cognitive abilities, including memory, language, and decision-making skills.)

Alzheimer disease typically becomes clinically apparent in one's 70s or later; **early onset Alzheimer disease** is the diagnosis when an individual develops symptoms before the age of 65. An AD diagnosis is often delayed due to confusion with other forms of cognitive impairment. Symptoms include slow, progressive loss of higher intellectual functions and changes in mood and behavior. AD gradually causes language deterioration, impaired visuospatial skills, indifferent attitude, and poor judgment, while leaving motor function intact. AD progresses relentlessly over months and years, and thus has come to be known as "the long goodbye." Eventually, it robs its victims of their memory, their former personality, and even the capacity to speak.

As people age, mental decline often appears to be related to altered or decreased numbers of synapses between neurons. Many different avenues of research suggest that the key to brain vitality is brain activity. Ways to stimulate an active brain include taking a daily walk, playing games, attending plays or lectures, gardening, working crosswords or other puzzles, reading and writing daily, or participating in community groups.

The underlying cause of AD remains a mystery, although both genetics and environment seem to play a role. Postmortem examinations of the brains of AD patients show marked and generalized cerebral atrophy. Microscopic examinations of brain tissue reveal a profound decrease in the number of cerebral cortical neurons, and a proliferation of two abnormal types of structures, **amyloid** (am'i-loyd) **plaques** and **neurofibrillary tangles.** Amyloid plaques are insoluble deposits of a protein called **beta amyloid,** along with portions of neurons and microglial cells. Neurofibrillary tangles are formed from a protein called **tau** that is hyperphosphorylated (i.e., contains excess amounts of phosphate). Researchers are not sure if the plaques and tangles are the cause of AD, or merely a by-product of the disease's manifestations. Biochemical alterations also occur, most significantly a decreased level of the neurotransmitter acetylcholine in the cerebrum.

At present, there is no cure for AD, although some medications help alleviate the symptoms and seem to slow the progress of the disease. In the meantime, researchers are trying to develop diagnostic tests that can better predict who may be at risk for AD. Until recently, the only way to definitively diagnose AD was at autopsy, when the brain could be macroscopically and microscopically examined. Now, positron emission tomography (PET) scans appear to be able to identify the early brain changes seen in AD. Unfortunately, PET scans are not widely available at health-care facilities and their cost may be prohibitive.

Research has suggested that difficulty or loss in identifying common smells (like lemon, cinnamon, etc.) is linked with an increased risk in developing AD. In fact, this loss of smell may be one of the first signs of developing the disease, presumably because the brain regions involved with smell are among the first regions to develop the neurofibrillary tangles of AD.

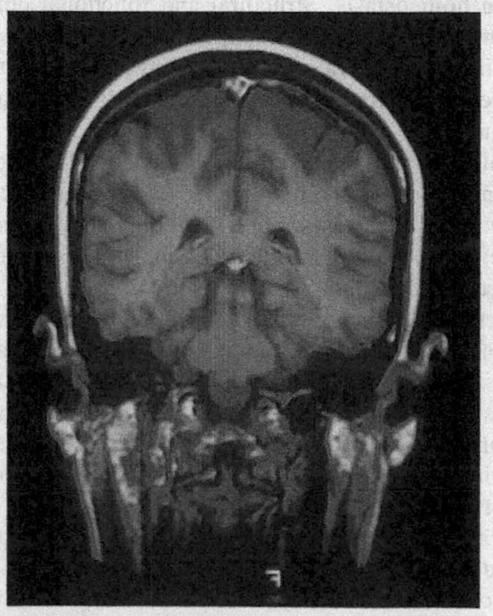

(a) Normal brain

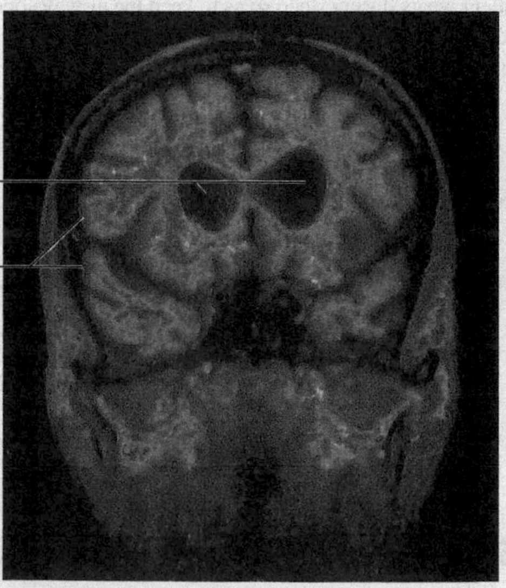
Enlarged ventricles
Cortical atrophy

(b) Alzheimer brain

MRIs show coronal sections of (a) a normal brain and (b) an Alzheimer brain. (Note the large ventricles and wide spaces between gyri in the AD brain.)

(a) Stevie Grand/Science Source; (b) James Cavallini/Custom Medical Stock Photo/Newscom

Clinical Terms

ataxia (ă-tak′s ē-ă; *a* = not, *taxis* = order) Inability to perform coordinated body movements.

delirium (dē-lir′ ē-ŭm; *deliro* = to be crazy) Altered state of consciousness consisting of confusion, distractibility, disorientation, disordered thinking and memory, defective perception, hyperactivity, agitation, and autonomic nervous system overactivity.

hemiballismus (hem′ē-bal-iz′m ŭs; *ballismos* = jumping about) Jerking, involuntary movement involving proximal limb musculature on only one side of the body.

Chapter Summary

17.1 General Characteristics of Nervous System Pathways	■ Sensory and motor pathways share the following characteristics: decussation, somatotopy, pairing, and usually two or three neurons within the CNS.
17.2 Sensory Pathways	■ Pathways of the somatosensory system mediate limb position, touch, temperature, and pain. **17.2a Functional Anatomy of Sensory Pathways** ■ Primary neurons conduct stimuli to the CNS; secondary neurons are interneurons that synapse either onto a tertiary neuron within the thalamus or in the cerebellum. Decussation occurs by axons of either the primary or secondary neurons. ■ The posterior funiculus–medial lemniscal pathway conducts stimuli of fine touch, precise pressure, and proprioception (posture). ■ The anterolateral pathway (anterior and posterior spinothalamic tracts) transports stimuli related to pain, pressure, temperature, and touch. Decussation of secondary neuron axons occurs in the spinal cord at the level of entry. ■ The spinocerebellar pathway (anterior and posterior spinocerebellar tracts) conducts stimuli to the cerebellum related to tendons, joints, and muscle posture.
17.3 Motor Pathways	■ The motor pathways of the brain and spinal cord work together to control skeletal muscle. **17.3a Functional Anatomy of Motor Pathways** ■ Somatic motor pathways involve an upper motor neuron and a lower motor neuron. ■ Somatic motor commands travel through either the direct system (conscious control) or the indirect system (unconscious control). ■ Pyramidal cells are primary motor cortex neurons; the pyramidal pathway provides a rapid, direct mechanism for conscious skeletal muscle control. It consists of two pairs of descending motor tracts: the corticobulbar tracts, the lateral corticospinal tracts, and the anterior corticospinal tracts. ■ The indirect pathway is composed of centers that issue motor commands at an unconscious level: the rubrospinal, reticulospinal, tectospinal, or vestibulospinal tracts. ■ The cerebral nuclei are processing centers for patterned background movement (such as arm swinging while walking). They adjust motor commands issued in other processing centers. ■ The cerebellum helps regulate the functions of the descending somatic motor pathways by influencing and controlling movement. **17.3b Levels of Processing and Motor Control** ■ Complex motor patterns are controlled and coordinated by the cerebellum, cerebral nuclei, midbrain, and frontal lobes of the cerebrum.
17.4 Higher-Order Processing and Integrative Functions	■ Higher-order mental functions encompass learning, memory, reasoning, and consciousness. **17.4a Development and Maturation of Higher-Order Processing** ■ Higher-order functions mature and increase in complexity as development proceeds. **17.4b Hemispheric Lateralization** ■ In most individuals, the left hemisphere is the categorical hemisphere, and the right is the representational hemisphere. **17.4c Language** ■ The Wernicke area is responsible for recognition of spoken and written language. The motor speech area initiates a specific motor program for the muscles of the cheeks, larynx, lips, and tongue to produce speech. **17.4d Cognition** ■ Mental processes such as awareness, perception, thinking, knowledge, and memory are collectively called cognition. **17.4e Memory** ■ Memory is a higher-order mental function involving the storage and retrieval of information gathered through previous activities. Memory classifications include sensory memory, short-term memory (STM), working memory, and long-term memory (LTM). **17.4f Consciousness** ■ The highest state of consciousness and cortical activity is alertness. Sleep is a natural, temporary absence of consciousness.

(continued on next page)

Chapter Summary *(continued)*

	17.4g Electroencephalogram ■ An electroencephalogram monitors brain activity by measuring brain waves through the use of electrodes. **17.4h Sleep** ■ Sleep is a period of rest for the brain and involves cycles of REM (rapid eye movement) and non-REM (non-rapid eye movement) activity.
17.5 Aging and the Nervous System	■ Both structural and functional changes accompany the aging of the brain. Some of these changes are reduced neuron population, including sensory neurons; reduced blood flow through the brain; and reduced cognition.

Challenge Yourself

Actively write or type your answers in a separate document to reinforce your learning, before checking your answers.

Multiple Choice

Select the best answer from the four choices provided.

1. The fasciculus cuneatus and fasciculus gracilis compose which of the following?
   a. spinocerebellar tracts
   b. posterior funiculi
   c. spinothalamic tracts
   d. anterior white commissure
2. Which motor tracts conduct impulses to regulate the skilled movements of the upper and lower limbs?
   a. reticulospinal tracts
   b. corticospinal tracts
   c. rubrospinal tracts
   d. tectospinal tracts
3. Which of the following spinal cord tracts does *not* transmit sensation from the lower limb?
   a. fasciculus gracilis
   b. anterior spinocerebellar tract
   c. posterior spinocerebellar tract
   d. lateral corticospinal tract
4. Which of these are *not* part of an indirect motor pathway?
   a. rubrospinal tracts
   b. tectospinal tracts
   c. corticobulbar tracts
   d. reticulospinal tracts
5. Pyramidal cell axons project through corticospinal tracts and synapse at which structures?
   a. motor nuclei of cranial nerves
   b. motor neurons in the anterior horns of the spinal cord
   c. motor neurons in the posterior horns of the spinal cord
   d. motor neurons in the lateral horns of the spinal cord
6. The right hemisphere tends to be dominant for which functions?
   a. mathematical calculations
   b. motor commands involved with speech
   c. musical and artistic skills
   d. analytic reasoning
7. Which type of brain waves are prevalent when an individual is in deep sleep?
   a. theta and alpha
   b. beta and delta
   c. theta and delta
   d. alpha and delta
8. Motor and sensory pathways share many characteristics. Of the following, which is seen only with sensory pathways?
   a. Most pathways decussate.
   b. The neurons utilized are called primary, secondary, and tertiary neurons.
   c. All pathways are composed of paired tracts.
   d. Neuron cell bodies are located in ganglia within the PNS, gray horns of the spinal cord, or brain nuclei.
9. Which of these is the least likely to affect information transfer from STM (short-term memory) to LTM (long-term memory)?
   a. emotional state
   b. repetition or rehearsal
   c. auditory association cortex
   d. cerebral nuclei
10. Where are tertiary neurons located?
    a. extending between the posterior horn and the anterior horn
    b. extending between the posterior horn and the brainstem
    c. extending between the thalamus horn and the primary somatosensory cortex
    d. extending between the primary motor cortex and the brainstem

Content Review

1. Describe the function of primary neurons, secondary neurons, and tertiary neurons in the sensory pathways of the nervous system.
2. Describe the sensory pathway by which the pressure applied to the right hand during a handshake is transmitted and perceived in the left primary somatosensory cortex.
3. What are the main differences between the indirect pathway and direct pathway tracts?
4. Identify and describe the distribution of the motor pathways that conduct conscious, voluntary motor impulses through the spinal cord.
5. Describe the relationship between the cerebral nuclei and the cerebellum in motor activities.
6. What are the roles of the Wernicke area, the motor speech area, and the angular gyrus with respect to producing speech?
7. Explain the process by which something may be committed to long-term memory. How does long-term memory differ from sensory memory and short-term memory?

8. Describe the activities of the reticular activating system. What role does it play in both consciousness and sleep?
9. Compare and contrast the amount of sleep infants, young children, teenagers, and adults typically need. What percentage of that sleep typically is non-REM sleep?
10. What is the consequence of reduction in the number of sensory neurons during aging?

Developing Critical Reasoning

1. Melissa had a horrible headache, restricted movement in her right arm, and slight slurring of her speech. After an MRI was performed, the ER physician suggested that Melissa had suffered a CVA (cerebrovascular accident). What structures in the brain were affected by this incident? What might be the cause of the problem and the expected outcome?
2. Randolph, a college professor, suffered a severe blow to the head while being robbed at an ATM. This trauma caused him to be unable to impart any emotion into his lectures, although he could still speak. Identify Randolph's condition, and locate the area of damage to his brain.
3. While undergoing surgery, George suffered complications and slipped into a pathologic state of unconsciousness. He cannot be awakened and does not respond at all to any stimuli. Based on this description, what state of unconsciousness do you think George is in, and why? What would you predict his EEG may show?

Answers to "What Do You Think?"

1. No one is quite sure why most pathways decussate. Some researchers have speculated that in more primitive brain systems, most pathways were bilateral (a combination of decussating and undecussating pathways), and as brains evolved, only one of the two pathways remained (typically, the decussating pathway). However, this hypothesis has not been proven and does not explain why the decussating pathways would remain.
2. If our brains were consciously aware of every single sensory stimulus, we would go on "sensory overload." There would be too many sensations to effectively process and interpret, and we would not be able to concentrate on the task at hand. For example, being able to "tune out" many sensory stimuli allows you to study in a crowded student lounge with the music blaring.
3. Study habits that repeat and reinforce the material are best for converting short-term memories into long-term memories. Rewriting your notes, making flashcards, reading the text, and reviewing the material on a regular basis (not just once or twice) all help form long-term memory.

Design Element: Pencil Icon: Slavojub Pantelic/Shutterstock

NERVOUS SYSTEM

18 Autonomic Nervous System

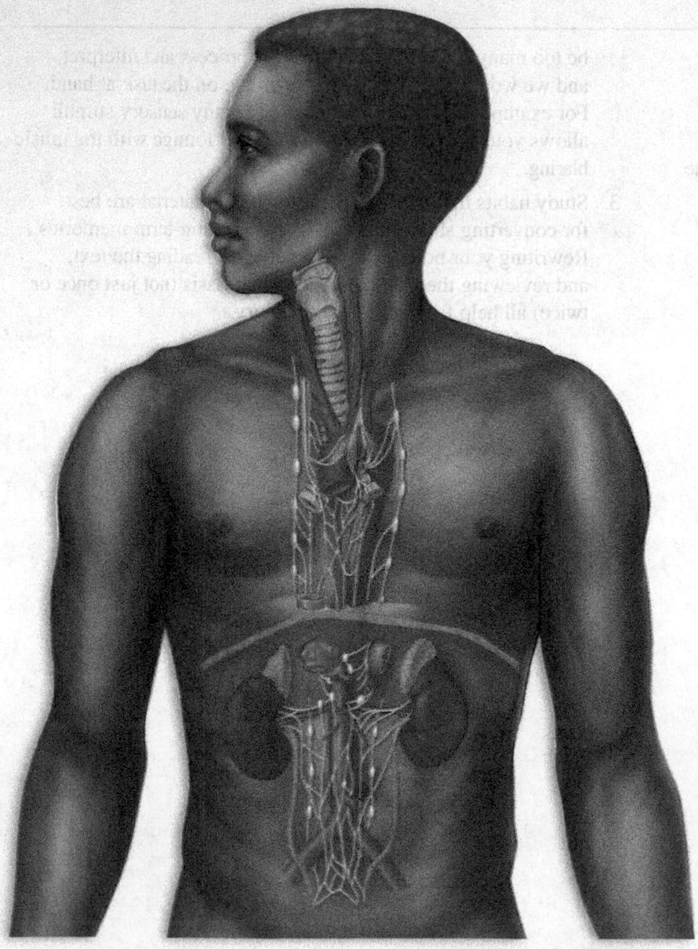

Outline

Anatomy & Physiology Revealed 4.0
MODULE 7: NERVOUS SYSTEM

On a twisting downhill slope, an Olympic skier is concentrating on controlling his body to negotiate the course faster than anyone else in the world. Compared to the spectators in the viewing areas, his pupils are more dilated, and his heart is beating faster and pumping more blood to his skeletal muscles. At the same time, organ system functions not needed in the race are practically shut down. Digestion, urination, and defecation can be delayed until the race is over. The skier exhibits a state of heightened readiness, called the "fight-or-flight" response, because the sympathetic division of the autonomic nervous system is dominant.

We introduce this chapter on the autonomic nervous system by first describing how the nervous system is organized into a somatic nervous system and an autonomic nervous system. We then compare their functional organizations and the CNS regions that control the autonomic nervous system.

18.1 Comparison of the Somatic and Autonomic Nervous Systems

✓ Learning Objectives

1. Compare and contrast the anatomy and functions of the SNS and the ANS.
2. Explain how the two-neuron pathway facilitates communication and control in the ANS.

Recall from section 14.1 that anatomists and physiologists have devised various ways to organize the nervous system both structurally and functionally. Here, we introduce a slightly different way of functionally organizing the nervous system into two systems that is based upon whether we are conscious of the process. The two components are the somatic nervous system and the autonomic nervous system (**figure 18.1**).

The **somatic nervous system (SNS)** includes processes that are perceived or consciously controlled (figure 18.1*a*). The **somatic sensory** portion includes detection of stimuli and transmission of nerve impulses from the *special senses* (i.e., vision, hearing, equilibrium, smell, and taste), *skin,* and *proprioceptors* (receptors in joints and muscles that detect body position) to the CNS. The sensory portion of the somatic nervous system, for example, allows us to see a beautiful mountain, smell a baby's skin, or taste a delicious dinner. The **somatic motor** portion involves initiation and transmission of nerve impulses from the CNS to control *skeletal muscles.* This is represented by voluntary activities such as getting out of a chair, picking up a ball, and throwing the ball for a dog to chase. Both the sensory nerve impulses we consciously perceive and the motor nerve impulses that we voluntarily initiate to skeletal muscle involve the cerebrum (see section 15.3b). Reflexive skeletal muscle activity is controlled by the brainstem and spinal cord (see section 16.5).

The **autonomic nervous system (ANS)** (aw-tō-nom′ik; *auto* = self, *nomos* = law), also called the **autonomic motor** or *visceral*

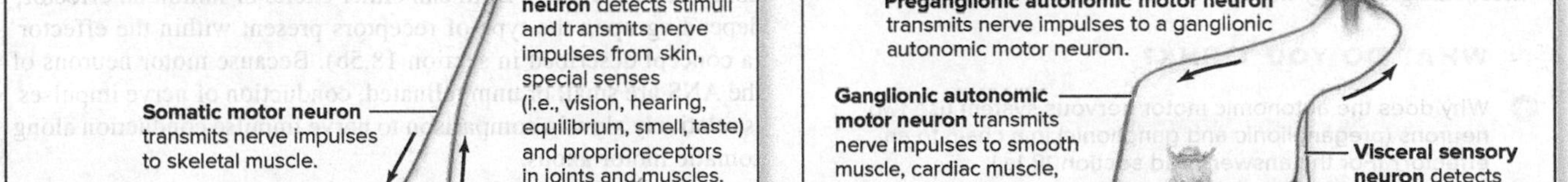

Figure 18.1

Comparison of Somatic and Autonomic Nervous Systems. The nervous system is functionally organized into the (*a*) somatic nervous system, which involves processes that we consciously perceive and control, and the (*b*) autonomic nervous system, which involves processes that occur below the conscious level. (Note that the visceral sensory structures are not part of the ANS per se.)

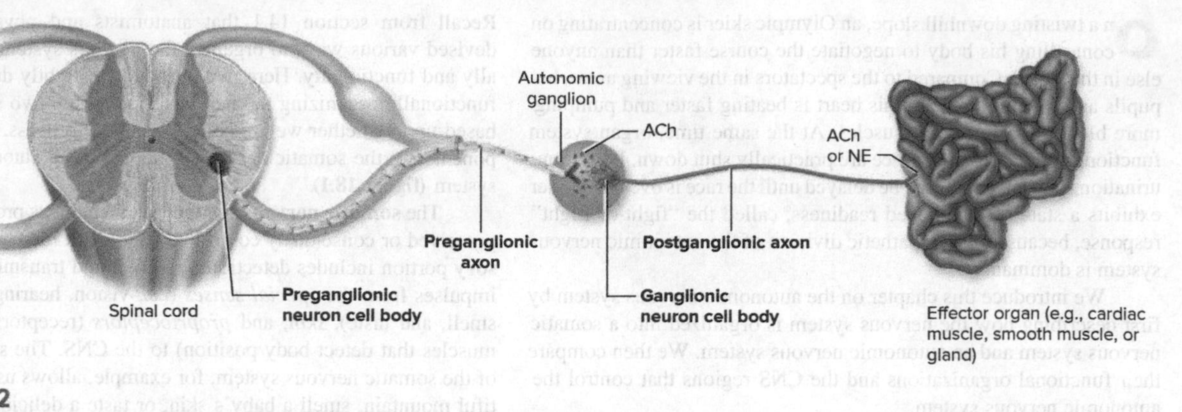

Figure 18.2

Lower Motor Neurons of the Autonomic Nervous System. The autonomic nervous system employs a chain of two lower motor neurons, a preganglionic neuron, and a ganglionic neuron. The dendrites and cell body of a preganglionic neuron are housed within the CNS (brain or spinal cord). The preganglionic axon synapses with a ganglionic neuron within an autonomic ganglion. The preganglionic axon always uses acetylcholine (ACh) to communicate, whereas the postganglionic axon uses either ACh or norepinephrine (NE) at the target organ.

motor system, includes processes regulated below the conscious level (figure 18.1*b*). This system is a motor system (see section 14.1b), which initiates and transmits nerve impulses from the CNS to cardiac muscle, smooth muscle, and glands. The autonomic nervous system often reflexively responds to input from **visceral sensory** components, such as receptors that monitor carbon dioxide concentration in the blood or detect pressure by measuring stretch in smooth muscles of visceral walls. The visceral sensory structures are not part of the ANS per se, but rather, simply transmit input from sensory receptors that may result in motor output by the ANS.

The function of the ANS is to maintain **homeostasis,** or a constant internal environment (see section 1.3a). Thus, the ANS regulates all physiological processes that must be maintained by the nervous system to keep the body alive, including the regulation of heart rate, blood pressure, body temperature, sweating, and digestion. The ANS keeps these processes within optimal ranges and adjusts the variables to meet changing body needs.

WHAT DO YOU THINK?

1. Why does the autonomic motor nervous system use two neurons (preganglionic and ganglionic) in a chain to an effector? (For the answer, read section 18.1a.)

18.1a Motor Neurons of the Somatic Versus Autonomic Nervous System

One significant anatomic difference between the somatic nervous system and autonomic nervous system is the number of lower motor neurons that extend from the CNS. A single lower motor neuron extends from the CNS to skeletal muscle fibers in the somatic nervous system (see figure 18.1*a*). The cell body of a lower motor neuron lies within the brainstem or the spinal cord, and its axon exits the CNS in either a cranial nerve or a spinal nerve to a skeletal muscle, respectively (see sections 15.8 and 16.4). Additionally, the motor neurons of the somatic nervous system (1) are composed of myelinated axons with a large diameter allowing for fast propagation of a nerve impulse; and (2) always release acetylcholine (ACh) neurotransmitter from its synaptic knobs to stimulate or excite the skeletal muscle fiber (see section 10.3b).

In comparison, a chain of two lower motor neurons extends from the CNS to innervate cardiac muscle, smooth muscle, and glands in the ANS (see figure 18.1*b*, **figure 18.2**). The first of the two ANS motor neurons is the **preganglionic** (prē′gang-l ē-on′ik) **neuron.** Its cell body lies within the brainstem or the spinal cord. A **preganglionic axon** extends from this cell body and exits the CNS in either a cranial nerve or a spinal nerve. This axon projects to an autonomic ganglion in the peripheral nervous system. Preganglionic neurons have myelinated axons that typically are small in diameter, and the nerve impulse always results in the release of ACh to excite the second neuron.

The second neuron in this pathway is called a **ganglionic neuron.** Its cell body resides within an autonomic ganglion. A **postganglionic axon** extends from the cell body to an effector (cardiac muscle, smooth muscle, or a gland). Ganglionic neurons have unmyelinated axons that are even smaller in diameter than preganglionic axons. The neurotransmitter released from the ganglionic neuron in response to a nerve impulse is either ACh or norepinephrine (NE). Both can either excite or inhibit an effector, depending upon the type of receptors present within the effector (a concept described in section 18.5b). Because motor neurons of the ANS are small or unmyelinated, conduction of nerve impulses is relatively slow in comparison to nerve impulse conduction along somatic motor axons.

One significant point must be made concerning the two-neuron motor pathway in the ANS: It has a distinctive advantage in that it allows for increasing communication and control. This occurs because there is neuronal convergence and neuronal divergence. **Neuronal convergence** (kon-ver′jens) occurs because axons from numerous preganglionic neurons synapse with and influence a single ganglionic cell. **Neuronal divergence** (di-ver′jens; *di* = two) occurs because axons from one preganglionic cell synapse with and influence numerous ganglionic cells.

Table 18.1 compares and contrasts the characteristics of the somatic and autonomic nervous systems.

WHAT DID YOU LEARN?

1. Draw and label the motor neuron structure for both the SNS and the ANS. Discuss their differences.
2. What organs are innervated by the ANS?
3. Where is a ganglionic neuron cell body located?

Table 18.1	Comparison of Somatic and Autonomic Motor Nervous Systems	
Feature	**Somatic Nervous System**	**Autonomic Nervous System**
Functional Organization		
Sensory Input	Special sense, skin; proprioceptors	Visceral senses (and some somatic senses)
Effectors	Skeletal muscle fibers	Cardiac muscle cells, smooth muscle cells, glands
CNS Region of Control	Cerebral cortex, cerebral nuclei, thalamus, cerebellum, brainstem, spinal cord	Hypothalamus, brainstem, spinal cord Cerebrum, thalamus, limbic system
Motor Neurons		
Number of Neurons in Pathway	One lower motor neuron from CNS: somatic motor neuron axon extends from CNS to effector	Two lower motor neurons from CNS: Preganglionic neuron has preganglionic axon that projects to ganglionic neuron; ganglionic neuron has postganglionic axon that projects to effector
Axon Properties	Myelinated and thicker in diameter; have fast nerve impulse propagation	Preganglionic axons are myelinated and thin in diameter Postganglionic axons are unmyelinated and are thinner in diameter; both have relatively slow nerve impulse propagation
Neurotransmitter Released	Acetylcholine (ACh)	Preganglionic axons release ACh Postganglionic axons release either ACh or norepinephrine (NE)
Response of Effector	Excitation only	Either excitation or inhibition
Ganglia Associated with Motor Neurons	None	Autonomic ganglia: Parasympathetic division: terminal ganglia, intramural ganglia Sympathetic division: sympathetic trunk ganglia, prevertebral ganglia

Learning Strategy 18.1

A good way to understand the two-neuron ANS chain is to compare it to the U.S. airline system, which uses connecting flights and "airport hubs" to transport the maximum number of people in the most cost-effective way. Imagine that you are flying from Indianapolis to Miami for spring break.

Your first flight from Indianapolis to Chicago is the **preganglionic axon.** Although flying north to Chicago is out of your way, the airline sends you to an airport hub because it is more efficient to send all Indianapolis passengers to this main location before they take different flights throughout the United States.

The airport hub in Chicago is the **autonomic ganglion,** the point where preganglionic and postganglionic "flights" meet up. Other preganglionic flights are arriving at the airport hub, and here all these passengers will connect with other flights.

Your connecting flight from Chicago to Miami is the **ganglionic neuron.** This flight will take you to your final destination, just as a postganglionic axon sends a nerve impulse to an effector organ. On the plane with you are people from other preganglionic flights who all want to go to Miami as well.

Is using two different flights the most *direct* way for you to get from Indianapolis to Florida? Of course not. But it is the most *cost-efficient* (or *energy-efficient*) way for the airlines to transport and disperse many passengers with a limited number of planes.

The connecting-flight arrangement also allows for the extensive convergence of passengers to an airport "hub," and for the extensive divergence of passengers from the "hubs" to the final destinations. Thus, the two motor neurons used in the ANS allow for neuronal convergence and divergence.

The autonomic nervous system is similar to connecting airline flights and "airport hubs" in that both try to group and disperse many different items (nerve impulses or passengers) with a limited number of neurons, impulse or flights.

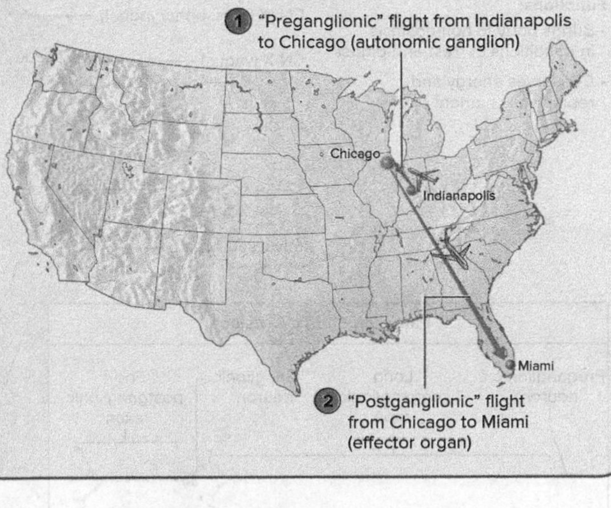

18.2 Divisions of the Autonomic Nervous System

✓ Learning Objectives

3. Describe the functional differences between the parasympathetic and the sympathetic divisions.
4. Compare and contrast the anatomic components of the parasympathetic and sympathetic divisions.

The ANS is subdivided into the parasympathetic division and the sympathetic division. Here we discuss both the general functional and anatomic differences between the two divisions.

18.2a Functional Differences

The divisions perform dramatically different functions—but instead of being thought of as antagonistic, they should be considered complementary. The **parasympathetic** (par-ă-sim-pa-thet'ik; *para* = alongside, *sympatheo* = to feel with) **division** functions to maintain homeostasis when we are at rest. This division is primarily concerned with conserving energy and replenishing nutrient stores. Because it is most active when the body is at rest or digesting a meal, the parasympathetic division has been nicknamed the "rest-and-digest" division.

The **sympathetic** (sim-p ă-thet′ik) **division** functions to maintain homeostasis during exercise or times of stress or emergency, which includes the release of nutrients from stores (e.g., glucose released from the liver). Because of its function in regulating the more active states the sympathetic division has been nicknamed the "fight-or-flight" division. During these fight-or-flight events, the sympathetic division exhibits a mass activation response, whereby all components receiving sympathetic innervation get stimulated.

Learning Strategy 18.2

To help identify when the parasympathetic nervous system is active, remember the three **D's**: **d**igestion, **d**iuresis, and **d**efecation. To remember when the sympathetic nervous system is active, remember the three **E's**: **e**xercise, **e**xcitement, and **e**mergency.

18.2b Anatomic Differences in Lower Motor Neurons

Anatomically, these two divisions are similar in that they typically both use a preganglionic neuron and a ganglionic neuron to innervate cardiac muscle, smooth muscle, or glands. Additionally, both divisions have autonomic ganglia that house the ganglionic neuron cell bodies. One of the major differences is where the preganglionic neuron cell bodies are housed in the CNS (**figure 18.3**). Parasympathetic preganglionic cell bodies are located in either the brainstem or the lateral gray matter of the S2–S4 spinal cord segments, and for this reason this division is also termed the *craniosacral* (krā′nē-ō-sā′krăl) *division*. In comparison, sympathetic preganglionic neuron cell bodies are located in the lateral horns of the T1–L2 spinal cord segments, and for this reason this division is also termed the *thoracolumbar* (thō′ră-kō-lŭm′bar) *division*. Other anatomic differences between the parasympathetic and sympathetic nervous systems include the following:

- **Length of preganglionic and postganglionic axons.** Parasympathetic preganglionic axons are longer, and postganglionic axons are shorter, when compared to their counterparts in the sympathetic division. In the sympathetic division, preganglionic axons are shorter and postganglionic axons are longer.

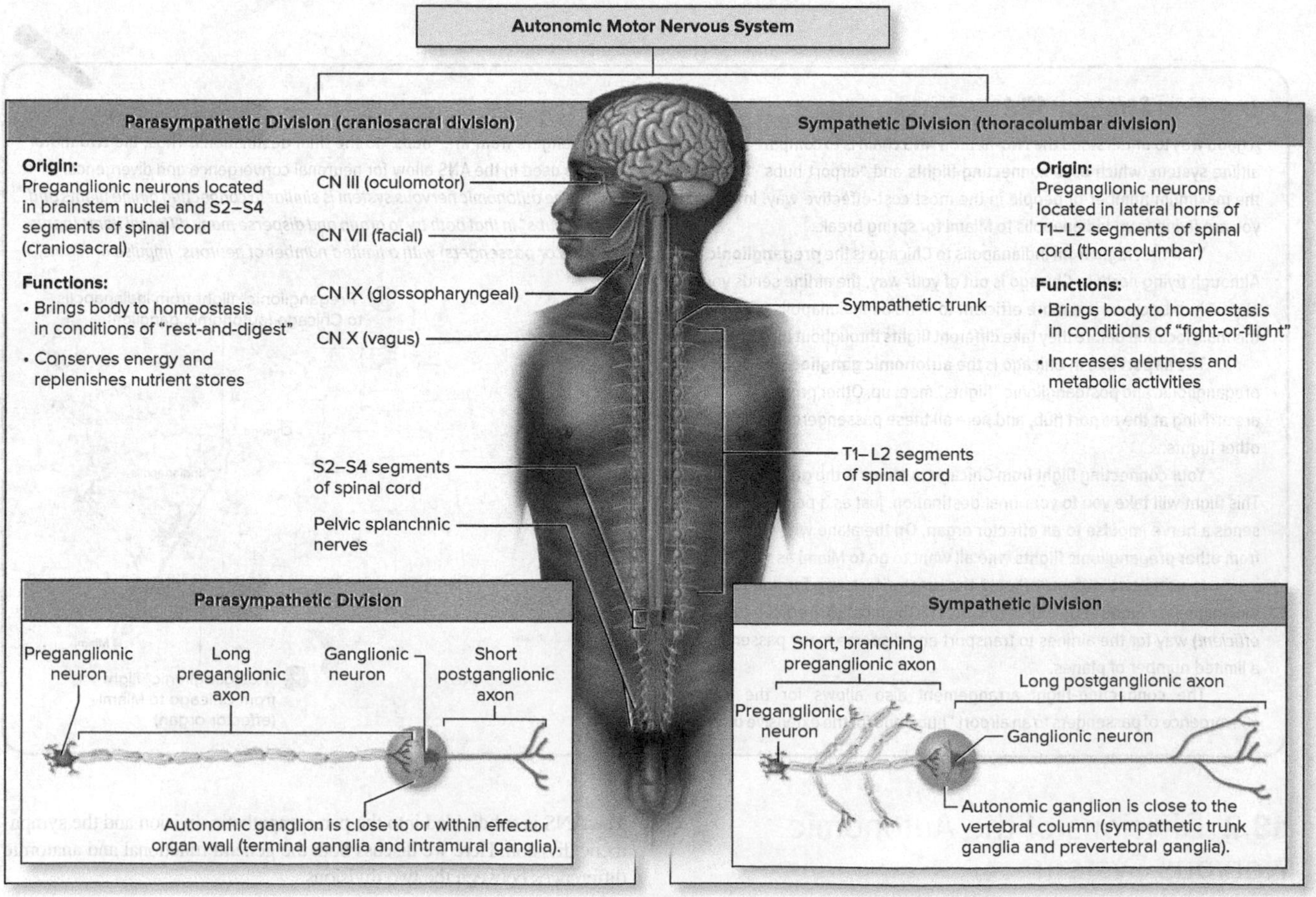

Figure 18.3

Comparison of Parasympathetic and Sympathetic Divisions. The neurons of the parasympathetic division extend from the brainstem and sacral region, whereas the neurons of the sympathetic division extend from the thoracic and lumbar regions of the cord. The parasympathetic division axons exhibit very little branching, and autonomic ganglia lie close to or within the effector organ. The sympathetic division axons of both neurons show much branching, and autonomic ganglia lie close to the vertebral column. APR

Table 18.2 Comparison of Parasympathetic and Sympathetic Divisions of the ANS

Feature	Parasympathetic Division	Sympathetic Division
Function	Maintains homeostasis; conserves energy and replenishes energy stores; "rest-and-digest" division	Prepares body to cope with emergencies; releases energy; "fight-or-flight" division
Location of Preganglionic Neuron Cell Bodies	Brainstem and lateral gray matter in S2–S4 segments of spinal cord; thus it is also called the craniosacral division	Lateral horns in T1–L2 segments of spinal cord; thus it is also called the thoracolumbar division
Divergence of Axons	Few (1 axon innervates < 4 ganglionic neurons)	Extensive (1 axon innervates > 20 ganglionic neurons)
Length of Preganglionic Axon and Number of Branches	Long and has relatively few branches	Short and has many branches (over 20)
Length of Postganglionic Axon	Short	Long
Location of Ganglia	Terminal ganglia located close to the target organ; intramural ganglia located within wall of the target organ	Sympathetic trunk (paravertebral) ganglia located on either side of vertebral column; prevertebral (collateral) ganglia located anterior to vertebral column and descending aorta
Rami Communicantes	None	White rami attach to T1–L2 spinal nerves; gray rami attach to all spinal nerves (see Section 18.4a)
Degree of Response	Local	Mass activation or local

- **Number of preganglionic axon branches.** Parasympathetic preganglionic axons tend to have few (less than 4) branches, whereas sympathetic preganglionic axons tend to have many branches (more than 20).
- **Location of ganglia.** Parasympathetic autonomic ganglia are either close to or within the effector (terminal ganglia and intramural ganglia, respectively). In comparison, sympathetic autonomic ganglia are relatively close to the spinal cord, and are on either side of the spinal cord or anterior to the spinal cord (sympathetic trunk ganglia and prevertebral ganglia, respectively). (These ganglia are described in section 18.4a.)

Figure 18.3 and **table 18.2** compare the parasympathetic and sympathetic divisions of the autonomic nervous system.

WHAT DID YOU LEARN?

4 Describe the anatomic differences between the postganglionic axons in the parasympathetic and sympathetic divisions.

18.3 Parasympathetic Division

✓ Learning Objectives

5. Describe the anatomy of the parasympathetic division.
6. Explain the relationship of the parasympathetic division to the brain, the cranial components, and the pelvic splanchnic nerves.
7. Identify the effects of parasympathetic innervation on effectors.

The parasympathetic division of the ANS is structurally simpler than the sympathetic division. The parasympathetic division is also termed the *craniosacral* (krā′nē-ō-sā′krăl) *division* because its preganglionic neurons are housed within nuclei in the brainstem and within the lateral gray matter of the S2–S4 spinal cord segments. The ganglionic neurons in the parasympathetic division are found in either **terminal** (ter′mi-n ăl; *terminus* = a boundary) **ganglia,** which are located close to the effector, or **intramural** (in′tr ă-myū′răl; *intra* = within, *murus* = wall) **ganglia,** which are located within the wall of the target organ.

18.3a Cranial Components

The cranial nerves associated with the parasympathetic division are the oculomotor (CN III), facial (CN VII), glossopharyngeal (CN IX), and vagus (CN X) (see figure 18.3). The first three of these nerves convey parasympathetic innervation to the head, whereas the vagus nerve is the source of parasympathetic stimulation for the thoracic and most abdominal organs (**figure 18.4**). Recall that these cranial nerves are paired; they are found on the left and right side of the body.

Review table 15.8 for illustrations of the cranial nerve pathways and the locations of their associated parasympathetic ganglia.

Oculomotor Nerve (CN III)

The **oculomotor nerve (CN III)** is formed by axons extending from some cell bodies housed in nuclei in the midbrain. The preganglionic axons extend from CN III to the **ciliary** (sil′ē-ar-ē; *ciliaris* = eyelash) **ganglion** within the orbit. Postganglionic axons project from this ganglion to the ciliary muscle and sphincter pupillae muscle of the iris of the eye (see section 19.5b and figure 19.11). Parasympathetic innervation to the ciliary muscle results in lens accommodation, which makes the lens more rounded so that we can see close-up objects. The postganglionic axons that travel to the pupillary constrictor muscle result in pupil constriction when the eye is exposed to bright light.

Facial Nerve (CN VII)

The **facial nerve (CN VII)** contains parasympathetic preganglionic axons that exit the pons and control the production and secretion of tears, nasal secretions, and saliva. Two branches of parasympathetic preganglionic axons, the *greater petrosal nerve* and the *chorda tympani nerve,* exit the facial nerve and terminate at one of two ganglia. The greater petrosal nerve terminates at the **pterygopalatine** (ter′i-g ō-pal′ă-tīn) **ganglion** near the junction of the maxilla and palatine bones. Postganglionic axons project to the lacrimal gland and small glands of the nasal cavity, oral cavity, and palate to increase secretion by these glands.

The other parasympathetic branch of the facial nerve, the chorda tympani nerve, terminates on ganglionic neurons in the **submandibular** (sŭb′man-dib′y ū-lăr; *sub* = under) **ganglion** near the angle of the mandible. Postganglionic axons projecting from this ganglion supply the submandibular and sublingual salivary glands in the floor of the mouth, causing an increase in salivary gland secretions (see section 26.2c). Thus, your mouth waters when you smell an aromatic meal due in part to these parasympathetic axons.

WHAT DO YOU THINK?

2 The pterygopalatine ganglion is sometimes nicknamed the *hay fever ganglion.* Why is this nickname appropriate?

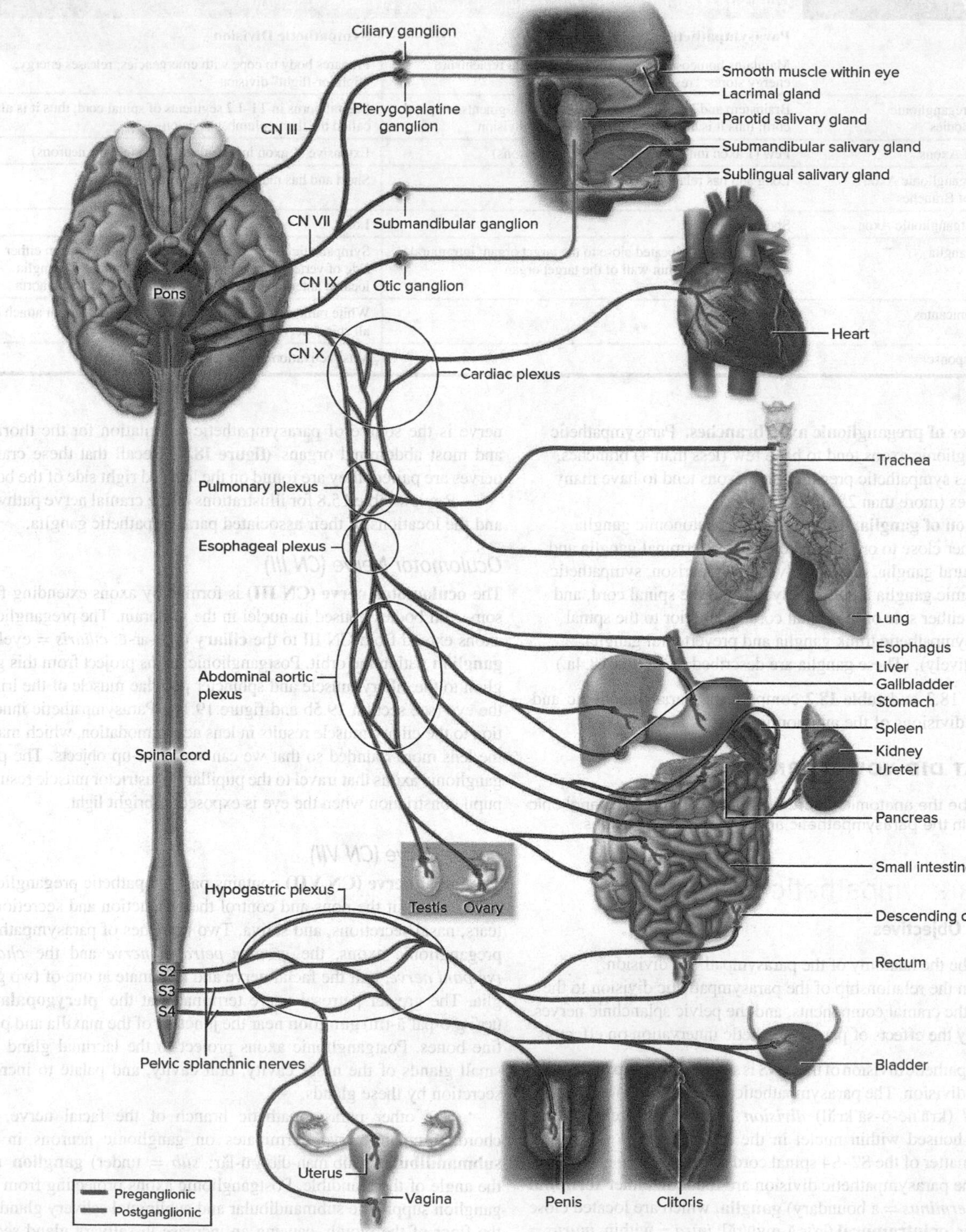

Ciliary ganglion
Smooth muscle within eye
Lacrimal gland
Pterygopalatine ganglion
CN III
Parotid salivary gland
Submandibular salivary gland
Sublingual salivary gland
CN VII
Submandibular ganglion
CN IX
Otic ganglion
Pons
CN X
Heart
Cardiac plexus
Trachea
Pulmonary plexus
Esophageal plexus
Lung
Esophagus
Liver
Gallbladder
Abdominal aortic plexus
Stomach
Spleen
Spinal cord
Kidney
Ureter
Pancreas
Small intestine
Hypogastric plexus
Testis
Ovary
Descending colon
Rectum
S2
S3
S4
Bladder
Pelvic splanchnic nerves
Uterus
Vagina
Penis
Clitoris
Preganglionic
Postganglionic

Figure 18.4

Overview of Parasympathetic Pathways. Preganglionic neurons of the parasympathetic division extend from the brain and sacral region of the spinal cord. Ganglionic neurons are located in terminal and intramural ganglia, and extend from these ganglia to innervate the viscera. APR

Table 18.3 Parasympathetic Division Outflow

Nerve(s)	CNS Origin of Preganglionic Neuron	Autonomic Ganglion	Effectors Innervated
CN III (Oculomotor)	Midbrain	Ciliary ganglion	Ciliary muscle to control lens for accommodation; sphincter pupillae muscle of eye to constrict pupil
CN VII (Facial)	Pons	Pterygopalatine ganglion	Lacrimal gland; glands of nasal cavity, palate, oral cavity
		Submandibular ganglion	Submandibular and sublingual salivary glands
CN IX (Glossopharyngeal)	Medulla oblongata	Otic ganglion	Parotid salivary gland
CN X (Vagus)	Medulla oblongata	Multiple terminal and intramural ganglia	Thoracic viscera and most abdominal viscera
Pelvic Splanchnic Nerves	S2–S4 segments of spinal cord	Terminal and intramural ganglia	Some abdominal viscera and most pelvic viscera

Glossopharyngeal Nerve (CN IX)

The **glossopharyngeal nerve (CN IX)** innervates the parotid salivary gland. Parasympathetic neurons extend from the brainstem in the glossopharyngeal nerve. From this nerve, the preganglionic parasympathetic axons branch and synapse on ganglionic neurons in the **otic** (ō′tik; *ous* = ear) **ganglion,** which is positioned anterior to the ear near the foramen ovale (see section 7.1a and figure 7.8 to review skull landmarks). Postganglionic axons from the otic ganglion cause an increase in secretion from the parotid salivary glands.

Vagus Nerve (CN X)

The **vagus nerve (CN X)** is responsible for supplying parasympathetic innervation to the thoracic organs and most of the abdominal organs, as well as the gonads (ovaries and testes).[1] Almost 80% of all parasympathetic preganglionic axons are transmitted through the vagus nerve. The term vagus means *wanderer,* which describes the wandering pathway of the vagus nerve as it projects inferiorly through the neck and travels throughout the trunk.

Left and right vagus nerves extend multiple branches to the thoracic organs. As these nerves travel inferiorly, their position changes slightly, and they are referred to as the anterior and posterior vagal trunks. In the thoracic cavity, parasympathetic innervation causes increased mucous production and decreased diameter in the airways (see section 25.7), as well as decreases in the heart rate (see section 22.5). These trunks pass through the diaphragm and associate with the descending abdominal aorta within the abdominal cavity, where they project to their ganglia located immediately adjacent to or within the wall of their target organs. This parasympathetic innervation also causes increased smooth muscle motility and secretory activity in digestive tract organs (see section 26.4). APR

18.3b Pelvic Splanchnic Nerves

The remaining preganglionic parasympathetic axons originate from preganglionic neuron cell bodies housed within the lateral gray matter of the S2–S4 spinal cord segments (figure 18.4). These preganglionic parasympathetic axons branch to form the **pelvic splanchnic** (splangk′nik; visceral) **nerves,** which contribute to the superior and inferior hypogastric plexus. The preganglionic parasympathetic axons that emanate from each plexus project to the ganglionic neurons within either the terminal or intramural ganglia.

The target organs innervated by pelvic splanchnic nerves include the distal portion of the large intestine, the rectum, most of the reproductive organs, the urinary bladder, and the distal part of the ureter. This parasympathetic innervation causes increased smooth muscle motility (muscle contraction) and secretory activity in the digestive organs (see chapter 26), contraction of smooth muscle in the bladder wall (see section 27.3b), and erection of the clitoris and the penis (see sections 28.2e and 28.3g).

[1] It is unclear what function, if any, these parasympathetic axons have on the gonads.

18.3c Effects and General Functions of the Parasympathetic Division

The parasympathetic division is most active during times when the body must process nutrients, conserve energy, and attempt to return to homeostasis. The lack of extensive divergence in preganglionic axons prevents the mass activation seen in the sympathetic division. Thus, the effects of the parasympathetic nervous system tend to be discrete and localized. In other words, parasympathetic activity can affect one group of organs without necessarily having to "turn on" all other organs. **Table 18.3** summarizes the effects of parasympathetic innervation.

WHAT DID YOU LEARN?

5. What are the differences between the terminal and intramural ganglia?
6. Create a three-column chart: In the first column, list the cranial nerves that are involved in the parasympathetic division of the ANS. In the second, identify the target organ for each cranial nerve. In the third, identify the effect of the parasympathetic division on that organ.

18.4 Sympathetic Division

✓ Learning Objectives

8. Describe the anatomy of the sympathetic division.
9. Explain the relationship of the sympathetic division to the spinal cord and the spinal nerves.
10. Describe the sympathetic function of the adrenal medulla.
11. Identify the effects of sympathetic innervation on effectors.

The sympathetic division is also called the *thoracolumbar* (thō′ră-kō-lŭm′bar) *division* because the preganglionic neuron cell bodies originate and are housed between the first thoracic (T1) and the second lumbar (L2) spinal segments.

18.4a Organization and Anatomy of the Sympathetic Division

The sympathetic division is much more complex than the parasympathetic division, both anatomically and functionally (see figure 18.3; **figure 18.5**). The sympathetic preganglionic neuron cell bodies are housed in the **lateral horn** of the T1–L2 segments of the spinal cord. From there, the preganglionic sympathetic axons travel with somatic

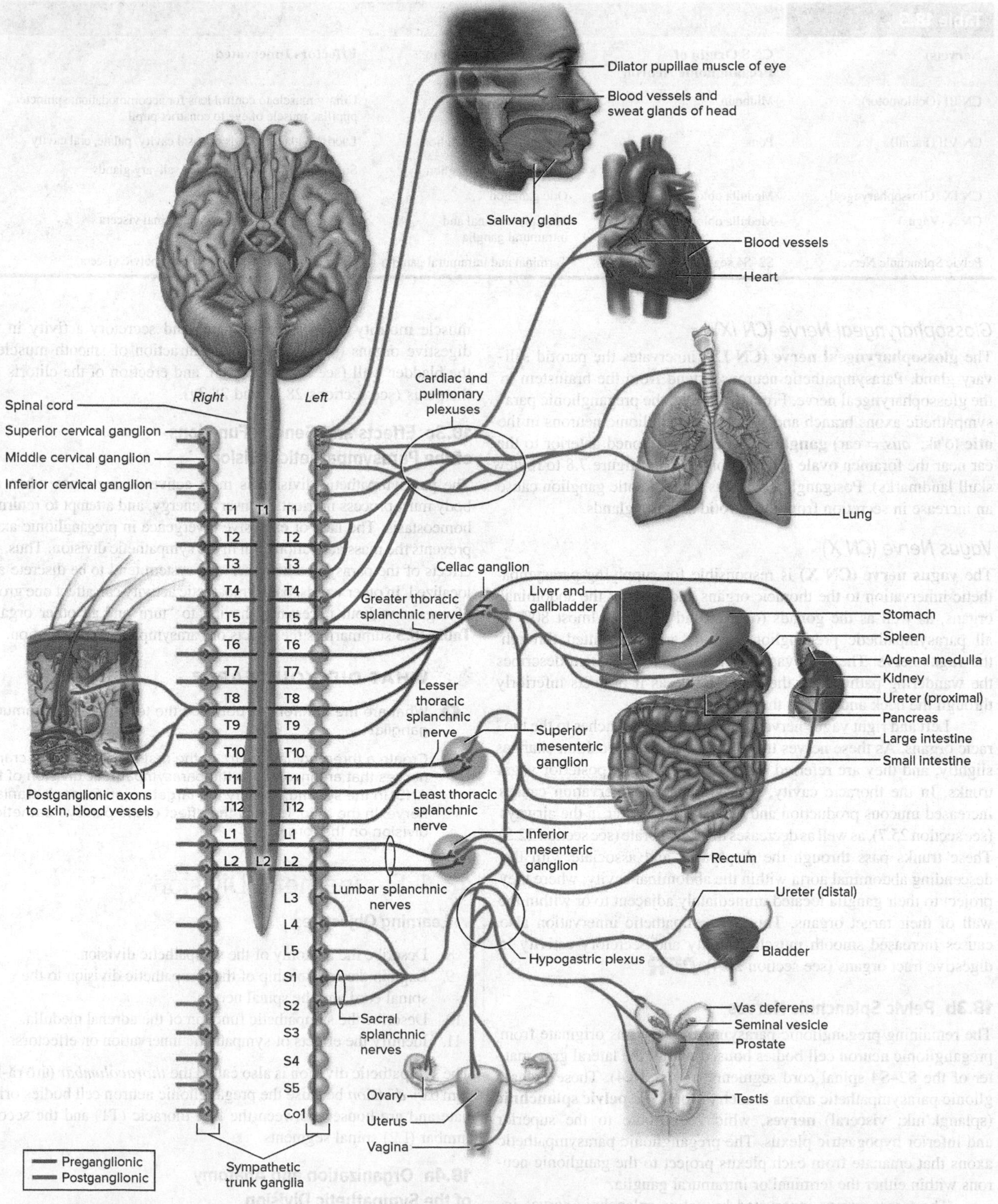
Dilator pupillae muscle of eye
Blood vessels and sweat glands of head
Salivary glands
Blood vessels
Heart
Cardiac and pulmonary plexuses
Lung
Right
Left
Spinal cord
Superior cervical ganglion
Middle cervical ganglion
Inferior cervical ganglion
T1 T1 T1
T2 T2
T3 T3
T4 T4
T5 T5
T6 T6
T7 T7
T8 T8
T9 T9
T10 T10
T11 T11
T12 T12
L1 L1
L2 L2 L2
L3
L4
L5
S1
S2
S3
S4
S5
Co1
Celiac ganglion
Greater thoracic splanchnic nerve
Liver and gallbladder
Stomach
Spleen
Adrenal medulla
Kidney
Ureter (proximal)
Pancreas
Large intestine
Small intestine
Lesser thoracic splanchnic nerve
Superior mesenteric ganglion
Postganglionic axons to skin, blood vessels
Least thoracic splanchnic nerve
Inferior mesenteric ganglion
Rectum
Lumbar splanchnic nerves
Ureter (distal)
Bladder
Hypogastric plexus
Vas deferens
Seminal vesicle
Prostate
Sacral splanchnic nerves
Ovary
Testis
Uterus
Vagina
Preganglionic
Postganglionic
Sympathetic trunk ganglia

Figure 18.5

Overview of Sympathetic Pathways. Preganglionic axons of the sympathetic division extend from the T1–L2 regions of the spinal cord. Ganglionic axons are located in the sympathetic trunk and prevertebral ganglia, and extend to the target organs. (*Left*) The outflow of preganglionic axons and the distribution of postganglionic axons innervating the skin. (*Right*) Sympathetic postganglionic axon pathways through the gray rami, spinal nerves, and splanchnic nerves. APR motor neuron axons to exit the spinal cord and enter first the anterior roots and then the T1–L2 spinal nerves. However, these preganglionic sympathetic axons remain with the spinal nerve for only a short distance before they leave the spinal nerve.

Sympathetic Trunks and Ganglia

Immediately lateral to the vertebral column and anterior to the paired spinal nerves are the left and right **sympathetic trunks (figure 18.6)**. A sympathetic trunk looks much like a pearl necklace. The "string" of the necklace is composed of bundles of axons, whereas the "pearls" are the **sympathetic trunk ganglia** (*paravertebral* or *chain ganglia*), which house sympathetic ganglionic neuron cell bodies.

One sympathetic trunk ganglion typically is associated with each spinal nerve. However, the cervical portion of each sympathetic trunk is partitioned into only three sympathetic trunk ganglia—the superior, middle, and inferior cervical ganglia—as opposed to the eight cervical spinal nerves. The **superior cervical ganglion** contains postganglionic sympathetic neuron cell bodies whose axons are distributed to structures within the head and neck. These sympathetic postganglionic axons innervate the sweat glands in the head and neck, the smooth muscle in blood vessels of the head and neck, the dilator pupillae muscle of the eye, and the superior tarsal muscle of the eye (which elevates the eyelid). The **middle** and **inferior cervical ganglia** house neuron cell bodies that extend postganglionic axons to the thoracic viscera. As is shown in figure 18.5, all three ganglia send branches to the cardiac plexus. APR

White and Gray Rami

Connecting the spinal nerves to each sympathetic trunk are rami communicantes (rā′mī kŏ-mū-ni-kan′t ēz; *communico* = to share with

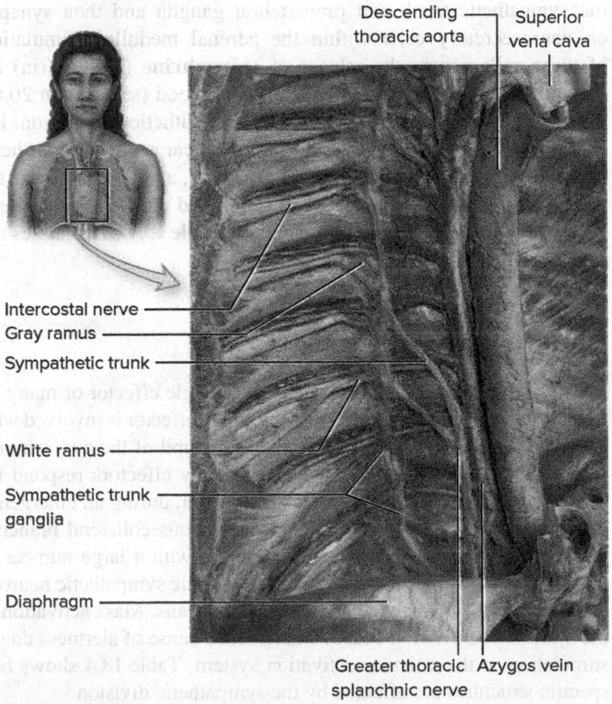

Descending thoracic aorta
Superior vena cava
Intercostal nerve
Gray ramus
Sympathetic trunk
White ramus
Sympathetic trunk ganglia
Diaphragm
Greater thoracic splanchnic nerve
Azygos vein

Figure 18.6

Sympathetic Trunk. An anterolateral cadaver photo of the right side of the thoracic cavity shows the sympathetic trunk, the gray and white rami communicantes, their attachment to the intercostal nerves, and the greater thoracic splanchnic nerve. APR

McGraw-Hill Education/Photo and Dissection by Christine Eckel

someone) (see figures 16.5 and 16.7). **White rami communicantes** (or simply **white rami**) are composed of *pre*ganglionic sympathetic axons from the T1–L2 spinal nerves to the sympathetic trunk. Thus, white rami are associated only with the T1–L2 spinal nerves. Since preganglionic axons are myelinated, the white ramus has a whitish appearance (hence, its name). White rami are similar to "entrance ramps" onto a highway.

Gray rami communicantes (or simply **gray rami**) are composed of *post*ganglionic sympathetic axons from the sympathetic trunk to the spinal nerve. Since the postganglionic axons are unmyelinated, the gray rami have a grayish appearance. Gray rami are similar to "exit ramps" off a highway. Gray rami connect to all spinal nerves: the cervical, thoracic, lumbar, sacral, and coccygeal spinal nerves. By these routes, the sympathetic information that originated in the thoracolumbar region of the spinal cord can be dispersed to all parts of the body.

Sympathetic Splanchnic Nerves

Sympathetic splanchnic nerves are composed of preganglionic sympathetic axons that did not synapse in a sympathetic trunk ganglion. They extend anteriorly from each sympathetic trunk to most of the abdominal and pelvic viscera. (These splanchnic nerves should not be confused with the pelvic splanchnic nerves associated with the parasympathetic division.) Some of the larger splanchnic nerves have specific names:

- The **greater thoracic splanchnic nerve** forms from preganglionic axons extending from the T5–T9 sympathetic trunk ganglia.
- The **lesser thoracic splanchnic nerve** forms from preganglionic axons extending from the T10–T11 sympathetic trunk ganglia.
- The **least thoracic splanchnic nerve** forms from preganglionic axons extending from the T12 sympathetic trunk ganglia.
- The **lumbar splanchnic nerves** originate from the L1 and L2 sympathetic trunk ganglia.

In addition to these, there also are small **sacral splanchnic nerves** that originate from the sacral sympathetic ganglia. Splanchnic nerves typically terminate in **prevertebral** (or *collateral*) **ganglia.** These ganglia are called prevertebral because they are immediately anterior to the vertebral column on the anterolateral wall of the abdominal aorta. Prevertebral ganglia typically cluster around the origins of the major abdominal arteries and are named for these arteries. For example, the celiac ganglion is located around the origin of the celiac trunk (an artery). Sympathetic postganglionic axons extend away from the ganglionic neuron cell bodies in these ganglia and innervate many of the abdominal organs.

Types of Prevertebral Ganglia

Splanchnic nerves typically terminate in **prevertebral** (*or collateral*) **ganglia.** The prevertebral ganglia differ from the sympathetic trunk ganglia segments in that (1) they are anterior to the vertebral column (hence, the name prevertebral) on the anterolateral surface of the aorta; and (2) they are located only in the abdominopelvic cavity. Prevertebral ganglia include the celiac, superior mesenteric, and inferior mesenteric ganglia.

The **celiac ganglia** are adjacent to the origin of the celiac artery. The left and right greater thoracic splanchnic nerves (composed of axons from the T5–T9 segment of the spinal cord) synapse on ganglionic neurons within the celiac ganglia. Postganglionic axons from these ganglia innervate the stomach, spleen, liver, gallbladder, and proximal part of the duodenum and part of the pancreas.

The **superior mesenteric** (mes′en-ter′ik; *mesos* = middle, *enteron* = intestine) **ganglia** are adjacent to the origin of the superior mesenteric artery. The lesser and least thoracic splanchnic nerves project to and terminate in the superior mesenteric ganglia. Thus, these ganglia receive preganglionic sympathetic neurons from the T10–T12 segments of the spinal cord. Postganglionic axons extending from the superior mesenteric ganglia innervate the distal half of the duodenum, part of the pancreas, the remainder of the small intestine, the proximal part of the large intestine, the kidneys, and the proximal parts of the ureters.

The **inferior mesenteric ganglia** are adjacent to the origin of the inferior mesenteric artery. They receive sympathetic preganglionic axons via the lumbar splanchnic nerves, which originate in the L1–L2 segments of the spinal cord. Its postganglionic axons project to and innervate the distal colon, rectum, urinary bladder, distal parts of the ureters, and most of the reproductive organs.

WHAT DID YOU LEARN?

7. Draw and label where the sympathetic division originates from on the spinal cord.
8. Distinguish between the sympathetic trunk ganglia and the prevertebral ganglia.
9. Describe the structural and functional differences between the white and gray rami communicantes. Do these structures contain myelinated or unmyelinated axons? Which carry preganglionic axons, and which carry postganglionic axons?

Learning Strategy 18.3

This can help you remember the splanchnic nerves: "**p**" is for **p**elvic and **p**arasympathetic, and "**s**" is for **s**acral and **s**ympathetic.

18.4b Sympathetic Pathways

All sympathetic preganglionic neurons originate in the lateral gray horns of the T1–L2 segments of the spinal cord. However, the sympathetic pathways of the axons of these neurons vary, depending upon the location and the type of effector organ being innervated. Recall that preganglionic axons extend from the preganglionic neuron cell bodies via the anterior roots and travel with the T1–L2 spinal nerves. The preganglionic axons immediately leave the spinal nerve and travel through white rami to enter the sympathetic trunk. Once inside the sympathetic trunk, the preganglionic axons may remain at the level of entry, or travel superiorly or inferiorly within the sympathetic trunk. Axons exit the sympathetic trunk ganglia by one of four pathways (**figure 18.7**).

Spinal Nerve Pathway

The **spinal nerve pathway** extends from the spinal cord to effectors of the skin of the neck, torso, and limbs. Skin effectors include sweat glands, smooth muscle forming arrector pili muscles (produce "goose bumps"), and smooth muscle cells within the walls of blood vessels (see section 5.3). In this pathway, a preganglionic neuron synapses with a ganglionic neuron in a sympathetic trunk ganglion (figure 18.7*a*). The postganglionic axon extends through a gray ramus that is at the same "level" as the ganglionic neuron. For example, if the preganglionic and ganglionic neurons synapse in the L4 ganglion, the postganglionic axon extends through the gray ramus at the level of the L4 spinal nerve. After the postganglionic axon extends through the gray ramus, it enters the spinal nerve and extends to its target organ.

Postganglionic Sympathetic Nerve Pathway

The **postganglionic sympathetic nerve pathway** extends from the spinal cord to the internal organs of the thoracic cavity (including the esophagus, heart, lungs, and thoracic blood vessels), effectors of the skin of the head and neck (sweat glands, arrector pili, and blood vessels of the skin), neck viscera, as well as the superior tarsal and dilator pupillae muscles in the eye (for increasing the amount of light entering the eye) (see section 19.5b). In this pathway, the preganglionic neuron synapses with a ganglionic neuron in a sympathetic trunk ganglion, but the postganglionic axon does *not* leave the trunk via a gray ramus (figure 18.7*b*). Instead, the postganglionic axon extends away from the sympathetic trunk ganglion and projects directly to the effector organ.

Splanchnic Nerve Pathway

The **splanchnic nerve pathway** extends from the spinal cord to the abdominal and pelvic organs (e.g., stomach, small intestines, kidney). In this pathway, a preganglionic neuron does not synapse with a ganglionic neuron in a sympathetic trunk ganglion. Rather, the preganglionic axons pass through the sympathetic trunk ganglia without synapsing and extend to the prevertebral ganglia (figure 18.7*c*). There, the preganglionic axon synapses with a ganglionic neuron. The postganglionic axon then projects to the effector organs.

Adrenal Medulla Pathway

The final pathway is the **adrenal medulla pathway** (figure 18.7 *d*). In this pathway, the internal region of the adrenal gland, called the **adrenal** (ă-drē′năl; *ad* = to, *ren* = kidney) **medulla,** is directly innervated by preganglionic sympathetic axons. (There is no ganglionic neuron.) The axons of the preganglionic neuron extend through both the sympathetic trunk and prevertebral ganglia and then synapse on neurosecretory cells within the adrenal medulla. Stimulation of these cells causes the release of **epinephrine** (ep′i-nef′rin) and **norepinephrine** (nōr′ep-i-nef′rin) into the blood (see section 20.6b). These hormones prolong the effects of sympathetic stimulation. For example, if you narrowly miss getting into a car accident, your heart continues to beat quickly, you breathe rapidly, and you feel tense and alert well after the event because of prolonged effects of the sympathetic stimulation of the adrenal medulla. **Table 18.4** summarizes the sympathetic division pathways.

18.4c Effects and General Functions of the Sympathetic Division

The sympathetic division may innervate a single effector or many effectors, simultaneously. For example, a single effector is involved when smooth muscle controls the diameter of the pupil of the eye, whereas during an emergency or crisis situation many effectors respond together, a phenomenon termed **mass activation,** during an emergency or crisis situation. In mass activation, numerous collateral branches of preganglionic sympathetic axons synapse with a large number of ganglionic neurons to stimulate many ganglionic sympathetic neurons and simultaneously activate many effector organs. Mass activation of the sympathetic division causes a heightened sense of alertness due to stimulation of the reticular activation system. Table 18.4 shows how specific structures are affected by the sympathetic division.

Mass activation often occurs simultaneously with an increase in tonus in skeletal muscle. However, this increased skeletal muscle tension is not due to activation of the ANS, but merely to changes in muscle tone. In addition, the affected individual experiences a feeling of excess energy, which is usually caused by mobilization of energy reserves in the liver. Some obvious systemic changes accompany

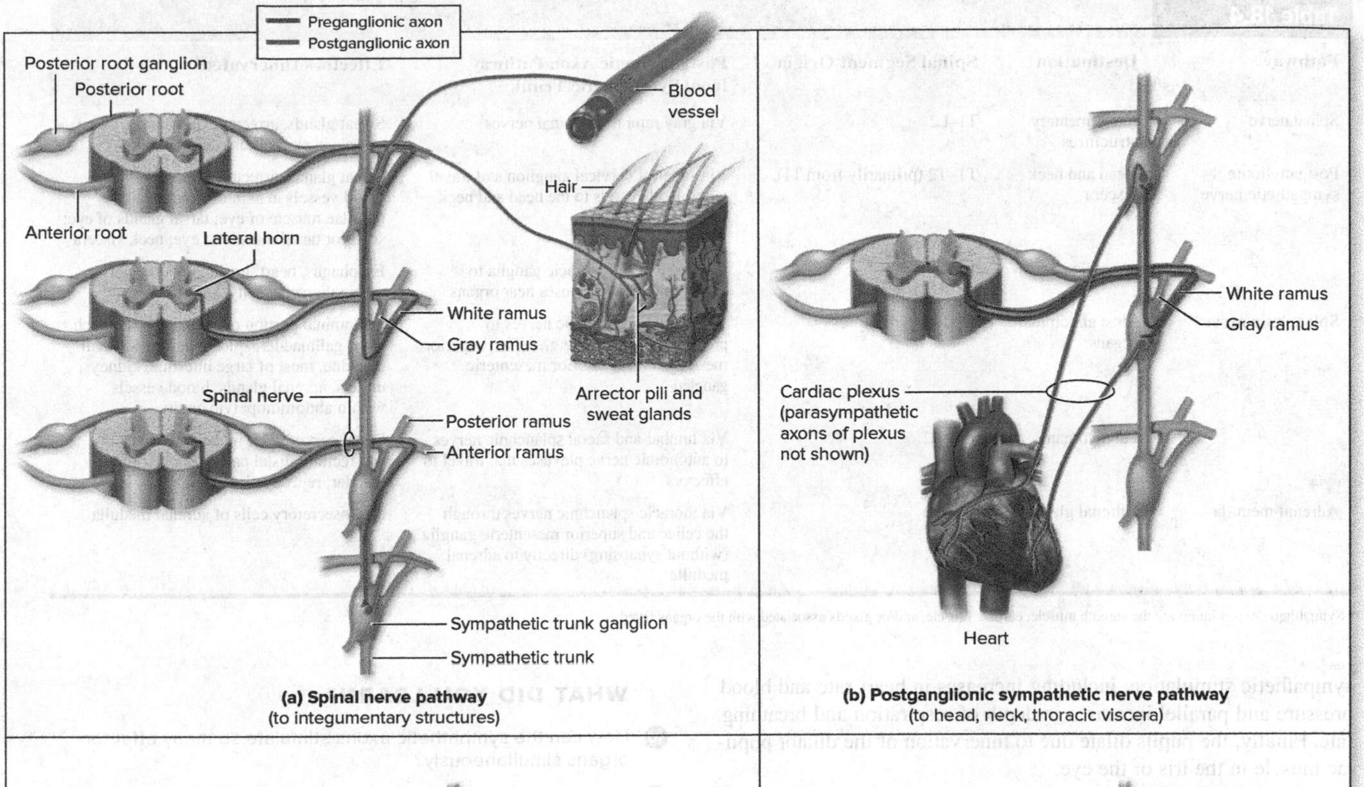
Preganglionic axon
Postganglionic axon
Posterior root ganglion
Posterior root
Anterior root
Lateral horn
Blood vessel
Hair
White ramus
Gray ramus
Spinal nerve
Arrector pili and sweat glands
Posterior ramus
Anterior ramus
Sympathetic trunk ganglion
Sympathetic trunk
(a) Spinal nerve pathway (to integumentary structures)
White ramus
Gray ramus
Cardiac plexus (parasympathetic axons of plexus not shown)
Heart
(b) Postganglionic sympathetic nerve pathway (to head, neck, thoracic viscera)
Sympathetic trunk ganglion
White ramus
Gray ramus
Intestine
Preganglionic axon
Splanchnic nerves
Prevertebral ganglion
(c) Splanchnic nerve pathway (to abdominal and pelvic viscera)
White ramus
Gray ramus
Splanchnic nerve
Adrenal medulla
Prevertebral ganglion (no synapse occurs)
(d) Adrenal medulla pathway

Figure 18.7

Types of Sympathetic Pathways. (*a*) Spinal nerve: the postganglionic axon leaves the grey rami at the same level as the ganglion, regardless of whether the preganglionic axon entered the white rami at that level (arrector pili) or at a different level (blood vessel). (*b*) Postganglionic sympathetic nerve: the postganglionic axon does not travel on a grey rami. (*c*) Splanchnic nerve: the preganglionic axon leaves the sympathetic trunk and synapses in a prevertebral ganglion. (*d*) Adrenal medulla: the preganglionic axon leaves the sympathetic trunk (without synapsing) and synapses with the cells of the adrenal medulla.

Table 18.4 Sympathetic Division Pathways

Pathway	Destination	Spinal Segment Origin	Postganglionic Axon Pathway from Sympathetic Trunk	Effectors Innervated[1]
Spinal nerve	Integumentary structures	T1–L2	Via gray rami to all spinal nerves	Sweat glands, arrector pili muscles, blood vessels in skin of torso, limbs, and neck
Postganglionic sympathetic nerve	Head and neck viscera	T1–T2 (primarily from T1)	Via superior cervical ganglion and travel with blood vessels to the head and neck viscera	Sweat glands, arrector pili muscles, and blood vessels in skin of head; dilator pupillae muscle of eye; tarsal glands of eye; superior tarsal muscle of eye; neck viscera
	Thoracic organs	T1–T5	Via cervical and thoracic ganglia to autonomic nerve plexuses near organs	Esophagus, heart, lungs, blood vessels within thoracic cavity
Splanchnic nerve	Most abdominal organs	T5–T12	Via thoracic splanchnic nerves to prevertebral ganglia (e.g., celiac, superior mesenteric, and inferior mesenteric ganglia)	Abdominal portion of esophagus, stomach, liver, gallbladder, spleen, pancreas, small intestine, most of large intestine, kidneys, ureters, adrenal glands, blood vessels within abdominopelvic cavity
	Pelvic organs	T10–L2	Via lumbar and sacral splanchnic nerves to autonomic nerve plexuses that travel to effectors	Distal part of large intestine, anal canal, and rectum; distal part of ureters; urinary bladder; reproductive organs
Adrenal medulla	Adrenal gland	T8–T12	Via thoracic splanchnic nerves through the celiac and superior mesenteric ganglia (without synapsing) directly to adrenal medulla	Neurosecretory cells of adrenal medulla

[1] Sympathetic axons innervate the smooth muscle, cardiac muscle, and/or glands associated with the organs listed.

sympathetic stimulation, including increases in heart rate and blood pressure and parallel increases in depth of respiration and breathing rate. Finally, the pupils dilate due to innervation of the dilator pupillae muscle in the iris of the eye.

WHAT DO YOU THINK?

3 When a person is very stressed and tense, his or her blood pressure typically rises. What aspect of the sympathetic nervous system causes this rise in blood pressure?

Clinical View 18.1

The Autonomic Nervous System and Cardiovascular Disease

The autonomic nervous system (ANS) affects the cardiovascular system by changing heart rate (see section 18.5e) and blood pressure (see section 18.5f and 18.5g). Irregularities in the function of the sympathetic division of the ANS are associated with the development of several cardiovascular disorders, such as heart failure, essential hypertension (high blood pressure from unknown cause), postural syncope (loss of consciousness due to change in position or standing for too long), and heart disease due to mental stress. Greater understanding of sympathetic mechanisms has led to improved treatments such as beta-blockers to reduce heart rate and, thus, blood pressure. A more recent intervention for essential hypertension is renal sympathetic nerve ablation which impacts the renin-angiotensin pathway (see sections 20.9a and 27.2f) to maintain lower blood pressure. A better understanding of how the sympathetic division affects the cardiovascular system will enable the development of additional targeted treatments.

WHAT DID YOU LEARN?

10 How can the sympathetic axons stimulate so many effector organs simultaneously?

11 What is the function of splanchnic nerves in the sympathetic division?

12 Draw a flow chart for each of the four sympathetic pathways used by the two lower neurons in the sympathetic division. Indicate what structures these neurons pass through and where the preganglionic axon synapses with the ganglionic neuron.

18.5 Other Features of the Autonomic Nervous System

Learning Objectives

12. Identify the structure and location of autonomic plexuses.
13. Describe the enteric nervous system (ENS).
14. Compare and contrast the types of neurotransmitters.
15. Explain dual innervation of the ANS.
16. Describe how autonomic reflexes help maintain homeostasis.

Both divisions of the autonomic nervous system innervate organs through specific axon bundles called autonomic plexuses. Communication between neurons and effectors in the autonomic nervous system is by chemical messengers, called neurotransmitters. These chemical messengers and the receptors on body organs to which they bind are specific in each division of the autonomic nervous system. Most organs are innervated by both divisions of the autonomic nervous system in what is called dual innervation. Autonomic reflexes help us maintain homeostasis. We discuss autonomic plexuses first.

18.5a Autonomic Plexuses

Autonomic plexuses are collections of sympathetic postganglionic axons and parasympathetic preganglionic axons, as well as some visceral sensory axons. These sympathetic and parasympathetic axons are close to one another, but they do not interact or synapse with one another. Although these plexuses look like disorganized masses of axons, they provide a complex innervation pattern to their target organs (**figure 18.8**).

In the mediastinum of the thoracic cavity, the **cardiac plexus** consists of postganglionic sympathetic axons that extend from the cervical and thoracic sympathetic trunk ganglia, as well as preganglionic axons from the vagus nerve. Increased sympathetic activity increases heart rate and blood pressure, whereas increased parasympathetic activity decreases heart rate (see section 22.5).

The **pulmonary plexus** consists of postganglionic sympathetic axons from the thoracic sympathetic trunk ganglia and preganglionic axons from the vagus nerve. The axons project to the bronchi and blood vessels of the lungs. Stimulation of this parasympathetic pathway causes a reduction in the diameter of the bronchi (called *bronchoconstriction*) and bronchioles and increased secretion from mucous glands of the bronchial tree. Sympathetic innervation causes bronchodilation (increase in the diameter of the bronchi and bronchioles) (see section 25.7).

The **esophageal plexus** consists of preganglionic axons from the vagus nerve. Smooth muscle activity in the inferior esophageal wall is coordinated by parasympathetic axons that control the swallowing reflex in the inferior region of the esophagus by innervating smooth muscle in the inferior esophageal wall and the inferior esophageal sphincter, a valve through which swallowed food and drink must pass (see section 26.5).

The **abdominal aortic plexus** consists of the **celiac plexus, superior mesenteric plexus,** and **inferior mesenteric plexus.** The abdominal aortic plexus is composed of postganglionic axons projecting from the prevertebral ganglia and preganglionic axons from the vagus nerve that enter the abdominopelvic cavity with the esophagus. Note that the celiac plexus also is known as the *solar plexus,* and it is partly responsible for the sensation of "getting the wind knocked out of you" when you are hit hard in the epigastric region.

The **hypogastric plexus** consists of a complex meshwork of postganglionic sympathetic axons (from the aortic plexus and the lumbar region of the sympathetic trunk) and preganglionic parasympathetic axons from the pelvic splanchnic nerve. Its axons innervate viscera within the pelvic region.

18.5b Enteric Nervous System

The **enteric nervous system (ENS)** is a weblike array of neurons (motor, sensory, and interneurons) that are arranged throughout the wall of the gastrointestinal (GI) tract from the esophagus through to the anus. It not only innervates the smooth muscle and glands of the GI tract but also mediates the complex coordinated reflexes for peristalsis. ENS neurons are located within both numerous small ganglia throughout the gastrointestinal tract wall, and two large plexuses: (1) the **submucosal plexus** (called *Meissner plexus*) and

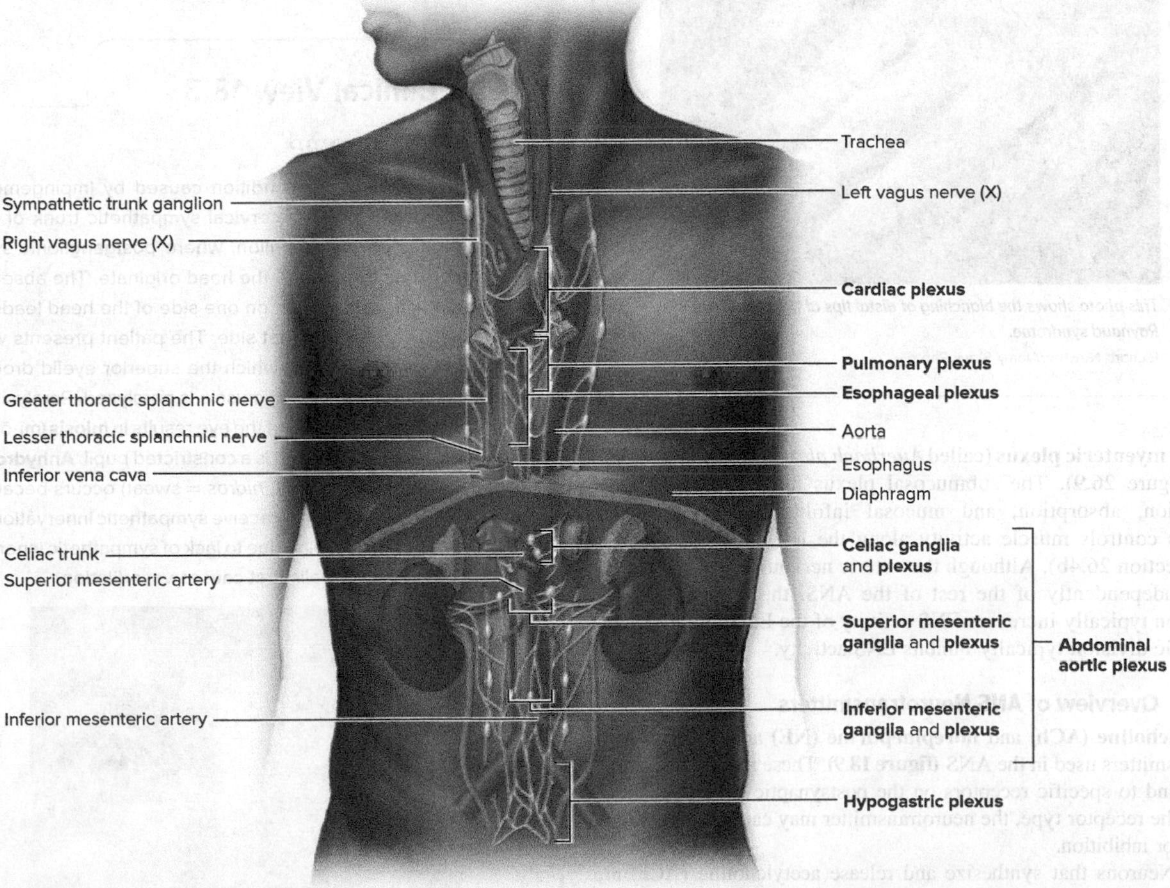

Figure 18.8

Autonomic Plexuses. Autonomic plexuses are located in both the thoracic and abdominopelvic cavities. This anterior view shows the cardiac, pulmonary, and esophageal plexuses in the thoracic cavity and the abdominal aortic plexus (celiac, superior mesenteric, inferior mesenteric plexuses) in the abdominopelvic cavity.

Clinical View 18.2

Raynaud Syndrome

Raynaud syndrome, or *Raynaud phenomenon*, is a sudden constriction of the small arteries of the digits. The immediate decrease in blood flow results in blanching (loss of the red hue) of the skin distal to the area of vascular constriction. The vascular constriction is accompanied by pain, which may even continue for a while after the vessels have dilated and restored the local blood flow. Episodes are typically triggered by exposure to cold, although emotional stress has been known to precipitate a Raynaud attack. This condition is more common in women than in men, and is believed to result from an exaggerated local sympathetic response. The severity of this medical condition depends upon the frequency and the length of time of each occurrence. Most people affected with Raynaud syndrome must avoid the cold and other triggering circumstances.

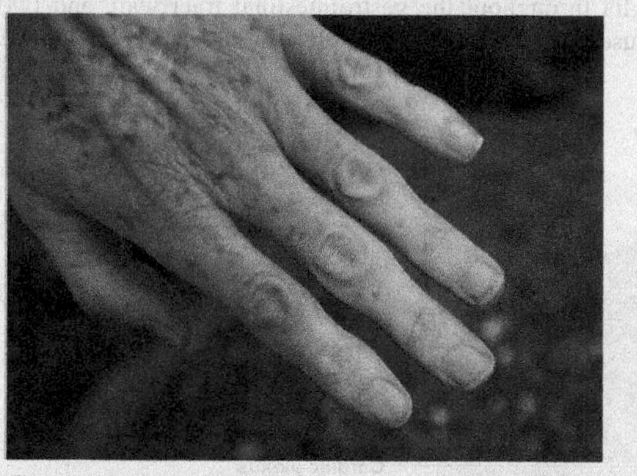

This photo shows the blanching of distal tips of fingers in primary Raynaud syndrome.

Richard Newton/Alamy Stock Photo

(2) the **myenteric plexus** (called *Auerbach plexus*) (see section 26.4b and figure 26.9). The submucosal plexus mainly controls local secretion, absorption, and mucosal infolding. The myenteric plexus controls muscle activity along the length of the GI tract (see section 26.4b). Although the enteric nervous system can function independently of the rest of the ANS, the parasympathetic division typically increases ENS activity of the ENS, and the sympathetic division typically inhibits ENS activity.

18.5c Overview of ANS Neurotransmitters

Acetylcholine (ACh) and **norepinephrine (NE)** are the main neurotransmitters used in the ANS (**figure 18.9**). These neurotransmitters will bind to specific receptors on the postsynaptic cell. Depending upon the receptor type, the neurotransmitter may cause either stimulation or inhibition.

Neurons that synthesize and release acetylcholine (ACh) are called **cholinergic** (kōl′in-er-jik; *ergon* = work) **neurons.** Receptors that bind ACh are called **cholinergic receptors.** Cholinergic neurons include the following:

- All sympathetic and parasympathetic preganglionic neurons
- All parasympathetic ganglionic neurons
- The specific sympathetic ganglionic neurons that innervate sweat glands of the skin

There are two types of cholinergic receptors (nicotinic and muscarinic), and each responds differently to binding of ACh. *Nicotinic receptors* were so named because they are sensitive to the drug nicotine. These receptors occur on the cell bodies of all ganglionic neurons (see figure 18.9), as well as on the cells of the adrenal medulla. *Muscarinic receptors* respond to muscarine, a mushroom toxin. They occur in all target plasma membranes in the parasympathetic division and in the few selected sympathetic target cells (e.g., sweat glands in the skin).

Neurons that synthesize and secrete norepinephrine (NE) are called **adrenergic** (ad-r ĕ-ner′jik) **neurons.** Most sympathetic ganglionic neurons are adrenergic. Receptors that bind NE (or a related molecule, like epinephrine) are called **adrenergic receptors.**

In summary, all autonomic preganglionic axons release ACh, which binds to nicotinic receptors in the ganglionic neuron's plasma membrane. These receptors excite the ganglionic cell. All postganglionic parasympathetic axons release ACh, which can excite or inhibit the effector cell, depending upon the type of cholinergic receptor and the tissue. In contrast, the ACh released from sympathetic axons is excitatory only. Most postganglionic sympathetic axons release NE, which can be excitatory or inhibitory, depending upon the type of adrenergic receptor and the tissue.

Clinical View 18.3

Horner Syndrome

Horner syndrome is a condition caused by impingement, injury, or severing of the cervical sympathetic trunk or the T1 sympathetic trunk ganglion, where postganglionic sympathetic axons traveling to the head originate. The absence of sympathetic innervation on one side of the head leads to certain clinical signs on that side. The patient presents with **ptosis** (tō′sis; a falling), in which the superior eyelid droops because the superior tarsal muscle is paralyzed. Paralysis of the dilator pupillae muscle of the eye results in **miosis** (mī-ō′sis; *meiosis* = lessening), which is a constricted pupil. **Anhydrosis** (an-hī-drō′sis; *an* = without, *hidros* = sweat) occurs because the sweat glands no longer receive sympathetic innervation. A fourth symptom is flushing due to lack of sympathetic innervation to blood vessel walls that causes vasodilation.

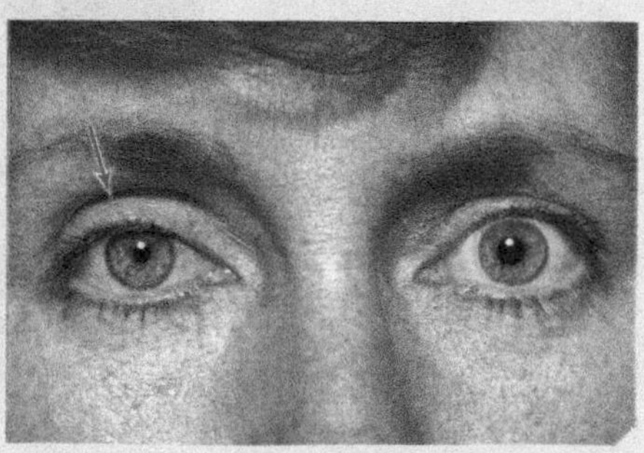

Horner syndrome in right eye. Note the ptosis (blue arrow) and constriction of the pupil.

Mediscan/Alamy Stock Photo

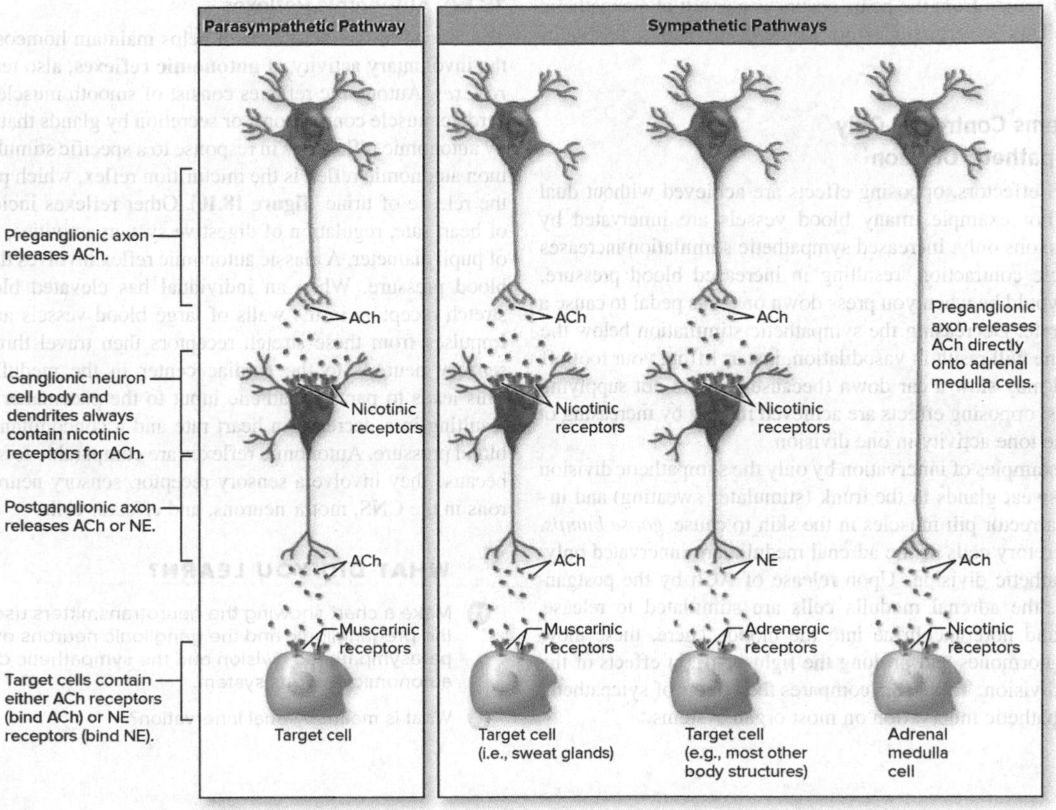

Figure 18.9

Comparison of Neurotransmitters in the Autonomic Nervous System. In the parasympathetic pathway, both the preganglionic and postganglionic axons release acetylcholine (ACh). In the sympathetic pathway, all preganglionic axons and a few specific postganglionic axons release ACh. Most postganglionic sympathetic axons release norepinephrine (NE).

18.5d Autonomic Tone

The parasympathetic and sympathetic divisions both continuously release neurotransmitter to regulate specific target organs for either sustained stimulation or inhibition; a process referred to as the **autonomic tone.** Activity of an organ may be controlled merely by the change in tone within a single ANS division. For example, the diameter of most blood vessels is maintained in a partially constricted state by the effects of sympathetic tone. A decrease in stimulation below the sympathetic tone causes vessel dilation, whereas an increase above sympathetic tone brings about vessel constriction. If the initial level of sympathetic tone were not present, then only vasoconstriction could occur as a result of sympathetic division activity.

18.5e Dual Innervation

Many ANS effectors have **dual innervation,** meaning that they are innervated by postganglionic axons from both parasympathetic and sympathetic divisions. The actions caused by activities of both the divisions on the same organ usually result in effects that are antagonistic or cooperative.

Antagonistic Effects

Generally, the effects of parasympathetic and sympathetic innervation to the same organ are antagonistic—that is, they oppose each other. Some variations occur in how antagonistic effects are expressed, as follows:

- **Control of heart rate.** Parasympathetic stimulation slows down the heart rate, whereas sympathetic stimulation speeds up the heart rate. The same heart muscle effector cells receive this opposing stimulation.
- **Control of muscular activity in the gastrointestinal tract.** Parasympathetic stimulation of smooth muscle cells in the gastrointestinal tract wall accelerates their rate of contraction and thus increases gastrointestinal tract motility, whereas sympathetic stimulation decreases motility.
- **Control of pupil diameter in the iris of the eye.** Here, different effectors are innervated by the ANS divisions. Parasympathetic stimulation of the sphincter pupillae (circular muscle layer) in the iris causes pupil constriction, whereas sympathetic stimulation of the dilator pupillae (radial muscle layer) in the iris causes pupil dilation.

Cooperative Effects

Cooperative effects are seen when both parasympathetic and sympathetic stimulation cause different responses that together produce a single, distinct result. The best example of cooperative effects occurs in the sexual function of the male reproductive system. The penis becomes erect as a result of parasympathetic innervation, and ejaculation of semen from the penis occurs as a result of sympathetic innervation. This synergistic effort of ANS divisions facilitates reproduction.

18.5f Systems Controlled Only by the Sympathetic Division

In some ANS effectors, opposing effects are achieved without dual innervation. For example, many blood vessels are innervated by sympathetic axons only. Increased sympathetic stimulation increases smooth muscle contraction, resulting in increased blood pressure. An analogy would be when you press down on a gas pedal to cause a car to accelerate. Decreasing the sympathetic stimulation below the autonomic tone will result in vasodilation, just as lifting your foot off the gas pedal may slow a car down (because you are not supplying the gas). Thus, opposing effects are achieved merely by increasing or decreasing the tone activity in one division.

Other examples of innervation by only the sympathetic division are noted in sweat glands in the trunk (stimulates sweating) and innervation of arrector pili muscles in the skin to cause *goose bumps.* The neurosecretory cells of the adrenal medulla are innervated only by the sympathetic division. Upon release of ACh by the postganglionic axon, the adrenal medulla cells are stimulated to release epinephrine and norepinephrine into the blood. There, these molecules act as hormones and prolong the fight-or-flight effects of the sympathetic division. **Table 18.5** compares the effects of sympathetic and parasympathetic innervation on most organ systems.

18.5g Autonomic Reflexes

The autonomic nervous system helps maintain homeostasis through the involuntary activity of **autonomic reflexes,** also termed *visceral reflexes.* Autonomic reflexes consist of smooth muscle contractions, cardiac muscle contractions, or secretion by glands that are mediated by autonomic reflex arcs in response to a specific stimulus. One common autonomic reflex is the micturition reflex, which partly controls the release of urine (**figure 18.10**). Other reflexes include alteration of heart rate, regulation of digestive system activities, and alteration of pupil diameter. A classic autonomic reflex involves the reduction of blood pressure. When an individual has elevated blood pressure, stretch receptors in the walls of large blood vessels are stimulated. Impulses from these stretch receptors then travel through visceral sensory neurons to the cardiac center in the medulla oblongata. This leads to parasympathetic input to the pacemaker of the heart, resulting in a decrease in heart rate and a concomitant decrease in blood pressure. Autonomic reflexes are comparable to spinal reflexes because they involve a sensory receptor, sensory neurons, interneurons in the CNS, motor neurons, and effector cells.

WHAT DID YOU LEARN?

13 Make a chart showing the neurotransmitters used by the preganglionic and the ganglionic neurons of the parasympathetic division and the sympathetic division of the autonomic nervous system.

14 What is meant by dual innervation?

Table 18.5 Effects of the Parasympathetic and Sympathetic Divisions

Effector	Parasympathetic Effect	Sympathetic Effect
CIRCULATORY SYSTEM		
Heart	Decreases heart rate	Increases heart rate
Blood vessels		
Coronary	Vasodilation	Vasoconstriction or vasodilation
Integumentary and most other blood vessels	None	Vasoconstriction (increase blood pressure)
DIGESTIVE SYSTEM		
GI tract gland secretion	Stimulates	Inhibits
Peristalsis (motility)	Stimulates	Inhibits
GI tract vasculature	Vasodilation	Vasoconstriction
Sphincters	Relaxation (open)	Contraction (close)
RESPIRATORY SYSTEM		
Bronchi and bronchioles of lungs	Bronchoconstriction (airway narrows)	Bronchodilation (airway widens)
URINARY SYSTEM		
Urinary bladder (smooth muscle wall)	Contraction	Relaxation
Internal urethral sphincter	Relaxation (open)	Contraction (close)
REPRODUCTIVE SYSTEM		
Penis	Stimulates erection	Stimulates ejaculation
Clitoris	Stimulates erection	Poorly understood
EYES		
Pupils	Constriction	Dilation
Ciliary muscle	Contraction for near vision	None
INTEGUMENTARY SYSTEM		
Arrector pili	None	Contraction to cause hair erection
Sweat glands	None	Secretion

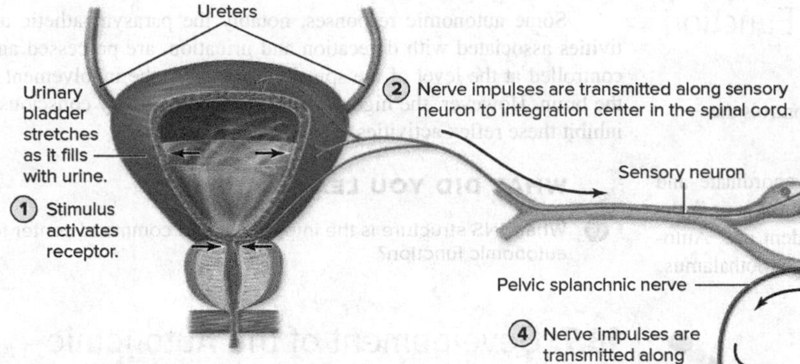
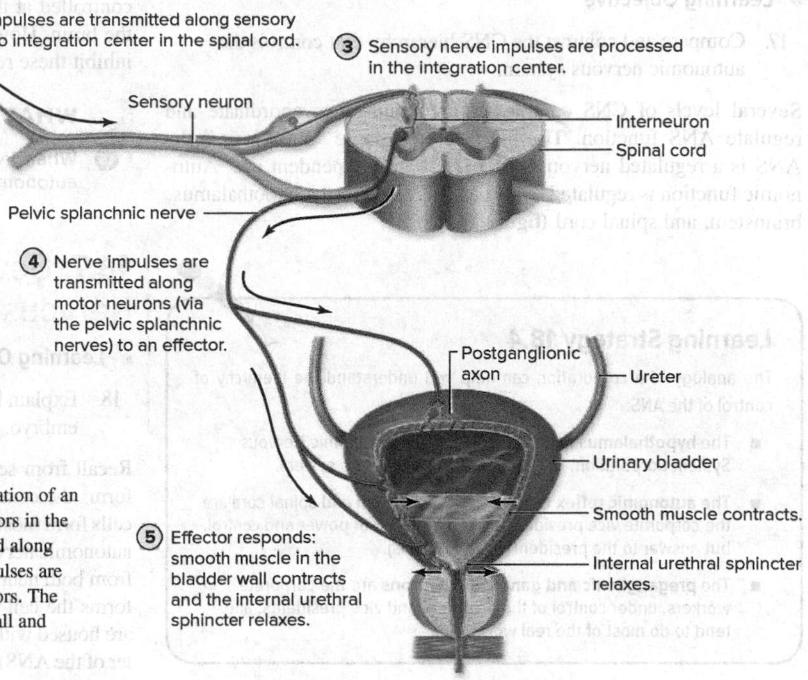
Ureters
Urinary bladder stretches as it fills with urine.
1 Stimulus activates receptor.
2 Nerve impulses are transmitted along sensory neuron to integration center in the spinal cord.
3 Sensory nerve impulses are processed in the integration center.
Sensory neuron
Interneuron
Spinal cord
Pelvic splanchnic nerve
4 Nerve impulses are transmitted along motor neurons (via the pelvic splanchnic nerves) to an effector.
Postganglionic axon
Ureter
Urinary bladder
Smooth muscle contracts.
5 Effector responds: smooth muscle in the bladder wall contracts and the internal urethral sphincter relaxes.
Internal urethral sphincter relaxes.

Figure 18.10

Autonomic Reflexes. An autonomic reflex involves stimulation of an automatic effector. Here, the reflex is initiated as baroreceptors in the bladder wall are stretched and nerve impulses are transmitted along sensory neurons to interneurons within the CNS. Nerve impulses are then transmitted along motor neurons to stimulate the effectors. The effector response is the contraction of the urinary bladder wall and relaxation of the internal urethral sphincter.

Clinical View 18.4

Autonomic Dysreflexia

Autonomic dysreflexia is a potentially dangerous vascular condition that causes blood pressure to rise profoundly, sometimes so high that blood vessels rupture. Specifically, it stimulates a sympathetic division reflex that causes systemic vasoconstriction and a marked increase in blood pressure. Autonomic dysreflexia is caused by hyperactivity of the autonomic nervous system in the weeks and months after a spinal cord injury at or above T_6. A strong stimulus, often an overly distended bladder or bowel, below the level of injury can result in a unbalanced autonomic response. There is a sympathetic spinal reflex, but the counterbalancing parasympathetic response does not occur below the level of the injury. Proper bladder and bowel care can reduce the incidence of autonomic dysreflexia.

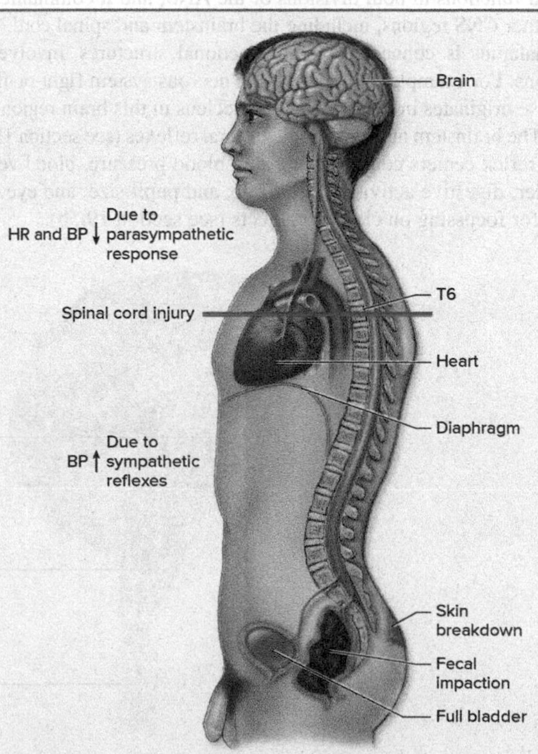
Brain
HR and BP ↓ Due to parasympathetic response
T6
Spinal cord injury
Heart
Diaphragm
BP ↑ Due to sympathetic reflexes
Skin breakdown
Fecal impaction
Full bladder

This illustration shows a spinal cord injury at level T_6 and possible stimuli of and effects due to autonomic dysreflexia.

18.6 CNS Control of Autonomic Function

✓ **Learning Objective**

17. Compare and contrast the CNS hierarchy that controls the autonomic nervous system.

Several levels of CNS complexity are required to coordinate and regulate ANS function. Thus, despite the name "autonomic," the ANS is a regulated nervous system, not an independent one. Autonomic function is regulated by three CNS regions: the hypothalamus, brainstem, and spinal cord (**figure 18.11**).

Learning Strategy 18.4

The analogy of a corporation can help you understand the hierarchy of control of the ANS:

- The **hypothalamus** is the president of the Autonomic Nervous System Corporation. It oversees all activity in this system.
- The **autonomic reflex centers** in the brainstem and spinal cord are the corporate vice presidents, who have a lot of power and control, but answer to the president (hypothalamus).
- The **preganglionic and ganglionic neurons** are the corporate workers, under control of the president and vice presidents, and tend to do most of the real work!

The hypothalamus is the integration and command center for autonomic functions (see section 15.4c). It contains nuclei that control visceral functions in both divisions of the ANS, and it communicates with other CNS regions, including the brainstem and spinal cord. The hypothalamus is connected to the functional structures involved in emotions. For example, the sympathetic nervous system fight-or-flight response originates in the sympathetic nucleus in this brain region.

The brainstem nuclei mediate visceral reflexes (see section 15.5). These reflex centers control changes in blood pressure, blood vessel diameter, digestive activities, heart rate, and pupil size, and eye lens shape for focussing on close-up objects (see section 19.5b).

Some autonomic responses, notably the parasympathetic activities associated with defecation and urination, are processed and controlled at the level of the spinal cord without the involvement of the brain. However, the higher centers in the brain may consciously inhibit these reflex activities.

WHAT DID YOU LEARN?

15. What CNS structure is the integration and command center for autonomic function?

18.7 Development of the Autonomic Nervous System

✓ **Learning Objective**

18. Explain how the autonomic nervous system develops in an embryo.

Recall from sections 3.4c and 15.1a that the embryonic **neural tube** forms the central nervous system structures, whereas the neural crest cells form most of the peripheral nervous system structures. Because the autonomic nervous system has both CNS and PNS components, it forms from both neural tube and neural crest cells. In general, the neural tube forms the cell bodies of preganglionic neurons (since these structures are housed within the CNS), the hypothalamus (the master control center of the ANS), the autonomic nervous system centers in the brainstem, the white rami, and the autonomic reflex centers within the spinal cord. In general, the neural crest cells form all autonomic ganglia, ganglionic neurons and their postganglionic axons, gray rami communicantes, the sympathetic trunk ganglia, and the adrenal medulla.

The neural crest cells begin to migrate during the fourth week of development. Those slated to form ANS structures differentiate soon thereafter. Preganglionic neurons begin to extend axons anteriorly from the neural tube during the fifth week of development (**figure 18.12**). These axons encounter the ganglionic neurons, and the sympathetic trunk begins to form during week 6. By the end of the eighth week, the rami communicantes have formed; the developing heart and lungs begin to receive autonomic innervation in the tenth week of development.

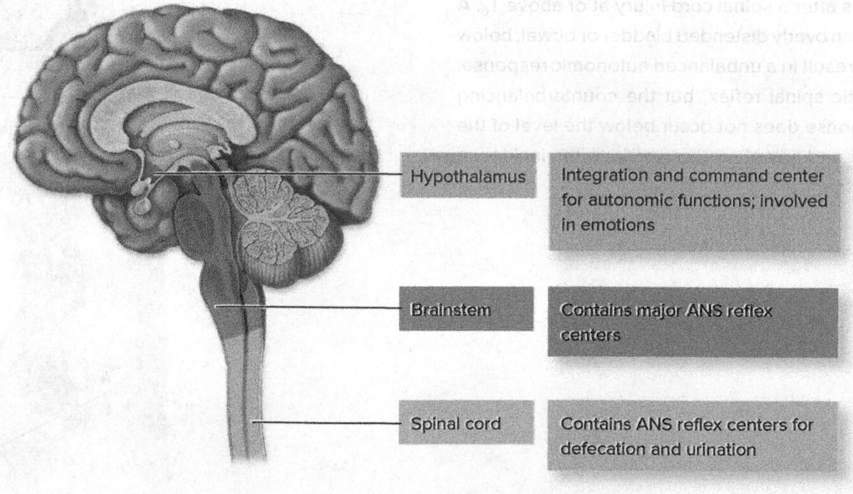
Hypothalamus
Integration and command center for autonomic functions; involved in emotions
Brainstem
Contains major ANS reflex centers
Spinal cord
Contains ANS reflex centers for defecation and urination

Figure 18.11

Control of Autonomic Functions by Higher Brain Centers. ANS functions are regulated by the hypothalamus, which in turn control ANS centers in the brainstem and spinal cord.

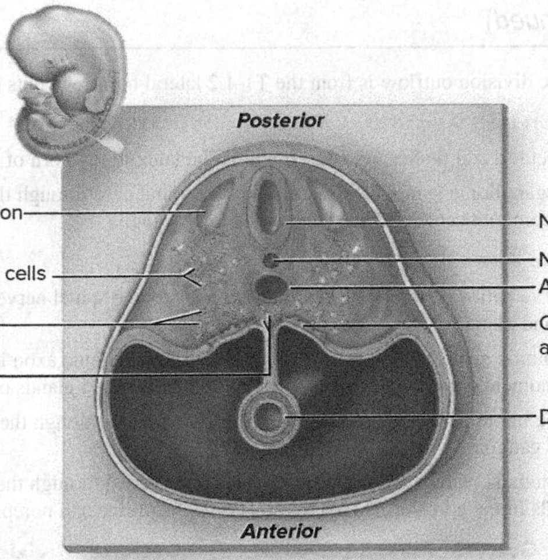

Figure 18.12

Neural Crest Cell Derivatives. A transverse section through a 5-week embryo shows structures that develop from migrating neural crest cells, including posterior root ganglia, many of the ANS structures, and the cells of the adrenal medulla.

Clinical Terms

Hirschsprung disease (congenital megacolon) Dilation and hypertrophy of the colon due to absence (aganglionosis) or marked reduction (hypoganglionosis) in the number of ganglion cells within the colon.

vagotomy (vā-got′ō-mē; *tome* = incision) Surgical separation or splitting of the vagus nerve, usually performed to reduce gastric acid secretion in ulcer patients when medications have failed.

Chapter Summary

18.1 Comparison of the Somatic and Autonomic Nervous Systems	■ The SNS innervates skeletal muscle. The ANS innervates smooth muscle, cardiac muscle, and glands, and controls involuntary motor activities. **18.1a Motor Neurons of the Somatic Versus Autonomic Nervous System** ■ A single lower motor neuron axon innervates skeletal muscle fibers in the SNS, whereas the ANS has a two-neuron pathway consisting of preganglionic neurons in the CNS and ganglionic neurons in the PNS.
18.2 Divisions of the Autonomic Nervous System	■ The ANS is composed of a parasympathetic division and a sympathetic division. **18.2a Functional Differences** ■ The parasympathetic division is primarily concerned with maintaining homeostasis when the body is at rest, which includes conserving energy and replenishing nutrient stores. ■ The sympathetic division is primarily concerned with maintaining homeostasis in conditions of "fight-or-flight." **18.2b Anatomic Differences in Lower Motor Neurons** ■ Parasympathetic preganglionic neurons reside in the brainstem and sacral regions of the spinal cord, whereas sympathetic preganglionic axons reside in the thoracic and lumbar regions of the spinal cord.
18.3 Parasympathetic Division	■ The parasympathetic preganglionic neurons are housed either within the brainstem or within the sacral region of the spinal cord. ■ The ganglionic neurons in the parasympathetic division are located within either terminal ganglia or intramural ganglia. **18.3a Cranial Components** ■ Parasympathetic preganglionic axons extend from cell bodies in brainstem nuclei through the oculomotor, facial, glossopharyngeal, and vagus cranial nerves. **18.3b Pelvic Splanchnic Nerves** ■ The remaining preganglionic parasympathetic cell bodies are housed within the S2–S4 segments of the spinal cord and form pelvic splanchnic nerves. **18.3c Effects and General Functions of the Parasympathetic Division** ■ The parasympathetic division of the ANS alters activities of effector organs to manage and control food processing, energy absorption, and relaxation activities.

(continued on next page)

Chapter Summary *(continued)*

18.4 Sympathetic Division	■ The sympathetic division outflow is from the T1–L2 lateral horn segments of the spinal cord. **18.4a Organization and Anatomy of the Sympathetic Division** ■ Preganglionic neuron cell bodies are housed within the lateral gray horn of the spinal gray matter. ■ Myelinated, preganglionic sympathetic axons exit the spinal cord through the anterior root of a spinal nerve and travel through the white rami communicantes to the sympathetic trunk ganglia. **18.4b Sympathetic Pathways** ■ In the spinal nerve pathway, the postganglionic axon enters the spinal nerve through the gray ramus and extends to target organs (blood vessels and glands of the skin). ■ In the postganglionic sympathetic nerve pathway, the postganglionic axon leaves the sympathetic trunk and extends directly to the target organs (thoracic organs, neck viscera, and blood vessels and glands of the head and neck). ■ In the splanchnic nerve pathway, the preganglionic axon passes through the sympathetic trunk without synapsing and travels to the prevertebral ganglia. ■ In the adrenal medulla pathway, the preganglionic axons extend through the autonomic ganglia without synapsing. They synapse on secretory cells in the adrenal medulla that release epinephrine and norepinephrine into the blood. **18.4c Effects and General Functions of the Sympathetic Division** ■ Sympathetic division pathways prepare the body for fight or flight.
18.5 Other Features of the Autonomic Nervous System	■ Both divisions of the autonomic nervous system innervate organs through specific axon bundles. **18.5a Autonomic Plexuses** ■ Autonomic plexuses are meshworks of postganglionic sympathetic axons, preganglionic parasympathetic axons, and visceral sensory neuron axons in the anterior body cavities that merge and intermingle but do not synapse with each other. **18.5b Enteric Nervous System** ■ The gastrointestinal tract has the enteric nervous system to regulate digestive functions. The enteric nervous system may operate independently, although ANS divisions may stimulate or inhibit this system. **18.5c Overview of ANS Neurotransmitters** ■ Both the preganglionic and postganglionic axons in the parasympathetic division release acetylcholine (ACh); the preganglionic axon and some postganglionic axons in the sympathetic division release acetylcholine; however, most of the postganglionic axons of the sympathetic division release norepinephrine (NE). **18.5d Autonomic Tone** ■ Both ANS divisions maintain some continual activity, which is called the autonomic tone for that division. **18.5e Dual Innervation** ■ Many visceral effectors have dual innervation, meaning they are innervated by axons from both ANS divisions. The actions of the divisions often oppose each other, and thus they exert antagonistic effects on the same organ. **18.5f Systems Controlled Only by the Sympathetic Division** ■ Some ANS effectors are innervated by the sympathetic division only, such as the smooth muscle in blood vessel walls. **18.5g Autonomic Reflexes** ■ Homeostasis in the human body is maintained through the activity of autonomic reflexes.
18.6 CNS Control of Autonomic Function	■ Autonomic function is influenced by three CNS regions: hypothalamus, brainstem, and spinal cord.
18.7 Development of the Autonomic Nervous System	■ The neural tube gives rise to most of the CNS structures of the ANS. ■ The neural crest cells give rise to most of the PNS structures of the ANS.

Challenge Yourself

Actively write or type your answers in a separate document to reinforce your learning, before checking your answers.

Multiple Choice

Select the best answer from the four choices provided.

1. Which statement about a splanchnic nerve in the sympathetic division of the ANS is true?
   a. It connects neighboring sympathetic trunk ganglia.
   b. It controls parasympathetic functions in the thoracic cavity.
   c. It is formed by preganglionic axons that travel to prevertebral ganglia.
   d. It travels through parasympathetic pathways in the head.

2. Where are some parasympathetic preganglionic neuron cell bodies housed?
   a. hypothalamus
   b. sacral region of the spinal cord
   c. cerebral cortex
   d. thoracolumbar region of the spinal cord

3. Which of the following is *not* a function of the sympathetic division of the ANS?
   a. increases heart rate and breathing rate
   b. prepares for emergency
   c. increases digestive system motility and activity
   d. dilates pupils
4. Postganglionic axons from the celiac ganglia innervate which of the following?
   a. stomach
   b. urinary bladder
   c. lung
   d. adrenal medulla
5. What are the sympathetic ganglia called that lie anterior to the vertebral column and the aorta?
   a. intramural
   b. sympathetic trunk
   c. prevertebral
   d. terminal
6. Which neurotransmitter is used by all parasympathetic division synapses?
   a. dopamine
   b. norepinephrine
   c. acetylcholine
   d. epinephrine
7. Which autonomic nerve plexus innervates the pelvic organs?
   a. cardiac plexus
   b. esophageal plexus
   c. hypogastric plexus
   d. inferior mesenteric plexus
8. Which of the following describes a sympathetic postganglionic axon?
   a. long, unmyelinated axon
   b. short, myelinated axon
   c. short, unmyelinated axon
   d. long, myelinated axon
9. What do neural crest cells form?
   a. the hypothalamus
   b. white rami communicantes
   c. autonomic ganglia
   d. autonomic reflex centers
10. Which of the following cranial nerves carry parasympathetic preganglionic nerve axons?
    a. CN III (oculomotor)
    b. CN V (trigeminal)
    c. CN IX (glossopharyngeal)
    d. CN X (vagus)

Content Review

1. What three CNS regions control the autonomic nervous system?
2. For the following ganglia, identify the location and the division of the ANS each is part of: sympathetic trunk ganglia, prevertebral ganglia, terminal and intramural ganglia.
3. Compare and contrast the postganglionic axons of the parasympathetic and sympathetic divisions. Examine the axon length, myelination (or lack thereof), and the neurotransmitter used.
4. Explain how adrenal medulla stimulation potentiates (prolongs) the effects of the sympathetic division of the autonomic nervous system.
5. Identify and describe the four basic pathways used in the sympathetic division.
6. Are the cell bodies of sympathetic and parasympathetic neurons located in the central nervous system, in the peripheral nervous system, or in both? Explain your answer.
7. Identify the types of axons that compose the gray and white rami communicantes, describe their anatomic arrangement and location, and discuss the reason for the differences in their color.
8. Describe how the general functions of the sympathetic and parasympathetic divisions of the ANS differ.
9. What may occur with the mass activation of the sympathetic division of the ANS?
10. Describe the embryonic components that form ANS structures.

Developing Critical Reasoning

1. Holly takes night classes at the local community college. After her lecture, she walks alone to her car and suddenly hears several dozen screeching birds fly away from the tree she is walking under. Holly immediately feels her heart pounding and notices that her breathing rate has increased. Minutes later, she still feels tense and "on edge." What happened internally to cause Holly's initial response? Why did Holly still feel tense minutes later?
2. Some faculty dislike teaching lecture classes after lunch, complaining that the students do not pay attention at this time. From an anatomic viewpoint, what is happening to these students?
3. Taylor was given epinephrine during an asthma attack. Why was epinephrine used to treat Taylor?

Answers to "What Do You Think?"

1. Compared to the somatic motor system, the autonomic motor system has a limited number of resources (nerves) to transmit the motor information throughout the body. By using a two-neuron pathway, nerve impulses are able to diverge to a larger number of resources. (Learning Strategy 18.1, which compares the ANS to the airline industry [see section 18.1a], also helps answer this question.)
2. The pterygopalatine ganglion is nicknamed the *hay fever ganglion* because when it is overstimulated, it causes some of the classic allergic reactions, including watery eyes, runny and itchy nose, sneezing, and scratchy throat.
3. Sympathetic innervation causes vasoconstriction of most blood vessels. When blood vessels are constricted, it takes more force and pressure to pump blood through the vessels, so blood pressure rises.

Design Element: Pencil Icon: Slavojub Pantelic/Shutterstock

NERVOUS SYSTEM

19 Senses: General and Special

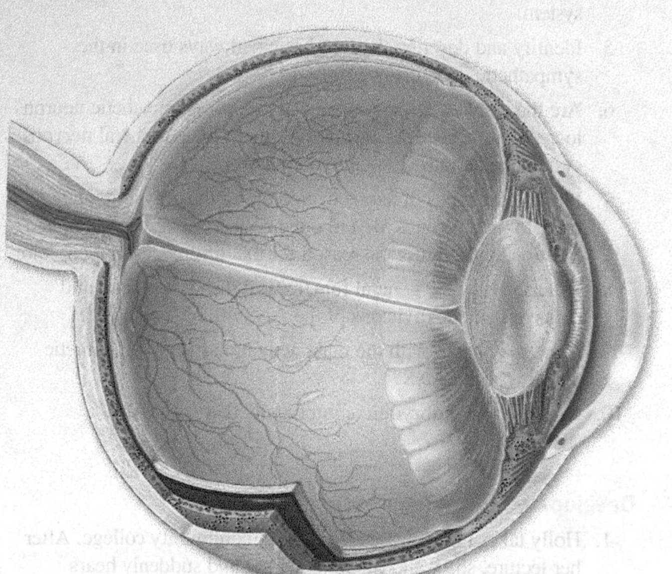

Outline

Anatomy & Physiology Revealed 4.0

MODULE 7: NERVOUS SYSTEM

We are continually exposed to an onslaught of sensory information, both externally (from the environment) and internally (within the body). **Stimuli** (stim′y ū-lī; *stimulus* = a goad) are the changes in the external or internal environment that are detected and processed as sensory information. Some of these stimuli may give us pleasure, as when we watch a funny movie, listen to a CD, touch a baby's face, or eat a tasty meal. Other stimuli may alert us to potential dangers, as when we see a stranger lurking in the dark, smell smoke upon walking into a room, or touch a hot pan on the kitchen stove. Still others may provide routine, moment-to-moment information about both our body's external surroundings and its internal state.

Our conscious awareness of incoming sensory information is called **sensation.** Only a stimulus that reaches the cerebral cortex of the brain results in a sensation of that stimulus. Thus, although our bodies are constantly bombarded by sensory stimuli, we are consciously aware of only a fraction of these stimuli.

Stimuli are detected by sensory receptors. This chapter focuses on the two classes of sensory receptors in our bodies: receptors for the **general senses** (temperature, pain, touch, stretch, and pressure) and receptors for the **special senses** (gustation, olfaction, vision, equilibrium, and hearing).

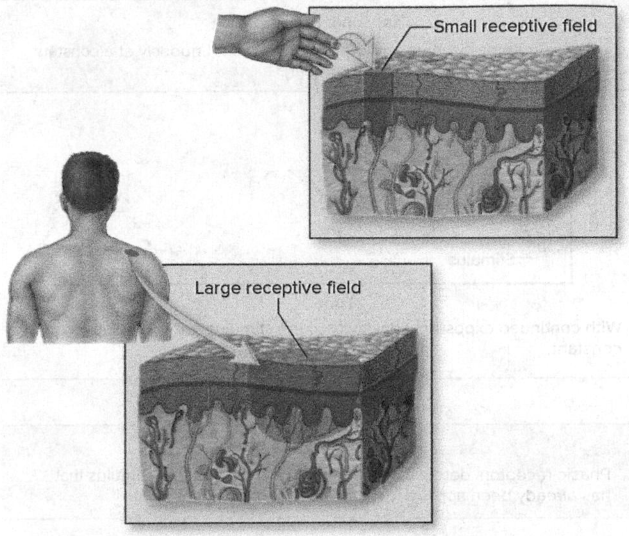

Figure 19.1

Receptive Fields. The specific area monitored by each sensory receptor is called its receptive field. A smaller receptive field offers greater specificity of localization than does a larger receptive field.

19.1 Introduction to Sensory Receptors

✓ **Learning Objective**

1. Identify and describe the properties and classification schemes for sensory receptors.

Sensory receptors (*recipio* = to receive) range in complexity from the relatively simple, bare dendritic ending of a single sensory neuron (e.g., touch receptors; see figure 19.5) to complex structures called *sense organs,* whose nerve endings are associated with epithelial tissue, connective tissue, or muscular tissue (e.g., the eye; see figure 19.13). The feature common to all sensory receptors is the ability to respond to a stimulus and initiate sensory input to the central nervous system (CNS). Here we define stimuli and sensations, provide an overview of the basic properties of sensory receptors, and describe how sensory receptors are classified.

19.1a Properties of Sensory Receptors

Important functional characteristics are associated with receptors including how they serve as transducers, the size of their receptive fields, and the two basic patterns of how the receptors communicate with the CNS.

Sensory Receptors as Transducers

Sensory receptors act as transducers. **Transducers** (tranz-d ū′sĕr; *trans* = across, *duco* = to lead) change one form of energy into a different form. The original energy form detected is specific to the type of receptor (e.g., those forms of energy are detected within the eye, ear, and blood vessels). However, the form the energy is transduced or changed to is always electrical energy, and it is conducted along a sensory neuron. This sensory information is relayed to the CNS for interpretation.

Receptive Field

The **receptive field** of a sensory receptor is the entire area through which the sensitive ends of the sensory receptor cell are distributed. This is most clearly shown with a comparison of receptive fields within the skin **(figure 19.1)**.

An inverse relationship exists between the size of the receptive field and our ability to identify the exact location of a stimulus. If the receptive field is small, precise localization of the stimulus and sensitivity are determined easily. In contrast, a broad receptive field detects only the general region of the stimulus.

Although it might seem advantageous for all sensory receptors to have small receptive fields, the number of receptors in the body would have to markedly increase to detect environmental stimuli if all receptive fields were very small. Not only would organ size and total body surface area need to increase markedly to accommodate all of these extra sensory receptors, but also the increase in energy costs to maintain activity in such a large number of sensory receptors would be enormous.

Tonic and Phasic Receptors

All sensory receptors become less sensitive to a constant stimulus and initiate a progressive decrease in the number of nerve impulses sent to the brain. This decrease in sensitivity to a continuous stimulus is called **adaptation.** However, the rate of decrease is different for each of the various types of sensory receptors. This difference in adaption is used to categorize sensory receptors as either tonic receptors or phasic receptors **(figure 19.2)**.

Tonic receptors *slowly* adapt to a constant stimulus. In response to a constant stimulus, tonic receptors continuously generate nerve impulses and slowly decrease the number relayed to the CNS. Examples of tonic receptors include receptors within the inner ear that determine head position, and proprioceptors in the joints and muscles that provide information of where your body is in space. In addition, pain receptors are tonic receptors, so as to provide the motivation to address the cause of the pain and hopefully eliminate it so that the pain will stop.

In comparison, **phasic receptors** *rapidly* adapt to a constant stimulus. Phasic receptors generate nerve impulses in response to a new (or changing) stimulus and then quickly decrease the number of nerve impulses relayed to the CNS. Examples include the deep-pressure receptors that sense the increased pressure when we first sit down in a chair. We are immediately aware of the pressure increase

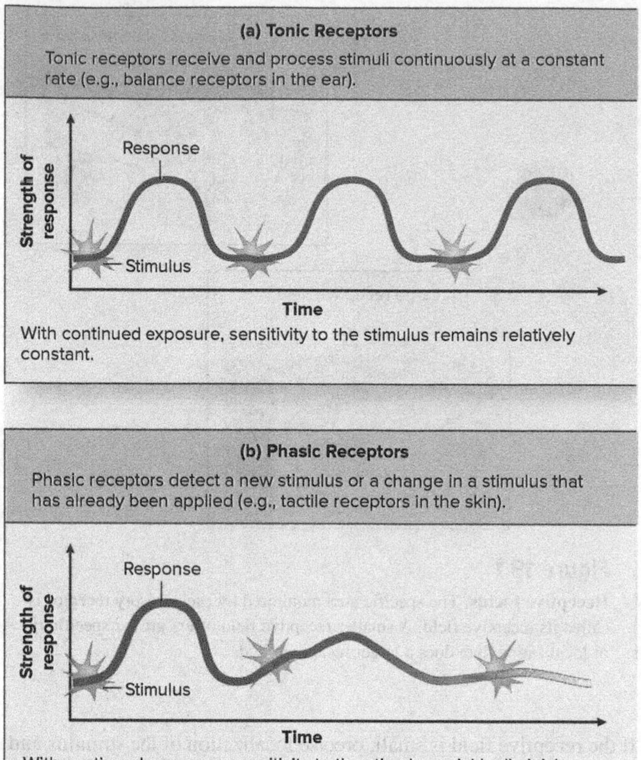
(a) Tonic Receptors
Tonic receptors receive and process stimuli continuously at a constant rate (e.g., balance receptors in the ear).
Response
Strength of response
Stimulus
Time
With continued exposure, sensitivity to the stimulus remains relatively constant.
(b) Phasic Receptors
Phasic receptors detect a new stimulus or a change in a stimulus that has already been applied (e.g., tactile receptors in the skin).
Response
Strength of response
Stimulus
Time
With continued exposure, sensitivity to the stimulus quickly diminishes, resulting in adaptation.

Figure 19.2

Sensory Receptor Responses. (*a*) Tonic receptor activity continuously responds to a constant stimulus, whereas (*b*) phasic receptor activity generate a response to a new or changing stimulus, and then rapidly adapt.

wherever our body contacts the chair. But soon, we do not notice this pressure because adaptation has occurred in these receptors. You may have experienced adaptation after placing your glasses on the top of your head and then forgetting that they were there. It is advantageous for us to not be continuously bombarded by this type of sensory information.

WHAT DID YOU LEARN?

1. How does a sensory receptor function as a transducer?
2. What is the difference between tonic and phasic receptors?

19.1b Classification of Sensory Receptors

General sense receptors are distributed throughout the skin and organs. Special sense receptors are housed within complex organs in the head. Three criteria are used to categorize sensory receptors—receptor dis - tribution, stimulus origin, and modality of stimulus **(table 19.1)**.

Sensory Receptor Distribution

General sense receptors are distributed throughout the body and are simple in structure. The receptors for general senses are sub - divided into two categories based upon their location in the body, and include somatic sensory receptors and visceral sensory receptors.

Table 19.1 Criteria for Classifying Sensory Receptors

Classification	Description	Examples
SENSORY RECEPTOR DISTRIBUTION (LOCATION OF RECEPTOR)		
General senses	Distributed throughout the body; structurally simple	
Somatic sensory receptors	Located in skin and mucous membranes Located in joints, muscles, and tendons	Tactile (touch receptors) Joint receptors, muscle spindles, Golgi tendon organs
Visceral sensory receptors	Located within walls of viscera and blood vessels	Stretch receptors in stomach wall, chemoreceptors in blood vessels
Special senses	Located only in the head; structurally complex sense organ	Sensory receptors for smell, taste, vision, hearing, and equilibrium
STIMULUS ORIGIN (LOCATION OF STIMULUS)		
Exteroceptors	Detect stimuli in the external environment	Sensory receptors within skin or mucous membranes Sensory receptors for smell, taste, vision, hearing, and equilibrium
Interoceptors	Detect stimuli within the body	Sensory receptors within walls of viscera and blood vessels
Proprioceptors	Detect stimuli within joint, skeletal muscles, and tendons that sense body or limb movement	Joint receptors, muscle spindles, Golgi tendon organs
MODALITY OF STIMULUS (STIMULATING AGENT)		
Chemoreceptors	Detect chemicals (molecules or ions) dissolved in fluid	Taste receptors, receptors in blood vessels that monitor hydrogen ions (H^+)
Thermoreceptors	Detect changes in temperature	Sensory receptors within skin and hypothalamus
Photoreceptors	Detect changes in light intensity, color, and movement	Eye
Mechanoreceptors	Detect physical deformation of the plasma membrane due to touch, pressure, vibration, and stretch; subtypes include baroreceptors, proprioceptors, tactile receptors, and other specialized cells such as the hair cells in the cochlea of the ear	Tactile receptors in the skin
Nociceptors	Detect painful stimuli	Pain receptors present in almost all organs

Somatic sensory (or *somatosensory*) **receptors** are tactile receptors housed within both the skin and mucous membranes, which line the nasal cavity, oral cavity, vagina, and anal canal. These sensory receptors monitor several types of stimuli including texture of an object, pressure, vibration, temperature, and pain. Somatic sensory receptors are also within joints, muscles, and tendons, and include joint receptors, muscle spindles, and Golgi tendon organs, respectively. These detect stretch and pressure relative to position and movement of the skeleton and skeletal muscles. A Golgi tendon organ, for example, monitors stretch of a tendon when a muscle contracts. **Visceral sensory receptors** are located in the walls of the viscera (internal organs) and blood vessels. These receptors detect stretch in the smooth muscle within the walls of internal organs (e.g., stretch of the stomach wall), chemical changes in the contents within their lumen (e.g., a change in carbon dioxide levels in the blood), temperature, and pain.

In comparison, **special sense receptors** are located only within the head and are specialized, complex sense organs. The five special senses are olfaction (smell), gustation (taste), vision (sight), hearing (audition), and equilibrium (head position and acceleration). The special sense receptors are discussed in detail in this chapter.

Stimulus Origin

Based upon where the stimulus originates, there are three types of sensory receptors: exteroceptors, interoceptors, and proprioceptors.

Exteroceptors (eks'ter- ō-sep'tŏr, -tōr; *exterus* = external) detect stimuli from the external environment. For example, the sensory receptors in your skin (called *cutaneous receptors*) are exteroceptors because external stimuli typically cause sensations to the skin. Likewise, receptors for your special senses are considered exteroceptors because they usually interpret external stimuli, such as the taste of the food you just ate or the sound of music on the radio. Exteroceptors are also found in the mucous membranes that open to the outside of the body, such as the nasal cavity, oral cavity, vagina, and anal canal.

Interoceptors (in'tĕr-ō-sep'tŏr; *inter* = between), also called *visceroceptors,* detect stimuli in internal organs (viscera). These sensory receptors are primarily stretch receptors in the smooth muscle of these organs. Most of the time we are unaware of these sensory receptors, but when the smooth muscle stretches to a certain point (e.g., when eating a large meal stretches our stomach wall), we may become aware of these sensations. Interoceptors also report on pressure, chemical changes in the visceral tissue, and temperature. When we feel pain in our internal organs, it is usually because a tissue has been deprived of oxygen (as in a heart attack), because the smooth muscle has been stretched so much that we are uncomfortable, or because the tissue has suffered trauma, and damaged cells have released chemicals that stimulate specific interoceptors.

Proprioceptors (prō'prē-ō-sep'tŏr; *proprius* = one's own) are located in muscles, tendons, and joints. These sensory receptors detect body and limb movements, skeletal muscle contraction and stretch, and changes in joint capsule structure. Thus, even if you are not looking at your body joints, you are aware of their positioning and the state of contraction of your skeletal muscles, because proprioceptors send this information to the CNS.

Modality of Stimulus

Sensory receptors also may be classified according to the stimulus they perceive, called the **modality of stimulus,** or the *stimulating agent.* For example, some sensory receptors respond only to temperature changes, whereas others respond to chemical changes. There are five groups of sensory receptors, based upon their modality of stimulus: chemoreceptors, thermoreceptors, photoreceptors, mechanoreceptors, and nociceptors.

- **Chemoreceptors** (kē'mō-rē-sep'tōr) detect chemicals such as specific molecules dissolved in fluid in our external and internal environments, including ingested food and drink, body fluids, and inhaled air. For example, the receptors in the taste buds on our tongue are chemoreceptors, because they respond to the specific molecules in ingested food. Likewise, chemoreceptors in some of our blood vessels monitor the concentration of oxygen and carbon dioxide molecules in our blood.
- **Thermoreceptors** (ther'm ō-rē-sep't ōr; *therme* = heat) respond to changes in temperature. Thermoreceptors are present in both the skin and the hypothalamus. These receptors initiate reflexes that regulate and maintain body temperature.
- **Photoreceptors** (fō'tō-rē-sep't ōr; *phot* = light) are located in the eye, where they detect changes in light intensity, color, and movement.
- **Mechanoreceptors** (me-k ăn'ō-rē-sep'tōr; *mechane* = machine) respond to distortion of the plasma membrane that occurs due to touch, pressure, vibration, and stretch. The various types of mechanoreceptors include baroreceptors, proprioceptors, tactile receptors, and other specialized cells such as the hair cells in the cochlea of the ear that move in response to sound waves. For example, **baroreceptors** (bar'ō-rē-sep'tōr; *baros* = weight) are a type of mechanoreceptor, which are stimulated by changes in stretch or distension within the wall of body structures. Baroreceptors located within blood vessel walls monitor stretch of these structures, as part of blood pressure regulation.
- **Nociceptors** (nō-si-sep'ter, -tōr; *noci* = pain) respond to painful stimuli, to inform the body of injury or other damage. *Somatic nociceptors* detect chemical, heat, or mechanical damage to the body surface or skeletal muscles. For example, exposure to acid, touching a hot pan, or suffering a sprained ankle stimulate somatic nociceptors. *Visceral nociceptors* detect internal body damage within the viscera due to excessive stretching of smooth muscle, oxygen deprivation of the tissue, or chemicals released from damaged tissue.

Clinically Significant Types of Pain **Phantom** (fan'tŏm) **pain** is a sensation associated with a body part that has been removed. Following the amputation of an appendage, the patient often continues to experience pain that feels like it is coming from the removed part. The stimulation of a sensory neuron pathway from the removed limb anywhere on the remaining intact portion of the pathway propagates nerve impulses and conducts them to the primary somatosensory cortex of the brain (see section 15.3b), where they are interpreted as originating in the amputated limb. In other words, the cell bodies of the sensory neurons that provided sensation to the leg remain alive because they were not part of the leg. This so-called **phantom limb syndrome** can be quite debilitating. Some people experience extreme pain, whereas others have an insatiable desire to scratch a nonexistent itch.

Referred pain occurs when impulses from certain viscera are perceived as originating not from the organ, but in dermatomes of the skin (see figure 16.6). Numerous cutaneous and visceral sensory neurons conduct nerve impulses through the same ascending tracts within the spinal cord (**figure 19.3**). As a result, impulses conducted along ascending pathways may be localized incorrectly. Consequently, the primary somatosensory cortex in the brain is unable to differentiate between the actual and false sources of the stimulus.

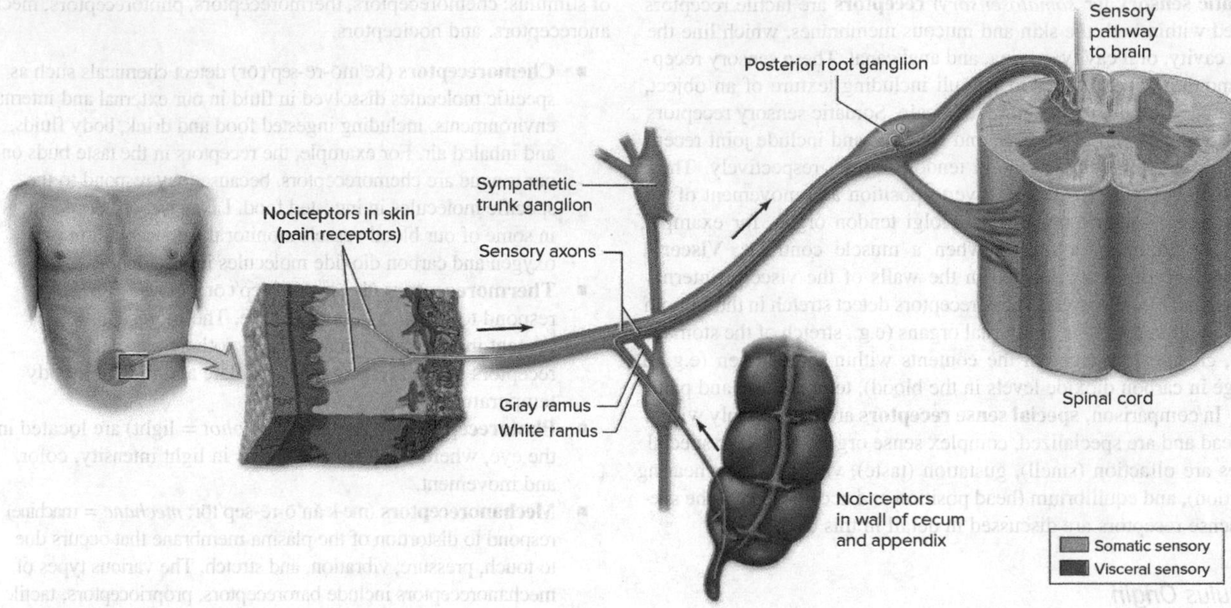
Sensory pathway to brain
Posterior root ganglion
Sympathetic trunk ganglion
Nociceptors in skin (pain receptors)
Sensory axons
Gray ramus
White ramus
Spinal cord
Nociceptors in wall of cecum and appendix
Somatic sensory
Visceral sensory

Figure 19.3

Source of Referred Pain. Misinterpretation of a pain source occurs when sensory impulses from two different organs are conducted to the brain via a common pathway. For example, pain that is perceived as originating from the umbilical region of the skin actually has its source within the appendix.

Learning Strategy 19.1

Here is one way to remember the differences between somatic nociceptors and visceral nociceptors: When you eat a very spicy meal, your mouth stings and burns because the nociceptors in your mouth are somatic nociceptors. They detect the spicy stimuli and send impulses to the brain where the stimuli are translated into the stinging, burning sensation. When you swallow that spicy meal and it travels through your GI tract, you may not experience the stinging, burning sensation because the nociceptors there are visceral nociceptors that respond only to abnormal muscle stretch, oxygen deprivation, or chemical imbalance in the tissue. Now, when the waste products from that spicy meal are expelled from the body, the anus may burn and sting because the nociceptors around the anus and lower anal canal are somatic nociceptors.

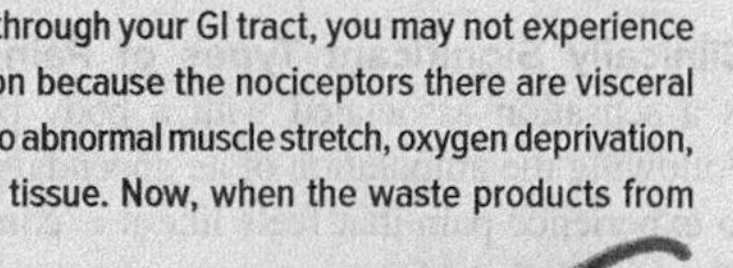

Skip ODonnell/Getty Images

Clinically, some common sites of referred pain are useful in medical diagnosis (**figure 19.4**). For example, cardiac problems are often a source of referred pain. The heart's visceral sensory pain pathway uses the same nervous system structures as its sympathetic innervation, which originates from T1–T5 segments of the spinal cord (see section 22.5). Pain associated with a myocardial infarction (heart attack) may be referred to the skin dermatomes innervated by the T1–T5 spinal nerves, which lie along the pectoral region and the medial side of the arm. Thus, some individuals who are experiencing heart problems may feel pain along the medial side of the left arm, where the T1 dermatome lies (see Clinical View 22.4: "Angina Pectoris and Myocardial Infarction" in section 22.3). By the same token, kidney and ureter pain may be referred along the T10–L2 dermatomes, which typically overlie the inferior abdominal wall in the groin and loin regions (see section 27.2c and Clinical View 27.3: "Renal Calculi" in section 27.3b).

Visceral pain pathways usually utilize the same nervous structures as sympathetic nerve pathways, but sometimes they can follow parasympathetic pathways as well. For example, referred pain from the urinary bladder can follow the parasympathetic pathways (via the pelvic splanchnic nerves). Because the pelvic splanchnic nerves lie in the S2–S4 segments of the spinal cord, pain may be referred to the S2–S4 dermatomes, which overlie the medial buttocks region.

WHAT DO YOU THINK?

1. Based upon stimulus origin, would a cutaneous pain receptor be classified as an exteroceptor, an interoceptor, or a proprioceptor? Based upon receptor distribution, would this same cutaneous receptor be classified as a general somatic, general visceral, or special sense? Finally, how would this pain receptor in the skin be classified based upon modality of stimulus?

WHAT DID YOU LEARN?

3. What is a sensation? How is a sensation related to a stimulus?
4. What are the three groups of receptors classified by stimulus origin?
5. What stimuli affect mechanoreceptors and thermoreceptors?

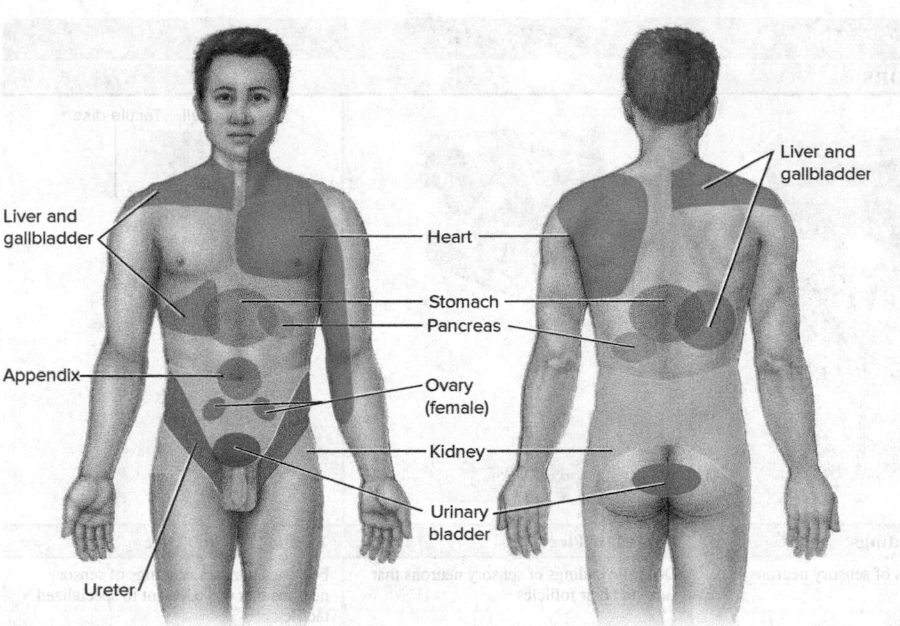
Liver and gallbladder
Heart
Stomach
Pancreas
Appendix
Ovary (female)
Kidney
Urinary bladder
Ureter
Liver and gallbladder

Figure 19.4
Common Sites of Referred Pain. This image illustrates the regions of skin where pain may be referred from selected organs. Note how pain from the heart may be referred to the left upper limb, and pain from the liver and gallbladder may be referred to the right shoulder.

19.2 Tactile Receptors

✓ Learning Objective

2. Describe the types of tactile receptors and their functions.

Tactile (tak'til; *tango* = to touch) **receptors** are the most numerous type of sensory receptor. They are mechanoreceptors that react to touch, pressure, and vibration stimuli. They are located in the dermis (see section 5.3) and the subcutaneous layer **(figure 19.5)**. Tactile receptors range from simple, dendritic ends that have no connective tissue wrapping (called unencapsulated) to complex structures that are wrapped with connective tissue or glial cells (called encapsulated) **(table 19.2)**.

19.2a Unencapsulated Tactile Receptors

Unencapsulated tactile receptors have no connective tissue wrapping around them and are relatively simple in structure. The three types of unencapsulated tactile receptors are free nerve endings, root hair plexuses, and tactile discs.

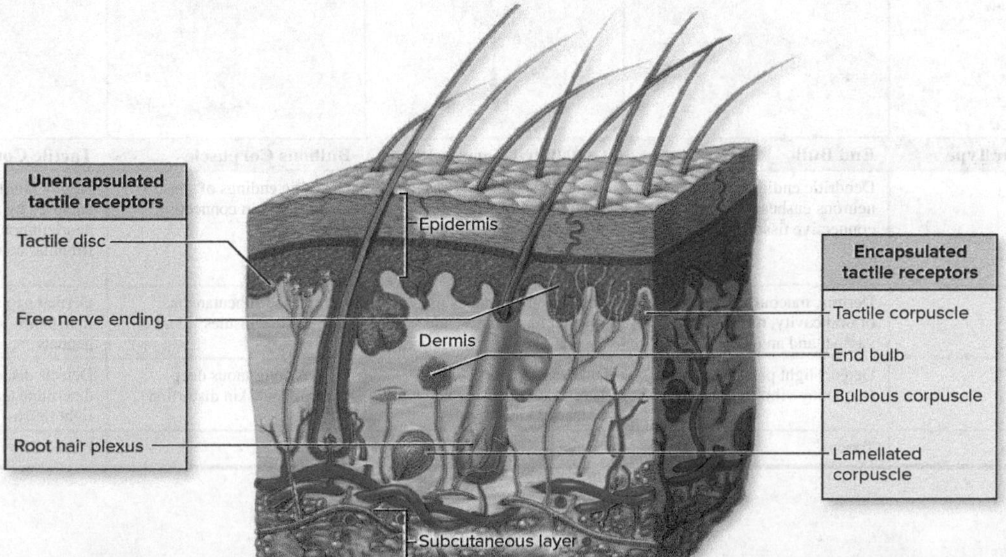
Unencapsulated tactile receptors
Tactile disc
Free nerve ending
Root hair plexus
Epidermis
Dermis
Subcutaneous layer
Encapsulated tactile receptors
Tactile corpuscle
End bulb
Bulbous corpuscle
Lamellated corpuscle

Figure 19.5
Tactile Receptors. Various types of tactile receptors in the skin receive information about touch, pressure, or vibration in our immediate environment. Unencapsulated tactile receptors have no connective tissue covering around them, whereas encapsulated tactile receptors are enclosed by either connective tissue or glial cells.

Table 19.2 Types of Tactile Receptors

UNENCAPSULATED TACTILE RECEPTORS

	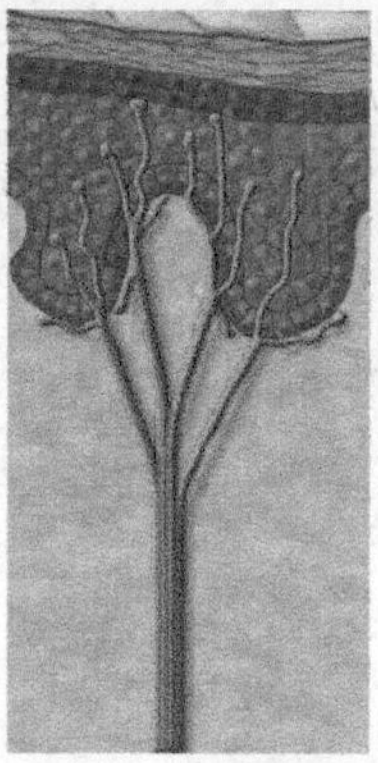	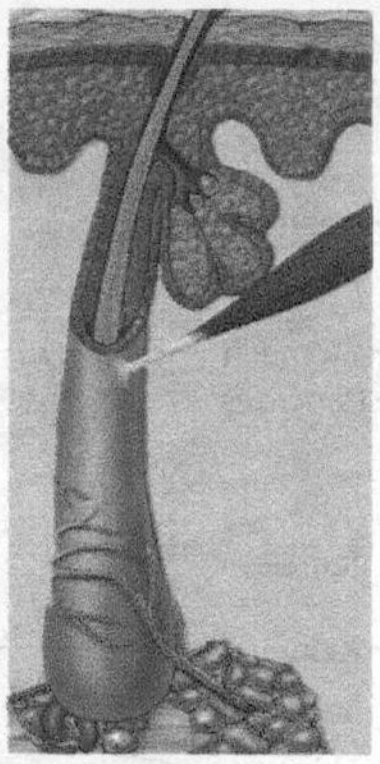	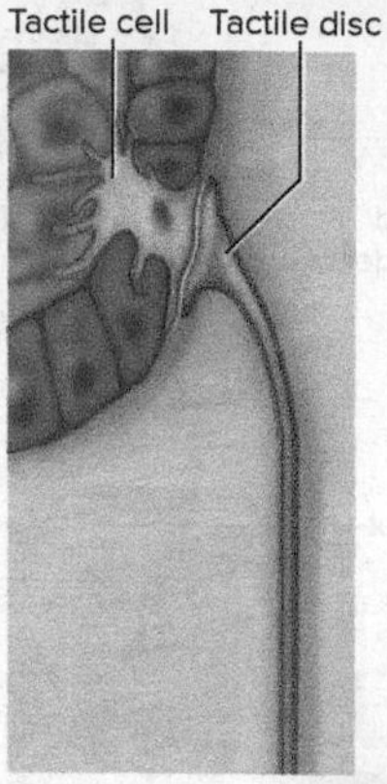
Tactile Receptor Type	**Free Nerve Endings**	**Root Hair Plexus**	**Tactile (Merkel) Disc**
Structure	Dendritic endings of sensory neurons	Dendritic endings of sensory neurons that surround hair follicles	Flattened dendritic endings of sensory neurons that end adjacent to specialized tactile cells
Location	Deep epidermis and papillary layer of the dermis; some dendritic endings extend into the deepest layers of the epidermal strata	Reticular layer of the dermis	Stratum basale of epidermis
Function	Detects temperature, pain; some detect light touch and pressure	Detects movement of the hair	Detects light touch
Rate of Adaptation	Phasic or tonic	Phasic	Tonic

ENCAPSULATED TACTILE RECEPTORS

	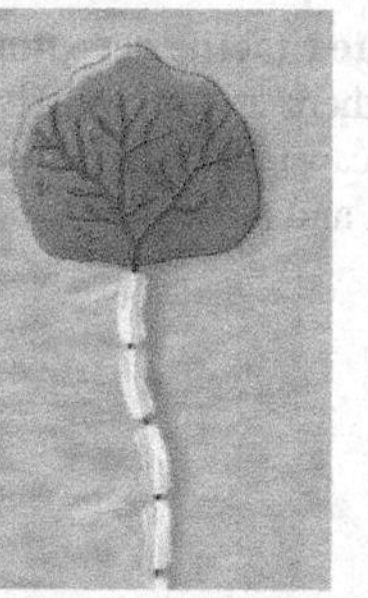		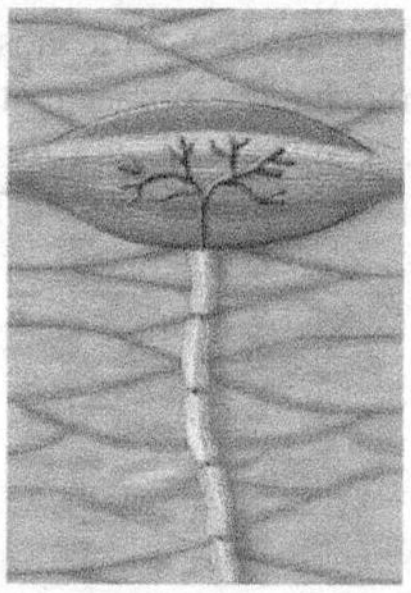	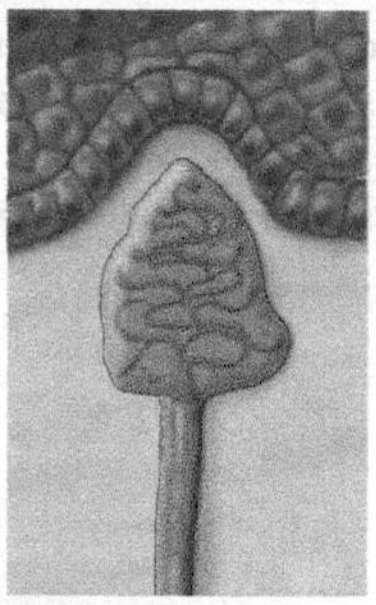
Tactile Receptor Type	**End Bulb**	**Lamellated Corpuscle**	**Bulbous Corpuscle**	**Tactile Corpuscle**
Structure	Dendritic endings of sensory neurons ensheathed in connective tissue	Dendritic endings of sensory neurons ensheathed with an inner core of neurolemmocytes and outer concentric layers of connective tissue	Dendritic endings of sensory neurons within connective tissue	Highly intertwined dendrites enclosed by modified neurlemmocytes and dense irregular connective tissue
Location	Dermis, mucous membranes of oral cavity, nasal cavity, vagina, and anal canal	Dermis, subcutaneous tissue, synovial membranes, and some viscera	Dermis and subcutaneous layer; joint capsules	Dermal papillae, especially in lips, palms, eyelids, nipples, genitals
Function	Detects light pressure and low-frequency vibration	Functions in coarse touch; detects deep pressure and high-frequency vibration	Detects continuous deep pressure and skin distortion	Detects discriminative touch to determine textures and shapes; light touch
Rate of Adaptation	Tonic	Phasic	Tonic	Phasic

Free nerve endings are terminal branches of dendrites. They are the least complex of the tactile receptors and reside closest to the surface of the skin, usually in the papillary layer of the dermis. Often, some dendritic branches extend into the deepest epidermal strata and terminate between the epithelial cells. These tactile receptors primarily detect pain and temperature stimuli, but some also detect light touch and pressure.

Root hair plexuses are specialized free nerve endings that form a weblike sheath around hair follicles in the reticular layer of the dermis. Any movement or displacement of the hair changes the arrangement of these branching dendrites, initiating a nerve impulse. These receptors quickly adapt; thus, although we feel the initial contact of a long-sleeved shirt on our arm hairs when we put on the garment, our conscious awareness subsides immediately until we move and the root hair plexuses are restimulated.

Tactile discs, previously called *Merkel discs,* are flattened nerve endings that function as tonic receptors for fine touch. These receptors are important in distinguishing the texture and shape of a stimulating agent. Tactile discs are associated with special **tactile cells** (*Merkel cells*), which are located in the stratum basale of the epidermis. Tactile cells exhibit a small receptive field and communicate directly with the dendrites of a sensory neuron. (Note that tactile cells are the only specialized receptor cells; other tactile receptors are simply the dendritic endings of primary sensory neurons.)

19.2b Encapsulated Tactile Receptors

As their name suggests, **encapsulated tactile receptors** are surrounded (encapsulated) by another structure. They may be either wrapped by connective tissue or covered by glial cells. Encapsulated tactile receptors include end bulbs, lamellated corpuscles, bulbous corpuscles, and tactile corpuscles.

End bulbs, previously called *Krause bulbs,* are dendritic endings of sensory neurons ensheathed in connective tissue. They are located in the dermis of the skin near the border of the stratified squamous epithelium, and in the mucous membranes of the oral cavity, nasal cavity, vagina, and anal canal. End bulbs detect light-pressure stimuli and low-frequency vibration.

Lamellated (lam'ĕ-lāt-ĕd) **corpuscles,** previously called *Pacinian corpuscles,* are composed of several dendritic endings ensheathed with an inner core of neurolemmocytes (see section 14.2b) and outer concentric layers of connective tissue. They occur deep within the reticular layer of the dermis of the skin; in the subcutaneous tissue of the palms of the hands, soles of the feet, breasts, and external genitalia; in the synovial membranes of joints; and in the walls of some organs. The structure and location of lamellated corpuscles allow them to function in coarse touch, as well as sense continuous deep-pressure and high-frequency vibration stimuli.

Bulbous corpuscles, previously called *Ruffini corpuscles,* are dendritic endings of sensory neurons ensheathed within connective tissue that are housed within the dermis and subcutaneous layer, as well as in joint capsules. They detect both continuous deep pressure and distortion in the skin. These are tonic receptors that do not exhibit adaptation.

Tactile corpuscles, previously called *Meissner corpuscles,* are large, encapsulated oval receptors. They are formed from highly intertwined dendrites enclosed by modified neurolemmocytes, which are then covered with dense irregular connective tissue. They are housed within the dermal papillae of the skin, especially in the lips, palms, eyelids, nipples, and genitals. Tactile corpuscles are phasic receptors for discriminative touch to determine textures and shapes of an object and for light touch.

WHAT DID YOU LEARN?

6 How do unencapsulated receptors differ from encapsulated receptors?

7 Write out your own table that lists the cutaneous receptor type, whether it is encapsulated or unencapsulated, and what sensations it detects.

19.3 Olfaction

✓ **Learning Objective**

3. Identify and describe the structure, location, and innervation pathway of olfactory receptors.

Olfaction (ol-fak 'shŭn; *olfacio* = to smell) is the sense of smell, whereby volatile molecules (called **odorants**) must be dissolved in the mucus in our nasal cavity to be detected. Thus, the receptors used in olfaction are chemoreceptors.

Compared to many other animals, our olfactory ability is vastly less sensitive and not as highly developed, because we do not rely as greatly on olfactory information to find food or communicate with others. Yet we do have the ability to distinguish one odor among thousands of different ones, a capability that we may appreciate as we walk through a garden of flowers.

Olfactory Organs

Within the nasal cavity, paired olfactory organs are the organs of smell. They are composed of several components (**figure 19.6**). In our nasal cavity, an **olfactory epithelium** lines the superior region of the nasal cavity, including both the superior nasal conchae and the inferior surface of the cribriform plate of the ethmoid bone. This specialized epithelium is composed of three distinct cell types:

- **Olfactory receptor cells** (also called *olfactory neurons*), which detect odors
- **Supporting cells** (also called *sustentacular cells*) that sandwich the olfactory neurons and sustain the receptors
- **Basal cells** (which function as neural stem cells) continually replace olfactory receptor cells

Internal to the olfactory epithelium is an areolar connective tissue layer called the **lamina propria** (lam 'i-nă prō 'prī-ă). Housed within the collagen fibers and ground substance of this layer are mucin-secreting **olfactory glands** (or *Bowman glands*) and many blood vessels and nerves. Secretions from both supporting cells and olfactory glands form the mucus that covers the exposed surface of the olfactory epithelium.

19.3a Olfactory Receptor Cells

Olfactory receptor cells are bipolar neurons that serve as the primary neuron in the sensory pathway for smell. Olfactory receptor cells have both a single dendrite and an unmyelinated axon. Projecting from the dendrites are numerous thin, nonmotile cilia called **olfactory hairs,** which extend into the layer of mucus. Olfactory hairs contain chemoreceptors within their plasma membrane that detect one specific odorant molecule.

Depending upon which olfactory receptor cells are stimulated, different smells will be perceived. Axons of olfactory receptor cells form bundles (fascicles) of the **olfactory nerves (CN I)** (see section 15.8). These fascicles project through foramina (holes) in the cribriform plate of the ethmoid bone to enter an olfactory bulb.

Olfactory receptor cells are one of the few types of neurons that are replaced. Olfactory receptor cells are regenerated every 40 to 60 days by basal cells within the olfactory epithelium. (This process of regeneration decreases with age, and the remaining olfactory neurons lose their sensitivity to odors. Thus, an elderly individual has a decreased ability to recognize odor molecules.)

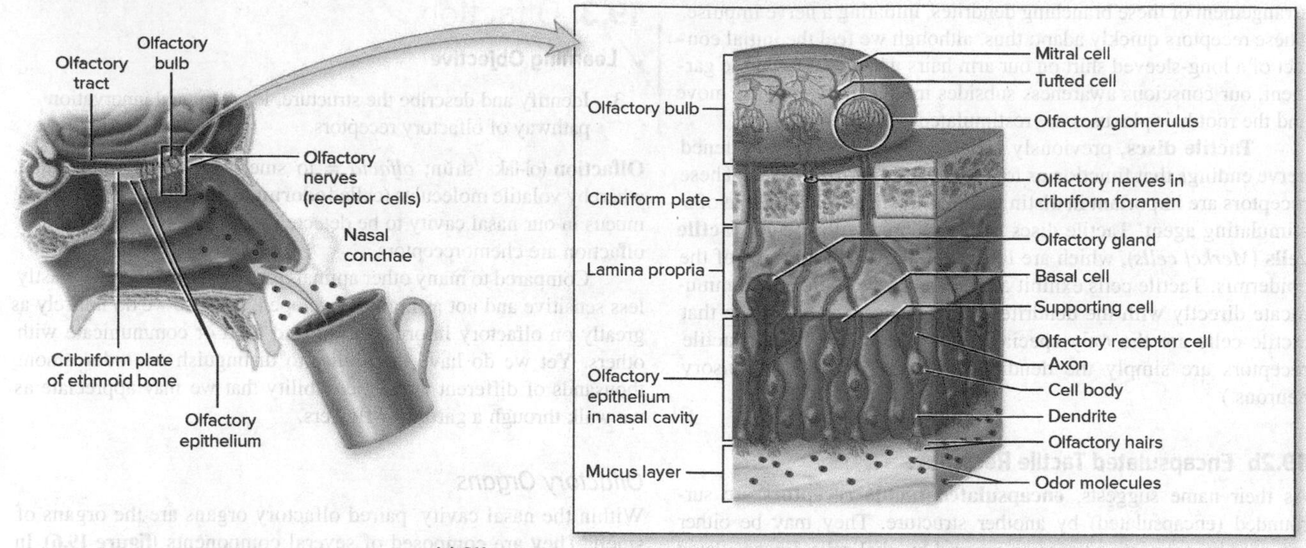
Olfactory tract
Olfactory bulb
Olfactory nerves (receptor cells)
Nasal conchae
Cribriform plate of ethmoid bone
Olfactory epithelium
Olfactory bulb
Cribriform plate
Lamina propria
Olfactory epithelium in nasal cavity
Mucus layer
Mitral cell
Tufted cell
Olfactory glomerulus
Olfactory nerves in cribriform foramen
Olfactory gland
Basal cell
Supporting cell
Olfactory receptor cell
Axon
Cell body
Dendrite
Olfactory hairs
Odor molecules

(a) Olfactory receptor cells

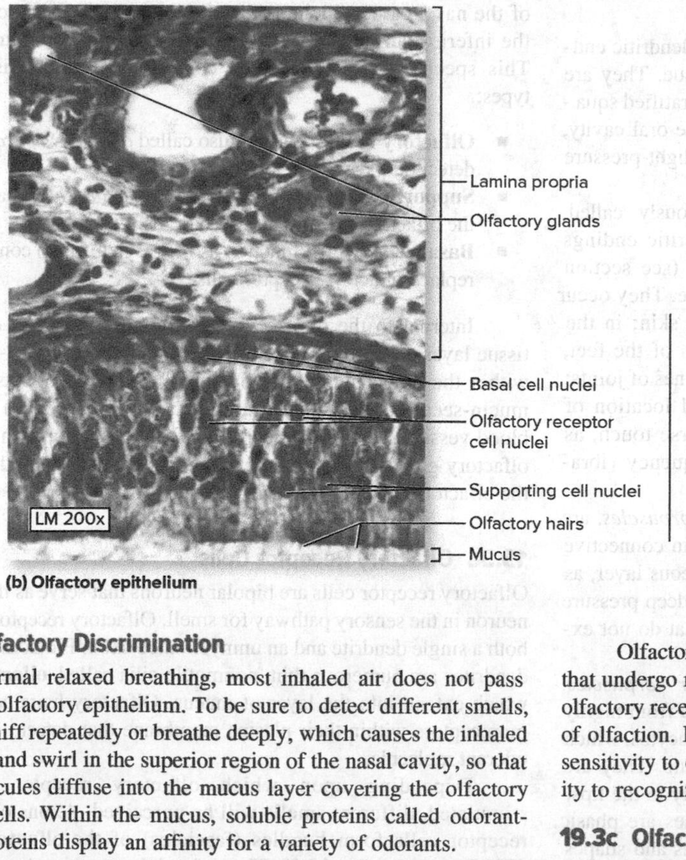
Lamina propria
Olfactory glands
Basal cell nuclei
Olfactory receptor cell nuclei
Supporting cell nuclei
Olfactory hairs
Mucus
LM 200x

(b) Olfactory epithelium

Figure 19.6

Olfactory Organs. Olfactory organs house olfactory receptor cells that detect chemical stimuli in the air we breathe. (*a*) When olfactory receptor cells within the olfactory epithelium are stimulated, they send nerve impulses in axons that pass through the cribriform plate of the ethmoid bone and synapse on neurons within the olfactory bulb. (*b*) A photomicrograph of the olfactory epithelium. **APR**

(b) ©Victor P. Eroschenko

19.3b Olfactory Discrimination

During normal relaxed breathing, most inhaled air does not pass across the olfactory epithelium. To be sure to detect different smells, we must sniff repeatedly or breathe deeply, which causes the inhaled air to mix and swirl in the superior region of the nasal cavity, so that odor molecules diffuse into the mucus layer covering the olfactory receptor cells. Within the mucus, soluble proteins called odorant-binding proteins display an affinity for a variety of odorants.

In contrast to the five basic taste sensations, the olfactory system can recognize as many as eight different primary odors as well as many thousands of other chemical stimuli. Primary odors are those that are detectable by a large number of people, such as camphorous, fishy, malty, minty, musky, and sweaty. Secondary odors are those produced by a combination of chemicals and not detected or recognized by everyone. For example, some flower blossoms exhibit almost 100 odoriferous compounds, and individuals in the general population vary widely in their ability to recognize some or all of these. However, there are no obvious structural differences between olfactory receptor cells.

Olfactory receptor cells are one of the few types of neurons that undergo mitosis to replace old or damaged cells. The number of olfactory receptor cells declines with age, thus diminishing the sense of olfaction. In addition, the remaining olfactory neurons lose their sensitivity to odors. Thus, an elderly individual has a decreased ability to recognize odor molecules.

19.3c Olfactory Pathways

The **olfactory bulbs** are the terminal ends of olfactory tracts located inferior to the frontal lobes of the brain (see figure 15.1*b*). Axons of olfactory nerves synapse with both *mitral cells* and *tufted cells* (both of which are secondary neurons) within the olfactory bulbs. The resulting spherical structures are called **olfactory glomeruli** (glō-mar′y ū-lī; sing., *glomerulus* = small ball). We have about 2000 glomeruli in our olfactory bulbs, and numerous olfactory receptor cells converge on each olfactory glomerulus. Thus, each glomerulus is collecting sensory information from many olfactory receptors, which enhances our ability to detect faint odors.

Axon bundles of the mitral and tufted cells form the paired **olfactory tracts** that project posteriorly along the inferior frontal lobe surface directly to the primary olfactory cortex in the temporal lobe (see table 15.3) and selected different regions of the brain, including the hypothalamus and limbic system (see section 15.7). Unlike other sensory information, olfactory pathways do not project to the thalamus and therefore do not undergo any thalamic processing prior to reaching the cerebrum. However, because olfactory pathways also travel to the hypothalamus and limbic system (see section 15.7), some smells may elicit behavioral and emotional reactions.

WHAT DID YOU LEARN?

8 What are the components and functions of the olfactory organs?

9 Draw a flowchart of the structures in the pathway by which odors are converted to nerve impulses and then detected by the brain.

19.4 Gustation

✓ **Learning Objective**

4. Describe the structure, location, and innervation pathway of gustatory receptors.

Our sense of taste, called **gustation** (gŭs-tā′shŭn; *gusto* = to taste), permits us to perceive the characteristics of what we eat and drink. Gustatory (taste) cells are chemoreceptors located within taste buds on the tongue and soft palate. The tongue and soft palate also house mechanoreceptors and thermoreceptors to provide information about the texture and temperature of the food we are eating.

19.4a Papillae and Taste Buds of the Tongue

On the dorsal surface of the tongue are epithelial and connective tissue elevations called **papillae** (pă-pil′ē; *papula* = a small nipple). There are four types of papillae: filiform, fungiform, vallate, and foliate (**figure 19.7*a, b***):

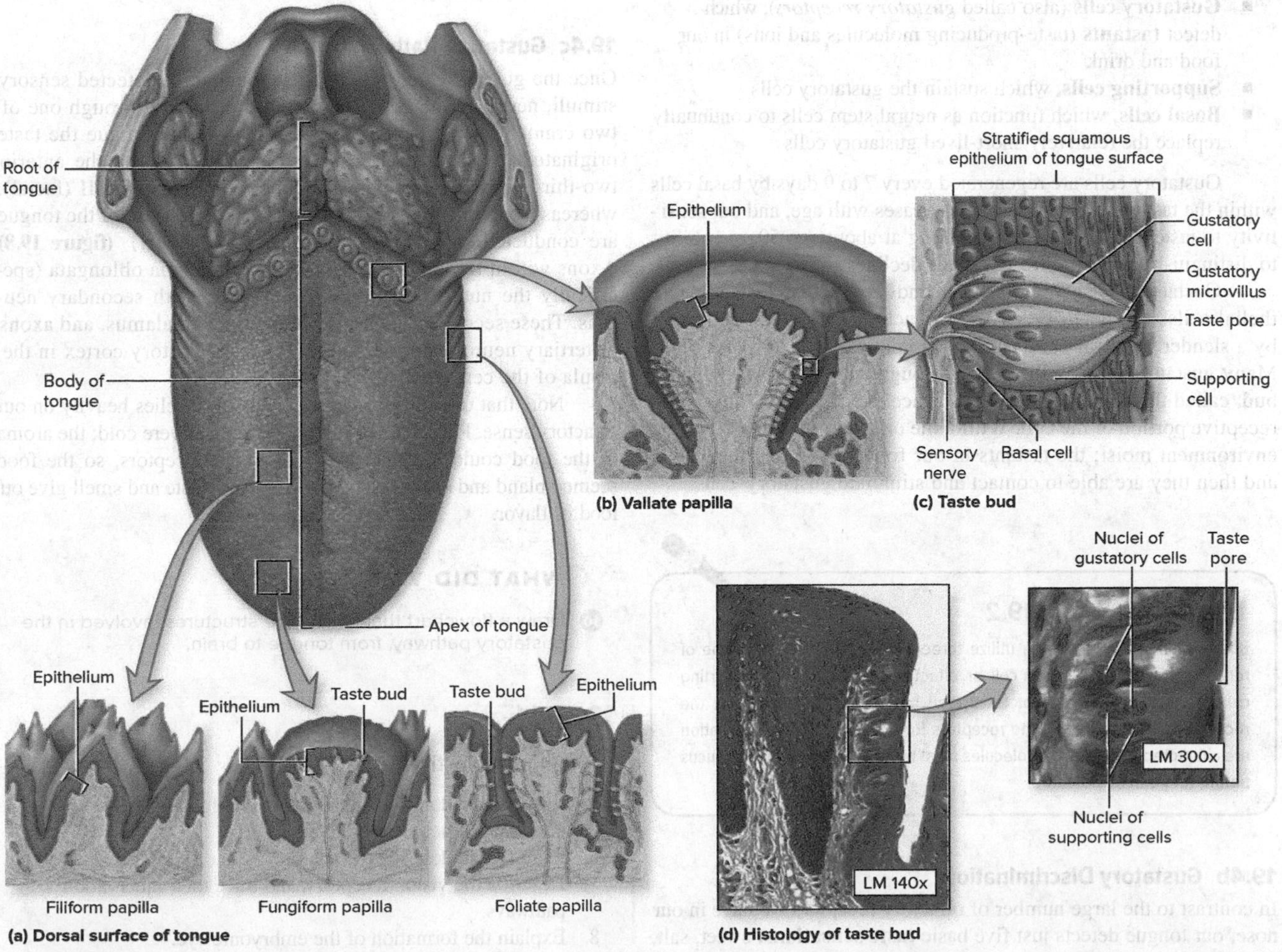

Root of tongue
Body of tongue
Apex of tongue
Epithelium
Epithelium
Taste bud
Taste bud
Epithelium
Filiform papilla
Fungiform papilla
Foliate papilla
(a) Dorsal surface of tongue
Epithelium
(b) Vallate papilla
Stratified squamous epithelium of tongue surface
Gustatory cell
Gustatory microvillus
Taste pore
Supporting cell
Sensory nerve
Basal cell
(c) Taste bud
Nuclei of gustatory cells
Taste pore
LM 140x
LM 300x
Nuclei of supporting cells
(d) Histology of taste bud

Figure 19.7

Tongue Papillae and Taste Buds. (*a*) Papillae are small elevations on the tongue surface that exist in four types: filiform, fungiform, foliate, and vallate (shown in [*b*]). (*b*) A vallate papilla exhibits many taste buds, one of which is shown in detail in (*c*). (*d*) Photomicrographs show the histological structure of a taste bud.

Filiform (fil'i-f ōrm; *filum* = thread) **papillae** are short and bristlelike; they are distributed on the anterior two-thirds of the tongue surface. These papillae do not house taste buds and thus, have no role in gustation. Instead, their bristlelike structure serves a mechanical function; they assist in detecting texture and manipulating food.

Fungiform (fŭn'ji-f ōrm; = mushroom-shaped) **papillae** are blocklike projections primarily located on the tip and sides of the tongue. Each contains only a few taste buds.

Vallate (val' āt; *vallo* = to surround) **papillae,** or *circumvallate papillae,* are the least numerous (about 10 to 12) yet are the largest papillae on the tongue. They are arranged in an inverted V shape on the posterior dorsal surface of the tongue. Each papilla is surrounded by a deep, narrow depression. Most of our taste buds are housed within the walls of these papillae along the side facing the depression.

Foliate (fō'lē-āt; leaflike) **papillae** are not well developed on the human tongue. They extend as ridges on the posterior lateral sides of the tongue and house only a few taste buds during infancy and early childhood.

Taste buds are cylindrical sensory organs which have the appearance of an onion (figure 19.7*c, d*). Each taste bud is composed of three distinct cell types:

- **Gustatory cells** (also called *gustatory receptors*), which detect **tastants** (taste-producing molecules and ions) in our food and drink
- **Supporting cells,** which sustain the gustatory cells
- **Basal cells,** which function as neural stem cells to continually replace the relatively short-lived gustatory cells

Gustatory cells are regenerated every 7 to 9 days by basal cells within the taste bud. This process decreases with age, and our sensitivity to taste also decreases. Beginning at about age 50, our ability to distinguish between different tastes declines.

Gustatory cells within the taste buds are specialized neuroepithelial cells. The dendritic ending of each gustatory cell is formed by a slender **gustatory microvillus,** sometimes called a *taste hair.* Many gustatory microvilli extend through an opening in the taste bud, called the **taste pore,** to the surface of the tongue. This is the receptive portion of the cell. Within the oral cavity, saliva keeps the environment moist; the tastants in our food dissolve in the saliva, and then they are able to contact and stimulate gustatory cells.

Learning Strategy 19.2

Both olfaction and gustation utilize three main types of cells: a type of receptor cell (i.e., gustatory cell or olfactory receptor cell), supporting cells (to sustain the receptor cells), and basal cells (which replace the receptor cells). In addition, the receptors for both olfaction and gustation are chemoreceptors, since molecules must be dissolved in saliva or mucus before they can be detected.

19.4b Gustatory Discrimination

In contrast to the large number of olfactory receptors we have in our nose, our tongue detects just five basic **taste sensations:** sweet, salt, sour, bitter, and umami:

- **Sweet** tastes are produced by organic compounds such as sugar or other molecules (e.g., artificial sweeteners).
- **Salt** tastes are produced by metal ions, such as sodium (Na^+) and potassium (K^+).
- **Sour** tastes are associated with acids in the ingested material, such as hydrogen ions (H^+) in vinegar.
- **Bitter** tastes are produced primarily by alkaloids such as quinine, unsweetened chocolate, nicotine, and caffeine.
- **Umami** stimuli: *Umami* is a Japanese word meaning "delicious flavor." It is a taste related to amino acids, such as glutamate and aspartate, to produce a savory or meaty flavor.

For the basic taste sensations, the threshold required to stimulate the receptor varies. Our taste receptors are more sensitive to bitter and sour stimuli, as those sensations might indicate something toxic or poisonous in our food. Employing a combination of taste modalities allows us to perceive a wide variety of tastes.

In the past, researchers thought certain tastes were best interpreted along specific regions of the tongue; however, research has found that these "taste maps" were incorrect and that taste sensations are spread over broader regions of the tongue than previously thought.

WHAT DO YOU THINK?

2 When a person has a stuffy nose from a "cold" or hay fever, he or she typically can't detect tastes as well. Why?

19.4c Gustatory Pathways

Once the gustatory cells within taste buds have detected sensory stimuli, nerve impulses are transmitted primarily through one of two cranial nerves, depending on where on the tongue the taste originated (see section 15.8). Taste sensations from the anterior two-thirds of the tongue are conducted through CN VII (facial), whereas taste sensations from the posterior one-third of the tongue are conducted through CN IX (glossopharyngeal) **(figure 19.8)**. Axons within these nerves project to the medulla oblongata (specifically the nucleus solitarius) to synapse with secondary neurons. These secondary neurons project to the thalamus, and axons of tertiary neurons project to the primary gustatory cortex in the insula of the cerebrum (see table 15.3).

Note that our ability to taste what we eat relies heavily on our olfactory sense. Recall the last time you had a severe cold; the aroma of the food could not reach your olfactory receptors, so the food seemed bland and almost tasteless. Together, taste and smell give our food its flavor.

WHAT DID YOU LEARN?

10 Draw a flowchart that shows the structures involved in the gustatory pathway, from tongue to brain.

19.5 Vision

✓ Learning Objectives

5. Identify and describe the structure and function of the accessory structures of the eye.
6. Identify and describe the anatomy of the eye.
7. Describe the vision receptors, and trace their innervation pathways.
8. Explain the formation of the embryonic eye.

Visual stimuli help us form specific detailed visual images of objects in our environment. The sense of vision uses visual receptors (photoreceptors) in the eyes to detect light, color, movement, and to perceive

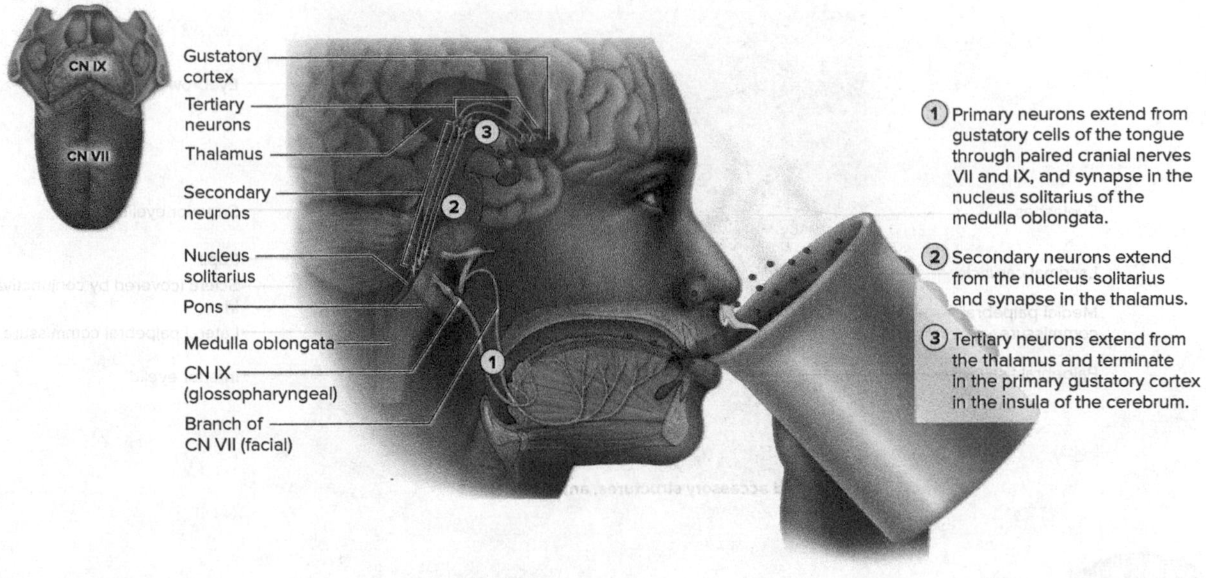
CN IX
CN VII
Gustatory cortex
Tertiary neurons
Thalamus
Secondary neurons
Nucleus solitarius
Pons
Medulla oblongata
CN IX (glossopharyngeal)
Branch of CN VII (facial)
3
2
1
1 Primary neurons extend from gustatory cells of the tongue through paired cranial nerves VII and IX, and synapse in the nucleus solitarius of the medulla oblongata.
2 Secondary neurons extend from the nucleus solitarius and synapse in the thalamus.
3 Tertiary neurons extend from the thalamus and terminate in the primary gustatory cortex in the insula of the cerebrum.

Figure 19.8

Gustatory Pathway. Taste sensations are transmitted by the paired facial nerves (CN VII) from the anterior two-thirds of the tongue and by the glossopharyngeal nerves (CN IX) from the posterior one-third of the tongue. These taste sensations are transmitted to the nucleus solitarius of the medulla oblongata before being conducted to the thalamus and finally entering the primary gustatory cortex of the cerebrum. APR

detailed visual images in our environment. Before describing the structures of the eye, we briefly examine the accessory structures that support and protect the eye's exposed surface.

19.5a Accessory Structures of the Eye

The accessory structures of the eye prevent foreign objects from coming into contact with the eye (eyebrows, eyelashes, and eyelids); keep the exposed surface moist, clean, and lubricated (lacrimal glands); and provide a superficial covering over its anterior exposed surface (conjunctiva) (**figure 19.9**).

External Accessory Structures

The **eyebrows** are slightly curved rows of thick, short hairs at the superior edge of the orbit of the eye along the supraorbital ridge. They function primarily to prevent sweat from dripping into the open eyes. **Eyelashes** extend from the margins of the eyelids and prevent large foreign objects from coming into contact with the anterior surface of the eye.

The **eyelids,** also called the *palpebrae* (pal-pē′brē; sing., *palpebra*), form the movable anterior protective covering over the surface of the eye. Each eyelid is formed by a fibrous core (termed the **tarsal plate**), tarsal muscles, tarsal glands, the palpebral part of the orbicularis oculi muscle, the palpebral conjunctiva, and a thin covering of skin. **Tarsal glands,** previously called *Meibomian glands,* are sebaceous glands that produce a secretion to prevent tear overflow from the open eye and keep the eyelids from adhering together. The eyelids' free margins are separated by a central **palpebral fissure** (or *eyeslit*).

The eyelids are united at the **medial** and **lateral palpebral commissures.** At the medial commissure is a small, reddish body called the **lacrimal caruncle** (kar′ŭng-kil; *caro* = flesh) that houses ciliary glands. Ciliary glands are modified sweat glands that form the thick secretory products that contribute to the gritty, particulate material often noticed around the eyelids after awakening.

Conjunctiva

A specialized stratified columnar epithelium termed the **conjunctiva** (kon-jŭnk-tī′vă) forms a continuous lining over the external, anterior surface of the eye (the **ocular conjunctiva**) and the internal surface of the eyelid (the **palpebral conjunctiva**). The space formed by the junction of the ocular conjunctiva and palpebral conjunctiva is called the **conjunctival fornix** (fōr′niks; = vault or arch).

The conjunctiva contains numerous goblet cells, which lubricate and moisten the eye. Additionally, the conjunctiva contains many blood vessels, which supply nutrients to the avascular sclera ("white") of the eye. The conjunctiva also contains abundant nerve endings that detect foreign objects as they contact the eye. The conjunctiva does not cover the surface of the cornea (the transparent center of the external eye), so no blood vessels interfere with passage of light into the eye.

Lacrimal Apparatus

Each eye is associated with a **lacrimal** (lak′ri-m ăl; *lacrima* = a tear) **apparatus** that produces, collects, and drains **lacrimal fluid,** more commonly known as *tears,* from the eye (**figure 19.10**). Lacrimal fluid lubricates the anterior surface of the eye to reduce friction from eyelid movement; continuously cleanses and moistens the eye surface; and helps prevent bacterial infection because it contains an antibiotic-like enzyme called **lysozyme.**

A **lacrimal gland** is located within the superolateral depression of each orbit. It is composed of an orbital or superior part and a palpebral or inferior part. The gland continuously produces tears. The blinking motion of the eyelids "washes" the lacrimal fluid released from excretory ducts over the eyes. Gradually, the lacrimal fluid is transferred to the **lacrimal caruncle** at the medial surface of the eye. On the superior and inferior sides of the lacrimal caruncle are two small openings called the **lacrimal puncta** (pungk′tă; sing., *punctum;* to prick). (If you examine your own eye, each punctum appears as a "hole" in the lacrimal caruncle.) Each lacrimal punctum has a **lacrimal canaliculus,**

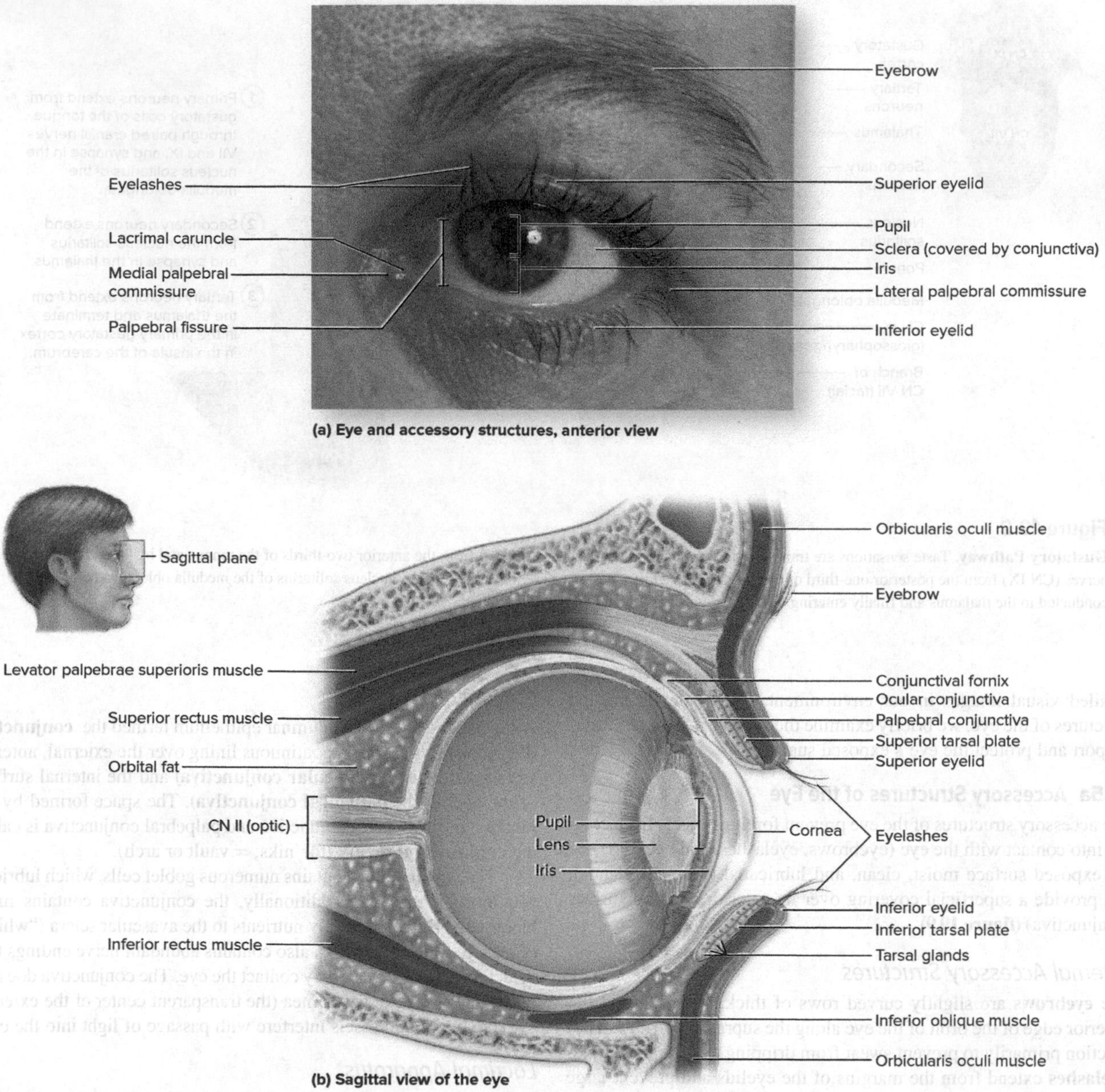

Eyebrow
Eyelashes
Superior eyelid
Lacrimal caruncle
Pupil
Sclera (covered by conjunctiva)
Medial palpebral commissure
Iris
Lateral palpebral commissure
Palpebral fissure
Inferior eyelid
Sagittal plane
Orbicularis oculi muscle
Eyebrow
Levator palpebrae superioris muscle
Conjunctival fornix
Ocular conjunctiva
Superior rectus muscle
Palpebral conjunctiva
Superior tarsal plate
Orbital fat
Superior eyelid
CN II (optic)
Pupil
Lens
Iris
Cornea
Eyelashes
Inferior eyelid
Inferior tarsal plate
Inferior rectus muscle
Tarsal glands
Inferior oblique muscle
Orbicularis oculi muscle

(a) Eye and accessory structures, anterior view

(b) Sagittal view of the eye

Figure 19.9

External Anatomy of the Eye and Surrounding Accessory Structures. *(a)* Accessory structures protect the eye. *(b)* A sagittal section shows the eye and its accessory structures.

(a) ©McGraw-Hill Education/Jw Ramsey, photographer

which is a small canal that drains lacrimal fluid into a rounded **lacrimal sac.** Finally, a **nasolacrimal duct** receives the lacrimal fluid from the lacrimal sac. This duct, which is along the lateral side of the nose, delivers the drained fluid into the nasal cavity, where it mixes with mucus.

WHAT DO YOU THINK?

3. When a person cries, tears spill onto the cheeks, and the person usually gets a temporary runny nose. Based upon your knowledge of the lacrimal apparatus, what is happening?

19.5b Eye Structure

The eye is an almost spherical organ that measures about 2.5 centimeters in diameter. Nearly 80% of the eye is receded into the orbit of the skull (see section 7.1g), a space also occupied by the lacrimal gland, extrinsic eye muscles, numerous blood vessels that supply nutrients, and the cranial nerves that innervate the eye and other structures in the face and orbit. **Orbital fat** (see figure 19.9) cushions the posterior and lateral sides of the eye, providing support, protection, and vasculature.

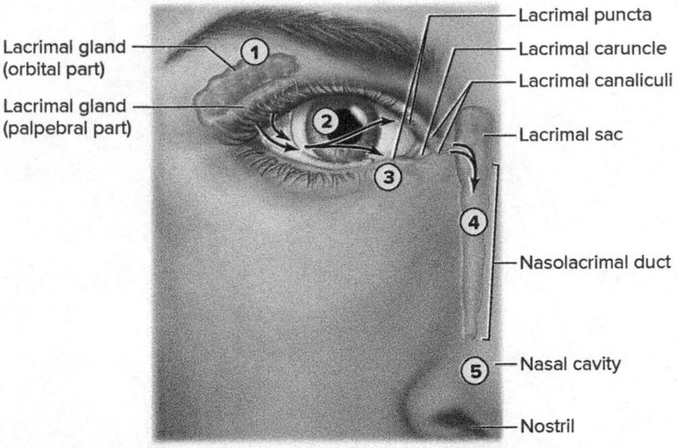
Lacrimal gland (orbital part)
Lacrimal gland (palpebral part)
Lacrimal puncta
Lacrimal caruncle
Lacrimal canaliculi
Lacrimal sac
Nasolacrimal duct
Nasal cavity
Nostril
1
2
3
4
5

(1) Lacrimal fluid (tears) is produced in the lacrimal gland.

(2) Lacrimal fluid is dispersed across eye surface when we blink.

(3) Lacrimal fluid enters the lacrimal puncta, drains into the lacrimal canaliculi, and collects in the lacrimal sac.

(4) Lacrimal fluid from the lacrimal sac drains through the nasolacrimal duct.

(5) Lacrimal fluid enters the nasal cavity.

Figure 19.10

Lacrimal Apparatus. The lacrimal apparatus continually produces lacrimal fluid that cleanses and maintains a moist condition on the anterior surface of the eye. Lacrimal fluid production and drainage occur in a series of steps.

Clinical View 19.1

Conjunctivitis

Conjunctivitis (kon-jŭnk-ti-vī′tis) is the most common nontraumatic eye complaint seen by physicians. It presents as inflammation and reddening of the conjunctiva, and is often called *pink eye*. Conjunctivitis frequently results from a viral infection, but also can be a response to a bacterial infection, airborne allergens (pollen or animal dander), chemicals, or physical irritants, such as contact lenses left in too long.

Trachoma is a chronic, contagious form of conjunctivitis caused by *Chlamydia trachomatis*. Infection by this bacterium results in inflammation because of hypertrophy of the conjunctiva. The condition is accompanied by the appearance of newly formed, minute gray-yellow granules in the conjunctiva. Trachoma is a common cause of neonatal blindness in developing countries; the newborn becomes infected as it passes through the birth canal. Blindness occurs when the inflammatory process causes scarring and thickening of the conjunctiva.

The interior of the eye consists of two fluid-filled cavities. These two cavities are separated by the lens, which is a transparent biconvex structure enclosed in a fibrous capsule (**figure 19.11**). The **posterior cavity,** which lies behind the lens, contains a permanent fluid called vitreous humor, and the **anterior cavity,** which is in front of the lens, contains a circulating fluid called aqueous humor. The lens and both fluids are described in detail later in this section.

Three principal layers form the wall of the eye: the fibrous tunic (outermost layer), the vascular tunic (middle layer), and the retina (innermost layer) (figure 19.11*b*).

Fibrous Tunic

The external layer of the eye wall, called the **fibrous tunic,** is composed of the anterior cornea and the posterior sclera.

The avascular, transparent **cornea** (kōr′nē-ă) forms the anterior surface of the fibrous tunic. It exhibits a convex shape, and thus it refracts (bends) light rays coming into the eye. The cornea is composed of an inner simple squamous epithelium, a middle layer of collagen fibers, and an outer stratified squamous epithelium, called the **corneal epithelium.** At its circumferential edge, this epithelium is continuous with the ocular conjunctiva, and it adjoins the sclera. The structural continuity between the cornea and sclera is called the **limbus** (lim′bŭs) or the *corneal scleral junction.*

The cornea contains no blood vessels; thus, both its external and internal epithelial surfaces must obtain nutrients by alternative means. Nutrients and oxygen are supplied to the external corneal epithelium by fluid from the lacrimal glands, whereas the internal epithelium obtains needed gases and nutrients from the fluid in the anterior chamber of the eye.

Most of the fibrous tunic is formed by tough **sclera** (sklē′ră; *skleros* = hard), a part of the outer layer that is called the "white" of the eye. It is composed of dense irregular connective tissue that includes both collagen and elastic fibers. The sclera provides for eye shape and protects the eye's delicate internal components.

Vascular Tunic

The middle layer of the eye wall is the **vascular tunic,** also called the *uvea* (yū′vē-ă; *uva* = grape). It is composed of three distinct regions; from posterior to anterior, they are the choroid, the ciliary body, and the iris (figure 19.11). The vascular tunic houses an extensive array of blood vessels, lymph vessels, and the intrinsic muscles of the eye.

The **choroid** (kor′oyd; *choroeides* = like a membrane) is the most extensive and posterior region of the vascular tunic. It houses a vast network of capillaries, which supply both nutrients and oxygen to the retina, the inner layer of the eye wall. Cells of the choroid are filled with pigment from the numerous melanocytes in this region. The melanin pigment is needed to absorb extraneous light that enters the eye, thus allowing the retina to clearly interpret the remaining light rays and form a visual image.

The **ciliary** (sil′ē-ar′ē; *cilium* = eyelid) **body** is located anterior to the choroid. The ciliary body is composed of **ciliary muscles** (bands of smooth muscle) and **ciliary processes** (folds of epithelium that cover the ciliary muscles). Extending from the ciliary body to the lens are suspensory ligaments. Relaxation and contraction of the ciliary muscles change the tension on the suspensory ligaments,

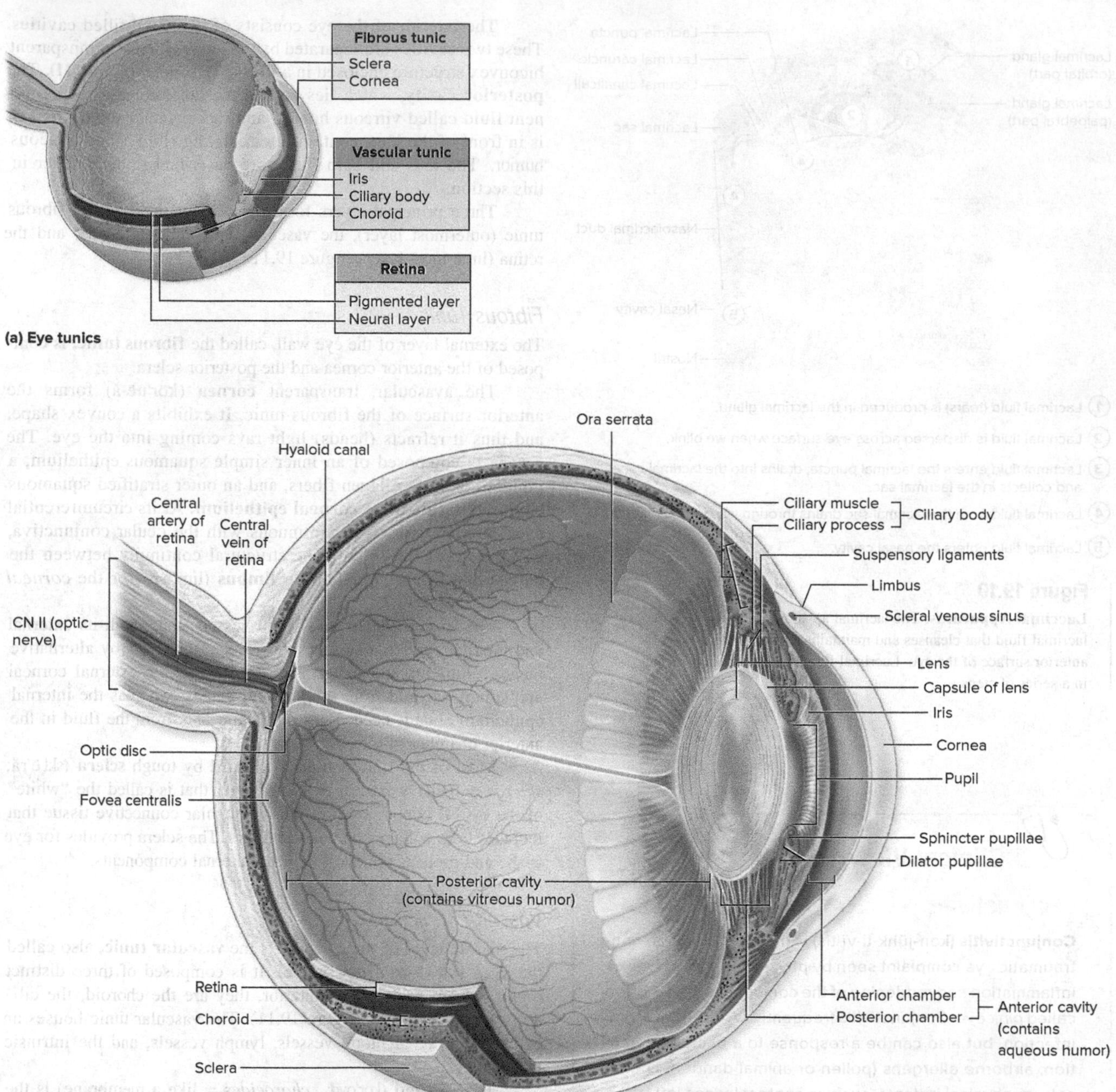
Fibrous tunic
Sclera
Cornea
Vascular tunic
Iris
Ciliary body
Choroid
Retina
Pigmented layer
Neural layer
(a) Eye tunics
Ora serrata
Hyaloid canal
Central artery of retina
Central vein of retina
CN II (optic nerve)
Optic disc
Fovea centralis
Ciliary muscle
Ciliary process
Ciliary body
Suspensory ligaments
Limbus
Scleral venous sinus
Lens
Capsule of lens
Iris
Cornea
Pupil
Sphincter pupillae
Dilator pupillae
Posterior cavity (contains vitreous humor)
Retina
Choroid
Sclera
Anterior chamber
Posterior chamber
Anterior cavity (contains aqueous humor)
(b) Sagittal view of the eye

Figure 19.11

Anatomy of the Internal Eye. Sagittal views depict (*a*) the three tunics of the eye, and (*b*) internal eye structures showing the relationships among the components of the vascular layer, the lens, and the cornea. APR

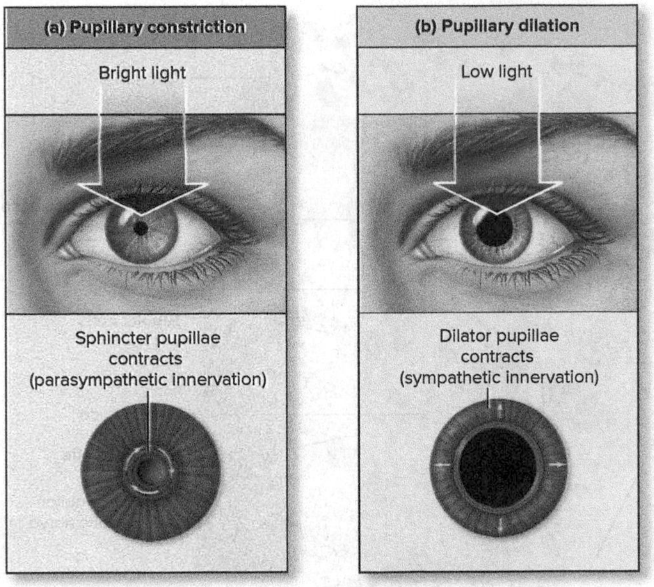

Figure 19.12

Pupil Diameter. Pupillary constriction decreases the diameter of the pupil to reduce the amount of light entering the eye. Pupillary dilation increases pupil diameter to increase light entry into the eye. (*a*) Pupillary constriction is controlled by the parasympathetic division of the ANS, and (*b*) pupillary dilation is controlled by the sympathetic division.

thereby altering the shape of the lens. In addition, the ciliary body epithelium secretes a fluid called aqueous humor (to be discussed later in this section).

The most anterior region of the vascular tunic is the **iris** (ī′ris; rainbow), which is the colored portion of the eye. In the center of the iris is a black hole called the **pupil** (pyū-pīl). The peripheral edge of the iris is continuous with the ciliary body. The iris is composed of two layers of pigment-forming cells (anterior and posterior layers), two groups of smooth muscle fibers, and an array of vascular and nervous structures. The iris controls pupil size or diameter—and thus the amount of light entering the eye—using its two smooth muscle layers: the sphincter pupillae and the dilator pupillae muscles (**figure 19.12**). The **sphincter pupillae** (or *pupillary constrictor*) muscle is arranged in a pattern that resembles concentric circles around the pupil. Under the control of the parasympathetic division of the ANS, it constricts the pupil. The **dilator pupillae** (or *pupillary dilator*) muscle is organized in a radial pattern extending peripherally through the iris. It is controlled by the sympathetic division of the ANS to dilate the pupil. Only one set of these smooth muscles can contract at any one time. When stimulated by bright lights, parasympathetic innervation (via CN III, oculomotor nerve) causes the sphincter pupillae to contract and thus constrict the pupil, whereas low light levels activate sympathetic stimulation to cause pupil dilation.

Retina

The internal layer of the eye wall, called the **retina** (ret′i-nă; *rete* = a net), or either the *internal tunic* or *neural tunic,* is composed of two layers: an outer pigmented layer and an inner neural layer (**figure 19.13*a***). The **pigmented layer** is immediately internal (deep) to the choroid. The choroid and pigmented layers are firmly attached to one another. The pigmented layer has three main functions. It provides vitamin A for photoreceptor cells. The pigmented layer also transports all nutrients and oxygen from the choroid to the neural layer. Light rays that pass through the inner layer are absorbed in this outer layer.

The inner **neural layer** houses all of the photoreceptors and their associated neurons. This layer of the retina is responsible for receiving light rays and converting them into nerve impulses that are transmitted to the brain.

The **ora serrata** (ōr′ă sē-ră′tă; *serratus* = sawtooth) is the jagged margin between the neural layer of the retina and the nonphotosensitive pigmented layer of the retina that continues anteriorly to cover the ciliary body and the posterior side of the iris (see figure 19.11*b*).

Table 19.3 summarizes the characteristics of the three tunics of the eye wall.

Organization of the Neural Layer Three distinct layers of cells form the neural layer: photoreceptor cells, bipolar cells, and ganglion cells. Incoming light must pass almost through the entire neural layer before reaching the photoreceptors.

The outermost layer of the neural layer is composed of **photoreceptor cells** of two types: **Rods** have a rod-shaped outer part and function in dim light, whereas **cones** have a cone-shaped outer part and function in high-intensity light and in color vision.

Rods are longer and narrower than cones. Rods are primarily located in the peripheral regions of the neural layer. There are more than 100 million rod cells per eye. Rods are especially important when the light is dim. They detect movement but exhibit poor visual acuity. In addition, rods pick up contrasting dark and light tones, but cannot distinguish color. Thus, when you are trying to see at night, it is primarily the rods that are working. The rods can perceive the object, but your vision may not be particularly sharp, and you may find it difficult to see any color variation.

In contrast, cones occur at a density of less than 10 million per eye. Cones are activated by high-intensity light and provide precise visual acuity and color recognition. Thus, when you notice the fine details in a colorful picture, the cones of your neural layer are responsible.

Learning Strategy 19.3

Use these study aids to remember the functions of cones and rods:

- **C**ones detect **C**olor (both start with the letter C).
- **R**ods work best in **R**educed light conditions.

Immediately internal (deep) to the photoreceptor layer is a layer of **bipolar cells,** a type of bipolar neuron. Rods and cones form synapses on the dendrites of bipolar cells. Sandwiched between the photoreceptor layer and the bipolar cells is a thin web of **horizontal cells** that form connections between the photoreceptor and bipolar cells. There are far fewer bipolar neurons than photoreceptors, and thus information must converge as nerve impulses are directed toward the brain from the stimulated photoreceptors.

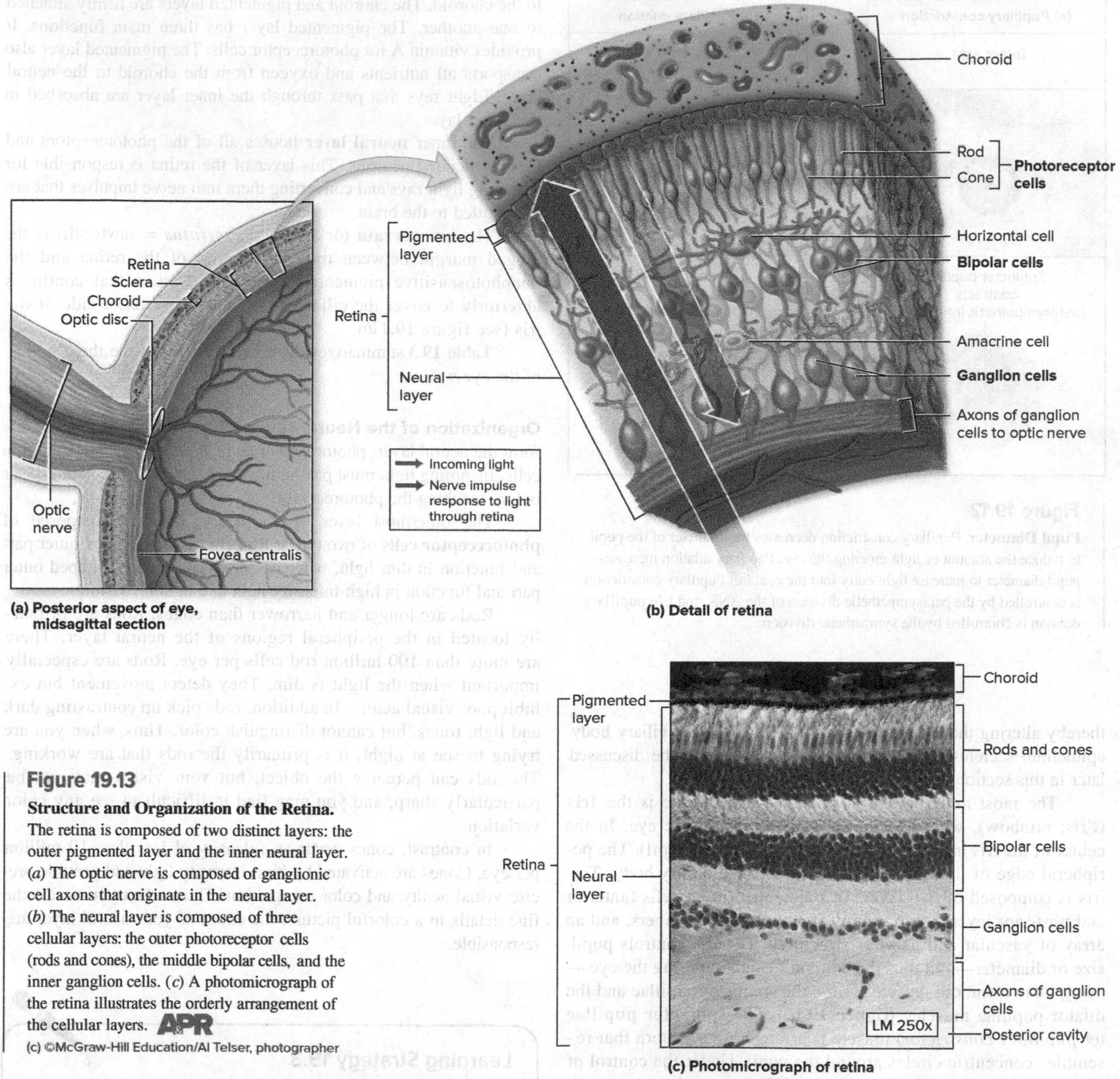
Retina
Sclera
Choroid
Optic disc
Optic nerve
Fovea centralis
(a) Posterior aspect of eye, midsagittal section
Pigmented layer
Retina
Neural layer
Incoming light
Nerve impulse response to light through retina
Choroid
Rod
Cone
Photoreceptor cells
Horizontal cell
Bipolar cells
Amacrine cell
Ganglion cells
Axons of ganglion cells to optic nerve
(b) Detail of retina
Choroid
Pigmented layer
Rods and cones
Retina
Neural layer
Bipolar cells
Ganglion cells
Axons of ganglion cells
LM 250x
Posterior cavity
(c) Photomicrograph of retina

Figure 19.13

Structure and Organization of the Retina. The retina is composed of two distinct layers: the outer pigmented layer and the inner neural layer. (*a*) The optic nerve is composed of ganglionic cell axons that originate in the neural layer. (*b*) The neural layer is composed of three cellular layers: the outer photoreceptor cells (rods and cones), the middle bipolar cells, and the inner ganglion cells. (*c*) A photomicrograph of the retina illustrates the orderly arrangement of the cellular layers. APR

(c) ©McGraw-Hill Education/Al Telser, photographer

Table 19.3	Tunics of the Eye Wall		
Tunic/Structures	**Components**	**Location**	**Function(s)**
FIBROUS TUNIC (*EXTERNAL LAYER*)			
Cornea	Two layers of epithelium with collagen fibers in the middle; avascular	Forms the anterior one-sixth of the external eye layer	Transmits and refracts incoming light
Sclera	Dense regular connective tissue	Posterior covering of the eye (forms the remaining five-sixths of the external eye layer); the "white" of the eye	Supports eye shape and protects it
VASCULAR TUNIC (*MIDDLE LAYER*)			
Choroid	Areolar connective tissue; highly vascularized	Forms posterior two-thirds of middle wall of eye	Supplies nourishment to retina
Ciliary body	Ciliary smooth muscles and an inner, secretory epithelium	Between choroid posteriorly and iris anteriorly	Holds suspensory ligaments that attach to the lens and change lens shape for far and near vision Epithelium secretes aqueous humor
Iris	Two layers of smooth muscle (sphincter pupillae and dilator pupillae) with a central opening called the pupil	Anterior region of middle layer	Controls pupil diameter and thus the amount of light entering the eye
RETINA (*INTERNAL LAYER*)			
Pigmented layer	Pigmented epithelial cells and supporting cells	Outermost portion of retina that directly adheres to choroid	Absorbs extraneous light Provides vitamin A for photoreceptor cells
Neural layer	Photoreceptors, bipolar neurons, and ganglion cells	Inner portion of retina	Detects incoming light rays; light rays are transduced or converted to nerve impulse and transmitted to brain

Clinical View 19.2

Detached Retina

A **detached retina** occurs when the outer pigmented and inner neural layers of the retina separate. Detachment may result from head trauma (soccer players and high divers are especially susceptible), or it may have no overt cause. Individuals who are nearsighted, due to a more elliptical eyeball, are at increased risk for detachment because their retina is typically thinned or "stretched" more than that of a normal eye. There is also increased risk for retinal detachment in diabetics and older individuals. A detached retina results in deprivation of nutrients for cells in the inner neural layer because it is pulled away from the vascularized choroid layer. Degeneration and death of the neural layer of the retina occur if the blood supply is not restored.

Symptoms of a detached retina include a large number of "floaters" (small, particle-like objects) in the vision; the appearance of a "curtain" in the affected eye; flashes of light; and decreased, watery, or wavy vision.

The treatment for a detached retina depends upon the location of the detachment and its severity. **Pneumatic retinopexy** is a treatment for upper retinal detachment. The physician inserts a needle into the anesthetized eye and injects a gas bubble into the vitreous humor. The gas bubble rises and pushes against the upper retinal detachment, forcing the two layers back together again. The gas bubble absorbs and disappears over 1–2 weeks, and then a laser may be used to "tack" the two layers of the retina together. The **scleral buckle** uses a silicone band to press inward on the sclera to hold the retina in place. A laser is then used to reattach the retina. The scleral buckle remains as a permanent fixture in the eye.

Individuals who have had a detached retina in one eye are at increased risk for developing a detachment in the other eye as well. Thus, the retinal detachment patient must be extra-vigilant in monitoring his or her vision.

Ganglion cells form the innermost layer in the neural layer that is adjacent to the vitreous humor in the posterior cavity. Neuronal convergence continues between the bipolar neurons and ganglionic neurons. **Amacrine** (ahm′ ă-krin) **cells** help process and integrate visual information as it passes between bipolar and ganglionic neurons. Axons extend from the ganglionic cells into and through the **optic disc.** These axons converge to form the optic nerve (CN II) as they exit the eye and extend toward the brain (see section 15.8) The optic disc lacks photoreceptors, and consequently it is called the **blind spot** because there are no receptors to detect an image that might fall there (**figure 19.14**).

Just lateral to the optic disc is a rounded, yellowish region of the neural layer called the **macula** (mak′y ū-lă) **lutea** (lū′te- ă; saffron-yellow). Within the macula lutea is a pit called the **fovea centralis** (fō′vē-ă, pit; sen-trā′lis, central), which contains the highest proportion of cones

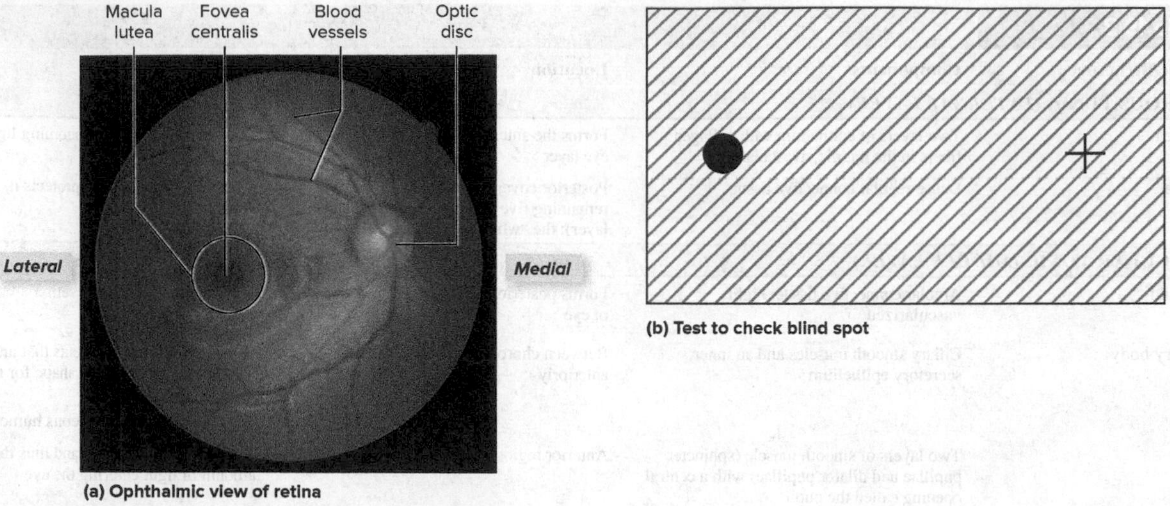

Figure 19.14

Internal View of the Retina Showing the Optic Disc (Blind Spot). An ophthalmoscope is used to view the retina through the pupil. (*a*) Blood vessels travel through the optic nerve to enter the eye at the optic disc. (*b*) Check your blind spot! Close your left eye. Hold this figure in front of your right eye, and stare at the black spot. Move the figure toward your open eye. At a certain point, when the image of the plus sign is over the optic disc, the plus sign seems to disappear.

(a) Nikom nik sunsopa/Shutterstock

and almost no rods. This pit is the area of sharpest vision; when you read the words in your text, they are precisely focused here.

Lens

The **lens** is a strong, yet deformable, transparent structure bounded by a dense, fibrous, elastic capsule. Internally, it is composed of precisely arranged layers of cells that have lost their organelles and are filled completely by a protein called *crystallin.* The lens focuses incoming light onto the retina, and its shape determines the degree of light refraction.

The **suspensory** (sŭs-pen′s ŏ-rē; *suspensio* = to hang up) **ligaments** attach to the lens capsule at its periphery, where they transmit tension that enables the lens to change shape. The tension in the suspensory ligaments varies according to the contraction and relaxation of the **ciliary muscles** in the ciliary body. When the ciliary muscles relax, the ciliary body moves posteriorly, away from the lens, and so the tension on the suspensory ligaments increases. This constant tension causes the lens to flatten **(figure 19.15a)**. A flattened lens is necessary for far vision

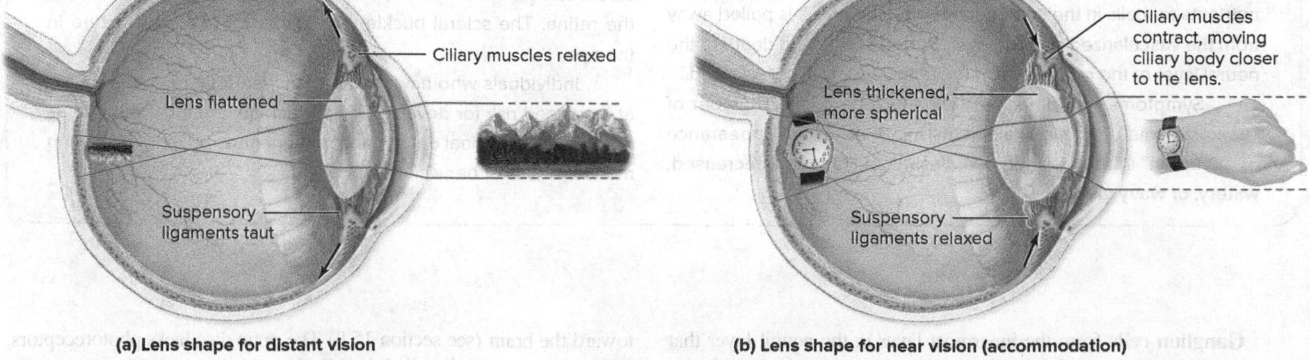

Figure 19.15

Lens Shape in Far Vision and Near Vision. (*a*) To focus a distant object on the retina, the ciliary muscles within the ciliary body relax, which tenses the suspensory ligaments and flattens the lens. (*b*) Accommodation occurs when a nearby object is focused on the retina. The ciliary muscles contract, causing the suspensory ligaments to relax and the lens to thicken (become more spherical).

Clinical View 19.3

Macular Degeneration

Macular degeneration, the physical degeneration of the macula lutea of the retina, has become a leading cause of blindness in developed countries. Although the majority of cases are reported in people over 55, the condition may occur in younger people as well. Most non-age-related cases are associated with an aggravating condition such as diabetes, an ocular infection, heredity, or trauma to the eye. People who smoke and those with hypertension are at increased risk for developing macular degeneration.

Macular degeneration occurs in two forms—*dry* or *wet*. About 70% of affected people have the dry form, which is characterized by photoreceptor loss and thinning of the pigmented layer. The remaining 30% of patients have the wet form, which has all of the dry form characteristics plus bleeding, capillary proliferation, and scar tissue formation. The wet form is the most advanced and aggressive type, and it accounts for most of the cases of blindness. The disease is often present in both eyes, although it may progress at different rates in each eye.

The first symptom of macular degeneration is typically the loss of visual acuity. Other common vision problems include straight lines appearing distorted or wavy; a dark, blurry area of visual loss in the center of the visual field; diminished color perception; "floaters"; dry eyes; and cataracts.

At present, there is no cure for macular degeneration. However, its progression may be slowed. Early detection has become an important element in treatment. To track the progression of the disease, doctors rely heavily on self-monitoring, in which the patient regularly performs a simple visual test using the *Amsler grid* (see figures *c, d*). While staring at the dot, the patient looks for wavy lines, blurring, or missing parts of the grid. If the lines of the grid do not appear straight and regular, or if parts seem to be missing, the patient should be examined for changes in the macula. The most effective treatment for macular degeneration uses laser photocoagulation to destroy the abnormally proliferating vessels in the macula. Although this procedure cannot restore lost vision, it does slow the pace of visual loss.

(a) Normal vision

(b) The same scene as viewed by a person with macular degeneration

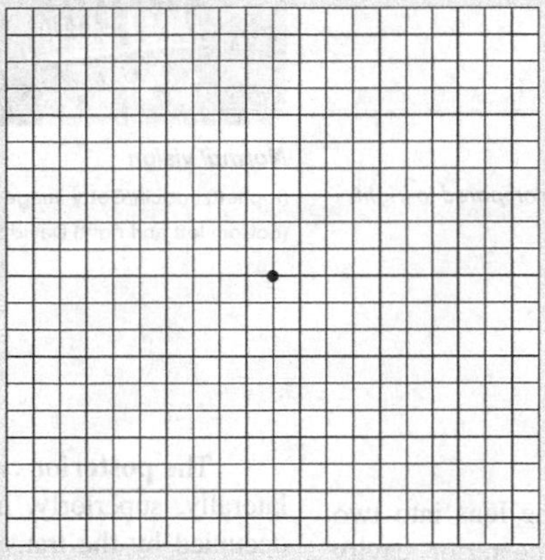

(c) Amsler grid, seen with normal vision

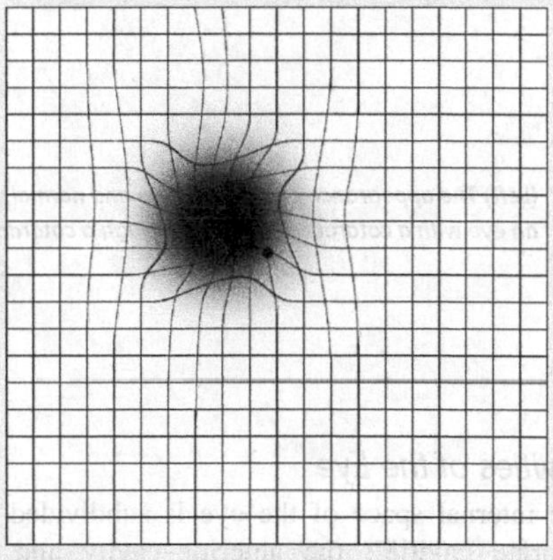

(d) Amsler grid, as viewed by a person with macular degeneration

Comparison showing differences between normal vision (left) and the vision of a person with macular degeneration (right).

(a, b) Steve Mason/Getty Images

(viewing distant objects). This shape of the lens is the "default" position of the lens.

In contrast, when we wish to see close objects (use our near vision), the lens must become more spherical to properly refract (bend) the light rays and focus an image on the retina. The process of making the lens more spherical to view close-up objects is called **accommodation** (ă-kom′ŏ-dā′shŭn; *accommodo* = to adapt) (figure 19.15*b*). Accommodation is controlled by the parasympathetic division of the ANS (see section 18.3); specifically, originating within the oculomotor nerve (see section 15.8). Stimulation of the ciliary muscles by parasympathetic axons causes the muscles to contract. When the ciliary muscles contract, the entire ciliary body moves anteriorly and thus moves closer to the lens itself. This process reduces the suspensory ligaments' tension and releases some of their "pull" on the lens, so the lens can become more spherical.

Clinical View 19.4

Cataracts

Cataracts (kat′ă-rakt) are small opacities within the lens that, over time, may coalesce to completely obscure the lens. Cataracts are a major cause of blindness worldwide. Most cases occur as a result of aging, although other causative factors include diabetes, intraocular infections, excessive ultraviolet light exposure, and glaucoma. The resulting vision problems include difficulty focusing on close objects, reduced visual clarity as a consequence of clouding of the lens, "milky" vision, and reduced intensity of colors.

A cataract needs to be removed only when it interferes with normal daily activities. Newer surgical techniques include **phacoemulsification** (or **phaco**), a process whereby the opacified center of the lens is fragmented using ultrasonic sound waves, thus making it easy to remove. The destroyed lens then typically is replaced with an artificial intraocular lens, which becomes a permanent part of the eye.

Cataract
Eye without a cataract
Eye with a cataract
Normal vision
Image seen through cataract

(Left) The appearance of a normal eye and normal vision compared to (right) an eye with a cataract and vision through a cataract.

(top left) cgouin/Getty Images; (top right) sruilk/Shutterstock; (bottom left and right) David Buffington/Getty Images

Cavities of the Eye

The internal space of the eye is subdivided by the lens into two separate cavities: the anterior cavity and the posterior cavity (**figure 19.16**). The **anterior cavity** is the space anterior to the lens and posterior to the cornea. The iris of the eye subdivides the anterior cavity further into two chambers: The **anterior chamber** is between the iris and cornea, whereas the **posterior chamber** is between the lens and the iris. APR

The anterior cavity contains a fluid called **aqueous** (ak′wē-ŭs; watery) **humor** (hyū′mŏr), which is a filtrate of plasma that resembles CSF and is produced by the epithelium covering the ciliary body. Aqueous humor removes waste products and helps maintain the chemical environment within the anterior and posterior chambers of the eye. The aqueous humor is secreted into the posterior chamber. From the posterior chamber, it flows through the pupil into the anterior chamber. The aqueous humor is continually resorbed across the covering epithelium into a vascular space, called the **scleral venous sinus** (previously called the *canal of Schlemm*), located in the limbus between the cornea and the sclera. The scleral venous sinus conducts the resorbed aqueous humor to the veins that drain the eye. Thus, as with cerebrospinal fluid, excess aqueous humor is removed from these eye chambers and transported into the venous circulation.

The **posterior cavity** is posterior to the lens and is surrounded laterally, superiorly, inferiorly, and posteriorly by the retina. It is occupied by the transparent, gelatinous **vitreous** (vit′rē-ŭs; glassy) **humor,** which completely fills the space between the lens and the retina. The vitreous humor helps maintain eye shape, support the retina, and transmit light from the lens to the retina. Within the vitreous humor is a thin **hyaloid** (hī′ă-loyd; *hyalos* = glass) **canal.** This canal is a remnant of embryonic hyaloid blood vessels that once supplied the retina and lens (see section 19.5d).

19.5c Visual Pathways

Figure 19.17 depicts the visual pathways. The visual pathways begin at the retina, where the photoreceptor cells convert light stimuli to a nerve impulse. The bipolar cells are the primary neurons, and the ganglion cells are the secondary neurons with the visual pathways (see sensory pathways from section 17.2). The axons of the ganglion cells form the optic nerve (see figure 19.13). Optic nerves project from each eye and converge at the **optic chiasm** (kī′azm) (figure 19.17). The optic chiasm is a flattened structure anterior to the infundibulum where many of the optic nerve axons decussate (cross) to the other side. The ganglionic axons originating from the medial region of each retina cross to the opposite side of the brain at the optic chiasm, whereas ganglionic axons

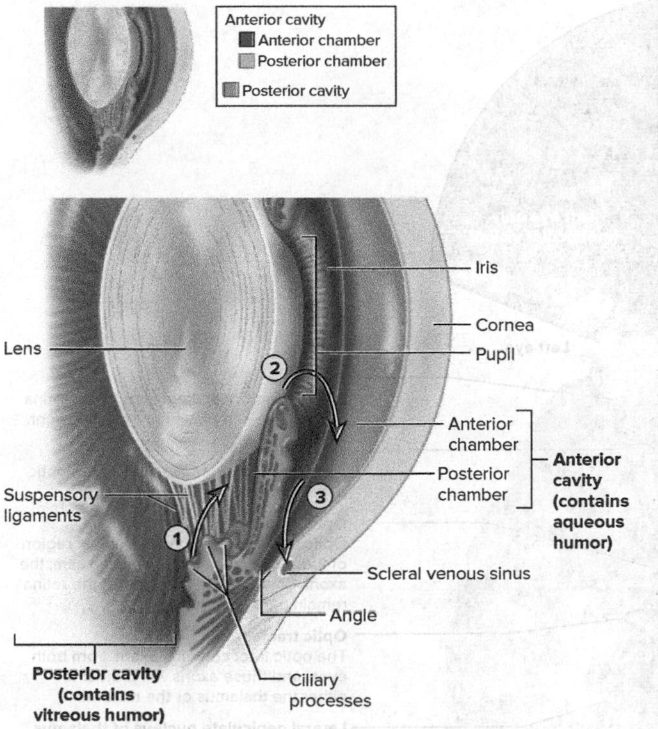

(1) Aqueous humor is secreted by the ciliary processes into the posterior chamber.

(2) Aqueous humor moves from the posterior chamber, through the pupil, to the anterior chamber.

(3) Excess aqueous humor is resorbed via the scleral venous sinus.

Figure 19.16

Aqueous Humor: Secretion and Reabsorption. Aqueous humor is a watery secretion that is continuously produced and circulated through the eye, helping to maintain the chemical environment and removing waste products.

originating from the lateral region of each retina remain on the same side of the brain and do not cross. **Optic tracts** extend laterally from the optic chiasm as a composite of ganglionic axons originating from the retina of each eye.

The majority of the optic tract axons extend to the thalamus, specifically to the **lateral geniculate** (je-nik′ū-lāt; *genu* = knee, referring to its appearance) **nucleus,** where visual information is processed within each thalamic body. Tertiary neurons project axons from the thalamus to the visual cortex of the occipital lobe for interpretation of incoming visual stimuli.

Note that the left and right eyes have somewhat overlapping visual fields. For the brain to interpret these two distinct visual images, it must process or unite them into one. These overlapping images then provide us with **stereoscopic vision,** or **depth perception,** which is the ability to determine how close or far away an object is. Animals that don't have overlapping visual fields (such as horses or deer) may have a greater visual range, but they cannot perceive visual depths.

Clinical View 19.5

Glaucoma

Glaucoma (glaw-kō′mă) is a disease that exists in three forms, all characterized by increased intraocular pressure: angle-closure glaucoma, open-angle glaucoma, and congenital glaucoma. Angle-closure and open-angle glaucoma both involve the angle formed in the anterior chamber of the eye by the union of the choroid and the limbus (see figure 19.11), or corneal-scleral junction. This angle is the important tract for draining the aqueous humor. If it narrows, fluid and pressure build up within the anterior chamber. About one-third of all cases of glaucoma develop as a direct consequence of the narrowing of this angle, a condition called *angle-closure glaucoma. Open-angle glaucoma* accounts for about two-thirds of glaucoma cases. In this instance, although the drain angles are adequate, fluid transport out of the anterior chamber is impaired. *Congenital glaucoma* occurs only rarely and is due to hereditary factors or intrauterine infection.

Regardless of the cause of glaucoma, fluid buildup causes a posterior dislocation of the lens and a substantial increase in pressure in the posterior chamber. Compression of the choroid layer may occur, constricting the blood vessels that nourish the retina. Retinal cell death and increased pressure may distort the axons within the optic nerve. Eventually, the patient may experience such symptoms as reduced field of vision, dim vision, and halos around lights.

A scene as viewed by someone with glaucoma.

Source: National Eye Institute, National Institutes of Health

In addition to the neural pathway that relays input to the visual cortex, a limited number of axons within each optic tract project to the midbrain. Those that extend to the **superior colliculi** (ko-lik′yū-lī) coordinate the reflexive movements of the extrinsic eye muscles, whereas those that extend to the **pretectal nuclei** of the midbrain function as the control centers in both the pupillary reflex to regulate the amount of the light that enters the eye and the accommodation reflex for focusing the lens.

19.5d Development of the Eye

Eye development begins during the fourth week of development when left and right **optic vesicles** evaginate from the diencephalic

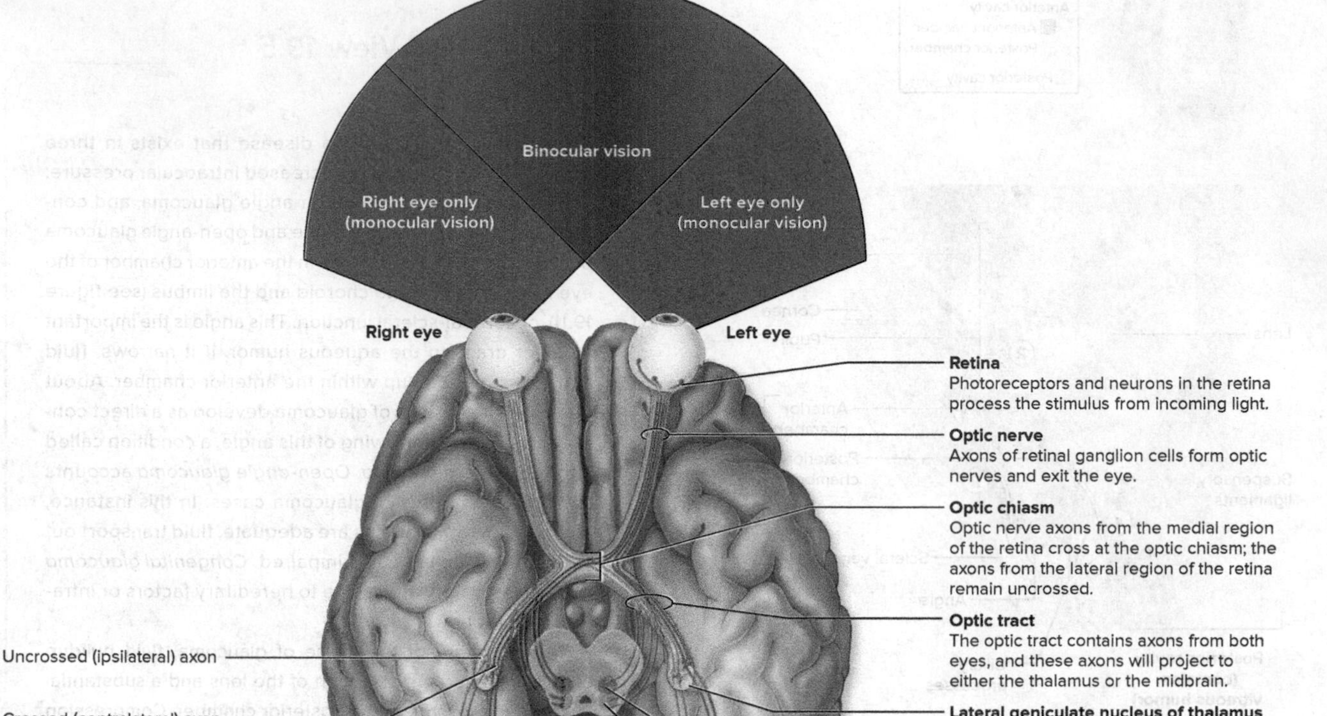
Binocular vision
Right eye only
(monocular vision)
Left eye only
(monocular vision)
Right eye
Left eye
Retina
Photoreceptors and neurons in the retina process the stimulus from incoming light.
Optic nerve
Axons of retinal ganglion cells form optic nerves and exit the eye.
Optic chiasm
Optic nerve axons from the medial region of the retina cross at the optic chiasm; the axons from the lateral region of the retina remain uncrossed.
Optic tract
The optic tract contains axons from both eyes, and these axons will project to either the thalamus or the midbrain.
Uncrossed (ipsilateral) axon
Crossed (contralateral) axon
Lateral geniculate nucleus of thalamus
The majority of the optic tract axons project to the lateral geniculate nucleus in the thalamus.
Pretectal nucleus of the midbrain
Limited number of optic tract axons project here for pupillary reflexes and accommodation.
Projection fibers (optic radiation)
Superior colliculus of midbrain
Some optic tract axons project here for reflexive movements of the extraocular eye muscles.
Primary visual cortex of occipital lobe
Receives processed information from the thalamus for vision.
Inferior view

Figure 19.17

Inferior View of the Brain Showing Visual Pathways. Each optic nerve conducts visual stimulus information. At the optic chiasm, some axons from the optic nerve decussate. The optic tract on each side then contains axons from both eyes. Visual stimulus information is processed by the thalamus and then interpreted by visual association areas in the cerebrum. APR

portion of the prosencephalon (**figure 19.18**). Thus, these optic vesicles (the future retina of the eye) are formed from the neural tube. As the optic vesicle nears the surface ectoderm, the vesicle invaginates (indents) so that it forms an **optic cup.** The optic cup contains an inner and outer layer, and is connected to the developing brain by an **optic stalk. Hyaloid vessels** (blood vessels) enter the optic cup through an opening in the optic stalk. The ectoderm overlying the optic cup forms a depression called a **lens pit.** This pit further indents and forms a circular structure called the **lens vesicle,** which will develop into the future lens of the eye. As mentioned earlier in this section the hyaloid vessels eventually regress, leaving the hollow cavity known as the **hyaloid canal** (see figure 19.11).

During the fifth and sixth weeks of development, the lens vesicle pinches off the surface of the ectoderm and becomes an internal structure (figure 19.18). Meanwhile, the inner and outer layers of the optic cup give rise to the inner neural layer and outer pigmented layer of the retina, respectively. Initially, a space exists between these two layers, but that space disappears, and the layers contact each other before birth.

Within the developing optic cup, a gelatinous material called the **primary vitreous body** begins forming; it eventually gives rise to the vitreous humor in the eye. The vitreous humor is not continuously secreted, so the vitreous humor in your eye right now is the same vitreous humor that was produced during this embryonic period.

During the sixth and seventh weeks of development, the mesenchyme around the optic cup forms the choroid and sclera. The iris, ciliary body, and suspensory ligaments form from the choroid beginning in the third month of development. Meanwhile,

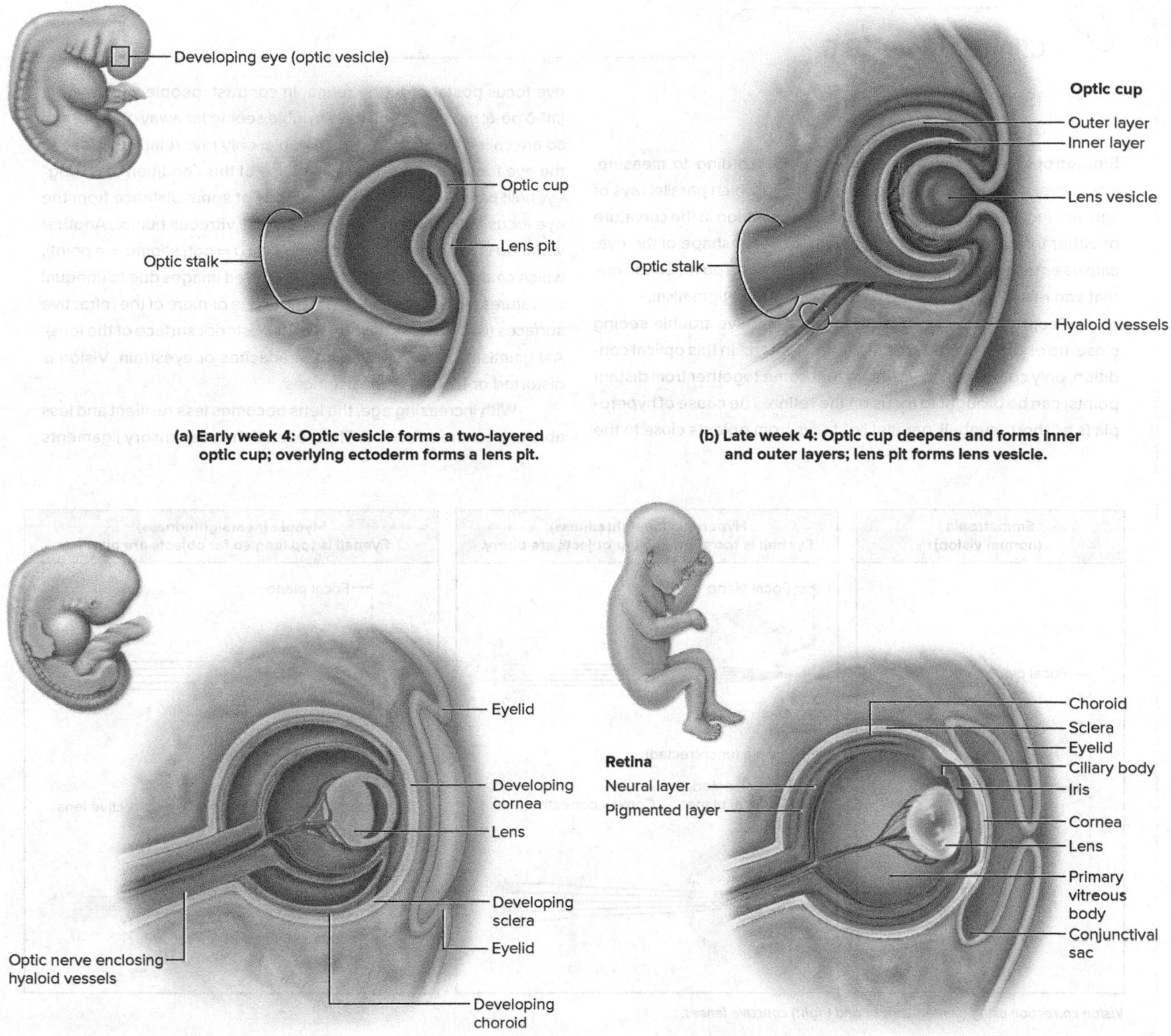
Developing eye (optic vesicle)
Optic cup
Lens pit
Optic stalk
Optic cup
Outer layer
Inner layer
Lens vesicle
Optic stalk
Hyaloid vessels
Eyelid
Developing cornea
Lens
Developing sclera
Eyelid
Optic nerve enclosing hyaloid vessels
Developing choroid
Choroid
Sclera
Eyelid
Ciliary body
Iris
Retina
Neural layer
Pigmented layer
Cornea
Lens
Primary vitreous body
Conjunctival sac

(a) Early week 4: Optic vesicle forms a two-layered optic cup; overlying ectoderm forms a lens pit.

(b) Late week 4: Optic cup deepens and forms inner and outer layers; lens pit forms lens vesicle.

(c) Week 6: Lens becomes an internal structure; corneas, sclera, and choroid start to form.

(d) Week 20: Three tunics of the eye have formed.

Figure 19.18

Eye Development. Development of the eye begins in the embryo during week 4 with the formation of optic vesicles lateral to the forebrain. (*a*) Early in week 4 of development, the optic vesicle forms a two-layered optic cup, and the overlying ectoderm forms a lens pit. (*b*) By late week 4, the lens pit becomes a lens vesicle, and hyaloid blood vessels begin to be incorporated into the forming optic nerve. (*c*) At week 6, the cornea, sclera, and choroid begin to develop. (*d*) By week 20, the three tunics of the eye, a lens, and primary vitreous body are present.

the cornea develops from the mesenchyme anterior to the lens as well as from part of the overlying ectoderm. These different tissue layers form the multiple tissue layers of the cornea by the eighth week of development.

Finally, the eyelids and the conjunctiva form from both the outer surface ectoderm and an underlying layer of mesenchyme. The lacrimal glands, which are essentially a type of exocrine gland, are formed from ectoderm that burrowed into the deeper connective tissue layers around the superolateral surface of the eye.

WHAT DID YOU LEARN?

11. How is lacrimal fluid spread across the eye and removed from the orbital region?
12. What are the three eye tunics; what is the primary function of each tunic?
13. Identify the three main cell layers in the neural layer of the retina, and discuss the function of each.
14. Make a flow chart of the structures light passes through before it reaches the retina. List the structures that refract the light rays.

Clinical View 19.6

How Vision Can Be Functionally Impaired

Emmetropia (em′ĕ-trō′pē-ă; *emmetros* = according to measure; *ops* = eye) is the condition of normal vision in which parallel rays of light are focused exactly on the retina. Any variation in the curvature of either the cornea or the lens, or in the overall shape of the eye, causes entering light rays to form an abnormal focal point. Conditions that can result include hyperopia, myopia, and astigmatism.

People with **hyperopia** (hī′pĕr-ō′pē-ă) have trouble seeing close-up objects, and so are called "farsighted." In this optical condition, only convergent rays (those that come together from distant points) can be brought to focus on the retina. The cause of hyperopia is a "short" eyeball; parallel light rays from objects close to the eye focus posterior to the retina. In contrast, people with **myopia** (mī-ō′pē-ă; *myo* = to shut) have trouble seeing far-away objects, and so are called "nearsighted." In myopia, only rays relatively close to the eye focus on the retina. The cause of this condition is a "long" eyeball; parallel light rays from objects at some distance from the eye focus anterior to the retina within the vitreous humor. Another variation is **astigmatism** (ă-stig′mă-tizm; *a* = not, *stigma* = a point), which causes unequal focusing and blurred images due to unequal curvatures along different meridians in one or more of the refractive surfaces (cornea, anterior surface, or posterior surface of the lens). Astigmatism can give a person headaches or eyestrain. Vision is distorted or blurred at all distances.

With increasing age, the lens becomes less resilient and less able to become spherical. Thus, even if the suspensory ligaments

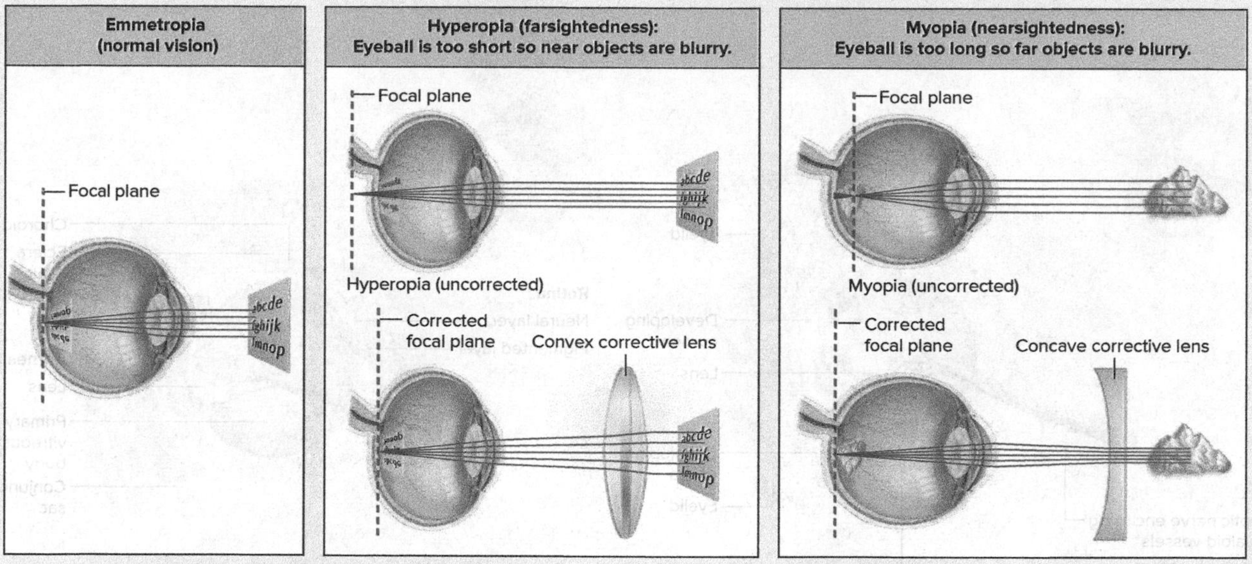

Vision correction using (center) convex and (right) concave lenses.

19.6 Equilibrium and Hearing

✓ Learning Objectives

9. Identify the structures, and describe the anatomy of the ear.
10. Describe the detection and processing of equilibrium sensations.
11. Explain the collection and processing of sound.
12. Describe the formation of the embryonic ear.

The ear is partitioned into three distinct anatomic regions: external, middle, and inner (**figure 19.19**). The external ear is located mostly on the outside of the body, and the middle and inner areas are housed within the petrous part of the temporal bone. Movements of the inner ear fluid result in the sensations of hearing and equilibrium (balance).

19.6a External Ear

The external ear is a skin-covered, primarily cartilaginous structure called the **auricle**, or *pinna* (pin′ă; wing). The auricle is funnel-shaped, and serves to protect the entry into the ear and to direct sound waves into the bony tube called the **external acoustic meatus** (see section 7.1c), which extends medially and slightly superiorly from the lateral surface of the head. The external acoustic meatus terminates at the **tympanic** (tim-pan′ik; *tympanon* = drum) **membrane,** or *eardrum,* a delicate, funnel-shaped epithelial sheet that is the partition between the external and middle ear. The tympanic membrane vibrates when sound waves hit it. These vibrations provide the means for transmission of sound wave energy into the middle and inner ear.

The narrow external opening in the external acoustic meatus prevents large objects from entering and damaging the tympanic relax, the lens may not be able to spring out of the flattened position into the more spherical shape needed for near vision, and reading close-up words becomes difficult. This age-related change is called **presbyopia** (prez-bē-ō′pē-ă; *presbys* = old man, *ops* = eye).

The typical treatment for vision disturbances is eyeglasses. A concave eyeglass lens is used to treat myopia, because the concave lens refracts (bends) the light rays to make the focused image appear directly on the retina, instead of too far in front of it. A lens that is convex is used to treat both hyperopia and presbyopia. The convex lens refracts the light rays so they can be better focused on the retina.

In more recent times, surgical techniques have been developed to treat vision problems. **Corneal incision** involves cutting the cornea to change its shape, and thereby change its ability to refract light. One type of corneal incision procedure, called a **radial keratotomy** (ker′ă-tot′ō-mē; *tome* = incision), or **RK,** treats nearsightedness. The ophthalmologist makes radial-oriented cuts in the cornea, much like the spokes of a wheel. These cuts flatten the cornea, and allow it to refract the light rays so that they focus on the retina.

Currently more common than corneal incision is **laser vision correction,** which uses a laser to change the shape of the cornea. Two of the more popular types of laser vision correction are photorefractive keratectomy and laser-assisted in situ keratomileusis.

Photorefractive keratectomy (PRK) is called a *photoablation procedure* because the laser removes (ablates) tissue directly from the surface of the cornea. The removal of tissue results in a newly shaped cornea that can focus better. This procedure is becoming less popular, because its regression rate is high—that is, the epithelial tissue that covers the surface of the cornea can regrow and regenerate, leading to partial return to uncorrected vision.

Laser-assisted in situ keratomileusis (ker′ă-tō-mī-lū′sis) (or **LASIK**) is rapidly becoming the most popular laser vision correction procedure. It can treat nearsightedness, farsightedness, and astigmatism. LASIK removes tissue from the inner, deeper layer of the cornea, which is less likely to regrow than surface tissue, so less vision regression occurs.

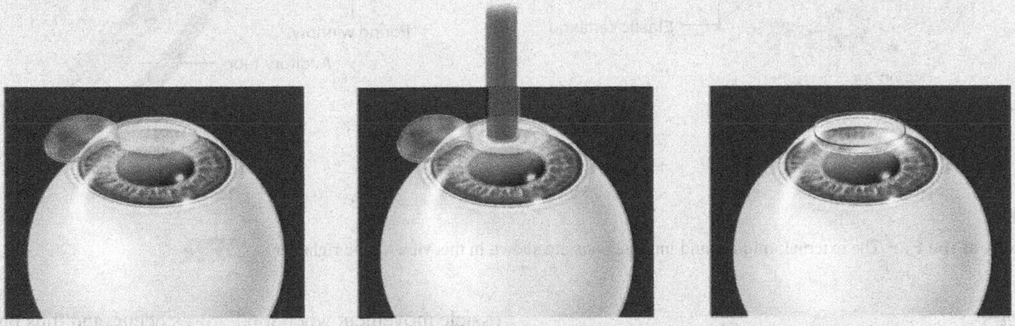

(1) Cornea is sliced with a sharp knife. Flap of cornea is reflected, and deeper corneal layers are exposed.

(2) A laser removes microscopic portions of the deeper corneal layers, thereby changing the shape of the cornea.

(3) Corneal flap is put back in place, and the edges of the flap start to fuse within 72 hours.

LASIK laser vision correction procedure.

membrane. Near its entrance, fine hairs help guard the opening. Deep within the canal, ceruminous glands produce a waxlike secretion called **cerumen,** which combines with dead, sloughed skin cells to form earwax. This material may help reduce infection within the external acoustic meatus by impeding microorganism growth.

19.6b Middle Ear

The middle ear contains an air-filled **tympanic cavity** (figure 19.19). Medially, a bony wall that houses the oval window and round window separates the middle ear from the inner ear. The tympanic cavity maintains an open connection with the atmosphere through the **auditory tube** (also called the *pharyngotympanic tube* or *Eustachian tube*). This passageway opens into the nasopharynx (upper throat) from the middle ear (see section 25.2c). It has a normally closed, slitlike opening at its connection to the nasopharynx. Air movement through this tube occurs as a result of chewing, yawning, and swallowing, which allows the pressure to equalize in the middle ear. Middle ear infections result when infectious agents (e.g., a cold virus) move from the nasopharynx through the auditory tube into the middle ear (see Clinical View 19.7: "Otitis Media and Otitis Externa" in section 19.6c).

WHAT DO YOU THINK?

4. When an airplane descends to a lower altitude, you may feel greater pressure in your ears, followed by a "popping" sensation, before more normal pressure resumes. What do you think happens anatomically?

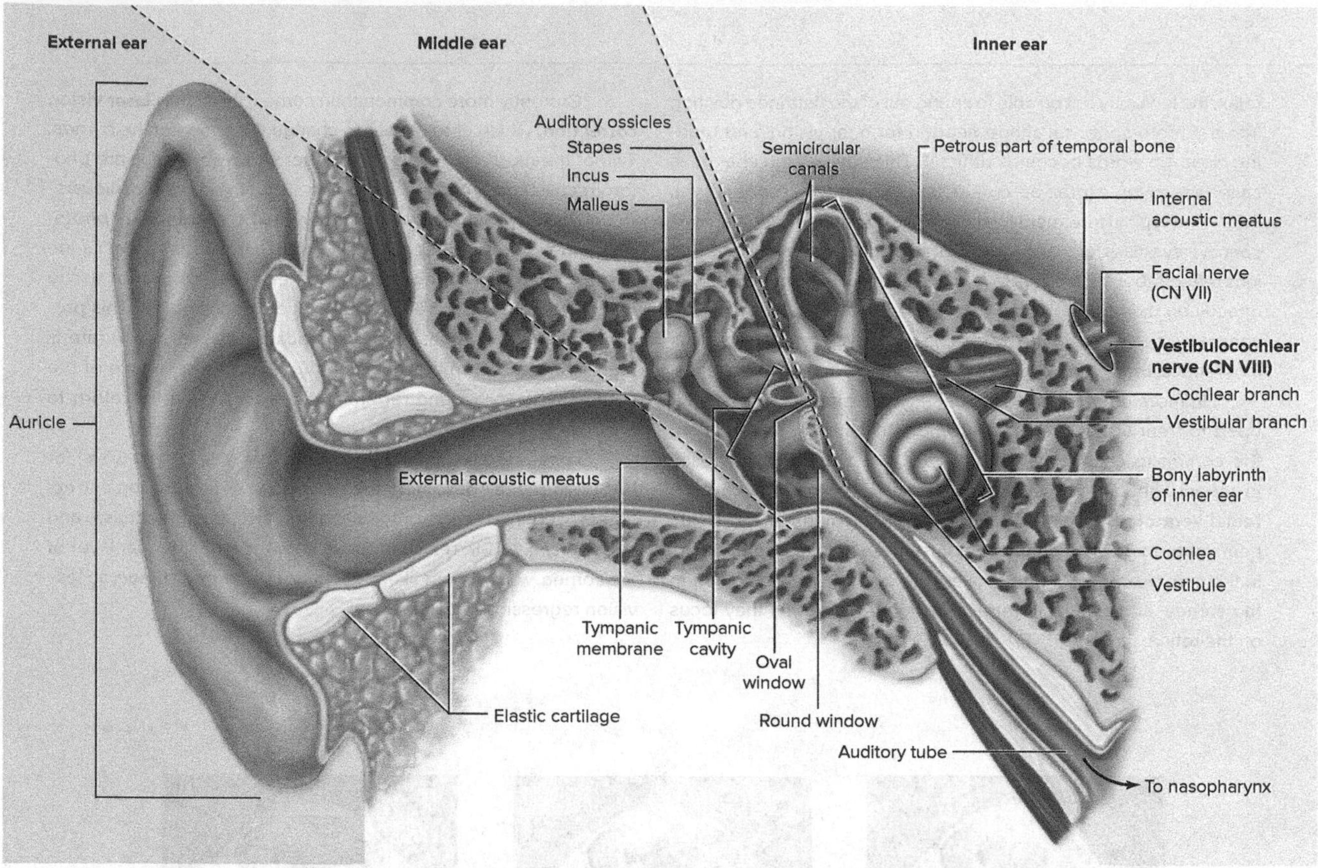

External ear
Middle ear
Inner ear
Auditory ossicles
Stapes
Incus
Malleus
Semicircular canals
Petrous part of temporal bone
Internal acoustic meatus
Facial nerve (CN VII)
Vestibulocochlear nerve (CN VIII)
Cochlear branch
Vestibular branch
Auricle
External acoustic meatus
Bony labyrinth of inner ear
Cochlea
Vestibule
Tympanic membrane
Tympanic cavity
Oval window
Elastic cartilage
Round window
Auditory tube
To nasopharynx

Figure 19.19

Anatomic Regions of the Ear. The external, middle, and inner regions are shown in this view of the right ear. APR

Auditory Ossicles

The tympanic cavity of the middle ear houses the three smallest bones of the body, called the **auditory ossicles** (os′i-k ēl) (**figure 19.20**; see also figure 19.19). These bones are, from lateral to medial, the malleus (hammer), the incus (anvil), and the stapes (stirrup). The **malleus** (mal′ ē-ŭs) is attached to the medial surface of the tympanic membrane, and suspended by ligaments bound to the wall of the tympanic cavity. It resembles a large hammer in shape. The **incus** (ing′kŭs) resembles an anvil and is the middle auditory ossicle. The **stapes** (stā′pēz) resembles a stirrup on a saddle. It has a cylindrical, disclike footplate that fits into the oval window, an opening that marks the lateral wall of the inner ear.

The auditory ossicles are responsible for amplifying sound waves and transmitting them into the inner ear via the oval window. When sound waves strike the tympanic membrane, the three middle ear ossicles vibrate along with the tympanic membrane, causing the footplate of the stapes to move in and out of the oval window. The movement of this ossicle initiates pressure waves in the fluid within the closed compartment of the inner ear. Because the tympanic membrane is 20 times greater in diameter than the stapes footplate in the oval window, sounds transmitted across the middle ear are amplified more than 20-fold, and we are able to detect very faint sounds.

Two tiny skeletal muscles, called the **stapedius** and the **tensor tympani,** are located within the middle ear. These muscles restrict ossicle movement when loud noises occur, and thus protect the sensitive receptors in the inner ear.

19.6c Inner Ear

The inner ear is located within the petrous part of the temporal bone, where there are spaces or cavities called the **bony labyrinth** (lab′i-rinth; an intricate, mazelike passageway) (**figure 19.21**; see also figure 19.19). Within the bony labyrinth are membrane-lined, fluid-filled tubes and spaces called the **membranous labyrinth.** Receptors for equilibrium and hearing are housed within the membranous labyrinth.

The space between the outer walls of the bony labyrinth and the membranous labyrinth is filled with a fluid called **perilymph** (per′i-limf), which is similar in composition to both extracellular fluid and cerebrospinal fluid (CSF). In the inner ear, the perilymph suspends, supports, and protects the membranous labyrinth from the wall of the bony labyrinth. The membranous labyrinth contains a unique fluid called **endolymph** (en′d ō-limf). Endolymph exhibits a low sodium and high potassium concentration similar to that of intracellular fluid.

The bony labyrinth is structurally and functionally partitioned into three distinct regions that include the cochlea, vestibule, and semicircular canals:

- The **cochlea** (kok′lē-ă = snail shell) houses a membranous labyrinth structure called the **cochlear duct** (or scala media).

- The **vestibule** (ves'ti-byūl; *vestibulum* = entrance court) contains two saclike, membranous labyrinth structures—the **utricle** (yū'tri-kĕl; *uter* = leather bag) and the **saccule** (sak'yūl; *saccus* = sack).
- The **semicircular canals** each contain a membranous labyrinth structure called the **semicircular duct.**

Structures and Mechanism of Equilibrium

The term **equilibrium** refers to our awareness and monitoring of head position. Sensory receptors in the utricle, saccule, and semicircular ducts—collectively called the **vestibular apparatus**—help monitor and adjust our equilibrium. Our brain receives this sensory input and, along with visual sensory input and input from our proprioceptors, integrates this information so we may keep our balance and make positional adjustments as necessary.

The utricle and saccule detect head position during **static equilibrium**—that is, when the head is stationary. So, for example, when you are standing in the anatomic position, it is the utricle and saccule that inform your brain that your head is upright. The utricle and saccule also detect **linear acceleration** changes of the head. This occurs, for example, when you tilt your head downward to look

Clinical View 19.7

Otitis Media and Otitis Externa

Otitis (ō-tī'tis; *itis* = inflammation) **media** (mē'dē-ă; *medius* = middle) is an infection of the middle ear. It is most often experienced by young children, whose auditory tubes are horizontal, relatively short, and undeveloped. If a young child has a respiratory infection, the causative agent may spread from the throat into the tympanic cavity and the mastoidal air cells. Fluid then accumulates in the middle ear cavity, resulting in pressure, pain, and sometimes impaired hearing.

Classic symptoms of otitis media include fever (sometimes over 104°F), pulling on or holding the affected ear, and general irritability. An **otoscope** (ō'tō-skōp; *skopeo* = to view) is an instrument used to examine the tympanic membrane, which normally appears white and "pearly," but in cases of severe otitis media is red and may even bulge due to fluid pressure in the middle ear.

Repeated ear infections, or a chronic ear infection that does not respond to antibiotic treatment, usually calls for a surgical procedure called a **myringotomy** (mir-ing-got'ō-mē; *myringa* = membrane), whereby a ventilation tube is inserted into the tympanic membrane. This procedure offers immediate relief from the pressure and allows the infection to heal and the pus and mucus to drain from the middle ear. Eventually, the inserted tube is sloughed, and the tympanic membrane heals.

Once a child is about 5 years old, the auditory tube has become larger, more angled, and better able to drain fluid and prevent infection from reaching the middle ear. Thus, the occurrence rate for ear infections drops dramatically at this time.

Otitis externa is an infection of the skin that covers the external acoustic meatus. It is commonly known as *swimmer's ear* because the infection is usually caused by excessive water exposure (e.g., from swimming or showering). When water collects in the external acoustic meatus, the skin can become soggy and serve as a culture medium for bacteria and fungi. Symptoms of otitis externa include pain or itching in the outer part of the ear (the pain is often worse when the auricle is pulled on or moves, as when chewing), swelling of the meatus and auricle, a stuffy or plugged-up feeling with decreased or muffled hearing in the affected ear, and, if infection is severe, pus draining from the affected ear. Otitis externa usually is not a dangerous condition and often clears up by itself within a few days. When more severe infections are present, topical antibiotics can be applied to the infected area.

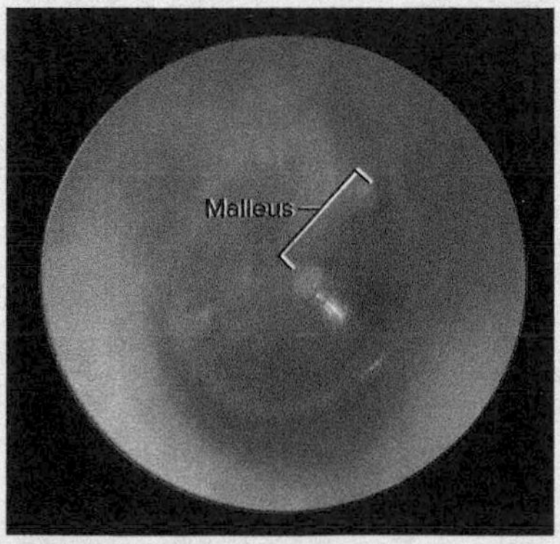

Normal tympanic membrane
ISM/Clinica CLAROS/Medical Images

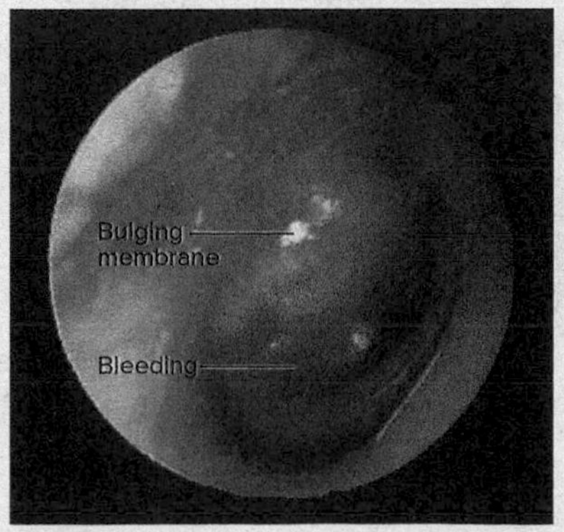

Otitis media present, bulging red tympanic membrane
Neal R. Chamberlin, PhD/McGraw-Hill Education

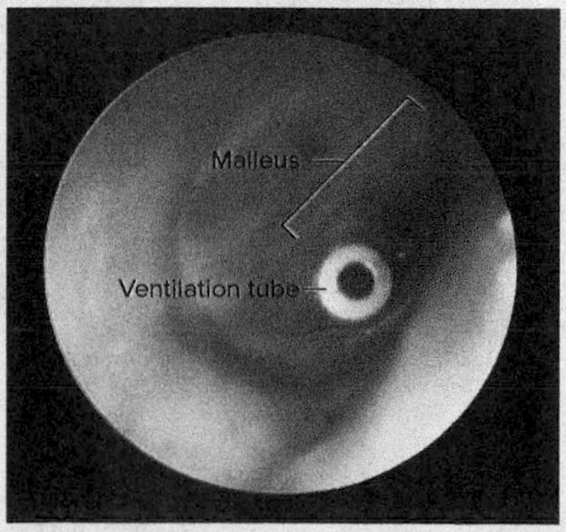

Myringotomy
ISM/Clinica CLAROS/Medical Images

Middle ear views as seen with an otoscope.

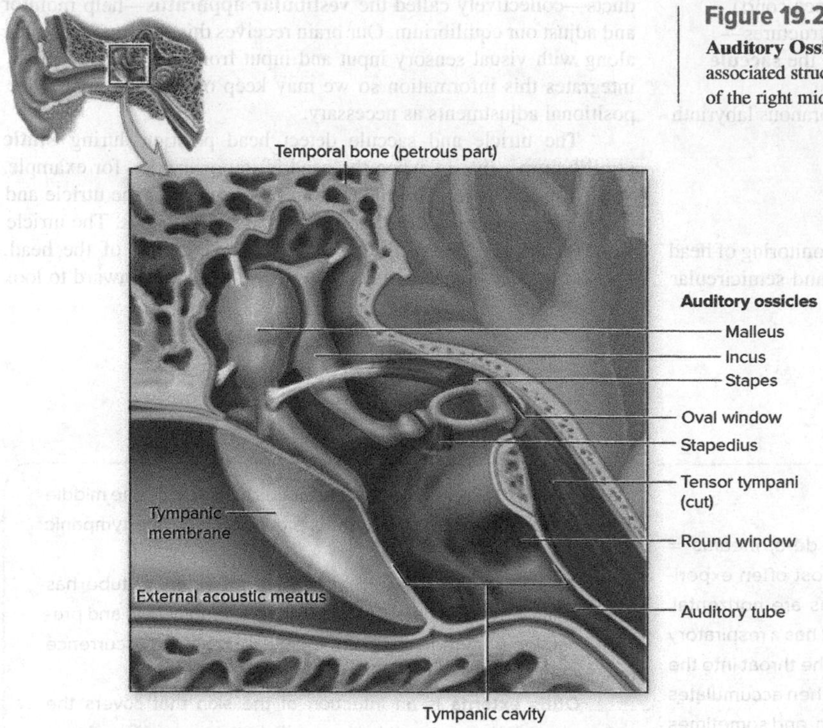
Temporal bone (petrous part)
Auditory ossicles
Malleus
Incus
Stapes
Oval window
Stapedius
Tensor tympani (cut)
Tympanic membrane
Round window
External acoustic meatus
Auditory tube
Tympanic cavity

Figure 19.20

Auditory Ossicles. The middle ear contains the auditory ossicles and associated structures within the tympanic cavity, as shown in this view of the right middle ear.

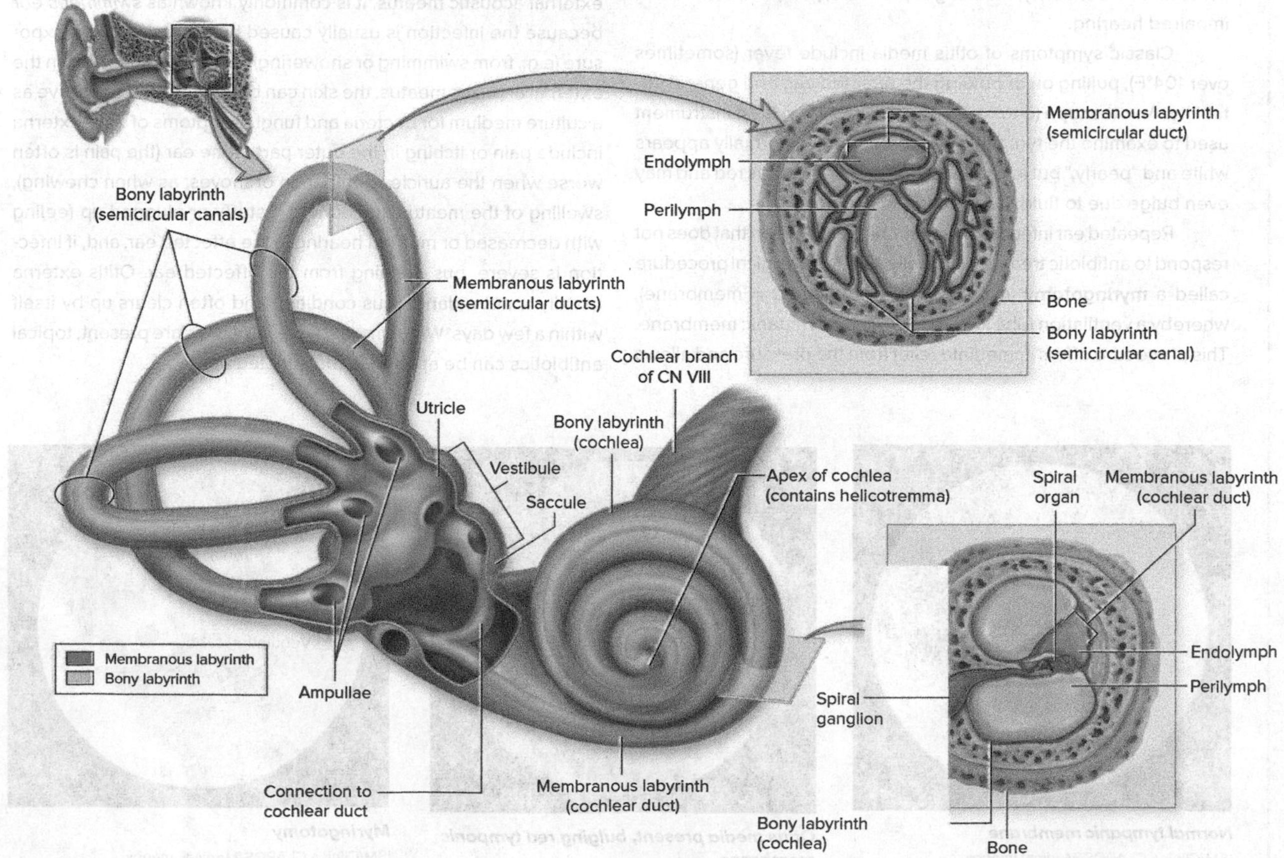
Membranous labyrinth (semicircular duct)
Endolymph
Perilymph
Bone
Bony labyrinth (semicircular canal)
Bony labyrinth (semicircular canals)
Membranous labyrinth (semicircular ducts)
Cochlear branch of CN VIII
Utricle
Bony labyrinth (cochlea)
Vestibule
Saccule
Apex of cochlea (contains helicotremma)
Spiral organ
Membranous labyrinth (cochlear duct)
Endolymph
Perilymph
Membranous labyrinth
Bony labyrinth
Ampullae
Spiral ganglion
Connection to cochlear duct
Membranous labyrinth (cochlear duct)
Bony labyrinth (cochlea)
Bone

Figure 19.21

Inner Ear. The inner ear is composed of a bony labyrinth cavity that houses a fluid-filled membranous labyrinth. Within the bony labyrinth are the portions of the membranous labyrinth for equilibrium and balance (saccule, utricle, and semicircular canals) and the cochlear duct for hearing.

at your shoes. The semicircular ducts, in contrast, are responsible for detecting **angular acceleration,** or rotational movements of the head. The sensory receptors in the semicircular ducts are stimulated when you shake your head "no," or when a figure skater does a spin on the ice.

Learning Strategy 19.4

Rotation may be defined as either a pivot about a central axis or a circular movement. Rotational movements of the head (i.e., angular acceleration) are detected by the circular-shaped structures called semicircular canals.

Both static equilibrium and linear acceleration are detected by the sensory receptors housed within the vestibule of the inner ear. The sensory receptor, called a **macula,** is located along the internal wall of both the utricle and saccule **(figure 19.22).** Each macula is composed of a mixed layer of **hair cells** and **supporting cells.** Hair cells are the sensory receptors of the inner ear for both equilibrium and hearing. They continuously release neurotransmitter molecules to the sensory neurons that monitor their activity. The apical surface of each hair cell has a covering of numerous (more than 50) long, stiff microvilli, termed **stereocilia** (ster′ ē-ō-sil′ē-ă; *stereos* = solid, *cilium* = eyelid). In the maculae of the utricle and saccule and in the semicircular ducts, each hair cell also has one long cilium, termed a **kinocilium** (kin′ ō-sil′ē-ŭm; *kino* = movement) on its apical surface (figure 19.22*c*). Both the stereocilia and kinocilia may be physically bent or displaced, resulting in changes in the amount and rate of neurotransmitter release from the hair cell.

Stereocilia and kinocilia projecting from the hair cells embed within a gelatinous mass that completely covers the apical surface of the epithelium. This gelatinous layer is embedded with a bunch of small calcium carbonate crystals called **otoliths** (ō′tō-lith; *lithos* = stone), or *statoconia*. Together, the gelatinous layer and the crystals form the **otolithic membrane** (or *statoconic membrane*). The otoliths push on the underlying gelatin, thereby increasing the weight of the otolithic membrane covering the hair cells. The position of the head influences the position of the otolithic membrane **(figure 19.23).** When the head is held erect, the otolithic membrane applies pressure directly onto the hair cells, and minimal stimulation of the hair cells occurs. However, tilting the head due to either acceleration or deceleration causes the otolithic membrane to shift its position on the macula surface, thus distorting the stereocilia. Bending of the stereocilia results in a change in the amount of neurotransmitter released from the hair cells and a simultaneous change in the stimulation of the sensory neurons. Thus, distortion of the hair cells in one particular

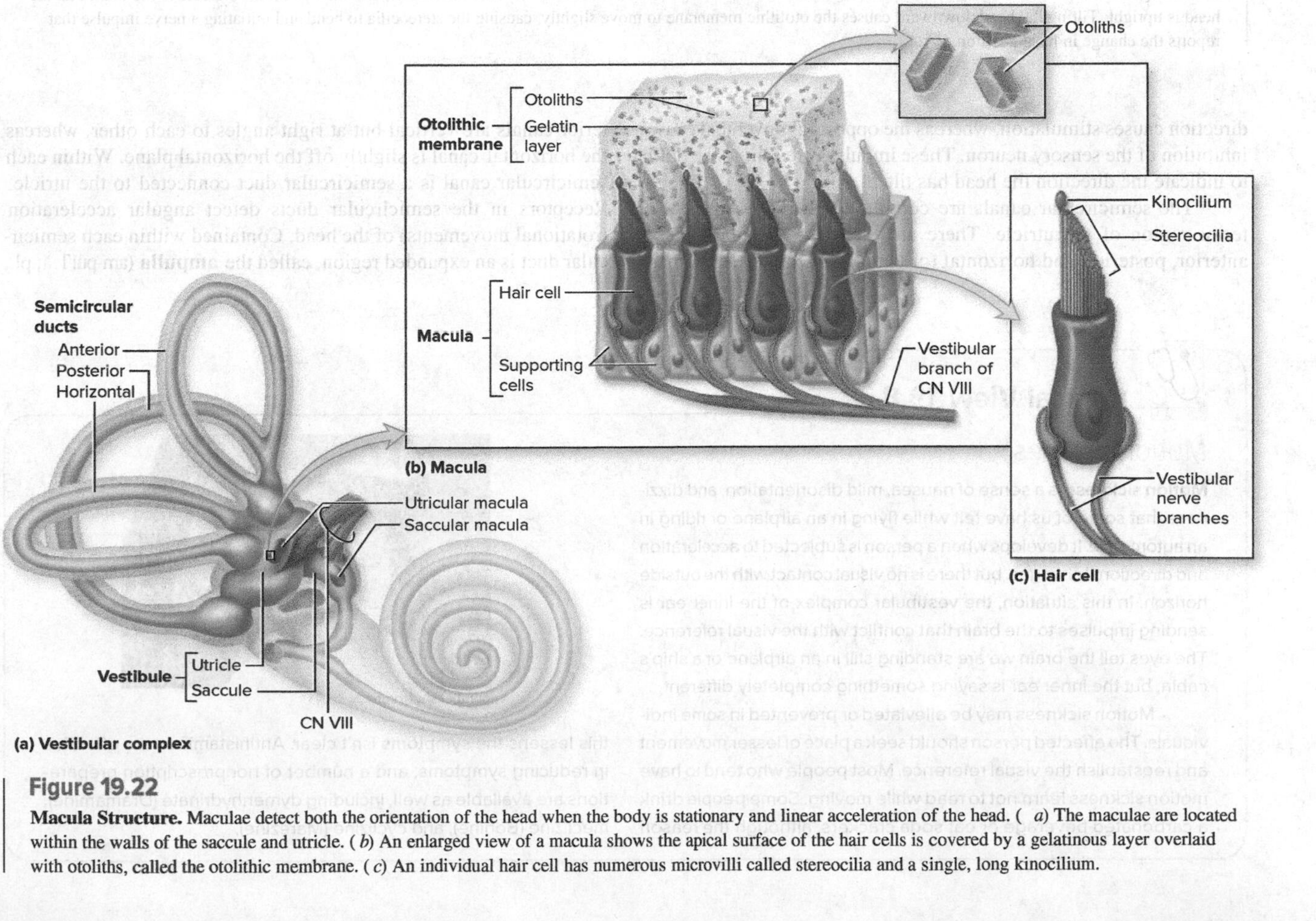

Figure 19.22

Macula Structure. Maculae detect both the orientation of the head when the body is stationary and linear acceleration of the head. (*a*) The maculae are located within the walls of the saccule and utricle. (*b*) An enlarged view of a macula shows the apical surface of the hair cells is covered by a gelatinous layer overlaid with otoliths, called the otolithic membrane. (*c*) An individual hair cell has numerous microvilli called stereocilia and a single, long kinocilium.

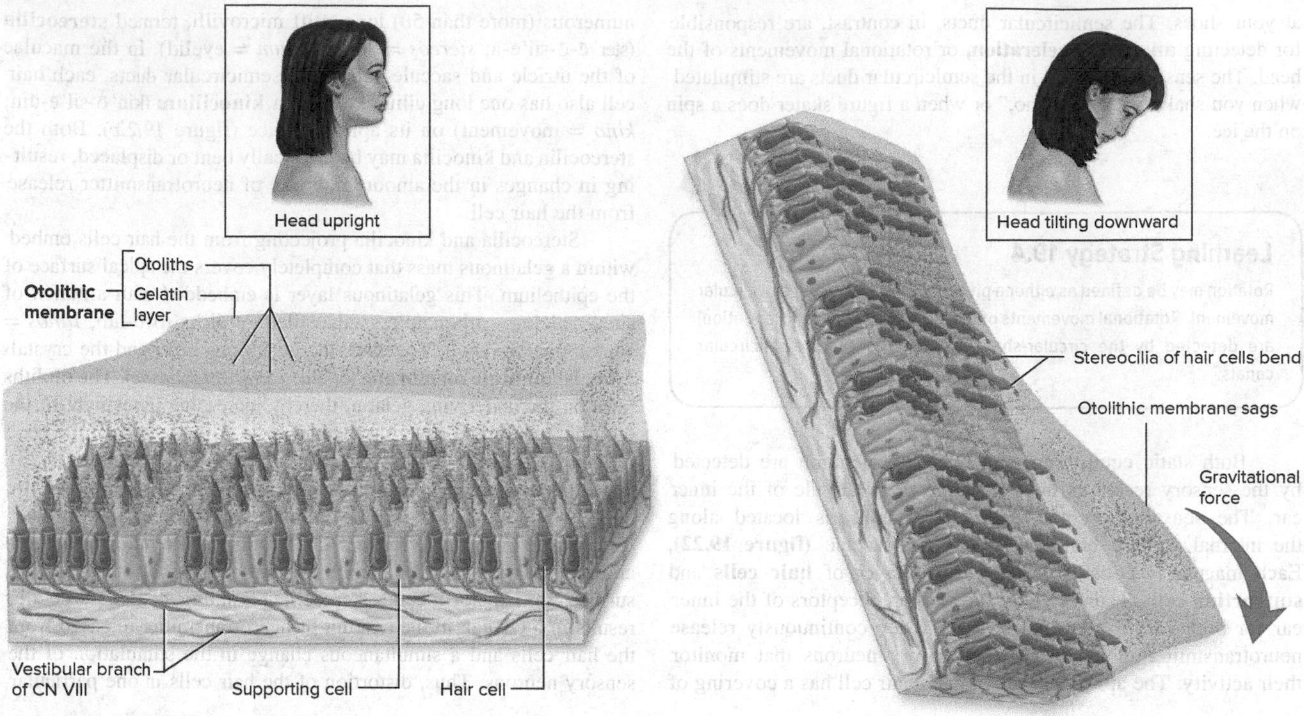

Head upright
Otoliths
Otolithic membrane
Gelatin layer
Vestibular branch of CN VIII
Supporting cell
Hair cell
Head tilting downward
Stereocilia of hair cells bend
Otolithic membrane sags
Gravitational force

Figure 19.23

Detecting Head Position. When the head is upright, the stereocilia are encased within the otolithic membrane, and their positions indicate to the brain that the head is upright. Tilting the head downward causes the otolithic membrane to move slightly, causing the stereocilia to bend and initiating a nerve impulse that reports the change in head position.

direction causes stimulation, whereas the opposing movement causes inhibition of the sensory neuron. These impulses are sent to the brain to indicate the direction the head has tilted.

The semicircular canals are continuous with the superoposterior region of the utricle. There are three semicircular canals: anterior, posterior, and horizontal (or lateral). The anterior and posterior canals are vertical but at right angles to each other, whereas the horizontal canal is slightly off the horizontal plane. Within each semicircular canal is a semicircular duct connected to the utricle. Receptors in the semicircular ducts detect angular acceleration (rotational movements) of the head. Contained within each semicircular duct is an expanded region, called the **ampulla** (am-pul'l ă; pl.,

Clinical View 19.8

Motion Sickness

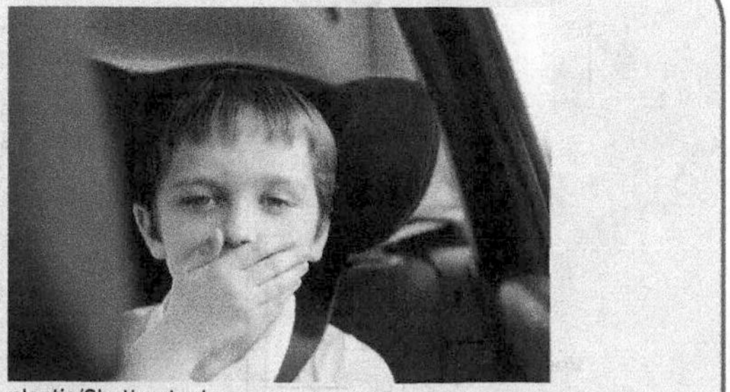

plantic/Shutterstock

Motion sickness is a sense of nausea, mild disorientation, and dizziness that some of us have felt while flying in an airplane or riding in an automobile. It develops when a person is subjected to acceleration and directional changes, but there is no visual contact with the outside horizon. In this situation, the vestibular complex of the inner ear is sending impulses to the brain that conflict with the visual reference. The eyes tell the brain we are standing still in an airplane or a ship's cabin, but the inner ear is saying something completely different.

Motion sickness may be alleviated or prevented in some individuals. The affected person should seek a place of lesser movement and reestablish the visual reference. Most people who tend to have motion sickness learn not to read while moving. Some people drink a carbonated beverage or eat soda crackers, although the reason this lessens the symptoms isn't clear. Antihistamines are effective in reducing symptoms, and a number of nonprescription preparations are available as well, including dymenhydrinate (Dramamine), meclizine (Bonine), and cyclizine (Marezine).

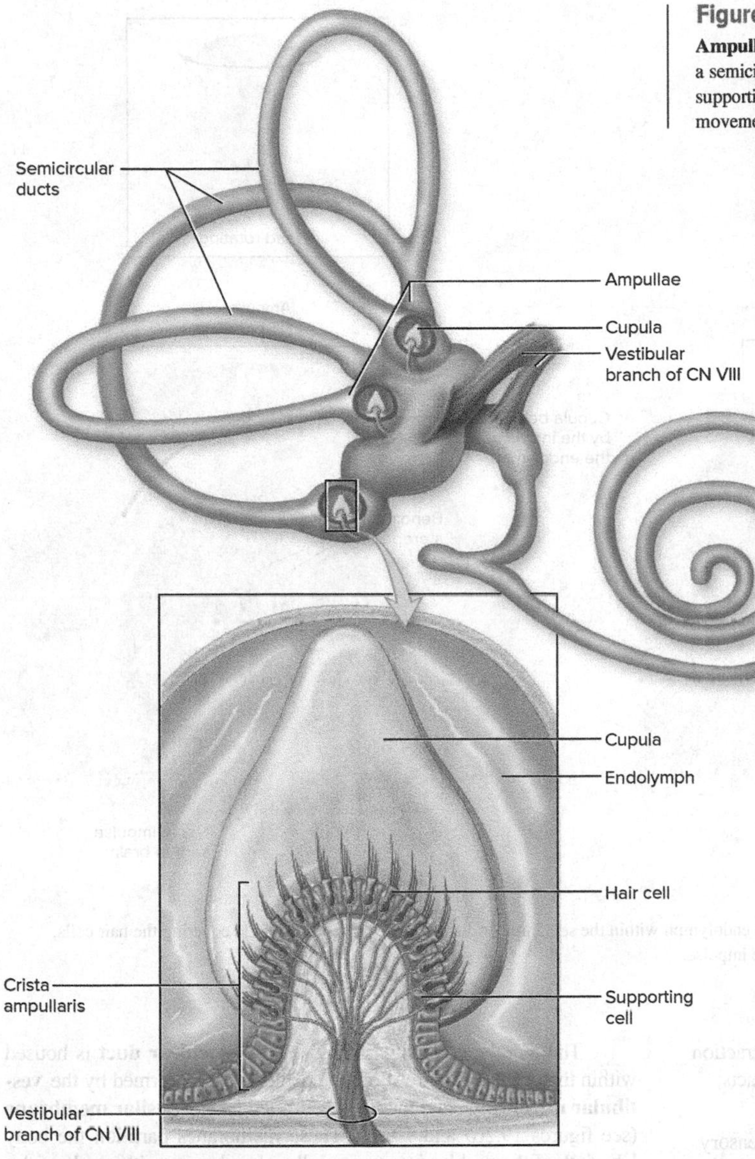

Semicircular ducts
Ampullae
Cupula
Vestibular branch of CN VIII
Cupula
Endolymph
Hair cell
Crista ampullaris
Supporting cell
Vestibular branch of CN VIII

Figure 19.24

Ampulla Structure. A diagrammatic section through an ampulla in a semicircular duct details the relationships among the hair cells and supporting cells, the cupula, and the endolymph in detecting rotational movement of the head.

ampullae, am-pul′lē), located at the end furthest from the utricle connection (**figure 19.24**). The ampulla contains an elevated region, called the **crista ampullaris** (or *ampullary crest*), that is covered by an epithelium of hair cells and supporting cells (**figure 19.25**). These hair cells embed both their kinocilia and stereocilia into an overlying gelatinous dome called the **cupula** (kū′pū-lă). This accessory structure extends completely across the semicircular duct to the roof over the ampulla.

When the head rotates, it causes endolymph within the semicircular ducts to move and push against the cupula, causing bending of the stereocilia. Stereocilia bending results in altered neurotransmitter release from the hair cells and simultaneous stimulation of the sensory neurons. As described earlier in this section, fluid movement in one direction causes distortion of the hair cells, resulting in stimulation, whereas the opposing movement causes distortion resulting in inhibition.

Vestibular Pathway The nerve pathway that relays sensory input from the vestibular apparatus is as follows:

1. When the stereocilia of either the maculae (within the utricle and saccule) or the crista ampullaris (within the ampulla of a semicircular duct) distort, nerve impulses are initiated through the vestibular branch of the vestibulocochlear nerve (CN VIII) (see section 15.8).
2. The sensory axons of the vestibular branch (the primary neurons in this sensory pathway) terminate at either the (a) medulla oblongata (vestibular nuclei) or (b) cerebellum.
   a) Thepaired **vestibular nuclei** within the superior region of the medulla oblongata (see section 15.5c) integrate the stimuli from the vestibular apparatus (as well as the eyes and proprioceptors) to reflexively control movements of the eye (via the oculomotor, trochlear, and abducens

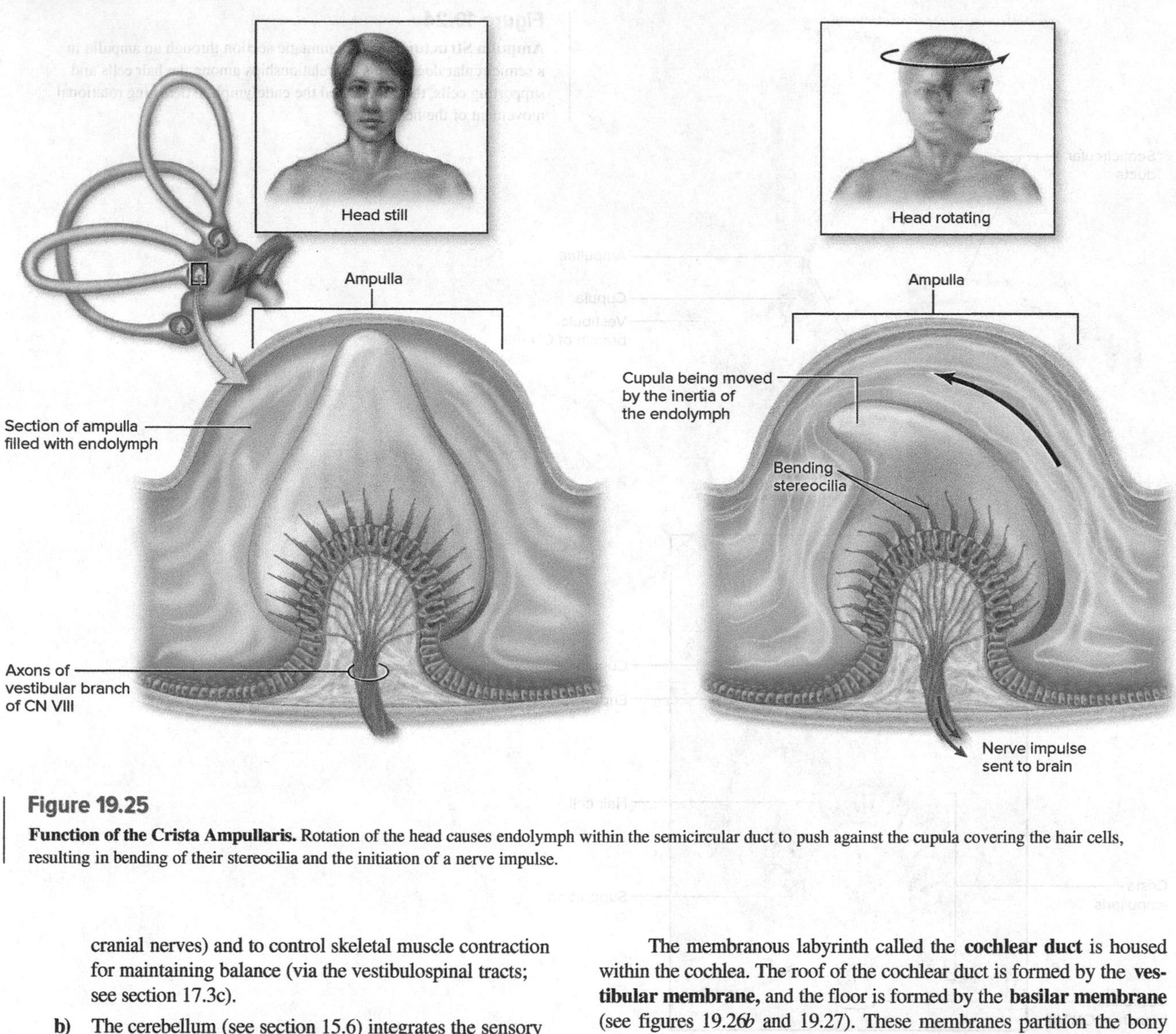
Head still
Head rotating
Ampulla
Ampulla
Section of ampulla filled with endolymph
Cupula being moved by the inertia of the endolymph
Bending stereocilia
Axons of vestibular branch of CN VIII
Nerve impulse sent to brain

Figure 19.25

Function of the Crista Ampullaris. Rotation of the head causes endolymph within the semicircular duct to push against the cupula covering the hair cells, resulting in bending of their stereocilia and the initiation of a nerve impulse.

cranial nerves) and to control skeletal muscle contraction for maintaining balance (via the vestibulospinal tracts; see section 17.3c).

b) The cerebellum (see section 15.6) integrates the sensory input from the vestibular apparatus (as well as input from the eyes, proprioceptors, and cerebrum) to coordinate skeletal muscle contraction to maintain balance and muscle tone (via the descending vestibulospinal motor tracts).

3. Nerve impulses are also sent from the vestibular nuclei and cerebellum to the thalamus and eventually the cerebral cortex for further processing and for our awareness of body position.

Structures for Hearing

Hearing organs are housed within the cochlea in both inner ears. View both **figure 19.26**, which is a cross section of the cochlea, and **figure 19.27**, which is a longitudinal section of a cochlea (partially "unrolled," so the structure can be viewed more easily), as you read through this section.

Cochlea The cochlea is a snail-shaped spiral chamber within the bone of the inner ear. Figure 19.26*a* depicts how the cochlea "wraps" about 2.5 times around a spongy bone axis called the **modiolus** (mō-dī′ō-lŭs = hub of a wheel), giving the cochlea its snail-shaped appearance.

The membranous labyrinth called the **cochlear duct** is housed within the cochlea. The roof of the cochlear duct is formed by the **vestibular membrane,** and the floor is formed by the **basilar membrane** (see figures 19.26*b* and 19.27). These membranes partition the bony labyrinth of the cochlea into two smaller chambers on either side of the cochlear duct; both are filled with perilymph. The chamber adjacent to the vestibular membrane is the **scala vestibuli** (*vestibular duct*), and the chamber adjacent to the basilar membrane is the **scala tympani** (*tympanic duct*). The scala vestibuli and scala tympani interconnect through a small channel called the **helicotrema** (hel′i-kō-trē′mă; *helix* = spiral, *trema* = hole) at the apex (tip) of the cochlea (figure 19.27).

Spiral Organ Protected within the membranous cochlear duct is the **spiral organ** (formerly called the *organ of Corti*), which is the sensory structure for hearing (see figures 19.26 and 19.27). The spiral organ is a thick sensory epithelium consisting of both hair cells and supporting cells that rest on the basilar membrane. Two categories of hair cells rest on the basilar membrane, including a single row of **inner hair cells** (which function as the sensory receptors for hearing) and three rows of **outer hair cells** (which alter the response of the spiral organ to sound). Like the hair cells of the macula, the apical surface of each hair cell also has numerous stereocilia and a single kinocilium. The stereocilia and kinocilium are embedded in an overlying gelatinous structure called the **tectorial** (tek-tō′rē-ăl; *tectus* = to cover) **membrane.** Extending from the

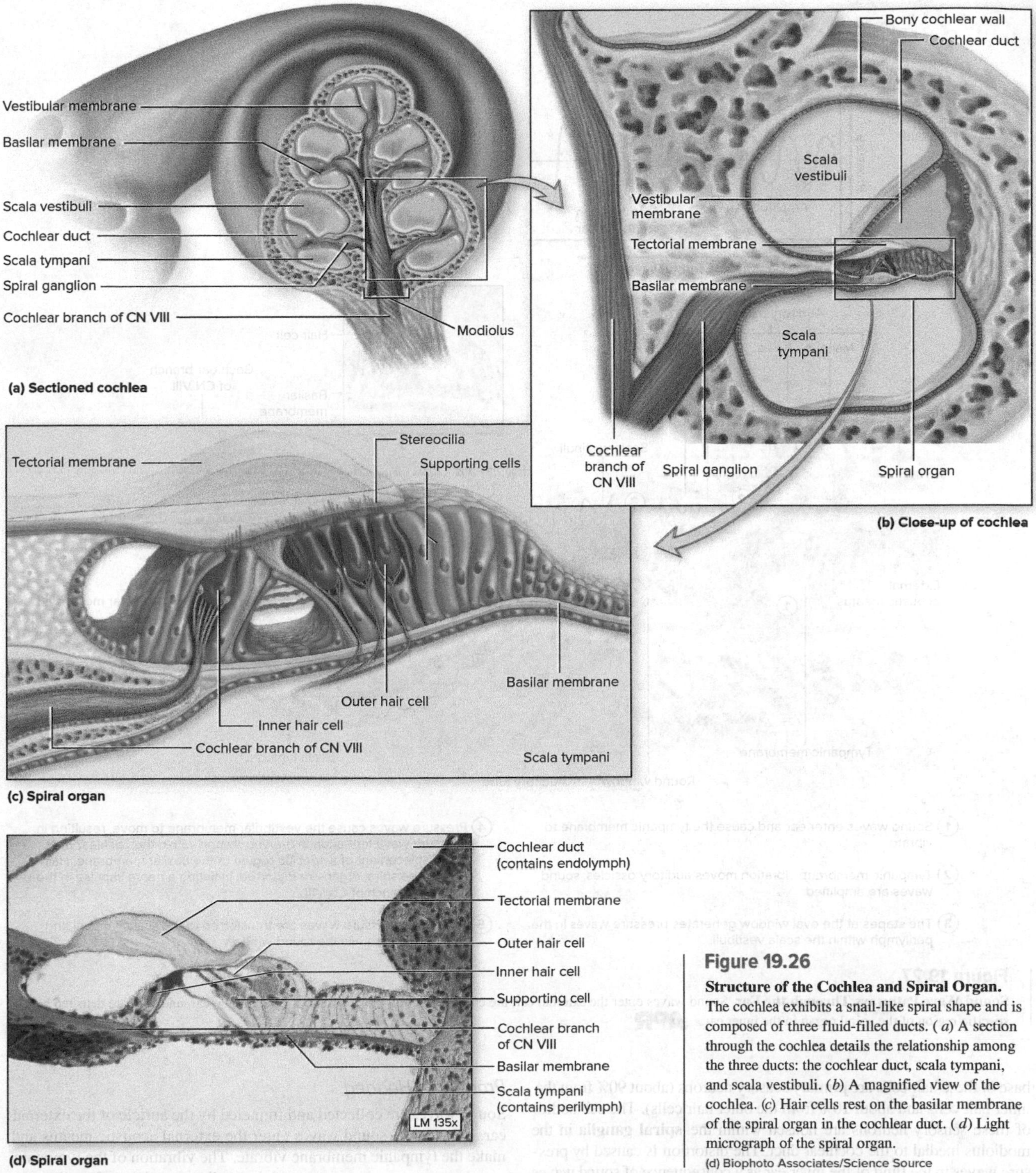
Vestibular membrane
Basilar membrane
Scala vestibuli
Cochlear duct
Scala tympani
Spiral ganglion
Cochlear branch of CN VIII
Modiolus
(a) Sectioned cochlea
Bony cochlear wall
Cochlear duct
Scala vestibuli
Vestibular membrane
Tectorial membrane
Basilar membrane
Scala tympani
Cochlear branch of CN VIII
Spiral ganglion
Spiral organ
(b) Close-up of cochlea
Stereocilia
Tectorial membrane
Supporting cells
Basilar membrane
Outer hair cell
Inner hair cell
Cochlear branch of CN VIII
Scala tympani
(c) Spiral organ
Cochlear duct
(contains endolymph)
Tectorial membrane
Outer hair cell
Inner hair cell
Supporting cell
Cochlear branch
of CN VIII
Basilar membrane
Scala tympani
(contains perilymph)
LM 135x
(d) Spiral organ

Figure 19.26

Structure of the Cochlea and Spiral Organ. The cochlea exhibits a snail-like spiral shape and is composed of three fluid-filled ducts. (*a*) A section through the cochlea details the relationship among the three ducts: the cochlear duct, scala tympani, and scala vestibuli. (*b*) A magnified view of the cochlea. (*c*) Hair cells rest on the basilar membrane of the spiral organ in the cochlear duct. (*d*) Light micrograph of the spiral organ.

(d) Biophoto Associates/Science Source

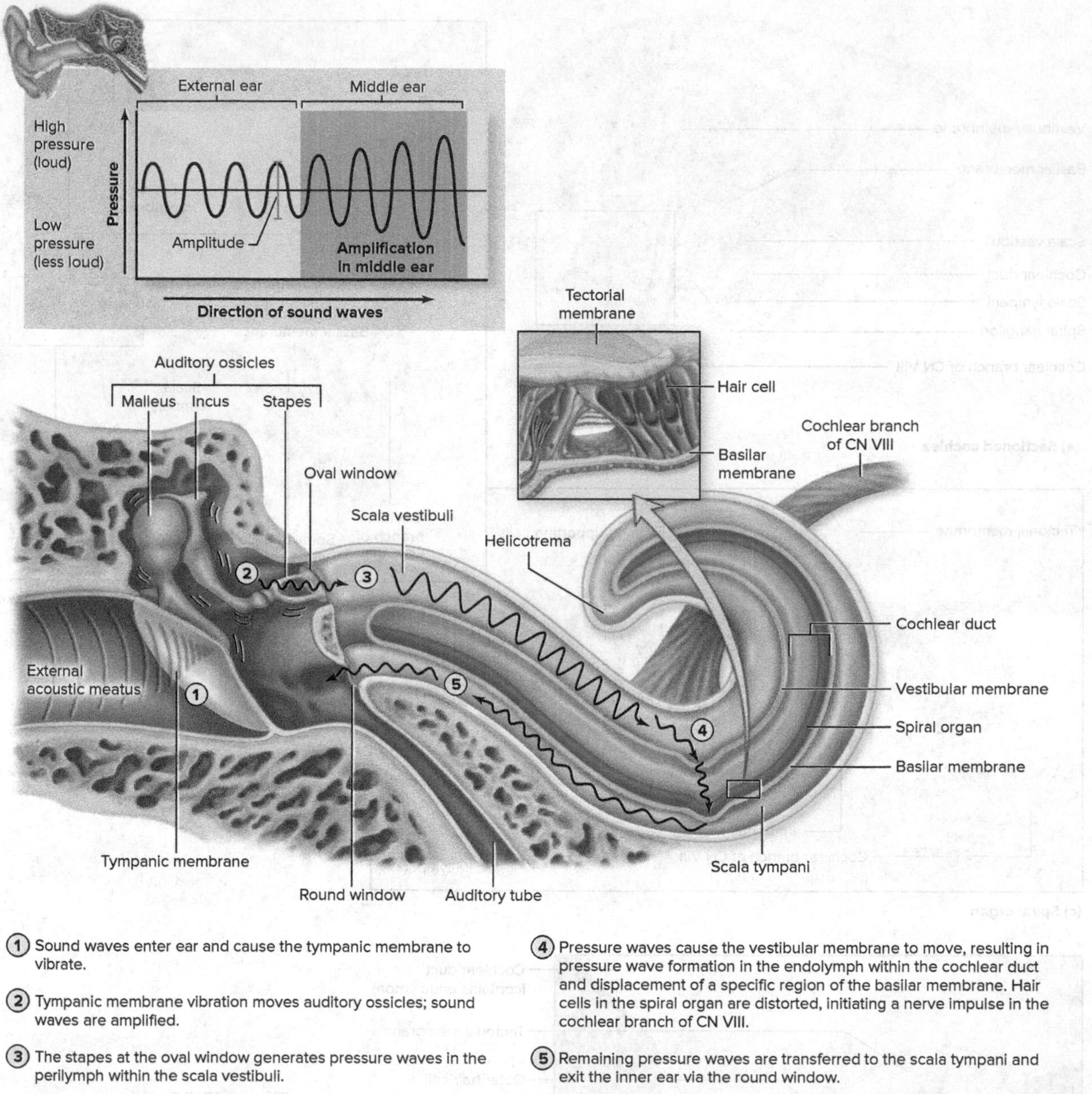
External ear
Middle ear
High pressure (loud)
Low pressure (less loud)
Pressure
Amplitude
Amplification in middle ear
Direction of sound waves
Auditory ossicles
Malleus
Incus
Stapes
Oval window
Scala vestibuli
Helicotrema
Tectorial membrane
Hair cell
Basilar membrane
Cochlear branch of CN VIII
Cochlear duct
Vestibular membrane
Spiral organ
Basilar membrane
External acoustic meatus
Tympanic membrane
Round window
Auditory tube
Scala tympani
1 Sound waves enter ear and cause the tympanic membrane to vibrate.
2 Tympanic membrane vibration moves auditory ossicles; sound waves are amplified.
3 The stapes at the oval window generates pressure waves in the perilymph within the scala vestibuli.
4 Pressure waves cause the vestibular membrane to move, resulting in pressure wave formation in the endolymph within the cochlear duct and displacement of a specific region of the basilar membrane. Hair cells in the spiral organ are distorted, initiating a nerve impulse in the cochlear branch of CN VIII.
5 Remaining pressure waves are transferred to the scala tympani and exit the inner ear via the round window.

Figure 19.27
Sound Wave Pathways Through the Ear. Sound waves enter the external ear, are conducted through the ossicles of the middle ear, and then are detected by a specific region of the spiral organ in the inner ear. APR

base of these hair cells are primary sensory neurons (about 90% from the inner hair cells and about 10% from the outer hair cells). The cell bodies of these sensory neurons are housed within the **spiral ganglia** in the modiolus medial to the cochlear duct. The distortion is caused by pressure waves in the fluid of the inner ear as a consequence of sound waves arriving at the tympanic membrane (see the next section). The pressure waves cause the basilar membrane to flutter or "bounce," resulting in distortion of the stereocilia (see figure 19.26).

Table 19.4 summarizes the structures of the inner ear and clarifies which ones are part of the bony labyrinth and which are part of the membranous labyrinth.

Process of Hearing

Sound waves are collected and funneled by the auricle of the external ear. From there, sound waves enter the external acoustic meatus and make the tympanic membrane vibrate. The vibration of the tympanic membrane causes movement of the auditory ossicles. Sound waves are amplified, allowing even faint sounds to cause vibration. The foot of the stapes moves like a piston in the oval window, thereby transmitting the effect of sound waves into pressure waves within the inner ear.

These pressure waves originate within the inner ear at the oval window and travel through the perilymph in the scala vestibuli.

Table 19.4	Inner Ear Structures		
Bony Labyrinth Structure	**Membranous Labyrinth Structure(s) Housed in Bony Labyrinth**	**Structure Housing Receptors**	**Function of Receptors**
Vestibule	Utricle, saccule	Macula	Detect head position during static equilibrium; detect linear acceleration of the head
Semicircular canals	Semicircular ducts	Crista ampullaris	Detect rotational movements of the head
Cochlea	Cochlear duct	Spiral organ	Hearing (transduction or conversion of sound and pressure waves to a nerve impulse)

Pressure waves in the scala vestibuli cause deformation of the cochlear duct. Pressure waves in the cochlear duct displace specific regions of the basilar membrane, relating to frequency (described later in this section). Hair cells in the spiral organ of this region are distorted, initiating nerve impulses in the cochlear branch of CN VIII. Simultaneously, the pressure wave vibrations in the cochlear duct are transmitted to the perilymph of the scala tympani, and are absorbed at the round window, as the window bulges slightly.

The sound waves that give rise to pressure waves in the inner ear are characterized by their frequency and intensity. **Frequency** is the number of waves that move past a point during a specific amount of time. Frequency is measured in *hertz (Hz)*, and is classified as high, medium, or low **(figure 19.28)**. Frequency is interpreted as the pitch of a sound. The region of the spiral organ stimulated by pressure waves in the perilymph varies according to the frequency of the sound: High-frequency sounds stimulate it near the oval window, whereas

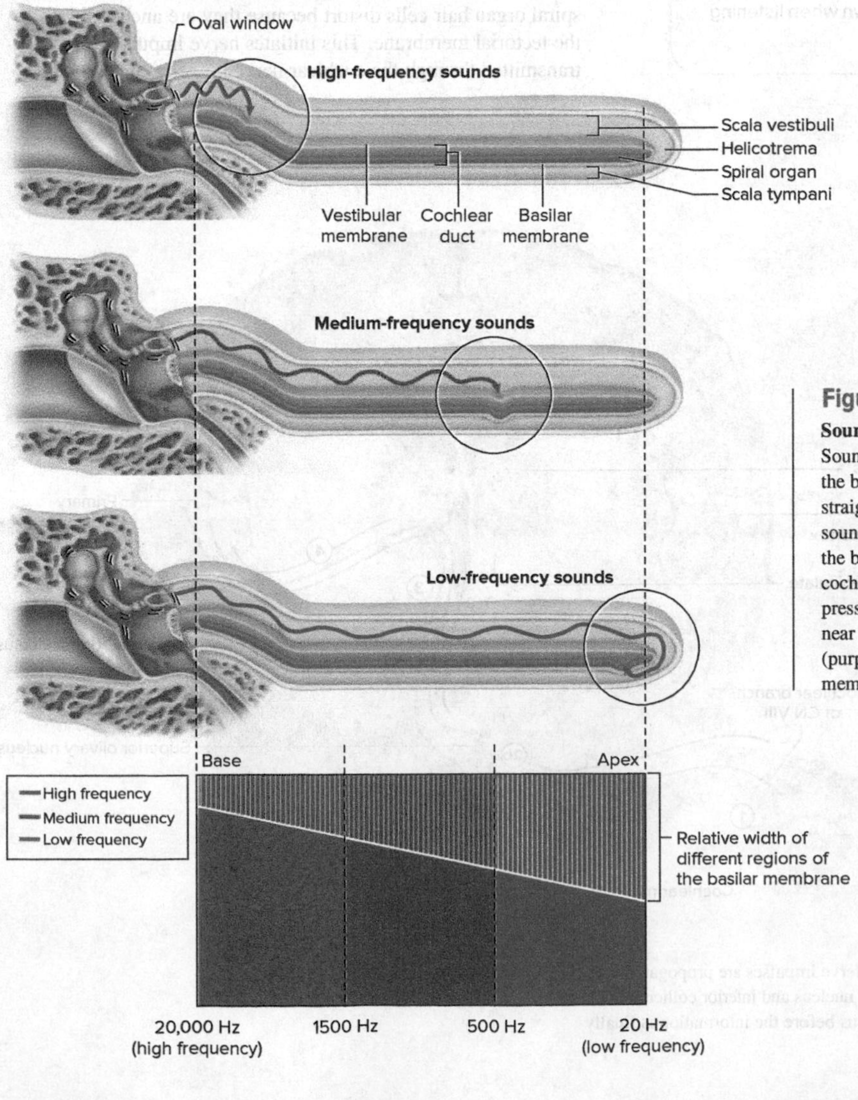
Oval window
High-frequency sounds
Scala vestibuli
Helicotrema
Spiral organ
Scala tympani
Vestibular membrane
Cochlear duct
Basilar membrane
Medium-frequency sounds
Low-frequency sounds
Base
Apex
High frequency
Medium frequency
Low frequency
Relative width of different regions of the basilar membrane
20,000 Hz (high frequency)
1500 Hz
500 Hz
20 Hz (low frequency)

Figure 19.28

Sound Wave Interpretation at the Basilar Membrane. Sound waves are interpreted at specific sites along the basilar membrane within a cochlea that has been straightened from its normal spiral shape. High-frequency sounds (red arrow) generate pressure waves that cause the basilar membrane to displace close to the base of the cochlea. Medium-frequency sounds (green arrow) generate pressure waves that cause the basilar membrane to displace near the center of the cochlea. Low-frequency sounds (purple arrow) generate pressure waves that cause the basilar membrane to displace near the helicotrema.

Clinical View 19.9

Are Earbuds Bad for Your Health?

Zhax/Shutterstock

Continuous or repeated exposure to loud noises is known to damage hearing, and studies report that the development of a benign tumor, called **acoustic neuroma,** often accompanies such hearing loss. The acoustic neuroma is a tumor of the vestibular branch of CN VIII. Its development was first reported as a consequence of cell phone use. Further investigations suggest that acoustic neuromas may develop in patients exposed to extended periods of loud noise from other sources, including plant machinery, motors, sporting events, power tools, and music. Thus, although there is no proven link between acoustic neuromas and exposure to loud music, there is a correlation between loud music and hearing loss. So, play it safe and keep the volume down when listening with your earbuds.

low-frequency sounds stimulate the spiral organ far away from the oval window. **Loudness,** or *sound intensity,* is measured in units called *decibels (dB)*. Soft sounds cause relatively small movements of the basilar membrane in a relatively smaller area of the spiral organ, whereas loud sounds cause relatively larger movement of the basilar membrane in a wider area of the spiral organ. The greater movement of the basilar membrane associated with louder sounds increases both the rate of nerve impulses that are initiated by the inner hair cells and the number of hair cells that are stimulated.

Figure 19.28 shows that high-frequency and upper medium-frequency pressure waves are transmitted across the vestibular membrane to cause the basilar membrane to vibrate, resulting in hair cell stimulation in that region. Low-frequency pressure waves travel around the helicotrema to the scala tympani to cause basilar membrane vibration.

Auditory Pathways

We discussed how sound waves travel through the inner ear earlier in this section. But what is the nerve pathway that the initiated nerve impulses travel through in the brain? This auditory pathway is shown in **figure 19.29** and described here:

1. When the basilar membrane moves, the stereocilia on the spiral organ hair cells distort because they are anchored by the tectorial membrane. This initiates nerve impulses that are transmitted through the cochlear nerve branches that attach

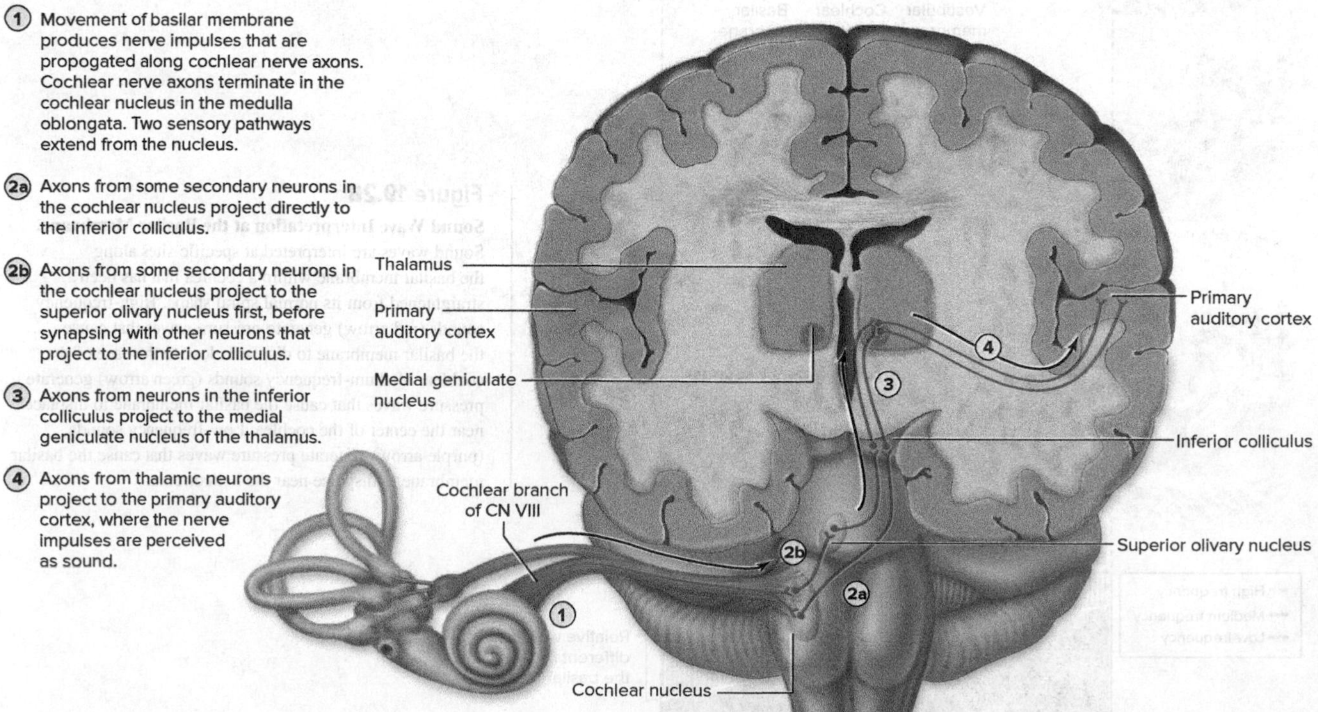

Figure 19.29

Central Nervous System Pathways for Hearing. Nerve impulses are propogated along the cochlear branch of CN VIII to the superior olivary nucleus and inferior colliculus of the brainstem, and then stimuli are sent to the thalamus before the information is finally transmitted to the primary auditory cortex.

to the hair cells. The sensory axons of the cochlear nerve (the primary neurons in this sensory pathway) terminate in the **cochlear nucleus** within the brainstem. These sensory neurons synapse with secondary neurons housed within this nucleus.

2. After integration and processing of the incoming information within the cochlear nucleus, axons from secondary neurons in this nucleus take one of two pathways: (a) the axons of some secondary neurons project directly to the inferior colliculi of the midbrain, whereas (b) axons from other secondary neurons first project to the superior olivary nucleus within the pons (see section 15.5b) and synapse with other sensory neurons that then project to the inferior colliculi.
   a) Nerve impulses arriving at the **inferior colliculi** (see section 15.5a) are also involved in a reflex to loud sounds; here nerve impulses are relayed to skeletal muscles of the body that cause us to jump and turn our head in response to loud sounds.
   b) Nerve impulses arriving at the **superior olivary nuclei** function to both localize the sound and are involved in the reflex to loud sounds that transmits nerve impulses to the tensor tympani and stapedius to contract and decrease the vibration of the ossicles.
3. Nerve impulses are transmitted from an inferior colliculus to the **medial geniculate nucleus** of the thalamus (see section 15.4b) for initial processing and filtering of auditory sensory information.
4. Axons from the tertiary neurons in the thalamus extend to the **primary auditory cortex** within the temporal lobe (see section 15.3b), where nerve impulses are perceived as sounds.

19.6d Development of the Ear

Ear development begins during the fourth week **(figure 19.30)**. All embryonic germ layers contribute to ear formation, including the surface ectoderm and the layer that is beginning to specialize as the neuroectoderm. Each part of the ear originates separately.

External and Middle Ear Development

The auricle of the external ear forms from the surface ectoderm. Masses of tissue from the first and second pharyngeal arches come together and fuse, forming the unique shape of the auricle. Each external acoustic meatus forms from an external indentation of the ectoderm called the **first pharyngeal cleft** (or *groove*). The tympanic cavity and the auditory tube of each middle ear are formed from an internal tubelike expansion of the pharynx called the **first pharyngeal pouch.** (Eventually, four pharyngeal clefts and pouches form, but only the first pharyngeal cleft and pouch develop into external and middle ear structures.) Specifically, as the first pharyngeal pouch grows, it develops into a trumpet-shaped structure called the **tubotympanic recess.** The narrow part of this structure forms the auditory tube, whereas the expanded end forms the tympanic cavity of the middle ear.

Clinical View 19.10

Cochlear Implants

A **cochlear implant** is an electronic device that assists some hearing-impaired people. It is not a hearing aid and does not restore normal hearing; rather, it compensates for damaged or nonfunctioning parts of the inner ear. The components of a cochlear implant include (1) an external microphone to detect sound (typically worn behind one ear), (2) a speech processor to arrange the sounds from the microphone, and (3) a transmitter connected to a receiver/stimulator (placed within the cochlea) to convert the processed sound into electrical impulses.

A cochlear implant parallels normal hearing by selecting sounds, processing them into electrical impulses, and then sending sound information to the brain for interpretation. However, this type of "hearing" is considerably different from normal hearing. Patients with implants report that voices sound squeaky and high-pitched, but this limitation does not prevent people with implants from having oral communication capabilities.

Although tens of thousands of people have received cochlear implants, some controversy accompanies their increasing use. First, any surgical installation procedure is always accompanied by a small risk for infection or complication. Second, cochlear implants do not always improve hearing quality. Cochlear implant opponents also have expressed concern that the implant represents a threat to the sign-based culture of deaf people. Others question the use of implants in children, who may not have made the decision for themselves.

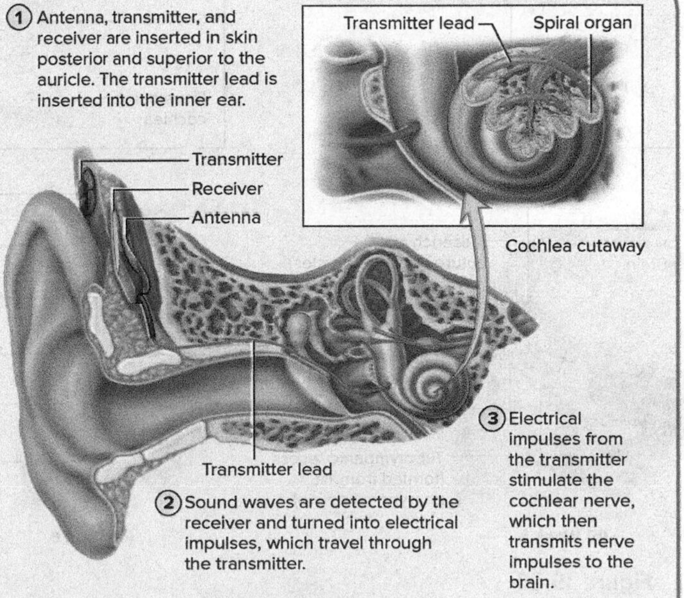
1 Antenna, transmitter, and receiver are inserted in skin posterior and superior to the auricle. The transmitter lead is inserted into the inner ear.
Transmitter lead
Spiral organ
Cochlea cutaway
Transmitter
Receiver
Antenna
Transmitter lead
2 Sound waves are detected by the receiver and turned into electrical impulses, which travel through the transmitter.
3 Electrical impulses from the transmitter stimulate the cochlear nerve, which then transmits nerve impulses to the brain.

The components of a cochlear implant.

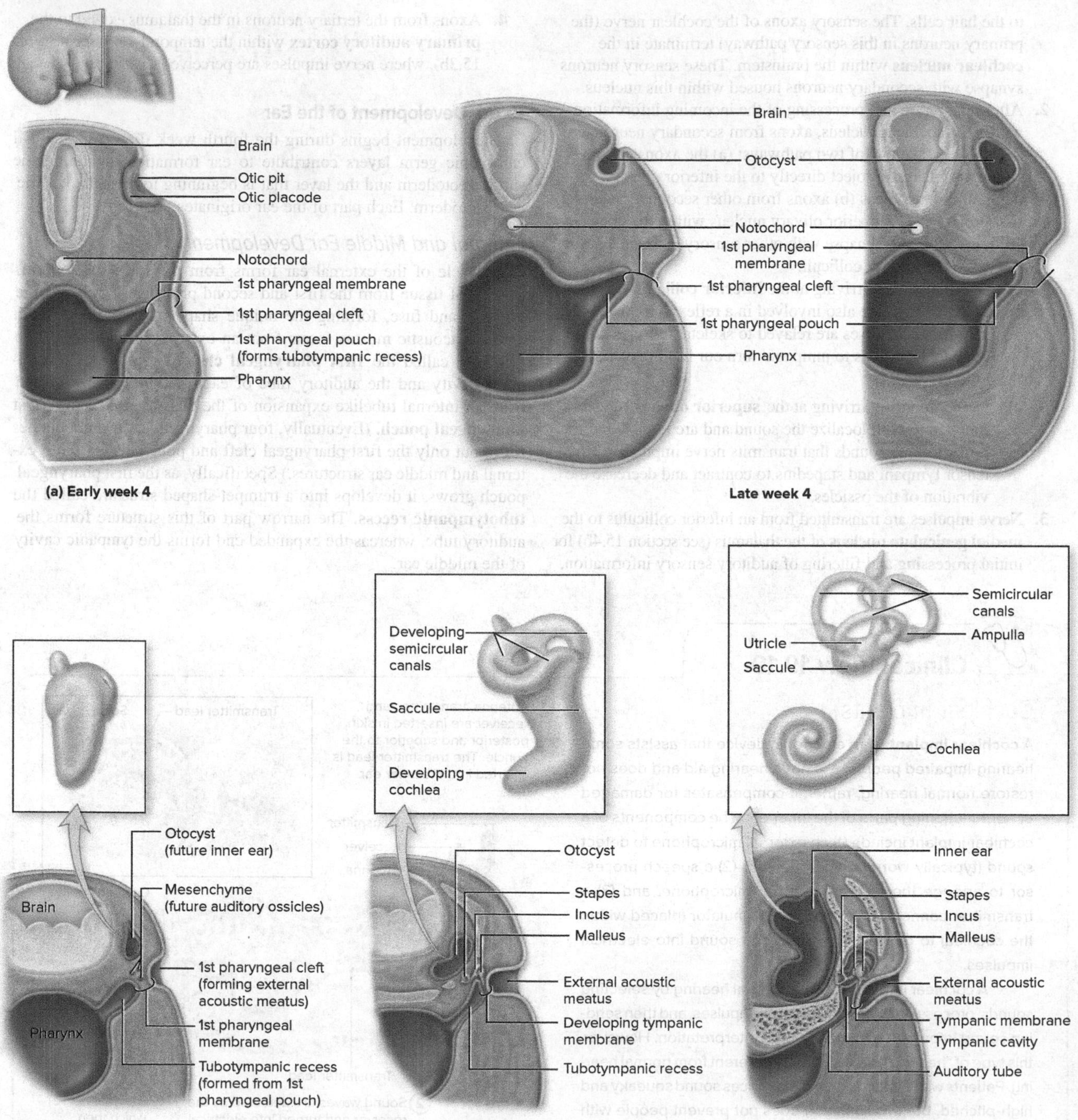

Figure 19.30

Development of the Ear. (*a*) Ear development begins during week 4, when the otic placode invaginates and turns into an otocyst (future inner ear). The first pharyngeal cleft, membrane, and pouch develop and form middle and external ear structures. (*b*) By week 5, a tubotympanic recess forms from the first pharyngeal pouch, and the first pharyngeal cleft begins to form the external acoustic meatus. (*c*) The auditory ossicles form beginning in week 6, and the first pharyngeal membrane forms the tympanic membrane (eardrum). (*d*) By week 8, the otocyst forms a recognizable inner ear, and the tubotympanic recess forms the auditory tube and tympanic cavity of the middle ear.

As the first pharyngeal pouch and the first pharyngeal cleft grow toward one another, their inner endoderm and outer ectoderm form the **first pharyngeal membrane,** which later thins and forms the tympanic membrane. The auditory ossicles develop from mesenchyme cells that are near, but not inside, the tympanic cavity. During the ninth month of development, the tympanic cavity expands and envelops the ossicles, thereby enclosing these ear bones within the tympanic cavity.

Inner Ear Development

Each inner ear forms from an **otic placode** (plak'ōd; *plax* = flat) that is formed from ectoderm and is at the level of the rhombencephalon (hindbrain). Each otic placode invaginates, forming an **otic pit.** Eventually, each otic pit closes off and becomes an internal structure called an **otocyst** (ō'tō-sist; *kystis* = bladder), or *otic vesicle.*

The otocyst is initially very primitive. During the fifth and sixth weeks of development, the otocyst begins to expand. Its anterior tip elongates and starts to form the future cochlear duct. The utricle and saccule become better differentiated. The hair cells of the spiral organ start to develop by week 7. Also during the seventh week, the three semicircular ducts form along with the ampulla structures within them. The shape of the membranous labyrinth is attained by the end of the eighth week. As the petrous part of the temporal bone (bony labyrinth) develops around the membranous labyrinth, the space between the two labyrinths fills with perilymph.

WHAT DID YOU LEARN?

15. Make a flowchart that lists the structures sound waves pass through before reaching the spiral organ.
16. What is the difference between the bony and membranous labyrinths?
17. What sensation does the macula detect, and how does it work?
18. In general, how are the hair cells in the spiral organ stimulated?
19. What embryonic structures form the external and middle ear?

Clinical Terms

conduction deafness Deafness due to middle ear conditions that prevent vibration transfer between the tympanic membrane and the oval window.

keratitis (ker'ă-tī'tis; *keras* = horn, *itis* = inflammation) Inflammation of the cornea.

Meniere disease An equilibrium disturbance characterized by vertigo, nausea, vomiting, tinnitus, and progressive hearing loss; it is caused by distortion of the membranous labyrinth of the endolymphatic duct due to excessive accumulation of fluid.

nystagmus (nis-tag'mŭs; a nodding) Involuntary, rhythmic oscillation of the eyeballs; may occur after damage to the brainstem.

otosclerosis (ō'tō-sklĕ-rō'sis; *sclerosis* = hardening) Condition in which abnormal, microscopic bone growth in the inner ear traps the stapes in the oval window.

papilledema (pap'il-ĕ-dē'mă) A swelling of the optic disc (the point where the optic nerve joins the eye). Papilledema is caused by an increase in CSF pressure in the extension of the subarachnoid space around the optic nerve and fluid pressure within the skull (intracranial pressure).

sensorineural deafness (sen's ōr-i-noor' ăl) Deafness caused by problems within the cochlea or along the auditory nerve pathway.

tinnitus (ti-nī'tŭs; *tinnio* = to jingle) Ear noises (ringing, roaring, or hissing).

vertigo (ver-tī'gō; *verto* = to turn) Sensation of rotation, such as spinning or whirling.

Chapter Summary

	■ The body detects numerous stimuli continuously. Stimuli may be pleasurable, alert us to danger, or provide information about moment-to-moment changes in our environment. ■ A stimulus is a change in the internal or external environment that is detected by a receptor and causes a response. Impulses caused by a stimulus arrive in the CNS and are perceived as a sensation.
19.1 Introduction to Sensory Receptors	■ Sensory receptors detect changes in the external and internal environments, and range in complexity from single-celled to multicellular. **19.1a Properties of Sensory Receptors** ■ Sensory receptors act as transducers, detecting specific stimuli, ultimately causing a nerve impulse to be propagated along a sensory neuron. ■ A receptive field encompasses the area of distribution of the sensory receptor's sensitive ends. A smaller receptive field allows a more precise identification of stimulus location. ■ Sensory impulses may be from either tonic (continuously stimulated) or phasic (on-and-off stimulation) receptors. **19.1b Classification of Sensory Receptors** ■ General sense receptors are housed in the skin, musculoskeletal organs, and viscera. Special sense receptors are housed within the head. ■ Sensory receptors are defined by stimulus origin (exteroceptors, interoceptors, proprioceptors); receptor distribution (general senses and special senses); and modality of stimulus. ■ General sense receptors have a specificity for chemicals (chemoreceptors); temperature (thermoreceptors); light (photoreceptors); touch, stretch, vibration, and pressure (mechanoreceptors and baroreceptors); and pain (nociceptors).

(continued on next page)

Chapter Summary *(continued)*

19.2 Tactile Receptors

- Tactile receptors react to touch, pressure, and vibration stimuli. Tactile receptors may be either unencapsulated or encapsulated.
- Free nerve endings are unencapsulated dendrites that detect pain and temperature stimuli, as well as some light touch and pressure.

19.2a Unencapsulated Tactile Receptors

- These tactile receptors are relatively simple in structure and have no connective tissue wrapping.

19.2b Encapsulated Tactile Receptors

- Tactile receptors covered either by connective tissue or glial cells.

19.3 Olfaction

- Olfaction is the chemical sense of smell. Paired olfactory organs are composed of a lining olfactory epithelium (olfactory receptor cells, supporting cells, and basal cells), a lamina propria, and olfactory glands.

19.3a Olfactory Receptor Cells

- Olfactory receptor cells are bipolar neurons with olfactory hairs.

19.3b Olfactory Discrimination

- The olfactory system recognizes different chemical stimuli. The number of olfactory receptors declines as we age.

19.3c Olfactory Pathways

- Olfactory receptor cell axons enter a pair of olfactory bulbs. Neurons within the olfactory bulbs project axon bundles called olfactory tracts to the olfactory cortex in the cerebrum.

19.4 Gustation

- Gustation is the chemical sense of taste.

19.4a Papillae and Taste Buds of the Tongue

- Gustatory cells are housed in taste buds that also have supporting cells and basal cells.

19.4b Gustatory Discrimination

- The five basic taste sensations are sweet, salt, sour, bitter, and umami.

19.4c Gustatory Pathways

- CN VII (facial) and CN IX (glossopharyngeal) are involved in conducting taste information through gustatory pathways.

19.5 Vision

- The eyes house photoreceptors that detect light, color, and movement.

19.5a Accessory Structures of the Eye

- Accessory structures that cover and protect the eye include the conjunctiva, eyebrows, eyelashes, eyelids, and lacrimal glands.
- Each lacrimal apparatus includes a lacrimal gland and a series of channels and ducts that distribute and drain thin, watery lacrimal fluid (tears) to cleanse the eye surface and moisten the conjunctiva.

19.5b Eye Structure

- The eye is an almost spherical, hollow organ that has three principal layers called tunics.
- The fibrous tunic (external layer), which has an anterior cornea and a posterior sclera, helps focus light on the retina; protects and maintains the shape of the eye; and provides the attachment site for the extrinsic eye muscles (sclera).
- The vascular tunic (middle layer) has three regions: the choroid, which distributes vascular and lymphatic vessels inside the eye; the ciliary body, which assists lens shape changes with the suspensory ligaments and secretes aqueous humor; and the iris, which controls pupil diameter.
- The retina is composed of an outer pigmented layer and an inner neural layer that houses all of the photoreceptors and their associated neurons.
- The three cell layers in the neural layer are (1) photoreceptors (rods and cones) that are stimulated by photons of light; (2) supporting cells and neurons that process and begin to integrate incoming visual stimuli; and (3) an inner layer of ganglion cells that conduct impulses to the brain.
- The retina has a posterior, yellowish region called the macula lutea, which houses a concentration of cones. Vision is most acute at a depression within the center of the macula lutea called the fovea centralis.
- The lens is a hard, deformable, transparent structure bounded by a dense fibrous, elastic capsule.

19.5c Visual Pathways

- The optic nerves formed by ganglionic axons that project from each eye through the paired optic foramina converge at the optic chiasm.
- The optic tract is the continuation of nerve fibers of ganglionic axons from the optic chiasm. Each optic tract is a composite of ganglionic axons originating from the retinas of each eye.

19.5d Development of the Eye

- Eye development begins during the fourth week with the evagination of the forebrain that forms optic vesicles.
- Optic vesicles invaginate and form a double-layered epithelium called the optic cup.
- The lens develops from the lens vesicle.

19.6 Equilibrium and Hearing	■ Receptors in the ear provide for the senses of equilibrium and hearing. **19.6a External Ear** ■ The external ear is a skin-covered, cartilage-supported structure called the auricle. ■ The external acoustic meatus directs sound waves to the tympanic membrane, a delicate epithelial sheet that partitions the spaces of the outer and middle ear. Its vibrations provide the means for transmission of sound wave energy to the inner ear. **19.6b Middle Ear** ■ The tympanic cavity (middle ear) is an air-filled space occupied by three small auditory ossicles: the malleus, the incus, and the stapes, which transmit sound wave energy from the outer to the inner ear. **19.6c Inner Ear** ■ The inner ear houses the structures for equilibrium and hearing. Specialized receptors called hair cells are housed in the membranous labyrinth, which lies within a cavernous space in dense bone called the bony labyrinth. ■ Hair cells are the sensory receptors for equilibrium and hearing. When their apical surface stereocilia, and sometimes kinocilia, are displaced, a change occurs in neurotransmitter release and the firing rate of the monitoring sensory neuron. ■ The saccule and utricle are membranous sacs of the vestibular complex that contain areas of hair cells called maculae, which detect acceleration or deceleration of the head in one direction. ■ The semicircular canals of the vestibular complex house the membranous semicircular ducts, each with an ampulla that houses the hair cells for detecting rotational movements of the head. ■ Equilibrium stimuli from the vestibule and semicircular canals are conducted through the vestibular branch of the vestibulocochlear nerve (CN VIII). ■ Hearing organs are housed within the cochlea. ■ Sound is perceived when impinging sound waves cause vibrations of the tympanic membrane, resulting in auditory ossicle vibrations that lead to vibrations of the basilar membrane. Movement of the basilar membrane causes stereocilia distortion, which is perceived as sound. ■ Sound waves transmitted in the fluid of the inner ear are detected by hair cells of the spiral organ. Impulses are conducted through the cochlear branch of the vestibulocochlear nerve (CN VIII) to the cochlear nuclei in the brainstem. **19.6d Development of the Ear** ■ Ear development begins during the fourth week. All embryonic germ layers contribute to the formation of the ear, including the surface ectoderm and the layer that is beginning to specialize as the neuroectoderm.

Challenge Yourself

Actively write or type your answers in a separate document to reinforce your learning, before checking your answers.

Multiple Choice

Select the best answer from the four choices provided.

1. Which type of cutaneous receptor consists of unencapsulated, terminal branches of dendrites?
   a. lamellated corpuscles
   b. free nerve endings
   c. bulbous corpuscles
   d. end bulbs
2. Baroreceptors are a class of mechanoreceptor that respond to what type of sensation?
   a. light touch
   b. pain stimuli
   c. increase in muscle tension
   d. changes in pressure
3. Which sensory structure has stereocilia of hair cells embedded in a gelatinous structure called a cupula?
   a. semicircular duct
   b. saccule
   c. cochlear duct
   d. utricle
4. Which photoreceptors perceive color and sharp vision?
   a. amacrine cells
   b. rods
   c. horizontal cells
   d. cones
5. Which statement accurately describes the receptor activity when you rotate your head?
   a. The otolithic membrane on the macula shifts, bending the kinocilium and increasing nerve impulse frequency.
   b. The otolithic membrane on the hair cells of the spiral organ shifts and changes the frequency of nerve impulse transmission.
   c. The cupula moves and bends the stereocilia and kinocilium, resulting in the generation of a nerve impulse.
   d. The otolithic membrane on the crista ampullaris shifts, resulting in the generation of a nerve impulse.
6. What is the arrangement of tunics in the eye, from the center of the eye to the periphery?
   a. retina, vascular, fibrous
   b. vascular, retina, fibrous
   c. vascular, fibrous, retina
   d. retina, fibrous, vascular
7. Because tastes must be dissolved in saliva before they are detected, gustatory cells are best classified as which of the following?
   a. gustatory receptors
   b. chemoreceptors
   c. thermoreceptors
   d. nociceptors

8. What is the only sensation that can reach the cerebral cortex without first processing through the synapses in the thalamus?
   a. pain
   b. olfaction
   c. proprioception
   d. touch
9. What is the correct pathway by which tears are produced, drained, and enter the nasal cavity?
   a. lacrimal gland → nasolacrimal duct → lacrimal punctum → lacrimal canaliculus → lacrimal sac → nasal cavity
   b. lacrimal gland → lacrimal sac → lacrimal canaliculus → lacrimal punctum → nasolacrimal duct → nasal cavity
   c. lacrimal gland → lacrimal punctum → lacrimal canaliculus → lacrimal sac → nasolacrimal duct → nasal cavity
   d. lacrimal gland → lacrimal canaliculus → lacrimal sac → lacrimal punctum → nasolacrimal duct → nasal cavity
10. Which statement is true about the cochlear duct?
   a. It is part of the bony labyrinth.
   b. It is filled with perilymph.
   c. It contains hair cells that convert sound waves into nerve impulses.
   d. It contains a spiral organ that rests on a vestibular membrane.

Content Review

1. What are the classifications of sensory receptors according to modality of stimulus? Give an anatomic example of each.
2. How are visceral nociceptors different from somatic nociceptors, and how do they relate to the phenomenon known as "referred pain"?
3. What are the pathways by which taste sensations reach the brain?
4. Describe the pathway by which olfactory stimuli travel from the nasal cavity to the brain.
5. Make a flowchart that shows the structures involved in converting light rays to nerve impulses, and then transmitting those nerve impulses to the occipital lobe.
6. How is the lens able to focus images from a book that you are reading, and then immediately also focus the image of children playing in your backyard?
7. Discuss the formation, circulation, and reabsorption of aqueous humor in the eye.
8. List the major structures of the middle ear and their functions.
9. Briefly describe the structural relationship between the membranous labyrinth and the bony labyrinth.
10. Describe the pathway by which sound waves enter and exit the ear, and how that sound is converted into a nerve impulse.

Developing Critical Reasoning

1. Savannah is an active 3-year-old who began to cough and sniffle. Then she experienced an earache and a marked decrease in hearing acuity. During a physical examination, her pediatrician noted the following signs: elevated temperature, a reddened tympanic membrane with a slight bulge, and some inflammation in the pharynx. What might the pediatrician call this condition, and how would it be treated? How does Savannah's age relate to her illness?
2. After Alejandro quit smoking, he discovered that foods seemed much more flavorful than when he had smoked. How are smoking and taste perceptions linked?
3. Louis entered an elevator and pressed the Up button. Which of Louis's receptors detected this vertical motion in the elevator (despite not having visual cues of moving upward), and how exactly did these receptors work?

Answers to "What Do You Think?"

1. A cutaneous pain receptor would be classified as an exteroceptor (based upon stimulus origin), general sense/somatic sensory receptor (based upon receptor distribution), and a nociceptor (based upon modality of stimulus).
2. Olfaction plays a major role in detecting tastes. Most taste is due to our perception of the odor, rather than the taste, of the food. If your nose is stuffed up and you can't smell the food, your taste perception is impaired as well.
3. When a person cries, tears flood the lacrimal apparatus. The lacrimal puncta are unable to collect all the tears, which then flow over the lower eyelids. In addition, the nasolacrimal duct pours many more tears than normal into the nasal cavity where they mix with mucus, resulting in the runny nose.
4. Air pressure increases when the airplane descends, which is why you may feel greater pressure in your ears. The "popping" noise results from your auditory tubes opening and releasing some of that pressure in your middle ear.

Design Element: Pencil Icon: Slavojub Pantelic/Shutterstock

ENDOCRINE SYSTEM

Endocrine System 20

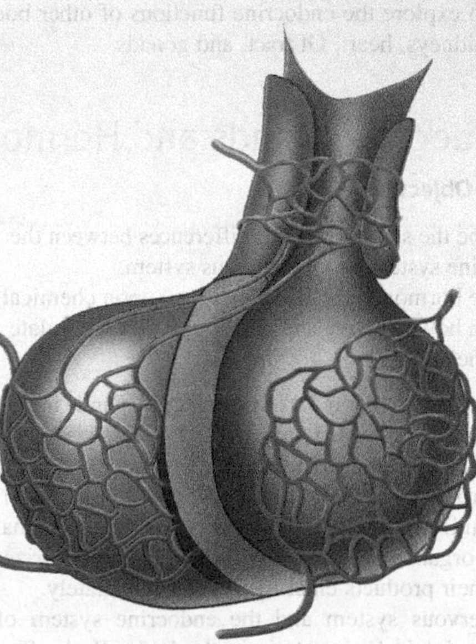

Outline

Anatomy & Physiology Revealed 4.0

MODULE 8: ENDOCRINE SYSTEM

Some days are just more hectic than others. We don't have time for breakfast and then perhaps have a class that meets over the lunch hour, allowing us only enough time to grab something from the snack machine before heading off to work or other classes in the afternoon. Finally, upon returning home for the evening, we are so hungry we eat rapidly and have a second helping. Fortunately, our endocrine system has come to our rescue, maintaining blood glucose levels within normal homeostatic limits during this period of erratic food intake. Through the release of hormones, the **endocrine system** provides the means to regulate and control many diverse metabolic processes of the body, including regulating blood sugar.

This chapter begins with an overview of the endocrine organs (called glands) and the endocrine cells, and then describes how they regulate body functions as well as what happens when they malfunction. We also explore the endocrine functions of other body organs, such as the kidneys, heart, GI tract, and gonads.

20.1 Endocrine Glands and Hormones

✓ Learning Objectives

1. Describe the similarities and differences between the endocrine system and the nervous system.
2. Outline hormone classification based upon chemical structure.
3. Explain how negative and positive feedback regulate hormone secretion.

We have learned in section 4.1f that exocrine glands usually produce secretions that are released into ducts opening onto an epithelial surface. In contrast, **endocrine glands** are ductless and secrete their molecular products directly into the blood. All endocrine cells, whether organized into a single organ or scattered in small clusters within other organs, are located within highly vascularized areas to ensure that their products enter the blood immediately.

The nervous system and the endocrine system often work together to maintain homeostasis in the body. Both affect specific target cells (see section 20.1a) using chemical messengers. However, their communication methods and their effects differ (**figure 20.1**). The nervous system uses nerve impulses along axons to release the neurotransmitter into the synaptic cleft right at the target cells. The endocrine system uses hormones as chemical messengers. These hormones are transported through the body to the target cells by the circulatory system. **Table 20.1** lists several similarities and differences between the nervous and endocrine systems.

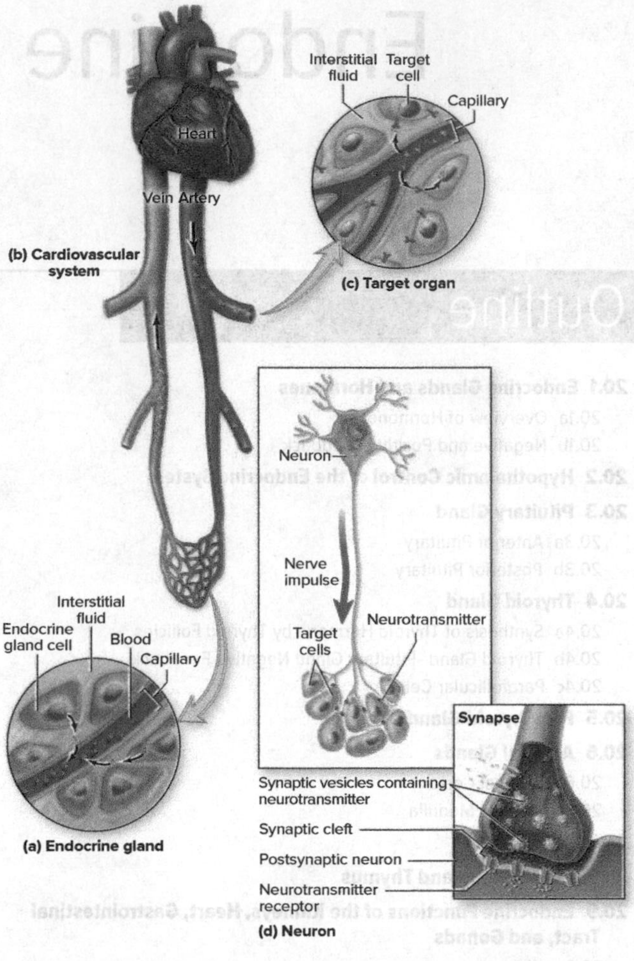

Figure 20.1

Nervous and Endocrine System Communication Methods. *(a–c)* In the endocrine system, hormones are secreted by endocrine cells. The hormones enter the blood and are transported throughout the body to reach their target cells. *(d)* In the nervous system, neurons release neurotransmitters into a synaptic cleft to stimulate their target cells.

20.1a Overview of Hormones

The endocrine glands release **hormones** (hōr′mōn; *hormao* = to rouse) into the blood (**figure 20.2**). Hormones are chemical messengers that change the metabolic activity of the target cells. Only cells with specific receptors for the hormone (enabling the hormone to bind to the cell) respond to that hormone. These cells are called **target cells,** and the organs that contain them are called **target organs.** In contrast, organs, tissues, or cells that do not have the specific receptor for a hormone do not bind or attach the hormone and do not respond to it. One example is prolactin, a hormone produced by the anterior pituitary. The target organ for this hormone is the mammary gland;

Table 20.1 Comparison of the Nervous System and the Endocrine System

Features	Nervous System	Endocrine System
Communication Method	A nerve impulse causes neurotransmitter release from a neuron into a synaptic cleft	Endocrine glands secrete hormones into blood; hormones are transported within the blood to target cells throughout body
Target of Stimulation	Other neurons, muscle cells, and gland cells	Any cell in the body with a receptor for the hormone
Response Time	Rapid reaction time: Typically milliseconds or seconds	Relatively slow reaction time: Seconds to minutes to hours
Range of Effect	Typically has localized, specific effects in the body	Typically has widespread effects throughout the body
Duration of Response	Short-term: Milliseconds; terminates with removal of stimulus	Long-lasting: Minutes to days to weeks; may continue after stimulus is removed

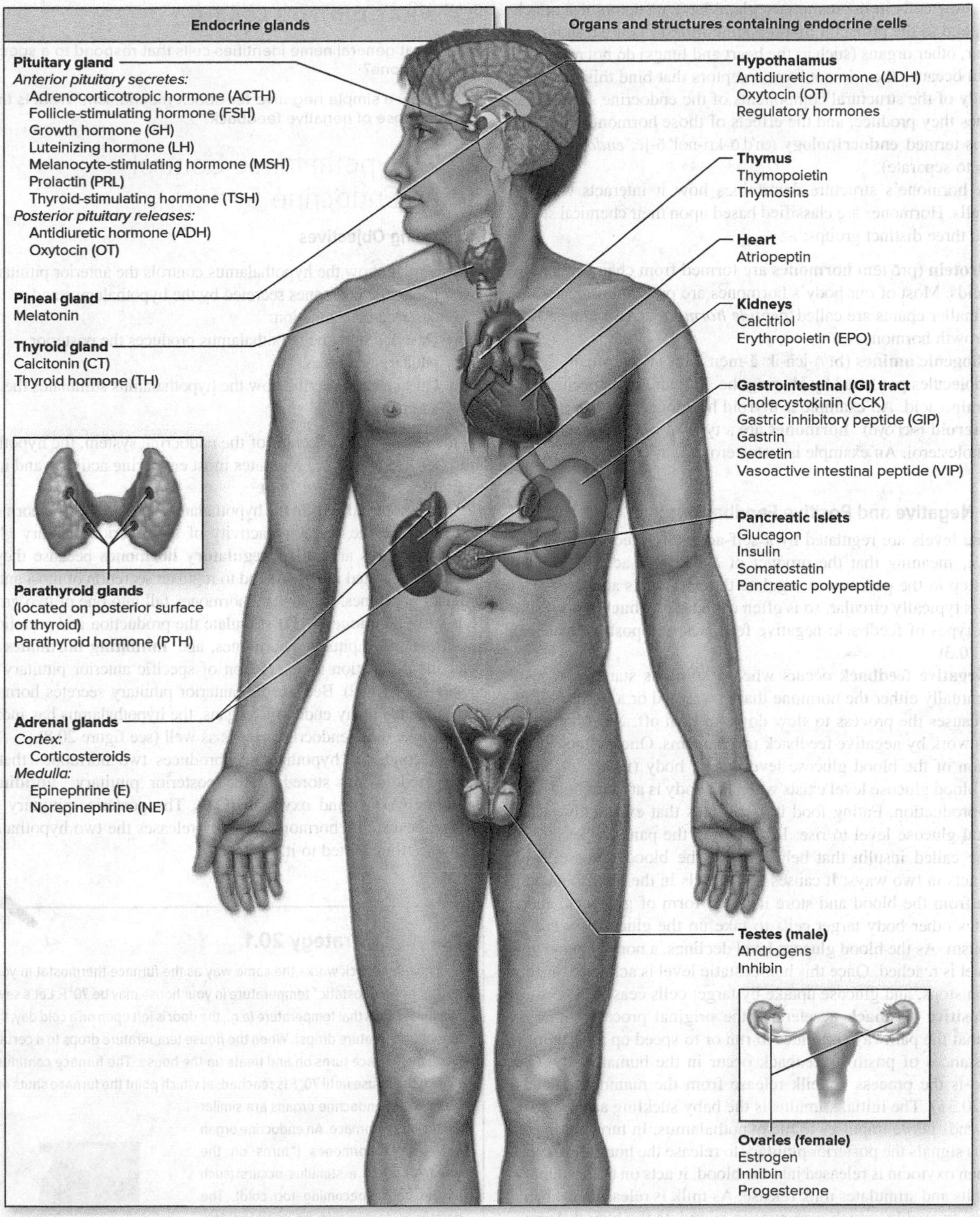
Endocrine glands
Organs and structures containing endocrine cells
Pituitary gland
Anterior pituitary secretes:
Adrenocorticotropic hormone (ACTH)
Follicle-stimulating hormone (FSH)
Growth hormone (GH)
Luteinizing hormone (LH)
Melanocyte-stimulating hormone (MSH)
Prolactin (PRL)
Thyroid-stimulating hormone (TSH)
Posterior pituitary releases:
Antidiuretic hormone (ADH)
Oxytocin (OT)
Pineal gland
Melatonin
Thyroid gland
Calcitonin (CT)
Thyroid hormone (TH)
Parathyroid glands
(located on posterior surface of thyroid)
Parathyroid hormone (PTH)
Adrenal glands
Cortex:
Corticosteroids
Medulla:
Epinephrine (E)
Norepinephrine (NE)
Hypothalamus
Antidiuretic hormone (ADH)
Oxytocin (OT)
Regulatory hormones
Thymus
Thymopoietin
Thymosins
Heart
Atriopeptin
Kidneys
Calcitriol
Erythropoietin (EPO)
Gastrointestinal (GI) tract
Cholecystokinin (CCK)
Gastric inhibitory peptide (GIP)
Gastrin
Secretin
Vasoactive intestinal peptide (VIP)
Pancreatic islets
Glucagon
Insulin
Somatostatin
Pancreatic polypeptide
Testes (male)
Androgens
Inhibin
Ovaries (female)
Estrogen
Inhibin
Progesterone

Figure 20.2

Endocrine System. Endocrine glands, other organs, and structures that contain endocrine cells occur throughout the body. They produce and release various types of hormones. The left side of this image identifies endocrine glands and the hormones they release. The right side of this image shows other organs and structures in the body that have endocrine cells and the hormones those cells release.

that is, some cells in the mammary gland have receptors that attach and respond to the prolactin by producing milk to nourish an infant. However, other organs (such as the heart and lungs) do not respond to prolactin because they do not have receptors that bind this hormone. The study of the structural components of the endocrine system, the hormones they produce, and the effects of those hormones on target organs is termed **endocrinology** (en′d ō-kri-nol′ ŏ-jē; *endo* = within, *krino* = to separate).

A hormone's structure determines how it interacts with the target cells. Hormones are classified based upon their chemical structure into three distinct groups:

- **Protein** (prō′tēn) **hormones** are formed from chains of amino acids. Most of our body's hormones are protein hormones. Smaller chains are called *peptide hormones.* An example is growth hormone.
- **Biogenic amines** (bī′ō-jen-ik ă-mēn′, am′in) are small molecules produced by altering the structure of a specific amino acid. An example is thyroid hormone.
- **Steroid** (ster′oyd) **hormones** are a type of lipid derived from cholesterol. An example is testosterone.

20.1b Negative and Positive Feedback

Hormone levels are regulated by a self-adjusting mechanism called *feedback,* meaning that the product of a pathway acts back at an earlier step in the pathway to regulate the pathway's activities. This pattern is typically circular, so is often called a **feedback loop.** There are two types of feedback: negative feedback and positive feedback (**figure 20.3**).

Negative feedback occurs when a stimulus starts a process, and eventually either the hormone that is secreted or a product of its effects causes the process to slow down or turn off. Most hormonal systems work by negative feedback mechanisms. One example is the regulation of the blood glucose level in the body (figure 20.3*a*). A normal blood glucose level exists when the body is at homeostasis for energy production. Eating food is a stimulus that eventually causes the blood glucose level to rise. In response, the pancreas secretes a hormone called insulin that helps reduce the blood glucose level. Insulin acts in two ways: It causes target cells in the liver to take up glucose from the blood and store it in the form of glycogen, and it stimulates other body target cells to take up the glucose for use in metabolism. As the blood glucose level declines, a normal blood glucose level is reached. Once this homeostatic level is achieved, insulin secretion stops, and glucose uptake by target cells ceases.

Positive feedback accelerates the original process, either to ensure that the pathway continues to run or to speed up its activities. Few instances of positive feedback occur in the human body. One example is the process of milk release from the mammary glands (figure 20.3*b*). The initial stimulus is the baby suckling at the breast, which sends nerve impulses to the hypothalamus. In turn, the hypothalamus signals the posterior pituitary to release the hormone oxytocin. When oxytocin is released into the blood, it acts on the mammary gland cells and stimulates milk release. As milk is released, the baby continues to suckle, which continues to stimulate the hypothalamus. This process goes on until the baby stops suckling or all the milk is expelled from the breast. Then milk release ceases.

Many of the body's feedback mechanisms are much more complex than the examples just given, usually involving multiple steps or multiple feedback loops. Complex loops are the most common self-adjusting regulatory mechanisms because they permit an exquisite fine-tuning of the process, not just an all-or-none effect.

WHAT DID YOU LEARN?

1. What general name identifies cells that respond to a specific hormone?
2. Draw a simple negative feedback mechanism. What is the purpose of negative feedback?

20.2 Hypothalamic Control of the Endocrine System

✓ Learning Objectives

4. Explain how the hypothalamus controls the anterior pituitary.
5. Name the hormones secreted by the hypothalamus and describe their function.
6. Describe how the hypothalamus produces the posterior pituitary hormones.
7. Outline and describe how the hypothalamus stimulates the adrenal gland.

As the master control center of the endocrine system, the hypothalamus (see section 15.4c) regulates most endocrine activity, and it does so in three ways (**figure 20.4**).

First, special cells in the hypothalamus secrete specific hormones that influence the secretory activity of the anterior pituitary gland. These hormones are called **regulatory hormones** because they are molecules secreted into the blood to regulate secretion of most anterior pituitary hormones. Regulatory hormones fall into one of two groups: **Releasing hormones (RH)** stimulate the production and secretion of specific anterior pituitary hormones, and **inhibiting hormones (IH)** deter the production and secretion of specific anterior pituitary hormones (**table 20.2**). Because the anterior pituitary secretes hormones that influence many endocrine organs, the hypothalamus has indirect control over these endocrine organs as well (see figure 20.8).

Second, the hypothalamus produces two hormones that are transported to and stored in the posterior pituitary: **antidiuretic hormone (ADH)** and **oxytocin (OT).** The posterior pituitary does not synthesize any hormones. It only releases the two hypothalamic hormones transported to it.

Learning Strategy 20.1

Negative feedback works the same way as the furnace thermostat in your house. A "homeostatic" temperature in your house may be 70°F. Let's say a stimulus affects that temperature (e.g., the door is left open on a cold day, the indoor temperature drops). When the house temperature drops to a certain level, the furnace turns on and heats up the house. The furnace continues to heat the house until 70°F is reached, at which point the furnace shuts off.

Most endocrine organs are similar to your house furnace. An endocrine organ secretes its hormones ("turns on the furnace") when a stimulus occurs (such as the house becoming too cold). The hormones continue to be secreted only until the stimulus ends and homeostasis occurs (the house returns to normal temperature). Thus, throughout the day, your endocrine organs are periodically releasing hormones and then stopping this release, depending upon the stimulus, just as your furnace may come on periodically during the day as the house cools.

Kim DeClaire/Getty Images

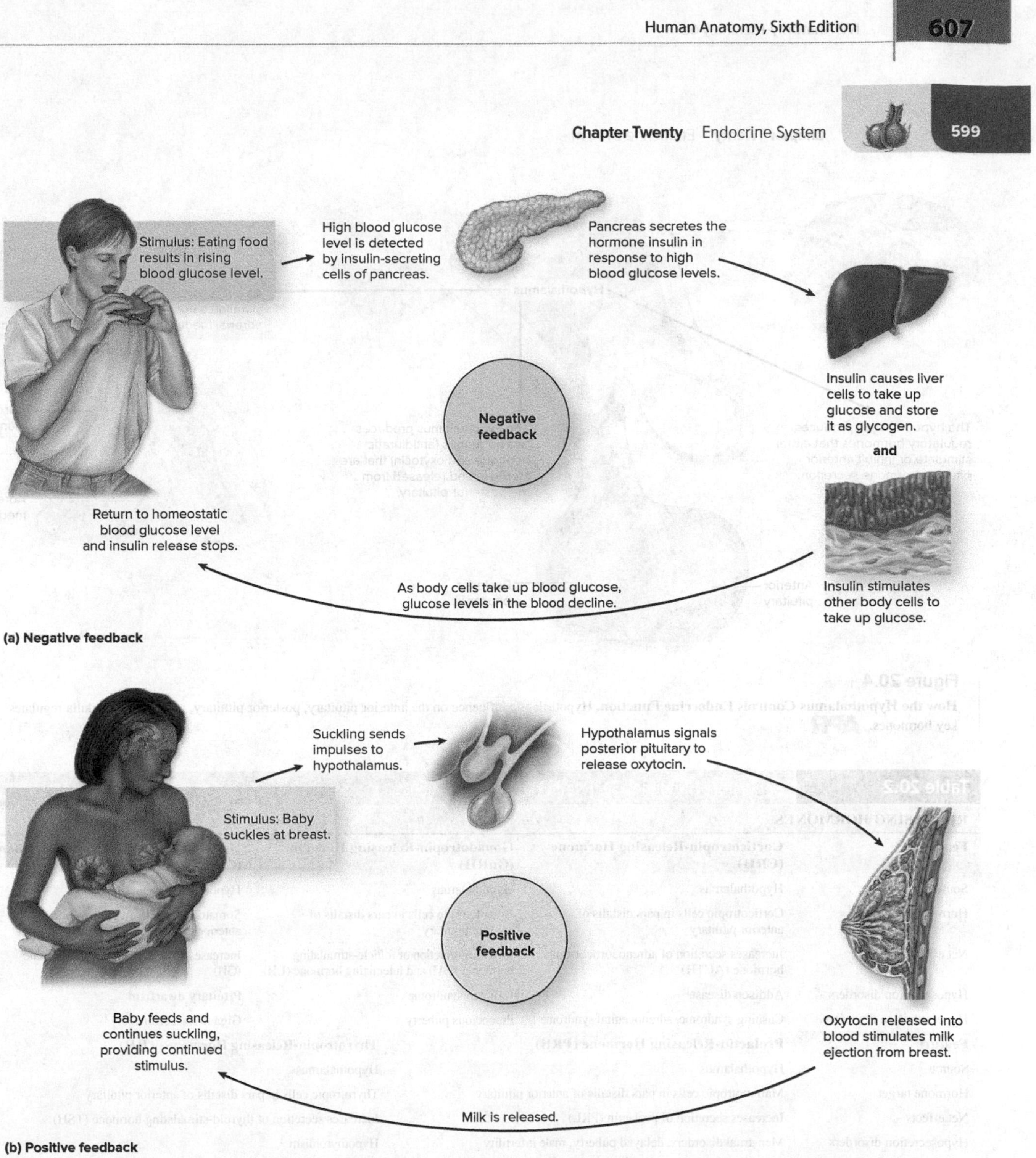
Stimulus: Eating food results in rising blood glucose level.
High blood glucose level is detected by insulin-secreting cells of pancreas.
Pancreas secretes the hormone insulin in response to high blood glucose levels.
Insulin causes liver cells to take up glucose and store it as glycogen.
and
Insulin stimulates other body cells to take up glucose.
As body cells take up blood glucose, glucose levels in the blood decline.
Return to homeostatic blood glucose level and insulin release stops.
Negative feedback
(a) Negative feedback
Stimulus: Baby suckles at breast.
Suckling sends impulses to hypothalamus.
Hypothalamus signals posterior pituitary to release oxytocin.
Oxytocin released into blood stimulates milk ejection from breast.
Milk is released.
Baby feeds and continues suckling, providing continued stimulus.
Positive feedback
(b) Positive feedback

Figure 20.3

Negative and Positive Feedback in the Endocrine System. The initial step in any feedback pathway is the stimulus. (*a*) Negative feedback occurs when the end product of a pathway acts to turn off or slow down the pathway. (*b*) Positive feedback is involved when the end product of a pathway stimulates further pathway activity.

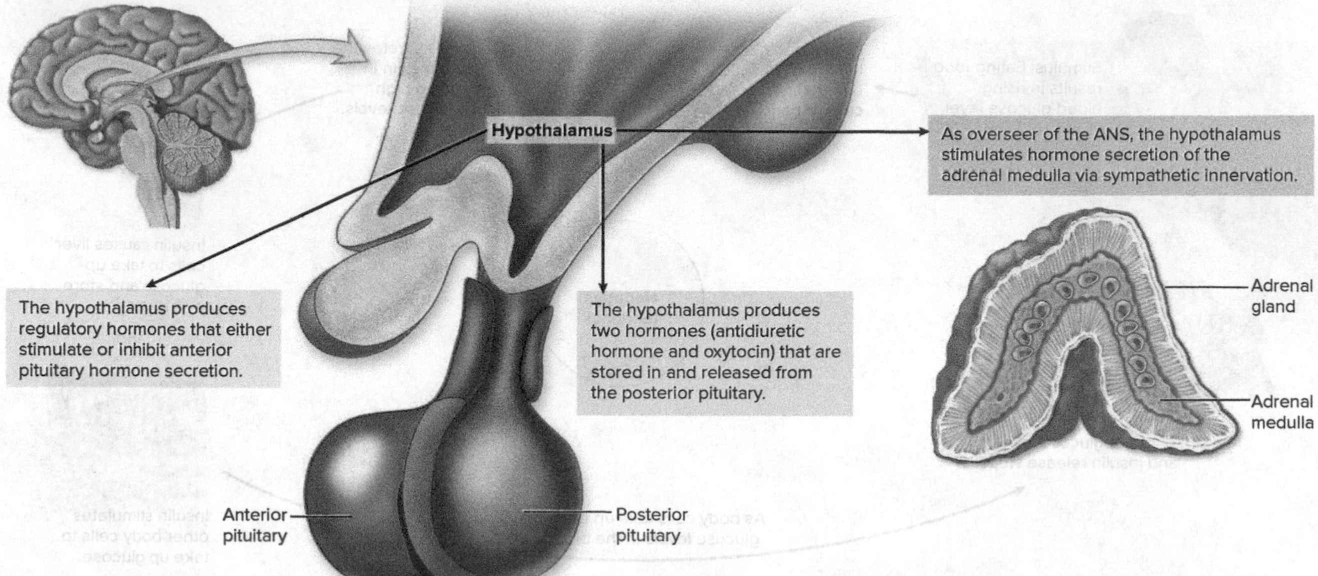
Hypothalamus
As overseer of the ANS, the hypothalamus stimulates hormone secretion of the adrenal medulla via sympathetic innervation.
The hypothalamus produces regulatory hormones that either stimulate or inhibit anterior pituitary hormone secretion.
The hypothalamus produces two hormones (antidiuretic hormone and oxytocin) that are stored in and released from the posterior pituitary.
Adrenal gland
Adrenal medulla
Anterior pituitary
Posterior pituitary

Figure 20.4

How the Hypothalamus Controls Endocrine Function. Hypothalamic influence on the anterior pituitary, posterior pituitary, and adrenal medulla regulates key hormones. APR

Table 20.2 Regulatory Hormones Secreted by the Hypothalamus

RELEASING HORMONES

Feature	Corticotropin-Releasing Hormone (CRH)	Gonadotropin-Releasing Hormone (GnRH)	Growth Hormone–Releasing Hormone (GHRH); Also Called Somatocrinin
Source	Hypothalamus	Hypothalamus	Hypothalamus
Hormone target	Corticotropic cells in pars distalis of anterior pituitary	Gonadotropic cells in pars distalis of anterior pituitary	Somatotropic cells in pars distalis of anterior pituitary
Net effects	Increases secretion of adrenocorticotropic hormone (ACTH)	Increases secretion of follicle-stimulating hormone (FSH) and luteinizing hormone (LH)	Increases secretion of growth hormone (GH)
Hyposecretion disorders	Addison disease[1]	Kallman syndrome	Pituitary dwarfism[3]
Hypersecretion disorders	Cushing syndrome, adrenogenital syndrome [1]	Precocious puberty	Gigantism, acromegaly[3]

Feature	Prolactin-Releasing Hormone (PRH)	Thyrotropin-Releasing Hormone (TRH)
Source	Hypothalamus	Hypothalamus
Hormone target	Mammotropic cells in pars distalis of anterior pituitary	Thyrotropic cells in pars distalis of anterior pituitary
Net effects	Increases secretion of prolactin (PRL)	Increases secretion of thyroid-stimulating hormone (TSH)
Hyposecretion disorders	Menstrual disorders, delayed puberty, male infertility	Hypothyroidism [2]
Hypersecretion disorders	Reduced menstruation, anovulatory infertility, male impotence	Hyperthyroidism [2]

INHIBITING HORMONES

Feature	Growth Hormone-Inhibiting Hormone (GHIH): Also Called Somatostatin[A]	Prolactin-Inhibiting Hormone (PIH); Also Called Dopamine[B]
Source	Hypothalamus	Hypothalamus
Hormone target	Somatotropic cells in pars distalis of anterior pituitary	Mammotropic cells in pars distalis of anterior pituitary
Net effects	Decreases secretion of growth hormone (GH)	Decreases secretion of prolactin (PRL)
Hyposecretion disorders	Gigantism, acromegaly[3]	Reduced menstruation, anovulatory infertility, male impotence
Hypersecretion disorders	Pituitary dwarfism[3]	Menstrual disorders, delayed puberty, male infertility

[1] See Clinical View 20.5: "Disorders of Adrenal Cortex Hormone Secretion" in section 20.6a.

[2] See Clinical View 20.3: "Disorders of Thyroid Hormone Secretion" in section 20.4c.

[3] See Clinical View 20.1: "Disorders of Growth Hormone Secretion" in section 20.3a.

[A] The term GHIH tends to be used in association with the hypothalamus, whereas somatostatin is used in other contexts such as the pancreas.

[B] The term PIH tends to be used in association with the hypothalamus, whereas dopamine is used when discussing a neurotransmitter.

Finally, because the hypothalamus is also the master control center of the autonomic nervous system (ANS), it directly oversees the stimulation and hormone secretion of the adrenal medulla. The adrenal medulla is an endocrine structure that secretes its hormones in response to stimulation by the sympathetic nervous system.

Although the hypothalamus regulates most endocrine activity, some endocrine cells secrete hormone without any input from the hypothalamus. For example, the parathyroid glands secrete their hormone in response to concentration of ions in the blood, rather than a regulatory hormone.

WHAT DO YOU THINK?

1. If a patient had a damaged hypothalamus, how might this affect the workings of the endocrine system?

WHAT DID YOU LEARN?

3. What types of hormones does the hypothalamus secrete to regulate the functioning of the anterior pituitary?

20.3 Pituitary Gland

✓ Learning Objectives

8. Describe the anatomy of the anterior and posterior pituitary.
9. Explain the types of cells that secrete the hormones of the anterior pituitary.
10. Name the hormones of the anterior pituitary, and describe their functions.
11. Name the hormones of the posterior pituitary and describe their functions.
12. Explain the relationships between the hypothalamus and the pituitary gland.

The **pituitary** (pi-tū′i-tār′ē) **gland,** or *hypophysis* (hī-pof′i-sis; undergrowth), lies inferior to the hypothalamus (**figure 20.5**). This small, slightly oval gland is housed within the hypophyseal fossa in the sella turcica of the sphenoid bone (see section 7.1c). It is connected to the hypothalamus by a thin stalk, the **infundibulum** (in′fŭn-dib′y ū-lŭm; a funnel). The infundibulum extends from the base of the hypothalamus at the **median eminence,** a conical projection sandwiched between the optic chiasm anteriorly and the mammillary bodies posteriorly. Superiorly, the pituitary gland is covered by the diaphragma sellae, which is a cranial dural septa that ensheathes the stalk of the infundibulum to restrict pituitary gland movement (see figure 15.5).

The pituitary gland is partitioned both structurally and functionally into an anterior pituitary and a posterior pituitary (sometimes referred to as just the *anterior lobe* and *posterior lobe,* respectively). Both regions are derived from different embryonic structures (see section 20.11b).

20.3a Anterior Pituitary

Most of the pituitary gland is composed of the **anterior pituitary,** or *adenohypophysis* (ad′ĕ-nō-hī-pof′i-sis; *adenos* = gland), which is the part of the pituitary gland that both produces and secretes hormones. It is partitioned into three distinct areas (figure 20.5). The **pars distalis** is the large anterior portion of the anterior pituitary. A thin **pars intermedia** is a scant region between the pars distalis and the posterior pituitary. The histology of the pituitary gland is shown in **figure 20.6**. The **pars tuberalis** is a thin wrapping around the infundibular stalk (a posterior pituitary structure), which is also called the infundibulum.

Like all endocrine glands, the anterior pituitary has an extensive distribution of many blood vessels to facilitate uptake and transport of hormones.

Control of Anterior Pituitary Secretions

Anterior pituitary secretions are controlled by regulatory hormones secreted by the hypothalamus (see figure 20.4). These regulatory hormones reach the anterior pituitary by traveling through a blood vessel network called the **hypothalamo-hypophyseal** (hī′pō-thal′ă-mō-hī-pō-fiz′ē-ăl) **portal system** (**figure 20.7**). Portal systems are composed of two different capillary beds (plexuses) connected by portal vessels. The hypothalamo-hypophyseal portal system is composed of a capillary plexus in the hypothalamus and portal veins that shunt the blood to a capillary plexus in the anterior pituitary before the blood is returned to the heart.

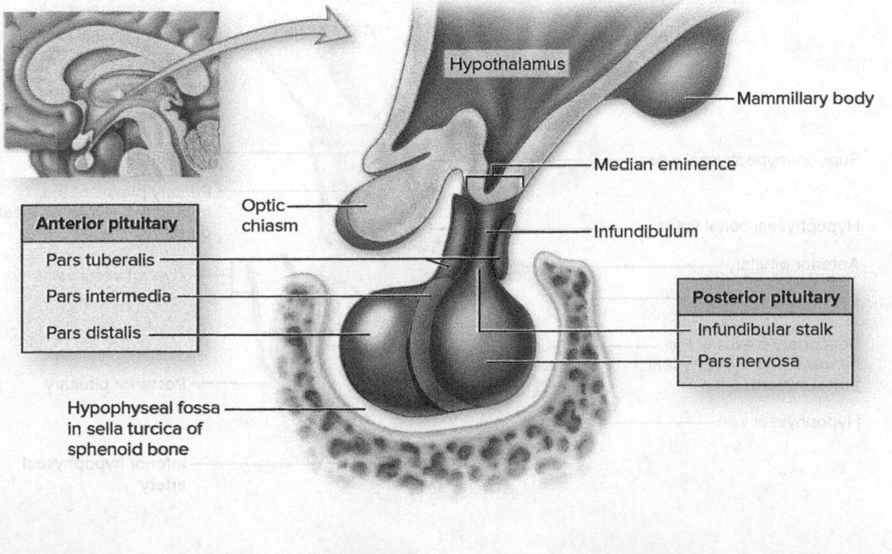

Hypothalamus
Mammillary body
Median eminence
Optic chiasm
Infundibulum
Anterior pituitary
Pars tuberalis
Pars intermedia
Pars distalis
Posterior pituitary
Infundibular stalk
Pars nervosa
Hypophyseal fossa in sella turcica of sphenoid bone

Figure 20.5

Pituitary Gland. The pituitary gland is composed of an anterior and a posterior part, which are attached to the hypothalamus by a stalk called the infundibulum. The pituitary gland occupies the hypophyseal fossa within the sella turcica of the sphenoid bone.

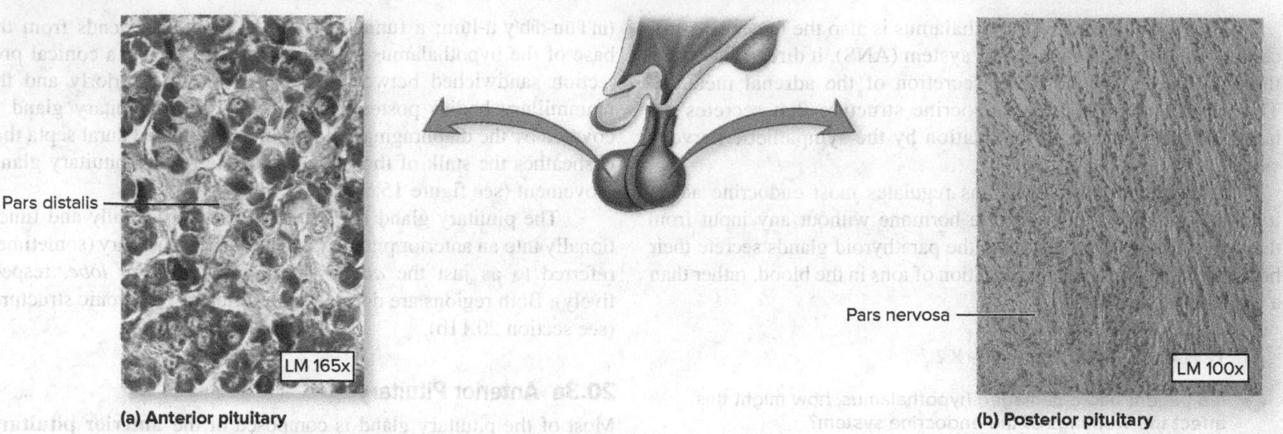

Figure 20.6

Microscopic Anatomy of the Pituitary Gland. Comparison of the anterior pituitary (pars distalis) and the posterior pituitary (pars nervosa).

(a) Victor P. Eroschenko; (b) Elizabeth Pennefather-O'Brien

The portal system functions in the following way:

1. The median eminence of the hypothalamus has a very porous capillary network called the **primary plexus** (or *primary capillary plexus*). Hypothalamic hormones enter the blood here. This plexus receives arterial blood from the superior hypophyseal artery and is drained by the **hypophyseal portal veins.**
2. The hypophyseal portal veins extend inferiorly from the median eminence of the hypothalamus through the infundibulum to the anterior pituitary. There, they disperse into a network of capillaries called the **secondary plexus** (or *secondary capillary plexus*). From this plexus, the hypothalamic hormones exit the blood and enter the interstitial spaces around the cells of the anterior pituitary, where they can affect the activities of these cells.
3. Blood from the anterior pituitary (along with the hormones the anterior pituitary releases) is drained by **anterior hypophyseal veins.** Blood carrying anterior pituitary hormones returns to the heart and from there is transported throughout the body to the target cells.

Thus, the hypothalamo-hypophyseal portal system provides a pathway for hypothalamic hormones to immediately reach the anterior pituitary. In addition, the veins that drain this portal system provide a pathway by which the anterior pituitary hormones reach the systemic blood.

Hormones of the Anterior Pituitary

The anterior pituitary secretes seven major hormones **(figure 20.8)**. Five of the seven hormones are **tropic** (trop′ik) **hormones.** Tropic hormonesstimulate hormone secretion from other endocrine glands or cells. The following specific cells in the anterior pituitary secrete these tropic hormones:

- **Thyrotropic** (thī-rō-trop′ik) **cells** in the pars distalis synthesize and secrete **thyroid-stimulating hormone (TSH),** also called *thyrotropin* (thī-rō-trō′pin). TSH regulates the release of thyroid hormone from the thyroid gland (see section 20.4a). Increased secretion of TSH results from pregnancy, stress, or exposure to low temperatures.
- **Gonadotropic** (gō′nad- ō-trōp′ik, gon′ ă-dō-) **cells** in the pars distalis synthesize and secrete both **follicle-stimulating hormone (FSH)** and **luteinizing** (lū′tē-i-nī-zing) **hormone (LH),** collectively called **gonadotropins.** These hormones influence reproductive system activities by regulating

Figure 20.7

Hypothalamo-Hypophyseal Portal System. The hypothalamus regulates the function of the anterior and posterior pituitary. The hypothalamo-hypophyseal portal system is the circulatory connection between the hypothalamus (source of regulatory hormones) and the anterior pituitary (contains target cells of the hypothalamic regulatory hormones).

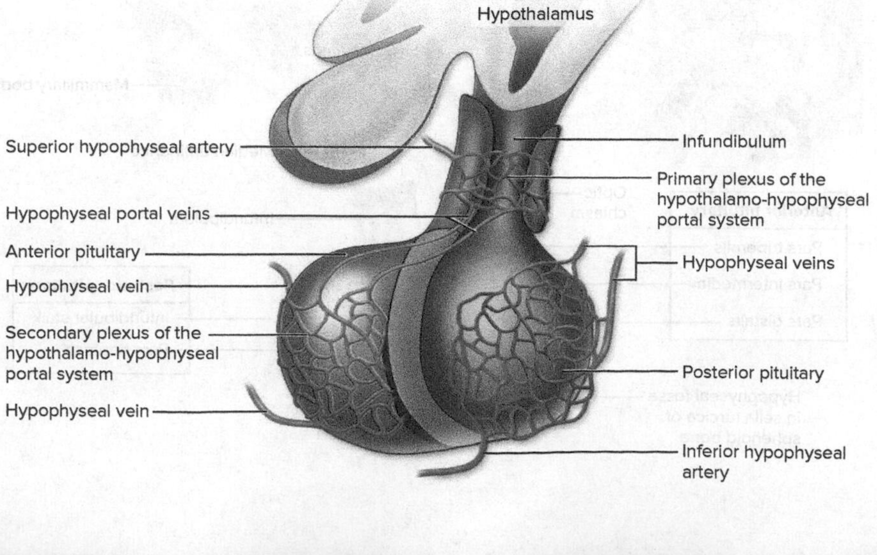

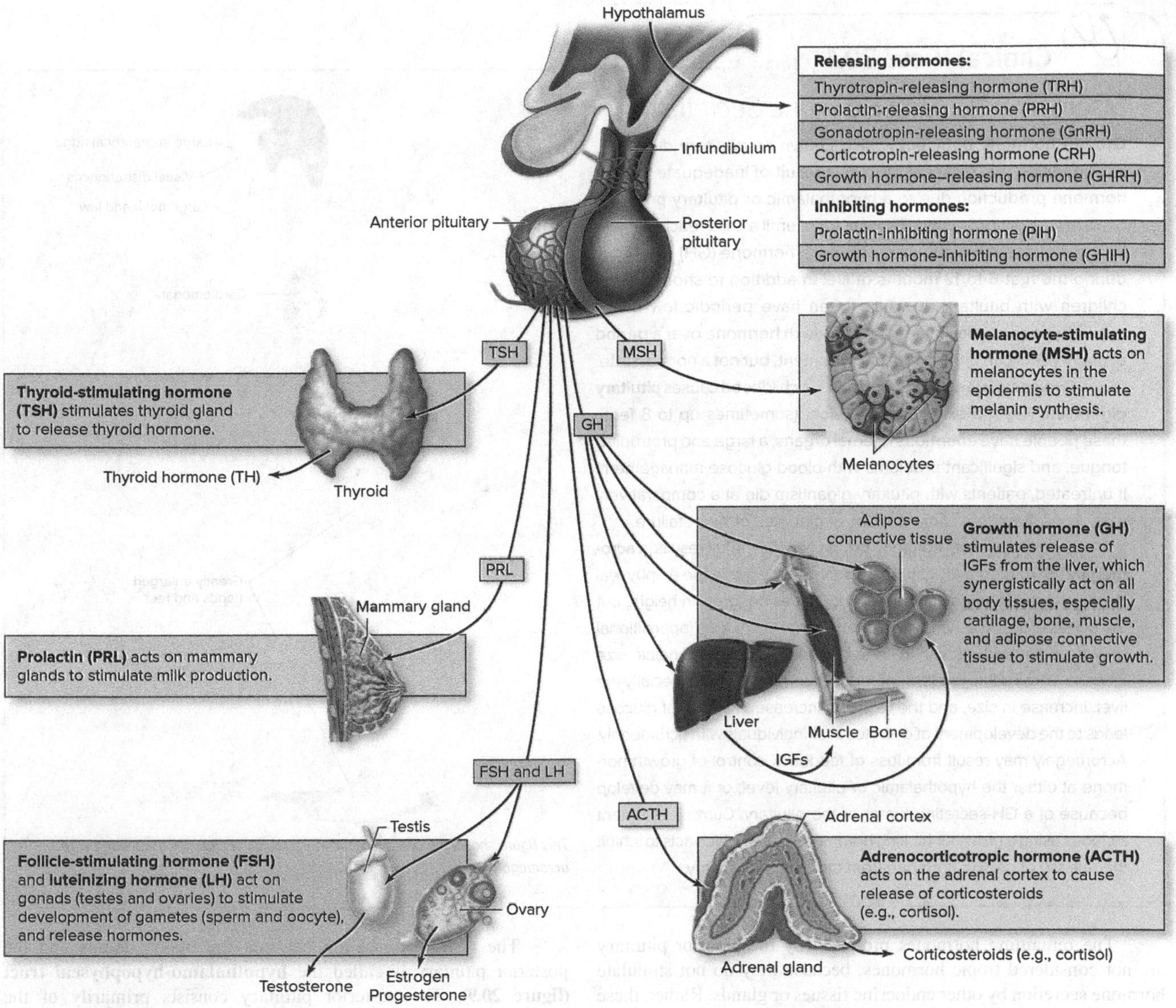
Hypothalamus
Releasing hormones:
Thyrotropin-releasing hormone (TRH)
Prolactin-releasing hormone (PRH)
Gonadotropin-releasing hormone (GnRH)
Corticotropin-releasing hormone (CRH)
Growth hormone–releasing hormone (GHRH)
Inhibiting hormones:
Prolactin-inhibiting hormone (PIH)
Growth hormone-inhibiting hormone (GHIH)
Infundibulum
Anterior pituitary
Posterior pituitary
TSH
MSH
GH
PRL
FSH and LH
ACTH
Thyroid-stimulating hormone (TSH) stimulates thyroid gland to release thyroid hormone.
Thyroid hormone (TH)
Thyroid
Melanocyte-stimulating hormone (MSH) acts on melanocytes in the epidermis to stimulate melanin synthesis.
Melanocytes
Adipose connective tissue
Growth hormone (GH) stimulates release of IGFs from the liver, which synergistically act on all body tissues, especially cartilage, bone, muscle, and adipose connective tissue to stimulate growth.
Liver
Muscle
Bone
IGFs
Mammary gland
Prolactin (PRL) acts on mammary glands to stimulate milk production.
Testis
Ovary
Follicle-stimulating hormone (FSH) and luteinizing hormone (LH) act on gonads (testes and ovaries) to stimulate development of gametes (sperm and oocyte), and release hormones.
Testosterone
Estrogen
Progesterone
Adrenal cortex
Adrenocorticotropic hormone (ACTH) acts on the adrenal cortex to cause release of corticosteroids (e.g., cortisol).
Adrenal gland
Corticosteroids (e.g., cortisol)

Figure 20.8

Anterior Pituitary Hormones. Six of the seven hormones released by the anterior pituitary are controlled by regulatory hormones from the hypothalamus (see corresponding colors). One hormone (MSH) is not. All seven of the hormones affect different areas of the body.

hormone synthesis by the gonads, as well as the production and maturation of gametes in both sexes (see sections 28.2a and 28.3c).

- **Corticotropic** (kōr′ti-k ō-trop′ik) **cells** are located in the pars distalis. These cells synthesize and secrete **adrenocorticotropic** (ă-drē′nō-kōr′ti-k ō-trō′pik) **hormone (ACTH),** also called *corticotropin.* ACTH stimulates the adrenal cortex to produce and secrete its own hormones (see section 20.6a).
- **Somatotropic** (sō′mă-tō-trop′ik) **cells** in the pars distalis synthesize and secrete **growth hormone (GH),** also called *somatotropin.* GH directly stimulates cell growth as well as cell division (mitosis) and affects most body cells, including adipose connective tissue, but specifically those of the skeletal and muscular systems. GH acts as a tropic hormone by stimulating the liver to produce **insulin-like growth factor 1 and 2** (IGF-1 and IGF-2), also called *somatomedin* (sō′mă-tō-mē′din), the hormone that stimulates growth at the epiphyseal plates of long bones (see section 6.4d).

Learning Strategy 20.2

Remember the anterior pituitary hormones with the **FLAT PIG** mnemonic:

- **F** is for FSH
- **L** is for LH
- **A** is for ACTH
- **T** is for TSH
- **P** is for Prolactin
- **I** is to be Ignored
- **G** is for GH

Clinical View 20.1

Disorders of Growth Hormone Secretion

Growth hormone deficiency, also known as *pituitary dwarfism,* is a condition that exists at birth as a result of inadequate growth hormone production due to a hypothalamic or pituitary problem. Growth retardation is typically not evident until a child reaches 1 year of age, because the influence of growth hormone (GH) is minimal during the first 6 to 12 months of life. in addition to short stature, children with pituitary dwarfism often have periodic low blood sugar (hypoglycemia). Injections of growth hormone over a period of many years can bring about improvement, but not a normal state.

Oversecretion of growth hormone in childhood causes **pituitary gigantism**. Beyond extraordinary height (sometimes up to 8 feet), these people have enormous internal organs, a large and protruding tongue, and significant problems with blood glucose management. If untreated, patients with pituitary gigantism die at a comparatively early age, often from complications of diabetes or heart failure.

Excessive growth hormone production in an adult results in **acromegaly** (ak′rō-meg′ă-lē) instead of gigantism because the epiphyseal plate is closed in an adult. The individual does not grow in height, but the bones of the face, hands, and feet enlarge and widen (appositional growth), along with growth in cartilage. An increase in mandible size leads to a protruding jaw (prognathism). Internal organs, especially the liver, increase in size, and the resulting increased release of glucose leads to the development of diabetes in all individuals with acromegaly. Acromegaly may result from loss of feedback control of growth hormone at either the hypothalamic or pituitary level, or it may develop because of a GH-secreting tumor of the pituitary. Current treatment includes using a growth-inhibiting hormone analog, which acts to inhibit the release of growth hormone from the anterior pituitary.

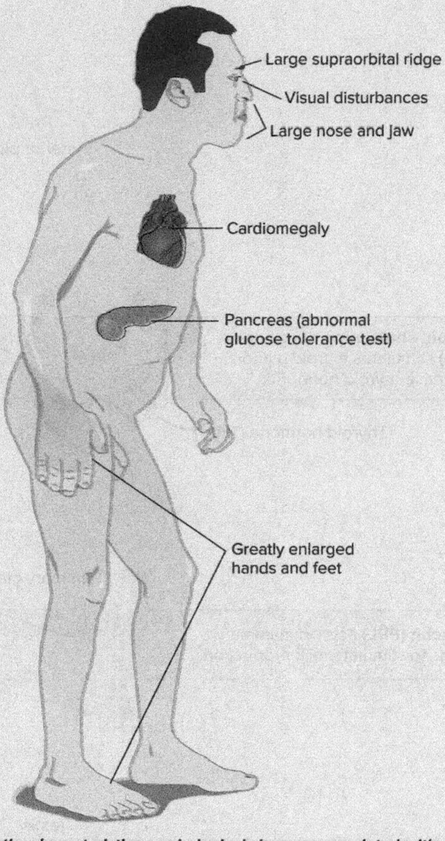
Large supraorbital ridge
Visual disturbances
Large nose and jaw
Cardiomegaly
Pancreas (abnormal glucose tolerance test)
Greatly enlarged hands and feet

This figure shows the characteristic morphological changes associated with acromegaly.

The remaining hormones produced by the anterior pituitary are not considered tropic hormones, because they do not stimulate hormone secretion by other endocrine tissues or glands. Rather, these hormones directly affect other activities in specific cells in the body. **Prolactin** (prō-lak′tin; *lac* = milk) **(PRL)** is secreted by cells in the pars distalis of the anterior pituitary. In females, prolactin regulates mammary gland growth and breast milk production (see section 28.2f). Because of this mammary gland stimulation, the cells that secrete prolactin are often called **mammotropic** (mam′ō-trop′ik) **cells.** Studies suggest that prolactin receptors occur on many body organs, and in males may influence the sensitivity of interstitial cells in the testes to the effects of luteinizing hormone for testosterone secretion.

Melanocyte-stimulating hormone (MSH) is secreted by the cells in the pars intermedia of the anterior pituitary. MSH stimulates both the rate of melanin synthesis by melanocytes in the integument and the distribution of melanocytes in the skin (see section 5.2a). Its secretion has little effect on humans and usually ceases prior to adulthood, except in specific diseases.

20.3b Posterior Pituitary

The **posterior pituitary** (*neurohypophysis*) is the neural part of the pituitary gland because it was derived from nervous tissue at the base of the diencephalon (see figures 20.4 and 20.5). The posterior pituitary is composed of a rounded lobe called the **pars nervosa** and the **infundibular stalk,** also called the **infundibulum.**

The neural connection between the hypothalamus and the posterior pituitary is called the **hypothalamo-hypophyseal tract (figure 20.9).** The posterior pituitary consists primarily of the endings of unmyelinated axons that extend through the hypothalamo-hypophyseal tract from neuron cell bodies housed in the hypothalamus. These hypothalamic neurons are called **neurosecretory** (nū′rō-sē′krĕ-tōr-ē) **cells** because they secrete hormones. The hormones they produce are transported through the unmyelinated axons and housed in their terminals within the posterior pituitary. These hormones are released from the posterior pituitary when a nerve impulse passes through the neuron to the ending in the posterior pituitary. Instead of releasing a neurotransmitter into a synaptic cleft, the posterior pituitary releases a hormone into the blood.

Two specific hypothalamic nuclei contain the neuron cell bodies whose axons extend via the hypothalamo-hypophyseal tract into the posterior pituitary. The **supraoptic** (sū′pră-op′tik) **nucleus** is located superior to the optic chiasm, and the **paraventricular** (par′ă-ven-trik′yū-lăr) **nucleus** is in the anterior-medial region of the hypothalamus adjacent to the third ventricle (see section 15.4c). The neuron cell bodies in both nuclei produce two closely related peptide hormones, **antidiuretic** (an′tē-dī-yū-ret′ik) **hormone (ADH)** and **oxytocin** (ok′sē-tō′sin; *okytokos* = swift birth).

ADH is released from the posterior pituitary in response to various stimuli, including a decrease in blood volume, a decrease in

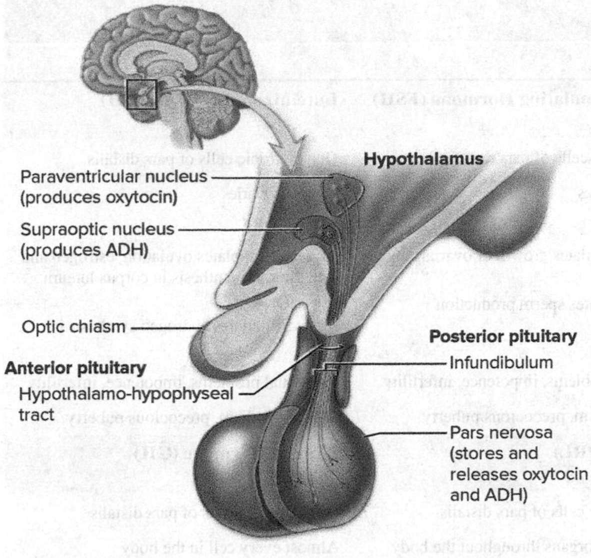
Hypothalamus
Paraventricular nucleus (produces oxytocin)
Supraoptic nucleus (produces ADH)
Optic chiasm
Anterior pituitary
Hypothalamo-hypophyseal tract
Posterior pituitary
Infundibulum
Pars nervosa (stores and releases oxytocin and ADH)

Figure 20.9

Hypothalamo-Hypophyseal Tract. The hypothalamus regulates the function of the anterior and posterior pituitary. The hypothalamo-hypophyseal tract is the nervous connection between nuclei in the hypothalamus and axonal endings in the posterior pituitary.

Learning Strategy 20.3

Use the following analogy to understand the complex interrelationships among the hypothalamus, anterior pituitary, and target organs.

The endocrine system is similar to the hierarchy of a corporation:

- The **hypothalamus** is the "president" of the endocrine system. It produces and secretes regulatory hormones that act on the anterior pituitary.
- The **anterior pituitary** is the "vice president" of the endocrine system. The vice president is pretty powerful, but usually it must receive orders (regulatory hormones) from the president before it can do its job. After receiving these hormones from the hypothalamus, the anterior pituitary secretes hormones that act on the target organs.
- The **target organs** are the "workers" in the endocrine system. They receive orders (hormones) from the vice president. These organs respond to the anterior pituitary hormones (either by secreting their own hormones or by performing some action that helps keep the body at homeostasis).

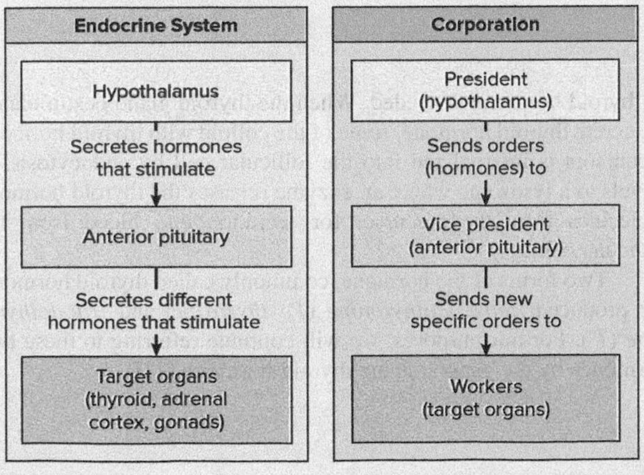
Endocrine System
Hypothalamus
Secretes hormones that stimulate
Anterior pituitary
Secretes different hormones that stimulate
Target organs (thyroid, adrenal cortex, gonads)
Corporation
President (hypothalamus)
Sends orders (hormones) to
Vice president (anterior pituitary)
Sends new specific orders to
Workers (target organs)

blood pressure, or an increase in the concentration of specific electrolytes (salts) in the blood. These conditions indicate that the body is dehydrated. ADH primarily increases water retention from kidney tubules during urine production, resulting in more concentrated urine and conservation of the body's water supply (see section 27.2d). Another consequence of its release is the vasoconstriction of blood vessels, resulting in increased blood pressure; thus, ADH is also referred to as **vasopressin** (vā′sō-pres′in; *vas* = vessel, *pressium* = to press down) (see section 23.2).

Oxytocin stimulates contraction of the uterine wall smooth musculature to facilitate labor and childbirth, and it is also responsible for milk ejection from the mammary gland (see sections 28.2c and 28.2f). Oxytocin induces smooth muscle contraction in male reproductive organs during ejaculation (release of semen during sexual activity, see sections 28.3d and 28.3g). Investigations suggest that oxytocin influences maternal behavior and pair bonding. Oxytocin receptors have been found throughout the body in a number of organs, including the reproductive organs, pancreas, cardiovascular system, kidney, and brain. One group of studies linked oxytocin to decreases in both heart rate and cardiac output. Interestingly, other studies suggest that oxytocin can modulate stress, social behaviors, and anxiety through the activity of the limbic system (see section 15.7).

Table 20.3 summarizes the hormones of the anterior and posterior pituitary gland and the effects of each hormone. APR

WHAT DID YOU LEARN?

4. Where is the pituitary gland located?
5. What are the anterior pituitary hormones and their functions?
6. Explain how the hypothalamus controls hormone release from both the anterior and posterior pituitary.

20.4 Thyroid Gland

✓ Learning Objectives

13. Describe the anatomy and location of the thyroid gland.
14. Explain how thyroid hormone is produced and stored.
15. Describe how thyroid hormone secretion is regulated by the anterior pituitary.
16. Identify the parafollicular cells, name the hormone they secrete, and describe the hormone's function.

The largest gland entirely devoted to endocrine activities is the **thyroid** (thī′royd; *thyreos* = an oblong shield) **gland (figure 20.10)**. The thyroid gland in an adult weighs between 25 and 30 grams and is located immediately inferior to the thyroid cartilage of the larynx and anterior to the trachea. It is covered by a connective tissue capsule.

The thyroid gland is butterfly-shaped, composed of **left** and **right lobes** connected at the anterior midline by a narrow **isthmus** (is′mŭs; constrict). Both lobes of the thyroid gland are highly vascularized, giving the gland an intense reddish coloration. The gland is supplied by the superior and inferior thyroid arteries. Thyroid veins return venous blood from the thyroid and also transport the thyroid hormones into the general circulation.

20.4a Synthesis of Thyroid Hormone by Thyroid Follicles

At the histologic level, the thyroid gland is composed of numerous microscopic, spherical structures called **thyroid follicles.** The wall of each follicle is formed by simple cuboidal epithelial cells, called **follicular cells,** that surround a central lumen. That lumen houses a

Table 20.3 Pituitary Gland Hormones

MAJOR HORMONES SECRETED BY THE ANTERIOR PITUITARY

Feature	Adrenocorticotropic Hormone (ACTH)	Follicle-Stimulating Hormone (FSH)	Luteinizing Hormone (LH)
Source	Corticotropic cells of pars distalis	Gonadotropic cells of pars distalis	Gonadotropic cells of pars distalis
Hormone target	Adrenal cortex	Female: Ovaries Male: Testes	Female: Ovaries Male: Testes
Net effects	Stimulates production of corticosteroid hormones	Female: Stimulates growth of ovarian follicles Male: Stimulates sperm production	Female: Stimulates ovulation, estrogen and progesterone synthesis in corpus luteum of ovary Male: Stimulates androgen synthesis in testes
Hyposecretion disorders	Addison disease[1]	Menstrual problems, impotence, infertility	Menstrual problems, impotence, infertility
Hypersecretion disorders	Cushing syndrome, adrenogenital syndrome [1]	Hypergonadism, precocious puberty	Hypergonadism, precocious puberty
Feature	**Thyroid-Stimulating Hormone (TSH); Also Called Thyrotropin**	**Prolactin (PRL)**	**Growth Hormone (GH)**
Source	Thyrotropic cells of pars distalis	Mammotropic cells of pars distalis	Somatotropic cells of pars distalis
Hormone target	Thyroid gland	Receptors on organs throughout the body Female: Mammary glands Male: Interstitial cells in testes	Almost every cell in the body
Net effects	Stimulates thyroid hormone synthesis and secretion	Female: Stimulates milk production in mammary glands Male: May play a role in the sensitivity of the interstitial cells to LH	Stimulates increased growth and metabolism in target cells; stimulates synthesis of somatomedin in the liver to stimulate growth at epiphyseal plate
Hyposecretion disorders	Hypothyroidism [2]	Menstrual disorders, delayed puberty, male infertility	Pituitary dwarfism[3]
Hypersecretion disorders	Hyperthyroidism [2]	Reduced menstruation, female infertility, male impotence	Gigantism, acromegaly[3]

HORMONES STORED IN THE POSTERIOR PITUITARY

Feature	Antidiuretic Hormone (ADH); Also Called Vasopressin	Oxytocin (OT)
Source	Supraoptic and paraventricular nuclei of hypothalamus	Supraoptic and paraventricular nuclei of hypothalamus
Hormone target	Kidney, smooth muscle in arteriole walls	Female: Uterus, mammary glands Male: Smooth muscle of male reproductive tract
Net effects	Stimulates reabsorption of water from tubular fluid in kidneys; stimulates vasoconstriction in arterioles of body, thereby raising blood pressure	Female: Stimulates smooth muscle contraction in uterine wall; stimulates milk ejection from mammary glands Male: Stimulates contraction of smooth muscle of male reproductive tract
Hyposecretion disorders	Diabetes insipidus	Reduced milk release from mammary glands
Hypersecretion disorders	Water retention	Rarely a problem

[1] See Clinical View 20.5: "Disorders of Adrenal Cortex Hormone Secretion" in section 20.6a.
[2] See Clinical View 20.3: "Disorders of Thyroid Hormone Secretion" in section 20.4c.
[3] See Clinical View 20.1: "Disorders of Growth Hormone Secretion" in section 20.3a.

viscous, protein-rich fluid termed **colloid** (kol'oyd). External to individual follicles are some cells called **parafollicular cells,** which we discuss later in this chapter.

The follicular cells are instrumental in producing **thyroid hormone.** Follicular cells synthesize a glycoprotein called **thyroglobulin (TGB)** and secrete it by exocytosis into the colloid. In brief, iodine molecules must be combined with the thyroglobulin in the colloid to produce thyroid hormone precursors, which are TGB molecules that contain immature thyroid hormone within their structure. The precursors are stored in the colloid until the secretion of thyroid hormone is needed. When the thyroid gland is stimulated to secrete thyroid hormone, some of the colloid with thyroid hormone precursors is internalized into the follicular cell by endocytosis. It travels to a lysosome where an enzyme releases the thyroid hormone molecules from the precursor for secretion into blood from the follicular cells.

Two forms of the hormone, commonly called thyroid hormone, are produced: *tetraiodothyronine* (*T_4; thyroxine*) and *triiodothyronine* (*T_3*). For our purposes, we will continue referring to these two hormones by the general name thyroid hormone (TH).

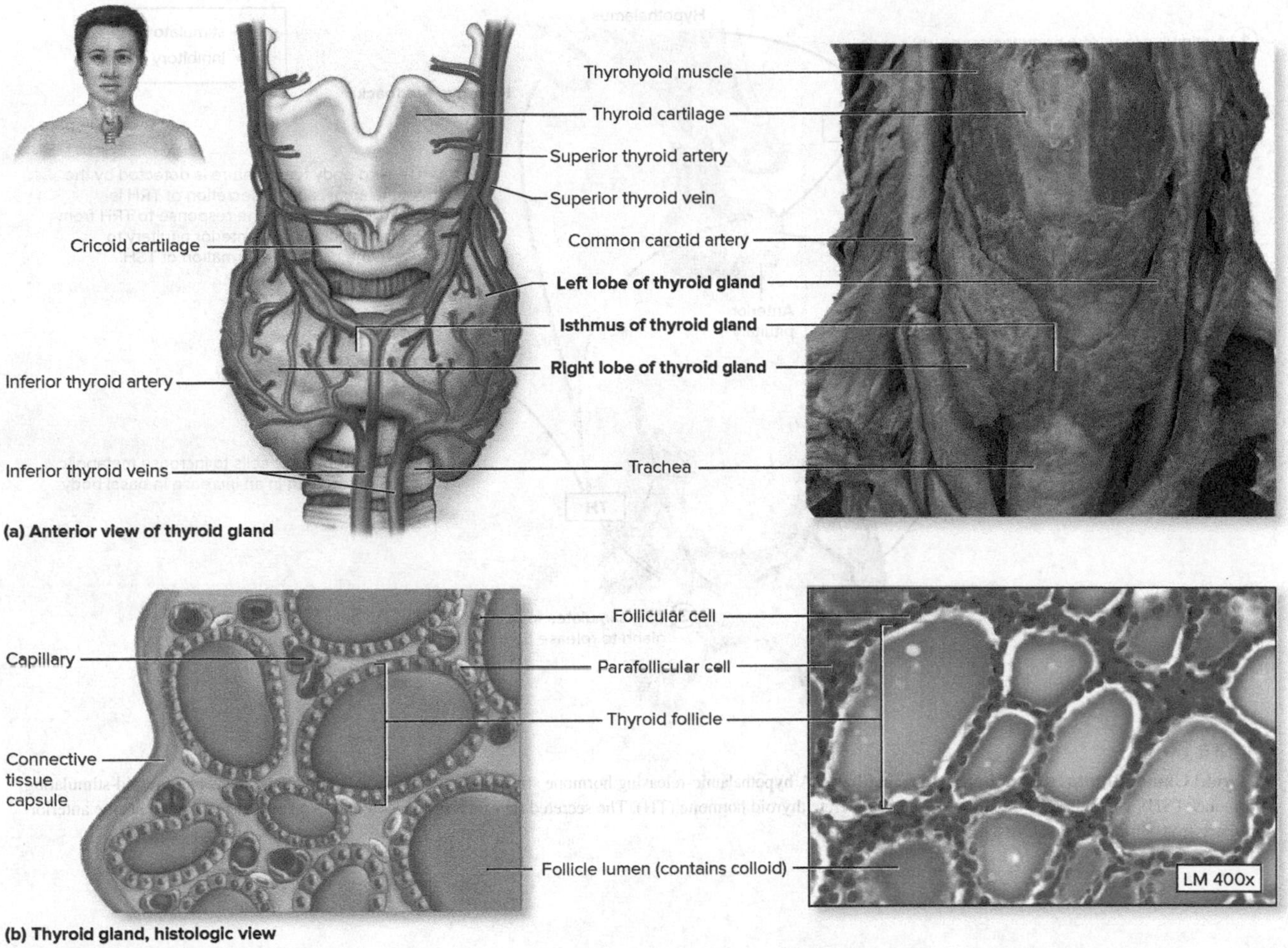
Thyrohyoid muscle
Thyroid cartilage
Superior thyroid artery
Superior thyroid vein
Cricoid cartilage
Common carotid artery
Left lobe of thyroid gland
Isthmus of thyroid gland
Right lobe of thyroid gland
Inferior thyroid artery
Inferior thyroid veins
Trachea
(a) Anterior view of thyroid gland
Follicular cell
Capillary
Parafollicular cell
Thyroid follicle
Connective tissue capsule
Follicle lumen (contains colloid)
LM 400x
(b) Thyroid gland, histologic view

Figure 20.10

Thyroid Gland. (*a*) Location, gross anatomy, and vascular connections of the thyroid gland. (*b*) Microscopic anatomy of thyroid follicles, illustrating the simple cuboidal epithelium of the follicular cells, colloid within the follicle lumen, and the relationship of parafollicular cells to a follicle. APR

(a) Christine Eckel/McGraw-Hill Education; (b) Dr. Alvin Telser/McGraw-Hill Education

WHAT DO YOU THINK?

2 Have you ever noticed that most of the salt you buy in the grocery store is labeled as "iodized"? Why is iodine added to our salt?

20.4b Thyroid Gland–Pituitary Gland Negative Feedback

The regulation of thyroid hormone secretion depends upon a complex thyroid gland–pituitary gland negative feedback process, shown in **figure 20.11** and described here:

1. A stimulus (such as low body temperature or a decreased level of thyroid hormone in the blood) starts the feedback process. This stimulus signals the hypothalamus and causes it to release **thyrotropin-releasing hormone (TRH).**
2. TRH travels through the hypothalamo-hypophyseal portal system to stimulate thyrotropic cells in the anterior pituitary, causing them to synthesize and release **thyroid-stimulating hormone (TSH).**
3. Increased levels of TSH stimulate the follicular cells of the thyroid gland to release **thyroid hormone (TH)** into the blood.
4. TH stimulates its target cells (many of the cells in the body), increasing cellular metabolism. Basal body temperature rises as a result of this stimulation.
5. The increased heat produced as a product due to increased metabolism elevates body temperature and inhibits the release of TRH by the hypothalamus. Also, TH reduces the response of anterior pituitary cells to TRH, thus inhibiting the interactions of the hypothalamus and anterior pituitary. As TH levels rise in the blood, the anterior pituitary stops secreting TSH, and so the thyroid gland is no longer stimulated to release TH.

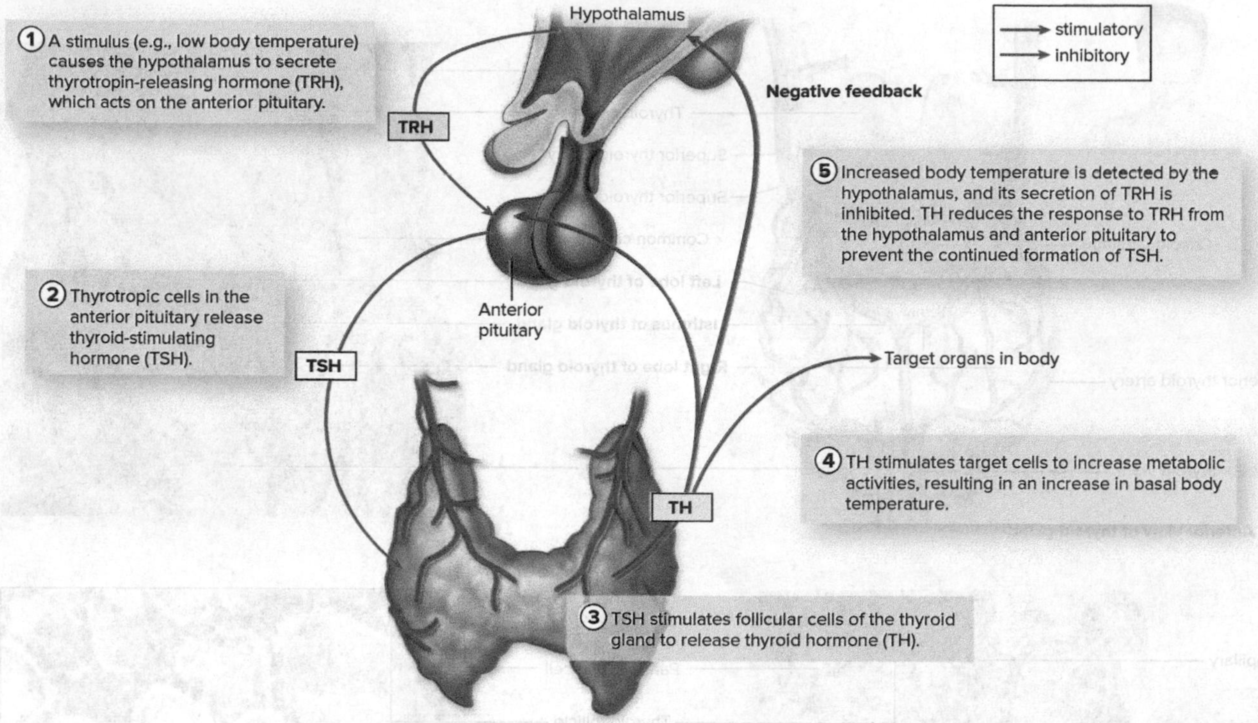

Hypothalamus
stimulatory
inhibitory
① A stimulus (e.g., low body temperature) causes the hypothalamus to secrete thyrotropin-releasing hormone (TRH), which acts on the anterior pituitary.
TRH
Negative feedback
⑤ Increased body temperature is detected by the hypothalamus, and its secretion of TRH is inhibited. TH reduces the response to TRH from the hypothalamus and anterior pituitary to prevent the continued formation of TSH.
② Thyrotropic cells in the anterior pituitary release thyroid-stimulating hormone (TSH).
Anterior pituitary
TSH
Target organs in body
④ TH stimulates target cells to increase metabolic activities, resulting in an increase in basal body temperature.
TH
③ TSH stimulates follicular cells of the thyroid gland to release thyroid hormone (TH).

Figure 20.11

Thyroid Gland–Pituitary Gland Negative Feedback. A hypothalamic-releasing hormone stimulates the anterior pituitary gland to secrete thyroid-stimulating hormone (TSH), which causes the thyroid gland to secrete thyroid hormone (TH). The secreted thyroid hormone stimulates target cells and prevents the anterior pituitary from further stimulating the hypothalamus.

Clinical View 20.2

Hypophysectomy

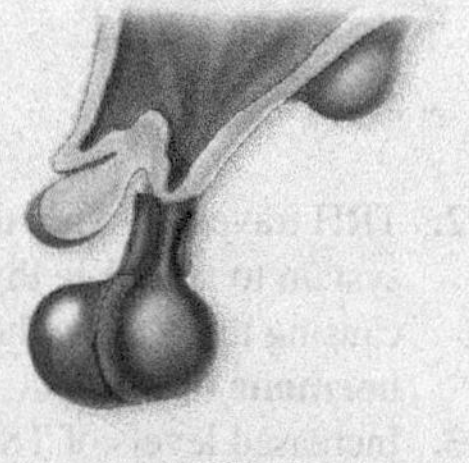

The surgical removal of the pituitary gland is called a **hypophysectomy** (hī′pof-i-sek′tō-mē). Although rarely performed today, this surgery was done in years past to treat advanced breast and prostate cancer, two malignancies that depend on hormone stimulation for their growth. Pituitary removal effectively shuts off the hormone source to these tumors, but medications are now available to block the hormone stimulation in these cancers instead.

Currently, a hypophysectomy is performed for tumors in the pituitary gland. Most pituitary tumors cause changes in a person's vision, because the optic chiasm is essentially draped around the anterior pituitary. The preferred route of entry in a hypophysectomy is through the nasal cavity and sphenoidal sinus, directly into the sella turcica. This approach requires very small instruments and allows complete removal of the pituitary with a minimum of trauma.

20.4c Parafollicular Cells

External to the thyroid follicles are some larger endocrine cells, called **parafollicular** (par′ă-fo-lik′y ū-lăr; *para* = alongside, *folliculus* = a small sac) **cells,** or *C cells,* which occur either individually or in small clusters (see figure 20.10*b*). Parafollicular cells secrete the hormone **calcitonin** (kal′si-t ō′nin; *tonos* = stretching) in response to an elevated level of blood calcium. Ultimately, calcitonin acts to reduce the blood calcium level. Calcitonin does this by inhibiting osteoclast activity, thus decreasing bone matrix resorption and increasing calcium ion loss in urine. The activity of calcitonin is antagonistic to the effects of parathyroid hormone (PTH), described next.

Table 20.4 lists the disorders that result from abnormal secretion of TH and calcitonin, and Clinical View 20.3: "Disorders of Thyroid Hormone Secretion" in section 20.4c discusses two of these. **APR**

WHAT DID YOU LEARN?

7 Draw and label a section of the thyroid gland. Include in your drawing: thyroid follicle, follicle cells, colloid, and parafollicular cells.

8 How does thyroid hormone affect the body?

Table 20.4	Thyroid and Parathyroid Gland Hormones		
Feature	**Thyroid Hormone (TH)**	**Calcitonin**	**Parathyroid Hormone (PTH)**
Source	Follicular cells of thyroid gland	Parafollicular cells of thyroid gland	Chief cells of parathyroid gland
Hormone target	Most body cells	Bone, kidney	Bone, small intestine, kidney
Net effects	Increases metabolism, oxygen use, growth, and energy use; supports and increases rate of development	Reduces calcium levels in body fluids; decreases bone resorption by osteoclasts and increases calcium loss through kidneys	Increases calcium levels in blood through bone resorption (so calcium may be delivered to tissues needing calcium ions, such as muscle tissue); increases calcium absorption by small intestine by calcitriol; decreases calcium loss through the kidneys
Hyposecretion disorders	Hypothyroidism, goiter[1]		Hypoparathyroidism [2]
Hypersecretion disorders	Hyperthyroidism, Graves disease[1]	Thyroid cancer; some association with lung, breast, and pancreatic cancers; chronic renal failure	Hyperparathyroidism [2]

[1] See Clinical View 20.3: "Disorders of Thyroid Hormone Secretion" in section 20.4c.

[2] See Clinical View 20.4: "Disorders of Parathyroid Gland Secretion" in section 20.5.

Clinical View 20.3

Disorders of Thyroid Hormone Secretion

Thyroid hormone (TH) adjusts and maintains the basal metabolic rate of many cells in our body. In the healthy state, TH release is very tightly controlled, but should the amount vary by even a little, a person may exhibit noticeable symptoms. Disorders of thyroid activity are among the most common metabolic problems clinicians see.

Hyperthyroidism (hī-per-thī′royd-izm) results from excessive production of TH, and is characterized by increased metabolic rate, weight loss, hyperactivity, and heat intolerance. Although there are a number of causes of hyperthyroidism, the more common ones are (1) ingestion of TH supplements (weight control clinics sometimes use TH to increase metabolic activity); (2) excessive stimulation of the thyroid by the pituitary gland; and (3) loss of feedback control by the thyroid itself. This last condition, called **Graves disease,** is an autoimmune disorder involving the formation of autoantibodies that mimic TSH hormone. The autoantibodies bind to TSH receptors on the follicular cells of the thyroid, causing an abnormally high level of TH release. Graves disease includes all the symptoms of hyperthyroidism plus a peculiar change in the eyes known as **exophthalmos** (protruding and bulging eyeballs). Hyperthyroidism is treated by removing the thyroid gland, either by surgery or intravenous injections of radioactive iodine. In the latter procedure, the thyroid literally "cooks itself" as it sequesters the radioactive iodine, but other organs are not damaged because they do not store iodine as the thyroid does. Patients whose thyroid glands have been removed must take hormone supplements on a daily basis.

Hypothyroidism (hī′pō-thī′royd-izm) results from decreased production of TH. It is characterized by low metabolic rate, lethargy, a feeling of being cold, weight gain (in some patients), and photophobia (an aversion and avoidance of light). Hypothyroidism may be caused by decreased iodine intake, lack of pituitary stimulation of the thyroid, post-therapeutic hypothyroidism (resulting from either surgical removal or radioactive iodine treatments), or destruction of the thyroid by the person's own immune system (**Hashimoto thyroiditis**). Oral replacement of TH is the treatment for this type of hypothyroidism.

A **goiter** refers to enlargement of the thyroid, typically due to an insufficient amount of the dietary iodine needed to produce TH. Although the pituitary releases more TSH in an effort to stimulate the thyroid, the lack of dietary iodine prevents the thyroid from producing the needed TH. The long-term consequence of the excessive TSH stimulation is overgrowth of the thyroid follicles and the thyroid itself. Goiter was a relatively common deformity in the United States until food processors began adding iodine to table salt. It still occurs in parts of the world where iodine is lacking in the diet, and as such is referred to as **endemic goiter.** Unfortunately, goiters do not readily regress once iodine is restored to the diet, and surgical removal is often required.

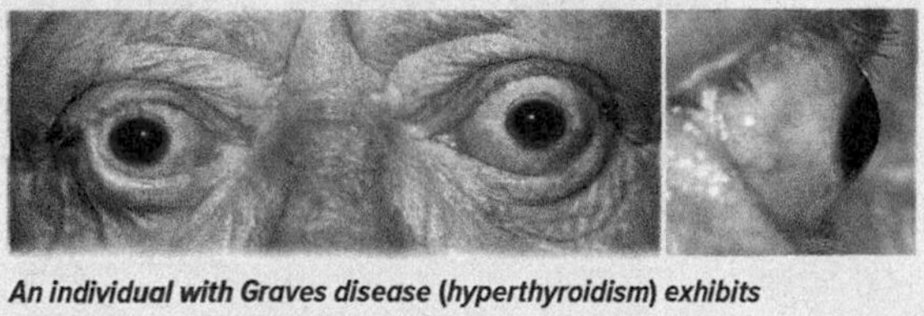

An individual with Graves disease (hyperthyroidism) exhibits exophthalmos: bulging and protruding eyeballs.
Chris Barry/Medical Images

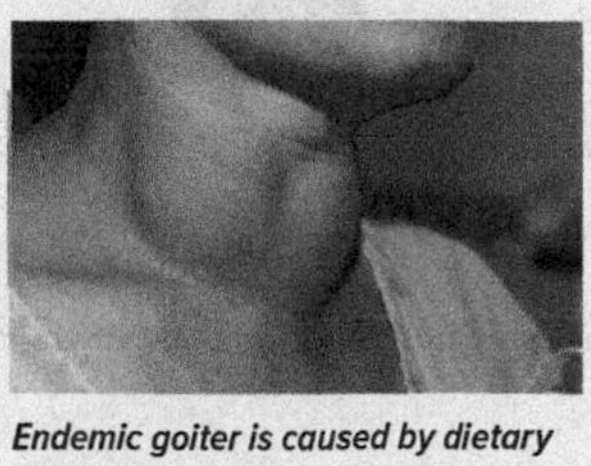

Endemic goiter is caused by dietary iodine deficiency.
Karan Bunjean/Shutterstock

20.5 Parathyroid Glands

✓ Learning Objectives

17. Describe the parathyroid glands' anatomy and location.
18. Name the hormone secreted by the parathyroid glands, and explain how it functions.

The small, brownish-red **parathyroid** (par'ă-thī'royd) **glands** are located on the posterior surface of the thyroid gland (**figure 20.12**). The parathyroid glands are usually four small nodules, but some individuals may have as few as two or as many as six of these glands. The inferior thyroid artery generally supplies all nodules of the parathyroid gland. Rarely, the superior thyroid artery may supply the superior pair of nodules.

There are two different types of cells in the parathyroid gland: chief cells and oxyphil cells. The **chief cells,** or *principal cells,* have a large, spherical nucleus and a relatively clear cytoplasm. They are the source of **parathyroid hormone (PTH). Oxyphil** (ok'sē-fil) **cells** are larger than chief cells, and each oxyphil has a granular, pink cytoplasm. The function of oxyphil cells is not known.

PTH is secreted into the blood in response to decreased blood calcium levels, which may result from normal events such as loss of electrolytes during sweating or urine formation. Because calcium ions are needed for many body functions, including activity at synapses and muscle contraction (see sections 14.6a and 10.3c), inadequate levels of calcium in the blood mean that the body cannot function properly. Thus, parathyroid hormone stimulates the release of calcium stores into the blood, ultimately raising blood calcium levels. PTH influences target organs in several ways:

- PTH stimulates osteoclasts to resorb bone and release calcium ions from bone matrix into the blood.
- PTH stimulates calcitriol synthesis from an inactive form of vitamin D as a result of increased calcium ions in the kidney. Calcitriol is a hormone that promotes calcium absorption of ingested nutrients in the small intestine.
- PTH prevents the loss of calcium ions during the formation of urine in the kidneys. Calcium ions are returned to the blood from filtrate of the blood that is later modified to form urine.

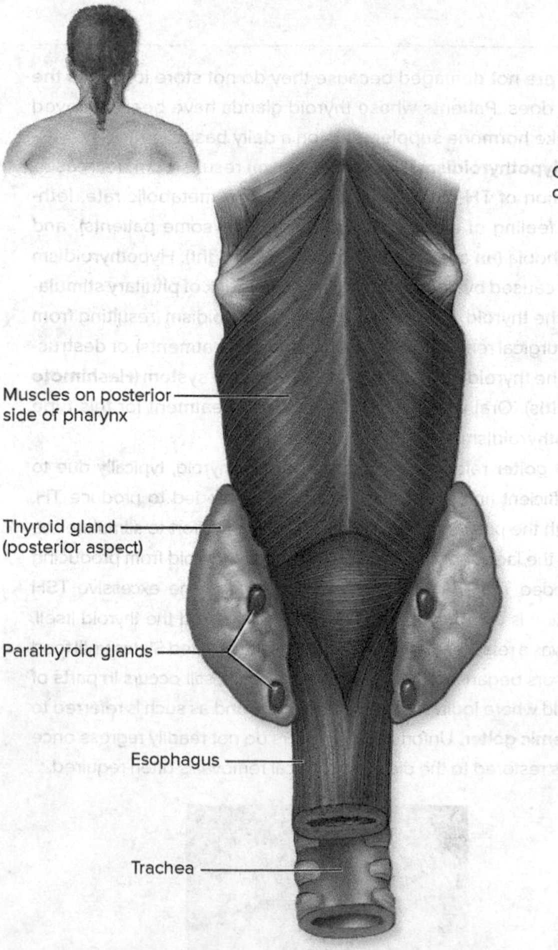
Muscles on posterior side of pharynx
Thyroid gland (posterior aspect)
Parathyroid glands
Esophagus
Trachea

(a) Posterior view of esophagus, thyroid, and parathyroid glands

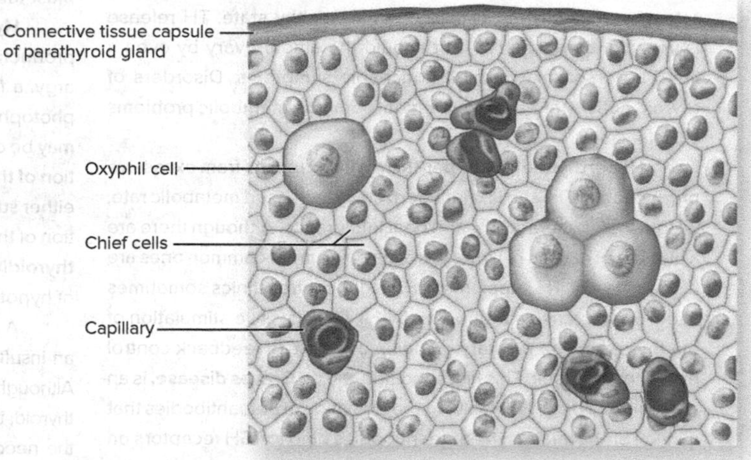
Connective tissue capsule of parathyroid gland
Oxyphil cell
Chief cells
Capillary
Chief cells
Oxyphil cells
LM 135x

(b) Microscopic views of a parathyroid gland

Figure 20.12

Parathyroid Glands. *(a)* The parathyroid glands are four small nodules attached to the capsule of the thyroid gland on its posterior surface. (*b)* A drawing shows that each parathyroid gland is enclosed by a connective tissue capsule. Both the drawing and the micrograph show chief cells and oxyphil cells.

(b) Victor P. Eroschenko

Clinical View 20.4

Disorders of Parathyroid Gland Secretion

The parathyroid glands are critical to the control of blood calcium levels. Over- or underactivity of the parathyroids can have serious, if not fatal, consequences. **Hyperparathyroidism** (hī′pěr-par′ă-thī′royd-izm) refers to overactivity of the parathyroid glands and is the most commonly encountered disorder of the parathyroid glands. Following are the major consequences of hyperparathyroidism: (1) Bones are depleted of calcium (and thus become more subject to fractures); (2) The extra resorption of calcium from the filtrate that becomes urine leads to an increased incidence of kidney stones; (3) High blood calcium levels cause a decrease in bowel motility, which leads to constipation; (4) High blood calcium levels cause psychological changes, such as depression, decreased mental activity, and eventually coma. Hyperparathyroidism usually results from just one of the four glands increasing in size and beginning to work on its own without control.

Hypoparathyroidism is underactivity of the parathyroid glands. It is a rare condition that results in abnormally low blood calcium levels (*hypocalcemia*). Most of the symptoms are neuromuscular, and range from mild tingling in the fingers and limbs to marked muscle cramps and contractions (tetany); in severe cases, convulsions may occur, and death may result if left untreated. Hypoparathyroidism is most commonly due to accidental removal or damage to the parathyroid glands during thyroid surgery. Less commonly, hypoparathyroidism occurs because of autoimmune destruction of glands. Therapy consists of dietary calcium and vitamin D supplements in people with hypoparathyroidism. Recombinant human PTH can be used if dietary supplements aren't sufficient.

Table 20.4 lists the hormones secreted by the thyroid and parathyroid glands, and the Clinical View 20.4: "Disorders of Parathyroid Gland Secretion" in this section focuses on two disorders that result from abnormal secretion of PTH. APR

WHAT DID YOU LEARN?

9 What are the main effects of parathyroid hormone?

20.6 Adrenal Glands

✓ Learning Objectives

19. Differentiate between the structure of the adrenal cortex and adrenal medulla.
20. Name the hormones produced in the adrenal cortex and describe their effects on target cells.
21. Name the hormones produced in the adrenal medulla and describe their effects on target cells.

The **adrenal** (ă-drē′năl; *ad* = to, *ren* = kidney) **glands** (or *suprarenal glands*) are paired, pyramid-shaped endocrine glands anchored on the superior surface of each kidney (**figure 20.13**). The adrenal glands are embedded in fat and fascia to minimize their movement. These endocrine glands are supplied by multiple suprarenal arteries that branch from larger abdominal arteries, including the inferior phrenic arteries, the aorta, and the renal arteries. Venous drainage enters the suprarenal veins. The adrenal gland has an outer **adrenal cortex** and an inner central core called the **adrenal medulla.** These two regions secrete different types of hormones (**table 20.5**).

20.6a Adrenal Cortex

The adrenal cortex exhibits a distinctive yellow color as a consequence of the stored lipids in its cells. These cells synthesize more than 25 different steroid hormones, collectively called **corticosteroids.** Corticosteroid synthesis is stimulated by the ACTH produced by the anterior pituitary. Corticosteroids are vital to our survival; trauma to or removal of the adrenal glands requires corticosteroid supplementation throughout life.

The adrenal cortex is partitioned into three separate regions: the zona glomerulosa, the zona fasciculata, and the zona reticularis (figure 20.13*d*). Different functional categories of steroid hormones are synthesized and secreted in the separate zones.

The **zona glomerulosa** (zō′nă glō-měr′yū-lōs′ă; *glomerulus* = ball of yarn) is the thin, outer cortical layer composed of dense, spherical clusters of cells. These cells synthesize **mineralocorticoids** (min′ěr-al-ō-kōr′ti-koyd), a group of hormones that help regulate the composition and concentration of electrolytes (ions) in body fluids. The principal mineralocorticoid is **aldosterone** (al-dos′t ěr-ōn), which regulates the ratio of sodium (Na^+) and potassium (K^+) ions in our blood by stimulating Na^+ retention and K^+ secretion. If the ratio of these electrolytes becomes unbalanced, body functions are dramatically affected; severe imbalances can result in death.

The **zona fasciculata** (fă-sik′y ū-lă′tă; *fascicle* = bundle of parallel sticks) is the middle layer and the largest region of the adrenal cortex. It is composed of parallel cords of lipid-rich cells that have a bubbly, almost pale appearance. **Glucocorticoids** (glū′kō-kōr′ti-koyd) are synthesized by these cells. Glucocorticoids stimulate metabolism of lipids and proteins, and help regulate glucose levels in the blood, especially as the body attempts to resist stress and repair injured or damaged tissues. The most common glucocorticoids are **cortisol** (kōr′ti-sol) (*hydrocortisone*) and **corticosterone** (kōr′ti-kos′ter- ōn).

The innermost region of the cortex, called the **zona reticularis** (re-tik′y ū-lăr′is; *reticulum* = network), is a narrow band of small, branching cells. These cells are capable of secreting minor amounts of sex hormones called **gonadocorticoids.** The primary gonadocorticoids secreted are **androgens,** which are male sex hormones. In females, some of the androgens are converted to estrogen. The amount of androgen secreted by the adrenal cortex is small compared to that secreted by the gonads.

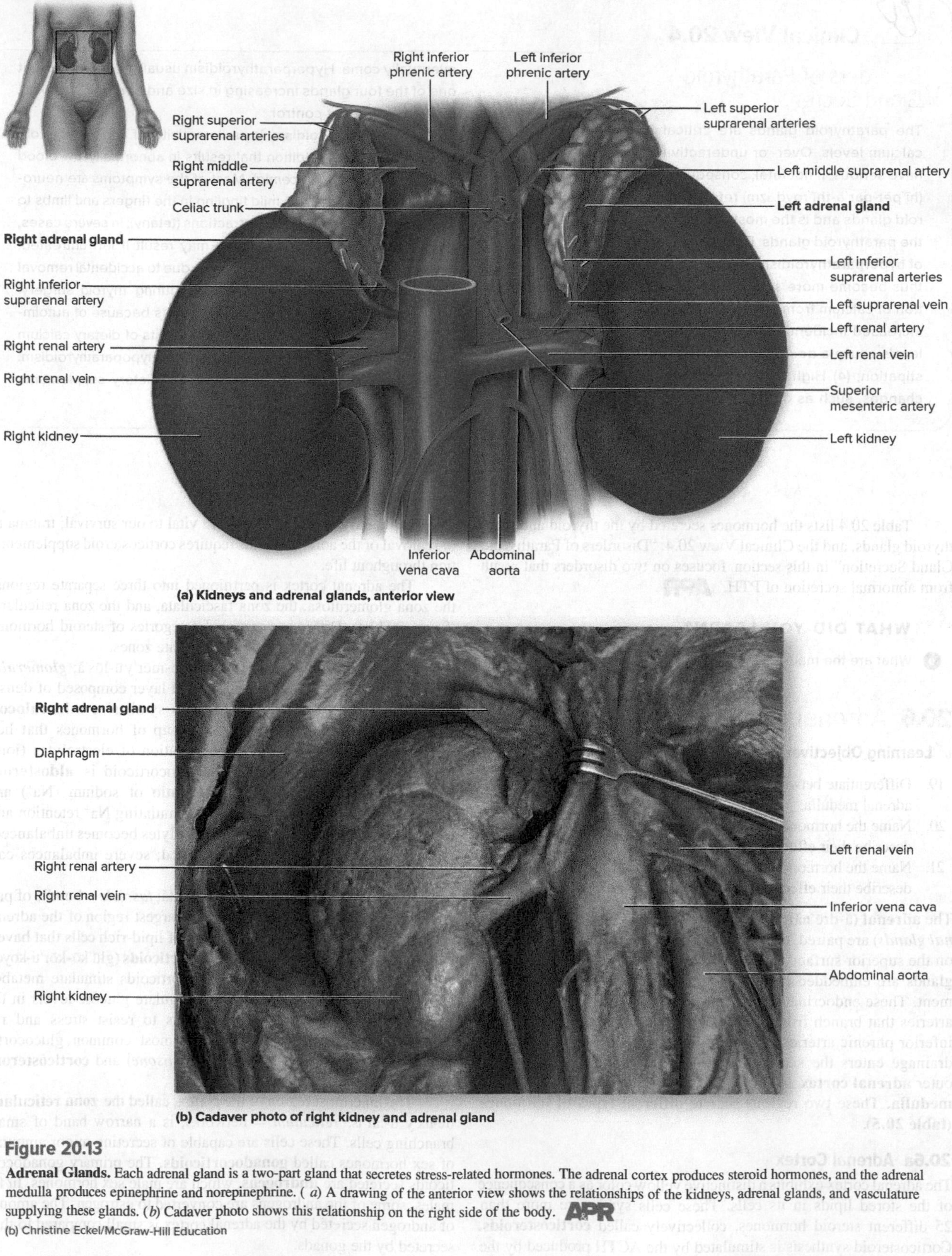

Right inferior phrenic artery
Left inferior phrenic artery
Right superior suprarenal arteries
Left superior suprarenal arteries
Right middle suprarenal artery
Left middle suprarenal artery
Celiac trunk
Left adrenal gland
Right adrenal gland
Left inferior suprarenal arteries
Right inferior suprarenal artery
Left suprarenal vein
Left renal artery
Right renal artery
Left renal vein
Right renal vein
Superior mesenteric artery
Right kidney
Left kidney
Inferior vena cava
Abdominal aorta
Right adrenal gland
Diaphragm
Left renal vein
Right renal artery
Right renal vein
Inferior vena cava
Abdominal aorta
Right kidney

(a) Kidneys and adrenal glands, anterior view

(b) Cadaver photo of right kidney and adrenal gland

Figure 20.13

Adrenal Glands. Each adrenal gland is a two-part gland that secretes stress-related hormones. The adrenal cortex produces steroid hormones, and the adrenal medulla produces epinephrine and norepinephrine. (*a*) A drawing of the anterior view shows the relationships of the kidneys, adrenal glands, and vasculature supplying these glands. (*b*) Cadaver photo shows this relationship on the right side of the body. APR

(b) Christine Eckel/McGraw-Hill Education

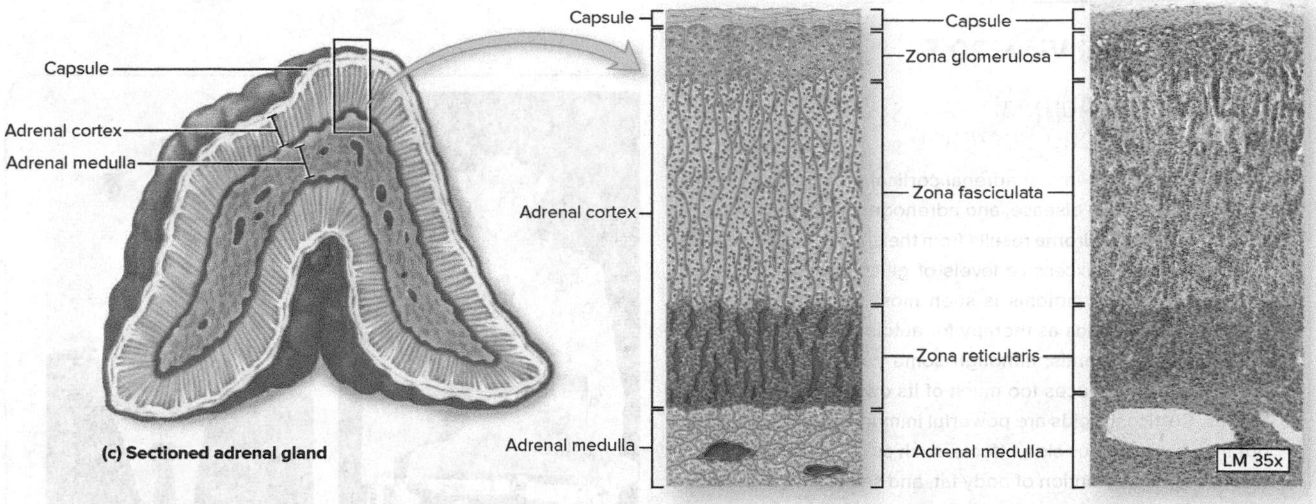

Figure 20.13

Adrenal Glands. (*continued*) (*c*) A sectioned adrenal gland shows the outer cortex and the inner medulla. (*d*) A diagram and a micrograph illustrate the three zones of the adrenal cortex, as well as the relationship of the cortex to the external capsule and the internal medulla.

(d) Dr. Alvin Telser/McGraw-Hill Education

Table 20.5 Comparison of Adrenal Cortex and Adrenal Medulla

Feature	Adrenal Cortex	Adrenal Medulla
Embryonic Derivative	Intermediate mesoderm	Neural crest cells
Adrenal Gland Location	Outer region of the gland	Inner region of the gland
Mode of Stimulation	Hormonal (stimulated by ACTH from anterior pituitary)	Nervous (stimulated by preganglionic axons from sympathetic division of ANS)
Hormones Produced	Corticosteroids: mineralocorticoids, glucocorticoids, gonadocorticoids	Epinephrine, norepinephrine
Effects of Hormones	Mineralocorticoids regulate the balance of electrolytes (e.g., Na^+ and K^+) in the body Glucocorticoids elevate blood glucose levels during long-term stressful situations (e.g., fasting, injury, anxiety), and stimulate the body to use fats and proteins as energy resources Gonadocorticoids (primarily androgens) are sex hormones	Prolongs fight-or-flight response of the sympathetic division of the ANS

Table 20.6 lists the adrenal gland hormones, and the Clinical View 20.5: "Disorders of Adrenal Cortex Hormone Secretion" in this section describes some disorders that result from abnormal se-cretion of adrenal gland hormones. In addition, the use and abuse of anabolic steroids is addressed in the Clinical View 10.5: "Anabolic Steroids and Other Performance-Enhancing Compounds" in section 10.4.

20.6b Adrenal Medulla

The **adrenal medulla** forms the inner core of each adrenal gland (figure 20.13*c, d*). It has a pronounced red-brown color due to its extensive vascularization. The adrenal medulla primarily consists of clusters of large, spherical cells called **chromaffin** (krō′maf-in; *chroma* = color, *affinis* = affinity) **cells**. These chromaffin cells were formed from neural crest cells, so they are essentially modified ganglionic cells of the sympathetic division of the autonomic nervous system. They are innervated by preganglionic sympathetic axons.

When stimulated by the sympathetic division of the ANS, one population of chromaffin cells secretes the hormone **epinephrine** (ep′i-nef′rin; *epi* = upon, *nephros* = kidney), also called *adrenaline* (ă-dren′ ă-lin). The other population secretes the hormone **norepinephrine** (nōr′ep-i-nef′rin), also called *noradrenaline* (nōr′ă-dren′ ă-lin). These hormones work with the sympathetic division of the autonomic nervous system to prepare the body for an emergency or fight-or-flight situation. Because hormones are released more slowly than nerve impulses and their effects are longer lasting, the secretion of epinephrine and norepinephrine helps prolong the effects of the sympathetic stimulation. Thus, long after the sympathetic axons have ceased to transmit nerve impulses, the

Clinical View 20.5

Disorders of Adrenal Cortex Hormone Secretion

Four abnormal patterns of adrenal cortical function are Cushing syndrome, Addison disease, and adrenogenital syndrome.

Cushing syndrome results from the chronic exposure of the body's tissues to excessive levels of glucocorticoid hormones. This complex of symptoms is seen most frequently in people taking corticosteroids as therapy for autoimmune diseases such as rheumatoid arthritis, although some cases result when the adrenal gland produces too much of its own glucocorticoid hormones. Corticosteroids are powerful immunosuppressant drugs, but they have serious side effects, such as osteoporosis, muscle weakness, redistribution of body fat, and salt retention (resulting in overall swelling of the tissues). Cushing syndrome is characterized by body obesity, especially in the face (called *moon face*) and back (referred to as *buffalo hump*). Other symptoms include hypertension, excess hair growth, kidney stones, and menstrual irregularities.

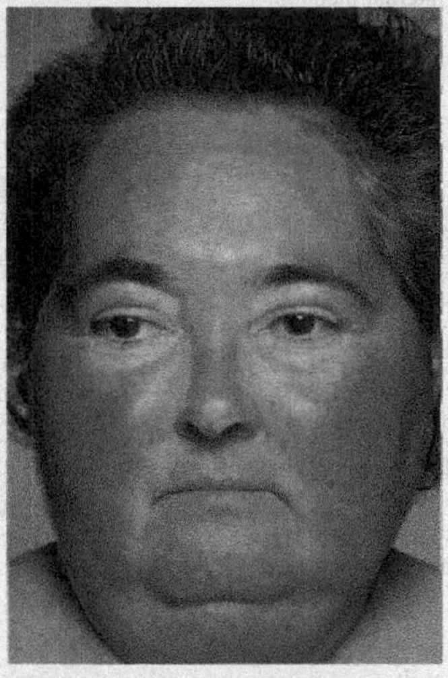

Photo of woman with Cushing syndrome. Symptoms include the excessive adipose deposits in the face, producing the characteristic moon face.
Clinical Photography, Central Manchester University Hospitals NHS Foundation Trust, UK/Science Source

Addison disease involves insufficient production of steroids (usually glucocorticoids and perhaps mineralocorticoids) from the adrenal cortex. Addison disease can result from (1) adrenal glands that were malformed during development, (2) impaired enzymatic pathways for steroid synthesis, and (3) destruction of the adrenal gland (typically by an autoimmune disorder that forms autoantibodies against the adrenal gland that results in its destruction). The symptoms include weight loss, general fatigue and weakness, hypotension, and hyperpigmentation (darkening) of the skin. Perhaps the most well-known person with Addison disease was John Fitzgerald Kennedy (JFK).

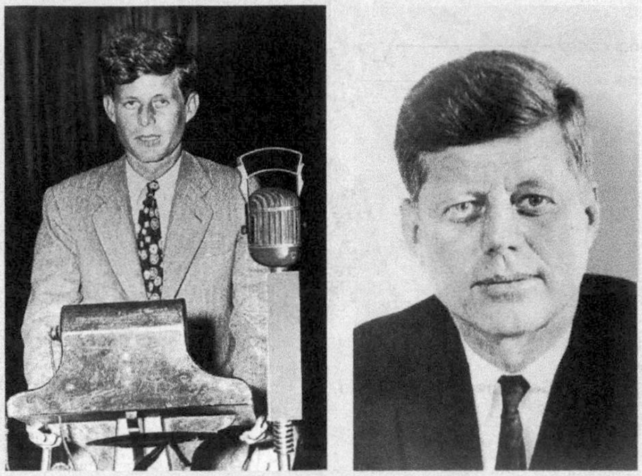

(a) (b)

(a) Photo of John F. Kennedy prior to being treated for Addison disease.
(b) Portrait of John F. Kennedy after being treated for Addison disease.
(a) AP Images; (b) Source: Library of Congress [LC-USZ62-117124]

Adrenogenital syndrome, also known as *androgen insensitivity syndrome* or *congenital adrenal hyperplasia,* first manifests in the embryo and fetus. It is characterized by the inability to synthesize corticosteroids. The pituitary, sensing the deficiency of corticosteroids, releases massive amounts of ACTH in an unsuccessful effort to bring the glucocorticoid content of the blood up to a healthy level. This large amount of ACTH produces *hyperplasia* (increased size) of the adrenal cortex and causes the release of intermediary hormones that have a testosterone-like effect. The result is **virilization** (masculinization) in a newborn. Virilization in girls means the clitoris is enlarged, sometimes to the size of a male penis. The effect may be so profound that the sex of a newborn female is questioned or even mistaken. A virilized male may have an enlarged penis and exhibit signs of premature puberty as early as age 6 or 7. (See Clinical View 28.9: "Intersex Conditions" in section 28.5.) About 75% of affected newborns also have a salt-losing problem, owing to their bodies' inability to manufacture mineralocorticoids and glucocorticoids. Treatment consists of oral corticosteroids, which boost the body's level of corticosteroids and inhibit the pituitary from releasing excessive amounts of ACTH.

Table 20.6 Adrenal Gland Hormones

Feature	Mineralocorticoids (e.g., aldosterone)	Glucocorticoids (e.g., cortisol, corticosterone)	Gonadocorticoids (e.g., androgens)	Epinephrine and Norepinephrine
Source	Zona glomerulosa of adrenal cortex	Zona fasciculata of adrenal cortex	Zona reticularis of adrenal cortex	Chromaffin cells of adrenal medulla
Hormone target	Kidney cells	Liver cells	Cells that respond to sex hormones	Various cells throughout the body
Net effects	Regulate electrolyte composition and concentration in body fluids	Stimulate lipid and protein metabolism; regulate blood glucose levels	Protein synthesis in cells that respond to sex hormones	Work with the sympathetic division of the ANS to stimulate fight-or-flight response
Hyposecretion disorders	Addison disease[1]	Addison disease[1]	Generally no effect; may see effect post-menopause	Inconsequential
Hypersecretion disorders	Hypertension, edema[2]	Cushing syndrome[1]	Adrenogenital syndrome	Pheochromocytoma (benign tumor in adrenal medulla)[1]

[1] See Clinical View 20.5: "Disorders of Adrenal Cortex Hormone Secretion" in this section.

[2] See Clinical View 23.3: "Hypertension and Hypotension" in section 23.2.

Learning Strategy 20.4

Here is how to remember the adrenal gland hormonal functions:

- The zona glomerulosa regulates the levels of sodium and potassium ions in the blood, so it regulates *salt.*
- The zona fasciculata secretes glucocorticoids, which keep blood glucose levels up, so it regulates *sugar.*
- Finally, the zona reticularis secretes small amounts of androgens, so it regulates *sex* (hormones).

Thus, the adrenal cortex regulates **salt, sugar,** and **sex!**

sympathetic responses continue to linger because the epinephrine and norepinephrine are still present in the blood and affecting their target cells. APR

WHAT DID YOU LEARN?

10 What is the primary function of aldosterone?

11 Draw a flow chart showing the stimulation of epinephrine.

WHAT DO YOU THINK?

3 A person who is extremely allergic to bee stings may carry an "EpiPen," which is an auto-injector of epinephrine. Why would the epinephrine help this individual?

20.7 Pancreas

Learning Objectives

22. Describe the anatomy and location of the pancreas.
23. Name the hormones produced by the pancreatic islets, and explain how they function.

The **pancreas** (pan′kr ē-as; *pan* = all, *kreas* = flesh) is an elongated, spongy, nodular organ situated posterior to the stomach between the duodenum of the small intestine and the spleen (**figure 20.14**). The pancreas performs both exocrine and endocrine activities, and thus it is considered a *heterocrine,* or mixed, gland. The pancreas is mostly composed of groups of cells called **pancreatic acini** (sing., *acinus* = grape). Acinar cells produce an alkaline pancreatic juice that is secreted through pancreatic ducts into the duodenum of the small intestine (see section 26.10c). This pancreatic juice aids digestion.

Scattered among the pancreatic acini are small clusters of endocrine cells called **pancreatic islets** (ī′let), also known as *islets of Langerhans* (figure 20.14*b*). Estimates of the number of islets range between 1.5 and 2 million; however, these endocrine cell clusters form only about 1% of the pancreatic volume. A pancreatic islet may be composed of four types of cells: two major types (called alpha cells and beta cells) and two minor types (called delta cells and F cells). Each type produces its own hormone (**table 20.7**).

Alpha cells secrete **glucagon** (glū′k ă-gon) when blood glucose levels drop. Glucagon causes target cells in the liver to break down glycogen into glucose and release glucose into the blood to increase blood glucose levels. Also, this hormone stimulates adipose cells to break down lipid and secrete it into the blood.

Beta cells secrete **insulin** (in′s ū-lin; *insula* = island) when blood glucose levels are elevated. Target cells respond to insulin by taking up the glucose, thus lowering blood glucose levels (see figure 20.3*a*). Insulin also promotes glycogen synthesis and lipid storage.

Delta cells are stimulated by high levels of nutrients in the blood. Delta cells synthesize **somatostatin** (sō′mă-tō-stat′in; *stasis* = standing still), also described as *growth hormone–inhibiting hormone* (*GHIH*) (see table 20.2). In this context it only acts within the pancreas, not systemically. Somatostatin slows the release of insulin and glucagon as well as the activity of the digestive organs, thereby also slowing the rate of nutrient entry into the blood. This process gives the other islet hormones the ability to control and coordinate nutrient uptake.

F cells are stimulated by protein digestion in the digestive tract. F cells secrete **pancreatic polypeptide (PP)** to suppress and regulate somatostatin secretion from delta cells. Together, these pancreatic hormones provide for orderly uptake and processing of nutrients. APR

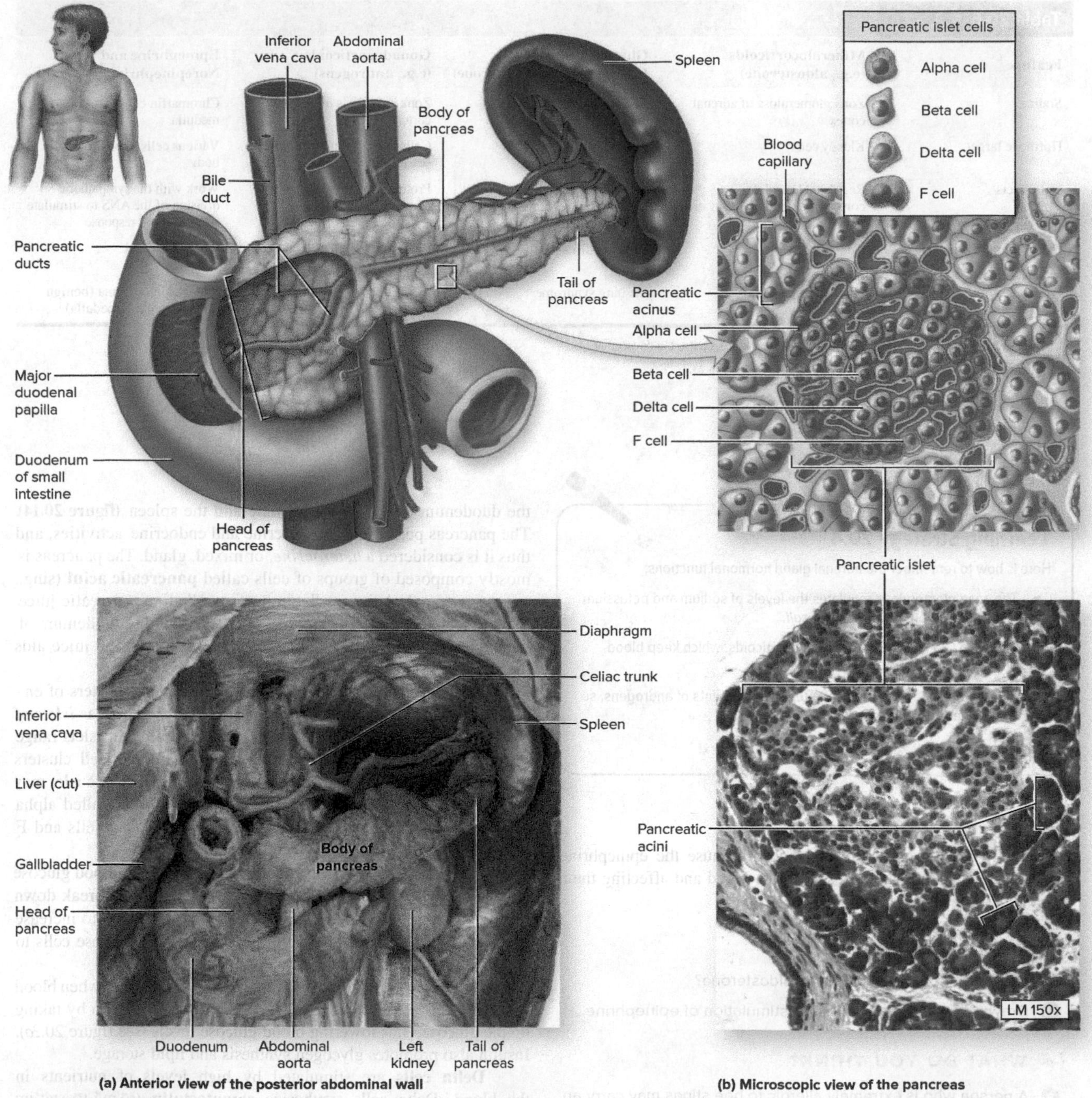

Figure 20.14

Pancreas. The pancreas performs both exocrine and endocrine activities. (*a*) A diagram and cadaver photo illustrate the relationship between the pancreas and the small intestine and spleen. (*b*) A diagram and micrograph reveal the histology of a pancreatic islet. Different types of islet cells are distinguished by a specific staining technique called *immunohistology* (not shown). APR

(a) Christine Eckel/McGraw-Hill Education; (b) Al Telser/McGraw-Hill Education

Table 20.7	Pancreatic Hormones			
Feature	**Glucagon**	**Insulin**	**Somatostatin**	**Pancreatic Polypeptide**
Source	Alpha cells of pancreatic islets	Beta cells of pancreatic islets	Delta cells of pancreatic islets	F cells of pancreatic islets
Hormone target	Liver, adipose cells	Liver, body cells	Alpha and beta cells of pancreatic islets	Delta cells of pancreatic islets
Net effects	Increases blood glucose levels, glycogen breakdown in liver cells, lipid breakdown in adipose cells	Decreases glucose levels in body fluids, glucose transport into target cells; promotes glycogen and lipid formation and storage	Slows release of insulin and glucagon to slow rate of nutrient absorption during digestion	Suppresses somatostatin secretion from delta cells
Hyposecretion disorders	Hypoglycemia	Diabetes mellitus[1]	No discernable effect as this is a local agent here	Excessive pancreatic enzyme secretion
Hypersecretion disorders	Hyperglycemia	Hyperinsulism	Suppresses insulin and glucagon release	Inhibits gallbladder secretion; suppresses pancreas secretion; overstimulates gastric secretion

[1] See Clinical View 20.6: "Conditions Resulting in Abnormal Blood Glucose Levels" in section 20.7.

Clinical View 20.6

Conditions Resulting in Abnormal Blood Glucose Levels

Diabetes (dī-ă-bē′tēz) **mellitus** (me-lī′tŭs; sweetened with honey) is a metabolic condition marked by inadequate uptake of glucose from the blood. The name "diabetes mellitus" is derived from the phrase "sweet urine" because some of the excess glucose is expelled into the urine, resulting in *glycosuria* (glucose in the urine). Chronically elevated blood glucose levels damage blood vessels, especially the smaller arterioles. Because of its damaging effects on the vascular system, diabetes is the leading cause of retinal blindness, kidney failure, and nontraumatic leg amputations in the United States. Diabetes is also associated with increased incidence of heart disease and stroke. In fact, heart disease or stroke is the cause of death in approximately 65% of individuals with diabetes.

Measuring the amount of glucose attached to hemoglobin molecules within erythrocytes (**hemoglobin A1C test**) is an accurate means for determining the degree of risk for developing diabetes. The greater the amount of attached glucose, the higher the risk.

Three categories of diabetes mellitus are type 1 diabetes, type 2 diabetes, and gestational diabetes.

Type 1 diabetes, also referred to as *insulin-dependent diabetes mellitus (IDDM)*, or *juvenile diabetes,* is characterized by absent or diminished production and release of insulin by the pancreatic islet cells. This type tends to occur in children and younger individuals, and is not directly associated with obesity. Type 1 diabetes may develop in a person who harbors a genetic predisposition, although some kind of triggering event is required to start the process. Often, the trigger is a viral infection; then the process continues as an autoimmune condition in which the beta cells of the pancreatic islets are destroyed. Research suggests lymphocytes that express characteristics of both T and B cells may have a role in type 1 diabetes. Treatment of type 1 diabetes requires daily injections of insulin. Research using transplanted islet cells and stem cells shows promise as an effective means in treating type 1 diabetes.

Ian Hooton/Science Source

Type 2 diabetes, also known as *insulin-independent diabetes mellitus (IIDM),* results from either decreased insulin release by the pancreatic beta cells or decreased insulin effectiveness at peripheral tissues. This type of diabetes was previously referred to as *adult-onset diabetes* because it tended to occur in people over the age of 30. However, type 2 diabetes is now rampant in adolescents and young adults. Obesity plays a major role in the development of type 2 diabetes, and more young people are considered overweight than ever before. Most type 2 diabetes patients can be successfully treated with a combination of diet, exercise, and medications that enhance insulin release or increase its sensitivity at the tissue level. In more severe cases, a person with type 2 diabetes must take insulin injections.

Gestational diabetes is seen in some pregnant women, typically in the latter half of the pregnancy. If untreated, gestational diabetes can pose a risk to the fetus as well as increase delivery complications. Most at risk for developing this condition are women who are overweight; those of African American, Native American, or Hispanic ancestry; or those who have a family history of diabetes. Although gestational diabetes usually resolves after giving birth, a woman who presents with the condition has a 20% to 50% chance of developing type 2 diabetes within 10 years.

Hypoglycemia

Hypoglycemia occurs when blood glucose levels drop below 60 mg/dL. Hypoglycemia is not a disease; however, it may be a nonspecific indicator of some underlying homeostatic imbalance. The causes of hypoglycemia are numerous and include insulin overdose, prolonged and intense exercise, drinking alcohol on an empty stomach, liver or kidney dysfunction, deficiency of either glucocorticoids or growth hormone, and certain genetic conditions. Symptoms may include hunger, dizziness, nervousness, confusion, feeling anxious or weak, sweating, sleepiness, or any combination of these. The symptoms are thought to occur from insufficient glucose to the brain or from the activation of the sympathetic nervous system in response to low blood glucose levels.

If an individual is unable to eat or drink safely, such as if unconscious, unresponsive, or having convulsions, glucagon can be administered by injection. This provides a safe means to offset the low blood glucose level.

WHAT DID YOU LEARN?

12. What hormones are produced in the pancreatic islets?

20.8 Pineal Gland and Thymus

✓ Learning Objective

24. Describe the anatomy, location, and endocrine functions of the pineal gland and thymus.

The **pineal** (pin′ē-al; *pineus* = relating to the pine) **gland,** also called the *pineal body,* is a small, cone-shaped structure attached to the posterior region of the epithalamus (see section 15.4a and figure 20.2). It is composed primarily of **pinealocytes,** which secrete **melatonin** (mel′ă-tōn′in; *melas* = dark hue, *tonas* = contraction), a hormone that makes us drowsy. Its production tends to be cyclic; it increases at night and decreases during the day. Melatonin secretion helps regulate a circadian rhythm (24-hour body clock).

Studies have linked low melatonin levels with mood (affective) disorders, such as *seasonal affective disorder (SAD),* a condition that may be treated with light therapy. Melatonin also appears to affect the synthesis of a hypothalamic hormone (gonadotropin-releasing hormone). This hormone is responsible for regulating synthesis of two hormones from the anterior pituitary (follicle-stimulating hormone and luteinizing hormone), which in turn regulate the reproductive system. The role of melatonin in sexual maturation is not well understood. However, excessive melatonin secretion is known to delay puberty in humans.

The **thymus** (thī′mŭs; *thymos* = sweetbread) is a bilobed structure located within the mediastinum superior to the heart and immediately posterior to the sternum (see figure 20.2). A connective tissue framework houses both the epithelial cells and maturing T-lymphocytes (a specific type of white blood cell) (see section 24.3a). The size of the thymus varies among individuals; however, it is always relatively large in infants, continues to grow until puberty, then diminishes in size and activity. The adult thymus is usually only one-third to one-fourth its pre-puberty size and weight. Most of the functional cells of the thymus are lost, and the ensuing space fills with adipose connective tissue.

The thymus functions principally in association with the lymphatic system to regulate and maintain body immunity. It produces **thymopoietin** (thī′mō-poy-ē′tin) and **thymosins** (thī′mō-sins) (a group of complementary hormones). These hormones act by stimulating and promoting the differentiation, growth, and maturation of T-lymphocytes. The thymus will be discussed in greater detail in section 24.4b.

WHAT DID YOU LEARN?

13. Where is the pineal gland located?

20.9 Endocrine Functions of the Kidneys, Heart, Gastrointestinal Tract, and Gonads

✓ Learning Objective

25. Explain how hormones secreted by the kidneys, heart, gastrointestinal tract, and gonads help regulate homeostasis.

Some of the organs of the urinary, cardiovascular, digestive, and reproductive systems contain their own endocrine cells, which secrete hormones. These hormones help regulate the following: electrolyte levels in the blood, erythrocyte production, blood volume, blood pressure, digestive system activities, and sexual maturation and activity (**table 20.8**).

20.9a Kidneys

Hormones secreted by endocrine cells in the kidneys help regulate electrolyte concentration in body fluids, the rate of erythrocyte production, and an increase in both blood volume and blood pressure. The specific hormones the kidneys secrete are calcitriol and erythropoietin. Renin is an enzyme released by the kidneys.

Calcitriol (kal′si-tr ī′ol) is an active form of vitamin D and is synthesized by specific endocrine cells of the kidneys when they are stimulated by increased blood levels of parathyroid hormone. Calcitriol stimulates the intestinal cells to increase their uptake of both calcium and phosphate, thus increasing calcium levels in body fluids.

Table 20.8 Organs with Endocrine Functions, Their Hormones, and Hormonal Effects

Gland/Endocrine Cells	Hormone(s)	Hormonal Effect(s)
Kidney[1]	Calcitriol	Promotes calcium absorption in small intestine
	Erythropoietin	Stimulates erythrocyte production and maturation
Heart	Atrial natriuretic peptide (ANP)	Increases sodium and water loss in urine, resulting in decreased blood pressure and volume
GI tract	Various hormones related to digestion	Controls overall secretory activity and motility in GI tract
Ovaries	Estrogen	Stimulates development of female reproductive organs, follicle maturation; regulates menstrual cycle; stimulates growth of mammary glands
	Progesterone	Regulates menstrual cycle; stimulates growth of uterine lining; stimulates growth of mammary glands
	Inhibin	Inhibits secretion of follicle-stimulating hormone (see section 28.2a)
Testes	Androgens (primarily testosterone)	Stimulates male reproductive organ development, production of sperm
	Inhibin	Inhibits secretion of follicle-stimulating hormone (see section 28.3c)

[1] Renin is released by the kidneys, but it is an enzyme, not a hormone. Renin helps in the production of angiotensin II, a hormone that stimulates the production of aldosterone.

The kidneys release **erythropoietin** (ĕ-rith′r ō-poy′ĕ-tin) **(EPO)** when the blood's oxygen content is low. EPO causes increases in the rates of erythrocyte production and maturation. The resulting elevated numbers of erythrocytes increase the blood's ability to transport oxygen.

Renin (rē′nin), an enzyme produced in the kidney, helps form a hormone (angiotensin II) that stimulates specific cells of the adrenal cortex to produce and secrete aldosterone (see section 20.6a). Renin is released in response to several stimuli including the sympathetic nervous system. Decrease in blood pressure and abnormal electrolyte concentration in the fluid being formed into urine in the kidneys also stimulate renin secretion.

20.9b Heart

Modified cardiac muscle cells in the wall of the right atrium secrete the hormone **atrial natriuretic** (nā′trē-yū-ret′ik; *natrium* = to carry, *ouron* = urine) **peptide (ANP),** also called *atriopeptin* (ā′trē-ō-pep′tin), in response to excessive stretch in the wall of the heart. This stretching is caused by a marked elevation in either blood volume or blood pressure. ANP reduces blood volume by causing water loss and sodium excretion from the blood into the urine. With less blood volume, blood pressure drops.

20.9c Gastrointestinal Tract

The **gastrointestinal (GI) tract,** or *digestive tract,* consists of the organs involved in ingesting and digesting food, which include the stomach, small intestine, and large intestine (see sections 26.2 through 26.9). Accessory organs include the liver, pancreas, and gallbladder (see section 26.10). Some of these organs have their own endocrine cells, which produce hormones that help regulate digestive activities, and stimulate the liver, gallbladder, and pancreas to release secretions needed for efficient digestion. These hormones will be further discussed in sections 26.7c, 26.8b, and 26.10c.

20.9d Gonads

The **gonads** (gō′nad; *gone* = seed) are the female and male primary sex organs—the ovaries in females and the testes in males (see sections 28.2a and 28.3c). In addition to producing gametes, the gonads also produce sex hormones. The **ovaries** produce the female sex hormones **estrogen** and **progesterone,** whereas the **testes** produce the male sex hormones called **androgens,** many of which are converted into **testosterone.** The gonads also produce **inhibin,** which inhibits follicle-stimulating hormone secretion. The specific functions of these hormones are discussed in sections 28.2a and 28.3c.

WHAT DID YOU LEARN?

14 What hormone is produced by cardiac muscle cells in the heart wall?

20.10 Aging and the Endocrine System

✓ Learning Objective

26. Describe how endocrine activity changes as people age.

Aging reduces the efficiency of endocrine system functions, resulting in decreased secretory activities of endocrine glands and reduced hormone levels in the blood. Many abnormalities or disorders experienced after middle age, such as abdominal weight gain or muscle loss, are directly related to endocrine gland dysfunction or imbalance. For example, the secretion of GH and sex hormones often changes. Reduction in GH levels leads to loss of weight and body mass in the elderly, although continued exercise reduces this effect. In addition, testosterone or estrogen levels decline as males and females age. Often hormone replacement therapy (HRT) attempts to supplement GH and sex hormone levels that have naturally diminished with age.

20.11 Development of the Endocrine System

✓ Learning Objective

27. Describe the developmental events in adrenal, pituitary, and thyroid gland development.

Endocrine organs originate at different times during development and are derived collectively from all three germ layers (ectoderm, mesoderm, and endoderm). Here, we describe the development of three representative endocrine organs (the adrenal glands, the pituitary gland, and the thyroid gland), whereas the development of other organs containing endocrine cells is discussed in sections 24.4b, 26.7c, 26.8b, 26.10c, 28.2a, and 28.3c.

20.11a Adrenal Glands

Early in the second month of embryonic development, the two future components of the adrenal gland begin to develop: (1) The adrenal cortex is derived from intermediate mesoderm located in a region called the **urogenital** (yūr′ō-jen′i-tăl) **ridge.** This urogenital ridge forms the future gonads and some components of the urinary system (see section 27.5a). (2) The adrenal medulla develops from neural crest cells that migrated from the developing neural tube (see section 18.7 and figure 18.12). Thus, the adrenal medulla has a neuroectodermal origin. These neural crest cells migrate to the urogenital ridge region, where they are engulfed by the intermediate mesoderm that forms the developing adrenal cortex. Maturation and development of the adrenal gland continue into early childhood.

20.11b Pituitary Gland

The anterior and posterior pituitary have different developmental origins (**figure 20.15**). The anterior pituitary develops as an outpocketing of the ectoderm from the stomodeum (future opening of the mouth). The posterior pituitary develops as a bud that grows from the developing hypothalamus.

Both parts of the pituitary gland start growing during the third week of development. A growth of tissue called the **hypophyseal pouch** (or *Rathke pouch*) forms in the stomodeum (the future mouth) and grows superiorly toward the future diencephalon. At the same time, a **neurohypophyseal bud** grows from the developing diencephalon toward the stomodeum. This bud later forms most of the adult infundibulum and the posterior pituitary. By late in the second month of development, the hypophyseal pouch loses its connection with the oral cavity as it grows superiorly toward the developing neurohypophyseal bud. Eventually, the hypophyseal pouch and neurohypophyseal bud adhere to one another, and the pituitary gland is formed.

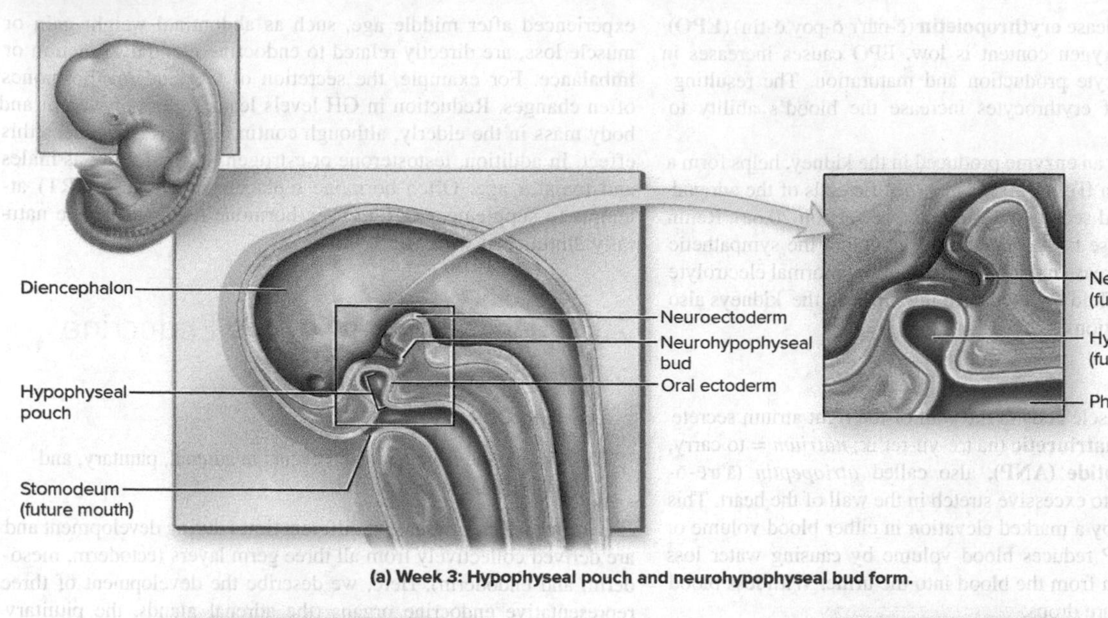
Diencephalon
Hypophyseal pouch
Stomodeum (future mouth)
Neuroectoderm
Neurohypophyseal bud
Oral ectoderm
Neurohypophyseal bud (future posterior pituitary)
Hypophyseal pouch (future anterior pituitary)
Pharynx
(a) Week 3: Hypophyseal pouch and neurohypophyseal bud form.
Infundibulum
Hypophyseal pouch
Neurohypophyseal bud
(b) Late second month: Hypophyseal pouch loses contact with roof of pharynx.
Anterior pituitary
Pars tuberalis
Pars intermedia
Pars distalis
Posterior pituitary
Median eminence
Pars nervosa
(c) Fetal period: Anterior and posterior pituitary have formed.

Figure 20.15

Pituitary Gland Development. The pituitary gland forms from two separate structures. (*a*) During the third week of development, a hypophyseal pouch (future anterior pituitary) grows from the roof of the pharynx, while a neurohypophyseal bud (future posterior pituitary) forms from the diencephalon. (*b*) By late in the second month, the hypophyseal pouch loses contact with the roof of the pharynx as it merges with the neurohypophyseal bud. (*c*) During the fetal period, the anterior and posterior pituitary develop fully.

Clinical View 20.7

Thyroid Gland Developmental Anomalies

Variations occur in how the developing thyroid gland migrates and how the thyroglossal duct regresses. Normally, the thyroid gland should migrate to a position inferior to the larynx, and the thyroglossal duct should regress completely. But sometimes, a portion of the thyroglossal duct persists and forms a variable median-placed **pyramidal lobe** of the thyroid gland.

Another developmental anomaly of the thyroid is an **ectopic thyroid gland,** in which some of the developing thyroid, or the entire gland, is located along its path of descent. Thus, tissue identifiable as thyroid gland may be found more superiorly in the neck or even along the base of the tongue. This condition is not very common.

Finally, a **thyroglossal cyst** may develop if part or all of the thyroglossal duct persists and doesn't form a pyramidal lobe. The remnant of this duct can gradually fill with fluid produced by the cells lining the thyroglossal duct, forming a painless, movable mass in the center of the neck. Thyroglossal duct cysts are typically painless and seen in children at about age 5. Such cysts may require surgical removal.

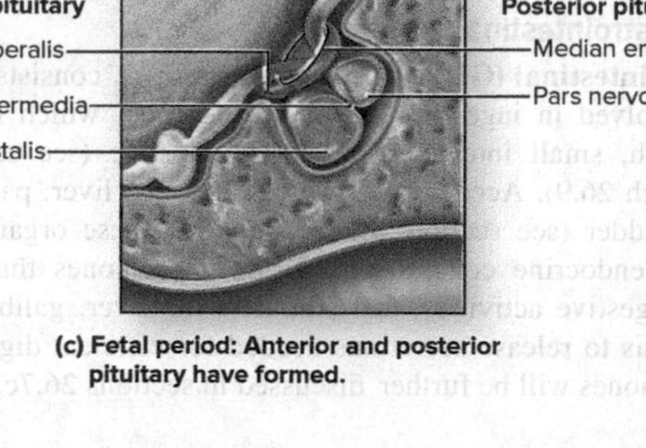

Pyramidal lobe (black arrow).
Electronic Publishing Services, Inc., NY/McGraw-Hill Education

20.11c Thyroid Gland

During the end of the fourth week, the thyroid gland begins to form from endodermal tissue (**figure 20.16**). The gland first forms as a mass called the **thyroid diverticulum** between the developing anterior two-thirds and the posterior one-third of the tongue. This is called the **foramen cecum** of the tongue. As the thyroid diverticulum develops, it migrates and descends through the developing neck, initially maintaining a connection with the tongue called the **thyroglossal duct.**

By the seventh week of development, the thyroid gland reaches its final position anterior to the trachea and immediately inferior to the thyroid cartilage of the larynx. The thyroid gland becomes functional by weeks 10–12 of development.

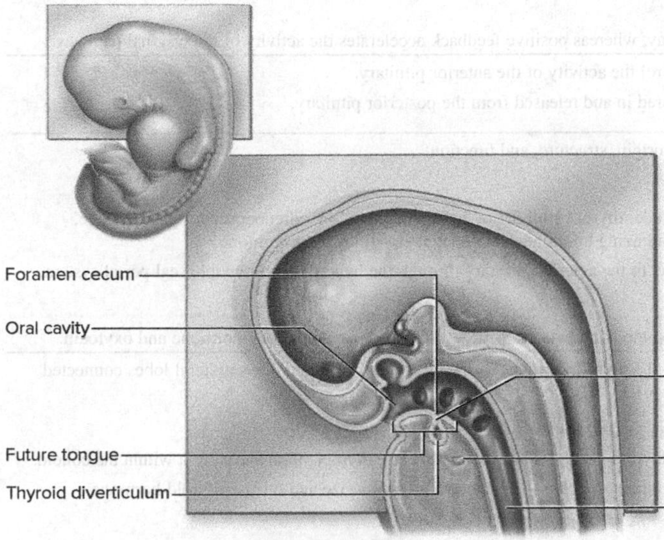
Foramen cecum
Oral cavity
Thyroglossal duct
Future tongue
Developing hyoid bone
Thyroid diverticulum
Esophagus

(a) Week 4: Thyroid diverticulum forms.

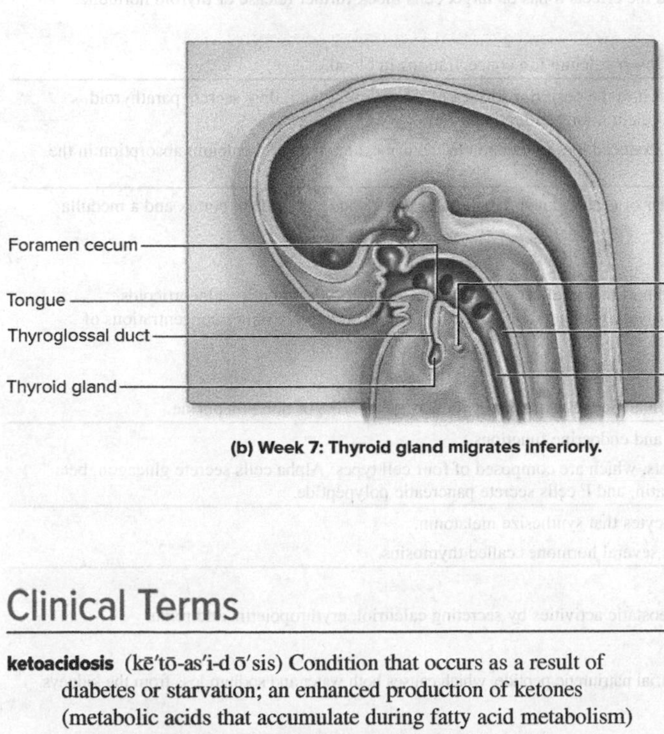
Foramen cecum
Hyoid bone
Tongue
Esophagus
Thyroglossal duct
Thyroid gland
Trachea

(b) Week 7: Thyroid gland migrates inferiorly.

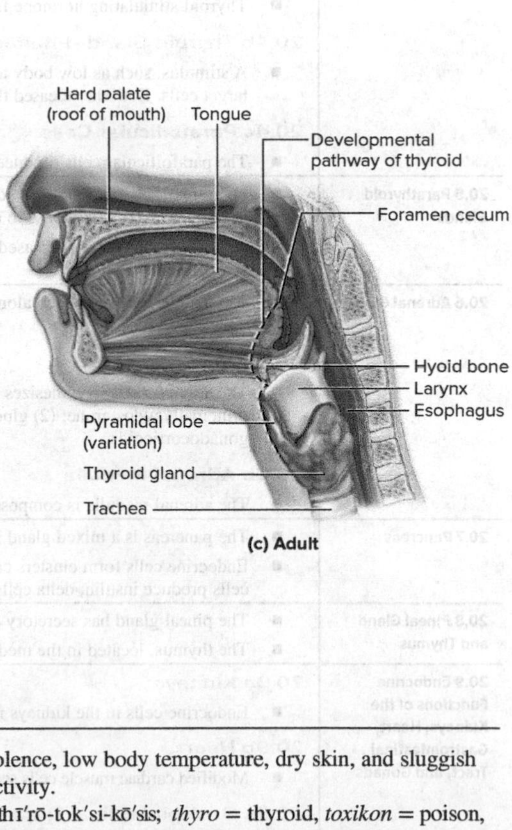
Hard palate (roof of mouth)
Tongue
Developmental pathway of thyroid
Foramen cecum
Hyoid bone
Larynx
Esophagus
Pyramidal lobe (variation)
Thyroid gland
Trachea

(c) Adult

Figure 20.16

Thyroid Gland Development. The thyroid gland begins to form in the fourth week as an invagination in the floor of the future tongue. The thyroid initially remains attached to the tongue via a thyroglossal duct. *(a)* Inferior extension of the thyroid diverticulum at development week 4. *(b)* By week 7, the thyroid gland migrates inferiorly, and the thyroglossal duct starts to regress. *(c)* In an adult, the thyroid is anterior to the trachea and inferior to the larynx.

Clinical Terms

ketoacidosis (kē'tō-as'i-d ō'sis) Condition that occurs as a result of diabetes or starvation; an enhanced production of ketones (metabolic acids that accumulate during fatty acid metabolism) in the blood leads to markedly lower blood pH, which can be life-threatening.

myxedema (miks'e-dē'mă; *myxa* = mucus, *oidema* = swelling) Type of hypothyroidism that occurs in adults and is characterized by somnolence, low body temperature, dry skin, and sluggish mental activity.

thyrotoxicosis (thī'rō-tok'si-kō'sis; *thyro* = thyroid, *toxikon* = poison, *osis* = condition) Condition resulting from excessive quantities of thyroid hormone; in its acute form, the patient experiences elevated temperature, rapid heart rate, and abnormal activity in a variety of other body systems.

Chapter Summary

- Homeostasis is maintained by nervous and endocrine system activities.

20.1 Endocrine Glands and Hormones

- Endocrine glands are ductless organs that secrete their molecular products directly into the blood.

20.1a Overview of Hormones

- Hormones are chemical messengers in the endocrine system. Upon release into the blood, these secretions affect intercellular activities.
- Target cells have receptors for specific hormones to which they will respond.
- The three groups of hormones based upon chemical structure are protein hormones, biogenic amines, and steroid hormones.

20.1b Negative and Positive Feedback

- Negative feedback inhibits the activity of a pathway, whereas positive feedback accelerates the activity of the original pathway.

20.2 Hypothalamic Control of the Endocrine System

- Regulatory hormones from the hypothalamus control the activity of the anterior pituitary.
- The hypothalamus produces the two hormones stored in and released from the posterior pituitary.

20.3 Pituitary Gland

- The anterior and posterior pituitary parts differ in origin, structure, and function.

20.3a Anterior Pituitary

- Hormones released from the anterior pituitary include: thyroid-stimulating hormone, prolactin, adrenocorticotropic hormone, growth hormone, follicle-stimulating hormone, luteinizing hormone, and melanocyte-stimulating hormone.
- Regulatory hormones from the hypothalamus travel to the anterior pituitary through the hypothalamo-hypophyseal portal system.

20.3b Posterior Pituitary

- The posterior pituitary houses axon endings from some hypothalamic neurons that produce antidiuretic hormone and oxytocin.

20.4 Thyroid Gland

- The thyroid gland, located immediately inferior to the thyroid cartilage of the larynx, is composed of two lateral lobes connected medially by a narrow isthmus.

20.4a Synthesis of Thyroid Hormone by Thyroid Follicles

- Thyroid follicles are fluid-filled spheres within the thyroid gland; follicle cells synthesize thyroglobulin and store it within the colloid.
- Thyroid-stimulating hormone from the anterior pituitary stimulates follicle cells to synthesize and release thyroid hormone.

20.4b Thyroid Gland–Pituitary Gland Negative Feedback

- A stimulus, such as low body temperature, causes thyroid hormone release. Thyroid hormone increases cellular metabolism at the target cells. Both the released thyroid hormone and the effects it has on target cells block further release of thyroid hormone.

20.4c Parafollicular Cells

- The parafollicular cells produce calcitonin to help lower calcium ion concentrations in blood.

20.5 Parathyroid Glands

- Four small, nodular parathyroid glands are embedded in the posterior surface of the thyroid gland; they secrete parathyroid hormone (PTH) in response to decreased levels of calcium ions within body fluids.
- PTH secretion causes increased osteoclast activity, reduced loss of calcium in the urine, and increased calcium absorption in the intestine.

20.6 Adrenal Glands

- Adrenal glands are located along the superior border of each kidney. Each adrenal gland has a peripheral cortex and a medulla core within its capsule.

20.6a Adrenal Cortex

- The adrenal cortex synthesizes and secretes steroid hormones collectively called corticosteroids: (1) mineralocorticoids, principally aldosterone; (2) glucocorticoids, primarily cortisol and corticosterone; and (3) relatively minor concentrations of gonadocorticoids.

20.6b Adrenal Medulla

- The adrenal medulla is composed of groups of chromaffin cells that secrete either epinephrine or norepinephrine.

20.7 Pancreas

- The pancreas is a mixed gland with both exocrine and endocrine functions.
- Endocrine cells form clusters called pancreatic islets, which are composed of four cell types: Alpha cells secrete glucagon, beta cells produce insulin, delta cells produce somatostatin, and F cells secrete pancreatic polypeptide.

20.8 Pineal Gland and Thymus

- The pineal gland has secretory cells called pinealocytes that synthesize melatonin.
- The thymus, located in the mediastinum, produces several hormones called thymosins.

20.9 Endocrine Functions of the Kidneys, Heart, Gastrointestinal Tract, and Gonads

20.9a Kidneys

- Endocrine cells in the kidneys regulate some homeostatic activities by secreting calcitriol, erythropoietin, and renin.

20.9b Heart

- Modified cardiac muscle cells secrete the hormone atrial natriuretic peptide, which causes both water and sodium loss from the kidneys.

20.9c Gastrointestinal Tract

- Hormones secreted by endocrine cells in the stomach and small intestine promote activity during digestion.

20.9d Gonads

- Ovaries synthesize and secrete estrogen and progesterone; testes produce androgens, primarily testosterone.

20.10 Aging and the Endocrine System	■ Usually, the secretory activity of endocrine glands decreases with age, especially the production and activities of GH and estrogen.
20.11 Development of the Endocrine System	■ Organs of the endocrine system develop individually at different times during the embryonic and fetal stages. **20.11a Adrenal Glands** ■ The adrenal cortex is derived from intermediate mesoderm, and the adrenal medulla develops from neural crest cells, beginning early in the second month. **20.11b Pituitary Gland** ■ The anterior pituitary develops as an outpocketing of the ectoderm from the stomodeum, whereas the posterior pituitary develops as a bud from the developing hypothalamus. **20.11c Thyroid Gland** ■ The thyroid begins to form from endoderm of the primitive tongue at the end of the fourth week of development.

Challenge Yourself

Actively write or type your answers in a separate document to reinforce your learning, before checking your answers.

Multiple Choice

Select the best answer from the four choices provided.

1. Retention of water from the kidney occurs as a result of the production and release of which hormone?
   a. epinephrine
   b. thyroid hormone
   c. antidiuretic hormone
   d. glucocorticoid
2. What occurs when glucose levels in the blood are elevated?
   a. glucagon is released
   b. insulin is released
   c. thyroid hormone is released
   d. aldosterone is released
3. Which of the following is a tropic hormone?
   a. glucagon
   b. epinephrine
   c. melatonin
   d. growth hormone
4. Follicle-stimulating hormone stimulates the production of which of the following?
   a. steroids in the adrenal cortex
   b. gametes (sperm and oocytes) in males and females
   c. hormones in parafollicular cells of the thyroid gland
   d. melanin in melanocytes
5. Which hormone is synthesized by cells in the posterior pituitary gland?
   a. adrenocorticotropic hormone
   b. growth hormone
   c. luteinizing hormone
   d. antidiuretic hormone
6. What is the function of glucocorticoids?
   a. maintain Na^+ levels
   b. develop the circadian rhythm
   c. lower calcium levels in the blood
   d. elevate blood glucose levels during periods of stress
7. Which hormone is antagonistic to parathyroid hormone?
   a. thyroid hormone
   b. insulin
   c. calcitonin
   d. norepinephrine
8. Parathyroid hormone is released from the parathyroid gland when blood levels of which ion fall?
   a. sodium
   b. calcium
   c. potassium
   d. iodine
9. What stimulates secretion of epinephrine and norepinephrine from the adrenal medulla?
   a. adrenocorticotropic hormone
   b. increased levels of growth hormone
   c. sympathetic nerve innervation
   d. increased levels of glucose in body fluids
10. What hormone is released from the kidneys?
    a. follicle-stimulating hormone
    b. erythropoietin
    c. glucagon
    d. growth hormone

Content Review

1. Describe the relationship between hormones and target organs.
2. Identify the three chemical classes of hormones, and give an example of each.
3. Explain how the hypothalamus regulates and controls endocrine system function.
4. Describe the structure of the hypothalamo-hypophyseal portal system, and briefly discuss the advantage of the structural arrangement.
5. What seven hormones are released by the anterior pituitary, what target organs do they affect, and what are the functions of these hormones?
6. What is the function of calcitonin, and under what conditions might the body release it?
7. What are the consequences of insufficient parathyroid hormone (PTH) secretion?
8. Describe the structure of the adrenal cortex. What hormones are secreted in each region?
9. Identify the cell types of the pancreatic islets and the hormones secreted by each type.
10. Explain why the kidneys, heart, GI tract, and gonads are considered part of the endocrine system.

Developing Critical Reasoning

1. The TV news reports that children and teenagers today are heavier than ever and that these populations are at increased risk for type 2 diabetes. Your father asks, "Isn't type 2 diabetes called adult-onset diabetes? If so, then why are children at risk?" How would you answer your father? Compare and contrast type 1 and type 2 diabetes, and discuss how the terms "adult-onset diabetes" and "juvenile diabetes" may no longer be appropriate.
2. Susan is a 35-year-old mother of two who works as an admissions officer at the university. Lately she has been extremely lethargic, sleeps for long periods of time, and feels mentally slow. Additionally, she feels cold most of the time and exhibits muscular weakness. What tests should be performed, and what problem should her physician suspect?
3. Explain why there are two systems of communication in the body that use chemical messengers—the nervous system and the endocrine system. What is the advantage to having both?

Answers to "What Do You Think?"

1. Damage to the hypothalamus could affect its secretion of oxytocin and antidiuretic hormone. Also, the hypothalamus might not be able to properly release its regulating hormones, so anterior pituitary function could be adversely affected. Finally, because the hypothalamus oversees the autonomic nervous system, adrenal medulla function (which is controlled by sympathetic innervation) might be affected as well.
2. Iodine is needed for normal thyroid hormone production. Without adequate dietary levels of iodine, an individual is at risk for developing a goiter (an enlarged thyroid gland). In the United States, iodine is added to most store-bought salt to ensure that we have adequate dietary levels of iodine.
3. Epinephrine is a treatment for anaphylactic shock, an immediate allergic reaction in which the blood vessels dilate and the airways constrict. Blood pressure drops, and breathing becomes difficult. Epinephrine counteracts these effects by constricting the blood vessels (and thereby raising blood pressure) and opening the airways. People who are extremely allergic may die if not treated promptly.

Design Element: Pencil Icon: Slavojub Pantelic/Shutterstock

Cardiovascular System

CARDIOVASCULAR SYSTEM

Blood 21

Outline

Anatomy & Physiology Revealed 4.0

MODULE 9: CARDIOVASCULAR SYSTEM

Within our bodies is a connective tissue so valuable that donating a portion of it to someone else can save that person's life. This tissue regenerates itself continuously and is responsible for transporting the gases, nutrients, and hormones our bodies need for proper functioning. Losing too much of this tissue can kill us, and yet it is something we frequently take for granted.

This essential connective tissue is blood. Blood is considered a fluid connective tissue because it contains cells, a liquid ground substance (called plasma), and dissolved proteins. In this chapter, we describe the components of blood, its functions, and how the body produces the various types of blood components.

21.1 General Composition and Functions of Blood

✓ Learning Objectives

1. List and describe the basic components of blood.
2. Explain how blood functions in transport, regulation, and protection.

Blood is a type of fluid connective tissue (see section 4.2d). Blood is about four times more viscous than water, meaning that blood is thicker and more stickier or gluey. The temperature of blood is about 1°C higher than measured body temperature; thus, if your body temperature is 37°C, your blood temperature is about 38°C.

21.1a Components of Blood

Whole blood can be separated into its liquid and cellular components by using a machine called a **centrifuge,** as shown in **figure 21.1.**

Figure 21.1 shows the three components separated by centrifugation, from bottom to top in the test tube:

- **Erythrocytes** (ĕ-rith′r ō-sīt; *erythros* = red, *kyte* = cell), sometimes called *red blood cells,* form the lower layer of the centrifuged blood. They typically average about 44% of a blood sample.
- A **buffy coat** makes up the middle layer. This thin, slightly gray-white layer is composed of cells called **leukocytes** (or *white blood cells*) and cell fragments called **platelets.** The buffy coat forms less than 1% of a blood sample.

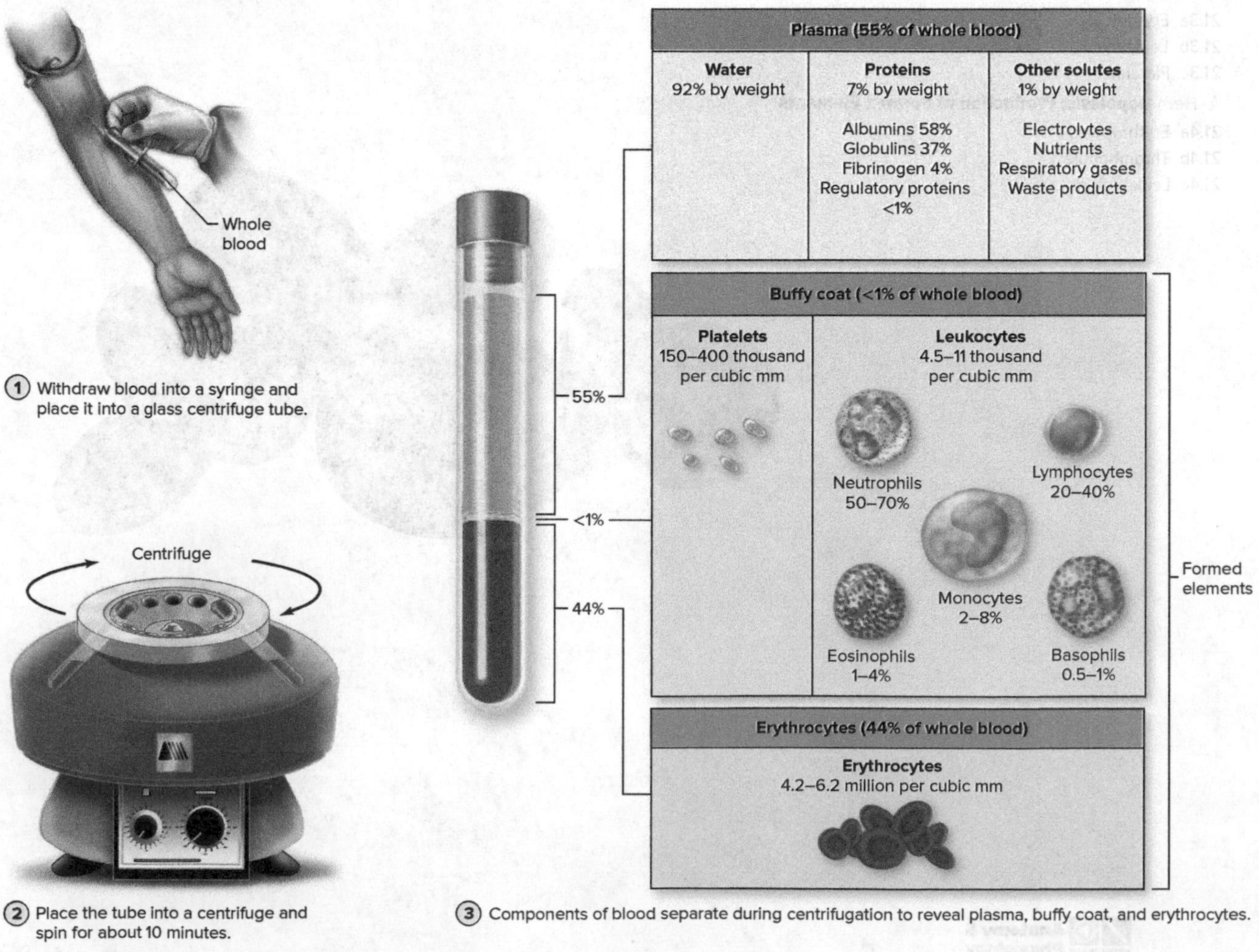
Whole blood
1 Withdraw blood into a syringe and place it into a glass centrifuge tube.
Centrifuge
2 Place the tube into a centrifuge and spin for about 10 minutes.
55%
<1%
44%
Plasma (55% of whole blood)
Water
92% by weight
Proteins
7% by weight
Albumins 58%
Globulins 37%
Fibrinogen 4%
Regulatory proteins <1%
Other solutes
1% by weight
Electrolytes
Nutrients
Respiratory gases
Waste products
Buffy coat (<1% of whole blood)
Platelets
150–400 thousand per cubic mm
Leukocytes
4.5–11 thousand per cubic mm
Neutrophils 50–70%
Lymphocytes 20–40%
Monocytes 2–8%
Eosinophils 1–4%
Basophils 0.5–1%
Formed elements
Erythrocytes (44% of whole blood)
Erythrocytes
4.2–6.2 million per cubic mm
3 Components of blood separate during centrifugation to reveal plasma, buffy coat, and erythrocytes.

Figure 21.1

Whole Blood Separation and Composition. Whole blood contains plasma (average is about 55%) and formed elements. The percentages presented in this figure are average numbers of cells, and the numbers for components of the buffy coat represent average ranges. A cubic millimeter of blood is equivalent to a microliter (μL).

- **Plasma** is a straw-colored liquid that lies above the buffy coat in the centrifuge tube; it generally makes up about 55% of blood.

Collectively, the erythrocytes and the components of the buffy coat (i.e., the leukocytes and platelets) are called the **formed elements.**

It is best to refer to these structures as formed elements, rather than cells, because platelets are merely fragments broken off from a larger cell. The formed elements, together with the liquid plasma, compose whole blood (the substance we most commonly refer to simply as "blood").

WHAT DO YOU THINK?

1. If your body becomes dehydrated, does the plasma percentage in whole blood increase or decrease?

21.1b Functions of Blood

Blood performs a variety of important functions related to transportation, regulation, and protection.

Transportation

Blood transports numerous elements and compounds throughout the body. For example, erythrocytes and plasma carry oxygen from the lungs to body cells and then transport the carbon dioxide produced by the cells back to the lungs to diffuse from the body (see section 25.1a). Blood plasma transports nutrients that have been absorbed from the GI tract (see section 26.1a). Plasma also transports hormones secreted by the endocrine glands (see section 20.1). Finally, plasma carries some waste products from the cells to organs such as the kidneys, where these waste products are removed (see section 27.1).

Regulation

Blood regulates many body functions including body temperature. Plasma absorbs and distributes heat throughout the body. If the body needs to be cooled, the blood vessels in the dermis dilate and dissipate the excess heat through the integument. Conversely, when the body needs to conserve heat, the dermal blood vessels constrict, and the warm blood is shunted to deeper blood vessels in the body (see section 5.1b).

Blood also helps regulate pH levels in the body's tissues. The term **pH** is a measure of how acidic or alkaline a fluid is. A neutral pH (neither acidic nor alkaline fluid, such as water) is measured at exactly 7, whereas **acidic** fluids (e.g., orange juice) are between 0 and 7, and **alkaline** fluids (e.g., milk) are between 7 and 14. Blood plasma contains compounds and ions that may be distributed to the fluid bathing cells within the tissues (interstitial fluid) to help maintain normal tissue pH. In addition, blood plasma pH is continuously regulated to try to maintain a value between 7.35 and 7.45 (slightly alkaline), which is the pH level required for normal functioning of all body cells. If the blood pH falls much below 7.35, the condition called **acidosis** results, and depresses the central nervous system; coma and death could occur. If the blood pH rises much above 7.45, **alkalosis** results, characterized by a hyperexcited nervous system and convulsions.

Blood maintains normal fluid levels in the cardiovascular system. A constant exchange of fluid takes place between the blood plasma and the interstitial fluid. If too much fluid is absorbed into the blood, high blood pressure results. Yet if too much fluid leaves the blood plasma and enters the interstitial fluid, blood pressure drops to unhealthy levels, and the tissues swell with excess fluid. To maintain a balance of fluid between the blood and the interstitial fluid, blood contains molecules (such as salts and some proteins) to prevent excess fluid loss from the plasma.

Protection

Leukocytes help guard against infection by mounting an immune response if a pathogen or an **antigen** (an'ti-jen; *anti* = opposite, *gen* = producing) (a substance perceived as foreign to the body) is found. **Antibodies** (an'tē-bod'ē; *body* = main part), which are molecules that can bind to antigens until the immune system destroys or removes the antigen, are transported in plasma. In addition, platelets and plasma proteins protect the body against blood loss by forming blood clots.

WHAT DID YOU LEARN?

1. What are the percentages of plasma and formed elements in the blood? Of the formed elements, what percentages are erythrocytes, leukocytes, and platelets?
2. What are the three main ways blood helps with regulation?

21.2 Blood Plasma

✓ **Learning Objective**

3. List and describe the components of plasma.

Blood plasma is a complex mixture of water, proteins, and other solutes (**table 21.1**). When the clotting proteins are removed from plasma, the remaining fluid is termed **serum** (sē'rum; whey).

Water is the most abundant compound in plasma, making up about 92% of plasma's total volume. Water facilitates the transport of materials in the plasma. The next most abundant compounds in plasma are the plasma proteins.

21.2a Plasma Proteins

Plasma proteins make up about 7% of the plasma (see figure 21.1). Measured amounts of plasma proteins usually range between 6 and 8 grams of protein in a volume of 100 milliliters of blood (referred to as grams per deciliter [g/dL]). The plasma proteins include albumins, globulins, fibrinogen, and regulatory proteins. All of these proteins buffer against pH changes, and so they regulate blood pH. Each protein also has additional specific functions.

Albumins (al-bū'min; *albumen* = white of egg) are the smallest and most abundant of the plasma proteins, making up about 58% of total plasma proteins. These proteins regulate water movement between the blood and interstitial fluid by providing some of the plasma solutes to drive osmosis. Secondarily, albumins act as transport proteins that carry ions, hormones, and some lipids in the blood.

Globulins (glob'y ū-lin; *globules* = globule) are the second-largest group of plasma proteins, forming about 37% of all plasma proteins. The smaller **alpha-globulins** and the larger **beta-globulins** primarily bind, support, and protect certain water-insoluble (hydrophobic) molecules, hormones, and ions. **Gamma-globulins,** also called *immunoglobulins* or antibodies, are soluble proteins produced by some of our immune cells to protect the body against pathogens that may cause disease.

Fibrinogen (fī-brin' ō-jen; *fibra* = fiber) makes up about 4% of all plasma proteins. Fibrinogen is responsible for blood clot formation. Following trauma to the walls of blood vessels, fibrinogen is converted into long, insoluble strands of **fibrin,** which helps form a blood clot.

Regulatory proteins form a very minor class of plasma proteins (less than 1% of total plasma proteins). These proteins include enzymes (proteins that accelerate chemical reactions) and proenzymes (inactive precursors of enzymes).

21.2b Other Solutes in Plasma

In addition to proteins, plasma contains a variety of other solutes, including electrolytes (such as sodium, potassium, and chloride ions), nutrients, respiratory gases (oxygen and carbon dioxide), some hormones, and waste products. These solutes make up less than 1% of blood plasma. The levels of these solutes will vary, depending on

Table 21.1 Composition of Blood Plasma

Plasma Component (percentage of plasma)	Functions
Water (~92% of plasma)	The solvent in which formed elements are suspended and proteins and solutes are dissolved
PLASMA PROTEINS (~7% OF PLASMA): All proteins serve to buffer against pH changes	
Albumin (~58% of plasma proteins)	Exerts osmotic force to retain fluid within the blood Contributes to blood's viscosity Responsible for some fatty acid and hormone transport
Globulins (~37% of plasma proteins)	Alpha-globulins transport lipids and some metal ions Beta-globulins transport iron ions and lipids in blood Gamma-globulins are antibodies that immobilize pathogens
Fibrinogen (~4% of plasma proteins)	Participates in blood coagulation (clotting)
Regulatory proteins (<1% of plasma proteins)	Consists of enzymes (which serve to speed up a chemical reaction) and proenzymes (the precursors of enzymes)
OTHER SOLUTES (~1% OF BLOOD PLASMA)	
Electrolytes (e.g., sodium, potassium, calcium, chloride, iron, bicarbonate, and hydrogen)	Help establish and maintain membrane potentials, maintain pH balance, and regulate osmosis (control of the percentages of water and salt in the blood)
Hormones (e.g., insulin, thyroid hormone, testosterone, estrogen)	Chemical messengers that travel in the blood and act on target cells in the body.
Nutrients (e.g., amino acids, glucose, cholesterol, vitamins, fatty acids)	Energy source; precursor for synthesizing other molecules
Respiratory gases (oxygen and carbon dioxide dissolved in plasma, and carbon dioxide carried as bicarbonate in plasma)	Oxygen is needed for aerobic cellular respiration; carbon dioxide is a waste product produced by cells during this process
Wastes (breakdown products of metabolism) (e.g., lactic acid, creatinine, urea, bilirubin, ammonia)	Serve no function in plasma; rather, wastes merely are being transported to the liver and kidneys to be removed from the blood

factors such as whether the blood is oxygenated or deoxygenated, and whether selected hormones are secreted into the blood.

21.2c Differences Between Plasma and Interstitial Fluid

Plasma is a type of *extracellular fluid (ECF)*, meaning it is a body fluid found outside cells. Plasma and interstitial fluid (the type of extracellular fluid that surrounds the outside of cells) have similar concentrations of most dissolved products, nutrients, and electrolytes, with the exception of the plasma proteins. The concentration of dissolved oxygen is higher in plasma than in interstitial fluid, because the cells take up and use the oxygen from the interstitial fluid during energy production. This difference in concentration ensures that oxygen will continue to diffuse from blood into the interstitial fluid. Similarly, the concentration of carbon dioxide is lower in blood than in interstitial fluid because cells produce carbon dioxide during energy production. This difference in concentration ensures that carbon dioxide will readily diffuse from the interstitial fluid into the blood, where it will be transported to the lungs and leave the body.

WHAT DID YOU LEARN?

3. What are the components of plasma?
4. List the four types of plasma proteins from most abundant to least abundant, and describe the primary functions of each.

21.3 Formed Elements in the Blood

✓Learning Objectives

4. Describe the structural and functional characteristics of erythrocytes.
5. Define hematocrit, and compare how hematocrit values may vary based on a person's age or sex.
6. Explain the erythrocyte life cycle, including the location to which erythrocyte components are recycled.
7. Explain the significance of the ABO and Rh blood groups.
8. Identify and describe the types of leukocytes and explain their functions.
9. Describe the structure and formation of platelets, and explain their role in blood clotting.

The formed elements have three components:

- Erythrocytes make up more than 99% of formed elements. Their primary function is to transport respiratory gases in the blood.
- Leukocytes make up less than 0.01% of formed elements. All leukocytes contribute to mounting an immune response and defending the body against pathogens.
- Platelets make up less than 1% of formed elements and help with blood clotting.

Table 21.2 summarizes the characteristics of the formed elements.

The percentage of the volume of all formed elements in the blood is called the **hematocrit** (hē′mat′ ō-krit, hem′ă-; *hemato* = blood, *krino* = to separate). This medical dictionary definition differs from the clinical definition, which equates the hematocrit to the percentage volume of erythrocytes only. In practice, the true hematocrit and the clinical hematocrit are virtually the same.

Table 21.2 Characteristics of the Formed Elements

Formed Element	Size (diameter)	Function	Life Span	Density (average number per mm³ of blood = µL)
Erythrocytes	7.5 µm	Transport oxygen and carbon dioxide	~120 days	Females: ~4.8 million Males: ~5.4 million
Leukocytes	1.5 to 3 times larger than an erythrocyte; 11.25–22.5 µm	Initiate immune response; defend against harmful substances	Varies from 12 hours (neutrophil) to years (lymphocyte)	4500–11,000
Platelets	Less than 1/4 the size of an erythrocyte; ~2 µm	Participate in blood clotting	~8–10 days	150,000–400,000

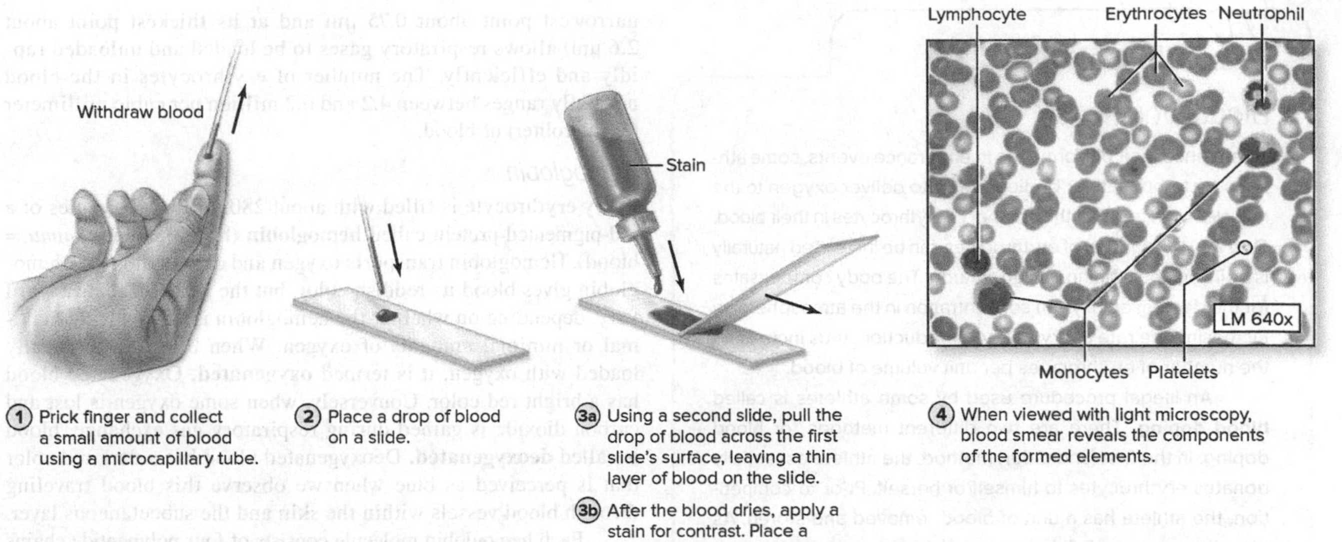
Withdraw blood
Stain
Lymphocyte
Erythrocytes
Neutrophil
LM 640x
Monocytes
Platelets
1 Prick finger and collect a small amount of blood using a microcapillary tube.
2 Place a drop of blood on a slide.
3a Using a second slide, pull the drop of blood across the first slide's surface, leaving a thin layer of blood on the slide.
3b After the blood dries, apply a stain for contrast. Place a coverslip on top.
4 When viewed with light microscopy, blood smear reveals the components of the formed elements.

Figure 21.2
Preparing a Blood Smear. APR
(4) ©McGraw-Hill Education/Al Telser, photographer

Hematocrit values vary somewhat and are dependent upon the age and sex of the individual. A very young child's hematocrit may vary from 30% to 60%, and that range will narrow to 35% to 50% as the child becomes older. Adults who produce significant levels of testosterone (typically, males) tend to have a hematocrit ranging between 42% and 56%, whereas adults who do not have high levels of testosterone (typically, females) hematocrits range from 38% to 46%. Testosterone influences hematocrit by stimulating the kidney to produce the hormone erythropoietin (EPO), which promotes erythrocyte production (see section 20.9a). An elevated hematocrit may indicate that the patient is either dehydrated or participating in blood doping (see Clinical View 21.1: "Blood Doping" in section 21.3a), whereas a lowered hematocrit often suggests the patient is suffering from anemia (see Clinical View 21.2: "Anemia" in section 21.3a).

All of the components of the formed elements can be viewed by preparing a **blood smear.** A blood smear and the steps to produce a smear are shown in **figure 21.2**. In the blood smear micrograph, notice the abundance of erythrocytes versus the smaller numbers of leukocytes and platelets.

21.3a Erythrocytes

Although erythrocytes are commonly referred to as red blood cells, or RBCs, the term "cell" is a misnomer because mature erythrocytes lack nuclei and organelles. It is more appropriate to call it a formed element.

Erythrocytes transport oxygen and carbon dioxide between the tissues and the lungs (see section 25.1a). Their structure enables them to carry these respiratory gases proficiently. A normal, mature erythrocyte is very small, with a diameter of about 7.5 micrometers (μm) (**figure 21.3**). Its unique, biconcave disc structure (at its

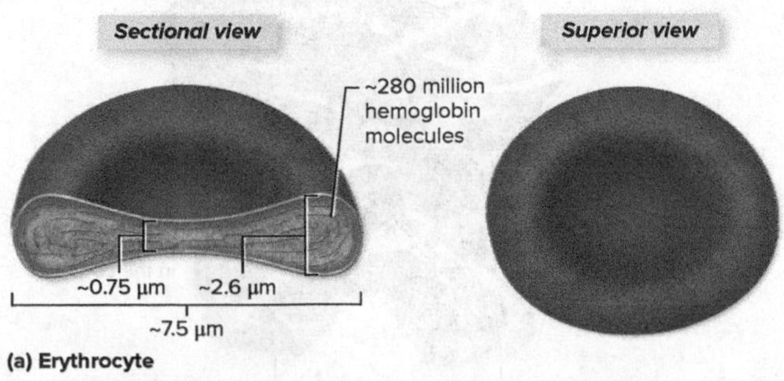
Sectional view
Superior view
~280 million hemoglobin molecules
~0.75 μm
~2.6 μm
~7.5 μm
(a) Erythrocyte

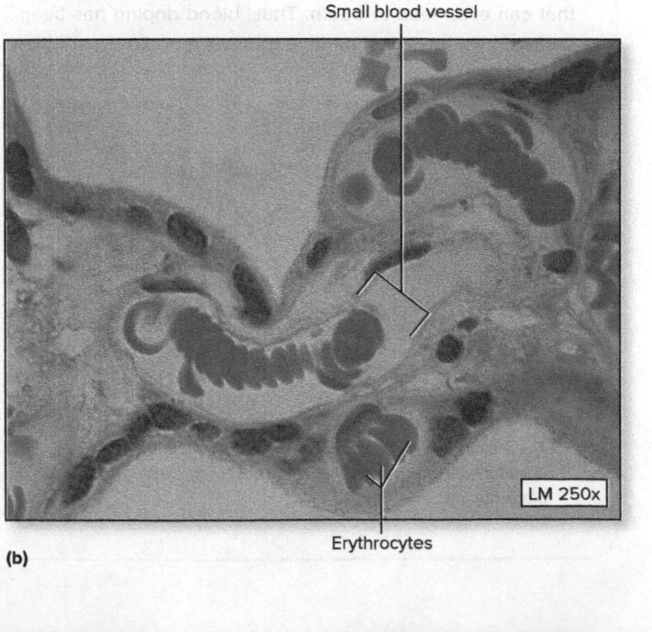
Small blood vessel
LM 250x
Erythrocytes
(b)

Figure 21.3
Erythrocyte Structure. *(a)* An erythrocyte has the gross structure of a biconcave disc, as shown here in sectional and superior views. *(b)* LM of erythrocytes shows their three-dimensional structure as they travel through a small blood vessel. APR
(b) ©Ed Reschke

Clinical View 21.1

Blood Doping

To enhance their performance in endurance events, some athletes try to boost their bodies' ability to deliver oxygen to the muscles by increasing the number of erythrocytes in their blood. One way the number of erythrocytes can be increased naturally is by living and training at high altitude. The body compensates for the decreased oxygen concentration in the atmosphere by increasing the rate of erythrocyte production, thus increasing the number of erythrocytes per unit volume of blood.

An illegal procedure used by some athletes is called **blood doping.** There are two different methods for blood doping. In the first (and older) method, the athlete essentially donates erythrocytes to himself or herself. Prior to competition, the athlete has a unit of blood removed and stored. As the kidneys detect the decreased blood oxygen, the hormone erythropoietin (EPO) is released by the kidneys (see section 20.9a) and the bone marrow responds by increasing production of erythrocytes to make up for the ones just removed. A few days before the competition, the erythrocytes from the donated unit are transfused back into the athlete's body. The increased number of erythrocytes increases the amount of oxygen transported in the blood and is thought to favorably affect muscle performance, thereby improving athletic performance. The second method of blood doping has occurred with the development of pharmaceutical EPO, which is used to treat anemia. In this method of blood doping, an athlete is injected with pharmaceutical EPO to further increase erythrocyte levels.

Potentially deadly dangers are inherent in blood doping. By increasing the number of erythrocytes per measured volume of blood, blood doping increases the viscosity of the blood. Thus, the heart must work harder to pump this "thicker," more cellular blood. Eventually, temporary athletic success may be overshadowed by permanent cardiovascular damage that can even lead to death. Thus, blood doping has been banned by athletic competition governing bodies.

The reputation of the Tour de France cycling tournament has been tarnished by reports that many past competitors used blood doping.

mike coleman/Alamy Stock Photo

narrowest point about 0.75 μm and at its thickest point about 2.6 μm) allows respiratory gases to be loaded and unloaded rapidly and efficiently. The number of erythrocytes in the blood normally ranges between 4.2 and 6.2 million per cubic millimeter (or microliter) of blood.

Hemoglobin

Every erythrocyte is filled with about 280 million molecules of a red-pigmented protein called **hemoglobin** (hē′mō-glō′bin; *haima* = blood). Hemoglobin transports oxygen and carbon dioxide. Hemoglobin gives blood its reddish color, but the shade of that red will vary, depending on whether the hemoglobin is transporting maximal or minimal amounts of oxygen. When blood is maximally loaded with oxygen, it is termed **oxygenated.** Oxygenated blood has a bright red color. Conversely, when some oxygen is lost and carbon dioxide is gained during respiratory gas exchange, blood is called **deoxygenated.** Deoxygenated blood has a dark red color that is perceived as blue when we observe this blood traveling through blood vessels within the skin and the subcutaneous layer.

Each hemoglobin molecule consists of four polypeptide chains called **globins.** Two of these globins are called **alpha (α) chains,** and the other two, which are slightly different, are called **beta (β) chains (figure 21.4).** These globin chains each contain a nonprotein (or **heme**) group that is in the shape of a ring, with an iron ion (Fe^{2+}) in its center.

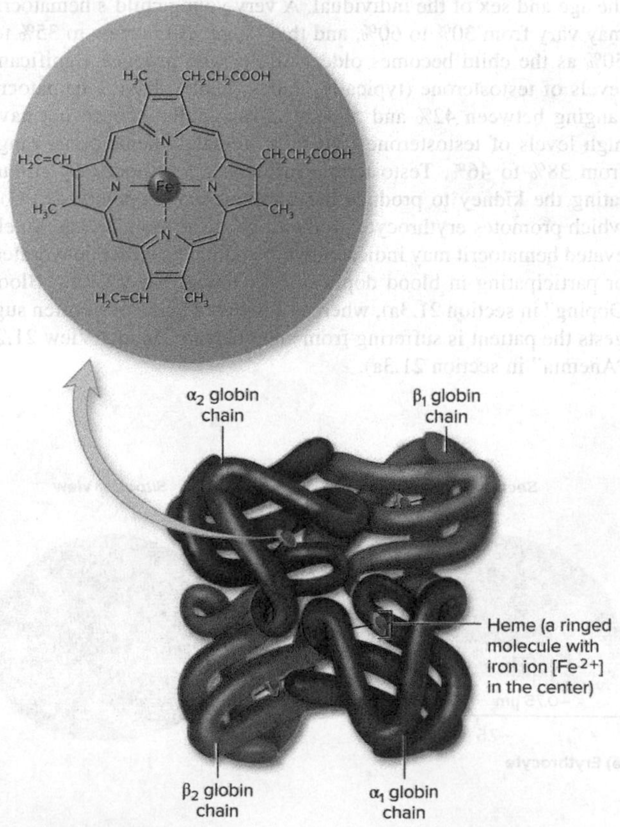

Figure 21.4

Molecular Structure of Hemoglobin. A single molecule of hemoglobin is composed of four protein subunits, called globins, each containing a heme group that holds a single iron ion (Fe^{2+}) in its center. Each hemoglobin molecule transports four oxygen molecules that are weakly attracted to the Fe^{2+}.

Oxygen binds to these iron ions for transport in the blood. Because each molecule of hemoglobin has four rings, each hemoglobin molecule has four iron ions and is capable of binding four molecules of oxygen. The oxygen binding is fairly weak to ensure rapid attachment and detachment of oxygen with hemoglobin. This weak attachment allows oxygen to diffuse between hemoglobin in the erythrocytes and body tissues when there is a difference in oxygen concentration. For example, oxygen is in higher concentration in the lungs compared to the blood, so oxygen diffuses from the lungs into the blood. Conversely, oxygen is in higher concentration in the blood compared to the interstitial fluid around body cells, so oxygen diffuses from the blood to the interstitial fluid. Carbon dioxide and the globin molecule (but not the iron ion) have a similar weak attachment relationship for the transport and exchange of carbon dioxide molecules.

Erythrocyte Life Cycle

The absence of both a nucleus and cellular organelles comes at a cost to the erythrocyte by reducing its life span. A mature erythrocyte cannot synthesize proteins to repair itself or replace damaged membrane regions. Aging and the wear-and-tear of circulation through blood vessels cause erythrocytes to become more fragile and less flexible. Therefore, the erythrocyte has a finite life span of about 120 days (**figure 21.5**). Every day, just under 1% of the oldest circulating erythrocytes are removed from circulation. The old erythrocytes are phagocytized in the liver and spleen by cells called macrophages. Some erythrocyte components are stored in other organs for recycling, whereas other components are excreted from the body, as shown in steps 4 and 5 of figure 21.5 and explained here:

- The heme group (minus the iron ion) in hemoglobin is converted first into a green pigment called **biliverdin** (bil′i-ver′din; *bilis* = bile). Biliverdin is eventually converted into a yellow-green pigment called **bilirubin** (bil′i-r ū′bin). Bilirubin is a component of a digestive secretion called *bile,* which is produced by liver cells (see section 26.10a). When bile enters the GI tract, it helps emulsify (break down) fats.
- The iron ion component in hemoglobin is removed and transported by a beta-globulin protein, called **transferrin** (trans-fer′in; *trans* = across, *ferrum* = iron), to the liver where the iron ion is passed to another protein, called **ferritin** (fer′i-tin) for storage. Ferritin is stored in the liver and will be transported to the red bone marrow, as needed, for erythrocyte production.
- Erythrocyte membrane proteins and globin proteins are broken down into free amino acids, some of which the body uses for protein synthesis to make new erythrocytes.

Blood Types

The plasma membrane of an erythrocyte has numerous molecules called **surface antigens** (or *agglutinogens*), that project from the plasma membrane. The most commonly identified group of antigens is the **ABO blood group.** This group has two surface antigens, called

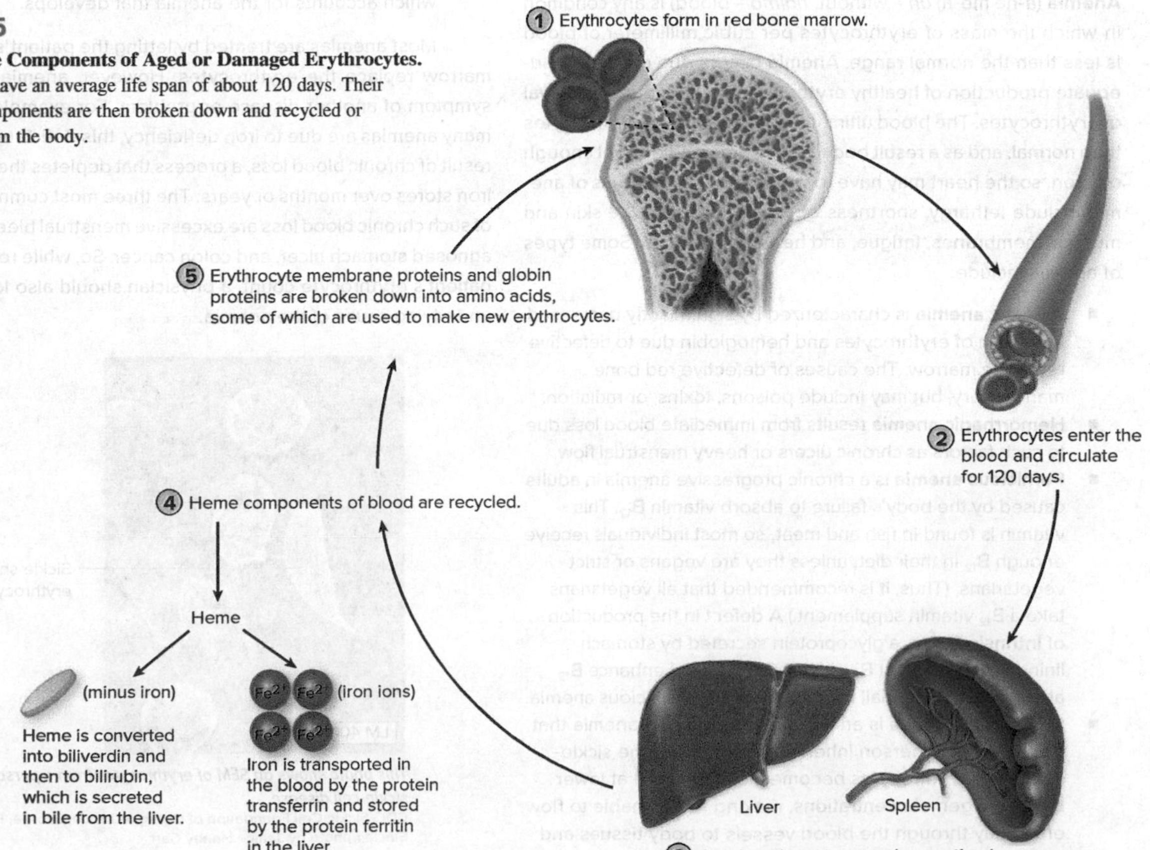

1 Erythrocytes form in red bone marrow.
2 Erythrocytes enter the blood and circulate for 120 days.
3 Aged erythrocytes are phagocytized in the liver and spleen.
Liver
Spleen
4 Heme components of blood are recycled.
5 Erythrocyte membrane proteins and globin proteins are broken down into amino acids, some of which are used to make new erythrocytes.
Heme
(minus iron)
(iron ions)
Heme is converted into biliverdin and then to bilirubin, which is secreted in bile from the liver.
Iron is transported in the blood by the protein transferrin and stored by the protein ferritin in the liver.

Figure 21.5

Recycling the Components of Aged or Damaged Erythrocytes. Erythrocytes have an average life span of about 120 days. Their molecular components are then broken down and recycled or eliminated from the body.

A and B. The presence or absence of either the A and/or B surface antigen on the erythrocyte are the criteria that determine your **ABO blood type,** as shown in **figure 21.6*a*** and listed here:

- **Type A** blood has erythrocytes with surface antigen A only.
- **Type B** blood has erythrocytes with surface antigen B only.
- **Type AB** blood has erythrocytes with both surface antigens A and B.
- **Type O** blood has erythrocytes with neither surface antigen A nor B.

The ABO surface antigens on erythrocytes are accompanied by specific **antibodies** (or *agglutinins*) that travel in the blood plasma. In general, an antibody is a protein that is produced by a leukocyte (specifically, a *B-lymphocyte*) and designed to recognize and attach to a specific antigen it perceives as foreign to the body. The ABO blood group has both **anti-A** and **anti-B antibodies** that react with the surface antigen A and the surface antigen B, respectively. Your blood plasma does not have antibodies that recognize the surface antigens on your erythrocytes. Within the ABO blood group, the following blood types and antibodies are normally associated:

- Type A blood has anti-B antibodies within its blood plasma.
- Type B blood has anti-A antibodies within its blood plasma.
- Type AB blood has *neither* anti-A nor anti-B antibodies within its blood plasma.
- Type O blood has *both* anti-A and anti-B antibodies within its blood plasma.

Blood types become clinically important when a patient needs a blood transfusion. If a person is transfused with blood of an incompatible type, antibodies in the plasma bind to surface antigens of the transfused erythrocytes, and clumps of erythrocytes bind together in a process termed **agglutination** (ă-glū-ti-nā′shŭn; *ad* = to, *gluten* = glue). Clumped erythrocytes can block blood vessels and prevent the normal circulation of blood. Eventually, some or all of the clumped erythrocytes may rupture, a process called **hemolysis** (hē-mol′i-sis; *lysis* = destruction). The release of erythrocyte contents and fragments into the blood often causes further reactions and

Clinical View 21.2

Anemia

Anemia (ă-nē′mē-ă; *an* = without, *haima* = blood) is any condition in which the mass of erythrocytes per cubic millimeter of blood is less than the normal range. Anemia occurs due either to inadequate production of healthy erythrocytes or decreased survival of erythrocytes. The blood ultimately contains fewer erythrocytes than normal, and as a result body tissues are unable to get enough oxygen, so the heart may have to work harder. Symptoms of anemia include lethargy, shortness of breath, pallor of the skin and mucous membranes, fatigue, and heart palpitations. Some types of anemia include:

- **Aplastic anemia** is characterized by significantly decreased formation of erythrocytes and hemoglobin due to defective red bone marrow. The causes of defective red bone marrow vary, but may include poisons, toxins, or radiation.
- **Hemorrhagic anemia** results from immediate blood loss due to such factors as chronic ulcers or heavy menstrual flow.
- **Pernicious anemia** is a chronic progressive anemia in adults caused by the body's failure to absorb vitamin B_{12}. This vitamin is found in fish and meat, so most individuals receive enough B_{12} in their diet, unless they are vegans or strict vegetarians. (Thus, it is recommended that all vegetarians take a B_{12} vitamin supplement.) A defect in the production of **intrinsic factor,** a glycoprotein secreted by stomach lining cells to protect B_{12} in the stomach and enhance B_{12} absorption in the small intestine, leads to pernicious anemia.
- **Sickle-cell disease** is an autosomal recessive anemia that occurs when a person inherits two copies of the sickle-cell gene. Erythrocytes become sickle-shaped at lower blood oxygen concentrations, making them unable to flow efficiently through the blood vessels to body tissues and more prone to destruction (a process called *hemolysis*). These erythrocytes typically survive only 10–20 days, which accounts for the anemia that develops.

Most anemias are treated by letting the patient's own bone marrow replace the erythrocytes. However, anemia is often a symptom of another disease or problem. For example, although many anemias are due to iron deficiency, this deficiency can be a result of chronic blood loss, a process that depletes the body of its iron stores over months or years. The three most common causes of such chronic blood loss are excessive menstrual bleeding, undiagnosed stomach ulcer, and colon cancer. So, while restoring the patient's erythrocyte count, a physician should also look for any underlying cause of the anemia.

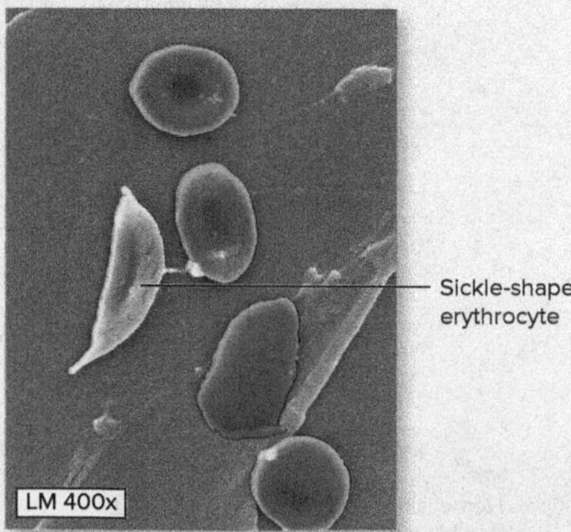
Sickle-shaped erythrocyte
LM 400x

This photo shows an SEM of erythrocytes from a person with sickle-cell disease.
CDC/Sickle Cell Foundation of Georgia: Jackie George, Beverly Sinclair/photo by Janice Haney Carr

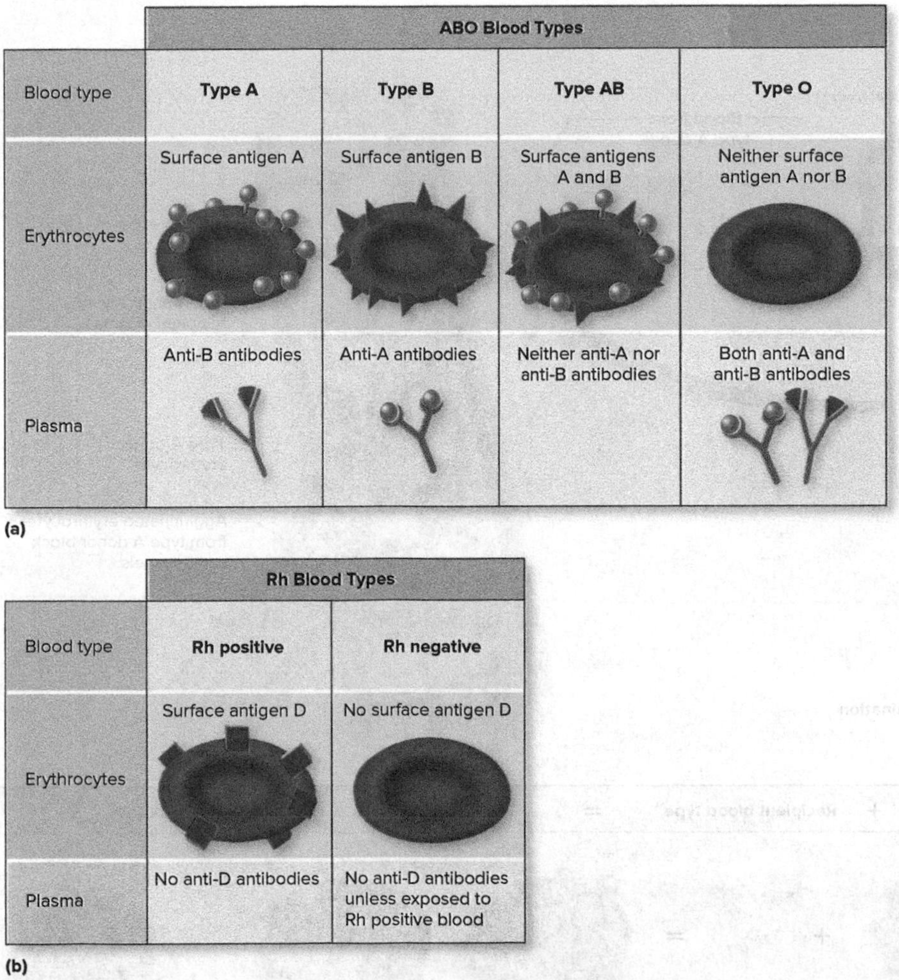

Figure 21.6

ABO Blood Types. The blood type of an individual is determined by the specific antigens exposed on the surface of the erythrocyte membrane. Likewise, plasma contains antibodies that attach to antigens from outside the body. (*a*) ABO blood types. (Note: The antibodies are shown here as already bound to the antigen, to clarify the differences between the different antibodies.) (*b*) Rh blood types.

Learning Strategy 21.1

To remember which ABO blood type is associated with which specific antibody, keep in mind that each blood type has an antibody of a different letter:

- Type A blood does *not* have anti-A antibodies (because anti-A antibodies and type A blood start with the same letter); it has only anti-B antibodies.
- Type B blood does *not* have anti-B antibodies. (It can't have anti-B antibodies, because the B antibodies and type B blood start with the same letter); it has only anti-A antibodies.
- Type AB blood has *both* A and B in its name, so it has no anti-A or anti-B antibodies.
- Type O blood has *neither* an A nor a B in its name, so it has both anti-A and anti-B antibodies.

ultimately may damage organs. Therefore, compatibility between donor and recipient must be determined prior to blood donations and transfusions using an agglutination test **(figure 21.7)**.

WHAT DO YOU THINK?

2 Why is an individual with type O blood sometimes referred to as a "universal donor"? Likewise, why is an individual with type AB blood sometimes referred to as a "universal recipient"?

Another common surface antigen on erythrocyte membranes is part of the Rh blood type. The **Rh blood type** is determined by the presence or absence of the Rh surface antigen, often called either **Rh factor** or **surface antigen D.** When the Rh factor is present, the individual is said to be **Rh positive (Rh$^+$).** Conversely, an individual is termed **Rh negative (Rh$^-$)** when the surface antigen is lacking from the membranes of his or her erythrocytes (see figure 21.6*b*).

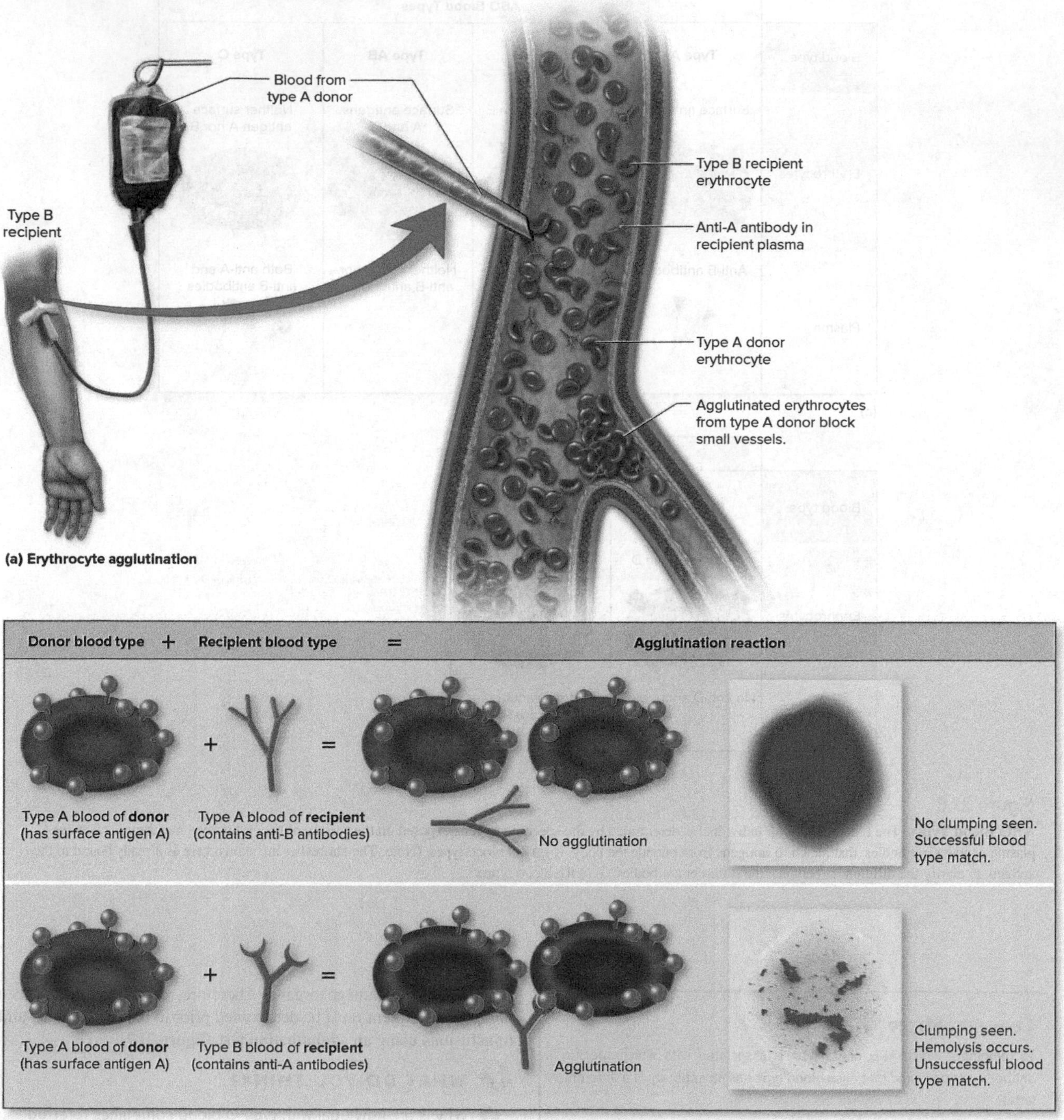
Blood from type A donor
Type B recipient
Type B recipient erythrocyte
Anti-A antibody in recipient plasma
Type A donor erythrocyte
Agglutinated erythrocytes from type A donor block small vessels.
(a) Erythrocyte agglutination
Donor blood type + Recipient blood type = Agglutination reaction
Type A blood of donor (has surface antigen A)
Type A blood of recipient (contains anti-B antibodies)
No agglutination
No clumping seen. Successful blood type match.
Type A blood of donor (has surface antigen A)
Type B blood of recipient (contains anti-A antibodies)
Agglutination
Clumping seen. Hemolysis occurs. Unsuccessful blood type match.
(b) Agglutination test

Figure 21.7

Agglutination Reaction. *(a)* If a person receives mismatched blood, antibodies in the blood plasma bind to their respective surface antigens within the erythrocyte plasma membranes; erythrocytes agglutinate (clump) and may block small blood vessels. (*b*) In a test between plasma and erythrocyte samples, a successful match (no clumping) is compared to an unsuccessful match (clumping).

(b, right top and bottom) Jarun011/iStock/Getty Images

In contrast to the ABO blood group, where antibodies may be found in the blood even without prior exposure to a foreign antigen, antibodies to the Rh factor termed **anti-D antibodies** appear in the blood only when an Rh negative individual is exposed to Rh positive blood. This exposure to Rh positive blood most often occurs as a result of an inappropriate blood transfusion. Therefore, individuals who are Rh positive never exhibit anti-D antibodies, because they possess the Rh antigen on their erythrocytes. Only individuals who are Rh negative can exhibit anti-D antibodies, and that can occur only after exposure to Rh antigens.

The ABO and Rh blood types are usually reported together. For example, types AB and Rh^+ together are reported as AB^+. However, remember that ABO and Rh blood types are independent of each other, and neither of them interacts with or influences the presence or activities of the other group.

WHAT DID YOU LEARN?

5. Why does an erythrocyte lack cellular organelles, and how is this related to its life span?
6. How do transferrin and ferritin participate in recycling erythrocyte components after the cells break down?
7. Should a person with blood type A donate blood to a person with blood type AB? Why or why not?

Clinical View 21.3

Rh Incompatibility and Pregnancy

The potential presence of anti-D antibodies is especially important in pregnant women who are Rh negative and have an Rh positive fetus. An Rh incompatibility may result during the pregnancy if the mother has previously been exposed to Rh positive blood (such as can occur with a previously carried Rh positive fetus, typically at the time of childbirth). As a result of the prior exposure, the mother has anti-D antibodies that may cross the placenta and destroy the fetal erythrocytes, resulting in severe illness or death. The illness that occurs in the newborn is called **hemolytic disease of the newborn (HDN),** or *erythroblastosis fetalis.* The newborn typically presents with *anemia* and *hyperbilirubinemia* (increased bilirubin in the blood) due to erythrocyte destruction. In severe cases, the infant may develop heart failure and must be given a blood transfusion to survive.

Giving a pregnant Rh negative woman special immunoglobulins (e.g., RhoGAM) between weeks 28–32 of her pregnancy and at birth prevents the mother from developing anti-D anitbodies. Specifically, these immunoglobulins bind to fetal erythrocyte surface antigens—and in so doing, prevent the mother's immune system from recognizing Rh antigens and being stimulated to produce anti-D antibodies.

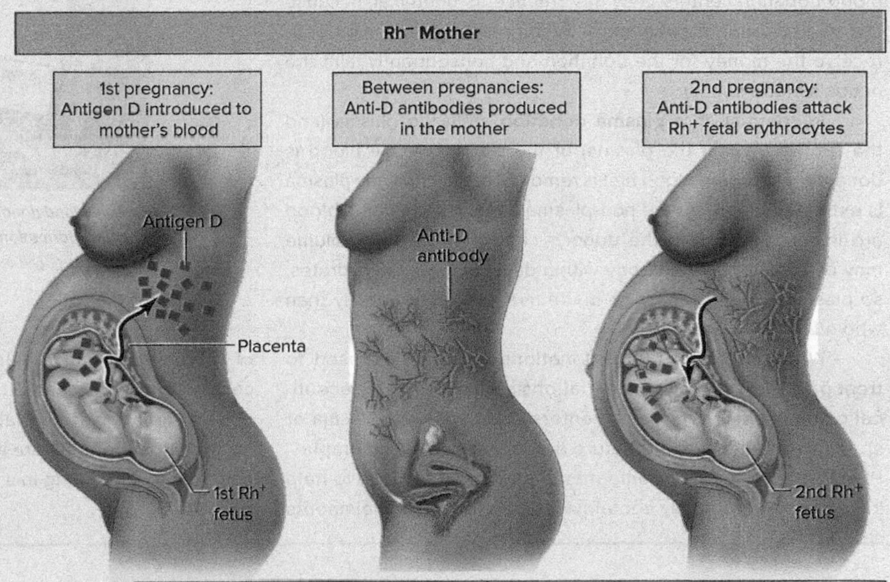
Rh⁻ Mother
1st pregnancy: Antigen D introduced to mother's blood
Between pregnancies: Anti-D antibodies produced in the mother
2nd pregnancy: Anti-D antibodies attack Rh⁺ fetal erythrocytes
Antigen D
Placenta
1st Rh⁺ fetus
Anti-D antibody
2nd Rh⁺ fetus

	Mother Rh Blood Types		Fetus Rh Blood Types	
	Pregnancy #1	Pregnancy #2	Pregnancy #1	Pregnancy #2
Blood type	Rh negative	Rh negative	Rh positive	Rh positive
Erythrocytes	No antigen D	No antigen D	Antigen D	Antigen D
Plasma	No anti-D antibodies	Anti-D antibodies (due to prior exposure)	No anti-D antibodies	No anti-D antibodies Anti-D antibodies from mother cross placenta and attack fetal erythrocytes causing **hemolytic disease of the newborn**

Hemolytic disease of the newborn.

Clinical View 21.4

Whole Blood Versus Plasma Donations: What's the Difference?

A **whole blood donation** is a donation of all the components of blood (i.e., formed elements and plasma) in a single donation visit. Most blood drives to collect whole blood donations are held by nonprofit organizations (such as the American Red Cross). Donations almost always are voluntary, and no cash compensation is given to donors. Whole blood donation is regulated by the Food and Drug Administration (FDA), which requires that any blood collected in a for-profit situation (i.e., where the donor is paid money to donate whole blood) must be labeled as such. Although it is not illegal to pay donors for a whole blood donation, the FDA and blood donation centers view the practice as unethical, because an infected donor may lie about their medical history in order to receive the money for the donation and consequently taint the nation's blood supply.

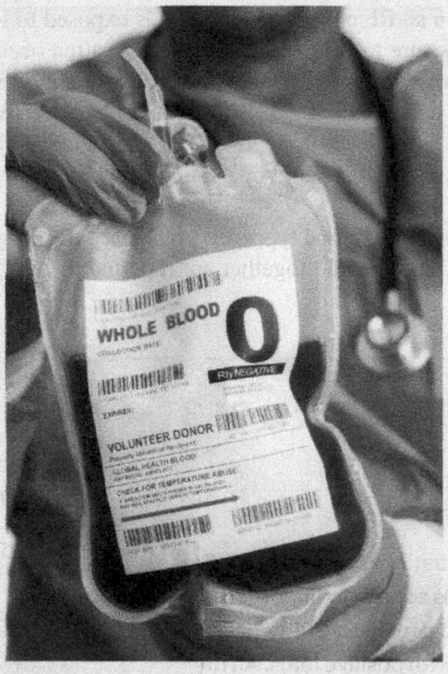

A whole blood donation is packaged with clear labeling information.

DieterMeyrl/iStock/Getty Images

In contrast, in a **plasma donation,** only the plasma (and the proteins within the plasma) of the donor's whole blood is donated. The whole blood first is removed as one unit, the plasma is extracted, and then the non-plasma components of the blood are injected back into the donor's circulation. Plasma volume may be replaced by the body within days as a person hydrates, so plasma donations may be made much more frequently than whole blood donations.

Whereas whole blood donations typically are used to treat patients, most plasma donations are sent to pharmaceutical companies and research centers, which use the plasma or specific proteins to manufacture drugs and test new therapies. Plasma and its protein components may be processed to help kill any pathogens they contain, whereas the formed elements of whole blood would be damaged if subjected to a similar process. Because of these differences, the FDA does not require plasma donations to be labeled if the donors have been paid for their donations. There is a great demand for plasma and its components, resulting in a variety of for-profit plasma donation centers.

21.3b Leukocytes

Leukocytes help initiate an immune response and defend the body against pathogens. Leukocytes are true cells in that they contain a nucleus and cellular organelles. Leukocytes also differ from erythrocytes in that leukocytes are about 1.5 to 3 times larger in diameter and they do not contain hemoglobin. The number of leukocytes in the blood normally ranges between 4500 and 11,000 per cubic millimeter (or microliter) of blood in adults. Infants normally have a higher number than children or adults.

Abnormal numbers of leukocytes result from various pathologic conditions. For example, a reduced number of leukocytes causes a serious disorder called **leukopenia** (lū′kō-pē′nē-ă; *penia* = poverty). This condition may result from viral or bacterial infection, certain types of leukemia (see Clinical View 21.5: "Leukemia" in section 21.3c.), or toxins that damage the red bone marrow. Conversely, **leukocytosis** (lū′kō-sī-tō′sis) results from an elevated leukocyte count (greater than 11,000 per cubic millimeter of blood) and is often indicative of infection, inflammatory reaction, or extreme physiologic stress.

Leukocytes are motile and remarkably flexible. In fact, most leukocytes function in body tissues (as opposed to the blood). Leukocytes enter the tissue by a process called **diapedesis** (dī′ ĕ-dē′sis; *dia* = through, *pedesis* = a leaping), whereby they leave the vessel by squeezing between the endothelial cells of the blood vessel wall. **Chemotaxis** (kē′mo-tak′sis; *taxis* = orderly arrangement) is a process whereby leukocytes are attracted to the site of infection by molecules released by damaged cells, dead cells, mast cells, or invading pathogens.

The five types of leukocytes are divided into two distinguishable classes—granulocytes and agranulocytes—based upon the presence or absence of visible organelles termed granules when stained **(table 21.3)**. When a normal blood smear is observed using light microscopy (see figure 21.2), erythrocytes outnumber leukocytes by 500- to 1000-fold.

Granulocytes

Granulocytes (gran′yū-lō-sīt; *granulum* = small grain) have granules in their cytoplasm that are clearly visible using light microscopy. When a blood smear is stained to provide contrast, three types of granulocytes can be distinguished: neutrophils, eosinophils, and basophils.

Table 21.3 Leukocytes

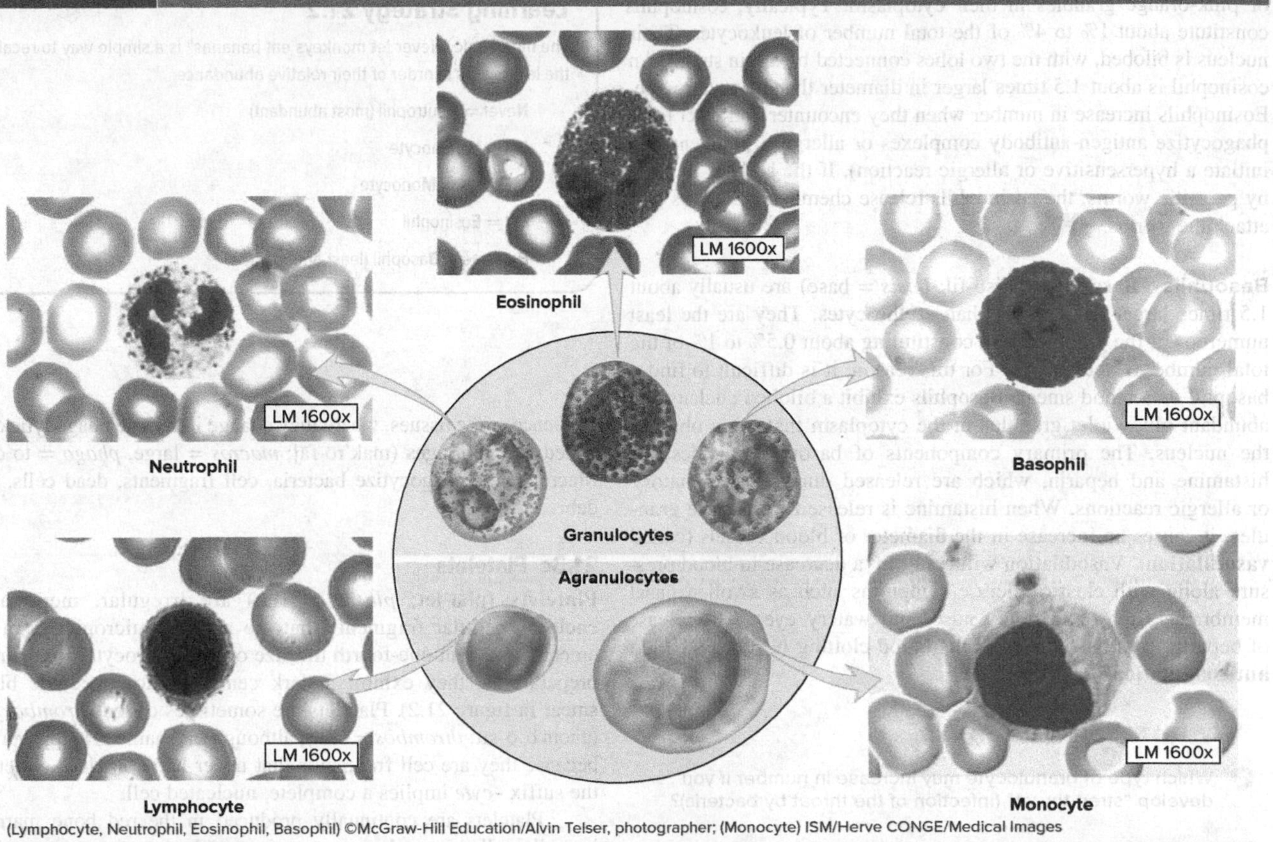
LM 1600x
Eosinophil
LM 1600x
Neutrophil
LM 1600x
Basophil
Granulocytes
Agranulocytes
LM 1600x
Lymphocyte
LM 1600x
Monocyte

(Lymphocyte, Neutrophil, Eosinophil, Basophil) ©McGraw-Hill Education/Alvin Telser, photographer; (Monocyte) ISM/Herve CONGE/Medical Images

Type	Characteristics	Functions	Approximate %
GRANULOCYTES			
Neutrophils	Nucleus is multilobed (as many as five lobes) Cytoplasm contains neutral or pale, distinct granules (when stained)	Phagocytize pathogens, especially bacteria Release enzymes that target pathogens	50–70% of total leukocytes (1800–7800 cells per microliter)
Eosinophils	Nucleus is bilobed Cytoplasm contains reddish or pink-orange granules (when stained)	Phagocytize antigen-antibody complexes and allergens Release chemical mediators to destroy parasitic worms	1–4% of total leukocytes (100–400 cells per microliter)
Basophils	Nucleus is bilobed Cytoplasm contains deep blue-violet granules (when stained)	Release histamine (vasodilator) and heparin (anticoagulant) during inflammatory or allergic reactions	0.5–1% of total leukocytes (20–50 cells per microliter)
AGRANULOCYTES			
Lymphocytes	Round or slightly indented nucleus (fills the cell in smaller lymphocytes) Nucleus is usually darkly stained Thin rim of cytoplasm surrounds nucleus	Attack pathogens and abnormal/infected cells Coordinate immune cell activity Produce antibodies	20–40% of total leukocytes (1000–4800 cells per microliter)
Monocytes	Kidney-shaped or C-shaped nucleus Nucleus is generally pale staining Abundant cytoplasm around nucleus	Can exit blood vessels and become macrophages Phagocytize pathogens (e.g., bacteria, viruses), cellular debris, dead cells	2–8% of total leukocytes (100–700 cells per microliter)

Neutrophils The most numerous leukocyte in the blood is the **neutrophil** (nū′trō-fil; *neuter* = neither), constituting about 50% to 70% of the total number of leukocytes. The neutrophil is named for its distinctive neutral- or pale-colored granules within a light lilac cytoplasm. They are about 1.5 times larger in diameter than an erythrocyte and exhibit a multilobed nucleus with as many as five lobes interconnected by thin strands. Because of the various shapes of their nuclei, neutrophils also may be called *polymorphonuclear* (*PMN*) *leukocytes*. Neutrophils usually remain in circulation for about 10 to 12 hours before they exit the blood vessels and enter the tissue spaces, where they phagocytize infectious pathogens, especially bacteria. The number of neutrophils in a person's blood rises dramatically during a bacterial infection as more neutrophils are produced to target the bacteria. APR

Eosinophils **Eosinophils** (ē′ō-sin′ō-fil; *eos* = dawn) have reddish or pink-orange granules in their cytoplasm. Typically, eosinophils constitute about 1% to 4% of the total number of leukocytes. Their nucleus is bilobed, with the two lobes connected by a thin strand. An eosinophil is about 1.5 times larger in diameter than an erythrocyte. Eosinophils increase in number when they encounter and react to or phagocytize antigen-antibody complexes or allergens (antigens that initiate a hypersensitive or allergic reaction). If the body is infected by parasitic worms, the eosinophils release chemical mediators that attack the worms. APR

Basophils **Basophils** (bā′sō-fil; *basis* = base) are usually about 1.5 times larger in diameter than erythrocytes. They are the least numerous of the granulocytes, constituting about 0.5% to 1% of the total number of leukocytes. For this reason, it is difficult to find a basophil on a blood smear. Basophils exhibit a bilobed nucleus and abundant blue-violet granules in the cytoplasm that often obscure the nucleus. The primary components of basophil granules are histamine and heparin, which are released during inflammatory or allergic reactions. When histamine is released from these granules, it causes an increase in the diameter of blood vessels (called **vasodilation**). Vasodilation will result in a decrease in blood pressure along with classic allergic symptoms such as swollen nasal membranes, itchy and runny nose, and watery eyes. The release of heparin from basophils inhibits blood clotting (a process called **anticoagulation**). APR

WHAT DO YOU THINK?

3. Which type of granulocyte may increase in number if you develop "strep throat" (infection of the throat by bacteria)?

Agranulocytes

Agranulocytes [illegible] ū-lō-sīt) are leukocytes that have such small granules in their cytoplasm that they are frequently overlooked—hence the name agranulocyte (*a* = without). Agranulocytes include both lymphocytes and monocytes.

Lymphocytes As their name implies, most **lymphocytes** (lim′fō-sīt) reside in lymphatic organs and structures. Typically, lymphocytes constitute about 20% to 40% of the total number of leukocytes. Their dark-staining nucleus is usually rounded or slightly indented, and smaller lymphocytes exhibit only a thin rim of blue-gray cytoplasm around the nucleus. When activated, lymphocytes grow larger and have proportionally more cytoplasm. Thus, some of the smaller, nonactivated lymphocytes may have a diameter less than that of an erythrocyte, whereas activated lymphocytes may be two times the diameter of an erythrocyte. APR

There are three categories of lymphocytes. **T-lymphocytes** (*T-cells*) manage and direct an immune response; some directly attack foreign cells and virus-infected cells. **B-lymphocytes** (*B-cells*) are stimulated to become plasma cells and produce antibodies. **Natural killer cells** (*NK cells*) attack abnormal and infected tissue cells. Lymphocytes are examined in detail in section 24.3.

Monocytes A **monocyte** (mon′ō-sīt; *monos* = single) can be up to three times the diameter of an erythrocyte. Monocytes usually constitute about 2% to 8% of all leukocytes. The pale-staining nucleus of a monocyte is kidney-shaped or C-shaped. After about 3 days in circulation, monocytes exit blood vessels and take up residence in the tissues, where they change into large phagocytic cells called **macrophages** (mak′rō-fāj; *macros* = large, *phago* = to eat). Macrophages phagocytize bacteria, cell fragments, dead cells, and debris. APR

> **Learning Strategy 21.2**
>
> The mnemonic "Never let monkeys eat bananas" is a simple way to recall the leukocytes in order of their relative abundance:
>
> **N**ever = **N**eutrophil (most abundant)
>
> **L**et = **L**ymphocyte
>
> **M**onkeys = **M**onocyte
>
> **E**at = **E**osinophil
>
> **B**ananas = **B**asophil (least abundant)

21.3c Platelets

Platelets (plāt′let; *platys* = flat) are irregular, membrane-enclosed cellular fragments that are about 2 micrometers in diameter (less than one-fourth the size of an erythrocyte). In stained preparations, they exhibit a dark central region (see the blood smear in figure 21.2). Platelets are sometimes called *thrombocytes* (throm′b ō-sīt; *thrombos* = clot), although that name is inappropriate because they are cell fragments that never had a nucleus, whereas the suffix *-cyte* implies a complete, nucleated cell.

Platelets are continually produced in the red bone marrow by cells called **megakaryocytes** (meg′a˘-kar̆ē-ō-sīt; *megas* = big) (**figure 21.8**). Megakaryocytes are easily distinguished both by their large size (about 100 micrometers in diameter) and their dense, multilobed nucleus. Megakaryocytes extend long processes (called proplatelets) through the blood vessel wall. These proplatelets are spliced by the force of the blood flow into platelets. Thus, megakaryocytes remain within the red bone marrow, whereas the fragments that become platelets enter the bloodstream.

Normally, the concentration of platelets in an adult ranges from 150,000 to about 400,000 per cubic millimeter (or microliter) of blood. Severe trauma to a blood vessel causes the blood to coagulate, or clot. The formation of a blood clot is a complex process. It involves platelets first forming a plug, which then is reinforced by fibrin strands from the blood plasma. These fibrin strands trap some erythrocytes and platelets in the area, thereby forming a blood clot (**figure 21.9**). If not used to help form blood clots, platelets circulate in the blood for 8 to 10 days. Thereafter, they are broken down, and their contents are recycled. An abnormally small number of platelets in circulating blood is termed **thrombocytopenia.**

WHAT DID YOU LEARN?

8. Draw the five types of leukocytes, and list the types from most common to least common in blood.
9. Make your own table that lists the five types of leukocytes and the specific functions of each.
10. Where are megakaryocytes located, and how do they form platelets?

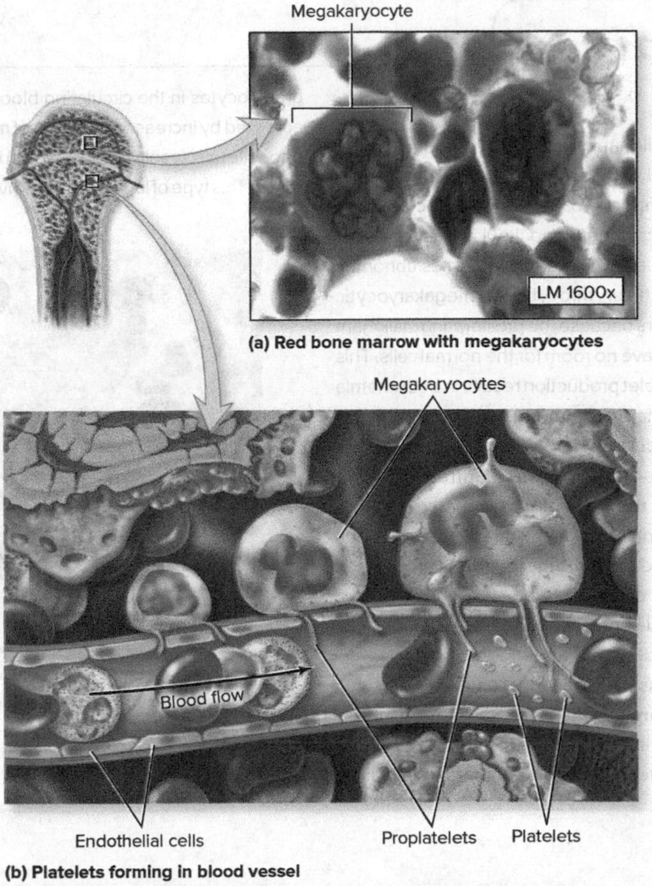
Megakaryocyte
LM 1600x
(a) Red bone marrow with megakaryocytes
Megakaryocytes
Blood flow
Endothelial cells
Proplatelets
Platelets
(b) Platelets forming in blood vessel

Figure 21.8
Platelet Formation. Platelets are derived from megakaryocytes in the red bone marrow. (*a*) Photomicrograph of megakaryocytes in red bone marrow. (*b*) Megakaryocytes extend long processes (called proplatelets) through the blood vessel wall. These proplatelets are spliced by the force of the blood flow into platelets, which then circulate in the blood.
(a) ©McGraw-Hill Education/Alvin Telser, photographer

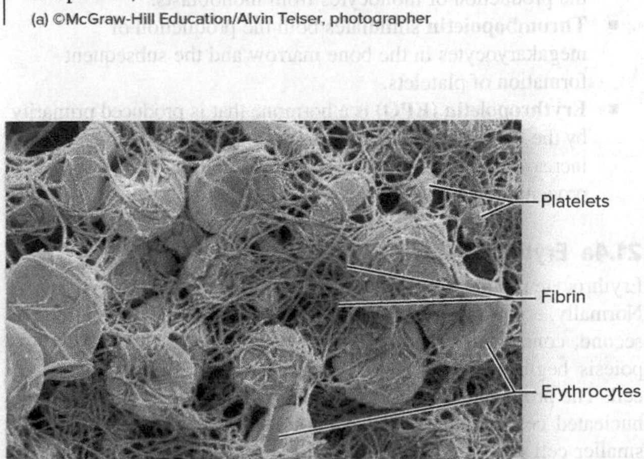
Platelets
Fibrin
Erythrocytes
SEM 5000x

Figure 21.9
Blood Clot. Severe trauma to a blood vessel causes the blood to coagulate, or clot. In a complex process, components in the plasma produce a web of fibrin that traps erythrocytes and platelets and halts blood flow. This SEM shows erythrocytes, fibrin, and platelets within a forming clot.
Steve Gschmeissner/Science Photo Library RF/Getty Images

21.4 Hematopoiesis: Production of Formed Elements

✓ Learning Objectives

10. Explain the general process of hematopoiesis, including the name of the hematopoietic stem cell and the substances (CSFs) involved in hematopoiesis.
11. Compare and contrast the development processes for erythrocytes, leukocytes, and platelets.

Hematopoiesis (hē′ma-t ō-poy-ē′sis; poiesis = a making), also called *hemopoiesis*, is the production of formed elements. Hematopoiesis begins during the embryonic period, when the yolk sac forms blood stem cells and primitive formed elements. Later in the embryonic period, the liver takes over the role of hematopoiesis and is the main site of prenatal blood cell formation. Eventually, hematopoietic stem cells populate the red bone marrow, and by the time the child is born, the red bone marrow (and not the liver) is the main site of hematopoiesis (see section 6.2a).

Clinical View 21.5

Leukemia

Leukemia (lū-kē′mē-ă) is a malignancy (cancer) in the leukocyte-forming cells. There are several categories of leukemia, but all are marked by abnormal development and proliferation of leukocytes, both in the bone marrow and the circulating blood. Leukemias represent a malignant transformation of a leukocyte cell line, and as abnormal leukocytes increase in number, the erythrocytic and megakaryocytic lines typically decrease in numbers because the proliferating malignant cells overtake the marrow and leave no room for the normal cells. This decrease in erythrocyte and platelet production results in both anemia and bleeding, which are often the first signs of leukemia. Leukemias are classified based upon their duration as either acute or chronic.

Acute leukemia progresses rapidly, and if untreated, death occurs within a few months after the onset of symptoms (severe anemia, hemorrhages, and recurrent infections). Acute leukemia tends to occur in children and young adults. **Chronic leukemia** progresses more slowly; survival typically exceeds 1 year from the onset of symptoms, which include anemia and a tendency to bleed. Chronic leukemia usually occurs in middle-aged and older individuals.

Leukemia can also be classified based upon the type of cell that has become malignant. **Granulocytic leukemia** is characterized by uncontrolled proliferation of immature cells in the myeloid stem cell lines, as well as by the presence of large numbers of immature granulocytes in the circulating blood. **Lymphocytic leukemia** is characterized by increased numbers of malignant lymphocytes and/or lymphocytic precursors (*lymphoblasts*) in the bone marrow and circulating blood. This type of leukemia often involves lymph nodes and the spleen.

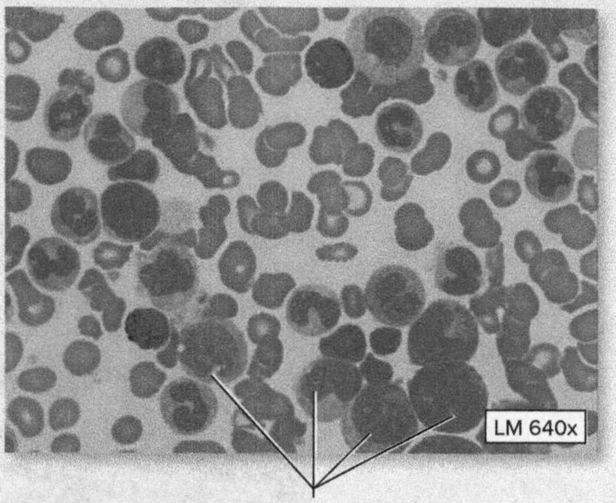
LM 640x
Malignant leukocytes

This photo shows a blood smear from a person with chronic myelogenous leukemia.

Dennis K. Burns, MD; Travis G. Brown, MD; Walter L. Kemp, MD/McGraw-Hill Education

The process of hematopoiesis starts with hematopoietic stem cells called **hemocytoblasts** (hē′mō-sī′tō-blast) (**figure 21.10**). Hemocytoblasts are considered multipotent cells, meaning that they can differentiate and develop into many different kinds of cells. Hemocytoblasts produce two lines for blood cell development: the **myeloid** (mī′ĕ-loyd; *myelos* = marrow) **line** forms erythrocytes, megakaryocytes, and all leukocytes except lymphocytes; the **lymphoid** (lim′foyd) **line** forms lymphocytes.[1]

The maturation and division of hematopoietic stem cells is influenced by **colony-stimulating factors (CSFs),** or *colony-forming units* (*CFUs*). These molecules are all growth factors (except erythropoietin, which is a hormone) and include the following. Review figure 21.10 as you read this section to see where each of the following growth factor acts.

- **Multi-colony-stimulating factor (multi-CSF)** increases the formation of erythrocytes, as well as all classes of granulocytes, monocytes, and platelets from myeloid stem cells.
- **Granulocyte-macrophage colony-stimulating factor (GM-CSF)** accelerates the formation of all granulocytes and monocytes from their progenitor cells.
- **Granulocyte colony-stimulating factor (G-CSF)** stimulates the formation of granulocytes from myeloblast cells.
- **Macrophage colony-stimulating factor (M-CSF)** stimulates the production of monocytes from monoblasts.
- **Thrombopoietin** stimulates both the production of megakaryocytes in the bone marrow and the subsequent formation of platelets.
- **Erythropoietin (EPO)** is a hormone that is produced primarily by the kidneys (small amounts are produced by the liver) to increase the rate of production and maturation of erythrocyte progenitor and erythroblast cells (see section 20.9a).

21.4a Erythropoiesis

Erythrocyte production is called **erythropoiesis** (ĕ-rith′r ō-poy-ē′sis). Normally, erythrocytes are produced at the rate of about 3 million per second, controlled by the hormone erythropoietin (EPO). Erythropoiesis begins with a **myeloid stem cell** that forms a progenitor cell. The progenitor cell forms a **proerythroblast,** which is a large, nucleated cell. This cell then becomes an **erythroblast,** a slightly smaller cell that is forming hemoglobin in its cytoplasm. The next stage, called a **normoblast,** is a still smaller cell with more hemoglobin in the cytoplasm; at the end of this stage, the nucleus is ejected. Eventually, a cell called a **reticulocyte** (re-tik′y ū-lō-sīt) is produced. The reticulocyte has lost all organelles except some ribosomes, but it continues to produce hemoglobin. The transformation from myeloid stem cell to reticulocyte takes about 5 days. Reticulocytes enter the circulation, and within 1 to 2 days the remaining organelles degenerate, and the reticulocyte becomes a mature erythrocyte.

[1] This discussion represents the classical model of hematopoiesis (where there are separate myeloid and lymphoid stem cells). A more recent (but still debated) *myeloid-based model* suggests that the lymphoid line of cells (T- and B-lymphocytes) *also* arises from the myeloid stem cell, instead of from a separate lymphoid stem cell. As there is still debate among scientists about these models, we present the classical model.

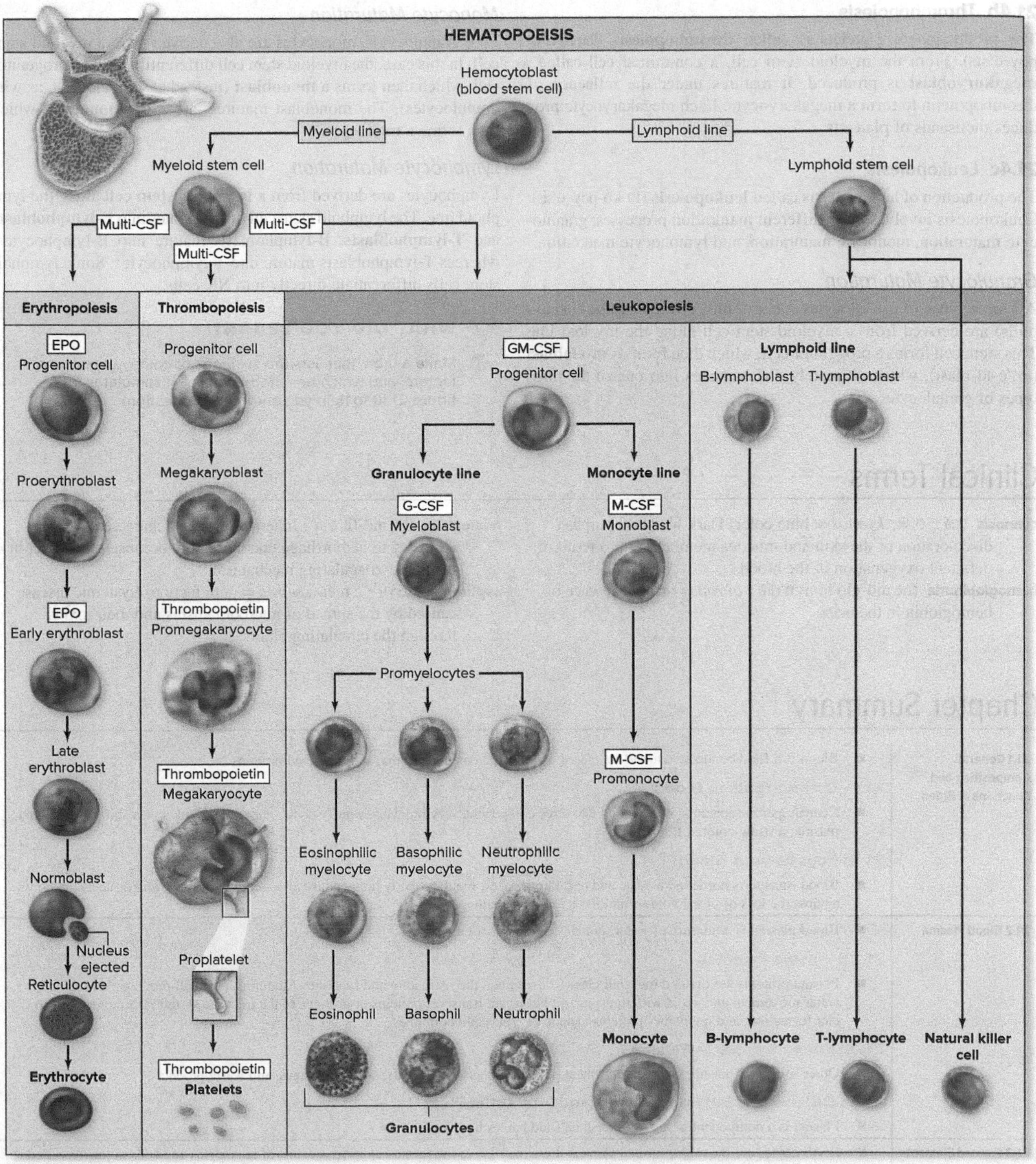
HEMATOPOIESIS
Hemocytoblast (blood stem cell)
Myeloid line
Lymphoid line
Myeloid stem cell
Lymphoid stem cell
Multi-CSF
Multi-CSF
Multi-CSF
Erythropoiesis
Thrombopoiesis
Leukopoiesis
EPO
Progenitor cell
Proerythroblast
EPO
Early erythroblast
Late erythroblast
Normoblast
Nucleus ejected
Reticulocyte
Erythrocyte
Progenitor cell
Megakaryoblast
Thrombopoietin
Promegakaryocyte
Thrombopoietin
Megakaryocyte
Proplatelet
Thrombopoietin
Platelets
GM-CSF
Progenitor cell
Granulocyte line
Monocyte line
G-CSF
Myeloblast
M-CSF
Monoblast
Promyelocytes
M-CSF
Promonocyte
Eosinophilic myelocyte
Basophilic myelocyte
Neutrophilic myelocyte
Eosinophil
Basophil
Neutrophil
Granulocytes
Monocyte
Lymphoid line
B-lymphoblast
T-lymphoblast
B-lymphocyte
T-lymphocyte
Natural killer cell

Figure 21.10

Hematopoiesis: The Origin, Differentiation, and Maturation of Formed Elements. All formed elements are derived from common hematopoietic stem cells, called hemocytoblasts. Both myeloid stem cells and lymphoid stem cells are derived from hemocytoblasts. Myeloid stem cells give rise to erythrocytes, platelets, and to all leukocytes except lymphocytes. Lymphoid stem cells give rise to lymphocytes and natural killer (NK) cells. APR

21.4b Thrombopoiesis

The production of platelets is called **thrombopoiesis** (throm′b ō-poy-ē′sis). From the myeloid stem cell, a committed cell called a **megakaryoblast** is produced. It matures under the influence of thrombopoietin to form a megakaryocyte. Each megakaryocyte pro - duces thousands of platelets.

21.4c Leukopoiesis

The production of leukocytes is called **leukopoiesis** (lū′kō-poy-ē′sis). Leukopoiesis involves three different maturation processes: granulocyte maturation, monocyte maturation, and lymphocyte maturation.

Granulocyte Maturation

All three types of granulocytes (neutrophils, basophils, and eosino - phils) are derived from a myeloid stem cell along the myeloid line. This stem cell forms a progenitor cell, which then forms a **myeloblast** (mī′ĕ-lō-blast), which ultimately differentiates into one of the three types of granulocytes.

Monocyte Maturation

Like granulocytes, monocytes are also derived from a myeloid stem cell. In this case, the myeloid stem cell differentiates into a progenitor cell, which then forms a **monoblast** (instead of a myeloblast, as with granulocytes). The monoblast matures into a **promonocyte,** which then forms a **monocyte.**

Lymphocyte Maturation

Lymphocytes are derived from a **lymphoid stem cell** along the lymphoid line. The lymphoid stem cell differentiates into **B-lymphoblasts** and **T-lymphoblasts.** B-lymphoblasts mature into B-lymphocytes, whereas T-lymphoblasts mature into T-lymphocytes. Some lymphoid stem cells differentiate directly into NK cells.

WHAT DID YOU LEARN?

11 Make a table that lists the six types of colony-stimulating factors, and which hematopoietic cell it stimulates (use figure 21.10 to help you answer this question).

Clinical Terms

cyanosis (sī′ă ō′sis; *kyanos* = blue color) Dark bluish or purplish discoloration of the skin and mucous membranes as a result of deficient oxygenation of the blood.

hemoglobinuria (hē′mō-glō′bi-nyū′rē ă ; *ouron* = urine) Presence of hemoglobin in the urine.

hemophilia (hē′mō-fil′ē-aˇ) Inherited disorder characterized by a tendency to hemorrhage uncontrollably because of a defect in the blood-coagulating mechanism.

septicemia (sep′ti-s ē′mē ă ; *sepsis* = putrefaction) Systemic disease caused by the spread of microorganisms and their toxins through the circulating blood.

Chapter Summary

21.1 General Composition and Functions of Blood

- Blood is a fluid connective tissue composed of formed elements, plasma, and dissolved proteins.

21.1a Components of Blood

- Centrifugation separates whole blood into three components: erythrocytes, a buffy coat composed of leukocytes and platelets, and plasma, a straw-colored fluid.

21.1b Functions of Blood

- Blood transports nutrients, wastes, and respiratory gases; regulates body temperature, pH, and water levels; and protects the body against the loss of blood volume and the activities of pathogens.

21.2 Blood Plasma

- Blood plasma is a mixture of water, proteins, and other solutes.

21.2a Plasma Proteins

- Plasma proteins are divided into four classes based upon their structure and function: Albumins are small proteins that regulate water movement and assist with transport; globulins are transport proteins or proteins of the immune system; fibrinogen aids in clot formation; and regulatory proteins include enzymes and hormones.

21.2b Other Solutes in Plasma

- Other solutes in plasma include electrolytes, respiratory gases, nutrients, some hormones, and waste products.

21.2c Differences Between Plasma and Interstitial Fluid

- Plasma is a component of blood; interstitial fluid bathes body cells.

21.3 Formed Elements in the Blood

- Erythrocytes are the major formed element. Less than 1% of the formed elements consist of leukocytes and cell fragments called platelets. A hematocrit is the percentage of the volume of all formed elements in the blood.

21.3a Erythrocytes

- Erythrocytes have a biconcave disc structure that facilitates the exchange of respiratory gases into and out of the cells.
- Hemoglobin is a pigmented protein that fills mature erythrocytes; it transports oxygen and carbon dioxide.
- Aged erythrocytes are broken down and their components recycled after about 120 days in the blood.
- Erythrocyte plasma membranes have molecules called surface antigens; blood plasma has antibodies.
- When antibodies bind to surface antigens, agglutination may result in hemolysis of the erythrocytes.
- The Rh blood group is determined by the presence or absence of the Rh surface antigen.

21.3 Formed Elements in the Blood *(continued)*	**21.3b Leukocytes** ■ Leukocytes are white blood cells that defend against invading pathogens; reduce the activities of abnormal cells; and remove damaged cells, debris, and antigen-antibody complexes. ■ A disorder in which leukocytes are reduced in number is called leukopenia; a slightly elevated leukocyte count is termed leukocytosis. ■ Leukocytes are either granulocytes (neutrophils, eosinophils, and basophils) or agranulocytes (lymphocytes and monocytes) based upon the presence (or lack) of granules in their cytoplasm. **21.3c Platelets** ■ Platelets are the smallest components of the formed elements. These membrane-enclosed packets of cytoplasm are derived from megakaryocytes. ■ An abnormal number of platelets causes a condition called thrombocytopenia.
21.4 Hematopoiesis: Production of Formed Elements	■ Formed elements have a relatively short life span. They are constantly renewed by the process of hematopoiesis. ■ Hematopoietic stem cells are pluripotent cells called hemocytoblasts located in red bone marrow. **21.4a Erythropoiesis** ■ Erythropoiesis is the production of erythrocytes. The hormone erythropoietin (EPO) controls the rate of proerythroblast maturation to become an erythrocyte. **21.4b Thrombopoiesis** ■ Thrombopoiesis is the production of platelets. A megakaryoblast is produced, and it matures under the influence of thrombopoietin to form a megakaryocyte. **21.4c Leukopoiesis** ■ The production of leukocytes is called leukopoiesis. This process begins in the bone marrow with the division of hemocytoblasts.

Challenge Yourself

Actively write or type your answers in a separate document to reinforce your learning, before checking your answers.

Multiple Choice

Select the best answer from the four choices provided.

1. In the adult, hematopoietic stem cells reside in which structure?
   a. blood
   b. red bone marrow
   c. liver
   d. muscle
2. Which type of leukocyte increases during allergic reactions and parasitic worm infections?
   a. basophil
   b. eosinophil
   c. lymphocyte
   d. neutrophil
3. Which kind of cell forms platelets?
   a. lymphocyte
   b. megakaryocyte
   c. eosinophil
   d. reticulocyte
4. Which of the following is *not* a function of blood?
   a. prevention of fluid loss
   b. nutrient and waste transport
   c. maintenance of constant pH levels
   d. production of hormones
5. A person with blood type A has what components in her blood plasma?
   a. anti-B antibodies in her blood plasma
   b. anti-A antibodies in her blood plasma
   c. both anti-A and anti-B antibodies in her blood plasma
   d. no antibodies in her blood plasma
6. The hematocrit is a measure of which of the following?
   a. water concentration in the plasma
   b. the percentage of formed elements in the blood
   c. the number of platelets in the blood
   d. antibody concentration in the plasma
7. Oxygen attaches to which ion in hemoglobin?
   a. calcium
   b. sodium
   c. iron
   d. potassium
8. During the recycling of erythrocyte components, what happens to the components that are broken down from globin?
   a. The globin components are used to synthesize new proteins to make new erythrocytes.
   b. The globin components are stored as iron in the liver.
   c. The globin components are eliminated from the body in the bile.
   d. The globin components are removed in the urine.
9. What type of leukocyte produces antibodies in response to exposure to a pathogen?
   a. eosinophil
   b. basophil
   c. T-lymphocyte
   d. B-lymphocyte
10. Which of the following is *not* a characteristic of a mature erythrocyte?
    a. biconcave disc shape
    b. absence of organelles
    c. life span of about 12 months
    d. filled with hemoglobin

Content Review

1. How does blood help regulate body temperature?
2. Make a table that lists the main components found in plasma, their relative percentages, and their general functions.
3. When blood is centrifuged, a thin, gray-white layer called the buffy coat covers the layer of packed erythrocytes. What are the components of the buffy coat?
4. Draw and then describe the shape of an erythrocyte. How is this shape advantageous to its function?
5. How are erythrocytes broken down, and to what location are their components recycled?
6. What are the anatomic characteristics of each type of leukocyte? How can you tell these leukocytes apart when viewing a blood smear under the microscope?
7. How do the functions of basophils differ from those of lymphocytes?
8. Briefly describe the origin, structure, and functions of platelets.
9. What is hematopoiesis? Briefly compare where hematopoiesis occurs in an embryo/fetus versus an adult, and describe the stem cells common to all types of formed elements.
10. Make a flowchart that lists the cell types involved in erythropoiesis, starting with a hematocytoblast and ending with a mature erythrocyte. During which phase of development is the nucleus ejected?

Developing Critical Reasoning

1. While taking a clinical laboratory class, Marilyn prepared and examined blood smears from several donors. One of the smears had an increased percentage (about 10% of observed leukocytes) of cells containing reddish-orange granules. Discuss the type of cell described and the condition that may have caused this increase in the donor.
2. Abby is a nurse on duty in a hospital emergency room when a critically injured patient is brought in. The physician calls for an immediate blood transfusion, but the patient's blood type is unknown. What blood type should the patient be given and why?
3. A physician sees a 25-year-old patient who has symptoms of extreme fatigue. Her skin is much paler than normal, and she says she doesn't have the energy she used to have. About a year ago she adopted a vegan diet. Blood work shows that the patient has a hematocrit of 25%. Is her hematocrit normal? If not, what do her hematocrit and symptoms suggest?

Answers to "What Do You Think?"

1. When you become dehydrated, the plasma percentage decreases because the primary component of plasma is water.
2. A person with type O blood sometimes is considered a "universal donor" because their erythrocytes have no surface antigens. Without surface antigens, the type O erythrocytes will not be destroyed through agglutination and hemolysis by antibodies in the recipient's plasma. Likewise, a person with type AB blood sometimes is considered a "universal recipient" because their blood plasma has no antibodies to the ABO blood types. Thus, the AB recipient may receive any type of blood and not worry about the donor's erythrocytes being destroyed.
3. Neutrophils increase in number when you get "strep throat" because they target bacteria.

Design Element: Pencil Icon: Slavojub Pantelic/ Shutterstock

CARDIOVASCULAR SYSTEM

Heart 22

Outline

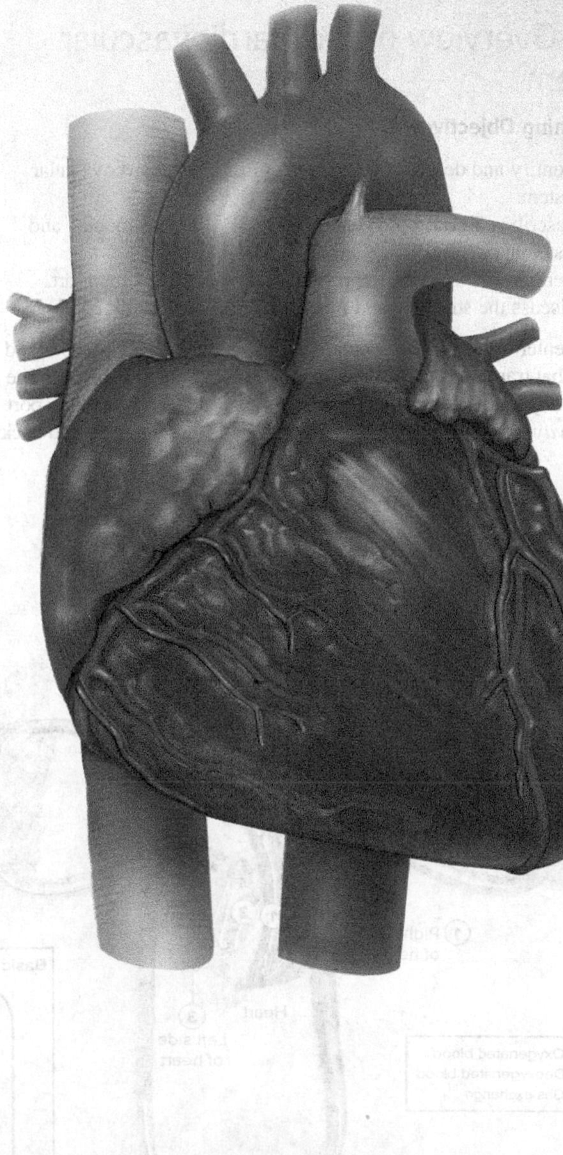

Anatomy & Physiology Revealed 4.0
MODULE 9: CARDIOVASCULAR SYSTEM

In chapter 21, we discovered the importance of blood and the myriad of substances it carries. To maintain homeostasis, blood must circulate continuously throughout the body. The nonstop pumping action of the heart is essential for maintaining blood circulation. If the heart fails to pump adequate volumes of blood, cells are deprived of needed oxygen and nutrients, waste products accumulate, and cell death may occur.

In a healthy, 80-kilogram resting adult, the heart beats about 75 times per minute (about 4500 times per hour or 108,000 times per day). The amount of blood pumped from one ventricle per minute (about 5.25 liters [L] at rest) is called the *cardiac output*. When the body is more active, and the cells need oxygen and nutrients delivered at a faster pace, the heart can increase its output up to five- or six-fold.

22.1 Overview of the Cardiovascular System

✓ Learning Objectives

1. Identify and describe the basic features of the cardiovascular system.
2. Describe and trace the general patterns of the pulmonary and systemic circulations.
3. Identify and describe the position and location of the heart.
4. Discuss the structure and function of the pericardium.

As the center of the cardiovascular system, the heart connects to blood vessels that transport blood between the heart and all body tissues. The two basic types of blood vessels are **arteries** (ar′ter- ē), which transport blood *away* from the heart, and **veins** (vān), which transport blood back *to* the heart. The differences between these types of vessels are discussed in section 23.1. Most arteries carry blood high in oxygen (except for the pulmonary arteries, as explained in section 22.1a), whereas most veins carry blood low in oxygen (except for the pulmonary veins). The arteries and veins entering and leaving the heart are called the **great vessels** because of their relatively large diameter. The heart exhibits several related characteristics and functions:

- The heart's anatomy ensures the **unidirectional flow** of blood through it. Backflow of blood is prevented by valves within the heart.
- The heart acts like two side-by-side pumps that work at the same rate and pump the same volume of blood; one directs blood to the lungs for respiratory gas exchange, whereas the other directs blood to body tissues for nutrient and respiratory gas delivery.
- The heart develops **blood pressure** through alternate cycles of heart wall contraction and relaxation. Blood pressure is the force of the blood pushing against the inside walls of the vessels. A minimum blood pressure is essential for pushing blood through the blood vessels.

22.1a Pulmonary and Systemic Circulations

The cardiovascular system consists of two circulations: the pulmonary circulation and the systemic circulation (**figure 22.1**). The **pulmonary** (pul′m ō-nār′ē; *pulmo* = lung) **circulation** conveys deoxygenated blood from the right side of the heart through blood vessels to the lungs for the pickup of oxygen and the release of carbon dioxide, and then back through blood vessels to the left side of the heart.

The **systemic** (sis-tem′ik) **circulation** moves oxygenated blood from the left side of the heart through blood vessels to the systemic cells

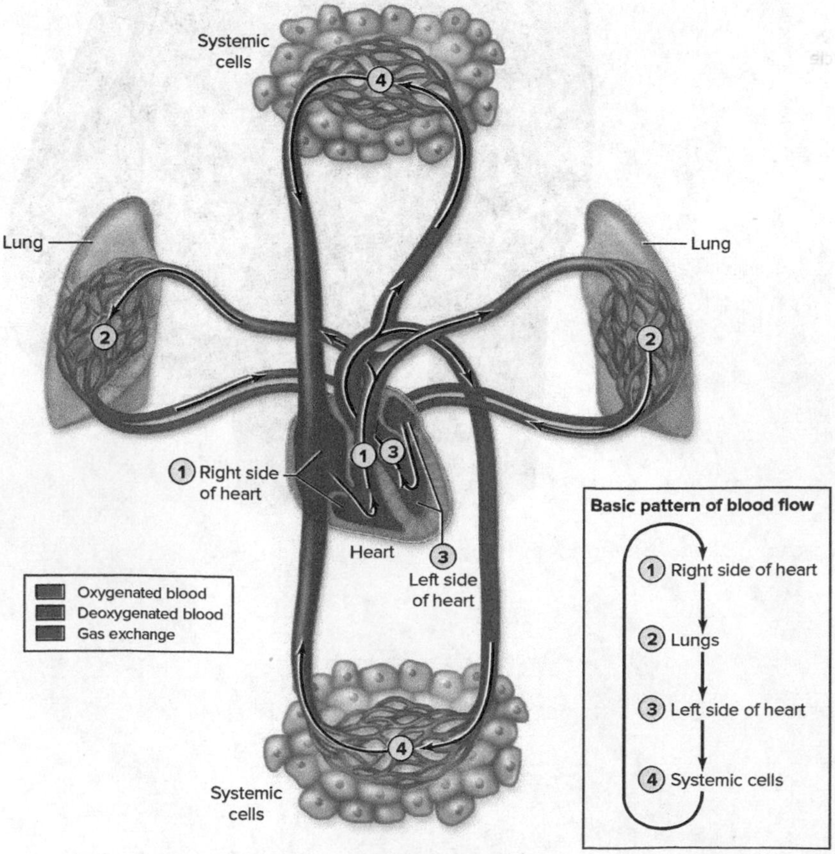

Figure 22.1

Cardiovascular System. The schematic drawing of the cardiovascular system is composed of the pulmonary circulation and the systemic circulation. The pulmonary circulation pumps blood from the right side of the heart through pulmonary vessels, to the lungs, and back to the left side of the heart (steps 1, 2, and 3). The systemic circulation pumps blood from the left side of the heart, through systemic vessels in peripheral tissues, and back to the right side of the heart (steps 3, 4, and back to 1). APR such as those of the liver, skin, muscle, and brain. Nutrients, respiratory gases, and wastes are exchanged with these systemic cells before blood is returned to the right side of the heart. Thus, the basic pattern of blood flow is the right side of the heart → lungs → the left side of the heart → systemic tissues of the body → back to the right side of the heart.

WHAT DO YOU THINK?

1. We previously mentioned that arteries tend to carry oxygenated blood, but the great vessels entering the lungs are the exception. Why are these vessels still called arteries?

22.1b Position of the Heart

The heart is located left of the body midline posterior to the sternum in the **mediastinum (figure 22.2)**. The heart is slightly rotated such that its right side or **right border** (primarily formed by the right atrium and ventricle) is located more anteriorly, whereas its left side or **left border** (primarily formed by the left atrium and ventricle) is located more posteriorly. The posterosuperior surface of the heart, formed primarily by the left atrium, is called the **base** (not shown in figure 22.2). The pulmonary veins that enter the left atrium border this base. The **superior border** is formed by the great arterial trunks (ascending aorta and pulmonary trunk) and the superior vena cava. The inferior, conical end is called the **apex** (ā′peks; tip). It projects slightly anteroinferiorly toward the left side of the body. The **inferior border** is formed by the right ventricle.

22.1c Characteristics of the Pericardium

The heart is contained within the **pericardium** (per′i-kar′dē-ŭm), a fibrous sac and serous lining **(figure 22.3**; see also figure 1.10). The pericardium restricts the heart's movements so that it doesn't bounce and move about in the thoracic cavity, and prevents the heart from overfilling with blood.

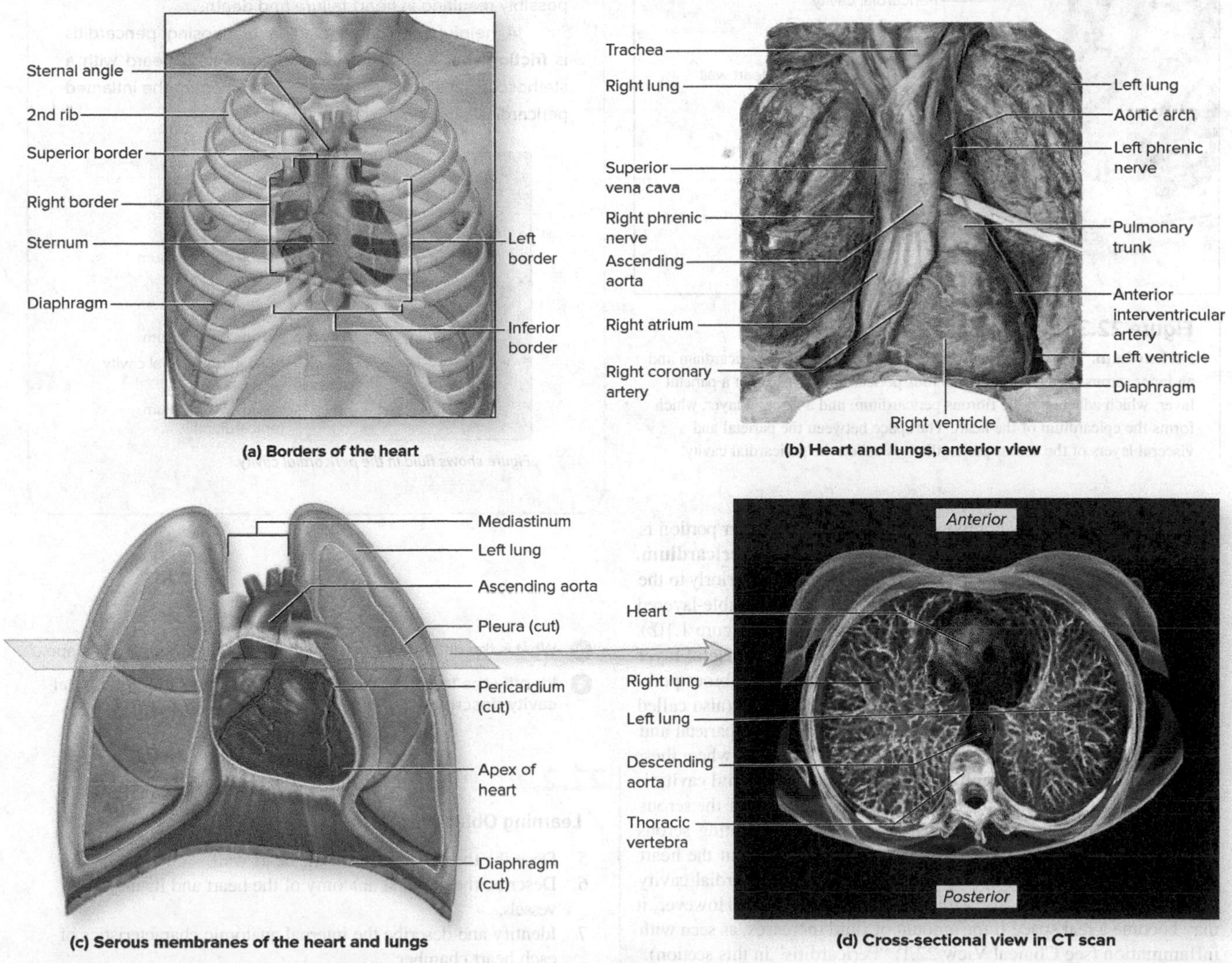
Sternal angle
2nd rib
Superior border
Right border
Sternum
Diaphragm
Left border
Inferior border
(a) Borders of the heart
Trachea
Right lung
Superior vena cava
Right phrenic nerve
Ascending aorta
Right atrium
Right coronary artery
Right ventricle
Left lung
Aortic arch
Left phrenic nerve
Pulmonary trunk
Anterior interventricular artery
Left ventricle
Diaphragm
(b) Heart and lungs, anterior view
Mediastinum
Left lung
Ascending aorta
Pleura (cut)
Pericardium (cut)
Apex of heart
Diaphragm (cut)
(c) Serous membranes of the heart and lungs
Anterior
Heart
Right lung
Left lung
Descending aorta
Thoracic vertebra
Posterior
(d) Cross-sectional view in CT scan

Figure 22.2

Heart Position Within the Thoracic Cavity. The heart is in the mediastinum of the thoracic cavity. *(a)* An anterior view shows the position of the heart posterior to the anterior thoracic cage. The borders of the heart are labeled. *(b)* Cadaver photo of the heart within the mediastinum (anterior view). *(c)* Serous membranes (pericardium and pleura) surround the heart and lungs, respectively. *(d)* A three-dimensional computed tomography (CT) cross-sectional view depicts the heart's relationship to the other organs in the thoracic cavity. CT scans are typically inferior views. APR

(b) ©McGraw-Hill Education/Christine Eckel, photographer; (d) Zephyr/Science Photo Library RF/Alamy Stock Photo

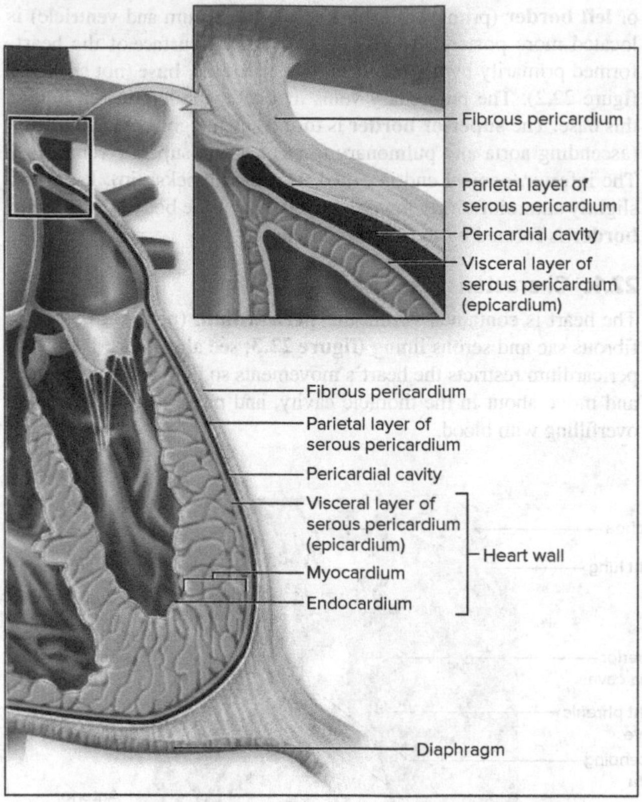

Figure 22.3

Pericardium. The pericardium consists of an outer fibrous pericardium and an inner serous pericardium. The serous pericardium consists of a parietal layer, which adheres to the fibrous pericardium, and a visceral layer, which forms the epicardium of the heart. The space between the parietal and visceral layers of the serous pericardium is called the pericardial cavity.

The pericardium is composed of two parts. The outer portion is a tough, dense connective tissue layer called the **fibrous pericardium.** This layer is attached inferiorly to the diaphragm and superiorly to the base of the great vessels. The inner portion is a thin, double-layered serous membrane called the **serous pericardium** (see figure 1.10*b*). The serous pericardium may be subdivided into (1) a **parietal layer** of serous pericardium that lines the inner surface of the fibrous pericardium, and (2) a **visceral layer** of serous pericardium (also called the **epicardium**) that covers the outside of the heart. The parietal and visceral layers reflect (fold back) along the great vessels, where these layers become continuous with one another. The **pericardial cavity** is a narrow space between the parietal and visceral layers of the serous pericardium. Both layers of pericardium secrete lubricating serous fluid into the pericardial cavity to decrease friction when the heart beats and the layers rub against one another. The pericardial cavity is a potential space with just a thin lining of serous fluid. However, it may become a real space if the amount of fluid increases, as seen with inflammation (see Clinical View 22.1: "Pericarditis" in this section).

WHAT DID YOU LEARN?

1. What is the basic distinction between arteries and veins?
2. Draw and label the arteries and veins for the pulmonary and systemic circulations.

Clinical View 22.1

Pericarditis

Pericarditis (per'i-kar-dī'tis; *itis* = inflammation) is an inflammation of the pericardium, typically caused by viruses, bacteria, or fungi. The inflammation is associated with an increase in permeability of the capillaries, which become more "leaky," resulting in fluid accumulation in the pericardial cavity. At this point, the potential space of the pericardial cavity becomes a real space as it fills with fluid. In severe cases, the excess fluid accumulation limits the heart's movement and keeps the heart chambers from filling with an adequate amount of blood. The heart is unable to pump blood, leading to a medical emergency called **cardiac tamponade** (tam'pŏ-nād') and possibly resulting in heart failure and death.

A helpful physical finding in diagnosing pericarditis is **friction rub,** a crackling or scraping sound heard with a stethoscope that is caused by the movement of the inflamed pericardial layers against each other.

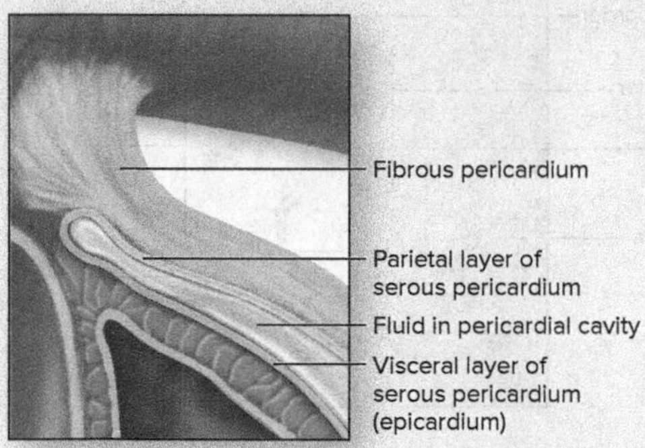

Figure shows fluid in the pericardial cavity.

3. What is the difference between the base of the heart and its apex?
4. Identify the layers of the pericardium. Why is the pericardial cavity described as a potential space?

22.2 Anatomy of the Heart

✓ Learning Objectives

5. Describe the three layers of the heart wall.
6. Describe the external anatomy of the heart and its major vessels.
7. Identify and describe the internal anatomic characteristics of each heart chamber.
8. Explain how valves regulate blood flow through the heart.

The heart is a relatively small, conical organ about the size of a person's clenched fist. In the average normal adult, it weighs about 250 to 350 grams, but certain diseases may cause heart size to increase dramatically.

> **Learning Strategy 22.1**
>
> To demonstrate the almost frictionless movement of the heart within the pericardial sac, try the following demonstration:
>
> 1. Obtain two glass microscope slides. Place them together and then try to slide them back-and-forth past each other. You will find that they stick together (even if they are very clean) and do not move relative to one another very easily!
> 2. Now, take two similar glass slides and place a very small drop of water onto the surface of one slide. Place the slides together, as before, and then try to slide them back-and-forth past each other.
>
> We predict that you have demonstrated to yourself that glass slides move easily past each other when a water drop is present between them. This ease of movement of two opposing surfaces parallels the sliding movement of the parietal and visceral pericardial surfaces when a thin layer of serous fluid is present between them.

22.2a Heart Wall Structure

The heart wall consists of three distinctive layers: an external epicardium, a middle myocardium, and an internal endocardium (**figure 22.4**).

The **epicardium** (ep′i-kar′dē-ŭm; *epi* = upon, *kardia* = heart) is the outermost heart layer and is also known as the *visceral layer of the serous pericardium*. The epicardium is composed of a serous membrane and areolar connective tissue (see section 4.3). As we age, more fat is deposited in the epicardium, and so this layer becomes thicker and more fatty.

The **myocardium** (mī′ō-kar′dē-ŭm; *mys* = muscle) is the middle layer of the heart wall and is composed of cardiac muscle tissue (see sections 4.4a and 10.9a). The myocardium is the thickest of the three heart wall layers. It lies deep to the epicardium and superficial to the endocardium. Contraction of cardiac muscle composing the myocardium generates the force necessary to pump blood. The ventricular myocardium may change in thickness as we age. For example, it hypertrophies in response to narrowing of systemic arteries because the heart must work harder to pump the blood. We consider the microscopic anatomy of cardiac muscle in section 22.4a.

The internal surface of the heart chambers and the external surfaces of the heart valves are covered by **endocardium** (en′dō-kar′dē-ŭm; *endon* = within). The endocardium, like the epicardium, is composed of a simple squamous epithelium and an underlying layer of areolar connective tissue. The epithelial layer of the endocardium is continuous with the epithelial layer called the endothelium, which lines the blood vessels (see section 23.1a).

22.2b External Heart Anatomy

The heart is composed of four hollow chambers: two smaller atria and two larger ventricles (**figure 22.5**). The thin-walled left and right **atria** (ā′trē-ă; sing., *atrium;* entrance hall) are the superior chambers. The anterior part of each atrium is a wrinkled, flaplike extension, called an **auricle** (aw′ri-kl; *auris* = ear) because it resembles an ear. The atria receive all blood returning to the heart. The right atrium receives blood from the systemic circulation, and the left atrium receives blood from the pulmonary circulation. Blood that enters an atrium is passed to the ventricle on the same side of the heart. The left and right **ventricles** (ven′tri-kěl; *venter* = belly) are the inferior chambers. Two large arteries, the **pulmonary trunk** and the **aorta** (ā-ōr′tă), exit the heart at its superior border. The pulmonary trunk transports blood from the right ventricle into the pulmonary circulation, whereas the aorta conducts blood from the left ventricle into the systemic circulation. Both ventricles pump the same volume of blood per minute.

The atria are separated from the ventricles externally by a relatively deep **coronary sulcus** (or *atrioventricular sulcus*) that extends around the circumference of the heart. An **interventricular** (in-ter-ven-trik′ū-lăr; *inter* = between) **sulcus** is a groove between the ventricles that extends inferiorly from the coronary sulcus toward the heart apex, and delineates the superficial boundary between the right and left ventricles. The **anterior interventricular sulcus** is located on the anterior side of the heart, and the **posterior interventricular sulcus** is located on the posterior side of the heart. Located within all of these sulci are coronary vessels associated with supplying blood to the heart wall. Coronary vessels are described in detail in section 22.3.

22.2c Internal Heart Anatomy: Chambers and Valves

Figure 22.6 depicts the internal anatomy and structural organization of the four heart chambers: the right atrium, right ventricle, left atrium,

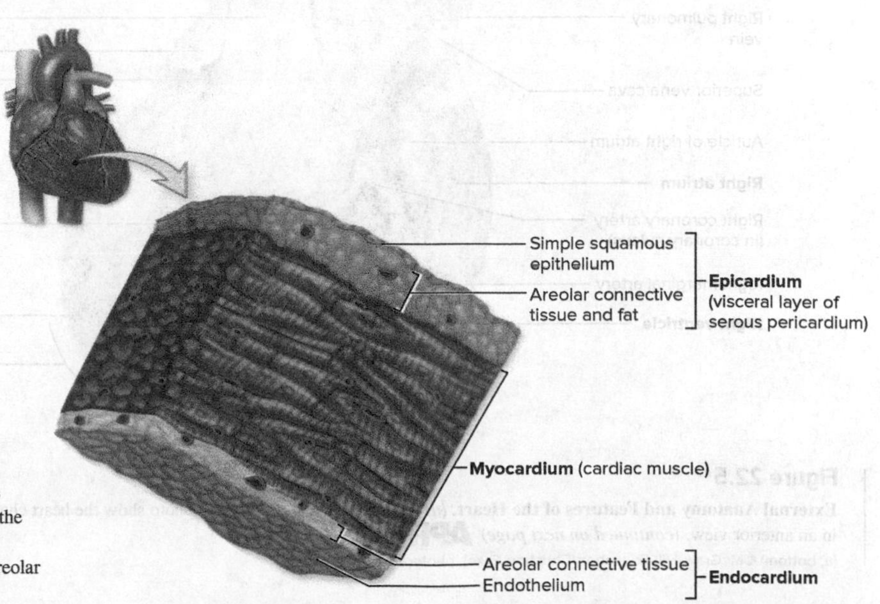

Figure 22.4

Organization of the Heart Wall. The heart wall is composed of an outer epicardium (visceral layer of the serous pericardium), a middle myocardium (cardiac muscle), and an inner endocardium (composed of areolar connective tissue and an endothelium).

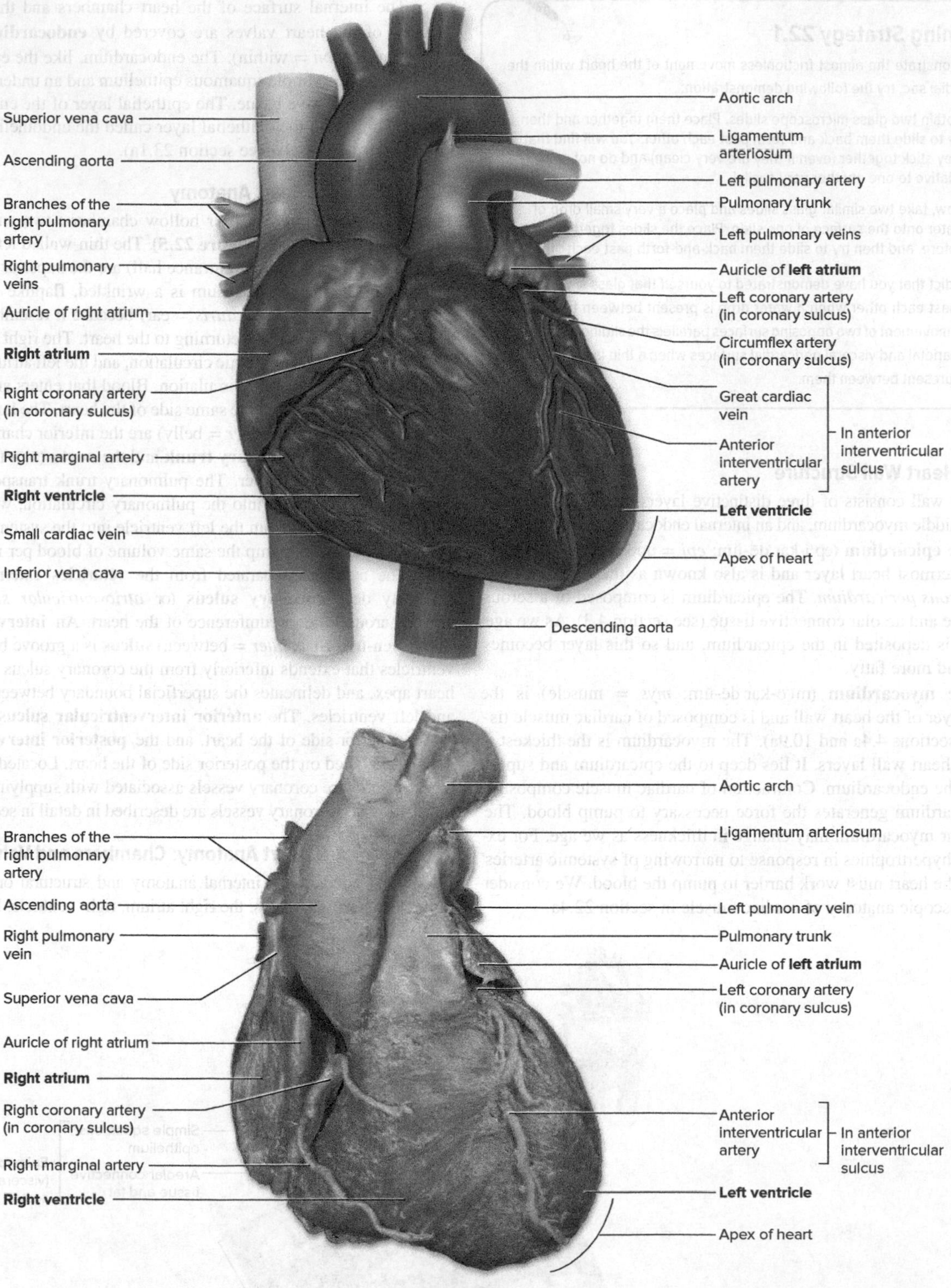
Superior vena cava
Ascending aorta
Branches of the right pulmonary artery
Right pulmonary veins
Auricle of right atrium
Right atrium
Right coronary artery (in coronary sulcus)
Right marginal artery
Right ventricle
Small cardiac vein
Inferior vena cava
Aortic arch
Ligamentum arteriosum
Left pulmonary artery
Pulmonary trunk
Left pulmonary veins
Auricle of left atrium
Left coronary artery (in coronary sulcus)
Circumflex artery (in coronary sulcus)
Great cardiac vein
Anterior interventricular artery
In anterior interventricular sulcus
Left ventricle
Apex of heart
Descending aorta
Aortic arch
Ligamentum arteriosum
Branches of the right pulmonary artery
Ascending aorta
Left pulmonary vein
Right pulmonary vein
Pulmonary trunk
Auricle of left atrium
Superior vena cava
Left coronary artery (in coronary sulcus)
Auricle of right atrium
Right atrium
Right coronary artery (in coronary sulcus)
Anterior interventricular artery
In anterior interventricular sulcus
Right marginal artery
Left ventricle
Right ventricle
Apex of heart
(a) Anterior view

Figure 22.5

External Anatomy and Features of the Heart. *(a)* An illustration and a cadaver photo show the heart chambers and associated vessels and the apex of the heart in an anterior view. *(continued on next page)* APR

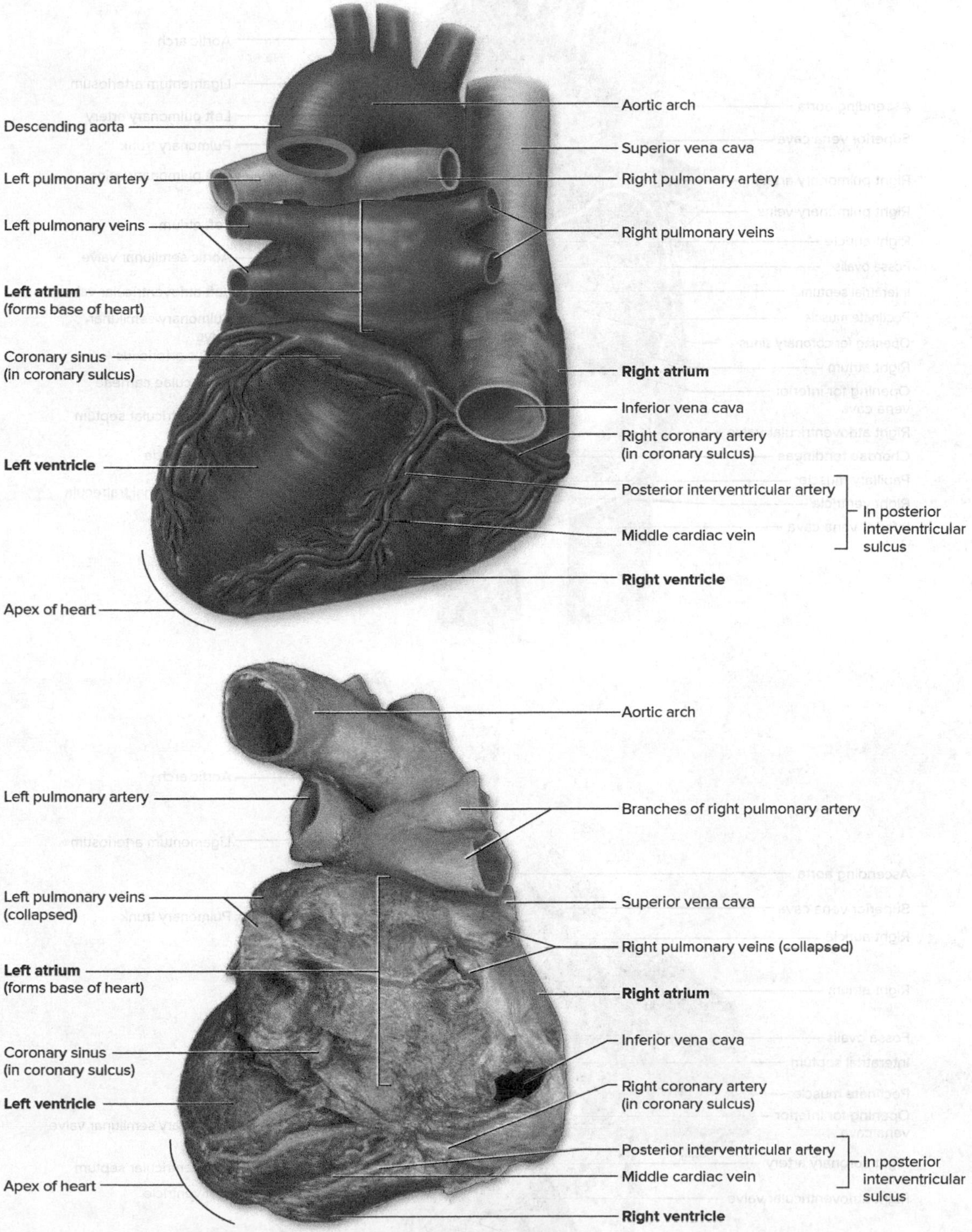
Aortic arch
Descending aorta
Superior vena cava
Left pulmonary artery
Right pulmonary artery
Left pulmonary veins
Right pulmonary veins
Left atrium
(forms base of heart)
Coronary sinus
(in coronary sulcus)
Right atrium
Inferior vena cava
Right coronary artery
(in coronary sulcus)
Left ventricle
Posterior interventricular artery
Middle cardiac vein
In posterior interventricular sulcus
Right ventricle
Apex of heart
Aortic arch
Left pulmonary artery
Branches of right pulmonary artery
Left pulmonary veins
(collapsed)
Superior vena cava
Right pulmonary veins (collapsed)
Left atrium
(forms base of heart)
Right atrium
Coronary sinus
(in coronary sulcus)
Inferior vena cava
Left ventricle
Right coronary artery
(in coronary sulcus)
Posterior interventricular artery
Middle cardiac vein
In posterior interventricular sulcus
Apex of heart
Right ventricle

(b) Posterior view

Figure 22.5

External Anatomy and Features of the Heart. ***(continued)*** *(b)* An illustration and a cadaver photo show the heart chambers and associated vessels and the base of the heart in a posterior view. APR

(b, bottom) ©McGraw-Hill Education/Christine Eckel, photographer

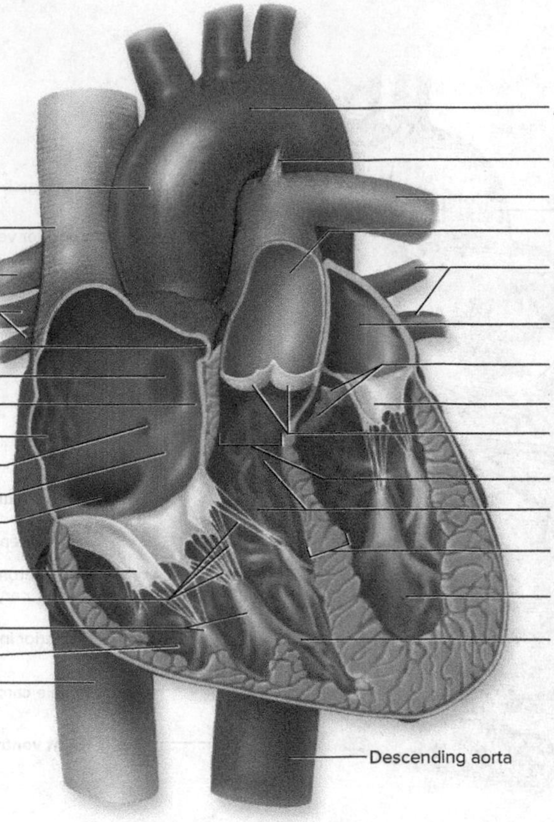

Aortic arch
Ligamentum arteriosum
Left pulmonary artery
Pulmonary trunk
Left pulmonary veins
Left atrium
Aortic semilunar valve
Left atrioventricular valve
Pulmonary semilunar valve
Conus arteriosus
Trabeculae carneae
Interventricular septum
Left ventricle
Septomarginal trabecula
Descending aorta
Ascending aorta
Superior vena cava
Right pulmonary artery
Right pulmonary veins
Right auricle
Fossa ovalis
Interatrial septum
Pectinate muscle
Opening for coronary sinus
Right atrium
Opening for inferior vena cava
Right atrioventricular valve
Chordae tendineae
Papillary muscle
Right ventricle
Inferior vena cava

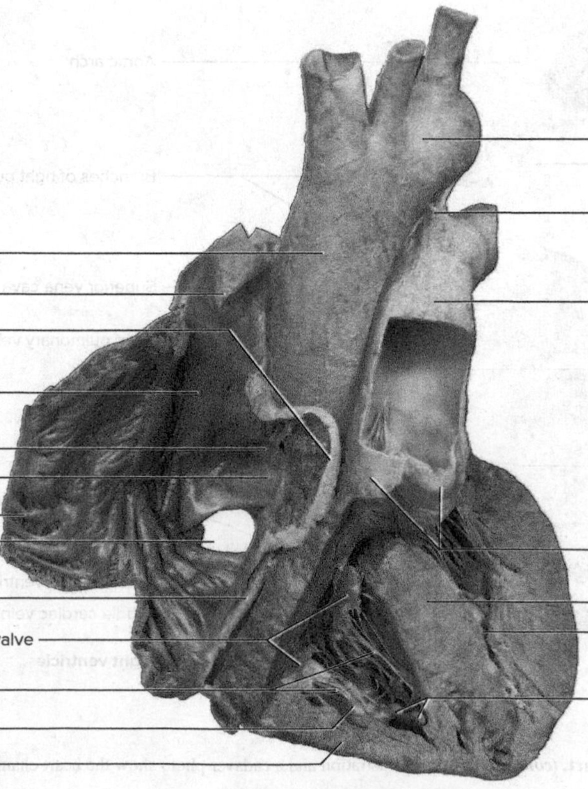

Aortic arch
Ligamentum arteriosum
Pulmonary trunk
Pulmonary semilunar valve
Interventricular septum
Left ventricle
Trabeculae carneae
Ascending aorta
Superior vena cava
Right auricle
Right atrium
Fossa ovalis
Interatrial septum
Pectinate muscle
Opening for inferior vena cava
Right coronary artery
Right atrioventricular valve
Chordae tendineae
Papillary muscle
Right ventricle

Coronal section, anterior view

Figure 22.6

Internal Anatomy of the Heart. An illustration and a cadaver photo reveal the internal structure of the heart, including the valves and the musculature of the heart wall. APR

Table 22.1 Heart Valves

Heart Valve	Location	Structure	Function
Right atrioventricular valve	Between right atrium and right ventricle	Three triangular-shaped cusps of dense connective tissue covered by endothelium; chordae tendineae attached to free edges	Prevents backflow of blood into right atrium when ventricles contract
Pulmonary semilunar valve	Between right ventricle and pulmonary trunk	Three semilunar cusps of dense connective tissue covered by endothelium; no chordae tendineae	Prevents backflow of blood into right ventricle when ventricles relax
Left atrioventricular valve	Between left atrium and left ventricle	Two triangular-shaped cusps of dense connective tissue covered by endothelium; chordae tendineae attached to free edges	Prevents backflow of blood into left atrium when ventricles contract
Aortic semilunar valve	Between left ventricle and ascending aorta	Three semilunar cusps of dense connective tissue covered by endothelium; no chordae tendineae	Prevents backflow of blood into left ventricle when ventricles relax

and left ventricle. Each of these chambers plays a role in the continuous process of blood circulation. Important to their function are valves, endothelium-lined dense connective tissue cusps that keep blood flowing in one direction by preventing its backflow **(table 22.1)**. Valve cusps are the tapering projection of a cardiac valve, also called *flaps* or *leaflets.* When the flaps of the valves are forced closed during the cardiac cycle, they produce the "lubb-dupp" heart sounds. The first sound heard with a stethoscope is the result of the **atrioventricular (AV) valves** closing, producing a "lubb" sound. The second sound is produced when the semilunar valves close, producing a "dupp" sound. (See Clinical View 22.2: "Heart Sounds and Heart Murmurs" in section 22.2c.)

Fibrous Skeleton

The fibrous skeleton of the heart is formed from dense regular connective tissue and is located between the atria and the ventricles **(figure 22.7)**. The fibrous skeleton performs the following functions:

- Provides structural support at the boundary between the atria and the ventricles
- Forms supportive fibrous rings to anchor the heart valves
- Provides a rigid framework for the attachment of cardiac muscle tissue
- Acts as an electrical insulator to prevent action potentials in the atria from passing to the ventricles, so that the ventricles do not contract at the same time as the atria

Notice that cardiac muscle cells are arranged in spiral bundles around the heart chambers attached to the fibrous skeleton (figure 22.7*b*). When the atria contract, they compress the wall of the chambers inward to move the blood into the ventricles. When the ventricles contract, the action is similar to the wringing of a mop that begins at the apex of the heart and compresses superiorly, moving the blood into the great arteries.

Right Atrium

The **right atrium** receives deoxygenated venous blood from the systemic circulation and the heart muscle itself. Three major vessels empty into the right atrium: (1) The **superior vena cava** (vē′nă kā′vă; pl: vē′nē ca′vē) drains blood from the head, neck, upper limbs, and superior regions of the trunk; (2) the **inferior vena cava** drains blood from the lower limbs and trunk; and (3) the **coronary sinus** drains blood from the heart wall.

The **interatrial** (in′ter- ā′trē-ăl) **septum** forms a thin wall between the right and left atria. The posterior atrial wall is smooth, but the auricle and anterior wall exhibit obvious muscular ridges, called **pectinate**

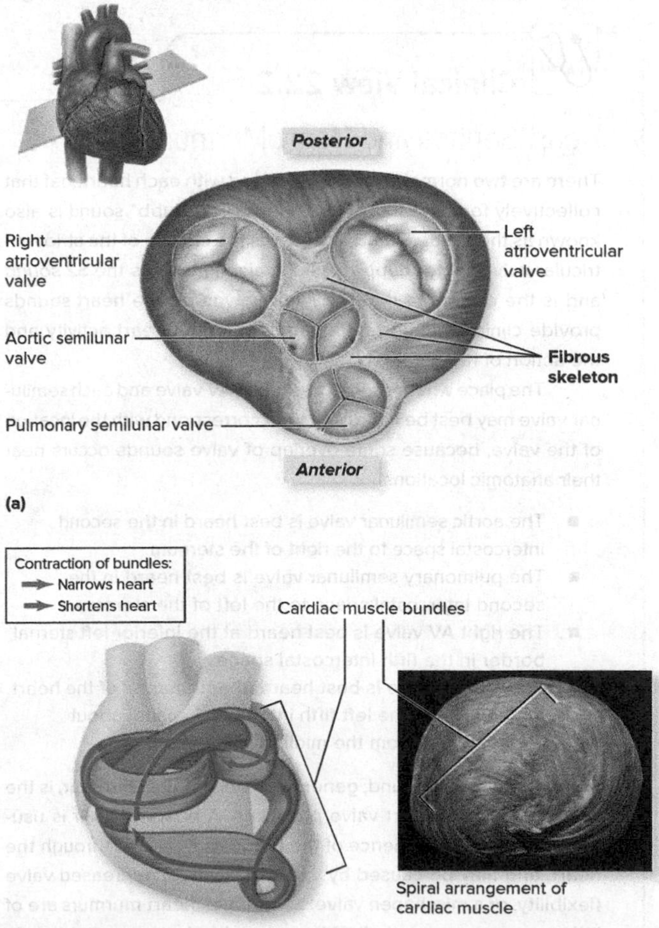

Figure 22.7

Fibrous Skeleton of the Heart. (*a*) The fibrous skeleton is composed of dense irregular connective tissue that provides both mechanical support and electrical insulation within the heart. Shown in superior view, its structural support of heart valves is especially evident. (*b*) Diagram and photo of spiral pattern of cardiac muscle attached to the fibrous skeleton.

(b, right) Dr. Carlos Baptista and Roy Schneider, University of Toledo HSC (pek'ti-nāt; teeth of a comb) **muscles.** The structural differences in the anterior and posterior walls occur because the two walls formed from separate structures during embryonic development. Inspection of the interatrial septum reveals an oval depression called the **fossa** (fos'ă; trench) **ovalis,** also called the *oval fossa.* It occupies the former location of the fetal foramen ovale, which shunted blood from the right atrium to the left atrium during fetal life, as described later in section 22.8.

Separating the right atrium from the right ventricle is the **right atrioventricular opening.** This opening is covered by a **right atrioventricular valve** (also called the *tricuspid valve,* because it has three triangular cusps). Blood flows from the right atrium, through the right atrioventricular opening when the valve is open, into the right ventricle. The right AV valve is forced closed when the right ventricle begins to contract, preventing blood from flowing back into the right atrium.

Right Ventricle

The right ventricle receives blood from the right atrium. An **interventricular septum** forms a thick wall between the right and left ventricles. The internal wall surface of each ventricle displays characteristic large, smooth, irregular muscular ridges, called the **trabeculae carneae** (tră-bek'y ū-lē; *trabs* = beam; kar'nē-ē; *carne* = flesh) (see figure 22.6).

The right ventricle typically has three cone-shaped, muscular projections called **papillary** (pap'i-lār'ē; *papilla* = nipple) **muscles,** which anchor numerous thin strands of collagen fibers called **chordae tendineae** (kōr'dē ten'di-nē-ē). The chordae tendineae attach to the lower surface of cusps of the right AV valve and prevent the valve from everting and flipping into the atrium when the right ventricle is contracting. A muscle bundle called the **septomarginal trabecula** (see figure 22.6), or *moderator band,* connects the base of the anterior papillary muscle to the interventricular septum. At its superior end, the right ventricle narrows into a smooth-walled, conical region called the **conus arteriosus.** Beyond the conus arteriosus is the **pulmonary semilunar valve,** which separates the right ventricle and the pulmonary trunk. The pulmonary trunk divides shortly into right and left **pulmonary arteries,** which carry deoxygenated blood to the lungs.

Semilunar valves are located within the walls of both ventricles immediately before the connections of the right and left ventricles to the pulmonary trunk and aorta, respectively (see figure 22.6). Each valve is

Clinical View 22.2

Heart Sounds and Heart Murmurs

There are two normal sounds associated with each heartbeat that collectively form the lubb-dupp sound. The "lubb" sound is also known as the *S1 sound* and represents the closing of the atrioventricular valves. The "dupp" sound is also known as the *S2 sound* and is the closing of the semilunar valves. These heart sounds provide clinically important information about heart activity and the action of heart valves.

The place where sounds from each AV valve and each semilunar valve may best be heard does not correspond with the location of the valve, because some overlap of valve sounds occurs near their anatomic locations.

- The aortic semilunar valve is best heard in the second intercostal space to the right of the sternum.
- The pulmonary semilunar valve is best heard in the second intercostal space to the left of the sternum.
- The right AV valve is best heard at the inferior left sternal border in the fifth intercostal space.
- The left AV valve is best heard near the apex of the heart (at the level of the left fifth intercostal space, about 9 centimeters from the midline of the sternum).

An abnormal heart sound, generally called a **heart murmur,** is the first indication of heart valve problems. A heart murmur is usually the result of turbulence of the blood as it passes through the heart, and may be caused by valvular leakage, decreased valve flexibility, or a misshapen valve. Sometimes heart murmurs are of little consequence, but all of them need to be evaluated to rule out a more serious heart problem. Two types of heart murmurs are valvular insufficiency and valvular stenosis.

Valvular insufficiency, also termed *valvular incompetence,* occurs when one or more of the cardiac valves leaks because the valve cusps do not close tightly enough. Inflammation or disease may cause the free edges of the valve cusps to become scarred and constricted, allowing blood to regurgitate back through the valve and may cause heart enlargement.

Valvular stenosis (ste-nō'sis; narrowing) is scarring of the valve cusps so that they become rigid or partially fused and cannot completely open. A stenotic valve is narrowed and presents resistance to the flow of blood, decreasing chamber output. Often the affected chamber undergoes hypertrophy and dilates—both conditions that may have dangerous consequences. A primary cause of valvular stenosis is **rheumatic** (rū-mat'ik) **heart disease,** which may follow a streptococcal infection of the throat.

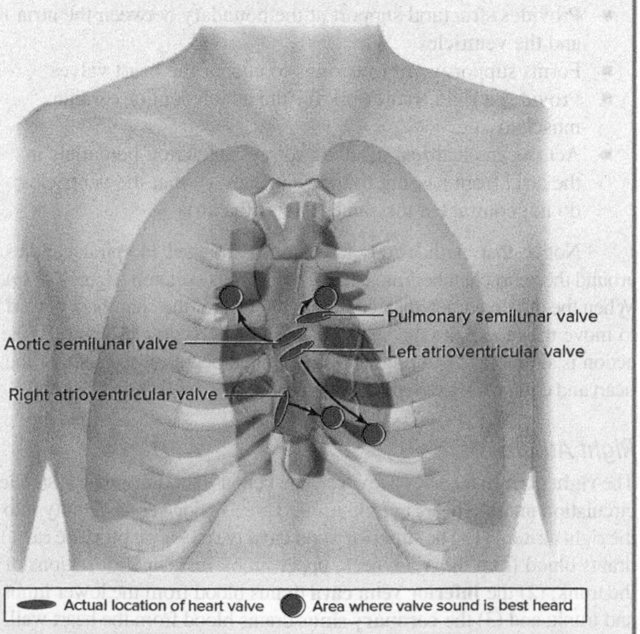

Locations of individual heart valves and the ideal listening sites for each valve are shown.

composed of three thin, half-moon-shaped, pocketlike semilunar cusps. As blood is pumped into the arterial trunks, it pushes against the cusps, forcing the valves open. When ventricular contraction ceases, blood is prevented from flowing back into the ventricles from the arterial trunk by first entering the pockets of the semilunar valves between the cusps and the chamber wall. This causes the cusps to "fill and expand" and meet at the artery center, effectively blocking blood backflow.

Left Atrium

Once gas exchange occurs in the lungs, the oxygenated blood travels through the **pulmonary veins** to the left atrium (see figure 22.6). The smooth posterior wall of the left atrium contains openings for typically four pulmonary veins. Sometimes two of these vessels fuse prior to reaching the left atrium, thus decreasing the number of openings through the atrial wall. Like the right atrium, the left atrium also has pectinate muscles along its anterior wall as well as an auricle.

Separating the left atrium from the left ventricle is the **left atrioventricular opening,** covered by the **left atrioventricular valve** (also called the *bicuspid valve,* because it has two triangular cusps). This valve is also sometimes called the *mitral* (mī'trăl) *valve,* because the two triangular cusps resemble a miter (the headpiece worn by a bishop). Oxygenated blood flows from the left atrium, through the left atrioventricular opening when the valve is open, into the left ventricle. The left AV valve is forced closed when the left ventricle contracts, preventing blood backflow into the left atrium.

Left Ventricle

The left ventricular wall is typically three times thicker than the right ventricular wall (**figure 22.8**). The left ventricle requires thicker walls to generate enough pressure to force the oxygenated blood that has returned to the heart from the lungs into the aorta and then through the entire systemic circulation. (The right ventricle, in contrast, merely has to pump blood to the nearby lungs.) The trabeculae carneae in the left ventricle are more prominent than in the right ventricle. Typically, two large papillary muscles project from the ventricle's inner wall and anchor the chordae tendineae that attach to the cusps of the left AV valve. At the superior end of the ventricular cavity, the **aortic semilunar valve** marks the end of the left ventricle and the entrance into the aorta (see figure 22.7).

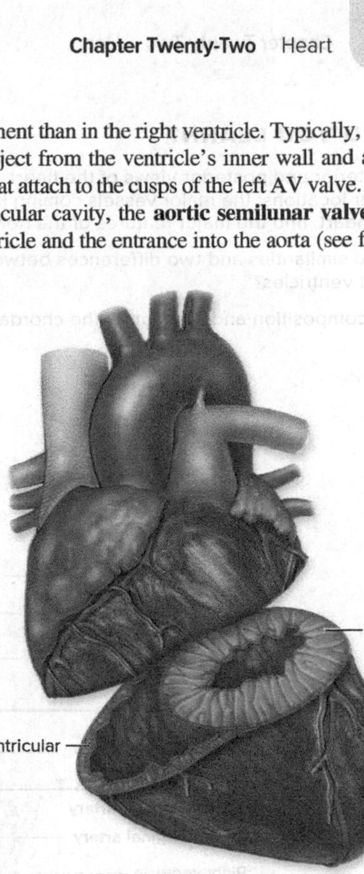

Figure 22.8

Comparison of Right and Left Ventricular Wall Thickness. The wall of the left ventricle is about three times thicker than that of the right ventricle, because the left ventricle must generate a force sufficient to push blood through the systemic circulation to capillary beds.

Clinical View 22.3

Teenage Athletes and Sudden Cardiac Death

Sudden deaths of high school athletes have occurred during athletic events. These deaths were apparently caused by underlying, previously undetected cardiovascular disease. Studies indicated that no forewarning of a problem preceded these deaths. Autopsies revealed that most deaths were due to congenital heart defects and coronary artery anomalies. The result from these anomalies was cardiomegaly, which led to sudden death.

Cardiomegaly is one term used to indicate an increase in the thickness of the heart muscle wall (*hypertrophy*) or an obvious increase or enlargement in heart size (*dilation*) due to stress applied to the heart. Many cardiovascular diseases can cause enlargement of the heart. However, the enlargement of the heart seen in young athletes is caused by a condition called **hypertrophic cardiomyopathy.** Other terms used are *hypertrophic heart, heart enlargement,* or *athlete's heart.* This condition involves both an enlargement of the heart walls (especially one or both ventricles) and a narrowing of the openings (outlets) for the blood to pass through, which results in a decrease in cardiac output. Strenuous exercise exacerbates the condition, and patients may develop symptoms of shortness of breath, chest pain, and fainting. In some cases, sudden death may occur, often while the individual is participating in a physically demanding activity.

A standard x-ray that may accompany a physical examination often reveals potential cardiomegaly. The confirmation of the cardiomegaly being associated with hypertrophic cardiomyopathy (athlete's heart) depends upon an echocardiogram (a specialized ultrasound of the heart) that is used to evaluate the heart's function and its structure.

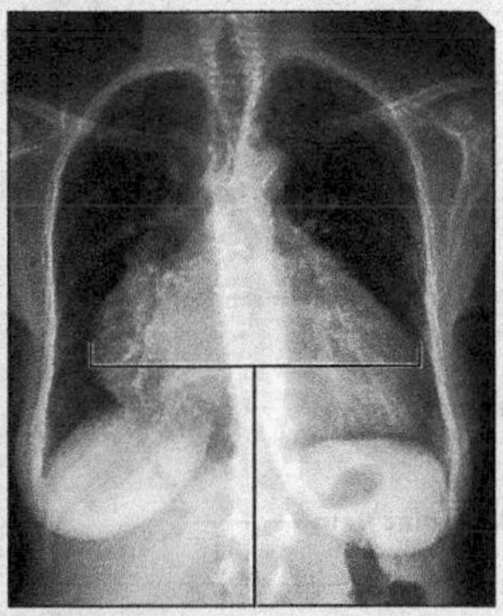

Cardiomegaly in an adult female. Note how the heart shadow (bracket) encompasses most of the width of the thorax.

ISM/SOVEREIGN/Medical Images

As a result, many school districts require student athletes to undergo a physical with an accompanying x-ray or echocardiogram prior to being approved to participate on athletic teams.

WHAT DID YOU LEARN?

5. Draw the anterior and posterior views of the heart. Label the four chamber locations, the major vessels coming into and leaving the heart, and the major features of the heart.
6. What are two similarities and two differences between the right and left ventricles?
7. What is the composition and function of the chordae tendineae?

22.3 Coronary Circulation

✓ Learning Objective

9. Identify and describe the location, origins, and branches of the coronary blood vessels.

Left and **right coronary arteries** travel within the coronary sulcus of the heart to supply blood to the cells of the heart wall **(figure 22.9a)**. These arteries are the only branches of the ascending aorta. The

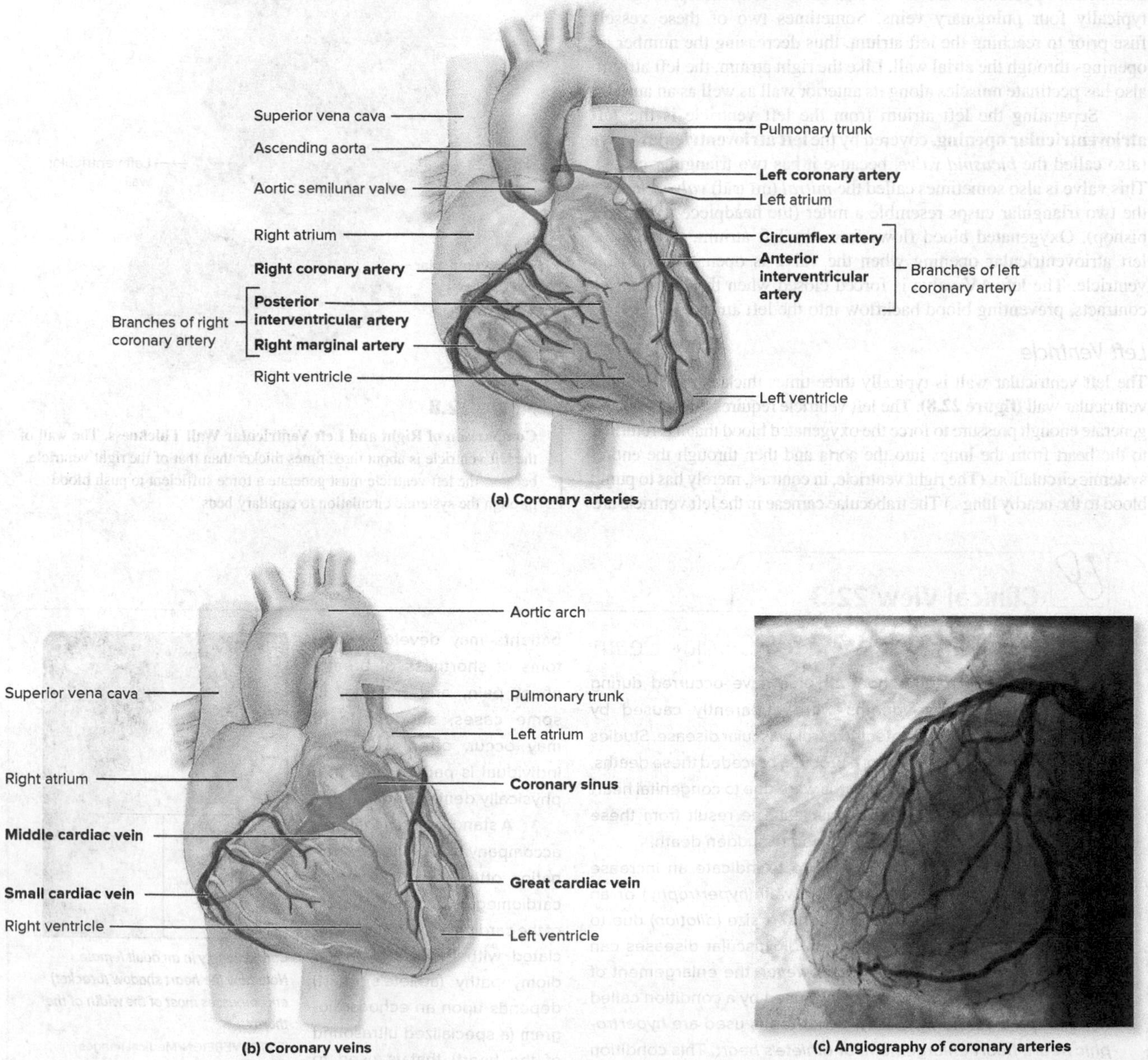
Superior vena cava
Ascending aorta
Aortic semilunar valve
Right atrium
Right coronary artery
Branches of right coronary artery
Posterior interventricular artery
Right marginal artery
Right ventricle
Pulmonary trunk
Left coronary artery
Left atrium
Circumflex artery
Anterior interventricular artery
Branches of left coronary artery
Left ventricle
Aortic arch
Superior vena cava
Pulmonary trunk
Left atrium
Right atrium
Coronary sinus
Middle cardiac vein
Great cardiac vein
Small cardiac vein
Right ventricle
Left ventricle

(a) Coronary arteries

(b) Coronary veins

(c) Angiography of coronary arteries

Figure 22.9

Coronary Circulation. Diagram of the (*a*) anterior view of coronary arteries that transport blood to cardiac muscle tissue and (*b*) coronary veins that transport blood from cardiac muscle tissue. (*c*) Angiography of normal left coronary artery and its branches.

(c) kalus/iStock/Getty Images

openings for these arteries are located in the wall of the ascending aorta immediately superior to the aortic semilunar valve.

The right coronary artery typically branches into the right **marginal artery,** which supplies the right border of the heart, and the **posterior interventricular artery,** which supplies the posterior surface of both the left and right ventricles. The left coronary artery typically branches into the **anterior interventricular artery** (also called the *left anterior descending artery*), which supplies the anterior surface of both ventricles and most of the interventricular septum, and the **circumflex** (ser′kŭm-fleks; around) **artery,** which supplies the left atrium and ventricle. This arterial pattern can vary greatly among individuals. For example, some people may have a posterior interventricular artery that is a branch of the left coronary artery. Knowledge of this variation is essential when treating individuals for coronary artery disease.

Learning Strategy 22.2

Note that an artery's name is associated with the artery's location. The right marginal artery is found on the margin of the right ventricle from an anterior view. The anterior interventricular and posterior interventricular arteries are found along the anterior and posterior interventricular sulci, respectively. The circumflex artery travels around to the posterior of the heart, as its name suggests.

The coronary arteries are considered **functional end arteries** (see section 23.1). In other words, whereas the left and right coronary arteries share some tiny connections, called **anastomoses,** function-

Clinical View 22.4

Angina Pectoris and Myocardial Infarction

Unhealthy coronary arteries may not be able to supply sufficient blood flow to the heart wall. Coronary arteries may become narrowed and occluded with plaques in a condition called **atherosclerosis** (ath′er-ō-skler-ō′sis; *athere* = gruel, *sclerosis* = hardness), or *coronary artery disease* (see Clinical View 23.5: "Atherosclerosis" in section 23.3h). In contrast, some individuals may experience coronary spasm, which is the sudden narrowing of the vessels caused by smooth muscle contraction in their wall. Either atherosclerosis or coronary spasm can lead to angina pectoris or the more severe myocardial infarction.

Angina (an′ji-nă, an-jī′nă) **pectoris** is a poorly localized pain sensation in the left side of the chest, the left arm and shoulder, or sometimes the jaw and the back (although these symptoms may vary, especially in women). Generally it results from strenuous activity, when workload demands on the heart exceed the ability of the narrowed coronary vessels to supply blood. The pain from angina is typically referred (referred pain; see section 19.1b) along the sympathetic pathways (T1–T5 spinal cord segments, see section 18.4b), so an individual may experience pain in the chest region or down the left arm, where the T1 dermatome (section 16.4a) is located. The pain diminishes shortly after the person stops the exertion, and normal blood flow to the heart is restored. Treatment may include medications that cause temporary vascular dilation, such as nitroglycerin. The prognosis and long-term therapy for angina depend upon the severity of the vascular narrowing or spasming.

The term **infarction** refers to death of tissue due to lack of blood supply. **Myocardial infarction (MI),** commonly called a *heart attack,* is a potentially lethal condition resulting from sudden and complete occlusion of a coronary artery. A region of the myocardium is deprived of oxygen, and some of this tissue may

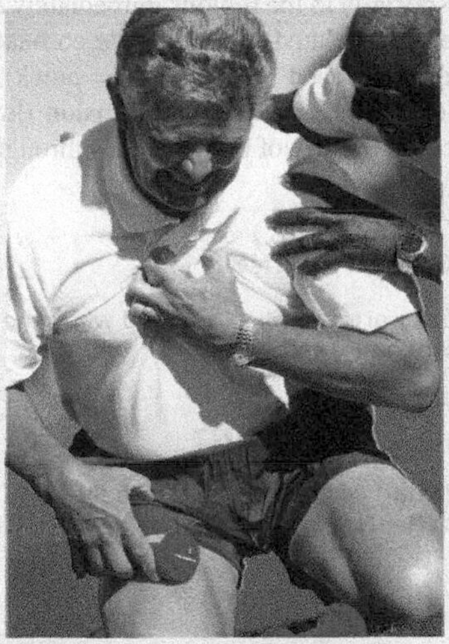

A classic symptom of a myocardial infarction is crushing chest pain.
Corbis/VCG/image100/Getty Images

die (undergo necrosis). Some people experiencing an MI report the sudden development of excruciating and crushing substernal chest pain that typically radiates into the left arm or left side of the neck. Women may not experience these symptoms but instead be overcome with incredible fatigue and flulike symptoms, and thus may be misdiagnosed. Other immediate symptoms include weakness, shortness of breath, nausea, vomiting, anxiety, and marked sweating. Mature cardiac muscle cells have little or no capacity to regenerate (i.e., they cannot undergo mitosis), so when an MI results in cell death, scar tissue forms to fill the gap. If a large amount of tissue is lost, the person may die within a few hours or days because the heart has been profoundly and suddenly weakened.

ally they act like end arteries, which have no anastomoses and are the "end of the line" when it comes to arterial blood flow. The anastomoses allow the coronary arteries to shunt a tiny amount of blood from one artery to another. However, if one of the arteries becomes blocked, as happens with coronary artery disease, these anastomoses are too tiny to shunt sufficient blood from one artery to the other. For example, if a branch of the left coronary artery becomes blocked, the right coronary artery cannot shunt enough blood to the part of the heart supplied by this branch. As a result, the part of the heart wall that was supplied by the branch of the left coronary artery dies due to lack of blood flow to the tissue.

Venous return occurs through one of several cardiac veins (figure 22.9*b*). The **great cardiac vein** runs alongside the anterior interventricular artery; the **middle cardiac vein** runs alongside the posterior interventricular artery; and the **small cardiac vein** travels close to the right marginal artery. These cardiac veins all drain into the **coronary sinus,** a large vein that lies in the posterior aspect of the coronary sulcus. The coronary sinus drains directly into the right atrium of the heart (see section 22.2c).

Because the ventricular myocardium is compressed during contraction, most coronary flow occurs during ventricular relaxation. Normally, flow is evenly distributed throughout the thickness of the myocardium. Under certain circumstances, however, coronary flow may be reduced, especially to the regions immediately external to the endocardium. Situations related to inadequate coronary blood flow include **tachycardia** (tak'i-kar'd ē-ă; *tachys* = quick), an increased heart rate that shortens diastole, and **hypotension** (low blood pressure), which reduces the ability of blood to flow through the ventricular myocardium.

WHAT DO YOU THINK?

2 Do the coronary arteries fill with blood when the ventricles contract or when they relax?

WHAT DID YOU LEARN?

8 Draw a flow chart of the different vessels blood flows through from the left ventricle to the heart wall to the right atrium.

22.4 How the Heart Beats: Electrical Properties of Cardiac Tissue

✓ Learning Objectives

10. Compare and contrast cardiac muscle and skeletal muscle.
11. Explain the conduction of muscle impulses along cardiac muscle cells.
12. Describe autorhymicity and the heart's conducting system.

The efficient pumping of blood through the heart and blood vessels requires precisely coordinated contractions of the heart chambers. These contractions are made possible by the properties of cardiac muscle tissue and by specialized cells in the heart, known collectively as its *conducting system.*

22.4a Characteristics of Cardiac Muscle Tissue

The myocardium is composed of cardiac muscle, which was described briefly in sections 4.4a (see table 4.14) and 10.9a (see table 10.6). Recall that cardiac muscle cells are relatively short, branched cells that usually house one or two central nuclei and numerous mitochondria for ATP supply (**figure 22.10**). Cardiac muscle cells are arranged in spiral bundles and wrapped around and between the heart chambers. Cardiac muscle tissue exhibits some characteristics that are similar to those of skeletal muscle and others that are different (**table 22.2**). For example, the cells in both tissue types are striated, with extensive capillary networks that supply needed nutrients and oxygen. However, cardiac and skeletal muscle tissue differ in the following ways:

- The sarcoplasmic reticulum in cardiac muscle is less extensive and not as organized as in skeletal muscle.
- Cardiac muscle has no terminal cisternae, whereas skeletal muscle does.
- Cardiac muscle lacks the extensive association of sarcoplasmic reticulum and transverse tubules (T-tubules) present in skeletal muscle.
- In cardiac muscle, T-tubules overlie Z discs instead of the junctions of A bands and I bands as seen in skeletal muscle.
- The T-tubules in cardiac muscle have a less extensive distribution and a reduced association with SR compared to those in skeletal muscle, allowing for both the delayed onset and prolonged contraction of cardiac muscle tissue.

22.4b Contraction of Heart Muscle

Cardiac muscle cells contract as a single unit because muscle impulses (changes in voltage across the sarcolemma [see section 10.3c]) are distributed immediately and simultaneously throughout all cells of first the atria and then the ventricles. Neighboring cardiac muscle cells in the walls of heart chambers have formed specialized cell–cell contacts called **intercalated** (in-ter'k ă-lā-tĕd) **discs** which electrically and mechanically link the cells together and permit the immediate passage of muscle impulses (figure 22.10).

Intercalated discs have numerous desmosomes and gap junctions. The desmosomes prevent cardiac muscle cells from pulling apart (see section 4.1c). The gap junctions provide a low-resistance pathway for ions to move between adjoining cardiac muscle cells. This path allows the muscle impulse to travel easily and instantaneously among cardiac muscle cells. Gap junctions are required for the synchronous beating of cardiac muscle cells (see section 4.1c). Therefore, cardiac muscle cells function as a single, coordinated unit; the precisely timed stimulation and response by cardiac muscle cells of both the atria and the ventricles are dependent upon these structural features.

22.4c The Heart's Conducting System

The heart exhibits **autorhythmicity,** meaning that the heart itself (not external nerves) is responsible for initiating the heartbeat. Certain cardiac muscle cells are specialized to initiate and conduct muscle impulses to the contractile muscle cells of the myocardium. Collectively, these specialized cells are called the heart's **conducting system (figure 22.11).**

The heartbeat is initiated by the specialized cardiac muscle cells of the **sinoatrial (SA) node,** which are located in the posterior wall of the right atrium, adjacent to the entrance of the superior vena cava. The cells of the SA node act as the **pacemaker,** the rhythmic center that establishes the pace for cardiac activity. Under the influence of parasympathetic innervation, SA node cells initiate impulses 70 to 80 times per minute.

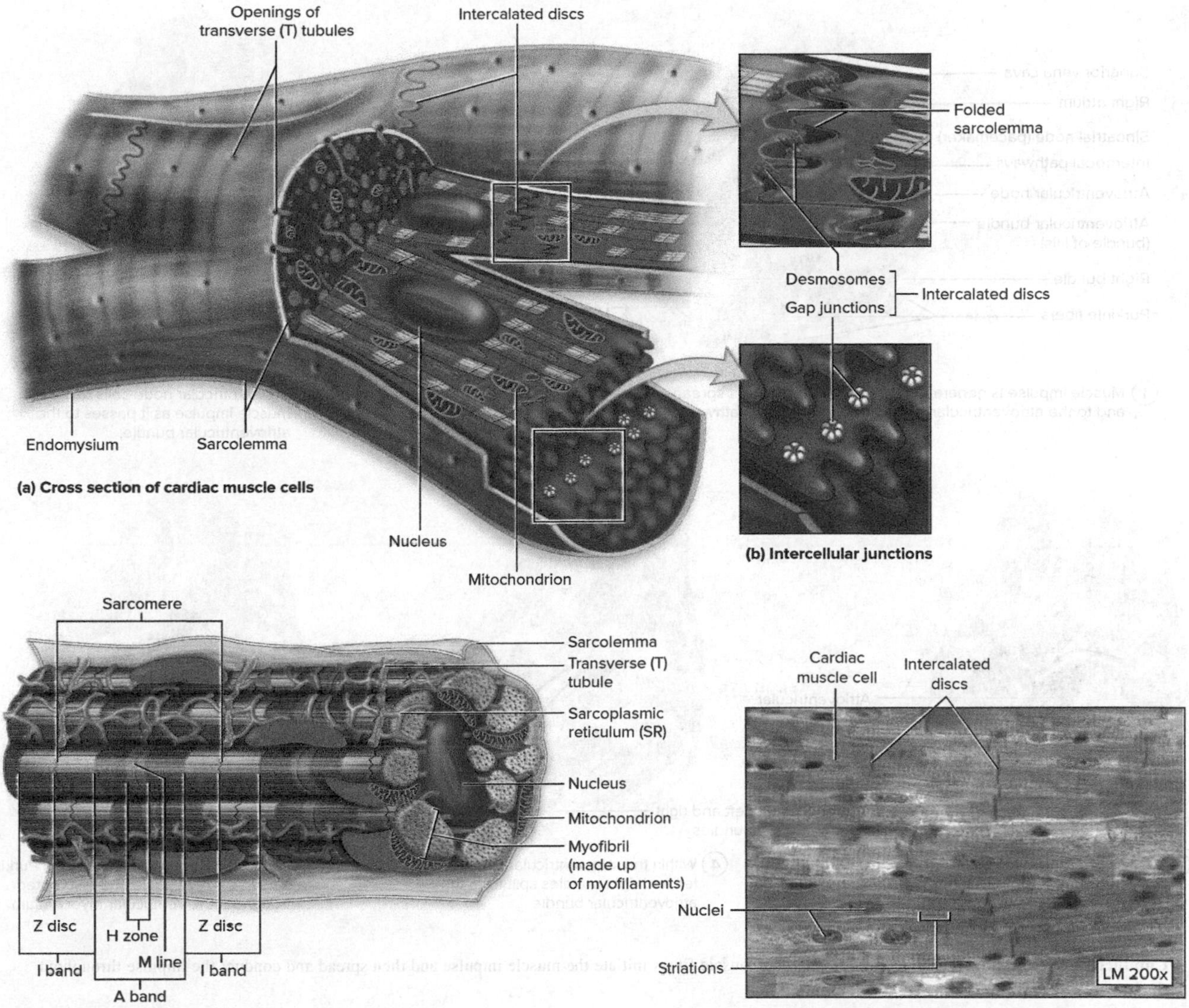
Openings of transverse (T) tubules
Intercalated discs
Folded sarcolemma
Desmosomes
Gap junctions
Intercalated discs
Endomysium
Sarcolemma
Nucleus
Mitochondrion
Sarcomere
Sarcolemma
Transverse (T) tubule
Sarcoplasmic reticulum (SR)
Nucleus
Mitochondrion
Myofibril (made up of myofilaments)
Z disc
H zone
M line
Z disc
I band
I band
A band
Cardiac muscle cell
Intercalated discs
Nuclei
Striations
LM 200x

(a) Cross section of cardiac muscle cells

(b) Intercellular junctions

(c) Longitudinal view of cardiac muscle cell

(d) Longitudinal section of cardiac muscle

Figure 22.10

Organization and Histology of Cardiac Muscle. Cardiac muscle cells form the myocardium. *(a)* Individual cells are relatively short, branched, and striated. *(b)* They are connected to adjacent cells by intercalated discs. *(c)* Transverse (T) tubules are invaginations of the sarcolemma that surround myofibrils and overlie the Z disc. The sarcoplasmic reticulum (SR) is sparse in cardiac muscle compared to its abundance in skeletal muscle. *(d)* Light micrograph of cardiac muscle in longitudinal section. APR

(d) Victor P. Eroschenko

Table 22.2 Comparison of Cardiac and Skeletal Muscle

Features	Cardiac Muscle	Skeletal Muscle
Cell structure	Short and branching	Long and cylindrical
Nuclei	One or two nuclei in the center of the cell	Multiple nuclei at the periphery of the fiber
Specialized intercellular junctions?	Yes, in intercalated discs	No
Functional units	Sarcomere	Sarcomere
T-tubule organization	Overlie Z discs	Overlie A band/I band junctions
Protein structure	Thick and thin filaments	Thick and thin filaments
Sarcoplasmic reticulum	Less than in skeletal muscle	More than in cardiac muscle
Mitochondria	More than skeletal muscle	Fewer than cardiac muscle

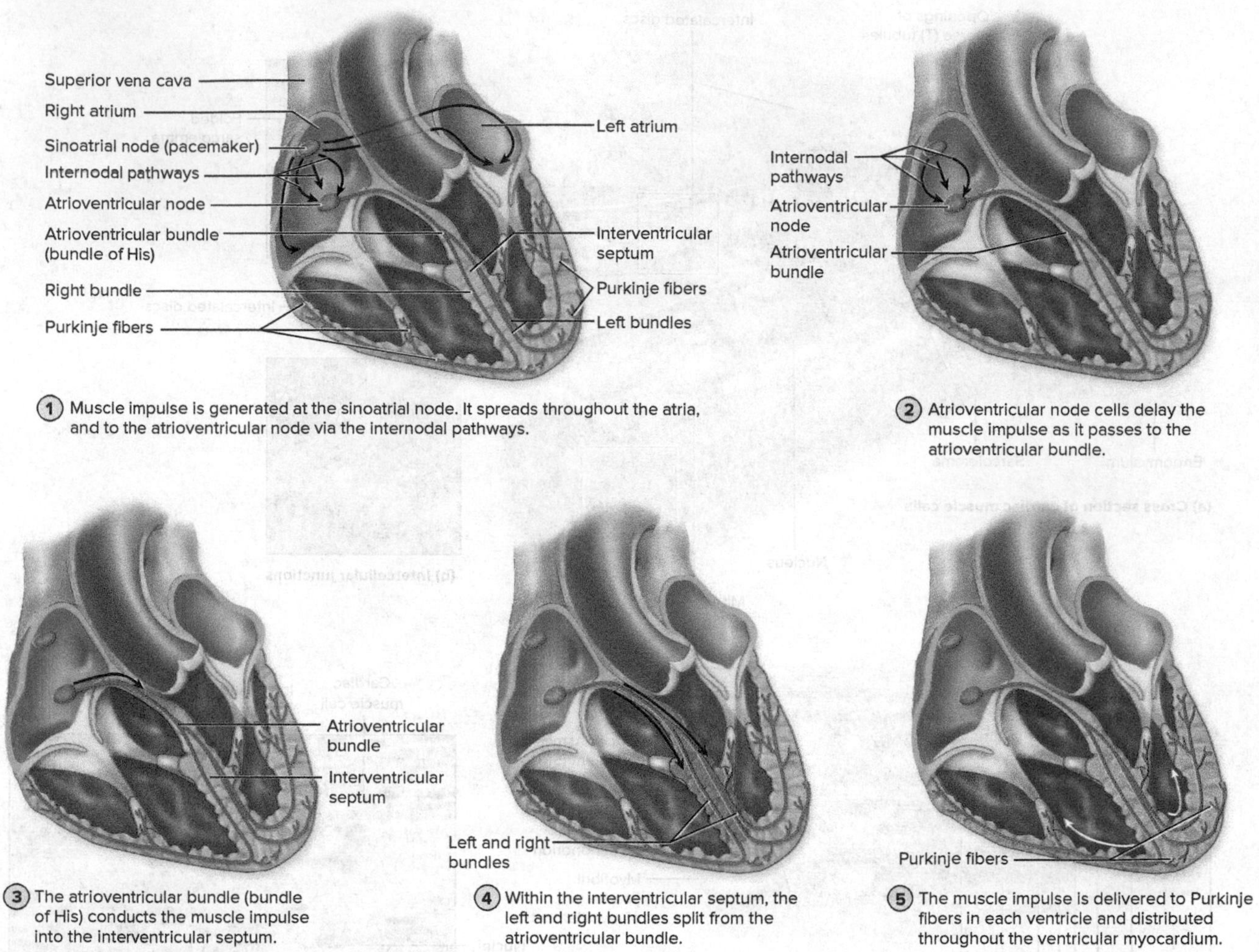

Figure 22.11

Conducting System of the Heart. Modified cardiac muscle fibers initiate the muscle impulse and then spread and conduct the impulse throughout the heart. APR

The muscle impulse spreads via gap junctions between cardiac muscle cells throughout both atria, and to the **atrioventricular (AV) node** via internodal pathways. The AV node is located in the floor of the right atrium between the right AV valve and the opening for the coronary sinus. The AV node normally slows conduction of the impulse as it travels from the atria to the ventricles, providing a delay between activation of the atria and the ventricles.

Recall that the fibrous skeleton electrically insulates the atria from the ventricles to prevent random muscle impulses from spreading between the atria and the ventricles. There is an opening in the fibrous skeleton that allows the AV node to communicate with the next part of the conduction system, the **atrioventricular (AV) bundle.** This bundle, also known as the *bundle of His,* receives the muscle impulse from the AV node and extends into the interventricular septum before dividing into **left** and **right bundles** (also known as *bundle branches*). These bundles conduct the impulse to conduction fibers called **Purkinje** (pŭr-kin′j ē) **fibers** that begin within the apex of the heart and extend through the walls of the ventricles. Purkinje fibers are larger than other cardiac muscle cells. Muscle impulse conduction along the Purkinje fibers is extremely rapid, consistent with the large size of the cells, and the impulse spreads immediately throughout the ventricular myocardium.

WHAT DID YOU LEARN?

9. What are three of the ways in which cardiac muscle differs from skeletal muscle?
10. Draw a flow chart outlining the path of the cardiac muscle impulse. Include all parts of the conducting system of the heart.
11. What is meant by the term *autorhythmic* when used to describe the heart?

Clinical View 22.5

The Electrocardiogram

Electrical currents within the heart can be detected during a routine physical examination using monitoring electrodes attached to the skin—usually at the wrist, ankles, and six separate locations on the chest. The electrical impulses are collected and charted as an **electrocardiogram** (ē-lek′trō-kar′dē-ō-gram; *gramma* = drawing), also called an **ECG** or *EKG*. When readings from the different electrodes are compared, they collectively provide an accurate, comprehensive assessment of the electrical activity of the heart.

An ECG provides a composite tracing of all muscle impulses generated by myocardial cells. It records the wave of change in voltage (potential) across the sarcolemma that (1) originates in the SA node, (2) radiates through both of the atria to the AV node, (3) passes through the AV node and the interventricular septum to the heart apex, and (4) stimulates the Purkinje fibers in the ventricular myocardium.

The progress of impulse transmission through the various parts of the conducting system is mirrored in an electrocardiogram. A typical ECG tracing for one heart cycle has three principal deflections: a P wave above the baseline, a QRS complex that begins (Q) and ends (S) with small downward deflection from the baseline and has a large deflection (R) above the baseline, and a T wave above the baseline (see figure). These waves are indicators of depolarization and repolarization within specific regions of the heart:

1. The **P wave** is generated when the impulse originating in the SA node depolarizes the cells of the atria.
2. The **QRS complex** identifies the beginning of depolarization of the ventricles. Simultaneously, the atria repolarize; however, this repolarization signal is masked by the electrical activity of the ventricles.
3. The **T wave** is a small, rounded peak that denotes ventricular repolarization.

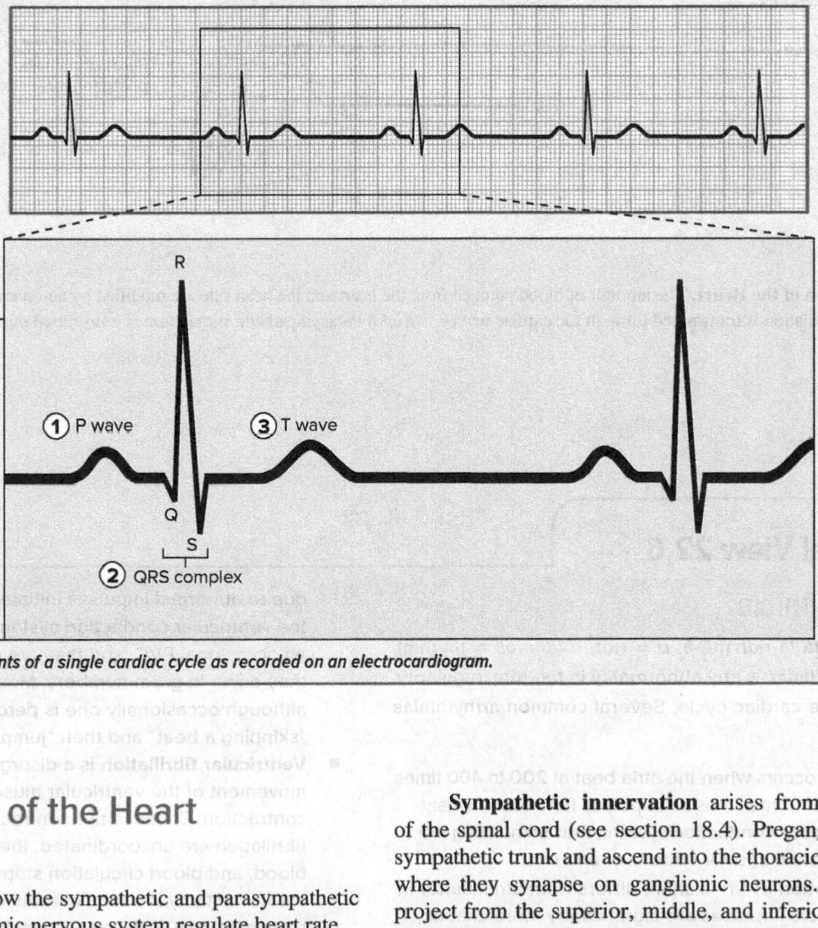

The events of a single cardiac cycle as recorded on an electrocardiogram.

22.5 Innervation of the Heart

✓ Learning Objective

13. Describe and explain how the sympathetic and parasympathetic divisions of the autonomic nervous system regulate heart rate.

The heart is innervated by the autonomic nervous system (**figure 22.12**). This innervation consists of sympathetic and parasympathetic components, collectively referred to as the **cardiac plexus** (see section 18.5a). The innervation by autonomic centers in the brainstem doesn't initiate a heartbeat, but it can increase or decrease the rate of the heartbeat.

Sympathetic innervation arises from the T1–T5 segments of the spinal cord (see section 18.4). Preganglionic axons enter the sympathetic trunk and ascend into the thoracic and cervical portions, where they synapse on ganglionic neurons. Postganglionic axons project from the superior, middle, and inferior cervical ganglia and the T1–T5 ganglia, and travel directly to the heart through cardiac nerves. Sympathetic innervation increases the rate and the force of heart contractions.

Parasympathetic innervation comes from the medulla oblongata via the left and right vagus nerves (CN X) (see section 18.3). As the vagus nerves descend into the thoracic cavity, they give off branches that supply the heart. Parasympathetic innervation

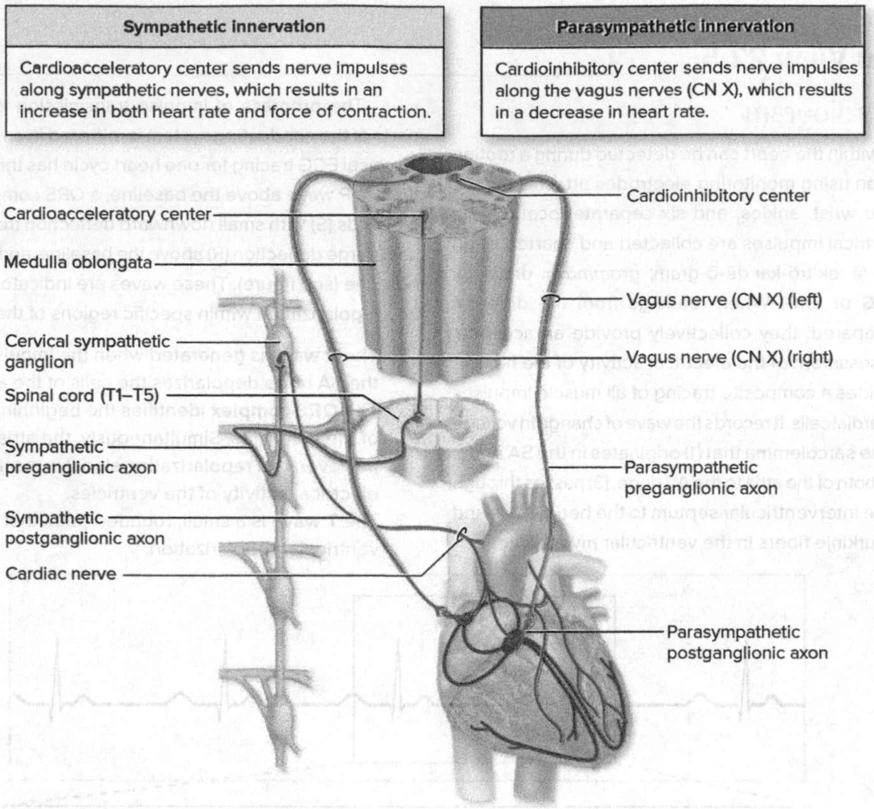
Sympathetic innervation
Cardioacceleratory center sends nerve impulses along sympathetic nerves, which results in an increase in both heart rate and force of contraction.
Parasympathetic innervation
Cardioinhibitory center sends nerve impulses along the vagus nerves (CN X), which results in a decrease in heart rate.
Cardioacceleratory center
Medulla oblongata
Cervical sympathetic ganglion
Spinal cord (T1–T5)
Sympathetic preganglionic axon
Sympathetic postganglionic axon
Cardiac nerve
Cardioinhibitory center
Vagus nerve (CN X) (left)
Vagus nerve (CN X) (right)
Parasympathetic preganglionic axon
Parasympathetic postganglionic axon

Figure 22.12

Autonomic Innervation of the Heart. The amount of blood pumped from the heart and the heart rate are modified by autonomic centers in the brainstem. *(Left)* Sympathetic stimulation is transmitted through the cardiac nerves. *(Right)* Parasympathetic stimulation is transmitted through the vagus nerves. APR

Clinical View 22.6

Cardiac Arrhythmia

Cardiac arrhythmia (ă-ridh′mē-ă; *a* = not, *rhythmos* = rhythm), also called *dysrhythmia,* is any abnormality in the rate, regularity, or sequence of the cardiac cycle. Several common arrhythmias are described:

- **Atrial flutter** occurs when the atria beat at 200 to 400 times per minute. Abnormal muscle impulses flow continuously through the atrial conduction system, thus stimulating the atrial musculature and AV node over and over.
- **Atrial fibrillation** (fī-bri-lā′shŭn) differs from atrial flutter in that the muscle impulses are significantly more chaotic, leading to an irregular heart rate. The ventricles respond by increasing and decreasing contraction activities, which may lead to serious disturbances in the cardiac rhythm.
- **Premature ventricular contractions (PVCs)** often result from stress, stimulants such as caffeine, or sleep deprivation. They occur either singly or in rapid bursts due to abnormal impulses initiated within the AV node or the ventricular conduction system. All of us experience an occasional PVC, and they are not detrimental unless they occur in great numbers. Most PVCs go unnoticed, although occasionally one is perceived as the heart "skipping a beat" and then "jumping" in the chest.
- **Ventricular fibrillation** is a disorganized, rapid, repetitious movement of the ventricular muscle that replaces normal contraction. Because the contractions of a heart in fibrillation are uncoordinated, the heart does not pump blood, and blood circulation stops. This cessation of cardiac activity is called **cardiac arrest.** Cardiopulmonary resuscitation (CPR) (see Clinical View 13.2: "Surface Anatomy and CPR" in section 13.3) can be used to continue circulation of blood during cardiac arrest. Attempts to resynchronize cardiac muscle cell electrical activity require use of an *automated external defibrillator (AED)* or paddle electrodes.

Learning Strategy 22.3

Here is one way to help you remember the effects of sympathetic and parasympathetic innervation on the heart:

Sympathetic innervation **S**peeds the heart rate.

Parasympathetic innervation does the o**P**posite (decreases the heart rate).

decreases the heart rate, but generally tends to have no effect on the force of contractions.

Although there is a particularly rich sympathetic and parasympathetic innervation of the SA and AV nodes, the working myocardial cells are also supplied by both types of autonomic axons.

WHAT DID YOU LEARN?

12 How does the sympathetic division of the autonomic nervous system affect the heart rate?

22.6 Tying It All Together: The Cardiac Cycle

✓ **Learning Objectives**

14. Identify and describe the events in the cardiac cycle.
15. Trace the pattern of blood flow through the heart.

A **cardiac cycle** includes all the events within the heart from the start of one heartbeat to the initiation of the next. During a single cardiac cycle, all chambers within the heart experience alternate periods of contraction and relaxation. The contraction of a heart chamber is called **systole** (sis'tō-lē). During this period, the contraction of the myocardium forces blood either into another chamber (from atrium to ventricle) or into a blood vessel (from a ventricle into the attached large artery). The relaxation phase of a heart chamber is termed **diastole** (dī-as'tō-lē; dilation). During this period between contraction phases, the myocardium of each chamber relaxes, and the chamber fills with blood.

At the beginning of the cardiac cycle, the left and right atria contract simultaneously. When the atria contract (atrial systole), blood is forced through the open AV valves into the ventricles. Blood continues to enter the atria via their associated veins (see section 22.2c). Left and right ventricular contraction (ventricular systole) occurs after the atria start to relax (atrial diastole) (**figure 22.13*a***). When the ventricles contract, blood pushes the cusps of the AV valves closed, their edges meet to form a seal. Papillary muscles and the chordae tendineae prevent these valve cusps from everting. The semilunar valves are forced open, and blood enters the pulmonary trunk and the aorta. When the ventricles relax (ventricular diastole), blood flows passively from the relaxed atria into the ventricles through open AV valves (figure 22.13*b*). The cardiac cycle ends with all four chambers in diastole.

WHAT DO YOU THINK?

3 What could happen if the AV valves were to evert into the atria?

22.6a Steps in the Cardiac Cycle

The events in a normal cardiac cycle are shown in **figure 22.14** and described here:

1. **Atrial contraction and ventricular filling** occur at the beginning of the cardiac cycle. There is a brief contraction of the atrial myocardium initiated by the SA node. Contraction of the atria finishes filling the ventricles through the open AV valves while the ventricles are in diastole. The semilunar valves remain closed.
2. **Isovolumic contraction** happens at the beginning of the ventricular contraction. The AV valves are forced closed (producing the "lubb" sound), and the semilunar valves remain closed. The atria remain in diastole.
3. **Ventricular ejection** takes place later in the ventricular contraction, when pressure on blood in the ventricles forces the semilunar valves to open, and blood is ejected into the arterial trunks. The atria remain in diastole, and the AV valves remain closed.
4. **Isovolumic relaxation** occurs at the start of ventricular relaxation. The semilunar valves close to prevent blood backflow into the ventricles (producing the "dupp" sound). The AV valves remain closed and the atria remain in diastole.
5. **Atrial relaxation and ventricular filling** happen during the continuation of ventricular relaxation. The atria remain in diastole. The AV valve opens, and passive filling of the ventricle from the atria begins and continues as most of the ventricular filling occurs. The semilunar valves remain closed.

22.6b Summary of Blood Flow During the Cardiac Cycle

As the heart chambers cyclically contract and relax, pressure on the blood in the chambers alternately increases and decreases. **Table 22.3** illustrates the flow of blood through the four heart chambers during the cardiac cycle. As you learn this sequence, keep the following general principles in mind:

- Blood flows from high pressure to low pressure.
- Heart valves keep blood flowing in one direction.
- Blood flows from veins into the atria under low pressure.
- About 70% of the ventricular filling occurs passively when both chambers are relaxed, atrial pressure is greater than the ventricular pressure, and the AV valves are open. Atrial systole fills the final 30% of the ventricles.
- Ventricular contraction (systole) increases pressure on the blood within the ventricles. This pressure continues to increase, first closing the AV valves, then forcing the semilunar valves open to eject blood into the great arteries.

Learning Strategy 22.4

Blood moves through the heart from high pressure to low pressure. Contraction of the wall of the heart chamber increases the pressure, which causes the blood to move.

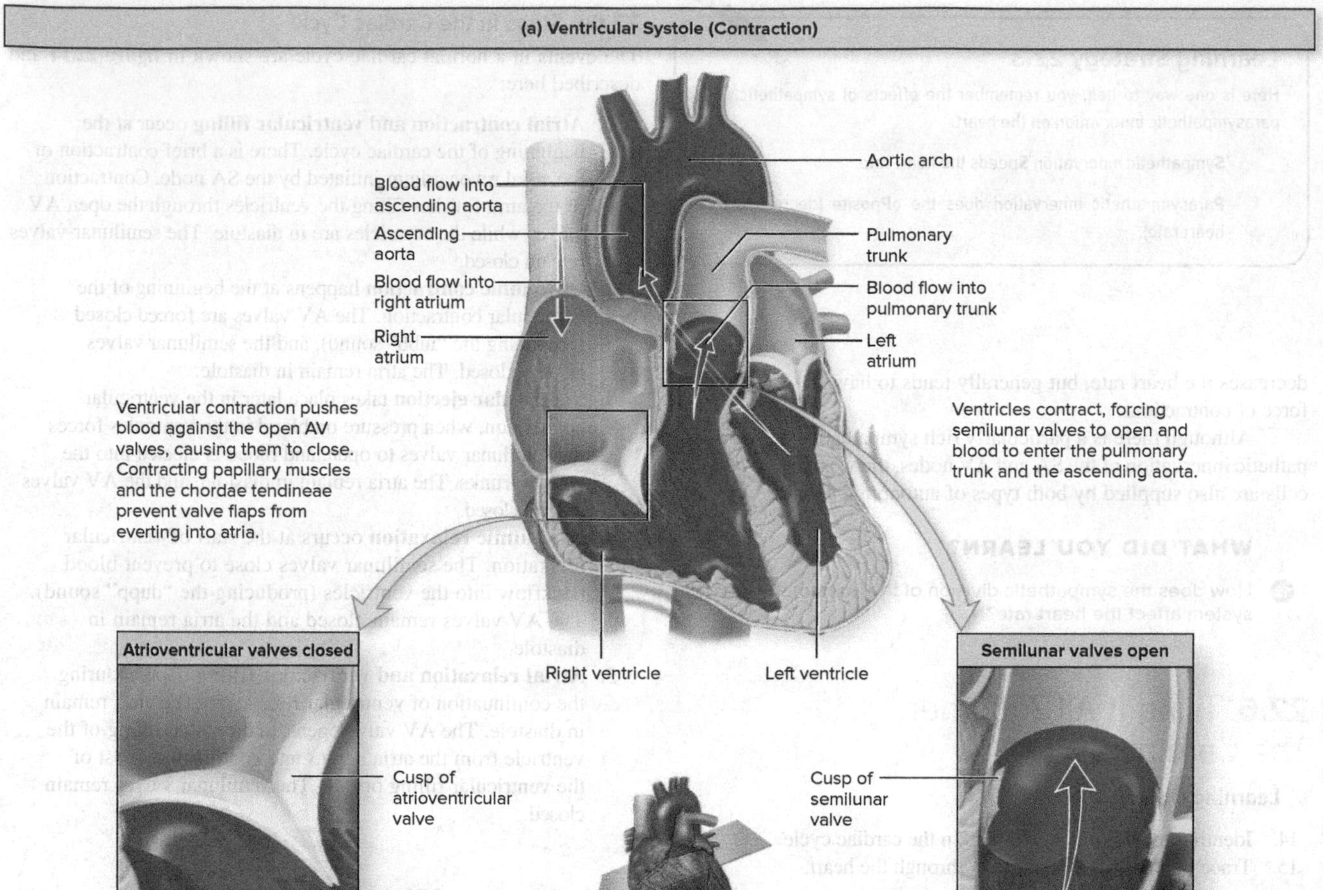

Figure 22.13

Ventricular Systole and Ventricular Diastole. *(a)* The semilunar valves open during ventricular systole to allow blood to flow into the large arteries; the AV valves close during ventricular systole to prevent backflow of blood into the atria. *(b)* During ventricular diastole, the AV valves open to allow blood to enter the ventricles from the atria; the semilunar valves remain closed to prevent backflow of blood into the ventricles from the large arteries. Transverse sections in both *(a)* and *(b)* show a superior view.

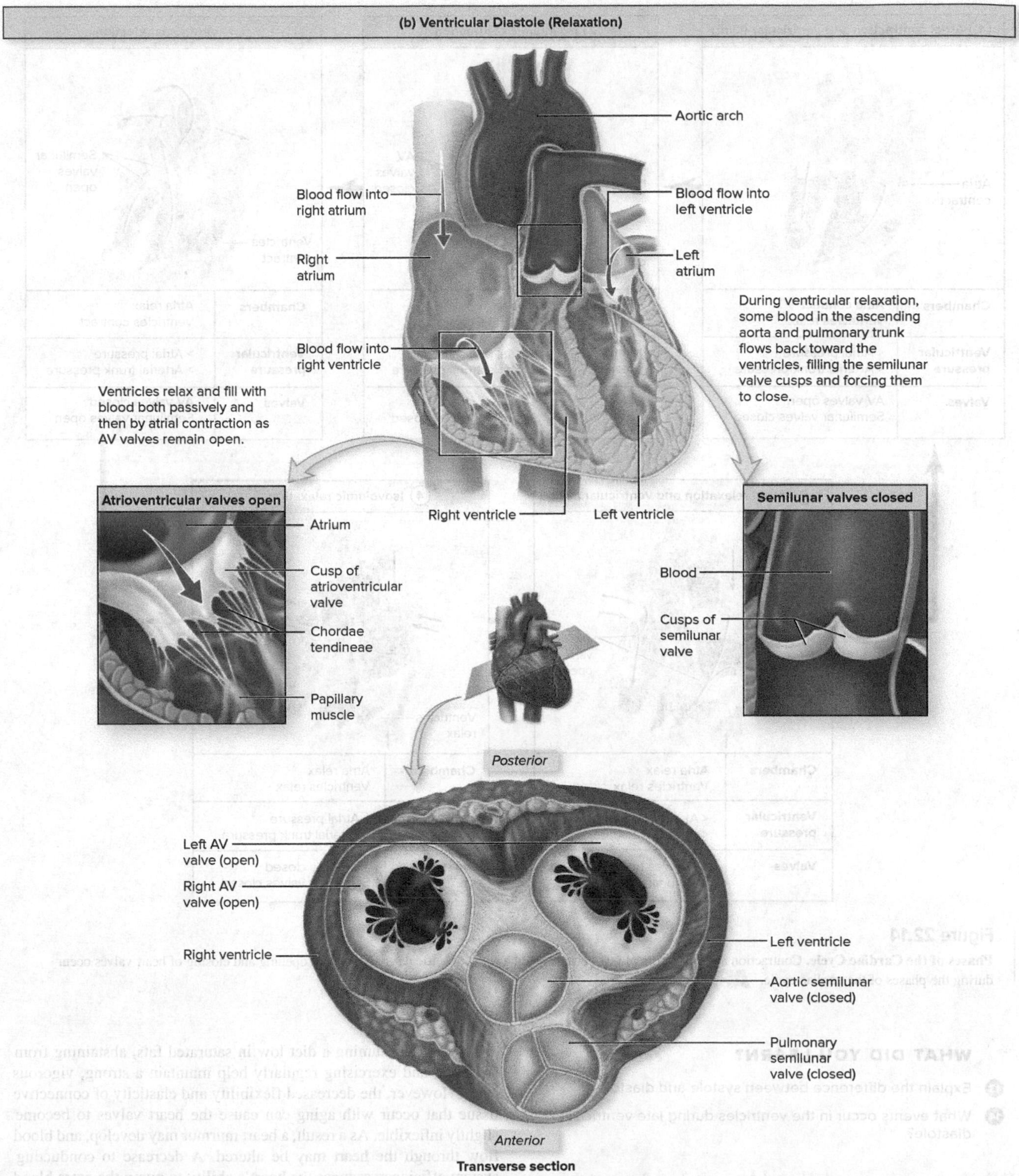
(b) Ventricular Diastole (Relaxation)
Aortic arch
Blood flow into right atrium
Blood flow into left ventricle
Right atrium
Left atrium
During ventricular relaxation, some blood in the ascending aorta and pulmonary trunk flows back toward the ventricles, filling the semilunar valve cusps and forcing them to close.
Blood flow into right ventricle
Ventricles relax and fill with blood both passively and then by atrial contraction as AV valves remain open.
Atrioventricular valves open
Atrium
Cusp of atrioventricular valve
Chordae tendineae
Papillary muscle
Right ventricle
Left ventricle
Semilunar valves closed
Blood
Cusps of semilunar valve
Posterior
Left AV valve (open)
Right AV valve (open)
Right ventricle
Left ventricle
Aortic semilunar valve (closed)
Pulmonary semilunar valve (closed)
Anterior
Transverse section

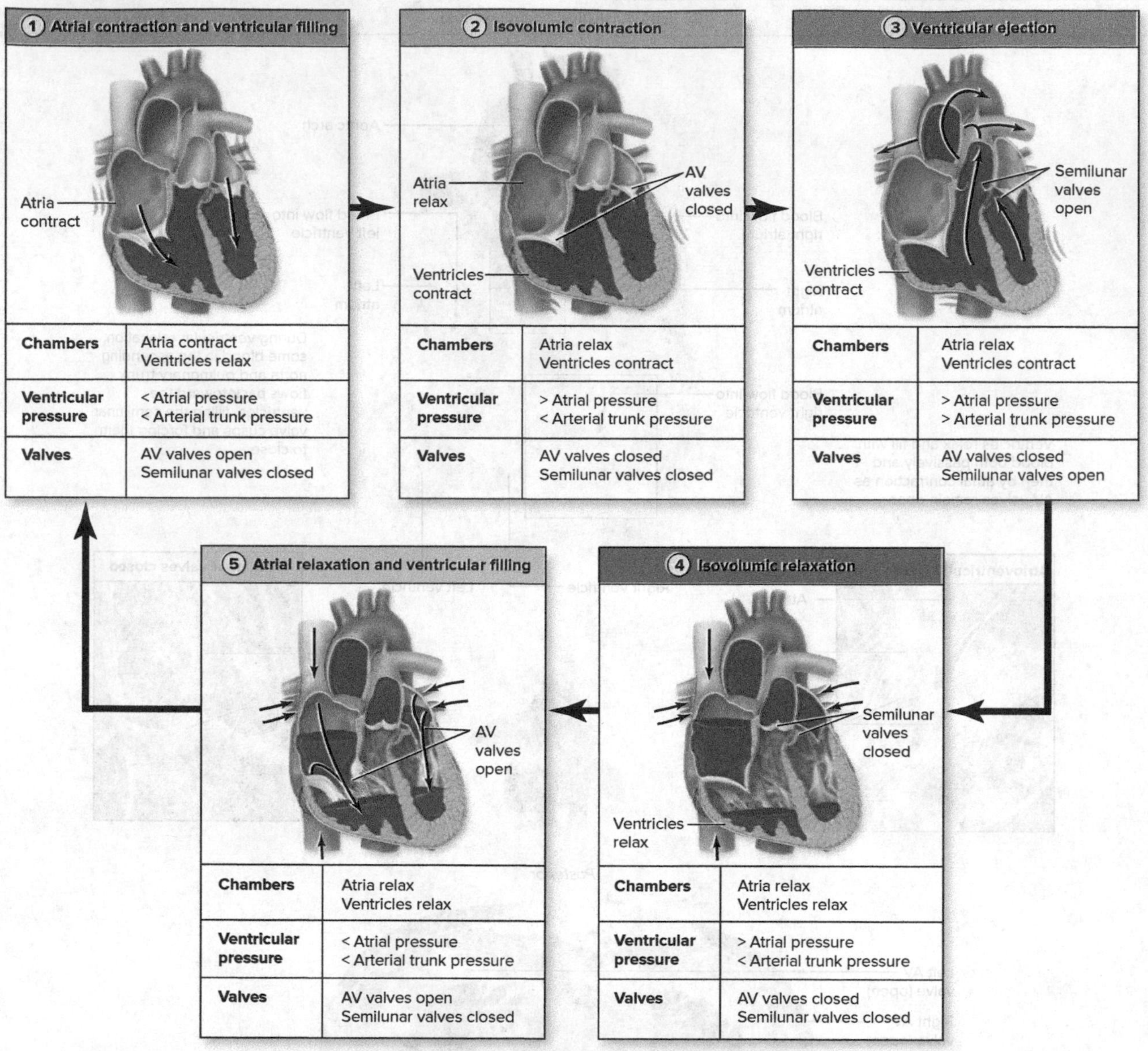
1 Atrial contraction and ventricular filling
Atria contract
Chambers: Atria contract; Ventricles relax
Ventricular pressure: < Atrial pressure; < Arterial trunk pressure
Valves: AV valves open; Semilunar valves closed
2 Isovolumic contraction
Atria relax
AV valves closed
Ventricles contract
Chambers: Atria relax; Ventricles contract
Ventricular pressure: > Atrial pressure; < Arterial trunk pressure
Valves: AV valves closed; Semilunar valves closed
3 Ventricular ejection
Semilunar valves open
Ventricles contract
Chambers: Atria relax; Ventricles contract
Ventricular pressure: > Atrial pressure; > Arterial trunk pressure
Valves: AV valves closed; Semilunar valves open
4 Isovolumic relaxation
Semilunar valves closed
Ventricles relax
Chambers: Atria relax; Ventricles relax
Ventricular pressure: > Atrial pressure; < Arterial trunk pressure
Valves: AV valves closed; Semilunar valves closed
5 Atrial relaxation and ventricular filling
AV valves open
Chambers: Atria relax; Ventricles relax
Ventricular pressure: < Atrial pressure; < Arterial trunk pressure
Valves: AV valves open; Semilunar valves closed

Figure 22.14

Phases of the Cardiac Cycle. Contraction and relaxation of heart chambers, changes in ventricular pressure, and opening and closing of heart valves occur during the phases of the cardiac cycle. APR

WHAT DID YOU LEARN?

13 Explain the difference between systole and diastole.

14 What events occur in the ventricles during late ventricular diastole?

22.7 Aging and the Heart

✓ Learning Objective

16. Explain how heart function changes as we age.

A healthy heart is capable of quickly and efficiently altering both the heartbeat rate and the volume of blood pumped during a change in activity. Consuming a diet low in saturated fats, abstaining from smoking, and exercising regularly help maintain a strong, vigorous heart. However, the decreased flexibility and elasticity of connective tissue that occur with aging can cause the heart valves to become slightly inflexible. As a result, a heart murmur may develop, and blood flow through the heart may be altered. A decrease to conducting system efficiency reduces the heart's ability to pump the extra blood needed during stress and exercise.

In addition, high blood pressure causes the ventricles to work harder to pump blood into the arterial trunks. This results in ventricular myocardium hypertrophy, which increases the thickness of the walls. This increase in cardiac muscle cell size interferes with the cell's functional arrangement, causing the heart to work less efficiently.

Table 22.3 Blood Flow Through the Heart

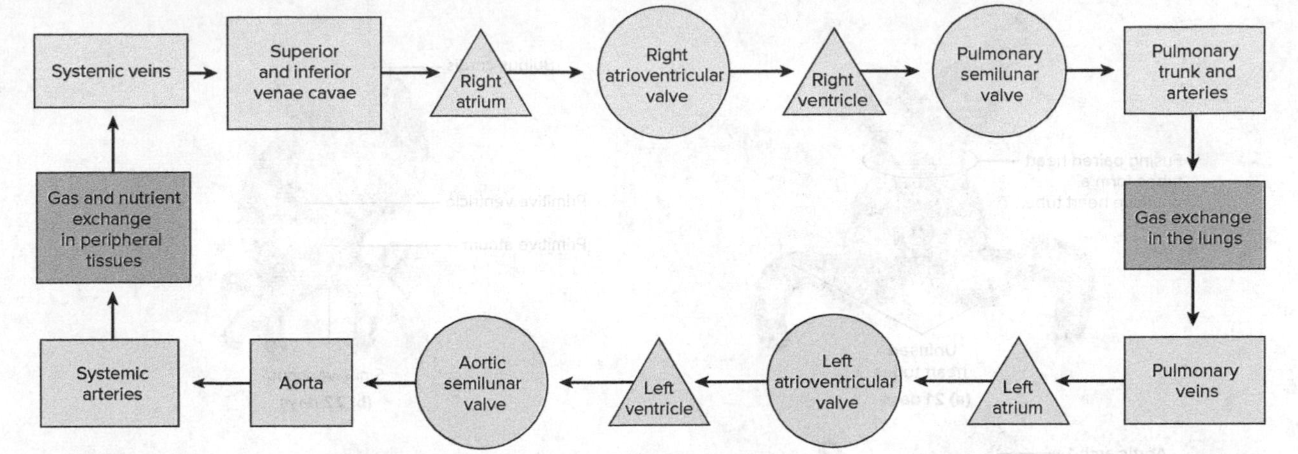

Chamber of the Heart	Receives Blood From	Sends Blood To	Valves Through Which Blood Flows
Right atrium	Superior vena cava, inferior vena cava, coronary sinus	Right ventricle	Right AV valve
Right ventricle	Right atrium	Pulmonary trunk (blood enters vessels of pulmonary circulation)	Pulmonary semilunar valve
Left atrium	Pulmonary veins	Left ventricle	Left AV valve
Left ventricle	Left atrium	Ascending aorta (blood enters vessels of systemic circulation)	Aortic semilunar valve

WHAT DID YOU LEARN?

15 What are some age-related changes that result in altered heart functions?

22.8 Development of the Heart

✓ Learning Objective

17. Trace and describe the formation of postnatal heart structures from the primitive heart tube.

Development of the heart commences in the third week, when the embryo becomes too large to receive its nutrients through diffusion alone. At this time, the embryo needs its own blood supply, heart, and blood vessels for transporting oxygen and nutrients through its growing body. The steps involved in heart development are complex, because the heart must begin working before its development is complete.

By day 19 (middle of week 3), two**heart tubes** (or *endocardial tubes*) form from mesoderm in the embryo. By day 21, these paired tubes fuse, forming a single primitive heart tube (**figure 22.15**). This tube develops the following named expansions that ultimately give rise to postnatal heart structures (listed from inferior to superior): **sinus venosus, primitive atrium, primitive ventricle,** and **bulbus cordis** (bŭl'bŭs kōr'dis). The sinus venosus and primitive atrium form parts of the left and right atria. The primitive ventricle forms most of the left ventricle. The bulbus cordis may be further subdivided into a trabeculated part of the right ventricle, which forms most of the right ventricle; the **conus cordis,** which forms the outflow tracts for the ventricles; and the **truncus arteriosus,** which forms the ascending aorta and pulmonary trunk (figure 22.15 *c*). **Table 22.4** lists these primitive heart tube components and their resulting structures.

By day 22, the primitive heart begins to beat and begins its process of bending and folding (figure 22.15*b*). The bulbus cordis is pulled inferiorly, anteriorly, and to the embryo's right, while the primitive ventricle moves left to reposition. The primitive atrium and sinus venosus reposition superiorly and posteriorly. Thus, by day 28 the heart tube is S-shaped (figure 22.15*c*).

The next major steps in heart development occur during weeks 5–8, when the single heart tube becomes partitioned into four chambers (two atria and two ventricles), and the great vessels form. The common atrium is subdivided into a left and right atrium by an interatrial septum, which consists of two parts (**septum primum** and **septum secundum**) that partially overlap. These two parts connect to tissue masses called **endocardial cushions.** An opening in the septum secundum (which is covered by the septum primum) is called the **foramen ovale** (ō-val'ē) (figure 22.15*d*). Because the embryonic lungs are not functional, much of the blood is shunted from the right atrium to the left atrium by traveling through the foramen ovale and pushing the septum primum into the left atrium. Blood cannot flow back from the left atrium to the right, because the septum primum's movement to the right is stopped when it comes against the septum secundum. Thus, the septum primum acts as a unidirectional flutter valve.

When the baby is born and the lungs are fully functional, the blood from the left atrium pushes the septum primum and secundum together, creating a closed interatrial septum. The only remnant of the embryonic opening is an oval-shaped depression in the interatrial septum called the fossa ovalis.

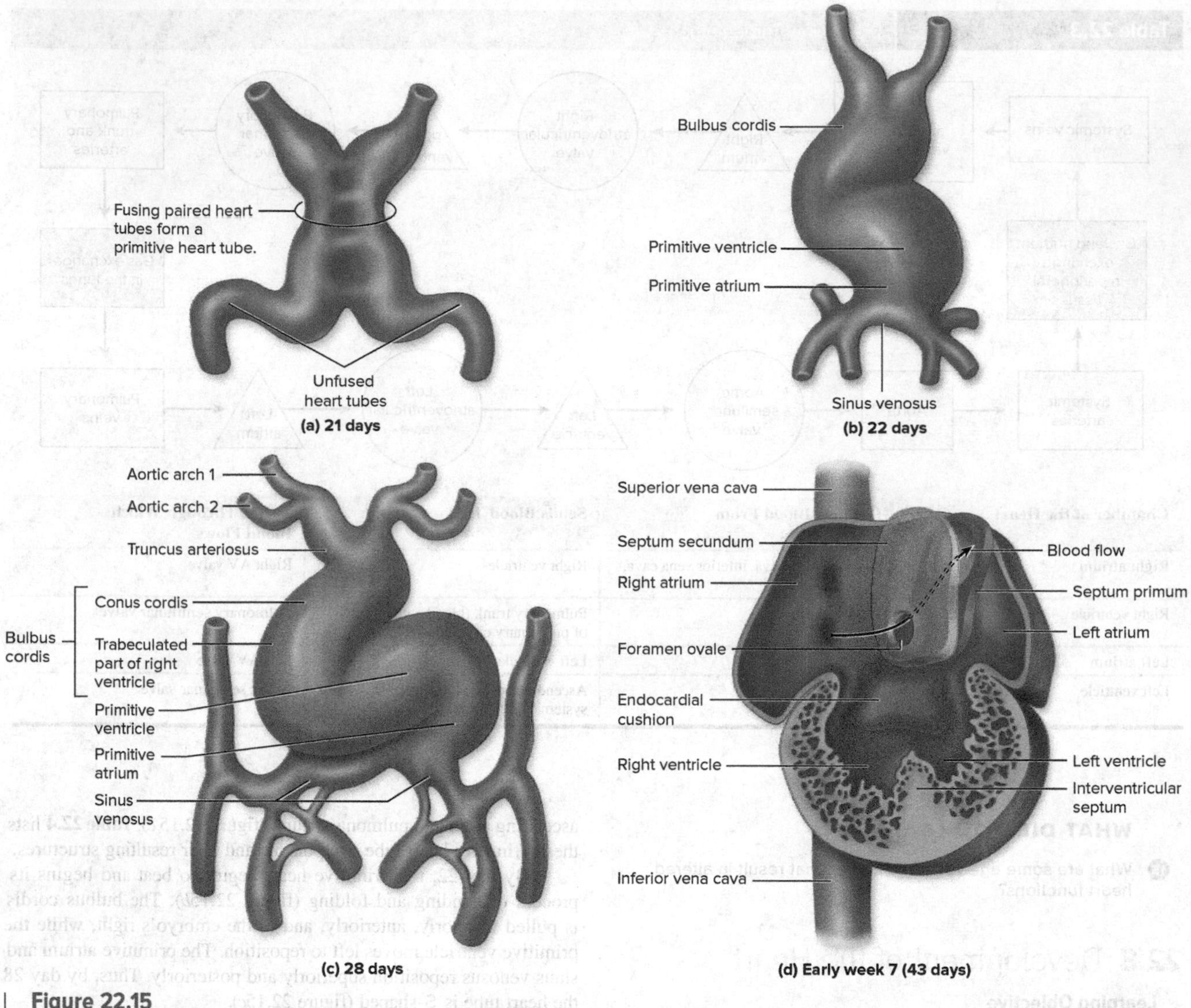
Fusing paired heart tubes form a primitive heart tube.
Unfused heart tubes
(a) 21 days
Bulbus cordis
Primitive ventricle
Primitive atrium
Sinus venosus
(b) 22 days
Aortic arch 1
Aortic arch 2
Truncus arteriosus
Bulbus cordis
Conus cordis
Trabeculated part of right ventricle
Primitive ventricle
Primitive atrium
Sinus venosus
(c) 28 days
Superior vena cava
Septum secundum
Right atrium
Foramen ovale
Endocardial cushion
Right ventricle
Inferior vena cava
Blood flow
Septum primum
Left atrium
Left ventricle
Interventricular septum
(d) Early week 7 (43 days)

Figure 22.15

Development of the Heart. The heart develops from mesoderm. By day 19, paired heart tubes are present in the cardiogenic region of the embryo. *(a)* These paired tubes fuse by day 21. *(b)* The single heart tube bends and folds upon itself, beginning on day 22. *(c)* By day 28, the heart tube is S-shaped. *(d)* By early week 7, the interatrial septum is formed by two overlapping septa. The foramen ovale is a passageway that detours blood away from the pulmonary circulation into the systemic circulation prior to birth.

Table 22.4 Primitive Heart Tube Components and Their Postnatal Structures

Heart Tube Component	Postnatal Derivative
Sinus venosus	Superior vena cava, coronary sinus, smooth posterior wall of right atrium
Primitive atrium	Anterior muscular portions of left and right atria
Primitive ventricle	Most of left ventricle
Bulbus cordis	
Trabeculated part of right ventricle	Most of right ventricle
Conus cordis	Outflow tracts from ventricles to aorta and pulmonary trunk
Truncus arteriosus	Ascending aorta, pulmonary trunk

Left and right ventricles are partitioned by an interventricular septum that grows superiorly from the floor of the ventricles. The AV valves, papillary muscles, and chordae tendineae all form from portions of the ventricular walls as well. The superior part of the interventricular septum develops from the **aorticopulmonary septum,** which is a spiral-shaped mass that also subdivides the truncus arteriosus into the pulmonary trunk and the ascending aorta.

Many congenital heart malformations result from incomplete or faulty development during these early weeks. For example, in an **atrial septal defect** the postnatal heart still has an opening between the left and right atria. Thus, blood from the left atrium (the higher-pressure system) is shunted to the right atrium (the lower-pressure system). This can lead to enlargement of the right side of the heart.

Ventricular septal defects can occur if the interventricular septum is incompletely formed. A common malformation called **tetralogy of Fallot** occurs when the aorticopulmonary septum divides the truncus arteriosus unevenly. As a result, the patient has a ventricular septal defect, a very narrow pulmonary trunk (termed *pulmonary stenosis*), an aorta that overlaps both the left and right ventricles, and an enlarged right ventricle (termed *right ventricular hypertrophy*).

Clinical Terms

bradycardia (brad′ē-kar′dē-ă; *bradys* = slow) Slowing of the heartbeat, usually described as less than 50 beats per minute.

cardiomyopathy (kar′dē-ō-mī-op′ă-thē) Another term for disease of the myocardium; causes vary and include thickening of the ventricular septum (hypertrophy), secondary disease of the myocardium, or sometimes a disease of unknown cause.

endocarditis (en′dō-kar-dī′tis) Inflammation of the endocardium. Types include bacterial (caused by the direct invasion of bacteria), chorditis (affecting the chordae tendineae), infectious (caused by microorganisms), mycotic (due to infection by fungi), and rheumatic (due to endocardial involvement as part of rheumatic heart disease).

ischemia (is-kē′mē-ă; *ischo* = to keep back) Inadequate blood flow to a structure caused by obstruction of the blood supply, usually due to arterial narrowing or disruption of blood flow.

myocarditis (mī′ō-kar-dī′tis) Inflammation of the muscular walls of the heart. This uncommon disorder is caused by viral, bacterial, or parasitic infections, exposure to chemicals, or allergic reactions to certain medications.

Chapter Summary

22.1 Overview of the Cardiovascular System	■ Arteries transport blood away from the heart, and veins return blood to the heart. ■ Heart functions include one-directional blood flow through the cardiovascular system, coordinated side-by-side pumps, and generation of pressure to drive blood through blood vessels. **22.1a Pulmonary and Systemic Circulations** ■ The pulmonary circulation conveys blood to and from the lungs, and the systemic circulation carries blood to and from all the organs and tissues. **22.1b Position of the Heart** ■ The heart is located posterior to the sternum in the mediastinum. ■ Its base is the posterosuperior surface formed primarily by the left atrium; the apex is in the conical, inferior end. **22.1c Characteristics of the Pericardium** ■ The pericardium that encloses the heart has an outer fibrous portion and an inner serous portion. ■ The pericardial cavity is a thin space between the layers of the serous pericardium. Pericardial fluid produced by the serous membranes lubricates the surfaces to reduce friction.
22.2 Anatomy of the Heart	■ The heart is a small, cone-shaped organ. **22.2a Heart Wall Structure** ■ The heart wall has an epicardium (visceral pericardium), myocardium (thick layer of cardiac muscle), and endocardium (thin endothelium and areolar connective tissue). **22.2b External Heart Anatomy** ■ The heart has four chambers: Two smaller atria receive blood returning to the heart, and two larger ventricles pump blood away from the heart. ■ Around the circumference of the heart, a deep coronary sulcus separates the atria and ventricles. Shallow sulci extend from the coronary sulcus on the anterior and posterior surfaces between the ventricles. Coronary vessels lie within the sulci.

(continued on next page)

Chapter Summary *(continued)*

22.2 Anatomy of the Heart *(continued)*	**22.2c Internal Heart Anatomy: Chambers and Valves** ■ Dense regular connective tissue forms the fibrous skeleton of the heart that separates the atria and the ventricles. This skeleton (1) separates atria and ventricles, (2) anchors heart valves, (3) provides for attachment of cardiac muscle tissue, and (4) electrically insulates atria and ventricles. ■ The right atrium receives blood from the superior vena cava, the inferior vena cava, and the coronary sinus. ■ Atria are separated by an interatrial septum, and ventricles are separated by an interventricular septum. ■ Four pulmonary veins empty into the left atrium. ■ Thick-walled ventricles receive blood from the atria through open AV valves. The free edges of the AV valve cusps are prevented from everting into the atria by the chordae tendineae. ■ Trabeculae carneae are large, irregular muscular ridges on the inside of the ventricle wall. ■ Papillary muscles are cone-shaped projections on the inner surface of the ventricles that anchor the chordae tendineae. ■ Semilunar valves are located within the wall of each ventricle near its connection to a large artery. The right ventricle houses the pulmonary semilunar valve, and the left ventricle houses the aortic semilunar valve.
22.3 Coronary Circulation	■ The major coronary artery branches are the anterior interventricular and circumflex arteries from the left coronary artery, and the right marginal and posterior interventricular arteries from the right coronary artery. ■ Venous return is through the cardiac veins into the coronary sinus, which drains into the right atrium of the heart.
22.4 How the Heart Beats: Electrical Properties of Cardiac Tissue	**22.4a Characteristics of Cardiac Muscle Tissue** ■ Cardiac muscle cells are small and branched. They form sheets of cardiac muscle tissue arranged into spiral bundles wrapped around and between the heart chambers. ■ Intercalated discs tightly link the muscle cells together and permit the immediate passage of muscle impulses. **22.4b Contraction of Heart Muscle** ■ The heart exhibits autorhythmicity. Its stimulus to contract is initiated by cells of the sinoatrial (SA) node in the roof of the right atrium. ■ Muscle impulses travel to the atrioventricular (AV) node and then through the AV bundle within the interventricular septum to Purkinje fibers in the heart apex. **22.4c The Heart's Conducting System** ■ The heart initiates its own heartbeat using specialized cardiac muscle cells of the sinoatrial node. ■ The conducting system includes sinoatrial (SA) node, atrioventricular (AV) node, AV bundle, and Purkinje fibers, which conduct the impulse throughout the heart.
22.5 Innervation of the Heart	■ Sympathetic and parasympathetic innervation of the heart have opposing influences on heart rate. Autonomic innervation increases or decreases the rate of the heartbeat, but does not initiate the heartbeat.
22.6 Tying It All Together: The Cardiac Cycle	■ A cardiac cycle is the period of time from the start of one heartbeat to the beginning of the next. ■ All chambers within the heart experience alternate periods of contraction (systole) and relaxation (diastole) during a single cycle. **22.6a Steps in the Cardiac Cycle** ■ The cardiac cycle involves five phases: atrial contraction and ventricular filling, isovolumic contraction, ventricular ejection, isovolumic relaxation, and atrial relaxation and ventricular filling. **22.6b Summary of Blood Flow During the Cardiac Cycle** ■ Cyclic contraction and relaxation of heart chambers result in the pumping of blood out of the chambers and the subsequent refilling of the chambers with blood for the next cycle.
22.7 Aging and the Heart	■ Decreased flexibility of heart structures as we age reduces the efficiency of cardiac function. Increased blood pressure results in hypertrophy of the myocardium.
22.8 Development of the Heart	■ Development of the heart commences in the third week; two heart tubes form and fuse to become a single primitive heart tube. ■ The primitive heart tube develops expansions that later form postnatal heart structures.

Challenge Yourself

Actively write or type your answers in a separate document to reinforce your learning, before checking your answers.

Multiple Choice

Select the best answer from the four choices provided.

1. Which structures allow muscle impulses to spread rapidly between cardiac muscle cells?
   a. sarcomeres
   b. intercalated discs
   c. chemical neurotransmitters
   d. AV valves
2. Venous blood from the heart wall enters the right atrium through which vessel?
   a. superior vena cava
   b. coronary sinus
   c. inferior vena cava
   d. pulmonary veins
3. How is blood prevented from flowing into the right ventricle from the pulmonary trunk?
   a. closing of the right AV valves
   b. opening of the pulmonary semilunar valve
   c. contraction of the right atrium
   d. closing of the pulmonary semilunar valve
4. Which of the following is the correct circulatory sequence for blood to pass through part of the heart?
   a. R. atrium → right AV valve → R. ventricle → pulmonary semilunar valve
   b. R. atrium → left AV valve → R. ventricle → pulmonary semilunar valve
   c. L. atrium → right AV valve → L. ventricle → aortic semilunar valve
   d. L. atrium → left AV valve → L. ventricle → pulmonary semilunar valve
5. The pericardial cavity is located between which two structures?
   a. fibrous pericardium and the parietal layer of the serous pericardium
   b. parietal and visceral layers of the serous pericardium
   c. visceral layer of the serous pericardium and the epicardium
   d. myocardium and the visceral layer of the serous pericardium
6. In the developing heart, the atria form from the primitive atrium and which other structure?
   a. sinus venosus
   b. bulbus cordis
   c. primitive ventricle
   d. conus cordis
7. What are the irregular muscular ridges in the ventricular walls called?
   a. papillary muscles
   b. trabeculae carneae
   c. chordae tendineae
   d. moderator bands
8. In what location does the sympathetic innervation of cardiac muscle originate?
   a. CN X (vagus nerve)
   b. L1–L2 segments of the spinal cord
   c. the AV node
   d. T1–T5 segments of the spinal cord
9. Which of the following does not occur when the ventricles contract?
   a. closing of the AV valves
   b. blood ejecting into the pulmonary trunk and aorta
   c. closing of the semilunar valves
   d. opening of the semilunar valves
10. What is the thickest part of the heart wall?
   a. the pericardium
   b. the epicardium
   c. the myocardium
   d. the endocardium

Content Review

1. What are the differences between the pulmonary and systemic circulations?
2. What chamber walls primarily form the anterior side of the heart? What chamber walls form the posterior side of the heart?
3. Compare the structure, location, and function of the parietal and visceral layers of the serous pericardium.
4. Where is the fibrous skeleton of the heart located? What are its functions?
5. Why are the chordae tendineae required for the proper functioning of the AV valves?
6. Explain why the walls of the atria are thinner than those of the ventricles, and why the walls of the right ventricle are relatively thin when compared to the walls of the left ventricle.
7. Identify and compare the branches of the right and left coronary arteries. In general, what portions of the heart does each branch supply?
8. Compare cardiac and skeletal muscle. In what ways are these muscle types similar? In which ways are they different?
9. Describe the functional differences in the effects of the sympathetic and parasympathetic divisions of the autonomic nervous system on the activity of cardiac muscle.
10. What are the phases of the cardiac cycle? Describe each phase with respect to which heart chambers are in systole or diastole, which valves are open or closed, and blood flow into or out of the chambers.

Developing Critical Reasoning

1. It was the end of the semester, and Huang had begun to prepare for his final examinations. Unfortunately, he still had to work his full-time job. To find sufficient time to study, he stayed up late and drank large amounts of coffee to stay alert. One evening during a very late study session, Huang felt a pounding in his chest and thought he was having a heart attack. His roommate took Huang to the emergency room. After an examination and interview by the physician, Huang was told that he probably had a cardiac arrhythmia. What was the most probable cause of the arrhythmia?

2. Josephine is a 55-year-old overweight woman who has a poor diet and does not exercise. One day while walking briskly, she experienced pain in her chest and down her left arm. Her doctor told her she was experiencing angina due to heart problems. Josephine asks you to explain what causes angina, and why she was feeling pain in her arm even though the problem was with her heart. What do you tell her?

3. Arthur was an 85-year-old man who had lived in the mountains his entire life. He went to see his doctor because he was getting tired more frequently. His doctor told him that he had a patent foramen ovale. How might this have happened, and why hadn't Arthur found out about it earlier?

Answers to "What Do You Think?"

1. The pulmonary arteries carry blood low in oxygen to the lungs because the lungs are responsible for replenishing the oxygen supplies in the blood. After deoxygenated blood travels to the lungs, the pulmonary capillaries are involved in gas exchange—that is, carbon dioxide leaves the blood, and oxygen enters the blood. Then the pulmonary veins carry the newly oxygenated blood back to the heart.
2. When the ventricles contract, they also constrict the coronary arteries. Thus, the coronary arteries can fill with blood only when the ventricles are relaxed.
3. If the AV valves were to evert into the atria, some of the blood from the ventricles would be pushed into the atria, resulting in inefficient pumping of blood. When the heart has to work harder to pump the blood out of the heart, clinical problems result (see Clinical View 22.2: "Heart Sounds and Heart Murmurs" in section 22.2c for further information).

Design Element: Pencil Icon: Slavojub Pantelic/Shutterstock

CARDIOVASCULAR SYSTEM

Vessels and Circulation 23

Outline

Anatomy & Physiology Revealed 4.0

MODULE 9: CARDIOVASCULAR SYSTEM

Blood vessels are analogous to highways—they are an efficient mode of transport for oxygen, carbon dioxide, nutrients, hormones, and waste products to and from body tissues. The heart is the mechanical pump that propels the blood through the vessels. Together, the heart and blood vessels form a closed-loop system, whereby blood is continuously pumped to and from all areas of the body.

Blood vessels are not rigid and immobile; rather, they can pulsate and change shape in accordance with the body's needs. This chapter examines the basic histologic structure common to all blood vessels and traces the flow of blood through all of the different body regions.

23.1 Anatomy of Blood Vessels

✓ Learning Objectives

1. Describe the tunics found in a typical blood vessel.
2. Compare and contrast the structure and function of arteries, capillaries, and veins.
3. Describe the path of blood flow from each type of artery to capillaries to veins.
4. Compare and contrast the structure and locations of the three types of capillaries.
5. Explain how the respiratory pump and the skeletal muscle pump help propel blood through veins.

The **systemic circulation** consists of the blood vessels that extend to all body regions. The **pulmonary circulation** consists of the vessels that take the blood to and from the lungs for the purpose of gas exchange. Both circulations work continuously and in tandem with each other.

The three classes of blood vessels are arteries, capillaries, and veins. In the systemic circulation, as the ventricles of the heart contract, arteries convey blood away from the heart to the body. Arteries branch into smaller and smaller vessels until they feed into the capillaries, where gas and nutrient exchange occurs. From the capillaries, veins return blood to the heart.

Arteries become progressively smaller as they branch and extend farther from the heart, whereas veins become progressively larger as they unite (or merge) and come closer to the heart. The site where two or more arteries (or two or more veins) converge to supply the same body region is called an **anastomosis** (ă-nas′tō-mō′sis; pl., *anastomoses*). An arterial anastomosis provides alternate blood supply routes to body tissues or organs. (For an example, see figure 23.12, which shows anastomoses among the superior and inferior epigastric arteries.) Some arteries do not form anastomoses; these so-called **end arteries** provide only one pathway through which blood can reach an organ. Examples of end arteries include the renal artery of the kidney and the splenic artery of the spleen. Other arteries (such as the coronary arteries in the heart wall) are called **functional end arteries,** meaning that their anastomoses are so tiny that the arteries may almost be considered end arteries.

A **venous anastomosis** includes two or more *veins* draining the same body region. Veins tend to form many more anastomoses than do arteries. Veins that drain the upper limb, including the basilic, brachial, and cephalic veins, provide an example of a venous anastomosis (see figure 23.19*b*).

Often, an artery travels with a corresponding vein. These vessels are called **companion vessels** because they supply the same body region and tend to lie next to one another.

23.1a Blood Vessel Tunics

Both artery and vein walls have three layers, called **tunics** (tū′nik; *tunica* = coat). The tunics surround the **lumen** (lū′men), or inside space, of the vessel through which blood flows. These tunics are the tunica intima, tunica media, and tunica externa (**figure 23.1**).

The innermost layer of a blood vessel wall is the **tunica intima** (tū′ni-k ă in-ti′mă; *intimus* = inmost), or *tunica interna*. It is composed of an **endothelium** (a simple squamous epithelium lining the blood vessel lumen) and a subendothelial layer made up of a thin layer of areolar connective tissue, and may have an internal elastic lamina. (Veins typically do not have this lamina.)

The **tunica media** (mē′dē-ă; *medius* = middle) is the middle layer of the vessel wall. It is composed of circularly arranged layers of smooth muscle cells and may have an external elastic lamina. (Veins typically do not have this lamina.) Sympathetic innervation causes the smooth muscle to contract, resulting in **vasoconstriction** (vā′sō-kon-strik′shŭn), or narrowing of the blood vessel lumen. When the smooth muscle cells relax, **vasodilation** (vā′sō-dī-lā′shŭn), or widening of the blood vessel lumen, results.

The **tunica externa** (eks-ter′n ă; *externe* = outside), or *tunica adventitia,* is the outermost layer of the blood vessel wall. It is composed of areolar connective tissue that contains elastic and collagen fibers. The tunica externa helps anchor the vessel to other structures. Very large blood vessels require their own blood supply to the tunica externa in the form of a network of small arteries called the **vasa vasorum** (vā′să vā-sōr′ŭm; vessels of vessels). The vasa vasorum extend through the tunica externa.

In arteries, the thickest layer is the tunica media. Conversely, the thickest layer in veins is the tunica externa. The lumen in an artery is narrower than in its companion vein of the same size (**figure 23.2**). Further, arteries tend to have more elastic and collagen fibers in all their tunics, which means that artery walls remain open (patent), can spring back to shape, and can withstand changes in blood pressure. In contrast, vein walls tend to collapse if there is no blood in the vein. **Table 23.1** compares the characteristics of arteries and veins.

Finally, capillaries contain only the tunica intima, but this layer consists of a basement membrane and endothelium only. Intercellular clefts are the thin spaces between adjacent cells in the capillary wall. Having only the tunica intima, without connective tissue and muscle layers, allows for rapid gas and nutrient exchange between the blood and the tissues.

23.1b Arteries

Arteries (ar′ter- ē) transport blood away from the heart. The arteries in the systemic circulation transport oxygenated blood to the body tissues. In contrast, the pulmonary arteries (part of the pulmonary circulation) transport deoxygenated blood to the lungs.

The three basic types of arteries are elastic arteries, muscular arteries, and arterioles (**figure 23.3**, *right*). In general, as an artery's diameter decreases, there is a corresponding decrease in the amount of elastic fibers and a relative increase in the amount of smooth muscle.

Note that all arteries are able to vasoconstrict, but the *amount* of vasoconstriction (which is regulated by sympathetic innervation; see section 18.5f) varies, based on the proportion of smooth muscle to elastic fibers in the wall. The greater the proportion of smooth muscle (versus elastic fibers), the greater the

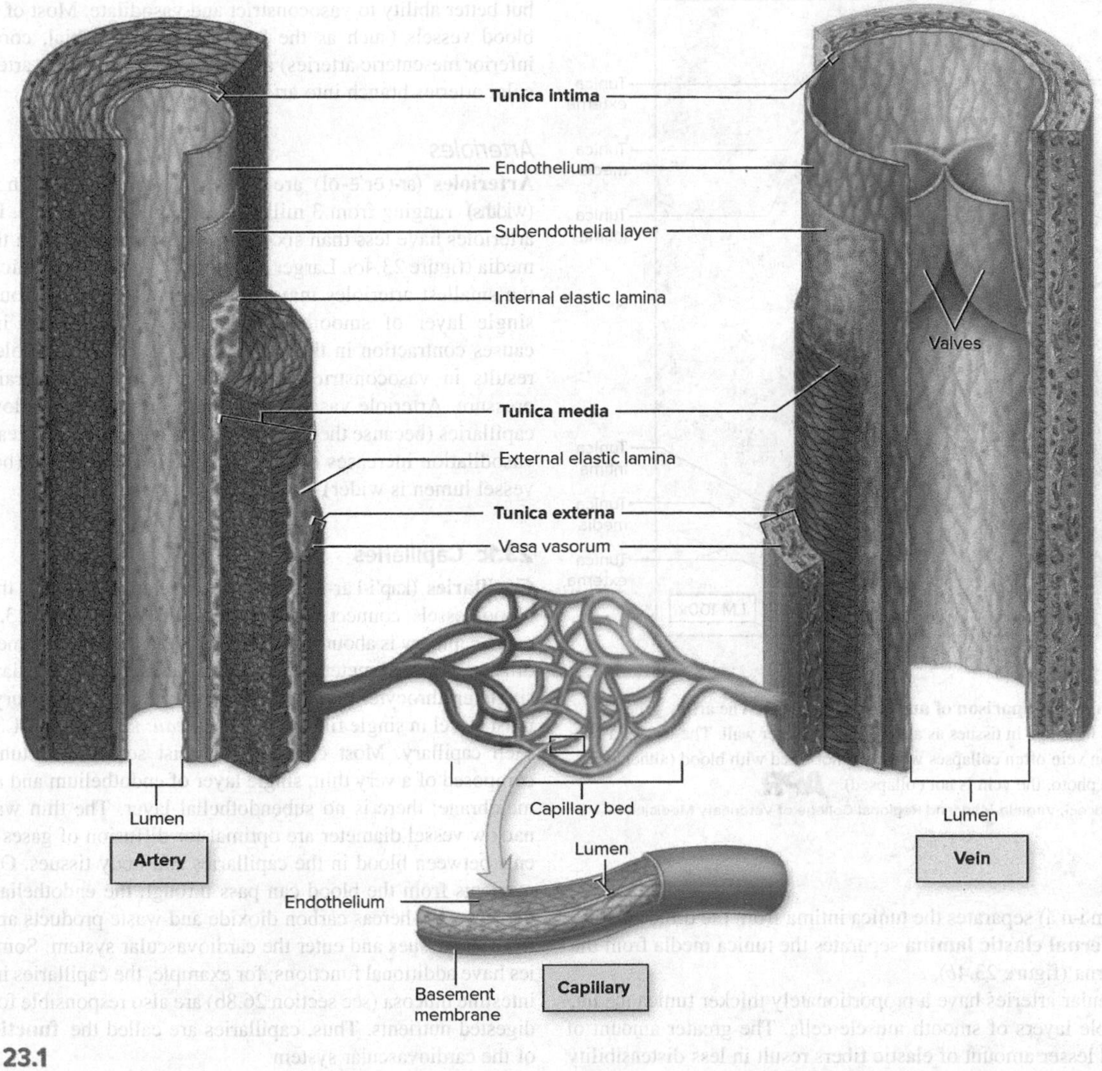

Figure 23.1

Walls of an Artery, a Capillary, and a Vein. Both arteries and veins have a tunica intima, tunica media, and tunica externa. However, an artery has a thicker tunica media and a relatively smaller lumen, whereas a vein's thickest layer is the tunica externa, and it has a larger lumen. Arteries typically will have internal and external elastic laminae, while these laminae are absent or very thin in veins. Some veins also have valves. Capillaries typically have only a tunica intima, but they do not have a subendothelial layer—just the endothelium and a basement membrane.

ability of the vessel to vasoconstrict. Thus, the smallest arteries (i.e., arterioles) have the greatest capacity for vasoconstriction (and so the arterioles have the greatest effect on regulating blood pressure; see section 23.2).

Elastic Arteries

Elastic arteries are the largest arteries, with diameters (widths) ranging from 2.5 centimeters to 1 centimeter. They are also called *conducting arteries* because they conduct blood away from the heart to the smaller muscular arteries. As their name suggests, these arteries have a large proportion of elastic fibers throughout all three tunics, especially in the tunica media **(figure 23.4*a*)**. The abundant elastic fibers allow the elastic artery to stretch when a heart ventricle ejects blood into the vessels. In this manner, the elastic arteries are able to withstand the strong pulsations of the ejected blood as well as reduce the force of the pulsations somewhat, so that the pressure of the arterial blood equalizes slightly as it reaches the smaller arteries and eventually the capillaries. Examples of elastic arteries include the aorta and the pulmonary, brachiocephalic, common carotid, subclavian, and common iliac arteries. Elastic arteries branch into muscular arteries.

Muscular Arteries

Muscular arteries typically have diameters (widths) ranging from 1 centimeter to 3 millimeters. These medium-sized arteries are also called *distributing arteries* because they distribute blood to body organs and tissues. Unlike elastic arteries, the elastic fibers in muscular arteries are confined to two circumscribed rings: The **internal elastic**

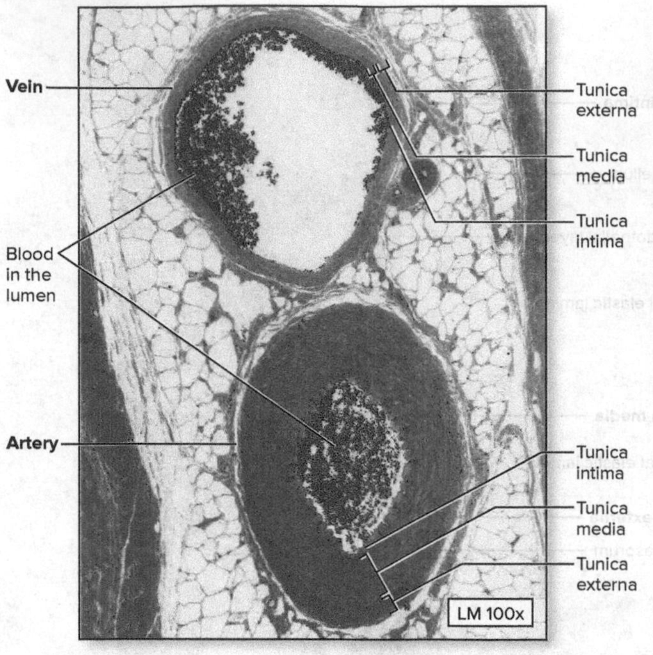

Figure 23.2

Microscopic Comparison of an Artery and Vein. The artery generally maintains its shape in tissues as a result of its thicker wall. The wall of a companion vein often collapses when it is not filled with blood (although in the above photo, the vein is not collapsed). APR

Thomas Caceci, Virginia-Maryland Regional College of Veterinary Medicine

lamina (lam′i-n ă) separates the tunica intima from the tunica media, and the **external elastic lamina** separates the tunica media from the tunica externa (figure 23.4*b*).

Muscular arteries have a proportionately thicker tunica media, with multiple layers of smooth muscle cells. The greater amount of muscle and lesser amount of elastic fibers result in less distensibility but better ability to vasoconstrict and vasodilate. Most of the named blood vessels (such as the brachial, anterior tibial, coronary, and inferior mesenteric arteries) are examples of muscular arteries. Muscular arteries branch into arterioles.

Arterioles

Arterioles (ar-t ēr′ē-ōl) are the smallest arteries, with diameters (widths) ranging from 3 millimeters to 10 micrometers. In general, arterioles have less than six layers of smooth muscle in their tunica media (figure 23.4*c*). Larger arterioles have all three tunics, whereas the smallest arterioles may have an endothelium surrounded by a single layer of smooth muscle cells. Sympathetic innervation causes contraction in the smooth muscle of the arteriole wall and results in vasoconstriction of the arteriole, which raises blood pressure. Arteriole vasoconstriction decreases blood flow into the capillaries (because the vessel lumen is narrower), whereas arteriole vasodilation increases blood flow into the capillaries (because the vessel lumen is wider).

23.1c Capillaries

Capillaries (kap′i-l ār-ē; *capillaris* = relating to hair), the smallest blood vessels, connect arterioles to venules (see figure 23.3). The average capillary is about 1 millimeter in length with a diameter (width) of 8 to 10 micrometers, just slightly larger than the diameter of a single erythrocyte. The narrow vessel diameter means erythrocytes must travel in single file (called a *rouleau;* see section 21.3a) through each capillary. Most capillaries consist solely of a tunica intima composed of a very thin, single layer of endothelium and a basement membrane; there is no subendothelial layer. The thin wall and the narrow vessel diameter are optimal for diffusion of gases and nutrients between blood in the capillaries and body tissues. Oxygen and nutrients from the blood can pass through the endothelial lining to the tissues, whereas carbon dioxide and waste products are removed from the tissues and enter the cardiovascular system. Some capillaries have additional functions; for example, the capillaries in the small intestine mucosa (see section 26.8b) are also responsible for receiving digested nutrients. Thus, capillaries are called the **functional units** of the cardiovascular system.

Table 23.1 Comparison of Arteries and Veins

Characteristic	Artery	Vein
Lumen Diameter	Narrower than vein lumen	Wider than artery lumen; often appears collapsed when cut in cross section
General Wall Thickness	Thicker than companion vein	Thinner than companion artery
Cross-Sectional Shape	Retains its circular cross-sectional shape	Cross section tends to flatten (collapse) if no blood is in the vein
Thickest Tunic	Tunica media	Tunica externa
Elastic and Collagen Fibers in Tunics	More than in vein	Less than in artery
Valves	None	Present in most veins
Blood Pressure	Higher than in veins (larger arteries typically > 90 mm Hg)	Lower than in arteries (about 2 mm Hg)
Blood Flow	Transports blood away from heart	Transports blood to heart
Blood Oxygen Levels	Systemic arteries transport blood high in O_2 Pulmonary arteries transport blood low in O_2	Systemic veins transport blood low in O_2 Pulmonary veins transport blood high in O_2

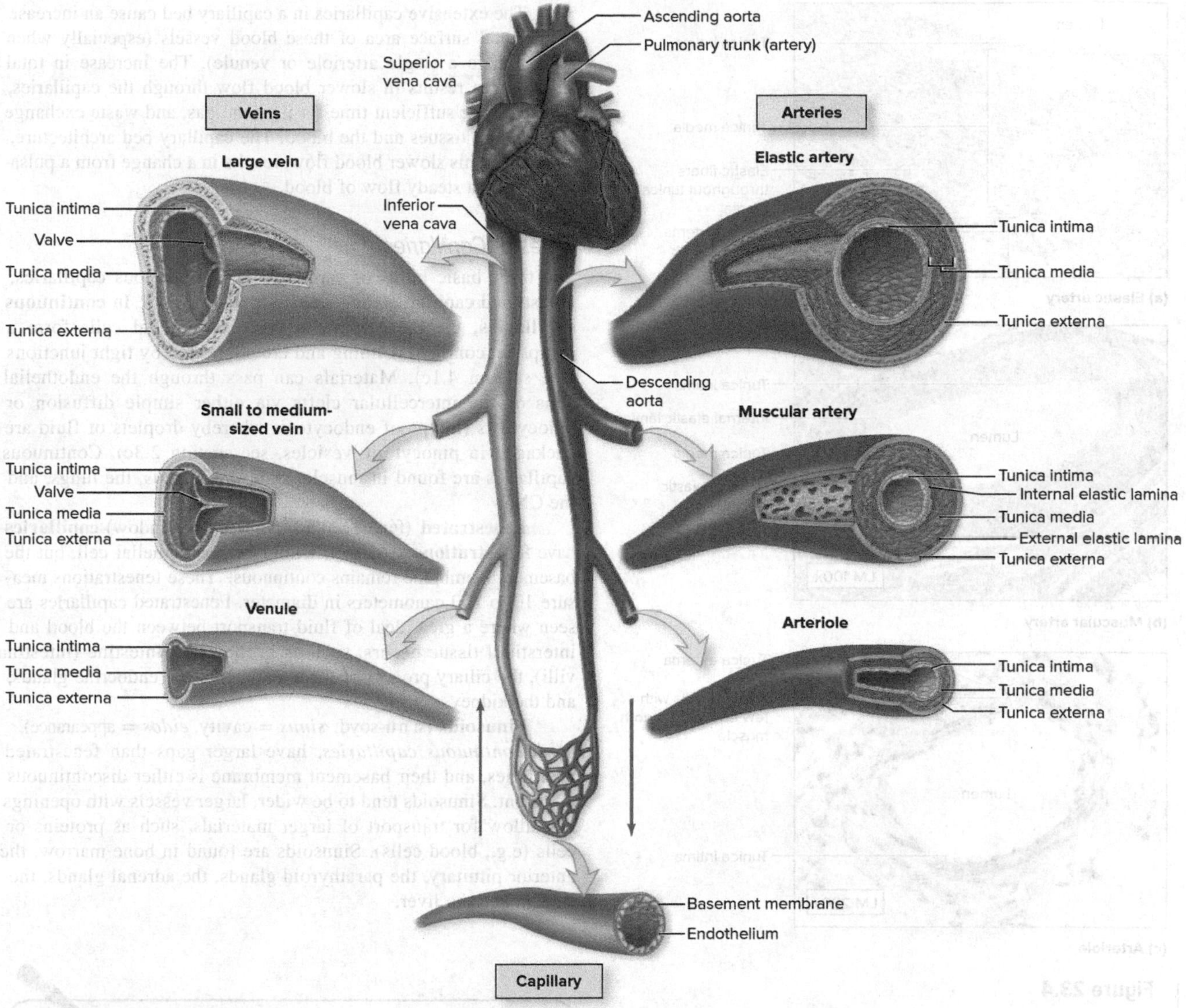
Ascending aorta
Pulmonary trunk (artery)
Superior vena cava
Veins
Arteries
Large vein
Elastic artery
Tunica intima
Valve
Tunica media
Tunica externa
Inferior vena cava
Tunica intima
Tunica media
Tunica externa
Descending aorta
Small to medium-sized vein
Muscular artery
Tunica intima
Valve
Tunica media
Tunica externa
Tunica intima
Internal elastic lamina
Tunica media
External elastic lamina
Tunica externa
Venule
Arteriole
Tunica intima
Tunica media
Tunica externa
Tunica intima
Tunica media
Tunica externa
Basement membrane
Endothelium
Capillary

Figure 23.3

Comparison of Companion Vessels. Arteries and veins supplying the same region are called companion vessels. The thickness of the tunics differs, depending upon the size of the vessels.

Learning Strategy 23.1

Is that a muscular artery or an arteriole you are examining using light microscopy? One easy way to figure this out is to count the smooth muscle layers in the tunica media (see figure 23.4 for reference):

- Arterioles have six or fewer layers of smooth muscle in their tunica media.
- Muscular arteries usually have many more layers of smooth muscle in their tunica media.

Capillary Beds

Capillaries do not function independently; rather, a group of capillaries (10–100) functions together and forms a **capillary bed** (**figure 23.5**). A capillary bed is fed by a **metarteriole** (met′ar-tēr′ē-ōl; *meta* = after), which is a vessel branch of an arteriole. The proximal part of the metarteriole is encircled by scattered smooth muscle cells, whereas the distal part of the metarteriole (called the **thoroughfare channel**) has no smooth muscle cells. The thoroughfare channel connects to a **postcapillary venule** (ven′yūl, vē′nool), which drains the capillary bed. Vessels called **true capillaries** branch from the metarteriole and make up the

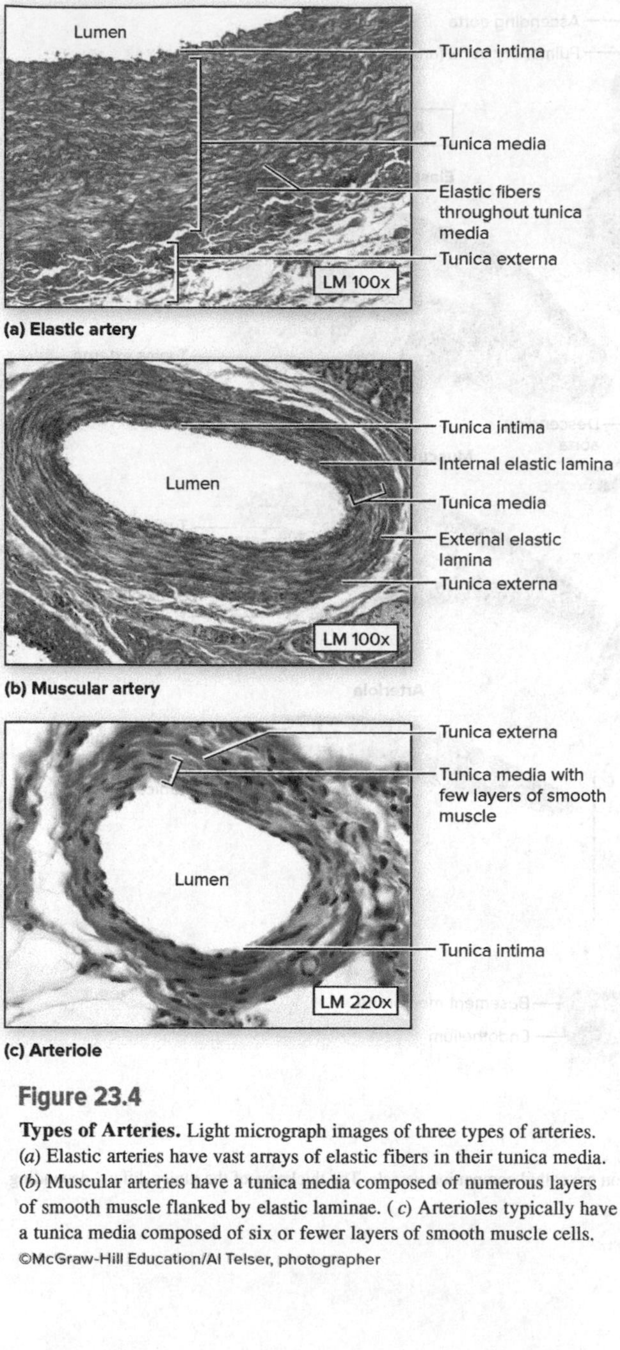
Lumen
Tunica intima
Tunica media
Elastic fibers throughout tunica media
Tunica externa
LM 100x
(a) Elastic artery
Tunica intima
Internal elastic lamina
Lumen
Tunica media
External elastic lamina
Tunica externa
LM 100x
(b) Muscular artery
Tunica externa
Tunica media with few layers of smooth muscle
Lumen
Tunica intima
LM 220x
(c) Arteriole

Figure 23.4

Types of Arteries. Light micrograph images of three types of arteries. (*a*) Elastic arteries have vast arrays of elastic fibers in their tunica media. (*b*) Muscular arteries have a tunica media composed of numerous layers of smooth muscle flanked by elastic laminae. (*c*) Arterioles typically have a tunica media composed of six or fewer layers of smooth muscle cells.

bulk of the capillary bed. For many capillary beds, a smooth muscle ring called the **precapillary sphincter** controls blood flow into the true capillaries. Relaxation of the precapillary sphincter permits blood to flow into the true capillaries. In contrast, precapillary sphincter contraction prevents blood from flowing into the capillaries, and instead reroutes blood flow from the metarteriole into the postcapillary venule via the thoroughfare channel. The precapillary sphincters open when the tissue needs nutrients, and they close when the tissue's needs have been met. These precapillary sphincters go through cycles of contracting and relaxing at a rate of about 5–10 cycles per minute. This cyclical process is called **vasomotion.**

The extensive capillaries in a capillary bed cause an increase in the total surface area of these blood vessels (especially when compared to a single arteriole or venule). The increase in total surface area results in slower blood flow through the capillaries, thus allowing sufficient time for nutrient, gas, and waste exchange between the tissues and the blood. The capillary bed architecture, along with this slower blood flow, results in a change from a pulsatile flow to a steady flow of blood.

Types of Capillaries

The three basic kinds of capillaries are continuous capillaries, fenestrated capillaries, and sinusoids (**figure 23.6**). In **continuous capillaries,** the most common type, endothelial cells form a complete, continuous lining and are connected by tight junctions (see section 4.1c). Materials can pass through the endothelial cells or the intercellular clefts via either simple diffusion or pinocytosis (a type of endocytosis whereby droplets of fluid are packaged in pinocytotic vesicles, see section 2.3c). Continuous capillaries are found in muscle, skin, the thymus, the lungs, and the CNS.

Fenestrated (fen′es-trāt′ĕd; *fenestra* = window) **capillaries** have **fenestrations** (or *pores*) within each endothelial cell, but the basement membrane remains continuous. These fenestrations measure 10 to 100 nanometers in diameter. Fenestrated capillaries are seen where a great deal of fluid transport between the blood and interstitial tissue occurs, such as in the small intestine (intestinal villi), the ciliary process of the eye, most of the endocrine glands, and the kidney.

Sinusoids (si′nŭ-soyd; *sinus* = cavity, *eidos* = appearance), or *discontinuous capillaries,* have larger gaps than fenestrated capillaries, and their basement membrane is either discontinuous or absent. Sinusoids tend to be wider, larger vessels with openings that allow for transport of larger materials, such as proteins or cells (e.g., blood cells). Sinusoids are found in bone marrow, the anterior pituitary, the parathyroid glands, the adrenal glands, the spleen, and the liver.

Learning Strategy 23.2

Arteries always transport blood *away* from the heart, whereas veins always transport blood back *to* the heart, regardless of whether the blood is oxygenated or deoxygenated.

23.1d Veins

Veins (vān) drain capillaries and return the blood to the heart. Compared with a corresponding artery, vein walls are relatively thin, and the vein lumen is larger (see figure 23.3, *left*). Systemic veins transport deoxygenated blood from the rest of the body to the right atrium of the heart, whereas pulmonary veins transport oxygenated blood from the lungs to the left atrium of the heart. Because blood pressure gradually decreases as blood travels through smaller arteries and into capillaries, the pressure has been substantially reduced by the time blood reaches the veins. At rest, the body's veins hold about 60% of the body's blood. Thus, veins function as **blood reservoirs.**

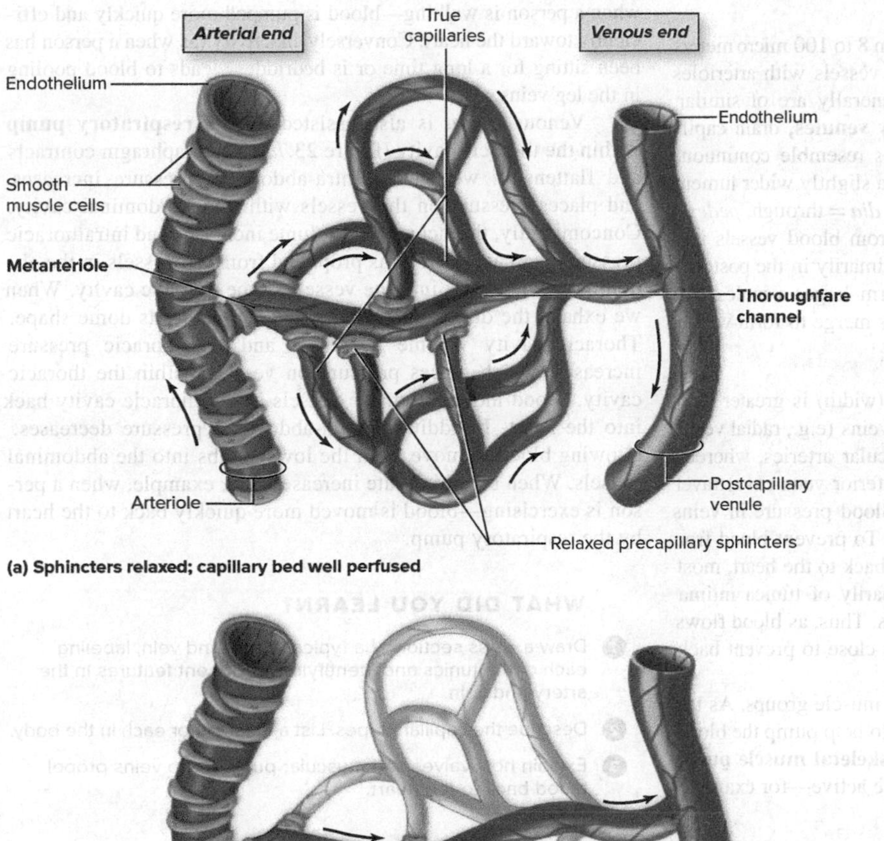
Arterial end
True capillaries
Venous end
Endothelium
Smooth muscle cells
Metarteriole
Endothelium
Thoroughfare channel
Postcapillary venule
Arteriole
Relaxed precapillary sphincters
(a) Sphincters relaxed; capillary bed well perfused
Contracted precapillary sphincters
(b) Sphincters contracted; blood bypasses capillary bed

Figure 23.5

Capillary Bed Structure. A capillary bed originates from a metarteriole. The distal part of the metarteriole is called the thoroughfare channel, and it directly connects to the postcapillary venule. True capillaries branch from the metarteriole, and blood flow into these true capillaries is regulated by the precapillary sphincters. (*a*) In a well-perfused capillary bed, with all of the precapillary sphincters relaxed, blood can travel through the capillary bed. (*b*) When the precapillary sphincters are contracted, blood is prevented from entering the capillary bed, and instead travels directly through the thoroughfare channel.

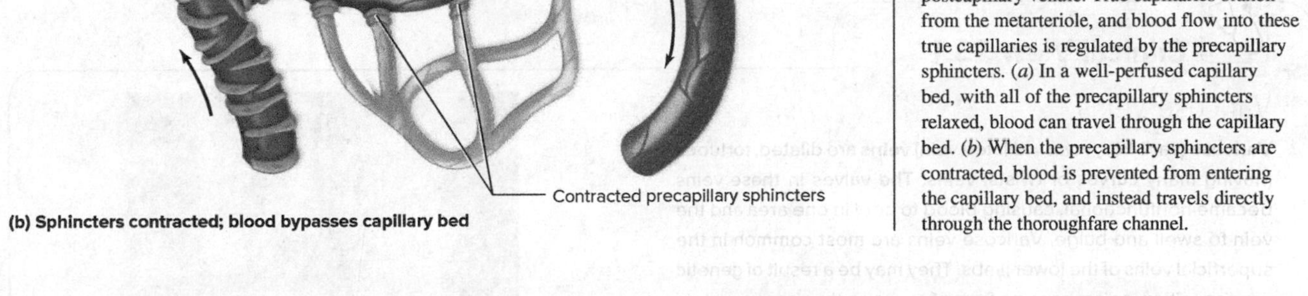
Basement membrane
Pinocytotic vesicles
Erythrocyte
Lumen
Intercellular cleft
Nucleus of endothelial cell
(a) Continuous capillary
Basement membrane
Fenestrations
Erythrocyte
Lumen
Intercellular cleft
Nucleus of endothelial cell
(b) Fenestrated capillary
Discontinuous basement membrane
Large openings
Erythrocyte
Lumen
Intercellular cleft
Nucleus of endothelial cell
(c) Sinusoid

Figure 23.6

Types of Capillaries. (*a*) Continuous capillaries have tight junctions between the endothelial cells that permit minimal fluid leakage. (*b*) Fenestrated capillaries have fenestrations (pores) in the endothelial cells to permit small molecules to move out of the vessel. (*c*) Sinusoids have big gaps between the endothelial cells and a discontinuous basement membrane that promotes transport of larger molecules.

Venules

Venules are the smallest veins, measuring from 8 to 100 micro meters in diameter (width). Venules are companion vessels with arterioles because both supply the same areas and generally are of similar size. The smallest ones, called **postcapillary venules,** drain capillaries (see figure 23.5). Postcapillary venules resemble continuous capillaries in structure, except that they have a slightly wider lumen. The mechanism of **diapedesis** (dī'ă-pĕ-dē'sis; *dia* = through, *pedesis* = a leaping), by which leukocytes migrate from blood vessels into interstitial fluid (see section 21.3b), occurs primarily in the postcapillary venules. Smaller venules merge to form larger venules, the largest of which have all three tunics. Venules merge to form veins.

Veins

A venule becomes a vein when its diameter (width) is greater than 100 micrometers. Smaller and medium-sized veins (e.g., radial veins, femoral vein) typically travel alongside muscular arteries, whereas the largest veins (e.g., common iliac veins, inferior vena cava) travel alongside elastic arteries (see figure 23.3). Blood pressure in veins is too low to overcome the forces of gravity. To prevent blood from pooling in the limbs and assist blood moving back to the heart, most veins contain numerous **valves** formed primarily of tunica intima and strengthened by elastic and collagen fibers. Thus, as blood flows superiorly in the limbs, these one-way valves close to prevent backflow (**figure 23.7**).

Many deep veins pass between skeletal muscle groups. As the skeletal muscles contract, veins are squeezed to help pump the blood toward the heart. This process is called the **skeletal muscle pump** (figure 23.7 *a*). When skeletal muscles are more active—for example, when a person is walking—blood is pumped more quickly and efficiently toward the heart. Conversely, inactivity (as when a person has been sitting for a long time or is bedridden) leads to blood pooling in the leg veins.

Venous return is also assisted by the **respiratory pump** within the thoracic cavity (figure 23.7*b*). The diaphragm contracts and flattens as we inhale. Intra-abdominal pressure increases and places pressure on the vessels within the abdominal cavity. Concomitantly, thoracic cavity volume increases and intrathoracic pressure decreases. Blood is propelled from the vessels in the abdominopelvic cavity into the vessels in the thoracic cavity. When we exhale, the diaphragm relaxes and returns to its dome shape. Thoracic cavity volume decreases and intrathoracic pressure increases, which places pressure on vessels within the thoracic cavity. Blood moves from the vessels in the thoracic cavity back into the heart. In addition, intra-abdominal pressure decreases, allowing blood to move from the lower limbs into the abdominal vessels. When breathing rate increases—for example, when a person is exercising—blood is moved more quickly back to the heart by the respiratory pump.

WHAT DID YOU LEARN?

1. Draw a cross section of a typical artery and vein, labeling each of the tunics and identifying prominent features in the artery and vein.
2. Describe the capillary types. List a location for each in the body.
3. Explain how valves and muscular pumps help veins propel blood back to the heart.

Clinical View 23.1

Varicose Veins

Varicose (var'i-kōs; *varix* = dilated vein) **veins** are dilated, tortuous (having many curves or twists) veins. The valves in these veins became nonfunctional, causing blood to pool in one area and the vein to swell and bulge. Varicose veins are most common in the superficial veins of the lower limbs. They may be a result of genetic predisposition, aging, or some form of stress on the venous system that inhibits venous return (such as standing for long periods of time, obesity, or pregnancy).

Symptoms of varicose veins may be alleviated by elevating the affected body part or wearing compression stockings (to promote blood movement in the lower limbs). In a procedure called **sclerotherapy,** an irritant is injected into small varicose veins to make them scar and seal off. Typically, a patient needs multiple sclerotherapy sessions before optimal results are seen. For larger varicose veins, an outpatient surgical procedure called stripping or vein removal (**phlebectomy**) may be performed.

Varicose veins in the anorectal region are called **hemorrhoids** (hem'ŏ-roydz; *haima* = blood, *rhoia* = a flow). Hemorrhoids occur due to increased intra-abdominal pressure, as when a person strains to have a bowel movement or is in labor during childbirth.

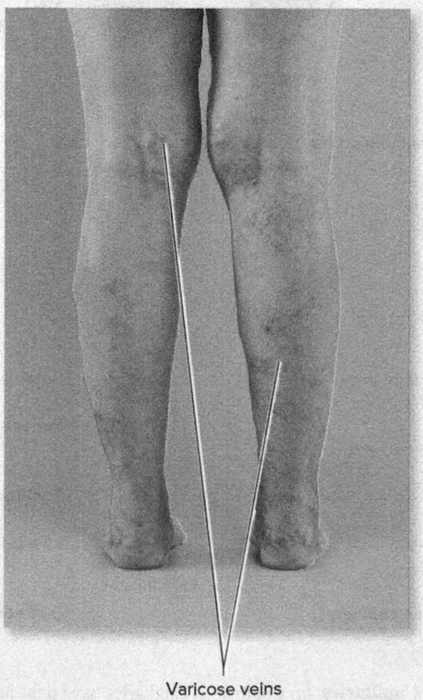

DIGIcal/Getty Images

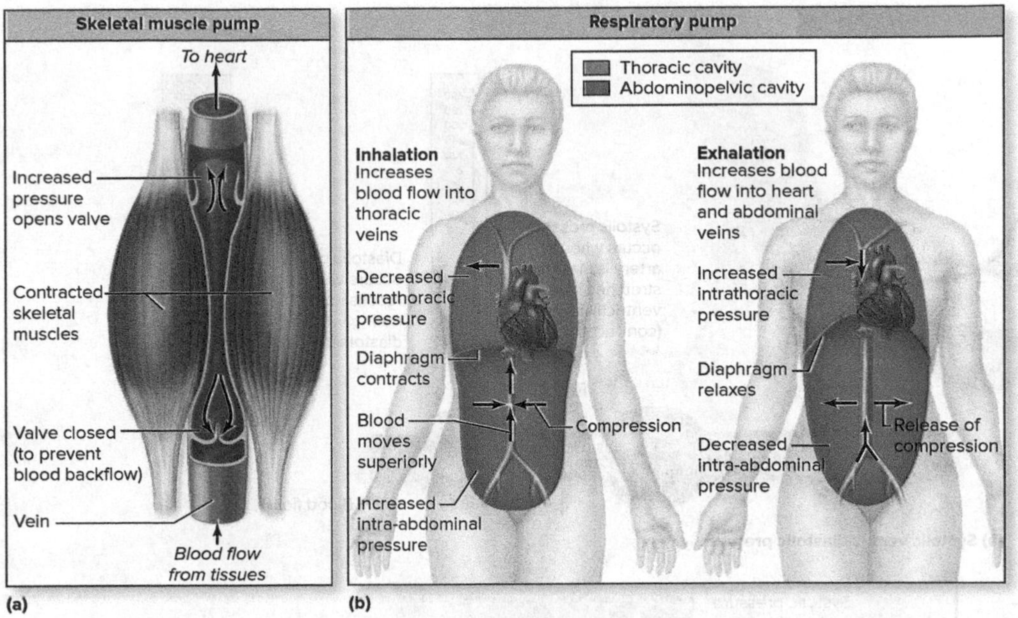

Figure 23.7

Factors That Influence Venous Return. To help overcome the small pressure gradient in veins, blood return to the heart via veins is facilitated by both (*a*) the skeletal muscle pump within the limbs, and (*b*) the respiratory pump within the torso.

Clinical View 23.2

Deep Vein Thrombosis

Deep vein thrombosis (throm-bō′sis; a clotting) **(DVT)** refers to a blood clot **(thrombus)** in a vein. The most common site for the thrombus is a vein in the calf (sural) region. DVT typically occurs in individuals with heart disease or those who are inactive or immobile for a long period of time, such as bedridden patients. Even healthy individuals who have been on a long airline trip may develop DVT.

Initial signs of DVT include fever, tenderness and redness in the affected area, severe pain and swelling in the areas drained by the affected vein, and rapid heartbeat. The most serious complication of DVT is a **pulmonary embolus** (em′bō-lŭs; a plug), in which a blood clot breaks free and travels to the lung, eventually blocking a branch of the pulmonary artery and potentially causing respiratory failure and death. If a DVT is diagnosed, the patient is given anticoagulation medication, such as low-molecular-weight heparin, to help prevent further clotting and break up the existing clot.

23.2 Blood Pressure

✓ Learning Objectives

6. Define blood pressure and explain how blood pressure measurements change as blood moves through arteries, capillaries, and veins.
7. Compare and contrast diastolic and systolic blood pressure.

The rhythmic pumping of blood through the heart produces a pulsation of blood through the arteries. When you check your **pulse** (pŭls; *pulsus* = a stroke), you are feeling these pulsations of blood. Arterial walls contain elastic connective tissue, which allows them to expand and recoil in response to the pulsating blood. Due to this pulsating blood, larger arteries tend to exhibit high pressure, which gradually decreases as blood travels into smaller and smaller arteries.

Blood pressure is the force per unit area that blood places on the inside wall of a blood vessel and is measured in millimeters of mercury, or mm Hg (**figure 23.8**). Arterial blood pressure is measured with a **sphygmomanometer** (sfig′m ō-mă-nom′ĕ-tĕr; *sphygmos* = pulse, *manos* = thin, *metron* = measure). A cuff is wrapped around the arm such that when inflated it completely compresses the brachial artery, temporarily stopping the flow of blood. Then air is gradually released from the cuff while a health-care practitioner places a stethoscope just distal to the compressed artery and listens for the sound of blood flow. Once the first pulsation is heard through the stethoscope, the sphygmomanometer is read. The reading on the dial at this time is the **systolic blood pressure,** the pressure in the vessel during ventricular systole (ventricular contraction). The health-care practitioner continues to listen to artery pulsations, and when the pulsations stop (because blood is flowing evenly through the blood vessel), the sphygmomanometer is read again for a measurement of **diastolic blood pressure,** the pressure during ventricular diastole (ventricular relaxation).

Systolic pressure is greater than diastolic pressure due to the greater force from ventricular contraction. Blood pressure is expressed as a ratio, in which the numerator (upper number) is the systolic pressure and the denominator (lower number) is the diastolic pressure. The average adult has a blood pressure of 120/80 mm Hg.

Blood pressure is produced in the ventricles of the heart, so pressure is highest in the arteries closest to the heart, such as the

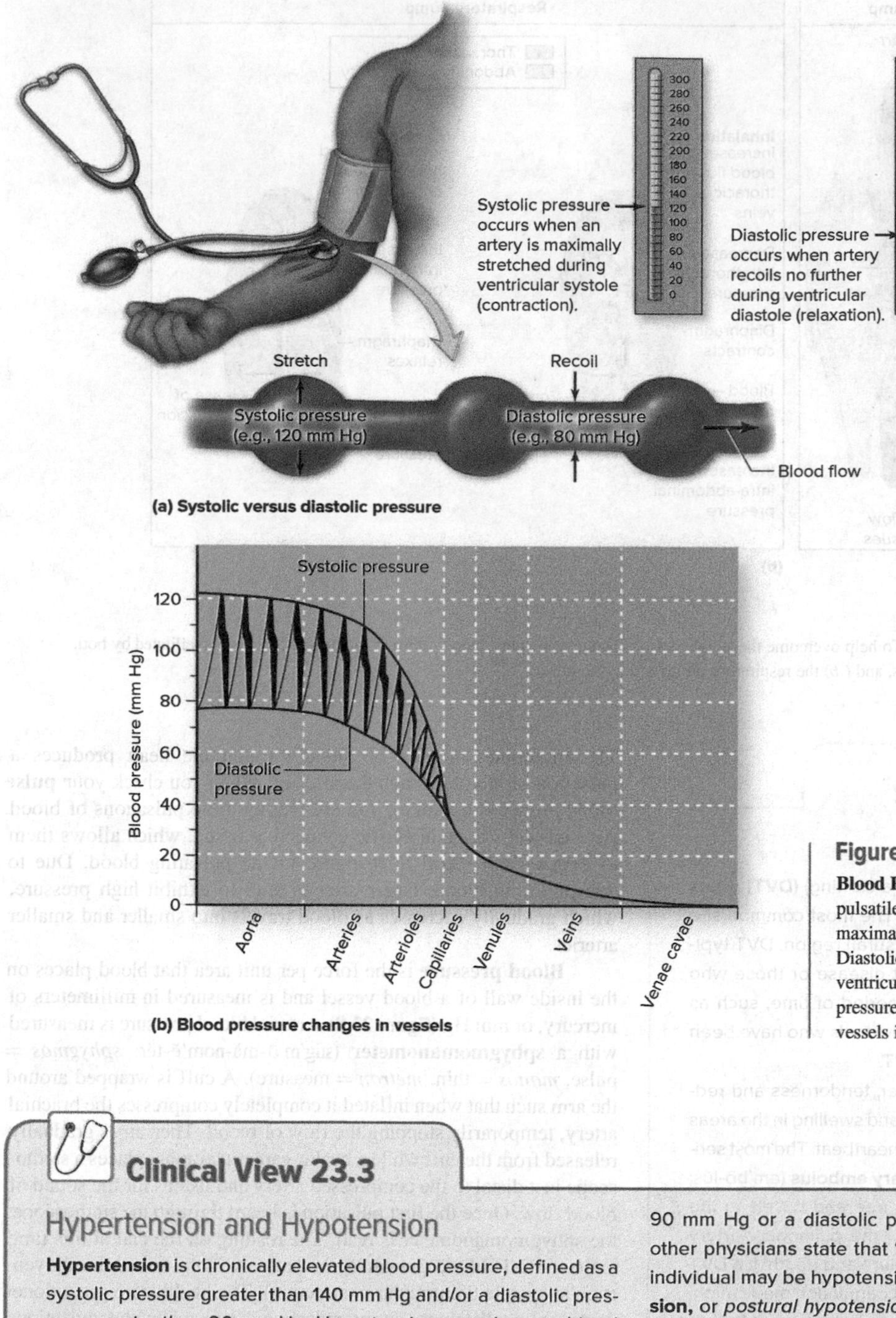
Systolic pressure occurs when an artery is maximally stretched during ventricular systole (contraction).
Diastolic pressure occurs when artery recoils no further during ventricular diastole (relaxation).
Stretch
Recoil
Systolic pressure (e.g., 120 mm Hg)
Diastolic pressure (e.g., 80 mm Hg)
Blood flow
(a) Systolic versus diastolic pressure
Systolic pressure
Diastolic pressure
Blood pressure (mm Hg)
120
100
80
60
40
20
0
Aorta
Arteries
Arterioles
Capillaries
Venules
Veins
Venae cavae
(b) Blood pressure changes in vessels

Figure 23.8

Blood Pressure. Blood pressure in the arteries is pulsatile. *(a)* systolic pressure is when the artery is maximally stretched during ventricular contraction. Diastolic pressure is when the artery recoils during ventricular relaxation. *(b)* tracing compares the blood pressure changes as blood flows through the different vessels in the cardiovascular system.

Clinical View 23.3

Hypertension and Hypotension

Hypertension is chronically elevated blood pressure, defined as a systolic pressure greater than 140 mm Hg and/or a diastolic pressure greater than 90 mm Hg. Hypertension may damage blood vessel walls, making arteries more likely to develop atherosclerosis, or it may thicken the arteriole walls and reduce their luminal diameter, a condition called **arteriolosclerosis** (see Clinical View 23.5: "Atherosclerosis" in section 23.3h). Hypertension also is a major cause of heart failure, owing to the extra workload placed on the heart.

In contrast, **hypotension** is a chronically low blood pressure that results in symptoms such as fatigue, dizziness, and fainting. Some physicians define hypotension as a systolic pressure below 90 mm Hg or a diastolic pressure below 60 mm Hg, whereas other physicians state that "normal" low blood pressure for one individual may be hypotensive for another. **Orthostatic hypotension,** or *postural hypotension,* is a drop in blood pressure when an individual suddenly changes position, such as when a person stands up after sitting or lying down. As a result, the person may experience dizziness, light-headedness, and fainting after this positional change. Essentially, orthostatic hypotension occurs when the nervous system responses that help regulate blood pressure do not function quickly enough, and mean arterial pressure (the average [or mean] measure of the blood pressure forces on the arteries) decreases below 60 mm Hg. Thus, the blood remains pooled in the veins and not enough reaches the cerebral vasculature, resulting in the above symptoms.

aorta. As the arteries branch into smaller vessels and travel greater distances from the ventricles, blood pressure decreases (figure 23.8). By the time the blood reaches the capillaries, fluctuations between systolic and diastolic blood pressure disappear. Blood pressure at this point is about 40 mm Hg, and once blood leaves the capillaries, pressure is below 20 mm Hg. Blood pressure drops from 20 mm Hg in the venules to almost 0 mm Hg by the time blood travels through the venae cavae to the right atrium of the heart.

Several factors can influence arterial blood pressure. Increased blood volume and increased cardiac output (the amount of blood pumped out of a ventricle in 1 minute) both can increase blood pressure. Vasoconstriction raises blood pressure, whereas vasodilation reduces blood pressure. Some medicines and drugs can either increase or decrease pressure as well. People who are overweight or less healthy tend to have increased blood pressure.

WHAT DO YOU THINK?

1. Nicotine stimulates the heart and raises cardiac output. It also causes arteriole vasoconstriction. Given this information, would you expect the blood pressure of a smoker to be high or relatively low?

WHAT DID YOU LEARN?

4. What is blood pressure? What are the similarities and differences between systolic pressure and diastolic pressure?

23.3 Systemic Circulation

✓ Learning Objectives

8. Identify and describe the general blood flow into and out of the heart.
9. Identify and describe the blood flow through the head and neck
10. Identify and describe the blood flow through the thorax, abdomen, and pelvis.
11. Identify and describe the blood flow through the upper limb.
12. Identify and describe the blood flow through the lower limb.

The systemic circulation consists of blood vessels that extend to all body regions. In this section, we discuss arterial and venous systemic blood flow according to body region. As you read these descriptions, it may help you to refer to **figure 23.9**, which shows the locations of the major arteries and veins.

Learning Strategy 23.3

Here are some tips to remember the names of blood vessels:

1. Blood vessels often are named for either the body region they traverse or the bone next to them. For example, the radial artery travels by the radius, and the axillary artery is in the axillary region.
2. Some blood vessels are named for the structure they supply. For example, the renal arteries supply the kidneys, the gonadal arteries supply the gonads, and the facial arteries supply the face.
3. Arteries and veins that travel together (called companion vessels) often share the same name. For example, the femoral artery is accompanied by the femoral vein.
4. Write out your own simplified flowchart of blood vessels for each body region.

23.3a General Arterial Flow Out of the Heart

Oxygenated blood is pumped out of the left ventricle of the heart and enters the **ascending aorta.** The **left** and **right coronary arteries** arise immediately from the wall of the ascending aorta and supply the heart. The ascending aorta curves toward the left side of the body and becomes the **aortic arch** (*arch of the aorta*). Three main arterial branches arise from the aortic arch: (1) the **brachiocephalic** (brā′kē-ō-se-fal′ik) **trunk** (also known as the *innominate artery*), which bifurcates into the **right common carotid** (ka-rot′id) **artery** supplying arterial blood to the right side of the head and neck, and the **right subclavian** (sŭb-klā′vē-ăn; *sub* = beneath; clavicle) **artery** supplying the right upper limb and some thoracic structures; (2) the **left common carotid artery** supplying the left side of the head and neck; and (3) the **left subclavian artery** supplying the left upper limb and some thoracic structures.

The aortic arch curves and projects inferiorly as the **descending thoracic aorta** that extends several branches to supply the thoracic wall. When this artery extends inferiorly through the aortic opening (hiatus) in the diaphragm, it is renamed the **descending abdominal aorta.** In the abdomen, arterial branches originate from the aorta wall to supply the abdominal wall and organs.

At the level of the fourth lumbar vertebra, the descending abdominal aorta bifurcates into **left** and **right common iliac** (il′ē-ak; *ileum* = groin) **arteries.** Each of these arteries further divides into an **internal iliac artery** (to supply pelvic and perineal structures) and an **external iliac artery** (to supply the lower limb).

23.3b General Venous Return to the Heart

Once oxygenated blood is distributed throughout the body, it returns to the heart through veins that often share the same names as their corresponding arteries (figure 23.9). The veins that drain the head, neck, and upper limbs merge to form the **left** and **right brachiocephalic veins,** which in turn unite (merge) to form the **superior vena cava.** The superior vena cava drains directly into the right atrium. The larger veins inferior to the diaphragm merge to eventually form the **inferior vena cava.** The inferior vena cava lies to the right side of the descending abdominal aorta, and is responsible for transporting venous blood toward the heart from the lower limbs, pelvis and perineum, and abdominal structures. The inferior vena cava extends through the caval opening in the diaphragm and also drains blood directly into the right atrium.

23.3c Blood Flow Through the Head and Neck

The left and right common carotid arteries supply most of the blood to the head and neck. They travel parallel immediately lateral to either side of the trachea (**figure 23.10*a***). At the superior border of the thyroid cartilage, each artery divides into an **external carotid artery** that supplies structures external to the skull, and an **internal carotid artery** that supplies internal skull structures. Prior to this bifurcation, the common carotid artery contains a structure called the carotid sinus, which is a receptor that detects changes in blood pressure.

Blood Flow Through the Neck and Superficial Head Structures

The external carotid artery supplies blood to several branches: (1) the **superior thyroid artery** supplies the thyroid gland, larynx, and some anterior neck muscles; (2) the **ascending pharyngeal** (fă-rin′j ē-ăl; *pharynx* = throat) **artery** supplies the pharynx;

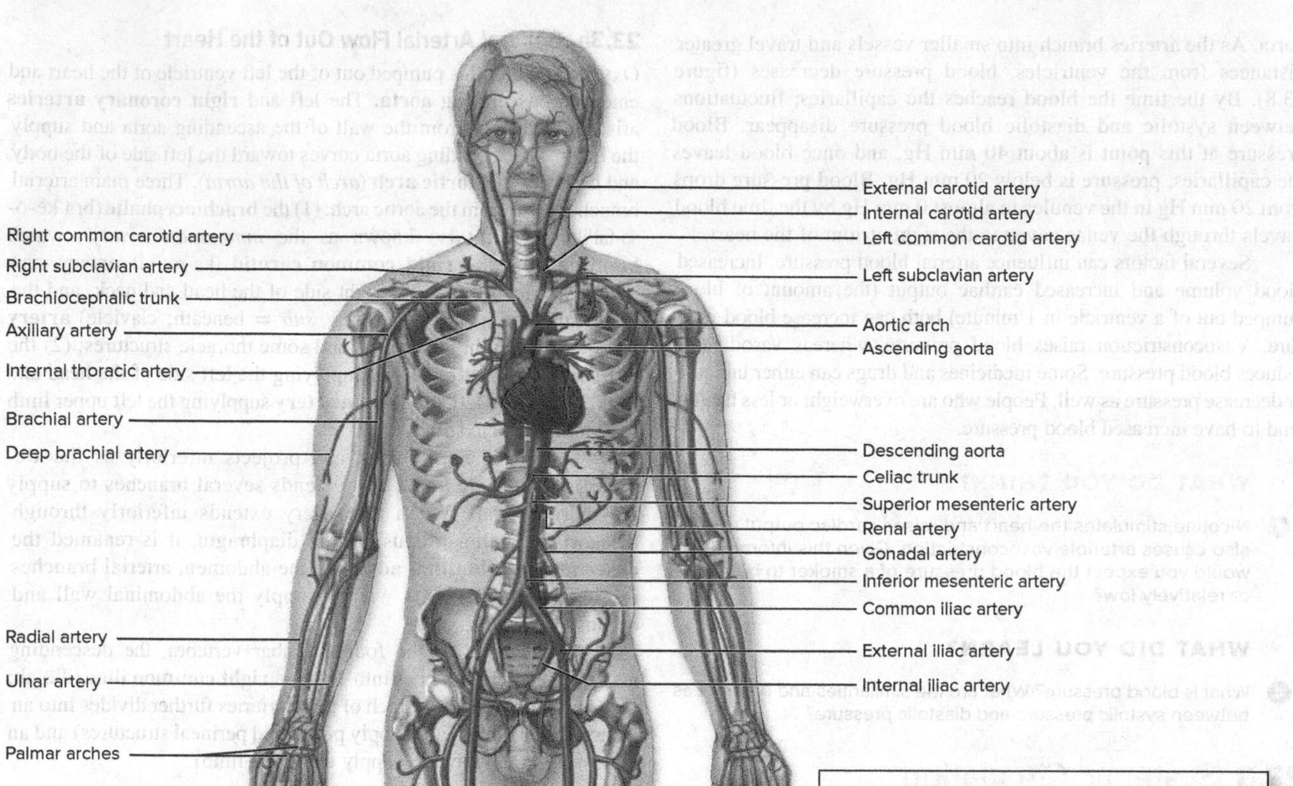
External carotid artery
Internal carotid artery
Right common carotid artery
Left common carotid artery
Right subclavian artery
Left subclavian artery
Brachiocephalic trunk
Axillary artery
Aortic arch
Ascending aorta
Internal thoracic artery
Brachial artery
Deep brachial artery
Descending aorta
Celiac trunk
Superior mesenteric artery
Renal artery
Gonadal artery
Inferior mesenteric artery
Common iliac artery
Radial artery
External iliac artery
Ulnar artery
Internal iliac artery
Palmar arches
Deep femoral artery
Femoral artery
Popliteal artery
Posterior tibial artery
Anterior tibial artery
Right subclavian artery
Right common carotid artery
Left common carotid artery
Left subclavian artery
Brachiocephalic trunk
Aortic arch
Ascending aorta
Left coronary artery
Right coronary artery
Descending thoracic
aorta (posterior to heart)
Diaphragm
Descending abdominal
aorta
Right common iliac artery
Left common iliac artery
(a) Arteries, anterior view

Figure 23.9

General Vascular Distribution. Arteries in the systemic circulation transport blood from the heart to systemic capillary beds; systemic veins return this blood to the heart. (*a*) Anterior view of the systemic arteries, with an inset of the heart and aorta. (*b*) Anterior view of the systemic veins, with an inset of the major veins that drain into the heart. APR

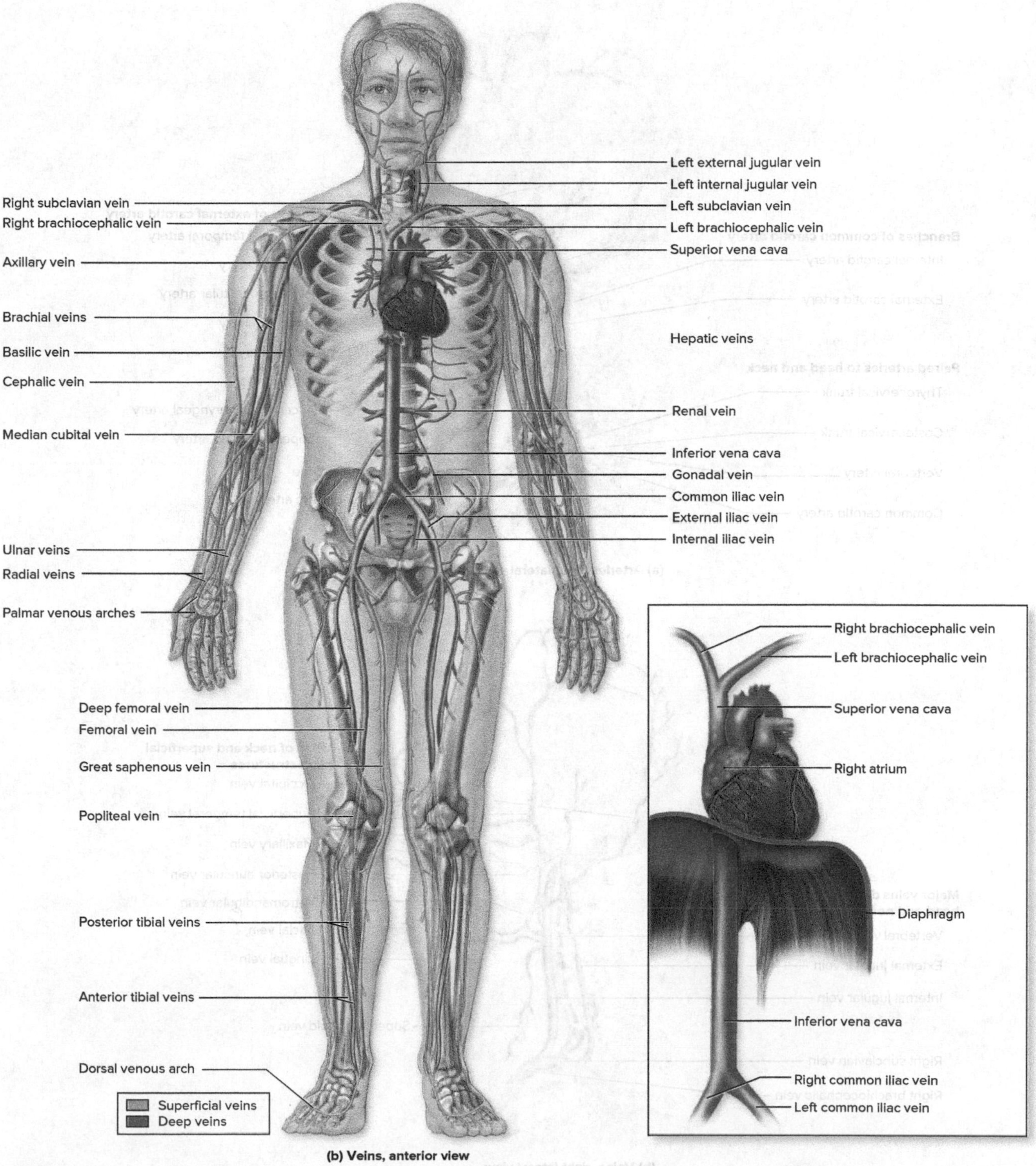
Left external jugular vein
Left internal jugular vein
Left subclavian vein
Left brachiocephalic vein
Superior vena cava
Right subclavian vein
Right brachiocephalic vein
Axillary vein
Brachial veins
Basilic vein
Cephalic vein
Median cubital vein
Hepatic veins
Renal vein
Inferior vena cava
Gonadal vein
Common iliac vein
External iliac vein
Internal iliac vein
Ulnar veins
Radial veins
Palmar venous arches
Deep femoral vein
Femoral vein
Great saphenous vein
Popliteal vein
Posterior tibial veins
Anterior tibial veins
Dorsal venous arch
Superficial veins
Deep veins
Right brachiocephalic vein
Left brachiocephalic vein
Superior vena cava
Right atrium
Diaphragm
Inferior vena cava
Right common iliac vein
Left common iliac vein
(b) Veins, anterior view

Figure 23.9
General Vascular Distribution. ***(Continued)***

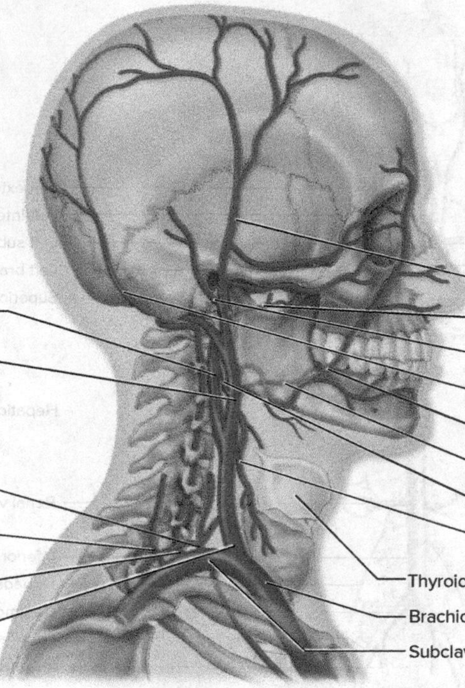
Branches of common carotid artery
Internal carotid artery
External carotid artery
Paired arteries to head and neck
Thyrocervical trunk
Costocervical trunk
Vertebral artery
Common carotid artery
Branches of external carotid artery
Superficial temporal artery
Maxillary artery
Posterior auricular artery
Occipital artery
Facial artery
Lingual artery
Ascending pharyngeal artery
Superior thyroid artery
Thyroid cartilage
Brachiocephalic artery
Subclavian artery

(a) Arteries, right lateral view

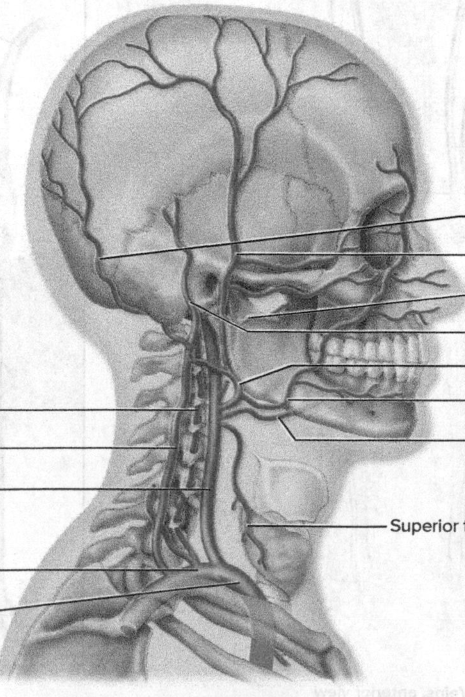
Veins of neck and superficial head structures
Occipital vein
Superficial temporal vein
Maxillary vein
Posterior auricular vein
Retromandibular vein
Facial vein
Lingual vein
Superior thyroid vein
Major veins draining head and neck
Vertebral vein
External jugular vein
Internal jugular vein
Right subclavian vein
Right brachiocephalic vein

(b) Veins, right lateral view

Figure 23.10

Blood Flow to the External Head and Neck. Right lateral views show (*a*) major arteries and (*b*) major veins of the head and neck. (*c*) A cadaver photo shows the major vessels of the head and neck. APR

(c) ©McGraw-Hill Education/Christine Eckel, photographer

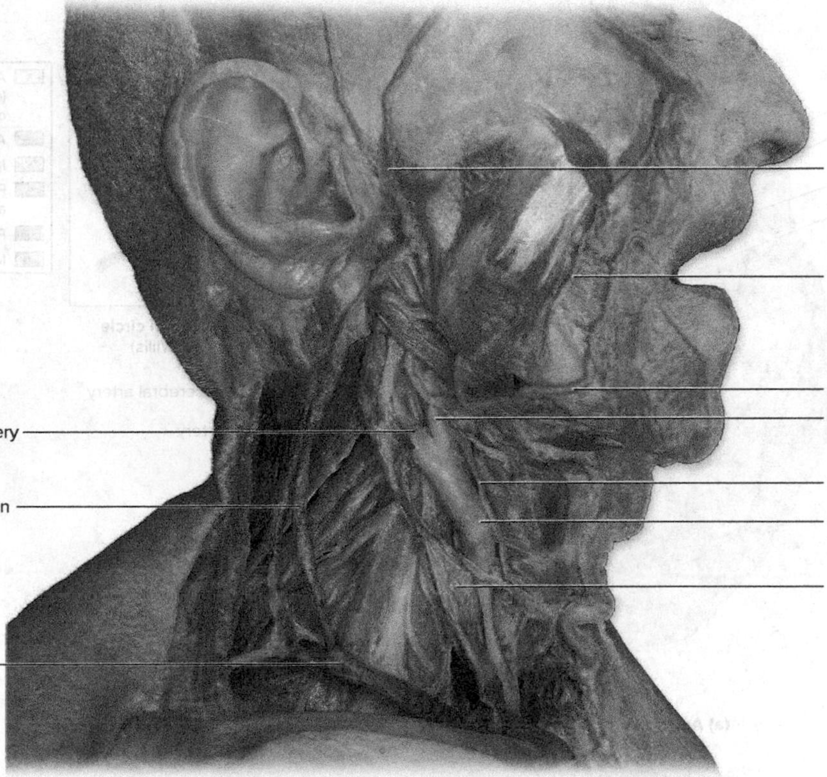
Superficial temporal artery
Facial vein (cut)
Facial artery
External carotid artery
Internal carotid artery
Superior thyroid artery
External jugular vein
Common carotid artery
Internal jugular vein
Subclavian vein

(c) Head and neck vessels, right lateral view

(3) the **lingual** (ling′gwăl) **artery** supplies the tongue; (4) the **facial artery** supplies most of the facial region; (5) the **occipital artery** supplies the posterior portion of the scalp; and (6) the **posterior auricular artery** supplies the ear and the scalp around the ear. Thereafter, the external carotid artery divides into the **maxillary artery,** which supplies the teeth, gums, nasal cavity, and meninges, and the **superficial temporal artery,** which supplies the side of the head and the parotid gland.

Venous return is through smaller veins that merge to form the **facial, superficial temporal,** and **maxillary** (mak′si-l ār-ē) **veins** (figure 23.10 *b*). Most of these veins drain into the **external jugular vein** that drains into the subclavian vein and then into the brachiocephalic vein. Figure 23.10*c* shows the major arteries and veins of the head and neck.

Blood Flow Through the Cranium

The internal carotid artery branches only after it enters the skull through the carotid canal. Once inside the skull, it forms multiple branches, including the **anterior** and **middle cerebral arteries,** which supply the brain, and the **ophthalmic** (of-thal′mik; *ophthalmos* = eye) **arteries,** which supply the eyes (**figure 23.11**).

The **vertebral arteries** arise from the subclavian arteries and travel through the transverse foramina of the cervical vertebrae before entering the skull through the foramen magnum, where they merge to form the **basilar** (bas′i-l ăr; *basis* = base) **artery.** The basilar artery travels immediately anterior to the pons and extends many branches prior to subdividing into the **posterior cerebral arteries,** which supply the posterior portion of the cerebrum.

The **cerebral arterial circle** (*circle of Willis*) is an important anastomosis of arteries around the sella turcica. The circle is formed from posterior cerebral arteries, **posterior communicating arteries** (branches of the posterior cerebral arteries), internal carotid arteries, **anterior cerebral arteries,** and **anterior communicating arteries** (which connect the two anterior cerebral arteries). This arterial circle equalizes blood pressure in the brain and can provide collateral channels should one vessel become blocked.

WHAT DO YOU THINK?

2 If both common carotid arteries were blocked, would any blood be able to reach the brain? Why or why not?

Some cranial venous blood is drained by the **vertebral veins** that extend through the transverse foramina of the cervical vertebrae and drain into the brachiocephalic veins. However, most of the venous blood of the cranium drains through several large veins collectively known as the **dural** (dū′r ăl) **venous sinuses** (figure 23.11 *b*). Recall that these large veins are formed between the two layers of dura mater and also receive excess CSF. There are no valves in the dural venous sinus system, so potentially the blood can flow in more than just one direction.

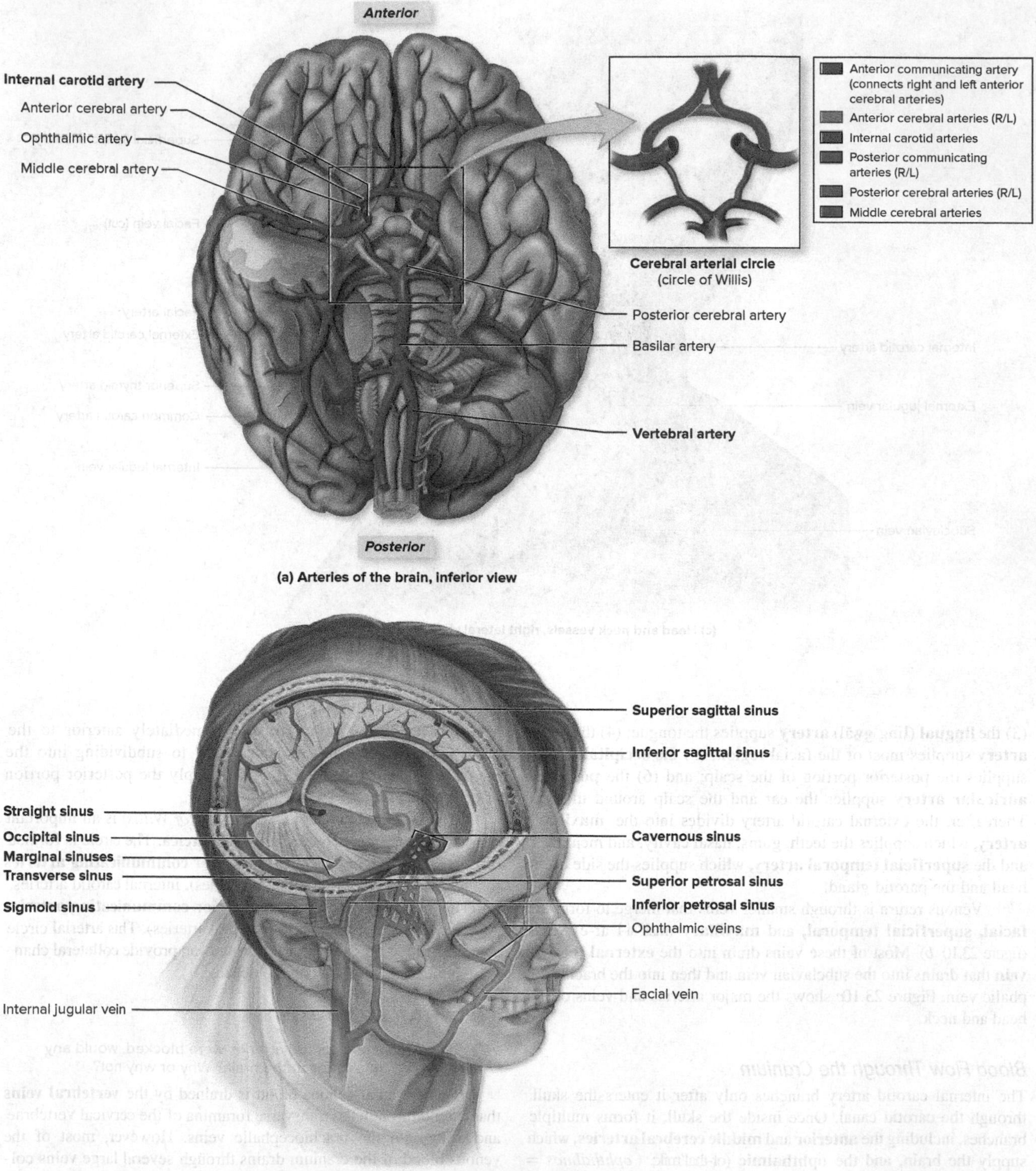

(a) Arteries of the brain, inferior view

(b) Venous drainage of cranium, right superior anterolateral view

Figure 23.11

Blood Flow Through the Cranium. The internal carotid and vertebral arteries supply blood to the cranium, and blood is drained from the cranium by the internal jugular veins. (*a*) The arterial circulation is revealed in an inferior view of the brain with a portion of the right temporal lobe and right cerebellar hemisphere removed. (*b*) Venous drainage of the cranium is shown from a superior anterolateral view. The dural venous sinuses are labeled in bold. APR

Clinical View 23.4

Detecting a Pulse Point

A pulse refers to the rhythmic throbbing of an arterial wall as blood is being pumped through it. Measuring the pulse is clinically significant for the following reasons:

1. It allows us to indirectly determine the rate of our heartbeat.
2. The force of the pulse can inform us about blood pressure, as high blood pressure will produce a more forceful pulse, and low blood pressure will produce a weaker pulse.
3. The absence of a pulse can allow us to determine if blood flow to a body part is lacking.

Pulse points can be found throughout the body and typically are located where an artery may be compressed against a bone or other solid structure. Two fingers are used to palpate the pulse, but the thumb is typically not used because it has a weak pulse of its own, which may interfere with pulse detection. Some common pulse points are shown.

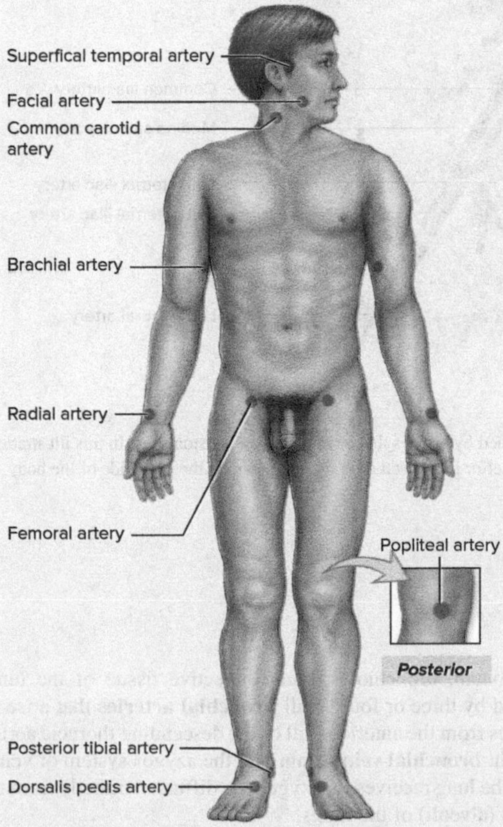
Superfical temporal artery
Facial artery
Common carotid artery
Brachial artery
Radial artery
Femoral artery
Popliteal artery
Posterior
Posterior tibial artery
Dorsalis pedis artery

The **dural venous sinus system** has several components (see also figure 15.5). The **superior sagittal sinus** is located superior to the longitudinal fissure of the brain; it drains into one of the transverse sinuses (usually the right one). The **inferior sagittal sinus** is found within the inferior free edge of the falx cerebri. The **straight sinus** is formed from the union (merging) of the inferior sagittal sinus and the great cerebral vein; this sinus drains into **left** and **right transverse sinuses** that travel horizontally along the internal margin of the occipital bone. Finally, the S-shaped **left** and **right sigmoid** (sig′moyd; = letter S) **sinuses** are a continuation of the transverse sinuses; they drain into the **internal jugular veins.** The internal jugular veins and subclavian veins merge to form the brachiocephalic veins that drain into the superior vena cava. Additional components of the dural venous sinus system include the **occipital** and **marginal sinuses,** the **superior** and **inferior petrosal sinuses,** and the **cavernous sinuses.** APR

23.3d Blood Flow Through the Thoracic and Abdominal Walls

The arterial flow to the thoracic and abdominal walls is supplied by several pairs of arteries (**figure 23.12**). A left and right **internal thoracic artery** arises from each subclavian artery to supply the mammary gland and anterior thoracic wall. Each internal thoracic artery has the following branches: the first six **anterior intercostal arteries** that supply the anterior intercostal spaces, and a **musculophrenic** (mŭs′kyū-lō-fren′ik; *phren* = diaphragm) **artery** that divides into anterior intercostal arteries 7–9. The internal thoracic artery then is renamed the **superior epigastric** (ep-i-gas′trik; *epi* = upon, *gastric* = stomach) **artery,** which transports blood to the superior abdominal wall. The **inferior epigastric artery,** a branch of the external iliac artery, supplies the inferior abdominal wall. Together, the superior and inferior epigastric arteries form extensive anastomoses.

The left and right **costocervical** (kos′tō-ser′vi-kal) **trunks** and **thyrocervical trunks** arise from each subclavian artery. The costocervical trunk has a branch called the **supreme intercostal artery,** which branches into the first and second **posterior intercostal arteries.** Posterior intercostal arteries 3–11 are branches of the descending thoracic aorta. The posterior and anterior intercostal arteries anastomose, and each pair forms a horizontal vessel arc that spans a segment of the thoracic wall.

Finally, five pairs of **lumbar arteries** branch from the descending abdominal aorta to supply the posterolateral abdominal wall.

In addition to the paired vessels just described, an unpaired **median sacral artery** arises at the bifurcation of the aorta in the pelvic region to supply the sacrum and coccyx.

Venous drainage of the thoracic and abdominal walls is a bit more complex than the arterial pathways (**figure 23.13**). **Anterior intercostal veins,** a **superior epigastric vein,** and a **musculophrenic vein** all empty into the **internal thoracic vein.** Each internal thoracic vein drains into its respective brachiocephalic vein. The **inferior epigastric vein** drains into the **external iliac vein.** The first and second **posterior intercostal veins** then merge with the **supreme intercostal vein** to drain into the brachiocephalic vein. Remember, the brachiocephalic veins merge to form the superior vena cava.

The **lumbar veins** and **posterior intercostal veins** drain into the azygos system of veins along the posterior thoracic wall. The **hemiazygos** (hem′ē-az′ī-gos) and **accessory hemiazygos veins** on the left side of the vertebrae drain the left-side veins. The **azygos vein** drains the right-side veins and also receives blood from the hemiazygos

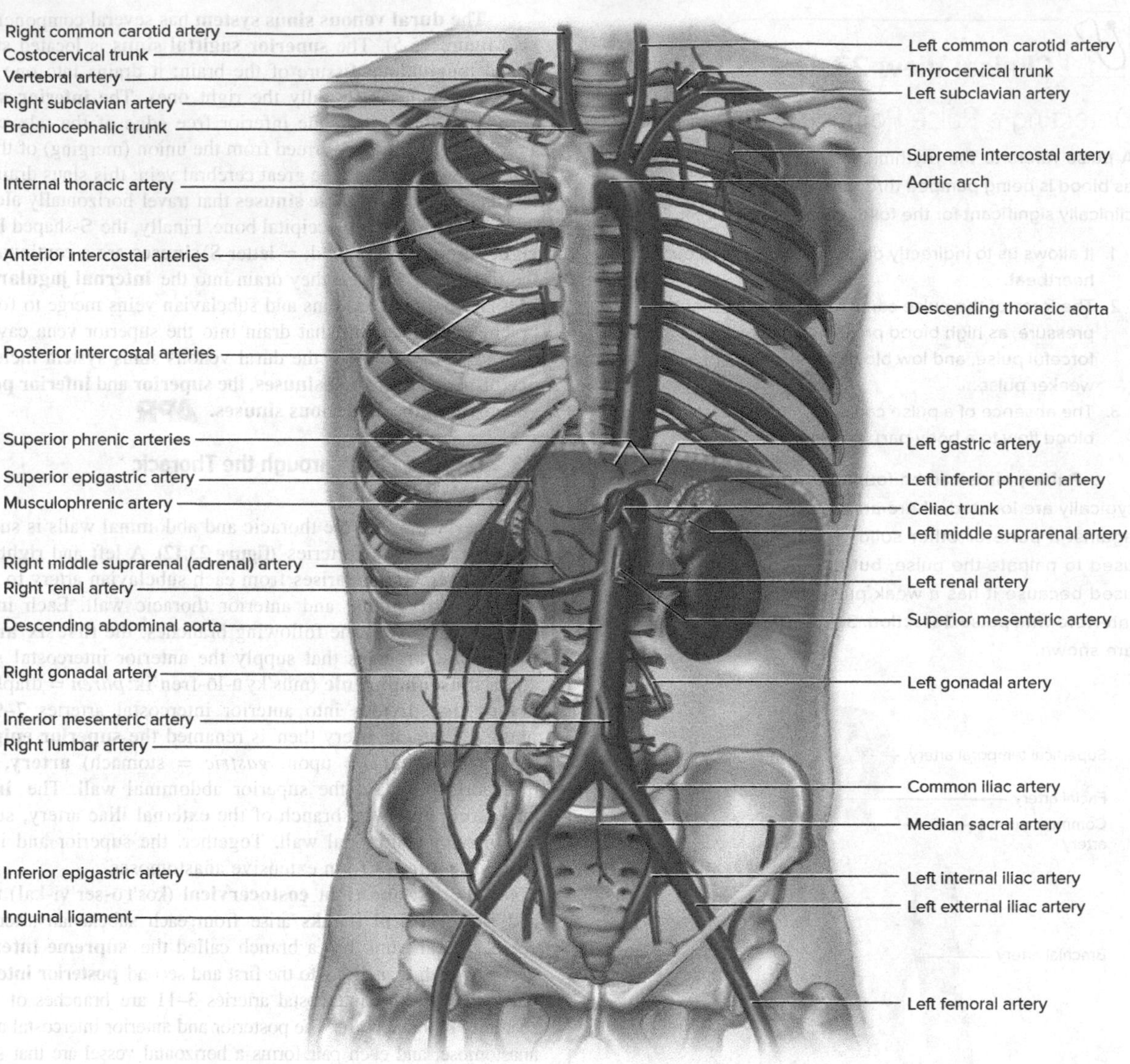
Right common carotid artery
Costocervical trunk
Vertebral artery
Right subclavian artery
Brachiocephalic trunk
Internal thoracic artery
Anterior intercostal arteries
Posterior intercostal arteries
Superior phrenic arteries
Superior epigastric artery
Musculophrenic artery
Right middle suprarenal (adrenal) artery
Right renal artery
Descending abdominal aorta
Right gonadal artery
Inferior mesenteric artery
Right lumbar artery
Inferior epigastric artery
Inguinal ligament
Left common carotid artery
Thyrocervical trunk
Left subclavian artery
Supreme intercostal artery
Aortic arch
Descending thoracic aorta
Left gastric artery
Left inferior phrenic artery
Celiac trunk
Left middle suprarenal artery
Left renal artery
Superior mesenteric artery
Left gonadal artery
Common iliac artery
Median sacral artery
Left internal iliac artery
Left external iliac artery
Left femoral artery

Figure 23.12
Arterial Circulation to the Thoracic and Abdominal Body Walls. The torso is supplied by arteries that have extensive anastomoses. In this illustration, the more anteriorly placed arteries as well as the "vessel arcs" formed by the anterior and posterior intercostal arteries are shown on the right side of the body. The left side of the body illustrates the deeper, posteriorly placed arteries only. APR

veins. The azygos vein also receives blood from the esophageal veins, bronchial veins, and pericardial veins. The azygos vein drains into the superior vena cava.

Figure 23.14 shows the arteries and veins of the posterior thoracic and abdominal walls.

23.3e Blood Flow Through the Thoracic Organs and Spinal Cord

The main thoracic organs include the heart, the lungs, the esophagus, and the diaphragm. The vasculature supplying the heart (coronary circulation) was discussed in section 22.3; the vessels of the other thoracic organs are discussed here (see figures 23.12 and 23.13).

Lungs

The bronchi, bronchioles, and connective tissue of the lungs are supplied by three or four small **bronchial arteries** that arise as tiny branches from the anterior wall of the descending thoracic aorta. Left and right **bronchial veins** drain into the azygos system of veins. The rest of the lung receives its oxygen via diffusion directly from the tiny air sacs (alveoli) of the lungs.

Esophagus

Several small **esophageal** (ē-sof′ă-jē′ăl, ē′sŏ-faj′ē-ăl) **arteries** arise from the anterior wall of the descending thoracic aorta and supply the esophagus. Additionally, the **left gastric artery** forms

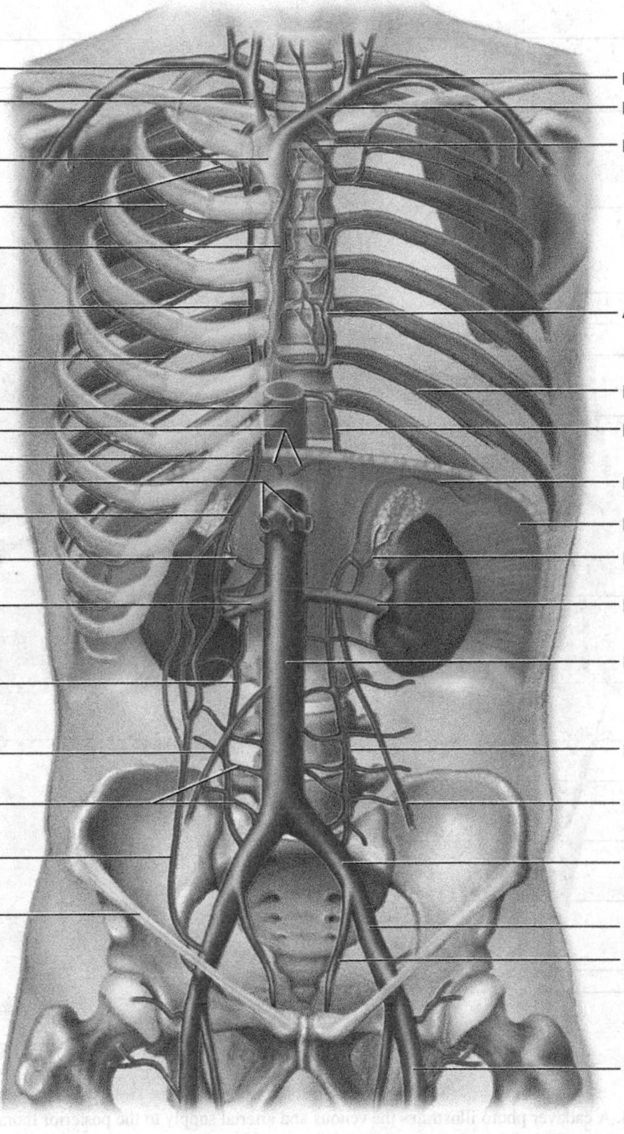
Right subclavian vein
Right brachiocephalic vein
Superior vena cava
Anterior intercostal veins
Azygos vein
Internal thoracic vein
Right posterior intercostal vein
Inferior vena cava
Superior phrenic veins
Musculophrenic vein
Hepatic veins
Right superior epigastric vein
Right suprarenal vein
Right renal vein
Right ascending lumbar vein
Right gonadal vein
Right lumbar veins
Right inferior epigastric vein
Inguinal ligament
Left subclavian vein
Left brachiocephalic vein
Left supreme intercostal vein
Accessory hemiazygos vein
Left posterior intercostal vein
Hemiazygos vein
Left inferior phrenic vein
Diaphragm
Left suprarenal vein
Left renal vein
Inferior vena cava
Left ascending lumbar vein
Left gonadal vein
Left common iliac vein
Left external iliac vein
Left internal iliac vein
Left femoral vein

Figure 23.13

Venous Circulation to the Thoracic and Abdominal Body Walls. The right side of this body primarily illustrates the more anteriorly placed veins as well as the vessel arcs formed by the anterior and posterior intercostal veins. The left side of the body illustrates the deeper, posteriorly placed veins only. APR

several **esophageal branches** that supply the abdominal portion of the esophagus. **Esophageal veins** drain the esophageal wall, and may take either of two routes: into the azygos vein or into the left gastric vein. The left gastric vein drains into the hepatic portal vein.

Diaphragm

Arterial blood is supplied to the diaphragm by paired vessels. **Superior phrenic** (fren′ik; *phren* = diaphragm) **arteries** arise from the descending thoracic aorta; both **musculophrenic arteries** and pericardiacophrenic arteries arise from the internal thoracic artery; and **inferior phrenic arteries** arise from the descending abdominal aorta to supply the diaphragm. Superior phrenic and inferior phrenic veins drain into the inferior vena cava, whereas the musculophrenic and pericardiacophrenic veins drain into the internal thoracic veins that empty into the brachiocephalic veins.

Spinal Cord

The superior part of the spinal cord is supplied primarily by an **anterior spinal artery** (formed from the union of branches from the vertebral arteries) and paired **posterior spinal arteries** (each is a branch of either the vertebral artery or the posterior inferior cerebellar artery) (see figure 16.2*b*). In addition, there are numerous

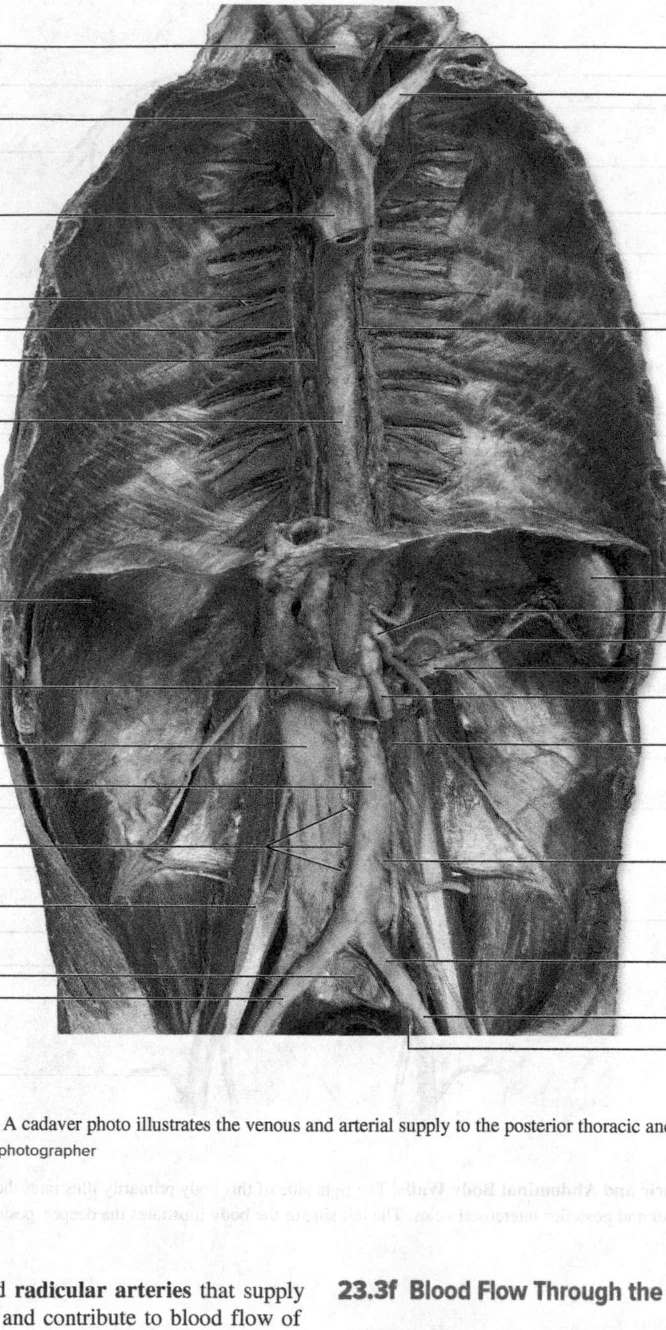
Trachea (cut)
Right brachiocephalic vein
Superior vena cava
Posterior intercostal vessels
Sympathetic trunk
Azygos vein
Descending thoracic aorta
Diaphragm
Hepatic portal vein
Inferior vena cava
Descending abdominal aorta
Lumbar arteries
Gonadal vein
Common iliac veins
Right common iliac artery
Thoracic duct
Left brachiocephalic vein
Hemiazygos vein
Spleen
Celiac trunk
Splenic artery
Splenic vein
Superior mesenteric artery
Superior mesenteric vein
Inferior mesenteric artery
Left common iliac artery
Left external iliac artery
Left internal iliac artery

Figure 23.14

Vessels of the Posterior Body Wall. A cadaver photo illustrates the venous and arterial supply to the posterior thoracic and abdominal walls. APR

segmental medullary arteries and **radicular arteries** that supply the inferior part of the spinal cord and contribute to blood flow of the superior part of the spinal cord. These segmental and radicular arteries are branches of larger segmental vessels, such as the posterior intercostal and lumbar arteries.

WHAT DID YOU LEARN?

5. What are the three main branches of the aortic arch, and which main body regions are supplied by each branch?
6. Make a flowchart to illustrate venous drainage from the dural venous sinuses to the heart.
7. Describe the route of the arterial supply to the anterior thoracic and anterior abdominal wall, beginning with the internal thoracic artery.

23.3f Blood Flow Through the Gastrointestinal Tract

Arterial Supply to the Abdomen

Three unpaired arteries arise from the anterior wall of the descending abdominal aorta to supply the gastrointestinal (GI) tract. From superior to inferior, these arteries are the celiac trunk, superior mesenteric artery, and inferior mesenteric artery.

The **celiac** (sē′lē-ak; *koilia* = belly) **trunk** is located immediately inferior to the aortic opening (hiatus) of the diaphragm (**figure 23.15*a***). It supplies the stomach, part of the duodenum, the liver, part of the pancreas, and the spleen. Three branches branch off this arterial trunk: the left gastric, splenic, and common hepatic arteries. (1) The **left gastric artery** supplies the lesser curvature of the stomach, and extends some esophageal branches. The left gastric artery anastomoses with the right

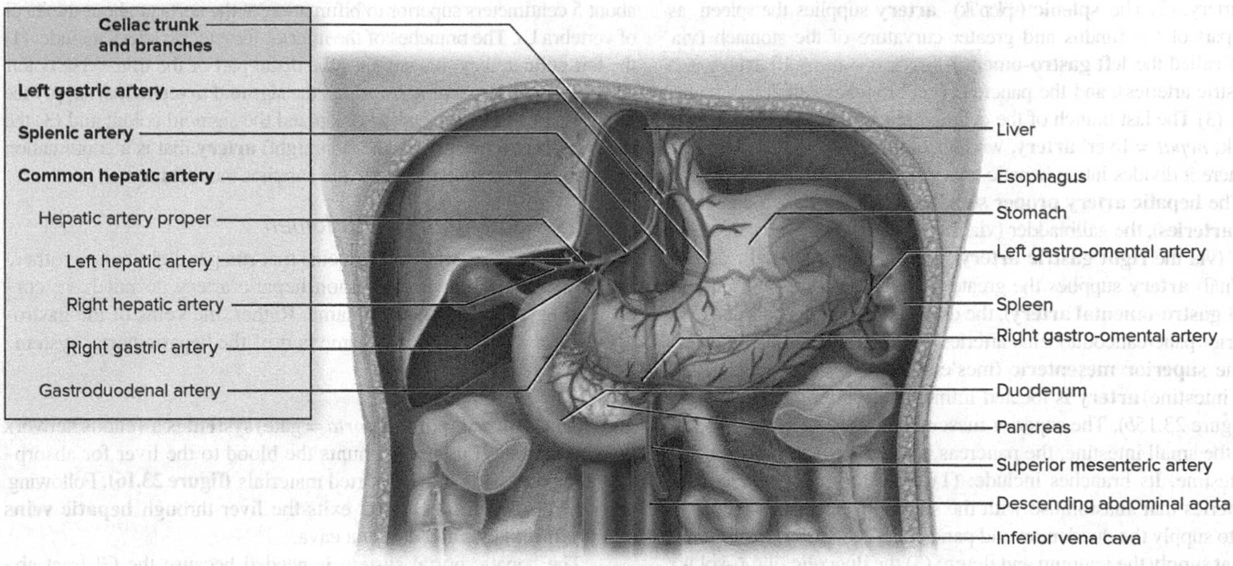
Celiac trunk and branches
Left gastric artery
Splenic artery
Common hepatic artery
Hepatic artery proper
Left hepatic artery
Right hepatic artery
Right gastric artery
Gastroduodenal artery
Liver
Esophagus
Stomach
Left gastro-omental artery
Spleen
Right gastro-omental artery
Duodenum
Pancreas
Superior mesenteric artery
Descending abdominal aorta
Inferior vena cava

(a) Celiac trunk branches

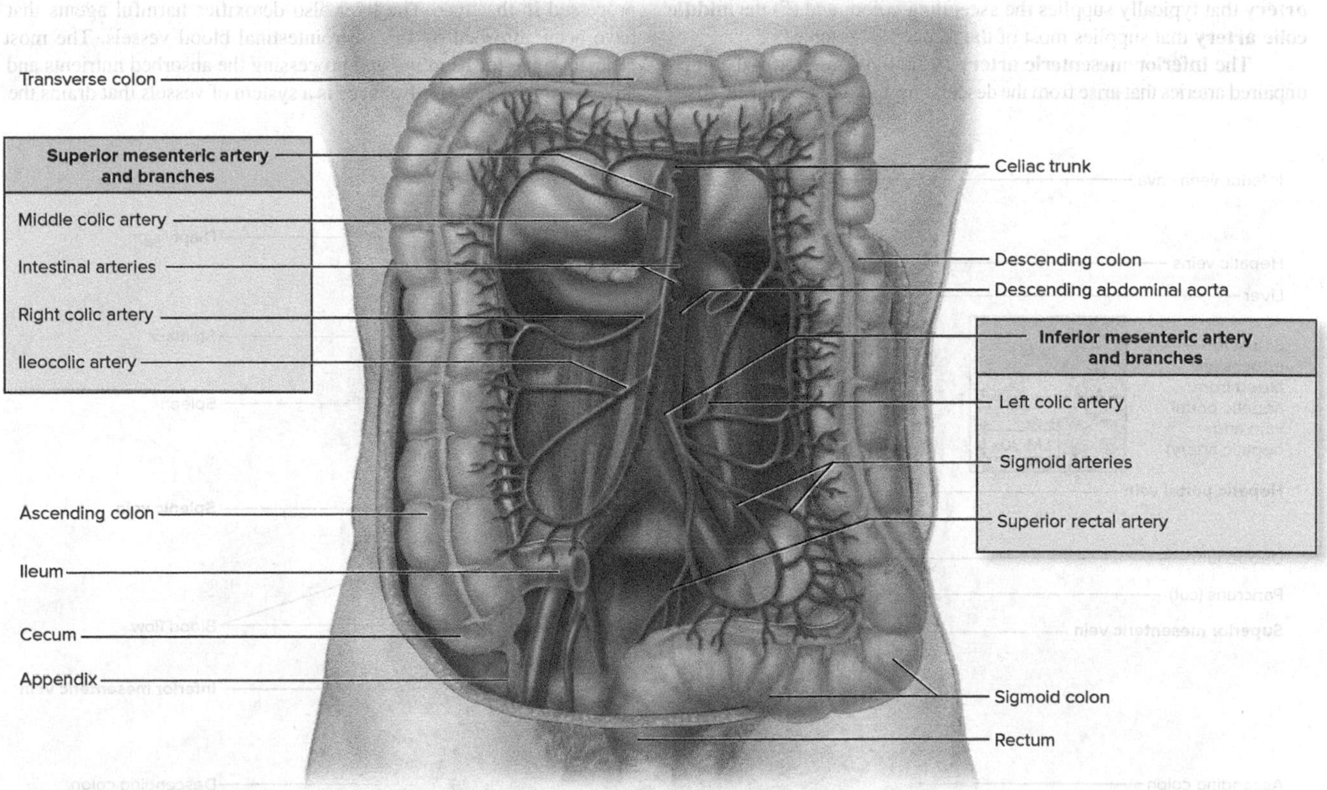
Transverse colon
Superior mesenteric artery and branches
Middle colic artery
Intestinal arteries
Right colic artery
Ileocolic artery
Ascending colon
Ileum
Cecum
Appendix
Celiac trunk
Descending colon
Descending abdominal aorta
Inferior mesenteric artery and branches
Left colic artery
Sigmoid arteries
Superior rectal artery
Sigmoid colon
Rectum

(b) Superior and inferior mesenteric arteries

Figure 23.15

Arterial Supply to the Gastrointestinal Tract and Abdominal Organs. The celiac trunk, superior mesenteric artery, and inferior mesenteric artery supply most of the abdominal organs. (*a*) Branches of the celiac trunk supply part of the esophagus, stomach, spleen, pancreas, liver, and gallbladder. (*b*) Branches of the superior mesenteric and inferior mesenteric arteries primarily supply the intestines. APR gastric artery. (2) The **splenic** (splen′ik) **artery** supplies the spleen, as well as part of the fundus and greater curvature of the stomach (via branches called the **left gastro-omental** [gas′tr ō-ō-men′t ăl] **artery** and short gastric arteries), and the pancreas (via branches called pancreatic arteries). (3) The last branch of the celiac trunk is the **common hepatic** (he-pat′ik; *hepat* = liver) **artery,** which extends to the right side of the body where it divides into a hepatic artery proper and a gastroduodenal artery. The **hepatic artery proper** supplies the liver (via **left** and **right hepatic arteries**), the gallbladder (via the **cystic artery**), and part of the stomach (via the **right gastric artery**). The **gastroduodenal** (gas′tr ō-dū′ ō-dē′năl) **artery** supplies the greater curvature of the stomach (via the **right gastro-omental artery**), the duodenum, and the pancreas (via the superior pancreaticoduodenal arteries).

The **superior mesenteric** (mes′en-ter′ik; *mesos* = middle, *enteron* = intestine) **artery** is located immediately inferior to the celiac trunk (figure 23.15*b*). The superior mesenteric artery supplies blood to most of the small intestine, the pancreas, and the proximal part of the large intestine. Its branches include: (1) the inferior pancreaticoduodenal arteries that anastomose with the superior pancreaticoduodenal arteries to supply the duodenum and pancreas; (2) 18–20 **intestinal arteries** that supply the jejunum and ileum; (3) the **ileocolic** (il′ē-ō-kol′ik) **artery** that supplies the ileum, cecum, and appendix; (4) the **right colic artery** that typically supplies the ascending colon; and (5) the **middle colic artery** that supplies most of the transverse colon.

The **inferior mesenteric artery** is the most inferior of the three unpaired arteries that arise from the descending abdominal aorta. It arises about 5 centimeters superior to bifurcation of the aorta at about the level of vertebra L_3. The branches of the inferior mesenteric artery include: (1) the **left colic artery** that supplies the distal part of the transverse colon and part of the descending colon; (2) the **sigmoid arteries** that supply the inferior part of the descending colon and the sigmoid colon; and (3) the **superior rectal** (rek′t ăl; *rectus* = straight) **artery** that is a continuation of the inferior mesenteric artery and supplies the rectum.

Venous Return from the Abdomen

In contrast to most arteries and veins that run parallel to one another, the celiac artery and the common hepatic artery do not have corresponding veins of the same name. Rather, the veins of the gastrointestinal tract all drain into some part of the hepatic portal system.

Hepatic Portal System

The **hepatic portal** (pōr′tăl; *porta* = gate) **system** is a venous network that drains the GI tract and shunts the blood to the liver for absorption and processing of transported materials **(figure 23.16)**. Following nutrient absorption, the blood exits the liver through **hepatic veins** that drain into the inferior vena cava.

The hepatic portal system is needed because the GI tract absorbs digested nutrients, and these nutrients must be absorbed and processed in the liver. The liver also detoxifies harmful agents that have been absorbed by the gastrointestinal blood vessels. The most efficient route for handling and processing the absorbed nutrients and any absorbed harmful substances is a system of vessels that drains the

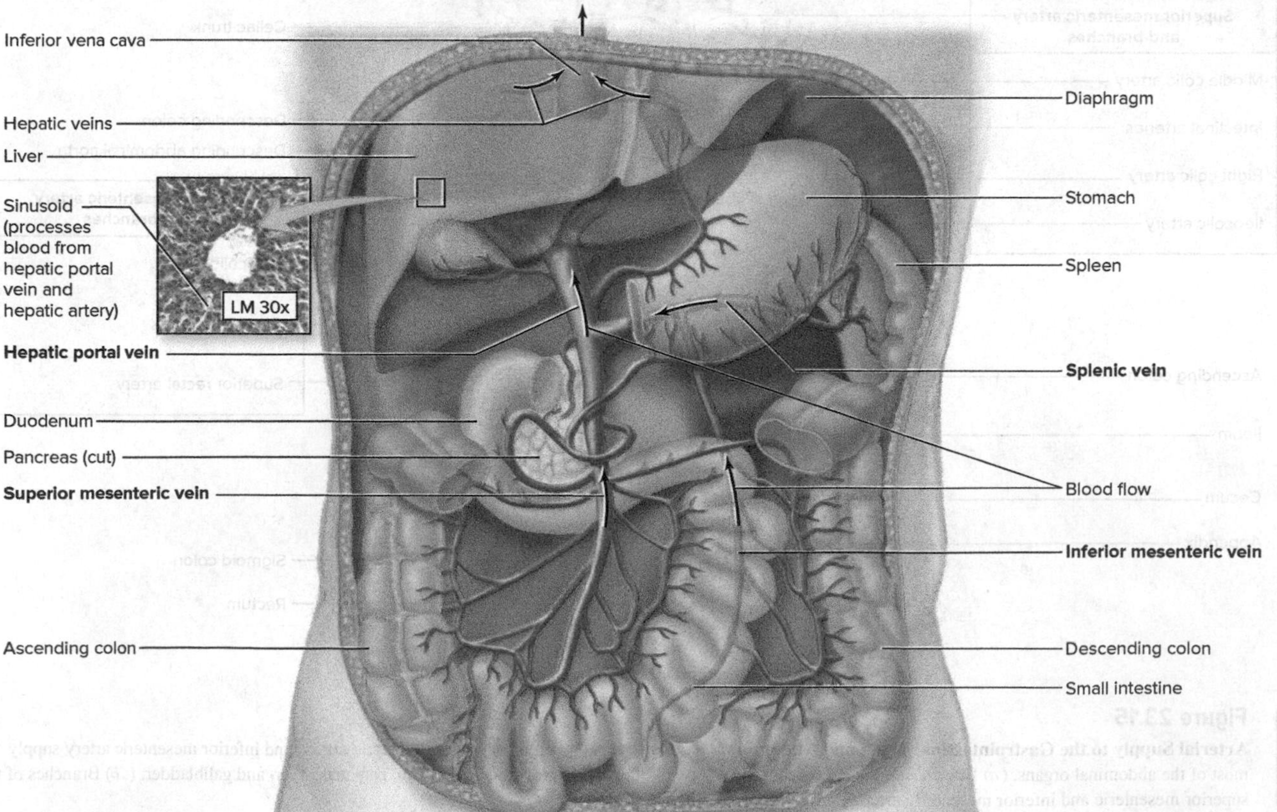
Inferior vena cava
Hepatic veins
Liver
Sinusoid (processes blood from hepatic portal vein and hepatic artery)
LM 30x
Hepatic portal vein
Duodenum
Pancreas (cut)
Superior mesenteric vein
Ascending colon
Diaphragm
Stomach
Spleen
Splenic vein
Blood flow
Inferior mesenteric vein
Descending colon
Small intestine

Figure 23.16

Hepatic Portal System. The hepatic portal system is a network of veins that transports venous blood from the GI tract to the liver for nutrient processing. APR

Photo: Victor P. Eroschenko

GI tract directly into the liver, rather than distributing these materials throughout the entire cardiovascular system. The hepatic portal system also receives products of erythrocyte destruction (e.g., from the spleen; see figure 21.5), so that the liver can recycle some of these products.

The **hepatic portal vein** is the large vein that receives deoxygenated (oxygen-poor) but nutrient-rich blood from the gastrointestinal organs. Three main venous branches merge to form this vein: (1) The **inferior mesenteric vein,** a vertically positioned vein draining the distal part of the large intestine, receives blood from the superior rectal vein, sigmoid veins, and left colic vein. In most individuals, the inferior mesenteric vein flows directly into the splenic vein, which then drains into the hepatic portal vein. (2) The **splenic vein,** a horizontally positioned vein draining the spleen, receives blood from pancreatic veins, short gastric veins, and the left gastro-omental vein. (3) The **superior mesenteric vein,** another vertically positioned vein on the right side of the body, drains the small intestine and part of the large intestine. It receives blood from the intestinal veins, pancreaticoduodenal veins, ileocolic vein, and right and middle colic veins. Some small veins, such as the left and right gastric veins, drain directly into the hepatic portal vein.

Figure 23.17 is a cadaver photo showing the arteries and veins of the posterior abdominal wall region. Note in this example that the inferior mesenteric vein drains into the superior mesenteric vein, not the splenic vein. This figure illustrates that the hepatic portal system can show great variation in some individuals.

The venous blood in the hepatic portal vein flows through the sinusoids of the liver for absorption, processing, and storage of nutrients. In these sinusoids, the venous blood mixes with some arterial blood entering the liver in the hepatic arteries. Thus, liver cells also receive oxygenated blood. Once nutrient absorption has occurred, blood leaves the liver through **hepatic veins** that drain into the inferior vena cava. APR

Learning Strategy 23.4

Although the pattern of the veins of the hepatic portal system can vary, together they typically resemble the side view of a chair. The front leg of the chair represents the inferior mesenteric vein, whereas the back leg represents the superior mesenteric vein. The seat of the chair is the splenic vein, whereas the back represents the hepatic portal vein.

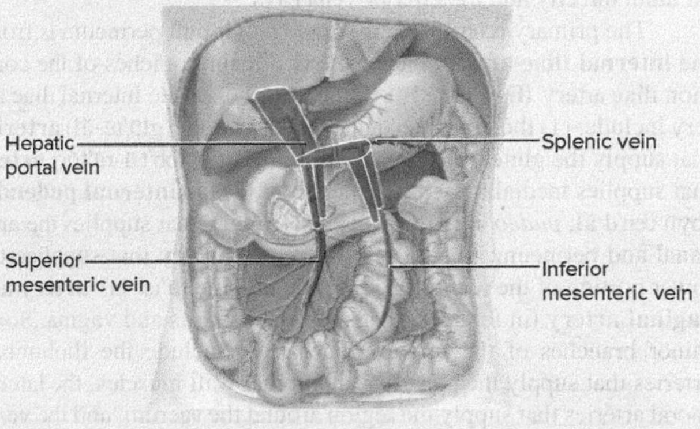
Hepatic portal vein
Splenic vein
Superior mesenteric vein
Inferior mesenteric vein

The configuration of the veins of the hepatic portal system resembles the side view of a chair.

23.3g Blood Flow Through the Posterior Abdominal Organs, Pelvis, and Perineum

In addition to the arteries already mentioned, three other paired arterial branches branch from the sides of the descending abdominal aorta: (1) The **middle suprarenal artery** supplies each adrenal gland;

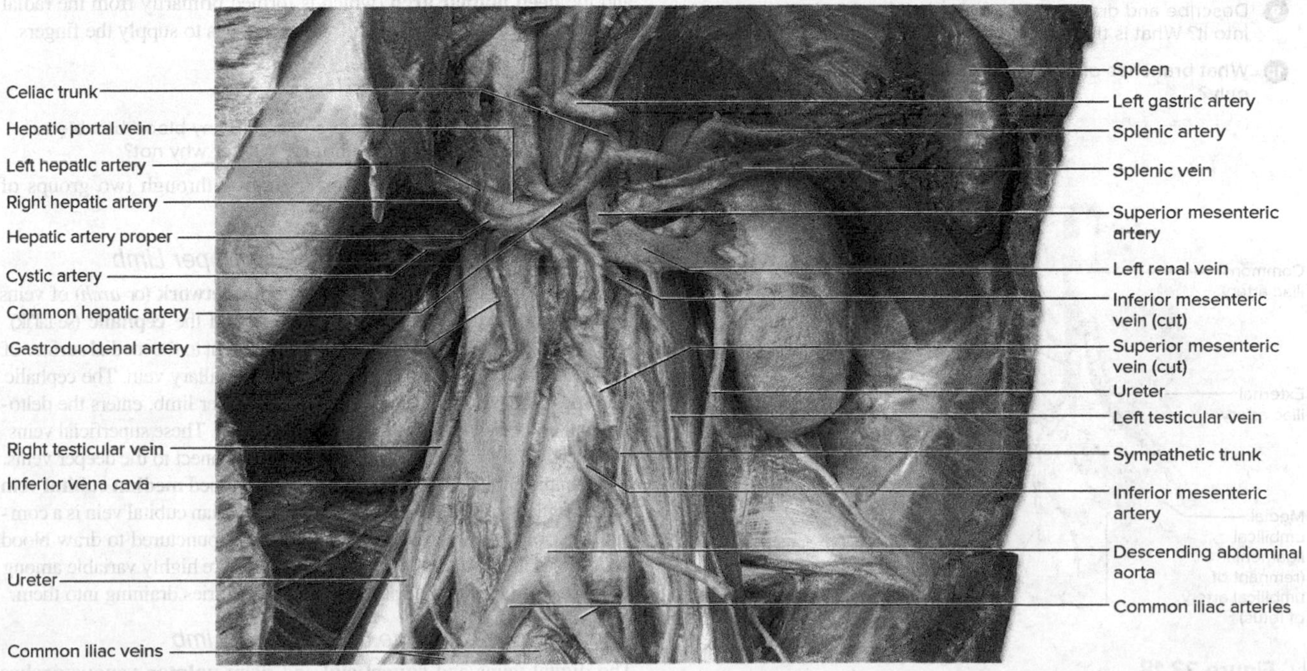
Celiac trunk
Hepatic portal vein
Left hepatic artery
Right hepatic artery
Hepatic artery proper
Cystic artery
Common hepatic artery
Gastroduodenal artery
Right testicular vein
Inferior vena cava
Ureter
Common iliac veins
Spleen
Left gastric artery
Splenic artery
Splenic vein
Superior mesenteric artery
Left renal vein
Inferior mesenteric vein (cut)
Superior mesenteric vein (cut)
Ureter
Left testicular vein
Sympathetic trunk
Inferior mesenteric artery
Descending abdominal aorta
Common iliac arteries

Figure 23.17

Major Vessels of the Posterior Abdominal Wall. In this cadaver photo, the inferior mesenteric vein varies from the "average" hepatic portal system pattern by draining into the superior mesenteric vein.

(2) the **renal** (rē′năl) **artery** supplies each kidney; and (3) the **gonadal** (gō-nad′ăl) **artery** supplies each gonad (testes or ovaries) (see figure 23.12). (Note: The right middle suprarenal artery may branch from the right renal artery in some individuals.) Subsequently, these organs are drained by veins having the same name as the arteries. The **left suprarenal vein** and **left gonadal vein** typically drain into the **left renal vein,** which then drains into the inferior vena cava. In contrast, the **right renal vein, right suprarenal vein,** and **right gonadal vein** all drain directly into the inferior vena cava.

The primary arterial supply to the pelvis and perineum is from the **internal iliac artery,** one of the two main branches of the common iliac artery (**figure 23.18**). Some branches of the internal iliac artery include: (1) the **superior** and **inferior gluteal** (glū′tē-ăl) **arteries** that supply the gluteal region; (2) the **obturator** (ob′tū-rā′tōr) **artery** that supplies medial muscles of the thigh; (3) the **internal pudendal** (pyū-den′d ăl; *pudeo* = to feel ashamed) **artery** that supplies the anal canal and perineum; (4) the **middle rectal artery** that supplies the lower portion of the rectum; and (5) the **uterine** (ū′ter-in) **artery** and **vaginal artery** (in females) that supply the uterus and vagina. Some minor branches of the internal iliac artery include the iliolumbar arteries that supply the posterior abdominal wall muscles, the lateral sacral arteries that supply the region around the sacrum, and the vesical arteries that supply the bladder and the prostate (in males).

The pelvis and perineum are drained by veins with the same name as the supplying arteries. The veins drain into the **internal iliac** vein. The internal and external iliac veins merge to form the **common iliac vein,** which subsequently drains into the inferior vena cava.

WHAT DID YOU LEARN?

8. Make a table that lists the three main arteries that supply the GI tract, their typical major branches, and the organs that each artery supplies.
9. Describe and draw the hepatic portal system. Which veins drain into it? What is the main function of the hepatic portal system?
10. What branches of the internal iliac artery are seen in females only?

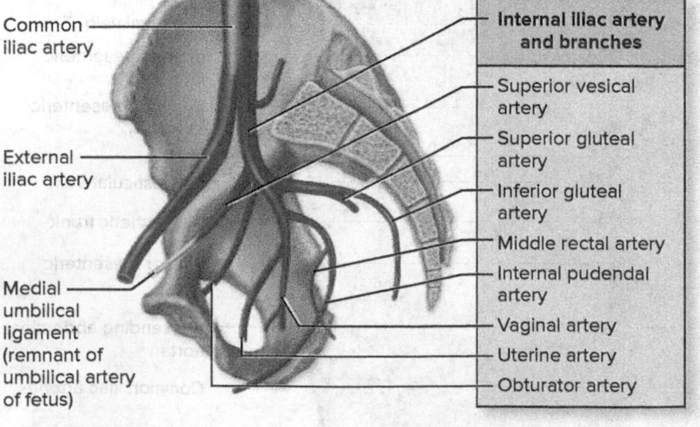
Common iliac artery
External iliac artery
Medial umbilical ligament (remnant of umbilical artery of fetus)
Internal iliac artery and branches
Superior vesical artery
Superior gluteal artery
Inferior gluteal artery
Middle rectal artery
Internal pudendal artery
Vaginal artery
Uterine artery
Obturator artery

Figure 23.18

Arterial Supply to the Pelvis. Branches of the right internal iliac artery distribute blood to the pelvic organs. Shown is a female pelvis; a male pelvis would have no uterine artery, and instead of a vaginal artery, would have an inferior vesical artery. APR

23.3h Blood Flow Through the Upper Limb

Blood flow through the upper limb closely mirrors its flow through the lower limb in many respects. Both the upper and lower limbs are supplied by a main arterial vessel: the subclavian artery for the upper limb and the femoral artery for the lower limb. This artery bifurcates at the elbow or knee. Arterial and venous arches are seen in both the hand and foot. Finally, both the upper limb and the lower limb have superficial and deep networks of veins.

Arterial Flow

A **subclavian artery** supplies blood to each upper limb (**figure 23.19*a***). The left subclavian artery arises directly from the aortic arch, whereas the right subclavian artery is a division of the brachiocephalic trunk. The subclavian artery extends multiple branches: (1) the vertebral artery, (2) the thyrocervical trunk (to supply the thyroid gland and some neck and shoulder muscles), (3) the internal thoracic artery, and (4) the costocervical trunk (see figure 23.12).

After the subclavian artery passes over the lateral border of the first rib, it is renamed the **axillary** (ak′sil- ār′ē) **artery.** The axillary artery extends many branches to the shoulder and thoracic region, including the superior thoracic artery (not to be confused with the supreme intercostal artery), the thoracoacromial artery, the lateral thoracic artery, the humeral circumflex arteries, and the subscapular artery. When the axillary artery passes the inferior border of the teres major muscle, it is renamed the **brachial** (brā′kē-ăl) **artery.** The brachial artery travels alongside the humerus. One of its branches is the **deep brachial artery** (also known as the *profunda brachii artery* or *deep artery of the arm*), which supplies blood to most brachial (arm) muscles. In the cubital fossa, the brachial artery divides into an **ulnar** (ŭl′năr) **artery** and a **radial** (rā′dē-ăl) **artery.** Both arteries supply the forearm and wrist before they anastomose and form two arterial arches in the palm: the **superficial palmar** (pahl′m ăr) **arch** (formed primarily from the ulnar artery) and the **deep palmar arch** (which is formed primarily from the radial artery). **Digital arteries** branch from the arches to supply the fingers.

WHAT DO YOU THINK?

3. If the left ulnar artery were cut, would any blood be able to reach the left hand and fingers? Why or why not?

Venous drainage of the upper limb is through two groups of veins: superficial and deep.

Superficial Venous Drainage of the Upper Limb

On the dorsum of the hand, a **dorsal venous network** (or *arch*) of veins drains into both the **basilic** (ba-sil′ik) **vein** and the **cephalic** (se-fal′ik) **vein** (figure 23.19 *b*). The basilic vein runs adjacent to the medial surface of the upper limb and eventually helps form the axillary vein. The cephalic vein runs alongside the lateral aspect of the upper limb, enters the deltopectoral triangle, and drains into the axillary vein. These superficial veins have perforating branches that allow them to connect to the deeper veins.

In the cubital region, an obliquely positioned **median cubital vein** connects the cephalic and basilic veins. The median cubital vein is a common site for **venipuncture,** in which a vein is punctured to draw blood or inject a solute. All of these superficial veins are highly variable among individuals and have multiple superficial tributaries draining into them.

Deep Venous Drainage of the Upper Limb

The digital veins and **superficial** and **deep palmar venous arches** drain into pairs of **radial veins** and **ulnar veins** that run parallel to arteries of the same name. (Paired veins that run alongside an artery are collectively known as *venae commitantes.*) At the level of the cubital fossa, the radial and ulnar veins merge to form a pair of

Clinical View 23.5

Atherosclerosis

Atherosclerosis (ath′er-ō-skler-ō′sis, *athere* = gruel, *sclerosis* = hardening) is a progressive disease of the elastic and muscular arteries. It is characterized by the presence of an **atheroma** (or *atheromatous plaque*), which leads to thickening of the tunica intima and narrowing of the arterial lumen. Atherosclerosis is linked to over 50% of all deaths in the United States, and it is a leading cause of morbidity and mortality in other countries of the Western world as well.

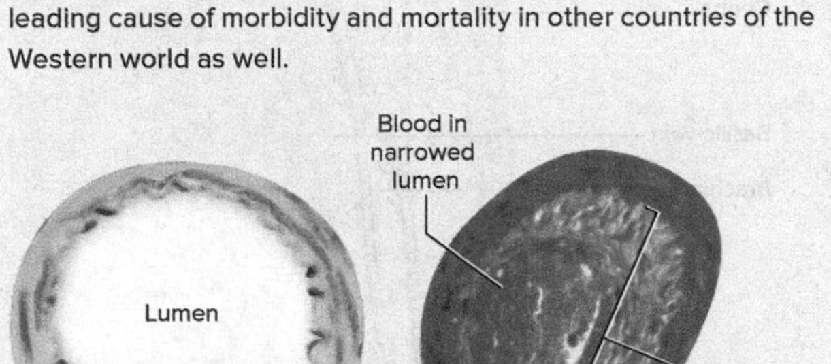
Blood in narrowed lumen
Lumen
Atheroma occluding lumen
LM 20x
LM 50x

(a) Normal artery **(b) Atherosclerotic artery**

(a) (Normal artery) Al Telser/McGraw-Hill Education; (b) (Atherosclerotic artery) Al Telser/McGraw-Hill Education

Etiology of Atherosclerosis

Although the cause of atherosclerosis is not completely understood, the **response-to-injury hypothesis** is the most widely accepted. This proposal states that injury (especially repeated injury) to the endothelium of an arterial wall results in an inflammatory reaction that eventually leads to the development of an atheroma. The injury could be caused by infection, trauma to the vessel, or hypertension. The injured endothelium becomes more permeable, which encourages leukocytes and platelets to adhere to the lesion and initiate an inflammatory response. Low-density lipoproteins (LDLs) and very-low-density lipoproteins (VLDLs) enter the tunica intima, combine with oxygen, and remain stuck to the vessel wall. This oxidation of lipoproteins attracts monocytes, which adhere to the endothelium and migrate into the wall. As the monocytes migrate into the wall, they digest the lipids and develop into structures called **foam cells.** Eventually, smooth muscle cells from the tunica media migrate into the atheroma and proliferate, which causes further enlargement of the atheroma. Atherosclerotic plaques cause narrowing of the lumen of the blood vessel, thereby restricting blood flow to the regions the artery supplies.

Risk Factors for Atherosclerosis

Hypercholesterolemia (an increased amount of cholesterol in the blood), which also tends to run in families, has been positively associated with the rate of development and severity of atherosclerosis. In addition, males tend to be affected more than females, and symptomatic atherosclerosis increases with age. Finally, smoking and hypertension both cause vascular injury, which increases the risk.

Treatment and Prevention Options

If an artery is occluded (blocked) in one or just a few areas, a treatment called **angioplasty** (an′jē-ō-plas′tē; *angeion* = vessel, *plastos* = formed) is used. A physician inserts a balloon-tip catheter into an artery, and positions it at the site where the lumen is narrowed. Then the balloon is inflated, forcibly expanding the narrowed area. To ensure that the area remains open, a stent may be placed at the site. A stent is a piece of wire-mesh that springs open to keep the vessel lumen open. For occluded coronary arteries, a much more invasive treatment known as **coronary bypass surgery** may be needed. A vein (e.g., great saphenous vein) or artery (e.g., internal thoracic artery) is detached from its original location and grafted from the aorta to the coronary artery system, thus bypassing the area(s) of atherosclerotic narrowing.

Ideally, the best treatment for atherosclerosis is to try to prevent it by:

- Maintaining a healthy diet and watching your cholesterol level.
- Not smoking.
- Monitoring your blood pressure regularly. If you have hypertension, seek treatment as soon as possible.

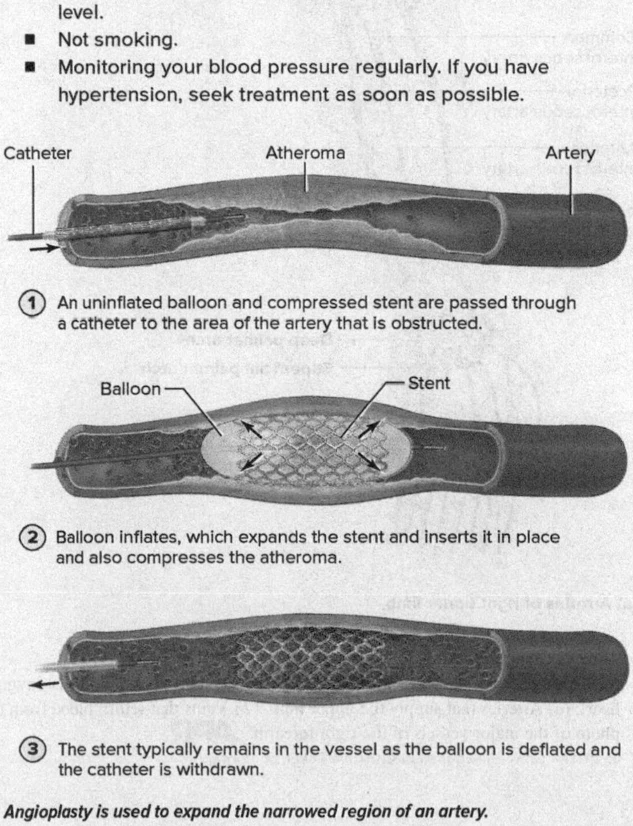
Catheter
Atheroma
Artery
(1) An uninflated balloon and compressed stent are passed through a catheter to the area of the artery that is obstructed.
Balloon
Stent
(2) Balloon inflates, which expands the stent and inserts it in place and also compresses the atheroma.
(3) The stent typically remains in the vessel as the balloon is deflated and the catheter is withdrawn.

Angioplasty is used to expand the narrowed region of an artery.

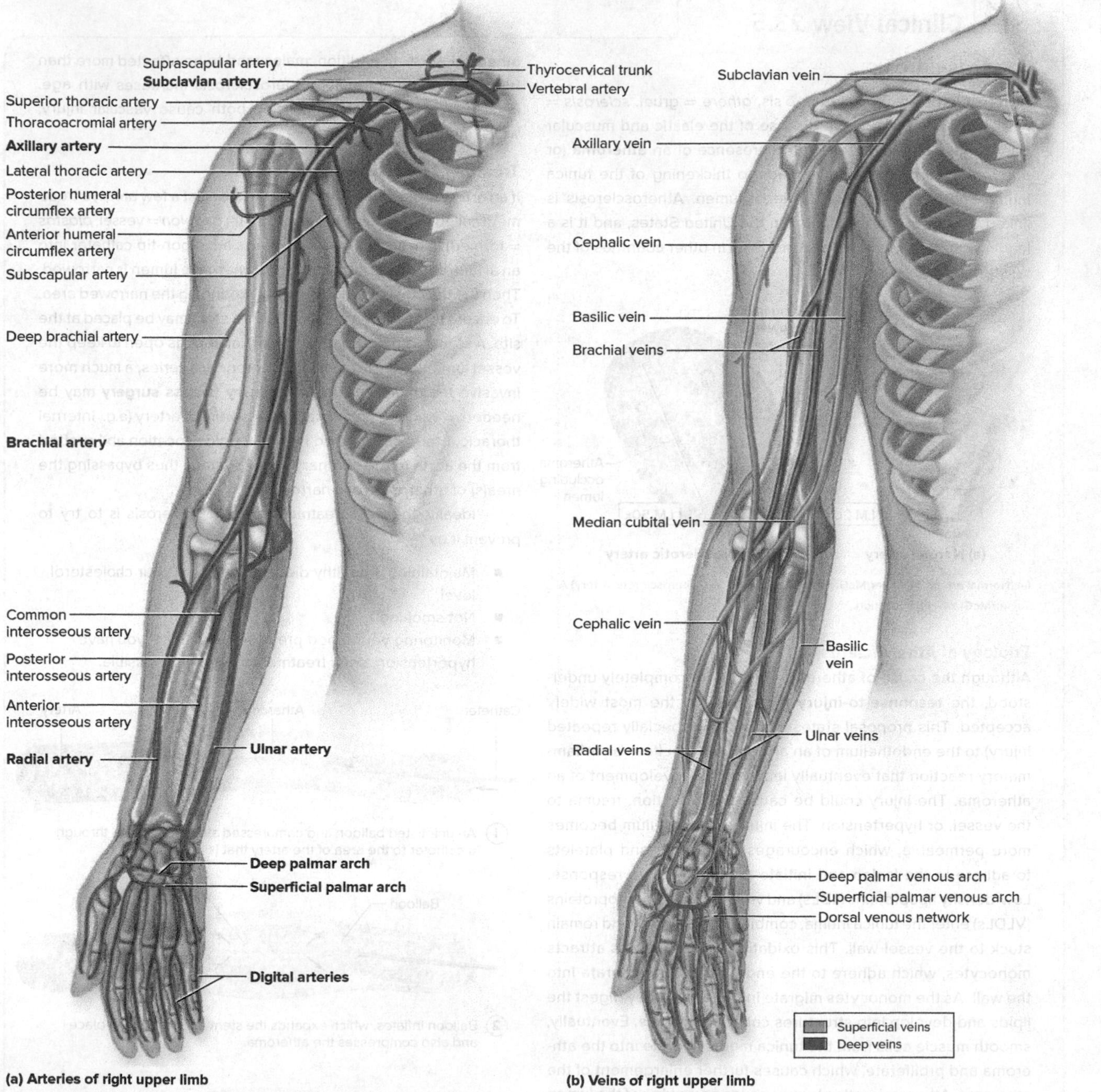
Suprascapular artery
Subclavian artery
Superior thoracic artery
Thoracoacromial artery
Axillary artery
Lateral thoracic artery
Posterior humeral circumflex artery
Anterior humeral circumflex artery
Subscapular artery
Deep brachial artery
Brachial artery
Common interosseous artery
Posterior interosseous artery
Anterior interosseous artery
Radial artery
Ulnar artery
Deep palmar arch
Superficial palmar arch
Digital arteries
Thyrocervical trunk
Vertebral artery
(a) Arteries of right upper limb
Subclavian vein
Axillary vein
Cephalic vein
Basilic vein
Brachial veins
Median cubital vein
Cephalic vein
Basilic vein
Ulnar veins
Radial veins
Deep palmar venous arch
Superficial palmar venous arch
Dorsal venous network
Superficial veins
Deep veins
(b) Veins of right upper limb

Figure 23.19

Vascular Supply to the Upper Limb. The subclavian artery transports oxygenated blood to the upper limb; veins merge to return deoxygenated blood to the heart. (*a*) Arteries that supply the upper limb. (*b*) Veins that return blood from the upper limb. (*c*) Cadaver photo of the major vessels of the right arm. (*d*) Cadaver photo of the major vessels of the right forearm. APR

brachial veins that travel with the brachial artery. Brachial veins and the basilic vein merge to form the **axillary vein.** Superior to the lateral border of the first rib, the axillary vein is renamed the **subclavian vein.** When the subclavian vein and internal jugular vein merge, they form the brachiocephalic vein. As we have seen, the left and right brachiocephalic veins form the superior vena cava.

The combined arteries and veins of the upper limbs are shown in cadaver photos in figure 23.19*c, d.*

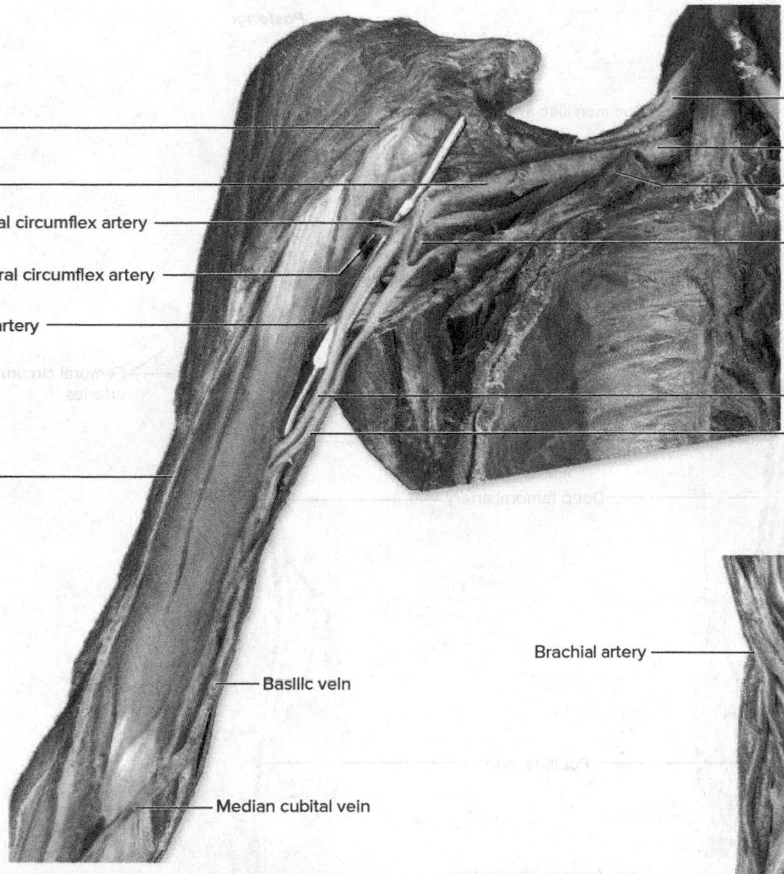
Cephalic vein
Axillary artery
Anterior humeral circumflex artery
Posterior humeral circumflex artery
Deep brachial artery
Cephalic vein
Basilic vein
Median cubital vein
Brachial plexus
Subclavian artery
Subclavian vein
Subscapular artery
Brachial artery
Median nerve

(c) Right axilla and arm, anterior view

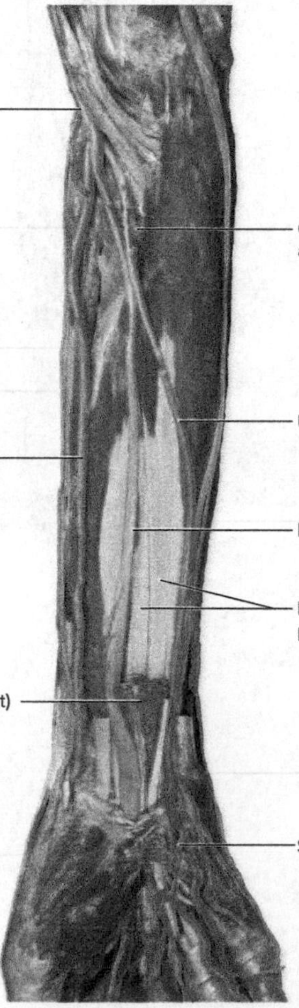
Brachial artery
Radial artery
Flexor muscles (cut)
Common interosseous artery
Ulnar artery
Median nerve
Flexor digitorum profundus tendons
Superficial palmar arch

(d) Right forearm, anterior view

Figure 23.19
Vascular Supply to the Upper Limb. (*Continued*)

23.3i Blood Flow Through the Lower Limb

The arterial and venous blood flow of the lower limb is very similar to that of the upper limb. As we discuss lower limb blood flow, compare it with that of the upper limb.

Arterial Flow

The main arterial supply for the lower limb is the external iliac artery, which is a branch of the common iliac artery (**figure 23.20*a***). The external iliac artery travels inferior to the inguinal ligament, where it is renamed the **femoral** (fem′ŏ-răl) **artery.** The **deep femoral artery** (*profunda femoris artery* or *deep artery of the thigh*) branches off the femoral artery to supply the hip joint (via **medial** and **lateral femoral circumflex arteries**) and many of the thigh muscles, before traversing posteromedially along the thigh. The femoral artery passes through an opening in the adductor magnus muscle and enters the posteriorly placed popliteal fossa, where the vessel is renamed the **popliteal** (pop-lit′ē-ăl, pop-li-tē′ăl) **artery.** The popliteal artery supplies the knee joint and muscles in this region.

The popliteal artery divides into an **anterior tibial** (tib′ē-ăl) **artery** that supplies the anterior compartment of the leg, and a **posterior tibial artery** that supplies the posterior compartment of the leg. The posterior tibial artery extends a branch called the **fibular** (fib′yū-lăr) **artery,** which supplies the lateral compartment leg muscles.

The posterior tibial artery continues to the plantar side of the foot, where it branches into **medial** and **lateral plantar arteries.** The anterior tibial artery crosses over the anterior surface of the ankle, where it is renamed the **dorsalis pedis artery** (*dorsal artery of the foot*). The dorsalis pedis artery and a branch of the lateral plantar artery unite to form the **plantar** (plan′tar) **arch** of the foot. **Digital arteries** extend from the plantar arch and supply the toes.

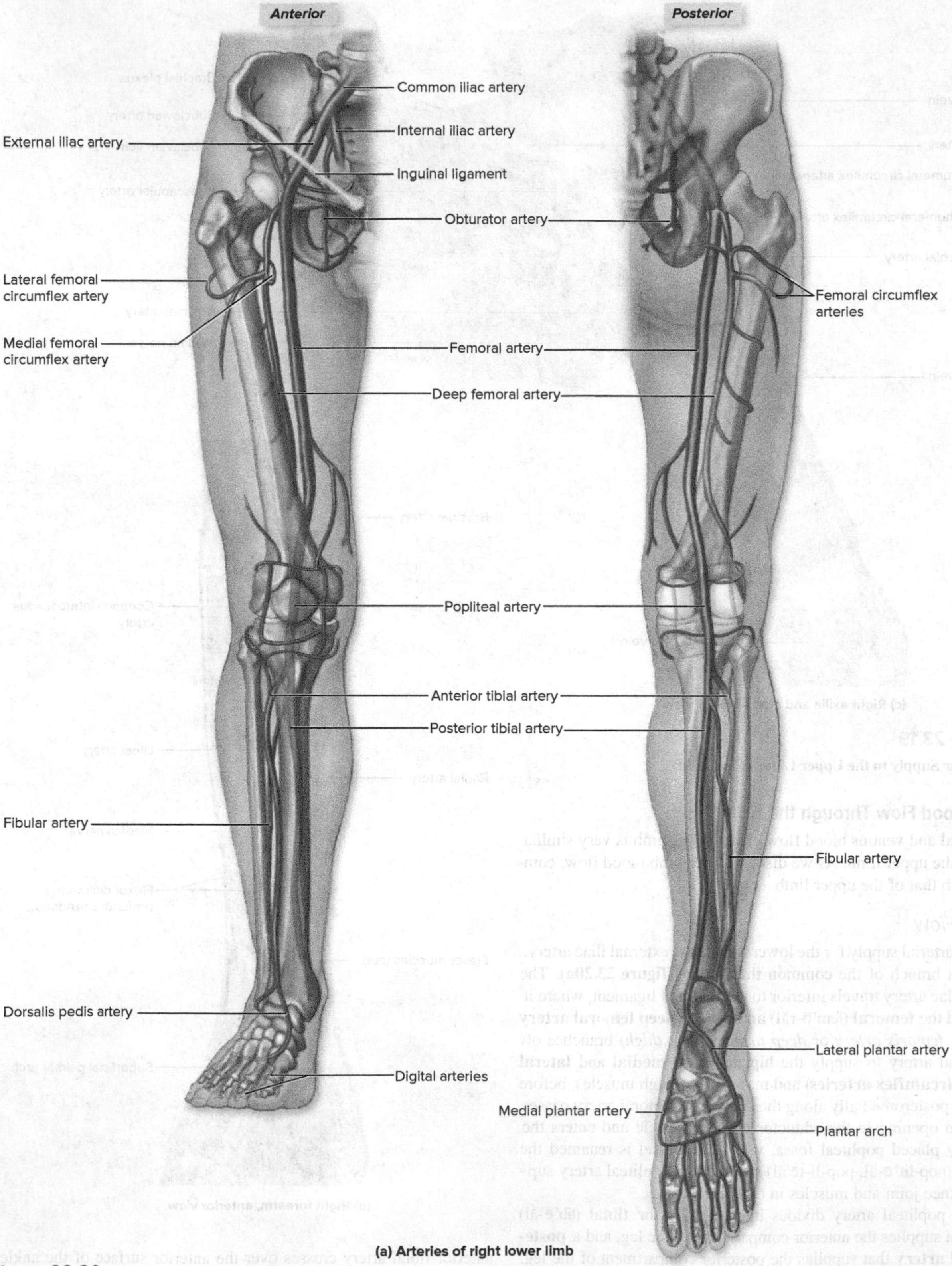
Anterior
Posterior
Common iliac artery
Internal iliac artery
External iliac artery
Inguinal ligament
Obturator artery
Lateral femoral circumflex artery
Medial femoral circumflex artery
Femoral circumflex arteries
Femoral artery
Deep femoral artery
Popliteal artery
Anterior tibial artery
Posterior tibial artery
Fibular artery
Fibular artery
Dorsalis pedis artery
Lateral plantar artery
Digital arteries
Medial plantar artery
Plantar arch

(a) Arteries of right lower limb

Figure 23.20

Vascular Supply to the Lower Limb. The external iliac artery transports oxygenated blood to the lower limb; veins merge to return deoxygenated blood to the heart. (*a*) Anterior and posterior views of arteries distributed throughout the right lower limb. (*b*) Anterior and posterior views of veins that return blood from the right lower limb. APR

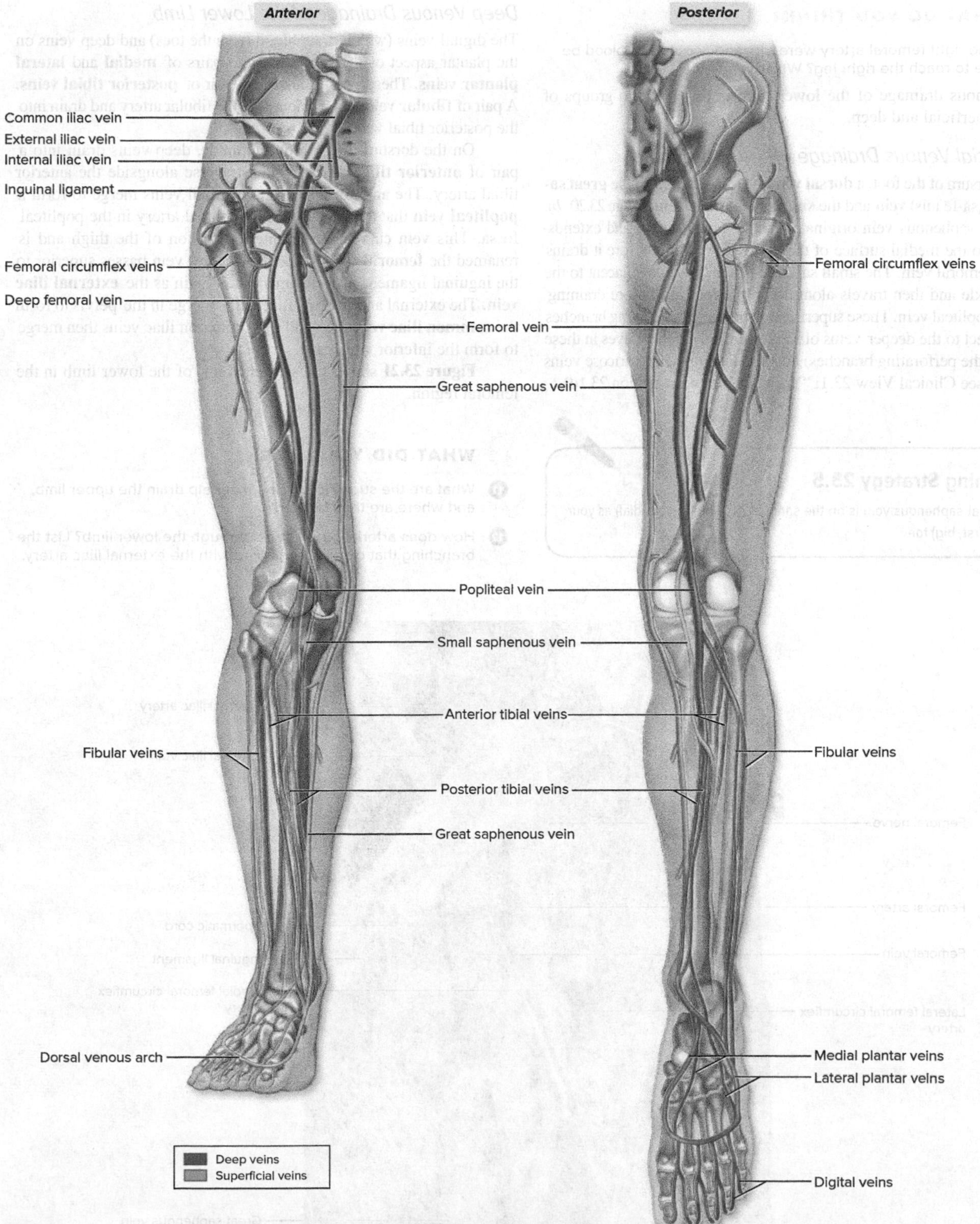
Anterior
Posterior
Common iliac vein
External iliac vein
Internal iliac vein
Inguinal ligament
Femoral circumflex veins
Deep femoral vein
Femoral vein
Great saphenous vein
Femoral circumflex veins
Popliteal vein
Small saphenous vein
Anterior tibial veins
Fibular veins
Fibular veins
Posterior tibial veins
Great saphenous vein
Dorsal venous arch
Medial plantar veins
Lateral plantar veins
Digital veins
Deep veins
Superficial veins

(b) Veins of right lower limb

Figure 23.20
Vascular Supply to the Lower Limb. ***(Continued)***

WHAT DO YOU THINK?

4. If the right femoral artery were blocked, would any blood be able to reach the right leg? Why or why not?

Venous drainage of the lower limb is through two groups of veins: superficial and deep.

Superficial Venous Drainage of the Lower Limb

On the dorsum of the foot, a **dorsal venous arch** drains into the **great saphenous** (să-fē′nŭs) **vein** and the **small saphenous vein** (figure 23.20 *b*). The great saphenous vein originates in the medial ankle and extends adjacent to the medial surface of the entire lower limb before it drains into the femoral vein. The small saphenous vein extends adjacent to the lateral ankle and then travels along the posterior calf, before draining into the popliteal vein. These superficial veins have perforating branches that connect to the deeper veins of the lower limb. If the valves in these veins (or the perforating branches) become incompetent, varicose veins develop (see Clinical View 23.1: "Varicose Veins" in section 23.1d).

Learning Strategy 23.5

The great saphenous vein is on the same side of the leg (medial) as your great (first, big) toe.

Deep Venous Drainage of the Lower Limb

The digital veins (which drain blood from the toes) and deep veins on the plantar aspect of the foot drain into pairs of **medial** and **lateral plantar veins.** These veins drain into a pair of **posterior tibial veins.** A pair of **fibular veins** travel alongside the fibular artery and drain into the posterior tibial veins.

On the dorsum of the foot and ankle, deep veins drain into a pair of **anterior tibial veins,** which traverse alongside the anterior tibial artery. The anterior and posterior tibial veins merge to form a **popliteal vein** that accompanies the popliteal artery in the popliteal fossa. This vein curves to the anterior portion of the thigh and is renamed the **femoral vein.** Once the femoral vein passes superior to the inguinal ligament, it is renamed once again as the **external iliac vein.** The external and internal iliac veins merge in the pelvis to form the **common iliac vein.** Left and right common iliac veins then merge to form the inferior vena cava.

Figure 23.21 shows arteries and veins of the lower limb in the femoral region.

WHAT DID YOU LEARN?

11. What are the superficial veins that help drain the upper limb, and where are they located?

12. How does arterial blood travel through the lower limb? List the branching that occurs, beginning with the external iliac artery.

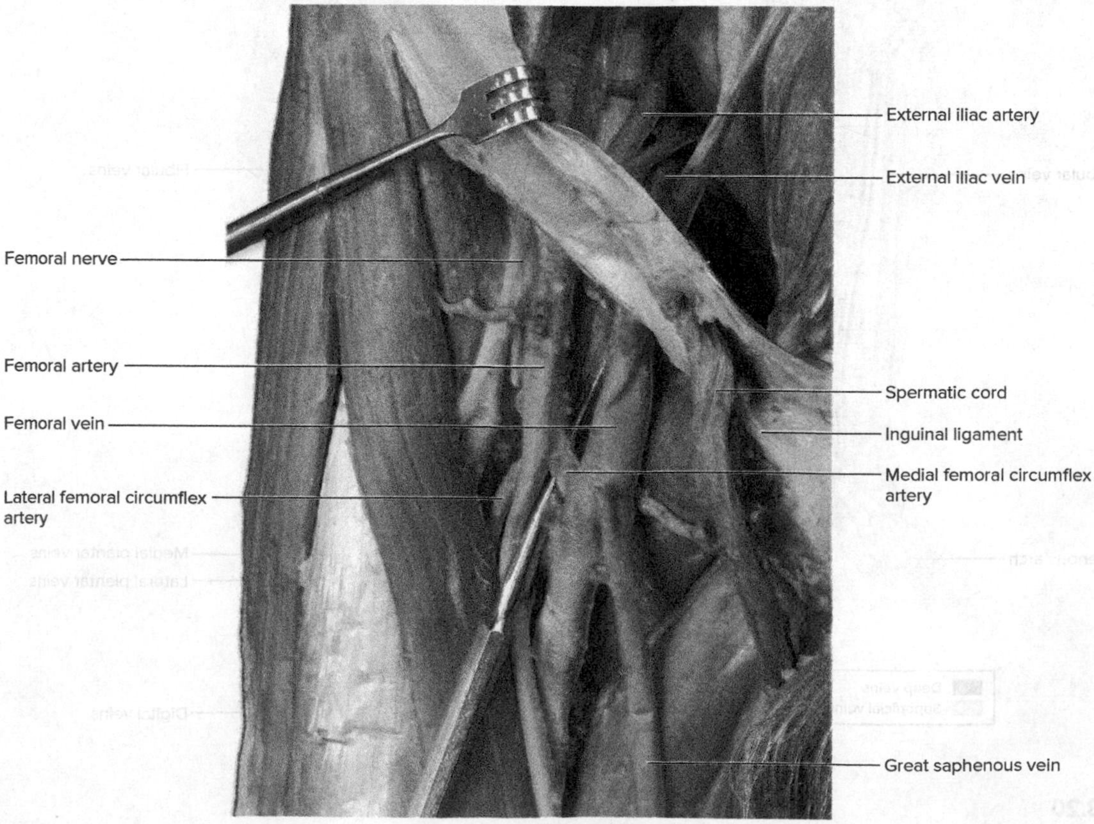
External iliac artery
External iliac vein
Femoral nerve
Femoral artery
Femoral vein
Lateral femoral circumflex artery
Spermatic cord
Inguinal ligament
Medial femoral circumflex artery
Great saphenous vein

Figure 23.21

Vascular Supply to the Lower Limb. A cadaver photo shows major vessels of the anterior thigh.

23.4 Pulmonary Circulation

✓ **Learning Objective**

13. List the pulmonary circulation vessels and trace their pathways.

The pulmonary circulation is responsible for transporting deoxygenated blood from the right side of the heart to the lungs, and then returning the newly oxygenated blood to the left side of the heart (**figure 23.22**). Blood low in oxygen is pumped out of the right ventricle into the **pulmonary trunk.** This vessel travels superiorly and slightly to the left before it bifurcates into a **left pulmonary artery** and a **right pulmonary artery** that go to the lungs. The pulmonary arteries divide into smaller arteries that continue to subdivide to form arterioles. These arterioles finally branch into pulmonary capillaries, where gas exchange occurs. Carbon dioxide is removed from the blood and enters the tiny air sacs (alveoli) of the lungs, whereas oxygen moves in the opposite direction, from the air sacs into the blood. The capillaries merge to form venules and then the **pulmonary veins.** Typically, two left and two right pulmonary veins transport the newly oxygenated blood to the left atrium of the heart.

Compared to the systemic circulation, the vessels that make up the pulmonary circulation are relatively short. Blood doesn't need to be pumped as far in the pulmonary circulation, because the lungs are close to the heart. In addition, the pulmonary arteries have less elastic connective tissue and wider lumens than systemic arteries. As a result, blood pressure is lower in the pulmonary arteries than in the systemic arteries, and pressure is correspondingly lower on the right side of the heart than on the left side.

WHAT DID YOU LEARN?

13 Compare the bronchial arteries and veins (discussed earlier in this chapter) with the pulmonary arteries and veins.

23.5 Review of Heart, Systemic, and Pulmonary Circulation

✓ **Learning Objective**

14. Trace and describe the flow of blood and oxygenation of blood in the systemic and pulmonary circulations.

A simplified flowchart of blood circulation is outlined in **figure 23.23.** Keep in mind that the outline provided in figure 23.23 is an oversimplification of complex events. For example, remember that both ventricles contract together. Thus, while some blood is traveling through the systemic vessels, blood is also traveling through the pulmonary vessels.

WHAT DID YOU LEARN?

14 Make a flowchart that shows the path of blood from the right atrium of the heart to the left ventricle of the heart and aorta, listing the specific vessels that transport blood to and from the lungs. Label which structures are transporting deoxygenated blood, and which are transporting oxygenated blood, and where gas exchange occurs.

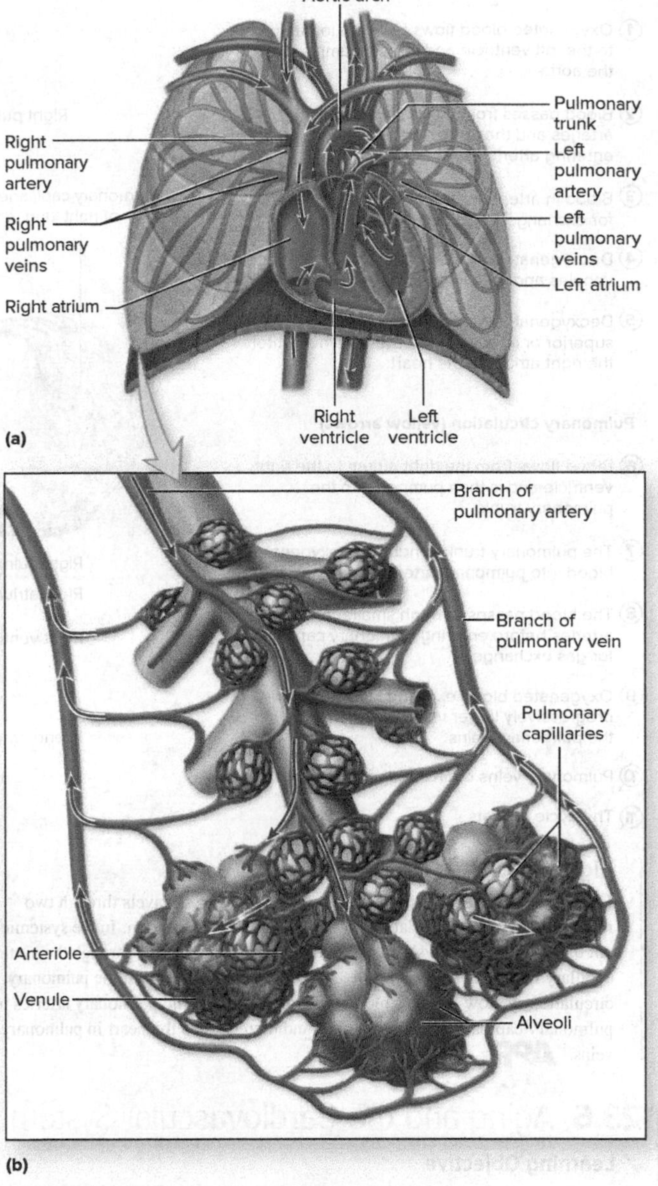

Figure 23.22

Pulmonary Circulation. The pulmonary circulation conducts blood from the heart to and from the gas exchange surfaces of the lungs. Blood circulation through the heart is indicated by colored arrows (blue = deoxygenated blood; red = oxygenated blood). *(a)* Deoxygenated blood is pumped from the right ventricle to the lungs through the pulmonary arteries. Oxygenated blood returns to the heart from the lungs within the pulmonary veins. *(b)* At the microscopic level, pulmonary capillaries are associated with the alveoli of the lungs.

Systemic circulation (black arrows)

1. Oxygenated blood flows from the left atrium to the left ventricle and then is pumped into the aorta.
2. Blood passes from the aorta into elastic arteries and then into muscular arteries before entering arterioles.
3. Blood in arterioles enters systemic capillaries for exchange of gases and nutrients.
4. Deoxygenated blood exits capillary beds into venules and then into veins.
5. Deoxygenated blood is conducted to either the superior or inferior vena cava and then enters the right atrium of the heart.

Pulmonary circulation (yellow arrows)

6. Blood flows from the right atrium to the right ventricle and is then pumped into the pulmonary trunk.
7. The pulmonary trunk conducts deoxygenated blood into pulmonary arteries to the lungs.
8. The blood passes through smaller and smaller arteries before entering pulmonary capillaries for gas exchange.
9. Oxygenated blood exits the lung via a series of progressively larger veins that merge to form the pulmonary veins.
10. Pulmonary veins drain into the left atrium.
11. The cycle repeats.

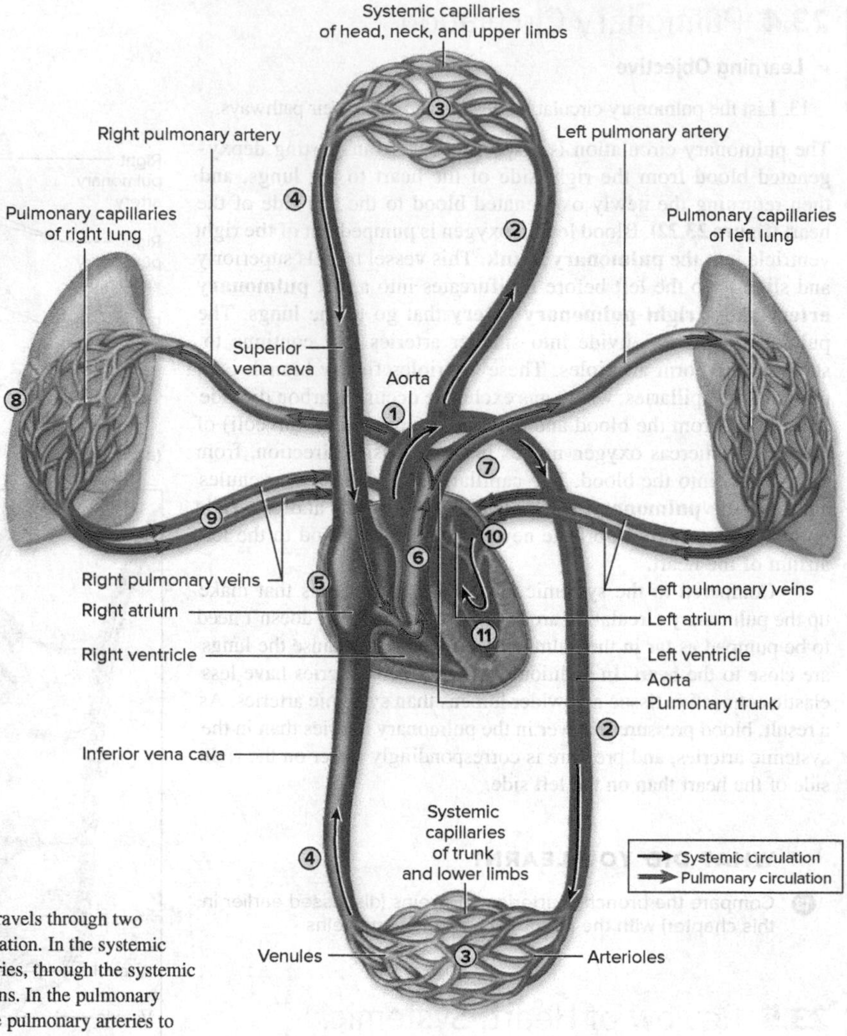

Figure 23.23

Cardiovascular System Circulatory Routes. Blood travels through two routes: the systemic circulation and the pulmonary circulation. In the systemic circulation (black arrows), blood is pumped into the arteries, through the systemic capillary beds, and then back to the heart in systemic veins. In the pulmonary circulation (yellow arrows), blood is pumped through the pulmonary arteries to pulmonary capillary beds in the lungs and then back to the heart in pulmonary veins. APR

23.6 Aging and the Cardiovascular System

✓ Learning Objective

15. Describe the effects of aging on blood vessel structure and function.

The amount of vascularization in a given tissue may change over time through the processes of angiogenesis and regression. **Angiogenesis** (an′jē-ō-jen′ĕ-sis; *angio* = vessel, *genesis* = production) is the formation of new blood vessels in tissues that require them. For example, angiogenesis is stimulated in skeletal muscle in response to aerobic training; in adipose tissue, angiogenesis occurs in adipose connective tissue when an individual gains weight in the form of fat deposits. **Regression** (or return to previous state) of vessels is also possible. For example, some skeletal muscle blood vessels regress when an individual who was physically active becomes sedentary, or blood vessels in adipose tissue regress when the amount of adipose tissue is decreased through restriction of food and increased physical activity.

As vessels age or become diseased, arteries lose their elasticity and so expand and recoil less readily, making it more difficult for the heart to pump blood. Thus, older individuals typically see a rise in their systolic blood pressure and may develop hypertension (see Clinical View 23.3: "Hypotension and Hypertension" in section 23.2). In addition, this reduction of vessel elasticity means older individuals are more apt to develop an **aneurysm,** whereby part of the arterial wall thins and balloons out, making it more prone to rupture (see Clinical View 23.6: "Aneurysms" in this section).

Atherosclerosis (described in detail in Clinical View 23.5: "Atherosclerosis" in section 23.3h) is a disease process that leads to plaque (atheroma) buildup in the arteries as we age. In addition to causing loss of vessel elasticity, atherosclerosis will reduce and potentially block blood flow to a part of an organ, resulting in tissue damage and possible tissue death. While we may not be able to prevent the development of atherosclerosis as we age, we can slow the process of plaque buildup by maintaining a healthy weight and diet, staying active, and not smoking.

WHAT DID YOU LEARN?

15. How are aging and blood pressure related?

Clinical View 23.6

Aneurysms

An **aneurysm** (an'yū-rizm; *aneurysma* = a dilation) is a localized, abnormal dilation of a blood vessel. Although an aneurysm can form in any type of vessel, aneurysms are particularly common in arteries, especially the aorta, because of the higher blood pressure on the arterial side of the circulation. After being initiated by a weakness in the wall of the vessel, an aneurysm tends to increase in size over a period of time (weeks to months to years) until it possibly ruptures.

An **abdominal aortic aneurysm** is most often a consequence of atherosclerosis. Most abdominal aortic aneurysms develop between the level of the renal arteries and the point near where the aorta bifurcates into the common iliac arteries. A ruptured aorta is a surgical emergency that few people survive. An abdominal aortic aneurysm may be detected during a physical exam as a pulsating abdominal mass. X-ray and ultrasound studies can confirm the diagnosis. To repair abdominal aneurysms, stent grafts can be inserted through an incision in the femoral artery, positioned in the area of the aneurysm using x-ray guidance, and then expanded to reinforce the weakened and dilated area of the aortic wall.

A **berry (cerebral** or **saccular) aneurysm** is a weak area in a cerebral blood vessel that balloons out and fills with blood. It is so named because it is a saclike outpocketing of a cerebral blood vessel that appears berry-shaped. All cerebral aneurysms have the potential to rupture and cause bleeding within the brain, which can cause serious complications such as hemorrhagic stroke, subarachnoid hemorrhage, nerve damage, or death. The disorder may result from congenital defects or from other conditions such as high blood pressure, atherosclerosis, head trauma, or infection. When a berry aneurysm ruptures, an individual may experience a sudden and extremely severe headache (described by patients as the "worst headache of my life"), double vision, nausea, vomiting, stiff neck, and/or loss of consciousness. Treatment of the aneurysm typically involves using sutures, clamps, or other materials to repair the ruptured site.

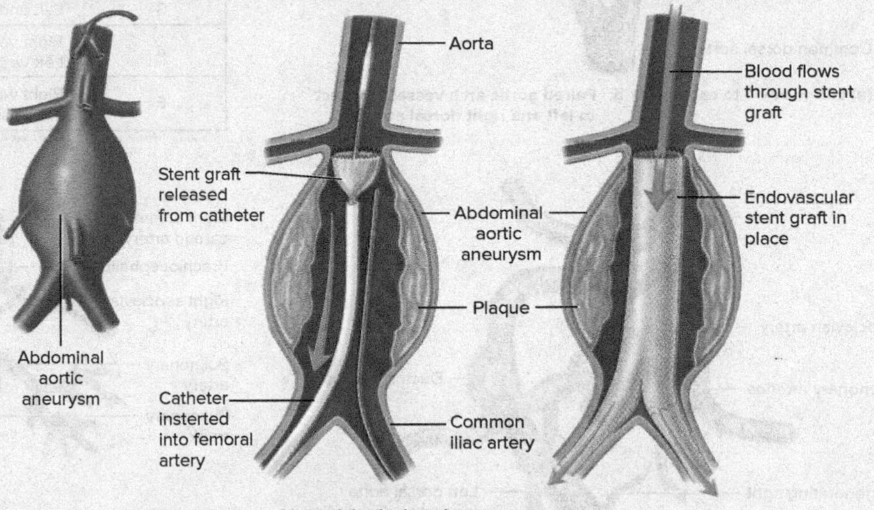

Placement of an endovascular stent for an abdominal aortic aneurysm.

23.7 Blood Vessel Development

✓ Learning Objectives

16. Explain the developmental fates of the embryonic vessels.
17. Compare and contrast the fetal and postnatal circulatory patterns.

The heart and its blood vessels begin to develop in the embryo during the third week. The blood vessels form by a process called **vasculogenesis** (vas'ky ū-lō-jen'ĕ-sis; *vasculum* = small vessel, *genesis* = production), whereby some of the mesoderm forms cells called angioblasts, and these angioblasts connect to form the first primitive blood vessels. These vessels then grow and invade developing tissues throughout the embryo.

23.7a Artery Development

The embryo initially has both a **left dorsal aorta** and **right dorsal aorta (figure 23.24*a*)**. These two vessels remain separate until the level of the fourth thoracic vertebra, where they fuse to form a **common dorsal aorta** that supplies blood to the inferior part of the body. Eventually, the superior part of the right dorsal aorta degenerates and disappears, leaving the left dorsal aorta and common dorsal aorta (figure 23.24). The left dorsal aorta and common dorsal aorta form the descending thoracic aorta.

Beginning the fourth week, the truncus arteriosus of the heart connects to the left and right dorsal aortae by a series of paired **aortic arch vessels** (figure 23.24). These vessels are numbered 1–6. Aortic arch vessels 1 and 2 primarily regress, and only a small portion of them remains to form small segments of arteries in the head. Aortic arch vessel 5 never forms in humans. The remaining aortic arch vessels—3, 4, and 6—develop into adult arteries (figure 23.24). In addition, the most superior part of the truncus arteriosus (called the **aortic sac**) forms the brachiocephalic trunk. The dorsal aorta (now part of the descending aorta) develops vascular "sprouts" that form many of the blood vessels in the body. These blood vessel sprouts grow and migrate to the areas that need vascularization.

23.7b Vein Development

The venous system of the embryo develops from three venous systems:the **vitelline** (vī-tel'in; *vitellus* = yolk) **system, the umbilical** (ŭm-bil'i-kăl) **system,** and the **cardinal** (kar'di-n ăl; *cardinalis* = principal) **system.** All three systems initially are bilateral and con - nect to the sinus venosus of the heart. However, these three systems

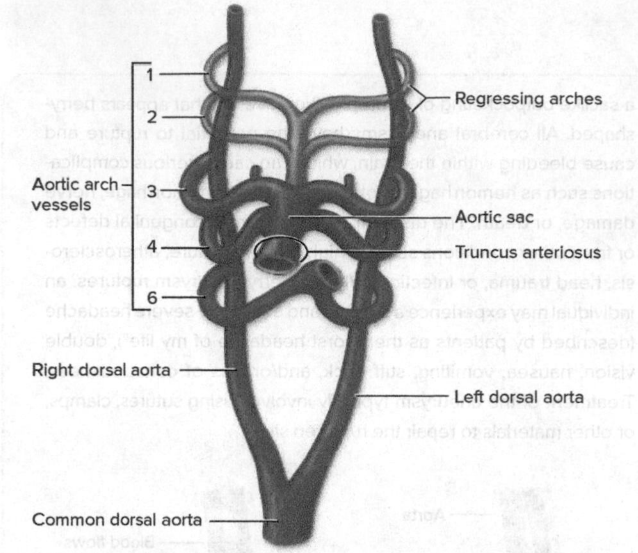

(a) Late week 4 to early week 5: Paired aortic arch vessels connect to left and right dorsal aortae

Figure 23.24

Thoracic Artery Development. Aortic arch vessels form most of the major thoracic and head and neck arteries. (*a*) By late week 4 to early week 5, paired aortic arch vessels arise from the truncus arteriosus and attach to paired left and right dorsal aortae. (*b*) During week 7, the right dorsal artery starts to degenerate, and the left dorsal aorta becomes the descending thoracic aorta. (*c*) By week 8, the aortic arch vessels have undergone remodeling to form the aortic arch, major branches of the arch, and the pulmonary arteries.

Aortic Arch Vessel	Postnatal Structure Formed by Vessels
1	Small part of maxillary arteries
2	Small part of stapedial arteries
3	Left and right common carotid arteries
4	Right vessel: proximal part of right subclavian artery Left vessel: aortic arch (connects to the left dorsal aorta)
6	Right vessel: right pulmonary artery Left vessel: left pulmonary artery and ductus arteriosus

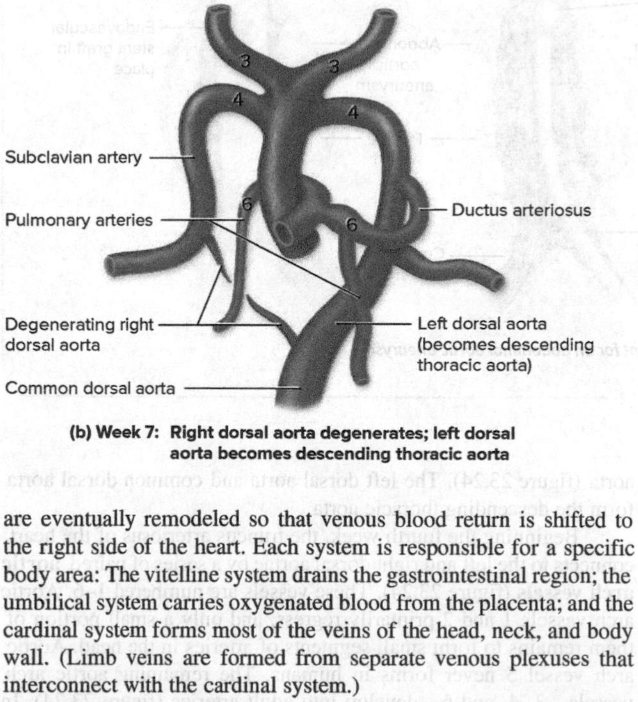

(b) Week 7: Right dorsal aorta degenerates; left dorsal aorta becomes descending thoracic aorta

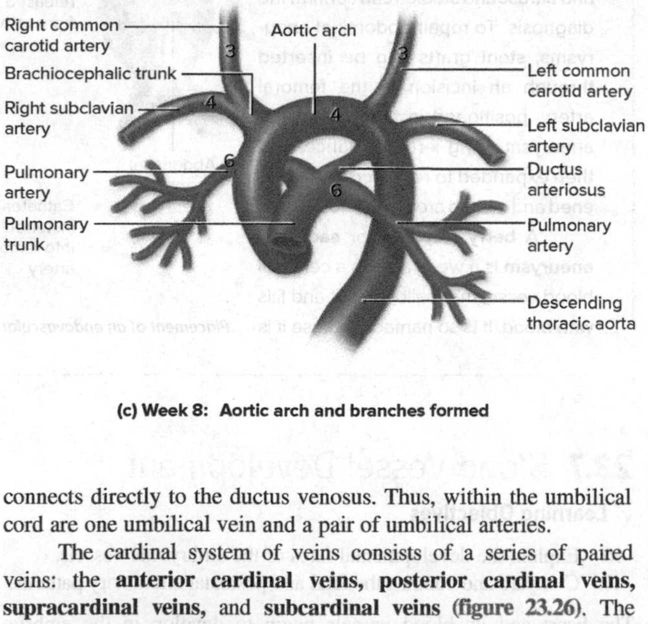

(c) Week 8: Aortic arch and branches formed

are eventually remodeled so that venous blood return is shifted to the right side of the heart. Each system is responsible for a specific body area: The vitelline system drains the gastrointestinal region; the umbilical system carries oxygenated blood from the placenta; and the cardinal system forms most of the veins of the head, neck, and body wall. (Limb veins are formed from separate venous plexuses that interconnect with the cardinal system.)

The vitelline system of veins consists of **left** and **right vitelline veins,** which are apparent through the fourth week (**figure 23.25**). Beginning in the fifth week and continuing through the twelfth week, the left vitelline vein primarily degenerates, and the right vitelline vein forms the hepatic portal system, the sinusoids of the liver, and the portion of the inferior vena cava between the liver and the heart. Also formed from the right vitelline vein is the **ductus venosus** (dŭk′tŭs vē-nō′sŭs), which connects the umbilical vein to the inferior vena cava and heart, and shunts blood away from the fetal liver.

The umbilical system of veins originally begins with a **left** and **right umbilical vein.** However, by the second month of development, the right umbilical vein disappears, and the left umbilical vein connects directly to the ductus venosus. Thus, within the umbilical cord are one umbilical vein and a pair of umbilical arteries.

The cardinal system of veins consists of a series of paired veins: the **anterior cardinal veins, posterior cardinal veins, supracardinal veins,** and **subcardinal veins** (**figure 23.26**). The anterior cardinal veins develop into the veins of the head and neck and the veins superior to the heart. By the eighth week of development, the posterior cardinal veins degenerate and are largely replaced by the supracardinal and subcardinal veins. The supracardinal and subcardinal veins undergo asymmetrical remodeling, whereby venous blood flow is shifted to the right side of the body. The subcardinal veins form veins that drain the posterior abdominal wall, whereas the supracardinal veins form the hemiazygos and azygos system of veins. The inferior vena cava is formed from parts of the right vitelline, right subcardinal, right supracardinal, and right posterior cardinal veins. The mature vessel pattern is formed well before birth and shown in figure 23.26*b*.

23.7c Comparison of Fetal and Postnatal Circulation

The cardiovascular system of the fetus is structurally and functionally different from that of the newborn. Whereas the fetus receives

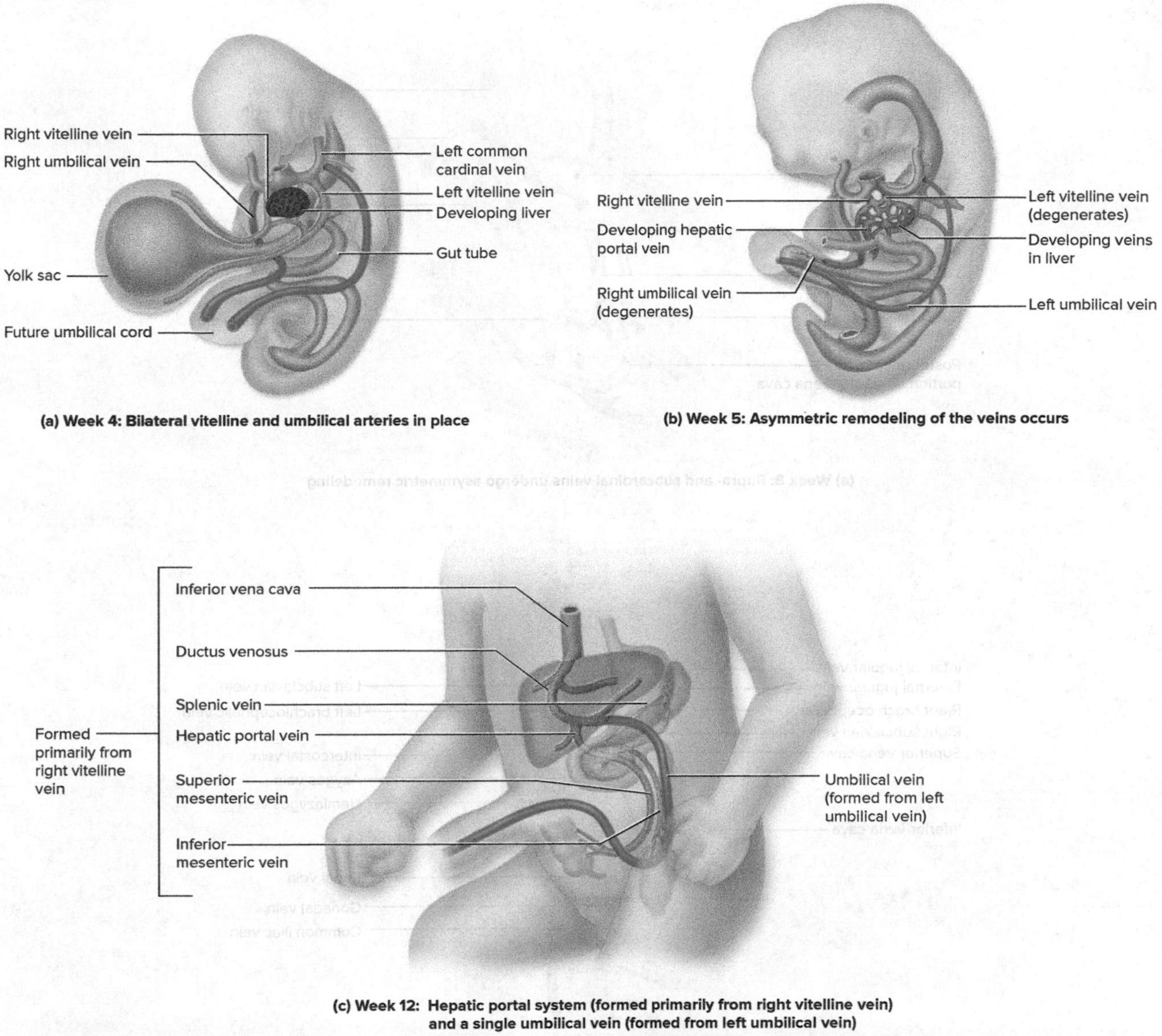
Right vitelline vein
Right umbilical vein
Left common cardinal vein
Left vitelline vein
Developing liver
Gut tube
Yolk sac
Future umbilical cord
(a) Week 4: Bilateral vitelline and umbilical arteries in place
Right vitelline vein
Developing hepatic portal vein
Right umbilical vein (degenerates)
Left vitelline vein (degenerates)
Developing veins in liver
Left umbilical vein
(b) Week 5: Asymmetric remodeling of the veins occurs
Inferior vena cava
Ductus venosus
Splenic vein
Hepatic portal vein
Superior mesenteric vein
Inferior mesenteric vein
Formed primarily from right vitelline vein
Umbilical vein (formed from left umbilical vein)
(c) Week 12: Hepatic portal system (formed primarily from right vitelline vein) and a single umbilical vein (formed from left umbilical vein)

Figure 23.25

Development of Vitelline and Umbilical Veins. The vitelline veins transport blood from the yolk sac, whereas the umbilical veins carry oxygenated blood to the embryo. (*a*) At week 4, the bilateral vessels are present. (*b*) By week 5, the vitelline vessels form the blood vessels in the liver, and the right vitelline vein forms the hepatic portal vein. (*c*) By week 12, the right vitelline vein forms most of the hepatic portal system, and the left vitelline vein regresses. Conversely, the right umbilical vein regresses, and the left umbilical vein persists as the single umbilical vein.

oxygen and nutrients directly from the mother through the placenta, its postnatal cardiovascular system is independent. In addition, because the fetal lungs are not functional, the blood pressure in the pulmonary arteries and right side of the heart is greater than the pressure in the left side of the heart. Finally, several fetal vessels help shunt blood directly to the organs in need and away from the organs that are not yet functional. As a result, the fetal cardiovascular system has some structures that are modified or that cease to function once the human is born. Figure 23.27 compares the fetal and postnatal circulation patterns.

Fetal circulation occurs as follows:

1. Oxygenated blood from the placenta enters the body of the fetus through the **umbilical vein.**
2. The blood from the umbilical vein is shunted away from the liver and directly toward the inferior vena cava through the **ductus venosus.**
3. Oxygenated blood in the ductus venosus mixes with deoxygenated blood in the inferior vena cava.
4. Blood from the superior and inferior venae cavae empties into the right atrium.
5. Because pressure is greater on the right side of the heart (compared to the left side), most of the blood is shunted from the right atrium to the left atrium via the **foramen ovale.** This blood flows into the left ventricle and then is pumped out through the aorta.

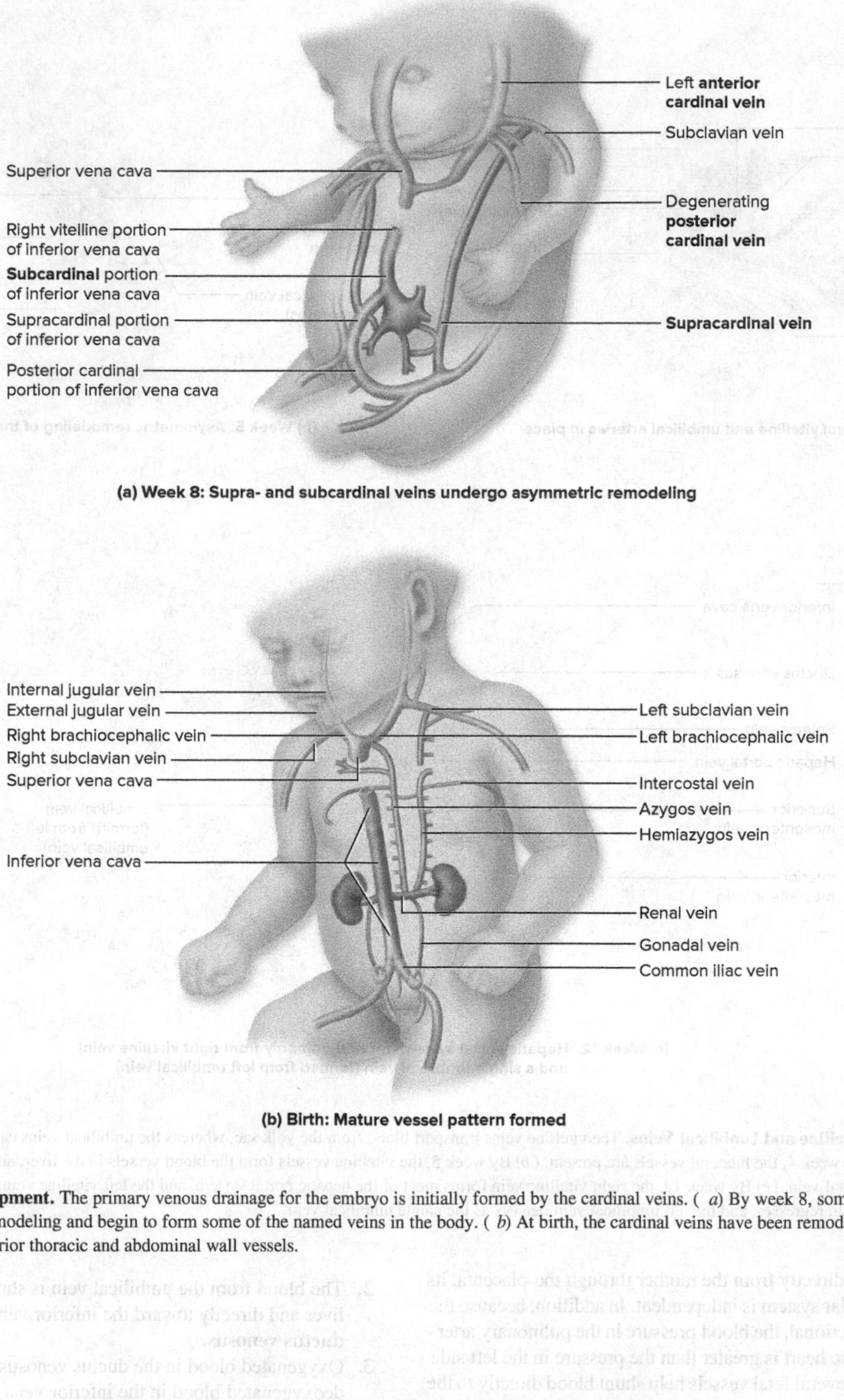
Left anterior cardinal vein
Subclavian vein
Superior vena cava
Degenerating posterior cardinal vein
Right vitelline portion of inferior vena cava
Subcardinal portion of inferior vena cava
Supracardinal portion of inferior vena cava
Supracardinal vein
Posterior cardinal portion of inferior vena cava
(a) Week 8: Supra- and subcardinal veins undergo asymmetric remodeling
Internal jugular vein
External jugular vein
Right brachiocephalic vein
Right subclavian vein
Superior vena cava
Left subclavian vein
Left brachiocephalic vein
Intercostal vein
Azygos vein
Hemiazygos vein
Inferior vena cava
Renal vein
Gonadal vein
Common iliac vein
(b) Birth: Mature vessel pattern formed

Figure 23.26

Cardinal Vein Development. The primary venous drainage for the embryo is initially formed by the cardinal veins. (*a*) By week 8, some of these cardinal veins undergo asymmetric remodeling and begin to form some of the named veins in the body. (*b*) At birth, the cardinal veins have been remodeled to form the inferior vena cava and the posterior thoracic and abdominal wall vessels.

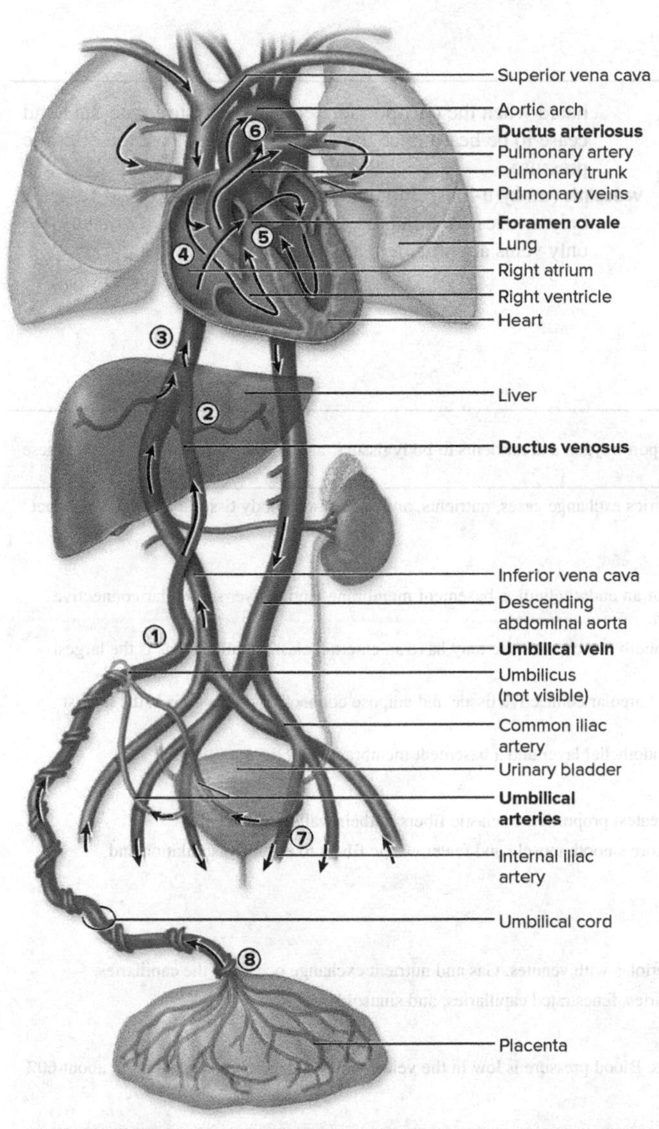
Superior vena cava
Aortic arch
Ductus arteriosus
Pulmonary artery
Pulmonary trunk
Pulmonary veins
Foramen ovale
Lung
Right atrium
Right ventricle
Heart
Liver
Ductus venosus
Inferior vena cava
Descending abdominal aorta
Umbilical vein
Umbilicus (not visible)
Common iliac artery
Urinary bladder
Umbilical arteries
Internal iliac artery
Umbilical cord
Placenta
1
2
3
4
5
6
7
8

Fetal Cardiovascular Structure	Postnatal Structure
Ductus arteriosus	Ligamentum arteriosum
Ductus venosus	Ligamentum venosum
Foramen ovale	Fossa ovalis
Umbilical arteries	Medial umbilical ligaments
Umbilical vein	Round ligament of liver (ligamentum teres)

Figure 23.27

Fetal Circulation. Structural changes in both the heart and blood vessels accommodate the different needs of the fetus and the newborn. The pathway of blood flow is indicated by black arrows. The numbers correspond to the steps listed in the text. The chart at the bottom of the drawing summarizes the fate of each of the fetal cardiovascular structures.

Clinical View 23.7

Patent Ductus Arteriosus

In some infants (especially premature infants), the ductus arteriosus fails to constrict and close after birth. This **patent** (open) **ductus arteriosus** occurs in about 8 per 10,000 births. Because the systemic circulation is under higher pressure than the pulmonary circulation, a patent ductus arteriosus serves as a conduit through which blood from the aorta can enter the pulmonary system. If left untreated, this shunting will, over a period of several years, result in high blood pressure in the pulmonary circuit. This pulmonary hypertension then leads to failure of the right ventricle. Because circulating chemicals called prostaglandins help keep the ductus arteriosus open during fetal life, the first form of treatment for a patent ductus arteriosus is prostaglandin-inhibiting medication. In the uncommon instance that medication does not work, the ductus arteriosus is surgically repaired.

6. A small amount of blood enters the right ventricle and pulmonary trunk, but much of this blood is shunted from the pulmonary trunk to the aorta through a vessel detour called the **ductus arteriosus** (ar-tēr'ē-ō'sŭs).
7. Blood travels to the rest of the body, and the deoxygenated blood returns to the placenta through a pair of **umbilical arteries.**
8. Nutrient and gas exchange occurs at the placenta, and the cycle repeats.

At birth, the fetal circulation begins to change into the postnatal pattern. When the baby takes its first breath, pulmonary resistance drops, and the pulmonary arteries dilate. As a result, pressure on the right side of the heart decreases so that the pressure is greater on the left side of the heart, which handles the systemic circulation.

The postnatal changes are as follows:

- The umbilical vein and umbilical arteries constrict and become nonfunctional. They turn into the **round ligament of the liver** (or *ligamentum* [lig'ă-men'tŭm; band] *teres*) and the **medial umbilical ligaments,** respectively.
- The ductus venosus ceases to be functional and constricts, becoming the **ligamentum venosum** (vē-nō'sŭm).
- Because pressure is now greater on the left side of the heart, the two flaps of the interatrial septum close off the foramen ovale. The only remnant of the foramen ovale is a thin, oval depression in the wall of the septum called the **fossa ovalis.**
- Within 10 to 15 hours after birth, the ductus arteriosus closes and becomes a fibrous structure called the **ligamentum arteriosum.**

WHAT DID YOU LEARN?

16 Make a flowchart that shows the path of blood flow in the fetus, starting with the placenta.

17 Each medial umbilical ligament is a remnant of what embryonic vessel?

Clinical Terms

edema Noticeable swelling from fluid accumulation in body tissues. Edema most commonly occurs in the feet and legs, where it is referred to as peripheral edema.

Korotkoff (kŏ-rot′kŏf) **sounds** Distinctive sounds heard through a stethoscope when taking a blood pressure reading, resulting from blood turbulence in the artery. The sounds are first heard when the cuff pressure equals the systolic pressure and cease to be heard once the cuff has deflated past the diastolic pressure.

vasculitis (vas-kyū-lī′tis) Inflammation of any type of blood vessel. If only arteries are inflamed, the condition is called *arteritis;* if only veins are inflamed, it is called *phlebitis.*

Chapter Summary

- Blood vessels form a closed supply system to transport oxygen and nutrients to body tissues, and remove waste products from these tissues.

23.1 Anatomy of Blood Vessels

- Arteries conduct blood away from the heart; capillaries exchange gases, nutrients, and wastes with body tissues; and veins conduct blood to the heart.

23.1a Blood Vessel Tunics

- The tunica intima (innermost layer) is composed of an endothelium, a basement membrane, and a layer of areolar connective tissue. It also may contain an internal elastic lamina.
- The tunica media (middle layer) is composed of smooth muscle and also may have an external elastic lamina. This is the largest tunic in an artery.
- The tunica externa (outermost layer) is composed of areolar connective tissue and adipose connective tissue. This is the largest tunic in a vein.
- Capillaries have a tunica intima, composed of an endothelial layer and a basement membrane only.

23.1b Arteries

- Elastic arteries have the largest diameter and the greatest proportion of elastic fibers in their walls.
- Muscular arteries are medium-sized arteries with more smooth muscle and fewer elastic fibers to ensure vasodilation and vasoconstriction.
- Arterioles are the smallest arteries.

23.1c Capillaries

- Capillaries, the smallest blood vessels, connect arterioles with venules. Gas and nutrient exchange occurs in the capillaries.
- The three types of capillaries are continuous capillaries, fenestrated capillaries, and sinusoids.

23.1d Veins

- Venules are small veins that merge into larger veins. Blood pressure is low in the veins, which act as reservoirs and hold about 60% of the body's blood at rest.
- One-way valves prevent blood backflow in veins.

23.2 Blood Pressure

- Blood pressure is the force exerted by the blood on the vessel wall. Systolic blood pressure is a measure of pressure during ventricular contraction, and diastolic pressure is a measure of pressure during ventricular relaxation.

23.3 Systemic Circulation

- The systemic circulation conducts oxygenated blood to and deoxygenated blood from peripheral capillary beds.

23.3a General Arterial Flow Out of the Heart

- The ascending aorta gives off the left and right coronary arteries to supply the heart.
- The aortic arch has three branches: the brachiocephalic trunk, the left common carotid artery, and the left subclavian artery.
- The descending thoracic aorta extends several branches to supply the thoracic wall.
- The descending abdominal aorta bifurcates into common iliac arteries; these vessels divide into internal and external iliac arteries.

23.3b General Venous Return to the Heart

- Deoxygenated blood returns to the heart via the superior and inferior venae cavae.

23.3 Systemic Circulation (*continued*)

23.3c Blood Flow Through the Head and Neck

- Common carotid arteries branch into the internal and external carotid arteries, which supply most of the blood to the head and neck.
- The cerebral arterial circle is an arterial anastomosis that supplies the brain.
- The internal and external jugular veins drain blood from the head and neck.
- Vertebral veins and the dural venous sinuses drain the cranium.

23.3d Blood Flow Through the Thoracic and Abdominal Walls

- The thoracic and abdominal walls are supplied by paired arteries.
- Hemiazygos and accessory hemiazygos veins drain the left side of the thorax, and the azygos vein drains the right side of the thorax.

23.3e Blood Flow Through the Thoracic Organs and Spinal Cord

- Bronchial arteries and bronchial veins supply the connective tissue, bronchi, and bronchioles of the lung.
- Esophageal arteries and veins supply the esophagus.
- Superior phrenic arteries, the musculophrenic arteries, and the inferior phrenic arteries and veins supply the diaphragm.
- The spinal cord is supplied by anterior and posterior spinal arteries, as well as by segmental medullary and radicular arteries.

23.3f Blood Flow Through the Gastrointestinal Tract

- Three unpaired arteries supply the gastrointestinal tract organs: the celiac trunk, the superior mesenteric artery, and the inferior mesenteric artery.
- The hepatic portal vein is a large vein that receives oxygen-poor but nutrient-rich blood from the gastrointestinal organs and takes it to the liver. Blood exits the liver via hepatic veins.

23.3g Blood Flow Through the Posterior Abdominal Organs, Pelvis, and Perineum

- Paired branches of the descending abdominal aorta supply the posterior abdominal organs and the pelvis and perineum. Venous drainage is by veins of the same name as the arteries.

23.3h Blood Flow Through the Upper Limb

- The subclavian artery continues as the axillary artery and then becomes the brachial artery. The brachial artery divides into an ulnar artery and a radial artery.
- Anastomoses of ulnar and radial arteries form the superficial palmar arch and the deep palmar arch; digital arteries branch off the arches to supply the fingers.
- The superficial group of veins contains the basilic, median cubital, and cephalic veins that drain into the axillary vein. The deep group of veins contains veins that bear the same names as the arteries.

23.3i Blood Flow Through the Lower Limb

- The external iliac artery extends inferior to the inguinal ligament and is renamed the femoral artery. It enters the popliteal fossa, and then becomes the popliteal artery before dividing into anterior and posterior tibial arteries. The posterior tibial artery gives off a fibular artery. The posterior tibial artery branches into medial and lateral plantar arteries.
- The superficial group of veins includes the great saphenous vein and the small saphenous vein. The deep group of veins consists of veins that bear the same names as the corresponding arteries.

23.4 Pulmonary Circulation

- The pulmonary circulation carries deoxygenated blood to the lungs and returns oxygenated blood to the heart.

23.5 Review of Heart, Systemic, and Pulmonary Circulation

- Oxygenated blood is pumped from the left ventricle through the systemic circulation and back to the right side of the heart. This deoxygenated blood is pumped from the right ventricle through the pulmonary circulation and returns as oxygenated blood to the left side of the heart.

23.6 Aging and the Cardiovascular System

- As adults age, the heart and blood vessels become less resilient, systolic blood pressure may rise, and the incidence and severity of atherosclerosis increase.

23.7 Blood Vessel Development

- The blood vessels form by a process called vasculogenesis beginning in the third week of development.

23.7a Artery Development

- The right dorsal aorta regresses, and the left dorsal aorta (plus the common aorta) form the descending aorta.
- Aortic arch vessels 1, 2, 3, 4, and 6 develop into parts of adult arteries in the head, neck, and thorax.

23.7b Vein Development

- Three bilateral venous systems connect the sinus venosus of the heart: the vitelline system, the umbilical system, and the cardinal system. These are the origin of the venous system.

23.7c Comparison of Fetal and Postnatal Circulation

- The fetal cardiovascular system contains some structures that are modified or cease to function once the baby is born.

Challenge Yourself

Actively write or type your answers in a separate document to reinforce your learning, before checking your answers.

Multiple Choice

Select the best answer from the four choices provided.

1. Which vessel type consists of a tunica intima with large gaps between the endothelial cells, and a discontinuous basement membrane?
   a. continuous
   b. arteriole
   c. sinusoid
   d. fenestrated
2. Some venous blood from the lower limb drains through which of the following veins?
   a. great saphenous vein
   b. basilic vein
   c. external jugular vein
   d. median cubital vein
3. Which of the following vessels supplies the stomach wall and is not a direct branch of the celiac trunk?
   a. splenic artery
   b. right gastric artery
   c. left gastric artery
   d. common hepatic artery
4. Which type of vessel has a large number of smooth muscle cell layers in its tunica media as well as elastic tissue confined to an internal elastic lamina and external elastic lamina?
   a. elastic artery
   b. muscular artery
   c. arteriole
   d. venule
5. Which statement is true about veins?
   a. Veins always transport deoxygenated blood.
   b. Veins drain into smaller vessels called venules.
   c. The largest tunic in a vein is the tunica externa.
   d. The lumen of a vein tends to be smaller than that of a comparably sized artery.
6. Which of the following is the pathway that blood follows through the upper limb arteries?
   a. subclavian → axillary → ulnar → radial → brachial
   b. subclavian → axillary → brachial → cephalic → basilic
   c. subclavian → ulnar → brachial → radial
   d. subclavian → axillary → brachial → radial and ulnar
7. Which of the following veins typically does *not* drain directly into the inferior vena cava?
   a. renal
   b. hepatic portal
   c. common iliac
   d. right gonadal
8. After birth, the umbilical vein becomes which structure?
   a. medial umbilical ligament
   b. ligamentum venosum
   c. ligamentum arteriosum
   d. round ligament of the liver
9. The left fourth aortic arch vessel in an embryo becomes which structure?
   a. left common carotid artery
   b. left subclavian artery
   c. aortic arch
   d. left pulmonary artery
10. Vasa vasorum are found in which tunic of a large blood vessel?
    a. intima
    b. media
    c. externa
    d. intermedia

Content Review

1. What are the respiratory and skeletal muscular pumps, and how do they assist in the return of venous blood to the heart?
2. Compare and contrast arteries and veins with respect to function, tunic size, and lumen size.
3. Trace the path of blood flow from the left ventricle of the heart to the right atrium of the heart. List the types of vessels (e.g., elastic arteries, arterioles) the blood travels through, and identify the type of blood vessel in which gas and nutrient exchange occur.
4. What is the main function of capillaries? What are the three kinds of capillaries?
5. Is blood pressure higher in arteries or veins? What are the consequences of hypertension?
6. Identify the three main branches of the aortic arch that receive oxygenated blood, and identify the areas of the body they supply.
7. How is blood flow through the upper and lower limbs similar?
8. Compare the systemic and pulmonary circulations. Discuss the function of arteries and veins in each system.
9. How does aging affect blood vessel anatomy and function?
10. What postnatal changes occur in the heart and blood vessels? Why do these occur?

Developing Critical Reasoning

1. Two 50-year-old men are trying to determine their risk for developing atherosclerosis. John jogs three times a week, maintains a healthy weight, and eats a diet low in saturated fats. Thomas rarely exercises, is overweight, and only occasionally eats healthy meals. Based on your knowledge of the cardiovascular system and atherosclerosis, which man do you think is more at risk for developing the disease? What other factors could put a person at risk for atherosclerosis?
2. Arteries tend to have a lot of vascular anastomoses around body joints (such as the elbow and knee). Propose a reason why this would be beneficial.
3. The internal thoracic artery is frequently used as a coronary bypass vessel (a replacement artery for a blocked coronary artery). What makes this vessel a good choice for this surgery? Will blood flow to the thoracic wall be compromised as a result? Why or why not?

Answers to "What Do You Think?"

1. A smoker would have elevated blood pressure, because nicotine increases cardiac output and causes vasoconstriction.
2. Blood could still reach the brain through the vertebral arteries. However, it is unlikely that these arteries could provide sufficient blood to the entire brain and head.
3. If the left ulnar artery were cut, the left hand and fingers could still receive blood via the left radial artery.
4. If the right femoral artery were blocked, blood flow to the right leg would be cut off; in other words, the popliteal artery and the branches to the leg would not receive any blood.

24 | Lymphatic System

Outline

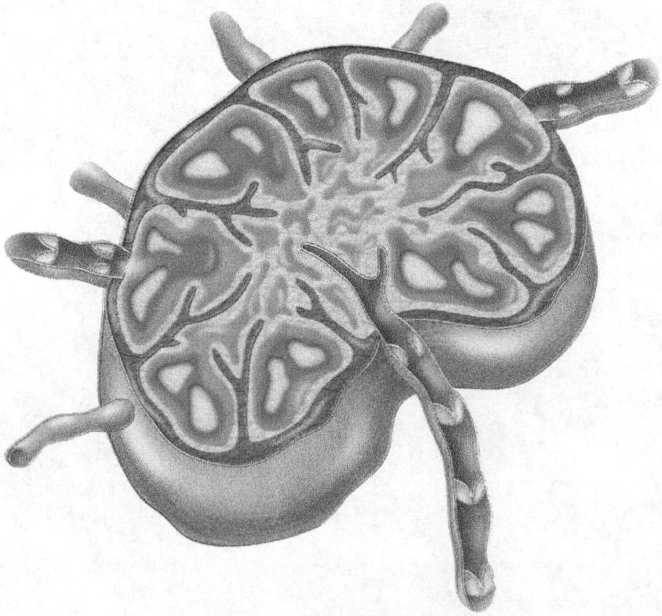

Anatomy & Physiology Revealed 4.0

MODULE 10: LYMPHATIC SYSTEM

We have seen in chapters 21–23 how the cardiovascular system transports blood throughout the body, where it exchanges gases and nutrients with the tissues. Another body system, called the **lymphatic** (lim-fat'ik) **system**, aids the cardiovascular system by transporting excess interstitial fluid through lymphatic vessels assisting in maintaining fluid homeostasis. Once this fluid enters the vessels, the fluid is renamed lymph, a type of fluid connective tissue (see section 4.2d). Along the way, lymph is filtered through lymphoid structures and checked for foreign or pathologic material, such as bacteria and cancer cells. Lymphoid structures contain certain cells that initiate an immune response to abnormal materials. Without the primary immune response by the lymphatic system, the body would be unable to fight infection and keep itself healthy.

We examine the lymphatic vessels, lymphoid cells, and lymphoid structures of the body in this chapter. Additionally, we learn how each of these components plays an important role in keeping us healthy.

24.1 Functions of the Lymphatic System

✓ Learning Objective

1. Explain how the lymphatic system aids fluid homeostasis and guards the health of body cells and tissues.

The lymphatic system involves several organs as well as an organized array of lymphoid cells and lymphatic vessels located throughout the body (**figure 24.1**). Together, these structures transport fluids and help the body fight infection. However, not all of these components of the lymphatic system are involved in each function.

At the arterial end of a capillary bed, blood pressure forces fluid from the blood into the interstitial spaces around cells. This fluid is called **interstitial fluid** (not to be confused with *extracellular fluid,* a term that encompasses both interstitial fluid and plasma [see section 2.3a]). Most of this fluid is reabsorbed at the venous end of the capillaries, but an excess of about 3 liters of fluid per day remains in the interstitial spaces. A network of **lymphatic vessels** (also called *lymph vessels*) (figure 24.1) reabsorbs this excess fluid and returns it to the venous circulation. If this excess fluid were not removed, body tissues would swell, a condition called **edema** (e-dē'mă; *oidema* = a swelling). Further, this excess fluid would accumulate outside the circulatory system, causing blood volume to drop precipitously. Thus, the lymphatic system prevents interstitial fluid levels from rising out of control and helps maintain blood volume levels.

Lymphatic vessels also transport dietary lipids. Although most nutrients are absorbed directly into the blood, some larger materials, such as lipids and lipid-soluble vitamins, are unable to enter the blood directly from the gastrointestinal (GI) tract. These materials are transported through tiny lymphatic vessels called lacteals, which drain into larger lymphatic vessels and eventually into the circulatory system (see section 26.4c).

Lymphoid organs house lymphocytes, a type of leukocyte (see section 21.3b). Although some lymphocytes circulate in the blood, most are located in the lymphoid structures and organs. Some lymphoid organs assist in these cells' maturation, whereas others serve as a site for lymphocyte replication (mitosis).

Finally, the lymphatic system cells generate an immune response and increase the lymphocyte population when necessary. Lymphoid structures contain T-lymphocytes, B-lymphocytes, dendritic cells, and macrophages (monocytes that have migrated from the blood into other tissues). These cells are constantly monitoring the blood and the interstitial fluid for**antigens** (an'ti-jen; *anti(body)* + *gen* = producing), which are substances that bind to components of adaptive immunity

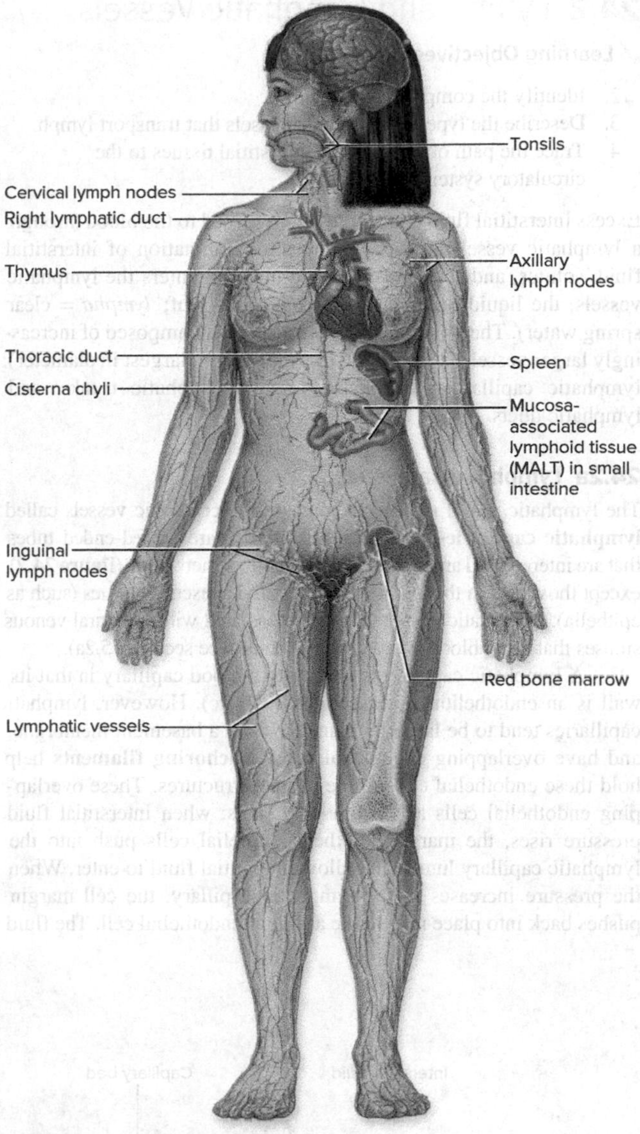

Figure 24.1

Lymphatic System. The lymphatic system consists of lymphatic vessels, lymphoid cells, and lymphoid organs that work together to pick up and transport interstitial fluid back to the blood and to mount an immune response when needed.

such as T-lymphocytes or antibodies. Many antigens are foreign or abnormal to the body, such as bacteria, viruses, and even cancer cells. If such antigens are discovered, lymphoid cells initiate a systematic defense against the antigens, called an **immune** (i-myūn') **response.** Some of the cells produce soluble proteins called **antibodies** that bind to the foreign or abnormal agent, thus damaging it or identifying it to other elements of the immune system. Other cells attack and destroy the antigen directly. Still other cells become memory cells, which remember the past antigen encounters and initiate an even faster and more powerful response should the same antigen appear again.

WHAT DID YOU LEARN?

1. Make a table of the structures in the lymphatic system and their functions.

24.2 Lymph and Lymphatic Vessels

✓ Learning Objectives

2. Identify the components of lymph.
3. Describe the types of lymphatic vessels that transport lymph.
4. Trace the path of lymph from interstitial tissues to the circulatory system.

Excess interstitial fluid and solutes are returned to the blood through a lymphatic vessel network. When the combination of interstitial fluid, solutes, and sometimes foreign material enters the lymphatic vessels, the liquid mixture is called **lymph** (limf; *lympha* = clear spring water). The lymphatic vessel network is composed of increasingly larger vessels, as follows (from smallest to largest in diameter): lymphatic capillaries, lymphatic vessels, lymphatic trunks, and lymphatic ducts.

24.2a Lymphatic Capillaries

The lymphatic vessel network begins with microscopic vessels called **lymphatic capillaries.** Lymphatic capillaries are closed-ended tubes that are interspersed among most blood capillary networks (**figure 24.2**), except those within the red bone marrow and avascular tissues (such as epithelia). Lymphatic vessels also are associated with the dural venous sinuses that drain blood away from the brain (see section 15.2a).

A lymphatic capillary is similar to a blood capillary in that its wall is an endothelium (see sections 23.1a, c). However, lymphatic capillaries tend to be larger in diameter, lack a basement membrane, and have overlapping endothelial cells. **Anchoring filaments** help hold these endothelial cells to the nearby structures. These overlapping endothelial cells act as one-way flaps; when interstitial fluid pressure rises, the margins of the endothelial cells push into the lymphatic capillary lumen and allow interstitial fluid to enter. When the pressure increases in the lymphatic capillary, the cell margin pushes back into place next to the adjacent endothelial cell. The fluid that is now "trapped" in the lymphatic capillary cannot be released back into the interstitial spaces.

The small intestine (part of the GI tract) contains special types of lymphatic capillaries called **lacteals** (lak'tē-ăl; *lactis* = milk) (see sections 26.4c and 26.8b). Lacteals pick up not only interstitial fluid, but also dietary lipids and lipid-soluble vitamins (vitamins that must be dissolved in lipids before they can be absorbed). The lymph from the GI tract has a milky color due to the lipid, and for this reason the GI tract lymph is also called **chyle** (kīl; *chylos* = juice).

> **Learning Strategy 24.1**
>
> Fluid enters into a lymphatic capillary in a manner analogous to entering a house through the front door. Imagine that the door is unlocked and you turn the knob. By pushing on the knob, you put pressure on the outside of the door, causing it to open so you can enter (just like the pressure of interstitial fluid on the outside of the lymphatic capillary wall causes the fluid to enter the capillary). Once inside, you apply pressure to the inside surface of the door, causing the door to close (just as fluid pressure against the inside of the lymphatic capillary surface causes that cell margin to close against the neighboring cell).

24.2b Lymphatic Vessels

Lymphatic capillaries merge to form larger structures called **lymphatic vessels.** Lymphatic vessels resemble small veins, in that both contain three tunics (intima, media, and externa) and both have **valves** within the lumen (see section 23.1d). Because the lymphatic vessel network is a low-pressure system, valves prevent lymph from pooling in the vessel and help prevent lymph backflow (**figure 24.3**). These valves are especially important in areas where lymph flow is against the direction of gravity. Contraction of nearby skeletal muscles also helps move lymph through the vessels.

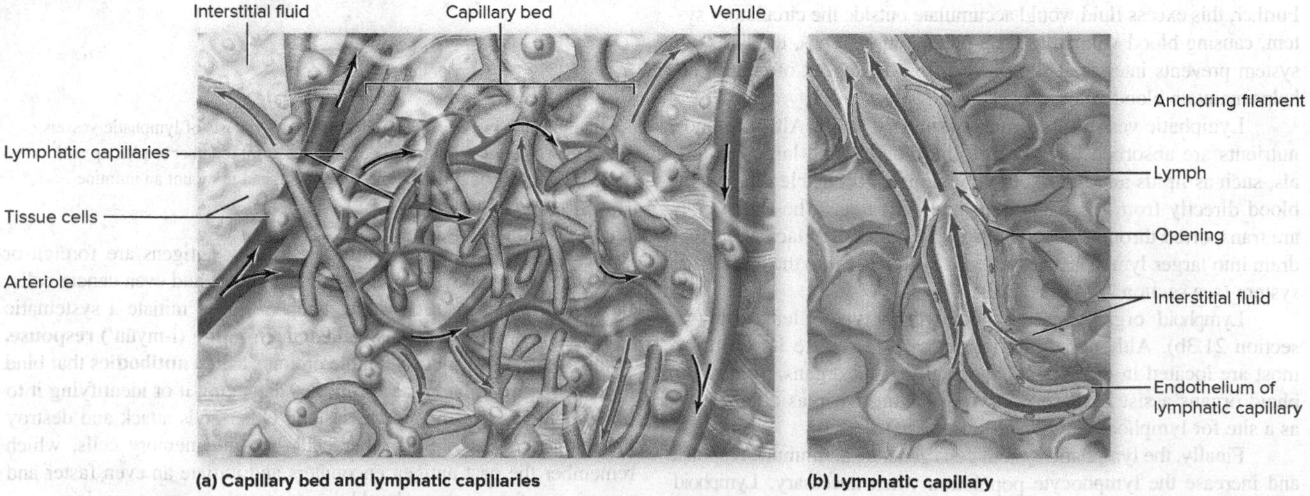
Interstitial fluid
Capillary bed
Venule
Lymphatic capillaries
Tissue cells
Arteriole
Anchoring filament
Lymph
Opening
Interstitial fluid
Endothelium of lymphatic capillary
(a) Capillary bed and lymphatic capillaries
(b) Lymphatic capillary

Figure 24.2

Lymphatic Capillaries. (*a*) Lymphatic capillaries arise as blind-end vessels within connective tissue among most blood capillary networks and absorb excess fluid left during capillary exchange. (*b*) A lymphatic capillary takes up excess interstitial fluid through overlapping endothelial cells. The fluid is then called lymph. Here, the black arrows show blood flow and the green arrows show lymph flow. APR

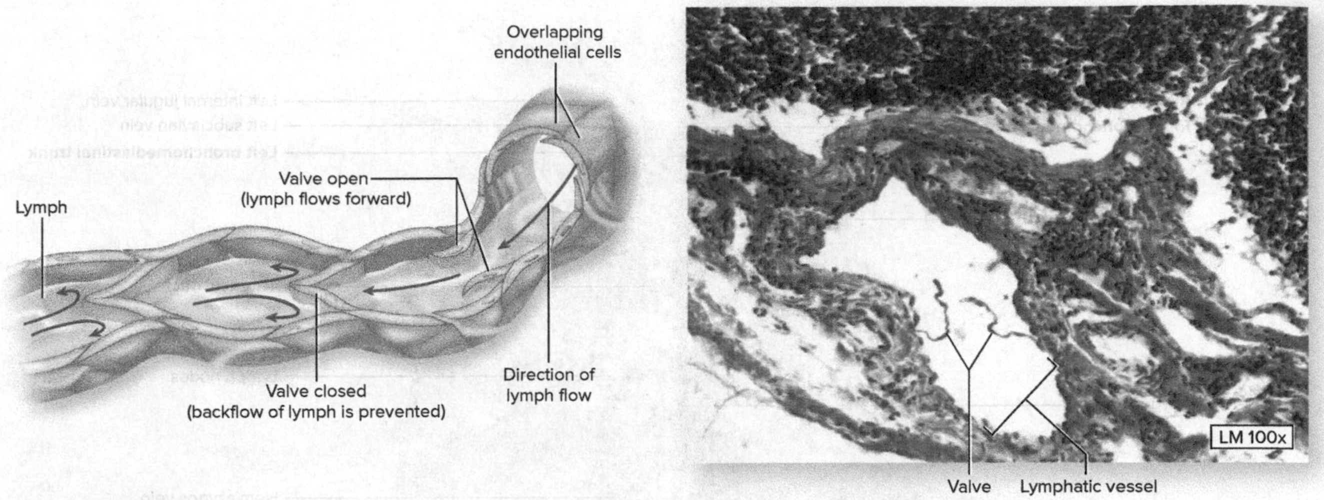

(a) Lymphatic vessel, longitudinal section **(b) Lymphatic vessel, cross section**

Figure 24.3

Lymphatic Vessels and Valves. (*a*) A drawing shows how lymphatic vessels contain valves to prevent backflow of lymph. (*b*) A light micrograph shows a cross section of a lymphatic vessel.

(b) ©McGraw-Hill Education/Alvin Telser, photographer

Some lymphatic vessels connect directly to lymphoid organs called lymph nodes. **Afferent lymphatic vessels** transport lymph to a lymph node where it is filtered for foreign or pathogenic antigens. Once filtered, the lymph exits the lymph node via **efferent lymphatic vessels.** Lymph nodes are often found in clusters, so after one lymph node receives and filters lymph, the lymph is passed to another lymph node in the cluster, then to another lymph node, and so on. Thus, lymph is repeatedly examined for the presence of foreign or pathogenic antigens.

24.2c Lymphatic Trunks

Left and right **lymphatic trunks** form from merging lymphatic vessels (figure 24.4). Each lymphatic trunk drains lymph from a major body region, as follows:

- **Jugular trunks** drain lymph from the head and neck.
- **Subclavian trunks** drain lymph from the upper limbs, breasts, and superficial thoracic wall.
- **Bronchomediastinal trunks** drain lymph from deep thoracic structures.
- A single **intestinal trunk** drains lymph from most abdominal structures.
- **Lumbar trunks** drain lymph from the lower limbs, abdominopelvic wall, and pelvic organs.

24.2d Lymphatic Ducts

Lymphatic trunks drain into one of two **lymphatic ducts.** The two lymphatic ducts empty lymph back into the venous circulation. The **right lymphatic duct,** located near the right clavicle, returns the lymph into the junction of the right subclavian vein and the right internal jugular vein. It receives lymph from the lymphatic trunks that drain the right side of the head and neck, right upper limb, and right side of the thorax (figure 24.4*b*).

The **thoracic duct** is the largest lymphatic vessel, with a length of about 37.5 to 45 centimeters (15 to 18 inches). At the base of the thoracic duct and anterior to the L_2 vertebra is a rounded, saclike structure called the **cisterna chyli** (sis-ter'n ă kī'lī; cistern) (figure 24.4 *a*). The cisterna chyli gets its name from the milky lymph called chyle it receives from the small intestine. Left and right intestinal and lumbar trunks drain into the cisterna chyli. The thoracic duct travels superiorly from the cisterna chyli and lies directly anterior to the vertebral bodies. It passes through the aortic opening of the diaphragm, and then it ascends to the left of the vertebral body midline. It drains lymph into the junction of the left subclavian vein and left internal jugular vein. The thoracic duct receives lymph from most regions of the body, including the left side of the head and neck, left upper limb, left thorax, and all body regions inferior to the diaphragm (including the right lower limb and right side of the abdomen).

WHAT DID YOU LEARN?

2. What is lymph?
3. Describe the structure of lymphatic capillaries. Into what structures do they drain?
4. Naming the lymphatic vessels and lymphoid structures involved, trace the flow of lymph from a capillary bed in a person's right foot back into venous circulation.

24.3 Lymphoid Cells

✓ Learning Objectives

5. List and describe the types of lymphoid cells.
6. Explain the function of lymphocytes in the body's immune response.
7. Outline and describe lymphocyte formation.

Lymphoid cells work together to elicit an immune response. Among the types of lymphoid cells are macrophages, some epithelial cells, dendritic cells, and lymphocytes.

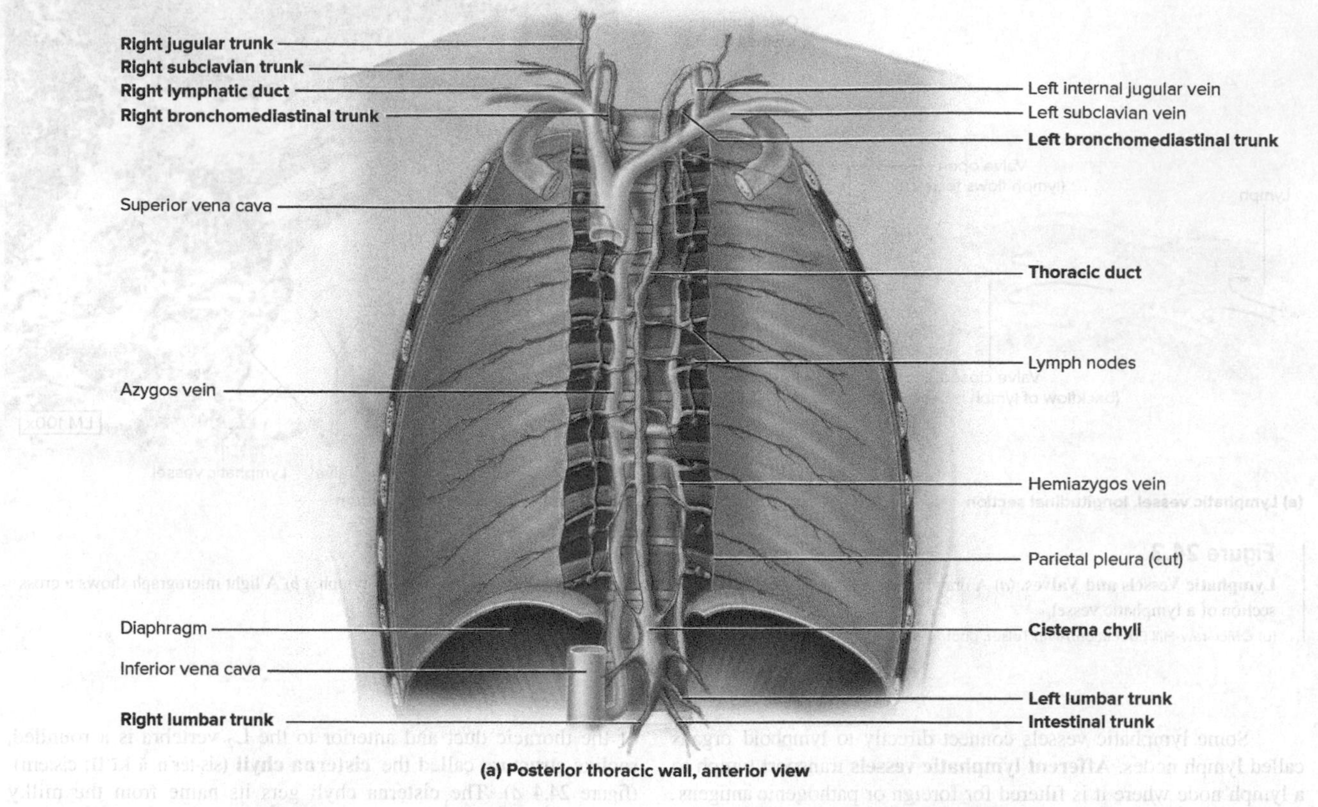
Right jugular trunk
Right subclavian trunk
Right lymphatic duct
Right bronchomediastinal trunk
Superior vena cava
Azygos vein
Diaphragm
Inferior vena cava
Right lumbar trunk
Left internal jugular vein
Left subclavian vein
Left bronchomediastinal trunk
Thoracic duct
Lymph nodes
Hemiazygos vein
Parietal pleura (cut)
Cisterna chyli
Left lumbar trunk
Intestinal trunk
(a) Posterior thoracic wall, anterior view
Area drained by right lymphatic duct
Area drained by thoracic duct
(b) Lymph drainage pattern
Thoracic duct
Thyroid gland
Trachea (cut)
Right brachiocephalic vein
Brachiocephalic trunk
Superior vena cava
Azygos vein
Left internal jugular vein
Left vertebral vein
Left subclavian vein
Left vertebral artery
Left brachiocephalic vein
Thoracic duct
Hemiazygos vein
(c) Thoracic duct

Figure 24.4

Lymphatic Trunks and Ducts. Lymph drains from lymphatic trunks into lymphatic ducts that each empty into the junctions of the internal jugular and subclavian veins. (*a*) An anterior view of the posterior thoracic wall illustrates the major lymphatic trunks and ducts. (*b*) Pattern of lymph drainage into the right lymphatic duct and the thoracic duct. (*c*) A cadaver photo of the thoracic duct. APR

Clinical View 24.1

Lymphedema

Lymphedema (limf′e-dē-mă) refers to an accumulation of interstitial fluid that occurs due to interference with lymphatic drainage in a part of the body. As the interstitial fluid accumulates, the affected area swells and becomes painful. If lymphedema is left untreated, the protein-rich interstitial fluid may interfere with wound healing and can even contribute to an infection by acting as a growth medium for bacteria.

Most cases of lymphedema are *obstructive*, meaning they are caused by blockage of lymphatic vessels. There are several causes of obstructive lymphedema:

- Any surgery that requires removal of a group of lymph nodes (e.g., breast cancer surgery when the axillary lymph nodes are removed)
- The spread of malignant tumors within the lymph nodes and/or lymphatic vessels
- Radiation therapy, which may cause scar formation
- Trauma or infection of the lymphatic vessels

Lymphedema has no cure, but it can be controlled. Patients may wear compression stockings or other compression garments to reduce swelling and assist interstitial fluid return to the circulation. Certain exercise regimens may improve lymphatic drainage as well.

Millions of individuals in Southeast Asia and Africa have developed lymphedema as a result of infection by threadlike parasitic filarial worms. **Lymphatic filariasis** (fil-ă-rī′ă-sis; *filum* = thread) is a type of lymphedema whereby filarial worms lodge in the lymphatic system, live and reproduce there for years, and eventually obstruct lymphatic drainage. Although filarial worms can gain entrance to the body through cracks in the skin of the foot, mosquitoes are the most common vector for transmitting filariasis. An affected body part can swell to many times its normal size. In these extreme cases, the condition also is known as **elephantiasis** (el′ĕ-fan-tī′ă-sis; *elephas* = elephant). Patients are treated with anti-parasitic medications to kill the filarial worms, although the damage to the lymphatic system may be irreversible.

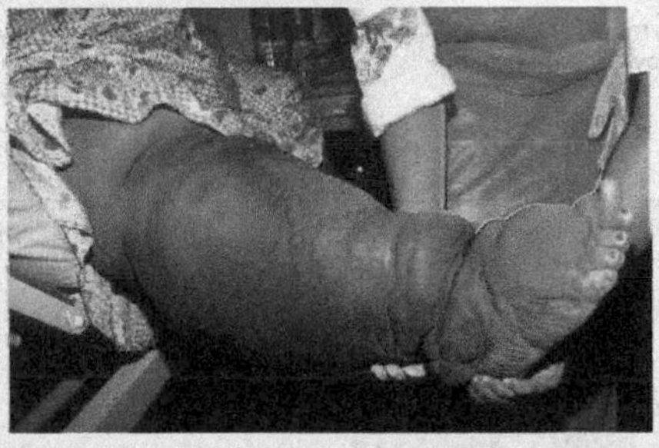

Elephantiasis (lymphatic filariasis) of the lower limb.
Andy Crump, TDR, World Health Organization/Science Source

Macrophages (mak′r ō-fāj; *macros* = large, *phago* = to eat) are monocytes that have migrated from the blood into other body tissues, including those of the lymphatic system. They are responsible for phagocytosis of foreign substances. They also may present antigens to other lymphoid cells. Special epithelial cells (also called **nurse cells**) occur in the thymus, where they secrete thymic hormones. **Dendritic** (den-drit′ik) **cells** occur throughout the body's tissues; they internalize antigens and present them to lymphocytes. These cells are the main antigen-presenting cell of the immune system. (Recall from section 5.1b that there are dendritic cells within the epidermis of the skin.) **Lymphocytes** are the most abundant cells in the lymphatic system. There are three types of lymphocytes, and each has a specific job in the overall immune response.

24.3a Types and Functions of Lymphocytes

The three types of lymphocytes are T-lymphocytes (also called *T-cells*), B-lymphocytes (also called *B-cells*), and natural killer (NK) cells. All three types migrate through the lymphatic system and search for antigens.

T-lymphocytes

T-lymphocytes make up about 70% to 85% of body lymphocytes. The lymphocyte plasma membrane contains a coreceptor that can recognize a particular antigen. (Coreceptors are named with the letters "CD" followed by a number.) There are several types of T-lymphocytes, each with a particular kind of coreceptor. The two main groups are helper T-lymphocytes and cytotoxic T-lymphocytes (**figure 24.5**).

Learning Strategy 24.2

Lymphocytes are identified according to the tissue or organ where they mature:

T-lymphocytes mature in the Thymus.

B-lymphocytes mature in the Bone marrow.

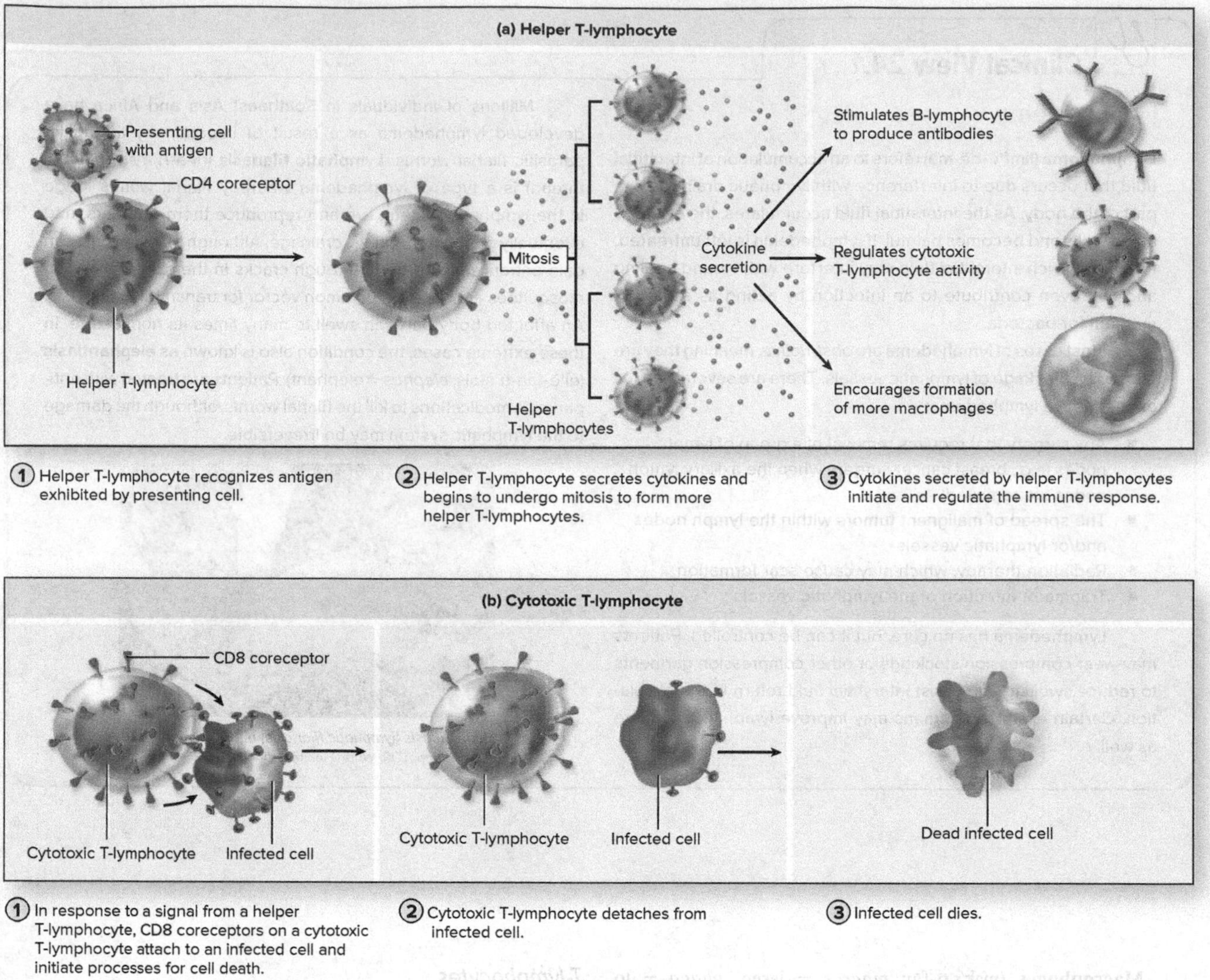
(a) Helper T-lymphocyte
Presenting cell with antigen
CD4 coreceptor
Helper T-lymphocyte
Mitosis
Helper T-lymphocytes
Cytokine secretion
Stimulates B-lymphocyte to produce antibodies
Regulates cytotoxic T-lymphocyte activity
Encourages formation of more macrophages
1 Helper T-lymphocyte recognizes antigen exhibited by presenting cell.
2 Helper T-lymphocyte secretes cytokines and begins to undergo mitosis to form more helper T-lymphocytes.
3 Cytokines secreted by helper T-lymphocytes initiate and regulate the immune response.
(b) Cytotoxic T-lymphocyte
CD8 coreceptor
Cytotoxic T-lymphocyte
Infected cell
Cytotoxic T-lymphocyte
Infected cell
Dead infected cell
1 In response to a signal from a helper T-lymphocyte, CD8 coreceptors on a cytotoxic T-lymphocyte attach to an infected cell and initiate processes for cell death.
2 Cytotoxic T-lymphocyte detaches from infected cell.
3 Infected cell dies.

Figure 24.5
Types of T-lymphocytes and Their Role in the Immune Response. *(a)* Helper T-lymphocytes are presented antigen by a presenting cell, activated, and then secrete cytokines to initiate both the maturation of immune defense cells and the immune response. (*b)* Activated cytotoxic T-lymphocytes recognize antigens on infected cells and directly attack and kill infected cells, thereby reducing threats by pathogens.

Helper T-lymphocytes are needed to mount an effective defense against antigens. They primarily contain the CD4 corecep-tor. For this reason, helper T-lymphocytes are also called *CD4+ cells,* or *T4 cells.* There are many kinds of helper T-lymphocytes in the body, and each is activated by and responds to one type of antigen only. For example, one type of helper T-lymphocyte may respond to the chickenpox virus, but this same helper T-lymphocyte will not be activated if it comes across *Streptococcus* bacteria. Helper T-lymphocytes initiate and oversee the immune response; in other words, they are the "conductors" in the immune response "symphony." Helper T-lymphocytes regulate the immune responseby secreting **cytokines** (sī′tō-kīn; *kinesis* = movement), which are chemical signals that bind to receptors on other lymphoid and immune system cells and help activate them. APR

Cytotoxic T-lymphocytes, also called *CD8+ cells* or *T8 cells,* primarily contain the CD8 coreceptor. These lymphocytes come in direct contact with infected or tumor cells and kill them. Each type of cytotoxic T-lymphocyte responds to one type of antigen only. Cytotoxic T-lymphocytes kill by secreting substances into abnormal cells that cause unregulated entry of material into the cell and directly triggers cell death. A cytotoxic T-lymphocyte acts only after it is activated by a helper T-lymphocyte. APR

Other subsets of T-lymphocytes include memory T-lymphocytes and regulatory T-lymphocytes. **Regulatory T-lymphocytes** often contain the CD4 coreceptor and appear to suppress potentially dangerous immune system activities, such as autoimmunity. **Memory T-lymphocytes** arise from T-lymphocytes that have encountered a foreign antigen. They patrol the body, and if they encounter the same

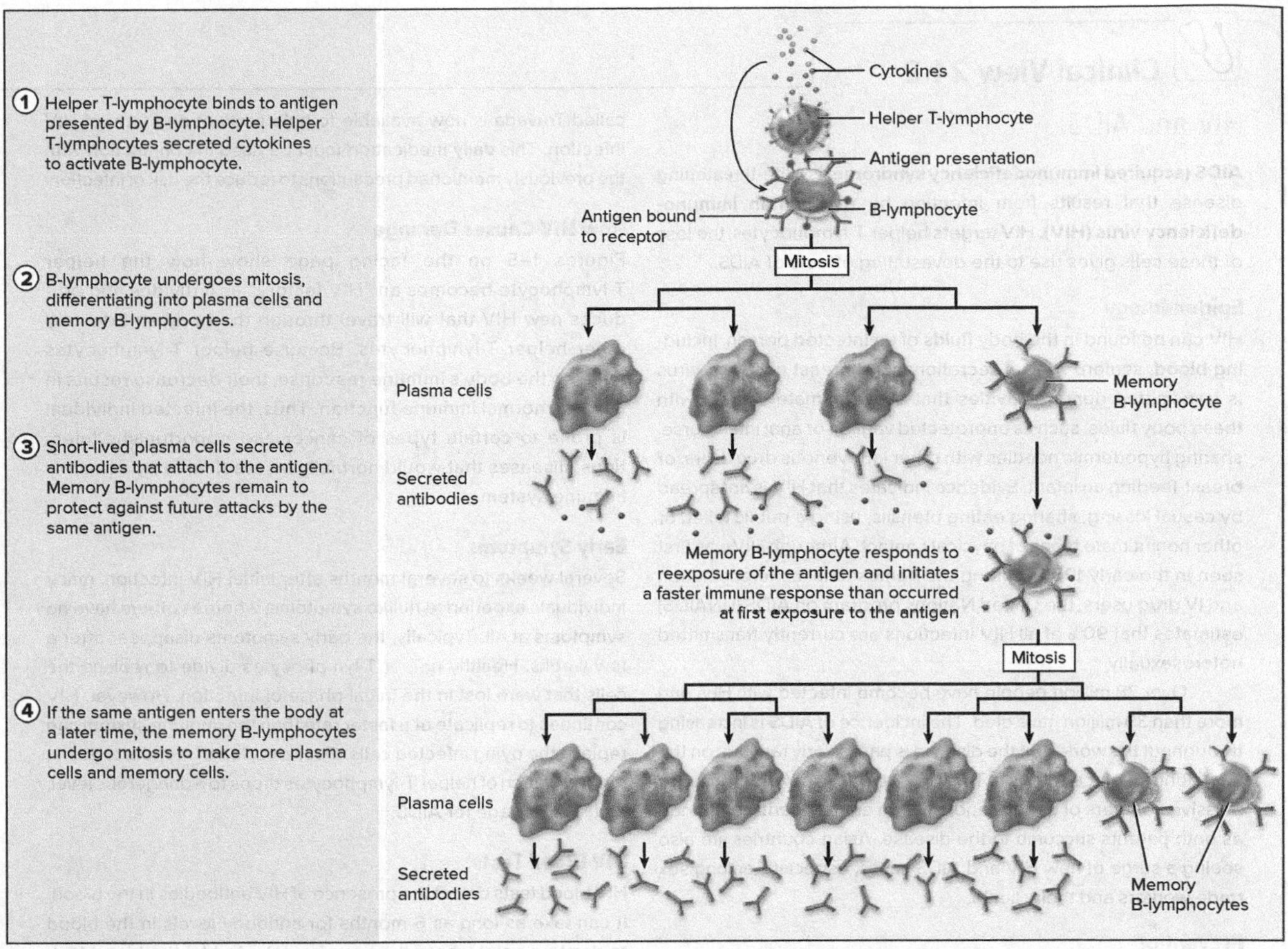

1 Helper T-lymphocyte binds to antigen presented by B-lymphocyte. Helper T-lymphocytes secreted cytokines to activate B-lymphocyte.
2 B-lymphocyte undergoes mitosis, differentiating into plasma cells and memory B-lymphocytes.
3 Short-lived plasma cells secrete antibodies that attach to the antigen. Memory B-lymphocytes remain to protect against future attacks by the same antigen.
4 If the same antigen enters the body at a later time, the memory B-lymphocytes undergo mitosis to make more plasma cells and memory cells.
Cytokines
Helper T-lymphocyte
Antigen presentation
B-lymphocyte
Antigen bound to receptor
Mitosis
Plasma cells
Memory B-lymphocyte
Secreted antibodies
Memory B-lymphocyte responds to reexposure of the antigen and initiates a faster immune response than occurred at first exposure to the antigen
Mitosis
Plasma cells
Secreted antibodies
Memory B-lymphocytes

Figure 24.6

B-lymphocytes and Their Role in the Immune Response. B-lymphocytes are activated by helper T-lymphocytes by cytokine secretion. Their response to primary and secondary exposure to an antigen is shown here in a series of steps.

antigen again, they mount an even faster immune response than occurred at the first exposure to the antigen.

B-lymphocytes

B-lymphocytes make up about 15% to 30% of the lymphocytes in the body. B-lymphocytes contain antigen receptors that respond to one particular antigen and stimulate the production of **immunoglobulins (Ig)** (im′yū-nō-glob′yū-lin), or **antibodies,** that respond to that particular antigen. There are five main classes of immunoglobulins based upon the order of amino acids in their composition. These classes, from most common in the plasma to least common, are IgG, IgA, IgM, IgD, and IgE. These immunoglobulins act by forming antigen-antibody complexes that help destroy or neutralize specific foreign antigens. B-lymphocytes are typically activated by a helper T-lymphocyte, but they can be activated independently by binding to antigen. Once it is activated, the B-lymphocyte undergoes cell division and differentiates into one of two types of B-lymphocytes: plasma cells or memory B-lymphocytes (**figure 24.6**).

Most of the activated lymphocytes become **plasma** (plaz′m ă) **cells,** mature cells that produce and secrete large amounts of antibodies. Plasma cells may be either short-lived or long-lived. The short-lived plasma cells have a life span of less than a week, whereas long-lived plasma cells can live for months or years.

A few of the activated B-lymphocytes do not differentiate into plasma cells and instead become **memory B-lymphocytes.** These cells "remember" the initial antigen attack and stand guard to mount a faster, more efficient immune response should the same antigen

Learning Strategy 24.3

Functions of lymphocytes can be thought of as being analogous to aspects of the armed forces:

Helper T-lymphocytes are generals of the army; they recruit and regulate other immune cells.

Cytotoxic T-lymphocytes are highly trained soldiers; they engage in "cell-to-cell" combat against a specific foe.

B-lymphocytes are the elite military forces that release "munitions" (antibodies), typically from a distance.

Clinical View 24.2

HIV and AIDS

AIDS (acquired immunodeficiency syndrome) is a life-threatening disease that results from infection by the **human immunodeficiency virus (HIV).** HIV targets helper T-lymphocytes; the loss of these cells gives rise to the devastating effects of AIDS.

Epidemiology

HIV can be found in the body fluids of an infected person, including blood, semen, vaginal secretions, and breast milk. The virus is transmitted during activities that allow intimate contact with these body fluids, such as unprotected vaginal or anal intercourse, sharing hypodermic needles with other intravenous drug users, or breast-feeding an infant. Evidence indicates that HIV is *not* spread by casual kissing, sharing eating utensils, using a public toilet, or other nonintimate types of physical contact. Although HIV was first seen in the early 1980s among the homosexual male population and IV drug users, the United Nations program on AIDS (UNAIDS) estimates that 90% of all HIV infections are currently transmitted heterosexually.

Over 78 million people have become infected with HIV, and more than 39 million have died. The incidence of AIDS is increasing throughout the world, but the disease is particularly rampant on the continents of Africa and Asia. The AIDS epidemic in Africa has led to massive numbers of deaths, and children are frequently orphaned as both parents succumb to the disease. Asian countries are also seeing a surge of new HIV and AIDS cases, especially among sex trade workers and their clients.

Prevention

The key to limiting the spread of HIV infection is to refrain from behaviors that allow the virus to be transmitted. Unprotected sexual intercourse (especially anal intercourse) can spread HIV, so individuals should either practice abstinence or protect themselves by using condoms. (Other contraceptives, such as birth control pills, do *not* protect an individual from HIV infection.) Both partners in a monogamous relationship should be tested for HIV via a simple blood test before engaging in sexual intercourse. Intravenous drug users should not share needles. Health-care workers should wear gloves and be careful around patients' body fluids. HIV-infected pregnant women need special prenatal care to keep from transmitting the virus to their fetuses, and HIV-infected mothers are discouraged from breast-feeding. A pre-exposure prophylactic medication called Truvada is now available to help prevent one form of HIV infection. This daily medication must be used in conjunction with the previously mentioned precautions to reduce the risk of infection.

How HIV Causes Damage

Figures 1–5 on the facing page show how the helper T-lymphocyte becomes an "HIV factory" as it divides and produces new HIV that will travel through the body and destroy other helper T-lymphocytes. Because helper T-lymphocytes oversee the body's immune response, their decrease results in a loss of normal immune function. Thus, the infected individual is prone to certain types of cancer and opportunistic infections, diseases that would normally be eradicated by a healthy immune system.

Early Symptoms

Several weeks to several months after initial HIV infection, many individuals experience flulike symptoms, whereas others have no symptoms at all. Typically, the early symptoms disappear after a few weeks. Healthy helper T-lymphocytes divide to replace the cells that were lost in the initial phase of infection. However, HIV continues to replicate at a faster rate than the immune system can replace the dying infected cells. Over a period of months to years, the population of helper T-lymphocytes drops to a dangerous level, setting the stage for AIDS.

HIV Blood Tests

HIV blood tests detect the presence of HIV antibodies in the blood. It can take as long as 6 months for antibody levels in the blood to rise to a point where they can be detected by the blood test. Thus, individuals who have been exposed to HIV, but are tested within the first 6 months, may receive a false-negative result simply because the antibodies have not yet reached the detectable level. Even though the antibody test is negative at this early stage, the person can still infect others.

When Does HIV Become AIDS?

HIV is diagnosed as AIDS when a person's helper T-lymphocyte count drops to below 200 cells per cubic milliliter (healthy individuals have between 800 and 1200 cells per cubic milliliter), when an opportunistic infection or illness develops. Common opportunistic infections include *Pneumocystis jiroveci* pneumonia and *histoplasmosis*. Malignancies that tend to occur in

strike again. If the antigen does strike again, the body responds so quickly that no symptoms may occur. Memory B-lymphocytes have a much longer life span than plasma cells; some live for months or even years.

Some vaccines (e.g., polio vaccine, flu vaccine) introduce modified or dead forms of an antigen so that memory cells may be formed and the body can fight and eliminate the illness before any symptoms ever develop. Depending upon the life span of the particular memory B-lymphocytes, the vaccine may provide lifelong immunity, or periodic **booster shots** may be needed to ensure continued protection against the antigen. APR

WHAT DO YOU THINK?

1. Tetanus (commonly known as *lockjaw*) is a severe illness that causes painful muscle spasms and convulsions and can lead to death. If adults are advised to get a tetanus booster shot about once every 10 years, what is the probable life span of the tetanus-detecting memory B-lymphocytes?

people whose immune systems are weakened include *Kaposi sarcoma* and *non-Hodgkin lymphoma*. Opportunistic infections and malignancies account for up to 80% of all AIDS-related deaths. In addition, many AIDS patients have some form of CNS complications, including meningitis, encephalitis, neurologic deficits, and neuropathies.

Treatment Options

HIV infection is a lifelong illness; there is no cure. Current pharmaceutic treatments alleviate symptoms or help prevent the spread of HIV infection in the body, but they cannot eradicate HIV from an infected individual. In addition, most of these drugs have numerous unpleasant side effects.

Drug treatment for HIV is *highly active antiretroviral therapy (HAART)*. There are six classes of antiretroviral agents. Patients taking a combination of drugs typically experience a dramatic reduction in viral load and even a slight rise in their helper T-lymphocyte count. However, they must take these drugs for life, or else the HIV and AIDS will progress.

Unfortunately, HIV drugs are expensive and not widely available in developing countries, where the need for them is greatest. One hopeful sign is that pharmaceutical companies are negotiating with the governments of developing countries to make cheaper forms of these drugs available. In addition, pharmaceutical companies are working together to create better and easier-to-use medications that patients will be more likely to use.

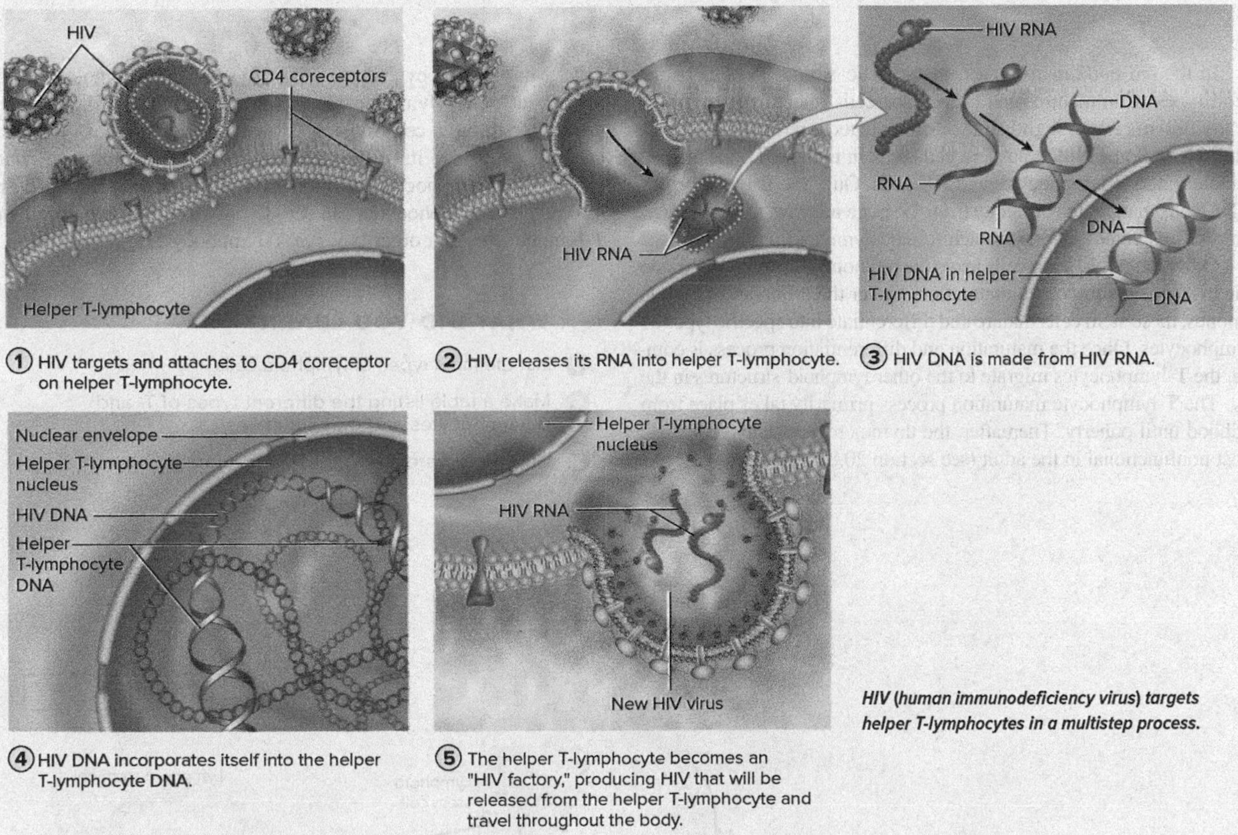

HIV
CD4 coreceptors
Helper T-lymphocyte
HIV RNA
HIV RNA
DNA
RNA
RNA
DNA
HIV DNA in helper T-lymphocyte
DNA
① HIV targets and attaches to CD4 coreceptor on helper T-lymphocyte.
② HIV releases its RNA into helper T-lymphocyte.
③ HIV DNA is made from HIV RNA.
Nuclear envelope
Helper T-lymphocyte nucleus
HIV DNA
Helper T-lymphocyte DNA
Helper T-lymphocyte nucleus
HIV RNA
New HIV virus
④ HIV DNA incorporates itself into the helper T-lymphocyte DNA.
⑤ The helper T-lymphocyte becomes an "HIV factory," producing HIV that will be released from the helper T-lymphocyte and travel throughout the body.

HIV (human immunodeficiency virus) targets helper T-lymphocytes in a multistep process.

NK Cells

NK (natural killer) cells, also called *large granular lymphocytes,* make up the remaining small percentage of body lymphocytes. NK cells tend to have CD16 receptors. Unlike T- and B-lymphocytes, which respond to one particular antigen only, NK cells can kill a wide variety of infected cells and some cancerous cells.

Table 24.1 reviews the main types of lymphocytes and their functions.

24.3b Lymphopoiesis

Hematopoiesis was shown to be the formation and maturation of all formed elements in the blood (see section 21.4 and figure 21.10). **Lymphopoiesis** (lim′f ō-poy-ē′sis) is the process of lymphocyte development and maturation. When a lymphocyte fully matures, it becomes **immunocompetent,** meaning that the lymphocyte is fully able to participate in the immune response. Immature lymphocytes cannot participate in the immune response. All lymphocyte types originate in the red bone marrow, but their maturation sites differ **(figure 24.7).**

Table 24.1 Types of Lymphocytes

Cell Type	Function	Type of Antigen Response
T-LYMPHOCYTE		
Helper T-lymphocyte	Initiates and oversees the immune response	Responds to a single antigen
Cytotoxic T-lymphocyte	Directly kills infected cells; must be activated by a helper T-lymphocyte first	Responds to a single antigen
Memory T-lymphocyte	A type of T-lymphocyte that has already encountered an antigen; patrols the body seeking the same antigen again	Responds to a single antigen
Regulatory T-lymphocyte	Helps "turn off" the immune response once it has been activated	Responds to a single antigen
B-LYMPHOCYTE		
Plasma cell	Produces and secretes antibodies	Responds to a single antigen
Memory B-lymphocyte	Remembers an initial antigen attack and mounts a faster, more efficient response should the same antigen type attack again	Responds to a single antigen
NK (NATURAL KILLER) CELL		
NK (natural killer) cell	Kills a wide variety of infected and cancerous cells	Responds to multiple antigens

In the red bone marrow, a hematopoietic stem cell gives rise to several types of immature blood precursor cells, including **lymphoid** (lim′foyd) **stem cells** (a slightly more differentiated type of stem cell) (see section 21.4). Some lymphoid stem cells remain in the red bone marrow and mature into B-lymphocytes and NK cells. Once the B-lymphocytes and NK cells mature, they migrate from the bone marrow, travel through the blood, and enter lymphoid structures and lymphoid organs.

Other lymphoid stem cells leave the red bone marrow and migrate to the thymus for subsequent maturation. Under the influence of thymic hormones, these stem cells mature and differentiate into specific types of T-lymphocytes. Once the maturation and differentiation process is complete, the T-lymphocytes migrate to the other lymphoid structures in the body. The T-lymphocyte maturation process primarily takes place from childhood until puberty. Thereafter, the thymus regresses and becomes almost nonfunctional in the adult (see section 20.8).

Most lymphocytes have long life spans, and some can live for many years. Once lymphocytes leave their maturation sites, they can proliferate through cell division. However, each type of lymphocyte can replicate only its own kind—that is, a B-lymphocyte cannot produce a T-lymphocyte, only other B-lymphocytes. Similarly, mature helper T-lymphocytes can divide only into other mature helper T-lymphocytes, not other types of T-lymphocytes.

WHAT DID YOU LEARN?

5. List the main types of lymphoid cells.
6. Make a table listing the different types of T- and B-lymphocytes and their functions.
7. How and where are lymphocytes formed?

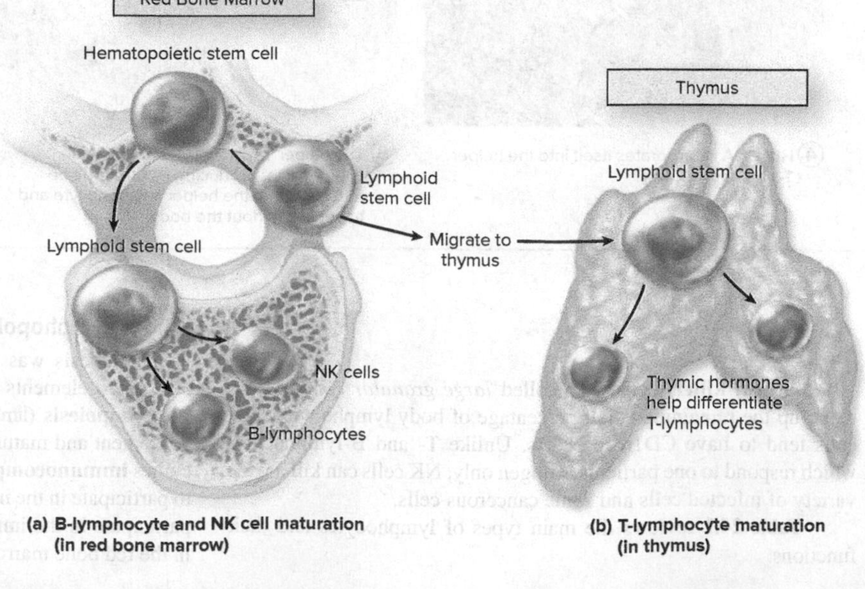

Figure 24.7

Lymphopoiesis. (*a*) B-lymphocytes and NK cells mature in the red bone marrow. (*b*) T-lymphocytes mature and differentiate in the thymus under the influence of thymic hormones.

24.4 Lymphoid Structures

✓ Learning Objectives

8. Describe the structure and functions of lymphoid nodules.
9. List the organs of the lymphatic system, and explain their functions.

In addition to the lymphatic vessels, the lymphatic system consists of lymphoid nodules and various lymphoid organs (see figure 24.1).

24.4a Lymphoid Nodules

Lymphoid nodules (nod′y ūl; *nodulus* = knot), or *lymphoid follicles,* are ovoid clusters of lymphoid cells with some extracellular connective tissue matrix that are *not* surrounded by a connective tissue capsule. The pale center of a lymphoid nodule is called the **germinal** (jer′mi-năl; *germen* = bud) **center;** it contains proliferating B-lymphocytes and some macrophages. T-lymphocytes are located outside the germinal center. Cells in the lymphoid nodules filter and attack antigens. Individually, a lymphoid nodule is small. However, in some areas of the body, many lymphoid nodules group together to form larger structures, such as mucosa-associated lymphoid tissue (MALT) or tonsils.

MALT (Mucosa-Associated Lymphoid Tissue)

Large collections of lymphoid nodules are located in the lamina propria of the mucosa of the gastrointestinal, respiratory, genital, and urinary tracts. Together, these collections of lymphoid nodules are called **MALT (mucosa-associated lymphoid tissue).** As food, air, and urine enter their respective tracts, the lymphoid cells in the MALT detect antigens and initiate an immune response. MALT is very prominent in the mucosa of the small intestine, primarily in the ileum. There, collections of lymphoid nodules called **Peyer patches** can become quite large and bulge into the gut lumen (**figure 24.8*a***; see also sections 26.4c and 26.8b). APR

Tonsils

Tonsils (ton′sil; *tonsilla* = a stake) are large clusters of lymphoid cells and extracellular connective tissue matrix that are not completely surrounded by a connective tissue capsule (figure 24.8*b, c*). Tonsils consist of multiple germinal centers and have invaginated outer edges called crypts. Crypts help trap material and facilitate its identification by lymphocytes. Several groups of tonsils occur in the pharynx (throat): A single **pharyngeal tonsil,** commonly referred to as *adenoids* (ad′ĕ-noydz; *aden* = gland), is in the posterior wall of the nasopharynx; **palatine tonsils** are in the posterolateral region of the oral cavity; and **lingual tonsils** are along the posterior one-third of the tongue.

WHAT DO YOU THINK?

2. If your tonsils are removed, how does your body develop an immune response against antigens in the throat? Are any other sources of lymphoid cells or structures located there?

24.4b Lymphoid Organs

A **lymphoid organ** consists of lymphoid cells within an extracellular connective tissue matrix, and is completely surrounded by a connective tissue capsule. The main lymphoid organs are the thymus, lymph nodes, and spleen.

Thymus

The **thymus** (thī′mŭs) is a bilobed organ located in the anterior mediastinum. In infants and young children, the thymus is quite large and extends into the superior mediastinum as well (**figure 24.9*a***). The thymus continues to grow until puberty, when it reaches a maximum weight of 30 to 50 grams. After reaching this size, cells of the thymus regress, and much of the functional thymus is eventually replaced by adipose connective tissue. In adults, the thymus atrophies and becomes almost nonfunctional.

In its prime, the thymus consists of two fused **thymic lobes,** each surrounded by a connective tissue capsule. Fibrous extensions of the capsule, called **trabeculae** (tră-bek′y ū-lē) or *septa,* subdivide the thymic lobes into **lobules;** each lobule has an outer **cortex** and an inner **medulla** (figure 24.9 *b*). These distinct zones support different stages of T-lymphocyte development. The cortex contains immature T-lymphocytes and some macrophages. The medulla contains epithelial cells and T-lymphocytes that have completed maturation. In addition, the medulla contains **thymic corpuscles** (or *Hassall corpuscles*), which are circular aggregations of aged, degenerated epithelial cells (also known as *nurse cells*) (figure 24.9*c*).

Clinical View 24.3

Tonsillitis and Tonsillectomy

Tonsils help protect the pharynx from infection. They frequently become inflamed and infected, a condition called **acute tonsillitis** (ton′si-lī′tis). The palatine tonsils are most commonly affected. The tonsils redden and enlarge; in severe cases, to the point that they partially obstruct the pharynx and may cause respiratory distress.

Tonsils may be infected by viruses, such as adenoviruses, or bacteria, such as *Streptococcus*. Streptococcal tonsillitis often results in very red tonsils that have whitish specks (called whitish exudate). The symptoms of tonsillitis include fever, chills, sore throat, and difficulty swallowing.

Persistent or recurrent infections can lead to permanent enlargement of the tonsils and a condition known as **chronic tonsillitis.** If medical treatment does not help the chronic tonsillitis, surgical removal of the tonsils **(tonsillectomy)** may be indicated. Medical guidelines suggest performing a tonsillectomy only if the person has had seven tonsillar infections in 1 year, five infections in 2 years, or three infections per year for 3 years running. Research indicates that tonsillectomy does not significantly affect the body's response to new infections.

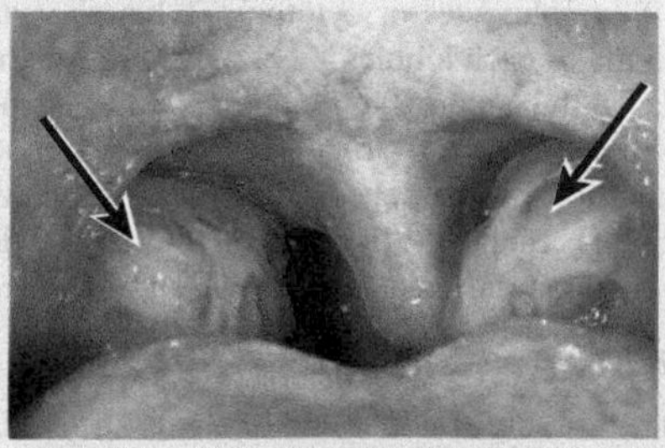

Enlarged tonsils (black arrows).

Science Photo Library/Alamy Stock Photo

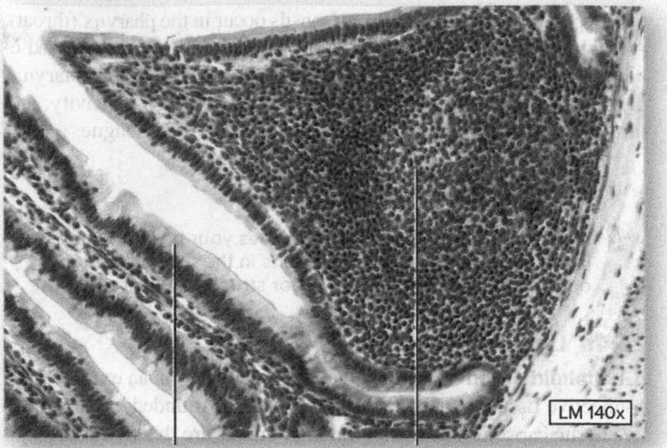
LM 140x
Simple columnar epithelium of small intestine
MALT (Peyer patches)

(a) MALT in small intestine

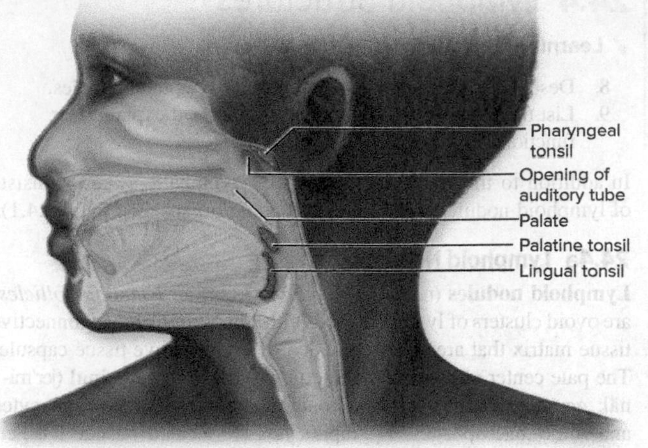
Pharyngeal tonsil
Opening of auditory tube
Palate
Palatine tonsil
Lingual tonsil

(b) Tonsils

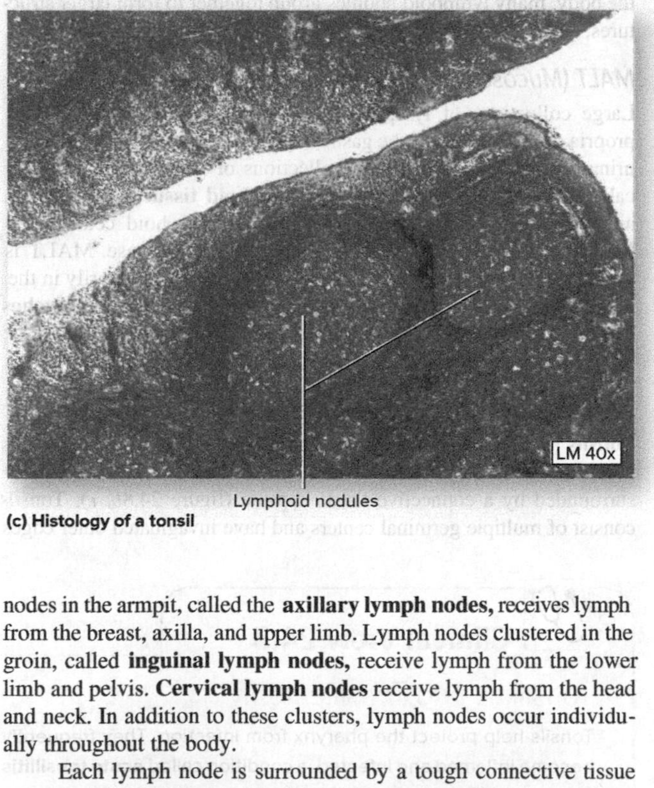
LM 40x
Lymphoid nodules

(c) Histology of a tonsil

Figure 24.8

Lymphatic Nodules. (*a*) MALT (mucosa-associated lymphoid tissue) in the ileum of the small intestine is called Peyer patches. (*b*) Tonsils reside in the wall of the pharynx and are composed of (*c*) lymphoid nodules. APR

(a, c) ©McGraw-Hill Education/Alvin Telser, photographer

The thymus functions as a site for T-lymphocyte maturation and differentiation. Immature lymphocytes migrate to the thymus during embryonic development. These immature cells then reside in the cortex of each lobule. The nurse cells in the cortex secrete several **thymic hormones** that stimulate T-lymphocyte maturation and differentiation. T-lymphocytes within the thymus do not participate in the immune response and are protected from antigens in the body by a well-formed **blood-thymus barrier** around the blood vessels in the cortex. When the T-lymphocytes differentiate (e.g., mature into helper T-lymphocytes or cytotoxic T-lymphocytes), they migrate to the medulla of each lobule. No blood-thymus barrier is present in the medulla, so the mature T-lymphocytes enter the blood and migrate to other lymphatic system structures. The T-lymphocyte maturation and differentiation process occurs primarily when we are young. Once adulthood is reached, differentiated T-lymphocytes can be produced by cell division only, not by maturation of new cells in the thymus.

Lymph Nodes

Lymph nodes are small, round or ovoid structures located along the pathways of lymphatic vessels (see figure 24.1). They range in length from 1 to 25 millimeters, and typically occur in clusters that receive lymph from selected body regions. For example, the cluster of lymph nodes in the armpit, called the **axillary lymph nodes,** receives lymph from the breast, axilla, and upper limb. Lymph nodes clustered in the groin, called **inguinal lymph nodes,** receive lymph from the lower limb and pelvis. **Cervical lymph nodes** receive lymph from the head and neck. In addition to these clusters, lymph nodes occur individually throughout the body.

Each lymph node is surrounded by a tough connective tissue **capsule** (kap′sūl) **(figure 24.10*a*)**. The capsule projects internal extensions called **trabeculae** into the node, subdividing the node into compartments. The trabeculae also provide a pathway through which blood vessels and nerves may enter the lymph node. Lymphoid cells surround the trabeculae, and channels called lymph sinuses provide a pathway through which lymph flows.

The lymph node regions deep to the capsule are subdivided into an outer **cortex** and an inner **medulla.** The cortex consists of lymphoid nodules and lymph sinuses called **cortical sinuses.** Remember that lymphoid nodules contain an outer region of T-lymphocytes surrounding an inner germinal center that houses proliferating B-lymphocytes and some macrophages. In addition, dendritic cells within these lymph nodes collect and present antigen to the helper T-lymphocytes. The lymph node medulla has strands of lymphoid cells (primarily B-lymphocytes and macrophages) supported by

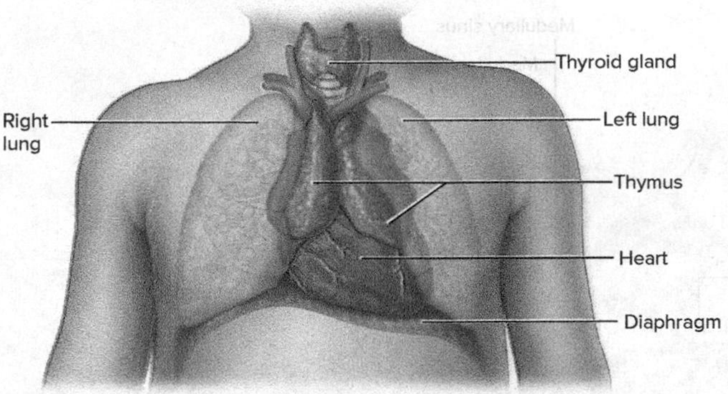
Thyroid gland
Right lung
Left lung
Thymus
Heart
Diaphragm

(a) Child's thorax, anterior view

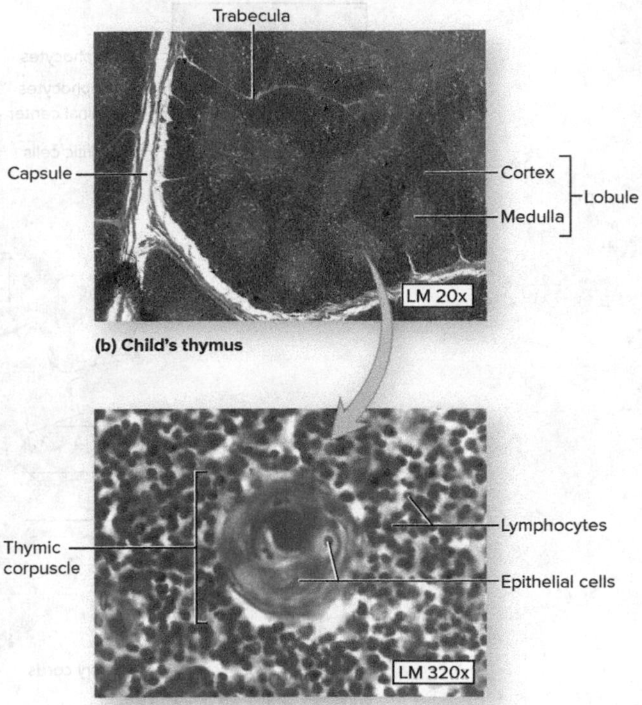
Trabecula
Capsule
Cortex
Medulla
Lobule
LM 20x
Thymic corpuscle
Lymphocytes
Epithelial cells
LM 320x

(b) Child's thymus

(c) Thymic corpuscle

Figure 24.9

Thymus. (*a*) The thymus is a bilobed lymphoid organ that is most prominent in children. (*b*) A micrograph of a child's thymus shows the arrangement of the cortex and the central medulla within a lobule. (*c*) A thymic corpuscle is visible within the medulla of the thymus in this micrograph. APR

(b, c) ©McGraw-Hill Education/Alvin Telser, photographer

Clinical View 24.4

Palpation of Lymph Nodes as Diagnostic Tool

Lymph nodes are lymphoid organs, which house T- and B-lymphocytes, our adaptive immune system cells. These nodes can be palpated in the head and neck, but are palpable in other areas (axillary and inguinal regions) only if they are enlarged. Enlargement (swelling) within the lymph node is a result of a response to infection (e.g., virus) or can be a site of metastases of cancer cells. The lymph node has a tight connective tissue capsule and becomes tender when it enlarges. Palpation of the lymph nodes evaluates size and motility of the nodes. If nodes are enlarged and tender for a prolonged period or become hard and fixed, further treatment may be prescribed. Location and number of enlarged nodes along with other symptoms can point to different diagnoses. For instance, a sore throat, fever, and generalized swelling of all lymph nodes are symptoms of mononucleosis, whereas swelling limited to the cervical region accompanied by a sore throat are symptoms of a cold.

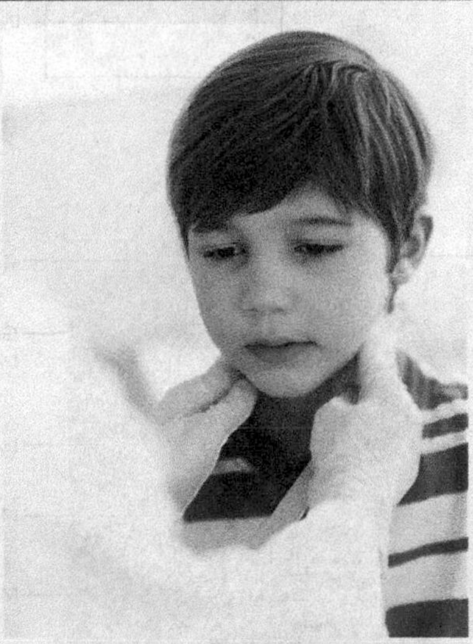

A physician palpates the cervical lymph nodes of a young patient.

Tom Grill/JGI/Blend Images LLC

connective tissue fibers called **medullary cords.** The medulla also contains lymph sinuses called **medullary sinuses.**

The primary function of a lymph node is to filter antigens from lymph and initiate an immune response when necessary. Afferent lymphatic vessels transport lymph to the lymph node, where it slowly percolates through the cortical sinuses and then the medullary sinuses. Macrophages line the lymph sinuses and remove foreign debris from the lymph. Lymph then exits the lymph node by way of one or two efferent lymphatic vessels. Efferent lymphatic vessels originate at the indented portion of the lymph node called the **hilum** (hī′lŭm) or *hilus.*

If antigens are presented to lymphocytes, an immune response is generated. The lymphocytes undergo cell division (especially in the germinal centers), and some of these new lymphocytes and antibodies eventually travel through the blood, where they can help fight infection. When a person is sick (e.g., influenza or strep throat), some of the lymph nodes are often swollen and tender to the touch. These symptoms indicate that lymphocytes are proliferating and beginning to fight the infection.

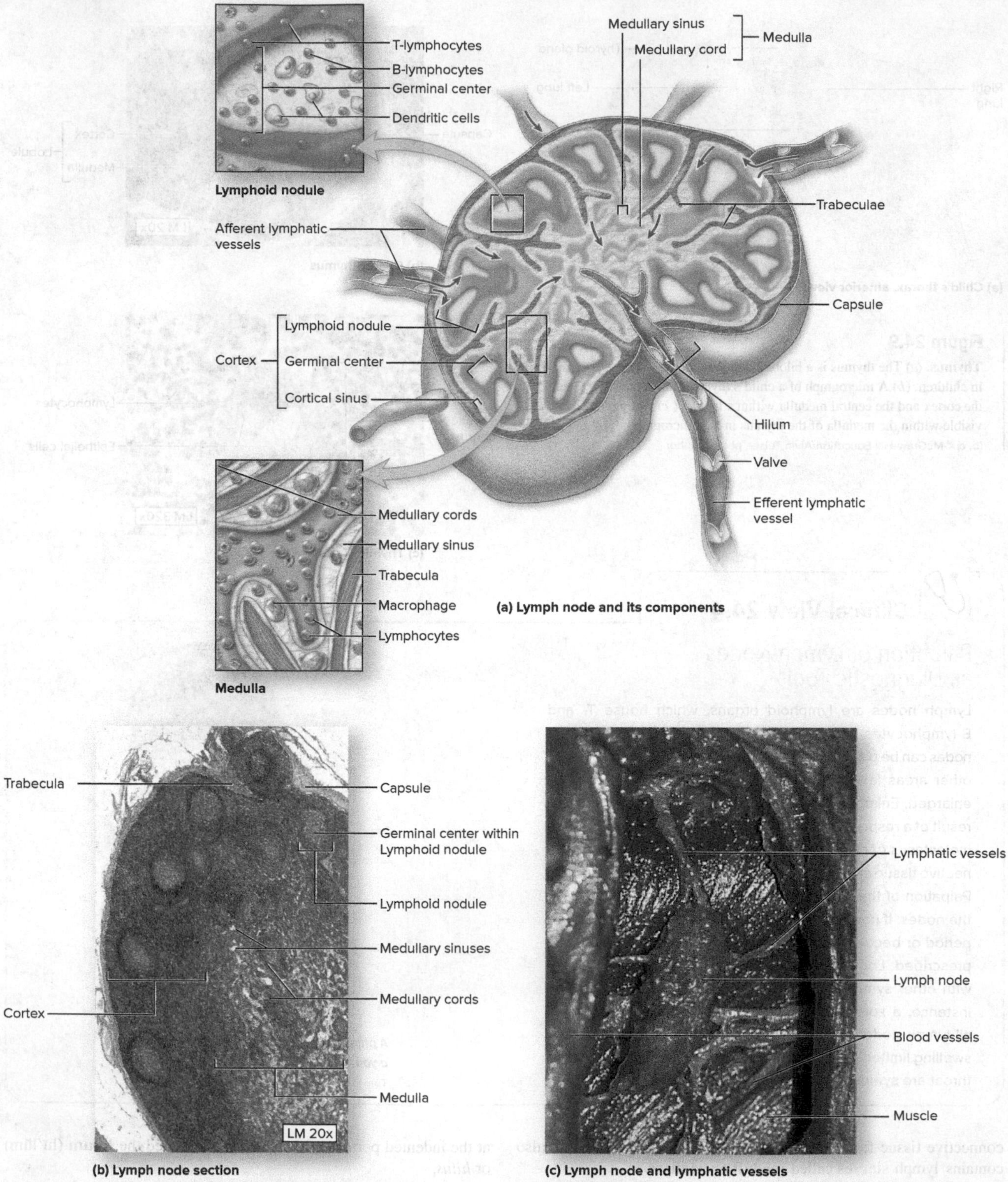
T-lymphocytes
B-lymphocytes
Germinal center
Dendritic cells
Lymphoid nodule
Medullary sinus
Medullary cord
Medulla
Trabeculae
Afferent lymphatic vessels
Capsule
Lymphoid nodule
Cortex
Germinal center
Cortical sinus
Hilum
Valve
Efferent lymphatic vessel
Medullary cords
Medullary sinus
Trabecula
Macrophage
Lymphocytes
Medulla
(a) Lymph node and its components
Trabecula
Capsule
Germinal center within Lymphoid nodule
Lymphoid nodule
Medullary sinuses
Medullary cords
Cortex
Medulla
LM 20x
(b) Lymph node section
Lymphatic vessels
Lymph node
Blood vessels
Muscle
(c) Lymph node and lymphatic vessels

Figure 24.10

Lymph Nodes. Lymph nodes are small, encapsulated structures that filter the lymph in lymphatic vessels. (*a*) Green arrows indicate the direction of lymph flow into and out of the lymph node. (*b*) A micrograph of a lymph node shows the cortex and medulla. (*c*) A cadaver photo of a lymph node and lymphatic vessels. APR

(b) ©McGraw-Hill Education/Alvin Telser, photographer; (c) Dr. Kent Van De Graaff

Clinical View 24.5

Lymphoma

A **lymphoma** (lim-fō′mă; *oma* = tumor) is a malignant neoplasm that develops from lymphoid structures. A lymphoma usually (but not always) presents as a nontender, enlarged lymph node, often in the neck or axillary region. Some patients have no further symptoms, whereas others may experience night sweats, fever, and unexplained weight loss in addition to the nodal enlargement. Lymphomas are grouped into two categories: Hodgkin lymphoma and non-Hodgkin lymphoma.

Hodgkin lymphoma (or *Hodgkin disease*) is characterized by the presence of the **Reed-Sternberg cell,** a large cell whose two nuclei resemble owl eyes, surrounded by lymphocytes within the affected lymph node. Hodgkin lymphoma affects young adults (ages 16–35) and people over 60. It arises in a lymph node and then spreads to other nearby lymph nodes. If caught early, Hodgkin lymphoma can be treated and cured by excision of the tumor, radiation, and/or chemotherapy.

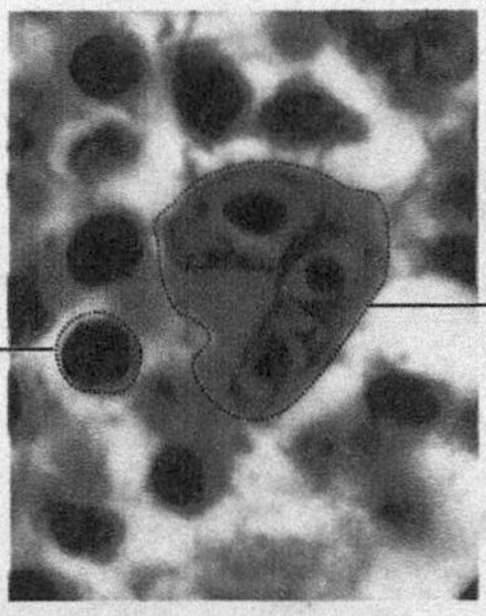
Normal lymphocyte
Reed-Sternberg cell, a characteristic of Hodgkin lymphoma

Light micrograph of Hodgkin Lymphoma
National Cancer Institute

Non-Hodgkin lymphomas are much more common than Hodgkin lymphomas. These lymphomas typically develop in lymphoid structures, usually from abnormal B-lymphocytes, and less commonly from T-lymphocytes. Some kinds of non-Hodgkin lymphoma are aggressive and often fatal, whereas others are slow-growing and more responsive to treatment. Treatment depends upon the type of non-Hodgkin lymphoma, the extent of its spread at the time of discovery, and the rate of progression of the malignancy.

Cancerous cells from other areas of the body can travel easily through the lymphatic system (a process called **metastasis,** see Clinical View 2.5: "Characteristics of Cancer Cells", in section 2.7), and become entrapped in lymph nodes. These cancerous cells can proliferate and also contribute to enlarged lymph nodes. A lymph node enlarged by cancer tends to be firm and nontender, as opposed to a lymph node that is swollen and tender due to an infection. If an individual is diagnosed with a cancer, the lymph nodes that drain the affected organ or body region are examined to determine if the cancer has spread. For example, if cancer is detected in a breast, the axillary lymph nodes are examined.

Spleen

The largest lymphoid organ in the body is the **spleen,** which is located in the left upper quadrant of the abdomen, inferior to the diaphragm and adjacent to ribs 9–11. This deep red organ lies lateral to the left kidney and posterolateral to the stomach. The spleen can vary considerably in size and weight, but typically is about 12 centimeters long and 7 centimeters wide. The spleen's posterolateral aspect (called the diaphragmatic surface) is convex and rounded, whereas the concave anteromedial border (the *visceral surface*) contains the hilum, where blood vessels and nerves enter and leave the spleen (**figure 24.11*a, d***). A **splenic** (splen′ik) **artery** delivers blood to the spleen, while blood returns to the circulation by way of a **splenic vein.**

The spleen is surrounded by a dense irregular connective tissue **capsule.** The capsule sends extensions called **trabeculae** into the organ. Within these trabeculae extend branches of the splenic artery and vein called **trabecular vessels.** The spleen lacks a cortex and medulla. Rather, the cells around the trabeculae are subdivided into white pulp and red pulp. Each cluster of white pulp is surrounded by red pulp (figure 24.11*b, c*).

The **white pulp** is associated with the arterial supply of the spleen and consists of circular clusters of lymphoid cells (T-lymphocytes, B-lymphocytes, and macrophages). In the center of each cluster is a **central artery.** As blood enters the spleen and flows through the central arteries, the white pulp lymphoid cells monitor the blood for foreign materials, bacteria, and other antigens. If antigens are found, the T- and B-lymphocytes elicit an immune response. Thus, while lymph nodes monitor *lymph* for antigens, the spleen monitors *blood* for antigens.

The **red pulp** is associated with the venous supply of the spleen, because blood that enters the spleen in the central arteries then travels through blood vessels in the red pulp. Red pulp consists of splenic cords and splenic sinusoids. The **splenic cords** (*cords of Bilroth*) contain erythrocytes, platelets, macrophages, and some plasma cells. One of the functions of the spleen is to serve as a blood reservoir, whereby the formed elements are stored in these splenic cords. In situations where more erythrocytes (and thus, greater oxygen delivery) are needed, such as during exercise, these erythrocytes reenter circulation. Because the spleen contains a large amount of blood, severe trauma to the spleen results in massive hemorrhage.

Among the splenic cords, the **splenic sinusoids** act like enlarged capillaries that carry blood. These vessels have a discontinuous basal lamina, so blood cells can easily enter and exit across the vessel wall. Macrophages lining the sinusoid lumen phagocytize (1) bacteria and foreign debris from the blood, and (2) old and defective erythrocytes and platelets (a process called **hemolysis** [hē-mol′i-sis; *lysis* = destruction]). Old erythrocytes can rupture or become trapped in the sinusoids, making them a target for these macrophages. Sinusoids merge to form small veins, and eventually the filtered blood leaves the spleen via the splenic vein.

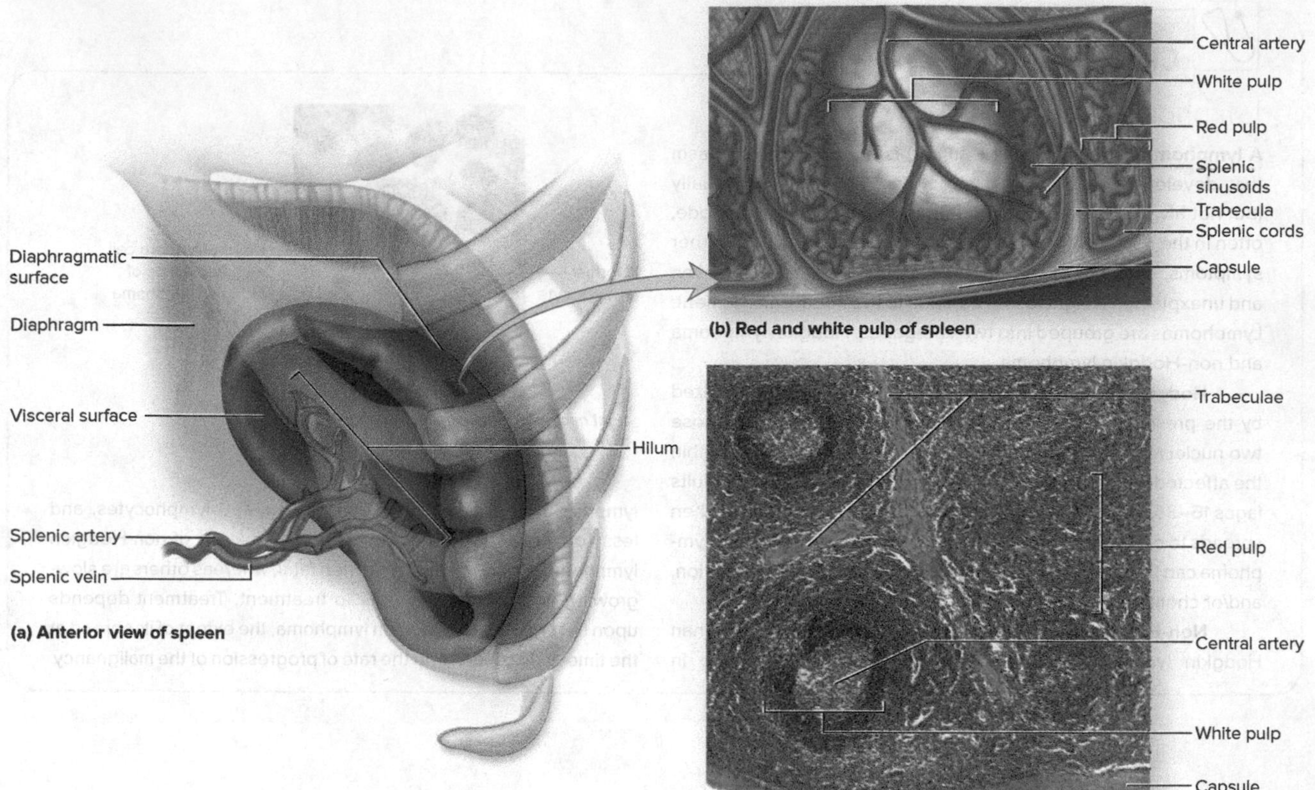
Diaphragmatic surface
Diaphragm
Visceral surface
Hilum
Splenic artery
Splenic vein
(a) Anterior view of spleen
Central artery
White pulp
Red pulp
Splenic sinusoids
Trabecula
Splenic cords
Capsule
(b) Red and white pulp of spleen
Trabeculae
Red pulp
Central artery
White pulp
Capsule
LM 40x
(c) Histology of spleen
Diaphragm
Inferior vena cava
Splenic artery
Hilum of spleen
Spleen
Splenic vein
Pancreas
Liver (cut)
Left kidney
(d) Abdominal cavity, anterior view

Figure 24.11

Spleen. (*a*) An anterior view illustrates the hilum as well as the splenic artery and vein. (*b*) A diagram depicts the microscopic arrangement of blood vessels, the red pulp, and the white pulp. (*c*) A micrograph of the spleen shows areas of white pulp and red pulp. (*d*) A cadaver photo shows the spleen and its relationship to the diaphragm, pancreas, and kidney. In this photo, the pancreas has been moved inferiorly to show the splenic vessels more clearly. APR

Table 24.2	Lymphoid Structures and Organs		
Component	**Structure or Organ[1]**	**Functions**	**Location**
Lymphoid nodules	Structure	Filter and attack antigens	Throughout body
MALT (mucosa-associated lymphoid tissue)	Structure	Filter and attack antigens in food, air, or urine	Within walls of GI, respiratory, genital, and urinary tracts
Tonsils	Structure	Protect against antigens in inhaled and ingested materials	Within pharynx
Thymus	Organ	Site of T-lymphocyte maturation and differentiation; stores maturing lymphocytes	Superior mediastinum (in adults); anterior and superior mediastinum (in children)
Lymph nodes	Organ	Filter lymph; mount immune response	Throughout body; frequently in clusters in the axillary, inguinal, and cervical regions
Spleen	Organ	Filters blood and recycles aged erythrocytes and platelets; serves as a blood reservoir; houses lymphocytes; mounts immune response to foreign antigens in the blood	In left upper quadrant of abdomen, near 9th–11th ribs and inferior to diaphragm

[1] A lymphoid structure is unencapsulated or has an incomplete connective tissue capsule, whereas a lymphoid organ has a complete connective tissue capsule encircling it.

In summary, the spleen performs the following functions:

- Initiates an immune response when antigens are found in the blood (a white pulp function)
- Serves as a reservoir for erythrocytes and platelets (a red pulp function)
- Phagocytizes old, defective erythrocytes and platelets (a red pulp function)
- Phagocytizes bacteria and other foreign materials

Table 24.2 summarizes the lymphoid structures and organs and their functions. **APR**

WHAT DO YOU THINK?

3 If your spleen were removed (splenectomy), would you be able to fight off illness and infections effectively? Why or why not?

WHAT DID YOU LEARN?

8 What is MALT, and where is it found?

9 Describe the main function of the thymus, and explain how the blood-thymus barrier supports this function.

10 Draw and label the structures of a lymph node.

11 How do the white pulp and red pulp of the spleen differ with respect to both cell population and function?

24.5 Aging and the Lymphatic System

✓ Learning Objective

10. Explain how aging affects the lymphatic system.

Some lymphatic system functions are not affected by aging. For example, the body effectively continues to transport lymph back to the blood and absorb dietary lipids from the small intestine. However, other functions change as we age. First, when an individual reaches adulthood, the thymus no longer matures and differentiates T-lymphocytes. New T-lymphocytes can be produced only by division (mitosis) of preexisting lymphocytes. Second, the lymphatic system's ability to provide immunity and fight disease decreases as we get older. Helper T-lymphocytes do not respond to antigens as well, and do not always reproduce rapidly. Reduced numbers of helper T-lymphocytes lead to fewer activated B-lymphocytes and T-lymphocytes. Therefore, the body's ability to acquire immunity and resist infection decreases, making elderly people more susceptible to illnesses and more likely to become sicker than younger adults. Older individuals are advised to get a pneumococcal vaccine and yearly influenza vaccinations because of their increased risk of developing *Streptococcus pneumoniae* infections or the flu, respectively. The faltering immune system may also be less able to target and eliminate malignant cells, suggesting one reason why the elderly tend to be more prone to cancer.

WHAT DID YOU LEARN?

12 Why are elderly individuals more prone to illnesses?

24.6 Development of the Lymphatic System

✓ Learning Objective

11. Outline the lymphatic system formation in the developing embryo and fetus.

The first lymphoid structures (called **primary lymph sacs**) appear during the sixth week of development. Six primary lymph sacs form: Two **jugular lymph sacs** develop near each junction of the subclavian and future internal jugular veins; two **posterior lymph sacs** develop near each junction of the external and internal iliac veins; a **retroperitoneal** (ret′rō-per′i-t ō-nē′ăl) **lymph sac** forms in the digestive system mesentery; and a **cisterna chyli** forms dorsal to the aorta (**figure 24.12*a***).

Paired lymphatic vessels connect the lymph sacs by the ninth week (figure 24.12*b*). Eventually, portions of the paired lymphatic vessels are obliterated, and a single thoracic duct forms that travels from the cisterna chyli, along the bodies of the vertebrae, and empties into the union of the left subclavian and left internal jugular veins. The right lymphatic duct is formed from some other lymphatic vessels. Additional smaller lymphatic vessels form during and after the embryonic period.

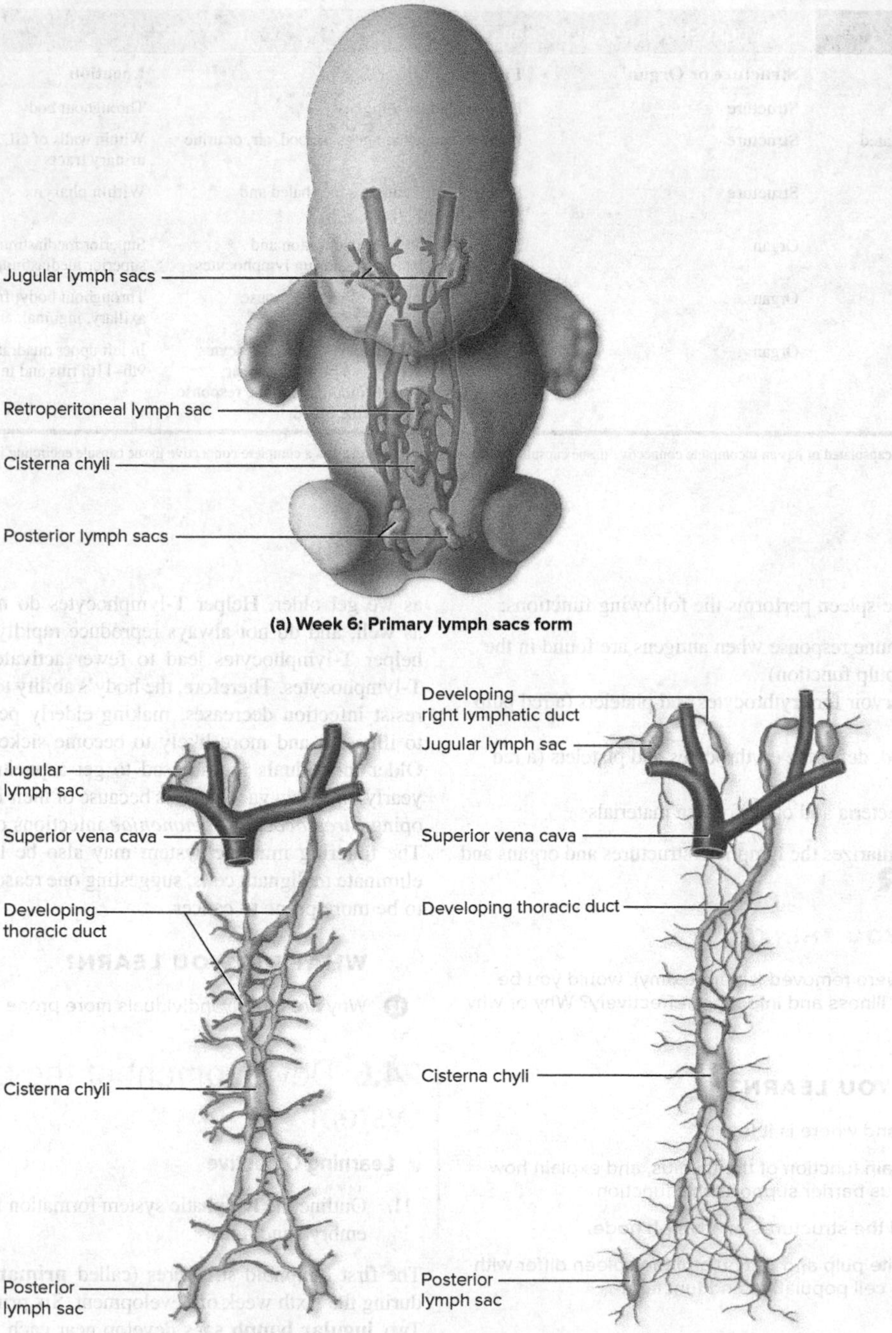
Jugular lymph sacs
Retroperitoneal lymph sac
Cisterna chyli
Posterior lymph sacs
(a) Week 6: Primary lymph sacs form
Jugular lymph sac
Superior vena cava
Developing thoracic duct
Cisterna chyli
Posterior lymph sac
(b) Week 9: Lymphatic vessels connect to the lymph sacs
Developing right lymphatic duct
Jugular lymph sac
Superior vena cava
Developing thoracic duct
Cisterna chyli
Posterior lymph sac
(c) Fetal period: Right lymphatic and thoracic ducts form; lymph sacs will form lymph nodes

Figure 24.12

Development of the Lymphatic System. (*a*) Lymph sacs appear by week 6 of development. (*b*) Paired lymphatic vessels develop by week 9. (*c*) During the fetal period, some of the lymphatic vessels enlarge and form the right lymphatic and thoracic ducts. Lymph sacs eventually develop into lymph nodes.

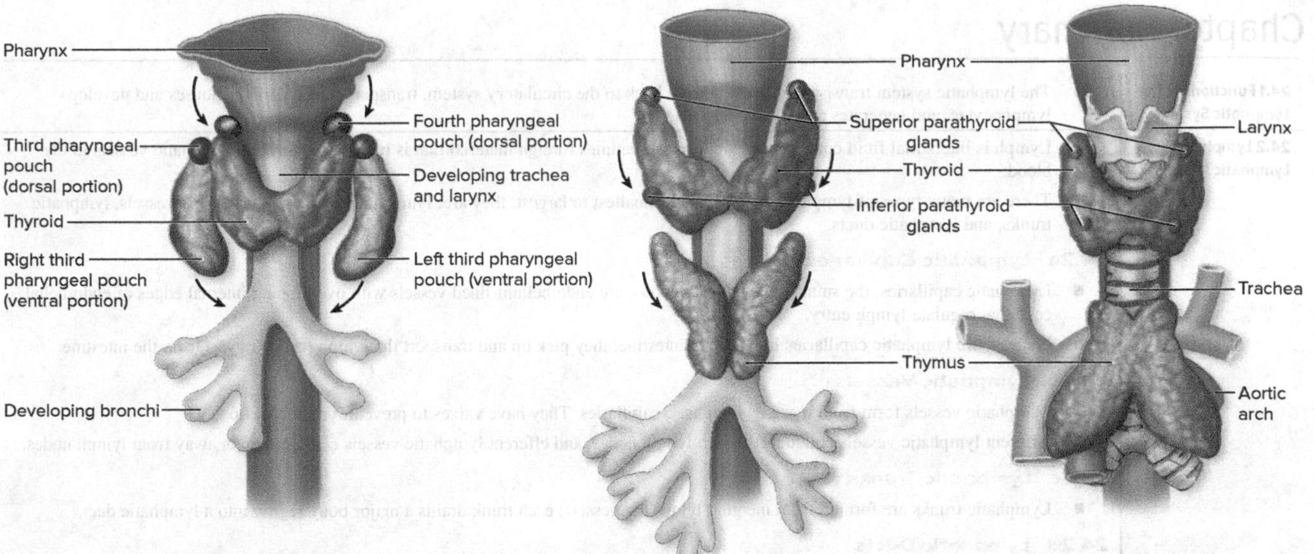
Pharynx
Third pharyngeal pouch (dorsal portion)
Thyroid
Right third pharyngeal pouch (ventral portion)
Developing bronchi
Fourth pharyngeal pouch (dorsal portion)
Developing trachea and larynx
Left third pharyngeal pouch (ventral portion)
Pharynx
Superior parathyroid glands
Thyroid
Inferior parathyroid glands
Thymus
Larynx
Trachea
Aortic arch

(a) Week 5: Ventral portions of left and right third pharyngeal pouches migrate inferiorly **(b) Week 7: Left and right third pharyngeal pouches fuse to form the bilobed thymus** **(c) Fetal period: Thymus is positioned in mediastinum**

Figure 24.13

Development of the Thymus. The thymus originates from the ventral portions of the third pharyngeal pouches. (*a*) These pouches branch off the pharynx and migrate inferiorly beginning in the fifth week. (*b*) The left and right pouches fuse in the future mediastinum during the seventh week, forming the bilobed thymus. (*c*) By the fetal period, the thymus gland is large and is positioned within the mediastinum.

During the fetal period, connective tissue subdivides the lymph sacs (except the cisterna chyli) into rounded structures that later become the lymph nodes (figure 24.12*c*). Lymphocytes within the developing lymph sacs eventually form the cortex and medulla of each lymph node.

The thymus forms from the *ventral* (anterior) portions of the left and right third pharyngeal pouches (**figure 24.13**). These pouches are the internal, endodermal portions of the third pharyngeal arches. During weeks 4–7 of development, the left and right third pouches migrate inferiorly from the pharynx to their final position posterior to the sternum. The two ventral portions fuse to form a single thymus gland. Lymphocytes begin infiltrating the gland shortly after its formation. By the fetal period, the thymus gland is large and located within the mediastinum, superior to the heart and anterior to the aortic arch and trachea.

The spleen is formed from mesoderm that condenses in the future greater omentum during the fifth week of development. Initially, the spleen functions solely as a blood cell–producing organ. During the second trimester, T-lymphocytes and B-lymphocytes enter the organ, helping form the characteristic red pulp and white pulp.

The palatine tonsils form from endoderm from the left and right second pharyngeal pouches and the second pharyngeal arch mesoderm. During months 3–5 of development, lymphoid cells enter the tonsils. Other tonsils (e.g., pharyngeal tonsil, lingual tonsils) and lymphoid structures such as MALT form from aggregations of lymphoid cells and connective tissue.

Clinical Terms

autoimmune disease Disease in which the body's immune system mistakenly attacks its own healthy tissues. Examples include systemic lupus erythematosus (SLE), multiple sclerosis (MS), rheumatoid arthritis, type 1 diabetes mellitus, and scleroderma.

lymphadenectomy (lim-fad′ĕ-nek′tŏ-mē; = gland) Removal or excision of lymph nodes.

lymphangitis (= vessel) Inflammation of the lymphatic vessels.

splenomegaly (splē′nō-meg′ă-lē; *mega* = large) Enlarged spleen, often seen in association with infection (e.g., mononucleosis).

Chapter Summary

24.1 Functions of the Lymphatic System	■ The lymphatic system transports interstitial fluid back to the circulatory system, transports dietary lipids, houses and develops lymphocytes, and generates an immune response.
24.2 Lymph and Lymphatic Vessels	■ Lymph is interstitial fluid containing solutes and sometimes foreign material that is transported through lymphatic vessels to the blood. ■ There are many types of lymphatic vessels. From smallest to largest, they are: lymphatic capillaries, lymphatic vessels, lymphatic trunks, and lymphatic ducts. **24.2a Lymphatic Capillaries** ■ Lymphatic capillaries, the smallest lymphatic vessels, are endothelium-lined vessels with overlapping internal edges of endothelial cells that regulate lymph entry. ■ Lacteals are lymphatic capillaries in the small intestine; they pick up and transport the lymph (called chyle) from the intestine. **24.2b Lymphatic Vessels** ■ Lymphatic vessels form from merging lymphatic capillaries. They have valves to prevent lymph backflow. ■ Afferent lymphatic vessels conduct lymph to lymph nodes, and efferent lymphatic vessels conduct lymph away from lymph nodes. **24.2c Lymphatic Trunks** ■ Lymphatic trunks are formed from merging lymphatic vessels; each trunk drains a major body region into a lymphatic duct. **24.2d Lymphatic Ducts** ■ The right lymphatic duct drains the right side of the head and neck, the right upper limb, and the right side of the thorax. It drains into the junction of the right subclavian vein and the right internal jugular vein. ■ The thoracic duct drains lymph from the left side of the head and neck, the left upper limb, the left thorax, and all body regions inferior to the diaphragm. It drains into the junction of the left subclavian vein and left internal jugular vein.
24.3 Lymphoid Cells	■ Lymphoid cells include macrophages that phagocytize foreign substances, epithelial cells that secrete thymic hormones, dendritic cells that filter antigens from lymph, and lymphocytes that perform specific functions in the immune response. **24.3a Types and Functions of Lymphocytes** ■ Each helper T-lymphocyte responds to one type of antigen only, and secretes cytokines, which are chemical signals that activate other lymphoid cells. ■ Cytotoxic T-lymphocytes kill infected cells following direct contact with them. ■ Memory T-lymphocytes arise from T-lymphocytes that have encountered an antigen, and cause a faster immune response than the first time. ■ Regulatory T-lymphocytes often "turn off" the immune response once it has been activated. ■ Activated B-lymphocytes respond to one particular antigen; they proliferate and differentiate into either plasma cells or memory B-lymphocytes. ■ Plasma cells produce and secrete large numbers of antibodies. ■ Memory B-lymphocytes mount an even faster and more powerful immune response upon reexposure to an antigen. ■ NK cells respond to multiple antigens; they destroy infected cells and some cancerous cells. **24.3b Lymphopoiesis** ■ Some hematopoietic stem cells remain in the red bone marrow and mature into B-lymphocytes and NK cells. Other stem cells exit the red bone marrow and migrate to the thymus for subsequent maturation into T-lymphocytes.
24.4 Lymphoid Structures	■ Lymphoid structures include lymphoid nodules and various lymphoid organs. **24.4a Lymphoid Nodules** ■ Lymphoid nodules are ovoid clusters of lymphoid cells and extracellular connective tissue matrix that are not contained within a connective tissue capsule. ■ MALT (mucosa-associated lymphoid tissue) is composed of lymphoid nodules housed in the walls of the GI, respiratory, genital, and urinary tracts. ■ Tonsils are large clusters of partially encapsulated lymphoid cells and extracellular connective matrix. **24.4b Lymphoid Organs** ■ The lymphoid organs are composed of lymphoid structures completely surrounded by a connective tissue capsule. ■ The thymus is where T-lymphocytes mature and differentiate under stimulation by thymic hormones. ■ Lymph nodes are small structures that filter lymph. ■ The spleen is partitioned into white pulp (consists of clusters of lymphoid cells that generate an immune response when exposed to antigens in the blood) and red pulp (consists of splenic cords that store blood and sinusoids containing macrophages that phagocytize foreign debris, old erythrocytes, and platelets).
24.5 Aging and the Lymphatic System	■ The lymphatic system's ability to provide immunity and fight disease decreases as we get older.

24.6 Development of the Lymphatic System	■ The primary lymph sacs eventually give rise to lymph nodes. ■ The thymus forms from the ventral portions of the left and right third pharyngeal pouches. ■ The spleen forms from mesodermal condensations during week 5 of development. ■ The palatine tonsils are derived from the second pharyngeal pouches.

Challenge Yourself

Actively write or type your answers in a separate document to reinforce your learning, before checking your answers.

Multiple Choice

Select the best answer from the four choices provided.

1. Lymph from which of the following body regions drains into the thoracic duct?
   a. right side of the thorax
   b. right upper limb
   c. right lower limb
   d. right side of the head
2. Which type of lymphoid cell is responsible for producing antibodies?
   a. macrophage
   b. helper T-lymphocyte
   c. plasma cell
   d. NK cell
3. Which statement is false about lymphoid nodules?
   a. The center has proliferating B-lymphocytes and some macrophages.
   b. T-lymphocytes are located along the periphery.
   c. Lymphoid nodules are completely surrounded by a connective tissue capsule.
   d. Lymphoid nodules in the ileum of the small intestine are called Peyer patches.
4. What is the function of the blood-thymus barrier?
   a. It protects maturing T-lymphocytes from antigens in the blood.
   b. It filters the blood and starts an immune response when necessary.
   c. It subdivides the thymus into a cortex and a medulla.
   d. It forms thymic corpuscles.
5. Which type of lymphatic vessel consists solely of an endothelium and has one-way flaps that allow interstitial fluid to enter?
   a. lymphatic vessel
   b. lymphatic capillary
   c. lymphatic duct
   d. lymphatic trunk
6. Which statement is true about lymph nodes?
   a. Cancerous lymph nodes are swollen and tender to the touch.
   b. The medulla of a lymph node contains lymphatic nodules.
   c. Lymph enters the lymph node through afferent lymphatic vessels.
   d. Lymphatic sinuses are located in the cortex of a lymph node only.
7. In an early *Streptococcus* infection of the throat, all of the following structures may swell *except* which structure?
   a. pharyngeal tonsil
   b. spleen
   c. cervical lymph node
   d. palatine tonsil
8. Which of the following is a function of the white pulp of the spleen?
   a. phagocytizes erythrocytes
   b. serves as a blood cell reservoir
   c. elicits an immune response if antigens are detected in the blood
   d. serves as a site for hematopoiesis during fetal life
9. The primary lymph sacs form which structures?
   a. thoracic duct
   b. right lymphatic duct
   c. spleen
   d. lymph nodes
10. What change occurs to the adult lymphatic system as we get older?
    a. The body produces and transports less lymph.
    b. Greater numbers of B-lymphocytes are produced.
    c. Helper T-lymphocytes do not respond as well to antigens.
    d. The lymph nodes enlarge.

Content Review

1. List the functions of the lymphatic system.
2. Describe what lymph is, and draw a flowchart that illustrates what structures the lymph travels through to return to the circulatory system.
3. Which body regions have their lymph drained to the thoracic duct?
4. Compare and contrast the types of lymphoid cells with respect to their appearance, function, and place of maturation.
5. Describe how the lymphoid cells elicit an immune response.
6. Describe the basic composition of a lymphoid nodule, and give examples in the body where lymphoid nodules may be found.
7. Describe how the thymus's anatomy and function change from infancy on.
8. Describe the basic anatomy of a lymph node, how lymph enters and leaves the node, and the functions of this organ.
9. Compare and contrast the red and white pulp of the spleen with respect to the anatomy and functions of each.
10. Describe how lymphatic vessels and lymph nodes develop.

Developing Critical Reasoning

1. Arianna was diagnosed with mononucleosis, an infectious disease that targets B-lymphocytes. When she went to the doctor, he palpated her left side, just below the rib cage. The doctor told Arianna she was checking to see if a certain organ was enlarged, a complication that can occur with mononucleosis. What lymphoid organ was the doctor checking, and why would it become enlarged? Include some explanation of the anatomy and histology of this organ in your answer.
2. Why is HIV infection so devastating to the body? In your answer, explain what cells are infected and why the body cannot produce more mature, noninfected cells. Also explain how AIDS affects the way the body fights infection, and give some examples of ailments that are common among AIDS patients.
3. Jordan has an enlarged lymph node along the side of his neck, and he is worried that the structure may be a lymphoma. What are some criteria to help distinguish between infected lymph nodes and malignant lymph nodes? If the lymph node were cancerous, how would a physician determine if the cancer has spread to other parts of the body?

Answers to “What Do You Think?”

1. If you need a booster shot about once every 10 years, that indicates a maximum 10-year life span of tetanus-detecting memory B-lymphocytes. Many of these cells may die off before the 10 years is up, which is why a physician gives you a tetanus booster earlier if you have been exposed to tetanus—for example, by piercing your foot on a rusty nail that could carry tetanus bacteria.
2. If the tonsils are removed, other lymphoid tissue and lymphoid organs in the head and neck, such as lymph nodes, can mount an immune response to antigens in the throat. Also, the lymphocytes circulating in the blood can detect antigens in the throat.
3. Most individuals who have their spleens removed can fight off illness and infections effectively, because the other lymphoid tissues and organs take over the immune functions previously handled by the spleen. However, the risk for severe bacterial infection is greater, because there is no spleen to filter bacteria from the blood. For this reason, individuals who have undergone splenectomies may need to be vaccinated against certain bacteria and undergo long-term (years or even lifelong) antibiotic therapy.

Respiratory System 25

Outline

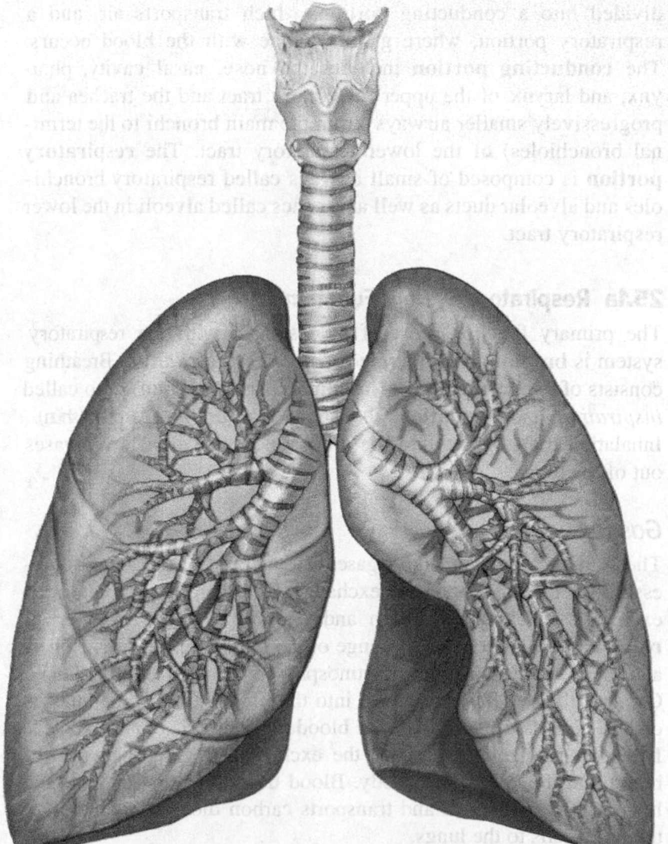

Anatomy & Physiology Revealed 4.0

MODULE 11: RESPIRATORY SYSTEM

The **respiratory** (res′pi-r ă-tōr′ē; *respiro* = to breathe) **system** provides the means for gas exchange required by living cells. Oxygen must be supplied without interruption, and carbon dioxide, a waste product generated by the cells, must be continuously expelled. The respiratory and cardiovascular systems are inseparable partners. While the respiratory system exchanges gases between the atmosphere and the blood, the cardiovascular system transports those gases between the lungs and the body cells. This chapter examines the cells, tissues, and organs involved in the complex and vital process of respiration.

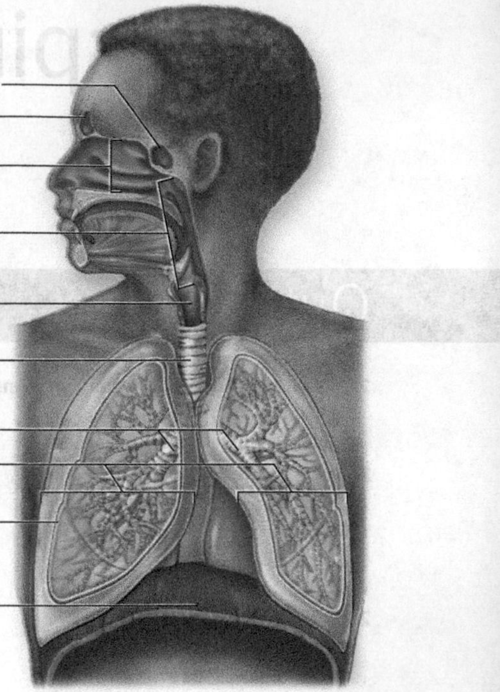

Figure 25.1

Gross Anatomy of the Respiratory System. The major components of the respiratory system are organized into the upper and lower respiratory tracts. The smaller air passageways of the lungs, which make up part of the lower respiratory tract, are not shown in this diagram.

25.1 General Organization and Functions of the Respiratory System

✓ Learning Objectives

1. Compare and contrast the general functions and structures of the conducting and respiratory portions of the respiratory system.
2. Explain the functions of the respiratory system.

Anatomically, the respiratory system consists of an upper respiratory tract (nose, nasal cavity, pharynx, and larynx) and a lower respiratory tract (trachea, bronchi, and progressively smaller air passageways in the lungs) (**figure 25.1**). Functionally, it can be divided into a conducting portion, which transports air, and a respiratory portion, where gas exchange with the blood occurs. The **conducting portion** includes the nose, nasal cavity, pharynx, and larynx of the upper respiratory tract and the trachea and progressively smaller airways (from the main bronchi to the terminal bronchioles) of the lower respiratory tract. The **respiratory portion** is composed of small airways called respiratory bronchioles and alveolar ducts as well as air sacs called alveoli in the lower respiratory tract.

25.1a Respiratory System Functions

The primary function most of us associate with the respiratory system is **breathing,** also termed *pulmonary ventilation.* Breathing consists of two cyclic phases: **inhalation** (in-hă-lā′shŭn), also called *inspiration,* and **exhalation,** also called *expiration* (eks-pi-rā′shŭn). Inhalation draws gases into the lungs, and exhalation forces gases out of the lungs.

Gas Exchange

The continuous movement of gases into and out of the lungs is necessary for the process of gas exchange. There are two types of gas exchange: external respiration and internal respiration. **External respiration** involves the exchange of gases between the atmosphere and the blood. Oxygen in the atmosphere is inhaled into the lungs. Oxygen diffuses from the lungs into the blood at the same time as carbon dioxide diffuses from the blood into the lungs to be exhaled. **Internal respiration** involves the exchange of gases between the blood and the cells of the body. Blood transports oxygen from the lungs to the body cells and transports carbon dioxide produced by the body cells to the lungs.

In addition to gas exchange, the respiratory system also functions in gas conditioning, sound production, olfaction, and defense.

Gas Conditioning

As inhaled gases pass through conducting airways, the gases are **conditioned** (i.e., warmed, humidified, and cleansed) prior to reaching the gas exchange surfaces of the lungs. Specifically, the gases are warmed to body temperature by being in close contact with the nasal blood vessels transporting warm blood. The gases are humidified (moistened), and cleansed of particulate matter through contact with the respiratory epithelium and its sticky mucous covering. Conditioning is facilitated by the twisted pathways through the nasal cavity and paranasal sinuses, which cause the inhaled air to become very turbulent during inhalation. This swirling of inhaled gases means the air remains in the nasal cavity and paranasal sinuses for a relatively longer time, providing greater opportunity for conditioning.

Sound Production

As air is forced out of the lungs and moves through the larynx, sound may be produced, such as speech or singing. Other anatomic structures aid sound production, including the nasal cavity, paranasal sinuses, teeth, lips, and tongue.

Olfaction

The superior region of the nasal cavity is covered with olfactory epithelium, which contains receptors for the sense of smell (see section 19.4). These receptors are stimulated when airborne molecules are inhaled and dissolved in the mucus covering this olfactory epithelium.

Defense

Finally, both the structure of the respiratory system and some of the cells within the respiratory epithelium protect the body against infection by airborne molecules. The entrance to the respiratory system (the nose) is inferiorly directed, is lined with coarse hairs, and has twisted passageways to prevent large particles, microorganisms, and insects from entering. Additionally, several structures in the respiratory system secrete mucus onto the epithelium. This mucus serves to trap inhaled dust, dirt particles, microorganisms, and pollen. The structures that secrete mucus include the goblet cells scattered throughout the pseudostratified ciliated columnar epithelium, and mucous glands housed in the lamina propria deep to the epithelium. The mucous glands also secrete **lysozyme,** an enzyme that helps defend against inhaled bacteria. If we are exposed to airborne allergens, large quantities of small particulate material, irritating gases, or pathogens, the rate of mucus production increases.

WHAT DID YOU LEARN?

1. Explain the functions carried out by the respiratory system in addition to gas exchange.
2. What components make up the conducting portion of the respiratory system? Which components make up the respiratory portion of the respiratory system?

Clinical View 25.1

Cystic Fibrosis

Cystic fibrosis (sis′tik fī-brō′sis) is the most common serious genetic disease in Caucasians, occurring with a frequency of approximately 1 in 3500 births in the United States. The condition is rare among people of Asian and African descent. The name cystic fibrosis refers to the characteristic scarring and cyst formation within the pancreas. Clinical View 2.1: "Cystic Fibrosis and Chloride Channels" in section 2.3c previously described how the disease's symptoms in multiple body systems all result from defective chloride channels. This lack of chloride secretion causes sodium and water to move from the mucus back into the secretory cell itself, thus dehydrating the mucus covering the epithelial surface. The mucus becomes thick and sticky, obstructing the airways of the lungs and the ducts of the pancreas and salivary glands. Pulmonary infections, secondary to airway obstruction, are common and can be life-threatening. In the case of the pancreas, the obstructed ducts lead to a backup of digestive enzymes that eventually destroy the pancreas itself.

Interestingly, the normal chloride transport protein works in the opposite direction in the sweat glands of the skin. Chloride and sodium are not reabsorbed from the sweat, and so they become concentrated on the skin in individuals with cystic fibrosis. Mothers of babies with cystic fibrosis often find that the baby tastes "salty" when kissed. Thus, clinically elevated chloride levels in sweat are one method of diagnosing the disease.

The primary treatment for cystic fibrosis involves agents that break up the thick mucus in the lungs, and antibiotics for the chronic pulmonary infections. Absorption problems caused by pancreatic damage are treated with orally administered digestive enzymes, vitamins, and caloric supplements. Because the gene responsible for cystic fibrosis has been identified, scientists have been investigating ways to insert copies of the healthy gene into the epithelial cells of the respiratory tracts of cystic fibrosis patients.

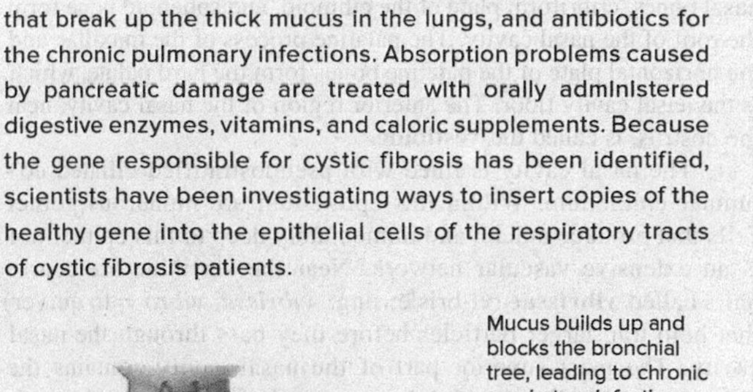
Mucus builds up and blocks the bronchial tree, leading to chronic respiratory infections.
Mucus buildup blocks the pancreatic ducts and prevents digestive enzymes from entering the small intestine.

Cystic fibrosis results in thickened mucus that obstructs both the respiratory passageways and ducts of glands such as the pancreatic ducts.

25.2 Upper Respiratory Tract

✓ Learning Objectives

3. Identify and describe the structure and function of the nose, nasal cavity, and paranasal sinuses.
4. Compare and contrast the three regions of the pharynx.
5. Describe the composition and functions of the larynx.
6. Explain how the larynx is involved in adjusting the pitch and loudness of sound.

The **upper respiratory tract** is composed of the nose and nasal cavity, paranasal sinuses, pharynx, and associated structures. These structures are all part of the conducting portion of the respiratory system. When an individual has an upper respiratory tract infection, some or all of these structures are involved.

25.2a Nose and Nasal Cavity

The **nose** is the main conducting airway for inhaled air (**figure 25.2**). The nose is supported superiorly by paired **nasal bones** that form the bridge of the nose (see section 7.1a). Anteroinferiorly from the bridge is the fleshy, cartilaginous **dorsum nasi.** The dorsum nasi contains one pair of **lateral cartilages** and two pairs of **alar cartilages.** Paired **nostrils,** or *nares* (nā′res; sing., nā′ris), open on the inferior surface of the nose.

Within the nose is the **nasal cavity.** The nasal cavity is continuous posteriorly with the nasopharynx via paired openings called **choanae** (kō′an-ē; sing., *choana*), or *internal nares.* The frontal bone, nasal bones, cribriform plate of the ethmoid, and sphenoid bone form the roof of the nasal cavity. The palatine process of the maxillae and the horizontal plate of the palatine bones form the hard palate, which is the nasal cavity floor. The anterior region of the nasal cavity, near the nostrils, is called the **vestibule.**

The nasal cavity is lined with pseudostratified ciliated columnar epithelium. Within this epithelium are numerous goblet cells that produce mucin, and immediately deep to this epithelium is an extensive vascular network. Near the vestibule are coarse hairs called **vibrissae** (vī-bris′ē; sing., *vibrissa; vibro* = to quiver) that help trap larger particles before they pass through the nasal cavity. The most superior part of the nasal cavity contains the **olfactory epithelium,** which is composed of both a pseudostratified ciliated columnar epithelium and olfactory receptor cells (see section 19.4).

The **nasal septum** divides the nasal cavity into left and right portions. It is formed anteriorly by **septal nasal cartilage.** A thin, bony sheet formed by the perpendicular plate of the ethmoid bone (superiorly) and the vomer bone (inferiorly) forms the posterior part of the nasal septum (see section 7.1e).

Along the lateral walls of the nasal cavity are three paired, bony projections: the **superior, middle,** and **inferior nasal conchae** (kon′kē; sing., *concha;* a shell). These conchae subdivide the nasal cavity into separate air passages, each called a **nasal meatus** (mē-ā′tŭs). The superior, middle, and inferior meatuses are located immediately inferior to their corresponding nasal conchae. As inhaled air passes over constricted, narrow grooves in each meatus, the inhaled air becomes turbulent. Increased turbulence ensures that the air remains in the nasal cavity for a longer time, so that the air becomes warmed and humidified. Because the conchae help produce this turbulence, they are sometimes called the "turbinate" bones.

Besides functioning in filtration, conditioning, and olfaction, the nasal cavity is a resonating chamber that contributes to sound production, discussed in section 25.3a.

WHAT DO YOU THINK?

1 What does it mean if someone has a "deviated septum"? What kinds of problems can arise with a deviated septum?

25.2b Paranasal Sinuses

Four bones of the skull contain paired air spaces called the **paranasal** (par- ă-nā′săl; *para* = alongside) **sinuses,** which together decrease skull bone weight (see section 7.1f). These spaces are named for the bones in which they are housed; thus, from a superior to inferior direction, they are the **frontal, ethmoidal, sphenoidal,** and **maxillary sinuses** (**figure 25.3**). All sinuses communicate with the nasal cavity by ducts and are lined with the same pseudostratified ciliated columnar epithelium as the nasal cavity. Like the nasal cavity, the paranasal sinuses also serve to warm and humidify inhaled air, and they also provide a resonance (deep, tonal quality) to the voice. APR

Learning Strategy 25.1

The nasal cavity and the paranasal sinuses are the primary structures that warm and humidify the air we inhale. To illustrate this, breathe through your mouth instead of your nose on a cold day. Your throat and trachea may feel "raw," and you may cough because the air entering the lungs from your mouth is not being properly conditioned.

25.2c Pharynx

The common space used by both the respiratory and digestive systems is the **pharynx** (far′ingks), commonly called the throat (see figure 25.2). The pharynx is funnel-shaped, meaning that it is slightly wider superiorly and narrower inferiorly. The pharynx originates posterior to the nasal and oral cavities and extends inferiorly to the level of the bifurcation of the larynx and esophagus. For most of its length, the pharynx is the common pathway for both inhaled and exhaled air (the respiratory system) and ingested food (the digestive system [see section 26.3]).

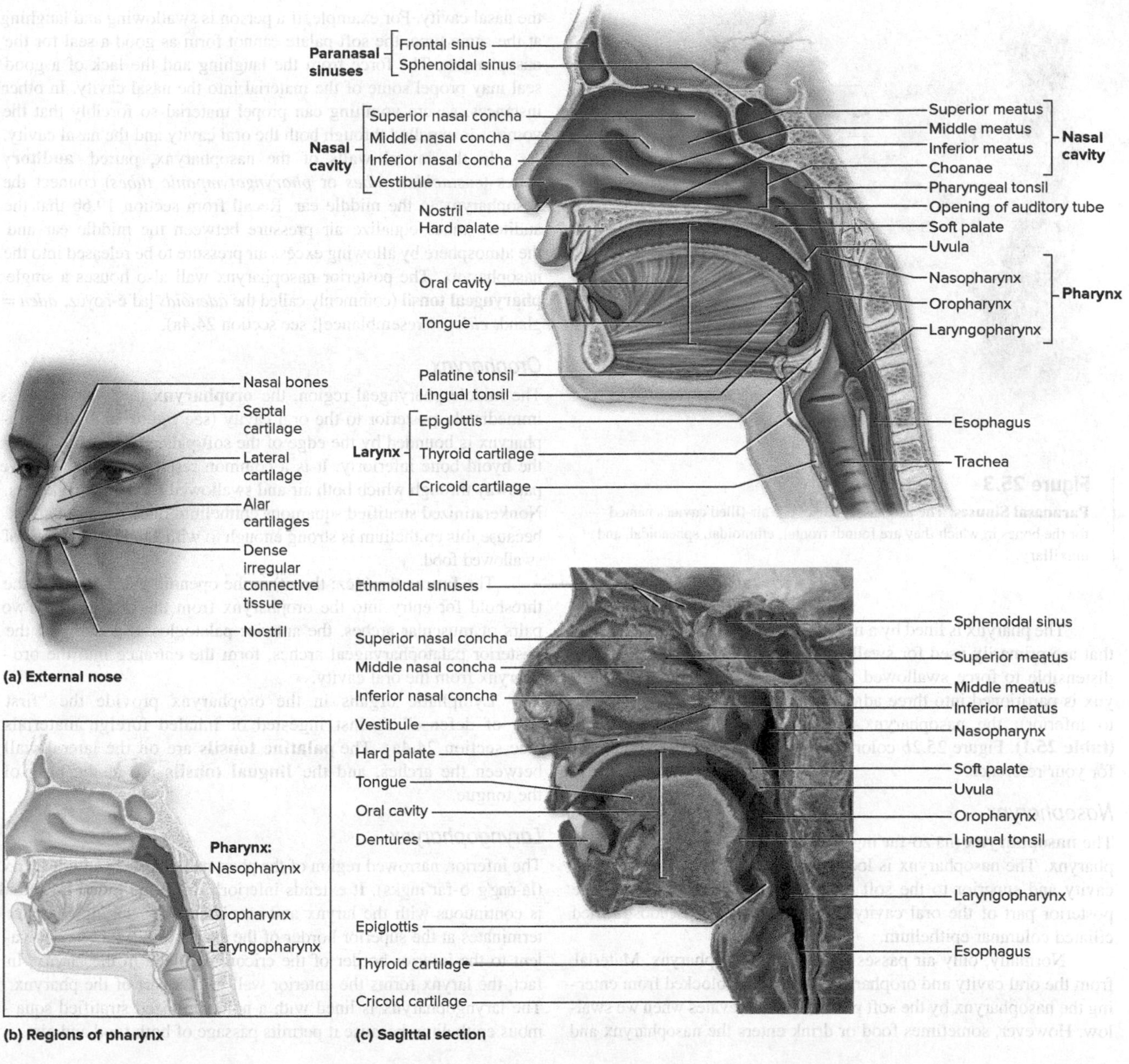
Paranasal sinuses
Frontal sinus
Sphenoidal sinus
Nasal cavity
Superior nasal concha
Middle nasal concha
Inferior nasal concha
Vestibule
Nostril
Hard palate
Oral cavity
Tongue
Palatine tonsil
Lingual tonsil
Larynx
Epiglottis
Thyroid cartilage
Cricoid cartilage
Superior meatus
Middle meatus
Inferior meatus
Choanae
Nasal cavity
Pharyngeal tonsil
Opening of auditory tube
Soft palate
Uvula
Nasopharynx
Oropharynx
Laryngopharynx
Pharynx
Esophagus
Trachea
Nasal bones
Septal cartilage
Lateral cartilage
Alar cartilages
Dense irregular connective tissue
Nostril
(a) External nose
Pharynx:
Nasopharynx
Oropharynx
Laryngopharynx
(b) Regions of pharynx
Ethmoidal sinuses
Superior nasal concha
Middle nasal concha
Inferior nasal concha
Vestibule
Hard palate
Tongue
Oral cavity
Dentures
Epiglottis
Thyroid cartilage
Cricoid cartilage
(c) Sagittal section
Sphenoidal sinus
Superior meatus
Middle meatus
Inferior meatus
Nasopharynx
Soft palate
Uvula
Oropharynx
Lingual tonsil
Laryngopharynx
Esophagus

Figure 25.2

Anatomy of the Upper Respiratory Tract. The upper respiratory tract includes the nose, nasal cavity, paranasal sinuses, pharynx , and larynx . (*a*) Supporting structures of the nose. (*b*) The three specific regions of the pharynx (nasopharynx, oropharynx, and laryngopharynx) are highlighted in a diagrammatic sagittal section. (*c*) A diagrammatic sagittal section and cadaver photo of the head show the upper respiratory tract structures and their relationship to the larynx, trachea and esophagus. APR

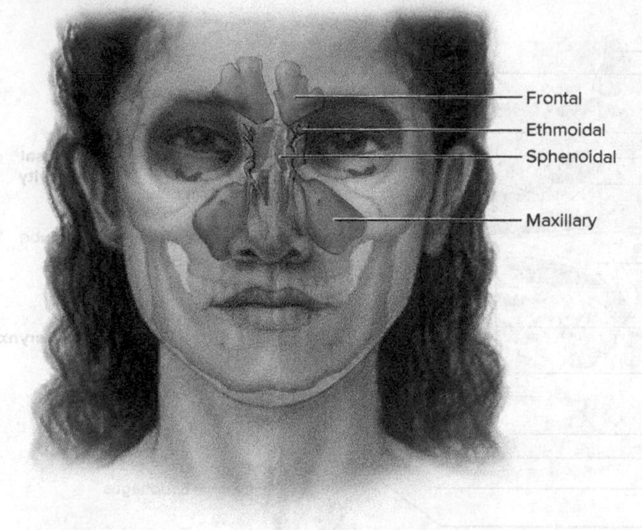

Figure 25.3

Paranasal Sinuses. The paranasal sinuses are air-filled cavities named for the bones in which they are found: frontal, ethmoidal, sphenoidal, and maxillary.

The pharynx is lined by a mucosa and contains skeletal muscles that are primarily used for swallowing. Its flexible lateral walls are distensible to force swallowed food into the esophagus. The pharynx is partitioned into three adjoining regions (listed from superior to inferior): the nasopharynx, oropharynx, and laryngopharynx (**table 25.1**). Figure 25.2*b* color-codes these regions of the pharynx for your reference.

Nasopharynx

The **nasopharynx** (nā′zō-far′ingks) is the superiormost region of the pharynx. The nasopharynx is located directly posterior to the nasal cavity and superior to the soft palate, which separates it from the posterior part of the oral cavity. It is lined with a pseudostratified ciliated columnar epithelium.

Normally, only air passes through the nasopharynx. Material from the oral cavity and oropharynx is typically blocked from entering the nasopharynx by the soft palate, which elevates when we swallow. However, sometimes food or drink enters the nasopharynx and the nasal cavity. For example, if a person is swallowing and laughing at the same time, the soft palate cannot form as good a seal for the nasopharynx. The force from the laughing and the lack of a good seal may propel some of the material into the nasal cavity. In other instances, severe vomiting can propel material so forcibly that the vomitus is expelled through both the oral cavity and the nasal cavity.

In the lateral walls of the nasopharynx, paired **auditory tubes** (*eustachian tubes* or *pharyngotympanic tubes*) connect the nasopharynx to the middle ear. Recall from section 19.6b that the auditory tubes equalize air pressure between the middle ear and the atmosphere by allowing excess air pressure to be released into the nasopharynx. The posterior nasopharynx wall also houses a single **pharyngeal tonsil** (commonly called the *adenoids* [ad′ĕ-noydz; *aden* = gland, *eidos* = resemblance]; see section 24.4a).

Oropharynx

The middle pharyngeal region, the **oropharynx** (ōr′ō-far′ingks), is immediately posterior to the oral cavity (see figure 25.2). The oropharynx is bounded by the edge of the soft palate superiorly and by the hyoid bone inferiorly. It is a common respiratory and digestive pathway through which both air and swallowed food and drink pass. Nonkeratinized stratified squamous epithelium lines the oropharynx because this epithelium is strong enough to withstand the abrasion of swallowed food.

The **fauces** (faw′s ēz; throat) is the opening that represents the threshold for entry into the oropharynx from the oral cavity. Two pairs of muscular arches, the anterior palatoglossal arches and the posterior palatopharyngeal arches, form the entrance into the oropharynx from the oral cavity.

Lymphatic organs in the oropharynx provide the "first line of defense" against ingested or inhaled foreign materials (see section 24.4a). The **palatine tonsils** are on the lateral wall between the arches, and the **lingual tonsils** are at the base of the tongue.

Laryngopharynx

The inferior, narrowed region of the pharynx is the **laryngopharynx** (lă-ring′g ō-far′ingks). It extends inferiorly from the hyoid bone and is continuous with the larynx and esophagus. The laryngopharynx terminates at the superior border of the esophagus, which is equivalent to the inferior border of the cricoid cartilage in the larynx. In fact, the larynx forms the anterior wall of this part of the pharynx. The laryngopharynx is lined with a nonkeratinized stratified squamous epithelium because it permits passage of both food and air.

Table 25.1 Regions of the Pharynx

Pharyngeal Region	Function(s)	Epithelial Lining	Characteristics
Nasopharynx	Conducts air	Pseudostratified ciliated columnar epithelium	Posterior to nasal cavity Pharyngeal tonsil on posterior wall Auditory tubes open into nasopharynx to equalize air pressure in the middle ear
Oropharynx	Conducts air; serves as passageway for food and drink	Nonkeratinized stratified squamous epithelium	Posterior to oral cavity Paired palatine tonsils on lateral walls Lingual tonsils on base of tongue (and thus in anterior region of oropharynx) Extends between soft palate and level of hyoid bone
Laryngopharynx	Conducts air; serves as passageway for food and drink	Nonkeratinized stratified squamous epithelium	Extends from level of hyoid bone to beginning of esophagus (posterior to level of cricoid cartilage in larynx)

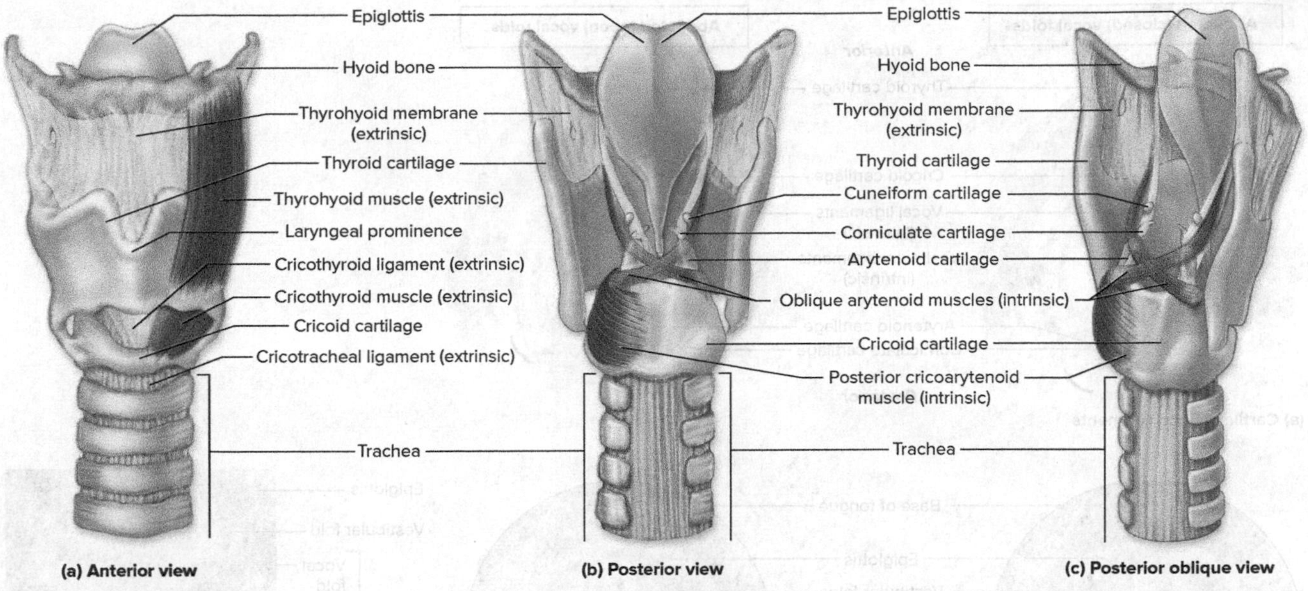
Epiglottis
Hyoid bone
Thyrohyoid membrane (extrinsic)
Thyroid cartilage
Thyrohyoid muscle (extrinsic)
Laryngeal prominence
Cricothyroid ligament (extrinsic)
Cricothyroid muscle (extrinsic)
Cricoid cartilage
Cricotracheal ligament (extrinsic)
Trachea
Cuneiform cartilage
Corniculate cartilage
Arytenoid cartilage
Oblique arytenoid muscles (intrinsic)
Posterior cricoarytenoid muscle (intrinsic)
(a) Anterior view
(b) Posterior view
(c) Posterior oblique view

Figure 25.4

Larynx. The larynx shown in (*a*) anterior view, (*b*) posterior view, and (*c*) posterior oblique view. It is composed of nine cartilages, various ligaments, and skeletal muscle. The nine cartilages, as well as extrinsic and intrinsic ligaments, form the flexible support of the larynx. Extrinsic muscles participate in the elevation of the larynx, and intrinsic muscles function in sound production. APR

25.2d Larynx

The **larynx** (lar′ingks), also called the voice box, is a somewhat cylindrical airway that averages about 4 centimeters (1.6 inches) in length (**figure 25.4**). It is located anteroinferiorly to the laryngopharynx and superiorly to the trachea.

Functions of the Larynx

The larynx has several major functions:

- **Serves as a passageway for air.** The larynx is normally open to allow the passage of air during pulmonary ventilation.
- **Prevents ingested materials from entering the trachea and bronchi.** During swallowing, the superior opening of the larynx is covered to prevent ingested materials from entering the trachea, the bronchi, and the rest of the airways in the lungs.
- **Produces sound for speech.** Ligaments within the larnyx, called vocal cords, vibrate as air is passed over them during an exhalation.
- **Assists in increasing pressure in the abdominal cavity.** The epiglottis (described later in this section) closes over the larynx so air cannot escape; simultaneously abdominal muscles contract to increase abdominal pressure. This action is referred to as the **Valsalva maneuver.** You can experience the increase in abdominal pressure associated with the Valsalva maneuver by holding your breath while forcefully contracting your abdominal muscles.
- **Participates in both a sneeze and cough reflex.** A sneeze and a cough both result in an explosive blast of exhaled air. This occurs when the abdominal muscles contract forcefully and the vocal cords are initially closed. They open abruptly as the pressure increases in the thoracic cavity. Sneezing is initiated by irritants in the nasal cavity and coughing by irritants in the trachea and bronchi.

Larynx Anatomy

The opening that connects the pharynx and larynx is called the **laryngeal inlet,** *laryngeal aperture,* or *laryngeal aditus.* The larynx is formed and supported by a framework of nine pieces of cartilage that are held in place by ligaments and muscles. The anatomic arrangement of the nine cartilages includes the single thyroid, cricoid, and epiglottis cartilages, and the paired arytenoid, corniculate, and cuneiform cartilages as shown in figure 25.4.

The **thyroid cartilage** is the largest laryngeal cartilage. Shaped like a shield, it forms the lateral and anterior walls of the larynx. The almost V-shaped anterior projection of the thyroid cartilage is called the **laryngeal** (lă-rin′j ē-ăl) **prominence** (commonly referred to as the *Adam's apple*). This protuberance is generally larger in males because (1) the laryngeal inlet is narrower in males (90 degrees) than in females (120 degrees), and (2) it enlarges at puberty due to testosterone-induced growth.

Inferior to the thyroid cartilage is the ring-shaped **cricoid** (krī′koyd; *kridos* = a ring) **cartilage.** The large, spoon- or leaf-shaped **epiglottis** (ep′i-glot′is; *epi* = on; *glottis* = mouth of windpipe) is anchored to the inner aspect of the thyroid cartilage and projects posterosuperiorly into the pharynx. It closes over the laryngeal inlet during swallowing. The three smaller, paired cartilages, the **arytenoid** (ar′i-t ē′noyd), **corniculate** (kōr′nik′y ū-lāt; *corniculatus* = horned), and **cuneiform** (kū′ne-i-f ōrm; *cuneus* = wedge) **cartilages** are located internally. All cartilages of the larynx, except the epiglottis, are composed of hyaline cartilage (see table 4.11a). The epiglottis, which opens and closes over

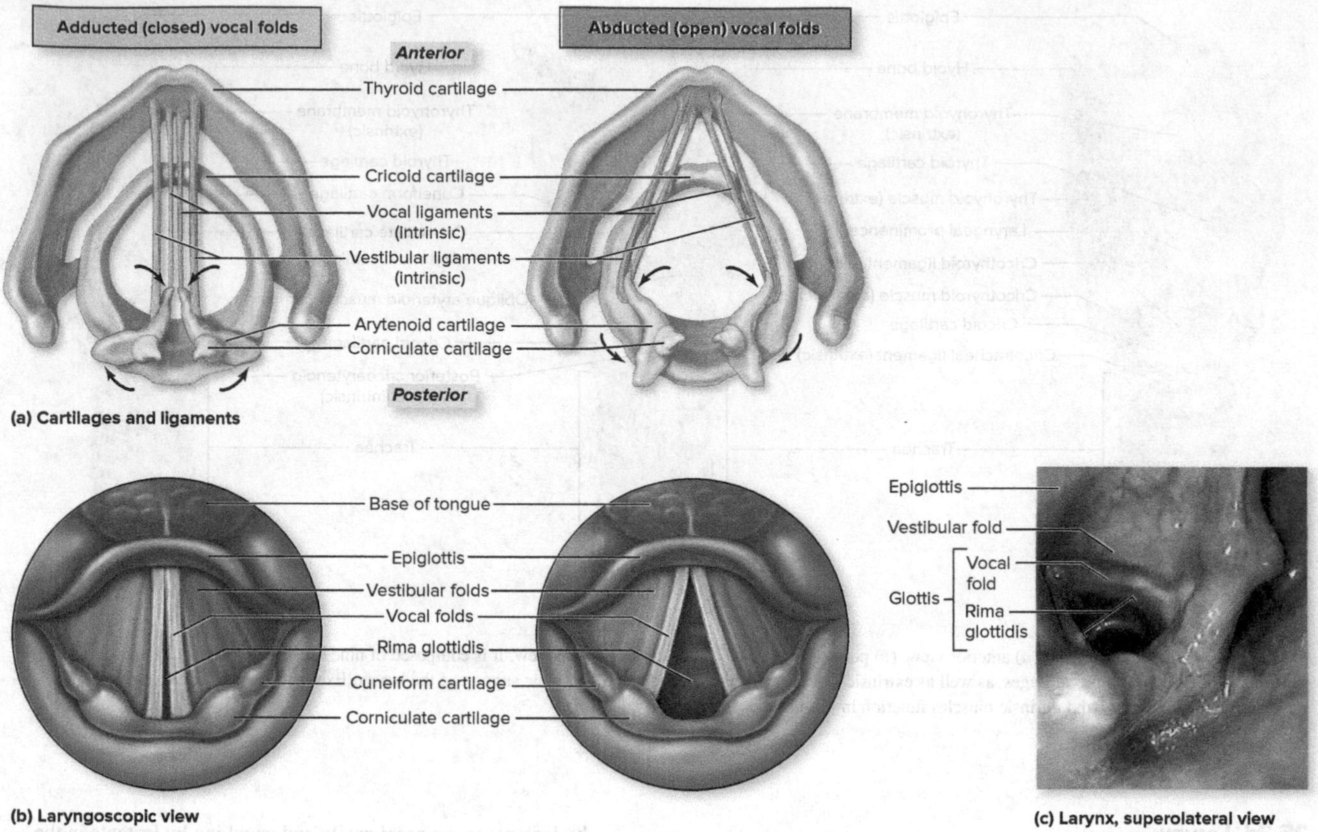

Figure 25.5

Vocal Folds. The vocal folds (true vocal cords) are elastic ligaments covered with a mucous membrane that extends between the thyroid and arytenoid cartilages. These folds surround the rima glottidis and are involved in sound production. Adducted (closed) and abducted (open) vocal folds are shown in (*a*) a superior view of the cartilages and ligaments only, and (*b*) a diagrammatic laryngoscopic view of the coverings around these cartilages and ligaments. (*c*) A photo of a superolateral laryngoscopic view, showing the vestibular folds, the vocal folds, and the rima glottidis opening into the trachea.

(c) ISM/CAMAL/Diomedia

the laryngeal inlet, is composed of the more flexible elastic cartilage (see table 4.11c).

Laryngeal ligaments are classified as either extrinsic ligaments or intrinsic ligaments. **Extrinsic ligaments** attach to the external surface of laryngeal cartilages of the larynx and extend to other structures that include the hyoid bone and trachea. These extrinsic ligaments include the **cricothyroid ligament** (extending from the cricoid cartilage to the thyroid cartilage) and the **thyrohyoid membrane** (extending from the thyroid cartilage to the hyoid bone).

The **intrinsic ligaments** are located within the larynx and include both vocal ligaments and vestibular ligaments (**figure 25.5**). The **vocal ligaments** are composed primarily of elastic connective tissue and extend anterior to posterior between the thyroid cartilage and the arytenoid cartilages. These ligaments are covered with a mucous membrane to form the **vocal folds.** Vocal folds also are called the *true vocal cords* because they produce sound when air passes between them. They are distinctive from the surrounding tissue because they are avascular and white in color. The opening between these folds is called the **rima glottidis** (rī′mă; slit; glo-tī′dis). Together the vocal folds and the rima glottidis form the **glottis.**

The **vestibular ligaments** form the other intrinsic ligaments. These extend between the thyroid cartilage to the arytenoid and corniculate cartilages. Together with the mucosa covering them, they form the **vestibular folds** located superior to the vocal folds. The opening between the vestibular folds is called the **rima vestibuli.** These folds also are called the *false vocal cords* because they have no function in sound production, but serve to protect the vocal folds.

Skeletal muscles compose part of the larynx wall and are classified as either extrinsic or intrinsic muscles. The **extrinsic muscles** of the larynx originate on either the hyoid bone or the sternum and insert on the thyroid cartilage. Extrinsic muscles normally stabilize the larynx and help move it during swallowing.

The **intrinsic muscles** of the larynx are located within the larynx and attach to both the arytenoid and corniculate cartilages. Contraction of the intrinsic muscles causes the arytenoid cartilages to pivot resulting in a change in the dimension of the rima glottidis. The opening becomes narrower as the vocal folds are adducted and becomes wider if the vocal folds are abducted. They

Clinical View 25.2

Laryngitis

Laryngitis (lar-in-jī′tis) is an inflammation of the larynx that may extend to its surrounding structures. Viral or bacterial infection is the number one cause of laryngitis. Less frequently, laryngitis follows overuse of the voice, such as yelling for several hours at a football game. Symptoms include hoarse voice, sore throat, and sometimes fever. Severe cases of laryngitis sometimes can produce inflammation and swelling extending to the epiglottis. Children's airways are proportionately smaller, and a swollen and inflamed epiglottis (called **epiglottitis**) may lead to sudden airway obstruction and become a medical emergency.

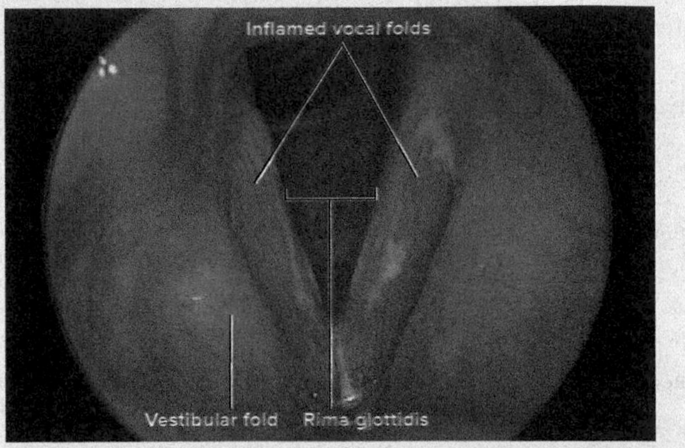

A laryngoscopic view shows the inflamed, reddened vocal folds characteristic of laryngitis.

C. Richard Stasney, M.D./Texas Voice Center

Learning Strategy 25.2

The vocal folds are comparable to the strings of a harp. The short strings produce the high notes, while the long strings produce the low notes. Thus, shorter vocal folds produce higher notes than longer vocal folds.

function in voice production and help close off the larynx when swallowing.

Sound Production

Sound production originates as the vocal folds begin to vibrate. This occurs when the intrinsic laryngeal muscles narrow the opening of the rima glottidis and air is forced past the vocal cords during an exhalation.

The characteristics of the sound include range, pitch, and loudness. The **range** of a voice (be it soprano or bass) is determined by the length and thickness of the vocal folds. Males generally have longer and thicker folds than do females, and thus males produce sounds that are in a lower range. Our vocal folds increase in length as we grow, which is why our voices become lower or deeper as we mature to adulthood.

Pitch refers to the frequency of sound waves. Pitch is determined by the amount of tension or tautness on the vocal folds as regulated primarily by the intrinsic laryngeal muscles. Increasing the tension on the vocal folds causes the vocal folds to vibrate more when air passes by them and thus to produce a higher sound. Conversely, the less taut the vocal folds, the less they vibrate, and the lower the pitch of the sound.

Loudness depends upon the force of the air passing across the vocal cords. A lot of air forced through the rima glottidis produces a loud sound, whereas a little air produces a soft sound. When you whisper, only the most posterior portion of the rima glottidis is open, and the vocal folds do not vibrate. Because the vocal folds are not vibrating, the whispered sounds are all of the same pitch.

Speech also requires the participation of the spaces in the pharynx, nasal and oral cavities, and the paranasal sinuses, which serve as resonating chambers for sound, and the structures of the lips, teeth, and tongue that help form different sounds. Young children tend to have high, nasal-like voices because their sinuses are not yet well developed, so they lack large resonant chambers. When you hold your nose and speak, your voice sounds quite different because air doesn't pass through the nasal cavity.

WHAT DID YOU LEARN?

3. What is the function of the nasal conchae?
4. How is swallowed food prevented from entering the nasopharynx?
5. What are the functions of the larynx?
6. Draw an anterior and lateral view of the laryngeal cartilages, and include the vocal and vestibular ligaments.

25.3 Lower Respiratory Tract

✓ Learning Objectives

7. Identify and describe the structure and function of the trachea.
8. Compare and contrast the composition and function of the bronchial tree, alveolar ducts, and alveoli.

The **lower respiratory tract** is made up of conducting airways (trachea, bronchi, bronchioles, and terminal bronchioles) as well as the respiratory portion of the respiratory system (respiratory bronchioles, alveolar ducts, and alveoli) (**table 25.2**; see figure 25.1). A lower respiratory tract infection affects some or all of these structures.

Table 25.2 Structures of the Lower Respiratory Tract

Structure[1]	Anatomic Description	Wall Support	Epithelial Lining	Function(s)
Trachea	Flexible, semirigid tubular organ connecting larynx to main bronchi	C-shaped cartilage rings keep trachea patent (open)	Pseudostratified ciliated columnar epithelium	Conducts air, participates in cough reflex
Bronchi	Largest airways of bronchial tree; consist of main, lobar, segmental, and smaller bronchi	Incomplete rings and irregular plates of cartilage; some smooth muscle	Larger bronchi lined by pseudostratified ciliated columnar epithelium; smaller bronchi lined by simple columnar epithelium	Conduct air
Bronchioles	Smaller conducting airways of bronchial tree; larger bronchioles branch into smaller bronchioles; terminal bronchioles are last part of conducting portion	No cartilage; proportionately greater amounts of smooth muscle in walls	Ranges from simple ciliated columnar epithelium (for largest bronchioles) to simple cuboidal epithelium (for smaller bronchioles)	Conduct air; smooth muscle in walls allows for bronchoconstriction and bronchodilation
Respiratory bronchioles	Smallest conducting airways; first structures of the respiratory portion	No cartilage; smooth muscle is scarce in walls	Simple cuboidal epithelium	Gas exchange
Alveolar ducts	Tiny airways that branch off respiratory bronchioles; multiple alveoli found along walls of alveolar duct	No cartilage, no smooth muscle	Simple squamous epithelium	Gas exchange
Alveoli	Tiny microscopic air sacs	No cartilage, no smooth muscle	Simple squamous epithelium	Gas exchange

[1] Structures are listed in the order that air passes through them during inhalation.

Clinical View 25.3

Aspiration of Foreign Bodies and the Heimlich Maneuver

A foreign object (e.g., a piece of meat, candy, chewing gum, or grape) may be **aspirated** (breathed in a foreign object) through the laryngeal opening into the vestibule of the larynx, where it becomes trapped. This will cause the laryngeal muscles to spasm, and the rima glottidis closes so no air can enter the trachea. As a result, asphyxiation occurs—and the person will die in about 4 to 5 minutes from lack of oxygen if the obstruction is not dislodged and removed.

The **Heimlich maneuver** (also known as *abdominal thrusts*) is based upon the concept that, because the lungs still contain air, sudden compression with quick thrusts of the abdomen just below the diaphragm causes the diaphragm to elevate and compress the lungs, expelling air through the trachea and into the larynx. This maneuver usually dislodges the foreign body from the larynx and propels the foreign object back up into the mouth.

To perform the Heimlich maneuver on a conscious adult, the rescuer stands behind the affected person and makes a fist with one hand and places it, thumb toward the person choking, below the xiphoid process and above the umbilicus. In a series of six to ten sharp and distinct thrusts superiorly and inward, the rescuer attempts to develop enough pressure to create an artificial cough, which will force the foreign object out of the larynx.

To apply the Heimlich maneuver to yourself, make a fist with one hand and place it in the middle of the body at a spot above the navel and below the sternum, then grasp the fist with the other hand and push sharply inward and upward. If this fails, the choking person should press the upper abdomen over the back of a chair, edge of a table, porch railing, or something similar, and thrust up and inward until the object is dislodged.

Heimlich maneuver performed on an individual who is choking.

25.3a Trachea

The **trachea** (trā′kē-ă; rough) is a flexible, slightly rigid tubular organ often referred to as the *windpipe*. The trachea extends through the mediastinum and lies immediately anterior to the esophagus, inferior to the larynx, and superior to the main bronchi of the lungs. The trachea averages about 2.5 centimeters in diameter and 12 to 14 centimeters in length.

The anterior and lateral walls of the trachea are supported by 15 to 20 C-shaped **tracheal cartilages (figure 25.6*a*)**. These hyaline cartilage "rings" reinforce and provide some rigidity to the tracheal wall to ensure that the trachea remains open (patent) at all times. The cartilage rings are connected by elastic connective tissue sheets called **anular** (an′yū-lăr; *anulus* = ring) **ligaments.** The open ends of each C-shaped piece are bound together by the **trachealis muscle** and an elastic, ligamentous membrane (figure 25.6*b*). The trachealis distends during swallowing and bulges into the lumen of the trachea to allow for expansion of the esophagus to accommodate larger materials being swallowed. During coughing, it contracts to reduce trachea diameter, thus facilitating the more rapid expulsion of air and helping to loosen material (foreign objects or food materials) from the air passageway.

The mucosa lining the trachea is a pseudostratified ciliated columnar epithelium with numerous mucin-secreting goblet cells and an underlying lamina propria that houses mucin-secreting glands (figure 25.6*d*). The movement of cilia propels mucus laden with dust and dirt particles toward the larynx and the pharynx, where it is swallowed. A submucosal layer deep to the mucosa contains many submucous glands.

At the level of the sternal angle (where the manubrium and body of the sternum unite; see section 7.5a), the trachea bifurcates into two smaller tubes, called the right and left **main bronchi** (brong′kī; *bronchos* = windpipe) (or *primary bronchi*). Each main bronchus projects inferiorly and laterally into a lung. The most

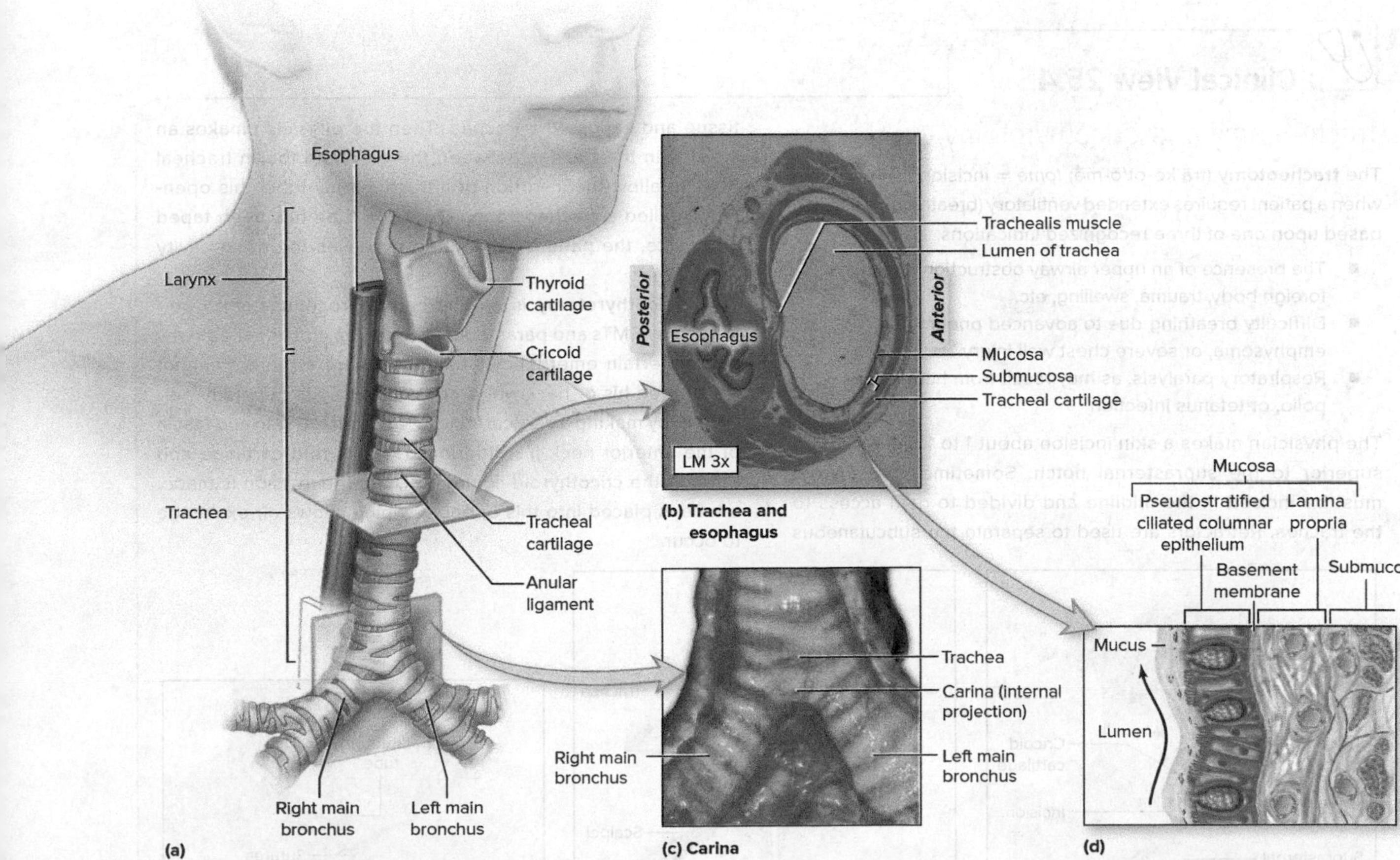

Figure 25.6

Trachea. (*a*) The trachea connects to the larynx superiorly and the main bronchi inferiorly. (*b*) A cross-sectional photomicrograph shows the relationship of the trachea and the esophagus. The wall of the trachea is supported by C-shaped rings of tracheal cartilage. (*c*) A photo of the trachea leading into the main bronchi. Located at this split is the carina, which houses sensory receptors that, when stimulated by irritants, induce a cough. (*d*) The inner surface of the tracheal wall, showing the upward movement of mucus toward the pharnyx. APR

(b) Lester V. Bergman/Corbis/Getty Images; (c) SPL/Science Source inferior tracheal cartilage separates the main bronchi at their origin and forms an internal ridge called the **carina** (kă-rī′nă; keel) (figure 25.6*c*). The right main bronchus enters the lung more vertically than the left main bronchus (figure 25.6*a*). The right bronchus is also wider and shorter than the left. This can be clinically significant because aspirated foreign objects are more likely to become lodged on the right side (see Clinical View 25.3: "Aspiration of Foreign Bodies and the Heimlich Maneuver" in section 25.3a).

WHAT DO YOU THINK?

2 In chronic smokers, the lining of the trachea and bronchi changes from a pseudostratified ciliated columnar epithelium to a stratified squamous epithelium. Why do you think this change occurs? What are some consequences of this epithelium in the trachea?

25.3b Bronchial Tree

The **bronchial tree** is a highly branched system of air passageways that originate from the left and right **main bronchi** and progressively branch into narrower tubes as they diverge throughout the lungs (**figure 25.7**). Incomplete rings of hyaline cartilage support the walls of the main bronchi to ensure that they remain open.

The main bronchi enter the hilum of each lung together with the pulmonary vessels, lymphatic vessels, and nerves. Each main bronchus then branches into **lobar bronchi** (or *secondary bronchi*). The left lung has two lobar bronchi because it has two lobes; the right lung has three lobes and three lobar bronchi. Lobar bronchi are smaller in diameter than main bronchi. They further divide into **segmental bronchi.** The right lung is supplied by 10 segmental bronchi, and the left lung is supplied by 8 to 10 segmental bronchi. (The difference in the number depends upon whether some of the left lung segmental bronchi are combined or separate structures.)

Clinical View 25.4

Tracheotomy and Cricothyrotomy

The **tracheotomy** (trā′kē-ot′ō-mē; *tome* = incision) is performed when a patient requires extended ventilatory (breathing) assistance based upon one of three recognized indications:

- The presence of an upper airway obstruction due to a foreign body, trauma, swelling, etc.
- Difficulty breathing due to advanced pneumonia, emphysema, or severe chest wall injury
- Respiratory paralysis, as may result from head injury, polio, or tetanus infection

The physician makes a skin incision about 1 to 1.5 centimeters superior to the suprasternal notch. Sometimes the thyroid must be incised in the midline and divided to gain access to the trachea. Retractors are used to separate the subcutaneous tissue and expose the trachea. Then the physician makes an incision in the trachea between the third and fourth tracheal rings to allow the insertion of a tracheotomy tube; this opening is called a **tracheostomy.** Once the tube has been taped into place, the patient's breathing bypasses the nasal cavity and larynx.

Cricothyrotomy is an alternative procedure often performed by EMTs and paramedics to open an individual's airway during certain emergency situations where a patient cannot breathe on his or her own. A cricothyrotomy is generally performed by making a vertical incision through the skin and fascia of the anterior neck just inferior to the thyroid cartilage and through the cricothyroid ligament. Once the incision is made, a tube is placed into this opening, which allows air exchange to occur.

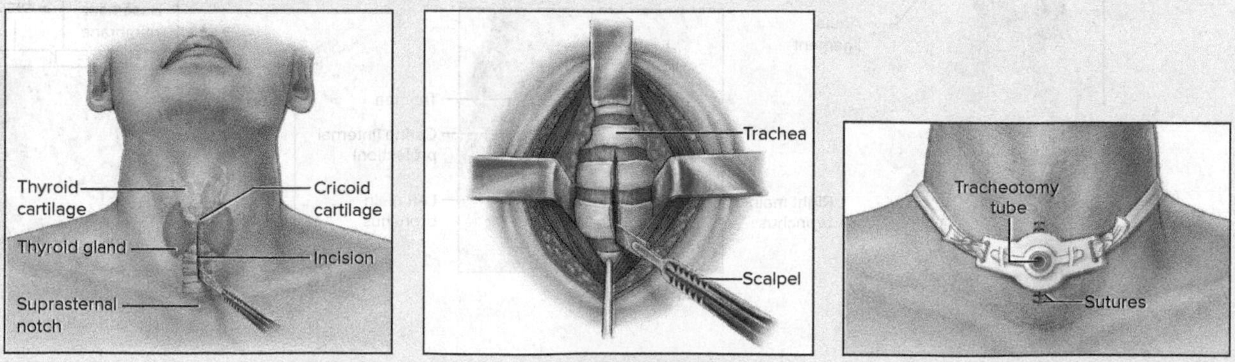

(1) Incision is made superior to suprasternal notch. Thyroid may have to be cut as well.

(2) Retractors separate the tissue, and an incision is made through the third and fourth tracheal rings.

(3) A tracheotomy tube is inserted, and the remaining incision is sutured closed.

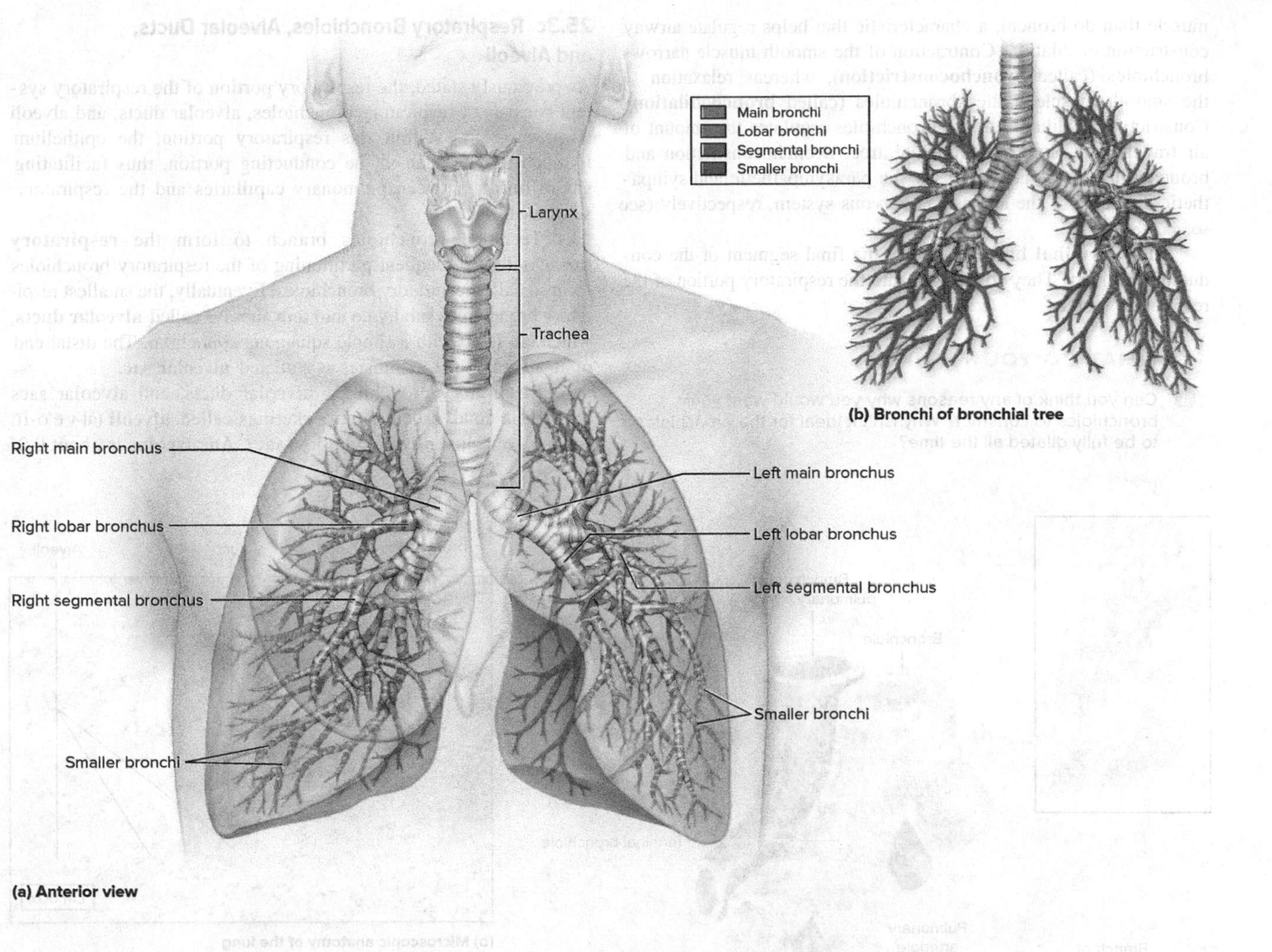
Main bronchi
Lobar bronchi
Segmental bronchi
Smaller bronchi
Larynx
Trachea
Right main bronchus
Right lobar bronchus
Right segmental bronchus
Smaller bronchi
Left main bronchus
Left lobar bronchus
Left segmental bronchus
Smaller bronchi
(a) Anterior view
(b) Bronchi of bronchial tree

Figure 25.7

Bronchial Tree. *(a)* The bronchial tree is composed of conducting passageways that originate at the main bronchi and end at the terminal bronchioles (not visible in this view). *(b)* The bronchi of the bronchial tree are color-coded. **APR**

Each segmental bronchus, also called a *tertiary bronchus,* supplies a part of the lung called a bronchopulmonary segment, discussed in section 25.4b.

There are about 9 to 12 different levels of bronchial branch division (not all shown in figure 25.7). Thus, the main, lobar, and segmental bronchi are the first, second, and third generations of bronchi, respectively. All types of bronchi exhibit some common characteristics:

- Incomplete rings of cartilage in the walls become less numerous and smaller, because the smaller the airway, the less cartilage needed to keep the airways open. Eventually, there are only scattered pieces of cartilage as the bronchi continue to divide and decrease in diameter.
- The largest branches of bronchi are lined by a pseudostratified ciliated columnar epithelium, whereas smaller branches of bronchi are lined by a ciliated columnar epithelium.
- A complete ring of smooth muscle is found between the mucosa of the airways and the cartilaginous support in the wall.

The bronchi branch into smaller and smaller tubules that eventually reach a diameter of less than 1 millimeter. These smaller tubules, called **bronchioles** (brong'kē-ōl), are no longer lined with pseudostratified ciliated columnar epithelium, but with simple columnar or simple cuboidal epithelium. Unlike the smallest bronchi, which have irregular plates of cartilage in their walls, the walls of bronchioles contain no cartilage, because their small diameter alone prevents collapse. Instead, they have a thicker layer of smooth muscle than do bronchi, a characteristic that helps regulate airway constriction or dilation. Contraction of the smooth muscle narrows bronchioles (called **bronchoconstriction**), whereas relaxation of the smooth muscle dilates bronchioles (called **bronchodilation**). Constriction or dilation of the bronchioles regulates the amount of air traveling through the bronchial tree. Bronchoconstriction and bronchodilation are controlled by the parasympathetic and sympathetic divisions of the autonomic nervous system, respectively (see section 18.5).

The **terminal bronchioles** are the final segment of the conducting pathway. They conduct air into the respiratory portion of the respiratory system.

WHAT DO YOU THINK?

5 Can you think of any reasons why you would want your bronchioles to constrict? Why isn't it ideal for the bronchioles to be fully dilated all the time?

25.3c Respiratory Bronchioles, Alveolar Ducts, and Alveoli

As previously stated, the respiratory portion of the respiratory system consists of respiratory bronchioles, alveolar ducts, and alveoli (**figure 25.8**). Within this respiratory portion, the epithelium is much thinner than in the conducting portion, thus facilitating gas diffusion between pulmonary capillaries and the respiratory structures.

Terminal bronchioles branch to form the **respiratory bronchioles.** Subsequent partitioning of the respiratory bronchioles forms smaller respiratory bronchioles. Eventually, the smallest respiratory bronchioles subdivide into thin airways called **alveolar ducts,** which are lined with a simple squamous epithelium. The distal end of an alveolar duct terminates as a dilated **alveolar sac.**

Respiratory bronchioles, alveolar ducts, and alveolar sacs all contain small saccular outpocketings called **alveoli** (al-vē'ō-lī; sing., al-vē'ō-lŭs; *alveus* = hollow sac). An alveolus is about 0.25

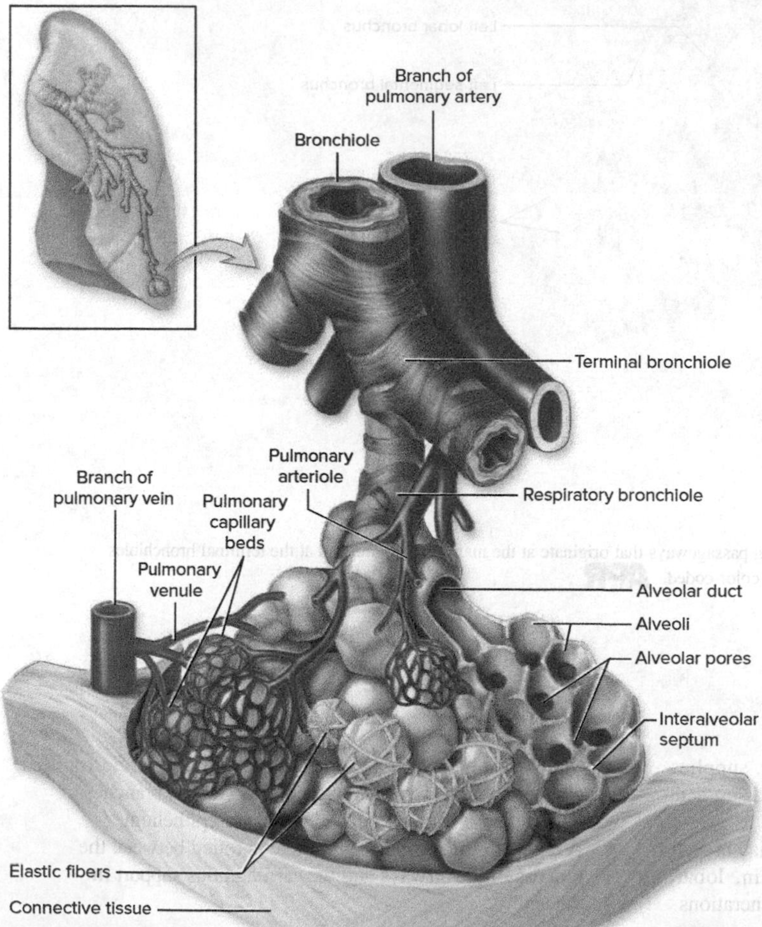

(a) Bronchioles and alveoli of the lung

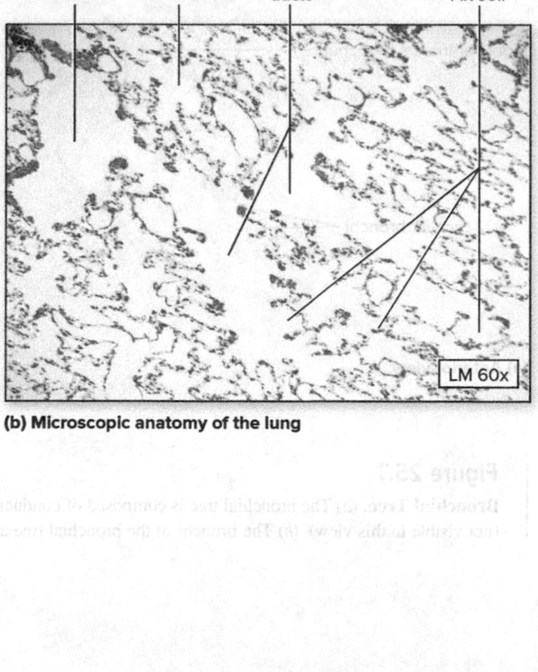

(b) Microscopic anatomy of the lung

Figure 25.8

Bronchioles and Alveoli. Bronchioles and alveoli form the terminal ends of the respiratory passageway. (*a*) Terminal bronchioles branch into respiratory bronchioles, which then branch into alveolar ducts and alveoli. A pulmonary vessel travels with the bronchioles, and the pulmonary capillaries wrap around the alveoli for gas exchange. Elastic tissue is also wrapped around alveoli. (*b*) A photomicrograph shows the relationship of respiratory bronchioles, alveolar ducts, and alveoli.

(b) ©McGraw-Hill Education/Alvin Telser, photographer

to 0.5 millimeter in diameter. Its thin wall is specialized to promote diffusion of gases between the alveolus and the blood in the pulmonary capillaries (**figure 25.9**). Each lung contains about 300 to 400 million alveoli. Alveoli abut one another, so their sides become slightly flattened. Thus, an alveolus in cross section actually looks more hexagonal or polygonal in shape than circular (see figure 25.8*a*). The small openings in the walls between adjacent alveoli, called **alveolar pores,** provide for collateral ventilation of alveoli. Blood capillaries surround each alveolus to facilitate gas exchange. The interalveolar septum contains elastic fibers that contribute to the ability of the lungs to stretch during inhalation and recoil during exhalation.

Two cell types form the alveolar wall. The predominant cell is an **alveolar type I cell,** also called a *squamous alveolar cell.* This simple squamous epithelial cell promotes rapid gas diffusion across the alveolar wall. The **alveolar type II cell,** called a *septal cell,* is part of a smaller population of cells within the alveolar wall. Typically, it displays an almost cuboidal shape. Alveolar type II cells secrete **pulmonary surfactant** (sŭr-fak´tănt), a fluid composed of lipids and proteins that coats the inner alveolar surface to reduce surface tension and prevent the collapse of the alveoli. **Alveolar macrophages,** or *dust cells,* may be either fixed or free. Fixed alveolar macrophages remain within the connective tissue of the alveolar walls, whereas free alveolar macrophages are migratory cells that continually crawl within the alveoli, engulfing any microorganisms or particulate material that has reached the alveoli. The alveolar macrophages are able to leave the lungs either by entering the alveolar lymphatics or by being coughed up in sputum (matter from the respiratory tract, such as mucus mixed with saliva).

The **respiratory membrane** is the thin wall between the alveolar lumen and the blood (figure 25.9). It consists of the plasma membranes of an alveolar type I cell, an endothelial cell of a capillary, and their fused basement membranes. Oxygen diffuses from the lumen of the alveolus across the respiratory membrane into the pulmonary capillary, thereby allowing the erythrocytes in the blood to become oxygenated again. Conversely, carbon dioxide diffuses from the blood in the capillary through the respiratory membrane to enter the alveolus. Once in the alveoli, carbon dioxide is exhaled from the respiratory system into the external environment. APR

WHAT DID YOU LEARN?

7. What are some anatomic differences between bronchi and bronchioles?
8. How do terminal and respiratory bronchioles differ in structure and function?

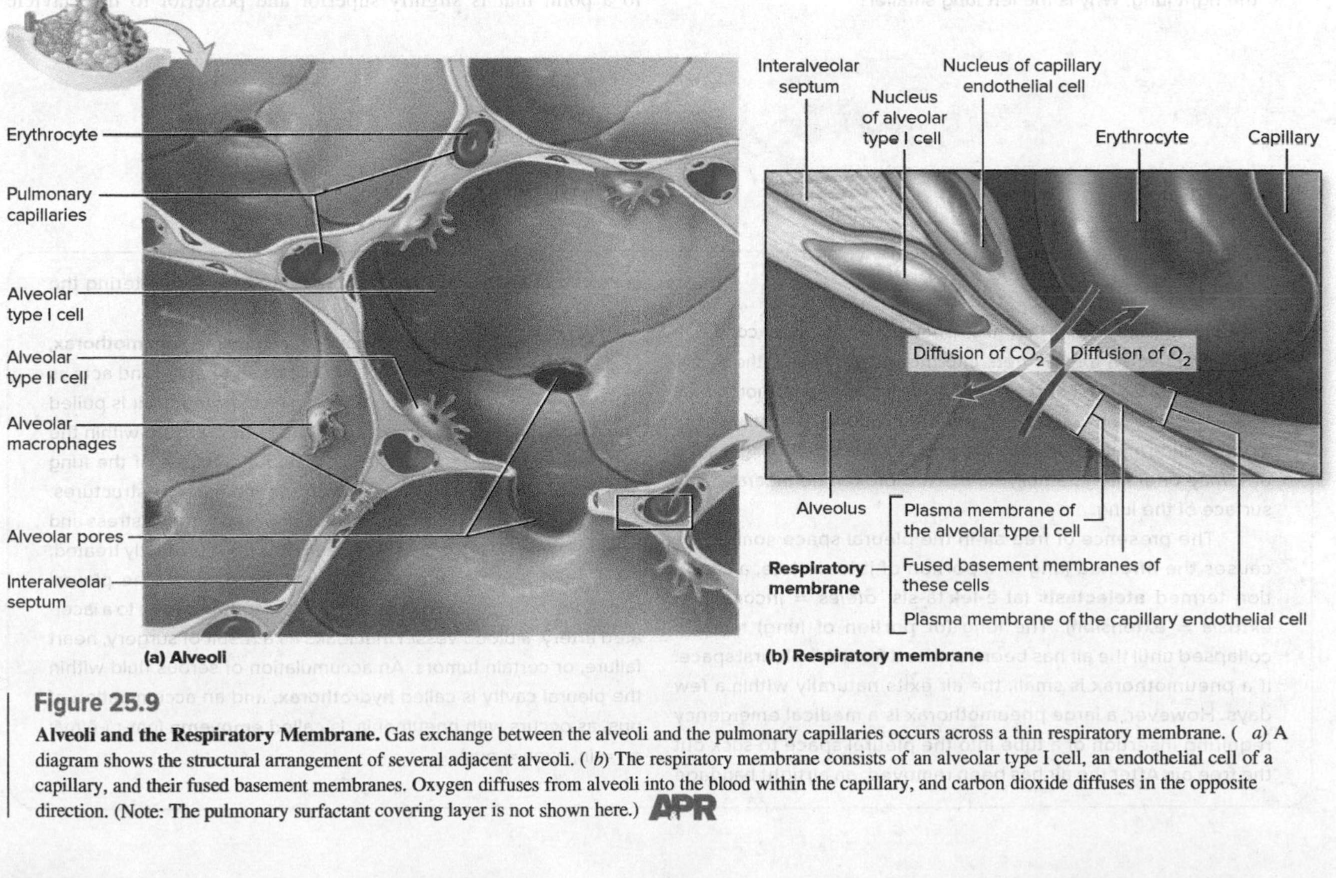
Erythrocyte
Pulmonary capillaries
Alveolar type I cell
Alveolar type II cell
Alveolar macrophages
Alveolar pores
Interalveolar septum
(a) Alveoli
Interalveolar septum
Nucleus of alveolar type I cell
Nucleus of capillary endothelial cell
Erythrocyte
Capillary
Diffusion of CO_2
Diffusion of O_2
Alveolus
Respiratory membrane
Plasma membrane of the alveolar type I cell
Fused basement membranes of these cells
Plasma membrane of the capillary endothelial cell
(b) Respiratory membrane

Figure 25.9

Alveoli and the Respiratory Membrane. Gas exchange between the alveoli and the pulmonary capillaries occurs across a thin respiratory membrane. (*a*) A diagram shows the structural arrangement of several adjacent alveoli. (*b*) The respiratory membrane consists of an alveolar type I cell, an endothelial cell of a capillary, and their fused basement membranes. Oxygen diffuses from alveoli into the blood within the capillary, and carbon dioxide diffuses in the opposite direction. (Note: The pulmonary surfactant covering layer is not shown here.) APR

Learning Strategy 25.3

To help understand the relationship between the respiratory bronchiole, alveolar duct, alveolar sac, and alveolus, visualize a building with multiple wings that radiate from a common atrium. A hallway connects each wing to the central atrium. Classrooms open into the hallways along their length. At the end of each hallway is an expanded common space lined with more classrooms. (1) The atrium is like the respiratory bronchiole . . . it distributes respiratory gases into every hallway. (2) The hallway leading to each wing is like the alveolar duct . . . it conducts respiratory gases into each wing. (3) The end of each alveolar duct (hallway) terminates in a large, expanded foyer (the alveolar sac) lined with multiple classrooms (alveoli). (4) Each classroom is like an alveolus . . . it is where gas exchange occurs.

25.4 Lungs

✓ Learning Objectives

9. Identify the structure and describe the function of the pleura.
10. Identify and describe the anatomy of the lungs, including their blood supply and lymphatic drainage.

The lungs house the bronchial tree and the respiratory portion of the respiratory system. The lungs are located on the lateral sides of the thoracic cavity and separated from each other by the mediastinum.

WHAT DO YOU THINK?

4 As you will soon learn, the left lung is physically smaller than the right lung. Why is the left lung smaller?

25.4a Pleura and Pleural Cavities

The outer lung surfaces and the adjacent internal thoracic wall are lined by a serous membrane called **pleura** (plūr′ă), which is formed from simple squamous epithelium called a mesothelium. The mesothelium is attached to a thin layer of areolar connective tissue. The outer surface of each lung is covered by the **visceral pleura,** whereas parietal pleura lines the internal thoracic walls, the lateral surfaces of the mediastinum, and the superior surface of the diaphragm are lined by the **parietal pleura (figure 25.10).** (These pleural layers may also be viewed in the transverse section of the thoracic cavity shown in figure 22.2*c*.) The visceral and parietal pleural layers meet at the hilum of each lung. The **pleural cavity** is a space located between the visceral and parietal serous membrane layers. When the lungs are fully inflated, the pleural cavity is considered a *potential space* because the visceral and parietal pleurae are almost in contact with each other. An oily, serous fluid is produced by the serous membranes and covers their surface within the pleural cavity. Serous fluid acts as a lubricant, ensuring the pleural surfaces slide by each other with minimal friction during breathing. The serous fluid also creates tension between the pleural membranes, so when the chest wall expands, pulling the parietal pleura with it, then the serous fluid creates tension and pulls the visceral pleura with it.

25.4b Gross Anatomy of the Lungs

The paired, spongy lungs are the primary organs of respiration. Each lung has a conical shape. Its wide, concave **base** rests inferiorly upon the muscular diaphragm, and its relatively blunt superior region, called the **apex** (or *cupola*), projects superiorly to a point that is slightly superior and posterior to the clavicle

Clinical View 25.5

Pneumothorax

Pneumothorax (nū-mō-thōr′aks; *pneuma* = air) is a condition that occurs when free air gets into the pleural cavity, the space between the parietal and visceral pleura. A pneumothorax may develop in one of two ways. Air may be introduced externally from a penetrating injury to the chest, such as a knife wound or gunshot, or it may originate internally as when a broken rib lacerates the surface of the lung.

The presence of free air in the pleural space sometimes causes the affected lung or a portion of it to deflate, a condition termed **atelectasis** (at-ĕ-lek′tă-sis; *ateles* = incomplete, *ektasis* = extension). The lung (or portion of lung) remains collapsed until the air has been removed from the pleural space. If a pneumothorax is small, the air exits naturally within a few days. However, a large pneumothorax is a medical emergency requiring insertion of a tube into the pleural space to suck out the free air. After the air has been removed, an airtight bandage is placed over the entry site to prevent air from reentering the pleural space.

A particularly dangerous condition is **tension pneumothorax,** in which a hole in the chest or lung allows air to enter and acts as a one-way valve. As the patient struggles to breathe, air is pulled in through the wound but cannot escape. Air pressure within the pleural space becomes greater, causing atelectasis of the lung and eventually displacing the heart and mediastinal structures. Both lungs then become compressed, and respiratory distress and death occur unless the tension pneumothorax is promptly treated.

Fluid also has the potential to accumulate in the pleural space. For example, blood may collect (**hemothorax**) due to a lacerated artery, a blood vessel that leaks as a result of surgery, heart failure, or certain tumors. An accumulation of serous fluid within the pleural cavity is called **hydrothorax,** and an accumulation of pus, as occurs with pneumonia, is called **empyema** (em-pī-ē′mă; *en* = in, *pyon* = pus).

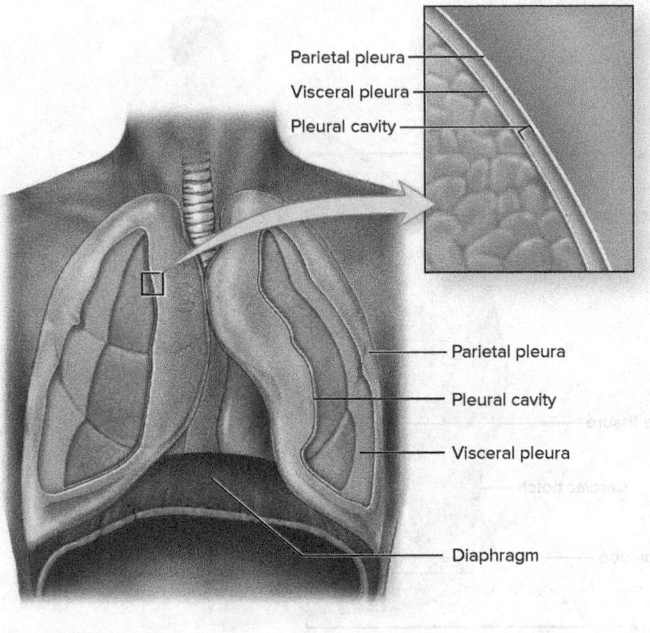
Parietal pleura
Visceral pleura
Pleural cavity
Parietal pleura
Pleural cavity
Visceral pleura
Diaphragm

Figure 25.10

Pleural Membranes. The serous membranes associated with the lungs are called the pleura. The parietal pleura lines the inner surface of the thoracic cavity, and the visceral pleura covers the outer surface of the lungs. The thin space between these layers is called the pleural cavity.

(**figure 25.11**). Both lungs are bordered by the thoracic wall anteriorly, laterally, and posteriorly, and supported by the rib cage. Toward the midline, the lungs are separated from each other by the mediastinum.

The relatively broad, rounded surface in contact with the thoracic wall is called the **costal surface** of the lung. The **mediastinal surface** of the lung is directed medially (facing the mediastinum) and is slightly concave in shape. This surface houses the vertical, indented **hilum** through which the main (primary) bronchi, pulmonary vessels, lymph vessels, and nerves pass. Collectively, all structures passing through the hilum are termed the **root** of the lung.

The right and left lungs exhibit some obvious structural differences. Because the heart projects into the left side of the thoracic cavity, the left lung is slightly smaller than the right lung. The left lung has a medial surface indentation, called the **cardiac impression,** that is formed by the heart. The left lung also has an anterior indented region called the **cardiac notch.** The descending thoracic aorta forms a groovelike impression on the medial surface of the left lung.

The right lung is subdivided into the **superior** (*upper*), **middle,** and **inferior** (*lower*) **lobes** by two fissures. The **horizontal fissure** separates the superior from the middle lobe, whereas the **oblique fissure** separates the middle from the inferior lobe. The left lung has only two lobes, superior and inferior, which are subdivided by an oblique fissure. The **lingula** of the left lung is located on the superior lobe. The lingula is homologous to the middle lobe of the right lung.

The left and right lungs may be partitioned into **bronchopulmonary segments**—10 in the right lung, and typically 8 to 10 in the left lung (**figure 25.12**). (The discrepancy in bronchopulmonary segment number for the left lung comes from the merging or lumping of some left bronchopulmonary segments into combined ones by some anatomists.) Each bronchopulmonary segment is supplied by its own segmental bronchus and a branch of the pulmonary artery and vein. In addition, each segment is surrounded by connective tissue, thereby encapsulating one segment from another and ensuring that each bronchopulmonary segment is an autonomous unit. Thus, if a portion of a lung is diseased, a surgeon can remove the entire bronchopulmonary segment that is affected, while the remaining healthy bronchopulmonary segments continue to function as before.

25.4c Blood Supply to and from the Lungs

Both the pulmonary circulation and the bronchial circulation supply the lungs. Recall from section 23.4 that the **pulmonary circulation** conducts blood to and from the gas exchange surfaces of the lungs to replenish its depleted oxygen levels and get rid of excess carbon dioxide (see figures 23.22 and 23.23). Deoxygenated blood is pumped from the right ventricle through the pulmonary trunk into pulmonary arteries, which enter the lung. Thereafter, continuous branching of these vessels leads to pulmonary capillaries that encircle all alveoli. The deoxygenated blood that enters these capillaries becomes oxygenated before it returns to the left atrium through a series of pulmonary venules and veins.

The **bronchial circulation** is a component of the systemic circulation. The bronchial circulation consists of tiny bronchial arteries and veins that supply the bronchi and bronchioles of the lung. This part of the circulatory system is much smaller than the pulmonary system, because most tiny respiratory structures (alveoli and alveolar ducts) exchange respiratory gases directly with the inhaled air. About three or four tiny **bronchial arteries** branch from the anterior wall of the descending thoracic aorta and divide to form capillary beds to supply structures in the bronchial tree. Increasingly larger **bronchial veins** collect venous blood and drain into the azygos and hemiazygous systems of veins.

25.4d Lymphatic Drainage

Lymph nodes and vessels are located within the connective tissue of the lung as well as around the bronchi and pleura (**figure 25.13**). The lymph nodes collect carbon, dust particles, and pollutants that managed not to get filtered out by the pseudostratified ciliated columnar epithelium. The lymph from the lung is conducted first to **pulmonary lymph nodes** within the lungs. Lymphatic vessels exit these lymph nodes and conduct lymph to **bronchopulmonary lymph nodes** located at the hilum of the lung. These vessels drain first into **tracheobronchial lymph nodes** and then into the **left** and **right bronchomediastinal trunks** (discussed in section 24.2c). The right bronchomediastinal trunk drains into the right lymphatic duct, whereas the left bronchomediastinal trunk drains into the thoracic duct.

WHAT DO YOU THINK?

5 The lymph nodes of the lung become black and darkened over time in both smokers and nonsmokers. Why do these lymph nodes turn black?

WHAT DID YOU LEARN?

9 Draw lateral and medial views of the left and right lungs. Label the lobes, fissures, and hilum of each lung.

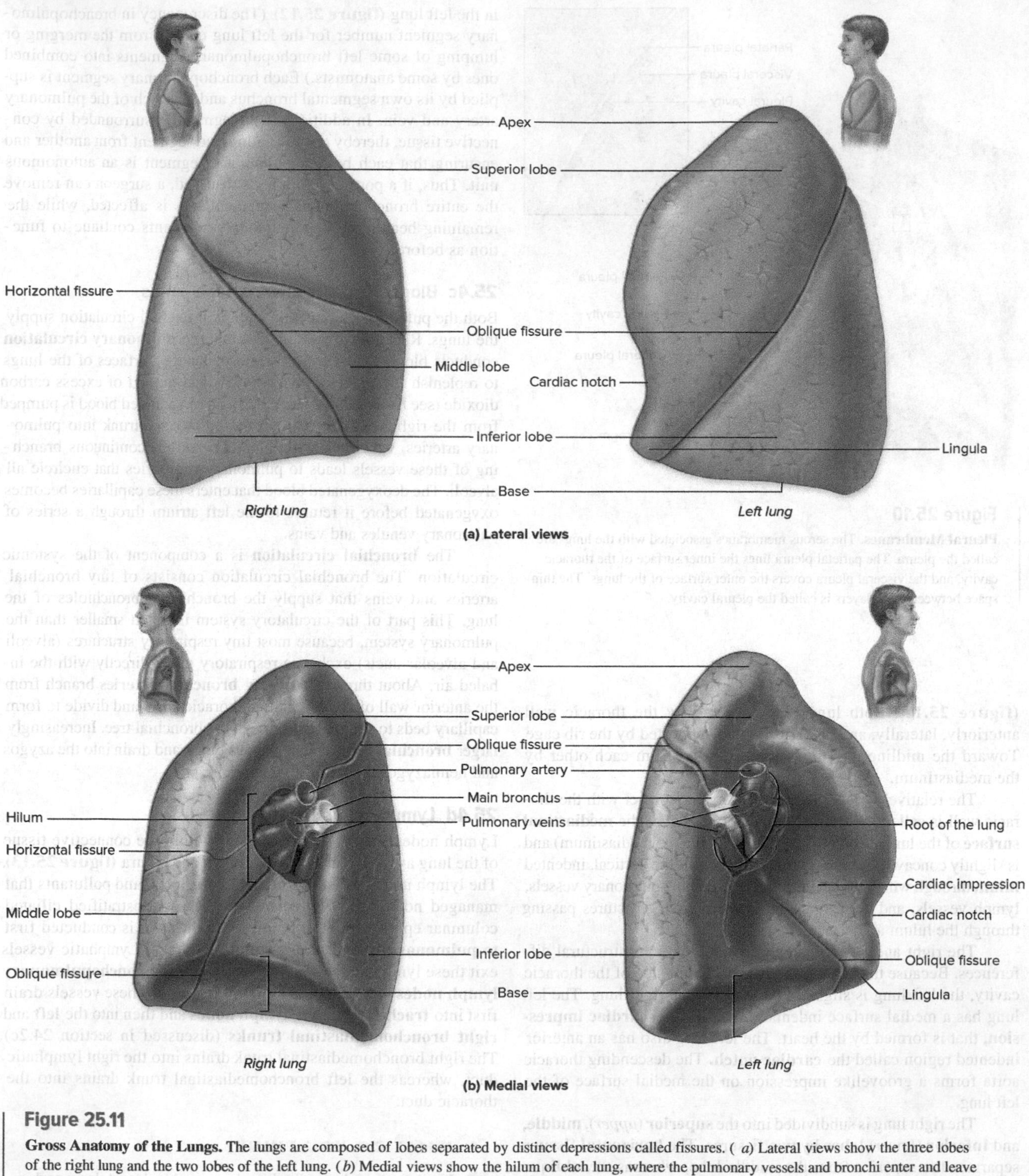
Apex
Superior lobe
Horizontal fissure
Oblique fissure
Middle lobe
Cardiac notch
Inferior lobe
Lingula
Base
Right lung
Left lung
(a) Lateral views
Apex
Superior lobe
Oblique fissure
Pulmonary artery
Main bronchus
Hilum
Pulmonary veins
Root of the lung
Horizontal fissure
Cardiac impression
Middle lobe
Cardiac notch
Inferior lobe
Oblique fissure
Oblique fissure
Base
Lingula
Right lung
Left lung
(b) Medial views

Figure 25.11

Gross Anatomy of the Lungs. The lungs are composed of lobes separated by distinct depressions called fissures. (*a*) Lateral views show the three lobes of the right lung and the two lobes of the left lung. (*b*) Medial views show the hilum of each lung, where the pulmonary vessels and bronchi enter and leave the lung.

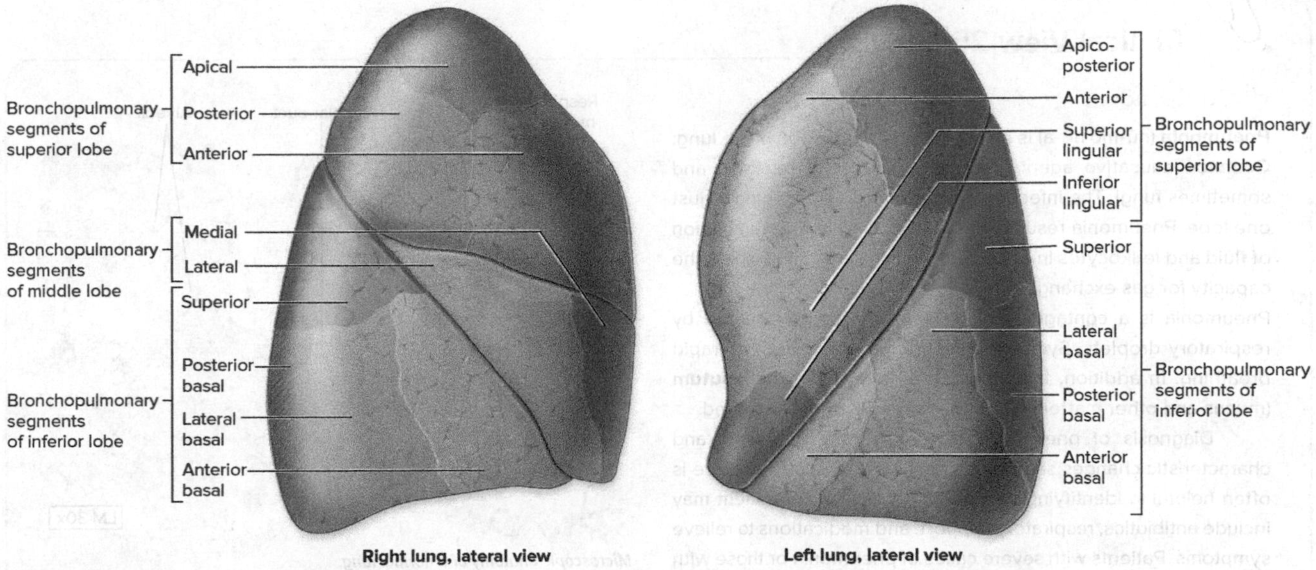
Apical
Posterior
Anterior
Bronchopulmonary segments of superior lobe
Medial
Lateral
Bronchopulmonary segments of middle lobe
Superior
Posterior basal
Lateral basal
Anterior basal
Bronchopulmonary segments of inferior lobe
Right lung, lateral view
Apico-posterior
Anterior
Superior lingular
Inferior lingular
Bronchopulmonary segments of superior lobe
Superior
Lateral basal
Posterior basal
Anterior basal
Bronchopulmonary segments of inferior lobe
Left lung, lateral view

Figure 25.12

Bronchopulmonary Segments of the Lungs. The portion of each lung supplied by each segmental bronchus (represented by different colors) is a bronchopulmonary segment. (The medial basal bronchopulmonary segment cannot be seen from this view.)

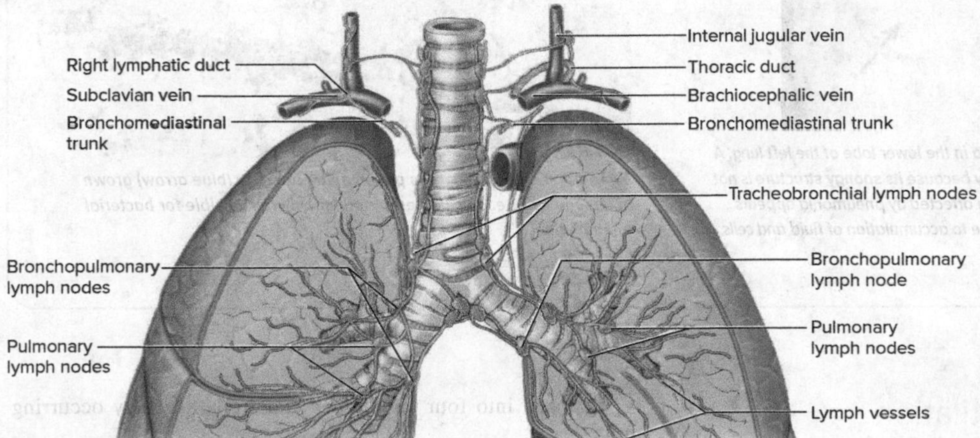
Right lymphatic duct
Subclavian vein
Bronchomediastinal trunk
Bronchopulmonary lymph nodes
Pulmonary lymph nodes
Internal jugular vein
Thoracic duct
Brachiocephalic vein
Bronchomediastinal trunk
Tracheobronchial lymph nodes
Bronchopulmonary lymph node
Pulmonary lymph nodes
Lymph vessels

Figure 25.13

Lung Lymphatic Drainage. Lymph vessels conduct lymph to the pulmonary, bronchopulmonary, and tracheobronchial lymph nodes. Lymph is then drained by the bronchomediastinal trunks into the right lymphatic duct or the thoracic duct.

Clinical View 25.6

Pneumonia

Pneumonia (nū-mō′nē-ă) is an infection of the alveoli of the lung. Common causative agents include viruses and bacteria, and sometimes fungi. The infection may involve an entire lung or just one lobe. Pneumonia results in tissue swelling and accumulation of fluid and leukocytes in the alveoli, thus greatly diminishing the capacity for gas exchange.

Pneumonia is a contagious disease that is usually spread by respiratory droplets. Symptoms include cough, fever, and rapid breathing. In addition, the bronchi produce and expel **sputum** (mucus and other matter), which may be rust- or green-tinged.

Diagnosis of pneumonia depends upon symptoms and characteristic changes seen on a chest x-ray. A sputum culture is often helpful in identifying the specific organism. Treatment may include antibiotics, respiratory support, and medications to relieve symptoms. Patients with severe cases of pneumonia or those with coexisting lung diseases, such as chronic bronchitis or emphysema, may require supplemental oxygen.

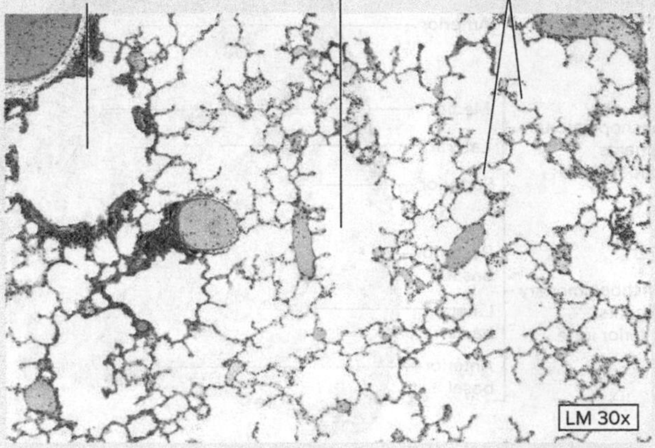

Microscopic anatomy of a normal lung.
©McGraw-Hill Education/Alvin Telser, photographer

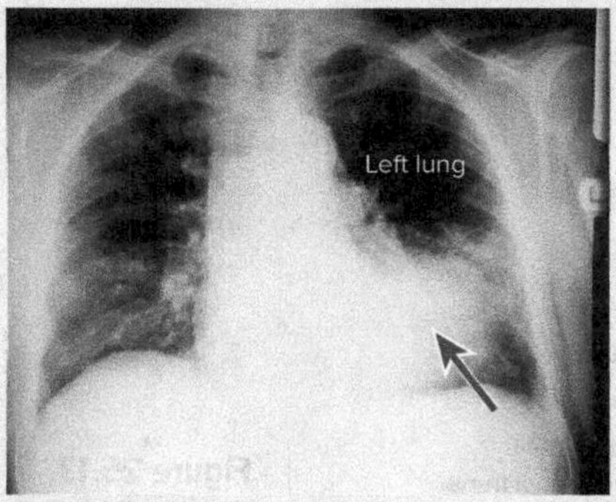

Chest x-ray of a patient with pneumonia in the lower lobe of the left lung. A normal lung appears darker on an x-ray because its spongy structure is not dense. In contrast, the portion of a lung affected by pneumonia appears white or opaque on an x-ray (arrow) due to accumulation of fluid and cells.
Anthony Ricci/Shutterstock

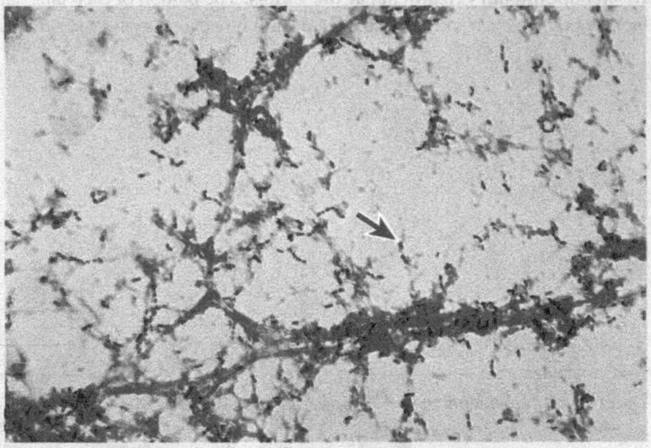

Micrograph of streptococcus pneumoniae bacteria (blue arrow) grown in a blood culture. This bacteria is commonly responsible for bacterial pneumonia.
Centers for Disease Control and Prevention (CDC)

25.5 Pulmonary Ventilation

✓ Learning Objective

11. Describe the process of pulmonary ventilation.

Breathing, also known as **pulmonary ventilation,** is the movement of air into and out of the respiratory system. Breathing may be either quiet or forced. **Quiet breathing** is the rhythmic breathing that occurs at rest; **forced breathing** is vigorous breathing that accompanies exercise or hard exertion. At rest, a normal adult breathes about 12 to 15 times per minute, and about 500 milliliters of air are exchanged with the atmosphere per breath. The airflow exchange is caused by the muscular actions associated with inhalation and exhalation, as well as by differences in atmospheric air pressure and lung (intrapulmonary) air pressure. Gas exchange is organized into four continuous and simultaneously occurring processes:

- **Pulmonary ventilation**—movement of respiratory gases between the atmosphere and the alveoli of the lungs
- **Pulmonary gas exchange** (*alveolar gas exchange* or *external respiration*)—exchange of respiratory gases between the alveoli and the blood
- **Gas transport**—transport of respiratory gases within the blood between the lungs and tissues of the body
- **Tissue gas exchange** (*systemic gas exchange* or *internal respiration*)—exchange of respiratory gases between the blood and tissues of the body

The movement of gases into and out of the respiratory system follows **Boyle's law,** which states, "The pressure of a gas decreases if the volume of the container increases, and vice versa." Thus, when the volume of the thoracic cavity increases even slightly during inhalation, the intrapulmonary pressure decreases slightly, and air flows into the lungs through the conducting airways. Therefore, the air flows from a region of higher pressure (the atmosphere) into a region of lower pressure within the lungs (the intrapulmonary region). Similarly, when the volume of the thoracic cavity decreases during exhalation, the intrapulmonary pressure increases and forces air out of the lungs into the atmosphere.

WHAT DID YOU LEARN?

10 What is pulmonary ventilation?

25.6 Mechanics of Breathing

✓ Learning Objectives

12. Describe the actions of the skeletal muscles of breathing.
13. Explain how the thoracic cavity changes in size and shape during respiration.

The mechanics of breathing involve coordinated movement of skeletal muscles, as well as dimensional changes in the thoracic cavity. Here we first discuss which muscles are involved with both quiet and forced breathing, and then we examine how the thoracic cavity changes shape as we inhale and exhale.

25.6a Skeletal Muscles of Breathing

The skeletal muscles of breathing are classified into the following three categories: muscles of quiet breathing, muscles of forced inhalation, and muscles of forced exhalation **(figure 25.14)**.

- **Muscles of quiet breathing** are involved in normal rhythmic breathing that occurs at rest. They are the diaphragm and the external intercostals. These muscles alternately contract and relax, resulting in movement of air into and out of the lungs (see section 11.3).
- **Muscles of forced inhalation** are used during a deep inhalation, such as occurs during heavy exercise. They include the sternocleidomastoid, scalenes, pectoralis minor, serratus posterior superior, and erector spinae (see sections 11.1g, 11.2, 11.3, and 12.1a).All of these muscles (except the erector spinae) are located in a more superior position relative to the thoracic cavity. They help elevate the ribs to increase the thoracic cavity volume more than occurs during quiet breathing.
- **Muscles of forced exhalation** contract during a hard exhalation when one blows up a balloon or coughs. These muscles include the internal intercostals, abdominal muscles, transversus thoracis, and serratus posterior inferior (see sections 11.3 and 11.4). They usually either move the rib cage inferiorly, medially, and posteriorly or compress the abdominal contents to move the diaphragm superiorly into the thoracic cavity. These movements cause a large decrease in thoracic cavity volume.

The muscles of forced inhalation and forced exhalation are collectively referred to as the *accessory muscles of breathing*.

25.6b Volume Changes in the Thoracic Cavity

Cyclic activity of breathing muscles causes thoracic cavity volume changes that occur in vertical, lateral, and anterior-posterior directions **(figure 25.15)**.

Vertical changes of the thoracic cavity result from diaphragm movement as it contracts and relaxes. It forms the rounded thoracic cavity "floor" and is dome-shaped when relaxed. Contraction flattens and moves its central portion inferiorly to press against the abdominal viscera—consequently, the vertical dimensions of the thoracic cavity increase. When the diaphragm relaxes and returns to its original position, the vertical dimensions decrease.

Only small movements of the diaphragm are required for breathing, and usually the changes in vertical dimension measure a few millimeters during quiet breathing. Greater changes in superior movement of the diaphragm occur during forced exhalation because the abdominal wall muscles also are contracting.

Lateral dimension changes occur either as the rib cage is elevated and the thoracic cavity widens, or as the rib cage depresses and thoracic cavity narrows. These lateral movements can be mimicked by placing your hands at the sides of your ribs and then abducting and adducting the hands relative to the ribs.

Anterior-posterior dimension changes occur as the inferior portion of the sternum moves anteriorly and then posteriorly. This action can be visualized by placing one hand on the front of your lower chest and lifting it outwardly away from the chest and then

Learning Strategy 25.4

To visualize rib movement during external respiration, think of the thoracic cavity as a bucket and the ribs as the bucket handles. When the bucket handles are lifted up, they move relatively farther away from the edges of the bucket. Thus, the measurement from the bucket handles (ribs) to the bucket (thoracic cavity) increases, just as the lateral dimensions of the thoracic cavity increase. When the bucket handles are depressed, they move next to the edges of the bucket, and so the distance from the bucket handle (ribs) to the bucket (thoracic cavity dimension) decreases.

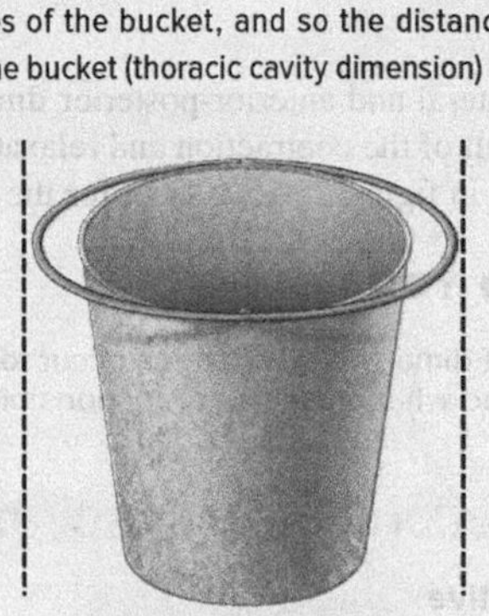

Inhalation: Ribs (bucket handles) elevated, lateral dimension increased

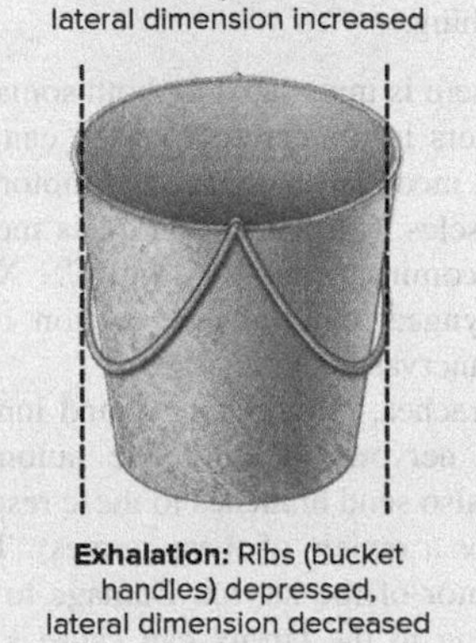

Exhalation: Ribs (bucket handles) depressed, lateral dimension decreased

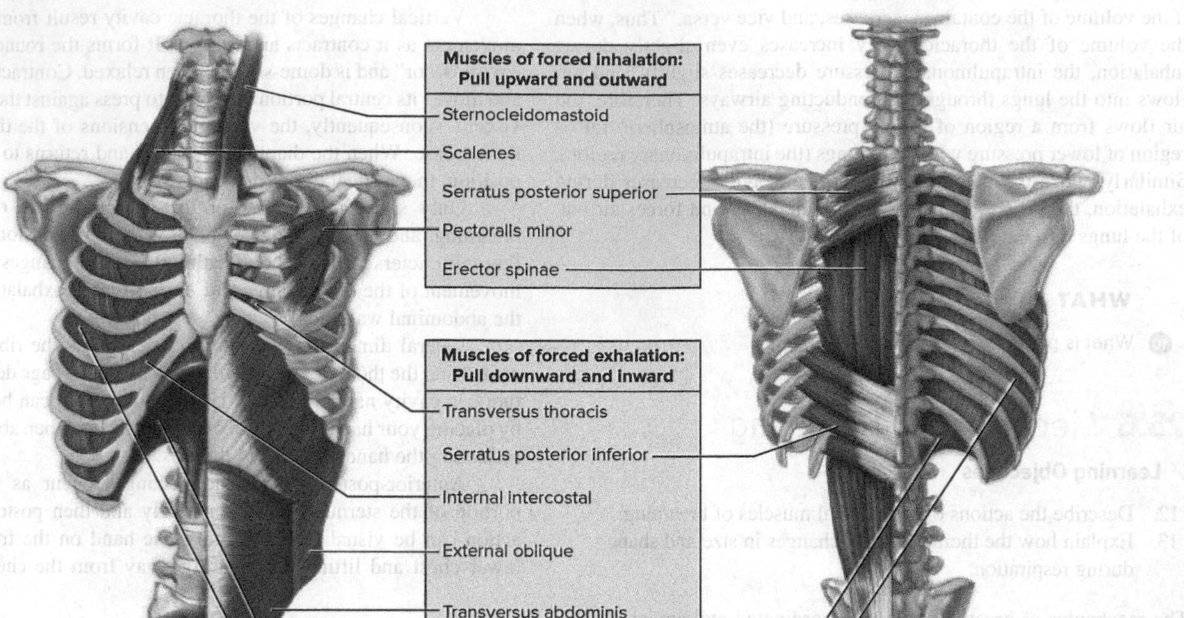
Muscles of forced inhalation: Pull upward and outward
Sternocleidomastoid
Scalenes
Serratus posterior superior
Pectoralis minor
Erector spinae
Muscles of forced exhalation: Pull downward and inward
Transversus thoracis
Serratus posterior inferior
Internal intercostal
External oblique
Transversus abdominis
Muscles of quiet breathing increase dimensions of thoracic cavity
Diaphragm
External intercostal
Anterior view
Posterior view

Figure 25.14
Skeletal Muscles of Breathing.

back. In general, lateral and anterior-posterior dimensional changes both occur as a result of the contraction and relaxation of all muscles of breathing shown in figure 25.15, except for the diaphragm.

WHAT DID YOU LEARN?

11 What types of dimensional changes occur to the thorax when you inhale, and what muscles are responsible?

25.7 Innervation of the Respiratory System

✓ Learning Objective

14. Describe the components of the autonomic nervous system that regulate breathing.

The respiratory system is innervated by both somatic and autonomic motor nerves. Centers in the cerebral cortex can affect respiratory centers of pons and medulla oblongata and motor neurons that control respiratory muscles. Conscious control is mediated by somatic motor innervation coming primarily from CN X (vagus) to move pharyngeal and laryngeal muscles (see section 15.8). Additionally, the phrenic nerve innervates the diaphragm.

The larynx, trachea, bronchial tree, and lungs are innervated by the autonomic nervous system. The autonomic nerves that innervate the heart also send branches to these respiratory structures (see figure 22.12 for a review of these nerves). The vagus nerve is the primary innervator of the larynx. Damage to one of the vagus nerve branches going to the larynx can cause a person to have a monotone or a permanently hoarse voice.

Sympathetic innervation to the lungs originates from the T1–T5 (or occasionally T2–T5) segments of the spinal cord (see section 18.4). These preganglionic fibers enter the sympathetic trunk and synapse with ganglionic neurons. The postganglionic sympathetic fibers (called the cardiac nerves) innervate both the heart and the lungs. The main function of the sympathetic innervation is to open up or dilate the bronchioles (bronchodilation). Parasympathetic innervation to the lungs is from the left and right vagus nerves (CN X). The main function of the parasympathetic innervation is to decrease the airway diameter of the bronchioles (bronchoconstriction).

Collectively, the sympathetic and parasympathetic axons form the **pulmonary plexus**, a weblike network of axons that surrounds the main bronchi and enters the lungs at the hilum (see section 18.5a). Sensory information about the "stretch" in smooth muscle around the bronchial tree is typically conducted by the vagus nerve to the brainstem and then relayed to centers involved with external respiration as well as to other reflex centers, such as those involved in coughing and sneezing.

WHAT DO YOU THINK?

6 When an asthma inhaler provides relief for bronchoconstriction, is it mimicking sympathetic or parasympathetic stimulation?

25.7a Ventilation Control by Respiratory Centers of the Brain

The involuntary, rhythmic activities that deliver and remove respiratory gases are regulated in the brainstem (**figure 25.16**). Regulatory respiratory centers are located within the reticular formation of the brain (see section 17.4f), through both the medulla oblongata and the pons.

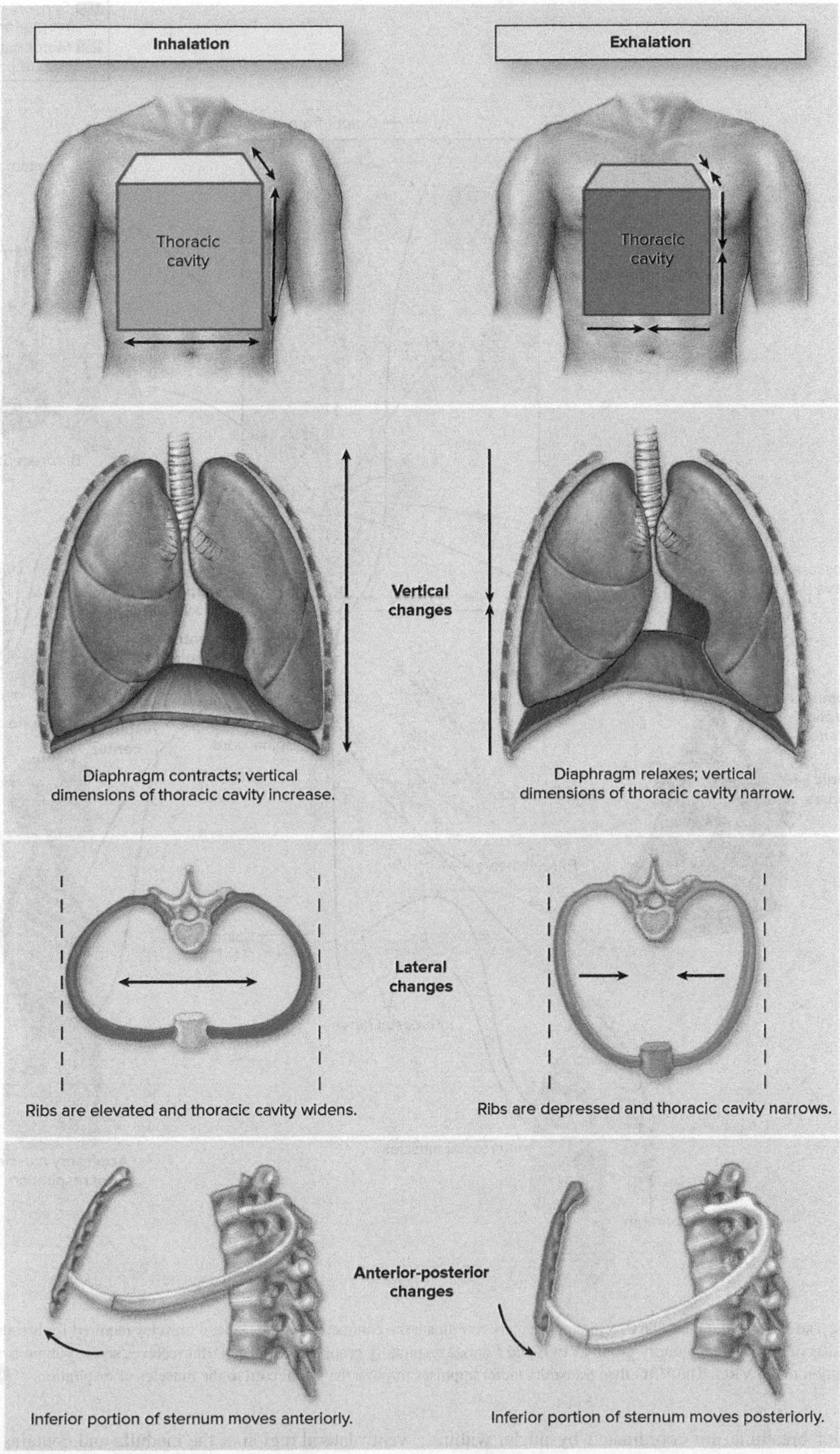

Inhalation
Exhalation
Thoracic cavity
Thoracic cavity
Vertical changes
Diaphragm contracts; vertical dimensions of thoracic cavity increase.
Diaphragm relaxes; vertical dimensions of thoracic cavity narrow.
Lateral changes
Ribs are elevated and thoracic cavity widens.
Ribs are depressed and thoracic cavity narrows.
Anterior-posterior changes
Inferior portion of sternum moves anteriorly.
Inferior portion of sternum moves posteriorly.

Figure 25.15

Thoracic Cavity Dimensional Changes Associated with Breathing. The boxlike thoracic cavity changes size upon inhalation and exhalation. During inhalation, the box increases in vertical, lateral, and anterior-posterior dimensions due to movement of the sternum, ribs, and diaphragm, respectively. Upon exhalation, these dimensions decrease, and the thoracic cavity becomes smaller. APR

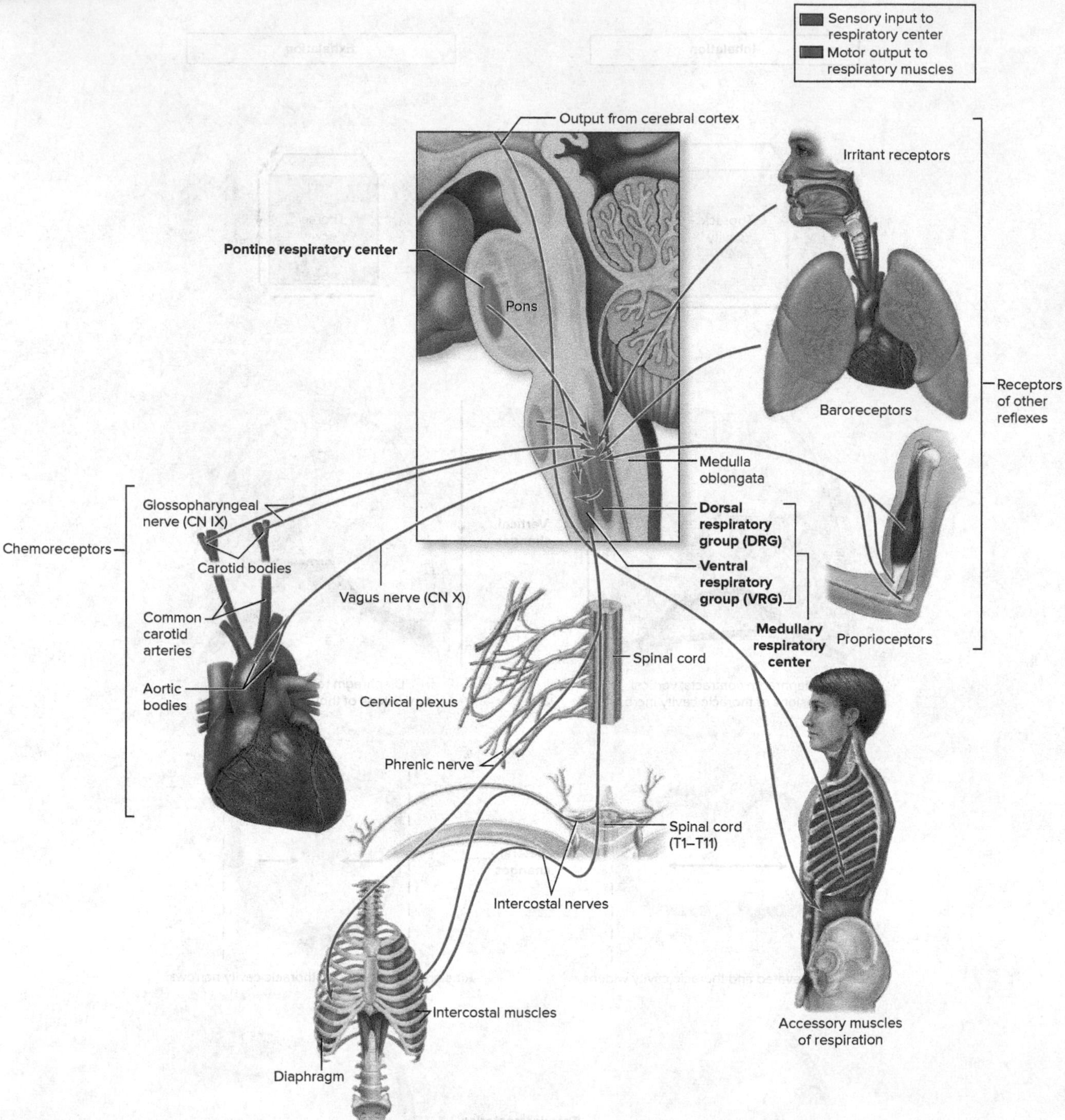

Sensory input to respiratory center
Motor output to respiratory muscles
Output from cerebral cortex
Irritant receptors
Pontine respiratory center
Pons
Baroreceptors
Receptors of other reflexes
Medulla oblongata
Dorsal respiratory group (DRG)
Ventral respiratory group (VRG)
Medullary respiratory center
Proprioceptors
Glossopharyngeal nerve (CN IX)
Chemoreceptors
Carotid bodies
Vagus nerve (CN X)
Common carotid arteries
Spinal cord
Aortic bodies
Cervical plexus
Phrenic nerve
Spinal cord (T1–T11)
Intercostal nerves
Intercostal muscles
Accessory muscles of respiration
Diaphragm

Figure 25.16

Respiratory Centers. The pontine and medullary respiratory centers coordinate the contraction of the skeletal muscles required for breathing. The medullary respiratory center consists of a ventral respiratory group (VRG) and a dorsal respiratory group (DRG). The DRG receives sensory input from multiple locations and relays this information to the VRG. The VRG then transmits motor impulses through the spinal cord to the muscles of respiration. APR

The skeletal muscles of breathing are coordinated by nuclei within the brainstem. These nuclei are housed specifically in the **medullary respiratory center** within the medulla oblongata and the **pontine respiratory center** (also called the *pneumotaxic center*) within the pons. These two centers are collectively called the **respiratory center.**

There are two distinct groups of nuclei in the medullary respiratory center. The **ventral respiratory group (VRG)** is located in the ventrolateral region of the medulla and contains neurons that control both inhalation and exhalation. Posterior to the VRG in the dorsomedial region of the medulla is the **dorsal respiratory group (DRG),** which relays its input to the VRG. The VRG initiates neural impulses for inhalation and exhalation; previously, physiologists thought the DRG controlled this activity. Axons from upper motor neurons extend from the VRG into the spinal cord. Axons from lower motor neurons

Clinical View 25.7

Asthma

Asthma (az′mă) is a chronic condition characterized by episodes of bronchoconstriction and wheezing, coughing, shortness of breath, and excess pulmonary mucus. Its incidence is increasing among young people, particularly those living in urban areas where airborne industrial pollutants and tobacco smoke are abundant. In most cases, the affected person develops a sensitivity to an airborne agent such as pollen, smoke, mold spores, dust mites, or particulate matter. Upon reexposure to this triggering substance, a localized immune reaction occurs in the bronchi and bronchioles, resulting in bronchoconstriction, swollen submucosa, and increased production of mucus. Episodes typically last an hour or two. Continual exposure to the triggering agent increases the severity and frequency of asthma attacks. Eventually, the walls of the bronchi and bronchioles may become permanently thickened, leading to chronic and unremitting airway narrowing and shortness of breath. If airway narrowing is extreme during a severe asthma attack, death could occur.

Today, the primary treatment for asthma consists of administering inhaled steroids (cortisone-related compounds) to reduce the inflammatory reaction, combined with bronchodilators to alleviate the bronchoconstriction. In severe cases, oral doses of steroids may control the allergic hyper-response and reduce the inflammation.

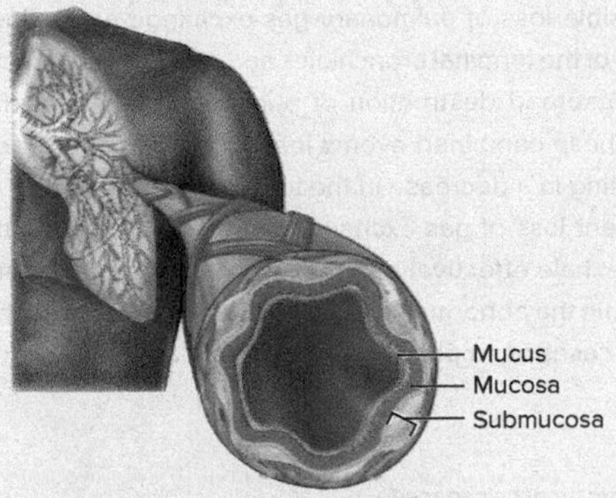
Mucus
Mucosa
Submucosa

Normal bronchiole

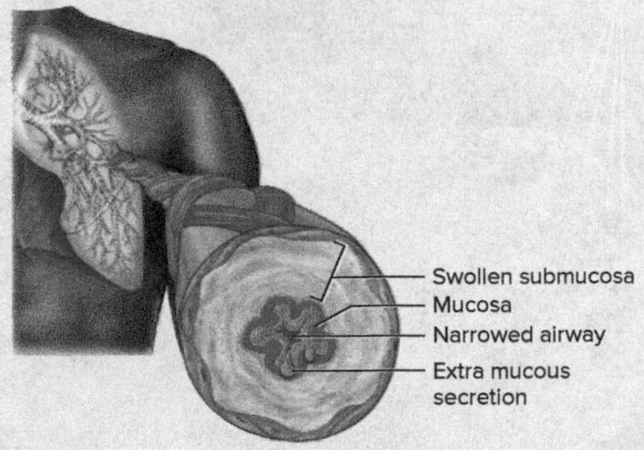
Swollen submucosa
Mucosa
Narrowed airway
Extra mucous secretion

Bronchiole during an asthma attack

Individuals suffering from asthma may need to use inhaled medications to dilate their constricted bronchioles.
sirtravelalot/Shutterstock

extend from the spinal cord and form both the **phrenic nerves** that innervate the diaphragm (see section 16.4d) and **intercostal nerves** that innervate the intercostal muscles (see section 16.4c).

The **pontine respiratory center** is located within the pons and modifies the activity of the nuclei in the medulla. Specifically, this center appears to provide for a smooth transition between inhalation and exhalation by sending impulses to the VRG. Erratic breathing results if this area is damaged.

For example, a breathing rhythm that involves 2 seconds of inhalation followed by 3 seconds of exhalation results in an average respiratory rate of 12 times per minute. The average range for the rate of quiet breathing is generally between 12 and 15 times per minute—a rate referred to as **eupnea** (yūp-nē′ă).

WHAT DID YOU LEARN?

12. What is the main function of sympathetic innervation to the lungs?
13. Compare the activities of the DRG and the VRG in the brain's respiratory centers.

25.8 Aging and the Respiratory System

✓ Learning Objective

15. List and describe the age-related respiratory system changes.

The respiratory system becomes less efficient with age due to several structural changes. First, aging results in a decrease in elastic connective tissue in the lungs and the thoracic cavity wall. This loss of elasticity reduces the amount of gas that can be exchanged with each breath and results in a decrease in the ventilation rate. In addition, a condition such as emphysema may cause a loss of alveoli or a decrease in their functionality. The resulting reduced capacity for gas exchange can cause an older person to become "short of breath" upon exertion.

Finally, as we get older, carbon, dust, and pollution material gradually accumulate in our lymph nodes and lungs. If a person also smokes regularly, the lungs become even darker and blacker throughout because of the deposition of carbon particles in the cells.

Clinical View 25.8

Smoking, Emphysema, and Lung Cancer

Smoking results in the inhalation of over 200 chemicals that blacken the respiratory passageways and cause respiratory changes that increase the risk of (1) respiratory infections, and (2) cellular and genetic damage to the lungs that may lead to emphysema or lung cancer.

Deleterious effects of smoking also include vasoconstriction in the cardiovascular system due to nicotine, interference with oxygen binding to hemoglobin by carbon monoxide, and increased risk and severity of atherosclerosis. Reduced blood flow results in decreased delivery of nutrients and oxygen to cells in systemic tissues.

Smoking increases the risk of both stomach ulcers caused by *Helicobacter pylori* infection and cancer of the esophagus, stomach, and pancreas. It also increases the risks associated with human papillomavirus (HPV) infection linked to increased risk of cervical cancer, and the risk of Alzheimer disease. Secondhand smoke is associated with an increased risk of bronchitis, asthma, and ear infections in children.

Emphysema (em′fi-sē′mă; *en* = in, *physema* = a blowing) is an irreversible loss of pulmonary gas exchange areas due to inflammation of the terminal bronchioles and alveoli, in conjunction with the widespread destruction of pulmonary elastic connective tissue. These combined events lead to dilation of individual alveoli, resulting in a decrease in the total number of alveoli, and the subsequent loss of gas exchange surface area. The patient is unable to exhale effectively, so that stagnant, oxygen-poor air builds up within the abnormally large (but numerically diminished) alveoli. Most cases of emphysema result from damage caused by

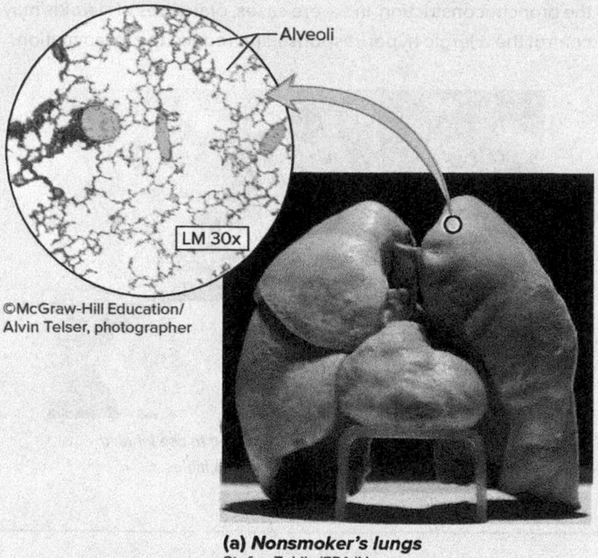

©McGraw-Hill Education/ Alvin Telser, photographer

(a) ***Nonsmoker's lungs***
Stefan Zaklin/EPA/Newscom

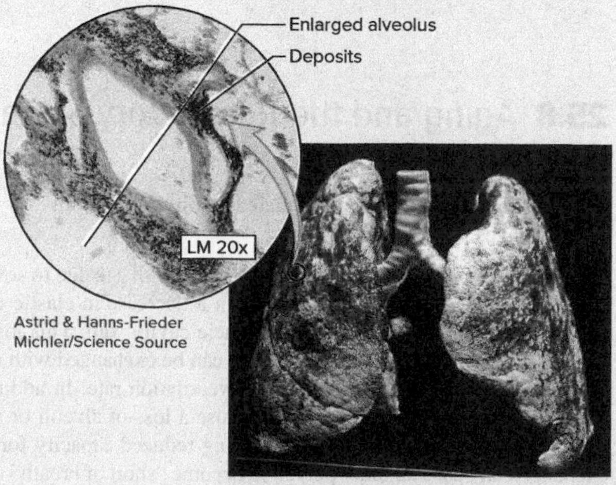

Astrid & Hanns-Frieder Michler/Science Source

(b) ***Smoker's lungs***
360b/Shutterstock

Smoking causes the lungs to become blackened. The alveoli become enlarged and less numerous, and contain black deposits. Compare the gross and microscopic anatomy of (a) a nonsmoker's lungs to (b) a smoker's lungs.

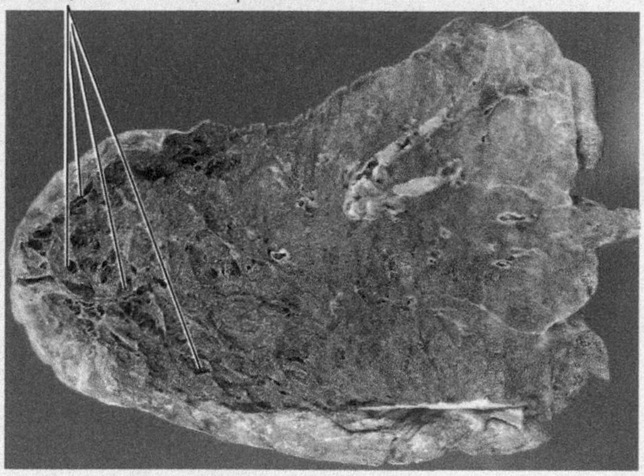

(c) ***Gross anatomy of lung with emphysema***
Dennis K. Burns, MD Travis G. Brown, MD Walter L. Kemp, MD/McGraw-Hill Education

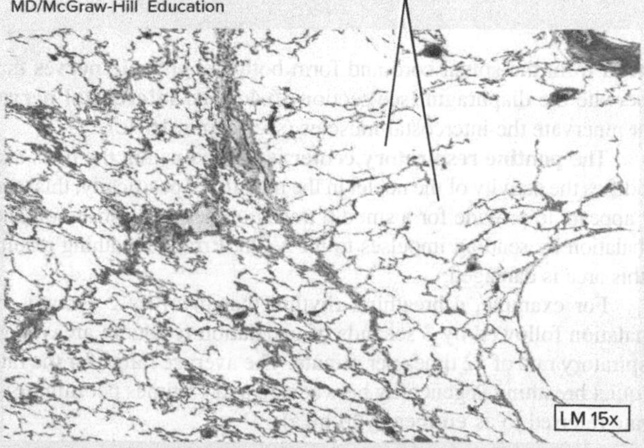

(d) ***Microscopic image of lung with emphysema***
Emphysema causes dilation of the alveoli and loss of elastic tissue, resulting in poorly functioning alveoli. (c) A gross section of an emphysemic lung shows the dilated alveoli. (d) Microscopically, the alveoli are abnormally large and nonfunctional.
©McGraw-Hill Education/Alvin Telser, photographer

smoking. Once the tissue in the lung has been destroyed, it cannot regenerate, and thus there is no cure for emphysema. The best therapy for an emphysema patient is to stop smoking and try to get optimal use from the remaining lung tissue by using a bronchodilator, seeking prompt treatment for pulmonary infections, and taking oxygen supplementation if necessary.

(e) *An individual with advanced emphysema must rely on a portable oxygen tank, such as this backpack tank.*
CHAD Therapeutics, Inc.

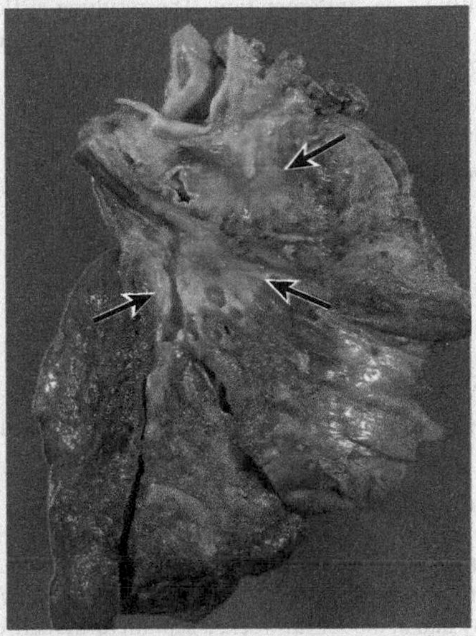

(f) *Gross section of a lung with squamous cell carcinoma (black arrows).*
Dennis K. Burns MD, Travis G. Brown MD, Walter L. Kemp MD/McGraw-Hill Education

Lung cancer is a highly aggressive and frequently fatal malignancy that originates in the epithelium of the respiratory system. Smoking causes about 85% of all lung cancers. Metastasis, the spread of cancerous cells to other tissues, occurs early in the course of the disease, making a surgical cure unlikely for most patients. Pulmonary symptoms include chronic cough, coughing up blood, excess pulmonary mucus, and increased likelihood of pulmonary infections. Some people are diagnosed based upon symptoms that develop after the cancer has already metastasized to a distant site. For example, lung cancer commonly spreads to the brain, so in some cases lung cancer is not discovered until the patient seeks treatment for a seizure disorder related to cancer in the brain.

Lung cancers are classified by their histologic appearance into three basic patterns: squamous cell carcinoma, adenocarcinoma, and small-cell carcinoma.

Squamous cell carcinoma (kar'si-nō'mă; *karkinos* = cancer, *oma* = tumor) may develop when the pseudostratified ciliated columnar epithelium lining the lungs changes to a sturdier stratified squamous epithelium to withstand the chronic inflammation and injury caused by tobacco smoke. If the chronic injury continues, these transformed epithelial cells may accumulate enough genetic damage to become overtly malignant.

Adenocarcinoma of the lung arises from the mucin-producing glands in the respiratory epithelium. It begins when DNA injury causes one of these cells to become malignant and begin to divide uncontrollably.

Small-cell carcinoma is a less common type of lung cancer; it originates in the main bronchi and eventually invades the mediastinum. This type of cancer arises from the small neuroendocrine cells in the larger bronchi; their secretions help regulate muscle tone in the bronchi and vessels. As a consequence of their endocrine heritage, some of these tumors secrete hormones. For example, a small-cell carcinoma of the lung occasionally releases ACTH, producing symptoms of Cushing syndrome (see Clinical View 20.5: "Disorders of Adrenal Cortex Hormone Secretion" in section 20.6a).

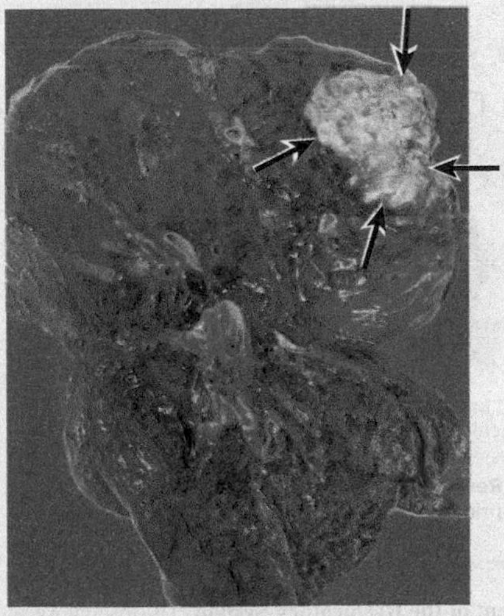

(g) *A lung exhibiting adenocarcinoma (black arrows).*
Dennis K. Burns MD, Travis G. Brown MD, Walter L. Kemp MD/McGraw-Hill Education

Two distinct diseases, *emphysema* and *chronic bronchitis,* together make up the more general disease classification of **chronic obstructive pulmonary disease (COPD).** COPD characterized by lung structural abnormalities resulting from inflammation. The resulting airflow obstruction makes it hard for the patient to exhale. COPD often is caused by smoking.

WHAT DID YOU LEARN?

14 What are some ways that aging can affect the respiratory system?

25.9 Development of the Respiratory System

✓ Learning Objective

16. Explain how the respiratory system forms in the embryo and fetus.

Early in the fourth week of development, a ventral outgrowth extends from the developing pharynx. This endodermal outgrowth is called the **respiratory diverticulum** (dī-ver-tik′ū-lŭm; byroad), or *lung bud,* and it initially maintains communication with the pharynx (**figure 25.17*a***). By late in the fourth week, a septum forms between the pharynx and the respiratory diverticulum, partitioning them into two separate tubes. The respiratory diverticulum, formed from endoderm, undergoes intricate branching to form the respiratory tree. Surrounding the respiratory diverticulum is mesoderm, which later differentiates into the vasculature, muscle, and cartilage of each lung.

The respiratory diverticulum grows inferiorly and forms the future trachea. At the end of the fourth week, the respiratory diverticulum branches into a **left** and **right primary bronchial bud.** Each bud forms the rudiments of the left and right main bronchi, respectively. Growing branches of the pulmonary arteries and veins travel with these developing bronchial buds. By the fifth week of development, the primary bronchial buds branch into **secondary bronchial buds**

Clinical View 25.9

Sudden Infant Death Syndrome (SIDS)

Sudden infant death syndrome (SIDS), also known as *crib death,* is the sudden and unexplained death of an infant younger than 1 year of age. Most SIDS deaths occur in infants between 2 and 4 months of age. To be counted as a SIDS death, the child must die for no apparent reason other than cessation of breathing. SIDS deaths are thoroughly evaluated through investigation of the death scene, examination of family history, and autopsy of the child.

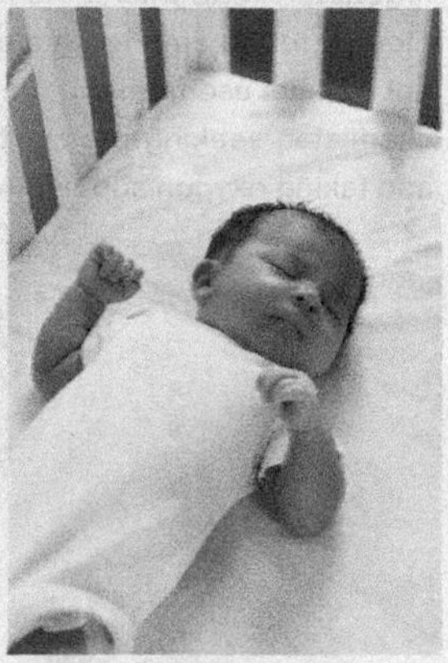

An infant should sleep on its back, and not the stomach, to reduce the risk of SIDS.

Lucy von Held/Blend Images/Getty Images

Although the definitive cause of SIDS is not known, current research indicates that SIDS babies have trouble regulating and maintaining blood pressure, breathing, and body temperature. Some form of stress, in combination with one or more of these three factors, appears to be involved in SIDS deaths. It is now known that babies sleeping on their stomachs are at greater risk for SIDS than those sleeping on their backs. The national Safe to Sleep Campaign (formerly called the Back to Sleep Campaign), significantly reduced the number of SIDS deaths in the United States.

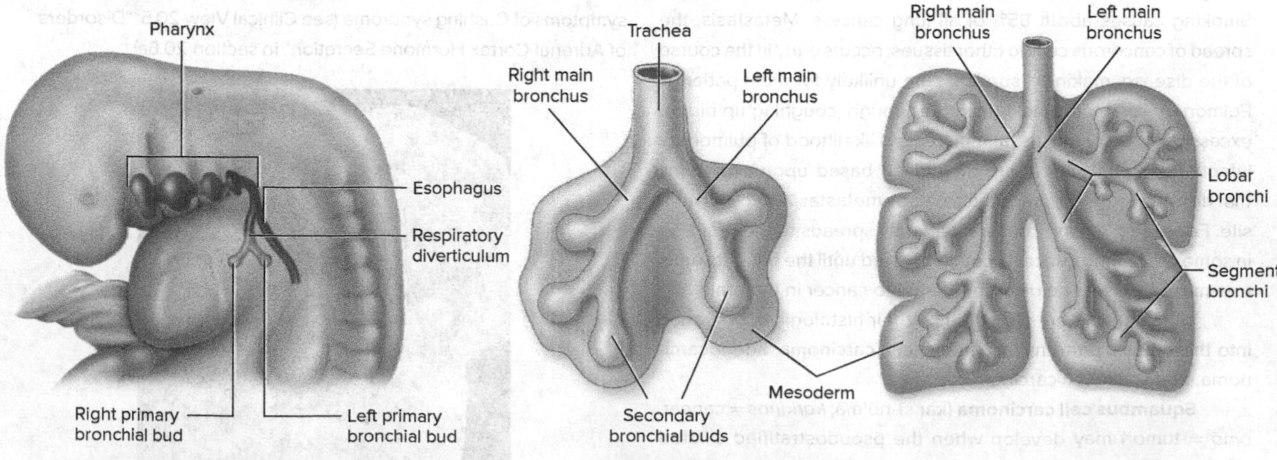

Figure 25.17

Development of the Respiratory System. The respiratory system forms as an outgrowth (called the respiratory diverticulum) from the developing pharynx beginning at week 4. (*a*) Primary bronchial buds appear later during week 4. (*b*) Secondary bronchial buds branch from the main bronchi during week 5 and grow into the surrounding mesoderm. (*c*) By week 6, the segmental bronchi of the left and right lungs have formed.

(figure 25.17 *b*). The secondary bronchial buds form the lobar bronchi of each lung. Thus, the left primary bronchial bud branches into two secondary bronchial buds (because the left lung has two lobar bronchi), and the right primary bronchial bud branches into three secondary bronchial buds (for the three lobar bronchi of the right lung).

In the following weeks, the secondary bronchial buds undergo further branching. Week 6 is marked by the development of segmental bronchi and the rudiments of the bronchopulmonary segments (figure 25.17 *c*). From week 6 to week 16, the respiratory tree forms smaller branches until finally the terminal bronchioles form. Thus, the conducting portion of the respiratory system has developed by week 16.

Weeks 16–28 mark the branching and development of respiratory bronchioles from the terminal bronchioles. From week 28 of development until birth, **primitive alveoli** (also called *terminal sacs*) develop more profusely. These primitive alveoli have a thick epithelial lining that must thin into simple squamous epithelium in order for the alveoli to become functional. It isn't until after week 28 that this epithelium becomes sufficiently thinned for respiration. In addition, by about week 28 the alveolar type II cells start to secrete pulmonary surfactant, which helps keep the alveoli patent (open) and facilitates inflation. Without sufficient surfactant, the alveoli collapse upon exhalation, and it becomes difficult to reinflate them. Prematurely born infants sometimes experience respiratory distress due to inadequate production of surfactant.

Prior to birth, the respiratory system is nonfunctional because gas exchange occurs between fetal blood and maternal blood at the placenta. The lungs and pulmonary vessels of the fetus are collapsed, and so most of the blood is shunted away from the lungs to the fetus's systemic circulation. At birth, the first contraction of the external intercostal muscles and diaphragm fills the lungs with air. (The pressure changes within the thoracic cavity drive the commencement of pulmonary circulation.) Blood is sent to the lungs, where gas exchange occurs, and the newborn relies on its own lungs (instead of the mother's placenta) for respiratory gas exchange.

Even after we are born, our lungs continue to produce additional primitive alveoli. Some research has indicated that alveoli continue to develop until we are about 8 years old, by which time each lung has about 300 to 400 million alveoli. **Table 25.3** summarizes the events in respiratory system development.

Table 25.3 Major Events of Respiratory System Development

Week of Development/Age	Respiratory System Structure Formed
Early week 4	Respiratory diverticulum forms
Late week 4	Primary bronchial buds form (each is the rudiment of the main bronchi)
Week 5	Lobar bronchial buds form
Week 6	Segmental bronchial buds form
Week 6–week 16	Successive branching of segmental bronchial buds forms smaller bronchi and bronchioles; eventually, terminal bronchioles form; conducting portion of respiratory system is complete
Week 16–week 28	Terminal bronchioles branch into respiratory bronchioles
Week 28–birth	Primitive alveoli form; pulmonary surfactant begins to be produced
Birth–8 years	Alveoli continue to develop; eventually, adult number of alveoli (300–400 million per lung) is attained

Clinical Terms

bronchitis Inflammation of the bronchi, due to either an infection or chronic exposure to irritants (such as cigarette smoke)

epistaxis (ep′i-stak′sis; *epi* = on, *stazo* = to fall in drops) Bleeding from the nose; may be caused by allergies, hypertension, infection, or nasal trauma. Also called nosebleed or nasal hemorrhage.

hyaline (hī′ă-lin; *hyalos* = glass) **membrane disease** Disease seen especially in premature neonates with reduced amounts of lung surfactant.

tuberculosis (TB) A potentially serious bacterial infection that primarily affects the lungs, but can also damage other parts of the body. TB is caused by the bacterium *Mycobacterium tuberculosis*.

Chapter Summary

25.1 General Organization and Functions of the Respiratory System	■ The respiratory system has a conducting portion to convey gas to and from the lungs and a respiratory portion for gas exchange with the blood. **25.1a Respiratory System Functions** ■ Respiratory system functions include gas exchange, gas conditioning, sound production, olfaction, and defense.

(continued on next page)

Chapter Summary (continued)

25.2 Upper Respiratory Tract	■ The conducting airways of the upper respiratory tract are the nose, nasal cavity, paranasal sinuses, pharynx, larynx, and their associated structures. **25.2a Nose and Nasal Cavity** ■ The nasal cavity is the primary site for conditioning inhaled air. It houses three pairs of nasal conchae that cause turbulence in inhaled air, which passes posteriorly into the nasopharynx through the choanae. **25.2b Paranasal Sinuses** ■ Paranasal sinuses are paired air spaces in the frontal, ethmoidal, and sphenoidal bones, and the maxillae. They decrease skull bone weight, help condition inhaled air, and contribute to sound resonance. **25.2c Pharynx** ■ The pharynx is composed of (1) the nasopharynx, with paired auditory openings on the lateral wall and a pharyngeal tonsil on the posterior wall; (2) the oropharynx, with paired palatine tonsils on the lateral walls and lingual tonsils at the base of the tongue; and (3) the laryngopharynx, which is continuous with the larynx and esophagus. **25.2d Larynx** ■ The larynx conducts air into the trachea and lower respiratory tract, and produces sound. ■ The larynx is composed of cartilage and has paired vocal folds that produce sound when air passes between them.
25.3 Lower Respiratory Tract	■ The conducting airways of the lower respiratory tract include the trachea, bronchi, bronchioles to the terminal bronchioles, and their associated structures. Its respiratory portions include respiratory bronchioles, alveolar ducts, and alveoli. **25.3a Trachea** ■ The trachea is lined by pseudostratified ciliated columnar epithelium and has C-shaped tracheal cartilage rings that support the tracheal wall and prevent its collapse. **25.3b Bronchial Tree** ■ The bronchial tree conducts respiratory gases from the main bronchi to the terminal bronchioles. ■ Bronchial tree passageways have cartilage and/or smooth muscle bands to support the walls. The passageway sequence is (1) main bronchi, (2) lobar bronchi, (3) segmental bronchi, (4) bronchioles, and (5) terminal bronchioles. **25.3c Respiratory Bronchioles, Alveolar Ducts, and Alveoli** ■ Respiratory bronchioles branch from terminal bronchioles and have alveoli outpocketings in their walls. ■ An alveolus is a small, thin sac with two types of cells in its wall. ■ Alveolar type I cells promote rapid gas diffusion; alveolar type II cells secrete pulmonary surfactant. ■ Alveolar macrophages remove inhaled particulate materials from alveolar surfaces. ■ The respiratory membrane consists of alveolar type I cells, an endothelial cell of a capillary, and their fused basement membranes.
25.4 Lungs	■ The lungs are lateral to the mediastinum in the thoracic cavity. **25.4a Pleura and Pleural Cavities** ■ The visceral pleura covers the lung outer surface, and the parietal pleura lines the internal thoracic walls; a pleural cavity is sandwiched between the pleural layers. The pleural membranes produce serous fluid. **25.4b Gross Anatomy of the Lungs** ■ Lung surfaces include the base (upon the diaphragm), the apex (superior surface), the costal surface (against the thoracic wall), and the mediastinal surface (facing the mediastinum). ■ The hilum is a medial opening through which bronchi, pulmonary vessels, lymph vessels, and nerves enter the lungs. **25.4c Blood Supply to and from the Lungs** ■ The pulmonary circulation transports blood to and from the gas exchange surfaces of the lungs, and the bronchial circulation supplies the bronchi and bronchioles. **25.4d Lymphatic Drainage** ■ The connective tissue in the lung houses lymph nodes and lymph vessels.
25.5 Pulmonary Ventilation	■ Breathing, called pulmonary ventilation, is the movement of air into and out of the respiratory tract. Change in air pressure between the atmosphere and the alveoli drives ventilation.
25.6 Mechanics of Breathing	■ Breathing involves coordinated movement of skeletal muscles and volume changes in the thoracic cavity. **25.6a Skeletal Muscles of Breathing** ■ The primary muscles that move the ribs for forced inhalation are: (1) scalenes, (2) external intercostals, and (3) serratus posterior superior. The primary muscles that move the ribs for forced exhalation are: (4) internal intercostals, (5) transversus thoracis, and (6) serratus posterior inferior. **25.6b Volume Changes in the Thoracic Cavity** ■ Inhalation causes the thoracic cavity space to increase vertically, laterally, and in an anterior-posterior direction; exhalation causes it to return to its original size.

25.7 Innervation of the Respiratory System	■ Sympathetic stimulation causes bronchodilation; parasympathetic stimulation causes bronchoconstriction. **25.7a Ventilation Control by Respiratory Centers of the Brain** ■ The medullary respiratory center has a dorsal respiratory group (DRG) for inhalation and a ventral respiratory group (VRG) for forced exhalation. ■ The apneustic and pneumotaxic centers within the pons influence the respiration rate by modifying the activity of the DRG.
25.8 Aging and the Respiratory System	■ The respiratory system becomes less efficient with age due to loss of elasticity and loss or decreased size and functionality of alveoli.
25.9 Development of the Respiratory System	■ Early in the fourth week of development, a respiratory diverticulum forms and leads to primary bronchial buds by late in that same week. ■ By the fifth week of development, the primary main bronchial buds branch into secondary bronchial buds. Once they branch, the primary buds become the main bronchi and the secondary buds become the lobar bronchi. These bronchial buds undergo further branching until terminal bronchioles are formed by week 16. Respiratory bronchioles form from the terminal bronchioles during weeks 16–28. ■ Alveoli continue to form from week 28 of development until about 8 years of age, when the adult number of 300 to 400 million alveoli per lung is attained.

Challenge Yourself

Actively write or type your answers in a separate document to reinforce your learning, before checking your answers.

Multiple Choice

Select the best answer from the four choices provided.

1. What structure does the visceral pleura cover?
   a. outer surface of the lung
   b. gas exchange surface of the alveoli
   c. inner wall of the thoracic cavity
   d. trachea
2. Which area is common to the respiratory system and the digestive system, and provides a passageway through which food, drink, or air can travel?
   a. nasopharynx
   b. trachea
   c. oropharynx
   d. glottis
3. Which statement correctly describes the trachea?
   a. It bifurcates into left and right main bronchi at the level of the sternal angle.
   b. It is located superior to the larynx.
   c. It is lined by nonkeratinized stratified squamous epithelium.
   d. It is a component of the upper respiratory tract.
4. Which structure is the last, smallest portion of the conducting portion of the respiratory system?
   a. nasopharynx
   b. terminal bronchiole
   c. respiratory bronchiole
   d. alveolus
5. Which is *not* a function of the paranasal sinuses?
   a. warm inhaled air
   b. responsible for sound resonance
   c. gas exchange
   d. humidify inhaled air
6. Which cartilage of the larynx forms the laryngeal prominence?
   a. arytenoid
   b. cuneiform
   c. thyroid
   d. cricoid
7. What is the function of the C-shaped cartilage rings in the trachea?
   a. serve as a point of attachment for some muscles of exhalation.
   b. support muscular attachments to the thyroid cartilage and epiglottis.
   c. prevent the trachea from collapsing.
   d. attach the trachea to the esophagus posteriorly.
8. Which term describes the exchange of respiratory gases between the alveoli and the blood?
   a. systemic gas exchange
   b. gas transport
   c. alveolar gas exchange
   d. pulmonary ventilation
9. What type of epithelium lines an alveolus?
   a. simple squamous epithelium
   b. pseudostratified ciliated columnar epithelium
   c. simple cuboidal epithelium
   d. transitional epithelium
10. The conducting portion of the respiratory system is completely formed by what week of embryonic/fetal development?
    a. 6
    b. 10
    c. 16
    d. 28

Content Review

1. What is the difference between the conducting portion and the respiratory portion of the respiratory tract, and what structures are found in which portion?
2. What are the main functions of the respiratory system, and which respiratory system structures are responsible for these functions?
3. What must happen to the vocal folds to produce a higher-pitched sound? A lower-pitched sound? What produces a louder sound?
4. What are the components of the bronchial tree, from largest to smallest? How does the structure (epithelium, presence of cartilage, abundance of smooth muscle) change in the bronchial tree?

5. What are the differences between the vocal folds and the vestibular folds?
6. Why are alveolar type II cells important in maintaining the inflation of the lungs?
7. How do the left and right lungs differ anatomically?
8. How do the dimensions of the thoracic cavity change when we inhale and exhale? What muscles assist with these dimensional changes?
9. Name the autonomic nervous system respiratory centers in the pons and the medulla oblongata, and describe their functions.
10. Describe the ways in which the respiratory system changes as we age.

Developing Critical Reasoning

1. Charlene has had a bad cold for the last few days. While preparing a presentation for her speech class, she records her talk so that she can critique it later. When she listens to the recording, her young daughter exclaims, "Mommy that doesn't even sound like you. What happened to your voice?" How is Charlene's cold related to the changes in her voice?
2. Your best friend George is an athletic 20-year-old who smokes regularly. George tells you, "Smoking doesn't affect me—I can still run and do the sports I like. All that talk about smoking being dangerous doesn't apply to me." Do you agree with George? What would you tell him about the dangers of smoking and some of the conditions he may expect to have later in life?
3. Elisa is pregnant with her first child and is at risk for a preterm delivery. She was told by her physician that preterm infants born after week 28 of development have a better chance at survival than those born before this date. She asks you why this is the case. What is your explanation?

Answers to "What Do You Think?"

1. A "deviated septum" is off-center, so one side of the nasal cavity is larger than the other. This alters the normal flow of air through the nose, and if the narrower side becomes blocked, nasal congestion or sinus problems may result.
2. The epithelium changes because a stratified squamous epithelium is more sturdy and protective against smoke than a pseudostratified ciliated columnar epithelium. Unfortunately, because stratified squamous epithelium lacks cilia and goblet cells, less mucus is produced, and no cilia are present to propel particles away from the bronchi toward the pharynx. Thus, the main way to eliminate these particles is by coughing, leading to the chronic "smoker's cough."
3. The constriction of the bronchioles allows for a more forceful expulsion of air from the lungs, which may help dislodge accumulated mucus or inhaled foreign particulate materials. If the bronchioles were dilated all the time, it would be more difficult to expel mucus or foreign particles.
4. The left lung is smaller because the heart projects into the left side of the thoracic cavity.
5. Lymph nodes darken and turn black as they accumulate the dust, particles, and pollution we inhale over a lifetime.
6. An asthma inhaler mimics sympathetic stimulation because it causes bronchodilation.

Design Element: Pencil Icon: Slavojub Pantelic/Shutterstock

Digestive System 26

Outline

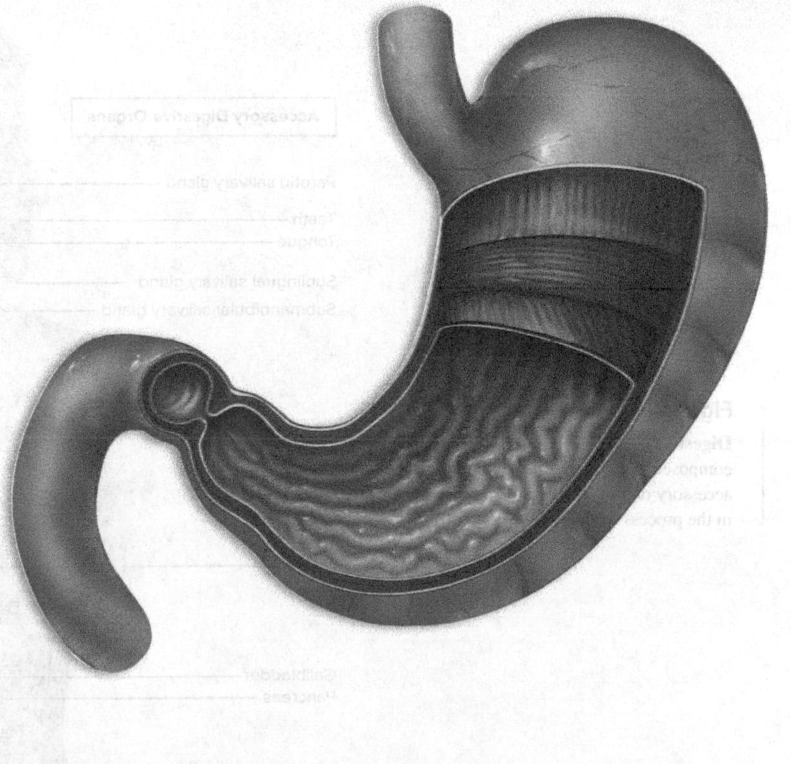

Anatomy & Physiology Revealed 4.0

MODULE 12: DIGESTIVE SYSTEM

Each time we eat a meal and drink fluids, our bodies take in the nutrients necessary for survival. However, these nutrients must be digested and processed—broken down both mechanically and chemically—into components small enough for our cells to use. These components are absorbed from the **digestive** (di-jes′tiv, dī-; *digestus* = to force apart, divide, dissolve) **system** into the blood and transported to the body tissues.

After the nutrients from foods are absorbed, some materials remain that cannot be digested or absorbed, such as cellulose and fiber. These materials are expelled from the body via a process called defecation. All of these functions are the responsibility of the digestive system.

26.1 General Structure and Functions of the Digestive System

✓ Learning Objectives

1. Identify and describe the digestive tract organs and accessory digestive organs.
2. Describe the basic functions of the digestive system.
3. Compare and contrast mechanical and chemical digestion.

The digestive system includes the organs that ingest the food, mix and transport the ingested material, digest the material into smaller usable components, absorb the necessary digested nutrients into the blood and expel the waste products from the body. When you eat, you put food into your mouth and it mixes with saliva as you chew. The chewed food mixed with saliva is called a **bolus** (bō′lŭs; lump), and it is the bolus that is swallowed. The stomach processes the bolus and turns it into a pastelike substance called **chyme.** Hereafter, we will simplify our discussion by referring to the ingested contents as "material."

The digestive system has two separate categories of organs: those composing the gastrointestinal tract, and the accessory digestive organs (**figure 26.1**). The **gastrointestinal** (gas′trō-in-tes′tin-ăl; *gastro* = the stomach) **(GI) tract** is also called either the *digestive tract* or *alimentary canal.* The GI tract organs essentially form a continuous tube that includes the oral cavity (mouth), pharynx (throat), esophagus, stomach, small intestine, large intestine, anal canal, and ends at the anus. The entire GI tract is lined by a mucous membrane. The contraction of muscle in the GI tract wall propels materials through the tract.

Accessory digestive organs are connected to the GI tract and typically develop as outgrowths from the tract. The accessory digestive organs assist the GI tract in the digestion of material. Accessory digestive organs include the teeth, tongue, salivary glands, liver, gallbladder, and pancreas.

26.1a Digestive System Functions

The digestive system performs six main functions: ingestion, motility, secretion, digestion, absorption, and elimination of wastes.

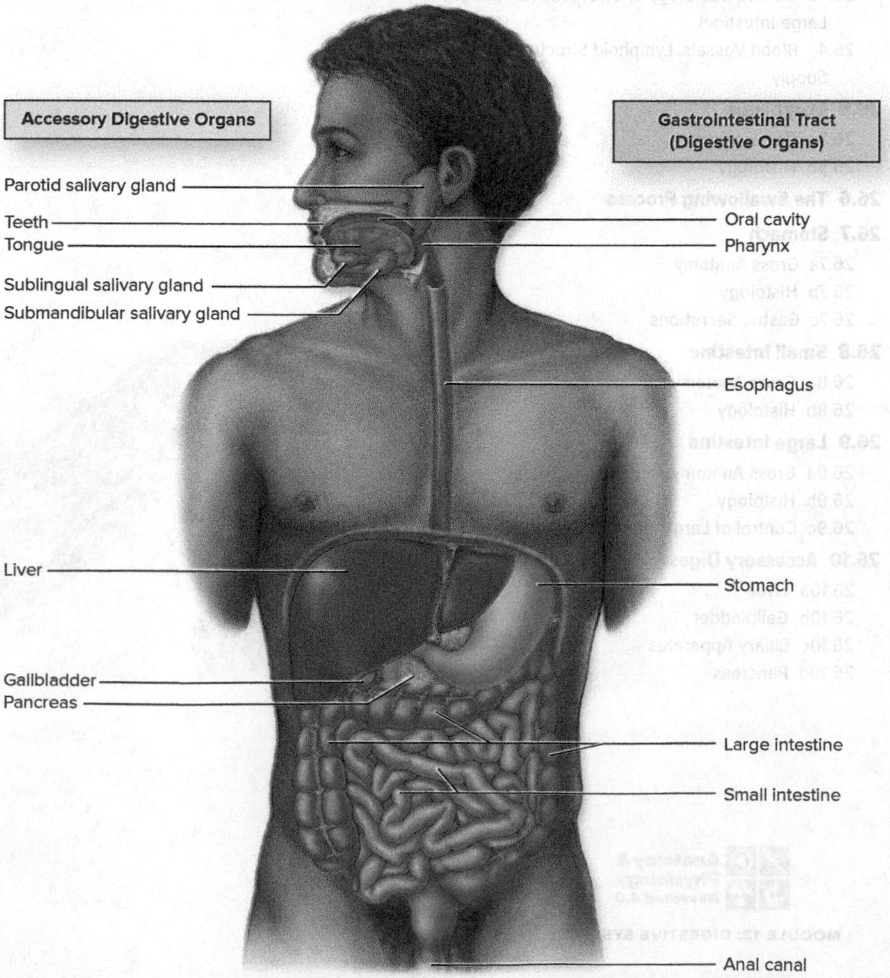
Accessory Digestive Organs
Gastrointestinal Tract (Digestive Organs)
Parotid salivary gland
Teeth
Tongue
Sublingual salivary gland
Submandibular salivary gland
Oral cavity
Pharynx
Esophagus
Liver
Stomach
Gallbladder
Pancreas
Large intestine
Small intestine
Anal canal

Figure 26.1

Digestive System. The digestive system is composed of the gastrointestinal (GI) tract and accessory digestive organs that assist the GI tract in the process of digestion.

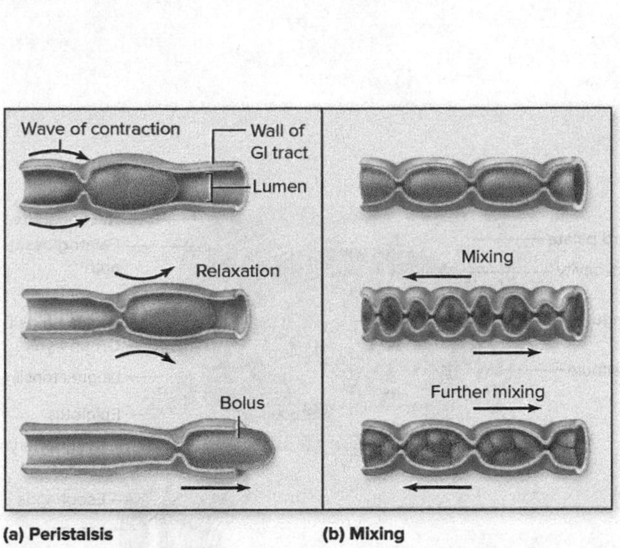

Figure 26.2

Peristalsis and Mixing. A swallowed bolus is propelled through the GI tract by the coordinated contraction and relaxation of the GI tract wall musculature. (*a*) Peristalsis is a wave of contraction that moves material ahead of the wave through the GI tract toward the anus. (*b*) Mixing is the back-and-forth muscular contractions in the small intestine whereby ingested material blends with secretory products to increase the efficiency of digestion and absorption.

Ingestion (in-jes'chŭn; *ingero* = to carry in) is the introduction of solid and liquid materials into the oral cavity (mouth). It is the first step in the process of digesting and absorbing nutrients.

After the materials are swallowed, voluntary and involuntary muscular contractions mix and move materials through the GI tract. These movements are termed **motility.** Motility involves peristalsis and mixing. **Peristalsis** (per'i-stal'sis; *stalsis* = constriction) is the process of muscular contraction that forms ripples along part of the GI tract and forces material to move further along the tract (**figure 26.2*a***). Peristalsis is like pushing toothpaste through a toothpaste tube: As you push on the flat end of the tube, a portion of toothpaste moves toward the opening. As you push the middle of the tube, the segment of toothpaste moves even closer to the opening. Churning movements in the small intestine, called **mixing** or *segmentation,* help disperse the material being digested and combine it with digestive organ secretions (figure 26.2*b*). The material within the lumen of the small intestine is moved back-and-forth to mix it with the secretory products that are being introduced into that region of the GI tract.

Secretion (se-krē'shŭn; *secerno* = to separate) is the process of producing and releasing mucin or fluids such as acid, bile, and digestive enzymes. When these products are secreted into the lumen of the GI tract, they facilitate chemical digestion and the passage of material through the GI tract. Some of these products (e.g., acid, bile, digestive enzymes) help digest food. Mucin secretions serve a protective function. Mucin mixes with water to form mucus, and the mucus coats the GI wall to protect and lubricate it against acidic secretions and abrasion by passing materials.

Digestion is the breakdown of large food items into smaller structures and molecules. There are two aspects to digestion: **Mechanical digestion** physically breaks down ingested materials into smaller pieces, and **chemical digestion** breaks down ingested material into smaller molecules by using enzymes. (Review enzymes in section 2.3a.) The first part of mechanical digestion is **mastication** (mas'ti-kā'shŭn; *mastico* = to chew), the chewing of ingested material by the teeth in the oral cavity.

Absorption (ab-sōrp'shŭn; *absorptio* = to swallow) involves either passive or active transport of electrolytes, digestion products, vitamins, and water across the GI tract epithelium and into GI tract blood and lymph vessels.

The final function of the digestive system is the **elimination** of wastes. Our bodies use most, but not all, of the components of what we eat. All undigestible materials as well as the waste products secreted by the accessory organs into the GI tract are compacted into **feces** (fē'sēz; *faex* = dregs), or *fecal material,* and then eliminated from the GI tract by the process of **defecation** (def'ĕ-kā'shŭn; *defaeco* = to remove the dregs).

Learning Strategy 26.1

The process of mixing (or segmentation) is like kneading bread dough or blending a smoothie. It combines ingested materials with digestive enzymes and mechanically breaks down larger digested particles into smaller ones so the enzymes have a greater effect.

WHAT DID YOU LEARN?

1. List the structures that compose the GI tract from mouth to anus.
2. How do secretion and absorption differ?

26.2 Oral Cavity

✓ **Learning Objective**

4. Identify and describe the structure and function of the tongue, salivary glands, and teeth.

The **oral cavity,** or *mouth,* is the entrance to the GI tract (**figure 26.3**). The mouth is the initial site of mechanical digestion (via mastication) and chemical digestion (via an enzyme in saliva). The epithelial lining of the oral cavity is a nonkeratinized stratified squamous epithelium that protects against the abrasive activities associated with digestion. This lining is moistened continuously by the secretion of saliva.

The oral cavity is bounded anteriorly by the teeth and lips and posteriorly by the oropharynx. The superior boundary of the oral cavity is formed by the hard and soft palates. The floor, or inferior surface, of the oral cavity is formed by the mylohyoid muscle covered with a mucous membrane. The tongue attaches to the floor of the oral cavity.

The oral cavity has two distinct regions: The **vestibule** is the space between the cheeks or lips and the gums. The **oral cavity proper** lies central to the alveolar processes of the mandible and maxillae.

26.2a Cheeks, Lips, and Palate

The lateral walls of the oral cavity are formed by the cheeks, which are covered externally by the integument and contain the buccinator muscles. The buccinator muscles compress the cheeks against the teeth to hold solid materials in place during chewing. The cheeks terminate at the fleshy **lips** (or *labia*), which form the anterior wall of the oral cavity. The lips are formed primarily by the orbicularis oris muscle and covered with keratinized stratified squamous epithelium. Lips have a reddish hue because of their abundant supply of superficial blood vessels and the reduced amount of keratin within their outer epithelial layer. The **gingivae** (jin'ji-vē), or *gums,* are composed of dense irregular connective tissue, with an overlying nonkeratinized stratified squamous epithelium that covers the alveolar processes of

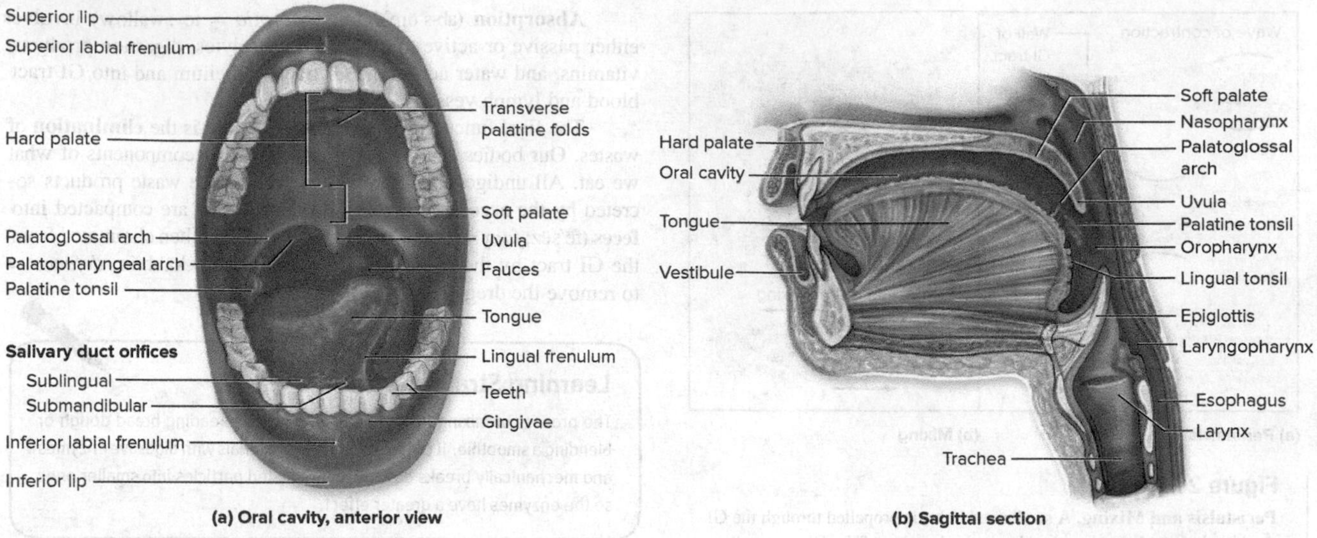

Figure 26.3

Oral Cavity. (*a*) Ingested food and drink enter the GI tract through the oral cavity, shown here in anterior view. (*b*) A diagrammatic sagittal section shows the structures of the oral cavity and the pharynx. APR

the upper and lower jaws and surrounds the necks of the teeth (see section 7.1d). The internal surfaces of the superior and inferior lips each are attached to the gingivae by a thin mucosa fold in the midline, called the **labial** (lā′bē-ăl) **frenulum** (fren′y ū-lŭm; *frenum* = bridle).

The **palate** (pal′ăt) forms the superior boundary, or "roof," of the oral cavity and acts as a barrier to separate it from the nasal cavity. The anterior two-thirds of the palate is hard and bony (called the hard palate), whereas the posterior one-third is soft and muscular (called the soft palate). The **hard palate** is formed by the palatine processes of the maxillae and the horizontal plates of the palatine bones. It is covered with dense connective tissue and nonkeratinized stratified squamous epithelium and exhibits prominent **transverse palatine folds,** or *friction ridges,* that assist the tongue in manipulating ingested materials prior to swallowing. The arching **soft palate** is primarily composed of skeletal muscle and covered with nonkeratinized stratified squamous epithelium. Extending inferiorly from the posterior part of the soft palate is a conical median projection called the **uvula** (yū′vy ū-lă; *uva* = grape). When you swallow, the soft palate and the uvula elevate to close off the posterior entrance into the nasopharynx and prevent ingested materials from entering the nasal region.

The **fauces** represent the opening between the oral cavity and the oropharynx. The fauces are bounded by paired muscular folds: the **palatoglossal arch** (the anterior fold containing the palatoglossus muscle) and the **palatopharyngeal arch** (the posterior fold containing the palatopharyngeal muscle). The **palatine tonsils** are housed between the arches (see section 24.4a). These tonsils serve as an "early line of defense" as they monitor ingested food and drink for antigens, and initiate an immune response when necessary.

26.2b Tongue

The **tongue** (tŭng) is an accessory digestive organ that is formed primarily from skeletal muscle and covered with stratified squamous epithelium. Numerous small projections, termed **papillae** (pă-pil′ē; sing., *papilla; papula* = pimple), cover the superior (dorsal) surface of the tongue (see section 19.3a). The tongue's stratified squamous epithelium is keratinized over the filiform papillae but nonkeratinized over the rest of the tongue. Sections 25.1a and 25.3a described the tongue as a participant in sound production. In addition, the tongue manipulates and mixes ingested materials during chewing and helps compress the materials against the palate to turn them into a bolus. The tongue also performs important functions in swallowing. The inferior surface of the tongue attaches to the floor of the oral cavity by a thin, vertical mucous membrane, the **lingual frenulum** (figure 26.3 *a*). In addition, the posteroinferior surface of the tongue contains **lingual tonsils.** Extrinsic and intrinsic skeletal muscles move the tongue (see section 11.1d, figure 11.6).

26.2c Salivary Glands

The salivary glands collectively produce and secrete **saliva** (să-lī′v ă), a fluid that assists in the initial activities of digestion. The volume of saliva secreted daily ranges between 1.0 and 1.5 liters. Most saliva is produced during mealtime, but smaller amounts are produced continuously to ensure that the oral cavity mucous membrane remains moist. Water makes up 99.5% of the volume of saliva and is its primary ingredient. Saliva also contains a mixture of other components **(table 26.1)**.

Saliva has various functions. It moistens ingested food and helps it become a slick, semisolid bolus that is more easily swallowed. Saliva also moistens, cleanses, and lubricates the oral cavity structures. The first step in chemical digestion occurs when **salivary amylase** starts the process of breaking down carbohydrates. Saliva contains antibodies and an antibacterial substance called **lysosyme** that help inhibit bacterial growth in the oral cavity. Finally, saliva is the watery medium into which food molecules are dissolved so that taste receptors on the tongue can be stimulated.

A small amount of saliva is produced by unicellular glands within the oral cavity, collectively known as **intrinsic salivary glands.** These intrinsic salivary glands are responsible for secreting **lingual lipase,** an enzyme that is activated by the low pH levels in the

Table 26.1 Saliva Characteristics

Production Rate	pH Range	Composition of Saliva	Solute Components	Neural Control of Saliva Secretion
1–1.5 L/day	Slightly acidic (pH 6.4 to 6.8)	99.5% water; 0.5% solutes	Ions (e.g., Na^+, K^+, chloride, bicarbonate) Immunoglobulin A (helps decrease bacterial infections) Lysozyme (antibacterial enzyme) Mucin Lingual lipase (from intrinsic salivary glands) Salivary amylase (enzyme that breaks down carbohydrates)	Parasympathetic axons in CN IX stimulate parotid salivary gland secretions Parasympathetic axons in CN VII stimulate submandibular and sublingual salivary gland secretions Sympathetic activation stimulates mucin secretion

stomach to break down lipids. Most saliva, however, is produced from multicellular exocrine glands outside the oral cavity called **extrinsic salivary glands.** Three pairs of multicellular salivary glands are located external to the oral cavity: the parotid, submandibular, and sublingual glands **(figure 26.4*a*).**

The **parotid** (pă-rot′id; *para* = beside, *ot* = ear) **salivary glands** are the largest salivary glands. Each parotid gland is located anterior and slightly inferior to the ear, partially overlying the masseter muscle. The parotid salivary glands produce about 25% to 30% of the saliva, which is conducted through the **parotid duct** to the

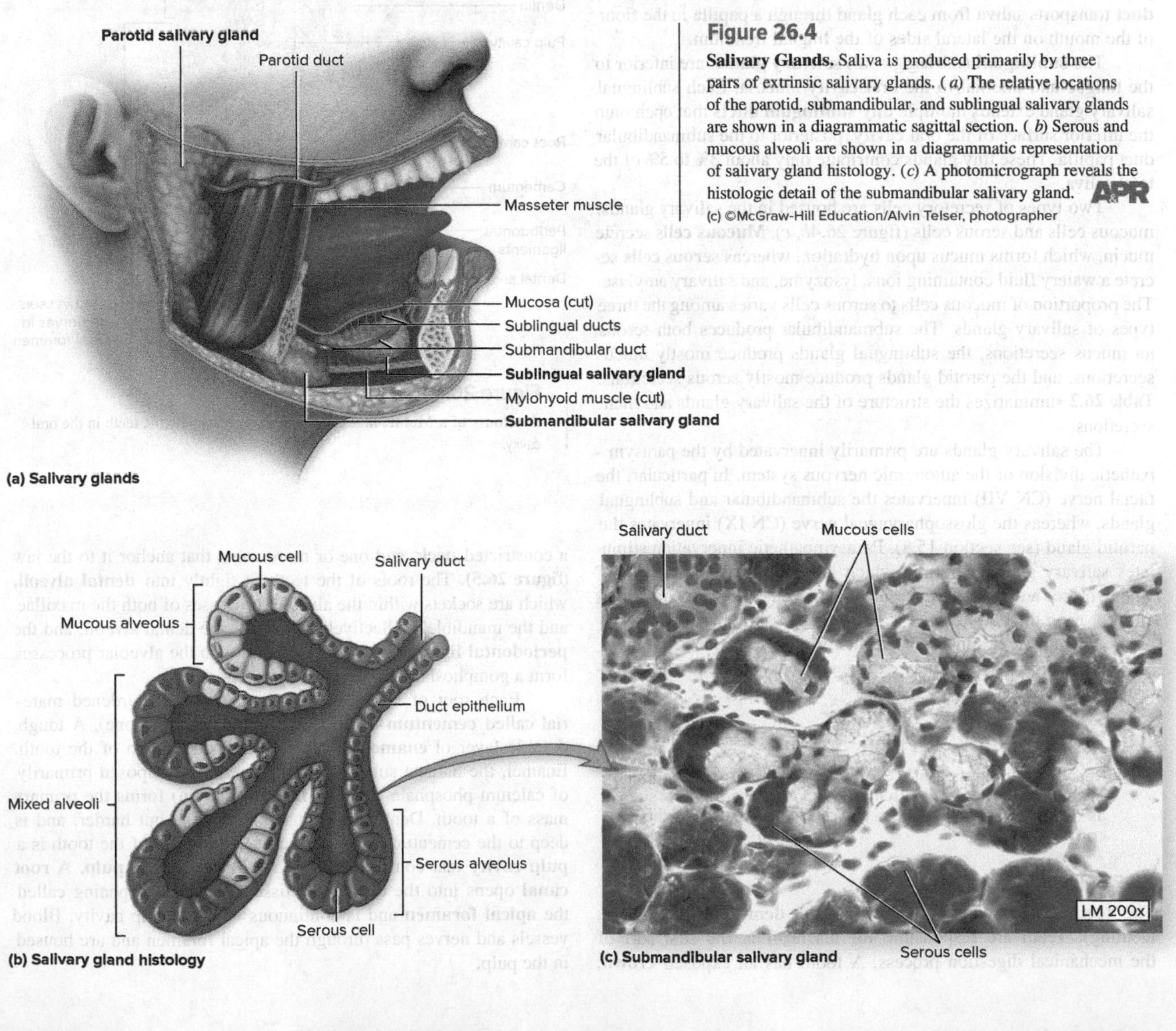
Parotid salivary gland
Parotid duct
Masseter muscle
Mucosa (cut)
Sublingual ducts
Submandibular duct
Sublingual salivary gland
Mylohyoid muscle (cut)
Submandibular salivary gland
(a) Salivary glands
Mucous cell
Salivary duct
Mucous alveolus
Duct epithelium
Mixed alveoli
Serous alveolus
Serous cell
(b) Salivary gland histology
Salivary duct
Mucous cells
LM 200x
Serous cells
(c) Submandibular salivary gland

Figure 26.4

Salivary Glands. Saliva is produced primarily by three pairs of extrinsic salivary glands. (*a*) The relative locations of the parotid, submandibular, and sublingual salivary glands are shown in a diagrammatic sagittal section. (*b*) Serous and mucous alveoli are shown in a diagrammatic representation of salivary gland histology. (*c*) A photomicrograph reveals the histologic detail of the submandibular salivary gland. APR

(c) ©McGraw-Hill Education/Alvin Telser, photographer

Table 26.2 Extrinsic Salivary Gland Characteristics

Salivary Gland	Structure and Location	Types of Secretion	Percentage of Saliva Produced
Parotid	Largest of the salivary glands; located anterior and slightly inferior to ears; parotid duct conducts secretions into the vestibule near upper 2nd molar	Mostly serous secretions	25–30%
Submandibular	Located inferior to mandibular body; submandibular duct opens lateral to lingual frenulum	Both mucus and serous secretions	60–70%
Sublingual	Smallest of the salivary glands; located inferior to tongue; tiny sublingual ducts open into floor of oral cavity	Mostly mucus secretions	3–5%

oral cavity. The parotid duct extends from the gland, parallel to the zygomatic arch, before penetrating the buccinator muscle and opening into the vestibule of the oral cavity near the second upper molar.

As their name suggests, the **submandibular** (sŭb′man-dib′yū-lăr) **salivary glands** are inferior to the body of the mandible. They produce most of the saliva (about 60% to 70%). A **submandibular duct** transports saliva from each gland through a papilla in the floor of the mouth on the lateral sides of the lingual frenulum.

The **sublingual** (sŭb-ling′gw ăl) **salivary glands** are inferior to the tongue and internal to the oral cavity mucosa. Each sublingual salivary gland extends multiple tiny **sublingual ducts** that open onto the inferior surface of the oral cavity, posterior to the submandibular duct papilla. These tiny glands contribute only about 3% to 5% of the total saliva.

Two types of secretory cells are housed in the salivary glands: mucous cells and serous cells (figure 26.4*b, c*). **Mucous cells** secrete mucin, which forms mucus upon hydration, whereas **serous cells** secrete a watery fluid containing ions, lysozyme, and salivary amylase. The proportion of mucous cells to serous cells varies among the three types of salivary glands. The submandibular produces both serous an mucus secretions, the sublingual glands produce mostly mucus secretions, and the parotid glands produce mostly serous secretions. **Table 26.2** summarizes the structure of the salivary glands and their secretions.

The salivary glands are primarily innervated by the parasympathetic division of the autonomic nervous system. In particular, the facial nerve (CN VII) innervates the submandibular and sublingual glands, whereas the glossopharyngeal nerve (CN IX) innervates the parotid gland (see section 15.8). Parasympathetic innervation stimulates salivary gland secretion, which is why your mouth "waters" when you see a delicious dinner in front of you. Your salivary glands are preparing the body for the start of the digestion process. In contrast, sympathetic stimulation inhibits normal secretion from these glands, which is why you may experience a dry mouth after a fight-or-flight response.

WHAT DO YOU THINK?

1. Research suggests that a "dry mouth" (inadequate production of saliva) is correlated with increased dental problems, such as caries (cavities). What are the possible reasons for this correlation?

26.2d Teeth

The **teeth** are collectively known as the **dentition** (den-tish′ŭn; teething). Teeth are responsible for mastication, the first part of the mechanical digestion process. A tooth has an exposed **crown,** a constricted **neck,** and one or more **roots** that anchor it to the jaw (**figure 26.5**). The roots of the teeth fit tightly into **dental alveoli,** which are sockets within the alveolar processes of both the maxillae and the mandible. Collectively, the roots, the dental alveoli, and the **periodontal ligaments** that bind the roots to the alveolar processes form a gomphosis joint (described in section 9.2a).

Each root of a tooth is ensheathed within hardened material called **cementum** (sē-men′tŭm; rough quarry stone). A tough, durable layer of **enamel** (ē-nam′ĕl) forms the crown of the tooth. Enamel, the hardest substance in the body, is composed primarily of calcium phosphate crystals. **Dentin** (den′tin) forms the primary mass of a tooth. Dentin is comparable to bone but harder, and is deep to the cementum and the enamel. The center of the tooth is a **pulp cavity** that contains a connective tissue called **pulp.** A **root canal** opens into the connective tissue through an opening called the **apical foramen** and is continuous with the pulp cavity. Blood vessels and nerves pass through the apical foramen and are housed in the pulp.

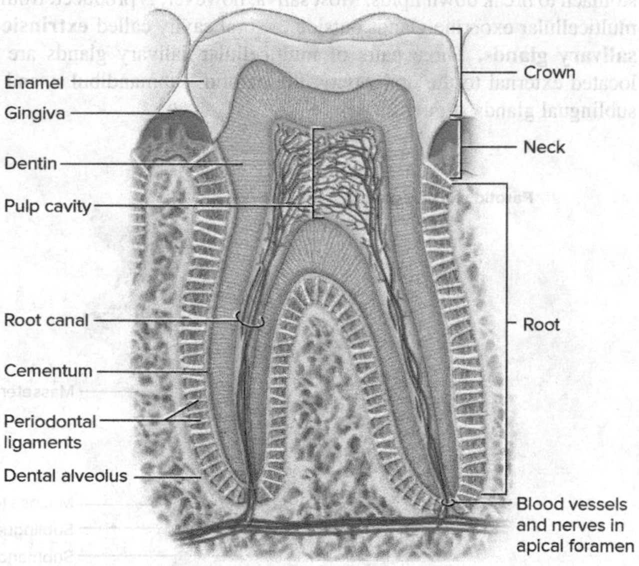
Enamel
Gingiva
Dentin
Pulp cavity
Root canal
Cementum
Periodontal ligaments
Dental alveolus
Crown
Neck
Root
Blood vessels and nerves in apical foramen

Figure 26.5

Anatomy of a Molar. Ingested material is chewed by the teeth in the oral cavity.

The **mesial** (mē′zē-ăl; *mesos* = middle) **surface** of the tooth is the surface closest to the midline of the mouth, while the **distal surface** of the tooth is farthest from the mouth midline. Other tooth surfaces include: the **buccal surface,** adjacent to the internal surface of the cheek; the **labial surface,** adjacent to the internal surface of the lip; the **lingual surface,** facing the tongue; and the **occlusal** (ŏ-klū′zăl) **surface,** where the teeth from the opposing superior and inferior arches meet.

Two sets of teeth develop and erupt during a normal lifetime. In an infant, 20 **deciduous** (dē-sid′y ū-ŭs; *deciduus* = falling off) **teeth,** also called *milk teeth* erupt between 6 months and 30 months after birth. These teeth are eventually lost and replaced by 32 **permanent teeth.** As **figure 26.6** shows, the more anteriorly placed permanent teeth tend to appear first, followed by the posteriorly placed teeth. (The exceptions to this rule are the first molars, which appear at about age 6 and are sometimes referred to as the *6-year molars.*) The last teeth to erupt are the third molars (also called *wisdom teeth*) in the late teens or early 20s. Often the jaw lacks space to accommodate these final molars, and they may either emerge only partially or grow at an angle and become impacted (wedged against another structure). Impacted teeth cannot erupt properly because of the angle of their growth.

WHAT DO YOU THINK?

2 If the deciduous teeth are eventually replaced by permanent teeth, why do humans have deciduous teeth in the first place?

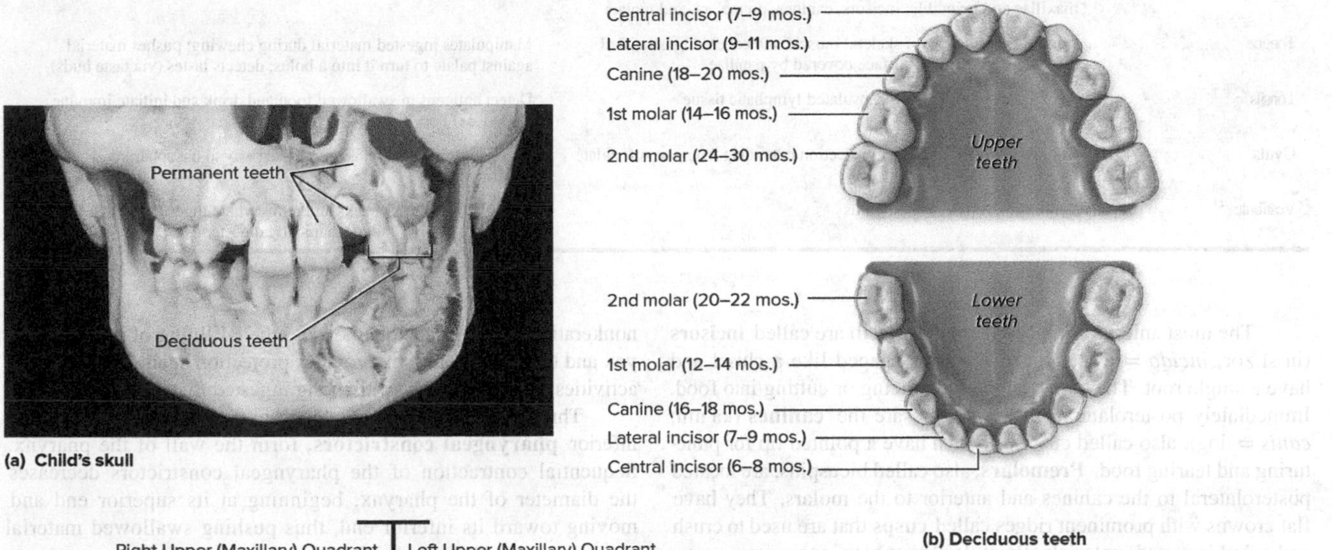
Permanent teeth
Deciduous teeth
(a) Child's skull
Central incisor (7–9 mos.)
Lateral incisor (9–11 mos.)
Canine (18–20 mos.)
1st molar (14–16 mos.)
2nd molar (24–30 mos.)
Upper teeth
2nd molar (20–22 mos.)
Lower teeth
1st molar (12–14 mos.)
Canine (16–18 mos.)
Lateral incisor (7–9 mos.)
Central incisor (6–8 mos.)
(b) Deciduous teeth
Right Upper (Maxillary) Quadrant
Left Upper (Maxillary) Quadrant
Central incisor (7–8 yrs.)
Lateral incisor (8–9 yrs.)
Canine (11–12 yrs.)
1st premolar (10–11 yrs.)
2nd premolar (10–12 yrs.)
1st molar (6–7 yrs.)
2nd molar (12–13 yrs.)
3rd molar (17–25 yrs.)
Upper teeth
Hard palate
3rd molar (17–25 yrs.)
2nd molar (11–13 yrs.)
1st molar (6–7 yrs.)
2nd premolar (11–12 yrs.)
1st premolar (10–12 yrs.)
Canine (9–10 yrs.)
Lateral incisor (7–8 yrs.)
Central incisor (6–7 yrs.)
Lower teeth
Right Lower (Mandibular) Quadrant
Left Lower (Mandibular) Quadrant
(c) Permanent teeth

Figure 26.6

Teeth. (*a*) Both deciduous teeth and unerupted permanent teeth are visible in this cutaway section of a child's skull. (*b, c*) Comparison of the dentition of deciduous and permanent teeth, including the approximate age at eruption for each tooth. Also shown in (*c*) are the dental quadrants, which are formed by a sagittal plane that passes between the central incisors in the maxilla and mandible. APR

Table 26.3 Oral Cavity Structures and Their Functions

Structure	Description	Function(s)
Gingivae	Composed of dense irregular connective tissue and nonkeratinized stratified squamous epithelium	Surround necks of teeth and cover alveolar processes
Hard palate	Anterior roof of mouth; bony shelf covered by dense connective tissue and nonkeratinized stratified squamous epithelium	Forms anterior two-thirds of roof of mouth; separates oral cavity from nasal cavity
Lips	Form part of anterior walls of oral cavity; covered with keratinized stratified squamous epithelium	Close oral cavity during chewing
Extrinsic salivary glands	Three pairs of large multicellular glands: parotid glands, sublingual glands, and submandibular glands	Produce saliva
Soft palate	Posterior roof of mouth formed from skeletal muscle and covered with nonkeratinized stratified squamous epithelium; the uvula hangs from it	Forms posterior one-third of roof of mouth; helps close off entryway to nasopharynx when swallowing
Teeth	Hard structures projecting from the alveolar processes of the maxillae and mandible: incisors, canines, premolars, and molars	Mastication (chewing food)
Tongue	Composed primarily of skeletal muscle and covered by stratified squamous epithelium; surface covered by papillae	Manipulates ingested material during chewing; pushes material against palate to turn it into a bolus; detects tastes (via taste buds)
Tonsils	Aggregates of partially encapsulated lymphatic tissue	Detect antigens in swallowed food and drink and initiate immune response if necessary
Uvula	Conical, median, muscular projection extending from the soft palate	Assists soft palate in closing off entryway to nasopharynx when swallowing
Vestibule	Space between cheek and gums	Space between lips/cheeks and gums where ingested materials are mixed with saliva and mechanically digested

The most anteriorly placed permanent teeth are called **incisors** (in-sī′zŏr; *incido* = to cut into). They are shaped like a chisel and have a single root. They are designed for slicing or cutting into food. Immediately posterolateral to the incisors are the **canines** (kā′nīn; *canis* = dog), also called cuspids, which have a pointed tip for puncturing and tearing food. **Premolars,** also called bicuspids, are located posterolateral to the canines and anterior to the molars. They have flat crowns with prominent ridges called **cusps** that are used to crush and grind ingested materials. Premolars may have one or two roots. The **molars** (mō′lăr; *molaris* = millstone) are the thickest and most posteriorly placed teeth. They have large, broad, flat crowns with distinctive cusps, and three or more roots. Molars are also adapted for grinding and crushing ingested materials. If the mouth is divided into quadrants, each quadrant contains the following number of permanent teeth: two incisors, one canine, two premolars, and three molars (figure 26.6).

Table 26.3 summarizes the structures of the oral cavity and their functions.

WHAT DID YOU LEARN?

3. What are the main components of saliva, and what functions do they serve?
4. Draw a generic tooth and label the following: Crown, root, neck, pulp cavity, root canal, enamel, dentin, cementum, alveolus, periodontal ligament.

26.3 Pharynx

✓ Learning Objectives

5. Identify and describe the structure of the pharynx.
6. Explain the process of swallowing (deglutition).

The common space used by both the respiratory and digestive systems is the **pharynx** (see section 25.2c and figure 26.1). The nonkeratinized stratified squamous epithelial lining of the oropharynx and the laryngopharynx provides protection against the abrasive activities associated with swallowing ingested materials.

Three skeletal muscle pairs, called the superior, middle, and inferior **pharyngeal constrictors,** form the wall of the pharynx. Sequential contraction of the pharyngeal constrictors decreases the diameter of the pharynx, beginning at its superior end and moving toward its inferior end, thus pushing swallowed material toward the esophagus. As the pharyngeal constrictors contract, the epiglottis of the larynx closes over the laryngeal opening to prevent ingested materials from entering the larynx and trachea (see section 25.3a).

The vagus nerves (CN X) innervate most pharyngeal muscles (see section 15.8). The main arteries supplying the pharynx are branches of the external carotid arteries. The pharynx is drained by the internal jugular veins (see section 23.3c).

WHAT DID YOU LEARN?

5. How do pharyngeal constrictors move swallowed material to the esophagus?

26.4 General Arrangement of Abdominal GI Organs

✓ Learning Objectives

7. Identify and describe the peritoneum and the mesenteries.
8. Compare and contrast the four tunics in the GI tract wall.
9. Describe the blood vessels, lymphoid structures, and nerves that supply the GI tract.

The abdominal organs of the GI tract are supported by serous membranes, and the walls of these organs have specific layers, called tunics.

26.4a Peritoneum, Peritoneal Cavity, and Mesentery

The abdominopelvic cavity is lined with moist serous membranes (**figure 26.7**). The portion of the serous membrane that lines the inside surface of the body wall is called the **parietal peritoneum** (per'i-tō-nē'ŭm; *periteino* = to stretch over). The portion of the serous membrane that folds back (reflects) to cover the surface of internal organs is called the **visceral peritoneum.** Between these two layers is the **peritoneal cavity,** a potential space where the peritoneal layers that face each other secrete a lubricating serous fluid. The thin layer of fluid in the peritoneal cavity lubricates both the body wall and the internal organ surfaces, allowing the abdominal organs to move freely, and reducing any friction resulting from this movement (see figure 1.10*d* and section 1.4e).

Learning Strategy 26.2

The peritoneum is similar to the pleura and the serous pericardium. All of these membranes have a parietal layer that lines the body wall and a visceral layer that covers the organ. The space between the parietal and visceral layers is where serous fluid is secreted, and this fluid acts as a lubricant to prevent friction as the organ moves.

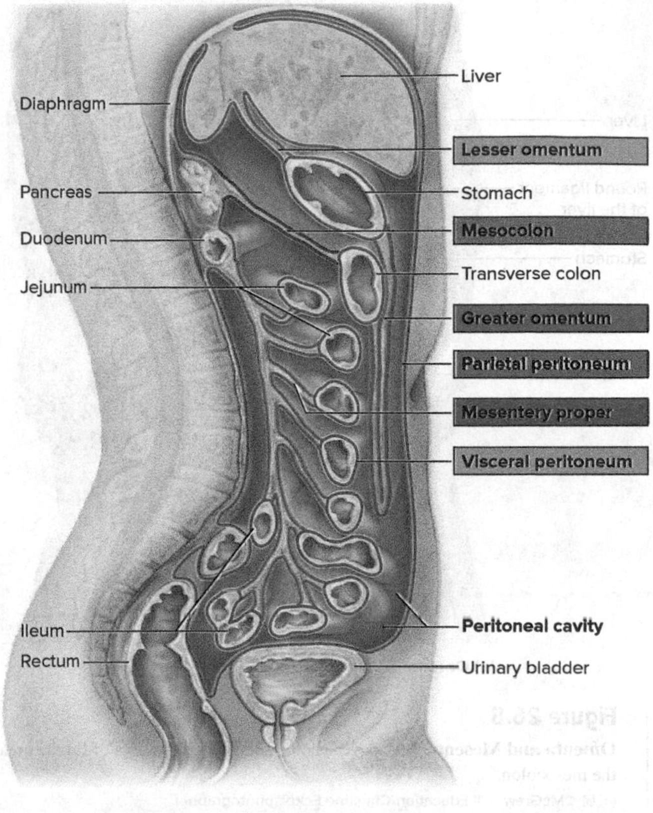

Figure 26.7

Peritoneum and Mesenteries. Many abdominal organs are held in place by double-layered serous membrane folds called mesenteries. The peritoneum is the serous membrane lining the internal abdominal wall (parietal layer) and covering the outer surface of the abdominal organs (visceral layer). This sagittal view through the abdominopelvic cavity shows the relationship between the peritoneal membranes and the abdominal organs they ensheathe. APR

Within the abdomen, organs that are completely surrounded by visceral peritoneum are called **intraperitoneal** (in'tră-per'i-tō-nē'ăl) **organs.** They include the stomach, part of the duodenum of the small intestine, the jejunum and the ileum of the small intestine, the cecum, the appendix, and the transverse and sigmoid colon of the large intestine. **Retroperitoneal** (re'trō-per'i-tō-nē'ăl) **organs** are covered by peritoneum on their anterolateral surfaces only, because they typically lie directly against the posterior abdominal wall. Retroperitoneal organs include most of the duodenum, the pancreas, the ascending and descending colon of the large intestine, and the rectum.

The **mesenteries** (mes'en-ter-ē; *mesos* = middle, *enteron* = intestine) are folds of peritoneum that support and stabilize the intraperitoneal GI tract organs. Blood vessels, lymphatic vessels, and nerves are sandwiched between the two folds and supply the digestive organs.

Because a mesentery contains multiple tissues and is a single unit, some anatomists have suggested classifying this structure as an organ in its own right. There are several different types of mesenteries. The **greater omentum** (ō-men'tŭm) extends inferiorly like an apron from the greater curvature of the stomach and covers most of the abdominal organs (**figure 26.8*a***). It often accumulates large amounts of adipose connective tissue. The **lesser omentum** connects the lesser curvature of the stomach and the proximal end of the duodenum to the liver. The lesser omentum may be subdivided into a hepatogastric ligament, which runs from the liver to the stomach, and a hepatoduodenal ligament, which runs from the liver to the duodenum.

The **mesentery proper** is a fan-shaped fold of peritoneum that suspends most of the small intestine from the internal surface of the posterior abdominal wall (figure 26.8*b*). The peritoneal fold that attaches parts of the large intestine to the internal surface of the posterior abdominal wall is called the **mesocolon** (mez'ō-kō'lon). Essentially, a mesocolon is a mesentery for parts of the large intestine. There are several distinct sections of the mesocolon, each named for the portion of the colon it suspends. For example, transverse mesocolon is associated with the transverse colon, whereas the sigmoid mesocolon is associated with the sigmoid colon.

A **peritoneal ligament** is a peritoneal fold that attaches one organ to another organ, or attaches an organ to the anterior or lateral abdominal wall. Some examples of peritoneal ligaments include the **coronary ligament,** a peritoneal fold attaching the superior surface of the liver to the diaphragm at the margins of the bare area of the liver; the **falciform** (fal'si-fōrm; *falx* = sickle) **ligament,** a peritoneal fold that attaches the liver to the anterior internal abdominal wall; and the **lienorenal ligament,** a fold of peritoneum between the spleen and the kidney.

26.4b General Histology of GI Organs (Esophagus to Large Intestine)

The GI tract from the esophagus through the large intestine is a tube composed of four concentric layers, called **tunics.** From deep (the lining of the lumen) to superficial (the external covering), these tunics are the mucosa, the submucosa, the muscularis, and the adventitia or serosa (**figure 26.9**). The general pattern of the tunics is

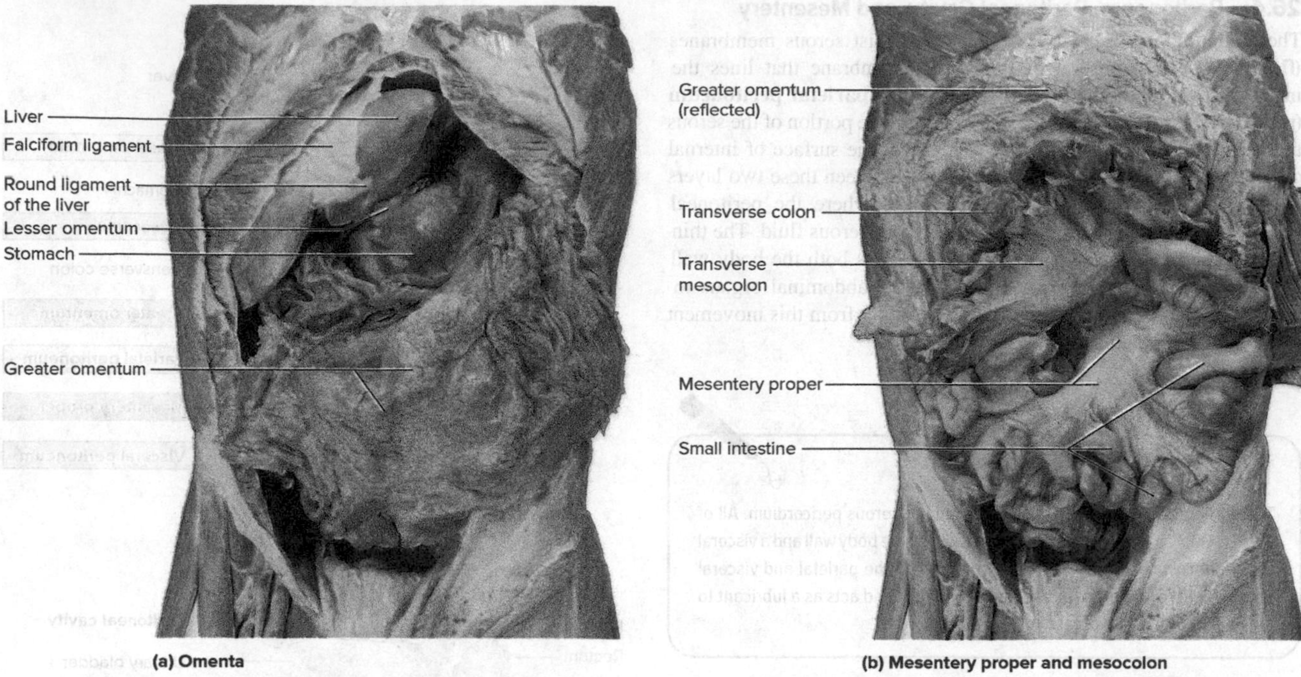
Liver
Falciform ligament
Round ligament of the liver
Lesser omentum
Stomach
Greater omentum
(a) Omenta
Greater omentum (reflected)
Transverse colon
Transverse mesocolon
Mesentery proper
Small intestine
(b) Mesentery proper and mesocolon

Figure 26.8

Omenta and Mesentery. Cadaver photos show anterior views of (*a*) the greater and lesser omenta, and (*b*) the mesentery proper and some of the mesocolon.

(a, b) ©McGraw-Hill Education/Christine Eckel, photographer

described next. There are variations in the general pattern, which will be described in detail when we discuss the specific organs in which they appear.

Mucosa

The **mucosa** (myū-kō′sǎ), or *mucous membrane* has three components: (1) an inner (superficial) epithelium lining the lumen of the GI tract; (2) an underlying areolar connective tissue, called the **lamina propria;** and (3) a relatively thin layer of smooth muscle, termed the **muscularis mucosae.** The muscularis mucosae is very thin (or absent) at the level of the laryngopharynx and thickens progressively as it approaches the stomach.

For most of the abdominal GI tract organs, the lining epithelium is a simple columnar epithelium. The portions of the GI tract that must withstand abrasion (such as the esophagus) are lined by a nonkeratinized stratified squamous epithelium (see section 4.1e).

Submucosa

The **submucosa** is composed of either areolar or dense irregular connective tissue and has far fewer cells than the lamina propria. Submucosa components include: accumulations of lymphoid tissue in some submucosal regions; mucin-secreting glands that project ducts across the mucosa and open into the lumen of the tract in the esophagus and duodenum; many large blood vessels and lymphatic vessels; and nerves that extend fine branches into both the mucosa and the muscularis. These nerve fibers and their associated ganglia are collectively referred to as the **submucosal nerve plexus** (or *Meissner plexus*). It contains sensory neurons, sympathetic postganglionic axons, and parasympathetic ganglia (see sections 14.2a, 18.4b, and 18.3, respectively). The submucosal nerve plexusis a component of the *enteric nervous system* (see section 18.5b).

Muscularis

The **muscularis** (mŭs′kyū-lā′ris) typically contains two layers of smooth muscle. Exceptions to this pattern include the esophagus (which contains a mixture of skeletal and smooth muscle) and the stomach (which contains three layers of smooth muscle). The fibers of the inner layer of smooth muscle are oriented circumferentially around the GI tract, and are called the **inner circular layer.** The fibers of the outer layer are oriented lengthwise along the GI tract, and are called the **outer longitudinal layer.**

If you think of the GI tract as a tube, then contractions of the circular layer constrict the diameter of the tube lumen, whereas contractions of the longitudinal layer shorten the tube. At specific locations along the GI tract, the inner circular muscle layer is greatly thickened to form a **sphincter.** A sphincter closes off the lumen opening at some point along the GI tract, and in so doing it can help control the movement of materials through the GI tract. The nerve fibers and the associated ganglia located between the two layers of smooth muscle control its contractions and are collectively referred to as the **myenteric** (mī′en-ter′ik; *mys* = muscle, *enteron* = intestine) **nerve plexus** (or *Auerbach plexus*). The myenteric nerve plexus is also a component of the enteric nervous system (see section18.5b).

Adventitia or Serosa

The outermost tunic may be either an adventitia or a serosa. An **adventitia** (ad-ven-tish′ǎ) is composed of areolar connective tissue

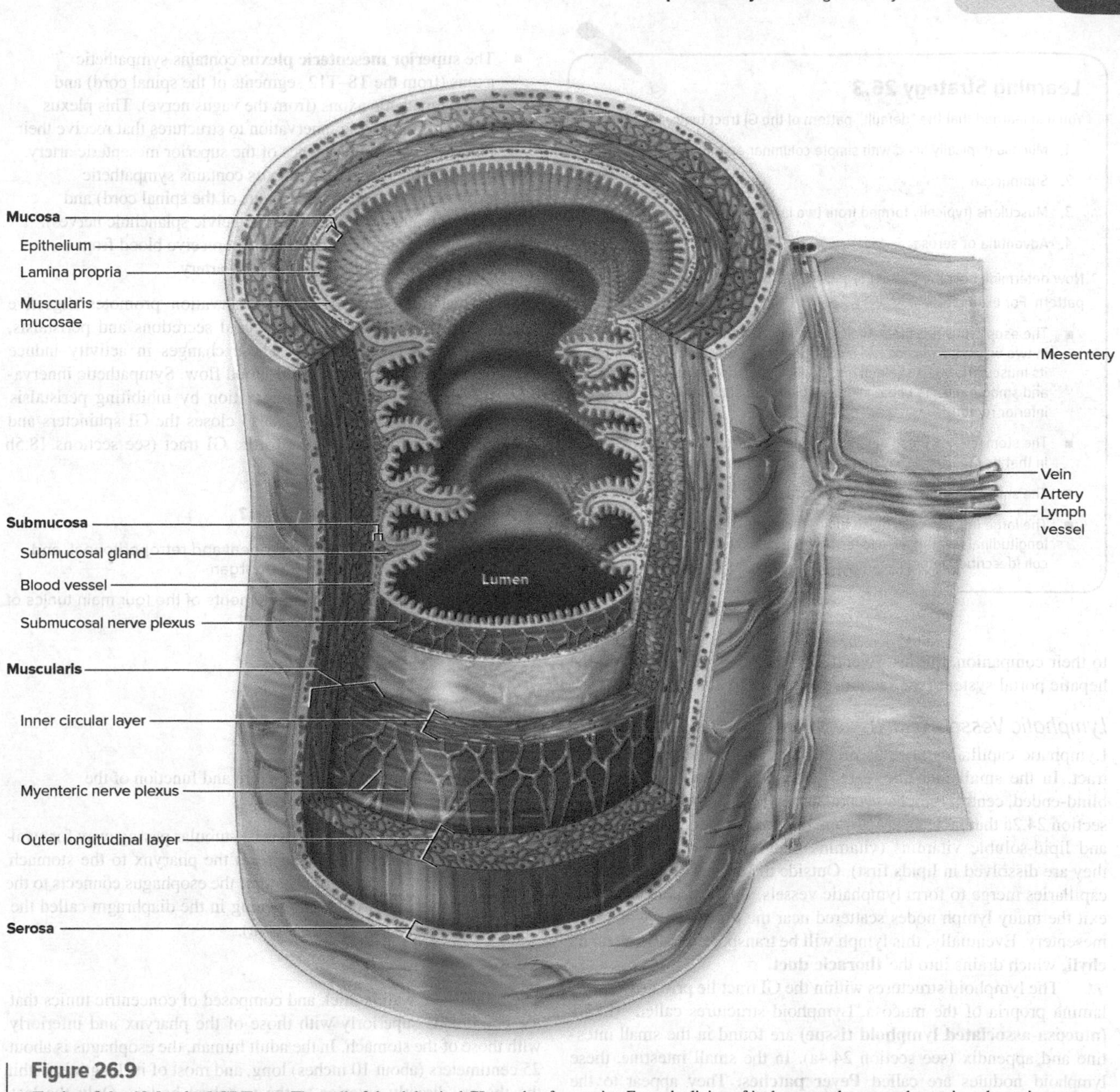
Mucosa
Epithelium
Lamina propria
Muscularis mucosae
Submucosa
Submucosal gland
Blood vessel
Submucosal nerve plexus
Muscularis
Inner circular layer
Myenteric nerve plexus
Outer longitudinal layer
Serosa
Lumen
Mesentery
Vein
Artery
Lymph vessel

Figure 26.9

Tunics of the Abdominal GI Tract. The wall of the abdominal GI tract has four tunics. From the lining of its lumen to the external covering, the tunics are the mucosa, submucosa, muscularis, and adventitia or serosa.

with dispersed collagen and elastic fibers. A **serosa** (se-r ō′să) has the same components as the adventitia, but is covered by a visceral peritoneum. Intraperitoneal organs have a serosa, because they are completely surrounded by visceral peritoneum. Retroperitoneal organs primarily have an adventitia, because these organs are only partially covered by visceral peritoneum. For example, the ascending colon (which is retroperitoneal) has an adventitia, whereas the stomach (an intraperitoneal organ) has a serosa.

26.4c Blood Vessels, Lymphoid Structures, and Nerve Supply

The GI tract has a rich blood and nerve supply. In addition, extensive lymphoid structures along the length of the GI tract act as sentinels to monitor for antigens that may have been ingested (see section 24.1). The blood vessels, lymphoid structures, and nerves enter the GI tract from either the surrounding structures (e.g., nearby organs, abdominal wall) or via the supporting mesentery.

Blood Vessels

The **celiac trunk, superior mesenteric artery,** and **inferior mesenteric artery** supply the abdominal GI tract (see section 23.3f). These arteries split into smaller branches that extend throughout the walls of the GI organs. Branches travel within the tunics, and the mucosa contains capillaries that have fenestrated endothelial cells to promote absorption. The veins arising in the mucosa form anastomoses in the submucosa before exiting the wall of the GI tract adjacent

Learning Strategy 26.3

You just learned that the "default" pattern of the GI tract tunics is:

1. Mucosa (typically lined with simple columnar epithelium)
2. Submucosa
3. Muscularis (typically formed from two layers of smooth muscle)
4. Adventitia or serosa

Now determine how the GI tract organs follow or deviate from this default pattern. For example:

- The esophagus has these tunics, but it deviates from the pattern in two ways: Its mucosa has a stratified squamous epithelium, and its muscularis has a skeletal muscle in its superior region, skeletal and smooth muscle in the middle region, and smooth muscle in its inferior region.
- The stomach has these tunics, but it deviates from the pattern in that its muscularis has three layers of smooth muscle, not two.
- The small intestine follows the basic "default" pattern of tunics.
- The large intestine has these tunics, but in its muscularis, the outer longitudinal layer of muscle forms three distinct bands called teniae coli (described later in section 26.9b).

to their companion arteries. Eventually, the veins merge to form the hepatic portal system (see sections 23.3f and 26.10a).

Lymphatic Vessels and Tissues

Lymphatic capillaries arise as blind tubes in the mucosa of the GI tract. In the small intestine, each villus usually contains a single, blind-ended, central lymphatic capillary called a **lacteal.** Recall from section 24.2a that lacteals are responsible for absorbing dietary lipids and lipid-soluble vitamins (vitamins that can be absorbed only if they are dissolved in lipids first). Outside the organ walls, lymphatic capillaries merge to form lymphatic vessels. These vessels enter and exit the many lymph nodes scattered near the organs and within the mesentery. Eventually, this lymph will be transported to the **cisterna chyli,** which drains into the **thoracic duct.**

The lymphoid structures within the GI tract lie primarily in the lamina propria of the mucosa. Lymphoid structures called **MALT (mucosa-associated lymphoid tissue)** are found in the small intestine and appendix (see section 24.4a). In the small intestine, these lymphoid nodules are called **Peyer patches.** They appear to the naked eye as oval bodies about the size of a pea, but are often much larger structures. Less commonly, lymphoid structures are found external to the simple epithelium throughout the stomach and intestines where they are known as diffuse lymphoid tissue. Also, solitary lymphoid nodules may occur in the esophagus, the pylorus of the stomach, and along the entire length of the small and large intestines.

Nerves

The nerves associated with the GI tract consist of both autonomic motor and visceral sensory axons (see sections 18.1 and 18.5a) which work with the *enteric nervous system* (see section 18.5b) There are three main groups of autonomic plexuses:

- The **celiac plexus** contains sympathetic axons (from the T5–T9 segments of the spinal cord) and parasympathetic axons (from the vagus nerve). This plexus supplies structures that receive their blood supply from branches of the celiac trunk.
- The **superior mesenteric plexus** contains sympathetic axons (from the T8–T12 segments of the spinal cord) and parasympathetic axons (from the vagus nerve). This plexus transmits autonomic innervation to structures that receive their blood supply from branches of the superior mesenteric artery.
- The **inferior mesenteric plexus** contains sympathetic axons (from the L1–L2 segments of the spinal cord) and parasympathetic axons (from the pelvic splanchnic nerves). This plexus supplies structures that receive blood from branches of the inferior mesenteric artery.

In general, parasympathetic innervation promotes digestive system activity by stimulating GI gland secretions and peristalsis, and by relaxing GI sphincters. These changes in activity induce vasodilation and an increase in GI blood flow. Sympathetic innervation opposes parasympathetic innervation by inhibiting peristalsis and some GI gland secretions. It also closes the GI sphincters and vasoconstricts the blood vessels to the GI tract (see sections 18.5b and 18.5e).

WHAT DID YOU LEARN?

6. Compare the terms intraperitoneal and retroperitoneal, and give examples of each type of organ.
7. Draw and label all the main elements of the four main tunics of the default pattern of the GI tract.

26.5 Esophagus

✓ Learning Objective

10. Identify and describe the structure and function of the esophagus.

The **esophagus** (ē-sof′ă-gŭs; gullet) is a tubular passageway for swallowed materials being conducted from the pharynx to the stomach (see figure 26.1). The inferior region of the esophagus connects to the stomach by passing through an opening in the diaphragm called the **esophageal hiatus** (hī- ā′tŭs; to yawn).

26.5a Gross Anatomy

The esophageal wall is thick and composed of concentric tunics that are continuous superiorly with those of the pharynx and inferiorly with those of the stomach. In the adult human, the esophagus is about 25 centimeters (about 10 inches) long, and most of its length is within the thorax, directly anterior to the vertebral bodies. Only the last 1.5 centimeters of the esophagus are located in the abdomen. The empty esophagus is flattened; the lumen only opening slightly with the passage of a food bolus.

26.5b Histology

The esophageal mucosa is different from that in the abdominal GI tract organs in that it is composed of thick, nonkeratinized stratified squamous epithelium (**figure 26.10**). This epithelium is better suited to withstand the abrasions of the bolus as it moves through the esophagus (see section 4.1e). Because the esophagus does not absorb any nutrients, this thicker, protective epithelium supports its function.

The submucosa is thick and composed of abundant elastic fibers that permit distension during swallowing. It houses numerous mucous glands that provide a thick, lubricating mucus for the epithelium.

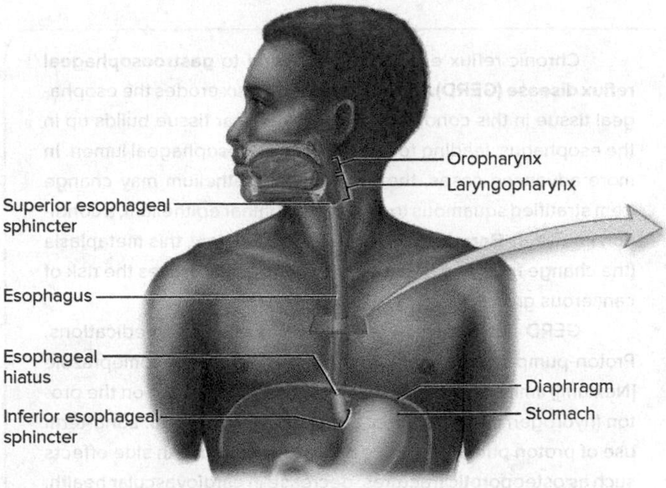

Oropharynx
Laryngopharynx
Superior esophageal sphincter
Esophagus
Esophageal hiatus
Diaphragm
Stomach
Inferior esophageal sphincter

(a) Pharynx and esophagus

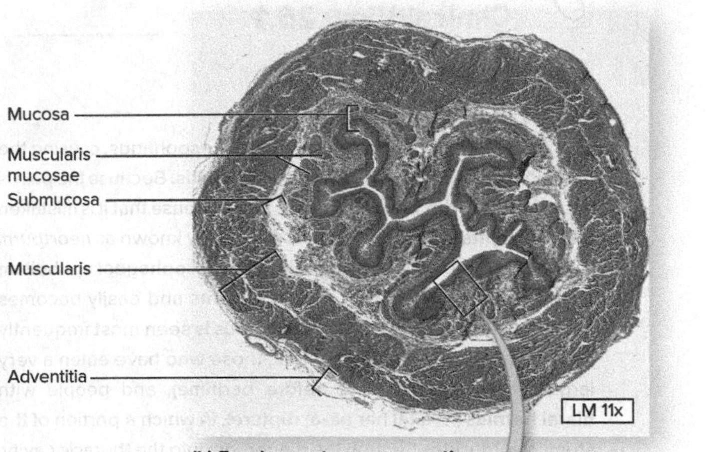

Mucosa
Muscularis mucosae
Submucosa
Muscularis
Adventitia
LM 11x

(b) Esophagus, transverse section

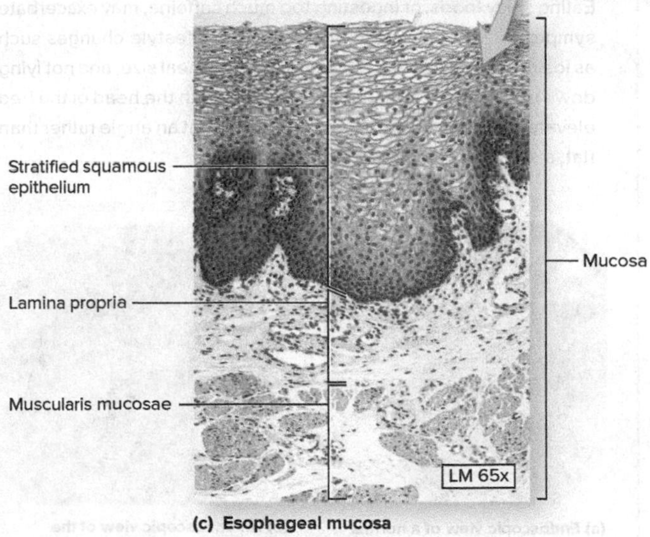

Stratified squamous epithelium
Mucosa
Lamina propria
Muscularis mucosae
LM 65x

(c) Esophageal mucosa

Figure 26.10
Histology of the Esophagus. (*a*) The esophagus extends inferiorly from the pharynx and conducts swallowed materials to the stomach. (*b*) A photomicrograph of a transverse section through the esophagus identifies the tunics in its wall. (*c*) A photomicrograph shows the esophageal mucosa. APR
(b) Alfred Pasieka/Getty Images; (c) ©McGraw-Hill Education/Alvin Telser, photographer

The muscularis is composed of an inner circular layer and an outer longitudinal layer. The muscularis of the esophagus is unique in that it contains both skeletal and smooth muscle. The two layers of muscle in the superior one-third of the muscularis layer are skeletal, rather than smooth, to ensure that the swallowed material moves rapidly out of the pharynx and into the esophagus before the next respiratory cycle begins. (Remember that smooth muscle contracts more slowly than does skeletal muscle; see section 10.9b.) Skeletal and smooth muscle fibers intermingle in the middle one-third of the esophagus, and only smooth muscle is found within the wall of the inferior one-third. This transition marks the beginning of a continuous smooth muscle muscularis that extends throughout the stomach and the small and large intestines to the anus. The outermost layer of the esophagus is an adventitia, which adheres it to the posterior body wall.

The **superior esophageal sphincter** (or *pharyngoesophageal sphincter*) is a contracted ring of circular skeletal muscle at the superior end of the esophagus. It is the area where the esophagus and the pharynx meet. This sphincter is closed during inhalation of air so it enters the larynx and trachea instead of the esophagus.

The **inferior esophageal sphincter** (*gastroesophageal,* or *cardiac sphincter*) is a contracted ring of circular smooth muscle at the inferior end of the esophagus. This sphincter isn't strong enough alone to prevent materials from refluxing back into the esophagus; instead, the muscles of the diaphragm at the esophageal opening contract to help prevent materials from regurgitating from the stomach into the esophagus.

WHAT DID YOU LEARN?

8. How do the esophageal tunics differ from the "default" tunic pattern?

26.6 The Swallowing Process

✓ Learning Objective

11. List and explain the three phases of swallowing.

Swallowing, also called *deglutition* (dē′glū-tish′ŭn; *degluto* = to swallow), is the process of moving ingested materials from the oral

Clinical View 26.1

Reflux Esophagitis and Gastroesophageal Reflux Disease

Sometimes acidic chyme refluxes into the esophagus, causing the burning pain and irritation of **reflux esophagitis.** Because the pain is felt posterior to the sternum and can be so intense that it is mistaken for a heart attack, this condition is commonly known as *heartburn.*

Unlike the stomach epithelium, the esophageal epithelium is poorly protected against acidic contents and easily becomes inflamed and irritated. Reflux esophagitis is seen most frequently in overweight individuals, smokers, those who have eaten a very large meal (especially just before bedtime), and people with **hiatal hernias** (hī-ā'tăl her'nē-ă; rupture), in which a portion of the stomach protrudes through the diaphragm into the thoracic cavity. Eating spicy foods, or ingesting too much caffeine, may exacerbate symptoms. Preventive treatment includes lifestyle changes such as losing weight, quitting smoking, limiting meal size, and not lying down until 2 hours after eating. Sleeping with the head of the bed elevated 4 to 6 inches, so that the body lies at an angle rather than flat, also helps alleviate symptoms.

Chronic reflux esophagitis can lead to **gastroesophageal reflux disease (GERD).** Frequent gastric reflux erodes the esophageal tissue in this condition, so over time scar tissue builds up in the esophagus, leading to narrowing of the esophageal lumen. In more advanced cases, the esophageal epithelium may change from stratified squamous to a simple columnar epithelium, a condition known as **Barrett esophagus.** Unfortunately, this metaplasia (the change from one type of cell to another) increases the risk of cancerous growths.

GERD may be treated with a series of medications. Proton-pump inhibitors (e.g., omeprazole [Prilosec], esomeprazole [Nexium]) limit acid secretion in the stomach by acting on the proton (hydrogen ion [H^+]) pumps that help produce acid. Long-term use of proton pump inhibitor's have been linked with side effects such as osteoporotic fractures, decrease in cardiovascular health, potential increase in bacterial infections of the digestive tract, and most recently, dementia. Histamine (H_2) blockers (e.g., famotidine [Pepcid], nizatidine [Axid], ranitidine [Zantac]) also help limit acid secretion in the stomach. Antacids (e.g., Tums, Rolaids) also help neutralize stomach acid.

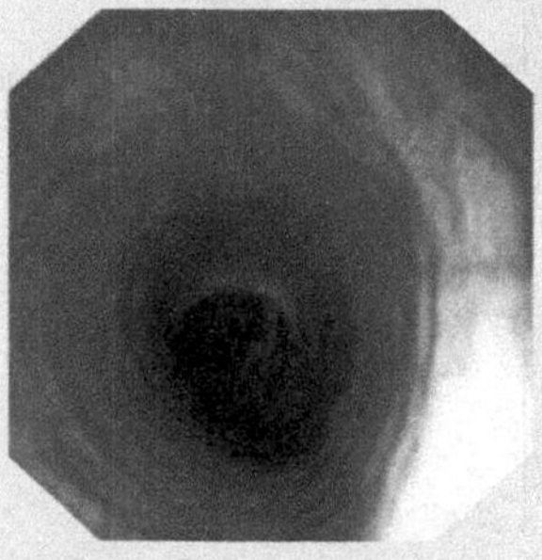

(a) Endoscopic view of a normal esophagus.

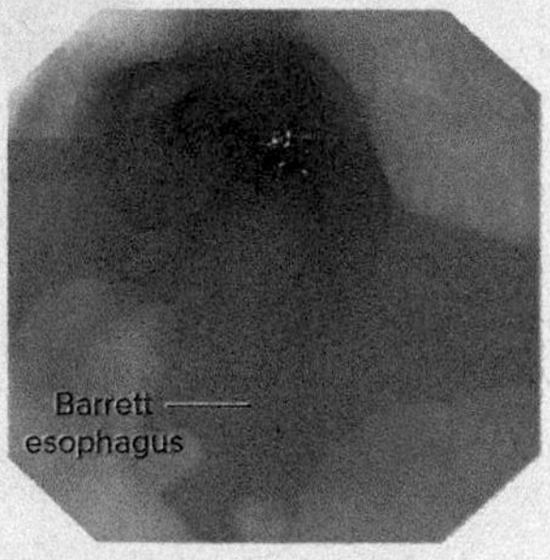
Barrett esophagus

(b) An endoscopic view of the esophagus shows the signs of Barrett esophagus.

(a) ©McGraw-Hill Education/Neal R. Chamberlin, photographer; (b) Gastrolab/Science Source

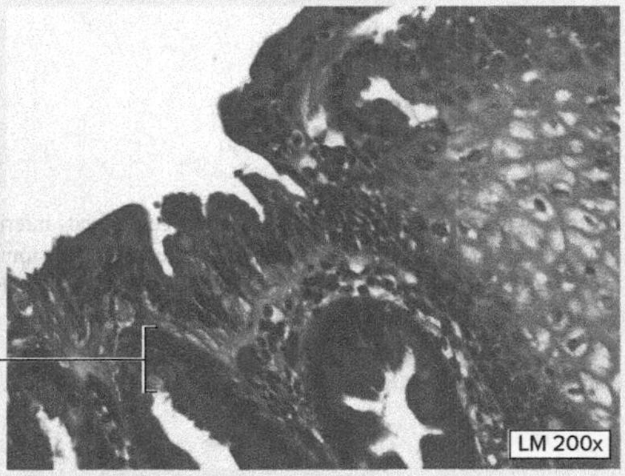
Columnar secretory epithelium
LM 200x

Microscopic appearance of Barrett esophagus.

©McGraw-Hill Education

cavity to the stomach. There are three phases of swallowing: the voluntary phase, the pharyngeal phase, and the esophageal phase (**figure 26.11**).

The **voluntary phase** occurs after ingestion. Food and saliva mix in the oral cavity. Chewing forms a bolus that is mixed and manipulated by the tongue and then pushed superiorly against the hard palate. Transverse palatine folds in the hard palate help direct the bolus posteriorly toward the oropharynx.

The arrival of the bolus at the entryway to the oropharynx initiates the **pharyngeal phase,** when tactile sensory receptors trigger the swallowing reflex, which is controlled by the swallowing center in the medulla oblongata (see section 15.5c). The bolus passes quickly and involuntarily through the pharynx to the esophagus. During this phase, (1) the soft palate and uvula elevate to block the passageway between the nasopharynx and oropharynx; (2) the bolus enters the oropharynx; and (3) the larynx and laryngeal opening elevate toward the epiglottis, ultimately covering and sealing the glottis to prevent swallowed materials from entering the trachea (see section 25.3a). Pharyngeal constrictors are skeletal muscle groups that contract involuntarily and sequentially to ensure that the swallowed bolus moves quickly (1 second elapses in this phase) through the pharynx and into the esophagus.

The **esophageal phase** is also involuntary. It is the time (about 5 to 8 seconds) during which the bolus passes through the esophagus and into the stomach. This phase begins when the superior esophageal sphincter relaxes to allow ingested materials into the esophagus. The presence of the bolus within the lumen of the esophagus stimulates peristaltic waves of muscular contraction that assist in propelling the bolus toward the stomach. The inferior sphincter contracts after the

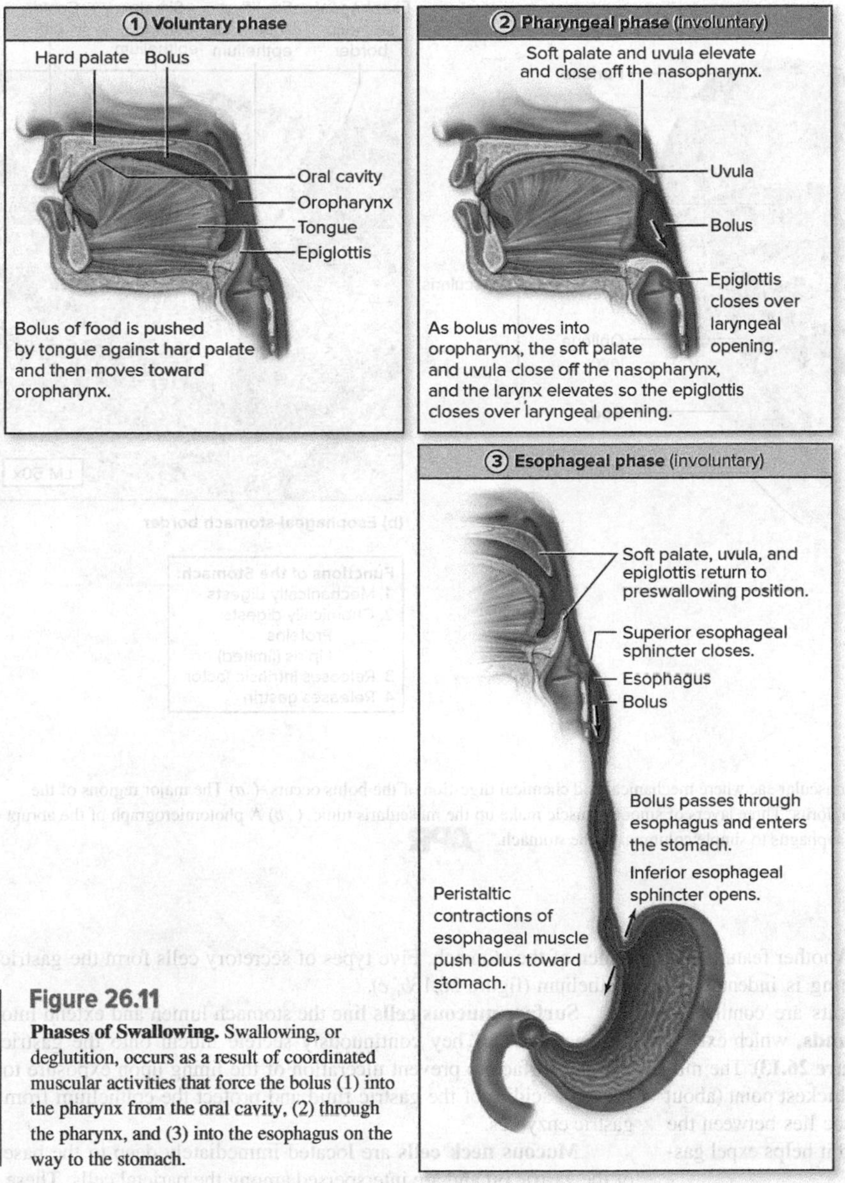
① Voluntary phase
Hard palate
Bolus
Oral cavity
Oropharynx
Tongue
Epiglottis
Bolus of food is pushed by tongue against hard palate and then moves toward oropharynx.
② Pharyngeal phase (involuntary)
Soft palate and uvula elevate and close off the nasopharynx.
Uvula
Bolus
Epiglottis closes over laryngeal opening.
As bolus moves into oropharynx, the soft palate and uvula close off the nasopharynx, and the larynx elevates so the epiglottis closes over laryngeal opening.
③ Esophageal phase (involuntary)
Soft palate, uvula, and epiglottis return to preswallowing position.
Superior esophageal sphincter closes.
Esophagus
Bolus
Bolus passes through esophagus and enters the stomach.
Inferior esophageal sphincter opens.
Peristaltic contractions of esophageal muscle push bolus toward stomach.

Figure 26.11
Phases of Swallowing. Swallowing, or deglutition, occurs as a result of coordinated muscular activities that force the bolus (1) into the pharynx from the oral cavity, (2) through the pharynx, and (3) into the esophagus on the way to the stomach.

bolus passes into the stomach to prevent reflux of materials and fluids back into the esophagus.

WHAT DID YOU LEARN?

9 Briefly describe the three phases of swallowing.

26.7 Stomach

✓ Learning Objectives

12. Identify and describe the gross anatomy of the stomach.
13. Identify and describe the histology of the stomach wall.
14. Compare and contrast the secretions of the stomach.

The **stomach** (stŭm′ăk; *stomachus* = belly) is a muscular, J-shaped sac that occupies the left upper quadrant of the abdomen, immediately inferior to the diaphragm (**figure 26.12**). It continues the mechanical and chemical digestion of the bolus. After the bolus has been completely processed in the stomach, the product is called **chyme** (kīm; *chymos* = juice). Chyme has the consistency of a paste-like soup. The stomach facilitates (1) mechanical digestion by contractions of its thick muscularis layer that churns and mixes the bolus with gastric secretions, and (2) chemical digestion through its gastric secretions of acid and enzymes.

26.7a Gross Anatomy

The stomach is composed of four regions:

- The **cardia** (kar′d ē-ă; heart) is the small, narrow, superior entryway into the stomach lumen from the esophagus. The internal opening where the cardia meets the esophagus is called the **cardiac orifice.**
- The **fundus** (fŭn′dŭs; bottom) is the dome-shaped region lateral and superior to the esophageal connection with the stomach. Its superior surface contacts the diaphragm.
- The **body** (corpus) is the largest region of the stomach; it is inferior to the cardiac orifice and the fundus.
- The **pylorus** (pī-l ōr′ŭs; gatekeeper) is a narrow, medially directed, funnel-shaped pouch that forms the terminal region of the stomach. The pylorus is divided into two parts: the **pyloric antrum** (the more expanded region near the body) and the **pyloric canal** (the more narrow region that attaches to the duodenum). Its opening into the duodenum of the small intestine is called the **pyloric orifice.** Surrounding this pyloric orifice is a thick ring of circular smooth muscle called the **pyloric sphincter.** The pyloric sphincter regulates the entrance of chyme into the small intestine: It closes upon sympathetic innervation and opens upon parasympathetic innervation.

The inferior convex border of the stomach is the **greater curvature,** whereas the superior concave border is termed the **lesser curvature.** The greater omentum attaches to the greater curvature edge of the stomach, and the lesser omentum extends between the lesser curvature and the liver.

Internally, the stomach lining is composed of numerous **gastric folds,** or *rugae* (rū′jē; *ruja* = wrinkle). They are seen only when the stomach is empty, allowing the stomach to expand greatly when it fills and then return to its normal J-shape when it empties.

26.7b Histology

The stomach is lined by a simple columnar epithelium, although little absorption occurs in the stomach. This epithelium does not contain goblet cells; instead, surface mucous cells (described later in this

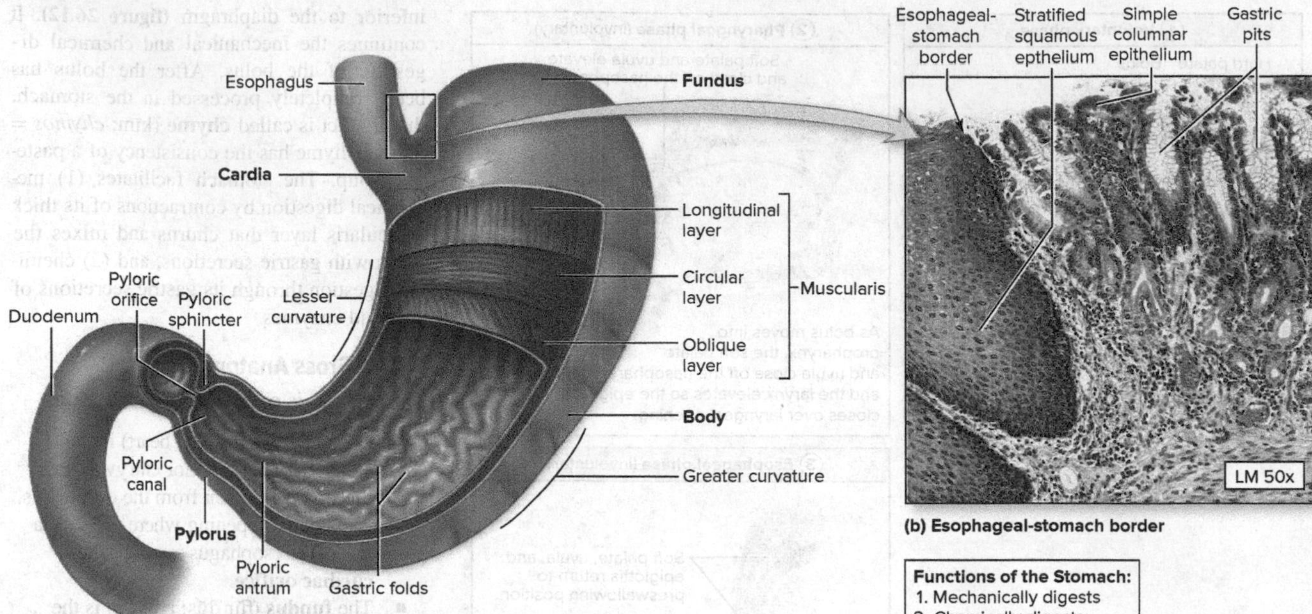

Esophagus
Fundus
Cardia
Longitudinal layer
Circular layer
Muscularis
Oblique layer
Body
Greater curvature
Pyloric orifice
Pyloric sphincter
Lesser curvature
Duodenum
Pyloric canal
Pylorus
Pyloric antrum
Gastric folds
Esophageal-stomach border
Stratified squamous epthelium
Simple columnar epithelium
Gastric pits
LM 50x

(a) Stomach regions, anterior view

(b) Esophageal-stomach border

Functions of the Stomach:
1. Mechanically digests
2. Chemically digests:
   Proteins
   Lipids (limited)
3. Releases intrinsic factor
4. Releases gastrin

Figure 26.12
Gross Anatomy of the Stomach. The stomach is a muscular sac where mechanical and chemical digestion of the bolus occurs. (*a*) The major regions of the stomach are the cardia, the fundus, the body, and the pylorus. Three layers of smooth muscle make up the muscularis tunic. (*b*) A photomicrograph of the abrupt transition from stratified squamous epithelium in the esophagus to simple columnar in the stomach. APR
(b) Victor P. Eroschenko

section) secrete mucin onto the epithelial lining. Another feature that distinguishes the stomach mucosa is that the lining is indented by numerous depressions called **gastric pits.** The pits are continuous with branched tubular glands, called **gastric glands,** which extend through the length of the mucosa to its base (**figure 26.13**). The mucosa of the stomach is only 1.5 millimeters at its thickest point (about the thickness of a nickel). The muscularis mucosae lies between the base of the gastric glands and the submucosa, and it helps expel gastric gland secretory products when it contracts.

The muscularis of the stomach is composed of three smooth muscle layers instead of two (the default pattern): an inner oblique layer, a middle circular layer, and an outer longitudinal layer. The oblique layer is best-developed at the cardia and the body of the stomach. The presence of a third layer of smooth muscle assists the continued churning and blending of the bolus. The outermost tunic of the stomach is a serosa, because the stomach is intraperitoneal.

WHAT DO YOU THINK?

3 The stomach secretes gastric juices, which are highly acidic and can break down and chemically digest food. What prevents the gastric juices from eating away at the stomach itself?

26.7c Gastric Secretions

Gastric juices are produced by cells in the gastric glands, and their secretions are released into gastric pits, which funnel them to the lumen of the stomach. Five types of secretory cells form the gastric epithelium (figure 26.13*b, c*).

Surface mucous cells line the stomach lumen and extend into the gastric pits. They continuously secrete mucin onto the gastric luminal surface to prevent ulceration of the lining upon exposure to the high acidity of the gastric fluid and protect the epithelium from gastric enzymes.

Mucous neck cells are located immediately deep to the base of the gastric pit and are interspersed among the parietal cells. These cells produce an acidic mucin that differs structurally and functionally from the mucin secreted by the surface mucous cells. The acidic mucin helps maintain the acidic conditions resulting from the secretion of hydrochloric acid by parietal cells.

Parietal cells (also called *oxyntic cells*) are located primarily in the proximal and middle parts of the gastric gland. Their distinctive features are small intracellular channels called canaliculi, which are lined by microvilli. Hydrochloric acid secreted across the parietal cells' vast internalized surface helps denature proteins to facilitate chemical digestion. Parietal cells also produce **intrinsic factor,** a molecule that binds vitamin B_{12} in the stomach lumen and assists in B_{12} absorption in the ileum of the small intestine.

Chief cells (also called *zymogenic cells* or *peptic cells*) are housed primarily in the distal part of the gastric gland. These cells synthesize and secrete enzymes, primarily inactive pepsinogen, into the lumen of the stomach. The acid content of the stomach then converts inactive pepsinogen into the active enzyme **pepsin,** which

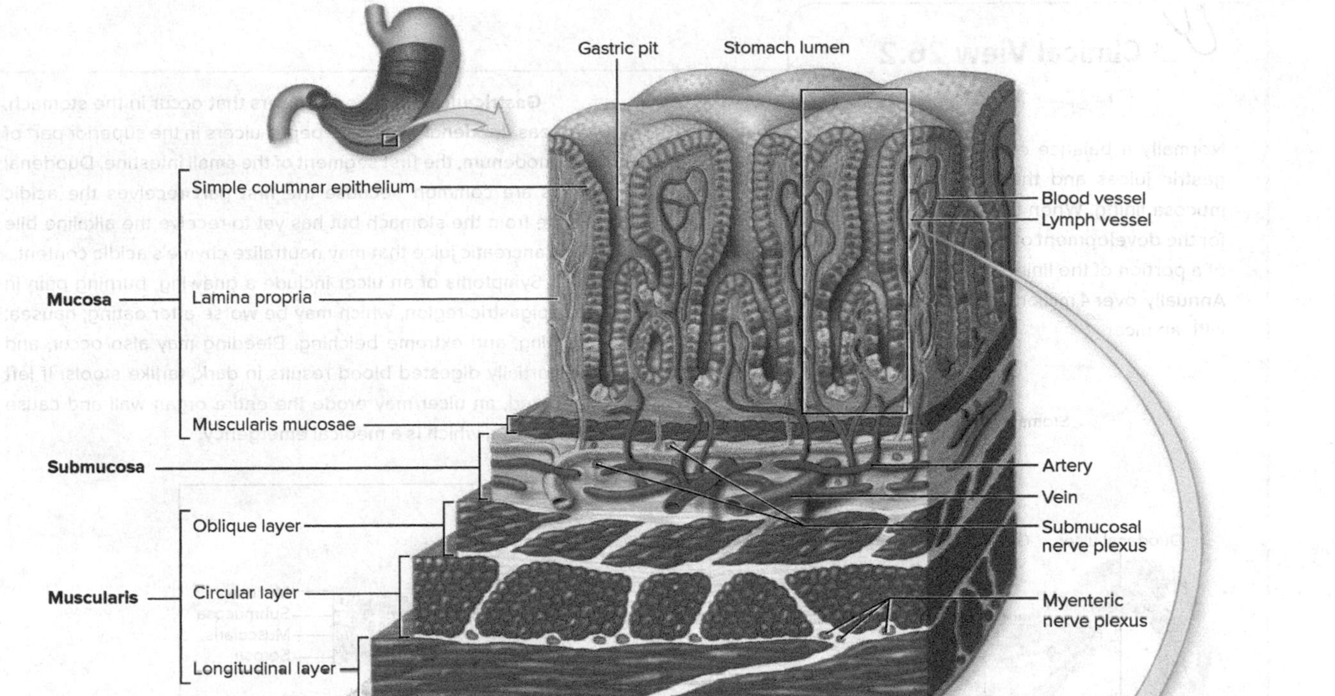

Gastric pit
Stomach lumen
Simple columnar epithelium
Mucosa
Lamina propria
Muscularis mucosae
Blood vessel
Lymph vessel
Submucosa
Artery
Vein
Submucosal nerve plexus
Oblique layer
Muscularis
Circular layer
Myenteric nerve plexus
Longitudinal layer
Serosa
(a) Stomach wall, sectional view
Stomach lumen
Gastric pit
Gastric glands
LM 60x
(b) Stomach mucosa
Simple columnar epithelium
Gastric pit
Gastric gland
Surface mucous cell (secretes alkaline fluid containing mucin)
Mucous neck cell (secretes acidic fluid containing mucin)
Parietal cell (secretes intrinsic factor and hydrochloric acid)
Chief cell (secretes pepsinogen and gastric lipase)
Enteroendocrine cell (secretes gastrin into blood)
(c) Gastric pit and gland

Figure 26.13

Histology of the Stomach Wall. *(a)* The stomach lumen contains invaginations within the mucosa called gastric pits that lead into gastric glands. (*b*) A photomicrograph shows gastric glands and the cells lining the gastric pit. (*c*) A diagrammatic section of a gastric pit and gland shows their structure and the distribution of different types of secretory cells.

(b) ©McGraw-Hill Education/Alvin Telser, photographer

Clinical View 26.2

Peptic Ulcers

Normally a balance exists in the stomach between the acidic gastric juices and the protective, regenerative nature of the mucosa lining. When this balance is thrown off, the stage is set for the development of a **peptic ulcer**—a chronic, solitary erosion of a portion of the lining of either the stomach or the duodenum. Annually, over 4 million people in the United States are diagnosed with an ulcer.

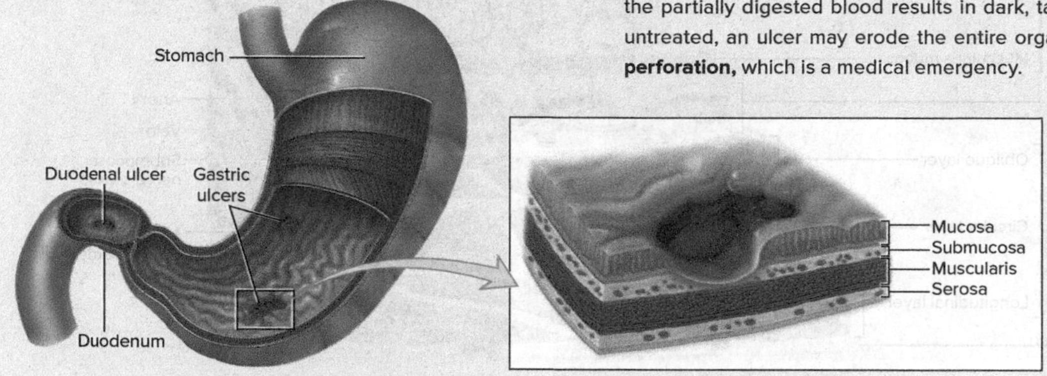
Stomach
Duodenal ulcer
Gastric ulcers
Duodenum
Mucosa
Submucosa
Muscularis
Serosa

(a) Common locations of gastric and duodenal ulcers

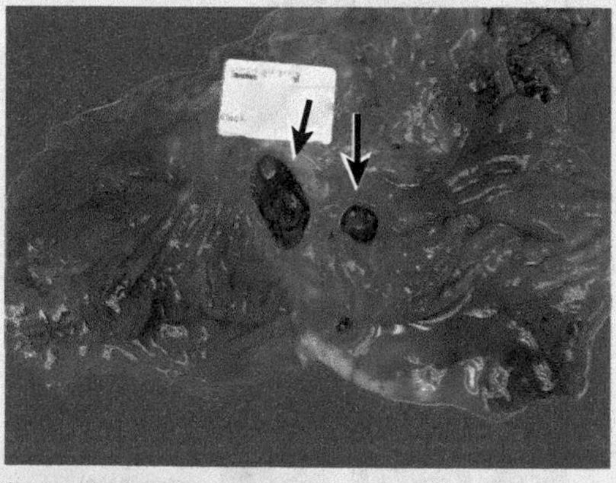

(b) Gastric ulcers (black arrows)

Courtesy of Dr. Jill Urban, Dallas County Medical Examiner's Office, Dallas, TX

Gastric ulcers are peptic ulcers that occur in the stomach, whereas **duodenal ulcers** are peptic ulcers in the superior part of the duodenum, the first segment of the small intestine. Duodenal ulcers are common because the first part receives the acidic chyme from the stomach but has yet to receive the alkaline bile and pancreatic juice that may neutralize chyme's acidic content.

Symptoms of an ulcer include a gnawing, burning pain in the epigastric region, which may be worse after eating; nausea; vomiting; and extreme belching. Bleeding may also occur, and the partially digested blood results in dark, tarlike stools. If left untreated, an ulcer may erode the entire organ wall and cause **perforation,** which is a medical emergency.

Irritation of the gastric mucosa **(gastritis)** has been linked to many cases of peptic ulcer. Nonsteroidal anti-inflammatory drugs (NSAIDs), such as ibuprofen and aspirin, are a common cause of gastritis, and these drugs also impair healing of the gastric lining. However, the major player in peptic ulcer formation is a bacterium called *Helicobacter pylori,* which is present in over 70% of gastric ulcer cases and well over 90% of duodenal ulcer cases. *H. pylori* resides in the stomach and produces enzymes that weaken the protective effects of the gastric mucus. As leukocytes enter the stomach to destroy the bacteria, they also destroy the mucous neck cells. This further irritates the stomach lining and creates an ideal environment for continued *H. pylori* colonization.

Categories of medications that help include an antibiotic taken for 2 weeks to eradicate *H. pylori,* and treatments that are similar for gastric reflux, including antacids, proton-pump inhibitors, a histamine (H_2) blocker, and antacids.

chemically digests denatured proteins in the stomach into smaller fragments.

Enteroendocrine (en'ter- ō-en'd ō-krin; *enteron* = gut, intestine) **cells** are endocrine cells widely distributed in the gastric glands of the stomach. These cells secrete **gastrin,** a hormone that enters the blood and stimulates the secretory activities of the chief and parietal cells and the contractile activity of gastric muscle. Enteroendocrine cells also produce other hormones, such as somatostatin, that modulate the function of nearby enteroendocrine and exocrine cells.

There are numerous gastric pits in the mucosa of the stomach, but the types of secretory cells differ in the various regions of the stomach. The glands of the fundus and body contain all five of the cell types discussed; however, the glands of the cardia and pylorus contain mostly mucous neck cells. Parietal cells are abundant in the glands of the fundus and body, but they are virtually absent in pyloric glands. Thus, the glands of the fundus and body produce highly acidic secretions, whereas those in the cardia and pylorus produce mainly protective, alkaline mucin. The alkaline mucus can help protect the adjacent regions of the digestive tract (esophagus and duodenum) from damage by stomach acid and digestive enzymes.

Saliva, mucin, and gastric secretions contribute substantially to the volume of ingested material. In fact, if a person eats 1 liter of food, the amount of chyme that enters the small intestine is 3 to 4 liters, due to the volume of the secretions. APR

WHAT DID YOU LEARN?

10. What are the four regions of the stomach, and where is each located?
11. Create a table of the five types of secretory cells in the stomach and what they secrete.

26.8 Small Intestine

✓ Learning Objectives

15. Identify and describe the gross anatomy of the small intestine.
16. Differentiate the histology of the small intestine.

The small intestine finishes the chemical digestion process and is responsible for absorbing up to 90% of the nutrients and water. Ingested nutrients spend at least 12 hours in the small intestine as chemical digestion and absorption are completed.

26.8a Gross Anatomy and Regions

The **small intestine,** also called the *small bowel,* is a coiled, thin-walled tube about 6 meters (20 feet) in length in the unembalmed cadaver. (It is much shorter in a living individual due to smooth muscle tone.) It extends from the pylorus of the stomach to the cecum of the large intestine, occupying a significant portion of the abdominal cavity. The small intestine receives its blood supply primarily from branches of the superior mesenteric artery, and it is innervated by the superior mesenteric plexus (see sections 23.3f and 18.5a, respectively). The small intestine consists of three specific segments: the duodenum, the jejunum, and the ileum (**figure 26.14**).

The **duodenum** (dū′ō-dē′nŭm, dū-od′ĕ-nŭm; breadth of twelve fingers) forms the initial or first segment of the small intestine. It is about 25 centimeters (10 inches) long and originates at the pyloric sphincter. The duodenum is arched into a C-shape around the head of the pancreas and becomes continuous with the jejunum at the **duodenojejunal flexure** (flek′sher; *fleksura* = bend). Most of the duodenum is retroperitoneal, although the very initial portion is intraperitoneal and connects to the liver by the lesser omentum. Within the wall of the duodenum is the **major duodenal papilla,** through which bile (secretions released from the liver and gallbladder) and pancreatic juice enter the duodenum (see figure 26.21*a*). A **minor duodenal papilla** also receives an additional small amount of pancreatic juice via an accessory pancreatic duct.

The **jejunum** (jĕ-jū′nŭm; *jejunus* = empty) is the middle region of the small intestine. Extending about 2.5 meters (7.5 feet), it makes up about two-fifths of the small intestine's total length. The jejunum is the primary region within the small intestine for chemical digestion and nutrient absorption. It is intraperitoneal and suspended within the abdomen by the mesentery proper.

The **ileum** (il′ē-ŭm; *eiles* = twisted) is the final or last region of the small intestine. At about 3.6 meters (10.8 feet) in length, the ileum forms about three-fifths of the small intestine. Its distal end terminates at the **ileocecal** (il′ē-ō-sē′kăl) **valve,** a sphincter that controls the entry of materials into the large intestine (see figure 26.16). The ileum is intraperitoneal and suspended in the abdomen by the mesentery proper.

Internally, the mucosal and submucosal tunics of the small intestine are thrown into **circular folds** (also called *plicae* [plī′kē; fold] *circulares*) (**figure 26.15*a, b***). Circular folds, which can be seen with the naked eye, help increase the surface area through which nutrients can be absorbed. In addition, the circular folds act like "speed bumps" to slow down the movement of chyme and ensure that it remains within the small intestine for maximal nutrient absorption. Circular folds are more numerous in the duodenum and jejunum, and least numerous in the ileum.

WHAT DO YOU THINK?

4. Why are the circular folds much more numerous in the duodenum than in the ileum? How does the abundance of circular folds relate to the main functions of the duodenum and ileum?

26.8b Histology

When circular folds are viewed at the microscopic level, smaller, fingerlike projections of mucosa only, called **villi,** can be seen along their surface. These villi further increase the surface area for absorption and secretion. Increasing the absorptive surface area even further are **microvilli** (mī-kr ō-vil′ī; *mikros* = small) along the free (apical) surface of the simple columnar cells (figure 26.15*e* and section 4.1e). Individual microvilli are not clearly visible in light micrographs of the small intestine; instead, they collectively appear as a **brush border** that resembles a brightly staining surface on the apical end of the simple columnar cells (figure 26.15*d*). Each villus contains an arteriole and a venule, with a rich capillary network between them. The capillaries absorb most nutrients. In the center of the villus is a lacteal, which is responsible for absorbing lipids and lipid-soluble vitamins, which are too large to be absorbed by the capillaries (see section 24.2a).

Between some of the intestinal villi are invaginations of mucosa called **intestinal glands** (also known as *intestinal crypts* or *crypts of Lieberkuhn*) (figure 26.15*c*). These glands extend to the base of the mucosa and slightly resemble the gastric glands of the stomach. Lining them are simple columnar epithelial cells (with goblet cells), unicellular glands, and enteroendocrine cells. The enteroendocrine cells release hormones such as **secretin, cholecystokinin,** and **gastric inhibitory peptide.** Some of these hormones temporarily slow down digestive activities as material from the stomach begins to enter the small intestine, thereby prolonging the time for stomach emptying into the small intestine. The goblet cells produce mucin to lubricate and protect the intestinal lining as materials being digested pass through.

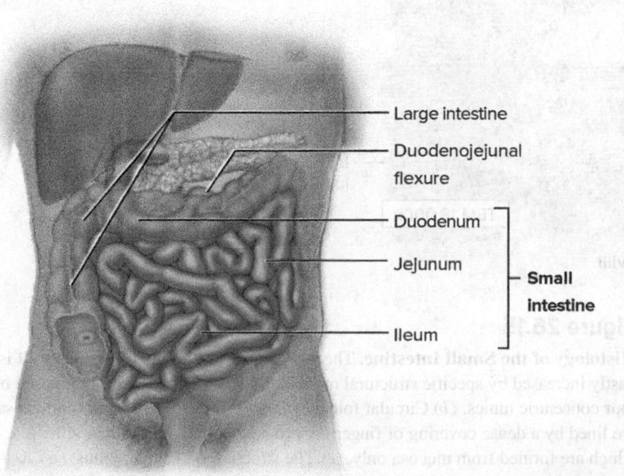

Figure 26.14

Gross Anatomy of the Small Intestine. The three regions of the small intestine—duodenum, jejunum, and ileum—are continuous and "framed" within the abdominal cavity by the large intestine.

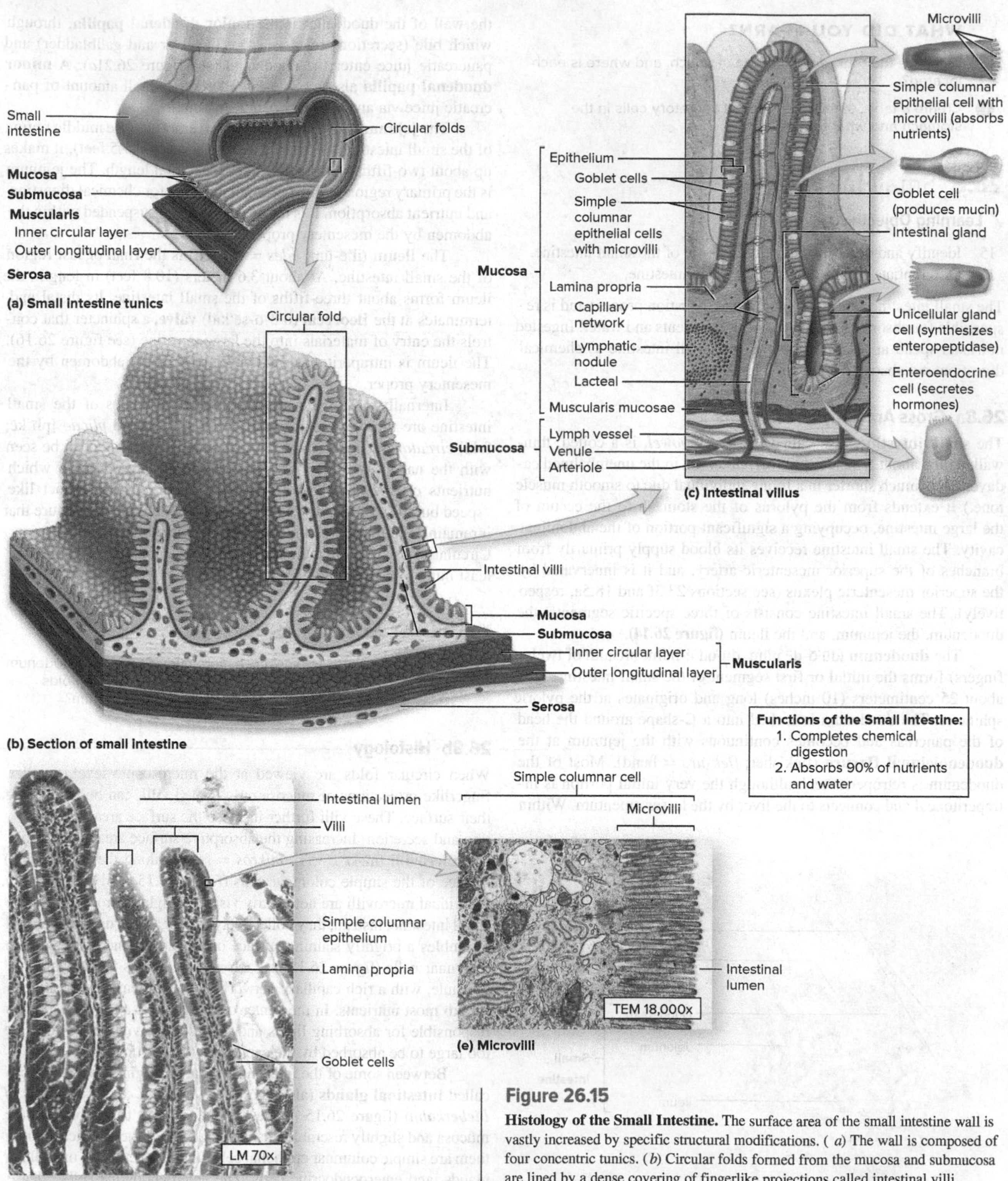
Small intestine
Circular folds
Mucosa
Submucosa
Muscularis
Inner circular layer
Outer longitudinal layer
Serosa
(a) Small intestine tunics
Circular fold
Intestinal villi
Mucosa
Submucosa
Inner circular layer
Outer longitudinal layer
Muscularis
Serosa
(b) Section of small intestine
Microvilli
Simple columnar epithelial cell with microvilli (absorbs nutrients)
Epithelium
Goblet cells
Simple columnar epithelial cells with microvilli
Goblet cell (produces mucin)
Intestinal gland
Mucosa
Lamina propria
Capillary network
Lymphatic nodule
Lacteal
Unicellular gland cell (synthesizes enteropeptidase)
Enteroendocrine cell (secretes hormones)
Muscularis mucosae
Submucosa
Lymph vessel
Venule
Arteriole
(c) Intestinal villus
Functions of the Small Intestine:
1. Completes chemical digestion
2. Absorbs 90% of nutrients and water
Intestinal lumen
Villi
Simple columnar epithelium
Lamina propria
Goblet cells
LM 70x
(d) Intestinal villi
Simple columnar cell
Microvilli
Intestinal lumen
TEM 18,000x
(e) Microvilli

Figure 26.15

Histology of the Small Intestine. The surface area of the small intestine wall is vastly increased by specific structural modifications. (*a*) The wall is composed of four concentric tunics. (*b*) Circular folds formed from the mucosa and submucosa are lined by a dense covering of fingerlike projections called intestinal villi, which are formed from mucosa only. (*c*) The structure of a single villus. (*d*) A photomicrograph shows the internal structure of villi projecting into the intestinal lumen. (*e*) A TEM photo shows the microvilli of the plasma membrane along the apical surface of the epithelium.

(d) ©McGraw-Hill Education/Alvin Telser, photographer; (e) Dr. Lee Peachey

Table 26.4 Small Intestine Structures Involved in Chemical Digestion and Absorption

Structure	Anatomy	Function(s)
Circular folds	Circular folds of mucosa and submucosa	Slow down the passage of materials undergoing digestion; increase surface area for both chemical digestion and absorption
Villi	Fingerlike projections of mucosa	Increase surface area for both absorption and chemical digestion
Microvilli	Folded, fingerlike projections of plasma membrane on apical surface of columnar epithelial cells	Increase surface area for both absorption and chemical digestion
Intestinal glands	Invaginations into mucosa between villi	Increase surface area for both absorption and chemical digestion; enteroendocrine cells lining intestinal glands secrete digestive hormones
Submucosal glands	Coiled tubular glands within submucosa with ducts opening into intestinal lumen	Secrete alkaline mucin to protect and lubricate lining of small intestine

Distinctive histologic features characterize the three small intestine regions. The proximal duodenum contains **submucosal glands** (or *Brunner glands*), which produce a viscous, alkaline mucus that protects the duodenum from the acidic chyme. Circular folds are best-developed in the jejunum and nearly absent in the ileum. Additionally, villi are larger and more numerous in the jejunum. The number of goblet cells in the mucosa increases from the duodenum to the ileum, due to the increased need for lubrication as digested materials are absorbed and undigested materials are left behind. Peyer patches are abundant primarily in the ileum (see sections 24.4a and 26.4c).

Table 26.4 summarizes all of the small intestine structures that aid in chemical digestion and absorption.

WHAT DID YOU LEARN?

12 Compare and contrast the gross anatomic and histologic characteristics that distinguish the duodenum, jejunum, and ileum.

26.9 Large Intestine

✓ Learning Objectives

17. Identify and describe the gross anatomy of the large intestine.
18. Identify and describe the microscopic structure of the large intestine.
19. Trace the movement of material through the large intestine.

The **large intestine,** also called the *large bowel,* forms a three-sided perimeter in the abdominal cavity around the centrally located small intestine (**figure 26.16**). From its origin at the ileocecal junction to its termination at the anus, the large intestine has an approximate length of 1.5 meters (5 feet) and a diameter of 6.5 centimeters (2.5 inches). It is called the "large" intestine because its diameter is greater than that of the small intestine. Recall from section 26.8 that the small intestine absorbs much, but not all, of the digested material. On average, about 1 liter of remaining material passes from the small intestine to the large intestine daily.

The large intestine absorbs most of the water and ions from the remaining digested material. In so doing, the watery material that first enters the large intestine soon solidifies and becomes **feces.** The large intestine stores the feces until the body is ready to defecate (expel the feces). The large intestine also absorbs a very small percentage of nutrients still remaining in the digested material.

26.9a Gross Anatomy and Regions

The initial or first region of the large intestine is a blind sac called the **cecum** (sē'kŭm; *caecus* = blind), which is located in the right lower abdominal quadrant. This pouch extends inferiorly from the ileocecal valve. Projecting inferiorly from the posteromedial region of the cecum is the **vermiform** (ver'mi-fōrm; *vermis* = worm) **appendix** (ă-pen'diks; appendage), a thin, hollow, fingerlike sac lined by lymphocyte-filled lymphatic nodules (see section 24.4a). Both the cecum and the vermiform appendix are intraperitoneal organs.

At the level of the ileocecal valve, the **colon** begins and forms an inverted U-shaped arch. The colon is partitioned into four segments: the ascending colon, transverse colon, descending colon, and sigmoid colon.

The **ascending colon** originates at the ileocecal valve and extends superiorly from the superior edge of the cecum along the right lateral border of the abdominal cavity. The ascending colon is retroperitoneal, because its posterior wall directly adheres to the posterior abdominal wall, and only its anterior surface is covered with peritoneum. As it approaches the inferior surface of the liver, the ascending colon makes a 90-degree turn toward the left side of the abdominal cavity. This bend in the colon is called the **right colic** (kol'ik) **flexure,** or the *hepatic flexure,* as it lies inferior to the liver (figure 26.16 *a*).

The **transverse colon** originates at the right colic flexure and curves slightly anteriorly as it projects horizontally across the anterior region of the abdominal cavity. A type of mesentery called the **transverse mesocolon** connects the transverse portion of the large intestine to the posterior abdominal wall. Hence, the transverse colon is intraperitoneal. As the transverse colon approaches the spleen in the left upper quadrant of the abdomen, it makes a 90-degree turn inferiorly. The resulting bend in the colon is called the **left colic flexure,** or the *splenic* (splen'ik) *flexure,* as it lies inferior to the spleen (figure 26.16 *a*).

The **descending colon** is retroperitoneal and found along the left side of the abdominal cavity. It originates at the left colic flexure and descends vertically until it terminates at the sigmoid colon. The **sigmoid** (sig'moyd; resembling letter S) **colon** originates at the **sigmoid flexure,** where the descending colon curves and turns inferomedially into the pelvic cavity. The sigmoid colon is intraperitoneal and has a mesentery called the **sigmoid mesocolon.** The sigmoid colon terminates at the rectum.

The **rectum** (rek'tŭm; *rectus* = straight) is a retroperitoneal structure that connects to the sigmoid colon. The rectum is a

Figure 26.16

Gross Anatomy of the Large Intestine. (*a*) Anterior view of the large intestine, which forms the distal end of the GI tract. (*b*) Details of the rectum and anal canal.

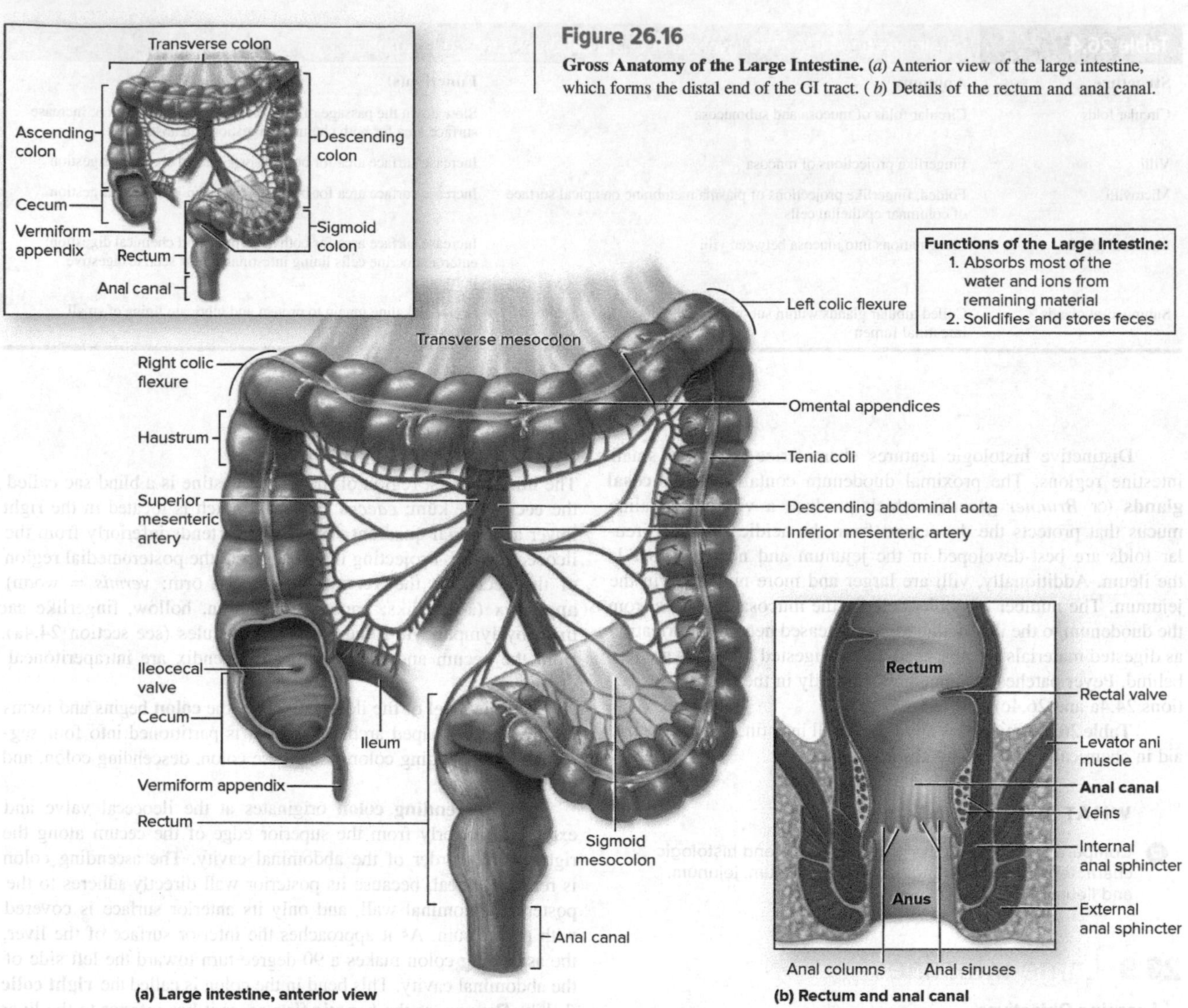
Transverse colon
Ascending colon
Descending colon
Cecum
Vermiform appendix
Sigmoid colon
Rectum
Anal canal
Functions of the Large Intestine:
1. Absorbs most of the water and ions from remaining material
2. Solidifies and stores feces
Left colic flexure
Transverse mesocolon
Right colic flexure
Omental appendices
Haustrum
Tenia coli
Superior mesenteric artery
Descending abdominal aorta
Inferior mesenteric artery
Ileocecal valve
Cecum
Ileum
Vermiform appendix
Rectum
Sigmoid mesocolon
Anal canal
Rectum
Rectal valve
Levator ani muscle
Anal canal
Veins
Internal anal sphincter
Anus
External anal sphincter
Anal columns
Anal sinuses

(a) Large intestine, anterior view

(b) Rectum and anal canal

muscular tube that readily expands to store accumulated fecal material prior to defecation. Three thick, transverse folds of the rectum, called **rectal valves,** ensure that fecal material is retained during the passing of gas (figure 26.16*b*). The rectum then terminates at the anal canal.

The terminal few centimeters of the large intestine are called the **anal** (ā′năl) **canal** (figure 26.16 *b*). The anal canal passes through an opening in the levator ani muscles of the pelvic floor and terminates at the anus. The internal lining of the anal canal contains relatively thin longitudinal ridges, called **anal columns,** between which are small depressions termed **anal sinuses.** As fecal material passes through the anal canal during defecation, pressure exerted on the anal sinuses causes their cells to release excess mucin. As a result, this extra mucus lubricates the anal canal during defecation. At the base of the anal canal are the **internal** and **external anal sphincters,** which close off the opening to the anal canal and relax (open) during defecation. The internal anal sphincter is involuntary, whereas the external anal sphincter is voluntary (see section 11.5).

Learning Strategy 26.4

Many of the segments of the colon are named for the direction in which materials travel. So material ascends (travels superiorly) in the *ascending colon,* material travels across in the *transverse colon,* and material descends (travels inferiorly) in the *descending colon.*

26.9b Histology

The mucosa of the large intestine is lined with simple columnar epithelium and goblet cells (**figure 26.17**). Unlike the small intestine, the large intestine mucosa lacks intestinal villi; however, it contains numerous intestinal glands that extend to the muscularis mucosae. The glands' goblet cells secrete mucin to lubricate the undigested material as it passes through, and the simple columnar epithelial cells continue to absorb nutrients that were not absorbed during passage through the small intestine. Many lymphatic nodules (see section 24.4a) and lymphatic cells occupy the lamina propria of the large intestine.

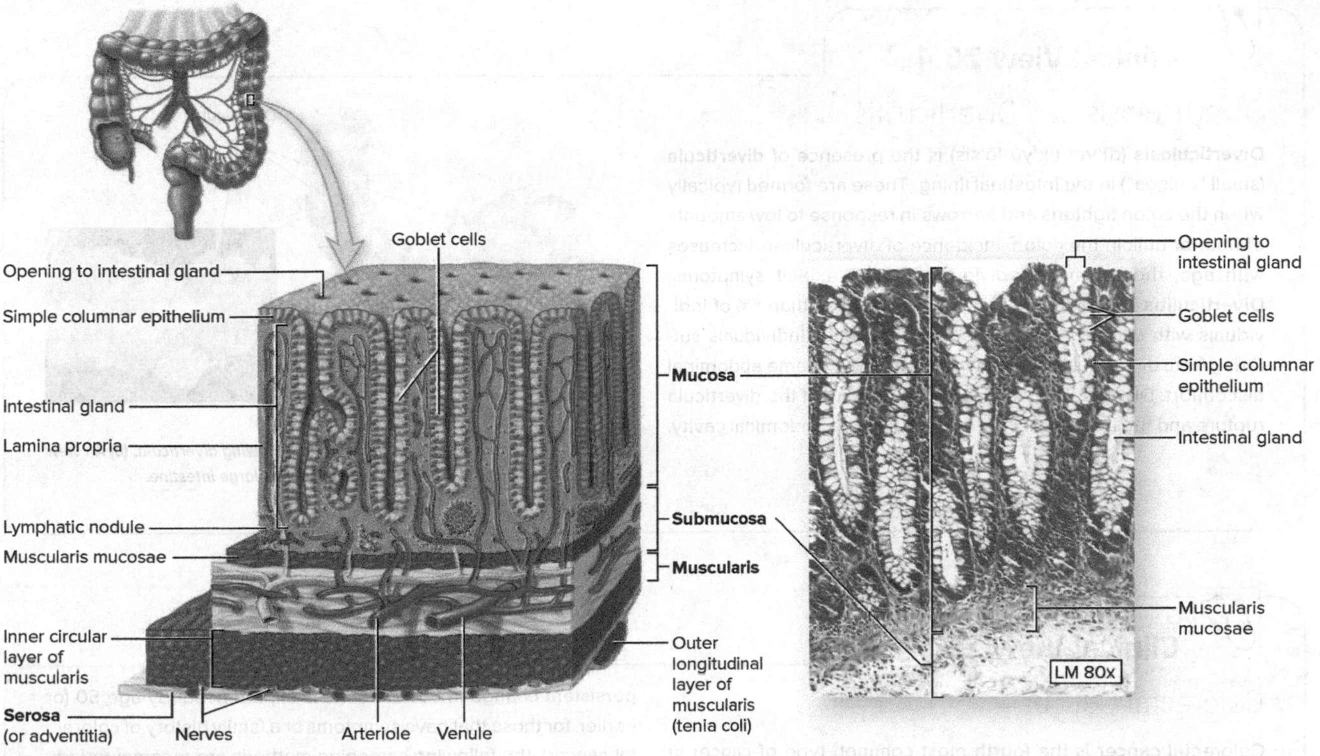
Goblet cells
Opening to intestinal gland
Simple columnar epithelium
Intestinal gland
Lamina propria
Lymphatic nodule
Muscularis mucosae
Inner circular layer of muscularis
Serosa
(or adventitia)
Nerves
Arteriole
Venule
Outer longitudinal layer of muscularis (tenia coli)
Mucosa
Submucosa
Muscularis
Opening to intestinal gland
Goblet cells
Simple columnar epithelium
Intestinal gland
Muscularis mucosae
LM 80x

(a) Large intestine tunics

(b) Large intestine mucosa and submucosa

Figure 26.17

Histology of the Large Intestine. *(a)* The luminal wall of the large intestine is composed of four tunics: mucosa, submocosa, muscularis, and serosa (or adventitia). *(b)* A photomicrograph shows the histology of the mucosa and submucosa of the large intestine wall.

(b) ©McGraw-Hill Education/Alvin Telser, photographer

Clinical View 26.3

Appendicitis

Inflammation of the appendix is called **appendicitis** (ă-pen-di-sī′tis). Most cases of appendicitis occur because fecal matter obstructs the appendix. As the tissue in its wall becomes inflamed, the appendix swells, the blood supply is compromised, and bacteria may proliferate in the wall. Untreated, the appendix may burst and release its contents into the peritoneum, causing a massive and potentially deadly infection called *peritonitis.*

During the early stages of appendicitis, the smooth muscle wall (innervated by the ANS) contracts and goes into spasms. This pain thus is referred to the T10 dermatome around the umbilicus (see section 19.1b and figures 19.3 and 19.4).

As the inflammation worsens and the parietal peritoneum becomes inflamed as well, the pain becomes sharp and localized to the right lower quadrant of the abdomen. Individuals with appendicitis typically experience nausea or vomiting, abdominal tenderness in the inferior right quadrant, a low fever, and an elevated leukocyte count. Acute appendicitis may be treated first with antibiotics. If the appendicitis fails to resolve, the inflamed appendix may be surgically removed in a procedure called an **appendectomy.**

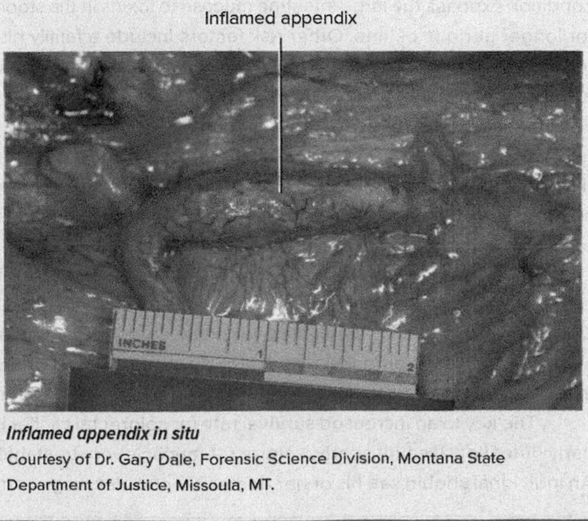
Inflamed appendix
INCHES

Inflamed appendix in situ

Courtesy of Dr. Gary Dale, Forensic Science Division, Montana State Department of Justice, Missoula, MT.

Clinical View 26.4

Diverticulosis and Diverticulitis

Diverticulosis (dī′ver-tik′yū-lō′sis) is the presence of **diverticula** (small "bulges") in the intestinal lining. These are formed typically when the colon tightens and narrows in response to low amounts of fiber or bulk in the colon. Incidence of diverticulosis increases with age, though many individuals do not exhibit symptoms. **Diverticulitis** is inflammation of diverticula. Less than 5% of individuals with diverticulosis develop diverticulitis. Individuals suffering from diverticulitis may have a fever and extreme abdominal discomfort. Diverticulitis may be life-threatening if the diverticula rupture and the intestinal contents leak into the abdominal cavity.

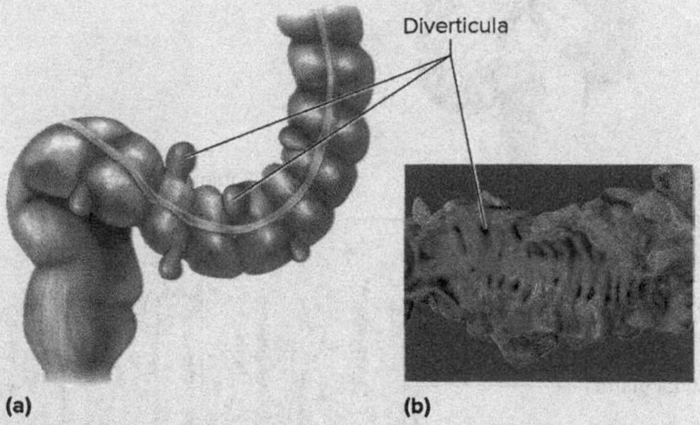
Diverticula
(a)
(b)

(a) An external view of the sigmoid colon showing diverticula. (b) An view of diverticula shown in a removed portion of large intestine.

(b) ©McGraw-Hill Education

Clinical View 26.5

Colorectal Cancer

Colorectal cancer is the fourth most common type of cancer in the United States, with over 140,000 cases occurring annually and 50,000 of those resulting in death. The term **colorectal cancer** refers to a malignant growth anywhere along the intestine (colon and rectum). The majority of colorectal cancers appear in the distal descending colon, sigmoid colon, and rectum, which are the segments of the large intestine that have the longest contact with fecal matter before it is expelled from the body. Most colorectal cancers arise from **polyps** (pol′ip), which are outgrowths from the colon mucosa. Note, however, that colon polyps are very common and most of them never become cancerous. Low-fiber diets have also been implicated in increasing the risk of colon cancer, because decreased dietary fiber leads to decreased stool bulk and longer time for stools to remain in the large intestine. Theoretically, this condition exposes the large intestine mucosa to toxins in the stools for longer periods of time. Other risk factors include a family history of colorectal cancer, personal history of ulcerative colitis, and increased age (most patients are over the age of 40).

Initially, most patients are asymptomatic. Later, they may notice rectal bleeding (often evidenced as blood in the stool or on the toilet paper) and a persistent change in bowel habits (typically constipation). Eventually, the person may experience abdominal pain, fatigue, unexplained weight loss, and anemia.

The cancerous growth in the colon must be removed surgically, and sometimes radiation or chemotherapy is used as well. Colorectal cancers that are limited to the mucosa have a 5-year survival rate, but the prognosis is poor for cancers that have spread into deeper colon wall tunics or metastasized to the lymph nodes.

The key to an increased survival rate for colorectal cancer is early detection. If caught early, colorectal cancer is very treatable. An individual should see his or her doctor if rectal bleeding or any persistent change in bowel habits is experienced. By age 50 (or earlier, for those that have symptoms or a family history of colorectal cancer), the following screening methods are recommended:

1. Take a yearly **fecal occult** (ŏ-kŭlt′, ok′ŭlt) **blood test,** which checks for the presence of blood in the stools.
2. A **sigmoidoscopy** (sig′moy-dos′kŏ-pē; *skopeo* = to view) every 5 years. In this procedure, which is done in the doctor's office, an endoscope is inserted into the rectum and sigmoid colon to check for polyps or cancer.
3. A **colonoscopy** (kō′lon-os′kŏ-pē) every 10 years. A colonoscopy is more extensive than a sigmoidoscopy. The endoscope is inserted into the large intestine at least up to the right colic flexure of the colon, and sometimes as far proximally as the ileocecal valve.

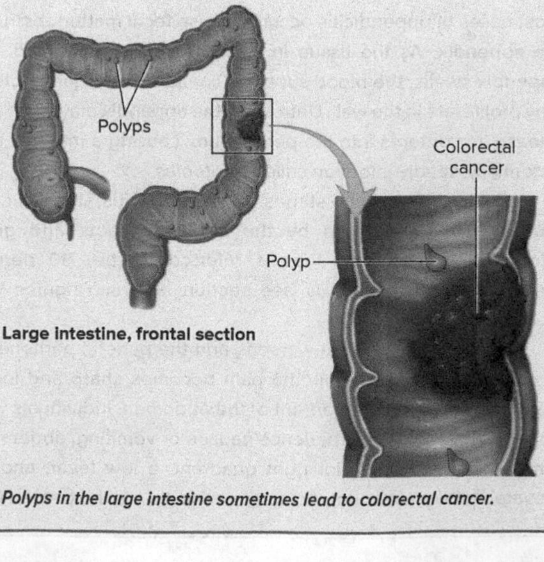
Polyps
Colorectal cancer
Polyp
Large intestine, frontal section

Polyps in the large intestine sometimes lead to colorectal cancer.

The muscularis of the colon and cecum has two layers of smooth muscle, but the outer longitudinal layer does not completely surround the colon and cecum. Instead, these longitudinal smooth muscle fibers form three thin, distinct, longitudinal bundles called **teniae** (tē′nē-ē; ribbons, band) **coli** (kō′lī). The teniae coli act like elastic in a waistband—they help bunch up the large intestine into many sacs, collectively called **haustra** (haw′str ă; sing., *haustrum; haustus* = to drink up) (see figure 26.16*a*). Hanging off the external surface of the haustra are lobules of fat called **omental appendices,** or *epiploic* (ep′i-pl ō′ik; membrane-covered) *appendages.*

26.9c Control of Large Intestine Activity

Large intestine movements are regulated by local reflexes in the autonomic nervous system. With the ingestion of more food, peristaltic movements in the ileum increase, as does the frequency of the opening of the ileocecal valve. This so-called **gastroileal reflex** results in the accumulation of more chyme in the cecum and ascending colon. Mixing movements are infrequent in the colon. Instead, three types of movements are typically associated with the passage of digested material through the large intestine: peristaltic movements, haustral churning, and mass movement.

Peristaltic movements of the large intestine are usually weak and sluggish, but otherwise they resemble those that occur in the wall of the small intestine. **Haustral churning** occurs after a relaxed haustrum fills with digested or fecal material until its distension stimulates reflex contractions in the muscularis, causing churning and movement of the material to more distal haustra. **Mass movements** are powerful, peristaltic-like contractions involving the teniae coli that propel fecal material toward the rectum. Generally, mass movements occur two or three times a day, often during or immediately after a meal. This is the **gastrocolic** (gas′tr ō-kol′ik) **reflex.**

Two common problems with defecation are constipation and diarrhea. **Constipation** is typically a temporary, impaired ability to defecate and generally results in compacted feces that are difficult to eliminate. Constipation may result from a combination of factors, including a diet low in fiber, dehydration, lack of exercise, and improper bowel habits (not defecating when the urge arises, allowing additional water to be absorbed from the feces). In contrast, **diarrhea** may result as a consequence of disruption in normal mechanisms to absorb intestinal water, or excessive amounts of osmotically active solutes that keep water in the intestinal lumen and prevent its reabsorption.

WHAT DID YOU LEARN?

13. Identify the retroperitoneal and intraperitoneal large intestine structures.
14. What specific movements and reflexes propel material through the large intestine?

26.10 Accessory Digestive Organs

✓ Learning Objectives

20. Identify and describe the gross anatomy and microscopic anatomy of the liver.
21. Identify and describe the gross anatomy and microanatomy of the pancreas.
22. Trace and describe the path of bile and pancreatic juice through the biliary apparatus to the duodenum.

The accessory digestive organs produce secretions that facilitate the chemical digestive activities of GI tract organs. Important accessory digestive organs are the liver, the gallbladder, and the pancreas.

26.10a Liver

The **liver** (liv′ĕr) lies in the right upper quadrant of the abdomen, immediately inferior to the diaphragm. Weighing 1 to 2 kilograms (2.25 to 4.5 pounds), it constitutes about 2% of an adult's body weight. The liver is covered by a connective tissue capsule and a layer of visceral peritoneum, except for a small region on its diaphragmatic surface called the bare area.

Gross Anatomy

The liver is composed of four incompletely separated lobes and supported by two ligaments **(figure 26.18)**. The major lobes are the **right lobe** and the **left lobe.** The right lobe is separated from the smaller

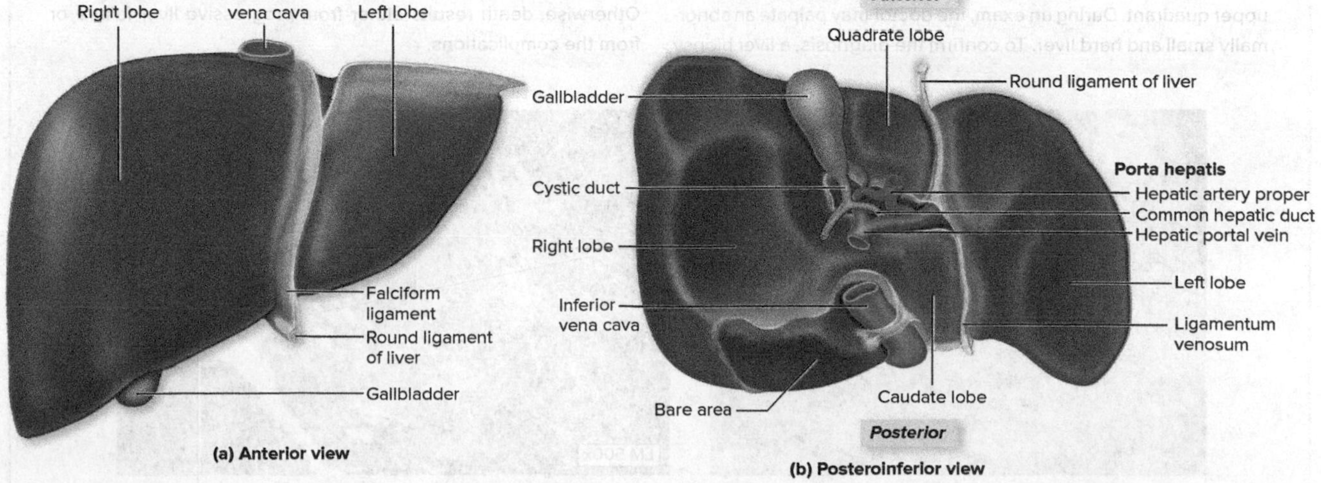

Figure 26.18
Gross Anatomy of the Liver. The liver is in the upper right quadrant of the abdomen. (*a*) Anterior and (*b*) posteroinferior views show the four lobes of the liver, as well as the gallbladder and the porta hepatis. APR

left lobe by the falciform ligament, a peritoneal fold that secures the liver to the anterior abdominal wall. In the inferior free edge of the falciform ligament lies the **round ligament of the liver** (or *ligamentum teres*), which represents the remnant of the fetal umbilical vein (see section 23.7c). Subdivisions of the right lobe include the **caudate** (kaw'd āt; *cauda* = tail) **lobe** and the **quadrate** (kwah'dr āt; *quadratus* = square) **lobe.** The caudate lobe is adjacent to the inferior vena cava, and the quadrate lobe is adjacent to the gallbladder (figure 26.18*b*).

Along the inferior surface of the liver are several structures that collectively resemble the letter H. The gallbladder and the round ligament of the liver form the vertical superior parts of the H; the **inferior vena cava** and the **ligamentum venosum** form the vertical inferior parts. (Recall from section 23.7c that the ligamentum venosum was a remnant of the ductus venosus in the embryo.) Finally, the **porta** (pōr'tă; gate) **hepatis** (hep'ă-tis) represents the horizontal crossbar of the H and is where blood and lymph vessels, bile ducts, and nerves enter and leave the liver.

Histology

A connective tissue capsule branches through the liver and forms septa that partition the liver into thousands of small, polyhedral **hepatic lobules,** which are the classic structural and functional units of the liver (**figure 26.19**). Within hepatic lobules are liver cells called **hepatocytes** (hep'a'tō-sīt). At the periphery of each lobule are several **portal triads,** composed of branches of the hepatic portal vein, the hepatic artery, and the bile duct.

A dual blood supply serves the liver. The **hepatic portal vein** carries blood from the capillary beds of the GI tract, spleen, and

Clinical View 26.6

Liver Cirrhosis

Liver cirrhosis (sir-rō'sis; *kirrhos* = yellow) results when hepatocytes have been destroyed and are replaced by fibrous scar tissue. This scar tissue often surrounds isolated nodules of regenerating hepatocytes. The scar tissue also compresses both (1) the blood vessels, resulting in **hepatic portal hypertension** (high blood pressure in the hepatic portal venous system); and (2) the bile ducts in the liver, which impedes bile flow.

Liver cirrhosis is caused by chronic injury to the hepatocytes, as may result from chronic alcoholism, liver disease, or certain drugs or toxins. **Chronic hepatitis** (hep-ă-tī'tis) is a long-term inflammation of the liver that leads to necrosis of liver tissue. Most frequently, viral infections from either **hepatitis B** or **hepatitis C** produce chronic hepatitis. Other disorders that result in liver cirrhosis include some inherited diseases, chronic biliary obstruction, and biliary cirrhosis.

Early stages of liver cirrhosis may be asymptomatic. However, once liver function begins to falter, the patient complains of fatigue, weight loss, and nausea, and may have pain in the right upper quadrant. During an exam, the doctor may palpate an abnormally small and hard liver. To confirm the diagnosis, a liver biopsy is done to obtain a small portion of liver tissue through a needle passed into the liver; the cells are then examined microscopically. The fibrosis and scarring of liver cirrhosis are irreversible.

Advanced liver cirrhosis may have a variety of complications:

- **Jaundice** (yellowing of the skin and sclerae of the eyes) occurs when the liver's ability to eliminate bilirubin is impaired.
- **Edema** (e-dē'mă), the accumulation of fluid in body tissues, is evident due to reduced formation and release of albumin.
- **Ascites** (ă-sī'tēz; fluid accumulation in the abdomen) develops because of decreased albumin production.
- Intense itching occurs when bile products are deposited in the skin.
- Toxins in the blood and brain accumulate because the liver cannot effectively process them.
- **Hepatic portal hypertension** (high blood pressure in the hepatic portal venous system) can lead to dilated veins of the inferior esophagus (esophageal varices).

End-stage liver cirrhosis can be treated only with a liver transplant. Otherwise, death results either from progressive liver failure or from the complications.

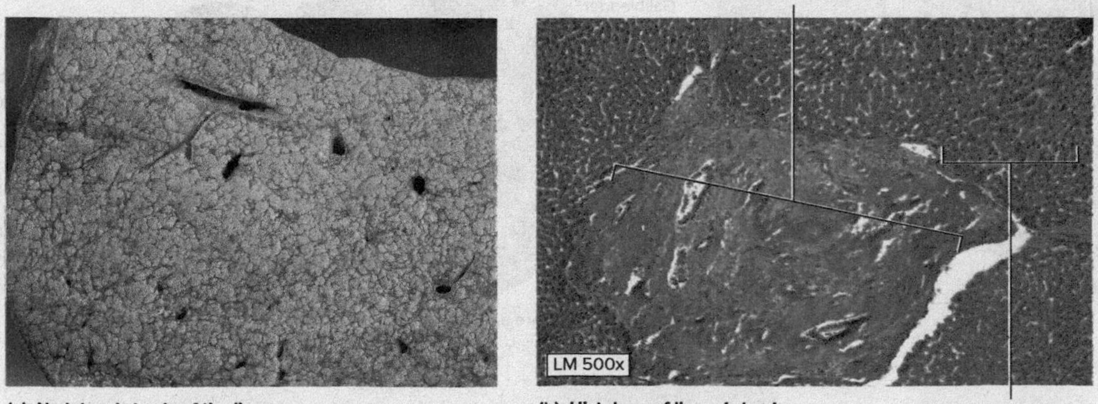

(a) Nodular cirrhosis of the liver (b) Histology of liver cirrhosis

(a) This gross specimen depicts a type of nodular cirrhosis of the liver. (b) A photomicrograph shows how scar tissue infiltrates and replaces hepatocytes.

(a) Dennis K. Burns, MD; Travis G. Brown, MD; Walter L. Kemp, MD/McGraw-Hill Education; (b) Centers for Disease Control and Prevention (CDC)

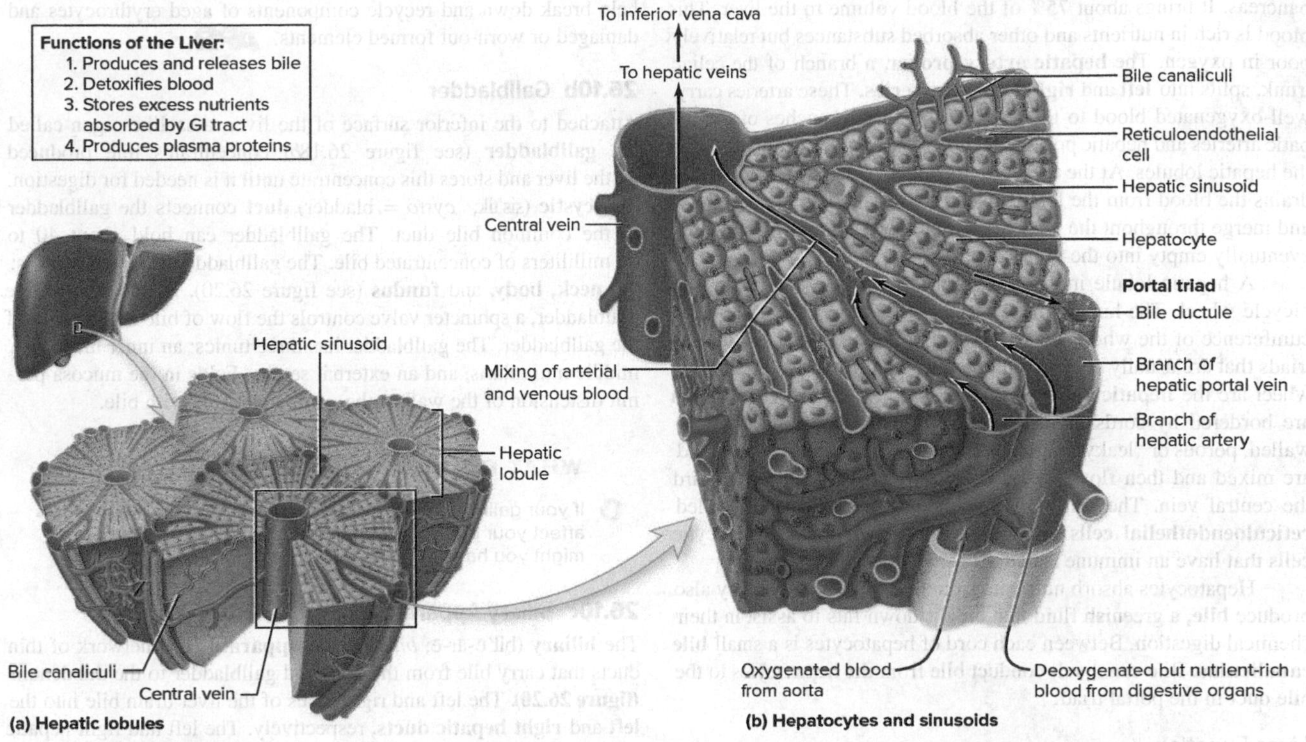
Functions of the Liver:
1. Produces and releases bile
2. Detoxifies blood
3. Stores excess nutrients absorbed by GI tract
4. Produces plasma proteins
Hepatic sinusoid
Hepatic lobule
Bile canaliculi
Central vein
(a) Hepatic lobules
To inferior vena cava
To hepatic veins
Central vein
Mixing of arterial and venous blood
Bile canaliculi
Reticuloendothelial cell
Hepatic sinusoid
Hepatocyte
Portal triad
Bile ductule
Branch of hepatic portal vein
Branch of hepatic artery
Oxygenated blood from aorta
Deoxygenated but nutrient-rich blood from digestive organs
(b) Hepatocytes and sinusoids
Portal triad
Bile ductule
Branch of hepatic portal vein
Branch of hepatic artery
LM 220x
Portal triad
Hepatic lobule
Hepatic sinusoid
Hepatocytes
LM 30x
(c) Liver lobule
Hepatic lobules
Right and left hepatic veins
Hepatic artery
Hepatic portal vein
From spleen
Vena cava
Central vein
From small and large intestine
(d) Hepatic portal system

Figure 26.19

Histology of the Liver. (*a*) The functional units of the liver are called hepatic lobules. (*b*) A central vein projects through the center of a hepatic lobule, and several portal triads define its periphery. (*c*) Photomicrgraphs depict a liver lobule at a lower magnification and a portal triad at higher magnification. (*d*) Diagram of the hepatic portal system. APR

(c, top) ©McGraw-Hill Education/Alvin Telser, photographer; (c, bottom) Victor P. Eroschenko pancreas. It brings about 75% of the blood volume to the liver. This blood is rich in nutrients and other absorbed substances but relatively poor in oxygen. The **hepatic artery proper,** a branch of the celiac trunk, splits into **left** and **right hepatic arteries.** These arteries carry well-oxygenated blood to the liver. Blood from branches of the hepatic arteries and hepatic portal vein mixes as it passes to and through the hepatic lobules. At the center of each lobule is a **central vein** that drains the blood from the lobule. Central veins collect venous blood and merge throughout the liver to form numerous **hepatic veins** that eventually empty into the inferior vena cava.

A hepatic lobule in cross section looks like a side view of a bicycle wheel. The hub of the wheel is the central vein. At the circumference of the wheel where the tire would be are several portal triads that are usually equidistant apart. The numerous spokes of the wheel are the **hepatic sinusoids** (sī′nŭ-soyd; *sinus* = cavity), which are bordered by cords of hepatocytes. Hepatic sinusoids are thin-walled, porous or "leaky" capillaries where venous and arterial blood are mixed and then flow slowly through the hepatic lobule toward the central vein. The sinusoids are lined with stellate cells called **reticuloendothelial cells** (or *Kupffer cells*), which are phagocytic cells that have an immune function.

Hepatocytes absorb nutrients from the sinusoids, and they also produce **bile,** a greenish fluid that breaks down fats to assist in their chemical digestion. Between each cord of hepatocytes is a small **bile canaliculus.** Bile canaliculi conduct bile from the hepatocytes to the bile duct in the portal triad.

Liver Function

The liver has numerous functions. Besides producing bile, hepatocytes detoxify drugs, metabolites, and poisons. Hepatocytes also store excess nutrients and vitamins and release them when they are needed. Finally, hepatocytes synthesize blood plasma proteins such as albumins, globulins, and blood clotting proteins . Reticuloendothelial cells in the liver sinusoids phagocytize debris in the blood as well as help break down and recycle components of aged erythrocytes and damaged or worn-out formed elements. APR

26.10b Gallbladder

Attached to the inferior surface of the liver, a saclike organ called the **gallbladder** (see figure 26.18*b*) concentrates bile produced by the liver and stores this concentrate until it is needed for digestion. The **cystic** (sis′tik; *cysto* = bladder) **duct** connects the gallbladder to the common bile duct. The gallbladder can hold about 40 to 60 milliliters of concentrated bile. The gallbladder has three regions: the **neck, body,** and **fundus** (see figure 26.20). At the neck of the gallbladder, a sphincter valve controls the flow of bile into and out of the gallbladder. The gallbladder has three tunics: an inner mucosa, a middle muscularis, and an external serosa. Folds in the mucosa permit distension of the wall as the gallbladder fills with bile.

WHAT DO YOU THINK?

5 If your gallbladder were surgically removed, how would this affect your digestion of fatty meals? What diet alterations might you have to make after this surgery?

26.10c Biliary Apparatus

The **biliary** (bil′ē-ār-ē; *bilis* = bile) **apparatus** is a network of thin ducts that carry bile from the liver and gallbladder to the duodenum **(figure 26.20)**. The left and right lobes of the liver drain bile into the **left** and **right hepatic ducts,** respectively. The left and right hepatic ducts merge to form a single **common hepatic duct.** The **cystic duct** is attached to the common hepatic duct and carries bile to and from the gallbladder. The cystic duct allows bile to enter and to leave the gallbladder; the direction of flow is controlled by hormonal influences. Bile travels from the common hepatic duct through the cystic duct to be stored in the gallbladder; stored bile travels back through the cystic duct for conduction to the small intestine. The union of the

Clinical View 26.7

Gallstones (Cholelithiasis)

High concentration of certain materials in the bile may lead to the eventual formation of **gallstones.** Gallstones occur twice as frequently in women as in men, and are more prevalent in developed countries. Obesity, increasing age, female sex hormones, Caucasian ethnicity, and lack of physical activity are all risk factors for developing gallstones.

The term **cholelithiasis** (kō′lē-li-thī′ă-sis; *chole* = bile, *lithos* = stone, *iasis* = condition) refers to the presence of gallstones in the gallbladder. If the gallstones leave the gallbladder and enter the biliary apparatus, the condition is called choledocholethiasis. Gallstones are typically formed from condensations of either cholesterol or calcium and bile salts. These stones can vary from the tiniest grains to structures almost the size of golf balls. The majority of gallstones are asymptomatic until a gallstone becomes lodged in the neck of the cystic duct, causing the gallbladder to become inflamed **(cholecystitis)** and dilated. The most common symptom is severe pain (called *biliary colic*) perceived in the right hypochondriac region, sometimes between the scapulae, or in the area of the right shoulder. Nausea and vomiting may occur, along with indigestion and bloating. Symptoms are typically worse after eating a fatty meal. Treatment consists of surgical removal of the gallbladder, called **cholecystectomy** (kō′lē-sis-tek′tō-mē; *kystis* = bladder, *ektome* = excision).

Following surgery, the liver continues to produce bile, even in the absence of the gallbladder, but concentrating bile no longer occurs.

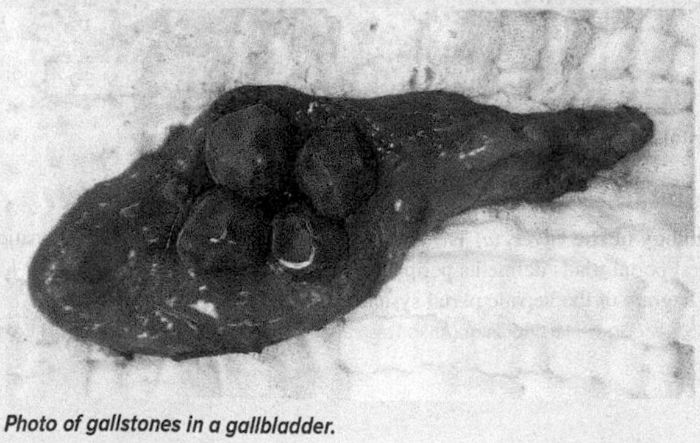

Photo of gallstones in a gallbladder.
Pthawatc/Shutterstock

Clinical View 26.8

Intestinal Disorders

The small and large intestine are prone to an array of medical conditions, known collectively as "intestinal disorders." Some of the more common intestinal disorders are described here.

Celiac disease (also known as *gluten-sensitive enteropathy*) is an autoimmune disorder that affects up to 1% of the population in the United States. Research indicates that some humans who are infected with a reovirus (a normally benign virus) will develop celiac disease if the immune response to this virus triggers intestinal changes that lead to gluten intolerance. **Gluten**—a protein common in wheat, rye, and barley (but not rice or corn)—stimulates an immune response in affected individuals that damages the villi of the small intestine, which interferes with absorption. Common foods that contain gluten include breads, pizza, pasta, and many processed foods. Symptoms include abdominal pain and chronic diarrhea, which leads to nutrient deficiencies because of malabsorption. Although there is no cure for celiac disease, it can be effectively managed by following a gluten-free diet. Gluten has been associated with non-celiac sensitivities. These disorders also are managed through diet.

The term **inflammatory bowel disease (IBD)** applies to two autoimmune disorders, Crohn disease and ulcerative colitis. In both of these disorders, selective regions of the intestine become inflamed.

Crohn disease is a condition of young adults characterized by intermittent and relapsing episodes of intense abdominal cramping and diarrhea. Although any region of the GI tract may be involved, the distal ileum is the most frequently and severely affected site. Inflammation involves the entire thickness of the intestinal wall, extending from the mucosa to the serosa. For reasons that are not clear, lengthy regions of the intestine having no trace of injury or inflammation may be followed abruptly by several inches of markedly diseased intestine.

The age distribution and symptoms of **ulcerative colitis** are similar to those of Crohn disease, but ulcerative colitis involves only the large intestine. The rectum and descending colon are the first to show signs of inflammation and are generally the most severely affected. Also, in ulcerative colitis the inflammation is confined to the mucosa, instead of the full thickness of the intestinal wall. Finally, unlike Crohn disease, ulcerative colitis is associated with a profoundly increased risk of colon cancer.

Treatment of inflammatory bowel disease is complex. Anti-inflammatory drugs, as well as stress reduction and possibly nutritional supplementation, help control symptoms. Surgery may be necessary.

Crohn disease, ulcerative colitis, and celiac disease are distinctly different from a much more common disorder called **irritable bowel syndrome (IBS).** IBS is characterized by abnormal function of the colon with symptoms of crampy abdominal pain, bloating, constipation, and/or diarrhea. It occurs in about one in every five people in the United States, and is more common in women than men. Irritable bowel syndrome may be diagnosed if a medical evaluation has ruled out Crohn disease and ulcerative colitis. Although neither a cause nor a cure for IBS is known, most people can control their symptoms by reducing stress, changing their diet, and using certain medicines.

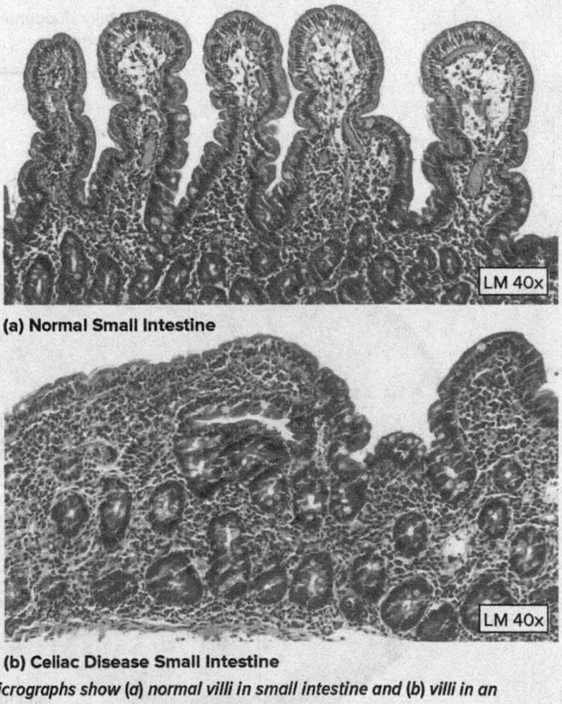

Micrographs show (a) normal villi in small intestine and (b) villi in an individual with celiac disease.

David Litman/Shutterstock

cystic duct and the common hepatic duct forms the **common bile duct** that extends inferiorly to the duodenum.

The **hepatopancreatic ampulla** is a posteriorly placed swelling in the duodenal wall where the common bile duct and main pancreatic duct merge and pierce the duodenal wall. Bile and pancreatic juice mix in the hepatopancreatic ampulla prior to emptying into the duodenum via the **major duodenal papilla.**

26.10d Pancreas

The **pancreas** is referred to as a mixed gland because it exhibits both endocrine and exocrine functions. The endocrine functions are performed by the cells of the pancreatic islets (see section 20.7). Exocrine activity results in the secretion of digestive enzymes and bicarbonate, collectively called **pancreatic juice,** into the duodenum.

The pancreas is a retroperitoneal organ that extends horizontally from the medial edge of the duodenum toward the left side of the abdominal cavity, where it touches the spleen. It exhibits a wide **head** adjacent to the curvature of the duodenum, a central, elongated **body** projecting toward the left lateral abdominal wall, and a **tail** that tapers as it approaches the spleen (**figure 26.21**).

The pancreas contains modified simple cuboidal epithelial cells called **acinar cells.** These cells, which are organized into large

Figure 26.20

Biliary Apparatus. Bile flows through the biliary apparatus (green), and pancreatic juice flows through the main pancreatic duct until the two vessels merge at the hepatopancreatic ampulla. Numbers indicate the pathway sequence for bile and pancreatic juice.

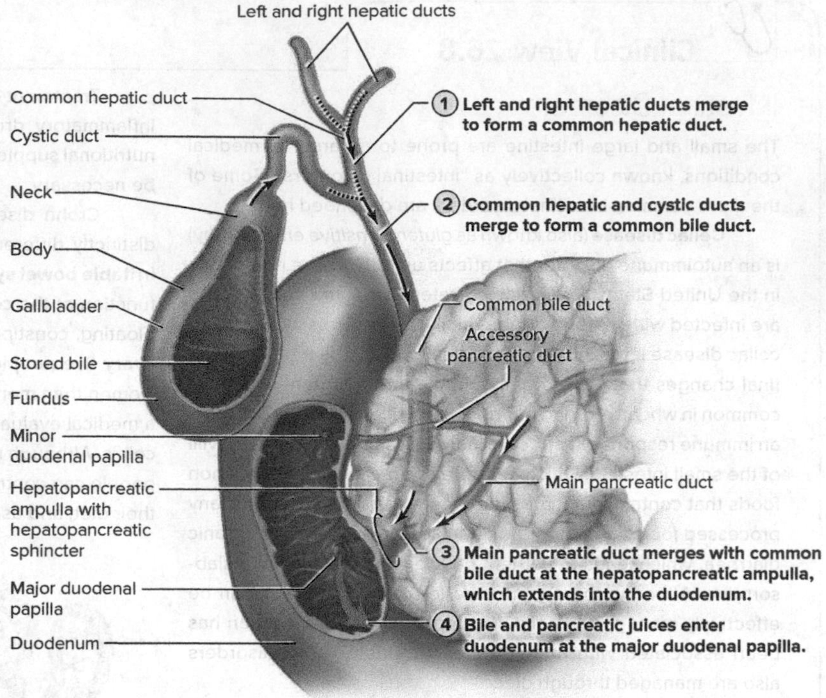
Left and right hepatic ducts
Common hepatic duct
Cystic duct
Neck
Body
Gallbladder
Stored bile
Fundus
Minor duodenal papilla
Hepatopancreatic ampulla with hepatopancreatic sphincter
Major duodenal papilla
Duodenum
1 Left and right hepatic ducts merge to form a common hepatic duct.
2 Common hepatic and cystic ducts merge to form a common bile duct.
Common bile duct
Accessory pancreatic duct
Main pancreatic duct
3 Main pancreatic duct merges with common bile duct at the hepatopancreatic ampulla, which extends into the duodenum.
4 Bile and pancreatic juices enter duodenum at the major duodenal papilla.

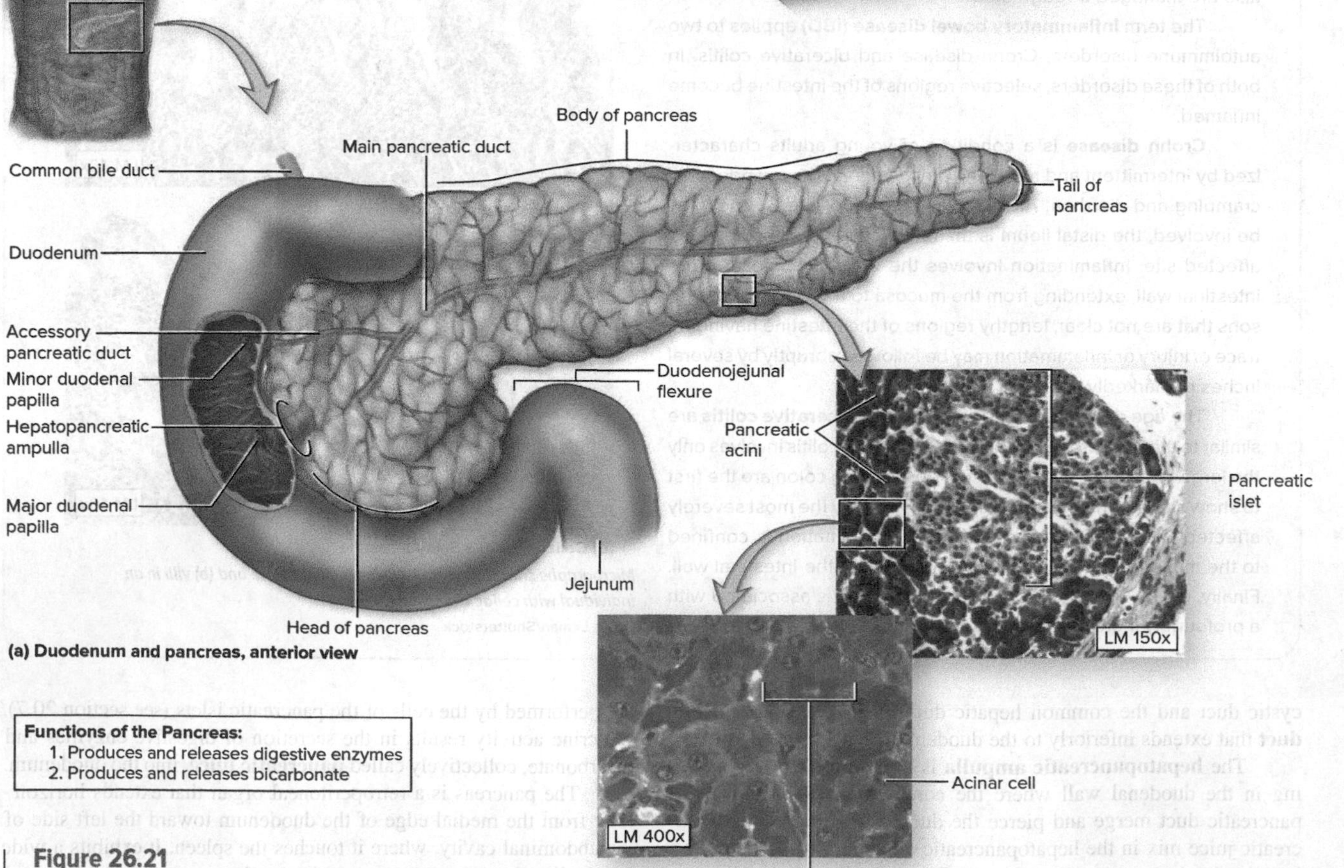
Body of pancreas
Main pancreatic duct
Common bile duct
Tail of pancreas
Duodenum
Accessory pancreatic duct
Minor duodenal papilla
Hepatopancreatic ampulla
Major duodenal papilla
Duodenojejunal flexure
Jejunum
Head of pancreas
(a) Duodenum and pancreas, anterior view
Pancreatic acini
Pancreatic islet
LM 150x
Acinar cell
LM 400x
Pancreatic acinus
(b) Histology of pancreas

Functions of the Pancreas:
1. Produces and releases digestive enzymes
2. Produces and releases bicarbonate

Figure 26.21

Anatomy and Histology of the Pancreas. (*a*) The components of the pancreas are shown in relationship to the pancreatic duct and the duodenum. (*b*) Photomicrographs depict the histology of acinar cells within the pancreas.

clusters termed **acini** (sing., *acinus*), or *lobules* secrete the mucin and digestive enzymes of the pancreatic juice. The simple cuboidal epithelial cells lining the pancreatic ducts secrete bicarbonate (alkaline fluid) to help neutralize the acidic chyme arriving in the duodenum from the stomach. Most of the pancreatic juice travels through ducts that merge to form the **main pancreatic duct,** which drains into the major duodenal papilla in the duodenum (see section 26.8a). A smaller accessory pancreatic duct drains a small amount of pancreatic juice into a minor duodenal papilla in the duodenum.

Both hormonal and neural mechanisms control pancreatic juice secretions. Enteroendocrine cells in intestinal glands release cholecystokinin to promote the secretion of pancreatic juices from acinar cells, and secretin to stimulate the release of alkaline fluid from pancreatic duct cells. Pancreatic juice secretion is also stimulated by parasympathetic (vagus nerve) innervation, whereas sympathetic innervation inhibits pancreatic juice secretion.

WHAT DID YOU LEARN?

15 Draw and label the structural components of a portal triad.

16 What is the function of the gallbladder?

17 What is the function of pancreatic acini?

26.11 Aging and the Digestive System

✓ Learning Objective

23. Explain how the digestive system changes as we age.

Age-related changes in digestion system function usually progress slowly and gradually. Overall, reduced secretions accompany normal aging. Mucin secretion decreases, reducing the thickness and amount of mucus in the layer that protects the GI tract and making internal damage to digestive organs more likely. Decreased secretion of enzymes and acid results in diminished effectiveness of chemical digestion, which in turn can diminish nutrient absorption. The reduction of glandular secretion is compounded by decreased replacement of epithelial cells.

Another change that occurs with age is a reduction in the thickness of the smooth muscle layers in the muscularis. Consequently, both muscular tone and GI tract motility may be lowered significantly. Additionally, smooth muscle ensheathing the GI tract may adversely affect the function of sphincters or valves that help move materials through the GI tract. As a result, significant changes in nutrient absorption, as well as gastroesophageal reflux disease (GERD), may occur (see Clinical View 26.1 "Reflux Esophagitis and Gastroesophageal Reflux Disease" in section 26.6).

Improper dental care or sometimes simply aging can result in either the loss of teeth or periodontal disease. Both conditions adversely affect normal eating habits and nutrition. As food intake dwindles, changes occur in GI tract motility, secretion, and absorption. Marked dietary alterations may also increase the chance of developing cancer in either the stomach or the intestines.

Finally, a direct result of aging is a reduction in olfactory and gustatory sensations. When a person loses the ability to smell or taste food, his or her dietary intake usually changes as a result.

WHAT DID YOU LEARN?

18 How might the decrease in mucin secretion due to aging affect GI tract organs?

26.12 Development of the Digestive System

✓ Learning Objective

24. Explain the major events in digestive system development.

At the end of the third week of development, the disc-shaped embryo undergoes lateral folding, which transforms the endoderm and some lateral plate mesoderm into a cylindrical primitive **gut tube.** The gut tube eventually connects to the primitive mouth and the developing anus, while still maintaining a connection to the yolk sac via a thin stalk called the **vitelline** (vī-tel'in, - ēn) **duct.** A double-layered membrane called **dorsal mesentery** wraps around the gut tube and helps anchor it to the posterior body wall. A portion of the gut tube called the abdominal foregut has **ventral mesentery** that attaches it to the anterior body wall.

The gut tube may be divided into three components: a superior or cephalic **foregut,** a centrally located **midgut,** and an inferior or caudal **hindgut (figure 26.22*a*). Table 26.5** lists the structures derived from the foregut, midgut, and hindgut. Portions of the gut tube expand to form some of the abdominal organs. Some accessory digestive system organs develop as buds, or outgrowths, from the gut tube. Many of these structures rotate or shift before assuming their final positions in the body.

26.12a Stomach, Duodenum, and Omenta Development

By the fourth week of development, a portion of the foregut expands and forms a spindle-shaped dilation that will become the stomach. Between the fifth and seventh weeks, the posterior (dorsal) part of this dilation grows faster than the anterior (ventral) part, so the anterior wall becomes the concave lesser curvature, and the posterior wall becomes the convex greater curvature (figure 26.22*b*). The dorsal mesentery will form the greater omentum, whereas the ventral mesentery that attaches to the lesser curvature will form the lesser omentum.

During the seventh week, the developing stomach rotates 90 degrees clockwise about a longitudinal axis, as viewed from the superior aspect of the organ (figure 26.22*c*). Thus, the posterior side of the stomach (the greater curvature) rotates so that it faces the left side of the body, while the anterior side (the lesser curvature) rotates and faces the right side. One week later, the stomach and duodenum rotate about an anterior-posterior axis. This rotation pulls the pyloric region of the stomach and the duodenum superiorly while moving the fundus and the cardia of the stomach slightly inferiorly (figure 26.22*d*).

26.12b Liver, Gallbladder, and Pancreas Development

The liver parenchyma, gallbladder, pancreas, and biliary apparatus develop from buds or outgrowths from the endoderm of the duodenum. (The liver stroma or connective tissue framework is formed from nearby mesoderm.) The **liver bud** appears first, during the third week, develops within the ventral mesentery, and grows superiorly toward the developing diaphragm. By the fourth week, the liver's attachment to the duodenum becomes a thinned tube that forms the common bile duct. An outgrowth forms off the bile duct that becomes the gallbladder and cystic duct. As the liver enlarges, the ventral mesentery thins and becomes the falciform ligament.

The pancreas starts to form at week 4 from two separate outgrowths of the bile duct, called the **ventral pancreatic bud** and the **dorsal pancreatic bud.** By week 6, the ventral pancreatic bud and the biliary apparatus rotate behind the duodenum. The ventral and dorsal pancreatic buds fuse to form the pancreas.

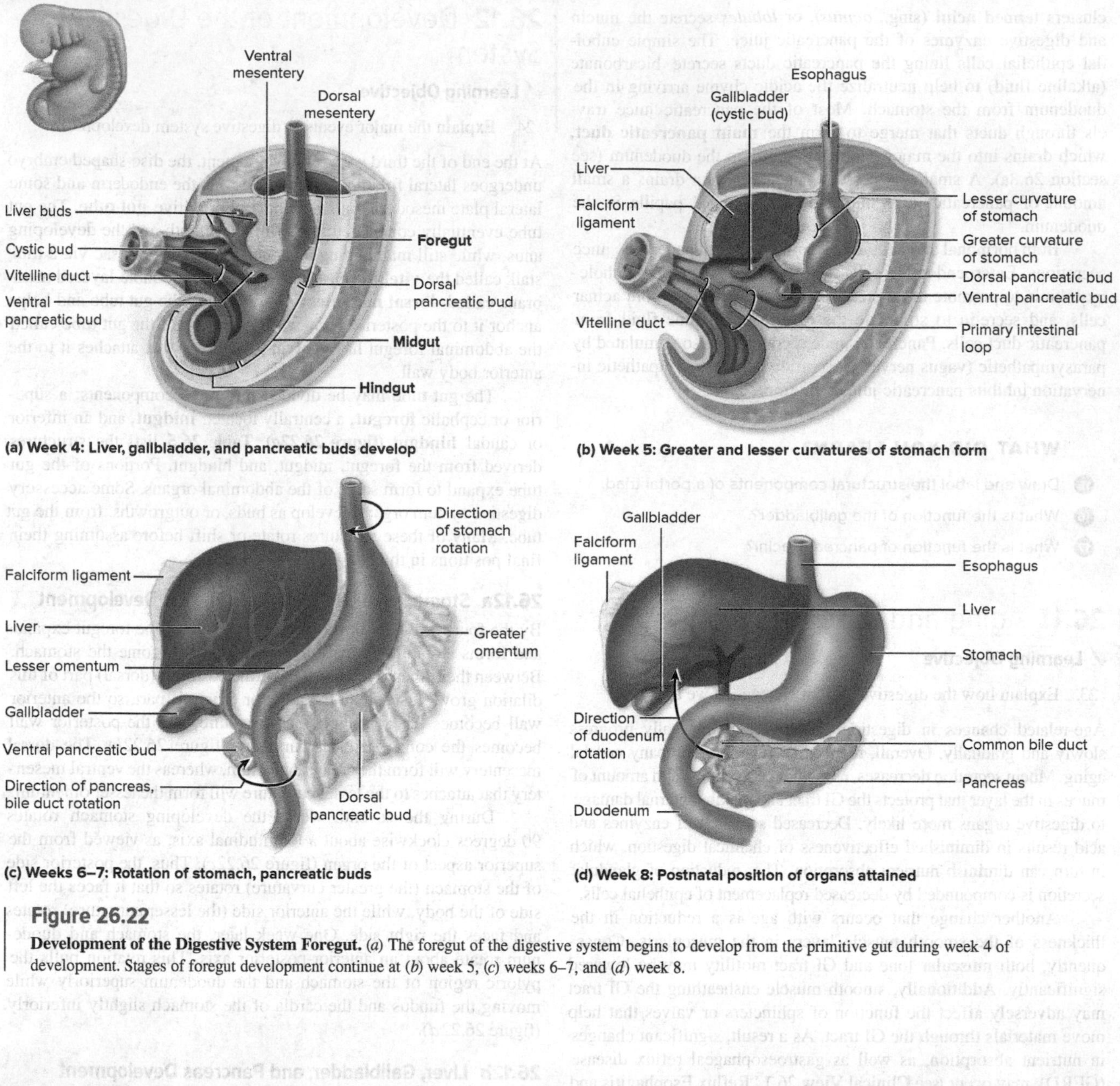
Ventral mesentery
Dorsal mesentery
Liver buds
Cystic bud
Foregut
Vitelline duct
Dorsal pancreatic bud
Ventral pancreatic bud
Midgut
Hindgut
(a) Week 4: Liver, gallbladder, and pancreatic buds develop
Esophagus
Gallbladder (cystic bud)
Liver
Falciform ligament
Lesser curvature of stomach
Greater curvature of stomach
Dorsal pancreatic bud
Ventral pancreatic bud
Vitelline duct
Primary intestinal loop
(b) Week 5: Greater and lesser curvatures of stomach form
Direction of stomach rotation
Falciform ligament
Liver
Greater omentum
Lesser omentum
Gallbladder
Ventral pancreatic bud
Direction of pancreas, bile duct rotation
Dorsal pancreatic bud
(c) Weeks 6–7: Rotation of stomach, pancreatic buds
Gallbladder
Falciform ligament
Esophagus
Liver
Stomach
Direction of duodenum rotation
Common bile duct
Pancreas
Duodenum
(d) Week 8: Postnatal position of organs attained

Figure 26.22

Development of the Digestive System Foregut. *(a)* The foregut of the digestive system begins to develop from the primitive gut during week 4 of development. Stages of foregut development continue at *(b)* week 5, *(c)* weeks 6–7, and *(d)* week 8.

Table 26.5 Anatomic Derivatives of the Primitive Gut Tube

Organs Formed	Foregut	Midgut	Hindgut
Digestive organs	Pharynx, esophagus, stomach, proximal half of duodenum	Distal half of duodenum; jejunum, ileum, cecum, appendix, ascending colon, proximal (right) two-thirds of transverse colon	Distal (left) one-third of transverse colon; descending colon, sigmoid colon, rectum, superior portion of anal canal
Accessory digestive organs	Most of liver; gallbladder, biliary apparatus, pancreas		
Non-digestive organs	Lungs, spleen		Urinary bladder epithelium, urethra epithelium

26.12c Intestine Development

The small and large intestines are formed from the midgut and hindgut, as shown in **figure 26.23**. During the fifth week, the midgut rapidly elongates and forms a **primary intestinal loop.** The cranial portion of the loop (*cranial loop*) forms the jejunum and most of the ileum, whereas the caudal portion of the loop (*caudal loop*) forms the very distal part of the ileum and much of the large intestine. The loop apex connects to the yolk sac via the vitelline duct.

Due to rapid growth of the liver and the resulting limited space in the developing abdominal cavity, the primary intestinal loop herniates into the umbilicus during the sixth week. As this loop herniates, it undergoes a 90-degree counterclockwise rotation, as viewed from the anterior surface of the body. The cranial loop rotates to the right of the body, while the caudal loop rotates to the left of the body. For the next several weeks, the intestinal loop grows and expands in the umbilicus because there is no available space inside the abdominal cavity.

By weeks 10 and 11, the midgut retracts into the abdomen as the abdominal cavity becomes spacious enough to house all the intestines. As the midgut retracts, it undergoes another 180-degree counterclockwise rotation, as viewed from the front of the body. Now the cranial loop is on the left side of the body, and the caudal loop is on the right. Thus, the net intestinal rotation is 270 degrees counterclockwise. The cranial loop (forming the jejunum and most of the ileum) retracts and positions itself in the left side of the abdominal cavity. The caudal loop (forming the distal ileum and the proximal part of the large intestine) is pulled to the right side of the abdominal cavity. The vitelline duct begins to regress and disappears before the baby is born.

WHAT DID YOU LEARN?

19 What structures develop from endoderm outgrowths of the duodenum?

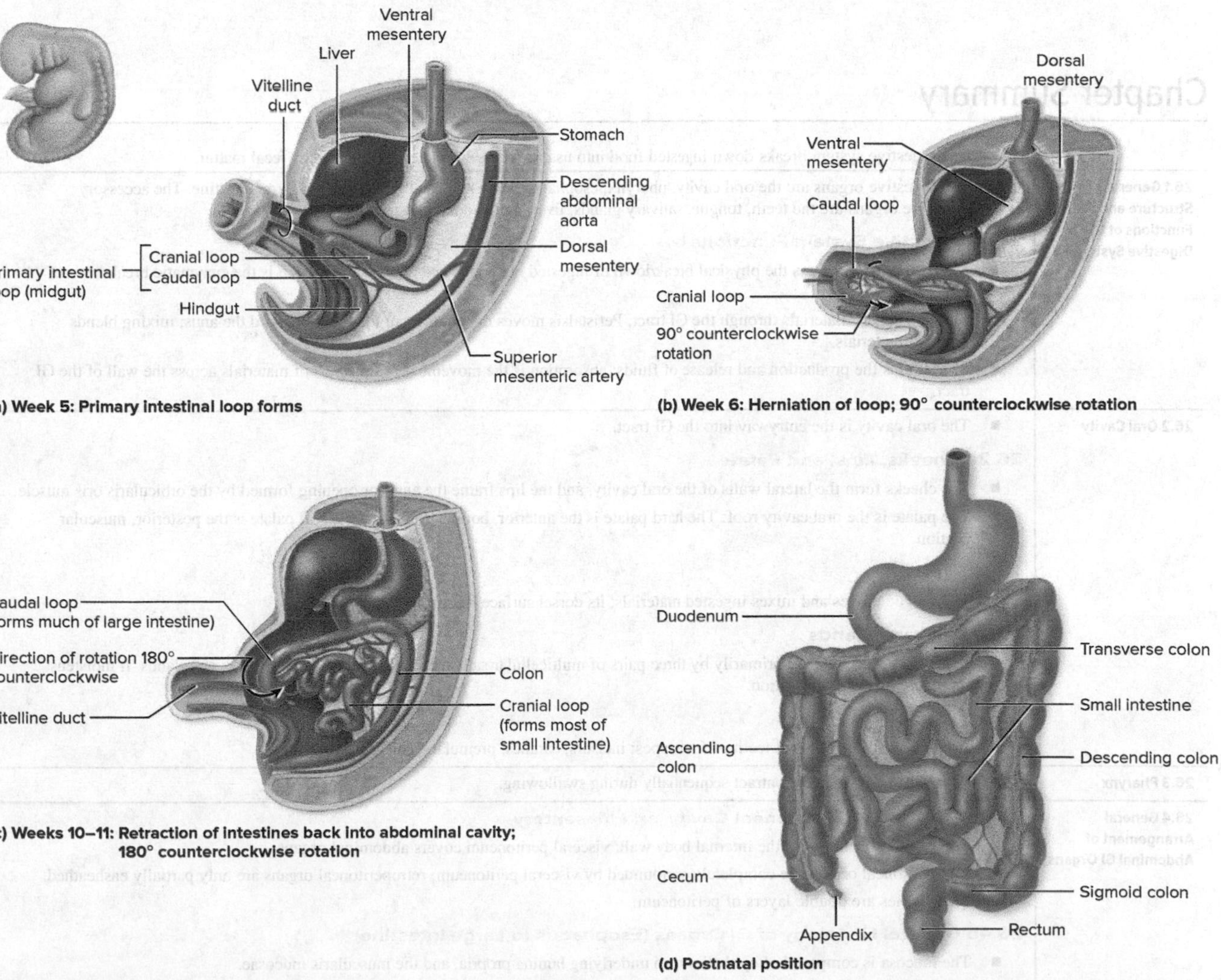

(a) Week 5: Primary intestinal loop forms

(b) Week 6: Herniation of loop; 90° counterclockwise rotation

(c) Weeks 10–11: Retraction of intestines back into abdominal cavity; 180° counterclockwise rotation

(d) Postnatal position

Figure 26.23

Development of the Digestive System Midgut. The midgut of the digestive system forms almost all of the small intestine and the proximal region of the large intestine. Development of these structures is shown at (*a*) week 5, (*b*) week 6, and (*c*) weeks 10–11. (*d*) The postnatal position of the digestive organs.

Clinical Terms

bariatric surgery (gastric bypass) Surgically narrowing or blocking off a large portion of the stomach; typically performed in severely obese people who have had trouble losing weight by more traditional methods.

colostomy A surgical procedure that moves and attaches a portion of the colon so it exits through the abdominal wall. Materials moving through the large intestine drain into a bag (ostomy pouch) attached to the abdomen.

dysentery (dis-en-tĕr-ē; *dys* = bad, *entera* = bowels) Painful, bloody diarrhea due to an infectious agent.

gastroenteritis (gas′tr ō-en-ter-ī′tis) Inflammation and irritation of the GI tract, often associated with vomiting and diarrhea.

hemorrhoids (hem′ŏ-roydz; *rhoia* = flow) Dilated, tortuous veins around the rectum and/or anus.

intussusception (in-tŭs-sŭ-sep′sh ŭn; *intus* = within, *suscipio* = to take up) Type of intestinal obstruction in which one part of the intestine constricts and gets pulled into the immediately distal segment of intestine; most commonly seen near the ileocecal junction. Symptoms include bloody stools and severe abdominal pain.

mumps (a lump) Viral infection of the parotid glands, resulting in painful swelling of the glands.

volvulus Twisting or torsion of an intestinal segment around itself. If left untreated, obstruction of digestive materials results, and the segment necroses due to poor blood supply. Symptoms include intense abdominal pain and vomiting.

Chapter Summary

	■ The digestive system breaks down ingested food into usable nutrients and expels the rest as fecal matter.
26.1 General Structure and Functions of the Digestive System	■ The digestive organs are the oral cavity, pharynx, esophagus, stomach, small intestine, and large intestine. The accessory digestive organs are the teeth, tongue, salivary glands, liver, gallbladder, and pancreas. **26.1a Digestive System Functions** ■ Mechanical digestion is the physical breakdown of ingested materials, and chemical digestion is the enzymatic breakdown of molecules. ■ Motility moves materials through the GI tract. Peristalsis moves materials from the mouth toward the anus; mixing blends ingested materials. ■ Secretion is the production and release of fluids; absorption is the movement or transport of materials across the wall of the GI tract.
26.2 Oral Cavity	■ The oral cavity is the entryway into the GI tract. **26.2a Cheeks, Lips, and Palate** ■ The cheeks form the lateral walls of the oral cavity, and the lips frame the anterior opening formed by the orbicularis oris muscle. ■ The palate is the oral cavity roof: The hard palate is the anterior, bony portion, and the soft palate is the posterior, muscular portion. **26.2b Tongue** ■ The tongue moves and mixes ingested materials; its dorsal surface has papillae. **26.2c Salivary Glands** ■ Saliva is a fluid secreted primarily by three pairs of multicellular salivary glands, called extrinsic salivary glands. It moistens food and provides lubrication. **26.2d Teeth** ■ Adults have 32 permanent teeth of four types: incisors, canines, premolars, and molars.
26.3 Pharynx	■ Pharyngeal constrictors contract sequentially during swallowing.
26.4 General Arrangement of Abdominal GI Organs	**26.4a Peritoneum, Peritoneal Cavity, and Mesentery** ■ Parietal peritoneum lines the internal body wall; visceral peritoneum covers abdominal organs. ■ Intraperitoneal organs are completely surrounded by visceral peritoneum; retroperitoneal organs are only partially ensheathed. ■ Mesenteries are double layers of peritoneum. **26.4b General Histology of GI Organs (Esophagus to Large Intestine)** ■ The mucosa is composed of epithelium, an underlying lamina propria, and the muscularis mucosae. ■ The submucosa is a dense irregular connective tissue layer containing blood vessels, lymphatic vessels, and nerves. ■ The muscularis usually has two smooth muscle layers: an inner circular layer and an outer longitudinal layer. ■ The adventitia is the outermost covering; when covered by visceral peritoneum, it is called a serosa. **26.4c Blood Vessels, Lymphoid Structures, and Nerve Supply** ■ GI tract organs have extensive blood vessels, lymphoid structures, and nerves.

26.5 Esophagus	**26.5a Gross Anatomy** ■ The esophagus conducts swallowed materials from the pharynx to the stomach. **26.5b Histology** ■ The esophagus is lined by nonkeratinized stratified squamous epithelium. ■ The muscularis has all skeletal fibers superiorly, changes to intermingled skeletal and smooth fibers in the middle, and contains all smooth fibers inferiorly.
26.6 The Swallowing Process	■ Swallowing has three phases: The voluntary phase moves a bolus into the pharynx; the pharyngeal phase moves the bolus through the pharynx into the esophagus; and the esophageal phase conducts the bolus to the stomach.
26.7 Stomach	**26.7a Gross Anatomy** ■ Mechanical digestion and chemical digestion occur in the stomach. ■ The four stomach regions are the cardia, fundus, body, and pylorus. **26.7b Histology** ■ The stomach mucosa is composed of a simple columnar epithelium containing gastric pits and gastric glands. ■ The muscularis has three smooth muscle layers: inner oblique, middle circular, and outer longitudinal. **26.7c Gastric Secretions** ■ Five types of secretory cells form the gastric glands: surface mucous cells (secrete mucin), mucous neck cells (secrete acidic mucin), parietal cells (secrete hydrochloric acid and intrinsic factor), chief cells (secrete pepsinogen), and enteroendocrine cells (secrete gastrin and other hormones).
26.8 Small Intestine	**26.8a Gross Anatomy and Regions** ■ The small intestine finishes chemical digestion and absorbs most of the nutrients. ■ The small intestine is divided into the duodenum, jejunum, and ileum. **26.8b Histology** ■ The small intestine has circular folds with fingerlike villi projecting from them. The villi are lined with cells with microvilli on their apical surface. The circular folds, villi, and microvilli increase the surface area of the small intestine.
26.9 Large Intestine	**26.9a Gross Anatomy and Regions** ■ The large intestine absorbs fluids and ions, and compacts undigestible wastes. ■ The large intestine is composed of the cecum, ascending colon, transverse colon, descending colon, sigmoid colon, rectum, and anal canal. **26.9b Histology** ■ The large intestine mucosa lacks villi, but contains intestinal glands. ■ The outer longitudinal layer of the muscularis forms three discrete bands called teniae coli. The teniae coli cause the wall of the colon to bunch into sacs called haustra. **26.9c Control of Large Intestine Activity** ■ Local autonomic reflexes regulate large intestine movements.
26.10 Accessory Digestive Organs	**26.10a Liver** ■ The liver receives venous blood from the hepatic portal vein and oxygenated blood from the hepatic artery proper. ■ Liver functions are bile production, drug detoxification, storage of nutrients and glycogen, and synthesis of plasma proteins. **26.10b Gallbladder** ■ The gallbladder stores and concentrates bile produced by the liver. **26.10c Biliary Apparatus** ■ The hepatic ducts drain bile into a single common hepatic duct, and the cystic duct merges with the common hepatic duct to form the common bile duct. ■ The common bile duct and the pancreatic duct merge to empty their contents into the duodenum via the major duodenal papilla. **26.10d Pancreas** ■ Pancreatic acini produce pancreatic juice that neutralizes acidic chyme.
26.11 Aging and the Digestive System	■ Age-related changes in the digestive system lead to reduced secretions and diminished absorption of nutrients.
26.12 Development of the Digestive System	■ The gut tube has a superior foregut, a central midgut, and an inferior hindgut. **26.12a Stomach, Duodenum, and Omenta Development** ■ Stomach formation begins by week 4 of development. Differential growth rates cause the greater and lesser curvatures of the stomach to form. **26.12b Liver, Gallbladder, and Pancreas Development** ■ The liver parenchyma, gallbladder, and pancreas develop from endoderm outgrowths of the duodenum. **26.12c Intestine Development** ■ The small and large intestines form from the midgut and hindgut beginning in week 5.

Challenge Yourself

Actively write or type your answers in a separate document to reinforce your learning, before checking your answers.

Multiple Choice

Select the best answer from the four choices provided.

1. Which organ is located in the right upper quadrant of the abdomen?
   a. liver
   b. spleen
   c. descending colon
   d. appendix
2. Which cells of the stomach secrete hydrochloric acid (HCl)?
   a. chief
   b. parietal
   c. mucous
   d. enteroendocrine
3. The material leaving the ascending colon next enters which structure?
   a. cecum
   b. descending colon
   c. sigmoid colon
   d. transverse colon
4. Which of these organs is retroperitoneal?
   a. stomach
   b. transverse colon
   c. descending colon
   d. ileum
5. Sympathetic innervation is responsible for which GI tract activities?
   a. closing the pyloric sphincter
   b. stimulating peristalsis
   c. stimulating secretion of the pancreatic acinar cells
   d. vasodilating the major digestive system blood vessels
6. Which structure is derived from the cranial part of the primary intestinal loop?
   a. jejunum
   b. cecum
   c. ascending colon
   d. appendix
7. Which structure merges with the main pancreatic duct so that their combined contents empty into the duodenum through the major duodenal papilla?
   a. left hepatic duct
   b. common bile duct
   c. cystic duct
   d. common hepatic duct
8. Which statement is false about pancreatic juice?
   a. It is secreted through the main pancreatic duct into the duodenum.
   b. It is responsible for emulsifying (breaking down) fats.
   c. It is produced by the acinar cells of the pancreas.
   d. The juice has an alkaline pH.
9. Which structure constitutes the "living" part of a tooth?
   a. dentin
   b. cementum
   c. pulp
   d. enamel
10. Where does most of the chemical digestion of our food occur?
    a. large intestine
    b. pancreas
    c. small intestine
    d. esophagus

Content Review

1. What initial stages of digestion occur in the oral cavity?
2. The GI tract from the esophagus to the anal canal is composed of four tunics. Describe the general histology of the tunics and the specific features of the stomach tunics.
3. Compare and contrast gastric juice and pancreatic juice with respect to their composition and function.
4. Compare the anatomy and functions of the circular folds, villi, and microvilli in the small intestine.
5. What are the teniae coli and haustra, and how are they associated?
6. What is the function of each structure in the portal triad of the hepatic lobule, and how do they work together to contribute to the overall functioning of the liver?
7. What is the function of the gallbladder, and what role does it play in digestion?
8. List in order the organs of the GI tract through which ingested material travels, and describe the type(s) of digestion (mechanical/chemical) that takes place in each organ. At what point is the material called a bolus, chyme, and feces?
9. Why are there so many mucin-producing glands along the length of the GI tract?
10. Describe how the small and large intestine form.

Developing Critical Reasoning

1. Alexandra experienced vomiting and diarrhea, and was diagnosed with gastroenteritis (stomach flu). What specific digestive system organs were affected by the illness, and how did the illness interfere with each organ's function?
2. Most cases of colorectal cancer occur in the most distal part of the large intestine (the rectum, sigmoid colon, and descending colon). Why do fewer instances of colon cancer tend to occur in the proximal part of the large intestine? Include the anatomy and function of the colon components in your explanation.
3. You are watching a television show where the doctor is operating on the small intestine. They pull it out of the abdomen and run their hands along it like it is a garden hose. Why is this depiction wrong?

Answers to "What Do You Think?"

1. Saliva cleanses the mouth in a variety of ways. As saliva washes over the tongue and teeth, it helps remove foreign materials and buildup. Lysozyme in saliva is an antibacterial enzyme. A person who has a dry mouth is not able to cleanse the mouth well and is more likely to develop dental problems as a result of built-up bacterial and foreign material.
2. A young child's mouth is too small to support adult-sized teeth. Deciduous teeth are much smaller and fit a child's mouth better. As the mouth increases in size by about age 6, it is able to support the first adult-sized teeth.
3. The stomach is lined with specialized surface mucous cells that secrete mucus onto the lining. This mucus prevents the acid from eating away the stomach wall. In addition, the stomach epithelial lining is constantly regenerating to replace any cells that are damaged.
4. The duodenum has many circular folds so that the digested materials can be slowed down and adequately mixed with pancreatic juice and bile. The jejunum also has many circular folds because the slowing down of the materials aids in absorbing the maximum amount of nutrients. By the time chyme reaches the distal ileum, most nutrient absorption has occurred, and so the circular folds are not as essential.
5. When the gallbladder is removed, bile is still produced by the liver, but it is secreted in a "slow drip." A fatty meal requires much more bile for digestion than the amount supplied by a "slow drip," causing the patient to experience gas, pain, bloating, and diarrhea. Thus, surgical patients are initially told to limit their fat intake. The body gradually adjusts so that more bile is secreted, and thus a person may eventually be able to introduce more fat back into his or her diet.

27 Urinary System

Outline

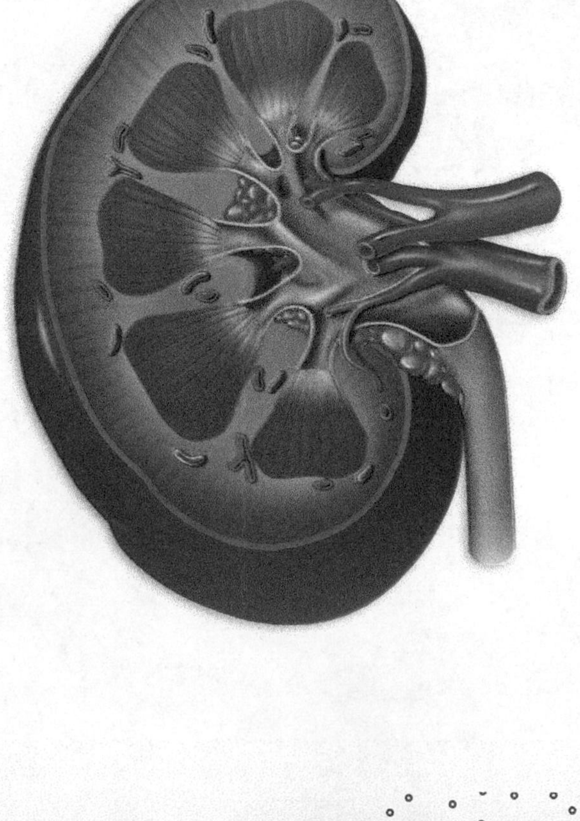

Anatomy & Physiology Revealed 4.0

MODULE 13: URINARY SYSTEM

In the course of carrying out their specific functions, the cells of all body systems produce waste products, and these waste products end up in the blood. In this case, the blood is analogous to a river that supplies drinking water to a nearby town. The river water may become polluted with sediment, animal waste, and motorboat fuel—but the town has a water treatment plant that removes these waste products and makes the water safe to drink. The **urinary** (yūr'i-nār'ē) **system** is the body's "water treatment plant." Without it, waste products could accumulate in the blood and kill us. This chapter focuses on the organs of the urinary system and how they work together to remove waste products from the blood and help maintain homeostasis.

27.1 General Structure and Functions of the Urinary System

✓ Learning Objectives

1. Identify and describe the primary organs of the urinary system.
2. Explain the functions of the urinary system.

The organs of the urinary systemare the kidneys, ureters, urinary bladder, and urethra (**figure 27.1**). The kidneys filter waste products from the blood and convert the filtrate into **urine** (yūr'in). The ureters, urinary bladder, and urethra are collectively known as the **urinary tract** because they transport the urine out of the body.

Besides removing waste products from the blood, the urinary system performs many other functions, including the following:

- **Storage of urine.** Urine is produced continuously, but it would be quite inconvenient if we were constantly excreting urine. The urinary bladder is an expandable, muscular sac that can store as much as 1 liter of urine.
- **Expulsion of urine.** The urethra transports urine from the urinary bladder and expels it outside the body. In section 27.3b, we discuss the expulsion of urine from the bladder, which is called micturition or urination.
- **Regulation of blood volume.** The kidneys control the volume of interstitial fluid and blood under the direction of certain hormones. Because changes in blood volume affect blood pressure, the kidneys also indirectly affect blood pressure.
- **Regulation of erythrocyte production.** As the kidneys filter the blood, they are also indirectly measuring the oxygen level in the blood. If blood oxygen levels are reduced, cells in the kidney secrete a hormone called **erythropoietin** (ĕ-rith'r ō-poy'ĕ-tin) (**EPO**; described in sections 20.9a and 21.4). Erythropoietin acts on stem cells in the bone marrow to increase erythrocyte production. Having more erythrocytes allows the blood to transport more oxygen.
- **Regulation of ion levels.** The kidneys help control the blood's ion balance, such as sodium ions (Na^+), potassium ions (K^+), calcium ions (Ca^{2+}), and phosphate ions (PO_4^{3-}) by eliminating varying amounts of these ions in the urine, depending upon dietary intake.
- **Regulation of acid-base balance.** The kidneys aid in maintaining acid-base balance by altering blood levels of both hydrogen ions (H^+) and bicarbonate ions (HCO_3^-) by also eliminating varying amounts of these ion s.

Learning Strategy 27.1

The main purpose of the kidneys is not to make urine, but to *make good blood.*

Table 27.1 summarizes the organs of the urinary system and their functions.

WHAT DID YOU LEARN?

1. What organs make up the urinary tract, and what is the main function of the urinary tract?
2. Describe the mechanisms by which the kidneys regulate blood volume and erythrocyte production.

Table 27.1 Urinary System Organs and Their Functions

Organ	Location	Description/Characteristics	Function
Kidneys	Posterior abdominal wall; right kidney placement is inferior to left kidney placement	Paired, bean-shaped organs; composed of outer cortex and inner medulla	Filter blood and process filtrate into tubular fluid, then urine
Ureters	Extend from kidneys to trigone of bladder, along posterior abdominopelvic wall	Paired thin, fibromuscular tubes composed of inner mucosa, middle muscularis of smooth muscle, and an outer adventitia	Transport urine from kidney to urinary bladder via peristalsis
Urinary bladder	Pelvic cavity, posterior to pubic symphysis (when full, it extends into inferior part of abdominal cavity)	Muscular distensible sac composed of inner mucosa, a submucosa, a muscularis, and an outer adventitia or serosa The neck of the bladder is the inferior constricted region where bladder and urethra meet; contains internal urethral sphincter	Reservoir for urine until micturition (urination) occurs
Urethra	Inferior to neck of urinary bladder; extends through muscles of pelvic floor and opens into perineum	Single muscular tube; 3–5 cm long in females; 18–20 cm long in males	Transports urine from urinary bladder to outside of body

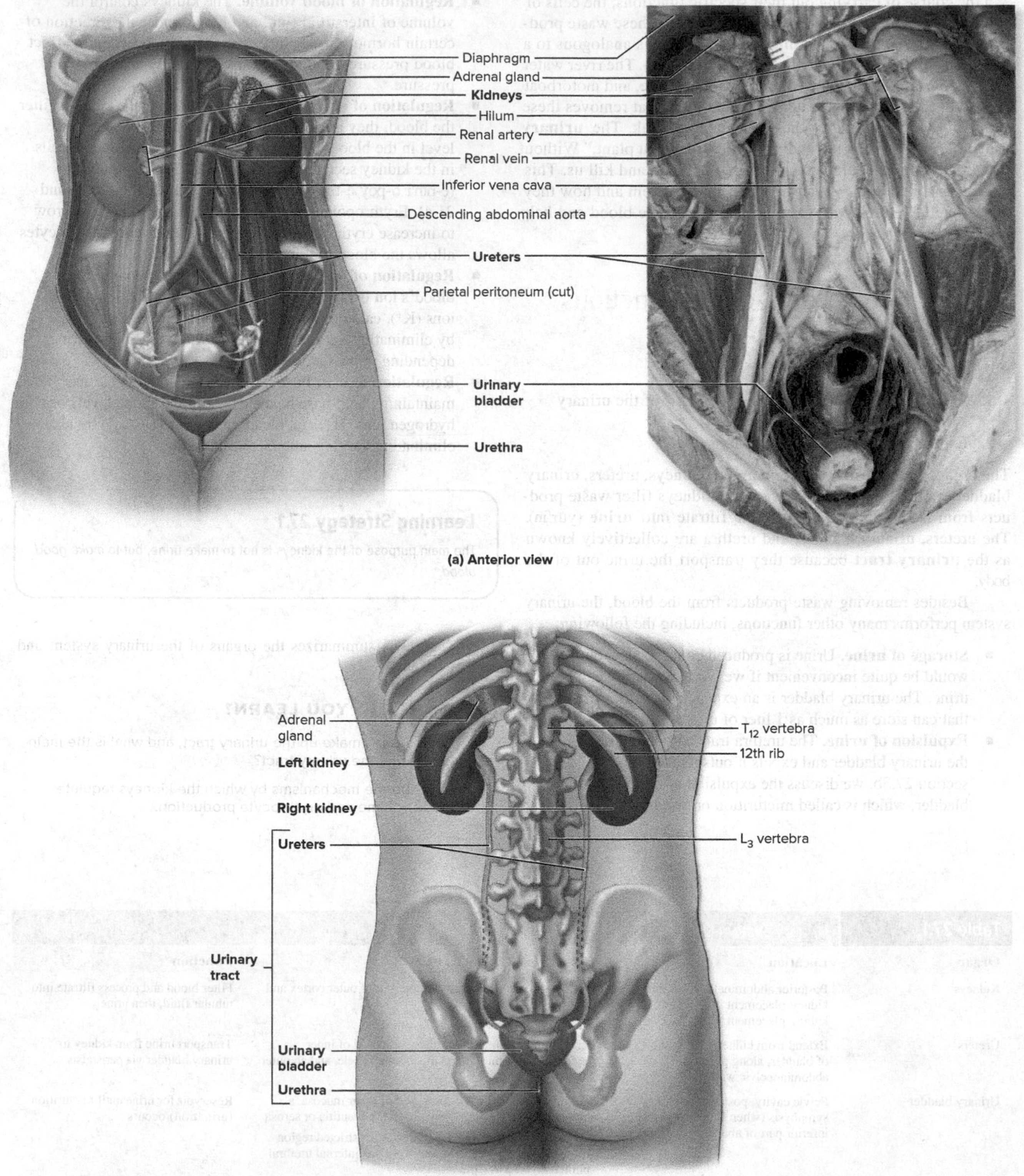
Diaphragm
Adrenal gland
Kidneys
Hilum
Renal artery
Renal vein
Inferior vena cava
Descending abdominal aorta
Ureters
Parietal peritoneum (cut)
Urinary bladder
Urethra
(a) Anterior view
Adrenal gland
Left kidney
Right kidney
Ureters
Urinary tract
Urinary bladder
Urethra
T_{12} vertebra
12th rib
L_3 vertebra
(b) Posterior view

Figure 27.1

Urinary System. The urinary system is composed of two kidneys, two ureters, a single urinary bladder, and a single urethra, shown here in (*a*) anterior and (*b*) posterior views. (Components of the urinary system are labeled in bold font.) APR

(a, right) ©McGraw-Hill Education/Christine Eckel, photographer

27.2 Kidneys

✓ Learning Objectives

3. Identify and describe the gross and microscopic anatomy of the kidney.
4. Trace the path of blood flow into and out of the kidney, listing where blood is filtered and where gas and nutrient exchange occur.
5. Compare and contrast the concepts of glomerular filtration, tubular reabsorption, and tubular secretion.
6. List the components of a nephron, and explain their roles in urine formation.

The kidneys are two symmetrical, bean-shaped, reddish-brown organs located along the posterior abdominal wall, lateral to the vertebral column (figure 27.1). Each kidney weighs about 100 grams and measures about 12 centimeters (cm) in length, 6.5 cm in width, and 2.5 cm in thickness.

WHAT DO YOU THINK?

1 A person must have at least one functioning kidney to survive. Why do you think a lack of kidneys is deadly?

27.2a Gross and Sectional Anatomy of the Kidney

The kidneys are **retroperitoneal,** because their anterior surface is covered with parietal peritoneum and the posterior aspect lies directly against the posterior abdominal wall. The **superior pole** (also called *superior extremity*) of the left kidney is at about the level of the T_{12} vertebra, and its **inferior pole** (also called *inferior extremity*) is at about the level of the L_3 vertebra. The superior pole of the right kidney is positioned about 2 cm inferior to the superior pole of the left kidney to accommodate the large size of the liver. An adrenal gland rests on the superior pole of each kidney.

The kidney has a concave medial border called the **hilum** (hī′lŭm; *hilum* = a small bit), where vessels, nerves, and the ureter enter and/or exit the kidney. The hilum is continuous with an internal space within each kidney called the **renal** (rē′năl; *ren* = kidney) **sinus.** The renal sinus houses renal arteries, renal veins, lymph vessels, nerves, the renal pelvis, renal calyces, and a variable amount of adipose connective tissue. The kidney's lateral border is convex.

Each kidney is surrounded and supported by several tissue layers. From innermost (closest to the kidney) to outermost, these layers are the fibrous capsule, perinephric fat, renal fascia, and paranephric fat (**figure 27.2**):

- The **fibrous capsule** (kap′s ūl; *capsa* = box) or *renal capsule,* directly adheres to the outer surface of the kidney and is composed of dense irregular connective tissue. The fibrous capsule maintains the kidney's shape, protects it from trauma, and helps prevent infectious pathogens from entering the kidney.
- The **perinephric fat** (*peri* = around, near; also called *perirenal fat,* or *adipose capsule*) is external to the fibrous capsule and contains adipose connective tissue that varies in thickness.

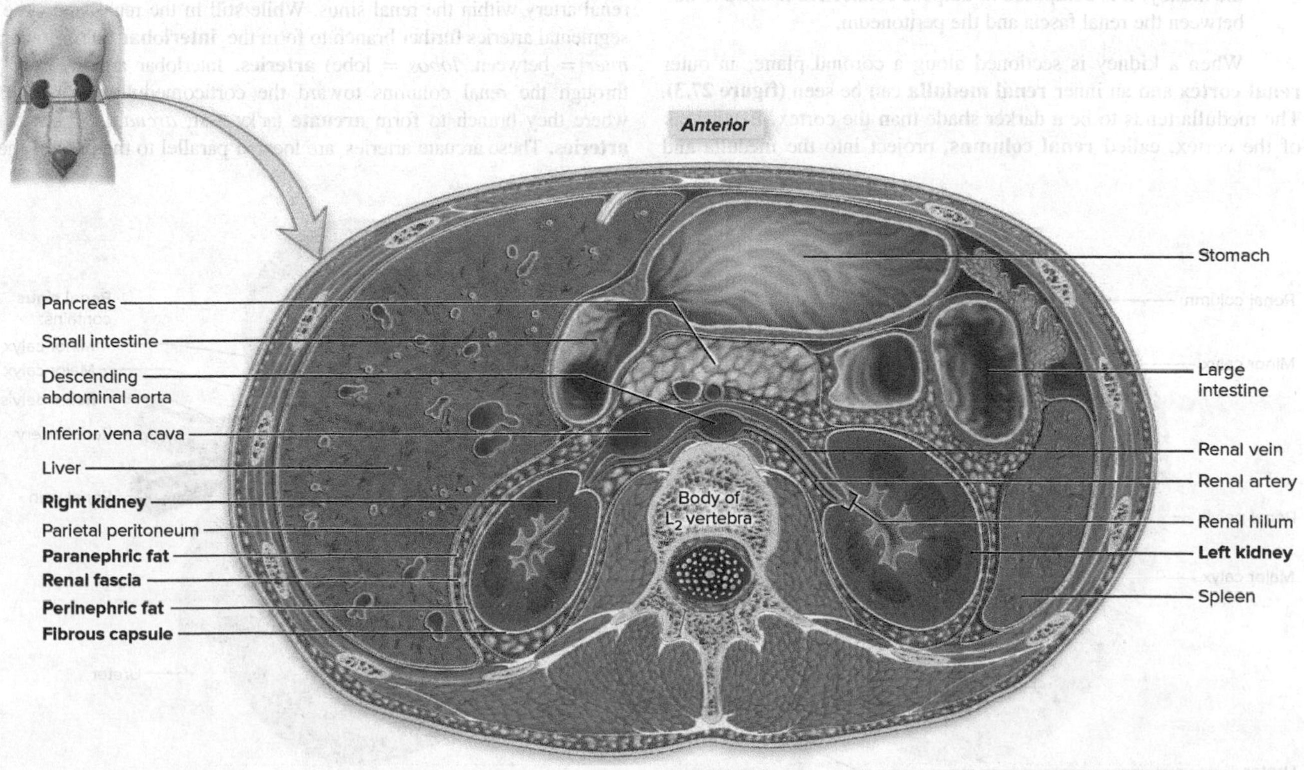
Anterior
Pancreas
Small intestine
Descending abdominal aorta
Inferior vena cava
Liver
Right kidney
Parietal peritoneum
Paranephric fat
Renal fascia
Perinephric fat
Fibrous capsule
Body of L_2 vertebra
Stomach
Large intestine
Renal vein
Renal artery
Renal hilum
Left kidney
Spleen
Posterior

Figure 27.2

Position and Stabilization of the Kidneys. An inferior cross-sectional view (which is the view typically used in CT scans) shows that the kidneys are positioned on the posterior abdominal wall and are covered on their anterior surface by the parietal peritoneum and surrounded by four concentric tissue layers (from innermost to outermost): fibrous capsule, perinepheric fat, renal fascia, and paranephric fat.

Learning Strategy 27.2

To understand the retroperitoneal position of the kidneys, imagine placing an eraser against a blackboard, which represents the posterior abdominal wall. Then hang a cloth (which represents the parietal peritoneum) so that the eraser is between the blackboard and the cloth. The eraser, which is located posterior to the cloth (the *parietal peritoneum*), is in the retroperitoneal region. Structures that would be in front of (and enclosed by) the cloth are described as being *intraperitoneal*.

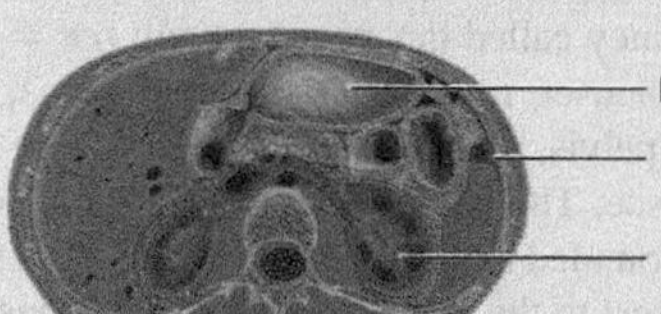

Intraperitoneal
Parietal peritoneum
Retroperitoneal

This layer, which is also called the *perirenal fat*, completely surrounds the kidney and offers cushioning and support.

- The **renal fascia** (fash′ ē-ă; a band) is external to the perinephric fat and is composed of dense irregular connective tissue. It anchors the kidney to the posterior abdominal wall and peritoneum.
- The **paranephric fat** (*para* = next to; also called *pararenal fat,* or *paranephric body*) is the outermost layer surrounding the kidney. It is composed of adipose connective tissue and lies between the renal fascia and the peritoneum.

When a kidney is sectioned along a coronal plane, an outer **renal cortex** and an inner **renal medulla** can be seen **(figure 27.3)**. The medulla tends to be a darker shade than the cortex. Extensions of the cortex, called **renal columns,** project into the medulla and subdivide the medulla into **renal pyramids** (or *medullary pyramids*). An adult kidney typically contains 8 to 15 renal pyramids. The wide base of a renal pyramid lies at the external edge of the medulla where the cortex and medulla meet, called the **corticomedullary junction** (or *corticomedullary border*). The apex (tip) of the renal pyramid (called the **renal papilla**) projects toward the renal sinus.

Each renal papilla projects into a funnel-shaped space called the **minor calyx** (kā′liks; pl., *calyces,* or *calices,* kal′i-s ēz; cup of a flower). There are between 8 and 15 minor calyces—in other words, one minor calyx for each renal papilla. Several minor calyces merge to form a larger space called a **major calyx**—each kidney typically contains two or three major calyces. Urine from the renal pyramids is collected by the minor calyces and then drained into the major calyces. The major calyces merge to form a large, funnel-shaped **renal pelvis,** which collects urine and transports it into the ureter.

A human kidney is divided into 8 to 15 **renal lobes.** A renal lobe consists of a medullary pyramid and some cortical substance immediately surrounding the renal pyramid.

27.2b Blood Supply to the Kidney

Because the kidneys' primary function is to filter the blood, at least 20% to 25% of the body's blood supply normally flows through the kidneys at any given moment. The blood pathway through the kidney is shown in **figure 27.4**. Blood is carried to a kidney in a **renal artery,** which generally arises and extends from the lateral region of the descending abdominal aorta at the level of the first or second lumbar vertebra. Up to five **segmental** (seg-men′t ăl) **arteries** branch from the renal artery within the renal sinus. While still in the renal sinus, the segmental arteries further branch to form the **interlobar** (in′tĕr-lō′bar; *inter* = between, *lobos* = lobe) **arteries.** Interlobar arteries travel through the renal columns toward the corticomedullary junction, where they branch to form **arcuate** (ar′ky ū-āt; *arcuatus* = bowed) **arteries.** These arcuate arteries are located parallel to the base of the

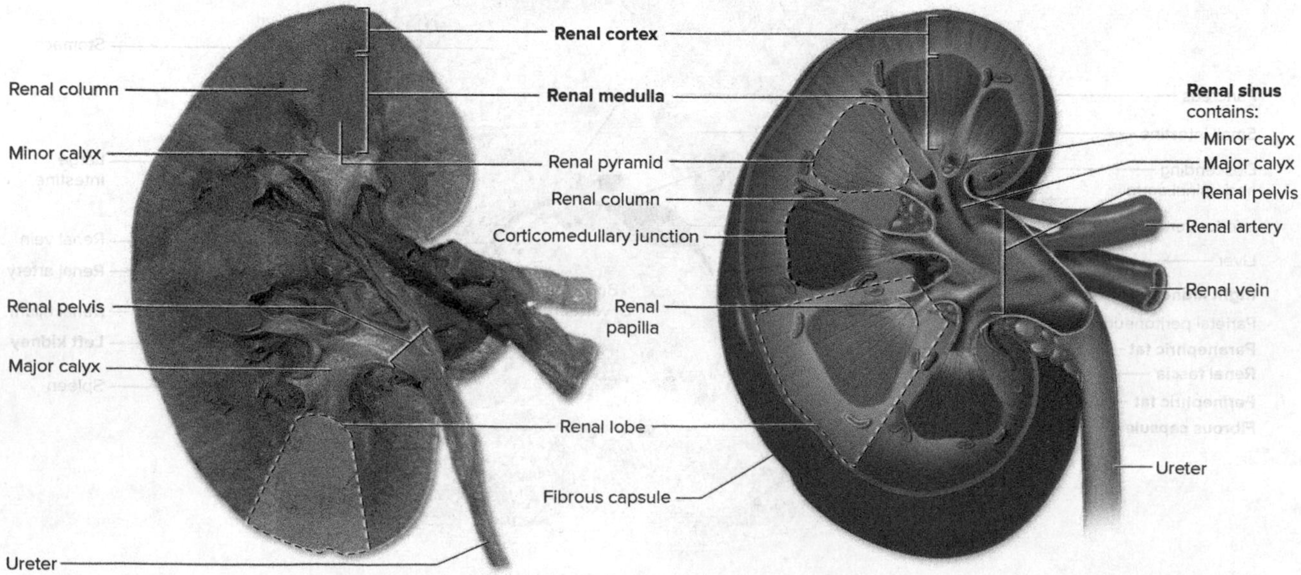

Renal cortex
Renal column
Renal medulla
Minor calyx
Renal pyramid
Renal column
Corticomedullary junction
Renal pelvis
Renal papilla
Major calyx
Renal lobe
Fibrous capsule
Ureter
Renal sinus contains:
Minor calyx
Major calyx
Renal pelvis
Renal artery
Renal vein
Ureter
Right kidney, coronal section

Figure 27.3

Kidney. A dissected right kidney and corresponding drawing of the kidney is shown. These coronal sections reveal the external cortex, the internal medulla, and urine drainage areas of the kidney. APR

(left) ©McGraw-Hill Education/Rebecca Gray, photographer

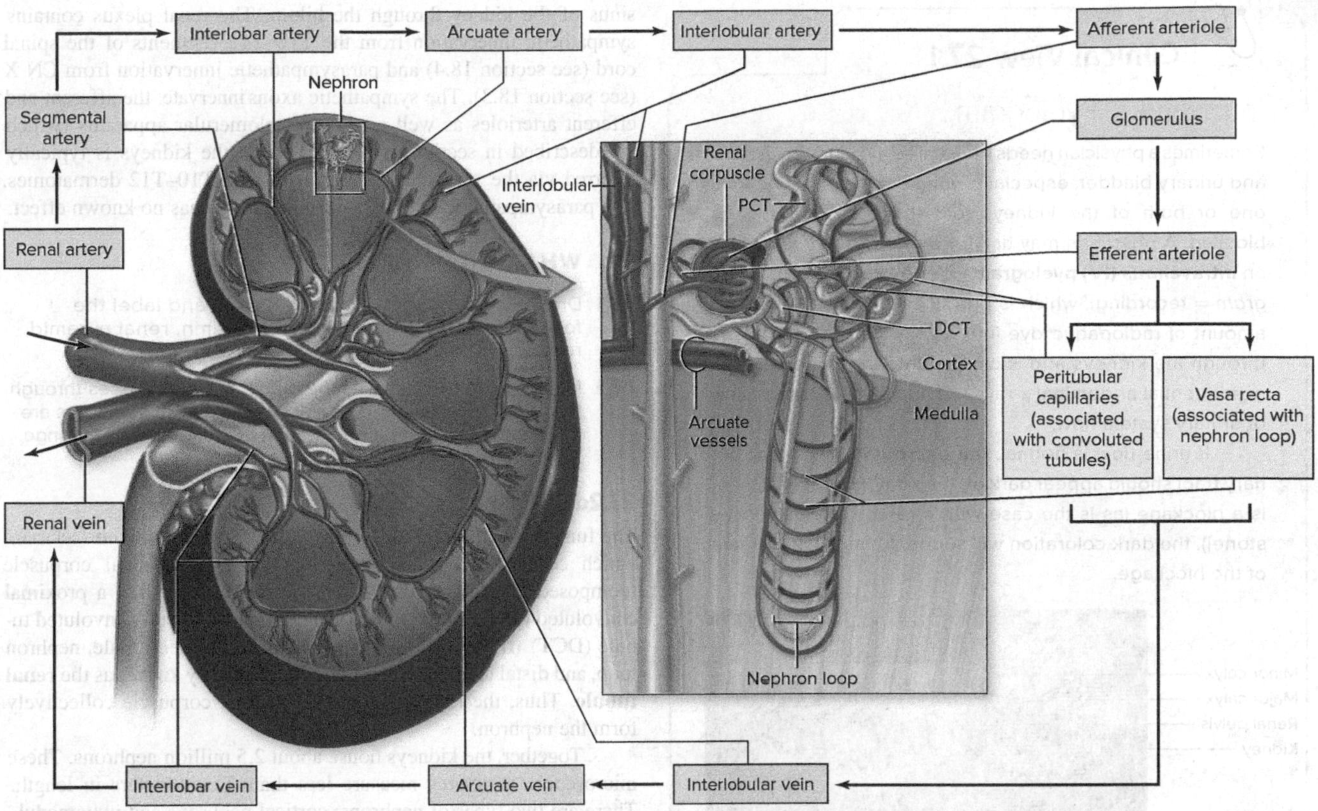

Figure 27.4

Blood Supply to the Kidneys. A coronal view depicts kidney circulation. An expanded view shows circulation to a nephron. Pink boxes indicate vessels with arterial blood; lavender boxes indicate vessels where reabsorbed materials reenter the blood; blue boxes indicate vessels returning blood to the general circulation.

medullary pyramid at the corticomedullary junction. The arcuate arteries give off branches called **interlobular** (in′tĕr-lob′y ū-lăr) **arteries** (or *cortical radiate arteries*) that project peripherally into the cortex.

As the interlobular arteries enter the cortex, they extend small branches called **afferent** (af′ĕr-ĕnt; *ad* = toward, *ferre* = to lead) **arterioles** (or *afferent glomerular arteriole*). An afferent arteriole then enters a structure called a renal corpuscle and forms a capillary network called the **glomerulus** (glō-mer′y ū-lŭs; *glomus* = ball of yarn, *ulus* = small). Some blood plasma is filtered through the fenestrated epithelium of the glomerulus into the capsular space within the renal corpuscle. Once some of the blood plasma has been filtered, the remaining blood leaves the glomerulus and enters an **efferent** (ef′ĕr-ent; *efferens* = to bring out) **arteriole** (or *efferent glomerular arteriole*). The efferent arteriole is still carrying oxygenated blood because gas and nutrient exchange with cells of the kidney has not yet occurred.

The efferent arterioles branch into one of two types of capillary networks: peritubular capillaries or vasa recta (figure 27.4). These capillary networks are responsible for the actual exchange of gases, nutrients, and waste materials within the kidney. **Peritubular capillaries** are intertwined with the convoluted tubules and primarily reside in the cortex of the kidney. **Vasa recta** (vā′să rek′t ă; *vasculum* = small vessel, *rectus* = straight) are intertwined with the nephron loop and primarily reside in the medulla of the kidney.

The peritubular capillaries and vasa recta then drain into a network of veins. The smallest of these veins are the **interlobular veins** (or *cortical radiate veins*) which travel alongside the interlobular arteries. Interlobular veins merge to form **arcuate veins** that project parallel to the base of each medullary pyramid near the corticomedullary junction. Arcuate veins merge to form **interlobar veins** that travel

Learning Strategy 27.3

The names of the blood vessels in the kidney can give you a clue as to their location or appearance:

- Interlobar vessels are located *between* ("inter") the lobes of the kidney.
- Arcuate vessels form vessel "arcs" at the corticomedullary junction.
- Interlobular vessels are located between the smaller lobules of the kidney cortex.
- Afferent arterioles carry blood *to* the glomerulus (remember, "afferent" means "toward").
- Efferent arterioles take blood *away from* the glomerulus (remember, "efferent" means to take away, or "exit").
- Peritubular capillaries are *around* ("peri") the tubules (proximal and distal convoluted tubules).
- Vasa recta means "straight vessels," and these vessels run parallel to the long, straight tubules of the nephron loop.

Clinical View 27.1

Intravenous Pyelogram

Sometimes a physician needs to visualize the kidneys, ureters, and urinary bladder, especially when the flow of urine from one or both of the kidneys into the bladder becomes blocked. A physician may ask for an x-ray study known as an **intravenous (IV) pyelogram** (pī′el-ō-gram′; *pyelos* = tub, *gram* = recording), which is produced by injecting a small amount of radiopaque dye into a vein. As the dye passes through the kidneys and is cleared into the urine, a series of sequential abdominal x-rays provide a "time-lapse" view of urinary system flow.

If urine flow is normal, the entire pathway of the urinary tract should appear dark on the x-ray. However, if there is a blockage (as is the case with a renal calculus [kidney stone]), the dark coloration will suddenly "stop" at the area of the blockage.

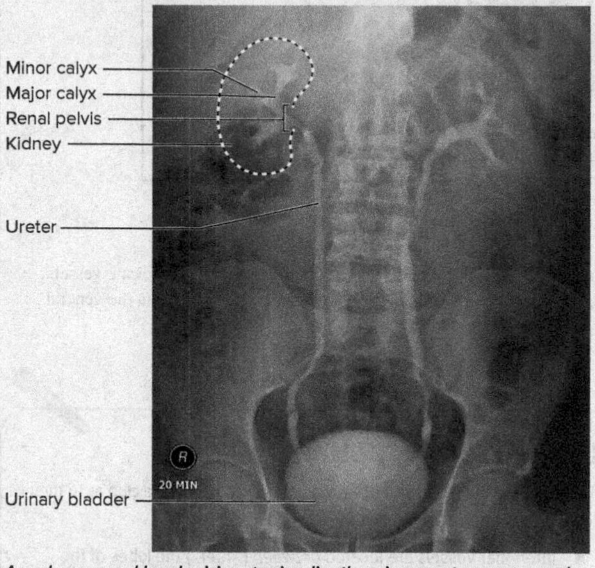

A pyelogram enables physicians to visualize the urinary system organs and identify the location of any blockages.
sphotography/123RF

through the renal columns from the corticomedullary junction toward the renal sinus. Interlobar veins merge in the renal sinus to form the **renal vein.** (Although many veins are associated with arteries of the same name, there are no segmental veins; rather, the interlobar veins merge to form the renal vein.) The renal veins leave the kidney at its hilum and traverse horizontally to drain into the inferior vena cava.

Blood filtration occurs at the glomerulus, and the blood remains highly oxygenated until it reaches the peritubular capillaries and vasa recta, where exchange of gases occurs. APR

27.2c Innervation of the Kidney

Each kidney is innervated by a mass of sensory and autonomic nervous system axons collectively called the **renal plexus.** The renal plexus accompanies each renal artery and enters the renal sinus of the kidney through the hilum. The renal plexus contains sympathetic innervation from the T10–T12 segments of the spinal cord (see section 18.4) and parasympathetic innervation from CN X (see section 18.3). The sympathetic axons innervate the afferent and efferent arterioles as well as the juxtaglomerular apparatus (which are described in section 27.2f). Pain from the kidneys is typically referred via the sympathetic pathway to the T10–T12 dermatomes. The parasympathetic innervation to the kidney has no known effect.

WHAT DID YOU LEARN?

3. Draw a coronal section of the kidney and label the following: cortex, medulla, renal column, renal pyramid, renal sinus, minor calyx, major calyx, renal pelvis.
4. Make a flowchart that lists the path that blood passes through the blood vessels of the kidney. Identify which structures are involved with either blood filtration or gas/nutrient exchange.

27.2d Nephrons

The functional filtration unit in the kidney is the **nephron** (nef′ron), which consists of the following components: a renal corpuscle (composed of a glomerulus and a glomerular capsule), a proximal convoluted tubule (PCT), a nephron loop, and a distal convoluted tubule (DCT) **(figure 27.5)**. The proximal convoluted tubule, nephron loop, and distal convoluted tubule are collectively known as the **renal tubule.** Thus, the renal tubule and the renal corpuscle collectively form the nephron.

Together, the kidneys house about 2.5 million nephrons. These microscopic structures measure less than 5 centimeters in length. There are two types of nephrons: cortical nephrons and juxtamedullary nephrons (figure 27.5). About 85% of the nephrons are termed **cortical nephrons** because the bulk of the nephron resides solely in the cortex, and their relatively short nephron loops just barely penetrate the medulla. The remaining 15% of nephrons are called **juxtamedullary** (jŭks′tă-med′y ŭ-lăr-ē; *juxta* = close to) **nephrons,** because their renal corpuscles lie close to the corticomedullary junction, and their long nephron loops extend deep into the medulla.

Urine Formation

The nephrons form urine through three interrelated processes: filtration, tubular reabsorption, and tubular secretion **(figure 27.6)**:

1. **Glomerular filtration** is the process by which water and some dissolved solutes in the blood plasma passively move out of the glomerulus into the capsular space of the renal corpuscle due to pressure differences across the filtration membrane. This separated fluid is called **filtrate,** which is essentially blood plasma minus large solutes (e.g., most proteins).
2. **Tubular reabsorption** occurs when substances in the filtrate move by diffusion or active transport across the wall of the renal tubules to return to the blood. Once filtrate begins to be modified, it is called **tubular fluid.** Usually, all needed solutes and most of the water that formed the filtrate are reabsorbed by the blood. As reabsorption occurs, some excess solutes, water, and waste products remain within the tubular fluid.
3. **Tubular secretion** is the active transport of solutes out of the blood (within the peritubular capillaries and vasa recta) into the tubular fluid (within the convoluted tubules and nephron loop).

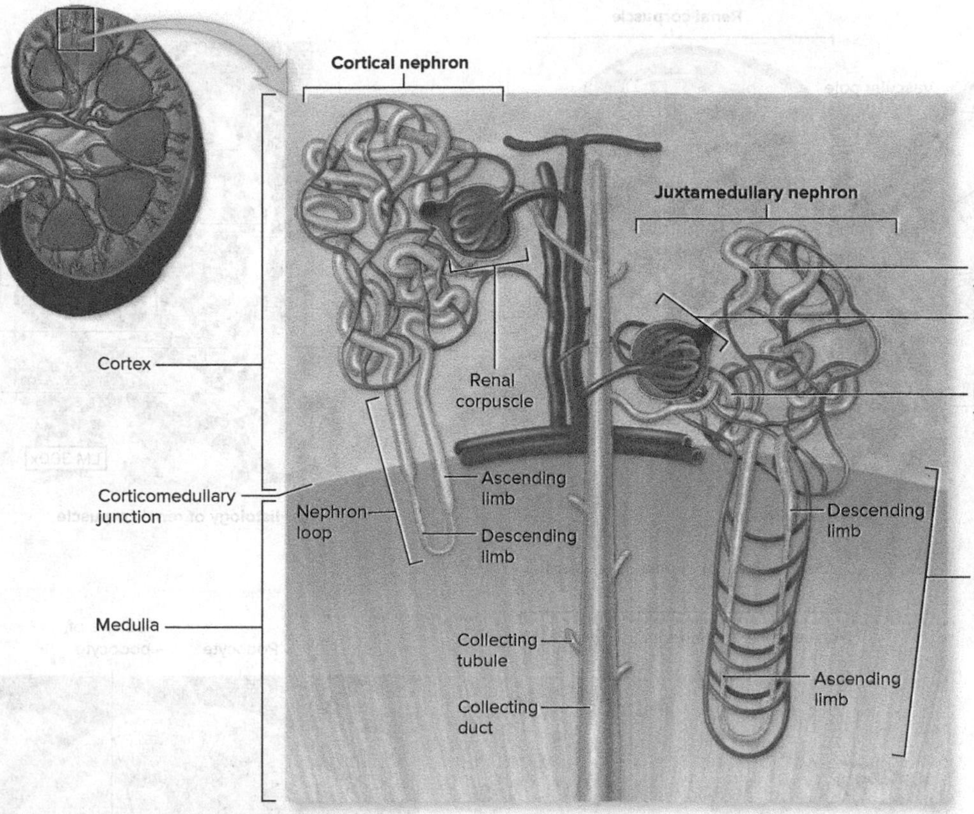

Figure 27.5

Two Types of Nephrons. Cortical nephrons are located almost completely in the cortex and have short nephron loops that barely penetrate into the medulla. Juxtamedullary nephrons lie close to the corticomedullary junction. These nephrons have relatively long nephron loops that extend deeper into the medulla.

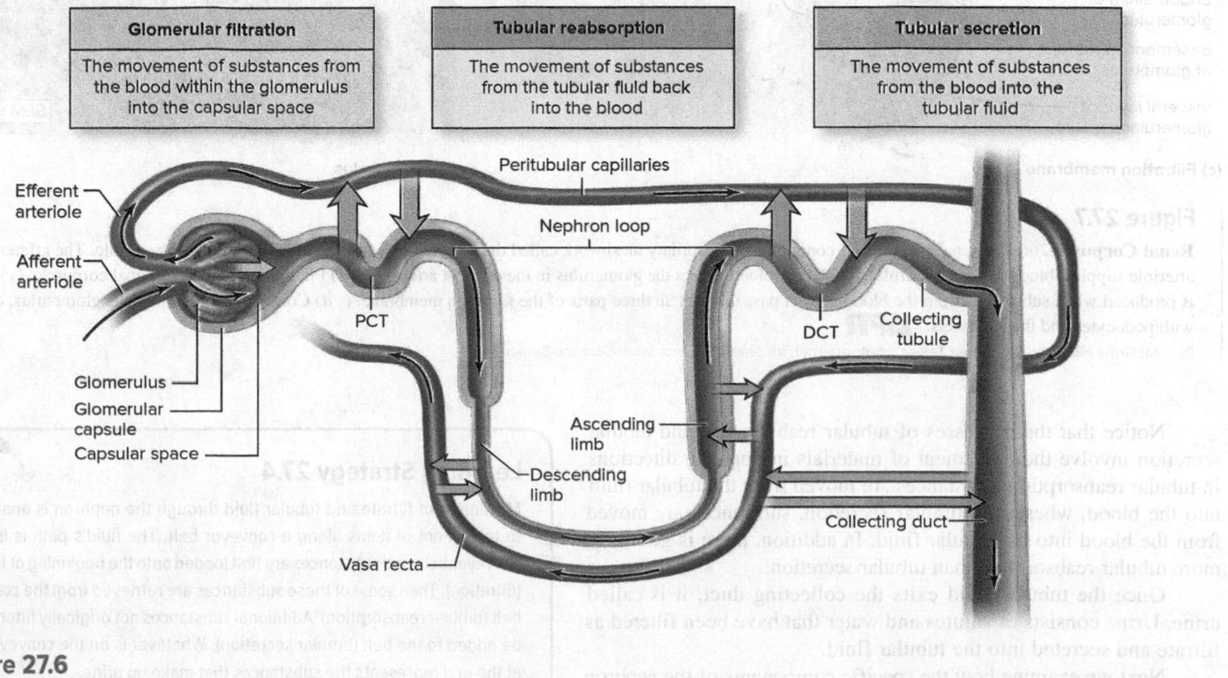

Figure 27.6

Overview of Processes of Urine Formation. The three major processes of urine formation include glomerular filtration, tubular reabsorption, and tubular secretion.

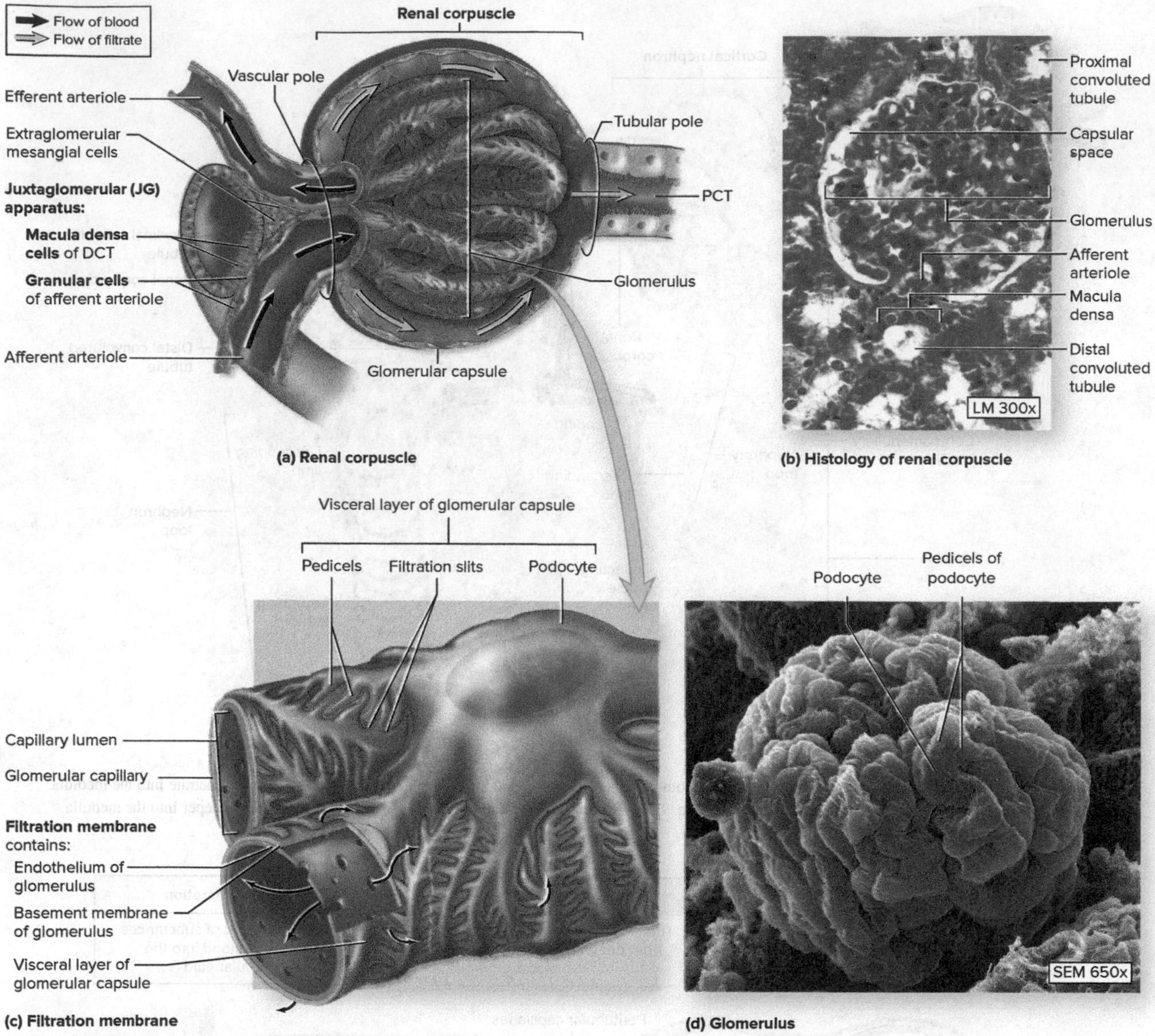

Flow of blood
Flow of filtrate
Renal corpuscle
Vascular pole
Efferent arteriole
Extraglomerular mesangial cells
Juxtaglomerular (JG) apparatus:
Macula densa cells of DCT
Granular cells of afferent arteriole
Afferent arteriole
Tubular pole
PCT
Glomerulus
Glomerular capsule
(a) Renal corpuscle
Proximal convoluted tubule
Capsular space
Glomerulus
Afferent arteriole
Macula densa
Distal convoluted tubule
LM 300x
(b) Histology of renal corpuscle
Visceral layer of glomerular capsule
Pedicels
Filtration slits
Podocyte
Capillary lumen
Glomerular capillary
Filtration membrane contains:
Endothelium of glomerulus
Basement membrane of glomerulus
Visceral layer of glomerular capsule
(c) Filtration membrane
Podocyte
Pedicels of podocyte
SEM 650x
(d) Glomerulus

Figure 27.7

Renal Corpuscle. *(a)* The renal corpuscle is composed of a capillary meshwork called the glomerulus housed within the glomerular capsule. The afferent arteriole supplies blood to the glomerular capillaries; blood leaves the glomerulus in the efferent arteriole. (*b*) Photomicrograph of a renal corpuscle. (*c*) Filtrate is produced when substances from the blood plasma pass through all three parts of the filtration membrane. (*d*) Colorized SEM shows the glomerulus, covered with podocytes and their pedicels. APR

(b) ©McGraw-Hill Education/Alvin Telser, photographer; (d) Steve Gschmeissner/Science Source

Notice that the processes of tubular reabsorption and tubular secretion involve the movement of materials in opposite directions. In tubular reabsorption, substances are moved from the tubular fluid into the blood, whereas in tubular secretion, substances are moved from the blood into the tubular fluid. In addition, there is generally more tubular reabsorption than tubular secretion.

Once the tubular fluid exits the collecting duct, it is called urine. Urine consists of solutes and water that have been filtered as filtrate and secreted into the tubular fluid.

Next we examine how the specific components of the nephron carry out these processes.

Learning Strategy 27.4

Movement of filtrate and tubular fluid through the nephron is analogous to movement of items along a conveyor belt. The fluid's path is like the conveyor belt, and substances are first loaded onto the beginning of the belt (filtration). Then some of these substances are retrieved from the conveyor belt (tubular reabsorption). Additional substances not originally filtered can be added to the belt (tubular secretion). Whatever is on the conveyor belt at the end represents the substances that make up urine.

Renal Corpuscle A **renal corpuscle** (kōr′pŭs-l; *corpus* = body, *cle* = tiny) is an enlarged, bulbous region of a nephron (**figure 27.7*a, b***). It is composed of two structures: the thick tangle of capillaries called the **glomerulus,** and an epithelial capsule surrounding the glomerulus called the **glomerular capsule** (*Bowman capsule*). The glomerular capsule has two layers: a visceral layer that directly overlies the glomerulus and a parietal layer. The visceral layer is composed of specialized cells called *podocytes* (to be discussed later in this section), whereas the parietal layer is formed from a simple squamous epithelium. Between these two layers is a capsular space. As blood flows through the glomerulus, the solutes and water within the blood are filtered from the glomerulus into the capsular space.

The renal corpuscle has two opposing poles: a **vascular pole,** where the afferent and efferent arterioles are found, and a **tubular pole,** where the proximal convoluted tubule attaches to the renal corpuscle.

The **filtration membrane** is a porous, thin (0.1 micrometer wide), and negatively charged structure that is formed by the glomerulus and visceral layer of the glomerular capsule (figure 27.7*c*). It is composed of three sandwiched layers. For a substance in the blood to become part of the filtrate, it must be able to pass through these three layers of the "filter," which are listed from innermost (closest to the lumen of the glomerulus) to outermost:

1. **Endothelium of glomerulus.** The endothelium of the glomerulus is fenestrated (see types of capillaries in section 23.1c). It allows plasma and its dissolved substances to be filtered, while restricting the passage of large structures, such as the formed elements (erythrocytes, leukocytes, and platelets).
2. **Basement membrane of glomerulus.** The porous basement membrane restricts the passage of large plasma proteins, while allowing smaller structures to pass through.
3. **Visceral layer of glomerular capsule.** The visceral layer of the glomerular capsule is composed of specialized cells called **podocytes** (pod′ō-sīt; *podos* = foot). Podocytes are octopus-shaped cells that have long, "footlike" processes called **pedicels** (ped′i-sel; *pedicellus* = little foot) that wrap around the glomerular capillaries to support the capillary wall but do not completely ensheathe it (figure 27.7*c, d*). The pedicels are separated by thin spaces called **filtration slits** that are covered with membrane. Pedicels of one podocyte interlock with pedicels of a different podocyte, similar to how the fingers of your hands can interlock. The membrane-covered filtration slits restrict the passage of most small proteins.

Several factors cause materials to be filtered from the glomerulus. First, the afferent arteriole is wider in diameter than the efferent arteriole, so the blood in the afferent arteriole enters the glomerulus under high pressure, which helps filter the plasma and solutes out of the glomerulus. Second, the glomerulus is designed to be "leaky" to allow some plasma and solutes to be filtered. Third, the filtration slits between pedicles permit the ready passage of filtered material into the capsular space.

Some nutrients, ions, plasma proteins, and vitamins are initally released into the filtrate and need to be returned to the blood. Therefore, the renal tubule (proximal convoluted tubule, nephron loop, and distal convoluted tubule) becomes responsible for modifying this filtrate. The filtrate is modified by reabsorbing the needed solutes and secreting unwanted substances. The filtrate first enters the proximal convoluted tubule, where it begins to be modified and becomes tubular fluid.

Proximal Convoluted Tubule The **proximal convoluted tubule (PCT)** originates at the tubular pole of the renal corpuscle (**figure 27.8**; see figure 27.7*a*). It is lined by a simple cuboidal epithelium with tall microvilli that markedly increase its reabsorption capacity. When viewed under a microscope, the lumen of the proximal convoluted tubule looks fuzzy due to the brush border formed by the tall microvilli. In addition, the cytoplasm of these cells stains brightly, due to an abundance of mitochondria in the cytoplasm.

The cells of the proximal convoluted tubule actively reabsorb all nutrients (such as glucose and amino acids). The cells also reabsorb most vitamins and any plasma proteins from the tubular fluid. About 60% to 65% of the water in the tubular fluid is reabsorbed by osmosis. The reabsorbed solutes and water enter the blood in the peritubular capillaries and are returned to the general circulation. The proximal convoluted tubule also secretes some hydrogen ions (H^+) into the tubular fluid.

Nephron Loop The **nephron loop** (or *loop of Henle*) originates from the end of the proximal convoluted tubule and projects toward and into the medulla (see figure 27.5). Each loop has two limbs: a **descending limb** extending from the cortex toward and into the medulla, and an **ascending limb** that returns back to the renal cortex. The descending limb is first lined with a simple cuboidal epithelium (this segment is called the thick descending limb) and then a simple squamous epithelium (this segment is called the thin descending limb). The ascending limb is first lined by a simple squamous epithelium (this segment is called the thin ascending limb) and then by a simple cuboidal epithelium (this segment is called the thick ascending limb). The ascending limb of the nephron loop returns to the renal cortex and terminates at the distal convoluted tubule.

The primary function of the nephron loop is to facilitate reabsorption of water and solutes from the tubular fluid. Sodium ions (Na^+) and chloride ions (Cl^-) are the primary solutes reabsorbed from the ascending limb, although other solutes may be reabsorbed as well. When these materials are reabsorbed from the nephron loop, they are returned to the blood via the vasa recta capillary network. The nephron loop also secretes some hydrogen ions (H^+) into the tubular fluid.

Distal Convoluted Tubule The **distal convoluted tubule (DCT)** originates in the renal cortex at the end of the thick ascending limb of the nephron loop and contacts the afferent arteriole wall at the vascular pole (figure 27.8). Like the proximal convoluted tubule, the distal convoluted tubule is also lined with simple cuboidal epithelium. However, the distal convoluted tubule cells are smaller and have only sparse, short microvilli (figure 27.8*c*). Thus, the distal convoluted tubule lumen does not appear fuzzy. In addition, the distal convoluted tubule cytoplasm stains more lightly than that of the proximal convoluted tubule, because the distal convoluted tubule has fewer mitochondria.

The primary function of the distal convoluted tubule is to secrete ions such as potassium (K^+) and hydrogen (H^+) into the tubular fluid. However, reabsorption of water and sodium ions (Na^+) also occurs here, primarily under the influence of antidiuretic hormone (ADH) and aldosterone (see sections 20.3b and 20.6a). **ADH** (posterior pituitary) and **aldosterone** (adrenal cortex) are secreted in response to low blood volume or low solute concentration in the tubular fluid within the kidney. These hormones cause the distal convoluted tubule cells to increase water and sodium reabsorption from tubular fluid.

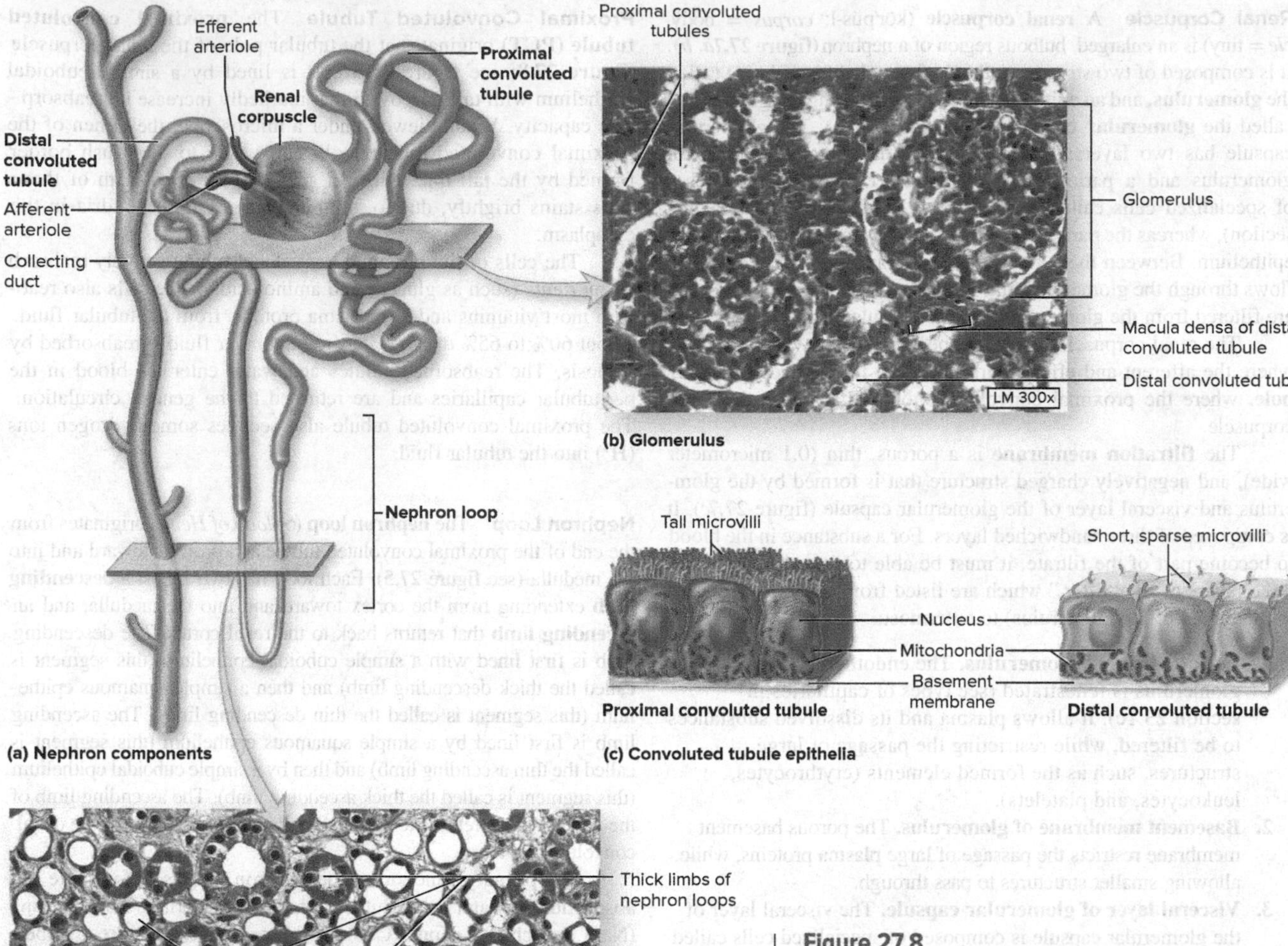
Efferent arteriole
Renal corpuscle
Proximal convoluted tubule
Distal convoluted tubule
Afferent arteriole
Collecting duct
Nephron loop
(a) Nephron components
Proximal convoluted tubules
Glomerulus
Macula densa of distal convoluted tubule
Distal convoluted tubule
LM 300x
(b) Glomerulus
Tall microvilli
Short, sparse microvilli
Nucleus
Mitochondria
Basement membrane
Proximal convoluted tubule
Distal convoluted tubule
(c) Convoluted tubule epithelia
Thick limbs of nephron loops
Collecting ducts
Thin limbs of nephron loops
Vasa recta
LM 100x
(d) Histology of renal medulla

Figure 27.8

Convoluted Tubules and Nephron Loop. The convoluted tubules and nephron loop carry tubular fluid that is being modified to form urine. (*a*) In this drawing, each of the components of the nephron is distinguished by a different color. (*b*) A photomicrograph of a section through the cortex compares transverse sections of the proximal and distal convoluted tubules. (*c*) Comparisons of the simple cuboidal epithelium lining the proximal and distal convoluted tubules show that proximal convoluted tubules have more microvilli and mitochondria than distal convoluted tubules. (*d*) A photomicrograph of a transverse section through the medulla compares the thick and thin limbs of the nephron loops, the collecting ducts, and vasa recta.

(b, d) ©McGraw-Hill Education/Alvin Telser, photographer

Once the tubular fluid leaves the distal convoluted tubule, it enters the collecting tubules.

Table 27.2 summarizes the parts of a nephron and their functions.

Learning Strategy 27.5

Use the phrase "***Al likes salt***" to remember that **al**dosterone helps our bodies retain sodium.

27.2e Collecting Tubules and Collecting Ducts: How Tubular Fluid Becomes Urine

When the tubular fluid leaves the distal convoluted tubules, it must travel through a series of small **collecting tubules** that empty into **collecting ducts.** Collecting tubules and collecting ducts project through the renal medulla toward the renal papilla (not shown) (see figures 27.5 and 27.8*d*). Both collecting tubules and collecting ducts are lined by a simple epithelium. The epithelial cells are cuboidal in the tubules, but very tall columnar cells in the ducts near the renal papilla.

Table 27.2 Parts of a Nephron and Their Functions

Structure	Description	Function(s)
Renal corpuscle	Capillary ball covered by podocytes and surrounded by an epithelial capsule; capsular space is between the parietal and visceral layers of the capsule	Produces a filtrate of blood that must be modified as it passes through the convoluted tubules and nephron loop
Proximal convoluted tubule	Tubule lined with simple cuboidal epithelium; has a prominent brush border (microvilli); cytoplasm tends to stain more brightly than DCT cells	Reabsorbs all nutrients (glucose and amino acids); reabsorbs most ions (especially Na^+), plasma proteins, vitamins, and water; secretes some H^+ ions
Nephron loop	Tubule that forms a hairpin/ U-shaped loop; has thick and thin ascending and descending portions; the most distal part of the loop often extends into the medulla	Reabsorbs water in tubular fluid; also reabsorbs Na^+ and Cl^-; secretes some H^+ ions
	Thick limbs are lined with simple cuboidal epithelium	
	Thin limbs are lined with simple squamous epithelium	
Distal convoluted tubule	Tubule lined with simple cuboidal epithelium with only a sparse brush border; cytoplasm of cells tends to be paler than that of PCT cells	Secretes H^+ and K^+ into tubular fluid; reabsorbs Na^+ and water from tubular fluid (in presence of aldosterone and ADH)

The collecting ducts are the last structures that have the capacity to modify the tubular fluid further, and can do so under the influence of ADH and aldosterone. Secretion of these hormones results in increased water and sodium absorption from the tubular fluid in the collecting ducts, thereby reducing water and sodium loss from the kidneys. ADH is secreted in response either to a rise in the concentration of ions in the blood or a fall in blood volume, as when the body is dehydrated and needs to conserve water. If an individual is well hydrated, the collecting ducts merely transport the tubular fluid and do not modify it. However, if an individual is dehydrated, water conservation must occur, and more-concentrated urine is produced. ADH acts on the collecting duct epithelium, making it more able to absorb water from the tubular fluid.

Once the tubular fluid leaves the collecting duct and enters the papillary duct, the tubular fluid now may be called **urine.** The remaining structures in the kidney simply transport the urine and cannot modify this fluid further.

Several collecting ducts empty into a papillary duct that opens at the apex (tip) of the renal papilla. Urine leaves the renal papillae and enters the minor calyces, which then transport the urine to major calyces, which in turn transport the urine to the renal pelvis. Because the calyces and the renal pelvis are in contact with urine, they are lined with transitional epithelium. The renal pelvis conducts urine into the ureter. APR

WHAT DO YOU THINK?

2 Is ADH secreted when the body is dehydrated or well hydrated?

27.2f Juxtaglomerular Apparatus

Associated with the nephron are some structures collectively referred to as the **juxtaglomerular** (jŭks′tă-glō-mer′y ū-lăr; *juxta* = near) **apparatus** (see figure 27.7*a*, *b*). Components of the juxtaglomerular apparatus are granular cells, macula densa, and extraglomerular mesangial cells. **Granular cells** (also called *juxtaglomerular epithelioid cells*) are modified smooth muscle cells of the afferent arteriole located near the entrance to the renal corpuscle. The **macula** (mak′yū-lă; spot) **densa** (den′s ă; dense) is a group of modified epithelial cells in a distal convoluted tubule that monitor ion concentrations in the tubular fluid. These cells, which are located only on the tubule side next to the afferent arteriole, are narrower and taller than other distal convoluted tubule epithelial cells. **Extraglomerular mesangial cells,** located between the granular cells and the arterioles, can contract and phagocytize filtered particles.

The structures of the juxtaglomerular apparatus work together to regulate blood pressure and **glomerular filtration rate (GFR,** the amount of filtrate the kidneys produce during a period of time). If GFR or blood pressure is reduced, the granular cells are stimulated to release the enzyme **renin**. Recall from section 20.9a that renin activates the renin-angiotensin pathway, resulting in aldosterone production, which causes increases in both sodium ion concentration in the blood and blood volume. This arrangement is important in maintaining blood volume and blood pressure homeostasis in the body.

Finally, recall from section 27.2c that the cells of the juxtaglomerular apparatus are innervated by sympathetic axons. Should there be a drop in blood pressure (for example, during hemorrhage), the sympathetic innervation will stimulate the granular cells to contract and release renin, thereby increasing blood pressure.

WHAT DID YOU LEARN?

5 Make a table that lists the components of the nephron and the main activities of each component.

6 Describe how glomerular filtration differs from tubular secretion.

7 List and describe the components of the filtration membrane in the order in which fluid passes by them as blood is filtered.

8 What cells make up the juxtaglomerular apparatus, and how do these cells work to regulate blood pressure?

27.3 Urinary Tract

✓ Learning Objectives

7. Identify and describe the gross and microscopic anatomy of the ureters.
8. Identify and describe the gross and microscopic anatomy of the urinary bladder.
9. Compare and contrast the anatomy of the female urethra and male urethra.
10. Explain the steps involved in micturition (urination).

The urinary tract consists of the ureters, urinary bladder, and urethra.

27.3a Ureters

The **ureters** (yū-rē′tĕr, yū′rē-ter) are long, fibromuscular tubes that conduct urine from the kidneys to the urinary bladder. Each ureter averages 25 centimeters in length and is retroperitoneal. The ureters originate at the renal pelvis as each exits the hilum of the kidney, and then extend inferiorly to enter the posterolateral wall of the base

Clinical View 27.2

Renal Failure, Dialysis, and Kidney Transplants

Renal failure refers to greatly diminished or absent renal function caused by the destruction of about 90% of the tissue in the kidney. Renal failure often results from a chronic disease that affects the glomerulus or the small blood vessels of the kidney, as a result of autoimmune conditions, high blood pressure, or diabetes. Once the kidneys have been destroyed, there is no chance they will regenerate or begin functioning again. Thus, the two main treatments are dialysis or a kidney transplant.

The term **dialysis** (dī-al′i-sis; *dialyo* = to separate) comes from a Greek word meaning "to separate agents or particles on the basis of their size." Two forms of dialysis are commonly used today: peritoneal dialysis and hemodialysis. In **peritoneal dialysis,** a catheter is permanently placed in the peritoneal cavity, to which a bag of dialysis fluid can be attached externally. As this fluid enters the peritoneal cavity, harmful waste products are transferred, or *dialyzed,* from the blood into the fluid. After several hours, the fluid is drained from the peritoneal cavity and replaced with fresh fluid.

In **hemodialysis,** the patient's blood is cycled through a machine that filters the waste products across a specially designed membrane. The patient must remain stationary for the time it takes to cycle the blood through the dialysis unit while the metabolic waste products are removed. Hemodialysis must be performed three to four times a week, and each treatment takes about 4 hours.

A **kidney transplant** from a genetically similar person may successfully restore renal function. The kidney is generally removed from the donor by a laparoscopic procedure that removes the kidney through the umbilicus (navel, or belly button) after making a single small incision. This decreases the donor's recovery time from about 3 months to just under a month. The replacement kidney is attached to an artery and vein in the inferior abdominopelvic region, where it is relatively easy to establish a vascular connection. The new kidney rests either on the superior surface of, or immediately lateral to, the urinary bladder. Because a pelvic artery and vein connect the donor kidney to the patient's blood supply, having the kidney near the bladder means only a short segment of a ureter is needed for connection to the bladder. The diseased kidney is not removed. Because the transplanted kidney is a foreign tissue, immunosuppressant drugs are administered to suppress the immune system's activity.

Donor kidneys may come through an organ procurement program or from a living person. Because most people have two kidneys, and normal renal function actually requires only one, some people have donated a kidney (while still alive) to a relative or even to a total stranger.

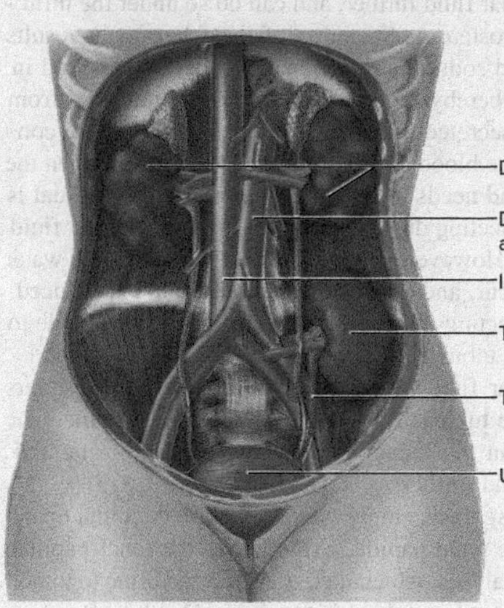

Location of a transplanted kidney in the abdominopelvic cavity.

of the urinary bladder. The wall of the ureter is composed of three concentric tunics. From innermost to outermost, these tunics are the mucosa, muscularis, and adventitia (**figure 27.9**). (The ureter does not have a submucosa.)

The **mucosa** is formed from transitional epithelium (see section 4.1e) , which is both distensible (stretchy) and impermeable to the passage of urine. External to the transitional epithelium of the mucosa is the lamina propria, composed of a fairly thick layer of dense irregular connective tissue. The continuous production of urine ensures that the ureters are rarely completely empty, but as peristaltic waves propel urine through the ureter, the ureter may be temporarily empty at specific places along its length. At these locations, the mucosa folds to fill the lumen. Thereafter, when the ureter is distended, the mucosa can be stretched; this folding of the mucosa allows for considerable increase in the luminal diameter when needed.

The middle **muscularis** consists of two smooth muscle layers: an inner longitudinal layer and an outer circular layer. (The arrangement of muscle layers is opposite that in the GI tract, where the circular layer is the inner layer.) The presence of urine within the renal pelvis causes these muscle layers to produce peristaltic waves that propel the urine through the ureters into the urinary bladder.

Learning Strategy 27.6

To help you identify transitional epithelium in a microscopic anatomy image, recall that this epithelium not only is stratified (has multiple layers) but also is the only epithelial type to contain some binucleated cells.

WHAT DO YOU THINK?

3 Why do the ureters use peristalsis to actively pump urine to the urinary bladder? Why don't the ureters rely on gravity to move the urine to the inferiorly located bladder?

The external layer of the ureter wall is the **adventitia,** which is formed from areolar connective tissue. Some extensions of this areolar connective tissue layer also anchor the ureter to the posterior abdominal wall.

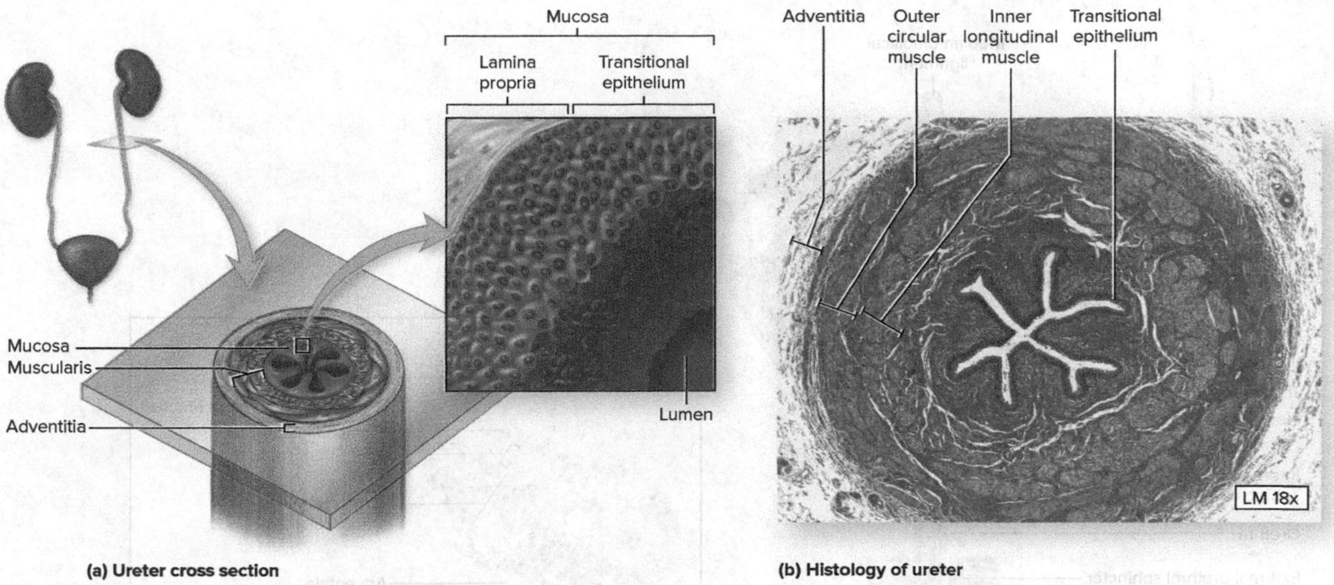

Figure 27.9

Ureters. The ureters conduct urine from the kidneys to the urinary bladder for storage prior to voiding from the body. (*a*) Features of a ureter in cross-sectional view. (*b*) A photomicrograph of a ureter in cross section shows its mucosal folds and thick muscularis.

(b) ©McGraw-Hill Education/Alvin Telser, photographer

The ureters project through the posteroinferior bladder wall obliquely, and some smooth muscle fibers of the inner longitudinal layer of the muscularis insert into the lamina propria of the bladder. Because of the oblique course the ureters take through the bladder wall, the ureteral walls are compressed as the bladder distends, decreasing the likelihood of urine refluxing into the ureters from the bladder.

Multiple blood vessels supply blood to the ureters. In general, a segment of ureter receives its blood supply from a branch of the nearest artery. Thus, the superior aspects of the ureter are supplied by the renal arteries, whereas the more inferior aspects may receive their arterial supply from the aorta, common iliac, and/or internal iliac arteries. Venous drainage is through the companion veins.

The ureters are innervated by the autonomic nervous system. Parasympathetic axons (see section 18.3) come from CN X (which supplies the superior region of the ureter) and from the pelvic splanchnic nerves (which supply the inferior region of the ureter). There are no known effects of this innervation. Sympathetic axons (see section 18.4) come from the T11–L2 segments of the spinal cord. Pain from the ureter (e.g., due to a kidney stone lodged in the ureter) is referred to the T11–L2 dermatomes. These dermatomes are along a "loin-to-groin" region, so pain along this region typically means ureter and/or kidney discomfort.

27.3b Urinary Bladder

The **urinary bladder** is an expandable, muscular container that serves as a reservoir for urine **(figure 27.10)**. The bladder is positioned immediately posterior to the pubic symphysis. In females, the urinary bladder is anteroinferior to the uterus and directly anterior to the vagina; in males, the bladder is anterior to the rectum and superior to the prostate gland. The urinary bladder is a retroperitoneal organ, because only its superior surface is covered with peritoneum.

When empty, the urinary bladder exhibits an upside-down pyramidal shape. Filling with urine distends it superiorly until it assumes an oval shape (figure 27.10*c*). A fibrous, cordlike **median umbilical ligament** extends toward the umbilicus from its origin on the anterosuperior border of the urinary bladder. It is a remnant of the embryologic structure called the urachus. Ureters enter the posterolateral wall of the urinary bladder through the **ureteral openings.** The constricted **neck** of the bladder is located inferiorly and connected to the urethra.

A posteroinferior triangular area of the urinary bladder wall, called the **trigone** (trī′gōn; *trigonum* = triangle), is formed by imaginary lines connecting the two ureteral openings and the urethral opening. The trigone does not move and remains in place as the urinary bladder fills and evacuates. It functions as a funnel to direct the stored urine into the urethra as the bladder wall contracts. The trigone is embryologically different from the rest of the urinary bladder. While the urinary bladder forms from a structure called the cloaca, the trigone forms from the distal parts of the ureters, which become incorporated into the posterior wall of the urinary bladder.

The four tunics that form the wall of the bladder are the mucosa, submucosa, muscularis, and adventitia. The **mucosa** lines the bladder lumen; it is formed by a transitional epithelium that accommodates the shape changes occurring with distension, and by a highly vascularized lamina propria that supports the mucosa. Additionally, mucosal folds, called **rugae,** allow for even greater distension. Within the trigone region, the mucosa is smooth, thick, and lacking rugae. The **submucosa** lies immediately external to the mucosa and is formed by dense irregular connective tissue that supports the urinary bladder wall.

The **muscularis** consists of three layers of smooth muscle, collectively called the **detrusor** (dē-trū′sŏr, -sōr; *detrudo* = to drive away) **muscle.** These smooth muscle bundles exhibit such complex orientations that it is difficult to delineate individual layers in random histologic sections. At the neck of the urinary bladder, an involuntary **internal urethral sphincter** is formed by the smooth muscle that encircles the urethral opening.

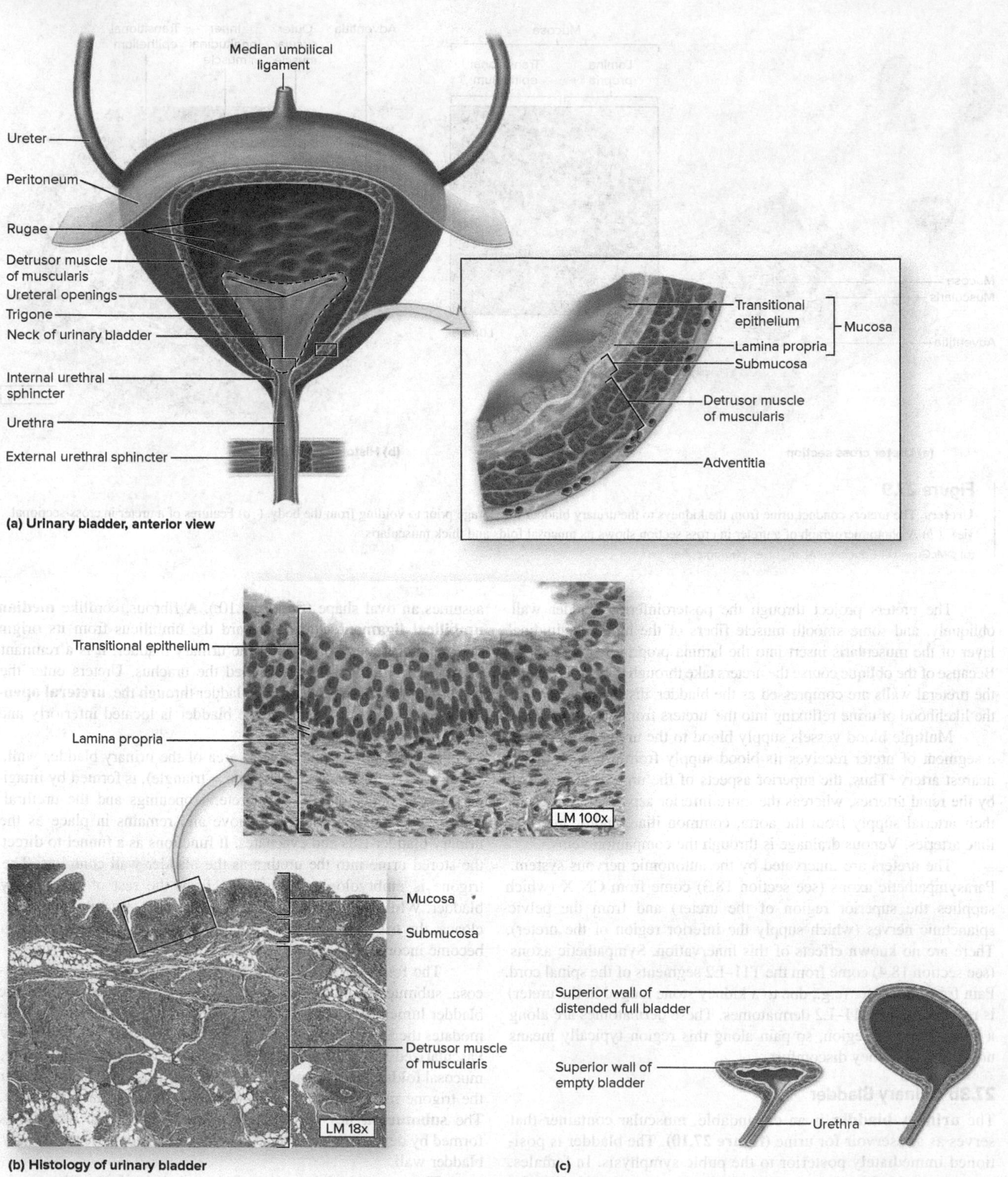
Median umbilical ligament
Ureter
Peritoneum
Rugae
Detrusor muscle of muscularis
Ureteral openings
Trigone
Neck of urinary bladder
Internal urethral sphincter
Urethra
External urethral sphincter
Transitional epithelium
Lamina propria
Mucosa
Submucosa
Detrusor muscle of muscularis
Adventitia
(a) Urinary bladder, anterior view
Transitional epithelium
Lamina propria
LM 100x
Mucosa
Submucosa
Detrusor muscle of muscularis
LM 18x
(b) Histology of urinary bladder
Superior wall of distended full bladder
Superior wall of empty bladder
Urethra
(c)

Figure 27.10

Urinary Bladder. (*a*) The urinary bladder is an expandable, muscular sac. This anterior view depicts the female bladder. (*b*) Photomicrographs of the urinary bladder wall show its mucosa, submucosa, and muscularis. (*c*) Sagittal views show that the urinary bladder expands superiorly and becomes more oval in shape as it fills with urine. APR

(b, top) ©Victor P. Eroschenko; (b, bottom) ©McGraw-Hill Education/Alvin Telser, photographer

Clinical View 27.3

Renal Calculi

A **renal calculus** (kal′kyū-lŭs, pl., *calculi;* pebbles), or *kidney stone,* is formed from crystalline minerals that build up in the kidney. Over 75% of calculi contain calcium, in combination with either oxalate or phosphate.

Causes and risk factors for kidney stone formation include inadequate fluid intake and dehydration, frequent urinary tract infections, reduced urinary flow and volume, and certain abnormal chemical or mineral levels in the urine. Males tend to develop stones more often than females.

If the renal calculi are very small, they are asymptomatic, and the person excretes them without ever realizing it. However, a larger stone can become obstructed in the kidney, renal pelvis, or ureter. The term **urolithiasis** (yūr′ō-li-thī′ă-sis; *lithos* = stone) refers to the presence of renal calculi anywhere along the urinary tract. Symptoms include severe, cramping pain along the "loin-to-groin" region and possibly nausea and vomiting. The epithelium of the ureter becomes inflamed as it tries to push the stone along its path, resulting in blood in the urine, called **hematuria** (hē′mă-tyū′rē-a).

Most stones smaller than about 4 millimeters in diameter eventually pass through the urinary tract on their own once the patient drinks plenty of water (2–3 quarts per day) to assist movement. But if the stone is too large (more than 8 millimeters in diameter) and doesn't pass on its own, medical intervention is required. The most common treatment is **lithotripsy** (lith′ō-trip′sē; *tresis* = boring), whereby ultrasound or shock waves are directed toward the stones to pulverize them into smaller particles that can be expelled in the urine. Alternatively, using **ureteroscopy,** a scope is inserted from the urethra into the urinary bladder and ureter to break up and remove the stone. If these treatments aren't viable, traditional surgery may be required.

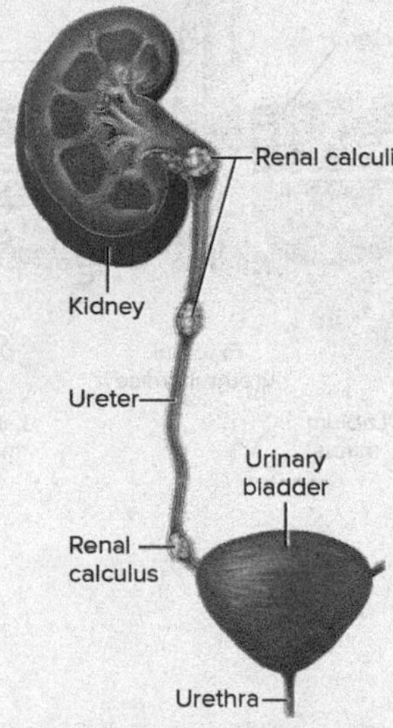

Renal calculi may become lodged at various sites along the urinary tract.

The **adventitia** is the outer layer of areolar connective tissue of the urinary bladder. A peritoneal membrane covers only the superior surface of the urinary bladder, and in this superior region, the peritoneum plus the connective tissue forms a serosa.

Arterial blood vessels extend to the urinary bladder and penetrate its wall from branches of the internal iliac artery. Venous blood drains into the internal iliac veins.

27.3c Urethra

The **urethra** (yū-rē′thr ă) is a fibromuscular tube that originates at the neck of the urinary bladder and conducts urine to the exterior of the body (**figure 27.11**). The luminal lining of the urethra is a protective mucous membrane that houses clusters of mucin-producing cells called urethral glands. Bundles of smooth muscle fibers surround the mucosa and help propel urine to the outside of the body.

Two urethral sphincters restrict the release of urine until the pressure within the urinary bladder is high enough and voluntary activities needed to release the urine are activated. The **internal urethral sphincter** is the involuntary, superior sphincter surrounding the neck of the bladder, where the urethra originates. This sphincter is a circular thickening of the detrusor muscle and is controlled by the autonomic nervous system. The **external urethral sphincter** is inferior to the internal urethral sphincter and is composed of circularly arranged skeletal muscle fibers. This sphincter is a voluntary sphincter controlled by the somatic nervous system. This is the muscle children learn to control when they become "toilet-trained."

The male and female urethras differ in length and morphology.

Female Urethra

The female urethra has a single function: to transport urine to the exterior of the body. The lumen of the female urethra is primarily lined with a stratified squamous epithelium. The urethra is 3 to 5 centimeters long, and opens to the outside of the body at the external urethral orifice located in the female perineum.

Male Urethra

The male urethra has two functions—urinary and reproductive—because it serves as a passageway for both urine and semen, but not at the same time. It is about 18 to 20 centimeters long and is partitioned into three segments: the prostatic urethra, the membranous urethra, and the spongy urethra.

The **prostatic** (pros-tat′ik) **urethra** (figure 27.11 *b*) is about 3 to 4 centimeters long and is the most dilatable portion of the urethra. It extends through the prostate gland, immediately inferior to the male bladder, where multiple small prostatic ducts enter it. The urethra in this region is lined by a transitional epithelium, with many blood vessels in the underlying dense irregular connective tissue. Two smooth muscle bundles surround the mucosa: an internal longitudinal bundle and an external circular bundle. The external circular muscular bundles are a continuation of the thickened circular region of smooth muscle forming the internal urethral sphincter at the bladder outlet.

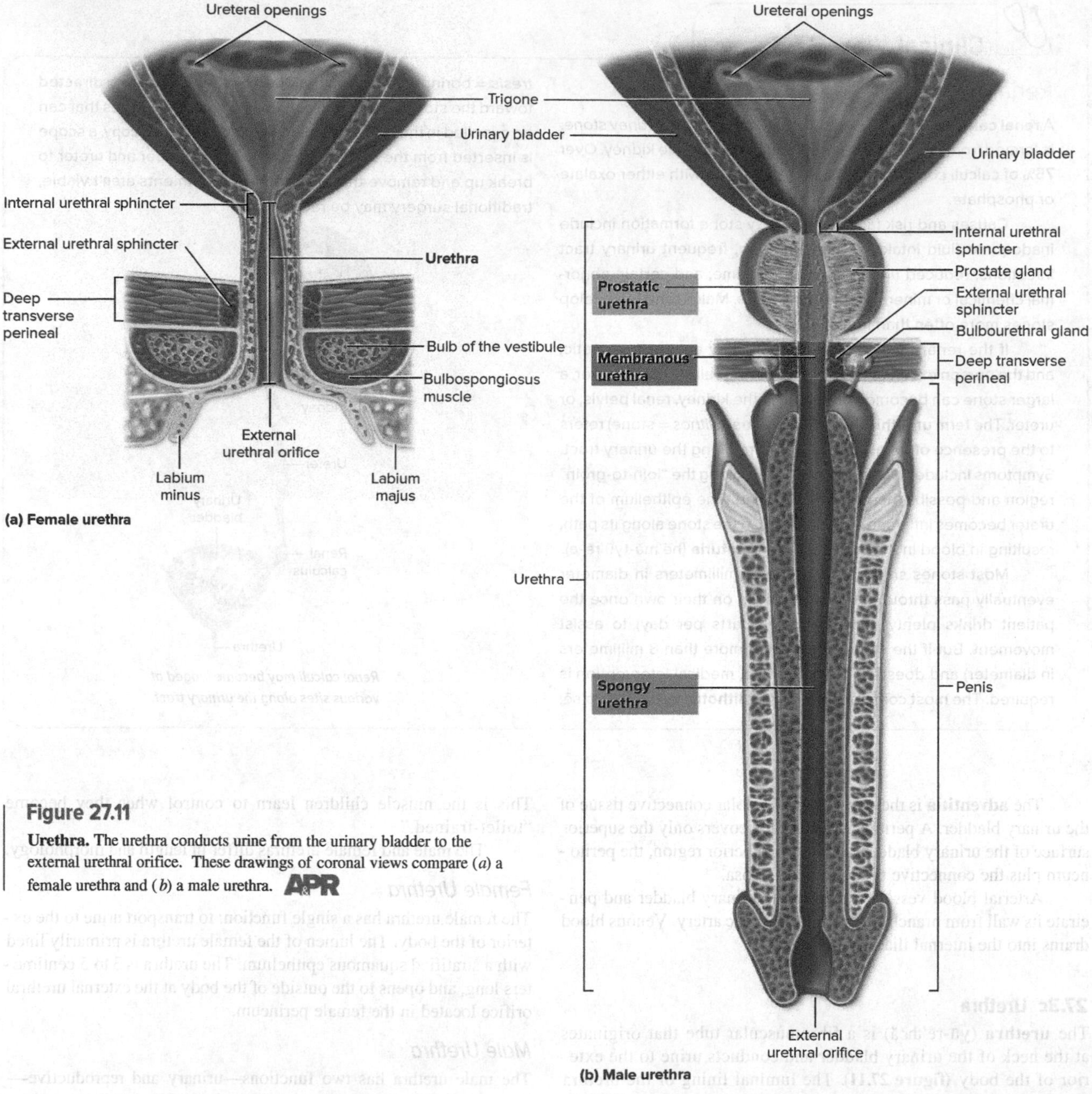
Ureteral openings
Trigone
Urinary bladder
Internal urethral sphincter
External urethral sphincter
Urethra
Deep transverse perineal
Bulb of the vestibule
Bulbospongiosus muscle
External urethral orifice
Labium minus
Labium majus
(a) Female urethra
Ureteral openings
Urinary bladder
Internal urethral sphincter
Prostate gland
Prostatic urethra
External urethral sphincter
Bulbourethral gland
Membranous urethra
Deep transverse perineal
Urethra
Spongy urethra
Penis
External urethral orifice
(b) Male urethra

Figure 27.11

Urethra. The urethra conducts urine from the urinary bladder to the external urethral orifice. These drawings of coronal views compare (*a*) a female urethra and (*b*) a male urethra. APR

The **membranous** (mem′bră-nŭs) **urethra** is the shortest and least dilatable portion of the male urethra. It extends from the inferior surface of the prostate gland and is surrounded by skeletal muscle fibers that form the external urethral sphincter of the urinary bladder. The epithelium in this region is often either stratified columnar or pseudostratified columnar.

The **spongy** (spŭn′jē) **urethra** is the longest part (15 centimeters) of the male urethra. It is encased within a cylinder of erectile tissue in the penis called the corpus spongiosum, and extends to the **external urethral orifice.** The proximal part of the spongy urethra is lined by a pseudostratified columnar epithelium, whereas the distal part has a lining of stratified squamous epithelium. APR

27.3d Micturition

The expulsion of urine from the bladder is called **micturition** (mik′ch ū-rish′ŭn; *micturio* = to desire to make water) or **urination** (yūr′i-nā′shŭn). Micturition is initiated by a complex sequence of events called the **micturition reflex.** Micturition is initiated when the bladder fills with at least 200–300 ml of urine. This volume distends

Clinical View 27.4

Urinary Tract Infections

A **urinary tract infection (UTI)** occurs when bacteria (most commonly *E. coli*) or fungi enter and multiply within the urinary tract. Women are more prone to UTIs because they have a short urethra that is close to the anus, allowing bacteria from the GI tract to more readily enter the female urethra. Sexual intercourse or medical use of a urinary catheter also increases the risk of UTIs in both sexes.

A UTI often develops first in the urethra, an inflammation called **urethritis** (yū′rĕ-thrī′tis). If the infection spreads to the urinary bladder, **cystitis** (sis-tī′tis) results. Occasionally, bacteria from an untreated UTI can spread up the ureters to the kidneys, a condition termed **pyelonephritis** (pī′ĕ-lō-ne-frī′tis).

Symptoms of a UTI include difficult and painful urination, called **dysuria** (dis-yū′rē-ă; *dys* = bad, difficult); frequent urination; and a feeling of uncomfortable pressure in the pubic region. If the infection spreads to the kidneys, then sharp back and flank pain, fever, and occasionally nausea and vomiting occur. A UTI can be diagnosed through **urinalysis** (yūr′i-nal′i-sis), a test of the urine that can reveal the presence of inflammatory cells, blood, and bacteria or fungi. Appropriate antibiotic therapy cures most UTIs caused by bacteria.

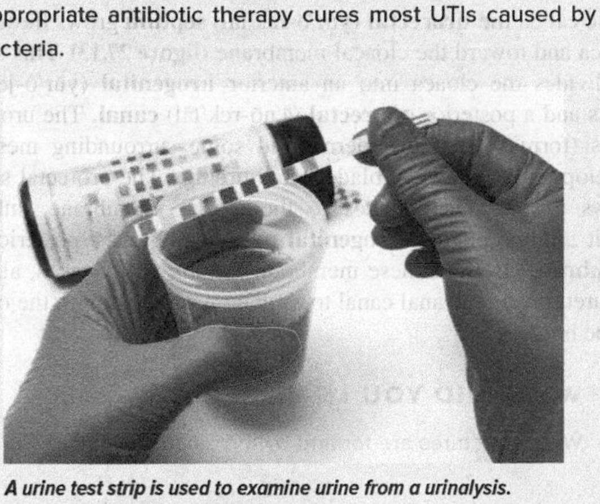

A urine test strip is used to examine urine from a urinalysis.

Alexander Raths/Shutterstock

the urinary bladder, activating baroreceptors (stretch receptors) in the bladder wall that signal the micturition center in the pons. This center oversees the autonomic innervation involved in micturition. Pelvic splanchnic nerves (parasympathetic nerves) from spinal cord segments S2–S4 stimulate the detrusor muscle to contract and the internal urethral sphincter to relax (open). Thus, parasympathetic innervation stimulates micturition.

In infants and individuals who have lost the conscious control of urination, the external urethral sphincter also opens and urine is expelled from the body. In contrast, individuals who are "toilet trained" are able to control the timing of urination via conscious decision (because the external urethral sphincter is controlled by the somatic nervous system). Once the urinary bladder is empty, the detrusor muscle relaxes and the sphincters (both internal and external) contract (close).

Sympathetic axons from the T11–L2 segments of the spinal cord inhibit contraction of the detrusor muscle and stimulate the contraction (closing) of the internal urethral sphincter. Thus, sympathetic innervation inhibits micturition.

WHAT DID YOU LEARN?

9. Draw a cross section of the ureter. Label the tunics and the type of epithelium lining its lumen.
10. What is the trigone of the bladder, and how is it different structurally from the rest of the bladder?
11. What are the three components of the male urethra, and where are they located?
12. How does an infant's micturition differ from the micturition of a toilet-trained individual?

27.4 Aging and the Urinary System

✓ Learning Objective

11. Describe the changes in the urinary system as we age.

Changes in the size and functioning of the kidneys normally begin in our third decade of life and continue thereafter. With age comes a reduced blood flow to the kidneys and a decrease in the number of functional nephrons. The reduction in blood flow contributes to a decreased glomerular filtration rate; consequently, both reabsorption and secretion are reduced. The loss of nephrons results in a diminished ability to filter and cleanse the blood as well as a decrease in the number of target cells within the kidneys that are capable of responding to stimulation by aldosterone or antidiuretic hormone. Thus, the ability to control blood volume and blood pressure is reduced.

Structural changes in the urinary bladder also affect the storage and voiding of urine. The bladder decreases in size, and smooth muscle tone in the bladder wall gradually diminishes, which may lead to more frequent urination. Sometimes, there is a delay in noticing the urge to urinate. Additionally, control of the urethral sphincters—and eventually even control of micturition—may be lost.

The inability to control the expulsion of urine is called **incontinence.** It most commonly occurs among the elderly, and most frequently in women. The extent of the incontinence ranges from occasional urine leakage to complete inability to retain urine. There are two categories of incontinence: (1) stress incontinence often occurs during vigorous exercise or strenuous coughing, and (2) urge incontinence results from immediate bladder contraction after feeling a strong need to urinate. Causes of incontinence include severe weight gain, complications following pelvic surgery, coincidence with uncontrolled diabetes, severe constipation, pelvic prolapse as a result of pregnancy, and enlarged prostate.

WHAT DID YOU LEARN?

13. What are the possible consequences of aging on urine production?

27.5 Development of the Urinary System

✓ Learning Objective

12. Explain the embryonic and fetal development of the urinary system.

Most of the urinary system and the reproductive system (discussed in section 28.5) form from the **intermediate mesoderm** of the embryo. Intermediate mesoderm is located between the somites (paraxial mesoderm) and the lateral plate mesoderm. Thus, the urinary system and the reproductive system are linked in both their development and their postnatal functions.

27.5a Kidney and Ureter Development

Some of the intermediate mesoderm forms bilateral longitudinal ridges, each called a **urogenital ridge.** The urogenital ridges ultimately will form parts of the urinary system and internal reproductive organs. The urinary parts of the urogenital ridges give rise to three sets of excretory organs, which become increasingly more advanced. The first excretory organs, each called a **pronephros** (prō-nef′ros; before kidney; pl., *pronephroi*), appear in the cervical region of the embryo and seem to be vestigial—that is, they have no known function in humans. They appear in the early fourth week and quickly degenerate by the end of that same week.

The second set of organs, each called a **mesonephros** (pl., *mesonephroi*), appears just before the pronephroi degenerate. These structures are formed from tissue comprising the urogenital ridge in the thoracic and lumbar regions. Each mesonephros is composed of multiple saclike segments. A **mesonephric** (mez′ō-nef′rik) **duct** drains urine from each mesonephros to the developing urinary bladder. The mesonephros (or "intermediate" kidney) persists until about week 10 of development.

Early in the fifth week, the final set of excretory organs, each called a **metanephros** (or *permanent kidney*), forms **(figure 27.12)**. Each metanephros (pl., *metanephroi*) forms a functional adult kidney and takes over urine production by week 10. The components of the metanephros form from two specific structures: the ureteric bud and the metanephric mesoderm **(table 27.3)**. The **ureteric** (yū′rē-ter′ik) **bud** forms as a separate outgrowth from the caudal end of the mesonephric duct and gives rise to the ureter, renal pelvis, calyces, and collecting ducts of the kidney. The **metanephric** (met′ă-nef′rik) **mesoderm** develops from intermediate mesoderm in the sacral region of the embryo, and forms the nephron components of the kidney: the glomerular capsule, the proximal convoluted tubule, the nephron loop, and the distal convoluted tubule. The metanephric mesoderm will not grow and develop unless the ureteric bud grows into and merges with it.

As the ureteric bud grows and merges with the metanephric mesoderm, the ureteric bud undergoes a branching pattern (figure 27.12 *b*). The first set of branches forms the major calyces in week 6, and the second set of branches forms the minor calyces in week 7. This branching pattern continues until the tiny collecting ducts are formed in the kidney, so that by week 32, well over 1 million collecting tubules have formed. As the calyces and collecting ducts form, they signal the metanephric mesoderm to grow and develop into the nephron components. By week 10 of development, the metanephros is able to both produce and expel urine. Fetal urine supplements amniotic fluid production.

During weeks 6–9, the developing kidneys migrate from their position in the pelvic cavity to a more superior position in the lumbar portion of the abdominal cavity (figure 27.12*c*). The mechanisms for this ascent are not known, but may be related to differential growth of the embryo. As the kidneys ascend, they obtain temporary blood vessels from the nearby vasculature. When the kidneys migrate further, the older temporary blood vessels regress and degenerate, and new blood vessels for the kidney form. Eventually, by week 9, the kidneys complete migration to the lumbar region and acquire their permanent renal arteries branching from the descending abdominal aorta.

27.5b Urinary Bladder and Urethra Development

The urinary bladder and urethra develop from the distal part of the hindgut called the **cloaca** (klō-ā′kă; sewer). The cloaca forms not only the epithelium of the urinary bladder and urethra, but also the rectum and anal canal. The cloaca is separated from the outside of the body by a thin **cloacal membrane.** Extending superiorly from the cloaca to the umbilicus is a thin, tubular hindgut extension called the **allantois** (ă-lan′tō-is). (By week 6, the allantois becomes a fibrous cord called the **urachus,** and in adults the remnant of this cord is called the median umbilical ligament.)

Between weeks 4 and 7 of development, a mass of mesodermal tissue called the **urorectal** (yur′ō-rek′tăl) **septum** grows through the cloaca and toward the cloacal membrane **(figure 27.13)**. This septum subdivides the cloaca into an anterior **urogenital** (yūr′ō-jen′i-tăl) **sinus** and a posterior **anorectal** (ā′nō-rek′tăl) **canal.** The urogenital sinus (formed from endoderm) and some surrounding mesoderm develop into the urinary bladder and urethra. The urorectal septum grows toward and attaches to the cloacal membrane, subdividing it into an anterior **urogenital membrane** and a posterior **anal membrane.** Both of these membranes rupture by week 8, allowing the urethra and the anal canal to each communicate with the outside of the body.

WHAT DID YOU LEARN?

14. What structures are formed by the cloaca?

Table 27.3	Embryonic Derivations of Ureter and Kidney Structures
Ureteric Bud Origin	**Metanephric Mesoderm Origin**
Ureter	Glomerular capsules
Renal pelvis	Proximal convoluted tubules
Major calyces	Nephron loops
Minor calyces	Distal convoluted tubules
Collecting tubules and ducts	

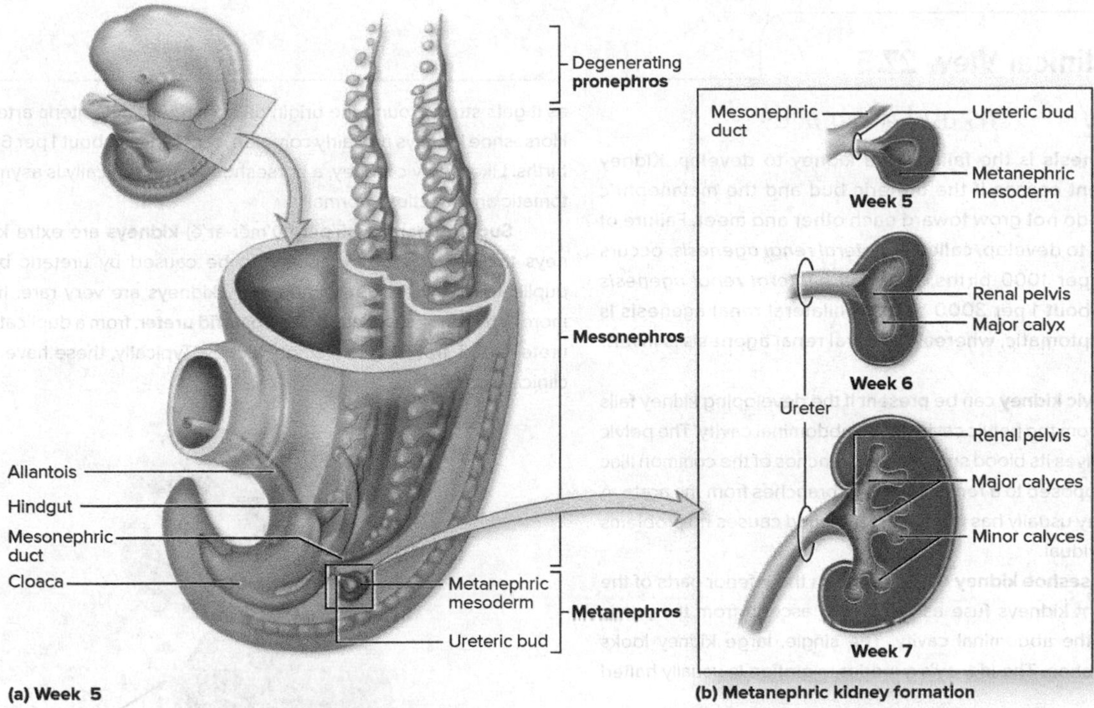

Degenerating pronephros
Mesonephros
Metanephros
Allantois
Hindgut
Mesonephric duct
Cloaca
Metanephric mesoderm
Ureteric bud
(a) Week 5
Mesonephric duct
Ureteric bud
Metanephric mesoderm
Week 5
Renal pelvis
Major calyx
Week 6
Ureter
Renal pelvis
Major calyces
Minor calyces
Week 7
(b) Metanephric kidney formation

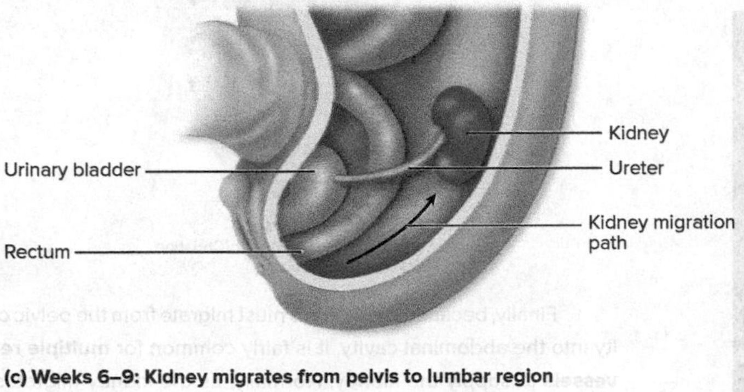

Kidney
Urinary bladder
Ureter
Kidney migration path
Rectum
(c) Weeks 6–9: Kidney migrates from pelvis to lumbar region

Figure 27.12

Kidney Development. The kidneys form from the urogenital ridges of the embryo. (*a*) By week 5, the pronephroi have regressed, and the mesonephroi begin producing urine. The metanephric kidneys, which eventually form the permanent kidneys, also begin to form. (*b*) The development of the metanephric kidney is shown between weeks 5 and 7. (*c*) Between weeks 6 and 9, the kidney migrates superiorly from the pelvic cavity to the lumbar region on the posterior abdominal wall.

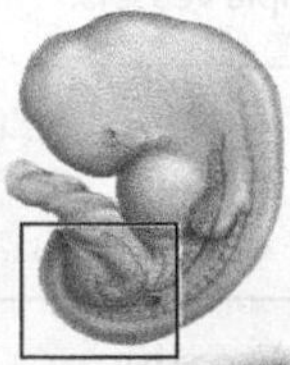

Figure 27.13

Bladder Development. (*a*) A common cloaca unites the distal part of the gut tube with the future urinary bladder. The cloaca is separated from the outside of the body by a thin cloacal membrane. (*b*) A tissue mass called the urorectal septum grows inferiorly and partitions the cloaca into an anteriorly located urogenital sinus (which forms the urinary bladder and urethra) and an anorectal canal.

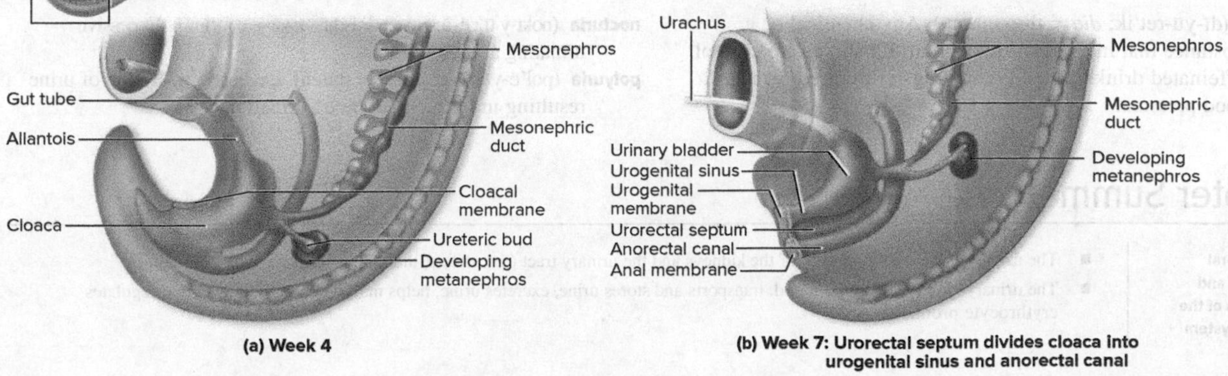

Mesonephros
Gut tube
Allantois
Mesonephric duct
Cloacal membrane
Cloaca
Ureteric bud
Developing metanephros
(a) Week 4
Urachus
Mesonephros
Mesonephric duct
Urinary bladder
Urogenital sinus
Urogenital membrane
Developing metanephros
Urorectal septum
Anorectal canal
Anal membrane
(b) Week 7: Urorectal septum divides cloaca into urogenital sinus and anorectal canal

Clinical View 27.5

Kidney Variations and Anomalies

Renal agenesis is the failure of a kidney to develop. Kidney development ceases if the ureteric bud and the metanephric mesoderm do not grow toward each other and meet. Failure of one kidney to develop, called *unilateral renal agenesis,* occurs in about 1 per 1000 births, whereas *bilateral renal agenesis* occurs in about 1 per 3000 births. Unilateral renal agenesis is often asymptomatic, whereas bilateral renal agenesis is invariably fatal.

A **pelvic kidney** can be present if the developing kidney fails to migrate from the pelvic cavity to the abdominal cavity. The pelvic kidney receives its blood supply from branches of the common iliac artery, as opposed to a renal artery that branches from the aorta. A pelvic kidney usually has normal function and causes no problems for the individual.

A **horseshoe kidney** develops when the inferior parts of the left and right kidneys fuse as they try to ascend from the pelvic cavity into the abdominal cavity. The single, large kidney looks like a horseshoe. The kidney's superior migration is usually halted as it gets stuck around the origin of the inferior mesenteric artery. Horseshoe kidneys are fairly common, occurring in about 1 per 600 births. Like a pelvic kidney, a horseshoe kidney typically is asymptomatic and functions normally.

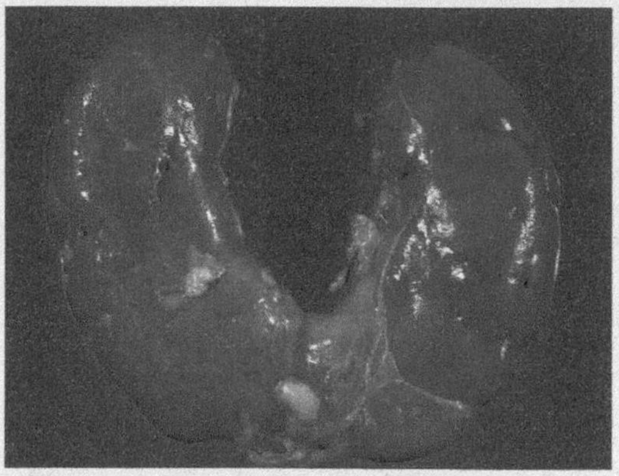

Horseshoe kidney is a fairly common anatomic variation.
©McGraw-Hill Education

Supernumerary (sū'pĕr-nū'mĕr-ār'ē) **kidneys** are extra kidneys that develop. They appear to be caused by ureteric bud duplication. However, supernumerary kidneys are very rare. It is more common to see a **duplicated** or **bifid ureter**, from a duplicated ureteric bud, traveling to a single kidney. Typically, these have no clinical significance.

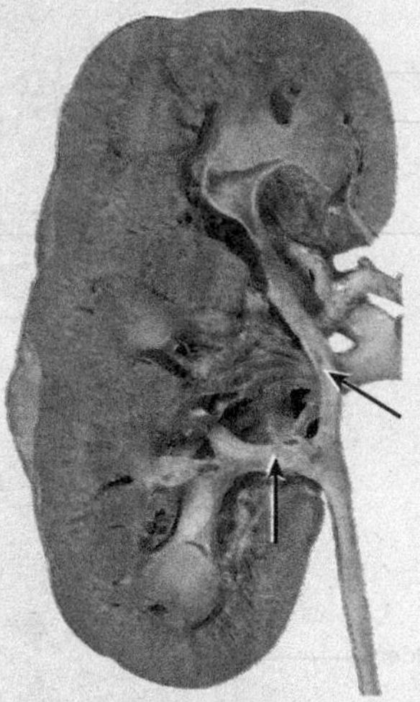

Bifid ureter (arrows).
©McGraw-Hill Education/Christine Eckel, photographer

Finally, because the kidneys must migrate from the pelvic cavity into the abdominal cavity, it is fairly common for **multiple renal vessels** to supply the kidney. Normally, as the kidney migrates, it acquires temporary vessels from the nearby blood supply, and its older, inferior vessels regress and degenerate. If these temporary vessels fail to degenerate, the kidney is left with multiple vessels.

Clinical Terms

diuretic (dī-yū-ret'ik; *dia* = throughout) Any chemical or substance that increases urine output. Examples are alcohol, caffeinated drinks, and diuretic drugs prescribed for high blood pressure.

nocturia (nokt-y ū'rē-ă; *nox* = night, *ouron* = urine) Excessive urinating at night.

polyuria (pol'ē-yū'rē-ă; *polys* = much) Excessive secretion of urine resulting in frequent, copious urination.

Chapter Summary

27.1 General Structure and Functions of the Urinary System	■ The urinary system is composed of the kidneys and the urinary tract (the ureters, the urinary bladder, and the urethra). ■ The urinary system filters the blood, transports and stores urine, excretes urine, helps maintain blood volume, and regulates erythrocyte production.

27.2 Kidneys

27.2a Gross and Sectional Anatomy of the Kidney

- The kidneys are surrounded by a strong fibrous capsule, perinephric fat, renal fascia, and paranephric fat.
- The kidney contains the renal cortex (peripheral) and the renal medulla (central). The renal medulla is subdivided into renal pyramids, each with an apex called a renal papilla that projects into the funnel-shaped minor calyx.
- Urine deposited within the minor calyx flows into the major calyx and then into the renal pelvis.

27.2b Blood Supply to the Kidney

- Blood is transported to the kidneys in renal arteries, which divide into segmental arteries that form interlobar arteries, which give rise to arcuate arteries. Arcuate arteries branch into interlobular arteries, which supply the glomerulus via the afferent arteriole.
- Blood leaving the glomerulus follows this path: efferent arteriole, peritubular capillaries or vasa recta, interlobular veins, arcuate veins, interlobar veins, and renal vein.

27.2c Innervation of the Kidney

- The renal plexus innervates each kidney with sympathetic and parasympathetic axons.

27.2d Nephrons

- The nephron is the structural and functional unit of the kidney. Nephrons are composed of a renal corpuscle and a renal tubule (i.e., proximal convoluted tubule, nephron loop and distal convoluted tubule).
- The renal corpuscle is the site of blood filtration.
- The renal tubule reabsorbs almost all plasma proteins, nutrients, and ions from the tubular fluid.

27.2e Collecting Tubules and Collecting Ducts: How Tubular Fluid Becomes Urine

- Distal convoluted tubules empty into collecting tubules that empty into collecting ducts, which merge to empty into the papillary duct that opens at the edge of the renal papilla and releases urine into the minor calyx.

27.2f Juxtaglomerular Apparatus

- The juxtaglomerular apparatus has granular cells (smooth muscle cells of the afferent arteriole) and a macula densa (distal convoluted tubule epithelial cells adjacent to the afferent arteriole). It releases renin to regulate blood pressure.

27.3 Urinary Tract

- The urinary tract consists of paired ureters, a urinary bladder, and a single urethra.

27.3a Ureters

- The ureters are retroperitoneal, fibromuscular tubes that conduct urine from the kidneys to the urinary bladder.
- The ureteral mucosa has a transitional epithelium; the muscularis consists of two layers of smooth muscle.

27.3b Urinary Bladder

- The urinary bladder stores urine.
- The mucosa is formed by a transitional epithelium; the submucosa is formed by dense irregular connective tissue, and the muscularis is composed of three layers of smooth muscle bundles (the detrusor muscle).
- The adventitia is the external layer of the urinary bladder.

27.3c Urethra

- The urethra conducts urine from the bladder to the exterior of the body.
- An internal urethral sphincter (involuntary) and an external urethral sphincter (voluntary) control the voiding of urine.
- The female urethra is relatively short, and has a single function: to transport urine.
- The male urethra is about 18–20 centimeters long and serves as a passageway for both urine and semen.

27.3d Micturition

- Parasympathetic innervation promotes micturition, and sympathetic innervation inhibits micturition.

27.4 Aging and the Urinary System

- Structural changes in the kidneys and urinary bladder affect the production, storage, and voiding of urine.
- Incontinence is the inability to control micturition.

27.5 Development of the Urinary System

- Most of the early urinary system and the reproductive system form from the intermediate mesoderm.

27.5a Kidney and Ureter Development

- The intermediate mesoderm condenses along the posterior body wall and forms a urogenital ridge on each side of the vertebral column.
- Three successive sets of excretory organs form: the pronephros, the mesonephros, and the metanephros (or permanent kidney).

27.5b Urinary Bladder and Urethra Development

- The urinary bladder and urethra develop from the distal part of the hindgut called the cloaca.

Challenge Yourself

Actively write or type your answers in a separate document to reinforce your learning, before checking your answers.

Multiple Choice

Select the best answer from the four choices provided.

1. Which urinary system organ is responsible for filtering the blood?
   a. ureter
   b. urinary bladder
   c. kidney
   d. urethra
2. Which statement correctly describes the urinary bladder anatomy?
   a. The bladder neck is surrounded by the external urethral sphincter.
   b. The detrusor muscle contains only two layers of smooth muscle.
   c. The bladder is lined with transitional epithelium.
   d. The bladder receives urine from the kidneys via the two urethras.
3. Tubular fluid from the proximal convoluted tubule next travels to which structure?
   a. capsular space
   b. collecting duct
   c. distal convoluted tubule
   d. nephron loop
4. What is the apex of the renal pyramid called?
   a. renal pelvis
   b. renal papilla
   c. renal column
   d. renal capsule
5. Which arteries are located at the corticomedullary junction of the kidney?
   a. arcuate arteries
   b. segmental arteries
   c. interlobar arteries
   d. renal arteries
6. Which urinary system structure is formed from the ureteric bud (and not from metanephric mesoderm)?
   a. glomerular capsule
   b. minor calyx
   c. nephron loop
   d. proximal convoluted tubule
7. Urine in a major calyx of the kidney next travels to which structure?
   a. ureter
   b. minor calyx
   c. urinary bladder
   d. renal pelvis
8. Which structure is controlled by the somatic motor nervous system?
   a. muscularis of the ureter
   b. external urethral sphincter
   c. internal urethral sphincter
   d. detrusor muscle of the urinary bladder
9. Reabsorption is the movement of fluid and solutes from which of the following?
   a. filtrate into the glomerular capillaries
   b. tubular fluid into the capsular space
   c. tubular fluid into the peritubular capillaries
   d. blood vessels into the collecting ducts
10. The micturition reflex controls which of the following?
    a. urine formation
    b. voiding of the filled bladder
    c. reabsorption of glucose from filtrate
    d. filling of the urinary bladder

Content Review

1. What are the basic functions of the urinary system?
2. Describe the connective tissue coverings that surround the kidney, from internal to external. Why are these coverings especially important to kidney structure and function?
3. Map the flow of blood into and out of the kidney. List which structures carry oxygenated blood and which carry deoxygenated blood. In addition, list the structures responsible for gas exchange and reabsorption of materials from the filtrate.
4. Describe the anatomic structure of the glomerulus and the visceral layer of the glomerular capsule.
5. What microscopic structures are located predominantly in the cortex of the kidney? Which structures are located primarily in the medulla of the kidney?
6. Describe the structure of the tunics of the ureter, and explain how those tunics function to transport urine.
7. What prevents urine stored in the urinary bladder from being forced back through the ureters to the kidney?
8. In what ways do the male and female urethras differ?
9. Trace the course of fluid movement, beginning with the production of filtrate in the renal corpuscle and ending with the expulsion of urine from the urethra.
10. What is incontinence, and why is it more prevalent in older individuals?

Developing Critical Reasoning

1. While drinking many beers one night, Jason noticed that he had to urinate more frequently. The following morning, Jason's mouth felt dry, and he had a headache. A friend told Jason that his symptoms were the result of dehydration. Based upon your knowledge of the urinary system, how and why did Jason become dehydrated? What hormone normally regulates the amount of water in the urine, and how did the alcohol interfere with this hormone's function?

2. Males who suffer from either benign prostatic hypertrophy (noncancerous prostate gland enlargement) or prostate cancer often have problems with urination. Based upon your knowledge of the male urethra, hypothesize why these urination problems occur.

3. In boxing, a punch to the lumbar region of the back is illegal because of the potential injury it can cause. What structure do you think could be injured by this type of punch, and what symptoms might develop?

Answers to "What Do You Think?"

1. Without functioning kidneys, the blood would not be able to be filtered, so waste products would accumulate. This accumulation of toxic material in the blood leads to death unless the materials are filtered out.
2. ADH is secreted when the body is dehydrated, so the body can conserve what remaining water it has.
3. When we are lying down, gravity is unable to passively transport urine to the urinary bladder. Thus, peristalsis is also needed so that urine can be actively pumped from the ureters to the urinary bladder no matter what position the body is in.

28 Reproductive System

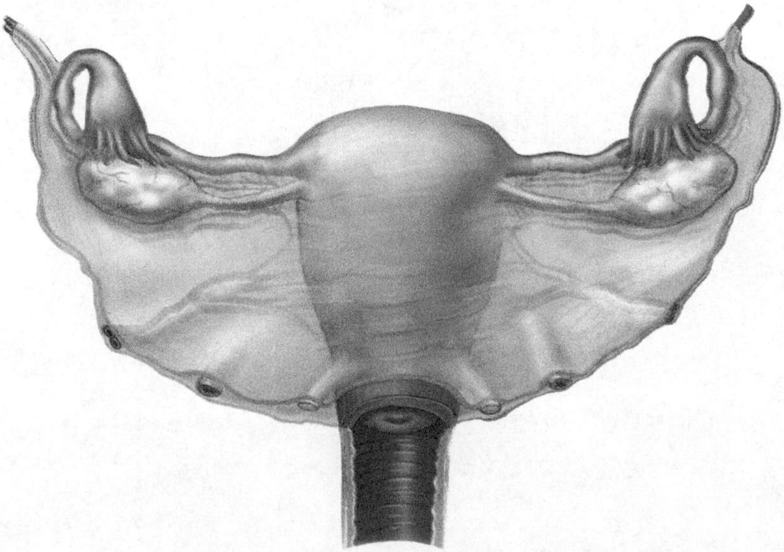

Outline

Anatomy & Physiology Revealed 4.0

MODULE 14: REPRODUCTIVE SYSTEM

The female and male reproductive systems provide the means for the sexual maturation of each individual and produce the special cells necessary to propagate the next generation. We first discuss the general similarities between the two reproductive systems and then focus upon the specific structures and functions of each system.

28.1 Comparison of the Female and Male Reproductive Systems

✓ **Learning Objectives**

1. Describe the similarities between the female and male reproductive systems.
2. Explain the events of puberty.
3. Identify and describe the components of the perineum in females and males.

The female and male reproductive systems have obvious differences, and yet they share several general characteristics. For example, some mature reproductive system structures are derived from common developmental structures (primordia) and serve a common function in adults. Such structures are called **homologues** (hōm′ō-log; *homo* = same or alike, *logos* = relation). The structures listed in **table 28.1** are described in detail in sections 28.2 and 28.3.

Both reproductive systems have primary sex organs called **gonads** (gō′nad; *gone* = seed)—ovaries in females and testes in males. The gonads produce sex cells called **gametes** (gam′ēt; wife or husband), which unite at fertilization to form a new individual. Female gametes are called oocytes, whereas male gametes are called sperm. In addition, the gonads produce large amounts of **sex hormones** (estrogen and progesterone in the female and androgens in the male), which affect maturation, development, and changes in the activity of the reproductive system organs.

Both sexes have accessory reproductive organs, including ducts to carry gametes away from the gonads toward the site of fertilization (in females) or simply to the outside of the body (in males). Fertilization occurs when female and male gametes fuse. Sexual union is known as **copulation** (kop′y ū-lā′shŭn; *copulatio* = a joining), **coitus** (kō′i′tŭs; to come together), or **sexual intercourse.** If fertilization occurs, then the support, protection, and nourishment of the developing human occurs within the female reproductive tract.

Both the female and male reproductive systems are primarily nonfunctional and dormant until a time in adolescence known as puberty. At **puberty** (pyū′bĕr-tē; *puber* = grown up), external sex characteristics become more prominent, such as breast enlargement, penis and scrotum enlargement, pubic hair growth, and the reproductive organs become fully functional. Also, the gametes begin to mature, and the gonads start to secrete their sex hormones.

Puberty is initiated when the hypothalamus significantly increases **GnRH (gonadotropin-releasing hormone)** secretion (see table 20.2). GnRH acts on specific cells in the anterior pituitary and stimulates them to release **FSH (follicle-stimulating hormone)** and **LH (luteinizing hormone).** (Prior to puberty, FSH and LH are virtually nonexistent.) As levels of FSH and LH increase, the gonads produce significant levels of sex hormones and start the processes of gamete maturation and sexual maturation.

Table 28.1 Reproductive System Homologues

Female Organ	Male Organ	Common Function(s)
Ovary	Testis	Produces gametes and sex hormones
Clitoris	Glans of penis	Contains erectile tissue that stimulates sexual arousal and climax
Labia minora	Body of penis	Contain erectile tissue that stimulates sexual arousal and climax
Labia majora	Scrotum	Protect and cover some reproductive structures
Greater vestibular gland	Bulbourethral gland	Secretes mucin for lubrication

Both reproductive systems produce gametes. However, the female reproductive tract typically releases a single gamete (secondary oocyte) monthly, whereas the male reproductive tract produces large numbers (100 million) of gametes (sperm) daily. Sperm are stored within the male reproductive tract for a short time, and if they are not expelled from the body within that period, they are resorbed.

Learning Strategy 28.1

A simplified flowchart of the endocrine pathway in puberty is as follows:

GnRH (from hypothalamus) → **FSH** and **LH** (from anterior pituitary) → Sex hormone release and gamete maturation (in the gonads).

28.1a Perineum

The **perineum** (per′i-nē′ŭm) is an area between the thighs that is bounded anteriorly by the pubic symphysis, laterally by the ischial tuberosities, and posteriorly by the coccyx (**figure 28.1**). This region appears diamond-shaped, with two distinct triangle bases formed by an imaginary horizontal line extending between the ischial tuberosities of the ossa coxae. Both triangles house specific structures in the floor of the trunk:

- The anterior triangle, called the **urogenital triangle,** contains the clitoris and the urethral and vaginal orifices in females and the base of the penis and the scrotum in males. Within the urogenital triangle are the muscles that surround the external genitalia, called the ischiocavernosus, bulbospongiosus, and superficial transverse perineal muscles (see section 11.5).
- The posterior triangle, called the **anal triangle,** is the location of the anus in both sexes. Surrounding the anus is the external anal sphincter.

The external anal sphincter, bulbospongiosus, and superficial transverse perineal muscles are partly anchored by a dense connective tissue structure called the **perineal body.** Review table 11.12 and figure 11.15 when learning these structures.

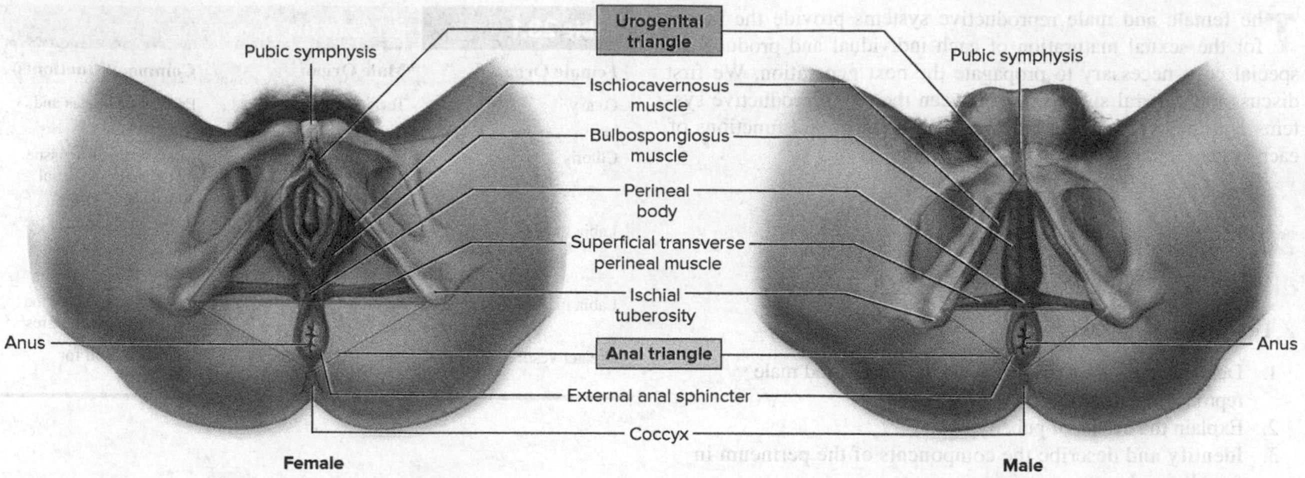

Figure 28.1
Perineum. The perineum is the diamond-shaped area between the thighs, extending from the pubis anteriorly to the coccyx posteriorly, and bordered laterally by the ischial tuberosities. An imaginary horizontal line extending from the ischial tuberosities subdivides the perineum into a urogenital triangle anteriorly and an anal triangle posteriorly. **APR**

WHAT DID YOU LEARN?

1. What is puberty?
2. Compare the structures in the female and male urogenital triangles.

28.2 Anatomy of the Female Reproductive System

✓ Learning Objectives

4. Describe the gross and microscopic anatomy of the ovaries.
5. Explain follicle development, the ovarian cycle, and the process of ovulation.
6. Describe the anatomy of the uterine tubes and their function.
7. Identify and describe the regions of the uterus, and outline the uterine cycle.
8. Describe the anatomy of the vagina and the external genitalia.
9. Identify and describe the gross and microscopic anatomy of the mammary glands.

A sagittal section through the female pelvis illustrates the internal reproductive structures and their relationships to the urinary bladder and rectum (**figure 28.2**). As the peritoneum folds around the various pelvic organs, it produces two major dead-end recesses, or pouches. The anterior **vesicouterine** (ves′i-k ō-yū′ter-in; *vesica* = bladder, *utero* = uterus) **pouch** forms the space between the urinary bladder and the uterus and the posterior **rectouterine** (rek′t ō-yū′ter-in) **pouch** forms the space between the uterus (anteriorly) and the rectum (posteriorly).

The primary sex organs of the female are the ovaries. The accessory reproductive organs include the uterine tubes, uterus, vagina, clitoris, and mammary glands.

28.2a Ovaries

The **ovaries** are paired, oval organs located within the pelvic cavity lateral to the uterus (**figure 28.3**). The ovaries in an adult are slightly larger than an almond—about 2 to 3 cm (centimeters) long, 2 cm wide, and 1 to 1.5 cm thick. Their size usually varies during each menstrual cycle as well as during pregnancy.

The ovaries are anchored within the pelvic cavity by specific cords and sheets of connective tissue. A double fold of peritoneum, called the **mesovarium** (mez′ō-vā′rē-ŭm; *mesos* = middle, *ovarium* = ovary), attaches to each ovary at its **hilum,** which is the anterior surface of the ovary where its blood vessels and nerves enter and leave the organ. The mesovarium secures each ovary to a **broad ligament,** which is a drape of peritoneum that hangs over the uterus. Each ovary is anchored to the lateral aspect of the uterus by an **ovarian ligament;** a **suspensory ligament** attaches to the lateral edge of each ovary and projects superolaterally to the pelvic wall. The ovarian blood vessels and nerves are housed within each suspensory ligament, and they join the ovary at its hilum. Smooth muscle fibers within both the mesovarium and the suspensory ligament contract at the time of ovulation to bring the ovaries into close proximity with the uterine tube openings.

Each ovary is supplied by an **ovarian artery** and an **ovarian vein.** The ovarian arteries are direct branches off the aorta, immediately inferior to the renal vessels. The ovarian veins exit the ovary and drain into either the inferior vena cava (right ovarian vein) or the left renal vein (left ovarian vein) (see section 23.3g). Traveling with the ovarian artery and vein are autonomic nerves. Sympathetic

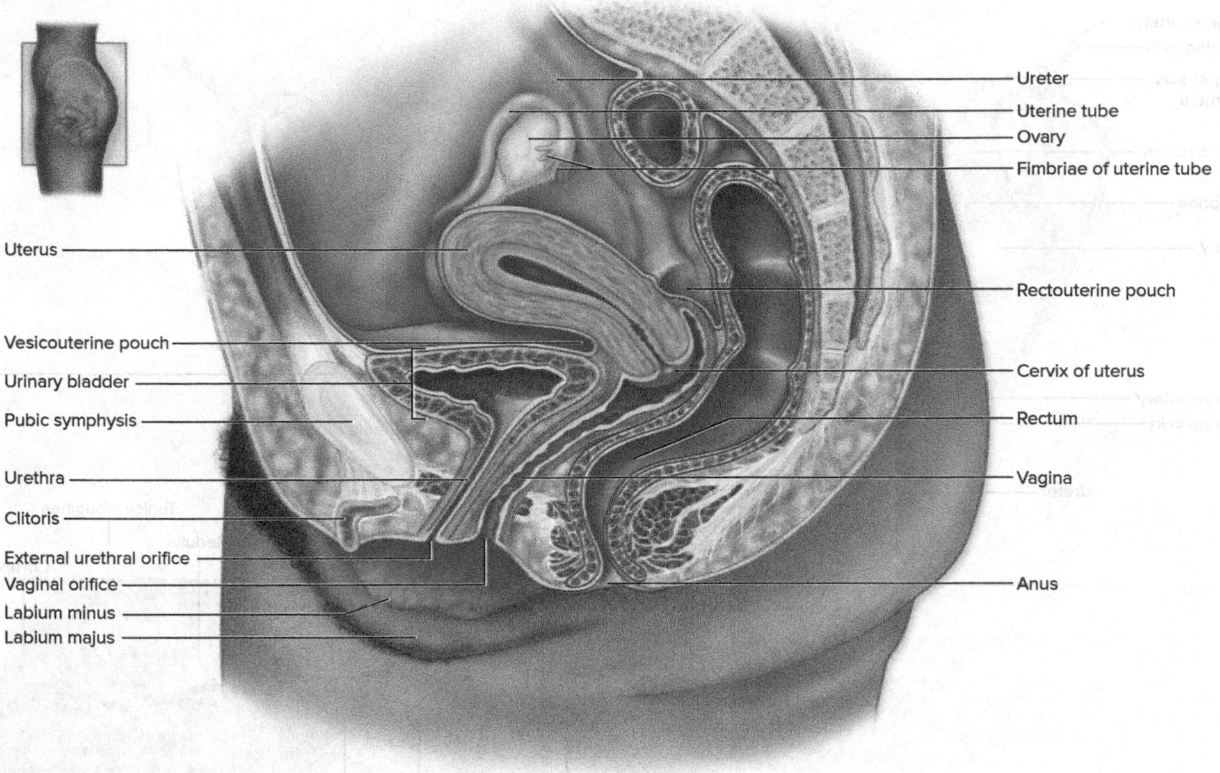
Ureter
Uterine tube
Ovary
Fimbriae of uterine tube
Uterus
Rectouterine pouch
Vesicouterine pouch
Urinary bladder
Cervix of uterus
Pubic symphysis
Rectum
Urethra
Vagina
Clitoris
External urethral orifice
Vaginal orifice
Anus
Labium minus
Labium majus

Figure 28.2

Sagittal Section of the Female Pelvic Region. A sagittal section of the female pelvis illustrates the position of the uterus with respect to the rectum and urinary bladder. APR

axons come from the T10 segments of the spinal cord, whereas parasympathetic axons come from CN X (vagus nerve) (see sections 18.4 and 18.3, respectively).

When an ovary is sectioned and viewed microscopically, many features are visible (**figure 28.4**). Surrounding the ovary is a thin, simple cuboidal epithelial layer called the **germinal epithelium,** so named because early anatomists erroneously thought it was the origin of the female germ (sex) cells. Deep to the germinal epithelium is a connective tissue capsule called the **tunica albuginea** (al-b ū-jin′ē-ă; *albugo* = white spot), which is homologous to the tunica albuginea of the testis. Deep to the tunica albuginea, the ovary can be partitioned into an outer **cortex** and an inner **medulla.** The cortex contains ovarian follicles, whereas the medulla is composed of areolar connective tissue and contains branches of the ovarian blood vessels, lymph vessels, and nerves.

Ovarian Follicles

Within the cortex are thousands of **ovarian follicles.** Ovarian follicles consist of an **oocyte** surrounded by **follicle cells** which support the oocyte. There are several different types of ovarian follicles, each representing a different stage of development (figure 28.4):

1. A **primordial follicle** is the most primitive type of ovarian follicle. Each primordial follicle consists of a **primary oocyte** surrounded by a single layer of *squamous* follicle cells. A primary oocyte is an oocyte that is arrested in the first meiotic prophase. About 1.5 million of these types of follicles are present in the ovaries at birth.
2. A **primary follicle** forms from a maturing primordial follicle. Each primary follicle consists of a primary oocyte surrounded by a single layer of *cuboidal* follicular cells, which are now called **granulosa cells.** A protective structure called the **zona** (zō′nă; zone) **pellucida** (pe-lū′sĭd-ă; *pellucidus* = allowing the passage of light) surrounds the oocyte. It is a translucent structure that is formed primarily by glycoproteins.
3. A **secondary follicle** forms from a primary follicle. Each secondary follicle contains a primary oocyte and many layers of granulosa cells. Some cells, called **thecal cells,** derived from connective tissue, develop around the periphery of the ovarian follicle.
4. An **antral follicle** (also called a *vesicular follicle,* or *tertiary ovarian follicle*) forms from a secondary follicle. A fluid-filled space called the **antrum** develops within the granulosa cells. The antrum contains a fluid that increases in volume as ovulation nears. Surrounding the primary oocyte and the zona pellucida is the corona radiata. The **corona** (kō-rō′nă; crown) **radiata** (rā-dē-ă′tă; radiating) is the innermost layer

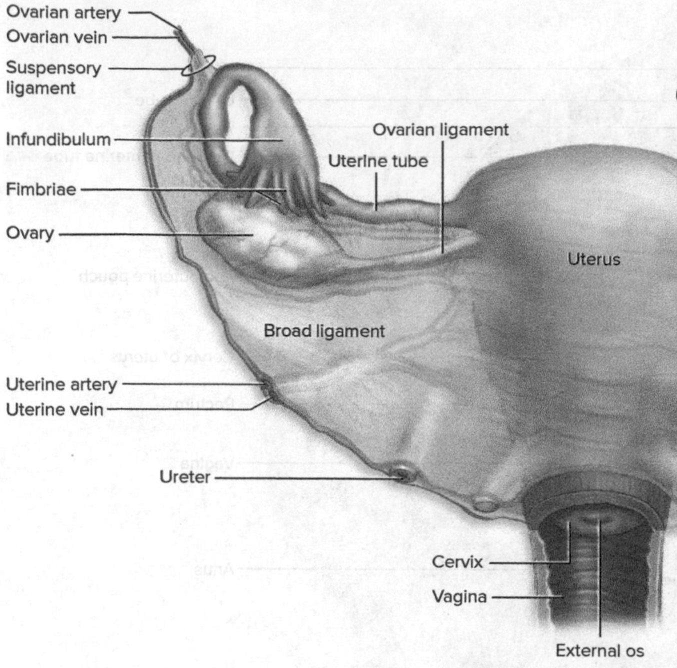
Ovarian artery
Ovarian vein
Suspensory ligament
Infundibulum
Fimbriae
Ovary
Ovarian ligament
Uterine tube
Mesosalpinx (part of broad ligament)
Uterus
Broad ligament
Uterine artery
Uterine vein
Ureter
Cervix
Vagina
External os

(a) Posterior view

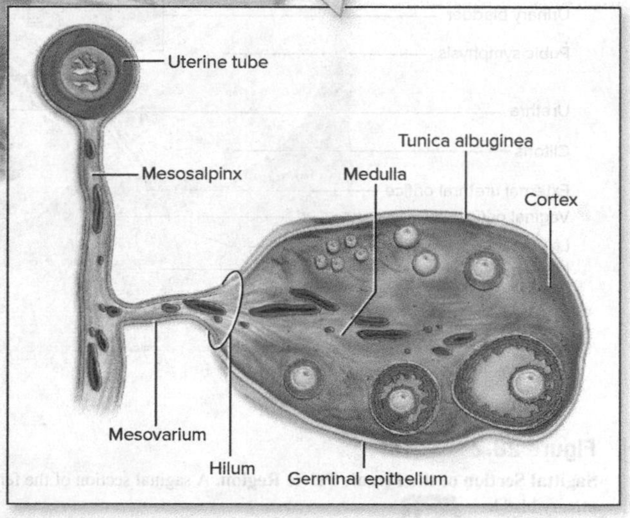
Uterine tube
Mesosalpinx
Tunica albuginea
Medulla
Cortex
Mesovarium
Hilum
Germinal epithelium

(b) Lateral sectional view

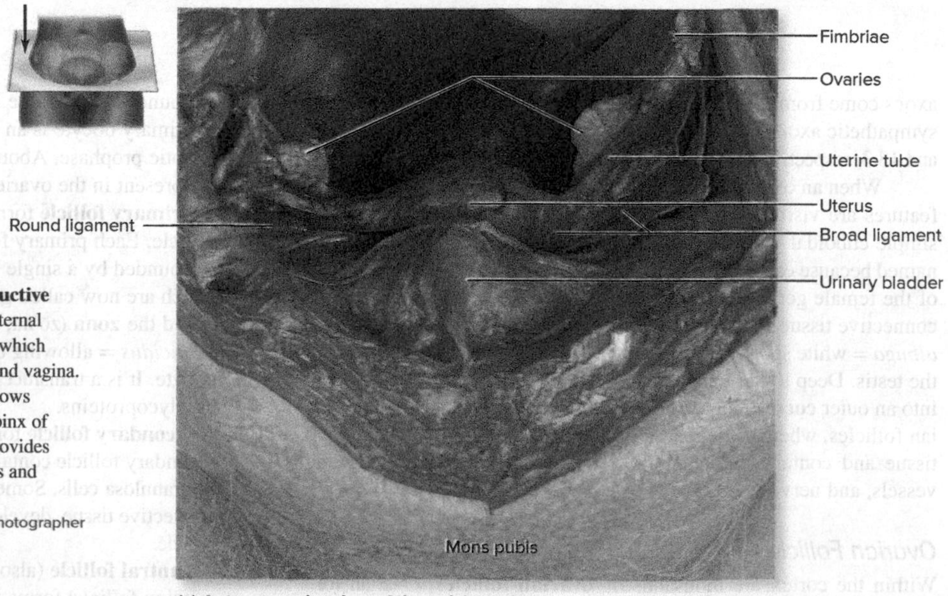
Fimbriae
Ovaries
Uterine tube
Uterus
Round ligament
Broad ligament
Urinary bladder
Mons pubis

(c) Anterosuperior view of the pelvic cavity

Figure 28.3

Internal Organs of the Female Reproductive System. (*a*) A posterior view shows the internal organs of the female reproductive system, which include the ovaries, uterine tubes, uterus, and vagina. (*b*) A lateral sectional view of the ovary shows the mesovarium in relation to the mesosalpinx of the broad ligament. (*c*) A cadaver photo provides an anterosuperior view of the female pelvis and reproductive organs. APR

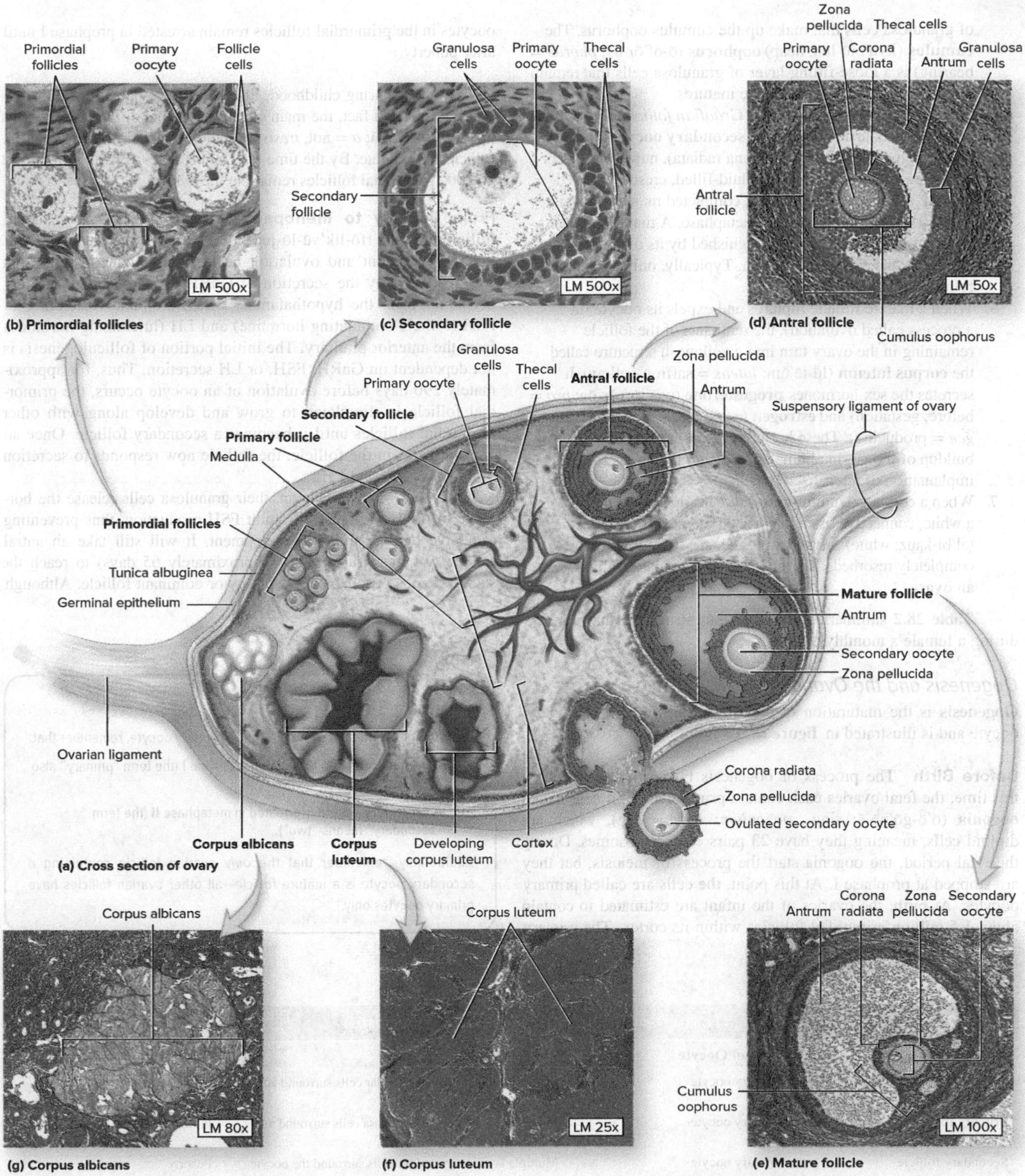

Primordial follicles
Primary oocyte
Follicle cells
LM 500x
(b) Primordial follicles
Granulosa cells
Primary oocyte
Thecal cells
Secondary follicle
LM 500x
(c) Secondary follicle
Zona pellucida
Thecal cells
Primary oocyte
Corona radiata
Granulosa cells
Antrum
Antral follicle
LM 50x
(d) Antral follicle
Cumulus oophorus
Granulosa cells
Thecal cells
Primary oocyte
Zona pellucida
Antral follicle
Antrum
Suspensory ligament of ovary
Secondary follicle
Primary follicle
Medulla
Primordial follicles
Tunica albuginea
Germinal epithelium
Mature follicle
Antrum
Secondary oocyte
Zona pellucida
Ovarian ligament
Corona radiata
Zona pellucida
Ovulated secondary oocyte
Corpus albicans
Corpus luteum
Developing corpus luteum
Cortex
(a) Cross section of ovary
Corpus albicans
LM 80x
(g) Corpus albicans
Corpus luteum
LM 25x
(f) Corpus luteum
Antrum
Corona radiata
Zona pellucida
Secondary oocyte
Cumulus oophorus
LM 100x
(e) Mature follicle

Figure 28.4

Stages of Follicle Development Within an Ovary. The ovary produces and releases both female gametes (secondary oocytes) and sex hormones. (*a*) A coronal view of the ovary contents depicts the different stages of follicle maturation, ovulation, and corpus luteum development and degeneration. Most of the follicles and structures shown in this image would appear at different times during the ovarian cycle—they do not occur simultaneously. Further, the follicles do not migrate through the ovary; rather, all follicles are shown together merely for comparative purposes. Histologic sections identify (*b*) primordial follicles, (*c*) a secondary follicle, (*d*) an antral follicle, and (*e*) a mature follicle. After ovulation, the remnant of the mature follicle forms (*f*) the corpus luteum, which then degenerates into (*g*) the corpus albicans.

of granulosa cells that make up the cumulus oophorus. The **cumulus** (kyū′mū-lŭs; heap) **oophorus** (ō-of′ōr-ŭs; *phorus* = bearing) is a loose-fitting layer of granulosa cells that remain around the oocyte as the follicle matures.

5. A **mature follicle** (also called a *Graafian follicle*) forms from an antral follicle and contains a **secondary oocyte** (surrounded by a zona pellucida and the corona radiata), numerous layers of granulosa cells, and a large, fluid-filled, crescent-shaped antrum. A secondary oocyte has completed meiosis I and is arrested in the second meiotic metaphase. A mature follicle becomes large and can be distinguished by its overall size as well as by the size of the antrum. Typically, only one mature follicle forms each month.
6. When a mature follicle ruptures and expels its oocyte (in a process called ovulation), the remnants of the follicle remaining in the ovary turn into a yellowish structure called the **corpus luteum** (lū-tē′ŭm; *luteus* = saffron-yellow). It secretes the sex hormones **progesterone** (prō-jes′tĕr-ōn; *pro* = before; gestation) and **estrogen** (es′tr ō-jen; *oistrus* = estrus, *gen* = producing). These hormones stimulate the continuing buildup of the uterine lining and prepare the uterus for possible implantation of a fertilized ovum.
7. When a corpus luteum regresses (breaks down), it turns into a white, connective tissue scar called the **corpus albicans** (al′bi-kanz; white). Most corpus albicans structures are completely resorbed, and only a few may remain within an ovary.

Table 28.2 summarizes the different structures that develop during a female's monthly cycle.

Oogenesis and the Ovarian Cycle

Oogenesis is the maturation of a primary oocyte to a secondary oocyte and is illustrated in **figure 28.5**.

Before Birth The process of oogenesis begins in the fetus. At this time, the fetal ovaries each contain primordial germ cells called **oogonia** (ō′ō-gō′nē-ă; sing., *oogonium; oon* = egg), which are diploid cells, meaning they have 23 pairs of chromosomes. During the fetal period, the oogonia start the process of meiosis, but they are stopped at prophase I. At this point, the cells are called primary oocytes. At birth, the ovaries of the infant are estimated to contain about 1.5 million primordial follicles within its cortex. The primary oocytes in the primordial follicles remain arrested in prophase I until after puberty.

Childhood During childhood, the ovaries are inactive, and no follicles develop. In fact, the main event that occurs during childhood is **atresia** (ă-trē′zē-ă; *a* = not, *tresis* = a hole), in which some primordial follicles degenerate. By the time the child reaches puberty, only about 400,000 primordial follicles remain in the ovaries.

From Puberty to Menopause When puberty is reached, **folliculogenesis** (fŏ-lik′yū-lō-jen′ĕ-sis) and a cyclic pattern of follicle development and ovulation begin. This cyclic pattern is in part regulated by the secretion of GnRH (gonadotropin-releasing hormone) from the hypothalamus, which stimulates secretion of FSH (follicle-stimulating hormone) and LH (luteinizing hormone) from the anterior pituitary. The initial portion of folliculogenesis is not dependent on GnRH, FSH, or LH secretion. Thus, for approximately 290 days before ovulation of an oocyte occurs, the primordial follicle is stimulated to grow and develop along with other primordial follicles until it becomes a secondary follicle. Once an antrum forms in the follicle, the follicle now responds to secretion of GnRH, FSH, and LH.

As the follicles develop, their granulosa cells release the hormone **inhibin,** which helps inhibit FSH production, thus preventing excessive ovarian follicle development. It will still take an antral follicle two menstrual cycles (approximately 65 days) to reach the stage where is becomes the ovulatory or dominant follicle. Although

Learning Strategy 28.2

To distinguish a primary oocyte from a secondary oocyte, remember that:

- A **primary** oocyte is arrested in prophase **I** (the term "primary" also means "one").
- A **secondary** oocyte is arrested in metaphase **II** (the term "secondary" means "two").

Additionally, remember that the *only* ovarian follicle containing a secondary oocyte is a mature follicle—all other ovarian follicles have primary oocytes only.

Table 28.2 Ovarian Follicles and Structures That Develop in the Ovary

Ovarian Structure	Type of Oocyte	Anatomic Characteristics	Time of First Appearance
Primordial follicle	Primary oocyte	Single layer of flattened follicular cells surround an oocyte	Fetal period
Primary follicle	Primary oocyte	Single layer of cuboidal granulosa cells surround an oocyte	Puberty
Secondary follicle	Primary oocyte	Multiple layers of granulosa cells surround the oocyte	Puberty
Antral follicle	Primary oocyte	Small, fluid-filled antrum develops within layers of granulosa cells	Puberty
Mature follicle	Secondary oocyte	Many layers of granulosa cells surround the oocyte and a very large antrum	Puberty
Corpus luteum	No oocyte	Yellowish, collapsed folds of granulosa cells	Puberty
Corpus albicans	No oocyte	Whitish connective tissue scar, remnant of a degenerated corpus luteum	Puberty

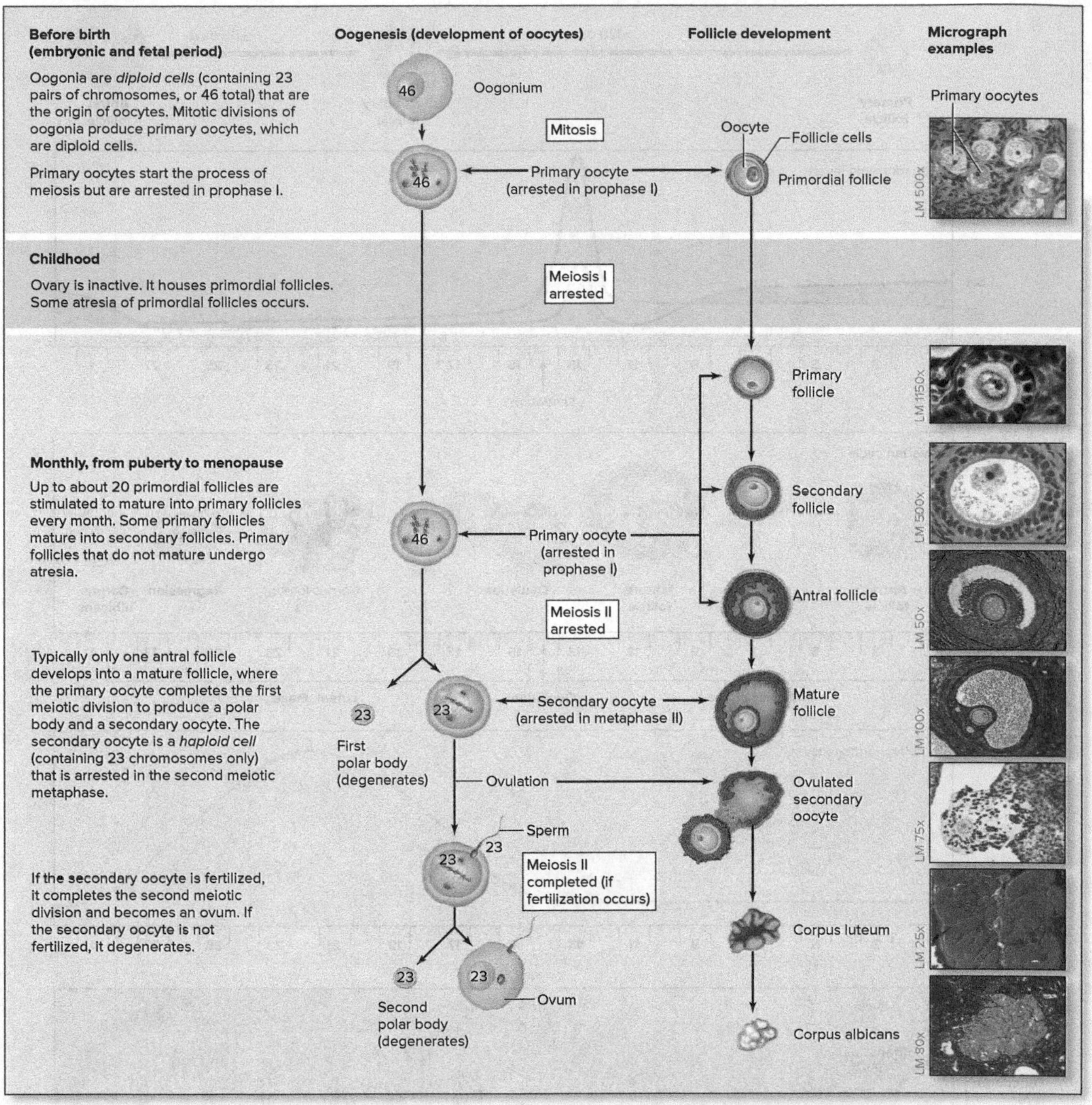
Before birth
(embryonic and fetal period)
Oogonia are *diploid cells* (containing 23 pairs of chromosomes, or 46 total) that are the origin of oocytes. Mitotic divisions of oogonia produce primary oocytes, which are diploid cells.
Primary oocytes start the process of meiosis but are arrested in prophase I.
Oogenesis (development of oocytes)
Follicle development
Micrograph examples
46
Oogonium
Mitosis
Oocyte
Follicle cells
Primary oocytes
46
Primary oocyte
(arrested in prophase I)
Primordial follicle
LM 500x
Childhood
Ovary is inactive. It houses primordial follicles. Some atresia of primordial follicles occurs.
Meiosis I
arrested
Primary
follicle
LM 1150x
Monthly, from puberty to menopause
Up to about 20 primordial follicles are stimulated to mature into primary follicles every month. Some primary follicles mature into secondary follicles. Primary follicles that do not mature undergo atresia.
Secondary
follicle
LM 500x
46
Primary oocyte
(arrested in
prophase I)
Antral follicle
Meiosis II
arrested
LM 50x
Typically only one antral follicle develops into a mature follicle, where the primary oocyte completes the first meiotic division to produce a polar body and a secondary oocyte. The secondary oocyte is a *haploid cell* (containing 23 chromosomes only) that is arrested in the second meiotic metaphase.
23
23
Secondary oocyte
(arrested in metaphase II)
Mature
follicle
LM 100x
First
polar body
(degenerates)
Ovulation
Ovulated
secondary
oocyte
LM 75x
Sperm
23
23
Meiosis II
completed (if
fertilization occurs)
If the secondary oocyte is fertilized, it completes the second meiotic division and becomes an ovum. If the secondary oocyte is not fertilized, it degenerates.
Corpus luteum
LM 25x
23
23
Ovum
Second
polar body
(degenerates)
Corpus albicans
LM 30x

Figure 28.5

Oogenesis. Oogenesis begins in the fetus, when primary oocytes develop in primordial follicles. The ovary and these follicles remain inactive during childhood. At puberty, a select number of primordial follicles each month are stimulated to develop into secondary follicles. Some of these secondary follicles will develop into antral follicles. Each month one dominant follicle will mature and undergo ovulation producing a female gamete (secondary oocyte).

(1, 3, 7, and 8) ©McGraw-Hill Education/Alvin Telser, photographer; (2) Jacques Testart/ARFIV/Science Source; (4–5) Ed Reschke/Getty Images; (6) Dr. Francisco Gaytan

many antral follicles respond to FSH and LH, it is the dominant follicle that is the focus of our discussion of the **ovarian cycle** and the three phases—follicular, ovulatory, and luteal—identified in this cycle **(figure 28.6)**.

Follicular Phase The **follicular phase** occurs during days 1–13 of an approximate 28-day ovarian cycle. At the beginning of each follicular phase, FSH and LH stimulate the dominant follicle to rapidly increase in size.

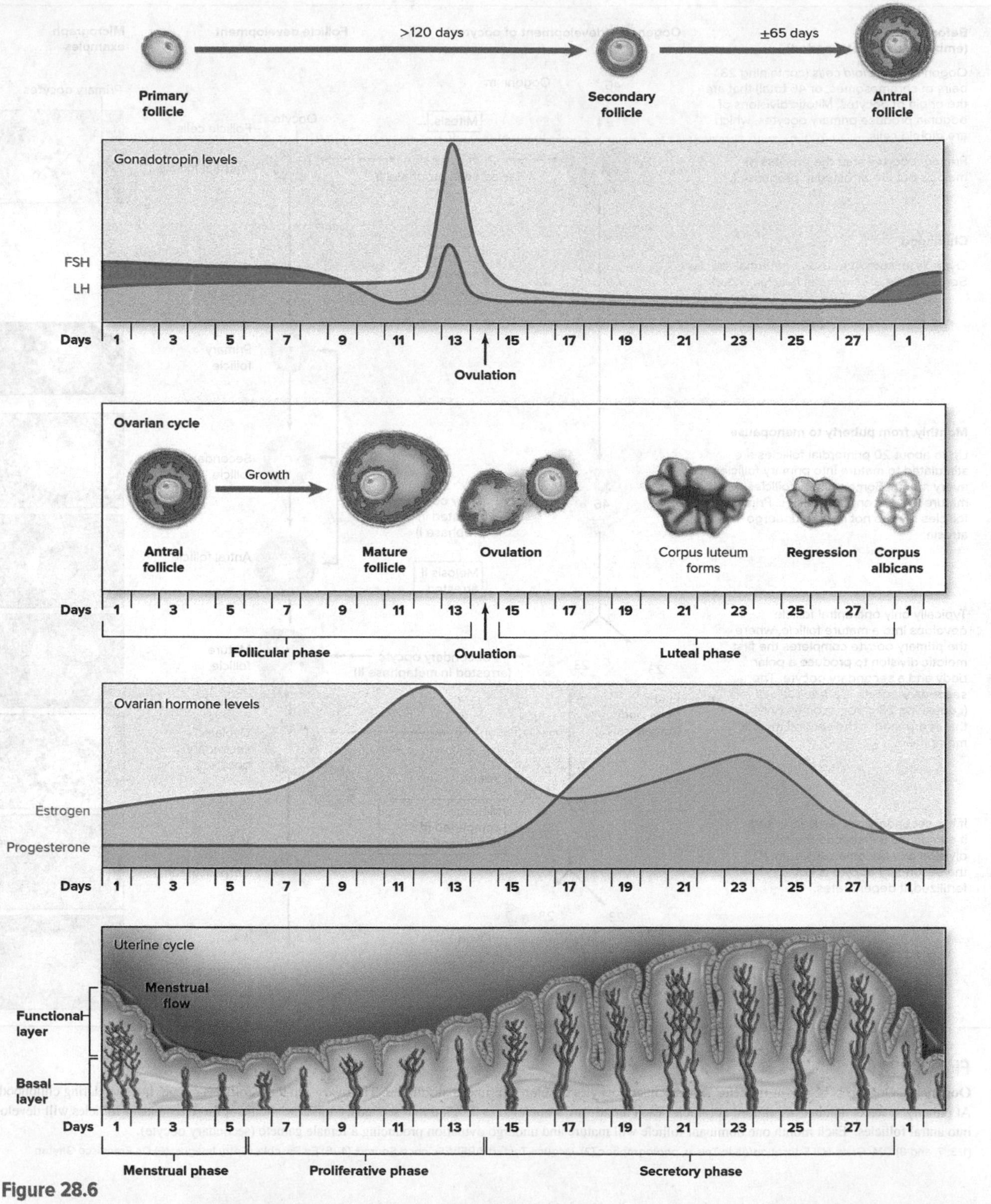

>120 days
±65 days
Primary follicle
Secondary follicle
Antral follicle
Gonadotropin levels
FSH
LH
Days 1 3 5 7 9 11 13 15 17 19 21 23 25 27 1
Ovulation
Ovarian cycle
Growth
Antral follicle
Mature follicle
Ovulation
Corpus luteum forms
Regression
Corpus albicans
Follicular phase
Ovulation
Luteal phase
Ovarian hormone levels
Estrogen
Progesterone
Uterine cycle
Menstrual flow
Functional layer
Basal layer
Menstrual phase
Proliferative phase
Secretory phase

Figure 28.6

Hormonal Changes in the Female Reproductive System. The topmost diagram depicts a portion of the 290 days it takes a primordial follicle to develop into a secondary follicle (non-hormonally dependent) and the approximately 65 days it takes a secondary follicle to become a dominant follicle (hormonally dependent). The remainder of the figure shows the relationship among FSH and LH secretion, their effect of the dominant follicle, and the hormonal relationship to the menstrual cycle. Follicle-stimulating hormone (FSH)and luteinizing hormone (LH) stimulate rapid growth of the dominant antral follicle during the follicular phase of the ovarian cycle. Estrogen secreted by the ovarian follicles stimulates the proliferative phase in the uterine cycle, whereas a peak in luteinizing hormone (LH) promotes both ovulation and the development of the corpus luteum, which produces both progesterone and estrogen to promote uterine lining development. APR

The volume of fluid increases within the antrum, and the oocyte is forced toward one side of the follicle, where it is surrounded by a cluster of granulosa cells termed the cumulus oophorus. The innermost layer of these cells is the corona radiata.

As the antral follicle develops into a mature follicle, its primary oocyte finishes meiosis I, and two cells form (see figure 28.5). One of these cells receives a minimal amount of cytoplasm and forms a **polar body,** which is a nonfunctional cell that later deteriorates. The other cell receives the bulk of the cytoplasm and becomes the secondary oocyte, which continues to develop and reaches metaphase II of meiosis before it is arrested again. This secondary oocyte does not complete meiosis unless it is fertilized by a sperm. If the oocyte is never fertilized, it breaks down and degenerates about 24 hours later.

Ovulation **Ovulation** (ov′yū-lā′shŭn) occurs on day 14 of a 28-day ovarian cycle and is defined as the release of the secondary oocyte from a mature follicle (figure 28.6). Typically, only one ovary ovulates each month. Ovulation is induced when there is a peak in LH secretion. As the time of ovulation approaches, the granulosa cells in the mature follicle increases their rate of fluid secretion, forming a larger antrum and causing further swelling within the follicle. The edge of the follicle that continues to expand at the ovarian surface becomes quite thin and eventually ruptures, expelling the secondary oocyte.

Luteal Phase The **luteal phase** occurs during days 15–28 of the ovarian cycle, when the remaining granulosa cells in the ruptured mature follicle turn into a corpus luteum. It secretes progesterone and estrogen that stabilize and build up the uterine lining, and prepare for possible implantation of a fertilized ovum.

The corpus luteum has a life span of about 10–13 days if the secondary oocyte is not fertilized. After this time, the corpus luteum regresses and becomes a corpus albicans. As the corpus luteum degenerates, its levels of secreted progesterone and estrogen drop, causing the uterine lining to be shed as **menstruation** (men-strū-ā′shŭn), also called **menses** or a **period.** This event marks the end of the luteal phase. The first menstrual cycle, called **menarche** (me-nar′kē; *men* = month, *arche* = beginning), is the culmination of female puberty and typically occurs around ages 11–12.

If the secondary oocyte is fertilized and successfully **implants** in the uterine lining, this fertilized structure (now a pre-embryo) begins its own development (as discussed in sections 3.3 and 3.4). The pre-embryo starts secreting **human chorionic gonadotropin (hCG),** a hormone that enters the mother's blood and acts on the corpus luteum. Essentially, hCG lets the corpus luteum know that implantation has occurred and that the corpus luteum should continue producing progesterone, which will build and stabilize the uterine lining. After 3 months, the placenta of the developing fetus starts producing its own progesterone and estrogen, so by the end of the third month, the corpus luteum has usually regressed and formed a corpus albicans.

Menopause The time when a woman is nearing menopause is called **perimenopause.** During perimenopause, estrogen levels begin to drop, and one may experience irregular periods, skip some periods, or have very light periods. When monthly menstrual cycles have stopped for 1 year without a pregnancy, one is said to be in **menopause** (men′ō-pawz; *pauses* = cessation). The age at onset of menopause varies considerably, but typically is between 45 and 55 years. Menopause is reached when there are no longer any ovarian follicles or the follicles that remain stop maturing. As a result, significant amounts of estrogen and progesterone are no longer secreted. Thus, the endometrial lining does not grow, and menstrual periods no longer occur.

WHAT DO YOU THINK?

1. If a woman has one ovary surgically removed, can she still become pregnant? Why or why not?

28.2b Uterine Tubes

The **uterine tubes,** also called the *fallopian* (fă-lō′pē-ăn) *tubes* or *oviducts* (ō′vi-dŭkt; *duco* = to lead), extend laterally from both sides of the uterus toward the ovaries (**figure 28.7**). Fertilization of the secondary oocyte occurs in the lateral part of these tubes, and the pre-embryo begins to develop as it travels toward the uterus. Usually it takes the pre-embryo about 3 to 4 days to reach the lumen of the uterus.

The uterine tubes are small in diameter, and reach their maximum length of between 10 and 12 centimeters after puberty. These tubes are covered and suspended by the **mesosalpinx** (mez′ō-sal′pinks; *salpinx* = trumpet), a specific superior part of the broad ligament of the uterus (see figure 28.3*a*). Each uterine tube is composed of contiguous segments that are distinguishable in both gross examination and histologic sections:

- The **infundibulum** (in′fŭn-dib′yū-lŭm; funnel) is the free, funnel-shaped, lateral margin of the uterine tube. Its numerous individual fingerlike folds are called **fimbriae** (fim′brē-ē; fringes). The fimbriae of the infundibulum are not attached to the ovary but enclose it at the time of ovulation.
- The **ampulla** (am-pul′ă; two-handled bottle) is the expanded region medial to the infundibulum. Fertilization of a secondary oocyte typically occurs there.
- The **isthmus** (is′mŭs) extends medially from the ampulla toward the lateral wall of the uterus. It forms about one-third of the length of the uterine tube.
- The **uterine part** (*intramural part* or *interstitial segment*) extends medially from the isthmus and is continuous with the wall of the uterus.

The wall of the uterine tube consists of a mucosa, a muscularis, and a serosa. The **mucosa** is formed from a ciliated columnar epithelium and a layer of areolar connective tissue. The mucosa has linear folds, which reduce the size of the uterine tube lumen. After ovulation, the cilia on the apical surface of the epithelial cells of both the infundibulum and the ampulla begin to beat in the direction of the uterus. This beating causes a slight current in the fluid within the uterine tube lumen, drawing the ovulated oocyte into the uterine tube and moving it toward the uterus.

Learning Strategy 28.3

One way to remember the segments of the uterine tubes is as follows:

- The infundibulum (the only segment with an "F" in it) has the fimbriae.
- The **am**pulla is the **arm** of the uterine tube.
- The **is**thmus **is** the longest.
- The uter**ine** part is **in** the uterus.

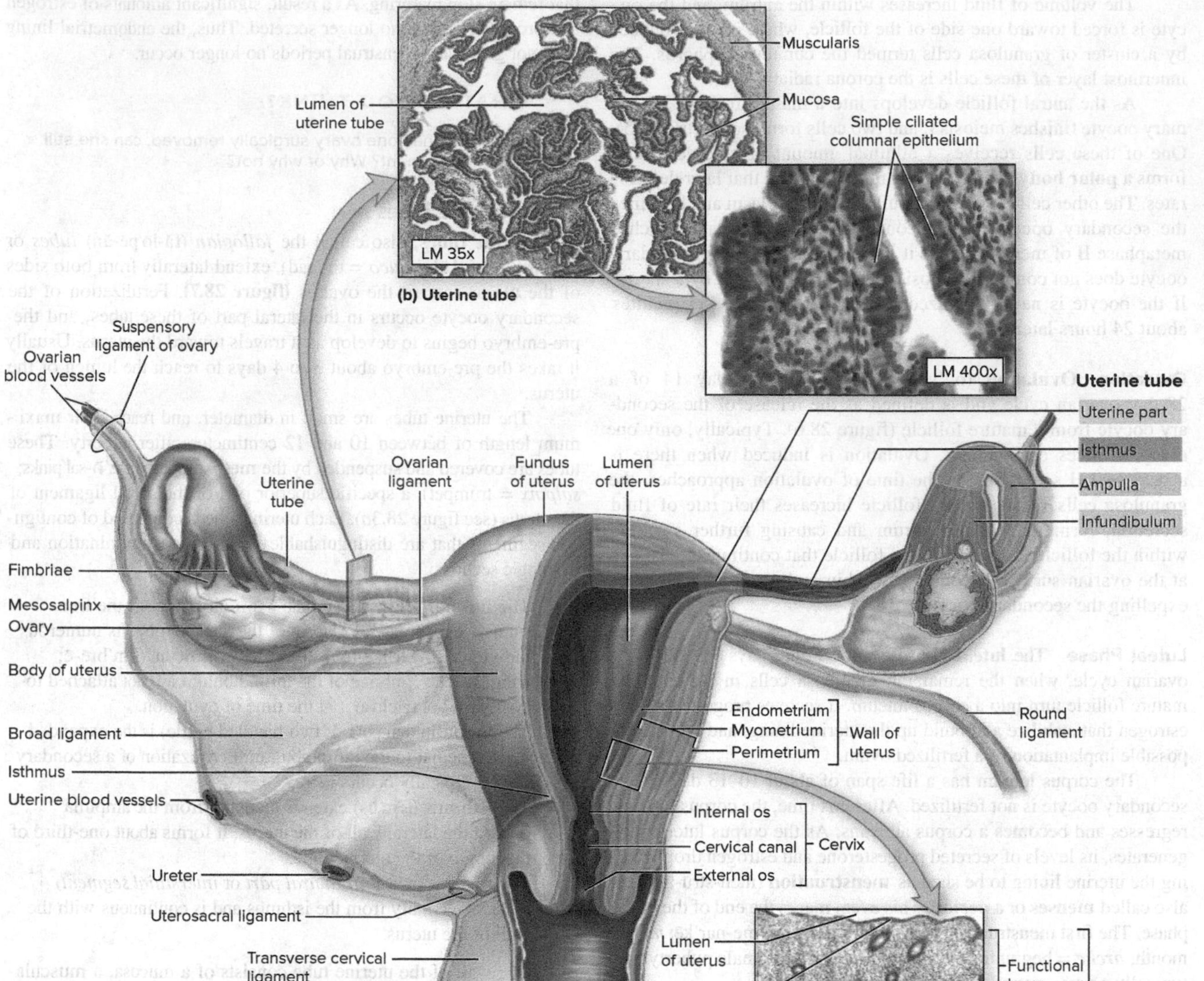
Lumen of uterine tube
Muscularis
Mucosa
Simple ciliated columnar epithelium
LM 35x
(b) Uterine tube
LM 400x
Uterine tube
Uterine part
Isthmus
Ampulla
Infundibulum
Suspensory ligament of ovary
Ovarian blood vessels
Uterine tube
Ovarian ligament
Fundus of uterus
Lumen of uterus
Fimbriae
Mesosalpinx
Ovary
Body of uterus
Broad ligament
Isthmus
Uterine blood vessels
Ureter
Uterosacral ligament
Transverse cervical ligament
Vagina
Endometrium
Myometrium
Perimetrium
Wall of uterus
Round ligament
Internal os
Cervical canal
External os
Cervix
(a) Posterior view
Lumen of uterus
Epithelium
Uterine glands
Functional layer
Basal layer
Endometrium
Myometrium
LM 45x
(c) Uterine wall

Figure 28.7

Uterine Tubes and the Uterus. The uterine tubes are paired passageways that capture the ovulated secondary oocyte, provide the site for fertilization, and transport the oocyte to the uterus. (*a*) The relationship between a uterine tube and the uterus is shown in a posterior view (*left*) and a partially cut-away diagram (*right*). (*b*) A photomicrograph shows a cross section of the uterine tube. (*c*) A photomicrograph shows the layers of the endometrium and part of the myometrium in the wall of the uterus.

(b, top and bottom, c) ©McGraw-Hill Education/Alvin Telser, photographer

The **muscularis** is composed of an inner circular layer and an outer longitudinal layer of smooth muscle cells. The muscular layer increases in relative thickness as the uterine tube approaches the lateral wall of the uterus. Some peristaltic contractions in the muscularis help propel the secondary oocyte, or pre-embryo if fertilization has occurred, through the uterine tube toward the uterus. The **serosa** is the external serous membrane covering the uterine tube.

WHAT DID YOU LEARN?

3. Draw and label the five different types of ovarian follicles.
4. What is ovulation?
5. What is menarche, and when does it occur?
6. Name the segments of the uterine tube. What type of epithelium lines the uterine tubes, and what is its function?

28.2c Uterus

The **uterus** (yū′tĕr-ŭs; womb) is a pear-shaped, thick-walled muscular organ within the pelvic cavity. It has a lumen (internal space) that connects to the uterine tubes superolaterally and to the vagina inferiorly (figure 28.7*a*). Normally, the uterus is angled anterosuperiorly across the superior surface of the urinary bladder, a position referred to as **anteverted** (an′te-vert′ed; *ante* = before, *versio* = a turning). If the uterus is positioned posterosuperiorly (so that it is projecting toward the rectum), this position is called **retroverted** (re′trō-ver-tĕd). As an individual ages, the uterus may shift from anteverted to retroverted.

The uterus serves many functions. Following fertilization, the pre-embryo makes contact with the uterine lining and implants in the inner uterine wall. The uterus then supports, protects, and nourishes the developing embryo/fetus by forming a vascular connection that later develops into the placenta. The uterus ejects the fetus at birth after maternal oxytocin levels increase to initiate the uterine contractions of labor (see section 20.3b). If a secondary oocyte is not fertilized, the muscular wall of the uterus contracts and sheds its inner lining as menses.

The uterus is partitioned into the following regions:

- The **fundus** (fŭn′dŭs) is the broad, curved superior region extending between the lateral attachments of the uterine tubes.
- The **body** is the major part of the uterus, it is the middle region composed of a thick wall of smooth muscle.
- The **isthmus** is a narrow, constricted inferior region of the body that is superior to the cervix.
- The **cervix** is the narrow inferior portion of the uterus that projects into the vagina.

Within the cervix is a narrow channel called the **cervical canal,** which connects to the vagina inferiorly. The superior opening of this canal is the **internal os** (*os* = mouth). The **external os** is the inferior opening of the cervix into the lumen of the vagina. The external os is covered with nonkeratinized stratified squamous epithelium. The cervix contains mucin-secreting glands that help form a thick mucus plug at the external os. This mucus plug is suspected to be a physical barrier that prevents pathogens from invading the uterus from the vagina. The mucus plug thins

Clinical View 28.1

Ovarian Cancer

Ovarian cancer refers to a primary malignancy in the ovaries. The cancer may originate from any ovarian structure, although 90% are epithelial tumors. Not all tumors that develop in the ovaries are malignant (or cancerous), but when the tumors are malignant, a diagnosis of ovarian cancer is made. Ovarian cancer is the fifth most common cancer in women.

Women that have the inherited mutation in the *BRCA1* and *BRCA2* genes (which normally produce tumor suppressor proteins) have a lifetime risk of about 10% to 40% of developing ovarian cancer (compared to a 1% to 2% risk for those without the mutation in these genes). Other risk factors for the disease include increasing age, obesity, infertility, and a family history of ovarian cancer, breast cancer, or colorectal cancer. Birth control medication (in premenopausal women) reduces the risk of ovarian cancer, whereas postmenopausal estrogen therapy increases the risk.

Ovarian cancer is difficult to diagnose early because initial symptoms may be nonspecific and because there is no reliable test for the disease. Initial symptoms may include constipation, increased need and urgency to urinate, abdominal swelling and bloating, pelvic pain, indigestion, nausea, unexplained back pain, and changes in weight. A blood test for CA-125 (a cancer antigen protein found on ovarian cancer cells) may indicate the likelihood of ovarian cancer, but because CA-125 levels also may be elevated in numerous other noncancerous conditions (such as endometriosis), a high CA-125 test alone is not considered reliable for a diagnosis of cancer.

If diagnosed early, 5-year survival-rate prognoses are very good. Unfortunately, many ovarian cancers are not detected until after the cancer has metastasized to other organs, which dramatically reduces the chances for good long-term survival rates.

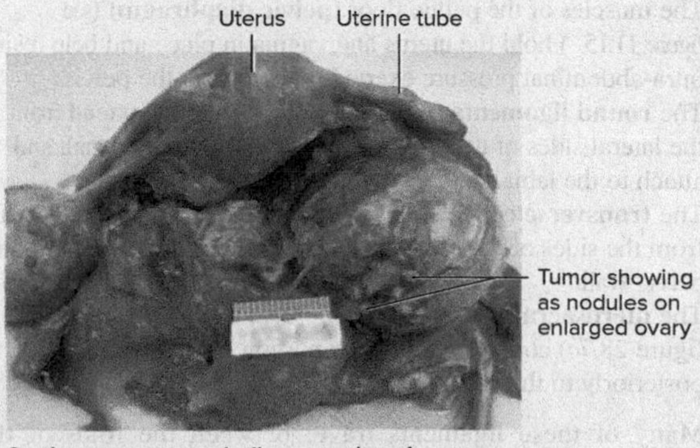

Ovarian cancer on surgically removed ovaries.

Dennis K. Burns, MD; Travis G. Brown, MD; Walter L. Kemp, MD/McGraw-Hill Education

Clinical View 28.2

Cervical Cancer

Cervical cancer is one of the most common malignancies in females worldwide. The most important risk factor is human papillomavirus (HPV) infection. A vaccine (i.e., Gardasil and Cervarix) has been developed for the four most common types of HPV. The vaccine is most effective if given before the individual, whether female or male, becomes sexually active. Thus, recommended age range for the vaccine is 11 to 13 years.

The **Papanicolaou (Pap) smear** is a diagnostic method of examining cervical epithelial cells for abnormalities and possible cervical cancer. A health-care professional inserts a metal or plastic instrument called a **speculum** (spek′yū-lŭm; mirror) into the vagina to keep the vagina open in order to examine the cervix. Epithelial cells are scraped from the edge of the cervix and examined for any abnormal cellular development (termed *dysplasia*). In addition, the cells may be tested to see if they have been infected with one of four strains of HPV most likely to cause cervical cancer (termed hrHPV, or high risk HPV). If a Pap smear is abnormal and the cells test positive for hrHPV, then the clinician follows up with a **colposcopy,** which is a procedure to more closely examine the cervix and possibly take **biopsy** samples of the cervix.

In 2018 the U.S. Preventative Services Task Force updated the guidelines for cervical cancer screening, due to the high correlation between cervical cancer and high-risk HPV strain infection. By ages 21 to 29, women should get a Pap smear once every three years (and more frequently if abnormal results occur). From age 30 to 65, women may continue to get a Pap smear every three years or get an HPV test every five years. After age 65, if all of these tests were normal in the past, women likely do not need to get further testing.

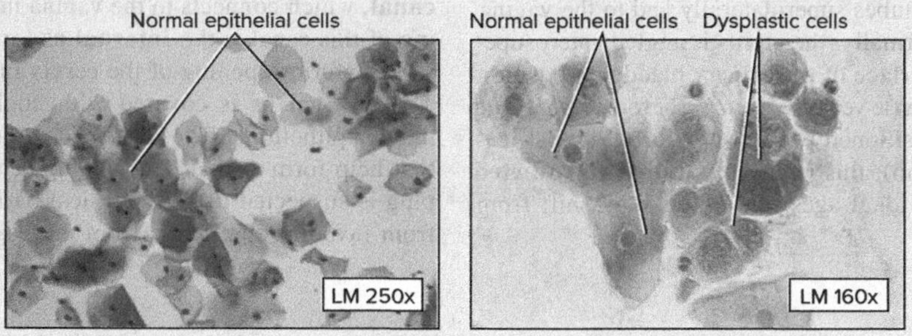

(a) ***Normal Pap smear.*** **(b)** ***Abnormal Pap smear.***

(a) Komsan Loonprom/Shutterstock; (b) Parviz M. Pour/Science Source

considerably around the time of ovulation, so sperm may more easily enter the uterus.

Support of the Uterus

Several structures support the uterus.

- The muscles of the pelvic floor **(pelvic diaphragm)** (see figure 11.15) hold the uterus and vagina in place and help resist intra-abdominal pressure exerted inferiorly on the pelvis.
- The **round ligaments** (figure 28.7) of the uterus extend from the lateral sides of the uterus, through the inguinal canal, and attach to the labia majora.
- The **transverse cervical ligaments** (or *cardinal ligaments*) run from the sides of the cervix and superior vagina laterally to the pelvic wall.
- The **uterosacral ligaments** (or *sacrocervical ligaments;* figure 28.7*a*) connect the inferior portion of the uterus posteriorly to the sacrum.

Many of these ligaments travel between the folds of the broad ligament. Weakness in either the pelvic floor muscles or these ligaments can lead to **prolapse** (prō-laps′; *prolapsus* = a failing) of the uterus, in which the uterus starts to protrude through the vagina. Despite its name, the broad ligament is not a strong support for the uterus, but rather a peritoneal drape over the uterus.

Blood Supply

Each internal iliac artery extends a branch called a **uterine artery** through the broad ligament to the lateral wall of the uterus (see figure 28.7). Numerous smaller branches from the uterine artery then penetrate the muscular wall of the uterus and further diverge into arcuate arteries. Thereafter, each arcuate artery gives rise to smaller vessels, called radial arteries, which extend into the innermost layer (endometrium) of the uterus. Here they branch into spiral arteries, which swirl throughout the endometrium, extending between and throughout the uterine glands toward the mucosal surface.

Wall of the Uterus

The uterine wall is composed of three concentric tunics: the perimetrium, myometrium, and endometrium (figure 28.7). The outer tunic of most of the uterus is a serosa called the **perimetrium** (per′i-mē′trē-ŭm; *metra* = uterus). The perimetrium is continuous with the broad ligament. The **myometrium** (mī′ō-mē′trē-ŭm; *mys* = muscle) is the thick, middle tunic of the uterine wall formed from three intertwining layers of smooth muscle. In the nonpregnant uterus, the muscle cells are less than 0.25 millimeter in length. During the course of a pregnancy, smooth muscle cells increase both in size (**hypertrophy;** hī-pĕr′trō-fē) and in number (**hyperplasia;** hī-pĕr-plā′zhē-ă). Some cells may exceed 5 millimeter in length by the end of gestation. The innermost tunic of the uterus, called the **endometrium** (en′dō-mē′trē-ŭm), is an intricate mucosa composed of a simple columnar epithelium and an underlying lamina propria. The lamina propria is filled with compound tubular glands (also called **uterine glands**), which enlarge during the uterine cycle.

Two distinct layers form the endometrium. The deeper layer is the **basal layer,** also called the *stratum basalis* (bā-sā′lis). The basal layer is immediately adjacent to the myometrium, and is a permanent layer that undergoes few changes during each uterine cycle. The more superficial of the two endometrial layers is the **functional layer,** or *stratum functionalis* (fŭnk′sh ŭn-ăl′is). Beginning at puberty, the functional layer grows from the basal layer under the influence of estrogen and progesterone secreted from the ovarian follicles. If fertilization and implantation do not occur, this lining is shed as menses.

Uterine (Menstrual) Cycle and Menstruation

The cyclical changes in the endometrial lining occur under the influence of estrogen and progesterone secreted by the ovary. The **uterine cycle** (or *menstrual cycle*) consists of three distinct phases of endometrium development: the menstrual phase, proliferative phase, and secretory phase (see figure 28.6, *bottom*).

The **menstrual** (men′str ū-āl; *menstrualis* = monthly) **phase** occurs about days 1–5 of the cycle. This phase is marked by sloughing of the functional layer and lasts through the period of menstrual bleeding. The **proliferative** (prō-lif′ĕr-ă-tiv; *proles* = offspring, *fero* = to bear) **phase** follows, spanning about days 6–14. The initial development of the functional layer of the endometrium overlaps the time of follicle growth and estrogen secretion by the ovary. The last phase is the **secretory** (se-kr ē′tō-rē) **phase,** which occurs between about days 15–28. During the secretory phase, increased progesterone secretion from the corpus luteum results in increased vascularization and development of uterine glands. If the secondary oocyte is not fertilized, the corpus luteum degenerates, and the progesterone level drops dramatically. Without progesterone, the functional layer lining sloughs off, and the next uterine cycle begins with the menstrual phase.

Table 28.3 compares the uterine cycle with the ovarian cycle and **table 28.4** summarizes the hormones that influence the ovarian and uterine cycles. The day ranges listed on figure 28.6 and table 28.3 are for a 28-day cycle, meaning ovulation occurs at day 14 and menses occurs every 28 days. With a longer cycle (say, menstruation occurs about every 35 days), the menstrual phase and/or proliferative phase is longer than average. Typically, ovulation occurs 14 days before menstruation, so the secretory phase day ranges do not vary as much.

Table 28.3 Comparison of Ovarian and Uterine Cycle Phases

Day[1]	Ovarian Cycle Phase	Uterine Cycle Phase
1–5	Follicular phase	Menstrual phase
6–13	Follicular phase	Proliferative phase
14	Ovulation	Proliferative phase
15–28	Luteal phase	Secretory phase

[1] This table assumes a 28-day cycle between menstrual periods. If a woman has a longer or shorter cycle, the day ranges for the follicular, menstrual, and proliferative phases will vary.

WHAT DO YOU THINK?

2. What factors could influence the length and timing of the uterine cycle?

28.2d Vagina

The **vagina** (vă-jī′nă) is a thick-walled, fibromuscular tube that forms the inferiormost region of the female reproductive tract and measures about 10 centimeters in length in an adult (see figure 28.2). The vagina connects the uterus with the outside of the body anteroventrally, and thus functions as the birth canal. The vagina is also the copulatory organ of the female, as it receives the penis during intercourse, and it serves as the passageway for menstruation.

The vaginal wall is heavily invested with both blood vessels and lymphatic vessels. Arterial supply comes from the vaginal arteries, and venous drainage is via vaginal veins. The lumen of the vagina is flattened anteroposteriorly. The vagina's relatively thin, distensible wall consists of three tunics: an inner mucosa, a middle muscularis, and an outer adventitia.

The **mucosa** consists of a nonkeratinized stratified squamous epithelium and a highly vascularized lamina propria (**figure 28.8**).

Table 28.4 Influence of Hormones on the Ovarian and Uterine Cycles

Hormone	Primary Source of Hormone	Effects
Gonadotropin-releasing hormone (GnRH)	Hypothalamus	Stimulates anterior pituitary to produce and secrete FSH and LH
Follicle-stimulating hormone (FSH)	Anterior pituitary	Stimulates development and maturation of ovarian follicles
Luteinizing hormone (LH)	Anterior pituitary	Stimulates ovulation (when there is a peak in LH)
Estrogen	Ovarian follicles (before ovulation), corpus luteum (after ovulation), or placenta (during pregnancy)	Initiates and maintains growth of the functional layer of the endometrium
Progesterone	Corpus luteum or placenta (during pregnancy)	Primary hormone responsible for functional layer growth after ovulation; causes increase in blood vessel distribution, uterine gland size, and nutrient production
Inhibin	Ovarian follicles	Inhibits FSH secretion, so as to prevent excessive follicular development

Clinical View 28.3

Endometriosis

Endometriosis (en′dō-mē-trē-ō′sis) occurs when part of the endometrium is displaced onto the external surface of organs within the abdominopelvic cavity. Scientists think that during the regular uterine (menstrual) cycle, some individuals expel endometrial tissue from the uterine tubes and it becomes implanted onto the surface of various abdominal and pelvic organs. This displaced endometrium may grow under the influence of hormones, but it cannot be expelled through the vagina during menses. Thus, the ensuing hemorrhage and breakdown of the displaced endometrium may cause considerable pain and scarring that often leads to deformities of the uterine tubes. Treatments include the use of hormones designed to retard the growth and cycling of the displaced endometrial tissue, as well as surgical removal of the ectopic endometrium.

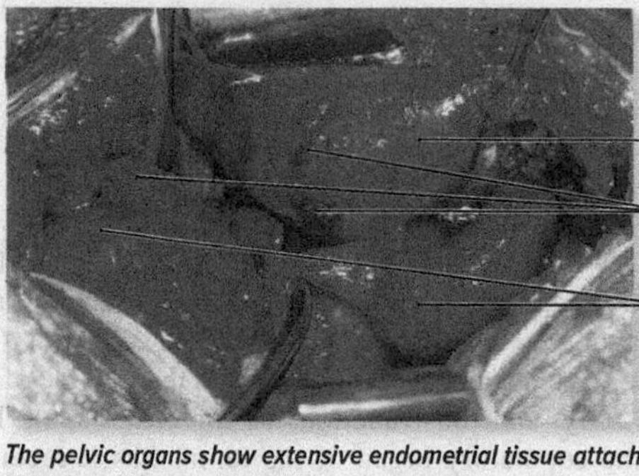
Uterus
Ectopic endometrial tissue
Intestines

The pelvic organs show extensive endometrial tissue attachments.

Source: *Operational Obstetrics & Gynecology –2nd Edition*. The Health Care of Women in Military Settings. CAPT Michael John Hughey, MC, USNR NAVMEDPUB 6300-2C, Bureau of Medicine and Surgery, Department of the Navy, 2300 E Street NW, Washington, D.C. 20372–5300, January 1, 2000. Original image courtesy CAPT Richard Stock, MC, USN

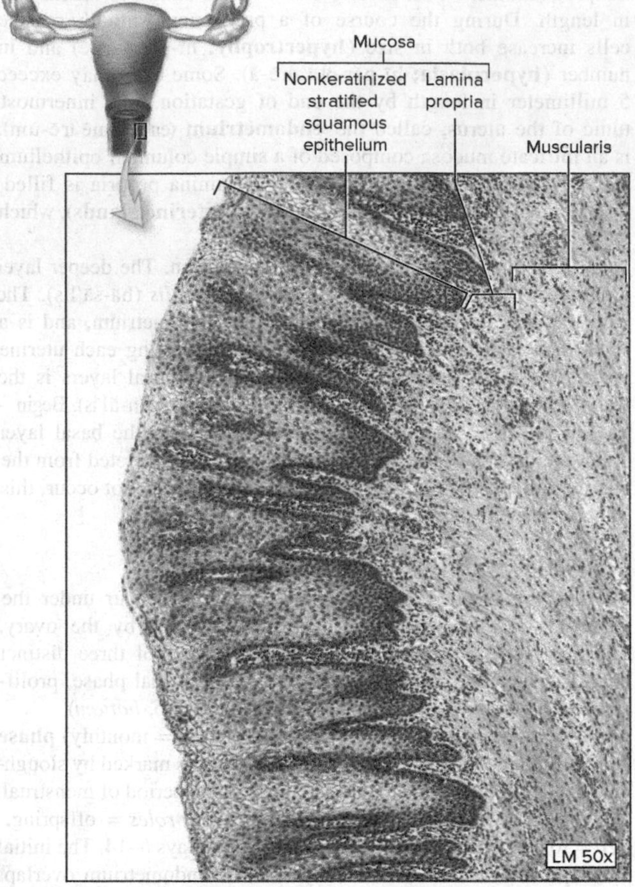
Mucosa
Nonkeratinized stratified squamous epithelium
Lamina propria
Muscularis
LM 50x

Figure 28.8

Histology of the Vagina. The epithelial lining of the vagina in a mature female is a stratified squamous epithelium. APR

©McGraw-Hill Education/Alvin Telser, photographer

Superficial cells of the vaginal epithelium contribute to the acidic environment that helps prevent bacterial and other pathogenic invasion. During each menstrual phase, large numbers of lymphocytes and granulocytes invade the lamina propria to help prevent infection during menstruation. The inferior region of the vaginal mucosa contains numerous transverse folds, or rugae. Near the external opening of the vagina, called the **vaginal orifice,** these mucosal folds project into the lumen to form a vascularized, membranous barrier called the **hymen** (hī′men; membrane). The hymen typically is perforated during the first instance of sexual intercourse, but also may be perforated by tampon use, medical exams, or very strenuous physical activity.

The **muscularis** of the vagina has both outer and inner layers of smooth muscle. The outer layer is composed of bundles of longitudinal smooth muscle cells that are continuous with corresponding muscle cells in the myometrium. The smooth muscle cells of the inner circular layer are interwoven with the outer longitudinal muscle fibers at the point where the two muscle layers meet. Near the vaginal orifice are some skeletal muscle fibers of the muscularis layer that cause partial narrowing of the vaginal orifice. The **adventitia** contains some inner elastic fibers and an outer layer of areolar connective tissue. APR

28.2e External Genitalia

The external sex organs of the female are termed the **external genitalia** or **vulva** (vŭl′vă; a covering) (**figure 28.9*a***). The **mons** (monz; mountain) **pubis** is an expanse of skin and subcutaneous connective tissue immediately anterior to the pubic symphysis. The mons pubis is covered with pubic hair in postpubescence. The **labia majora** (lā′bē-ă mă-jōr′ă; sing., *labium majus; labium* = lip, *majus* = larger) are paired, thickened folds of skin and connective tissue. The labia majora are homologous to the scrotum. In adulthood, their outer surface is covered with coarse pubic hair; they contain numerous sweat and sebaceous glands. The **labia minora** (mī-nōr′ă; sing., *labium minus; minus* = smaller) are paired folds immediately internal to the labia majora. They are devoid of hair and contain a

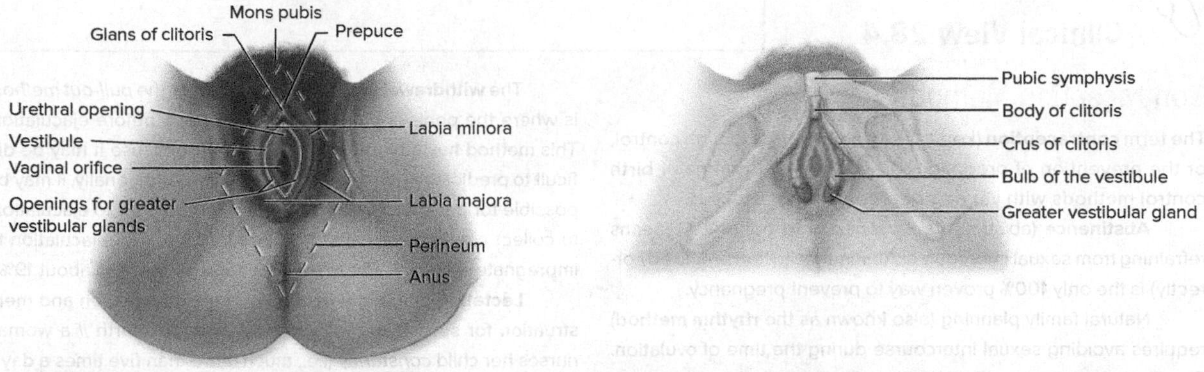
Mons pubis
Glans of clitoris
Prepuce
Urethral opening
Vestibule
Vaginal orifice
Openings for greater vestibular glands
Labia minora
Labia majora
Perineum
Anus
Pubic symphysis
Body of clitoris
Crus of clitoris
Bulb of the vestibule
Greater vestibular gland

(a) Superficial structures of external genitalia **(b) Deep structures of external genitalia**

Figure 28.9

Female External Genitalia. (*a*) Inferior view of the external genitalia, illustrating the urethral opening and the vaginal opening, which are within the vestibule and bounded by the labia minora. (*b*) Deep structures associated with the external genitalia.

highly vascular layer of areolar connective tissue. Sebaceous glands are located in these folds, as are numerous melanocytes, resulting in enhanced pigmentation of the folds.

The space between the labia minora is called the **vestibule.** Within the vestibule are the **urethral opening** and the vaginal orifice. On either side of the vaginal orifice is an erectile body called the **bulb of the vestibule** (figure 28.9*b*), which becomes erect and increases in sensitivity during sexual intercourse. A pair of **greater vestibular glands** (previously called *glands of Bartholin*) are housed within the posterolateral walls of the vestibule. These are tubuloacinar glands that secrete mucin, which forms mucus to act as a lubricant for the vagina. Secretion increases during sexual intercourse, when additional lubrication is needed. These secretory structures are homologous to the bulbourethral glands.

The **clitoris** (klit′ō-ris) is a small erectile body, usually less than 2 centimeters in length, located at the anterior regions of the labia minora. It is homologous to the penis of the male. Two small erectile bodies called **corpora cavernosa** form its **body.** Pelvic splanchnic nerve innervation results in increased blood flow and erection of the clitoris upon stimulation (see section 18.3b). Extending from each of these bodies posteriorly are elongated masses, each called the **crus** (krūs) **of the clitoris,** which attach to the pubic arch. Capping the body of the clitoris is the **glans** (glanz; acorn). The many specialized sensory nerve receptors housed in the clitoris provide pleasure to the female during sexual intercourse. The **prepuce** (prē′pūs; foreskin) is an external fold of the labia minora that forms a hoodlike covering over the clitoris.

28.2f Mammary Glands

Each **mammary gland,** or *breast,* is located within the anterior thoracic wall and is composed of a compound tubuloalveolar exocrine gland (**figure 28.10**). The gland's complex secretory product (called breast milk) contains proteins, fats, and a sugar to provide nutrition to infants.

The **nipple** (nip′ĕl; beak) is a cylindrical projection on the center of the breast. It contains multiple tiny openings of the excretory ducts that transport breast milk. The **areola** (ă-rē′ō-lă; small area) is the pigmented, rosy or brownish ring of skin around the nipple. Its surface often appears uneven and grainy due to the numerous sebaceous glands, called **areolar glands,** immediately internal to the surface. The color of the areola may vary, depending upon whether or not a woman has given birth. In a **nulliparous** (nŭl-ip′ă-rŭs; *nullus* = none, *pario* = to bear) woman—one who has never given birth—the areola is rosy or light brown in color. In a **parous** (par′ŭs) woman—one who has given birth—the areola may change to a darker rose or brown color.

Internally, the breasts are supported by fibrous connective bands called **suspensory ligaments.** These thin bands extend from the skin and attach to the deep fascia overlying the pectoralis major muscle. Thus, the breast and the pectoralis major muscle are structurally linked.

The mammary glands are subdivided into **lobes,** which are further subdivided into smaller compartments called **lobules.** Lobules contain secretory units termed **alveoli** that produce milk in the lactating female. Alveoli become more numerous and larger during pregnancy. Tiny ducts drain milk from the alveoli and lobules. The tiny ducts of the lobules merge and form 10 to 20 larger channels called **lactiferous** (lak-tif′ĕr-ŭs; *lact* = milk, *fero* = to bear) **ducts.** A lactiferous duct drains breast milk from a single lobe. As each lactiferous duct approaches the nipple, its lumen expands to form a **lactiferous sinus,** a space where milk is stored prior to release from the nipple.

During pregnancy, the levels of estrogen, progesterone, and prolactin rise dramatically. Recall from section 20.3a that the hormone **prolactin** is produced in the anterior pituitary and is responsible for milk production. Thus, when the amount of prolactin increases, the mammary gland grows and forms more expanded and numerous alveoli. In the last trimester of pregnancy, a precursor to breast milk (called colostrum) is produced and a few days after birth, colostrum is replaced by **breast milk.**

Breast milk is released by a process called **lactation** (lak-tā′shŭn; lactatio = to suckle), which occurs in response to a complex sequence of internal and external stimuli.

Clinical View 28.4

Contraception Methods

The term **contraception** (kon′tră-sep′shŭn) refers to birth control, or the prevention of pregnancy. There is a wide range of birth control methods with varying degrees of effectiveness.

Abstinence (ab′sti-nents; *abstineo* = to hold back) means refraining from sexual intercourse. Abstinence (when practiced correctly) is the only 100% proven way to prevent pregnancy.

Natural family planning (also known as the **rhythm method**) requires avoiding sexual intercourse during the time of ovulation. The rhythm method requires that a woman know when she is ovulating, which may be difficult to determine consistently. As a result, this method has a high failure rate (25%).

The **withdrawal method,** also known as the *pull-out method,* is where the penis is pulled out of the vagina before ejaculation. This method has a high failure rate, in part because it may be difficult to predict the point prior to ejaculation. Additionally, it may be possible for pre-ejaculate (emissions secreted prior to ejaculation) to collect enough sperm in the urethra from a prior ejaculation to impregnate a female. The failure rate for withdrawal is about 19%.

Lactation (nursing a baby) can prevent ovulation and menstruation for several to many months after childbirth *if* a woman nurses her child *constantly* (i.e., much more than five times a day!). The frequent lactation sends signals to the hypothalamus to prevent FSH and LH from being secreted, thus preventing ovulation. Failure rate in the first 6 months is 2%.

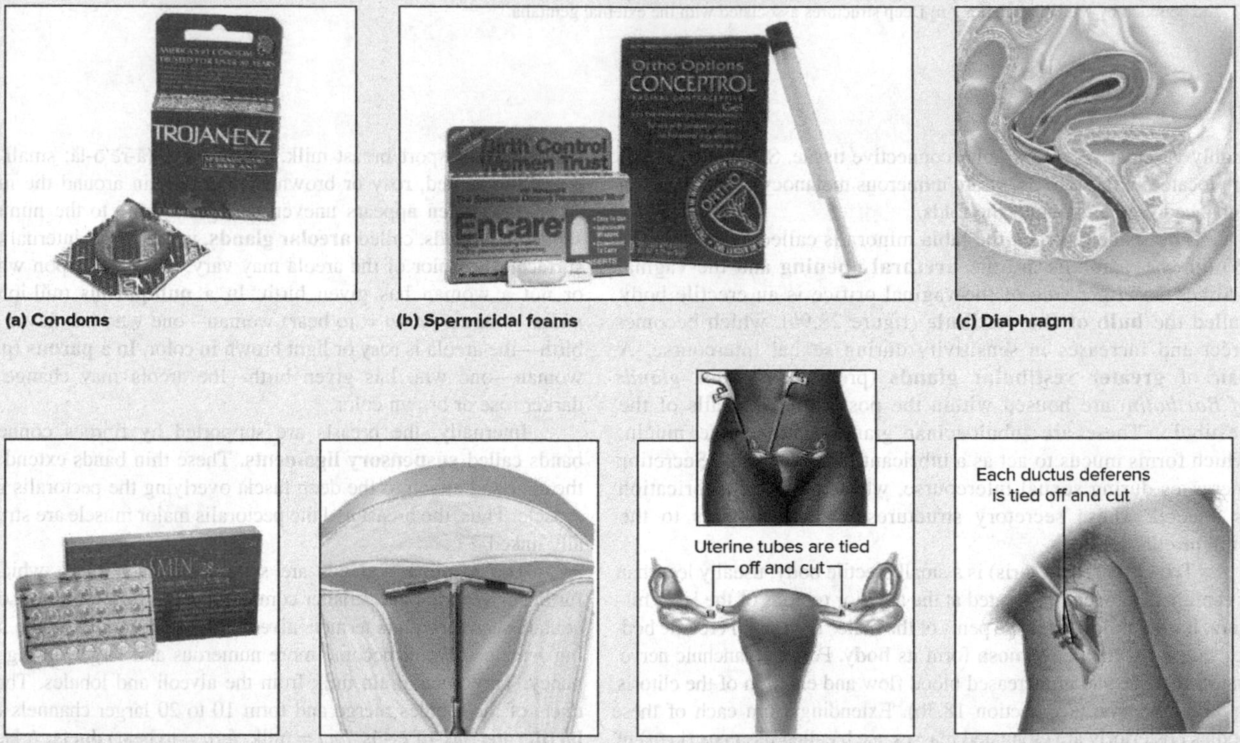

(a) Condoms (b) Spermicidal foams (c) Diaphragm (d) Oral contraceptive (e) Intrauterine device (IUD) (f) Tubal ligation (g) Vasectomy

Contraception includes barrier, chemical, and surgical methods.

(a, b, d) ©McGraw-Hill Education/Jill Braaten, photographer

Barrier methods of birth control use a physical barrier to prevent sperm from reaching the uterine tubes. Barrier methods include the following:

- **Condoms,** when used properly, collect the sperm and prevent them from entering the female reproductive tract. They are also the only birth control method that helps protect against sexually transmitted viruses and infections, such as human papillomavirus, herpes, and HIV. Condoms for males fit snugly on the erect penis, whereas **vaginal condoms** are placed in the vagina prior to sexual intercourse. The typical use failure rate for condoms is about 15%.
- **Spermicidal foams and gels** are chemical barrier methods that kill sperm before they travel to the uterine tubes. They are inserted into the vagina and/or placed on the penis prior to sexual intercourse. With a failure rate of about 25%, foams and gels should be used in conjunction with physical barrier methods.
- **Diaphragms** and **cervical caps** are circular, rubbery structures that are inserted into the vagina and placed over the cervix prior to sexual intercourse. Spermicidal gel is used around the edges to help prevent sperm from entering the cervix. The failure rate for these products is as high as 20% in the first year of use.

Intrauterine devices (IUDs) are T-shaped, flexible plastic structures inserted into the uterus by a health-care provider. Once in place, the IUD prevents fertilization from occurring. The IUD may contain copper or levonorgestrel. IUDs containing copper are effective for up to 10 years, and those containing levonorgestrel (e.g., Skyla or Mirena) are effective for 3 to 5 years. Although few women in North America use IUDs, their failure rate typically is low (1% to 2%).

Chemical methods of birth control are very effective if used properly. They include the following:

- **Oral contraceptives**, commonly called *birth control pills*, come in packets varying from 21 to 91 days. These daily pills contain low levels of estrogen and/or progestins. Some packets include a week of non-hormone-containing pills, during which circulating levels of estrogen and progestins drop, and menstruation occurs. (*Note:* Progesterone is one type of progestin.) The low levels of estrogen and progestins prevent the LH "spike" needed for ovulation. Thus, oral contraceptives prevent ovulation. Typical use failure rate depends upon the product and is between 0.1% and 7%.
- **Estrogen/progestin** (prō-jes′tin; *pro* = before, gestation) **patches** are alternatives to the daily oral contraceptive. A patch placed on the body delivers a regular amount of estrogen/progestin through the skin (transdermally). The patch is replaced each week. The typical use failure rate is 1%.
- **Injected/implanted progestins** help prevent pregnancy by preventing ovulation and thickening the mucus around the cervix (thus creating a slight physical barrier to the sperm). Medroxyprogesterone (Depo-Provera) is an injectable contraceptive given once every 3 months, whereas etonogestrel (Implanon) is an implantable contraceptive that lasts for up to 3 years. The typical use failure rate for these products is 0.3%.
- **Morning-after pills** containing levonorgestrel (e.g., Preven or Plan B One-Step) must be taken within 48 to 72 hours after having unprotected intercourse and is most effective when taken within 24 hours. These pills work by inhibiting ovulation, altering the menstrual cycle to delay ovulation, or irritating the uterine lining to prevent implantation.
- **Mifepristone** (Mifeprex in the United States; RU-486 in Europe) was approved for use during the first 7 weeks of pregnancy. Mifepristone blocks progesterone receptors, so progesterone cannot attach to these receptors and thereby maintain a pregnancy. When taken with a prostaglandin drug, mifepristone induces a miscarriage.

Surgical methods of contraception are **tubal ligation** for women and **vasectomy** (va-sek′tō-mē) for men. A tubal ligation requires that uterine tubes are cut and the ends are tied off or cauterized shut to prevent both sperm from reaching the oocyte and the oocyte from reaching the uterus. The uterine tubes are ligated either laparoscopically (shown in the adjacent figure) or via entry through the uterus. A vasectomy is an outpatient procedure whereby each ductus deferens is cut, a short segment is removed, and then the ends are tied off. Sperm cannot leave the testis and thus are broken down and resorbed. Both surgeries are effective birth control methods, but they are usually permanent and irreversible.

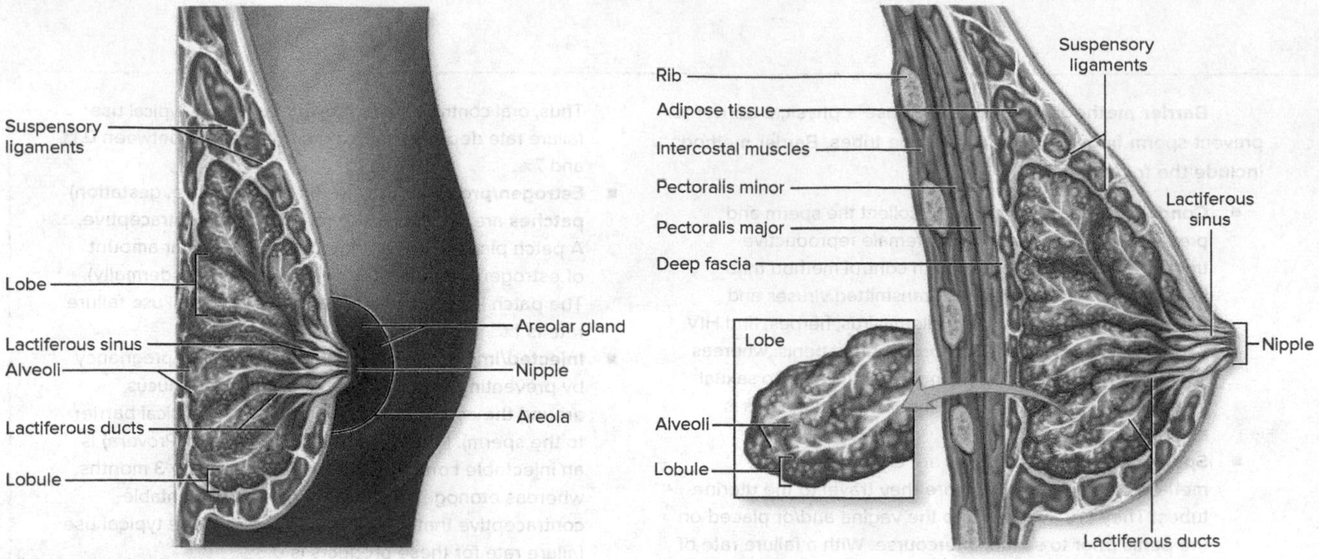

(a) Anteromedial view **(b) Sagittal view**

Figure 28.10

Mammary Glands. The mammary glands are composed of glandular tissue and a variable amount of fat. (*a*) An anterior view is partially cut away to reveal internal structures. (*b*) A diagrammatic sagittal section of a mammary gland shows the distribution of alveoli within lobules and the extension of ducts to the nipple. **APR**

Clinical View 28.5

Breast Cancer

Breast cancer affects about 1 in every 8 women in the United States, and it also occurs in males, although infrequently. Some well-documented risk factors for breast cancer include: maternal relatives with breast cancer, longer reproductive span (early menarche coupled with delayed menopause), obesity, nulliparity (never having been pregnant), late age at first pregnancy, and the presence of mutations in genes (*BRCA1* and *BRCA2*). Except for the genetic influence, all of the risk factors are related to increased exposure to estrogen over a long period of time.

Almost all breast cancers are carcinomas, meaning the cancer is derived from epithelium (in this case, the epithelium that lines the lactiferous ducts and lobules of the breast). Monthly self-examination has proved to be one of the most important means of early detection of breast malignancies. **Mammography,** which is an x-ray of the breast that can detect small areas of increased tissue density, can identify many small malignancies that are not yet palpable in a self-examination. Recommendations vary, but most physicians agree that women 40 and over should have a mammogram done every 1 to 2 years.

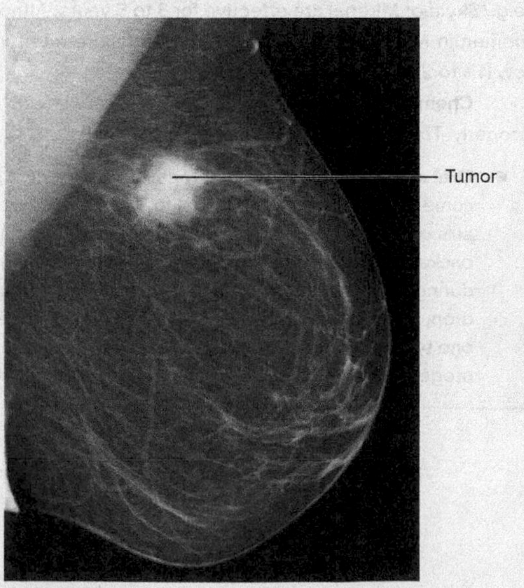

Mammogram showing a tumor in the breast.
ksass/Getty Images

While prolactin stimulates production of breast milk, the hormone **oxytocin** is responsible for milk ejection. Recall from section 20.3b that oxytocin is secreted by the hypothalamus and stored in the posterior lobe of the pituitary, and is also responsible for uterine contractions during labor. In response to a stimulus, such as a baby crying or sucking the nipple, oxytocin is released, and milk is ejected from the nipple. As milk drains from the alveoli, increased levels of prolactin are released so the breast can produce more milk. Once a baby stops nursing, the levels of oxytocin drop, and milk ejection ceases. This release of oxytocin is regulated by positive feedback (see section 20.1b, figure 20.3).

During the first few weeks of breast-feeding, the mother may experience uterine contractions called **afterpains,** which are caused by the increased levels of oxytocin in her blood. These uterine contractions help shrink the uterus to its prepregnancy size. Afterpains typically become less noticeable and cease a few weeks after birth, by which time the uterus has shrunk considerably.

WHAT DID YOU LEARN?

7. Identify and describe the ligaments that support the uterus and hold it in place.
8. What name is given to the innermost tunic of the uterus? What are the two distinct layers that form this tunic?
9. What mammary gland structures produce and drain milk from each lobe?

28.3 Anatomy of the Male Reproductive System

✓ Learning Objectives

10. Describe the gross and microscopic anatomy of the testes.
11. Explain both spermatogenesis and spermiogenesis.
12. Outline the male reproductive duct system, and explain the function of each component.
13. Describe the anatomy and function of the male accessory reproductive organs.
14. Identify and describe the components of the penis.

In the male, the primary sex organs are the **testes** (tes'tēz; sing., *testis*). The accessory reproductive organs include a complex set of ducts and tubules leading from the testes to the penis, a group of male accessory glands, and the penis, which is the organ of copulation (**figure 28.11**).

28.3a Scrotum

The ideal temperature for producing and storing sperm is about 2°–3° Celsius lower than internal body temperature. The **scrotum** (skrō'tŭm), which is a skin-covered sac between the thighs, provides the cooler environment needed for normal sperm development and maturation (**figure 28.12**). The scrotum is homologous to the labia majora.

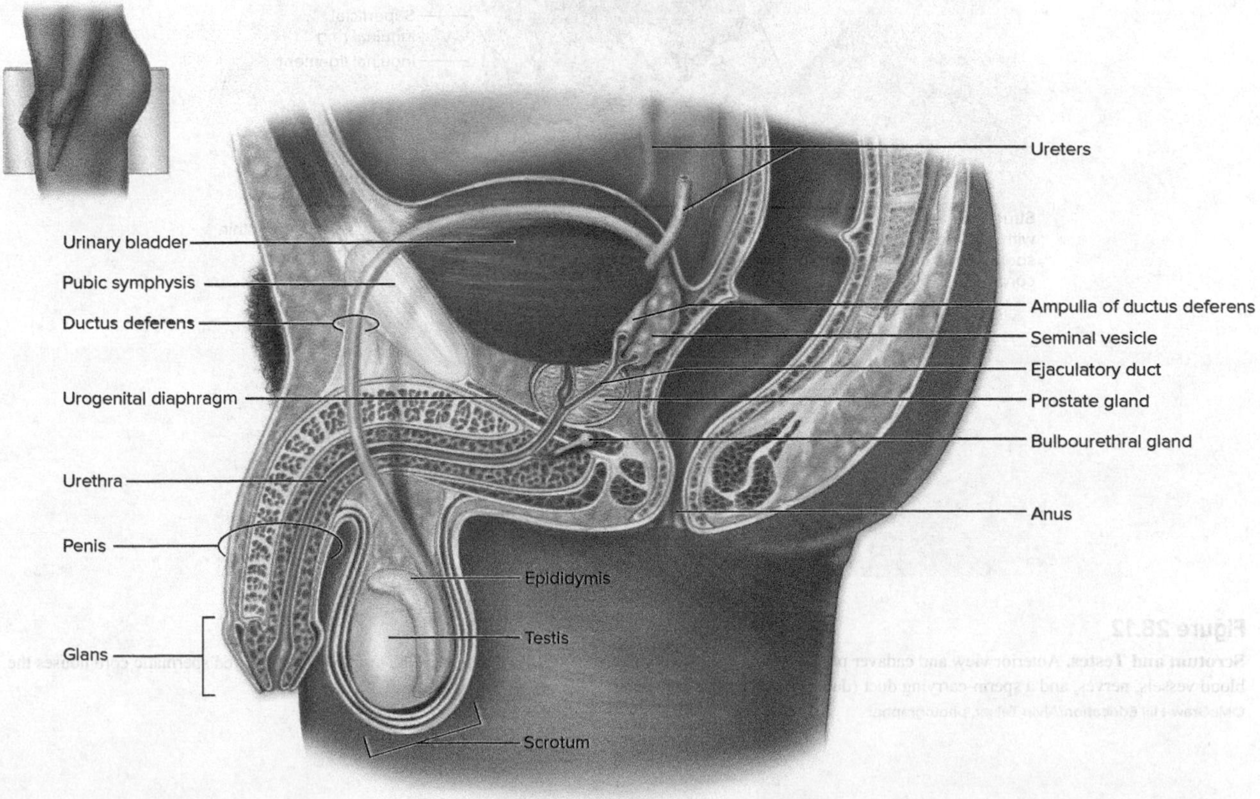

Figure 28.11
Male Pelvic Region. A diagrammatic sagittal section shows the locations and relationships of the male pelvic structures. APR

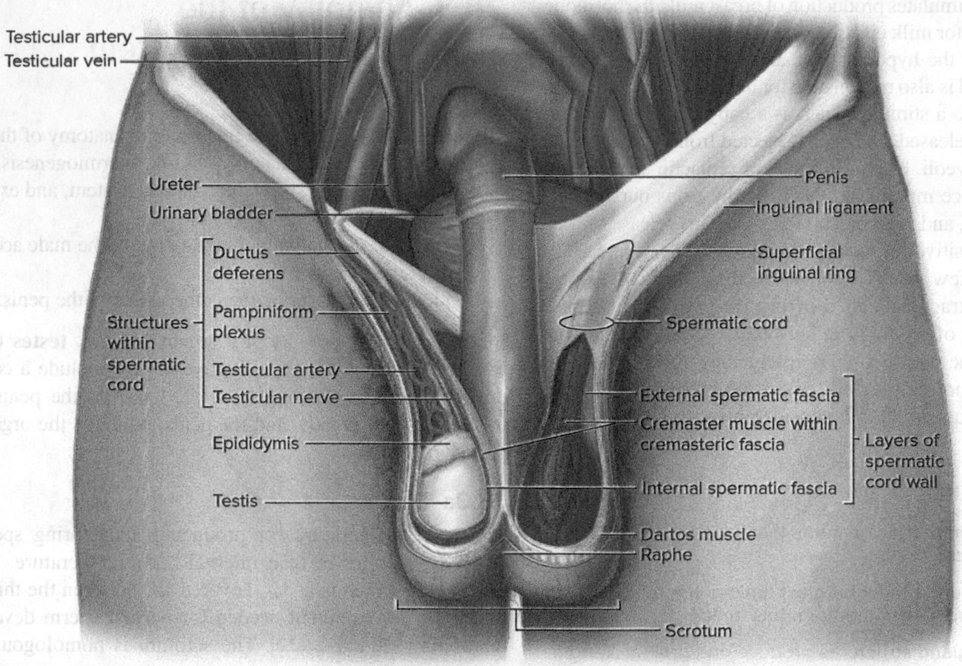

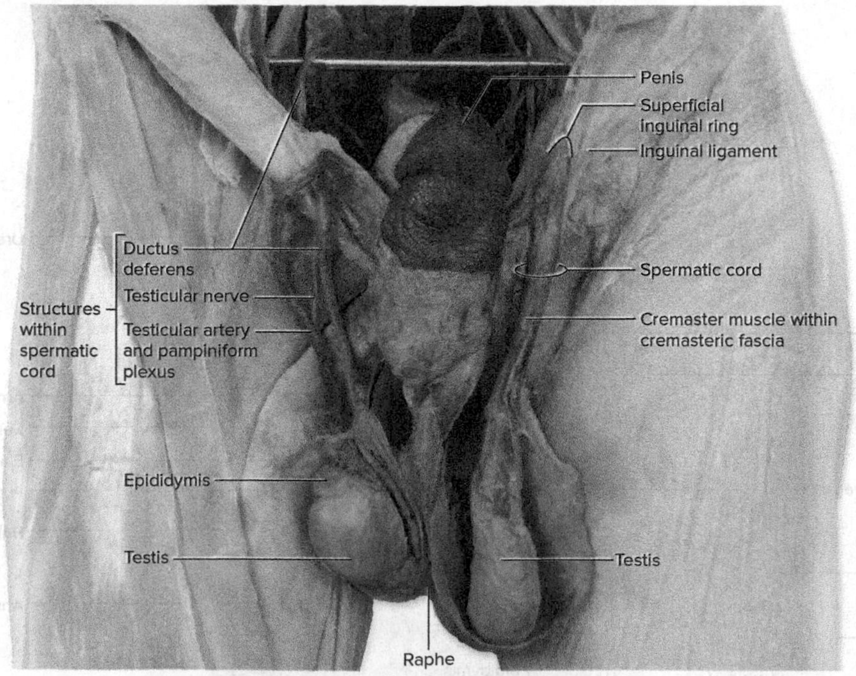

Figure 28.12

Scrotum and Testes. Anterior view and cadaver photo show the scrotum, a skin-covered sac that houses the testes. A multilayered spermatic cord houses the blood vessels, nerves, and a sperm-carrying duct (ductus deferens) for each testis. APR

Externally, the scrotum contains a distinct, ridgelike seam at its midline, called the **raphe** (rā′fē; *rhaphe* = seam). The raphe persists in an anterior direction along the inferior surface of the penis and in a posterior direction to the anus. The wall of the scrotum is composed of an external layer of skin, a thin layer of superficial fascia immediately internal to the skin, and a smooth muscle layer, the **dartos** (dar′t ōs; skinned) **muscle,** immediately internal to the fascia.

When the testes are exposed to elevated temperatures, the dartos muscle relaxes, which unwrinkles the skin of the scrotum and allows the testes to move further away from the body. This inferior movement away from the body cools the testes. At the same time, another muscle (the cremaster muscle) also relaxes to allow the testes to move inferiorly away from the body. The opposite occurs if the testes are exposed to cold. In this case, the dartos and cremaster muscles contract, pulling the testes and scrotum closer to the body to conserve heat.

28.3b Spermatic Cord

The blood vessels and nerves to the testis travel from within the abdomen to the scrotum in a multilayered structure called the **spermatic cord** (figure 28.12; see **figure 28.13***a*). The spermatic cord originates in the **inguinal canal,** a tubelike passageway through the inferior abdominal wall (see section 13.4b). This canal can be the site of inguinal hernias as discussed in Clinical View 11.5 "Hernias" in section 11.4.

The spermatic cord wall consists of three layers:

- An **internal spermatic fascia** is formed from fascia deep to the abdominal muscles.
- The **cremaster** (krē-mas′ter; a suspender) **muscle** and **cremasteric fascia** are formed from muscle fiber extensions of the internal oblique muscle and its aponeurosis, respectively.
- An **external spermatic fascia** is formed from the aponeurosis of the external oblique muscle.

Within the spermatic cord is a singular **testicular artery** that is a direct branch from the abdominal aorta (see section 23.3g). The testicular artery is surrounded by a plexus of veins called the **pampiniform** (pam-pin′i-f ōrm; *pampinus* = tendril, *forma* = form) **plexus.** This venous plexus is a means to provide thermoregulation by pre-cooling arterial blood prior to reaching the testes. Autonomic nerves travel with these vessels and innervate the testis (see section 18.4a).

28.3c Testes

In an adult, each testis is an oval organ housed within the scrotum (see figure 28.12). Each weighs about 10–12 grams, and displays average dimensions of 4 centimeters (cm) in length, 2 cm in width, and 2.5 cm in anteroposterior diameter. The testes produce sperm and androgens (male sex hormones).

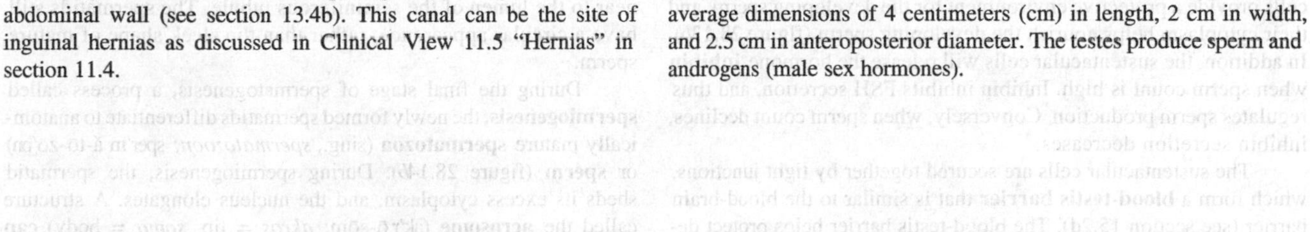
Spermatic cord
Blood vessels and nerves
Head of epididymis
Duct of epididymis
Seminiferous tubule
Ductus deferens
Efferent ductule
Mediastinum testis (housing rete testis)
Septum
Lobule
Body of epididymis
Visceral layer of tunica vaginalis
Parietal layer of tunica vaginalis
Tunica albuginea
Tail of epididymis
(a) Testis
Seminiferous tubule
Sustentacular cells
Sperm
Spermatids
Germ cells
Spermatogonia
Interstitial cell
Tubule lumen
LM 40x
(b) Seminiferous tubule, cross section

Figure 28.13

Testes and Seminiferous Tubules. (*a*) The gross anatomy of a testis is shown diagrammatically in a cut-away, partial sagittal section. (*b*) A photomicrograph reveals a cross section of a seminiferous tubule in the testis.

(b) Dr. Thomas Caceci, Virginia-Maryland Regional College of Veterinary Medicine

Each testis is covered both anteriorly and laterally by a serous membrane, the **tunica vaginalis** (văj-in-ăl'ĭs; ensheathing). This membrane is derived from the peritoneum of the abdominal cavity. The tunica vaginalis has an outer **parietal layer** and an inner **visceral layer** that are separated by serous fluid. A thick, whitish, fibrous capsule called the **tunica albuginea** covers the testis and lies immediately deep to the visceral layer of the tunica vaginalis (figure 28.13*a*). At the posterior margin of the testis, the tunica albuginea thickens and projects into the interior of the organ as the **mediastinum testis.** Blood vessels, a system of ducts, lymphatic vessels, and some nerve fibers enter or leave each testis through the mediastinum testis.

The tunica albuginea projects internally into the testis and forms delicate connective tissue **septa,** which subdivide the internal space into about 250 separate **lobules.** Each lobule contains up to four extremely convoluted, thin and elongated **seminiferous** (sem'i-nif' ĕr-ŭs; *semen* = seed, *fero* = to carry) **tubules.** The seminiferous tubules contain two types of cells: (1) a group of nondividing support cells called the **sustentacular** (sŭs'ten-tak'yū-lăr; *sustento* = to hold upright) (*Sertoli* or *nurse*) **cells,** and (2) a population of dividing germ cells that continuously produce sperm beginning at puberty.

The sustentacular cells assist with sperm development. These cells provide a protective environment for the developing sperm, and their cytoplasm helps nourish the developing sperm (figure 28.13*b*). In addition, the sustentacular cells will release the hormone **inhibin** when sperm count is high. Inhibin inhibits FSH secretion, and thus regulates sperm production. Conversely, when sperm count declines, inhibin secretion decreases.

The sustentacular cells are secured together by tight junctions, which form a **blood-testis barrier** that is similar to the blood-brain barrier (see section 15.2d). The blood-testis barrier helps protect developing sperm from materials in the blood. It also protects the sperm from the body's leukocytes, which may perceive the sperm as foreign because they have different chromosome numbers and arrangements from the other body cells.

The spaces surrounding the seminiferous tubules are called **interstitial spaces.** Within these spaces reside the **interstitial cells** (or *Leydig cells*). Luteinizing hormone stimulates the interstitial cells to produce hormones called **androgens** (an'dr ō-jen; *andros* = male human). There are several types of androgens, the most common one being testosterone. Although the adrenal cortex secretes a small amount of androgens, the vast majority of androgen release is via the interstitial cells in the testis, beginning at puberty.

WHAT DO YOU THINK?

3. If a male's testes were removed, would he still be able to produce androgens?

Development of Sperm: Spermatogenesis and Spermiogenesis

Spermatogenesis (sper'm ă-tō-jen'ĕ-sis; *genesis* = origin) is the process of sperm development that occurs within the seminiferous tubule of the testis. Spermatogenesis does not begin until puberty, when GnRH secretion releases FSH and LH, which stimulate the testis to begin gamete development.

The process of spermatogenesis is shown in **figure 28.14*a*.** All sperm develop from primordial germ (stem) cells called **spermatogonia** (sper'm ă-tŏ-gō'nē-ă; sing., *spermatogonium; sperma* = seed, *gone* = generation). Spermatogonia are diploid cells (meaning they have 23 pairs of chromosomes for a total of 46). These cells lie near the base of the seminiferous tubule, surrounded by the cytoplasm of sustentacular cells. To produce sperm, spermatogonia first divide by mitosis (see section 2.6). One of the cells produced is a new spermatogonium (a new germ cell), to ensure that the numbers of spermatogonia never become depleted, and the other cell is a "committed cell" which becomes a **primary spermatocyte.** A primary spermatocyte is diploid and an exact copy of a spermatogonium. It is the primary spermatocytes that undergo meiosis.

When a primary spermatocyte undergoes meiosis I, the two cells produced are called **secondary spermatocytes.** Secondary spermatocytes are haploid, meaning they have 23 chromosomes only. These cells remain surrounded by the sustentacular cells, but move relatively closer to the lumen of the seminiferous tubule as opposed to the base of the seminiferous tubule.

Secondary spermatocytes complete meiosis (go through meiosis II) and form **spermatids** (sper 'mă-tid). A spermatid is a haploid cell and is surrounded by the sustentacular cell, very near to the lumen of the seminiferous tubule. The spermatids still have a circular appearance, rather than the sleek shape of mature sperm.

During the final stage of spermatogenesis, a process called **spermiogenesis,** the newly formed spermatids differentiate to anatomically mature **spermatozoa** (sing., *spermatozoon;* sper'm ă-tō-zō'on) or **sperm** (figure 28.14*b*). During spermiogenesis, the spermatid sheds its excess cytoplasm, and the nucleus elongates. A structure called the **acrosome** (ak'r ō-sōm; *akros* = tip, *soma* = body) **cap** forms over the nucleus. This acrosome cap contains digestive enzymes that help penetrate the secondary oocyte for fertilization. As the spermatid elongates, a **tail** (*flagellum*) forms from the organized microtubules. The tail attaches to a **midpiece** (*neck*) region containing mitochondria and a centriole. These mitochondria provide the energy to move the tail.

Learning Strategy 28.4

Use these hints to help identify the various testis cells microscopically:

1. Spermatogonia are closest to the seminiferous tubule base. As spermatogenesis occurs and the cells mature, more mature cells are found closer to the lumen of the seminiferous tubule. Note how close the spermatozoa are to the lumen.
2. Sometimes it is difficult to distinguish an entire sustentacular cell because its cytoplasm is pale and surrounds the developing sperm. You can identify sustentacular cells by their nucleus, which is oval or flattened and usually has a prominent nucleolus.
3. The interstitial cells are not located within the seminiferous tubule but external to it, usually in clumps of three or more cells.

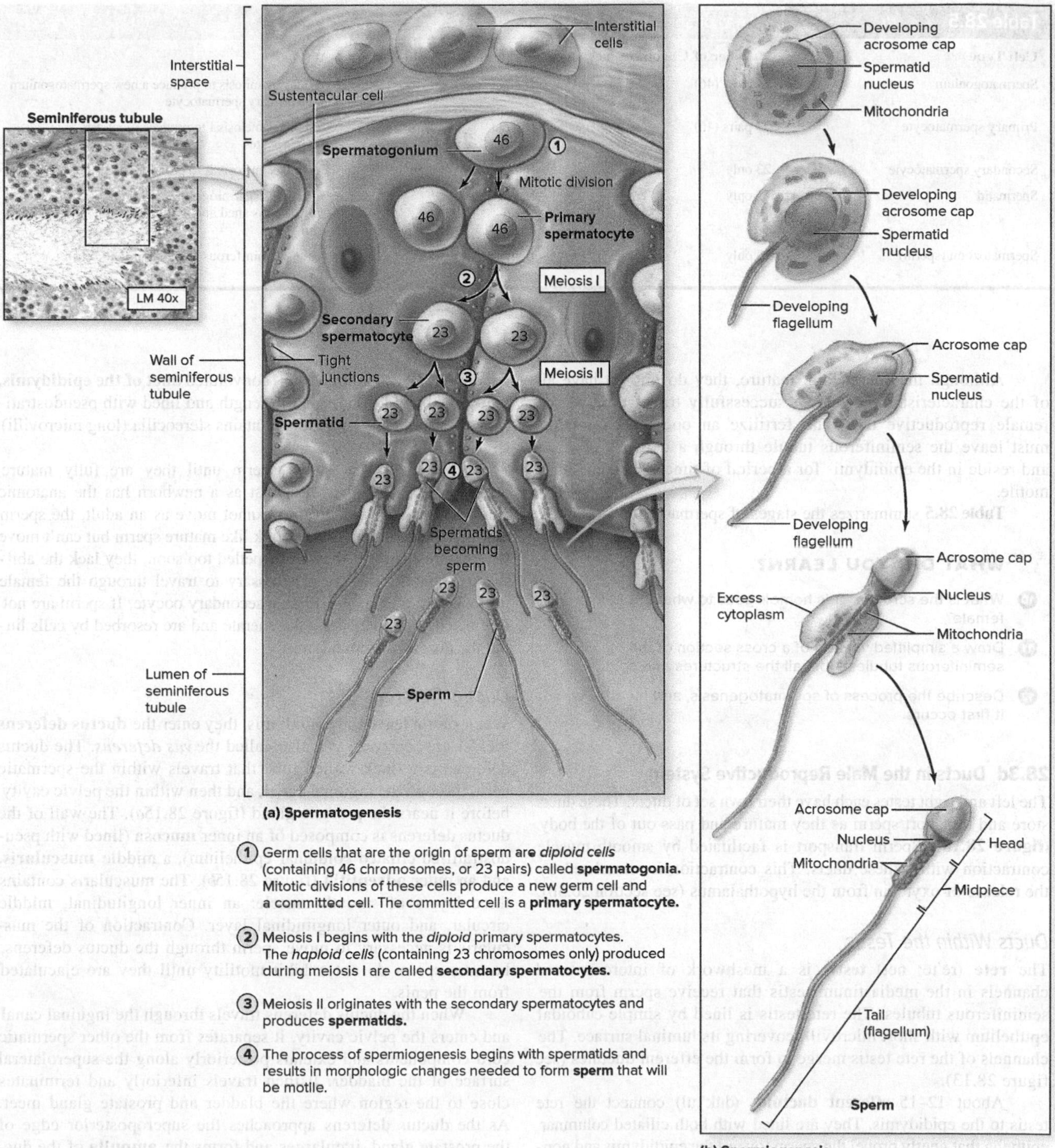
Seminiferous tubule
LM 40x
Interstitial space
Sustentacular cell
Interstitial cells
Spermatogonium
46
1
Mitotic division
46
46
Primary spermatocyte
2
Meiosis I
Secondary spermatocyte
23
23
Wall of seminiferous tubule
Tight junctions
3
Meiosis II
Spermatid
23
4
Spermatids becoming sperm
Lumen of seminiferous tubule
Sperm
(a) Spermatogenesis
1 Germ cells that are the origin of sperm are *diploid cells* (containing 46 chromosomes, or 23 pairs) called **spermatogonia.** Mitotic divisions of these cells produce a new germ cell and a committed cell. The committed cell is a **primary spermatocyte.**
2 Meiosis I begins with the *diploid* primary spermatocytes. The *haploid cells* (containing 23 chromosomes only) produced during meiosis I are called **secondary spermatocytes.**
3 Meiosis II originates with the secondary spermatocytes and produces **spermatids.**
4 The process of spermiogenesis begins with spermatids and results in morphologic changes needed to form **sperm** that will be motile.
Developing acrosome cap
Spermatid nucleus
Mitochondria
Developing acrosome cap
Spermatid nucleus
Developing flagellum
Acrosome cap
Spermatid nucleus
Developing flagellum
Acrosome cap
Nucleus
Excess cytoplasm
Mitochondria
Acrosome cap
Nucleus
Mitochondria
Head
Midpiece
Tail (flagellum)
Sperm
(b) Spermiogenesis

Figure 28.14

Spermatogenesis and Spermiogenesis. (*a*) The processes of spermatogenesis and spermiogenesis take place within the wall of the seminiferous tubule. (*b*) Structural changes occur during spermiogenesis as a sperm forms from a spermatid. APR

(a) Dr. Thomas Caceci, Virginia-Maryland Regional College of Veterinary Medicine

Table 28.5 Stages of Spermatogenesis

Cell Type	Number of Chromosomes	Haploid or Diploid	Action
Spermatogonium	23 pairs (46)	Diploid	Divides by mitosis to produce a new spermatogonium and a primary spermatocyte
Primary spermatocyte	23 pairs (46)	Diploid	Completes meiosis I to produce secondary spermatocytes
Secondary spermatocyte	23 only	Haploid	Completes meiosis II to produce spermatids
Spermatid	23 only	Haploid	Undergoes spermiogenesis, where most of its cytoplasm is shed and a midpiece, tail, and head form
Spermatozoon (sperm)	23 only	Haploid	Leaves seminiferous tubule and matures in epididymis

Although the sperm look mature, they do not yet have all of the characteristics needed to successfully travel through the female reproductive tract and fertilize an oocyte. The sperm must leave the seminiferous tubule through a network of ducts and reside in the epididymis for a period of time to become fully motile.

Table 28.5 summarizes the stages of spermatogenesis.

WHAT DID YOU LEARN?

10. What is the scrotum? It is homologous to what structure in the female?
11. Draw a simplified version of a cross section of the seminiferous tubule. Label all the structures and cells.
12. Describe the process of spermatogenesis, and mention when it first occurs.

28.3d Ducts in the Male Reproductive System

The left and right testes each have their own set of ducts. These ducts store and transport sperm as they mature and pass out of the body **(figure 28.15)**. Sperm transport is facilitated by smooth muscle contraction within these ducts. This contraction is stimulated by the release of oxytocin from the hypothalamus (see section 20.3b).

Ducts Within the Testis

The **rete** (rē'tē; net) **testis** is a meshwork of interconnected channels in the mediastinum testis that receive sperm from the seminiferous tubules. The rete testis is lined by simple cuboidal epithelium with short microvilli covering its luminal surface. The channels of the rete testis merge to form the efferent ductules (see figure 28.13).

About 12–15 **efferent ductules** (dŭk'tūl) connect the rete testis to the epididymis. They are lined with both ciliated columnar epithelia that gently propel the sperm toward the epididymis and nonciliated columnar epithelia that absorb excess fluid secreted by the seminiferous tubules. The efferent ductules drain into the epididymis.

Epididymis

The **epididymis** (ep'i-did'i-mis; pl.,*epididymides; epi* = upon, *didymis* = twin) is a comma-shaped structure composed of an internal duct and an external covering of connective tissue. Its **head** lies on the superior surface of the testis, whereas the **body** and **tail** are on the posterior surface of the testis (see figure 28.13*a*). Internally, the epididymis contains a long, convoluted **duct of the epididymis,** which is about 4 to 5 meters in length and lined with pseudostratified columnar epithelium that contains stereocilia (long microvilli) (figure 28.15*c*).

The epididymis stores sperm until they are fully mature and capable of being motile. Just as a newborn has the anatomic characteristics of an adult, but cannot move as an adult, the sperm that first enter the epididymis look like mature sperm but can't move like mature sperm. If they are expelled too soon, they lack the ability to be motile, which is necessary to travel through the female reproductive tract and fertilize a secondary oocyte. If sperm are not ejaculated, the older sperm degenerate and are resorbed by cells lining the duct of the epididymis.

Ductus Deferens

When sperm leave the epididymis, they enter the **ductus deferens** (dĕf'er-ens; carry away), also called the *vas deferens.* The ductus deferens is a thick-walled tube that travels within the spermatic cord, through the inguinal canal, and then within the pelvic cavity before it nears the prostate gland (figure 28.15*a*). The wall of the ductus deferens is composed of an inner **mucosa** (lined with pseudostratified ciliated columnar epithelium), a middle **muscularis,** and an outer **adventitia** (figure 28.15*b*). The muscularis contains three layers of smooth muscle: an inner longitudinal, middle circular, and outer longitudinal layer. Contraction of the muscularis is necessary to move sperm through the ductus deferens, because sperm do not exhibit motility until they are ejaculated from the penis.

When the ductus deferens travels through the inguinal canal and enters the pelvic cavity, it separates from the other spermatic cord components and extends posteriorly along the superolateral surface of the bladder. It then travels inferiorly and terminates close to the region where the bladder and prostate gland meet. As the ductus deferens approaches the superoposterior edge of the prostate gland, it enlarges and forms the **ampulla** of the ductus deferens (figure 28.15*a*). The ampulla of the ductus deferens unites with the proximal region of the seminal vesicle to form the terminal portion of the reproductive duct system, called the ejaculatory duct.

Ejaculatory Duct

Each **ejaculatory duct** is between 1 and 2 centimeters long. The epithelium of the ejaculatory duct is a pseudostratified ciliated columnar epithelium. The ejaculatory duct conducts sperm (from the

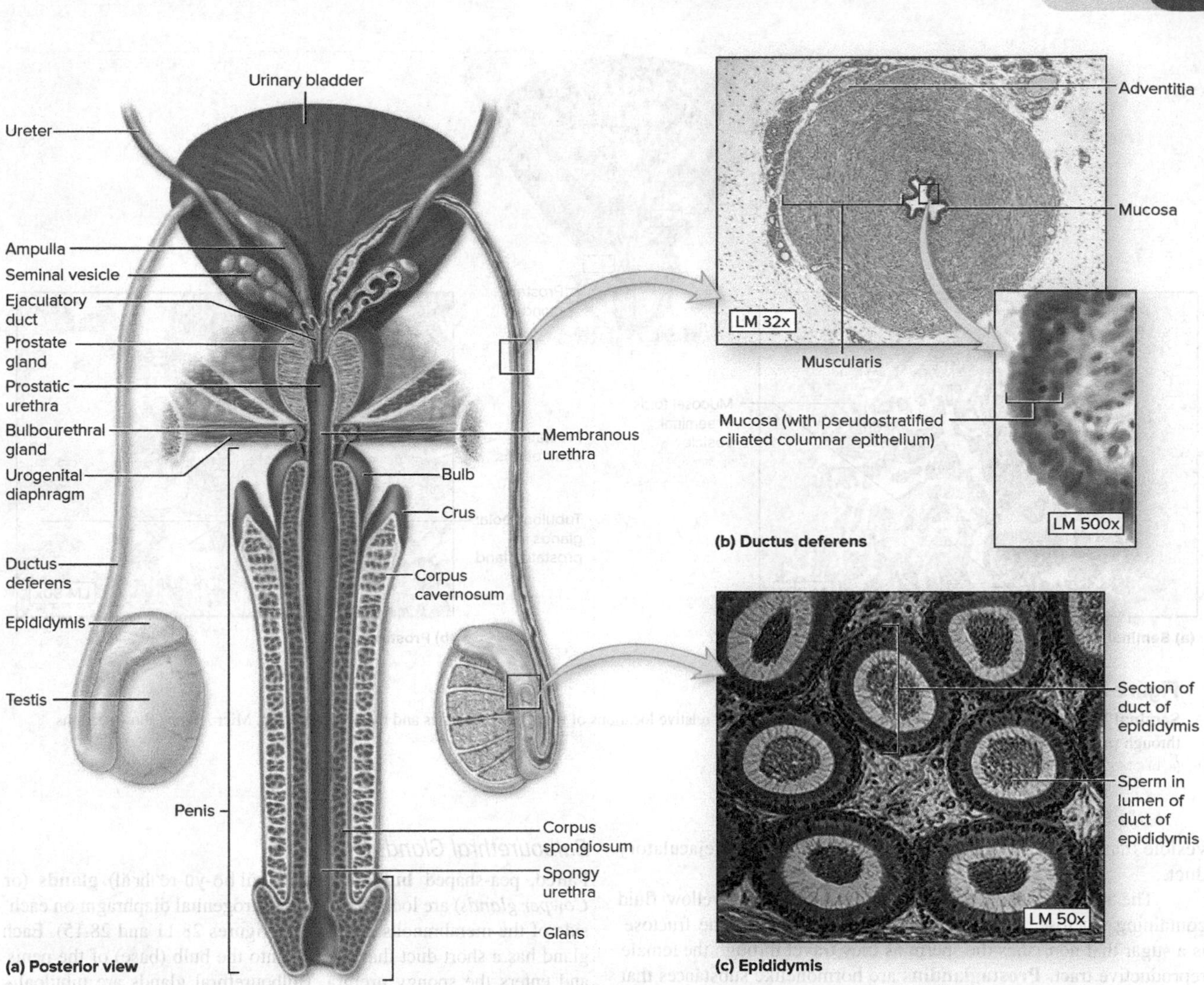
Urinary bladder
Ureter
Ampulla
Seminal vesicle
Ejaculatory duct
Prostate gland
Prostatic urethra
Bulbourethral gland
Urogenital diaphragm
Ductus deferens
Epididymis
Testis
Penis
Membranous urethra
Bulb
Crus
Corpus cavernosum
Corpus spongiosum
Spongy urethra
Glans
(a) Posterior view
Adventitia
Mucosa
LM 32x
Muscularis
Mucosa (with pseudostratified ciliated columnar epithelium)
LM 500x
(b) Ductus deferens
Section of duct of epididymis
Sperm in lumen of duct of epididymis
LM 50x
(c) Epididymis

Figure 28.15

Duct System in the Male Reproductive Tract. (*a*) A posterior view depicts the structural components of the male reproductive ducts and accessory glands. (*b*) Micrographs show a cross section through the ductus deferens. (*c*) A micrograph shows a cross section through the epididymis. APR

(b, top and bottom) ©McGraw-Hill Education/Alvin Telser, photographer; (c) Ed Reschke/Getty Images

ductus deferens) and a component of seminal fluid (from the seminal vesicle) toward the urethra. Each ejaculatory duct opens into the prostatic urethra.

Urethra

The **urethra** transports semen from both ejaculatory ducts to the outside of the body. Recall from section 27.3c that the urethra is subdivided into a **prostatic** (pros-tat′ik) **urethra** that extends through the prostate gland (figure 28.15), a **membranous urethra** that travels through the urogenital diaphragm, and a **spongy urethra** that extends through the penis.

28.3e Accessory Glands

Recall from section 28.2d that the vagina has a highly acidic environment to prevent bacterial growth. Sperm cannot survive in this type of environment, so a slightly alkaline (pH 7–8) secretion called **seminal** (sem′i-n ăl) **fluid** is needed to neutralize the acidity of the vagina. In addition, as the sperm travel through the female reproductive tract (a process that can take hours to several days), they are nourished by nutrients within the seminal fluid. The components of seminal fluid are produced by accessory glands: the seminal vesicles, the prostate gland, and the bulbourethral glands.

Seminal Vesicles

The paired **seminal vesicles** are located on the posterior surface of the urinary bladder lateral to the ampulla of the ductus deferens (figure 28.15*a*). Each seminal vesicle is an elongated, hollow organ about 5–8 centimeters long. The wall of each vesicle contains mucosal folds of pseudostratified columnar epithelium (**figure 28.16*a***). It is the medial (proximal) portion of the seminal

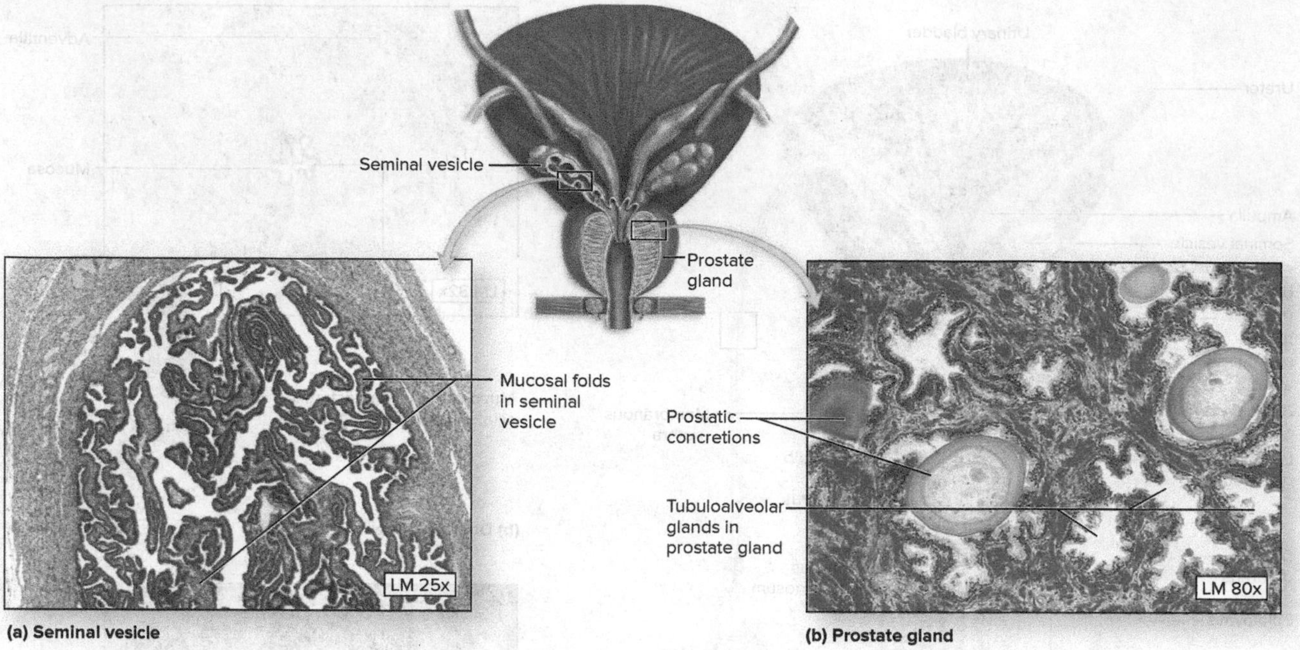

Figure 28.16

Seminal Vesicles and Prostate Gland. A drawing depicts the relative locations of the seminal vesicles and the prostate gland. Micrographs show sections through (*a*) a seminal vesicle and (*b*) the prostate gland.

(a, b) ©McGraw-Hill Education/Alvin Telser, photographer

vesicle that merges with a ductus deferens to form the ejaculatory duct.

The seminal vesicles secrete a viscous, whitish-yellow fluid containing fructose, prostaglandins, and bicarbonate. The fructose is a sugar that nourishes the sperm as they travel through the female reproductive tract. **Prostaglandins** are hormonelike substances that promote the widening and slight dilation of the external os of the cervix, which facilitates sperm entry into the uterus. Bicarbonate helps maintain the pH of the existing fluid.

Prostate Gland

The **prostate** (pros′tāt; one who stands before) **gland** is a compact, encapsulated organ that weighs about 20 grams and is shaped like a walnut, measuring about 2 cm by 3 cm by 4 cm. It is located immediately inferior to the bladder. The prostate gland includes submucosal glands that produce mucin and more than 30 tubuloalveolar glands that open directly through numerous ducts into the prostatic urethra (figure 28.16*b*). Together, these glands contribute a component to the seminal fluid.

The prostate gland secretes a slightly milky fluid that is weakly acidic and rich in citric acid, seminalplasmin, and **prostate-specific antigen (PSA).** The citric acid is a nutrient for sperm health, the seminalplasmin is an antibiotic that combats urinary tract infections in the male, and the PSA acts as an enzyme to help liquify semen following ejaculation. (Note that the slightly acidic secretion of the prostate does not cause the seminal fluid to be acidic, and thus the seminal fluid still functions to neutralize the acidity of the vagina.) Some components of prostatic fluid solidify into spherical bodies called *prostatic concretions* (kon-krē′shŭn) in the lumens of the glands (figure 28.16*b*).

Bulbourethral Glands

Paired, pea-shaped **bulbourethral** (bŭl′bō-yū-rē′thr ăl) **glands** (or *Cowper glands*) are located within the urogenital diaphragm on each side of the membranous urethra (see figures 28.11 and 28.15). Each gland has a short duct that projects into the bulb (base) of the penis and enters the spongy urethra. Bulbourethral glands are tubuloalveolar glands that have a simple columnar and pseudostratified columnar epithelium. Their secretory product is a clear, viscous mucin that forms mucus. As a component of the seminal fluid, this mucus lubricates the urethra prior to ejaculation.

28.3f Semen

Seminal fluid from the accessory glands combines with sperm from the testes to make up **semen** (sē′mĕn; seed). When released during intercourse, semen is called the **ejaculate** (ē-jak′y ū-lāt), and it normally measures about 3 to 5 milliliters in volume and contains about 200 to 500 million spermatozoa. The average transit time of human spermatozoa—from their release into the lumen of the seminiferous tubules, passage through the duct system, and appearance in the ejaculate—is about 2 weeks. Because semen is composed primarily of seminal fluid, a male who is very active sexually may have a reduced sperm count because there are fewer sperm to be released from the epididymis; however, the total semen volume remains close to normal for that individual.

WHAT DO YOU THINK?

4 If a male has a vasectomy, is he still able to produce sperm? If so, what happens to those sperm? How is the composition of semen changed in an individual who has had a vasectomy?

Clinical View 28.6

Benign Prostatic Hyperplasia and Prostate Cancer

Benign prostatic hyperplasia (BPH) is a noncancerous enlargement of the prostate gland. BPH is a common disorder in older men, caused by hormonal changes.

In BPH, large, discrete nodules form within the prostate and compress the prostatic urethra. Thus, the patient has difficulty starting and stopping a stream of urine, and often complains of **nocturia** (excessive urinating at night), **polyuria** (more-frequent urination), and **dysuria** (painful urination). Some drug regimens help inhibit hormones that cause prostate enlargement, but when medications are no longer effective, surgical removal of the prostatic enlargement is indicated. The most commonly performed surgical procedure is called a **TURP (transurethral resection of the prostate),** in which an instrument called a **resectoscope** (rē-sek′tō-skōp) is inserted into the urethra to cut away the problematic enlargement.

Prostate cancer is one of the most common malignancies among men over 50, and the risk of developing it increases with age. Prostate cancer forms hard, solid nodules, most often in the posterior part of the prostate gland. Early stages of the cancer are generally asymptomatic, but as it progresses, urinary symptoms may develop. Untreated prostate cancer can metastasize to other body organs.

Early diagnosis and treatment of prostate cancer are vital for cure and long-term survival. A very effective screening tool is a **digital rectal exam,** whereby a physician inserts a finger into the rectum and palpates adjacent structures (including the prostate gland). In addition, most physicals for men over the age of 50 now include a test for **prostate-specific antigen (PSA)** in the blood. An elevated PSA level can indicate either benign prostatic hyperplasia or prostate cancer.

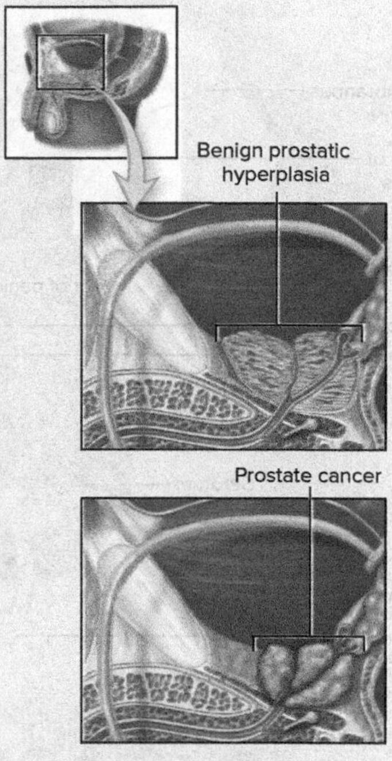

For earlier stages of the disease, radiation therapy may be beneficial—either traditional external-beam radiation or **interstitial radiotherapy,** in which radioactive palladium or iodine "seeds" are permanently implanted in the prostate. For patients with a more aggressive cancer, the entire prostate and some surrounding structures are surgically removed, a procedure called a **radical prostatectomy.**

28.3g Penis

The **penis** (pē′nis; tail) and the scrotum form the external genitalia in males (**figure 28.17*a***). Internally, the attached portion of the penis is the **root,** which is dilated internal to the body surface, forming both the **bulb** and the **crura of the penis.** The bulb attaches the penis to the bulbospongiosus muscle in the urogenital triangle, and the crura attach the penis to the pubic arch. The **body,** or *shaft,* of the penis is the elongated, movable portion. The tip of the penis is called the **glans,** and it contains the **external urethral orifice.** The skin of the penis is thin and elastic. At the distal end of the penis, the skin is attached to the raised edge of the glans and forms a circular fold called the **prepuce** (*foreskin*) (see Clinical View 28.7: "Circumcision" in this section).

Within the shaft of the penis are three cylindrical erectile bodies (figure 28.17*b*). The paired **corpora cavernosa** (kav′er-n ō-sa′; sing., *corpus cavernosum; caverna* = grotto) are located dorsolaterally. Ventral to them along the midline is the single **corpus spongiosum** (spŭn′jē-ō-sŭm), which contains the spongy urethra. Each corpus cavernosum terminates in the shaft of the penis, whereas the corpus spongiosum continues within the glans. The erectile bodies are ensheathed by the tunica albuginea, which also provides an attachment to the skin over the shaft of the penis.

The erectile bodies are composed of a complex network of **venous spaces** surrounding a central artery. During sexual excitement, blood enters the erectile bodies via the central artery and fills in the venous spaces. As these venous spaces become engorged with blood, the erectile bodies become rigid, a process called **erection** (ē-rek′shŭn; *erecto* = to set up). The rigid erectile bodies compress the veins that drain blood away from the venous spaces. Thus, the spaces fill with blood, but the blood cannot leave the erectile bodies until the sexual excitement ceases. Parasympathetic innervation (via the pelvic splanchnic nerves) is responsible for increased blood flow and thus the erection of the penis (see section 18.3b).

Ejaculation (ē-jak′y ū-lā′shŭn; *eiaculatus* = to shoot out) is the process by which semen is expelled from the penis with the help of rhythmic contractions of the smooth muscle in the wall of the urethra. In the early stages of ejaculation, the hypothalamus releases a burst of oxytocin, which induces smooth muscle contraction in the male duct system and facilitates semen release (see section 20.3b). Sympathetic innervation (from the lumbar splanchnic nerves) is responsible for ejaculation (see section 18.4a).

Learning Strategy 28.5

One way to remember the autonomic innervation for the penis is this phrase: **Point and Shoot!** The **p** in **p**oint (erection) also stands for **p**arasympathetic innervation, whereas the **s** in **s**hoot (ejaculation) stands for **s**ympathetic innervation.

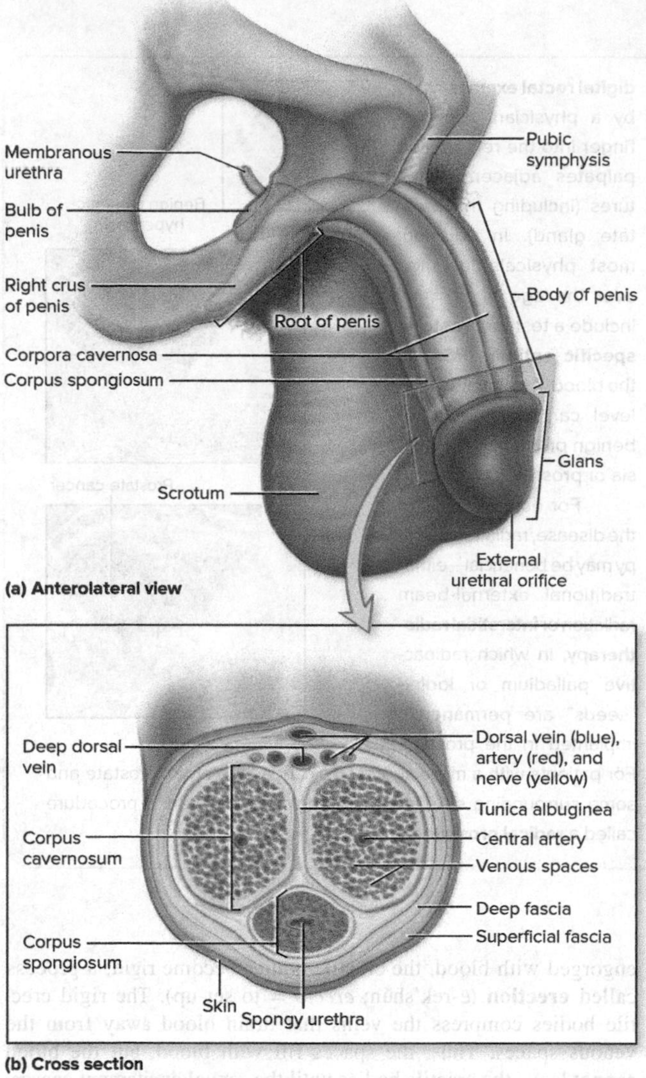

Membranous urethra
Pubic symphysis
Bulb of penis
Right crus of penis
Root of penis
Body of penis
Corpora cavernosa
Corpus spongiosum
Glans
Scrotum
External urethral orifice
(a) Anterolateral view
Deep dorsal vein
Dorsal vein (blue), artery (red), and nerve (yellow)
Tunica albuginea
Corpus cavernosum
Central artery
Venous spaces
Deep fascia
Superficial fascia
Corpus spongiosum
Skin
Spongy urethra
(b) Cross section

Figure 28.17

Anatomy of the Penis. (*a*) An anterolateral view of the circumcised penis. (*b*) A diagrammatic, transverse section shows the arrangement of the erectile bodies.

Although in most body systems sympathetic and parasympathetic innervation tend to perform opposite functions, the male reproductive system is an exception. Here, parasympathetic innervation is necessary to achieve an erection, whereas sympathetic innervation promotes ejaculation (see section 18.5e). Relaxation of autonomic activity after sexual excitement reduces blood flow to the erectile bodies and shunts most of the blood to other veins, thereby returning the penis to its flaccid condition. APR

WHAT DID YOU LEARN?

13 List the structures, starting with the testes, that the sperm must travel through to be released from the body.

14 What is the composition of semen, and what organs contribute to semen?

15 Specifically, how do both parasympathetic and sympathetic innervation work on penile function during sexual arousal?

Clinical View 28.7

Circumcision

Circumcision (ser'kŭm-sizh'ŭn; *circum* = around, *caedo* = to cut) is the surgical removal of the prepuce (foreskin) of the penis. The drawings here compare a circumcised penis (a) with an uncircumcised penis (b). It is practiced in many cultures.

Circumcision has several health benefits: Circumcised males appear less likely to develop urinary tract infections in the first year of life, because the bacteria that cause these infections tend to stick to the foreskin. Circumcision may also protect against penile inflammation (because the glans of a circumcised penis can be kept clean more easily) and penile cancer. Finally, some research has suggested that circumcised males have a reduced risk of acquiring and passing on sexually transmitted infections (STIs), including HIV.

The drawbacks to circumcision include the following: Infants are sometimes circumcised without anesthesia, subjecting them to pain and elevated stress levels. Circumcision also carries a risk of complications, including infection, excessive bleeding, and in rare cases, subsequent surgery. Finally, some individuals have suggested that circumcision may affect sensation during sexual intercourse, although this hypothesis has not been systematically tested or proven.

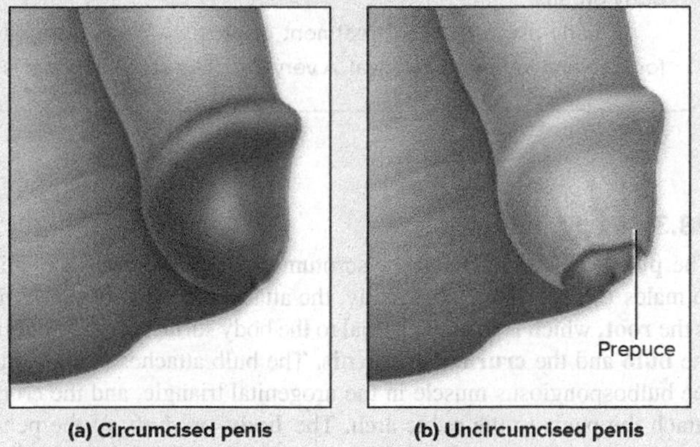

Prepuce

(a) Circumcised penis **(b) Uncircumcised penis**

28.4 Aging and the Reproductive Systems

✓ Learning Objective

15. Describe the age-related changes that occur in the female and male reproductive systems.

Our reproductive systems are basically nonfunctional for several years following birth. When we reach puberty, hormonal changes in the hypothalamus and anterior pituitary stimulate the gonads to begin producing sex hormones. Thereafter, changes occur in many body structures, the reproductive organs mature, and the gonads begin to produce gametes. The time of onset of puberty varies among individuals, but it clearly occurs at a younger average age today than it did 40 or 50 years ago.

Clinical View 28.8

Sexually Transmitted Infections

Sexually transmitted infections (STIs), also known as *sexually transmitted diseases,* or *venereal diseases,* are a group of infectious diseases that are usually transmitted via sexual contact. Often the symptoms of STIs are not immediately noticeable, so infected individuals may spread the disease to someone else without realizing it. Mothers also may transmit STIs to their newborns, either directly across the placenta or at the time of delivery. Condoms, when properly used, have been shown to help prevent the spread of STIs, but they are not 100% effective.

STIs are a leading cause of **pelvic inflammatory disease** in women, in which the pelvic organs become infected. Should bacteria from an STI infect the uterus and uterine tubes, scarring is likely to follow, leading to blockage of the tubes and infertility. We've already discussed two types of STIs, human papillomavirus (see Clinical View 28.2: "Cervical Cancer" in section 28.2c and Clinical View 24.2: "HIV and AIDS" in section 24.3a). We now explore other common STIs.

Chlamydia (kla-mid'ē-ă) is the most frequently reported bacterial STI in the United States. The responsible agent is *Chlamydia trachomatis.* Most infected people are asymptomatic, whereas the rest develop symptoms within 1 to 3 weeks after exposure. These symptoms include abnormal vaginal discharge, painful urination (in both males and females), and low back pain. Chlamydia is treated with antibiotics.

Genital herpes (her'pēz; *herpo* = to creep) is caused by herpes simplex virus type 1 (HSV-1) or type 2 (HSV-2). Infected individuals undergo cyclic outbreaks of blister formation in the genital and anal regions; the blisters are filled with fluid containing millions of infectious viruses. The blisters then break and turn into tender sores that remain for 2–4 weeks. Typically, future cycles of blistering are less severe and shorter in duration than the initial episode. There is no cure for herpes, but antiviral medications can lessen the severity and length of an outbreak.

Gonorrhea (gon'ō-rē'ă) is caused by the bacterium *Neisseria gonorrhoeae,* and is spread either by sexual contact or from mother to newborn at the time of delivery. Symptoms include painful urination and/or a yellowish discharge from the penis or vagina. Gonorrhea is treated with antibiotics, although many gonorrhea strains have become resistant to some antibiotics. If untreated, women may develop pelvic inflammatory disease, and men may develop epididymitis, a painful condition of the epididymis that can lead to infertility. If a newborn acquires the disease, then blindness, joint problems, and/or a life-threatening blood infection may result.

Syphilis (sif'i-lis) is caused by the corkscrew-shaped bacterium *Treponema pallidum.* The bacterium is spread sexually via contact with a syphilitic sore (called a **chancre** [shan'ker]), or a newborn may acquire it *in utero.* Babies can acquire congenital syphilis from their mothers and are often stillborn, but if they live, they have a high incidence of skeletal malformities and neurologic problems. Syphilis can be treated with antibiotics.

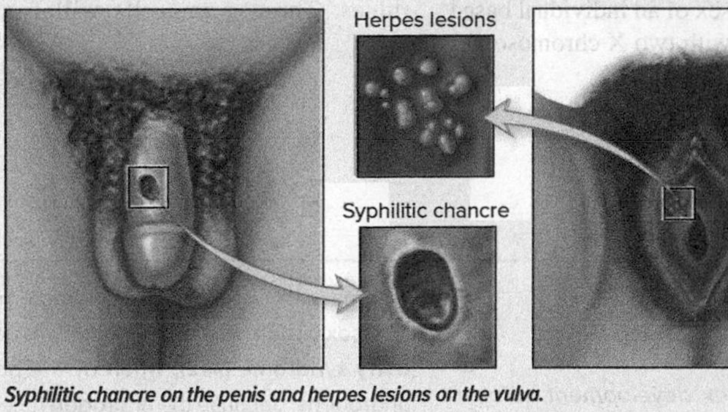

Syphilitic chancre on the penis and herpes lesions on the vulva.

After reaching sexual maturity, the female and male reproductive systems exhibit marked differences in their response to aging. Gametes typically stop maturing in females by their late 40s or 50s, and menopause occurs. A reduction in hormone production that accompanies menopause causes some atrophy of the reproductive organs and the breasts. The vaginal wall thickness decreases, as do glandular secretions for maintaining a moist, lubricated lining. The uterus shrinks and atrophies, becoming much smaller than it was before puberty.

The lack of significant amounts of estrogen and progesterone in a menopausal woman also affects other organs and body systems. Women may experience *hot flashes,* in which their bodies perceive periodic elevations in body temperature, and they may develop thinning scalp hair and/or an increase in facial hair. Menopausal women are at greater risk for osteoporosis (thinning, brittle bones) and heart disease due to the drop in estrogen and progesterone levels. **Hormone replacement therapy (HRT),** in the form of estrogen and progesterone supplements primarily, can be prescribed to peri- and postmenopausal women to help diminish these symptoms and risks. However, the potential risks associated with HRT (e.g., increased risk of breast cancer, stroke, heart attack, and blood clots) may outweigh the benefits, so physicians assess each individual for her suitability for HRT. Studies regarding HRT continue.

In contrast, males do not experience the relatively abrupt change in reproductive system function that females do. A slight decrease in the size of the testes parallels a reduction in the size of the seminiferous tubules and the number of interstitial cells. The resulting decreased testosterone levels in males in their 50s signal a change called the **male climacteric** (klī-mak'ter-ik, klī-mak-ter'ik).

However, males generally do not stop producing gametes as females do following menopause.

Most males experience prostate enlargement (either benign or cancerous) as they age. This prostate enlargement can interfere with sexual and urinary functions. Also associated with aging are **erectile dysfunction** and **impotence,** which refer to the inability to achieve or maintain an erection. Besides aging, other risk factors for this condition include heart disease, diabetes, smoking, and prior prostate surgery. Many drugs have entered the market (e.g., sildenafil [Viagra]) that treat erectile dysfunction by prolonging vasodilation of the penile arteries and thus inhibiting relaxation of the erectile bodies.

WHAT DID YOU LEARN?

16. What are some body changes that accompany menopause?

28.5 Development of the Reproductive Systems

✓ Learning Objective

16. Describe the development of the female and male reproductive systems.

The female and male reproductive structures originate from the same basic primordia, which differentiate into female or male structures, depending upon the signals the primordia receive. To better explain this process, we must first distinguish between the genetic and phenotypic sex of an individual.

28.5a Genetic Versus Phenotypic Sex

Genetic sex (or *genotypic sex*) refers to the sex of an individual based upon the sex chromosomes. An individual with two X chromosomes is a genetic female, whereas an individual with one X and one Y chromosome is a genetic male. Genetic sex is determined at fertilization.

In contrast, **phenotypic** (fē′nō-tip′ik, fen-ō-) **sex** refers to the appearance of an individual's internal and external genitalia. A person with ovaries and female external genitalia (labia) is a phenotypic female, whereas a person with testes and male external genitalia (penis, scrotum) is a phenotypic male. Phenotypic sex starts to become apparent no earlier than the seventh week of development.

How does the primordial tissue know whether to develop into female reproductive organs or male reproductive organs? In males, the **sex-determining region Y (SRY) gene** is located within the larger **testis-determining factor (TDF) region** on the Y chromosome. If the Y chromosome is present, the SRY gene produces proteins to stimulate the production of hormones (e.g., testosterone and other androgens) that initiate male phenotypic development. If a Y chromosome is absent (e.g., the individual is a genetic female), or if the Y chromosome is either lacking or has an abnormal SRY gene, a female phenotypic sex results. Although undoubtedly more complicated, the female phenotypic sex may be thought of as the organism's default pattern. This pattern is not changed unless SRY and its proteins are present.

28.5b Formation of Indifferent Gonads and Genital Ducts

Early in the fifth week of embryonic development, paired **genital ridges** (or *gonadal ridges*) form from **intermediate mesoderm.** The genital ridges will form the gonads. These longitudinal ridges are medial to the developing kidneys at about the level of the tenth thoracic vertebra (**figure 28.18**, *top*). Between weeks 5 and 6, primordial **germ cells** migrate from the yolk sac to the genital ridges. These germ cells will form the future gametes (either

Clinical View 28.9

Intersex Conditions (Disorders of Sex Development)

Intersex conditions, or *disorders of sex development,* refer to a series of disorders where there is a discrepancy between a person's genotype (and gonad development) and their external genitalia. (The previous term used to describe this condition is *hermaphrodite* (her-maf′rō-dīt), which is derived from the Greek name Hermaphroditus, the mythological son of the Greek god Hermes and the goddess Aphrodite.)

True gonadal intersex, previously known as *true hermaphroditism,* refers to an individual with both ovarian and testicular structures (which typically does not have the potential for fertility) and ambiguous (or female) external genitalia. The person may be a genetic male (XY) or a genetic female (XX). True hermaphroditism is very rare.

A **46 XY intersex** individual, previously known as a *male pseudohermaphrodite,* is a genetic male (XY) whose external genitalia resemble those of a female (female phenotypic sex). The 46 XY intersex condition most commonly is caused by **androgen insensitivity syndrome (AIS),** whereby the body cells cannot respond to androgens, because the androgen receptors do not form or function properly. Another cause may be from either a reduction or lack of male hormones (e.g., testosterone) during development.

A **46 XX intersex** individual, previously known as a *female pseudohermaphrodite,* is a genetic female (XX) with external genitalia that resemble those of a male (male phenotypic sex). The clitoris may be enlarged and look like a small penis, and the two labia may become partially fused to resemble a scrotum. The 46XX intersex condition may result if the female fetus is exposed to excessive androgens (e.g., if the pregnant mother was given certain medications to help prevent miscarriage). More commonly, this condition is caused by **congenital adrenal hyperplasia,** in which the fetus's adrenal glands produce excessive amounts of androgens.

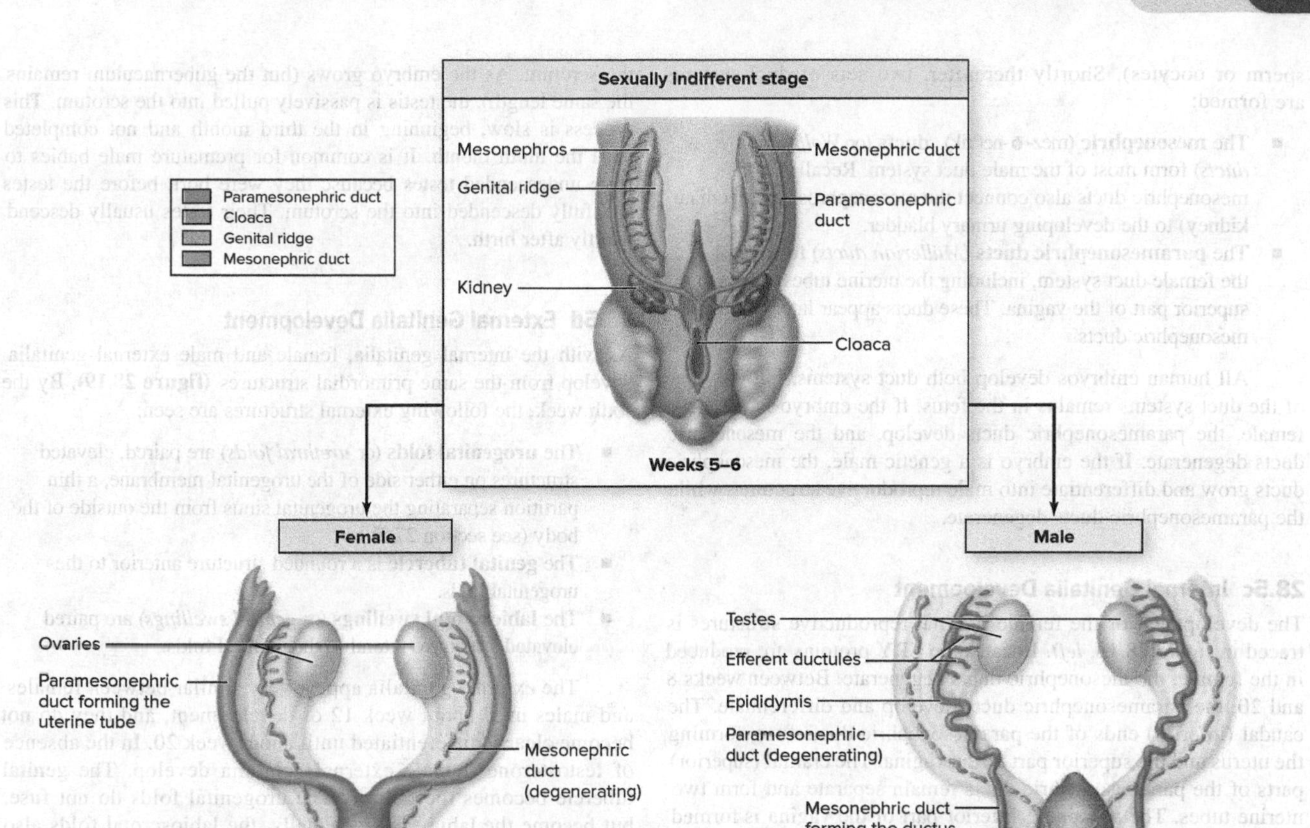
Sexually indifferent stage
Paramesonephric duct
Cloaca
Genital ridge
Mesonephric duct
Mesonephros
Genital ridge
Kidney
Mesonephric duct
Paramesonephric duct
Cloaca
Weeks 5–6
Female
Male
Ovaries
Paramesonephric duct forming the uterine tube
Mesonephric duct (degenerating)
Fused paramesonephric ducts forming the uterus
Urinary bladder (moved aside)
Urogenital sinus forming the urethra and inferior vagina
Weeks 10–12
Testes
Efferent ductules
Epididymis
Paramesonephric duct (degenerating)
Mesonephric duct forming the ductus deferens
Urinary bladder
Seminal vesicle
Urogenital sinus forming the urethra
Weeks 10–12
Uterine tube
Ovary
Uterus
Urinary bladder (moved aside)
Vagina
Hymen
Urethra
At birth
Urinary bladder
Seminal vesicle
Prostate gland
Bulbourethral gland
Ductus deferens
Urethra
Epididymis
Efferent ductules
Testis
At birth

Figure 28.18

Embryonic Development of the Female and Male Reproductive Tracts. Through the first 6 weeks of development, the embryo is termed "sexually indifferent." Thereafter, genetic expression determines sex differentiation.

sperm or oocytes). Shortly thereafter, two sets of duct systems are formed:

- The **mesonephric** (mez-ō-nef′rik) **ducts** (or *Wolffian ducts*) form most of the male duct system. Recall that the mesonephric ducts also connect the mesonephros (intermediate kidney) to the developing urinary bladder.
- The **paramesonephric ducts** (*Müllerian ducts*) form most of the female duct system, including the uterine tubes, uterus, and superior part of the vagina. These ducts appear lateral to the mesonephric ducts.

All human embryos develop both duct systems, but only one of the duct systems remains in the fetus. If the embryo is a genetic female, the paramesonephric ducts develop, and the mesonephric ducts degenerate. If the embryo is a genetic male, the mesonephric ducts grow and differentiate into male reproductive structures, while the paramesonephric ducts degenerate.

28.5c Internal Genitalia Development

The development of the female internal reproductive structures is traced in figure 28.18, *left*. Because no SRY proteins are produced in the female, the mesonephric ducts degenerate. Between weeks 8 and 20, the paramesonephric ducts develop and differentiate. The caudal (inferior) ends of the paramesonephric ducts fuse, forming the uterus and the superior part of the vagina. The cranial (superior) parts of the paramesonephric ducts remain separate and form two uterine tubes. The remaining inferior part of the vagina is formed from the urogenital sinus (which also forms the urinary bladder and urethra).

By about week 7 of development, the *SRY* gene on the Y chromosome begins influencing the indifferent gonad to become a testis, which then forms sustentacular cells and interstitial cells. Once the sustentacular cells form, they begin secreting **anti-Müllerian hormone (AMH)** (also known as *Müllerian inhibiting substance*), which inhibits the development of the paramesonephric ducts (figure 28.18, *right*). These paramesonephric ducts degenerate and, between weeks 8 and 12, the mesonephric ducts form the male duct system—efferent ductules, epididymides, ductus deferens, seminal vesicles, and ejaculatory ducts.

The prostate and bulbourethral glands do not form from the mesonephric ducts. Instead, they begin to form as endodermal "buds" or outgrowths of the developing urethra between weeks 10 and 13. As the prostate gland and bulbourethral glands develop, they incorporate mesoderm into their structures as well.

Finally, note that the indifferent gonad originates near the level of the T_{10} vertebra. Throughout prenatal development, the developing testis descends from the abdominal region toward the developing scrotum. A thin band of connective tissue called the **gubernaculum** (gū′ber-nak′yū-lŭm; helm) attaches to the testis and pulls it from the abdomen, through the developing inguinal canal, to its placement in the scrotum. As the embryo grows (but the gubernaculum remains the same length), the testis is passively pulled into the scrotum. This process is slow, beginning in the third month and not completed until the ninth month. It is common for premature male babies to have undescended testes because they were born before the testes had fully descended into the scrotum. Their testes usually descend shortly after birth.

28.5d External Genitalia Development

As with the internal genitalia, female and male external genitalia develop from the same primordial structures (**figure 28.19**). By the sixth week, the following external structures are seen:

- The **urogenital folds** (or *urethral folds*) are paired, elevated structures on either side of the urogenital membrane, a thin partition separating the urogenital sinus from the outside of the body (see section 27.5b).
- The **genital tubercle** is a rounded structure anterior to the urogenital folds.
- The **labioscrotal swellings** (or *genital swellings*) are paired elevated structures lateral to the urethral folds.

The external genitalia appear very similar between females and males until about week 12 of development, and they do not become clearly differentiated until about week 20. In the absence of testosterone, female external genitalia develop. The genital tubercle becomes the clitoris. The urogenital folds do not fuse, but become the labia minora. Finally, the labioscrotal folds also remain unfused and become the labia majora. In the presence and circulation of testosterone, the primitive external genitalia structures will differentiate. The genital tubercle enlarges and elongates, forming the glans of the penis and part of the dorsal side of the penis. The urogenital folds grow and fuse around the developing urethra and form the ventral side of the penis. Finally, the labioscrotal swellings fuse at the midline, forming the scrotum.

WHAT DID YOU LEARN?

17 What is the difference between genetic and phenotypic sex?

Learning Strategy 28.6

You may be aware that the sex of an unborn child can typically be determined with an ultrasound sometime between weeks 18 and 22. You now know why the physician waits until this time—it is when the external genitalia first become clearly distinguishable.

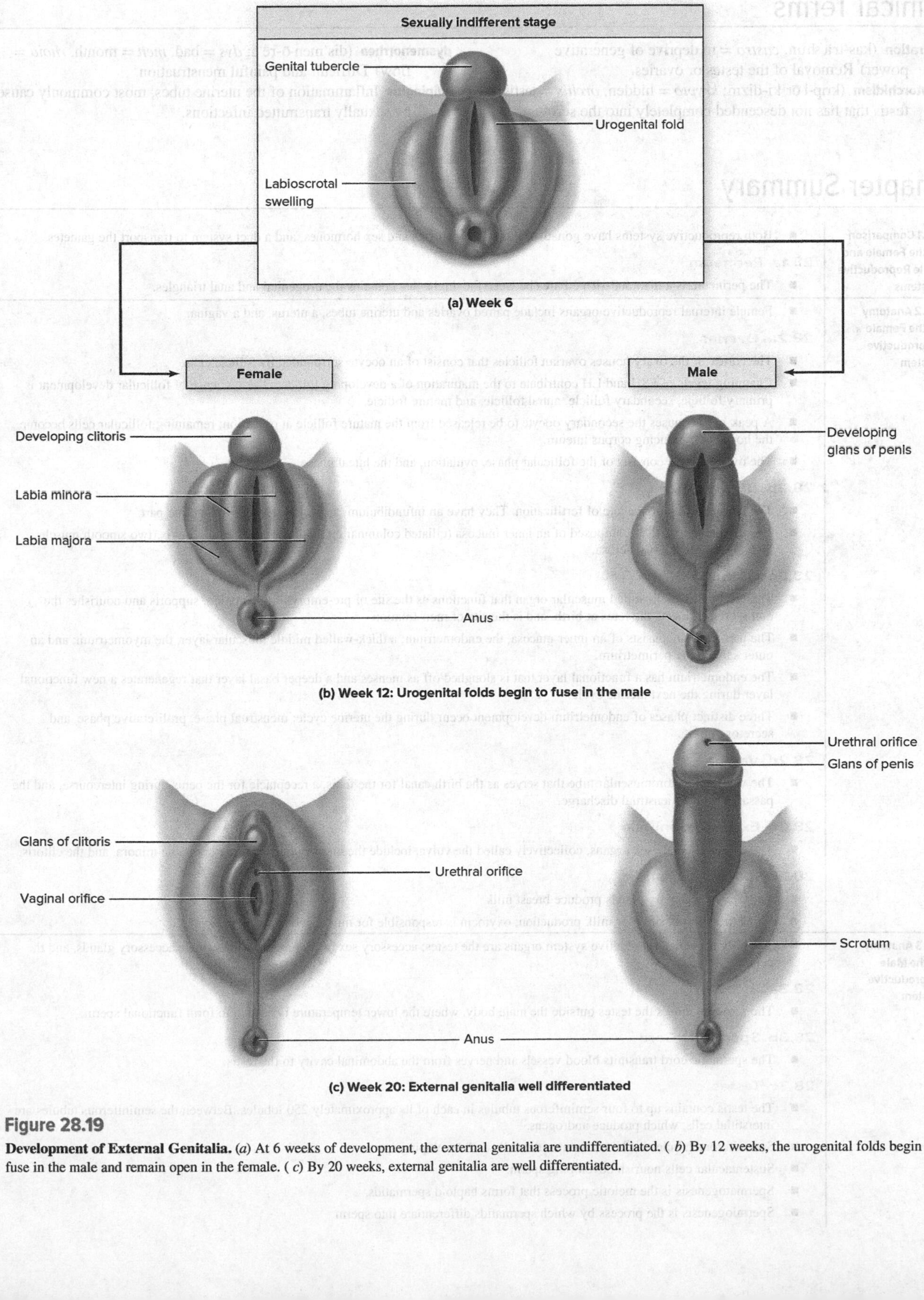
Sexually indifferent stage
Genital tubercle
Urogenital fold
Labioscrotal swelling
(a) Week 6
Female
Male
Developing clitoris
Labia minora
Labia majora
Developing glans of penis
Anus
(b) Week 12: Urogenital folds begin to fuse in the male
Urethral orifice
Glans of penis
Glans of clitoris
Urethral orifice
Vaginal orifice
Scrotum
Anus
(c) Week 20: External genitalia well differentiated

Figure 28.19

Development of External Genitalia. (*a*) At 6 weeks of development, the external genitalia are undifferentiated. (*b*) By 12 weeks, the urogenital folds begin to fuse in the male and remain open in the female. (*c*) By 20 weeks, external genitalia are well differentiated.

Clinical Terms

castration (kas-trā′shŭn; *castro* = to deprive of generative power) Removal of the testes or ovaries.

cryptorchidism (krip-tōr′ki-dizm; *krypto* = hidden, *orchis* = testis) A testis that has not descended completely into the scrotum.

dysmenorrhea (dis′men-ō-rē′ă; *dys* = bad, *men* = month, *rhoia* = flow) Difficult and painful menstruation.

salpingitis Inflammation of the uterine tubes, most commonly caused by sexually transmitted infections.

Chapter Summary

28.1 Comparison of the Female and Male Reproductive Systems	■ Both reproductive systems have gonads that produce gametes and sex hormones, and a duct system to transport the gametes. **28.1a Perineum** ■ The perineum is a diamond-shaped area between the thighs that contains the urogenital and anal triangles.
28.2 Anatomy of the Female Reproductive System	■ Female internal reproductive organs include paired ovaries and uterine tubes, a uterus, and a vagina. **28.2a Ovaries** ■ The cortex of the ovary houses ovarian follicles that consist of an oocyte surrounded by follicle cells. ■ Changing levels of FSH and LH contribute to the maturation of a developing follicle. The sequence of follicular development is primary follicle, secondary follicle, antral follicle, and mature follicle. ■ A peak in LH causes the secondary oocyte to be released from the mature follicle at ovulation; remaining follicular cells become the hormone-producing corpus luteum. ■ The ovarian cycle consists of the follicular phase, ovulation, and the luteal phase. **28.2b Uterine Tubes** ■ The uterine tubes are the site of fertilization. They have an infundibulum, ampulla, isthmus, and uterine part. ■ The uterine tube wall is composed of an inner mucosa (ciliated columnar epithelium), middle muscularis (two smooth muscle layers), and an external serosa. **28.2c Uterus** ■ The uterus is a thick-walled muscular organ that functions as the site of pre-embryo implantation, supports and nourishes the embryo/fetus, ejects the fetus at birth, and is the site of menstruation. ■ The uterine wall consists of an inner mucosa, the endometrium; a thick-walled middle muscular layer, the myometrium; and an outer serosa, the perimetrium. ■ The endometrium has a functional layer that is sloughed off as menses and a deeper basal layer that regenerates a new functional layer during the next uterine cycle. ■ Three distinct phases of endometrium development occur during the uterine cycle: menstrual phase, proliferative phase, and secretory phase. **28.2d Vagina** ■ The vagina is a fibromuscular tube that serves as the birth canal for the fetus, a receptacle for the penis during intercourse, and the passageway for menstrual discharge. **28.2e External Genitalia** ■ The external female sex organs, collectively called the vulva, include the mons pubis, labia majora, labia minora, and the clitoris. **28.2f Mammary Glands** ■ The paired mammary glands produce breast milk. ■ Prolactin is responsible for milk production; oxytocin is responsible for milk ejection.
28.3 Anatomy of the Male Reproductive System	■ The primary male reproductive system organs are the testes; accessory sex organs include ducts, male accessory glands, and the penis. **28.3a Scrotum** ■ The scrotum houses the testes outside the male body, where the lower temperature is needed to form functional sperm. **28.3b Spermatic Cord** ■ The spermatic cord transmits blood vessels and nerves from the abdominal cavity to the testis. **28.3c Testes** ■ The testis contains up to four seminiferous tubules in each of its approximately 250 lobules. Between the seminiferous tubules are interstitial cells, which produce androgens. ■ Seminiferous tubules contain sustentacular cells and developing sperm. ■ Sustentacular cells nourish developing sperm. ■ Spermatogenesis is the meiotic process that forms haploid spermatids. ■ Spermiogenesis is the process by which spermatids differentiate into sperm.

	28.3d Ducts in the Male Reproductive System ■ Ducts store and transport sperm. They include the rete testis, the efferent ductules, the epididymis, the ductus deferens, and the ejaculatory duct. ■ The male urethra carries urine or semen at any one time. **28.3e Accessory Glands** ■ Accessory glands produce seminal fluid, a nutrient-rich, alkaline fluid that supports sperm. Accessory glands include seminal vesicles, the prostate gland, and the bulbourethral glands. **28.3f Semen** ■ Semen is a mixture of seminal fluid and sperm. **28.3g Penis** ■ The penis is the copulatory organ. ■ The body of the penis contains three parallel erectile bodies and the urethra.
28.4 Aging and the Reproductive Systems	■ Females undergo a change in reproductive structure and fertility called menopause. Males undergo a male climacteric in which the production of testosterone is measurably reduced.
28.5 Development of the Reproductive Systems	■ Both female and male reproductive structures originate from the same basic primordia. Gene expression determines how they differentiate. **28.5a Genetic Versus Phenotypic Sex** ■ Genetic sex is based upon chromosome type; phenotypic sex refers to the appearance of the internal and external genitalia. **28.5b Formation of Indifferent Gonads and Genital Ducts** ■ Early in development, genital ridges form from intermediate mesoderm. Primordial germ cells migrate from the yolk sac to the genital ridges and form the future gametes. **28.5c Internal Genitalia Development** ■ In the absence of the sex-determining region Y (*SRY*) gene, the female reproductive pattern develops. The male reproductive pattern develops as a result of the *SRY* gene and its proteins. **28.5d External Genitalia Development** ■ The external genitalia appear very similar until about week 12; external genitalia become fully differentiated about week 20.

Challenge Yourself

Actively write or type your answers in a separate document to reinforce your learning, before checking your answers.

Multiple Choice

Select the best answer from the four choices provided.

1. Which portion of the penis contains the urethra and has only corpus spongiosum erectile tissue?
   a. body
   b. glans
   c. root
   d. prepuce
2. Which organ does not produce a component of seminal fluid?
   a. bulbourethral glands
   b. testes
   c. seminal vesicles
   d. prostate gland
3. The vestibule is bounded by which of the following structure(s)?
   a. vaginal opening
   b. urethral opening
   c. labia minora
   d. labia majora
4. Which structure are sperm stored in until they are fully mature and capable of motility?
   a. epididymis
   b. seminiferous tubule
   c. ductus deferens
   d. rete testis
5. Which structure is the female homologue to the penis?
   a. labia majora
   b. labia minora
   c. clitoris
   d. vagina
6. Ovulation occurs due to a dramatic "peak" in which hormone?
   a. progesterone
   b. LH
   c. FSH
   d. prolactin
7. Which statement is true about the uterus?
   a. The basal layer of the endometrium is shed each month during menses.
   b. The myometrium is composed of several layers of skeletal muscle.
   c. The cervix projects into the vagina.
   d. The round ligament is peritoneum that drapes over the uterus.
8. Which structure contains a primary oocyte, several layers of granulosa cells, and an antrum?
   a. primary follicle
   b. secondary follicle
   c. antral follicle
   d. mature follicle

9. Which structure is the most anteriorly placed structure in the female perineum?
   a. vaginal orifice
   b. urethral orifice
   c. labia minora
   d. clitoris
10. The paramesonephric ducts in the embryo form which of the following?
    a. uterine tubes and uterus
    b. ovary
    c. ductus deferens
    d. seminal vesicle

Content Review

1. What are some similarities between the female and male reproductive systems? What are the anatomic homologues between these systems?
2. Describe the events that occur during puberty in males and females.
3. Identify the regions of the uterine tube.
4. How does aging affect the male and female reproductive systems?
5. Compare and contrast the ovarian cycle phases and the uterine cycle phases. When do they occur? What specific events are associated with each phase?
6. Describe these parts of the mammary gland: nipple, areola, lobe, lobule, and alveoli.
7. What is the function of sustentacular cells in the production of spermatozoa?
8. Describe the process of spermatogenesis, including which cells are diploid and which are haploid.
9. Compare the secretions of the seminal vesicles, the prostate gland, and the bulbourethral glands.
10. What changes occur in the penis to allow a male to attain an erection?

Developing Critical Reasoning

1. Caitlyn had unprotected sex with her fiancé about 2 weeks after her last period, and is worried that she might have become pregnant. She asks her physician if there are times during her monthly menstrual cycle when she might be more likely to become pregnant. She also asks how birth control pills prevent a woman from becoming pregnant. What will the physician tell Caitlyn?
2. If parents wish to know the sex of their unborn baby, they usually have to wait until weeks 18–22 of development before a sonogram determining the sex can be performed. Based upon your knowledge of reproductive system development, explain why the sex of the unborn baby can't be determined easily before this time.
3. An adult male over 50 visits his doctor because he is having problems with urination. He has an increased urge to urinate, but has difficulty starting and stopping urination. Tests show no urinary tract infection or kidney stones. What is another possibility? Discuss why it would have an impact on urination.

Answers to "What Do You Think?"

1. A woman can become pregnant as long as she has one remaining functioning ovary.
2. Stress, age, medications, and body weight all can affect a woman's monthly uterine (menstrual) cycle. Stress and excessively lean body mass can lead to amenorrhea (absence of periods).
3. If a male's testes were removed, the adrenal glands could still produce a small amount of androgens. However, because the testes produce the overwhelming majority of androgens, the small amount produced by the adrenal glands would have little effect on the male.
4. If a male has a vasectomy, sperm still form in the seminiferous tubule and then mature in the epididymis. However, because the sperm are not ejaculated, they die, and their components are broken down and resorbed in the epididymis. An individual who has had a vasectomy ejaculates seminal fluid only, not semen (which contains sperm).

Design Element: Pencil Icon: Slavojub Pantelic/Shutterstock

ANSWERS

Appendix A

The Content Review questions from each Challenge Yourself question set are answered on the Human Anatomy Online Learning Center at www.mhhe.com/mckinley4.

CHAPTER ONE

Challenge Yourself

Multiple Choice

1. d
2. b
3. b
4. b
5. c
6. a
7. c
8. d
9. a
10. b

Developing Critical Reasoning

1. The level of anatomic study would be microscopic—either cytologic or histologic—or pathologic. Cytologic studies would examine the blood itself, while histologic studies would examine muscle tissue removed during biopsy. Cytologic studies and histologic studies look in blood and muscle samples for pathogens as well as any increase in white blood cells, results of inflammatory responses, and the presence of cellular debris. Pathologic studies look for anatomic changes in organs as a result of infection.

2. Antebrachial = forearm; patellar = kneecap; sacral = posterior region between the hips; brachial region= the arm.

3. The best techniques would be computed tomography and MRI, but they are expensive. Sonography may provide some information; it would probably not be very precise, but it is inexpensive. Radiography would provide some information only if used in conjunction with radiopaque dyes.

CHAPTER TWO

Challenge Yourself

Multiple Choice

1. c
2. c
3. b
4. b
5. c
6. d
7. b
8. b
9. c
10. a

Developing Critical Reasoning

1. The cells have lost their water by the process of osmosis. Water from inside the cell has moved by diffusion across the plasma membrane to the outside of the cell. As a result of the loss of intracellular water, the cells have shrunk.

2. Enclosure of some organelles within a membrane ensures that the contents of the organelle are isolated from the rest of the cytoplasm. Thus, each membrane-bound organelle is able to maintain its specific organization and conduct its own specific function(s) without interference from other cellular activities.

3. Longtime smokers develop "smoker's cough." There is a lot of debris inhaled with the tobacco smoke that is trapped by mucus, and the mucus is moved by the cilia on the cells of the respiratory system. Smoking damages these cilia. Without the cilia, the mucus is not easily cleared from the air passages, so smokers will cough to help move the mucus.

CHAPTER THREE

Challenge Yourself

Multiple Choice

1. b
2. d
3. b
4. a
5. c
6. c
7. a
8. b
9. c
10. c

Developing Critical Reasoning

1. The procedure used to check for trisomy in the fetus is called amniocentesis, and it is usually performed during the fourth month of pregnancy. Analysis of the chromosomes in cells from the amniotic fluid may reveal the presence of trisomy. The most common cause of this abnormality is nondisjunction of chromosomes, meaning that sister chromatids for chromosome 21 did not separate during anaphase II of meiosis, thus producing a gamete with 24, not 23, chromosomes.

2. Thalidomide was used to alleviate morning sickness in newly pregnant women, so it affected organogenesis during the embryonic period, especially limb bud formation (see table 3.2).

3. The young woman should be concerned because her pregnancy was likely in the embryonic period when she engaged in binge drinking. Exposure to alcohol during the embryonic period can result in the malformation of some or all organ systems or the death of the embryo.

Appendix A

CHAPTER FOUR

Challenge Yourself

Multiple Choice

1. d	6. a
2. b	7. c
3. b	8. b
4. c	9. c
5. a	10. b

Developing Critical Reasoning

1. The type of tissue specimen being observed is an areolar (loose) connective tissue. The "open spaces" are apparently due to abundant ground substance. The different types of protein fibers include both collagen (long, straight, and unbranched) and elastic (small and branched) fibers. The different connective tissue cell types probably include fibroblasts, mesenchymal cells, and macrophages.
2. The pain in the knee may be due to degeneration of the cartilage on the surfaces of the bones that form the knee joint. By taking chemical supplements that may help in the regrowth or support of cartilage, the man with the knee joint problems may obtain relief.
3. Older adults' skin is thinner and more fragile because as we age, the amount of protein in the epithelium decreases. The process of cell replacement also becomes less effective, resulting in a decrease in the collagen and elastin in the connective tissue below the epithelium.

CHAPTER FIVE

Challenge Yourself

Multiple Choice

1. c	6. b
2. d	7. b
3. a	8. b
4. b	9. c
5. c	10. d

Developing Critical Reasoning

1. When the body is cold and needs to conserve heat, the blood vessels in the dermis vasoconstrict—that is, the vessel diameter narrows to allow for less blood flow. In an effort to conserve heat, blood is shunted to deeper body tissues, and relatively less blood flow occurs in the dermal blood vessels. The skin appears pale. When the body becomes too warm, it needs to dissipate heat. Blood vessels in the dermis respond by undergoing vasodilation—that is, the vessel diameter becomes larger to allow for more blood flow. As relatively more blood flows through these vessels, the warmth from the blood dissipates through the skin, and the body cools off. Due to relatively more blood in these dermal blood vessels, your face becomes flushed.
2. Teri's acne is probably caused by plugged sebaceous ducts. At puberty, increased hormone levels stimulate sebaceous gland secretion, making the pores more prone to blockage and leading to various types of acne lesions.
3. John has been chronically overexposed to UV rays from sunlight. This exposure may have damaged the DNA in his epidermal cells and accelerated the process of aging. Because excessive UV exposure is the predominant factor in the development of nearly all skin cancers, the growths removed from John's face were probably cancerous.

CHAPTER SIX

Challenge Yourself

Multiple Choice

1. b	6. a
2. c	7. a
3. b	8. b
4. b	9. b
5. d	10. b

Developing Critical Reasoning

1. The bone in Marty's leg was undergoing the final phase of fracture repair. The hard callus formed earlier in the repair process persists for several months as an obvious bump composed of excess bony material. Eventually, osteoclasts remove most of the excess bony material from both the external and internal surfaces of the bone.
2. Elise most likely has a low level of calcium in her blood as a result of lack of vitamin D. Her depressed calcium level will naturally slow the bone building process because mineralization of new bone lags behind the formation of osteoid by osteoblasts. Vitamin D is required to stimulate the absorption and transport of calcium from the gastrointestinal tract into the blood. The source of vitamin D is either diet or synthesis in the skin upon exposure to UV radiation. Elise's nutrition was poor, and she tended to remain indoors, away from normal amounts of UV light, making lack of vitamin D likely in her case.
3. The physician was concerned because the fracture apparently occurred across the epiphyseal plate, the site for growth of the long bones of the limbs. If the epiphyseal plate is altered or disrupted, bones do not grow normally. Using screws to align the fractured bone ensures that the growth plate has the correct structure and that normal growth will continue.

CHAPTER SEVEN

Challenge Yourself

Multiple Choice

1. c
2. a
3. c
4. c
5. a
6. b
7. b
8. c
9. b
10. a

Developing Critical Reasoning

1. The cause of the lower back pain is probably a herniated disc in the lumbar region. The construction worker twists and flexes the vertebral column and lifts heavy objects, putting him at risk for herniation. The overweight teen has probably overextended the lumbar curve due to altered posture, resulting in a herniation.

2. At birth, the cranium is not completely formed. The flat bones of the skull are connected by flexible areas of dense regular connective tissue called fontanelles. This flexibility allows the cranial bones to overlap as the skull is temporarily deformed to facilitate passage through the birth canal. Fontanelles also allow the skull to return to normal shape in a few days. The cranial bones continue to grow, and the fontanelles have usually been replaced by bone by the age of 15 months.

3. The forensic anthropologist could examine various features of the skull to determine the sex of the individual. A larger, more robust skull with a prominent external occipital protuberance and a squared-off mental protuberance would indicate a male skull. A female skull may be smaller, more gracile, have a more triangular mental protuberance, a more rounded external occipital protuberance, and less pronounced superciliary arches.

CHAPTER EIGHT

Challenge Yourself

Multiple Choice

1. b
2. c
3. c
4. b
5. a
6. c
7. c
8. b
9. c
10. b

Developing Critical Reasoning

1. She should not be prescribed thalidomide. If a pregnant female takes thalidomide during weeks 4–8 of embryonic development (the time when the limbs are developing), limb development can be severely disrupted.

2. There are several differences between the pelvis of a female and that of a male. The female ilium flares more laterally, while the male ilium projects more superiorly (thus giving males narrower hips). The female pelvis is wider, the acetabulum is smaller, and the greater sciatic notch is much wider. The sacrum tends to be shorter and wider in females. The female pelvis has a wider, larger pelvic inlet and pelvic outlet. The body of the pubis in females is much longer and almost rectangular in shape, compared to the shorter, triangular-shaped appearance of the male pubic body. The female subpubic angle is wider and convex, while the male subpubic angle is much narrower and typically does not extend past 90 degrees. The relative age can be determined from the os coxae. Between the ages of 13 and 15 years, the ilium, ischium, and pubis fuse to form the os coxae of the pelvic girdle. Further, the morphology of the pubic symphysis can be used to estimate the age at death.

3. The young male has a condition called "flat feet," meaning that the medial longitudinal arch is flattened and the entire sole may touch the ground. As a result, long walks or running result in very painful feet because the structures on the sole of the foot are compressed. Since the Army requires standing for a long time and perhaps long marches, individuals with pes planus are ineligible for service.

CHAPTER NINE

Challenge Yourself

Multiple Choice

1. c
2. c
3. b
4. c
5. c
6. c
7. a
8. b
9. d
10. d

Developing Critical Reasoning

1. Erin experienced a dislocation of the glenohumeral joint. Immediately following the initial blow, the head of the humerus pushed into the inferior part of the capsule. Next, the head of the humerus tore the inferior part of the capsule and dislocated the humerus, so the humerus was then inferior to the glenoid cavity. Once the humeral head became dislocated from the glenoid fossa, the pulling action of the chest muscles displaced it superiorly and medially, causing the humeral head to lie just inferior to the coracoid process.

2. The knee joint is at risk in "clipping" in a football game. The parts of the joint injured may include the tibial collateral ligament, the medial meniscus, and the anterior cruciate ligament (ACL). When all three are affected, the condition is known as the "unhappy triad" of injuries. First, the leg is forcibly abducted and laterally rotated. If the blow is severe enough, the tibial collateral ligament tears, followed by tearing of the medial meniscus, since these two structures are connected. The force that tears the tibial collateral ligament and medial meniscus is thus transferred to the ACL. Since the ACL is relatively weak, it tears as well.

3. The term "double-jointed" is a misnomer. Carla should instead say that she has extensively mobile joints. Some individuals do display greater mobility within their joints than other individuals. The thumb movement that Carla demonstrated may be referred to as hyperextension, because the movement is beyond the typical normal mobility of the joint.

CHAPTER TEN

Challenge Yourself

Multiple Choice

1. d	6. c
2. d	7. c
3. d	8. a
4. b	9. b
5. c	10. d

Developing Critical Reasoning

1. Paul experienced atrophy in the muscles of his left forearm due to the lack of stimulation those muscles received during the 6 weeks his arm was in the cast. Atrophy is a reduction in muscle size, tone, and power. If a muscle experiences a marked decrease in use, the muscle becomes flaccid, and its fibers decrease in size and become weaker.
2. Myofilaments are protein filaments consisting of the contracting proteins actin and myosin and some regulatory proteins. The actin proteins and regulatory proteins form the thin filaments, while the myosin proteins make up the thick filaments. The thin filaments insert into and extend between thick filament proteins within a band. The proximity of thick and thin filament proteins permits the interaction of myofilaments within myofibrils when the muscle fiber is stimulated. Stimulation of the muscle fiber results in the shortening of the entire cell. During a contraction, crossbridges form, binding thick filaments to thin, and the myosin heads pivot toward the M line in the center of the sarcomere. This action pulls the thin filaments toward the center of the sarcomere, causing the sarcomere to shorten. Upon the shortening of all sarcomeres, the skeletal muscle fiber itself is shortened.
3. Savannah's 59-year-old grandfather has less tolerance for exercise than Savannah due to many factors. Older individuals experience muscle atrophy, caused by a decrease in cell proliferation, cell volume, and cell number. The decreased muscle strength is compounded by the tendency toward rapid fatigue. The atrophy of muscle secondarily results in a lesser amount of tension generated by that muscle. Consequently, the muscle fatigues more readily while performing a specific amount of work. As a result, the individual has a reduced ability to eliminate the heat generated during muscular contraction. In addition, each skeletal muscle fiber decreases in diameter. The consequences of decreased fiber diameter include the following: a cutback in oxygen storage capacity because of less myoglobin, reduced glycogen reserves, and a decreased ability to produce ATP. Overall, muscle strength and endurance are impaired, and the individual tends to become fatigued quickly. Depreciated cardiovascular performance also occurs as a result of aging, and thus blood flow to active muscles does not increase with exercise as rapidly as it does in younger people. Finally, after exercising, the muscles in an older individual have a reduced capacity to recover. As we get older, the number of satellite cells in skeletal muscle steadily decreases, resulting in diminished repair capabilities as well.

CHAPTER ELEVEN

Challenge Yourself

Multiple Choice

1. c	6. b
2. a	7. c
3. c	8. c
4. b	9. b
5. a	10. c

Developing Critical Reasoning

1. When Albon strained to lift the heavy furniture, rising pressure in his abdominopelvic cavity provided the force to push a segment of the intestine into the inguinal canal, causing the inguinal hernia. The inguinal region is one of the weakest areas of the abdominal wall. Males are more likely to develop inguinal hernias than females, because their inguinal canals, and superficial inguinal rings, are larger to allow room for the spermatic cord. Albon's hernia was most likely a direct inguinal hernia, in which herniation occurs through the superficial inguinal ring, but not down the entire length of the inguinal canal. It typically is seen in middle-aged males with poorly developed abdominal muscles and protruding abdomens.
2. Pat might have injured her external urethral sphincter, which assists in urination in females and in both urination and ejaculation in males. This sphincter is under voluntary control, and injury to this muscle could result in the loss of voluntary control over urination.
3. "Crow's-feet" (the horizontal wrinkles that may develop at the lateral corners of the eyes) may develop from repeated contraction of the orbicularis oculi muscle. The wrinkles develop perpendicular to the direction of the muscle fibers after years of repeated use of the muscles to blink, close the eyes, squint, and so on.

CHAPTER TWELVE

Challenge Yourself

Multiple Choice

1. b	6. b
2. c	7. d
3. b	8. c
4. d	9. c
5. b	10. b

Developing Critical Reasoning

1. Most of the muscles in the anterior compartment of the thigh cause extension of the knee, but three muscles cause flexion of the hip. Paralysis of these muscles would therefore compromise both knee extension and hip flexion.
2. Two movements are associated with the elbow joint: extension and flexion. If working out in an exercise facility, Karen could do the following exercises. (1) Arm curls: While standing, pick up a dumbbell. With the arm fully extended at the side, lift the weight toward the shoulder. This would improve flexion. Then slowly let the weight return to the side. (2) Barbell lift: While standing, lift a barbell and curl it up to the chest. Then push the barbell over the head. This would improve flexion and extension. All exercises are performed for 10–12 repetitions, followed by a short rest and a repeat of the exercises three times.
3. The prime mover in elbow flexion is the brachialis. Its movement is not affected by pronation or supination of the forearm. However, the biceps brachii, which is also a forearm flexor, is ineffective in forearm flexion if the forearm is pronated. Thus, pronation of the forearm prevents the biceps brachii from helping with forearm flexion.

CHAPTER THIRTEEN

Challenge Yourself

Multiple Choice

1. c	6. c
2. b	7. c
3. a	8. b
4. c	9. c
5. a	10. b

Developing Critical Reasoning

1. The health-care worker may have accidentally pierced Marcie's sciatic nerve. Usually, injections are administered in the upper lateral quadrant of the buttock, because the sciatic nerve and gluteal nerves and vessels are located primarily in the medial and inferior lateral part of the buttock.
2. The doctor was able to tell which rib Javier had fractured by locating the sternal angle at the level of the second rib, which facilitates the identification and counting of individual ribs.
3. The doctor was palpating Louisa's cervical lymph nodes, which can become swollen as a result of an infection such as the flu.

CHAPTER FOURTEEN

Challenge Yourself

Multiple Choice

1. c	6. c
2. b	7. c
3. d	8. c
4. c	9. b
5. c	10. b

Developing Critical Reasoning

1. Marianne may be showing symptoms of multiple sclerosis, in which progressive demyelination of neurons in the central nervous system (accompanied by the destruction of oligodendrocytes) interferes with nerve impulse conduction. The result is impaired sensory perception and motor coordination.
2. The lining of the blood vessels is an epithelium, which continually replaces itself, but nervous tissue does not replace itself readily. Growth of new nervous tissue in the amputated limb must occur by Wallerian degeneration, a relatively slow process.
3. Your body cannot make new neurons (except in a few localized areas of the brain), but it can make new synapses, which can enable different areas of the brain to take on some of the functions of other parts of the brain. This process becomes slower as we age and takes some time. See Clinical View: 14.1 "Neuroplasticity and Neurogenesis" in section 14.2a.

CHAPTER FIFTEEN

Challenge Yourself

Multiple Choice

1. c	6. c
2. c	7. c
3. b	8. a
4. d	9. b
5. c	10. a

Developing Critical Reasoning

1. Shannon apparently survived a cerebrovascular accident (stroke) in the left frontal lobe of her cerebrum. Damage occurred to the specific regions in the primary motor cortex that control movement of the right upper limb and also to areas of the speech center.
2. Surrounding the brain is the blood-brain barrier. It protects the nervous tissue of the brain from drugs, waste products, and other solutes in the blood by restricting or preventing the movement of these materials out of the blood capillaries into the nervous tissue of the brain. The drug dopamine could alleviate the symptoms of Parkinson disease, but it is not allowed past the blood-brain barrier. The barrier that keeps the drug from reaching the brain is formed by the perivascular feet of astrocytes and the endothelial cells of the capillaries. On the other hand, these same barrier structures prevent materials that could adversely affect the brain from reaching its nervous tissue.
3. Dustin would have been less likely to survive if he had been shot in the brainstem because numerous brainstem structures are involved in involuntary control of heart rate, blood pressure, and respiration. Without the control afforded by these vital structures, survival is not possible.

CHAPTER SIXTEEN

Challenge Yourself

Multiple Choice

1. a	6. c
2. d	7. a
3. b	8. a
4. c	9. c
5. d	10. c

Developing Critical Reasoning

1. Because Arthur is paralyzed in both the upper and lower limbs, his injury must have occurred in the cervical region of the spinal cord, superior to the cervical enlargement. The likelihood of recovery is not good, since severed axons within the CNS generally do not regenerate (review Wallerian degeneration in section 14.4).
2. Jessica may have damaged her ulnar nerve. Ulnar nerve injuries often accompany elbow fractures because the nerve is close to the medial epicondyle of the humerus. Damage to the ulnar nerve may paralyze most of the intrinsic hand muscles, so Jessica may be unable to adduct or abduct her fingers.
3. Morgan's tendon reflex failed. Normally this reflex responds to increased tension in the tendon because of increased contraction and force generation in the muscle. The reflex acts to relax the muscle.

CHAPTER SEVENTEEN

Challenge Yourself

Multiple Choice

1. b
2. b
3. d
4. c
5. b
6. c
7. c
8. b
9. c
10. c

Developing Critical Reasoning

1. Melissa has suffered a cerebrovascular accident, or stroke, due to reduced supply of blood to a specific part of the brain. The diminished supply of nutrients quickly results in damage or death to neurons in the area, with a coincidental loss of functions normally controlled by that brain region. The areas affected in Melissa's brain would be in the left frontal lobe: the motor speech area and the region of the precentral gyrus that controls motor activity of the right upper limb. The extent of Melissa's recovery depends on the location and duration of the cut-off blood supply.

2. Randolph has apparently incurred damage to the cortical region of the representational hemisphere opposite the motor speech area in the categorical hemisphere. Damage to this part of the representational hemisphere results in aprosody, which causes dull, emotionless speech.

3. Because George no longer responds to any stimuli, he most likely is in either a coma or a persistent vegetative state. (He is not in a stupor, because individuals in a stupor ARE able to respond to extreme stimuli.) A detailed neurologic exam would be needed to better determine if he is experiencing a coma versus a persistent vegetative state. There are variations in EEG results for these states, but George's EEG might show a decrease or lack of alpha and beta waves (which are the predominant waves when we are awake and alert), and a greater propensity of delta and/or theta waves (which predominate during sleeping or during pathologic states of unconsciousness).

CHAPTER EIGHTEEN

Challenge Yourself

Multiple Choice

1. c
2. b
3. c
4. a
5. c
6. c
7. c
8. a
9. c
10. b

Developing Critical Reasoning

1. Holly has had a fight-or-flight experience resulting from the sudden, unexpected screeching of the birds. An immediate increase in sympathetic division activity caused noticeable increases in heart rate and respiratory rate, as well as heightened alertness, pupil dilation, and increased metabolic activities. She continues to experience some of these effects even though the noise is gone and she no longer feels frightened, because the initial response to activation of the fight-or-flight process caused the adrenal medulla to release epinephrine and norepinephrine into her bloodstream. These hormones prolong the effects of the sympathetic division stimulation.

2. Students typically have a hard time paying attention in class immediately after a meal because the parasympathetic division of the autonomic nervous system is dominant at this time. This is the "rest-and-digest" division. Energy stores are being replenished, and digestive activities are predominant. A person tends to be less alert during parasympathetic-dominant times.

3. Taylor was given epinephrine because epinephrine acts like norepinephrine and dilates smooth muscle of the bronchi and bronchioles, allowing for better air passage into and out of the lungs.

CHAPTER NINETEEN

Challenge Yourself

Multiple Choice

1. b
2. d
3. a
4. d
5. c
6. a
7. b
8. b
9. c
10. c

Developing Critical Reasoning

1. The pediatrician would call this condition otitis media, a middle ear infection often experienced by young children, whose auditory tubes are horizontal, relatively short, and undeveloped. As a child ages, the auditory tube becomes larger and more angled, which helps drain the middle ear; thus, infections decrease.

2. Gustation and olfaction are linked, so the smell of a food contributes more to taste than the food itself. When olfaction is impaired (as occurs with chronic smoking), gustation is also impaired since a person can't detect the odors from the food. When a person quits smoking, the sense of smell gradually improves, and so taste perceptions also improve.

3. The vertical movement in the elevator is a type of angular acceleration, so this movement is detected by Louis's maculae within the utricle and saccule of the inner ear. As Louis ascends in the elevator, the otolithic membrane shifts against the stereocilia and kinocilium of the maculae, causing them to bend. The bending of the stereocilia results in a change in the amount of neurotransmitter released from the hair cells of the maculae, which changes the stimulation of the sensory neurons. As a result, the frequency of nerve impulses is changed. This change in nerve impulses travels through the vestibular branch of the cochlear nerve to the vestibular nuclei of the medulla oblongata and the cerebellum (which reflexively control movements of the eye and balance). The vestibular nuclei also transmit nerve impulses to the thalamus and the cerebral cortex, so Louis is aware that his body is ascending in the elevator.

CHAPTER TWENTY

Challenge Yourself

Multiple Choice

1. c
2. b
3. d
4. b
5. d
6. d
7. c
8. b
9. c
10. b

Developing Critical Reasoning

1. Type 2 diabetes is also known as insulin-independent diabetes mellitus (IIDM). It results from either decreased insulin release by the pancreatic beta cells or decreased insulin effectiveness in target cells. This type of diabetes was previously called adult-onset diabetes because it tended to occur in people over the age of 30. However, type 2 diabetes is now rampant in adolescents and young adults, since obesity plays a major role in the development of IIDM and many young people are overweight. Type 1 diabetes, also referred to as insulin-dependent diabetes mellitus (IDDM), is characterized by absent or diminished production and release of insulin by the pancreatic islet cells. This type tends to occur in children and younger individuals, and is not directly associated with obesity. Type 1 diabetes develops in a person who harbors a genetic predisposition, although some kind of triggering event is required to start the process. Often, the trigger is a viral infection, and then the process continues as an autoimmune condition in which the beta cells of the pancreatic islets are the primary focus of destruction.
2. Susan's physician should suspect that she has hypothyroidism, a condition that results from decreased production of thyroid hormone and is characterized by low metabolic rate, lethargy, and a feeling of being cold. Her physician should run tests to check for levels of thyroid hormone in the blood and to ensure that iodine is being taken up by the cells of the thyroid gland.
3. Having two communication systems enables the body to have variable responses to the environment. The nervous system transmits nerve impulses directly to the target cells to elicit a response for a relatively short period of time—a longer response would require constant input from the nervous system, which would require a lot of energy and deplete the neurotransmitters. The endocrine system, on the other hand, can use the bloodstream to affect many different regions of the body over a longer period of time, providing a stronger and more prolonged response.

CHAPTER TWENTY-ONE

Challenge Yourself

Multiple Choice

1. b
2. b
3. b
4. d
5. a
6. b
7. c
8. a
9. d
10. c

Developing Critical Reasoning

1. Marilyn observed an increased number of eosinophils in the blood smear. Usually these cells are present in concentrations of 1–4% of the blood. The higher percentage may indicate either an increase in the number of antigen-antibody complexes in the body or the presence of a parasitic worm.
2. With no prior knowledge of the blood type of the recipient, the physician should call for a transfusion with type O negative blood. This blood type does not exhibit surface antigens of either the ABO system or the Rh system. Thus, the chance of a transfusion reaction would be minimal.
3. Normal hematocrit levels for an adult female range from 38% to 46%. The patient's hematocrit level of 25%, coupled with her symptoms of extreme fatigue and pale skin, is strongly suggestive of some type of anemia. More tests would need to be done, but her history suggests she may have pernicious anemia (which is an anemia that develops when the body fails to absorb B_{12}). B_{12} is primarily found in fish and meat, so individuals who have adopted a vegan diet but have not properly supplemented it with added B_{12} are at risk for developing pernicious anemia.

CHAPTER TWENTY-TWO

Challenge Yourself

Multiple Choice

1. b
2. b
3. d
4. a
5. b
6. a
7. b
8. d
9. c
10. c

Developing Critical Reasoning

1. Huang probably suffered from premature ventricular contractions, which cause the heart to skip beats and/or make it feel as if it is jumping in the chest. The premature ventricular contractions most likely resulted from the stress of studying and working, sleep deprivation, and caffeine, the stimulant in the coffee Huang was drinking.
2. Josephine should be told that angina is a poorly localized pain sensation in the left side of the chest, left arm and shoulder, or sometimes the jaw and/or the back. Strenuous activity generally causes angina when workload demands on the heart exceed the ability of the narrowed coronary vessels to supply blood. Her pain diminished shortly after the brisk walking stopped because normal blood flow to the heart had been restored.
3. Arthur's foramen ovale did not completely close after his birth. When the septum primum and secundum were pushed together, they probably did not fuse completely. Because it was mostly closed, it probably did not bother him enough for him to notice until he became older.

CHAPTER TWENTY-THREE

Challenge Yourself

Multiple Choice

1. c	6. d
2. a	7. b
3. b	8. d
4. b	9. c
5. c	10. c

Developing Critical Reasoning

1. Thomas is at greater risk for developing atherosclerosis. Males tend to be affected more than females, and although we are comparing the risks for two males, the risk for Thomas is greater because he is overweight and does not follow a healthy diet. Without a healthy diet, the possibility of developing hypertension and vascular injury increases, thus increasing the risk for atherosclerosis. Thomas's diet may also result in increased cholesterol in the blood, which is associated with the rate of development and severity of atherosclerosis.
2. An anastomosis occurs where two or more arteries (or veins) merge and supply the same body region. Vascular anastomoses occur in joints to ensure that the tissues and organs beyond the joint have an uninterrupted supply of blood. When the joint is flexed, some vessels may be pinched. If only one supplying vessel went through a joint (elbow or knee), the part of the limb beyond the joint could potentially lose its blood supply if the joint were flexed and maintained in that state. The anastomosis ensures that there will always be another pathway through which the blood can move beyond the joint, no matter the position of the joint.
3. The internal thoracic artery is an ideal coronary bypass vessel for many reasons. Unlike the great saphenous vein (another vessel sometimes used for bypass surgery), the internal thoracic artery is an artery (not a vein), so it is more structurally similar to the coronary arteries. The internal thoracic artery is immediately adjacent to the heart, so a surgeon does not have to create a completely new incision to remove this artery from its original location. Once this artery has been removed and attached to the heart, blood flow to the thoracic wall is not compromised, because there are extensive anastomoses in this region. The thoracic wall may be supplied by the superior epigastric artery (via its anastomoses with the inferior epigastric artery) as well as by the anterior intercostal arteries (which have anastomoses with the posterior intercostal arteries that extend from the descending thoracic aorta).

CHAPTER TWENTY-FOUR

Challenge Yourself

Multiple Choice

1. c	6. c
2. c	7. b
3. c	8. c
4. a	9. d
5. b	10. c

Developing Critical Reasoning

1. Antigens associated with mononucleosis are found within the blood. Arianna's doctor was palpating her spleen to see if it was enlarged. When antigens are present in the blood, lymphoid cells in the white pulp of the spleen detect those antigens, and T-lymphocytes and B-lymphocytes initiate an immune response. One result is that the number of lymphocytes increases dramatically to fight the infection. This increase in lymphocyte number causes enlargement of the spleen.
2. HIV, the human immunodeficiency virus, binds to and then infects helper T-lymphocytes. This causes the helper T-lymphocytes to become HIV factories and prevents them from initiating and overseeing immune responses in the body. Other lymphoid cells target and destroy the infected helper T-lymphocytes, decreasing their numbers. Over a period of time, the helper T-lymphocyte population decreases, and the infected individual is unable to mount immune responses to normal infections. Opportunistic infections (e.g., *Pneumocystis jiroveci* pneumonia [PCP] and histoplasmosis) and cancers (e.g., Kaposi sarcoma and non-Hodgkin lymphoma) often occur and may result in death.
3. Both cancerous and infected lymph nodes can become enlarged. However, while an infected lymph node is tender or painful to the touch, a cancerous lymph node tends to be hard and painless. A biopsy (in which cells are taken from the lymph node) could confirm the diagnosis. If the lymph node is cancerous, a physician could check to see if other lymph nodes are also hard, nontender, and enlarged. Biopsies of suspicious-looking nodes can help determine if the cancer has spread.

CHAPTER TWENTY-FIVE

Challenge Yourself

Multiple Choice

1. a	6. c
2. c	7. c
3. a	8. c
4. b	9. a
5. c	10. b

Developing Critical Reasoning

1. Charlene's cold has had several effects that cause changes in her voice. Inflammation in the nasal cavity alters the volume of space available for sound resonance. Likewise, the accumulation of mucus and fluid in the paranasal sinuses alters sound resonance for voice production. Finally, inflammation in the larynx affects the vocal folds, making the voice sound hoarse and gravelly.
2. Smoking is always dangerous. It significantly increases the risk and severity of atherosclerosis and is directly related to the development of cancers of the lung, esophagus, and stomach. The most common smoking-related diseases are emphysema and cancer. Emphysema is an irreversible loss of pulmonary gas exchange area due to inflammation of the terminal bronchioles and alveoli, in conjunction with widespread destruction of pulmonary elastic connective tissue. Proper exhalation fails, and once these lung structures have been destroyed, no regeneration is possible.
   Smoking accounts for about 85% of all lung cancers. Metastasis, the spread of cancerous cells to other tissues, occurs early in the course of the disease, making surgical cure unlikely for most patients. Pulmonary symptoms include chronic cough, coughing up blood, excess pulmonary mucous production, and increased likelihood of pulmonary infections. Some people are diagnosed only after the lung cancer has metastasized to distant sites.
3. The lungs are among the last of the organs to fully develop. The immediate danger from a preterm birth is respiratory failure, because the lungs are so underdeveloped. Respiratory bronchioles (the first part of the respiratory portion of the respiratory system) aren't formed until week 28, which is also when alveolar type II cells start to produce pulmonary surfactant, which helps keep alveoli patent and facilitates inflation. Thus, children born at week 28 or later are more likely to have alveoli that can remain open, and therefore are more likely to be able to breathe on their own.

CHAPTER TWENTY-SIX

Challenge Yourself

Multiple Choice

1. a
2. b
3. d
4. c
5. a
6. a
7. b
8. b
9. c
10. c

Developing Critical Reasoning

1. Due to Alexandra's vomiting, the epithelial lining of the esophagus, pharynx, and oral cavity was exposed to acidic materials that could "burn" it. Additionally, the volume of fluid loss may have contributed to dehydration. The diarrhea caused rapid expulsion of materials from the intestines through the anal canal, so that appropriate nutrient and water absorption did not occur.
2. Colorectal cancer is a malignant growth anywhere along the large intestine or rectum. However, most cases occur in the distal descending colon, the sigmoid colon, and the rectum, regions that are in contact with fecal material longer than the regions of the proximal part of the large intestine. Small outgrowths from the mucosal lining, called polyps, are often the focal point for cancer origin. Often, nutrition may increase a patient's risk for cancer. A reduced-fiber diet results in decreased stool bulk, a greater concentration of toxins in the stools, and longer transit time for fecal materials. An individual's genetic history may also increase the risk for colorectal cancer development.
3. The small intestine is connected to the posterior abdominal wall by the mesentery, so it cannot be pulled out of the abdomen entirely, nor can it be seen separate from the mesentery.

CHAPTER TWENTY-SEVEN

Challenge Yourself

Multiple Choice

1. c
2. c
3. d
4. b
5. a
6. b
7. d
8. b
9. c
10. b

Developing Critical Reasoning

1. Jason experienced more frequent urination because his body was "clearing" the excess fluid from the numerous beers he had consumed. Normally, as our body loses fluid through urination or sweating, we produce ADH to prevent excess fluid loss that leads to dehydration. However, alcohol inhibits the secretion of ADH from the posterior pituitary, and thus excess fluid is lost during urination. This causes the "dry mouth" that is indicative of dehydration.
2. The prostatic urethra extends through the prostate gland, immediately inferior to the male bladder. A patient with benign prostatic hypertrophy has an enlarged prostate that causes constriction of the prostatic urethra, and thus urine cannot be voided normally.
3. A punch to the lumbar region of the back could injure a kidney (thus, the punch has the nickname "kidney punch"). Even though the kidney is enveloped in multiple protective layers of connective tissue and fat, a direct hit can bruise or severely damage this organ. Common symptoms are pain in the lumbar region, or blood in the urine if the kidney 's filtration system has been damaged. In more severe cases, torn blood vessels to and from the kidney can result in severe hemorrhage (since the kidneys receive 20% to 25% of the body's blood at any given time).

CHAPTER TWENTY-EIGHT

Challenge Yourself

Multiple Choice

1. b
2. b
3. c
4. a
5. c
6. b
7. c
8. c
9. d
10. a

Developing Critical Reasoning

1. If Caitlyn has regular 28-day ovarian and uterine cycles, then at 2 weeks since her last period she would have been close to the time of ovulation. Sperm can live for several days in the female reproductive tract, and thus viable sperm may have been present either before, during, or immediately after ovulation, increasing her risk of becoming pregnant significantly. The physician would tell Caitlyn that birth control pills typically come in 28-day packets. The first 21 days of pills contain low levels of estrogen and/or progestins, which prevent the LH "spike" needed for ovulation. Thus, birth control pills prevent ovulation.
2. The external genitalia appear very similar in males and females until about week 12 of development, and do not become clearly differentiated until about week 20. An ultrasound is typically delayed until sometime between weeks 18 and 22 because the external genitalia are not clearly distinguishable until then.
3. Given that there is no urinary tract infection or kidney stones, it is possible that the prostate gland is enlarged. Because the urethra passes through the prostate, if this gland is enlarged it can impinge on the urethral lumen, making it more difficult and painful to urinate.

Glossary

Pronunciation Key

Pronouncing a word correctly is as important as knowing its spelling and its contextual meaning. The mastery of all three allows a student to take ownership of the word. The system employed in this text is basic and consists of the following conventions.

1. Vowels marked with a line above the letter are pronounced as follows:

ā	day, base
ē	be, feet
ī	pie, ivy
ō	so, pole
ū	unit, cute

2. Vowels marked with the breve (˘) are pronounced as follows:

ă	above, about
ĕ	genesis, bet
ĭ	pit, sip
ŏ	collide
ŭ	cut, bud

3. Vowels not marked are pronounced as follows:

a	mat
o	not, ought
e	term

4. Other phonetic symbols used include:

ah	father
aw	fall
oo	food
ow	cow
oy	void

5. For consonants, the following key was employed:

b	bad	n	no
ch	child	ng	ring
d	dog	p	put
dh	this	r	right
f	fit	s	so
g	got	sh	shoe
h	hit	t	tight
j	jive	th	thin
k	keep	v	very
ks	tax	w	wet
kw	quit	y	yes
l	learn	z	zero
m	mice	zh	measure

6. The principal stressed syllables are followed by a prime (′); single-syllable words do not have a stress mark. Nonstressed syllables are separated by a hyphen.

7. Acceptable alternate pronunciations are given as needed.

A

abduction (ab-dŭk′shŭn) Movement of a body part away from the midline of the body.
achondroplasia (ā-kon′drō-plā′zē-ă) Disease characterized by abnormal conversion of cartilage to bone.
acrosome (ak′rō-sōm) Membranous cap on the anterior two-thirds of the sperm nucleus that contains digestive enzymes for penetrating an oocyte.
adaptation (ad′ap-t ā′shŭn) Advantageous change of an organ or tissue to meet new conditions.
adduction (ă-dŭk′shŭn) Medial movement of a body part toward the midline.
adipocyte (ad′i-p ō-sīt) Fat storage cell.
adrenergic (ad-r ĕ-ner′jik) Relating to nerve cells that use norepinephrine as their neurotransmitter.
afferent (af′ĕr-ĕnt) Inflowing or going toward a center.
agglutination (ă-glū-ti-nā′shŭn) Process by which erythrocytes adhere and form into clumps that can block blood vessels and disrupt normal blood circulation.
agonist (ag′on-ist) Muscle that contracts to produce a particular movement; also called *prime mover.*
albumin (al-bū′min) Plasma protein important in regulating fluid balance.
alimentary (al-i-men′ter-ē) Relating to food or nutrition.
alopecia (al′ō-pē′shē-ă) Thinning or loss of hair.
alveolus (al-vē′ ō-lŭs; pl., alveoli, -ō-lī) Small hollow or cavity. Air sac in the lungs; also, a milk-secreting portion of a mammary gland.
amblyopia (am′bl ē-ō′p ē-ă) Suppression of central vision or visual acuity in one eye due to the two eyes pointing in different directions so that the two scenes cannot be fused into a single image.
amnion (am′n ē-on) Extraembryonic membrane that envelops the embryo and secretes amniotic fluid .
amphiarthrosis (am′fē-ar-thrō′sis) A slightly movable joint.
ampulla (am-pul′l ă; pl., ampullae, -lē) Saccular dilation of a canal or duct, such as the ductus deferens in the male reproductive system.
anastomosis (ă-nas′t ō-mō′sis; pl., anastomoses, -sez) Union of two structures, such as blood vessels, to supply the same region.
androgen (an′dr ō-jen) Male sex hormone; one type of androgen is testosterone.
anemia (ă-nē′m ē-ă) Any condition in which the number of erythrocytes is below normal.
angioplasty (an′j ē-ō-plas′t ē) The reopening of a blood vessel through a variety of means.
antagonist (an-tag′ō-nist) Muscle that opposes or resists the action of another.
antebrachium (an′t ē-brā′k ē-ŭm) Forearm.
antigen (an′ti-jen) Any substance that can bind to a component of the adaptive immune system, such as T-lymphocytes or antibodies.
aorta (ā-ōr′tă) Main trunk of the systemic arterial system, beginning at the left ventricle and ending when it divides to form the common iliac arteries.
aperture (ap′er-ch ūr) Open gap or hole.
apex (ā′peks) Extremity of a conical or pyramidal structure, e.g., the inferior, conical end of the heart.
apical (ap′i-k ăl) Related to the tip or extremity of a conical or pyramidal structure.
aponeurosis (ap′ō-nū-rō′sis; pl., aponeuroses, -sēz) Flattened, sheet-like tendon.
apoptosis (ap′op-tō′sis, ap′ō-tō′sis) Programmed cell death.
appendicular (ap′en-dik′-y ū-lăr) Relating to an appendage or limb, e.g., the appendicular skeleton.
appositional (ap′ō-zish′ŭn-ăl) Being placed or fitted together, e.g., appositional growth of bone.
arachnoid (ă-rak′noyd) **granulation** A collection of arachnoid villi.
arachnoid mater Meninx lying external to the pia mater.
arachnoid villi Fingerlike extensions of the arachnoid mater that project through the dura mater into the dural venous sinuses.
arcuate (ar′ky ū-āt) Having a shape that is arched or bowed.
artery (ar′ter- ē) Blood vessel conveying blood away from the heart.
arthrology (ar-throl′ ō-jē) Branch of anatomy concerned with joints.
articular (ar-tik′y ū-lăr) Relating to a joint.
articulation (ar-tik-y ū-lā′sh ŭn) Joint or connection between bones.
astrocyte (as′tr ō-sīt) Largest and most abundant glial cell of the nervous system.
atlas (at′las) The first cervical vertebra.
atrium (ā′trē-ŭm; pl., atria, ā′trē-ă) Chamber or cavity to which are connected other chambers or passageways, e.g., the heart has a left atrium and a right atrium.
atrophy (at′r ō-fē) Wasting of tissues, organs, or the entire body.
auricle (aw′ri-kl) The external ear; also called the *pinna.*
auscultation (aws′k ŭl-tā′shŭn) Listening to the sounds made by various body structures to help diagnose medical conditions.
autolysis (aw-tol′i-sis) Digestion of cells by enzymes present within the cell itself.

Glossary

autophagy (aw-tof'ă-jē) Segregation and disposal of damaged organelles within a cell.
axial (ak'sē-ăl) Relating to or situated in the central part of the body—the head, neck, and trunk, e.g., the axial skeleton.
axis (ak'sis) The second cervical vertebra.
axolemma (ak'sō-lem'ă) Plasma membrane of an axon.
axon (ak'son) Process of a nerve cell that conducts the impulse away from the cell body.
axoplasm (ak'sō-plazm) Cytoplasm within the axon.

B

baroreceptor (bar'ō-rē-sep'ter, -tōr) A sensory receptor that detects changes in pressure.
basal nuclei (nū'klē'ī) see *cerebral nuclei*.
benign (bē-nīn') Term that denotes the mild character of an illness or the nonmalignant character of a neoplasm.
bile (bīl) Fluid secreted by the liver and discharged from the gallbladder into the duodenum.
biomechanics (bī'ō-me-kan'iks) Analysis of biological systems in mechanical terms.
bolus (bō'lŭs) A single quantity of something, such as a mass of food swallowed.
bursa (ber'să; pl., bursae, ber'sē) Closed, fluid-filled sac lined with a synovial membrane; usually found in areas subject to friction.

C

calcification (kal'si-fi-kā'shŭn) Process in which structures in the body become hardened as a result of deposited calcium salts; normally occurs only in the formation of bone and teeth.
callus (kal'ŭs) Composite mass of cells and extracellular matrix that forms at a fracture site to establish continuity between the bone ends.
calyx (kā'liks; pl., calyces or calices, kal'i-sēz) Cup-shaped structure.
canaliculus (kan'ă-lik'yū-lŭs; pl., canaliculi, -lī) Small canal or channel.
capacitation (kă-pas'i-tā'shŭn) A period of conditioning whereby the sperm coat is modified while in the female reproductive tract prior to being able to fertilize the secondary oocyte.
carotene (kar'ō-tēn) Class of yellow-red pigments widely distributed in plants and animals.
carpal (kar'păl) Relating to the wrist.
cartilaginous (kar'ti-laj'i-nŭs) Relating to or consisting of cartilage.
cataract (kat'ă-rakt) Complete or partial opacity of the lens.
cauda equina (kaw'dă ē-kwī'nă) Groups of axons within the vertebral canal inferior to the tapered inferior end of the spinal cord proper.
caudal (caw-dăl) Pertaining to the tail or rear end.
cecum (sē'kŭm) Blind pouch forming the first part of the large intestine.
centriole (sen'trē-ōl) Organelle that participates in the separation of chromosome pairs during cell division.
centromere (sen'trō-mēr) The nonstaining constriction of a chromosome that is the point of attachment of the spindle fiber.
cephalic (se-fal'ik) Cranial; relating to the cranium or head.
cerebellum (ser'e-bel'ŭm) The second largest part of the brain; develops posteriorly to the pons in the metencephalon.
cerebral nuclei (ser'ĕ-brăl nū'klē-ī) Collections of gray matter buried deep within central white matter in the basal region of the brain.
cerumen (sĕ-rū'men) Soft, waxy secretion of the ceruminous gland; found in the external auditory meatus.
chemotaxis (kē'mo-tak'sis) Movement in response to chemicals.
choana (kō'an-ă) Opening into the nasopharynx on either side of the nasal cavity.
cholecalciferol (kō'lē-kal-sif'er-ol) Vitamin D of animal origin found in human skin and in the fur and feathers of animals and birds exposed to sunlight.
cholinergic (kol'in-er'jik) Relating to nerve cells that use acetylcholine as their neurotransmitter.
chondroblast (kon'drō-blast) Actively mitotic form of a matrix-forming cell found in growing cartilage.
chondrocyte (kon'drō-sīt) Mature, nondividing cartilage cell.
chordamesoderm (kōr'dă-mes'ō-derm) Mesodermal cells that form the notochord.
chorion (kō'rē-on) Multilayered, outermost fetal membrane through which nourishment passes and attachment to the uterus occurs.
chromatid (krō'mă-tid) One of the two strands of a chromosome joined by a centromere.
chromatin (krō'ma-tin) Genetic material of the nucleus.
chromosome (krō'mō-sōm) The most organized level of genetic material; a single long molecule of DNA and associated proteins; becomes visible only when cell is dividing.
chyle (kīl) Lymph drained from gastrointestinal tract.
chyme (kīm) Liquefied, partly digested food expelled from the stomach into the duodenum.
cilium (sil'ē-ŭm; pl., cilia, -ă) Motile extension of a cell surface, containing cytoplasm and microtubules.
circumduction (ser'kŭm-dŭk'shŭn) Cone-like movement of a body part.
cisterna (sis-ter'nă; pl., cisternae, -ter'nē) Ultramicroscopic spaces between the membranes of the flattened sacs of various organelles.
cleavage (klēv'ij) Series of mitotic cell divisions occurring in the zygote immediately following its fertilization.
clonus (klō'nŭs) Movement marked by rapid, successive contractions and relaxations of a muscle.
coccyx (kok'siks) The end of the vertebral column, formed from four fused vertebrae; the tailbone.
cognition (kog-ni'shŭn) Mental activities associated with thinking, learning, and memory.
coitus (kō'i-tŭs) Sexual union or intercourse.
commissure (kom'i-shūr) Bundle of axons passing from one side to the other in the brain or spinal cord.
conjunctiva (kon'jŭnk-tī'vă) Mucous membrane covering the anterior surface of the eyeball and the posterior surface of the eyelids.
connexon (kō-neks'ōn) Complex protein assembly that traverses the lipid bilayer of the plasma membrane and may join with those of another cell to form a gap junction.
contralateral (kon'tră-lat'er-ăl) Relating to the opposite side.
conus medullaris (kō'nŭs med'yul-ār'is) Inferior end of the spinal cord.
cornea (kōr'nē-ă) Transparent structure making up the anterior surface of the eye.
coronal (kōr'ō-năl) A vertical plane that divides the body into anterior and posterior parts; also called frontal plane.
coronary (kōr'o-nār-ē) Denoting the blood vessels or other structures and activities related to the heart.
corpus callosum (kōr'pŭs kal-lō-sŭm) White matter tract between the cerebral hemispheres.
costal (kos'tăl) Relating to a rib.
craniosynostosis (krā'nē-ō-sin'os-tō'sis) Premature ossification of one or more skull sutures.
cubital (kyū'bi-tăl) Relating to the elbow.
cutaneous (kyū-tā'nē-ŭs) Relating to the skin.
cytokine (sī'tō-kīn) Protein that regulates the intensity and duration of an immune response.
cytokinesis (sī'tō-ki-nē'sis) Division of the cytoplasm during cell division.
cytology (sī-tol'ō-jē) Study of cells.
cytoplasm (sī'tō-plazm) All the materials contained between the plasma membrane and the nucleus; includes cytosol, organelles, and inclusions.
cytosol (sī'tō-sol) The viscous, syruplike fluid of the cytoplasm.

D

deciduous (dē-sid'yū-ŭs) Not permanent, e.g., deciduous teeth.
decussation (dē-kŭ-sā'shŭn) Any crossing over or intersection of parts.
defecation (def'ĕ-kā'shŭn) Discharge of feces from the rectum.
deglutition (dē-glū-tish'ŭn) Swallowing.
dendrite (den'drīt) Process of a neuron that conducts impulses toward the cell body.
dentition (den-tish'ŭn) Natural teeth in the dental arch, considered collectively.
depression (dĕ-presh'ŭn) Inferior displacement of a body part.
dermatology (der'mă-tol'ō-jē) Branch of medicine concerned with all aspects of the skin.
dermatome (der'mă-tōm) Area of skin supplied by a single spinal nerve. Also, during embryonic development, the cells that form the connective tissue of the skin.
dermis (der'mis) Layer of skin internal to the epidermis; contains blood and lymph vessels, nerves and nerve endings, glands, and usually hair follicles.
desmosome (dez'mō-sōm) One type of adhesion between two epithelial cells; a type of intercellular junction.

detrusor (dĕ-trū'sŏr) Muscle that acts to expel urine from the bladder.
diapedesis (dī' ă-pĕ-dē'sis) Passage of leukocytes (white blood cells) through the intact blood vessel wall.
diaphysis (dī-af'i-sis; pl., diaphyses, -sēz) Elongated, rodlike part of a long bone between its two ends; the shaft of a long bone.
diarthrosis (dī'ar-thr ō'sis; pl., diarthroses, -sēz) A freely movable (synovial) joint.
diastole (dī-as't ō-lē) The relaxation phase of a heart chamber.
diffusion (di-fy ū'zh ŭn) Random movement of molecules or particles down their concentration gradient.
diploë (dip'l ō-ē) Central layer of spongy bone between the two layers of compact bone (outer and inner plates) of the flat cranial bones.
diploid (dip'loyd) State of a cell containing pairs of homologous chromosomes. In humans, the diploid number of chromosomes is 46, 23 pairs.
dislocation (dis'l ō-kā'shŭn) A joint injury where there is complete displacement of a bone from its normal position.
diuretic (dī'y ū-ret'ik) Agent that increases the excretion of urine.
dizygotic twins (dī'zī-got'ik) Nonidentical twins occurring when two secondary oocytes become fertilized and are implanted in the uterine wall at about the same time.
dorsiflexion (dōr'si-flek'sh ŭn) Movement of the foot whereby the dorsum of the foot is brought closer to the anterior leg.
duodenum (dū'ō-dē'nŭm, dū-od'ĕ-nŭm) First section of small intestine.
dura mater (dū'ră mā'tĕr) Tough, fibrous membrane forming the outer covering of the central nervous system.
dyskinesia (dis'ki-n ē'zē-ă) Difficulty performing voluntary movements.

E

ectoderm (ek'tō-d'ĕrm) Outermost of the three primary germ layers of the embryo.
ectopic (ek-top'ik) Out of place, e.g., in an ectopic pregnancy, the pre-embryo implants in the uterine tube rather than in the uterus.
edema (e-d ē-mă) Accumulation of excess fluid in cells or tissues.
effector (ē-fek'tŏr, -tōr) Peripheral tissue or organ that receives nerve impulses and then reacts.
efferent (ef'ĕr-ent) Outgoing or moving away from a center.
ejaculation (ē-jak'y ū-lā'shŭn) Expulsion of semen from the penis.
elevation (el'ĕ-vā'shŭn) Superior movement of a body part.
embryo (em'brē-ō) Organism in the early stages of development; in humans, the embryonic stage extends from the third to the eighth week of development.
embryology (em'brē-olŏ-jē) Study of the origin and development of the organism, from fertilization of the secondary oocyte until birth.
enamel (ē-nam'ĕl) Hard substance covering the exposed portion of the tooth.
endocardium (en'd ō-kar'd ē-ŭm) Innermost covering of the heart wall.
endocrine (en'd ō-krin) Secrete internally, such as hormones that are transported by the circulation.
endocrinology (en'd ō-kri-nol' ŏ-jē) Medical specialty concerned with hormonal secretions and their physiologic and pathologic consequences.
endocytosis (en'd ō-sī-t ō'sis) Movement of substances from the extracellular environment into the cell.
endoderm (en'd ō-dĕrm) Innermost of the three primary germ layers of the embryo.
endolymph (en'd ō-limf) Fluid within the membranous labyrinth of the inner ear.
endometrium (en'd ō-mē'trē-ŭm) Mucous membrane forming the inner layer of the uterine wall.
endomysium (en'd ō-miz'ē-ŭm, -mis' ē-ŭm) Areolar connective tissue layer surrounding a muscle fiber.
endoneurium (en'd ō-nū'rē-ŭm) Areolar connective tissue of a peripheral nerve that surrounds the axons.
endosteum (en-dos't ē-ŭm) Layer of cells lining the inner surface of bone in the medullary cavity.
ependymal (ĕ-pen'di-măl) Relating to the cellular lining of the brain ventricles and central canal of the spinal cord.
epicardium (ep'i-kar'd ē-ŭm) The visceral layer of serous pericardium.
epidermis (ep'i-d ĕrm'is) Superficial epithelial portion of the skin.
epimysium (ep'i-mis'ē-ŭm) Fibrous connective tissue envelope surrounding a skeletal muscle.
epineurium (ep'i-n ū'rē-ŭm) Outermost supporting connective tissue layer of peripheral nerves.
epiphyseal line (ep'i-fiz'ē-ăl) Portion of the epiphyseal plate that remains when long bone growth ceases.
epiphysis (e-pif'i-sis; pl., epiphyses, -sēz) Expanded, knobby region at the end of a long bone.
eponychium (ep'ō-nik'ē-ŭm) Corneal layer of epidermis found proximal and lateral to the nail plate.
erection (ē-rek'shŭn) Erectile tissues in the penis fill with blood and cause the penis to enlarge and become firm.
erythrocyte (ĕ-rith'r ō-sīt) Mature red blood cell.
erythropoiesis (ĕ-rith'r ō-poy-ē'sis) Formation of erythrocytes.
erythropoietin (ĕ-rith'r ō-poy'ĕ-tin) Protein that stimulates erythropoiesis.
esophagus (ĕ-sof'ă-gŭs) Portion of the gastrointestinal tract between the pharynx and the stomach.
eversion (ē-ver'zh ŭn) Turning the sole of the foot outward or laterally.
exhalation (eks-h ă-lā'shŭn) Forcing air from the lungs.
exocrine (ek's ō-krin) Glandular secretions delivered to an apical or luminal surface through a duct.
exocytosis (ek's ō-sī-to'sis) Process whereby secreting granules or droplets are exported out of a cell.
extension (eks-ten'shŭn) Movement of a joint in an anterior-posterior plane that increases the articulating angle.
exteroceptor (eks'ter- ō-sep't ŏr, -tōr) Sensory receptor in the skin, in a mucous membrane, or in one of the special senses that responds to external stimulation.

F

facet (fas'et, f ă-set') Small, smooth area on a bone.
falciform (fal'si-fōrm) Having a sickle shape.
falx cerebri (fawlks se-ē'bri) Portion of the dura mater septa that projects into the longitudinal fissure between the right and left hemispheres of the brain.
fascia (fash' ē-ă; pl., fasciae, -ē-ē) Sheath of dense connective tissue that envelops the body beneath the skin, encloses muscles, and separates their various layers or groups.
fascicle (fas'i-k ĕl) Band or bundle of muscle or nerve fibers.
fauces (faw's ēz) Space between the oral cavity and the pharynx.
feces (fē'sēz) Material discharged from the GI tract during defecation.
fertilization (fer'til-i-z ā'shŭn) Process of sperm penetration of the secondary oocyte.
fetal (fē'tăl) Relating to the fetus; in humans, the fetal period extends from the ninth week of development until birth (typically at 38 weeks).
fibroblast (fī'brō-blast) Large, flat, connective tissue cells with tapered ends that produce the fibers and ground substance components of the extracellular matrix.
fibrosis (fī-brō'sis) Formation of fibrous connective tissue as a repair or reactive process.
filtrate (fil'tr āt) Whatever materials get through a filter.
fimbria (fim'brē-ă; pl., fimbriae, -brē-ē) Any fringelike struc ture, e.g., the fimbriae of the infundibulum enclose the ovary at the time of ovulation.
fissure (fish' ŭr) Deep furrow, cleft, or slit.
flagellum (flă-jel'- ŭm; pl., flagella, -ă) Whiplike locomotory organelle that arises from within the cell and extends outside it.
flexion (flek'shŭn) Movement of a joint in an anterior-posterior plane that decreases the angle between the articulating bones.
flexure (flek'shŭr) Bend in an organ or structure.
folliculitis (fō-lik'y ū-lī'tis) Inflammation of a hair follicle.
fontanelle (fon'tă-nel') One of several membranous intervals at the margins of the cranial bones in an infant.
fornix (fōr'niks; pl., fornices, -ni-sēz) Arch-shaped structure.
fossa (fos'ă; pl., fossae, -fos'ē) Depression, often more or less longitudinal in shape, below the level of the surface of a part.
furuncle (fū'rŭng-kĕl) Localized pyrogenic infection; also called a *boil.*

G

gamete (gam'ēt) A sex cell with the haploid number of chromosomes.
gametogenesis (gam'ĕ-tō-jen'ĕ-sis) Formation and development of gametes (sex cells).
ganglion (gang'gl ē-on; pl., ganglia, -glē-ă) Group of neuron cell bodies in the peripheral nervous system.
gastrulation (gas'tr ū-lā'shŭn) Formation of the three primary germ layers.
genotype (jen' ō-tīp) The genetic constitution of an individual that, along with environmental influences, contributes to the phenotype.

glabella (glă-bel′ă) The smooth part of the frontal bone that is in between the superciliary arches.
glycocalyx (glī′k ō-kā′liks) Filamentous coating on the apical surface of certain epithelial cells.
goblet cell Mucin-secreting cell.
gomphosis (gom-fō′sis; pl., gomphoses, -sēz) Fibrous joint in which a peglike process fits into a hole.
gonad (gō′nad) Organ that produces sex cells and sex hormones; the ovaries in a female and the testes in a male.
gustation (gŭs-tā′shŭn) Sense of taste.
gyrus (jī′r ŭs; pl., gyri, -rī) Elevated fold of cerebral cortex.

H

hapalonychia (hap′ă-lō-nik′ē-ă) Thinning of nails that results in bending and breaking of their free edge.
haploid (hap′loyd) The number of chromosomes in a sperm or secondary oocyte. In humans, the haploid number is 23.
hemangioma (hē-man′j ē-ō′mă) Congenital anomaly characterized by a proliferation of blood vessels forming a neoplasm-like mass.
hematocrit (hē-mat′ō-krit, hem′ ă-) Percentage of whole blood attributed to all formed elements (erythrocytes, leukocytes, and platelets).
hematopoiesis (hē′mat′ō-poy-ē′sis) Formation and development of blood cells.
hemoglobin (hē′mō-glō′bin) A red pigmented protein that transports oxygen and carbon dioxide; responsible for characteristic bright red color of arterial blood.
hemolysis (hē-mol′i-sis) Alteration or destruction of erythrocytes.
hemorrhage (hem′ŏ-răj) Abnormal escape of blood from a blood vessel.
hernia (her′n ē-ă) Protrusion of a part through the structures normally surrounding or containing it.
hiatus (hī- ā′tŭs) Opening.
hillock (hil′lok) Any small elevation or prominence.
hilum (hī′l ŭm) The part of an organ where structures such as blood vessels, nerves, and lymph vessels enter or leave.
histology (his-tol′ŏ-jē) Study of tissues.
homeostasis (hō′mē-ō-stā′sis, -os′tă-sis) State of equilibrium in the body with respect to various functions and the chemical composition of bodily fluids.
homologous (hō-mol′ŏ-gŭs) Alike in certain critical attributes.
hormone (hōr′mōn) Chemical formed in one part of the body and transported by the blood to another where it can affect cellular activity.
hyaline (hī′ ă-lin, -lēn) Clear, homogeneous substance; a type of cartilage.
hydroxyapatite (hī-drok′s ē-ap-ă-tīt) Natural mineral structure that the crystal lattice of bone and teeth closely resembles.
hyperextension (hī′p ĕr-eks-ten′shŭn) Extension of a body part beyond its normal range of motion.
hyperkyphosis (hī′p ĕr-kī-fō′sis) Exaggerated convex curvature of the thoracic vertebral column.
hyperlordosis (hī′p ĕr-lor-d ō′sis) Exaggerated concave curvature of the lumbar vertebral column.
hypogastric (hī′p ō-gas′trik) Relating to the hypogastrium, or pubic region.

I

idiopathic (id′ē-ō-path′ik) Describing a disease of unknown cause.
infundibulum (in′f ŭn-dib′y ū-lŭm) Funnel-shaped structure or passage.
ingestion (in-jes′ch ŭn) Introduction of food and drink into the GI tract.
inhalation (in′hă-lā′shŭn) Drawing in a breath.
innervation (in′ĕr-vā′shŭn) Supply of nerves to a body structure.
insertion (in-sĕr′sh ŭn) The usually distal and more movable attachment of a muscle. (This term typically is replaced by the phrase *inferior attachment* or *distal attachment* in this text.)
integument (in-teg′yū-ment) Cover enveloping the body; includes the epidermis, dermis, and all derivatives of the epidermis; also called skin or the cutaneous membrane.
intercalated disc (in-ter′k ă-lā-tĕd disk) Complex cellular junction that interconnects cardiac muscle cells in the heart wall.
interneuron (intĕr-nū′ron) Type of neuron that resides within the CNS and coordinates activity between sensory and motor neurons.
interoceptor (in′tĕr-ō-sep′t ŏr) Small sensory receptors within the walls of the viscera (organs). Also known as a *viceroceptor*.
interstitial (in′tĕr-stish′ ăl) Relating to spaces within a tissue or organ, but not a body cavity, e.g., interstitial fluid occupies the extracellular matrix of tissues.
intervertebral (in′tĕr-ver′t ĕ-brăl) Between vertebrae.
intramembranous ossification (in′tr ă-mem′brā-nŭs) Bone formation that takes place within a membrane; the formation of the flat bones of the skull.
intramural (in′tr ă-myū′răl) Within the substance of the wall of a cavity or hollow organ.
intraperitoneal (in′tr ă-per′i-t ō-nē′ăl) Location of a structure or organ that is completely covered with visceral peritoneum.
invaginate (in-vaj′i-n āt) To infold or insert a structure within itself.
inversion (in-ver′zh ŭn) Turning inward of the foot.
ipsilateral (ip′si-lat′ĕr-ăl) On the same side.
isometric (ī′s ō-met′rik) Condition in which the ends of a contracting muscle are held fixed and the muscle generates tension but does not change length.
isotonic (ī′s ō-ton′ik) Condition in which a contracting muscle generates tension and changes length.

K

keratinization (ker′ă-tin′i-zā′shŭn) Development of a horny layer due to cells filled with the protein keratin.
keratinocyte (ke-rat′i-nō-sīt) The most abundant cell type in the epidermis and found throughout the epidermis; cells that produce keratin.
kyphosis (kī-fō′sis) Convex curvature of the thoracic part of the vertebral column.

L

lacrimal (lak′ri-m ăl) Relating to tears.
lactation (lak-tā′shŭn) Production of milk.
lacteal (lak′t ē-ăl) Tiny vessel that transports lymph with lipids and lipid-soluble vitamins from the small intestine.
lacuna (lă-kū′nă; pl., lacunae, -kū′nē) Small space, cavity, or depression.
lamella (lă-mel′ă; pl., lamellae, -mel′ē) Layer of bone connective tissue.
lanugo (lă-nū′gō) Fine, soft, unpigmented fetal hair.
larynx (lar′ingks) Organ of voice production that lies between the pharynx and the trachea.
lateralization (lat′ĕr-al-ī-z ā′shŭn) Process whereby certain asymmetries of structure and function occur.
lemniscus (lem-nis′k ŭs; pl., lemnisci, -nis′ī) Bundle of axons ascending from sensory relay nuclei to the thalamus.
leptomeninges (lep′t ō-mĕ-nin′j ēz) Term used in medicine to refer to the pia mater and arachnoid mater together.
lesion (lē′zhŭn) Pathologic change in a tissue.
lethargy (leth′ăr-jē) Mild impairment of consciousness characterized by reduced awareness and alertness.
leukocyte (lū′kō-sīt) Any one of several types of white blood cells.
leukopoiesis (lū′kō-poy-ē′sis) Formation and development of leukocytes.
ligament (lig′ă-ment) Band or sheet of dense regular fibrous tissue that connects bones, cartilage, or other structures.
lobe (lōb) Subdivision of an organ, bounded by some structural demarcation.
lordosis (lor-d ō′sis) Concave curvature of the lumbar vertebral column.
lumen (lū′men) The space inside a structure, such as where blood is transported within a blood vessel.
lunula (lū′nū-lă) Pale, arched area at the proximal end of the nail plate.
lymph (limf) Usually transparent fluid found in lymph vessels; derived from interstitial fluid.
lymphoblast (lim′f ō-blast) Immature cell that becomes a lymphocyte.
lymphopoiesis (lim′f ō-poy-ē′sis) Formation of lymphatic cells.
lysosome (lī′s ō-sōm) Organelle containing digestive enzymes.

M

malignant (mă-lig′n ănt) In reference to a neoplasm, having the property of invasiveness and spread.
MALT Mucosa-associated lymphoid tissue, found in the lining of the gastrointestinal tract, urinary system, and respiratory system.
mastication (mas′ti-k ā′shŭn) Chewing of food.

matrix (mā′triks; pl., matrices, mā′tri-sēz) Surrounding substance within which cells or structures are contained or embedded.
mechanoreceptor (mek′ă-nō-rē-sep′tŏr) Sensory receptor that responds to touch, vibration, pressure, or distortion.
mediastinum (me′dē-as-tī′nŭm) Median space of the thoracic cavity.
meiosis (mī-ō′sis) Sex-cell division that produces gametes, each of which contains the haploid number of chromosomes.
melanin (mel′ă-nin) Any of the dark brown to black pigments that occur in the skin, hair, and retina.
melanocyte (mel′ă-nō-sīt) Pigment-producing cell in the basal layer of the epidermis.
menarche (me-nar′kē) Time of the first menstrual period.
meninx (mē′ninks; pl., meninges, -jēz) Any one of the membranes covering the brain and spinal cord.
meniscus (mě-nis′kŭs; pl., menisci, mě-nis′sī) Crescent-shaped fibrocartilage found in certain joints.
menopause (men′ō-pawz) Permanent cessation of menses.
menses (men′sēz) Periodic physiologic hemorrhage from the uterine mucous membrane; commonly referred to as the menstrual period.
menstruation (men-strū-ā′shŭn) Cyclic endometrial shedding and discharge of menses.
mesenchyme (mes′eng-kīm) An embryonic connective tissue.
mesoderm (mez′ō-derm) The middle of the three primary germ layers of the embryo.
mesothelium (mez′ō-thē′lē-ŭm) The simple squamous epithelium that lines serous cavities.
metaphysis (mě-taf′i-sis; pl., metaphyses, -sēz) Section of a long bone between the epiphysis and the diaphysis.
metaplasia (met′ă-plā′zē-ă) Abnormal change in a tissue.
metastasis (mě-tas′tă-sis) Spread of cancerous cells from one part of the body to another.
metopic (me-top′ik) Relating to the forehead.
microfilament (mī′krō-fil′ă-ment) Smallest structural element of the cytoskeleton.
microglial cell (mī-krog′lē-ăl) Category of small glial cells in the central nervous system.
microscopy (mī-kros′kŏ-pē) Investigation of very small objects by means of a microscope.
microtubule (mī′krō-tū′byūl) Hollow, cylindrical cytoplasmic element.
micturition (mik′chū-rish′ŭn) Urination.
mitochondrion (mī′tō-kon′drē-on; pl., mitochondria, -ă) Organelle associated with the production of ATP.
mitosis (mī-tō′sis) Process of somatic cell division.
monozygotic twins (mon′ō-zī-got′ik) Identical twins arising from a single oocyte fertilized by a single sperm.
mons (monz) Anatomic prominence or slight elevation above the general level of the surface, e.g., mons pubis.
mucin (myū′sin) An often protective secretion containing carbohydrate-rich glycoproteins.
mucosa (myū-kō′să) Mucous membrane that lines various body structures.
muscularis (mŭs-kyū-lā′ris) Muscular layer in the wall of a hollow organ or tubular structure.
myelin (mī′ě-lin) Lipoproteinaceous material of the myelin sheath.
myelinated (mī′ě-li-nāt′ed) Covered by a myelin sheath.
myenteron (mī-en′ter-on) Muscle coat of the intestine; also called the tunica muscularis.
mylohyoid (mī′l ō-hī′oyd) Pertaining to the molar teeth or the posterior portion of the mandible and hyoid.
myoblast (mī′ō-blast) Undifferentiated muscle cell with the potential of becoming a muscle fiber.
myocardium (mī′ō-kar′dē-ŭm) Middle layer of the heart wall, consisting of cardiac muscle.
myofibril (mī′ō-fī′bril) One of the longitudinal fibrils found in skeletal and cardiac muscle fibers.
myofilament (mī′ō-fil′ă-ment) A protein filament that makes up the myofibrils in skeletal muscle.
myoglobin (mī′ō-glō′bin) Oxygen-carrying and -storing molecule in muscle.
myometrium (mī′ō-mē′trē-ŭm) Middle tunic (muscular wall) of the uterus.
myotome (mī′ō-tōm) Part of the somite that develops into skeletal muscle.

N

naris (nā′ris; pl., nares, -res) Anterior opening to the nasal cavity; also known as a *nostril*.
necrosis (ně-krō′sis) Pathologic death of cells or a portion of a tissue or organ.
neoplasia (nē′ō-plā′zē-ă) Process that results in the formation of a neoplasm or abnormal growth.
neoplasm (nē′ō-plazm) An abnormal tissue that grows by cell proliferation more rapidly than normal.
nephron (nef′ron) Convoluted tubular functional unit of the kidney.
neurilemma (nū′ri-lem′ă) The delicate outer membrane sheath around an axon.
neurofibril (nū′rō-fī′bril) Filamentous structure in a neuron.
neurofilament (nū′rō-fil′ă-ment) Group of intermediate-sized filaments in a neuron.
neuromuscular (nū′rō-mus′kyū-lăr) Relationship between a nerve and a muscle, e.g., a neuromuscular junction.
neuron (nū′ron) Nervous system cell that transmits and receives nerve impulses.
neuropore (nū′rō-pōr) Opening in the embryo leading from the central canal of the neural tube to the exterior.
neurulation (nū′rū-lā′shŭn) Formation of the neural plate and its closure to form the neural tube.
nociceptor (nō′si-sep′tŏr, -tōr) Peripheral sensory receptor for the detection of painful stimuli.
nucleolus (nū-klē′ō-lŭs; pl., nucleoli, -lī) Spherical, dark body within the nucleus where subunits of ribosomes are made.

O

oblique (ob-lēk′) Slanted, at an angle.
occult (ŏ-kŭlt′, ok′ŭlt) Hidden or concealed.
olfaction (ol-fak′shŭn) Sense of smell.
oligodendrocyte (ol′i-gō-den′drō-sīt) Category of large glial cells in the central nervous system.
omentum (ō-men′tŭm) Fold of peritoneum from the stomach to another abdominal organ.
oogenesis (ō′ō-jen′ě-sis) Formation and development of oocytes.
oogonium (ō′ō-gō′nē-ŭm; pl., oogonia, -ă) Diploid germ cell that forms oocytes.
opposition (op′pō-si′shŭn) Movement of the thumb across the palm to touch the palmar side of the fingertips.
organelle (or′gă-nel) Complex, organized structures in the cytoplasm of a cell with unique characteristic shapes; called "little organs."
organogenesis (ōr′gă-nō-jen′ě-sis) Formation of organs during development.
orifice (or′i-fis) Aperture or opening.
origin (ōr′i-jin) The less movable of the two points of attachment of a muscle. (This term typically is replaced with the phrase *superior attachment* or *proximal attachment* in this text.)
os (oz; pl., os′sis, osă) An opening into a hollow organ or canal.
osmosis (os-mō′sis) A type of simple diffusion in which water diffuses from one side of a selectively permeable membrane to the other side.
osseous (os′ē-ŭs) Bony.
ossicle (os′i-kěl) Small bone.
osteoblast (os′tē-ō-blast′) Bone-forming cell.
osteoclast (os′tē-ō-klast′) Large cell type that functions in the absorption and removal of bone connective tissue.
osteocyte (os′tē-ō-sīt′) Bone cell in a lacuna.
osteogenesis (os′tē-ō-jen′ě-sis) Production of new bone.
osteolysis (os′tē-ol′i-sis) Softening, absorption, and destruction of bone connective tissue.
osteon (os′tē-on) Functional unit of compact bone tissue; also called a Haversian system.
osteopenia (os′tē-ō-pē′nē-ă) Decreased calcification or density of bone.
osteoporosis (os′tē-ō-pō-rō′sis) Medical condition characterized by decreased bone mass and increased susceptibility to fracture.
osteoprogenitor (os′tē-ō-prō-jen′i-ter) Precursor to bone cells.
ovulation (ov′yū-lā′shŭn) Release of a secondary oocyte from the mature follicle.
ovum (ō′vŭm; pl., ova, -vă) Female sex cell that has been fertilized and has completed meiosis II.

P

palate (pal′ăt) Partition between the oral and nasal cavities; the roof of the mouth.
palpation (pal-pā′shŭn) Using the sense of touch to identify or examine internal body structures.
papilla (pă-pil′ă; pl., papillae, -pil′ē) Small, nipplelike process.
parenchyma (pă-reng′ki-mă) Specific functional cells of a gland or organ.
parietal (pă-rī′ ĕ-tăl) Relating to the wall of any cavity.
patellar (pa-tel′ăr) Relating to the kneecap.
pathologic (path′ō-loj′-ik) Pertaining to disease.
pedal (ped′ăl) Relating to the foot.
percussion (per-k ŭsh′ŭn) Using sounds produced by tapping the surface of the body to help diagnose medical conditions.
pericardium (per′i-kar′dē-ŭm) Fibroserous membrane covering the heart.
perichondrium (per′i-kon′dr ē-ŭm) Layer of dense irregular connective tissue around the surface of cartilage.
perilymph (per′i-limf) Fluid within the osseous labyrinth, surrounding and protecting the membranous labyrinth.
perimetrium (per′i-mē′trē-ŭm) Serous coat of the uterus.
perimysium (per′i-mis′ē-ŭm, -miz′ē-ŭm) Fibrous sheath enveloping each of the fascicles of skeletal muscle fibers.
perineurium (per′i-nū′rē-ŭm) Fibrous sheath of peripheral nerves that surrounds the nerve fascicles.
periosteum (per′ē-os′t ē-ŭm) Thick, fibrous membrane covering the entire external surface of a bone, except for the articular cartilage.
peritoneum (per′i-t ō-nē′ŭm) Serous sac that lines the abdominopelvic cavity and covers most of the viscera within.
peroxisome (pĕ-rok′si-sōm) Membrane-bound organelle containing oxidative enzymes.
Peyer patches Lymphoid nodules found primarily in small intestine and appendix.
phagocytosis (fag′ō-sī-t ō′sis) Process by which cells ingest and digest solid substances.
phalanx (fă′langks; pl., phalanges, -jēz) Long bone of a digit.
phenotype (fē′nō-tīp) Observable characteristics of an individual.
philtrum (fil′tr ŭm) Groove in the midline of the upper lip.
pinna (pin′ ă) Another name for the auricle or outer ear.
pinocytosis (pin′ō-sī-tō′sis) Cellular process of actively engulfing liquid.
placenta (plă-sen′t ă) Organ of exchange between the embryo or fetus and the mother.
plantar flexion (plan′tar flek′shŭn) The extension of the foot as in pointing the foot and toes downward.
plasmalemma (plaz′m ă-lem′ă) The plasma (cell) membrane.
platelet (plāt′let) Irregularly shaped cell fragment that participates in blood clotting.
pleura (plūr′ă; pl., pleurae, plūr′ē) Serous membranes enveloping the lungs and lining the walls of the pleural cavity.
plexus (plek′sŭs) Network of nerves, blood vessels, or lymph vessels.
pollex (pol′eks) Thumb.
polycythemia (pol′ē-sī-th ē′mē-ă) Greater than the normal number of erythrocytes.
polyspermy (pol′ē-sper′m ē) Entrance of more than one sperm into the oocyte.
postsynaptic (pōst′sin-ap′tik) On the distal side of a synaptic cleft.
prepuce (prē′pūs) Free fold of skin that covers the glans of the penis; also known as the *foreskin*.
presynaptic (prē′sin-ap′tik) On the proximal side of a synaptic cleft.
pronation (prō-nā′shŭn) Rotational movement of the forearm causing the hand to be directed posteriorly or inferiorly.
proprioceptor (prō′prē-ō-sep′tŏr) Sensory end organ that senses position or state of contraction.
protraction (prō-trak′sh ŭn) Movement of a body part anteriorly in a horizontal plane.
protuberance (prō-tū′bĕr-ăns) Swelling or knoblike outgrowth.
pulmonary (pul′m ō-nār′ē) Relating to the lung.
pulse (pŭls) Rhythmic dilation of an artery resulting from increased blood volume during heart contraction.
pupil (pyū′pĭl) Circular hole in the center of the iris of the eye.

R

ramus (rā′mŭs; pl., rami, rā′mī) One of the primary divisions of a nerve or blood vessel. Also, part of an irregularly shaped bone that forms an angle.
raphe (rā′fē) Line of union between two contiguous, bilateral symmetrical structures, e.g., the raphe of the scrotum.
reticulocyte (re-tik′y ū-lō-sīt) Young erythrocyte.
retraction (rē-trak′sh ŭn) Posteriorly directed movement of a body part.
retroperitoneal (ret′rō-per′i-t ō nē′ăl) Posterior to the peritoneum.
ribosome (rī′b ō-sōm) Ribonucleoprotein structure that is the site of protein synthesis; organelle in the cytoplasm.
rotation (rō-tā′shŭn) Movement of a part around its axis.
ruga (rū′gă; pl., rugae, rū′jē) Fold, ridge, or crease.

S

sacroiliac (sā′krō-il′ē-ak) Pertaining to the sacrum and the ilium.
sacrum (sā′krŭm) Next-to-last bone of the vertebral column; formed of five fused vertebrae.
sagittal (saj′i-tăl) Being in an anteroposterior direction.
sarcolemma (sar′k ō-lem′ă) Plasma membrane of a muscle fiber.
sarcomere (sar′k ō-mēr) Functional unit of skeletal muscle.
sarcoplasm (sar′k ō-plazm) Cytoplasm of a muscle fiber.
sclera (skl ē′ră) Portion of the fibrous layer forming the outer covering of the eyeball, except for the cornea.
sclerotome (skl ē′rō-tōm) The portion of a somite that gives rise to vertebrae and ribs.
scoliosis (skō′lē-ō′sis) Abnormal lateral curvature of the vertebral column.
sebum (sē′bŭm) Secretion of a sebaceous gland.
semen (sē′mĕn) Secretion composed of sperm and seminal fluid.
semipermeable (sem′ ē-per′m ē-ă-bĕl) Freely permeable to some molecules, but relatively impermeable to other molecules.
sensation (sen-s ā′shŭn) Translation into consciousness of the effects of a stimulus.
septum (sep′tŭm) A thin wall that separates two cavities or two soft tissue masses.
serosa (se-r ō′să) Outermost coat of a visceral structure that lies in a closed body cavity.
serous (sē′rŭs) Producing a substance that has a watery consistency.
serum (sē′rum) Clear, watery fluid that remains after clotting proteins are removed from plasma.
sinus (sī′n ŭs) Cavity or hollow space; also, a channel for the passage of blood or lymph.
sinusoid (sī′nū-soyd) Resembling a sinus; a microscopic space or passage for blood in certain organs, such as the liver or the spleen.
skeleton (skel′ ĕ-tŏn) Bony framework of the body; collectively, all the bones of the body.
somatomedin (sō′mă-tō-mē′din) Peptide that stimulates certain anabolic processes in bone and cartilage.
somite (sō′mīt) One of the paired segments consisting of cell masses formed in the early embryonic mesoderm on the sides of the neural tube.
spermatid (sper′m ă-tid) Late stage of the development of the sperm.
spermatogenesis (sper′m ă-tō-jen′ĕ-sis) Process by which stem cells become sperm.
spermatogonium (sper′m ă-tō-gō′nē-ŭm; pl., spermatogonia, -ă) Diploid germ cell that produces sperm.
spermiogenesis (sper′m ē-ō-jen′ĕ-sis) Stage of spermatogenesis during which immature spermatids become sperm, or spermatozoa.
sphincter (sfingk′t ĕr) Muscle that encircles a duct, tube, or orifice such that its contraction constricts the lumen or orifice.
sphygmomanometer (sfig′m ō-mă-nom′ĕ-tĕr) Instrument for measuring arterial blood pressure.
strabismus (stra-biz′m ŭs) Lack of parallelism of the visual axes of the eye.
stria (strī′ ă; pl., striae, strī′ ē) Stripes, bands, streaks, or lines distinguished by a difference in color, texture, or elevation from surrounding tissue.
stupor (stū′pŏr) State of impaired consciousness from which the individual can be aroused only by continual stimulation.
subcutaneous (sŭb′kyū-tā′nē-ŭs) Beneath the skin.
subluxation (sŭb′lŭk-sā′shŭn) Incomplete dislocation of a body part.
sulcus (sŭl′kŭs; pl., sulci, sŭl′sī) Groove on the surface of the brain.
supernumerary (sū′pĕr-nū′mĕr-ār′ē) Exceeding the normal number.
supination (sū′pi-n ā′shŭn) Rotation of the forearm such that the hand faces anteriorly or superiorly.
suture (sū′chūr) Synarthrosis in which bones are united by a dense regular connective tissue membrane.

symphysis (sim′fi-sis; pl., symphyses, -sēz) Cartilaginous joint in which the two bones are separated by a pad of fibrocartilage.
synapse (sin′aps) Functional contact of a nerve cell with another nerve cell, effector, or receptor.
synarthrosis (sin′ar-thr ō′sis; pl., synarthroses, -sēz) Immovable joint.
synchondrosis (sin′kon-dr ō′sis; pl., synchondroses, -sēz) Cartilaginous joint in which the bones are joined by hyaline cartilage.
syncytiotrophoblast (sin-sit′ē-ō-trōf-ō-blast) Outer layer of the trophoblast that produces the hormone human chorionic gonadotropin (hCG).
syndesmosis (sin′dez-mō′sis; pl., syndesmoses, -sēz) Fibrous joint in which the opposing surfaces of articulating bones are united by ligaments.
synergist (sin′ĕr-jist) Structure, muscle, agent, or process that aids the action of another.
synostosis (sin′os-t ō′sis; pl., synostoses, -sēz) Osseous union between two bones that were initially separate.
systemic (sis-tem′ik) Relating to the entire organism as opposed to any of its individual parts.
systole (sis′t ō-lē) Contraction of the heart.

T

tactile (tak′til) Relating to touch.
tendon (ten′d ŏn) Cord of dense regular connective tissue that connects muscle to bone.
teratology (ter′ ă-tol′ō-jē) Branch of science concerned with congenital malformations.
testis (tes′tis; pl., testes, -tēz) Male organ for producing gametes and androgens.
thenar (thē′nar) A structure related to the base of the thumb or the thumb's underlying connective components.
thermoreceptor (ther′m ō-rē-sep′t ŏr, -tōr) Receptor that detects changes in temperature.
thoracic (thō-ras′ik) Relating to the thorax, the area between the neck and the abdomen.
thrombopoiesis (throm′b ō-poy-ē′sis) Formation of blood platelets.
trabecula (tră-bek′y ū-lă; pl., trabeculae, -lē) Meshwork; a small piece of the spongy substance of bone, usually interconnected with other similar pieces.
transducer (tranz-d ū′sĕr) Device or organ designed to convert energy from one form to another.
transudate (tranz′y ū-dāt) Fluid that has passed through a membrane.
trophoblast (trof′ ō-blast, trō′fō-blast) Cell layer covering the blastocyst that will allow the embryo to receive nourishment from the mother.
tubercle (tū′bĕr-kĕl) Nodule or slight elevation from the surface of a bone that allows attachment of a tendon or ligament.
tuberosity (tū′bĕr-os′i-t ē) Large tubercle or rounded elevation, as on the surface of a bone.
tunic (tū′nik) One of the covering layers of a body part, especially a blood vessel or other tubular structure.

U

ultrasound (ŭl′tră-sound) A medical imaging method that uses sound waves to visualize internal structures, also known as *sonography.*
ultrastructure (ŭl′tră-strŭk′ch ūr) Cell structure viewable via the electron microscope.
umbilical (ŭm-bil′i-kăl) Relating to the umbilicus (navel).
ureter (yū-rē′tĕr, yū′rē-ter) Tubes that connect the kidney to the urinary bladder.
urethra (yū-rē′thr ă) Canal leading from the bladder to externally discharge urine.
urinalysis (yūr′i-nal′i-sis) Analysis of the urine to help assess the state of a person's health.
urine (yūr′in) Fluid and dissolved substances excreted by the kidney.

V

vasculogenesis (vas′ky ū-lō-jen′ĕ-sis) Formation of the vascular system.
vein (vān) Blood vessel carrying blood toward the heart.
vellus (vel′ ŭs) Fine, nonpigmented hair covering most of the fetal body.
ventricle (ven′tri-k ĕl) Cavity within an organ such as the heart or the brain.
vertebra (ver′t ĕ-bră; pl., vertebrae, -brē) Segment of the spinal column.
vertebral (ver′t ĕ-brăl) Relating to a vertebra or the vertebral column.
vesicle (ves′i-k ăl) Closed cellular structure in the cytoplasm surrounded by a single membrane.
vibrissa (vī-bris′ă; pl., vibrissae, vī-bris′ē) Hair in the vestibule of the nose.
viscera (vis′ ĕr-ă) Organs of the digestive, respiratory, urinary, and endocrine systems.
vulva (vŭl′vă) External genitalia of the female.

X

xiphoid (zi′foyd) Sword-shaped.

Z

zygote (zī′gōt) Diploid cell resulting from the union of a sperm and an ovum.

Index

Note: Page numbers followed by *f* and *t* indicate figures and tables.

A

B

C

D

F

H

J

K

M

N

O

U

V

W

X

Y

Z

Credits

Online Supplements

McGraw Hill Education connect®

Connect APR & PHILS Access Card for Human Anatomy, Sixth Edition

McGraw-Hill Connect is a digital teaching and learning environment that improves performance over a variety of critical outcomes. With Connect, instructors can deliver assignments, quizzes and tests easily online. Students can practice important skills at their own pace and on their own schedule.

HOW TO REGISTER

Using a Print Book?
To register and activate your Connect account, simply follow these easy steps:

1. **Go to the Connect course web address provided by your instructor or visit the Connect link set up on your instructor's course within your campus learning management system.**
2. **Click on the link to register.**
3. **When prompted, enter the Connect code found on the inside back cover of your book and click Submit. Complete the brief registration form that follows to begin using Connect.**

Using an eBook?
To register and activate your Connect account, simply follow these easy steps:

1. **Upon purchase of your eBook, you will be granted automatic access to Connect.**
2. **Go to the Connect course web address provided by your instructor or visit the Connect link set up on your instructor's course within your campus learning management system.**
3. **Sign in using the same email address and password you used to register on the eBookstore. Complete your registration and begin using Connect.**

**Note: Access Code is for one use only. If you did not purchase this book new, the access code included in this book is no longer valid.*

Need help? Visit mhhe.com/support